Standard & Poor's Stock and Bond Guide

Standard & Poor's Stock and Bond Guide

2000 Edition

Standard & Poor's

McGraw-Hill

New York San Francisco Washington, D.C. Auckland Bogotá Caracas Lisbon London Madrid Mexico City Milan Montreal New Delhi San Juan Singapore Sydney Tokyo Toronto

International Standard Serial Number: 1074–2786

This book is printed on recycled paper containing a minimum of 50% total recycled fiber with 10% postconsumer de-inked fiber.

McGraw-Hill

*A Division of The **McGraw-Hill** Companies*

Standard & Poor's

The Publisher of the *Stock Guide* and the *Bond Guide* is Shauna Morrison. The Editor is Frank LoVaglio.

1 2 3 4 5 6 7 8 9 0 MAL/MAL 0 9 8 7 6 5 4 3 2 1 0

ISBN 0-07-135888-9

The sponsoring editor for this book was Griffin Hansbury, and the production supervisor was Modestine Cameron. The front matter, introduction, and section opening materials were set by North Market Street Graphics.

Printed and bound by Malloy Lithographers, Inc.

CONTENTS

ABOUT THE AUTHOR

Standard & Poor's, a division of The McGraw-Hill Companies, is the nation's leading securities information company. It provides a broad range of services, including the respected bond and stock ratings, advisory services, data guides, and the most closely watched and widely reported gauge of stock market activity—the S&P 500 Stock Index. Standard & Poor's products are marketed around the world and used extensively by financial professionals and individual investors.

Standard & Poor's Stock and Bond Guide

INTRODUCTION

by Alan J. Miller, C.F.A.

The world's most inspired artist could not produce a great oil painting without brushes and palette, paints and canvas. The head chef at the most outstanding four-star restaurant on Paris' right bank could not cook a top-flight meal without the tools of the trade and proper ingredients: pots, pans and cutlery, fruits and vegetables, seasonings and spices. Even a cobbler could not manufacture a pair of first-class boots without hammer and nails, leather and twine.

Similarly, the most intelligent and serious investors could not select appropriate investments nor construct efficient portfolios for themselves without the right tools.

But what are the right tools for such serious investors?

The answer is more obvious than you might think. It is *information.* In today's information economy, what paints and brushes are to the artist, what spices and seasonings are to the cook, what leather and twine are to the cobbler, that is what comprehensive economic and financial information are to serious investors. Information which provides the investor with answers to such questions as:

What business is a company in?

How is the company capitalized and how well is it financed?

Is it highly leveraged?

What is its earnings growth record?

What has been its dividend-paying policy?

Are major institutions owners of its shares?

If one were to decide to invest in the company, how might that be accomplished?

Are its common shares listed and, if so, on which exchange?

Does it have any bonds outstanding?

What about preferred stocks?

Are any of these issues convertibles?

Are options available?

And what about mutual funds?

And annuities?

These, and dozens of questions like them, are the sort which serious investors, individual or institutional, must address if they are truly to do an effective job in managing their own assets or those entrusted to them.

To be sure, investors could, if they wanted, choose a random route of ignorance, hoping to get lucky by relying solely on a tip from a friend or neighbor, or they might throw darts at a page of stock market quotations, or they could buy the securities of companies whose names simply tickled their fancy. And from time to time they might even get lucky and generate a profit.

But over the long run, there is little doubt that such an approach would leave them worse off than when they started. Indeed, it is likely that they would be no more successful than would a painter who merely splattered paint on a canvas and wished for the best, or a chef who dumped a slew of meats, vegetables, and spices in a pot and hoped, thereby, to create a flavorful stew.

Sure, it *might* happen—just as a million monkeys randomly typing away at a million typewriters might someday produce a play of equivalent stature to Shakespeare's *Hamlet.* But don't bet on it.

No, a much better idea, and one adopted by virtually all investment professionals, is to attempt to seek out the most comprehensive and significant economic and financial information available, and to base investment decisions on a reasoned interpretation, evaluation, and analysis of such data. After all, in a rational world governed by the laws of cause and effect, that is the approach destined to maximize an investor's probability of success.

Which is where Standard & Poor's comes in.

Standard & Poor's

For generations, Standard & Poor's has been recognized as the leading purveyor of financial, economic, and business data to the investment community. The S&P 500 is among the most important and most widely reported benchmark indexes for investment professionals worldwide. Its products include *The Outlook,* one of the nation's leading investment advisory services; MarketScope, a respected, real-time investment advisory service for brokers; the Standard & Poor's Stock Market Encyclopedia; the Earnings Guide; the Trendline Chart Guide; and a whole host of other services that have proven all but indispensable to investment professionals. And not least of these are the Standard & Poor's monthly Stock and Bond Guides which provide hundreds of thousands of bits of information on more than 14,000 different securities—including common stocks, preferred stocks, annuities, mutual funds, and domestic and foreign bonds.

The Stock and Bond Guides have long been available only by subscription to individuals and institutions alike, but never before have individuals been able to purchase a combined year-end Stock and Bond Guide directly through a retail bookstore. Now all that has changed. *Standard & Poor's Stock and Bond Guide,* the first combined Standard & Poor's investment guide available to serious individual investors directly through retail outlets, is what you now hold in your hands.

This is an exceptional product, containing in just one source, a wealth of information designed to enable you to select the most appropriate securities for your own portfolio, no matter what your objectives.

The Common and Convertible Preferred Stock Guide

The first section of this book contains 51 columns of information on more than 5000 common and convertible preferred stocks—or approximately a quarter of a million bits of information on most of the equities in which you might be considering investing. Specifically:

1. The first column provides index numbers as a visual guide to the columnar data and indicates whether particular common stocks are components of the S&P 500 Stock Index, S&P MidCap 400, or S&P SmallCap 600. Also included are statistical data on each index, as well as on the S&P Super Composite 1500 Index. We have indicated where options are traded, along with footnotes indicating the exchanges on which those options trade and their monthly cycle.

2. The next column indicates the ticker symbols of stocks for the primary exchanges on which they trade. Supplementary symbols which appear on the ticker tape, such as "Pr" for preferred stocks, are also provided.

3. The name of the company appears here. This is not necessarily the exact corporate title of the company and may include abbreviations because of space limitations. When the name of the company is not followed by the designation of any particular issue of stock, it is the common stock which is being referred to.

This column also provides considerable additional information. For preferred stocks, call prices are shown in parentheses after the names of issues. Footnoted data indicate the years in which call prices decline. And various abbreviations indicate other provisions, for example, conversion terms of a preferred stock; whether or not it is participating or cumulative; when a stock is nonvoting; when a security is an American Depository Receipt; or the exercise terms of warrants.

Units of trading on the New York and American Stock Exchanges generally are 100 shares. When the unit is different for a particular issue (say 10, 25, or 50 shares), that fact is also indicated here.

4. This column indicates the markets in which the security trades. The primary exchange is the first market listed.

5. This column provides Standard & Poor's rankings for common stocks and ratings for convertible preferred stocks. These rankings and ratings represent some of the most valuable information in this book and merit special discussion.

Standard & Poor's Earnings and Dividend Rankings for Common Stocks

The investment process involves assessment of various factors—such as product and industry position, corporate resources, and financial policy—with results that make some common stocks more highly esteemed than others. In this assessment, Standard & Poor's believes that earnings and dividend performance is the end result of the interplay of those factors and that, over the long run, the record of this performance has a considerable bearing on relative quality. The rankings, however, do not pretend to reflect all the factors, tangible or intangible, that bear on stock quality. Even so, they are highly regarded, and many institutional investors will only buy stocks that carry Standard & Poor's highest rankings.

Relative quality of bonds or other debt—that is, degrees of protection for principal and interest—called *creditworthiness,* cannot be applied to common stocks; therefore, rankings are not to be confused with Standard & Poor's ratings which are arrived at by a necessarily different approach.

Growth and stability of earnings and dividends are key elements in establishing Standard & Poor's earnings and dividend rankings for common stocks, which are designed to capsulize the nature of the record in a single symbol. It should be noted, however, that the process also takes into consideration certain adjustments and modifications deemed desirable in establishing such rankings.

The point of departure in arriving at these rankings is a computerized scoring system based on per share earnings and dividend records of the most recent ten years. This is a period considered long enough to measure significant time segments of secular growth, to capture indications of basic change in trend as they develop, and to encompass the full peak-to-peak range of the business cycle.

Basic scores are computed for earnings and dividends, then adjusted by a set of predetermined modifiers for growth, stability within long-term trend, and cyclicality. Adjusted scores for earnings and dividends are then combined to yield a final score.

Further, the ranking system makes allowance for the fact that, in general, corporate size imparts certain recognized advantages from an investment standpoint. Conversely, minimum size limits (in terms of corporate sales volume) are set for the various rankings, but the system provides for making exceptions where the score reflects an outstanding earnings-dividend record.

The final score for each stock is measured against a scoring matrix determined by analysis of the scores of a large and representative sample of stocks. The range of scores in the array of this sample has been aligned with the following ladder of rankings:

A+ Highest

A High

A− Above Average

B+ Average

B Below Average

B− Lower

C Lowest

D In Reorganization

NR No ranking because of insufficient data or because the stock is not amenable to the ranking process

The positions as determined above may be modified in some instances by special considerations, such as natural disasters, massive strikes, and nonrecurring accounting adjustments.

Bear in mind, however, that a ranking is not a forecast of future market performance, but is basically an appraisal of past performance of earnings and dividends, and relative current standing. Hence, these rankings should not be used as market recommendations: a high-score stock may at times be so overpriced as to justify its sale, while a low-score stock may be attractively priced for purchase.

Moreover, rankings based upon earnings and dividend records are no substitute for complete analysis. They cannot take into account potential effects of management changes, internal company policies not yet fully reflected in the earnings and dividend record, public relations standing, recent competitive shifts, and a host of other factors that may be relevant to investment status and decision. But they are an excellent place for the conscientious investor to begin.

Standard & Poor's Ratings for Preferred Stocks

Standard & Poor's preferred stock ratings are determined in an entirely different fashion. Unlike Standard & Poor's common stock rankings, these ratings are assessments of the capacity and willingness of an issuer to pay preferred stock dividends and any applicable sinking-fund obligations.

A preferred stock rating also differs from a bond rating inasmuch as it is assigned to an equity issue, which issue is intrinsically different from, and subordinated to, a debt issue. To reflect this difference, the preferred stock rating symbol will normally not be higher than the bond rating symbol assigned to, or that would be assigned to, the senior debt of the same issuer.

The preferred stock ratings are based on the following considerations:

1. Likelihood of payment, that is, the capacity and willingness of the issuer to meet the timely payment of preferred stock dividends and any applicable sinking-fund requirements in accordance with the terms of the obligation
2. Nature and provisions of the issue
3. Relative position of the issue in the event of bankruptcy, reorganization, or other arrangements affecting creditors' rights

Preferred stock ratings array as follows:

AAA This is the highest rating assigned by Standard & Poor's to a preferred stock issue and indicates an extremely strong capacity to pay the preferred stock obligations.

AA A preferred stock issue rated AA also qualifies as a high-quality fixed income security. The capacity to pay preferred stock obligations is very strong, although not as overwhelming as for issues rated AAA.

A An issue rated A is backed by a sound capacity to pay the preferred stock obligations, although it is somewhat more susceptible to the adverse effects of changes in circumstances and economic conditions.

BBB An issue rated BBB is regarded as backed by an adequate capacity to pay the preferred stock obligations. Whereas it normally exhibits adequate protection parameters, adverse economic conditions or changing circumstances are more likely to lead to a weakened capacity to make payments for a preferred stock in this category than for issues in the A category.

BB, B, CCC Preferred stocks rated BB, B, and CCC are regarded, on balance, as predominately speculative with respect to the issuer's capacity to pay preferred stock obligations. BB indicates the lowest degree of speculation and CCC the highest degree of speculation. While such issues will likely have some quality and protective characteristics, these are outweighed by large uncertainties or major risk exposures to adverse conditions.

CC This rating is reserved for a preferred stock issue in arrears on dividends or sinking-fund payments, but that is currently paying.

C A preferred stock rated C is a nonpaying issue.

D A preferred stock rated D is a nonpaying issue with the issuer in default on debt instruments.

NR This designation indicates that no rating has been requested, that there is insufficient information on which to base a rating, or that Standard & Poor's does not rate a particular type of obligation as a matter of policy.

Plus (+) or Minus (–) To provide more detailed indications of preferred stock quality, the ratings from AA to CCC may be modified by the addition of a plus or minus sign to show relative standing within the major rating categories.

Changes in Standard & Poor's common stock rankings and preferred stock ratings are highlighted by arrows showing the direction of change, up or down.

Now let's return to an explanation of the remaining columns in the Common and Convertible Preferred Stock Guide.

6–7. These columns indicate the number of financial institutions that hold the stock and the number of shares, in thousands, held. The data cover almost 4500 institutions, including investment companies, banks, insurance companies, college endowments, and money managers, as obtained from Vickers Stock Research Corporation.

8. In this column, the company's principal business is briefly described. Where a company is engaged in several lines of business, an attempt is made to list that line from which it obtains the greatest proportion of its revenues. In addition, an indication of the company's rank within its industry is given where possible.

9–14. The next six columns show the stock's price ranges during three discrete periods: for the 27 years 1971–1997 (columns 9–10); for the year 1998 (columns 11–12); and for the year 1999 (columns 13–14).

15. This column indicates the number of shares traded in December, 1999.

16–18. The next three columns show the stock's high, low, and closing prices in December, 1999. Prices for Canadian issues are quoted in Canadian dollars, when the primary exchanges on which these issues are traded are Canadian exchanges. When the closing quotation is a bid price, a "B" will follow the price in the "Last" column.

19. This column presents dividend yields, calculated by dividing the total indicated annual dividend rate by the closing price of the stock on December 31, 1999. The dividend rate used for this calculation is based upon the latest dividends paid which may or may not include extras or stock dividends as indicated by the footnotes.

20. This column indicates the stock's latest price-earnings (or P-E) ratio, derived by dividing the closing price of the stock on December 31, 1999 by estimated 1999 earnings (where estimates are available) or by the last 12 months earnings (where 1999 estimates are not available).

21. The EPS 5 Year Growth Rate is the compounded annual rate of per-share earnings growth for the last five years, expressed as a percentage.

22–24. The total return value represents the price appreciation of a stock plus any cash dividends. To make the figures as close as possible to real portfolios, dividends are reinvested on the payment date, at that day's price. The total return figure, expressed as an annualized percentage, covers three time periods on a trailing basis: 12 months (column 22), 36 months (column 23), and 60 months (column 24).

25. This column (the first on the right-hand page) again provides index numbers as a visual guide to the columnar data. In addition, details of all stock dividends and stock splits effected during the previous five years are reported through symbols and footnotes. Adjustments are made for all stock dividends and splits.

26. This column indicates that one or more cash dividends have been paid in each calendar year, without interruption, through 1999, beginning with the year listed.

27–33. The next seven columns provide data relating to the company's dividend policy. Where payments are being made at a regular established rate, that fact is noted in column 27 (Period) as follows: M = Monthly; Q = Quarterly; S = Semiannually; A = Annually. The amount of that regular payment is indicated in column 28 ($). The date of the latest payment appears in column 29 (Date) and the date on which the stock sells "ex dividend" (that is, the date on which the stock sells without the right to receive the latest declared dividend) appears in column 30 (Ex. Div.). Where stock dividends, no dividends, or dividends at no regular rate are being paid, those facts also appear in columns 27–30.

Column 31 provides total dividends paid in calendar 1999, including both regular and extras. Column 32 shows the latest total annual indicated rate based on the most recent quarterly or semiannual rate or on dividends paid during the last 12 months. And column 33 presents the total paid, including extras, in calendar 1998.

34–37. The next four columns provide important balance sheet information. Columns 34, 35, and 36 present Cash and Equivalents, Current Assets (including cash and equivalents), and Current Liabilities in millions of dollars. Column 37 indicates the date of that latest balance sheet information.

Where current balance sheet elements are not of analytical significance, other pertinent data are presented according to the industry in which the company operates, such as Total Deposits for banks and Total Assets for industrial and other finance companies. Amounts are presented in millions of dollars.

38–40. The next three columns describe the company's capitalization: long-term debt in millions of dollars in column 38; preferred shares in thousands in column 39; and outstanding common shares in thousands in column 40.

41–50. The next ten columns present a record of the company's earnings per share for the last five years. Earnings per share are presented on a *"Diluted"* basis pursuant to FASB 128, which became effective December 15, 1997, and are generally reported including discontinued operations, before extraordinary items. This reflects a change from previously reported *Primary* earnings per share.

Column 41 indicates the month in which the fiscal year ends so that you can tell exactly which periods you're looking at. Columns 42–46 present earnings per share for the years 1995–1999 and column 47 shows earnings per share for the last 12 months. Earnings for fiscal years ending March 31 or earlier are shown under the column of the preceding calendar year and "Last 12 Months" earnings indicate earnings through the period shown in the interim earnings column, when available, or annual, if not.

Where Standard & Poor's estimates are shown, they are the final product of careful analysis by industry specialists of available relevant information. They are unofficial, however, and responsibility for their accuracy cannot be assumed. Arrows denote changes in current estimates.

Interim earnings are shown, when available, for the longest accounting interval since the last fiscal year-end. Column 48 indicates the period for which interim earnings are being shown. Column 50 presents figures for that period in 1999 while column 49 presents figures for the same period in 1998 for comparative purposes.

51. Finally, the last column on the right-hand page again provides index numbers as a visual guide to the columnar data.

How to Use the Standard & Poor's Common and Convertible Preferred Stock Guide

We have outlined the wealth of information that is available on more than 5000 common and convertible preferred stocks in the Standard & Poor's Stock Guide—information relating to balance sheet data, stock price history, earnings records, dividend records, institutional ownership, and on and on. But how might an individual investor actually make use of all that? Let's look at two examples.

Suppose you were convinced that the timing was right to increase the amount of your funds committed to common or convertible preferred stocks and were interested primarily in ample and secure current income. Once you decided what you considered an adequate return, you'd thumb through the Stock Guide and select stocks yielding as much or more than your desired rate, as shown in the "% Dividend Yield" column near the extreme right of the left-hand page. By that one operation, alone, you would have run stocks through a preliminary screen and come up with a much more manageable list.

Now you'd probably want to know the prospects for maintaining dividends. By reference to the "Cash Dividends Each Year Since" column, adjacent on the next page, you could weed out those stocks whose record of consecutive dividend payments did not meet the standards you considered desirable.

Next you would have to decide if the stocks remaining on your list had adequate current protection. Among the various factors you would study in this connection would be annual and interim earnings and the company's financial position. In so doing, you'd be seeking answers to such questions as:

Do recent earnings cover dividend payments?

Have earnings been increasing or declining?

Is the company's balance sheet relatively clean with little long-term debt or is the company highly leveraged?

The measurement of earnings and dividends stability and growth provided by Standard & Poor's earnings and dividend rankings for common stocks and its ratings for preferred stocks are other helpful tools in the selection process. The fifth column on the left-hand page provides these rankings and ratings which have been discussed and explained at some length earlier in this introduction. Depending on the degree of conservatism you might wish to exercise, preferred stocks rated below A or common stocks ranked below B+ might be weeded out.

Having subjected your list to these various screenings, you might have perhaps a handful of issues remaining for further study. These securities should then be investigated in as thorough a fashion as possible. You'd still have a lot of work to do, but you'd have a huge head start in having eliminated hundreds, if not thousands, of companies which would not suit your needs. One place to begin the final phase of your search might be a Standard & Poor's Stock Report. Look for a check mark before the company name in order to find out companies for which reports are available.

Alternatively, suppose your objective was to invest for long-term capital appreciation rather than high current income. Again the Standard & Poor's Stock Guide will be of tremendous help to you in getting started.

Instead of beginning with the dividend yield column, you might start by looking at the array of earnings-per-share statistics on the right-hand page. What you'd be looking for would be companies with consistent records of earnings growth, those whose earnings rose annually over the last five years, and those whose interim earnings for 1999 were greater than for the comparable period in 1998.

But just because a company's earnings were growing wouldn't necessarily mean that its common stock was attractive for purchase; the stock still might be overpriced. So you'd also want to look at the final column on the left-hand page to assure yourself that the stock's price-earnings ratio wasn't inordinately high.

Next, you'd want to look at the stock's Standard & Poor's ranking. And you'd probably want to review some of the balance sheet statistics to get a feeling for just how highly leveraged the company was.

In this situation (unlike the first in which you were seeking stocks providing ample, secure current income), you would end up with a small and manageable list of companies with good historic earnings growth records, selling at reasonable price-earnings multiples, and boasting satisfactory financial strength. Again you'd still have to do further research to ferret out the most attractive growth stocks to meet your objectives, but a good part of your job will have been done.

What have been outlined here are only two investor approaches: one suitable for an investor seeking high current income and the other appropriate for an investor more interested in long-term capital appreciation. But the data presented provide the basis for many other applications as well, which will become increasingly apparent to you as you use this book.

Standard & Poor's Preferred Stock Summary

The next section of this Standard & Poor's Guide provides data on more than 400 other nonconvertible preferred issues, including ticker symbols; exchanges on which these issues trade; call features; prices; dividend rates; payment dates; and yields. Perhaps most important, also included are the proprietary Standard & Poor's Preferred Stock Ratings, which have been discussed at some length earlier in this introduction.

Standard & Poor's Closed-End Fund Summary

The closed-end fund summary presents uniform data on over 500 closed-end funds to make comparisons easy. You'll find all these facts on each closed-end fund: ticker symbol, fund name, exchange; fund type—24 kinds in all; dividends—latest payment, date, ex-dividend, year-to-date, regular distributions, capital gains distributions, indicated rate, yield %; price range—prior and current year to date, current month high / low and last; net assets—NAV premium/ discount, latest NAV, common shares outstanding.

Standard & Poor's Mutual Fund Summary

Mutual funds are ideal investment vehicles for many investors who prefer to delegate the tasks of stock selection, asset allocation, and market timing to professional portfolio managers and who appreciate the additional benefits of broad diversification and liquidity which mutual funds provide. But how is one to determine *which* mutual fund may be most appropriate? Fortunately this guide can be of help to you on that score as well.

The next section of the Standard & Poor's Guide contains extensive information on nearly 700 mutual funds arrayed in 25 columns. Here's what you'll be able to determine:

1. The name of the fund and the year in which it was originated or initially offered to the public.

2. The fund's principal objective: Growth, Income, Return on Capital, Stability or Preservation of Capital, or whether all objectives are treated equally.

3. The fund's type: Balanced, Bond, Common, Convertible Bond and Preferred, Flexible, Long-Term Governments (including GNMA, etc.), Global, Hedge, International, Leverage, Preferred, Precious Metals, Options, Specialized, Tax Free, or Short-Term Investments.

4. The fund's total net assets at market value less current liabilities (including cash equivalents) expressed in millions of dollars as of September 30, 1999.

5. The fund's cash and receivables plus U.S. Government securities, short-term commercial paper and short-term municipal and corporate bonds and notes, less current liabilities, expressed in millions of dollars as of September 30, 1999.

6. Whether or not the fund has IRA and Keogh plans available.

7–11. Performance results for the fund for each of the last five years, that is, the annual percentage change in net asset value per share in each of the years 1995–1999 after adjustment for all capital gains and dividends distributions, but excluding sales charges.

12. The minimum required initial purchase of shares exclusive of contractual plans (which is usually lower for retirement plans).

13. The maximum percentage sales charge, that is, the charge added to net asset value in computing the offering price.

18. The results of a $10,000 investment in the fund, assuming that all dividends and capital gains are reinvested. The calculation excludes any sales charge.

Standard & Poor's Variable Annuity/Life Investment Summary

An annuity is a contract between an insurance company and an annuitant whereby the insurance company guarantees to make fixed or variable payments to the annuitant at a future time, in exchange for a single or flexible premium.

Traditionally, annuities provided fixed payments over the course of an annuitant's lifetime in exchange for a single lump-sum premium payment, but a combination of rising inflation rates and increased life expectancies reduced the appeal of such products. As a result, in the late 1950s, the variable annuity was invented: This product is invested in assets (such as common stocks) which might be expected to rise in line with the rate of inflation, thereby providing some protection against declining purchasing power but at some increase in risk.

Variable annuities are variable in two senses:

1. they vary in what they are invested in (usually stocks, bonds, or money-market instruments); and
2. they vary in what they pay based upon fluctuations in their market value.

Since annuities are variable in both these senses, those who may be interested in purchasing them (usually for retirement) obviously need to find out something about the underlying terms of different annuities, the insurance companies marketing them, performance records, and so on. The Standard & Poor's Guide can help you in this area too.

The next section of the Standard & Poor's Guide contains information on 170 annuity vehicles arrayed in 14 columns. Here's what you'll be able to determine:

1. The name of the contract and the issuing company.

2. The investment vehicle, that is, what the underlying investment is.

3. Who the manager or submanager is.

4. The investment objective.

5. When the annuity was first offered.

6. Total assets (expressed in millions of dollars).

7–9. Fees and expenses, including separate account, fund, administrative, surrender, and sales charges.

10–13. Performance results, that is, annual percentage changes in unit values from 1996 through 1999.

14. Unit values as of December 28, 1999.

The Standard & Poor's Bond Guide

The next section of this book contains voluminous information on more than 6500 corporate bonds issued by more than 1500 different companies. Data relating to companies (including name, industry, fixed charges coverage, balance sheet figures, long-term debt outstanding, capitalization and debt-to-equity ratios) are referenced to the boldface headings at the top of the page. Data relating to individual issues (including exchanges where traded, descriptions, interest payment dates, recent rating history, redemption provisions, and others) are referenced to the second set of headings in lightface type.

Specifically, the following information is provided for *companies:*

1. The first company column provides the name of the issuing company and is footnoted to provide additional information relating to control, name changes, subsidiaries, and so on.

2. The next company column references the issuing company's principal business by industry code.

3–5. The next three company columns indicate fixed charges coverage for each of the three years 1996, 1997, and 1998. Figures represent the number of times available earnings (before income taxes and extraordinary charges or credits) cover fixed charges. Fixed charges include interest on funded debt, other interest, amortization of debt discount and expense, and similar charges.

6. The sixth company column indicates the month in which the fiscal year ends. For fiscal years ending March 31 or earlier, figures are shown under the columns of the preceding calendar year.

7–10. The next four company columns provide balance sheet data [cash and equivalents, current assets (including cash and equivalents), and current liabilities] in millions of dollars as of the annual or interim balance sheet date shown. (Note that utilities with a reasonable debt-to-property ratio often may report current liabilities in excess of current assets but that, in many instances, this is of no real significance since utilities have constant tax deferrals, high current debt maturity, and the ability to forecast revenues.)

11. The next company column shows the company's long-term debt in millions of dollars, that is, debt and certain obligations due after one year, including bonds, debentures, mortgages, and capitalized lease obligations. Increased debt resulting from new financing and offered subsequent to the latest balance sheet date is indicated by a five-pointed star (★).

12. The twelfth company column presents the company's capitalization in millions of dollars, that is, the sum of the stated values of common shareholders' equity, preferred and preference stock, total debt, and minority interest.

13. Finally, the last company column calculates total debt as a percentage of total capitalization, that is, total debt (including short-term debt) divided by total capital. This provides a measurement of the degree to which a company is leveraged.

Additionally, the following information is provided for *issues:*

1. The first issue column describes the specific bond, including coupon and maturity date. If the bond is traded on either the New York or American Stock Exchanges, that fact is noted as well.
2. The second issue column indicates the dates on which interest is payable. Symbols following interest dates note foreign issues payable in U.S. funds or currency of the issuing country and issues in default.
3. The next issue column presents Standard & Poor's ratings. These ratings differ from both common stock rankings and preferred stock ratings (previously described) and merit special discussion.

Standard & Poor's Corporate Ratings

A Standard & Poor's rating is a current assessment of the creditworthiness of an obligor with respect to a specific obligation. This assessment may take into consideration obligors such as guarantors, insurers, or lessees.

Ratings are based on the following considerations:

1. Likelihood of default as evidenced by the capacity and willingness of the obligor as to the timely payment of interest and repayment of principal in accordance with the terms of the obligation
2. Nature and provisions of the obligation
3. Protection afforded by, and relative position of, the obligation in the event of bankruptcy, reorganization, or other arrangement under the laws of bankruptcy and other laws affecting creditors' rights.

Investment Grades: AAA, AA, A, BBB The top four categories (AAA, AA, A, and BBB) are commonly known as "Investment Grade" ratings. Under present commercial bank regulations issued by the Comptroller of the Currency, bonds rated in these categories are generally regarded as eligible for bank investments. (In addition, however, the Legal Investment Laws of various states may impose certain rating or other standards for obligations eligible for investment by savings banks, trust companies, insurance companies, and fiduciaries in general.)

AAA Debt rated AAA has the highest rating assigned by Standard & Poor's. Capacity to pay interest and repay principal is extremely strong.

AA Debt rated AA has a very strong capacity to pay interest and repay principal and differs from the higher rated issues only in small degree.

A Debt rated A has a strong capacity to pay interest and repay principal although it is somewhat more susceptible to the adverse effects of changes in circumstances and economic conditions than debt in higher rated categories.

BBB Debt rated BBB is regarded as having an adequate capacity to pay interest and repay principal. Whereas it normally exhibits adequate protection parameters, adverse economic conditions or changing circumstances are more likely to lead to a weakened capacity to pay interest and repay principal for debt in this category than in higher rated categories.

Speculative Grades: BB, B, CCC, CC, C Debt rated BB, B, CCC, CC, and C is regarded, on balance, as predominantly speculative with respect to capacity to pay interest and repay principal in accordance with the terms of the obligation. BB indicates the lowest degree of speculation and C the highest degree. Although such debt will likely have some quality and protective characteristics, these are outweighed by large uncertainties or major risk exposure to adverse conditions.

BB Debt rated BB has less near-term vulnerability to default than other speculative issues. However, it faces major ongoing uncertainties or exposure to adverse business, financial, or economic conditions which could lead to inadequate capacity to meet timely interest and principal payments. The BB rating category is also used for debt subordinated to senior debt that is assigned an actual or implied BBB– rating.

B Debt rated B has a greater vulnerability to default but currently has the capacity to meet interest payments and principal repayments. Adverse business, financial, or economic conditions will likely impair capacity or willingness to pay interest and repay principal. The B rating category is also used for debt subordinated to senior debt that is assigned an actual or implied BB or BB– rating.

CCC Debt rated CCC has a currently identifiable vulnerability to default and is dependent upon favorable business, financial, and economic conditions to meet the requirements of timely payment of interest and repayment of principal. In the event of adverse business, financial, or economic conditions, it is not likely to have the capacity to pay interest and repay principal. The CCC rating category is also used for debt subordinated to senior debt that is assigned an actual or implied B or B– rating.

CC The rating CC is typically applied to debt subordinated to senior debt that is assigned an actual or implied CCC rating.

C The rating C is typically applied to debt subordinated to senior debt that is assigned an actual or implied CCC– rating. The C rating may be used to cover a situation where a bankruptcy petition has been filed, but debt service payments are continued.

CI The rating CI is reserved for income bonds on which no interest is being paid.

D Debt rated D is in payment default. The D rating category is used when interest payments or principal repayments are not made on the date due even if the applicable grace period has not expired, unless Standard & Poor's believes that such payments will be made during such grace period. The D rating also is used upon the filing of a bankruptcy petition, if debt service payments are jeopardized.

Plus (+) or Minus (–) The ratings from AA to CCC may be modified by the addition of a plus (+) or minus (–) sign to show relative standing within the major categories.

r The 'r' is attached to highlight derivative, hybrid, and certain other obligations that Standard & Poor's believes may experience high volatility or high variability in expected returns due to noncredit risks. Examples of such obligations are: securities whose principal or interest return is indexed to equities, commodities, or currencies; certain swaps and options; and interest only and principal only mortgage securities. The absence of an 'r' symbol should not be taken as an indication that an obligation will exhibit no volatility or variability in total return.

NR This designation indicates that no public rating has been requested, that there is insufficient information on which to base a rating, or that Standard & Poor's does not rate a particular type obligation as a matter of policy.

Let's now return to an explanation of the remaining *issue* columns in the Bond Guide:

4–5. The next two issue columns indicate the date of the latest rating change and the previous rating.

6. The sixth issue column indicates whether or not the bond is eligible for purchase by banks.

7. The next issue column indicates the bond's form: Book-entry; Coupon only; Registered only; or Coupon or Registered, interchangeably.

8–13. The following six issue columns provide information regarding redemption provisions: the regular call price with beginning date (in parentheses) or ending date (columns 8–9); sinking-fund price with beginning date (in parentheses) or ending date (columns 10–11); and refund price with beginning date (in parentheses) or ending date (columns 12–13).

14. The next issue column indicates the amount of the issue outstanding (in millions of dollars) as of the latest available complete balance sheet date.

15–16. The next two issue columns reference the original underwriter and the year the issue was originally offered.

17–19. The following three issue columns indicate the bond's high and low price in 1999 and its last sale price as of December 31, 1999 (for listed issues) or bid price or Standard & Poor's valuation for over-the-counter issues or listed issues not traded on the last business day of the year.

20–21. Finally, the last two issue columns provide the bond's current yield and yield to maturity computed on the basis of the year-end price shown in column 19.

How to Use the Standard & Poor's Bond Guide

We have described the data available on more than 6500 corporate bonds in the Standard & Poor's Bond Guide—information relating to descriptions of corporate issuers and issues alike, balance sheet data, fixed charges coverage, long-term debt, capitalizations, redemption provisions, interest payment dates, debt ratings, underwritings, price history, current yields, yields to maturity and much, much more. But how can an individual investor actually use this information? Two examples follow.

A conservative investor might start with a consideration of Standard & Poor's bond ratings. Being conservative, she might limit her interest to investment grade bonds, those rated BBB or higher. Or she might set her sights even higher than that, screening out all bonds rated below A or even AA.

In addition to limiting her credit risk, however, she might want to limit her interest rate risk as well. So she might cut her list even further, eliminating those issues with maturities of longer than, say, seven years.

From among those issues, she next might search for those which provide the highest yields to maturity. As a preliminary cut, these are the issues which would appear to provide the greatest value within the context of her particular risk parameters.

Once she did these three things, the investor might check redemption provisions to make sure that what appear to be bargains aren't just fool's gold likely to be called away from her. Then, depending on her personal requirements (for liquidity, perhaps, or current income), she might check out the size of the issue, whether or not it was listed, current yield and interest payment dates.

Even once this was done, however, the investor still wouldn't know whether or not to place an order to purchase any particular issue—but she'd surely be a lot closer to making an intelligent decision. With just a few issues remaining after she completed these initial screens, she'd know exactly which bonds to investigate further and her project would be manageable.

An aggressive speculator, on the other hand, might address this issue the other way around: rather than starting out by screening for quality, he might screen for yield to maturity, looking for those issues providing the biggest payoffs—assuming they don't default. And he might want to increase his bet even further by assuming a big interest rate risk as well, screening out any issues with *less* than ten years to go to maturity.

But will these issues default? The investor now would examine such statistical data as fixed charges coverage, total debt as a percentage of capital, and the other balance sheet information provided in these tables. He, after all, would be looking for bargains too—but at the other end of the spectrum: poorly rated issues which would *not* be likely to default.

Not surprisingly, the issues this investor would be likely to come up with probably would carry low Standard & Poor's ratings—and that's when he'd have to be prepared to do a lot more work. Why are these bonds' ratings as low as they are, if fixed charges coverage, debt/capital ratios, and balance sheet data appear acceptable? Is there something qualitative he's missing?

Further research could provide the answers. Screening the Bond Guide wouldn't be the end of the job, but by reducing the number of issues to be investigated in depth down to a manageable number, it certainly would make the total job a whole lot easier.

The final sections of this Guide also provide extensive information on more than 550 Canadian and other foreign issues and nearly 300 convertible bonds.

Foreign Bonds

Information on foreign bonds is arrayed in 19 columns like this:

1–5. The first five columns provide a description of the bond, the coupon rate, the maturity date, and interest payment dates.

6. The next column indicates the Standard & Poor's Rating. Debt obligations of issuers outside the United States and its territories are rated on the same basis as domestic corporate and municipal issues. The ratings measure the creditworthiness of the obligor but do not take into account currency exchange and related uncertainties.

7–9. The next three columns provide information relating to redemption provisions: callability, sinking fund, and refunding and other provisions.

10–12. In these three columns, you can determine who the underwriter of the issue was, the price at which the bonds initially were sold, and the year of the underwriting.

13. This column indicates the dollar amount of the issue outstanding (in millions).

14–18. Here's where you'll discover the bond's price history: the range from 1988 through 1998 in columns 14–15; the 1999 range in columns 16–17; and the closing price (or closing bid) in 1999 in column 18.

19. The last column provides a calculation of yield to maturity.

Convertible Bonds Statistical Analysis

Finally, the Guide provides considerable statistical data on nearly 300 different convertible bonds, arrayed in 24 columns. Here is what you'll be able to find out:

1–4. From these columns, you'll be able to determine the name of the issue, whether or not it's listed on the New York or American Stock Exchange, the coupon rate, interest payment dates, and maturity date.

5. The next column presents the Standard & Poor's rating, determined in the same manner as for all other bonds, as discussed earlier.

6. The next column indicates whether the bond is in bearer, registered, or book-entry form.

7. The seventh column shows the dollar amount of bonds outstanding (in millions).

8–11. The next four columns relate to the conversion feature. Column 8 indicates the year in which the conversion feature expires. Column 9 indicates the number of common shares into which each $1,000 bond is convertible. Column 10 is an alternative way of looking at the information in column 9: It shows the conversion price per common share. And column 11 indicates the annual dividend income which bondholders would receive, in lieu of interest income, if they were to convert their bonds into common stock (based upon current dividend rates).

12–14. The next three columns provide price information on the bond: the high and low prices at which the bond sold in 1999 (columns 12–13) and the last sale (or bid or asked price) for the bond in 1999.

15–16. The next two columns show current bond yields and yields to maturity based upon latest prices and bond coupon rates.

17–18. These two columns deal with the conversion value of the bond. Column 17 indicates the stock value of the bond, that is, the present market value of the total number of shares of common stock into which each $1,000 bond may be converted. Column 18 indicates the price at which the common stock would have to sell to equal the bond price.

19–20. The next two columns relate to the value of the underlying common stock into which the bond is convertible. Column 19 shows the common stock's last price (and indicates, incidentally, if the stock is traded on the New York or American Stock Exchange). Column 20 shows the stock's current price-earnings ratio, that is, the stock's latest price divided by the last 12 months earnings per share.

21–24. Finally, the last four columns provide earnings data on the underlying common stock: columns 22–24 indicate earnings per share in fiscal 1998, 1999, and the latest 12 months, respectively, while column 21 indicates the month in which the fiscal year ends.

How to Use the Convertible Bond Guide

The investor in convertible bonds typically seeks the best of two different worlds: (1) the assured income and more secure creditor position which attach to bond investment; and (2) the growth and inflation hedge characteristics which attach to equity ownership. In effect, he looks for the reward potential which attracts investors in common stocks while hoping to avoid at least some of the risk inherent in equity ownership.

Of course, in convertible bond investing, as in most human activities, "there ain't no such thing as a free lunch," and it is seldom that one can find the opportunity to acquire an attractive convertible bond selling at conversion value and providing a yield greater than that which would be available from the underlying common stock.

Nonetheless, there frequently are good opportunities among convertibles, even if there are no *perfect* investments. To find them, an investor should look for convertible bonds with the following two important characteristics:

1. They should be convertible into common stocks which themselves are attractive investments. (After all, what is the value of an option to acquire something you won't want?)

2. They should be selling at reasonable prices, that is, at prices which do not put too great a premium on the conversion privilege.

Turning first to the question of the underlying value of the common stock, the investor might peruse the last six columns on the convertible bond page. This would show whether or not the company was profitable, whether earnings rose or fell last year, the price at which the stock is selling, and whether that price represented a high or low multiple of earnings.

Such information is valuable but it is, admittedly, scanty, and the investor then would be well advised to turn to the data relating to the common stock in the Stock Guide section of this book. There he or she would be able to determine much more regarding the stock's earnings trend, its performance history, the company's capitalization, dividend-paying ability, and so on.

Once that is done and the investor decides that the stock is a possible candidate for investment, he or she must consider whether the company's convertible bond might provide a more attractive way to make that investment. In an ideal world, of course, the investor would be able to buy the bond at conversion value (rather than at a lesser value, because arbitrage activities would not allow a spread to persist), and the bond would be yielding more than the underlying common. But this is unlikely. More likely, he or she will have to pay *some* premium for the conversion privilege (although often a higher yield will be realized than could have been received on the common stock itself).

To evaluate this, the investor should investigate the column headed Stock Value of Bond. If the bond is not selling for too much more than this, then the conversion premium is small; but if the bond price is well above the stock value, then a big premium is being demanded for the conversion privilege. He or she could also get a feel for this by looking at the Conversion Parity column: If the stock is selling at close to its conversion price, then it wouldn't have too far to go before the bond would necessarily have to rise too; but if the gap is substantial, it would be possible that the stock could appreciate substantially while the bond did not.

Additionally, the investor ought to compare the bond's current yield and yield to maturity to the yield on the stock. If the yield on the bond is much higher than that on the stock, he or she might be willing to pay some significant premium for the convertible since, in effect, it would be possible to amortize the premium over time through the receipt of incremental interest income (relative to dividend income on the stock).

Summary

This is just a brief outline of what this Stock and Bond Guide contains and some of the ways in which it may be used by the individual investor. But the possibilities really are much greater than can be touched on in a short introduction. Thus, as you use this book, combining data from one section with information from another, and using it as the starting point for a more thorough investigation of the investment opportunities available to you, we have little doubt that you will discover a wealth of new uses and applications which will enable you to be an increasingly successful investor.

Good luck!

THE STOCK GUIDE

HOW TO USE THE STOCK GUIDE

It is necessary to read carefully the following instructions and those on Pages 4 and 5 to correctly interpret abbreviations and data in the Guide.

Column	Explanation
INDEX	The index numbers are a visual guide to the columnar data. Stocks with options are indicated by ●; stocks in the S&P Indices are flagged with: ¶ for the S&P 500; # for the S&P MidCap 400; ✣ for the S&P SmallCap 600.
Ticker Symbol	Ticker symbols are those of the exchange first listed in "Market" column. Supplementary symbols as would appear on the ticker tape after symbol, such as "Pr" for preferred stocks, etc., are indented.
STOCKS NAME OF ISSUE (Call Price of Pfd. Stocks) Market	Issues for which **STOCK REPORTS** are available are flagged with a ✔ Names shown in this column are not necessarily the exact corporate title of the company. Also, because of space limitation, the occasional use of abbreviations has been necessary. Where the name of the company is not followed by the designation of any particular issue of its stock, it is the common or capital stock that is referred to. The Call Price of preferred stocks is shown in parentheses after the name of the issue; the footnoted data indicates year in which the call price declines. Abbreviations of various provisions, etc. are shown on Page 5. Unit of Trading for stocks on the New York Stock Exchange and American Stock Exchange is indicated as follows: 10—10 shares; 25—25 shares; 50—50 shares; all others 100 shares. The markets for each issue are indicated by standard abbreviations, as shown on Page 5. The primary exchange is the first market shown.
Com Rank & Pfd. Rating	Standard & Poor's Rankings and Ratings are explained on pages xiv and xv. Directional arrows denote changes in the last 3 months.
Inst. Hold Shs Cos (1,000)	The number of financial institutions—banks, investment, insurance, college endowments and "13F" money managers—that hold this stock and the number of shares (000 omitted) held. See explanation on Page 4.
PRINCIPAL BUSINESS	This is the principal business of the company. Where a company is engaged in several lines of business every effort has been made to list that line from which it obtains the greatest proportion of its revenue. In addition, an indication of the company's rank in the industry is given where possible.
PRICE RANGE: Historical (High Low), Last Year (High Low), Current Year (High Low)	High and Low price ranges are for the calendar years indicated. Price ranges are not exclusive for the exchange on which the stock is currently traded, but are based on the best available data covering the period of the column head. Historical price ranges may be based on the best available high and low bid prices during the period, and should be viewed as reasonable approximations.
Month Sales in 100s	Trading volume is for the month indicated in hundreds of shares. NYSE & ASE companies are based on composite tape, all others are for primary exchange shown.
Last Month Prices (High Low Last)	Last sales are closing quotations for the month indicated. When the closing quotation is a bid price, a 'B' will follow the 'Last' price. In the case of Canadian issues, prices are quoted in Canadian dollars provided the first exchange listed is a Canadian exchange.
% Div. Yield	Yields are derived by dividing total indicated dividend rate by price of stock. Such rate is based on latest dividend paid including (†), or excluding (e) extras as indicated by footnote. Additional symbols used: (s) including stock; and (‡) including extras and stock.
P-E Ratio	P-E Ratio (Price-Earnings Ratio)—See explanation on Page 4.
EPS 5 Yr Growth	The EPS 5-Year Growth Rate is the annualized, per-year percentage growth rate for the preceding five-year period (through the trailing 12 months). The computation uses the least-squares method, which is suitable for this type of analysis. This growth rate should be used in conjunction with the company's actual earnings in order to determine the possibility of an erratic earnings history. Values between -49 and 99 are shown. NM=over 99, Neg=less than -49, ...= No data.
Total Return %	Total Return value represents the price appreciation of a stock with cash dividends reinvested on the pay date. Where an issue has had a stock distribution of another issue, no return has been calculated for the time period involved. The three values given are the annual compounded rate per year for the prior 12, 36 and 60 month period.

ALSO SEE OPPOSITE PAGE

HOW TO USE THE STOCK GUIDE

It is necessary to read carefully the following instructions and those on Pages 4 and 5 to correctly interpret abbreviations and data in the Guide.

INDEX	Cash Divs. Ea. Yr. Since	DIVIDENDS — Latest Payment: Per / $	Date	Ex. Div.	-$- This Year	Total Ind. rate	-$- Last Year	FINANCIAL POSITION — Mil. $: Cash & Curr. Equiv. / Assets / Curr. Liabs. / Balance Sheet Date	CAPITALIZATION — Long Term Debt Mil. $ / Shs. 000 Pfd. / Com.	Yrs. End / ANNUAL EARNINGS — -$- Per Share -$- Latest Five Years / Last 12 Mos.	INTERIM EARNINGS OR REMARKS — Period / $ - Per Share - $ Comparison	INDEX
Detaiils of stock dividends and stock splits, effected dring the past five years, are reported by symbol ◆ and footnotes which carry numerals corresponding to those in "Index" column. Adjustments have been made for all stock dividends.	One or more cash dividends have been paid each calendar year to date, without interruption, beginning with year listed.	Latest dividend payment, if at a regular established rate, it is so noted by M—Monthly, Q—Quarterly, S—Semi-Annually, or A—Annually.	Date of disbursement of the latest payment. If an extra or stock dividend also is being paid, it is so indicated by footnote.	The date shown is that on which the stock sells "ex-dividend"; that is the date on which it sells without the right to receive the latest declared dividend.	Payments made or declared payable thus far in the current calendar year, including both regular and extras, if any.	Indicated Rates are usually based on most recent quarterly or semi-annual payments, or on dividends paid during the last 12 months.	Total dividend payments, including extras if any, made in the preceding calendar year. For preferred dividend accumulations to latest payment due date, see "Financial Position" or Remarks column.	Cash & Equivalent, Current Assets, (includes cash/equiv) and Current Liabilities are given in millions of dollars (000,000) omitted, as $17.00—$17,000,000, 1.75—$1,750,000, 0.18—$175,000, etc. Where current balance sheet items are not of analytical significance, special calculations pertinent to the industry in which the company operates are presented, as tangible "Book Value per Share" for Banks, "Net Asset Value per Share" for Investment Trusts, and tangible "Equity per Share" (stockholders) for Insurance and Finance Companies. Intagibles such as goodwill, debt discount or pfd liquidating value have been deducted.	Long Term Debt is in millions of dollars, as 25.0—$25,000,000; 2.58—$2,580,000; 0.20—$200,000. It includes funded debt, long term bank loans, etc. Preferred and common stocks are in shares to the nearest thousands (000 omitted), as 150—150,000; 30—30,000; 2—1,500 (due to rounding). Outstanding shares exclude treasury stock. Figure shown under preferred shares column on company name line represents the combined number of preferred shares outstanding.	Earnings are presented on a "Diluted" basis (indicated with a footnote "V") as available by company, including discontinued operations but excluding extraordinary items. More detailed information on method of reporting and usage of standard footnotes can be found on Page 4. **Earnings for fiscal years ending March 31 or earlier are shown under the column of the preceding calendar year.** S&P Earnings Estimates are the final product of careful analysis by industry specialists of available relevant information. They are unofficial, however, and responsibility for their accuracy cannot be assumed. An arrow denotes changes in current estimate. Last 12 Mos. indicates 12 months earnings through period shown in interim earnings column, when available, or annual, if not.	Interim earnings are shown, when available, for the longest accounting interval since the last fiscal year-end. Also published in this column from time to time are references to SF provisions & divd arrears of pfds. See also Financial Position column for such notations.	The index numbers are a visual guide to the columnar data.

◆ **Stock Splits & Divs By Page Reference Index.**

ALSO SEE INSIDE FRONT COVER

UNIFORM FOOTNOTE EXPLANATIONS

To provide for consistency, eliminate repetition, and allow space for situations requiring further explanation, items recurring frequently that demand footnote explanation have been designated with specific symbols, which are explained on this page. Additional explanatory notations appear at the bottom of respective pages.

EARNINGS PER SHARE are presented on a "Diluted" basis (indicated with a footnote "v") as available by company, excluding extraordinary items. This policy change from old "Primary" earnings is reflective of all earnings reported after December 15, 1997 (FASB 128). Net asset values are shown for mutual funds. Foreign issues traded ADR are in dollars, converted at prevailing exchange rate. Specific footnotes used in earnings columns:

- ★ — Interim not comparable with annual earnings
- § — Net asset value
- △ — Excludes extraordinary income
- ▲ — Includes extraordinary income
- □ — Excludes extraordinary charge
- ■ — Includes extraordinary charge
- ∫ — Primary earnings(includes dilutive common equivalents)
- * — Before tax loss carryforward
- ± — Combined various classes
- △ — Comparison 1997-1998
- ® — Fully diluted earnings
- ⌶ — Partial year
- b — Fixed charges & Pfd. & Pref. dividends Times Earned
- c — Company only
- d — Deficit
- E — S&P estimate
- f — Net investment income
- j — Currency of country of origin
- k — Net gain from operations
- p — Pro forma reflecting acquisitions, mergers, etc.
- P — Preliminary
- v — Diluted

LAST 12 MOS. indicates earnings computed through period shown in interim earnings column, unless otherwise footnoted. Where no interim period has been reported, last annual is given.

CHANGES IN S&P EARNINGS ESTIMATES are denoted by arrows showing the direction of change, up or down (↑↓). The indicator appears in the issue of the Stock Guide for the month in which the change occurred.

P-E RATIO—Ratio is derived by dividing current price by estimated new year earnings or last 12 months earnings if no estimate is available.

INSTITUTIONAL HOLDINGS — Figures in these columns show how many financial institutions hold the stock in question, and how many shares (000 omitted) are so held. This data cover almost 4,500 institutions, including investment companies, banks, insurance companies, college endowments, "13F" money managers, obtained from Vickers Stock Research Corporation, 226 New York Ave., Huntington, NY 11743.

CHANGES IN S&P COMMON STOCK RANKINGS AND PREFERRED STOCK RATINGS are highlighted by arrows showing the direction of changed, up or down (↑↓). When a change is made, the indicator appears in the next three issues of the Stock Guide.

DIVIDENDS frequently include extra cash payments, stock, capital gains, payments on arrears for Pfd shares, or may be before deduction of foreign income taxes. These and other situations dictate the use of uniform footnotes, as follows:

- ⑦ — Previous record(if any) not available
- © — Dividend from capital gains
- ⊙ — Excludes circled c type
- ‡ — Includes extras and stock
- ◆ — Divd. converted to U.S. funds
- † — Includes extras
- a — Dividend paid a/c arrears
- e — Excluding extras
- g — In Canadian funds, subject to 15% non-residence tax
- h — Stock of another company
- s — Also stock
- t — Less tax country of origin
- y — Based on last year's payment

OTHERS used in various columns:

- ± — Combined various classes
- ★ — Giving effect to new financing
- p — Pro forma reflecting acquisitions, mergers, etc.

STOCKS WITH OPTIONS are indicated by ● in the index column preceding the ticker symbol. Numeric footnotes are used to show the exchanges on which the option trades and the cycle: 1—Jan, Apr, Jul, Oct; 2—Feb, May, Aug, Nov; 3—Mar, Jun, Sep, Dec.

STOCKS IN THE S&P Indices are flagged in the index column preceding the ticker symbol with: ¶ for the S&P 500; # for the MidCap400; ✣ for the SmallCap 600.

STOCK SPLITS & DIVIDENDS are indicated by ◆ in the "Index" column preceding the Dividend data. Details appear in footnotes which carry numerical symbols corresponding to those in the "Index" column. Adjustments of per share price ranges, dividends paid, book value, and earnings have been made for all stock splits and stock dividends.

ABBREVIATIONS USED

A — Asked Price
ADR — American Depositary Receipts
ADS — American Depositary Shares
B — Bid Price
Cl — Class
cm — Cumulative
Com — Common
Ctf — Certificates
Cv — Convertible
Dep — Depositary Receipts
Gtd — Guaranteed
L.P. — Ltd.Partnership
NC — Non-Callable
non-cm — Non-Cumulative
non-vtg — Non-Voting
Ord — Ordinary
Pfd — Preferred
Pr — Prior
Pref — Preference
Ptc — Participating
Red — Redeemable
Red restr — Redemption restriction
REIT — Real Estate Investment Trust
SBI — Shares of Beneficial Interest
Ser — Series
SF — Sinking Fund
shs — Shares
vtc — Voting Trust Certificates
Vtg — Voting

EXCHANGES REPRESENTED

Am — Amsterdam
AS — American
Au — Australian
B — Boston
BEL — Belgium
BSPA — Brazilian
Ch — Chicago
C — Cincinnati
CBOE — Chicago Board Options Exch
ECM — Emerging Company Marketplace
IDX — Index
Lo — London
MA — Madrid
ME — Mexican
Mo — Montreal
ML — Milan
NNM — Nasdaq National Market
NSC — Nasdaq SmallCap
NY — New York
P — Pacific
Pa — Paris
Ph — Philadelphia
Ro — Rome
To — Toronto
Vc — Vancouver

Unit of Trading for stocks on the New York Stock Exchange and the American Stock Exchange is indicated as follows: (10)-10 shares; (25)-25 shares; (50)-50 shares; all others 100 shares.

¶ S&P 500
\# MidCap 400
✣ SmallCap 600
• Options

Index	Ticker	Name of Issue (Call Price of Pfd. Stocks)	Market	Com. Rank. & Pfd. Rating	Inst. Hold Cos	Inst. Hold Shs. (000)	Principal Business	Price Range 1971-97 High	1971-97 Low	1998 High	1998 Low	1999 High	1999 Low	Dec. Sales in 100s	December, 1999 Last Sale Or Bid High	Low	Last	%Div Yield	P-E Ratio	EPS 5 Yr Growth	% Annualized Total Return 12 Mo	36 Mo	60 Mo
1	SPSC	S&P Super Composite 1500 Index	IDX	....[51]	..	...	U.S. equity perform indicator	212.05	111.17	261.73	193.53	315.02	254.39	....	315.02	291.50	308.89	1.1	28	...	20.3	24.6	...
2•[1]	SPIC	S&P 500 Index	IDX	....[52]	..	...	Broad large-cap indicator	986.25	60.96	1244.93	912.83	1473.13	1205.46	....	1473.13	1387.48	1469.25	1.1	29	6	21.0	27.6	28.6
3•[1]	SPMC	S&P MidCap 400 Index	IDX	....[53]	..	...	Broad mid-cap indicator	340.40	119.43	392.31	268.65	445.10	352.35	....	445.10	409.28	444.67	1.1	23	9	14.7	21.8	23.1
4•[1]	SPYC	S&P SmallCap 600 Index	IDX	....[54]	..	...	Broad small-cap indicator	192.98	92.45	206.31	126.15	197.80	154.14	....	197.80	180.70	197.79	0.7	22	10	12.4	11.7	17.0
5	AAM	Aames Financial	NY,P	NR	48	3659	Mortgage brokerage svcs	40¾	1 15/16	15 11/16	1	3¾	11/16	83347	1⅛	11/16	¾	...	d	Neg	–76.5	–68.3	–26.6
6	AAON	✓AAON Inc	NNM	B	9	1685	Mfr air-condition'g/heat'g eqp	16 9/16	7/16	11¾	6⅝	16⅜	8⅛	4047	14½	12¼	14⅜	...	11	17	54.4	43.4	6.2
✣7•[2]	AIR	✓AAR Corp	NY,Ch,Ph	B+	198	22466	Mkts aviation parts/service	27	13/16	32 7/16	17 7/16	24	14⅝	26850	20	15¼	17 15/16	1.9	11	30	–23.5	–2.3	17.3
✣8	RNT	✓Aaron Rents	NY	A–	87	10371	Rents & sells furniture	20¼	3½	24 5/16	11⅛	22¼	12⅞	6006	18¼	17 1/16	17¾	0.2	14	16	17.6	14.6	24.7
9	RNT.A	✓ Cl 'A'	NY	A–	23	917		18½	1⅝	26	10 9/16	20	11⅝	895	20	15⅝	18¼	0.2	15	16	22.5	9.5	23.7
10•[3]	AATT	Aavid Thermal Technologies	NNM	NR	74	5027	Thermal mgmt prds	38¼	6 3/16	36¾	8½	25	11⅜	10079	24¾	23	24 9/16	...	19	NM	45.6	31.7	...
11	ABAX	✓Abaxis Inc	NNM	NR	13	816	Dvlp stge:blood analyzer sys	17½	2 1/16	3¾	1⅛	8¼	1 7/16	21426	8¼	4¼	7¾	...	d	36	300	24.7	19.9
¶12•[4]	ABT	✓Abbott Laboratories	NY,B,C,Ch,P,Ph	A+	1610	845874	Diversified health care prod	34⅞	¼	50 1/16	32½	53 5/16	33	1169897	40 1/16	33	36 5/16	1.9	22	17	–24.7	14.5	19.5
13	ABCR	✓ABC-NACO Inc	NNM	NR	62	8706	Mfr orig'l&replace'mt rail prd	27⅝	12	20¼	8	21	8	10277	11 7/16	8	8¼	...	d	Neg	–32.3	–25.4	–17.8
#14•[5]	ANF	✓Abercrombie & Fitch Co'A'	NY,Ch,Ph	NR	537	89364	Retail casual apparel	18 1/16	6¼	36⅛	14 7/16	50¾	21	289845	32 9/16	23⅜	26 11/16	...	20	70	–24.6	47.9	...
15•[6]	ABY	✓Abitibi-Consolidated	NY,To,Mo,P,Vc	B–	139	103237	Newsprint,paper prods	28⅝	2 5/16	16 13/16	7⅝	13 13/16	7⅝	30949	12 3/16	10⅜	11⅞	◆2.3	d	Neg	32.6	–6.0	0.0
✣16•[7]	ABM	✓ABM Industries Inc	NY,B,Ch,P,Ph	A+	142	14333	Janitorial & building maint	31½	¾	37	25	34½	20	19205	22 11/16	20	20⅜	3.0	12	15	–40.0	5.2	14.2
17	ABN	✓ABN AMRO Holding ADS[58]	NY,Ph	NR	44	19311	Bank'g operations, Netherlands	24 7/16	18¼	27 9/16	14¼	25 13/16	19	9695	25 5/16	23⅝	25 5/16	2.1	16	10	19.6	...	...
18	BOUT	✓About.com Inc	NNM	NR	79	3390	Internet based news,info svcs	....	....	....	....	100	19½	61616	94¾	40½	89¾	...	d	...	...	...	...
19	ABRI	✓Abrams Industries	NNM	B	16	547	Construct'n/mfg, real estate	8⅜	¾	8 13/16	4⅛	6⅞	3	228	4½	3¾	4¼	3.8	9	NM	–12.0	–2.6	1.4
20	AKR	✓Acadia Realty Trust	NY,Ph,P	NR	27	4342	Real estate investment trust	20⅜	8¾	9 5/16	4¾	5¾	4⅜	5006	4 15/16	4⅜	4⅝	10.4	12	Neg	–5.6	–18.3	–12.1
21	ANA	✓Acadiana Bancshares	AS	NR	10	246	Savings bank, Louisiana	24¾	11⅜	25¾	14¾	20⅞	17⅜	84	20⅞	19⅝	19⅝	2.6	13	...	16.1	12.2	...
22	AIF	✓Acceptance Insur Cos	NY,B,Ch,P,Ph	B–	86	6596	Hldg co: prop & casualty insur	54 11/16	6	25¾	16¾	20 7/16	4⅞	22995	7	4⅞	5¾	...	d	Neg	–71.6	–33.7	–17.5
23•[6]	AKLM	✓Acclaim Entertainment	NNM	↑B–	147	28955	Dvlp video game cartridges	31¾	1 15/16	12 5/16	3⅝	13	4¾	260470	6 13/16	4¾	5⅛	...	9	–13	–58.2	16.4	–18.6
24•[8]	ACL	✓ACE Limited	NY,Ph	NR	365	187607	Provides liability insurance	33 11/16	6 15/16	43	24⅜	35¼	15½	185540	18½	16	16 11/16	2.6	7	NM	–50.7	–4.6	18.2
25	AK	✓Ackerley Group	NY	B–	79	10567	Brdcstg:pro basketball:adv	18½	⅝	24⅞	14⅝	20	11⅛	3914	18½	16	18⅛	0.1	59	81	–0.6	15.7	40.2
26	ACME	✓Acme Communications	NNM	NR	36	3578	Own,oper TV stations	....	....	....	....	39⅝	23	11290	37½	31½	33¼	...	..	...	...	...	...
27	ACEE	✓Acme Electric	NNM,P	B–	34	1293	Mfr pwr conversion eqp	38¾	⅜	6½	3 15/16	7⅛	4	3867	7	5 7/16	5¾	...	9	NM	21.1	–5.2	–14.7
28	ACU	✓Acme United	AS,Ch	C	11	666	Medic eq:shears,scissors	19 9/16	1⅜	6½	1⅞	2½	13/16	3526	1½	13/16	1⅛	...	14	53	–50.0	–41.1	–19.1
#29•[9]	ART	✓ACNielsen Corp	NY	NR	331	51981	Marketing/info analysis	24⅝	14	29⅝	19⅛	32¾	19⅞	47006	25⅜	21¾	24⅝	...	19	...	–12.8	17.3	...
30	ACRG	ACR Group	NSC	B–	3	390	Dstr heating & cooling equip	20 13/16	5/16	2 13/16	1	2⅜	1	4475	1 7/16	1⅛	1⅜	...	8	39	37.5	–9.8	12.9
31	ACRO	Acrodyne Communications	NSC	NR	6	271	Dvlp,mfr transmitter equip	7¾	1⅞	5¾	2⅝	4 11/16	1¼	14581	3¼	1⅞	2⅞	...	d	–45	–27.0	–21.5	...
32	AYS	✓ACSYS Inc	AS	NR	12	1082	Temporary staffing svcs	....	....	20½	2½	5⅝	1 5/16	8112	2	1 5/16	1 11/16	...	15	...	–56.5	...	...
33•[6]	ANET	✓ACT Networks	NNM	C	48	5453	Mfr data commun ntwk prd	48½	5¾	15¼	4¼	25⅝	4 15/16	71640	10½	6 9/16	9 5/16	...	d	Neg	–24.0	–36.6	...
34•[10]	ACTL	✓Actel Corp	NNM	NR	116	15809	Dvlp programmable gate arrays	29⅛	7¼	21½	7¼	24½	11	30904	24¼	21	24	...	34	81	20.0	0.3	23.8
✣35•[6]	ACTN	✓Action Performance Cos	NNM	NR	202	15220	Motorsports replicas/merch	38½	1½	39¼	17	48¼	9	225947	16 15/16	9	11½	...	7	80	–67.5	–13.9	35.7
36•[11]	IATV	✓ACTV Inc	NNM	C	53	6694	Interactive TV programming	9	⅝	4½	1⅜	51¾	3 13/16	211595	51¾	19	45 11/16	...	d	–9	1099	141	66.0
#37•[12]	ACN	✓Acuson Corp	NY,P	B–	131	14275	Medical ultrasound imaging	40	5	20 11/16	13 7/16	18 1/16	9 13/16	17100	12 11/16	10 5/16	12 9/16	...	20	41	–15.2	–19.8	–5.0
38	ACX	✓ACX Technologies	NY,Ch	NR	100	11505	Mfr packag'g ceramic,alum'n pd	31⅜	5⅜	25 13/16	9 5/16	16 11/16	7½	13222	11¼	9 3/16	10 11/16	...	7	47	...	...	...
#39	ACXM	✓Acxiom Corp	NNM	B	336	60136	Computer-based mkting svcs	25	1	31¼	16½	31	14 9/16	275523	24⅞	16¾	24	...	29	–33	–22.6	0.0	28.4
✣40•[9]	ADAC	✓ADAC Laboratories	NNM	↓B–	108	11774	Nuclear medicine comput sys	82⅛	1½	31⅝	16⅞	24½	5⅝	26672	12¾	9⅞	10¾	...	d	Neg	–46.2	–23.4	8.1
41	ADGO	✓Adams Golf	NNM	NR	20	455	Dgn/mfr golf clubs	....	....	18⅞	3	5 9/16	1 9/16	23646	2 3/16	1 9/16	1⅝	...	d	...	–60.3	...	...
42	AE	✓Adams Res & Energy	AS,B,Ch,Ph	B	17	782	Oil&gas explor,dev,prod'n	70½	1¾	14¾	5¼	11⅜	5 13/16	461	8⅞	8¼	8½	1.2	7	15	49.7	–10.4	–2.0
¶43•[13]	ADPT	✓Adaptec Inc	NNM	B+	391	84588	Mfr computer data flow sys	54¼	9/16	39½	7⅞	57¾	17 7/16	230778	56⅞	46⅛	49⅞	...	28	–40	184	7.6	33.4
✣44•[14]	ADAP	✓Adaptive Broadband	NNM	B	110	10359	Electr commun transmiss eq	39¾	¼	24¼	6¾	76⅝	8⅜	91098	76⅝	37⅞	73 13/16	...	63	NM	687	70.6	15.1
¶45•[8]	ADCT	✓ADC Telecommunications	NNM	B	500	105303	Telecommunications equip	45	1/64	42	15¾	75¾	34⅜	380702	75¾	52¾	72 9/16	...	..	15	109	32.6	42.2
46	ADEX	✓ADE Corp	NNM	NR	39	5556	Mfr semiconductor mfg eqp	45½	8¼	21	6½	19½	8 1/16	10065	19½	15½	16½	...	d	Neg	26.9	–1.0	...
47	ABIZ	✓Adelphia Business Solutions'A'	NNM	NR	88	10186	Telecommunication svcs	....	....	20⅛	3½	54⅞	8⅜	122791	54⅞	30½	48	...	d	...	217	...	...
48•[15]	ADLAC	✓Adelphia Communic'A'	NNM	C	246	37511	Cable TV operations in U.S.	28½	4½	48⅛	16⅜	87	44⅞	251813	67	56⅛	65⅝	...	..	...	43.4	125	50.1
49	ADFC	✓AdForce Inc	NNM	NR	48	2291	Internet ad services	....	....	....	....	74⅛	12 9/16	68718	74⅛	36¼	71⅜	...	d	...	...	...	...
50	ASF	✓Administaff Inc	NY,Ch,Ph	NR	55	4642	Professional employment svcs	26½	13¾	52 15/16	21⅝	34½	11⅛	19026	30¾	15	30¼	...	55	26	21.0	...	...
51	PVD	✓Administradora de Fondos ADS[66]	NY,Ph,P	NR	39	3078	Pension fund administ'r/Chile	28¾	12¾	19 7/16	11¾	24 7/16	12⅜	3048	21½	20 7/16	21½	4.1	14	7	72.8	12.7	9.9

Uniform Footnote Explanations-See Page 4. Other: [1]CBOE. [2]Ph:Cycle 1. [3]ASE,CBOE:Cycle 3. [4]ASE,CBOE,P,Ph:Cycle 2. [5]CBOE,P:Cycle 2. [6]CBOE:Cycle 1. [7]P:Cycle 3. [8]P:Cycle 2. [9]ASE:Cycle 2. [10]P,Ph:Cycle 3. [11]P,Ph:Cycle 2. [12]P:Cycle 1. [13]ASE,CBOE,P:Cycle 1. [14]ASE:Cycle 1. [15]CBOE,Ph:Cycle 1. [51]Inst. hold 56.78%(by $). [52]Inst. hold 56.27%(by $). [53]Inst. hold 62.45%(by $). [54]Inst. hold 59.91%(by $). [55]12 Mo Dec,'95. [56]12 Mo Dec'95. [57]Pfd in $M. [58]Ea ADS rep 1 ord 1.25NLG. [59]5 Mo Dec'96. [60]®$1.96,'96. [61]Stk dstr of Coorstek Inc. [62]Mar'98 & prior. [63]12 Mo Dec'98. [64]Fiscal Mar'98 & prior. [65]9 Mo Dec,'98. [66]Ea ADS rep 15 com,no par.

Index	Cash Divs. Ea.Yr. Since	Dividends: Latest Payment Period $	Date	Ex. Div.	Total $ So Far 1999	Ind. Rate	Paid 1998	Financial Position Mil-$: Cash& Equiv.	Curr. Assets	Curr. Liab.	Balance Sheet Date	Capitalization: Lg Trm Debt Mil-$	Shs. 000 Pfd.	Com.	Earnings $ Per Shr. Years End	1995	1996	1997	1998	1999	Last 12 Mos.	Interim Earnings Period	$ per Shr. 1998	1999	Index
1	....	**888 issues pay divs**			**3.44**	**3.48**	**3.314**	**Market Value $13498B**				....	...	...	**Dc**	**7.12**	**8.15**	**v8.36**	**8.00**	**E11.09↓**	**9.35**	**12 Mo Sep**		**9.35**	1
2	....	**402 issues pay divs**			**16.69**	**16.76**	**16.195**	**Market Value $12234B**				....	...	...	**Dc**	**33.96**	**38.73**	**v39.72**	**37.77**	**E51.47↓**	**43.96**	**12 Mo Sep**	**38.09**	**43.96**	2
3	....	**233 issues pay divs**			**4.74**	**4.95**	**4.168**	**Market Value $901B**				....	...	...	**Dc**	**10.77**	**11.10**	**v11.92**	**12.51**	**E19.29↓**	**15.53**	**12 Mo Sep**		**15.53**	3
4	....	**253 issues pay divs**			**1.39**	**1.37**	**1.403**	**Market Value $363B**				....	...	...	**Dc**	**4.00**	**5.34**	**v5.75**	**5.29**	**E8.82↓**	**6.18**	**12 Mo Sep**		**6.18**	4
5◆	1992	Div Omitted 11-17-98			...	Nil	0.099	Total Assets $869.94M			9-30-99	281	102	31032	Je	0.74	v1.14	v0.60	v1.23	vd8.00	d7.95	3 Mo Sep	vd0.07	vd0.02	5
6◆	....	None Paid			...	Nil	....	0.75	35.7	17.2	9-30-99	8.11	...	6259	Dc	v0.33	v0.33	v0.48	v0.82	....	1.32	9 Mo Sep	v0.59	v1.09	6
7◆	1973	Q0.08½	12-3-99	10-29	0.34	0.34	0.34	1.44	497	156	8-31-99	181	...	27401	My	0.44	v0.66	v0.91	v1.27	v1.49	1.58	6 Mo Nov	v0.70	v0.79	7
8◆	1993	S0.02	1-3-00	12-1	0.04	0.04	0.04	Total Assets $297.65M			9-30-99	67.8	...	±19909	Dc	v±[55]0.66	v±0.77	±v0.94	v±1.04	E1.27	1.22	9 Mo Sep	v±0.76	v±0.94	8
9◆	1986	S0.02	1-3-00	12-1	0.04	0.04	0.04	....	...	...		....	...	3830	Dc	v±[56]0.66	v±0.77	±v0.94	±v1.04	....	1.22	9 Mo Sep	v±0.76	v±0.94	9
10	....	None Since Public			...	Nil	....	23.8	87.1	42.3	10-02-99	9.28	...	9608	Dc	vd2.83	v□0.02	v0.98	v0.86	....	1.28	9 Mo Sep	v0.55	v0.97	10
11	....	None Since Public			...	Nil	....	3.24	9.58	6.10	9-30-99	0.60	4	13976	Mr	vd0.65	vd0.72	vd0.44	vd0.31	....	d0.25	6 Mo Sep	vd0.15	vd0.09	11
12◆	1926	Q0.17	2-15-00	1-12	0.66	0.68	0.58½	630	5878	4329	9-30-99	1336	...	p1537311	Dc	v0.71	v1.19	v1.34	v1.51	E1.68	1.56	9 Mo Sep	v1.10	v1.15	12
13	....	None Since Public			...	Nil	....	3.19	206	128	10-31-99	249	...	19061	Jl	□1.46	0.81	v□0.41	v□0.81	v□d0.33	d0.63	3 Mo Oct	v□0.20	vd0.10	13
14◆	....	None Since Public			...	Nil	....	140	251	158	10-30-99	....	...	102002	Ja	±pv0.17	±v0.27	±v0.47	v±0.96	E1.33	1.21	9 Mo Oct	v±0.40	v±0.65	14
15	1949	gQ0.10	1-4-00	12-14	g0.40	0.40	g0.40	23.0	1028	899	j6-30-99	2736	...	190569	Dc	3.24	pv1.37	vd0.62	vd0.16	....	jd1.47	9 Mo Sep	v0.22	vd1.09	15
16◆	1965	Q0.15½	2-3-00	1-12	0.56	0.62	0.48	2.05	353	176	7-31-99	24.9	[57]6	22341	Oc	0.92	v1.05	v1.22	v1.44	E1.65	1.59	9 Mo Jul	v0.95	v1.10	16
17◆	1992	0.262	9-17-99	8-23	0.526	0.53	0.544	Total Deposits $246279M			6-30-99	46153	362500	1438000	Dc	1.19	1.23	v1.29	v1.43	....	1.63	6 Mo Jun	v0.73	v0.93	17
18	....	None Since Public			...	Nil	....	47.8	54.6	15.3	9-30-99	0.59	...	★15348	Dc	...	...	...	vpd1.98	....	d4.92	9 Mo Sep	vpd1.22	vpd4.16	18
19	1960	Q0.04	1-4-00	12-8	0.18	0.16	0.18	3.62	47.2	33.9	10-31-99	63.4	...	2936	Ap	d0.11	vd0.10	v0.80	v1.02	vd0.23	0.45	6 Mo Oct	vd0.21	v0.47	19
20	1999	0.12	1-15-00	12-29	0.36	0.48	....	Total Assets $554.02M			9-30-99	309	...	25955	Dc	v0.44	v□d0.06	vd0.18	□vd0.86	....	0.39	9 Mo Sep	vd1.05	v0.20	20
21	1996	Q0.13	1-14-00	12-29	0.50	0.52	0.44	Total Deposits $214.29M			9-30-99	53.9	...	1500	Dc	pd0.29	‡v[59]0.07	v1.20	v1.17	....	1.46	9 Mo Sep	v0.84	v1.13	21
22	....	5%Stk	12-17-84	11-26	...	Nil	....	Total Assets $1338.34M			9-30-99	p94.9	...	14254	Dc	v0.28	v[60]1.99	v2.30	v0.37	....	d0.03	9 Mo Sep	v1.66	v□1.26	22
23	....	None Since Public			...	Nil	....	74.4	189	160	8-31-99	51.7	...	55525	Au	0.86	d4.47	vd3.21	v0.37	v0.57	0.57				23
24◆	1993	Q0.11	1-14-00	12-29	0.40	0.44	0.34	Total Assets $9668M			6-30-99	650	...	p217799	Sp	1.68	v2.00	v2.69	v2.96	....	2.24	9 Mo Jun	v2.93	v2.21	24
25◆	1995	A0.02	4-15-99	3-23	0.02	0.02	0.02	2.57	86.9	72.0	9-30-99	395	...	±34890	Dc	v±□d0.09	□±v0.51	±v1.04	v□0.75	....	0.31	9 Mo Sep	v±0.73	±□0.29	25
26	....	None Since Public			...	Nil	....	1.67	22.1	20.2	6-30-99	p198	...	★16750	Dc	...	...	...	vpd1.37	....	....	6 Mo Jun	n/a	vpd1.38	26
27	....	0.08	12-3-90	11-5	...	Nil	....	0.22	25.0	10.0	10-02-99	7.83	...	5074	Je	0.20	d0.06	v0.03	v0.50	v0.53	0.61	3 Mo Sep	v0.10	v0.18	27
28	....	0.05	3-5-93	2-8	...	Nil	....	....	17.4	16.3	9-30-99	0.36	...	3377	Dc	vd2.61	vd0.95	v0.06	vd0.49	....	0.08	9 Mo Sep	v0.03	v0.60	28
29	....	None Since Public			...	Nil	....	100	434	469	9-30-99	....	...	57912	Dc	pd4.09	vp0.28	v0.62	v0.96	E1.28	1.20	9 Mo Sep	v0.60	v□0.84	29
30	....	None Paid			...	Nil	....	0.13	37.3	20.3	8-31-99	16.6	...	10671	Fb	v0.02	v0.10	v0.08	v0.12	....	0.18	6 Mo Aug	v0.14	v0.20	30
31	....	None Since Public			...	Nil	....	1.80	10.1	5.68	9-30-99	0.02	7	6770	Dc	Nil	vd0.48	vd0.65	vd1.04	....	d1.19	9 Mo Sep	vd0.05	vd0.20	31
32	....	None Since Public			...	Nil	....	....	27.1	12.0	9-30-99	38.4	...	14503	Dc	...	pv0.14	vd0.18	vd0.09	....	0.11	9 Mo Sep	vd0.10	v0.10	32
33	....	None Since Public			...	Nil	....	46.7	74.5	5.84	9-30-99	....	...	10249	Je	0.24	d0.78	v0.15	vd2.11	vd0.32	d0.47	3 Mo Sep	vd0.10	vd0.25	33
34	....	None Since Public			...	Nil	....	84.1	152	55.7	10-03-99	....	...	21920	Dc	vd0.07	v0.70	v0.76	v0.68	....	0.70	9 Mo Sep	v0.50	v0.52	34
35◆	....	None Since Public			...	Nil	....	53.1	156	54.0	6-30-99	109	...	16925	Sp	0.27	v0.46	v0.69	v1.48	Pv1.65	1.65				35
36	....	None Paid			...	Nil	....	12.9	16.1	1.04	9-30-99	4.74	...	41971	Dc	v∆d0.67	vd0.75	vd0.61	vd0.98	....	d0.94	9 Mo Sep	vd0.51	vd0.47	36
37	....	None Since Public			...	Nil	....	16.1	303	109	10-02-99	74.2	...	26722	Dc	v0.25	vd0.39	v0.73	v0.73	E0.62↓	0.74	9 Mo Sep	v0.49	v0.50	37
38◆	....	h[61]....	12-31-99	12-29	h[61]...	Nil	....	42.3	414	606	9-30-99	665	...	28523	Dc	v0.87	vd3.23	v0.96	v0.73	....	1.56	9 Mo Sep	v0.36	v1.19	38
39◆	....	None Since Public			...	Nil	....	13.3	327	147	9-30-99	310	...	85927	Mr	0.35	v0.47	v0.60	vd0.22	....	0.84	6 Mo Sep	vd0.64	v0.42	39
40	....	0.12	10-7-96	9-25	...	Nil	....	4.87	133	119	7-04-99	....	...	20542	Sp	0.65	0.90	v0.69	v0.36	Pvd1.64	d1.64				40
41	....	None Since Public			...	Nil	....	30.4	66.0	5.99	9-30-99	....	...	22480	Dc	...	...	vpd0.37	v0.61	....	d0.50	9 Mo Sep	v0.83	vd0.28	41
42	1994	A0.10	12-15-99	11-29	0.10	0.10	0.10	38.2	208	192	9-30-99	6.00	...	4218	Dc	v0.29	v1.34	v1.36	v0.55	....	1.27	9 Mo Sep	v0.38	v1.10	42
43◆	....	None Since Public			...	Nil	....	703	935	163	9-30-99	230	...	102111	Mr	0.94	v0.93	v□1.54	vd0.12	E1.80	1.51	6 Mo Sep	vd0.75	v0.88	43
44	....	None Since Public			...	Nil	....	31.7	119	36.3	9-30-99	58.7	...	16065	Je	d0.51	0.72	vd3.48	vd0.47	v0.78	1.17	3 Mo Sep	vd0.65	vd0.26	44
45◆	....	None Since Public			...	Nil	....	82.8	713	293	7-31-99	12.3	...	p149596	Oc	0.47	v0.67	v0.81	v1.08	vP0.57	0.57				45
46	....	None Since Public			...	Nil	....	39.4	91.0	17.7	10-31-99	12.2	...	13390	Ap	v0.48	v0.98	v1.48	v0.61	vd1.89	d2.20	6 Mo Oct	vd0.67	vd0.98	46
47	....	None Since Public			...	Nil	....	126	195	49.9	9-30-99	1141	[57]236	★±69436	Dc	...	pd2.72	v[62]d2.33	v[63]d2.53	....	d3.17	9 Mo Sep	vd1.82	vd2.46	47
48	....	None Paid			...	Nil	....	Total Assets $4941.36M			9-30-99	3968	...	±★123856	Dc	±d4.56	±□d4.50	v□±[64]d6.07	Pv±[65]d3.63	....	....	9 Mo Sep	□vd4.12	v□d2.56	48
49	....	None Since Public			...	Nil	....	70.6	73.8	9.05	9-30-99	5.25	...	19988	Dc	...	...	...	vpd1.44	....	d1.40	9 Mo Sep	vpd1.05	vpd1.01	49
50	....	None Since Public			...	Nil	....	53.1	98.3	66.4	9-30-99	....	...	13425	Dc	v0.10	v0.24	v0.53	v0.62	....	0.55	9 Mo Sep	v0.35	v0.28	50
51	1995	0.114	12-27-99	12-6	1.051	0.89	0.903	0.80	12.0	18.9	12-31-97	....	...	16734	Dc	1.51	1.42	v1.51	....	....	1.51				51

◆Stock Splits & Divs By Line Reference Index [5]3-for-2,'96,'97. [6]10%,'95. [7]3-for-2,'98. [8]2-for-1,'96. [9]2-for-1 in Cl'B','96. [12]2-for-1,'98. [14]2-for-1,'99. [16]2-for-1,'96. [17]4-for-1,'97. [24]3-for-1,'98. [25]2-for-1,'96. [35]2-for-1,'96. [38]2-for-1,'95. [39]2-for-1,'95,'96. [43]2-for-1,'94,'96. [45]2-for-1,'95,'96.

¶ S&P 500
# MidCap 400
✣ SmallCap 600
• Options

Index	Ticker	Name of Issue (Call Price of Pfd. Stocks)	Market	Com. Rank. & Pfd. Rating	Inst. Hold Cos	Inst. Hold Shs. (000)	Principal Business	Price Range 1971-97 High	1971-97 Low	1998 High	1998 Low	1999 High	1999 Low	December, 1999 Dec. Sales in 100s	Last Sale Or Bid High	Last Sale Or Bid Low	Last Sale Or Bid Last	%Div Yield	P-E Ratio	EPS 5 Yr Growth	% Annualized Total Return 12 Mo	36 Mo	60 Mo
¶1•[1]	ADBE	✔Adobe Systems	NNM,Ch	B+	550	95904	Print,graphic software sys	37⅛	¾	25 15/16	11 13/16	79	18 13/16	589319	71⅞	59⅞	67¼	0.1	46	66	189	...	...
#2•[2]	ADTN	✔Adtran Inc	NNM	B	100	8174	Dgn/svc digital transmiss'n pd	75¼	9	34¾	15⅝	55½	15¾	70055	55½	37 5/16	51 7/16	...	41	13	181	7.4	17.6
3	ADG	✔Advanced Communications Grp	NY	NR	35	4050	Telecommunications svcs	....	....	17½	3	13 15/16	3 15/16	37703	13 15/16	7⅞	13⅝	...	d	...	225	...	...
4	AESP	✔Advanced Elect Support Pds	NSC,Ch,Ph	NR	..	...	Dgn/mfr computer network pds	9	2 15/16	4 11/16	1¼	3 7/16	1 5/16	4125	2 3/16	1½	1⅝	...	d	...	26.2	...	...
5•[3]	AEIS	✔Advanced Energy Indus	NNM	NR	128	10453	Semiconductor/thin film prd eq	38⅛	2⅞	25¾	5⅝	49⅞	17⅞	51060	49⅞	32½	49¼	...	..	Neg	97.0	109	...
6•[4]	AFCI	✔Advanced Fibre Communic	NNM	NR	177	44027	Dgn digital loop telecom sys	43¼	12½	44¾	4	47½	6¾	331271	47½	26½	44 11/16	...	..	NM	309	17.2	...
7	AMVC	✔Advanced Mach Vision Cl'A'	NSC	B–	8	2334	Mfr machine vision systems	6⅜	⅝	2½	1	1½	11/16	30370	1½	11/16	¾	...	78	NM	–34.2	–22.6	–2.2
8	AVM	✔Advanced Magnetics	AS	C	15	1576	Mfr medical diagnostic prd	31¼	2 13/16	14⅞	5	7¾	3	5502	4 11/16	3 9/16	4⅛	...	d	Neg	–43.6	–35.7	–22.1
9	ADMS	✔Advanced Marketing Svcs	NNM	B+	46	3457	Warehouse club book supplier	12	11/16	13 13/16	7 15/16	28⅝	10¾	6376	28⅝	20	28 7/16	0.3	18	30	256	89.4	62.9
10	ADMG	✔Advanced Matls Group	NSC	NR	5	121	Mfr ind'l use foam products	8¼	¼	3⅞	¾	1⅝	⅝	11805	1	¾	⅞	...	d	–7	–30.0	–14.0	5.0
¶11•[5]	AMD	✔Advanced Micro Dev	NY,B,Ch,Ph,P	C	310	67125	Major semiconductor mfr	48½	⅛	32¾	12¾	33	14 9/16	591155	31 15/16	26½	28 15/16	...	d	Neg	–0.2	4.0	3.1
12	API	✔Advanced Photonix'A'	AS	NR	3	175	Dvlp radiation detection prd	10	⅞	1¾	½	3½	7/16	34018	3½	⅝	2 13/16	...	d	99	309	1.5	10.0
13	ARTT	✔Advanced Radio Telecom	NNM	NR	50	8482	Dvp stg:microwave telecom	16½	5¾	17¾	1⅞	25	6	110297	25	12¾	24	...	d	...	220	28.7	...
14	ATPX	✔Advanced Technical Products	NNM	NR	14	1328	Mfr metal & fiber prod	18	3/16	15 5/16	5½	14¼	7½	1166	13 15/16	13¼	13 15/16	...	11	NM	52.7	146	86.1
✣15	ATIS	✔Advanced Tissue Sciences	NNM	C	78	8342	Human cell tissue technology	21¼	1¼	15⅝	1¾	6	1¾	131671	3⅝	2⅛	2½	...	d	1	–3.6	–36.1	–21.2
16•[6]	ADVNA	✔ADVANTA Corp Cl'A'	NNM	B+	94	7461	Mkts consumer fin'l prod	58¼	13/16	32¾	7⅛	23 15/16	9⅝	23087	20⅜	17	18¼	1.4	10	9	40.0	–23.5	–5.8
17•[7]	ADVNB	✔ Cl'B'	NNM	B+	44	6524		53⅝	7¾	31¼	5¼	19⅛	7⅝	16133	14⅞	12	14 1/16	2.1	7	9	30.3	–28.3	–9.5
18	AMM	✔Advantage Marketing Sys	AS	B–	1	3	Prd promotion/mkt svcs	11½	1	4 5/16	1½	5¾	1⅞	2997	5¾	4⅛	5 9/16	...	22	50	170	...	...
19	WS	RedmWrrt(Pur1com at$3.40)	AS	....	1	16		1	11/16	1¾	½	2⅛	⅝	1220	2⅛	1¼	1 15/16	...	..	...	...	...	...
20	WS.A	Wrrt(Pur1com at$3.40)	AS	....	..	...		¼	.01	¼	⅛	1½	⅛	90	1¼	⅞	1⅛B	...	..	...	...	...	...
21	ADV	✔Advest Group	NY,B,Ch,Ph	B	64	2339	Fin'l services hldg co	27½	1⅝	33¾	14⅛	26	16	3714	18⅜	16	18⅜	1.1	12	35	0.3	20.4	29.7
✣22•[8]	AD	✔ADVO Inc	NY,Ph	B	177	18554	Direct mail advertis'g svcs	27½	3	33⅝	19	27½	14 15/16	20846	23¾	20¼	23¾	...	13	18	–10.0	19.3	20.3
23	AER	✔Aegis Realty	AS	NR	16	729	Real estate investment trust	12	10	12⅝	8⅜	10⅜	8 9/16	5122	9 3/16	8 9/16	8 13/16	10.9	13	...	–0.8	...	...
24•[9]	AEG	✔AEGON N.V. Ord[56]	NY,Ph	NR	280	17719	Life/health ins, invest prods	45⅝	2½	125¾	44 7/16	130⅛	69⅝	24643	97⅛	89 3/16	95½	1.0	37	16	–20.8	47.2	53.6
25•[10]	AERL	✔Aerial Communications	NNM	NR	80	8157	Dvlp stge:licensee commun svcs	17¾	3⅞	9¼	1⅝	61⅝	5	54927	61⅝	38⅛	60⅞	...	d	Neg	936	95.7	...
26	ACY	✔Aerocentury Corp	AS	NR	2	197	Aircraft leasing svcs	....	....	9¾	4	10¼	5¼	598	6⅛	5¼	6⅛	...	7	...	–27.4	...	...
27	ARX	✔Aeroflex Inc	NY,Ch,Ph	B	131	13324	Mfr military/ind'l products	14⅛	1/16	15¼	6¼	22⅜	5 5/16	36055	10⅜	7⅝	10⅜	...	19	NM	–31.4	29.7	22.6
28	AIM	✔Aerosonic Corp	AS	B–	9	197	Mfg,overhaul aircraft instr	14⅞	1/16	20⅛	6½	15 5/16	10	1985	12	10	12	...	..	NM	11.0	41.3	45.0
29	ARVX	✔Aerovox Inc	NNM	C	22	1558	Mfr AC/DC pwr capacitors	12¼	2⅛	4¾	1⅜	3¼	2 1/16	3489	3¼	2½	3⅛	...	12	–15	47.1	–13.0	–16.3
¶30•[11]	AES	✔AES Corp	NY,Ch,Ph	B+	615	122107	Oper pwr generat'g facilities	49⅝	5 5/16	58	23	76⅜	32 13/16	164171	76⅜	57 9/16	74¾	...	56	17	57.8	47.6	50.3
31	Pr C	AES Tr III 6.75% Cv Pfd([57]52.11)	NY	B	..	...		....	....	....	....	62	47¼	9717	62	51	61⅝	5.5	..	...	...	...	...
32	Pr T	AES Tr I $2.6875[59]'TECONS'([60]50)	NY	↓B	11	479	Subsid of AES Corp	73⅝	48	85¼	40	105 5/16	53⅝	12033	105 5/16	81⅛	105	2.6	..	...	...	...	...
33	AETH	✔Aether Systems	NNM	NR	..	...	Wireless data services	....	....	....	....	89⅜	16	77281	78 7/16	50	71⅝	...	..	...	...	...	...
¶34•[7]	AET	✔Aetna Inc	NY,B,C,Ch,P,Ph	B	719	120100	Multiline insurance business	118⅛	10 1/16	89⅜	60 3/16	99⅞	46½	200800	60	49⅜	55 13/16	1.4	12	12	–28.3	–10.4	5.5
35	ATRM	✔Aetrium Inc	NNM	B–	22	3842	Mfr integrated circuit mfr eq	28¼	5 11/16	19	3⅝	12 7/16	5⅛	16706	7⅝	5¼	6⅝	...	d	Neg	–40.1	–20.8	–3.0
#36	ACS	✔Affiliated Computer Services'A'	NY,Ch,Ph	B+	302	39591	Information processing svc	32	8	45	22⅜	53	31¾	42989	46	35 13/16	46	...	26	21	2.2	15.6	33.7
37	AMG	✔Affiliated Managers Grp	NY	NR	163	20933	Investment advisory svcs	30 3/16	23½	39½	13⅜	40⅞	22	16698	40⅞	28 13/16	40 7/16	...	24	...	35.4	...	...
38	AFFX	✔Affymetrix Inc	NNM	NR	179	10905	Dvp stg: DNA probe arrays	49⅜	9	35¼	16⅛	195⅛	23¾	95550	195⅛	95	169 11/16	...	d	–6	596	103	...
¶39•[8]	AFL	✔AFLAC Inc	NY,B,Ch,P,Ph	A+	608	139497	Insurance & broadcasting	28 15/16	⅛	45 5/16	22 11/16	56¾	39	113023	50 7/16	43½	47 3/16	0.6	24	18	8.2	31.2	35.9
40	ATAC	✔Aftermarket Technology	NNM	NR	50	5622	Re-mfr auto drive train prd	27¼	13½	27¼	3⅞	12⅝	4½	18300	12⅝	7¾	11 15/16	...	d	...	51.6	–11.5	...
41	ASV	✔Ag Services of America	NY	B+	27	1573	Svcs to agricultural ind	20¼	3 11/16	18½	11⅝	18 1/16	13	1809	15	13⅞	14 15/16	...	10	19	4.4	–3.5	13.3
#42•[12]	AG	✔AGCO Corp	NY,Ph,P	NR	174	45096	Mfr/dstr farm equipment	36 5/16	1 11/16	30 15/16	5¼	14⅛	6	79713	14⅛	11¾	13 7/16	0.3	..	Neg	71.3	–22.1	–2.2
43	ACOM	AGENCY.com Ltd	NNM	NR	..	...	Internet professional svcs	....	....	....	....	98	26	235386	98	26	51	...	d	...	...	...	...
44•[13]	A	✔Agilent Technologies	NY	NR	..	...	Test,measur't inst/commun pd	....	....	....	....	80	30	478350	80	41	77 5/16	...	57	...	...	...	...
#45•[14]	ATG	✔AGL Resources	NY,P	B+	217	21494	Natural gas utility,Georgia	22	2⅛	23⅜	17 11/16	23⅜	15 9/16	28687	19	16 9/16	17	6.4	13	11	–21.9	–1.7	8.6
46•[15]	AEM	✔Agnico Eagle Mines[64]	NY,To,Ch,Mo,Ph,P	B–	77	20761	Silver & gold mining prop	34¼	1⅝	8	2⅝	9 11/16	4	22151	7 9/16	6½	7 7/16	0.3	..	...	81.1	–18.6	–6.3
47	ADC	✔Agree Realty	NY,Ch,P	NR	12	185	Real estate investment trust	22⅜	13½	22⅞	17⅛	19⅛	13⅜	5321	15	13⅜	14¼	12.9	9	4	–14.4	–4.0	8.6
48•[3]	ABTX	✔AgriBioTech Inc	NNM	NR	60	14015	Mfr chemical agricultural prd	17⅜	1¼	29½	7⅝	17⅞	1 15/16	156224	3¼	1 15/16	2⅜	...	d	–10	–81.6	2.8	...
✣49•[10]	AGX	✔Agribrands Intl	NY	NR	167	7068	Animal food/agricultural pds	....	....	43⅜	21⅜	53 9/16	30	5728	47 11/16	45 3/16	46	...	11	...	53.3	...	...
50	AGTO	✔Agritope Inc	NSC	NR	13	76	Agricultural biotech R&D	7½	6	8	⅞	4⅛	¾	7696	1 7/16	15/16	1⅛	...	d	...	–16.6	...	...
51•[3]	AGU	✔Agrium Inc	NY,Ch,Ph	NR	99	46744	Produces nitrate/fertilizer prd	16¼	8 11/16	15¾	7⅞	10⅝	7½	25472	8⅝	7½	7⅞	◆1.0	13	–15	–8.3	–16.1	...

Uniform Footnote Explanations-See Page 4. Other: [1]P:Cycle 1. [2]ASE,P,Ph:Cycle 2. [3]CBOE:Cycle 1. [4]ASE:Cycle 3. [5]ASE,CBOE,P,Ph:Cycle 1. [6]ASE,CBOE:Cycle 1. [7]ASE:Cycle 1. [8]ASE:Cycle 2. [9]CBOE,Ph:Cycle 1. [10]CBOE:Cycle 3. [11]CBOE,P:Cycle 2. [12]P:Cycle 2. [13]ASE,CBOE,Ph:Cycle 2. [14]P:Cycle 3. [15]ASE,CBOE,Mo,P:Cycle 2. [51]Spl div. [52]Pfd in $M. [53]If com exceeds $6.80 for 20 con trad days. [54]®$1.54,'97. [55]©$0.075,'99. [56]Amer Reg Ctf. [57]Fr 10-17-2002,scale to *50 in 2006. [58]AES Corp com. [59]Term Cv Sec Sr'A'. [60]Fr 3-31-2000(earlier for'Tax Event're-spec cond). [61]Into AES Corp com. [62]84% owned by Hewlett-Packard. [63]Subsid pfd in $M. [64]Canadian funds prior to'99. [65]12 Mo Jun,'95. [66]Pfd in M$.

Splits ◆ Index	Cash Divs. Ea.Yr. Since	Dividends: Latest Payment Period $	Date	Ex. Div.	Total $ So Far 1999	Ind. Rate	Paid 1998	Financial Position Mil-$ Cash& Equiv.	Curr. Assets	Curr. Liab.	Balance Sheet Date	Capitalization Lg Trm Debt Mil-$	Shs. 000 Pfd.	Com.	Earnings $ Per Shr. Years End	1995	1996	1997	1998	1999	Last 12 Mos.	Interim Earnings Period	$ per Shr. 1998	1999	Index
1◆	1988	Q0.02½	1-11-00	12-23	0.10	0.10	0.10	480	647	251	9-03-99	....	...	120198	Nv	0.63	1.02	v1.26	v0.78	E1.45	1.46	9 Mo Aug	v0.40	v1.09	1
2◆	....	None Since Public			...	Nil	....	60.3	191	27.9	9-30-99	50.0	...	39476	Dc	v0.80	v1.03	v1.03	v1.03	E1.26	1.11	9 Mo Sep	v0.80	v0.88	2
3	....	None Since Public			...	Nil	....	1.41	25.4	64.4	9-30-99	....	...	20084	Dc	...	p0.18	vpd0.28	vpd0.54	....	d3.25	9 Mo Sep	vd0.32	vd3.03	3
4	....	None Since Public			...	Nil	....	1.06	11.8	6.16	9-30-99	....	...	3230	Dc	p0.64	pv0.95	vp0.30	vd1.99	....	d1.21	9 Mo Sep	vd0.54	v0.24	4
5	....	None Since Public			...	Nil	....	28.5	95.9	21.8	9-30-99	0.20	...	★28191	Dc	v0.69	v0.24	v0.47	vd0.36	....	0.17	9 Mo Sep	vd0.22	v0.31	5
6◆	....	None Since Public			...	Nil	....	166	269	42.3	9-30-99	....	...	77813	Dc	pv0.05	pv0.11	v0.48	v0.34	....	0.23	9 Mo Sep	v0.27	v0.16	6
7	....	None Since Public			...	Nil	....	3.24	16.6	6.18	9-30-99	3.80	...	±12822	Dc	v±0.11	v±d0.49	v±0.49	v±0.18	....	0.01	9 Mo Sep	v±0.10	v±d0.07	7
8	....	None Since Public			...	Nil	....	21.9	22.8	0.76	9-30-99	....	...	6752	Sp	Δ0.32	vd1.44	vΔ0.32	vd0.93	vd0.66	d0.66				8
9◆	1998	Q0.02	3-15-00	2-28	0.057	0.08	0.05	42.7	284	214	10-02-99	....	...	8630	Mr	v0.73	v0.75	v1.07	v1.43	....	1.60	6 Mo Sep	v0.45	v0.62	9
10	....	None Since Public			...	Nil	....	0.40	9.11	8.20	8-29-99	0.84	...	8519	Nv	d0.32	Δ0.34	v0.27	vd0.27	....	d0.54	9 Mo Aug	v0.13	vd0.14	10
11	....	[51]0.01	5-24-95	4-27	...	Nil	....	377	1160	753	9-26-99	1441	...	147211	Dc	v1.57	d0.51	vd0.15	vd0.72	Ed3.11	d0.89	9 Mo Sep	vd0.88	d1.05	11
12	....	None Since Public			...	Nil	....	2.33	4.78	0.98	9-26-99	....	80	±10917	Mr	vd0.07	vd0.17	vNil	v0.04	....	d0.03	6 Mo Sep	v±0.02	v±d0.05	12
13	....	None Since Public			...	Nil	....	197	206	17.1	9-30-99	109	3138	27484	Dc	pvd0.54	p□vd3.80	vd3.23	vd1.89	....	d6.81	9 Mo Sep	vd1.33	vd6.25	13
14◆	....	None Since Public			...	Nil	....	0.25	80.2	52.2	10-01-99	24.4	1000	5297	Dc	Δ0.03	□0.07	v0.95	v1.01	....	1.29	9 Mo Sep	v0.60	v0.88	14
15	....	None Since Public			...	Nil	....	22.1	28.3	21.8	9-30-99	9.64	[52]5	56599	Dc	vd0.72	vd0.61	vd0.96	vd1.11	....	d0.51	9 Mo Sep	vd0.89	vd0.29	15
16	1989	Q0.063	12-16-99	11-26	0.252	0.25	0.252	Total Deposits $1704.18M			9-30-99	950	1	±28506	Dc	v±3.20	v±3.89	±v1.50	±v15.71	E1.87	2.13	9 Mo Sep	v±14.88	v±1.30	16
17	1992	Q0.076	12-16-99	11-26	0.302	0.30	0.302	....	...	...		....	...	18040	Dc	v±3.20	v±3.89	±v1.50	±v15.71	....	2.13	9 Mo Sep	v±14.88	v±1.30	17
18	....	None Paid			...	Nil	....	3.41	4.92	1.49	9-30-99	0.12	...	4143	Dc	v0.09	v0.26	v0.04	v0.09	....	0.25	9 Mo Sep	v0.05	v0.21	18
19	....	Terms&trad. basis should			be checked in detail			Wrrts expire 11-6-2002				....	...	1300	Dc	...	...	...	....	....	....	Callable at 25¢[53]			19
20	....	Terms&trad. basis should			be checked in detail			Wrrts expire 11-6-2002				....	...	1300	Dc	...	...	...	....	....	....	Callable at $0.0001			20
21	1997	Q0.05	1-17-00	12-29	0.19	0.20	0.16	Total Assets $1462.62M			9-30-99	48.9	...	8925	Sp	0.73	1.35	v[54]1.62	v1.92	v1.48	1.48				21
22	....	†10.00	3-5-96	3-6	...	Nil	....	9.34	118	120	9-25-99	177	...	20632	Sp	□1.14	0.13	v1.09	v1.55	v1.79	1.79				22
23	1998	Q0.24	2-14-00	12-29	[55]1.035	0.96	0.96	Total Assets $194M			9-30-99	59.0	...	8047	Dc	...	p0.72	pv0.75	v0.82	....	0.69	9 Mo Sep	v0.66	v0.53	23
24◆	1987	0.457	9-17-99	8-16	0.987	0.99	0.881	Equity per shr $15.79			12-31-98	2210	115000	p657425	Dc	1.57	1.76	v1.91	v2.35	....	2.62	9 Mo Sep	v1.67	v1.94	24
25	....	None Since Public			...	Nil	....	7.56	51.8	149	9-30-99	857	...	±94728	Dc	pvd0.11	vd0.56	vd3.45	vd4.71	....	d2.52	9 Mo Sep	vd3.56	vd1.37	25
26	....	None Since Public			...	Nil	....	Total Assets $51.41M			9-30-99	....	...	1607	Dc	...	pNil	n/a	v0.74	....	0.87	9 Mo Sep	v0.57	v0.70	26
27	....	5%Stk	5-27-86	5-7	...	Nil	....	0.91	82.9	29.8	9-30-99	23.1	...	18391	Je	0.57	d1.46	v0.34	v0.51	v0.51	0.54	3 Mo Sep	v0.12	v0.15	27
28	....	0.00¾	2-25-77	2-24	...	Nil	....	1.25	16.8	5.13	10-31-99	3.89	...	3986	Ja	vd0.50	v0.24	v0.31	v0.09	....	0.06	9 Mo Oct	v0.10	v0.07	28
29	....	None Since Public			...	Nil	....	1.23	38.5	20.4	10-02-99	18.7	...	6105	Dc	v0.30	vd0.25	vd2.15	v0.33	....	0.26	9 Mo Sep	v0.30	v0.23	29
30◆	....	3%Stk	3-28-94	3-4	...	Nil	....	751	1866	1878	9-30-99	7387	...	206384	Dc	v0.70	v0.81	v□1.11	vΔ1.67	E1.34	1.10	9 Mo Sep	vΔ1.18	v0.61	30
31	....	Plan qtly div			...	3.37	....	Cv into 0.7108 com[58]				....	9000	...	Dc	...	...	...	....	....	....				31
32	1997	Q0.672	12-31-99	12-28	2.687	2.688	2.68¾	Cv into 0.6906 com, $72.40[61]				....	5000	...	Dc	...	...	...	....	....	....	Mand red 3-31-2027			32
33	....	None Since Public			...	Nil	....	4.41	4.70	1.03	6-30-99	....	...	★26067	Dc	...	...	...	vpd0.31	....	....	6 Mo Jun	n/a	vpd0.20	33
34	1934	0.20	2-15-00	1-26	0.80	0.80	0.80	Total Assets $109463.00M			9-30-99	2958	11613	149674	Dc	v2.20	v4.72	v5.60	v5.41	E4.60	5.05	9 Mo Sep	v4.10	v3.74	34
35◆	....	None Since Public			...	Nil	....	15.0	35.6	7.14	9-30-99	....	...	9436	Dc	v0.46	v1.08	v0.14	vd1.00	....	d0.96	9 Mo Sep	vd0.81	vd0.77	35
36◆	....	None Since Public			...	Nil	....	12.4	439	239	9-30-99	422	...	±49343	Je	0.69	v0.85	v±1.05	±v1.11	v±1.66	1.76	3 Mo Sep	v±0.37	v±0.47	36
37	....	None Since Public			...	Nil	....	35.5	89.2	50.8	9-30-99	158	...	±23084	Dc	...	n/a	□vp0.41	v1.33	....	1.70	9 Mo Sep	v±0.85	v±1.22	37
38	....	None Since Public			...	Nil	....	23.0	256	20.9	9-30-99	★150	[52]50	25918	Dc	pvd0.84	vd0.62	vd0.99	vd1.11	Ed0.40	d1.14	9 Mo Sep	vd0.80	vd0.83	38
39◆	1973	Q0.07½	12-1-99	11-16	0.29	0.30	0.25¼	Total Assets $35225.00M			9-30-99	1079	...	266118	Dc	v1.17	v1.37	v2.08	v1.76	E2.00	2.12	9 Mo Sep	v1.34	v1.70	39
40	....	None Since Public			...	Nil	....	2.10	211	113	9-30-99	239	...	20417	Dc	pv0.65	v1.02	v□1.19	v□d0.36	....	d0.64	9 Mo Sep	v□0.61	v0.33	40
41◆	....	None Since Public			...	Nil	....	0.03	305	258	8-31-99	13.9	...	5234	Fb	v0.73	v0.84	v0.96	v1.20	....	1.43	9 Mo Nov	v1.13	v1.36	41
42◆	1992	Q0.01	12-1-99	11-10	0.04	0.04	0.04	18.0	1619	680	9-30-99	851	...	59546	Dc	v2.31	v□2.26	v□2.74	v0.99	ENil	d0.09	9 Mo Sep	v1.35	v0.27	42
43	....	None Since Public			...	Nil	....	3.12	42.3	23.1	p9-30-99	p47.5	...	★33748	Dc	...	...	...	vpd0.82	....	d0.86	9 Mo Sep	vpd0.56	vpd0.60	43
44	....	None Since Public			...	Nil	....	1080	3443	973	p7-31-99	....	...	[62]★452000	Oc	...	...	...	pv0.56	Pv1.35	1.35				44
45◆	1939	Q0.27	12-1-99	11-17	1.08	1.08	1.08	14.0	224	230	6-30-99	610	[63]74	56912	Sp	0.50	v1.36	v1.36	v1.41	vP1.29	1.29				45
46	1983	t0.02	2-25-00	2-14	t0.02	0.02	t0.02	117	164	20.4	j12-31-98	161	...	55253	Dc	v0.50	v0.01	vd2.83	vd0.23	....	....	9 Mo Sep	n/a	vd0.18	46
47	1994	Q0.46	1-6-00	12-21	1.84	1.84	1.84	Total Assets $152.92M			9-30-99	77.4	...	4365	Dc	v1.23	v1.41	v1.41	v□1.46	....	1.53	9 Mo Sep	v1.10	v1.17	47
48	....	None Since Public			...	Nil	....	1.40	140	135	9-30-99	11.4	...	49878	Je	[65]d0.35	vd0.76	vd0.38	v0.01	v□d1.12	d1.20	3 Mo Sep	v0.01	vd0.07	48
49	....	None Since Public			...	Nil	....	178	341	155	8-31-99	11.5	...	10379	Au	...	...	p0.77	v1.29	v4.11	4.11				49
50	....	None Since Public			...	Nil	....	1.66	7.29	3.96	6-30-99	0.01	214	4070	Sp	pd4.25	pvd0.93	pvd3.23	vd1.42	Pvd1.15	d1.15				50
51◆	1995	gS0.05½	1-10-00	12-21	g0.11	0.11	g0.11	146	743	453	6-30-99	477	[66]171	113378	Dc	v1.72	v1.07	v1.40	v0.94	....	0.59	9 Mo Sep	v0.79	v0.44	51

◆**Stock Splits & Divs By Line Reference Index** [1]2-for-1,'99. [2]2-for-1,'95. [6]2-for-1,'97. [9]3-for-2,'99:To split 3-for-2,ex Jan 19,'00. [14]No adj for reorg,'97. [24]5-for-2,'95:2-for-1,'98. [30]3-for-2,'94:2-for-1,'97. [35]3-for-2,'95. [36]2-for-1,'96. [39]3-for-2,'96:2-for-1,'98. [41]2-for-1,'94. [42]3-for-2,'94:2-for-1,'96. [45]2-for-1,'95. [51]3-for-1,'96.

¶ S&P 500
# MidCap 400
✤ SmallCap 600
• Options

Index	Ticker	Name of Issue (Call Price of Pfd. Stocks)	Market	Com. Rank. & Pfd. Rating	Inst. Hold Cos	Inst. Hold Shs. (000)	Principal Business	Price Range 1971-97 High	1971-97 Low	1998 High	1998 Low	1999 High	1999 Low	December, 1999 Dec. Sales in 100s	Last Sale Or Bid High	Low	Last	%Div Yield	P-E Ratio	EPS 5 Yr Growth	% Annualized Total Return 12 Mo	36 Mo	60 Mo
1•[1]	AHO	✔Ahold Ltd ADR[51]	NY,Ch	NR	75	4300	Retail food,Netherlands & U.S.	31 15/16	6⅜	37 5/16	24 13/16	41⅞	25⅝	17480	32⅜	25⅝	29 15/16	1.1	24	13	−18.1	15.1	26.
2	AHTC	AHT Corp	NNM	NR	23	2373	Med mgmt/clinical info sys	28¼	6⅝	18 13/16	1 1/16	6 15/16	1¾	33273	5⅝	3 7/16	4 11/16	. . .	d	−10	168	−27.9	. .
3	AGT	✔AimGlobal Technologies[52]	AS,To	NR	6	542	Mfr safety & detection prod	29 5/16	3/16	17 11/16	6⅝	13½	3⅛	16079	6 3/16	3⅛	5 15/16	. . .	. .	. . .	−47.0	−31.2	−10.
✤4•[2]	AEIC	✔Air Express Intl[54]	NNM,Ch	B+	204	26085	Air freight forwarding	37⅛	1/32	31⅜	14¼	32 11/16	14⅛	73832	32 7/16	31 3/16	32 5/16	0.9	22	11	50.2	15.7	20.
¶5•[3]	APD	✔Air Products & Chem	NY,B,Ch,P,Ph	A	715	178100	Indust'l gases,eq,chemicals	44 13/16	1¼	45 5/16	29	49¼	25 11/16	138903	33⅞	28½	33 9/16	2.1	16	15	−14.4	0.7	10.
#6•[4]	ABF	✔Airborne Freight	NY,B,Ch,P,Ph	B+	256	32559	Int'l air express/freight	37 3/16	11/16	42⅞	14¼	42 9/16	19½	98631	25⅜	20 5/16	22	0.7	11	37	−38.6	24.2	17.
7	BOS	✔Airboss of America	To	NR	. .	. . .	Mfr rubber-based products	8 13/16	⅜	3 13/16	1 13/16	5½	2 15/16	4838	4⅛	3½	3⅞	. . .	12	NM	21.9	26.3	17.
#8•[5]	ARG	✔Airgas Inc	NY,Ch,Ph,P	B	191	37841	Dstr ind'l,medical,splty gases	27⅛	⅞	18 13/16	8	14	7⅞	43081	9 15/16	8 1/16	9½	. . .	12	11	6.3	−24.4	−2.
9	PCSA	✔AirGate PCS	NNM	NR	48	3155	Dvp stg:wireless communic svcs	. . . .	. . . .	. . . .	. . . .	54¾	17	34537	54¾	39½	52¾	. . .	. .	. . .	. . .	. . .	. . .
10	FLY	✔Airlease Ltd L.P.	NY,Ch	NR	12	1222	Leases commercial aircraft	20¾	8⅛	14½	12⅜	12¾	10 11/16	2385	11⅞	10⅞	11⅛	14.7	11	−8	1.3	4.7	12.
11	ANCC	AirNet Communications	NNM	NR	. .	. . .	Telecom infrastructure prd	. . . .	. . . .	. . . .	. . . .	45	14	285734	45	14	36⅜	. . .	. .	. . .	. . .	. . .	. . .
12	ANS	✔AirNet Systems	NY	NR	46	4763	Integrated air transport svcs	27 1/16	10¾	29½	11 11/16	14⅜	4⅝	6405	8	4⅝	7 1/16	. . .	21	. . .	−50.9	−21.8	. .
13	ASY	✔Airport Systems Intl	AS	NR	4	874	Mfr radio navigation equip	11⅛	2¾	10	1¾	4⅛	1½	1083	2⅝	2	2⅛	. . .	d	Neg	15.2	−25.4	−16.
14•[6]	AAIR	✔AirTran Hldgs	NNM	NR	86	9329	Oper low fare airline	34¾	3⅛	9 7/16	2⅛	7¼	2¾	113604	5	3½	4½	. . .	7	Neg	72.6	−11.0	−2.
#15•[6]	AKS	✔AK Steel Holding	NY,P	NR	285	54893	Integrated steel producer	24	9⅝	23¾	13⅝	29⅝	13¾	135625	19 1/16	15½	18⅞	2.6	27	−23	−17.7	0.7	6.
16	Pr	$3.625cmCv[57]'B'Pfd(51.45)	NY	B–	14	1261		65¼	39	54¾	39⅛	54 7/16	42 11/16	96	53⅝	52 3/16	128B	2.8	. .	. . .	. . .	. . .	. . .
17	AKAM	✔Akamai Technologies	NNM	NR	. .	. . .	Internet speed&reliability svcs	. . . .	. . . .	. . . .	. . . .	344⅞	26	93702	344⅞	201	327⅝	. . .	. .	. . .	. . .	. . .	. . .
18	AKRN	✔Akorn Inc	NNM	B–	22	2589	Dstr pharmaceutical products	4½	1⅛	9 3/16	2⅝	5 9/16	3½	14577	4⅞	3⅞	4⅞	. . .	14	23	0.0	36.0	8.
19•[7]	AKZOY	✔Akzo Nobel N.V. ADS[61]	NNM	NR	106	12946	Chemical,fiber,hlthcare prod	47⅜	9 7/16	63 11/16	31 9/16	52¼	33⅝	28574	52¼	43½	49¾	1.8	22	−2	14.2	16.8	14.
20	ALQ	Alabama Pwr 6.75% Sr Notes'J'	NY	. . . .[62]	. .	. . .	Electric utility, Georgia	. . . .	. . . .	. . . .	. . . .	24½	19⅞	4625	21¾	19⅞	20¼	8.3	. .	. . .	. . .	. . .	. . .
21	ACA	Alabama Pwr 7.00% Sr Notes	NY	. . . .[64]	5	181	Electric utility, Georgia	. . . .	. . . .	25¾	23⅞	25 7/16	19¼	5409	21 5/16	19¼	19 13/16	8.8	. .	. . .	−15.0	. . .	. .
22	ABJ	Alabama Pwr 7.00% Sr Notes'C'	NY	. . . .[64]	1	6	Electric utility, Georgia	. . . .	. . . .	25¾	24 1/16	25½	19⅛	4957	21½	19⅛	20	8.8	. .	. . .	−14.2	. . .	. .
23	ALZ	Alabama Pwr 7.125% Sr Notes	NY	. . . .[65]	2	29	Electric utility, Georgia	25⅛	24¾	25 11/16	24	25¾	20	3887	21 9/16	20	20¼	8.8	. .	. . .	−13.7	. . .	. .
24	ALG	✔Alamo Group	NY	B	40	3960	Mfr mowing/grounds mainten eq	23¾	11⅜	21 13/16	10⅝	12⅝	6⅞	5002	10¼	8¾	10¼	2.3	. .	−36	−7.3	−13.4	−6.
25	AMI	✔Alaris Medical	AS,Ch,P	C	32	3422	Mfr infusion pumps/drug R&D	19¼	⅜	7½	3	6½	1⅜	14987	2½	1⅜	1⅞	. . .	d	Neg	−68.1	−20.6	−1.
#26•[8]	ALK	✔Alaska Air Group	NY,B,Ch,P,Ph	B–	304	18907	Scheduled/charter airline sv	40⅛	1¾	62 9/16	26	54 11/16	33 3/16	60493	38 9/16	33 3/16	35⅛	. . .	7	35	−20.6	18.7	18.
27	ALSK	✔Alaska Communic Sys Grp	NNM	NR	. .	. . .	Telecommun svc,Alaska	. . . .	. . . .	. . . .	. . . .	16	12	61765	14⅜	12	12⅜	. . .	. .	. . .	. . .	. . .	. . .
#28	AIN	✔Albany Intl 'A'	NY,Ph,P	B	143	21914	Mfr paper machine belt prod	26⅛	7⅝	28¾	15 7/16	24½	13½	12513	16 9/16	14	15½	s. . .	16	2	−14.9	−7.8	−0.
#29•[9]	ALB	✔Albemarle Corp	NY,Ph,P	NR	154	12482	Mfg ind'l chemicals	27¼	12¼	26 3/16	16	25 5/16	16⅝	9825	19½	17 5/16	19 3/16	2.1	11	14	−17.7	3.6	8.
30	AOG	✔Alberta Energy	NY,Ch,To	B	102	40554	Oil&gas explor, dvlp prod'n	25⅞	15	26¼	17⅜	32¾	20 5/16	3984	32¾	26⅝	31 5/16	◆0.9	25	−18	47.4	10.9	. .
¶31•[10]	ACV	✔Alberto-Culver Cl'B'	NY,B,Ch,Ph,P	†A+	219	11831	Hair care,health,beauty aids,	32 9/16	5/16	32 7/16	19¾	27⅞	21 9/16	14714	27⅝	25 3/16	25 13/16	1.0	17	14	−2.3	3.6	14.
32•[7]	ACV.A	✔ Class'A'(1/10 vtg)	NY,Ph	†A+	87	17403	oper beauty supply stores	27⅞	3 3/16	28½	17 15/16	26⅛	19 7/16	8717	23⅝	21¾	21¾	1.2	14	14	−12.9	3.1	13.
¶33•[3]	ABS	✔Albertson's, Inc	NY,B,Ch,P	A+	960	276865	Food supermkts: food-drug	48⅝	5/16	67⅛	44	66⅝	29	482757	33½	29	32¼	2.2	21	−2	−48.6	−1.8	3.
¶34•[11]	AL	✔Alcan Aluminium Ltd	[12]NY,To,B,C,Ch,Mo,P,Ph	B–	422	126395	Aluminum mfr/finished prod	40 5/16	3 5/16	34½	18 11/16	42	22 15/16	257391	42	33⅞	41⅜	1.5	24	22	55.8	9.3	12.
35•[6]	ALA	✔Alcatel ADS[66]	NY,Ph,P	B	168	73463	Commun sys, energy, transp'tn	30¾	14¼	47⅛	15 15/16	46 1/16	20⅜	135571	46 1/16	37½	45	0.8	45	NM	86.9	42.9	23.
36	ALCD	✔Alcide Corp	NNM	B	23	380	R&D microbiocidal chemistry	82½	3⅛	65	12 1/16	25½	10½	2318	14¾	11½	12¾	. . .	d	Neg	−15.7	−15.0	13.
¶37•[10]	AA	✔Alcoa Inc	NY,B,C,Ch,P,Ph	B	1033	311707	Leading U.S. aluminum prod'r	44 13/16	3	40⅝	29	83⅜	35 15/16	436843	83⅜	65 9/16	83	e1.0	31	13	127	40.0	33.
#38•[3]	ALEX	✔Alexander & Baldwin	NNM	B	185	25742	Shipping,R.E.,agribusiness	39½	1 11/16	31⅛	18 13/16	27⅛	18⅝	30238	23⅜	21⅜	22 13/16	3.9	13	−11	2.1	0.6	4.
39	ALX	✔Alexander's, Inc	NY,B,Ch,Ph	NR	48	1610	Real estate investment trust	92⅜	2	95¼	72⅛	84⅛	66	256	79½	73⅝	79	. . .	43	−48	1.0	−0.1	8.
40	ARE	✔Alexandria R.E. Equities	NY	NR	108	10892	Real estate investment trust	31⅞	20	34 9/16	25 3/16	33	24⅞	7418	32	27⅞	31 13/16	5.4	21	. . .	8.9	. . .	. .
41	ALFA	✔Alfa Corp	NNM	A–	57	3383	Insurance holding company	18¼	7/16	24⅜	16	25⅜	14 13/16	5539	18⅛	14 13/16	16 5/16	2.9	11	20	−30.9	11.8	11.
42	ALGO	✔Algos Pharmaceutical	NNM	NR	55	4250	Dvp stge:pain mgmt pds	33	9⅞	39½	18½	33⅝	7⅝	28844	15½	9⅛	11	. . .	d	. . .	−57.7	−0.7	. .
43	ALCO	Alico, Inc	NNM	B	32	1630	Citrus fruit: cattle-Florida	39	1½	23½	16	19	13¾	1664	18⅛	15⅜	16¾	1.8	29	−8	−5.0	−1.3	1.
44	ALKS	✔Alkermes Inc	NNM	NR	206	22838	Drug delivery systems R&D	29⅝	1⅞	27⅝	10⅛	57½	21⅝	67351	57½	39¾	49⅛	. . .	d	−16	121	28.3	87.
45•[13]	ALLR	✔Allaire Corp	NNM	NR	93	7353	Computer software & svcs	. . . .	. . . .	. . . .	. . . .	188¼	20	54067	188¼	131⅞	146 5/16	. . .	88	. . .	. . .	. . .	. . .
46	Y	✔Alleghany Corp	NY,B,Ch,Ph	B+	125	4786	Prop&casualty insur:fin'l svcs	284 5/16	4¾	371 1/16	168⅝	206⅝	173½	627	206⅝	184 1/16	185½	s. . .	13	−2	2.7	−1.6	7.
#47•[9]	AYE	✔Allegheny Energy	NY,B,C,Ch,P,Ph	A–	355	51144	Electric utility hldg co	32⅝	5⅞	34 15/16	26⅝	35 3/16	26 3/16	54515	29 5/16	26 3/16	26 15/16	6.4	10	5	−16.3	2.1	10.
¶48•[10]	ATI	✔Allegheny Technologies	NY,Ph	NR	382	52221	Spec metals	65¾	39¾	59⅛	28	48⅜	20¼	115666	25 3/16	20¼	22 7/16	5.7	7	51	. . .	. . .	. .
49•[3]	ALGX	✔Allegiance Telecom	NNM	NR	169	35863	Telecommunication svcs	. . . .	. . . .	15 11/16	5	92⅝	11 9/16	47533	92⅝	62 15/16	92¼	. . .	. .	. . .	661	. . .	. .
✤50•[1]	ALN	✔Allen Telecom	NY,B,Ch,P,Ph	B	125	21798	Elec telecom equip	39⅜	15/16	21⅛	4 11/16	12⅜	4½	20229	12⅜	8¾	11 9/16	. . .	. .	Neg	72.9	−19.6	. .
¶51•[5]	AGN	✔Allergan, Inc	NY,P	B+	530	115068	Ophthalmic/dermatologic pd	21	6⅛	33¼	15⅞	57 13/16	31 11/16	181603	52	40 9/16	49¾	0.6	40	Neg	. . .	. . .	. . .

Uniform Footnote Explanations-See Page 4. Other: [1]ASE:Cycle 3. [2]P:Cycle 2. [3]Ph:Cycle 3. [4]CBOE:Cycle 2. [5]Ph:Cycle 1. [6]CBOE:Cycle 3. [7]ASE,CBOE:Cycle 1. [8]ASE:Cycle 1. [9]P:Cycle 3. [10]CBOE:Cycle 1. [11]ASE:Cycle 3,To:Cycle 2. [12]Vc [13]CBOE,P:Cycle 1. [51]Each ADR rep 1 com,NLG 1.25. [52]Mar'99 & prior pricing in $Cdn. [53]13 Mo Mar'98. [54]Deutsche Post AG plan acq,$33. [55]Excl shs held in trust. [56]Fiscal Sep'96 & prior. [57]Thru 10-14-99,scale to $50 in 2002. [58]4 Mo Dec,'98. [59]Fiscal Jun'95 & prior. [60]12 Mo Dec:Fiscal Jun'96 earned $0.05. [61]Each ADS rep 1 com shr, NLG 5. [62]Rated'AAA'by S&P. [63]Total issue amt in $M. [64]Rated 'A' by S&P. [65]Rated 'A' by S & P. [66]Ea ADS rep 0.2 ord FF40. [67]Stk dstr of Chicago Title Corp. [68]Excl subsid pfd. [69]Stk dstr of Teledyne Tech & Water Pik Tech. [70]8 Mo Dec'97. [71]Stk dstr of TransPro Inc. [72]Stk dstr of Allergan Specialty Therapeutics.

Splits ◆ Index	Cash Divs. Ea. Yr. Since	Dividends: Latest Payment Period $	Date	Ex. Div.	Total $ So Far 1999	Ind. Rate	Paid 1998	Financial Position Mil-$ Cash& Equiv.	Curr. Assets	Curr. Liab.	Balance Sheet Date	Capitalization Lg Trm Debt Mil-$	Shs. 000 Pfd.	Com.	Earnings $ Per Shr. Years End	1995	1996	1997	1998	1999	Last 12 Mos.	Interim Earnings Period	$ per Shr. 1998	1999	Index
1◆	1983	0.11	10-7-99	9-3	0.32	0.32	0.298	1145	8869	10153	j1-03-99	8646	...	628097	Dc	0.78	0.85	v0.90	v1.09	....	1.24	9 Mo Sep	v0.69	v0.84	1
2	....	None Since Public			...	Nil	....	4.20	5.08	5.37	9-30-99	....	...	10711	Dc	vd1.67	vd0.28	v0.81	vd7.46	....	d5.33	9 Mo Sep	vd2.99	vd0.86	2
3	....	None Paid			...	Nil	....	1.71	40.9	20.5	j6-30-99	4.99	...	11088	Mr	...	...	v[53]0.45	n/a	....	....	3 Mo Jun	vNil	vd0.26	3
4◆	1991	Q0.07	10-29-99	10-6	0.26	0.28	0.22	46.8	457	323	9-30-99	51.3	...	33598	Dc	v0.99	v1.16	v1.41	v1.26	E1.50	1.37	9 Mo Sep	v1.04	v1.15	4
5◆	1954	Q0.18	2-14-00	12-31	0.70	0.72	0.64	61.6	1782	1858	9-30-99	1462	...	[55]229305	Sp	1.65	1.87	v1.91	v2.48	v2.09	2.09				5
6◆	1974	Q0.04	12-7-99	11-19	0.16	0.16	0.15¾	20.6	451	294	9-30-99	299	...	48642	Dc	v0.55	v0.64	v2.44	v2.72	E2.00↓	2.28	9 Mo Sep	v1.94	v1.50	6
7◆	....	None Paid			...	Nil	....	....	42.9	36.0	j9-30-99	26.0	...	22631	Dc	d0.24	v0.08	v0.20	v0.26	....	j0.32	9 Mo Sep	v0.20	v0.26	7
8◆	....	None Since Public			...	Nil	....	....	386	187	9-30-99	835	...	70210	Mr	v0.60	v0.34	v0.57	v0.72	....	0.82	6 Mo Sep	v0.30	v□0.40	8
9	....	None Since Public			...	Nil	....	2.91	3.66	12.5	6-30-99	p154	...	★10826	Dc	...	...	...	vd1.54	....	....	6 Mo Jun	n/a	vd2.21	9
10	1987	Q0.41	2-15-00	12-29	1.64	1.64	1.68	Total Assets $70.20M			9-30-99	11.7	...	4625	Dc	v1.46	v1.85	v1.17	v1.04	....	1.00	9 Mo Sep	v0.79	v0.75	10
11	....	None Since Public			...	Nil	....	27.0	44.2	14.0	9-30-99	0.23	p...	★22224	Dc	...	...	...	vpd1.44	....	....	9 Mo Sep	n/a	vpd1.38	11
12	....	None Since Public			...	Nil	....	1.09	31.0	11.2	9-30-99	36.4	...	11411	Dc	p0.74	vp[56]d0.23	v1.04	v0.46	....	0.33	9 Mo Sep	v0.56	v□0.43	12
13	....	None Since Public			...	Nil	....	0.19	11.7	5.14	10-31-99	1.16	...	2231	Ap	0.50	d0.10	v0.25	v0.40	vd1.59	d1.22	6 Mo Oct	vd0.31	v0.06	13
14◆	....	None Since Public			...	Nil	....	55.1	117	107	9-30-99	266	...	65172	Dc	v1.13	vd0.76	vd1.72	vd0.63	E0.65	0.13	9 Mo Sep	vd0.16	v0.60	14
15◆	1995	Q0.12½	11-17-99	10-19	0.50	0.50	0.50	203	1568	1112	9-30-99	1304	p2700	103057	Dc	4.78	v2.35	v2.43	v1.92	E0.70	1.46	9 Mo Sep	v∆1.22	v□0.76	15
16	1992	Q0.90⅝	12-31-99	11-26	3.62½	3.625	3.62½	Cv into 6.78 com				....	2700	...	Dc	b1.11	...	...	....	....	....				16
17	....	None Since Public			...	Nil	....	92.0	93.6	9.74	9-30-99	12.3	p...	★91442	Dc	...	...	...	p[58]d0.05	....	....	9 Mo Sep	n/a	vpd0.59	17
18	....	0.017	7-1-91	5-24	...	Nil	....	0.71	32.0	14.0	9-30-99	24.7	...	18413	Dc	[59]0.15	v[60]Nil	v0.11	v0.25	....	0.34	9 Mo Sep	v0.17	v0.26	18
19◆	1989	0.263	11-22-99	10-25	0.882	0.88	0.883	1180	12450	11409	j12-31-98	5888	...	285000	Dc	∆2.87	v2.67	v2.83	v2.36	....	2.31	6 Mo Jun	v1.45	v1.40	19
20	1999	Q0.422	12-31-99	12-14	1.003	1.688	....	Co option redm 5-26-2004 at $25				[63]200	...	...	Dc	...	...	...	....	....	....	Mature 6-30-2039			20
21	1998	Q0.43¾	12-31-99	12-14	1.75	1.75	1.483	Co option redm fr 2-26-2003 at $25				[63]200	...	...	Dc	...	...	...	....	....	....	Mature 12-31-2047			21
22	1998	Q0.43¾	12-31-99	12-14	1.75	1.75	0.763	Co option redm fr 4-23-2003 at $25				★190	...	...	Dc	...	...	...	....	....	....	Mature 3-31-2048			22
23	1997	Q0.445	12-31-99	12-14	1.336	1.781	1.781	Co option redm fr 12-1-2002 at $25				194	...	...	Dc	...	...	...	....	....	....	Mature 12-1-2047			23
24	1993	Q0.06	11-3-99	10-14	0.34	0.24	0.43	5.89	102	22.0	9-30-99	19.7	...	9736	Dc	v1.35	v0.91	v1.41	v0.42	....	0.10	9 Mo Sep	v0.87	v0.55	24
25	....	None Since Public			...	Nil	....	22.2	209	78.5	9-30-99	527	...	59297	Dc	∆v0.38	v□d3.27	vd0.16	vd0.42	....	d0.18	9 Mo Sep	vd0.42	vd0.18	25
26	....	0.05	11-5-92	10-8	...	Nil	....	246	495	600	9-30-99	154	...	26403	Dc	1.28	v2.05	v3.53	v4.81	E5.20↓	5.45	9 Mo Sep	v3.79	v4.43	26
27	....	None Since Public			...	Nil	....	113	175	41.9	9-30-99	608	...	★31829	Dc	...	...	...	vd0.54	....	....	9 Mo Sep	n/a	vpd0.48	27
28◆	1987	2%Stk	1-12-00	12-8	2%Stk	Stk	s0.20	24.9	521	158	9-30-99	554	...	±30409	Dc	v±1.28	v□±1.54	±v1.49	v±1.01	....	0.99	9 Mo Sep	v1.04	v1.02	28
29	1994	Q0.10	1-1-00	12-13	0.40	0.40	0.36	45.6	321	137	9-30-99	146	...	46748	Dc	v1.18	v2.65	v1.44	v1.63	E1.72	1.83	9 Mo Sep	v1.16	v1.36	29
30	1985	gA0.40	6-30-99	6-7	g0.40	0.40	g0.40	n/a	629	410	j6-30-99	2721	★6000	140029	Dc	v1.44	Pv0.65	v1.73	v0.21	....	j0.88	9 Mo Sep	v0.15	v0.82	30
31◆	1967	Q0.06½	11-20-99	11-4	0.26	0.26	0.24	57.8	646	336	9-30-99	225	...	±55726	Sp	±0.95	±1.11	■±∆1.25	v±1.37	v±1.51	1.51				31
32◆	1986	Q0.06½	11-20-99	11-4	0.26	0.26	0.24	....	...	...		....	...	23372	Sp	±0.95	±1.11	±1.49	±v1.37	Pv±1.51	1.51				32
33	1960	Q0.18	2-10-00	1-12	0.71	0.72	0.67	219	4665	4163	10-28-99	4961	...	423628	Ja	v1.83	v1.95	v2.08	v2.30	E1.55	1.24	9 Mo Oct	v1.45	v□0.39	33
34	1939	tQ0.15	12-20-99	11-17	t0.60	0.60	t0.60	616	3271	1554	6-30-99	1318	9000	219148	Dc	v□2.30	v1.74	v∆2.02	v1.71	E1.70	1.57	9 Mo Sep	v1.33	v1.19	34
35	1903	0.35	7-22-99	6-28	0.35	0.35	0.321	Equity per shr $7.52			j12-31-98	2318	...	185000	Dc	d7.00	0.67	v0.99	v3.08	E1.00	0.56	6 Mo Jun	v2.77	v0.25	35
36	....	None Since Public			...	Nil	....	4.74	9.96	1.75	8-31-99	0.32	73	2518	My	0.60	v0.82	v1.04	v1.16	vd0.38	d1.02	6 Mo Nov	v0.40	vd0.24	36
37◆	1939	†0.201	11-25-99	11-3	†0.80½	0.805	†0.75	297	4754	3176	9-30-99	2669	558	366407	Dc	2.22	1.47	v2.31	v2.42	E2.65	2.50	9 Mo Sep	v1.83	v1.91	37
38	1902	Q0.22½	12-2-99	11-8	0.90	0.90	0.90	3.79	184	155	9-30-99	231	...	43124	Dc	v1.23	v1.44	v1.80	v□0.69	E1.75↑	0.98	9 Mo Sep	v□1.04	v1.33	38
39	....	0.10	9-9-80	8-20	...	Nil	....	Total Assets $313M			9-30-99	274	...	5001	Dc	v0.49	v4.94	v1.49	vd1.21	....	1.85	9 Mo Sep	vd1.98	v1.08	39
40	1997	Q0.43	1-14-00	12-31	1.66	1.72	1.60	Total Assets $620.08M			9-30-99	333	1544	13741	Dc	...	p0.39	vp1.00	v1.58	....	1.55	9 Mo Sep	v1.19	v1.16	40
41	1974	Q0.12	12-1-99	11-10	0.47¼	0.48	0.43¾	Total Assets $1333.79M			9-30-99	11.2	...	39638	Dc	v0.55	v0.79	v1.29	v1.38	....	1.53	9 Mo Sep	v1.05	v1.20	41
42	....	None Since Public			...	Nil	....	37.4	38.1	2.98	9-30-99	....	...	17404	Dc	pvd0.35	pvd0.36	vd0.56	vd0.98	....	d1.01	9 Mo Sep	vd0.76	vd0.79	42
43	1973	0.30	11-5-99	10-14	0.30	0.30	0.50	15.8	45.2	8.74	8-31-99	45.6	...	7028	Au	1.27	0.63	v1.59	v0.97	v0.58	0.58				43
44	....	None Since Public			...	Nil	....	167	173	25.3	9-30-99	25.6	2304	25384	Mr	vd0.93	vd1.03	vd0.47	vd1.98	....	d2.18	6 Mo Sep	vd0.88	vd1.08	44
45	....	None Since Public			...	Nil	....	56.8	123	27.4	9-30-99	0.68	...	★13094	Dc	...	...	vpd1.38	Pvd1.51	....	1.66	9 Mo Sep	vd3.70	vd0.53	45
46◆	....	2%Stk	4-26-99	3-30	2%Stk	Stk	[67]....	Total Assets $4469M			9-30-99	417	...	7301	Dc	v11.35	v11.58	v14.07	v12.76	....	14.32	9 Mo Sep	v10.98	v12.54	46
47	1935	Q0.43	12-30-99	12-9	1.72	1.72	1.72	24.3	602	1253	9-30-99	2058	[68]...	110436	Dc	v2.00	v1.73	v2.30	v□2.15	E2.59	2.37	9 Mo Sep	v□1.76	v□1.98	47
48◆	1996	Q0.32	12-14-99	11-18	h[69]1.28	1.28	1.28	49.0	1290	637	9-30-99	257	...	93558	Dc	p□v3.06	v□2.54	v3.34	v2.44	E3.40	2.36	9 Mo Sep	v1.70	v∆1.62	48
49	....	None Since Public			...	Nil	....	609	665	91.9	9-30-99	506	...	★64917	Dc	...	...	p[70]d4.31	vpd4.73	....	....	9 Mo Sep	n/a	vd2.62	49
50	....	h[71]....	10-10-95	10-11	...	Nil	....	14.2	211	62.7	9-30-99	118	...	27649	Dc	v1.22	v0.48	□v0.88	vd0.38	....	Nil	9 Mo Sep	vd0.25	v0.13	50
51◆	1989	Q0.07	12-9-99	11-16	0.28	0.28	h[72]0.26	264	767	427	9-24-99	248	...	131490	Dc	v0.56	v0.59	v0.98	vd0.69	E1.25	1.17	9 Mo Sep	vd0.91	v0.95	51

◆**Stock Splits & Divs By Line Reference Index** [1]3-for-1,'97. [4]3-for-2,'94,'97. [5]2-for-1,'98. [6]2-for-1,'98. [7]1-for-4 REVERSE,'98. [8]2-for-1,'96. [14]2-for-1,'95(twice). [15]2-for-1,'97. [19]2-for-1,'98. [28]Adj for 2%,'99. [31]2-for-1,'97. [32]2-for-1,'97. [37]2-for-1,'95,'99. [46]Adj for 2%,'99:No adj for stk dstr,'98. [48]1-for-2 REVERSE,'99. [51]2-for-1,'99.

¶ S&P 500
\# MidCap 400
✣ SmallCap 600
• Options

Index	Ticker	Name of Issue (Call Price of Pfd. Stocks)	Market	Com. Rank. & Pfd. Rating	Inst. Hold Cos	Inst. Hold Shs. (000)	Principal Business	Price Range 1971-97 High	1971-97 Low	1998 High	1998 Low	1999 High	1999 Low	December, 1999 Dec. Sales in 100s	Last Sale Or Bid High	Low	Last	%Div Yield	P-E Ratio	EPS 5 Yr Growth	% Annualized Total Return 12 Mo	36 Mo	60 Mo
1	AACB	✔Alliance Atlantis Communic'B'	NNM,To	NR	33	5920	Produce/dev filmed entertain't	13 5/8	7 7/8	22 1/8	11 1/8	18 1/2	7 1/2	2231	9	7 1/2	8 1/4	...	4	Neg	-49.8	-2.9	...
2	ANE	✔Alliance Bancorp New England	AS	B–	10	112	Savings bank, Connecticut	12 3/16	1 3/8	16 11/16	9	12 3/4	8 3/4	995	9 3/4	8 3/4	8 7/8	2.7	7	NM	-22.7	17.6	20.7
3•[1]	AC	✔Alliance Cap Mgmt Holding L.P.	NY,Ph,P	NR	167	108602	Investment management svcs	19 15/16	2 7/16	29	18 3/4	34	24 1/8	20666	32 1/4	29 1/2	29 15/16	6.9	13	18	24.7	41.0	36.6
4	PFA	Alliance Forest Prod[51]	NY,To	NR	40	12590	Mfr lumber products	37 1/8	16 1/4	33	8 1/2	13 7/8	9 1/8	381	12 3/16	9 11/16	11 13/16	...	d	...	26.0	-21.3	-13.2
5	ALLY	✔Alliance Gaming	NSC	C	24	2156	Coin gam'g machine operator	155 5/16	3 5/16	21 7/16	5 11/16	9 13/16	2 3/8	35772	3 7/8	2 3/8	2 3/4	...	d	48	-60.3	-42.8	-36.4
✣6	ALLP	✔Alliance Pharmaceutical	NNM	C	67	13707	Dvlp,mfr med'l/pharmac'l prod	44	2	11 3/8	2 3/16	8 1/2	2 1/4	126615	8 1/2	4 3/16	7 3/8	...	d	-11	125	-18.5	4.2
7	ARLP	✔Alliance Resource Ptnrs LP	NNM	NR	3	233	Coal mining U.S.	....	....	....	....	19 1/16	12	26503	13 3/4	12	12 1/4	16.3	..	...	...	...	...
8•[2]	ALSC	✔Alliance Semiconductor	NNM	NR	59	16767	Mfr hi performance memory pd	48 1/4	3 5/16	9 15/16	1 15/16	17 1/2	2 1/2	97635	17 1/2	13	16 11/16	...	13	-39	311	32.8	4.1
#9•[3]	LNT	✔Alliant Energy	NY,B,Ch,P	B+	200	20891	Utility hldg:Wisconsin Pwr/Lt	36 3/4	6 3/4	35 3/8	28	32 3/8	25 3/16	23700	28 3/16	25 11/16	27 1/2	7.3	12	-3	-8.5	6.2	7.0
✣10•[4]	ATK	✔Alliant Techsystems	NY,Ph,P	NR	238	8546	Mfr munitions/defense prod	69	8 5/8	83 1/16	55	88	51	24582	62 5/16	51	62 5/16	...	10	NM	-24.4	4.2	8.9
11•[5]	ALLC	✔Allied Capital	NNM	B+	137	21442	Loans to small business	22 3/4	9 1/2	29 1/4	12	24	16 1/2	82813	20 5/16	16 3/4	18 5/16	e8.7	13	6	16.9	15.7	21.8
12	AHPI	✔Allied Healthcare Prod	NNM	C	21	4743	Mfr medical gas equipment	19 1/2	5 3/8	8	1 1/8	3	1 1/8	1838	3	2 3/8	2 3/8	...	d	Neg	46.2	-31.5	-31.7
13	AHI	✔Allied Holdings	NY	NR	20	2426	Auto/truck motor carrier	24	5 1/2	24	10	14 1/2	5	7693	7 1/8	5 3/4	6 1/8	...	36	-28	-57.4	-8.5	-12.6
14	AIB	✔Allied Irish Banks ADS[54]	NY,Ch,P	NR	85	11098	Major banking corp, Ireland	20 3/16	5 7/16	36 15/16	19 1/16	41 11/16	20 7/8	15509	26 3/16	20 7/8	21 1/8	3.1	12	15	-41.1	20.8	24.8
15	ADP	✔Allied Products	NY,B,Ch,P	B–	36	1835	Metalwk'g/farm & indl mach	30 5/16	1	25 3/16	5 7/8	7 1/2	2 1/2	10491	3 7/8	3 3/16	3 9/16	e4.5	d	Neg	-41.0	-42.4	-16.7
16	ALR	✔Allied Research Corp	AS	B–	20	1084	Subsid mfrs defense prod	17 1/2	1/8	13 1/2	6	8 1/4	4 3/8	2800	6 15/16	5 7/8	6 15/16	...	d	NM	-15.9	4.2	6.8
17	ARCC	✔Allied Riser Communic	NNM	NR	..	...	Voice & video communic svcs	....	....	....	....	26 1/8	15 1/8	137276	22 7/8	15 1/8	20 11/16	...	..	...	...	...	...
¶18•[6]	AW	✔Allied Waste Ind	NY,Ph	C	333	118843	Integrated waste disposal	37 1/2	5/8	31 5/8	16 1/8	24 1/16	6 1/2	220469	8 7/8	6 1/2	8 13/16	...	9	Neg	-62.7	-1.6	17.1
#19•[7]	AFC	✔Allmerica Financial	NY,Ch,Ph,P	NR	312	32701	Prop&casualty insur/finl svc	51	21	75 1/4	38 3/8	64 13/16	46 1/16	29752	55 5/8	48 7/16	55 5/8	0.4	11	21	-3.5	18.9	...
20	ALU	✔Allou Health&Beauty'A'	AS	B	27	1061	Dstr hlth & beauty aid prod	11 3/8	1 3/4	16	3 3/8	14 1/4	5 5/8	7969	8	6 1/16	6 5/8	...	3	5	-38.4	-0.3	-3.1
21	MDRX	✔Allscripts Inc	NNM	NR	53	12325	Internet based physician svcs	....	....	....	....	52 3/8	10 3/4	64216	52 3/8	31 7/8	44	...	d	...	...	...	...
22	ALLS	✔Allstar Systems	NSC	NR	3	212	Computer&telecom hrdwr/softwr	8	3 5/8	5 1/2	1 1/4	2 7/8	1	5143	1 5/8	1	1 5/16	...	d	Neg	-30.0	...	...
¶23•[8]	ALL	✔Allstate Corp	NY,P	NR	1192	488778	Prop,liability life insurance	47 3/16	11 5/16	52 3/8	36 1/16	41	22 7/8	715033	28	22 7/8	24 1/16	2.5	9	41	-36.4	-4.7	17.1
24	ALJ	Allstate Cp 7.125% 'QUIBS'	NY	A–[56]	8	148	Sr Qtly Interest Bonds	24 15/16	24 3/4	26 1/4	24 1/2	25 7/8	19 13/16	8737	21 7/8	19 13/16	20 7/16	8.7	..	...	-13.0	...	...
¶25•[9]	AT	✔ALLTEL Corp	NY,B,Ch,P,Ph	A	981	170096	Telecommun/data process svc	41 5/8	2	61 3/8	38 1/4	91 13/16	56 5/16	163281	91 13/16	76 7/16	82 11/16	1.5	35	9	40.8	41.7	26.0
26	Pr	$2.06 cm Cv C Pfd(27.50)	NY	BBB+	1	.2	dstr tel eqp/materials	237	18	292	250	480	362	....	....	....	493 1/8B	0.4	..	...	...	...	...
27	ALC	✔Alltrista Corp	NY	NR	61	5157	Mfr home canning products	29 3/4	12	29 1/4	19	34	19 7/16	3044	24 3/4	20 9/16	22 1/8	...	5	17	-7.8	-4.9	2.3
✣28•[4]	AHAA	✔Alpha Indus	NNM,B,P	B–	189	16659	Microwave comp. & devices	18 3/4	1/8	24 13/16	5 3/4	67 5/8	13 1/2	39661	66 1/4	52	57 5/16	...	44	87	141	123	69.3
29	ATGI	✔Alpha Technologies Grp	NNM	C	13	977	Mapping database mgmt sys	18 3/4	13/16	5 1/2	1 1/4	7	1 1/2	4894	6 15/16	5 5/8	6	...	10	Neg	292	15.7	2.2
✣30•[10]	ALO	✔Alpharma Inc'A'	NY,Ch,Ph	B–	..	...	Pharmac'ls:animal health prod	29 3/8	2 7/16	36 15/16	18 15/16	43 3/8	24 9/16	44601	33 1/8	26 3/8	30 3/4	0.6	24	NM	-12.4	29.2	9.6
31•[4]	AGI	✔Alpine Group	NY,Ch,P	B	66	6315	Mfr telecom cable/refractory	21 1/4	1/4	22 1/4	13 1/8	18 5/8	9 3/8	8301	12 7/8	10 1/2	12 7/8	...	4	NM	-14.2	23.3	...
32	ALS	ALSTOM ADS[60]	NY	NR	9	780	Power generation sys/eqp	....	....	34 1/16	19	35 9/16	22 1/2	532	34 1/8	28 1/2	33 3/8	1.3	22	...	46.2	...	...
33	ATON	✔Alteon WebSystems	NNM	NR	26	1171	E-commerce internet svcs	....	....	....	....	138	19	54149	138	75	87 3/4	...	d	...	...	...	...
#34•[9]	ALTR	✔Altera Corp	NNM,Ch	B	616	166262	Mfrs integrated circuits	32 7/8	1/2	30 15/16	14 1/8	68 9/16	23 15/16	873762	62 5/8	45	49 9/16	...	46	49	63.2	39.8	56.9
35	ALRC	✔Alternative Resources	NNM	B–	52	8264	Provide info svcs personnel	44 1/2	7	26	4 5/8	15 1/4	3 9/16	17909	6 1/16	4 1/16	5 1/2	...	10	Neg	-48.2	-31.8	-18.8
36•[11]	ALI	✔Alterra Healthcare	AS,Ch	NR	89	9605	Assisted living residences	29 9/16	10 5/8	35 1/4	16	34 1/8	5 3/8	40666	8 3/8	6	8 5/16	...	9	...	-75.6	-16.7	...
37	IAM	Altos Hornos de Mexico ADS[61]	NY,Ch,Ph	NR	..	...	Largest steel producer Mexico	15 1/8	9 5/8	12	2 7/8	4 3/4	1 3/8	....	....	....	....	...	..	NM	...	...	...
¶38•[9]	AZA	✔ALZA Corp	NY,B,Ch,P	B–	525	75983	Drug delivery system	55 1/8	11/16	54	30 7/8	55 3/4	26 1/2	675830	43 1/2	26 1/2	34 5/8	...	22	-17	-33.7	...	...
39•[2]	AMZN	✔Amazon.com	NNM	NR	396	87854	Online book retailer	5 1/2	1 5/16	60 5/16	4 1/8	113	41	2464605	113	76	76 1/8	...	d	Neg	42.9	...	...
40	AMB	✔AMB Property	NY	NR	145	49763	Real estate investment trust	25 1/8	21	26	20 3/4	23 1/2	18	42798	20 1/8	18	19 15/16	7.0	12	...	-1.6	...	...
#41•[12]	ABK	✔Ambac Financial Group	NY,Ph,P	NR	486	68310	Muni bond insurance co	47 9/16	10 1/16	65 15/16	40 7/8	63	44 11/16	63132	58 1/2	50 11/16	52 3/16	0.8	12	14	-12.6	17.4	24.2
42	AKB	Ambac Finl Grp 7.08% Debs	NY	....[63]	3	97	Unsecured debt obligations	....	....	26	24 1/4	25 3/4	19 3/8	6973	22 1/8	19 3/8	20 1/2	8.6	..	...	-12.5	...	...
43	AMBI	✔AMBI Inc	NNM	C	16	1201	Natural/pharm'l prd	8 3/16	1 1/8	2 1/4	5/8	3 7/8	1 1/16	31779	2 11/16	1 7/8	2 1/2	...	12	NM	133	-4.9	-4.6
44	AEN	✔AMC Entertainment	AS,Ch,P,Ph	B–	69	7010	Operates movie theatres	34 1/2	3	29	10 1/4	20 13/16	8	16462	10 3/8	8	8 5/8	...	d	Neg	-59.0	-15.7	-3.4
✣45	AIZ	✔Amcast Industrial	NY,Ch,Ph	B	104	4442	Mfr metal/flow control prod	27 1/2	3 11/16	24 1/2	13 7/8	22	12 3/8	13686	17	13	16 3/8	3.4	14	-6	-11.1	-10.1	-2.0
✣46•[10]	ACO	✔AMCOL Intl	NY	A	117	10202	Produce specialty chem&min prd	22	1 5/8	16 3/8	8	17 7/8	8 1/4	9982	17 3/4	15 1/8	16 1/8	1.7	15	14	66.8	17.6	13.5
47	DIT	AMCON Distributing	AS	NR	4	7	Dstr consumer prod	4 3/8	1 1/4	9 3/4	3 1/8	10 1/4	5 11/16	1172	10	7 1/4	8B	1.0	5	31	16.6	66.6	...
48•[1]	DOX	✔Amdocs Ltd	NY	NR	153	45136	Computer software/svcs	....	....	17 1/2	8 3/16	37 15/16	13 1/2	108919	37 15/16	33 5/16	34 1/2	...	70	...	102	...	...
49	AAE	Amdocs Ltd $1.51'TRACES'	NY	NR	10	1221	Trust Auto Com Exch Secur	....	....	....	....	35	20 3/16	13919	35	30 9/16	32 1/8	4.7	..	...	...	...	...
¶50•[4]	AHC	✔Amerada Hess	NY,To,B,C,Ch,P,Ph,Mo	B–	487	67497	Oil explor,prod,refining,mktg	64 1/2	5 5/8	61 1/16	46	66 5/16	43 3/4	78342	59 7/16	53 1/2	56 3/4	1.1	25	Neg	15.3	0.4	5.6
¶51•[10]	AEE	✔Ameren Corp	NY,B,C,Ch,P,Ph	A–	396	53194	Electricity in Mo,Ill&Iowa	44 5/8	8 7/8	44 5/16	35 9/16	42 15/16	32	107577	34 7/8	32	32 3/4	7.8	11	1	-18.1	0.5	4.6

Uniform Footnote Explanations-See Page 4. Other: [1]CBOE:Cycle 1. [2]ASE,CBOE,P,Ph:Cycle 1. [3]Ph:Cycle 1. [4]Ph:Cycle 2. [5]ASE,CBOE:Cycle 2. [6]CBOE:Cycle 3. [7]ASE:Cycle 2. [8]ASE,CBOE,Ph:Cycle 1. [9]P:Cycle 1. [10]Ph:Cycle 3. [11]CBOE:Cycle 2. [12]P:Cycle 2. [51]Mar'98 & prior pricing $Cdn. [52]Incl 6.42M sub units. [53]Pfd in $M. [54]Ea ADS rep 2 Ord,IR 25p. [55]Approx. [56]Rated A+ by S&P. [57]or earlier upon'Tax Event're-sec cond. [58]Stk dstr of Polyvision Corp. [59]Accum on Pfd. [60]Ea ADS rep 1 ord,40 FF. [61]Ea ADS rep 5 com,no par. [62]Stk dstr of Crescendo Pharmaceuticals Corp. [63]Rate AA by S&P. [64]Or earlier upon'Tax Event're-spec cond. [65]Accum on pfd. [66]Special divd.

Index	Cash Divs. Ea.Yr. Since	Dividends: Latest Payment Period $	Date	Ex. Div.	Total $ So Far 1999	Ind. Rate	Paid 1998	Financial Position Mil-$ Cash& Equiv.	Curr. Assets	Curr. Liab.	Balance Sheet Date	Capitalization Lg Trm Debt Mil-$	Shs. 000 Pfd.	Com.	Earnings $ Per Shr. Years End	1995	1996	1997	1998	1999	Last 12 Mos.	Interim Earnings Period	$ per Shr. 1998	1999	Index
1	....	None Paid			...	Nil	....	Total Assets $1599M			j6-30-99	524	1856	±23752	Mr	v±1.99	±v1.44	v±1.54	vd1.44	....	j1.43	6 Mo Sep	v±d2.34	v±0.53	1
2◆	1996	Q0.06	11-23-99	11-5	0.23	0.24	0.167	Total Deposits $244M			9-30-99	46.5	...	2300	Dc	vd0.49	v0.61	v0.82	v1.03	....	1.20	9 Mo Sep	v0.75	v0.92	2
3◆	1988	0.56	11-15-99	10-26	2.07	2.07	1.60	Total Assets $1554.99M			9-30-99	....	...	p171266	Dc	v0.94	v1.13	v0.74	v1.66	E2.25	2.11	9 Mo Sep	v1.22	v1.67	3
4	....	None Since Public			...	Nil	....	133	269	202	j6-30-99	432	...	36566	Dc	v4.56	v3.21	v0.79	v0.68	....	jd0.06	9 Mo Sep	v0.37	vd0.37	4
5◆	....	....			...	Nil	....	22.1	179	54.6	9-30-99	317	153	9706	Je	d3.33	vd16.24	vd0.67	□vd3.89	vd1.09	d0.77	3 Mo Sep	vd0.28	v0.04	5
6	....	None Paid			...	Nil	....	9.17	11.8	11.0	9-30-99	9.22	500	44649	Je	d1.35	d0.91	vd0.63	vd1.04	vd1.89	d1.81	3 Mo Sep	vd0.33	vd0.25	6
7	1999	0.23	11-12-99	10-27	0.23	2.00	....	87.3	113	50.4	p3-31-99	232	...	[52]★15405	Dc	...	...	...	vpd0.43	....	....	3 Mo Mar	n/a	vpd0.03	7
8◆	....	None Since Public			...	Nil	....	61.9	101	22.5	10-02-99	0.48	...	42159	Mr	v0.26	vd0.43	vd0.15	vd0.53	....	1.33	6 Mo Sep	vd0.50	v1.36	8
9	1946	0.50	11-15-99	10-27	2.00	2.00	2.00	64.0	419	672	9-30-99	1597	[53]114	78737	Dc	1.90	v2.34	pv2.02	v1.26	....	2.27	9 Mo Sep	v0.93	v1.94	9
10	....	None Since Public			...	Nil	....	28.9	352	265	10-03-99	305	...	9979	Mr	v3.56	v4.41	v5.10	v□5.52	E6.25	6.83	6 Mo Sep	v□2.51	v3.82	10
11	1994	Q0.40	12-30-99	12-15	†1.63	1.60	†1.57	Total Assets $1170M			9-30-99	508	...	62492	Dc	v1.37	v1.17	v1.24	v1.50	....	1.45	9 Mo Sep	v1.19	v1.14	11
12	....	0.07	7-15-96	6-26	...	Nil	....	0.47	32.6	9.78	9-30-99	16.7	...	7807	Je	1.45	0.25	vd0.58	□vd0.88	vd0.53	d0.49	3 Mo Sep	vd0.16	vd0.12	12
13	....	None Since Public			...	Nil	....	51.1	219	120	9-30-99	349	...	8036	Dc	v0.80	□v0.64	v0.31	v1.08	....	0.17	9 Mo Sep	v0.44	vd0.47	13
14◆	1991	[55]0.256	9-29-99	8-18	[55]0.656	0.66	0.527	Book Value $23.11			12-31-98	3835	250	859881	Dc	1.09	1.28	v1.32	v1.74	....	1.83	6 Mo Jun	v0.80	v0.89	14
15◆	1995	Q0.04	12-31-99	12-2	†0.17	0.16	0.16	0.91	162	193	9-30-99	1.80	...	11847	Dc	v2.34	v1.39	v1.62	vd1.19	....	d2.77	9 Mo Sep	v0.44	vd1.14	15
16	....	5%Stk	11-6-92	10-8	...	Nil	....	25.7	56.7	29.4	9-30-99	3.12	...	4846	Dc	vd0.46	v1.08	v1.85	v1.90	....	d0.94	9 Mo Sep	v1.38	vd1.46	16
17	....	None Since Public			...	Nil	....	24.3	24.7	7.82	6-30-99	3.49	p...	★61357	Dc	...	...	...	n/a	....	....	6 Mo Jun	n/a	vd1.01	17
18	....	None Since Public			...	Nil	....	101	2850	3221	9-30-99	9242	...	188848	Dc	v0.16	v□d1.06	□v0.57	v□d0.54	E0.94	d2.24	9 Mo Sep	v□0.29	v□d1.41	18
19	1996	A0.25	11-15-99	10-28	0.25	0.25	0.20	Total Assets $29080.00M			9-30-99	500	...	54256	Dc	□p2.91	v3.63	v3.82	v3.33	....	5.16	9 Mo Sep	v2.24	v4.07	19
20	....	None Since Public			...	Nil	....	0.26	240	173	9-30-99	0.61	...	±6644	Mr	v0.65	v0.70	v0.72	v0.20	....	2.25	6 Mo Sep	v±0.15	v±2.20	20
21	....	None Since Public			...	Nil	....	63.1	72.1	7.03	9-30-99	0.06	p...	★24147	Dc	...	...	...	vpd1.15	....	d0.79	9 Mo Sep	v□d1.19	vpd0.83	21
22	....	None Since Public			...	Nil	....	3.79	48.1	37.9	9-30-99	....	...	4171	Dc	v0.19	v0.60	v0.52	vd0.25	....	d0.38	9 Mo Sep	v0.11	vd0.02	22
23◆	1993	Q0.15	1-3-00	11-26	0.58½	0.60	0.52½	Total Assets $90322.00M			9-30-99	2106	...	805396	Dc	v2.12	v2.32	v3.55	v3.94	E2.70↓	3.77	9 Mo Sep	v3.01	v2.84	23
24	1998	Q0.44½	12-15-99	11-26	1.78	1.78	1.76	Co option redm fr 12-19-2002 at $25				....	...	★10000	Dc	...	...	...	...	....	....	Due 12-15-2097[57]			24
25	1961	Q0.32	1-3-00	12-7	1.22	1.28	1.16	37.0	1170	1179	9-30-99	3813	300	p313930	Dc	1.86	v1.52	v2.70	v1.89	E2.40	2.24	9 Mo Sep	v1.39	v1.74	25
26	1977	Q0.51½	12-15-99	11-24	2.06	2.06	2.06	Cv into 5.963 common, $4.61				....	32	...	Dc	...	...	...	...	....	....				26
27	....	None Since Public			...	Nil	....	32.2	140	74.2	9-26-99	130	...	6764	Dc	v1.44	v1.84	v1.96	v2.19	....	4.74	9 Mo Sep	v1.88	v□4.43	27
28◆	....	0.017	8-12-85	7-16	...	Nil	....	128	170	17.3	9-26-99	0.43	...	19529	Mr	v0.29	vd1.05	v0.65	v1.31	....	1.31	6 Mo Sep	v0.51	v0.51	28
29	....	None Since Public			...	Nil	....	0.40	18.0	8.35	5-02-99	8.77	...	6942	Oc	0.57	d0.05	vd0.50	vd0.41	Pv0.58	0.58				29
30	1984	Q0.04½	1-21-00	1-5	0.18	0.18	0.18	23.3	385	182	9-30-99	648	...	±★29590	Dc	v±0.87	v±d0.53	±v0.76	v±0.92	....	1.26	9 Mo Sep	v±0.59	v±0.93	30
31	....	h[58]....	6-13-95	6-14	...	[59]Nil	....	48.0	687	504	10-31-99	1372	20	14517	Ap	vd0.38	v□0.23	v□2.60	v□0.89	v□0.76	2.94	6 Mo Oct	v0.62	v□2.80	31
32	1999	0.454	10-25-99	9-29	0.454	0.45	....	Equity per shr $10.67			3-31-98	38.0	...	★238327	Mr	...	...	pv0.95	Pv1.50	....	1.50				32
33	....	None Since Public			...	Nil	....	29.8	36.6	11.2	6-30-99	1.92	p...	★38268	Je	...	...	...	....	vpd0.44	d1.25	3 Mo Sep	vd0.39	vd1.20	33
34◆	....	None Since Public			...	Nil	....	786	1036	259	9-30-99	....	...	199475	Dc	v0.48	v0.58	v□0.77	v0.78	E1.09	0.95	9 Mo Sep	v0.57	v0.74	34
35◆	....	None Since Public			...	Nil	....	0.58	83.7	32.0	9-30-99	52.0	...	15516	Dc	v0.65	v0.82	v0.88	vd1.13	....	0.58	9 Mo Sep	vd1.33	v0.38	35
36	....	None Since Public			...	Nil	....	33.0	104	80.4	9-30-99	696	...	22085	Dc	pd0.40	vd0.57	vd0.44	v0.92	....	0.96	9 Mo Sep	v0.64	v□0.68	36
37	....	None Since Public			...	Nil	....	60.5	786	624	12-31-97	1548	...	384083	Dc	0.91	Δ5.20	v2.65	....	....	2.65				37
38	....	h[62]....	9-30-97	10-1	...	Nil	....	253	515	110	9-30-99	934	...	102125	Dc	v0.88	v1.08	vd3.07	v1.26	E1.55	1.21	9 Mo Sep	v0.83	v0.78	38
39◆	....	None Since Public			...	Nil	....	905	1080	357	9-30-99	1462	...	340787	Dc	v...	vd0.03	vd0.11	vd0.42	Ed1.05	d1.38	9 Mo Sep	vd0.27	vd1.23	39
40	1997	Q0.35	12-28-99	12-15	1.74¼	1.40	1.028	Total Assets $3647.95M			9-30-99	1278	4000	86577	Dc	...	pn/a	pv1.16	v1.26	v....	1.68	9 Mo Sep	v0.97	v□1.39	40
41◆	1991	Q0.11	12-1-99	11-8	0.42	0.44	0.38	Total Assets $11325.66M			9-30-99	424	...	69920	Dc	v2.37	v3.91	v3.13	v3.56	E4.30	4.02	9 Mo Sep	v2.68	v3.14	41
42	1998	Q0.44¼	12-31-99	12-13	1.77	1.77	1.303	Co option redeem fr 3-31-2003 at $25[64]				★200	...	....	Dc	...	...	...	...	...	....	Mature 3-31-2098			42
43	....	None Paid			...	[65]Nil	....	2.01	8.88	5.68	9-30-99	3.00	1	30518	Je	0.01	d0.27	vd0.38	vd0.04	v0.19	0.20	3 Mo Sep	v0.05	v0.06	43
44	....	[66]1.14	9-8-92	8-18	...	Nil	....	10.4	102	194	9-30-99	700	...	±23469	Mr	□1.21	v0.75	vd1.59	vd0.69	....	d1.38	6 Mo Sep	v0.21	v□d0.48	44
45	1936	Q0.14	12-22-99	12-3	0.56	0.56	0.56	6.93	203	134	8-31-99	174	...	8955	Au	2.02	1.85	v1.48	□v1.81	v2.11	1.19	3 Mo Nov	v1.09	v0.17	45
46◆	1937	Q0.07	1-3-00	12-2	0.26	0.28	0.22½	5.47	164	62.2	9-30-99	99.4	...	26796	Dc	v0.60	v0.52	v0.72	v0.78	....	1.07	9 Mo Sep	v0.55	v0.84	46
47◆	1999	0.03	1-21-00	12-29	0.08	0.08	....	0.35	37.0	21.5	6-30-99	15.8	...	2480	Sp	0.33	0.51	v0.79	v0.93	Pv1.48	1.48				47
48	....	None Since Public			...	Nil	....	25.4	142	226	9-30-98	9.22	...	p205238	Sp	...	...	pd0.05	□v0.19	Pv0.49	0.49				48
49	1999	0.379	12-13-99	12-8	0.757	1.51	....	6-11-2002 exch For Amdocs Ltd com re-spec cond				....	...	★10000	Sp	...	...	...	...	...	....				49
50	1922	Q0.15	1-4-00	12-9	0.60	0.60	0.60	25.5	2053	1866	9-30-99	2336	...	90695	Dc	vd4.26	v7.09	v0.08	vd5.12	E2.28	d1.27	9 Mo Sep	vd0.45	v3.40	50
51	1906	Q0.63½	12-31-99	12-6	2.54	2.54	2.54	331	1150	1198	9-30-99	2302	3596	137215	Dc	v2.72	v2.71	□v2.82	v2.82	E2.97	3.04	9 Mo Sep	v□2.63	v2.85	51

◆**Stock Splits & Divs By Line Reference Index** [2]4-for-3,'97:3-for-2,'98. [3]2-for-1,'93,'98. [5]1-for-3.5 REVERSE,'99. [8]3-for-2,'95(twice). [14]3-for-1,'99. [15]3-for-2,'97. [23]2-for-1,'98. [28]3-for-2,'99. [34]2-for-1,'95,'97,'99. [35]2-for-1,'95. [39]3-for-1,'99:2-for-1,'98,'99. [41]2-for-1,'97. [46]3-for-2,'97. [47]Vote 10% stk div,ex Jan 21,'00.

¶ S&P 500
\# MidCap 400
✣ SmallCap 600
• Options

Index	Ticker	Name of Issue (Call Price of Pfd. Stocks)	Market	Com. Rank. & Pfd. Rating	Inst. Hold Cos	Inst. Hold Shs. (000)	Principal Business	Price Range 1971-97 High	1971-97 Low	1998 High	1998 Low	1999 High	1999 Low	Dec. Sales in 100s	December, 1999 Last Sale Or Bid High	Low	Last	%Div Yield	P-E Ratio	EPS 5 Yr Growth	% Annualized Total Return 12 Mo	36 Mo	60 Mo
1	MFA	America First Mtg Investments	NY	NR	9	82	Real estate investment trust	....	....	9 15/16	4 5/16	5 13/16	4	2146	5 1/16	4½	4 9/16	14.7	..	...	17.9	...	...
¶2•[1]	AOL	✔America Online	NY,Ch,Ph	B–	1599	958925	Provides online computer svcs	5 11/16	1/16	40	5 3/16	95 13/16	32½	5125852	95 13/16	72 1/16	75⅞	...	..	NM	96.2	233	145
3•[2]	AWA	✔America West Holdings'B'	NY,P	NR	179	28512	Regional airline service	23¾	6⅜	31 5/16	9 9/16	24⅛	16	36228	21¾	19	20¾	...	7	68	22.1	9.3	21.0
4	AATK	✔Amer Access Technologies	NSC	NR	8	107		12¾	2½	23¼	15	22¾	4¼	7231	7½	4 9/16	5⅛	...	d	...	–73.7	...	...
5	AIRS	✔Amer Aircarriers Support	NNM	NR	13	365	Aircraft components/parts	....	....	9¾	3⅞	12½	6⅝	4549	8½	6⅝	7¾	...	..	...	–20.5	...	...
6	AAG	✔Amer Annuity Group	NY,P	B	63	41063	Multiline insurance co	23⅞	3	25¼	21¾	25	15⅝	2944	18	15⅝	18	0.6	11	12	–21.3	9.0	13.9
7	AXL	✔Amer Axle & Manufacturing	NY	NR	43	4439	Dgn/mfr auto driveline sys	....	....	....	....	17⅜	11⅜	5944	13 9/16	11⅜	12⅛	...	..	...	...	...	...
8	BKC	✔Amer Bank, Conn	AS	B+	27	649	Savings bank, Connecticut	24¾	¾	33	17⅞	25⅝	19½	1089	25¼	21⅜	23⅞B	e3.9	12	14	9.5	24.5	24.7
9	ABL	✔Amer Biltrite	AS,B,Ph	B+	24	603	Floor cover'g/elec tape prod	35¼	1¾	31¾	20½	26⅜	12⅜	2176	14⅝	12⅜	14¼	3.5	6	1	–28.6	–12.0	–10.9
10	BNGO	✔Amer Bingo & Gaming	NSC	NR	3	16	Manage bingo centers	10½	1⅛	6¾	1¼	1⅞	⅜	23091	⅞	½	⅞	...	d	43	–42.8	–15.2	...
11	ABP	✔Amer Business Prod	NY,Ch	A–	68	4654	Business supplies/printing	28½	1¼	24⅛	16 1/16	23⅝	10¼	7108	12½	10¼	11 11/16	5.6	16	–13	–48.0	–19.9	–1.6
12•[3]	ACAS	✔Amer Capital Strategies	NNM	NR	68	8085	Investment banking svcs	20¾	15	24⅝	9 3/16	23⅛	14	13652	23⅛	19 13/16	22¾	e7.7	10	...	45.3	...	...
13	APO	✔Amer Community Properties Tr	AS	NR	7	151	Real estate development	....	....	7⅛	3¾	5⅞	3	351	3⅜	3⅛	3 3/16	...	32	...	–24.2	...	...
#14•[4]	AEOS	✔Amer Eagle Outfitters	NNM	NR	248	22853	Retail casual apparel/footwear	8 11/16	1¼	33 15/16	7 3/16	58½	29 7/16	135816	50½	41⅝	45	...	28	NM	35.4	196	72.7
15	ECGO	✔Amer Eco	NNM,To,Ch	B–	7	196	Industrial & ecological svcs	46¼	1⅝	12¼	1 9/16	2⅝	⅝	50886	1	⅝	11/16	...	d	Neg	–58.5	–53.6	–23.1
¶16•[3]	AEP	✔Amer Electric Pwr	NY,B,C,Ch,P,Ph	B+	476	89223	Utility holding co	52	13½	53 5/16	42 1/16	48 3/16	30 9/16	96190	32 13/16	31	32⅛	7.5	12	–1	–27.2	–2.5	5.6
¶17•[5]	AXP	✔Amer Express	NY,To,B,C,Ch,P,Ph,Mo	B+	1611	334573	Travel & invest sv,insur,bk'g	91½	4 7/16	118⅝	67	168⅞	94⅞	324229	168⅞	149¼	166¼	0.5	31	14	63.4	44.7	...
#18•[6]	AFG	✔Amer Finl Group	NY,B,Ch,P,Ph	B	147	20525	Property & casualty insurance	49¼	4⅝	45¾	30½	43⅝	24½	16803	27¼	24½	26⅜	3.8	17	93	–38.1	–8.8	3.4
✣19•[7]	AFWY	✔Amer Freightways	NNM	B	149	13918	Motor carrier-general freight	24⅞	3⅜	13⅛	6	24⅜	9¼	36923	17 15/16	12 9/16	16 3/16	...	11	15	40.4	13.3	–4.0
¶20•[2]	AGC	✔Amer General	NY,B,C,Ch,P,Ph	B+	884	180135	Hldg co:diversified fin'l	56¼	1 3/16	79	52 5/16	82 3/16	61⅞	96592	76¼	67¼	75⅞	2.1	17	5	–0.6	26.0	25.4
21	PrC	6.00%'A'[56]Cv[57] 'MIPS'([58]50)	NY	A	47	2147		72¾	49½	98¾	67½	101 3/16	78⅜	2376	94⅛	84	94⅛	3.2	..	...	...	...	...
22	Pr D	7% cm[60] Cv Pfd(37.41)	NY	NR	12	1207		49	36½	65	45	69½	52	335	60½	55¾	62¾B	4.1	..	...	...	...	...
¶23•[8]	AM	✔Amer Greetings Cl'A'	NY,Ph	A	387	48573	Cards & gift wrappings	40⅛	1⅝	53¾	35	44 5/16	22	72300	25 11/16	22⅞	23⅝	3.4	12	...	–40.7	–3.8	–0.4
¶24•[8]	AHP	✔Amer Home Products	NY,B,C,Ch,P,Ph	A+	1836	882332	Drugs, food,household prd	42 7/16	2 11/16	58¾	37¾	70¼	36½	869801	52	36½	39¼	2.3	22	Neg	–29.1	12.5	23.2
25	Pr	$2.00 cm Cv Pfd (60) vtg	NY	NR	4	.7	pkgd medicine,med prod	1400	101	1926	1725	1800	1400	2	1800	1400	1413B	0.1	..	...	...	...	...
26	HSTR	✔Amer Homestar	NNM	NR	46	7678	Mfr,sell-manufactured homes	17 3/16	3 7/16	26⅛	10⅞	15⅞	3 1/16	18534	4 1/16	3⅛	3 15/16	...	..	...	–73.8	–30.8	–0.1
27	IND	✔Amer Industrial Prop	NY,Ch	NR	30	4745	REIT:self-liquid'g	76⅞	5⅝	14⅜	9⅛	15	9 9/16	2145	12 15/16	11 1/16	12⅜	7.1	d	98	13.6	7.5	16.2
28	AIA	✔Amer Ins Mtge Inv L.P.	AS,Ph	NR	3	867	Mortgage invest mgmt services	18⅝	3 1/16	4¼	2 9/16	2 15/16	2¼	2961	2½	2 5/16	2⅜	10.1	7	2	1.5	8.5	8.0
29	AII	✔Amer Ins Mtge Inv Ser 85[64]	AS,Ph	NR	11	298	Originate/acquire mtge loans	20¼	10	14 15/16	11½	12 11/16	7⅞	2591	8 11/16	7⅞	8⅜	e12.3	9	–6	–10.7	2.7	8.1
30	AIJ	✔Amer Ins Mtge Inv Ser 86[64]	AS	NR	10	443	Originate/acquire mtge loans	14⅜	9⅛	10⅛	7⅝	8¾	4¾	2461	5 3/16	4 13/16	4 15/16	9.9	13	–21	–4.3	13.1	13.0
31	AIK	✔Amer Ins Mtge Inv Ser 88[64]	AS	NR	9	177	Originate/acquire mtge loans	15⅛	11	14¼	10 11/16	11⅝	5 15/16	1888	6⅝	5 15/16	6⅜	e14.3	8	–9	–7.9	5.8	12.9
¶32•[3]	AIG	✔Amer Intl Group	NY,B,Ch,P	A+	2123	883838	Major int'l insur hldg co	60 1/16	⅝	82⅛	51⅞	112⅞	76½	453493	112⅞	100½	108⅛	0.2	34	15	40.2	41.6	36.5
33	AIP	✔Amer Israeli Paper Ord	AS,B,Ch,Ph,P	NR	..	...	Paper mfg fr imported pulp	59¾	4	45	28¾	65½	31⅛	81	65½	56¾	59¾	10.6	13	1	146	35.8	20.7
34•[9]	PLB	✔Amer Italian[72]Pasta'A'[73]	NY,Ph	NR	143	15578	Produce/market pasta	26	18	39½	17⅝	31⅛	22¼	15137	31⅛	27 3/16	30¾	...	24	...	16.6	...	...
✣35•[2]	AMSY	✔Amer Mgmt Systems	NNM	B+	282	29430	Computer sys mgmt/admin	37⅛	½	40¼	18¾	39¾	19¾	72196	36¼	27⅞	31⅜	...	24	19	–21.6	8.6	19.7
36	AMZ	✔Amer Medical Security Grp	NY	NR	41	7956	Small group medl insur prod	....	....	15 1/16	6⅜	16¼	4	12934	6 5/16	4 15/16	6	...	d	...	–58.1	...	...
37•[10]	SKYC	✔Amer Mobile Satellite	NNM	NR	79	19004	Dvlp stg:satellite comm svc	33¼	6 3/16	16⅛	3½	23½	3 15/16	120738	23⅛	12 9/16	21 1/16	...	d	–25	301	19.8	10.6
38	AMC	✔Amer Mortgage Acceptance SBI	AS	NR	3	14	Real estate investment trust	....	....	....	....	13⅞	8½	1854	9⅜	8½	8⅞	16.3	6	...	...	...	...
39	CAN	✔Amer Natl Can Group	NY	NR	64	20980	Mfr beverage cans	....	....	....	....	17¼	11⅜	44231	13½	12 3/16	13	e4.3	..	...	...	...	...
40	ANAT	✔Amer Natl Insur	NNM	A	105	4751	Insurance:Life,hlth,prop	105	5⅜	109⅞	73	89⅜	60⅝	2438	69⅛	60⅝	63¾	4.5	7	2	–19.8	–1.6	10.1
#41•[11]	APCC	✔Amer Power Conversion	NNM	B+	445	105608	Mfr constant pwr supply prod	17 3/16	⅛	24¾	11¾	29⅜	13 1/16	239367	29⅜	20¾	26⅜	...	25	22	9.1	24.7	26.4
42	APR	✔Amer Precision Indus	NY,Ch,Ph	B	32	2557	Ind'l process eq: electr comp	26	¼	21	9½	12⅝	8¼	6577	10⅞	8½	8½	...	11	8	–17.6	–24.7	2.9
43	AFV	✔Amer Quantum Cycles	AS	NR	2	15	Dvlp stge:mfr motorcycles	45½	22	32	1⅝	18	1¼	7896	2⅝	1¼	1⅝	...	d	Neg	377	...	...
44	ACP	✔Amer R.E.Ptnrs L.P.	NY,Ch	NR	22	39920	Acquire,manage real estate	17½	6⅛	11 9/16	7⅛	10¼	7⅜	3584	7 13/16	7⅜	7⅝	...	5	...	–24.2	–5.8	0.3
45	ARB	✔Amer Realty Tr SBI	NY,Ch,P	NR	7	173	Inv,RE,loans/own rental prop	22¼	3/16	16⅜	13⅞	17⅝	14⅞	898	17 5/16	16⅞	17	...	d	–38	4.5	39.7	42.2
46	INV	✔Amer Residential Inv Trust	NY,Ph	NR	10	376	Real estate investment trust	16¾	11⅜	14⅜	3⅝	8¾	5 5/16	5037	7 13/16	5⅜	6⅞	17.5	d	...	44.7	...	...
47	ACR	✔Amer Retirement	NY,Ph	NR	58	9667	Senior living/health care svcs	21⅞	14	23⅜	12¾	18½	4	21222	8⅞	4 3/16	7 15/16	...	13	...	–49.4	...	...
48	ASI	✔Amer Safety Ins Grp	NY	NR	..	...	Casualty insurance	....	....	15 1/16	6¾	10⅜	6	2072	6 15/16	6	6½	...	6	10	–32.5	...	...
49	ASE	✔Amer Science & Engr	AS,B	C	13	576	X-ray prod:rsch&engr svc	18¾	11/16	16½	9⅜	12	6	3114	8½	6⅝	7¼	...	23	NM	–37.0	–18.7	3.4
50	AMS	✔Amer Shared Hosp Sv	AS,P	B–	4	58	Medical diagnostic imag'g eq	12⅛	3/16	2	9/16	7⅛	15/16	3129	4⅝	3⅜	4¼	...	1	NM	258	32.9	53.4
51	SKI	✔Amer Skiing	NY	NR	28	7185	Own/oper ski resorts	18¼	13 15/16	17	5 3/16	8 1/16	2⅜	19483	4	2⅞	3 3/16	...	d	...	–58.5	...	...

Uniform Footnote Explanations-See Page 4. Other: [1]ASE,CBOE,P,Ph:Cycle 2. [2]CBOE:Cycle 1. [3]CBOE:Cycle 2. [4]CBOE,Ph:Cycle 2. [5]ASE,CBOE:Cycle 1. [6]Ph:Cycle 3. [7]Ph: Cycle 1. [8]ASE:Cycle 1. [9]ASE:Cycle 3. [10]CBOE:Cycle 3. [11]ASE,CBOE:Cycle 3. [51]8 Mos Dec'98. [52]Spl div. [53]Incl current amts. [54]12 Mo Jan'96:Jul'95 earn $0.30. [55]Subsid Pfd in $M. [56]Monthly Income Preferred Shrs. [57]Fr 5-31-2003. [58]Issued by subsid,Amer Genl Del L.L.C.. [59]Co opt conv right expire 5-31-2000 re-spec cond. [60]Fr 3-1-2000. [61]Fiscal May'99 & prior. [62]Incl $0.12 return of cap,'99. [63]Incl $0.99 return of cap,'98. [64]L.P. Units. [65]Incl $0.17 return of cap,'00. [66]Incl $1.54 return of cap,'99. [67]Incl $1.35 return of cap,'98. [68]Incl $2.46 return of cap,'99. [69]Incl return of cap,'98. [70]Indl $3.47 return of cap,'99. [71]Incl $2.45 return of cap,'98. [72]Cv into Cl 'B'. [73]Plan SmallCap 600 listing: eff Jan 4. [74]9 Mo Sep'96. [75]10 Mo Dec'97.

Common and Convertible Preferred Stocks

Index	Splits ◆ Cash Divs. Ea. Yr. Since	Dividends Latest Payment Period $	Date	Ex. Div.	Total $ So Far 1999	Ind. Rate	Paid 1998	Financial Position Mil-$ Cash& Equiv.	Curr. Assets	Curr. Liab.	Balance Sheet Date	Capitalization Lg Trm Debt Mil-$	Shs. 000 Pfd.	Com.	Earnings $ Per Shr. Years End	1995	1996	1997	1998	1999	Last 12 Mos.	Interim Earnings Period	$ per Shr. 1998	1999	Index
1	1998	0.14	2-18-00	12-30	0.79½	0.67	0.53	Total Assets $468M			9-30-99	....	...	9063	Dc	...	p0.58	n/a	v†[51]0.32	....	....	9 Mo Sep	n/a	v0.66	1
2◆	1998	[52]0.00	6-12-98	5-28	...	Nil	[52]0.00	1759	2408	2011	9-30-99	341	...	2235486	Je	d0.03	0.02	vd0.33	v0.04	v0.30	0.34	3 Mo Sep	v0.03	v0.07	2
3	....	None Since Public			...	Nil	....	247	481	661	9-30-99	156	...	±37145	Dc	±□v1.18	±v□0.20	±v1.63	v2.40	E2.80	2.78	9 Mo Sep	v1.88	v2.26	3
4	....	None Paid			...	Nil	....	3.27	6.04	0.38	9-30-99	....	11	4064	Dc	...	d0.02	d0.14	vd0.43	....	d0.53	9 Mo Sep	v0.05	vd0.05	4
5	....	None Since Public			...	Nil	....	0.29	60.0	57.2	9-30-99	2.76	...	7190	Dc	...	pv0.28	pv0.59	vp0.76	....	....	9 Mo Sep	n/a	v0.62	5
6	1989	A0.10	12-16-99	11-30	0.10	0.10	0.10	Net Asset Val $13.20			9-30-99	200	...	42372	Dc	v1.37	v□1.39	□v1.61	v□2.23	....	1.60	9 Mo Sep	v□1.93	v□1.30	6
7	....	None Since Public			...	Nil	....	173	561	468	9-30-99	795	...	46357	Dc	v0.50	v0.43	v0.43	n/a	....	....	9 Mo Sep	vd0.35	v1.78	7
8◆	1982	†0.29	12-23-99	12-8	†0.94	0.92	†0.88	Book Value $13.11			12-31-98	[53]113	...	4703	Dc	1.00	1.42	v1.69	v2.24	....	2.05	9 Mo Sep	v1.74	v1.55	8
9◆	1979	Q0.12½	1-3-00	12-14	0.50	0.50	0.42½	38.7	178	90.3	10-02-99	111	...	3573	Dc	v1.61	v1.69	v2.18	□v2.67	....	2.52	9 Mo Sep	v□1.68	v1.53	9
10	....	None Since Public			...	Nil	....	3.41	5.83	0.69	9-30-99	1.33	...	9911	Dc	d0.58	v0.15	Δv0.16	vd0.29	....	d0.23	9 Mo Sep	vd0.12	vd0.06	10
11◆	1941	Q0.16½	12-15-99	11-29	0.66	0.66	0.63	33.7	135	59.0	9-30-99	34.9	...	14744	Dc	v1.57	v1.28	v1.16	v0.74	....	0.73	9 Mo Sep	v0.83	v0.82	11
12	1997	†0.03	1-11-00	12-28	†1.82	1.76	1.23	Total Assets $326.23M			9-30-99	[53]69.8	...	18224	Dc	...	p0.30	n/a	v1.48	....	2.32	9 Mo Sep	v0.97	v1.81	12
13	1999	Div Omitted 6-24-99			0.05	Nil	....	Total Assets $120M			9-30-99	[53]83.6	...	5192	Dc	...	...	v0.10	v0.23	....	0.10	9 Mo Sep	v0.37	v0.24	13
14◆	....	None Since Public			...	Nil	....	116	230	92.7	10-30-99	....	...	46658	Ja	v[54]d0.03	v0.13	v0.42	v1.13	....	1.62	9 Mo Oct	v0.61	v1.10	14
15	....	None Since Public			...	Nil	....	18.2	149	39.4	5-31-99	133	...	21710	Nv	0.40	0.81	1.08	vd1.44	....	d2.01	9 Mo Aug	v0.18	vd0.39	15
16	1909	Q0.60	12-10-99	11-8	2.40	2.40	2.40	274	2828	3907	9-30-99	6219	[55]169	194103	Dc	v2.85	v3.14	□v3.28	v2.81	E2.70	2.51	9 Mo Sep	v2.44	v2.14	16
17◆	1870	Q0.22½	2-10-00	1-5	0.90	0.90	0.90	Total Assets $132616.00M			9-30-99	6720	...	447673	Dc	v3.10	v3.89	v4.15	v4.63	E5.40	5.25	9 Mo Sep	v3.47	v4.09	17
18	1987	Q0.25	10-25-99	10-13	1.00	1.00	1.00	Total Assets $16018.55M			9-30-99	738	...	58407	Dc	vΔ3.83	v□4.26	□v3.28	v□2.01	....	1.56	9 Mo Sep	v□2.63	v□2.18	18
19	....	None Since Public			...	Nil	....	2.08	181	143	9-30-99	225	...	32096	Dc	v0.42	v0.25	v0.56	v0.87	E1.45↑	1.32	9 Mo Sep	v0.60	v1.05	19
20	1929	Q0.40	12-1-99	11-10	1.60	1.60	1.50	Total Assets $111275M			9-30-99	8717	2318	247117	Dc	v2.66	v2.63	v2.19	v2.96	E4.55	3.40	9 Mo Sep	v2.95	v3.39	20
21	1995	0.25	12-31-99	12-28	3.25	3.00	3.00	Cv into 1.2288 com,Amer Gen Cp,$40.69[59]				....	5000	...	Dc	...	...	...	....	....	....				21
22	1996	Q0.643	12-1-99	11-10	2.573	2.573	2.573	Cv into 0.8264 com				....	2300	...	Dc	...	...	...	....	....	....	Mand conv into 1 com 3-1-2001			22
23	1950	Q0.20	12-9-99	11-22	0.78	0.80	0.74	28.5	1103	550	8-31-99	455	...	±64518	Fb	±1.54	v±2.22	v±2.55	v±2.53	E2.05	1.40	9 Mo Nov	v±1.71	v±0.58	23
24◆	1919	Q0.23	12-1-99	11-9	0.90½	0.92	0.87	2583	9596	7549	9-30-99	3622	25	1305721	Dc	v1.35	v1.46	v1.55	v1.85	E1.78	d1.13	9 Mo Sep	v1.59	vd1.39	24
25	1966	Q0.50	1-1-00	12-9	2.00	2.00	2.00	Cv into 36 com				....	25	...	Dc	b3.01	...	...	....	....	....				25
26◆	....	None Since Public			...	Nil	....	41.2	210	152	9-30-99	127	375	18424	Je	0.52	0.65	v0.86	v□1.01	v[61]0.96	....	3 Mo Sep	n/a	vd0.08	26
27◆	1998	Q0.22	1-14-00	1-4	0.84	0.88	0.58	Total Assets $633.6M			9-30-99	346	...	20903	Dc	□vd2.50	vΔd2.50	Δvd0.26	v□d0.35	....	d0.10	9 Mo Sep	v□0.31	v□0.56	27
28	1985	0.09	2-1-00	12-29	[62]0.36	0.24	[63]1.28	Total Assets $26.76M			9-30-99	....	...	10000	Dc	v0.30	v0.27	v0.28	v0.39	....	0.32	6 Mo Jun	v0.16	v0.09	28
29	1986	[65]0.25	2-1-00	12-29	†[66]2.54	1.03	[67]3.41	Total Assets $145.49M			9-30-99	....	...	12080	Dc	v1.27	v1.26	v1.20	v1.11	....	0.95	9 Mo Sep	v0.85	v0.69	29
30	1994	0.02	2-1-00	12-29	[68]2.88	0.49	[69]4.44	Total Assets $71.19M			9-30-99	0.67	...	9576	Dc	v1.16	v1.30	v0.94	v0.53	....	0.39	9 Mo Sep	v0.43	v0.29	30
31	1994	1.04	2-1-00	12-29	[70]4.23	0.91	†[71]4.51	Total Assets $84.09M			9-30-99	....	...	8802	Dc	v1.49	v1.11	v1.09	v0.99	....	0.83	9 Mo Sep	v0.77	v0.61	31
32◆	1969	Q0.05	3-17-00	3-1	0.19	0.20	0.17	Total Assets $259786.00M			9-30-99	20052	...	1548242	Dc	v1.88	v2.18	v2.52	v2.86	E3.20	3.22	9 Mo Sep	v2.03	v2.39	32
33	1999	t9.30	12-29-99	12-10	t22.027	6.35	....	37.0	213	111	12-31-98	15.7	...	3855	Dc	5.76	v6.61	v3.13	v3.91	....	4.51	6 Mo Jun	v1.46	v2.06	33
34	....	None Since Public			...	Nil	....	3.09	55.3	26.1	9-30-99	81.5	...	18177	Sp	...	□[74]d0.24	p0.57	v□0.98	v1.26	1.26				34
35◆	....	None Since Public			...	Nil	....	80.3	370	181	9-30-99	18.1	...	40858	Dc	v0.72	v0.37	v0.74	v1.21	E1.32	1.28	9 Mo Sep	v0.83	v0.90	35
36	....	0.12	9-25-98	9-4	...	Nil	0.36	Total Assets $516.85M			9-30-99	[53]52.9	...	16278	Dc	...	...	pv0.29	v0.42	....	d1.98	9 Mo Sep	v0.81	vd1.59	36
37	....	None Since Public			...	Nil	....	61.4	162	69.4	9-30-99	604	...	48496	Dc	vd2.69	vd5.38	vd4.74	vd4.52	....	d4.92	9 Mo Sep	vd3.39	v□d3.79	37
38	1999	0.36¼	2-14-00	12-29	0.36¼	1.45	....	Equity per shr $14.17			6-30-99	....	...	p4214	Dc	...	v0.83	v0.92	v0.88	....	1.53	9 Mo Sep	v0.70	v1.35	38
39	1999	†Q0.14	2-29-00	1-27	†0.28	0.56	....	163	717	646	9-30-99	1133	...	55000	Dc	...	...	...	pv2.00	....	....	9 Mo Sep	n/a	v□1.75	39
40	1923	Q0.71	12-17-99	12-1	2.78	2.84	2.70	Equity per shr $110.07			12-31-98	....	...	26479	Dc	7.79	v8.14	v9.38	v7.45	....	9.09	9 Mo Sep	v5.83	v7.47	40
41◆	....	None Since Public			...	Nil	....	330	818	190	9-26-99	....	...	192595	Dc	v0.37	v0.49	v0.64	v0.76	E1.04	0.95	9 Mo Sep	v0.52	v0.71	41
42	....	0.06½	1-15-97	12-24	...	Nil	....	4.23	93.4	47.6	9-30-99	58.5	1236	7067	Dc	v0.65	v0.88	v0.97	v0.68	....	0.81	9 Mo Sep	v0.48	v0.61	42
43◆	....	None Since Public			...	Nil	....	1.07	3.39	0.67	10-31-99	0.08	...	★5273	Ap	Nil	Nil	vNil	vd5.24	vd5.60	d5.14	6 Mo Oct	vd0.73	vd0.27	43
44	....	0.12½	2-14-94	12-27	...	Nil	....	Total Assets $1214.77M			9-30-99	189	8060	46098	Dc	v1.33	v□2.02	v2.13	v1.28	....	1.61	9 Mo Sep	v1.01	v1.34	44
45◆	1996	Div Omitted 8-11-99			0.10	Nil	0.15	Total Assets $939.33M			9-30-99	791	3401	10564	Dc	vΔd0.31	Δvd0.46	vd0.22	vd2.24	....	d2.36	9 Mo Sep	v0.14	v0.02	45
46	1998	Q0.30	1-31-00	12-29	0.87	1.20	0.84	Total Assets $1298.11M			9-30-99	1192	...	8056	Dc	...	n/a	v[75]0.82	vd0.15	....	d0.12	9 Mo Sep	v0.69	v0.72	46
47	....	None Since Public			...	Nil	....	29.6	61.1	30.1	9-30-99	405	...	17138	Dc	...	p□v0.31	□v0.35	v□0.51	....	0.62	9 Mo Sep	v□0.41	v0.52	47
48	....	None Since Public			...	Nil	....	Total Assets $93M			6-30-99	....	...	6045	Dc	1.07	v0.98	Pv1.08	v1.04	....	1.04	9 Mo Sep	v0.74	v0.74	48
49	....	5%Stk	8-25-81	8-3	...	Nil	....	1.13	32.0	16.7	9-30-99	0.01	...	4915	Mr	0.18	v0.40	v0.95	v0.40	....	0.31	6 Mo Sep	v0.21	v0.12	49
50	....	None Since Public			...	Nil	....	11.0	12.7	3.09	9-30-99	18.1	...	3829	Dc	vΔd2.96	vd0.08	v0.24	v3.15	....	3.32	9 Mo Sep	v0.15	v0.32	50
51	....	None Since Public			...	Nil	....	7.83	48.7	140	10-24-99	414	37	±30404	Jl	...	...	pd0.17	vpd0.49	vd1.07	d1.28	3 Mo Oct	vd0.67	v□d0.88	51

◆Stock Splits & Divs By Line Reference Index [2]2-for-1,'95(twice),'98(twice),'99(twice). [8]2-for-1,'98. [9]2-for-1,'94. [11]3-for-2,'95. [14]3-for-2,'98(twice):2-for-1,'99. [17]No adj for Lehman Bros dstr(0.20 com)'94. [24]2-for-1,'96,'98. [26]5-for-4,'97:3-for-2,'97. [27]1-for-5 REVERSE,'97. [32]3-for-2,'95,'97,'98:5-for-4,'99. [35]3-for-2,'94,'96. [41]2-for-1,'99. [43]1-for-4 REVERSE,'99. [45]2-for-1,'96,'97.

¶ S&P 500
# MidCap 400
✢ SmallCap 600
• Options

Index	Ticker	Name of Issue (Call Price of Pfd. Stocks)	Market	Com. Rank. & Pfd. Rating	Inst. Hold Cos	Inst. Hold Shs. (000)	Principal Business	Price Range 1971-97 High	1971-97 Low	1998 High	1998 Low	1999 High	1999 Low	December, 1999 Dec. Sales in 100s	Last Sale Or Bid High	Last Sale Or Bid Low	Last Sale Or Bid Last	%Div Yield	P-E Ratio	EPS 5 Yr Growth	% Annualized Total Return 12 Mo	36 Mo	60 Mo
#1•[1]	ASD	✓Amer Standard	NY,Ch,Ph,P	NR	239	49879	Air condit'g,bath fix,brake sy	51⅝	19⅝	49¼	21⅝	49 7/16	31⅛	52125	46	38 15/16	45⅞	...	13	NM	27.4	6.2	...
✢2	AWR	✓Amer States Water	NY	B+	92	2511	Water supply, some elec	25⅝	4¼	29¼	21⅛	39¾	22 3/16	3287	39¾	35	36	3.6	18	5	37.5	24.1	21.8
3	AMK	✓Amer Techl Ceramics	AS,Ch	B	18	384	Mfrs ceramic capacitors	22¼	1	17½	5⅞	17	5⅜	1393	17	12	16	...	20	9	142	35.0	35.5
4	AMT	✓Amer Tower'A'	NY,Ph	NR	322	102168	Oper wireless communic towers	....	....	29⅝	13¼	33¼	17⅛	206355	33¼	25 11/16	30 9/16	...	d	...	3.4	...	...
5	AVD	✓Amer Vanguard	AS	B	8	152	Mfr agric-chem/dstr ind'l eqp	15½	⅜	9⅞	4½	8	4½	661	6⅜	5⅛	6⅛	1.0	5	11	5.5	−3.5	0.4
6	BETM	✓Amer Wagering	NNM	NR	10	151	Own/oper hotel & casino	15¼	5	8¾	3¾	10½	3½	5567	6¼	5	6⅛	...	d	...	−24.0	−21.7	...
#7•[2]	AWK	✓Amer Water Works	NY,B,Ch,Ph,P	A	222	30912	Water utility holding co	29 11/16	13/16	33¾	25¼	34¾	20½	50005	25 9/16	20½	21¼	4.0	15	5	−35.1	4.1	14.8
✢8•[3]	ACF	✓AmeriCredit Corp	NY,Ch,P	B–	219	65156	Provides used-car financing	17 3/16	1 1/16	18⅝	6⅝	18 15/16	9 13/16	54987	18 15/16	16	18½	...	15	28	33.9	21.9	44.0
9	APU	✓AmeriGas Partners L.P.	NY,Ch,P	NR	28	836	Real propane distributor	27¼	20¾	27	21	25⅛	12¾	28794	17⅛	12¾	15 1/16	14.6	d	Neg	−26.4	−3.6	...
10	HOST	✓Amerihost Properties	NNM	C	10	2014	Own/oper limited svc motels	12¼	1½	5 15/16	2 9/16	4½	2 9/16	4465	3½	2 9/16	3⅜	...	d	Neg	−11.5	−18.4	−1.1
11•[4]	AAS	✓AmeriSource Health'A'	NY,Ph	NR	283	46742	Wholesale dstr drug,hlth prod	33⅛	9⅞	40⅜	22¼	41⅜	11	72509	15½	11 9/16	15 3/16	...	11	NM	−53.0	−14.1	...
12•[3]	AMTD	✓AmeriTrade Holding'A'	NNM	NR	87	16528	Brokerage/financial svcs	3¼	1	6½	1⅞	62 13/16	5	818937	29¼	20½	21 11/16	...	..	−1	316	...	...
13	AMN	✓Ameron Intl	NY,P	B+	81	1924	Mfr concrete & steel pipes	70	4¼	63½	33⅜	47 15/16	34½	1148	43⅜	38¾	39 9/16	3.2	6	18	10.2	−6.0	9.5
14	AMH	✓AmerUs Life Holdings'A'	NY	NR	104	9945	Life insurance/annuity prd	38⅛	16½	36¾	14⅜	28 13/16	16 5/16	6990	25	22⅞	23	1.7	11	...	4.6	...	...
15	AHB	AmerUs Life Hldgs 7% 'ACES'[53]	NY	BB+	5	615	Adj Convers'n-rate Equity Sec Units	....	....	31 15/16	17	27 11/16	18¼	2566	24⅝	22½	22¾	9.7	..	...	3.2	...	...
✢16•[5]	AMES	✓Ames Department Stores	NNM	NR	258	23518	Discount department stores	19⅝	1	29⅝	10½	48⅞	22⅜	134611	34 15/16	25	28 13/16	...	d	Neg	6.7	88.3	63.1
#17•[6]	AME	✓AMETEK, Inc	NY,B,Ch,P,Ph	B+	159	21205	Mfr instruments/elec mtrs	28	1⅛	31⅜	15¾	25¾	16½	8761	20 5/16	18	19 1/16	1.3	12	9	−13.5	−4.0	3.7
18	PIN	✓AMF Bowling	NY,Ph	NR	44	31171	Oper bowling centers	25 3/16	19½	31	3⅞	8¾	2 5/16	24980	3¼	2 5/16	3⅛	...	d	...	−39.0	...	...
19•[7]	AFM	✓AMFM Inc[55]	NY	NR	505	125747	Own, operates radio stations	37⅜	3 15/16	57⅜	18⅝	79¾	39½	196150	79¾	69⅞	78¼	...	d	−23	63.4	84.7	68.3
¶20•[8]	AMGN	✓Amgen Inc	NNM	B	1355	641115	Res/dev of biological prod	17⅜	1/16	27¼	11 11/16	66 7/16	25 11/16	1656377	66 7/16	42⅝	60 1/16	...	62	30	140	66.4	53.4
21•[9]	AMKR	✓Amkor Technology	NNM	NR	139	53667	Mfr semiconductor eqp	....	....	14	3	29 9/16	7⅛	180328	29 9/16	22⅞	28¼	...	44	26	161	...	...
22	AML	✓Amli Residential Prop	NY,Ch	NR	96	7659	Real estate investment trust	24¾	17	24⅜	18 7/16	23	18⅞	10900	21⅝	19 7/16	20 3/16	9.1	12	11	−1.2	3.1	10.1
23	AIS	✓Ampal-Amer Israel'A'	AS,B	NR	23	1979	Loans/investments in Israel	13⅛	⅜	6⅛	3¼	9⅝	3⅞	7843	9⅝	6⅝	9¼	...	9	49	115	24.3	7.7
24	AP	✓Ampco-Pittsburgh	NY,B,Ch,Ph	B–	55	5260	Air&liquid hndlg eq:metal pr	26 11/16	4 7/16	19⅝	9⅞	14⅛	9 3/16	1880	12 5/16	9 13/16	10⅛	4.0	7	15	−3.7	−2.9	2.7
25	AXC	✓Ampex Corp'A'	AS,Ch,Ph,P	NR	50	8268	Produce magnetic record'g sys	15¾	11/16	3¼	11/16	7½	1 1/16	120532	6⅜	3 13/16	5 7/16	...	d	Neg	412	−16.6	38.6
26	APH	✓Amphenol Corp'A'	NY,P	NR	81	3212	Mfr elec&fiberoptic connectors	56⅝	5⅛	64	27	71½	29 7/16	56411	71½	63½	66 9/16	...	31	18	121	44.1	22.6
27	AMPI	✓Amplicon, Inc	NNM	B+	39	2691	Lease/sell computers,elec eq	17½	3⅜	24	11¾	16⅜	8	1943	12	10¼	10⅞B	1.5	7	11	−26.9	5.0	4.8
¶28•[10]	AMR	✓AMR Corp	NY,B,C,Ch,P,Ph	B–	672	134331	Hldg co:American Airlines	66¼	2 7/16	89 15/16	45⅝	75 7/16	52 9/16	177001	70	59	67	...	14	46	12.8	15.0	20.3
29	AAR	AMR Corp 7.875%'PINES'	NY	....[59]	3	37	Public Income NOTES	....	....	....	....	25	19 9/16	5603	22 3/16	19 9/16	20 9/16	9.6	..	...	...	...	...
30	AXR	✓AMREP Corp	NY,B,Ch,P,Ph	B–	24	1163	Land develop: dstr mag,books	23 7/16	7/16	10½	5½	8	3⅜	2310	4 13/16	3⅜	4¾	...	6	16	−25.5	7.0	−5.3
31	AMCT	✓AMRESCO Capital Tr	NNM	NR	38	3726	Real estate investment trust	....	....	15 1/16	5⅞	11 1/16	8	13755	9	8¼	8½	18.7	..	...	5.6	...	...
✢32	AMMB	✓AMRESCO INC	NNM	B	114	12042	Specialty financial svcs	37⅞	⅛	39¾	1 5/16	12 13/16	1¼	257239	3⅛	1¼	1⅜	...	d	Neg	−83.9	−62.5	−26.6
¶33•[11]	ASO	✓AmSouth Bancorp	NY,B,Ch,Ph,P	A–	403	92779	Comm'l bkg,Alabama,Florida	25⅜	1	30 7/16	20 7/16	34 9/16	18¾	178594	23 1/16	18¾	19 5/16	4.1	12	19	−34.6	13.6	24.6
34	ATC	✓AmTec Inc	AS	NR	11	852	Dvp stg:Telecom svcs, China	6¼	½	2½	9/16	3½	13/16	76035	2¼	1 3/16	1 13/16	...	d	8	107	−16.0	...
35	AVZ	✓AMVESCAP PLC[63]ADS	NY,Ch,Ph	NR	28	3172	Investment management svcs	43⅛	15 11/16	62¼	21½	58½	36	3233	58½	51	56½	1.2	28	12	49.3	39.1	...
36•[12]	AAP	✓Amway Asia Pacific[64]	NY,Ch,Ph	NR	19	1501	Dstr vehicle for Amway prd	49⅝	16¼	22 15/16	8¼	18	6⅞	10763	18	17¼	17 15/16	...	82	−45	96.6	−23.2	−9.1
37	AJL	✓Amway Japan Ltd[65]ADS[66]	NY,Ch,Ph,P	NR	22	3458	Dstr Amway products in Japan	25¾	8½	11⅝	3½	7¼	3¾	23563	7¼	5 15/16	6 9/16	5.8	20	−17	33.1	−22.3	−12.2
38	AMW	✓Amwest Insur Group	AS,Ch,P	B	24	1636	Hldg co:underwrite surety bds	15 1/16	6⅜	15 5/16	11 13/16	13 3/16	6⅜	981	7 7/16	6¾	7¼	5.0	13	21	−36.3	−5.0	1.2
¶39•[3]	APC	✓Anadarko Petroleum	NY,B,P	B	566	96017	Oil & gas explor,dev,prod'n	38⅜	9 3/16	44⅞	24¾	42¾	26¼	151474	34 7/16	28⅜	34⅛	0.6	..	Neg	11.2	2.3	12.8
40•[13]	ANAD	✓ANADIGICS Inc	NNM	NR	112	11855	Dstr microwave commun eqp	54¼	8	35½	4⅝	55⅜	11 3/16	57932	55⅜	43¼	47 3/16	...	d	Neg	313	21.8	...
¶41•[9]	ADI	✓Analog Devices	NY,B,Ch,P,Ph	B	556	139287	Electronic measure/contr pr	36 11/16	1/16	39⅝	12	94½	24⅜	350467	94½	58¾	93	...	85	12	196	54.4	52.0
✢42	ALOG	✓Analogic Corp	NNM	B+	96	5959	Data conversion products	41	1/16	48	31	40½	23	3567	33	27	33	0.8	24	8	−11.5	0.2	12.5
✢43	ANLY	✓Analysts Intl	NNM	A+	123	11835	Computer program'g serv's	36½	1/32	36	13¼	19¾	8⅝	18664	12 15/16	11½	12½	3.2	14	15	−33.0	−10.7	15.3
44	ANLT	✓Analytical Surveys	NNM,NSC	B+	40	1563	Computerized maps/info files	36	⅝	54½	15⅛	37⅝	11 1/16	20410	14¼	11 1/16	11 7/16	...	7	53	−62.9	5.0	28.7
✢45•[1]	SLOT	✓Anchor Gaming	NNM	NR	153	5029	Oper gaming machines,CO,NV	99½	10½	94¾	42	64 7/16	33	11093	57	40½	43 7/16	...	12	24	−22.9	2.6	23.3
46	ANCR	✓Ancor Communications	NNM	NR	78	10671	Mfr,sell communic network prd	41⅜	2½	9⅛	1	94⅛	4	201768	94⅛	58	67⅞	...	d	7	1597	69.2	64.6
47	AXL	✓Anderson Exploration	To	↑B	20	8543	Oil & gas explor,dvlp,prod'n	20¼	3½	19⅜	12½	22⅝	11⅝	99571	17⅜	14¾	17¼	...	31	56	24.1	−0.9	6.4
48	ANDN	Andover.Net Inc	NNM	NR	..	...	Oper network of web sites	....	....	....	....	90	18	277665	90	18	35⅝	...	d	...	...	...	...
49•[12]	AND	✓Andrea Electronics	AS,Ch,P	C	15	662	Devlp electr communic sys/eq	34¼	⅛	26⅛	4	12¾	5	34367	10	7¼	7 11/16	...	d	−2	−21.7	11.9	−8.4
¶50•[1]	ANDW	✓Andrew Corp	NNM	B	295	44660	Telecomm antennas & lines	42 9/16	⅞	30 1/16	10⅜	22⅞	11	191326	20½	13	18 15/16	...	51	−1	14.8	−18.7	4.2
51	ADRX	✓Andrx Corp	NNM	NR	166	10678	Pharmaceutical products	23½	5½	25 13/16	12¼	78	22¼	70049	52¼	38½	42 5/16	...	17	NM	65.3	73.8	...

Uniform Footnote Explanations-See Page 4. Other: [1]CBOE:Cycle 1. [2]Ph:Cycle 2. [3]CBOE:Cycle 2. [4]CBOE,Ph:Cycle 2. [5]ASE,CBOE:Cycle 1. [6]Ph:Cycle 1. [7]ASE,P:Cycle 1. [8]ASE,CBOE,P,Ph:Cycle 1. [9]Ph:Cycle 3. [10]ASE:Cycle 2. [11]ASE,Ph:Cycle 3. [12]ASE,CBOE:Cycle 2. [13]ASE,CBOE,Ph:Cycle 1. [51]Excl subsid pfd. [52]Incl 9.9M Subordinated Units. [53]AmerUs Life Pur contract & 6.86% 'QUIPS'. [54]Re-spec cond. [55]Clear Channel plan acq,stk. [56]Redempt'n of Stk Pur Rt. [57]Spl div. [58]Incl common privately held. [59]Rated BBB- by S&P. [60]Approx. [61]Issue debt only. [62]®$1.05,'96. [63]Ea ADS rep 5 Ord shr,par 25p. [64]New AAP Limited plan acq,$18. [65]Ea ADS rep 0.5 com, no par. [66]NAJ Co Ltd plan acq,cash. [67]Pfd in $M.

Common and Convertible Preferred Stocks

Index	Splits ◆ Cash Divs. Ea. Yr. Since	Dividends: Latest Payment Period $	Date	Ex. Div.	Total $ So Far 1999	Ind. Rate	Paid 1998	Financial Position Mil-$: Cash & Equiv.	Curr. Assets	Curr. Liab.	Balance Sheet Date	Capitalization: Lg Trm Debt Mil-$	Shs. 000 Pfd.	Com.	Earnings $ Per Shr. Years End	1995	1996	1997	1998	1999	Last 12 Mos.	Interim Earnings Period	$ per Shr. 1998	1999	Index
1	....	None Since Public			...	Nil	....	45.0	1880	2343	9-30-99	1944	...	70733	Dc	v□1.87	vd0.60	v□1.57	v□0.46	E3.53	1.30	9 Mo Sep	v□2.02	v2.86	1
2	1931	Q0.32	12-1-99	11-4	1.28	1.28	1.26	Total Assets $520.57M			9-30-99	160	82	8958	Dc	v1.54	v1.69	v1.56	v1.62	....	1.97	12 Mo Sep	v1.62	v1.97	2
3	....	None Since Public			...	Nil	....	5.60	25.2	5.84	9-30-99	3.66	...	3827	Je	Δ0.45	0.53	v0.87	v1.05	v0.56	0.79	3 Mo Sep	vd0.02	v0.21	3
4	....	None Since Public			...	Nil	....	41.7	120	77.6	9-30-99	376	...	±155703	Dc	...	...	vpd0.14	□vd0.48	....	d0.33	9 Mo Sep	v□d0.37	vd0.22	4
5◆	1996	0.06	4-19-99	4-6	0.06	0.06	0.07	0.70	33.7	13.9	9-30-99	14.9	...	2475	Dc	v1.23	v0.65	v0.81	v0.85	....	1.15	9 Mo Sep	v0.01	v0.31	5
6	....	None Since Public			...	Nil	....	3.50	5.22	5.03	10-31-99	1.88	17	7825	Ja	p0.06	v0.02	vd1.13	vd0.21	....	d0.06	9 Mo Oct	vd0.22	vd0.07	6
7◆	1948	Q0.21½	11-15-99	10-27	0.86	0.86	0.82	46.0	284	397	9-30-99	2397	[51]2067	96915	Dc	v1.32	v1.31	v1.45	v1.58	....	1.45	9 Mo Sep	v1.20	v1.07	7
8◆	....	None Since Public			...	Nil	....	Total Assets $1323.51M			9-30-99	375	...	73570	Je	0.48	v0.34	v0.48	v0.76	v1.11	1.23	3 Mo Sep	v0.23	v0.35	8
9	1995	0.55	11-18-99	11-8	2.20	2.20	2.20	8.08	114	135	6-30-99	706	...	[52]41969	Sp	p0.04	p0.24	v1.04	v0.51	Pvd0.68	d0.68				9
10	....	None Since Public			...	Nil	....	6.46	11.3	15.4	9-30-99	59.8	...	5107	Dc	v0.34	v0.49	vd0.19	vd0.20	....	d0.09	9 Mo Sep	v□d0.03	v0.08	10
11◆	....	None Since Public			...	Nil	....	100	1795	1185	6-30-99	567	...	±48746	Sp	±□0.77	v±□0.93	±□v0.98	v±1.04	Pv□1.38	1.38				11
12◆	....	None Since Public			...	Nil	....	Total Assets $2652M			6-25-99	58.0	...	±174437	Sp	0.05	0.07	v±0.08	vNil	Pv0.07	0.07				12
13	1939	Q0.32	11-16-99	10-26	1.28	1.28	1.28	9.68	253	118	8-31-99	142	...	3992	Nv	3.15	v3.87	v4.73	v5.08	....	6.45	9 Mo Aug	v2.37	v3.74	13
14	1997	Q0.10	11-30-99	11-17	0.40	0.40	0.40	Total Assets $10924M			9-30-99	367	...	±30099	Dc	pv2.99	pv3.20	v2.46	v1.86	....	2.08	9 Mo Sep	v1.43	v1.65	14
15	1998	0.552	7-27-99	7-22	1.657	2.21	0.552	7-27-2001 exch for AmerUs Life com[54]				....	...	★4150	Dc	...	...	...	....	....	....	Mand redemption 7-27-2003			15
16	....	None Paid			...	Nil	....	42.3	1287	816	10-30-99	800	...	29134	Ja	vd0.08	v□0.85	v1.46	v1.40	Ed0.46	d1.51	9 Mo Oct	v0.47	vd2.44	16
17◆	1942	Q0.06	12-23-99	12-7	0.24	0.24	0.24	18.7	296	313	9-30-99	227	...	32174	Dc	v□1.62	v1.54	v1.49	v□1.50	....	1.58	9 Mo Sep	v□1.31	v1.39	17
18	....	None Since Public			...	Nil	....	30.1	192	137	9-30-99	1199	...	83598	Dc	...	pvd0.55	□vd0.71	vd2.11	....	d3.69	9 Mo Sep	vd1.21	vΔd2.79	18
19◆	....	None Since Public			...	Nil	....	86.5	680	444	9-30-99	5646	4886	209779	Dc	vd0.26	vd0.33	□vd0.41	v□d0.54	....	d0.75	9 Mo Sep	v□d0.31	vd0.52	19
20◆	....	[56]0.00	3-21-97	3-24	...	Nil	....	1524	2126	818	9-30-99	223	...	1021516	Dc	v0.30	v0.61	v0.59	v0.81	E0.97	0.97	9 Mo Sep	v0.59	v0.75	20
21	....	None Since Public			...	Nil	....	288	553	338	9-30-99	842	...	124781	Dc	pv0.62	pv0.36	pv0.48	vp0.66	....	0.64	9 Mo Sep	vp0.49	v0.47	21
22	1994	Q0.46	11-23-99	11-9	1.81	1.84	1.76	Total Assets $828.35M			9-30-99	410	3975	16985	Dc	v1.18	□v1.20	□v1.44	v1.49	....	1.70	9 Mo Sep	v0.96	v1.17	22
23	....	[57]0.21	12-28-95	12-13	...	Nil	....	Total Assets $324M			9-30-99	139	943	[58]18268	Dc	0.08	vd0.38	v0.50	v0.07	....	1.05	9 Mo Sep	vd0.04	v0.94	23
24	1966	Q0.10	1-31-00	1-12	0.40	0.40	0.36	17.9	116	36.8	9-30-99	14.7	...	9590	Dc	v0.94	v1.29	v1.73	v1.64	....	1.50	9 Mo Sep	v1.27	v1.13	24
25	....	None Since Public			...	Nil	....	15.3	83.0	31.9	9-30-99	45.7	26	54519	Dc	1.78	v0.28	v0.32	v0.20	....	d0.18	9 Mo Sep	v0.19	vd0.19	25
26	....	None Since Public			...	Nil	....	8.97	340	147	9-30-99	938	...	★20616	Dc	v1.33	1.45	v□1.83	v2.03	....	2.12	9 Mo Sep	v1.58	v1.67	26
27◆	1994	Q0.04	1-7-00	12-21	0.16	0.16	0.16	Total Assets $439.14M			9-30-99	235	...	11640	Je	0.99	v1.09	v1.31	v1.55	v1.60	1.58	3 Mo Sep	v0.37	v0.35	27
28◆	....	0.05	2-15-80	1-28	...	Nil	....	1965	5112	6509	9-30-99	5217	...	148083	Dc	v□1.25	v□6.08	v5.39	v7.52	E4.95	5.57	9 Mo Sep	v6.39	v4.44	28
29	1999	Q0.492	10-31-99	10-13	[60]0.591	1.969	....	Co opt to redm fr 7-13-2004 at $25				[61]★150	...	...	Dc	...	...	...	....	....	....	Due 7-13-2039			29
30	....	None Paid			...	Nil	....	Total Assets $185.79M			10-31-99	49.7	...	7240	Ap	v0.55	v0.38	v0.99	v1.11	v1.02	0.85	6 Mo Oct	v0.44	v0.27	30
31	1998	0.44	1-27-00	12-29	1.55	1.59	0.34	Total Assets $261.21M			9-30-99	113	...	10015	Dc	...	...	...	n/a	....	....	9 Mo Sep	n/a	v0.74	31
32	....	0.05	10-15-95	9-27	...	Nil	....	Total Assets $2624.74M			9-30-99	1881	...	48771	Dc	v0.85	v[62]1.06	v1.53	vd1.61	....	d3.66	9 Mo Sep	v0.80	vd1.25	32
33◆	1943	Q0.20	1-3-00	12-13	0.673	0.80	0.533	Total Deposits $12947.29M			9-30-99	4239	...	p391088	Dc	v0.88	0.96	v1.21	v1.45	E1.68	1.64	9 Mo Sep	v1.06	v1.25	33
34	....	None Since Public			...	Nil	....	0.74	0.84	0.80	9-30-99	....	...	35530	Mr	d0.21	vd0.14	vd0.23	vd0.23	....	d0.16	6 Mo Sep	vd0.12	vd0.05	34
35◆	1995	0.289	10-15-99	9-1	0.678	0.68	0.989	199	679	544	j12-31-98	686	...	670023	Dc	1.15	1.52	v1.69	v1.25	....	1.99	9 Mo Sep	v0.85	v1.59	35
36	1994	Div Suspended 10-14-98			...	Nil	0.66	157	277	175	8-31-98	....	...	56442	Au	1.50	1.37	v1.76	v0.03	Pv0.22	0.22				36
37	1994	0.207	12-8-99	8-26	0.382	0.38	0.332	177	494	324	8-31-98	....	...	144026	Au	0.79	0.86	v0.65	v0.33	Pv0.33	0.33				37
38◆	1986	Q0.09	1-14-00	12-29	0.361	0.36	0.364	Total Assets $228.43M			9-30-99	14.5	...	4325	Dc	v0.90	vd0.67	v1.32	v1.44	....	0.56	9 Mo Sep	v1.19	v0.31	38
39◆	1986	Q0.05	12-22-99	12-6	0.20	0.20	0.18¾	14.8	259	232	9-30-99	1405	200	127519	Dc	v0.18	v0.85	v0.89	vd0.41	E0.22	d0.44	9 Mo Sep	v0.06	v0.03	39
40◆	....	None Since Public			...	Nil	....	37.3	86.6	32.6	10-03-99	3.32	...	★18406	Dc	v0.64	v0.93	v1.02	vd0.65	....	d0.38	9 Mo Sep	vd0.39	vd0.12	40
41◆	....	5%Stk	4-10-78	3-20	...	Nil	....	637	1249	357	7-31-99	100	...	174459	Oc	0.75	1.03	v1.04	v□0.71	vP1.10	1.10				41
42	1995	Q0.07	11-4-99	10-19	0.28	0.28	0.24	121	244	37.3	10-31-99	6.34	...	12800	Jl	v1.02	v1.04	v1.58	v1.87	v1.53	1.36	3 Mo Oct	v0.37	v0.20	42
43◆	1988	Q0.10	2-15-00	1-27	0.40	0.40	0.34	35.0	136	54.5	9-30-99	20.0	...	22558	Je	0.51	0.56	v0.73	v0.99	v1.00	0.90	3 Mo Sep	v0.27	v0.17	43
44◆	....	None Paid			...	Nil	....	2.91	69.5	20.7	6-30-99	26.3	...	6932	Sp	0.27	0.38	v0.60	v1.06	Pv1.60	1.60				44
45	....	None Since Public			...	Nil	....	26.9	102	50.8	9-30-99	213	...	11994	Je	1.40	1.84	v2.63	v5.20	v3.82	3.64	3 Mo Sep	v1.48	v1.30	45
46	....	None Paid			...	Nil	....	71.9	78.7	5.57	9-30-99	5.82	...	27756	Dc	vd0.44	vd0.60	vd0.93	vd1.04	....	d0.16	9 Mo Sep	vd1.11	vd0.23	46
47	....	None Paid			...	Nil	....	....	99.8	117	6-30-99	618	...	125130	Sp	d0.05	0.40	0.72	v0.20	Pv0.56	j0.56				47
48	....	None Since Public			...	Nil	....	9.87	10.5	2.97	9-30-99	0.76	p...	★15000	Sp	...	...	...	....	vpd1.44	d1.44				48
49◆	....	0.013	1-15-90	12-20	...	Nil	....	9.35	21.4	5.77	9-30-99	0.71	[67]7	13243	Dc	vd0.20	vd0.05	v0.39	vd0.61	....	d0.70	9 Mo Sep	vd0.31	vd0.40	49
50◆	....	None Since Public			...	Nil	....	53.8	394	103	6-30-99	51.1	...	82049	Sp	□0.77	0.99	v0.97	v1.18	vP0.37	0.37				50
51◆	....	None Since Public			...	Nil	....	107	273	110	9-30-99	....	...	31467	Dc	vd0.28	vd0.17	vd0.27	v0.27	....	2.46	9 Mo Sep	v0.07	v2.27	51

◆Stock Splits & Divs By Line Reference Index [5]10%,'96. [7]2-for-1,'96. [8]2-for-1,'98. [11]2-for-1,'99. [12]2-for-1,'98,'99:3-for-1,'99. [17]No adj for Culligan stk dstr,'97. [19]3-for-2,'96:2-for-1,'98. [20]2-for-1,'95,'99(twice). [27]2-for-1,'97. [28]2-for-1,'98. [33]3-for-2,'97,'98,'99. [35]2-for-1,'98. [38]10%,'98,'99. [39]2-for-1,'98. [40]3-for-2,'97. [41]3-for-2,'95,'96:4-for-3,'97. [43]2-for-1,'96:3-for-2,'97. [44]3-for-2,'96. [49]2-for-1,'97. [50]3-for-2,'94,'95,'96,'97. [51]2-for-1,'99.

¶ S&P 500
# MidCap 400
✣ SmallCap 600
• Options

Index	Ticker	Name of Issue (Call Price of Pfd. Stocks)	Market	Com. Rank. & Pfd. Rating	Inst. Hold Cos	Inst. Hold Shs. (000)	Principal Business	Price Range 1971-97 High	1971-97 Low	1998 High	1998 Low	1999 High	1999 Low	December, 1999 Dec. Sales in 100s	Last Sale Or Bid High	Low	Last	%Div Yield	P-E Ratio	EPS 5 Yr Growth	% Annualized Total Return 12 Mo	36 Mo	60 Mo
✣1	AGL	✓Angelica Corp	NY,Ch,Ph	B–	92	5204	Mfr/rental career apparel	40¼	2 9/16	24½	14⅛	19⅜	8 11/16	8333	11 1/16	8 11/16	9¾	9.8	13	–16	–44.2	–15.7	–14.8
2•[1]	AU	✓Anglogold Ltd ADS[51]	NY,Ph	NR	99	14236	South Africa gold mining	....	....	31	16	37	18 1/16	47903	26 7/16	23 9/16	25 11/16	5.4	15	...	38.5	...	...
¶3•[2]	BUD	✓Anheuser-Busch Cos	NY,B,Ph,P	A	1264	286655	Largest U.S. brewer:baking	48¼	1 7/16	68¼	42 15/16	84	64 7/16	306244	75½	66⅛	70⅞	1.7	24	12	9.6	...	...
4•[3]	ANIC	✓Anicom Inc	NNM	NR	51	8493	Dstr commun wires,cable eqp	18⅝	3	17⅛	5⅞	11	3½	53605	5	4	4¼	...	d	Neg	–53.7	–22.8	...
✣5•[1]	AXE	✓Anixter Intl	NY,Ch,Ph,P	B	175	19988	Dstr wiring sys/networking prd	22 1/16	⅛	22¾	11⅞	23¾	10⅝	14843	22	19⅛	20⅝	...	7	31	1.5	8.6	3.6
6	NLY	✓Annaly Mortgage Mgmt	NY,Ph	NR	39	4554	Real estate investment trust	13⅛	10	11¾	6⅛	11 9/16	7 15/16	8973	9 3/16	8 5/16	8¾	16.0	7	...	21.5	...	...
✣7•[4]	ANN	✓AnnTaylor Stores	NY,Ch,Ph,P	B–	..	...	Retail women's apparel/shoes	44⅞	9¼	40¼	11¼	53 1/16	31 3/16	115722	44 7/16	32 11/16	34 7/16	...	18	82	–12.7	25.3	0.0
8•[5]	ALRE	✓Annuity & Life Re (Holdings)	NNM	NR	123	21489	Life reinsurance,annuity pds	....	....	27	15	29⅛	18⅝	17451	28¾	20⅞	26⅛	0.6	..	...	–2.6	...	...
9	ANSS	✓ANSYS Inc	NNM	NR	43	10289	Dvp engineering softwr	15½	5⅜	12¾	5½	12 1/16	6⅜	23306	12 1/16	9⅛	11	...	13	...	0.0	–6.6	...
10•[5]	ANTC	✓ANTEC Corp	NNM	NR	264	30932	Dvlp CATV transmission pd	38½	7⅜	25	10⅜	60¼	18	366626	55 15/16	23¼	36½	...	26	43	81.4	59.5	14.7
11•[6]	AHR	✓Anthracite Capital	NY,Ph	NR	50	10076	Real estate investment trust	....	....	15½	3⅝	7 15/16	6	19072	6 15/16	6⅛	6⅜	18.2	..	...	–3.3	...	...
12	ANH	✓Anworth Mortgage Asset	AS	NR	4	235	Real estate investment trust	....	....	9⅛	3⅛	5½	3¾	1537	4 13/16	4 7/16	4½	12.4	..	...	23.6	...	...
13	ANU Pr	ANZ Exch Pfd Tr[57]	NY	A–	2	21	Closed-end mgmt inv co	....	....	26	24½	25⅞	20 11/16	8841	23	20 11/16	21⅝	9.2	..	...	–8.1	...	...
14	TNT	✓A.O.Tatneft ADS[59]	NY	NR	16	3044	Oil & gas explor,dev,prod'n	....	....	23¾	1¼	9⅝	1 5/16	37857	9⅝	4¼	9½	0.6	9	...	405	...	...
¶15•[7]	AOC	✓Aon Corp	NY,B,Ch,P	B+	473	136983	Insur hldg:accid,health,life	39¼	¾	50⅜	32 3/16	46 11/16	26 1/16	142633	41 1/16	33½	40	2.1	17	6	15.2	17.0	27.0
16	APAT	APA Optics	NSC	C	3	115	Dvlp optic/optoelectronic sys	9¼	1½	8	4	19½	3½	9348	19½	7	15½	...	d	–47	218	52.4	34.7
17•[8]	APAC	✓APAC Customer Services	NNM	NR	50	6994	Provides marketing svcs	59	8	16¼	2¾	14 1/16	2 3/16	150798	14 1/16	5½	14 1/16	...	d	Neg	272	–28.4	...
¶18•[9]	APA	✓Apache Corp	NY,B,Ch,P	B	628	96411	Oil,gas explor'n & prod'n	45 1/16	1 11/16	38¾	21 1/16	49 15/16	17⅝	207735	37⅝	30	36 15/16	0.8	27	Neg	47.3	2.6	9.1
19	Pr C	$2.015'C' Cv Pfd(NC)	NY	BBB–	50	5882		....	....	....	....	44¾	29 11/16	13525	35½	29 11/16	35½	5.7	..	...	...	...	...
20	AIV	✓Apartment Investment & Mgmt'A'	NY,Ch,Ph,P	NR	278	54710	Real estate investment trust	38	16¼	41	30	44⅛	34 1/16	43906	40 3/16	34 1/16	39 3/16	6.3	..	–8	14.1	19.3	26.8
21	Pr K	8.0% cm Cv Sr'K'Pfd([63]25.50)	NY	NR	20	4630		....	....	....	....	27¾	22 13/16	2622	24½	22 13/16	24½B	8.2	..	...	...	...	...
✣22	APEX	✓Apex Inc	NNM	NR	129	17343	Mfr/dgn switching systems	27 13/16	4 9/16	23½	7 9/16	35⅝	11	74880	34	23¼	32¼	...	36	...	111	...	...
23	AXM	✓Apex Mortgage Capital	NY	NR	17	543	Real estate investment trust	15	13 11/16	14 1/16	7⅛	14	9 9/16	4668	11⅝	9¾	10 3/16	18.1	5	...	20.1	...	...
24	SIL	✓Apex Silver Mines	AS	NR	30	8242	Explore/dvp silver prop	13 1/16	11	14⅛	6¾	15¼	7⅞	7720	12⅝	11⅜	12	...	d	...	45.5	...	...
25	APHT	✓Aphton Corp	NNM	NR	29	3141	Immune sys biopharmaceutl R&D	29¼	5	18⅛	6¼	17¾	9 13/16	7439	15⅝	12	15¼	...	d	–18	19.6	–7.9	10.2
✣26•[10]	APOG	✓Apogee Enterprises	NNM	B–	106	15077	Auto glass: alum window sys	25¼	⅛	15½	8⅛	14 5/16	4¾	28333	6⅛	4¾	5 1/16	4.1	7	–17	–53.9	–35.5	–8.6
#27•[5]	APOL	✓Apollo Group'A'	NNM	B	226	48175	Adult higher education svcs	32¾	1⅝	43¼	20½	34¼	17 9/16	150680	29⅝	20	20 1/16	...	25	36	–40.8	–3.4	70.2
28	AJA	Appalachian Pwr 8.00% Jr Debs[66]	NY	....[67]	5	123	Subsid of Amer Elec Pwr	26	23¾	26½	25	26⅛	21	1463	23 9/16	21	21¼	9.4	..	...	–10.2	...	...
29	APJ	Appalachian Pwr 8.25% Jr Debs[68]	NY	....[67]	4	116	Subsid of Amer Elec Pwr	26 5/16	24½	26½	25⅜	26½	21 7/16	532	24 3/16	21 7/16	22¼	9.3	..	...	–6.3	4.2	...
30	AJB	Appalachian Pwr 7.20% Sr Notes'A'	NY	NR	2	274	Subsid of Amer Elec Pwr	....	....	25 5/16	23 15/16	25¼	19	2034	21½	19	19⅞	9.1	..	...	–13.9	...	...
31	AJC	Appalachian Pwr 7.30% Sr Notes'B'	NY	NR	1	75	Subsid of Amer Elec Pwr	....	....	25½	24 3/16	25⅝	19⅛	4016	21⅝	19⅛	19¾	9.2	..	...	–14.8	...	...
¶32•[11]	AAPL	✓Apple Computer	NNM	B–	649	101931	Personal computer systems	73¼	5⅝	43¾	13½	118	32	840841	118	91 1/16	102 13/16	...	29	...	151	70.1	21.7
33	AOI	✓Apple Orthodontix'A'	AS	NR	9	695	Dental practice mgmt svcs	16¼	7	16½	2¼	4⅞	⅜	23241	⅝	⅜	7/16	...	d	...	–86.6	...	...
✣34•[5]	APPB	✓Applebee's Intl	NNM	A–	209	20149	Franchised restaur't operator	34¼	2	26	16⅛	35	20⅛	86147	30⅝	23	29½	0.3	17	22	43.6	2.8	17.6
35	AAII	✓Applied Analytical Industries	NNM	NR	36	6170	Pharmaceutical/biotech svcs	30¼	11¼	19⅛	9	28	4 15/16	11143	9¼	7⅛	9⅛	...	d	–48	–47.5	–21.9	...
36	ADSX	Applied Digital Solutions	NNM	NR	16	432	Dvlp software/hardware prod	9¾	2⅝	5½	1½	16	1⅝	713585	9	5	7½	...	d	59	111	12.6	...
37	AGTX	✓Applied Graphics Tech	NNM	NR	77	12949	Provide digital prepress svcs	62	10	61	7⅛	17 7/16	5⅞	23795	10 5/16	8 1/16	8⅝	...	d	...	–47.7	–33.3	...
✣38•[7]	APZ	✓Applied Indus Technologies	NY,Ch,Ph	B	117	13602	Dstr bearings & pwr transm'n	43 11/16	2	29 5/16	12	19 1/16	11⅛	5005	17⅛	16	16⅝	2.9	15	...	23.6	–1.2	4.9
39•[12]	APM	✓Applied Magnetics	NY,B,P,Ph	C	66	8424	Computer eq & components	60½	5/16	13 15/16	3 3/16	8 7/16	5/16	304247	¾	⅜	⅜	...	d	Neg	–93.9	–76.8	–36.0
¶40•[7]	AMAT	✓Applied Materials	NNM	B	1181	266356	Reactors to mfr thin films	54 3/16	1/32	47	21 9/16	129	42⅞	1159343	129	98⅛	126 11/16	...	67	9	197	92.1	64.8
41	AMCC	✓Applied Micro Circuits	NNM	NR	319	41103	Mfr integrated circits	6¾	4⅛	20 5/16	6⅛	128⅜	16 7/16	188947	128⅜	83½	127¼	...	..	...	650	...	...
✣42•[1]	APW	✓Applied Power Cl'A'	NY,Ph	↑B+	285	32243	Mfr hydraulic ind'l/constr eq	35 1/16	2½	40 3/16	20⅜	38⅞	21⅜	49652	36¾	30½	36¾	0.2	17	15	–1.8	23.2	24.1
43	APSG	✓Applied Signal Technology	NNM	B	21	2066	Mfr reconnaissance equipment	16¼	3¼	19¾	9 1/16	14⅝	5	8747	14½	11⅜	14 1/16	1.8	12	47	32.4	45.5	28.9
44	ATHY	✓AppliedTheory Corp	NNM	NR	29	2589	Internet technology prd	....	....	....	....	29¼	10	51266	29¼	17½	27¾	...	d	...	...	...	...
45	AOP	✓AppOnline.com Inc	AS	NR	4	26	Mortgage & brokerage svcs	7¾	3/16	3⅝	⅝	5 13/16	13/16	9447	2 1/16	1¼	1 7/16	...	d	...	–32.4	44.6	...
#46•[13]	AHG	✓Apria Healthcare Grp	NY,Ch	NR	174	38190	Home hlth care svcs/products	41⅝	9½	14⅛	2 9/16	22 1/16	7⅛	37675	18	13 7/16	17 15/16	...	..	–30	101	–1.5	–5.1
47	ATS	✓APT Satellite Hldg Ltd ADS[70]	NY,Ch	NR	20	3471	Satellite svcs,Asia-Pac region	19⅜	9⅞	14	2	7⅛	2⅜	17786	5	3⅞	4⅝	...	15	...	13.9	–30.9	...
✣48•[14]	ATR	✓AptarGroup Inc	NY,Ph	NR	261	29557	Mfr pkg compon'ts:pumps,valves	29 9/16	8	33 7/16	19 11/16	31½	22½	19161	28¼	24 11/16	25⅛	0.8	15	16	–9.9	13.3	12.6
✣49	WTR	✓Aquarion Co[71]	NY,Ch,Ph	B+	123	3644	Water util/enviro test'g labs	24⅝	5 5/16	27 7/16	20¾	37 5/16	22⅛	6927	37 5/16	36 9/16	37	3.0	17	13	40.8	32.2	25.6
50•[5]	ARA	✓Aracruz Celulose S.A.ADS[73]	NY,Ph,P	NR	118	23109	Produce eucalyptus kraft pulp	27½	7⅞	16¾	4 11/16	26½	7 15/16	54256	26½	20⅜	26¼	0.5	39	NM	231	17.9	8.4
51	ATV	✓ARC Intl	AS,To,Ch,P	B–	13	1540	Cable TV/movie theatre equip	7⅜	¼	6½	1	2¼	⅜	13893	15/16	⅜	¾	...	d	Neg	–52.0	–41.5	–25.4

Uniform Footnote Explanations-See Page 4. Other: [1]CBOE:Cycle 1. [2]P,Ph:Cycle 3. [3]Ph:Cycle 3. [4]P:Cycle 3. [5]CBOE:Cycle 2. [6]CBOE,Ph:Cycle 2. [7]P:Cycle 1. [8]Ph:Cycle 1. [9]CBOE,Ph:Cycle 1. [10]P,Cycle 2. [11]ASE,CBOE,P,Ph:Cycle 1. [12]CBOE,P:Cycle 1. [13]ASE:Cycle 2. [14]ASE:Cycle 1. [51]Ea ADS rep 0.5 Ord,.50R. [52]®$2.34,'96. [53]Pfd in $M. [54]19 Wks Jun '97. [55]10 Mo Dec'97. [56]9 Mo Dec'98. [57]Trust Units Exch for Pref Shs. [58]Or earlier re-spec cond. [59]Ea ADS rep 20 ord, 10 Roubles. [60]Approx. [61]To 5-15-2002. [62]0.8197 - 1 com re-spec cond. [63]Fr 2-18-2002. [64]Fiscal Apr'96 & prior. [65]9 Mo Jan'98:Fiscal Apr'97 earned d$0.44. [66]Jr Sub Deferrable Int Deb Sr'B'. [67]Rated BBB+ by S&P. [68]Jr Sub Deferrable Int Deb Sr'A'. [69]Excl subsid pfd shrs. [70]Ea ADS rep 8 Ord shr, HK$0.10. [71]Kelda Group plc plan acq,$37.05. [72]Final div. [73]Ea ADS rep 10 Cl'B' pref,no par. [74]Incl 575M Cl'B'pref.

Index	Splits ◆ Cash Divs. Ea.Yr. Since	Dividends Latest Payment Period $	Date	Ex. Div.	Total $ So Far 1999	Ind. Rate	Paid 1998	Financial Position Mil-$ Cash& Equiv.	Curr. Assets	Curr. Liab.	Balance Sheet Date	Capitalization Lg Trm Debt Mil-$	Shs. 000 Pfd.	Com.	Earnings $ Per Shr. Years End	1995	1996	1997	1998	1999	Last 12 Mos.	Interim Earnings Period	$ per Shr. 1998	1999	Index
1	1954	Q0.24	1-1-00	12-13	0.96	0.96	0.96	14.2	190	48.3	10-30-99	88.9	...	8676	Ja	0.13	v0.88	vd0.75	v0.99	....	0.73	9 Mo Oct	v0.77	v0.51	1
2	1998	0.741	10-4-99	8-18	1.379	1.38	0.607	14.9	149	172	12-31-97	85.9	2779	p97670	Dc	...	2.34	1.73	...	....	1.73				2
3◆	1932	Q0.30	12-9-99	11-5	1.16	1.20	1.08	131	1684	1822	9-30-99	4835	...	465290	Dc	v1.24	v[52]2.34	v2.36	v2.53	E2.93	2.88	9 Mo Sep	v2.18	v2.53	3
4◆	....	None Since Public			...	Nil	....	0.10	249	114	9-30-99	91.9	[53]20	25121	Dc	v0.14	v0.19	vNil	v0.30	....	d0.28	9 Mo Sep	v0.22	vd0.36	4
5◆	....	0.10	5-18-79	4-30	...	Nil	....	15.7	1128	450	10-01-99	557	...	36152	Dc	v0.70	v0.72	v0.95	v1.45	....	2.98	9 Mo Sep	v1.32	v2.85	5
6	1998	Q0.35	1-27-00	12-29	1.33½	1.40	0.91	Total Assets $1409M			9-30-99	....	...	13344	Dc	...	...	v[54][55]0.83	v1.19	....	1.33	9 Mo Sep	v0.91	v1.05	6
7	....	None Since Public			...	Nil	....	50.5	315	119	10-30-99	114	...	31538	Ja	d0.04	v0.36	v□0.47	v1.44	....	1.95	9 Mo Oct	v1.07	v□1.58	7
8	1998	Q0.04	12-2-99	11-16	0.16	0.16	0.04	Total Assets $1707M			12-31-98	....	...	25500	Dc	...	...	...	v0.76	....	....	9 Mo Sep	n/a	v0.95	8
9	....	None Since Public			...	Nil	....	54.8	65.8	15.5	9-30-99	....	...	16228	Dc	pvd0.17	v□0.09	v0.45	v0.68	....	0.82	9 Mo Sep	v0.49	v0.63	9
10	....	None Since Public			...	Nil	....	7.97	379	162	9-30-99	189	...	36715	Dc	vd0.23	v0.67	vd0.55	v0.15	....	1.43	9 Mo Sep	v0.10	v1.38	10
11	1998	Q0.29	1-31-00	12-29	1.16	1.16	0.63	Total Assets $669.67M			9-30-99	....	...	20964	Dc	...	...	n/a	v[56]d0.07	....	....	9 Mo Sep	n/a	v0.99	11
12	1998	Q0.14	1-18-00	12-30	0.51	0.56	0.25	Total Assets $171.95M			9-30-99	....	...	2278	Dc	...	...	n/a	v[56]0.38	....	....	9 Mo Sep	n/a	v0.39	12
13	1999	Q0.50	1-18-00	12-29	2.00	2.00	....	Exch for ANZ Pref Shs or cash re-spec cond				....	16000	...	Sp	...	...	...	...	....	....	Mand exch 10-15-2047[58]			13
14	1999	[60]0.026		5-25	[60]0.065	0.06	....	2335	9533	7498	j12-31-97	1788	1475	21457	Dc	0.26	d3.06	pv1.01	...	....	1.01				14
15◆	1950	Q0.21	11-15-99	10-29	0.813	0.84	0.733	Total Assets $21113.00M			9-30-99	1617	1000	256634	Dc	v1.53	v1.27	v1.12	v2.07	E2.30	1.81	9 Mo Sep	v1.54	v1.28	15
16	....	None Since Public			...	Nil	....	2.10	2.61	0.36	9-30-99	2.98	...	8824	Mr	d0.01	vNil	vd0.12	vd0.30	....	d0.39	6 Mo Sep	vd0.13	vd0.22	16
17◆	....	None Since Public			...	Nil	....	0.25	112	70.4	10-03-99	120	...	47563	Dc	pv0.18	v0.64	□v0.02	vd1.63	....	d1.67	9 Mo Sep	v0.10	v0.06	17
18	1965	Q0.07	1-31-00	12-29	0.28	0.28	0.28	16.6	355	342	9-30-99	1422	240	114083	Dc	v0.28	v1.38	v1.65	vd1.34	E1.36	d0.76	9 Mo Sep	v0.30	v0.88	18
19	1999	Q0.50⅝	2-15-00	1-27	0.991	2.015	....	Conv into 0.8197 com[61]				....	7000	...	Dc	...	...	...	...	....	....	Mand Cv 5-15-2002[62]			19
20	1994	Q0.62½	11-15-99	11-4	2.50	2.50	2.25	Total Assets $4507.17M			9-30-99	1581	p22824	66763	Dc	v0.86	v1.04	v1.08	v0.80	....	0.24	9 Mo Sep	v0.79	v0.23	20
21	1999	0.50	11-18-99	10-28	1.50	2.00	....	Cv into 0.59524 Cl'A'com $42				....	5700	...	Dc	...	...	...	...	....	....				21
22◆	....	None Since Public			...	Nil	....	60.0	89.3	4.93	10-01-99	....	...	20784	Dc	pv0.19	pv0.29	v□0.55	v0.75	....	0.89	9 Mo Sep	v0.52	v0.66	22
23	1998	Q0.46	1-21-00	12-29	1.56	1.84	0.81	Total Assets $766.64M			9-30-99	....	...	5753	Dc	...	...	n/a	v0.90	....	1.92	9 Mo Sep	v0.50	v1.52	23
24	....	None Since Public			...	Nil	....	26.2	27.5	1.98	12-31-98	1.97	...	26251	Dc	d0.20	vd0.66	vd0.72	vd0.42	....	d0.40	9 Mo Sep	vd0.28	vd0.26	24
25	....	None Since Public			...	Nil	....	14.4	15.1	3.01	10-31-99	....	...	15235	Ja	d0.32	[64]d0.37	v[65]d0.48	vd0.68	....	d0.66	9 Mo Oct	vd0.49	vd0.47	25
26◆	1974	Q0.05¼	11-9-99	10-21	0.21	0.21	0.20¼	7.25	202	104	8-28-99	170	...	27796	Fb	v0.65	v0.93	vd1.84	v0.91	....	0.74	9 Mo Nov	v0.73	v0.56	26
27◆	....	None Since Public			...	Nil	....	108	198	109	8-31-99	4.22	...	±76438	Au	±0.18	v±0.28	v±0.43	v±0.59	v±0.75	0.80	3 Mo Nov	v±0.17	v±0.22	27
28	1997	Q0.50	12-31-99	12-28	2.00	2.00	2.00	Co option redm fr 3-18-2002 at $25				★90.0	...	...	Dc	...	...	...	...	....	....	Mature 3-31-2027			28
29	1996	Q0.516	12-31-99	12-28	2.062	2.063	2.06¼	Co option redm fr 9-17-2001 at $25				★75.0	...	...	Dc	...	...	...	...	....	....	Mature 9-30-2026			29
30	1998	Q0.45	12-31-99	12-14	1.80	1.80	1.49	Co option redm fr 3-3-2003 at $25				★100	...	...	Dc	...	...	...	...	....	....	Mature 3-31-2038			30
31	1998	Q0.45⅝	12-31-99	12-28	1.82½	1.825	0.801	Co option redm fr 4-22-2003 at $25				★100	...	...	Dc	...	...	...	...	....	....	Mature 6-30-2038			31
32	....	0.12	12-15-95	11-21	...	Nil	....	3226	4285	1549	9-30-99	300	150	160880	Sp	3.45	d6.59	vd8.29	v2.10	v3.61	3.61				32
33	....	None Since Public			...	Nil	....	10.2	10.6	4.04	9-30-99	25.1	...	±13900	Dc	...	pvd7.24	±v0.09	v±d0.75	....	d0.78	9 Mo Sep	v±0.07	v±0.04	33
34◆	1991	A0.10	1-28-00	12-22	0.09	0.10	0.07	5.97	53.8	68.2	9-26-99	129	...	27231	Dc	vp0.92	v1.21	v1.43	v□1.67	E1.75	1.68	9 Mo Sep	v□1.28	v1.29	34
35	....	None Since Public			...	Nil	....	0.63	58.6	42.5	9-30-99	5.55	...	17205	Dc	pv0.20	vd0.26	v0.08	v0.35	....	d0.39	9 Mo Sep	v0.26	vd0.48	35
36	....	None Since Public			...	Nil	....	9.03	131	105	9-30-99	40.9	...	44709	Dc	v0.09	v0.15	v0.15	v0.13	....	d0.04	9 Mo Sep	v0.15	vd0.02	36
37	....	None Since Public			...	Nil	....	13.4	285	124	9-30-99	436	[69]...	22475	Dc	pvd0.80	v0.77	v0.83	v0.39	....	d0.14	9 Mo Sep	v0.60	v0.07	37
38◆	1957	Q0.12	11-30-99	11-10	0.48	0.48	0.60	15.2	374	134	9-30-99	101	...	20939	Je	0.98	v1.25	v1.44	v1.38	v0.93	1.15	3 Mo Sep	v0.06	v0.28	38
39	....	5%Stk	4-10-89	3-6	...	Nil	....	6.05	20.9	109	7-03-99	115	...	43737	Sp	0.08	1.35	v3.37	vd6.49	Pvd6.29	d6.29				39
40◆	....	None Since Public			...	Nil	....	2259	4404	1402	8-01-99	612	...	378415	Oc	1.28	v1.63	v1.32	v0.61	vP1.89	1.89				40
41◆	....	None Since Public			...	Nil	....	105	142	21.4	9-30-99	6.50	...	53951	Mr	...	p0.17	v0.38	v0.31	....	0.43	6 Mo Sep	v0.16	v0.28	41
42◆	1987	Q0.01½	11-30-99	11-15	0.06	0.06	0.06	22.3	409	324	8-31-99	808	...	38978	Au	□0.91	1.21	v1.47	v0.66	v1.98	2.16	3 Mo Nov	v0.41	v0.59	42
43	1999	Q0.06¼	5-12-00	4-26	0.12½	0.25	....	16.6	59.8	17.1	7-30-99	....	...	8454	Oc	0.12	0.23	v0.91	v1.15	Pv1.14	1.14				43
44	....	None Since Public			...	Nil	....	54.9	63.1	11.8	9-30-99	5.08	...	21340	Dc	...	...	vd0.62	vd0.56	....	d0.67	9 Mo Sep	vd0.29	vd0.40	44
45	....	None Paid			...	Nil	....	Total Assets $113.8M			6-30-99	0.52	6	29954	Dc	...	...	vd0.10	v0.01	....	d0.11	9 Mo Sep	v0.03	vd0.09	45
46	....	None Since Public			...	Nil	....	36.6	206	159	9-30-99	399	...	52042	Dc	v□d1.58	v0.64	vd5.30	vd4.02	E0.10	1.03	9 Mo Sep	vd4.07	v0.98	46
47	....	None Since Public			...	Nil	....	12.4	15.3	55.4	12-31-97	66.3	...	420000	Dc	□0.28	0.25	v0.32	...	....	0.32				47
48◆	1993	Q0.05	11-23-99	10-29	0.18	0.20	0.16	32.0	363	169	9-30-99	235	...	36451	Dc	v0.99	v1.03	v1.27	v1.65	....	1.68	9 Mo Sep	v1.14	v1.17	48
49◆	1890	[72]0.28	1-4-00	12-21	0.834	1.12	1.097	3.37	54.6	27.1	9-30-99	141	...	11508	Dc	v1.26	v0.86	v1.39	v1.74	....	2.24	9 Mo Sep	v1.16	v1.66	49
50◆	1995	0.134	4-29-99	3-25	0.134	0.13	0.189	34.2	203	716	3-31-98	738	[74]616000	454908	Dc	±3.60	±1.20	□v0.67	...	....	0.67				50
51	....	None Since Public			...	Nil	....	1.86	23.9	24.6	6-30-99	33.7	...	14279	Dc	0.61	v0.70	v0.69	vd0.85	....	d1.07	6 Mo Jun	vd0.14	vd0.36	51

◆Stock Splits & Divs By Line Reference Index [3]2-for-1,'96:No adj for dstr of Earthgrains, '96. [4]2-for-1,'96. [5]2-for-1,'95. [15]3-for-2,'97,'99. [17]2-for-1,'96. [22]3-for-2,'99. [26]2-for-1,'97. [27]4-for-3,'95:3-for-2,'95,Feb,Jun,'96,'98. [34]3-for-2,'94. [38]3-for-2,'95,'97. [40]2-for-1,'95,'97. [41]2-for-1,'99. [42]2-for-1,'98. [48]2-for-1,'98. [49]3-for-2,'99. [50]3-for-2,'94:4-for-3,'95:1-for-2 REVERSE,'97.

¶ S&P 500
# MidCap 400
✣ SmallCap 600
• Options

Index	Ticker	Name of Issue (Call Price of Pfd. Stocks)	Market	Com. Rank. & Pfd. Rating	Inst. Hold Cos	Inst. Hold Shs. (000)	Principal Business	Price Range 1971-97 High	1971-97 Low	1998 High	1998 Low	1999 High	1999 Low	Dec. Sales in 100s	December, 1999 Last Sale Or Bid High	Low	Last	%Div Yield	P-E Ratio	EPS 5 Yr Growth	% Annualized Total Return 12 Mo	36 Mo	60 Mo
1•[1]	AAC	✔Arcadia Financial Ltd	NY,Ch,Ph,P	NR	84	16683	Purchases,sells,svc auto loans	30⅝	3	10½	3	9 13/16	3⅜	52015	4 9/16	4¼	4 7/16	...	4	Neg	22.4	–32.2	–5.5
2	ARJ	✔Arch Chemicals	NY,Ph	NR	123	14970	Specialty chemical svcs	....	....	....	....	25 5/16	12 5/16	14153	21⅝	15½	20 15/16	3.8	13	...	...	...	...
3	ACI	✔Arch Coal	NY	NR	61	5260	Mining,mkt bituminous coal	30½	24⅜	29¼	14 7/16	16⅞	8 9/16	2656	11⅜	8 9/16	11 5/16	4.1	d	...	–31.4	...	...
4•[2]	APGR	✔Arch Communications Group	NNM	C	49	27228	Provides paging services	92¼	11¼	20 13/16	2 1/16	11⅝	3 3/16	64956	6¾	5¼	6⅝	...	d	–46	67.7	–36.4	–32.8
¶5•[3]	ADM	✔Archer-Daniels-Midland	NY,B,Ch,P,Ph	B+	540	348481	Process soybeans:flour mill'r	22 5/16	5/16	21 7/16	14⅛	16¼	11 7/16	313941	13 5/16	11 11/16	12⅛	s1.6	38	–23	–20.8	–8.7	–0.3
6•[4]	ASN	✔Archstone Communities Tr	NY,Ch,Ph,P	NR	234	65707	Real estate investment trust	25⅛	1½	24½	17⅞	23½	18 15/16	44935	21	18 15/16	20½	7.5	13	15	8.7	...	...
7	Pr A	7% cm Cv Sr'A'Pfd([51]25)	NY	↓BBB	31	2605		33⅞	20	32⅞	24	31⅝	25½	1841	28⅛	25½	28⅛	6.8	..	...	...	...	...
✣8•[5]	ACAT	✔Arctic Cat	NNM	B+	106	10003	Mfr snowmobiles&accessories	21¾	2⅛	10⅞	8	10½	7½	23279	10 5/16	9⅞	10	2.4	37	–15	0.8	3.0	–10.3
9	ARDNA	Arden Group Cl'A'	NNM	B	16	695	West Coast food supermkts	27¼	5/16	60	23 1/16	43⅞	33	243	38⅜	33⅛	36	...	11	33	–10.0	35.5	27.4
10	ARI	✔Arden Realty	NY,Ph	NR	218	50927	Real estate investment trust	32⅜	20	31⅛	19¾	27 3/16	17⅝	62862	20 7/16	17⅝	20 1/16	8.9	13	...	–6.6	–4.0	...
11•[6]	ARDT	✔Ardent Software	NNM	B–	127	11797	Dvlp softwr for UNIX oper sys	23¼	5¼	23⅞	7	40⅛	13¼	160187	40⅛	29¼	39	...	..	NM	69.6	73.2	17.1
12	AGR	✔Argentaria Banco Hipotecario ADS[52]	NY,P	NR	43	7912	General banking, Spain	32¼	14	51¾	29½	58	41¼	1583	47	44¼	46½	1.8	28	–1	–7.5	31.1	26.0
13	AGII	✔Argonaut Group	NNM	B–	99	7375	Ins hldg:workers comp,liab	38⅛	5	37½	21¼	27 15/16	18 11/16	9579	24	18 11/16	19⅞	8.3	17	22	–13.4	–8.4	–1.8
14	AGY	✔Argosy Gaming	NY,Ch,Ph	NR	78	13910	Operates riverboat casino	36¾	2¾	4½	1⅞	17 7/16	2⅝	66112	17 7/16	14	15 9/16	...	15	11	479	49.8	5.6
15	ARBA	✔Ariba Inc	NNM	NR	123	14457	Internet based business svcs	....	....	....	....	211	30½	747068	211	87¾	177⅜	...	d	...	...	...	...
16	AZL	✔Arizona Land Income'A'	AS	NR	6	596	Real estate investment trust	10⅝	2⅝	7 3/16	5	6¾	4¼	993	4⅞	4½	4⅝	e8.6	10	43	1.8	13.3	18.7
17	AZD	Arizona Pub Svc 10%'[54]MIDS'[55]	NY	....[56]	..	...	Electric utility, Arizona	28¾	24¾	28 3/16	26	26 11/16	24⅞	1285	25⅝	24⅞	25	10.0	..	...	...	...	...
✣18•[7]	ABFS	✔Arkansas Best	NNM	NR	92	10608	Genl truck'g:tire retreading	17⅛	4⅛	11 15/16	4 7/16	14¾	5	20431	14⅛	12	12	...	7	NM	105	40.0	–0.1
19	ARMHY	✔ARM Holdings ADS[57]	NNM	NR	38	3666	Dgn computer microprocessors	....	....	16⅞	8¾	205	15¼	14058	205	142	191½	...	..	...	1173	...	...
20	AH	✔Armor Holdings	NY,Ph	NR	55	12069	Mfr bullet resistant vests	13½	5 1/16	12½	8⅞	14 15/16	8½	9225	13⅛	11¼	13⅛	...	22	63	14.8	17.3	...
¶21•[8]	ACK	✔Armstrong World Indus	NY,B,Ch,P,Ph	B	388	29131	Mfr floor cover'gs/bldg prd	75⅝	6 3/16	90	46 15/16	64 5/16	29	60969	34¾	29	33⅝	5.8	6	Neg	–42.3	–19.2	0.1
22	AKK	Armstrong World Ind 7.45%'QUIBS'	NY	A–	7	340	Senior Qtly Interest Bonds	....	....	26⅛	24¾	25¾	19⅞	4551	22 3/16	19⅞	20⅜	9.1	..	...	–13.6	...	...
#23	AIND	✔Arnold Indus	NNM	A	116	14260	Trucking-gen'l commodities	25⅝	⅛	18⅛	11⅝	17	8	13255	14 7/16	10⅜	14 1/16	3.1	10	5	–10.2	–1.2	–4.9
24•[7]	ARQL	✔ArQule Inc	NNM	NR	31	4697	Pharmaceutical R&D	29¼	9	25½	4	12⅛	3½	38137	12⅛	5¼	10¼	...	d	...	108	–13.3	...
25	HRT	✔Arrhythmia Research Tech	AS,Ph	B–	2	198	Mkt cardiological medical prd	12¼	¾	2⅛	⅞	2⅞	1⅛	1064	2 3/16	1⅜	1⅝	...	27	51	23.9	–13.4	–8.3
#26•[9]	ARW	✔Arrow Electronics	NY,B,Ch,P	B–	291	89638	Dstr electronic components	36	7/16	36¼	11¾	26 9/16	13 3/16	59264	26½	19¾	25⅝	...	20	–3	–4.9	–1.6	7.3
27•[10]	ARRO	✔Arrow International	NNM	NR	103	6857	Mfr disposable catheters	48¾	17½	41¾	20⅞	31⅜	18⅝	10294	30⅛	25 7/16	29	0.8	19	–4	–6.8	1.0	–2.6
✣28•[7]	ATSN	✔Artesyn Technologies	NNM	B–	159	28361	Dvp/mfr pwr conv eq	33 7/16	⅛	26⅞	11¾	26	11 13/16	78012	23⅝	18¼	21	...	21	23	50.0	2.5	44.1
29	SRS	✔ARV Assisted Living	AS	NR	16	3919	Oper assisted living facilities	20¾	7¾	16⅛	2¾	6⅜	1⅜	22974	1 15/16	1⅜	1½	...	d	–38	–75.5	–49.5	...
#30•[11]	ARV	✔Arvin Indus	NY,B,Ch,P,Ph	B+	259	16676	Auto pts,exhaust/ride ctrl sy	41⅝	2 7/16	44⅛	31	42⅞	24⅝	28383	29⅛	24⅝	28⅜	3.1	8	NM	–30.3	7.2	6.9
31	GOAL	✔Ascent Entertainment Grp	NNM	NR	104	21368	Diverse entmt/media co	25¼	8⅛	12¾	5 11/16	17½	7¼	46990	13 1/16	11 13/16	12 11/16	...	d	Neg	72.0	–7.7	...
32	ASTSF	✔ASE Test Ltd	NNM	NR	47	9868	Integrated circuit testing	23	2½	28¼	10	26 15/16	15⅛	33818	25	17¼	24⅜	...	23	...	51.6	71.5	...
33•[12]	ASL	✔Ashanti Goldfields Ltd GDS[61]	NY,Ch,Ph	NR	88	28019	Gold mining,Ghana, Africa	25¾	6½	12	5¼	10 11/16	2 7/16	55509	3 7/16	2 7/16	2⅝	3.4	5	–20	–71.6	–39.2	...
34	ASFD	✔Ashford.com Inc	NNM	NR	13	2805	Web retailer - luxury items	....	....	....	....	35	9⅛	163622	25½	10½	11	...	d	...	...	...	...
¶35•[13]	ASH	✔Ashland Inc	NY,B,C,Ch,P,Ph	↑B+	400	45883	Petro/refining/chem/constr'n	55	5⅛	57 15/16	42¼	50⅝	30 5/16	47412	34	31⅛	32 15/16	3.3	9	41	–29.9	–6.8	1.8
36	ASTN	✔Ashton Tech Group	NSC	NR	23	1832	Info technology svcs	15½	13/16	4⅜	1⅛	18	1½	96117	8¼	5	6 7/16	...	d	...	296	6.2	...
37	ARH	✔Asia Pac Resources Intl'A'	NY,Ch,Ph	NR	10	10892	Pulp,paper,rayon fiber	10	1¾	3⅛	¼	1 13/16	5/16	28075	1 13/16	1⅛	1¾	...	d	–37	...	...	...
38	AWC	Asia Pacific Wire & Cable	NY,Ph	NR	8	2505	Mfr telecomun wire prod-Asia	14 1/16	7⅛	8¾	1⅞	4¾	2	1577	4⅛	3 7/16	4 1/16	...	d	...	1.6	...	...
39•[9]	PAP	✔Asia Pulp & Paper ADS[64]	NY,Ch,P	NR	107	77320	Mfr pulp & paper products	17⅛	7¼	16⅜	4¾	11⅞	5½	91245	8¾	7⅛	7⅞	...	13	31	–4.5	–11.4	...
40	WS	Wrrt(Pur 1 ADS at $9.36)	NY	....	27	3034		....	....	....	....	3⅞	⅝	9066	1 7/16	¾	15/16	...	..	...	...	...	...
41	SAT	✔Asia Satellite Telecom ADS[65]	NY,Ch	NR	22	1683	Satellite transponder capacity	33½	16½	22	9¾	36	13¾	3167	36	28	35	0.7	18	65	102	15.6	...
42	ASKJ	✔ASK Jeeves	NNM	NR	53	2242	Internet question,answering svc	....	....	....	....	190½	14	107277	144	102⅞	112 15/16	...	..	...	...	...	...
43•[14]	ASMI	✔ASM Intl N.V.	NNM	NR	7	2238	Eq to mfr semicond devices	20⅝	3/16	13⅛	2 7/16	24⅜	3⅝	126635	24⅜	16⅜	23	...	d	–37	338	33.7	71.7
44•[15]	ASML	✔ASM Lithography Hldg NV	NNM	NR	..	...	Dvlp photolithography proj sys	53⅞	4½	49 1/16	12 15/16	114⅞	31¼	118846	114⅞	90¾	113¾	...	..	...	273	110	...
✣45•[4]	ASPT	✔Aspect Communications[66]	NNM	B	149	29014	Mfr phone call process'g sys	33⅝	1 7/16	37 3/16	11¼	43½	6	190772	42¼	29	39⅛	...	d	Neg	127	7.2	36.1
46	ASDV	✔Aspect Development	NNM	NR	140	15853	Dvp client/server software	26 9/16	8⅜	45	15½	73¾	6¼	93887	73¾	44⅛	68½	...	..	NM	54.6	71.5	...
✣47	AZPN	✔Aspen Technology	NNM	B	146	16712	Chem engineer'g software prd	46¼	6½	56⅞	6⅛	30½	8⅛	76673	30½	20⅞	26 7/16	...	d	Neg	82.3	–13.0	21.9
48	AIC	✔Asset Investors Corp	NY,Ch,P	NR	24	1134	Mtge investments REIT	96¼	8⅛	21 3/16	12	15½	10 11/16	3830	13	10 11/16	11⅛	9.0	27	Neg	–6.2	–8.0	13.5
49	ALF	✔Assisted Living Concepts	AS,Ph	NR	54	9121	Own/oper sr citizen housing	22⅜	3¾	21⅝	9½	14⅝	¾	31242	2⅜	1⅛	2⅛	...	d	...	–83.8	–33.1	–11.7
#50•[16]	ASBC	✔Associated Banc-Corp	NNM	A	184	20605	Commercial banking,IL&WI	47⅜	½	44 3/16	25⅜	45	30 3/16	34969	40⅜	33⅜	34¼	3.4	14	8	3.5	10.7	16.6
51	AEC	✔Associated Estates Realty	NY	NR	65	3449	Real estate investment trust	24¾	17	24⅜	11½	12⅞	6 15/16	16795	7 15/16	6 15/16	7 13/16	19.2	13	–14	–23.4	–23.0	–9.4

Uniform Footnote Explanations-See Page 4. Other: [1]ASE,CBOE:Cycle 1. [2]CBOE:Cycle 3. [3]P,Ph:Cycle 3. [4]P:Cycle 3. [5]CBOE,Ph:Cycle 1. [6]ASE:Cycle 2. [7]CBOE:Cycle 1. [8]Ph:Cycle 3. [9]ASE:Cycle 3. [10]Ph:Cycle 2. [11]CBOE:Cycle 2. [12]ASE,CBOE:Cycle 2. [13]Ph:Cycle 1. [14]ASE,CBOE:Cycle 3. [15]P:Cycle 1. [16]CBOE,Ph:Cycle 3. [51]Fr 11-30-2003. [52]Ea ADS rep 0.5 com,125 Spanish Pesetas. [53]Approx. [54]Monthly Income Debt Securities. [55]Jr Sub Deferrable Int Debs Sr'A'. [56]Rated BBB- by S&P. [57]Ea ADS rep 3 ord, 1p. [58]®$3.81,'96. [59]Fiscal Mar'96 & prior. [60]9 Mo Dec'97. [61]Global Depositary shr ea rep 1 ord no par. [62]Excludes preference shr hld by Ghana govt.. [63]Stk dstr of PT Indorayon Utama. [64]Ea ADS rep 4 ord shrs,US$0.50. [65]Ea ADS rep 10 com, HK$0.10. [66]Formerly Aspect Telecommunications.

Common and Convertible Preferred Stocks

Splits ◆ Index	Cash Divs. Ea.Yr. Since	Dividends Latest Payment Period $	Date	Ex. Div.	Total $ So Far 1999	Ind. Rate	Paid 1998	Financial Position Mil-$ Cash& Equiv.	Curr. Assets	Curr. Liab.	Balance Sheet Date	Capitalization Lg Trm Debt Mil-$	Shs. 000 Pfd.	Com.	Earnings $ Per Shr. Years End	1995	1996	1997	1998	1999	Last 12 Mos.	Interim Earnings Period	$ per Shr. 1998	1999	Index
1	....	None Since Public			...	Nil	....	Total Assets $855M			9-30-99	453	...	39444	Dc	v□1.11	v1.65	v□d1.08	vd2.13	....	1.01	9 Mo Sep	vd2.26	v□0.88	1
2	1999	0.20	12-10-99	11-8	0.60	0.80	....	19.2	377	202	9-30-99	81.5	...	23003	Dc	...	...	Pvp2.26	Pvp1.55	....	1.57	9 Mo Sep	vp1.65	v1.67	2
3	1997	Q0.11½	12-15-99	11-12	0.46	0.46	0.46	4.14	330	313	9-30-99	1181	...	38187	Dc	...	pv1.21	vp1.30	v□0.79	....	d0.05	9 Mo Sep	v□0.79	vΔd0.05	3
4◆	....	None Since Public			...	Nil	....	21.9	107	160	6-30-99	1362	250	48061	Dc	v□d2.13	v□d16.59	vd26.31	v□d29.34	....	d30.92	9 Mo Sep	v□d7.55	□vd9.13	4
5◆	1927	Q0.05	11-29-99	11-3	s0.193	0.20	s0.136	1110	6304	4481	9-30-99	3200	...	608360	Je	1.22	1.10	v0.60	v0.65	v□0.45	0.32	3 Mo Sep	v0.19	v0.06	5
6◆	1970	Q0.38½	2-28-00	2-10	1.48	1.54	1.39	Total Assets $5299.71M			9-30-99	1995	11997	139400	Dc	v0.93	v□1.45	v0.65	□v1.50	....	1.54	9 Mo Sep	v□1.06	v□1.10	6
7	1993	0.498	12-31-99	12-9	1.994	1.913	1.872	Cv into 1.3469 com,$18.561				....	3797	...	Dc	...	...	...	....	....	....				7
8◆	1992	Q0.06	12-2-99	11-15	0.24	0.24	0.24	86.2	249	108	9-30-99	....	...	±25632	Mr	±0.56	v±0.78	v±0.88	v±0.84	....	0.27	6 Mo Sep	v0.73	v0.16	8
9◆	....	0.07½	8-24-87	8-11	...	Nil	....	30.8	49.9	25.9	10-02-99	5.32	...	±3585	Dc	v±1.37	v±0.79	v±1.44	v±2.81	....	3.32	9 Mo Sep	v2.04	v2.55	9
10	1997	Q0.44½	1-27-00	12-29	1.75½	1.78	1.66	Total Assets $2513.86M			9-30-99	977	...	63350	Dc	p1.16	p1.33	v1.41	v1.54	....	1.56	9 Mo Sep	v1.14	v1.16	10
11	....	None Since Public			...	Nil	....	37.9	83.6	61.6	9-30-99	....	...	19385	Dc	vd0.49	□vd0.33	v0.40	v0.10	....	0.37	9 Mo Sep	vd0.21	v0.06	11
12	1993	[53]0.046		12-8	0.82	0.82	0.782	Book Value $14.15			12-31-97	1523	...	122500	Dc	2.43	□1.86	v1.69	....	....	1.69				12
13	1989	Q0.41	11-23-99	11-5	1.64	1.64	1.64	Total Assets $1649M			9-30-99	....	...	22790	Dc	v2.32	d3.92	v2.02	v2.61	....	1.20	9 Mo Sep	v2.32	v0.91	13
14	....	None Since Public			...	Nil	....	37.7	72.9	106	9-30-99	346	...	28161	Dc	0.29	□vd0.98	vd1.65	v0.23	....	1.03	9 Mo Sep	v0.07	v□0.87	14
15◆	....	None Since Public			...	Nil	....	16.3	32.3	26.8	p3-31-99	0.69	...	90870	Sp	...	...	...	vpd0.24	Pvd0.84	d0.84				15
16	1988	Q0.10	1-14-00	12-28	†1.30	0.40	0.40	Total Assets $12.56M			9-30-99	....	...	±2344	Dc	±0.18	v±0.20	±v0.33	±v0.42	....	0.46	9 Mo Sep	v±0.28	v±0.32	16
17	1995	M0.208	12-31-99	12-28	2.50	2.50	2.50	Co option redm fr 1-31-2000 at $25				75.0	...	...	Dc	...	...	...	....	....	....	Mature 1-31-2025			17
18	....	0.01	2-28-96	2-12	...	Nil	....	4.37	242	279	9-30-99	202	1495	19735	Dc	vd1.90	vd2.10	v0.56	v1.21	....	1.84	9 Mo Sep	v0.80	v1.43	18
19◆	....	None Since Public			...	Nil	....	65.7	86.6	20.3	12-31-98	....	...	188856	Dc	...	...	v0.03	v0.17	....	0.24	9 Mo Sep	v0.11	v0.18	19
20	....	None Paid			...	Nil	....	24.0	84.2	25.5	9-30-99	2.57	...	23547	Dc	v0.08	v0.08	v0.21	v0.50	....	0.60	9 Mo Sep	v0.35	v0.45	20
21	1934	Q0.48	12-2-99	11-3	1.92	1.92	1.88	63.1	429	848	9-30-99	1586	...	40062	Dc	v2.68	□v[58]3.82	v4.50	vd0.23	E6.00	0.49	9 Mo Sep	v4.06	v4.78	21
22	1999	Q0.46½	1-18-00	12-30	1.793	1.86	....	Co option redm fr 10-28-2003 at $25				★180	...	...	Dc	...	...	...	....	....	....	Mature 10-15-2038			22
23	1972	Q0.11	12-3-99	11-17	0.44	0.44	0.44	17.9	77.5	57.6	9-30-99	0.16	...	24628	Dc	v1.13	v0.94	v1.22	v1.36	....	1.37	9 Mo Sep	v0.98	v0.99	23
24	....	None Since Public			...	Nil	....	41.0	45.0	11.7	9-30-99	9.53	...	12838	Dc	pd0.33	pd0.39	v0.02	vd0.54	....	d1.12	9 Mo Sep	vd0.32	vd0.90	24
25	....	None Since Public			...	Nil	....	0.70	3.94	1.21	9-30-99	0.65	...	3439	Dc	v0.31	v0.17	v0.01	vd0.04	....	0.06	9 Mo Sep	v0.01	v0.11	25
26◆	....	0.02½	10-13-86	9-18	...	Nil	....	49.2	3130	1340	9-30-99	1517	...	95990	Dc	v2.03	v1.98	v1.64	v1.50	E1.29	1.17	9 Mo Sep	v1.16	v0.83	26
27	1992	Q0.05½	12-15-99	11-26	0.22	0.22	0.20	3.94	167	58.7	8-31-99	11.1	...	22852	Au	1.52	1.41	v1.58	v0.37	v1.54	1.50	3 Mo Nov	v0.44	v0.40	27
28	....	None Since Public			...	Nil	....	40.9	226	101	10-01-99	46.2	...	37228	Dc	□v0.52	v0.79	v0.75	v0.67	....	1.02	9 Mo Sep	v0.42	v0.77	28
29	....	None Since Public			...	Nil	....	12.7	35.9	25.6	9-30-99	127	...	15873	Dc	d0.21	□[59]d0.15	v[60]d1.98	vd2.90	....	d3.39	9 Mo Sep	vd0.82	v□d1.31	29
30	1925	Q0.22	12-31-99	12-1	0.85	0.88	0.81	45.6	859	734	10-03-99	506	...	25829	Dc	v0.85	v2.03	v2.85	v3.23	....	3.72	9 Mo Sep	v2.40	v□2.89	30
31	....	None Since Public			...	Nil	....	72.8	212	63.6	9-30-99	332	...	29756	Dc	vd0.87	v□d1.20	vd1.40	vd1.67	....	d1.64	9 Mo Sep	vd1.36	vd1.33	31
32◆	....	None Since Public			...	Nil	....	20.3	60.4	49.8	12-31-98	73.5	...	77686	Dc	p0.23	0.31	v0.54	v1.14	....	1.08	6 Mo Jun	v0.29	v0.23	32
33	1995	0.09	6-7-99	4-1	0.09	0.09	0.068	113	276	282	12-31-98	414	[62]...	109338	Dc	1.22	v0.64	v0.50	v0.37	....	0.58	9 Mo Sep	v0.19	v0.40	33
34	....	None Since Public			...	Nil	....	24.6	31.4	1.79	6-30-99	....	p...	★36864	Mr	...	...	...	pvd0.10	....	d0.49	6 Mo Sep	vpd0.01	vpd0.40	34
35	1936	Q0.275	12-15-99	11-18	1.10	1.10	1.10	110	2059	1396	9-30-99	1627	...	72177	Sp	0.08	v2.96	□v3.76	v2.63	v3.89	3.89				35
36	....	None Since Public			...	Nil	....	28.0	29.6	18.8	9-30-99	....	233	25178	Mr	...	d0.49	vd1.46	vd1.80	....	d0.49	6 Mo Sep	vd1.68	vd0.37	36
37	1999	0.309	2-15-99	2-17	h[63]0.309	Nil	....	130	292	1126	12-31-98	555	...	±318500	Dc	0.23	vd0.42	vd0.59	vd0.13	....	d0.17	3 Mo Mar	v0.02	vd0.02	37
38	....	None Since Public			...	Nil	....	28.6	82.4	39.1	12-31-97	16.4	...	★10733	Dc	...	p1.62	vd0.60	Pv0.38	....	d0.18	9 Mo Sep	v0.36	vd0.20	38
39	....	0.037	8-11-97	7-14	...	Nil	....	1373	3925	2129	12-31-98	7714	...	★1151582	Dc	v1.16	v0.75	v1.06	v0.60	....	0.60				39
40	....	Terms&trad. basis should			be checked in detail			Wrrts expire 7-27-2000				....	...	191860	Dc	...	...	...	....	....	....				40
41	1997	0.077	12-1-99	10-7	0.257	0.26	0.206	....	...	...	12-31-97	7714	...	390000	Dc	0.56	v1.30	v1.90	....	....	1.90				41
42	....	None Since Public			...	Nil	....	54.8	63.7	12.3	9-30-99	2.20	...	26805	Dc	...	...	...	vpd0.48	....	....	9 Mo Sep	n/a	vpd1.49	42
43◆	....	None Since Public			...	Nil	....	41.9	390	276	j12-31-98	189	...	34541	Dc	1.46	1.25	vd2.38	v0.02	....	d0.04	9 Mo Sep	v0.08	v0.02	43
44◆	....	None Since Public			...	Nil	....	333	1737	358	j12-31-98	600	...	138000	Dc	0.63	0.92	n/a	v0.52	....	0.11	6 Mo Jun	v0.44	v0.03	44
45◆	....	None Since Public			...	Nil	....	225	360	128	9-30-99	161	...	48635	Dc	v0.52	v0.75	v0.67	v0.61	Ed0.68	d0.50	9 Mo Sep	v0.50	vd0.61	45
46◆	....	None Since Public			...	Nil	....	71.7	97.1	31.5	9-30-99	....	...	28904	Dc	vd0.14	v0.03	vd0.17	v0.48	....	0.27	9 Mo Sep	v0.31	v0.10	46
47◆	....	None Since Public			...	Nil	....	102	223	71.1	9-30-99	89.5	...	25175	Je	0.35	d0.96	v0.63	v0.59	vd1.04	d0.89	3 Mo Sep	vd0.26	vd0.11	47
48◆	1987	Q0.25	11-18-99	11-2	1.00	1.00	0.75	Equity per shr $15.20			6-30-99	48.6	...	5633	Dc	v2.96	v1.95	v1.43	v0.04	....	0.41	9 Mo Sep	vd0.04	v0.33	48
49◆	....	None Since Public			...	Nil	....	23.9	36.5	24.5	9-30-99	233	...	17121	Dc	vd0.10	v0.01	v0.34	v□d1.18	....	d1.78	9 Mo Sep	v□d0.74	vd1.34	49
50◆	1970	Q0.29	11-15-99	10-29	1.16	1.16	1.044	Total Deposits $8978.53M			9-30-99	25.7	...	63977	Dc	v1.79	□v1.67	v0.82	v2.46	....	2.48	9 Mo Sep	v1.86	v1.88	50
51	1994	Q0.37½	11-1-99	10-13	1.59	1.50	1.86	Total Assets $864.76M			9-30-99	552	225	21540	Dc	v□1.09	v0.99	Δv0.88	□v0.60	....	0.59	9 Mo Sep	v□0.53	vΔ0.52	51

◆Stock Splits & Divs By Line Reference Index [4]1-for-3 REVERSE,'99. [5]Adj for 5%,'99. [6]No adj for stk dstr Homestead Village. [8]3-for-2,'94. [9]4-for-1,'98. [15]2-for-1,'99. [19]4-for-1,'99. [26]2-for-1,'97. [32]2-for-1,'98,'99. [43]3-for-1,'96. [44]2-for-1,'97,'98. [45]2-for-1,'95,'97. [46]2-for-1,'98. [47]2-for-1,'97. [48]1-for-5 REVERSE,'97:No adj for stk dstr,'93. [49]2-for-1,'97. [50]6-for-5,'97:5-for-4,'95,'98.

¶ S&P 500
\# MidCap 400
✣ SmallCap 600
• Options

Index	Ticker	Name of Issue (Call Price of Pfd. Stocks)	Market	Com. Rank. & Pfd. Rating	Inst. Hold Cos	Inst. Hold Shs. (000)	Principal Business	Price Range 1971-97 High	1971-97 Low	1998 High	1998 Low	1999 High	1999 Low	December, 1999 Dec. Sales in 100s	Last Sale Or Bid High	Low	Last	%Div Yield	P-E Ratio	EPS 5 Yr Growth	% Annualized Total Return 12 Mo	36 Mo	60 Mo
¶1•[1]	AFS	✔Associates First Capital'A'	NY	NR	1157	554023	Consumer/commercial finance	36¼	14½	43 11/16	22⅝	49	26 3/16	646079	34⅝	26 3/16	27 7/16	0.9	13	18	-34.8	8.3	...
2	ATEA	Astea Intl	NNM	NR	14	443	Customer interaction software	30¼	1 11/16	4 7/16	1⅜	6⅛	1 11/16	37023	6⅛	3¾	5⅝	...	13	31	219	-1.9	...
✣3	ASTE	✔Astec Industries	NNM	B	176	9888	Asphalt mix plants,pav'g eqp	10 1/16	½	28¾	7 9/16	43¾	14¾	69283	25 7/16	14¾	18 13/16	...	11	26	-32.3	58.3	24.2
#4•[2]	ASFC	✔Astoria Financial	NNM	NR	275	37243	Savings & loan, New York	58⅞	12½	63⅜	26¾	51⅞	28⅜	102945	31⅞	28⅜	30 7/16	3.2	13	-2	-31.8	-4.5	20.3
5•[3]	AZN	✔AstraZeneca ADR[51]	NY,P	NR	181	89334	R&D ethical pharmaceuticals	38⅜	8 15/16	50	31	48 15/16	35 5/16	81744	45⅝	39½	41¾	1.6	30	18	-5.3	18.6	29.4
6	ALOT	✔Astro-Med	NNM	B-	20	887	Specialty hi-speed printers	21½	¼	8⅜	5	8¼	4¾	1085	6⅜	5⅛	6⅛	2.6	47	-22	15.9	-8.4	-9.0
7	ASYT	✔Asyst Technologies	NNM	C	129	9424	Semiconductor mfr envro sys	47 15/16	4½	33½	5¾	67 7/16	13¼	67724	67 7/16	39⅜	65 9/16	...	d	Neg	222	97.1	41.1
8•[4]	ATHM	✔At Home Corp'A'	NNM	NR	486	69747	Provide Internet svcs	15 5/16	5¼	42⅜	10¼	99	33⅛	1899848	54½	40 13/16	42⅞	...	d	...	15.6	...	...
9	ATJ	✔AT Plastics	AS	NR	16	12337	Polymers/films & packaging	14	7 11/16	9	5¼	6⅛	1 15/16	575	3	1 15/16	2⅜	...	5	-25	-58.5	-36.2	...
10	ATTC	✔AT&T Canada'B'[53]	NNM,To	NR	141	29297	Telecommunication svcs	8 15/16	7½	22½	7¼	45⅞	14 13/16	52538	45⅞	36 9/16	40¼	...	..	...	141	...	...
11	NCD	AT&T Capital 8.25% 'PINES'	NY	....[54]	5	240	Senior Public Income Notes	....	....	26⅛	25	26 9/16	21 11/16	7680	24⅞	21 11/16	22¾	9.1	..	...	-4.2	...	...
12	NCF	AT&T Capital 8.125%'PINES'	NY	....[55]	..	...	Senior Public Income Notes	....	....	....	....	26⅜	21 9/16	16623	24¾	21 9/16	22 13/16	8.9	..	...	...	...	...
¶13•[4]	T	✔AT&T Corp	NY,B,C,Ch,P,Ph	B+	2283	1430369	Telecom svcs/business sys	45 15/16	9 15/16	52 11/16	32¼	66 11/16	41½	2115443	58 11/16	49⅞	50 13/16	1.7	25	38	2.7	...	...
14•[4]	LMG.A	✔AT&T Corp-Liberty Media'A'	NY,Ph	NR	805	809354	Produces cable TV programs	12 5/16	4	23 5/16	11 1/16	56 13/16	21⅞	486296	56 13/16	40¾	56 13/16	...	..	...	147	108	...
15	LMG.B	Cl'B'[58]	NY,Ph	NR	23	1099		12½	5⅛	24 1/16	11 1/16	68¾	22¼	2386	68¾	45⅜	68¾	...	..	...	190	121	...
16	ATL	✔Atalanta/Sosnoff Capital	NY,Ch	B	22	752	Inv't mgmt/brokerage svcs	15½	1⅞	11⅞	6 13/16	11⅛	6¾	185	9	8⅜	8½B	2.9	7	6	3.0	1.2	10.8
17	FDY	✔Atchison Casting	NY,Ch	NR	43	4841	Produce iron/steel castings	22¼	10¾	20⅛	8⅜	12⅛	7½	2703	10	8½	9⅛	...	7	-13	-1.4	-20.3	-11.7
18	AAME	✔Atlantic American	NNM	B-	20	1502	Life,accident,health insur	15 13/16	¼	5½	3⅝	4 11/16	2¼	3718	2⅞	2¼	2 5/16	...	18	60	-52.6	-8.9	0.5
✣19•[5]	ACAI	✔Atlantic Coast Airlines Hldgs	NNM	NR	125	12873	Regional airline U.S.	15 15/16	¾	35½	11¾	35⅞	15	23975	24	20⅛	23¾	...	17	NM	-5.0	57.1	90.9
20	ABR	✔Atlantic Premium Brands	AS	NR	6	857	Wholesale non-alcoholic bev	7	1 1/16	4	1¾	3	1⅝	1307	2⅛	1 7/16	2	...	33	NM	6.7	-11.6	-7.4
¶21•[2]	ARC	✔Atlantic Richfield[60]	NY,To,B,C,Ch,P,Ph	B	1231	213234	Oil&gas explor, dvlp, prod'n	87¼	5 15/16	84 11/16	56¼	98⅜	52½	373074	92⅝	83 9/16	86½	3.3	20	-38	37.1	13.5	15.9
22	Pr A	$3.00 cm Cv Pref (82)vtg	NY,B,P,Ph	BBB+	5	.7	strong interest in Alaskan	1500	81	1047⅛	900	1200	734	1	1200	1200	1176½B	0.3	..	...	...	...	...
23	Pr C	$2.80 cm Cv Pref(70)vtg	NY,B,Ch,P,Ph	BBB+	29	15	north slope: copper	408	42½	392	288	460	259	8	448¼	410	415¼B	0.7	..	...	...	...	...
24	ANK	✔Atlantic Tele-Network	AS,Ph	B	22	1111	Tele svc Virgin Islands/Guyana	27½	6	16¼	6¾	12	7¾	1350	9⅜	8½	9⅛	6.6	5	17	7.5	-13.9	2.6
25	AGH	✔Atlantis Plastics	AS,Ch,P	B-	17	1377	Hldg:Mfr plastics,furniture	11⅜	¾	9⅛	4¾	16¾	8	641	14⅞	13½	14	...	12	NM	75.0	11.4	18.9
26•[2]	CGO	✔Atlas Air	NY,Ph	NR	133	13163	Int'l air cargo carrier	42 13/16	8	33 7/16	13¾	36	18⅞	15596	28¼	23 13/16	27 7/16	...	16	40	-14.2	-4.2	...
27	ATP	Atlas Pacific Limited[61]	Au	NR	..	...	Gold mining/pearling	1¼	⅛	5/16	3/16	⅜	⅛	....	⅜	¼	5/16	...	d	20	...	...	...
#28•[6]	ATML	✔Atmel Corp	NNM,Ch	B	312	121869	Dvlp/mfr integrated circuits	24 7/16	⅞	10⅝	3	31½	6 13/16	932368	31½	22 5/16	29 9/16	...	80	Neg	288	21.5	28.8
29	ATMI	✔ATMI Inc	NNM	B-	152	16628	Dvlp diamond semiconductors	42¼	4¼	33¾	10⅞	38	16⅞	41629	35	28	33 1/16	...	..	-3	30.9	24.2	41.0
✣30	ATO	✔Atmos Energy Corp	NY	B+	138	10563	Natural gas utility	31	5 1/16	32¼	24¾	33	19⅝	11140	22 11/16	19⅝	20 7/16	5.6	35	-5	-33.6	-1.0	8.3
✣31•[7]	ATW	✔Atwood Oceanics	NY,Ph	B-	135	10005	Contract offshore drilling	61⅝	1¼	61⅜	15 1/16	38 13/16	16⅛	18098	38 13/16	32 15/16	38⅝	...	19	43	127	6.8	45.8
32	VOX	✔Audiovox Cl'A'	AS,Ch,Ph	B	66	9978	Auto sound/telephone equip	18⅜	1	7 13/16	3⅝	36½	5¾	40859	36½	25	30¼	...	30	NM	410	74.6	31.3
33•[3]	AOR	✔Aurora Foods	NY	NR	80	15530	Produce/mkt processed foods	....	....	22⅝	9½	20	7 9/16	50644	9⅝	7¾	9 5/16	...	d	...	-53.0	...	...
✣34	ASPX	✔Auspex Systems	NNM	B-	80	17214	Mfr client/server computer sys	25½	3⅞	10 13/16	1⅝	15¼	3¾	98397	13 13/16	6⅞	10¼	...	d	Neg	137	-4.1	8.7
35	ANZ	✔Australia & N.Z. Bk ADS[62]	NY,Ch	NR	32	1364	General banking/Fin'l svcs	41⅝	15⅛	38 15/16	24¼	40⅜	31⅜	1348	37 3/16	35¼	35 13/16	4.8	12	4	18.8	10.9	24.5
36	ABTL	✔autobytel.com inc	NNM	NR	43	3341	Internet based vehicle buy sv	....	....	....	....	58	11⅛	100800	19½	13½	15 3/16	...	d	...	...	...	...
37	ACAM	✔Autocam Corp	NNM	NR	15	956	Mfr specialty metal components	17 7/16	4	20⅛	10⅜	18⅞	8	5411	18 3/16	17	18 1/16	0.4	16	7	10.1	27.5	20.1
¶38•[8]	ADSK	✔Autodesk, Inc	NNM,Ch	B+	346	44397	Computer-aid design/draftg	53	1 15/16	50 1/16	21⅝	49 7/16	17	241900	34⅛	28⅞	33¾	0.7	..	-18	-20.2	7.2	-2.4
39	ALV	✔Autoliv Inc	NY,Ch	NR	117	11048	Mfr auto safety systems	45½	30½	37¼	24 7/16	41⅞	27¼	7029	30⅝	27¼	29¼	1.5	15	...	-20.3	...	...
¶40•[9]	AUD	✔Automatic Data Proc	NY,B,Ch,P,Ph	A+	1092	454017	Computer services	31 5/16	5/16	42⅛	28¾	54 13/16	36¼	216990	54 13/16	48⅜	53⅞	0.6	48	11	35.3	37.1	31.2
41•[10]	AN	✔AutoNation Inc	NY,Ph	B-	190	120818	Retail auto dealer/waste mgmt	44⅜	3/16	30	10	18⅜	7½	422026	10⅛	7½	9¼	...	14	NM	-37.8	-33.3	...
42	TTE	✔Autotote Corp Cl'A'	AS,Ph	C	32	14085	Pari-mutuel wagering sys	29¼	⅞	3 1/16	1⅛	4⅞	1¼	47626	4⅞	2½	3¼	...	..	NM	73.3	31.3	-22.2
43	AWEB	✔Autoweb.com Inc	NNM	NR	42	1211	Internet based auto buy svc	....	....	....	....	50	8 1/16	124344	14⅛	9⅞	10⅞	...	d	...	...	...	...
¶44•[11]	AZO	✔AutoZone Inc	NY,Ph,P	B+	408	88678	Retail auto parts stores	37⅝	5¾	38	20½	37 5/16	22 9/16	97346	32⅝	27⅛	32 5/16	...	19	13	-1.9	5.5	5.9
45•[12]	AVDO	✔Avado Brands	NNM	B+	80	18151	Oper full svc restaurants	28⅜	2 3/16	16	7	9 15/16	3⅞	35240	4 15/16	4	4¼	1.4	6	21	-48.8	-31.8	-20.0
46	AWX	✔Avalon Holdings'A'	AS,Ph	NR	15	1097	Transportation/environ svcs	....	....	9½	5 11/16	7¼	4 13/16	4639	5¼	4 13/16	5	...	d	...	-29.2	...	...
47	AVB	✔AvalonBay Communities	NY,Ch,Ph,P	NR	238	54048	Real Estate Invest Trust	40⅝	16¾	39¼	30½	37	30 13/16	26597	35	30⅞	34⅝	6.0	25	16	7.6	4.1	18.3
48	AVNT	✔Avant Corp	NNM	NR	135	28429	Dvlp circuit dsgn softwr prd	51	9¾	29¾	10 7/16	25¼	10½	39094	15 11/16	14½	15	...	13	NM	-6.3	-22.1	...
49	AVAN	✔Avant Immunotherapeutics	NNM	C	29	4747	Dvlp diagnostic/therap'tc prd	14⅛	1 3/16	4 9/16	1	3½	1	27664	2½	1¾	2½	...	d	20	41.1	15.0	-0.2
50•[13]	AVE	✔Aventis[64]ADR[65]	NY,Ch,P	NR	96	36515	Biotech/pharma/agric	47	19⅜	58⅝	35 13/16	68 9/16	43⅜	41909	68 9/16	55 9/16	56⅞	0.8	56	-25	14.8	20.4	21.8
51	WS	Wrrt(Pur Ord'A'shrs[67])	NY	....	8	1046		4 3/16	1⅜	7	2	7⅝	2⅜	6082	7⅝	4½	5⅛	...	..	...	...	...	...

Uniform Footnote Explanations-See Page 4. Other: [1]ASE,CBOE:Cycle 3. [2]CBOE:Cycle 1. [3]CBOE,Ph:Cycle 1. [4]ASE,CBOE,P,Ph:Cycle 1. [5]ASE,CBOE,Ph:Cycle 2. [6]CBOE:Cycle 2. [7]Ph:Cycle 1. [8]P:Cycle 1. [9]Ph:Cycle 2. [10]ASE,CBOE:Cycle 1. [11]CBOE:Cycle 3. [12]ASE:Cycle 3. [13]ASE,CBOE,P:Cycle 1. [51]Ea ADS rep 1 ord shrs. [52]Approx. [53]Dep Receipts. [54]Rated'BBB'by S&P. [55]Rated 'BBB' by S&P. [56]Total issue amt in $M. [57]5 Mo Dec'95. [58]Cv into 1 Cl'A'shr. [59]Spl div. [60]BP Amoco plan acq,0.82 ADS. [61]All data reported in Australian dollars. [62]Ea ADS rep 5 ord shrs, A $1.00 par. [63]Stk dstr of Republic Environmental Systems Inc. [64]Ea ADR rep 1 ord shr FF 25. [65]Formerly Rhone-Poulenc ADR. [66]Excl subsid Pfd. [67]3 Wrrts to pur 1 ord'A'shr,FF303.

Index (◆ Splits)	Cash Divs. Ea. Yr. Since	Dividends: Latest Payment Period $	Date	Ex. Div.	Total $ So Far 1999	Ind. Rate	Paid 1998	Financial Position Mil-$ Cash& Equiv.	Curr. Assets	Curr. Liab.	Balance Sheet Date	Capitalization Lg Trm Debt Mil-$	Shs. 000 Pfd.	Com.	Earnings $ Per Shr. Years End	1995	1996	1997	1998	1999	Last 12 Mos.	Interim Earnings Period	$ per Shr. 1998	1999	Index
1◆	1996	Q0.06½	12-1-99	10-28	0.23	0.26	0.20½	Total Assets $84959.00M			9-30-99	42879	...	728245	Dc	pv1.05	v1.24	v1.49	v1.75	E2.05	1.95	9 Mo Sep	v1.28	v1.48	1
2	....	None Since Public			...	Nil	....	41.0	55.1	9.81	9-30-99	0.32	...	13996	Dc	vp0.45	vpd1.50	vpd1.40	v2.53	....	0.43	9 Mo Sep	v1.97	vd0.13	2
3◆	....	None Since Public			...	Nil	....	2.59	177	71.4	9-30-99	70.8	...	19112	Dc	v0.23	v0.22	v0.71	v1.26	....	1.67	9 Mo Sep	v0.97	v1.38	3
4◆	1995	Q0.24	12-1-99	11-10	0.96	0.96	0.80	Total Deposits $9440.22M			9-30-99	1410	2000	54384	Dc	v2.10	v1.79	v3.04	v□0.94	....	2.36	9 Mo Sep	v1.82	v3.24	4
5◆	1993	[52]0.23	10-25-99	9-8	[52]0.676	0.68	0.682	371	2689	2003	j12-31-98	451	...	p1779007	Dc	0.55	1.13	v1.26	v1.24	....	1.38	9 Mo Sep	v1.06	v1.20	5
6	1991	Q0.04	1-4-00	12-15	0.16	0.16	0.16	12.4	32.9	8.18	10-30-99	0.13	...	4418	Ja	0.26	v0.46	v0.21	v0.11	....	0.13	9 Mo Oct	v0.07	v0.09	6
7◆	....	None Since Public			...	Nil	....	30.7	107	26.4	9-30-99	....	...	★14956	Mr	0.50	vd0.31	v1.36	vd1.80	....	d3.36	6 Mo Sep	v1.11	vd0.45	7
8◆	....	None Since Public			...	Nil	....	449	535	189	9-30-99	300	...	±380255	Dc	...	pvd0.13	vpd1.06	pvd0.63	Ed0.04	d2.75	9 Mo Sep	vd0.35	vd2.47	8
9	1994	Div Omitted 9-29-99			g0.135	Nil	g0.18	0.26	93.4	56.7	j6-30-99	233	...	20014	Dc	1.92	v0.98	v0.68	v0.62	....	j0.35	6 Mo Jun	v0.29	v0.02	9
10◆	....	None Since Public			...	Nil	....	488	775	323	j6-30-99	2614	...	±92520	Dc	pd0.20	pvd0.84	vd5.71	vd3.02	....	j0.09	9 Mo Sep	vd2.14	v0.97	10
11	1999	Q0.516	1-18-00	12-30	1.927	2.063	....	Co option redm 11-15-2003 at $25				★500	...	...	Dc	...	...	...	....	....	....	Mature 11-15-2028			11
12	1999	Q0.508	11-15-99	10-27	1.843	2.031	....	Co option redm 12-15-2003 at $25				....	...	[56]650	Dc	...	...	...	....	....	....	Mature 12-15-2028			12
13◆	1881	Q0.22	2-1-00	12-29	0.88	0.88	0.88	....	13040	23515	9-30-99	28419	...	3195347	Dc	v0.06	v2.44	v1.89	v□2.42	E2.05	2.14	9 Mo Sep	v1.67	v1.39	13
14◆	....	None Since Public			...	Nil	....	4897	5363	2255	6-30-99	1493	...	±1265147	Dc	±[57]d0.04	±v1.29	±v0.16	±v0.19	....	....	4 Mo Jun	n/a	v±d0.48	14
15◆	....	None Since Public			...	Nil	....	....	...	...		....	...	108431	Dc	±[57]d0.04	±v1.29	v±0.16	Pv±0.19	....	....	4 Mo Jun	n/a	v±d0.48	15
16	1995	[59]0.25	12-30-98	12-16	...	0.25	[59]0.25	Total Assets $96.27M			9-30-99	....	...	9075	Dc	v1.14	v1.00	v1.08	v0.81	....	1.20	9 Mo Sep	v0.64	v1.03	16
17	....	None Since Public			...	Nil	....	2.82	176	89.8	9-30-99	106	...	7644	Je	1.73	3.87	v1.67	v1.55	v1.26	1.30	3 Mo Sep	v0.04	v0.08	17
18	....	0.02	8-15-88	6-24	...	Nil	....	Total Assets $344.95M			9-30-99	51.0	134	21024	Dc	vd0.39	v0.09	v0.35	v0.37	....	0.13	9 Mo Sep	v0.27	v0.03	18
19◆	....	None Since Public			...	Nil	....	43.4	100	46.3	9-30-99	80.1	...	18551	Dc	Δv0.65	v1.08	v0.80	v1.42	....	1.42	9 Mo Sep	v1.07	v□1.07	19
20	....	None Since Public			...	Nil	....	0.82	16.9	17.2	9-30-99	15.8	...	6812	Dc	vd1.22	v0.17	v0.05	□v0.07	....	0.06	9 Mo Sep	v□0.16	v0.15	20
21◆	1927	Q0.71¼	12-15-99	11-17	2.85	2.85	2.85	991	3146	4296	9-30-99	5691	109	322732	Dc	4.21	v5.09	v□5.77	v1.40	E4.25	0.18	9 Mo Sep	v3.81	v2.59	21
22	1966	Q0.75	12-20-99	11-17	3.00	3.00	3.00	Cv into 13.6 common				....	52	...	Dc	b2.80	...	...	....	....	....				22
23	1969	Q0.70	12-20-99	11-17	2.80	2.80	2.80	Cv into 4.8 common				....	5730	...	Dc	b2.80	...	...	....	....	....				23
24	1999	Q0.15	1-7-00	12-29	0.60	0.60	....	34.5	60.9	24.0	9-30-99	8.81	...	4659	Dc	1.40	1.47	pv1.69	v3.23	....	1.89	9 Mo Sep	v2.53	v1.19	24
25	....	0.02½	10-18-95	10-2	...	Nil	....	3.63	58.8	29.9	9-30-99	81.9	...	±7593	Dc	Δ±□d1.86	v□±1.05	±v0.05	v□0.87	....	1.19	9 Mo Sep	v±□0.60	v±0.92	25
26◆	....	None Since Public			...	Nil	....	448	518	185	9-30-99	1322	...	34341	Dc	v0.71	v1.15	Δv0.20	v1.37	E1.70	1.63	9 Mo Sep	v0.83	v□1.09	26
27◆	....	None Paid			...	Nil	....	No Recent Finls				0.27	...	31511	Dc	d0.02	d0.03	...	....	....	jd0.03				27
28◆	....	None Since Public			...	Nil	....	343	973	430	9-30-99	718	...	201604	Dc	v0.58	v1.00	v0.01	vd0.25	E0.37	0.29	9 Mo Sep	vd0.30	v□0.24	28
29	....	None Since Public			...	Nil	....	86.5	142	31.6	9-30-99	4.40	...	26201	Dc	v0.30	v0.65	v0.24	v0.29	....	0.33	9 Mo Sep	v0.17	v0.21	29
30◆	1984	Q0.285	12-10-99	11-22	1.11	1.14	1.07	8.59	135	287	9-30-99	377	...	31248	Sp	v1.06	v1.42	v0.81	v1.84	v0.58	0.58				30
31◆	....	None Paid			...	Nil	....	20.1	50.5	19.0	9-30-99	54.0	...	13675	Sp	0.54	v0.84	v1.14	v2.84	v2.01	2.01				31
32	....	None Since Public			...	Nil	....	5.87	277	100	8-31-99	25.6	50	±19888	Nv	±d1.02	v±d2.82	±v1.05	v±0.16	....	1.00	9 Mo Aug	v±d0.02	v±0.82	32
33	....	None Since Public			...	Nil	....	1.42	238	212	6-30-99	689	...	67031	Dc	...	...	pv0.38	vpd1.30	....	d1.20	9 Mo Sep	v0.31	v0.41	33
34	....	None Since Public			...	Nil	....	34.5	71.7	31.6	9-30-99	....	...	27496	Je	v0.51	v0.77	v0.52	vd0.69	vd1.50	d1.69	3 Mo Sep	vd0.26	vd0.45	34
35	1980	[52]0.963	12-30-99	11-16	1.823	1.71	2.412	Total Deposits $63110M			9-30-99	5018	124	1565428	Sp	2.65	2.92	v2.46	v2.34	v2.95	2.95				35
36	....	None Since Public			...	Nil	....	90.1	95.5	16.9	9-30-99	....	...	18212	Dc	...	vpd0.68	vpd1.53	vpd1.49	....	d0.87	9 Mo Sep	vd1.85	vd1.23	36
37◆	1996	Q0.02	11-15-99	10-28	0.08	0.08	s0.076	4.01	60.0	40.6	9-30-99	106	...	6313	Je	0.82	0.88	v0.85	v1.18	v0.96	1.16	3 Mo Sep	v0.03	v0.23	37
38◆	1989	Q0.06	10-22-99	10-6	0.24	0.24	0.24	393	593	288	10-31-99	....	...	61600	Ja	v1.76	v0.88	v0.31	v1.85	E0.14	0.35	9 Mo Oct	v1.25	vd0.25	38
39	1997	0.11	3-2-00	2-1	0.44	0.44	0.44	120	1192	1107	9-30-99	537	...	102313	Dc	...	pv1.69	vd6.71	v1.84	....	1.91	9 Mo Sep	v1.28	v1.35	39
40◆	1974	Q0.08¾	1-1-00	12-8	0.30½	0.35	0.26½	1372	2443	1323	9-30-99	141	...	625108	Je	0.69	v0.77	v0.86	v0.99	v1.10	1.13	3 Mo Sep	v0.20	v0.23	40
41◆	....	h[63]....	4-26-95	4-27	...	Nil	....	398	3981	2735	9-30-99	2106	...	402895	Dc	v0.07	v□d0.04	v1.02	v1.06	E0.66↓	1.77	9 Mo Sep	v0.82	v1.53	41
42	....	None Since Public			...	Nil	....	14.5	44.7	48.1	7-31-99	154	...	36266	Oc	d1.72	vd1.09	□vd0.50	vd0.44	Pv0.01	0.01				42
43	....	None Since Public			...	Nil	....	60.3	72.0	9.72	9-30-99	0.43	...	25043	Dc	...	...	...	vpd0.69	....	d0.40	9 Mo Sep	vd0.78	vd0.49	43
44◆	....	None Since Public			...	Nil	....	5.92	1225	1001	8-28-99	888	...	144353	Au	0.93	v1.11	v1.28	v1.48	v1.63	1.69	12 Wk Nov	v0.34	v0.40	44
45◆	1992	Q0.01½	11-30-99	11-10	0.05¾	0.06	0.04¾	3.27	31.7	84.6	10-03-99	306	...	25310	Dc	v0.30	v0.30	v0.73	□v1.65	E0.70	0.58	9 Mo Sep	v1.58	v0.51	45
46	....	None Since Public			...	Nil	....	20.2	41.1	12.5	9-30-99	....	...	±3803	Dc	...	...	vpd0.27	pvd0.17	....	d0.05	9 Mo Sep	vp0.15	v0.27	46
47	1994	Q0.52	1-18-00	12-29	2.05	2.08	1.86	Total Assets $4215.96M			9-30-99	1674	18323	65738	Dc	0.91	v□1.06	v1.40	v1.37	....	1.39	9 Mo Sep	v1.03	v1.05	47
48	....	None Since Public			...	Nil	....	226	300	101	9-30-99	....	...	38524	Dc	v0.45	v0.47	v0.24	v0.81	....	1.16	9 Mo Sep	v0.57	v0.92	48
49	....	None Paid			...	Nil	....	15.8	17.6	2.03	9-30-99	0.35	...	48011	Dc	vd0.47	vd0.50	vd0.52	vd1.56	....	d0.09	9 Mo Sep	vd1.65	vd0.18	49
50	1993	0.479	6-15-99	5-28	0.479	0.48	0.468	6305	51920	54398	j12-31-98	25369	[66]927	p812876	Dc	1.37	v1.63	vd2.47	v2.03	....	1.01	6 Mo Jun	v1.60	v0.58	50
51	....	Terms&trad. basis should			be checked in detail			Wrrts expire 11-5-2001				....	...	25475	Dc	...	...	...	....	....	....				51

◆**Stock Splits & Divs By Line Reference Index** [1]2-for-1,'98. [3]2-for-1,'99. [4]2-for-1,'96. [5]3-for-1,'98. [7]2-for-1,'97. [8]2-for-1,'99. [10]2-for-1,'99. [13]No adj for stk dstr, '96:3-for-2,'99. [14]3-for-2,'97,'98:2-for-1,'99. [15]3-for-2 in Cl'A','97:3-for-2,'98:2-for-1,'99. [19]2-for-1,'98. [21]2-for-1,'97. [26]3-for-2,'99. [27]1-for-4 REVERSE'93. [28]2-for-1,'95,'99. [30]3-for-2,'94. [31]2-for-1,'97. [37]3-for-2,'94:Adj for 5%,'98. [38]2-for-1,'94. [40]2-for-1,'96,'99. [41]2-for-1,'96. [44]2-for-1,'94. [45]3-for-2,'94.

¶ S&P 500 · # MidCap 400 · ✣ SmallCap 600 · • Options

Index	Ticker	Name of Issue (Call Price of Pfd. Stocks)	Market	Com. Rank. & Pfd. Rating	Inst. Hold Cos	Inst. Hold Shs. (000)	Principal Business	1971-97 High	1971-97 Low	1998 High	1998 Low	1999 High	1999 Low	Dec. Sales in 100s	December, 1999 Last Sale Or Bid High	Low	Last	%Div Yield	P-E Ratio	EPS 5 Yr Growth	% Annualized Total Return 12 Mo	36 Mo	60 Mo
1	PIX	✔Avenue Entertainment Grp	AS	NR	3	76	Prod films/TV programs	10¼	5 1/16	7½	1⅝	3¾	⅜	1877	15/16	⅜	⅝	...	d	...	-70.6	...	..
¶2•[1]	AVY	✔Avery Dennison Corp	NY,Ch,P	A	600	79131	Adhesives,labels,office prd	45¾	1 9/16	62 1/16	39 7/16	73	39⅜	69108	73	58	72⅞	1.5	35	16	64.5	29.5	35.3
3•[2]	AVL	✔Aviall Inc	NY,P	NR	94	9599	Turbine engine overhaul, svcs	19	5⅜	15⅝	9¾	19	7	29387	8 13/16	7	8 3/16	...	3	NM	-30.3	-4.0	1.5
✣4	AVS	✔Aviation Sales	NY,Ph	NR	130	9261	Aircraft spare parts dstr	38 15/16	18	44 11/16	24	47⅝	13 9/16	36872	18	14½	16½	...	7	...	-59.4	-7.0	..
✣5•[3]	AVID	✔Avid Technology	NNM	NR	128	11859	Sell audio/video editing sys	49¼	9	47¾	11 1/16	34¼	9 7/16	56513	13¾	9⅝	13 1/16	...	d	Neg	-44.1	8.0	-16.5
6•[4]	AVIR	✔Aviron	NNM	NR	86	9054	Biopharmaceutical R&D	32¾	6¾	33	11½	34 1/16	14 13/16	63259	17¼	14 15/16	15 13/16	...	d	...	-38.9	28.2	..
7•[5]	AVI	✔Avis Rent A Car	NY,Ph	NR	195	23484	Auto rental services	36 9/16	17	38¼	11⅜	37⅞	17	42478	25 11/16	18⅞	25 9/16	...	10	...	5.7	...	..
8•[6]	AVA	✔Avista Corp	NY,B,Ch,P,Ph	B	133	14714	Hydroelectric pwr, nat'l gas	24 13/16	7 9/16	24⅞	16⅛	19 9/16	14⅝	32062	16 7/16	15	15 7/16	3.1	12	...	-17.5	-1.5	8.4
#9•[7]	AVT	✔Avnet, Inc	NY,B,Ch,P,Ph	A	299	33431	Distributor elec components	74½	1⅞	66¼	34 15/16	60 15/16	34	45993	60½	54⅞	60½	1.0	12	7	1.4	2.5	11.7
¶10•[6]	AVP	✔Avon Products	NY,B,C,Ch,P,Ph	B+	696	216345	Cosmetics,jewelry,gift prod	39	4½	46¼	25	59⅛	23 5/16	238354	36¾	30½	33	2.2	28	6	-24.2	7.0	20.1
11•[8]	AVX	✔AVX Corp	NY,P	NR	125	19374	Mfr passive electronic comp'ts	39⅝	16	23⅜	13½	50 7/16	12 9/16	35358	50 7/16	39¼	49 15/16	0.5	76	-13	198	33.9	..
12•[9]	AWRE	✔Aware Inc	NNM	NR	116	8827	Dvlp telecommun softwr	19	8½	27¾	4¼	87⅛	20½	113128	47	30⅛	36⅜	...	..	NM	33.8	53.2	..
13	AXA	✔AXA ADS[55]	NY,Ch	NR	92	8119	Insurance & Financial svcs	39⅞	25¾	72½	36 3/16	80¼	53¾	9689	73⅝	67¾	71	1.1	..	...	-0.3	33.3	..
14•[10]	AXF	✔AXA Financial	NY,P	NR	456	382051	Insurance/financial services	26½	3 9/16	42 1/16	14⅛	38¾	25½	137086	36¼	31¼	34	0.3	16	28	18.2	41.0	31.1
15	AXNT	✔AXENT Technologies	NNM	NR	87	7681	Dvlp info security softwr	25½	9⅜	32⅝	12	40½	7 11/16	107568	24	16¼	21	...	..	-22	-31.3	11.9	..
16	AXG	✔Axogen Ltd[58]	AS	NR	17	2946	Dvp stg:drug formulat'n R&D	....	....	....	....	34½	28½	4728	34½	34 3/16	34⅜B	...	d	...	...	...	..
17	AXPH	✔Axys Pharmaceuticals	NNM	NR	57	7654	Small molecule therapeutics	19½	4	10¾	3⅜	8⅛	2 11/16	72048	5	3⅛	4 1/16	...	d	-13	-30.9	-33.0	-9.0
18	AZC	✔Azco Mining	AS,P	C	5	336	Acq,explor,dvlp mineral prop	2⅞	11/16	1⅝	5/16	1 5/16	½	22378	13/16	⅝	11/16	...	d	-42	37.4	-20.6	-20.2
✣19•[11]	AZR	✔Aztar Corp	NY,P	B-	152	27779	Oper casino hotel facilities	14⅛	2⅜	9 15/16	2⅞	11⅛	4 3/16	29558	11	9⅞	10⅞	...	27	56	115	14.5	12.6
20	AZZ	✔Aztec Mfg Co	NY	B+	25	1438	Mfr electr prds/galvanizing	25 7/16	⅛	15½	6⅝	13¼	7 13/16	2651	12½	9	12¼	1.0	11	31	35.3	14.6	26.9
21	AZX	✔Azurix Corp	NY	NR	103	29189	Water resource services	....	....	....	....	24¼	6 9/16	106823	8 15/16	6 9/16	8 15/16	...	..	...	...	...	..
22	BHO	✔B&H Ocean Carriers	AS,Ch,P	B-	8	499	Own/oper bulk cargo vessels	20¼	1⅞	9	2⅝	4	1	904	1¾	1⅜	1⅝	...	d	NM	-60.6	-20.6	-4.7
23•[11]	BAANF	✔Baan Co NV	NNM	NR	47	13492	Dvlp ntwk/mgmt software	40 13/16	5 5/16	55½	9½	17 13/16	6⅞	99600	15 1/16	13	14⅛	...	d	Neg	34.5	-6.2	..
24	BYBI	Back Yard Burgers	NSC	NR	3	70	Oper fast-food restaurants	11¾	1½	3 13/16	1⅞	2½	1 7/16	3778	1¾	1 7/16	1½	...	11	76	-24.2	-10.7	-13.3
25•[12]	BWEB	✔BackWeb Technologies	NNM	NR	52	4688	Internet communic software	....	....	....	....	51 7/16	12	216785	42⅞	27¾	42⅛	...	d	...	...	...	..
26	BAU	✔Bacou USA	NY	NR	59	3541	Dgn/mfr protective eqp	19⅛	14¾	25⅜	15	24	12⅜	837	16¼	14¾	15 1/16	...	10	...	-29.9	-3.2	..
27	BMI	✔Badger Meter	AS,Ch	B+	28	1201	Fluid meters/accessories	57½	2⅛	40⅝	25	41	29⅜	600	30⅞	29⅜	30⅛	2.4	12	23	-13.6	18.4	23.3
28	BZ	✔Bairnco Corp	NY,Ch,Ph,P	B	33	3038	Electr/ind'l prd/food svc eqp	42¼	11/16	11½	5½	8	4⅝	1425	7 5/16	5⅞	6	3.3	14	-17	-13.1	-0.6	11.1
✣29•[13]	JBAK	✔Baker(J.) Inc	NNM	B-	75	10987	Self-svc footwear retailer	25⅞	3	13⅝	3 7/16	9¼	3⅜	17583	6	4⅝	6	1.0	22	NM	5.4	5.1	-16.0
30	BKR	✔Baker (Michael)	AS,Ch,Ph	B-	27	3182	Engr,oper & maint,constr	15 3/16	⅝	10⅝	6 9/16	9⅞	5	1822	6⅝	5⅝	6⅝	...	d	-45	-32.1	1.3	12.1
¶31•[14]	BHI	✔Baker Hughes Inc	NY,B,P	B-	742	264582	Oil,gas,mining equip/svcs	49⅝	11⅛	44⅛	15	36¼	15	892215	26 13/16	15	21 1/16	2.2	..	Neg	21.7	-13.8	4.6
32	BAL	✔Balanced Care	AS	NR	19	2261	Senior living/care svcs	....	....	10⅝	4⅜	8½	⅞	16198	1¾	1⅛	1 5/16	...	d	...	-83.6	...	..
33	BCP	✔Balchem Corp	AS	B+	13	659	Mfr specialty chemicals	13½	11/16	15 15/16	4 15/16	8¾	5	1954	8¾	7⅝	8	0.6	13	16	49.7	12.8	15.4
✣34•[15]	BEZ	✔Baldor Electric	NY,Ch,Ph	A	148	13019	Industrial electric motors	23 13/16	3/16	27 3/16	19 1/16	21 11/16	17	10621	19¾	17	18⅛	2.6	16	11	-8.5	1.3	8.2
35	BWINB	✔Baldwin & Lyons Cl'B'	NNM	B+	48	2412	Insurance agent/broker	28¾	3 11/16	25	18½	26	19⅝	1235	23 15/16	20⅛	22⅛	1.8	17	-4	-8.9	8.4	10.6
36	BWINA	Baldwin & Lyons Cl'A'	NNM	B+	5	138		28¾	⅜	25⅛	16⅛	25 11/16	19¾	7	22 5/16	20½	21¼B	1.9	17	-4	2.0	9.8	10.8
37	BPAO	✔Baldwin Piano & Organ	NNM	B-	22	1984	Mfrs pianos & electr organs	20	5½	17	8½	11½	6	6938	9⅛	7¾	8½B	...	d	Neg	-11.7	-8.9	-5.0
38	BLD	✔Baldwin Technology'A'	AS,Ch,Ph	B-	44	8492	Mfrs eqp for printing indus	15⅜	1¾	6½	4¼	6⅜	1 11/16	9114	2⅝	2	2⅛	...	9	35	-62.2	-5.3	-17.3
¶39•[16]	BLL	✔Ball Corp	NY,B,Ch,P,Ph	B	337	24138	Containers: metal:aerospace	48½	2	48 15/16	28⅝	59⅛	35⅜	23096	39 15/16	35⅜	39⅜	1.5	13	NM	-12.7	16.4	6.5
40	BTN	✔Ballantyne of Omaha	NY	NR	31	2421	Mfr motion pic't proj/restr eq	14 5/16	2½	13¾	5 11/16	10½	4¾	12662	5 15/16	4 15/16	5¾	s...	10	26	-28.1	-10.1	..
41	BLDP	✔Ballard Power Systems	NNM	B-	55	4548	R&D fuel cell power systems	27½	3¼	44 3/16	16	40½	21¾	39218	30⅛	25¼	28 3/16	...	d	25	2.5	61.3	..
42•[16]	BFT	✔Bally Total Fitness Holding	NY,Mo,Ph	NR	115	18958	Oper fitness centers	22	3¾	37 9/16	10½	34⅜	19⅛	30690	29⅜	22⅝	26 11/16	...	22	...	7.3	49.8	..
43	BTEK	✔Baltek Corp	NNM	B-	20	313	Balsa wood pd/shrimp farm'g	19⅜	⅝	12	7½	10¾	7	194	8	7 3/16	7⅝B	...	6	25	-22.8	1.7	3.2
44	BALT	Baltimore Technologies ADS[63]	NNM	NR	..	...	Info security prd & svcs	....	....	....	....	89	24 13/16	5697	89	47¼	88	...	..	...	...	...	..
45•[6]	BBV	✔Banco Bilbao Vizcaya ADS[64]	NY,Ch,P	NR	38	7157	Commercial banking,Spain	10 15/16	2⅛	21 1/16	9 1/16	17½	11⅝	5633	14 15/16	13½	14 3/16	2.3	34	10	-9.1	38.5	44.8
46	BPC	✔Banco Coml Portugues ADS[67]	NY,P	NR	13	1542	Commercial bank, Portugal	22½	10½	36¾	19⅜	33⅛	24¼	311	28½	26 13/16	26 15/16	1.8	10	18	-9.4	29.6	19.9
47	AED	✔Banco de A Edwards ADS[69]	NY	NR	26	2020	Commercial banking, Chile	22¾	15¼	17¼	6⅝	17 5/16	8¾	4869	17 5/16	14⅞	16⅜B	2.5	15	18	54.7	1.1	..
48•[17]	BGALY	✔Banc Galicia-Buenos AiresADR[70]	NNM	NR	82	17764	Commercial banking,Argentina	27 7/16	3 9/16	23¾	7⅞	26¼	10 5/16	66790	20 15/16	18 9/16	19 13/16	1.7	13	11	16.3	7.1	26.1
49•[10]	BFR	✔Banco Frances del Rio ADS[71]	NY,Ph,P	NR	58	6542	Commercial bank, Argentina	38⅛	7	31⅛	14	27	14¼	20007	24¼	21	23 11/16	3.8	..	...	15.8	-2.7	16.2
50	BGA	✔Banco Ganadero ADS[74]	NY,Ph	NR	10	448	Commercial banking-Colombia	43 13/16	15⅝	44¼	16⅞	21¼	15¼	1380	16¾	15⅞	15¾B	6.2	15	-8	-17.4	-12.1	-4.7
51	BLX	✔Banco Latinoamer de Export'E'	NY,Ph	NR	..	...	Multi-national bank, Panama	58¼	20⅛	44	12 15/16	34⅛	16 3/16	4821	24 5/16	21	23⅜	4.1	7	5	48.2	-20.3	-3.2

Uniform Footnote Explanations-See Page 4. Other: [1]Ph:Cycle 1. [2]ASE,Ph:Cycle 3. [3]ASE:Cycle 3. [4]ASE,CBOE:Cycle 2. [5]ASE,CBOE:Cycle 3. [6]CBOE:Cycle 1. [7]ASE,P:Cycle 2. [8]ASE,CBOE,P:Cycle 2. [9]P,Ph:Cycle 1. [10]ASE,CBOE:Cycle 1. [11]CBOE:Cycle 2. [12]ASE,CBOE,P,Ph:Cycle 3. [13]CBOE:Cycle 3. [14]P:Cycle 1. [15]CBOE,P:Cycle 3. [16]ASE:Cycle 2. [17]Ph:Cycle 2. [51]5 Mo Dec'96. [52]Excl 15M ESOP. [53]®$1.62,'96. [54]77% owned by Kyocera Corp. [55]Each ADS rep 0.5 ord shr. [56]Incl curr amts. [57]Pfd in $M. [58]Elan Corp plan acq,$34.56. [59]Incl 12000 special shs. [60]5 Mo Dec '95. [61]Fiscal Sep'97 & prior. [62]Restated fr d$3.38,'96. [63]Ea ADS rep 1 ord shr 0.01 P. [64]Each ADS equals one Ord shr,700 Pesetas. [65]Approx. [66]Incl return of cap. [67]Ea ADS rep 5 ord,Escudos 1000. [68]Incl shrs hld by subsid. [69]Ea ADS rep 165 Sr A com,no par. [70]Ea ADS rep 4 ord Cl'B' shrs,Ps1.00. [71]Ea ADS rep 3 ord Ps.100. [72]Fiscal Jun'97 & prior. [73]6 Mo Dec'98 & Fiscal Jun'98 earn $1.56. [74]Ea ADS rep 100 Cl'B'Ord,PS10.00.

Index	Cash Divs. Ea. Yr. Since	Dividends: Latest Payment: Period $	Date	Ex. Div.	Total $ So Far 1999	Ind. Rate	Paid 1998	Financial Position Mil-$: Cash & Equiv.	Curr. Assets	Curr. Liab.	Balance Sheet Date	Capitalization: Lg Trm Debt Mil-$	Shs. 000: Pfd.	Com.	Earnings $ Per Shr.: Years End	1995	1996	1997	1998	1999	Last 12 Mos.	Interim Earnings: Period	$ per Shr. 1998	1999	Index
1	....	None Paid			...	Nil	....	Total Assets $5.55M			9-30-99	0.84	...	4589	Dc	...	‡[51]d0.02	vd0.41	vd0.50	....	d0.39	9 Mo Sep	vd0.34	vd0.23	1
2◆	1964	Q0.27	12-15-99	11-29	0.99	1.08	0.87	5.80	963	786	10-02-99	653	...	[52]112676	Dc	v1.32	v[53]1.63	v1.93	v2.15	E2.10	2.01	9 Mo Sep	v1.60	v1.46	2
3	....	0.01	1-2-96	12-13	...	Nil	....	3.91	184	73.4	9-30-99	40.3	...	18272	Dc	vd12.41	v□0.72	v1.45	v3.32	....	2.66	9 Mo Sep	v1.22	v0.56	3
4	....	None Since Public			...	Nil	....	8.73	552	325	9-30-99	169	...	15049	Dc	pv1.00	□pv1.32	v1.77	v□2.06	....	2.43	9 Mo Sep	v□1.42	v1.79	4
5	....	None Since Public			...	Nil	....	83.0	203	109	9-30-99	11.6	...	23830	Dc	v0.77	vd1.80	v1.08	vd0.15	....	d1.31	9 Mo Sep	vd0.20	vd1.36	5
6	....	None Since Public			...	Nil	....	48.9	51.3	16.2	9-30-99	100	...	15887	Dc	pvd1.70	pvd1.94	vd1.94	vd3.49	....	d3.52	9 Mo Sep	vd2.46	vd2.49	6
7	....	None Since Public			...	Nil	....	Total Assets $11.20M			9-30-99	8716	7240	31130	Dc	...	pv0.28	pv1.16	v1.82	....	2.52	9 Mo Sep	v1.70	v2.40	7
8	1899	Q0.12	12-15-99	11-19	0.48	0.48	1.05	180	1350	1218	9-30-99	788	1890	35645	Dc	v1.41	v1.35	v1.96	v1.28	....	1.29	9 Mo Sep	v0.97	v0.98	8
9	1961	Q0.15	1-3-00	12-8	0.60	0.60	0.60	92.9	2342	805	10-01-99	819	...	p41945	Je	3.32	v4.31	v4.25	v3.80	v4.86	5.07	3 Mo Sep	v0.42	v0.63	9
10◆	1919	Q0.18	12-1-99	11-12	0.72	0.72	0.68	101	1398	1651	9-30-99	205	...	242304	Dc	v0.94	v1.18	v1.27	v1.02	E1.17	1.17	9 Mo Sep	v0.46	v0.61	10
11	1995	Q0.06½	11-8-99	10-28	0.26	0.26	0.25½	221	748	240	9-30-99	17.9	...	[54]86773	Mr	v1.58	v1.38	v1.53	v0.48	....	0.66	6 Mo Sep	v0.32	v0.50	11
12	....	None Since Public			...	Nil	....	33.9	40.1	1.26	9-30-99	....	...	21785	Dc	pvd0.29	v0.01	vd0.23	vd0.11	....	0.16	9 Mo Sep	vd0.14	v0.13	12
13	1997	0.767	6-7-99	5-6	0.767	0.77	0.647	Equity per shr $18.29			12-31-97	6427	...	331350	Dc	1.69	1.94	v1.90	n/a	....	....	6 Mo Jun	v1.32	v1.58	13
14◆	1992	Q0.02½	12-23-99	12-2	0.10	0.10	0.10	Total Assets $188976.90M			9-30-99	[56]7805	[57]533	450191	Dc	v0.88	v□0.25	v1.24	v1.81	E2.20	2.21	9 Mo Sep	v1.42	v1.82	14
15	....	None Since Public			...	Nil	....	107	140	40.0	9-30-99	....	...	28003	Dc	v0.28	v0.54	vd1.63	v0.30	....	0.06	9 Mo Sep	vd0.06	vd0.30	15
16	....	None Since Public			...	Nil	....	2.19	15.6	5.08	7-31-98	....	...	[59]5302	Jl	...	...	vd4.73	vd10.03	....	d10.03				16
17	....	None Since Public			...	Nil	....	43.2	51.1	26.6	9-30-99	23.4	...	30442	Dc	vd2.71	vd0.45	vd0.73	vd5.25	....	d1.54	9 Mo Sep	vd5.06	vd1.35	17
18	....	None Paid			...	Nil	....	10.1	10.6	0.29	9-30-99	....	...	29832	Je	vd0.19	v0.67	vd0.32	vd0.12	vd0.17	d0.15	3 Mo Sep	vd0.03	vd0.01	18
19	....	None Since Public			...	Nil	....	56.0	115	109	9-30-99	461	[57]7	43705	Dc	vd0.15	v0.46	v0.08	v□0.23	....	0.40	9 Mo Sep	v□0.20	v□0.37	19
20	1969	A0.12	3-26-99	3-3	0.12	0.12	0.10	0.41	25.2	13.1	8-31-99	13.7	...	4749	Fb	0.46	v0.74	v1.19	v0.86	....	1.15	9 Mo Nov	v0.71	v1.00	20
21	....	None Since Public			...	Nil	....	415	603	1239	9-30-99	1007	...	117100	Dc	...	...	...	pv0.74	....	....	9 Mo Sep	n/a	v□0.51	21
22	....	0.15	3-14-95	2-28	...	Nil	....	12.2	27.7	21.8	12-31-98	126	...	4314	Dc	d0.21	v0.98	v0.04	Δvd0.23	....	d0.23				22
23◆	....	None Since Public			...	Nil	....	216	534	224	12-31-97	201	...	193699	Dc	0.09	v0.19	v0.37	Pvd1.59	....	d1.74	9 Mo Sep	vd0.10	d0.25	23
24	....	None Since Public			...	Nil	....	0.50	1.29	1.87	10-02-99	5.35	...	4613	Dc	d0.65	v0.08	v0.04	v0.25	....	0.14	9 Mo Sep	v0.16	v0.05	24
25	....	None Since Public			...	Nil	....	11.1	18.0	8.96	3-31-99	....	[57]3	★35042	Dc	...	...	...	vpd0.69	....	d0.45	9 Mo Sep	vd0.58	vd0.34	25
26	....	None Since Public			...	Nil	....	4.83	97.8	55.0	9-30-99	126	...	17630	Dc	p‡[60]0.30	v1.18	v0.83	v1.19	....	1.50	9 Mo Sep	v0.88	v1.19	26
27◆	1934	Q0.18	12-15-99	11-29	0.72	0.72	0.60	0.92	45.6	35.9	9-30-99	12.4	...	3348	Dc	v±1.04	v±1.39	v±1.65	v2.12	....	2.46	9 Mo Sep	v1.61	v1.95	27
28	1972	Q0.05	1-4-00	12-3	0.20	0.20	0.20	0.95	63.5	30.5	10-02-99	29.9	...	7878	Dc	0.75	v0.85	v0.94	v0.18	....	0.44	9 Mo Sep	v0.56	v0.82	28
29	1987	Q0.01½	1-31-00	1-19	0.06	0.06	0.06	2.12	262	101	10-30-99	212	...	14067	Ja	vd2.79	vd8.02	v0.27	v0.14	....	0.27	9 Mo Oct	v0.27	v0.40	29
30	....	0.01	11-1-83	10-12	...	Nil	....	2.89	109	86.2	9-30-99	4.90	...	±8181	Dc	v0.35	v0.50	v0.60	vd0.30	....	d1.05	9 Mo Sep	v0.54	vd0.21	30
31	1987	0.11½	11-26-99	11-4	0.46	0.46	0.46	34.1	2315	979	9-30-99	2777	...	329209	Dc	□0.67	1.23	□[61]0.71	vd0.92	E0.21↓	0.40	9 Mo Sep	vd0.95	v0.37	31
32	....	None Since Public			...	Nil	....	4.73	19.2	16.1	9-30-99	14.8	...	16723	Je	...	vpd0.34	pvd0.66	pv0.28	vd1.41	d1.74	3 Mo Sep	v0.11	□d0.22	32
33◆	1986	A0.05	1-14-00	12-22	0.033	0.05	0.033	5.75	8.81	2.56	9-30-99	1.15	...	4827	Dc	0.33	v0.40	v0.57	v0.60	....	0.60	9 Mo Sep	v0.44	v0.44	33
34◆	1938	Q0.12	1-4-00	12-10	0.43	0.48	0.40	36.1	259	75.9	10-02-99	56.5	...	p35902	Dc	v0.84	v0.97	v1.09	v1.17	....	1.16	9 Mo Sep	v0.90	v0.89	34
35	1986	Q0.10	11-30-99	11-12	0.40	0.40	0.40	Total Assets $524.40M			9-30-99	....	...	±13198	Dc	v±1.96	v±1.51	±v1.75	±v1.22	....	1.29	9 Mo Sep	v±1.10	v±1.17	35
36	1974	Q0.10	11-30-99	11-12	0.40	0.40	0.40	....	...	...		....	...	2326	Dc	v±1.96	v±1.51	±v1.75	±v1.22	....	1.29	9 Mo Sep	v±1.10	v±1.17	36
37	....	None Since Public			...	Nil	....	1.17	72.2	35.1	9-30-99	33.7	...	3453	Dc	v1.15	v0.59	v1.28	v0.21	....	d1.37	9 Mo Sep	v0.18	vd1.40	37
38	....	0.003	3-31-92	3-9	...	Nil	....	12.8	104	71.7	9-30-99	17.8	...	±15790	Je	0.32	±v0.14	v±d2.21	±v0.52	v±0.33	0.24	3 Mo Sep	v±0.11	v±0.02	38
39	1958	Q0.15	12-15-99	11-29	0.60	0.60	0.60	30.6	1022	639	10-03-99	1230	1587	30270	Dc	vd0.64	v0.68	v1.74	v□0.91	E3.10	1.70	9 Mo Sep	v□1.76	v2.55	39
40◆	....	5%Stk	3-1-99	2-10	5%Stk	Stk	....	1.10	44.0	10.0	9-30-99	11.1	...	12476	Dc	v0.27	v0.40	v0.52	v0.57	....	0.59	9 Mo Sep	v0.38	v0.40	40
41◆	....	None Paid			...	Nil	....	411	439	38.3	j6-30-99	0.39	...	83786	Dc	d0.24	vd0.14	v0.04	v0.01	....	jd0.60	9 Mo Sep	v0.03	vd0.58	41
42	....	None Since Public			...	Nil	....	12.5	280	448	9-30-99	549	...	23819	Dc	vd3.25	vΔ[62]d2.04	□vd1.51	v0.51	....	1.22	9 Mo Sep	v0.32	v□1.03	42
43	....	0.07½	1-18-91	1-7	...	Nil	....	1.95	33.4	18.5	9-30-99	0.71	...	2523	Dc	v0.78	v0.18	v0.73	v1.29	....	1.29	9 Mo Sep	v0.85	v0.85	43
44	....	None Since Public			...	Nil	....	26.0	35.6	13.3	6-30-99	8.90	...	★36604	Dc	...	...	...	vpd0.96	....	....	6 Mo Jun	n/a	vd0.91	44
45◆	1989	[65]0.014	12-20-99	12-7	[66][65]0.319	0.32	0.315	Book Value $2.04			12-31-97	1931	...	2028000	Dc	0.34	0.40	v0.42	....	....	0.42				45
46◆	1994	0.488	4-26-99	4-7	0.488	0.49	0.396	Book Value $1.21			12-31-97	874	...	[68]779795	Dc	1.24	1.19	v1.35	Pv1.72	....	2.80	6 Mo Jun	v0.58	v1.66	46
47	1996	0.41¼	5-5-99	4-30	0.41¼	0.41	†0.554	Total Deposits $3070M			12-31-98	1089	...	5789520	Dc	1.15	1.37	1.35	v1.10	....	1.10				47
48◆	1993	0.338	10-12-99	9-29	0.338	0.34	s0.208	Total Deposits $7850.4M			6-30-99	869	...	405417	Je	0.79	0.94	Pv1.25	v1.13	v1.49	1.49				48
49◆	1994	0.005	8-2-99	7-21	0.305	0.90	0.602	Book Value $8.91			12-31-98	....	...	186632	Dc	0.91	1.56	[72]2.17	v‡[73]0.87	....	....	6 Mo Jun	n/a	v0.56	49
50	1995	[65]0.234		12-27	0.971	0.98	1.006	Book Value $19.18			12-31-97	257	479760	3140498	Dc	2.00	1.80	v1.07	....	....	1.07				50
51	1993	A0.96	3-5-99	2-16	0.96	0.96	0.96	Total Deposits $1750.86M			6-30-99	1464	1724	20313	Dc	3.44	v3.95	v3.87	Pv3.47	....	3.62	3 Mo Mar	v1.02	v1.17	51

◆**Stock Splits & Divs By Line Reference Index** [2]2-for-1,'96. [10]2-for-1,'96,'98. [14]2-for-1,'99. [23]2-for-1,'96,'97. [27]2-for-1,'97. [33]3-for-2,'98. [34]6-for-5,'94:3-for-2,'95:4-for-3,'97. [40]10%,'96:3-for-2,'97,'98:Adj for 5%,'99. [41]3-for-1,'98. [45]3-for-1,'97,'98. [46]6-for-5,'93. [48]18%,'95:19%,'96:17.5%,'98:9%,'98:Vote 15.6% stk div,hldrs Nov 12. [49]15%,'95,'96.

¶ S&P 500
# MidCap 400
✣ SmallCap 600
• Options

Index	Ticker	Name of Issue (Call Price of Pfd. Stocks)	Market	Com. Rank. & Pfd. Rating	Inst. Hold Cos	Inst. Hold Shs. (000)	Principal Business	Price Range 1971-97 High	1971-97 Low	1998 High	1998 Low	1999 High	1999 Low	December, 1999 Dec. Sales in 100s	Last Sale Or Bid High	Low	Last	%Div Yield	P-E Ratio	EPS 5 Yr Growth	% Annualized Total Return 12 Mo	36 Mo	60 Mo
1	BRS	✓Banco Rio De La Plata ADS[51]	NY	NR	34	50229	Commercial banking, Argentina	16¾	9¾	14⅝	4¾	14¼	7⅞	16023	13 7/16	11⅝	12 3/16	1.5	23	...	-4.5	...	...
2•[1]	STD	✓Banco Santander Cent Hispano ADS	NY,Ch,P	NR	82	18422	Gen'l bkg,Spain & worldwide	8 3/16	2⅝	14¼	6 5/16	12 5/16	8 1/16	27528	12 5/16	10⅝	11 11/16	1.4	6	50	21.4	48.3	43.0
3	BSB	✓Banco Santander-Chile ADS	NY,Ch	NR	33	40227	General banking-Chile	18½	8½	15½	8½	19⅝	11	3641	17¾	15 1/16	15¼	5.6	18	1	11.2	4.9	10.8
4	SBP	✓Banco Santander-Puerto Rico	NY	NR	33	3055	General banking-Puerto Rico	....	....	23½	21⅜	22⅝	15	6199	17	15	15 7/16	2.9	8	13	-28.3	...	...
5	SAN	✓Banco Santiago[55]ADS	NY,Ch	NR	28	1971	Commercial bank,Chile	28⅝	20¼	23 15/16	11	22⅝	13½	1302	21¾	20 1/16	21⅜	4.4	14	...	55.5	...	...
6	BWP	✓Banco Wiese ADS	NY,Ch,Ph,P	NR	12	2165	Commercial banking, Peru	12½	4¾	5¾	1¾	3⅜	11/16	8516	1 11/16	1 1/16	1 3/16	4.2	4	-2	-36.6	-40.9	-32.7
7	BKCT	✓Bancorp Connecticut	NNM	NR	9	326	General banking, Connecticut	26	1 3/16	22½	13⅝	18¼	13	886	17⅝	14	15½	4.0	12	14	7.2	15.0	30.3
8	BXS	✓BancorpSouth	NY	A	71	4853	Commercial banking, Tupelo	24 3/16	1 1/16	24	16 13/16	19 7/16	15⅜	4977	17 3/16	16 3/16	16 5/16	3.2	15	7	-7.2	8.6	17.8
9•[2]	BWE	✓BancWest Corp	NY	A-	155	27040	Commercial bkg/fin'l svcs	21 15/16	13/16	24	13 13/16	24¼	18½	16643	22 3/16	19 1/16	19½	3.5	13	-3	-15.8	7.3	14.6
#10	BDG	✓Bandag, Inc.	NY,B,Ch,Ph,P	A-	134	5149	Tread rubber: tire recap eqp	73¼	2½	59¾	28 5/16	41⅝	23½	8432	25¼	23½	25	4.7	9	-5	-35.2	-17.0	-14.3
11	BDG A	Cl'A'	NY,Ph	A-	46	4706		71	43½	54⅜	27⅜	37¾	19 15/16	4757	21 5/16	19 15/16	21¼	5.6	8	-5	-36.4	-20.2	-14.8
12	BMCC	✓Bando McGlocklin Capital	NNM	NR	11	448	Real estate investment trust	16 13/16	5	11 13/16	7¼	12¼	7¼	5650	9	7¼	8 11/16	7.5	8	-31	6.1	...	...
✣13	BGR	✓Bangor Hydro Electric	NY,Ph	B	62	2740	Electric utility in Maine	24⅛	4⅞	12 13/16	6⅛	17 5/16	11⅞	3062	17 5/16	16	16 7/16	3.7	8	1	30.6	21.6	15.5
¶14•[3]	BAC	✓Bank of America	NY,B,Ch,P	A-	1898	970420	Comm'l bkg:Southeast,N.C.,CA	71 11/16	1 11/16	88 7/16	44	76⅜	47⅝	1471002	59	47⅝	50 3/16	4.0	11	4	-13.9	4.9	21.7
15	IRE	Bank of Ireland(Governor&Co)ADS[58]	NY,Ch	NR	8	423	Banking/fin'l svcs,Ireland	31	15⅝	45	29¾	50 5/16	30½	2454	34	30½	31½	2.6	16	31	-27.5	23.2	...
16•[4]	BMO	✓Bank of Montreal[60]	NY,To,Ch,Mo,Ph,Vc	A	135	69130	General bkg,Canada	47 11/16	4 15/16	60 11/16	33 7/16	46 1/16	33	2440	35 13/16	33	34⅛	◆3.8	5	10	-10.6	6.8	18.6
¶17•[5]	BK	✓Bank of New York	NY,B,CS,Ch,Ph,P	A-	1053	464436	Commercial bkg,New York	29¼	15/16	40⅝	24	45 5/16	31 13/16	448394	41 1/16	36	40	1.6	24	17	1.0	36.3	43.9
18•[6]	BNS	✓Bank of Nova Scotia	To,Mo,Vc	A-	49	30966	General Banking, Canada	34⅝	1¾	44 11/16	22 13/16	36⅞	28⅝	189374	32⅛	30 7/16	31 1/16	3.1	11	24	-5.5	13.5	22.2
19	MBK	✓Bank of Tokyo-Mitsubishi[61]ADS	NY,Ch,Ph,P	NR	90	38199	Commercial banking, Japan	27⅞	10	16	5 15/16	17 1/16	9⅜	67447	15⅝	13½	13 15/16	0.4	d	Neg	33.4	-9.1	-8.2
¶20•[7]	ONE	✓Bank One Corp	NY,B,Ch,P,Ph	A	1559	647358	Comml bkg,Ohio,midwest	54 7/16	1 5/16	65⅝	36 1/16	63 5/16	29¾	1137462	35 11/16	29¾	32	5.3	9	7	-35.2	-0.3	16.9
21•[5]	BPLS	Bank Plus Corp	NNM	NR	35	8928	General banking,California	13⅞	8⅝	16⅝	2⅛	6⅝	2½	31517	3⅞	2½	2⅞	...	d	NM	-34.3	-37.0	...
22•[3]	BNKU	✓Bank United 'A'	NNM	NR	245	25602	General banking, Texas	49⅞	20	56½	23⅝	44	26⅝	63720	35⅞	26⅝	27¼	2.7	8	6	-29.1	2.4	...
23	BKP	Bank United 8%[63]'PIES'[64]	NY	....[65]	3	131	Premium Income Equity Sec	....	....	....	....	53½	39	2161	47⅝	39	39¼	10.2	..	...	...	...	...
24•[8]	BBX	✓BankAtlantic Bancorp 'A'	NY,Ph	B	53	8273	Savings bank, Florida	11 7/16	4 1/16	12 13/16	4⅜	7 13/16	3¾	39114	4 13/16	3¾	4⅛	2.4	14	-49	-14.0	-4.8	...
25	BKUNA	✓BankUnited Financial'A'	NNM	B-	43	6515	Savings bank,Coral Gables, Fl	16	2⅜	18¾	6 9/16	11¾	6	14370	9	6¾	7 15/16	...	d	Neg	-0.8	-7.4	10.2
#26•[9]	BN	✓Banta Corp	NY	B+	188	19671	Printing/graphic/video svcs	30 11/16	7/16	35¼	21 13/16	27⅝	16¾	16493	23	20⅞	22 9/16	2.7	35	-16	-15.6	1.6	4.3
27•[10]	BNYN	✓Banyan Systems	NNM	C	40	3845	Dvlp networking softwr prd	26½	1 3/16	13⅝	2⅛	23⅞	6¼	160598	23⅞	12	20	...	..	69	125	64.4	2.3
28	BHB	✓Bar Harbor Bankshares	AS	NR	12	652	Commercial banking, Maine	31	23⅝	29½	16¼	23¾	17¼	459	19⅝	17¼	17¾	4.3	10	5	-22.4	...	...
29	BCS	✓Barclays plc ADS[68]	NY,B,Ch,Ph,P	NR	48	818	Comm'l bkg,U.K.,world wide	115⅝	18 13/16	130⅞	58⅜	130	85	741	119	105¼	115⅛	2.5	20	28	31.4	22.5	29.1
¶30•[11]	BCR	✓Bard (C.R.)	NY,B,Ch,P	A-	429	39153	Hospital, surgical specialties	39	1⅝	50¼	28½	59⅞	41 11/16	60104	54 1/16	47½	53	1.5	23	30	8.7	26.1	16.8
✣31	B	✓Barnes Group	NY,Ch	B+	116	9352	Mfr prec mech springs:dstr	30⅜	1 13/16	34	21¼	30	15¼	8300	17¾	15¼	16 5/16	4.7	10	10	-42.1	-3.7	8.7
#32•[10]	BKS	✓Barnes & Noble	NY,Ch,P	NR	183	27067	Retail bookstores/superstrs	33 15/16	10	48	22 3/16	44⅜	20 1/16	149804	24⅞	20⅜	20⅝	...	15	NM	-51.5	15.6	5.9
33	BNBN	✓barnesandnoble.com inc 'A'	NNM	NR	81	7383	Retail books,info online	....	....	....	....	26⅝	14 1/16	180672	21	14 1/16	14 3/16	...	..	...	...	...	...
34	BNTT	✓Barnett Inc	NNM	NR	54	6580	Dstr plumbing/elect/hardwr pds	29½	14	25⅞	7⅞	17⅝	7¼	11020	11½	8 11/16	10⅜	...	11	...	-24.5	-27.5	...
35	BRN	✓Barnwell Indus	AS,To,Ch	C	12	115	O&G dev Cdn/water sys Hawaii	37½	3⅝	17⅝	10⅞	13¼	9¾	164	12¾	11¾	12¾	...	33	Neg	9.7	-14.5	-7.5
✣36•[12]	BRL	✓Barr Laboratories	NY,Ph	B	187	8512	Mfr generic pharmaceuticals	49⅞	1¾	49¾	24⅝	48 9/16	28 5/16	28219	35	28 9/16	31⅜	...	15	56	-34.6	22.9	23.0
✣37•[13]	BRR	✓Barrett Resources	NY,Ch,Ph	C	279	24639	Oil&gas explor,dev,prod'n	46⅞	2	39 11/16	16⅜	41¼	15 7/16	46033	30	23 1/16	29 7/16	...	d	Neg	22.7	-11.6	7.5
¶38•[14]	ABX	✓Barrick Gold	NY,To,P,Ph,Mo	A-	541	166164	Gold prod'n U.S./Canada	32⅞	11/16	23 11/16	12⅞	26	16⅛	290306	18¾	17 3/16	17 11/16	1.1	21	-19	-8.3	-14.1	-3.7
39	BIS	✓Barrister Info Sys	AS	C	5	80	Info sys to legal profession	108/16	5/16	1½	11/16	4⅝	¾	8418	1½	15/16	1 1/16	...	d	4	13.3	-14.3	16.3
40	RGB	✓Barry (R.G.)	NY,Ch,P	B	38	4576	Slippers, comfort footwear	18⅞	15/16	17 11/16	10	13⅛	3½	6892	4 9/16	3½	4	...	6	11	-63.6	-28.6	-9.1
41	BAS	✓Bass ADS[70]	NY,P	NR	26	2193	Oper brewery,hotel,restaur'ts	15¾	6¾	20 1/16	10½	17	10¼	3008	12 13/16	10¼	11 13/16	4.4	9	11	-14.2	5.8	16.8
✣42	BSET	✓Bassett Furniture	NNM	B-	115	5993	Mfr wood furniture for home	44	4 1/16	34	15¼	25	15⅜	7794	18	15 9/16	16	5.0	11	-28	-31.0	-10.1	-7.8
43•[5]	BMG	✓Battle Mtn Gold	NY,To,Ch,P,Ph	C	232	58275	Operates gold & silver mines	29 15/16	4⅜	7½	3 1/16	4 15/16	1 11/16	168744	2 9/16	2 1/16	2 1/16	...	d	Neg	-49.2	-32.6	-28.0
44	Pr	$3.25 cm Cv Pfd([71]51.626)	NY,Ch	B-	18	550		70½	43⅝	50½	35	42 3/16	23 5/16	2407	29 13/16	23 5/16	25 11/16	12.7	..	...	...	...	...
¶45•[15]	BOL	✓Bausch & Lomb	NY,B,Ch,P,Ph	B-	493	45428	Vision care & instruments	60½	2⅛	60	37¾	84¾	51⅜	111625	71¼	58⅝	68 7/16	1.5	29	25	15.9	27.8	17.9
¶46•[2]	BAX	✓Baxter International[72]	NY,B,C,Ch,Ph,P	B	1055	219819	Mfr,dstr hospital/lab prod	60¼	6	66	48½	76	56 13/16	206569	68½	58 9/16	62 13/16	1.8	24	...	-0.5	...	...
47	BYS	✓Bay State Bancorp	AS	NR	6	349	Savings bank, MA	....	....	33¾	18⅝	23⅝	19	1688	20	19	19⅜B	1.7	19	...	-17.9	...	...
48	BVC	✓Bay View Capital	NY	B+	102	14336	Commercial banking/finl sv,CA	37¼	5⅜	38¼	10⅞	22	11½	25651	16 13/16	13¼	14 3/16	2.8	9	NM	-33.0	-10.8	10.5
49	MWH	✓Baycorp Holdings	AS	NR	14	6670	Electric generating, NH	10⅜	6⅛	7½	3¼	10½	1⅞	3688	10½	8⅛	9 11/16	...	d	...	177	6.6	...
50	BYX	✓Bayou Steel'A'	AS	B-	27	2305	Operates a steel minimill	13	1⅛	9 9/16	2⅝	4 9/16	3	7412	4	3	4	...	9	33	-3.0	15.1	0.6
¶51•[9]	BBT	✓BB&T Corp	NY,Ph,P	A-	395	66748	Comm'l bkg,North&So.Carolina	32½	1⅜	40¾	26¼	40⅝	27 3/16	123969	34 3/16	27 3/16	27⅜	2.9	14	17	-30.7	17.5	27.0

Uniform Footnote Explanations-See Page 4. Other: [1]ASE:Cycle 3. [2]CBOE:Cycle 2. [3]Ph:Cycle 2. [4]Mo:Cycle 1. [5]CBOE:Cycle 1. [6]To:Cycle 3. [7]P:Cycle 2. [8]ASE,P,Ph:Cycle 3. [9]CBOE,Ph:Cycle 3. [10]ASE,CBOE:Cycle 1. [11]Ph:Cycle 1. [12]ASE:Cycle 2. [13]P:Cycle 3. [14]ASE:Cycle 1,To:Cycle 3. [15]ASE:Cycle 1. [51]Ea ADS rep 2 Cl'B' ord, PS1. [52]Fiscal Jun'97 & prior. [53]Approx. [54]Incl proceeds from sale of rts. [55]Ea ADS rep 1,039 Ord shrs. [56]Incl: 11,400M'B'/3,293M'C'/40,986M'D'Pfd. [57]Jun'95 & prior reported on Net Asset basis. [58]Ea ADS rep 4 Ord Units,IR 1 par. [59]Incl current amts. [60]Prices prior to 10-27-94 in Cdn $. [61]Each ADS rep 1 ord,par 50y. [62]Excl subsid pfd. [63]Ea Unit consist of stk pur contract & 1 pfd shr. [64]Pfd redm by Co fr 8-16-2002 at $50. [65]Rated BBr. [66]$3.625 pfd div&$0.375 contract adj pymt. [67]Re-spec cond. [68]Each ADS equals 4 Ord shrs. [69]Excl 115M members units. [70]Ea ADS rep 1 ord,25 pence. [71]To 3-15-99,scale to $50 in 2003(in com stk). [72]Plan spin-off cardiovascular bus.

Splits ◆ Index	Cash Divs. Ea. Yr. Since	Dividends: Latest Payment Period $	Date	Ex. Div.	Total $ So Far 1999	Ind. Rate	Paid 1998	Financial Position Mil-$ Cash& Equiv.	Curr. Assets	Curr. Liab.	Balance Sheet Date	Capitalization Lg Trm Debt Mil-$	Shs. 000 Pfd.	Com.	Earnings $ Per Shr. Years End	1995	1996	1997	1998	1999	Last 12 Mos.	Interim Earnings Period	$ per Shr. 1998	1999	Index
1	1998	0.181	5-24-99	5-17	0.181	0.18	0.123	Book Value $6.30			12-31-98	797	. . .	±335268	Dc	. . .	. . .	pv[52]0.80	v0.60	. . . .	0.52	6 Mo Jun	v0.39	v0.31	1
2◆	1942	[53]0.041	2-7-00	1-26	0.159	0.16	s0.193	Book Value $1.35			12-31-97	11190	. . .	p3134416	Dc	0.32	0.34	v2.03	. . . .	. . . .	2.04	3 Mo Mar∆	v0.78	v0.80	2
3	1995	0.851	5-13-99	4-27	0.851	0.85	[54]0.34½	Book Value $5.74			12-31-97	1146	. . .	25189000	Dc	0.69	v1.71	v1.26	Pv0.78	. . . .	0.83	9 Mo Sep	v0.43	v0.48	3
4	1999	Q0.11	1-3-00	12-9	0.33	0.44	. . . .	Book Value $12.96			12-31-98	420	2610	38623	Dc	v1.08	v1.23	v1.80	v1.78	. . . .	2.03	9 Mo Sep	v1.19	v1.44	4
5	1997	0.953	4-12-99	3-23	0.953	0.95	0.771	. . . .	. . .	. . .		p2304	. . .	[56]p9108217	Dc	p2.08	v1.57	Pv1.45	. . . .	. . . .	1.50	3 Mo Mar∆	v0.37	v0.42	5
6◆	1995	[53]0.003	1-5-99	12-23	[53]0.003	0.05	0.047	Total Deposits $2189M			12-31-98	57.4	. . .	342626	Dc	0.68	0.60	v0.50	v0.34	. . . .	0.34				6
7◆	1986	Q0.15½	11-16-99	10-28	0.59½	0.62	0.53½	Total Deposits $345.12M			9-30-99	72.8	. . .	5191	Dc	v0.77	v0.89	v1.08	v1.14	. . . .	1.28	9 Mo Sep	v0.90	v1.04	7
8◆	1945	Q0.13	1-3-00	12-13	0.48	0.52	0.42½	Total Deposits $4.73M			9-30-99	153	. . .	57190	Dc	v0.85	v1.02	v1.01	v1.01	. . . .	1.08	9 Mo Sep	v0.81	v0.88	8
9◆	1929	Q0.17	12-15-99	11-29	0.63½	0.68	0.62	Total Deposits $12987.9M			9-30-99	807	. . .	±124546	Dc	v1.28	1.28	v1.32	v1.07	E1.48	1.08	9 Mo Sep	v0.98	v0.99	9
10	1976	Q0.29½	1-21-00	12-16	1.14	1.18	1.10	69.5	447	159	9-30-99	109	. . .	±21912	Dc	v±3.82	v±3.44	±v5.33	v±2.63	. . . .	2.85	9 Mo Sep	v±1.79	v±2.01	10
11	1992	Q0.29½	1-21-00	12-16	1.14	1.18	1.37½	. . . .	. . .	. . .		. . . .	. . .	10782	Dc	±3.82	±3.44	±v5.33	v±2.63	. . . .	2.80	6 Mo Jun	v±1.02	v±1.19	11
12◆	1987	†0.12	1-31-00	12-29	0.655	0.65	0.655	0.50	9.03	3.30	9-30-99	52.3	675	3985	Dc	§[57]5.07	v0.75	v0.86	v0.93	. . . .	1.08	9 Mo Sep	v0.61	v0.76	12
13	1999	Q0.15	1-20-00	12-29	0.30	0.60	. . . .	37.3	51.9	40.1	9-30-99	206	133	7363	Dc	v0.36	v1.33	vd0.24	v1.33	. . . .	2.09	12 Mo Sep	v0.88	v2.09	13
14◆	1903	Q0.50	12-23-99	12-1	1.85	2.00	2.04	Total Deposits $337.01M			9-30-99	54352	1829	1707184	Dc	vp2.98	pv3.36	pv3.61	v2.90	E4.80	4.03	9 Mo Sep	v2.24	v3.37	14
15◆	1997	[53]0.304	1-21-99	11-23	0.79¼	0.83	0.637	Book Value $8.27			3-31-98	[59]1394	15500	1028200	Mr	1.31	1.63	v1.93	. . . .	. . . .	1.93				15
16	1829	gQ0.47	11-29-99	11-3	g1.88	1.88	g1.76	Total Deposits $143983M			j10-31-98	4791	70000	264433	Oc	3.45	4.21	v4.62	v4.66	Pv4.72	j4.72				16
17◆	1785	Q0.16	11-4-99	10-20	0.58	0.64	0.54	Total Deposits $44795.00M			9-30-99	2416	17	736398	Dc	v1.09	v1.20	v1.35	v1.53	E1.70	2.24	9 Mo Sep	v1.13	v1.84	17
18◆	1834	gQ0.24	1-27-00	12-30	g0.87	0.96	g0.80	Total Deposits $156498M			j7-31-99	5451	61007	493513	Oc	1.69	2.04	v2.95	v2.64	. . . .	j2.84	9 Mo Jul	v1.97	v2.17	18
19◆	1989	0.035	12-20-99	9-27	0.065	0.06	0.052	Book Value $4.33			3-31-99	72295	81400	4675456	Mr	0.09	0.06	vd1.24	vd0.62	. . . .	d0.62				19
20◆	1935	Q0.42	1-1-00	12-13	1.64	1.68	1.485	Total Deposits $156900.00M			9-30-99	33157	. . .	1146880	Dc	v2.20	pv2.52	v1.99	v2.61	E3.50	2.77	9 Mo Sep	v2.42	v2.58	20
21	. . . .	None Since Public			. . .	Nil	. . . .	Total Deposits $2480.45M			9-30-99	346	. . .	19442	Dc	vd8.83	vd0.85	v0.66	vd2.90	. . . .	d0.76	9 Mo Sep	vd2.96	vd0.82	21
22	1996	Q0.18½	12-28-99	12-13	0.71½	0.74	0.64	Total Deposits $7213.26M			6-30-99	6387	[62]. . .	31704	Sp	±1.35	±3.87	□±v2.47	v±3.54	Pv3.28	3.28				22
23	1999	1.087	11-16-99	11-10	1.087	[66]4.00	. . . .	Pur contract for Bank United com to8-16-2002[67]				. . . .	. . .	★2000	Sp	. . .	. . .	. . .	. . . .	. . . .	. . . .	Mand pfd redm at $50 8-16-2004			23
24◆	1996	0.025	1-18-00	12-31	0.096	0.10	0.093	Total Deposits $2140.10M			6-30-99	921	. . .	±42608	Dc	v0.54	v±0.50	v±0.68	vd0.19	. . . .	0.29	9 Mo Sep	v0.05	v0.53	24
25	. . . .	0.02½	6-30-94	6-14	. . .	Nil	. . . .	Total Deposits $2228.75M			6-30-99	1460	953	±18363	Sp	±1.77	v±0.10	v±0.54	v±0.39	Pv±d0.24	d0.24				25
26◆	1927	Q0.15	2-1-00	1-12	0.56	0.60	0.51	31.2	370	241	10-02-99	115	. . .	26591	Dc	v1.75	v1.63	v1.44	v1.80	E0.65	0.45	9 Mo Sep	v1.37	v0.02	26
27	. . . .	None Since Public			. . .	Nil	. . . .	78.4	92.4	26.9	9-30-99	. . . .	. . .	24393	Dc	vd1.27	vd1.59	vd0.97	v0.05	. . . .	0.20	9 Mo Sep	v0.01	v0.16	27
28◆	1984	Q0.19	12-10-99	11-17	0.72	0.76	0.67	Total Deposits $293M			9-30-99	104	. . .	3644	Dc	v1.72	v1.95	v1.86	v1.92	. . . .	1.86	9 Mo Sep	v1.39	v1.33	28
29	1986	1.149	10-1-99	8-18	2.928	2.93	2.793	Total Deposits 143225M			j12-31-98	3734	. . .	1511000	Dc	5.18	6.50	v4.89	v5.78	. . . .	5.78				29
30	1960	Q0.20	2-4-00	1-20	0.78	0.80	0.74	59.5	509	344	9-30-99	159	. . .	51189	Dc	v1.52	v1.61	v1.26	v4.51	E2.27	4.59	9 Mo Sep	v1.56	v1.64	30
31◆	1934	Q0.19	12-10-99	11-29	0.75	0.76	0.694	39.0	221	114	9-30-99	140	. . .	19014	Dc	v1.38	v1.61	v1.96	v1.69	. . . .	1.72	9 Mo Sep	v1.33	v1.36	31
32◆	. . . .	None Since Public			. . .	Nil	. . . .	19.2	1429	967	10-30-99	575	. . .	69455	Ja	v■d0.85	v0.75	v□0.93	v1.29	E1.35	1.24	9 Mo Oct	vd0.45	vd0.50	32
33	. . . .	None Since Public			. . .	Nil	. . . .	561	585	41.3	9-30-99	. . . .	. . .	[69]29215	Dc	. . .	. . .	. . .	n/a	. . . .	. . . .	9 Mo Sep	vd0.45	vd0.50	33
34	. . . .	None Since Public			. . .	Nil	. . . .	6.83	100	26.9	9-30-99	33.0	. . .	16247	Je	. . .	□0.61	v0.75	v0.87	v0.94	0.95	3 Mo Sep	v0.21	v0.22	34
35	. . . .	0.07½	3-24-95	3-6	. . .	Nil	. . . .	2.22	5.06	5.98	6-30-99	13.1	. . .	1317	Sp	0.49	v0.93	v0.79	vd2.95	Pv0.39	0.39				35
36◆	. . . .	None Since Public			. . .	Nil	. . . .	88.6	285	128	9-30-99	29.9	. . .	22837	Je	□0.31	□0.33	v0.87	v□1.45	v2.09	2.10	3 Mo Sep	v0.48	v0.49	36
37	. . . .	None Paid			. . .	Nil	. . . .	14.6	190	176	9-30-99	306	. . .	32579	Dc	vd0.09	v1.02	v0.92	vd2.95	. . . .	d2.79	9 Mo Sep	v0.33	v0.49	37
38	1987	tS0.10	12-15-99	11-26	t0.20	0.20	t0.18	565	783	196	6-30-99	525	. . .	394278	Dc	0.83	v0.60	vd0.33	v0.79	E0.85	0.84	9 Mo Sep	v0.58	v0.63	38
39	. . . .	None Since Public			. . .	Nil	. . . .	0.16	5.13	3.49	9-30-99	1.34	. . .	11662	Mr	v∆d0.11	vd0.05	vd0.08	vNil	. . . .	d0.09	9 Mo Dec	v0.01	vd0.08	39
40◆	. . . .	0.018	12-1-81	11-6	. . .	Nil	. . . .	4.95	101	43.8	10-02-99	8.57	. . .	9328	Dc	v0.65	v0.84	v1.03	v0.98	. . . .	0.65	9 Mo Sep	vd0.37	vd0.70	40
41◆	1990	[53]0.365	2-18-00	12-21	0.521	0.52	1.72	456	1396	1989	j9-30-98	2012	. . .	796000	Sp	0.69	0.78	0.46	v1.33	. . . .	1.33				41
42	1935	Q0.20	11-30-99	11-12	0.80	0.80	0.80	0.88	123	45.4	8-28-99	4.00	. . .	12261	Nv	1.63	v1.39	vd1.50	v1.20	. . . .	1.50	9 Mo Aug	v0.80	v1.10	42
43	1985	Div Omitted 2-2-99			. . .	Nil	0.05	39.2	182	75.4	9-30-99	177	2300	229866	Dc	0.09	vd0.36	□vd0.05	vd1.08	Ed0.25↓	d1.17	9 Mo Sep	vd0.11	vd0.20	43
44	1993	Q0.81¼	11-15-99	10-28	3.25	3.25	3.25	. . . .	. . .	. . .		. . . .	2000	. . .	Dc	. . .	. . .	. . .	. . . .	. . . .	. . . .				44
45	1952	Q0.26	1-3-00	11-29	1.04	1.04	1.04	951	1914	811	9-25-99	977	. . .	±57710	Dc	±v1.93	v±1.47	v±0.89	v±0.45	E2.33	6.53	9 Mo Sep	±1.21	v±7.29	45
46	1934	Q0.291	1-3-00	12-8	1.164	1.16	1.164	825	4255	2550	9-30-99	2716	. . .	290931	Dc	v2.31	v2.41	v1.06	v1.09	E2.67↓	2.75	9 Mo Sep	v0.36	v□2.02	46
47	1999	Q0.08	11-19-99	11-5	0.25	0.32	. . . .	Total Deposits $224M			9-30-99	135	. . .	2267	Mr	. . .	p0.97	n/a	v0.95	. . . .	1.05	6 Mo Sep	v0.48	v0.58	47
48◆	1989	Q0.10	10-22-99	10-6	0.40	0.40	0.40	Total Deposits $3676.35M			9-30-99	2090	. . .	18684	Dc	v□d0.15	v0.79	v1.06	v1.12	. . . .	1.63	9 Mo Sep	v0.74	v1.25	48
49	. . . .	None Paid			. . .	Nil	. . . .	10.7	19.9	4.44	9-30-99	. . . .	. . .	8232	Dc	vd0.76	v0.51	vd1.35	vd0.82	. . . .	d0.74	9 Mo Sep	vd0.75	v□d0.67	49
50	. . . .	None Since Public			. . .	Nil	. . . .	25.5	138	21.3	6-30-99	119	. . .	±12891	Sp	±0.73	±d0.17	v±0.09	v□2.28	Pv±0.47	0.47				50
51◆	1934	Q0.20	2-1-00	1-12	0.75	0.80	0.66	Total Deposits $25704.75M			9-30-99	6322	. . .	p330969	Dc	v0.80	1.28	v1.30	v1.71	E1.95	1.84	9 Mo Sep	v1.23	v1.36	51

◆Stock Splits & Divs By Line Reference Index [2]3-for-1,'97:2-for-1,'98,'99. [6]2.06192-for-1,'95. [7]6-for-5,'96:2-for-1,'97. [8]2-for-1,'95,'98. [9]2-for-1,'99. [12]10%,'99. [14]2-for-1,'97. [15]2-for-1,'99. [17]2-for-1,'94,'96,'98. [18]2-for-1,'98. [19]Adj for 5%,'96. [20]5-for-4,'93:10%,'92,'94,'96,'98. [24]5-for-4,'96,'97(twice),'98:15%,'99. [26]3-for-2,'96. [28]2-for-1,'99. [31]3-for-1,'97. [32]2-for-1,'97. [36]3-for-2,'96,'97. [40]4-for-3,'94,'95:5-for-4,'96. [41]1.7857-for-1 & dstr'B'shr,'98. [48]2-for-1,'97. [51]2-for-1,'98.

¶ S&P 500
# MidCap 400
✣ SmallCap 600
• Options

Index	Ticker	Name of Issue (Call Price of Pfd. Stocks)	Market	Com. Rank. & Pfd. Rating	Inst. Hold Cos	Inst. Hold Shs. (000)	Principal Business	Price Range 1971-97 High	1971-97 Low	1998 High	1998 Low	1999 High	1999 Low	Dec. Sales in 100s	December, 1999 Last Sale Or Bid High	Low	Last	%Div Yield	P-E Ratio	EPS 5 Yr Growth	% Annualized Total Return 12 Mo	36 Mo	60 Mo
1	BB	✓BBV Banco BHIF ADS[51]	NY	NR	5	655	Commercial bank, Chile	22⅜	15⅞	16 1/16	7¾	17½	7	191	15⅛	13 1/16	14⅞B	0.1	15	−7	92.3	0.0	...
2	BCG	✓BC Gas	To,Mo,Vc	B	10	1031	Natural gas: Brit Columbia	28	3 5/16	34	25½	31⅜	20 7/16	20727	25⅜	20 7/16	25⅜	4.6	13	12	−13.1	12.2	18.9
3•[1]	BCE	✓BCE Inc	NY,To,C,Mo,Vc,B,Ch,P,Ph	B+	287	110958	Telecommun svcs & eq,Canada	34	6 7/16	46⅝	25⅝	98 5/16	37 5/16	127059	98 5/16	66¾	90 3/16	◆1.0	34	46	145	61.9	49.1
4	BTS	✓BCT.TELUS Communications	To	B+	18	4977	Telecommunication svcs, Canada	46½	6⅛	61	35	44¾	28 3/16	57067	37½	31	35⅛	4.0	23	1	−12.6	9.8	12.6
✣5•[2]	BEAV	✓BE Aerospace	NNM	C	165	14046	Airline audio/video ctrl sys	41½	4¾	35¾	13	22¼	5¾	108612	8⅞	6⅜	8 7/16	...	60	NM	−59.8	−32.2	2.7
6	BFRE	✓Be Free	NNM	NR	..	...	e-business promotion svcs	....	....	....	....	87 1/16	24⅛	136907	87 1/16	40½	71⅞	...	..	...	...	...	...
7	BESI	✓BE Semiconductor Indus	NNM	NR	5	1216	Mfr semiconductor mfg eqp	19½	9½	12 11/16	4⅛	15	5⅝	462	15	12	13½	...	..	...	140	2.6	...
8•[3]	BEAS	✓BEA Systems	NNM	NR	189	58832	Dgn computer software	12½	3	14 13/16	4 5/16	74⅝	5⅝	835539	74⅝	39⅞	69 15/16	...	d	...	1043	...	...
¶9•[4]	BSC	✓Bear Stearns Cos	NY,B,Ch,P	A	497	74908	Investment bank'g,brokerage	44 1/16	3 11/16	58 1/16	23 9/16	50½	31⅞	108352	42⅞	38⅞	42¾	s1.3	9	24	40.4	28.7	37.4
10	BOC	✓Beard Co	AS	NR	9	791	Carbon dioxide oper enviro svc	6¼	1⅝	5 15/16	3¼	4⅜	1¾	512	2⅝	1¾	1⅞	...	d	Neg	−42.3	−13.3	2.9
11	BUTI	BeautiControl Cosmetics	NNM	B−	14	644	Mfr/mkt cosmetics,toiletries	21¾	2	10¼	5 3/16	6⅝	2⅛	3293	3 3/16	2⅛	2 3/16	2.7	d	Neg	−58.4	−45.9	−28.1
12	BZH	✓Beazer Homes USA[53]	NY,Ch	NR	70	6388	Single family homebuilders	21	11⅛	27⅛	16½	27⅜	15⅝	5048	20⅛	17 3/16	19¼	...	5	19	−23.0	1.3	10.6
#13•[5]	BEC	✓Beckman Coulter	NY,Ch,P	B	235	17671	Mfr med'l lab analysis equip	52 5/16	11⅞	64 15/16	40 1/16	55¾	39½	18390	51	44 9/16	50⅞	1.3	15	−27	−5.0	11.3	14.3
¶14•[1]	BDX	✓Becton, Dickinson	NY,B,C,Ch,P,Ph	A	701	200021	Health care pr:ind'l safety	27 13/16	1¼	49⅝	24⅜	44 3/16	22⅜	250987	28 9/16	22⅜	26 15/16	1.4	26	5	−36.3	8.7	19.1
¶15•[6]	BBBY	✓Bed Bath & Beyond	NNM	NR	456	133423	Domestics/home prd superstrs	19⅝	1¾	35 3/16	17⅛	39⅜	25½	402327	36	29⅛	34¾	...	41	31	1.8	42.1	36.1
16	BED	✓Bedford Prop Investors	NY,Ch,P,Ph	NR	104	10389	Invests in commercial RE	40	4	22	15	18 7/16	14½	9692	17 5/16	15 11/16	17 1/16	9.8	9	44	10.6	6.4	15.6
17	BMED	✓BEI Medical Systems	NNM	C	17	1539	Mfr medical diagnostic prd	17	2⅞	5½	1 1/16	3½	⅝	8005	1¾	1 1/16	1¾	...	d	−22	−9.7	...	...
18	BEIQ	✓BEI Technologies	NNM	NR	33	3235	Electrical components	13⅞	10½	20¾	5 5/16	18¾	7¼	7511	18¾	11½	15¼	0.5	21	...	63.8	...	...
19	BYH	Beijing Yanhua Petrochem'H'ADS[54]	NY	NR	14	1178	Prod resins/plastics/ethylene	25⅞	8 11/16	10⅛	2 9/16	11⅞	3	2439	7 9/16	6⅛	6⅞	1.7	46	...	74.1	...	...
20	BELFA	✓Bel Fuse Inc'A'	NNM	B−	43	1416	Mfr/sale of electronic parts	11 1/16	⅞	20 5/16	5⅝	37⅜	13⅜	7200	37⅜	24 5/16	27⅞	...	14	NM	39.8	58.2	46.6
21	BELFB	✓ Cl'B'	NNM	B−	29	1013		....	....	17 3/16	5⅝	35	12½	18610	35	21 5/16	23 15/16	0.8	12	NM	41.5	...	...
22	BOG	✓Belco Oil & Gas	NY,P	NR	49	3600	Oil & gas explor,dvlp, prod'n	37¼	18⅛	19	4⅜	7 15/16	4¾	5765	6 3/16	4 15/16	5½	...	d	Neg	−1.1	−41.4	...
23	Pr	6.50% Cv Pfd ([56]26.1375)	NY	B−	25	2334		....	....	26¼	13½	18¼	14½	3518	16⅛	14½	15 3/16	10.7	..	...	...	...	...
✣24•[7]	BWC	✓Belden Inc	NY,Ch,P	NR	201	20927	Mfr electrical wire,cable	39⅞	14¼	43⅞	11¼	25½	15 9/16	16559	21½	17 1/16	21	1.0	21	−7	0.1	−16.6	−0.3
¶25•[8]	BEL	✓Bell Atlantic Corp	NY,B,Ch,P,Ph	B+	1655	660229	Tel sv:Northeast USA	45⅞	8⅛	61 3/16	40 7/16	69½	50⅝	717203	67¼	59 3/16	61 9/16	2.5	21	8	16.9	30.3	25.9
26	BCICF	Bell Canada Intl	NNM,To	NR	17	3399	Provide telecommunicat'n svcs	22 15/16	13¾	26 9/16	6⅛	25⅜	9⅝	7055	25⅜	16⅜	22 11/16	...	d	...	102	...	...
27	BHW	✓Bell & Howell	NY,P	NR	157	18011	Info access/dissemin'tn sys,sv	35⅜	15½	37 13/16	21½	39¾	27 3/16	13348	34 3/16	29½	31 13/16	...	17	NM	−15.9	10.2	...
28	BI	✓Bell Industries	NY,B,Ch,P,Ph	C	40	2968	Dstr electronic components	22 9/16	¾	14⅝	8 15/16	12¼	4⅜	105961	9⅛	4 13/16	7 7/16	...	d	Neg	80.6	5.4	7.9
29•[9]	BELM	✓Bell Microproducts	NNM	NR	33	4791	Mkt computer products	16	5¾	11	5¼	11	5½	15893	11	6 7/16	11	...	15	−1	18.9	7.4	0.5
¶30•[10]	BLS	✓BellSouth Corp	NY,B,Ch,P,Ph	B+	1450	847373	Tel sv:south,so central U.S.	29 1/16	4 9/16	50	27 1/16	51 5/16	39¾	591562	48 9/16	44	46 13/16	1.6	24	16	−4.6	35.5	32.1
31	BLB	BellSouth Cap Fdg 7.375%'QUIBS'	NY	AAA	2	20	Qtly Interest Bonds	....	....	....	....	26	21 13/16	6070	24⅜	21 13/16	22¼	8.3	..	...	...	...	...
32	KTB	BellSouth 7% CorTS Tr Debs	NY	NR	..	...	Corporate-Backed Trust Sec	....	....	....	....	24¼	20 1/16	786	21½	20 1/16	20 3/16	...	..	...	...	...	...
33•[8]	BELW	✓Bellwether Exploration	NNM	C	37	4859	Oil&gas explor'n,dvlp prod'n	34 9/16	2	11⅛	3 13/16	6 5/16	2½	23798	5 1/16	3¾	4 13/16	...	d	Neg	−2.5	−15.1	−0.8
#34•[6]	BLC	✓Belo (A.H.)Cl'A'	NY,Ch,Ph,P	B+	268	73662	Newspaper publishing:brdcstg	28 1/16	2 1/16	28 7/16	13 15/16	24½	16⅜	50243	19 15/16	17 11/16	19 1/16	1.5	16	−3	−3.1	4.3	7.4
35	BGO	✓Bema Gold	AS,P	C	23	2177	Explr,dvlp mineral properties	9½	1 5/16	2 13/16	11/16	1⅝	½	70585	13/16	9/16	⅝	...	d	−32	−23.0	−52.8	−18.0
¶36•[11]	BMS	✓Bemis Co	NY,Ch,Ph,P	A	351	32165	Packaging,adhesive products	47 15/16	11/16	46 15/16	33½	40⅜	30 3/16	21279	35	30 13/16	34⅞	2.6	16	9	−5.7	0.3	10.2
✣37	BHE	✓Benchmark Electronics	NY,Ch,P	B+	190	13243	Mfrs circuit boards	30½	1 13/16	37½	17⅝	43 13/16	12	24805	27⅛	19⅛	22 15/16	...	19	14	−37.4	15.2	13.8
38	BNV	✓Benckiser N.V.'B'	NY	NR	5	35	Mfr detergents/cleaning agents	42¾	33½	67¼	38	71¼	49	....	....	....	....	...	..	14	...	...	...
39	BNG	✓Benetton Group ADS[64]	NY,Ch,Ph,P	NR	17	1612	Int'l mfr of casual apparel	35 7/16	11 1/16	48 7/16	28¼	46 9/16	30⅞	453	46 9/16	39¾	45 7/16	3.7	25	5	20.7	29.2	19.2
40	BTON	Benetton Group[65]S.p.A[66]	ML	NR	3	4041	Int'l mfr of casual apparel	2990	755	4295	2250	2⅜	1⅜	....	2⅜	1 15/16	2¼	...	..	6	...	...	...
41	BE	Benguet Corp Cl'B'	NY,B,Ch,P,Ph	NR	6	196	Engin'g eq:Philippine gold	6⅛	⅛	15/16	⅛	¼	1/32	33307	3/16	1/32	⅛	...	..	...	−39.7	−36.9	−31.5
42	BTHS	✓Benthos Inc	NSC	NR	2	65	Cont'r inspect'n/undersea sys	20	9½	16½	4⅝	10⅛	5⅞	387	8¾	7¼	8	...	13	38	39.1	...	...
43	BNT	✓Bentley Pharmaceuticals	AS,Ph,P	C	8	391	Dvlp stage:pharmaceut'l prod	210	2	3⅜	13/16	6 7/16	1⅜	19501	6 7/16	4⅛	6 3/16	...	d	44	313	33.1	8.2
44	WS.B	Wrrt'B'(Pur1com at$5)	AS	....	3	258		....	....	3/16	1/32	15/16	1/32	3573	15/16	⅜	⅞	...	..	...	...	...	...
✣45	BNO	✓Benton Oil & Gas[68]	NY,Ch,Ph	C	77	9501	Oil & gas explor,dev,prod'n	28⅝	1¼	13 11/16	2 7/16	5 3/16	1 7/16	40124	2 1/16	1 7/16	1 15/16	...	d	Neg	−35.4	−55.9	−26.7
#46•[12]	BBC	✓Bergen Brunswig 'A'	NY,Ch,B,Ch,P,Ph	A−	319	78918	Drug and health care dstr	23	⅛	35	16 13/16	37¾	6 7/16	205775	9 3/16	7 7/16	8 5/16	3.6	14	−23	−75.7	−8.4	3.3
47•[2]	BKLY	✓Berkley (W.R.)	NNM	B+	125	17845	Regional insurance co's	46⅜	7/16	49⅞	25¼	36¼	19 13/16	20989	22¼	19 13/16	20⅞	2.5	20	−24	−37.5	−13.4	−2.1
48	BRK.A	✓Berkshire Hathaway'A'[69]	NY([10]),Ch	B	460	256	Insurance,shoes,investments	48600	38	88400	45800	81100	52000	104	58200	52000	56100B	...	40	32	−34.1	10.6	17.7
49	BRK.B	Cl'B' (0.005 vtg)[71]	NY,Ch	NR	538	3266		1624	990	2795	1529	2713	1700½	4519	1888	1700½	1830	...	38	...	−22.1	18.1	...
50	BTZ	✓Berlitz International	NY,P,BB	NR	50	1796	Language instruction svcs	27 5/16	12	30⅝	25½	29	16 7/16	936	19¾	16 7/16	17 3/16	...	d	Neg	−40.7	−5.1	5.7
51	BRY	✓Berry Petroleum'A'	NY,Ch,Ph,P	B−	70	8055	Oil & gas dvlpmt prod'n	21⅜	8	17 9/16	10½	15 7/16	8 11/16	4775	15 7/16	13 7/16	15⅛	2.6	38	94	9.8	4.5	13.2

Uniform Footnote Explanations-See Page 4. Other: [1]Ph:Cycle 3. [2]Ph:Cycle 2. [3]ASE,CBOE:Cycle 3. [4]CBOE,P:Cycle 1. [5]ASE,Ph:Cycle 2. [6]CBOE:Cycle 2. [7]ASE:Cycle 3. [8]CBOE:Cycle 1. [9]P:Cycle 3. [10]ASE:Cycle 1. [11]Ph:Cycle 1. [12]CBOE:Cycle 3. [51]Ea ADS rep 10 Sr'G'com,no par. [52]Excl subsid pfd. [53]Instl. hldgs over 90%. [54]Ea ADS rep 50 ord'H'shs,RMB1. [55]70% owned by China Natl Petrochem. [56]Fr 3-15-2001,scale to $25 in 2008. [57]Subsid pfd in $M. [58]Or earlier upon'Tax Event're-spec cond. [59]Total issue amt. [60]To be determined. [61]Fiscal June'96 & prior. [62]12 Mo Dec'97:Fiscal June'97 earned $0.44. [63]Fiscal Dec'95 & prior,Cdn$. [64]Each ADS rep 20 Ord,Lire 250. [65]Data reported in Billion of Italian Lire. [66]No adj for conv to Euro Dollar eff 1999. [67]If com exceeds $6.50 for 20 con trad days. [68]Plan SmallCap 600 delisting: eff Jan 4. [69]Cv into 30 shrs Cl'B'. [70]Incl 177 'B' shares equiv. [71]Each share equals 1/30 Cl'A'.

Index	Cash Divs. Ea.Yr. Since	Dividends Latest Payment Period $	Date	Ex. Div.	Total $ So Far 1999	Ind. Rate	Paid 1998	Financial Position Mil-$ Cash& Equiv.	Curr. Assets	Curr. Liab.	Balance Sheet Date	Capitalization Lg Trm Debt Mil-$	Shs. 000 Pfd.	Com.	Earnings $ Per Shr. Years End	1995	1996	1997	1998	1999	Last 12 Mos.	Interim Earnings Period	$ per Shr. 1998	1999	Index
1	1997	0.013	4-5-99	3-17	0.013	0.01	0.527	Book Value $9.44			12-31-97	12.5	...	203187	Dc	2.77	1.55	v1.00	....	....	1.00				1
2	1964	gQ0.29½	11-30-99	11-15	g1.16½	1.18	g1.09	n/a	249	686	j9-30-99	1118	...	42912	Dc	v1.16	v2.53	v1.27	v1.85	....	j1.90	9 Mo Sep	v0.95	v1.00	2
3◆	1881	gQ0.34	1-15-00	12-13	g1.36	1.36	g1.36	5652	8234	6558	j6-30-99	8256	68000	643140	Dc	v1.12	v1.70	□v2.11	v7.07	E1.85	j7.75	9 Mo Sep	v6.57	v7.25	3
4◆	1993	gQ0.35	1-1-00	12-8	g1.05	1.40	g1.38	n/a	1311	1924	j9-30-99	1503	[52]...	±177450	Dc	2.00	v1.90	v2.29	□v2.82	....	j1.56	9 Mo Sep	v□1.88	v0.62	4
5	....	None Since Public			...	Nil	....	29.8	326	169	8-28-99	581	...	24826	Fb	□d3.71	v0.72	v□1.30	vd3.36	....	0.14	6 Mo Aug	vd2.49	v1.01	5
6	....	None Since Public			...	Nil	....	19.3	21.6	10.8	9-30-99	5.45	p...	★26218	Dc	...	...	...	vpd0.49	....	....	9 Mo Sep	n/a	vpd0.78	6
7	....	None Since Public			...	Nil	....	75.0	242	102	j12-31-97	34.7	...	26394	Dc	d0.50	v0.83	v0.40	n/a	....	....	3 Mo Mar	v0.04	vd0.06	7
8◆	....	None Since Public			...	Nil	....	277	415	185	10-31-99	260	...	±158380	Ja	...	pvd1.13	vd0.22	v±d0.37	....	d0.06	9 Mo Oct	±d0.35	±d0.04	8
9◆	1986	sQ0.143	11-26-99	11-9	s0.565	0.57	0.544	Total Assets $157880.20M			9-24-99	15841	3729	119177	Je	1.40	v2.96	v3.81	v4.17	v4.27	4.86	3 Mo Sep	v0.36	v0.95	9
10	....	None Since Public			...	Nil	....	1.71	3.06	1.40	9-30-99	2.48	28	2439	Dc	vd0.17	vd0.11	v1.86	vd1.52	....	d1.83	9 Mo Sep	vd0.47	vd0.78	10
11	1989	Q0.01½	10-14-99	9-28	0.33	0.06	0.42	6.12	26.0	13.9	8-31-99	9.26	...	7231	Nv	0.70	0.90	v0.02	vd0.49	....	d0.79	9 Mo Aug	vd0.24	vd0.54	11
12	....	None Since Public			...	Nil	....	Total Assets $622.59M			6-30-99	215	p...	p8924	Sp	1.23	v2.01	v1.15	v2.66	Pv4.15	4.15				12
13	1989	Q0.16	12-2-99	11-9	0.64	0.64	0.61	30.0	933	567	9-30-99	1017	...	29052	Dc	v1.70	v2.58	vd9.58	v1.14	E3.51	2.90	9 Mo Sep	v0.51	v2.27	13
14◆	1926	Q0.09¼	1-7-00	12-10	0.34	0.37	0.29	64.6	1684	1329	9-30-99	954	1017	250798	Sp	0.90	1.06	v1.15	v0.90	v1.04	1.04				14
15◆	....	None Since Public			...	Nil	....	131	578	283	8-28-99	....	...	139839	Fb	v0.29	v0.39	v0.51	v0.68	E0.84	0.81	9 Mo Nov	v0.44	v0.57	15
16◆	1993	Q0.42	1-14-00	12-29	1.50	1.68	1.26	Total Assets $663M			9-30-99	181	...	20444	Dc	v0.05	v1.14	v1.94	v1.38	....	1.86	9 Mo Sep	v1.02	v□1.50	16
17◆	....	Div Discontinued 3-2-98			...	Nil	....	2.43	7.29	2.21	7-03-99	1.00	...	7867	Sp	d0.65	v0.28	v0.03	vd0.68	Pvd0.92	d0.92				17
18	1997	Q0.02	12-17-99	11-30	0.08	0.08	0.08	9.73	71.7	30.4	7-03-99	39.8	...	7477	Sp	...	p0.35	v0.64	v0.37	Pv□0.74	0.74				18
19	1998	0.12	7-22-99	5-25	0.12	0.12	0.369	43.1	281	219	12-31-98	108	...	[55]±3374000	Dc	...	pv0.03	v0.03	v0.15		0.15				19
20◆	....	None Since Public			...	Nil	....	23.1	68.9	13.1	9-30-99	....	...	±10522	Dc	v0.80	v0.76	±v0.86	±v1.45	....	1.93	9 Mo Sep	v±0.93	v±1.41	20
21◆	1999	Q0.05	11-1-99	10-13	0.20	0.20	....	....	...	...		....	...	5266	Dc	v0.80	±v0.76	±v0.86	±v1.45	....	1.93	9 Mo Sep	v±0.93	v±1.41	21
22	....	None Since Public			...	Nil	....	4.97	38.8	52.9	9-30-99	302	4239	31673	Dc	pv1.15	vp1.42	vd1.80	vd4.85	....	d2.36	9 Mo Sep	vd3.27	vd0.78	22
23	1998	Q0.40⅝	12-15-99	11-29	1.62½	1.625	0.831	Cv into 1.1292				....	3000	...	Dc	...	...	...	...	...	...				23
24	1994	Q0.05	1-5-00	12-7	0.20	0.20	0.20	1.62	252	91.0	9-30-99	288	...	24358	Dc	v1.76	v2.11	v2.30	v1.35	....	0.98	9 Mo Sep	v1.27	v0.90	24
25◆	1984	Q0.38½	2-1-00	1-6	1.54	1.54	1.54	299	8897	11369	9-30-99	17463	[57]200	1552786	Dc	□v1.84	vΔ2.01	v1.56	v□1.87	E2.95	2.85	9 Mo Sep	v□1.22	v2.20	25
26	....	None Since Public			...	Nil	....	35.0	2019	4206	j6-30-99	7093	4000	78800	Dc	d1.35	vd0.57	vd0.92	vd0.83	....	jd3.26	9 Mo Sep	vd1.53	vd3.96	26
27	....	None Since Public			...	Nil	....	8.25	371	332	10-02-99	477	...	23613	Dc	v□1.15	v□1.38	□vd0.18	v1.58	....	1.89	9 Mo Sep	v0.97	v1.28	27
28◆	1999	1.30	12-17-99	12-20	7.00	Nil	....	3.85	80.6	47.2	6-30-99	....	...	9608	Dc	v1.67	v1.75	□v1.07	vd6.67	....	d5.94	9 Mo Sep	vd0.28	v0.45	28
29	....	None Since Public			...	Nil	....	3.41	307	137	9-30-99	90.5	...	9183	Dc	v0.48	v0.92	v0.53	v0.68	....	0.75	9 Mo Sep	v0.42	v0.49	29
30◆	1984	0.19	2-1-00	1-11	0.76	0.76	0.72	1140	6941	13614	9-30-99	8786	...	1882319	Dc	v□0.79	v1.44	v1.64	v1.78	E1.95	1.87	9 Mo Sep	v1.27	v1.36	30
31	1999	Q0.46	2-1-00	1-12	0.44	1.844	....	Co opt to redm fr 8-1-2004 at $25[58]				[59]★500	...	...	Dc	...	...	...	...	...	....	Mature 8-1-2039			31
32	1999	0.83⅛	12-1-99	11-26	0.832 [60]	....	....	....	...	...		★50.0	...	...	Dc	...	...	...	...	...	....	Due 12-1-2095			32
33◆	....	None Paid			...	Nil	....	2.23	22.5	17.3	9-30-99	118	...	13854	Dc	0.12	[61]0.11	v[62]0.51	vd5.50	....	d5.56	9 Mo Sep	vd0.02	vd0.08	33
34◆	1939	Q0.07	3-3-00	2-9	0.19	0.28	0.24	30.7	289	181	9-30-99	1654	...	±118440	Dc	±0.84	±v1.06	v±0.71	v±0.52	E1.19	1.01	9 Mo Sep	v±0.42	v±0.91	34
35	....	None Paid			...	Nil	....	13.5	25.8	14.4	6-30-99	20.0	...	122899	Dc	v[63]d0.08	vd0.06	vd0.07	vd0.40	....	d0.33	9 Mo Sep	vd0.09	vd0.02	35
36	1922	Q0.23	12-1-99	11-9	0.92	0.92	0.88	25.0	596	266	9-30-99	367	...	52310	Dc	v1.63	v1.90	v2.00	v2.09	E2.20	2.23	9 Mo Sep	v1.41	v1.55	36
37◆	....	None Since Public			...	Nil	....	21.6	466	272	9-30-99	165	...	16221	Dc	v0.75	v0.96	v1.25	v1.35	....	1.22	9 Mo Sep	v0.96	v0.83	37
38	1998	0.324	8-24-99	8-6	0.605	0.60	0.311	50.8	529	733	12-31-98	242	...	±52720	Dc	p±1.44	p±1.86	vp1.44	v2.34	....	2.34				38
39◆	1990	1.248	12-8-99	11-17	1.673	1.67	0.398	297	2237	908	12-31-97	67.7	...	1820000	Dc	1.53	1.78	v1.80	....	....	1.80				39
40◆	....	30.00	5-18-92	5-18	...	Nil	....	n/a	3958	3000	j12-31-97	p352	...	1815588	Dc	126.20	140.70	p163.00	....	....	j163.00				40
41	....	t0.018	2-4-90	12-15	...	Nil	....	177	1526	2127	j12-31-97	154	220	±114111	Dc	±0.01	±d0.06	vd0.43	n/a	....	....	3 Mo Mar	vd0.02	vd0.02	41
42◆	....	None Since Public			...	Nil	....	4.41	9.74	2.20	6-30-99	....	...	1361	Sp	0.12	v0.90	v1.14	v0.52	Pv0.60	0.60				42
43◆	....	None Since Public			...	Nil	....	5.92	11.7	5.10	9-30-99	5.45	...	10123	Dc	vd0.83	v□d0.79	vd0.97	vd0.35	....	d0.20	9 Mo Sep	vd0.29	vd0.14	43
44	....	Terms&trad. basis should be checked in detail						Wrrts expire 2-14-2001				....	...	...	Dc	...	...	...	...	....	....	Callable at 5¢[67]			44
45	....	None Since Public			...	Nil	....	39.7	76.3	38.7	9-30-99	276	...	29577	Dc	v0.40	v□1.29	v0.59	vd6.21	....	d4.57	9 Mo Sep	vd2.67	vd1.03	45
46◆	1978	Q0.07½	12-1-99	11-12	0.30	0.30	0.25½	113	3781	2924	6-30-99	1075	★12000	134207	Sp	0.64	0.73	v0.81	v0.03	Pv0.59	0.59				46
47◆	1975	Q0.13	1-3-00	12-15	0.51	0.52	0.47	Total Assets $4818.11M			9-30-99	593	...	25616	Dc	v1.90	v2.53	v3.02	v□1.76	E1.05	0.14	9 Mo Sep	v□1.85	v□0.23	47
48	....	0.10	1-3-67	11-29	...	Nil	....	Total Assets $126592M			9-30-99	2448	...	[70]±1342	Dc	611.00	v2065.00	v1542.00	v2262.00	E1400.00	1449.00	9 Mo Sep	v1822.00	v1009.00	48
49	....	None Paid			...	Nil	....	....	...	...		....	...	5342	Dc	...	v69.00	v51.40	v75.40		48.30	9 Mo Sep	v60.73	v33.63	49
50	....	None Since Public			...	Nil	....	29.3	113	99.8	9-30-99	211	...	9530	Dc	v0.23	v0.40	□v0.56	v0.22	....	d0.37	9 Mo Sep	v0.17	v□d0.42	50
51	1987	Q0.10	12-29-99	12-8	0.40	0.40	0.40	4.30	19.7	10.7	9-30-99	60.0	...	±22011	Dc	v±0.56	v±0.80	v±0.87	v±0.18	....	0.40	9 Mo Sep	v±0.23	v±0.45	51

◆Stock Splits & Divs By Line Reference Index [3]2-for-1,'97. [4]Dec'98 & prior data of BC TELECOM. [8]2-for-1,'99. [9]Adj for 5%,'99(twice). [14]2-for-1,'96,'98. [15]2-for-1,'96,'98. [16]1-for-2 REVERSE,'96. [17]No adj for stk dstr,'97. [20]2-for-1 in C'l'B','99. [21]2-for-1,'99. [25]2-for-1,'98. [28]6-for-5,'97. [30]2-for-1,'95,'98. [33]1-for-8 REVERSE,'94. [34]2-for-1,'95,'98. [37]2-for-1,'97. [39]Adj to 4%,'97. [40]10-for-1,'98. [42]3-for-2,'97. [43]1-for-10 REVERSE,'95. [46]5-for-4,'97:2-for-1,'98. [47]3-for-2,'97.

¶ S&P 500
# MidCap 400
✣ SmallCap 600
• Options

Index	Ticker	Name of Issue (Call Price of Pfd. Stocks)	Market	Com. Rank. & Pfd. Rating	Inst. Hold Cos	Inst. Hold Shs. (000)	Principal Business	1971-97 High	1971-97 Low	1998 High	1998 Low	1999 High	1999 Low	Dec. Sales in 100s	Last Sale Or Bid High	Last Sale Or Bid Low	Last Sale Or Bid Last	%Div Yield	P-E Ratio	EPS 5 Yr Growth	Total Return 12 Mo	Total Return 36 Mo	Total Return 60 Mo
¶1•[1]	BBY	✔Best Buy	NY,Ch,P,Ph	B	617	133146	Electronic/appliance stores	11 5/16	1/64	31⅛	9	80½	30⅞	1003112	66 9/16	42 9/16	50¼	...	32	55	64.2	167	45.2
¶2•[2]	BFO	✔Bestfoods	NY,B,C,Ch,P,Ph	A	882	190305	International food processor	54⅜	1 7/16	60⅞	43¼	60	45¼	119924	55⅝	51⅛	52 9/16	2.0	21	17	...	...	...
3	BSTW	✔Bestway Inc	NSC	B–	1	2	Rents household products	11½	6	9¼	5	11½	5	816	7½	5	5	...	17	–11	–4.8	–8.4	...
4	BET	✔Bethlehem Corp	AS,Ch	B–	2	1	Energy & environmental pr	9 1/16	5/16	4	1 3/16	3⅛	⅝	1632	1	⅝	11/16	...	d	–41	–65.7	–32.7	–6.0
¶5•[3]	BS	✔Bethlehem Steel	NY,B,C,Ch,P,Ph	B–	314	72885	Integrated steel company	48	4⅝	17⅛	7	10 15/16	5⅞	284307	8½	6 3/16	8⅜	...	d	Neg	0.0	–1.9	–14.2
6	Pr	$5 cm Cv Pfd(50)	NY,Ph	B–	22	143	serv'g heavy construction &	59⅞	12¾	56	50	55¾	39	2518	49 5/16	39	46	10.9	..	...	...	...	...
7	Pr B	$2.50 cm Cv Pfd(25)	NY,Ch,Ph	B–	17	50	capital goods markets	29¾	6⅝	29⅜	25½	27 11/16	19½	2430	24⅜	19½	23¼	10.8	..	...	...	...	...
#8•[4]	BEV	✔Beverly Enterprises	NY,B,Ch,P,Ph	B–	193	75932	Health care facilities	22½	3/16	16¼	5¼	8 3/16	3½	84507	4⅝	3⅝	4⅜	...	10	Neg	–35.2	–29.0	–20.5
9	BYND	✔Beyond.com Corp	NNM	NR	94	13219	Computer software svcs	....	....	32	6 3/16	41 5/16	7¼	297896	11 11/16	7⅜	7 13/16	...	..	...	–62.4	...	...
10	BNC	✔BFC Construction[52]	AS,To,Mo,B,Ph,P	B–	13	3163	Constr:util,PL,civil&ind'l	35½	3⅜	11	5½	9⅛	6⅜	834	9	7⅞	7⅝B	e...	d	Neg	25.6	–5.6	–4.3
11	BFX	✔BFX Hospitality Group	AS	↓C	7	364	Oper casual dining restaurants	9⅛	½	3⅛	1 1/16	1 15/16	9/16	1883	13/16	9/16	⅝	...	d	Neg	–47.3	–34.1	–14.6
12	BRG	✔BG Group plc[54]ADS[55]	NY,B,Ch,P,Ph	NR	27	5139	Major gas supplier in UK	34 11/16	5½	40 1/16	25 11/16	37 15/16	26⅞	1938	31⅝	26⅞	30⅞	2.5	16	27	–13.8	37.2	18.6
13	BHAG	✔BHA Group	NNM	B+	44	5396	Aftermkt envir air poll'n ctrl	18 13/16	2 1/16	19	10¼	13⅝	6¼	8655	9¼	7⅜	7⅞	1.5	53	–15	–42.5	–10.0	2.5
14	BHC	✔BHC Communications'A'	AS,P	B–	84	3596	Own/oper VHF/UHF TV stations	133	40⅛	145 5/16	102 9/16	169	107	668	162	153	160	...	..	–4	32.3	17.4	17.7
15	YFM	✔Big City Radio 'A'	AS	NR	11	2062	Own/oper radio stations	8¾	7	13⅜	3	5½	3 3/16	6441	4⅞	4	4¾	...	d	...	16.9	...	...
✣16•[5]	BILL	✔Billing Concepts	NNM	NR	104	16994	Bill'g clearinghse/telecom svc	25	8	30	7⅝	14 13/16	3⅞	99797	8 3/16	5	6½	...	16	...	–40.9	–22.5	...
✣17•[6]	BDY	✔Bindley Western Indus	NY,Ch,Ph,P	B+	212	19266	Wholesaler of ethical drugs	18¼	3⅛	36 15/16	15 3/16	25 13/16	11¾	37523	15 3/16	11¾	15 1/16	0.4	25	–2	...	...	...
18	BIO.A	✔Bio-Rad Labs Cl'A'[58]	AS,Ch	B	64	4723	Research chems:med test:kits	37	1 1/16	34⅛	19½	29	18⅞	2438	25¼	22½	23⅜	...	10	7	11.3	–8.0	4.9
19	BIO.B	Class B Cv	AS,Ch	B	3	13	hi technology instr	36¾	⅛	33¾	19¾	27½	19⅜	4	24⅝	23⅛	23⅛B	...	10	7	13.5	–8.1	4.7
✣20•[3]	BTGC	✔Bio-Technology Genl	NNM	B–	110	8826	Health prod thru biotechn'y	23¼	1	13 13/16	4 3/16	17⅞	5⅝	199571	17⅞	10½	15¼	...	34	NM	120	5.1	47.9
21•[3]	BCHE	✔BioChem Pharma	NNM,Ch,Mo,To	B–	155	38327	R&D therapeutic prod	32¾	3 13/16	28⅞	14½	30¼	17⅜	120126	23½	19 7/16	21¾	...	12	NM	...	...	...
22	BCRX	✔BioCryst Pharm'l	NNM	NR	38	3166	R&D Pharmaceutical products	20¾	3⅜	9½	4⅜	35 5/16	6⅜	40527	30¼	18½	29½	...	d	24	321	21.7	44.9
#23•[7]	BGEN	✔Biogen Inc	NNM	B	745	108705	Research/dev of biotech'gy	26⅜	15/16	43¾	16⅜	90 7/16	38¾	430217	85½	66¾	84½	...	65	NM	104	63.4	52.0
24	BJCT	✔Bioject Medl Technologies	NSC	NR	8	241	Dvlp stge:medl syringe R&D	45	2 3/16	12½	4¼	15	1	36377	15	3 1/16	8⅛	...	d	21	84.0	53.3	–3.8
25	BLTI	✔BIOLASE Technology	NSC	C	7	85	Mfr dental laser,endodontic eq	25	½	4⅜	1¾	3¾	1 13/16	22028	2¾	2	2 11/16	...	d	–2	26.4	–12.4	21.9
✣26•[8]	BXM	✔Biomatrix Inc	NY,Ph	B–	162	8046	Therapeutic biomaterial R&D	20 15/16	1½	30½	11 9/16	45	17⅝	45209	23¾	17⅝	19¼	...	21	NM	–33.8	34.1	61.6
¶27•[9]	BMET	✔Biomet, Inc	NNM,Ph	B+	515	70380	Mfr surgical implant devices	32⅜	3/16	41 3/16	23⅜	45¾	24⅝	213083	40 3/16	29 13/16	40	0.4	35	10	–0.2	38.9	23.8
28	BVA	Bionova Holding	AS	NR	11	847	Agribusiness biotechnology	7	3 1/16	4⅞	2½	4	1	2291	2⅛	1	1½	...	d	–12	–57.1	–24.6	...
29	BSTC	BioSpecifics Technologies	NNM	NR	13	267	Pharmaceutical R&D	19	2½	8¼	3¼	4 15/16	1⅜	4432	3 3/16	1⅜	2⅛	...	24	92	–46.9	–23.5	–24.2
30	BBH	Biotech HOLDRs Tr Dep Receipt	AS	NR	..	...	Investment co-Biotech ind	....	....	....	....	150½	102	51260	150½	102	143½	...	..	...	...	...	...
31•[10]	BTX	✔BioTime Inc	AS	NR	24	1541	Dvlp stge: blood substitutes	27	7/16	19¾	5½	21½	8⅛	11718	11⅜	8½	8⅞	...	d	...	–48.9	–1.7	67.8
32•[3]	BVF	✔Biovail Corp Intl	NY,P	B–	83	6216	R&D ctrl released pharma'l pd	40	1 7/16	49½	20 7/16	94⅝	32⅜	53493	94⅝	68⅛	93¾	...	40	42	148	54.1	103
33	WS	Wrrt(Pur 1 com at $40)	NY	....	..	...		....	....	....	....	57⅜	23	8674	57⅜	35½	57¼	...	..	...	...	...	...
✣34	BIR	✔Birmingham Steel	NY,Ch,Ph,P	↓C	101	13409	Mini-mills:steel/steel pr	32⅝	5 3/16	18	3½	9 1/16	3¼	63036	7¾	3¼	5 5/16	...	d	Neg	29.0	–33.1	–21.5
✣35•[6]	BSYS	✔BISYS Group	NNM	NR	279	24073	Data processing svc to banks	43⅜	9⅞	52¼	32½	65½	41⅜	35714	65½	52⅛	65¼	...	30	NM	26.4	20.7	24.1
#36•[3]	BJS	✔BJ Services	NY,Ch,Ph,P	↓B–	..	...	O&G well pressure pump'g svc	45⅜	5	43 13/16	11⅞	43 7/16	13 7/16	196738	43 7/16	31 3/16	41 13/16	...	d	Neg	168	17.9	37.7
37	WS	Wrrt(Pur 2 com at $15)	NY	....	19	1225		64½	3	56½	5½	57	6 15/16	7223	57	33¼	54¼	...	..	...	...	...	...
#38•[1]	BJ	✔BJ's Wholesale Club	NY	NR	382	63633	Wholesale cash & carry mdsg	16	13	23⅛	14⅝	38¾	20¼	68868	38¾	34¼	36½	...	26	...	58.0	...	...
✣39	BBOX	✔Black Box Corp[64]	NNM	NR	185	15983	Mkt computer communic/ntwk eq	46	8⅝	41	21½	68¾	26⅜	33720	68¾	59 5/16	67	...	26	22	76.9	17.5	...
¶40•[11]	BDK	✔Black & Decker Corp	NY,B,C,Ch,P,Ph	B	490	74186	Mfr power tools/home prod	44¼	8	65½	37 15/16	64⅝	41	131000	52¼	43¼	52¼	0.9	16	Neg	–6.2	21.3	18.4
#41	BKH	✔Black Hills Corp	NY,B,Ch,Ph	A	137	6461	Electric utility:coal mining	24 5/16	1¼	27 15/16	20 11/16	26½	20 5/16	8757	23	21½	22 3/16	4.7	17	2	–12.1	10.6	14.8
42	BLK	✔BlackRock Inc'A'	NY	NR	..	...	Investment management svcs	....	....	....	....	19⅜	12½	7071	19⅜	16 11/16	17 3/16	...	..	...	...	...	...
43	BL	✔Blair Corp	AS,B,Ch,P,Ph	B–	61	3965	Mail order:apparel&furnish'gs	70¾	3⅛	34⅛	17⅛	27½	12½	4617	15⅝	12½	14	4.3	9	–14	–34.7	–7.2	–15.5
44	BCL	✔BLC Financial Svcs	AS	NR	2	24	Small business loans	....	....	5¼	1 13/16	2 15/16	1½	7094	1¾	1½	1¾	...	14	62	–22.2	...	...
45	BLM	✔Blimpie Int'l	AS	NR	17	888	Franchise Blimpie trademarks	16	15/16	4½	1¾	3½	⅞	5601	1⅞	⅞	1⅞	3.7	19	–23	–11.3	–42.1	–24.6
¶46•[12]	HRB	✔Block (H & R)	NY,B,Ch,P,Ph	A–	560	75099	Tax,computer & personal serv	48⅞	11/16	49 1/16	35 5/16	59½	38	65705	47¼	41¼	43¾	2.5	23	19	–0.6	17.3	6.2
47	BLOCA	✔Block Drug'A'non-vtg	NNM	A–	87	5960	Denture, dental care pr: drugs	48⅛	1 7/16	43⅜	30⅝	45⅝	24 7/16	7553	33⅞	24 7/16	31	s4.0	14	1	–21.8	–4.3	4.7
48•[13]	BBI	✔Blockbuster Inc 'A'	NY	NR	58	22665	Retail videocassettes,DVD/games	....	....	....	....	17⅛	11⅜	81134	16 7/16	12½	13⅜	0.6	..	...	...	...	...
49	BDR	✔Blonder Tongue Labs	AS,Ch,Ph	NR	16	796	'Private Cable' ind electr sys	19½	6⅛	16⅛	5⅛	9¾	4¾	6030	6¼	4¾	5	...	12	2	–24.5	–17.0	...
50	BLT	✔Blount Intl	NY,Ch	B+	29	439	Mfr timber cutting prds,	26⅞	9/16	34⅜	18 15/16	29 15/16	10½	2446	17	13	15 15/16	...	24	–4	–35.6	–4.9	1.8
51	BSI	✔Blue Square-Israel ADS[67]	NY,Ph	NR	29	3778	Supermkt,dept,spl strs Israel	19⅝	9¼	16⅜	10	16⅞	10 7/16	2602	13¼	11½	12¾	7.3	20	1	34.6	0.6	...

Uniform Footnote Explanations-See Page 4. Other: [1]CBOE:Cycle 3. [2]P:Cycle 1. [3]CBOE:Cycle 1. [4]P:Cycle 3. [5]P:Cycle 2. [6]Ph:Cycle 3. [7]ASE,CBOE,P:Cycle 1. [8]Ph:Cycle 2. [9]ASE,CBOE:Cycle 1. [10]ASE,CBOE,Ph:Cycle 2. [11]CBOE:Cycle 2. [12]ASE:Cycle 1. [13]ASE,CBOE,P,Ph:Cycle 1. [51]Stk dstr of Corn Prods Intl. [52]Armbro Enterprises plan acq,$8.30. [53]Spl div. [54]Full pay't ADS's equal 5 Ord par 25p. [55]Formerly BG plc ADS. [56]Special divd. [57]Stk dstr of Priority Healthcare Corp. [58]1/10 vtg. [59]Stk dstr of CliniChem Development'A'. [60]To be determined. [61]As defined. [62]Fiscal Jun'97 & prior. [63]6 Mo Dec'98:Fiscal Jun'98 earn d$0.35. [64]Instl. hldgs over 90%. [65]90.4% owned by Lehman Brothers Merch Banking. [66]Fiscal Feb'96&prior:12 Mo Dec'95 earned $2.53. [67]Ea ADS rep 1 ord shr, NIS 100.

Splits ◆ Index	Cash Divs. Ea. Yr. Since	Dividends: Latest Payment Period $	Date	Ex. Div.	Total $ So Far 1999	Ind. Rate	Paid 1998	Financial Position Mil-$ Cash& Equiv.	Curr. Assets	Curr. Liab.	Balance Sheet Date	Capitalization Lg Trm Debt Mil-$	Shs. 000 Pfd.	Com.	Earnings $ Per Shr. Years End	1995	1996	1997	1998	1999	Last 12 Mos.	Interim Earnings Period	$ per Shr. 1998	1999	Index
1◆	....	None Paid			...	Nil	....	473	2055	1374	8-28-99	25.7	...	205270	Fb	v0.28	v0.01	v0.52	v1.07	E1.55↑	1.41	9 Mo Nov	v0.52	v0.86	1
2◆	1920	Q0.26½	1-25-00	12-30	†1.00¼	1.06	h[51]0.92	127	2251	2159	9-30-99	1884	1700	278933	Dc	v1.68	v1.93	v□1.18	v□2.15	E2.47	2.31	9 Mo Sep	v1.58	v1.74	2
3	....	None Paid			...	Nil	....	Total Assets $24270.14M			10-31-99	10.9	...	1757	Jl	1.99	0.09	0.10	v0.44	v0.35	0.29	3 Mo Oct	v0.07	v0.01	3
4	....	0.062	5-15-76	4-9	...	Nil	....	0.21	10.2	13.6	8-31-99	1.93	...	2379	My	0.08	0.14	v0.22	v0.15	v0.12	d0.04	3 Mo Aug	v0.03	vd0.13	4
5	....	0.10	12-10-91	11-5	...	Nil	....	103	1301	1056	9-30-99	724	14661	131152	Dc	v1.23	vd3.15	v2.03	v0.64	Ed1.75	d1.63	9 Mo Sep	v0.92	vd1.35	5
6	1983	Q1.25	12-10-99	11-8	5.00	5.00	5.00	Cv into 1.7699 com,$28.25				....	2500	...	Dc	...	...	...	....	....	....				6
7	1983	Q0.62½	12-10-99	11-8	2.50	2.50	2.50	Cv into 0.8403 com,$29.75				....	4000	...	Dc	...	...	...	....	....	....				7
8◆	....	0.05	1-11-88	12-24	...	Nil	....	17.5	492	345	9-30-99	776	...	102496	Dc	vd0.16	v□0.50	□v0.57	v□d0.24	E0.44	d1.82	9 Mo Sep	v□0.58	vd1.00	8
9	....	None Since Public			...	Nil	....	87.0	132	38.6	9-30-99	63.3	...	36250	Dc	...	...	vpd0.30	vpd1.28	....	....	9 Mo Sep	n/a	vd2.73	9
10	1999	g[53]0.75	12-22-99	12-15	g[53]0.75	Nil	....	103	292	178	j6-30-99	30.0	...	8275	Dc	v0.07	v1.07	v0.12	v1.83	....	jd0.87	9 Mo Sep	v1.57	vd1.13	10
11	....	None Since Public			...	Nil	....	3.36	3.89	1.76	6-30-99	0.97	...	3984	Sp	d0.22	v0.22	v0.96	vd0.47	Pvd0.44	d0.44				11
12◆	1987	3.046	12-29-99		3.806	0.76	0.826	544	1620	3445	j12-31-98	3199	145000	3520893	Dc	1.15	d0.42	vd1.25	v1.90	....	1.90				12
13◆	1993	Q0.03	12-1-99	11-18	0.12	0.12	0.114	1.80	61.6	16.5	6-30-99	30.2	...	6987	Sp	0.78	v0.90	v1.06	v0.97	Pv0.15	0.15				13
14	1997	[56]1.00	2-19-99	2-10	[56]1.00	Nil	[56]1.00	1332	1586	249	9-30-99	95.0	...	±22512	Dc	v±1.50	v±0.17	±v5.61	v±1.75	....	1.23	9 Mo Sep	v±1.60	v±1.08	14
15	....	None Since Public			...	Nil	....	11.9	21.1	3.79	9-30-99	148	...	±14069	Dc	vd0.66	pvd0.39	□vd1.74	v□d1.21	....	d1.63	9 Mo Sep	v□d0.89	vd1.31	15
16◆	....	None Since Public			...	Nil	....	0.53	78.1	4.00	6-30-99	....	...	37353	Sp	p0.45	p0.58	v0.11	v0.74	Pv0.42	0.42				16
17◆	1990	Q0.01½	12-10-99	11-24	0.061	0.06	h[57]0.056	23.0	1403	1140	9-30-99	13.8	...	33739	Dc	v0.72	v0.77	v0.89	v0.63	....	0.61	9 Mo Sep	v0.78	v0.76	17
18◆	....	None Paid			...	Nil	....	11.8	240	92.0	9-30-99	35.4	...	±12463	Dc	v±2.06	v□±2.23	±v1.33	v±1.98	....	2.43	9 Mo Sep	v±1.44	v±1.89	18
19◆	....	None Since Public			...	Nil	....	Cv into 1 Cl'A'				....	...	2488	Dc	v±2.06	v□±2.23	v±1.33	v±1.98	....	2.41	9 Mo Sep	v±1.46	v±1.89	19
20	....	None Since Public			...	Nil	....	80.9	136	15.1	9-30-99	....	...	52912	Dc	vΔ0.08	v0.47	v0.28	v0.36	E0.45	0.40	9 Mo Sep	v0.26	v0.30	20
21◆	....	h[59]....	6-26-98	6-18	...	Nil	h[59]....	164	379	72.5	j6-30-99	9.15	...	108954	Dc	vd0.05	v0.31	v0.74	v1.06	E1.27	j1.26	9 Mo Sep	v0.72	v0.92	21
22	....	None Since Public			...	Nil	....	6.23	19.9	1.21	9-30-99	0.01	...	★17239	Dc	vd0.96	vd0.69	vd0.77	vd0.34	....	d0.42	9 Mo Sep	vd0.24	vd0.32	22
23◆	....	None Since Public			...	Nil	....	672	879	128	9-30-99	53.7	...	150242	Dc	v0.04	v0.28	v0.59	v0.90	E1.30	1.23	9 Mo Sep	v0.63	v0.96	23
24◆	....	None Paid			...	Nil	....	3.82	5.08	1.04	9-30-99	....	1085	5802	Mr	d1.95	vd1.30	vd3.60	vd1.25	....	d0.60	6 Mo Sep	vd0.67	vd0.02	24
25◆	....	None Since Public			...	Nil	....	1.38	3.34	2.91	9-30-99	....	...	17733	Dc	vd0.21	vd0.21	vd0.21	vd0.69	....	d0.26	9 Mo Sep	vd0.59	vd0.16	25
26◆	....	None Since Public			...	Nil	....	27.7	50.6	12.5	9-30-99	17.1	...	23000	Dc	vd0.01	v0.13	v0.70	v0.51	....	0.90	9 Mo Sep	v0.20	v0.59	26
27	1996	0.14	8-6-99	7-7	0.14	0.14	0.12	236	747	231	8-31-99	....	...	112822	My	0.69	0.82	v0.93	v1.11	v1.03	1.13	6 Mo Nov	v0.61	v0.71	27
28	....	None Paid			...	Nil	....	6.15	61.8	47.1	9-30-99	103	...	23588	Dc	pvd0.35	vd1.19	vd1.11	vd0.80	....	d1.07	9 Mo Sep	vd0.77	vd1.04	28
29	....	None Paid			...	Nil	....	4.93	10.0	1.61	10-31-99	....	...	4530	Ja	d0.07	v0.23	v0.17	v0.26	....	0.09	9 Mo Oct	v0.17	vNil	29
30	....	Plan qtly div			...	[60]....	....	Receipt Val based on 20 Biotech Ind Co's[61]				....	...	★4500	Dc	...	...	...	...	....	....	Expire 12-31-2039			30
31◆	....	None Since Public			...	Nil	....	6.60	6.70	0.49	9-30-99	....	...	10861	Dc	d0.30	d0.25	v[62]d0.35	v[63]d0.21	....	d0.29	9 Mo Sep	vd0.30	vd0.38	31
32◆	....	None Since Public			...	Nil	....	86.4	144	31.0	6-30-99	126	...	p25943	Dc	v0.23	v0.92	v1.38	v1.63	E2.35	2.02	9 Mo Sep	v1.14	v1.53	32
33	....	Terms&trad. basis should			be checked in detail			Wrrts expire 9-30-2002				....	...	3738	Dc	...	...	...	...	....	....				33
34	1988	Div Postponed 12-7-99			0.10	Nil	0.32½	0.98	311	156	9-30-99	499	...	29735	Je	1.74	d0.08	v0.50	v0.05	vd7.61	d7.45	3 Mo Sep	v0.03	v0.19	34
35	....	None Since Public			...	Nil	....	40.8	166	151	9-30-99	....	...	27273	Je	d0.27	v0.72	v1.55	v1.46	v1.36	2.15	3 Mo Sep	vd0.35	v0.44	35
36◆	....	None Since Public			...	Nil	....	3.92	439	445	9-30-99	423	...	71177	Sp	0.23	0.65	v1.31	v1.44	vd0.42	d0.42				36
37	....	Terms&trad. basis should			be checked in detail			Wrrts expire 4-13-2000				....	...	4800	Sp	...	...	...	...	....	....				37
38◆	....	None Since Public			...	Nil	....	9.22	578	471	10-30-99	2.10	...	73512	Ja	...	p0.81	v0.91	v□1.07	E1.43	1.33	9 Mo Oct	v□0.58	v0.84	38
39◆	....	None Since Public			...	Nil	....	4.05	139	53.5	9-30-99	49.0	...	19141	Mr	v1.10	v1.40	v1.75	v2.09	E2.56	2.32	6 Mo Sep	v0.95	v1.18	39
40	1937	Q0.12	12-31-99	12-15	0.48	0.48	0.48	142	2059	1649	10-03-99	1058	...	86860	Dc	□2.77	v2.39	v2.35	vd8.22	E3.32	2.93	9 Mo Sep	vd9.06	v2.09	40
41◆	1942	Q0.26	12-1-99	11-9	1.04	1.04	1.00	25.3	174	169	9-30-99	161	...	21350	Dc	v1.19	v1.40	v1.49	v1.19	....	1.30	9 Mo Sep	v1.18	v1.29	41
42	....	None Since Public			...	Nil	....	Equity per shr $0.92			6-30-99	....	...	±★63983	Dc	...	...	...	pv0.64	....	....	6 Mo Jun	vp0.43	vp0.77	42
43	1931	0.15	12-15-99	11-15	0.60	0.60	0.60	7.56	272	76.4	9-30-99	25.0	...	8210	Dc	v2.72	v1.58	v1.45	v2.49	....	1.58	9 Mo Sep	v1.70	v0.79	43
44	....	None Since Public			...	Nil	....	Total Assets $75.1M			9-30-99	50.1	...	20289	Je	0.01	Δ0.04	Δv0.11	v0.15	v0.14	0.13	3 Mo Sep	v0.03	v0.02	44
45◆	1993	S0.035	10-15-99	9-29	0.07	0.07	0.07	9.16	13.2	3.58	9-30-99	....	...	9471	Je	0.27	0.43	v0.34	v0.26	v□0.12	0.10	3 Mo Sep	v□0.05	v0.03	45
46	1962	Q0.275	1-3-00	12-9	1.025	1.10	0.85	212	1108	868	10-31-99	353	...	98336	Ap	1.01	v1.67	v0.45	v3.65	v2.14	1.88	6 Mo Oct	vd0.58	vd0.84	46
47◆	1971	sQ0.311	1-3-00	11-29	s1.224	1.24	s1.179	83.6	429	392	9-30-99	104	...	±23580	Mr	v±3.79	v±0.37	±v2.20	v±2.19	....	2.29	6 Mo Sep	v1.05	v1.15	47
48	1999	Q0.02	11-22-99	10-28	0.02	0.08	....	122	639	916	p3-31-99	p1157	...	★±175003	Dc	...	...	...	vpd2.20	....	....	9 Mo Sep	n/a	vpd0.42	48
49	....	None Since Public			...	Nil	....	0.22	40.6	13.3	9-30-99	17.1	...	7562	Dc	vp0.64	vp0.47	v0.77	v0.84	....	0.42	9 Mo Sep	v0.60	v0.18	49
50◆	1983	0.071	7-1-99	6-10	0.21⅜	Nil	0.285	30.0	378	145	9-30-99	857	...	[65]30796	Dc	±v[66]1.27	v±1.41	v±1.53	v□1.65	....	0.67	9 Mo Sep	v±0.61	v±d0.37	50
51	1997	0.01⅞	6-28-99	6-11	0.76⅞	0.93	0.18	73.0	280	334	12-31-98	77.6	...	36900	Dc	0.86	v1.05	v0.86	v0.82	....	0.65	9 Mo Sep	v0.55	v0.38	51

◆Stock Splits & Divs By Line Reference Index [1]2-for-1,'94,'98,'99. [2]2-for-1,'98. [8]No adj for stk dstr,'97. [12]1-for-1.125 REVERSE,'99. [13]10%,'96,'97,'98. [16]2-for-1,'98. [17]4-for-3,'98,'99:No adj for stk dstr,'99. [18]3-for-2,'96. [19]3-for-2,'96. [21]2-for-1,'97. [23]2-for-1,'96,'99. [24]1-for-5 REVERSE:eff Oct 13:1-for-5 REVERSE,'99. [25]1-for-4 REVERSE,'94. [26]2-for-1,'99. [31]3-for-1,'97. [32]3-for-1,'96:To split 2-for-1,ex Jan 20,'00. [36]2-for-1,'98. [38]2-for-1,'99. [39]No adj for stk dstr MICOM Commun,'94. [41]3-for-2,'98. [45]3-for-2,'94. [47]Adj for 3%,'99. [50]3-for-2,'95:2-for-1,'97:No adj for merger/recap,'99.

¶ S&P 500
# MidCap 400
✣ SmallCap 600
• Options

Index	Ticker	Name of Issue (Call Price of Pfd. Stocks)	Market	Com. Rank. & Pfd. Rating	Inst. Hold Cos	Inst. Hold Shs. (000)	Principal Business	Price Range 1971-97 High	1971-97 Low	1998 High	1998 Low	1999 High	1999 Low	Dec. Sales in 100s	December, 1999 Last Sale Or Bid High	Low	Last	%Div Yield	P-E Ratio	EPS 5 Yr Growth	% Annualized Total Return 12 Mo	36 Mo	60 Mo
1	BXG	✓Bluegreen Corp	NY,Ch,P	B	43	7453	Sells undeveloped rural land	15 5/8	5/16	12	4 1/4	7 3/4	4 1/4	13171	5 15/16	4 1/4	5	...	8	49	−33.9	22.1	14.2
#2•	BTH	✓Blyth Industries	NY,Ch	NR	181	25068	Mfr,mkt candle products	39 1/2	5 1/2	38 1/16	22	34 15/16	21 1/8	40069	27 7/8	22 1/16	24 9/16	...	14	40	−21.4	−6.7	21.0
✣3•[1]	BMC	✓BMC Industries	NY,Ch,Ph,P	B+	123	15741	Mfg:mashs for color TV/optics	35 5/8	5/8	22 1/4	3 13/16	13 7/16	3 15/16	27379	5 7/16	4 7/16	4 7/8	1.2	d	Neg	−21.3	−46.0	−8.2
¶4•[2]	BMCS	✓BMC Software	NNM	B+	963	217746	Dvlp IBM compatible sys softwr	35 5/8	11/16	60 1/4	29 1/4	84 1/16	30	610094	80 3/8	66 1/4	79 15/16	...	50	29	79.4	58.4	63.3
#5•[3]	BOBE	✓Bob Evans Farms	NNM	A–	180	20394	Restaurants sausage prod	23 1/2	5/16	26 7/8	18	26 3/8	12 3/4	63025	15 5/8	14 11/16	15 7/16	2.3	11	9	−39.6	6.4	−3.8
6•[4]	BOX	✓BOC Group ADS[51]	NY,Ch	NR	27	10706	Indl gases,pharm'l pd,food dst	39	26 7/8	35 3/4	22 1/8	44	26	2085	43	40 15/16	42 5/8	2.5	46	−3	61.5	17.3	...
7	BOCI	✓Boca Research	NNM	C	23	1267	Mfr computer peripheral prod	36 1/2	4 1/4	6 3/8	1 5/16	11 1/8	3	14703	8 3/4	6 3/8	6 5/8	...	d	Neg	112	−13.9	−5.9
8•[1]	RST	✓Boca Resorts	NY,Ph	NR	42	4869	Own/oper resorts NHL hockey team	32 1/2	10	22 7/8	7 1/8	11 5/16	7 3/8	10704	10 1/8	8 1/4	9 3/4	...	..	...	4.7	−17.3	...
9	BNP	✓Boddie-Noell Properties	AS,Ch	NR	20	521	REIT: Hardee's Food System	17 1/8	8 1/2	15 1/8	9 7/8	12	8	5306	9 1/2	8	8 3/8	14.8	16	−5	−10.0	−3.3	1.8
¶10•[5]	BA	✓Boeing Co	NY,B,C,Ch,P,Ph	B	1024	474500	Mfr jet airplanes: missiles	60 1/2	3/8	56 1/4	29	48 1/2	32 9/16	822238	42 1/8	37 1/16	41 7/16	1.4	18	46	28.8	−6.8	13.6
¶11•[5]	BCC	✓Boise Cascade	NY,B,C,Ch,P,Ph	B–	402	49764	Leading mfr of forest prod	52 5/16	5	40 3/8	22 1/4	47 3/16	28 3/4	92675	41 1/8	33 1/16	40 1/2	1.5	16	84	32.8	10.4	10.5
12•[5]	BOP	✓Boise Cascade Office Products	NY,Ch,Ph,P	NR	64	10092	Distribute office products	49 1/2	10 7/8	20 1/2	7 1/16	15 3/4	9 1/4	30960	15 5/16	14	15	...	16	14	11.1	−10.3	...
13	BOKF	✓BOK Financial	NNM	NR	58	2089	Commercial banking, Oklahoma	25 7/16	2 9/16	24 3/16	17 9/16	25 3/16	18 13/16	3774	21 1/4	19 1/4	20 3/16	s...	13	13	−8.6	20.3	18.4
14	BLE	✓Bolle Inc	AS	NR	16	1515	Dgn&mfr sunglasses/eyewear	....	....	10 1/8	1 5/8	5 1/8	1 7/8	7009	5 1/8	4 3/4	5 1/16	...	d	...	153	...	...
15	BTJ	✓Bolt Technology	AS,Ch	B–	15	732	Dvlp/mkt geophysical equip	10	2 5/8	10 3/4	5	8 15/16	3 3/8	3720	4 3/8	3 3/8	3 7/8	...	7	20	−41.5	−4.0	...
16	BBD.B	✓Bombardier Inc Cl'B'	To,Mo	A	45	20088	Mfr aircraft/transport eq	17	1/8	22 9/16	13 1/4	32 1/8	18 15/16	252667	32 1/8	27 7/8	29 5/8	e0.7	34	26	36.0	34.4	38.7
✣17•[4]	BBA	✓Bombay Company	NY,Ch,Ph,P	B–	90	23562	Sell furniture/leather goods	32 15/16	1/8	6 13/16	3 3/4	8 1/8	3 1/2	23446	5 7/8	4 1/4	4 1/2	...	25	NM	−18.2	−0.9	−14.8
18	BNSO	✓Bonso Electronics Intl	NNM	B–	1	2	Mfr electronics scales/prod	12 3/4	3/8	11 11/16	3 1/8	9 1/8	5 3/8	1766	8 11/16	8	8 3/8	...	60	−39	52.8	61.4	10.9
✣19•[6]	BAMM	✓Books-A-Million	NNM	B	55	3669	Book retailer so'eastern U.S.	18 5/8	4 1/8	47	2 1/4	17	7	104264	11 1/8	7 7/8	8 5/16	...	21	−6	−36.1	6.5	−13.2
20	WEL	✓Boots&Coots Intl Well Control	AS	NR	5	1647	Oilwell control svcs	....	....	7 15/16	1 7/8	3 1/16	1/4	66368	9/16	7/16	7/16	...	d	...	−85.4	...	...
21•[5]	BCU	✓Borden Chem/Plastics L.P.	NY,Ch,P	NR	35	3438	Produces chem & PVC resins	26 3/8	7 1/2	9 1/4	2 5/8	9 7/16	3 1/4	37955	5 11/16	4 1/4	4 13/16	...	d	Neg	2.7	−13.9	−19.6
#22•[7]	BGP	✓Borders Group	NY,Ch,Ph,P	NR	232	53857	Operates book superstores	32 5/16	6 15/16	41 3/4	17 7/8	25 3/4	11 3/4	104314	16 1/2	14 9/16	16 1/4	...	14	NM	−34.8	−3.2	...
#23•[4]	BWA	✓Borg-Warner Automotive	NY,Ch	NR	306	24937	Auto powertrain components	61 1/2	20 1/2	68 3/8	33 1/16	60	36 3/4	26440	41 1/8	38 5/8	40 1/2	1.5	8	14	−26.5	3.0	11.7
24•[8]	BLPG	✓Boron LePore & Assoc	NNM	NR	42	5651	Pharmaceutical industry svcs	28 1/2	17	43 1/4	23 1/8	36	4 15/16	19958	7 1/2	5 7/8	6 1/2	...	54	...	−81.2	...	...
25•[9]	SAM	✓Boston Beer 'A'	NY,Ph,P	NR	47	5469	Largest craft brewer U.S.	33	7 13/16	12 3/4	6 1/2	11 1/8	6 15/16	17881	7 9/16	6 15/16	7 3/16	...	14	10	−15.4	−11.2	...
26	BOS	✓Boston Celtics L.P.	NY,B,Ch,Ph	NR	11	8	Professional basketball team	28 7/8	10 3/8	21 1/2	7	17 1/2	9 1/8	908	10 1/16	9 1/8	10	...	d	Neg	−3.0	−19.3	−8.3
27	BXP	✓Boston Properties	NY,Ph	NR	274	57398	Real estate investment trust	35 1/4	25	36 1/16	23 7/16	37 1/2	27 1/4	40013	31 7/16	27 1/4	31 1/8	5.8	11	...	7.6	...	...
¶28•[10]	BSX	✓Boston Scientific	NY,Ph,P	B–	635	215286	Dvlp,mfr medical devices	39 3/16	4 11/16	40 13/16	20 1/8	47 1/16	17 9/16	390509	22 1/2	18 9/16	21 7/8	...	23	−11	−18.4	−9.7	20.5
29	BFD	✓BostonFed Bancorp	AS	NR	27	2476	Savings bank, Massachusetts	22 1/2	10	25 1/8	13 1/2	19	13 15/16	1822	16 1/4	14	15 7/8	3.0	10	...	−7.5	4.5	...
30	BND	✓Boundless Corp	AS	NR	10	268	Dgn computer terminals	93 3/4	6 1/4	11 1/4	2 7/8	10 3/4	3 5/16	9179	10 1/2	6 3/4	8 3/8	...	9	NM	67.5	−18.5	−12.2
31	BWG	✓Bouygues Offshore ADS[58]	NY,Ph	NR	17	605	Intl oil&gas ind services	29 7/8	11 1/2	25 1/4	10 1/4	20 1/2	10 3/8	1134	19 11/16	17 1/2	18 3/8	2.1	10	14	77.7	14.5	...
#32•[11]	BOW	✓Bowater, Inc.	NY,B,Ch,P,Ph	B–	299	48695	Mfrs newsprint,coated paper	57	14 7/8	60 1/2	31 3/16	60 9/16	36 15/16	66505	54 3/4	46 9/16	54 5/16	1.5	d	50	33.4	15.1	17.4
33	BWL.A	✓Bowl America Cl'A'	AS,B,Ch	B	14	367	Bowling centers	12 1/8	1/4	9 3/8	6 7/8	7 3/4	6 3/8	495	7 3/8	7	7	6.3	10	6	4.1	7.5	2.8
34	BWN	✓Bowlin Outdoor Adv/Travel	AS	NR	16	1044	Oper travel,ctrs,outdoor ad sv	8 7/8	3 3/8	10 7/8	3 1/2	7 1/4	3 7/16	3437	5 7/8	3 7/16	5 1/8B	...	39	1	0.0	−12.4	...
✣35•[12]	BNE	✓Bowne & Co.	NY,B,Ch,P,Ph	B+	185	25656	Fin'l,corp,legal printing	20 5/16	3/16	23 7/8	10 1/8	19 1/2	10 1/4	21500	13 13/16	11 3/16	13 1/2	1.6	28	−7	−23.3	4.6	11.0
36	BOYD	✓Boyd Bros.Transport'n	NNM	B	16	650	Flatbed trucking services	13	4 1/4	12 1/4	5	11 7/8	6	870	7 7/8	6 1/8	6 1/2B	...	4	23	4.0	−2.4	−7.8
37•[13]	BYD	✓Boyd Gaming	NY,Ch	NR	73	10724	Own,operate casino-hotels	26	5	8 3/8	2 1/2	7 3/8	3 1/16	17845	6 3/4	5 1/2	5 13/16	...	9	−9	75.5	−11.0	−11.6
38	FOB	✓Boyds Collection	NY	NR	58	13506	Design,import giftware prod	....	....	....	....	18 11/16	6 1/2	26152	8 3/4	6 1/2	6 15/16	...	6	...	...	...	...
39	BOY	✓Boykin Lodging	NY,Ch	NR	77	3166	Real estate investment trust	27 3/4	20	28 1/2	11 3/8	15 7/8	10 13/16	24293	12 7/16	10 13/16	10 15/16	17.2	9	...	1.3	−14.9	...
40•[14]	BPA	✓BP Amoco ADS[63]	NY,B,Ch,P,Ph	NR	1243	502209	Major integrated world oil	46 1/2	1 1/8	48 5/8	36 1/2	62 5/8	40 3/16	571717	62 5/8	58 7/16	59 5/16	2.1	31	−3	36.2	23.5	29.0
41	BPT	✓BP Prudhoe Bay Royalty[64]	NY,Ch,Ph,P	NR	33	1820	Royalties of oil/gas prop	35 1/2	13	16 7/8	4 5/16	11	4 7/16	10923	9 15/16	8 1/4	9 1/16	12.6	41	−29	106	−12.3	−3.5
42	BTR	✓Bradley Real Estate	NY,Ch	NR	122	16618	Real estate investment trust	32 1/2	13/16	22 3/4	18 3/8	21 11/16	15 5/8	22031	17 7/8	15 5/8	17 7/16	8.7	14	12	−8.2	5.5	10.4
43	Pr A	8.40% cm Cv Pfd 'A'([65]25)	NY	BBB+	19	642		....	....	25	21 3/8	24	19	1164	21 7/8	19	19 1/2	10.8	..	...	...	...	...
✣44	BRC	✓Brady Corp'A'	NY	A–	151	12902	Mfrs adhesives & coatings	35	3 5/16	35 3/4	16 1/4	36 5/16	19 1/2	6655	34 9/16	28 9/16	33 15/16	2.0	18	8	28.8	13.8	18.4
45•[15]	BDN	✓Brandywine Rlty Trust SBI	NY,Ph	NR	194	25125	Real estate investment trust	33 3/8	15/16	27 3/8	15 3/4	20 7/16	14 3/4	32229	16 15/16	14 3/4	16 3/8	9.8	20	NM	0.0	1.5	10.2
46	BRE	✓BRE Properties Cl'A'	NY,Ch,P	NR	133	19598	Real estate investment trust	30	1 7/16	28 11/16	21 1/2	26 3/8	20 1/2	27469	23 3/8	20 1/2	22 11/16	6.9	15	7	−2.1	2.9	15.0
47	BWAY	✓Breakaway Solutions	NNM	NR	..	...	Provide e-business solutions	....	....	....	....	77	14	38484	77	50 3/4	73	...	d	...	...	...	...
48	BRBK	✓Brenton Banks	NNM	A–	53	3146	Commercial bkg,Iowa	16 13/16	3/4	22 1/16	13 7/8	17 1/4	9	4622	11 3/4	9	10 1/8	3.5	12	18	−25.0	9.2	18.7
49	BVB	✓Bridge View Bancorp	AS	NR	4	17	Commercial banking, New Jersey	25 3/16	8 1/2	36 1/4	16 9/16	28 1/8	14 3/4	679	18	14 3/4	15 3/4	s1.3	15	...	−2.5	21.1	...
50	BDS	✓Bridgestreet Accommodations	AS	NR	15	1061	Extended stay housing svcs	14 1/8	9	13	2 3/8	5	1 1/8	4545	2	1 1/8	1 1/2	...	9	11	−52.9	...	...
¶51•[1]	BGG	✓Briggs & Stratton	NY,B,Ch,Ph,P	A–	376	17476	Mfr small gas engines:locks	53 5/8	6 7/8	52 7/16	33 5/8	71 1/8	46 11/16	19045	53 11/16	49 3/4	53 5/8	2.2	10	10	9.9	9.4	...

Uniform Footnote Explanations-See Page 4. Other: [1]Ph:Cycle 1. [2]CBOE,P:Cycle 2. [3]P:Cycle 1. [4]Ph:Cycle 3. [5]CBOE:Cycle 2. [6]ASE,CBOE,Ph:Cycle 2. [7]CBOE,Ph:Cycle 2. [8]CBOE:Cycle 2,Ph:Cycle 1. [9]ASE,P:Cycle 3. [10]ASE,CBOE,P,Ph:Cycle 2. [11]P:Cycle 3. [12]ASE:Cycle 1. [13]Ph:Cycle 2. [14]CBOE,P:Cycle 1. [15]P,Ph:Cycle 2. [51]Ea ADS rep 2 Ord shrs,25p. [52]Approx. [53]Incl 0.255M equiv'B'shrs. [54]80.9% owned by Boise Cascade. [55]Stk dstr of Tandy Brands Accessories. [56]Incl curr amts. [57]6 Mo Dec'97. [58]Ea ADS rep 0.5 com, FF10. [59]Oct'96 & prior. [60]12 Mo Dec'97. [61]Fiscal Jun'96 & prior. [62]12 Mo Dec'97:Fiscal Jun'97 earnd$1.19. [63]Ea ADS rep 6 ord shs,par$0.50. [64]Units of Beneficial Int. [65]Fr 8-7-2003. [66]Pfd in $M. [67]Incl current amts. [68]Fiscal Jul '95 & prior.

Splits ◆ Index	Cash Divs. Ea. Yr. Since	Dividends: Latest Payment Period $	Date	Ex. Div.	Total $ So Far 1999	Ind. Rate	Paid 1998	Financial Position Mil-$ Cash& Equiv.	Curr. Assets	Curr. Liab.	Balance Sheet Date	Capitalization Lg Trm Debt Mil-$	Shs. 000 Pfd.	Com.	Earnings $ Per Shr. Years End	1995	1996	1997	1998	1999	Last 12 Mos.	Interim Earnings Period	$ per Shr. 1998	1999	Index
1◆	....	5%Stk	3-28-96	3-5	...	Nil	....	Total Assets $380.72M			10-03-99	185	...	22962	Mr	0.30	vd0.21	v0.46	□v0.72	....	0.67	6 Mo Sep	v□0.43	v0.38	1
2◆	....	None Since Public			...	Nil	....	13.5	370	171	10-31-99	196	...	48075	Ja	v0.55	v0.88	v1.10	v1.50	....	1.78	9 Mo Oct	v1.05	v1.33	2
3◆	1994	Q0.01½	1-5-00	12-20	0.06	0.06	0.06	0.83	163	60.7	9-30-99	177	...	27370	Dc	v0.87	v1.24	v1.25	vd1.13	....	d0.10	9 Mo Sep	vd1.31	vd0.28	3
4◆	....	None Since Public			...	Nil	....	400	906	1048	9-30-99	....	...	242351	Mr	v0.50	v0.77	v0.77	v□1.47	E1.61	1.16	6 Mo Sep	0.61	v0.30	4
5	1964	Q0.09	12-1-99	11-17	0.36	0.36	0.33	9.65	51.1	122	10-29-99	0.87	.1	38478	Ap	v1.26	v0.69	v0.86	v1.09	v1.39	1.42	6 Mo Oct	v0.71	v0.74	5
6	1997	[52]0.499	2-8-00	12-21	1.047	1.05	1.031	268	1278	1055	j9-30-98	992	...	489000	Sp	1.65	1.78	1.89	v0.84	....	0.92	9 Mo Jun	v1.10	v1.18	6
7	....	None Since Public			...	Nil	....	14.7	26.9	8.35	9-30-99	....	...	11460	Dc	v1.07	v0.72	vd1.71	vd1.67	....	d1.37	9 Mo Sep	vd1.69	vd1.39	7
8	....	None Since Public			...	Nil	....	56.8	102	168	9-30-99	558	...	[53]±40861	Je	...	pd1.97	±vd0.74	v±0.04	v□±0.26	0.07	3 Mo Sep	vd0.57	vd0.76	8
9	1987	Q0.31	11-16-99	10-28	1.24	1.24	1.24	Total Assets $227.57M			9-30-99	149	...	5951	Dc	v0.54	v0.56	□v0.59	v□0.63	....	0.51	9 Mo Sep	v□0.48	v0.36	9
10◆	1942	Q0.14	3-3-00	2-9	0.56	0.56	0.56	2773	16720	14171	9-30-99	5909	...	934540	Dc	vd0.04	pv1.85	vd0.18	v1.15	E2.25	2.24	9 Mo Sep	v0.67	v1.76	10
11	1935	Q0.15	1-15-00	12-29	0.60	0.60	0.60	67.9	70.1	1204	9-30-99	1721	5032	57138	Dc	v5.39	vd0.63	vd1.19	v□d0.85	E2.55↑	1.63	9 Mo Sep	v□d0.60	v1.88	11
12◆	....	None Since Public			...	Nil	....	19.5	730	547	9-30-99	281	...	[54]65800	Dc	pv0.70	v0.88	v0.89	v0.81	....	0.96	9 Mo Sep	v0.66	v0.81	12
13◆	....	3%Stk	10-18-99	10-6	3%Stk	Stk	3%Stk	Total Deposits $5147.24M			9-30-99	149	...	49014	Dc	v0.94	v1.03	v1.22	v1.40	....	1.52	9 Mo Sep	v1.06	v1.18	13
14	....	None Since Public			...	Nil	....	2.08	32.6	29.8	9-30-99	9.37	74	6895	Dc	...	p0.59	n/a	vd4.98	....	d4.91	9 Mo Sep	v0.04	v0.11	14
15	....	None Paid			...	Nil	....	3.18	12.2	4.25	9-30-99	4.88	...	5370	Je	0.38	0.24	v0.41	v0.97	v0.80	0.57	3 Mo Sep	v0.29	v0.06	15
16◆	1984	g†0.056	1-31-00	1-12	g†0.211	0.22	†g0.168	Total Assets $15006M			j7-31-99	2471	12000	±681455	Ja	±0.23	v±0.58	v±0.58	±v0.76	....	j0.87	6 Mo Jul	v±0.32	v±0.43	16
17◆	....	h[55]....	1-11-91	1-14	...	Nil	....	5.50	129	36.6	10-30-99	....	...	36300	Ja	v0.33	vΔd0.07	v0.12	v0.11	....	0.18	9 Mo Oct	vd0.19	vd0.12	17
18◆	....	None Paid			...	Nil	....	1.28	7.31	3.99	3-31-99	0.24	...	3119	Mr	0.21	v0.19	v0.73	vNil	....	0.14	6 Mo Sep	v0.03	v0.17	18
19◆	....	None Since Public			...	Nil	....	5.84	248	160	10-30-99	36.9	...	18077	Ja	v0.42	v0.33	v0.40	v0.26	....	0.40	9 Mo Oct	vd0.11	v0.03	19
20	....	None Since Public			...	Nil	....	1.25	37.0	47.8	9-30-99	28.1	172	35244	Dc	...	...	□vd0.02	vd0.12	....	d0.48	9 Mo Sep	vNil	vd0.36	20
21	....	Div Omitted 4-21-98			...	Nil	0.10	6.91	131	77.4	9-30-99	258	...	36750	Dc	v□4.07	v0.13	v0.15	vd1.09	....	d1.01	9 Mo Sep	vd0.67	vd0.59	21
22◆	....	None Since Public			...	Nil	....	48.8	1354	1273	10-24-99	5.70	...	77323	Ja	pd2.53	v0.70	v0.98	v1.12	E1.20	0.95	9 Mo Oct	v0.07	vd0.10	22
23	1994	Q0.15	11-15-99	10-28	0.60	0.60	0.60	25.2	668	563	9-30-99	777	...	27040	Dc	±v3.15	v±1.75	±v4.31	v±4.00	....	5.06	9 Mo Sep	v2.65	v3.71	23
24	....	None Since Public			...	Nil	....	37.8	77.8	26.1	9-30-99	....	...	12455	Dc	...	pn/a	v0.72	v0.84	....	0.12	9 Mo Sep	v0.61	vd0.11	24
25	....	None Since Public			...	Nil	....	51.9	91.6	23.9	9-25-99	....	...	±20533	Dc	vp±0.33	v±0.41	±v0.37	v0.39	....	0.52	9 Mo Sep	v0.34	v0.47	25
26	1998	1.00	6-30-98		...	Nil	2.00	2.42	86.6	5.61	9-30-99	83.5	...	2704	Je	2.43	8.89	v0.06	v2.17	□vd2.85	d2.83	3 Mo Sep	v□d1.17	vd1.15	26
27	1997	Q0.45	1-28-00	12-28	1.72½	1.80	1.64	Total Assets $5354.78M			9-30-99	[56]3278	2000	67905	Dc	...	p1.19	v[57]0.70	v□1.61	E2.87	1.64	9 Mo Sep	v□1.17	v1.20	27
28◆	....	None Since Public			...	Nil	....	72.0	1095	1042	9-30-99	761	...	414701	Dc	vd0.05	v0.42	v0.40	vd0.68	E0.95	0.82	9 Mo Sep	vd0.86	v0.64	28
29	1996	Q0.12	11-16-99	10-29	0.46	0.48	0.37	Total Deposits $736M			9-30-99	391	...	5010	Dc	...	v0.48	v1.24	v1.43	....	1.64	9 Mo Sep	v1.04	v1.25	29
30◆	....	None Paid			...	Nil	....	....	32.8	16.0	9-30-99	14.5	...	4438	Dc	□v0.04	vd0.44	v0.86	v0.90	....	0.90	9 Mo Sep	v0.44	v0.44	30
31	1997	0.392	7-15-99	6-21	0.392	0.39	0.265	Equity per shr $4.90			12-31-98	33.1	...	17000	Dc	1.02	v1.37	v1.21	v1.46	....	1.85	6 Mo Jun	v0.66	v1.05	31
32	1984	Q0.20	1-3-00	12-8	0.80	0.80	0.80	70.0	648	378	9-30-99	1494	...	51667	Dc	v□5.48	v□4.64	v1.25	vd0.44	Ed0.35	1.62	9 Mo Sep	vd1.02	v1.04	32
33◆	1969	Q0.11	2-9-00	1-10	0.42	0.44	0.40	9.00	10.3	2.05	9-26-99	....	...	±5255	Je	±0.57	±0.45	v±0.44	±v0.54	v±0.61	0.67	3 Mo Sep	v±0.01	v±0.07	33
34	....	None Since Public			...	Nil	....	2.03	8.56	5.00	10-31-99	19.5	...	4385	Ja	0.11	v0.28	v0.24	v0.15	....	0.13	9 Mo Oct	v0.19	v0.17	34
35◆	1941	Q0.05½	11-24-99	11-9	0.22	0.22	0.20	28.1	345	165	9-30-99	114	...	36911	Dc	0.67	[59]1.21	v[60]1.87	v0.72	....	0.48	9 Mo Sep	v0.79	v0.55	35
36	....	None Since Public			...	Nil	....	1.20	24.7	23.1	9-30-99	30.0	...	3454	Dc	v0.56	v0.22	v0.62	v1.42	....	1.60	9 Mo Sep	v0.68	v0.86	36
37	....	None Since Public			...	Nil	....	63.9	125	114	9-30-99	714	...	62221	Dc	0.64	□[61]0.52	v[62]d1.04	v0.46	....	0.65	9 Mo Sep	v0.31	□v0.50	37
38	....	None Since Public			...	Nil	....	8.66	61.4	12.6	6-30-99	256	...	59913	Dc	...	...	...	pv0.90	....	1.12	9 Mo Sep	v0.59	v0.81	38
39	1997	Q0.47	2-7-00	12-29	1.88	1.88	1.86	Total Assets $614.92M			9-30-99	293	...	17104	Dc	p1.03	vp1.29	□v1.60	v□1.32	....	1.23	9 Mo Sep	v□1.06	v0.97	39
40◆	1917	0.30	12-10-99	11-17	1.519	1.22	1.21	875	17226	18166	12-31-98	10918	12706	19366020	Dc	0.93	v2.13	v2.13	v1.02	E1.93	1.03	9 Mo Sep	v1.01	v1.02	40
41	1989	0.404	10-20-99	10-13	0.57	1.14	0.679	Total Assets $23.47M			9-30-99	....	...	21400	Dc	v1.60	v1.94	v2.05	v0.68	....	0.22	9 Mo Sep	v0.63	v0.17	41
42◆	1961	Q0.38	12-31-99	12-9	1.49	1.52	1.42	Total Assets $967M			9-30-99	399	3478	24060	Dc	v0.85	v1.54	□v1.36	v2.37	....	1.26	9 Mo Sep	v2.07	v0.96	42
43	1998	0.52½	12-31-99	12-9	2.10	2.10	1.05	Cv into 1.0208 com				....	3480	...	Dc	...	...	...	....	....	....				43
44◆	1984	Q0.17	1-31-00	1-5	0.65	0.68	0.61	65.1	205	67.0	10-31-99	1.01	[66]3	±22650	Jl	1.28	1.27	v1.43	v1.23	v1.73	1.89	3 Mo Oct	v0.38	v0.54	44
45◆	1994	Q0.40	1-14-00	12-28	1.56	1.60	1.50	Total Assets $1822.3M			9-30-99	[67]881	2208	37500	Dc	vd1.33	vd0.44	v0.95	□v0.95	....	0.81	9 Mo Sep	v0.75	v0.61	45
46◆	1970	Q0.39	12-23-99	12-2	1.56	1.56	1.38	Total Assets $1613M			6-30-99	684	2150	44676	Dc	v[68]1.00	v2.92	v2.11	v1.41	....	1.51	9 Mo Sep	v1.03	v1.13	46
47	....	None Since Public			...	Nil	....	1.81	6.49	7.81	6-30-99	2.24	p...	★16866	Dc	...	...	...	vpd0.31	....	d0.58	6 Mo Jun	vpd0.11	vpd0.38	47
48◆	1988	0.087	10-26-99	10-12	0.347	0.35	0.317	Total Deposits $1502.35M			9-30-99	23.8	...	20423	Dc	v0.45	v0.63	v0.84	v0.95	....	0.83	9 Mo Sep	v0.70	v0.58	48
49◆	1997	0.05	2-1-00	1-12	s0.198	0.20	s0.188	Total Deposits $187M			9-30-99	....	...	2782	Dc	1.03	v0.63	v0.76	v0.90	....	1.03	9 Mo Sep	v0.64	v0.77	49
50	....	None Since Public			...	Nil	....	0.77	13.1	8.88	9-30-99	10.5	...	8005	Dc	v0.13	pv0.42	v0.08	v0.18	....	0.17	9 Mo Sep	v0.12	v0.11	50
51◆	1929	Q0.30	1-3-00	11-29	1.17	1.20	1.13	12.9	497	332	9-26-99	113	...	23134	Je	3.62	3.19	v2.15	v2.85	v4.52	5.43	3 Mo Sep	v0.19	v1.10	51

◆Stock Splits & Divs By Line Reference Index [1]Adj to 5%,'96. [2]2-for-1,'95:3-for-2,'97. [3]2-for-1,'94,'95. [4]2-for-1,'95,'96,'98. [10]2-for-1,'97. [12]2-for-1,'96. [13]2-for-1,'99:Adj for 3%,'99. [16]2-for-1,'95,'98. [17]3-for-2,'94. [18]1-for-6 REVERSE,'94. [19]2-for-1,'94. [22]2-for-1,'97. [28]2-for-1,'98. [30]1-for-10 REVERSE,'98. [33]2-for-1,'95. [35]2-for-1,'98. [40]2-for-1,'97,'99. [42]1-for-2 REVERSE,'94. [44]3-for-1,'95. [45]1-for-3 REVERSE,'96. [46]2-for-1,'96. [48]2-for-1,'98:10%,'96,'97,'98,'99. [49]2-for-1,'97:Adj for 5%,'99. [51]2-for-1,'94.

¶ S&P 500 # MidCap 400 ✚ SmallCap 600 • Options

Index	Ticker	Name of Issue (Call Price of Pfd. Stocks)	Market	Com. Rank. & Pfd. Rating	Inst. Hold Cos	Inst. Hold Shs. (000)	Principal Business	1971-97 High	1971-97 Low	1998 High	1998 Low	1999 High	1999 Low	Dec. Sales in 100s	December, 1999 Last Sale Or Bid High	Low	Last	%Div Yield	P-E Ratio	EPS 5 Yr Growth	% Annualized Total Return 12 Mo	36 Mo	60 Mo
✚1•[1]	CELL	✓Brightpoint Inc	NNM	B+	129	15776	Wholesale cellular phones	24¼	1¼	21⅝	5	19 15/16	3½	351146	16⅝	10 7/16	13⅛	...	d	Neg	−4.5	3.4	32.0
2	CBA	✓Brilliance China Automotive	NY,Ph	NR	12	2038	Minibus manufacturer in China	4⅝	7/16	1 9/16	11/16	5 15/16	13/16	41577	4	2 15/16	3 3/16	0.3	11	32	354	99.3	36.5
3	BDE	✓Brilliant Digital Entertain't	AS	NR	9	293	Digital entertain't programs	9⅞	3½	6⅜	1 1/16	7 15/16	1¾	21334	4½	2½	3 15/16	...	d	...	125	1.6	...
#4•[2]	EAT	✓Brinker Intl	NY,Ch,Ph	B+	356	59408	Limited menu restaurants	33 11/16	1 11/16	29¼	15	30⅝	19⅞	62295	24⅛	19⅞	24⅛	...	18	15	−16.5	14.7	5.9
5	BH	✓Bristol Hotel & Resorts	NY	NR	27	5897	Oper full-svc hotels	....	....	7¾	3¼	10	3⅞	8771	5 1/16	4⅝	5 1/16	...	..	...	−17.4	...	...
¶6•[1]	BMY	✓Bristol-Myers Squibb	NY,B,C,Ch,P,Ph	A	2187	1228258	Pharmaceutical,medical prod	49 1/16	15/16	67⅝	44⅛	79¼	57¼	871028	74 9/16	59 15/16	64 3/16	1.5	31	16	−2.8	35.5	38.3
7	Pr	$2 cm Cv Pfd (50)vtg	NY,B,P	NR	6	.9	non-prescp hlth pr: toiletries	450	25	906	906	1000	1000	....	....	....	1088⅝B	0.2	..	...	...	...	...
8	BWT	✓BriteSmile Inc	AS,Ch,P	C	22	1187	Dental cosmetic pds	30⅞	3/16	3 13/16	11/16	17¼	2 1/16	7219	11 3/16	7½	8⅛	...	d	Neg	177	−9.6	70.6
9•[3]	BAB	✓British Airways ADS[53]	NY,Ch,P,Ph	NR	75	9448	Major int'l U.K. airline	125⅛	16⅛	114¾	52⅛	88½	49	6590	68⅜	58	64⅜	4.5	17	−10	−0.6	−11.2	6.3
10•[4]	BTI	✓British Amer Tobacco ADS[55]	AS,B,Ch,Mo,P	NR	48	30865	Tobacco prod,fin'l svcs, insur	20¼	15/16	23 13/16	15	22¼	10 3/16	35822	12 11/16	10 3/16	10¼	9.8	13	−11	−37.8	−9.8	−1.0
11	BGY	British Energy ADS[56]	NY	NR	..	...	Electric utility,U.K.	....	....	....	....	24⅜	23	13	24⅜	23	22¾B	...	15	...	...	...	...
12•[5]	BSY	✓British Sky Bdcstg Gp ADS	NY,Ch,Ph,P	NR	15	546	Pay TV svcs U.K./Ireland	66¾	22⅞	54½	34⅛	95 13/16	40⅝	870	95 13/16	76¼	91⅝B	0.7	76	6	98.7	21.9	32.3
13•[6]	BTY	✓British Telecommn ADR[58]	NY,P	NR	132	5506	Telecomm'n svcs in UK	83¼	5 15/16	154 7/16	79 9/16	245	143	3486	245	208 11/16	238	1.2	39	6	60.6	62.5	40.7
14	BBSW	✓Broadbase Software	NNM	NR	31	1727	Customer info softwr prd	....	....	....	....	142¾	14	56132	142¾	80⅞	112½	...	..	...	...	...	...
15•[7]	BRCM	✓Broadcom Corp 'A'	NNM	NR	294	20953	Dvp silicon semiconductors	....	....	67½	12	289	46¼	330717	289	180 1/16	272⅜	...	..	NM	352	...	...
16	BVSN	✓BroadVision Inc	NNM	NR	246	42855	Dvp stg:World Wide Web software	3 7/16	1 7/16	14¾	2	179	9 1/16	492797	179	90	170 1/16	...	..	...	1496	302	...
#17•[5]	BRW	✓Broadwing Inc	NY,C,Ch	B	363	71398	Telecommun/internet svcs	33¾	15/16	38⅝	13⅜	37⅞	16 1/16	194934	37⅞	28½	36⅞	...	46	NM	...	...	...
18	Pr B	6.75% cm[60]Dep Pfd([61]52.365)	NY	NR	10	264		....	....	....	....	59	40⅛	4672	59	52	58½B	5.8	..	...	...	...	...
19•[8]	BRCD	✓Brocade Communic Sys	NNM	NR	123	14078	Storage area network sys	....	....	....	....	177	9½	353669	177	110⅛	177	...	..	...	...	...	...
20	BHP	✓Broken Hill Prop ADR[62]	NY,Ch,Ph,P	NR	62	12449	Steel,petroleum,minerals	31 13/16	1 13/16	21½	12 15/16	26 9/16	14 7/16	9624	26 9/16	21¾	26 9/16	2.4	d	Neg	90.0	1.3	3.3
21•[7]	BGL	✓Brooke Group Ltd	NY,Ch	B−	40	2802	Major cigarette mfr	13 5/16	1 9/16	23 9/16	3⅝	25⅝	13⅛	6073	17¾	14⅜	14 15/16	s6.7	1	NM	29.7	55.9	...
22	BPO	Brookfield Properties[63]	NY,To	NR	53	29100	Real estate development	150	3¼	25⅛	13½	22½	9 7/16	3033	11 1/16	9 7/16	10⅜	3.5	7	...	−43.8	−3.2	14.2
23	BRKL	✓Brookline Bancorp	NNM	NR	66	3072	General banking, MA	....	....	18½	9⅜	15¾	9½	16385	10⅛	9¾	9¾	2.5	..	...	−13.6	...	...
24•[8]	BRKS	✓Brooks Automation	NNM	C	105	8366	Dvp/mfr semiconductor eqp	41⅛	8	19¼	8	34¼	14½	22521	34¼	23⅝	32 9/16	...	d	Neg	123	25.8	...
25•[9]	BRKT	✓Brooktrout Inc	NNM	NR	47	2584	Mfr computer hardwr/softwr prd	42¼	4	22¾	9⅝	20 13/16	9⅞	39807	19⅜	15¼	18 9/16	...	31	−14	8.4	−12.8	29.8
26	BRO	✓Brown & Brown	NY	A−	78	6720	General insurance agency	31 5/16	1¾	42½	28 13/16	40⅝	29 5/16	3394	40⅝	35½	38 5/16	1.4	20	14	11.1	31.6	23.7
¶27	BF.B	✓Brown-Forman Cl'B'[65]	NY,B,Ch,P	A	298	28080	Mkt whisky,wine prd/Lenox china	55⅜	13/16	76⅞	51¾	77¼	54 15/16	13951	64 1/16	54 15/16	57¼	2.2	19	7	−23.0	9.9	16.1
28	BF.A	✓ Class 'A' vtg	NY,B,Ch	A	44	15688	imported wines,Lenox china	52¾	13/16	70¼	49	71	50 15/16	1265	58 15/16	50 15/16	53 15/16	2.3	18	7	−21.2	8.2	14.4
29	BNS	✓Brown & Sharpe Mfg'A'	NY,Ch,P	B−	61	7377	Measuring instr: mach tools	26⅛	2 11/16	16⅛	6⅝	8½	1⅞	12268	2½	2	2⅛	...	d	−6	−73.4	−46.7	−20.3
✚30•[10]	BWS	✓Brown Shoe	NY,Ch,Ph,P	B−	145	12682	Mfr/retailer shoes: fabric	44¼	4 7/16	20	12 7/16	21¾	12 11/16	12033	15⅞	12 11/16	14⅛	2.8	8	−12	−17.7	−4.7	−11.3
31	BRT	✓BRT Realty Trust SBI	NY,Ch	NR	9	182	Real estate investment trust	27⅜	1 5/16	8⅝	5 7/16	9	5⅞	1295	8	6⅝	8	...	5	NM	25.5	6.5	16.4
¶32•[1]	BC	✓Brunswick Corp	NY,B,C,Ch,P,Ph	B	394	67920	Marine, recreation products	37	⅞	35 11/16	12	30	18 1/16	46252	22¾	20	22¼	2.2	10	9	−8.1	−0.4	5.6
✚33•[11]	BW	✓Brush Wellman	NY,B,Ch,Ph	B	114	10521	Beryllium products & eq comp	44½	1 1/16	30	10 15/16	19 1/16	12⅞	6075	16 15/16	15 7/16	16 13/16	2.9	56	Neg	−0.6	3.5	1.7
34	BSQR	✓BSQUARE Corp	NNM	NR	..	...	Provides software solutions	....	....	....	....	56½	15	68727	45¼	30⅛	41 15/16	...	..	...	...	...	...
35	BPL	✓Buckeye Ptnrs L.P.	NY,Ch	NR	81	2680	Refined petrol'm pipeline sys	30	8⅞	31⅛	26	29½	25	5314	28¼	25	26	8.5	10	3	−2.9	15.2	17.3
✚36	BKI	✓Buckeye Technologies	NY,Ph,P	NR	119	15662	Mfr,mkt cellulose pulps	23⅜	9¼	25⅜	11¾	17⅞	12⅛	8609	15 15/16	14 7/16	14⅞	...	11	9	−0.4	4.1	...
37•[12]	BKE	✓Buckle Inc	NY	NR	90	4958	Oper casual apparel str chain	25 3/16	3½	39⅛	12¼	32 9/16	12 9/16	23588	15⅝	12 9/16	14 13/16	...	9	38	−38.3	21.3	32.9
38•[11]	BD	✓Budget Group'A'	NY,Ph	NR	117	22648	Oper Budget RentaCar franch's	37¾	6 3/16	39½	11	17¼	6	47483	9¼	7 5/16	9 1/16	...	d	Neg	−42.9	−17.5	−0.9
39	GBI	✓Bufete Industrial S.A. ADS[66]	NY,Ph,P	NR	3	900	Engineer,constr'n svcs-Mexico	54¾	5	9 15/16	2 15/16	4 9/16	⅜	4293	1 3/16	⅜	⅝	...	d	Neg	−84.6	−69.1	−53.7
#40•[13]	BOCB	✓Buffets Inc	NNM	B+	168	32405	Operates buffet-style rest'ts	27½	1 1/16	17⅛	8⅜	12 1/16	7 13/16	24801	11	9 5/16	10	...	11	32	−16.2	3.1	0.3
✚41•[14]	BMHC	✓Building Materials Hldg	NNM	NR	99	8621	Dstr/retail bldg materials	30½	3 13/16	15	8⅝	13½	7⅛	14771	11⅞	7⅛	10¼	...	6	3	−15.5	−5.8	−6.0
42	BOSS	✓Building One Services	NNM	NR	89	7949	Building maintenance svcs	21½	20	25 15/16	7⅞	21	7⅝	21416	10¾	7⅝	9 7/16	...	6	...	−54.8	...	...
43	BULL	Bull Run	NNM	B−	14	5946	Mfr computer printers	7⅜	3/16	5⅛	2⅞	7⅞	3¼	33772	7⅞	4	5⅞	...	d	−37	74.1	40.4	29.3
44	BNL	Bunzl PLC ADS[69]	NY	NR	1	51	Mfr paper & plastic prod	....	....	23½	19¾	28½	18½	5	27½	26⅜	26⅞B	2.2	17	...	34.6	...	...
45•[3]	BCF	✓Burlington Coat Factory	NY,Ch,Ph,P	B+	126	17378	Off-price apparel stores	23⅝	2 15/16	28 1/16	12¾	20¾	10¾	22230	13⅞	11¾	13⅞	0.1	12	27	−14.8	8.9	7.1
#46•[15]	BUR	✓Burlington Industries	NY,Ch,Ph,P	NR	149	43754	Mfr fabrics/textile prod	17⅛	9¼	18⅞	7½	11	3½	56028	4 3/16	3½	4	...	d	Neg	−64.0	−28.6	−16.5
¶47•[5]	BNI	✓Burlington Northn Santa Fe	NY,B,C,Ch,P,Ph	NR	869	356629	Railroad sys operations U.S.	33⅝	2¼	35 11/16	26⅞	37 15/16	22⅞	386597	29 15/16	22⅞	24¼	2.0	10	21	−28.1	−4.2	10.3
¶48•[16]	BR	✓Burlington Resources	NY,Ch,Ph,P	B	772	146669	Oil & gas,explor,dvlp	54½	23⅜	49⅝	29 7/16	47⅝	29½	323230	34 5/16	29½	33 1/16	1.7	50	NM	−6.4	−12.0	0.2
49	BPP	✓Burnham Pacific Prop	NY,Ch,Ph,P	NR	101	12570	Real estate investment trust	21½	5 11/16	15¾	11⅛	12 15/16	8 11/16	26613	9 13/16	8 11/16	9⅜	11.2	20	86	−14.8	−7.6	2.1
50	BOR	✓Burns Intl Services	NY,Ch,Ph,P	NR	98	11190	Provides protective services	22⅞	5½	24¾	13 1/16	22 1/16	8¼	34164	11⅞	8¼	10 13/16	...	9	66	−42.3	0.2	2.1
✚51•[5]	BBRC	✓Burr-Brown Corp	NNM	B	212	36715	Mfr microelec data devices	17 7/16	13/16	21½	7⅝	36¾	11¾	69309	36¾	29 7/16	36⅛	...	52	28	131	68.4	69.3

Uniform Footnote Explanations-See Page 4. Other: [1]CBOE:Cycle 3. [2]P:Cycle 1. [3]Ph:Cycle 1. [4]ASE,Ph:Cycle 1. [5]CBOE:Cycle 1. [6]ASE,CBOE:Cycle 1. [7]CBOE,Ph:Cycle 2. [8]ASE,CBOE,Ph:Cycle 1. [9]ASE,P:Cycle 1. [10]ASE:Cycle 3. [11]Ph:Cycle 2. [12]P,Ph:Cycle 2. [13]CBOE:Cycle 2. [14]P:Cycle 2. [15]ASE:Cycle 1. [16]CBOE,P,Ph:Cycle 2. [51]6 Mo Dec,'96:Fiscal Jun'96 earned d$0.11. [52]9 Mo Dec,'98. [53]Full paym't ADR's equal 10 Ord par 25p. [54]Approx. [55]Each Sponsored ADR rep 2 ord, 25p. [56]Ea ADS rep 4 ord,par 44.651 pence. [57]To be determined. [58]Full pay't ADR's equal 10 Ord par 25p. [59]Stk dstr of Convergys Corp. [60]Dep for 0.05 shr cm Cv Pfd. [61]Fr 4-5-2000,red restrn to 4-1-2002 re-spec cond. [62]ADR's represent'g 2 com par A$1. [63]May'99 & prior pricing in $Cdn. [64]9 Mo Dec'98. [65]Non-vtg. [66]Ea ADS rep 3 Ord Ptc Ctf(3'L'shrs&1'B'shr). [67]Fiscal Dec'98 & prior. [68]12 Mo Jun'99. [69]Ea ADS rep 5 ord shrs,25p. [70]Fiscal Jun'97 & prior. [71]11 Mo May'98.

Index	Cash Divs. Ea. Yr. Since	Dividends: Latest Payment Period $	Date	Ex. Div.	Total $ So Far 1999	Ind. Rate	Paid 1998	Financial Position Mil-$: Cash& Equiv.	Curr. Assets	Curr. Liab.	Balance Sheet Date	Capitalization: Lg Trm Debt Mil-$	Shs. 000 Pfd.	Com.	Earnings $ Per Shr. Years End	1995	1996	1997	1998	1999	Last 12 Mos.	Interim Earnings Period	$ per Shr. 1998	1999	Index
1◆	....	None Since Public			...	Nil	....	47.3	450	196	9-30-99	226	...	53381	Dc	pv0.21	vp0.30	v0.53	v0.38	....	d1.80	9 Mo Sep	v0.51	v□d1.67	1
2◆	1993	S0.005	11-3-99	10-13	0.011	0.01	0.011	823	2165	1435	j12-31-98	....	...	±130435	Dc	0.03	v0.05	v0.16	v0.29	....	0.29				2
3	....	None Since Public			...	Nil	....	1.94	4.80	2.75	9-30-99	0.33	...	12451	Dc	...	†v[51]d0.78	vd0.31	vd1.00	....	d0.97	9 Mo Sep	vd0.67	vd0.64	3
4◆	....	None Since Public			...	Nil	....	17.7	103	194	9-29-99	192	...	65420	Je	0.98	v0.44	v0.81	v1.02	□v1.25	1.35	3 Mo Sep	v□0.30	v0.40	4
5	....	Plan qtly div			...	....	....	15.9	107	66.1	9-30-99	....	...	17809	Dc	...	...	pv0.27	v†[52]0.15	....	....	9 Mo Sep	n/a	v0.42	5
6◆	1900	Q0.24½	2-1-00	1-5	0.86	0.98	0.78	2690	8957	5401	9-30-99	1331	11	1983692	Dc	v0.89	v1.40	v1.57	v1.55	E2.05	1.75	9 Mo Sep	v1.34	v1.54	6
7	1968	Q0.50	3-1-00	2-2	2.00	2.00	2.00	Cv into 16.96 common				....	12	...	Dc	...	...	...	....	....	....				7
8	....	None Paid			...	Nil	....	9.06	9.95	5.00	9-30-99	....	...	18825	Mr	0.01	vd0.15	vd1.62	vd1.13	....	d0.95	6 Mo Sep	vd0.76	vd0.58	8
9	1987	[54]0.821	2-7-00	11-17	3.687	2.89	2.883	1163	2583	3081	j3-31-99	6182	...	1073000	Mr	7.54	8.33	v7.01	v3.09	....	3.72	3 Mo Jun	v1.99	v2.62	9
10◆	1928	[54]0.128	10-8-99	8-11	[54]1.002	1.00	0.856	Equity per shr $0.27			12-31-98	3094	...	1571000	Dc	1.48	1.61	v1.06	v0.90	....	0.81	6 Mo Jun	v0.65	v0.56	10
11	....	Plan annual div			...	[57]....	....	271	1424	653	j9-30-99	2442	...	720339	Mr	...	...	v1.74	v1.70	....	1.51	6 Mo Sep	v0.62	v0.43	11
12	1995	0.264	4-13-99	2-24	0.264	0.61	0.633	64.7	628	520	j6-30-99	583	...	1723341	Je	0.83	1.30	1.66	v1.44	v1.51	1.20	3 Mo Sep	0.21	d0.10	12
13	1985	[54]1.401	2-22-99	1-4	3.38	2.78	3.35	3380	7534	8029	j3-31-99	3386	...	6469000	Mr	4.84	v5.38	v4.37	v7.25	E6.15	5.43	6 Mo Sep	v4.71	v2.89	13
14	....	None Since Public			...	Nil	....	28.0	30.7	9.30	6-30-99	0.78	p...	★17204	Dc	...	...	...	vpd1.51	....	....	9 Mo Sep	n/a	vd6.80	14
15◆	....	None Since Public			...	Nil	....	226	323	90.3	9-30-99	0.87	...	±104141	Dc	vNil	v0.05	vd0.02	v0.39	....	0.62	9 Mo Sep	v0.17	v0.40	15
16◆	....	None Since Public			...	Nil	....	79.5	106	29.4	9-30-99	5.03	...	★80684	Dc	pvd0.12	vd0.18	vd0.12	v0.05	....	0.15	9 Mo Sep	v0.03	v0.13	16
17◆	1879	Div Discontinued 7-21-99			0.30	Nil	h[59]0.40	3.40	212	437	9-30-99	766	p1446	p216251	Dc	v□d0.19	v1.35	v□1.41	v□1.09	E0.80	0.86	9 Mo Sep	v0.82	v0.59	17
18	2000	0.84⅜	1-1-00	12-13	...	3.37	....	Cv into 0.6874 com				....	2700	...	Dc	...	...	...	....	....	....				18
19◆	....	None Since Public			...	Nil	....	8.67	21.9	16.8	4-30-99	p0.23	p...	★51370	Oc	...	...	...	vpd0.42	Pv0.05	0.05				19
20◆	1959	0.306	12-2-99	11-2	0.634	0.63	0.635	1152	7218	6175	j5-31-98	12801	...	2055940	My	1.14	1.04	v0.38	vd1.10	....	d1.10				20
21◆	1995	sQ0.25	12-28-99	12-17	s0.631	1.00	0.286	57.4	233	198	9-30-99	157	...	21990	Dc	□d0.38	vd3.12	vd2.61	v1.06	....	10.73	9 Mo Sep	vd1.95	v□7.72	21
22	1996	S0.18	12-31-99	12-8	0.32	0.36	0.14	Total Assets $7.89M			6-30-99	4616	20312	133072	Dc	vd1.30	vd0.43	v0.67	v1.04	....	j1.08	6 Mo Jun	v0.54	v0.58	22
23	1998	0.06	11-12-99	10-27	0.27	0.24	0.10	Total Deposits $505M			9-30-99	111	...	28430	Dc	...	...	n/a	v[64]0.54	....	....	9 Mo Sep	n/a	v0.55	23
24	....	None Since Public			...	Nil	....	68.1	123	24.9	6-30-99	....	...	11108	Sp	0.72	1.04	vd0.27	vd1.84	vPd0.76	d0.76				24
25◆	....	None Since Public			...	Nil	....	55.5	89.8	29.1	9-30-99	....	...	10823	Dc	v0.52	v0.63	v0.23	v0.03	....	0.60	9 Mo Sep	v0.48	v1.05	25
26◆	1986	Q0.13	11-18-99	11-2	0.46	0.52	0.41	45.5	104	112	9-30-99	3.28	...	13601	Dc	v1.13	v1.27	v1.48	v1.72	....	1.94	9 Mo Sep	v1.25	v1.47	26
27◆	1960	Q0.31	1-1-00	12-1	1.18	1.24	1.12	187	1175	668	10-31-99	46.6	...	±68510	Ap	±2.15	v±2.31	v±2.45	v2.67	v±2.93	3.04	6 Mo Oct	v±1.51	v±1.62	27
28◆	1945	Q0.31	1-1-00	12-1	1.18	1.24	1.12	....	...	...		....	...	28988	Ap	±2.15	v±2.31	P±v2.45	v±2.67	v±2.93	3.04	6 Mo Oct	v±1.51	v±1.62	28
29◆	....	0.08	12-31-90	12-6	...	Nil	....	19.4	202	181	9-30-99	12.6	...	±13473	Dc	v±0.22	v±0.79	v±d0.79	±v0.88	....	d1.45	9 Mo Sep	v±0.39	v±d1.94	29
30	1923	Q0.10	1-3-00	12-9	0.40	0.40	0.40	47.7	522	255	10-30-99	162	...	18258	Ja	0.19	v1.15	vd1.19	v1.32	....	1.88	9 Mo Oct	v1.18	v1.74	30
31	....	0.16	10-2-90	9-10	...	Nil	....	Total Assets $88.16M			6-30-99	10.2	...	7165	Sp	0.37	v0.26	v0.86	v1.71	Pv1.61	1.61				31
32	1969	Q0.12½	12-15-99	11-22	0.50	0.50	0.50	122	1586	1048	9-30-99	627	...	91827	Dc	v1.32	v1.88	v□1.51	v1.88	E2.35	2.12	9 Mo Sep	v1.46	v1.70	32
33	1972	Q0.12	1-4-00	12-16	0.48	0.48	0.48	5.06	225	102	10-01-99	42.3	...	16328	Dc	v1.27	v1.53	v1.56	vd0.44	....	0.30	9 Mo Sep	vd0.42	v0.32	33
34	....	None Since Public			...	Nil	....	9.28	14.9	4.21	6-30-99	0.21	p...	★32197	Dc	...	...	...	pv0.09	....	....	6 Mo Jun	n/a	v0.03	34
35◆	1987	Q0.55	11-30-99	11-1	2.175	2.20	1.83¾	14.1	49.0	32.1	9-30-99	266	...	26791	Dc	v2.05	v2.02	v□1.91	v1.92	....	2.57	9 Mo Sep	v1.44	v2.09	35
36◆	....	None Since Public			...	Nil	....	6.08	205	64.7	9-30-99	433	...	35178	Je	p0.84	□1.12	v1.38	v1.45	v1.32	1.33	3 Mo Sep	v0.36	v0.37	36
37◆	....	None Since Public			...	Nil	....	72.3	146	40.5	10-30-99	....	...	21216	Ja	v0.47	v0.63	v1.05	v1.47	E1.65	1.59	9 Mo Oct	v0.94	v1.06	37
38	....	None Since Public			...	Nil	....	Total Assets $5681M			6-30-99	4471	...	±36911	Dc	±0.05	v±0.47	±v1.60	v□d0.12	....	d1.06	9 Mo Sep	v□1.78	v0.84	38
39	....	0.088	7-25-94	7-12	...	Nil	....	42.4	400	327	12-31-97	106	...	262596	Dc	d2.74	Δd0.07	vΔd0.16	....	....	d0.16				39
40	....	None Since Public			...	Nil	....	92.3	120	102	10-06-99	41.5	...	42059	Dc	v0.73	vd0.16	v0.62	v0.83	....	0.91	9 Mo Sep	v0.67	v0.75	40
41◆	....	None Since Public			...	Nil	....	7.27	225	78.1	9-30-99	167	...	12675	Dc	v0.79	v□0.97	v0.78	v1.20	....	1.67	9 Mo Sep	v0.98	v1.45	41
42	....	None Since Public			...	Nil	....	14.5	454	269	9-30-99	541	...	26099	Dc	...	...	n/a	v1.16	....	1.47	9 Mo Sep	v0.77	v1.08	42
43	....	None Since Public			...	Nil	....	0.16	11.6	72.7	9-30-99	66.8	...	22516	Je	v0.03	□v0.25	vd0.08	v[67]0.10	v[68]0.06	d0.09	3 Mo Sep	v0.17	v0.02	43
44	1999	[54]0.221	1-21-00	12-1	0.583	0.60	....	35.9	521	307	j12-31-98	120	...	453778	Dc	...	v1.40	v1.47	v1.56	....	1.56				44
45◆	1997	A0.02	11-2-99	10-5	0.02	0.02	0.02	5.75	8.81	2.56	8-28-99	8.54	...	46406	My	0.31	0.59	[70]1.17	v[71]1.34	v1.02	1.13	6 Mo Nov	v0.40	v0.51	45
46	....	None Since Public			...	Nil	....	35.7	634	202	10-02-99	881	...	±52066	Sp	±1.05	□±0.66	v±0.95	v±1.32	v±d0.57	d0.57				46
47◆	1940	Q0.12	1-3-00	12-9	0.48	0.48	0.42	24.0	1115	2070	9-30-99	5619	...	456949	Dc	v□0.56	v1.91	v1.88	v2.43	E2.40	2.38	9 Mo Sep	v1.80	v1.75	47
48	1988	Q0.138	1-3-00	12-8	0.55	0.55	0.55	....	467	448	9-30-99	1979	...	p217493	Dc	vd1.47	v1.88	v1.79	v0.48	E0.66	0.26	9 Mo Sep	v0.48	v0.26	48
49	1966	Q0.26¼	12-31-99	12-20	1.05	1.05	1.05	Total Assets $1086.1M			9-30-99	406	2800	32268	Dc	vd0.75	v□0.71	v0.87	v0.44	....	0.48	9 Mo Sep	v0.39	v□0.43	49
50	....	None Since Public			...	Nil	....	11.0	122	118	9-30-99	114	...	p19669	Dc	v□0.25	vd0.62	v0.79	v□1.47	....	1.23	9 Mo Sep	v□1.12	v□0.88	50
51◆	....	None Since Public			...	Nil	....	143	273	62.1	10-02-99	2.18	...	55476	Dc	v0.55	v0.53	v0.57	v0.63	....	0.69	9 Mo Sep	v0.47	v0.53	51

◆**Stock Splits & Divs By Line Reference Index** [1]5-for-4,'97:2-for-1,'97. [2]3-for-2,'99:5-for-1,'99. [4]3-for-2,'94. [6]2-for-1,'97,'99. [10]No adj for stk dstr,'98:ADR rep 1 ord prior to 3-15-94. [15]2-for-1,'99. [16]3-for-1,'99. [17]2-for-1,'97:No adj for stk dstr,'99. [19]2-for-1,'99. [20]10%,'95:2-for-1,'96. [21]Adj for 5%,'99. [25]3-for-2(twice),'96. [26]3-for-2,'98. [27]3-for-1,'94. [28]3-for-1,'94. [29]4-for-3 in new Cl'B','88. [35]2-for-1,'98. [36]2-for-1,'98. [37]2-for-1,'97:3-for-2,'98. [41]3-for-2,'94. [45]6-for-5,'97. [47]3-for-1,'98. [51]3-for-2,'95,'97,'98,'99.

¶ S&P 500
# MidCap 400
✣ SmallCap 600
• Options

Index	Ticker	Name of Issue (Call Price of Pfd. Stocks)	Market	Com. Rank. & Pfd. Rating	Inst. Hold Cos	Inst. Hold Shs. (000)	Principal Business	Price Range 1971-97 High	1971-97 Low	1998 High	1998 Low	1999 High	1999 Low	Dec. Sales in 100s	December, 1999 Last Sale Or Bid High	Low	Last	%Div Yield	P-E Ratio	EPS 5 Yr Growth	% Annualized Total Return 12 Mo	36 Mo	60 Mo
1	BOA	✓Bush Boake Allen	NY,Ch	NR	82	5972	Produce flavors & fragrances	35 11/16	15¼	35½	25	35⅛	22⅛	2094	25 3/16	24	24 9/16	...	18	1	–30.3	–2.7	–1.9
2	BSH	✓Bush Indus Cl'A'	NY,Ch	B+	61	6547	Ready-to-assemble furniture	28⅜	1	30⅝	12	18 3/16	10	2518	18 3/16	14¾	17 3/16	1.2	..	–30	40.3	–2.7	11.0
3•[1]	BOBJ	✓Business Objects ADS[51]	NNM	NR	114	13065	Dvp decision support software	55½	6⅝	33	6⅛	153½	16⅜	54169	153½	86	133⅝	...	..	5	311	115	48.7
✣4	BBR	✓Butler Mfg	NY	B	105	3456	Pre-engrd bldgs: agric eq	41⅞	4⅜	37 11/16	20	29 15/16	21	2298	22½	21 5/16	22 5/16	2.9	10	–9	2.3	–16.4	1.9
5	BY	✓BWAY Corp	NY,Ch	NR	48	4976	Mfr steel containers	25⅝	7 11/16	26 15/16	11½	16	5½	6586	7¼	5½	6⅛	...	10	–10	–59.3	–21.5	...
6	CBIS	C-bridge Internet Solutions	NNM	NR	..	...	eBusiness solution svcs	....	....	....	....	65	38¼	122208	65	38¼	48⅝	...	d	...	...	...	...
✣7•[2]	CCBL	✓C-COR.net Corp	NNM	B	106	5689	CATV equip-amplifiers	36½	15/16	20	8⅞	90⅞	13¾	56279	90⅞	50¼	76⅝	...	72	40	457	79.5	19.8
✣8•[3]	CUBE	✓C-Cube Microsystems	NNM,Ch	NR	239	23715	Video compression solutions	73½	7 7/16	30⅞	13¼	65⅜	17¼	152408	65⅜	44 1/16	62¼	...	51	85	130	19.0	45.7
✣9	CHP	✓C&D Technologies	NY,Ph	B+	158	12108	Mfrs battery power systems	24 9/16	1⅝	32⅜	19⅞	42½	20 3/16	8093	42½	33⅜	42½	0.3	21	22	55.5	41.1	36.6
10	CFON	C-Phone Corp	NNM	NR	9	236	Desktop video conferencing sys	19⅜	2¼	15½	2	4½	¾	33414	1¾	1	1⅛	...	d	11	–58.3	–34.4	–32.0
11	BFH	CABCO Tr BellSouth 6.75% Debs	NY	....[52]	..	...	Corporate Asset Backed Corp	....	....	....	....	24 11/16	19½	1506	21½	19½	20	8.5	..	...	...	...	...
12	PFH	CABCO Tr J.C.Penney 7.625% Debs	NY	....[53]	5	216	Corporate Asset Backed Corp	....	....	....	....	25⅝	16¾	3095	21⅛	16¾	18⅛	10.5	..	...	...	...	...
✣13•[4]	CDT	✓Cable Design Technologies	NY,Ch,Ph	NR	173	19372	Mfr elec data transmisn cables	34	4 5/16	32¼	9⅝	24 15/16	10⅞	32907	24¼	20 7/16	23	...	16	23	24.3	3.7	26.0
14•[5]	CWP	✓Cable & Wireless ADS[55]	NY,Ch,Ph,P	NR	124	15523	Intl telecommunications svcs	31¼	10 13/16	42 15/16	23¼	53¾	32	61233	53¾	39¼	52 15/16	1.2	33	25	46.8	31.9	27.6
15•[6]	CWZ	✓Cable&Wireless Communic ADS[56]	NY	NR	38	1166	Telecommunication Svcs	28	17¾	59⅛	21⅛	70½	44½	5362	70½	56 11/16	70	...	d	...	54.3	...	...
16•[7]	HKT	✓Cable & Wireless HKT ADR[57]	NY,Ch,P	NR	86	5876	Telecommun svcs,Hong Kong	26½	5 9/16	22 11/16	16 1/16	31⅛	15⅞	29277	31⅛	27 1/16	29⅛	3.8	18	11	75.0	28.2	14.4
17	TTV	✓Cabletel Communications	AS,Ph,P	C	2	108	Dstr communications equip	9⅝	2½	4⅛	½	5 13/16	1⅛	6088	4⅝	2⅝	4⅝	...	d	Neg	270	–5.6	–9.2
¶18•[8]	CS	✓Cabletron Systems	NY,Ch,Ph,P	B	324	81856	Mfr computer interconnectn eq	46½	1⅜	17⅛	6⅝	29 5/16	7 3/16	572549	29 5/16	21 5/16	26	...	74	Neg	210	–7.9	2.5
19•[9]	CVC	✓Cablevision Sys'A'	NY,Ch,P	C	323	57821	Operates CATV Systems	24 9/16	2½	50¼	21 13/16	91⅞	49⅞	100014	80⅛	68⅞	75½	...	d	6	50.6	115	43.0
#20•[1]	CBT	✓Cabot Corp	NY,B,Ch,P	↓B	197	45130	Carbon black: oil & gas	31⅝	9/16	39 15/16	21¾	29 13/16	17 15/16	21160	20¾	17 15/16	20⅜	2.2	16	–1	–25.6	–5.2	9.4
21	CTR	✓Cabot Industrial Tr	NY,Ph	NR	96	20457	Real estate investment trust	....	....	25⅛	16⅞	23	17⅜	11232	19⅝	17⅜	18⅜	7.4	..	...	–3.9	...	...
✣22•[10]	COG	✓Cabot Oil & Gas 'A'	NY,Ch,Ph,P	B–	199	22783	Oil & gas explor,dev,prod'n	27	10¼	24	12⅝	20	10¾	17709	16 7/16	13 3/16	16 1/16	1.0	d	NM	8.2	–1.2	3.1
23	CFLO	✓CacheFlow Inc	NNM	NR	..	...	Internet info flow appliances	....	....	....	....	182 3/16	24	66867	182 3/16	121	130 11/16	...	..	...	...	...	...
24	CACI	✓CACI Int'l	NNM	B+	76	6614	Prof svs,analysis/computer	23⅝	1/16	22¼	14⅝	24	16	10220	22⅞	19⅞	22⅝	...	17	11	34.1	2.5	17.4
25•[11]	CSG	✓Cadbury Schweppes ADS[61]	NY,Ch	NR	81	16766	Soft drinks,candy,food prod	21 15/16	3⅜	35 1/16	20⅛	34⅝	22¼	10916	25¼	22¼	24 3/16	2.6	21	11	–27.9	15.6	16.7
26	CADE	✓Cade Industries[62]	NNM	B–	13	540	Aircraft engineer'g,mfg svcs	3⅞	½	4⅜	1 15/16	5	2	3368	5	4 15/16	5	...	21	NM	124	55.9	49.9
#27•[3]	CDN	✓Cadence Design Sys	NY,Ch,Ph,P	B–	397	158084	Softwr for computer-aid-eng'g	29⅛	13/16	39	19⅛	34⅛	9 9/16	363732	24 1/16	17⅜	24	...	89	–1	–19.3	6.7	40.0
28	CDF	✓Cadillac Fairview	NY,To	NR	43	32033	Real estate development	25⅛	22¼	23½	15 15/16	23	16 7/16	2482	23	22 5/16	23	...	14	...	23.1	...	...
29	CDMS	✓Cadmus Communication	NNM	B+	42	3187	Print'g & graphic arts svcs	29⅞	4 3/16	28	15⅝	19¼	6⅛	14193	8⅝	6⅛	8½	2.4	..	–13	–54.1	–17.1	–10.5
30	CAE	✓CAE Inc	To	NR	13	6195	Mfr flight/visual simulat'n sy	15½	1⅝	13⅝	7 15/16	10⅝	7 5/16	74626	10⅝	9 3/16	9⅞	2.0	13	31	24.0	0.1	7.4
31•[12]	CAER	✓Caere Corp	NNM	B–	47	5795	Mfr info recognit'n softwr	24½	5½	15⅜	7½	18¾	5⅛	35890	8¼	6 7/16	7 5/16	...	10	47	–47.8	–14.0	–16.6
32	CGL.A	✓Cagle's Inc 'A'	AS,Ch	B	18	726	Poultry producer: food dstr	24⅝	5/16	20 15/16	10¼	21⅜	10⅞	1055	14	10⅞	11⅜	1.1	3	14	–41.2	–6.7	–8.0
33	CAIS	✓CAIS Internet	NNM	NR	52	2357	Internet access service	....	....	....	....	41½	9⅞	150550	41½	13¼	35½	...	d	...	...	...	...
34•[10]	CCC	✓Calgon Carbon	NY,Ph,P	B–	98	16811	Mkts activated carbons/svcs	30¾	5½	13⅞	5 13/16	7¾	5 1/16	23637	7 1/16	5 7/16	5⅞	3.4	25	NM	–17.6	–18.8	–6.3
35	CLIC	✓Calico Commerce	NNM	NR	..	...	e-commerce software/svcs	....	....	....	....	75¾	14	96184	67⅜	42 5/16	53	...	d	...	...	...	...
36	COOK	✓Calif Culinary Academy	NNM	NR	8	127	Oper chef training school	8⅞	4⅜	10	6¾	8½	3⅜	13850	4 15/16	3⅜	4 9/16	...	d	Neg	–46.3	–18.7	–9.8
37	CIBN	✓Calif Indep Bancorp	NNM	NR	12	48	General banking,Yuba City,CA	24 11/16	16⅞	26¾	17⅛	22⅜	16	293	18¼	16	17⅛	s2.6	17	–23	–3.5	0.0	...
38	CWT	✓Calif Water Svc Grp	NY	A–	72	2199	Water service in California	29 9/16	2 11/16	33¾	20¾	32	22 9/16	2329	32	29 9/16	30 5/16	3.6	19	6	0.8	18.1	19.5
39	CALP	Caliper Technologies	NNM	NR	..	...	Lab-on-chip technologies	....	....	....	....	73	16	114819	73	16	66¾	...	..	...	...	...	...
40	CNEBF	Call-Net Enterprises'B'[63]	NNM	NR	31	22300	Long-dist telecomn,Canada	21½	3⅜	20	5¾	9⅞	2⅞	12343	4 3/16	2⅞	3⅜	...	d	–3	–60.9	–35.6	–3.5
#41•[3]	ELY	✓Callaway Golf	NY,Ph,P	B	207	30074	Develop,mfr golf clubs	38½	2¼	33 15/16	9⅜	18 3/16	9 5/16	139261	18 3/16	13 11/16	17 11/16	1.6	22	Neg	76.2	–13.6	2.8
42	CPE	✓Callon Petroleum	NY	NR	49	3738	Oil&gas explor,dev.prod'n	22	9	18⅜	7⅞	15⅜	8⅞	12391	14 13/16	11 15/16	14 13/16	...	d	Neg	27.4	–8.0	6.4
43	Pr A	$2.125 cm CvEx[64]'A'Pfd([65]26.488)	NY	NR	9	314		49¼	24½	42½	23½	35	24	2240	34	28¾	34	6.3	..	...	...	...	...
#44	CPN	✓Calpine Corp	NY,Ch,Ph	NR	311	53543	Dvlp pwr generat'n facilities	11 7/16	6 3/16	13 13/16	6⅜	65½	12⅝	92909	64¾	54⅜	64	...	41	43	407	85.7	...
45	CN	✓Calton,Inc	AS,Ch,P,Ph	NR	11	1358	Homebldg ind services	153¾	¼	1¼	7/16	1⅞	1	14080	1¾	1½	1⅝	...	5	71	44.4	63.0	10.2
46	CADA	✓CAM Data Systems	NSC	↑B	3	61	Cash register/inventory ctr sy	6	½	3¾	2 3/16	27½	3⅛	24417	27½	14¾	17⅞	...	30	8	420	64.7	45.4
47	CBJ	✓Cambior Inc[68]	AS,Ch,To,Mo	B–	62	29833	Gold exploration/mining	16⅜	4⅝	8¼	4⅛	5 13/16	⅞	19437	1½	1	1 7/16	...	d	Neg	–70.7	–53.4	–33.2
✣48•[13]	CBM	✓Cambrex Corp	NY	B+	213	19145	Producer of specialty chems	26 3/16	1 5/16	29¾	19 5/16	35⅞	20½	9364	34½	30⅛	34 7/16	0.3	21	17	44.1	29.1	32.7
#49•[14]	CATP	✓Cambridge Technology Ptnrs	NNM	NR	183	22462	Info tech/software dvlp	43⅝	2 5/16	58⅜	13⅜	32¼	10⅝	438695	27	13 15/16	26¼	...	..	34	18.6	–7.9	28.8
50	CAC	✓Camden National	AS	NR	8	154	General banking, Maine	20¼	14	29	16 5/16	24	16¼	378	18½	16¼	16¾	3.6	11	7	–15.7	...	...
51	CPT	✓Camden Property Trust	NY	NR	201	28706	Real estate investment trust	33 3/16	20⅛	31 1/16	24½	28¼	23⅞	35788	27¾	25 3/16	27¾	7.5	22	13	15.2	6.2	10.1

Uniform Footnote Explanations-See Page 4. Other: [1]CBOE:Cycle 1. [2]ASE,CBOE:Cycle 3. [3]ASE,CBOE:Cycle 2. [4]Ph:Cycle 1. [5]CBOE:Cycle 2. [6]CBOE,Ph:Cycle 2. [7]ASE,CBOE:Cycle 1. [8]ASE,P:Cycle 1. [9]CBOE,P,Ph:Cycle 3. [10]Ph:Cycle 2. [11]ASE,Ph:Cycle 3. [12]ASE:Cycle 2. [13]P:Cycle 1. [14]Ph:Cycle 3. [51]Ea ADS rep 1 com,FF/1.00 par. [52]Rated'AAA'by S&P. [53]Rated 'A' by S&P. [54]Plus'Redm'Premium,re-spec cond. [55]Each ADS rep 3 ord shrs,50p. [56]Ea ADS rep 5 ord shrs,50p. [57]Each ADR represent 10 ord, HK$0.50. [58]Incl current amts. [59]Subsid pfd in $M. [60]®$1.19,'97. [61]Each ADS rep 4 Ord par 25p. [62]United Technologies(87%)plan mgr,$5.05. [63]Non-vtg. [64]Exch for $25 8.5% Cv Debs. [65]To 12-31-99. [66]Cvn subj to adj/spl cvn priv re spec cond. [67]Dstr of 0.1 Cl B ptnrshp. [68]Results prior to'96 in Cdn funds.

Splits ◆ Index	Cash Divs. Ea. Yr. Since	Dividends: Latest Payment Period $	Date	Ex. Div.	Total $ So Far 1999	Ind. Rate	Paid 1998	Financial Position Mil-$ Cash& Equiv.	Curr. Assets	Curr. Liab.	Balance Sheet Date	Capitalization Lg Trm Debt Mil-$	Shs. 000 Pfd.	Com.	Earnings $ Per Shr. Years End	1995	1996	1997	1998	1999	Last 12 Mos.	Interim Earnings Period	$ per Shr. 1998	1999	Index
1	....	None Since Public			...	Nil	....	3.64	209	87.0	9-25-99	8.61	...	19300	Dc	v1.57	v1.63	v1.60	v1.74	....	1.36	9 Mo Sep	v1.26	v0.88	1
2◆	1992	Q0.05	11-19-99	11-3	0.20	0.20	0.18½	2.33	99.4	60.3	10-02-99	129	...	±13880	Dc	v±0.95	v±1.31	±v1.52	v±0.78	....	0.08	9 Mo Sep	v±0.70	v±Nil	2
3◆	....	None Since Public			...	Nil	....	63.9	103	57.5	9-30-98	....	...	★18929	Dc	v0.49	v0.30	v0.17	Pv0.58	....	1.00	9 Mo Sep	v0.32	v0.74	3
4◆	1994	Q0.16	1-11-00	12-22	0.61	0.64	0.57	42.0	298	194	9-30-99	62.1	...	7036	Dc	v3.07	v3.35	v4.43	v0.92	....	2.17	9 Mo Sep	v1.67	v2.92	4
5◆	....	None Since Public			...	Nil	....	0.70	18.0	104	9-30-99	147	...	9309	Sp	1.23	v□0.40	v1.31	□v0.27	v0.60	0.60				5
6	....	None Since Public			...	Nil	....	....	4.59	6.40	9-30-99	0.32	...	★17303	Dc	...	...	...	vd0.39	....	d0.31	9 Mo Sep	vd0.35	vd0.27	6
7◆	....	None Since Public			...	Nil	....	0.94	76.3	41.8	9-24-99	3.82	...	★15176	Je	0.84	v0.60	vd0.64	v0.88	Pv1.14	1.07	3 Mo Sep	v0.07	vNil	7
8◆	....	None Since Public			...	Nil	....	277	377	73.6	9-30-99	20.2	...	40584	Dc	v0.74	vd2.15	v1.15	v△1.11	....	1.23	9 Mo Sep	v△0.79	v0.91	8
9◆	1987	Q0.02¾	2-25-00	2-9	0.11	0.11	0.069	6.39	160	90.5	10-31-99	93.8	...	12982	Ja	v1.09	v1.16	v1.56	v1.88	....	2.02	9 Mo Oct	v1.45	v1.59	9
10	....	None Since Public			...	Nil	....	3.20	4.66	0.79	8-31-99	....	...	8374	Fb	vd0.96	vd0.69	vd1.49	vd0.63	....	d0.56	6 Mo Aug	vd0.31	vd0.24	10
11	1999	0.717	10-15-99	9-29	0.717	1.69	....	Co opt to redm at $25 plus'Redm'Premium,re-spec				★45.0	...	...	Dc	...	...	...	...	....	....	Due 10-15-2033			11
12	1999	0.826	9-1-99	8-11	0.826	1.91	....	Co opt to redm at $25[54]				....	...	★2106	Ja	...	...	...	....	....	....	Due 3-1-2097			12
13◆	....	None Since Public			...	Nil	....	13.5	317	144	10-31-99	166	...	28249	Jl	0.57	□0.57	v1.17	v1.29	v1.36	1.40	3 Mo Oct	v0.41	v0.45	13
14	1990	0.452	9-9-99	7-21	0.648	0.65	0.611	1979	4324	4114	j3-31-99	4876	...	2410726	Mr	1.29	1.46	v2.86	v1.81	E1.60	1.81				14
15	....	None Since Public			...	Nil	....	270	957	1486	3-31-98	4326	...	1490000	Mr	p0.05	1.49	vd0.19	....	....	d0.19				15
16	1989	0.496	1-5-00	11-23	1.097	1.10	1.098	17240	22274	14973	j3-31-99	....	...	11959000	Mr	1.15	1.25	v1.86	v1.24	E1.65	1.24				16
17	....	None Since Public			...	Nil	....	0.01	19.7	14.8	j6-30-99	....	...	6545	Dc	v0.14	v0.18	vd0.09	vd1.19	....	jd1.02	9 Mo Sep	vd0.12	v0.05	17
18◆	....	None Since Public			...	Nil	....	196	772	365	8-31-99	....	...	180557	Fb	v0.93	v1.40	vd0.81	vd1.47	E0.35	d0.62	6 Mo Aug	vd0.90	vd0.05	18
19◆	....	None Since Public			...	Nil	....	Total Assets $7083.30M			9-30-99	[58]5881	[59]1685	±172935	Dc	v±d3.55	v±d4.63	±vd0.12	v±d3.16	Ed4.89	d5.10	6 Mo Jun	vd1.90	vd3.84	19
20◆	1931	Q0.11	12-10-99	11-23	0.44	0.44	0.43	19.2	655	475	6-30-99	422	75	66112	Sp	2.18	2.60	v[60]1.19	v1.61	vP1.31	1.31				20
21	1998	Q0.34	1-19-00	12-29	1.34½	1.36	0.852	Total Assets $1463M			9-30-99	360	...	40619	Dc	...	p1.07	n/a	v1.17	....	....	9 Mo Sep	n/a	v0.99	21
22	1990	Q0.04	11-26-99	11-9	0.16	0.16	0.16	1.47	104	90.5	9-30-99	319	1134	25073	Dc	vd4.05	v0.66	v0.97	v0.08	....	d0.01	9 Mo Sep	v0.11	v0.02	22
23	....	None Since Public			...	Nil	....	17.8	21.7	5.18	7-31-99	2.81	p...	★32671	Ap	...	...	...	vpd0.79	....	....	3 Mo Jul	n/a	vpd0.30	23
24	....	None Since Public			...	Nil	....	0.05	119	48.3	9-30-99	62.1	...	11001	Je	0.77	0.92	v0.92	v1.05	v1.26	1.32	3 Mo Sep	v0.28	v0.34	24
25◆	1985	1.966	11-29-99	8-11	0.617	0.62	0.597	520	1689	1689	j1-02-99	551	...	2036000	Dc	1.02	1.17	v2.28	v1.14	....	1.14				25
26	....	None Paid			...	Nil	....	0.98	40.3	26.1	9-30-99	8.72	...	21606	Dc	vd0.02	v0.05	v0.11	v0.19	....	0.24	9 Mo Sep	v0.14	v0.19	26
27◆	....	8.6%Stk	6-7-88	5-26	...	Nil	....	120	514	374	10-02-99	38.8	...	p243507	Dc	v0.51	v0.16	v□0.83	v0.14	....	0.27	9 Mo Sep	vd0.10	v0.03	27
28	....	None Since Public			...	Nil	....	Total Assets $4782M			j4-30-99	[58]2931	...	75779	Oc	...	v0.53	v0.53	v0.75	....	j1.13	9 Mo Jul	v0.50	v0.88	28
29	1941	Q0.05	12-17-99	12-2	0.20	0.20	0.20	7.07	135	81.6	9-30-99	65.2	...	9014	Je	1.21	□0.87	vd0.65	v1.11	v□1.76	0.05	3 Mo Sep	v0.31	vd1.40	29
30	1972	gQ0.05	12-31-99	12-14	g0.18	0.20	g0.16	38.4	595	437	j9-30-99	296	...	111034	Mr	0.54	v0.55	v0.64	v0.70	....	j0.76	6 Mo Sep	v0.28	v0.34	30
31	....	None Since Public			...	Nil	....	49.6	60.4	6.48	9-30-99	....	...	12086	Dc	v0.18	v0.03	v0.24	v0.78	....	0.72	9 Mo Sep	v0.51	v0.45	31
32◆	1992	Q0.03	12-15-99	11-29	0.12	0.12	0.12	0.11	55.6	28.8	10-02-99	35.5	...	4747	Mr	v1.73	v0.41	v0.53	v4.41	....	3.58	6 Mo Sep	v2.22	v1.39	32
33	....	None Since Public			...	Nil	....	69.5	73.5	41.1	9-30-99	....	...	22428	Dc	...	...	vd0.48	vd1.17	....	d2.64	9 Mo Sep	vd0.75	v□d2.22	33
34	1987	Q0.05	1-11-00	12-28	0.32	0.20	0.32	3.84	130	61.8	9-30-99	71.0	...	38802	Dc	v0.53	v0.54	v0.54	v0.21	....	0.24	9 Mo Sep	v0.15	v0.18	34
35	....	None Since Public			...	Nil	....	5.37	15.6	15.6	9-30-99	1.17	...	33686	Mr	...	...	...	vpd0.74	....	d0.91	6 Mo Sep	vd1.04	vd1.21	35
36	....	None Since Public			...	Nil	....	0.69	5.92	9.35	9-30-99	2.12	...	3815	Je	0.05	d0.32	v0.04	vd0.22	vd0.23	d0.40	3 Mo Sep	v0.11	vd0.06	36
37◆	1995	Q0.11	11-19-99	11-3	s0.424	0.44	s0.399	Total Deposits $260M			9-30-99	....	...	1901	Dc	v1.75	v2.00	vd0.10	v1.54	....	1.03	9 Mo Sep	v1.10	v0.59	37
38◆	1931	Q0.27⅛	11-15-99	10-28	1.08½	1.085	1.07	3.30	37.9	52.6	9-30-99	156	139	12884	Dc	v1.16	v1.50	v1.83	v1.45	....	1.59	9 Mo Sep	v1.12	v1.26	38
39	....	None Since Public			...	Nil	....	27.8	29.2	5.90	9-30-99	3.48	p...	★19405	Dc	...	...	...	vpd0.21	....	....	9 Mo Sep	n/a	vpd0.53	39
40	....	None Since Public			...	Nil	....	585	857	557	j6-30-99	2110	...	±90300	Dc	±d1.58	±d0.14	v±0.31	v±d3.32	....	jd4.34	9 Mo Sep	±vd2.42	±vd3.44	40
41◆	1993	Q0.07	12-23-99	11-30	0.28	0.28	0.28	75.4	310	118	9-30-99	....	...	76073	Dc	v1.40	v1.73	v1.85	vd0.38	E0.80	d0.13	9 Mo Sep	v0.53	v0.78	41
42	....	None Paid			...	Nil	....	7.94	18.5	15.5	9-30-99	107	1045	★11764	Dc	v0.14	v0.45	v0.88	vd4.17	....	d4.29	9 Mo Sep	v0.10	vd0.02	42
43	1996	Q0.53⅛	1-17-00	12-29	2.12½	2.13	2.12½	Cv into 2.273 com, $11[66]				....	1380	...	Dc	...	...	...	....	....	....				43
44◆	....	None Since Public			...	Nil	....	173	333	162	9-30-99	1552	...	★62895	Dc	pv0.34	v0.63	v0.83	□v1.10	....	1.56	9 Mo Sep	v□0.77	v□1.24	44
45◆	....	[67]....	12-28-87	12-29	...	Nil	....	30.5	32.9	1.97	8-31-99	....	...	21800	Nv	d0.12	v0.02	△vNil	v0.16	....	0.34	9 Mo Aug	v0.02	v0.20	45
46	....	None Paid			...	Nil	....	5.05	9.32	4.31	9-30-99	....	...	2213	Sp	0.21	v0.39	v0.08	v0.08	v0.59	0.59				46
47	1987	Div Omitted 10-28-99			g0.02½	Nil	g0.05	19.6	76.7	31.4	6-30-99	186	...	70563	Dc	vd0.13	v0.08	v0.12	vd0.16	....	d0.70	9 Mo Sep	v0.17	vd0.37	47
48◆	1989	Q0.03	11-26-99	11-9	0.12	0.12	0.11	30.8	231	79.9	9-30-99	227	...	24604	Dc	v0.98	v1.19	v0.73	v1.54	....	1.65	9 Mo Sep	v1.14	v1.25	48
49◆	....	None Since Public			...	Nil	....	72.4	316	112	9-30-99	....	...	60408	Dc	v0.28	v0.42	v0.57	v0.83	E0.14	0.58	9 Mo Sep	v0.57	v0.32	49
50◆	1997	Q0.15	1-31-00	1-12	0.60	0.60	0.553	Total Deposits $535M			9-30-99	86.3	...	p8063	Dc	v1.03	v1.14	v1.31	v1.41	....	1.59	9 Mo Sep	v1.01	v1.19	50
51	1993	Q0.52	1-17-00	12-16	2.06½	2.08	2.00½	Total Assets $2468.67M			9-30-99	1086	...	40213	Dc	v0.86	v0.58	v1.41	v1.12	....	1.27	9 Mo Sep	v0.79	v0.94	51

◆**Stock Splits & Divs By Line Reference Index** [2]5-for-4,'95:3-for-2,'94,'96. [3]2-for-1,'96. [4]3-for-2,'95. [5]3-for-2,'97. [7]To split 2-for-1,ex Jan 7, 2000. [8]2-for-1,'95. [9]2-for-1,'98. [13]3-for-2,'96,'98. [18]2.5-for-1,'95:2-for-1,'96. [19]2-for-1,'98(twice). [20]2-for-1,'94,'96. [25]2-for-1,'99. [27]3-for-2,'95,'96:2-for-1,'97. [32]5-for-4,'94:2-for-1,'95. [37]Adj for 5%,'99. [38]2-for-1,'98. [41]2-for-1,'94,'95. [44]2-for-1,'99. [45]Reorg,1-for-20 REVERSE,'93. [48]3-for-2,'96:2-for-1,'98. [49]3-for-1,'96. [50]3-for-1,'98.

¶ S&P 500
# MidCap 400
✣ SmallCap 600
• Options

Index	Ticker	Name of Issue (Call Price of Pfd. Stocks) Market	Com. Rank. & Pfd. Rating	Inst. Hold Cos	Inst. Hold Shs. (000)	Principal Business	Price Range 1971-97 High	1971-97 Low	1998 High	1998 Low	1999 High	1999 Low	Dec. Sales in 100s	December, 1999 Last Sale Or Bid High	Low	Last	%Div Yield	P-E Ratio	EPS 5 Yr Growth	% Annualized Total Return 12 Mo	36 Mo	60 Mo
		Camden Property Trust (Cont.)																				
1	Pr A	$2.25 Sr'A'cm Cv Pfd([51]25) ....NY	NR	28	880		27¾	23⅛	28½	23 7/16	26⅜	21¾	1598	23¼	21¾	22 7/16	10.0	..	...	...	...	...
2	CCJ	✔Cameco Corp....NY,Ch,Ph,To	B	41	10339	Mines,refines uranium	55⅛	28¼	33⅞	15 9/16	26 11/16	14⅜	1244	16	14⅜	15⅛	NM	15	−19	−13.0	−26.3	...
3	CAB	✔Cameron Ashley Bldg Prod....NY	NR	52	5397	Building materials distrib	20	7½	22 9/16	9½	13⅜	7¼	14279	12	7¼	10	...	5	8	−23.4	−10.6	−7.3
4	CCH	Campbell Resources....NY,To,B,Ch,P,Mo	C	23	31573	Natural resources, Canada	16 15/16	¼	15/16	¼	⅜	⅛	90285	¼	⅛	3/16	...	d	Neg	−31.2	−43.2	−21.1
¶5•[1]	CPB	✔Campbell Soup....NY,To,B,Ch,P,Ph	A−	558	113161	Canned soup & other foods	59 7/16	1⅜	62⅞	46 11/16	55¾	37 7/16	127200	46	37 7/16	38 11/16	2.3	24	2	...	...	...
6	CSPLF	✔Canada South'n Petrol....NSC,P,Mo,B,Ph,To	C	16	440	Engaged in oil exploration	26½	1 5/16	8½	3 5/16	11½	4½	8905	6¾	5⅛	5⅞	...	d	−14	17.5	−6.2	4.9
7	CDX	✔Canadex Resources....To	NR	..	...	Busing,leasing,freight,O&G	4 3/16	⅛	1½	15/16	1⅛	⅝	69	13/16	11/16	11/16B	...	4	20	...	...	−26.0
8	EEE	✔Canadian 88 Energy....AS,To	NR	35	29353	Oil&gas explor,dev,prod'n	7 1/16	⅜	7 9/16	2⅞	4 7/16	1 1/16	31403	1 9/16	1 1/16	1 5/16	...	..	−29	−58.8	−39.8	−8.1
9•[2]	BCM	✔Canadian Imperial Bk Commerce[55]...NY,Mo,Vc	B+	99	71904	Gen'l bkg,Canada & worldwide	41¾	4 1/16	41 5/16	15 13/16	29 3/16	19 1/16	4441	24¼	21	23¾	5.1	7	5	1.1	−3.8	11.5
10	CMW	✔Canadian Marconi....AS,To,B,Mo,Ch,Ph	B	20	2695	Avionics, telecommunications	23½	⅝	15⅞	11	13⅜	10¾	280	13¼	12 1/16	13⅛	2.1	9	44	11.9	8.6	5.4
11•[3]	CNI	✔Canadian Natl Railway....NY	NR	337	112850	Railroad oper Canada & U.S.	28 7/16	7¼	33 9/16	20 11/16	36⅝	22 9/16	163460	31 9/16	25½	26½	◆1.6	5	NM	4.4	14.1	...
12	Pr	5.25% Cv Pfd(NC[56])....NY	NR	40	2494		....	....	....	....	57 1/16	41	8111	49⅜	41	42	6.2	..	...	...	...	...
13	CNQ	✔Canadian Natural Resources....To	B	35	7665	Oil & gas explor,dvlp,prod'n	44¼	1/32	31½	18¼	38⅝	19 13/16	71363	36¾	30 9/16	35¼	...	28	5	53.3	−2.1	20.7
14•[4]	CXY	✔Canadian Occ Petrol....AS,To,B,Ch,P	B	89	30534	Oil,gas,chemical: metal	29¾	½	22 13/16	9⅞	21⅞	8 11/16	1903	20 11/16	18	19¾	◆1.0	d	Neg	93.5	9.2	14.0
15•[5]	CP	✔Canadian Pac,Ord....NY,To,Mo,Vc,B,C,Ch,P,Ph	B−	247	163357	Transportation/Natural Res	31 11/16	3 9/16	31 9/16	17⅞	27⅛	17	81105	22⅜	21	21 9/16	◆1.8	10	NM	17.1	−4.7	9.8
16	CTR.A	✔Canadian Tire'A'[58]....To	B	24	7091	Sells home,auto,prd/gasoline	31 15/16	4 9/16	45	29	46	32½	64443	37¾	33⅛	34⅜	1.2	15	75	−13.6	16.2	24.6
✣17•[6]	CDB	✔Canandaigua Brands[59]Cl'A'....NY,Ch	B+	231	11216	Domestic wine producer	57⅝	3	59¾	35¼	61½	42⅞	18596	54 7/16	46¾	51	...	13	38	−11.8	21.4	6.1
18	CDB.B	Cl B[60]....NY,Ch	B+	12	105		58	7/16	59¾	37¼	62¼	44¼	42	57¾	56 3/16	55⅞B	...	16	38	0.7	18.6	7.5
19	CAND	✔Candies Inc....NNM	B−	23	2499	Mfr athletic/casual footwear	7⅞	⅞	8⅝	2⅝	4⅛	9/16	55960	1	⅝	⅞	...	d	Neg	−75.8	−29.0	−2.6
20	AB	✔Cannon Express....AS	B−	12	447	Trucking-gen'l commodities	16	1 9/16	12⅛	4⅞	6⅜	2	1412	3⅛	2	2⅝	...	d	Neg	−47.5	−31.0	−28.2
21	CANNY	✔Canon Inc ADR[61]....NNM	NR	95	23606	Business mach, cameras,optic	32⅛	3/16	24 15/16	17	40 15/16	19¼	13204	40 15/16	29¾	40 9/16	0.3	46	20	89.7	25.7	21.1
22	CWG	CanWest Global Commun....NY	NR	15	1124	International TV broadcstg	20 7/16	8¾	19 13/16	10⅞	16⅛	10¼	797	11 5/16	10 5/16	11 3/16	◆1.9	8	23	−6.5	5.1	...
23	CAU	✔Canyon Resources....AS,Ch,Ph	C	11	5640	Gold,silver,mineral expl&dvl	4 7/16	¾	1 5/16	3/16	⅝	⅛	30258	⅜	3/16	5/16	...	..	14	24.8	−50.8	−27.5
24	CAA	✔Capital Alliance Income Tr....AS	NR	1	2	Real estate investment trust	....	....	8	4	5⅝	2⅜	608	3 9/16	2⅜	2 7/16	14.0	9	...	−47.1	...	...
25•[7]	CARS	✔Capital Automotive REIT....NNM	NR	77	15912	Real estate investment trust	....	....	19¾	8 13/16	15 3/16	11¼	17062	13⅝	11⅞	12 3/16	11.3	13	...	−9.4	...	...
26	CCBG	✔Capital City Bank Grp....NNM	NR	16	117	General banking, Florida	28 5/16	18	33⅛	19	30	20 3/16	1304	23⅞	20 3/16	21½	2.5	15	8	−20.5	...	...
¶27•[8]	COF	✔Capital One Financial....NY,P	NR	636	129035	Bank card issuer/svcs	18⅛	4⅝	43 5/16	16⅞	60¼	35 13/16	191553	51½	44 11/16	48 3/16	0.2	28	27	26.0	59.7	56.4
28	CPH	✔Capital Pacific Hldgs....AS,Ph	NR	14	3844	Builds single family homes	14⅞	¾	5 1/16	2⅛	3⅞	1⅞	1323	2⅝	2 3/16	2½	...	9	−1	−2.4	−7.2	1.0
29	CPI	✔Capital Properties....AS	NR	6	32	Leases prop/oper park'g facil	6⅞	5⅜	8⅞	5⅞	9	5 7/16	233	9	7½	8¾B	1.4	80	...	48.4	...	...
30	CSU	✔Capital Senior Living....NY	NR	77	8793	Opr assisted living communit's	17½	9 13/16	15½	5⅛	15	4¾	18598	5⅞	4¾	5 1/16	...	6	...	−63.7	...	...
31	CT	✔Capital Trust 'A'....NY,B,P,Ch	NR	14	4558	Offer consumer loans/svcs	15⅛	1⅛	11⅞	4⅜	6	3⅝	5715	5	3 15/16	5	...	12	NM	−16.7	22.1	25.2
32	CFFN	✔Capitol Federal Financial....NNM	NR	47	9048	Savings bank, Kansas	....	....	....	....	10 9/16	8⅝	61764	10⅜	9 9/16	9¾	4.1	14	...	...	...	...
33	CATA	✔Capitol Transamerica....NNM	B+	37	1395	Ins hldg:property & casualty	28⅛	1/16	22¾	15	19½	9½	2902	11¾	9½	10 1/16	2.8	6	14	−44.9	−19.5	3.2
34	CMO	✔Capstead Mortgage....NY,Ch,Ph,P	NR	77	6748	Mtge investments REIT	27 13/16	5¼	21 11/16	2⅛	6 3/16	3 11/16	65280	4⅜	3 11/16	4 3/16	14.3	5	Neg	12.0	−37.6	−1.4
35	Pr A	$1.60 cm Cv Pfd(16.40)....NY	NR	1	2		56	10½	43	10⅝	17	11⅛	144	14	11⅛	11¾	13.6	..	...	...	...	...
36	Pr B	$1.26 cm Cv Pfd(12.50)....NY	NR	17	2028		19¾	9¾	16	6 7/16	12 7/16	8 13/16	6342	10⅛	8 13/16	9½	13.3	..	...	...	...	...
37	CRRR	Captec Net Lease Realty....NNM	NR	32	2496	Real estate investment trust	18 1/16	15½	18 1/16	10⅞	13⅞	6	47670	11½	6	7½	...	5	...	−32.1	...	...
✣38	CSAR	✔Caraustar Industries....NNM	A−	146	15405	Mfr recycled paperboard/prd	38⅛	13¼	36	20½	30¼	19¾	13825	24½	21 11/16	24	3.0	14	5	−13.5	−8.2	3.8
39	CGGI	✔Carbide/Graphite Group....NNM	NR	52	5537	Mfr graphite electrode pds	39 15/16	12¼	37	7¾	17⅛	5⅜	10728	7¼	5⅜	6½	...	17	Neg	−55.9	−30.8	...
¶40•[9]	CAH	✔Cardinal Health....NY,Ch,P	A−	1024	221348	Wholesale dstr drug,hlth prod	52½	1½	76⅜	46 7/16	83¼	37	257455	52 7/16	42¾	47⅞	0.2	28	18	−36.8	7.6	18.8
41	CTE	✔Cardiotech Intl....AS,Ph	NR	3	170	Vascular grafts/med'l prod	5⅜	1⅜	2⅞	1	2	¼	5169	11/16	¼	9/16	...	d	−5	−62.5	−35.8	...
42	CARI	✔CareInsite Inc....NNM	NR	88	4181	Dvp stg:Internet hlthcare ntwk	....	....	....	....	85¼	18	25088	85¼	52 5/16	80½	...	..	...	...	...	...
43•[10]	CMX	✔Caremark Rx....NY,Ch	NR	126	65560	Multi-state HMO services	36	13	22⅜	1⅝	9	2⅞	267659	5¼	3 15/16	5 1/16	...	16	−45	−3.6	−37.5	...
44•[11]	CMDC	✔CareMatrix Corp....NNM,Ch,Ph	NR	94	6373	Oper assisted living commun	30 11/16	9 1/16	35	13	30¾	1⅞	69920	2⅞	2	2½	...	3	NM	−91.8	−42.5	−26.2
45	CSA	✔Careside Inc....AS	NR	2	109	Dvlp stg:blood test'g sys	....	....	....	....	10¼	4¾	5979	10¼	5⅜	9¾	...	d	...	...	...	...
46	WS	Wrrt(Pur 1 com at $9)....AS	....	1	48		....	....	....	....	3	⅞	4133	3	1⅜	3	...	..	...	...	...	...
47	CTND	✔Caretenders Healthcorp....NSC	NR	4	426	Home health svcs/adult care	36¼	4 11/16	8⅞	1¾	4⅛	1½	1728	3	2	2¼	...	d	Neg	−18.2	−25.8	−22.1
48	CDC	✔Carey Diversified LLC....NY,Ph	NR	40	713	Real estate investments	....	....	22 15/16	18 3/16	20	15⅝	9275	17 15/16	15⅝	16⅞	9.9	12	...	−6.1	...	...
49•[12]	CWC	✔Caribiner International....NY,Ph	NR	54	12930	Business training/commun svc	46 11/16	8½	44¼	5	10 9/16	3⅜	68303	9⅛	3⅜	3⅝	...	d	...	−60.3	−47.5	...
#50•[13]	CSL	✔Carlisle Cos....NY,Ch,Ph	A−	226	14800	Rubber, plastics, metal prod	47¾	⅝	53 1/16	32 9/16	52 15/16	30⅝	29226	36 1/16	32¾	36	2.0	12	23	−29.1	7.6	16.8

Uniform Footnote Explanations-See Page 4. Other: [1]CBOE:Cycle 2. [2]Vc:Cycle 3. [3]CBOE:Cycle 1. [4]ASE:Cycle 1. [5]Ph:Cycle 1,To:Cycle 2. [6]ASE,CBOE:Cycle 1. [7]CBOE,Ph:Cycle 1. [8]CBOE:Cycle 3. [9]ASE:Cycle 3. [10]ASE,CBOE,Ph:Cycle 3. [11]Ph:Cycle 3. [12]CBOE,Ph:Cycle 3. [13]P:Cycle 3. [51]Fr 4-30-2001. [52]Com or cash re-spec cond.. [53]Stk dstr of Vlassic Foods Intl. [54]Stk dstr of Prize Energy Inc. [55]Oct'97 & prior pricing in $Cdn. [56]Can be redm anytime due to'Tax Event're-spec cond. [57]Co opt to extinguish Cv right 7-1-2002. [58]Non-vtg. [59]0.10 vtg. [60]Cv into 1 Cl'A'. [61]ADRs rep 1 shrs com par 50 yen. [62]Approx. [63]Southmark Corp owns 87.3%. [64]Incl current amts. [65]To be determined. [66]If com exceeds $14 for 10 con trad days.

Index (Splits ◆)	Cash Divs. Ea. Yr. Since	Dividends: Latest Payment Period $	Date	Ex. Div.	Total $ So Far 1999	Ind. Rate	Paid 1998	Financial Position Mil-$ Cash& Equiv.	Curr. Assets	Curr. Liab.	Balance Sheet Date	Capitalization Lg Trm Debt Mil-$	Shs. 000 Pfd.	Com.	Earnings $ Per Shr. Years End	1995	1996	1997	1998	1999	Last 12 Mos.	Interim Earnings Period	$ per Shr. 1998	1999	Index
1	1998	Q0.56¼	2-15-00	12-16	2.25	2.25	1.68¾	Cv into 0.7701 com,$32.4638				....	4165	...	Dc	...	...	...	....	....	....	Co opt red fr 4-30-2001[52]			1
2	1991	gQ0.12½	1-14-00	12-29	g0.50	0.50	g0.50	20.2	539	120	j6-30-99	600	...	57656	Dc	v1.95	v2.60	v1.51	v0.76	....	j0.72	9 Mo Sep	v0.97	v0.93	2
3	....	None Since Public			...	Nil	....	3.57	312	138	7-31-99	169	...	8680	Oc	1.15	□1.31	v1.20	v1.61	Pv1.94	1.94				3
4	....	2%Stk	6-8-84	5-21	...	Nil	....	33.4	40.1	3.31	j6-30-99	4.97	...	155690	Dc	v0.09	v0.06	vd0.27	vd0.14	....	jd0.17	9 Mo Sep	vd0.05	vd0.08	4
5◆	1902	Q0.22½	1-31-00	1-5	0.90	0.90	h[53]0.84	34.0	1547	3373	10-31-99	1328	...	426424	Jl	1.40	1.61	v1.49	v□1.46	v1.63	1.59	3 Mo Oct	v0.58	v0.54	5
6	....	None Paid			...	Nil	....	4.25	4.95	0.54	j9-30-99	....	...	14284	Dc	d0.09	vd0.11	vd0.12	vd0.19	....	jd0.18	9 Mo Sep	vd0.17	vd0.16	6
7	....	None Paid			...	Nil	....	....	1.18	15.0	j6-30-99	3.24	7529	4861	Je	0.11	0.17	v0.29	v0.30	v0.18	j0.18				7
8	....	h[54]....	1-14-00	12-30	...	Nil	....	2.04	34.4	33.4	6-30-99	225	...	105429	Dc	v0.03	v0.12	0.18	v0.02	....	0.01	9 Mo Sep	v0.03	v0.02	8
9◆	1890	gQ0.30	1-28-00	12-27	g1.20	1.20	g1.20	Total Deposits $160315M			j7-31-99	4407	70000	412879	Oc	2.09	3.02	v3.50	v2.25	....	j2.27	9 Mo Jul	v2.22	v2.24	9
10	1996	gS0.14	12-17-99	11-30	g0.28	0.28	g0.35	274	377	90.8	j6-30-99	9.15	...	23601	Mr	0.38	v0.21	v1.16	v1.06	....	j0.99	6 Mo Sep	v0.40	v0.33	10
11◆	1996	gQ0.15	12-29-99	12-6	g0.75	0.60	g0.53	175	1021	1137	j6-30-99	3518	...	194800	Dc	p■d6.75	v4.89	v2.31	vΔ1.21	E3.70↑	j3.66	9 Mo Sep	vΔ0.23	vΔ2.68	11
12	1999	0.65⅝	12-31-99	12-13	1.364	2.62	....	Cv into 0.6498 shrs $76.95[57]				....	4000	...		...	...	...	....	....	....	Mature 6-30-2029			12
13	....	None Paid			...	Nil	....	....	25.0	1176	j9-30-99	1320	...	109859	Dc	v0.61	v1.14	v1.14	v0.59	....	j1.26	9 Mo Sep	v0.36	v1.03	13
14◆	1975	gQ0.07½	1-1-00	12-8	g0.30	0.30	g0.30	82.0	609	553	j6-30-99	1394	...	137800	Dc	v1.05	v1.40	v1.02	vd0.83	....	jd0.54	9 Mo Sep	vd0.28	v0.01	14
15	1944	gQ0.14	1-28-00	12-21	g0.56	0.56	g0.52	613	2636	4074	j12-31-98	3300	...	333000	Dc	d2.41	v2.52	v3.64	v2.39	E1.55	j1.62	9 Mo Sep	v1.60	v0.83	15
16	1996	gQ0.10	3-1-00	1-27	g0.40	0.40	g0.40	308	1506	1055	j1-02-99	816	...	±76955	Dc	±1.38	v±1.51	±v1.79	v±2.09	....	j2.29	9 Mo Sep	v±1.53	v±1.73	16
17	....	None Since Public			...	Nil	....	4.34	1025	499	8-31-99	1274	...	±18055	Fb	±1.20	v±1.42	±v2.62	v±□3.30	E4.07	3.47	6 Mo Aug	v±1.56	v±1.73	17
18	....	None Since Public			...	Nil	....	....	...	...		....	...	3158	Fb	±1.20	v±1.42	v±2.62	□v±3.30	....	3.47	6 Mo Aug	v±1.56	v±1.73	18
19	....	None Paid			...	Nil	....	0.47	33.4	19.1	10-31-99	2.30	...	17897	Ja	v0.11	v0.11	v0.33	vd0.04	....	d0.68	9 Mo Oct	v0.08	vd0.56	19
20	....	None Since Public			...	Nil	....	5.93	26.2	22.5	9-30-99	33.3	...	3205	Je	±1.35	±0.67	v0.44	v0.56	vd0.15	d0.01	3 Mo Sep	v0.02	v0.16	20
21◆	1949	[62]0.07		12-28	0.127	0.14	0.113	4363	14357	8977	12-31-98	1554	...	870306	Dc	0.61	0.92	v1.04	v1.07	....	0.89	6 Mo Jun	v0.48	v0.30	21
22◆	1996	gS0.15	10-15-99	9-28	g0.30	0.30	g0.30	n/a	396	259	j2-28-99	470	...	±p149347	Au	0.57	0.73	v0.95	v1.33	Pv0.97	j0.97				22
23◆	....	None Paid			...	Nil	....	2.82	11.2	12.6	9-30-99	5.21	...	46497	Dc	vd0.24	vd0.21	vd0.13	v□d0.06	....	Nil	9 Mo Sep	v□d0.03	v0.03	23
24	1998	0.08½	1-15-00	12-29	0.34	0.34	0.17	Total Assets $16M			9-30-99	0.41	632	1485	Dc	...	...	...	v0.34	....	0.28	9 Mo Sep	v0.18	v0.12	24
25	1998	0.36	1-31-00	12-29	1.34	1.38	0.556	Total Assets $918.5M			9-30-99	493	...	21607	Dc	...	p0.43	n/a	v0.79	....	0.95	9 Mo Sep	v0.56	v0.72	25
26◆	1996	Q0.13¼	12-20-99	12-2	0.49¼	0.53	0.45	Total Deposits $1223.3M			9-30-99	14.4	...	10179	Dc	v1.11	v1.31	v1.42	v1.49	....	1.43	9 Mo Sep	v1.13	v1.07	26
27◆	1995	Q0.027	11-22-99	11-16	0.107	0.107	0.107	Total Deposits $3576.40M			9-30-99	4328	...	197180	Dc	v0.64	v0.77	v0.93	v1.32	E1.70	1.61	9 Mo Sep	v0.97	v1.26	27
28	....	None Since Public			...	Nil	....	Total Assets $330.21M			8-31-99	206	...	[63]13880	Fb	v0.17	v0.23	vd0.15	v0.23	....	0.29	6 Mo Aug	v0.06	vΔ0.12	28
29◆	1993	Q0.03	11-23-99	11-5	0.11	0.12	0.10	Total Assets $14.39M			9-30-99	....	...	3000	Dc	0.03	v0.11	v0.02	vd0.07	....	0.11	9 Mo Sep	vd0.09	v0.09	29
30	....	None Since Public			...	Nil	....	21.8	45.7	5.87	9-30-99	58.3	...	19717	Dc	...	pv0.17	pv0.25	v0.61	....	0.83	9 Mo Sep	v0.40	v0.62	30
31	....	0.05	8-26-94	8-8	...	Nil	....	Total Assets $810.32M			9-30-99	[64]479	12268	21989	Dc	vd0.30	vd0.05	vd0.63	v0.44	....	0.41	9 Mo Sep	v0.35	v0.32	31
32	1999	0.10	11-19-99	11-3	0.30	0.40	....	Total Deposits $3942M			6-30-99	900	...	91512	Sp	...	...	...	vp0.68	....	0.68				32
33◆	1984	Q0.07	12-23-99	12-7	0.28	0.28	0.28	Total Assets $264.03M			9-30-99	....	...	11268	Dc	v1.24	v1.62	v1.35	v1.72	....	1.81	9 Mo Sep	v1.18	v1.27	33
34◆	1985	0.12	1-20-00	12-29	0.48	0.60	1.00	Total Assets $9137.62M			9-30-99	3413	17133	56901	Dc	v1.09	v2.07	v2.35	vd4.22	E0.80	0.56	9 Mo Sep	vd4.30	v0.48	34
35	1989	Q0.40	12-31-99	12-20	1.60	1.60	1.60	Cv into 2.0421 com				....	550	...	Dc	...	...	...	....	....	....				35
36	1992	0.10½	12-31-99	12-20	0.26	1.26	1.26	Cv into 0.7246 com				....	17081	...	Dc	...	...	...	....	....	....				36
37	1998	0.38	10-15-99	10-4	1.51½	[65]....	1.32	Total Assets $258.1M			9-30-99	121	...	9508	Dc	...	pv0.54	pv1.05	v1.21	....	1.46	9 Mo Sep	v0.92	v□1.17	37
38	1993	Q0.18	1-6-00	12-14	0.72	0.72	0.64	13.3	232	113	9-30-99	436	...	25484	Dc	v1.66	v2.28	v2.03	v2.04	....	1.77	9 Mo Sep	v1.54	v1.27	38
39	....	None Since Public			...	Nil	....	....	133	52.6	10-31-99	113	...	8313	Jl	3.71	□1.67	v□2.09	v□d0.58	v0.05	0.39	3 Mo Oct	vd0.23	v0.11	39
40◆	1983	Q0.02½	1-15-00	12-29	0.10	0.10	0.082	185	6160	3657	9-30-99	1520	...	280250	Je	0.89	0.77	v1.13	v1.45	v1.64	1.74	3 Mo Sep	v0.33	v0.43	40
41	....	None Since Public			...	Nil	....	0.79	1.35	1.17	9-30-99	2.18	...	6585	Mr	vd0.77	vd0.42	vd0.42	vd0.55	....	d0.56	6 Mo Sep	vd0.23	vd0.24	41
42	....	None Since Public			...	Nil	....	55.8	70.6	11.5	9-30-99	....	...	70410	Je	...	...	...	vd0.21	n/a	....	3 Mo Sep	vd0.04	vd0.10	42
43	....	None Since Public			...	Nil	....	20.1	573	1224	9-30-99	680	...	199566	Dc	Δpvd0.66	vd0.85	□vd4.25	v□d6.61	E0.31↓	d7.23	9 Mo Sep	vd0.21	vd0.83	43
44◆	....	None Paid			...	Nil	....	11.6	94.1	22.8	9-30-99	217	...	18033	Dc	d3.55	vd0.59	v0.38	v0.99	....	0.91	9 Mo Sep	v0.69	v0.61	44
45	....	None Since Public			...	Nil	....	8.53	8.77	3.37	9-30-99	1.27	163	7084	Dc	...	...	vd2.04	vd1.93	....	d1.84	9 Mo Sep	vd1.48	vd1.39	45
46	....	Terms&trad. basis should be checked in detail						Wrrts expire 6-16-2004				....	...	2000	Dc	...	...	...	....	....	....	Callable fr 12-16-99 at 5¢[66]			46
47◆	....	None Since Public			...	Nil	....	0.41	16.3	3.84	9-30-99	[64]15.6	...	3120	Mr	0.50	v0.56	v0.45	v□d1.88	....	d1.49	6 Mo Sep	vd1.89	vd1.50	47
48	1998	Q0.41¾	1-15-00	12-13	1.66½	1.67	1.23¾	Total Assets $863.85M			9-30-99	[64]322	...	25682	Dc	...	p1.81	pv1.58	v□1.57	....	1.47	9 Mo Sep	v□1.23	v1.13	48
49◆	....	None Since Public			...	Nil	....	14.4	161	91.7	6-30-99	437	...	23697	Sp	p0.25	p0.52	v0.83	v□0.04	Pvd2.21	d2.21				49
50◆	1950	Q0.18	12-1-99	11-12	0.68	0.72	0.60	10.7	538	253	9-30-99	282	...	30129	Dc	v1.41	v1.80	v2.28	v2.77	....	3.05	9 Mo Sep	v2.15	v2.43	50

◆Stock Splits & Divs By Line Reference Index [5]2-for-1,'97. [9]2-for-1,'97. [11]2-for-1,'99. [14]2-for-1,'96. [21]5-for-1,'98. [22]3-for-1,'96. [23]Propose 1-for-10 REVERSE split. [26]2-for-1,'97:3-for-2,'98. [27]3-for-1,'99. [29]3-for-1,'97. [33]10%,'95:3-for-2,'97. [34]3-for-2,'95,'96. [40]5-for-4,'94:3-for-2,'96,'98. [44]1-for-5 REVERSE,'96. [47]1-for-5 REVERSE,'95. [49]2-for-1,'97. [50]2-for-1,'97.

¶ S&P 500
\# MidCap 400
✣ SmallCap 600
• Options

Index	Ticker	Name of Issue (Call Price of Pfd. Stocks)	Market	Com. Rank. & Pfd. Rating	Inst. Hold Cos	Inst. Hold Shs. (000)	Principal Business	Price Range 1971-97 High	1971-97 Low	1998 High	1998 Low	1999 High	1999 Low	December, 1999 Dec. Sales in 100s	Last Sale Or Bid High	Low	Last	%Div Yield	P-E Ratio	EPS 5 Yr Growth	% Annualized Total Return 12 Mo	36 Mo	60 Mo
1	CCTVY	✓Carlton Communic ADS[51]	NNM	NR	24	2480	Mfrs TV prod in U.K./U.S.	47¼	10⅞	48¾	29¾	54½	33⅞	1354	51	42¼	47⅝	2.5	27	2	6.7	5.4	14.2
2	CCMPr	Carlton Commun[53]'X-CAPS'([54]26)	NY	A–	2	42	Mfr TV prod in U.K./U.S.	25 11/16	19⅛	26⅛	24 7/16	25⅝	19½	2171	22 11/16	19½	20⅛	9.9	..	...	...	...	...
3	KML	✓Carmel Container Sys	AS,Ch,P	NR	7	17	Israeli packaging mfr	17	1¾	9¾	5 3/16	8⅞	5⅛	202	8⅞	7⅜	8B	...	9	–35	39.1	0.5	1.6
✣4	CKE	✓Carmike Cinemas'A'	NY	C	108	6694	Oper motion picture theatres	35⅝	5	33 3/16	15	21 11/16	6½	17915	12⅜	6½	7 13/16	...	d	Neg	–61.5	–32.5	–19.4
5	CGY	Carnegie Intl[56]	AS	NR	9	39	Bankcard svcs/non-grip tech	2½	¼	3⅜	½	8¾	2⅛	....	....	....	....	...	..	...	...	...	...
¶6•[1]	CCL	✓Carnival Corp	NY,Ch,P,Ph	A	891	279200	Cruise ships,hotel,casino	27 15/16	2 1/16	48½	19	53½	38⅛	268018	50½	43 7/16	47 13/16	0.9	29	20	0.4	44.0	36.7
✣7	CAFC	✓Carolina First Corp	NNM	B+	92	4406	Bank hldg co, South Carolina	25¼	5 5/16	30⅝	16 13/16	30 13/16	14⅞	21220	20⅜	14⅞	18¼	2.2	13	NM	–26.8	6.0	13.3
¶8•[2]	CPL	✓Carolina Pwr & Lt	NY,B,C,Ch,P,Ph	A–	458	62892	Utility:elec & gas svc	42 11/16	5¼	49⅝	39 3/16	47⅞	29¼	104129	30⅞	29¼	30 7/16	6.8	11	4	–32.0	–1.1	8.1
9	CPD	Carolina Pwr & Lt 8.55%[57]'QUICS'[58]	NY	....[59]	4	3	Elec serv No & So Carolinas	27 5/16	25	27⅜	25½	26 7/16	23⅜	1492	24⅞	23⅜	23½	9.1	..	...	–2.7	4.6	...
#10•[3]	CRS	✓Carpenter Technology	NY,Ch,P,Ph	B+	190	13013	Stainless,high-alloy steels	52 7/16	3 13/16	58 15/16	30	37⅛	22 3/16	14362	27 13/16	24 13/16	27 7/16	4.8	18	–14	–14.9	–5.7	3.4
11	CRE	✓CarrAmerica Realty	NY	NR	169	28434	Real estate investment trust	33 7/16	16¾	31 11/16	19	26¾	17¾	35932	21 7/16	17¾	21⅜	8.7	16	8	–3.4	–3.4	11.5
12	CSV	✓Carriage Services 'A'	NY	NR	71	7872	Funeral services/products	26	13½	28¾	16	29¼	4⅝	18785	6	4⅝	5 15/16	...	12	NM	–79.1	–35.7	...
13	CARN	Carrington Laboratories	NNM,Ch	C	17	1166	Mfr pharmac'l prod/drug R&D	50⅞	3¼	6 7/16	2	4¼	1½	14298	2⅜	1 11/16	2	...	d	–28	–5.9	–36.3	–28.6
14	CIC	✓Carson Inc'A'	NY,Ch,Ph	NR	25	2230	Mfr, mkt hair care products	17	6	10¾	1½	5⅛	2½	8259	4⅜	2 15/16	3¼	...	d	...	–18.8	–38.4	...
#15•[1]	CAR	✓Carter-Wallace	NY,B,Ch,Ph,P	B	112	15276	Drug and toiletry products	45 13/16	13/16	19 11/16	14⅜	19⅝	15½	8457	18¼	17 7/16	17 15/16	1.3	23	NM	–7.6	6.0	8.0
16	CNY	✓Carver Bancorp	AS	NR	12	461	Savings bank, New York	17½	6⅛	16⅝	7⅞	11⅜	6½	777	11⅛	9⅛	11⅛	...	d	Neg	27.1	10.8	12.4
17•[4]	CAE	✓Cascade Corp	NY	B+	59	4290	Hydraulically actuated equip	20 7/16	⅜	18 7/16	11⅝	17 7/16	8 5/16	8802	10	8 5/16	9 3/16	4.4	9	6	–39.8	–14.6	–2.0
✣18	CGC	✓Cascade Natural Gas	NY,Ch,Ph,P	↑B+	92	3547	Nat'l gas dstr: Wash, Ore	19½	3⅜	18 11/16	14⅝	19¾	14⅜	3803	17 13/16	15⅜	16⅛	6.0	13	11	–5.8	4.1	8.1
19•[5]	CWST	✓Casella Waste Sys 'A'	NNM	NR	121	11491	Non-hazardous solid waste svc	26⅜	18	39	23¾	35⅞	12¾	25239	19 5/16	16⅜	18⅞	...	24	...	–49.2	...	...
✣20•[1]	CASY	✓Casey's Genl Stores	NNM	A+	204	31479	Convenience-style gen'l strs	12 13/16	⅞	18¼	12¼	16¾	9 11/16	158607	12⅝	9 11/16	10 7/16	0.6	13	13	–19.5	4.2	7.4
✣21•[6]	PWN	✓Cash Amer Intl	NY,Ch,Ph,P	A–	116	19644	Acquire,operate pawnshops	13¾	3 3/16	20⅞	9	15 15/16	6¾	17583	9¾	7½	9¾	0.5	23	–2	–35.5	5.2	0.3
22	CSDS	Casino Data Systems	NNM	NR	28	5531	Dvp casino act'g/playr info sy	21 5/16	2½	4 13/16	1¼	8	1½	35759	4	2¾	4	...	13	–33	100	–16.5	–10.2
✣23	CAS	✓Castle (A.M.)	AS,Ch	B	85	7444	Metals service dstr centers	30⅞	11/16	24⅞	14	18¼	10¾	2832	12½	11	11¾	6.6	19	–11	–17.3	–11.7	4.9
24	CCS	✓Castle & Cooke Inc	NY,P	NR	72	8929	Real estate dvlp't/resorts	21 1/16	11¾	21⅝	13½	18	11 15/16	3710	13	11 15/16	12 11/16	...	16	NM	–14.0	–7.4	...
25	CECX	✓Castle Energy Corp	NNM	B–	28	1158	Oil & gas explor,dev,prod'n	87½	3	20⅝	13⅜	29	15	3876	29	16¾	25⅜	2.4	9	3	50.3	37.3	19.4
26	LTG	✓Catalina Lighting	NY,Ch,Ph	↑B–	22	2773	Mkts light'g prod/ceil'g fans	15¼	1⅝	4¾	1 15/16	5¾	2⅛	5537	5 11/16	4⅝	4 13/16	...	6	–9	114	–0.4	–10.2
✣27•[7]	POS	✓Catalina Marketing	NY	NR	290	15681	Electronic coupon mktg sys	60	10	70½	39⅜	122½	60 9/16	18412	122½	95 3/16	115¾	...	50	22	69.3	28.1	33.0
28•[1]	CTAL	✓Catalytica Inc	NNM	NR	..	...	Pollution ctrl catalysts,sys	15⅞	2	20⅞	9⅝	18 3/16	9⅜	56508	14 13/16	9⅜	13 9/16	...	40	NM	–24.7	50.5	36.5
29•[8]	CDX	✓Catellus Development	NY,Ch,P	B–	231	75242	Real estate development	22	5¼	20⅜	10 3/16	16⅜	10¾	44264	13 9/16	11¾	12 13/16	...	23	NM	–10.5	4.0	16.9
¶30•[1]	CAT	✓Caterpillar Inc	NY,B,C,Ch,P,Ph	B	847	232689	Earthmoving mchy: diesel eng	61⅝	6⅜	60¾	39 1/16	66 7/16	42	383320	49 3/16	43⅛	47 1/16	2.8	15	7	4.8	10.1	13.7
31	CAV	✓Cavalier Homes	NY,Ch,Ph	B+	49	8950	Produce factory built homes	19 3/16	⅝	13 3/16	7 13/16	11⅜	3 11/16	17376	4 7/16	3 11/16	3 15/16	4.1	7	–8	–64.5	–28.9	–0.1
32	CVH	✓Cavanaughs Hospitality	NY	NR	30	4598	Own/oper full svc hotels	....	....	17 11/16	6 9/16	12 1/16	6⅜	6459	8⅝	6⅜	8¼	...	12	...	–23.3	...	...
33	CAVN	✓Cavion Technologies[64]	NSC	NR	..	...	Internet sv to credit unions	....	....	....	....	9	5 5/16	10720	8 1/16	5½	7¾	...	..	...	...	...	...
34	CBG	✓CB Richard Ellis Svcs	NY	NR	69	10771	Real estate svcs	39½	18	40½	12 7/16	24⅞	10 9/16	4546	14	12¼	12⅜	...	13	–47	–31.7	–14.8	...
35	CBL	✓CBL & Associates Prop	NY,Ch	NR	136	17891	Real estate investment trust	27⅝	16⅞	27	23⅜	27	19¼	12994	22⅛	19¼	20⅝	9.5	11	12	–13.6	–0.2	7.7
#36•[9]	CBRL	✓CBRL Group	NNM	A	219	28512	Restaurant & gift stores	34⅝	7/16	43	20⅛	24¼	9 1/16	201327	11 1/16	9 1/16	9 11/16	0.2	10	...	–58.3	–27.4	–12.0
¶37•[10]	CBS	✓CBS Corp[66]	NY,B,C,Ch,P,Ph	B–	1014	466631	TV/radio entertainment	39⅜	2	36⅝	18	64	31 11/16	380268	64	51 5/16	63 15/16	...	..	NM	94.9	48.1	40.1
38	SMTF	✓CBT Group ADS[67]	NNM	NR	149	31608	Dvp info tech education softwr	41 3/16	4	63⅞	6 11/16	38¼	8 9/16	83373	38¼	24 7/16	33½	...	..	23	125	7.4	...
39	CCAM	✓CCA Industries	NNM	B	11	460	Mfr,dstr hlth & beauty aid prd	9⅛	¼	3 7/16	1 1/16	2¼	1	13190	1¾	1⅛	1⅛	...	d	–26	–10.0	–21.3	–22.2
#40	CCB	✓CCB Financial	NY,Ch,Ph	A	182	14339	Comm'l bkg,North Carolina	55	1 3/16	58½	43⅛	59⅛	40	20580	46¼	40 7/16	43 9/16	2.7	12	13	–21.9	13.6	25.2
41	CCBT	✓CCBT Financial Companies	NNM	B+	20	1886	Comm'l bkg,Massachusetts	20½	⅝	24½	13½	19⅝	14¾	2903	15⅞	14⅞	15⅝	3.6	10	13	–11.9	14.5	22.4
42	CCCG	✓CCC Information Svcs	NNM	NR	55	13572	Auto claims mgmt softwr,sys	24¼	11½	29	9¼	18	8 15/16	15206	18	9⅞	17⅛	...	d	73	–0.7	2.3	...
✣43	CDI	✓CDI Corp	NY,Ch,Ph	B	143	7690	Engr'g & technical services	45¾	1/16	47 15/16	15	36	19½	5241	26⅝	23	24⅛	...	9	38	19.5	–5.3	4.0
44•[11]	CDNW	✓CDnow Inc	NNM	NR	76	5245	Online retail music pds	....	....	39¼	7	24 15/16	9⅞	163170	15⅞	9⅞	9⅞	...	d	...	–45.1	...	...
#45•[1]	CDWC	✓CDW Computer Centers	NNM	NR	204	18005	Direct mkt computer products	39	2 1/16	51 15/16	18	80	27 15/16	48144	80	61¼	78⅝	...	40	46	64.0	38.4	47.3
46	CFK	✓CE Franklin Ltd	AS,Mo	B–	4	517	Dstr oil field supplies	16¾	1⅛	9⅛	1½	5⅛	1 7/16	5714	4⅜	3	3 3/16	...	d	Neg	88.9	–10.0	6.1
✣47•[9]	CEC	✓CEC Entertainment	NY,Ph	B–	226	24822	Family restr/enter'nt ctrs	18¼	1	27 7/16	11¾	36 9/16	15 3/16	37729	31	23½	28¼	...	19	NM	52.9	32.8	53.3
48	CGS	✓CEC Resources	AS	NR	1	13	O&G acq,dvlp,prodn-Cdn	7¼	3⅞	5 11/16	4⅛	5¼	4⅛	348	4⅞	4¼	4⅞	...	d	Neg	14.7	–2.4	...
49	FUN	✓Cedar Fair L.P.	NY,Ch,Ph,P	NR	120	10909	Own,operate amusement parks	28¼	2⅞	30⅞	21¾	26	18 7/16	20224	19¾	18 7/16	19⅝	7.5	12	3	–20.9	7.7	12.2
50	HIV	✓Cel-Sci Corp	AS,Ph	C	10	271	Finances biomed/tec research	91⅞	2¼	6⅝	1½	3⅞	1⅝	21443	2½	2 3/16	2 5/16	...	d	12	32.1	–18.4	–6.8
51	WS.A	Wrrt(Pur 1 com at $10)[69]	AS	....	..	...		....	....	2½	3/16	1¼	¼	10	¼	¼	⅛B	...	..	...	...	...	...

Uniform Footnote Explanations-See Page 4. Other: [1]CBOE:Cycle 1. [2]Ph:Cycle 1. [3]Ph:Cycle 3. [4]P,Cycle 2. [5]CBOE:Cycle 3. [6]ASE,CBOE,Ph:Cycle 1. [7]ASE:Cycle 2. [8]ASE,CBOE:Cycle 3. [9]P:Cycle 3. [10]ASE:Cycle 1. [11]Ph:Cycle 2. [51]ADS's equal 5 Ord par 5p. [52]Approx. [53]Co opt exch for pref shrs re-specified cond. [54]To 10-7-99,scale to $25 in 2003. [55]Incl shrs hld by subsid. [56]ASE trading halted 4-30-99. [57]Quarterly Income Capital Securities. [58]Sr'A' Subordinated Deferrable Int Debs. [59]Rated A- by S&P. [60]Pfd in $M. [61]9 Mo Dec'96. [62]Fiscal Dec'95 & prior. [63]Fiscal Oct'97. [64]d/b/a Cavion.com. [65]®$1.03,Δ$4.03,'96. [66]Viacom Inc plan acq,1.085 com. [67]Ea ADS rep 1 ord, par IR 37.5p. [68]Accum on pfd. [69]Co can accel exp date re-spec cond.

Index	Cash Divs. Ea. Yr. Since	Dividends: Latest Payment Period $	Date	Ex. Div.	Total $ So Far 1999	Ind. Rate	Paid 1998	Financial Position Mil-$ Cash & Equiv.	Curr. Assets	Curr. Liab.	Balance Sheet Date	Capitalization Lg Trm Debt Mil-$	Shs. 000 Pfd.	Com.	Earnings $ Per Shr. Years End	1995	1996	1997	1998	1999	Last 12 Mos.	Interim Earnings Period	$ per Shr. 1998	1999	Index
1	1987	[52]0.73¼	4-13-00	12-21	1.131	1.21	1.125	288	1039	600	j9-30-98	328	356498	610532	Sp	2.05	2.48	2.84	v2.35	....	1.79	6 Mo Mar	v1.36	v0.80	1
2	1993	Q0.50	12-15-99	12-10	2.00	2.00	2.00	....	...	...		....	6000	...	Sp	...	...	...	....	....	....				2
3	....	t0.18	5-2-88	4-11	...	Nil	....	0.13	43.1	38.9	12-31-98	14.5	...	[55]2520	Dc	2.01	1.63	vd1.05	v0.65	....	0.88	9 Mo Sep	v0.51	v0.74	3
4	....	None Since Public			...	Nil	....	6.12	32.0	106	9-30-99	450	550	±11369	Dc	±1.16	v±d0.65	±v1.78	±d2.73	....	d3.18	9 Mo Sep	v±1.13□	±v0.68	4
5◆	....	None Paid			...	Nil	....	0.79	6.41	3.25	12-31-98	0.98	475	51743	Dc	...	...	v0.07	v0.06	....	0.06				5
6◆	1988	Q0.10½	12-14-99	11-26	0.37½	0.42	0.31½	940	1222	1225	8-31-99	1184	...	p616920	Nv	±0.80	±0.98	v1.12	v1.40	vP1.66	1.66				6
7◆	1994	Q0.10	2-1-00	1-12	0.36	0.40	0.32	Total Deposits $2398.09M			9-30-99	299	...	25719	Dc	v0.84	v0.92	v1.18	v1.19	....	1.37	9 Mo Sep	v0.98	v1.16	7
8	1937	Q0.51½	2-1-00	1-6	2.00	2.06	1.94	76.7	1032	903	9-30-99	2800	587	159590	Dc	v2.48	v2.66	v2.66	v2.75	E2.80	2.47	12 Mo Sep	v2.91	v2.47	8
9	1995	Q0.534	12-31-99	12-28	2.137	2.138	2.138	Co option redm fr 4-21-2000 at $25				125	...	...	Dc	...	...	...	....	....	....	Mature 6-30-2025			9
10◆	1907	Q0.33	12-2-99	11-2	1.32	1.32	1.32	5.70	424	319	9-30-99	345	[60]27	21930	Je	2.81	v3.38	v3.16	v3.84	v1.58	1.51	3 Mo Sep	v0.51	v0.44	10
11	1993	Q0.46¼	12-3-99	11-17	1.85	1.85	1.85	Total Assets $3636.88M			9-30-99	1680	9480	66823	Dc	v0.90	□v0.90	□v1.23	v1.32	....	1.38	9 Mo Sep	v1.25	v1.31	11
12	....	None Since Public			...	Nil	....	4.10	30.4	18.0		175	...	±11060	Dc	vd0.99	v□d0.09	□v0.34	Pv0.65	....	0.51	9 Mo Sep	v□0.57	v0.43	12
13	....	None Since Public			...	Nil	....	5.78	12.9	4.09	9-30-99	....	...	9395	Dc	vd0.22	vd0.74	v0.02	vd0.17	....	d0.33	9 Mo Sep	v0.03	vd0.13	13
14	....	None Since Public			...	Nil	....	20.6	90.6	31.2	9-30-99	136	...	±15209	Dc	...	[61]n/a	□v0.25	vΔNil	....	d1.06	9 Mo Sep	v±0.97	v±d0.09	14
15	1883	Q0.06	12-1-99	11-5	0.24	0.24	0.20	78.8	345	165	9-30-99	65.0	...	±44982	Mr	0.16	v0.58	v0.59	v0.62	....	0.77	6 Mo Sep	v0.34	v0.49	15
16	1997	0.05	9-21-98	8-19	...	Nil	0.05	Total Deposits $279M			9-30-99	65.7	...	2314	Mr	v0.35	vd0.80	v0.48	vd2.02	....	d1.59	6 Mo Sep	v0.23	v0.66	16
17◆	1954	Q0.10	12-17-99	12-1	0.40	0.40	0.40	17.9	136	54.0	10-31-99	114	[60]16	11440	Ja	v0.88	v1.48	v1.60	v1.63	....	1.03	9 Mo Oct	v1.39	v0.79	17
18	1964	Q0.24	2-15-00	1-12	0.96	0.96	0.96	4.28	28.8	23.7	6-30-99	125	102	11045	Sp	[62]0.80	0.84	v0.93	v0.82	Pv1.23	1.23				18
19	....	None Since Public			...	Nil	....	4.83	42.1	33.4	10-31-99	118	...	±p23157	Ap	...	...	p±0.07	v±d0.39	v±0.58	0.78	6 Mo Oct	v±0.28	v±0.48	19
20◆	1990	Q0.01½	2-15-00	1-28	0.06	0.06	0.06	23.1	84.3	103	10-31-99	120	...	52739	Ap	0.44	v0.51	v0.51	v0.63	v0.76	0.80	6 Mo Oct	v0.48	v0.52	20
21	1988	Q0.01¼	11-16-99	10-29	0.05	0.05	0.05	3.02	257	29.5	9-30-99	203	...	25385	Dc	v□0.45	v0.54	v0.66	v0.48	....	0.43	9 Mo Sep	v0.32	v0.27	21
22◆	....	None Since Public			...	Nil	....	14.7	68.8	17.9	9-30-99	0.03	...	18389	Dc	v0.34	v0.28	vd2.20	v0.14	....	0.31	9 Mo Sep	v0.04	v0.21	22
23◆	1934	Q0.19½	11-19-99	11-9	0.78	0.78	0.75½	3.29	278	109	9-30-99	157	...	14048	Dc	v1.93	v1.86	v1.69	v1.32	....	0.62	9 Mo Sep	v1.22	v0.52	23
24	....	None Since Public			...	Nil	....	Total Assets $1093.71M			9-30-99	279	...	17053	Dc	vd4.31	v0.25	vd0.01	v0.58	....	0.80	9 Mo Sep	v0.42	v0.64	24
25◆	1997	Q0.15	10-15-99	10-6	0.60	0.60	0.60	28.3	37.1	12.1	6-30-99	....	...	2579	Sp	2.20	3.73	v4.64	v3.66	Pv2.97	2.97				25
26	....	None Since Public			...	Nil	....	4.00	60.8	28.3	6-30-99	23.9	...	7011	Sp	0.05	v0.21	vd0.44	v0.15	Pv0.80	0.80				26
27◆	....	None Since Public			...	Nil	....	10.5	96.3	119	9-30-99	1.78	...	18240	Mr	1.10	v1.33	v1.73	v1.98	....	2.34	6 Mo Sep	v0.69	v1.05	27
28	....	Wrrt	8-22-97	8-25	...	Nil	....	57.8	190	75.4	9-30-99	68.3	...	57677	Dc	vd0.55	vd0.27	vd0.10	v0.33	....	0.34	9 Mo Sep	v0.24	v0.25	28
29	....	None Since Public			...	Nil	....	Total Assets $1820M			6-30-99	925	...	107142	Dc	vd0.78	v0.03	v0.24	v□0.55	E0.55	0.73	9 Mo Sep	v0.31	v0.49	29
30◆	1914	Q0.32½	2-19-00	1-18	1.25	1.30	1.10	283	11977	7600	9-30-99	10106	...	355553	Dc	v2.84	v3.50	□v4.37	v4.11	E3.10	2.80	9 Mo Sep	v3.28	v1.97	30
31◆	1989	Q0.04	11-15-99	10-27	0.16	0.16	0.13	22.3	133	100	10-01-99	6.18	...	17853	Dc	v1.03	v1.39	v0.51	v0.93	....	0.58	9 Mo Sep	v0.66	v0.31	31
32	....	None Since Public			...	Nil	....	7.85	17.2	16.8	9-30-99	124	...	12786	Dc	...	...	p[63]0.49	□v0.71	....	0.68	9 Mo Sep	v□0.61	v□0.58	32
33	....	None Since Public			...	Nil	....	....	6.42	0.81	p6-30-99	0.25	29	★4606	Dc	...	...	...	vpd0.77	....	....	6 Mo Jun	n/a	vd0.75	33
34	....	None Since Public			...	Nil	....	25.1	197	185	9-30-99	405	...	20684	Dc	pv0.55	vΔ[65]4.99	□v1.34	vd0.38	....	0.99	9 Mo Sep	vd1.07	v0.30	34
35	1994	Q0.48¾	1-14-00	12-29	1.92¾	1.95	1.83¾	Total Assets $2006.6M			9-30-99	1346	2875	24730	Dc	v□1.12	v□1.68	□v1.49	v□1.56	....	1.91	9 Mo Sep	v□1.16	v1.51	35
36	1972	Q0.00½	1-3-00	12-15	0.02	0.02	0.02	18.2	153	142	10-29-99	342	...	58633	Jl	1.09	1.04	v1.41	v1.65	v1.16	0.99	3 Mo Oct	v0.42	v0.25	36
37	1935	Div suspended 3-1-98			...	Nil	0.05	185	2401	1809	9-30-99	2346	...	p762395	Dc	vd0.25	v□0.35	v0.84	v□d0.02	E0.25	0.75	9 Mo Sep	vd0.02	v□0.75	37
38◆	....	None Since Public			...	Nil	....	102	152	35.0	12-31-98	....	...	48734	Dc	0.17	v0.30	v0.53	v0.36	....	0.13	6 Mo Jun	v0.25	v0.02	38
39	....	None Paid			...	Nil	....	1.91	20.0	8.11	8-31-99	....	...	±7267	Nv	±d0.23	v±0.13	v±0.25	±v0.21	....	d0.11	9 Mo Aug	v±0.20	v±d0.12	39
40◆	1934	Q0.29	1-3-00	12-13	1.07	1.16	0.96½	Total Deposits $6514.84M			9-30-99	167	...	p40485	Dc	1.94	v2.08	v2.27	v2.93	....	3.68	9 Mo Sep	v2.16	v2.91	40
41◆	1938	Q0.14	10-29-99	10-18	0.56	0.56	0.50	Total Deposits $799M			9-30-99	373	...	9061	Dc	v0.97	v1.05	v1.46	v1.38	....	1.55	9 Mo Sep	v1.01	v1.18	41
42	....	None Since Public			...	Nil	....	1.05	38.2	41.8	9-30-99	26.5	...	21899	Dc	pvd0.11	v□0.43	v0.62	vNil	....	d0.10	9 Mo Sep	v0.08	vd0.02	42
43	....	0.013	11-2-70	10-16	...	Nil	....	6.67	371	147	9-30-99	56.0	...	19053	Dc	v0.26	v1.58	v1.89	v2.32	....	2.76	9 Mo Sep	v1.63	v2.07	43
44	....	None Since Public			...	Nil	....	28.0	40.7	51.1	9-30-99	1.62	...	30355	Dc	...	...	vpd0.91	vd2.79	....	d3.87	9 Mo Sep	vd2.10	vd3.18	44
45◆	....	None Since Public			...	Nil	....	92.7	435	128	9-30-99	....	...	43214	Dc	v0.48	v0.79	v1.17	v1.51	....	1.97	9 Mo Sep	v1.09	v1.55	45
46	....	None Since Public			...	Nil	....	....	82.3	28.0	j6-30-99	41.7	...	16411	Dc	0.15	v0.40	v0.65	v0.14	....	jd0.32	9 Mo Sep	v0.15	vd0.31	46
47◆	....	None Since Public			...	[68]Nil	....	5.87	21.9	45.3	7-04-99	13.6	49	27189	Dc	vd0.01	v0.47	v0.89	v1.20	....	1.51	9 Mo Sep	v0.98	v1.29	47
48	....	None Since Public			...	Nil	....	....	0.97	0.79	j8-31-99	4.85	...	1521	Nv	v0.58	v0.35	v0.38	v0.16	....	jd0.13	9 Mo Aug	v0.17	vd0.12	48
49◆	1987	Q0.36¼	2-15-00	1-3	1.38¾	1.45	1.28½	5.88	40.7	10.8	9-26-99	197	...	51980	Dc	v1.45	v1.59	v1.47	v1.58	....	1.65	9 Mo Sep	v1.71	v1.78	49
50◆	....	None Since Public			...	Nil	....	7.28	7.93	0.20	6-30-99	....	...	16351	Sp	d0.89	d0.98	vd1.00	vd0.74	....	d0.56	9 Mo Jun	vd0.57	vd0.39	50
51	....	Terms&trad. basis should	be checked in detail					Wrrts expire 2-7-2000				....	...	5175	Sp	...	...	...	....	....	....				51

◆Stock Splits & Divs By Line Reference Index [5]1-for-10 REVERSE,'96. [6]2-for-1,'94,'98. [7]Adj to 5%,'95:6-for-5,'97. [10]2-for-1,'95. [17]2-for-1,'95. [20]2-for-1,'94,'98. [22]3-for-2,'95,'96. [23]3-for-2,'94:5-for-4,'96. [25]To split 3-for-1,hldrs Jan 12,'00. [27]2-for-1,'96. [30]2-for-1,'94,'97. [31]3-for-2,'96:5-for-4,'95,'96. [38]2-for-1,'96,'98. [40]2-for-1,'98. [41]2-for-1,'96,'98. [45]3-for-2,'96:2-for-1,'99. [47]3-for-2,'96,'99. [49]2-for-1,'97. [50]1-for-10 REVERSE,'95.

¶ S&P 500
\# MidCap 400
✣ SmallCap 600
• Options

Index	Ticker	Name of Issue (Call Price of Pfd. Stocks)	Market	Com. Rank. & Pfd. Rating	Inst. Hold Cos	Inst. Hold Shs. (000)	Principal Business	Price Range 1971-97 High	1971-97 Low	1998 High	1998 Low	1999 High	1999 Low	Dec. Sales in 100s	December, 1999 Last Sale Or Bid High	Low	Last	%Div Yield	P-E Ratio	EPS 5 Yr Growth	% Annualized Total Return 12 Mo	36 Mo	60 Mo
1	CZ	Celanese AG	NY	NR	..	...	Mfr industrial chemicals	....	....	....	....	19	14¾	2132	19	15⅛	18⅛	...	..	...	...	...	...
2	CLS	Celestica Inc[51]	NY,To	NR	146	25518	Computer svcs/electr mfr	....	....	13¾	5 3/16	57	12 1/16	144452	57	34⅜	55½	...	..	...	350	...	...
3	CNDS	✔CellNet Data Systems	NNM	NR	49	4158	Own/oper wireless networks	21⅜	6 9/16	14⅜	4⅜	11⅛	1⅛	247713	2	1⅛	1⅛	...	d	37	-77.5	-57.5	...
4•[1]	CLST	✔CellStar Corp	NNM	NR	90	16137	Dstr/sell cellular phones	24 15/16	1 15/16	18 13/16	3	13½	5	164978	11⅞	8¼	9⅞	...	24	22	45.0	18.4	5.7
5	CEMX	✔CEM Corp	NNM	B	22	1360	Mfr microwave test equip	15½	4⅜	13¾	8¾	10 15/16	5½	1507	10 15/16	8 5/16	10¾	...	16	-3	11.7	10.4	-0.5
6	CX	CEMEX S.A. ADS[52]	NY	NR	63	30789	Produce,dstr cement	....	....	....	....	28⅛	19¼	67725	28⅛	24¼	27⅞	...	..	...	...	...	...
7	WS	Wrrt[54]	NY	....	..	...		....	....	....	....	4⅛	2 9/16	15416	4⅛	2 9/16	4⅛B	...	..	...	...	...	...
¶8•[2]	CD	✔Cendant Corp	NY,Ch,Ph	B	669	499535	Member based consumer svcs	34⅜	13/16	41 11/16	6½	26 15/16	13⅝	1556362	26 15/16	16 1/16	26 9/16	...	d	17	37.5	3.1	13.4
9	CYCL	✔Centennial Cellular 'A'	NNM	NR	50	2275	Oper cellular telephone sys	8 1/16	2⅞	13 13/16	5½	119	13 9/16	17190	119	47¾	82⅞	...	d	-12	507	174	71.1
10	CTA	✔Center Trust	NY,Ch	NR	54	5392	Real estate investment trust	18⅞	10⅝	18	9½	13	9 1/16	5673	11	9 1/16	9 11/16	14.9	26	7	-10.3	-8.4	-6.5
11	CNT	✔CenterPoint Prop TrSBI	NY,Ch	NR	139	14451	Real estate investment trust	37 1/16	17½	37	30 9/16	38 9/16	30⅞	10225	36⅜	31 9/16	36⅜	5.5	19	32	13.6	9.2	20.6
12	Pr B	7.50% Cv Redm Pfd([60]50)	NY	BBB–	1	28		....	....	....	....	50⅛	37	425	42	37	40⅞	9.2	..	...	...	...	...
13	CXP	✔Centex Construction Prod	NY,Ph,P	NR	156	6881	Produce/mkt cement & wallboard	32⅝	8⅞	45⅛	29⅛	41 13/16	33	5001	39	33 1/16	39	0.5	8	37	-3.5	30.3	26.6
¶14•[3]	CTX	✔Centex Corp	NY,B,Ch,P	A–	429	54798	Home bldg,constr'n prd,S & L	33	11/16	45¾	26⅜	45¾	22⅜	86601	24¾	22⅜	24 11/16	0.6	6	31	-45.0	10.0	17.4
¶15•[4]	CSR	✔Central & So. West[61]	NY,B,C,Ch,P,Ph	A–	460	142202	Integ elec utility hldg co	34¼	5⅜	30¾	24⅞	28	19¼	124220	20 9/16	19½	20	8.7	10	-2	-21.4	-1.1	4.6
16•[5]	CENT	✔Central Garden & Pet	NNM	NR	103	13361	Dstr lawn,garden,pet,pool prd	32⅛	3¼	40½	10⅞	18½	6¾	30886	10 11/16	7⅜	10⅜	...	12	NM	-27.8	-21.0	20.3
17	ECP	✔Central Newspapers 'A'	NY,Ch,Ph	A–	198	23749	Newspaper publishing	38 7/16	6 15/16	37 7/16	27⅜	45 11/16	29⅞	17563	40¼	36⅝	39⅜	1.3	19	22	11.8	23.1	24.9
✣18•[6]	CPC	✔Central Parking	NY,Ph,P	NR	159	11748	Oper parking facilities	46 13/16	8	53⅜	25 7/16	37¼	14½	91513	22¼	14½	19⅛	0.3	..	-8	-40.9	-4.3	...
✣19	CV	✔Central VT Pub Svc	NY,Ch,Ph	B	61	3466	Electricity in Vt., N.H.	25¾	3½	15 7/16	9 9/16	14 7/16	9 9/16	4070	12¾	10 3/16	10⅝	8.3	10	-18	9.7	2.9	1.7
✣20	CBC	✔Centura Banks	NY,Ch,Ph	A	163	7157	Comm'l bkg, No Carolina	69 1/16	11⅝	76	54¾	74⅛	39 5/16	17996	49⅜	41 11/16	44⅛	2.9	12	11	-39.2	1.7	15.3
21	CNTR	✔Centura Software	NSC	B–	18	4759	Dvlp database softwr prod	35¼	⅞	3	⅞	11	9/16	448672	6⅞	3 10/16	5 7/16	...	d	NM	412	25.5	-13.5
22	CENX	✔Century Aluminum	NNM	NR	42	9724	Produce aluminum pds	20	12⅜	20¾	6	15⅛	4 3/16	15384	15⅛	9¾	15	1.3	28	49	62.4	-2.9	...
23	CBIZ	✔Century Business Svcs	NNM	NR	94	13764	Provides business svcs	20⅞	1¼	25⅜	8⅞	16⅛	8	154742	11½	8	8 7/16	...	14	NM	-41.3	-11.4	...
¶24•[7]	CTL	✔CenturyTel Inc	NY,Ch,Ph,P	A	591	94499	Tel svc in parts of 14 states	22 7/16	7/16	45 3/16	21 9/16	49	35 3/16	92906	48 11/16	44⅝	47⅜	0.4	28	18	5.8	52.2	30.4
✣25•[5]	CEPH	✔Cephalon Inc	NNM	C	151	20621	R&D neurodegenerative diseases	41½	5¾	16⅛	3⅞	37⅛	7¼	142685	37⅛	20⅜	34 9/16	...	d	-1	284	19.0	33.2
26	CERG	Ceres Group	NNM	C	15	575	Life,small group health ins	14⅛	5/16	11⅜	4 13/16	11⅝	5 15/16	4051	7¼	5 15/16	7	...	15	Neg	-32.5	-3.3	-1.3
¶27•[5]	CEN	✔Ceridian Corp	NY,To,B,C,Ch,P,Ph	B–	481	130549	Computer serv/eq: finance co	32 3/16	2⅜	36	21¾	40½	16⅝	146197	22⅞	19½	21 9/16	...	21	26	-38.2	2.1	9.9
✣28•[8]	CERN	✔Cerner Corp	NNM	B	135	15177	Devl,mkts clinical info sys	36	13/16	31⅞	18½	28 9/16	10 1/16	40309	21 13/16	18¼	19 11/16	...	76	-12	-26.4	8.3	-2.2
29	CRPB	✔Cerprobe Corp	NNM	B–	23	1955	Dvp/mfg circuit testing prods	27¼	5/16	22	8⅜	18¼	4 7/16	17332	10 15/16	6¾	7⅜	...	d	Neg	-45.1	-19.9	6.0
30	ENV	✔CET Environmental Svcs	AS,P	NR	2	28	Enviro consult'g/engin'g svc	13⅜	3¾	7¼	½	2⅛	¼	11621	2⅛	¾	2⅛	...	9	-12	70.0	-28.2	...
31	CITZ	✔CFS Bancorp	NNM	NR	36	3939	General banking, Indiana	....	....	12⅜	8	11½	8¾	10964	10	8¾	9 5/16	3.9	..	...	-4.5	...	...
32	GIB	✔CGI Group[66]	NY,To,Ph	NR	32	11341	Computer software & svcs	24⅛	5/16	34⅞	10½	54 9/16	17	12749	54 9/16	25¾	42 13/16	...	47	...	116	156	...
✣33	CHG	✔CH Energy Group[67]	NY,B,Ch,P,Ph	B+	174	6519	Hldg co:elec & gas svcs	43⅞	11	47 1/16	38⅞	45	30 9/16	11829	34¼	30 9/16	33	6.5	11	2	-22.1	7.7	11.3
34	CHRW	✔C.H. Robinson Worldwide	NNM	NR	171	19057	Motor freight transportat'n	26½	18	27	14⅜	42 1/16	24	33403	42 1/16	32⅞	39¾	0.8	33	14	54.7	...	...
35	CTU	✔Chad Therapeutics	AS,P	B–	11	674	Mfr respiratory care devices	20⅞	....	9⅝	1 7/16	3 1/16	½	7346	15/16	⅝	¾	...	d	Neg	-53.8	-62.4	-30.1
36	CCCFF	Chai-Na-Ta Corp	BB,To	NR	1	72	Produce,process,dstr Ginseng	26⅞	1⅜	2 5/16	⅝	1	3/16	1704	5/16	3/16	¼	...	d	Neg	-66.7	-64.6	-49.3
✣37•[9]	CHB	✔Champion Enterprises	NY,B,Ch,P,Ph	B	202	35320	Mfr'd homes/midsize buses	32½	½	30	17½	27⅜	7⅞	42182	9 9/16	7⅞	8½	...	6	12	-68.9	-24.2	3.2
38	CHMP	✔Champion Industries	NNM	NR	9	452	Commercial print'g/office prd	19¾	4⅛	17¼	9¼	10½	3 11/16	4107	4⅞	3 11/16	4 3/16	4.8	13	2	-57.7	-38.0	-19.3
¶39•[8]	CHA	✔Champion Intl	NY,B,C,Ch,P,Ph	B–	460	86892	Building mtls,paper prod	66½	9⅜	58 7/16	25 11/16	64½	33⅜	142529	63 11/16	54 5/16	61 15/16	0.3	28	-27	53.6	13.2	11.6
40	MPH	✔Championship Auto Racing	NY,Ph	NR	80	9314	Car racing/track oper svcs	....	....	29¾	16	35⅝	18¾	6615	24¾	22 1/16	23	...	19	...	-22.4	...	...
41	CHANF	✔Chandler Insurance Ltd	NNM	B–	2	20	Casualty re-insur-truck'g ind	13¼	2⅛	8⅞	5	10	6½	997	8⅝	7 3/16	8⅜	...	d	Neg	12.6	12.5	12.0
42	CHNL	✔Channell Commercial	NNM	NR	26	2668	Dgn thermoplastic enclosures	16½	9	13⅞	5¾	13⅝	6¾	2664	12⅝	9	11 7/16	...	11	...	36.6	-2.6	...
43•[10]	CHRS	✔Charming Shoppes	NNM,Ph	C	131	82431	Women's specialty stores	19½	1/32	5¾	3¼	7⅞	2 13/16	127163	7⅞	6	6⅝	...	27	26	53.6	9.4	0.2
44	CHT	✔Chart House Enterpr	NY,Ch,Ph,P	C	22	3361	Full-svc restaurant chain	15¾	4⅛	9 9/16	4	7 7/16	4	6222	5 9/16	4⅛	4 7/16	...	23	28	-27.6	-3.9	-13.9
45•[6]	CTI	✔Chart Industries	NY	NR	63	6447	Mfr custom-built indl equip	17⅝	1 5/16	23 5/16	5⅛	10¾	3 5/16	22671	4	3 5/16	4	...	d	-23	-46.9	-17.1	21.1
46	CHTR	✔Charter Communic'A'	NNM	NR	..	...	Operate cable TV systems	....	....	....	....	27¾	19	1353682	26⅜	20¼	21⅞	...	d	...	...	...	...
47	CHC	✔Charter Muni Mtg Acceptance	AS	NR	42	1532	Invest tax exempt bonds	13⅜	11	14 9/16	11	13½	11¼	6363	12 11/16	11¼	11¾	9.0	11	...	4.6	...	...
#48•[2]	CF	✔Charter One Finl	NY	A–	403	111803	Savings bank,Ohio	29	1⅜	33¼	16 13/16	30⅝	17½	195583	22 1/16	17½	19⅛	s3.3	9	37	-22.2	8.7	26.3
49	CHRT	✔Chartered Semiconductor ADS[69]	NNM	NR	..	...	Water fabrication svcs	....	....	....	....	73	20	117292	73	43⅞	73	...	d	...	...	...	...
50	CCF	✔Chase Corp	AS,Ph	↓B+	14	478	Protective coatings & tapes	15	½	19	8⅞	13⅝	8¾	935	12⅛	9 13/16	10⅞	2.9	8	35	-14.8	9.4	28.1
51	CSI	✔Chase Industries	NY,Ch,Ph	NR	46	5252	Mfr,dstr brass rod	20 1/16	5¾	21 15/16	10 3/16	11 1/16	7⅜	2733	9 1/16	7⅞	8⅛	...	8	1	-22.2	-14.8	5.0

Uniform Footnote Explanations-See Page 4. Other: [1]ASE,CBOE:Cycle 2. [2]Ph:Cycle 2. [3]CBOE:Cycle 1. [4]P:Cycle 2. [5]CBOE:Cycle 2. [6]Ph:Cycle 3. [7]P:Cycle 1. [8]CBOE:Cycle 3. [9]ASE:Cycle 1. [10]Ph:Cycle 1. [51]Sub vtg shrs. [52]Ea ADS rep 5 ord ptcp ctfs. [53]To be determined. [54]Pur CPO units based on Apprec Value re-spec cond. [55]Based on CPO Value,re-spec cond. [56]Spl $ dstr,excl dstr of $3.111CvNote,'89. [57]Excl pfd subsid shares. [58]Fiscal Jan'97 & prior. [59]Incl current amts. [60]Fr 6-30-2004,or earlier to preserve'REIT'status. [61]Approve Amer Electric mgr,0.6 com. [62]Subsid pfd in $M. [63]12 Mo Sep'95. [64]Stk dstr of Control Data Systems,'92. [65]Special dividend. [66]Sep'98 & prior pricing in Cdn$. [67]Formerly Central Hudson Gas & El. [68]®$1.29,'96. [69]Ea ADS rep 10 ord shrs,S$0.26par.

Common and Convertible Preferred Stocks

Index	Cash Divs. Ea.Yr. Since	Dividends: Latest Payment Period $	Date	Ex. Div.	Total $ So Far 1999	Ind. Rate	Paid 1998	Financial Position Mil-$ Cash& Equiv.	Curr. Assets	Curr. Liab.	Balance Sheet Date	Capitalization Lg Trm Debt Mil-$	Shs. 000 Pfd.	Com.	Earnings $ Per Shr. Years End	1995	1996	1997	1998	1999	Last 12 Mos.	Interim Earnings Period	$ per Shr. 1998	1999	Index
1	....	None Since Public			...	Nil	....	68.0	3266	2810	6-30-99	1184	...	p55915	Dc	...	...	...	vpd0.80	....	....	6 Mo Jun	n/a	vpd5.01	1
2◆	....	None Since Public			...	Nil	....	31.7	983	627	12-31-98	133	...	±149080	Dc	...	...	pvd0.08	vd0.47	....	0.27	9 Mo Sep	vd0.49	v0.25	2
3	....	None Since Public			...	Nil	....	18.3	34.7	21.0	9-30-99	441	...	43408	Dc	pvd13.93	vpd6.08	□vd2.53	vd3.40	....	d3.92	9 Mo Sep	vd2.43	vd2.95	3
4◆	....	None Since Public			...	Nil	....	83.6	566	259	8-31-99	150	...	60047	Nv	0.41	d0.11	v0.89	v0.24	....	0.42	9 Mo Aug	v0.55	v0.73	4
5	....	None Since Public			...	Nil	....	6.20	22.1	5.63	9-30-99	0.17	...	3043	Je	0.85	v0.78	v0.52	v0.70	v0.66	0.69	3 Mo Sep	v0.09	v0.12	5
6	....	Plan annual div				[53]...	....	3578	15445	17888	j3-31-99	32215	...	3669000	Dc	...	...	...	pv1.05	....	....	3 Mo Mar	n/a	vp1.25	6
7	....	Terms&trad. basis should	be checked in detail					Wrrts expire 12-13-2002				....	...	...	Dc	...	...	...	....	....	....	Mand redm[55]			7
8◆	....	[56]0.658	6-6-89	6-7	...	Nil	....	624	3489	2506	9-30-99	6138	[57]...	711025	Dc	0.56	[58]0.41	v0.06	v0.61	Ed0.56↓	1.86	9 Mo Sep	v0.50	v1.75	8
9◆	....	None Since Public			...	Nil	....	87.4	146	105	8-31-99	1475	...	31201	My	d0.64	±d0.38	v±d0.61	vd0.62	v□d1.20	d0.78	6 Mo Nov	vd0.03	v0.39	9
10	1994	Q0.36	1-20-00	12-29	1.44	1.44	1.44	Total Assets $962.63M			9-30-99	681	...	26145	Dc	vd0.20	vd0.17	□vd0.32	vd0.38	....	0.38	9 Mo Sep	v0.33	v□1.09	10
11	1994	Q0.503	2-7-00	1-20	1.90	2.01	1.75	Total Assets $1031.2M			9-30-99	[59]504	4000	20620	Dc	v□0.84	±□v1.22	v±1.41	v±1.50	....	1.95	9 Mo Sep	v±1.03	v□±1.48	11
12	1999	Q0.93¾	12-30-99	12-15	2.146	3.75	....	Cv into 1.1494 com				....	1000	...	Dc	...	...	...	....	....	....				12
13	1996	Q0.05	1-27-00	1-4	0.20	0.20	0.20	69.9	156	69.2	9-30-99	0.40	...	19048	Mr	v1.47	v1.89	v2.56	v3.71	....	4.73	6 Mo Sep	v1.85	v2.87	13
14◆	1973	Q0.04	1-12-00	12-13	0.16	0.16	0.15½	Total Assets $4605.4M			9-30-99	565	...	59267	Mr	0.92	v1.80	v2.36	v3.75	E4.35	4.08	6 Mo Sep	v1.69	v2.02	14
15	1947	Q0.43½	11-30-99	11-3	1.74	1.74	1.74	160	2169	3427	9-30-99	4319	[62]176	212648	Dc	v2.10	v2.07	□v1.55	v2.07	E2.00	1.97	9 Mo Sep	v1.88	v□1.78	15
16	....	None Since Public			...	Nil	....	2.69	589	369	6-26-99	126	...	±24927	Sp	[63]d0.33	±v0.71	v±1.07	±v1.15	±vP0.89	0.89				16
17◆	1949	Q0.13	1-10-00	12-21	0.49	0.52	0.43½	46.8	164	196	9-26-99	185	...	±88681	Dc	v1.01	v1.14	v1.54	v1.78	....	2.12	9 Mo Sep	v1.25	v1.59	17
18◆	1996	Q0.01½	1-14-00	12-29	0.06	0.06	0.06	40.9	128	154	6-30-99	460	...	36722	Sp	0.43	v0.53	v0.77	v0.94	Pv□0.12	0.12				18
19	1944	Q0.22	2-15-00	1-27	0.88	0.88	0.88	66.6	131	71.2	9-30-99	182	271	11467	Dc	v1.53	v1.51	□v1.32	v0.18	....	1.04	12 Mo Sep	v□0.38	v□1.04	19
20	1990	Q0.32	12-15-99	11-26	1.25	1.28	1.14	Total Deposits $6034M			9-30-99	787	...	28070	Dc	v2.45	v2.60	v3.15	v3.60	....	3.55	9 Mo Sep	v2.62	v2.57	20
21	....	None Since Public			...	Nil	....	4.18	22.2	23.7	9-30-99	....	...	p35421	Dc	vd3.62	v0.15	vd0.04	v0.08	....	d0.07	9 Mo Sep	v0.07	vd0.08	21
22	1996	Q0.05	12-31-99	12-21	0.20	0.20	0.20	117	210	81.4	9-30-99	112	...	20203	Dc	pv2.56	v0.79	v0.05	v0.89	....	0.54	9 Mo Sep	v0.78	v□0.43	22
23◆	....	None Since Public			...	Nil	....	65.5	313	85.1	9-30-99	117	...	p91279	Dc	v0.20	v0.18	v0.24	v0.53	....	0.60	9 Mo Sep	v0.39	v0.46	23
24◆	1974	0.04½	12-17-99	12-1	0.09	0.18	0.173	37.2	285	316	9-30-99	2042	324	139679	Dc	v0.87	v0.95	v1.87	v1.63	E1.70	1.64	9 Mo Sep	v1.26	v1.27	24
25	....	None Since Public			...	Nil	....	213	222	17.8	9-30-99	39.2	...	32401	Dc	vd1.63	vd2.19	vd2.36	vd1.95	Ed0.80	d2.07	9 Mo Sep	vd1.45	vd1.57	25
26	....	0.13	12-28-96	12-16	...	Nil	....	Total Assets $713.61M			9-30-99	48.5	...	13686	Dc	v1.07	vd2.29	vd5.01	vd0.49	....	0.46	9 Mo Sep	vd0.44	v0.51	26
27◆	....	h[64]....	8-31-92	9-1	...	Nil	....	97.6	683	486	9-30-99	622	...	144643	Dc	v□0.37	v1.13	v2.96	v1.29	E1.01	1.37	9 Mo Sep	v0.68	v0.76	27
28	....	None Since Public			...	Nil	....	71.9	243	72.1	10-02-99	100	...	33622	Dc	v0.72	v0.25	v0.45	v0.61	....	0.26	9 Mo Sep	v0.46	v□0.11	28
29	....	[65]0.03	5-23-94	4-19	...	Nil	....	15.7	37.7	8.25	9-30-99	3.94	...	7898	Dc	v0.53	vd0.30	v0.27	vd0.06	....	d0.28	9 Mo Sep	vd0.09	vd0.31	29
30	....	None Since Public			...	Nil	....	0.71	16.3	13.6	9-30-99	0.28	...	6284	Dc	v0.49	vd0.74	vd0.06	v0.09	....	0.23	9 Mo Sep	vd0.67	vd0.53	30
31	1998	Q0.09	1-28-00	1-5	0.33	0.36	0.08	Total Deposits $927M			9-30-99	383	...	19547	Dc	...	...	v0.37	v0.14	....	....	9 Mo Sep	n/a	v0.49	31
32	....	None Since Public			...	Nil	....	121	329	265	j9-30-98	5.73	...	133436	Sp	...	0.16	v0.10	v0.30	Pv0.63	j0.63				32
33	1903	Q0.54	2-1-00	1-6	2.16	2.16	2.15	7.18	236	219	9-30-99	347	560	16862	Dc	v2.74	v2.99	v2.97	v2.90	....	2.89	12 Mo Sep	v2.89	v2.89	33
34	1997	Q0.08	1-3-00	12-8	0.28	0.32	0.18	131	436	281	9-30-99	....	...	41175	Dc	0.72	v0.83	v0.67	v1.04	....	1.21	9 Mo Sep	v0.77	v0.94	34
35◆	....	3%Stk	10-15-96	9-27	...	Nil	....	1.80	11.3	1.29	9-30-99	....	...	10019	Mr	v0.42	v0.49	v0.08	vd0.15	....	d0.22	6 Mo Sep	v0.01	vd0.06	35
36◆	....	2½%Stk	5-22-97	5-6	...	Nil	....	1.07	31.5	10.4	j11-30-98	28.2	...	4022	Nv	1.33	[68]1.56	vd2.64	vd1.84	....	jd2.07	6 Mo May	vd0.33	vd0.56	36
37◆	....	0.01¼	7-15-74	6-24	...	Nil	....	25.1	552	527	10-02-99	225	...	47675	Dc	v1.14	v1.09	v1.54	v1.91	....	1.36	9 Mo Sep	v1.45	v0.90	37
38◆	1993	Q0.05	12-27-99	12-2	0.20	0.20	0.20	7.37	42.6	9.48	4-30-99	11.6	...	9714	Oc	0.37	0.40	v0.45	v0.45	Pv0.33	0.33				38
39	1940	Q0.05	10-15-99	9-15	0.20	0.20	0.20	606	1651	1125	9-30-99	2572	...	96199	Dc	v7.67	v1.48	vd5.72	v0.78	E2.25	1.57	9 Mo Sep	v0.85	v□1.64	39
40	....	None Since Public			...	Nil	....	100	109	12.8	9-30-99	0.09	...	15587	Dc	...	p0.45	pv0.45	v1.05	....	1.20	9 Mo Sep	v0.84	v0.99	40
41	....	None Since Public			...	Nil	....	Equity per shr $11.24			12-31-98	9.41	...	6942	Dc	v0.54	v0.14	vd0.16	v0.53	....	d0.03	9 Mo Sep	v0.41	vd0.15	41
42	....	None Since Public			...	Nil	....	1.54	46.6	21.1	9-30-99	29.1	...	9099	Dc	p0.70	pv1.06	pv0.91	v0.88	....	1.01	9 Mo Sep	v0.67	v0.80	42
43	....	0.02¼	7-15-95	6-27	...	Nil	....	55.4	371	231	10-30-99	96.1	...	98637	Ja	d1.35	vd0.07	v0.18	vd0.20	....	0.25	9 Mo Oct	vd0.11	vΔ0.34	43
44	....	None Since Public			...	Nil	....	0.37	6.66	18.3	9-27-99	21.1	...	11775	Dc	vd0.32	vd0.66	vd2.91	v0.05	....	0.19	9 Mo Sep	v0.05	v0.19	44
45◆	1993	Div Postponed 8-25-99			0.10	Nil	0.20	3.01	135	100	9-30-99	6.62	...	23750	Dc	v0.31	v0.66	v0.99	v1.16	....	d1.00	9 Mo Sep	v0.89	v□d1.27	45
46	....	None Since Public			...	Nil	....	135	279	5745	p6-30-99	p7774	...	★±170050	Dc	...	...	...	vpd3.16	Ed2.60	....	6 Mo Jun	n/a	vpd1.57	46
47	1998	Q0.26½	2-14-00	12-29	0.97	1.06	0.92	Total Assets $636M			9-30-99	....	[62]90	20581	Dc	...	p0.77	n/a	v0.98	....	1.06	9 Mo Sep	v0.73	v0.81	47
48◆	1988	Q0.16	11-22-99	11-4	s0.598	0.64	s0.501	Total Deposits $15059.84M			9-30-99	7803	...	p212171	Dc	v0.47	v1.14	v1.05	v□1.54	E2.14	1.78	9 Mo Sep	v1.30	v1.54	48
49	....	None Since Public			...	Nil	....	53.4	190	240	p6-30-99	451	...	★1238848	Dc	...	...	...	vd2.42	....	d2.03	6 Mo Jun	vd0.88	vd0.49	49
50	1993	A0.32	12-3-99	10-27	0.32	0.32	0.28	0.19	17.0	11.3	8-31-99	6.51	...	3906	Au	0.43	v0.61	v0.84	v1.56	v1.30	1.30				50
51◆	....	None Since Public			...	Nil	....	11.2	97.7	45.3	9-30-99	27.2	...	±15235	Dc	±1.11	v±1.37	±v1.54	v±1.01	....	0.98	9 Mo Sep	v±0.93	v±0.90	51

◆Stock Splits & Divs By Line Reference Index [2]2-for-1,'99. [4]3-for-2,'97:2-for-1,'98. [8]3-for-2,'95,'96. [9]3-for-1,'99. [14]2-for-1,'98. [17]2-for-1,'99. [18]3-for-2,'96,'97. [23]2-for-1,'96. [24]3-for-2,'98,'99. [27]2-for-1,'99. [35]3-for-2,'95:Adj to 3%,'96. [36]1-for-4 REVERSE,'96:Adj to 2.5%,'97. [37]2-for-1,'95,'96. [38]5-for-4,'94,'95,'96,'97. [45]3-for-2,'97,'98. [48]2-for-1,'98:Adj for 5%,'99. [51]3-for-2,'98.

¶ S&P 500
# MidCap 400
✣ SmallCap 600
• Options

Index	Ticker	Name of Issue (Call Price of Pfd. Stocks)	Market	Com. Rank. & Pfd. Rating	Inst. Hold Cos	Inst. Hold Shs. (000)	Principal Business	Price Range 1971-97 High	1971-97 Low	1998 High	1998 Low	1999 High	1999 Low	December, 1999 Dec. Sales in 100s	Last Sale Or Bid High	Low	Last	%Div Yield	P-E Ratio	EPS 5 Yr Growth	% Annualized Total Return 12 Mo	36 Mo	60 Mo
¶1•[7]	CMB	✔Chase Manhattan	NY,B,C,Ch,P	B	1725	576777	Commercial bkg,NYC&Texas	63¼	4 13/16	77 9/16	35 9/16	91⅛	65 13/16	652022	83⅜	72 1/16	77 11/16	2.1	14	17	11.6	23.0	37.8
2	CPJ	✔Chateau Communities	NY	NR	123	14076	Real estate investment trust	31 9/16	18	32	25 11/16	31	24 13/16	8661	27	25	25 15/16	7.5	22	1	−5.2	6.8	11.3
3•[2]	CHTT	✔Chattem Inc	NNM	B	109	5770	Consumer prod/spec'lty chem	32	1 3/16	48	12⅞	50¼	16 13/16	18764	23 7/16	16 13/16	19	. . .	10	24	−60.3	28.3	31.3
4	CHS	✔Chaus (Bernard) Inc	NY,B,Ch,Ph	B–	11	1900	Designs women's apparel	251¼	2 1/16	6⅜	1⅝	3 7/16	1⅝	13475	2¾	2 1/16	2 7/16	. . .	6	NM	0.0	−44.9	−44.2
5	CTIX	✔Cheap Tickets	NNM	NR	106	8523	Sell discount airline tickets	. . . .	. . . .	. . . .	. . . .	66⅝	11⅞	174231	20 11/16	11⅞	13 11/16	. . .	53	. . .	. . .	. . .	. . .
6•[3]	CHKP	✔Check Point Software Tech	NNM	NR	196	18832	Security software prod	50½	13¼	47¾	10⅞	223½	23	130582	223½	140⅝	198¾	. . .	88	NM	334	109	. . .
7	CTCQ	Check Technology	NNM	↓C	14	1170	Computerized check print'g	15¼	1½	5½	1½	4 9/16	1½	10506	4 9/16	2⅛	4	. . .	d	Neg	36.9	−19.3	−5.7
#8•[4]	CKFR	✔Checkfree Holdings	NNM	C	191	30912	Electronic commerce mkt serv	31 7/16	9½	31½	5¾	107½	20⅝	210934	107½	64⅝	104½	. . .	. .	NM	347	82.7	. . .
✣9•[5]	CKP	✔Checkpoint Systems	NY,P	B	139	18396	Electronic detection sys	39	1/16	22 3/16	6½	12¾	7	54800	10 9/16	7 9/16	10 9/16	. . .	18	9	−16.8	−25.6	1.2
✣10•[6]	CAKE	✔Cheesecake Factory	NNM	NR	156	14662	Oper casual dining restaurants	22 11/16	8⅞	30⅝	14¼	35½	19	27808	35½	26¾	35	. . .	37	16	18.0	42.6	27.3
11	CCG	✔Chelsea GCA Realty	NY,Ch,Ph	NR	117	10033	Real estate investment trust	42¼	23⅛	40 13/16	30½	39⅜	27⅞	28434	31 5/16	28 11/16	29¾	9.7	7	−3	−6.9	3.3	10.4
12•[7]	CMDX	✔Chemdex Corp	NNM	NR	55	5278	On-line health care svcs	. . . .	. . . .	. . . .	. . . .	143	15	95205	143	60 5/16	111	. . .	d	. . .	. . .	. . .	. . .
✣13	CHE	✔Chemed Corp	NY,Ch,Ph,P	B	129	3875	Plumbing/home hlthcare svcs	44⅝	3	42⅜	25⅛	34 1/16	24⅝	13263	30¼	25⅝	28⅝	7.4	17	−14	−8.3	−1.8	3.0
14	CFA	✔Chemfab Corp	NY	B	41	2814	Hi-performance coat'd fabrics	24¾	1	25¼	16 3/16	21⅝	14⅝	3052	15⅞	14⅝	15⅝	. . .	15	9	−24.5	3.7	14.6
✣15•[8]	CEM	✔ChemFirst Inc	NY,Ch	NR	89	9140	Mfr agricultural,pharma chem	28⅝	20⅜	28⅜	15 9/16	28	18⅛	10053	23⅞	19⅞	21⅞	1.8	20	. . .	12.7	−0.1	. . .
16	DDD	✔Chequemate Intl	AS	NR	2	175	Dvlp software,web sites	7¼	2¼	4	11/16	3 9/16	⅞	57253	3 7/16	1⅝	2⅝	. . .	d	−11	−22.2	−25.1	. . .
17	CHER	✔Cherry Corp	NNM	B	19	2898	Electro-mechanical products	19½	2½	19	9⅜	15¾	9¾	3940	12	10½	10⅝	. . .	9	3	−23.4	−12.3	−5.4
#18•[9]	CSK	✔Chesapeake Corp	NY,Ch,Ph,P	B	168	10402	Kraft paper, board: containers	39	2 13/16	41¾	31¾	38⅝	25¾	18374	34 7/16	27 11/16	30½	2.9	7	7	−15.0	1.5	1.0
19	CHK	✔Chesapeake Energy	NY,Ch,Ph,P	NR	90	22551	Oil & gas developm't/prod'n	35⅛	½	7¾	¾	4⅛	⅝	112425	3 1/16	2⅛	2⅜	. . .	d	Neg	154	−55.5	−6.8
20	Pr	7.0% cm Cv Pfd([57]52.45)	NY	D	19	5590		. . . .	. . . .	25	10	33	9	2257	30¾	25⅞	25½B	. . .	. .	. . .	. . .	. . .	. . .
21	CPK	✔Chesapeake Utilities	NY	B+	32	642	Natural gas dstr Del & Md	21¾	1½	20½	16½	19 13/16	14⅞	1563	19⅝	18	18⅜	5.7	13	−8	6.2	8.7	13.9
¶22•[1]	CHV	✔Chevron Corp	NY,B,C,Ch,P,Ph,Vc	B+	1569	332613	Major integrated int'l oil	89 3/16	5 1/16	90 3/16	67¾	104 15/16	73⅛	276458	92¾	83 15/16	86⅝	3.0	26	−3	7.3	13.3	17.9
23	JNS	✔Chic by H.I.S. Inc	NY,Ch,Ph	NR	22	4851	Design,mfr casual apparel	16	3⅞	9½	2½	4¾	9/16	16904	⅞	9/16	⅝	. . .	d	Neg	−80.4	−49.1	−42.0
24	CBI	✔Chicago Bridge & Iron N.V.	NY,Ph	NR	30	7750	Global engineer'g/const'n	23⅝	14½	17¾	8	15¼	9⅜	5352	14	11⅝	13¾	1.3	9	. . .	14.9	. . .	. . .
25	CVR	✔Chicago Rivet & Mach	AS,Ch	B+	20	164	Mfr rivets, fasteners: mchy	39 15/16	5⅜	49½	21	28⅜	19⅛	279	23 7/16	21⅜	22 15/16	e3.1	8	15	−5.0	20.9	18.9
26	CTZ	✔Chicago Title	NY	NR	147	11010	Title insurance svcs	. . . .	. . . .	51 7/16	35	48 3/16	31¾	10675	46½	43	46¼	3.1	10	. . .	2.2	. . .	. . .
27	CHCS	✔Chico's FAS	NNM	NR	95	5602	Retail private label clothing	19	2 11/16	26	6⅜	44¾	17⅝	18852	44¾	37½	37⅝	. . .	24	40	61.0	107	49.7
28	CFCM	Chief Consol Mining	NSC,P	C	10	224	Mine leasing operations,Utah	15⅜	13/16	5⅝	1 7/16	5⅛	1¾	7345	3	1¾	2 11/16	. . .	d	−3	13.1	−29.4	−12.1
29	CID	✔Chieftain Intl	AS,To,P	B–	77	9355	Oil & gas explor'n/prod'n	28⅛	10	24¾	13 15/16	22¾	9 9/16	19024	17 5/16	14 1/16	17¼	. . .	d	−1	20.0	−12.8	11.2
30	GSSPr	Chieftain Intl Fd $1.8125 Cv Pfd[60]	AS	NR	19	1132	Subsid of Chieftain Intl	35	19¼	32½	22⅜	29⅞	20¼	2217	25 9/16	23⅛	25½	7.1	. .	. . .	. . .	. . .	. . .
31	KIDS	✔Children's Comp Svcs	NNM	B–	35	4655	Educ/treatment/corrections	27	⅜	22½	7	15¾	5	5649	6⅞	5⅜	5⅝	. . .	9	19	−60.2	−24.6	7.8
32	PLCE	✔Children's Place Retail Stores	NNM	NR	141	10844	Children apparel stores	16⅛	4⅜	27¼	4 15/16	53⅞	13⅜	140728	27	13⅜	16 7/16	. . .	14	. . .	−34.6	. . .	. . .
33•[10]	CHINA	✔China.com Corp	NNM	NR	27	5209	Internet access svcs,Asian	. . . .	. . . .	. . . .	. . . .	107⅛	10	451757	107⅛	51⅝	78⅝	. . .	d	. . .	. . .	. . .	. . .
34	CEA	✔China Eastern Airlines ADS[62]	NY,Ch,Ph	NR	7	305	Scheduled airline svc,China	39⅞	15 13/16	16⅝	4	15 7/16	5	3819	13 7/16	11	11¼	. . .	7	NM	80.0	. . .	. . .
35	CHRB	✔China Resource Dvlmt	NSC	NR	. .	. . .	Dstrb rubber in China	687½	15	31¼	3⅛	49	2	9766	15½	5	8⅜	. . .	d	Neg	132	−18.5	. . .
36	ZNH	✔China Southern Airlines'H'ADS[64]	NY	NR	5	1847	Regional airline svc, China	36¾	12	14¾	3 1/16	13 15/16	3⅞	4191	12⅜	10	11 5/16	. . .	d	Neg	148	. . .	. . .
37	CHL	✔China Telecom(Hong Kong)ADS[65]	NY,Ph	NR	70	2296	Cellular telecomum svc, China	38¼	26⅜	42¾	22 1/16	129	32¼	19582	129	96	128⅝	. . .	90	. . .	270	. . .	. . .
38	TIR	China Tire Holdings Ltd	NY	NR	5	1817	Mfr motor vehicle tires	29	4¾	9⅞	4⅛	11⅝	3 9/16	7810	10⅛	5⅞	10 1/16	0.8	. .	Neg	144	2.3	−3.2
39	CYD	China Yuchai Intl	NY,Ch,Ph	NR	7	7413	Mfr diesel engines	13¾	2 7/16	3 3/16	⅜	3 15/16	⅜	17854	2	1 1/16	1 3/16	. . .	59	. . .	111	−37.0	−35.2
✣40•[2]	CQB	✔Chiquita Brands Intl	NY,B,Ch,P,Ph	B–	131	43350	Meat packing,bananas	50¾	13/16	16¼	9 5/16	12 1/16	3⅜	102679	5⅞	3⅜	4¾	4.2	d	−45	−48.7	−26.6	−17.5
41	Pr A	$2.875 cm[67]Cv'A'Pfd(NC)	NY	B	19	2133		59¼	39¼	51¾	33¼	39	15¾	2089	20⅜	15¾	19½	14.7	. .	. . .	. . .	. . .	. . .
42	Pr B	$3.75 cm [68]Cv'B'Pfd(NC)	NY	B–	16	989		66¼	49¾	61¼	40 7/16	46¾	19⅛	1774	24⅞	19⅛	24⅞	15.1	. .	. . .	. . .	. . .	. . .
#43•[3]	CHIR	✔Chiron Corp	NNM,Ch	B–	282	60983	Therapeutic/diagnostic prod	29 13/16	1⅛	26⅝	13¾	44 3/16	18½	416879	44 3/16	32 9/16	42⅜	. . .	70	NM	61.8	31.5	16.2
✣44	CHZ	✔Chittenden Corp	NY	A–	130	11761	General banking, Vermont	36	1½	40	25 7/16	33⅝	26	13455	32¾	29⅜	29⅝	3.0	. .	−19	−4.7	20.2	27.4
45	CHH	✔Choice Hotels Intl	NY	NR	76	26736	Hotel Franchisor/services	20	15 11/16	18½	9⅝	19¾	12	9510	17 3/16	15⅛	17⅛	. . .	18	. . .	25.1	. . .	. . .
✣46	CPS	✔ChoicePoint Inc	NY,Ph	NR	176	20009	Insurance industry svcs	24 1/16	15⅜	32¼	18 11/16	41 15/16	22 11/16	12888	41 15/16	32⅞	41⅜	. . .	31	. . .	29.0	. . .	. . .
#47•[11]	CCN	✔Chris-Craft Indus	NY,B,Ch,P,Ph	B–	185	17671	TV stations,video,chemicals	51 13/16	1/16	58⅝	38⅝	78¼	40⅛	11817	74⅛	68⅜	72⅛	s. . .	91	−2	58.8	27.7	22.7
48	Pr B	$1.40 cm Cv Pfd(40)vtg	NY,P	NR	1	.1	plastic:foam rubber	1730	3⅝	. . . .	. . . .	. . . .	. . . .	. . . .	. . . .	. . . .	2371½B	0.1	. .	. . .	. . .	. . .	. . .
49	CRC	✔Chromcraft Revington	NY,Ph	NR	29	9601	Design,mfr furniture	16 5/16	5	20⅛	13 11/16	17⅞	10⅛	1809	11⅜	10⅛	10½	. . .	7	9	−36.6	−8.8	−0.9
50	HS	✔CHS Electronics	NY,Ph	NR	91	10085	Wholesale computer equip/pd	30¾	4 11/16	24 13/16	4½	19¾	7/16	258515	2	9/16	1⅛	. . .	d	−35	−93.4	−53.7	. . .
¶51•[11]	CB	✔Chubb Corp	NY,B,Ch,P,Ph	A–	753	123013	Property-casualty insurance	78½	2	88 13/16	55⅜	76⅜	44	94239	57	51¼	56 5/16	2.3	17	5	−11.2	3.5	10.0

Uniform Footnote Explanations-See Page 4. Other: [1]ASE:Cycle 3. [2]Ph:Cycle 3. [3]ASE,CBOE,P,Ph:Cycle 1. [4]ASE,CBOE:Cycle 2. [5]P:Cycle 2. [6]ASE,P:Cycle 3. [7]ASE,P,Ph:Cycle 3. [8]P,ASE:Cycle 1. [9]ASE:Cycle 2. [10]ASE,CBOE,Ph:Cycle 2. [11]CBOE:Cycle 1. [51]Fiscal Dec '95 & prior. [52]6 Mo Jun '96. [53]Redemption of Stk Pur Rt. [54]6 Mo Dec'96. [55]Fiscal Jun'96 & prior. [56]12 Mo Dec'97:Jun'97 earned d$2.69. [57]Fr 5-1-2001,cash and/or com. [58]Fiscal Dec'95 & prior. [59]Excl subsid pfd. [60]Cm:Callable$25.6042 to 1-1-00,scale to$25in2001. [61]Fiscal Mar'96 & prior. [62]Ea ADS rep 100 ord'H'shrs RMB 1.00. [63]68.2% owned by Govt of China. [64]Ea ADS rep 50 ord H shs, 1 RMB. [65]Ea ADS rep 20 ord shrs, HK$0.10. [66]75.1% owned by Govt of China. [67]Co opt to 2-15-2001 Cv into com re-spec cond. [68]Co opt fr 9-10-99 to 9-10-2003 Cv into com re-spec cond. [69]Fiscal May'96 & prior. [70]7 Mo Dec'97:Fiscal May'97 earned $0.52. [71]Remption stk purch rt,'99. [72]Redemption stk pur rt,'99.

Splits ◆ Index	Cash Divs. Ea. Yr. Since	Dividends Latest Payment Period $	Date	Ex. Div.	Total $ So Far 1999	Ind. Rate	Paid 1998	Financial Position Mil-$ Cash& Equiv.	Curr. Assets	Curr. Liab.	Balance Sheet Date	Capitalization Lg Trm Debt Mil-$	Shs. 000 Pfd.	Com.	Earnings $ Per Shr. Years End	1995	1996	1997	1998	1999	Last 12 Mos.	Interim Earnings Period	$ per Shr. 1998	1999	Index
1◆	1827	Q0.41	1-31-00	1-4	1.59	1.64	1.39	Total Deposits $219623.00M			9-30-99	19182	★49600	824777	Dc	□v3.04	v2.47	v4.01	v4.24	E5.60	5.61	9 Mo Sep	v2.93	v4.30	1
2	1994	0.48½	1-15-00	12-22	1.91	1.94	1.79½	Total Assets $983.98M			9-30-99	462	...	28387	Dc	v□0.94	v1.08	v0.91	v0.97	....	1.18	9 Mo Sep	v0.72	v0.93	2
3	....	†20.00	6-11-93	6-14	...	Nil	....	10.5	89.0	72.9	8-31-99	364	...	9822	Nv	□1.69	□v0.47	□v0.80	v□1.86	....	1.93	9 Mo Aug	v□1.58	v□1.65	3
4◆	....	None Since Public			...	Nil	....	0.09	66.0	32.9	9-30-99	12.5	...	27116	Je	d14.00	vd3.91	vd2.46	v0.28	v0.40	0.43	3 Mo Sep	v0.13	v0.16	4
5	....	None Since Public			...	Nil	....	162	169	20.6	9-30-99	4.01	...	23869	Dc	vNil	v0.05	vd0.09	v0.03	....	0.26	9 Mo Sep	v0.06	v0.29	5
6◆	....	None Since Public			...	Nil	....	82.7	116	35.5	12-31-98	....	...	34773	Dc	0.14	v0.43	v1.07	v1.81	E2.27	2.09	9 Mo Sep	v1.34	v1.62	6
7	....	None Since Public			...	Nil	....	1.34	18.4	3.35	6-30-99	0.03	...	6161	Sp	0.33	0.35	v0.05	v0.03	Pvd0.26	d0.26				7
8	....	None Since Public			...	Nil	....	15.4	80.7	63.2	9-30-99	3.81	...	★54779	Je	[51]d0.01	□[52]d3.69	vd3.44	vd0.07	Pv0.18	0.13	3 Mo Sep	vd0.03	vd0.08	8
9◆	....	[53]0.00½	4-8-97	3-25	...	Nil	....	83.7	288	93.0	9-26-99	160	...	30163	Dc	v0.42	v0.60	v0.23	v0.53	....	0.57	9 Mo Sep	v0.35	v0.39	9
10◆	....	None Since Public			...	Nil	....	43.4	64.0	32.8	9-28-99	....	...	20094	Dc	v0.52	v0.35	v0.58	v□0.68	....	0.96	9 Mo Sep	v□1.34	v1.62	10
11	1994	Q0.72	12-30-99	12-21	2.88	2.88	2.76	Total Assets $787M			9-30-99	337	1000	15881	Dc	v1.75	v□1.81	□v1.88	v□1.12	E4.10	1.58	9 Mo Sep	v1.02	v1.48	11
12	....	None Since Public			...	Nil	....	126	133	15.0	9-30-99	0.59	...	32788	Dc	...	...	...	vpd0.85	....	d1.96	9 Mo Sep	vpd0.47	vpd1.58	12
13	1971	Q0.53	12-10-99	11-17	2.12	2.12	2.12	20.2	109	86.5	9-30-99	84.8	...	10448	Dc	2.35	v3.26	v3.02	v1.97	....	1.74	9 Mo Sep	v1.65	v1.42	13
14◆	....	None Since Public			...	Nil	....	6.45	58.8	31.3	9-30-99	....	...	7686	Je	v0.66	v0.94	v1.10	v1.33	v1.11	1.08	3 Mo Sep	v0.30	v0.27	14
15	1997	Q0.10	12-27-99	12-7	0.40	0.40	0.40	11.3	165	38.2	9-30-99	29.2	...	18218	Dc	v2.75	v[54]11.95	v1.86	v0.52	....	1.08	9 Mo Sep	v0.31	v0.87	15
16	....	None Paid			...	Nil	....	0.06	4.24	2.36	9-30-99	3.25	...	23867	Mr	vd0.15	vd0.12	vd0.59	vd0.23	....	d0.32	6 Mo Sep	vd0.08	vd0.17	16
17◆	....	0.03	10-5-90	9-17	...	Nil	....	7.24	137	61.5	8-31-99	68.0	...	±10165	Fb	v±0.91	v±1.28	±v1.39	v±1.55	....	1.20	9 Mo Nov	v±1.27	v±0.92	17
18	1933	Q0.22	2-15-00	1-12	0.88	0.88	0.80	36.0	436	296	9-30-99	643	...	17516	Dc	v3.88	v1.27	v□2.18	vΔ1.57	E4.45	3.96	9 Mo Sep	vΔ1.48	vΔ3.87	18
19◆	1997	Div Postponed 9-23-98			...	Nil	0.06	29.9	97.8	88.5	9-30-99	921	...	97249	Dc	0.21	[55]0.40	v[56]d3.52	v□d9.83	....	d4.47	9 Mo Sep	v□d5.34	v0.02	19
20	1998	Div Omitted 12-16-98			...	Nil	0.87½	Cv into 7.1942 com				....	4600	...	Dc	...	...	...	....	....	....	Arrears $3.50 to 11-1-99			20
21	1960	Q0.26	1-5-00	12-8	1.02	1.04	1.24¼	1.51	30.2	41.1	9-30-99	35.1	...	5163	Dc	v1.70	v1.67	v1.24	v1.04	....	1.39	12 Mo Sep	v1.08	v1.39	21
22◆	1912	Q0.65	12-10-99	11-17	2.48	2.60	2.44	1465	7335	9841	9-30-99	4857	...	656266	Dc	v1.43	v3.98	v4.95	v2.04	E3.35	1.60	9 Mo Sep	v2.35	v1.91	22
23	....	None Since Public			...	Nil	....	2.42	119	72.7	8-07-99	43.4	...	9871	Oc	0.10	vd2.62	v□d1.11	vd2.82	....	d1.34	9 Mo Jul	vd2.30	vd0.82	23
24	1997	0.04½	12-30-99	12-16	0.18	0.18	0.18	5.64	208	175	12-31-98	5.00	...	11415	Dc	...	p1.23	v0.43	v1.40	....	1.60	9 Mo Sep	v0.97	v1.17	24
25◆	1932	Q0.18	12-20-99	12-1	†1.07	0.72	†1.12	4.11	18.9	6.05	9-30-99	1.80	...	1151	Dc	v1.91	v1.66	v3.30	v2.90	....	2.95	9 Mo Sep	v2.08	v2.13	25
26	1998	Q0.36	12-15-99	11-29	1.42	1.44	0.68	Total Assets $2017.87M			9-30-99	21.4	...	21881	Dc	...	...	pv2.54	v4.44	....	4.80	9 Mo Sep	v3.24	v3.60	26
27◆	....	None Since Public			...	Nil	....	20.0	40.1	13.4	10-30-99	5.24	...	8529	Ja	[58]0.22	v0.24	v0.34	v1.07	....	1.58	9 Mo Oct	v0.88	v1.39	27
28	....	0.05	12-1-49	11-3	...	Nil	....	0.91	0.91	0.02	9-30-99	....	5	7952	Dc	d0.25	vd0.26	vd0.16	vd0.26	....	d0.31	9 Mo Sep	vd0.10	vd0.15	28
29	....	None Since Public			...	Nil	....	3.16	18.3	13.4	6-30-99	45.0	[59]...	★15849	Dc	vd0.54	v0.37	v0.38	vd0.67	....	d1.23	9 Mo Sep	vd0.27	vd0.83	29
30	1992	Q0.453	12-31-99	12-13	1.359	1.813	1.81¼	Cv into 1.25 Chieftain Intl com,$20				....	2400	...	Dc	...	...	...	....	....	....				30
31◆	....	None Since Public			...	Nil	....	2.96	31.4	12.8	9-30-99	24.1	...	7296	Je	□[61]0.46	v0.15	v□0.86	v0.84	□v0.66	0.64	3 Mo Sep	v0.08	v0.06	31
32	....	None Since Public			...	Nil	....	1.84	77.9	61.1	10-31-99	....	...	25592	Ja	...	pv1.28	p□v0.29	v0.80	....	1.19	9 Mo Oct	v0.42	v0.81	32
33◆	....	None Since Public			...	Nil	....	2.05	5.83	2.08	p12-31-98	....	...	★42214	Dc	...	...	...	vpd0.46	....	d0.46				33
34	....	None Since Public			...	Nil	....	128	461	438	12-31-97	1862	...	[63]±4866950	Dc	p2.53	2.36	v1.71	....	....	1.71				34
35◆	....	None Since Public			...	Nil	....	7.75	31.1	11.0	9-30-99	....	320	593	Dc	19.00	11.50	v3.70	vd10.60	....	d10.79	9 Mo Sep	vd0.82	vd1.01	35
36	....	None Since Public			...	Nil	....	496	747	640	12-31-98	2038	...	±3374000	Dc	0.62	1.98	v2.83	v±d0.97	....	d0.45	6 Mo Jun	v±d0.12	v±0.40	36
37	....	Plan annual div			...	....	....	2270	2782	1927	12-31-98	120	...	[66]11780788	Dc	...	p1.10	pv1.34	v1.43	....	1.43				37
38	1993	Q0.02	12-31-99	12-14	0.08	0.08	0.08	61.6	244	170	12-31-98	7.85	...	±9100	Dc	0.29	v0.20	v0.26	vNil	....	Nil				38
39	....	0.05		4-18	...	Nil	....	20.9	144	79.8	12-31-98	....	...	35340	Dc	0.73	d0.24	n/a	v0.02	....	0.02				39
40	1985	Q0.05	12-7-99	11-17	0.20	0.20	0.20	132	932	473	9-30-99	1195	5259	65866	Dc	v□0.16	v□d0.72	vd0.29	vd0.55	....	d1.48	9 Mo Sep	v1.03	v0.10	40
41	1994	Q0.719	12-7-99	11-17	2.875	2.875	2.875	Cv into 2.6316 com,$19				....	2000	...	Dc	...	...	...	....	....	....				41
42	1996	Q0.93¾	12-7-99	11-17	3.75	3.75	3.75	Cv into 3.3333 com				....	2000	...	Dc	...	...	...	....	....	....				42
43◆	....	None Since Public			...	Nil	....	905	1276	371	9-30-99	351	...	181650	Dc	vd2.15	v0.31	v0.40	v2.90	E0.61	2.68	9 Mo Sep	v0.91	v0.69	43
44◆	1992	Q0.22	11-19-99	11-3	0.86	0.88	0.78	Total Deposits $3595.46M			9-30-99	....	...	28335	Dc	v1.47	v1.72	v1.94	v2.09	....	0.23	9 Mo Sep	1.27	vd0.59	44
45	....	None Since Public			...	Nil	....	8.73	45.1	81.5	6-30-99	277	...	54043	Dc	...	[69]...	pv[70]0.45	vΔ0.81	....	0.98	9 Mo Sep	v0.60	v0.77	45
46◆	....	None Since Public			...	Nil	....	12.6	139	81.9	9-30-99	192	...	29514	Dc	...	p0.71	pv0.96	v1.18	....	1.33	9 Mo Sep	v0.80	v0.95	46
47	....	3%Stk	4-1-99	3-16	3%Stk	Stk	3%Stk	1353	1626	293	9-30-99	39.0	308	±33635	Dc	v0.49	v...	v2.13	v0.67	E0.80	0.36	9 Mo Sep	v0.67	v0.36	47
48	1977	S0.70	9-30-99	9-14	1.40	1.40	1.40	Cv into 32.88039				....	276	...	Dc	...	...	...	....	....	....				48
49◆	....	None Since Public			...	Nil	....	....	92.8	25.8	10-02-99	....	...	10162	Dc	v1.03	v1.19	v1.24	v1.41	....	1.43	9 Mo Sep	v1.03	v1.05	49
50◆	....	None Since Public			...	Nil	....	163	1025	1796	9-30-99	281	...	59557	Dc	v0.37	v0.78	v1.32	v0.82	....	d5.19	9 Mo Sep	v0.61	vd5.40	50
51◆	1902	[71]Q0.32	1-11-00	12-22	[72]1.27¼	1.28	1.22	Total Assets $23710.00M			9-30-99	793	...	p175936	Dc	v3.90	v2.88	v4.39	v4.19	E3.35	3.68	9 Mo Sep	v3.24	v2.73	51

◆Stock Splits & Divs By Line Reference Index [1]2-for-1,'98. [4]1-for-10 REVERSE,'97. [6]To split 2-for-1,hldrs Jan 23,'00. [9]2-for-1,'96. [10]3-for-2,'94,'98. [14]3-for-2,'96. [17]2-for-1 in Cl'A','94. [19]3-for-2,'95,'96:2-for-1,'94,'97. [22]2-for-1,'94. [25]2-for-1,'97. [27]To split 2-for-1,ex Jan 18,'00. [31]1-for-2 REVERSE,'96. [33]2-for-1,'99. [35]1-for-10 REVERSE,'97,'99. [43]4-for-1,'96. [44]5-for-4,'95,'96,'97. [46]2-for-1,'99. [49]2-for-1,'98. [50]1-for-2 REVERSE,'96:3-for-2,'97. [51]2-for-1,'96.

¶ S&P 500
# MidCap 400
✣ SmallCap 600
• Options

Index	Ticker	Name of Issue (Call Price of Pfd. Stocks)	Market	Com. Rank. & Pfd. Rating	Inst. Hold Cos	Inst. Hold Shs. (000)	Principal Business	Price Range 1971-97 High	1971-97 Low	1998 High	1998 Low	1999 High	1999 Low	Dec. Sales in 100s	December, 1999 Last Sale Or Bid High	Low	Last	%Div Yield	P-E Ratio	EPS 5 Yr Growth	% Annualized Total Return 12 Mo	36 Mo	60 Mo
#1	CHD	✔Church & Dwight	NY,Ch,Ph,P	A–	187	22253	Arm&Hammer,sodium bicarb	17⅞	½	18	13¼	30 3/16	16½	23732	29	25 9/16	26 11/16	1.0	24	45	50.4	34.6	26.5
2	CHY	✔Chyron Corp	NY,Ch,Ph,P	NR	23	3503	Electr TV titling,graphic eq	35	3/16	4 15/16	1¼	4¼	⅝	40024	4¼	11/16	1½	...	d	Neg	–20.0	–43.9	0.3
✣3	CBR	✔CIBER Inc	NY	B+	196	19989	Computer info tech sys/svs	29	1 15/16	40⅞	13 5/16	29 13/16	13¾	82128	29 13/16	21½	27½	...	30	50	–1.1	22.6	62.0
4	CDCO	✔CIDCO Inc	NNM	NR	43	3427	Dgn/Dvp network svcs tel equip	42½	11¾	20⅝	1¼	16⅛	2¾	134105	8⅜	3⅞	5 7/16	...	d	Neg	89.1	–32.3	–28.5
5•[1]	CIEN	✔CIENA Corp	NNM	NR	276	70182	Dgn fiberoptic telecom netwrks	63⅝	22¼	92⅜	8⅛	74 9/16	13⅝	1218777	74 9/16	43 1/16	57½	...	d	...	293	...	...
¶6•[2]	CI	✔CIGNA Corp	NY,B,Ch,P,Ph	B+	889	156699	Multi-line insur hldg co	66 15/16	4 15/16	82⅜	56	98⅝	63 7/16	134466	83⅜	73¾	80 9/16	1.5	16	40	5.7	23.2	33.8
¶7•[3]	CINF	✔Cincinnati Financial	NNM	A	340	63931	Insurance holding co	47 3/16	¼	46 15/16	30½	42½	30⅛	68402	33 11/16	30⅛	31 3/16	2.2	21	5	–13.3	18.1	19.9
8	JRL	Cincinnati G&E8.28%Jr SubDebs	NY	BBB+	3	14	Subsid of CINergy Corp	26½	24⅜	26½	25 5/16	26 5/16	21⅜	1013	24⅜	21⅜	21⅞	9.5	..	...	–7.4	3.2	...
¶9•[4]	CIN	✔CINergy Corp	NY,B,C,Ch,P,Ph	B	489	102490	Hldg:elec & natural gas	39⅛	5 15/16	39⅞	30 13/16	34⅞	23 7/16	114565	25 11/16	23 7/16	23 15/16	7.5	9	7	–25.9	–5.3	6.3
#10•[5]	CTAS	✔Cintas Corp	NNM	A+	407	50733	Sales & rental of uniforms	42½	1 7/16	71¼	39	78⅜	39	207414	55	39	53⅛	0.4	40	15	–24.3	22.9	25.4
11	CRCL	✔Circle International Group	NNM	B	98	13104	Int'l ocean/air freight fwdg	34	1 9/16	29⅝	12⅞	26¾	13¾	28824	24 1/16	18¾	22¼	1.2	20	1	10.0	–1.0	8.4
12	CIR	✔CIRCOR International	NY	NR	1	70	Mfr fluid-control devices	....	....	....	....	12 7/16	8 15/16	6244	11 3/16	9⅞	10 5/16	...	14	...	...	...	...
13	KMX	✔Circuit City Strs-CarMax[53]Grp[54]	NY,Ch,Ph	NR	30	15155	Retail used/new cars & trucks	22	8⅝	13½	3⅝	7⅛	1¾	36142	3¼	1 15/16	2 5/16	...	d	...	–57.0	...	...
¶14•[6]	CC	✔Circuit City Strs-CrctCtyGrp	NY,P,Ph	A–	650	161874	Retailer:video eq,appliances	22¾	1/64	27¼	14⅜	53⅞	23 11/16	651696	51 7/16	35 7/16	45 1/16	0.2	29	–7	80.9	44.6	32.8
15	CSYI	✔Circuit Systems	NNM	B–	13	371	Mfr printed circuit boards	9⅛	⅞	5	1⅝	3¾	1	2149	2⅛	1 1/16	1¼	...	d	Neg	–66.7	–30.7	–23.0
#16•[7]	CRUS	✔Cirrus Logic	NNM	C	124	15748	Mkt semiconductor controllers	61⅛	3 15/16	13 3/16	5 9/16	16½	6	146185	15⅝	11 13/16	13 5/16	...	..	Neg	35.7	–4.9	3.5
¶17•[8]	CSCO	✔Cisco Systems	NNM,Ch	B+	2381	1950651	Mfr computer network prod	20 3/16	⅛	48⅞	17 3/16	107 3/16	44 15/16	4215371	107 3/16	89 3/16	107⅛	...	..	28	131	96.6	94.1
18•[9]	CIT	✔CIT Group 'A'	NY,To	NR	279	93719	Commercial, consumer financing	32 13/16	27	37½	18⅜	34 3/16	17 11/16	180362	22⅞	19 7/16	21⅛	1.9	9	...	–32.5	...	...
19	CITC	✔Citadel Communications	NNM	NR	159	23572	Own/oper radio stations	....	....	29⅜	14⅞	65¼	19⅞	25215	65¼	44	64⅞	...	..	...	151	...	...
20	CDL	✔Citadel Holding	AS,B,Ch,P	NR	12	506	Own,manage real estate prop	60¾	2	5⅛	3⅛	5 7/16	2 11/16	4069	3½	2 11/16	3 7/16	...	2	NM	–12.7	...	...
¶21•[10]	C	✔Citigroup Inc	NY,B,Ch,P,Ph	A	2209	2089618	Diversified financial svcs	38¼	1⅞	49	19	58¼	32 11/16	1883472	57 9/16	53	55 11/16	1.0	20	29	70.0	41.9	...
22	CBK	✔Citizens First Finl	AS	NR	6	9	Savings bank,Illinois	20⅝	9½	22⅜	13	16	11 9/16	814	12½	11⅝	12	1.7	16	...	–12.9	–5.6	...
23	CIZ	✔Citizens Holding	AS	NR	..	...	General banking,Mississippi	....	....	....	....	29¼	20	96	21	20	20⅝	...	13	...	...	...	...
24	CIA	✔Citizens Inc'A'	AS,Ch	C	15	969	Life Insurance hldg co	14⅝	3/16	6⅝	4 15/16	7¼	2 9/16	2283	7⅛	5¾	6 15/16	s...	58	–45	32.0	–4.4	–2.1
25	CZN	✔Citizens Util	NY	A	229	94305	Telecommun/pub utility svcs	15 5/16	⅞	11 3/16	6⅞	14 5/16	7¼	110658	14 5/16	12¼	14 3/16	...	46	–24	80.7	16.4	18.2
26	CZNPr	Citiz Util Tr 5%'EPPICS'[57](50)	NY	A–	49	3206	Subsid of Citizens Utilities	52	42	50¼	39⅛	56⅜	38⅝	578	56⅜	52½	56⅜	4.4	..	...	...	...	...
¶27•[7]	CTXS	✔Citrix Systems	NNM	NR	527	78615	Multi-user applicat'n svr sys	28 3/16	2½	48⅞	18 3/16	130	26½	461960	130	93 15/16	123	...	93	...	154	112	...
#28•[4]	CYN	✔City National	NY,Ch,Ph,P	B	251	23289	Comm'l bkg,Beverly Hills,Calif	37½	7/16	41⅝	25¾	41 9/16	29⅝	34709	37⅝	30 5/16	32 15/16	2.0	15	22	–19.4	17.0	27.8
29	CTEL	City Telecom(H.K.)ADS[59]	NNM	NR	..	...	Telecommun svcs Hong Kong	....	....	....	....	23	14 3/16	1482	23	19⅞	20½	...	..	...	...	...	...
#30•[11]	CNW	✔CK Witco	NY,Ch,Ph,P	A–	328	84192	Spec chemicals,ind'l mchy	27⅜	5/16	32 13/16	12⅞	21⅜	7¼	124321	13⅞	9 9/16	13⅜	1.5	10	56	–35.4	–11.1	–2.6
✣31	CKR	✔CKE Restaurants	NY,Ch	B	215	34178	Fast svc restaurant chain	37½	1 5/16	42 1/16	15	30 5/16	5 11/16	70876	6⅜	5 11/16	5⅞	1.4	7	82	–77.9	–28.0	14.6
#32•[4]	CLE	✔Claire's Stores	NY,B,Ch,P	A–	262	27024	Women's specialty retail strs	26⅝	1/32	24⅛	14 5/16	36⅞	14¾	66931	24⅜	19 5/16	22⅜	0.7	13	24	9.9	20.3	34.3
✣33	CLC	✔CLARCOR Inc	NY	A–	170	14701	Mfr filtration/consumer prod	20 13/16	11/16	24 11/16	14¼	21⅜	14¼	9266	19 3/16	16⅞	18	2.6	13	9	–7.8	10.1	8.1
34	CLRN	✔Clarent Corp	NNM	NR	68	4872	Internet protocol systems	....	....	....	....	110¼	15	79654	95¼	57 15/16	77¾	...	..	...	...	...	...
✣35•[4]	CLFY	✔Clarify Inc	NNM	NR	212	20536	Dvp client/server software	59¼	6½	25	6⅜	138 5/16	16⅞	83244	138 5/16	92½	126	...	..	NM	416	37.9	...
36	CLR	✔Clarion Commercial Hldgs'A'	NY	NR	12	456	Real estate investment trust	....	....	20	1⅞	8	4⅜	2130	8	7⅜	7¾	12.1	..	...	106	...	...
37	CLSC	✔Classic Communications'A'	NNM	NR	..	...	Operate cable TV Sys,U.S.	....	....	....	....	39	25	183120	39	25	36 9/16	...	..	...	...	...	...
#38•[12]	CMH	✔Clayton Homes	NY,Ch,Ph,P	A–	233	63532	Produces/finances mfrd hms	15⅝	7/16	18⅛	10⅝	15 7/16	8¼	117281	10 11/16	8⅝	9 3/16	0.7	8	13	–33.1	–4.7	3.6
¶39•[2]	CCU	✔Clear Channel Commun	NY,Ch	B	910	261415	Oper TV/radio stations	39 15/16	5/16	62 5/16	31	91½	52	277835	91½	79¼	89¼	...	..	12	63.8	70.3	69.9
40	CLNTF	✔Clearnet Communic 'A'[63]	NNM,To	NR	74	20561	Wireless communic svc,Canada	20⅞	5	18¾	5¾	34½	8⅛	45169	34½	25½	34⅜	...	d	Neg	323	46.2	34.3
#41•[13]	CNL	✔Cleco Corp	NY,B,Ch,Ph,P	A–	174	10808	Hldg co:electric service in La.	33⅛	6⅜	36⅛	28⅝	35½	28¼	9495	33½	31⅛	32 1/16	5.2	13	4	–1.6	10.9	12.8
#42	CLF	✔Cleveland-Cliffs	NY,Ch,P	B	164	9147	Produce/process iron ore	47⅛	6	57 11/16	36 1/16	43 9/16	26 13/16	18854	31 11/16	27⅜	31⅛	4.8	18	–10	–19.3	–8.6	0.0
43	CCRO	✔ClinTrials Research	NNM	C	30	3021	Clinical research svcs	33 11/16	3 11/16	8½	2⅜	6⅞	3	11191	4¼	3	4⅛	...	d	Neg	4.8	–43.4	–7.6
¶44•[14]	CLX	✔Clorox Co	NY,B,C,Ch,P,Ph	A	808	126697	Household pr: spec foods	40 3/16	11/16	58¾	37 3/16	66 7/16	37½	251799	56	44¼	50⅜	1.6	52	1	–12.4	28.2	30.6
45	LNK	✔Clublink Corp	To	NR	1	473	Own/oper golf courses,Canada	18½	5	16⅛	8⅜	10⅞	6⅝	7261	8 1/16	6⅝	7¾	...	16	NM	–27.2	–6.2	2.1
46•[15]	CMGI	✔CMGI Inc	NNM	B–	309	35575	Invest in,dvlp internet cos	6 5/16	¼	33⅞	3⅜	288	27 1/16	1217268	288	144⅝	276⅞	...	88	NM	943	...	...
47	CMI	✔CMI Corp Cl'A'	NY,B,Ph,P	B–	46	5247	Automated roadbldg eq,dstr	22½	⅝	10	4½	12⅝	6 1/16	6833	8	6 1/16	7 1/16	0.8	16	–21	–10.5	18.1	2.1
#48	CTP	✔CMP Group[66]	NY,B,Ch,Ph,P	B	154	17476	Utility supplies electricity	24½	7⅞	20½	15¼	27⅝	16¼	9601	27⅝	26⅝	27 9/16	3.3	14	NM	52.1	40.8	22.4
¶49•[7]	CMS	✔CMS Energy	NY,B,C,Ch,P,Ph	B	452	78224	Hldg:elec&gas in Michigan	44 1/16	4⅛	50⅛	38¾	48 7/16	30 5/16	91581	34 5/16	30 5/16	31 3/16	4.7	11	1	–33.3	0.7	10.0
50	CMP	CMS Ener 8.75%Adj[68]Cv[69]Tr Sec[70]	NY	....	26	5317	Stock Purchase Units	....	....	....	....	41⅝	33⅛	16061	36⅞	33⅛	33⅞	10.7	..	...	...	...	...
51•[5]	CNA	✔CNA Financial	NY,B,Ch,P,Ph	B–	125	179832	Insurance holding company	44 1/16	¾	53 5/16	34½	45 5/16	33	15461	42⅛	38	38 15/16	...	37	19	–3.3	3.0	12.5

Uniform Footnote Explanations-See Page 4. Other: [1]ASE,CBOE,P:Cycle 1. [2]CBOE:Cycle 1. [3]ASE:Cycle 1. [4]CBOE:Cycle 2. [5]ASE:Cycle 2. [6]P:Cycle 1. [7]CBOE:Cycle 3. [8]CBOE,Ph:Cycle 1. [9]ASE,CBOE:Cycle 1. [10]CBOE,Ph:Cycle 3. [11]P:Cycle 2. [12]CBOE,Ph:Cycle 2. [13]P:Cycle 3. [14]CBOE,P,Ph:Cycle 1. [15]ASE,CBOE,P:Cycle 3. [51]Subsid pfd in $M. [52]To be determined. [53]Co opt Cv into Circuit City Stk-re-spec cond. [54]Co opt Redm for subsid stk re-spec cond. [55]Pfd in $M. [56]Stk dstr of Big 4 Ranch,'97. [57]Equity Providing Preferred Income Cv Sec. [58]Pay in com(Citzn Utl)or cash(Co or hldr option). [59]Not yet public. [60]Approx. [61]7 Mo Dec'98. [62]Special divd. [63]non-vtg. [64]12 Mo Dec'95:Fiscal Apr'95 earn d$0.17. [65]Stk dstr of Lycos Inc. [66]Energy East plan acq,$29.50. [67]Excl subsid pfd. [68]Stock Purchase date 7-1-2002. [69]Call option privilege to 4-1-2000 re-spec cond. [70]Dstr rate can be reset,re-spec cond. [71]Incl $0.052 pur contract div. [72]0.783-1.2121 CMS com & 1 pfd CMS Energy Tr II. [73]Loews Corp holds 84%.

Splits ◆ Index	Cash Divs. Ea. Yr. Since	Dividends: Latest Payment Period $	Date	Ex. Div.	Total $ So Far 1999	Ind. Rate	Paid 1998	Financial Position Mil-$ Cash& Equiv.	Curr. Assets	Curr. Liab.	Balance Sheet Date	Capitalization Lg Trm Debt Mil-$	Shs. 000 Pfd.	Com.	Earnings $ Per Shr. Years End	1995	1996	1997	1998	1999	Last 12 Mos.	Interim Earnings Period	$ per Shr. 1998	1999	Index
1◆	1901	Q0.07	12-1-99	11-5	0.26	0.28	0.24	24.1	185	130	9-30-99	30.0	...	38848	Dc	v0.26	v0.54	v0.62	v0.75	E1.12	1.05	9 Mo Sep	v0.54	v0.84	1
2◆	....	2%Stk	3-1-90	2-1	...	Nil	....	2.82	35.1	13.9	9-30-99	20.2	...	32088	Dc	v0.25	v0.27	vd0.02	vd0.14	....	d0.90	9 Mo Sep	vd0.11	vd0.87	2
3◆	....	None Since Public			...	Nil	....	51.5	214	78.1	9-30-99	....	...	59148	Je	0.14	0.25	vp0.40	vp0.65	v0.95	0.93	3 Mo Sep	v0.20	v0.18	3
4	....	None Since Public			...	Nil	....	48.2	96.3	22.3	9-30-99	....	...	13724	Dc	v1.51	v1.21	v0.90	vd3.66	....	d0.05	9 Mo Sep	vd3.33	v0.28	4
5	....	None Since Public			...	Nil	....	262	533	105	10-31-99	....	...	134605	Oc	...	p0.15	pv1.11	v0.49	vd0.03	d0.03				5
6◆	1867	Q0.30	1-10-00	12-21	1.187	1.20	1.137	Total Assets $92773.00M			9-30-99	1360	...	185952	Dc	v0.96	v4.64	v4.88	v6.05	E5.15↑	8.88	9 Mo Sep	v4.90	v□7.73	6
7◆	1954	Q0.17	1-14-00	12-15	0.663	0.68	0.597	Total Assets $10405.49M			9-30-99	546	...	164113	Dc	v1.33	v1.31	v1.77	v1.41	E1.50	1.50	9 Mo Sep	v1.15	v1.24	7
8	1996	Q0.518	12-31-99	12-28	2.07	2.07	2.07	Co option redm fr 6-30-2000 at $25				★100	...	...	Dc	...	...	...	....	....	....	Mature 6-30-2025			8
9	1853	Q0.45	11-15-99	10-28	1.80	1.80	1.80	57.5	1241	1823	9-30-99	2723	[51]93	158917	Dc	v2.20	v1.99	v□2.28	v1.65	E2.55	2.38	9 Mo Sep	v1.20	v1.93	9
10◆	1984	A0.22	3-3-99	2-3	0.22	0.22	0.18	82.2	630	203	8-31-99	267	...	111091	My	0.67	0.80	v1.05	v1.19	v1.23	1.33	6 Mo Nov	v0.71	v0.81	10
11	1977	S0.135	9-15-99	8-12	0.27	0.27	0.27	52.9	340	233	9-30-99	27.4	...	17309	Dc	v1.16	v1.34	v1.58	v1.07	....	1.11	9 Mo Sep	v0.74	v0.78	11
12	....	Plan qtly div			...	[52]....	....	6.71	184	58.2	6-30-99	p112	...	13368	Je	...	...	...	....	pv0.88	0.74	3 Mo Sep	v0.27	v0.13	12
13	....	None Since Public			...	Nil	....	35.7	466	232	8-31-99	140	...	23960	Fb	pd0.02	d0.01	vd0.35	vd0.24	....	d0.12	6 Mo Aug	vd0.06	v0.06	13
14◆	1979	Q0.018	1-14-00	12-29	0.07	0.07	0.07	206	2195	1147	8-31-99	111	...	203347	Fb	v0.92	v0.70	v0.57	v0.74	E1.57↑	0.61	9 Mo Nov	v0.31	v0.18	14
15	....	None Paid			...	Nil	....	0.30	28.1	52.0	10-31-99	20.4	...	4591	Ap	0.42	v0.58	v0.40	vd0.20	vNil	d0.64	6 Mo Oct	v0.17	vd0.47	15
16◆	....	None Since Public			...	Nil	....	123	345	183	9-25-99	316	...	65576	Mr	vd0.58	vd0.71	v0.52	vd6.77	E0.03	d7.18	6 Mo Sep	vd1.85	vd2.26	16
17◆	....	None Since Public			...	Nil	....	1765	4892	3029	10-30-99	....	...	3421222	Jl	0.17	0.30	v0.34	v0.42	v0.62	0.60	3 Mo Oct	v0.15	v0.13	17
18	1998	Q0.10	11-30-99	11-8	0.40	0.40	0.30	Total Assets $26739.00M			9-30-99	20293	...	p237556	Dc	...	pv1.64	v1.95	v2.08	....	2.30	9 Mo Sep	v1.54	v1.76	18
19	....	None Since Public			...	Nil	....	8.80	86.8	16.0	9-30-99	268	[55]121	31320	Dc	...	...	vpd1.17	vd1.51	....	0.16	9 Mo Sep	vd2.22	vd0.55	19
20	....	h[56]....	12-30-97	12-31	...	Nil	....	Total Assets $34.8M			9-30-99	....	...	6670	Dc	v0.16	v0.80	v0.24	v0.85	....	2.11	9 Mo Sep	v0.12	v1.38	20
21◆	1986	0.14	11-24-99	10-28	0.54	0.56	0.37	Total Deposits $247714.00M			9-30-99	53462	p8140	3371666	Dc	v1.24	v1.61	v1.69	v1.62	E2.75	2.30	9 Mo Sep	v1.43	v□2.11	21
22	1999	0.05	11-29-99	11-10	0.10	0.20	....	Total Deposits $220M			9-30-99	47.2	...	2033	Dc	...	n/a	v0.74	v0.84	....	0.73	9 Mo Sep	v0.58	v0.47	22
23	....	None Since Public			...	Nil	....	Book Value $10.81			6-30-99	10.0	...	3309	Dc	...	...	...	v1.42	....	1.54	6 Mo Jun	v0.75	v0.87	23
24◆	....	....	12-31-99	11-29	7%Stk	Stk	....	Total Assets $252.73M			9-30-99	....	...	±23535	Dc	v±0.15	v±0.10	v±0.15	v±d0.29	....	0.12	9 Mo Sep	v±d0.36	v±0.05	24
25◆	1998	Stk	12-31-98	11-27	...	Nil	....	35.9	291	472	9-30-99	2080	...	261266	Dc	v±0.64	v±0.68	v±0.03	□v±0.23	....	0.31	9 Mo Sep	v□±0.21	v±0.29	25
26	1996	Q0.62½	1-31-00	12-13	2.50	[58]2.50	2.50	Cv into 3.252 Citzn Utl 'A' com $15.375				....	3500	...	Dc	...	...	...	....	....	....				26
27◆	....	None Since Public			...	Nil	....	317	412	116	9-30-99	310	...	89611	Dc	vp0.03	v0.23	v0.47	v0.67	E1.32	1.11	9 Mo Sep	v0.43	v0.87	27
28	1994	Q0.16½	11-22-99	11-8	0.66	0.66	0.56	Total Deposits $5310.74M			9-30-99	303	...	45404	Dc	v1.06	v1.47	v1.68	v2.00	E2.25	2.22	9 Mo Sep	v1.48	v1.70	28
29	2000	[60]0.041	1-21-00	12-21	...	[52]....	....	275	438	274	j5-31-99	12.4	...	★473450	Au	...	...	...	v0.24	Pv0.18	0.18				29
30	1933	Q0.05	11-26-99	11-3	0.10	0.20	0.05	88.4	1293	853	9-30-99	1453	...	p118936	Dc	□v0.84	vd0.31	v□1.22	v□2.42	E1.30	2.27	9 Mo Sep	v□1.34	v□1.19	30
31◆	1988	S0.04	10-28-99	9-30	0.08	0.08	0.073	40.4	134	193	11-01-99	740	...	50501	Ja	0.33	v0.33	v0.97	vΔ1.39	....	0.86	9 Mo Oct	vΔ1.15	vΔ0.62	31
32◆	1984	Q0.04	11-27-99	11-9	0.16	0.16	0.15	118	248	67.0	10-30-99	....	...	±51215	Ja	±0.66	v±0.95	v±1.21	v±1.22	E1.72	1.49	9 Mo Oct	v±0.65	v±0.92	32
33◆	1921	Q0.11½	1-28-00	1-12	0.45¼	0.46	0.44¼	39.3	177	62.5	8-28-99	31.5	...	23980	Nv	0.99	1.12	v1.11	v1.30	....	1.42	9 Mo Aug	v0.89	v1.01	33
34	....	None Since Public			...	Nil	....	57.6	79.9	23.6	9-30-99	0.09	...	★30458	Dc	...	...	...	vpd0.42	....	....	9 Mo Sep	n/a	vd2.17	34
35◆	....	None Since Public			...	Nil	....	68.7	141	70.2	9-30-99	....	...	23713	Dc	v0.09	v0.38	v0.18	v0.32	....	0.62	9 Mo Sep	v0.17	v0.47	35
36	1998	0.20	1-17-00	12-29	0.75	0.94	0.59	Total Assets $99.72M			9-30-99	....	...	±4469	Dc	...	...	n/a	v↕[61]d9.93	....	....	9 Mo Sep	n/a	v1.26	36
37	....	None Since Public			...	Nil	....	Equity per shr Neg			9-30-99	p505	...	★±15990	Dc	...	...	...	vpd6.82	....	....	9 Mo Sep	n/a	vpd4.44	37
38◆	1995	Q0.016	1-19-00	12-27	0.064	0.06	0.064	Total Assets $1411.6M			9-30-99	95.7	...	139938	Je	0.59	v0.71	v0.80	v0.92	vP1.06	1.09	3 Mo Sep	v0.22	v0.25	38
39◆	....	[62]0.128	7-14-89	6-26	...	Nil	....	82.7	930	675	9-30-99	4404	...	338500	Dc	v0.23	v0.26	v0.33	v0.22	E0.68	0.34	9 Mo Sep	v0.19	v0.31	39
40	....	None Since Public			...	Nil	....	355	470	176	j6-30-99	1914	...	±500230	Dc	[64]d0.68	vd2.07	vd7.03	vd10.88	....	jd10.37	9 Mo Sep	v±d8.14	v±d7.63	40
41	1935	Q0.41½	11-15-99	11-2	1.65	1.66	1.61	40.2	228	367	9-30-99	362	[55]29	22509	Dc	2.08	v2.16	v2.18	v2.24	....	2.39	9 Mo Sep	v1.87	v2.02	41
42	1989	Q0.37½	12-1-99	11-17	1.50	1.50	1.65	33.0	223	77.0	9-30-99	70.0	...	11053	Dc	v□5.08	v5.23	v4.80	v5.06	....	1.74	9 Mo Sep	v3.30	vd0.02	42
43◆	....	None Since Public			...	Nil	....	6.75	45.5	29.6	9-30-99	0.34	...	18237	Dc	v0.26	v0.40	vd0.35	vd1.22	....	d0.50	9 Mo Sep	vd0.93	vd0.21	43
44◆	1968	Q0.20	11-15-99	10-27	0.76	0.80	0.68	209	1154	1314	9-30-99	704	...	236403	Je	0.95	1.07	v1.19	v1.41	v1.03	0.97	3 Mo Sep	v0.42	v0.36	44
45	....	None Since Public			...	Nil	....	2.59	67.3	59.2	j7-04-99	56.8	...	p21770	Dc	d0.41	v0.20	v0.40	v0.58	....	j0.49	6 Mo Jun	v0.22	v0.13	45
46◆	....	h[65]....	7-31-97	6-3	...	Nil	....	2481	2626	945	10-31-99	234	410	122971	Jl	0.38	0.19	vd0.29	v0.18	v4.60	3.14	3 Mo Oct	v0.38	vd1.08	46
47	1996	Q0.01½	12-1-99	11-18	0.04½	0.06	0.04	13.0	162	30.7	9-30-99	86.9	...	±21552	Dc	v0.82	v0.25	v0.15	v0.29	....	0.44	9 Mo Sep	v0.26	v0.41	47
48	1943	Q0.22½	1-31-00	1-6	0.90	0.90	0.90	225	379	268	9-30-99	123	629	32443	Dc	v0.86	v1.57	v0.16	v1.63	....	1.99	12 Mo Sep	v1.18	v1.99	48
49	1989	Q0.36½	11-22-99	11-1	1.39	1.46	1.26	234	1961	1991	9-30-99	8036	[67]...	p115801	Dc	v2.26	v2.44	v2.61	vΔ2.22	E2.90↓	2.28	9 Mo Sep	v2.19	v2.25	49
50	1999	0.907	1-1-00	12-13	0.837	[71]3.63	....	Ea unit rep pur contract for com&pfd[72]				....	...	★7250	Dc	...	...	...	....	....	....	Due 7-1-2004			50
51◆	....	0.048	6-3-74	5-6	...	Nil	....	Total Assets $63899.00M			9-30-99	2894	...	[73]184397	Dc	v4.05	v5.17	v5.17	v1.49	E1.05	1.07	9 Mo Sep	v2.29	v□1.87	51

◆Stock Splits & Divs By Line Reference Index [1]2-for-1,'99. [2]1-for-3 REVERSE,'97. [3]2-for-1,'96,'98. [6]3-for-1,'98. [7]3-for-1,'98. [10]2-for-1,'97. [14]2-for-1,'99. [16]2-for-1,'95. [17]3-for-2,'97,'98:2-for-1,'96,'99. [21]4-for-3,'96:3-for-2,'96,'97,'99. [24]Adj for 7%,'99. [25]Adj for 0.75%,'98(four times). [27]3-for-2,'98:2-for-1,'96,'99. [31]3-for-2,'97:10%,'98(twice). [32]3-for-2(twice),'96. [33]3-for-2,'98. [35]2-for-1,'96. [38]5-for-4,'94,'95,'96,'98. [39]5-for-4,'94:2-for-1,'95,'96,'98. [43]3-for-2,'96. [44]2-for-1,'97,'99. [46]3-for-2,'95:2-for-1,'96,'98,'99(twice):To split 2-for-1,ex Jan 12,'00. [51]3-for-1,'98.

¶ S&P 500 · # MidCap 400 · ✣ SmallCap 600 · • Options

Index	Ticker	Name of Issue (Call Price of Pfd. Stocks)	Market	Com. Rank. & Pfd. Rating	Inst. Hold Cos	Inst. Hold Shs. (000)	Principal Business	Price Range 1971-97 High	1971-97 Low	1998 High	1998 Low	1999 High	1999 Low	Dec. Sales in 100s	December, 1999 Last Sale Or Bid High	Low	Last	%Div Yield	P-E Ratio	EPS 5 Yr Growth	% Annualized Total Return 12 Mo	36 Mo	60 Mo
1	SUR	✔CNA Surety	NY,Ph	NR	94	40915	Property casualty insur	16½	12⅞	16¾	12 9/16	16	9¾	15799	13	9 13/16	13	2.5	11	...	−15.5	...	...
2	Pr A	CNB Cap Tr6.0%[51]'SPuRS'([52]25)	NY	BB+	12	724		....	....	28¾	24¾	35⅜	24½	3471	34¾	31	34¾	4.3	..	...	...	...	...
3•[1]	CNET	✔CNET Inc	NNM	NR	188	26023	Internet svc/TV programming	11⅝	2 15/16	18⅝	5⅞	79⅞	12	486164	79⅞	50	56¾	...	70	NM	328	98.8	...
#4•[2]	CNF	✔CNF Transportation	NY,B,Ch,P,Ph	B−	365	40250	Trucking: air freight	50⅞	2⅞	49 15/16	21 9/16	45⅞	28⅜	82715	34½	28½	34½	1.2	12	30	−7.2	...	...
5	Pr T	CNF Trust I$2.50[54]'TECONS'(51.625)	NY	BB+	37	1849	Subsid CNF Transportation	70	51¾	69¾	42⅞	63½	43¾	1580	48	43¾	48	5.2	..	...	...	...	...
6•[3]	CNH	✔CNH Global N.V.	NY,Ph	NR	95	31117	Mfr agricultural equipment	31 11/16	19	28 13/16	9 9/16	18⅞	8⅝	30307	13⅞	11⅜	13 5/16	4.1	11	...	0.8	−11.6	...
7	CNXS	✔CNS Inc	NNM	B−	23	3393	Mfr nasal breathing device	25⅞	11/16	7⅞	3⅜	8 7/16	2¾	22160	5 1/16	4	4⅛	...	d	−26	20.0	−34.0	−1.4
8	CEI	✔Co-Steel Inc[56]	To	B−	2	276	Mfr,mkt steel products	32	10⅛	25	12 5/16	17	10	10859	17	14⅜	17	2.4	d	Neg	37.4	−9.0	−8.2
✣9•[4]	COA	✔Coachmen Indus	NY,Ch,Ph	B	128	12075	Mfr recreational vehicles	30⅜	¼	31½	15 11/16	26⅞	13¼	11127	15⅞	13½	15⅛	1.3	8	15	−41.7	−18.1	16.0
10	CRV	✔Coast Distribution Sys	AS,Ch	C	11	562	Wholesale distr R.V.parts	11	1½	5	2	3⅜	1⅞	1303	2½	1⅞	2½	...	d	Neg	−9.1	−11.6	−20.0
¶11•[5]	CGP	✔Coastal Corp	NY,B,C,Ch,P,Ph	B	738	157939	Refining & marketing of oil	32½	½	38¾	25¼	45¼	29 7/16	165813	36 5/16	31¼	35 7/16	0.7	15	16	1.6	14.0	23.5
12	Pr A	$1.19 cm Cv A Pfd (33)vtg	NY,B	BB+	2	.2	natural gas, oil & gas,	228¾	10¼	275	268¼	275	260	....	....	....	270B	0.4	..	...	...	...	...
13	Pr B	$1.83 cm Cv B Pfd (50)vtg	NY	BB+	2	.4	coal mining, chemicals	235	14½	263 9/16	209 1/16	290	252	....	....	....	285B	0.6	..	...	...	...	...
14	PAR	✔Coastcast Corp	NY,Ch,Ph	NR	32	1906	Mfr metal golf clubheads	33⅞	7½	25	6⅝	16 13/16	6⅞	6285	16 13/16	12⅛	16⅝	...	20	3	90.0	4.7	7.2
15	COBT	✔Cobalt Networks	NNM	NR	..	...	Provide server appliances	....	....	....	....	172	22	83547	170	100¾	108⅜	...	..	...	...	...	...
16	COBR	✔Cobra Electronics	NNM	B−	31	2140	Consumer & ind'l electronics	23½	⅜	8⅝	3½	6⅜	3	12825	6⅜	4	4 15/16	...	2	NM	5.3	13.5	21.4
✣17	COKE	✔Coca-Cola Bott Consol	NNM	B	94	2206	Soft drink distributor	69	1⅞	75¾	56	60	45	3550	51½	45	47⅜	2.1	48	−6	−16.1	0.8	14.9
¶18•[6]	KO	✔Coca-Cola Co	NY,B,C,Ch,P,Ph	A+	1548	1231105	Major soft drink/juice co	72⅝	15/16	88 15/16	53⅝	70⅞	47 5/16	1154450	69	57⅜	58¼	1.1	45	6	−12.1	4.4	19.0
¶19•[7]	CCE	✔Coca-Cola Enterprises	NY,B,P,Ph	B	390	143734	Largest Coca-Cola bottler	36	3½	41 9/16	22⅞	37½	16 13/16	349347	21¼	16 13/16	20⅛	0.8	..	35	−43.3	8.1	27.9
20•[1]	KOF	✔Coca-Cola FEMSA ADS	NY,Ch,P	NR	87	15069	Coca-Cola bottler,mkt,Mexico	19 13/16	4 5/16	20 15/16	10¾	22½	9¾	37885	18⅜	15 5/16	17 9/16	0.6	38	8	33.6	23.5	17.4
✣21•[7]	CDE	✔Coeur d'Alene Mines	NY,Ch,Ph,P	C	79	5046	Mining claims:gold & silver	36	1 1/16	13⅝	4 1/16	6¼	3 1/16	43059	4 1/16	3 1/16	3 7/16	...	d	Neg	−25.7	−39.0	−26.6
22	Pr	Mandatory Adj Redeemable Cv Sec	NY	....[59]	15	1610		22½	11 11/16	15¾	5⅜	8⅛	3⅜	6130	4⅝	3⅜	3⅝	...	..	...	...	...	...
23•[5]	CXIPY	✔Coflexip ADS[61]	NNM	NR	88	8779	Mfr offshore flexible pipe	65½	11⅞	79½	29	50⅞	26⅜	12391	43 5/16	35½	38	1.3	13	NM	19.9	14.1	11.2
✣24•[8]	CGNX	✔Cognex Corp	NNM	B+	226	31833	Mfr machine vision systems	39 15/16	1¼	27 7/16	9	39 1/16	19	75859	39 1/16	29½	39	...	65	−1	95.0	28.2	24.9
25	COGN	✔Cognos Inc	NNM,To	B−	64	16149	Dvlp development tools softwr	39½	1 3/16	30½	14¾	48¾	19⅜	50438	48¾	33⅜	46⅛	...	37	36	84.5	17.9	50.6
26	CGN	✔Cognitronics Corp	AS,Ch	B	20	806	Voice processing equipment	14½	⅛	14	4 11/16	18⅝	4⅞	7152	18	13 13/16	16⅞	...	17	NM	178	93.5	64.2
✣27•[9]	COHR	✔Coherent, Inc	NNM	B	140	17174	Laser sys: optical, medical	29½	13/16	24¾	7½	30 9/16	11½	35573	30 9/16	24 7/16	26¾	...	56	−3	115	8.2	25.6
28	COHT	Cohesant Technologies	NSC	NR	1	23	Dvp spray finishing eqp	4¾	13/16	2⅜	1 1/16	3	1¼	1858	3	2⅛	2½	...	9	11	35.0	28.7	...
29	COHU	✔Cohu Inc	NNM,Ch	A−	99	8637	Electronic devices & TV eq	28⅞	⅛	24 5/16	6	31¾	10 9/16	38763	31¾	22⅞	31	0.6	56	−6	186	40.2	42.2
30	WDRY	✔Coinmach Laundry	NNM	NR	53	8812	Coin-oper laundry eqp/svcs	24¾	13	31½	5½	16⅞	8⅝	5761	12	10⅝	10⅝	...	d	...	−18.3	−16.1	...
31	CLQ	✔Cold Metal Products	AS,Ch	NR	21	2027	Intermediate steel processor	10½	4¼	5 9/16	2	4 5/16	1⅝	390	3⅝	3⅜	3⅛B	6.4	d	Neg	40.9	−19.7	−14.7
32	CWTR	✔Coldwater Creek	NNM	NR	53	2215	Direct mail catalog sales	35	10	41⅝	9 1/16	29¾	9⅞	8988	28¼	19⅞	20½	...	16	...	49.1	...	...
33•[10]	CNJ	✔Cole National	NY,Ph	NR	66	9192	Retail:gift/eyewear prod	48¼	8¼	41	13 3/16	18⅝	3⅞	13771	5½	3⅞	5	...	d	Neg	−70.7	−42.4	−12.2
34	CLN	✔Coleman Co[66]	NY,Ph,P	NR	49	4821	Mfr outdoor recreat'n prod	26	9¾	35 9/16	7 7/16	10⅝	6⅝	5674	9¾	8 15/16	9 9/16	...	22	Neg	2.0	−12.2	−11.8
35	CM	✔Coles Myer Ltd ADR[67]	NY,Ch,P	NR	13	534	Supermkt/dept strs,Australia	42¾	19⅛	42½	27⅜	48	39	289	41	39	40⅜B	3.3	22	−10	0.3	10.5	13.6
¶36•[7]	CL	✔Colgate-Palmolive	NY,B,C,Ch,P,Ph	A−	1175	377619	Household & personal care	39 5/16	1⅜	49 7/16	32½	65	36 9/16	238331	65	53½	65	1.0	44	22	41.7	43.3	35.1
37	CKC	✔Collins & Aikman	NY,Ch	NR	47	5308	Auto prd/interior furnish'g	12⅜	5⅝	9 11/16	4⅞	7⅝	3 15/16	3857	6 7/16	5 1/16	5¾	...	..	14	28.9	1.9	−4.9
38•[11]	CNB	✔Colonial BancGroup	NY,Ch,Ph	B+	148	26063	Commercial bkg,Alabama	17 13/16	1 3/16	18 15/16	10 1/16	15	9⅞	31843	11¾	9⅞	10⅜	3.7	14	6	−10.9	4.2	19.6
39	CLP	✔Colonial Properties Tr	NY,Ch,Ph	NR	128	9546	Real estate investment trust	31⅞	20½	32 3/16	24	28⅞	21¾	21033	25	21¾	23 3/16	10.0	14	6	−5.2	−1.1	8.9
40•[1]	COLT	✔COLT Telecom Group ADS[72]	NNM	NR	82	8147	Telecommunication svcs	11 11/16	4⅜	65½	10½	210⅞	60 1/16	14361	210⅞	145	204	...	d	...	241	249	...
41	COLB	✔Columbia Banking System	NNM	B−	43	1636	Commercial banking, Washington	17 15/16	4 13/16	25⅞	13 11/16	18 5/16	11⅝	9643	17⅛	13⅛	13⅛	s...	13	NM	−21.8	13.2	22.8
¶42•[12]	CG	✔Columbia Energy Group[73]	NY,To,B,C,Ch,P,Ph	B−	528	58654	Utility holding co:nat'l gas	52 7/16	8 9/16	60⅜	47 9/16	66¼	43⅞	80422	63¼	56⅜	63¼	1.4	17	NM	11.2	16.0	33.7
¶43•[13]	COL	✔Columbia/HCA Hlthcare	NY,P	NR	688	419554	Health care facilities/svcs	44⅞	6½	34⅝	17	29 7/16	17¼	469036	29 7/16	27¼	29 5/16	0.3	23	−34	...	...	...
44•[5]	COB	✔Columbia Laboratories	AS,Ph,P	C	62	6256	Dvlp,mkt pharmaceutical prod	20⅛	1⅜	15¾	2¼	9⅝	2¾	33034	8	6⅜	7½	...	d	10	145	−19.7	7.9
45	COLM	✔Columbia Sportswear	NNM	NR	69	9583	Dgn/mtr outdoor apparel	....	....	25 1/16	9⅝	21 11/16	11½	10459	21 11/16	16⅜	21½	...	18	...	27.4	...	...
46	EGY	✔Columbus Energy	AS	B−	14	990	Oil & gas explor, dev, prod'n	8 5/16	2	8 3/16	6¼	6¾	5¼	732	5¾	5½	5¾	...	d	Neg	−13.2	−3.3	3.9
47	CMCO	✔Columbus McKinnon	NNM	NR	84	8095	Dgn/mfr material handling pds	26½	13¼	31	13¾	30	9¾	14218	12⅛	9⅞	10⅛	2.8	7	7	−43.0	−12.3	...
48	CJA	Columbus SoPwr 7.92% Sub Db[75]	NY	....[76]	4	44	Electric utility, Ohio	26¼	23½	26⅞	24 15/16	26⅛	20⅜	827	23¼	20¾	21	9.4	..	...	−11.1	...	...
49	CSJ	Columbus SoPwr 8.375% Sub Db[77]	NY	....[76]	1	.8	Electric utility,Ohio	26⅞	24	26⅜	25⅜	26	22 1/16	558	24 5/16	22 1/16	22 5/16	9.4	..	...	−5.9	4.3	...
50•[2]	COMR	✔Comair Holdings	NNM	A+	287	40598	Passenger/pkge air transp	17 7/16	⅛	23½	13 15/16	29	15 9/16	22707	23 7/16	23¼	23⅜	0.5	15	36	4.3	30.8	47.9
51	CMRO	Comarco Inc	NNM	B+	26	2062	High technology computer sys	24¼	1/16	24	16¾	25	17	3265	23¾	18 7/16	23½	...	34	4	−2.1	8.8	22.9

Uniform Footnote Explanations-See Page 4. Other: [1]CBOE:Cycle 1. [2]CBOE:Cycle 3. [3]ASE,Ph:Cycle 3. [4]ASE:Cycle 3. [5]ASE,CBOE:Cycle 3. [6]ASE,CBOE,P,Ph:Cycle 2. [7]CBOE:Cycle 2. [8]P,Ph:Cycle 2. [9]P:Cycle 2. [10]Ph:Cycle 2. [11]Ph:Cycle 3. [12]ASE:Cycle 2. [13]ASE,CBOE:Cycle 2. [51]Shared Preference Redeem Securities. [52]Fr 6-23-2001. [53]Of CNB Bancshares. [54]Fr 6-1-2000,scale to $50 in 2005. [55]Into CNF Transportation. [56]Sub-vtg shrs. [57]Excl subsid pfd. [58]Coca-Cola Co owns 40%. [59]Rated CCCr by S&P. [60]To be determined. [61]Ea ADS rep 0.5 ord shr FF10. [62]In cash or stk. [63]1996 & prior in $Cdn. [64]6 Mo Mar'96. [65]Redemption of stk purch rts. [66]Sunbeam Corp plan acq,$6.44 in cash&0.57 com. [67]Ea new ADR rep 8 ord shrs A$0.50(old ADR rep 3). [68]Spl div. [69]Fiscal Jan'96 & prior. [70]Fiscal Dec'96. [71]Incl current amts. [72]Ea ADR rep 4 ord shs par,10p. [73]NiSource Inc offer $74 to Feb 11. [74]Stk dstr of LifePoint Hosps&Triad Hosps,'99. [75]Jr Sub Deferrable Int Debs Sr'B'. [76]Rated BBB+ by S&P. [77]Jr Sub Deferrable Int Debs Sr'A'. [78]®$0.85,'97.

Splits ◆ Index	Cash Divs. Ea. Yr. Since	Dividends: Latest Payment Period $	Date	Ex. Div.	Total $ So Far 1999	Ind. Rate	Paid 1998	Financial Position Mil-$: Cash& Equiv.	Curr. Assets	Curr. Liab.	Balance Sheet Date	Capitalization: Lg Trm Debt Mil-$	Shs. 000 Pfd.	Com.	Earnings $ Per Shr. Years End	1995	1996	1997	1998	1999	Last 12 Mos.	Interim Earnings Period	$ per Shr. 1998	1999	Index
1	1998	Q0.08	12-30-99	12-13	0.32	0.32	0.08	Total Assets $844M			9-30-99	102	...	43583	Dc	...	pv0.52	pv0.79	v1.04	....	1.23	9 Mo Sep	v0.74	v0.93	1
2	1998	Q0.37½	12-31-99	12-28	1.50	1.50	0.779	Cv into 0.46051 com[53]				....	6000	...	Dc	...	...	...	....	....	....				2
3◆	....	None Since Public			...	Nil	....	358	393	108	9-30-99	179	...	73476	Dc	vd0.80	vd0.53	vd0.46	v0.03	....	0.81	9 Mo Sep	vd0.02	v0.76	3
4◆	1995	Q0.10	12-15-99	11-10	0.40	0.40	0.40	133	1167	945	9-30-99	559	843	48376	Dc	v1.04	v0.42	v2.19	v2.45	E3.00	3.00	9 Mo Sep	v1.83	v2.38	4
5	1997	Q0.62½	12-1-99	11-26	2.50	2.50	2.50	Cv into 1.25 com, $40[55]				....	2200	...	Dc	...	...	...	....	....	....				5
6	1997	0.55	6-11-99	6-2	0.55	0.55	0.46¾	Equity per shr $10.10			12-31-98	928	...	149000	Dc	p1.79	v1.68	v3.20	Δv2.01	....	1.22	9 Mo Sep	vΔ2.07	v1.28	6
7◆	....	None Paid			...	Nil	....	51.6	70.1	14.0	9-30-99	....	...	14681	Dc	v0.76	v0.78	v0.44	v0.16	....	d0.52	9 Mo Sep	v0.08	vd0.60	7
8	1986	gQ0.10	12-7-99	11-10	g0.40	0.40	g0.40	12.6	393	336	9-30-99	331	...	30576	Dc	3.44	vd0.21	v0.87	vd2.78	....	jd2.59	9 Mo Sep	v0.19	v0.38	8
9◆	1982	Q0.05	12-2-99	11-8	0.20	0.20	0.20	40.4	210	71.6	9-30-99	8.77	...	15722	Dc	v1.17	vΔ1.76	v1.42	v1.92	....	2.03	9 Mo Sep	v1.48	v1.59	9
10	....	None Paid			...	Nil	....	0.80	54.9	9.27	9-30-99	24.5	[57]...	4313	Dc	v0.64	vd0.03	vd1.01	v0.02	....	d0.03	9 Mo Sep	v0.33	v0.28	10
11◆	1977	Q0.06¼	1-1-00	11-26	0.25	0.25	0.22½	56.0	2560	2558	9-30-99	4945	...	±213612	Dc	v±1.20	v□±2.26	±□v1.74	v±2.03	E2.31	2.16	9 Mo Sep	v±1.39	v±1.52	11
12	1968	Q0.29¾	12-15-99	11-26	1.19	1.19	1.19	Cv into 3.6125 com & 0.1 Cl'A'				....	63	...	Dc	...	...	...	....	....	....				12
13	1973	Q0.45¾	12-15-99	11-26	1.83	1.83	1.83	Cv into 3.6125 com & 0.1 Cl'A'				....	84	...	Dc	...	...	...	....	....	....				13
14	....	None Since Public			...	Nil	....	44.7	66.2	8.42	9-30-99	....	...	7875	Dc	v0.36	v1.67	v1.22	v0.87	....	0.84	9 Mo Sep	v0.94	v0.91	14
15	....	None Since Public			...	Nil	....	25.7	32.2	12.4	10-01-99	0.05	p...	★27298	Dc	...	...	...	vpd1.43	....	....	9 Mo Sep	n/a	vpd0.85	15
16	....	3%Stk	6-1-84	5-8	...	Nil	....	0.73	50.0	23.6	9-30-99	....	...	5988	Dc	vd0.18	v0.10	v0.73	v2.20	....	2.15	9 Mo Sep	v0.33	v0.28	16
17	1967	Q0.25	12-3-99	11-17	1.00	1.00	1.00	8.38	159	133	10-03-99	734	...	±8733	Dc	v±□1.67	±v1.73	±v1.79	v±1.75	....	0.98	9 Mo Sep	v1.64	v0.87	17
18◆	1893	Q0.16	12-15-99	11-29	0.64	0.64	0.60	1637	6124	9686	9-30-99	1108	...	2469981	Dc	v1.18	v1.38	v1.64	v1.42	E1.30	1.24	9 Mo Sep	v1.18	v1.00	18
19◆	1986	Q0.04	12-15-99	12-1	0.16	0.16	0.145	94.0	2483	3625	10-01-99	9762	489	[58]425475	Dc	0.21	v0.28	v0.43	v0.35	E0.08	0.95	9 Mo Sep	vd0.43	v0.17	19
20◆	1994	0.112	8-30-99	8-13	0.112	0.11	0.105	19.0	143	242	12-31-98	305	...	±1426000	Dc	0.30	0.43	v0.60	v0.46	....	0.46				20
21	....	0.15	4-19-96	4-3	...	Nil	....	126	200	32.5	9-30-99	240	7078	29181	Dc	v0.07	vd2.93	vd1.12	vd11.73	Ed1.05↑	d8.87	9 Mo Sep	vd3.53	vd0.67	21
22	1996	Q0.372	12-15-99	11-10	1.488	[60]....	1.488	Cv into 0.826 com $25.713				....	6588	...	Dc	...	...	...	....	....	....	Mand Conv 3-15-2000 into 1.111 com			22
23	1997	0.514	6-30-99	6-7	0.514	0.51	[62]0.525	285	772	541	12-31-98	156	...	15821	Dc	d0.61	v0.46	v2.63	v3.22	....	2.86	3 Mo Mar	v0.63	v0.27	23
24◆	....	None Since Public			...	Nil	....	200	248	32.5	10-03-99	....	...	41437	Dc	v0.65	v0.69	v0.91	v0.47	E0.60	0.47	9 Mo Sep	v0.42	v0.42	24
25◆	....	None Paid			...	Nil	....	149	228	97.4	5-31-99	2.50	...	43214	Fb	v[63]0.40	v0.80	v0.71	v1.31	....	1.25	9 Mo Nov	v0.92	v0.86	25
26◆	....	None Paid			...	Nil	....	13.9	27.8	4.50	9-30-99	0.11	...	5829	Dc	v0.25	v0.21	v0.62	v0.78	....	0.98	9 Mo Sep	v0.58	v0.78	26
27◆	....	None Since Public			...	Nil	....	68.9	318	123	9-30-99	74.7	...	24142	Sp	0.88	v1.31	v1.12	v0.79	v0.48	0.48				27
28	....	None Since Public			...	Nil	....	0.12	6.89	3.48	8-31-99	....	...	2337	Nv	0.16	d0.32	vd0.54	v0.26	Pv0.28	0.28				28
29◆	1978	Q0.04½	1-14-00	11-29	0.17½	0.18	0.15	74.2	181	48.2	9-30-99	....	...	19831	Dc	v1.23	v1.25	v1.47	v0.59	....	0.55	9 Mo Sep	v0.70	v0.67	29
30	....	None Since Public			...	Nil	....	Total Assets $891.81M			9-30-99	692	...	±13172	Mr	□p[64]d0.33	v□d1.11	vd1.32	vd0.91	....	d0.95	6 Mo Sep	vd0.51	vd0.55	30
31	1999	0.05	11-15-99	10-27	0.05	0.20	....	2.45	65.1	38.0	9-30-99	36.6	...	6368	Mr	v0.43	v0.47	v0.33	vd1.80	....	d1.35	6 Mo Sep	vd0.09	v0.36	31
32	....	None Since Public			...	Nil	....	2.84	61.6	38.3	8-28-99	....	...	10229	Fb	pv0.77	vp1.41	v1.10	v1.02	....	1.25	9 Mo Nov	v0.55	v0.78	32
33	1999	[65]0.01	12-20-99	12-2	[65]0.01	Nil	....	22.7	230	163	10-30-99	285	...	14859	Ja	v1.31	v□d2.44	v□0.43	v0.94	....	d0.42	9 Mo Oct	v1.64	v0.28	33
34◆	....	None Since Public			...	Nil	....	20.3	556	582	9-30-99	0.04	...	55827	Dc	v□0.75	v□d0.78	vd0.05	v□d0.73	....	0.42	9 Mo Sep	v□d0.06	v1.09	34
35◆	1983	0.638	11-16-99	10-15	1.327	1.33	1.212	281	3427	2746	j7-31-99	1866	...	1156799	Jl	2.20	1.49	2.01	v1.74	v1.82	1.82				35
36◆	1895	Q0.15¾	11-15-99	10-22	0.59	0.63	0.55	273	2431	2361	9-30-99	2187	5721	582581	Dc	v0.26	v0.98	v1.14	v1.31	E1.47	1.42	9 Mo Sep	v0.94	v1.06	36
37	1999	†0.71	5-28-99	5-18	[68]0.81	Nil	....	24.4	529	355	9-25-99	917	...	61914	Dc	[69]2.90	v□[70]2.55	□v2.35	vNil	....	0.02	9 Mo Sep	vNil	v0.02	37
38◆	1982	Q0.09½	11-12-99	10-27	0.38	0.38	0.34	Total Deposits $7601.21M			9-30-99	963	...	111938	Dc	v0.61	v0.63	v0.89	v0.49	....	0.75	9 Mo Sep	v0.53	v0.79	38
39	1994	Q0.58	11-8-99	10-27	2.32	2.32	2.20	Total Assets $1799.57M			9-30-99	[71]955	5000	22712	Dc	v1.29	□v1.60	□v1.66	v□1.47	....	1.62	9 Mo Sep	v1.15	v1.30	39
40◆	....	None Since Public			...	Nil	....	....	...	...		227	20000	★552324	Dc	d0.10	d0.24	Pvd1.91	Pvd0.66	....	d0.89	9 Mo Sep	vd0.48	vd0.71	40
41◆	....	5%Stk	5-26-99	5-10	5%Stk	Stk	....	Total Deposits $1072.91M			9-30-99	41.3	...	10601	Dc	v0.53	v0.59	v0.87	v0.93	....	0.98	9 Mo Sep	v0.69	v0.74	41
42◆	1996	Q0.22½	12-15-99	11-24	0.87½	0.90	0.767	21.6	1158	1657	9-30-99	1951	...	81264	Dc	Δ□d5.71	2.75	v3.27	v3.21	E3.80	2.89	9 Mo Sep	v2.17	v1.85	42
43◆	1993	0.02	3-1-00	1-28	h[74]0.08	0.08	0.08	124	3515	3149	9-30-99	5522	...	±563277	Dc	□v1.58	v2.22	v□d0.38	v0.59	E1.29	0.89	9 Mo Sep	v0.65	v0.95	43
44	....	None Since Public			...	Nil	....	4.23	9.21	3.87	9-30-99	10.0	3	29025	Dc	vd0.04	vd0.47	v0.03	vd0.48	....	d0.18	9 Mo Sep	vd0.30	vNil	44
45	....	None Since Public			...	Nil	....	8.60	299	166	9-30-99	26.7	...	25314	Dc	...	...	pv0.99	v1.36	....	1.22	9 Mo Sep	v1.08	v0.94	45
46◆	....	None Paid			...	Nil	....	1.40	4.27	2.81	8-31-99	5.60	...	3819	Nv	d0.35	v0.49	v0.49	vd0.29	....	d0.07	9 Mo Aug	vd0.23	vd0.01	46
47	1988	Q0.07	1-6-00	12-21	0.28	0.28	0.28	20.1	301	113	10-03-99	430	...	14877	Mr	p1.41	□v1.39	□v1.75	v1.92	....	1.56	6 Mo Sep	v0.85	v0.49	47
48	1997	Q0.49½	12-31-99	12-28	1.98	1.98	1.98	Co option redm fr 3-5-2002 at $25				★40.0	...	...	Dc	...	...	...	....	....	....	Mature 3-31-2027			48
49	1995	Q0.523	12-31-99	12-28	2.094	2.094	2.094	Co option redm fr 9-27-2000 at $25				75.0	...	...	Dc	...	...	...	....	....	....	Mature 9-30-2025			49
50◆	1987	Q0.03	8-12-99	7-29	0.084	0.12	0.107	330	385	143	9-30-99	94.7	...	95526	Mr	v0.60	v0.75	v1.01	v1.33	E1.55	1.45	6 Mo Sep	v0.68	v0.80	50
51	....	0.003	4-1-85	3-19	...	Nil	....	5.87	32.9	10.5	10-31-99	....	...	4285	Ja	v0.75	v[78]0.86	v0.89	v1.13	....	0.70	9 Mo Oct	v0.73	v0.30	51

◆**Stock Splits & Divs By Line Reference Index** [3]2-for-1,'99(twice). [4]No adj for stk dstr Consol Freightways Corp. [7]2-for-1,'95. [9]2-for-1,'96. [11]2-for-1,'98. [18]2-for-1,'96. [19]3-for-1,'97. [20]3-for-1,'98. [24]2-for-1,'95. [25]3-for-1,'96. [26]3-for-2,'99. [27]2-for-1,'98. [29]2-for-1,'95,'99. [34]2-for-1,'96. [35]0.84 new ADR-for-1 old,'93:Adj for 2%,'95. [36]2-for-1,'97,'99. [38]2-for-1,'97,'98. [40]4-for-1,'98. [41]3-for-2,'98:Adj for 5%,'99. [42]3-for-2,'98. [43]3-for-2,'96. [46]5-for-4,'97:10%,'94,'95,'98. [50]3-for-2,'95,'96,'97,'99.

¶ S&P 500
\# MidCap 400
✣ SmallCap 600
• Options

Index	Ticker	Name of Issue (Call Price of Pfd. Stocks)	Market	Com. Rank. & Pfd. Rating	Inst. Hold Cos	Inst. Hold Shs. (000)	Principal Business	Price Range 1971-97 High	1971-97 Low	1998 High	1998 Low	1999 High	1999 Low	Dec. Sales in 100s	December, 1999 Last Sale Or Bid High	Low	Last	%Div Yield	P-E Ratio	EPS 5 Yr Growth	% Annualized Total Return 12 Mo	36 Mo	60 Mo
¶1•[1]	CMCSK	✓Comcast Cl'A'Spl(non-vtg)	NNM	B–	793	518652	CATV,sound communic sys	16½	2 1/16	30⅛	14¾	57 11/16	28⅞	1064065	57 11/16	42⅝	50 9/16	0.1	d	NM	72.9	79.0	45.7
2•[1]	CMCSA	✓ Cl'A'vtg	NNM,Ch	B–	218	12421	music,telecom sys	16 9/16	1/64	29½	14¾	54⅝	28 1/16	60609	54⅝	39 9/16	47⅞	0.1	22	NM	67.3	76.4	44.8
3	CCZ	Comcast Cp 2.0%[51]Exch[52]'ZONES'[53]	NY	....[54]	..	...	Subordinated Debt Sec	....	....	....	....	108⅜	81⅝	16238	108⅜	90 11/16	95B	1.7	..	...	...	...	...
4	CMDL	✓Comdial Corp	NNM	B	40	4945	Mfr of telecomm systems	99⅜	1⅛	14⅝	6½	10¾	5⅜	18602	10¾	7 11/16	9 15/16	...	17	13	12.8	16.7	2.7
#5•[2]	CDO	✓Comdisco, Inc	NY,B,Ch,P	B+	291	72734	Remarket/lease IBM comp eq	17 1/16	1/64	23¼	12 7/16	43	10¾	332970	43	23 3/16	37¼	0.3	..	7	122	53.6	50.5
¶6•[3]	CMA	✓Comerica Inc	NY,P	A	638	91608	Comm'l Bkg,Detroit,Michigan	61⅞	1½	73	46½	70	44	137612	55 11/16	44	46 11/16	3.1	11	14	–29.9	12.8	27.2
7	CFS	✓Comforce Corp	AS	C	16	1321	Employment staffing svcs	123¾	⅝	11½	3½	6¼	1	13452	3	1 5/16	2⅞	...	d	NM	–46.5	–41.3	0.0
8	FIX	✓Comfort Systems USA	NY	NR	104	11911	HVAC installat'n/maint svcs	21 9/16	13	26⅝	14 3/16	18⅝	6 7/16	28251	8 7/16	6½	7⅜	...	6	...	–58.7	...	...
9•[4]	CLT	✓Cominco Ltd	AS,To,B,Mo,Ph,Vc	B–	54	11653	Lead, zinc mines: fertilizer	30	6⅛	19¼	8⅝	21⅞	11 5/16	4188	21⅞	17 7/16	21⅛	◆1.0	77	Neg	87.7	–3.8	4.9
✣10	CBH	✓Commerce Bancorp	NY,Ch,Ph	A	183	9797	Commercial banking, New Jersey	37 11/16	2⅝	50½	31⅝	50	38¾	15457	43⅞	39¾	40 7/16	s2.4	18	14	–13.4	28.9	34.8
11•[5]	CBSH	✓Commerce Bancshares	NNM	A+	153	23549	Commercial bkg,Missouri	42½	1¼	46 13/16	30 13/16	41 9/16	32 3/16	14843	38⅛	32⅜	33⅞	s1.7	13	12	–10.7	14.9	25.8
12	CGI	✓Commerce Group Inc	NY	B+	84	6188	Prop & casualty insur/mtg fin	36	13¼	39⅝	22 11/16	35 1/16	20¾	8904	28⅛	25¼	26⅛	4.3	11	–4	–22.8	5.1	13.0
13	CMRC	✓Commerce One	NNM	NR	70	4339	Electronic commerce solutions	....	....	....	....	331	8 13/16	702710	331	107 3/16	196½	...	d	...	...	...	...
14	CAX	✓Commercial Assets	AS	NR	10	466	Real estate investment trust	7¾	5½	7 1/16	5	6⅛	4⅛	4858	5	4⅛	4⅝	11.2	16	–11	–16.0	–1.1	7.6
✣15•[6]	CFB	✓Commercial Federal	NY,Ch,Ph	B–	260	35497	Svgs bank,Nebraska,Colorado	37½	¾	39	18¾	25 7/16	16 1/16	41692	18½	16 1/16	17 13/16	1.6	10	9	–22.3	–4.6	14.9
16	TEC	✓Commercial Intertech	NY,Ch,P	B+	102	6434	Engineered metal components	30	1⅜	24 9/16	12⅜	16 7/16	10½	4917	12⅞	10⅞	12¾	4.7	11	–3	3.2	...	...
✣17	CMC	✓Commercial Metals	NY,Ch	↑A	146	7463	Metal processor, steel mfg	33⅞	1	36	21 9/16	34 3/16	19 11/16	6470	33 15/16	29⅛	33 15/16	1.5	11	4	24.7	5.9	6.6
18	NNN	✓Commercial Net Lease Rlty	NY,Ph,P	NR	79	11344	Real estate investment trust	18 3/16	7	18 5/16	12½	13 15/16	9 7/16	29437	10¾	9 7/16	9 15/16	12.5	9	1	–16.8	–6.6	4.7
19	CXI	✓Commodore Applied Tech	AS,Ph	NR	10	1224	Dvlp stge:Enviro tech R&D	11⅝	1½	6¾	3/16	1½	3/16	19005	⅞	⅝	13/16	...	27	83	117	–45.4	...
20	WS	Wrrt(Pur1com at$8.40)	AS	....	2	226		5	⅛	2 1/16	1/32	⅝	1/64	7369	¼	1/16	⅛	...	..	...	...	...	...
21	CTCO	✓Commonwealth Tel Enterp	NNM	B–	127	7522	Tel svc in Penna/Cable TV	74 15/16	2 3/16	33½	18 13/16	61⅞	27½	10311	60½	52	52⅞	...	94	Neg	57.8	...	...
✣22•[7]	CTV	✓Commscope Inc[58]	NY	NR	311	42788	Mfr/sale electronic cable	19	10⅜	20¾	8¾	46⅜	15⅞	120967	44 5/16	35¾	40 5/16	...	34	...	140	...	...
23	CSII	✓Communic Sys	NNM	A–	42	3282	Telephone eq:tel sys:CATV	22¾	1⅝	19¼	10½	14¾	8½	4765	14¾	11¼	13	3.1	15	2	14.1	–2.0	3.3
24	CBU	✓Community Bank System	NY	A	60	2628	General banking,Upstate NY	34	3⅜	38¼	24 13/16	33⅝	22⅝	1560	26 3/16	22 11/16	23⅛	4.3	10	5	–18.2	9.7	16.5
25	CTY	✓Community Banks (PA)	AS	A+	15	294	Banking,financial svcs, PA	28¾	6 3/16	27 1/16	20½	25½	19⅝	746	23	21	22⅞	s2.8	14	10	3.2	20.3	18.8
26	SCB	✓Community Bankshares S.C.	AS	NR	2	90	General banking,South Carolina	19½	5⅞	17 7/16	13	14⅞	11¾	269	13	11⅞	13	s1.7	20	7	–6.2	30.3	...
27	CYL	✓Community Capital	AS	NR	4	29	General banking,South Carolina	14⅝	10½	18	9½	11	6⅞	1158	10⅜	8 1/16	8½	...	34	–23	–10.5	...	...
28	INB	✓Community Independent Bank	AS	NR	2	3	General banking, Penn	....	....	16	12	14½	11	18	11¼	11	10⅞B	2.6	15	...	–2.4	...	...
29	GGY	✓Compagnie Genl Geophy ADS[59]	NY	NR	13	1037	Geophysical equip mfr/svcs	31⅝	16	37	10	13½	7⅛	381	10½	9¼	9⅝	...	d	2	–11.5	...	...
30	CBD	✓Companhia Brasileira ADS[60]	NY	NR	60	7952	Food supermarkets, Brazil	25⅝	12	27	8	35¼	9 5/16	27598	35¼	26½	32 5/16	0.8	19	...	112	...	...
31	BRH	✓Comp Cervejaria Brahma Pfd ADS[62]	NY	NR	68	71075	Beef/soft drink prod'n,Brazil	16 3/16	10⅛	15¾	6⅜	14⅝	6¾	48939	14⅝	12¾	14	1.8	5	...	52.2	...	...
32	BRH.C	Com ADS[65]	NY	NR	4	266		16	10⅜	13¾	6⅝	10¼	7½	3	10¼	10	9½B	2.4	9	...	15.0	...	...
33	BVN	✓Comp de Minas Buenaventura ADS	NY,Ph	NR	73	12139	Gold & silver mining, Peru	24¼	12 5/16	17⅛	6⅝	19	11¼	6323	16¾	15½	16 1/16	0.9	..	...	24.8	–0.5	...
34	ELP	✓Comp Paranaense Energia'B'ADS[66]	NY	NR	..	...	Electric utility, Brazil	19 9/16	8⅞	15⅞	2 15/16	9⅜	3 9/16	72975	9⅜	7 9/16	9 5/16	2.8	..	...	36.1	...	...
35•[8]	VNT	✓Compania Anonima Tele 'D'ADS[68]	NY,Ch,Ph	NR	101	35344	Telecomun svc, Venezuela	49⅜	23	42 15/16	10⅛	32	14½	57498	26⅛	21⅛	24⅝	7.1	14	NM	47.6	1.1	...
36	CU	✓Compania Cervecerias Unidas ADS[69]	NY	NR	57	6532	Mfr,bottle,dstr beer in Chile	36¼	12⅜	31⅛	13	32 3/16	13¼	29751	32 3/16	27⅝	32 1/16	1.3	25	1	72.1	29.1	7.7
37•[9]	CTC	✓Compania de Telecom Chile ADS	NY,Ch,Ph,P	NR	145	55021	Telecommunications svc,Chile	38⅛	3	30	12⅛	28⅜	15⅛	51138	19 3/16	17 1/16	18¼	0.8	8	...	–11.3	–6.8	2.3
38	SID	✓Comp Siderurgica Nacional ADS[70]	NY	NR	23	9716	Steel mfr,Brazil	32⅝	25½	32¾	13 7/16	37	8⅜	5676	37	31⅜	36¾	3.4	..	...	79.8	...	...
¶39•[10]	CPQ	✓Compaq Computer	NY,B,Ch,P	B–	1278	686445	Mfr,svc computer systems	39¾	⅛	44¾	22 15/16	51¼	18¼	3790271	29⅛	24 7/16	27 1/16	0.4	90	Neg	–35.4	22.4	28.1
#40	CBSS	✓Compass Bancshares	NNM	A+	222	32474	Commercial bkg,Alabama,TX	31 11/16	¾	36	18¾	30¾	20½	81282	26 3/16	20½	22 5/16	3.6	13	9	–9.0	11.8	22.2
41	CTT	✓Competitive Technologies	AS,B,P	↑B–	10	468	Technology mgmt,education sv	25 5/16	2 3/16	11⅜	2 13/16	8¾	4 13/16	3779	5⅞	5	5¼	...	10	82	12.0	–19.3	–3.4
42•[11]	CBSI	✓Complete Business Solutions	NNM	NR	124	15150	Info technology svcs	22⅛	4 3/16	43¾	14 1/16	34¾	13⅛	86339	27⅝	17¼	25⅛	...	29	...	–25.8	...	...
43	CTK	✓Comptek Research Inc	AS	C	21	797	Electr tactical sys-US Navy	25½	1⅞	10	6⅞	14¾	7½	5052	13⅞	11⅝	13⅞	...	20	NM	58.6	35.6	–4.5
44	CCRT	✓CompuCredit Corp	NNM	NR	37	3807	Credit card services	....	....	....	....	39 1/16	12	9784	39 1/16	27⅜	38½	...	41	...	...	...	...
#45•[12]	CPU	✓CompUSA Inc	NY,P	B–	161	21196	Oper computer superstores	38	1 11/16	35⅜	10 9/16	14 15/16	5	306334	7	5	5 1/16	...	d	Neg	–61.2	–37.5	6.3
¶46•[9]	CA	✓Computer Assoc Intl	NY,B,Ph,P	B+	947	327994	Dsgn systems software products	57½	3/16	61 15/16	26	70⅝	32⅛	430035	70⅝	57 15/16	69 15/16	0.1	45	NM	64.3	28.5	37.8
47•[13]	CHRZ	✓Computer Horizons	NNM	B	132	11958	Data processing svs	46½	1/64	53½	17¼	30	9¼	93478	19½	13½	16 3/16	...	18	33	–39.2	–14.2	32.5
48•[12]	CLCX	✓Computer Learning Ctrs	NNM	NR	43	5602	Provides info tech educ svcs	31 9/16	2 5/16	39⅜	4½	7⅜	1¾	57204	3½	1¾	2⅜	...	d	Neg	–64.0	–36.6	...
49•[14]	CMNT	✓Computer Network Technology	NNM	B–	109	12742	Computer sys info transm'n eq	12¾	1	14¼	3½	30⅝	7⅜	139100	27⅝	18¾	22 15/16	...	66	NM	83.5	66.2	27.5
¶50•[13]	CSC	✓Computer Sciences	NY,B,Ch,P,Ph	B+	792	113429	Provides computer services	43⅞	¼	74⅞	39 15/16	94⅝	52⅜	191495	94⅝	64 15/16	94⅝	...	37	25	47.3	32.1	30.0
✣51	TSK	✓Computer Task Group	NY,Ph	B+	138	11739	Computer svs:mkt systems	49⅜	1/32	45	18½	29½	12 5/16	15286	15¾	13 7/16	14 13/16	0.3	12	37	–45.2	–11.5	27.8

Uniform Footnote Explanations-See Page4. Other: [1]Ph:Cycle 1. [2]P:Cycle 1. [3]Ph:Cycle 2. [4]To:Cycle 3. [5]P:Cycle 2. [6]Ph:Cycle 3. [7]ASE:Cycle 1. [8]ASE,CBOE:Cycle 1. [9]CBOE:Cycle 1. [10]ASE,CBOE,P,Ph:Cycle 1. [11]CBOE,P,Ph:Cycle 1. [12]CBOE:Cycle 2. [13]CBOE:Cycle 3. [14]CBOE,Ph:Cycle 1. [51]Hldrs opt to exch for cash,re-spec cond. [52]Co redm opt anytime,re-spec cond. [53]Zero Opt Nts Exch Sec. [54]Rated BBB-r by S&P. [55]re-spec cond. [56]If com exceeds $18 for 20 of 30 con trad days. [57]Stk dstr of RCN Corp & Cable Mich. [58]Formed from dstr Genl Instrument,'97. [59]Ea ADS rep 0.20 ord shr FF10. [60]Ea ADS rep 1000 Pfd shs,no par. [61]Shs in millions. [62]Ea ADS rep 20 Pfd shs,No Par. [63]Approx. [64]Incl 4610M Pfd shrs. [65]Ea ADS rep 20 com shs,No Par. [66]Ea ADS rep 1000 ord 'B'. [67]Shrs in millions. [68]Ea ADS rep 7 Cl'D' shrs. [69]Each ADS rep 5 ord,no par. [70]Ea ADS rep 100 ord. [71]®$0.93,'96. [72]Stk dstr of University Genetics. [73]Redemption of stk purch rt.

Splits ◆ Index	Cash Divs. Ea.Yr. Since	Dividends: Latest Payment Period $	Date	Ex. Div.	Total $ So Far 1999	Ind. Rate	Paid 1998	Financial Position Mil-$ Cash& Equiv.	Curr. Assets	Curr. Liab.	Balance Sheet Date	Capitalization Lg Trm Debt Mil-$	Shs. 000 Pfd.	Com.	Earnings $ Per Shr. Years End	1995	1996	1997	1998	1999	Last 12 Mos.	Interim Earnings Period	$ per Shr. 1998	1999	Index
1◆	1987	0.012	3-25-99	3-2	0.012	0.05	0.047	6236	7341	4092	9-30-99	6778	562	±751689	Dc	v□d0.08	±d0.11	□vd0.33	v1.21	Ed0.17	2.09	9 Mo Sep	±v0.69	v±□1.57	1
2◆	1977	0.012	3-25-99	3-2	0.012	0.05	0.047	....	...	...		....	...	63218	Dc	v±□d0.08	v±d0.11	□v±d0.33	v□1.21	....	2.14	9 Mo Sep	v±0.69	v□±1.62	2
3	2000	0.358	2-18-00	12-29	...	1.63	....	At mat amt based on Sprint Cp PCS Stk[55]				....	...	7000	Dc	...	...	...	....	....	....	Due 11-15-2029			3
4◆	....	None Since Public			...	Nil	....	2.27	56.2	16.1	10-03-99	26.0	...	8937	Dc	v1.27	v0.21	v0.65	v1.89	....	0.57	9 Mo Sep	v1.71	v0.39	4
5◆	1977	Q0.02½	12-13-99	11-9	0.10	0.10	0.10	Total Assets $7807M			9-30-99	5056	...	153140	Sp	0.58	v0.67	v0.78	v0.93	v0.30	0.30				5
6◆	1936	Q0.36	10-1-99	9-13	1.40	1.44	1.247	Total Deposits $22900.30M			9-30-99	8356	5000	156392	Dc	v2.37	v2.38	v3.19	v3.72	E4.15	4.03	9 Mo Sep	v2.75	v3.06	6
7	....	1.20	7-1-73	6-11	...	Nil	....	4.91	99.7	33.6	9-30-99	177	...	16395	Dc	Δvd4.69	v0.03	vd0.33	v0.05	....	d0.06	9 Mo Sep	v0.02	vd0.09	7
8	....	None Since Public			...	Nil	....	0.68	405	226	6-30-99	220	...	37814	Dc	...	pv0.64	pv0.76	vp1.07	....	1.19	9 Mo Sep	v0.74	v0.86	8
9	1995	gS0.15	12-31-99	12-14	g0.30	0.30	g0.30	64.3	722	317	j6-30-99	724	1342	85409	Dc	1.22	v1.78	vd0.87	vd0.27	....	j0.19	9 Mo Sep	vd0.13	v0.33	9
10◆	1984	sQ0.24½	1-21-00	1-5	s0.87	0.98	s0.916	Total Deposits $5504.73M			9-30-99	23.0	...	28050	Dc	v1.28	v1.30	v1.71	v1.98	....	2.22	9 Mo Sep	v1.44	v1.68	10
11◆	1936	sQ0.143	12-17-99	11-26	s0.571	0.571	s0.526	Total Deposits $9244.60M			9-30-99	26.0	...	62782	Dc	v1.56	1.79	v2.03	v2.30	E2.57	2.50	9 Mo Sep	v1.69	v1.89	11
12	1994	Q0.28	12-17-99	12-1	1.11	1.12	1.07	Net Asset Val $16.05			9-30-99	....	...	34565	Dc	v2.93	v2.04	v2.67	v2.68	....	2.45	9 Mo Sep	v2.07	v1.84	12
13◆	....	None Since Public			...	Nil	....	116	132	28.9	9-30-99	0.44	...	72186	Dc	...	...	...	vpd0.87	....	d0.83	9 Mo Sep	vpd0.67	vpd0.63	13
14	1993	Q0.13	11-16-99	10-29	0.52	0.52	0.39	Total Assets $96M			9-30-99	18.1	...	10368	Dc	v0.63	0.68	v1.32	v0.33	....	0.29	9 Mo Sep	v0.24	v0.20	14
15◆	1995	Q0.07	1-14-00	12-28	0.26	0.28	0.22	Total Deposits $7352.91M			9-30-99	4241	...	58988	Je	0.94	v1.59	□v1.35	v1.62	v1.54	1.73	3 Mo Sep	v0.25	v□0.44	15
16◆	1936	Q0.15	12-15-99	11-29	0.60	0.60	0.58½	21.5	188	117	4-30-99	102	893	14600	Oc	1.82	□v1.23	v1.56	v1.90	Pv1.14	1.14				16
17	1964	Q0.13	1-27-00	1-5	0.52	0.52	0.52	44.7	662	372	11-30-99	266	...	14407	Au	2.52	3.01	v2.54	v2.82	v3.22	3.17	3 Mo Nov	v0.75	v0.70	17
18	1985	Q0.31	11-15-99	10-27	1.24	1.24	1.23	Total Assets $744M			6-30-99	265	...	30407	Dc	v1.09	v1.18	v1.25	v1.10	....	1.13	9 Mo Sep	v0.82	v0.85	18
19	....	None Since Public			...	Nil	....	0.56	4.07	3.84	9-30-99	0.77	...	23702	Dc	pvd0.26	vd0.31	vd0.73	Δvd0.32	....	0.03	9 Mo Sep	vd0.45	vd0.10	19
20	....	Terms&trad. basis should			be checked in detail			Wrrts expire 6-28-2001				....	...	5000	Dc	...	...	...	....	....	....	Callable at 1¢[56]			20
21◆	....	h[57]....	9-30-97	10-1	...	Nil	....	15.1	84.8	83.6	9-30-99	201	...	±22108	Dc	v±1.23	□±v0.45	v±d0.97	v±0.36	....	0.56	9 Mo Sep	v0.54	v0.74	21
22	....	None Since Public			...	Nil	....	6.82	199	86.7	9-30-99	167	...	50803	Dc	...	pv1.06	vp0.70	v0.79	....	1.18	9 Mo Sep	v0.53	v0.92	22
23	1985	Q0.10	1-3-00	12-15	0.40	0.40	0.47	15.4	56.9	24.5	9-30-99	....	...	8549	Dc	v0.99	v0.88	v1.17	v0.87	....	0.87	9 Mo Sep	v0.72	v0.72	23
24◆	1986	Q0.25	1-10-00	12-13	0.94	1.00	0.83	Total Deposits $1372.00M			9-30-99	200	...	7105	Dc	1.70	1.83	v2.02	Δv2.03	....	2.24	9 Mo Sep	vΔ1.52	v1.73	24
25◆	1988	Q0.16	10-1-99	9-14	s0.625	0.64	0.571	Total Deposits $693.03M			9-30-99	161	...	6819	Dc	v1.00	v1.17	v1.23	v1.43	....	1.62	9 Mo Sep	v1.06	v1.25	25
26◆	1997	5%Stk	1-31-00	1-12	0.20	0.22	0.16	Total Deposits $178M			9-30-99	11.4	...	3039	Dc	v0.54	v0.30	v0.45	□v0.54	....	0.65	9 Mo Sep	v0.41	v0.52	26
27◆	....	5%Stk	10-31-98	9-28	...	Nil	5%Stk	Total Deposits $256M			9-30-99	22.1	...	3116	Dc	v0.50	v0.52	v0.27	v0.24	....	0.25	9 Mo Sep	v0.33	v0.34	27
28◆	1998	Q0.07	11-15-99	10-20	0.25	0.28	0.12	Total Deposits $85.9M			9-30-99	5.00	...	698	Dc	...	v0.99	v0.84	v0.78	....	0.72	9 Mo Sep	v0.65	v0.59	28
29	....	None Since Public			...	Nil	....	35.3	361	280	12-31-98	88.3	...	5075	Dc	d1.31	0.25	v1.07	vd1.71	....	d3.60	6 Mo Jun	v0.62	vd1.27	29
30	1996	0.275	7-6-99	4-28	0.275	0.27	0.399	381	927	719	12-31-97	283	[61]★28050	[61]50066	Dc	0.87	v1.41	v1.74	....	....	1.74				30
31	1996	[63]0.163	3-27-00	12-28	0.22¼	0.25	0.262	657	1457	1181	12-31-97	678	...	[64]±7336296	Dc	±0.80	±1.04	±2.80	....	....	2.80				31
32	1997	[63]0.148	3-27-00	12-28	0.202	0.23	0.238	....	...	...		....	...	2713837	Dc	±0.80	±1.04	...	....	....	1.04				32
33	1996	0.06	12-2-99	11-8	0.15	0.15	0.153	365	475	193	j12-31-97	2.45	...	±117423	Dc	0.34	p0.11	n/a	....	....	....				33
34	1997	0.262	5-28-99	5-23	0.262	0.26	0.197	670	1114	687	j12-31-97	744	...	[67]±272918	Dc	...	±0.92	n/a	....	....	....				34
35	1997	1.096	12-3-99	11-22	1.746	1.75	1.556	202	1170	771	12-31-98	598	...	±1000000	Dc	0.62	3.22	v3.69	v1.77	....	1.73	3 Mo Mar	v0.53	v0.49	35
36	1993	0.152	1-18-00	12-31	0.482	0.42	0.424	131	367	121	6-30-99	140	...	p310829	Dc	1.18	0.82	v1.37	v1.33	....	1.29	6 Mo Jun	v0.52	v0.48	36
37◆	1990	0.01	8-20-99	8-4	0.036	0.14	0.339	101	927	903	12-31-98	2067	...	±873995	Dc	±1.25	n/a	v0.35	v1.03	E2.25	1.03				37
38	1997	[63]0.448	1-18-00	1-3	1.767	1.24	3.016	1627	2693	2215	j12-31-97	1843	...	75226361	Dc	...	pd1.59	n/a	....	....	....				38
39◆	1998	Q0.02½	1-20-00	12-29	0.08	0.10	0.07½	3697	14706	12008	9-30-99	....	...	1700000	Dc	v0.60	v[71]0.87	v1.19	vd1.71	E0.30	0.65	9 Mo Sep	vd2.21	v0.15	39
40◆	1939	Q0.20	1-3-00	12-13	0.77½	0.80	0.683	Total Deposits $12744.52M			9-30-99	2151	...	113658	Dc	v1.22	v1.35	v1.56	v1.57	....	1.74	9 Mo Sep	v1.23	v1.40	40
41	....	h[72]....	6-2-86	5-23	...	Nil	....	6.26	6.92	1.39	10-31-99	....	2	6004	Jl	0.34	d0.10	vd0.27	vd0.21	v0.49	0.52	3 Mo Oct	vd0.05	vd0.02	41
42◆	....	None Since Public			...	Nil	....	77.9	213	41.9	9-30-99	....	...	37328	Dc	pv0.08	pv0.20	pv0.35	v0.18	....	0.88	9 Mo Sep	vd0.03	v0.67	42
43	....	0.04	9-3-93	8-9	...	Nil	....	2.36	49.1	31.4	10-01-99	53.8	...	5116	Mr	vd1.90	v0.42	v0.51	v0.65	....	0.69	6 Mo Sep	v0.28	v0.32	43
44	....	None Since Public			...	Nil	....	Total Assets $183M			9-30-99	....	...	40051	Dc	...	...	vpd0.02	pv0.77	....	0.95	9 Mo Sep	v0.59	v0.77	44
45◆	....	None Since Public			...	Nil	....	128	996	846	9-25-99	186	...	92712	Je	0.30	v0.65	v0.99	v0.33	vd0.50	d0.72	3 Mo Sep	v0.09	vd0.13	45
46◆	1990	S0.04	1-10-00	12-20	0.08	0.08	0.08	356	2361	2761	9-30-99	4870	...	539025	Mr	vd0.10	v0.64	v2.06	v1.11	E1.55	1.27	6 Mo Sep	vd0.34	vd0.18	46
47◆	....	5%Stk	4-5-82	3-12	...	Nil	....	7.67	211	67.3	9-30-99	4.33	...	31165	Dc	v0.44	v0.46	v0.84	v1.35	....	0.92	9 Mo Sep	v0.93	v0.50	47
48◆	....	None Since Public			...	Nil	....	3.41	65.4	62.8	10-31-99	....	...	18512	Ja	p0.17	v0.37	v0.56	vd0.02	....	d0.53	9 Mo Oct	v0.25	vd0.26	48
49	....	None Paid			...	Nil	....	22.8	84.6	33.7	9-30-99	1.48	...	23471	Dc	v0.17	v0.06	v□d0.10	v0.21	....	0.35	9 Mo Sep	v0.14	v0.28	49
50◆	1998	[73]0.001	4-13-98	3-26	...	Nil	[73]0.001	262	2555	1740	10-01-99	667	...	p166489	Mr	v0.71	v1.23	v1.64	v2.11	E2.55	2.29	6 Mo Sep	v0.85	v1.03	50
51◆	1976	A0.05	5-28-99	5-6	0.05	0.05	0.05	13.2	109	65.3	9-24-99	38.3	...	20876	Dc	v0.62	v0.63	v1.01	v1.42	....	1.28	9 Mo Sep	v1.01	v0.87	51

◆Stock Splits & Divs By Line Reference Index [1]2-for-1,'99. [2]3-for-2 in Cl'A' spl stk,'94:2-for-1 in Cl'A'spl stk,'99. [4]1-for-3 REVERSE,'95. [5]3-for-2,'95,'97:2-for-1,'98. [6]3-for-2,'98. [10]5-for-4,'98:Adj for 5%,'99. [11]3-for-2,'98:Adj for 5%,'99. [13]3-for-1,'99. [15]3-for-2,'97(twice). [16]No adj for stk dstr Cuno Inc,'96:3-for-2,'94. [21]2-for-3 REVERSE,'97:No adj for stk dstr,'97. [24]2-for-1,'97. [25]6-for-5,'94:10%,'96:3-for-2,'98:Adj for 5%,'99. [26]2-for-1,'97. [27]Adj for 5%,'98. [28]2-for-1,'98. [37]4.25-for-1,'97. [39]3-for-1,'94:5-for-2,'97:2-for-1,'98. [40]3-for-2,'97,'99. [42]2-for-1,'98. [45]2-for-1(twice),'96. [46]3-for-2,'95,'96,'97. [47]3-for-2,'94,'95,'96,'97. [48]3-for-2,'97:2-for-1,'98. [50]2-for-1,'98. [51]2-for-1,'97.

¶ S&P 500
# MidCap 400
✣ SmallCap 600
• Options

Index	Ticker	Name of Issue (Call Price of Pfd. Stocks)	Market	Com. Rank. & Pfd. Rating	Inst. Hold Cos	Inst. Hold Shs. (000)	Principal Business	Price Range 1971-97 High	1971-97 Low	1998 High	1998 Low	1999 High	1999 Low	Dec. Sales in 100s	December, 1999 Last Sale Or Bid High	Low	Last	%Div Yield	P-E Ratio	EPS 5 Yr Growth	% Annualized Total Return 12 Mo	36 Mo	60 Mo
1	LLB	✓Computrac Inc	AS,Ch	C	5	862	Software for legal profess'n	11⅝	7/16	1 3/16	⅜	1¼	½	4487	15/16	½	¾	...	13	−27	−14.3	−29.3	−9.7
2	CFW	✓Computron Software	AS	NR	13	896	Dgn/dvp data mgmt software	21¾	1 5/16	3⅛	11/16	4	⅜	37556	4	⅝	3½	...	d	−27	274	32.6	...
¶3•[1]	CPWR	✓Compuware Corp	NNM,Ch	NR	756	249917	Dvlp systems software prod	19¾	1 15/16	39⅞	15 9/16	40	16⅜	1030212	40	32 5/16	37¼	...	31	57	−4.5	81.9	53.0
4	CIX	✓CompX Intl 'A'	NY	NR	52	4563	Mfr office furniture&sys	...	...	28	14 9/16	26 11/16	12⅛	3849	19⅝	17½	18⅜	2.7	12	...	−30.3	...	...
#5•[2]	CQ	✓Comsat Corp[51]	NY,B,Ch,P,Ph	B	227	21948	Global telecommunications	35¼	5 11/16	42¾	21⅝	37 1/16	15⅜	35680	20	17½	19⅞	1.0	31	−37	−44.4	...	...
6•[1]	CRK	✓Comstock Resources	NY,Ch,Ph	B−	57	7582	Oil/gas explor & devel	24	⅞	13½	2 13/16	5⅞	2 3/16	28369	3 9/16	2⅝	2⅞	...	d	−23	−6.1	−39.5	−2.8
7	CMTL	Comtech Telecommns	NNM	B	16	504	Mfr communic'ns-related eqp	47 1/16	1 1/16	7½	2 13/16	29½	3 13/16	24372	21	14⅛	14¾	...	13	NM	153	100	56.3
8•[3]	CMTO	✓Com21 Inc	NNM	NR	83	6196	Mfr cable modems/communic sys	...	...	25	8⅜	37½	10⅜	239235	30	19	22 7/16	...	..	...	6.8	...	...
¶9•[4]	CMVT	✓Comverse Technology	NNM	B+	576	61541	Dvlp,mkt computer systems	36 9/16	3/16	47 11/16	19 9/16	145	43 5/16	262345	145	113	144¾	...	68	41	206	79.1	78.8
¶10•[5]	CAG	✓ConAgra Inc	NY,B,Ch,P,Ph	A	697	266342	Prepared foods:agri-products	38¾	1/16	33⅝	22 9/16	34⅜	20⅝	315385	24 7/16	20⅝	22 11/16	3.6	34	−1	−25.9	−0.6	10.4
11•[3]	CNCX	✓Concentric Network	NNM	NR	166	23471	Internet network svcs	8	3 15/16	20½	4 7/16	57⅝	15 15/16	258709	33¾	24	30 13/16	...	d	...	85.5	...	...
12	LENS	✓Concord Camera	NNM	B−	24	2148	Mfr,import camera/photo eqp	11¼	1⅜	7 7/16	2⅜	24¼	3½	42206	24¼	14⅞	22¾	...	29	NM	355	135	60.7
✣13	CCRD	✓Concord Communications	NNM	NR	185	13908	Dvp network mgmt software	23⅞	14	57⅜	14 13/16	69¾	29⅝	87341	57¾	38½	44⅜	...	53	...	−21.8	...	...
#14•[6]	CEFT	✓Concord EFS	NNM	B+	445	167331	Computer svcs to retail strs	14½	1/16	29¼	8⅞	33½	16 15/16	321910	29 9/16	23¾	25¾	...	64	35	−8.1	27.5	51.6
✣15	COE	✓Cone Mills	NY,Ph,P	NR	83	7654	Prod apparel fabrics/home prd	19⅝	7	10¼	3 13/16	7 3/16	4⅛	13889	5	4⅛	4½	...	d	Neg	−20.0	−17.0	−17.6
#16•[7]	CIV	✓Conectiv Inc[54]	NY	NR	206	28538	Holding co:electric & gas	...	...	24½	19 11/16	25½	16¼	56650	18⅛	16¼	16 13/16	5.2	d	...	−27.6	...	...
17•[7]	CIV.A	Cl'A'	NY	NR	36	472		...	...	39⅞	29 9/16	43	26½	2738	30 11/16	26½	29⅝	10.8	15	...	−18.3	...	...
18•[4]	CNXT	✓Conexant Systems	NNM	NR	397	93819	Mfr Semiconductor pds	...	...	11	6½	76 3/16	6 13/16	629713	76 3/16	59½	66⅜	...	..	...	694	...	...
19	CGM	✓Congoleum Corp 'A'	NY,Ph	NR	21	2885	Mfr resilient vinyl flooring	15⅝	8	11¼	6	9 7/16	2⅝	10385	4	2⅝	4	...	6	−12	−52.9	−33.9	...
✣20•[8]	CNMD	✓Conmed Corp	NNM	B	163	11357	Mfr disposable medical prod	34¾	1¼	33¼	19¾	35¾	22⅛	28329	29⅜	22⅛	25⅞	...	16	−7	−21.6	8.1	14.3
✣21	CNE	✓Connecticut Energy[56]	NY,Ph	A−	112	4084	Gas utility in south'n Conn	30 7/16	4 9/16	32¼	25 1/16	40 13/16	24¼	5224	40 13/16	38 3/16	38⅞	3.4	24	2	32.9	28.3	20.9
22	CTWS	✓Connecticut Wtr Svc	NNM	A−	34	447	Hldg co,water utility,Conn	22 11/16	5 3/16	28½	20	37	19	1269	37	30	32	3.7	20	3	23.5	24.4	23.0
¶23	COC.B	✓Conoco Inc'B'	NY	NR	384	309417	Oil & gas expl,dev,prod'n	...	...	...	...	29⅜	20¾	457949	27 1/16	20¾	24⅞	3.1	21	...	...	...	...
24•[7]	COC.A	Cl'A'	NY,Ph	NR	..	...		...	...	25¾	19⅜	31¼	19¼	226439	27⅛	20 15/16	24¾	3.1	d	...	22.6	...	...
¶25•[5]	CNC	✓Conseco Inc	NY,Ch,Ph,P	B+	659	237979	Hldg co:life insurance	50 1/16	7/16	58⅛	21 15/16	37⅞	16 9/16	599668	21⅛	16 9/16	17 13/16	3.4	6	12	−40.4	−16.5	11.6
26	CDV	✓Consol Delivery & Logistics	AS	NR	18	450	Ground/air delivery	13½	1⅝	5 11/16	2⅜	4⅞	2¾	4179	4⅛	3½	3⅝	...	9	NM	14.9	−7.0	...
27	CNX	✓CONSOL Energy	NY	NR	52	16223	Coal mining, U.S.	...	...	...	...	16	9⅝	38515	12 13/16	9⅝	10	11.2	..	...	...	...	...
¶28•[8]	ED	✓Consolidated Edison	NY,B,C,Ch,P,Ph	A	561	89060	Utility:el,gas,steam-NYC	41½	1½	56⅛	39 1/16	53 7/16	33 9/16	139684	35 7/16	33 9/16	34½	6.2	11	1	−31.4	11.5	12.5
29	EDL	Consolidated Ed 7.75%'QUICS'	NY	....[58]	8	117	Quarterly Income Capital Sec	26¼	22½	26½	25	26 3/16	21 9/16	6058	23	21 9/16	22 1/16	8.8	..	...	−7.3	4.4	...
30	EPI	Consolidated Ed 7.35%'PINES'	NY	....[59]	1	69	Sr Public Income Notes	...	...	...	...	24⅝	20 9/16	6964	22⅛	20 9/16	20⅞	8.8	..	...	...	...	...
31•[4]	CFWY	✓Consolidated Freightways	NNM	NR	113	11599	Trucking:air freight	18½	6	19¾	7½	18 7/16	6¾	52427	9⅜	6¾	7 15/16	...	8	...	−50.0	−3.7	...
✣32	CGX	✓Consolidated Graphics	NY,Ch,Ph	NR	223	10854	Commercial printing services	56 3/16	4¾	67⅝	31½	74½	13 5/16	58052	23¾	13 5/16	14 15/16	...	6	53	−77.9	−18.8	21.6
¶33•[9]	CNG	✓Consolidated Nat Gas[60]	NY,To,B,C,Ch,P,Ph	B+	528	55216	Integrated natural gas sys	60 15/16	4 3/16	60½	41 11/16	65 7/16	48½	85936	65 7/16	64	64 15/16	3.0	33	20	24.2	9.2	17.2
#34•[10]	CDP	✓Consolidated Papers	NY,Ch,Ph,P	B	195	30633	Enamel printing paper	32 11/16	9/16	35 1/16	21¾	32⅞	20 1/16	24874	32 7/16	28⅞	31 13/16	2.8	40	19	19.4	12.5	10.5
✣35	COP	✓Consolidated Products	NY,Ph	B+	109	10398	Drive-in type restaurants	12¼	⅜	18¾	11 3/16	19 3/16	7⅝	16104	10¾	7⅝	10⅛	...	16	10	−46.0	1.7	20.6
¶36•[7]	CNS	✓Consolidated Stores	NY,B,Ch,P,Ph	B	420	106984	Retails close-out mdse	50	1 3/16	46⅛	15½	38⅛	13 11/16	157124	17⅜	13 11/16	16¼	...	16	2	−19.5	−14.3	6.4
37	CTO	✓Consolidated Tomoka Land	AS,Ph	B	42	1732	Fla citrus,resorts,RE devel	28	1½	21⅝	11½	17¼	11 11/16	3397	13⅛	12	12¾	...	6	−5	−7.6	−4.5	4.5
38•[1]	DIN	Consorcio G Grupo Dina ADS[62]	NY,Ph	NR	8	2030	Mfr trucks & buses in Mexico	31	1⅜	5 7/16	1	1¾	½	17980	1 1/16	½	⅝	...	..	...	−58.3	−34.8	−41.9
39	DIN.L	Cl'L'ADS[63]	NY,Ph	NR	6	1741		13⅛	⅞	4 3/16	⅝	1	5/16	5031	⅝	5/16	⅜	...	d	...	−60.0	−38.7	−45.0
¶40•[7]	CEG	✓Constellation Energy Group	NY,B,C,Ch,P,Ph	B+	436	66351	Hldg co:elec & gas serv	34 5/16	4 1/16	35¼	29¼	31½	24 11/16	79073	30 11/16	27½	29	5.8	14	1	−0.4	8.6	11.8
41	CFN	ContiFinancial Corp	NY,Ch,P,Ph	NR	45	6206	Consumer/commercial financing	40½	21	38 9/16	2 15/16	8¾	⅛	59591	5/16	⅛	¼	...	d	Neg	−96.7	−81.4	...
42•[11]	CAL	✓Contl Airlines'B'	NY,Ph	NR	206	52474	Domestic/int'l air service	50 3/16	3¼	65⅛	28⅞	48	30	83428	44 7/16	36⅞	44⅜	...	8	NM	32.5	16.2	57.4
43	CAL.A	✓ Cl'A'	NY,Ch,Ph	NR	9	124		50½	3½	64¾	30⅞	48	31 13/16	928	44 11/16	36¾	44⅛	...	8	NM	27.2	16.5	56.9
44	CISC	✓Contl Information Sys	NSC	NR	3	649	Lease aircraft & equip	3 9/16	1½	3	1¼	1⅝	1⅛	2383	1⅜	1 3/16	1⅜	...	d	Neg	−8.5	−12.4	...
45	CUO	✓Contl Materials	AS,Ch	B−	19	352	Bldg mtls: mineral pr: mfg	19⅛	1¼	19⅛	12¾	23¼	15½	433	23	21	22⅝B	...	9	47	24.0	28.7	31.2
46	CNU	✓Continucare Corp	AS	NR	9	3342	Provides outpatient healthcare	13⅛	1½	6½	1 9/16	2	3/16	11976	1	½	¾	...	d	Neg	−55.5	−55.5	...
47	MCM	✓Controladora Comer'l Mex GDS[66]	NY	NR	9	463	Oper retail strs/restr Mexico	26⅝	13⅜	26 15/16	8¼	26¼	10 7/16	1812	26¼	21⅛	25⅛B	0.7	16	17	78.8	12.9	...
48	CONV	✓Convergent Communications	NNM	NR	33	7263	Data & voice transport prod	...	...	...	...	21 7/16	8½	123268	18¾	9⅜	15⅞	...	..	...	...	...	...
#49•[4]	CVG	✓Convergys Corp	NY	NR	316	82335	Provide billing/mgmt svcs	...	...	23¾	9⅝	31¾	14½	140172	31¾	24 15/16	30¾	...	31	...	37.4	...	...
50	CVE	✓Converse Inc	NY,Ch,P	NR	24	12929	Mfr athletic footwear,apparel	28	3½	8 5/16	1¾	5½	1⅜	13884	2⅛	1⅜	1⅜	...	d	Neg	−42.1	−56.8	−35.0
51	CGR	✓Cooker Restaurant	NY,Ch	B+	31	3117	Owns/operates restaurants	24	2 13/16	12¼	5½	7⅞	2⅜	15240	3½	2⅜	2⅞	3.5	d	Neg	−51.3	−36.6	−13.0

Uniform Footnote Explanations-See Page 4. Other: [1]CBOE:Cycle 2. [2]CBOE,P,Ph:Cycle 1. [3]CBOE,Ph:Cycle 1. [4]CBOE:Cycle 1. [5]ASE:Cycle 3. [6]P,Ph:Cycle 3. [7]Ph:Cycle 1. [8]ASE:Cycle 2. [9]ASE:Cycle 1. [10]P:Cycle 1. [11]ASE,CBOE:Cycle 3. [51]Lockheed Martin plan acq,$45.50 or 1 com. [52]Fiscal Dec'97 & prior. [53]Excl. subsidiary pfd. stk.. [54]Formed in mgr of Delmarva P&L & Atlantic Energy. [55]Excl subsid pfd. [56]Energy East plan acq,$42 in cash & stk. [57]Fiscal Jun'98 & prior. [58]Rated'A'by S&P. [59]Rated 'A' by S&P. [60]Dominion Res plan acq,$66.60 in cash or stk. [61]Excl $3 in sub debs,'90. [62]Ea ADS rep 4 com, no par. [63]Ea ADS rep 4'L' shrs,no par. [64]®$4.19,'96. [65]6 Mo May'95. [66]Ea Global Dep Shr rep 20 Uts(3Sr'B',1Sr'C'Shrs). [67]Incl 768M Cl'B' Units.

Splits ◆ Index	Cash Divs. Ea.Yr. Since	Dividends: Latest Payment Period $	Date	Ex. Div.	Total $ So Far 1999	Ind. Rate	Paid 1998	Financial Position Mil-$ Cash& Equiv.	Curr. Assets	Curr. Liab.	Balance Sheet Date	Capitalization Lg Trm Debt Mil-$	Shs. 000 Pfd.	Com.	Earnings $ Per Shr. Years End	1995	1996	1997	1998	1999	Last 12 Mos.	Interim Earnings Period	$ per Shr. 1998	1999	Index
1	....	0.05	1-22-88	12-29	...	Nil	....	2.65	4.07	0.59	10-31-99	....	...	6407	Ja	0.11	vd0.11	vd0.17	vd0.10	....	0.06	9 Mo Oct	vd0.12	v0.04	1
2	....	None Since Public			...	Nil	....	1.51	13.8	22.9	9-30-99	0.98	...	23914	Dc	pd0.46	vd1.53	vd0.65	vd0.38	....	d0.12	9 Mo Sep	vd0.39	vd0.13	2
3◆	....	None Since Public			...	Nil	....	208	875	542	9-30-99	515	...	357851	Mr	0.12	v0.27	v0.50	v0.87	E1.19	1.02	6 Mo Sep	v0.32	v0.47	3
4	1999	Q0.12½	12-31-99	12-22	0.12½	0.50	....	18.5	76.4	24.6	9-30-99	20.5	...	±16147	Dc	...	...	pv1.11	v1.37	....	1.52	9 Mo Sep	v0.97	v1.12	4
5◆	1970	Q0.05	12-13-99	11-9	0.20	0.20	0.20	75.0	251	191	9-30-99	379	...	53033	Dc	v0.79	v0.18	vd1.21	v0.50	E0.65	0.39	9 Mo Sep	v0.27	v0.16	5
6	....	None Since Public			...	Nil	....	6.09	27.9	26.0	9-30-99	254	...	25037	Dc	d2.24	v1.32	v0.85	vd0.71	....	d0.82	9 Mo Sep	vd0.17	vd0.28	6
7◆	....	None Paid			...	Nil	....	1.40	20.9	9.62	10-31-99	0.83	...	4571	Jl	d0.39	0.02	v0.13	v0.27	v1.15	1.17	3 Mo Oct	v0.09	v0.11	7
8	....	None Since Public			...	Nil	....	111	131	13.7	9-30-99	0.48	...	21501	Dc	...	...	vpd1.27	pvd0.83	....	....	9 Mo Sep	n/a	vd0.30	8
9◆	....	None Paid			...	Nil	....	726	1080	282	10-31-99	307	...	76347	Ja	v0.50	v0.77	v[52]1.07	v1.55	E2.13↑	1.96	9 Mo Oct	v1.12	v1.53	9
10◆	1976	Q0.204	3-1-00	1-26	0.739	0.814	0.647	10.7	6973	6554	8-29-99	2560[53]	...	492259	My	1.03	0.40	v□1.34	□v1.36	v0.75	0.66	6 Mo Nov	v0.69	v0.60	10
11◆	....	None Since Public			...	Nil	....	296	324	52.8	9-30-99	153	...	42120	Dc	...	pvd6.73	pvd2.82	vd3.34	Ed2.70	d2.91	9 Mo Sep	v∆d2.46	vd2.03	11
12	....	None Since Public			...	Nil	....	33.9	78.4	38.6	10-02-99	17.1	...	11686	Je	0.12	d0.16	d0.08	v0.52	v0.67	0.79	3 Mo Sep	v0.21	v0.33	12
13	....	None Since Public			...	Nil	....	60.7	71.5	18.2	9-30-99	....	...	p14352	Dc	pvd0.84	pvd0.57	pv0.01	v0.64	....	0.84	9 Mo Sep	v0.39	v0.59	13
14◆	....	None Since Public			...	Nil	....	560	733	255	9-30-99	80.0	...	205660	Dc	v0.14	v0.20	v0.30	v0.42	....	0.40	9 Mo Sep	v0.32	v0.30	14
15	....	None Since Public			...	Nil	....	3.93	181	158	10-03-99	119	396	25486	Dc	vd0.22	vd0.19	vd0.47	vd0.37	....	d1.18	9 Mo Sep	v0.20	v□d0.61	15
16	1998	Q0.22	1-31-00	1-7	1.21	0.88	1.15½	140	861	1499	9-30-99	1907[55]	...	±93008	Dc	...	...	n/a	v1.50	....	d1.62	9 Mo Sep	v1.27	vd1.85	16
17	1998	Q0.80	1-31-00	1-7	3.20	3.20	2.40	....	...	...		....	...	6561	Dc	...	...	n/a	v1.82	....	2.00	3 Mo Mar	v0.02	v0.20	17
18◆	....	None Since Public			...	Nil	....	411	900	268	6-30-99	350	...	194936	Sp	...	...	...	vpd1.33	Pv0.07	0.07				18
19	....	None Since Public			...	Nil	....	32.7	118	55.2	9-30-99	99.6	...	±8419	Dc	v±0.94	v±1.21	v□0.72	v□1.09	....	0.71	9 Mo Sep	v□0.77	v0.39	19
20◆	....	None Since Public			...	Nil	....	2.82	173	67.0	9-30-99	375	...	15299	Dc	0.94	v1.12	vd0.47	v□1.26	....	1.61	9 Mo Sep	v□0.84	v1.19	20
21	1850	Q0.33½	12-31-99	12-15	1.34	1.34	1.33½	6.65	50.7	53.9	9-30-99	148	...	10389	Sp	1.60	1.70	v1.81	v1.88	v1.61	1.61				21
22◆	1956	Q0.297	12-15-99	11-29	1.18	1.187	1.167	1.94	13.6	15.7	9-30-99	65.5	44	4839	Dc	v1.45	v1.46	v1.49	v1.53	....	1.62	9 Mo Sep	v1.16	v1.25	22
23	1999	0.19	12-10-99	11-8	0.38	0.76	....	318	2882	3517	9-30-99	★4717	...	±626255	Dc	...	...	pv1.52	±v0.71	E1.16	d0.26	9 Mo Sep	v±1.63	v±0.66	23
24	1999	0.19	12-10-99	11-8	0.71	0.76	....	....	...	...		....	...	189711	Dc	...	...	pv1.52	±v0.71	....	d0.26	9 Mo Sep	v±1.63	v±0.66	24
25◆	1988	Q0.15	1-3-00	12-16	0.57	0.60	0.51½	Total Assets $46987.30M			9-30-99	6829	...	327119	Dc	□v2.14	v□2.01	v□2.67	v□1.53	E3.15	3.24	9 Mo Sep	□v0.67	v2.38	25
26	....	None Since Public			...	Nil	....	1.44	32.2	27.2	9-30-99	22.9	...	7311	Dc	pvd0.10	vd0.10	v0.07	v0.34	....	0.41	9 Mo Sep	v0.19	v0.26	26
27	1999	0.28	11-22-99	11-4	0.56	1.12	....	21.5	610	834	9-30-99	312	...	79995	Je	...	...	...	pv[57]2.18	n/a	....	3 Mo Sep	v0.17	v0.13	27
28	1885	Q0.53½	12-15-99	11-15	2.14	2.14	2.12	189	1620	1757	9-30-99	4359	2746	221020	Dc	v2.93	v2.93	v2.95	v3.04	E3.15	3.12	12 Mo Sep	v3.07	v3.12	28
29	1996	Q0.484	12-31-99	12-13	1.453	1.938	1.93¾	Co option redm fr 3-31-2001 at $25				★275	...	...	Dc	...	...	...	....	....	....	Mature 3-31-2031			29
30	1999	Q0.459	1-3-00	12-15	0.464	1.838	....	Redeemable at $25 fr 7-1-2004				★275	...	...	Dc	...	...	...	....	....	....	Due 7-1-2039			30
31	....	None Since Public			...	Nil	....	95.6	499	397	9-30-99	15.1	...	21729	Dc	pvd1.36	vd2.52	v0.89	v1.12	E0.95	0.73	9 Mo Sep	v1.00	v0.61	31
32◆	....	None Since Public			...	Nil	....	7.35	149	87.4	9-30-99	207	...	15760	Mr	0.36	v0.81	v1.40	v2.28	....	2.62	6 Mo Sep	v1.03	v1.37	32
33	1944	Q0.48½	2-15-00	1-12	1.94	1.94	1.94	114	944	1189	9-30-99	1763	...	95928	Dc	v0.23	v3.13	v3.15	v2.49	E2.00	1.70	9 Mo Sep	v1.51	v0.72	33
34◆	1934	Q0.22	11-12-99	10-28	0.88	0.88	0.87	2.17	385	259	9-30-99	1431	...	90762	Dc	v0.07	v2.00	v1.31	v□1.18	E0.79	0.68	9 Mo Sep	v□0.98	v0.48	34
35◆	....	†[61]1.395	11-27-90	11-28	...	Nil	....	8.94	34.2	42.8	7-07-99	30.3	...	29273	Sp	0.45	0.49	v0.59	v0.67	vP0.64	0.64				35
36◆	....	None Since Public			...	Nil	....	93.3	1914	846	10-30-99	531	...	110825	Ja	0.85	v□1.19	v0.77	v□0.97	E1.00	0.85	9 Mo Oct	vd0.09	vd0.21	36
37	1976	Div Omitted 7-21-99			0.35	Nil	0.70	Total Assets $64.66M			9-30-99	10.4	...	6376	Dc	v1.26	v1.04	v0.64	v0.20	....	2.23	9 Mo Sep	v0.09	v2.12	37
38	....	0.047	1-10-95	12-21	...	Nil	....	165	4305	2010	j12-31-97	5109	...	±258026	Dc	d0.92	∆d0.01	n/a	....	....	....				38
39	....	0.047	1-10-95	12-21	...	Nil	....	....	...	...		....	...	54226	Dc	d0.92	∆d0.01	...	....	....	d0.01				39
40	1910	Q0.42	1-3-00	12-8	1.68	1.68	1.66	56.4	1653	2087	9-30-99	2588	1970	149556	Dc	v2.02	v1.85	v1.72	v2.06	E2.15	2.01	9 Mo Sep	v1.97	v1.92	40
41	....	None Since Public			...	Nil	....	Total Assets $978.17M			9-30-99	699	...	46662	Mr	vp2.00	v2.40	v2.86	vd9.21	....	d19.18	6 Mo Sep	vd2.33	vd12.30	41
42◆	....	None Since Public			...	Nil	....	1299	2520	2694	9-30-99	3030	...	±69251	Dc	v3.37	□±v[64]4.25	v□5.03	v□5.06	E5.35	5.42	9 Mo Sep	v±□4.15	v□±4.51	42
43◆	....	None Since Public			...	Nil	....	....	...	...		....	...	11407	Dc	v3.37	□v±[64]4.25	v□±5.03	v□5.06	....	5.42	9 Mo Sep	v□4.15	v□4.51	43
44	....	None Paid			...	Nil	....	Total Assets $30.7M			8-31-99	5.81	...	6824	My	‡[65]d0.23	v0.01	v0.15	vd0.77	vd0.99	d1.10	3 Mo Aug	v0.02	vd0.09	44
45◆	....	None Paid			...	Nil	....	0.14	36.6	21.9	10-02-99	3.12	...	1970	Dc	v0.30	v1.06	v1.39	v2.11	....	2.59	9 Mo Sep	v1.59	v2.08	45
46	....	None Paid			...	Nil	....	2.25	2.89	61.5	9-30-99	1.66	...	14540	Je	p□d0.23	p0.06	v0.16	vd1.20	□vd3.50	d3.55	3 Mo Sep	∆vd0.19	∆vd0.24	46
47	1997	0.179	5-4-99	4-21	0.179	0.18	0.165	130	486	519	12-31-97	p200	...	[67]±1086000	Dc	2.20	1.90	1.62	....	....	1.62				47
48	....	None Since Public			...	Nil	....	104	174	68.0	9-30-99	180	...	27965	Dc	...	...	...	vpd4.34	....	....	9 Mo Sep	n/a	vd3.92	48
49	....	....			...	Nil	....	42.4	451	789	9-30-99	....	...	152712	Dc	...	...	pv0.54	v0.57	E1.00	0.91	9 Mo Sep	v0.34	v0.68	49
50	....	None Since Public			...	Nil	....	1.71	129	138	10-02-99	102	...	17479	Dc	vd4.30	vd1.10	□vd0.25	v∆d1.36	....	d1.92	9 Mo Sep	vd0.44	vd1.00	50
51	1991	A0.10	2-26-99	2-3	0.10	0.10	0.07	1.55	6.65	20.3	10-03-99	82.6	...	5986	Dc	v0.61	v0.72	□v0.63	v0.65	....	d0.38	9 Mo Sep	0.49	vd0.54	51

◆**Stock Splits & Divs By Line Reference Index** [3]2-for-1,'97(twice),'99. [5]No adj for stk dstr Ascent Entmt Grp,'97. [7]3-for-2,'99. [9]3-for-2,'99. [10]2-for-1,'97. [11]2-for-1,'99. [14]3-for-2,'95,'96(twice),'98,'99:To split 3-for-2,ex Sep 23. [18]2-for-1,'99. [20]3-for-2,'94,'95. [22]3-for-2,'98. [25]2-for-1,'96,'97. [32]2-for-1,'97. [34]2-for-1,'98. [35]5-for-4,'97,'98:10%,'95,'97,'99. [36]5-for-4,'96,'97. [42]2-for-1,'96. [43]2-for-1,'96. [45]1-for-50 REVERSE,'99,100-for-1,'99.

¶ S&P 500
# MidCap 400
✤ SmallCap 600
• Options

Index	Ticker	Name of Issue (Call Price of Pfd. Stocks)	Market	Com. Rank. & Pfd. Rating	Inst. Hold Cos	Inst. Hold Shs. (000)	Principal Business	1971-97 High	1971-97 Low	1998 High	1998 Low	1999 High	1999 Low	Dec. Sales in 100s	December, 1999 Last Sale Or Bid High	Low	Last	%Div Yield	P-E Ratio	EPS 5 Yr Growth	% Annualized Total Return 12 Mo	36 Mo	60 Mo
1	CAM	✔Cooper Cameron	NY,P	NR	352	45465	Oil & gas ind services/prod	81¾	9¼	71	20⅛	50	22¼	100643	49¼	38	48 15/16	...	43	NM	99.7	8.6	...
✤2•[1]	COO	✔Cooper Cos	NY,P	B–	130	8262	Mfrs health care products	86¼	13/16	51 11/16	14	31⅞	11¾	18323	30 7/16	24 15/16	30⅛	0.3	17	NM	45.8	20.5	34.9
¶3•[2]	CBE	✔Cooper Indus	NY,B,Ch,P	A–	483	71214	Mfr elec equip&auto prod	59⅜	2¼	70⅜	36⅞	56¾	39⅝	46451	43 15/16	39⅝	40 7/16	3.3	12	NM	–12.8	1.4	...
¶4•[3]	CTB	✔Cooper Tire & Rubber	NY,Ch,Ph,P	A	343	49512	Auto/truck tires,rubber prd	39⅝	3/16	26¼	15 7/16	25	13¼	72284	15¾	13¼	15¾	2.7	9	5	–21.1	–5.5	–6.3
¶5•[4]	RKY	✔Coors (Adolph)Cl'B'[51]	NY,Ph	B	366	14500	Western beer brewer	41¼	9½	56¾	29¼	65 13/16	45¼	31879	53⅞	47 15/16	52½	1.3	22	13	–5.9	42.5	28.2
✤6	CPRT	✔Copart Inc	NNM	NR	137	15156	Auctions salvage vehicles	15⅛	5⅛	16¼	7½	51¾	13	43975	51¾	25	43½	...	49	23	179	90.1	38.6
7	PNE	Copene-Petroquimica[52]ADS[53]	NY	NR	4	201	Mfr petrochemical products	....	....	5¼	5	16 3/16	3 11/16	1196	16 3/16	11⅝	15⅞	6.8	..	...	267	...	...
8•[5]	CMTN	✔Copper Mtn Networks	NNM	NR	146	8865	Mfr telecommunic equip	....	....	....	....	67½	10½	406615	49⅜	38⅜	48¾	...	..	...	...	...	...
9	COPY	CopyTele Inc	NNM	NR	23	3947	Dvlp stge:data display sys	10⅜	11/16	4⅝	⅝	3 5/16	11/16	92281	1¼	¾	13/16	...	d	–12	–36.6	–45.2	–22.8
✤10•[4]	CORR	✔Cor Therapeutics	NNM	C	137	16043	Cardiovascular biopharma R&D	26⅛	7	24⅞	6 11/16	30⅝	8⅛	59586	30⅝	19	26⅞	...	d	–4	103	39.6	19.6
11	CRH	✔Coram Healthcare	NY,P	NR	41	7642	Health care services	26¾	1¼	3⅜	1 5/16	2⅞	⅜	80734	1⅛	⅝	1	...	d	NM	–46.7	–41.0	–42.9
#12•[6]	CDD	✔Cordant Technologies	NY,B,Ch,P,Ph	A–	328	29674	Aerospace propulsion sys	68 7/16	4 3/16	55¾	31⅜	52⅜	25½	33639	33⅛	28¾	33	1.2	8	29	–11.1	15.0	20.4
13	CDA	✔Cordiant Communic Grp[57]ADS	NY,Ch,Ph,P	NR	15	4703	Int'l advertising services	343¾	3¾	12¼	7	24½	9¼	12488	24½	19¾	22 7/16	0.5	36	NM	118	66.0	27.6
14	CLB	✔Core Laboratories N.V.	NY,Ph	NR	80	11705	Oil & gas industry svcs	22⅞	4¾	30¼	11⅝	26¼	11¾	48312	21 15/16	17 1/16	20	...	..	11	4.6	33.9	...
15	CME	✔Core Materials	AS,Ch,Ph	B–	14	1327	Sheet mold'g compound comp'ts	12⅜	⅝	7	1¾	3⅞	1 7/16	2812	2⅞	1⅝	2 5/16	...	15	77	–33.9	0.9	19.9
16	CORL	Corel Corp	NNM	C	45	6646	Dvlp PC applications software	19½	1⅜	4⅜	1 1/16	44½	2	3277848	44½	12	15⅛	...	d	Neg	278	27.1	1.8
17	CRM	Corimon ADS[58]	NY,Ch,P	NR	7	368	Mfr constr prd,chem,food prd	167⅞	⅞	6¼	11/16	1¾	9/16	3240	1 1/16	13/16	⅞	...	d	Neg	–26.3	–48.1	–57.8
18	CRXA	✔Corixa Corp	NNM	NR	49	3134	Dvp stg:Biopharmaceutical R&D	14⅛	8¾	10½	3 5/16	18⅛	7⅜	15134	17¼	14⅝	17	...	d	...	83.8	...	...
✤19•[4]	CPO	✔Corn Products Intl	NY	NR	310	24865	Corn refining/pds	32	28⅞	39½	21¾	35¼	21 9/16	18051	33 13/16	30 9/16	32¾	1.2	16	...	9.1	...	...
20	CRN	✔Cornell Corrections	NY	NR	81	7667	Oper correctional facilities	20¾	8⅞	25 7/16	8	22¾	8	12151	11⅞	8	8⅜	...	11	NM	–55.9	–1.9	...
21	CBN	✔Cornerstone Bancorp	AS	B	3	76	General banking, Connecticut	19 5/16	7¾	23½	17 3/16	19	11	291	12	11	11¼	e3.2	9	NM	–36.9	–7.8	...
22	CNO	✔Cornerstone Propane Ptnrs L.P.	NY,Ch	NR	18	2375	Propane retail marketer	23 15/16	19¾	23⅜	16	19	10	21374	13 7/16	10	11⅜	19.0	..	...	–22.0	–10.1	...
23	CPP	✔Cornerstone Properties	NY	NR	140	44207	Real estate investment trust	20	14	19 13/16	13¼	17	13	36687	15 7/16	13	14⅝	8.2	15	...	1.2	...	...
24	TCR	✔Cornerstone Realty Income Tr	NY,Ch,Ph	NR	53	5879	Real estate investment trust	12½	10⅛	13¼	10¼	11⅛	9	20390	10	9 1/16	9¾	11.1	17	...	3.0	...	...
¶25•[7]	GLW	✔Corning Inc	NY,B,Ch,P,Ph	B	840	174533	Sp'lty mat,commun,csmr prd/sv	65⅛	3⅛	45 11/16	22⅞	129 1/16	44¾	359092	129 1/16	93	128 15/16	0.6	70	NM	191	...	...
26	EXBD	✔Corporate Executive Board	NNM	NR	111	9734	Management services	....	....	....	....	57⅛	19	16224	57⅛	43⅞	55⅞	...	..	NM	...	...	...
27	OFC	✔Corporate Office Prop Tr SBI	NY,Ph	NR	42	3502	Real estate investment trust	11¾	4½	14¾	6⅛	9	5⅞	6292	8¼	7 5/16	7⅝	10.0	6	42	17.6	22.7	10.9
28	CPV	✔Correctional Properties Tr	NY,Ph	NR	43	4673	Real estate investment trust	....	....	23 7/16	13⅝	19 9/16	10⅝	11326	12¾	10⅝	12¼	11.9	..	...	–25.4	...	...
29	CO	✔Corrpro Co	NY,Ch	NR	37	3226	Corrosion ctrl engineer'g svc	19⅜	4⅛	13⅛	9¼	12⅝	5	4074	7⅛	5	5⅞	...	17	NM	–51.8	–7.2	–12.9
30	CBZ	✔Cort Business Services	NY	NR	93	10923	Rental furniture/access	43¼	12	48	14⅛	25⅝	15½	6537	19¾	16¼	17 7/16	...	10	18	–28.1	–5.4	...
31•[8]	CGA	✔Corus Group ADS	NY,Ch,P	NR	81	26761	Largest steel producer in U.K.	31½	7	28 11/16	14 1/16	28 15/16	15 5/16	23863	27⅞	20	25⅞	e6.3	52	Neg	150	16.5	15.2
32	CRVL	✔CorVel Corp	NNM	B–	46	4087	Workers compensation services	21⅜	4⅜	20 7/16	16¼	26¼	16 15/16	3840	24	20¼	23½	...	17	16	33.5	17.5	11.1
¶33•[9]	COST	✔Costco Wholesale	NNM	B–	871	171846	Wholesale cash & carry mdsg	65¼	11/16	76⅛	41¼	98¾	65⅜	513288	98¾	86	91¼	...	39	27	26.4	53.7	...
34	CGZ	✔Cotelligent Inc	NY,Ph	NR	64	4588	Computer consulting svcs	26¾	7¼	29⅞	10 7/16	21 11/16	2⅞	31301	6 15/16	3½	5⅜	...	d	Neg	–74.8	–39.4	...
35	COTT	Cott Corp[62]	NNM,To	C	38	24136	Mfr beverages/snack foods	37¾	4⅜	9¾	3	6¼	2	31110	6⅛	4⅞	5¼	...	..	...	48.7	–9.8	–11.2
36	CSLI	Cotton States Life Ins	NNM	A–	28	1344	Insurance: life,health	16	¾	19 9/16	8⅞	14½	7½	2229	9⅛	7½	8⅝	1.9	8	18	–41.2	6.4	21.2
37•[7]	CLTR	✔Coulter Pharmaceutical	NNM	NR	102	7095	Dvp stg:pharmaceutical R&D	23½	6½	35⅛	13¼	34⅝	11⅝	53337	24¾	16¼	22 11/16	...	d	...	–24.4	...	...
38	KTZ	Countrywide Cap I 8% CorTS	NY	....[65]	..	...	Corporate-Backed Trust Sec	....	....	....	....	25	21½	790	23⅝	21½	23⅛	8.6	..	...	...	...	...
¶39•[6]	CCR	✔Countrywide Credit Indus	NY,B,Ch,P	A–	533	93274	Services mtge loans	43¼	1/32	56¼	28⅝	51 7/16	24⅝	169998	29¼	24⅝	25¼	1.6	7	27	–49.2	–3.2	15.7
40	CUZ	✔Cousins Properties	NY,Ph	NR	123	13035	Real estate develop: jt vent	33¾	3/16	32 9/16	24 3/16	38¼	28 9/16	23552	35½	32⅝	33 15/16	5.3	11	22	10.7	11.9	20.3
41•[5]	COVD	✔Covad Communications Grp	NNM	NR	214	30502	Local communication svcs	....	....	....	....	81	12	365109	63½	49½	55 15/16	...	d	...	...	...	...
#42•[7]	CVD	✔Covance Inc	NY,Ph	NR	293	42324	Pharm'l prd dvlp research svcs	25	14½	29 11/16	17 11/16	32⅞	8⅛	64904	11 3/16	9	10 13/16	...	14	...	–62.9	–19.9	...
43	CVTI	✔Covenant Transport 'A'	NNM	B	70	5890	Long-haul trucking svcs	21	10⅝	23 5/16	9 3/16	20⅝	11⅛	15008	18¼	13⅜	17⅜	...	12	18	–2.8	6.5	–2.3
✤44•[6]	CVTY	✔Coventry Health Care	NNM,Ch	C	136	23081	Hlth benefit svcs/oper HMO's	31	3½	19¼	3⅞	15 5/16	5	36273	7⅝	5 13/16	6¾	...	11	–7	–23.4	–10.0	–22.7
45•[10]	COX	✔Cox Communications'A'	NY,Ch,Ph,P	NR	466	143925	Cable TV/communic svcs	20⅛	7	35⅜	17 3/16	52	32	105916	52	46	51½	...	43	NM	49.7	64.8	...
46	PRI	Cox[68]Communic[69]'PRIZES'[70]	NY	NR	..	...	Exch Sub Debs	....	....	....	....	105	87½	41212	105	87½	97¼	1.8	..	...	...	...	...
47•[8]	CXR	✔Cox Radio 'A'	NY,Ch,Ph	NR	149	8295	Own,oper radio stations	43½	15½	51⅜	26¼	107	37 5/16	6247	107	73½	99¾	...	54	...	136	78.6	...
48	CPBI	✔CPB Inc	NNM	A–	34	2366	Commercial banking, Hawaii	22⅞	4⅛	21	15	29⅛	16 9/16	1880	29⅛	25⅜	28½	2.0	18	4	67.2	27.7	20.5
✤49	CPY	✔CPI Corp	NY,Ch,Ph	B	119	6453	Photo studio/lab,elec publ'g	34¾	3⅜	27 7/16	18⅛	34⅞	17 11/16	15002	24 15/16	17 11/16	22 9/16	2.5	22	6	–13.1	13.1	7.7
50	CRG	✔Craig Corp[72]	NY,B,Ch,P,Ph	B–	24	802	Entertainment/movie theatres	13 5/16	⅜	14 1/16	6 11/16	8⅜	5⅝	1094	6⅞	5 11/16	6¾	...	d	Neg	–16.3	–1.8	9.0
51	Pr	Cl'A' com[74]Pref (1 Vote)	NY	B–	12	1620	banking investment in Calif	9¾	3 5/16	13½	6 9/16	7⅞	5 3/16	1213	6¼	5 3/16	6¼	...	..	...	...	...	...

Uniform Footnote Explanations-See Page 4. Other: [1]ASE:Cycle 2. [2]ASE:Cycle 1. [3]P,Ph:Cycle 2. [4]P:Cycle 1. [5]ASE,CBOE,P,Ph:Cycle 3. [6]Ph:Cycle 1. [7]CBOE:Cycle 2. [8]CBOE:Cycle 1. [9]ASE,P:Cycle 1. [10]CBOE:Cycle 3. [51]Non-vtg. [52]Ea ADS rep 50 Cl'A'Pfd,No Par. [53]Non-cm/non callable Cl'A'Pfd. [54]Incl 1.08 Billion Cl'A'Pfd. [55]Fiscal Jun'96 & prior. [56]12 Mo Dec'97. [57]ADS's represent'g 5 Ord shr par 25p. [58]Ea ADS rep 250 Com Bs10. [59]Pfd shs in millions. [60]Incl 6.6M Sub Units. [61]10 Mo Dec'98. [62]Cdn$ prior to Dec'98. [63]®$0.55,'96. [64]For 11 mos. [65]Rated BBB+ bySandP. [66]Or earlier upon'Tax Event're-spec cond. [67]Incl current amts. [68]Ptcp Redm Index Zero Prem Exch Sec. [69]Hldrs opt to exch cash,re-spec cond. [70]Co redm opt anytime,re-spec cond. [71]Re-spec cond. [72]Entitled to 30 votes. [73]Fiscal Sep'95 & prior. [74]$5.00 liquidation preference.

Index	Cash Divs. Ea. Yr. Since	Dividends: Latest Payment Period $	Date	Ex. Div.	Total $ So Far 1999	Ind. Rate	Paid 1998	Financial Position Mil-$ Cash& Equiv.	Curr. Assets	Curr. Liab.	Balance Sheet Date	Capitalization Lg Trm Debt Mil-$	Shs. 000 Pfd.	Com.	Earnings $ Per Shr. Years End	1995	1996	1997	1998	1999	Last 12 Mos.	Interim Earnings Period	$ per Shr. 1998	1999	Index
1◆	....	None Since Public			...	Nil	....	135	821	448	9-30-99	208	...	53928	Dc	vd9.98	v1.21	v2.53	v2.48	....	1.15	9 Mo Sep	v1.98	v0.65	1
2◆	1999	Q0.02	1-5-00	12-13	0.04	0.08	....	11.7	96.6	46.6	7-31-99	56.5	...	14024	Oc	0.01	v1.41	v∆2.28	v2.61	Pv1.75	1.75				2
3	1947	Q0.33	1-3-00	12-1	1.32	1.32	1.32	11.9	1410	971	9-30-99	717	...	94160	Dc	0.84	v2.77	v3.26	v3.69	E3.48	3.85	9 Mo Sep	v2.45	v2.61	3
4	1950	Q0.10½	12-24-99	11-26	0.42	0.42	0.39	40.3	644	216	9-30-99	205	...	75848	Dc	v1.35	v1.30	v1.55	v1.64	E1.85	1.87	9 Mo Sep	v1.14	v1.37	4
5	1970	Q0.16½	12-15-99	11-26	0.64½	0.66	0.60	260	615	412	9-26-99	105	...	±36860	Dc	v±1.13	v±1.14	v2.16	v1.81	E2.41	2.39	9 Mo Sep	v±1.56	v±2.14	5
6◆	....	None Since Public			...	Nil	....	33.0	91.2	29.1	10-31-99	7.54	...	26849	Jl	0.33	0.43	v0.45	v0.57	v0.80	0.88	3 Mo Oct	v0.15	v0.23	6
7	1997	0.269	11-30-99	10-28	1.083	1.08	1.762	277	607	428	12-31-97	759	[54]1090208	646693	Dc	...	...	...	....	....	....				7
8◆	....	None Since Public			...	Nil	....	111	139	23.1	9-30-99	3.09	...	47018	Dc	...	...	...	pvd0.31	....	....	9 Mo Sep	n/a	v0.12	8
9◆	....	None Since Public			...	Nil	....	2.84	7.20	1.59	7-31-99	....	...	60057	Oc	vd0.06	vd0.10	vd0.10	vd0.12	....	d0.11	9 Mo Jul	vd0.09	vd0.08	9
10	....	None Since Public			...	Nil	....	58.3	94.5	56.2	9-30-99	3.09	...	25139	Dc	vd0.39	vd1.86	vd1.60	vd1.14	Ed1.10	d1.47	9 Mo Sep	vd0.51	vd0.84	10
11	....	None Since Public			...	Nil	....	9.01	160	90.4	9-30-99	289	...	49597	Dc	vd8.39	vd2.05	v2.30	vd0.44	....	d1.06	9 Mo Sep	vd0.46	vd1.08	11
12◆	1925	Q0.10	12-13-99	11-26	0.40	0.40	0.40	20.3	606	766	9-30-99	357	...	36715	Dc	□1.39	[55]1.57	□v[56]3.34	v3.79	....	4.21	9 Mo Sep	v2.99	v3.41	12
13◆	1997	0.111	8-9-99	4-21	0.111	0.11	0.099	62.0	325	314	j12-31-98	36.0	...	225500	Dc	d0.60	0.47	v0.28	v0.56	....	0.62	6 Mo Jun	v0.16	v0.22	13
14◆	....	None Since Public			...	Nil	....	8.17	126	61.2	12-31-98	68.4	...	29298	Dc	v□0.26	v0.36	v0.65	v0.71	....	0.20	9 Mo Sep	v0.53	v0.02	14
15	....	0.003	9-29-95	9-18	...	Nil	....	2.26	33.8	21.0	9-30-99	26.8	...	9779	Dc	d0.15	v0.13	v0.28	v0.37	....	0.16	9 Mo Sep	v0.26	v0.05	15
16◆	....	None Paid			...	Nil	....	16.5	73.7	85.5	5-31-99	11.6	1503	62790	Nv	0.30	d0.05	vd3.84	vd0.51	....	d0.06	9 Mo Aug	vd0.63	vd0.18	16
17◆	....	0.168	6-15-94	5-20	...	Nil	....	4449	78193	67541	j3-31-98	38247	[59]4136	7238190	Mr	d48.07	0.54	d0.62	....	....	d0.62				17
18	....	None Since Public			...	Nil	....	55.4	58.6	16.7	9-30-99	11.5	...	p18332	Dc	vpd0.58	pvd0.55	pvd0.31	vd1.75	....	d1.77	9 Mo Sep	vd1.93	vd1.95	18
19	1998	Q0.10	1-25-00	12-30	0.34	0.40	0.08	51.0	493	313	9-30-99	325	...	37244	Dc	pv3.79	pv0.64	□vd2.02	v1.19	E2.05	1.93	9 Mo Sep	v0.87	v1.61	19
20	....	None Since Public			...	Nil	....	0.26	46.2	37.9	9-30-99	107	...	9583	Dc	pvd0.32	vd0.65	v0.46	v0.62	....	0.77	9 Mo Sep	v0.42	v□0.57	20
21◆	1995	Q0.09	1-15-00	12-29	†0.42	0.36	†0.314	Total Deposits $124M			9-30-99	....	...	1129	Dc	v1.14	v1.30	v1.25	v1.60	....	1.22	9 Mo Sep	v1.25	v0.87	21
22	1997	Q0.54	11-15-99	11-3	2.16	2.16	2.16	7.72	135	111	9-30-99	417	...	[60]±23389	Je	...	±p0.87	p±v0.46	v±0.50	v±0.23	0.07	3 Mo Sep	vd0.46	vd0.62	22
23	1997	Q0.30	11-30-99	10-27	1.20	1.20	1.20	Total Assets $4155M			9-30-99	1502	3030	129600	Dc	...	p□v0.39	□v0.63	v□0.84	....	0.98	9 Mo Sep	v□0.62	v□0.76	23
24	1997	Q0.27	1-25-00	12-28	1.07	1.08	1.03	Total Assets $867.33M			9-30-99	255	12666	38845	Dc	...	pd0.01	v0.59	v0.62	....	0.56	9 Mo Sep	v0.46	v0.40	24
25◆	1881	Q0.18	12-15-99	11-29	0.72	0.72	0.72	102	1632	1219	9-30-99	1287	p222	244785	Dc	vd0.23	v0.78	v1.89	v1.67	E1.85	1.83	9 Mo Sep	v1.23	v1.39	25
26	....	None Since Public			...	Nil	....	8.83	35.1	46.7	9-30-99	....	...	13570	Dc	vpd0.50	vpd0.01	pv0.05	pv0.14	....	0.42	9 Mo Sep	v0.35	v0.63	26
27	1992	Q0.19	1-14-00	12-29	0.73	0.76	0.60½	Total Assets $633M			6-30-99	337	984	17174	Dc	0.19	v0.21	vp0.34	v0.47	....	1.26	9 Mo Sep	vd0.26	v□0.53	27
28	1998	Q0.36½	11-18-99	11-2	1.43	1.46	0.60	Total Assets $204.73M			9-30-99	....	...	7130	Dc	...	...	pv0.09	v[61]0.97	....	....	9 Mo Sep	n/a	v0.92	28
29◆	....	None Since Public			...	Nil	....	4.78	88.8	28.9	9-30-99	67.7	...	7610	Mr	□d0.66	vd0.02	v0.82	□v0.55	....	0.35	6 Mo Sep	v0.10	vd0.10	29
30	....	None Since Public			...	Nil	....	Total Assets $381M			9-30-99	....	...	13099	Dc	p□v1.11	v1.31	v1.67	v□1.92	....	1.78	9 Mo Sep	v1.59	v□1.45	30
31	1989	†5.821	10-26-99	10-27	†7.554	1.64	1.724	1369	3691	1359	j4-03-99	852	...	1982000	Mr	5.86	2.42	v1.84	vd0.66	E0.50	d0.66				31
32◆	....	None Since Public			...	Nil	....	10.8	47.8	11.8	9-30-99	....	...	8116	Mr	0.79	v0.91	v1.11	v1.26	....	1.36	6 Mo Sep	v0.61	v0.71	32
33	....	None Since Public			...	Nil	....	716	3868	3426	11-21-99	921	...	222312	Au	0.68	1.24	v1.47	v2.03	v□2.23	2.33	12 Wk Nov	v□0.46	v0.56	33
34	....	None Since Public			...	Nil	....	0.22	76.1	35.1	9-30-99	48.1	...	15126	Mr	p0.46	pv0.60	vp0.85	v1.08	....	d0.64	6 Mo Sep	v0.52	vd1.20	34
35	1991	Div Omitted 9-15-98			...	Nil	g0.05	109	519	268	j1-02-99	633	...	63283	Dc	d0.49	v[63]0.50	vd0.12	v[64]d1.59		....	9 Mo Sep	n/a	v□0.26	35
36◆	1974	Q0.04	1-3-00	12-9	0.16	0.16	0.153	Total Assets $186.72M			9-30-99	....	...	6321	Dc	v0.63	v0.74	v0.96	v1.10	....	1.09	9 Mo Sep	v0.78	v0.77	36
37	....	None Since Public			...	Nil	....	93.1	101	11.0	9-30-99	9.71	...	16854	Dc	pvd1.28	vpd2.65	vd2.58	vd0.13	....	d0.34	9 Mo Sep	vd1.96	vd2.17	37
38	....	Plan semi annual div			...	2.00	....	Co opt to redm fr 12-15-2006 $25[66]				....	...	★1000	Fb	...	...	...	....	....	....				38
39◆	1979	Q0.10	1-31-00	1-10	0.38	0.40	0.32	Total Assets $16231.45M			8-31-99	11330	...	113165	Fb	1.95	v2.44	v3.09	v3.29	E3.56↓	3.51	9 Mo Nov	v2.43	v2.65	39
40	1980	Q0.45	12-22-99	12-7	1.68	1.80	1.49	Total Assets $852M			9-30-99	227	...	32157	Dc	v0.94	v1.43	v1.26	v1.41	....	3.15	9 Mo Sep	v1.06	v2.80	40
41◆	....	None Since Public			...	Nil	....	219	248	63.0	9-30-99	369	...	±★96573	Dc	...	...	vpd0.15	vd5.62	Ed2.95	....	9 Mo Sep	n/a	v±d1.90	41
42	....	None Since Public			...	Nil	....	12.4	300	187	9-30-99	209	...	58381	Dc	p0.40	vp0.22	v0.69	v0.83	....	0.77	9 Mo Sep	v0.62	v0.56	42
43	....	None Since Public			...	Nil	....	0.66	70.7	22.3	9-30-99	84.8	...	±14912	Dc	v±0.70	v±0.67	±v1.03	v1.27	....	1.44	9 Mo Sep	v±0.89	v±1.06	43
44◆	....	None Since Public			...	Nil	....	256	412	464	9-30-99	....	4710	59213	Dc	vNil	vd1.87	v0.36	vd0.22	E0.62	0.60	9 Mo Sep	vd0.36	v0.46	44
45◆	....	None Since Public			...	Nil	....	Total Assets $22415M			9-30-99	[67]5941	4836	±598579	Dc	vp0.21	±vd0.10	±vd0.25	v±2.30	E1.20	1.90	9 Mo Sep	v±1.75	v±1.35	45
46	....	Plan qtly div			...	1.71	....	At mat amt based on Sprint PCS Stk[71]				....	...	12500	Dc	...	...	...	....	....	....	Due 11-15-2029			46
47	....	None Since Public			...	Nil	....	7.82	79.2	40.5	9-30-99	420	...	±28887	Dc	±p0.07	v±0.69	±v1.75	v±0.80	....	1.86	9 Mo Sep	v0.56	v1.62	47
48◆	1958	Q0.14	1-21-00	12-29	0.54	0.56	0.52	Total Deposits $1259.63M			9-30-99	114	...	9382	Dc	v1.31	v1.33	v1.40	v1.45	....	1.60	9 Mo Sep	v1.08	v1.23	48
49	1985	Q0.14	11-29-99	11-18	0.56	0.56	0.56	48.3	109	50.6	11-13-99	59.6	...	9040	Ja	1.02	v1.06	v1.07	v2.15	....	1.04	9 Mo Oct	v0.68	vd0.43	49
50◆	....	0.01	1-31-80	12-21	...	Nil	....	24.6	27.3	18.0	9-30-99	3.62	...	±10606	Dc	v[73]0.29	v3.76	v0.26	vd0.08	....	d0.14	9 Mo Sep	vd0.07	vd0.13	50
51◆	....	None Since Public			...	Nil	....	....	...	...		....	7007	...	Dc	...	...	...	....	....	....				51

◆**Stock Splits & Divs By Line Reference Index** [1]2-for-1,'97. [2]1-for-3 REVERSE,'95. [6]2-for-1,'99:To split 2-for-1,ex Jan 25,'00. [8]2-for-1,'99. [9]2-for-1,'96. [12]2-for-1,'98. [13]No adj for Demerger,'97. [14]2-for-1,'97. [16]3-for-2,'94. [17]0.14-for-1 REVERSE,'97. [21]10%,'98. [25]No adj for stk dstr Covance Inc,'96. [29]5-for-4,'98. [32]2-for-1,'99. [36]5-for-4,'96,'97:3-for-2,'98. [39]3-for-2,'94. [41]3-for-2,'99. [44]2-for-1,'94. [45]2-for-1,'99. [48]2-for-1,'97. [50]2-for-1 in Cl'A','98. [51]2-for-1,'98.

¶ S&P 500 # MidCap 400 ✤ SmallCap 600 • Options

Index	Ticker	Name of Issue (Call Price of Pfd. Stocks)	Market	Com. Rank. & Pfd. Rating	Inst. Hold Cos	Inst. Hold Shs. (000)	Principal Business	Price Range 1971-97 High	1971-97 Low	1998 High	1998 Low	1999 High	1999 Low	Dec. Sales in 100s	December, 1999 Last Sale Or Bid High	Low	Last	%Div Yield	P-E Ratio	EPS 5 Yr Growth	% Annualized Total Return 12 Mo	36 Mo	60 Mo
¶1•[1]	CR	✓**Crane Co**	NY,B,Ch,P,Ph	B+	361	35136	Mfr industrial,consumer prd	31½	¾	37 9/16	21¾	32¾	16 1/16	66964	19 15/16	16 1/16	19⅞	2.0	12	19	...	...	...
2	CRD.B	✓**Crawford & Co Cl'B'**	NY,Ch,Ph	A–	50	17743	Insur co claim,risk,mgmt svcs	22⅞	⅛	20⅝	12	16⅝	10⅛	1092	14½	12⅝	13⅝	3.8	20	–3	–8.2	–0.6	8.5
3	CRD.A	✓ **Class'A' (non-vtg)**	NY	A–	25	14348		21¼	6 11/16	19¾	12	14 1/16	10	788	11⅝	10⅞	11⅜	4.6	17	–3	–11.1	–4.4	5.2
4	CAP.EC	**Creative Computer Appl**	ECM	B–	1		Hlthcare ind info sys/svcs	11	¼	1⅞	⅜	3 1/16	11/16	1605	2½	1¾	1⅞	...	9	–8	150	–5.0	–7.4
5	MALL	✓**Creative Computers**	NNM	NR	40	2260	Direct mkt computer products	33	3	63	4⅝	48⅞	5	27173	10 15/16	6¾	7 5/16	...	d	Neg	–76.8	0.0	...
6•[2]	CREAF	✓**Creative Technology**[52]	NNM	B–	57	16833	IBM compatible audio/video pd	29⅜	3½	25 5/16	7⅞	19	8⅞	81438	19	14 7/16	17⅜	1.4	15	NM	22.4	16.0	5.2
7•[3]	CMOS	✓**Credence Systems**	NNM	↓C	191	21055	Mfr semiconductor test eqp	55	6 11/16	34	9 5/16	87 11/16	17¼	83892	87 11/16	57¾	86½	...	d	Neg	368	62.6	50.3
8	BAP	✓**Credicorp Ltd**	NY,Ph	NR	58	16492	Banking,insur,fin'l svc Peru	21 15/16	9½	17⅝	5 13/16	13 9/16	7½	13188	12⅛	10⅝	12	1.7	9	...	36.0	0.8	...
9	CACC	✓**Credit Acceptance**	NNM	NR	60	16986	Auto dealers financial svcs	29¼	2 3/16	12⅝	4⅝	10¼	3	24042	4 1/16	3	3 1/16	...	d	Neg	–49.6	–46.1	–27.0
10•[4]	CREE	✓**Cree Research**	NNM	B–	160	17515	Mfr elec silicon carbide pd	15¾	1 5/16	24⅛	5¼	89¼	15⅛	100897	89¼	55¼	85⅜	...	..	NM	257	163	111
11•[5]	CEI	✓**Crescent Real Estate Eq**	NY,Ph,P	NR	303	74360	Real estate investment trust	40⅞	12¼	40⅜	21 1/16	25½	15⅛	100390	18 7/16	16 15/16	18⅜	12.0	7	–10	–11.0	...	...
12	Pr A	6.75% Sr'A'Cv Pfd([54]25)	NY	BB–	27	3018		....	....	25⅞	15⅛	18 3/16	13	6670	15⅛	14	15⅛	11.2	..	...	...	...	...
13	CRS	✓**Crestar Energy**	To	NR	21	9446	Oil & gas explor,dvlp prodn	32½	12	24	11½	24½	9¾	21967	20¼	17 9/16	19⅞	...	d	Neg	52.7	–12.0	6.5
14•[1]	CLJ	✓**Crestline Capital**	NY,Ph	NR	84	11096	Oper hotels/senior facilities	....	....	16 1/16	14½	24⅛	9 13/16	6520	22 1/16	19 5/16	20⅝	...	29	...	41.0	...	...
15	CMM	✓**CRIIMI MAE**	NY	D	46	7612	Real estate investment trust	18⅛	6¼	16¼	13/16	4⅛	1	91387	1⅞	1 1/16	1 7/16	...	16	–29	83.9	–14.2	7.5
16	Pr B	10.875% Sr'B'cm Cv Pfd([55]25)	NY	NR	5	809		41	25	36⅞	3½	19	12⅜	688	17⅞	16⅜	16½	...	..	...	...	...	...
17	Pr F	12% Cv'F'Pfd([57]10)	NY	NR	..	...		....	....	....	....	10	8⅛	420	9	8⅛	8⅜	14.3	..	...	...	...	...
18	CGW	✓**Cristalerias de Chile ADS**[59]	NY,Ch,Ph	NR	33	3172	Mfr glass containers,Chile	31	12½	15¼	10⅝	16½	12¼	12569	14½	13⅛	14⅜	3.7	11	–2	14.7	–4.0	1.3
19	CPTH	✓**Critical Path**	NNM	NR	121	9393	e-mail hosting sevices	....	....	....	....	150¼	28 1/16	227015	95⅛	52⅛	94⅜	...	d	...	...	...	...
20	CRNS	**Cronos Group**	NNM	NR	8	496	Leases marine containers	11⅞	2¾	7¼	3⅝	6⅛	2¾	1420	5¾	4 7/16	5	...	d	Neg	–21.6	–10.6	...
✤21	ATX	✓**Cross (A.T.) Cl'A'**	AS,B,Ch,P,Ph	C	62	3998	Fine writing instruments	41	1 13/16	14⅞	4¾	7⅞	3⅞	7060	5⅝	4 1/16	4½	...	d	Neg	–16.3	–25.2	–17.1
✤22•[6]	XTO	✓**Cross Timbers Oil**	NY,Ph	NR	152	32013	Oil & gas dvlpmt, prod'n	19⅛	5 5/16	21⅛	5 1/16	15⅛	4 9/16	47804	10 5/16	8 3/16	9 1/16	0.4	d	Neg	21.8	–5.7	7.8
23	Pr A	$1.5625 Sr'A'cm Cv Pfd([61]26.09)	NY,Ch	B–	5	640		40½	26	46½	18 3/16	33 1/16	18	2048	25	23	23⅛B	6.8	..	...	...	...	...
24	CRT	✓**Cross Timbers Royalty Tr**	NY,Ph	NR	16	810	Royalty interest O&G prop	18½	9½	17 11/16	7⅝	13⅞	8 7/16	2460	10¾	9¼	9 15/16	10.4	11	...	23.6	–4.1	10.1
25	CRDS	✓**Crossroads Systems**	NNM	NR	..	...	Provide storage routers	....	....	....	....	102¼	18	69670	102¼	58⅜	84½	...	d	...	...	...	...
26	CWN	✓**Crown Amer Realty Tr**	NY,Ch,P	NR	63	9155	Real estate investment trust	17½	6½	10 13/16	7 7/16	8	5¼	19820	6 5/16	5¼	5½	14.9	d	Neg	–19.9	–0.2	–7.4
27•[1]	TWRS	✓**Crown Castle Intl**	NNM	NR	151	42714	Wireless communication svcs	....	....	23½	6	33½	14 11/16	217097	33½	19¾	32⅛	...	d	...	36.7	...	...
28	CNP.A	✓**Crown Centl Pet 'A'**	AS,Ch	C	12	488	Independent producer,refiner	43⅞	3¼	22	7 1/16	12⅝	4¾	1346	6½	4¾	5⅝	...	d	33	–21.1	–23.1	–15.1
29	CNP.B	✓ **Class B (1/10 vtg)**	AS,Ch	C	19	2112	&marketer of petrol prd	40⅜	7⅝	20⅜	6¾	11¼	4 9/16	2994	6	4 9/16	5¼	...	d	33	–25.0	–24.1	–15.2
¶30•[1]	CCK	✓**Crown Cork & Seal**	NY,B,Ch,P,Ph	B	456	87803	Metal cans,closures:mchy	59¾	1½	55 9/16	24	37½	19 11/16	142900	23¾	19 11/16	22⅜	4.5	10	...	–24.7	–23.6	–8.1
31	Pr	4.50% cm Cv Pfd (NC)	NY,Ch	BB+	34	5889		55⅞	41¼	51	23½	34 15/16	18¼	6250	21½	18¼	20¾	9.1	..	...	...	...	...
32	CRW	✓**Crown Crafts**	NY,Ch,P	B	25	3419	Mfr home furnishings prod	21⅞	⅛	22⅝	5⅝	7 11/16	2¼	4538	3⅛	2¼	2⅞	4.2	d	Neg	–51.9	–32.8	–27.1
33	CNGR	✓**Crown Group**	NNM	B–	7	355	Oper gaming casino,Lousiana	11¼	5/16	6⅛	3	7⅞	4	9228	5½	4 11/16	4 15/16	...	2	NM	–13.2	28.8	7.9
34	CRO	✓**Crown Pac Partners L.P.**	NY,Ch,Ph	NR	31	659	Mfr dstr lumber products	27	17	29⅜	19⅝	24½	17	20029	19⅝	17	17⅞	12.6	16	1	–6.7	2.5	5.8
35	CRRS	✓**Crown Resources Corp**	NNM,To	C	24	4100	Gold,silver,mineral mining	11⅛	⅝	4⅞	1⅝	4¾	13/16	9533	2¼	1⅝	1⅞	...	d	Neg	–7.7	–32.8	–14.6
36	CRY	✓**CryoLife Inc**	NY,Ph	B	40	3915	Provides cryopreservat'n svcs	20¾	2⅜	18¼	9 3/16	15 15/16	9¾	7521	14	11¾	11¾	...	24	30	–1.1	–2.0	29.3
37	COR	✓**Crystal Gas Storage**	AS,P	B–	19	2090	Oil & gas explor prod'n	76500	12½	44	36	57¼	31	2492	57¼	55½	56 13/16	...	65	–3	50.5	16.4	13.8
38	KRY	✓**Crystallex Intl**[63]	AS,To	NR	14	301	Acq/dvp mineral prop	6 5/16	1⅞	8 5/16	5/16	1¾	½	52030	1¾	¾	1 5/16	...	9	...	200	–19.3	...
39	CSGS	✓**CSG Systems Intl**	NNM	NR	289	39701	Computer sys mgmt/svc	24⅞	7⅛	39½	17½	46¼	20¼	99100	45⅝	36 3/16	39⅞	...	22	...	1.1	73.2	...
40	CAO	✓**CSK Auto**	NY,Ph	NR	146	15918	Oper auto parts stores	....	....	29	19 7/16	37⅝	13	27035	20	13	17½	...	12	...	–34.4	...	...
41	CSPI	✓**CSP Inc**	NNM	B–	22	1425	Array processor,software pkg	17 7/16	3⅜	11 5/16	5 1/16	17	4 9/16	89982	17	4 11/16	7⅝	...	22	–5	16.2	16.9	11.9
42	CSS	✓**CSS Industries**	NY,Ph	B	57	3499	Seasonal prd,business forms	39¼	3/16	36	26⅜	31 1/16	20⅜	1472	21½	20⅝	21⅝	...	16	21	–29.5	–6.3	4.4
¶43•[7]	CSX	✓**CSX Corp**	NY,B,C,Ch,P,Ph	B	597	146507	RR hldg:Transportation	62 7/16	3 1/16	60⅜	36½	53 15/16	28 13/16	150194	36⅝	28 13/16	31⅜	3.8	52	–18	–22.2	–7.2	0.4
44	CFS	**CT Finl Services**	To,Mo	B+	1	175	Savings & loan svcs Cdn	55	2 11/16	69	47½	67	50½	596	64 15/16	63⅝	64¾B	1.7	24	11	17.8	28.4	32.9
45	CPTL	✓**CTC Communications Group**	NNM	B	48	3547	Network communic svcs	19½	1/16	14 15/16	4	41¾	8⅜	37864	41¾	24⅛	39	...	d	Neg	366	69.6	65.5
46	CTG	✓**CTG Resources**[64]	NY,Ch	↓B	74	2432	Gas Service, Connecticut	32⅜	4⅞	26¾	21 15/16	37 13/16	22⅛	4834	36¼	34⅜	34¾	3.0	22	–3	36.8	16.0	13.1
✤47•[8]	CTS	✓**CTS Corp**	NY,Ch,Ph	B+	256	18504	Electronic components/subsys	18⅝	1 1/16	21 5/16	11 3/16	86¼	20⅞	81190	86¼	59 3/16	75⅜	0.2	50	28	248	121	76.8
48	CUB	✓**Cubic Corp**	AS,B,Ch,Ph	B–	65	2249	Electronics:elevator:fare sys	40	9/16	33¾	16½	26	15¾	2389	22⅜	18¾	21⅞	1.7	17	8	18.8	–0.3	15.3
✤49	CFR	✓**Cullen/Frost Bankers**	NY,Ph	B	290	33306	Commercial bkg,Texas	31⅝	1 3/16	30 9/16	20 7/16	30⅝	22 11/16	28283	30¼	24¼	25¾	2.7	16	13	–3.1	18.7	30.7
50•[9]	CFI	✓**Culp Inc**	NY,Ph	A	45	7428	Mfr textile upholstery fabric	22 9/16	2 1/16	21¾	5 15/16	11 1/16	5⅛	3853	6¾	5⅞	6 5/16	2.2	9	–13	–18.5	–24.6	–7.7
¶51•[10]	CUM	✓**Cummins Engine**	NY,B,Ch,P	B	332	24560	Mfr diesel engines,components	83	5 13/16	62¾	28 5/16	65 11/16	34 9/16	49239	48½	38½	48 9/16	2.5	10	Neg	39.5	3.9	3.7

Uniform Footnote Explanations-See Page 4. Other: [1]Ph:Cycle 1. [2]CBOE:Cycle 1. [3]ASE,CBOE,Ph:Cycle 2. [4]ASE,CBOE:Cycle 3. [5]P:Cycle 1. [6]Ph:Cycle 2. [7]P:Cycle 2. [8]P:Cycle 3. [9]ASE,P:Cycle 3. [10]CBOE:Cycle 3. [51]Stk dstr of Huttig bldg Prods. [52]Ord shrs, par $0.25(Singapore dollars). [53]Incl current amts. [54]Fr 2-18-2003. [55]Fr 8-7-2006. [56]To be determined. [57]Fr 11-5-2000,in cash or Parity Cap Stk. [58]During 10 bus day pds beg 11-15-1999&1-21-2000. [59]Ea ADS rep 3 ord, no par. [60]Approx. [61]Fr 10-16-99,scale to $25 in 2006. [62]Or earlier if less than 30% of init issued shs. [63]May'97 & prior pricing in Cdn$. [64]Energy East plan acq,$41 in cash or stk. [65]Excl 3.6M ESOP shs.

Index	Splits ◆ Cash Divs. Ea. Yr. Since	Dividends: Latest Payment Period $	Date	Ex. Div.	Total $ So Far 1999	Ind. Rate	Paid 1998	Financial Position Mil-$ Cash& Equiv.	Curr. Assets	Curr. Liab.	Balance Sheet Date	Capitalization Lg Trm Debt Mil-$	Shs. 000 Pfd.	Com.	Earnings $ Per Shr. Years End	1995	1996	1997	1998	1999	Last 12 Mos.	Interim Earnings Period	$ per Shr. 1998	1999	Index
1◆	1939	h[51]....	12-16-99	12-27	h[51]0.40	0.40	0.267	15.0	684	256	9-30-99	313	...	65891	Dc	v1.11	v1.34	v1.63	v2.00	E1.65	1.90	9 Mo Sep	v1.49	v1.39	1
2◆	1965	Q0.13	11-19-99	11-3	0.52	0.52	0.50	25.7	268	156	9-30-99	0.02	...	±50754	Dc	□±v0.68	v±0.82	±v0.93	v±0.54	....	0.69	9 Mo Sep	v±0.42	v±0.57	2
3◆	1990	Q0.13	11-19-99	11-3	0.52	0.52	0.50	....	...	...		....	...	25931	Dc	v±0.68	v±0.82	±v0.93	v±0.54	....	0.69	9 Mo Sep	v±0.42	v±0.57	3
4	....	None Paid			...	Nil	....	0.65	4.76	3.27	8-31-99	....	...	3131	Au	Nil	0.32	v0.30	vd0.22	v0.21	0.21				4
5◆	....	None Since Public			...	Nil	....	16.9	94.1	70.9	9-30-99	0.32	...	10403	Dc	v0.66	vd0.62	v0.41	vd1.75	....	d1.38	9 Mo Sep	vd1.20	vd0.83	5
6◆	1999	0.25	12-17-99	11-29	0.75	0.25	....	417	688	203	6-30-98	32.0	...	92914	Je	0.30	d0.43	v1.84	v1.42	Pv1.25	1.15	3 Mo Sep	v0.23	v0.13	6
7◆	....	None Since Public			...	Nil	....	118	228	50.4	7-31-99	96.6	...	21723	Oc	v1.45	v1.72	v0.47	vd1.22	□Pd0.12	d0.12				7
8◆	1996	0.20	4-30-99	4-6	0.20	0.20	0.409	Equity per shr $7.39			12-31-97	....	...	94382	Dc	1.52	1.23	v1.36	....	....	1.36				8
9◆	....	None Since Public			...	Nil	....	Total Assets $661.55M			9-30-99	[53]158	...	46071	Dc	v0.68	v0.89	v0.03	v0.53	....	d0.20	9 Mo Sep	v0.42	vd0.31	9
10◆	....	None Since Public			...	Nil	....	44.9	66.7	11.1	9-26-99	....	...	29500	Je	vNil	v0.01	v0.14	v0.24	v0.45	0.51	3 Mo Sep	v0.09	v0.15	10
11◆	1994	0.55	11-16-99	10-22	2.20	2.20	1.69	Total Assets $5060M			9-30-99	2682	8000	120349	Dc	vp0.65	□v0.70	v1.20	v1.21	E2.65	0.15	9 Mo Sep	v0.85	vd0.21	11
12	1998	Q0.422	11-15-99	10-27	1.688	1.688	0.83	Cv into 0.6119, $40.86				....	8000	...	Dc	...	...	...	....	....	....				12
13	....	None Paid			...	Nil	....	....	131	132	j9-30-99	556	...	57442	Dc	0.16	v1.05	v0.62	vd3.51	....	jd2.30	9 Mo Sep	vd0.70	v0.51	13
14	....	Plan qtly div			...	....	....	Total Assets $1037M			6-18-99	285	...	20682	Dc	...	...	pv0.64	vp1.19	....	0.72	9 Mo Sep	vp0.85	v0.38	14
15	1989	Div Omitted 4-13-99			Stk	Nil	1.17	Total Assets $2347.15M			9-30-99	1913	1797	53553	Dc	v0.65	v1.03	v1.25	v0.74	....	0.09	9 Mo Sep	v0.98	v0.33	15
16	1996	0.91½	9-30-98	9-16	...	[56]....	2.67½	Cv into 2.2844 com,$10.94				....	1594	...	Dc	...	...	...	....	....	....				16
17	....	Plan qtly div			...	1.20	....	Conv into com at var rates[58]				....	1607	...	Dc	...	...	...	....	....	....				17
18	1994	[60]0.091		1-3	0.51	0.53	0.501	83.9	218	74.7	12-31-97	32.9	...	64000	Dc	1.18	1.22	v1.26	....	....	1.26				18
19	....	None Since Public			...	Nil	....	147	171	15.7	9-30-99	4.66	...	43046	Dc	...	...	...	vpd0.81	....	d1.29	9 Mo Sep	vd1.78	vd2.26	19
20	....	None Since Public			...	Nil	....	Total Assets $245M			9-30-99	114	...	9158	Dc	v1.21	v0.90	vd2.60	vd1.86	....	d1.27	9 Mo Sep	vd0.47	v0.12	20
21	1952	Div Omitted 12-8-98			...	Nil	0.32	34.8	92.1	43.5	10-02-99	....	...	±17037	Dc	v0.81	v0.40	vd0.40	vd0.33	....	d0.70	9 Mo Sep	vd0.25	vd0.62	21
22◆	1993	Q0.01	1-14-00	12-29	0.07	0.04	0.077	3.73	101	68.0	9-30-99	999	1139	48776	Dc	vΔd0.29	v0.48	v0.59	vd1.65	....	d0.09	9 Mo Sep	vd0.71	v0.85	22
23	1997	Q0.391	1-14-00	12-29	1.481	1.563	1.56¼	Cv into 2.16 com				....	1139	...	Dc	...	...	...	....	....	....				23
24	1992	0.152	1-14-00	12-29	1.028	1.03	1.177	Total Assets $34.97M			9-30-99	....	...	6000	Dc	v0.93	v1.35	v1.73	v1.15	....	0.94	9 Mo Sep	v0.92	v0.71	24
25	....	None Since Public			...	Nil	....	18.5	24.1	5.87	p7-31-99	0.94	...	★25383	Oc	...	...	...	vpd0.32	Pvpd0.26	d0.26				25
26	1993	Q0.20½	12-17-99	12-1	0.81½	0.82	0.80	Total Assets $872.87M			9-30-99	708	2500	26208	Dc	Δvd0.72	v□0.23	vd0.11	□vd0.18	....	d0.50	9 Mo Sep	v□0.06	vd0.26	26
27	....	None Since Public			...	Nil	....	492	575	105	9-30-99	1479	220	±156255	Dc	...	...	vpd0.39	vd1.02	....	d0.30	9 Mo Sep	vd1.38	v□d0.66	27
28	....	0.10	5-22-92	4-28	...	Nil	....	10.0	192	216	9-30-99	129	...	±10071	Dc	v□±d6.95	v±d0.28	±v1.94	v±d2.99	....	d4.62	9 Mo Sep	v±d1.30	v±d2.93	28
29	....	0.10	5-22-92	4-28	...	Nil	....	....	...	...		....	...	5254	Dc	v□±d6.95	±vd0.28	±v1.94	v±d2.99	....	d4.62	9 Mo Sep	v±d1.30	v±d2.93	29
30	1996	Q0.25	2-22-00	1-31	1.00	1.00	1.00	219	3329	4290	9-30-99	3398	8000	121862	Dc	v0.83	v2.14	v□2.15	v0.71	E2.20	1.55	9 Mo Sep	v1.06	v1.90	30
31	1996	Q0.471	2-22-00	1-31	1.885	1.885	1.885	Cv into 0.911 com				....	12432	...	Dc	...	...	...	....	....	....	Mand conversion 2-26-2000[62]			31
32	1989	Q0.03	12-29-99	12-13	0.12	0.12	0.12	0.61	145	124	9-26-99	42.9	...	8609	Mr	v0.48	v0.45	v0.92	vd1.37	....	d1.76	6 Mo Sep	vd0.27	vd0.66	32
33	....	None Paid			...	Nil	....	Total Assets $177.60M			10-31-99	97.4	...	8846	Ap	d2.01	1.03	v0.80	v0.04	v1.68	2.59	6 Mo Oct	v0.08	v0.99	33
34	1995	Q0.564	11-12-99	11-2	2.243	2.256	2.191	18.1	207	106	9-30-99	560	...	27415	Dc	v0.94	v0.94	v1.01	v1.02	....	1.11	9 Mo Sep	v0.77	v0.86	34
35	....	None Paid			...	Nil	....	5.71	5.85	0.26	9-30-99	15.0	...	14533	Dc	vd0.13	vd0.12	vd0.38	vd0.13	....	d0.15	9 Mo Sep	vd0.10	vd0.12	35
36◆	....	None Since Public			...	Nil	....	31.0	70.5	9.41	9-30-99	5.97	...	12248	Dc	v0.23	v0.40	v0.48	v0.53	....	0.49	9 Mo Sep	v0.42	v0.38	36
37	....	180.00	7-3-84	6-11	...	Nil	....	8.18	9.59	9.15	9-30-99	36.3	7361	2668	Dc	v0.52	v0.91	v0.76	v▲1.15	....	0.87	9 Mo Sep	v0.32	v0.04	37
38	....	None Paid			...	Nil	....	5.68	19.0	10.6	j6-30-99	22.9	...	37015	Dc	0.18	vd0.30	vd0.34	vd0.20	....	j0.10	9 Mo Sep	vd0.17	v0.13	38
39◆	....	None Since Public			...	Nil	....	31.0	116	89.0	9-30-99	65.8	...	51830	Dc	pd0.43	v□d0.07	v□d2.00	v1.62	....	1.84	9 Mo Sep	v0.54	v0.76	39
40	....	None Since Public			...	Nil	....	13.5	723	274	10-31-99	606	...	27834	Ja	...	pd0.13	□v0.12	v□0.99	....	1.48	9 Mo Oct	v□0.70	v□1.19	40
41◆	....	....			...	Nil	....	13.8	29.6	6.18	8-27-99	....	...	3576	Au	0.11	0.03	vd0.22	v0.37	v0.35	0.35				41
42	....	0.05	4-30-70	4-14	...	Nil	....	2.04	290	176	9-30-99	6.77	...	9473	Dc	v0.15	v2.03	v3.81	v2.21	....	1.33	9 Mo Sep	v0.71	vd0.17	42
43◆	1922	Q0.30	12-15-99	11-22	1.20	1.20	1.20	619	2527	3771	10-01-99	6096	...	218338	Dc	v2.91	v3.96	v3.62	v2.51	E0.60↓	0.87	9 Mo Sep	v2.00	v□0.36	43
44	1865	gQ0.28	12-31-99	12-15	g1.12	1.12	g1.00	Total Deposits $42.22M			j9-30-99	359	8000	119374	Dc	v2.02	v2.53	v4.20	v2.46	....	j2.74	9 Mo Sep	v1.88	v2.16	44
45◆	....	None Paid			...	Nil	....	44.6	81.9	43.3	9-30-99	83.2	...	14555	Mr	v0.38	v0.43	vd0.29	vd5.24	....	d5.67	6 Mo Sep	vd1.90	vd2.33	45
46	1851	Q0.26	12-22-99	12-6	1.04	1.04	1.01	36.0	92.1	46.4	6-30-99	218	129	8648	Sp	1.71	1.87	v1.60	v1.70	Pv1.57	1.57				46
47◆	1930	Q0.03	1-28-00	12-29	0.12	0.12	0.12	9.06	215	145	10-03-99	136	...	27530	Dc	v0.55	v0.67	v0.72	v1.28	....	1.52	9 Mo Sep	v0.90	v1.14	47
48◆	1971	S0.19	9-9-99	8-18	0.38	0.38	0.38	34.2	241	87.4	6-30-99	55.0	...	8907	Sp	0.60	1.23	v1.23	v0.10	....	1.32	9 Mo Jun	vd0.14	v1.08	48
49◆	1993	Q0.17½	12-15-99	11-26	0.67½	0.70	0.575	Total Deposits $5820.67M			9-30-99	98.5	...	53091	Dc	v1.02	v1.20	v1.37	v1.38	....	1.57	9 Mo Sep	v1.14	v1.33	49
50◆	1984	Q0.035	1-11-00	12-23	0.14	0.14	0.14	0.79	157	64.8	10-31-99	134	...	11320	Ap	0.87	0.98	v1.15	v1.19	v0.24	0.73	6 Mo Oct	vd0.10	v0.39	50
51	1948	Q0.30	12-15-99	11-29	1.12½	1.20	1.10	60.0	2242	1295	9-26-99	1166	...	[65]41400	Dc	v5.52	v4.01	v5.48	vd0.55	E5.00	4.23	9 Mo Sep	vd1.30	v3.48	51

◆Stock Splits & Divs By Line Reference Index [1]3-for-2,'96,'98. [2]3-for-2,'97. [3]3-for-2,'97. [5]No adj for stk dstr,'99. [6]2-for-1,'94. [7]3-for-2,'95. [8]17.5%,'96:6-for-5,'97:10%,'98. [9]2-for-1,'94. [10]2-for-1,'95,'99. [11]2-for-1,'97. [22]3-for-2,'98. [36]2-for-1,'96. [39]2-for-1,'99. [41]10%,'98(twice),'99. [43]2-for-1,'95. [45]5-for-4,'95:3-for-2,'95:2-for-1,'95. [47]3-for-1,'97:2-for-1,'99. [48]3-for-2,'96. [49]2-for-1,'96,'99. [50]13-for-10,'92:5-for-4,'93:3-for-2,'94.

¶ S&P 500
\# MidCap 400
✛ SmallCap 600
• Options

Index	Ticker	Name of Issue (Call Price of Pfd. Stocks)	Market	Com. Rank. & Pfd. Rating	Inst. Hold Cos	Inst. Hold Shs. (000)	Principal Business	Price Range 1971-97 High	1971-97 Low	1998 High	1998 Low	1999 High	1999 Low	December, 1999 Dec. Sales in 100s	Last Sale Or Bid High	Low	Last	%Div Yield	P-E Ratio	EPS 5 Yr Growth	% Annualized Total Return 12 Mo	36 Mo	60 Mo
1	CMLS	✓Cumulus Media 'A'	NNM	NR	..	...	Own/oper radio stations	....	....	17 7/8	4 7/8	55 7/16	9 1/8	85547	55 7/16	36 1/2	50 3/4	...	d	...	205	...	...
2	CW	✓Curtiss-Wright	NY,B,Ch,P,Ph	B–	77	8295	Process eq,aerospace,nuclear	39 7/8	2 1/2	48 3/8	33 1/16	40 5/8	30 3/8	494	37 7/8	35 5/8	36 7/8	1.4	10	...	–1.9	15.1	17.1
3	CVI	✓CV REIT	NY,Ch	NR	11	155	Real estate investment trust	27	7/16	15 1/4	11 1/2	13 5/8	8 7/8	5220	11 1/8	8 7/8	9	12.9	5	17	–21.4	–5.0	10.1
4	CVB	✓CVB Financial	AS	A–	38	1779	Comm'l bkg,California	22 5/8	7/16	26 3/8	16 1/2	29 5/8	18 3/8	2268	25 1/8	22 1/2	23 1/8	2.1	17	18	15.4	35.5	35.4
5	CNV	✓CVF Technologies	AS	NR	5	716	Information & enviro tech	....	....	8 1/8	2 5/8	6 3/4	2	6067	4	2 1/2	3 15/16	...	d	...	5.0	...	...
¶6•[1]	CVS	✓CVS Corp	NY,B,Ch,P,Ph	B–	965	323241	Oper drug/health stores	35	5/8	56	30 7/16	58 3/8	30	642876	40 3/16	30	39 7/8	0.6	26	NM	–27.1	...	...
7	CTF	CVS Corp $4.23'TRACES'	NY	NR	14	1012	Trust Auto Com Exch Secur	....	....	100 9/16	69 1/2	102 7/8	57 1/2	4397	72 3/4	57 1/2	71 1/4	5.9	..	...	–25.1	...	...
8	CYAN	✓Cyanotech Corp	NNM	B–	3	232	Dvlp algae related products	15	1/4	4 7/16	7/8	2 1/4	1/2	27920	2 1/4	1/2	1 9/16	...	d	Neg	47.1	–37.6	2.1
9•[2]	CYCH	✓CyberCash Inc	NNM	NR	34	1131	Internet fin'l svc/softwr	64 3/4	10 1/2	27 3/4	5 7/8	24	6 11/16	107069	11 7/8	9	9 1/4	...	d	...	–38.3	–26.2	...
10•[3]	CYBX	✓Cyberonics Inc	NNM	C	82	8548	Epilepsy treatment svcs	16 1/2	1 7/8	32 5/8	4 1/2	20 7/8	7 1/8	38891	18 1/4	13 7/8	15 15/16	...	d	16	18.1	65.7	35.4
11	CYSP	✓Cybershop.com Inc	NNM	NR	12	609	On-line retail svcs	....	....	30	2 3/4	17 1/2	5 1/8	111747	11 3/8	5 1/8	5 1/2	...	d	...	–51.6	...	...
✛12•[4]	CBXC	✓Cybex Computer Products	NNM	NR	101	6896	Dvlp/mkt computer eqp	13 9/16	4 11/16	29 3/8	9 7/8	52 3/8	14 7/8	29941	46 3/8	34 1/2	40 1/2	...	35	25	37.9	92.7	...
13	CYB	✓Cybex Intl	AS	C	22	1382	Mfr exercise/sports eqp	33 3/8	1/4	14 3/8	3 7/8	5 5/8	2	3076	2 7/8	2	2 5/8	...	11	19	–38.2	–35.6	–27.1
✛14•[5]	CYGN	✓Cygnus Inc	NNM	C	82	10606	Transdermal drug delivery sys	32 1/4	5 1/2	21	2 7/16	20	4 1/4	353087	20	8 7/16	18 1/4	...	d	–13	274	8.0	22.0
15•[4]	CYLK	✓Cylink Corp	NNM	NR	33	6997	Info security pds	28 3/4	6 5/8	15 7/8	2 15/16	14 15/16	3 3/8	49305	14 15/16	10 1/8	13 1/2	...	d	–15	272	1.3	...
16•[6]	CYMI	✓Cymer Inc	NNM	NR	171	17639	Mfg photolithography eq	49 1/4	4 3/4	29 7/8	5 7/8	48 7/8	14 1/2	95844	48 7/8	37 7/16	46	...	d	...	215	24.2	...
#17•[7]	CY	✓Cypress Semiconductor	NY,P	C	284	77407	Mfrs integrated circuits	27 3/4	3	12	5 1/2	33 1/2	7 3/8	340323	33 1/2	25 1/8	32 3/8	...	47	Neg	290	31.8	22.9
18	CYSV	✓Cysive Inc	NNM	NR	..	...	e-business software prd	....	....	....	....	85 1/8	17	38911	75 1/2	45	72 1/16	...	..	...	...	...	...
#19•[8]	CYT	✓Cytec Industries	NY,Ph,P	NR	246	29338	Integrated chemical prod'n	50 15/16	4 3/16	58 9/16	14 7/8	31 15/16	19 1/2	35209	24 1/4	21 3/4	23	...	8	24	8.2	–17.3	12.3
20•[6]	CYTC	✓Cytyc Corp	NNM	NR	177	16453	Dgn/dvp sample preparation sys	34 1/2	11 3/4	27 7/8	7 3/8	62 9/16	10	69012	62 9/16	40 3/8	61 1/16	...	..	NM	137	31.3	...
✛21•[1]	DHI	✓D.R.Horton	NY	NR	265	41395	Single-family home constr'n	21	4	24 15/16	10 5/8	23	10	55052	14 9/16	11 3/4	13 13/16	0.9	6	31	–39.5	9.0	24.2
22	DTII	✓D T Industries	NNM	NR	66	7637	Mfr spcl machines/metal prd	43 3/4	8 1/2	39	14 3/4	19 1/16	5 1/8	11507	8 5/16	7 3/16	7 7/8	...	d	Neg	–49.8	–39.0	–5.6
23	DAJ	Daimler-Benz 5.75% Sub Notes	NY	NR	1	15	Sub Mand Conv Notes	89	72 1/2	108	65	106 1/2	66	209	76 15/16	66	73 1/2	4.0	..	...	–20.4	...	...
24•[9]	DCX	✓DaimlerChrysler AG	NY	NR	475	37913	Mfr auto,electr/aerospc prd	....	....	99 1/16	74 1/2	108 5/8	65 5/16	134782	78 1/4	66 1/8	78	...	12	...	–16.6	...	...
✛25•[1]	DRC	✓Dain Rauscher	NY,B,Ch	B	136	5034	Brokerage/investm't bkg svcs	70 1/4	7/8	69	25 9/16	59 1/8	27 13/16	11084	49	41 3/4	46 1/2	1.9	13	–5	60.7	11.7	28.5
26	DMC.B	✓Dairy Mart Conven Str'B'	AS	C	6	78	Retail self-service strs	12 5/16	2 1/4	4 3/4	2 3/4	5 1/2	2 3/4	205	4 1/2	3 1/4	3 7/16	...	19	NM	1.8	–7.7	–4.2
27	DMC.A	Cl'A'	AS	C	9	183		12 1/8	2 1/2	5	2 7/8	5 5/8	2 3/8	2404	4 1/4	2 7/8	3 3/8	...	19	NM	–6.9	–9.1	–3.3
28	DZTK	✓Daisytek Intl	NNM	NR	93	11248	Dstr office/computer access eq	24	7 1/2	28 1/4	12 3/4	24 1/2	9	134192	24 1/2	18	23 5/16	...	30	7	22.7	4.5	...
29	DAKT	Daktronics Inc	NNM	NR	16	381	Mfg info display sys	10	3 1/4	16 1/2	5	29 3/4	8 1/4	14724	29 3/4	18	25 1/4	...	18	NM	113	84.8	36.9
30•[3]	DTL	✓Dal-Tile Intl	NY	NR	103	23210	Mfr,dstr,mkt ceramic tile	21 5/8	9 1/4	15 3/16	6	13 1/8	6 3/4	17979	10 1/2	8 15/16	10 1/8	...	9	...	–2.4	–20.8	...
✛31•[10]	DS	✓Dallas Semiconductor	NY,Ph	B+	305	23549	Mfrs hi performance circuits	56	4 1/8	50 1/16	22 11/16	64 15/16	33 1/16	26123	64 15/16	56 1/8	64 7/16	0.3	31	14	58.8	41.6	31.7
✛32•[4]	DMRK	✓Damark International'A'	NNM	C	49	2483	Direct market catalog sales	31	3 3/4	13 3/8	5 1/8	16 1/2	6 1/8	12552	16 1/2	9 1/2	15 3/4	...	d	Neg	93.8	18.4	13.8
33	DRF	✓Dan River 'A'	NY	NR	53	8989	Mfr, mkt textile products	16 7/8	15	21 1/2	8 1/16	11 3/4	4 3/8	8015	5 5/8	4 3/8	5 1/8	...	11	...	–56.4	...	...
¶34•	DCN	✓Dana Corp	NY,B,Ch,P	B+	642	122676	Mfr parts for auto industry	54 3/8	2 5/16	61 1/2	31 5/16	54 1/16	26	161797	30 3/16	26 11/16	29 15/16	4.1	7	9	–24.2	0.0	8.1
¶35•[11]	DHR	✓Danaher Corp	NY,B,Ch,P	B+	506	69943	Mfr hand tools,auto parts	32	1/8	55 1/4	28	69	42 3/4	79998	51 3/16	42 3/4	48 1/4	0.1	27	16	–11.1	27.7	30.2
36	DHC	✓Danielson Holding	AS,Ch	NR	36	3876	Investment co/insurance	14	2 3/8	8 1/8	3	7 1/2	2 7/8	3344	5 3/4	4 5/8	5 3/4	...	72	8	61.4	4.8	–5.5
37•[1]	DANKY	✓Danka Business Systems ADR[57]	NNM,Ch	NR	45	21823	Dstr office eq N.Amer&Europe	51 7/8	4 3/8	23 3/4	1 3/4	14 1/8	4 1/8	88592	14 1/8	11 3/8	12 1/16	...	d	Neg	203	–28.4	–9.5
¶38•[3]	DRI	✓Darden Restaurants	NY	NR	423	102188	Oper family style restaurants	14	6 3/4	18 15/16	11 3/4	23 3/8	15 5/8	69464	18 3/8	15 7/8	18 1/8	0.4	16	64	1.1	28.2	...
39	DAR	✓Darling International	AS	NR	26	13063	Processes animal-by-prd/grease	11 13/16	3	9 1/8	2 1/2	3 1/2	7/8	804	2 1/8	1 7/8	2 1/8	...	d	Neg	–30.6	–39.9	–13.2
40	DASTY	✓Dassault Systems ADS[58]	NNM	NR	21	1065	Dvp CAD/CAM software pds	36 7/8	11 1/2	55	25 5/8	65	30 1/16	11167	65	44 15/16	63	0.3	..	...	34.8	40.5	...
41•[12]	DBCC	✓Data Broadcasting	NNM	NR	73	3493	Provide stock quotes,finl info	15	1	18 9/16	2 9/16	50 5/8	6 1/8	200178	11 3/8	7 1/2	8 1/4	...	d	Neg	–53.8	5.6	14.9
42•[13]	DDIM	✓Data Dimensions	NNM	NR	17	595	Millennium data consult'g svcs	40 3/4	4 1/4	19	6 7/8	9 3/8	1 1/8	107559	5	2 1/2	2 9/16	...	11	56	–70.1	–39.9	...
43	DRAI	✓Data Research Associates	NNM	↓B	17	1217	Provides library automat'n sys	16 3/16	4 11/16	19 3/4	11 3/4	14 5/8	6 3/4	1666	9 5/8	6 3/4	8	1.5	18	–2	–42.3	–18.2	5.3
44	DRTN	✓Data Return	NNM	NR	..	...	Internet hosting svcs	....	....	....	....	67 1/8	13	98094	67 1/8	25	53 1/2	...	d	...	...	...	...
45	DTLN	Data Transmission Ntwk	NNM	C	64	8389	Agricultural market info svc	33 1/4	1 13/16	46	22 1/4	33 1/4	16 1/8	16283	21 1/2	16 1/2	17 1/4	...	d	–3	–40.3	–8.1	27.9
46	DKEY	Datakey Inc	NSC	C	5	751	Mfrs electronic access keys	12	1 7/8	7 1/2	1 15/16	5 5/8	1	16883	3 7/8	1 1/2	3 3/16	...	d	Neg	6.2	2.0	–0.4
47	DLK	Datalink.net Inc	AS	NR	1	40	Personalized info svcs	45	2 1/2	4 5/16	5/8	12 1/8	1 1/16	68110	12 1/8	3 3/8	10 7/8	...	d	...	1022	–26.6	...
48	DC	✓Datametrics Corp	AS,P	C	6	516	Mfr computer printers/periph'ls	11 3/4	1/16	2 11/16	3/4	2 3/8	13/16	7820	1 3/4	1 3/16	1 5/16	...	d	–23	–36.4	7.3	–23.5
49	DTM	✓Dataram Corp	AS,B,Ph	B	14	700	Computer memory products	6 9/16	....	7 5/16	2 15/16	24 1/4	4 7/16	23797	24 1/4	12 1/16	22 7/16	...	32	NM	257	99.7	61.5
✛50•[14]	DSCP	✓Datascope Corp	NNM	B+	139	9851	Electronic medical instru't'n	41 3/4	9/16	30 1/2	16	41	19 1/8	12091	41	36 5/8	40	0.4	27	7	73.9	26.0	18.7
51	DTSI	✓Datron Systems	NNM	B	17	1389	Satellite commun/radar sys	20 1/2	2	10 1/2	3 1/2	10 1/2	4 7/8	2855	10 1/2	7 3/4	8 1/2	...	13	45	56.3	2.0	–7.4

Uniform Footnote Explanations-See Page 4. Other: [1]P:Cycle 2. [2]CBOE,Ph:Cycle 3. [3]CBOE:Cycle 1. [4]CBOE:Cycle 2. [5]P:Cycle 3. [6]ASE,CBOE:Cycle 2. [7]CBOE,P:Cycle 3. [8]ASE:Cycle 2. [9]ASE,CBOE,P,Ph:Cycle 1. [10]Ph:Cycle 1. [11]Ph:Cycle 3. [12]CBOE:Cycle 3. [13]CBOE,Ph:Cycle 2. [14]P,Ph:Cycle 3. [51]Incl curr amt. [52]®$0.62,'96. [53]Re-spec cond. [54]To be determined. [55]Incl curr amts. [56]®$4.39,'96. [57]Ea ADR rep 4 ord, 5p. [58]Ea ADS rep 1 ord Par 10 FF.

Splits ◆ Index	Cash Divs. Ea.Yr. Since	Dividends: Latest Payment Period $	Date	Ex. Div.	Total $ So Far 1999	Ind. Rate	Paid 1998	Financial Position Mil-$ Cash& Equiv.	Curr. Assets	Curr. Liab.	Balance Sheet Date	Capitalization Lg Trm Debt Mil-$	Shs. 000 Pfd.	Com.	Earnings $ Per Shr. Years End	1995	1996	1997	1998	1999	Last 12 Mos.	Interim Earnings Period	$ per Shr. 1998	1999	Index
1	....	None Since Public			...	Nil	....	202	258	15.4	9-30-99	[51]285	129	★±34724	Dc	...	...	vpd2.50	v□d1.59	....	d1.85	9 Mo Sep	v□d0.93	vd1.19	1
2◆	1974	Q0.13	12-15-99	11-29	0.52	0.52	0.52	34.6	176	71.5	9-30-99	20.1	...	10083	Dc	v1.78	v1.58	v2.71	v2.82	....	3.73	9 Mo Sep	v2.04	v2.95	2
3	1976	Q0.29	1-13-00	12-31	1.16	1.16	1.16	Total Assets $258.41M			9-30-99	157	...	7967	Dc	v1.18	v1.20	v1.07	v1.99	....	1.75	9 Mo Sep	v0.89	v0.65	3
4◆	1990	Q0.12	2-15-00	1-28	0.349	0.48	0.364	Total Deposits $1245.9M			9-30-99	0.38	...	19630	Dc	v0.68	v0.79	v1.01	v1.21	....	1.38	9 Mo Sep	v0.87	v1.04	4
5	....	None Since Public			...	Nil	....	1.25	5.50	4.11	9-30-99	0.57	...	6720	Dc	d0.22	vd0.03	Pv1.47	vd0.75	....	d0.67	9 Mo Sep	vd0.57	v□d0.49	5
6◆	1916	Q0.05¾	11-3-99	10-20	0.23	0.23	0.22½	169	4646	2977	9-25-99	575	5300	391884	Dc	□vd1.80	v0.49	v0.12	v0.98	E1.53	1.47	9 Mo Sep	v0.61	v1.10	6
7	1998	1.058	11-15-99	10-28	4.23	4.23	1.974	5-21-2001 exch for CVS Corp com re-spec cond				....	...	★3048	Dc	...	...	...	...	....	....				7
8	....	None Paid			...	Nil	....	0.22	3.08	2.63	9-30-99	....	595	13766	Mr	0.17	v0.25	vd0.02	vd0.21	....	d0.21	6 Mo Sep	vd0.09	vd0.09	8
9	....	None Since Public			...	Nil	....	13.4	19.0	5.57	9-30-99	....	...	22958	Dc	pd1.39	vd2.77	vd2.43	vd2.15	....	d2.05	9 Mo Sep	vd1.71	vd1.61	9
10	....	None Since Public			...	Nil	....	17.2	27.0	4.57	9-30-99	....	...	17715	Je	d0.79	d1.06	vd0.93	vd0.88	vd0.72	d0.36	3 Mo Sep	vd0.27	vΔ0.09	10
11	....	None Since Public			...	Nil	....	5.71	8.25	5.31	9-30-99	0.07	...	9398	Dc	pvd0.11	pvd0.10	pvd0.26	vd1.22	....	d1.42	9 Mo Sep	vd0.53	vd0.73	11
12◆	....	None Since Public			...	Nil	....	37.9	67.4	13.2	10-01-99	....	...	12785	Mr	v0.41	v0.47	v0.28	v0.95	....	1.17	6 Mo Sep	v0.47	v0.69	12
13	....	0.02	8-20-90	7-16	...	Nil	....	1.84	43.5	28.0	9-25-99	33.8	...	8673	Dc	vd0.38	v0.45	vd0.76	v0.12	....	0.25	9 Mo Sep	vd0.01	v0.12	13
14	....	None Since Public			...	Nil	....	21.9	25.0	13.3	9-30-99	45.4	...	24774	Dc	d0.79	vd0.60	vd2.67	vd1.95	....	d1.42	9 Mo Sep	vd1.23	vd0.70	14
15	....	None Since Public			...	Nil	....	38.2	65.7	16.2	9-26-99	0.11	...	29730	Dc	vd0.06	v0.05	vd2.20	v0.18	....	d0.51	9 Mo Sep	v0.41	vd0.28	15
16◆	....	None Since Public			...	Nil	....	152	302	96.7	9-30-99	173	...	28277	Dc	p0.01	v0.29	v0.86	v0.09	....	d0.11	9 Mo Sep	v0.19	vd0.01	16
17◆	....	None Since Public			...	Nil	....	202	398	159	10-03-99	160	...	109290	Dc	v1.09	v[52]0.62	v0.21	vd1.24	E0.69↓	0.17	9 Mo Sep	vd1.01	v0.40	17
18	....	None Since Public			...	Nil	....	....	4.48	2.35	p6-30-99	....	...	★11127	Dc	...	...	...	v0.06	....	....	6 Mo Jun	n/a	vpd1.55	18
19◆	....	None Since Public			...	Nil	....	14.1	480	360	9-30-99	415	4	42224	Dc	v1.50	v2.03	v2.39	v2.68	....	2.75	9 Mo Sep	v1.98	v2.05	19
20◆	....	None Since Public			...	Nil	....	70.5	95.8	17.1	9-30-99	....	...	17999	Dc	vpd0.71	vpd0.92	vd1.31	vd0.66	....	0.36	9 Mo Sep	vd0.87	v0.15	20
21◆	1997	Q0.03	10-28-99	10-19	0.12	0.12	0.09	Total Assets $2362M			9-30-99	1191	...	62783	Sp	0.74	0.87	v1.15	v1.56	v2.50	2.50				21
22	1994	Div Omitted 9-28-99			0.04	Nil	0.08	8.37	209	90.8	9-26-99	120	...	10107	Je	0.94	1.50	v□2.42	□v2.49	vd0.17	d0.57	3 Mo Sep	v0.37	vd0.03	22
23	1997	1.451	11-24-99	11-10	4.609	2.96	7.96	Amt paid mat based on DaimlerChrysler shrs[53]				jp1000	...		Dc	...	...	...	...	....	....	Due 6-14-2002			23
24	1999	2.50	5-19-99	5-19	2.50	[54]....	....	Equity per shr $27.75			p12-31-98	[55]43999	...	p1003200	Dc	vpd1.83	pv5.42	pv7.30	v6.54	E6.33	6.81	9 Mo Sep	v4.65	v4.92	24
25◆	1992	Q0.22	11-24-99	11-8	0.88	0.88	0.88	Total Assets $2476M			9-30-99	108	...	12484	Dc	v2.85	v[56]4.49	v3.77	v0.61	....	3.69	9 Mo Sep	v1.01	v4.09	25
26	....	0.024	2-28-89	2-6	...	Nil	....	5.57	57.9	62.6	10-31-99	112	...	±4747	Ja	±vd1.12	v±d0.42	v±d0.37	v±0.01	....	0.18	9 Mo Oct	v±0.20	v±0.37	26
27	....	0.024	2-28-89	2-6	...	Nil	....	....	...	...		....	...	3223	Ja	±d1.12	v±d0.42	v±d0.37	v±0.01	....	0.18	9 Mo Oct	v±0.20	v±0.37	27
28◆	....	None Since Public			...	Nil	....	2.59	281	114	9-30-99	71.1	...	17174	Mr	v0.80	v0.97	v1.13	v□1.08	....	0.77	6 Mo Sep	v□0.60	v0.29	28
29◆	....	None Since Public			...	Nil	....	0.39	48.5	27.1	10-30-99	7.73	...	4397	Ap	0.23	vd0.05	v0.35	v0.78	v0.94	1.40	6 Mo Oct	v0.44	v0.90	29
30	....	None Since Public			...	Nil	....	0.86	266	161	10-01-99	383	...	54388	Dc	pv0.07	□v0.69	vd2.06	v0.45	....	1.15	9 Mo Sep	v0.30	v1.00	30
31	1995	Q0.05	12-1-99	11-10	0.20	0.20	0.16	177	327	56.5	10-03-99	....	...	28879	Dc	v1.32	v1.37	v2.19	v1.85	....	2.07	9 Mo Sep	v1.37	v1.59	31
32	....	None Since Public			...	Nil	....	8.39	83.2	91.6	10-02-99	....	...	5508	Dc	vd0.20	v0.70	v0.74	vd2.71	....	d2.21	9 Mo Sep	vd1.34	vΔd0.84	32
33	....	None Since Public			...	Nil	....	1.58	281	89.3	10-02-99	304	...	±22816	Dc	±pv0.02	p±v0.40	v□0.89	v□0.85	....	0.46	9 Mo Sep	v0.93	v0.54	33
34	1936	Q0.31	12-15-99	11-29	1.24	1.24	1.14	185	5091	4021	9-30-99	2574	...	164510	Dc	v2.83	v2.99	v3.49	v3.20	E4.05	3.88	9 Mo Sep	v2.39	v3.07	34
35◆	1993	Q0.01½	1-31-00	12-29	0.06	0.06	0.05¼	280	1208	801	10-01-99	341	...	142346	Dc	v0.91	v1.74	v1.28	v1.32	E1.76	1.69	9 Mo Sep	v0.91	v1.28	35
36	....	None Since Public			...	Nil	....	Total Assets $184.06M			9-30-99	....	...	17576	Dc	v0.14	vd0.53	v0.28	v0.14	....	0.08	9 Mo Sep	v0.11	v0.05	36
37◆	1993	0.108	7-28-98	6-24	...	Nil	0.21½	74.0	1044	605	9-30-99	980	...	228068	Mr	□0.90	v□0.73	v0.90	vd5.18	....	d4.70	6 Mo Sep	vd0.15	v0.33	37
38	1995	S0.04	11-1-99	10-6	0.08	0.08	0.08	30.2	358	526	8-29-99	313	...	131419	My	p0.31	v0.46	vd0.59	v0.67	v0.99	1.17	6 Mo Nov	v0.35	v0.53	38
39◆	....	None Since Public			...	Nil	....	2.76	39.0	44.1	10-02-99	115	...	15587	Dc	v0.90	v0.46	v0.33	vd2.06	....	d2.27	9 Mo Sep	vd0.70	vd0.91	39
40◆	1997	0.169	7-22-99	6-28	0.169	0.17	0.142	1229	2051	925	j12-31-97	96.5	...	110930	Dc	p0.38	p0.63	vd0.14	n/a	....	....	9 Mo Sep	v0.57	v0.62	40
41	....	None Since Public			...	Nil	....	39.9	58.4	32.7	9-30-99	....	...	34464	Je	0.68	v0.27	vd0.54	vd0.14	vd0.12	d0.21	3 Mo Sep	vNil	vd0.09	41
42◆	....	None Since Public			...	Nil	....	6.60	35.7	13.2	9-30-99	1.24	...	13657	Dc	0.10	v0.15	vNil	v0.69	....	0.24	9 Mo Sep	v0.47	v0.02	42
43◆	1997	0.12	1-25-00	1-6	0.12	0.12	0.12	16.0	24.6	6.11	6-30-99	....	...	5045	Sp	0.66	v0.80	v0.81	v0.67	Pv0.45	0.45				43
44	....	None Since Public			...	Nil	....	3.12	4.14	1.85	6-30-99	p....	...	★34461	Mr	...	...	...	vd0.07	....	d0.13	6 Mo Sep	vd0.04	vd0.10	44
45◆	....	None Since Public			...	Nil	....	0.36	20.1	35.7	9-30-99	28.9	...	11961	Dc	vd0.03	vd0.09	v0.19	v□d0.24	....	d0.16	9 Mo Sep	v□d0.18	vd0.10	45
46	....	None Paid			...	Nil	....	0.02	2.38	1.19	10-02-99	....	224	★5792	Dc	v0.06	vd0.60	vd1.45	vd0.94	....	d0.99	9 Mo Sep	vd0.66	vd0.71	46
47◆	....	None Paid			...	Nil	....	2.13	2.21	1.94	9-30-99	0.04	p237	3498	Mr	d3.50	vd3.01	vd7.53	vd2.12	....	d1.20	6 Mo Sep	vd1.37	vd0.45	47
48	....	7½%Stk	3-21-80	2-26	...	Nil	....	0.78	8.14	3.61	7-25-99	5.16	...	19007	Oc	d0.84	d1.39	vd0.24	vd0.22	....	d0.19	9 Mo Jul	vd0.12	vd0.09	48
49◆	....	None Since Public			...	Nil	....	8.39	30.4	12.3	10-31-99	....	...	7922	Ap	vd0.11	v0.13	v0.37	v0.39	v0.60	0.70	6 Mo Oct	v0.29	v0.39	49
50	2000	Q0.04	1-14-00	12-15	...	0.16	....	52.6	169	44.5	9-30-99	....	...	14989	Je	v1.07	v1.24	v0.86	v1.32	v1.36	1.49	3 Mo Sep	v0.17	v0.30	50
51	....	None Since Public			...	Nil	....	5.00	32.4	10.7	9-30-99	3.13	...	2701	Mr	vd0.48	v0.10	vd1.18	v0.63	....	0.67	6 Mo Sep	v0.20	v0.24	51

◆Stock Splits & Divs By Line Reference Index [2]2-for-1,'97. [4]3-for-2,'98:10%,'95,'96,'97,'98:To split 5-for-4,ex Feb 1. [6]2-for-1,'98. [12]3-for-2,'98(twice). [16]2-for-1,'97. [17]2-for-1,'95. [19]3-for-1,'96. [20]To split 2-for-1,ex Jan 31. [21]7-for-5,'95:Adj to 8%,'96. [25]3-for-2,'95. [28]2-for-1,'98. [29]To split 2-for-1,ex Jan 10, 2000. [35]2-for-1,'95,'98. [37]2-for-1,'94. [39]3-for-1,'97. [40]2-for-1,'97. [42]3-for-1,'97. [43]3-for-2,'96. [45]3-for-1,'96. [47]1-for-300 REVERSE,'96:1-for-10 REVERSE,'97. [49]2-for-1,'98:3-for-2,'99.

¶ S&P 500 · # MidCap 400 · ✣ SmallCap 600 · • Options

Index	Ticker	Name of Issue (Call Price of Pfd. Stocks)	Market	Com. Rank. & Pfd. Rating	Inst. Hold Cos	Inst. Hold Shs. (000)	Principal Business	Price Range 1971-97 High	1971-97 Low	1998 High	1998 Low	1999 High	1999 Low	Dec. Sales in 100s	December, 1999 Last Sale Or Bid High	Low	Last	%Div Yield	P-E Ratio	EPS 5 Yr Growth	% Annualized Total Return 12 Mo	36 Mo	60 Mo
1•[1]	DAB	✓Dave & Buster's	NY	NR	95	5048	Restaurants/entertainment	27⅝	7 7/16	27¾	10½	29⅜	5 1/16	90509	10⅜	5 1/16	8 3/16	...	10	45	-64.5	-15.0	...
2	DABR	✓David's Bridal	NNM	NR	53	9601	Retail bridal gowns	....	....	....	....	16	6¼	52690	12½	7⅛	11 3/16	...	19	...	...	...	...
3	DAVX	✓Davox Corp	NNM	B–	50	6509	Computer-aid commun'n sys	39¾	¾	35½	4¾	25½	5 15/16	67620	25½	16¼	19⅝	...	32	NM	157	-10.6	40.6
4	DAWK	✓Daw Technologies	NNM	NR	13	1705	Dgn cleanroom sys/svc	10⅝	1	3¼	⅝	2 1/16	7/16	14261	¾	½	⅝	...	d	Neg	-44.4	-39.0	-35.8
5	DWSN	✓Dawson Geophysical	NNM	B–	26	1670	Seismic data for oil/gas ind	27⅜	3	19¾	6⅝	12 7/16	6 1/16	3437	9½	8⅜	8 13/16	...	d	Neg	22.6	-7.8	-3.2
6	DXR	✓Daxor Corp	AS	C	12	430	Operates human sperm bank	37	1/16	16⅜	11½	18½	11¾	1482	15½	14	14½	...	d	Neg	-2.5	3.5	21.6
7	DAYR	✓Day Runner	NNM	B+	52	7208	Mfr personal organizer prd	21½	3¾	25½	11½	15½	3⅝	26643	7 7/16	3⅝	3⅞	...	d	Neg	-73.1	-26.3	-12.8
¶8•[2]	DH	✓Dayton Hudson	NY,B,Ch,P,Ph	A	1301	386718	Depart/disc/spec stores	37	¼	54¼	31 7/16	77	50 1/16	389293	77	65⅞	73 7/16	0.5	29	15	36.2	57.1	46.5
9	DAY	✓Dayton Mining	AS,Ch,Ph	NR	10	3338	Precious metal explor,dvlp	8	1 5/16	2	3/16	5/16	1/32	237965	⅛	1/16	⅛	...	..	...	-62.4	-75.9	...
10	DSD	✓Dayton Superior'A'	NY	NR	63	5127	Concrete/masonry accessory prd	19 7/16	9⅛	22⅛	14⅜	23½	11¾	3865	19 11/16	14½	16¼	...	7	NM	-16.1	7.4	...
11	Pr	10% Cap Tr Cv Pfd([51]21.40)	NY	NR	..	...		....	....	....	....	20⅝	16¾	749	20⅝	16¾	17¼	11.6	..	...	...	...	...
✣12	DBT	✓DBT Online	NY	NR	82	7128	On-line computer svcs	34¾	11¼	33⅜	12⅜	39 15/16	17⅜	13873	25⅞	17⅜	24 5/16	...	70	...	-2.5	17.9	...
13	DER	✓De Rigo ADS[53]	NY,Ch,P,Ph	NR	6	1351	Mfr sunglasses/eyeglass frames	31¾	5⅞	9 15/16	3¼	8½	4⅝	5928	6 1/16	4 15/16	5⅛B	...	47	-23	-7.5	-17.1	...
#14•[3]	DF	✓Dean Foods	NY,Ch,P	B+	243	19056	Milk & dairy: food items	59¾	⅜	60 11/16	39½	46 9/16	32 15/16	39759	40⅜	34⅝	39¾	2.2	20	NM	-0.4	9.3	8.9
15	DBRSY	✓DeBeers Consol Mines ADR[55]	NSC	NR	150	70625	Diamond mining	37¾	2⅛	27⅜	11 7/16	31¾	12¾	67951	31¾	27	28 15/16	2.5	25	-4	134	4.9	8.2
16	DII	✓Decorator Indus	AS	B	26	1275	Mfr & dstr of draperies	8 13/16	3/16	11 13/16	6¾	8¼	5	1524	5 5/16	5	5 5/16	5.3	7	5	-28.4	-5.2	13.9
17	DET	DECS Trust 8.50% 2000	NY	NR	3	314	Exch Notes For Com Stock	25⅞	23⅞	25½	8⅝	10 5/16	3⅜	3215	4 15/16	3⅜	4	...	..	...	-41.7	...	...
18	RYD	DECS Trust II 6.875% 2000	NY	NR	1	.3	Exch Notes For Com Stock	26⅜	23⅛	32¼	16½	27	18	2062	22¼	20⅞	21⅜	8.5	..	...	5.4	...	...
¶19•[4]	DE	✓Deere & Co	NY,B,C,Ch,P,Ph	B+	726	181785	Lgst mfr farm eq:constr mchy	60½	3 5/16	64⅛	28⅜	45 15/16	31 9/16	207550	43⅞	39 11/16	43⅜	2.0	43	-7	35.1	4.3	17.0
20	DGTC	✓Del Global Technologies	NNM,Ch	B+	33	3830	Mfr medical imaging sys	18⅞	1/16	12⅞	6⅛	11¾	7 3/16	7621	8 13/16	7 3/16	7¾	...	9	18	-32.6	-3.0	12.2
21	DLI	✓Del Laboratories	AS	A	22	1311	Drugs and cosmetics	30⅛	⅜	33 3/16	15 11/16	24½	7½	2281	9⅞	7½	7⅞	s1.7	d	Neg	-66.6	-18.9	-4.1
22•[5]	DLM	✓Del Monte Foods	NY,Ph	NR	80	21459	Mfr canned vegetables/fruit	....	....	....	....	17	9	32916	13⅜	9	12 5/16	...	11	...	...	...	...
23	RMY	✓Delco Remy Intl'A'	NY,Ph	NR	31	5234	Dgn/mfr auto & truck parts	13 1/16	12	17½	9⅛	11⅛	8	4101	9 7/16	8	8¼	...	7	...	-15.9	...	...
24•[6]	DZB	✓Delhaize America Cl'B'	NY	B+	87	7112	Oper food supermarket chain	54½	⅛	34⅛	23⅝	37 11/16	18¾	14445	23 7/16	20⅛	20⅞	2.4	11	13	-29.6	-10.3	8.0
25•[6]	DZA	✓ Class'A'non-vtg	NY	B+	125	14832		54½	¼	34 5/16	25⅛	38¼	17¼	44358	22¼	19 9/16	20 5/16	2.5	11	13	-35.1	-10.0	7.5
26	DLIA	✓dELiAs Inc	NNM	NR	50	3875	Direct marketing apparel	26⅛	11	32	4⅛	40	5½	64365	10⅝	7¼	7¼	...	d	...	-42.0	-28.5	...
¶27•[7]	DELL	✓Dell Computer Corp	NNM	B	1308	1060850	Dvlp/mfr IBM compatible PC's	13	1/16	37⅞	9 15/16	55	31⅜	6420231	54	40½	51	...	68	69	39.8	150	141
¶28•[8]	DPH	✓Delphi Automotive Systems	NY,Ph	NR	691	346171	Supply automotive parts	....	....	....	....	22¼	14	424307	16 3/16	14	15¾	1.8	8	...	...	...	...
✣29•[6]	DFG	✓Delphi Fin'l Group 'A'	NY,Ch,Ph	B+	192	8314	Ins hldg:life,disability,accid	42 3/16	4 5/16	59⅜	30 7/16	55 13/16	26 7/16	15780	30¼	26⅝	30	s...	12	15	-38.1	7.3	18.9
¶30•[9]	DAL	✓Delta Air Lines	NY,B,C,Ch,P,Ph	B–	623	101435	Domestic, Int'l air service	60 5/16	6⅜	71 13/16	40⅞	72	45 11/16	189008	53	47⅜	49 13/16	0.2	7	47	-4.0	12.3	14.8
31	DNT	Delta Air Lines 8.125% Nts	NY	....[56]	4	95	Equity note securities	....	....	....	....	25⅜	20	15170	23 11/16	20	20 15/16	9.7	..	...	...	...	...
✣32•[10]	DLP	✓Delta and Pine Land[57]	NY	B	146	20186	Produce cotton planting seed	33 11/16	3⅜	54	25⅞	38¾	14⅛	104054	25 13/16	14⅛	17⅜	0.7	97	-20	-52.8	0.4	30.5
33	DFC	✓Delta Financial	NY	NR	53	5371	Consumer finance svcs	25⅝	13	20⅝	2⅝	8⅝	3½	8081	5	3½	4⅛	...	9	41	-30.5	-38.8	...
34	DGAS	✓Delta Natural Gas	NNM	B	19	245	Dstr nat'l gas,Kentucky	23½	5¾	19¼	16 7/16	19	14⅛	963	15⅝	14⅜	15½B	7.4	18	-5	-11.0	0.7	6.0
35	DPTR	✓Delta Petroleum	NSC	NR	1	36	Oil&gas explor,dvlp,prod'n	9⅜	1⅝	4½	1⅛	3¾	1⅝	4410	2¾	2	2¾	...	d	23	42.0	-16.3	-16.7
36•[11]	DLW	✓Delta Woodside Ind	NY,Ch,Ph	C	61	10872	Mfr/sale fabrics & apparel	25¼	3⅝	6⅝	3⅛	7⅜	1 7/16	13474	2½	1 7/16	1 15/16	...	d	Neg	-67.5	-31.9	-28.5
37	DDDC	✓deltathree.com Inc	NNM	NR	..	...	Internet telephony svcs	....	....	....	....	33¾	15	109745	30¾	24½	25¾	...	d	...	...	...	...
38	DEL	✓Deltic Timber	NY	NR	87	7157	Timber harvest'g/lumber mfg	33⅛	18½	30 5/16	17⅞	28⅝	19½	1818	26 1/16	21 7/16	21⅞	1.1	32	...	8.5	1.4	...
¶39•[2]	DLX	✓Deluxe Corp	NY,B,Ch,P,Ph	B	446	57815	Imprinted bank checks: forms	49	1½	38 3/16	26 1/16	40½	24 7/16	73068	29 1/16	26	27 7/16	5.4	11	10	-21.6	-1.5	5.4
40	DNR	✓Denbury Resources	NY,To	NR	29	8298	Oil&gas explor,dvlp/prod'n	24¾	5	20⅝	3 7/16	6 11/16	3⅜	7876	4⅜	3 11/16	4¼	...	d	Neg	-1.4	-33.4	...
✣41	DRTE	✓Dendrite International	NNM	NR	206	33155	Manage large sales forces	11 13/16	2¼	19 11/16	6 5/16	39	13 3/16	168096	35	25	33⅞	...	..	...	148	147	...
#42•[10]	XRAY	✓DENTSPLY International	NNM	B+	289	45373	Mfr dental supplies & equip	31¾	1⅜	35⅛	20	29 5/16	20½	63313	24¾	22⅝	23⅝	1.1	21	-3	-7.4	0.7	9.4
✣43	DFS	✓Department 56	NY	NR	170	15278	Design,dstr collectibles/gifts	48	16⅞	39 5/16	22 15/16	37⅞	18 5/16	22267	23 7/16	18 5/16	22⅝	...	9	6	-39.8	-2.8	-10.7
44	DMI	✓Depomed Inc	AS	NR	7	614	Dvp stg:Pharmaceutical R&D	4 11/16	2½	14¼	4	14⅜	1 15/16	16958	6 15/16	3 13/16	6	...	d	...	-23.8	...	...
45	WS	Wrrt(Pur1com at $7.625)	AS	....	3	59		2⅝	¼	8¼	13/16	8⅞	⅝	3355	2⅝	⅝	1½	...	..	...	...	...	...
46	DES	✓Desc S.A. ADS[59]	NY,Ch,P	NR	61	9984	Auto pts,chemicals,R.E.,Finl	43¼	5 9/16	37 11/16	8⅞	29⅛	14 1/16	17509	18½	15¾	16¾	6.4	4	...	-12.7	-6.3	-4.8
47	EDG	Design Automation Sys	AS	NR	..	...	Computer system integration	....	....	....	....	17⅝	2½	7558	17⅝	7 5/16	13 15/16	...	..	...	...	...	...
48	DSHPrA	Designer FinTr 6%Cv'TOPrS'([60]51.80[61])	NY	BBB–			Trust Orig Preferred Sec	51⅛	31	47¾	35¼	38½	24	683	27¼	24	24½	12.2	..	...	...	...	...
49•[11]	DDC	✓Detroit Diesel	NY,Ch	NR	80	6159	Mfr heavy-duty diesel engines	36⅞	15½	25¾	15½	25½	17⅞	10610	19 9/16	18⅛	19 3/16	2.8	10	6	-5.7	-5.3	-1.8
50	DTH	Detroit Edison 7.375% 'QUIDS'[63]	NY	....[64]	3	213	Quraterly Income Debt Sec	....	....	25⅝	24⅞	25 7/16	18	2615	21¾	18	19	9.7	..	...	-18.7	...	...
51	DTB	Detroit Edison 7.54% 'QUIDS'[66]	NY	....[64]	2	107	Qtly Income Debt Securities	....	....	26⅜	24¾	25⅝	18½	2004	22 7/16	18½	19⅞	9.5	..	...	-15.4	...	...

Uniform Footnote Explanations-See Page 4. Other: [1]ASE,CBOE:Cycle 2. [2]P:Cycle 1. [3]P:Cycle 2. [4]ASE:Cycle 3. [5]Ph:Cycle 1. [6]ASE:Cycle 1. [7]Ph:Cycle 2. [8]Ph:Cycle 3. [9]ASE,CBOE,P,Ph:Cycle 1. [10]CBOE:Cycle 2. [11]CBOE:Cycle 3. [51]Fr 10-1-2002,earlier at premium re-spec cond. [52]Cl'A'com of Dayton Superior. [53]Ea ADS rep 1 Ord Shr,Lit 500. [54]To be determined. [55]ADR equal DeBeers/Centenary linked unit. [56]Rated BBB- by S&P. [57]Approve Monsanto Co mgr,0.86 com. [58]If com exceeds $15.25 for 20 of 30 con trad days. [59]Ea ADS rep 20 Sr'C' shrs,no par. [60]Fr 12-31-99. [61]Designer FinTr 6%Cv'TOPrS'(*51.80*). [62]Into shrs of Designer Holdings. [63]Jr Sub Deferrable Int Debs. [64]Rated'BBB'by S&P. [65]Can be deferred by co re-spec cond. [66]Jr Sub Deferrable Int Deb.

Index (Splits ◆)	Cash Divs. Ea.Yr. Since	Dividends: Latest Payment Period $	Date	Ex. Div.	Total $ So Far 1999	Ind. Rate	Paid 1998	Financial Position Mil-$ Cash& Equiv.	Curr. Assets	Curr. Liab.	Balance Sheet Date	Capitalization Lg Trm Debt Mil-$	Shs. 000 Pfd.	Com.	Earnings $ Per Shr. Years End	1995	1996	1997	1998	1999	Last 12 Mos.	Interim Earnings Period	$ per Shr. 1998	1999	Index
1◆	....	None Since Public			...	Nil	....	1.43	22.1	20.3	10-31-99	80.0	...	12953	Ja	v0.34	v0.58	v0.76	v1.03	....	0.84	9 Mo Oct	v0.64	v□0.45	1
2	....	None Since Public			...	Nil	....	13.4	59.7	20.5	10-02-99	2.16	...	19366	Dc	...	...	...	pv0.35	....	0.58	9 Mo Sep	v0.33	v0.56	2
3◆	....	None Since Public			...	Nil	....	57.6	84.5	23.5	9-30-99	....	...	13207	Dc	v0.42	v0.74	v1.45	v0.58	....	0.61	9 Mo Sep	v0.50	v0.53	3
4	....	None Paid			...	Nil	....	1.52	25.5	17.4	9-30-99	0.23	...	12513	Dc	v0.02	v0.27	vd0.18	vd0.32	....	d0.23	9 Mo Sep	vd0.32	vd0.23	4
5	....	None Since Public			...	Nil	....	19.2	26.2	1.09	6-30-99	....	...	5407	Sp	0.54	v0.45	v1.08	v1.27	Pvd1.19	d1.19				5
6	....	0.50	5-30-97	4-28	...	Nil	....	38.0	38.5	7.15	9-30-99	....	...	4713	Dc	v0.26	vd0.02	vd0.03	vd0.09	....	d0.02	9 Mo Sep	vd0.04	v0.03	6
7◆	....	None Since Public			...	Nil	....	9.33	117	41.9	9-30-99	110	...	11901	Je	0.63	0.90	v0.95	v1.27	vd0.34	d0.58	3 Mo Sep	v0.29	v0.05	7
8◆	1965	Q0.10	12-10-99	11-17	0.40	0.40	0.36	246	7104	5970	10-30-99	5263	p338	438176	Ja	0.67	v□30.00	v□1.70	v□2.04	E2.52	2.37	9 Mo Oct	v□1.09	v□1.42	8
9	....	None Paid			...	Nil	....	3.89	19.4	11.5	j6-30-99	5.98	...	★351400	Dc	d0.12	vd0.10	vd0.78	vd1.73	....	....	9 Mo Sep	n/a	vNil	9
10	....	None Since Public			...	Nil	....	3.58	106	46.3	9-30-99	129	...	5943	Dc	pv0.02	±p□0.94	v±1.17	v1.65	....	2.19	9 Mo Sep	v1.47	v2.01	10
11	1999	0.48	12-31-99	12-14	0.48	2.00	....	Cv into 0.80 com[52]				....	1063	...	Dc	...	...	...	....	....	....				11
12◆	....	None Paid			...	Nil	....	26.1	42.0	7.19	9-30-99	....	...	★19084	Dc	p0.05	v0.04	v0.33	v0.35	....	0.35	9 Mo Sep	v0.26	v0.26	12
13	1999	0.069	7-12-99	6-2	0.069	[54]....	....	92.0	214	124	12-31-98	2.31	...	44500	Dc	1.15	0.75	v0.25	v0.11	....	0.11				13
14	1941	Q0.22	12-15-99	11-17	0.86	0.88	0.82	20.8	617	456	8-29-99	658	...	39130	My	2.01	d1.24	v2.15	v2.57	v3.74	2.00	6 Mo Nov	v3.12	v1.38	14
15	1941	0.251	11-4-99	9-8	0.72	0.72	0.964	596	1566	3108	j12-31-98	....	3800	386000	Dc	1.77	1.93	v2.12	v1.21	....	1.17	6 Mo Jun	v0.88	v0.84	15
16◆	1993	Q0.07	12-15-99	12-1	0.28	0.28	0.252	1.64	13.1	6.31	10-02-99	1.84	...	3257	Dc	v0.56	v0.78	v0.74	v0.79	....	0.74	9 Mo Sep	v0.64	v0.59	16
17	1997	0.502	11-15-99	10-28	2.008	[54]....	2.008	Amt pay maturity based on DiMon Inc com stk				....	...	★3100	Je	...	...	...	....	....	....	Due 8-15-2000			17
18	1998	Q0.453	11-15-99	10-28	1.813	1.81	1.879	Amt pay maturity based on Royal Grp Tech com stk				....	...	★3278	Dc	...	...	...	....	....	....	Due 11-15-2000			18
19◆	1937	Q0.22	2-1-00	12-29	0.88	0.88	0.88	Total Assets $18731M			7-31-99	3628	...	233686	Oc	2.71	3.14	v3.74	v4.16	vP1.02	1.02				19
20◆	....	3%Stk	12-23-96	12-2	...	Nil	....	1.77	63.2	13.9	10-30-99	2.08	...	7815	Jl	0.38	0.48	v0.61	v0.71	Pv0.82	0.83	3 Mo Oct	v0.18	v0.19	20
21◆	1973	2%Stk	12-28-99	11-26	s0.137	0.137	0.129	2.55	120	64.1	9-30-99	60.0	...	7512	Dc	v0.84	v1.12	v1.56	v1.33	....	d0.59	9 Mo Sep	v1.37	vd0.55	21
22	....	None Since Public			...	Nil	....	11.0	893	706	9-30-99	487	...	52180	Je	...	...	...	pv0.25	□v0.68	1.15	3 Mo Sep	vd0.34	v0.13	22
23	....	None Since Public			...	Nil	....	11.7	470	206	10-31-99	451	...	±24396	Jl	...	...	pvd0.83	v□d0.11	v1.09	1.19	3 Mo Oct	v0.21	v0.31	23
24◆	1971	0.125	10-26-99	10-7	0.498	0.498	0.444	89.8	1455	1051	6-19-99	921	...	±156678	Dc	±v1.08	v±1.38	v±1.11	v±1.71	E1.90	1.80	6 Mo Jun	v±0.72	v±0.81	24
25◆	1983	0.126	10-26-99	10-7	0.504	0.504	0.45	....	...	...		....	...	80956	Dc	v±1.08	v±1.38	±v1.11	v±1.71	....	1.79	9 Mo Sep	v±1.18	v±1.26	25
26	....	None Since Public			...	Nil	....	70.5	136	45.7	10-30-99	6.97	...	14906	Ja	pNil	vp0.22	v0.34	v0.41	....	d0.10	9 Mo Oct	vNil	vd0.51	26
27◆	....	None Since Public			...	Nil	....	5857	9709	5324	10-29-99	508	...	2565160	Ja	0.08	v□0.17	v0.32	v0.53	E0.75	0.61	9 Mo Oct	v0.37	v0.45	27
28	1999	0.07	1-13-00	12-14	0.14	0.28	....	1258	8944	4764	9-30-99	1647	...	565000	Dc	...	...	p0.75	vpd0.04	E1.88	1.19	9 Mo Sep	vp0.25	v1.48	28
29◆	....	2%Stk	12-15-99	11-29	4%Stk	Stk	2%Stk	Total Assets $3385.98M			9-30-99	422	...	±20668	Dc	v±1.92	v±2.32	v±3.52	v±3.97	....	2.62	9 Mo Sep	v±3.23	v±1.88	29
30◆	1949	Q0.02½	12-1-99	11-8	0.10	0.10	0.10	1604	3536	5373	9-30-99	2276	6520	132866	Je	Δ2.04	0.71	5.65	v6.34	vP7.20	7.50	3 Mo Sep	v2.08	v2.38	30
31	1999	Q0.508	1-3-00	12-13	0.429	2.031	....	Co redm opt from 7-1-2004				★500	....	...	Je	...	...	...	....	....	....	Due 7-1-2039			31
32◆	1993	Q0.03	12-13-99	11-26	0.12	0.12	0.12	7.55	218	172	8-31-99	17.0	1067	38551	Au	0.29	0.40	v0.17	v0.04	v0.18	0.18				32
33	....	None Since Public			...	Nil	....	Total Assets $548.78M			9-30-99	275	...	15884	Dc	pv0.21	pv1.46	v1.98	v0.74	....	0.44	9 Mo Sep	v0.42	v0.12	33
34	1964	Q0.285	12-15-99	11-29	1.14	1.14	1.14	0.18	7.31	20.1	9-30-99	51.6	...	2428	Je	1.04	v1.41	v0.75	v1.04	v0.90	0.86	3 Mo Sep	vd0.29	vd0.33	34
35	....	None Paid			...	Nil	....	0.04	0.31	0.98	9-30-99	2.70	...	6679	Je	Δd1.33	d0.81	vd0.49	vd0.18	vd0.51	d0.51	3 Mo Sep	vd0.08	vd0.08	35
36	1988	Div Suspended 8-19-99			0.05	Nil	0.10	32.0	185	36.1	10-02-99	154	...	23719	Je	0.42	vd2.56	v0.30	vd1.78	vd1.63	d1.77	3 Mo Sep	v0.15	v0.01	36
37	....	None Since Public			...	Nil	....	1.29	4.23	8.12	9-30-99	12.3	...	★±27588	Dc	...	...	...	vd0.37	....	d1.02	9 Mo Sep	vd0.24	vd0.89	37
38	1997	0.06¼	12-15-99	11-29	0.25	0.25	0.25	6.38	29.7	7.91	9-30-99	53.0	...	12394	Dc	p0.70	pv1.03	v1.29	v0.48	....	0.69	9 Mo Sep	v0.40	v0.61	38
39	1921	Q0.37	12-6-99	11-18	1.48	1.48	1.48	113	418	376	9-30-99	120	...	73403	Dc	v1.06	v0.79	v0.55	v1.80	E2.60	2.59	9 Mo Sep	v1.06	v1.85	39
40◆	....	None Since Public			...	Nil	....	6.45	24.3	17.4	9-30-99	153	...	45647	Dc	v0.10	v0.62	v0.70	vd11.08	....	d6.20	9 Mo Sep	vd4.88	vNil	40
41◆	....	None Since Public			...	Nil	....	52.7	89.4	21.8	9-30-99	0.23	...	39144	Dc	v0.15	vd0.06	v0.13	v0.31	....	....	9 Mo Sep	n/a	v0.31	41
42◆	1994	Q0.06¼	1-7-00	12-27	0.22½	0.25	0.20½	9.43	325	188	9-30-99	170	...	52800	Dc	v0.99	v1.25	v1.37	v0.65	....	1.12	9 Mo Sep	v0.69	v1.16	42
43	....	None Since Public			...	Nil	....	0.45	186	163	10-02-99	20.0	...	17364	Dc	Δ□v2.28	v2.11	v2.05	v2.45	....	2.47	9 Mo Sep	v2.06	v2.08	43
44	....	None Since Public			...	Nil	....	6.00	6.19	0.82	9-30-99	0.47	...	6475	Dc	...	pvd0.12	pvd0.28	vd0.44	....	d0.72	9 Mo Sep	vd0.28	vd0.56	44
45	....	Terms&trad. basis should			be checked in detail			Wrrts expire 11-4-2002				....	...	1250	Dc	...	...	...	....	....	....	Callable at 10¢[58]			45
46◆	1997	0.512	12-30-98	12-16	...	1.08	1.077	1009	7984	6708	j12-31-98	6866	...	±1492363	Dc	0.60	□±3.48	...	v4.58	....	3.92	3 Mo Mar	v2.84	v2.18	46
47	....	None Paid			...	Nil	....	0.01	3.92	5.41	9-30-99	....	...	21584	Dc	...	...	...	pv0.02	....	....	9 Mo Sep	n/a	vd0.05	47
48	1996	Q0.75	12-31-99	12-13	3.00	3.00	3.00	Cv into 2.126 com$23.52[62]				....	2000	...	Dc	...	...	...	....	....	....	Mand redm 12-31-2016			48
49	1999	0.12½	1-20-00	12-16	0.50	0.53	....	2.60	779	592	9-30-99	39.3	...	24706	Dc	v1.62	v0.16	v1.21	v1.13	....	1.92	9 Mo Sep	v0.71	v1.50	49
50	1998	Q0.461	12-31-99	12-28	1.844	1.844	0.297	Co option redm fr 12-31-2003 at $25[65]				★100	...	...	Dc	...	...	...	....	....	....	Mature 12-31-2028			50
51	1998	Q0.47⅛	12-31-99	12-28	1.88½	1.885	0.733	Co option redm fr 6-30-2003 at $25				★100	...	...	Dc	...	...	...	....	....	....	Mature 6-30-2028[65]			51

◆Stock Splits & Divs By Line Reference Index [1]3-for-2,'97. [3]3-for-2,'97. [7]2-for-1,'98. [8]3-for-1,'96:2-for-1,'98. [12]2-for-1,'97. [16]4-for-3,'96:5-for-4,'97,'98. [19]3-for-1,'95. [20]Adj to 3%,'96(twice). [21]2-for-1,'95:4-for-3,'96,'98:Adj for 2%,'99. [24]1-for-3 REVERSE,'99. [25]1-for-3 REVERSE,'99. [27]2-for-1,'95,'96,'97,'98(twice),'99. [29]6-for-5,'96:Adj for 2%,'99(twice). [30]2-for-1,'98. [32]3-for-2,'96:4-for-3,'95,'97(twice). [40]1-for-2 REVERSE,'96. [41]2-for-1,'98:3-for-2,'99. [42]2-for-1,'97. [46]Adj to 1%,'97.

¶ S&P 500
# MidCap 400
✤ SmallCap 600
• Options

Index	Ticker	Name of Issue (Call Price of Pfd. Stocks)	Market	Com. Rank. & Pfd. Rating	Inst. Hold Cos	Inst. Hold Shs. (000)	Principal Business	Price Range 1971-97 High	1971-97 Low	1998 High	1998 Low	1999 High	1999 Low	December, 1999 Dec. Sales in 100s	Last Sale Or Bid High	Low	Last	%Div Yield	P-E Ratio	EPS 5 Yr Growth	% Annualized Total Return 12 Mo	36 Mo	60 Mo
1	DTA	Detroit Edison 7.625% 'QUIDS'[51]	NY	....[52]	1	2	Quarterly Income Debt Sec	25 15/16	22	25 15/16	24½	25⅝	20¼	3099	22 9/16	20¼	20 5/16	9.4	..	...	−13.5	2.9	...
2•[1]	DT	✔Deutsche Telekom ADS[54]	NY,Ch,Ph	NR	74	23755	Telecommunications svcs Europe	25	16⅛	33⅝	17	71 15/16	35⅞	33912	71 15/16	55 15/16	71	0.7	51	−1	120	54.4	...
3	DDR	✔Developers Diversified Rlty	NY,Ch,P	NR	180	38921	Real estate investment trust	20⅝	11	21 7/16	15⅞	18½	12 5/16	48180	14	12 5/16	12⅞	10.9	14	9	−20.9	−5.3	3.2
#4•[2]	DVN	✔Devon Energy	AS,Ph	B	427	54982	Oil & gas devel prod'n	49⅛	3⅝	41⅛	26⅛	44 15/16	20⅛	113527	36⅝	29½	32⅞	0.6	42	Neg	7.8	−1.3	13.1
#5•[3]	DV	✔DeVry Inc	NY,Ph	B	280	52570	Tech'l/MBA degree schools	16½	1⅛	30⅝	14	31⅞	15⅝	46089	21¼	15¾	18¾	...	32	22	−38.8	17.2	37.5
6	DWL	✔DeWolfe Cos	AS,Ph	NR	15	216	Sell residential prop/mtg svc	7⅛	3	8½	4 15/16	8½	6¼	352	6⅞	6 5/16	6½B	...	5	78	−13.4	8.0	5.2
#7•[4]	DEX	✔Dexter Corp	NY,B,Ch,P	B+	234	19259	Specialty chemicals:fiber	43 15/16	2 1/16	43⅜	23½	42⅜	26⅝	32629	42¼	32⅜	39¾	2.6	11	11	30.3	10.8	16.5
8	DMM.B	✔Dia Met Minerals'B'	AS	NR	16	1586	Nonmetallic mineral explor	23⅝	7⅝	21⅜	9⅞	17⅝	11¼	334	16⅛	13⅝	15 13/16	...	d	−30	20.5	1.2	...
9	DMM.A	✔ Cl'A'	AS	NR	12	1164		20	7⅜	17⅝	10⅜	16¼	9¾	96	14¼	12⅜	13⅛	...	11	71	23.5	−1.5	...
10•[5]	DEO	✔Diageo plc[58]ADS	NY,Ch,Ph,P	NR	170	72994	Food & drink prod/retailing	42¼	22⅜	51¾	33	49 9/16	31 9/16	80050	37 3/16	31 9/16	32	3.9	19	1	−28.4	3.9	9.0
✤11•[6]	DP	✔Diagnostic Products	NY,Ch,Ph	B+	115	5182	Medical immunodiagnostic kits	53¾	3 1/16	32⅞	20⅜	35 5/16	21⅞	3486	25¼	22½	24½	2.0	17	1	−19.8	−0.1	0.2
#12•[4]	DL	✔Dial Corp	NY	NR	402	66035	Mfr consumer products	21 13/16	11⅛	30¼	19⅜	38⅜	19½	100416	28	23	24 5/16	1.3	20	...	−14.9	20.3	...
13	DIAL	Dialog Corp[61]ADS	NNM	NR	4	405	Supply business info	21	8¾	16¼	3	9¾	3½	12824	7	4⅞	6⅜	...	32	NM	41.7	−22.8	...
14•[7]	DO	✔Diamond Offshore Drilling	NY,Ch,Ph	NR	352	124377	Contract drilling O&G wells	67½	11 11/16	54⅝	20 1/16	41	20¼	212749	32 9/16	27 1/16	30 9/16	1.6	26	NM	31.4	3.7	...
15	DIA	DIAMONDS Trust,Series 1[62]	AS	NR	45	2757	Long-term investment trust	...	...	94⅛	73⅞	115¾	90⅜	115677	115¾	108⅝	115 5/16	1.3	..	...	27.6	...	...
#16•[8]	DBD	✔Diebold, Inc	NY,B,Ch,P	A	306	37335	Auto teller machines/sec sys	50 15/16	13/16	55 5/16	19⅛	39⅞	19 11/16	93116	23⅝	19 11/16	23½	2.6	12	11	−32.5	−16.0	8.8
17	DIGX	✔Digex Inc'A'	NNM	NR	..	...	Internet web site svcs	...	...	...	...	90	14⅝	95763	90	33⅞	68¾	...	d	...	...	...	...
✤18•[9]	DGII	✔Digi International	NNM	B−	72	5308	Data commun hardwr/softwr	30¾	2 15/16	29½	8 9/16	17¾	6	60116	17¾	10 1/16	10 7/16	...	47	Neg	−6.2	3.2	−11.1
19	DMRC	Digimarc Corp	NNM	NR	..	...	Digital water marking tech	...	...	...	...	88	20	152302	88	20	50	...	..	...	...	...	...
20	DIGI	✔Digital Impact	NNM	NR	..	...	Internet direct mktg svcs	...	...	...	...	65	15	61018	65	43⅞	50⅛	...	..	...	...	...	...
21	DGIN	✔Digital Insight	NNM	NR	39	443	Internet banking svcs	...	...	...	...	52⅝	19	30567	46⅛	28½	36⅝	...	..	...	...	...	...
22	ISLD	✔Digital Island	NNM	NR	47	7625	Global network internet svc	...	...	...	...	156 15/16	8⅝	325729	156 15/16	42	95⅛	...	..	...	...	...	...
23	DGV	✔Digital Lava	AS	NR	12	572	Computer software & svcs	...	...	...	...	17¼	2¾	17277	7¼	3 1/16	7	...	d	...	...	...	...
24	WS	Wrrt(Pur 1 com at $9)[64]	AS	....	3	81		...	...	...	...	7 15/16	⅝	5871	2 3/16	⅝	2 3/16	...	..	...	...	...	...
25	DIGL	✔Digital Lightwave	NNM	NR	21	876	Telecommun svc/eqp	23¾	3¼	16 13/16	1⅛	69¼	2 5/16	123648	69¼	31 7/16	64	...	d	−34	2668	...	...
✤26•[6]	DMIC	✔Digital Microwave	NNM	B	187	44606	Microwave radio/fiber optics	25⅝	2¼	21⅝	2 5/16	25 13/16	6⅜	206165	25 13/16	15 5/16	23 7/16	...	d	Neg	242	18.9	17.9
27	DPW	✔Digital Power	AS,Ph	NR	..	...	Prov switching power supplies	11⅜	4⅛	7	1⅜	2⅜	1¼	1506	1 11/16	1¼	1 7/16	...	d	Neg	−17.9	−37.7	...
28•[10]	DIIG	✔DII Group	NNM	NR	293	30010	Contract electronics mfr	33½	7⅜	29⅞	9⅞	75½	21¾	194818	75½	61 13/16	71	...	53	−42	209	83.0	40.8
29	DDT	Dillard's Cap Tr 7.50% Cap Sec	NY	BB+	2	475	Sub Deferrable Int Debs	...	...	26 1/16	24⅜	25¾	15⅝	5373	18	15⅝	17⅛	10.9	..	...	−27.3	...	...
¶30•[3]	DDS	✔Dillard's Inc'A'	NY,Ch,P	A	397	84590	Dept stores in southwest US	52⅞	5/16	44½	26½	37 7/16	17¾	136677	20 15/16	17 15/16	20 3/16	0.8	8	−3	−28.4	−12.8	−5.0
#31•[10]	DME	✔Dime Bancorp	NY,Ch,Ph	B−	330	68745	Savings bank, New York	30⅜	1½	33 1/16	17⅛	27 3/16	14¾	155112	18⅜	14¾	15⅛	1.6	7	23	−41.7	1.7	14.9
32	DCOM	✔Dime Community Bancshares	NNM	NR	85	7214	Savings bank, New York	25¾	10	29½	14¾	25⅜	16⅝	9222	20⅜	16⅝	18½	3.7	10	...	−7.9	9.6	...
✤33	DMN	✔DIMON Inc	NY	NR	124	24691	Tobacco dealer/cut flowers	26¾	13¾	26 5/16	6 9/16	7 15/16	2 13/16	24767	3 9/16	2 13/16	3¼	6.2	d	−45	−53.8	−45.7	...
34	DIO	✔Diodes, Inc	AS,Ch	B−	20	1119	Semiconductor devices	19⅝	¼	11¾	3¾	22¼	4	6920	22¼	14½	21½	...	32	2	330	43.7	33.9
✤35•[11]	DNEX	✔Dionex Corp	NNM	B+	205	15362	Mfr ion chromatography sys	27½	2⅜	39⅝	18¾	51	32	17665	44½	37	41 3/16	...	33	13	12.5	33.8	34.8
✤36	DAP	✔Discount Auto Parts	NY,P	B+	92	8478	Auto parts stores, Florida	33⅞	12⅞	27½	19	26 7/16	11	9915	18 7/16	12½	18 1/16	...	11	5	−17.7	−8.2	−0.9
¶37•[12]	DIS	✔Disney (Walt) Co[67]	NY,B,C,Ch,P,Ph	↓B+	1476	913111	Amusement parks: films, TV	33 7/16	5/16	42 13/16	22½	38 11/16	23⅜	1646204	30	27⅛	29¼	0.7	47	...	−1.8	8.7	14.5
38•[13]	GO	✔ go.com Common Stk[68]	NY	NR	..	...		...	...	...	...	37 11/16	21½	225151	28 15/16	21½	23¾	...	..	...	...	...	...
39	RPD	✔Dispatch Management Svcs	AS	NR	22	5817	Freight transportation svcs	...	...	28	3	4½	1½	17227	4 5/16	2⅜	2 15/16	...	d	...	−27.7	...	...
40	DYS	✔Distribucion y Servicio ADS[71]	NY	NR	43	12942	Oper supermarkets, Chile	19	14 5/16	18¾	6½	19¾	8¼	28798	19½	17⅝	19B	0.4	..	9	66.4	...	...
41	HIR	✔Diversified Corp Resources	AS	NR	9	580	Employment svcs	10 9/16	7⅜	14¾	3 9/16	8⅛	2⅜	1740	3 3/16	2⅜	2⅞	...	9	86	−42.5	...	...
42	DVNT	Diversinet Corp	NSC	NR	20	3177	Mkt compact desktop unit	33 15/16	9/16	5⅜	11/16	29	1⅞	402648	29	14 3/16	22	...	..	...	967	455	...
43	DXT	✔Dixon Ticonderoga	AS,Ch,Ph	B−	17	528	Writ'g/art prod:indust'l prod	18⅝	⅛	15 9/16	7⅞	12⅛	5⅞	2612	8¼	5⅞	6½	...	4	21	−41.6	−5.2	−6.8
44	DCTM	✔Documentum Inc	NNM	NR	100	10953	Document mgmt software	46½	13¾	59⅝	16¾	63½	9⅜	74151	63½	34¾	59⅞	...	d	...	12.0	21.1	...
45•[14]	DFS	✔Dofasco, Inc	To,Mo,P	B	15	5697	Canadian steel producer	32⅝	6 9/16	26⅝	15¼	29½	17¾	69159	29½	26½	28½	3.5	12	1	52.1	7.8	13.3
#46•[6]	DOL	✔Dole Food Co	NY,B,Ch,P	B	205	31755	Processed/fresh foods: R.E.	50 1/16	5 7/16	57 5/16	28 1/16	34⅛	13¾	71531	16 5/16	13¾	16¼	2.5	13	Neg	−44.8	−20.7	...
¶47•[3]	DG	✔Dollar General	NY,Ph,P	A+	500	145424	Self-service discount stores	20½	1/32	30¼	16	32⅝	18⅞	324635	27 3/16	22 1/16	22¾	0.6	27	24	22.9	31.7	31.3
48	DGS	Dollar Gen'l 8.50%'STRYPES'	NY	NR	18	695	Struct Yld Prd Exch For Stk	...	...	43⅜	30 11/16	44¼	35⅝	4173	40½	35⅝	36⅛	9.3	..	...	10.4	...	...
49•[15]	DTG	✔Dollar Thrifty Auto Grp	NY	NR	155	22781	Vehicle rental services	21⅞	19⅝	24½	8½	26¼	10½	17958	24¼	19 7/16	23 15/16	...	11	...	85.9	...	...
#50•[3]	DLTR	✔Dollar Tree Stores	NNM	NR	290	48356	Operates discount stores	31 9/16	4 7/16	49½	23	52¼	28¾	94945	52¼	44⅛	48 7/16	...	41	42	10.9	42.6	...
¶51•[16]	D	✔Dominion Resources	NY,B,C,Ch,P,Ph	B	545	88189	Hldg co:elec service in Va	49½	6⅞	48 15/16	37 13/16	49⅜	36 9/16	168776	45 9/16	39¼	39¼	6.6	13	−8	−10.8	7.1	8.5

Uniform Footnote Explanations-See Page 4. Other: [1]ASE,CBOE,P:Cycle 1. [2]ASE,CBOE:Cycle 1. [3]P:Cycle 2. [4]ASE:Cycle 1. [5]ASE,P:Cycle 1. [6]P:Cycle 3. [7]CBOE:Cycle 3. [8]P,Ph:Cycle 2. [9]ASE,Ph:Cycle 1. [10]ASE:Cycle 3. [11]P:Cycle 1. [12]ASE,CBOE,P,Ph:Cycle 1. [13]ASE,CBOE,Ph:Cycle 1. [14]Mo:Cycle 3. [15]CBOE:Cycle 1. [16]Ph:Cycle 1. [51]Jr Sub Deferrable Int Debs. [52]Rated BBB by S&P. [53]Can be deferred by co re-spec cond.. [54]Ea ADS rep 1 ord shr,DM5. [55]Approx. [56]®$1.66,'96. [57]®$1.52,'96. [58]Ea ADS rep 4 ord,50 pence. [59]Fiscal Sep'96 & prior. [60]6 Mo Jun,'97. [61]Ea ADS rep 4 ord shrs par 0.01P. [62]Based on Dow Jones Ind'l Average-as defined. [63]or earlier re-spec cond. [64]Fr 2-17-2000. [65]If com exceeds $40.17 for 20 of 30 con trad days. [66]Or earlier for'Tax Event're-spec cond. [67]Disney common stock. [68]Cv into Disney Com Stk - re-spec cond. [69]To be determined. [70]73% owned by Disney(Walt) Co. [71]Ea ADS rep 15 ord, no par. [72]Re-spec cond. [73]Incl current amts. [74]Subsid Pfd in $M.

Splits ◆ Index	Cash Divs. Ea. Yr. Since	Dividends: Latest Payment: Period $	Date	Ex. Div.	Total $: So Far 1999	Ind. Rate	Paid 1998	Financial Position: Mil-$: Cash& Equiv.	Curr. Assets	Curr. Liab.	Balance Sheet Date	Capitalization: Lg Trm Debt Mil-$	Shs. 000: Pfd.	Com.	Earnings $ Per Shr.: Years: End	1995	1996	1997	1998	1999	Last 12 Mos.	Interim Earnings: Period	$ per Shr.: 1998	1999	Index
1	1996	Q0.477	12-31-99	12-28	1.90⅝	[53]1.91	1.906	Co option redm fr 3-31-2001 at $25				★185	...	...	Dc	...	...	...	....	....	....	Mature 3-31-2026			1
2	1997	0.472	6-4-99	5-25	[55]0.472	0.47	0.499	7554	13916	n/a	12-31-98	40068	...	2743700	Dc	■1.81	0.53	v0.67	v0.96	E1.40	0.96				2
3◆	1993	Q0.35	1-6-00	12-21	1.37¾	1.40	0.98¼	Total Assets $2267.38M			9-30-99	1111	1216	59765	Dc	v□0.74	v[56]0.84	v1.02	v□1.00	....	0.95	9 Mo Sep	v□0.76	v0.71	3
4	1993	Q0.05	12-31-99	12-13	0.20	0.20	0.20	380	597	541	p9-30-99	1933	1500	p85793	Dc	v0.65	v[57]1.52	v2.17	vd1.25	....	0.79	9 Mo Sep	vd1.18	v0.86	4
5◆	....	None Since Public			...	Nil	....	61.0	114	118	9-30-99	29.0	...	69442	Je	0.22	v0.29	v0.35	v0.44	Pv0.55	0.58	3 Mo Sep	v0.11	v0.14	5
6	1999	0.15	1-4-00	12-3	0.12	Nil	....	7.48	49.9	38.1	9-30-99	14.8	...	3371	Dc	v0.03	v0.57	v0.32	v0.95	....	1.42	9 Mo Sep	v0.92	v1.39	6
7	1957	Q0.26	1-10-00	12-13	1.04	1.04	1.00	81.7	454	228	9-30-99	212	...	23042	Dc	v1.66	v2.03	v2.41	v1.35	....	3.49	9 Mo Sep	v1.92	v4.06	7
8	....	None Since Public			...	Nil	....	0.27	30.7	1.17	j4-30-99	....	...	±30178	Ja	±vd0.08	v±d0.06	v±d0.10	vd0.21	....	jd0.06	3 Mo Apr	vd0.01	v0.14	8
9	....	None Since Public			...	Nil	....	....	...	...		....	...	8471	Ja	±vd0.08	v±d0.06	v±d0.10	vd0.21	....	j0.85	9 Mo Oct	vd0.05	v1.01	9
10	1988	0.756	11-19-99	10-6	1.257	1.26	1.543	1097	6558	7437	j6-30-99	3395	...	3428000	Je	1.80	[59]0.15	‡p[60]0.87	v1.52	v1.70	1.70				10
11	1988	Q0.12	11-17-99	11-1	0.48	0.48	0.48	14.5	130	44.0	9-30-99	....	...	13672	Dc	v1.75	v1.65	v1.32	v1.46	....	1.45	9 Mo Sep	v1.06	v1.05	11
12	1996	Q0.08	1-17-00	12-13	0.32	0.32	0.32	7.92	287	304	10-02-99	239	...	105376	Dc	pd0.42	pv0.33	v0.89	v1.02	E1.19	1.13	9 Mo Sep	v0.75	v0.86	12
13	....	None Since Public			...	Nil	....	7.46	80.5	97.7	12-31-98	140	...	151467	Dc	d0.27	d0.81	vd1.37	v0.19	....	0.20	9 Mo Sep	v0.30	v0.31	13
14◆	1997	Q0.12½	12-1-99	10-28	0.50	0.50	0.50	680	916	157	9-30-99	400	...	135824	Dc	p0.10	v1.18	v1.93	v2.66	E1.20	1.60	9 Mo Sep	v2.07	v1.01	14
15	1998	0.19	12-13-99	11-19	1.456	1.46	1.21	Net Asset Val $85.84			10-31-98	....	...	4150	Oc	...	...	...	§85.94	....	....	Mand terminate 1-13-2123[63]			15
16◆	1954	Q0.15	12-3-99	11-9	0.60	0.60	0.56	60.2	580	266	9-30-99	20.8	...	68953	Dc	v1.10	v1.40	v1.76	v1.10	E1.90	1.85	9 Mo Sep	v0.60	v1.35	16
17	....	None Since Public			...	Nil	....	133	148	11.4	9-30-99	18.1	...	±61500	Dc	...	...	...	vpd0.33	....	d0.89	9 Mo Sep	vpd0.25	vpd0.81	17
18	....	None Since Public			...	Nil	....	25.7	88.2	35.4	6-30-99	9.07	...	14910	Sp	1.38	v0.68	vd1.18	vd1.65	Pv0.22	0.22				18
19	....	None Since Public			...	Nil	....	8.00	10.7	3.50	9-30-99	0.18	p...	★10983	Dc	...	...	...	vpd0.53	....	....	9 Mo Sep	n/a	vpd0.12	19
20	....	None Since Public			...	Nil	....	7.18	8.85	3.47	9-30-99	0.91	p...	★23549	Mr	...	...	...	vpd0.39	....	....	6 Mo Sep	n/a	vpd0.62	20
21	....	None Since Public			...	Nil	....	10.8	12.3	4.61	6-30-99	0.56	p...	★14143	Dc	...	...	...	vpd0.50	....	....	6 Mo Jun	n/a	vpd0.37	21
22	....	None Since Public			...	Nil	....	50.7	55.0	11.0	3-31-99	2.22	p...	★33966	Sp	...	...	...	vpd1.39	....	....	6 Mo Mar	n/a	vpd0.81	22
23	....	None Since Public			...	Nil	....	6.43	7.09	0.63	9-30-99	0.02	...	4637	Dc	...	...	vd31.14	vd25.22	....	d1.75	9 Mo Sep	vd24.80	v□d1.33	23
24	....	Terms&trad. basis should be checked in detail						Wrrts expire 2-17-2004				....	...	1200	Dc	...	...	...	....	....	....	Callable fr 8-17-2000 at 10¢[65]			24
25	....	None Since Public			...	Nil	....	4.78	23.4	17.9	9-30-99	....	...	27018	Dc	vd0.08	vd1.00	vd0.25	vd1.13	....	d0.20	9 Mo Sep	vd0.89	v0.04	25
26◆	....	None Since Public			...	Nil	....	31.0	156	64.0	9-30-99	1.88	...	★67998	Mr	d0.20	v0.35	v0.42	vd1.57	....	d1.12	6 Mo Sep	vd0.43	v0.02	26
27	....	None Since Public			...	Nil	....	0.53	9.01	3.73	9-30-99	0.10	...	2771	Dc	0.80	v0.62	v0.41	vd0.21	....	d0.33	9 Mo Sep	v0.12	vNil	27
28◆	....	None Since Public			...	Nil	....	27.1	348	290	10-03-99	330	...	36772	Dc	v□0.95	v0.40	v1.26	vd0.68	....	1.33	9 Mo Sep	vd0.78	v1.23	28
29	1998	Q0.46⅞	2-1-00	1-12	1.87½	1.875	0.411	Co option redm fr 8-1-2013[66]				★200	...	...	Ja	...	...	...	....	....	....	Mature 8-01-2038			29
30	1969	Q0.04	2-1-00	12-29	0.16	0.16	0.16	43.6	4002	1534	10-30-99	3554	4	±104901	Ja	v±1.48	v±2.09	±v2.31	v±1.26	E2.47	1.99	9 Mo Oct	v±0.56	v±1.29	30
31	1997	Q0.06	12-1-99	11-17	0.23	0.24	0.19	Total Deposits $13293.75M			9-30-99	1365	...	110840	Dc	v0.57	v0.96	v1.13	v□2.09	E2.15	2.16	9 Mo Sep	v□1.54	v□1.61	31
32	1997	Q0.17	11-9-99	10-27	0.61	0.68	0.39	Total Deposits $1214M			9-30-99	370	...	12638	Je	...	...	v0.95	v1.09	v1.68	1.78	3 Mo Sep	v0.35	v0.45	32
33	1995	Q0.05	12-12-99	11-29	0.24	0.20	0.60	21.8	1082	633	9-30-99	534	...	44525	Je	d0.79	Δv0.98	v1.77	v0.98	vd0.12	d0.64	3 Mo Sep	v0.32	vd0.20	33
34	....	None Paid			...	Nil	....	1.71	32.4	16.3	9-30-99	5.45	...	5206	Dc	v0.90	v0.55	v0.93	v0.50	....	0.68	9 Mo Sep	v0.42	v0.60	34
35◆	....	None Since Public			...	Nil	....	11.4	76.1	40.8	9-30-99	0.48	...	22245	Je	0.67	0.88	v1.03	v1.18	v1.20	1.25	3 Mo Sep	v0.26	v0.31	35
36	....	None Since Public			...	Nil	....	6.78	249	96.8	8-31-99	254	...	16691	My	1.48	1.44	v0.77	v1.63	v□1.61	1.65	6 Mo Nov	v□0.76	v0.80	36
37◆	1957	A0.21	12-7-99	11-12	0.21	0.21	0.202	414	10200	7707	9-30-99	9278	...	2035000	Sp	0.87	0.65	v0.95	v0.89	v0.62	0.62				37
38	....	Plan annual div			...	[69]....	....	....	...	...		....	...	[70]p150000	Sp	...	...	...	....	....	....	No EPS Reported			38
39	....	None Since Public			...	Nil	....	1.46	35.5	34.5	9-30-99	69.3	...	12113	Dc	...	pv0.20	v0.25	v□d1.88	....	d2.14	9 Mo Sep	v□0.27	v0.01	39
40	1998	[55]0.08¼	1-11-00	12-21	0.092	0.08	0.02½	69.6	254	252	12-31-97	84.9	...	1378256	Dc	0.44	0.60	Δv0.15	....	....	0.15				40
41	....	None Since Public			...	Nil	....	1.14	12.0	6.11	9-30-99	2.77	...	2788	Dc	Δv0.16	Δv0.87	Δv1.25	v0.55	....	0.34	9 Mo Sep	v0.43	v0.22	41
42◆	....	None Paid			...	Nil	....	7.87	7.98	2.47	j7-31-99	2.22	...	15620	Oc	d0.20	d2.44	vd0.07	vd0.22	....	....	9 Mo Jul	n/a	vd0.31	42
43	....	0.02½	12-1-89	11-13	...	Nil	....	1.17	83.9	52.2	6-30-99	20.5	...	3401	Sp	0.33	□0.36	v1.05	v0.85	Pv1.87	1.87				43
44	....	None Since Public			...	Nil	....	78.5	121	51.3	9-30-99	0.15	...	16403	Dc	pv0.10	v0.30	v0.49	vd1.45	....	d0.24	9 Mo Sep	vd1.72	vd0.51	44
45	1994	gQ0.25	1-1-00	12-13	g1.00	1.00	g1.00	166	1317	591	j9-30-99	525	127	80446	Dc	1.98	v2.12	v2.12	v2.04	....	j2.40	9 Mo Sep	v1.68	v2.04	45
46◆	1991	Q0.10	12-9-99	11-16	0.40	0.40	0.40	34.5	1134	721	10-09-99	1240	...	55835	Dc	v0.39	v1.47	v2.65	v0.20	E1.30	d0.43	9 Mo Sep	v1.98	v1.35	46
47◆	1975	Q0.032	12-20-99	12-2	0.122	0.13	0.102	35.6	1213	673	10-29-99	1.53	1716	264317	Ja	0.33	v0.43	v0.54	v0.68	E0.85	0.77	9 Mo Oct	v0.39	v0.48	47
48	1998	0.838	11-15-99	10-28	3.353	3.354	1.55½	At maturity Dollar General com or cash[72]				....	...	★7500	Ja	...	...	...	....	....	....	Mature 5-15-2001			48
49	....	None Since Public			...	Nil	....	Total Assets $2400.95M			9-30-99	[73]1803	...	24148	Dc	...	pvd7.36	v0.90	v1.56	....	2.29	9 Mo Sep	v1.42	v2.15	49
50◆	....	None Since Public			...	Nil	....	19.1	283	121	9-30-99	54.3	...	62025	Dc	v0.34	v0.53	v0.75	v1.03	....	1.17	9 Mo Sep	v0.47	v0.61	50
51	1925	Q0.64½	12-20-99	11-23	2.58	2.58	2.58	357	2629	3346	9-30-99	6502	[74]1074	190808	Dc	2.45	v2.65	v2.15	v2.75	E3.00	1.49	12 Mo Sep	v3.01	v□1.49	51

◆**Stock Splits & Divs By Line Reference Index** [3]2-for-1,'98. [5]2-for-1,'95,'96,'98. [14]2-for-1,'97. [16]3-for-2,'94,'96,'97. [26]2-for-1,'97. [28]2-for-1,'97. [35]2-for-1,'96,'98. [37]3-for-1,'98. [42]1-for-4 REVERSE,'97. [46]No adj for stk dstr of Castle & Cooke,'95. [47]5-for-4,'95,'96,'97(twice),'98(twice),'99. [50]3-for-2,'97,'98.

¶ S&P 500
# MidCap 400
✣ SmallCap 600
• Options

Index	Ticker	Name of Issue (Call Price of Pfd. Stocks)	Market	Com. Rank. & Pfd. Rating	Inst. Hold Cos	Inst. Hold Shs. (000)	Principal Business	Price Range 1971-97 High	1971-97 Low	1998 High	1998 Low	1999 High	1999 Low	December, 1999 Dec. Sales in 100s	Last Sale Or Bid High	Low	Last	%Div Yield	P-E Ratio	EPS 5 Yr Growth	% Annualized Total Return 12 Mo	36 Mo	60 Mo
1	DOM	✔Dominion Res Black Warrior Tr	NY,Ch,Ph	NR	14	115	Invest trust/royalty interest	25¼	16⅞	22¾	12⅞	16¾	10¼	16220	13¼	10¼	11	...	5	...	–9.6	–5.3	6.5
2•[1]	DTC	✔Domtar, Inc	NY,To,B,Ch,Mo,Vc	B–	61	64790	Pulp/paper,constr mtls:chem	18¾	2 5/16	8 15/16	4⅜	12 13/16	5 11/16	13696	12 3/16	10¾	11¾	1.2	13	–16	104	14.7	12.9
#3	DCI	✔Donaldson Co	NY,B,Ch	A+	196	26661	Engine air cleaners, mufflers	27 11/16	5/16	26¾	13½	25 15/16	17 1/16	21057	25⅛	22	24 1/16	1.2	17	15	17.3	14.0	16.3
4•[2]	DLJ	✔Donaldson,Lufkin&Jenrette	NY,Ch,Ph	NR	167	109846	Sec underwrit'g/merchant bkg	44	13½	63¾	20⅜	100¾	36½	85547	51½	45½	48⅜	0.5	15	26	18.5	40.0	...
5	DIR	✔Donald,Luf&Jen-DLJdirect	NY	NR	69	2808	Online discount brokerage svc	....	....	....	....	45⅝	12 9/16	86778	17½	13 7/16	13 9/16	...	..	...	...	...	...
6	DCS	✔DONCASTERS plc ADS[54]	NY,Ch	NR	36	5095	Tolerance-critical compnts	31⅝	16½	34⅝	8⅛	21	6 9/16	14878	9	6 9/16	9	...	4	...	–44.4	...	...
7•[3]	DK	✔Donna Karan Intl	NY,Ch	NR	43	1759	Design,mkt,dstr clothing	30⅛	8⅞	16¾	5 1/16	11	5 9/16	16722	8⅜	6⅛	6 9/16	...	d	...	–13.9	–22.6	...
¶8•[4]	DNY	✔Donnelley(RR)& Sons	NY,B,Ch,P,Ph	B+	489	106876	Large commercial printer	41¾	2	48	33¾	44¾	21½	105847	25⅝	23	24 13/16	3.5	11	34	–41.7	–5.3	–1.3
9	DON	✔Donnelly Corp Cl'A'	NY,Ch	B+	38	3704	Mfrs automotive glass prod	23	4 15/16	22⅜	12½	17½	12⅛	1527	15⅛	13 9/16	14	2.9	..	...	10.8	–8.3	4.7
10	DHC.A	✔Donohue Inc'A'	To	B	26	7502	Dvlp,sell forest products	23 3/16	4 5/16	24½	15 5/16	26⅝	19 3/16	32331	26 7/16	22	26 3/16	1.7	18	3	38.8	19.6	24.5
11	DIIBF	Dorel Industries'B'	NNM,To	NR	32	4536	Mfr furniture/home furnishings	....	....	17½	10⅜	22¾	15	1278	18	15	16⅝B	...	7	37	3.1	22.5	35.1
12	HIL	✔Dot Hill Systems	NY,Ph	NR	19	1339	Dgn/mfr data storage sys	21⅛	9	14 5/16	4⅛	8⅛	4	17982	6 11/16	4¾	4 15/16	...	d	...	–8.1	...	...
13	DCLK	✔DoubleClick Inc	NNM	NR	282	27342	Internet advertising svcs	....	....	38 9/16	6¾	255 7/16	22	391347	255 7/16	160	253 1/16	...	d	...	1042	...	...
¶14•[4]	DOV	✔Dover Corp	NY,B,Ch,P,Ph	A	583	157983	Elevators:petrol eq:ind'l pr	36 11/16	⅜	39 15/16	25½	47 15/16	29 5/16	121535	47 15/16	44	45⅜	1.0	28	29	25.3	23.0	30.3
15	DVD	✔Dover Downs Entertainment	NY	NR	62	5794	Gaming/motorsports	13 7/16	8 1/16	16 13/16	9⅝	20⅜	12 1/16	5164	20	17¾	18¾	1.0	23	38	57.2	29.9	...
¶16•[5]	DOW	✔Dow Chemical	NY,B,C,Ch,P,Ph	B	1071	150937	Chem/metals/plastics/pkg	102⅝	8	101 7/16	74 11/16	138	85½	252023	136 3/16	115½	133⅝	2.6	23	5	51.5	23.7	19.0
¶17•[6]	DJ	✔Dow Jones & Co	NY,B,Ch,P,Ph	B+	366	48948	Business pubs & fin'l news	56¼	2 7/16	59	41 9/16	71⅜	43⅝	77187	71⅜	59⅜	68	1.4	22	–49	43.9	28.7	19.6
✣18	DSL	✔Downey Financial	NY,B,Ch,P	B	147	11085	Savings & loan,California	27¾	¼	35¼	17¼	26¼	17 11/16	8579	21⅛	19	20 3/16	s1.8	10	26	–19.3	9.2	35.6
#19•[7]	DPL	✔DPL Inc	NY,B,C,Ch,Ph	A–	292	56419	Hldg co:Dayton Pwr & Lt	19 3/16	3⅛	21¾	16⅝	22	16 5/16	55532	18⅝	16 7/16	17 5/16	5.4	13	5	–15.8	19.2	17.5
#20•[8]	DQE	✔DQE	NY,B,C,Ch,P,Ph	A–	279	32245	Hldg: Duquesne Light	35 3/16	7 1/16	44⅛	31 9/16	44¼	33⅝	38042	37⅜	33⅝	34⅝	4.6	14	5	–18.2	10.5	17.1
21	DCA	DQE Corp 8.375%'PINES'	NY	NR	1	20	Public Income Notes	....	....	....	....	25¼	22	2013	24 11/16	22	22½	9.3	..	...	...	...	...
✣22	DBRN	✔Dress Barn	NNM	B+	109	14206	Women's apparel stores	28⅜	1¼	32⅜	11¼	19⅝	12⅜	19580	18⅛	15 7/16	16⅝	...	10	17	9.5	3.5	9.1
23	DW	✔Drew Industries	AS	B	32	3736	Mfr specialty building prod	14⅜	⅜	15⅛	10⅛	13¼	8 7/16	1640	9¾	9	9	...	6	19	–22.6	–6.4	...
24•[9]	DRXR	✔Drexler Technology	NNM	C	19	1421	Optical data products	26 5/16	5/16	19½	7¼	13¾	6½	9629	10¾	7⅝	9¾	...	22	NM	–18.8	–2.4	13.2
#25•[8]	DRYR	✔Dreyer's Gr Ice Cr	NNM	B–	90	10155	Ice cream mfr & dstr	27½	1½	26¾	9	19 15/16	11 5/16	8796	17	15	17	0.7	d	Neg	13.3	6.3	7.4
✣26	DRQ	✔Dril-Quip Inc	NY,Ph	NR	106	4413	Mfr offshore drilling eqp	40 7/16	24	37	11¾	30⅞	11¾	7019	30⅞	24⅛	30⅜	...	39	47	71.1	...	...
27	DRH	✔Driver-Harris	AS	B–	3	16	Elec & heat resisting alloys	13¾	1 15/16	11	2¾	4¾	2	547	3½	3	3¼	...	d	Neg	–10.3	–28.3	–8.7
28	KOOP	✔drkoop.com Inc	NNM	NR	46	2687	Dvp stge:Internet hlth svc	....	....	....	....	45¾	9	125472	19⅞	11¾	11⅞	...	d	...	...	...	...
29	DRS	✔DRS Technologies	AS	B	27	3169	Anti-sub warfare comput sys	17	1⅛	15⅜	7	11	6⅞	3794	10	8	9⅝	...	16	–1	–12.0	–8.3	17.8
30	DEMP	Drug Emporium	NNM	B–	45	5459	Discount drug store chain	16 5/16	3¼	5⅝	3 3/16	12 15/16	3½	81880	6½	3½	4 7/16	...	d	...	–13.4	1.4	–4.2
31	DSCM	✔drugstore.com Inc	NNM	NR	51	3278	Internet based drug store	....	....	....	....	70	18	59518	55	32 5/16	36 3/16	...	d	...	...	...	...
32	DCU	DRYCLEAN USA[64]	AS	B	1	22	Dstr laundry/drycleaning eqp	8 7/16	1/16	3 9/16	⅝	3⅜	1	1954	2	1	1 7/16	...	11	9	–55.8	8.5	10.4
33	DSGIF	DSG International Ltd	NNM	NR	7	750	Mfr disposable diapers	29¾	7⅜	9½	2 13/16	10⅝	2¾	1796	7	5½	5⅞	...	6	–21	88.0	–26.4	–19.8
34•[9]	DSPG	✔DSP Group	NNM	NR	93	6603	Digital signal process equip	42¼	6¾	26⅞	9⅝	96¼	12⅝	43461	96¼	68	93	...	73	34	346	122	36.7
#35•[10]	DST	✔DST Systems	NY,Ch	NR	317	29642	Info processing/softwr svcs	45 7/16	21	70 9/16	34	76⅜	50 15/16	37965	76⅜	62 13/16	76 5/16	...	38	...	33.7	34.5	...
¶36•[11]	DTE	✔DTE Energy	NY,B,C,Ch,Ph	A–	464	67158	Electric & steam utility	37¼	7½	49¼	33 7/16	44 11/16	31 1/16	155590	33¾	31 1/16	31⅝	6.5	9	5	–22.5	5.1	10.5
37•[10]	DRD	✔Duane Reade	NY,Ph	NR	..	...	Operates drug store chain,NYC	....	....	45	16½	38½	19	44772	28	19	27 9/16	...	25	...	–28.4	...	...
38	DMH	✔Ducati Motor Hldg ADS[65]	NY	NR	5	56	Mfr motorcycles, Italy	....	....	....	....	33⅛	25 1/16	620	28⅛	25 1/16	25 5/16	...	d	...	...	...	...
39	DCO	✔Ducommun Inc	NY,B,P	B+	54	5877	Mfg svcs to aerospace indus	31 11/16	9/16	23 15/16	12⅞	15⅜	8½	6064	10⅞	8¾	10⅞	...	8	38	–21.3	–8.8	26.8
40	DCR	Duff & Phelps Credit Rating	NY	NR	98	3248	Financial credit rating svcs	41 13/16	7⅝	59 7/16	36⅜	89¼	50¾	4169	89¼	78⅜	88 15/16	0.1	25	29	62.6	54.9	55.9
¶41•[11]	DUK	✔Duke Energy	NY,B,C,Ch,P,Ph	A–	985	185400	Electric utility-Carolinas	56 9/16	5	71	53⅛	65 5/16	46¾	204422	51	46¾	50⅛	4.4	14	4	–18.6	6.9	10.2
42	DUT	Duke Energy 6.60% Sr Notes'C'	NY	...[69]	2	4	Electric utility, Carolina's	....	....	....	....	25⅛	19½	9275	21½	19½	20 1/16	8.2	..	...	...	...	...
43	DRE	✔Duke-Weeks Realty	NY,Ch,Ph	NR	309	76355	Real estate inv trust	25	5	25	19½	24¼	16⅝	99616	19½	16⅝	19½	8.0	15	11	–10.2	7.4	13.9
¶44•[12]	DNB	✔Dun & Bradstreet	NY,B,Ch,P,Ph	NR	557	133297	Financial/publishing svcs	71¾	3⅜	36 11/16	21¾	40	23⅜	164888	30¼	25 11/16	29½	2.5	18	11	–4.3	...	...
45	DNCC	✔Dunn Computer	NNM	NR	9	350	Mfr custom computer sys	10½	5	10⅜	1 15/16	6¼	¾	187386	6	1¼	3¼	...	d	...	–21.2	...	...
46	DUP.A	✔duPont of Canada Cl'A'	To,Mo	B+	11	555	Owned 75% by du Pont (E.I.)	36	1	47½	31½	60	40	5183	60	52⅛	59⅜	1.2	19	14	40.0	28.8	30.5
¶47•[3]	DD	✔duPont(EI)deNemours	NY,B,C,Ch,P,Ph	B+	1651	864037	Large chemical co:oil & gas	69¾	4 11/16	84 7/16	51 11/16	75 3/16	50 1/16	578482	69 7/16	58 1/16	65⅞	2.1	33	30	26.9	14.5	21.7
48•[6]	DPMI	✔DuPont Photomasks	NNM	NR	131	5934	Semiconductor mfr eqp	74⅛	17	58	16⅞	70 15/16	36	82527	70 15/16	40 9/16	48¼	...	37	5	13.7	2.1	...
49	DQZ	Duquesne Light 7.375% Bonds	NY	NR	2	20	Electric utility	....	....	25¾	24¾	25⅝	19 15/16	2101	22	19 15/16	20⅜	9.0	..	...	–13.4	...	...
50	DRRA	✔Dura Automotive Sys'A'	NNM	NR	147	12064	Mfr parts for auto industry	35¾	15⅝	40¾	19¼	35	15⅛	22874	20¾	15¾	17 7/16	...	6	25	–48.9	–8.1	...
✣51•[3]	DURA	✔Dura Pharmaceuticals	NNM	C	202	29462	Mkt respiratory ailment drugs	53	2	48⅝	8	17 11/16	9¾	87282	14 13/16	12 1/16	13 15/16	...	20	38	–8.2	–33.7	14.8

Uniform Footnote Explanations-See Page 4. Other: [1]Mo:Cycle 2. [2]ASE,CBOE,Ph:Cycle 1. [3]ASE,CBOE:Cycle 1. [4]ASE:Cycle 3. [5]CBOE:Cycle 3. [6]Ph:Cycle 3. [7]CBOE,Ph:Cycle 1. [8]P:Cycle 3. [9]CBOE:Cycle 1. [10]Ph:Cycle 2. [11]Ph:Cycle 1. [12]ASE:Cycle 2. [51]To be determined. [52]Incl 18M restricted shrs. [53]85M shrs owned by Donald,Luf&Jenrette. [54]Ea ADS rep 2 ord shrs, 25 pence. [55]Fiscal Jun'99 & prior. [56]11 Mo Dec'96. [57]Incl 24.263M equiv'A'shrs. [58]Fiscal Jul'96 & prior. [59]Subsid pfd. [60]Excl subsid pfd. [61]Total issue amt. [62]Stk dstr of Leslie Bldg Prods,'94. [63]9 Mo Dec'98. [64]Formerly Metro Tel Corp. [65]Ea ADS rep 10 ord 1000 Lit.. [66]Incl current amts. [67]Stk dstr of Arrow Electronics. [68]Pfd in $M. [69]Rated 'AAA' by S&P. [70]Total issue amt in $M.

Splits ◆ Index	Cash Divs. Ea. Yr. Since	Dividends: Latest Payment Period $	Date	Ex. Div.	Total $ So Far 1999	Ind. Rate	Paid 1998	Financial Position Mil-$ Cash& Equiv.	Curr. Assets	Curr. Liab.	Balance Sheet Date	Capitalization Lg Trm Debt Mil-$	Shs. 000 Pfd.	Com.	Earnings $ Per Shr. Years End	1995	1996	1997	1998	1999	Last 12 Mos.	Interim Earnings Period	$ per Shr. 1998	1999	Index
1	1994	0.694	12-9-99	11-24	2.463	[51]....	2.832	Total Assets $77.42M			9-30-99	....	...	7850	Dc	v2.67	v3.24	v3.10	v2.83	....	2.38	9 Mo Sep	v2.22	v1.77	1
2	1996	gQ0.035	1-1-00	11-29	g0.14	0.14	g0.14	43.0	861	645	j6-30-99	1187	2290	183925	Dc	2.32	v0.68	v0.15	v0.42	....	j0.63	9 Mo Sep	v0.31	v0.52	2
3◆	1956	Q0.07	12-16-99	12-1	0.25	0.28	0.21	56.4	350	176	10-31-99	92.6	...	46029	Jl	0.73	v0.84	v0.99	v1.14	v1.31	1.39	3 Mo Oct	v0.28	v0.36	3
4◆	1996	Q0.06¼	1-31-00	1-12	0.25	0.25	0.25	Total Assets $98115M			9-30-99	4661	7500	[52]144319	Dc	v1.55	v2.30	v3.16	v2.65	....	3.31	9 Mo Sep	v2.18	v2.84	4
5	....	None Since Public			...	Nil	....	....	...	...		....	...	[53]125919	Dc	...	...	...	pv0.01	....	....	9 Mo Sep	n/a	vp0.09	5
6	....	None Since Public			...	Nil	....	7.66	110	53.0	j12-31-98	111	...	17619	Dc	p0.68	v1.47	v1.93	v2.19	....	2.03	9 Mo Sep	v1.52	v□1.36	6
7	....	None Since Public			...	Nil	....	....	222	135	10-03-99	4.07	...	21600	Dc	pv0.91	vp0.59	vd3.78	v0.01	....	d0.06	9 Mo Sep	vd1.44	vd1.51	7
8	1911	Q0.22	12-1-99	11-4	0.86	0.88	0.82	66.7	1265	927	6-30-99	1300	...	126441	Dc	v1.92	vd1.04	v0.89	v2.08	E2.22	2.06	9 Mo Sep	v1.41	v1.39	8
9◆	1988	Q0.10	1-1-00	12-13	0.40	0.40	0.40	6.57	178	153	10-02-99	104	53	±10144	Dc	±1.14	±0.86	v±1.00	v±1.29	v±[55]1.04	....	9 Mo Sep	v±0.48	v□±2.18	9
10◆	1993	g0.11	12-1-99	11-15	g0.437	0.44	g0.413	n/a	776	544	j9-30-99	1238	p162	±135210	Dc	2.05	v1.51	v1.16	v1.70	....	j1.49	9 Mo Sep	v1.18	v0.97	10
11◆	....	None Since Public			...	Nil	....	6.80	324	113	j6-30-99	124	...	±27560	Dc	v0.44	v0.63	v1.00	v0.97	....	j1.75	9 Mo Sep	v0.55	v1.33	11
12	....	None Since Public			...	Nil	....	47.0	92.8	32.0	9-30-99	0.28	...	23870	Dc	...	pv0.32	vp0.57	v0.39	....	d0.12	9 Mo Sep	v0.06	vd0.45	12
13◆	....	None Since Public			...	Nil	....	363	397	47.8	9-30-99	250	...	p55474	Dc	...	‡v[56]d0.12	pvd0.28	vd0.56	....	d0.57	9 Mo Sep	vd0.44	vd0.45	13
14◆	1947	Q0.11½	12-15-99	11-26	0.44	0.46	0.48½	174	1618	1195	9-30-99	609	...	203630	Dc	v1.22	v1.69	v1.79	v1.69	E1.65	4.25	9 Mo Sep	v1.27	v3.83	14
15◆	1997	Q0.04½	12-10-99	11-8	0.18	0.18	0.16½	14.2	33.5	36.7	9-30-99	41.1	...	[57]±35901	Je	0.15	[58]0.35	v0.54	v0.70	v0.74	0.82	3 Mo Sep	v0.23	v0.31	15
16	1911	Q0.87	1-28-00	12-29	3.48	3.48	3.48	1041	8167	6124	9-30-99	4130	1361	219297	Dc	v7.61	v7.60	v7.70	v5.76	E5.90	5.40	9 Mo Sep	v5.10	v4.74	16
17	1906	Q0.24	12-1-99	10-28	0.96	0.96	0.96	35.3	363	543	9-30-99	150	...	±89471	Dc	v1.94	v1.95	vd8.36	v0.09	E3.04	1.07	9 Mo Sep	v1.34	v2.32	17
18◆	1986	Q0.09	11-30-99	11-9	0.35	0.36	s0.316	Total Deposits $6311.31M			9-30-99	1597	...	28148	Dc	v0.75	v0.73	v1.61	v2.05	....	2.01	9 Mo Sep	v1.60	v1.56	18
19◆	1919	Q0.23½	12-1-99	11-15	0.94	0.94	0.94	27.0	417	406	9-30-99	1337	[59]229	158630	Dc	v1.09	v1.15	v1.20	v1.24	E1.38	1.32	9 Mo Sep	v1.00	v1.08	19
20◆	1913	Q0.40	1-1-00	12-8	1.52	1.60	1.44	99.2	419	443	9-30-99	1369	[60]...	75313	Dc	v2.17	v2.29	v2.54	v□2.48	E2.46	2.43	12 Mo Sep	v□2.53	v2.43	20
21	1999	0.518	12-15-99	12-13	0.518	2.09	....	Co option redm 9-16-2004 at $25				[61]100	...	...	Dc	...	...	...	....	....	....	Mature 9-15-2039			21
22	....	None Since Public			...	Nil	....	171	281	112	10-30-99	....	...	19265	Jl	0.82	0.84	v1.33	v1.70	v1.53	1.61	3 Mo Oct	v0.39	v0.47	22
23◆	....	h[62]....	8-5-94	7-25	...	Nil	....	5.26	60.8	31.6	9-30-99	45.3	...	11351	Dc	v0.81	v1.15	v1.19	v1.34	....	1.48	9 Mo Sep	v1.03	v1.17	23
24	....	None Since Public			...	Nil	....	7.06	11.9	1.61	9-30-99	....	...	9815	Mr	vd0.18	vd0.26	v0.19	v0.41	....	0.44	6 Mo Sep	v0.20	v0.23	24
25◆	1990	Q0.03	1-4-00	12-21	0.12	0.12	0.12	2.35	203	156	9-25-99	125	1008	27706	Dc	vd0.13	v0.07	v0.17	vd1.75	....	d1.05	9 Mo Sep	vd0.29	v0.41	25
26	....	None Since Public			...	Nil	....	9.15	107	24.7	9-30-99	0.09	...	17245	Dc	v0.46	v0.63	v0.87	v1.01	....	0.77	9 Mo Sep	v0.76	v0.52	26
27	....	0.05	7-7-71	6-9	...	Nil	....	0.09	13.6	11.7	9-30-99	2.01	...	1372	Dc	v1.03	v1.86	vd0.42	vd1.55	....	d0.51	9 Mo Sep	vd1.10	vd0.06	27
28	....	None Since Public			...	Nil	....	4.10	75.0	15.8	9-30-99	....	...	30304	Dc	...	...	...	vpd0.74	....	d2.94	9 Mo Sep	vpd0.51	vpd2.71	28
29	....	None Since Public			...	Nil	....	6.83	160	142	9-30-99	106	...	9717	Mr	v±0.69	v0.84	±v0.93	v□0.44	....	0.60	6 Mo Sep	v0.06	v0.22	29
30	....	0.04	7-1-92	5-26	...	Nil	....	0.72	208	144	8-28-99	49.8	...	13193	Fb	v0.18	v0.09	v0.13	v0.29	....	d0.58	9 Mo Nov	v0.25	vd0.62	30
31	....	None Since Public			...	Nil	....	160	175	20.7	10-03-99	1.01	...	43367	Dc	...	...	...	‡p[63]d0.98	....	d3.19	9 Mo Sep	vpd0.45	vpd2.66	31
32	....	s0.029	9-26-86	8-29	...	Nil	....	0.58	6.58	1.93	9-30-99	1.52	...	6925	Je	0.06	0.06	v0.01	vd0.17	v0.12	0.13	3 Mo Sep	v0.02	v0.03	32
33	....	0.25	7-12-94	6-8	...	Nil	....	18.6	71.9	41.0	12-31-97	21.3	...	6675	Dc	0.58	v1.18	v0.15	Pv0.24	....	0.96	9 Mo Sep	vd0.33	v0.39	33
34	....	None Since Public			...	Nil	....	115	132	15.3	9-30-99	....	...	12454	Dc	v0.75	v0.62	v1.08	v1.44	E1.27	2.06	9 Mo Sep	v1.08	v1.70	34
35	....	None Since Public			...	Nil	....	96.0	453	265	9-30-99	47.6	...	63408	Dc	pv1.18	v3.32	v1.18	v1.11	E2.03	1.66	9 Mo Sep	v1.01	v1.56	35
36	1909	Q0.51½	1-15-00	12-16	2.06	2.06	2.06	54.0	1454	1691	9-30-99	4103	...	145045	Dc	v2.80	v2.13	v2.88	v3.05	E3.40	3.39	9 Mo Sep	v2.32	v2.66	36
37	....	None Since Public			...	Nil	....	0.90	183	87.0	6-27-99	330	...	17145	Dc	vd1.77	pvd1.77	vd1.45	v□1.07	E1.12	1.35	9 Mo Sep	v□0.50	v0.78	37
38	....	None Since Public			...	Nil	....	9.24	140	122	12-31-98	[66]p131	...	★157000	Dc	...	...	v0.21	vd0.10	....	d0.10				38
39◆	....	h[67]....	3-24-88	3-25	...	Nil	....	0.09	48.3	22.4	10-02-99	5.61	...	10353	Dc	v0.59	v0.89	v1.20	v2.04	....	1.37	9 Mo Sep	v1.63	v0.96	39
40	1994	Q0.03	12-10-99	11-22	0.12	0.12	0.12	7.38	20.4	9.44	9-30-99	....	...	4646	Dc	v1.28	v1.54	v2.00	v3.16	....	3.61	9 Mo Sep	v2.36	v2.81	40
41	1926	Q0.55	12-16-99	11-9	2.20	2.20	2.20	1060	6272	5966	9-30-99	8092	[68]333	365683	Dc	v2.67	□pv2.88	v2.50	v□3.42	E3.55	3.40	9 Mo Sep	v□2.82	vΔ2.80	41
42	1999	Q0.41¼	12-31-99	12-14	1.325	1.65	....	Co option redm fr 3-11-2004 at $25				[70]200	...	...	Dc	...	...	...	....	....	....	Mature 12-31-2038			42
43◆	1988	Q0.39	11-30-99	11-17	1.46	1.56	1.28	Total Assets $5336.19M			9-30-99	1669	1600	125212	Dc	v0.77	v0.90	v0.98	v1.12	....	1.28	9 Mo Sep	v0.84	v1.00	43
44◆	1934	Q0.18½	3-10-00	2-16	0.74	0.74	0.81	70.8	690	1343	9-30-99	....	...	160883	Dc	v1.87	vd0.26	pv1.27	v1.63	E1.64	1.68	9 Mo Sep	v1.12	v1.17	44
45	....	None Since Public			...	Nil	....	....	19.5	13.3	7-31-99	....	...	9341	Oc	0.06	0.31	0.25	v0.13	....	d2.80	9 Mo Jul	v0.31	vd2.62	45
46◆	1979	gQ0.18	1-31-00	12-30	g0.68	0.72	g0.64	750	1383	522	j9-30-99	....	...	93050	Dc	1.96	v2.16	v2.29	v3.21	....	j3.17	9 Mo Sep	v2.30	v2.26	46
47◆	1904	Q0.35	12-14-99	11-10	1.40	1.40	1.36½	2599	12107	10654	9-30-99	4622	2700	p1044525	Dc	v2.77	v3.18	v2.08	v□4.08	E2.00	10.98	9 Mo Sep	v1.29	v8.19	47
48	....	None Since Public			...	Nil	....	50.6	130	73.7	9-30-99	103	...	15430	Je	p0.70	p1.65	Δv2.37	v2.15	v1.09	1.29	3 Mo Sep	v0.21	v0.41	48
49	1998	Q0.461	2-1-00	1-12	1.844	1.844	0.932	Co option redm fr 5-1-2003 at $25				★100	...	...	Dc	...	...	...	....	....	....	Mature 4-15-2038			49
50	....	None Since Public			...	Nil	....	17.7	732	551	9-30-99	1130	...	±17413	Dc	p±v2.03	v±1.57	±v1.88	□v±2.42	....	3.19	9 Mo Sep	v±□1.58	v□±2.35	50
51◆	....	None Since Public			...	Nil	....	266	322	81.8	9-30-99	288	...	44225	Dc	vd1.53	v0.60	vd1.93	v0.06	E0.71	0.10	9 Mo Sep	v0.37	v0.41	51

◆**Stock Splits & Divs By Line Reference Index** [3]2-for-1,'94,'98. [4]2-for-1,'98. [9]5-for-4,'97. [10]3-for-2,'99. [11]2-for-1,'98. [13]2-for-1,'99:To split 2-for-1,ex Jan 11,'00. [14]2-for-1,'95,'97. [15]2-for-1,'98. [18]3-for-2,'96:Adj for 5%,'98. [19]3-for-2,'98. [20]3-for-2,'95. [23]2-for-1,'97. [25]2-for-1,'97. [39]3-for-2,'98. [43]2-for-1,'97. [44]No adj for stk dstr Cognizant, AC Nielsen'96:No adj for spin-off,'98. [46]3-for-1,'94. [47]2-for-1,'97. [51]2-for-1,'96.

¶ S&P 500
\# MidCap 400
✣ SmallCap 600
• Options

Index	Ticker	Name of Issue (Call Price of Pfd. Stocks)	Market	Com. Rank. & Pfd. Rating	Inst. Hold Cos	Inst. Hold Shs. (000)	Principal Business	Price Range 1971-97 High	1971-97 Low	1998 High	1998 Low	1999 High	1999 Low	Dec. Sales in 100s	December, 1999 Last Sale Or Bid High	Low	Last	%Div Yield	P-E Ratio	EPS 5 Yr Growth	% Annualized Total Return 12 Mo	36 Mo	60 Mo
1	DRA	✔Duraswitch Indus	AS	NR	4	918	Dgn/mfr electric switch pds	...	...	...	...	10	1⅛	11354	10	5⅛	6¾	...	..	...	...	...	...
2	DVI	✔DVI Inc	NY,Ch,Ph	B	68	8928	Finance/lease medical equip	21	⅞	27¼	9½	18⅞	11¼	7962	15⅜	12½	15 3/16	...	11	18	−16.2	5.3	7.7
✣3•[1]	DY	✔Dycom Industries	NY,Ch,Ph	B	265	19195	Telecommun & electrical svcs	18 11/16	¼	39½	14 3/16	56⅝	29 15/16	54889	47½	37 11/16	44 1/16	...	26	40	16.1	92.8	92.6
4	DBG	✔Dyersburg Corp	NY	NR	20	2218	Mfr/mkt fleece fabrics	14⅞	3⅞	12	2½	3⅞	¼	13876	1 1/16	½	15/16	...	d	Neg	−65.8	−48.6	−30.6
5	DDN	✔Dynamex Inc[51]	AS	NR	21	2292	Same-day delivery svcs	11⅞	5¼	14½	3¾	4⅜	1 15/16	...	...	...	...	...	...	...	...	...	...
6	BOOM	Dynamic Materials	NNM	B−	8	637	Explosion metal working	26¼	5/16	10⅞	3 7/16	6 7/16	⅞	5190	1 11/16	1	1 3/16	...	d	Neg	−68.3	−49.8	−11.0
7	DRCO	✔Dynamics Research	NNM,B	B−	17	894	Mfr encoders: computer svs	11⅞	1/16	12¾	4⅛	9½	2⅞	5501	9½	5	8½	...	d	Neg	44.7	16.4	39.6
8•[2]	DYN	✔Dynegy Inc[52]	NY	NR	133	28380	Integrated natural gas svcs	24¾	8	17½	9⅜	24¾	10⅛	36661	24¾	20⅛	24 5/16	0.2	30	...	123	1.8	18.7
9	DX	✔Dynex Capital	NY,Ch,Ph,P	B+	36	3473	Real estate investment trust	65	3¾	54½	16¼	22¼	5¼	12778	8 3/16	5 15/16	6 7/16	...	d	Neg	−63.1	−47.4	−14.0
10	EELN	✔E-Loan Inc	NNM	NR	33	4019	Online mortgage provider	...	...	...	...	74⅜	14	58120	25⅞	15½	16¼	...	49	...	...	...	...
11	EPNY	✔E.piphany Inc	NNM	NR	39	2359	Sales,mktg software products	...	...	...	...	275	16	46370	275	148⅛	223⅛	...	d	...	...	...	...
12	EIM	✔E-Sim Ltd	AS	NR	3	249	Dgn/dvp computer software	...	...	7⅛	1⅜	16¼	3⅛	44239	16¼	9⅜	13 11/16	...	d	...	321	...	...
13	ESPI	✔e.spire Communications	NNM	NR	79	7057	Telecommun svcs/equip	16	3¼	23⅜	4⅝	18⅛	4 5/16	232049	7⅝	5 1/16	5 13/16	...	d	−16	−8.8	−18.5	...
14	ESTM	✔E-Stamp Corp	NNM	NR	..	...	Dvp stg:net based postage sv	...	...	...	...	44⅞	17	95849	40⅜	20	22¼	...	..	...	...	...	...
#15•[3]	EGRP	✔E Trade Group	NNM	NR	270	53593	Online discount brokerage svc	12	2 1/16	16¼	2½	72¼	12¾	1405334	36	25 11/16	26⅛	...	d	−37	126	109	...
16	EZM.A	✔E-Z EM Inc'A'	AS	C	16	763	Mfr diagnostic imag'g prod	15¾	3	9¾	5⅞	8	4⅛	451	8	5¾	7¾	...	15	2	26.5	−9.8	18.1
17	EZM.B	Cl'B'(non-vtg)	AS	C	13	763		14½	3 5/16	9	4⅜	7⅝	4⅜	1614	7⅝	5½	7⅝	...	15	2	48.8	−10.0	19.2
18	EPII	Eagle Pacific Indus	NSC	B−	6	574	Mfr PVC pipe/tubing	5¼	¼	2½	1⅜	5⅛	1¼	8481	5	4 1/16	4¼	...	5	87	113	15.6	...
✣19	EUSA	✔Eagle USA Airfreight	NNM	NR	155	14582	Air freight forwarding svcs	25½	5½	24 7/16	8	49	13 15/16	46401	49	32½	43⅛	...	44	...	165	35.2	...
✣20•[1]	EGR	✔Earthgrains Co	NY	NR	290	29036	Mfr,dstr packaged bakery prd	23¾	6⅜	37¼	20¼	33½	15 5/16	43391	18⅝	15 5/16	16⅛	1.2	15	...	−47.5	8.0	...
21•[4]	ELNK	✔Earthlink Network[59]	NNM	NR	128	9074	Internet svc provider	13	4 5/16	78½	12¼	99⅜	35	201155	65	42¼	42½	...	d	...	−25.4	...	...
22•[5]	ERTH	✔EarthShell Corp	NNM	NR	53	8941	Dvp stg:disposable food pkg	...	...	24 3/16	5	18	1⅜	189049	7⅛	2¼	4⅛	...	d	...	−65.4	...	...
23	EWBX	✔EarthWeb Inc	NNM	NR	41	3406	Internet on-line svcs	...	...	85 1/16	14	89	25⅜	69506	55 5/16	33½	50 5/16	...	..	...	29.4	...	...
24	NGT	Eastern AmerNatlGasTr'SPERs'[60]	NY	NR	11	66	Secure Principal Ener Receipt	26¼	14¼	20¼	13¾	15 7/16	9¾	6383	12	9¾	10 5/16	13.6	6	...	−16.8	−5.1	2.4
25	EML	✔Eastern Co	AS,Ch	B+	29	1082	Mfrs locks & metal products	13 5/16	1½	19	12½	19½	14	404	15 13/16	14¾	15⅝	2.8	10	29	−3.2	25.5	16.5
¶26•[6]	EFU	✔Eastern Enterprises	NY,B,C,Ch,P,Ph	B	321	18092	Boston Gas/river barging	45⅝	5 9/16	45⅝	37⅝	57 7/16	33½	18646	57 7/16	55½	57 7/16	3.0	23	−11	36.7	22.5	22.1
✣27•[7]	EUA	✔Eastern Util Assoc[61]	NY,B,Ch,P	B	130	10438	Util hldg co: Mass & RI elec	41¾	8	28⅜	23 9/16	31⅝	26½	6464	30 11/16	30⅛	30 5/16	5.5	34	−13	13.5	29.0	14.7
28	EGP	✔EastGroup Properties Inc	NY,Ph	NR	96	5325	Real estate investment trust	26 11/16	2 7/16	22⅛	16 5/16	21⅞	15⅜	10738	18 13/16	16¼	18½	8.2	8	13	8.8	8.7	18.1
¶29•[8]	EMN	✔Eastman Chemical	NY,Ph,P	NR	437	58103	Mfr chemical plastic,fiber prd	76¼	39½	72 15/16	43½	60 5/16	36	83216	49	38 11/16	47 11/16	3.7	29	−4	10.8	−1.6	2.0
¶30•[3]	EK	✔Eastman Kodak	NY,B,C,Ch,P,Ph	B	1053	193201	Photograph apparatus,chem	94¾	18¼	88 15/16	57 15/16	80⅜	56⅝	366228	67 13/16	56⅝	66¼	2.7	16	−4	−5.6	−3.9	9.5
31	EZR	✔Easyriders Inc	AS	NR	8	124	Pub,entertain,rest,apparel	...	...	4¼	1⅛	2¾	⅝	6309	2	11/16	13/16	...	d	...	−53.6	...	...
¶32•[5]	ETN	✔Eaton Corp	NY,B,Ch,P,Ph	B+	549	52310	Electronic/electric sys,eqp:	103⅜	4	99⅝	57½	103½	62	57269	78⅜	69⅜	72⅝	2.4	12	6	5.0	3.6	10.6
✣33	EV	✔Eaton Vance[63]	NY,B,Ph	†A	163	11593	Advisor to mutual funds,dstr	19⅛	1/16	25 1/16	17 7/16	40	18 11/16	17250	38 7/16	33 15/16	38	1.0	27	10	84.2	49.3	...
34•[9]	EBAY	✔eBay Inc	NNM	NR	233	21212	Online trading services	...	...	103¾	6	234	55 5/16	688237	181⅞	125	125 3/16	...	..	...	55.7	...	...
35	EBNX	eBenX Inc	NNM	NR	..	...	e-commerce solutions	...	...	...	...	53⅞	20	418932	53⅞	20	45¼	...	..	...	...	...	...
36	EBKR	ebookers.com plc ADS[64]	NNM	NR	..	...	Travel prod & svcs online	...	...	...	...	43	16⅞	32971	25	16⅞	17 5/16	...	..	...	...	...	...
37	ECC	✔ECC International	NY,Ch,Ph	C	15	1606	Computer-contr simulators	17½	1/16	3 9/16	1 9/16	4½	2⅛	5057	3 7/16	3	3¼	...	d	Neg	30.0	−26.7	−21.6
38	EIN	✔Echelon International	NY,Ch	NR	72	3387	Real estate/financial svcs	25¼	12½	27 15/16	18¾	26⅛	18½	6693	25¾	21 15/16	23	...	13	...	3.1	13.8	...
39	ECO	✔Echo Bay Mines	AS,To,B,Ch,P,Mo,Vc	C	64	5235	Mining:gold & silver	30⅛	2	3 15/16	1¼	2⅝	1⅛	80191	1 9/16	1⅛	1 3/16	...	d	Neg	−32.2	−43.5	−35.2
40•[10]	DISH	✔EchoStar Communications'A'	NNM	NR	259	59379	Mfr satellite TV prod	10⅛	2¾	12¼	4 1/16	98¾	10¾	747411	98¾	63⅞	97½	...	d	Neg	708	161	...
41•[11]	ECIL	✔ECI Telecom Ltd	NNM	NR	186	34665	Electronic telecommun sys	35	3/16	40 5/16	19¾	45	23¾	172362	32⅞	24⅜	31⅝	0.6	14	7	−10.7	14.9	19.2
42•[1]	ESSI	✔Eco Soil Systems	NNM	NR	33	4784	Soil/cropcare mgmt sys	8⅛	3⅞	12⅝	3½	9	2 13/16	33546	4 5/16	2 13/16	4 5/16	...	d	...	−50.7	...	...
43	EECN	✔Ecogen Inc	NNM	C	13	449	Dvlps biological pesticides	72½	1¾	3¾	⅞	3 9/16	13/16	11634	1 11/16	13/16	1¼	...	d	25	−25.9	−20.6	−39.7
¶44•[5]	ECL	✔Ecolab Inc	NY,Ch,Ph	A−	456	61846	Comm'l cleaning&sanitizing	28	2	38	26⅛	44 7/16	31 11/16	89224	39¼	32⅞	39⅛	1.2	30	18	9.3	29.4	32.3
45	ECLG	✔eCollege.com	NNM	NR	..	...	Online college course svcs	...	...	...	...	17½	10¾	137561	17½	10¾	10 15/16	...	d	...	...	...	...
46	EEI	✔Ecology/Environment'A'	AS,Ch	B−	12	490	Evironm'l consult'g/test'g	28 7/16	7	12	9 1/16	9¼	5¼	819	5 15/16	5¼	5 5/16	6.0	48	−25	−40.2	−8.8	−6.7
47	ECSGY	✔ECsoft Group ADR[65]	NNM	NR	14	1820	Computer systems/svcs	19⅛	8	40½	11⅜	36¼	9½	2215	20	15½	18½	...	31	...	−47.5	24.3	...
¶48•[12]	EIX	✔Edison Intl	NY,B,C,Ch,P,Ph	B	656	181157	Hldg co for So'n Cal Edison	27 13/16	3 11/16	31	25⅛	29⅝	21⅝	310019	27¼	24 3/16	26 3/16	4.1	13	5	−2.2	14.1	17.8
49	EDSN	✔Edison Schools'A'	NNM	NR	..	...	Private mgmt public schools	...	...	...	...	18 7/16	14½	35600	18 1/16	14½	15¾	...	d	...	...	...	...
50	EDO	✔EDO Corp	NY,B,Ch	B−	37	2060	Electr eq:military,marine	23	7/16	10⅞	6 11/16	9⅜	5⅛	5653	6⅛	5⅛	5⅞	2.0	23	NM	−28.6	−5.0	12.6

Uniform Footnote Explanations-See Page 4. Other: [1]Ph:Cycle 3. [2]ASE,Ph:Cycle 3. [3]ASE,CBOE,P,Ph:Cycle 1. [4]CBOE,Ph:Cycle 1. [5]CBOE:Cycle 1. [6]Ph:Cycle 1. [7]Ph:Cycle 2. [8]CBOE:Cycle 3. [9]ASE,CBOE,P:Cycle 1. [10]CBOE,Ph:Cycle 3. [11]CBOE:Cycle 2. [12]P:Cycle 1. [51]ASE trading halted 9-16-99. [52]Plan comb w/Illinova Corp,$16.50 or 0.69 new. [53]®$1.48,'96. [54]12 Mo Jan'98. [55]Pfd in $M. [56]Fiscal Jun'95 & prior. [57]12 Mo Dec'96. [58]Fiscal Dec'95 & prior. [59]Plan comb/w MindSpring Ent,1.615 new. [60]Dep Unit int E.AmerNatGasTr&$20U.S.GvtObl(2013). [61]Approve New England Elec mgr, $31. [62]Excl subsid pfd. [63]Non-vtg. [64]Ea ADS rep 1 Ord shr,0.28P. [65]Ea ADR rep 1 ord,par .50p. [66]Subsid pfd in $M.

Index	Cash Divs. Ea. Yr. Since	Dividends: Latest Payment Period $	Date	Ex. Div.	Total $ So Far 1999	Ind. Rate	Paid 1998	Financial Position Mil-$ Cash& Equiv.	Curr. Assets	Curr. Liab.	Balance Sheet Date	Capitalization Lg Trm Debt Mil-$	Shs. 000 Pfd.	Com.	Earnings $ Per Shr. Years End	1995	1996	1997	1998	1999	Last 12 Mos.	Interim Earnings Period	$ per Shr. 1998	1999	Index
1◆	....	None Since Public			...	Nil	....	7.26	8.28	0.97	9-30-99	0.14	...	7496	Dc	...	...	...	vd0.13	....	....	9 Mo Sep	n/a	vd0.36	1
2	....	None Since Public			...	Nil	....	Total Assets $1221.49M			9-30-99	540	...	14214	Je	0.61	0.81	v0.74	v1.03	v1.30	1.37	3 Mo Sep	v0.30	v0.37	2
3◆	....	5%Stk	12-21-87	12-1	...	Nil	....	78.4	238	74.7	10-30-99	9.90	...	25761	Jl	0.35	pv0.49	pv0.73	vp1.01	v1.55	1.70	3 Mo Oct	v0.33	v0.48	3
4	1992	Div Omitted 5-11-99			0.01	Nil	0.04	0.17	116	99.5	7-03-99	133	...	13347	Sp	0.46	0.62	v□1.00	v0.53	Pv□d1.28	d1.28				4
5	....	None Since Public			...	Nil	....	1.35	36.5	22.7	4-30-99	45.8	...	10207	Jl	0.20	0.23	v□0.56	v0.71	Pvd0.16	d0.16				5
6	....	None Paid			...	Nil	....	0.34	9.93	20.4	9-30-99	0.01	...	2829	Dc	0.27	v0.59	v0.70	v0.49	....	d0.62	9 Mo Sep	v0.50	vd0.61	6
7◆	....	s0.007	4-13-84	3-26	...	Nil	....	9.41	77.7	66.0	9-30-99	....	...	7363	Dc	v0.08	v0.23	v0.53	vd0.77	....	d1.30	9 Mo Sep	vd0.03	vd0.56	7
8	1994	Q0.01¼	12-21-99	12-1	0.05	0.05	0.05	28.3	2743	2184	9-30-99	1416	7815	155970	Dc	pv0.40	v0.83	□vd0.58	v0.66	....	0.82	9 Mo Sep	v0.48	v0.64	8
9◆	1988	Div Omitted 12-15-98			...	Nil	4.80	Total Assets $4678.42M			9-30-99	4237	5061	11444	Dc	v3.40	v[53]5.96	v5.48	v□0.64	....	d1.99	9 Mo Sep	v2.37	□vd0.26	9
10	....	None Since Public			...	Nil	....	47.0	98.1	54.0	9-30-99	2.89	...	41717	Dc	...	...	...	vpd0.41	....	0.33	6 Mo Jun	vpd0.88	vpd0.14	10
11	....	None Since Public			...	Nil	....	19.8	22.3	4.06	6-30-99	8.10	p...	★25834	Dc	...	...	...	vpd1.17	....	d0.45	9 Mo Sep	vd3.62	vpd2.90	11
12	....	None Since Public			...	Nil	....	8.94	10.8	2.60	1-31-99	....	...	10185	Ja	...	...	[54]d0.49	vd0.39	....	d0.55	9 Mo Oct	vd0.20	vd0.36	12
13	....	None Since Public			...	Nil	....	92.8	217	215	9-30-99	767	[55]271	51123	Dc	v[56]d3.30	v[57]d8.54	vd4.65	vd4.45	....	d5.85	9 Mo Sep	vd2.97	vd4.37	13
14	....	None Since Public			...	Nil	....	1.92	2.41	2.74	6-30-99	0.01	p...	★37358	Dc	...	...	...	vpd0.57	....	....	9 Mo Sep	n/a	vpd1.23	14
15◆	....	None Since Public			...	Nil	....	189	3333	3013	9-30-99	....	...	244434	Sp	0.03	...	v0.11	vd0.01	vd0.23	d0.23				15
16◆	....	3%Stk	3-16-98	2-24	...	Nil	3%Stk	16.5	67.3	17.2	8-28-99	0.50	...	±10066	My	0.16	±2.04	v±d0.33	v±d0.60	v±0.47	0.51	3 Mo Aug	v±0.14	v±0.18	16
17◆	....	3%Stk	3-16-98	2-24	...	Nil	3%Stk	....	...	...		....	...	6031	My	0.16	2.04	v±d0.33	v±d0.60	v±0.47	0.51	3 Mo Aug	v±0.14	v±0.18	17
18	....	None Paid			...	Nil	....	1.75	75.1	73.6	9-30-99	9.98	19	7235	Dc	vd0.27	□v0.49	v0.06	v□0.14	....	0.82	9 Mo Sep	v□0.17	v0.85	18
19◆	....	None Since Public			...	Nil	....	59.4	149	47.4	6-30-99	....	...	28574	Sp	p0.34	p0.44	v0.60	v0.72	Pv0.98	0.98				19
20◆	1996	Q0.05	11-30-99	11-9	0.18	0.20	0.13	30.6	402	289	9-14-99	382	...	42514	Mr	p[58]d0.63	v0.40	v□0.89	v0.89	....	1.07	24 Wk Sep	v0.49	v0.67	20
21◆	....	None Since Public			...	Nil	....	338	361	78.9	9-30-99	9.20	4103	32598	Dc	vd0.80	vd2.57	vd1.49	vd2.58	Ed1.48	d3.72	9 Mo Sep	vd1.64	vd2.78	21
22	....	None Since Public			...	Nil	....	51.2	51.6	6.90	9-30-99	....	...	100045	Dc	...	...	pvd0.27	vd0.29	....	d0.43	9 Mo Sep	vd0.19	vd0.33	22
23	....	None Since Public			...	Nil	....	29.1	34.5	18.9	9-30-99	5.62	...	p9763	Dc	...	...	vpd1.63	vpd1.53	....	....	9 Mo Sep	n/a	vd2.78	23
24	1993	0.416	12-15-99	11-26	1.452	1.40	1.60	Liq date 5-15-2013				....	...	5900	Dc	1.58	v1.76	v1.66	v1.60	....	1.60				24
25◆	1940	Q0.11	12-15-99	11-23	0.43	0.44	†0.393	6.61	31.5	8.37	10-02-99	8.71	...	3652	Dc	v0.59	v0.21	v0.92	v1.43	....	1.64	9 Mo Sep	v1.05	v1.26	25
26	1974	Q0.43	1-4-00	11-30	1.68	1.72	1.64	30.7	223	208	9-30-99	517	...	p27020	Dc	v□2.98	v2.98	v2.54	vΔ2.24	E2.52	1.33	9 Mo Sep	vΔ2.07	v1.16	26
27	1928	Q0.41½	11-15-99	10-28	1.66	1.66	1.66	Total Assets $1481.03M			9-30-99	307	[62]...	20436	Dc	v1.61	v1.50	v1.86	v1.70	E0.90	0.84	12 Mo Sep	v1.80	v0.84	27
28◆	1978	Q0.38	12-30-99	12-17	1.48	1.52	1.40	Total Assets $626.71M			9-30-99	229	4525	15918	Dc	v1.21	v1.43	v1.56	v1.66	....	2.23	9 Mo Sep	v1.19	v□1.76	28
29	1994	Q0.44	1-3-00	12-13	1.76	1.76	1.76	75.0	1391	940	9-30-99	2090	...	78227	Dc	v0.68	v4.79	v3.63	v3.13	E1.64	1.25	9 Mo Sep	v3.15	v1.27	29
30◆	1902	Q0.44	1-3-00	11-29	1.76	1.76	1.76	604	6220	6570	9-30-99	920	...	315604	Dc	v3.62	v3.76	v0.01	v4.24	E4.09	3.67	9 Mo Sep	v3.41	v2.84	30
31	....	None Paid			...	Nil	....	0.11	9.68	15.6	9-30-99	35.9	...	23829	Dc	...	...	pd0.34	vd1.04	....	d0.67	9 Mo Sep	vd0.78	vd0.41	31
32	1923	Q0.44	11-24-99	11-4	1.76	1.76	1.76	71.0	2773	2817	9-30-99	1946	...	73600	Dc	v5.08	v4.46	v□5.93	v4.80	E5.95	6.36	9 Mo Sep	v3.79	v5.35	32
33◆	1976	Q0.09½	11-8-99	10-27	0.32	0.38	0.25½	105	108	53.2	7-31-99	28.6	...	±35875	Oc	±0.82	Δ±v0.94	v±1.04	v±0.81	vP□1.41	1.41				33
34◆	....	None Since Public			...	Nil	....	386	439	72.4	9-30-99	5.86	...	129338	Dc	...	...	vpd0.02	v0.02	E0.09	0.02	9 Mo Sep	v0.04	v0.04	34
35	....	None Since Public			...	Nil	....	7.29	11.3	2.16	9-30-99	....	p...	★15054	Dc	...	...	...	vpd0.16	....	....	9 Mo Sep	n/a	vpd0.33	35
36	....	None Since Public			...	Nil	....	n/a	6.30	4.43	p6-30-99	....	...	★17023	Dc	...	...	...	n/a	....	....	6 Mo Jun	n/a	vpd0.18	36
37	....	0.05	7-28-92	6-22	...	Nil	....	....	28.8	15.4	9-30-99	....	...	8424	Je	0.93	0.36	vd1.07	vd1.57	Pvd0.42	d0.14	3 Mo Sep	vd0.21	v0.07	37
38	....	None Since Public			...	Nil	....	24.0	75.5	59.3	9-30-99	152	...	6720	Dc	pvd0.77	Δvd4.51	v□1.40	Δv1.28	....	1.82	9 Mo Sep	vΔ0.10	v0.64	38
39	....	t0.03¾	12-31-96	12-4	...	Nil	....	7.42	62.9	85.2	9-30-99	40.4	...	140607	Dc	vd0.43	vd1.31	vd3.06	vd0.23	Ed0.10	d0.38	9 Mo Sep	vd0.15	vd0.30	39
40◆	....	None Since Public			...	Nil	....	198	594	607	9-30-99	1522	2659	±227846	Dc	vd0.09	vd0.63	vd1.92	vd1.65	Ed1.90	d3.55	9 Mo Sep	vd0.97	v□d2.88	40
41	1990	tQ0.05	11-18-99	11-2	t0.20	0.20	t0.20	442	896	273	12-31-98	100	...	76346	Dc	v1.16	v1.33	v1.70	v1.97	E2.32	1.10	9 Mo Sep	v1.38	v0.51	41
42	....	None Since Public			...	Nil	....	5.95	70.9	63.4	9-30-99	16.7	...	17921	Dc	pd0.29	vd0.72	vd0.10	vd0.61	....	d0.99	9 Mo Sep	v0.11	vd0.27	42
43◆	....	None Since Public			...	Nil	....	1.19	10.2	5.11	7-31-99	1.57	32	9978	Oc	d4.34	d0.40	d1.23	vd0.39	....	d0.89	9 Mo Jul	vd0.20	vd0.70	43
44◆	1936	Q0.12	1-18-00	12-29	0.42	0.48	0.38	26.4	584	479	9-30-99	184	...	129580	Dc	v0.73	v0.85	v1.00	v1.44	E1.32	1.29	9 Mo Sep	v1.14	v0.99	44
45	....	None Since Public			...	Nil	....	2.26	4.86	4.93	9-30-99	....	p...	★14696	Dc	...	...	...	vpd1.02	....	d1.65	9 Mo Sep	vpd0.60	vpd1.23	45
46◆	1987	S0.16	1-8-00	12-16	0.32	0.32	0.32	9.15	36.8	9.27	10-30-99	0.50	...	±3966	Jl	±0.52	±0.29	v±0.03	v±0.12	v±0.08	0.11	3 Mo Oct	v0.05	v0.08	46
47	....	None Since Public			...	Nil	....	22.3	38.8	19.5	12-31-97	0.65	...	★10556	Dc	pd0.21	v0.41	v0.56	Pv0.85	....	0.60	9 Mo Sep	v0.57	v0.32	47
48	1909	Q0.27	1-31-00	1-3	1.07	1.08	1.03	1218	3636	6182	9-30-99	11890	[66]535	347207	Dc	v1.65	v1.63	v1.73	v1.84	E2.00	1.97	12 Mo Sep	v1.74	v1.97	48
49	....	None Since Public			...	Nil	....	27.9	51.1	28.5	6-30-99	8.26	p...	★±42237	Je	...	...	...	....	vpd1.77	d1.91	3 Mo Sep	vd0.32	vd0.46	49
50	1997	Q0.03	1-6-00	12-15	0.12	0.12	0.11	29.0	79.1	38.9	9-25-99	27.8	58	6747	Dc	v0.20	v0.46	v0.81	v0.94	....	0.26	9 Mo Sep	v0.74	v0.06	50

◆**Stock Splits & Divs By Line Reference Index** [1]1-for-4.25 REVERSE,'99. [3]3-for-2,'99. [7]10%,'94,'97. [9]2-for-1,'97:1-for-4 REVERSE,'99. [15]2-for-1,'99(twice). [16]Adj for 3%,'98. [17]Adj for 3%,'98. [19]2-for-1,'96:3-for-2,'99. [20]2-for-1,'97,'98. [21]2-for-1,'98. [25]3-for-2,'99. [28]3-for-2,'97. [30]No adj for stk dstr 0.25 of Eastman Chem,'94. [33]No adj for stk dstr Inv Finl Svcs,'95:2-for-1,'97,'98. [34]3-for-1,'99. [40]2-for-1,'99(twice). [43]1-for-5 REVERSE,'96. [44]2-for-1,'94,'98. [46]Adj for 5%,'94.

¶ S&P 500
# MidCap 400
✣ SmallCap 600
• Options

Index	Ticker	Name of Issue (Call Price of Pfd. Stocks)	Market	Com. Rank. & Pfd. Rating	Inst. Hold Cos	Inst. Hold Shs. (000)	Principal Business	Price Range 1971-97 High	1971-97 Low	1998 High	1998 Low	1999 High	1999 Low	December, 1999 Dec. Sales in 100s	Last Sale Or Bid High	Last Sale Or Bid Low	Last Sale Or Bid Last	%Div Yield	P-E Ratio	EPS 5 Yr Growth	% Annualized Total Return 12 Mo	36 Mo	60 Mo
1	EDP	✔EDP-Electricidade Portugal ADS[51]	NY,Ph	NR	17	1142	Electric Utility-Portugal	39⅝	30½	54½	38⅜	50 1/16	29	1570	36⅛	30½	34⅞	3.7	21	...	−18.6	...	...
2	EBC	✔EdperBrascan Corp'A'	AS,Ph	NR	67	46327	Financial mgmt svcs	19⅝	16⅛	20⅞	12	16⅛	11¼	2483	13½	11⅞	13½	7.3	7	...	4.3	...	...
3	EDMC	✔Education Management	NNM	NR	128	17319	Provide postsecondary educat'n	16	7½	24	13⅝	31¾	8⅝	33798	15	9⅝	14	...	22	...	−40.7	10.1	...
4	EVCI	✔Educational Video Conferencing	NSC	NR	3	91	Provide video training pds	...	...	...	...	21	6	4212	21	17¼	20¼	...	d	...	...	...	...
#5•[1]	AGE	✔Edwards(AG)Inc	NY,B,Ch,P	A	319	41085	Security broker: inv banker	39 15/16	1/16	48 13/16	22⅝	41	24¼	87355	32⅞	26¾	32 1/16	1.9	8	22	−12.3	15.6	24.9
6	EEX	✔EEX Corp	NY,B,P,Ph	C	121	28803	Oil & gas explor,dev prod'n	64⅞	17¼	31⅞	5 1/16	7 11/16	2½	57411	3 5/16	2½	2 15/16	...	d	−9	−58.0	−56.2	−36.9
7•[2]	EFAX	✔eFax.com Inc	NNM	NR	25	809	Dvp print,tax,copy,scan softw	11	5	8	1 7/16	33	2½	182258	13⅝	6⅝	7¼	...	d	...	163	...	...
8	EFC	✔EFC Bancorp	AS	NR	5	668	Savings & loan, Illinois	...	...	15¼	9	12	9⅛	2219	10⅞	9¾	10	4.0	..	...	−5.4	...	...
9	EFNT	✔Efficient Networks	NNM	NR	60	4482	Telecommunication services	...	...	...	...	88½	15	74865	88½	55¼	68	...	..	...	...	...	...
10•[3]	ETV	✔E4L Inc	NY,Ch,P	C	57	10194	Provides direct market'g svcs	31 13/16	½	12 9/16	15/16	11⅜	1 5/16	77594	3⅜	2 3/16	2½	...	d	Neg	−76.6	−29.1	−13.4
11	EGAN	✔eGain Communications	NNM	NR	32	1848	e-commerce business svcs	...	...	...	...	63 7/16	12	85999	63 7/16	34¾	37¾	...	d	...	...	...	...
12•[4]	EGGS	✔Egghead.com Inc	NNM	NR	73	5598	Sells computers on internet	35¼	4⅝	108	10⅝	60⅝	11 5/16	808500	23⅞	11 5/16	16 3/16	...	d	...	−59.6	...	...
13	EGRT	Egreetings Network	NNM	NR	..	...	Internet based greeting svcs	...	...	...	...	16¼	7¾	206227	16¼	7¾	10⅛	...	..	...	...	...	...
14	EIDSY	✔Eidos PLC ADR[54]	NNM	NR	26	932	Dvp interactive softw pds	17½	6¼	21¾	9	105	15⅝	4179	105	83	83	...	86	...	417	90.5	...
15	AXA	✔Eiger Technology	To	NR	..	...	Mfr/dstr lighting fixtures	⅞	⅜	15/16	¼	4¼	¼	65508	4¼	1½	3½	...	..	−16	624	84.9	...
16•[1]	EGHT	✔8X8 Inc	NNM	NR	13	625	Dgn/dvp semiconductors	16⅛	6⅝	14½	1¾	7 9/16	2¾	78488	6⅞	4⅛	5⅛	...	..	...	−8.9	...	...
17•[1]	ENBXC	✔Einstein/Noah Bagel	NSC	NR	30	1154	Oper/franchise bagel stores	36½	5	6⅞	15/16	2 3/16	¼	76502	15/16	¼	⅜	...	d	...	−67.5	−76.1	...
18	EIR	Eircom plc ADS[55]	NY	NR	7	170	Telecommun svc,Ireland	...	...	...	...	...	14¾	7041	18¼	15¾	16	...	..	...	...	...	...
19	EKC	Ek Chor China Motorcycle	NY	NR	4	33	Joint venture motorcycle mfr	38⅞	2½	3⅝	1⅞	4 15/16	1 13/16	5148	3¼	2 1/16	2 3/16	...	d	Neg	14.8	−24.1	−24.7
20	EE	✔El Paso Electric	AS,Ch	NR	147	46809	Electr utility,Texas,N.Mexico	7 15/16	4¾	10⅜	6⅜	9 13/16	7	45890	9 13/16	8¾	9 13/16	...	18	...	12.1	14.7	...
¶21•[5]	EPG	✔El Paso Energy	NY,Ph,P	NR	503	93565	Natural gas pipeline system	33¾	9½	38 15/16	24 11/16	43 7/16	30 11/16	135431	39¾	33⅜	38 13/16	2.1	18	11	14.0	18.1	24.2
22	Pr C	4.75% cm'C'Pfd([59]50)	NY	BBB−	69	5345		...	...	54 1/16	42	55½	45⅛	3897	51¼	46½	50⅝	4.7	..	...	...	...	...
23	EPN	✔El Paso Energy Partners[61]LP[62]	NY	NR	40	974	Oper nat'l gas pipeline systems	...	...	28½	19¾	25⅛	16¾	13437	20 3/16	16¾	19	11.1	31	−45	3.4	...	...
24	EPN.P	Preference Unit	NY,Ch	NR	10	130		33⅛	10¼	34	17⅜	24½	16⅞	182	19¾	16⅞	16⅝B	6.7	26	−45	−7.4	−3.1	15.9
25	LCTO	El Sitio	NNM	NR	..	...	Spanish/Portuguese web sites	...	...	...	...	44⅞	16	272695	44⅞	16	36¾	...	..	...	...	...	...
26•[6]	ELN	✔Elan Corp ADS[64]	NY,Ch,Ph,P	NR	519	167559	Res/dev drug formulat'n tech	28 7/16	¾	38⅝	24 1/16	43 15/16	21¼	389325	30 1/16	24 1/16	29½	...	24	92	−14.3	21.7	27.5
27	WS A	Wrrt(Pur 2 ADS for $37.54)	NY	....	9	1727		...	...	...	...	56¼	20⅛	4280	32¾	23¼	29	...	..	...	...	...	...
28	WS B	Wrrt(Pur 2 ADS for $65.01)	NY	....	4	626		...	...	...	...	21½	16 15/16	6	21½	20¼	21½	...	..	...	...	...	...
29	ELBTF	Elbit Ltd	NNM	NR	8	359	Mfr computerized sys/prod	54	2	4⅜	2	18	3 3/16	36665	18	13 11/16	17 11/16	...	d	Neg	405	...	...
30•[2]	ELCO	✔Elcom Intl	NNM	NR	21	1818	Electr commerce softwr/svcs	16½	4½	7⅛	1 1/16	50	1 9/16	796459	50	10⅛	34	...	d	−36	1655	62.8	...
✣31	ELK	✔Elcor Corp	NY,B,Ch,Ph	B	181	13059	Roofing & industrial products	17 5/16	⅛	21 15/16	12⅞	34 15/16	19 3/16	24209	32⅞	28	30⅛	0.7	22	27	41.1	48.4	35.8
32	ETT	✔ElderTrust SBI	NY	NR	21	2053	Real estate investment trust	...	...	19⅝	9¼	11⅝	4 15/16	17267	6¼	4 15/16	6 1/16	...	67	...	−37.2	...	...
33	ELIX	✔Electric Lightwave'A'	NNM	NR	60	4286	Telecommunication svcs	16⅛	13⅛	23⅛	3½	20	7⅜	14128	20	14⅝	18¾	...	d	...	129	...	...
34	ELRC	Electro Rent	NNM	B+	70	18464	Rental/lease electr test eq	19⅞	3/16	28	9⅛	15 11/16	9	5150	12 1/16	11	11⅝	...	11	10	−27.9	−2.2	16.5
✣35•[4]	ESIO	✔Electro Scientific Ind	NNM	B−	178	9741	Computer-control laser sys	63¾	2½	45⅝	13⅛	73	34 3/16	34715	73	57	73	...	63	−17	61.1	41.1	27.7
36	EIL	✔Electrochemical Ind(1952)	AS	NR	..	...	Mfr/dstr chemical products	3 15/16	½	1⅛	9/16	1¼	⅝	588	1¼	1 1/16	1B	...	d	Neg	77.9	...	...
✣37•[7]	EGLS	✔Electroglas Inc	NNM	NR	144	13932	Mfr semicondctor mfg equip	40¼	6⅞	19⅝	7¾	29⅜	11½	36065	29⅜	24⅛	25⅝	...	..	Neg	116	16.3	9.4
#38•[4]	ERTS	✔Electronic Arts	NNM	B+	382	57746	Dvlp/mkt entertain't softwr	42¼	1 9/16	57⅛	33¼	124 7/16	38	394604	124 7/16	78¼	84	...	42	13	49.7	41.0	34.3
¶39•[8]	EDS	✔Electronic Data Systems	NY,B,Ph	A+	908	298292	Computer systems/svcs	63⅜	7/16	51 5/16	30 7/16	70	44⅛	359838	70	58	66 15/16	0.9	50	−8	34.8	17.3	13.2
40	ELBO	✔Electronics Boutique Hldgs	NNM	NR	46	3652	Special'y retail/elect games	...	...	25¾	6⅝	26 5/16	12⅛	52412	23½	15⅝	18	...	..	...	−11.7	...	...
41•[7]	EFII	✔Electronics For Imaging	NNM	NR	363	50714	Dvlp publish'g system softwr	57⅞	3 3/16	40⅜	13½	64⅞	32	160618	59½	44¾	58⅛	...	36	22	45.3	12.2	53.3
42	ELSI	✔Electrosource Inc	NSC	C	5	14	Mfr rechg storage batteries	71¼	1¾	3⅛	⅜	5¾	⅝	27561	5¾	2⅛	2¾	...	d	NM	340	−23.8	−37.7
43•[9]	ELF	✔Elf Aquitaine[71]ADS[72]	NY,Ch	B−	233	40369	Int'l integrated oil & gas co	69	27½	74⅝	48 5/16	99¼	50 1/16	5279	80½	73⅜	76⅝	1.3	26	NM	37.1	21.3	19.6
44	PERY	✔Ellis (Perry) Intl	NNM	B	37	1802	Designs, mkt men's sportswear	15⅝	5 11/16	18	6½	17¼	8½	1739	11⅞	10¾	11⅝	...	8	17	−3.1	6.6	12.5
45	ELT	Elscint Ltd	NY,Ch,Ph	NR	12	1654	Scient/nuclear medical/instr	143¾	2 9/16	13	6¼	13 7/16	5½	2898	6⅝	5½	6 1/16	...	3	16	−50.5	−1.0	−7.1
46	ENL	✔Elsevier NV[73] ADS[74]	NY,P	NR	19	1742	Publishing/information svcs	37⅝	18⅞	38⅜	24 5/16	33⅝	18⅝	4344	24⅛	19⅜	23⅞	2.9	52	...	−11.8	−8.1	5.9
47	ELXS	✔ELXSI Corp	NNM	B	21	576	Restaurants/video inspect eq	300	¾	17¾	8⅛	14¾	8½	655	13¾	12½	12 9/16B	...	3	29	2.4	25.0	19.7
48	AKO.A	✔Embotelladora Andina ADS[76]	NY,Ch,P	NR	47	9359	Produce soft drinks,Chile	27⅛	8 15/16	23½	10¼	20¾	12 9/16	3214	18 7/16	17¼	17 13/16	1.2	23	...	25.1	6.7	7.2
49	AKO.B	Cl'B' ADS[77]	NY	NR	38	9853		25	19	21	8⅜	16¾	10¼	4885	14 11/16	13 11/16	14⅝	1.6	19	...	15.2	...	...
50	EMT	✔Embratel Participacoes ADS[78]	NY	NR	117	57435	Telecommunication svcs	...	...	18 7/16	12⅝	27⅜	9⅛	140426	27⅜	18⅛	27¼	0.8	..	...	99.3	...	...

Uniform Footnote Explanations-See Page 4. Other: [1]CBOE:Cycle 2. [2]Ph:Cycle 2. [3]ASE,CBOE,P:Cycle 3. [4]CBOE:Cycle 3. [5]ASE:Cycle 1. [6]CBOE,P,Ph:Cycle 1. [7]CBOE:Cycle 1. [8]CBOE,Ph:Cycle 3. [9]ASE,CBOE:Cycle 1. [51]Ea ADS rep 2 ord,PTE 1000. [52]9 Mo Dec'96. [53]9 Mo Dec'98. [54]Ea ADR rep 1 ord,par .10p. [55]Ea ADS rep 4 ord shrs. [56]Approx. [57]To be determined. [58]11 Mo Dec'96. [59]Fr 3-31-2002. [60]El Paso Energy com. [61]Common Units. [62]Formerly Leviathan Gas PL. [63]Incl 1M Pref units. [64]Each ADS rep 1 ord shr P.IR 0.04. [65]Excl Executive shrs. [66]Fiscal Mar'95 & prior. [67]Incl current amts. [68]11 Mo Dec'98. [69]Stk dstr of Frutarom Indus. [70]Excl subsid Pfd. [71]Each ADS rep 0.5 ord shr FF50. [72]Total Fina(94%)plan acq,stk. [73]Ea ADS rep 2 ord, DF1.10. [74]Own 50% interest in Reed Elsevier plc. [75]Proportionate shr of Reed Elsevier(in pounds). [76]Ea ADS rep 6 Sr'A' com,no par. [77]Ea ADS rep 6 Sr'B'com,no par. [78]Ea ADS rep 1000 pfd shrs,no par.

Splits ◆ Index	Dividends: Cash Divs. Ea.Yr. Since	Latest Payment: Period $	Date	Ex. Div.	Total $: So Far 1999	Ind. Rate	Paid 1998	Financial Position Mil-$: Cash& Equiv.	Curr. Assets	Curr. Liab.	Balance Sheet Date	Capitalization: Lg Trm Debt Mil-$	Shs. 000: Pfd.	Com.	Earnings $ Per Shr. Years: End	1995	1996	1997	1998	1999	Last 12 Mos.	Interim Earnings: Period	$ per Shr. 1998	1999	Index
1	1998	1.278	6-14-99	5-20	1.278	1.28	1.17	1.84	609	876	12-31-97	2977	...	600000	Dc	1.47	1.54	v1.68	....	....	1.68				1
2	1997	Q0.24½	2-29-00	1-28	0.98	0.98	0.98	Equity per shr $20.87			12-31-98	2525	21000	281319	Dc	...	p1.28	v3.34	v2.12	....	j1.26	9 Mo Sep	v1.93	v1.07	2
3◆	....	None Since Public			...	Nil	....	5.08	34.0	59.2	9-30-99	14.9	...	29183	Je	...	p0.23	v0.36	v0.48	v0.61	0.63	3 Mo Sep	v0.01	v0.03	3
4	....	None Since Public			...	Nil	....	9.92	10.5	0.80	9-30-99	....	...	4347	Dc	...	...	...	vd1.03	....	d1.16	9 Mo Sep	vd0.74	vd0.87	4
5◆	1971	Q0.15	1-3-00	12-1	0.59	0.60	0.54	Total Assets $4352M			8-31-99	....	...	92092	Fb	1.77	v2.24	v2.75	v3.00	E3.80↑	3.75	9 Mo Nov	v2.22	v2.97	5
6◆	....	0.225	1-3-94	12-9	...	Nil	....	97.6	138	62.6	9-30-99	206	...	42471	Dc	vd1.14	vd0.87	vd5.13	vd0.97	....	d1.40	9 Mo Sep	vd0.83	vd1.26	6
7	....	None Since Public			...	Nil	....	11.0	17.2	5.40	9-30-99	....	...	12901	Dc	...	p[52]d0.14	vd0.61	vd0.13	....	d1.26	9 Mo Sep	vd0.10	vd1.23	7
8	1999	Q0.10	1-11-00	12-29	0.30	0.40	....	Total Deposits $309M			9-30-99	94.2	...	5366	Dc	...	p0.50	...	v‡[53]d0.08	....	....	9 Mo Sep	n/a	v0.53	8
9	....	None Since Public			...	Nil	....	56.1	85.5	16.4	9-30-99	....	...	37507	Je	...	...	...	vpd0.41	Ppd0.97	....	3 Mo Sep	n/a	vd0.25	9
10	....	0.02½	1-15-91	12-24	...	Nil	....	3.25	68.6	44.1	9-30-99	15.4	44	34556	Mr	0.74	vd2.07	vd2.31	v□d1.88	....	d1.82	6 Mo Sep	vd0.48	vd0.42	10
11	....	None Since Public			...	Nil	....	1.27	2.48	3.24	6-30-99	0.22	p...	★27816	Je	...	...	...	....	pvd0.93	d1.84	3 Mo Sep	vpd0.31	vpd1.22	11
12	....	None Since Public			...	Nil	....	26.3	47.5	32.5	9-30-99	....	...	p37102	Dc	vd0.04	v0.03	vd0.16	vd0.77	....	d1.88	9 Mo Sep	vd0.61	vd1.72	12
13	....	None Since Public			...	Nil	....	2.38	4.60	8.41	9-30-99	3.59	p...	★34441	Dc	...	...	...	vpd0.94	....	....	9 Mo Sep	n/a	vpd1.51	13
14	....	None Since Public			...	Nil	....	48.2	112	58.0	j3-31-99	30.8	...	17282	Mr	d0.57	0.73	v1.07	v2.01	....	0.97	6 Mo Sep	vd1.37	vd2.41	14
15	....	None Since Public			...	Nil	....	2.05	6.78	2.42	j6-30-99	1.50	...	18815	Sp	0.02	0.02	0.01	v0.01	....	0.01	9 Mo Jun	vNil	vNil	15
16	....	None Since Public			...	Nil	....	16.5	21.1	7.27	9-30-99	....	...	18525	Mr	...	pn/a	v0.25	vd1.28	....	....	6 Mo Sep	n/a	vd0.09	16
17	....	None Since Public			...	Nil	....	5.62	17.4	45.6	10-03-99	153	...	34084	Dc	d2.20	v0.27	vd0.04	vd6.18	....	d5.71	9 Mo Sep	vd0.81	vd0.34	17
18	2000	[56]0.065	1-21-00	12-1	...	[57]....	....	24.1	546	1021	4-01-99	178	...	★2207827	Mr	...	...	...	v0.15	....	0.15				18
19	1993	0.60	6-29-99	5-27	0.60	[57]....	0.60	15.8	16.3	0.51	12-31-97	2.34	...	17098	Dc	1.23	0.20	vd3.13	....	....	d3.13				19
20	....	None Since Public			...	Nil	....	50.1	156	120	9-30-99	815	1357	57838	Dc	p0.20	‡[58]n/a	v□0.69	vΔ0.70	....	0.55	9 Mo Sep	v0.65	v□0.50	20
21◆	1992	Q0.20	1-11-00	12-8	0.79⅛	0.80	0.75⅝	92.0	2161	2123	9-30-99	4045	...	p228320	Dc	v1.23	v0.52	v1.59	v1.85	E2.11	1.55	9 Mo Sep	v1.36	v□1.06	21
22	1998	Q0.59⅜	12-31-99	12-13	2.37½	2.375	1.867	Cv into 1.2022[60]				....	6500	...	Dc	...	...	...	....	....	....				22
23	1998	Q0.52½	11-12-99	10-27	2.10	2.10	0.52½	9.16	16.4	22.6	9-30-99	447	...	[63]±27028	Dc	±v0.97	±v1.57	v±d0.06	v±0.02	....	0.62	9 Mo Sep	vd0.06	v0.54	23
24◆	1993	Q0.275	11-12-99	10-27	1.10	1.10	1.82½	....	...	...		....	...	26737	Dc	0.97	v1.57	vd0.06	v0.02	....	0.62	9 Mo Sep	vd0.06	v0.54	24
25	....	None Since Public			...	Nil	....	34.5	36.7	6.83	p9-30-99	0.47	p1111	★38574	Dc	...	...	...	vpd5.19	....	....	9 Mo Sep	n/a	vpd2.18	25
26◆	....	0.008	6-11-84	5-14	...	Nil	....	820	1185	233	12-31-98	1235	...	[65]p232056	Dc	[66]0.60	vd3.16	v0.79	v0.56	E1.22	6.32	9 Mo Sep	vd4.89	v0.87	26
27	....	Terms&trad. basis should			be checked in detail			Wrrts expire 12-31-2001				....	...	5290	Dc	...	...	...	....	....	....				27
28	....	Terms&trad. basis should			be checked in detail			Wrrts expire 1-14-2003				....	...	1250	Dc	...	...	...	....	....	....				28
29◆	1986	t0.05	1-5-98	12-18	...	Nil	t0.05	n/a	82.2	20.2	12-31-97	9.57	...	21387	Dc	0.86	vd0.53	vd0.51	vPd0.53	....	d0.45	9 Mo Sep	vd0.38	vd0.30	29
30	....	None Since Public			...	Nil	....	33.4	113	72.6	9-30-99	....	...	28025	Dc	pvd0.05	v0.19	v0.35	vd0.94	....	d1.60	9 Mo Sep	vd0.48	vd1.14	30
31◆	1995	Q0.05	2-16-00	1-4	0.193	0.20	0.167	2.26	104	43.6	9-30-99	44.2	...	19566	Je	0.48	0.52	v0.61	v0.91	v□1.27	1.38	3 Mo Sep	v□0.39	v0.50	31
32	1998	0.36½	11-12-99	10-27	1.46	[57]....	0.973	Total Assets $267.89M			9-30-99	[67]72.2	...	7201	Dc	...	p0.24	n/a	v‡[68]0.54	....	0.09	9 Mo Sep	v0.41	v□d0.04	32
33	....	None Since Public			...	Nil	....	24.2	60.1	110	9-30-99	561	...	±49935	Dc	...	...	vd0.80	v□d1.35	....	d2.42	9 Mo Sep	v□d0.91	vd1.98	33
34◆	....	None Since Public			...	Nil	....	Total Assets $354.19M			8-31-99	79.4	...	24504	My	0.60	0.88	v0.97	v1.29	v0.96	1.07	3 Mo Aug	v0.15	v0.26	34
35	....	None Since Public			...	Nil	....	43.4	181	21.0	8-31-99	....	...	13093	My	v1.90	v1.79	p2.27	v1.47	v0.57	1.16	6 Mo Nov	v0.28	v0.87	35
36◆	....	h[69]....	5-28-96	5-28	...	Nil	....	6.17	70.6	62.5	12-31-98	60.5	...	33693	Dc	0.34	vd0.45	vd0.03	vd0.02	....	d0.04	9 Mo Sep	vNil	vd0.02	36
37◆	....	None Since Public			...	Nil	....	133	178	24.9	9-30-99	....	...	19921	Dc	v2.05	v1.36	vd0.86	vd1.62	E0.15↑	d1.10	9 Mo Sep	vd0.58	vd0.06	37
38	....	None Since Public			...	Nil	....	230	635	260	9-30-99	....	...	63206	Mr	0.75	v0.86	v1.19	v1.15	E2.02↓	1.83	6 Mo Sep	vd0.36	v0.32	38
39	1984	Q0.15	12-10-99	11-9	0.60	0.60	0.60	812	5884	4342	9-30-99	2287	[70]...	470782	Dc	□v1.94	v0.88	v1.48	v1.50	E1.34	1.03	9 Mo Sep	v1.22	v0.75	39
40	....	None Since Public			...	Nil	....	10.0	164	174	10-31-99	....	...	22214	Ja	...	...	pv0.74	pv1.11	....	....	9 Mo Oct	n/a	v0.36	40
41◆	....	None Since Public			...	Nil	....	433	547	81.9	9-30-99	3.63	...	55476	Dc	v0.71	v1.13	v1.15	v0.85	E1.60	1.55	9 Mo Sep	v0.53	v1.23	41
42◆	....	None Paid			...	Nil	....	0.01	1.24	2.74	9-30-99	0.01	...	11277	Dc	vd9.76	vd2.13	vd1.91	v□d0.95	....	d0.16	9 Mo Sep	vΔd1.07	vd0.28	42
43	1960	1.002	7-12-99	6-16	1.002	1.00	1.058	1672	14104	12700	12-31-98	4167	...	275000	Dc	1.93	v2.50	v1.81	v1.24	E3.00	3.11	6 Mo Jun	v1.49	v3.36	43
44◆	....	None Since Public			...	Nil	....	0.40	95.5	14.1	10-31-99	144	...	6738	Ja	0.75	v0.89	v1.08	v1.27	....	1.55	9 Mo Oct	v0.96	v1.24	44
45◆	....	None Paid			...	Nil	....	32.2	262	145	12-31-97	12.8	...	15922	Dc	0.90	v0.51	v0.04	Pv1.75	....	2.05	9 Mo Sep	vd0.11	v0.19	45
46	1995	0.214	10-8-99	8-16	0.686	0.69	0.82½	220	314	444	[75]j12-31-97	24.0	...	670764	Dc	1.24	1.30	v0.46	....	....	0.46				46
47	....	None Since Public			...	Nil	....	1.54	26.2	11.6	9-30-99	8.76	...	4282	Dc	v0.89	v1.51	v2.88	v0.95	....	3.90	9 Mo Sep	v0.69	v3.64	47
48◆	1994	0.041	11-19-99	11-29	0.214	0.22	0.19	393	601	175	12-31-97	351	...	±760275	Dc	0.63	0.77	v0.79	....	....	0.79				48
49	1997	0.045	11-19-99	11-2	0.235	0.24	0.208	....	...	...		....	...	380137	Dc	0.63	...	v0.79	....	....	0.79				49
50	1999	[56]0.209		12-29	0.215	0.21	....	....	...	...		....	...	p115491	Dc	...	...	...	....	....	....				50

◆**Stock Splits & Divs By Line Reference Index** [3]2-for-1,'98. [5]5-for-4,'94:3-for-2,'97. [6]1-for-3 REVERSE,'98. [21]2-for-1,'98. [24]2-for-1,'97. [26]2-for-1,'96,'99. [29]No adj for stk dstr Elbit Sys,Elbit Med'l,'96. [31]3-for-2,'97,'99. [34]3-for-2,'94,'96:2-for-1,'98. [36]6-for-5,'96. [37]2-for-1,'95. [41]2-for-1,'95,'97. [42]1-for-10 REVERSE,'96. [44]3-for-2,'97. [45]1-for-5 REVERSE,'96. [48]2-for-1 in Cl'B','97.

¶ S&P 500 # MidCap 400 ✣ SmallCap 600 • Options

Index	Ticker	Name of Issue (Call Price of Pfd. Stocks)	Market	Com. Rank. & Pfd. Rating	Inst. Hold Cos	Inst. Hold Shs. (000)	Principal Business	1971-97 High	1971-97 Low	1998 High	1998 Low	1999 High	1999 Low	Dec. Sales in 100s	December, 1999 Last Sale Or Bid High	Low	Last	%Div Yield	P-E Ratio	EPS 5 Yr Growth	% Annualized Total Return 12 Mo	36 Mo	60 Mo
¶1•[1]	EMC	✔EMC Corp	NY,P	B	1747	720098	Mfr computer storage prod	16 5/16	1/8	43 5/16	12	111	42	922303	111	83 5/16	109 1/4	...	..	30	157	138	82.5
2	EMCG	✔EMCOR Group	NNM	NR	80	8995	Mechanical/electric constr	22 1/4	9 3/8	23 1/8	12 1/2	26	16 1/16	12722	20 1/8	16 7/8	18 1/4	...	10	NM	13.2	12.0	...
3	ESC	✔Emeritus Corp	AS,Ch,Ph	NR	16	1889	Oper long-term care communit's	21 3/4	10	13 9/16	8 1/2	15 1/2	5	14834	7 1/8	5	6 1/2	...	d	−21	−38.5	−21.6	...
¶4•[2]	EMR	✔Emerson Electric	NY,B,C,Ch,P,Ph	A+	1298	316848	Mfr electric/electronic prdts	60 5/8	3 1/2	67 7/16	54 1/2	71 7/16	51 7/16	209481	60 13/16	53 1/16	57 3/8	2.5	19	9	−3.1	8.5	15.8
5	MSN	✔Emerson Radio	AS	NR	10	1961	Consumer electronic prod	3 3/4	3/8	11/16	1/4	7/8	7/16	17633	5/8	1/2	1/2	...	d	−4	−20.0	−25.0	−27.9
6	EMR	Emgold Mining	Vc,P	NR	1	19	Gold/mineral mining explor'n	7 1/2	1/16	9/16	1/8	3/8	1/32	3955	1/8	1/16	1/16B	...	d	...	−59.1	−68.9	−37.0
7•[3]	EMMS	✔Emmis Communications'A'	NNM	NR	..	...	Own/oper FM radio stations	53 1/2	11	57 7/8	22 1/8	124 11/16	39	57178	124 11/16	78 1/2	124 5/8	...	d	Neg	187	56.1	56.0
8	EDE	✔Empire Dist Elec[51]	NY,B,Ch	B+	79	4020	Utility:El svc in MO,KS,OK,AK	24 7/8	4 7/8	26 1/8	18 3/8	26 3/4	20 11/16	5212	24 1/8	21 11/16	22 5/8	5.7	20	1	−3.6	13.1	14.3
9	EMP	✔Empire of Carolina	AS,B,Ch	C	8	350	Design,mfr toys/seasonal pd	15	5/8	2 1/4	7/16	1 3/16	3/16	33873	5/16	3/16	1/4	...	d	Neg	−65.0	−62.8	−49.4
10	Pr A	Sr'A'cm CvPfd(NC)	AS	NR	1	16		....	....	10 3/4	6	8	2	2	4 1/4	2	1 7/8B	...	..	...	...	...	...
11	WS	Wrrt(Pur1com at$1.375)	AS	....	1	10		....	....	15/16	1/4	9/16	1/32	1289	1/8	1/32	1/8B	...	..	...	...	...	...
12	ERS	✔Empire Resources	AS	NR	1	19	Dvlp internet communicn prd	5 5/8	7/8	1 13/16	1 1/8	2 3/4	1	2342	1 5/8	1 1/4	1 5/8	...	81	NM	4.0	−13.4	...
13	WS	Wrrt(Pur 1 com at $9)	AS	....	1	100		1	1/16	1/8	1/64	1/4	1/16	932	1/4	1/16	1/4	...	..	...	...	...	...
14	EOC	✔Empresa Nac'l De El(Chile)ADS[55]	NY,Ch,P	NR	79	19185	Major elec utility in Chile	29	15 1/8	19 5/8	7 7/8	15 11/16	9	19548	14 3/8	13 3/16	14 3/16	0.6	..	...	26.1	−0.6	−7.6
15•[4]	ICA	✔Empresas ICA Sociedad ADS[56]	NY,Ph,P	NR	33	5143	Largest contrust'n co,Mexico	34 1/2	3 7/8	16 5/8	4 5/16	7 3/4	2 5/16	24426	3 13/16	2 15/16	3 1/4	7.1	d	Neg	−22.9	−38.5	−26.0
16	TL	Empresas Telex-Chile ADS[57]	NY,Ch,P	NR	7	553	Telecommunications svc-Chile	21 1/4	3 1/2	4 1/8	1/4	1 11/16	5/8	8292	1 1/16	3/4	3/4	...	d	Neg	−14.3	−45.3	−40.8
17•[5]	ELMG	✔EMS Technologies	NNM	B	50	6194	Wireless communications sys	29	3/16	24 3/4	10 1/4	18	6 5/8	16487	13	9 5/8	11 3/4	...	22	6	−16.1	−15.2	−0.6
18	EMLX	✔Emulex Corp	NNM	C	164	29415	Network access products	13 7/8	13/16	10	1 5/16	115	6 5/8	263764	115	72	112 1/2	...	..	81	1026	206	102
19	ENCD	✔ENCAD Inc	NNM	NR	24	1267	Mfr color inkjet printers	46 3/4	2 5/16	28 1/2	1 7/8	9 1/2	3 1/2	23207	5 7/8	4 7/16	4 3/4	...	d	Neg	31.9	−51.2	−5.0
20	ECA	Encal Energy[58]	NY,To,Ph	B−	30	13872	Oil&gas explor,dvlp,prod'n	7 1/2	1/8	4 7/16	2 7/8	5 15/16	3 7/16	652	4 3/4	3 7/8	4 1/8B	...	20	24	20.0	−1.3	6.6
21•[6]	WIRE	✔Encore Wire	NNM	NR	44	2964	Mfr copper electrical wire	25 11/16	2 7/8	27 5/16	6 3/4	12 13/16	6 1/2	21532	7 15/16	6 1/2	7 5/8	...	22	65	−17.6	0.0	−0.3
22•[7]	ELE	✔Endesa SA[59]ADS	NY,Ch,Ph	NR	127	36950	Major elec utility in Spain	22 7/16	3	27 15/16	16 7/8	30 1/4	18 7/16	23043	21	18 13/16	20 3/16	2.1	16	4	−23.4	7.5	17.7
23	DOR	✔Endorex Corp	AS	NR	4	2862	Dvp stg:biotechnology R&D	....	....	3 1/4	1 7/8	3 1/8	1 1/4	6103	3 1/8	1 15/16	2 3/4	...	d	...	33.4	...	...
24	EN	✔ENEL S.p.A. ADS[61]	NY	NR	..	...	Electric service,Italy	....	....	....	....	45 3/8	41	3057	44 1/8	41	41 1/4	...	..	...	...	...	...
✣25	EGN	✔Energen Corp	NY,Ch,Ph	A	173	15327	Gas serv in central Alabama	20 5/8	1 3/16	22 1/2	15 1/8	21 1/4	13 1/8	7674	19 1/4	15 3/4	18 1/16	3.7	13	7	−3.9	10.0	15.1
26	ENGSY	✔Energis PLC ADS[63]	NNM	NR	4	33	Communication svcs	24 3/8	21 1/4	118 1/4	21	240	111	36	240	194	235B	...	..	...	110	...	...
27•[8]	ENER	✔Energy Conv Devices	NNM	C	29	1748	Alt energy:syn mtls:info sys	46 1/2	2	15 3/8	4 5/8	15	7 1/2	10693	10 11/16	8 5/8	9 1/4	...	d	Neg	27.6	−12.1	...
#28•[9]	NEG	✔Energy East	NY,B,Ch,Ph,P	B	335	62982	Utility: electric & gas	19 1/4	5	29	16 1/2	28 5/8	20 9/16	70248	23 15/16	20 9/16	20 13/16	4.0	11	9	−23.8	29.8	22.9
29	EGAS	✔Energy Search	NSC	NR	..	...	Oil&gas dvlp/prod'n	11 1/2	6 1/2	11 1/2	3 15/16	5 5/8	3 3/8	1791	5 5/8	4 3/8	5 1/4	...	d	...	5.0	...	...
30	EWST	✔Energy West	NNM	B+	8	70	Gas utility in Montana	9 3/4	7/8	9 5/8	8 3/8	10 5/8	7	318	8 13/16	8 3/16	8 7/16B	5.7	13	1	−6.3	6.6	6.2
31	EI	✔EnergyNorth Inc[64]	NY,Ch	A−	31	622	Hldg co:dstr nat'l gas N.H.	28 13/16	3 11/16	29 3/4	25 1/4	55 1/4	26 5/8	591	55 1/16	54 1/8	55 1/16	2.5	40	−1	100	42.9	34.7
32	ENI	✔Enersis S.A. ADS[65]	NY,Ch,Ph,P	NR	94	9483	Electric utility - S. America	39	16 3/4	32 1/8	15 7/8	28 3/4	17 5/16	15447	23 13/16	22 9/16	23 1/8	1.9	17	9	−8.5	−2.9	−0.1
✣33•[10]	ENC	✔Enesco Group	NY,B,Ch,P,Ph	B−	126	10894	Consumer prd/household items	44 3/4	1	35	19 3/16	24 3/4	9 1/2	14996	12 1/2	9 1/2	11 1/16	10.1	d	Neg	−49.7	−21.8	−15.5
34	ENGA	✔Engage Technologies	NNM	NR	60	4747	Web visitor monitoring prd	....	....	....	....	73 15/16	15	72970	73 15/16	45	60	...	d	...	...	...	...
¶35•[11]	EC	✔Engelhard Corp	NY,B	B+	398	105290	Specialty chemical	32 1/2	3 3/8	22 13/16	15 3/4	23 11/16	16 1/4	93903	18 7/8	16 5/16	18 7/8	2.1	13	7	−1.2	1.6	7.1
36•[2]	EAII	✔Engineering Animation	NNM	NR	72	2188	Dvp 3D animation pds	33 5/16	10 11/16	72	28 5/16	63 3/8	6 1/2	51264	10 3/4	6 1/2	8 3/4	...	d	−49	−83.8	−18.5	...
✣37	EFS	✔Enhance Financial Svcs Grp	NY,Ph	B+	227	30729	Muni/asset-backed debt reinsr	31 1/16	7 3/4	37 9/16	17 5/16	30 1/8	15 1/2	21476	17 13/16	15 1/2	16 1/4	1.5	7	21	−45.1	−2.8	15.1
38	E	✔ENI S.p.A. ADS[66]	NY,Ch	NR	125	22191	Oil&gas explor,dvlp,prod'n	63 15/16	30 1/2	74 1/2	50 3/8	69 3/4	52 1/4	28391	55 7/8	52 1/4	55 1/8	2.1	16	58	−16.6	4.7	...
39	EBF	✔Ennis Business Forms	NY,Ch,Ph	B+	66	7913	Business forms: paper items	21 3/8	3/16	12 5/8	9 1/4	10 11/16	7 1/2	12427	9	7 1/2	7 3/4	8.0	8	−6	−16.6	−6.1	−3.8
¶40•[12]	ENE	✔Enron Corp	NY,To,B,C,Ch,P,Ph	A−	1164	455984	Major nat'l gas pipeline sys	23 3/4	1 1/16	29 3/8	19 1/16	44 7/8	28 3/4	426703	44 7/8	35 1/8	44 3/8	1.1	37	−1	57.6	29.6	26.3
41	Pr J	$10.50 cm Cv 2nd Pfd(100[68])	NY	BBB−	16	105	oil & gas explor & prod'n	620	117 1/4	732 1/2	565	1200 1/16	1089	12	1170 1/8	1170 1/8	1211 5/8B	1.1	..	...	...	...	...
42	EXG	Enron Cp 7.00% Exch Nts 2002	NY	NR	9	2138	Exch Notes For com	....	....	....	....	24 15/16	16 3/8	20229	20	16 3/8	18 3/4	8.3	..	...	...	...	...
#43•[2]	ESV	✔ENSCO Intl	NY,Ph,P	B	378	90566	Offshore contract drill'g	60 1/2	1/4	33 9/16	8 11/16	25	8 3/4	195970	22 7/8	18 5/16	22 7/8	0.4	d	10	115	−1.4	30.3
44	ETM	✔Entercom Communications'A'	NY	NR	151	16289	Own/oper radio stations	....	....	....	....	67 3/4	22 1/2	21690	67 3/4	57	66 1/4	...	d	...	...	...	...
¶45•[3]	ETR	✔Entergy Corp	NY,B,C,Ch,P	B	545	189455	Owns five operating utilities	39 7/8	7 3/4	32 7/16	23 1/4	33 1/2	23 11/16	148295	27 1/2	23 11/16	25 3/4	4.7	12	13	−13.8	3.1	9.7
46	ETP	✔Enterprise Oil ADS[71]	NY	NR	4	1289	Oil & gas explor dev prod'n	36 7/8	15 5/8	30	14	25 1/4	10 3/4	1786	22 1/4	19 1/8	19 9/16	0.7	..	−15	37.9	−14.6	4.6
47	EPD	✔Enterprise Products Partners	NY	NR	16	440	Oil & gas processing svcs	....	....	22 1/16	13 3/4	20 11/16	14 15/16	8687	20	17	18 7/16	9.8	12	...	36.5	...	...
48	EPR	✔Entertainment Properties Tr	NY,Ph	NR	87	8826	Real estate investment trust	20	18 7/8	20 1/8	14	20	12 1/2	16500	13 11/16	12 1/2	13 3/16	12.7	9	...	−14.2	...	...
49•[13]	ETA	✔Entrade Inc	NY,B,Ch,P,Ph	C	8	345	e-commerce service provider	41 3/4	2 1/2	4 3/8	2 1/8	43	4 1/4	52597	43	22 1/2	40 7/8	...	11	NM	876	85.8	48.0
50•[14]	ENMD	✔EntreMed Inc	NNM	NR	79	2997	Biopharmaceutical R&D	18 5/8	6 1/2	85	9 3/4	35 5/16	12	51042	33 7/8	22	25 5/8	...	d	−6	22.0	16.4	...

Uniform Footnote Explanations-See Page 4. Other: [1]ASE,CBOE,P,Ph:Cycle 1. [2]ASE:Cycle 3. [3]CBOE:Cycle 3. [4]ASE,CBOE:Cycle 1. [5]P:Cycle 1. [6]Ph:Cycle 2. [7]ASE,CBOE:Cycle 3. [8]ASE,Ph:Cycle 3. [9]P:Cycle 2. [10]ASE:Cycle 2. [11]CBOE:Cycle 1. [12]CBOE,P:Cycle 1. [13]Ph:Cycle 3. [14]CBOE:Cycle 2. [51]Approve Utilicorp United mgr,$29.50 cash or stk. [52]Payable in common. [53]Re-spec cond. [54]If com exceeds $15 - 20 out of 30 con trad days. [55]Ea ADS rep 30 com, no par. [56]Ea ADS rep 6 ord Participat'g ctf. [57]Ea ADS rep 2 com, no par. [58]May'97 & prior pricing in $Cdn. [59]ADS's represent 1 shr nominal value 800 Ptas. [60]Approx. [61]Ea ADS rep 10 ord,Lit 1000. [62]To be determined. [63]Ea ADS rep 5 ord, 50p. [64]Eastern Enterprises plan acq,$61.13. [65]Ea ADS rep 50 com,no par. [66]Ea ADS rep 10 ord, Lit. 1,000. [67]Excl subsid Pfd. [68]If com exceeds $5.49 for 30 con trad days. [69]3 Mo Dec'98. [70]Pfd in $M. [71]Ea ADS rep 3 ord shrs, 25p.

Splits ◆ Index	Cash Divs. Ea.Yr. Since	Dividends: Latest Payment Period $	Date	Ex. Div.	Total $ So Far 1999	Ind. Rate	Paid 1998	Financial Position Mil-$ Cash& Equiv.	Curr. Assets	Curr. Liab.	Balance Sheet Date	Capitalization Lg Trm Debt Mil-$	Shs. 000 Pfd.	Com.	Earnings $ Per Shr. Years End	1995	1996	1997	1998	1999	Last 12 Mos.	Interim Earnings Period	$ per Shr. 1998	1999	Index
1◆	....	None Since Public			...	Nil	....	1257	3197	816	9-30-99	506	...	1017505	Dc	v0.34	v0.40	v0.52	v0.74	E1.05	0.99	9 Mo Sep	v0.51	v0.76	1
2	....	None Paid			...	Nil	....	37.8	906	713	9-30-99	116	...	9685	Dc	vd1.13	v1.96	□v0.84	v□1.46	....	1.89	9 Mo Sep	v□0.90	v1.33	2
3	....	None Since Public			...	Nil	....	13.0	38.5	41.1	9-30-99	162	25	10412	Dc	□vd0.95	vd0.75	vd2.60	v□d2.96	....	d1.39	9 Mo Sep	v□d2.32	v□d0.75	3
4	1947	Q0.35¾	12-10-99	11-17	1.33¼	1.43	1.21	266	5124	4590	9-30-99	1317	...	433100	Sp	□2.08	2.27	v2.50	v2.77	v3.00	3.00				4
5	....	None Since Public			...	Nil	....	2.42	33.5	25.9	10-01-99	20.8	4	47828	Mr	vd0.35	vd0.61	vd0.04	vd0.01		d0.01	6 Mo Sep	v0.02	v0.02	5
6◆	....	None Since Public			...	Nil	....	....	0.02	0.86	j6-30-99	....	...	13904	Dc	...	vd0.11	vd0.10	vd0.05	....	jd0.05	6 Mo Jun	vd0.02	vd0.02	6
7◆	....	None Since Public			...	Nil	....	3.06	89.5	77.2	8-31-99	637	...	★±19434	Fb	±0.92	v±1.37	±v0.79	v□0.19	....	d0.25	9 Mo Nov	v±□0.62	v±0.18	7
8	1944	Q0.32	12-15-99	11-29	1.28	1.28	1.28	0.87	46.6	98.5	9-30-99	246	3263	17283	Dc	v1.18	v1.23	v1.29	v1.53	....	1.16	12 Mo Sep	v1.58	v1.16	8
9	....	0.12½	11-15-89	10-25	...	Nil	....	1.97	36.2	51.6	10-03-99	0.63	1565	19184	Dc	vd0.96	vd7.39	vd6.04	vd0.59	....	d0.39	9 Mo Sep	vd0.43	vd0.23	9
10	....	....			...	[52]....	....	Cv into 8 com				....	2100	...	Dc	...	...	...	...	....	....				10
11	....	Terms&trad. basis should			be checked in detail			Wrrts expire 5-6-2003				....	...	10200	Dc	...	...	...	...	....	....	Callable fr 5-5-2000[53]			11
12	....	None Since Public			...	Nil	....	1.55	45.6	35.8	9-30-99	....	...	p11700	Dc	d0.54	v□d0.74	vd0.57	vNil	....	0.02	6 Mo Jun	vp0.03	vp0.05	12
13	....	Terms&trad. basis should			be checked in detail			Wrrts expire 10-1-2001				....	...	3000	Dc	...	...	...	...	....	....	Callable at 1¢[54]			13
14	1994	0.087	5-21-99	5-5	0.087	0.09	0.235	345	859	807	12-31-98	4757	...	8201755	Dc	1.36	1.22	v0.98	v0.35	....	....	6 Mo Jun	vd0.32	vd0.67	14
15	1997	0.149	5-24-99	5-10	0.149	0.23	0.084	953	1753	1343	12-31-98	656	...	618311	Dc	0.82	0.65	vd0.18	v0.18	....	d1.00	6 Mo Jun	v0.04	vd1.14	15
16	....	0.034	6-3-97	5-15	...	Nil	....	2.29	101	175	12-31-97	116	...	111684	Dc	0.27	0.15	vd0.82	....	....	d0.82				16
17	....	None Since Public			...	Nil	....	11.7	105	37.6	10-01-99	37.5	...	8713	Dc	v0.32	v0.66	v0.84	v0.70	....	0.53	9 Mo Sep	v0.69	v0.52	17
18◆	....	None Since Public			...	Nil	....	98.4	129	19.6	9-26-99	....	...	35390	Je	0.16	d0.39	v0.06	vd0.44	v0.19	0.35	3 Mo Sep	v0.02	v0.18	18
19◆	....	None Since Public			...	Nil	....	1.01	47.4	13.2	9-30-99	....	...	11760	Dc	v0.70	v1.08	v1.45	vd1.58	....	d1.14	9 Mo Sep	vd0.28	v0.16	19
20	....	None Paid			...	Nil	....	n/a	38.4	39.9	j6-30-99	263	...	107938	Dc	vd0.01	v0.11	v0.12	v0.03	....	j0.14	9 Mo Sep	v0.01	v0.12	20
21◆	....	None Since Public			...	Nil	....	1.27	94.7	29.8	9-30-99	55.3	...	15377	Dc	vd0.03	v0.45	v1.31	v1.07	....	0.35	9 Mo Sep	v1.02	v0.30	21
22◆	1989	[60]0.162	1-28-00	12-29	0.43	0.43	0.377	644	3578	6168	12-31-98	8791	...	955000	Dc	1.19	1.25	v1.05	v1.29	....	1.29	9 Mo Sep	v0.90	v0.90	22
23	....	None Since Public			...	Nil	....	9.04	9.71	1.03	9-30-99	0.88	164	10353	Dc	...	...	vd1.03	vd2.26	....	d1.66	9 Mo Sep	vd1.23	vd0.63	23
24	....	Plan semi-annual div			...	[62]....	....	1622	6883	10522	6-30-99	9043	...	★12126150	Dc	...	...	...	v1.90	....	....	6 Mo Jun	n/a	v1.00	24
25◆	1943	Q0.16½	12-1-99	11-10	0.65	0.66	0.63	4.45	130	259	6-30-99	372	...	29823	Sp	0.89	0.98	v1.14	v1.23	Pv1.38	1.38				25
26	....	None Since Public			...	Nil	....	5.58	95.1	135	j3-31-99	233	...	294121	Mr	...	d2.53	...	v0.18	....	0.18	No Recent Reporting			26
27	....	None Paid			...	Nil	....	14.9	24.5	9.23	9-30-99	2.98	...	±12952	Je	0.81	0.10	vd1.67	vd1.50	vd1.06	d0.93	3 Mo Sep	vd0.41	vd0.28	27
28◆	1910	Q0.21	11-15-99	10-21	0.84	0.84	0.77½	1167	1490	449	9-30-99	1387	p3844	114407	Dc	1.25	v1.19	v1.28	v1.51	E1.96	1.94	12 Mo Sep	v1.50	v1.94	28
29	....	None Since Public			...	Nil	....	0.93	1.90	1.18	9-30-99	13.4	176	4277	Dc	...	□vd0.60	vd0.14	vd0.11	....	d0.37	9 Mo Sep	vd0.01	vd0.27	29
30◆	1960	Q0.12	1-6-00	12-8	0.47	0.48	0.45	0.56	15.1	13.1	9-30-99	16.8	...	2456	Je	0.68	0.61	v0.55	v0.64	v0.66	0.67	3 Mo Sep	vd0.28	vd0.27	30
31	1983	Q0.35	12-15-99	11-29	1.38½	1.40	1.32½	0.85	28.4	44.4	9-30-99	45.7	...	3320	Sp	1.30	1.89	v2.01	v1.64	v1.37	1.37				31
32	1993	0.313	5-28-99	5-12	0.313	0.45	0.577	376	1323	1405	12-31-98	2918	...	6800000	Dc	1.85	1.85	v1.73	v1.40	....	1.40				32
33	1943	Q0.28	1-1-00	12-13	1.12	1.12	1.12	11.1	223	185	9-30-99	....	...	13478	Dc	v2.23	v2.12	vd1.60	vd1.38	....	d1.57	9 Mo Sep	v1.32	v1.13	33
34	....	None Since Public			...	Nil	....	101	109	16.0	10-31-99	0.33	...	48739	Jl	...	...	...	vpd0.82	vpd0.89	d0.94	3 Mo Oct	vd0.17	vd0.22	34
35◆	1981	Q0.10	12-31-99	12-13	0.40	0.40	0.40	38.6	1211	1370	9-30-99	444	...	125839	Dc	v0.94	v1.03	v0.33	v1.29	E1.48†	1.41	9 Mo Sep	v0.96	v1.08	35
36◆	....	None Since Public			...	Nil	....	19.8	53.3	22.9	9-30-99	1.13	...	11965	Dc	vd0.39	v0.30	vd0.20	v0.03	....	d1.81	9 Mo Sep	vd0.18	vd2.02	36
37◆	1992	Q0.06	12-23-99	12-15	0.24	0.24	0.23	Total Assets $1434.86M			9-30-99	75.0	...	38056	Dc	v1.37	v1.52	v1.78	v2.10	E2.37	2.15	9 Mo Sep	v1.59	v1.64	37
38	1996	1.168	7-7-99	6-16	1.168	1.17	1.052	2545	16445	16197	12-31-98	5288	...	8000161	Dc	3.41	3.66	v3.62	v3.41	....	3.41				38
39	1973	Q0.15½	11-1-99	10-14	0.62	0.62	0.62	4.40	40.7	9.82	11-30-99	0.54	...	16392	Fb	1.13	v0.82	v0.62	v0.87	....	0.95	9 Mo Nov	v0.60	v0.68	39
40◆	1935	Q0.12½	12-20-99	11-29	0.50	0.50	0.48⅛	316	7567	6669	9-30-99	9593	[67]1320	715613	Dc	v0.97	v1.08	v0.16	v1.01	E1.19	1.20	9 Mo Sep	v0.77	v□0.96	40
41	1983	3.413	1-3-00	12-8	13.652	13.652	12.97	Cv into 27.304 common				....	1375	...	Dc	b2.40	...	...	...	....	....				41
42	1999	Q0.389	1-31-00	1-12	0.32	1.558	....	At maturity exch for Enron O&G Com,re-spec cond				....	...	★10000	Dc	...	...	...	...	....	....	Mature 7-31-2002			42
43◆	1997	Q0.02½	12-15-99	11-29	0.10	0.10	0.10	194	298	124	9-30-99	372	...	137308	Dc	v0.40	v0.72	v□1.64	v1.81	Ed0.09	0.20	9 Mo Sep	v1.60	vd0.01	43
44	....	None Since Public			...	Nil	....	9.81	68.4	28.6	9-30-99	159	...	★±45177	Dc	...	...	...	pv[69]0.64	....	d2.07	9 Mo Sep	vp0.88	vpd1.83	44
45	1988	Q0.30	12-1-99	11-8	1.20	1.20	1.50	1242	3953	2425	9-30-99	6952	[70]579	246834	Dc	vΔ2.13	v1.83	v1.03	v3.00	E2.15	3.18	12 Mo Sep	v1.68	v3.18	45
46	1993	0.138	11-9-99	9-21	0.138	0.14	[60]0.918	535	748	494	j12-31-97	880	5100	497702	Dc	0.87	1.29	v1.03	Pv0.15	....	0.15				46
47	1998	0.45	11-10-99	10-27	1.80	1.80	0.32	3.96	161	99.9	6-30-99	145	...	±66963	Dc	...	...	pv1.30	□v±0.62	....	1.59	9 Mo Sep	v±d0.04	v±0.93	47
48	1998	Q0.42	1-14-00	12-29	1.66	1.68	1.38	Total Assets $496M			9-30-99	216	...	14987	Dc	...	p1.28	n/a	v1.39	....	1.56	9 Mo Sep	v1.02	v1.19	48
49◆	....	0.05½	9-5-86	7-25	...	Nil	....	10.7	15.6	12.1	p6-30-99	....	p...	p11039	Dc	Δvd2.70	vΔ0.34	vd0.04	v4.16	....	3.75	9 Mo Sep	vd0.33	vd0.74	49
50	....	None Since Public			...	Nil	....	39.9	40.7	5.28	9-30-99	....	...	14706	Dc	pvd1.41	vd0.50	vd0.54	vd1.07	....	d1.99	9 Mo Sep	vd0.71	vd1.63	50

◆**Stock Splits & Divs By Line Reference Index** [1]2-for-1,'97,'99. [6]1-for-5 REVERSE,'92. [7]Propose 2-for-1 stk split. [18]2-for-1,'99(twice). [19]2-for-1,'96. [21]3-for-2,'97,'98. [22]4-for-1,'97. [25]2-for-1,'98. [28]2-for-1,'99. [30]2-for-1,'94. [35]3-for-2,'95. [36]3-for-2,'98. [37]2-for-1,'98. [40]2-for-1,'99. [43]1-for-4 REVERSE,'94:2-for-1,'97. [49]2-for-1,'96,'97.

¶ S&P 500
# MidCap 400
✣ SmallCap 600
• Options

Index	Ticker	Name of Issue (Call Price of Pfd. Stocks)	Market	Com. Rank. & Pfd. Rating	Inst. Hold Cos	Inst. Hold Shs. (000)	Principal Business	1971-97 High	1971-97 Low	1998 High	1998 Low	1999 High	1999 Low	Dec. Sales in 100s	Last Sale Or Bid High	Last Sale Or Bid Low	Last Sale Or Bid Last	%Div Yield	P-E Ratio	EPS 5 Yr Growth	Total Return 12 Mo	Total Return 36 Mo	Total Return 60 Mo
1•[1]	ENTU	✔Entrust Technologies	NNM	NR	110	13979	On-line security pds & svcs	....	....	29 7/16	9	70 5/8	16 7/8	370475	70 5/8	35	59 15/16	...	..	...	151	...	...
2	EEC	✔Environmental Elements	AS	C	12	1117	Design air pollut'n ctrl sys	22 1/2	1 5/8	6 7/8	2 7/16	4 7/16	1 13/16	1728	2 7/16	1 7/8	2 5/16	...	d	60	-41.3	-0.9	-6.6
3	EVV	✔Environmental Safeguards	AS	NR	1	13	Environmental mgmt svcs	....	....	8 3/8	1 1/8	2 1/8	11/16	4222	1 1/16	11/16	13/16	...	d	...	-35.0	...	...
4	ETC	✔Environmental Tectonics	AS,Ch	C	11	862	Mfr specialty systems	5 7/8	5/16	6 7/16	3 5/16	15 1/2	4 13/16	3087	15 1/2	9 1/4	15 1/8	...	45	NM	203	67.8	52.3
✣5•	ENZ	✔Enzo Biochem	NY,Ph,P	B–	90	3163	Enzymes: DNA research	24 5/8	1/2	16 1/2	6 3/8	48 5/8	8	47169	48 5/8	25 5/8	46	...	..	87	346	40.9	40.6
6•[2]	ENZN	✔ENZON Inc	NNM	C	120	21064	Biopharm:develop,mfg,mktg	17	1 1/4	14 5/8	3 5/8	47 1/4	11 1/4	85802	47 1/4	32 3/16	43 3/8	...	d	11	226	145	90.0
7•[3]	EOG	✔EOG Resources	NY,Ch,P	B+	329	92910	Oil & gas explor,dev,prod'n	30 5/8	8 1/8	24 1/2	11 3/4	25 3/8	14 3/8	231891	19	14 3/8	17 9/16	0.7	5	13	2.4	-10.9	-0.7
8	EOT	✔EOTT Energy Partners L.P.	NY,Ch,Ph,P	NR	28	450	Gather/mkt crude oil	22 3/8	12 3/4	20	11 1/4	19 1/4	12 1/4	17563	14 1/2	12 1/4	13	14.6	52	-18	-7.7	-6.3	7.8
9	EPC	EPCOS AG ADS[52]	NY	NR	..	...	Mfr electronic components	....	....	....	....	85 1/8	33 5/16	9556	85 1/8	60	74 1/2	...	..	...	...	...	...
✣10•[3]	EPIC	✔Epicor Software	NNM	C	99	13055	Dvlp finl mgmt,info softwr pd	39 3/4	3 1/8	27 1/4	5 3/8	14	3 1/2	145173	6 1/4	4	5 1/16	...	d	NM	-60.5	-24.7	-17.2
11	EBI	✔Equality Bancorp	AS	NR	1	.6	Savings & loan, Missouri	16 1/8	13 3/8	16	9 1/8	10 5/8	6	756	8 1/8	6	6 1/4	3.8	14	29	-32.2	...	...
12•[2]	ENT	✔EQUANT N.V. ADS[56]	NY,Ph	NR	148	43593	Data network svcs	....	....	69	27	113 5/8	67	125455	113 5/8	92 1/4	112	...	d	...	65.2	...	...
¶13•[4]	EFX	✔Equifax Inc	NY,Ch,Ph	A–	535	88969	Risk mgmt & fin'l ctrl svs	37 3/16	1/2	45	29 3/4	39 7/8	20 1/8	113161	24 7/8	20 1/8	23 9/16	1.6	15	12	-30.2	...	...
14	EQT	✔Equitable Resources	NY,B,Ch,Ph	B	222	22864	Oil & gas expl:Nat'l gas dstr	44 1/4	2 1/16	35 1/4	20 9/16	39	23 1/4	16611	36 1/16	32 9/16	33 3/8	3.5	d	Neg	18.9	8.1	8.5
15	ATF	Equity Income Fund[57]	AS,P	NR	93	509	1st exch series-AT&T shrs	121 3/8	19 5/16	188 1/2	114 1/4	219 1/8	174	1657	219 1/8	200 5/8	202 7/8	1.5	..	13	11.4	37.9	29.5
16	ENN	✔Equity Inns	NY,Ch	NR	87	9210	Real estate investment trust	16 9/16	8 7/8	16 1/16	8 3/4	10 3/16	6 1/4	61076	7 1/4	6 1/4	6 3/4	18.4	10	3	-19.5	-10.9	-0.1
17	EOP	✔Equity Office Properties Tr	NY,Ph	NR	370	180333	Real estate investment trust	34 11/16	21	32	20 3/16	29 3/8	20 13/16	130070	24 3/4	20 13/16	24 5/8	6.0	10	...	9.4	...	...
18	Pr B	5.25% Sr'B'cmCvPfd([58]51.1667)	NY	BBB	32	4718		....	....	41 1/2	38	44	35 3/4	6243	39 1/2	35 3/4	39B	6.4	..	...	...	...	...
19	EQTY	✔Equity Oil	NNM	C	22	2905	Expl & prod crude oil & gas	27	1	3 1/16	5/8	1 11/16	7/8	14983	1 3/8	15/16	1 1/8	...	d	-29	16.1	-28.4	-21.9
20	EQY	✔Equity One	NY	NR	22	1364	Real estate investment trust	....	....	11	8 1/4	12 1/8	8 9/16	2793	10 1/2	9 1/2	10 7/16	10.0	9	...	27.7	...	...
21•[5]	EQR	✔Equity Residential Prop Tr	NY,Ch,Ph	NR	444	98733	Real estate investment trust	55	24 7/8	52 9/16	34 11/16	48 3/8	38 1/8	59410	42 11/16	38 1/8	42 11/16	6.7	10	6	13.4	7.3	14.5
22	Pr E	Sr'E'cm CvPfd([60]25.875)	NY	BBB	24	1978		30 3/4	16 1/2	29 7/16	20 3/4	26 3/4	21 5/8	5094	23 5/8	21 5/8	23 5/8	7.4	..	...	...	...	...
23	Pr G	7.25%Sr'G'cmCv[62]Dep([63]25.90625)	NY	BBB	24	1523		26 1/16	23 1/2	26 7/16	18 1/2	24	18	9593	20 11/16	18	19 3/4	9.2	..	...	...	...	...
24	Pr H	$1.75 Sr'H'cm Cv Pfd([64]Stk)	NY	BBB	1	80		32 7/8	22	32 3/8	25	34 5/8	28 15/16	833	30 1/2	28 15/16	57 1/4B	3.1	..	...	...	...	...
25	Pr J	$2.15 Sr'J'cm Cv Pfd([65]Stk)	NY	BBB	33	2102		30 1/4	24 1/4	28 11/16	23 1/2	30 1/4	24	4105	26 1/16	24	26 1/16	8.2	..	...	...	...	...
26•[6]	ERICY	✔Ericsson(LM)Tel'B'ADS[66]	NNM	NR	428	191723	Worldwide telecommunic'ns	25 5/16	5/16	34	15	67 1/4	20 1/2	997406	67 1/4	48 3/4	65 11/16	0.3	97	20	177	64.8	58.7
27	ESAT	✔Esat Telecom Group ADS[67]	NNM	NR	77	9073	Telecommun svcs, Ireland	15 3/8	12 15/16	44 1/4	13 7/16	96 5/8	32 3/4	33095	96 5/8	71 1/4	91 1/2	...	d	...	138	...	...
28	ESCM	✔ESC Medical Systems	NNM	NR	25	3326	Develops medical devices	46 1/2	10	39 1/8	5 3/4	11 13/16	3 11/16	76704	9 5/8	4 13/16	9 9/16	...	d	Neg	-8.9	-27.9	...
29	ESE	✔ESCO Electronics[68]	NY,P	B–	85	8955	Mfr electronic/defense prod	19 15/16	2 5/8	20 3/4	8 1/2	13 15/16	8 9/16	7944	11 15/16	9 1/2	11 5/8	...	3	NM	28.3	4.7	15.8
30	ESREF	✔ESG Re Ltd	NNM	NR	43	7629	Accident,health life insur	25	20 7/8	28 7/8	12 3/4	22 1/4	5 1/8	29899	7	5 5/16	6 15/16	4.6	d	...	-64.7	...	...
31	ESPD	eSpeed Inc'A'	NNM	NR	..	...	Net based finl instr trad sv	....	....	....	....	63 3/4	22	317536	63 3/4	22	35 9/16	...	..	...	...	...	...
32	ESP	✔Espey Mfg & Electr	AS	B–	10	178	Electronic pwr supply,syst's	38	3/4	17	12 3/8	15 1/4	11 1/4	158	15	14	14 5/8	1.4	24	-11	17.0	0.1	6.4
33	ESF	Espirito Santo Finl ADS[70]	NY,Ch,Ph,P	NR	32	3144	Financial Svcs-Portugal	22 1/2	8 1/2	27 7/16	12 1/2	20 1/8	14 5/16	16450	16 1/8	15 1/16	15 3/4	4.1	10	10	-16.0	9.5	7.4
34	ESST	✔ESS Technology	NNM	NR	70	10517	Dvlp mixed signal semiconductors	39 5/8	7 3/8	9	1 7/8	23 3/4	4 15/16	72746	23 7/16	18 3/4	22 3/16	...	30	Neg	344	-7.6	...
35	ESX	✔Essex Bancorp	AS	NR	2	10	Savings bank,VA,NC	40	5/8	6 3/4	1 5/16	3 3/4	1 1/8	982	1 1/2	1 1/8	1 3/8	...	d	79	-4.3	-14.3	-21.1
36	ESS	✔Essex Property Trust	NY,Ch,Ph	NR	130	13600	Real estate investment trust	37 1/2	14 5/8	34 15/16	26 15/16	35 1/2	25 11/16	11389	34	29 1/16	34	6.5	16	11	22.1	11.4	26.3
✣37	ESL	✔Esterline Technologies	NY,Ch,Ph,P	B	137	12383	Printed circuits mfr equip	21 3/4	5/8	24 1/2	15 1/2	24 1/8	10 1/4	12348	12 1/2	10 1/4	11 9/16	...	7	20	-46.8	-3.8	11.1
✣38•[7]	ETEC	✔Etec Systems	NNM	NR	248	18938	Mask pattern generation eqp	69 1/8	7 3/4	62 3/8	14 7/8	55	21 5/8	50516	47 1/2	38	44 7/8	...	d	Neg	12.2	5.5	...
✣39•[8]	ETH	✔Ethan Allen Interiors	NY,Ph,P	NR	317	34968	Mfr,retail home furniture	28 9/16	5 7/16	44 7/16	15 3/4	37 3/4	24 11/16	43015	33 11/16	28 15/16	32 1/16	0.5	16	35	18.1	36.4	32.2
#40•[4]	EY	✔Ethyl Corp	NY,B,Ch,P,Ph	NR	148	27906	Mfr fuel additives	33	1 3/16	8 1/2	3 7/16	6 11/16	3 1/2	38066	4 3/16	3 1/2	3 1/2	7.1	5	-1	-34.6	-24.8	...
41	ETW	✔E'town Corp	NY	B+	98	2242	Water service in New Jersey	40 3/4	6 3/16	48 1/4	33 9/16	63 3/8	37	7029	62 7/8	61 1/2	62 1/4	3.3	22	7	37.0	32.0	26.1
42	ETYS	✔eToys Inc	NNM	NR	135	19491	Internet retail childrens prd	....	....	....	....	86	20	983061	61 1/2	24 1/2	26 1/4	...	d	...	...	...	...
43	ETZ	✔Etz Lavud Ltd Ord	AS,Ch	NR	1	84	Laminates & wood products	18 3/8	5/8	10 1/8	5 7/8	13	6 5/8	213	7 1/2	6 5/8	7 3/8	...	d	-31	-8.7	13.3	2.2
44	ETZ.A	Cl'A'vtg	AS	NR	2	33		13 1/4	3 7/8	8	4 1/4	7 13/16	4 3/4	110	5 1/8	4 3/4	5 1/8	...	d	...	-10.2	8.2	-2.5
45•[9]	ESCC	✔Evans&Sutherl'd Computer	NNM	C	68	6009	Computer graphics/softw sys	50 1/2	3 5/16	32	11 5/8	19	10 7/16	11002	13 3/16	10 7/16	11 7/16	...	d	Neg	-35.1	-22.9	...
#46•[10]	RE	✔Everest Reinsurance Hldgs	NY,Ch,P	NR	..	...	Treaty&facultative reinsurance	43	16 3/4	45 1/4	28 3/4	38 15/16	20 1/2	65027	24 7/8	21 1/2	22 5/16	1.1	7	NM	-42.2	-7.5	...
47	EVER	✔Evergreen Resources	NNM	B–	125	9971	Oil & gas explor,dev,prod'n	325	1 1/4	26 1/4	12 7/8	28 1/2	14 1/2	28590	21	14 7/8	19 3/4	...	58	NM	11.3	33.8	30.3
48	EVRT	✔EverTrust Financial Grp	NNM	NR	..	...	Commercial banking,Washington	....	....	....	....	11 1/8	9 3/16	12139	9 7/8	9 3/16	9 3/8	...	27	...	...	...	...
✣49	EWB	✔E.W. Blanch Holdings	NY	B+	193	9014	Reinsurance intermediary	35 11/16	15 3/4	48 1/4	33	71 3/4	45 3/8	19922	62 9/16	51 5/8	61 1/4	0.9	22	24	30.2	46.6	26.2
✣50•[11]	EXBT	✔Exabyte Corp	NNM,Ch	C	78	13840	Mfr 8mm cartridge tape subsys	40 5/8	5 5/8	12 3/4	4 1/2	9 1/8	3 3/8	44291	9 1/8	6 3/4	7 1/2	...	25	Neg	36.4	-17.5	-18.9

Uniform Footnote Explanations-See Page 4. Other: [1]Ph:Cycle 1. [2]CBOE:Cycle 2. [3]CBOE:Cycle 1. [4]P:Cycle 1. [5]P. Cycle 1. [6]CBOE,Ph:Cycle 1. [7]ASE,Ph:Cycle 3. [8]Ph:Cycle 2. [9]P:Cycle 3. [10]ASE:Cycle 1. [11]ASE,CBOE:Cycle 2. [51]Incl 9M subord units. [52]Ea ADS rep 1 ord,no par. [53]To be determined. [54]Fiscal Jun'97 & prior. [55]12 Mo Dec'98:Fiscal Jun'98 earned $0.45. [56]Ea ADS rep 1 Ord,0.02NLG. [57]Unit Invest't Tr. [58]Fr 2-15-2003,or earlier for chge in'REIT'status. [59]If com exceeds $41.055 20(out 30)trad days. [60]To 11-1-99,scale to $25 in 2003. [61]If com 150% Cv price-20 trad.days. [62]Dep for 0.10 shr 7.25% Sr G cm Pfd. [63]Fr 9-15-2002,scale to $25 in 2007. [64]Redeemable for 1.34 com re-spec cond. [65]Fr 3-31-2000 redeem for 1.136 com re-spec cond. [66]ADR equal 1 ord Cl'B'. [67]Ea ADS rep 2 ord,IR 0.01p. [68]Trust Receipts. [69]Spl div. [70]Ea ADS rep 1 ord,$10 par. [71]Excl subsid pfd. [72]Subsid pfd in $M. [73]Stk dstr of Tripos Inc,'94. [74]Fiscal Mar'96 & prior. [75]12 Mo Dec'96.

Splits ♦ Index	Cash Divs. Ea.Yr. Since	Dividends: Latest Payment Period $	Date	Ex. Div.	Total $ So Far 1999	Ind. Rate	Paid 1998	Financial Position Mil-$ Cash& Equiv.	Curr. Assets	Curr. Liab.	Balance Sheet Date	Capitalization Lg Trm Debt Mil-$	Shs. 000 Pfd.	Com.	Earnings $ Per Shr. Years End	1995	1996	1997	1998	1999	Last 12 Mos.	Interim Earnings Period	$ per Shr. 1998	1999	Index
1	....	None Since Public			...	Nil	....	87.6	111	24.7	9-30-99	0.02	...	±49851	Dc	...	...	pv0.01	vd0.68	....	0.08	9 Mo Sep	vd0.70	v0.06	1
2	....	0.03	6-1-92	4-24	...	Nil	....	0.64	26.0	15.7	9-30-99	9.93	...	7094	Mr	vd0.51	vd0.58	v0.01	v0.18	....	d0.05	6 Mo Sep	v0.08	vd0.15	2
3	....	None Since Public			...	Nil	....	1.87	6.12	3.61	9-30-99	4.87	...	10111	Dc	d0.26	Δvd0.11	□vd0.61	vd0.17	....	d0.09	9 Mo Sep	vd0.21	vd0.13	3
4♦	....	None Paid			...	Nil	....	3.04	29.5	14.9	8-27-99	4.18	25	6855	Fb	v0.05	vd0.01	v0.23	v0.29	....	0.34	6 Mo Aug	v0.09	v0.14	4
5♦	....	5%Stk	1-23-98	1-7	...	Nil	5%Stk	44.2	64.6	2.64	10-31-99	....	...	25100	Jl	0.24	d0.32	v0.06	v0.13	v0.26	0.29	3 Mo Oct	v0.03	v0.06	5
6	....	None Since Public			...	Nil	....	24.6	31.3	8.27	9-30-99	0.73	107	36814	Je	d0.26	vd0.20	vd0.16	vd0.12	vd0.14	d0.16	3 Mo Sep	vd0.03	vd0.05	6
7♦	1990	Q0.03	1-31-00	1-12	0.12	0.12	0.12	18.8	202	212	9-30-99	1165	...	119182	Dc	v0.88	v0.87	v0.77	v0.36	E3.93	3.70	9 Mo Sep	v0.30	v3.64	7
8	1994	Q0.47½	11-12-99	10-27	1.90	1.90	1.90	2.03	1053	1159	9-30-99	0.18	...	[51]±27476	Dc	□vd3.46	v1.50	vd0.75	vd0.21	....	0.25	9 Mo Sep	vd0.25	vΔ0.21	8
9	....	Plan annual div			...	[53]....	....	6.86	410	420	6-30-99	95.1	...	★65300	Sp	...	...	...	pv0.99	....	....	9 Mo Jun	n/a	vp0.75	9
10	....	None Since Public			...	Nil	....	34.5	128	74.9	9-30-99	....	1602	40830	Dc	d0.44	d2.23	v[54]d0.20	Pv[55]0.27	....	d0.40	9 Mo Sep	v0.49	vd0.18	10
11	1998	Q0.06	12-17-99	12-1	0.24	0.24	0.24	Total Deposits $130M			9-30-99	163	...	2532	Mr	v0.27	pv0.21	v0.51	v0.47	....	0.46	6 Mo Sep	v0.23	v0.22	11
12	....	None Since Public			...	Nil	....	452	726	226	12-31-98	20.3	...	201477	Dc	d0.21	d0.21	vd0.13	vd0.19	....	d0.14	9 Mo Sep	v□d0.19	vΔd0.14	12
13♦	1914	Q0.09¼	12-15-99	11-22	0.36¼	0.37	0.35¼	137	538	398	9-30-99	939	...	141436	Dc	v0.96	v1.19	□v1.26	v1.34	E1.58	1.41	9 Mo Sep	v1.03	v1.10	13
14	1950	Q0.29½	1-31-00	12-27	1.18	1.18	1.18	6.83	255	289	9-30-99	298	...	33036	Dc	v0.04	v1.69	v2.16	v□d0.97	....	d0.40	9 Mo Sep	v0.66	v1.23	14
15	1983	0.252	1-1-00	12-13	2.973	2.97	2.853	Total Assets $2596M			9-30-99	....	...	13188	Dc	§88.47	§83.10	§119.63	....	....	....				15
16	1994	Q0.31	1-31-00	12-29	1.24	1.24	1.22	Total Assets $852.78M			9-30-99	387	2750	37243	Dc	v0.70	v0.69	v□0.88	v0.78	....	0.67	9 Mo Sep	v0.70	v0.59	16
17	1997	0.42	12-29-99	12-13	1.58	1.48	1.38	Total Assets $14403.04M			9-30-99	5492	18600	252170	Dc	...	p0.75	p□v1.11	□v1.27	E2.55	1.33	9 Mo Sep	v□0.93	v□0.99	17
18	1998	Q0.65⅝	11-15-99	10-28	2.62½	2.479	1.932	Cv into 1.40056 com				....	6000	...	Dc	...	...	...	....	....	....	Fr 2-15-2003 Co opt redm for com[59]			18
19	....	0.05	4-5-93	3-8	...	Nil	....	0.66	4.25	1.02	9-30-99	16.5	...	12643	Dc	vd0.10	vd0.43	vd0.02	vd0.46	....	d0.24	9 Mo Sep	vd0.22	vNil	19
20	1998	Q0.26	12-30-99	12-15	1.02	1.04	0.62	Total Assets $206M			9-30-99	109	...	11391	Dc	...	...	vp0.76	vp1.11	....	1.11	9 Mo Sep	vp0.67	v0.67	20
21	1993	0.76	12-31-99	12-16	2.94	2.84	3.39	Total Assets $11049M			9-30-99	4755	26107	p126415	Dc	v1.67	v1.69	v1.76	v1.63	E4.45	2.08	9 Mo Sep	v1.22	v1.67	21
22	1994	Q0.43¾	1-3-00	12-16	1.75	1.75	1.75	Cv into 0.8122 com,$30.78				....	3000	...	Dc	...	...	...	....	....	....	Red opt 11-1-96 to 11-1-98[61]			22
23	1997	Q0.453	1-18-00	12-16	1.812	1.813	1.81¼	Cv into 0.4268 com,$58.58				....	12650	...	Dc	...	...	...	....	....	....				23
24	1993	Q0.43¾	12-31-99	12-16	1.75	1.75	1.75	Cv into 1.34 com,$34.55				....	4000	...	Dc	...	...	...	....	....	....				24
25	1995	Q0.53¾	12-31-99	12-16	2.15	2.15	2.15	Cv into 1.136 com,$40.76				....	4000	...	Dc	...	...	...	....	....	....				25
26♦	1967	0.204	4-13-99	3-24	0.204	0.20	0.188	18233	126532	66941	j12-31-98	10711	...	±1951000	Dc	±0.43	±0.53	v0.76	v0.82	E0.68	0.68	6 Mo Jun	v0.34	v0.20	26
27	....	None Since Public			...	Nil	....	112	131	47.2	j12-31-98	202	...	★40947	Dc	d0.38	d1.79	vd7.64	vd3.51	....	d4.67	3 Mo Mar	vd0.84	vd2.00	27
28♦	....	None Since Public			...	Nil	....	106	165	30.0	12-31-97	115	...	28764	Dc	0.23	v0.74	v1.06	Pv0.15	....	d4.72	9 Mo Sep	v0.18	vd4.69	28
29	....	[69]3.00	9-27-96	9-30	...	Nil	....	5.49	137	99.7	6-30-99	44.0	...	12375	Sp	d2.76	v2.26	v0.95	v0.90	Pv□4.00	4.00				29
30	1998	0.08	12-8-99	11-18	0.32	0.32	0.30	Total Assets $616M			6-30-99	....	...	13916	Dc	...	...	pvd0.37	v1.03	....	d0.84	9 Mo Sep	v0.74	vd1.13	30
31	....	None Paid			...	Nil	....	Equity per shr $1.95			9-30-99	....	...	±★50000	Mr	...	...	...	n/a	....	....	29 Wk Sep	n/a	vd0.15	31
32	1999	Q0.05	6-30-00	5-26	0.30	0.20	....	6.87	22.2	1.80	9-30-99	....	...	1049	Je	0.37	v0.41	v0.51	vd0.67	v0.66	0.62	3 Mo Sep	v0.08	v0.04	32
33♦	1994	0.65	6-15-99	6-8	0.65	0.65	0.63	Book Value $10.66			12-31-98	2783	[71]...	47593	Dc	v1.16	v1.32	v1.57	v1.53	....	1.56	6 Mo Jun	v0.76	v0.79	33
34	....	None Since Public			...	Nil	....	109	185	66.8	9-30-99	....	...	40962	Dc	v0.79	v0.52	vd0.27	vd0.68	....	0.75	9 Mo Sep	vd0.80	v0.63	34
35	....	0.50	2-14-92	12-26	...	Nil	....	Total Deposits $206M			9-30-99	34.8	2250	1061	Dc	vΔd4.31	vd8.39	vd1.83	vd0.73	....	d0.48	9 Mo Sep	vd0.91	vd0.66	35
36	1994	0.55	1-17-00	12-29	2.10	2.20	1.90	Total Assets $1130M			9-30-99	437	185	18055	Dc	□1.71	v□1.61	v□1.94	v□1.64	....	2.08	9 Mo Sep	v□1.21	v□1.65	36
37♦	....	0.09	7-31-86	6-30	...	Nil	....	63.3	227	92.4	7-31-99	117	...	17342	Oc	1.27	v1.31	v1.44	v1.70	Pv1.69	1.69				37
38	....	None Since Public			...	Nil	....	63.2	258	72.2	10-31-99	....	...	21571	Jl	p0.61	□2.07	v1.57	v2.05	v0.05	d0.41	3 Mo Oct	v0.43	vd0.03	38
39♦	1996	Q0.04	1-21-00	1-5	0.133	0.16	0.093	13.4	228	112	9-30-99	9.73	...	40792	Je	Δ□0.52	0.64	v1.11	v□1.63	v1.92	1.99	3 Mo Sep	v0.38	v0.45	39
40♦	1957	Q0.06¼	1-1-00	12-13	0.25	0.25	0.25	7.34	380	202	9-30-99	432	...	83465	Dc	v0.62	v0.78	v0.71	v0.85	....	0.66	9 Mo Sep	v0.73	v0.54	40
41	1881	Q0.51	12-17-99	12-1	2.04	2.04	2.04	5.49	59.6	125	6-30-99	268	[72]12	8574	Dc	v2.14	v1.96	v2.41	v2.66	....	2.82	12 Mo Sep	v2.64	v2.82	41
42	....	None Since Public			...	Nil	....	141	211	76.4	9-30-99	6.37	...	119756	Mr	...	...	v...	vpd0.74	....	d1.27	6 Mo Sep	vpd0.07	vpd0.60	42
43	1999	t0.25	12-15-99	10-28	t0.25	[53]....	....	16.7	375	334	j12-31-98	145	...	±3568	Dc	d1.27	d1.17	vd0.91	v0.52	....	d0.51	9 Mo Sep	v0.30	vd0.73	43
44	1999	t0.25	12-15-99	10-28	t0.25	[53]....	....	....	...	...		....	...	1804	Dc	d1.27	d1.17	...	....	....	d1.17				44
45	....	h[73]....	6-1-94	6-2	...	Nil	....	18.0	192	74.2	10-01-99	18.0	1500	9398	Dc	Δv2.33	v1.12	v0.53	vd1.70	....	d2.06	9 Mo Sep	vd1.87	vd2.23	45
46	1995	Q0.06	12-22-99	11-29	0.24	0.24	0.20	Total Assets $5783.05M			9-30-99	35.0	...	46958	Dc	v0.01	v2.21	v3.05	v3.26	....	3.20	9 Mo Sep	v2.47	v2.41	46
47	....	None Paid			...	Nil	....	1.70	6.40	6.67	9-30-99	7.00	...	14667	Dc	[74]d0.10	v[75]0.10	v0.51	v0.47	....	0.34	9 Mo Sep	v0.38	v0.25	47
48	....	None Since Public			...	Nil	....	Book Value $14.68			3-31-99	18.9	...	8596	Mr	...	...	...	v0.35	....	0.35				48
49	1993	Q0.14	12-1-99	10-29	0.50	0.56	0.46	3.04	65.5	50.1	9-30-99	0.41	...	13151	Dc	v1.34	v0.48	v1.99	v2.42	....	2.85	9 Mo Sep	v1.62	v2.05	49
50	....	None Since Public			...	Nil	....	41.4	116	33.4	10-02-99	5.80	...	22753	Dc	vd0.57	v0.39	vd1.38	vd0.12	E0.30	d1.93	9 Mo Sep	v0.11	vd1.70	50

♦Stock Splits & Divs By Line Reference Index [4]2-for-1,'99. [5]Adj for 5%,'98. [7]2-for-1,'94. [13]2-for-1,'95. [26]4-for-1,'95:2-for-1,'98. [28]3-for-2,'96. [33]2-for-1,'94. [37]2-for-1,'98. [39]2-for-1,'97,'99. [40]No adj for stk dstr of Albemarle Corp,'94:No adj for stk dstr of First Colony Corp,'93.

¶ S&P 500
# MidCap 400
✤ SmallCap 600
• Options

Index	Ticker	Name of Issue (Call Price of Pfd. Stocks)	Market	Com. Rank. & Pfd. Rating	Inst. Hold Cos	Inst. Hold Shs. (000)	Principal Business	Price Range 1971-97 High	1971-97 Low	1998 High	1998 Low	1999 High	1999 Low	Dec. Sales in 100s	December, 1999 Last Sale Or Bid High	Low	Last	%Div Yield	P-E Ratio	EPS 5 Yr Growth	% Annualized Total Return 12 Mo	36 Mo	60 Mo
1	XACT	✓Exactis.com Inc	NNM	NR	..	...	Outsourced email mktg svcs	....	....	....	....	36⅜	14	72514	32¾	20⅛	24 5/16	...	..	...	...	...	...
2	XLG	✓Excel Legacy	AS	NR	57	15078	Real estate development	....	....	4	2¾	5 11/16	2⅞	8179	3⅞	3	3 5/16	...	..	...	−17.2	...	...
3	EXM	✓Excel Maritime Carriers	AS,Ch	NR	..	...	Own/oper dry&tank vessels	350	11¼	3 11/16	1¼	3	1	43	2¾	1⅞	1⅞	...	d	NM	50.0	−46.9	−39.2
4	ELOT	✓Executone Info Sys	NNM	B	40	9512	Dev/dstr communicat'ns sys	13⅝	⅜	2⅞	⅝	12	1½	392894	6⅞	2⅜	5 7/16	...	d	Neg	211	31.8	10.8
5•[1]	EX	✓Exide Corp	NY,P	NR	82	16059	Mfr starting, ignit'n batteries	57½	14⅝	26 9/16	5⅜	21½	7 7/16	50768	9¾	7 7/16	8 5/16	1.0	d	Neg	−48.5	−28.5	−31.5
6•[2]	EXDS	✓Exodus Communications	NNM	NR	375	132840	Internet software svcs	....	....	8¾	1 15/16	93 7/16	6⅞	1304081	93 7/16	52 11/16	88 13/16	...	d	...	1010	...	...
7	EXPE	✓Expedia Inc	NNM	NR	..	...	Online travel services	....	....	....	....	65⅞	14	64313	55¾	34¾	35	...	..	...	...	...	...
✤8	EXPD	✓Expeditors Intl,Wash	NNM	B+	288	33498	Int'l air freight forward'g	24⅜	⅝	24⅛	12 7/16	46⅜	20 5/16	52961	46⅜	38¼	43 13/16	0.2	43	33	109	56.7	52.4
#9•[3]	ESRX	✓Express Scripts 'A'	NNM	NR	311	20245	Health care management svcs	32⅜	3⅛	69	27	105½	44⅜	117820	66 3/16	44⅜	64	...	37	28	−4.7	53.0	28.5
10•[4]	ESA	✓Extended Stay Amer	NY	NR	151	65611	Own/oper lodging facilities	23	6½	15¼	6	12 11/16	6 15/16	30662	8⅞	7 7/16	7 9/16	...	16	...	−28.0	−27.8	...
11	EXE.A	✓Extendicare Inc[52]	NY	NR	14	7438	Long-term hlth care facilities	16⅝	10⅞	13⅝	4 15/16	6	1½	693	3 5/16	2½	3	...	d	Neg	−44.8	−36.1	...
12	EXTR	✓Extreme Networks	NNM	NR	128	10694	Local area netwk switch'g prd	....	....	....	....	104¼	17	295949	90	60	83½	...	..	...	...	...	...
13	EXX.A	✓EXX Inc 'A'	AS	C	3	23	Toys,machinery,electr mtrs	34⅞	3/16	4½	1 7/16	8⅝	1⅝	3874	8⅝	3⅞	6 5/16	...	7	−5	237	17.7	−17.0
14	EXX.B	Cl'B'	AS	C	1	.1		34	1⅞	3 11/16	1½	7⅝	1⅝	727	7⅝	4	6⅛	...	7	−5	227	17.8	−17.7
¶15•[5]	XOM	✓Exxon Mobil[53]	NY,B,C,Ch,P,Ph	A	2322	1702145	World's leading oil co	67¼	3 7/16	77 5/16	56⅝	87¼	64 5/16	1110325	86 9/16	79¼	80 9/16	2.2	34	1	12.5	20.9	25.2
16•[5]	EZEN	✓Ezenia Inc	NNM	NR	53	8240	Supplies data commun ntwk prd	55	9⅝	19	6⅝	20 7/16	4⅝	31118	8¾	6	7 15/16	...	35	52	−56.8	−42.8	...
17	FMN	✓F&M National Corp	NY,Ch	A	63	2366	Commercial bkg,Virginia	35⅜	2 13/16	35 3/16	24⅛	32½	23 3/16	3190	28⅝	27 5/16	27 9/16	s3.4	16	9	0.6	14.2	16.7
18	FIT	✓Fab Indus	AS,Ph	B	27	2656	Warp knit textile producer	36¾	¼	33½	18¼	21	9⅞	1319	11¾	9⅞	10 13/16	6.5	83	−36	−47.0	−24.2	−16.6
19	FTUS	✓Factory 2-U Stores	NNM	C	65	4302	Oper off-price retail stores	94½	½	9	1 3/16	34⅛	8⅛	14721	30	20¾	28⅜	...	8	NM	244	133	62.6
✤20	FDS	✓FactSet Research Systems	NY,Ch	NR	162	6451	On-line fin'l database svcs	22 7/16	10 5/16	42 5/16	17 5/16	83½	35 9/16	5286	83½	60 1/16	79⅝	0.3	68	33	95.5	79.1	...
21	FVH	✓Fahnestock Viner Hldgs'A'	NY,Ph	B	27	3768	Securities brokerage svcs	21½	1 1/16	22 3/16	13 5/16	19 15/16	13¼	3943	15¼	14 5/16	14 15/16	1.9	17	−6	−13.0	2.6	21.5
✤22	FIC	✓Fair Isaac & Co.	NY	↑A	137	6252	Dvlp credit evaluation sys	50	1¾	46½	28 3/16	55⅝	26¼	8770	55⅝	39⅝	53	0.2	25	20	15.0	10.9	13.8
23•[6]	FA	✓Fairchild Corp 'A'	NY,Ch,P	B−	92	12154	Aerospace fasteners/Ind prd	28 11/16	⅝	24⅞	10⅜	16 3/16	6 13/16	22182	9¼	7	9 1/16	...	d	Neg	−42.5	−15.0	19.3
24•[7]	FCS	✓Fairchild Semiconductor Intl	NY	NR	64	19864	Dvlp,mfg semiconductors	....	....	....	....	34⅛	18½	107584	34⅛	24¾	29¾	...	..	...	...	...	...
25	FFD	✓Fairfield Communities	NY	NR	112	22100	Dvlp/oper resort,home dvlpm'ts	24⅜	15/16	24⅞	6½	17⅛	7	33536	11⅞	9⅝	10¾	...	9	28	−2.8	9.9	43.0
26	FFD	✓Fairfield Minerals	To	NR	..	...	Expl/dvp minerals properties	5	⅝	1¼	⅜	¾	¼	576	⅜	5/16	⅜B	...	d	Neg	−30.9	−39.3	−38.7
27	FCP	✓Falcon Products	NY	B+	38	4363	Contract furniture:food sv eq	17	⅜	14 3/16	9 15/16	12¾	7⅛	2096	9⅜	8⅝	8⅝	1.9	..	−27	−27.5	−14.5	−1.5
28	FL	✓Falconbridge Ltd	To	NR	27	9837	Mineral explor'n,mining Canada	33	17	23⅛	11¼	26 5/16	14¾	41427	26 5/16	22½	25 13/16	1.6	..	Neg	59.5	−2.2	2.8
29	FAL	✓Fall River Gas	AS	NR	14	235	Natural gas utility,Mass	16⅝	13¼	17½	14¼	22	16⅞	849	21⅞	21	21¼	4.5	22	−4	32.5	...	...
30	FCB	✓Falmouth Bancorp	AS	NR	2	1	Savings banking Cape Cod, MA	22⅝	10	24	12	17⅞	13	481	17¼	14½	14¼B	2.0	19	...	−3.3	4.3	...
#31•[8]	FDO	✓Family Dollar Stores	NY,B,Ch,P,Ph	A	401	126011	Self-service retail stores	15 1/16	1/32	22 7/16	11½	26¾	14	266491	18 1/16	14	16 5/16	1.2	20	18	−25.2	35.6	33.9
32•[9]	FGCI	✓Family Golf Centers	NNM	NR	84	13961	Golf-related rec'n facilities	24 5/16	3 5/16	31 9/16	10	19 13/16	¾	101738	1 13/16	1¼	1⅜	...	d	Neg	−92.9	−58.8	−18.9
33	FNL	✓Fansteel Inc	NY,Ch	B−	30	7207	Mfrs specialty metal prod	19⅜	1 1/16	9 9/16	5	6¼	3⅝	1527	4 7/16	3⅝	3⅞	...	7	−15	−32.6	−14.7	−10.4
34	FTMTF	✓Fantom Technologies	NNM,To	NR	14	1988	Mfr vacuum cleaners/floor pds	11	3½	11⅝	6⅞	16¼	9 1/16	235	14	11⅛	13¼B	◆1.0	6	27	37.5	25.9	...
35	FFH	✓Farm Family Holdings	NY	NR	46	2409	Property & casualty insurance	32¾	16	42⅝	28	43¾	31½	676	43¾	40 7/16	42¼	...	13	18	24.3	29.4	...
36	FTG	✓Farmstead Tel Group	AS	B	5	26	Resells used tel,mfr voice sys	18⅛	⅝	3½	1 1/16	2¾	⅞	3322	1¼	⅞	1 1/16	...	6	48	−57.5	−28.8	−25.9
37	WS.A	Wrrt'A'(Pur 1com at$2)	AS	....	2	19		¾	⅛	¾	1/16	⅞	⅛	211	⅜	⅛	⅛	...	..	...	...	...	...
38	WS.B	Wrrt'B' (Pur 1com at$2)	AS	....	1	21		½	1/16	¾	1/32	¾	⅛	151	3/16	⅛	⅛B	...	..	...	...	...	...
39	WS	Wrrt(Pur com[57])	AS	....	..	...		1	1/32	1⅛	5/16	13/16	¼	22	¼	¼	⅛B	...	..	...	...	...	...
40	FARC	✓Farr Co	NNM	B−	38	3381	Filters & filtration systems	13	3/16	14 5/16	8	11	7½	2843	10⅛	8½	9¾	...	11	NM	−3.7	10.0	29.3
#41•[3]	FAST	✓Fastenal Co	NNM	A	221	22571	Fasteners/constrn supply strs	60½	¾	56⅞	20½	60 9/16	33⅝	65613	46⅜	35	44 15/16	0.1	26	27	2.2	−0.5	17.2
42	FFG	✓FBL Financial Group 'A'	NY,Ph	NR	95	8075	Mtk,dstr insurance, investmts	20¾	8¾	30 11/16	17⅝	24½	12⅜	5094	20	12⅜	20	1.7	12	11	−16.2	18.9	...
43	FB	✓FBR Asset Investment	AS	NR	4	745	Real estate investment trust	....	....	....	....	15	10¾	10593	15	12⅝	14	8.3	26	...	...	...	...
¶44•[5]	FDX	✓FDX Corp	NY,B,Ch,P	B	685	173585	Pkg deliv sys/logistics mgmt svs	42¼	¾	46 9/16	21 13/16	61⅞	34⅞	364730	42 15/16	38	40 15/16	...	20	17	−8.2	22.6	22.2
✤45	FJC	✓Fedders Corp	NY,B,Ch,P,Ph	B−	89	8051	Air conditioners:heat transf	26 11/16	1 5/16	7 7/16	3⅞	7 1/16	5	8946	6	5 1/16	5½	2.2	10	−10	−3.5	−2.6	1.3
46	FJA	Cl'A' (non-vtg)	NY,Ph	B−	37	5791		6½	3 3/16	7 1/16	3 5/16	6 13/16	4⅝	5174	5¼	4⅝	5⅛	2.3	9	−18	−0.3	2.6	6.5
47	AGM.A	Federal Agricultural Mtge'A'	NY	NR	7	258	Agricultural financial svcs	35	3½	21½	16¼	18¾	14 13/16	149	18⅝	16 1/16	16⅛	...	29	NM	−7.2	−15.5	29.1
48	AGM	✓ Class C(non-vtg)	NY	NR	49	3559		22 13/16	1 5/16	26 11/16	9 1/16	26	12⅜	4215	23⅝	18⅝	20 3/16	...	41	NM	64.1	25.6	68.4
¶49•[10]	FRE	✓Federal Home Loan	NY,Ch,P	A+	1338	555323	Provides Residential Mtg fds	44 9/16	2½	66⅜	38 11/16	65¼	45⅜	416922	49⅞	45⅜	47 1/16	1.3	16	16	−26.2	20.9	31.8
#50•[11]	FMO	✓Federal-Mogul	NY,Ch,P,Ph	B−	320	57753	Mfr bearings:transmis'n pr	47⅝	2 15/16	72	33	65¼	16⅞	195034	22½	16⅞	20⅛	0.0	5	NM	−66.2	−2.3	1.3

Uniform Footnote Explanations-See Page 4. Other: [1]P,Ph:Cycle 2. [2]CBOE,Ph:Cycle 3. [3]ASE:Cycle 2. [4]CBOE:Cycle 3. [5]CBOE:Cycle 1. [6]Ph:Cycle 3. [7]CBOE,P,Ph:Cycle 2. [8]Ph:Cycle 1. [9]CBOE:Cycle 2. [10]ASE,CBOE,P,Ph:Cycle 3. [11]P:Cycle 1. [51]5 Mo Dec'98. [52]Sub Vtg Shrs. [53]Formerly Exxon Corp. [54]Special divd. [55]Incl current amts. [56]If com exceeds $2.90 for 20 con trad days. [57]1.07 com at $4.67 per sh. [58]If com exceeds $11.25 for 10 con trad days.

Index (Splits ◆)	Cash Divs. Ea. Yr. Since	Dividends: Latest Payment Period $	Date	Ex. Div.	Total $ So Far 1999	Ind. Rate	Paid 1998	Financial Position Mil-$: Cash& Equiv.	Curr. Assets	Curr. Liab.	Balance Sheet Date	Capitalization: Lg Trm Debt Mil-$	Shs. 000 Pfd.	Com.	Earnings $ Per Shr. Years End	1995	1996	1997	1998	1999	Last 12 Mos.	Interim Earnings Period	$ per Shr. 1998	1999	Index
1	....	None Since Public			...	Nil	....	0.56	3.83	4.28	6-30-99	0.30	p...	★11836	Dc	...	...	...	vpd0.68	....	....	6 Mo Jun	n/a	vpd0.56	1
2	....	None Paid			...	Nil	....	Total Assets $246.28M			9-30-99	75.2	21281	★36836	Dc	...	...	...	v[51]0.01	....	....	9 Mo Sep	n/a	v0.02	2
3◆	....	Stk		12-9	...	Nil	....	5.78	7.45	1.12	12-31-98	....	...	6572	Dc	d8.60	p0.49	v0.50	vd3.15	....	d3.15				3
4	....	None Paid			...	Nil	....	1.22	57.7	38.7	9-30-99	30.1	...	63005	Dc	vd0.79	□v0.46	vNil	vd0.74	....	d0.79	9 Mo Sep	vd0.13	vd0.18	4
5	1994	Q0.02	12-2-99	11-18	0.08	0.08	0.08	28.0	1026	584	10-03-99	1244	...	21374	Mr	□0.05	v□0.90	v□0.87	v□d6.11	....	d6.17	6 Mo Sep	v□d0.18	vd0.24	5
6◆	....	None Since Public			...	Nil	....	164	230	82.6	9-30-99	566	...	170452	Dc	...	...	pvd0.32	vd0.55	....	d0.57	9 Mo Sep	vd0.42	vd0.44	6
7	....	None Since Public			...	Nil	....	....	5.90	3.29	9-30-99	....	...	★38200	Je	...	...	...	vpd0.59	....	....	3 Mo Sep	n/a	vpd0.15	7
8◆	1993	S0.05	12-15-99	11-29	0.10	0.10	0.07	61.7	382	245	9-30-99	....	...	50446	Dc	v0.35	v0.48	v0.73	v0.89	....	1.01	9 Mo Sep	v0.63	v0.75	8
9◆	....	None Since Public			...	Nil	....	60.4	816	842	9-30-99	674	...	±38521	Dc	v±0.60	v±0.80	v±1.01	v±1.27	E1.75	1.42	9 Mo Sep	v±0.91	v±□1.06	9
10◆	....	None Since Public			...	Nil	....	8.79	51.7	76.3	9-30-99	818	...	96196	Dc	pvd0.05	v0.10	v0.03	v0.29	....	0.48	9 Mo Sep	v0.21	v□0.40	10
11	....	None Since Public			...	Nil	....	6.50	358	291	j6-30-99	1017	988	±74912	Dc	v0.92	v1.02	v0.92	v0.84	....	jd0.27	9 Mo Sep	v0.79	vd0.32	11
12	....	None Since Public			...	Nil	....	116	147	36.6	9-30-99	....	...	53420	Je	...	...	...	vpd0.44	vd0.04	0.12	3 Mo Sep	vpd0.08	v0.08	12
13◆	....	0.01½	10-1-82	9-13	...	Nil	....	7.55	14.5	3.93	9-30-99	1.71	...	±2537	Dc	v±0.86	v±d0.60	v±d0.08	v±0.29	....	0.89	9 Mo Sep	v±0.17	v±0.77	13
14◆	....	None Since Public			...	Nil	....	....	...	...		....	...	625	Dc	v±0.86	±vd0.60	v±d0.08	v±0.29	....	0.89	9 Mo Sep	v±0.17	v±0.77	14
15◆	1882	Q0.44	12-10-99	11-9	1.67	1.76	1.64	1190	18048	21579	9-30-99	4497	2428	p3453556	Dc	v2.58	v2.99	v3.37	v□2.61	E2.40↑	2.14	9 Mo Sep	v□1.99	v1.52	15
16	....	None Since Public			...	Nil	....	54.0	68.6	13.0	9-30-99	....	...	13591	Dc	vd0.37	v0.77	vd0.37	v0.13	....	0.23	9 Mo Sep	v0.02	v0.12	16
17◆	1970	sQ0.23½	1-25-00	12-21	s0.842	0.94	0.728	Total Deposits $2450.07M			9-30-99	25.7	...	22984	Dc	v1.21	v1.38	v1.49	v1.60	....	1.78	9 Mo Sep	v1.16	v1.34	17
18	1976	Q0.17½	12-21-99	12-3	0.70	0.70	0.70	59.7	110	12.4	8-28-99	0.43	...	5404	Nv	1.57	v1.51	v1.63	v1.06	....	0.13	9 Mo Aug	v1.01	v0.08	18
19◆	....	None Paid			...	Nil	....	4.34	63.0	69.8	10-30-99	13.8	...	12377	Ja	d0.51	vd9.07	vd1.27	vd0.77	....	3.76	9 Mo Oct	v□d4.28	v0.25	19
20◆	1999	Q0.05	12-21-99	11-26	0.20	0.20	....	54.8	76.6	23.5	8-31-99	....	...	15817	Au	0.32	0.40	v0.55	vΔ0.77	v1.11	1.17	3 Mo Nov	v0.26	v0.32	20
21	1993	Q0.07	11-19-99	11-3	0.28	0.28	0.28	Total Assets $762.17M			9-30-99	....	...	±12490	Dc	v±1.68	v±2.41	v2.08	v0.96	....	0.88	9 Mo Sep	v1.60	v1.52	21
22◆	1989	Q0.02	12-20-99	12-1	0.08	0.08	0.08	20.1	101	43.0	6-30-99	0.47	...	14021	Sp	1.00	1.27	v1.46	v1.68	Pv2.09	2.09				22
23	....	[54]0.20	10-11-91	9-24	...	Nil	....	59.6	461	213	10-03-99	481	...	±24821	Je	Δd2.12	±□v12.35	v±0.08	±v□5.48	□vd2.41	d1.74	3 Mo Sep	v0.05	v0.72	23
24	....	None Since Public			...	Nil	....	62.4	406	199	5-30-99	[55]p715	p...	★±88149	My	...	...	...	....	vpd1.39	....	9 Mo Nov	n/a	v0.15	24
25◆	....	None Paid			...	Nil	....	Total Assets $481.89M			9-30-99	....	...	44498	Dc	v0.35	v0.51	v□0.51	v0.93	....	1.16	9 Mo Sep	v0.72	v0.95	25
26	....	None Paid			...	Nil	....	0.89	2.35	0.04	j4-30-99	....	...	7243	Ja	Nil	vd0.47	vd0.12	vd0.16	....	jd0.17	3 Mo Apr	vd0.01	vd0.02	26
27◆	1994	Q0.04	1-18-00	12-30	0.08	0.16	0.16	7.32	111	60.7	7-31-99	17.0	...	8643	Oc	0.77	v0.86	v1.28	v0.68	Pv0.07	0.07				27
28	1995	gQ0.10	11-12-99	10-27	g0.40	0.40	g0.40	114	873	355	j9-30-99	1608	...	176971	Dc	1.89	v1.40	v0.75	vd0.24	....	j0.13	9 Mo Sep	vd0.08	v0.29	28
29	1880	Q0.24	11-15-99	10-28	0.96	0.96	0.96	0.47	8.78	6.82	6-30-99	19.5	...	2196	Sp	0.91	v0.80	v0.91	v0.97	Pv0.96	0.96				29
30	1996	Q0.07	12-21-99	12-3	0.28	0.28	0.25	Total Deposits $87.8M			6-30-99	5.55	...	1194	Sp	p0.55	0.32	v0.55	v0.84	Pv0.77	0.77				30
31◆	1976	Q0.05	1-14-00	12-13	0.19½	0.20	0.17½	95.3	720	379	8-28-99	....	...	172884	Au	0.34	0.36	0.43	v0.60	v0.81	0.81				31
32◆	....	None Since Public			...	Nil	....	5.62	36.7	34.5	9-30-99	282	...	26038	Dc	v□0.16	v0.36	v0.56	v□0.08	....	d2.44	9 Mo Sep	v□0.05	vd2.47	32
33	....	0.10	9-12-95	8-30	...	Nil	....	0.04	45.2	22.6	9-30-99	2.31	...	8599	Dc	v0.39	v0.50	vd0.97	v0.63	....	0.54	9 Mo Sep	v0.49	v0.40	33
34	1998	gQ0.05	1-1-00	11-26	g0.14	0.20	g0.03	9.44	67.7	33.9	j6-30-99	....	...	9021	Je	0.48	0.72	v0.86	v1.11	v1.51	j1.52	3 Mo Sep	v0.35	v0.36	34
35	....	None Since Public			...	Nil	....	Total Assets $1241.60M			9-30-99	....	163	6111	Dc	v3.20	□v2.13	v3.51	v3.52	....	3.23	9 Mo Sep	v2.67	v2.38	35
36◆	....	None Paid			...	Nil	....	0.34	15.7	5.26	9-30-99	4.47	...	3273	Dc	d0.30	v0.35	vd0.57	v0.17	....	0.17	9 Mo Sep	v0.14	v0.14	36
37	....	Terms&trad. basis should			be checked in detail			Wrrts expire 8-12-2001				....	...	1000	Dc	...	...	...	....	....	....	Callable at 10¢[56]			37
38	....	Terms&trad. basis should			be checked in detail			Wrrts expire 8-12-2001				....	...	1000	Dc	...	...	...	....	....	....	Callable at 10¢[56]			38
39	....	Terms&trad. basis should			be checked in detail			Wrrts expire 6-30-02				....	...	184	Dc	...	...	...	....	....	....	Callable at 5¢[58]			39
40◆	....	0.027	3-6-92	2-14	...	Nil	....	6.18	38.4	15.4	10-02-99	....	...	7960	Dc	v0.38	v0.71	v0.88	v0.86	....	0.88	9 Mo Sep	v0.66	v0.68	40
41◆	1991	A0.04	3-12-99	2-24	0.04	0.04	0.02	24.2	222	36.0	9-30-99	....	...	37939	Dc	v0.72	v0.86	v1.08	v1.40	E1.75	1.64	9 Mo Sep	v1.07	v1.31	41
42◆	1996	Q0.08¼	12-31-99	12-13	0.33	0.33	0.30	Total Assets $3631.73M			9-30-99	137	5000	±31767	Dc	p±v1.27	v±1.86	±v1.99	v±1.56	....	1.63	9 Mo Sep	v±1.17	v±1.24	42
43	1999	0.50	1-14-00	12-29	0.40	1.16	....	Equity per shr $17.85			6-30-99	....	...	7112	Dc	...	...	...	v0.16	....	0.54	6 Mo Jun	v0.43	v0.81	43
44◆	....	None Since Public			...	Nil	....	380	3153	2678	8-31-99	1360	...	298566	My	1.32	v0.96	v0.66	v1.68	v2.10	2.09	6 Mo Nov	v1.11	v1.10	44
45◆	1995	Q0.03	3-1-00	2-9	0.11	0.12	0.09	118	212	99.5	8-31-99	157	...	±35997	Au	±0.72	±0.74	±v0.39	v0.07	v±0.56	0.58	3 Mo Nov	vd0.08	vd0.06	45
46◆	1995	Q0.03	3-1-00	2-9	0.11	0.12	0.09	....	...	...		....	...	17596	Au	±0.72	±v0.74	±v0.39	±v0.07	±v0.56	0.56				46
47	....	None Since Public			...	Nil	....	Total Assets $2681M			9-30-99	707	...	±10871	Dc	±vd0.14	Δv0.07	v0.46	v0.52	....	0.55	9 Mo Sep	v0.42	v0.45	47
48◆	....	None Since Public			...	Nil	....	....	...	...		....	...	9321	Dc	±vd0.14	Δv0.07	v0.46	v0.52	....	0.49	6 Mo Jun	v0.32	v0.29	48
49◆	1989	Q0.15	12-31-99	12-9	0.60	0.60	0.48	Equity per shr $11.55			12-31-98	93525	62000	695179	Dc	1.42	v□1.65	v1.88	v2.31	E2.95	2.81	9 Mo Sep	v1.68	v□2.18	49
50	1936	Q0.00¼	12-10-99	11-26	0.01	0.01	0.12¾	65.0	2326	1771	9-30-99	3826	p773	73827	Dc	vd0.42	vd6.20	v□1.67	v□1.67	E4.15	5.55	9 Mo Sep	vd1.06	v2.82	50

◆Stock Splits & Divs By Line Reference Index [3]1-for-20 REVERSE,'98. [6]2-for-1,'99(three times). [8]2-for-1,'96,'99. [9]2-for-1,'94,'98. [10]2-for-1,'96. [13]To split 5-for-1,hldrs Dec 16. [14]To split 5-for-1 in Cl'A',hldrs Dec 16. [15]2-for-1,'97. [17]Adj for 3%,'99. [19]1-for-6 REVERSE,'94. [20]3-for-2,'99. [22]2-for-1,'95. [25]3-for-2,'97:2-for-1,'98. [27]10%,'95. [31]3-for-2,'97:2-for-1,'98. [32]3-for-2,'98. [36]1-for-10 REVERSE,'96. [40]3-for-2,'97,'98. [41]2-for-1,'95. [42]2-for-1,'98. [44]2-for-1,'96,'99. [45]3-for-2 in Cl'A':5-for-4 in Cl'A','95. [46]5-for-4,'95. [48]3-for-1,'99. [49]4-for-1,'97.

¶ S&P 500
\# MidCap 400
✤ SmallCap 600
• Options

Index	Ticker	Name of Issue (Call Price of Pfd. Stocks)	Market	Com. Rank. & Pfd. Rating	Inst. Hold Cos	Inst. Hold Shs. (000)	Principal Business	Price Range 1971-97 High	1971-97 Low	1998 High	1998 Low	1999 High	1999 Low	Dec. Sales in 100s	December, 1999 Last Sale Or Bid High	Low	Last	%Div Yield	P-E Ratio	EPS 5 Yr Growth	% Annualized Total Return 12 Mo	36 Mo	60 Mo
¶1•[1]	FNM	✔Federal Natl Mtge[51]	NY,B,C,Ch,P,Ph	A	1990	846835	Provides residential mtg fds	57 5/16	9/16	76 3/16	49 9/16	75⅞	58 9/16	476645	68 7/16	60 1/16	62 7/16	1.7	17	14	−14.3	20.4	32.6
2	FRT	✔Federal Rlty Inv Tr SBI	NY,Ch,P	NR	176	23900	Real estate investment trust	30¼	1 11/16	25 15/16	19⅜	24⅞	16⅜	41739	19⅛	16⅜	18 13/16	9.6	19	9	−13.6	−4.9	5.6
#3•[2]	FSS	✔Federal Signal	NY,B,Ch,P,Ph	A+	205	26294	Special trucks,tools,signals	28¼	3/16	27½	20	28⅛	15 1/16	53678	17 3/16	15 1/16	16 1/16	4.6	13	4	−39.5	−12.2	−2.1
¶4•[3]	FD	✔Federated Dept Stores	NY,Ph,P	NR	..	...	Operates department strs-U.S.	48⅞	11¼	56 3/16	32 13/16	57 1/16	36 7/16	244168	50¾	43⅛	50 9/16	...	14	38	16.1	14.0	21.3
5	WS.D	Wrrt'D'(Pur1com $29.92)	NY,Ph	....	23	2715		24⅞	4¼	29 13/16	9⅝	30⅜	12¼	5459	24½	18	24½	...	..	...	...	...	...
6•[4]	FII	✔Federated Investors 'B'	NY,Ph	NR	142	22425	Mutual fd mgmt/advisory svcs	....	....	20 3/16	11	21 3/16	15 1/16	25866	21 3/16	17	20 1/16	0.8	15	NM	11.7	...	...
7	FCH	✔FelCor Lodging Trust	NY,Ph	NR	224	27509	Real estate investment trust	42⅞	17	39½	17⅜	26⅛	16¼	54930	18⅛	16 15/16	17½	e12.6	5	1	−14.0	−14.0	5.7
8	Pr A	$1.95 Sr'A'cm Cv Pfd([52])	NY	BB−	18	2958		33 5/16	23⅜	31	17¾	23	14 13/16	4397	15⅝	14 13/16	15½	e12.6	..	...	...	...	...
9	FGP	✔Ferrellgas Partners L.P.	NY,Ch,Ph,P	NR	26	2124	Retail marketer of propane	24¾	19¾	22¾	16⅞	20⅛	11⅜	23661	14 13/16	11⅜	12⅝	15.8	34	−17	−16.9	−7.2	0.3
#10•[5]	FOE	✔Ferro Corp	NY,B,Ch,P	B	202	25818	Chemical specialties	26 11/16	1⅜	30⅛	18	30 15/16	19 9/16	17327	22¼	20⅝	22	2.6	12	−14	−13.4	7.3	8.9
11	FMM	✔FFP Marketing	AS	NR	2	12	Oper convenience stores	2¾	2 5/16	9¼	2½	6 15/16	1¼	2572	2⅝	1⅝	2⅝	...	d	...	−59.6	...	...
12	FFP	✔FFP Partners L.P.	AS	NR	1	1	Land development	12¾	13/16	4	⅜	1½	⅝	877	1⅛	11/16	1⅛	...	19	Neg	...	...	...
13	FIA	✔Fiat SpA ADR[54]	NY,Ch,Ph	NR	20	1956	Mfr automobiles,farm equip	82¼	18 7/16	49	24¼	41¾	27	4014	32¼	27	30⅛	1.6	..	NM	−10.4	12.0	3.7
14	FMK	✔FiberMark Inc	NY,Ch,Ph	NR	59	6226	Produce heavyweight pressboard	22½	3 11/16	26 5/16	10 15/16	15	9 11/16	8802	13¼	11 7/16	11¾	...	14	...	−13.8	−3.8	9.6
15	FBCI	✔Fidelity Bancorp	NNM	NR	16	617	Savings bank, Illinois	25¾	9¼	26	15¼	25 3/16	15	1605	18	16	16¾B	2.6	10	15	−28.7	1.5	12.1
✤16•[4]	FNF	✔Fidelity Natl Finl	NY,Ph	A−	184	12927	Title insurance/services	28 9/16	⅞	39 11/16	20⅞	30¾	13 7/16	35558	15½	13¾	14⅜	3.1	5	56	−47.4	15.9	24.0
¶17•[6]	FITB	✔Fifth Third Bancorp	NNM	A+	591	141360	Comm'l bkg,Cincinnati,Ohio	55 11/16	⅜	74⅛	47½	75 7/16	57⅞	188933	73 15/16	63½	73⅜	1.3	31	15	4.2	40.3	41.8
18•[7]	FLH	✔Fila Holdings ADS	NY,P	NR	23	2861	Market athletic footwear & pd	106⅞	12⅛	28	7⅛	16⅝	7¾	11286	12½	10	11	...	..	Neg	41.9	−41.8	−10.1
✤19•[4]	FILE	✔FileNet Corp	NNM	B−	123	13576	Document mgmt systems	33½	2½	32⅞	3 11/16	26⅜	6	85118	26⅜	18 3/16	25½	...	43	−23	122	17.2	13.8
20	FIF	✔Financial Federal	NY	B+	99	8918	Equipment financing/leasing	23⅝	4 7/16	28⅝	17⅛	24¾	15⅝	6894	23⅛	18⅛	22 13/16	...	17	21	−7.8	27.0	23.7
21	FSA	✔Financial Sec Assurance Hldg	NY,Ph	B	196	23459	Insure asset-backed securities	48 11/16	18¾	61⅛	38⅛	60¼	46⅛	9850	53¾	47⅞	52⅛	0.9	14	13	−3.0	17.7	21.2
22	FSE	Finl Sec Assurance 6.95%Sr'QUIDS'	NY	AA	2	14	Quarterly Income Debt Sec	....	....	25¼	24⅞	25 7/16	19⅜	3506	21⅛	19⅜	20	8.7	..	...	−14.7	...	...
23	FSD	Finl Sec Assurance 7.375%Sr'QUIDS'[8]		NR	2	54	Quarterly Income Debt Sec	25⅝	24 7/16	26⅛	24¾	25⅞	19¾	3009	22⅞	19¾	20⅞	8.8	..	...	−11.4	...	...
24	FNCM	✔Finet.com Inc	NSC	NR	41	8586	Computer software/svcs	5¾	4	5 1/16	⅜	18¼	13/16	375071	2⅜	1	1 5/16	...	d	...	5.0	...	...
25	FNSR	✔Finisar Corp	NNM	NR	..	...	Fiber optic subsystems	....	....	....	....	127	19	114658	117⅛	74½	89⅞	...	..	...	...	...	...
26•[9]	FINL	✔Finish Line 'A'	NNM	NR	96	10185	Sells athletic footwr/activewr	28	2 13/16	31 1/16	7	15⅞	4 7/16	84399	6¾	4 7/16	5 7/16	...	9	12	−32.0	−36.4	7.7
27	FTT	✔Finning Intl	To	B	11	3677	Heavy equip sales,svc,lease	21	1¼	18½	10¼	15⅝	9	15685	13⅝	12⅛	13½	1.5	44	−34	25.1	0.2	8.8
#28•[10]	FNV	✔FINOVA Group	NY,Ph,P	NR	355	47898	R.E. financing/insurance	50	8 15/16	65⅛	35 9/16	62 7/16	32½	69210	37⅝	32½	35½	2.0	10	16	−33.3	4.7	19.3
29	Pr A	FINOVA Fin Tr 5.50%Cv[57]TOPrS([58]50)[8]		BBB	33	1231		70	49¾	84⅝	59	81	49⅛	2399	53 9/16	49⅛	50	5.5	..	...	...	...	...
30	FACO	✔First Alliance 'A'	NNM	NR	19	3806	Sell/svc mortgage loans	24 3/16	11 5/16	18½	2⅜	5¾	1⅛	3511	2 13/16	1½	1⅞	...	5	−20	−50.0	−54.7	...
✤31	FAF	✔First Amer Finl	NY,Ch,Ph	B+	227	30378	Title insurance	16⅝	⅛	43	15 15/16	35 3/16	11½	45723	13⅞	11⅝	12 7/16	1.9	6	68	−60.7	12.6	29.0
32	FAH	✔First Amer Hlth Concepts	AS	†B	4	153	Eyecare cost mgmt svcs	12	¾	5½	3¼	5	2⅜	661	3⅝	2½	2¾B	...	16	−2	−27.9	−4.2	−17.0
✤33	FBP	✔First Bancorp	NY	B	83	5903	Comml bank,Puerto Rico	18 13/16	11/16	30½	16½	30⅜	19¼	8079	21⅝	19¼	20¾	1.7	11	11	−30.2	18.5	30.8
34	FBA	✔First Banks America	NY,B,Ch,P	B−	6	31	Commercial bkg,Dallas, Texas	31878⅜16	1⅞	25 3/16	16½	20⅝	16⅝	380	18¼	18	18B	...	14	NM	−7.7	21.1	13.3
35	FCF	✔First Commonwealth Finl	NY	A−	71	9776	General banking, Pennsylvania	17 11/16	4¼	17⅜	11¼	14⅞	10 1/16	4722	13 9/16	11 9/16	12	4.7	17	1	2.1	13.0	16.6
¶36•[2]	FDC	✔First Data	NY,Ph,P	B+	1067	360339	Credit-card processing svcs	46⅛	10⅝	36 1/16	19 11/16	51½	31 5/16	337932	50⅞	42¾	49 5/16	0.2	28	NM	55.0	10.8	16.0
37	FTFC	✔First Federal Capital	NNM	B+	47	3472	Savings Bank,Wisconsin	17	½	18¾	10⅞	18⅜	10½	11021	15½	12¼	14⅝	2.5	13	17	−8.6	26.2	25.3
38	FFCH	✔First Finl Hldgs	NNM	A−	51	2036	Svgs & loan,Charleston S.C.	26¾	1⅛	27⅜	14	21	14½	3671	18¼	15¼	16	3.5	11	12	−13.5	15.1	18.0
#39•[11]	FHCC	✔First Health Group	NNM	B+	195	37237	Hlthcare utiliz'n review svc	32¾	15/16	30⅞	13⅝	27 11/16	13⅝	54777	27 11/16	23 15/16	26⅞	...	20	5	62.3	8.3	9.5
40	FISB	✔First Indiana Corp	NNM	A−	44	2311	Commercial bkg,Indiana	26 7/16	1 3/16	30	17	26⅛	17¾	1519	23⅞	20⅝	21¾	2.4	13	NM	10.8	15.1	27.2
41•[12]	FR	✔First Industrial Rlty Tr	NY,Ch,Ph,P	NR	191	24351	Real estate investment trust	37½	17	37 13/16	21⅝	28⅜	22½	36776	28⅝	24⅜	27 7/16	9.0	14	17	12.1	4.1	16.1
42	FRME	✔First Merchants Corp	NNM	A+	38	2006	Commercial banking, Indiana	25 5/16	2 15/16	31 13/16	21½	29¼	21½	1358	28	25¾	26¼	3.4	17	7	4.0	18.1	16.8
✤43	FMBI	✔First Midwest Bancorp	NNM	A−	128	10939	Comm'l bkg,Illinois	30 3/16	1 5/16	34 11/16	22¾	30⅛	23 1/16	20007	29 1/16	24⅜	26½	2.7	16	9	7.6	9.5	18.9
44	FMSB	✔First Mutual Bancshares	NNM	NR	15	754	Savings bank, State of Wash	18 11/16	1⅜	17¾	10 13/16	13	9	915	12⅞	10½	12	e1.7	10	12	14.6	16.6	31.1
45	FNC	✔First National Corp	AS,Mo	NR	7	169	Commercial banking,S. Carolina	25⅝	14 9/16	32	20 11/16	31	22	239	23⅞	22	22⅛B	2.4	..	...	−19.4	...	...
46	FRC	✔First Republic Bank	NY,P	B	105	6263	Commercial bkg,Calif	32¼	4	38¼	19	30⅛	21	6071	24	21	23½	...	11	42	−6.2	11.9	15.9
#47•[9]	FSCO	✔First Security	NNM	A	280	73047	Comm'l bkg,UT,ID,WY,OR	28 7/16	1¼	27 15/16	15½	31	17½	214329	31	24¾	25½	2.2	18	14	11.9	22.6	34.5
48	SRCE	✔First Source Corp	NNM	A+	51	10885	Commercial bkg,Indiana	27½	¾	36 11/16	24 9/16	35¾	23⅞	3902	26 15/16	24⅞	25	1.3	14	13	−8.8	24.4	26.3
49	FSNM	✔First State Bancorporation	NNM	NR	19	907	General banking, New Mexico	14 11/16	5 7/16	18½	11	17 3/16	12 1/16	1452	14⅜	13	13¾	1.7	14	8	1.7	12.9	18.4
50	FTSP	✔First Team Sports	NNM	B−	15	961	Mfr in-line roller skates	31¾	7/16	4	¾	3 5/16	1⅛	11858	2 15/16	1 5/16	2 5/16	...	d	Neg	68.1	−29.6	−24.9

Uniform Footnote Explanations-See Page 4. Other: [1]Ph:Cycle 3. [2]ASE:Cycle 2. [3]CBOE:Cycle 2. [4]CBOE:Cycle 1. [5]Ph:Cycle 1. [6]Ph:Cycle 2. [7]CBOE,Ph:Cycle 1. [8]NY [9]ASE,CBOE:Cycle 3. [10]ASE:Cycle 1. [11]CBOE,P:Cycle 2. [12]P:Cycle 3. [51]d/b/a Fannie Mae. [52]Fr 4-30-2001 Red for cash or com re-spec cond. [53]Stk dstr of FFP Marketing Inc. [54]Ea ADR rep 1 ord shr,lit.1000. [55]Excl 799M savings shares. [56]Or earlier upon'Tax Event're-spec cond. [57]Trust Originated Preferred Securities. [58]Fr 12-31-99,(or earlier)re-spec cond. [59]Com of FINOVA Group Inc (can terminate re-spec cond). [60]Inc current amts. [61]p$0.88,'96.

Index	Cash Divs. Ea.Yr. Since	Latest Payment Period $	Date	Ex. Div.	Total $ So Far 1999	Ind. Rate	Paid 1998	Cash& Equiv.	Curr. Assets	Curr. Liab.	Balance Sheet Date	Lg Trm Debt Mil-$	Shs. 000 Pfd.	Com.	End	1995	1996	1997	1998	1999	Last 12 Mos.	Interim Period	$ per Shr. 1998	1999	Index
1◆	1956	Q0.27	11-25-99	10-27	1.08	1.08	0.96	Equity per shr $13.95			12-31-98	254878	23000	1025000	Dc	□1.96	□2.50	v□2.84	v□3.26	E3.70	3.60	9 Mo Sep	□v2.40	v2.74	1
2	1962	Q0.45	1-14-00	12-30	1.77	1.80	1.73	Total Assets $1541.88M			9-30-99	925	...	40348	Dc	v0.72	v0.86	v1.14	v0.94	....	0.99	9 Mo Sep	v0.67	v0.72	2
3◆	1948	Q0.18½	1-4-00	12-10	0.73¼	0.74	0.70	22.4	356	289	9-30-99	164	...	46100	Dc	v1.13	v1.35	v1.29	v1.30	....	1.24	9 Mo Sep	v0.94	v0.88	3
4	....	None Since Public			...	Nil	....	595	9498	5850	10-30-99	4658	...	209973	Ja	v0.39	v1.24	□v2.58	v□3.06	E3.50	3.40	9 Mo Oct	v□1.24	v1.58	4
5	....	Terms&trad. basis should be checked in detail						Wrrts expire 12-19-2001				....	...	8983	Ja	...	...	...	....	....	....				5
6	1998	Q0.042	11-15-99	10-28	0.164	0.168	0.076	213	254	87.4	9-30-99	402	...	±82810	Dc	v0.24	v0.13	v0.61	v1.07	....	1.33	9 Mo Sep	v0.76	v1.02	6
7	1994	Q0.55	1-31-00	12-28	†2.54½	2.20	2.20	Total Assets $4271M			9-30-99	1708	6108	65941	Dc	v1.69	□v1.53	v1.65	v□1.92	E3.80	1.61	9 Mo Sep	v□1.63	v1.32	7
8	1996	Q0.48¾	1-31-00	12-28	†2.157	1.95	1.95	Cv into 0.7752 com,$32.25				....	6000	...	Dc	...	...	...	....	....	....				8
9	1994	0.50	12-14-99	11-26	2.00	2.00	2.00	12.3	167	190	10-31-99	593	...	31307	Jl	0.76	□0.77	v0.74	v0.16	v□0.47	0.37	3 Mo Oct	vd0.35	vd0.45	9
10◆	1939	Q0.145	3-10-00	2-11	0.55	0.58	0.49½	11.9	482	297	9-30-99	257	1521	35288	Dc	v1.04	v1.21	vd1.08	v1.67	....	1.79	9 Mo Sep	v1.25	v1.37	10
11	....	None Since Public			...	Nil	....	16.5	70.5	61.1	9-26-99	39.5	...	3819	Dc	...	p0.39	pv0.03	vd0.12	....	d0.52	9 Mo Sep	v0.19	□vd0.21	11
12◆	....	h[53]. . . .	1-13-98	1-14	...	Nil	h[53]. . . .	....	1.45	2.39	9-30-99	21.6	...	2234	Dc	1.07	vd0.04	v0.03	vd0.08	....	0.06	9 Mo Sep	vd0.08	v0.06	12
13◆	1995	0.476	8-4-99	7-14	0.476	0.48	0.457	Equity per shr $6.60			12-31-98	11651[55]	1033000	367400	Dc	2.51	2.90	v2.52	▲□v0.26		0.26				13
14◆	....	None Since Public			...	Nil	....	8.81	110	51.8	9-30-99	156	...	7745	Dc	v1.30	v□1.19	v0.95	v1.43	....	0.87	9 Mo Sep	v1.41	v0.85	14
15	1995	Q0.11	11-15-99	10-27	0.44	0.44	0.40	Total Deposits $357.02M			9-30-99	30.0	...	2207	Sp	0.94	0.72	v0.33	v1.33	v1.76	1.76				15
16◆	1987	0.11	1-17-00	12-29	0.28	0.44	0.255	Total Assets $1000.05M			9-30-99	190	...	28494	Dc	v□0.45	v1.22	v□1.89	v3.23	....	2.82	9 Mo Sep	v2.36	v1.95	16
17◆	1952	Q0.24	1-14-00	12-29	0.84	0.96	0.657	Total Deposits $19538.24M			9-30-99	1658	...	p308703	Dc	v1.26	v1.41	v1.69	v1.76	E2.40	2.31	9 Mo Sep	v1.21	v1.76	17
18	1994	0.189	7-10-98	6-29	...	Nil	0.189	124	653	493	12-31-98	107	...	134000	Dc	2.37	4.34	v1.17	vd5.60	ENil	d4.18	9 Mo Sep	vd2.83	vd1.41	18
19◆	....	None Since Public			...	Nil	....	67.8	154	89.9	9-30-99	....	...	32379	Dc	v0.26	vd0.09	vd0.18	v0.03	E0.59	0.31	9 Mo Sep	v0.04	v0.32	19
20◆	....	None Since Public			...	Nil	....	Total Assets $977.06M			10-31-99	696	...	14862	Jl	0.54	v0.68	v0.80	v1.03	v1.30	1.36	3 Mo Oct	v0.30	v0.36	20
21	1994	Q0.12	12-8-99	11-22	0.46½	0.48	0.44	Total Assets $2639.06M			9-30-99	230	2000	★33518	Dc	v2.13	v2.61	v3.25	v3.82	....	3.66	9 Mo Sep	v2.83	v2.67	21
22	1999	Q0.434	2-1-00	1-12	1.68	1.738	....	Co option redm 11-1-2003 at $25[56]				★100	...	...	Dc	...	...	...	....	....	....	Mature 11-1-2098			22
23	1997	Q0.461	12-31-99	12-13	1.383	1.844	1.383	....	...	...		★130	...	...	Dc	...	...	...	....	....	....	Mature 9-30-2097			23
24	....	None Since Public			...	Nil	....	Total Assets $84.47M			10-31-99	38.1	...	93433	Ap	...	...	Δvd0.21	vd0.31	vd0.79	d0.73	6 Mo Oct	vd0.23	vd0.17	24
25	....	None Since Public			...	Nil	....	5.40	21.1	7.13	7-31-99	p....	p...	★50157	Ap	...	...	...	....	pv0.07	....	3 Mo Jul	n/a	pv0.03	25
26◆	....	None Since Public			...	Nil	....	36.0	202	85.9	8-28-99	....	...	±24843	Fb	v±0.47	v±0.80	±v1.02	v±0.80	....	0.62	9 Mo Nov	v±0.54	v±0.36	26
27◆	1981	gQ0.05	11-26-99	11-9	g0.20	0.20	g0.20	Total Assets $2048M			j9-30-99	509	100	78506	Dc	1.00	1.13	v1.27	v0.04	....	j0.31	9 Mo Sep	v0.20	v0.47	27
28◆	1992	Q0.18	1-3-00	11-26	0.66	0.72	0.58	Total Assets $12723M			9-30-99	10289	...	61227	Dc	v1.76	v2.09	v2.42	v2.70	E3.40	3.17	9 Mo Sep	v2.05	v2.52	28
29	1997	Q0.68¾	12-31-99	12-28	2.75	2.75	2.75	Cv into 0.6387 com $78.28[59]				....	2000	...	Dc	...	...	...	....	....	....	Mand redm 12-31-2016			29
30◆	....	None Since Public			...	Nil	....	Total Assets $117.54M			9-30-99	4.65	...	18139	Dc	pv1.91	±pv1.72	v±1.49	v0.73	....	0.35	9 Mo Sep	v0.60	v0.22	30
31◆	1909	Q0.06	1-14-00	12-29	0.24	0.24	0.204	Total Assets $1984.18M			9-30-99	248	...	65242	Dc	v0.15	v1.03	v1.21	v3.32	....	2.06	9 Mo Sep	v2.39	v1.13	31
32	....	None Paid			...	Nil	....	1.78	4.74	1.02	10-31-99	....	...	2605	Jl	0.25	0.14	v0.12	v0.14	v0.21	0.17	3 Mo Oct	vd0.02	v□d0.06	32
33◆	1995	Q0.09	12-31-99	12-13	0.36	0.36	0.30	Total Deposits $2330.3M			9-30-99	179	3600	28496	Dc	v1.58	v1.22	v1.57	v1.74	....	1.93	9 Mo Sep	v1.28	v1.47	33
34◆	....	37.504	12-1-84	11-20	...	Nil	....	Total Deposits $774.74M			9-30-99	44.2	...	±5688	Dc	vd0.99	v0.40	pv0.89	v0.90	....	1.25	9 Mo Sep	v0.71	v1.06	34
35◆	1987	Q0.14	1-14-00	12-28	0.49	0.56	0.44	Total Deposits $2934.69M			9-30-99	673	...	58236	Dc	v0.58	v0.63	v0.70	□v0.55	....	0.70	9 Mo Sep	v0.51	v0.66	35
36◆	1992	Q0.02	1-14-00	12-30	0.08	0.08	0.08	Total Assets $16131.00M			9-30-99	2195	...	419068	Dc	vd0.19	v1.37	v0.79	v1.04	E1.76	1.47	9 Mo Sep	v0.81	v1.24	36
37◆	1990	0.09	12-9-99	11-16	0.25	0.36	0.27	Total Deposits $1466.54M			9-30-99	333	...	18841	Dc	v0.57	v0.68	v0.88	v0.98	....	1.13	9 Mo Sep	v0.72	v0.87	37
38◆	1986	Q0.14	11-26-99	11-9	0.50	0.56	0.43½	Total Deposits $1208.05M			6-30-99	547	...	13340	Sp	0.74	0.56	v1.07	v□1.20	Pv1.40	1.40				38
39◆	....	None Since Public			...	Nil	....	102	170	170	9-30-99	220	...	49065	Dc	v0.95	v1.12	v0.10	v1.40	E1.35	1.33	9 Mo Sep	v1.07	v1.00	39
40◆	1987	Q0.13	9-15-99	9-1	0.39	0.52	0.48	Total Deposits $1272.99M			9-30-99	372	...	12513	Dc	vd1.39	v1.06	v1.36	v1.44	....	1.65	9 Mo Sep	v1.06	v1.27	40
41	1994	0.62	1-24-00	12-29	2.40	2.48	2.12	Total Assets $2526M			9-30-99	[60]1054	1710	38095	Dc	v0.63	v□1.37	□v1.70	v□1.25	....	1.91	9 Mo Sep	v□1.23	v1.89	41
42◆	1894	Q0.22	12-20-99	12-2	1.06	0.88	0.773	Total Deposits $1057.98M			9-30-99	205	...	12051	Dc	v1.21	v1.32	v1.43	v1.51	....	1.57	9 Mo Sep	v1.11	v1.17	42
43◆	1983	Q0.18	1-25-00	12-29	0.64	0.72	0.60	Total Deposits $4022.23M			9-30-99	....	...	41048	Dc	v1.02	v1.30	v1.28	v1.23	E1.67	1.63	9 Mo Sep	v0.83	v1.23	43
44◆	1988	Q0.05	1-5-00	12-13	†0.555	0.20	†0.50	Total Deposits $403M			9-30-99	99.3	...	4681	Dc	0.75	v0.85	v0.97	v1.09	....	1.21	9 Mo Sep	v0.81	v0.93	44
45◆	1997	Q0.13	11-19-99	11-10	0.52	0.52	0.436	Total Deposits $659M			9-30-99	34.2	...	7027	Dc	v0.88	v1.02	v1.14	v1.29	....	....	9 Mo Sep	n/a	v0.85	45
46◆	....	3%Stk	3-15-94	2-14	...	Nil	....	Book Value $18.27			12-31-98	1019	...	9078	Dc	0.15	v1.40	v1.71	v2.05	....	2.19	6 Mo Jun	v1.00	v1.14	46
47◆	1935	Q0.14	12-6-99	11-9	0.56	0.56	0.52	Total Deposits $13212.97M			9-30-99	2582	9	195756	Dc	v0.70	v1.02	v1.17	v1.28	E1.43	1.40	9 Mo Sep	v0.93	v1.05	47
48◆	1973	Q0.08	11-15-99	11-3	0.313	0.32	0.278	Total Deposits $2112.27M			9-30-99	56.7	...	18953	Dc	v1.08	v1.23	v1.35	v1.60	....	1.76	9 Mo Sep	v1.15	v1.31	48
49◆	1994	Q0.06	12-15-99	11-22	0.227	0.24	0.167	Total Deposits $446.23M			9-30-99	11.2	...	4920	Dc	v0.52	v[61]0.60	v0.81	v0.85	....	0.97	9 Mo Sep	v0.61	v0.73	49
50◆	....	None Since Public			...	Nil	....	2.38	27.3	10.5	8-31-99	4.99	...	5852	Fb	v1.30	v0.46	vd0.45	vd1.01	....	d0.15	6 Mo Aug	vd0.92	vd0.06	50

◆Stock Splits & Divs By Line Reference Index [1]4-for-1,'96. [3]4-for-3,'94. [10]3-for-2,'97. [12]No adj for stk dstr,'98. [13]10%,'97:1-for-2 REVERSE,'99. [14]3-for-2,'97. [16]3-for-2,'96:10%,'97,'98. [17]3-for-2,'96,'97,'98. [19]2-for-1,'98. [20]3-for-2,'97. [26]2-for-1,'96. [27]2-for-1,'97. [28]2-for-1,'97. [30]3-for-2,'97. [31]3-for-2,'98:3-for-1,'98. [33]3-for-2,'95:2-for-1,'98. [34]1-for-15 REVERSE,'95. [35]2-for-1,'99. [36]2-for-1,'96. [37]10$,'94:3-for-2,'97:2-for-1,'98. [38]2-for-1,'98. [39]2-for-1,'98. [40]4-for-3,'94:5-for-4,'97:6-for-5,'96,'98. [42]3-for-2,'95,'98. [43]5-for-4,'96:3-for-2,'99. [44]15%,'94:6-for-5,'96:3-for-2,'97:10%,'95,'97,'99. [45]2-for-1,'97:10%,'98. [46]Adj for 3%,'94. [47]3-for-2,'97,'98. [48]5-for-4,'97:10%,'98,'99. [49]5-for-4,'95:3-for-2,'99. [50]3-for-2,'95.

¶ S&P 500
# MidCap 400
✣ SmallCap 600
• Options

Index	Ticker	Name of Issue (Call Price of Pfd. Stocks)	Market	Com. Rank. & Pfd. Rating	Inst. Hold Cos	Inst. Hold Shs. (000)	Principal Business	Price Range 1971-97 High	1971-97 Low	1998 High	1998 Low	1999 High	1999 Low	December, 1999 Dec. Sales in 100s	Last Sale Or Bid High	Low	Last	%Div Yield	P-E Ratio	EPS 5 Yr Growth	% Annualized Total Return 12 Mo	36 Mo	60 Mo
#1•[1]	FTN	✔First Tenn Natl	NY	A+	358	47843	Comm'l bkg,Tennessee	34 13/16	5/8	38 3/8	23 3/8	45 3/8	27 3/8	84881	32 1/2	27 3/8	28 1/2	3.1	15	11	−23.5	17.7	26.4
¶2•[2]	FTU	✔First Union Corp	NY,Ph,P	A	1247	481736	Comml bkg,NC,southeast	53	1 1/8	65 15/16	40 15/16	65 3/4	32	679966	39 1/8	32	32 15/16	5.7	10	8	−43.3	−0.5	13.6
3•[3]	FUR	✔First Union RE EqSBI	NY,Ch,Ph	NR	59	28666	Ohio real estate invest trust	27 3/8	2 1/2	16 15/16	3 3/8	6 1/4	3 7/8	19215	5 1/16	4 1/2	4 3/4	...	d	Neg	−14.9	−25.6	−2.7
4	Pr A	Sr'A' cm Cv Pfd(NC[52])	NY	B−	10	466		54	25	54	15 1/2	24	19 1/2	141	21	19 3/4	20 1/4	10.4	..	...	...	...	...
5	UNTD	✔First United Bancshrs	NNM	A	41	2302	Commercial bkg,Arkansas	24 5/8	3 1/2	28 1/2	16 1/2	20 1/8	13 3/8	4157	15 13/16	13 3/8	13 3/8	3.7	10	7	−22.5	−3.2	9.5
#6•[4]	FVB	✔First Virginia Banks	NY,B,Ch,Ph	A	209	13412	Commercial bkg,Virginia	53 3/8	1 3/4	59 7/16	39 11/16	52 5/8	40 1/2	17993	46 1/2	40 1/2	43	3.3	16	5	−5.9	13.5	18.6
7	FRW	✔First Wash Realty Trust	NY	NR	67	4070	Real estate investment trust	27 3/4	17	28	20	24 3/16	17 3/4	8594	19 1/8	17 3/4	18 11/16	10.4	15	NM	−13.5	0.8	...
8	Pr	9.75% Sr'A'cm Ptcp Pfd([54]27.44)	NY	NR	9	2212		33 1/2	20 1/2	34 11/16	25 9/16	30 5/8	22 3/4	5461	24 3/8	23	23 7/8	10.2	..	...	...	...	...
9	FWV	✔First West Virginia Bancorp	AS,Ph	NR	6	98	Commerc'l banking,Wheeling WV	21 3/8	7 5/16	25 1/8	19 1/4	23 5/16	16 3/8	88	17 1/2	16 3/8	16 3/8B	3.4	11	13	−22.7	13.0	...
¶10•[4]	FSR	✔Firstar Corp	NY,Ph	NR	719	456644	Commercial banking,WI,IL,MN,AZ	....	....	31 5/16	23 1/2	35 5/16	19 9/16	700011	26 15/16	19 9/16	21 1/8	3.1	17	...	−30.7	...	...
¶11•[5]	FE	✔FirstEnergy Corp	NY,B,C,Ch,P,Ph	B	452	121067	Electric utility - Ohio	29	9 3/8	34 1/16	27 1/16	33 3/16	22 1/8	117144	24	22 3/8	22 11/16	6.6	9	2	−26.5	6.2	10.7
12	FAB	✔FirstFed Amer Bancorp	AS,Ph	NR	14	1592	Savings bank,MA,RI	22 1/2	12 7/8	23 1/2	10 1/4	14 15/16	11 1/2	1920	13	11 1/2	11 5/8	2.4	10	...	−13.6	...	...
13	FED	✔FirstFed Financial	NY,Ch	B−	121	12694	Svgs&loan,California	19 13/16	15/16	27	12	20	12 3/4	10739	15 11/16	12 3/4	14 1/16	...	8	NM	−21.3	8.7	17.5
#14•[6]	FMER	✔FirstMerit Corp	NNM	A−	182	23552	Comm'l bkg,Akron,Ohio	30 3/4	1 1/8	34 3/8	20 3/4	29 1/8	22 9/16	42557	26 1/2	22 9/16	23	3.5	18	14	−11.9	12.1	16.8
15	TIM	FIRSTPLUS Finl 7.25%'TIMES'[56]	AS	NR	4	201	Mandatory Exch Securities	57 1/4	25	51 15/16	6	7 7/8	2	183	2 1/2	2	2 1/2	...	..	...	−41.3	...	...
16	FSPT	✔FirstSpartan Financial	NNM	NR	13	398	Savings & loan,South Carolina	40 1/4	20	47 1/4	22 3/8	37	17 1/4	1714	18 5/8	17 5/8	18	e4.4	13	...	−6.4	...	...
#17•[4]	FISV	✔Fiserv Inc	NNM	B+	413	93207	Data process'g services	22 7/8	1 1/2	35 3/4	20	40 3/4	24 1/8	156645	40 1/4	34 3/4	38 5/16	...	37	NM	12.6	33.3	32.3
18•[3]	FSH	✔Fisher Scientific Intl	NY,Ph,P	C	40	33698	Mfr/dstr scientific equip	10 1/4	2 3/4	22 1/2	9 1/2	44	16 1/8	3412	44	25 7/16	36 1/8	...	d	Neg	...	...	...
19	FLGS	✔Flagstar Bancorp	NNM	NR	102	4477	Savings & loan, Michigan	22 1/4	12 15/16	30 1/2	17 1/2	30 1/8	12 5/8	12555	17 1/4	14 3/4	17 1/4	2.1	6	19	−32.9	...	...
20	BDL	✔Flanigan's Enterprises	AS,Ch	B	8	236	Liquor strs:cocktail lounges	10 1/4	5/16	6 3/4	3 9/16	8	3 3/4	478	5 1/8	4 1/4	4 9/16	...	6	31	−7.5	27.7	33.0
21	FLAS	✔FlashNet Communications	NNM	NR	25	699	Consumer internet access svcs	....	....	....	....	51 1/2	6	112368	9 3/4	6 1/8	6 3/16	...	d	...	...	...	...
¶22•[7]	FBF	✔FleetBoston Financial	NY,B,Ch,Ph,P	B+	944	322385	Comm'l bkg,RI,ME,NY,CT,MA	37 9/16	1 3/16	45 3/8	30	46 13/16	33 1/4	526733	39 13/16	33 1/4	34 13/16	3.4	12	21	−20.0	15.0	20.6
23	WS	Wrrt(Pur com[59])	NY	....	12	288		33 7/8	3 1/8	51	22	49 15/16	27 1/2	1791	36 7/16	27 1/2	29	...	..	...	...	...	...
¶24•[8]	FLE	✔Fleetwood Enterpr	NY,B,Ch,P,Ph	B+	288	25621	Recreat'l vehicle/Mfr hous'g	42 13/16	7/8	48	25	39 13/16	18	50099	21 7/8	18 7/8	20 5/8	3.7	7	11	−38.8	−7.0	4.4
✣25•[9]	FLM	✔Fleming Cos	NY,B,Ch,Ph,P	B−	146	26462	Whlse food to affil stores	45 7/8	4 1/4	20 3/4	8 5/8	13 7/16	7 3/16	23789	12 3/16	10	10 1/4	0.8	d	Neg	−0.4	−15.4	−13.7
26	FLB	✔Fletcher Challenge Bldg ADS[60]	NY,P,Ph	NR	13	2156	Buildings products division	34 3/16	18 1/4	24 1/2	9	17 7/8	11	12481	14 5/8	11	14 1/16	5.7	..	...	0.9	...	...
27	FCC.A	✔Fletcher Challenge Cda'A'	To,Mo,Vc	B−	6	2501	Canadian mfr timber products	25 7/8	1 13/16	24 1/4	14 5/16	18 1/2	12 3/4	13007	17 1/4	16	16 3/4	3.6	64	−25	2.4	−5.1	1.8
28	FEG	✔Fletcher Challenge Ener ADS[61]	NY,P	NR	17	2394	Energy division	53 3/4	19 3/4	40 1/2	14 5/8	32	16 9/16	12789	26 1/8	20 7/16	25 3/4	3.7	4	...	43.7	...	...
29	FFS	✔Fletcher Challenge Forest ADS	NY,P	NR	20	945	Oper wood/forestry division	19 7/8	7 7/8	8 7/8	2	6	3 1/8	34928	4 1/4	3 1/8	3 3/4	...	3	...	20.0	−37.9	−17.7
30	FLP	✔Fletcher Challenge Paper ADS[62]	NY,P	NR	8	110	Pulp & paper division	24 1/16	11 1/2	16 11/16	4 5/8	9 3/4	5 3/8	1309	7	5 3/8	6 3/4	3.0	..	...	7.7	...	...
31	FLXS	✔Flexsteel Indus	NNM	B+	51	2477	Quality upholstered furniture	18 1/2	11/16	15	8 3/4	14 5/8	11 3/8	1859	13 15/16	12 1/2	13 3/8	3.9	8	21	7.8	4.9	4.7
32•[10]	FLEX	✔Flextronics Intl	NNM	NR	226	73344	Electronic manufacturing svcs	12 3/8	2 3/16	21 7/8	5 1/2	49 3/8	16 3/8	504426	49 3/8	40 7/16	46	...	53	NM	122	90.0	65.7
33	FSW	✔flightserv.com	AS	NR	2	84	Computer software/svcs	3 3/4	3/8	2 3/8	3/16	11 7/8	1/4	35021	11 7/8	7 3/8	8 7/8	...	d	...	3450	76.1	...
34	FLIR	✔FLIR Systems	NNM	NR	57	6619	Mfr thermal imaging systems	22	8 1/2	23 3/4	10 3/8	23 3/4	11	5039	17	13 3/16	16 1/4	...	71	−36	−30.1	5.7	4.6
35	FLA	✔Florida East Coast Indus	NY,B,Ch	B	91	10044	Hldg co:Fla RR,land hldgs	29	7/8	36	23	45 3/8	25 7/8	2741	45 3/8	40 3/16	41 3/4	0.2	39	7	19.0	24.6	20.9
36	ELB	Florida P&L 7.05% CABCO Tr Debs	NY	....[64]	..	...	Corporate-Backed Trust Sec	....	....	....	....	24 1/8	18 5/8	1508	22 1/4	18 5/8	20 1/2	8.6	..	...	...	...	...
¶37•[11]	FPC	✔Florida Progress	NY,B,C,Ch,P,Ph	B+	410	51956	Hldg co:electric utility	39 1/4	3 5/8	47 1/8	37 11/16	48	35 7/8	38480	43 15/16	41 3/16	42 5/16	5.2	14	2	−0.7	...	...
38	FPU	✔Florida Public Utilities	AS,Ch,Ph	A−	23	723	Elec svc,natural/propane gas	12 5/16	1 1/2	17 5/8	11 9/16	20	14 5/8	165	18 1/4	16 3/4	16 7/8	4.0	15	12	2.4	23.6	22.3
✣39	FRK	✔Florida Rock Indus	NY	↑A−	160	9195	Concrete & aggregates	30	7/16	31 1/2	19 7/16	45 1/2	27 1/8	9281	34 3/4	30 3/4	34 7/16	1.2	14	21	12.2	29.5	21.9
40	FCIN	Flour City Intl	NNM	NR	4	224	Dgn custom exterior walls	....	....	8 1/8	2 15/16	5 5/16	1 5/16	7959	4 7/16	2 5/8	3 5/8	0.6	d	...	5.5	...	...
✣41	FLOW	✔Flow International	NNM	B	71	7735	Mfrs waterjet cutt'g systems	13 1/4	1	13 1/2	7 7/8	13 1/4	8 3/8	14322	12 1/2	10 1/4	11 3/8	...	31	...	17.4	7.6	10.2
#42•[1]	FLO	✔Flowers Indus	NY,B,Ch,Ph,P	B+	250	44101	Baked,convenience,snack food	21 1/2	5/16	26 5/16	16 1/2	25 1/2	13 5/16	65317	17 5/8	15 5/16	15 15/16	3.3	d	Neg	−31.5	6.9	18.6
#43•[9]	FLS	✔Flowserve Corp	NY,Ph	B+	176	28402	Corrosion resist process eq	36 11/16	13/16	33 3/4	15 3/8	21 9/16	15	14138	17 13/16	15 3/8	17	3.3	15	−3	6.0	−12.2	1.5
¶44•[3]	FLR	✔Fluor Corp	NY,B,C,Ch,P,Ph	↓B+	402	51861	Engr'g & constrn: coal,lead	75 7/8	3 5/8	52 1/2	34 1/8	46 1/2	26 3/16	88017	46 1/2	40 1/2	45 7/8	2.2	34	−8	10.2	−8.3	2.8
45	FCST	✔Flycast Communications[68]	NNM	NR	51	1756	Web-based advertising svcs	....	....	....	....	133 15/16	15 3/8	45025	133 15/16	67	129 15/16	...	d	...	...	...	...
¶46•[9]	FMC	✔FMC Corp	NY,B,C,Ch,P,Ph	B	325	21030	Chemicals/machinery	91 7/16	9	82 3/16	48 1/4	75 1/4	39 1/4	34758	57 5/16	46 1/4	57 5/16	...	9	−1	2.3	−6.5	−0.2
47•[12]	FMXI	✔Foamex International	NNM	NR	39	7030	Mfr polyurethane foam prd	22 1/8	6 3/8	18 3/8	9 7/8	13 3/8	4	19568	8 3/4	6 5/8	8 5/16	...	d	Neg	−32.8	−20.3	−3.6
48	FCOM	✔Focal Communications	NNM	NR	43	7558	Local communication svcs	....	....	....	....	29 3/4	13	14823	26 7/8	22 3/4	24 1/8	...	d	...	...	...	...
49	FOGD	Fogdog Inc	NNM	NR	..	...	Online retail sporting goods	....	....	....	....	22	8 1/2	220457	22	8 1/2	9 1/2	...	..	...	...	...	...
50•[3]	FMX	✔Fomento Economico ADS[69]	NY,Ph	NR	118	21089	Beverage producer,S. America	....	....	36 9/16	14 3/4	44 7/8	18 1/16	31328	44 7/8	37	44 1/2	0.8	..	...	68.7	...	...

Uniform Footnote Explanations-See Page 4. Other: [1]Ph:Cycle 2. [2]ASE,CBOE,P:Cycle 1. [3]CBOE:Cycle 1. [4]Ph:Cycle 3. [5]P:Cycle 1. [6]P:Cycle 2. [7]ASE:Cycle 1. [8]ASE:Cycle 2. [9]CBOE:Cycle 2. [10]Ph:Cycle 1. [11]ASE:Cycle 3. [12]CBOE:Cycle 3. [51]Spl div. [52]Fr 10-29-2001 red for 3.31 com,re-spec cond. [53]Pfd in $M. [54]Fr 7-15-99,scale to $25 in 2004. [55]Subsid pfd in $M. [56]ASE trading halted 11-8-99. [57]To be determined. [58]Stk dstr of ProcureNet Inc,'99. [59]2 com at $21.9375 per sh. [60]Ea ADS rep 10 Building Division shrs. [61]Ea ADS rep 10 Energy Division shrs. [62]Ea ADS rep 10 Paper Division shrs. [63]6 Mo Jun'96. [64]Rated AA- by S&P. [65]Subsid pfd. [66]Fiscal June'96 & prior. [67]12 Mos Dec'97:Fiscal June'97 earned $0.72. [68]CMGI Inc plan acq,0.4738 com. [69]Ea ADS rep 1 unit(1'B'shr,2 D-Bshrs,2 D-Lshr).

Index	Cash Divs. Ea. Yr. Since	Dividends: Latest Payment Period $	Date	Ex. Div.	Total $ So Far 1999	Ind. Rate	Paid 1998	Financial Position Mil-$ Cash& Equiv.	Curr. Assets	Curr. Liab.	Balance Sheet Date	Capitalization Lg Trm Debt Mil-$	Shs. 000 Pfd.	Com.	Earnings $ Per Shr. Years End	1995	1996	1997	1998	1999	Last 12 Mos.	Interim Earnings Period	$ per Shr. 1998	1999	Index
1◆	1895	Q0.22	1-1-00	12-8	0.76	0.88	0.66	Total Deposits $12423.4M			9-30-99	477	...	130374	Dc	v1.20	v1.32	v1.50	v1.72	E1.94	1.87	9 Mo Sep	v1.22	v1.37	1
2◆	1914	Q0.47	12-15-99	11-26	1.88	1.88	1.58	Total Deposits $133903M			9-30-99	31910	...	987743	Dc	v2.38	v2.58	v2.99	v2.95	E3.45	3.34	9 Mo Sep	v2.08	v2.47	2
3	1962	0.15½	1-28-00	12-29	[51]0.15½	Nil	0.22	Total Assets $605M			9-30-99	361	1349	42460	Dc	v□1.06	□v0.21	v□0.13	v□d2.73	....	d1.61	9 Mo Sep	vd0.89	v0.23	3
4	1997	Q0.52½	1-28-00	12-29	2.10	2.10	2.10	Cv into 3.311 com, $7.5625				....	2000	...	Dc	...	...	...	....	....	....				4
5◆	1979	Q0.12½	12-31-99	12-8	0.49	0.50	0.44½	Total Deposits $2227.42M			9-30-99	24.5	...	25296	Dc	v0.99	v1.14	v1.21	v1.20	....	1.29	9 Mo Sep	v0.90	v0.99	5
6◆	1960	Q0.36	1-10-00	12-29	1.32	1.44	1.16	Total Deposits $7846.77M			9-30-99	2.47	[53]496	49689	Dc	v2.18	v2.32	v2.45	v2.53	E2.72	2.99	9 Mo Sep	v1.85	v2.31	6
7	1995	Q0.48¾	11-15-99	10-28	1.95	1.95	1.95	Total Assets $556.17M			9-30-99	271	2692	9465	Dc	vd1.19	vd0.46	□v0.51	□v1.25	....	1.29	9 Mo Sep	v1.02	v1.06	7
8	1995	Q0.609	11-15-99	10-28	2.438	2.438	2.438	Cv into 1.282 com,$19.50				....	1920	...	Dc	...	...	...	....	....	....				8
9◆	1995	Q0.14	12-15-99	11-29	0.548	0.56	s0.361	Total Deposits $162M			9-30-99	....	...	1509	Dc	v0.98	v1.09	v1.28	v1.35	....	1.56	9 Mo Sep	v1.02	v1.23	9
10◆	1999	Q0.16¼	1-15-00	12-29	0.40	0.65	....	Total Deposits $50709.1M			9-30-99	5598	...	980187	Dc	pv0.58	pv0.64	pv0.78	pv0.81	E1.23	0.70	9 Mo Sep	v0.71	v0.60	10
11	1930	Q0.37½	12-1-99	11-3	1.50	1.50	1.50	116	1254	2494	9-30-99	5938	[55]809	233024	Dc	v2.05	v2.10	v1.94	v□1.95	E2.50	2.38	9 Mo Sep	v□1.54	v1.97	11
12	1998	Q0.07	11-16-99	10-27	0.24	0.28	0.10	Total Deposits $668M			9-30-99	653	...	7077	Mr	...	n/a	v0.84	v1.09	....	1.21	6 Mo Sep	v0.45	v0.57	12
13◆	....	None Since Public			...	Nil	....	Total Deposits $2004M			9-30-99	1154	...	18359	Dc	v0.31	v0.39	v1.07	v1.60	....	1.79	9 Mo Sep	v1.18	v□1.37	13
14◆	1939	Q0.20	12-20-99	11-24	0.76	0.80	0.66	Total Deposits $6868.76M			9-30-99	....	164	89802	Dc	vΔ0.38	v1.08	v1.36	v1.34	....	1.27	9 Mo Sep	v0.99	□v0.92	14
15	1997	Q0.886	11-15-99	10-28	3.544	[57]....	3.544	At Maturity FIRSTPLUS Com/Cash re-spec cond				....	...	2205	Sp	...	...	...	...	...	...	Mature 8-15-2000			15
16	1997	0.25	11-16-99	10-29	†12.85	0.80	0.65	Total Deposits $408M			9-30-99	59.0	...	3788	Je	...	...	n/a	v1.85	v1.36	1.35	3 Mo Sep	v0.42	v0.41	16
17◆	....	None Since Public			...	Nil	....	Total Assets $5063M			9-30-99	534	...	122626	Dc	vd0.41	v0.68	v0.76	v0.90	E1.05	1.04	9 Mo Sep	v0.67	v0.81	17
18◆	....	h[58]....	4-15-99		h[58]...	Nil	....	33.9	583	485	9-30-99	1019	...	40051	Dc	v0.04	v0.38	vd0.30	vd1.24	....	d0.01	9 Mo Sep	vd0.82	v0.41	18
19	1997	0.10	11-15-99	10-27	0.36	0.36	0.28	Total Deposits $2118.66M			9-30-99	1118	...	13128	Dc	v1.37	v1.51	v1.68	v2.90	....	3.04	9 Mo Sep	v2.00	v2.14	19
20◆	1999	0.10	2-1-99	12-30	0.10	[57]....	....	1.76	3.94	2.14	7-03-99	0.55	...	1976	Sp	0.30	0.40	0.58	v0.68	....	0.81	9 Mo Jun	v0.58	v0.71	20
21	....	None Since Public			...	Nil	....	26.0	29.7	32.2	9-30-99	1.80	...	14227	Dc	...	...	...	vd1.66	....	d1.59	9 Mo Sep	vd1.69	v□d1.62	21
22◆	1791	Q0.30	1-1-00	12-1	1.08	1.20	0.98	Total Deposits $63974.00M			9-30-99	19789	[53]691	p915564	Dc	v0.79	v1.99	v2.37	v2.52	E2.90	2.87	9 Mo Sep	v1.90	v2.25	22
23	....	Terms&trad. basis should			be checked in detail			Wrrts expire 1-26-2001				....	...	2500	Dc	...	...	...	...	...	....				23
24	1965	Q0.19	2-9-00	1-5	0.74	0.76	0.70	177	792	521	10-31-99	343	...	32653	Ap	1.82	1.71	v3.19	v3.01	v2.94	2.80	6 Mo Oct	v1.70	v1.56	24
25	1927	Q0.02	12-10-99	11-18	0.08	0.08	0.08	39.6	1567	1249	10-02-99	1557	...	38821	Dc	v1.12	v0.71	v1.02	vd13.48	Ed0.13	d15.25	9 Mo Sep	v0.70	vd1.07	25
26	1996	0.397	10-8-99	9-15	0.804	0.80	0.938	91.0	1037	793	6-30-98	521	...	322138	Je	2.13	2.21	2.55	n/a	....	....				26
27	1995	gQ0.15	12-15-99	11-26	g0.60	0.60	g0.60	746	1164	440	j9-30-99	....	1573	124189	Je	0.97	1.24	v0.96	v2.40	v0.30	j0.26	3 Mo Sep	v0.12	v0.08	27
28	1996	0.464	10-8-99	9-15	0.938	0.94	1.067	9.00	155	244	6-30-97	304	...	388440	Je	1.06	0.86	5.91	....	....	5.91				28
29	1994	0.07	4-9-98	3-11	...	Nil	0.07	64.0	129	64.0	6-30-97	373	...	880859	Je	0.62	0.63	□1.28	....	....	1.28				29
30	1996	0.099	10-8-99	9-15	0.201	0.20	0.21	1086	2340	950	j6-30-98	3299	...	636175	Je	1.49	1.55	d4.61	n/a	....	....				30
31	1938	Q0.13	1-3-00	12-17	0.49	0.52	0.48	10.4	78.8	27.8	9-30-99	....	...	6507	Je	0.73	0.63	v0.86	v1.08	v1.51	1.61	3 Mo Sep	v0.26	v0.36	31
32◆	....	None Since Public			...	Nil	....	173	654	413	3-31-99	197	...	★112604	Mr	d0.35	v0.17	v0.26	v0.56	E0.88	0.64	6 Mo Sep	v0.28	v0.35	32
33	....	None Since Public			...	Nil	....	Total Assets $13.11M			9-30-99	7.80	...	29493	Je	...	‡[63]0.05	v0.07	vd0.05	vd0.78	d1.12	3 Mo Sep	vd0.02	vd0.36	33
34	1999	0.40	10-15-99		0.40	Nil	....	4.14	171	109	9-30-99	1.70	...	14348	Dc	v0.70	v0.91	vd5.23	v1.45	....	0.23	9 Mo Sep	v0.68	vd0.54	34
35◆	1980	Q0.02½	12-17-99	12-1	0.10	0.10	0.10	108	150	39.9	9-30-99	....	...	36392	Dc	v0.74	v0.84	v1.11	v1.20	....	1.08	9 Mo Sep	v0.91	v0.79	35
36	1999	0.818	12-1-99	11-10	0.818	1.76	....	Redm fr 12-1-2003 at $25				....	...	★25	Dc	...	...	...	...	...	....	Due 12-1-2026			36
37◆	1937	Q0.545	12-20-99	12-2	2.18	2.18	2.14	11.3	1016	839	6-30-99	2478	[65]335	98203	Dc	v2.50	v2.32	v0.56	v2.90	E3.12	3.25	12 Mo Sep	v1.75	v3.25	37
38◆	1942	Q0.17	1-3-00	12-8	0.66	0.68	0.62	0.84	12.7	23.2	9-30-99	23.5	6	3021	Dc	v0.83	v0.93	v1.06	v1.02	....	1.11	12 Mo Sep	v1.04	v1.11	38
39◆	1978	Q0.10	1-3-00	12-9	0.35	0.40	0.25	4.55	127	121	6-30-99	97.7	...	18895	Sp	1.26	1.43	v1.99	v2.02	Pv2.42	2.42				39
40	....	Plan annual div			...	0.02	....	14.0	31.0	11.1	7-31-99	....	...	6268	Oc	...	...	p1.26	v0.78	....	d0.33	9 Mo Jul	v0.64	vd0.47	40
41	....	None Since Public			...	Nil	....	8.56	125	35.3	10-31-99	66.5	...	14727	Ap	0.53	v0.47	v0.05	v0.32	v0.45	0.37	6 Mo Oct	v0.26	v0.18	41
42◆	1971	Q0.13¼	12-17-99	12-1	0.51½	0.53	0.47½	23.0	704	714	10-09-99	1116	...	100308	Dc	v0.49	v[66]0.35	v[67]0.60	v□0.47	....	d0.27	9 Mo Sep	v□0.62	vd0.12	42
43◆	1935	Q0.14	12-3-99	11-3	0.56	0.56	0.56	17.9	458	179	9-30-99	213	...	37324	Dc	v1.30	v1.72	v1.26	vΔ1.20	E1.15	0.83	9 Mo Sep	vΔ1.00	v0.63	43
44	1974	Q0.25	1-12-00	12-20	0.80	1.00	0.80	219	2033	2304	7-31-99	318	...	75964	Oc	2.78	v3.21	v1.75	v2.97	vP1.37	1.37				44
45	....	None Since Public			...	Nil	....	71.4	84.8	18.5	9-30-99	3.41	...	15165	Dc	...	...	...	vpd1.40	....	d2.22	9 Mo Sep	pvd0.79	vpd1.61	45
46	....	0.55	3-31-86	3-3	...	Nil	....	76.0	1618	1392	9-30-99	1396	...	30590	Dc	v5.72	v5.54	□v4.53	v□4.08	E6.60†	5.38	9 Mo Sep	□v4.24	v5.54	46
47	1998	0.05	1-19-98	1-12	...	Nil	0.05	4.24	336	230	9-30-99	737	...	25053	Dc	vd2.01	v□d3.19	v□0.08	v□d2.79	....	d2.85	9 Mo Sep	v□0.67	v0.61	47
48	....	None Since Public			...	Nil	....	222	246	27.5	9-30-99	242	...	60665	Dc	...	...	vd0.07	vd0.18	....	d0.32	9 Mo Sep	vd0.13	vd0.27	48
49	....	None Since Public			...	Nil	....	21.9	23.5	5.61	9-30-99	0.34	p...	★35665	Dc	...	...	...	vpd0.43	....	....	9 Mo Sep	n/a	vd1.33	49
50	1998	0.355	7-9-99	6-28	0.355	0.36	0.322	2211	8175	6596	j12-31-98	7739	...	5341340	Dc	v0.07	v0.42	v0.38	v0.13	....	0.13				50

◆**Stock Splits & Divs By Line Reference Index** [1]2-for-1,'96,'98. [2]2-for-1,'97. [5]3-for-2,'96:2-for-1,'98. [6]3-for-2,'97. [9]3-for-2,'97:6-for-5,'99. [10]3-for-1,'99. [13]2-for-1,'98. [14]2-for-1,'97. [17]3-for-2,'98,'99. [18]5-for-1,'98. [20]2-for-1,'99. [22]2-for-1,'98. [32]2-for-1,'99(twice). [35]4-for-1,'98. [37]No adj for stk dstr Echelon Intl,'96. [38]2-for-1,'98. [39]2-for-1,'97. [42]3-for-2,'95,'97. [43]3-for-2,'94.

¶ S&P 500
\# MidCap 400
✣ SmallCap 600
• Options

Index	Ticker	Name of Issue (Call Price of Pfd. Stocks)	Market	Com. Rank. & Pfd. Rating	Inst. Hold Cos	Inst. Hold Shs. (000)	Principal Business	Price Range 1971-97 High	1971-97 Low	1998 High	1998 Low	1999 High	1999 Low	Dec. Sales in 100s	December, 1999 Last Sale Or Bid High	Low	Last	%Div Yield	P-E Ratio	EPS 5 Yr Growth	% Annualized Total Return 12 Mo	36 Mo	60 Mo
1	FSM	✔Foodarama Supermkts	AS,Ch	B–	20	225	Shop-Rite food chain	38⅝	2	43	23	32⅝	19⅞	518	26½	19⅞	19⅞	...	12	NM	–37.9	11.1	12.3
2	FOOT	✔Foothill Independent Banc	NNM	B+	21	1110	Commercial banking, Calif	15 3/16	2½	18¼	9¼	15⅞	11¾	1858	14⅛	12½	13	...	13	8	–11.2	22.3	27.8
✣3•[1]	FTS	✔Footstar Inc	NY,Ch	NR	181	15192	Retail footwear/apparel	31¾	18½	49¼	19¼	42⅛	22⅞	13594	33⅛	25⅞	30½	...	18	...	22.0	7.0	...
¶4•[2]	F	✔Ford Motor	NY,To,B,C,Ch,P,Ph,Mo	B+	1565	589650	Second largest auto maker	50¼	1¾	65 15/16	37½	67⅞	46¼	595544	53 15/16	48½	53 5/16	3.8	9	20	...	...	...
5	FOM	✔Foremost Corp,Amer	NY,Ch,Ph	B	90	18121	Mobile home & RV insurance	23 11/16	⅜	25 15/16	15⅛	28½	18	14363	28 7/16	27½	28⅜	1.3	15	...	37.2	14.3	21.2
6	FCE.A	✔Forest City Enterp Cl'A'	NY,Ch	NR	87	11453	R.E. dev & const	31¼	7/16	30⅝	17¾	28¾	19⅞	2280	28¼	23 13/16	28	0.7	33	NM	7.4	18.4	27.6
7	FCE.B	Class B Cv	NY,Ch	NR	21	1938		30½	4 5/16	30⅝	18	31 7/16	20 11/16	306	31 7/16	27 1/16	30½B	0.7	36	NM	19.3	22.4	29.8
#8•[3]	FRX	✔Forest Labs	NY,B,Ch,P,Ph	B+	415	70039	Pharmaceutical mfr & dstr	27⅞	1/32	53¼	24 5/16	61¾	41¼	130374	61¾	50	61 7/16	...	48	23	15.5	55.9	21.6
9•[3]	FST	✔Forest Oil	NY,Ph	C	164	29820	Oil & natural gas explor/dev	149 11/16	5	17⅜	7 9/16	18⅛	5⅜	73740	13 3/16	9	13 3/16	...	d	51	55.1	–9.2	3.5
10	FORR	✔Forrester Research	NNM	NR	74	2893	Independent research svcs	32⅞	15½	44	18½	72⅞	21	11772	72⅞	49	68⅞	...	68	32	57.4	38.8	...
¶11•[4]	FJ	✔Fort James	NY,B,Ch,P	B–	522	182654	Chem treated spec paper prod	47⅛	1 1/16	53	26½	42 3/16	23 15/16	166617	28⅝	25⅝	27⅜	2.2	13	NM	–30.3	–4.6	...
¶12•[5]	FO	✔Fortune Brands	NY,B,C,Ch,P,Ph	B	648	101317	Hardware,home improvmt prd	56	3½	42¼	25¼	45⅞	29⅜	66512	35 1/16	31 5/16	33 1/16	2.8	d	Neg	7.2	...	...
13	Pr A	$2.67 cm Cv Pfd(30.50)vtg	NY,B	BBB+	7	1	distilled bev,leisure prd	230	28¾	253½	170	273	185	8	204¾	201½	205¼B	1.3	..	...	...	...	...
¶14•[6]	FWC	✔Foster Wheeler	NY,B,Ch,P,Ph	B+	252	24583	Engineering/constr'n svcs	48⅛	1 9/16	32¼	11¾	16 1/16	7⅞	63686	10 7/16	7⅞	8⅞	2.7	9	Neg	–29.8	–35.6	–19.1
#15•[7]	FHS	✔Foundation Health Systems'A'	NY	NR	226	106138	Manage HMO's western U.S.	37⅛	19⅜	32⅝	5⅞	20 1/16	6¼	81561	10¼	8 5/16	9 15/16	...	9	Neg	–16.3	–26.2	–20.0
16	FDRY	✔Foundry Networks	NNM	NR	51	2256	Internet svc provider ntwk pd	....	....	....	....	332⅞	25	54705	332⅞	218⅝	301 11/16	...	..	...	...	...	...
17	FPWR	✔Fountain Powerboat Ind	NNM,Ch	B–	9	180	Mfr/sells sport/fishing boats	19	1	13⅞	3⅞	7	2	4020	3⅛	2½	2⅞	...	d	Neg	–39.5	–37.6	–3.8
18	KIDE	✔4 Kids Entertainment	NNM	B–	40	3836	Licenses commercial rights	5 15/16	5/16	4 7/16	13/16	93¼	2 7/16	289444	56¾	24¾	28	...	29	NM	681	341	88.3
19	FS	Four Seasons Hotels[54]	NY,Ch,Ph,To	NR	95	11251	Oper luxury hotels/resorts	43 9/16	7⅜	37 9/16	15	54	28⅝	20622	54	48⅝	53¼	◆0.1	16	NM	82.6	24.7	27.4
20•[8]	FOX	✔Fox Entertainment Grp 'A'	NY,Ph	NR	320	102399	Entertain,TV,film,CATV	....	....	25¾	19⅜	30	19½	144616	26 5/16	20⅞	24 15/16	...	86	...	–0.7	...	...
21	FPIC	✔FPIC Insurance Grp	NNM	NR	76	3746	Medical profession liab insur	30¾	10	48⅜	22½	50⅞	13 13/16	17939	19¼	15⅞	16 11/16	...	8	21	–65.1	7.3	...
¶22•[9]	FPL	✔FPL Group	NY,B,C,Ch,P,Ph	B+	774	102571	Hldg co:Fla Pwr & Lt	60	6¾	72 9/16	56 1/16	61 15/16	41⅛	127795	45⅛	41⅛	42 13/16	4.9	11	6	–27.7	1.3	8.2
23	FTE	✔France Telecom ADS[56]	NY,Ph	NR	46	1713	Telecommunicat'n svcs France	38⅛	31 11/16	83	35 7/16	134½	67	3110	134½	107⅜	133½	0.7	50	16	71.4	...	...
24	FFA	✔Franchise Finance Cp Amer	NY,Ch,Ph,P	NR	141	16022	Real estate investment trust	27⅞	16½	28⅝	21¾	25 9/16	20⅛	24281	24½	21¼	23 15/16	8.9	10	26	8.6	2.8	15.4
25	FN	✔Franco-Nevada Mining	To	B+	29	5321	Royalty interests gold mines	39⅛	⅛	38⅞	20⅝	35¾	19¾	97782	27	22⅛	22⅛	1.4	33	–5	–23.6	–9.9	7.8
26	FELE	✔Franklin Electric	NNM	B+	76	1951	Mfr special purpose elec mtrs	64¼	4¼	72½	40	74⅞	59	1015	73⅝	69½	70 3/16	1.1	16	13	5.2	15.8	16.9
27	FEP	✔Franklin Electronic Pub	NY	B–	24	1448	Dvlp,mkt computers/elec prd	44¼	1⅜	14 3/16	7¼	11⅞	1¼	5502	6¼	4⅜	5 15/16	...	d	Neg	–49.5	–21.2	–22.4
✣28	FC	✔Franklin Covey	NY,Ph,P	B	105	9365	Provides training seminars&prd	40½	14⅝	25¾	16 5/16	17 13/16	5 15/16	11862	7¾	6 13/16	7¼	...	d	Neg	–56.7	–29.8	–24.7
¶29•[1]	BEN	✔Franklin Resources	NY,B,Ch,P	A+	475	94936	Mut'l fd inv advisory & svcs	51⅞	....	57⅞	25¾	45	27	116664	32 9/16	30	32 1/16	0.7	19	15	0.9	12.7	22.8
30	FSN	✔Franklin Select Realty Tr	AS	NR	17	2102	Real estate investment trust	7	3	8⅛	5⅜	7½	5¼	4671	7¼	6¾	6⅞	7.0	..	–20	7.3	14.1	21.2
31	FCM	✔Franklin Telecommunications	AS	NR	4	47	Mfr hi-speed communic prd	....	....	....	....	5	1⅛	133095	4¾	2⅛	2½	...	d	–25	...	...	...
32	FWG	FREDDIE MAC 6.688%'98 Debs	NY	NR	2	98	Sr'A'debentures	....	....	25¾	23⅞	25¾	20⅜	1201	22½	20⅜	22¼	7.5	..	...	–5.1	...	...
33•[9]	FSI	✔Freedom Securities	NY,Ph	NR	61	10307	Retail brokerage/investments	....	....	23⅛	9⅜	19	10¼	10354	13 13/16	10¼	11¼	1.8	8	...	–24.7	...	...
34	FMKT	✔FreeMarkets Inc	NNM	NR	...	...	Business-business web auction	....	....	....	....	367⅞	48	162106	367⅞	48	341 5/16	...	..	...	...	...	...
¶35•[10]	FCX	✔Freep't McMoRan Copper&Gold'B'	NY,Ph,P	B	333	67931	Explor'n/mining in Indonesia	36⅛	14 15/16	21 7/16	9 13/16	21⅜	9⅛	102384	21⅜	15 9/16	21⅛	...	38	5	102	–9.5	...
36•[9]	FCX.A	✔ Cl'A'	NY,Ph	B	125	30908		34⅞	2 3/16	20 5/16	9 3/16	18¾	9	26387	18¾	13 7/16	18 9/16	...	28	34	91.6	–11.5	–0.6
37	Pr A	$1.25 cm Cv[59]Dep Pfd([60]25)	NY	BB	43	6235		30¾	19¾	24	14	19 5/16	14⅝	8605	19 1/16	15⅛	19 1/16	9.2	..	...	...	...	...
38	FREE	✔Freeserve plc ADS[61]	NNM	NR	6	852	Internet access svc, UK	....	....	....	....	102¾	21½	16345	102¾	45⅞	92	...	d	...	...	...	...
✣39•[10]	FMT	✔Fremont Genl	NY,Ph	A	213	29235	Insur hldg: workers compen	27⅝	9/16	31 1/16	18	25 11/16	4 11/16	137587	7¾	4 11/16	7⅜	4.3	31	–13	–70.1	–20.6	3.6
40	FEI	✔Frequency Electrs	AS,Ch,P,Ph	B–	29	2532	Electronic control prod	24	1/16	19⅜	5 9/16	13	6 3/16	5269	10⅜	8⅛	10⅜	1.9	d	–6	6.1	12.5	29.9
41•[11]	FMS	✔Fresenius Medical AG ADS[62]	NY,Ch,Ph	NR	60	6105	Mfr,dstr pharma'l/medl prd	32¾	20	26 15/16	12½	30⅜	15 11/16	6284	30⅜	27⅛	28⅜	0.5	..	...	22.1	1.0	...
42	FMSPr	Pref ADS[64]	NY	NR	3	31		27⅞	18	21⅛	12¼	16¾	11¼	50	14½	14	13½B	1.2	..	...	–14.7	–18.5	...
43	FRES	✔Fresh America	NNM	NR	21	684	Food distribution mgmt svc	27⅞	4 3/16	24¼	9½	23½	3⅜	15370	6	3⅞	4⅞	...	d	Neg	–70.9	–33.4	–8.1
44	SALD	✔Fresh Choice	NNM	C	18	1125	Oper casual restaurants, Calif	33¼	2⅞	4 5/16	1	3⅜	1⅜	6011	2½	1⅜	2⅜	...	d	Neg	55.1	–16.0	–24.2
45	FDP	✔Fresh Del Monte Produce	NY	NR	65	14835	Grow,dstr,mkt fresh produce	18	13⅛	23⅝	10½	21	6 5/16	24388	9¼	6 5/16	9	...	11	...	–58.5	...	...
✣46•[12]	FGH	✔Friede Goldman Halter	NY,Ph	NR	54	4233	Offshore oil rig repair svc	48	8½	44	9¾	20⅛	6 5/16	85950	8¾	6 5/16	6 15/16	...	8	36	–39.0	...	...
47	FBR	✔Friedman Billings Ramsey Gp'A'	NY,Ph	NR	47	2122	Investment banking svcs	21¾	17 11/16	21¼	3⅝	21¼	4⅜	29997	7 15/16	5 5/16	7⅞	...	d	Neg	21.2	...	...
48	FRD	✔Friedman Indus	AS	B	20	1204	Steel coils into plate/sheet	8⅝	⅝	8	4 3/16	5⅛	3¼	1315	3⅞	3¼	3⅜	s5.9	8	–1	–18.2	–3.2	11.4
49•[10]	FRDM	✔Friedman's Inc'A'	NNM	NR	69	9072	Retail fine jewelry	29¾	9	22⅜	4¼	13½	5⅞	10276	8⅝	6⅝	7½	0.7	7	7	–26.5	–20.1	–15.3
50	FRS	✔Frisch's Restaurants	AS,Ch,Ph,P	B	31	1799	Operates restaurants/hotels	31⅝	1	13⅞	8¼	11 3/16	8¼	3377	10	8¼	8 13/16	3.6	11	27	–14.2	–16.1	5.2

Uniform Footnote Explanations-See Page 4. Other: [1]P:Cycle 2. [2]ASE,CBOE,P,Ph:Cycle 3. [3]CBOE:Cycle 2. [4]CBOE:Cycle 3. [5]ASE:Cycle 3. [6]P:Cycle 1. [7]CBOE:Cycle 1. [8]Ph:Cycle 1. [9]Ph:Cycle 3. [10]Ph:Cycle 2. [11]ASE,CBOE:Cycle 2. [12]ASE,CBOE,Ph:Cycle 2. [51]To be determined. [52]Stk dstr of Associates First Cap Corp. [53]Incl curr amts. [54]Limited Vtg shrs. [55]Subsid pfd in $M. [56]Ea ADS rep 1 ord FF25. [57]Approx. [58]76.8% owned by Govt of France. [59]Dep for 0.05 shr Step-Up Cv Pfd stk. [60]To 8-1-99 red re-spec cond,aft at $25. [61]Ea ADR rep 10 ord shs,0.01 par. [62]Ea ADS rep 0.33 Ord shr,DM 5 par. [63]Pfd in $M. [64]Ea ADS rep 0.33 Pref shr, DM 5 par.

Splits ◆ Index	Cash Divs. Ea.Yr. Since	Dividends: Latest Payment Period $	Date	Ex. Div.	Total $ So Far 1999	Ind. Rate	Paid 1998	Financial Position Mil-$ Cash& Equiv.	Curr. Assets	Curr. Liab.	Balance Sheet Date	Capitalization Lg Trm Debt Mil-$	Shs. 000 Pfd.	Com.	Earnings $ Per Shr. Years End	1995	1996	1997	1998	1999	Last 12 Mos.	Interim Earnings Period	$ per Shr. 1998	1999	Index
1	....	0.12½	10-2-79	9-17	...	Nil	....	4.18	53.4	64.1	7-31-99	46.5	...	1117	Oc	□0.73	v1.13	v0.90	v1.59	....	1.62	9 Mo Jul	v1.16	v1.19	1
2◆	1999	0.08	1-31-00	1-12	0.33	[51]....	....	Total Deposits $415.38M			9-30-99	0.03	...	5875	Dc	v0.65	v0.75	v0.78	v0.80	....	0.97	9 Mo Sep	v0.58	v0.75	2
3	....	None Since Public			...	Nil	....	10.0	415	288	10-02-99	.....	...	20839	Dc	p0.94	pn/a	v2.72	v1.32	....	1.74	9 Mo Sep	v1.60	v2.02	3
4◆	1983	Q0.50	12-1-99	10-28	1.88	2.00	h[52]1.72	Total Assets $267390M			9-30-99	[53]144038	4	±1207885	Dc	v3.33	v3.64	v5.62	v17.76	E5.74	5.25	9 Mo Sep	v16.90	v4.39	4
5◆	1978	Q0.09	12-15-99	11-10	0.36	0.36	0.36	Total Assets $771.08M			9-30-99	84.0	...	26615	Dc	v1.46	v0.78	v1.79	v□1.68	....	1.92	9 Mo Sep	v□1.04	v1.28	5
6◆	1994	Q0.05	3-15-00	2-28	0.18	0.20	0.15	Total Assets $3633.47M			10-31-99	2717	...	±30030	Ja	vΔ±0.26	vΔ±0.35	vΔ0.04	vΔ1.27	....	0.85	9 Mo Oct	v±Δ0.98	vΔ±0.56	6
7◆	1994	Q0.05	3-15-00	2-28	0.18	0.20	0.15	Cv into 1 Cl'A'				.....	...	10698	Ja	±Δ0.26	vΔ±0.35	vΔ0.04	vΔ1.27	....	0.85	9 Mo Oct	v±Δ0.98	vΔ±0.56	7
8◆	....	2%Stk	7-2-73	5-30	...	Nil	....	210	466	128	9-30-99	.....	...	83568	Mr	v1.12	vd0.27	v0.44	v0.90	E1.28↓	1.31	6 Mo Sep	v0.20	v0.61	8
9◆	....	3%Stk	6-10-91	5-14	...	Nil	....	3.26	70.3	64.3	9-30-99	384	...	53806	Dc	vd2.74	vΔd0.04	v□0.08	vΔd4.83	....	d1.00	9 Mo Sep	vΔd3.62	v□0.21	9
10	....	None Since Public			...	Nil	....	87.4	117	57.8	9-30-99	.....	...	9163	Dc	pv0.34	pv0.43	v0.63	v0.81	....	1.01	9 Mo Sep	v0.52	v0.72	10
11	1973	Q0.15	12-31-99	12-15	0.60	0.60	0.60	8.00	1924	1548	9-26-99	2877	...	216372	Dc	□v0.62	v1.47	□v0.35	v□2.27	E2.13	1.98	9 Mo Sep	v□1.84	v□1.55	11
12	1905	Q0.23	12-1-99	11-8	0.89	0.92	0.85	69.3	2276	2071	9-30-99	970	345	164082	Dc	v□2.87	v□2.82	v□0.61	v□1.67	Ed5.62	d5.37	9 Mo Sep	v□1.12	vd5.92	12
13	1979	Q0.66¾	12-10-99	11-8	2.67	2.67	2.67	Cv into 6.205 common				....	461	...	Dc	b4.48	...	...	.....	.....	....				13
14	1960	Q0.06	12-15-99	11-10	0.54	0.24	0.84	211	1726	1451	9-24-99	880	...	40726	Dc	v0.78	v2.02	vd0.26	vd0.77	E1.00	0.46	9 Mo Sep	vd1.18	v0.05	14
15	....	None Since Public			...	Nil	....	1201	2138	1512	9-30-99	1084	...	±122255	Dc	±v1.55	v±0.67	±vd1.52	v±d1.35	E1.09	d0.02	9 Mo Sep	vd0.50	v□0.83	15
16◆	....	None Since Public			...	Nil	....	12.3	36.0	14.7	6-30-99	....	p...	★55636	Dc	...	...	...	pvd0.27	....	0.54	9 Mo Sep	pd0.64	pv0.17	16
17◆	....	None Since Public			...	Nil	....	0.90	14.4	12.9	9-30-99	9.98	...	4733	Je	0.45	v0.77	v0.24	v0.54	vd0.27	d0.31	3 Mo Sep	vd0.04	vd0.08	17
18◆	....	None Paid			...	Nil	....	33.5	63.4	26.5	9-30-99	.....	...	11602	Dc	vd0.11	vd0.03	v0.08	v0.27	....	0.98	9 Mo Sep	v0.07	v0.78	18
19	1986	gS0.05½	1-17-00	12-29	g0.11	0.11	g0.11	10.2	62.1	48.8	j6-30-99	180	...	±33910	Dc	±d2.62	±v1.04	v±1.24	v±2.06	....	j2.24	6 Mo Jun	v±0.76	v±0.94	19
20	....	None Since Public			...	Nil	....	Total Assets $17177M			9-30-99	888	...	±724060	Je	...	...	...	pv0.24	v±0.33	0.29	3 Mo Sep	v±0.10	v±0.06	20
21	....	None Since Public			...	Nil	....	Total Assets $590.24M			9-30-99	.....	...	9700	Dc	v1.47	v1.53	v1.76	v2.11	....	2.21	9 Mo Sep	v1.56	v1.66	21
22	1944	Q0.52	12-15-99	11-23	2.08	2.08	2.00	370	1618	2257	9-30-99	3091	[55]226	179241	Dc	v3.16	v3.33	v3.57	v3.85	E3.95	3.90	12 Mo Sep	v3.83	v3.90	22
23	1998	0.874	7-9-99	6-15	[57]0.874	0.87	0.95	2436	12330	14390	12-31-98	14155	...	[58]1024000	Dc	1.87	Δ0.39	v2.47	v2.69	....	2.69				23
24	1994	Q0.53	2-18-00	2-8	1.96	2.12	1.88	Total Assets $1800.53M			9-30-99	501	...	56034	Dc	□v1.33	v1.69	v1.76	v2.00	....	2.47	9 Mo Sep	v1.49	v1.96	24
25◆	1989	gA0.30	3-29-99	3-11	g0.30	0.30	g0.30	272	310	11.8	j6-30-99	.....	...	80506	Mr	0.79	v0.85	v0.70	v0.55	....	j0.68	6 Mo Sep	v0.21	v0.34	25
26	1993	Q0.20	11-19-99	11-3	0.77	0.80	0.66	35.3	107	46.0	10-02-99	18.1	...	5437	Dc	v2.35	v3.22	v4.01	v4.02	....	4.52	9 Mo Sep	v2.67	v3.17	26
27	....	None Paid			...	Nil	....	9.64	52.6	46.5	9-30-99	1.60	...	7854	Mr	v1.25	v0.82	v0.18	vd3.81	....	d3.59	6 Mo Sep	vd0.08	v0.14	27
28	....	None Since Public			...	Nil	....	26.8	212	204	8-31-99	6.54	750	20380	Au	1.71	1.53	v1.76	v□1.70	vd0.51	d0.75	3 Mo Nov	v0.50	v0.26	28
29◆	1981	Q0.06	1-14-00	12-29	0.22	0.24	0.20	819	1486	486	9-30-99	396	...	251007	Sp	1.08	v1.25	v1.71	v1.98	v1.69	1.69				29
30	1994	0.12	1-15-00	12-29	0.36	0.48	0.48	Total Assets $132M			9-30-99	26.5	...	±12996	Dc	v0.32	v0.28	v0.34	v0.41	....	0.05	9 Mo Sep	v0.28	vd0.08	30
31	....	None Paid			...	Nil	....	1.19	4.69	2.30	9-30-99	0.76	...	28258	Je	vd0.02	vd0.14	vd0.23	vd0.29	vd0.11	d0.17	3 Mo Sep	vd0.06	vd0.12	31
32	1998	S0.836	8-18-99	7-30	1.672	1.67	0.836	....	....	....		.....	...	....	Dc	...	...	...	.....	.....	....	Due 2-18-2013			32
33	1998	Q0.05	11-30-99	11-8	0.19	0.20	0.08	Total Assets $809M			9-30-99	36.1	...	21658	Dc	...	...	pv1.17	v□1.34	....	1.37	9 Mo Sep	v□1.00	v1.03	33
34	....	None Since Public			...	Nil	....	32.5	39.7	5.94	9-30-99	1.98	p...	★33855	Dc	...	...	...	pv0.01	....	....	9 Mo Sep	n/a	vpd0.51	34
35	1995	Div Omitted 12-9-98			...	Nil	0.20	3.36	588	586	9-30-99	2094	700	±163484	Dc	v±0.98	v±0.89	v±1.06	v±0.67	E0.55	0.63	9 Mo Sep	v±0.43	v±0.39	35
36	1988	Div Omitted 12-9-98			...	Nil	0.20	....	....	....		.....	...	64809	Dc	±0.98	P±v0.89	±v1.06	±v0.67	....	0.67				36
37	1993	Q0.43¾	11-1-99	10-13	1.75	1.75	1.75	Cv into 0.813 com,$30.75				.....	14000	14000	Dc	...	...	...	...	.....	....				37
38	....	None Since Public			...	Nil	....	....	3.80	8.25	5-01-99	.....	...	★1007325	Ap	...	...	...	....	vpd0.32	d0.32				38
39◆	1977	Q0.08	1-31-00	12-29	0.32	0.32	0.30	Total Assets $8545.85M			9-30-99	1107	...	70039	Dc	v1.09	v1.37	v1.61	v1.90	....	0.24	9 Mo Sep	v1.41	vd0.25	39
40◆	1997	S0.10	12-1-99	10-27	0.20	0.20	0.20	38.9	62.6	3.63	10-31-99	.....	...	7689	Ap	Δd0.56	v0.40	v0.66	v0.01	v0.15	d0.20	6 Mo Oct	v0.47	v0.12	40
41	1998	0.148	6-11-99	5-28	0.148	0.15	0.136	37.5	1342	905	12-31-97	1643	[63]28	70000	Dc	p0.21	vp0.19	v0.39	n/a	....	....	6 Mo Jun	v□d1.08	v0.33	41
42	1998	0.161	6-11-99	5-28	0.161	0.16	0.176	....	....	....		.....	...	5000	Dc	...	...	...	....	....	....				42
43	....	None Since Public			...	Nil	....	2.68	73.5	66.7	10-01-99	22.5	...	5241	Dc	v0.63	v1.04	v1.17	v1.20	....	d1.11	9 Mo Sep	v0.59	vd1.72	43
44	....	None Since Public			...	Nil	....	3.34	4.62	7.64	9-05-99	3.27	1188	5742	Dc	vd5.05	vd0.36	v0.05	vd1.13	....	d1.02	9 Mo Sep	vd0.19	v□d0.08	44
45	....	None Since Public			...	Nil	....	32.8	396	219	1-01-99	337	...	53764	Dc	...	pd2.57	vp0.84	v□1.44	....	0.82	9 Mo Sep	v□2.02	v1.40	45
46◆	....	None Since Public			...	Nil	....	9.87	111	96.2	9-30-99	44.2	...	p39883	Dc	pv1.70	pv0.10	vp0.91	v1.43	....	0.88	9 Mo Sep	v0.95	v0.40	46
47	....	None Since Public			...	Nil	....	Total Assets $202.11M			9-30-99	1.50	...	±48882	Dc	p±v0.17	pv±0.40	±pv0.85	v±d0.33	....	d0.43	9 Mo Sep	v±d0.25	v±d0.35	47
48◆	1972	0.05	2-25-00	1-19	s0.224	0.20	s0.274	0.71	36.0	11.9	9-30-99	4.00	...	7188	Mr	v0.40	v0.50	v0.66	v0.49	....	0.40	6 Mo Sep	v0.28	v0.19	48
49	1999	Q0.01¼	1-17-00	12-29	0.03¾	0.05	....	1.10	218	93.8	6-30-99	.....	...	±14415	Sp	±0.97	□±1.19	±v1.33	v±0.76	Pv±1.13	1.13				49
50◆	1956	Q0.08	1-10-00	12-28	0.29	0.32	0.28	0.07	8.20	17.7	9-19-99	30.1	...	5824	My	0.34	0.33	v0.17	v0.73	Δv0.74	0.81	3 Mo Aug	v0.23	v0.30	50

◆**Stock Splits & Divs By Line Reference Index** [2]10%,'95,'96,'97:15%,'98. [4]2-for-1,'94:No adj for stk dstr,'98. [5]3-for-1,'98. [6]3-for-2,'97:2-for-1,'98. [7]3-for-2,'97:2-for-1,'98. [8]2-for-1,'98. [9]1-for-5 REVERSE,'96. [16]To split 2-for-1,ex Jan 10,'00. [17]1-for-2 REVERSE,'94:3-for-2,'97. [18]3-for-2,'98:2-for-1,'99. [25]2-for-1,'96,'97. [29]3-for-2,'97:2-for-1,'98. [39]10%,'94:3-for-2,'96:2-for-1,'98. [40]3-for-2,'97. [46]2-for-1,'97. [48]Adj for 5%,'99. [50]Adj to 4%,'96.

¶ S&P 500
# MidCap 400
✤ SmallCap 600
• Options

Index	Ticker	Name of Issue (Call Price of Pfd. Stocks)	Market	Com. Rank. & Pfd. Rating	Inst. Hold Cos	Inst. Hold Shs. (000)	Principal Business	Price Range 1971-97 High	1971-97 Low	1998 High	1998 Low	1999 High	1999 Low	December, 1999 Dec. Sales in 100s	Last Sale Or Bid High	Low	Last	%Div Yield	P-E Ratio	EPS 5 Yr Growth	% Annualized Total Return 12 Mo	36 Mo	60 Mo
✤1•[1]	FRTZ	✔Fritz Companies	NNM	NR	130	19501	Freight transportation svcs	43¾	7½	16 13/16	5⅞	13	6¾	16003	11⅛	9⅝	10½	...	31	6	−2.9	−6.3	−14.8
2	FAJ	Frontier Adjusters of Amer	AS,Ch	B	2	88	Franchises insurance adjusters	6⅛	1⅜	3⅜	2	4⅜	1	1399	1⅜	1	1 5/16	...	13	−17	−11.7	−10.1	−1.6
✤3•[2]	FTR	✔Frontier Insurance Gr	NY,Ch,Ph	B	183	20202	Property & casualty insur	35 11/16	1 1/16	25 11/16	11 1/16	17¼	2⅜	106346	3½	2⅜	3 7/16	...	d	Neg	−72.7	−38.9	−13.9
4	FTO	✔Frontier Oil	NY,B,Ch,P	C	50	17348	Oil & gas expl,dev,prod	43⅜	½	9 5/16	4	8¼	4 9/16	11028	7	4⅞	6¾	...	23	NM	36.7	29.3	7.3
5•[1]	FTL	✔Fruit of The Loom'A'	NY,Ch,P,Ph	D	205	35556	Global mfr of family apparel	49⅝	3⅞	38 3/16	11½	19	9/16	913470	3⅛	9/16	1 7/16	...	d	Neg	−89.6	−66.4	−44.4
6	FCN	✔FTI Consulting	AS	NR	20	1154	Litigation support svcs	14¾	5½	20¾	2⅜	6⅜	2 9/16	2810	5⅝	4⅝	5	...	10	...	48.1	−20.0	...
7	FCL	✔FuelCell Energy	AS	B−	14	942	Electrochemical research	14 13/16	5	19 5/16	6 5/16	30⅝	5⅜	3552	30⅝	21	25 1/16	...	d	Neg	...	...	...
#8•[3]	FULL	✔Fuller (HB)	NNM	B+	166	8571	Industrial adhesives	60¼	1 1/16	65	34	72⅞	38⅛	8940	60⅜	51⅝	55 15/16	1.5	17	−3	18.0	7.5	12.2
#9•[4]	FBN	✔Furniture Brands Intl	NY,Ph,P	NR	312	46477	Mfr residential furniture	54	5½	34⅛	12 15/16	28 7/16	17	50464	22¼	18 3/16	22	...	10	27	−19.3	16.3	...
10	CHI	✔Furr's/Bishop's Inc(New)	NY	NR	8	4705	Oper cafeteria restaurants	23⅜	2 3/16	7½	2 3/16	7 3/16	2½	1783	3¾	2 11/16	3 1/16	...	d	67	−50.9	−17.0	...
11•[1]	FVCX	✔FVC.com Inc	NNM	NR	35	3057	Internet Video networking	....	....	19	7½	20½	3¾	40404	12⅜	9	11 11/16	...	d	...	−25.8	...	...
✤12	GKSRA	✔G & K Services Cl'A'	NNM	A	186	12765	Rents & launders textile prod	42¼	3/16	54⅝	35⅜	56¼	29	41249	34⅛	29	32⅜	0.2	17	16	−39.1	−4.8	14.5
13	GLR	✔G & L Realty Corp	NY,Ch,Ph	NR	18	320	Real estate investment trust	21¾	8⅛	21⅝	12⅝	15 3/16	7⅜	3245	9	8⅛	8 13/16	5.7	d	Neg	−23.6	−11.7	2.4
14	GAF	✔GA Financial	AS	NR	28	1937	Savings & loan, Pittsburgh, PA	20	10	22 7/16	11⅜	16⅜	12½	1576	13⅝	12¾	13¼	4.8	11	...	−10.8	−1.2	...
15	GBL	✔Gabelli Asset Management'A'	NY	NR	33	3181	Invest advisory svcs	....	....	....	....	18¾	13 1/16	4916	17⅝	14 15/16	16¼	...	...	...	...	...	...
16	GBP	✔Gables Residential Trust	NY,Ch	NR	122	16719	Real estate investment trust	29	17½	28 5/16	21¾	25¾	20¼	22439	24⅜	20¼	24	8.8	17	2	13.0	1.5	10.8
17•[5]	GADZ	✔Gadzooks Inc	NNM	NR	51	4367	Spcl retailer casual apparel	41	9 5/16	29⅞	5½	16⅝	6	16964	10	8⅜	9 13/16	...	61	−28	26.6	−18.7	...
18	ZOOX	✔Gadzoox Networks	NNM	NR	74	2058	Computer sys connection pds	....	....	....	....	109⅞	21	119066	86¾	42	43 9/16	...	d	...	...	...	...
19	GNA	✔Gainsco Inc	NY,Ph,Ch,P	B	49	6154	Property & casualty insur	14 9/16	⅝	10	5¾	6 15/16	3 15/16	7454	6	5⅜	5⅜	1.3	22	Neg	−11.1	−16.9	−3.9
20	GXY	✔Galaxy Foods	AS	NR	4	29	Dvlp cheese substitute prds	61¼	3 1/16	8 15/16	2 7/16	7¼	2½	8302	3 11/16	2½	2 15/16	...	13	NM	−15.2	−14.4	−21.2
21	GNL	✔Galey & Lord Inc	NY	NR	57	8313	Mfr cotton apparel fabrics	23½	8½	28⅞	8	8 15/16	1¼	8543	2½	1¾	1 15/16	...	d	Neg	−77.5	−49.3	−33.0
22•[6]	GLC	✔Galileo Intl	NY,Ph	NR	301	64781	Global travel svcs	29⅜	22	46⅛	24¾	59 5/16	25 5/16	86791	32 9/16	25 5/16	29 15/16	1.2	14	...	−30.6	...	...
23•[4]	GALT	✔Galileo Technology	NNM	NR	135	24155	Dvp semiconductor devices	23¼	11 3/16	21	3 5/16	34 9/16	8¾	169998	27⅜	21⅝	24⅛	...	47	...	79.8	...	...
✤24	AJG	✔Gallagher(Arthur J.)	NY,Ch	A	225	10665	Ins brokerage,risk mgmt svc	39½	6⅞	46¾	33 9/16	66¼	42¼	9606	66¼	53	64¾	2.5	19	10	51.5	32.2	18.9
25•[7]	GLH	✔Gallaher Group ADS[56]	NY	NR	169	16379	Mfr tobacco pds	24	16	31¼	19½	29½	14 3/16	16749	21⅛	14 3/16	15⅜	8.7	6	...	−39.9	...	...
¶26•[8]	GCI	✔Gannett Co	NY,B,Ch,P,Ph	A	1015	210901	Newspapers: TV/radio:adv	61 13/16	1 13/16	75⅛	47⅝	83⅝	60⅝	161415	83⅝	70 15/16	81 9/16	1.0	24	17	28.0	31.4	27.3
¶27•[5]	GPS	✔Gap Inc	NY,B,Ch,P,Ph	A+	968	396548	Apparel specialty stores	17⅛	1/32	40 15/16	15 5/16	52 11/16	30 13/16	633528	46⅞	39¾	46	0.2	38	30	23.2	74.1	60.6
28	GAN	✔Garan Inc	AS,Ch	B+	41	2837	Knitted/woven apparel	37⅜	1⅞	29¾	21½	33	24⅛	1127	31⅞	28¼	28⅝	†6.3	8	20	8.0	20.5	18.6
29•[4]	GRDG	✔Garden Ridge	NNM	NR	31	2862	Retail home & seasonal prd	30¼	6¼	22½	4¾	11¾	4⅝	10763	11½	11 3/16	11 7/16	...	72	−8	26.2	9.9	...
30	GDEN	✔Garden.com Inc	NNM	NR	11	1083	Online gardening svcs	....	....	....	....	24⅛	8	53319	15	8	8 11/16	...	d	...	...	...	...
31	GBUR	✔Gardenburger Inc	NNM	NR	23	2080	Mfr frozen meatless burgers	30¾	1 11/16	16⅛	8	12½	5	22478	9¼	5½	6⅝	...	d	Neg	−42.4	2.0	−10.4
✤32	GDI	✔Gardner Denver	NY,Ph	NR	121	8697	Mfr air compressors/blowers	28 7/16	2½	30 7/16	10⅜	21¾	11	7334	16 13/16	14⅞	16 11/16	...	11	NM	13.1	14.1	38.5
#33	IT.B	✔Gartner Group'B'	NY	NR	172	25271	Res'r/analysis of info tech	....	....	....	....	26	9⅜	38165	13 13/16	10¾	13 13/16	...	16	45	...	...	...
34•[4]	IT	✔ Cl'A'	NY,Ph	NR	218	36893		43⅛	2¾	41¾	17 5/16	25¾	9 9/16	137098	15 7/16	11 7/16	15¼	...	18	45	−24.2	−25.5	10.7
35•[8]	GSNX	✔GaSonics International	NNM	↓C	51	8689	Dvlp photoresist removal eq	27	6½	15	3 5/16	19¾	8 3/16	13798	19¾	14 11/16	19¾	...	d	Neg	126	24.4	12.8
¶36•[9]	GTW	✔Gateway Inc	NY,Ph	NR	552	128485	Direct mkt personal computers	23⅛	2 5/16	34⅜	15½	84	25 9/16	515268	77 5/16	64¼	72 1/16	...	51	28	182	75.4	67.9
#37•[10]	GMT	✔GATX Corp	NY,B,Ch,P,Ph	B+	268	37984	Railcar leas'g/equip financ'g	36 11/16	5⅛	47 9/16	26¼	40⅞	28 1/16	32280	33¾	30⅞	33¾	3.3	11	−19	−8.1	15.2	12.5
38	Pr	$2.50 cm Cv Pfd (63)vtg	NY,Ch	NR	5	5	tank terminals, shipping	180	28½	238	150	200	160	1	160	160	165B	1.5	..	...	...	...	...
39•[5]	GCR	✔Gaylord Container'A'	AS,Ch,P	C	122	34596	Mfr paper packaging prod	22	1⅞	10¾	2	8¾	5½	28983	7⅜	5 11/16	6 13/16	...	d	Neg	12.4	3.6	−5.7
40	WS	Wrrt(Pur 1 com)[57]	AS	....	10	798		11⅞	1⅜	10½	2½	8	5¾	61	6⅜	5¾	6⅜B	...	..	...	...	...	...
41•[5]	GET	✔Gaylord Entertainment	NY	NR	82	13681	Hotel management svc	33¼	28⅜	37½	22	33 1/16	23⅜	2953	31½	29 7/16	29 15/16	2.7	10	...	2.1	...	...
✤42	GCX	✔GC Companies	NY,Ch,P	NR	103	5227	Oper motion picture theatres	47 15/16	24¾	53	36	42	23	2915	28 1/16	23	25⅞	...	d	Neg	−37.8	−9.3	−0.3
43	GEHL	✔Gehl Co	NNM	B−	51	2865	Mfr farm,constr'n,indus equip	24 15/16	2¼	22½	11	23½	14	4552	19	16¾	18	...	6	26	17.1	18.3	23.6
44	GELX	✔GelTex Pharmaceuticals	NNM	NR	107	9715	Dvp stage:pharmaceutical R&D	32	9½	30½	13½	29	9⅛	85824	13½	9⅞	12 13/16	...	d	−13	−43.4	−19.2	...
45•[9]	GMST	✔Gemstar Intl Group	NNM	NR	289	93635	TV/video recording prods	10 7/16	2 7/16	17 5/16	5 3/16	79½	13⅞	546317	79½	54½	71¼	...	..	43	400	154	...
46	GX	✔Gencor Indus[59]	AS	B	29	778	Mfrs ind'l combustion sys	10 13/16	⅛	27½	7¼	10	5 15/16	....	....	....	....	...	..	49	...	...	...
✤47•[5]	GY	✔GenCorp	NY,B,C,Ch,P,Ph	B	197	30482	Aerospace,auto,polymer prods	40	2 9/16	31 3/16	16 7/16	26½	7⅝	34119	11 1/16	7⅝	9⅞	6.1	4	NM	...	...	...
48	GNLB	Genelabs Technologies	NNM	C	32	5398	Disease/cancer prevent'n prd	13⅛	15/16	4⅝	1½	6	1 7/16	130607	6	3½	5½	...	d	23	100	−3.5	35.9
49•[11]	DNA	✔Genentech Inc	NY	NR	127	37141	Biotechnology R&D	....	....	....	....	143	48½	138773	143	81⅛	134½	...	..	...	...	...	...
50	CHR	✔Gener S.A. ADS[61]	NY	NR	56	11917	Electricity generation, Chile	34⅞	18¾	24⅝	10½	22¼	12 13/16	8827	15 15/16	14 9/16	15½	2.8	14	...	−0.1	−5.9	−5.1

Uniform Footnote Explanations-See Page 4. Other: [1]CBOE:Cycle 2. [2]Ph:Cycle 1. [3]Ph:Cycle 2. [4]CBOE:Cycle 1. [5]CBOE:Cycle 3. [6]CBOE,Ph:Cycle 1. [7]ASE:Cycle 1. [8]P:Cycle 1. [9]ASE,CBOE,P:Cycle 3. [10]Ph:Cycle 3. [11]CBOE,Ph:Cycle 3. [51]12 Mo May'95. [52]Spl div. [53]Redemption of stkhldrs value rt. [54]Stk dstr of Evercel Inc. [55]Stk dstr of Converse & Florsheim Shoe,'94. [56]Ea ADS rep 4 ord shs. [57]1 Cl'A' com at $0.0001. [58]Exchangeable for Cl'A'com re-spec cond. [59]ASE trading halted 2-19-99. [60]Stk dstr of Omnova Solutions Inc. [61]Ea ADS rep 68 com, no par.

Splits ◆ Index	Cash Divs. Ea. Yr. Since	Dividends: Latest Payment Period $	Date	Ex. Div.	Total $ So Far 1999	Ind. Rate	Paid 1998	Financial Position Mil-$ Cash& Equiv.	Curr. Assets	Curr. Liab.	Balance Sheet Date	Capitalization Lg Trm Debt Mil-$	Shs. 000 Pfd.	Com.	Earnings $ Per Shr. Years End	1995	1996	1997	1998	1999	Last 12 Mos.	Interim Earnings Period	$ per Shr. 1998	1999	Index
1◆	....	None Since Public			...	Nil	....	51.0	554	390	8-31-99	129	...	36660	My	[51]0.34	v0.71	v0.01	v0.50	v0.37	0.34	3 Mo Aug	v0.19	v0.16	1
2	1984	Div Omitted 11-2-98			[52]1.60	Nil	0.11¼	1.74	3.69	1.24	9-30-99	....	...	8958	Je	v0.22	v0.25	v0.21	v0.13	v0.12	0.10	3 Mo Sep	v0.06	v0.04	2
3◆	1992	Div Postponed 12-17-99			0.28	Nil	0.26	Total Assets $2683.10M			9-30-99	299	...	34746	Dc	v0.98	v1.24	v0.92	vd1.34	....	d6.59	9 Mo Sep	v1.20	vd4.05	3
4	....	[53]0.10	6-1-87	4-21	...	Nil	....	26.0	84.2	47.9	9-30-99	★311	...	27311	Dc	vd0.70	vd0.25	□v0.83	□v0.65	....	0.30	9 Mo Sep	v□0.62	v0.27	4
5	....	None Since Public			...	Nil	....	File bankruptcy Chapt 11				1121	...	66905	Dc	v□±d3.00	v±1.90	v±d6.55	v±1.88	....	d2.76	9 Mo Sep	v±2.03	v±d2.61	5
6	....	None Since Public			...	Nil	....	2.45	27.5	9.04	9-30-99	40.9	...	4914	Dc	v0.24	v0.42	v0.70	v0.51	....	0.50	9 Mo Sep	v0.41	v0.40	6
7◆	....	h[54]....	2-22-99	2-17	h[54]...	Nil	....	5.32	10.8	4.51	7-31-99	1.66	...	6276	Oc	0.07	0.09	v0.07	vd0.06	Pvd0.16	d0.16				7
8	1953	Q0.20½	2-10-00	1-19	0.81½	0.82	0.78½	5.56	441	265	8-28-99	281	46	14037	Nv	□2.22	3.22	v□2.88	v1.15	E3.23	2.78	9 Mo Aug	v0.50	v2.13	8
9◆	....	h[55]....	11-18-94	11-21	...	Nil	....	10.0	693	183	9-30-99	540	...	49363	Dc	v□0.67	v□0.88	v1.15	v1.82	E2.14	2.02	9 Mo Sep	v1.36	v1.56	9
10◆	....	None Since Public			...	Nil	....	6.42	15.7	28.0	9-28-99	58.0	...	9758	Dc	vΔd3.80	v0.85	vd0.55	vd0.15	....	d0.20	9 Mo Sep	v0.55	v0.50	10
11	....	None Since Public			...	Nil	....	9.89	38.6	10.3	9-30-99	0.13	...	16730	Dc	...	...	vpd0.39	vd0.69	....	d0.60	9 Mo Sep	vd0.48	vd0.39	11
12◆	1968	Q0.018	12-30-99	12-7	0.07	0.07	0.08¾	0.91	155	96.4	9-25-99	183	...	±20520	Je	±0.90	±1.11	v±1.42	v1.57	v±1.81	1.86	3 Mo Sep	v±0.42	v±0.47	12
13	1994	Q0.12½	1-15-00	12-29	1.29½	0.50	1.56	Total Assets $232.83M			9-30-99	161	2875	2847	Dc	v□0.91	Δv0.09	v0.89	v0.70	....	d1.46	9 Mo Sep	v0.48	vd1.68	13
14	1996	Q0.16	11-19-99	11-3	0.64	0.64	0.54	Total Deposits $482M			9-30-99	307	...	6147	Dc	...	v0.71	v1.15	v1.23	....	1.25	9 Mo Sep	v0.92	v0.94	14
15	....	None Since Public			...	Nil	....	Total Assets $255M			9-30-99	5.88	...	±29752	Dc	...	...	pv0.75	n/a	....	....	9 Mo Sep	v0.73	v0.01	15
16	1994	Q0.53	12-31-99	12-15	2.08	2.12	2.02	Total Assets $1479.07M			9-30-99	739	4600	25444	Dc	v□1.25	v□1.36	v□1.53	v1.16	....	1.45	9 Mo Sep	v0.81	v1.10	16
17◆	....	None Since Public			...	Nil	....	6.47	54.5	21.8	10-30-99	....	...	8922	Ja	v0.60	v0.87	v0.91	v0.04	....	0.16	9 Mo Oct	v0.14	v0.26	17
18	....	None Since Public			...	Nil	....	8.30	97.2	8.11	9-30-99	5.44	...	25664	Mr	...	...	...	vpd0.91	....	d0.73	6 Mo Sep	vpd0.42	vpd0.24	18
19◆	1991	Q0.018	1-14-00	12-29	0.07	0.07	0.07	Total Assets $367.62M			9-30-99	18.0	...	20920	Dc	v0.81	v0.74	v0.56	vd0.56	....	0.25	9 Mo Sep	vd0.56	v0.25	19
20◆	....	None Paid			...	Nil	....	0.96	14.9	11.6	9-30-99	2.16	...	9184	Mr	d0.91	vd0.84	v0.07	v0.14	....	0.22	6 Mo Sep	v0.07	v0.15	20
21	....	None Since Public			...	Nil	....	29.7	422	126	7-03-99	687	...	11903	Sp	□0.44	v0.80	v1.14	v□0.97	....	d0.14	9 Mo Jun	v□0.71	vd0.40	21
22	1997	Q0.09	11-19-99	11-3	0.34½	0.36	0.285	12.8	279	309	9-30-99	434	...	90463	Dc	...	pv1.12	pv1.30	v1.86	....	2.18	9 Mo Sep	v1.59	v1.91	22
23◆	....	None Since Public			...	Nil	....	86.4	96.2	11.8	12-31-98	0.01	...	40954	Dc	...	pvd0.03	v0.27	v0.36	....	0.51	9 Mo Sep	v0.26	v0.41	23
24	1985	Q0.40	1-14-00	12-29	1.55	1.60	1.36	65.7	586	573	9-30-99	....	...	18371	Dc	v2.43	v2.52	v3.13	v3.10	....	3.41	9 Mo Sep	v2.24	v2.55	24
25	1997	0.469	11-29-99	9-22	1.344	1.34	1.145	65.6	1910	1415	j12-31-98	1180	...	681229	Dc	...	p0.12	v2.32	v2.09	....	2.42	6 Mo Jun	v0.87	v1.20	25
26◆	1929	Q0.21	1-3-00	12-15	0.81	0.84	0.77	54.3	982	916	9-26-99	2497	...	278771	Dc	v1.59	v3.33	v2.50	v3.50	E3.40	3.26	9 Mo Sep	v2.59	v2.35	26
27◆	1976	Q0.022	12-31-99	12-20	0.089	0.09	0.089	485	2617	2223	10-30-99	809	...	850895	Ja	v0.37	v0.47	v0.58	v0.91	E1.20	1.14	9 Mo Oct	v0.56	v0.79	27
28	1963	†1.05	11-30-99	11-18	†1.80	1.80	†1.50	12.2	105	32.1	6-30-99	2.03	...	5305	Sp	1.08	1.36	v1.92	v2.73	Pv3.49	3.49				28
29◆	....	None Since Public			...	Nil	....	1.24	122	61.6	10-31-99	....	...	15917	Ja	v0.46	v0.45	v0.62	v0.57	....	0.16	9 Mo Oct	v0.01	vd0.40	29
30	....	None Since Public			...	Nil	....	61.8	65.9	4.13	9-30-99	0.02	...	★17507	Je	...	...	...	....	vpd1.71	d1.86	3 Mo Sep	vd0.26	vd0.41	30
31◆	....	None Since Public			...	Nil	....	4.87	43.1	19.1	6-30-99	15.0	...	8840	Dc	0.29	v0.12	vd0.16	vd1.16	....	d2.47	9 Mo Sep	vd1.20	vd2.51	31
32◆	....	None Since Public			...	Nil	....	21.1	157	57.8	9-30-99	94.6	...	15012	Dc	v0.79	v1.11	v1.74	v2.22	....	1.52	9 Mo Sep	v1.56	v0.86	32
33	....	None Since Public			...	Nil	....	256	549	396	3-31-99	....	...	±p87990	Sp	±v0.28	±v0.17	±v0.71	±v0.83	±Pv0.84	0.84				33
34◆	1999	[52]1.20	7-22-99	7-19	[52]1.20	Nil	....	....	...	...		....	...	p52929	Sp	±0.28	±0.17	±0.71	v0.83	vP0.84	0.84				34
35◆	....	None Since Public			...	Nil	....	28.9	71.6	21.9	6-30-99	....	...	14555	Sp	1.21	0.65	v0.21	vd0.41	Pvd0.98	d0.98				35
36◆	....	None Since Public			...	Nil	....	1215	2573	1668	9-30-99	1.97	...	316535	Dc	v0.55	v0.80	v0.35	v1.09	E1.42	1.35	9 Mo Sep	v0.68	v0.94	36
37◆	1919	Q0.275	12-31-99	12-13	1.10	1.10	1.00	Total Assets $5359.00M			9-30-99	2874	...	49156	Dc	2.15	v2.10	vd1.27	v2.62	E3.05	2.87	9 Mo Sep	v2.11	v2.36	37
38	1969	Q0.62½	12-1-99	11-10	2.50	2.50	2.50	Cv into 2.50 common				....	49	...	Dc	...	...	...	....	....	....				38
39	....	None Since Public			...	Nil	....	8.70	233	151	6-30-99	925	...	53457	Sp	2.44	v□0.22	v□d1.40	v□d1.08	Pvd0.87	d0.87				39
40	....	Terms&trad. basis should			be checked in detail			Wrrts expire 11-2-2002				....	...	18009	Sp	...	...	...	....	....	....	Callable at $16.65[58]			40
41	1997	Q0.20	12-20-99	12-2	0.80	0.80	0.65	8.88	186	105	9-30-99	302	...	33029	Dc	...	pv2.26	v□p3.24	v0.94	....	2.89	9 Mo Sep	v0.50	v2.45	41
42	....	None Since Public			...	Nil	....	144	187	181	7-31-99	1.28	...	7796	Oc	1.11	v2.19	v1.90	vd5.39	....	d5.23	9 Mo Jul	v0.14	v0.30	42
43	....	0.04	6-30-91	6-10	...	Nil	....	3.97	129	59.5	10-02-99	9.14	...	5803	Dc	v1.44	v1.54	v1.95	v2.29	....	3.02	9 Mo Sep	v1.79	v2.52	43
44	....	None Since Public			...	Nil	....	62.1	81.1	3.74	9-30-99	3.95	...	p17900	Dc	vd0.85	vd1.60	vd1.80	vd0.72	....	d0.76	9 Mo Sep	vd1.54	vd1.58	44
45◆	....	None Since Public			...	Nil	....	214	227	37.0	3-31-99	....	...	200014	Mr	0.13	vd0.04	v0.19	v0.33	....	0.37	6 Mo Sep	v0.13	v0.17	45
46◆	1996	A0.03	1-22-99	12-29	0.03	0.03	0.02½	8.85	106	48.3	9-30-98	89.5	...	±9312	Sp	Δ±0.30	±0.39	v±0.74	v±1.52	....	1.52				46
47	1937	0.03	11-30-99	10-28	h[60]0.48	0.60	0.60	21.0	530	453	8-31-99	341	...	41798	Nv	1.17	1.24	v3.40	v1.99	....	2.43	9 Mo Aug	v1.22	v1.66	47
48	....	None Since Public			...	Nil	....	11.1	11.7	6.28	9-30-99	0.65	10	40011	Dc	d0.38	vd0.32	vd0.33	vd0.17	....	d0.25	9 Mo Sep	vd0.12	vd0.20	48
49◆	....	None Since Public			...	Nil	....	689	1173	355	9-30-99	150	...	256677	Dc	...	...	...	vpd0.88	....	....	9 Mo Sep	n/a	vd7.59	49
50	1994	0.201	4-30-99	4-14	0.338	0.44	0.504	72.7	291	140	j12-31-98	638	...	5586821	Dc	1.83	1.59	n/a	v1.13	....	1.13				50

◆**Stock Splits & Divs By Line Reference Index** [1]2-for-1,'95. [3]3-for-2,'94:2-for-1,'97:10%,'96,'98. [7]3-for-2,'99. [9]No adj for stk dstr Converse & Florsheim Shoe,'94. [10]1-for-15 REVERSE,'96:2-for-1&1-for-10 REVERSE,'99. [12]3-for-2,'94. [17]3-for-2,'96. [19]Adj to 5%,Sep'95. [20]1-for-7 REVERSE,'99. [23]2-for-1,'99. [26]2-for-1,'97. [27]2-for-1,'96:3-for-2,'97,'98,'99. [29]2-for-1,'96. [31]3-for-2,'94. [32]2-for-1,'97:3-for-2,'97. [34]2-for-1,'95,'96. [35]3-for-2,'95. [36]2-for-1,'97,'99. [37]2-for-1,'98. [45]2-for-1,'99(twice). [46]2-for-1,'97,'98. [49]2-for-1,'99.

¶ S&P 500
# MidCap 400
✣ SmallCap 600
• Options

Index	Ticker	Name of Issue (Call Price of Pfd. Stocks)	Market	Com. Rank. & Pfd. Rating	Inst. Hold Cos	Inst. Hold Shs. (000)	Principal Business	Price Range 1971-97 High	1971-97 Low	1998 High	1998 Low	1999 High	1999 Low	December, 1999 Dec. Sales in 100s	Last Sale Or Bid High	Low	Last	%Div Yield	P-E Ratio	EPS 5 Yr Growth	% Annualized Total Return 12 Mo	36 Mo	60 Mo
1	GBND	✔Genl Binding	NNM	B+	50	3971	Mfr business machines & sup	33¼	2 1/16	42½	26½	40	6	5870	11¾	6⅝	11¾	...	d	Neg	-68.0	-25.6	-8.1
2•[1]	BGC	✔Genl Cable	NY	NR	145	28634	Dvp copper wire/cable pds	26 1/16	13 9/16	32 15/16	11½	22⅞	6 7/16	58466	8 1/16	6 7/16	7 9/16	2.6	5	68	-62.5	...	...
3	GCG	✔Genl Chemical Group	NY,Ch	NR	42	6126	Produce inorganic chemicals	33⅜	16⅝	30⅞	12 15/16	19 15/16	1⅞	5571	2 13/16	2	2 5/16	...	1	...	...	...	...
4•[2]	MPP	✔Genl Cigar 'A'	NY,Ch,Ph	NR	60	9052	Mfr premium cigars	34	18	21¾	5½	10⅝	5⅝	10873	9 1/16	6⅞	8 5/16	...	2	...	-4.3	...	...
✣5	GNCMA	✔Genl Communication'A'	NNM	B	103	19113	Long distance telecom svcs	9¼	⅞	8⅜	2½	8	3¾	74697	5 13/16	3⅞	4⅜	...	d	Neg	7.7	-18.6	2.5
6	GDC	✔Genl DataComm Ind	NY,B,Ch,P	B	29	4493	Data communic'n netwk/eq	35⅞	1/16	6⅜	2	7¼	2 1/16	42562	7 3/16	5½	6⅝	...	d	-31	187	-14.2	-27.2
¶7•[3]	GD	✔Genl Dynamics	NY,B,C,Ch,P,Ph,Mo	B+	658	129572	Armored/space launch vehicles	45¾	11/16	62	40¼	75 7/16	46 3/16	187574	53¼	46 3/16	52¾	1.8	17	14	-9.2	16.6	22.2
¶8•[4]	GE	✔Genl Electric	NY,B,C,Ch,P,Ph	A+	2401	1716646	Consumer/ind'l prod,broad'cst	76 9/16	1⅞	103 15/16	69	159½	94 1/16	1300039	159½	130 1/16	154¾	1.1	48	16	53.6	48.5	46.2
9	JOB	✔Genl Employ Enterpr	AS,Ch	B	11	296	Personnel placement service	16⅝	¼	15⅛	4¼	6 3/16	3½	2568	5	4 5/16	4¾	1.1	8	35	-6.2	10.4	16.7
10	GGP	✔Genl Growth Properties	NY,P	NR	196	38191	Real estate investment trust	38⅜	18⅛	39¼	32½	38⅝	25	68073	30	25	28	7.3	15	16	-21.6	0.7	11.1
11	Pr A	7.25%'A'cm[53]Dep'PIERS'([54]25.8055)	NY	BB+	27	6805		....	....	25⅞	22 7/16	25 9/16	17¾	7522	21	17¾	20	9.1	..	...	...	...	...
¶12•[5]	GIC	✔Genl Instrument[56]	NY	NR	624	112491	Mfr communication pds	21½	12⅝	36 15/16	16 7/16	85 11/16	28⅛	229080	85 11/16	65⅛	85	...	90	...	151	...	...
13•[6]	GMGC	Genl Magic	NNM	NR	37	2341	Dvlp stge:spcl softwr tech	32	15/16	15 7/16	1¼	7 15/16	1 5/16	603514	4¾	2⅝	3⅞	...	d	-8	-23.0	18.8	...
¶14•[7]	GIS	✔Genl Mills	NY,B,C,Ch,P,Ph	B+	847	211372	Consumer foods,restaurants	39⅛	1¾	39 13/16	29 9/16	43 15/16	32½	296916	38 9/16	32½	35¾	3.1	19	8	11.7	13.2	...
¶15•[4]	GM	✔Genl Motors	NY,To,B,C,Ch,P,Ph,Mo	B	1249	406007	Largest mfr automotive prods	72 7/16	14 7/16	76 11/16	47 1/16	94⅞	59¾	541650	79 1/16	69¾	72 11/16	2.8	9	3	...	...	...
16•[2]	GMH	✔Genl Motors Cl'H'[59]	NY,B	B	393	81619	High technology electronics	68 15/16	13⅛	57⅞	30⅜	97⅝	38½	156676	97⅝	83⅝	96	...	d	-17	142	20.2	23.8
✣17	SEM	✔Genl Semiconductor[56]	NY	NR	..	...	Power semiconductors	17½	9⅞	15 3/16	5 13/16	15¼	5¾	96740	15¼	12⅜	14 3/16	...	44	...	73.3	...	...
18	GCO	✔Genesco Inc	NY,B,Ch,Ph,P	B–	112	15080	Apparel & footwear:shoe strs	39¾	1⅝	18⅞	3 15/16	14⅝	5⅜	25553	13⅞	10 13/16	13	...	7	NM	129	12.0	43.7
19	GNWR	✔Genesee & Wyoming'A'	NNM	NR	34	1839	Provide rail freight trans	37¾	17	27½	11⅜	15¼	7¾	3563	13 7/16	11⅝	12⅞	...	4	...	1.0	-28.2	...
20	GEL	✔Genesis Energy L.P.	NY,Ch	NR	15	378	Crude oil gathering,mkt'g	21½	16⅜	20⅜	13⅝	16 5/16	6⅝	13037	9⅜	6⅝	8 1/16	...	18	...	-34.7	-17.6	...
✣21•[8]	GHV	✔Genesis Hlth Ventures	NY,Ch,Ph,P	C	109	8985	Provide geriatric hlth svcs	39¾	4 3/16	30 9/16	7	9½	1 9/16	76094	2 15/16	1 13/16	2 1/16	...	d	Neg	-75.7	-59.5	-37.1
22•[4]	GNSS	✔Genesis Microchip	NNM	NR	76	9008	Dgn/dvp digital image sys	....	....	24 13/16	5⅞	35 13/16	15	296405	27⅞	17 15/16	21⅛	...	..	...	-12.9	...	...
23	GWO	✔Genesis Worldwide	NY,B,Ch,P	B–	28	1281	Lathes for metal-wkg indy	32¾	2⅛	8 15/16	6¼	9⅜	3⅛	5711	4⅜	3⅛	3 3/16	...	16	NM	-52.2	-25.6	-18.8
24	GCTI	✔Genesys Telecommunications	NNM	NR	129	11446	Telecommunication software	39⅝	18	39¾	9⅛	54½	10 11/16	52681	54½	50⅝	54	...	d	...	143	...	...
25	GEB	✔Genetronics Biomedical	AS,To	NR	6	773	Biotechnology R&D	4 7/16	2 9/16	6 5/16	2⅜	4⅛	2¼	7928	3½	2¾	3¼	...	d	...	-1.9	...	...
26•[5]	GECM	✔Genicom Corp	NNM	C	15	1760	Mfrs/mkts computer printers	16½	⅞	13⅛	2	4 1/16	¼	46210	1¾	11/16	¾	...	d	Neg	-67.6	-42.3	-22.1
27	GEN	✔GenRad, Inc	NY,B,Ch,P,Ph	B–	110	19179	Electr test & measurement pr	46⅜	1½	33 1/16	10 3/16	22⅜	13¼	27615	18½	14 15/16	16⅛	...	14	-33	2.4	-11.5	21.9
28	GENXY	✔Genset ADR[63]	NNM	NR	26	4353	R&D human gene pds	25⅜	13¼	38	17⅝	29	7⅞	17669	20⅜	9½	19 1/16	...	d	-17	-31.0	6.0	...
29	GK	✔GenTek Inc	NY	NR	51	6651	Auto parts & accessories	....	....	....	....	15 15/16	7 3/16	3029	11⅝	10 3/16	10 7/16	1.9	5	...	...	...	...
✣30•[9]	GNTX	✔Gentex Corp	NNM	B+	276	47764	Mfr optical/elec devices	14⅛	⅛	22	10¾	34⅞	16	151568	29 1/16	18½	27¾	...	32	31	38.8	40.4	35.8
¶31•[10]	GPC	✔Genuine Parts	NY,B,Ch,P	A+	487	125676	Distrib auto replacement parts	35⅞	2¼	38¼	28¼	35¾	22¼	103158	26¼	22¼	24 13/16	4.2	12	6	-23.2	-2.4	4.1
#32•[11]	GENZ	✔Genzyme Corp-Genl Div	NNM	B–	480	70227	Biological health care prod	38½	2⅞	50	23½	63⅛	30¾	270012	48⅜	33 9/16	45	...	24	52	...	...	...
✣33•[12]	GON	✔Geon Co	NY,P	NR	201	22415	Mfr polyvinyl chloride resins	31⅝	17¾	26	16¼	37	21 9/16	15329	33 3/16	27½	32½	1.5	8	3	43.7	20.9	5.7
#34•[12]	GGC	✔Georgia Gulf Corp	NY,Ch,Ph,P	B–	124	17964	Integrated chemical producer	59⅞	4⅞	36¾	14½	31⅛	10	44822	31⅛	24 11/16	30 7/16	1.1	28	-23	93.6	5.9	-3.5
¶35•[13]	GP	✔Georgia-Pacific (Ga-Pac Grp)	NY,B,C,Ch,P,Ph	B–	709	129121	Plywood,lumber,paper,gyps'm	54¼	6⅝	40½	18 11/16	54⅛	29 5/16	267614	50⅞	38 11/16	50¾	1.0	13	-26	75.9	...	...
#36	TGP	✔Georgia-Pacific (Timber Grp)	NY	NR	273	59633	Grow,sell timber/wood fiber	28½	22½	27¼	17⅜	27 3/16	19⅞	23534	25 13/16	23¾	24⅝	4.1	9	...	7.8	...	...
37	GPW	Georgia-Pacific 7.50%'PEPS'Units[66]	NY	NR	19	3189	Premium Equity Part Sec	....	....	....	....	53⅝	40½	22741	51⅛	41⅝	51	7.4	..	...	...	...	...
38	GPD	Georgia Power 6.875%'PINES'	NY	....[68]	2	3	Sr Public Income Notes	....	....	25⅜	23⅜	25¼	18⅞	3472	21	18⅞	19 7/16	8.8	..	...	-16.2	...	...
39	GPB	Georgia Power 6.60% Sr Notes'B'	NY	....[69]	1	.1	Electric utility,Georgia	....	....	25 7/16	25	26 3/16	19 9/16	4977	21½	19 9/16	20	8.3	..	...	-16.5	...	...
40	GPF	Georgia Power 6.625% Sr Notes 'D'	NY	....[71]	1	1	Electric utility, Georgia	....	....	....	....	25 7/16	19⅜	3529	21¼	19⅜	20⅛	8.2	..	...	...	...	...
41	GCW	✔Gerber Childrenswear	NY	NR	18	1733	Infant/toddler apparel prod	....	....	16⅝	5¼	8¾	3¾	4965	5	4	5	...	6	...	-42.4	...	...
✣42•[5]	GRB	✔Gerber Scientific	NY,B,Ch,P,Ph	B	160	16101	Automated manufacturing sys	24½	1/16	29 15/16	17 11/16	24⅞	17⅜	12063	21 15/16	18	21 15/16	1.5	16	11	-6.4	15.6	13.0
43	GGB	✔Gerdau S.A. ADS[72]	NY	NR	5	260	Mfr long rolled steel,Brazil	....	....	....	....	27	8 5/16	2148	27	19 9/16	26⅛B	2.8	..	...	...	...	...
44•[4]	GERN	Geron Corp	NNM	NR	41	1498	Biopharmaceutical R&D	18½	5⅜	24½	3½	20	9¼	207202	20	10 5/16	12⅝	...	d	-3	16.1	-1.6	...
45	GTHR	✔GetThere.com Inc	NNM	NR	..	...	Internet based travel svcs	....	....	....	....	52¼	16	100371	52¼	24	40¼	...	..	...	...	...	...
46	GPM	✔Getty Petroleum Mktg	NY,Ch	NR	26	2421	Petroleum products mkt/dstr	7⅜	3¼	6¾	2⅝	3½	2 3/16	3082	3 1/16	2 3/16	2 7/16	...	6	...	-17.0	...	...
47	GTY	✔Getty Realty	NY,B,Ch,Ph	B–	45	4011	Property leasing R/E dvlp	25	3/16	24¾	12⅛	16½	10 13/16	1767	12¾	10 13/16	11 3/16	3.6	15	21	-21.3	...	...
48	Pr A	$1.775 Series'A'Cv Pfd([74]25)	NY	NR	4	14		....	....	29	18¼	22	19 1/16	107	19½	19¼	19¼B	9.2	..	...	...	...	...
49	GPO	✔GIANT Group	NY,B,Ch	B–	16	586	Oper fast food restaurants	20½	2 13/16	9¾	5⅛	9 13/16	2½	3685	4 11/16	2½	3½	...	d	Neg	-61.6	-25.2	-12.3
50	GI	✔Giant Industries	NY	B–	51	4586	Oil & gas explor,devel,prod'n	20⅝	3⅜	23 11/16	8 9/16	12 9/16	5⅝	5738	8⅞	6 13/16	8⅜	...	9	-39	-10.7	-15.0	3.5

Uniform Footnote Explanations-See Page 4. Other: [1]ASE,CBOE:Cycle 2. [2]CBOE:Cycle 1. [3]CBOE:Cycle 2. [4]CBOE:Cycle 3. [5]Ph:Cycle 3. [6]ASE,CBOE,P:Cycle 2. [7]P:Cycle 1. [8]ASE:Cycle 3. [9]P:Cycle 3. [10]P:Cycle 2. [11]ASE,CBOE:Cycle 1. [12]Ph:Cycle 2. [13]Ph:Cycle 1. [51]Stk dstr of GenTek Inc,'99. [52]Incl current amts. [53]Dep for 0.025 shr 7.25% Sr'A"PIERS'. [54]Preferred Income Equity Redeem Stk. [55]Co opt fr 7-15-2003 redm for com,re-spec cond. [56]Formed from dstr Genl Instrument,'97. [57]Stk dstr of Delphi Automotive Sys. [58]Incl curr amts. [59]Vtg:co option to exch for com. [60]To be determined. [61]Fiscal May'98 & prior. [62]Fiscal Feb'97 & prior. [63]Ea ADR rep 0.333 ord shr FF 17. [64]Stk dstr of Genzyme Surgical Products. [65]Stk dstr of Genzyme Molecular Oncology,'98. [66]Sr Deferrable Notes & Purchase Contract. [67]To 8-16-2002 re-spec cond. [68]Rated 'A' by S&P. [69]Rated'AAA'by S&P. [70]Total issue amt in $M. [71]Rated 'AAA' by S&P. [72]Ea ADS rep 1000 Pfd Shrs,no par. [73]Approx. [74]Fr1-31-2001,if com exceeds$22.10 10(out90)days.

Splits ◆ Index	Cash Divs. Ea. Yr. Since	Dividends Latest Payment Period $	Date	Ex. Div.	Total $ So Far 1999	Ind. Rate	Paid 1998	Financial Position Mil-$ Cash& Equiv.	Curr. Assets	Curr. Liab.	Balance Sheet Date	Capitalization Lg Trm Debt Mil-$	Shs. 000 Pfd.	Com.	Earnings $ Per Shr. Years End	1995	1996	1997	1998	1999	Last 12 Mos.	Interim Earnings Period	$ per Shr. 1998	1999	Index
1	1975	Div Omitted 11-2-99			0.30	Nil	0.45	76.9	433	157	9-30-99	540	...	±15737	Dc	±v1.36	v±1.59	v±1.80	v±1.50	....	d1.66	9 Mo Sep	v±1.14	v±d2.02	1
2◆	1997	0.05	11-11-99	10-27	0.20	0.20	0.167	88.2	1147	584	9-30-99	827	...	34659	Dc	v0.69	pv1.08	v1.44	v1.90	....	1.54	9 Mo Sep	v1.43	v1.07	2
3	1996	Div Discontinued 4-30-99			h[51]0.05	Nil	0.20	35.0	121	56.7	9-30-99	151	...	±20818	Dc	pv1.07	±v2.13	±v2.50	v□2.35	....	2.15	9 Mo Sep	v±0.40	v±0.20	3
4	....	None Since Public			...	Nil	....	104	305	90.2	8-28-99	10.4	...	±26555	Nv	...	±p0.70	p±1.26	v0.92	....	4.17	9 Mo Aug	v0.69	v3.94	4
5	....	None Paid			...	Nil	....	13.4	63.6	47.2	9-30-99	341	...	±50628	Dc	v0.32	v0.28	v□d0.04	vd0.14	....	d0.15	9 Mo Sep	v±d0.12	v±d0.13	5
6	....	None Since Public			...	Nil	....	4.58	72.6	51.3	6-30-99	64.1	800	±21921	Sp	d1.40	vd0.83	vd2.11	vd1.64	Pv±d1.12	d1.12				6
7◆	1979	Q0.24	2-11-00	1-12	0.94	0.96	0.86½	69.0	3744	3638	10-03-99	233	...	200973	Dc	v2.54	v2.12	v2.49	v2.86	E3.20	4.12	9 Mo Sep	v2.12	v3.38	7
8◆	1899	Q0.41	1-25-00	12-22	1.40	1.64	1.20	Total Assets $380224M			9-30-99	66338	...	p3280992	Dc	v1.93	v2.16	v2.46	v2.80	E3.20	3.10	9 Mo Sep	v1.99	v2.29	8
9◆	1996	0.05	1-18-99	12-15	0.043	0.05	0.039	10.9	15.0	4.50	6-30-99	....	...	5088	Sp	0.22	0.33	v0.48	v0.58	Pv0.59	0.59				9
10	1993	0.51	1-31-00	1-4	1.94	2.04	1.86	Total Assets $5256.53M			9-30-99	[52]3378	338	51697	Dc	v1.69	v□2.20	□v2.76	v□1.59	....	1.87	9 Mo Sep	v1.04	v□1.32	10
11	1998	Q0.453	1-14-00	1-4	1.812	1.812	0.559	Cv into 0.6297 com				....	12000	...	Dc	...	...	...	...	....	....	Mand Redm 7-15-2008 at $25[55]			11
12◆	....	None Since Public			...	Nil	....	631	1257	483	9-30-99	....	...	174024	Dc	...	pvd0.65	vd0.11	v0.33	E0.94	0.79	9 Mo Sep	v0.06	v0.52	12
13	....	None Since Public			...	Nil	....	14.1	15.5	10.0	9-30-99	....	1	41254	Dc	vd0.84	vd1.74	vd1.06	vd2.09	....	d1.51	9 Mo Sep	vd1.58	vd1.00	13
14◆	1898	Q0.275	2-1-00	1-6	1.10	1.10	1.06	46.0	1253	2018	8-29-99	1687	...	303840	My	1.17	v1.47	v1.38	v1.30	v1.70	1.90	6 Mo Nov	v0.92	v1.12	14
15◆	1915	Q0.50	12-10-99	11-8	h[57]2.00	2.00	2.00	Total Assets $261942M			9-30-99	[58]123209	p28051	640208	Dc	v□7.28	v6.02	v8.62	v4.18	E8.51	9.90	9 Mo Sep	v1.60	v7.32	15
16◆	....	0.25	12-10-97	11-10	...	Nil	....	158	3639	2596	9-30-99	1929	...	135138	Dc	pv0.07	pv0.46	□pv1.23	v□0.70	Ed0.25↓	0.15	9 Mo Sep	v□0.38	vd0.17	16
17	....	None Since Public			...	Nil	....	5.85	132	60.7	9-30-99	290	...	36835	Dc	p0.47	vd0.50	v0.17	v0.50	....	0.32	9 Mo Sep	v0.60	v0.42	17
18	....	0.17	4-30-73	4-9	...	Nil	....	38.5	211	75.9	10-30-99	104	176	22002	Ja	v0.40	v0.39	□v0.32	v□1.90	....	1.89	9 Mo Oct	v□0.61	v0.60	18
19	....	None Since Public			...	Nil	....	16.7	70.3	58.1	9-30-99	120	...	±4299	Dc	p□v0.92	v1.49	v1.47	v2.19	....	3.13	9 Mo Sep	v1.04	v1.98	19
20	1997	0.50	11-15-99	10-27	2.00	[60]....	2.00	2.44	259	277	9-30-99	....	...	8604	Dc	p1.92	pv1.81	v0.90	v0.80	....	0.46	9 Mo Sep	v0.59	v0.25	20
21◆	....	None Since Public			...	Nil	....	38.8	606	236	6-30-99	1469	...	p48646	Sp	□1.13	1.35	v□1.34	v□d0.68	Pv□d8.11	d8.11				21
22	....	None Since Public			...	Nil	....	36.1	53.3	4.05	2-28-99	0.60	...	14439	Mr	d0.48	d0.59	vd0.62	v[61]0.29	....	....	3 Mo Jun	n/a	v0.27	22
23	1913	Div Omitted 8-4-99			0.10	Nil	0.20	1.45	66.5	143	9-30-99	15.6	15	4283	Dc	v0.21	vd1.47	vd1.12	v0.55	....	0.20	9 Mo Sep	v0.42	v0.07	23
24	....	None Since Public			...	Nil	....	72.7	132	43.4	9-30-99	0.06	...	25458	Je	...	pd0.18	v0.04	v0.30	vd0.11	d0.05	3 Mo Sep	v0.15	v0.21	24
25	....	None Since Public			...	Nil	....	12.7	14.4	1.71	9-30-99	0.09	...	22233	Mr	vd0.17	v[62]d0.24	vd0.43	vd0.33	....	d0.31	6 Mo Sep	vd0.26	vd0.24	25
26	....	None Since Public			...	Nil	....	0.01	0.13	0.19	10-03-99	105	...	11735	Dc	v0.51	v□0.17	v0.63	vd1.91	....	d3.71	9 Mo Sep	vd1.32	vd3.12	26
27	....	0.05	10-15-85	9-25	...	Nil	....	7.00	176	75.3	10-02-99	4.17	...	29746	Dc	v0.56	v1.11	v1.43	vd0.32	....	1.15	9 Mo Sep	vd0.25	v1.22	27
28	....	None Since Public			...	Nil	....	58.8	74.6	21.5	12-31-98	8.99	...	7420	Dc	d0.54	vd0.75	vd0.75	vd0.79	....	d1.06	9 Mo Sep	vd0.47	vd0.74	28
29	1999	0.05	12-30-99	12-14	0.15	0.20	....	34.5	417	295	9-30-99	712	...	±20818	Dc	...	...	...	pv±2.47	....	2.12	9 Mo Sep	v□1.72	v□1.37	29
30◆	....	None Since Public			...	Nil	....	79.8	129	24.2	9-30-99	....	...	73286	Dc	v0.28	v0.34	v0.49	v0.68	....	0.87	9 Mo Sep	v0.45	v0.64	30
31◆	1948	Q0.26	1-3-00	12-1	1.03	1.04	0.99	76.5	2857	921	9-30-99	675	...	177810	Dc	v1.68	v1.81	v1.90	v1.98	E2.14	2.08	9 Mo Sep	v1.40	v1.50	31
32◆	....	h[64]....	6-28-99	6-29	h[64]...	Nil	h[65]....	424	717	203	9-30-99	272	...	84130	Dc	v0.68	vd0.45	v0.98	v1.48	E1.85	1.29	9 Mo Sep	v1.57	v1.38	32
33	1993	Q0.12½	12-15-99	11-29	0.50	0.50	0.50	62.0	394	461	9-30-99	127	...	23709	Dc	v1.24	v0.50	v0.95	v0.58	E4.29	3.67	9 Mo Sep	v0.71	v□3.80	33
34	1995	Q0.08	1-10-00	12-16	0.32	0.32	0.32	3.21	144	108	9-30-99	397	...	30967	Dc	v4.73	v1.98	v2.39	v1.78	E1.10	0.81	9 Mo Sep	v1.36	v0.39	34
35◆	1927	Q0.12½	11-29-99	11-10	0.50	0.50	0.50	64.0	4410	3953	10-02-99	5010	...	170988	Dc	5.65	□v0.19	vd0.47	v□0.61	E4.00↓	3.22	9 Mo Sep	v□0.46	v3.07	35
36	1998	Q0.25	11-29-99	11-10	1.00	1.00	1.00	64.0	4410	3953	10-02-99	[52]4588	...	82858	Dc	...	pv1.40	v2.35	v□1.96	....	2.83	9 Mo Sep	v□1.42	v2.29	36
37	1999	1.344	11-16-99	11-10	1.344	3.75	....	Pur contract for Georgia-Pacific Com[67]				....	...	★15000	Dc	...	...	...	...	....	....	Note matures 8-16-2004			37
38	1998	Q0.43	12-31-99	12-14	1.72	1.718	1.596	Redeemable at $25 fr 1-27-2003				★145	...	...	Dc	...	...	...	...	....	....	Due 12-31-2047			38
39	1999	Q0.41¼	12-31-99	12-14	1.65	1.65	....	Co option redm fr 11-2-2003 at $25				....	...	[70]200	Dc	...	...	...	...	....	....	Mature 12-31-2038			39
40	1999	Q0.414	12-31-99	12-14	1.339	1.656	....	Co option redm fr 3-9-2004 at $25				[70]100	...	...	Dc	...	...	...	...	....	....	Mature 3-31-2035			40
41	....	None Since Public			...	Nil	....	4.82	144	55.2	10-02-99	14.6	...	±16999	Dc	...	...	pv0.50	±v□0.87	....	0.80	9 Mo Sep	v□0.64	v0.57	41
42	1978	Q0.08	11-30-99	11-10	0.32	0.32	0.32	20.2	254	121	10-31-99	189	...	22177	Ap	0.76	v0.84	v0.69	v0.32	v1.29	1.38	6 Mo Oct	v0.62	v0.71	42
43	1999	[73]0.505	3-10-00		0.551	0.73	....	156	971	488	12-31-98	769	...	56513000	Dc	...	...	n/a	n/a	....	....				43
44	....	None Since Public			...	Nil	....	41.7	42.9	6.75	9-30-99	21.8	...	16788	Dc	pvd1.34	pvd1.26	vd0.91	vd1.00	....	d2.92	9 Mo Sep	vd0.63	vd2.55	44
45	....	None Since Public			...	Nil	....	7.40	8.85	10.2	p7-31-99	p5.36	p...	★31345	Ja	...	...	...	vpd1.05		....	3 Mo Jul	n/a	vpd1.26	45
46	....	None Since Public			...	Nil	....	12.3	58.4	70.3	10-31-99	....	...	13949	Ja	...	n/a	v0.09	v0.04	....	0.42	9 Mo Oct	vd0.35	v0.03	46
47◆	1995	Q0.10	1-13-00	12-28	0.40	0.40	0.30	Total Assets $261.93M			10-31-99	43.1	2889	13567	Ja	v□1.06	vd0.72	v0.60	v0.36	....	0.75	9 Mo Oct	v0.17	v0.56	47
48	1998	Q0.44⅜	2-14-00	1-27	1.77½	1.775	0.85¾	Cv into 1.1312 com				....	2889	...	Ja	...	...	...	...	....	....				48
49	....	60.50	10-1-79	9-10	...	Nil	....	10.6	28.4	11.2	9-30-99	1.52	...	3990	Dc	vd4.37	v4.07	vd1.42	v0.15	....	d0.62	9 Mo Sep	v0.55	vd0.22	49
50	1995	Div suspended 10-1-98			...	Nil	0.20	30.6	181	115	9-30-99	258	...	10433	Dc	v0.68	v1.52	v1.37	vd0.20	....	0.93	9 Mo Sep	vd0.05	v1.08	50

◆**Stock Splits & Divs By Line Reference Index** [2]3-for-2,'98. [7]2-for-1,'94,'98. [8]2-for-1,'97:Vote Apr 26,'00 on 3-for-1. [9]3-for-2,'97:10%,'98:15%,'95,'96,'99. [12]No adj for stk dstr,'99. [14]2-for-1,'99. [15]No adj for stk dstr,'99. [16]No adj for spin-off,'97. [21]3-for-2,'96. [30]2-for-1,'96,'98. [31]3-for-2,'97. [32]2-for-1,'96:No adj for stk dstr,'97. [35]No adj for stk dstr,'97:2-for-1,'99. [47]No adj for stk dstr Getty Pete Mktg'97.

¶ S&P 500
# MidCap 400
✣ SmallCap 600
• Options

Index	Ticker	Name of Issue (Call Price of Pfd. Stocks)	Market	Com. Rank. & Pfd. Rating	Inst. Hold Cos	Inst. Hold Shs. (000)	Principal Business	Price Range 1971-97 High	1971-97 Low	1998 High	1998 Low	1999 High	1999 Low	December, 1999 Dec. Sales in 100s	Last Sale Or Bid High	Last Sale Or Bid Low	Last Sale Or Bid Last	%Div Yield	P-E Ratio	EPS 5 Yr Growth	% Annualized Total Return 12 Mo	36 Mo	60 Mo
1	ROCK	✓Gibralter Steel	NNM	NR	81	6021	Processor value-added steel pd	28	9¾	25¾	14⅜	26	17	2518	25¾	22	23⅜	e0.4	12	17	3.2	−3.6	16.9
✣2•[1]	GIBG	✓Gibson Greetings	NNM	B−	83	7006	Mfr greet'g cards/wrappings	32	8	29¼	8¾	12⅜	3¾	24868	9 13/16	8 9/16	9	...	d	99	−24.5	−23.0	−9.5
3•[2]	GILTF	✓Gilat Satellite Networks	NNM	NR	161	13551	Mfr satellite stations & hubs	41½	8	57¼	21¼	125¼	41¾	72368	125¼	76 15/16	118¾	...	d	Neg	115	68.9	58.2
4	GIL	✓Gildan Activewear'A'	NY,To	NR	47	4592	Mfr/dstr basic activewear	....	....	9⅝	6	24¼	7⅜	12367	23⅝	16⅝	18⅛	...	9	...	116	...	...
#5•[3]	GILD	✓Gilead Sciences	NNM	C	265	33221	Nucleotide pharmaceut'l R&D	47¼	6⅝	44¼	18	95½	35¼	158589	55⅞	37	54⅛	...	d	−10	31.8	29.4	41.6
¶6•[4]	G	✓Gillette Co	NY,B,C,Ch,P,Ph	A	1381	641232	Shaving, personal care: pens	53 3/16	9/16	62⅝	35 5/16	64⅜	33 1/16	688765	45 7/16	39⅝	41 3/16	1.4	36	7	−12.8	3.0	18.5
7	GISH	✓Gish Biomedical	NNM	C	9	317	Mfr disposable medical prod	17⅜	¼	5	2	3⅞	2	2584	3⅞	3 1/16	3⅜	...	d	Neg	28.6	−22.0	−11.9
8	GBCI	✓Glacier Bancorp	NNM	A+	28	1381	Savings bank,Montana	20 11/16	11/16	24⅜	17 3/16	24⅜	14⅞	1403	17⅝	15¼	16⅛	e3.7	13	8	−9.9	13.0	24.9
9	HOO	✓Glacier Water Services	AS	NR	16	1926	Oper drink'g wtr vending sys	31¼	8	32	24½	26¾	15⅛	375	16¼	15⅛	15¾B	...	d	Neg	−39.4	−11.7	−3.9
10•[5]	GLG	✓Glamis Gold Ltd	NY,Ch,Ph,P	C	39	11087	Explor,dev gold mineral prop	10⅛	1/16	4 15/16	1 11/16	3 5/16	1¼	51198	2 1/16	1⅝	1 13/16	...	d	Neg	−3.4	−36.1	−26.8
#11•[6]	GLT	✓Glatfelter (P. H.)	NY,Ch,P	B−	150	29303	Mfr printing/writing paper	29 13/16	5/16	19⅛	11 3/16	16½	9 1/16	13971	16⅛	12¼	14 9/16	4.8	20	NM	24.1	−2.4	3.1
12•[7]	GLX	✓Glaxo Wellcome plc[52] ADR	NY,Ch,P,Ph	NR	357	44213	Ethical pharmaceuticals	48½	¼	69 11/16	47⅛	76 3/16	48 1/16	84932	61 15/16	51⅜	55⅞	2.1	33	10	−17.8	23.7	26.3
13	GLE	✓Gleason Corp[54]	NY,Ch,P	B	78	5676	Bevel gear mchy: tooling	29⅝	2 3/16	35½	14¼	23⅝	15⅞	10842	23⅝	17¾	23¼	1.1	14	13	30.1	13.5	27.6
14•[5]	GEMS	✓Glenayre Technologies	NNM,Ch	B	81	24139	Mfr telecommunications eqp	53¾	⅝	17	4	13	2¼	641358	13	5½	11 5/16	...	..	Neg	155	−19.3	−7.6
15	GLB	✓Glenborough Realty Trust	NY,P	NR	176	23040	Real estate investment trust	30⅜	12	32¼	18	19 15/16	11 9/16	44583	13 9/16	12	13⅜	12.6	16	NM	−27.4	−1.8	...
16	Pr A	7.75%'A'cm Cv Pfd(25.97[55])	NY	NR	38	7947		....	....	27 5/16	16¾	20 3/16	13 1/16	7466	14 15/16	13⅛	13 15/16	13.9	..	...	...	...	...
17	GRT	✓Glimcher Realty Trust	NY,Ch,P	NR	99	9642	Real estate investment trust	23 5/16	15⅛	23⅛	14¾	18⅛	12 5/16	21967	14¼	12 5/16	12⅞	14.9	13	1	−7.0	−7.2	−0.3
¶18•[8]	GBLX	✓Global Crossing Ltd	NNM	NR	426	233732	Diversified telecommunication svcs	....	....	24¼	8	64¼	18 15/16	2154086	55¾	42	50	...	d	...	122	...	...
19•[9]	GIX	✓Global Industrial Tech[58]	NY,P	NR	137	13282	Minerals&refract'y prd/ind eq	25	6⅜	18⅝	5 9/16	13½	8½	20000	12 15/16	11⅞	12⅞	...	..	...	20.5	−16.5	−2.0
20•[1]	GLBL	✓Global Industries	NNM	NR	209	45834	Provides offshore O&G svcs	23½	1⅝	25¾	4¾	13¼	4 15/16	198114	8¾	6 3/16	8⅝	...	..	−20	40.8	−2.0	25.2
21	GBT	✓Global Light Telecommun	AS	NR	17	4979	Worldwide telecommun svcs	....	....	5⅛	2 15/16	14	3⅝	32312	14	10	12⅜	...	d	...	175	...	...
#22•[8]	GLM	✓Global Marine	NY,P	B−	315	83479	Oil & gas contract drilling	36 13/16	⅜	26¾	8¼	19⅞	7½	441994	17⅛	14	16⅝	...	32	NM	84.7	−6.9	35.6
23	GLO	✓Global Ocean Carriers	AS,P	NR	2	202	Ocean shipping fleet	15½	1½	3⅞	⅝	15/16	¼	1190	⅞	5/16	⅜	...	d	Neg	−50.0	−48.0	−34.7
24	GAI	✓Global-Tech Appliances	NY	NR	5	2763	Mfr household appliances	....	....	21⅝	3⅞	7 1/16	3⅞	2860	7 1/16	5 1/16	6⅞	...	13	16	41.0	...	...
25	GTN	✓Global Technovations[62]	AS,P	C	15	1983	Transportation related tech	9 3/16	⅛	1½	½	1¾	½	31866	1⅛	½	⅞	...	6	7	−12.5	−29.5	−33.0
26•[10]	GTS	✓Global TeleSystems Grp	NY	NR	339	130158	Telecommunications svcs	....	....	32⅛	10 9/16	45 13/16	17 15/16	289451	35⅞	28⅞	34¾	...	d	−32	25.0	...	...
27	GVG	✓Global Vacation Grp	NY	NR	17	1158	Provide vacation pds/svcs	....	....	15⅝	5⅜	14½	2¾	2329	3 15/16	2¾	2⅞	...	14	...	−66.2	...	...
28	GLBN	✓GlobalNet Financial.com	NNM	NR	2	46	Online financial info/svcs	....	....	....	....	41⅛	9 9/16	58483	41⅛	22½	28 13/16	...	d	...	...	...	...
29•[11]	GSTRF	✓Globalstar Telecommunications	NNM	NR	134	36623	Global telecommunications	29¾	2⅞	37⅛	8 5/16	49½	12⅝	986945	49½	20	44	...	d	...	119	41.0	...
30	GLBE	✓Globe Business Resources	NNM	NR	11	423	Rent/sell office hme furniture	26⅜	8	21¼	9¾	15	9¾	2527	13½	12⅛	12⅞	...	13	−1	3.0	7.9	...
31	GBIX	✓Globix Corp	NNM	NR	60	8870	Sale/svc computer sys & softwr	6 15/16	2	7 15/16	2	61⅜	5 1/16	226774	61⅜	19¼	60	...	d	Neg	1108	132	...
32	GLCBY	✓Globo Cabo ADS[64]	NNM	NR	10	2045	Cable T.V. oper, Brazil	15¾	3⅛	6¼	1¾	19⅝	1	312330	19⅝	6⅞	18	...	..	...	713	12.6	...
33	GG.A	Goldcorp Inc 'A'[65]	NY,To,Ch,Mo	NR	31	9112	Gold mining, exploration	10 9/16	2 7/16	5 15/16	2 9/16	8 3/16	4	1878	5 15/16	4⅞	5¾	...	d	Neg	0.0	−12.2	16.7
34	GG	Class'B'[66]	NY,Ch	NR	1	10		10¼	2¾	5⅞	3 7/16	8⅜	4⅝	83	6¼	5¾	5⅞	...	..	Neg	9.3	−11.1	15.1
35	GLDC	✓Golden Enterprises	NNM	B	15	853	Snack foods:bolts&fasteners	16½	5/16	7¼	5	5 9/16	2 5/16	2937	2 15/16	2 5/16	2½	9.6	21	−24	−50.5	−26.6	−12.9
36	GSR	✓Golden Star Resources	AS,Ch,P,Ph	NR	34	6812	Explor,mine gold S. America	21	2 3/16	4 13/16	15/16	2⅛	⅜	38488	1⅛	11/16	15/16	...	d	−21	−11.8	−58.4	...
37•[8]	GSB	✓Golden State Bancorp	NY,P	NR	238	51927	Savings & loan,California	37¾	5⅛	42 1/16	10	26 9/16	16¼	74041	19 5/16	16⅝	17¼	...	8	NM	3.8	−9.1	12.7
38	GTII	✓Golden Triangle Ind	NSC	NR	2	.1	Envir/ener sv,oil royl US&Aust	421⅞	4 15/16	14⅜	5 1/16	9¾	1¾	937	3	2	2	...	d	Neg	−74.8	−38.6	−23.9
¶39•[6]	GDW	✓Golden West Finl	NY,B,Ch,P	A−	452	116449	Savings&loan,CA,CO,KS,TX	32⅝	3/16	38 3/16	23¼	38 7/16	28 15/16	101490	34 5/16	30⅝	33½	0.6	12	19	16.0	19.5	25.4
40	GV	✓Goldfield Corp	AS,Ch	C	7	231	Elect'l constr,silver min'g	4⅜	¼	7/16	3/16	⅜	3/16	8876	⅜	¼	⅜	...	5	70	50.0	14.5	3.7
41•[12]	GS	✓Goldman Sachs Group	NY,Ph	NR	359	52425	Investment banking/asset mgmt	....	....	....	....	94 13/16	53	170034	94 13/16	74¾	94 3/16	0.5	17	...	...	...	...
42	GECC	Golf Entertainment	NSC	C	5	11	Golf course/range construction	88	2⅜	5	½	3⅝	½	2234	1	11/16	1	...	d	7	41.0	−6.3	−20.2
43	GTA	✓Golf Trust of America	AS	NR	84	5514	Real estate investment trust	29⅜	21	35½	24	27¾	14½	13616	17⅜	14½	16 15/16	10.4	14	...	−33.9	...	...
44•[5]	GGUY	✓Good Guys Inc	NNM	C	37	8097	Retails consumer electr prod	30	1 1/16	15¾	2 11/16	11	2¾	59437	11	8⅛	9 5/16	...	d	Neg	44.7	12.7	−4.7
¶45•[9]	GR	✓Goodrich (B.F.)	NY,B,C,Ch,P,Ph	B	527	86421	Aerospace prd/spcl chemicals	48¼	6¼	56	26½	45 11/16	21	179738	27 9/16	21	27½	4.0	9	6	−20.9	−9.6	8.2
46	GDP	✓Goodrich Petroleum	NY,B,Ch,P,Ph	C	7	3	Oil, gas explor & develop	436	4	8½	1 1/16	3⅛	11/16	4556	3 1/16	2¼	2 5/16	...	d	−36	76.2	−23.3	−18.8
¶47•[13]	GT	✓Goodyear Tire & Rub	NY,B,C,Ch,P,Ph	A−	529	96272	Mfr tire & rubber products	71¼	5⅜	76¾	45⅞	66¾	25½	303595	34 3/16	25½	28 1/16	4.3	16	−3	−42.8	−16.4	−1.4
✣48	GDYS	✓Goody's Family Clothing	NNM	B	121	10836	Sells Moder'tly-priced apparel	19⅞	3⅜	29	7⅝	14⅝	4⅞	48546	6¾	4⅞	5⅜	...	7	33	−46.4	−15.5	3.7
49	GNCNF	✓Goran Capital	NNM,To	NR	5	345	Non-std auto&crop insur	40	3½	32¼	6	13¼	1 13/16	2208	2¾	1 13/16	2	...	d	Neg	−80.7	−52.9	−17.9
50	GRC	✓Gorman-Rupp	AS	A−	50	3915	Mfr pumps:constr'n,ind'l use	22¼	1 3/16	21½	13¼	18⅛	14¼	1121	18	16	17½	3.4	12	6	8.4	12.4	3.1

Uniform Footnote Explanations-See Page 4. Other: [1]Ph:Cycle 3. [2]ASE,CBOE,P:Cycle 2. [3]P:Cycle 2. [4]ASE:Cycle 3. [5]CBOE:Cycle 3. [6]Ph:Cycle 2. [7]ASE,CBOE,P,Ph:Cycle 2. [8]CBOE:Cycle 1. [9]CBOE:Cycle 2. [10]ASE,CBOE,Ph:Cycle 1. [11]ASE,CBOE,P:Cycle 3. [12]ASE,CBOE,P,Ph:Cycle 1. [13]ASE:Cycle 1. [51]6 Mo Dec'95,fiscal June'95 earned $0.10. [52]Sponsored ADR's rep 2 Ord shrs 50p. [53]6 Mo Dec'95:Fiscal Jun'95 earn $1.60. [54]Vestar Capital Partners IV plan acq,$23. [55]Fr 1-16-2003,scale to $25 in 2008. [56]Incl current amts. [57]9 Mo Dec'97. [58]RHI AG plan acq,$13. [59]Fiscal Oct'97 & prior. [60]9 Mo Dec'98. [61]To be determined. [62]Formerly Top Source Technol. [63]12 Mo Sep,'95. [64]Ea ADS rep 10 Pfd shs, no par. [65]Sub vtg shrs. [66]Multi vtg shrs. [67]Stk dstr of Guyanor Resources Ltd S.A.. [68]Fiscal Dec'98:Jun'98 earned $1.78. [69]Incl 30M Restrict Stk,excl 33M Discretionary Stk. [70]Excl 4M Operating Partnership Units. [71]Spl div. [72]Fiscal 1995 & prior:Can$.

Index	Cash Divs. Ea.Yr. Since	Dividends: Latest Payment Period $	Date	Ex. Div.	Total $ So Far 1999	Ind. Rate	Paid 1998	Financial Position Mil-$ Cash& Equiv.	Curr. Assets	Curr. Liab.	Balance Sheet Date	Capitalization Lg Trm Debt Mil-$	Shs. 000 Pfd.	Com.	Earnings $ Per Shr. Years End	1995	1996	1997	1998	1999	Last 12 Mos.	Interim Earnings Period	$ per Shr. 1998	1999	Index
1	1999	†Q0.02½	1-3-00	12-20	†0.10	0.10	....	3.82	194	79.2	9-30-99	205	...	12570	Dc	v0.95	v1.39	v1.30	v1.57	....	1.90	9 Mo Sep	v1.19	v1.52	1
2	....	0.10	12-15-94	11-23	...	Nil	....	1.70	188	103	9-30-99	10.1	...	15847	Dc	d2.86	v1.34	v1.27	v0.13	....	d1.99	9 Mo Sep	vd0.26	vd2.38	2
3	....	None Since Public			...	Nil	....	8.66	120	35.7	9-30-98	....	...	★20164	Dc	0.95	v0.50	v1.51	Pvd7.38	....	d7.06	9 Mo Sep	v1.36	v1.68	3
4	....	None Since Public			...	Nil	....	....	152	118	1-03-99	35.8	...	★±13394	Sp	...	...	pv0.69	vp1.46	Pv2.00	2.00				4
5	....	None Since Public			...	Nil	....	307	387	56.8	9-30-99	85.4	...	43926	Dc	vd1.29	vd0.78	vd0.95	vd1.85	Ed1.80	d2.57	9 Mo Sep	vd0.64	vd1.36	5
6◆	1906	Q0.14¾	3-3-00	1-28	0.57	0.59	0.49	60.0	5445	3652	9-30-99	3270	148	1072658	Dc	v0.95	v0.83	v1.24	v0.95	E1.15	1.21	9 Mo Sep	v0.56	v0.82	6
7	....	None Since Public			...	Nil	....	3.27	13.7	2.01	9-30-99	....	...	3474	Je	0.52	0.10	vd0.57	vd0.59	vd0.49	d0.88	3 Mo Sep	vd0.08	vd0.47	7
8◆	1985	†0.20	1-20-00	1-7	†0.627	0.60	†0.465	Total Deposits $502.78M			9-30-99	194	...	9546	Dc	v0.98	v0.90	v1.09	v1.16	....	1.24	9 Mo Sep	v0.86	v0.94	8
9	....	None Since Public			...	Nil	....	20.1	26.0	7.88	10-03-99	83.5	...	2834	Dc	v0.80	v0.98	v0.13	vd1.05	....	d2.65	9 Mo Sep	vd0.18	v□d1.78	9
10	....	t0.05	3-28-97	3-12	...	Nil	....	31.7	53.2	15.8	6-30-99	....	...	68889	Dc	↕[51]d0.07	v0.15	vd0.27	vd0.06	....	d0.21	9 Mo Sep	v0.01	vd0.14	10
11	1946	Q0.17½	2-1-00	1-5	0.70	0.70	0.70	64.3	260	129	9-30-99	312	...	42225	Dc	v1.49	v1.41	v1.07	v0.86	....	0.73	9 Mo Sep	v0.77	v0.64	11
12	1959	0.494	10-12-99	8-11	1.176	1.18	1.16	2101	6055	4537	j6-30-99	1619	...	3668000	Dc	↕[53]0.86	1.77	v1.72	v1.69	E1.72↓	1.72	6 Mo Jun	v0.77	v0.80	12
13◆	1990	Q0.06¼	11-19-99	11-3	0.25	0.25	0.25	7.47	177	105	9-30-99	24.4	...	9586	Dc	v2.91	v1.84	v2.32	v2.43	....	1.70	9 Mo Sep	v1.63	v0.90	13
14◆	....	None Paid			...	Nil	....	33.0	201	74.1	9-30-99	....	...	62212	Dc	v1.22	v1.11	□vd1.28	vd0.65	E0.08	d2.73	9 Mo Sep	v0.09	vd1.99	14
15	1996	Q0.42	1-15-00	12-29	1.68	1.68	1.68	Total Assets $1818M			9-30-99	902	11500	31055	Dc	pv0.66	v□d0.21	□v1.09	v□0.79	....	0.84	9 Mo Sep	v0.67	vΔ0.72	15
16	1998	Q0.484	1-15-00	12-21	1.933	1.938	1.309	Cv into .7615 com				....	8000	...	Dc	...	...	...	....	....	....				16
17	1994	Q0.481	1-14-00	12-29	1.923	1.92	1.923	Total Assets $1.55M			9-30-99	[56]1091	5118	23760	Dc	v1.27	v1.27	v1.12	v□0.90	....	0.97	9 Mo Sep	v0.64	v□0.71	17
18◆	....	None Since Public			...	Nil	....	881	1008	248	p12-31-98	p1114	p...	★p758876	Dc	...	...	p↕[57]d0.04	v□d0.32	Ed0.10	0.45	9 Mo Sep	v□d0.49	v□0.28	18
19	....	None Since Public			...	Nil	....	8.00	478	372	9-30-99	166	...	22437	Dc	1.70	2.01	[59]d0.20	vd1.64	....	....	9 Mo Sep	n/a	v□0.15	19
20◆	....	None Since Public			...	Nil	....	36.3	187	173	9-30-99	193	...	91147	Dc	v0.27	v0.42	v0.61	v↕[60]0.42	....	0.04	9 Mo Sep	v0.41	v0.03	20
21	....	None Paid			...	Nil	....	41.5	56.9	26.3	9-30-98	92.9	...	18809	Dc	...	vd0.25	vd0.94	Pvd2.32	....	d3.65	9 Mo Sep	vd0.99	vd2.32	21
22	....	None Since Public			...	Nil	....	35.1	173	113	9-30-99	811	...	174419	Dc	v0.31	v1.03	□v1.79	v1.27	E0.52	0.65	9 Mo Sep	v1.07	v0.45	22
23	....	0.08	5-30-97	4-18	...	[61]....	....	8.96	11.4	17.2	12-31-98	178	...	4047	Dc	v1.00	v0.25	v0.51	vd3.33	....	d3.16	3 Mo Mar	vd0.31	vd0.14	23
24	....	None Since Public			...	Nil	....	1.61	34.5	31.7	12-31-97	0.56	...	★12200	Mr	0.57	v0.64	Pv1.71	Pv0.65	....	0.55	6 Mo Sep	v0.48	v0.38	24
25	....	None Paid			...	Nil	....	0.54	5.03	3.82	6-30-99	0.71	4	29799	Sp	d0.12	d0.24	vd0.12	vd0.21	Pv0.14	0.14				25
26	....	None Since Public			...	Nil	....	979	1452	664	9-30-99	1972	100	180099	Dc	d0.81	vpd1.17	vpd1.63	v□d1.71	....	d2.97	9 Mo Sep	v□d1.08	vd2.35	26
27	....	None Since Public			...	Nil	....	52.0	87.7	131	9-30-99	30.0	...	14776	Dc	...	...	pv0.29	vp0.42	....	0.21	9 Mo Sep	vp0.15	□vd0.06	27
28◆	....	None Paid			...	Nil	....	15.6	28.3	0.84	9-30-99	....	...	11359	Dc	...	...	vd0.42	vd0.72	....	d1.50	9 Mo Sep	vd0.37	vd1.15	28
29◆	....	None Since Public			...	Nil	....	Total Assets $580M			12-31-98	....	...	82020	Dc	vd0.31	vd0.37	vd0.43	vd0.67	....	d0.67				29
30	....	None Since Public			...	Nil	....	Total Assets $133.83M			8-31-99	69.7	...	4795	Fb	pv1.03	v0.89	v0.89	v1.10	....	1.02	6 Mo Aug	v0.59	v0.51	30
31◆	....	None Since Public			...	Nil	....	142	159	27.8	6-30-99	161	...	★16600	Sp	[63]0.03	d0.36	vd0.51	vd1.54	Pvd3.45	d3.45				31
32	1999	0.207	12-24-99	12-10	0.207	[61]....	....	No Recent Finls				....	★492307	★507693	Dc	pd0.32	n/a	...	....	....	....	No Recent Reporting			32
33◆	....	g0.02½	5-23-95	5-11	...	Nil	....	45.6	71.0	12.2	6-30-99	....	...	±77892	Dc	v±d0.04	v±0.13	v±d1.38	±vd0.03	....	d0.01	6 Mo Jun	v±d0.01	v±0.01	33
34◆	....	g0.02½	5-23-95	5-11	...	Nil	....	....	...	...		....	...	5334	Dc	v±d0.04	v±0.13	vd1.38	v±d0.03	....	0.01	9 Mo Sep	vd0.02	v0.02	34
35	1968	Q0.06	10-27-99	10-6	0.24	0.24	0.48	1.53	18.1	6.02	8-31-99	1.65	...	12160	My	0.42	0.28	v0.29	v0.30	v0.09	0.12	6 Mo Nov	v0.06	v0.09	35
36	....	h[67]....		3-14	...	Nil	....	2.40	15.4	6.07	9-30-99	5.36	...	36931	Dc	vd0.54	vd0.31	vd0.92	vd0.74	....	d1.40	9 Mo Sep	vd0.13	vd0.79	36
37	....	Wrrt	5-29-98	6-1	...	Nil	Wrrt	Total Deposits $23676M			9-30-99	22969	...	126100	Dc	Δ1.28	0.36	v0.72	□v[68]4.88	E2.20	0.40	9 Mo Sep	v□6.15	v1.67	37
38◆	....	None Paid			...	Nil	....	0.21	1.91	0.48	9-30-99	0.28	56	622	Dc	v0.62	v0.44	v0.46	v0.43	....	d1.69	9 Mo Sep	v0.42	vd1.70	38
39◆	1977	Q0.05¼	12-10-99	11-10	0.19¼	0.21	0.172	Total Deposits $26549.8M			9-30-99	8922	...	161610	Dc	v1.31	v□2.10	v2.04	v□2.58	E2.81	2.79	9 Mo Sep	v□1.93	v2.14	39
40	....	0.05	8-31-63		...	Nil	....	3.67	8.63	1.70	9-30-99	....	339	26855	Dc	vd0.03	vd0.01	v0.01	vd0.02	....	0.08	9 Mo Sep	vd0.05	v0.05	40
41	1999	0.12	2-24-00	1-20	0.24	0.48	....	Total Assets $236273M			8-27-99	22745	...	[69]±474686	Nv	...	...	...	pv±2.62	vP±5.57	5.57				41
42◆	....	Wrrt	8-7-95	7-27	...	Nil	....	Total Assets $5.48M			9-30-99	0.88	229	2642	Dc	d0.04	vd1.80	v0.08	vd2.63	....	d1.44	9 Mo Sep	vd1.56	vd0.37	42
43	1997	Q0.44	1-15-00	12-29	1.76	1.76	1.70	Total Assets $434.75M			9-30-99	223	...	[70]7736	Dc	p0.99	pv1.04	v1.03	v1.34	....	1.24	9 Mo Sep	v1.08	v0.98	43
44	....	None Since Public			...	Nil	....	10.1	176	104	6-30-99	55.7	...	16347	Sp	1.06	vd0.46	vd0.89	vd0.64	Pvd2.54	d2.54				44
45◆	1939	Q0.275	1-3-00	12-2	1.10	1.10	1.10	65.0	2145	1484	9-30-99	1527	...	110149	Dc	2.15	v2.48	v□2.66	v3.02	E3.10	1.55	9 Mo Sep	v□2.40	v0.93	45
46◆	....	Wrrt	1-25-80	1-9	...	Nil	....	6.05	8.39	7.69	9-30-99	34.1	1546	5342	Dc	□pv0.14	vd0.05	vd0.50	vd1.71	....	d0.79	9 Mo Sep	vd1.34	vd0.42	46
47	1937	Q0.30	12-15-99	11-12	1.20	1.20	1.20	233	5628	4534	9-30-99	1673	...	156331	Dc	v3.97	v0.65	v3.53	v4.31	E1.81	2.04	9 Mo Sep	v3.53	v1.26	47
48◆	....	[71]0.00½	6-6-95	4-27	...	Nil	....	28.2	323	219	10-30-99	0.32	...	33124	Ja	v0.32	v0.53	v0.99	v0.81	....	0.81	9 Mo Oct	v0.57	v0.57	48
49	....	None Paid			...	Nil	....	Equity per shr $0.58			12-31-98	13.7	...	5876	Dc	[72]1.96	v7.19	v2.12	vd2.04	....	d4.41	6 Mo Jun	v1.40	vd0.97	49
50◆	1935	Q0.15	12-10-99	11-9	0.60	0.60	0.58	10.3	85.3	21.3	9-30-99	1.98	...	8592	Dc	v1.10	v1.15	v1.23	v1.37	....	1.43	9 Mo Sep	v1.12	v1.18	50

◆Stock Splits & Divs By Line Reference Index [6]2-for-1,'95,'98. [8]3-for-2,'97:10%,'95,'96,'98,'99. [13]2-for-1,'97. [14]3-for-2,'95(twice),'96. [18]2-for-1,'99. [20]2-for-1,'96(twice),'97. [28]1-for-6 REVERSE,'99. [29]2-for-1,'97,'98. [31]2-for-1,'99. [33]2-for-1,'96. [34]2-for-1,'96. [38]1-for-2.5 REVERSE,'95:1-for-3 REVERSE,'97. [39]3-for-1,'99. [42]1-for-8 REVERSE,'94:1-for-4 REVERSE,'98. [45]2-for-1,'96. [46]1-for-8 REVERSE,'98. [48]2-for-1,'98. [50]3-for-2,'94.

¶ S&P 500
# MidCap 400
✤ SmallCap 600
• Options

Index	Ticker	Name of Issue (Call Price of Pfd. Stocks)	Market	Com. Rank. & Pfd. Rating	Inst. Hold Cos	Inst. Hold Shs. (000)	Principal Business	Price Range 1971-97 High	1971-97 Low	1998 High	1998 Low	1999 High	1999 Low	December, 1999 Dec. Sales in 100s	Last Sale Or Bid High	Last Sale Or Bid Low	Last Sale Or Bid Last	%Div Yield	P-E Ratio	EPS 5 Yr Growth	% Annualized Total Return 12 Mo	36 Mo	60 Mo
1•[1]	GOTO	✔GoTo.com Inc	NNM	NR	66	9631	Online market place services	....	....	....	....	114½	15	84993	108 15/16	57½	58¾	...	d	...	...	...	...
✤2	GOT	✔Gottschalks Inc	NY,Ch,Ph,P	B–	49	3715	Retail dept str chain,Calif	26⅜	4¾	9¼	6¼	9 5/16	6¾	4216	9 1/16	6⅞	7 7/16	...	11	NM	–2.5	12.3	0.2
3	GNET	✔go2net Inc	NNM	NR	110	5466	Internet navigational svc	2¾	1 5/16	12 15/16	1¾	111¾	8⅞	175121	111¾	71⅜	87	...	d	...	890	...	...
4	GOV	✔Gouverneur Bancorp	AS	NR	2	121	Savings & loan, N.Y.	....	....	....	....	5½	3¾	2158	5⅛	4 5/16	5	...	..	...	...	...	...
5	GPX	✔GP Strategies	NY,B,Ch,P,Ph	B–	47	6658	Environmental technol & svs	268	5½	17 11/16	9⅛	19⅛	5¾	5183	8	5¾	6⅛	...	d	–30	–59.2	–7.3	...
¶6•[2]	GPU	✔GPU Inc	NY,B,C,Ch,P,Ph	B+	555	90336	Util hldg co: N.J. & Penna.	42¾	1 11/16	47 3/16	35 3/16	45	28¾	79140	32 3/16	28¾	29¾	7.1	8	13	–28.8	1.4	8.5
¶7•[3]	GRA	✔Grace (W.R.) & Co	NY,B,C,Ch,P,Ph	B–	358	56060	Special chemical prds	83	9	86 15/16	10	21	11 13/16	52094	14 7/16	12 13/16	14⅛	...	9	Neg	–10.0	...	...
✤8•[4]	GGG	✔Graco Inc	NY,Ch	A–	168	13712	Specialized pump & spray eq	26 7/16	⅜	36½	19⅞	36 3/16	19⅞	8930	36⅛	31½	35⅞	1.6	13	33	23.4	32.4	32.8
9	GHM	✔Graham Corp	AS,Ch	B–	21	274	Vacuum & heat transfer eq	27 5/16	1⅝	18½	6¾	11⅛	6	504	7½	6⅛	6⅝	...	5	NM	–14.5	–10.9	–1.5
¶10•[5]	GWW	✔Grainger (W.W.)	NY,B,Ch,P,Ph	A	504	59823	Natl dstr indus/comm'l prod	49⅞	1 7/16	54 11/16	36 7/16	58⅛	36⅞	85528	50⅝	45 9/16	47 13/16	1.3	22	12	16.4	7.5	12.2
11•[6]	GBTVK	✔Granite Broadcasting[56]	NNM	NR	58	13207	Acquire/oper TV stations	15	2	13⅝	3½	14½	5¾	30608	14 1/16	8¾	10⅛	...	9	NM	68.8	–1.6	10.6
#12	GVA	✔Granite Construction	NY,Ch,Ph	B+	191	14957	Heavy constr contractor U.S.	18 3/16	6⅞	34⅜	14¼	37¾	16¾	24016	19¾	16¾	18 7/16	1.5	10	18	–44.2	15.2	17.4
13	GCS	✔Gray Communications Systems	NY,Ch	B	34	1168	TV broadcstg/newspaper publish	103⅛	3 9/16	22	16	20⅛	15⅛	973	18¾	17⅛	17 11/16	0.5	d	Neg	–3.0	12.6	20.4
14	GCS.B	✔ Cl'B'	NY,Ch	NR	25	4528		17 7/16	9 15/16	21½	12½	15⅜	11⅝	1469	13½	11⅝	13½	0.6	4	–21	–0.8	6.6	...
15	GRH	✔GRC International	NY,B,Ch,P	B–	34	2340	Research svcs/testing, softwr	45⅜	5/16	11⅜	3⅞	11⅞	5 15/16	8085	11⅞	9 15/16	11⅞	...	15	NM	88.1	13.5	0.9
¶16•[5]	GAP	✔Great Atl & Pac Tea	NY,B,C,Ch,P,Ph	B–	275	14050	Food supermarkets	65⅝	3½	34⅜	21⅞	37 11/16	24½	31827	28 3/16	24½	27⅞	1.4	..	Neg	–4.7	–3.1	10.2
17	GAJ	Great A&P Tea 9.375%'QUIBS'	NY	NR	2	18	Qtly Interest Bonds	....	....	....	....	25¾	20	4341	24¼	20	21	11.2	..	...	...	...	...
¶18•[7]	GLK	✔Great Lakes Chemical	NY,B,Ch,P	A–	423	44056	Specialty chemical prod	84	5/16	54 3/16	36 11/16	50	33 3/16	61318	38½	33 7/16	38 3/16	e0.8	16	–22	...	...	...
19	GL	✔Great Lakes REIT	NY,Ph	NR	66	7012	Real estate investment trust	19 15/16	15⅜	20 3/16	14 3/16	16 15/16	13 5/16	6112	15	13⅝	14⅜	9.5	10	...	–0.2	...	...
20	GNI	✔Great North'n Iron Ore[61]	NY,Ch	NR	12	40	Royalty income from mines	80¼	8¾	65½	50	64¼	53 9/16	445	57¾	54	54½	11.2	9	8	9.2	11.2	17.4
✤21	GPSI	✔Great Plains Software	NNM	NR	134	7402	Client/server softwr,svcs	35½	20⅜	49⅞	24⅞	78 15/16	25⅜	44293	78 15/16	52⅜	74¾	...	75	...	54.9	...	...
✤22	GMP	✔Green Mountain Pwr	NY,Ph	B	46	883	Electricity in Vermont	36⅝	3⅜	20 1/16	10	14½	7 1/16	4364	8 11/16	7 1/16	7 7/16	7.4	d	Neg	–25.4	–27.4	–17.7
23	GBR	✔Greenbriar Corp	AS,Ph	NR	6	1008	Hlth care svcs,retirement ctrs	23½	1¼	17⅜	1	3¼	5/16	586	15/16	5/16	11/16	...	d	Neg	–73.2	–63.4	–36.3
24	GBX	✔Greenbrier Cos	NY,Ch	NR	40	3613	Railroad transp'n eqp/leas'g	19½	7¾	19	12⅝	14⅜	8 3/16	8880	10⅝	8 3/16	8⅝	e4.2	6	–16	–36.4	–3.6	–10.2
#25•[8]	GPT	✔GreenPoint Finl	NY,Ch,Ph,P	NR	305	71954	Savings bank, New York	36¾	8¾	42⅞	24	37⅛	23 5/16	68580	26⅝	23 5/16	23 13/16	3.7	11	15	–30.1	2.3	21.1
26	GMAI	Greg Manning Auctions	NNM	NR	9	452	Conducts public auction svs	4⅞	1⅛	21¾	1⅛	28½	7½	16068	17½	11¾	13¾	...	d	27	46.7	104	43.6
27	GBCOA	✔Greif Bros[62] Cl'A'	NNM	B+	79	6807	Ship'g containers/containerbrd	36¼	1⅛	41¼	27⅜	30 9/16	20⅝	4148	30⅛	27⅝	29¾	1.6	17	–4	3.9	3.4	8.3
28	GREY	Grey Advertising	NNM	B+	85	598	Advertising agency	367	2¾	480	263	408	284	336	404¾	332	400	1.0	..	NM	11.2	18.4	23.3
29	GW	✔Grey Wolf	AS,Ch,Ph	C	98	52333	Onshore contract drilling	26¾	⅜	5½	11/16	3¾	¾	136696	3	2 7/16	2⅞	...	d	–18	283	0.7	30.8
30	GRIC	GRIC Communications	NNM	NR	..	...	Internet telephony communic sv	....	....	....	....	29	14	153912	29	14	25⅜	...	..	...	...	...	...
✤31	GFF	✔Griffon Corp	NY,B,Ch,Ph,P	B	121	22232	Home furnish'gs,electr equip	123¾	⅞	17 7/16	7⅝	11 5/16	6¼	15227	7⅞	6¾	7 13/16	...	12	1	–26.5	–13.9	–1.4
32	GRI	✔Gristede's Foods	AS,B	B–	5	172	Operates supermkt chain N.Y.	23¾	9/16	4½	1 13/16	3 15/16	1¾	420	2⅜	2¼	2⅛B	...	43	–44	13.3	0.0	–15.3
33	MAK	✔Group Maintenance Amer	NY	NR	83	13708	Air-condition'g/heat'g svcs	17 3/16	13	20⅝	10 5/16	15 7/16	7	17374	10 11/16	7	10 11/16	...	9	...	–11.9	...	...
✤34	GPI	✔Group 1 Automotive	NY	NR	78	6143	Own/oper auto dealerships	13 15/16	7¾	26	8⅝	30	12¾	6200	17⅛	12¾	13 15/16	...	9	...	–46.4	...	...
35	ABG	✔Groupe AB ADS[66]	NY,Ch	NR	13	2066	Prod,dstr TV programs,France	21¼	4¾	6 15/16	1⅞	5¾	1¾	6190	5¾	4 5/16	5⅝	...	d	...	190	–26.9	...
36•[8]	DA	✔Groupe Danone ADS[67]	NY,Ph	NR	69	4262	Produce pkg foods/beverages	37½	30 13/16	61⅜	33⅞	59	43	5718	47 11/16	43	46 9/16	1.1	28	–4	–16.2	...	...
37	GVE	✔Grove Property Trust	AS	NR	29	5198	Real estate investment trust	12⅜	6⅛	11¾	8¾	14	10 7/16	998	13¼	12½	13¼	5.4	..	–45	19.7	49.1	33.4
38	GBE	✔Grubb & Ellis	NY,B,Ch,P	B–	36	5045	R.E.broker: mtge: R.E.	63⅛	1⅝	16½	7¼	8⅛	4⅜	2889	6	4 9/16	4 11/16	...	11	NM	–41.9	1.4	18.6
39	GMK	✔Gruma S.A. ADS[70]	NY	NR	10	1978	Corn refining/products	....	....	10⅜	9⅜	10½	3⅞	3844	4½	3⅞	4 1/16	...	9	...	–58.6	...	...
40	ATY	✔Grupo Casa Autrey ADS[71]	NY,Ch,Ph,P	NR	9	1814	Dstr pharmac'l/consumer prd	36½	8	22	3 11/16	9⅜	2¾	4224	8⅞	7⅜	8¼	...	..	...	21.1	–24.3	–17.5
41	EKT	Grupo Elektra GDS[72]	NY,Ch,Ph	NR	20	2298	Specialty retailer, Mexico	18 9/16	1⅞	18⅛	2¾	10	3 1/16	31616	10	6⅜	9¾	0.9	13	62	97.5	9.5	8.4
42	IMY	✔Grupo Imsa ADS[73]	NY	NR	23	1772	Steel process/auto,constr pd	32⅛	19	23¾	5⅞	19 3/16	8 1/16	2862	17 3/16	14⅞	16¾B	1.8	5	36	68.9	–1.7	...
43	GID	✔Grupo Indl Durango ADS[74]	NY,Ch,P	NR	9	1126	Corrugated containers/paper pd	26½	3⅞	15¼	4 5/16	11⅞	4 9/16	3036	11⅞	10 7/16	11⅞	...	..	...	116	3.8	–3.4
44	MSK	✔Grupo Indl Maseca ADS[75]	NY,Ch,P	NR	23	4731	Producer of corn flour	30¼	6⅞	15½	6 1/16	14⅞	6¼	2732	7⅜	6½	7¼	3.4	7	8	–40.1	–25.6	–13.1
45	CEL.Y	✔Grupo Iusacell S.A.'L'ADS	NY,Ch,Ph,P	NR	8	748	Wireless telecommun,Mexico	33½	6½	23	4⅛	18¼	6⅜	1370	18¼	10	14⅜B	...	d	...	102	23.5	–5.0
46	GMD.B	Grupo Mex Desarr 'B'ADS	NY,Ph	NR	3	98	Infrastructure projects,Mexico	27⅝	⅛	⅜	⅛	....	....	....	....	....	....	...	..	Neg	...	...	...
47	GMD	✔ Series'L'ADS[76]	NY,Ch,Ph,P	NR	9	106		28⅛	½	⅝	3/16	....	....	....	....	....	....	...	..	Neg	...	...	...
48	RC	✔Grupo Radio Centro ADS[77]	NY,Ch,Ph,P	NR	21	3354	Radio broadcasting-Mexico	29⅝	6	15⅝	3¾	10 7/16	3 11/16	20520	10 7/16	5½	8⅜	9.1	..	...	55.8	10.7	–7.6
49	SIM	✔Grupo Simec ADS[78]	AS	NR	1	43	Oper steel mini-mill, Mexico	33¾	2¾	5	1⅛	5	¾	1236	4⅞	4	4⅝	...	d	–7	253	14.0	–21.1
50•[9]	TV	✔Grupo Televisa S.A.GDS[79]	NY,Ch,Ph,P	NR	217	52380	TV/radio production,Mexico	73¾	12⅛	43¼	14⅞	72¼	18¼	152276	72¼	48 13/16	68¼	...	..	–23	177	38.6	16.6

Uniform Footnote Explanations-See Page 4. Other: [1]ASE,CBOE:Cycle 2. [2]CBOE:Cycle 2. [3]ASE:Cycle 2. [4]P:Cycle 2. [5]ASE:Cycle 1. [6]Ph:Cycle 3. [7]CBOE:Cycle 3. [8]CBOE:Cycle 1. [9]ASE,CBOE:Cycle 1. [51]7 Mo Sep'96. [52]Stk dstr of 1 com & 1 wrrt of American Drug Co. [53]Subsid pfd in $M. [54]Fiscal Dec'95 & prior. [55]12 Mo Mar'97:Fiscal Dec'96 earned $1.90. [56]non-vtg. [57]Accum on Pfd. [58]Or earlier upon'Tax Event're-spec cond. [59]Total issue amt. [60]Stk dstr of Octel Corp. [61]Tr Ctfs. [62]Non-vtg. [63]®$20.19,'96. [64]Fiscal Feb'97 & prior. [65]39 Wk Nov'97. [66]Ea ADS rep 0.5 Ord shr, FF 10. [67]Ea ADS rep 0.20 ord shr, FF10. [68]®$1.81,'96. [69]Redemption of stk purch rt. [70]Ea ADS rep 4 ord,'B' No Par. [71]Ea ADS rep 10 ord shrs,no par. [72]Ea GDS rep 10 ord Ptc Ctf(ea rep 2'B'&1'L'shr). [73]Ea ADS rep 9uts (ea rep 3Sr'B'/2Sr'C'shrs no par). [74]Ea ADS rep 2 ord ptcf ctf. [75]Ea ADS rep 15 sr'B'com,no par. [76]Ea ADS rep 1 Sr L Shr,no par. [77]Ea ADS rep 9 non-Redm Ord Ptc ctf. [78]Ea ADS rep 20 series'B' shrs,no par. [79]Global Dep Shrs,rep 2 ord Ptc Ctf rep 1A,L&D shr.

Common and Convertible Preferred Stocks

Splits ◆ Index	Cash Divs. Ea. Yr. Since	Dividends: Latest Payment Period $	Date	Ex. Div.	Total $ So Far 1999	Ind. Rate	Paid 1998	Financial Position Mil-$ Cash& Equiv.	Curr. Assets	Curr. Liab.	Balance Sheet Date	Capitalization Lg Trm Debt Mil-$	Shs. 000 Pfd.	Com.	Earnings $ Per Shr. Years End	1995	1996	1997	1998	1999	Last 12 Mos.	Interim Earnings Period	$ per Shr. 1998	1999	Index
1	....	None Since Public			...	Nil	....	111	120	12.2	9-30-99	0.99	...	45532	Dc	...	...	...	vpd0.75	....	d0.87	9 Mo Sep	vpd0.48	vpd0.60	1
2	....	None Since Public			...	Nil	....	2.46	216	113	10-30-99	91.1	...	12576	Ja	vd0.54	v0.18	v0.36	v0.46	....	0.66	9 Mo Oct	vd0.27	vd0.07	2
3◆	....	None Since Public			...	Nil	....	267	272	7.60	6-30-99	....	168	27815	Sp	...	‡v[51]d0.10	vd0.10	vd0.10	Pvd6.44	d6.44				3
4	....	None Since Public			...	Nil	....	Total Deposits $45.1M			6-30-99	4.34	...	2304	Sp	...	...	...	pv0.30	....	....	9 Mo Jun	n/a	v0.08	4
5◆	....	h[52]....	8-15-94	8-16	...	Nil	....	4.90	90.8	78.2	9-30-99	15.2	...	±11544	Dc	v□0.15	v1.54	v0.31	vd0.19	....	d0.78	9 Mo Sep	vd0.23	vd0.82	5
6	1987	Q0.53	2-23-00	1-26	2.10½	2.12	2.04½	284	1558	3000	9-30-99	7301	[53]449	123425	Dc	v3.79	v2.47	v2.77	v□3.03	E3.60	3.70	12 Mo Sep	v2.95	v3.70	6
7◆	....	0.145	12-9-97	11-24	...	Nil	....	85.7	592	691	9-30-99	8.10	...	71785	Dc	d3.40	v30.57	v3.45	vd1.99	E1.50↑	d1.57	9 Mo Sep	v□0.76	v1.18	7
8◆	1970	Q0.14	2-2-00	1-12	0.44	0.56	0.44	2.08	132	69.3	9-24-99	82.1	...	20416	Dc	v1.06	v1.38	v1.71	v2.01	....	2.78	9 Mo Sep	v1.35	v2.12	8
9◆	....	0.047	1-4-93	11-9	...	Nil	....	4.91	20.4	8.02	9-30-99	0.32	...	1516	Mr	[54]0.72	[55]2.07	v2.21	v1.46	....	1.29	6 Mo Sep	v0.62	v0.45	9
10◆	1965	Q0.16	12-1-99	11-4	0.63	0.64	0.58½	47.6	1392	794	9-30-99	128	...	93383	Dc	v1.82	v2.02	v2.27	v2.44	E2.20	2.31	9 Mo Sep	v1.75	v1.62	10
11	....	None Since Public			...	[57]Nil	....	55.0	113	79.9	9-30-99	314	9033	±18139	Dc	±vd0.74	±□vd1.09	v±d2.93	□v±1.27	....	1.15	9 Mo Sep	v□d1.43	vd1.55	11
12◆	1990	Q0.07	1-14-00	12-28	0.27	0.28	†0.28	73.0	401	274	9-30-99	64.9	...	27026	Dc	v1.08	v1.02	v1.03	v1.70	....	1.79	9 Mo Sep	v1.33	v1.42	12
13◆	1992	Q0.02	12-16-99	11-29	0.08	0.08	0.06	3.87	33.8	25.3	9-30-99	285	1	±15422	Dc	v0.14	v±□0.63	±vd0.24	v3.25	....	d0.43	9 Mo Sep	v3.23	vd0.45	13
14◆	1996	Q0.02	12-16-99	11-29	0.08	0.08	0.06	....	...	...		....	...	5111	Dc	0.14	v□±0.63	±vd0.24	....	....	3.16	9 Mo Sep△	v±d0.17	v±3.23	14
15	....	None Paid			...	Nil	....	0.09	53.9	24.4	9-30-99	16.5	...	12370	Je	0.54	d1.92	vd1.76	v1.14	v0.87	0.78	3 Mo Sep	v0.30	v0.21	15
16	1986	Q0.10	2-1-00	1-7	0.40	0.40	0.40	144	1179	1123	9-11-99	885	...	38367	Fb	v1.50	v1.91	v□1.66	vd1.75	E0.02	d2.12	40 Wk Nov	v0.56	v0.19	16
17	1999	Q0.586	2-1-00	1-12	0.521	2.344	....	Co opt to redm fr 8-11-2004 at $25[58]				[59]★175	...	...	Fb	...	...	...	....	....	....	Mature 8-1-2039			17
18◆	1973	†Q0.08	1-31-00	12-29	†0.32¼	0.32	h[60]0.48	400	1098	343	9-30-99	732	...	57511	Dc	v4.48	v3.91	v0.94	v1.50	E2.41	1.85	9 Mo Sep	v1.50	v1.85	18
19	1997	Q0.34	12-31-99	12-15	1.34	1.36	1.24	Total Assets $454M			9-30-99	204	...	16295	Dc	v0.88	pv1.32	v0.91	v0.98	....	1.48	9 Mo Sep	v0.73	v1.23	19
20	1934	1.60	1-31-00	12-29	6.30	6.10	6.00	5.02	7.81	2.49	9-30-99	....	...	1500	Dc	v5.43	v5.99	v5.66	v6.77	....	6.12	9 Mo Sep	v5.16	v4.51	20
21	....	None Since Public			...	Nil	....	124	150	48.6	8-31-99	....	...	15559	My	...	p0.75	pP0.36	v0.32	v0.86	1.00	6 Mo Nov	v0.37	v0.51	21
22	1951	Q0.138	12-31-99	12-14	0.55	0.55	0.96¼	0.46	28.5	22.2	9-30-99	86.8	160	5382	Dc	v2.26	v2.22	v1.57	vd0.80	....	d1.12	9 Mo Sep	vd0.16	vd0.48	22
23◆	....	None Since Public			...	Nil	....	4.37	6.50	4.64	9-30-99	63.0	2975	6733	Dc	1.57	vd0.99	vd0.92	vd1.86	....	d1.54	9 Mo Sep	vd1.06	vd0.74	23
24	1994	Q0.09	12-15-99	11-17	†0.42	0.36	0.24	Total Assets $551M			8-31-99	173	...	14255	Au	1.18	v1.29	vd0.29	v1.42	v□1.43	1.43				24
25◆	1994	Q0.22	12-3-99	11-17	0.88	0.88	0.64	Total Deposits $11669.09M			9-30-99	921	...	107829	Dc	v1.14	v1.51	v1.86	v1.92	....	2.13	9 Mo Sep	v1.40	v1.61	25
26	....	None Since Public			...	Nil	....	0.35	19.1	11.9	9-30-99	1.79	...	6356	Je	d0.28	0.12	v0.15	vd0.05	v0.10	d0.02	3 Mo Sep	v0.05	vd0.07	26
27◆	1926	Q0.12	1-1-00	12-13	0.50	0.48	0.48	30.9	228	103	7-31-99	270	...	±22813	Oc	2.39	v1.48	v0.63	v1.15	Pv1.78	1.78				27
28	1965	Q1.00	12-15-99	11-29	4.00	4.00	4.00	163	1156	1205	9-30-99	78.0	30	±1247	Dc	v±16.32	v±[63]20.45	v±21.89	v±18.98	....	3.55	9 Mo Sep	v±14.37	v±d1.06	28
29	....	None Since Public			...	Nil	....	20.7	51.3	29.2	9-30-99	250	...	165159	Dc	vd0.35	vd0.18	v0.07	vd0.50	....	d0.68	9 Mo Sep	vd0.02	v□d0.20	29
30	....	None Since Public			...	Nil	....	10.2	13.0	6.99	9-30-99	1.12	p...	★17723	Dc	...	...	...	vpd2.27	....	....	9 Mo Sep	n/a	vpd1.42	30
31	....	None Paid			...	Nil	....	21.2	327	138	9-30-99	128	...	30348	Sp	0.71	v0.72	v1.06	v0.94	v0.66	0.66				31
32◆	....	None Since Public			...	Nil	....	0.07	32.9	18.9	8-29-99	31.7	...	19637	Nv	□0.58	[64]0.37	‡v[65]0.01	vd0.01	....	0.05	9 Mo Aug	vd0.04	v0.02	32
33	....	None Since Public			...	Nil	....	6.50	412	234	9-30-99	353	...	38346	Dc	...	pv0.51	vp0.49	v0.93	....	1.18	9 Mo Sep	v0.65	v0.90	33
34	....	None Since Public			...	Nil	....	103	442	347	9-30-99	102	...	21246	Dc	...	pv0.63	vp0.76	v1.16	....	1.50	9 Mo Sep	v0.87	v1.21	34
35	....	None Since Public			...	Nil	....	487	1636	1003	j12-31-98	230	...	25327	Dc	p0.65	0.55	△vd0.38	vd0.83	....	d0.26	6 Mo Jun	vd0.49	v0.08	35
36	1998	0.524	7-14-99	5-21	0.524	0.52	0.471	7221	29509	23047	j12-31-97	21543	...	73072	Dc	1.25	[68]1.85	v1.66	....	....	1.66				36
37◆	1994	0.18	1-17-00	12-28	0.71	0.72	0.672	Total Assets $327.22M			9-30-99	194	...	8175	Dc	v0.55	v0.42	v0.61	v□0.09	....	0.01	9 Mo Sep	v□0.45	v△0.37	37
38	....	[69]0.05	1-29-93		...	Nil	....	8.87	25.6	25.5	9-30-99	....	...	19991	Je	[54]d0.14	d0.10	△v0.97	v0.98	v0.37	0.42	3 Mo Sep	v0.11	v0.16	38
39	....	None Paid			...	Nil	....	327	4722	1585	j12-31-98	5329	...	350565	Dc	...	v1.91	v0.52	v0.48	....	0.48				39
40◆	1994	0.167	5-28-98	5-15	...	Nil	0.167	58.5	2829	1595	j12-31-97	500	...	280149	Dc	0.50	0.89	n/a	n/a	....	....	3 Mo Mar	v0.14	v0.10	40
41◆	1995	0.094	4-12-99	3-26	0.094	0.09	0.097	50.0	529	403	12-31-97	105	...	864970	Dc	0.11	△v0.61	v△0.67	Pv0.34	....	0.74	9 Mo Sep	v0.15	v0.55	41
42	1997	0.296	12-29-99	12-20	0.621	0.30	0.283	359	5604	3594	j12-31-97	3174	...	2813000	Dc	±0.45	*±3.65	v3.19	....	....	3.19				42
43	....	None Since Public			...	Nil	....	59.0	233	109	12-31-97	501	...	53678	Dc	1.28	4.69	v3.71	n/a	....	....	3 Mo Mar	v0.19	v1.31	43
44	1995	0.252	5-19-99	5-10	0.252	0.25	0.301	495	1717	208	j12-31-97	324	...	918405	Dc	0.96	1.38	v1.04	....	....	1.04				44
45	....	None Since Public			...	Nil	....	....	...	...		....	...	150209	Dc	d0.75	...	vd0.09	....	....	d0.09				45
46	....	None Since Public			...	Nil	....	4.70	283	808	12-31-97	90.0	...	±45252	Dc	d1.11	2.00	d3.24	....	....	d3.24				46
47	....	None Since Public			...	Nil	....	....	...	...		....	...	±42293	Dc	d1.11	v2.20	Pvd3.24	....	....	d3.24				47
48	1997	0.212	12-30-98	12-18	...	0.76	0.761	2.02	18.2	14.1	12-31-98	1.15	...	p193134	Dc	0.18	v0.25	v0.84	v0.16	....	....	3 Mo Mar	n/a	v0.17	48
49	....	None Since Public			...	Nil	....	21.0	92.8	38.7	12-31-98	292	...	±414301	Dc	d1.01	2.48	v1.21	vd0.55	....	d0.55				49
50	....	0.072	2-21-95	2-6	...	Nil	....	572	2176	344	12-31-98	1004	...	927000	Dc	±0.96	±d0.49	v4.79	v0.50	E0.45	0.50				50

◆Stock Splits & Divs By Line Reference Index [3]2-for-1,'99(twice). [5]1-for-4 REVERSE, '95. [7]No adj for dstr of Fresenius Med.'96:No adj for stk dstr,'98. [8]3-for-2,'94,'96,'98. [9]3-for-2,'96. [10]2-for-1,'98. [12]3-for-2,'96,'98. [13]3-for-2,'95,'98. [14]3-for-2,'98. [18]No adj for stk dstr,'98. [23]1-for-5 REVERSE,'95. [25]2-for-1,'98. [27]2-for-1,'95. [32]10%,'94. [37]1.125-for-1,5%,'97. [40]2.5-for-1,'96. [41]2-for-1,'98.

¶ S&P 500 # MidCap 400 ✣ SmallCap 600 • Options

Index	Ticker	Name of Issue (Call Price of Pfd. Stocks)	Market	Com. Rank. & Pfd. Rating	Inst. Hold Cos	Inst. Hold Shs. (000)	Principal Business	Price Range 1971-97 High	1971-97 Low	1998 High	1998 Low	1999 High	1999 Low	Dec. Sales in 100s	December, 1999 Last Sale Or Bid High	Low	Last	%Div Yield	P-E Ratio	EPS 5 Yr Growth	% Annualized Total Return 12 Mo	36 Mo	60 Mo
1	GTR	✓Grupo Tribasa S.A. ADS[51]	NY,Ch,Ph,P	NR	20	4137	Highway constr'n, Mexico	40¼	3⅛	7 7/16	1 3/16	1⅞	5/16	33785	13/16	5/16	5/16	...	..	...	-81.5	-60.0	-54.8
2	GSA	GS Finl Prd LP E-SIGNS 2002	NY	NR	2	150	Enhanced Stk Index Growth Nts	33 5/16	25	41¼	31⅝	45 11/16	40	196	45 11/16	45⅝	45¾B	...	..	...	10.9	18.1	...
3	GVP	✓GSE Systems	AS	NR	13	1315	Dvlp/dgn energy/mfr software	17¾	3	5½	1½	6¾	2⅝	631	3⅝	3	3⅛B	...	8	-39	25.0	-30.4	...
4•[1]	GSTX	✓GST Telecommunications	NNM,Ch,P	NR	115	20849	Telecommunications sys/svcs	17⅝	3¼	17 9/16	3⅝	17 15/16	5½	180701	9 11/16	6	9 1/16	...	d	-41	38.1	0.7	16.7
5•[2]	GTIS	GT Interactive Software	NNM	NR	57	15347	Publish/distrib software	26¾	5⅞	11½	3 9/16	6⅛	1 9/16	87448	2¼	1 9/16	1⅝	...	..	...	-66.9	-38.5	...
¶6•[3]	GTE	✓GTE Corp[56]	NY,B,C,Ch,P,Ph	B+	1689	495033	Lgst indep telephone sys:mfg	52¼	5⅝	71 13/16	46 9/16	78½	57	480607	76 15/16	67 9/16	70 9/16	2.7	18	7	11.6	19.9	23.2
#7•[1]	GTK	✓GTECH Holdings	NY,P	NR	173	26455	Computerized lottery systems	45⅞	15⅛	40 11/16	21 9/16	28 9/16	19⅝	20362	22⅝	19⅝	22	...	8	10	-14.1	-11.7	1.5
8	GIG	✓GTR Group	AS,To	NR	5	598	Refurbish old video games	3 7/16	5/16	1¼	⅜	6⅛	⅞	2615	3	2½	2⅞	...	7	...	200	...	...
9	GSH	✓Guangshen Railway ADS[57]	NY,Ph,P	NR	44	6322	Railroad operations, China	25⅝	10¾	13⅝	4⅛	7⅝	4 11/16	4024	6 1/16	5 7/16	5 9/16	10.8	6	...	1.9	-30.1	...
10•[4]	GUC	✓Gucci Group N.V.	NY,Ph,P	NR	85	23953	Mfr personal luxury accessor's	80½	22	57⅞	31½	120⅝	48 9/16	35874	120⅝	83⅞	114½	0.3	33	46	137	22.3	...
11	GES	✓Guess Inc	NY,Ch,Ph	NR	51	4121	Dsg,mkt casual apparel acces'r	18¼	6¼	8⅜	3⅝	22 15/16	4⅞	16635	22 15/16	16¾	21¾	...	23	...	352	14.8	...
12	GSY	✓Guest Supply	NY	↑B	22	1812	Personal care prod for hotels	23¾	1 9/16	19¼	7⅞	16½	8¼	4154	15 1/16	13 9/16	15	...	14	7	25.7	-5.2	3.7
¶13•[5]	GDT	✓Guidant Corp	NY,Ph,P	NR	912	235454	Dgn/mfr cardiological equip	34¾	3⅝	56½	25½	69⅞	41	383794	52½	42½	47	...	39	18	-14.5	49.0	63.9
✣14•[6]	GFD	✓Guilford Mills	NY,Ch,Ph	B+	102	11544	Knit fabric mfr	28¼	⅛	29⅝	11½	18	5⅝	13882	7 7/16	5⅝	7¼	6.1	15	-14	-54.5	-23.5	-10.8
15•[7]	GTRC	✓Guitar Center	NNM	NR	73	12247	Own/oper music pds stores	27⅝	13½	33¼	13⅝	30⅝	7 7/16	23309	10⅞	9	10 1/16	...	8	...	-59.1	...	...
16•[8]	GOU	✓Gulf Canada Resources	NY,To,Mo,P	C	115	165283	Oil/gas explor,dev,prod,mktg	21	2 1/16	7	2⅛	4⅞	2 3/16	128972	3 11/16	3 1/16	3⅜	...	d	1	14.9	-22.9	1.6
17•[9]	GRL	Gulf Indonesia Resources	NY	NR	58	15812	Oil/gas explor,dev,prod,mktg	26¼	19¼	22	5 13/16	13 7/16	6 3/16	21174	8 9/16	7⅛	8⅛	...	74	...	25.0	...	...
18	GSE	✓Gundle/SLT Environmental	NY,Ch,Ph,P	B–	28	4946	Mfg polyethylene lining prod	25	3⅞	6⅛	2½	5⅛	2¾	3185	4 3/16	3⅜	3½	...	7	66	-12.5	-19.2	-7.8
✣19•[10]	GYMB	✓Gymboree Corp	NNM,Ch	B	130	15182	Retail young childrens apparel	37¼	10	28⅞	3¾	13⅞	4¾	45263	6½	4 13/16	5⅝	...	43	Neg	-11.8	-37.4	-27.8
✣20•[1]	HMK	✓HA-LO Industries	NY,Ph	B	153	18935	Dstr specialty advertising pd	21 7/16	1 5/16	25 9/16	14 5/16	25 11/16	4 7/16	91930	9	5½	7½	...	d	-43	-69.8	-25.6	30.3
✣21•[10]	HDC	✓Hadco Corp	NY	C	154	11249	Mfrs printed circuits	75⅝	2⅞	54	17½	51	23⅝	13720	51	42¼	51	...	32	Neg	45.7	1.3	41.5
22	HAE	✓Haemacure Corp	To	NR	3	650	Dvlp stg:biological adhesives	5 7/16	1¾	7½	2 5/16	5½	1 13/16	2183	2 1/16	1 13/16	1⅞	...	d	...	-62.0	-22.0	...
23	HAE	✓Haemonetics Corp	NY,Ch,Ph	B+	130	22597	Mfr blood collection systems	28½	11	23⅜	13⅝	24¼	12 1/16	12379	24	20 9/16	23 13/16	...	28	-30	4.7	8.1	6.7
24	HBIX	✓Hagler Bailly	NNM	NR	27	3350	Mgmt consulting/advisory svcs	27	14	30¾	13½	22 9/16	4	10702	5⅞	4	5	...	6	...	-75.0	...	...
25	HAHN	✓Hahn Automotive Warehouse	NSC	NR	7	245	Retail/wholesale auto parts	14¾	5	6	2	6¼	½	10335	2½	1 1/16	1⅛	...	19	-11	-50.0	-47.2	-38.1
26•[9]	HAIN	✓Hain Food Group	NNM	NR	90	8013	Dvlp/mkt natural foods	12 13/16	2½	28⅝	9	28⅝	14 15/16	18850	24¾	22	22⅝	...	29	31	-10.5	87.9	37.1
27	HLY	✓Haley Industries	To	NR	1	108	Aerospace alloy casting pds	15 7/16	1	7½	3½	4⅜	2 5/16	840	2 15/16	2⅜	2½	...	42	NM	-40.5	-8.8	8.0
28	HX	✓Halifax Corp[60]	AS	B	8	121	Electric svc/facility support	15	2 7/16	10	5¼	11	4½	834	6 3/16	4½	6 3/16	...	d	Neg	-32.7	-14.4	8.6
¶29•[10]	HAL	✓Halliburton Co	NY,To,B,CS,Ch,Ph,P	B–	1169	335222	Oil well svcs:engr & constr	63¼	3⅞	57¼	25	51¾	28⅛	497486	41⅝	34	40¼	1.2	66	-38	37.6	11.6	21.9
30	HAF.EC	Hallmark Finl Svcs	ECM	NR	4	1691	Retail non-standard auto insur	9½	3/16	1 7/16	⅜	11/16	3/16	327	⅜	5/16	⅜B	...	8	-30	-14.2	-24.6	8.4
31	HWG	✓Hallwood Group	NY,B,Ch,Ph,P	B–	11	354	Investment co/merchant bank'g	1143 13/16	4 5/16	25	10 15/16	13¼	10 13/16	277	12⅝	11 11/16	12 9/16	...	4	NM	-1.6	4.9	21.4
32	HRY	✓Hallwood Rlty Ptnrs L.P.(New)	AS	NR	5	249	Acquire,manage real estate	55½	3⅛	70	44½	61¾	47¾	79	53½	50	51¼	...	17	NM	-13.9	27.9	34.0
33	HDG	✓Halsey Drug	AS,Ch,P	C	11	1393	Mfrs generic drug products	11 5/16	1⅛	3⅝	1	3¼	¾	13954	1¾	¾	15/16	...	d	-13	-31.9	-46.5	-15.1
34	JQH	✓Hammons(John Q)Hotels'A'	NY,Ch	NR	19	1393	Own,manage upscale hotels	16⅞	7½	9	3⅛	5½	3 5/16	5655	4 1/16	3 5/16	3⅞	...	28	-44	5.1	-23.0	-22.7
35	HAI	✓Hampton Indus	AS	B–	18	1039	Mens/boys shirts: casual wear	11⅞	¼	7 7/16	5 7/16	6	2	1013	2½	2	2 5/16	...	d	-28	-54.8	-16.4	-7.2
✣36	HKF	✓Hancock Fabrics	NY,P	B–	79	7966	Fabric retailer/wholesaler	27¾	5⅝	17⅛	7½	8 15/16	2⅞	26824	3 15/16	2⅞	3⅛	3.2	78	-34	-59.9	-29.8	-15.4
37	HBHC	✓Hancock Holding	NNM	B+	47	1597	Commercial banking, Miss	63½	12⅝	63½	39¾	48	37⅛	2555	40½	37⅛	38¾	2.6	14	2	-12.8	0.7	14.0
38•[11]	HDL	✓Handleman Co	NY,B,Ch,P	C	107	20367	Dstr recorded music & books	24	7/16	15	5 13/16	17	9⅝	18153	15½	11¼	13⅝	...	13	8	-3.6	15.7	4.4
✣39•[12]	HGR	✓Hanger Orthopedic Grp	NY,Ch,P	B–	171	15720	Ortho prosthetic rehab svc	17½	1½	25⅞	12¼	27½	8¾	20335	10 9/16	8¾	10	...	14	NM	-55.6	15.4	27.2
#40•[13]	MAH	✓Hanna(M.A.)Co	NY,B,Ch,P	B	207	35090	Polymers/specialty chemical	30	4 11/16	25 9/16	9¾	17⅜	9⅛	40452	11¾	9½	10 15/16	4.6	12	-12	-7.5	-18.2	-4.7
#41•[14]	HRD	✓Hannaford Bros	NY,B,Ch,Ph,P	A	249	15216	Food dstr: partner supermkts	44⅛	5/16	53	38¾	73⅜	43⅝	34987	72 15/16	65 15/16	69 9/16	1.0	30	8	32.3	28.5	24.0
42	HCM	✓Hanover Capital Mtg	AS	NR	8	1614	Real estate investment trust	....	....	17½	3⅝	6	3⅛	3969	3¾	3⅛	3⅝	16.0	d		-7.9	...	...
43	WS	Wrrt(Pur 1 com at $15)	AS	....	7	1919				4	1/64	¼	1/64	333	1/32	1/64	1/64				...	...	...
44	HCM.U	Unit[65]	AS	NR	..	...		19¼	14⅞	21⅞	3 3/16	6⅛	3	511	3⅝	3	3⅛	12.8	..	...	...	...	...
#45	HC	✓Hanover Compressor	NY,Ph	NR	119	10036	Natr'l gas compres'n rental/svcs	26	17⅛	29⅝	17 5/16	38⅝	19¼	36375	38⅛	28 1/16	37¾	...	32	39	47.0	...	...
46	HNV	✓Hanover Direct	AS,B,Ch,P,Ph	C	59	75117	Direct mkt catalog sales	29 5/16	9/16	3⅝	1⅞	3⅞	1 9/16	123232	3⅞	2¾	3⅝	...	d	Neg	5.5	69.1	0.0
47•[13]	HAN	✓Hanson plc ADR[66]	NY,B,Ch,P	NR	94	17202	Indust'l mgmt co:U.K. & U.S.	186	22	41⅞	20 13/16	50 15/16	31⅞	6830	44⅛	38⅞	40 9/16	2.6	8	-21	6.1	...	...
✣48•[3]	HRBC	✓Harbinger Corp	NNM	NR	142	16890	Dvp elec commerce softwr & svcs	28 5/16	5⅝	27 9/16	3½	34	5 1/16	195481	34	16¾	31 3/16	...	71	68	298	39.9	...
¶49•[9]	H	✓Harcourt General	NY,B,Ch,P	↑B+	384	45643	Retail stores, publishing,	57	5/16	61 15/16	41⅞	55½	32 13/16	93117	40½	32⅞	40¼	2.1	16	-25	...	...	...
50	Pr A	Ser[70]A cm Cv Stk(NC)	NY,Ch	NR	4	220	theatres,insurance	61	6⅝	67½	45	60	42½	83	51 11/16	43¾	51	1.9	..	...	...	...	...

Uniform Footnote Explanations-See Page 4. Other: [1]ASE,CBOE:Cycle 3. [2]CBOE,Ph:Cycle 1. [3]ASE:Cycle 3. [4]ASE,CBOE,Ph:Cycle 1. [5]ASE,P,Ph:Cycle 1. [6]P:Cycle 2. [7]Ph:Cycle 1. [8]Mo:Cycle 2. [9]CBOE:Cycle 2. [10]CBOE:Cycle 1. [11]CBOE,Ph:Cycle 3. [12]Ph:Cycle 3. [13]CBOE:Cycle 3. [14]P:Cycle 1. [51]Ea ADS rep 2 ord shrs, no-par. [52]Fiscal Sep'96 & prior. [53]12 Mo Dec:Fiscal Sep'97 earned d$4.59. [54]Fiscal Dec'96 & prior. [55]12 Mo Mar'98:Fiscal Dec'97 earned d$0.37. [56]Bell Atlantic plan mgr,1.22 com. [57]Ea ADS rep 50 Cl'H'Ord shrs RMB 1.00. [58]70% owned by Govt of China. [59]Approx. [60]ASE trading halted 3-16-99. [61]Dstr of $10 amt debs. [62]12 Mo Dec:Fiscal July'95 earn d$3.60. [63]Excl 16M LP units. [64]6 Mo Dec'97. [65]Ea unit rep 1 com & 1 wrrt. [66]ADR's representing 5 Ord shrs par 25p. [67]15 Mo Dec'97. [68]Stk dstr of Neiman Marcus Group Inc. [69]Pfd in $M. [70]Divd rt $0.03 plus amt pd on com.

Index	Cash Divs. Ea.Yr. Since	Dividends Latest Payment Period $	Date	Ex. Div.	Total $ So Far 1999	Ind. Rate	Paid 1998	Financial Position Mil-$ Cash& Equiv.	Curr. Assets	Curr. Liab.	Balance Sheet Date	Capitalization Lg Trm Debt Mil-$	Shs. 000 Pfd.	Com.	Earnings $ Per Shr. Years End	1995	1996	1997	1998	1999	Last 12 Mos.	Interim Earnings Period	$ per Shr. 1998	1999	Index
1	....	None Since Public			...	Nil	....	201	484	1161	12-31-98	454	...	203769	Dc	d0.62	0.11	d4.51	vd1.93	....	....	6 Mo Jun	n/a	vd0.12	1
2	....	....			...	....	....	Amt at matur based on S&P500 re-spec cond				★73.0	...	...	Dc	...	...	...	...	....	....	Mature 8-9-2002			2
3	....	None Since Public			...	Nil	....	3.60	28.6	24.9	9-30-99	0.12	...	5066	Dc	1.08	v0.82	vd1.72	v0.27	....	0.41	9 Mo Sep	v0.03	v0.17	3
4	....	None Since Public			...	Nil	....	45.2	217	123	9-30-99	1154	.5	37714	Dc	vd0.82	v[52]d3.24	v[53]d5.08	vd4.52	....	d4.80	9 Mo Sep	vd2.60	vd2.88	4
5	....	None Since Public			...	Nil	....	4.44	272	305	9-30-99	....	...	74634	Mr	p0.34	v[54]0.37	v[55]d0.43	n/a	....	....	6 Mo Sep	v0.05	vd0.84	5
6	1936	Q0.47	1-1-00	11-18	1.88	1.88	1.88	3555	11526	13662	9-30-99	14278	...	971795	Dc	v□2.61	v2.88	v2.90	v2.57	E4.00	4.00	9 Mo Sep	v□1.69	v□3.12	6
7	....	None Since Public			...	Nil	....	7.75	244	192	11-27-99	386	...	34799	Fb	v1.53	v1.80	v0.64	v2.16	E2.61	2.28	9 Mo Nov	v1.61	v1.73	7
8	....	None Since Public			...	Nil	....	13.0	35.0	6.88	j6-30-99	0.38	...	29174	Mr	...	...	vd0.19	v0.21	....	j0.28	6 Mo Sep	vd0.04	v0.03	8
9	1997	0.601	7-27-99	5-11	0.601	0.60	0.709	274	330	145	12-31-98	....	...	[58]4335550	Dc	p2.50	v1.68	v1.15	v0.91	....	0.91				9
10	1996	0.30	7-26-99	7-12	0.30	0.30	[59]0.30	168	539	279	1-31-99	17.3	...	58511	Ja	v1.68	v2.76	v2.86	v3.28	E3.44	3.63	9 Mo Oct	v2.16	v2.51	10
11	....	None Since Public			...	Nil	....	44.9	209	82.0	9-25-99	95.3	...	43079	Dc	pv0.96	vp1.18	Δv0.78	v0.59	....	0.96	9 Mo Sep	v0.49	v0.86	11
12◆	....	None Since Public			...	Nil	....	2.93	107	54.4	7-02-99	49.9	...	6551	Sp	0.70	v0.45	v0.55	v0.51	Pv1.10	1.10				12
13◆	1995	0.006	12-15-98	11-27	...	Nil	0.02½	26.0	873	781	9-30-99	570	...	p307361	Dc	v0.32	v0.18	□v0.50	v0.14	E1.20	1.10	9 Mo Sep	vd0.15	v□0.81	13
14◆	1973	Q0.11	11-29-99	11-10	0.44	0.44	0.44	22.6	339	211	10-03-99	146	...	19200	Sp	1.61	v1.47	v1.78	v□1.30	v0.47	0.47				14
15	....	None Since Public			...	Nil	....	0.40	167	105	9-30-99	69.8	...	22073	Dc	...	pvd0.34	v0.42	v1.31	....	1.27	9 Mo Sep	v0.26	v□0.22	15
16	....	g0.10	4-1-92	2-27	...	Nil	....	257	672	637	j6-30-99	2197	85505	348950	Dc	vd0.32	v0.03	v0.62	vd1.70	....	jd0.88	9 Mo Sep	vd1.31	vd0.49	16
17	....	None Since Public			...	Nil	....	66.5	139	90.5	12-31-98	228	...	87907	Dc	...	p0.19	v0.11	vd0.34	....	0.11	9 Mo Sep	vd0.27	v0.18	17
18	....	None Since Public			...	Nil	....	11.8	110	50.3	9-30-99	26.7	...	12865	Dc	vd0.13	v0.67	v0.29	v0.30	....	0.51	9 Mo Sep	v0.19	v0.40	18
19◆	....	None Since Public			...	Nil	....	32.7	93.4	35.3	10-30-99	11.0	...	24346	Ja	v1.04	v1.24	v1.41	v0.26	E0.13	d0.23	9 Mo Oct	v0.13	vd0.36	19
20◆	....	None Since Public			...	Nil	....	14.8	241	99.2	9-30-99	5.90	...	48718	Dc	v0.15	v0.26	v0.43	v0.53	....	d0.11	9 Mo Sep	v0.32	vd0.32	20
21	....	None Since Public			...	Nil	....	12.3	223	137	7-31-99	314	...	13629	Oc	1.98	2.89	vd3.18	vd4.09	Pv1.60	1.60				21
22	....	None Since Public			...	Nil	....	15.2	19.6	3.09	j7-31-99	0.91	...	15587	Oc	d0.72	d0.58	vd0.79	vd1.24	....	jd1.55	9 Mo Jul	vd0.65	vd0.96	22
23◆	....	None Since Public			...	Nil	....	56.2	223	66.9	10-02-99	52.9	...	25885	Mr	1.30	v1.20	vd0.93	v0.78	....	0.84	6 Mo Sep	v0.38	v0.44	23
24	....	None Since Public			...	Nil	....	13.5	82.4	31.1	9-30-99	0.67	...	17911	Dc	...	vd0.67	v0.70	vp0.93	....	0.80	9 Mo Sep	v0.36	v0.23	24
25◆	....	4%Stk	5-1-97	4-8	...	Nil	....	0.77	64.9	20.9	6-30-99	5.06	...	4745	Sp	d0.29	v0.39	vd4.45	v0.22	Pv0.06	0.06				25
26	....	None Paid			...	Nil	....	0.53	57.3	40.0	9-30-99	42.7	...	18049	Je	0.28	v0.24	v0.12	v□0.39	v0.71	0.76	3 Mo Sep	v0.12	v□0.17	26
27	....	None Paid			...	Nil	....	....	25.8	15.4	j6-30-99	24.4	...	10506	Dc	0.04	v0.16	v0.27	v0.33	....	j0.06	9 Mo Sep	v0.28	v0.01	27
28◆	1984	Div Postponed 5-4-99			0.05	Nil	0.20	....	25.0	21.6	9-30-99	15.3	...	2015	Mr	v0.43	v0.47	v0.21	vd2.63	....	d0.12	6 Mo Sep	vd2.38	v0.13	28
29◆	1947	Q0.12½	12-22-99	11-29	0.50	0.50	0.50	295	5761	3722	9-30-99	1059	...	441754	Dc	0.74	v1.19	v1.75	vd0.03	E0.61	0.65	9 Mo Sep	vd0.18	v□0.50	29
30	....	None Since Public			...	Nil	....	Total Assets $57.37M			9-30-99	7.05	...	11048	Dc	0.11	v0.09	vΔd0.08	vNil	....	0.05	9 Mo Sep	v0.01	v0.06	30
31◆	....	[61]....	5-3-89	5-16	...	Nil	....	Total Assets $102.32M			9-30-99	64.2	250	1883	Dc	Δ[62]d1.60	v3.26	Δv5.75	vΔ2.84	....	3.10	9 Mo Sep	v□1.41	v1.67	31
32◆	....	0.62½	2-14-92	12-24	...	Nil	....	Total Assets $221M			9-30-99	164	...	1673	Dc	□vd5.55	vd5.50	v1.35	v□3.55	....	3.09	9 Mo Sep	v□2.53	v2.07	32
33	....	5%Stk	12-15-89	11-9	...	Nil	....	2.39	8.43	7.53	9-30-99	42.8	...	14390	Dc	d0.28	vd1.49	vd1.12	vd0.92	....	d1.12	9 Mo Sep	vd0.64	vd0.84	33
34	....	None Since Public			...	Nil	....	39.7	53.4	67.8	10-01-99	809	...	[63]±5596	Dc	v□0.82	v0.81	±v0.38	v□±Nil	....	0.14	9 Mo Sep	v±□d0.22	±□d0.08	34
35◆	....	0.02	12-31-73	12-4	...	Nil	....	0.24	121	73.3	9-25-99	14.3	...	5554	Dc	vd0.39	v0.48	v0.19	v0.43	....	d0.41	9 Mo Sep	v0.29	vd0.55	35
36	1987	Q0.02½	1-15-00	12-29	0.40	0.10	0.50	10.9	162	66.9	10-31-99	37.0	...	18990	Ja	0.42	v0.58	v0.72	v0.18	....	0.04	9 Mo Oct	v0.30	v0.16	36
37◆	1937	Q0.25	12-15-99	12-1	1.00	1.00	1.00	Total Deposits $2444.83M			9-30-99	2.84	...	10911	Dc	v2.65	v3.08	v2.82	Δv2.78	....	2.74	9 Mo Sep	v2.18	v2.14	37
38	....	0.05	1-10-96	12-22	...	Nil	....	0.70	432	304	10-30-99	45.4	...	29108	Ap	v0.26	d0.67	v0.16	v0.01	vd1.11	1.02	6 Mo Oct	vd1.67	v0.46	38
39	....	None Paid			...	Nil	....	9.07	187	78.1	9-30-99	405	...	19084	Dc	v0.25	□v0.12	□v0.58	v0.75	....	0.72	9 Mo Sep	v0.53	v0.50	39
40◆	1944	Q0.12½	12-13-99	11-22	0.48½	0.50	0.45¾	47.5	697	417	9-30-99	426	...	48900	Dc	v2.14	v□1.26	v1.40	v□0.67	E0.95	0.82	9 Mo Sep	v□0.62	v0.77	40
41	1948	Q0.16½	12-23-99	12-8	0.66	0.66	0.60	52.6	313	290	10-02-99	251	...	42252	Dc	v1.66	v1.76	v1.40	v2.21	....	2.28	9 Mo Sep	v1.55	v1.62	41
42	1998	0.10	2-1-00	12-29	0.51	0.58	0.59	Total Assets $387M			9-30-99	274	...	5827	Dc	...	...	v[64]0.14	vd0.77	....	d3.11	9 Mo Sep	v0.15	vd2.19	42
43	....	Terms&trad. basis should be checked in detail						Wrrts expire 9-15-2000				....	...	5000	Dc	...	...	...	...	....	....				43
44	1998	Q0.10	2-1-00	12-29	0.51	0.40	0.75	....	...	...		....	...	★5000	Dc	...	...	...	...	....	....				44
45	....	None Since Public			...	Nil	....	9.09	190	60.5	9-30-99	125	...	28724	Dc	v0.31	pv0.16	v0.66	v1.01	....	1.20	9 Mo Sep	v0.71	v0.90	45
46	....	5%Stk	9-12-84	8-15	...	Nil	....	6.41	122	86.2	9-25-99	55.0	635	211255	Dc	□d0.30	v□d0.93	vd0.06	vd0.13	....	d0.13	9 Mo Sep	vd0.06	vd0.06	46
47◆	1986	0.34	9-24-99	8-18	1.052	1.05	1.049	1675	2288	1260	j12-31-98	1007	...	651504	Dc	12.24	P[52]17.04	v[67]9.81	v4.50	....	5.07	6 Mo Jun	v0.78	v1.35	47
48◆	....	None Since Public			...	Nil	....	67.2	121	47.2	9-30-99	....	...	38714	Dc	0.05	vd0.46	□vd0.95	vd0.35	E0.45	0.55	9 Mo Sep	vd0.55	v0.35	48
49◆	1953	Q0.21	1-31-00	1-12	h[68]0.81	0.84	0.77	248	1847	1319	7-31-99	1644	[69]894	±71156	Oc	2.16	±v2.62	v±d1.64	v±1.96	vP±2.55	2.55				49
50	1982	0.283	1-31-00	1-12	0.929	0.984	0.877	Cv into 1 common				....	1504	...	Oc	...	...	...	...	....	....				50

◆**Stock Splits & Divs By Line Reference Index** [12]3-for-2,'95. [13]2-for-1,'97,'99. [14]3-for-2,'97. [19]2-for-1,'94. [20]3-for-2,'96,'99:5-for-4,'96. [23]2-for-1,'93. [25]Adj to 4%,'97. [28]3-for-2,'96. [29]2-for-1,'97. [31]1-for-4 REVERSE,'95:3-for-2,'99. [32]1-for-5 REVERSE,'95. [35]10%,'98,'99. [37]15%,'96. [40]3-for-2,'94,'96. [47]No adj for stk dstr Millenium Chem,'96:1-for-8 REVERSE,'97. [48]3-for-2,'97,'98. [49]No adj for stk dstr of GC Co's,'93.

¶ S&P 500
# MidCap 400
✣ SmallCap 600
• Options

Index	Ticker	Name of Issue (Call Price of Pfd. Stocks)	Market	Com. Rank. & Pfd. Rating	Inst. Hold Cos	Inst. Hold Shs. (000)	Principal Business	Price Range 1971-97 High	1971-97 Low	1998 High	1998 Low	1999 High	1999 Low	Dec. Sales in 100s	December, 1999 Last Sale Or Bid High	Low	Last	%Div Yield	P-E Ratio	EPS 5 Yr Growth	% Annualized Total Return 12 Mo	36 Mo	60 Mo
1	HRDG	✔Harding Lawson Assoc Grp	NNM	B–	27	2491	Hazardous waste consult svcs	26	4 13/16	10½	5⅛	9	5	3606	7¾	6 15/16	7¾	...	d	Neg	26.5	3.5	6.6
2	HEC	✔Harken Energy	AS,P	C	71	27230	Oil & gas expl,dev,prod'n	25½	¾	7⅜	1 9/16	3 3/16	11/16	225549	1	11/16	13/16	...	d	–30	–59.4	–35.3	–17.5
✣3•[1]	JH	✔Harland (John H.)	NY,B,Ch,P	B	150	20798	Bank stationer: checks, etc.	33	1 1/16	21⅞	12¼	21¼	12⅜	14951	19 7/16	17¾	18 5/16	1.6	15	Neg	17.9	–16.5	0.9
#4•[2]	HDI	✔Harley-Davidson	NY,Ch,Ph,P	B+	542	94558	Manufactures motorcycles	31¼	7/16	47½	24 15/16	64 1/16	42¾	99877	64 1/16	55¾	64 1/16	0.3	38	20	35.7	41.1	36.7
5	HGIC	✔Harleysville Group	NNM	B+	98	9595	Insur hldg:prop/casualty	27½	3 13/16	28½	17¼	26⅛	12⅝	9969	15¼	12⅝	14¼	3.8	9	19	–43.0	0.6	6.2
✣6•[3]	HAR	✔Harman International	NY,Ch,Ph	B	214	16110	Audio video sys components	57 1/16	4 5/16	46 13/16	31½	56⅛	34¼	13570	56⅛	49 9/16	56⅛	0.4	..	–32	47.9	0.8	11.3
✣7	HRMN	✔Harmon Indus	NNM	B	79	6413	Railroad communic/ctrl prod	19 11/16	3/16	26½	16 13/16	23½	8¼	9394	13	11⅝	12⅛	1.0	19	3	–47.0	–0.1	–0.6
8•[4]	HLIT	✔Harmonic Inc	NNM	NR	186	24460	Dvlp CATV transmission prd	13⅜	3⅞	9½	3 13/16	100⅞	7 7/16	216069	100⅞	57½	94 15/16	...	..	32	915	131	...
9	HLD	✔Harold's Stores	AS,NSC	B+	12	1869	Retail:ladies&mens apparel	15 9/16	1⅜	8⅜	5⅛	8¼	3⅜	1112	4⅜	3⅜	3¾	...	16	–17	–49.2	–31.9	–10.8
¶10•[3]	HET	✔Harrah's Entertainment	NY,Ph,P	B	428	93103	Hotel & casino operations	55¼	2 15/16	26⅜	11 1/16	30¾	14 3/16	172591	27 7/16	22⅝	26 7/16	...	16	NM	68.5	10.0	...
#11•[3]	HRS	✔Harris Corp	NY,B,Ch,P,Ph	↓B+	395	57934	Gov't Sys/communications	50	1⅝	55 5/16	27 9/16	40⅝	15½	100707	26 13/16	21 5/16	26 11/16	0.7	59	–27	...	...	...
12	HPOL	Harris Interactive	NNM	NR	..	...	Marketing research svcs	....	....	....	....	24	13	163469	24	13	13 1/16	...	d	...	...	...	...
#13•[5]	HSC	✔Harsco Corp	NY,B,Ch,P,Ph	A–	210	21658	Industrial service,engin prd	47⅞	1 7/16	47¼	22 5/16	34⅜	23 1/16	14961	31⅞	28 13/16	31¾	3.0	15	8	7.5	0.1	12.1
#14	HHS	✔Harte-Hanks Inc	NY,Ph	B	203	30172	Direct marketing svcs/publish	19 5/16	5 1/16	28½	17 5/16	29¼	19 1/16	21021	21¾	19⅞	21¾	0.4	22	26	–23.4	16.5	27.8
¶15•[6]	HIG	✔Hartford Finl Svcs Gp	NY,P	NR	800	167744	Multi-line insurance	47¼	22¼	60	37⅝	66 7/16	36½	180677	48	41⅜	47⅜	2.0	13	49	–12.1	14.1	...
16•[6]	HLI	✔Hartford Life 'A'	NY,Ph	NR	227	18528	Life insurance/annuity prd	46⅝	32	63	32	60 5/16	37 1/16	40134	47¾	37¾	44	0.8	14	...	–23.9	...	...
✣17	HMX	✔Hartmarx Corp	NY,B,Ch,P	B–	93	15094	Apparel manufacturing/mktg	34¾	2 3/16	9	3 15/16	6	3¼	12155	4 1/16	3¼	4 1/16	...	34	–10	–27.8	–10.3	–7.1
18	HRVY	Harvey Entertainment	NNM	NR	11	594	Film entertain't/merchandis'g	19½	5¼	15¼	5	8¼	2⅞	4326	6¼	3⅝	3 13/16	...	d	Neg	–50.8	–13.7	–23.2
¶19•[5]	HAS	✔Hasbro Inc	NY,B,P	B+	572	149575	Mfrs toys & games	24 5/16	1/32	27 5/16	18 11/16	37	16⅞	314617	23	16⅞	18 15/16	1.3	21	7	–19.7	4.5	9.2
20	HMF	✔Hastings Mfg	AS	B–	7	86	Mfr automotive replace't parts	26⅝	2 3/16	24¾	16½	21¼	8	497	9⅝	8	7⅞B	e2.5	7	NM	–52.1	–12.4	–4.6
21	HAUP	✔Hauppauge Digital	NNM	NR	12	173	Mfr digital vidco prod	8	1 9/16	16	4 3/16	38⅛	7¼	27653	29	19 9/16	20⅛	...	31	...	118	72.3	...
22	HAVN	✔Haven Bancorp	NNM	NR	40	3756	General banking, New York	23	4⅝	29¾	9⅛	19	10½	8716	16½	14⅜	15 7/16	1.9	12	NM	5.1	4.5	20.3
23	HVT	✔Haverty Furniture	NY	A–	126	11900	Retail furniture stores	9 13/16	⅝	12	6½	19 5/16	9⅛	10138	13⅝	11½	12⅝	1.6	12	14	22.2	33.0	19.1
24	HVT.A	Cl'A'	NY	A–	9	481		9⅝	2 11/16	12 15/16	6⅜	18½	8½	129	13¼	12 11/16	12⅞	1.5	13	12	48.5	33.3	21.6
25	HA	✔Hawaiian Airlines	AS,Ph,P	NR	18	5982	Regional airline service	13½	1⅝	3 13/16	1½	3 3/16	2	13075	2⅜	2	2⅛	...	14	NM	–34.6	–14.3	...
#26•[7]	HE	✔Hawaiian Elec Indus	NY,B,Ch,P,Ph	B+	168	9312	Hldg:electric/finl svc,Hawaii	44⅝	7 1/16	42 9/16	36⅜	40½	28 1/16	24540	30⅝	28 1/16	28⅞	8.6	11	1	–22.8	–0.7	4.5
27	HWK	✔Hawk Corp 'A'	NY	NR	38	4453	Aerospace friction pds	....	....	19 15/16	6¼	11¾	3 13/16	5357	6 3/16	5	5 13/16	...	6	...	–30.6	...	...
28	HAZ	✔Hayes Lemmerz Intl	NY	NR	73	6741	Dsgn, mfr car & truck wheels	37¾	13⅞	41¼	23½	33½	14 9/16	21152	18	14 9/16	17 7/16	...	9	NM	–42.2	–3.2	...
29	HBS	✔Haywood Bancshares	AS,Ph	NR	3	54	Savings bank,North Carolina	22⅝	15⅝	23	15¾	21⅜	13⅜	135	21 3/16	20⅛	20¼B	3.2	17	–13	38.4	7.1	...
30•[8]	HCC	✔HCC Insurance Hldgs	NY,Ch,Ph	NR	208	33949	Prop & casualty insur,agency	32¾	3 3/16	23 15/16	15⅝	25⅛	8	40882	13 5/16	10⅜	13 3/16	1.5	14	11	–23.9	–17.5	10.0
31	HDWY	✔Headway Corporate Res	NNM	NR	17	1853	Human resources services	6¼	1½	12¾	4⅛	6 11/16	3 1/16	10104	4⅜	3 1/16	4⅜	...	10	...	–28.6	–1.8	...
32	HCP	✔Health Care Prop Inv	NY,B,Ch,P	NR	158	14675	Real estate investment trust	40⅜	9½	40	28¼	33⅛	21 11/16	46727	26⅜	21 11/16	23⅞	11.9	9	4	–14.1	–4.4	3.0
33	HCN	✔Health Care REIT	NY,Ch,P	NR	112	5371	Real estate investment trust	28¾	6 3/16	29¼	20	26⅝	14 11/16	36882	16 5/16	14 11/16	15⅛	15.2	7	7	–34.9	–6.6	3.9
#34•[3]	HMA	✔Health Management Assoc	NY,Ph,P	B+	400	193348	Oper acute care hospitals	17 11/16	15/16	25¾	14 15/16	21⅝	7	228469	13½	11 7/16	13⅜	...	22	25	–38.2	10.3	22.4
35	HR	✔Healthcare Realty Tr	NY,Ph	NR	169	14652	Real estate investment trust	30	17¾	29 15/16	21	23¼	14½	64870	16 7/16	14½	15⅝	14.0	8	8	–21.1	–8.6	2.8
36	HCRI	✔Healthcare Recoveries	NNM	NR	38	6848	Health insurance subrogation	26	14	24 9/16	8 9/16	17⅛	2 9/16	12046	3¾	2⅝	3⅝	...	7	...	–78.7	...	...
37	HCEN	HealthCentral.com	NNM	NR	..	...	Dvlp stge:online hlth care sv	....	....	....	....	12¾	6⅞	213041	12¾	6⅞	7 5/16	...	..	...	...	...	...
38	HLTH	✔Healtheon/WebMD Corp	NNM	NR	93	6314	Internet health svc	....	....	....	....	126 3/16	8	575209	51½	36½	37½	...	d	...	...	...	...
39	HPS	✔HealthPlan Services	NY,Ph	NR	47	5497	Managed healthcare services	29¼	13⅝	27	8	11½	3	23855	7	3	3½	15.7	27	–3	–67.2	–42.8	...
¶40•[9]	HRC	✔HEALTHSOUTH Corp	NY,Ch,Ph,P	B	623	245381	Medical rehabilitation svc	28 15/16	1	30 13/16	7 11/16	17¾	4 9/16	789712	5¾	4 11/16	5⅜	...	6	–26	–65.2	–34.7	–9.5
41	HPP	✔Healthy Planet Prod	AS,Ch	B–	3	89	Dsgn,mkt stationery/card prd	134	¼	3¾	7/16	1⅞	5/16	2944	11/16	⅜	⅝	...	d	Neg	–9.0	–45.0	–40.5
42	HTV	✔Hearst-Argyle Television 'A'	NY,Ph	NR	134	11520	Own/oper T.V. stations	32⅝	26¼	41¼	24	35¼	19 15/16	11278	27 1/16	20 7/16	26⅝	...	42	...	–19.3	...	...
43	HTL	✔Heartland Partners L.P. 'A'[54]	AS	NR	6	79	Real estate development	16	6¼	18¾	11⅞	23¼	13¾	132	20½	18⅝	20¼B	...	..	55	19.1	38.1	16.2
44•[10]	HPRT	✔Heartport Inc	NNM	NR	48	3843	Dvlp stg:heart surgery sys	43¾	16	23¾	2⅜	8⅞	1⅞	84032	7 13/16	3⅞	4¾	...	d	...	–19.1	–40.8	...
45	EAR	✔HEARx Ltd	AS,Ch	NR	12	342	Oper hearing care centers	73¾	10⅝	19⅜	5	7½	3¼	12839	4⅞	3 9/16	4 11/16	...	d	–11	0.3	–41.5	...
46•[11]	HL	✔Hecla Mining	NY,B,Ch,P,Ph	C	93	10644	Silver producer: lead,gold	35 13/16	3 1/16	7⅛	3 3/16	4⅜	1 7/16	119273	2⅛	1 7/16	1 9/16	...	d	32	–56.9	–34.8	–31.2
47	Pr B	Sr'B'cm Cv Pfd([57]51.40)	NY,Ch	CCC+	16	681		59⅛	38¾	49⅛	36	39½	22 3/16	1989	30 15/16	22 3/16	23⅞	14.7	..	...	...	...	...
48	HCT	✔Hector Communications	AS	B	27	1132	Oper tel cos,cable TV:WI,MN	10½	2¾	12⅝	7⅜	17¼	8	2180	15⅞	12	14	...	10	82	68.4	24.5	14.9
49	HEI	✔HEICO Corp	NY,B,Ch,P,Ph	B	39	1554	Mfr jet aircraft engine parts	19½	1/16	34¾	15 3/16	31 1/16	14¼	8400	22¾	14 13/16	21 13/16	0.2	24	44	–30.7	30.6	69.7
50	HEI.A	Cl'A'	NY	B	56	3576		....	....	31¼	12⅛	24⅝	12 7/16	3775	22	14⅜	21⅛	0.2	29	44	–8.4	...	...

Uniform Footnote Explanations-See Page 4. Other: [1]CBOE,Ph:Cycle 3. [2]P,Ph:Cycle 2. [3]CBOE:Cycle 2. [4]ASE,CBOE,Ph:Cycle 1. [5]P:Cycle 1. [6]CBOE:Cycle 3. [7]P:Cycle 2. [8]Ph:Cycle 1. [9]CBOE:Cycle 1. [10]CBOE,Ph:Cycle 1. [11]ASE:Cycle 3. [51]Stk dstr of Promus Hotel Corp,'95. [52]Stk dstr of Lanier Worldwide Inc. [53]Excl subsid pfd shares. [54]Units. [55]To be determined. [56]Excl Cl'B' L.P.. [57]Thru 6-30-2000,scale to $50 in 2003.

Index	Cash Divs. Ea. Yr. Since	Dividends: Latest Payment Period $	Date	Ex. Div.	Total $ So Far 1999	Ind. Rate	Paid 1998	Financial Position Mil-$: Cash& Equiv.	Curr. Assets	Curr. Liab.	Balance Sheet Date	Capitalization: Lg Trm Debt Mil-$	Shs. 000 Pfd.	Com.	Earnings $ Per Shr. Years End	1995	1996	1997	1998	1999	Last 12 Mos.	Interim Earnings Period	$ per Shr. 1998	1999	Index
1	....	None Since Public			...	Nil	....	12.0	64.4	29.6	8-31-99	....	...	4998	My	0.62	0.20	v0.49	v0.49	vd0.17	d0.15	3 Mo Aug	v0.20	v0.22	1
2	....	None Since Public			...	Nil	....	61.6	67.9	37.6	9-30-99	96.8	...	153588	Dc	vd0.02	vNil	vNil	vd0.42	....	d0.28	9 Mo Sep	vd0.24	vd0.10	2
3	1932	Q0.07½	12-2-99	11-16	0.30	0.30	0.30	57.6	168	100	10-01-99	107	...	30247	Dc	v1.50	vd0.45	v0.56	vd0.66	E1.20	d0.08	9 Mo Sep	v0.46	v1.04	3
4◆	1993	Q0.04½	12-30-99	12-16	0.17½	0.18	0.15½	163	929	562	9-26-99	280	...	151320	Dc	v0.74	v1.09	v1.13	v1.38	E1.68	1.63	9 Mo Sep	v0.99	v1.24	4
5◆	1986	Q0.135	12-30-99	12-13	0.52	0.54	0.48	Total Assets $1990.93M			9-30-99	96.8	...	29070	Dc	v1.51	v1.02	v1.86	v2.15	....	1.65	9 Mo Sep	v1.51	v□1.01	5
6◆	1994	Q0.05	11-24-99	11-9	0.20	0.20	0.20	11.7	669	262	9-30-99	331	...	17262	Je	□2.72	3.16	v2.90	v□2.86	v0.65	0.48	3 Mo Sep	v0.45	v0.28	6
7◆	1994	S0.06	12-17-99	12-1	0.12	0.12	0.11	7.16	165	76.7	9-30-99	70.8	...	11348	Dc	v0.67	v0.91	v1.06	v1.25	....	0.65	9 Mo Sep	v0.93	v0.33	7
8◆	....	None Since Public			...	Nil	....	52.8	121	33.2	10-01-99	....	...	30302	Dc	v0.20	v0.26	v0.22	vd0.93	E0.67↓	0.46	9 Mo Sep	vd0.95	v0.43	8
9◆	....	5%Stk	1-30-98	1-14	...	Stk	5%Stk	1.21	55.3	9.53	10-30-99	29.0	...	6075	Ja	v0.51	v0.61	v0.01	□v0.47	....	0.24	9 Mo Oct	v□0.26	v0.03	9
10	....	h[51]....	6-30-95	7-3	...	Nil	....	189	392	368	9-30-99	2515	...	128593	Dc	v□d1.00	v0.95	v□1.06	v□1.19	E1.66	1.39	9 Mo Sep	v□1.05	v□1.25	10
11◆	1941	0.05	12-3-99	11-17	h[52]0.77	0.20	0.92	283	1213	656	10-01-99	415	...	79569	Je	1.98	2.29	v2.63	v1.66	v□0.79	0.45	3 Mo Sep	v0.36	v0.02	11
12	....	None Since Public			...	Nil	....	19.3	29.5	14.5	p9-30-99	....	...	★31247	Je	...	...	...	....	vpd0.41	d0.54	3 Mo Sep	vpd0.04	vpd0.17	12
13◆	1939	Q0.23½	2-15-00	1-12	0.90	0.94	0.88	50.0	599	387	9-30-99	443	...	40141	Dc	v1.91	v2.37	v5.67	v2.34	E2.15	2.13	9 Mo Sep	v1.78	v1.57	13
14◆	1995	Q0.02	12-15-99	11-29	0.08	0.08	0.06	126	295	128	9-30-99	....	...	68666	Dc	v0.53	v0.53	□v4.37	v0.90	....	1.00	9 Mo Sep	v0.63	v0.73	14
15◆	1996	Q0.24	1-3-00	11-29	0.90	0.96	0.83	Total Assets $153553.00M			9-30-99	2798	...	221620	Dc	2.39	vd0.42	v5.58	v4.30	E3.70	4.09	9 Mo Sep	v3.00	v2.79	15
16	1997	Q0.09	1-3-00	11-29	0.36	0.36	0.27	Total Assets $125581.00M			9-30-99	900	...	±139970	Dc	...	pv0.19	vp2.28	v±2.75	....	3.19	9 Mo Sep	v±1.98	v±2.42	16
17	....	0.15	11-15-91	10-28	...	Nil	....	2.05	371	86.1	8-31-99	202	...	30581	Nv	0.10	Δ0.72	v0.74	v0.42	....	0.12	9 Mo Aug	v0.25	vd0.05	17
18	....	None Since Public			...	Nil	....	Total Assets $25.51M			9-30-99	....	190	4187	Dc	0.21	v0.33	v0.80	vd2.77	....	d3.13	9 Mo Sep	vd1.34	vd1.70	18
19◆	1981	Q0.06	2-15-00	1-28	0.233	0.24	0.213	108	2267	1839	9-26-99	408	...	193764	Dc	v0.77	v0.98	v0.68	v1.01	E0.91↓	1.29	9 Mo Sep	v0.36	v0.64	19
20◆	1940	†0.08	12-15-99	11-17	†0.32	0.20	†0.31½	0.09	18.5	7.51	9-30-99	3.63	...	790	Dc	vd3.93	vd1.15	v1.24	v2.24	....	1.16	9 Mo Sep	v1.55	v0.47	20
21	....	....			...	....	....	6.35	25.6	13.7	6-30-99	....	...	4332	Sp	d0.60	0.09	v0.22	v0.42	Pv0.66	0.66				21
22◆	1995	Q0.07½	1-21-00	12-29	0.30	0.30	0.30	Total Deposits $2015.51M			9-30-99	....	...	8967	Dc	v0.96	v1.08	v1.24	v0.89	....	1.25	9 Mo Sep	v0.61	v0.97	22
23◆	1935	Q0.05	11-24-99	11-8	0.19	0.20	0.16½	0.74	265	87.8	9-30-99	134	...	±22084	Dc	v±0.53	v±0.52	±v0.57	±v0.72	....	1.09	9 Mo Sep	v±0.43	v±0.80	23
24◆	1986	Q0.04¾	11-24-99	11-8	0.18	0.19	0.15½	....	...	...		....	...	4812	Dc	±0.53	±0.53	±v0.57	v±0.72	....	0.99	6 Mo Jun	v±0.22	v±0.49	24
25	....	None Since Public			...	Nil	....	55.6	105	104	9-30-99	26.5	...	40997	Dc	vd0.59	Δvd0.08	vd0.02	v0.19	....	0.15	9 Mo Sep	v0.19	v0.15	25
26	1901	Q0.62	12-10-99	11-8	2.48	2.48	2.48	Total Assets $8242M			9-30-99	2261	[53]...	32213	Dc	v2.65	v2.59	v2.75	v2.64	....	2.68	9 Mo Sep	v1.98	v2.02	26
27	....	None Since Public			...	Nil	....	2.94	64.9	33.0	9-30-99	94.3	2	8541	Dc	...	...	pv0.74	v□1.51	....	0.91	9 Mo Sep	v□1.23	v0.63	27
28◆	....	None Paid			...	Nil	....	50.6	499	610	10-31-99	1571	...	30339	Ja	vd0.81	□vd2.36	v1.12	v□1.60	....	1.86	9 Mo Oct	v□1.29	v1.55	28
29	1989	Q0.16	1-5-00	12-14	0.64	0.64	0.60	Total Deposits $116.96M			9-30-99	7.00	...	1250	Dc	v1.08	v0.87	v1.52	v0.21	....	1.19	9 Mo Sep	vd0.17	v0.81	29
30◆	1996	Q0.05	1-11-00	12-30	0.19	0.20	0.15	Total Assets $2154M			9-30-99	190	...	48792	Dc	v0.76	vp0.87	v1.07	v1.48	....	0.92	9 Mo Sep	v1.16	v0.60	30
31	....	None Paid			...	Nil	....	0.56	55.3	28.4	9-30-99	64.5	1	11248	Dc	d0.20	vd0.11	v0.28	v□0.47	....	0.43	9 Mo Sep	v□0.35	v0.31	31
32	1985	Q0.71	11-19-99	10-19	2.78	2.84	2.62	Total Assets $1505M			9-30-99	813	7400	51498	Dc	v2.78	v2.10	v2.19	v2.54	....	2.53	9 Mo Sep	v1.81	v1.80	32
33	1971	Q0.575	11-22-99	10-29	2.27	2.30	2.19	Total Assets $1261.86M			9-30-99	529	3000	28491	Dc	1.16	v2.17	v2.12	v2.24	....	2.29	9 Mo Sep	v1.65	v1.70	33
34◆	....	None Since Public			...	Nil	....	11.7	372	179	6-30-99	308	...	253357	Sp	0.26	v0.34	v0.43	v0.54	Pv0.60	0.60				34
35	1993	Q0.545	11-16-99	11-3	2.15	2.18	2.07	Total Assets $1628M			9-30-99	587	3000	39992	Dc	v1.41	v1.49	v1.68	v1.65	....	2.04	9 Mo Sep	v1.03	v1.42	35
36	....	None Since Public			...	Nil	....	1.12	32.6	21.3	9-30-99	12.3	...	11209	Dc	...	pv0.52	v0.37	v0.77	....	0.56	9 Mo Sep	v0.57	v0.36	36
37	....	None Since Public			...	Nil	....	16.2	17.9	2.74	9-30-99	0.26	p...	★19721	Dc	...	...	...	vpd0.10	....	....	9 Mo Sep	n/a	vpd3.21	37
38	....	None Since Public			...	Nil	....	27.7	53.2	30.3	9-30-99	2.08	...	p80856	Dc	...	...	vpd0.56	vd1.54	....	d1.09	9 Mo Sep	vd1.24	vd0.79	38
39	1997	Q0.138	10-19-99	10-6	0.55	0.55	0.52½	12.9	42.9	175	9-30-99	5.51	...	13665	Dc	v0.84	vd0.47	v0.71	v0.67	....	0.13	9 Mo Sep	v0.64	v0.10	39
40◆	....	None Since Public			...	Nil	....	161	1641	493	9-30-99	3011	...	386256	Dc	□v0.35	v0.55	v0.91	v0.11	E0.86	0.08	9 Mo Sep	v0.55	v0.52	40
41◆	....	None Paid			...	Nil	....	1.79	3.51	0.78	9-30-99	....	31	3835	Dc	1.05	v0.12	vd0.97	vd1.39	....	d0.63	9 Mo Sep	vd1.08	vd0.32	41
42	....	None Since Public			...	Nil	....	2.55	495	154	9-30-99	1564	22	±92792	Dc	...	pv0.81	vp0.96	v□1.08	....	0.63	9 Mo Sep	v□0.68	v□0.23	42
43	1997	0.75	1-7-98	12-29	...	[55]....	0.75	Total Assets $43.2M			9-30-99	27.3	...	[56]2142	Dc	vd1.86	v0.18	vd0.99	vd2.76	....	Nil	9 Mo Sep	vd2.86	vNil	43
44	....	None Since Public			...	Nil	....	47.9	52.5	25.2	9-30-99	52.9	...	25453	Dc	pvd0.78	vpd1.79	vd2.29	vΔd2.39	....	d0.95	9 Mo Sep	vd2.22	vd0.78	44
45◆	....	None Since Public			...	Nil	....	4.72	12.9	9.55	10-01-99	0.38	11	10999	Dc	vd0.50	vd2.50	vd1.20	vd1.30	....	d0.86	9 Mo Sep	vd0.69	vd0.25	45
46	....	0.05	12-21-90	11-15	...	Nil	....	6.10	63.0	28.5	9-30-99	51.9	2300	66781	Dc	vd2.28	vd0.79	vd0.16	vd0.15	Ed0.65	d0.75	9 Mo Sep	vd0.02	v□d0.62	46
47	1993	Q0.87½	1-1-00	12-8	3.50	3.50	3.50	Cv into 3.2154 com, $15.55				....	2300	...	Dc	...	...	...	...	....	....				47
48	....	None Paid			...	Nil	....	16.9	24.6	12.0	9-30-99	86.1	341	3505	Dc	vd0.04	v0.53	v0.93	v1.15	....	1.45	9 Mo Sep	v0.71	v1.01	48
49◆	1976	S0.02½	1-20-00	1-6	0.05	0.05	0.05	11.5	82.9	22.8	7-31-99	58.6	...	±15824	Oc	0.22	0.75	v0.49	v0.68	Pv0.93	0.93				49
50	1998	S0.02½	1-20-00	1-6	0.05	0.05	0.02½	....	...	...		....	...	★7132	Oc	0.17	0.75	±v0.49	v±0.68	....	0.74	3 Mo Jan	v±0.15	v±0.21	50

◆Stock Splits & Divs By Line Reference Index [4]2-for-1,'94,'97. [5]2-for-1,'97. [6]Adj for 5%,'95. [7]3-for-2,'98. [8]2-for-1,'99. [9]10%,'94:Adj for 5%,'98. [11]2-for-1,'97:No adj for stk dstr,'99. [13]2-for-1,'97. [14]3-for-2,'95:2-for-1,'98. [15]2-for-1,'98. [19]3-for-2,'97,'99. [20]2-for-1,'98. [22]2-for-1,'97. [23]2-for-1,'99. [24]2-for-1,'99. [28]2-for-1,'97. [30]3-for-2,'94:5-for-2,'96. [34]3-for-2,'94,'95,'96,'97,'98. [40]3-for-2,'92:2-for-1,'95,'97. [41]3-for-2,'96:10%,'95,'96(twice). [45]1-for-10 REVERSE,'99. [49]10%,'96(twice),'97:3-for-2,'96,'97:3-for-2 in Cl'A','98.

¶ S&P 500
# MidCap 400
✣ SmallCap 600
• Options

Index	Ticker	Name of Issue (Call Price of Pfd. Stocks)	Market	Com. Rank. & Pfd. Rating	Inst. Hold Cos	Inst. Hold Shs. (000)	Principal Business	Price Range 1971-97 High	1971-97 Low	1998 High	1998 Low	1999 High	1999 Low	December, 1999 Dec. Sales in 100s	Last Sale Or Bid High	Low	Last	%Div Yield	P-E Ratio	EPS 5 Yr Growth	% Annualized Total Return 12 Mo	36 Mo	60 Mo
#1•[1]	HMY	✔Heilig-Meyers	NY,Ch,P,Ph	B+	137	38479	Retail furniture stores	39	3/16	15 15/16	5⅝	8¼	2¼	145376	3⅝	2¼	2¾	2.9	d	Neg	–57.3	–43.0	–34.2
¶2•[2]	HNZ	✔Heinz (H.J.)	NY,B,Ch,Ph,P	A–	981	215202	Major mfr of processed foods	56 11/16	1	61¾	48½	58 13/16	39½	209785	44¼	39½	39 13/16	3.7	22	2	–27.6	6.4	13.8
3	Pr	$1.70 3d cm Cv 1st Pfd(28.50)[51]	NY,B	NR	..	...	ketchup,soups,baby foods	580	25½	805	702	760	580	....	....	....	537½B	0.3	..	...	...	...	...
4	HST	✔Heist(C.H.)Corp	AS	B–	17	339	Indl maintenance/temp svc	11½	1⅞	8⅝	6¼	7¼	5⅝	207	6⅛	5¾	5⅝B	...	51	–1	–6.3	–10.1	–4.6
5•[3]	HELE	✔Helen of Troy Ltd	NNM	B+	92	13351	Hair care appliances	20½	1/64	26½	12	20	7⅛	104461	10 11/16	7⅛	7¼	...	7	21	–50.6	–12.9	11.3
✣6•[4]	HELX	✔Helix Technology	NNM	B+	183	15797	Mfr of cryogenic equipment	33⅜	⅛	25⅛	6 13/16	49½	12⅞	62385	49½	38⅞	44 13/16	1.1	69	–47	252	50.6	44.0
7	OTE	Hellenic Telecommunic ADS[52]	NY	NR	91	31607	Telecommunication svc,Greece	....	....	13⅜	10⅞	16½	9½	104574	12 3/16	9⅞	11 15/16	...	..	...	–7.5	...	...
8	HF	✔Heller Financial 'A'	NY	NR	230	40698	Provide financial svcs	....	....	31 7/16	15½	31 15/16	18	63253	22 15/16	18	20 1/16	2.0	9	...	–30.1	...	...
9	HELO	✔Hello Direct	NNM	NR	14	1788	Mkt telecommunications eqp	18½	3⅝	13	4 1/16	21	7⅜	9889	15⅞	11	14⅞	...	22	9	47.8	46.3	...
#10•[2]	HP	✔Helmerich & Payne	NY,B,Ch,Ph,P	B	349	35229	Contract driller:o&g prod'n	45 9/16	1 3/16	34⅛	16⅛	30⅝	16	106978	25	18⅝	21¾	1.3	25	35	13.7	–4.8	12.6
11	HLM	✔Helmstar Group	AS,Ch	C	2	18	Merchant banking	13⅜	¼	3⅛	⅝	9½	1	1639	5⅛	4	5⅛	...	d	–30	413	89.8	59.3
12•[1]	HEB	✔Hemispherx BioPharma	AS,Ph	NR	19	1610	Pharmaceutical R&D	5½	1⅝	13 3/16	2⅝	10½	4 11/16	43477	10½	8	9 15/16	...	d	–3	44.5	64.1	...
13	WS	Wrrt(Pur 1 com at $4)	AS	....	2	188		2⅜	½	9	¾	6½	1⅝	8778	6½	3⅞	5⅞	...	..	...	...	...	...
✣14	JKHY	✔Henry(Jack) & Assoc	NNM	A–	184	8117	Data process'g svcs to banks	30¼	¼	55	24¾	56½	26 7/16	38585	56½	35	53 11/16	0.6	36	32	8.8	32.2	54.1
15•[5]	HERBA	✔Herbalife Intl'A'	NNM	B	73	3538	Weight ctrl/hlth care prod	37⅜	⅜	29	7½	16¼	10	2526	15	13⅝	14⅜	4.2	9	10	5.8	–20.5	1.7
¶16•[5]	HPC	✔Hercules, Inc	NY,B,Ch,P,Ph	A–	398	82252	Spcl chemicals/food prod	66¼	4 1/16	51⅜	24⅝	40 11/16	22⅜	84732	28	22⅜	27⅞	3.9	14	Neg	6.1	–11.0	–3.9
17	HPG	✔Heritage Propane Ptnrs L.P.	NY	NR	5	61	Propane retail marketer	25½	19¾	24⅞	20 13/16	24	16¾	6491	19½	16¾	18⅜	12.2	17	...	–10.3	5.6	...
18	HT	✔Hersha Hospitality Trust	AS	NR	2	218	Real estate investment trust	....	....	....	....	6⅜	4 13/16	790	5½	4 13/16	5	14.4	..	...			
¶19•[6]	HSY	✔Hershey Foods	NY,B,Ch,P,Ph	A	552	56565	Mfr chocolate,candy,pasta	63⅞	1/16	76⅜	59 11/16	64⅞	45¾	125760	54 3/16	45¾	47 7/16	2.2	23	22	–22.3	4.4	16.5
20•[2]	HRZ	✔Hertz Corp'A'	NY,Ch,Ph	NR	239	18777	Auto/constr'n eqp rental svcs	41¾	24	51⅞	27 9/16	64⅜	36⅞	32866	51⅛	41½	50⅛	0.4	17	31	10.3	...	...
¶21•[7]	HWP	✔Hewlett-Packard	NY,B,C,Ch,P,Ph	↑A+	1798	574884	Mfr computer products	72 15/16	15/16	82⅜	47 1/16	118 7/16	63⅜	779822	117 15/16	95 1/16	113¾	0.6	34	14	67.8	32.5	36.8
22	HXL	✔Hexcel Corp	NY,Ch,P	NR	75	12492	Honeycomb cores: plastics	43	1⅞	31⅜	7 1/16	11 7/16	4 13/16	23557	5 13/16	4 13/16	5 9/16	...	d	NM	–33.6	–30.0	4.3
23	HSR	✔Hi-Shear Technology	AS,Ch,Ph,P	NR	5	245	Electr/ordnance prod&sys	15	3⅜	9½	3⅞	7¾	2⅜	2841	3¼	2⅜	2⅝	...	8	NM	–47.5	–21.9	–27.1
24	HIBB	✔Hibbett Sporting Goods	NNM	NR	62	3990	Own/oper sporting goods stores	32¾	11	41¼	17⅜	31	12½	15198	18	12⅝	17	...	14	30	–29.9	5.4	...
#25•[8]	HIB	✔Hibernia Corp Cl'A'	NY,Ch,Ph,P	B	253	48847	Commercial bkg,Louisiana	26	1 9/16	22	12¼	17½	10¼	118339	12 11/16	10¼	10⅝	4.5	10	6	–37.0	–4.8	9.2
26	HICKA	✔Hickok Inc 'A'	NSC	↓B	2	.7	Mfr auto diagnostic equip	22½	2	14¼	6	8	5	194	6⅛	5	5	3.0	d	Neg	–28.3	–19.2	–20.5
27	HSAC	✔High Speed Access	NNM	NR	74	5811	Cable modem internet-access sv	....	....	....	....	49 9/16	13	221728	24	16¼	17⅝	...	..	...	...	...	...
28	HIC	✔Highlands Insurance Group	NY,Ch,P	NR	74	6285	Prop & casualty insurance	29⅜	16⅝	28⅞	9¾	14 15/16	6¾	16910	9 11/16	6¾	9 7/16	...	..	NM	–27.8	–22.5	...
29	HWYM	✔HighwayMaster Communic	NSC	NR	16	1141	Wireless communic svcs-trucking	22¾	5	8	13/16	3¾	1 1/16	31532	3 1/16	1¾	2¼	...	d	11	100	–50.1	...
30	HIW	✔Highwoods Properties	NY,Ch,Ph	NR	218	45701	Real estate investment trust	37⅞	18½	37 7/16	22¾	28	20¼	59180	23⅝	20¼	23⅝	9.4	13	14	0.4	–4.5	9.3
✣31	HRH	✔Hilb,Rogal & Hamilton	NY	B+	92	9099	Operates insurance agencies	20⅝	5⅝	19⅞	15⅝	29⅛	15 9/16	3767	29⅛	26¾	28¼	2.3	21	12	46.7	33.4	22.9
#32•[5]	HB	✔Hillenbrand Indus	NY,B,Ch,Ph,P	A	228	21663	Hosp eq,burial caskets,locks	51½	11/16	64 11/16	44⅜	56 13/16	26⅛	27266	35⅞	31⅛	31 11/16	2.5	14	17	–43.1	–2.8	4.5
¶33•[9]	HLT	✔Hilton Hotels	NY,B,Ch,P,Ph	B+	401	142673	Own/manage hotels	35 13/16	¼	35½	12	17⅛	8⅜	645318	11½	8⅜	9 9/16	0.8	12	4	...	...	...
34	HORT	✔Hines Horticulture	NNM	NR	18	4777	Oper commercial nurseries	....	....	11⅜	5	10¾	7⅜	3348	9	7½	8 7/16	...	14	...	–4.9	...	...
35	HRSH	✔Hirsch Intl Corp'A'	NNM	B	19	1247	Distrib embroidery machines	26¼	4 7/16	22¾	2	5⅝	13/16	17508	1 13/16	1⅛	1⅛	...	d	Neg	–62.1	–60.7	–27.7
#36•[8]	HBCCA	✔Hispanic Broadcasting'A'	NNM	NR	266	29988	Spanish language radio brdcst	47½	4¾	51¾	27 11/16	99⅝	40 9/16	53824	99⅝	78	92¼	...	..	NM	87.2	80.2	79.1
37•[8]	HIT	✔Hitachi,Ltd ADR[62]	NY,B,Ch,P,Ph	NR	115	12513	Elec eq, ind mchy: Japan	145	2⅜	84 11/16	40 3/16	164½	59 15/16	9330	164½	128⅝	161⅞	0.4	..	...	170	21.4	11.4
38	HMG	✔HMG/Courtland Prop	AS	NR	2	2	Real estate investment trust	25¼	2⅛	5⅞	3⅝	5	2 1/16	201	5	4⅛	4¾	...	2	NM	5.6	0.9	–10.5
39•[10]	HMTT	✔HMT Technology	NNM	NR	65	22582	Supply thin film disks	28¾	9½	15⅛	5⅝	16¼	2¼	86749	4 3/16	3¼	4	...	d	...	–68.8	–35.7	...
✣40	HNCS	✔HNC Software	NNM	NR	187	23862	Decision applications softwr	51	7	47⅛	22½	130	13¾	165470	130	71½	105¾	...	..	19	162	50.1	...
41•[8]	HLR	✔Hollinger Intl'A'	NY,Ch	NR	180	51782	Newspaper publishing	15	8⅞	18⅝	11 3/16	16 13/16	9¾	38775	13⅝	12 1/16	12 15/16	4.3	6	55	–3.2	7.8	6.3
42	Pr P	9.75% [63]Dep'PRIDES'([64]$9.988)	NY	CALL	5	191		13	9½	16¾	10¾	14⅜	8⅜	484	11¼	10 3/16	10⅞	...	..	...	...	...	...
43	HOC	✔Holly Corp	AS,Ph	B	49	5453	Petroleum refin'g & mktg	41	½	33⅜	14	17¼	12¼	2239	14⅜	12⅝	13 5/16	5.1	5	8	–17.4	–18.2	–10.3
44	HWD	✔Hollywood Casino'A'	AS	C	17	2151	Casino gaming operations	32¾	1¾	2 5/16	1	4⅝	1	6636	4⅝	3 9/16	4 5/16	...	54	–33	318	...	...
45•[11]	HLYW	✔Hollywood Entertainment	NNM	C	139	22332	Oper video rental superstores	35	2 5/16	29⅞	8	34 11/16	11⅝	125939	17 3/16	13⅜	14½	...	d	Neg	–46.8	–7.8	–0.8
✣46•[2]	HPK	✔Hollywood Park	NY	NR	122	13834	Horse racing track	35	2¼	22⅝	8	24 1/16	8	18797	24 1/16	19⅜	22 7/16	...	13	NM	170	14.4	15.3
✣47	HOLX	✔Hologic Inc.	NNM	B–	76	7093	Dvlp/mfr x-ray systems	49½	1 11/16	30¾	9⅞	13⅜	3	44109	7¼	5¼	5¾	...	d	Neg	–52.6	–38.5	–5.1
¶48•[12]	HD	✔Home Depot	NY,B,Ch,P,Ph	A+	1817	140677	Bldg mtls,home improv strs	20 3/16	1/32	41 5/16	18 7/16	69¾	34 9/16	1378031	69¾	52 15/16	68¾	0.3	70	26	69.1	84.2	47.0
49	HME	✔Home Properties of NY	NY,Ch,Ph	NR	115	13892	Real estate investment trust	28 5/16	16½	28 1/16	21 3/16	29⅛	22¼	9574	28⅛	25¼	27 7/16	7.7	22	16	15.0	15.0	15.8
50	HSI	✔Home Security Intl	AS	NR	7	2507	Sell/install/svc alarm sys	15	8⅞	13⅞	7⅜	11½	1¼	3115	3½	1 11/16	3¼	...	8	...	–71.1	...	...

Uniform Footnote Explanations-See Page 4. Other: [1]CBOE:Cycle 2. [2]CBOE:Cycle 3. [3]P:Cycle 2. [4]ASE,CBOE,P:Cycle 1. [5]ASE:Cycle 3. [6]ASE:Cycle 2. [7]ASE,CBOE,P,Ph:Cycle 2. [8]CBOE:Cycle 1. [9]ASE,CBOE,P,Ph:Cycle 3. [10]CBOE,Ph:Cycle 1. [11]ASE,CBOE:Cycle 1. [12]Ph:Cycle 2. [51]0.50 vtg. [52]Ea ADS rep 0.50 ord,750 Drs. [53]To be determined.. [54]If com exceeds $9 for 20 con trad days. [55]Incl 2.7M Sub Units. [56]Incl 4M units. [57]Ford Motor Co owns 55.4%. [58]Spl div. [59]Stk dstr of Park Place Entmt,'98. [60]Fiscal Sep'95&prior. [61]12 Mo Dec'96. [62]ADR's represent'g 10 com par yen 50. [63]Dep for 0.50 shr Sr'B'Cv Pfd. [64]Pfd Redeemable Increased Div Equity Sec. [65]Stk dstr of Pratt Hotel Corp. [66]Incl current amts.

Splits ◆ Index	Cash Divs. Ea.Yr. Since	Dividends: Latest Payment Period $	Date	Ex. Div.	Total $ So Far 1999	Ind. Rate	Paid 1998	Financial Position Mil-$ Cash& Equiv.	Curr. Assets	Curr. Liab.	Balance Sheet Date	Capitalization Lg Trm Debt Mil-$	Shs. 000 Pfd.	Com.	Earnings $ Per Shr. Years End	1995	1996	1997	1998	1999	Last 12 Mos.	Interim Earnings Period	$ per Shr. 1998	1999	Index
1	1975	Q0.02	11-20-99	11-1	0.23	0.08	0.28	4.91	976	425	8-31-99	536	...	59874	Fb	v0.84	v0.80	vd0.98	vd0.03	Ed1.02↓	d1.50	9 Mo Nov	v0.42	vd1.05	1
2◆	1911	Q0.36¾	1-10-00	12-16	1.39½	1.47	1.28¾	169	3107	2496	10-27-99	2825	...	354664	Ap	1.59	1.75	v0.81	v2.15	v1.29	1.79	6 Mo Oct	v1.21	v1.71	2
3	1976	Q0.42½	1-1-00	12-16	1.70	1.70	1.70	Cv into 13.5 common				....	20	...	Ap	b3.81	...	...	....	....	....				3
4	....	None Paid			...	Nil	....	2.51	27.4	9.12	9-26-99	16.9	...	2881	Dc	v0.56	v0.24	v0.31	v0.45	....	0.11	9 Mo Sep	v0.34	vNil	4
5◆	....	0.04	8-3-77	7-15	...	Nil	....	35.4	204	45.3	8-31-99	55.5	...	29287	Fb	v0.49	v0.62	v0.77	v0.96	....	1.00	6 Mo Aug	v0.42	v0.46	5
6◆	1987	Q0.12	11-2-99	10-21	0.48	0.48	0.75	21.7	65.5	18.3	10-01-99	....	...	22342	Dc	v1.05	v1.10	v1.07	vd0.09	E0.65↑	0.40	9 Mo Sep	vd0.09	v0.40	6
7	1999	0.324	9-10-99	6-22	0.324	[53]....	....	183	1395	889	6-30-98	475	...	★504054	Dc	...	...	v0.68	....	....	....	6 Mo Jun△	n/a	v0.34	7
8	1998	Q0.10	11-15-99	10-28	0.37	0.40	0.09	Total Assets $17693.00M			9-30-99	8253	7750	±97091	Dc	...	...	pv1.70	v1.91	E2.24↓	1.79	9 Mo Sep	v1.80	v1.68	8
9	....	None Since Public			...	Nil	....	6.67	23.4	5.56	9-30-99	....	...	5223	Dc	△□v0.48	v0.15	v0.35	v0.51	....	0.67	9 Mo Sep	v0.36	v0.52	9
10◆	1959	Q0.07	3-1-00	2-11	0.28	0.28	0.28	27.4	174	95.5	6-30-99	50.0	...	49497	Sp	0.20	v1.46	v1.67	v2.00	vP0.86	0.86				10
11	....	None Since Public			...	Nil	....	Total Assets $94.1M			9-30-99	72.8	...	5436	Dc	0.20	vd0.43	v0.31	vd0.11	....	d0.36	9 Mo Sep	vd0.04	vd0.29	11
12	....	None Since Public			...	Nil	....	7.78	7.89	2.12	9-30-99	....	...	26367	Dc	pvd0.18	vd0.29	vd0.35	vd0.32	....	d0.38	9 Mo Sep	vd0.22	vd0.28	12
13	....	Terms&trad. basis should			be checked in detail			Wrrts expire 11-2-2000				....	...	4620	Dc	...	...	...	....	....	....	Callable at 5¢[54]			13
14◆	1990	Q0.08	12-9-99	11-16	0.32	0.32	0.26	9.06	61.0	80.5	9-30-99	....	...	20142	Je	0.44	0.51	v0.80	v1.09	v1.50	1.48	3 Mo Sep	v0.42	v0.40	14
15	1992	Q0.15	11-12-99	10-26	0.60	0.60	0.60	119	294	160	9-30-99	2.48	...	±28652	Dc	v0.65	v1.43	±v1.72	v±1.60	....	1.66	9 Mo Sep	v±1.24	v±1.30	15
16◆	1913	Q0.27	12-29-99	12-1	1.08	1.08	1.08	88.0	1328	1118	9-30-99	3227	...	106321	Dc	v2.87	v2.98	v□3.18	v0.10	E2.07↓	d0.23	9 Mo Sep	v1.80	v1.47	16
17	1996	Q0.56¼	1-14-00	12-31	2.20	2.25	2.00	1.68	29.3	47.7	8-31-99	196	...	[55]±9842	Au	p0.35	pd0.69	0.64	v1.04	v1.11	1.11				17
18	1999	0.18	1-31-00	12-27	0.49	0.72	....	Total Assets $55.9M			9-30-99	23.9	...	[56]6481	Dc	...	...	...	n/a	....	....	9 Mo Sep	n/a	vp0.39	18
19◆	1930	Q0.26	12-15-99	11-18	1.00	1.04	0.92	42.9	1354	859	10-03-99	878	...	±138371	Dc	v±1.69	v±1.75	v±2.23	±v2.34	E2.05↓	3.30	9 Mo Sep	v±1.59	v±2.55	19
20	1997	Q0.05	12-10-99	11-10	0.20	0.20	0.20	Total Assets $10159.37M			9-30-99	6566	...	[57]±107923	Dc	v0.97	pv1.46	v1.86	v2.55	....	2.98	9 Mo Sep	v2.11	v2.54	20
21◆	1965	Q0.16	1-12-00	12-20	0.64	0.64	0.60	6106	20685	12349	7-31-99	1824	...	1019000	Oc	2.31	2.46	v2.95	v2.77	vP3.34	3.34				21
22	....	0.11	11-16-92	10-27	...	Nil	....	7.82	393	217	9-30-99	777	...	36522	Dc	v0.17	vd0.58	v1.74	v1.24	....	d0.47	9 Mo Sep	v1.15	vd0.56	22
23	....	None Since Public			...	Nil	....	0.19	11.1	5.10	8-31-99	1.21	...	6670	My	0.01	d0.20	v0.15	□v0.28	v0.31	0.32	3 Mo Aug	v0.02	v0.03	23
24	....	None Since Public			...	Nil	....	0.59	69.2	29.1	10-30-99	8.00	...	6434	Ja	v0.42	v□0.61	v0.93	v1.04	....	1.21	9 Mo Oct	v0.75	v0.92	24
25	1993	Q0.12	11-22-99	10-28	0.43½	0.48	0.37½	Total Deposits $11459.55M			9-30-99	1045	2000	160316	Dc	v1.00	v0.85	v0.98	v1.10	E1.12	1.06	9 Mo Sep	v0.80	v0.76	25
26◆	1989	[58]0.15	1-22-99	12-30	[58]0.15	0.15	0.10	0.43	10.3	2.06	6-30-99	0.43	...	±1200	Sp	±1.50	±v0.79	v±0.50	v±0.85	Pv±d0.22	d0.22				26
27	....	None Since Public			...	Nil	....	199	203	15.2	9-30-99	6.67	...	54184	Dc	...	...	...	vpd0.76	....	....	6 Mo Jun	n/a	vpd0.67	27
28	....	None Since Public			...	Nil	....	Total Assets $2133.70M			9-30-99	117	...	13957	Dc	vpd10.55	vd0.47	v1.09	v0.20	....	0.02	9 Mo Sep	v0.34	v0.16	28
29	....	None Since Public			...	Nil	....	25.4	58.4	18.6	9-30-99	92.0	...	24987	Dc	v□d1.43	v□d1.39	vd1.25	v△d2.17	....	d0.62	9 Mo Sep	vd1.77	vd0.22	29
30	1994	Q0.555	11-19-99	11-8	2.19	2.22	2.10	Total Assets $4121M			9-30-99	1828	7425	62053	Dc	v□1.54	v□1.58	□v1.65	□v1.74	....	1.78	9 Mo Sep	v□1.34	v□1.38	30
31	1987	Q0.16½	12-31-99	12-14	0.65½	0.66	0.63½	42.5	116	131	9-30-99	110	...	13121	Dc	v0.82	v0.84	v0.97	v1.18	....	1.35	9 Mo Sep	v1.06	v1.23	31
32	1948	Q0.19½	11-26-99	10-20	0.78	0.78	0.72	198	767	332	8-28-99	302	...	65467	Nv	1.27	2.02	v2.19	v2.73	E2.20	2.35	9 Mo Aug	v1.93	v1.55	32
33◆	1946	Q0.02	12-17-99	12-1	0.08	0.08	h[59]0.32	93.0	517	414	9-30-99	3415	...	p368816	Dc	v0.89	v□0.79	v0.94	v1.12	E0.79	0.71	9 Mo Sep	v0.98	v□0.57	33
34	....	None Since Public			...	Nil	....	....	173	100	9-30-99	203	...	22073	Dc	...	...	pv0.50	v□0.32	....	0.59	9 Mo Sep	v□0.57	v0.84	34
35◆	....	5%Stk	8-10-94	7-13	...	Nil	....	0.64	59.7	14.5	10-31-99	8.01	...	±9483	Ja	v1.09	v1.10	v0.89	vd0.49	....	d1.15	9 Mo Oct	v0.19	vd0.47	35
36◆	....	None Since Public			...	Nil	....	8.63	49.5	34.0	9-30-99	1.48	...	±★54349	Dc	□±v[60]d1.90	v±□[61]d0.12	v±0.45	v±0.54	....	0.61	9 Mo Sep	v±0.39	v±0.46	36
37	1951	0.246	12-20-99	9-27	0.628	0.63	0.335	14494	47243	30607	3-31-98	974	...	3337895	Mr	3.78	v2.06	v0.08	n/a	....	....	6 Mo Sep	vd3.98	v0.10	37
38	....	0.15	9-28-90	9-10	...	Nil	....	Total Assets $29.08M			9-30-99	9.67	...	1083	Dc	d3.04	vd1.82	v0.47	vd0.82	....	2.09	9 Mo Sep	vd0.18	v2.73	38
39	....	None Since Public			...	Nil	....	50.9	103	24.5	9-30-99	230	...	45794	Mr	□v1.31	v1.35	v1.40	vd0.48	....	d1.24	6 Mo Sep	v0.04	vd0.72	39
40◆	....	None Since Public			...	Nil	....	52.9	141	31.1	9-30-99	100	...	24558	Dc	vp0.28	v0.47	v0.68	v0.39	....	0.43	9 Mo Sep	v0.30	v0.34	40
41	1994	Q0.138	1-15-00	12-29	0.55	0.55	0.43¾	61.1	405	444	9-30-99	1488	3070	±102345	Dc	v±0.09	v□±0.42	v±0.87	v□1.47	....	2.16	9 Mo Sep	v□±1.33	v±□2.02	41
42	1996	0.844	1-3-00		0.951	Call	0.951	Cv into com 0.8439 Cl'A'com,$11.55				....	18000	...	Dc	...	...	...	....	....	....	Called Jan 3,'00 at $0.8439			42
43	1988	Q0.17	1-3-00	12-21	0.65	0.68	0.61	10.7	217	201	10-31-99	56.6	...	8254	Jl	△1.51	2.33	v1.59	v1.84	v2.42	2.49	3 Mo Oct	v0.32	v0.39	43
44	....	h[65]....	12-31-96	12-20	...	Nil	....	142	201	53.0	9-30-99	535	...	24950	Dc	□0.26	vpd1.18	vd0.60	v□d0.05	....	0.08	9 Mo Sep	v0.02	v□0.15	44
45◆	....	None Since Public			...	Nil	....	3.95	116	144	9-30-99	487	...	45795	Dc	v□0.36	v0.59	v□0.15	vd1.30	Ed0.38	d2.32	9 Mo Sep	v0.52	v□d0.50	45
46	....	0.048	3-31-92	3-9	...	Nil	....	259	320	143	9-30-99	618	...	26108	Dc	vd0.17	vd0.33	v0.32	v0.50	....	1.70	9 Mo Sep	v0.34	v1.54	46
47◆	....	None Since Public			...	Nil	....	58.1	115	27.8	6-26-99	....	...	p15303	Sp	0.22	0.91	v1.30	v0.75	Pvd0.26	d0.26				47
48◆	1987	Q0.06	12-16-99	11-30	0.133	0.24	0.077	976	7058	4164	10-31-99	735	...	2302364	Ja	v0.34	v0.43	v0.51	v0.70	E0.98	0.93	9 Mo Oct	v0.52	v0.75	48
49	1994	0.53	11-24-99	11-12	1.97	2.12	1.83	Total Assets $1471.68M			9-30-99	[66]640	...	19299	Dc	v□0.52	v0.74	□v0.98	v□1.40	....	1.27	9 Mo Sep	v□1.06	v□0.93	49
50	....	None Since Public			...	Nil	....	1.16	14.1	16.4	9-30-99	3.42	...	5151	Je	...	v0.37	v0.51	v1.04	v0.68	0.42	3 Mo Sep	v0.31	v0.05	50

◆**Stock Splits & Divs By Line Reference Index** [2]3-for-2,'95. [5]2-for-1,'96,'97. [6]2-for-1,'94,'97. [10]2-for-1,'98. [14]4-for-3,'94:3-for-2,'97. [16]3-for-1,'95. [19]2-for-1,'96. [21]2-for-1,'95,'96. [26]2-for-1,'95. [33]4-for-1,'96:No adj for stk dstr,'99. [35]5-for-4,'95,'96. [36]2-for-1,'97. [40]2-for-1,'96. [45]3-for-2,'94:2-for-1,'95. [47]2-for-1,'96. [48]2-for-1,'98:3-for-2,'97,'99.

¶ S&P 500 # MidCap 400 ✣ SmallCap 600 • Options

Index	Ticker	Name of Issue (Call Price of Pfd. Stocks)	Market	Com. Rank. & Pfd. Rating	Inst. Hold Cos	Inst. Hold Shs. (000)	Principal Business	Price Range 1971-97 High	1971-97 Low	1998 High	1998 Low	1999 High	1999 Low	Dec. Sales in 100s	December, 1999 Last Sale Or Bid High	Low	Last	%Div Yield	P-E Ratio	EPS 5 Yr Growth	% Annualized Total Return 12 Mo	36 Mo	60 Mo
1•[1]	HBI	✓HomeBase Inc	NY,P	B	85	27293	Home improvement stores	36	4⅝	10 7/16	4 15/16	6 15/16	2 13/16	80955	3½	2 13/16	3 1/16	...	8	−32	−52.0	−50.0	−28.8
¶2•[2]	HM	✓Homestake Mining	NY,B,Ch,P,Ph	B−	396	111376	Mining:gold,lead,zinc	24⅞	1⅜	15	7 11/16	11 7/16	7 3/16	307062	8½	7½	7 13/16	0.6	..	Neg	−13.6	−17.4	−13.6
3	HSD	✓Homestead Village	NY	NR	49	7842	Extended-stay lodg'g facilit's	20⅞	13⅝	16⅛	3⅜	5⅛	1⅞	16606	2½	2	2⅛	...	d	...	−52.8	−50.9	...
4	HOMS	✓homestore.com Inc	NNM	NR	55	7458	Net based real estate info svcs	....	....	....	....	109	19¾	41958	109	64¾	74¼	...	..	...	...	...	...
#5•[3]	HNI	✓HON Indus	NY	A	197	24397	Mfr office furn/hm bldg prod	32⅛	¼	37 3/16	20	29⅞	18¾	19931	23¾	20¼	21 15/16	1.7	15	18	−6.9	11.5	12.1
6•[4]	HMC	✓Honda Motor ADR[52]	NY,B,Ch,P,Ph	NR	84	2237	Autos,trucks,motorcycles	76 9/16	7/16	80	51 5/16	94	64 1/16	5338	87⅛	70¼	76½	0.4	14	36	15.2	11.1	17.2
¶7•[5]	HON	✓Honeywell Intl[53]	NY,To,B,C,Ch,P,Ph	B+	1541	591614	Aerospace,automotive,fibers	47⅛	3 13/16	47 9/16	32⅝	68⅝	37 13/16	786385	64	53 15/16	57 11/16	1.2	21	15	31.8	21.5	29.6
✣8	HH	✓Hooper Holmes	AS	B+	187	20859	Health care/info services	8 1/16	11/16	15 3/16	6¼	27½	11¾	15311	27½	23⅜	25¾	0.2	45	NM	81.5	83.4	75.6
9	HOOV	✓Hoover's Inc	NNM	NR	13	398	Net based company info svc	....	....	....	....	33	8⅛	26660	11 3/16	8¾	8¾	...	d	...	...	...	...
#10	HMN	✓Horace Mann Educators	NY,Ph	NR	226	36803	Insur hldg:prop,cslty,life	29 11/16	8 11/16	37⅝	26 1/16	33	19⅛	43749	22 5/16	19⅛	19⅝	2.1	19	3	−30.1	2.1	15.7
11	HRZB	✓Horizon Financial	NNM	A−	30	940	Savings bank,Bellingham,Wash	18½	2⅞	19⅜	12	15¼	9	3267	11	9	9½	5.1	9	3	−21.9	1.4	6.2
12	HMP	✓Horizon Medical Products	AS	NR	7	303	Dvp vascular-access pds	....	....	17⅛	1¾	8⅞	2	5616	3⅜	2	2½	...	13	...	−42.9	...	...
13	HZP	✓Horizon Pharmacies	AS	NR	14	589	Own/oper pharmacies	13½	3 5/16	16¼	5½	11⅞	2 5/16	7067	3	2 5/16	2⅝	...	d	...	−75.9	...	...
#14•[6]	HRL	✓Hormel Foods	NY,Ch,Ph,P	A	238	19609	Meat & food processing	33 1/16	15/16	39⅜	25 11/16	46 3/16	31	29705	45⅛	40	40⅝	1.7	18	8	26.2	17.1	12.8
15•[1]	HPT	✓Hospitality Properties Trust	NY,Ph,P	NR	158	12398	Real estate investment trust	38 5/16	24⅜	36¾	23 13/16	29⅞	17 15/16	73048	19⅛	17 15/16	19 1/16	14.5	9	...	−11.6	−4.9	...
16	HFD	✓Host Funding 'A'	AS	NR	2	9	Operate/lease hotels	10¾	5	8	1 9/16	3	1⅞	489	2¾	1⅞	2¼	...	d	Neg	0.0	−30.5	...
17•[4]	HMT	✓Host Marriott	NY,B,Ch,P,Ph	B−	227	157926	Real estate investment trust	43¾	1 3/16	22⅛	9⅞	14 13/16	7⅜	253012	9 7/16	7⅜	8¼	10.2	10	NM	...	...	...
18	HWS	✓Hotelworks.com Inc[56]	AS,Ph	NR	17	3157	Renovation/procurement svcs	14 3/16	½	13⅝	1¾	6¾	1½	28798	5	1 15/16	5	...	d	−29	2.6	−9.5	20.1
#19•[7]	HTN	✓Houghton Mifflin	NY,B,Ch,P	B+	236	23447	Publ textbooks: trade books	40¼	¾	47¼	26¾	52½	34⅞	38535	42⅞	36¼	42 3/16	1.2	30	97	−9.6	15.9	15.1
¶20•[8]	HI	✓Household Intl	NY,B,Ch,P	B+	905	393950	Finance & banking services	43 5/16	1⅝	53 11/16	23	52 5/16	35 13/16	296485	42 7/16	35 13/16	37¼	1.8	12	11	−4.5	8.3	27.0
21•[9]	THX	✓Houston Exploration	NY,Ch,Ph	NR	95	7545	Oil & Gas explor,dvlp,prod'n	27⅞	11½	24 9/16	14⅛	23⅛	12	6027	20⅛	17 11/16	19 13/16	...	d	...	−0.3	4.2	...
22	HXT	Houston Industries 7% 'ACES'	NY	NR	47	4765	Automatic Com Exch Securities	57¼	46⅜	106¾	54⅜	131 15/16	97¼	8775	120½	101 5/16	120½	2.7	..	...	16.6	...	...
23	HOV	✓Hovnanian Enterpr Cl'A'	AS,Ch,P,Ph	B	39	4309	Multifamily home builder	19¼	1¾	11½	6	9½	5¼	4702	6½	5¼	6⅜	...	5	−1	−26.1	−5.3	3.5
24	HWL	✓Howell Corp	NY,Ch	B−	15	1393	Oil & gas explor,devel,prod	33	⅝	17¼	2	7½	1 11/16	2937	6¼	5 5/16	5¾	2.8	d	Neg	190	−25.2	−11.9
25	HWM	✓Howmet International	NY,Ph	NR	83	12678	Mfr cast turbine engine parts	16⅛	14 9/16	18⅝	9¾	20⅝	11 3/16	15022	18¼	17½	18 1/16	...	15	...	12.0	...	...
26	HRP	✓HRPT Properties Tr SBI	NY,Ch,Ph,P	NR	165	24298	Real estate investment trust	20¾	6¾	21	13 13/16	15 15/16	7¼	226756	9⅛	7¼	9	14.2	8	3	...	...	...
✣27	HSE	✓HS Resources	NY,Ch	NR	113	10421	Oil & gas dvlp,prod'n/pipeline	29	9¼	17½	6⅛	17½	5¼	11822	17¼	12⅜	17¼	...	d	Neg	128	1.5	−0.4
#28•[10]	HSB	✓HSB Group	NY,Ch,Ph,P	B	184	13798	Insurance/engineering svcs	42½	1	59 9/16	34¾	42¼	30⅞	18034	35 11/16	30⅞	33 13/16	5.2	13	15	−14.0	7.5	9.8
29•[11]	HBC	✓HSBC Holdings ADS[60]	NY	NR	76	21288	Intl banking, Hong Kong	....	....	....	....	71½	53⅛	12731	71½	65	71⅜	...	9	...	...	...	...
30	HNP	✓Huaneng Power Intl ADS[63]	NY,Ph,P	NR	61	17623	Dvp,oper coal-fired pwr plants	29¼	12¼	26¼	6 5/16	17½	8⅜	18762	11 1/16	9¼	10 9/16	...	6	24	−25.1	−21.6	−5.9
#31	HUB.B	✓Hubbell Inc Cl'B'	NY,Ch,Ph	A−	327	38174	Electrical wiring devices:	51⅛	1¼	52¾	33⅞	49 3/16	26¼	37133	28 5/16	26¼	27¼	4.7	11	9	−25.8	−11.8	5.1
32	HUB.A	Class A com (20 votes)	NY,Ph	A−	62	6800	industrial controls & gear	48 5/16	1¼	49 1/16	33⅝	45¾	25¾	1915	28⅛	25¾	28⅛	4.6	12	9	−23.5	−6.8	6.7
33•[5]	HRBT	✓Hudson River Bancorp	NNM	NR	30	2955	Savings & loan, New York	....	....	13¾	8¾	12⅛	9¾	13918	11	9¾	10⅛	1.2	..	...	−9.8	...	...
34	HDSN	Hudson Technologies	NNM	NR	9	264	Refrigerant recovery svcs	24½	2⅞	5¾	1½	4 7/16	1¼	5540	2	1¼	1½	...	d	Neg	0.0	−35.6	...
✣35•[2]	HU	✓Hudson United Bancorp	NY,Ph	B+	226	20393	Commercial bkg,New Jersey	37 15/16	7/16	37	20½	35 5/16	24 15/16	42480	31 1/16	24 15/16	25 9/16	s3.8	10	8	−7.8	10.4	20.6
36	HBC	✓Hudson's Bay Co	To,Mo	B	21	7135	Retail dept stores,Canada	41⅛	9¾	35⅛	17⅞	23⅞	14	36478	19¾	17	17 3/16	2.1	28	−38	−8.7	−6.7	−4.3
✣37	HUF	✓Huffy Corp	NY,Ch	B−	74	6074	Mfr/dstr consumer products	24⅜	11/16	19 15/16	11 1/16	16¾	5 3/16	16374	7¼	5 3/16	5¼	...	d	Neg	−67.6	−26.9	−17.0
✣38	HUG	✓Hughes Supply	NY,Ph	B+	174	14068	Fla distr elect, plumb'g:mfg	36⅛	13/16	39 13/16	25⅛	30	17⅞	10338	24⅜	19⅝	21 9/16	1.6	8	17	−25.2	−8.0	13.3
39	HGT	✓Hugoton Royalty Trust	NY	NR	22	6743	Oil & gas royalty trust	....	....	....	....	10⅞	7½	17345	9	7½	8⅛	11.1	18	...	...	...	...
40•[7]	HGSI	✓Human Genome Sciences	NNM	NR	170	14605	R&D human gene products	49¾	12	45⅞	22¾	172 9/16	28¾	93458	172 9/16	108¼	152⅝	...	d	Neg	329	55.3	59.6
¶41•[12]	HUM	✓Humana Inc	NY,B,Ch,P,Ph	B−	354	137376	Provides managed hlth plans	35 1/16	3/16	32⅛	12¼	20¾	5⅞	220316	8 3/16	6¾	8 3/16	...	13	−6	−54.0	−24.5	−18.4
42•[2]	HUMC	Hummingbird Communications	NNM,To	B	19	1858	Dvlp,mkt computer software	60½	12¼	40¼	14¾	33⅝	14	6629	33⅝	22⅝	30½	...	..	−43	55.4	2.4	8.4
43	HTC	✓Hungarian Tel & Cable	AS	NR	6	46	Dvp stage:telecomm svcs	41½	7	11⅛	2⅛	9	3¼	4115	9	4 13/16	7¼	...	d	−9	123	−8.2	−7.1
44	HUN	✓Hunt Corp	NY,Ph	B+	44	4518	Mfr/dstr office & art prod	24⅞	⅜	25 3/16	9¼	12 3/16	6⅝	4885	9½	8 1/16	9½	4.3	13	−5	−6.6	−17.1	−4.3
#45•[3]	JBHT	✓Hunt(JB)Transport	NNM	B	119	10786	Motor carrier,gen'l freight	26¾	5 3/16	38⅞	12 5/16	26¼	11⅞	15759	14 3/16	12⅜	13⅞	1.4	15	73	−39.1	0.7	−0.8
46	HCO	✓Huntco Inc'A'	NY,Ch	B−	18	1527	Intermediate steel processor	42½	10	16⅝	3¼	6	2 1/16	5842	3 9/16	2⅛	3 3/16	...	d	Neg	−17.1	−39.3	−31.4
47	HTD	Huntingdon Life[66]Sciences ADR	NY,Ch,Ph,P	NR	11	3083	Biological safety evaluat'n	34¼	1¾	3 15/16	11/16	2 3/16	13/16	7219	1 1/16	13/16	15/16	...	d	18	−25.0	−49.4	−18.6
¶48•[13]	HBAN	✓Huntington Bancshares	NNM	A	375	59465	Commercial bkg,Ohio	32⅛	⅝	31⅜	20	34	21 7/16	122065	28 13/16	21 7/16	23⅞	3.4	14	4	−1.4	19.2	29.1
49	HWY	✓Huntway Refining	NY,Ch	B−	9	6598	Refines liquid asphalt prd	13⅞	¼	2 13/16	1	2⅛	15/16	5967	1 9/16	15/16	1 3/16	...	7	NM	−29.6	13.5	3.5
50	HURC	✓Hurco Companies	NNM	B−	26	2844	Machine tools-microproc'r	28½	1¾	9¼	5⅛	7	3	5095	3⅞	3 3/16	3½	...	12	NM	−33.3	−13.3	−2.6

Uniform Footnote Explanations-See Page 4. Other: [1]CBOE:Cycle 3. [2]CBOE:Cycle 1. [3]P:Cycle 2. [4]Ph:Cycle 1. [5]Ph:Cycle 3. [6]Ph:Cycle 2. [7]P:Cycle 1. [8]ASE:Cycle 1. [9]ASE,P,Ph:Cycle 3. [10]P:Cycle 3. [11]ASE,CBOE,Ph:Cycle 3. [12]CBOE:Cycle 2. [13]CBOE,Ph:Cycle 1. [51]Stk dstr of BJ's Wholesale Club Inc. [52]ADRs represent'g 2 com,par yen 50. [53]Formerly AlliedSignal Inc. [54]Stk dstr of Host Marriot Corp(New),'99. [55]Stk dstr of Crestline Cap Corp,'98. [56]Formerly Hospitality Worldwide Svcs. [57]Pfd in $M. [58]or earlier for 'Tax Event'. [59]Stk dstr of Senior Housing Properties Tr. [60]Ea ADS rep 5 ord shrs,$0.50. [61]To be determined. [62]Ord shrs. [63]Ea ADS rep 40 N ord shrs,par Rmb 1.00. [64]Stk dstr of Galen Health Care,'93. [65]Fiscal Apr'96 & prior. [66]ADR rep 5 ord shares. [67]15 Mo Dec'95.

Index (Splits ◆)	Cash Divs. Ea.Yr. Since	Dividends: Latest Payment Period $	Date	Ex. Div.	Total $ So Far 1999	Ind. Rate	Paid 1998	Financial Position Mil-$ Cash& Equiv.	Curr. Assets	Curr. Liab.	Balance Sheet Date	Capitalization Lg Trm Debt Mil-$	Shs. 000 Pfd.	Com.	Earnings $ Per Shr. Years End	1995	1996	1997	1998	1999	Last 12 Mos.	Interim Earnings Period	$ per Shr. 1998	1999	Index
1◆	....	h[51]....	7-28-97	7-29	...	Nil	....	86.1	523	249	10-30-99	108	...	37875	Ja	v2.20	v2.31	□v0.55	v0.54	....	0.39	9 Mo Oct	v0.51	v0.36	1
2	1946	S0.02½	11-17-99	10-27	0.07½	0.05	0.10	270	422	169	9-30-99	464	...	260264	Dc	v0.22	v0.21	vd1.15	vd1.02	E0.01↑	Nil	9 Mo Sep	vd1.02	vNil	2
3	....	None Since Public			...	Nil	....	23.4	31.3	54.9	9-30-99	552	...	120031	Dc	p∫d0.11	vp0.27	v0.18	□vd0.11	....	d1.17	9 Mo Sep	v0.19	v□d0.87	3
4	....	None Since Public			...	Nil	....	144	171	40.5	9-30-99	1.33	...	70063	Dc	...	...	...	vpd1.79	....	....	9 Mo Sep	n/a	vd2.00	4
5◆	1955	Q0.09½	12-1-99	11-16	0.38	0.38	0.32	18.9	332	237	10-02-99	153	...	60355	Dc	v0.67	v1.13	v1.45	v1.72	....	1.51	9 Mo Sep	v1.24	v1.03	5
6	1949	0.18	12-17-99	9-27	0.32	0.32	0.279	3133	19659	18791	3-31-99	5583	...	974414	Mr	1.36	v3.67	v4.04	v5.20	....	5.49	6 Mo Sep	v2.37	v2.66	6
7◆	1887	Q0.17	12-10-99	11-17	0.68	0.68	0.60	981	5867	4784	9-30-99	1287	...	p791613	Dc	v1.52	v1.76	v2.02	v2.32	E2.70	2.60	9 Mo Sep	v1.70	v1.98	7
8◆	1974	Q0.01¼	11-26-99	11-9	0.05	0.05	0.035	40.5	70.8	15.7	9-30-99	....	...	29076	Dc	vd0.49	v0.15	v0.30	v0.43	....	0.57	9 Mo Sep	v0.34	v0.48	8
9	....	None Since Public			...	Nil	....	62.4	65.6	7.65	9-30-99	0.06	...	12167	Mr	...	vd0.26	vd0.39	vd0.42	....	d0.65	6 Mo Sep	vd0.32	vd0.55	9
10◆	1992	Q0.10½	12-15-99	11-26	0.38¼	0.42	0.33¼	Total Assets $4224.92M			9-30-99	99.7	...	41028	Dc	v1.33	v1.54	v1.80	v1.95	....	1.05	9 Mo Sep	v1.43	v0.53	10
11◆	1988	Q0.12	2-4-00	1-4	0.45	0.48	†0.84	Total Deposits $537.50M			9-30-99	7.00	...	8559	Mr	v0.95	v1.03	v1.09	v1.14	....	1.09	6 Mo Sep	v0.54	v0.49	11
12	....	None Since Public			...	Nil	....	0.70	42.9	11.7	9-30-99	46.9	...	13366	Dc	...	...	pv0.30	vΔ0.08	....	0.19	9 Mo Sep	vΔ0.06	v0.17	12
13◆	....	None Since Public			...	Nil	....	1.62	36.4	17.4	9-30-99	16.1	...	5883	Dc	...	pv0.13	pv0.11	vd0.43	....	d0.55	9 Mo Sep	v0.15	v0.03	13
14◆	1928	Q0.17½	2-15-00	1-19	0.66	0.70	0.64	236	734	294	7-31-99	209	...	72458	Oc	v1.57	v1.04	v1.43	v1.85	vP2.22	2.22				14
15	1995	Q0.69	2-17-00	1-13	2.73	2.76	2.58	Total Assets $2198.96M			9-30-99	415	3000	56450	Dc	p2.20	v2.23	v2.15	□v2.08	....	2.05	9 Mo Sep	v□1.54	v1.51	15
16	....	Div postponed 3-31-98			...	Nil	....	Total Assets $31.7M			9-30-99	25.4	...	1720	Dc	±pvd0.04	v±d0.12	vd0.68	vd0.58	....	d1.14	9 Mo Sep	vd0.20	vd0.76	16
17	1999	0.21	1-17-00	12-29	[54]0.63	0.84	h[55]....	Total Assets $8330.00M			9-10-99	5700	★4160	229012	Dc	v□d0.78	vd0.07	v0.23	v□0.85	E0.87	1.29	9 Mo Sep	v0.22	v0.66	17
18	....	None Since Public			...	Nil	....	6.86	62.2	67.5	9-30-99	2.49	40	14664	Dc	d0.20	v0.26	vd0.13	vd0.02	....	d3.96	9 Mo Sep	v0.38	vd3.56	18
19◆	1908	Q0.13	11-24-99	11-8	0.51	0.52	0.50	9.41	522	357	9-30-99	305	...	31096	Dc	vd0.26	v1.56	v1.73	vΔ1.57	....	1.40	9 Mo Sep	vΔ2.28	vΔ2.11	19
20◆	1926	Q0.17	1-15-00	12-29	0.66	0.68	0.59	Total Assets $57585.50M			9-30-99	33170	[57]640	470140	Dc	v1.44	v1.77	v2.17	v1.03	E3.05	2.86	9 Mo Sep	v0.32	v2.15	20
21	....	None Since Public			...	Nil	....	2.94	51.8	125	9-30-99	260	...	23919	Dc	p0.16	v0.49	v0.97	vd3.05	....	d2.97	9 Mo Sep	v0.50	v0.58	21
22	1997	0.804	1-3-00	12-13	3.216	3.216	3.216	7-1-2000 exch for Time Warner com re spec cond[58]				....	...	★20000	Dc	...	...	...	...	....	....				22
23	....	None Since Public			...	Nil	....	Total Assets $612.09M			7-31-99	315	...	±21924	Oc	0.61	v0.75	vd0.31	□v1.19	Pv□1.43	1.43				23
24	1975	Q0.04	11-24-99	11-8	0.16	0.16	0.16	0.50	12.7	13.3	9-30-99	81.0	690	5472	Dc	v0.59	v1.97	v0.31	vd12.79	....	d4.22	9 Mo Sep	vd8.37	v0.20	24
25	....	None Since Public			...	Nil	....	9.60	340	351	6-30-99	73.0	7	100025	Dc	vNil	pv0.21	v□p0.67	v1.05	....	1.22	9 Mo Sep	v0.86	v1.03	25
26	1987	0.32	2-15-00	1-6	h[59]1.46	1.28	1.51	Total Assets $3325.21M			9-30-99	1430	...	131908	Dc	v1.08	v□1.16	□v1.25	v□1.22	....	1.08	9 Mo Sep	v0.91	v0.77	26
27	....	None Since Public			...	Nil	....	3.94	77.5	89.0	9-30-99	539	...	18798	Dc	v0.02	v0.61	v0.64	vd1.00	....	d0.34	9 Mo Sep	vd0.39	v0.27	27
28◆	1871	Q0.44	1-27-00	1-6	1.70	1.76	1.62	Total Assets $2289M			9-30-99	462	...	29115	Dc	v2.05	v1.77	v2.19	v4.21	E2.55	2.74	9 Mo Sep	v3.57	v2.10	28
29	1999	0.66½	10-7-99	8-16	0.66½	[61]....	....	Book Value $154.35			12-31-98	27361	...	[62]883000	Dc	...	...	v10.20	v7.95	....	8.10	6 Mo Jun	v1.50	v1.65	29
30	1999	0.386	7-22-99	5-4	0.386	[61]....	....	541	1027	1013	12-31-97	1384	...	±5000000	Dc	±1.16	±1.28	v1.65	Pv1.59	....	1.66	6 Mo Jun	v0.68	v0.75	30
31◆	1934	Q0.32	1-11-00	12-16	1.26	1.28	1.20	35.4	601	380	9-30-99	99.6	...	±64750	Dc	v±1.83	v±2.10	v±1.89	v±2.50	....	2.42	9 Mo Sep	v±1.87	v±1.79	31
32◆	1934	Q0.32	1-11-00	12-16	1.26	1.28	1.20	....	....	....		....	...	10421	Dc	v±1.83	v±2.10	v±1.89	v±2.50	....	2.42	9 Mo Sep	v±1.87	v±1.79	32
33	1999	Q0.03	11-18-99	10-26	0.09	0.12	....	Total Deposits $751M			9-30-99	30.6	...	16435	Mr	...	...	n/a	n/a	....	....	6 Mo Sep	n/a	v0.29	33
34◆	....	None Since Public			...	Nil	....	2.53	7.16	4.39	9-30-99	2.01	67	5086	Dc	0.46	vd0.47	vd3.26	vd0.52	....	d0.87	9 Mo Sep	vd0.17	vd0.52	34
35◆	1952	sQ0.243	12-1-99	11-23	s0.971	0.971	s0.855	Total Deposits $4829M			9-30-99	200	...	p50484	Dc	v1.35	v0.83	v1.98	v0.54	E2.48	2.38	9 Mo Sep	vd0.02	v1.83	35
36	1938	gQ0.09	1-31-00	1-5	g0.45	0.36	g0.72	8.00	2688	1231	j1-31-99	1290	...	74634	Ja	0.59	v0.61	vd1.47	v0.55	....	j0.61	9 Mo Oct	vd0.06	vNil	36
37	1950	Div Postponed 12-9-99			0.34	Nil	0.34	18.3	172	161	10-02-99	3.75	...	10160	Dc	vd0.77	v0.48	v0.78	vd0.05	....	d1.95	9 Mo Sep	v0.24	vd1.66	37
38◆	1976	Q0.08½	11-19-99	11-3	0.34	0.34	0.32½	8.03	968	323	10-31-99	529	...	23523	Ja	v1.77	v2.09	v2.30	v2.55	....	2.76	9 Mo Oct	v2.10	v2.31	38
39	1999	0.114	1-14-00	12-29	0.065	0.90		....	...	...		....	...	★40000	Dc	...	...	...	pv0.45	....	0.45				39
40	....	None Since Public			...	Nil	....	281	287	15.7	9-30-99	126	...	23133	Dc	vd1.98	vd0.42	vd0.99	vd1.03	....	d1.61	9 Mo Sep	vd0.48	vd1.06	40
41	....	h[64]....	3-5-93	3-8	...	Nil	....	2012	2681	2787	9-30-99	667	...	167523	Dc	v1.16	v0.07	v1.05	v0.77	E0.65	0.54	9 Mo Sep	v0.43	v0.20	41
42	....	None Since Public			...	Nil	....	138	176	22.9	9-30-98	....	...	15508	Sp	1.64	2.25	v1.84	v1.68	Pv0.02	0.02				42
43	....	None Paid			...	Nil	....	19.6	30.1	148	9-30-99	16.5	...	11982	Dc	vd6.30	□vd11.38	vd7.97	vd9.53	....	d3.41	9 Mo Sep	vd7.90	vΔd1.78	43
44	1965	Q0.10¼	1-6-00	12-23	0.41	0.41	0.41	28.7	91.8	26.7	8-29-99	57.0	...	10401	Nv	0.96	□1.33	v1.27	v1.05	....	0.74	9 Mo Aug	v0.97	v0.66	44
45	1985	Q0.05	11-22-99	10-29	0.20	0.20	0.20	2.82	266	240	9-30-99	417	...	35637	Dc	vd0.06	v0.58	v0.31	v1.28	E0.95	1.03	9 Mo Sep	v0.98	v0.73	45
46	1993	0.035	3-1-99	2-10	0.035	Nil	0.10½	0.02	113	47.0	9-30-99	106	...	±8942	Dc	v±0.12	±v[65]0.72	±v0.29	v±d0.50	....	d1.30	9 Mo Sep	vd0.01	v□d0.81	46
47	....	0.072	7-13-94	6-10	...	Nil	....	23.4	47.3	39.0	12-31-98	89.3	...	291010	Dc	[67]d2.28	0.58	vd0.39	vd1.20	....	d0.54	9 Mo Sep	vd0.82	vd0.16	47
48◆	1912	Q0.20	1-3-00	12-14	0.745	0.80	0.678	Total Deposits $19241.81M			9-30-99	4425	...	229757	Dc	v1.17	1.36	v1.25	v1.28	E1.77	1.45	9 Mo Sep	v1.15	v1.32	48
49	....	0.10	8-29-90	8-8	...	Nil	....	11.4	30.1	19.6	9-30-99	35.3	...	15003	Dc	vd1.24	Δ□vd0.01	v0.04	v0.15	....	0.16	9 Mo Sep	v0.11	v0.12	49
50	....	0.02	11-23-92	10-20	...	Nil	....	3.18	52.7	20.8	7-31-99	12.3	...	5951	Oc	0.04	0.72	v2.06	v1.39	Pv0.30	0.30				50

◆**Stock Splits & Divs By Line Reference Index** [1]No adj for stk dstr of BJ's Wholesale Club,'97. [5]2-for-1,'98. [7]2-for-1,'94,'97. [8]2-for-1,'97,'99. [10]2-for-1,'97. [11]15%,'97. [13]3-for-2,'97. [14]To split 2-for-1,ex Feb 16. [19]2-for-1,'97. [20]3-for-1,'98. [28]3-for-2,'98. [31]Adj to 5%,'95:2-for-1,'96. [32]Adj to 5%,'95:2-for-1,'96. [34]1-for-2 REVERSE,'94. [35]3-for-2,'95:Adj for 3%,'99. [38]3-for-2,'97. [48]10%,'96,'97,'98,'99.

¶ S&P 500
# MidCap 400
✣ SmallCap 600
• Options

Index	Ticker	Name of Issue (Call Price of Pfd. Stocks)	Market	Com. Rank. & Pfd. Rating	Inst. Hold Cos	Inst. Hold Shs. (000)	Principal Business	Price Range 1971-97 High	1971-97 Low	1998 High	1998 Low	1999 High	1999 Low	Dec. Sales in 100s	December, 1999 Last Sale Or Bid High	Low	Last	%Div Yield	P-E Ratio	EPS 5 Yr Growth	% Annualized Total Return 12 Mo	36 Mo	60 Mo
1•[1]	HSM	✓Hussmann Intl	NY	NR	169	37452	Commercial refrigeration sys	....	....	20⅛	11⅝	19	12⅝	56515	18 3/16	12⅝	15 1/16	0.5	d	...	-21.9	...	...
✣2•[2]	HTCH	✓Hutchinson Technology	NNM	B–	164	17533	Mfr computer disk drive parts	39	1 11/16	36 3/16	11⅞	51¼	17⅝	85301	21½	17⅝	21¼	...	28	Neg	-40.4	-5.6	20.9
3	HBP	Huttig Building Products	NY	NR	..	...	Dstr doors/windows,building pds	....	....	....	....	5⅛	3 7/16	35100	5⅛	3 7/16	4 15/16	...	..	...	...	...	...
4•[3]	HYC	✓Hypercom Corp	NY	NR	54	7544	Dvlp/mfr payment sys,ntwk pd	17 5/16	12¾	18 15/16	4¼	14¼	5	18347	10 1/16	8	10	...	50	-15	0.6	...	...
5•[4]	HYPR	✓HyperFeed Technologies	NNM,Ph,P	C	13	755	Stock price data-base svc	27½	⅝	5	⅝	15 11/16	1⅞	83714	7½	4⅛	4⅝	...	d	Neg	118	20.8	25.3
✣6•[5]	HYSL	✓Hyperion Solutions	NNM	NR	164	23535	Dvp multi-dimensional softwr	82¾	17	50¾	12	44	9⅞	78499	44	26⅛	43½	...	56	10	142	21.5	...
7	ICAB	✓i-CABLE Communic ADS[53]	NNM	NR	..	...	Pay TV operator,Hong Kong	....	....	....	....	37½	22	69976	32⅞	22	25 1/16	...	..	...	...	...	...
8	IFLO	✓I-Flow Corp	NSC	B–	11	575	Dvlp,mfr infusion systems	14 1/16	1¼	3¾	1 1/16	5	1 3/16	14622	4 7/16	3⅝	4	...	18	NM	226	-10.0	14.7
9	ITWO	✓i2 Technologies	NNM	NR	189	26420	Supply chain mgmt softwr	29¼	10	42¼	9¼	218	17¾	401021	218	83¾	195	...	..	57	542	117	...
10	IBAS	✓iBasis Inc	NNM	NR	..	...	Internet telephony svcs	....	....	....	....	45	16	91884	41⅞	24⅛	28¾	...	..	...	...	...	...
#11•[6]	IBP	✓IBP, Inc	NY,Ch,P,Ph	B	321	68903	Produces beef/pork products	33⅝	5⅝	29 7/16	16 9/16	29 3/16	16¾	90382	22¼	17 1/16	18	0.6	6	5	-37.9	-9.0	4.0
12•[7]	ICGX	✓ICG Communications	NNM,Ch,P,Vc	C	194	35681	Telecommunications services	28⅝	2½	44¼	11⅛	28 9/16	13 15/16	210506	19⅞	14⅝	18¾	...	d	-22	-12.8	2.1	7.2
13	IH	✓ICH Corp	AS	NR	11	161	Oper fast food chain	4⅞	3	5½	3⅛	15½	3⅝	1827	11⅛	8 7/16	11	...	7	...	203	...	...
14	IC.D	ICICI Limited ADS[57]	NY	NR	11	1991	Financial svcs,India	....	....	....	....	19	9 13/16	29849	19	11	13⅞	...	..	...	...	...	...
15	IC	Full Divd ADS[59]	NY	NR	..	...		....	....	....	....	18	10⅝	4902	18	11¼	14¾	...	..	...	...	...	...
#16•[8]	ICN	✓ICN Pharmaceuticals	NY,Ch,P	NR	212	31831	Mfr specialty/generic prod	37 5/16	1 7/16	52¼	13 13/16	36⅜	16 9/16	89782	26⅞	22⅜	25 9/16	1.1	18	Neg	13.0	25.8	20.1
17	ICOC	ICO Inc	NNM	↓C	25	5252	Prod'n,explor,svcs to oil ind	7½	1¼	6¼	1⅞	2½	¾	24575	1 13/16	1⅜	1½	...	d	Neg	-22.9	-35.0	-14.2
18•[9]	ICOS	✓ICOS Corp	NNM,Ch	NR	119	6874	Dvlp stge:biopharmaceut'l R&D	21½	3⅜	29⅞	12⅛	48½	24	60027	31⅞	25½	29¼	...	61	NM	-1.7	56.5	51.3
19	IDBE	✓ID Biomedical	NSC,Vc,To	NR	5	80	Medical products R&D	12⅝	2⅛	5 1/16	1⅞	3⅛	1 3/16	23671	2 13/16	1 5/16	2½	...	..	...	21.2	-16.6	-11.0
#20•[4]	IDA	✓Idacorp Inc	NY,B,Ch,P	B+	201	11333	Hydroelectric utility	37¾	9⅛	38 1/16	29⅞	36½	26	20939	28 3/16	26	26 13/16	6.9	11	6	-21.4	0.8	9.1
✣21•[3]	IDPH	✓IDEC Pharmaceuticals	NNM,Ch	C	287	18879	Dvlp stge:immune sys pharma'ls	23⅛	1 1/16	24 1/16	8⅝	105	19 13/16	321640	105	55	98¼	...	..	NM	318	102	147
22•[10]	IDX	✓Identix Inc	AS,Ch,Ph,P	C	40	3246	Mfr computerized ID systems	19¼	1¼	10 9/16	4 7/16	12½	5¼	30962	9 9/16	6⅞	9⅛	...	d	-39	8.2	3.7	23.4
✣23	IEX	✓IDEX Corp	NY,Ch,Ph	B+	155	19733	Mfr fluid handl'g/indl prod	36 11/16	4¼	38¾	19½	34⅛	21⅝	11642	31 7/16	25¾	30⅜	1.8	17	10	26.7	6.5	12.2
✣24•[7]	IDXX	✓IDEXX Laboratories	NNM	B–	242	30724	Mfr animal biomedical test prd	53¾	3⅜	28⅝	12¼	28⅛	14¼	78081	18¾	14 7/16	16⅛	...	d	Neg	-40.1	-23.5	-2.2
25•[11]	IDTC	✓IDT Corp	NNM	NR	95	6364	Internet access svcs	25¼	4	40¼	11⅞	35	9½	143314	25½	18½	18⅞	...	..	80	22.8	19.7	...
26•[6]	IDXC	✓IDX Systems	NNM	NR	97	9496	Health care info sys/svcs	44¼	18	55¾	33¼	46⅝	12 7/16	41549	32¾	21 3/16	31¼	...	..	5	-29.0	3.0	...
27	IEU	IES Util 7.875%JrSubDebs[61]	NY	NR	3	38	Subsid of IES Industries	26⅛	23⅜	26⅛	25	26	21⅞	238	23¾	21⅞	21⅞	9.0	..	...	-7.2	4.5	...
28	IFRS	✓IFR Systems	NNM	C	31	3592	Mfrs communic'ns test eqp	23½	2 13/16	25½	3⅛	13	2 15/16	20069	13	3⅝	10 1/16	...	11	-30	118	-1.2	9.8
29	IGEN	✓IGEN Intl	NNM	NR	65	4392	Mfr/mkt diagnostic systems	15 9/16	4⅝	46⅝	12¼	35¼	20⅞	22960	31¼	22⅝	29¾	...	d	-20	-2.9	81.2	40.8
30	IG	✓IGI Inc	AS,B,Ch,P	B–	12	875	Mfr animal health prod	32	⅝	4¼	1 5/16	2¼	1 1/16	4225	2	1 3/16	1 15/16	...	d	-47	0.0	-34.0	...
31	IGOC	✓iGo Corp	NNM	NR	..	...	Net retail electr device pd	....	....	....	....	26⅛	8½	67874	21½	8½	9 1/16	...	d	...	...	...	...
✣32•[11]	IHP	✓IHOP Corp	NY	B+	129	15824	Oper Intl House Pancake restr	18 11/16	4 11/16	23¼	14¾	26	14 15/16	11905	16¾	15	16 11/16	...	11	14	-16.3	12.3	4.2
¶33•[1]	IKN	✓Ikon Office Solutions	NY,B,Ch,Ph,P	B–	316	92254	Office technology/tech edu	66	13/16	36¼	5	16⅝	5⅝	181239	7 9/16	5⅜	6 13/16	2.3	10	Neg	-19.3	...	...
¶34•[11]	ITW	✓Illinois Tool Works	NY,B,Ch,P	A+	816	191200	Fasteners,tools, plastic items	60⅛	⅞	73 3/16	45 3/16	82	58⅛	166615	69	62 3/16	67 9/16	0.3	22	19	17.5	20.3	26.6
#35•[8]	ILN	✓Illinova Corp[65]	NY,B,C,Ch,P,Ph	B	281	54616	Hldg co: Illinois Power	44¾	12¾	31	23⅜	34⅞	20¾	47060	34⅞	28 11/16	34¾	3.6	d	Neg	45.2	13.3	14.7
36	ILUM	✓Illuminet Holdings	NNM	NR	..	...	Oper telecommun signaling sy	....	....	....	....	62⅛	19	17124	55	42 11/16	55	...	63	...	...	...	...
37	ILX	✓ILX Resorts	AS	B–	10	155	Dvlp,mkt resort properties	12 13/16	3⅛	7¼	1⅝	2½	1¼	3228	1 15/16	1 7/16	1½	...	d	Neg	-27.3	-31.8	-22.3
38•[12]	DISK	✓Image Entertainment	NNM	B–	19	1504	Dstr home video programs	14⅞	⅛	10½	3	12 11/16	3 9/16	27314	7⅜	4¾	5⅝	...	80	-44	-46.7	18.3	-5.7
39	IMON	ImaginOn Inc	NSC	NR	6	153	Dvlp stge:CD-ROM software	6⅞	13/16	2⅝	⅜	15¼	1 3/16	258106	6⅜	3 1/16	4¼	...	d	-45	209	45.7	...
40	IMAN	✓iManage Inc	NNM	NR	..	...	e-business software prd	....	....	....	....	40 1/16	11	71192	40 1/16	28¾	32⅛	...	..	...	...	...	...
41•[13]	IMS	✓Imasco Ltd	To,Mo,Vc	A–	36	12185	Tobacco,food,retail,fin'l svc	27⅛	½	33⅛	22	40⅞	30½	437241	40⅜	39	39 15/16	2.0	20	23	24.8	37.3	36.4
#42•[14]	IMN	✓Imation Corp	NY,Ph	NR	224	27139	Mfr data storage/imaging sys	33⅝	15⅛	19 15/16	13 9/16	34¼	15	22747	34¼	29⅞	33 9/16	...	20	NM	91.8	6.1	...
43	IMAT	Imatron Inc	NNM,Ch	C	32	3300	Cardiac diagnostic scanners	8⅝	⅜	4	13/16	4¾	13/16	383954	3 1/16	2	2½	...	d	-49	81.8	-8.9	18.0
44•[4]	IMAX	✓Imax Corp	NNM,To	NR	101	10828	Design,dstr project'n/sound sy	28¾	3¼	32¼	17	33⅝	15	25465	28⅝	23¼	27⅜	...	d	7	-13.4	21.6	45.7
#45•[15]	IGL	✓IMC Global	NY,Ch,Ph,P	B–	331	83936	Mfrs chemical fertilizer	44½	11¼	39½	17 13/16	27⅛	12¾	123704	17 1/16	14¾	16⅜	2.0	12	Neg	-22.0	-24.2	-4.6
46	WS	Wrrt(Pur1com at $44.50)	NY	....	42	1765		4⅛	3	6⅝	⅜	1⅜	1/16	9690	3/16	1/16	⅛	...	..	...	...	...	...
✣47	IMR	✓IMCO Recycling	NY,Ch,Ph	B+	139	9332	Aluminum can recycling svcs	24⅝	1	20	10¼	18	10¼	15291	12 13/16	10¼	12⅝	1.9	10	11	-16.9	-3.6	-2.4
48	ICCC	✓ImmuCell Corp	NSC	B–	4	9	Antibody-base prevention prd	6⅛	⅝	2¾	1	2⅝	1	6910	2⅝	1⅝	2⅜	...	20	80	90.0	0.0	17.5
✣49•[5]	IMNR	✓Immune Response	NNM	C	62	3494	R&D:immune sys pharmac'ls	62¾	2⅝	19 11/16	7⅜	13¼	3	117589	4 11/16	3	4⅝	...	d	7	-60.1	-19.2	-6.3
50•[16]	IMNX	✓Immunex Corp	NNM	C	251	57530	Immunological bio products	20⅛	1	31⅝	11 13/16	120½	28¾	300549	120½	61	109½	...	..	NM	248	182	96.7

Uniform Footnote Explanations-See Page 4. Other: [1]CBOE:Cycle 3. [2]ASE,CBOE,Ph:Cycle 2. [3]Ph:Cycle 1. [4]Ph:Cycle 2. [5]CBOE:Cycle 2. [6]ASE,Ph:Cycle 2. [7]ASE,CBOE:Cycle 3. [8]ASE:Cycle 3. [9]CBOE:Cycle 1. [10]ASE,CBOE,Ph:Cycle 3. [11]Ph:Cycle 3. [12]CBOE,Ph:Cycle 3. [13]Mo:Cycle 1. [14]ASE,CBOE:Cycle 1. [15]CBOE,P:Cycle 1. [16]ASE,CBOE,P,Ph:Cycle 3. [51]Fiscal Mar'98 & prior. [52]12 Mo Jun'98. [53]Ea ADS rep 20 ord shrs,HK$1. [54]Fiscal Sep'95 & prior. [55]12 Mo Dec'96:Fiscal Sep'96 earned d$6.70. [56]8 Mo Dec'97. [57]Ea ADS 5 Equity shrs,Rs.10. [58]To be determined. [59]Ea ADS rep 5 Equity shrs,Rs.10. [60]9 Mo Dec'98. [61]Jr Sub Deferrable Int Debs Sr'A'. [62]Fiscal Jun'97 & prior. [63]12 Mo Mar'99:Fiscal Jun'98 earn d$1.95. [64]Stk dstr of Novavax Inc. [65]Plan comb w/Dynergy Inc,1 new. [66]Subsid Pfd in $M. [67]Pfd in $M.

Index	Splits ◆ Cash Divs. Ea. Yr. Since	Dividends Latest Payment Period $	Date	Ex. Div.	Total $ So Far 1999	Ind. Rate	Paid 1998	Financial Position Mil-$ Cash& Equiv.	Curr. Assets	Curr. Liab.	Balance Sheet Date	Capitalization Lg Trm Debt Mil-$	Shs. 000 Pfd.	Com.	Earnings $ Per Shr. Years End	1995	1996	1997	1998	1999	Last 12 Mos.	Interim Earnings Period	$ per Shr. 1998	1999	Index
1	1998	Q0.02	1-4-00	12-13	0.08	0.08	0.06	43.0	514	239	9-30-99	343	...	50909	Dc	...	p0.95	pv1.01	pv1.11	....	d0.41	9 Mo Sep	v0.77	vd0.75	1
2◆	....	None Since Public			...	Nil	....	262	394	77.3	6-27-99	216	...	24741	Sp	1.28	v0.82	v2.21	vd2.46	Pv0.75	0.75				2
3	....	None Since Public			...	Nil	....	....	250	108	p9-30-99	101	...	p21600	Dc	...	...	...	pv1.02	....	....	9 Mo Sep	n/a	vp0.76	3
4	....	None Since Public			...	Nil	....	59.6	206	44.7	9-30-99	1.40	...	33196	Je	0.51	v0.33	v0.60	v0.44	v0.27	0.20	3 Mo Sep	v0.17	v0.10	4
5	....	None Paid			...	Nil	....	2.06	7.75	8.72	9-30-99	0.35	48	15001	Dc	v0.21	vd0.45	vd1.33	vd0.57	....	d0.58	9 Mo Sep	vd0.40	vd0.41	5
6	....	None Since Public			...	Nil	....	280	404	163	9-30-99	100	...	31175	Je	0.27	v0.50	v[51]0.58	v[52]0.67	v0.26	0.78	3 Mo Sep	vd0.33	v0.19	6
7	....	None Since Public			...	Nil	....	2.25	153	3138	p6-30-99	p232	...	★1960000	Dc	...	...	...	vpd0.73	....	....	6 Mo Jun	n/a	vpd0.28	7
8	....	None Paid			...	Nil	....	0.81	14.4	5.66	9-30-99	1.57	...	14487	Dc	v0.12	vd0.68	v0.03	v0.08	....	0.22	9 Mo Sep	v0.03	v0.17	8
9◆	....	None Since Public			...	Nil	....	189	369	174	9-30-99	....	...	76923	Dc	v0.06	v0.12	v0.10	v0.26	E0.38	0.34	9 Mo Sep	v0.02	v0.10	9
10	....	None Since Public			...	Nil	....	3.45	6.49	7.54	6-30-99	4.51	p...	★30417	Dc	...	...	...	vpd0.44	....	....	6 Mo Jun	n/a	vpd0.41	10
11◆	1988	Q0.02½	1-17-00	12-9	0.10	0.10	0.10	28.0	1507	1364	9-25-99	588	...	92265	Dc	□v2.92	v2.07	v1.25	v□2.19	E2.80	3.46	9 Mo Sep	v□1.21	v2.48	11
12	....	None Paid			...	Nil	....	170	339	158	9-30-99	1917	2590	47514	Dc	v[54]d6.83	v[55]d1.56	vd10.11	vd9.25	....	d10.57	9 Mo Sep	vd6.66	v∆d7.98	12
13	....	None Since Public			...	Nil	....	7.54	15.5	25.6	9-30-99	65.9	...	2836	Dc	...	p0.26	v‡[56]d0.31	v1.14	....	1.51	9 Mo Sep	v0.59	v0.96	13
14	....	Plan annual div			...	[58]....	....	Total Deposits $1427M			6-30-99	10163	...	★785312	Mr	...	...	...	v1.50	....	....	3 Mo Jun	n/a	v0.45	14
15	....	Plan annual div			...	[58]....	....	....	...	...		....	...	785312	Mr	...	...	...	v1.50	....	....	3 Mo Jun	n/a	v0.45	15
16◆	1985	Q0.07	10-27-99	10-8	0.27	0.28	0.233	180	570	150	9-30-99	595	1	78365	Dc	v1.44	v1.51	v1.69	vd4.78	E1.45	d2.03	9 Mo Sep	vd1.77	v0.98	16
17	1995	Div Omitted 3-5-99			...	Nil	0.16½	27.8	110	50.7	6-30-99	131	323	22114	Sp	0.41	vd0.24	v0.19	v0.17	Pv∆d1.01	d1.01				17
18	....	None Since Public			...	Nil	....	58.6	74.8	15.3	9-30-99	....	...	44212	Dc	vd0.73	vd0.77	vd0.30	v0.67	....	0.48	9 Mo Sep	vd0.68	vd0.87	18
19◆	....	None Paid			...	Nil	....	0.48	0.82	1.57	j6-30-99	1.30	...	15818	Dc	0.04	vd0.43	v[51]d0.69	v‡[60]d0.57	....	....	6 Mo Jun	n/a	vd0.24	19
20	1917	Q0.46½	11-19-99	10-21	1.86	1.86	1.86	17.2	305	364	9-30-99	742	568	37612	Dc	v2.10	v2.21	v2.32	v2.37	....	2.43	12 Mo Sep	v2.39	v2.43	20
21◆	....	None Since Public			...	Nil	....	230	267	18.2	9-30-99	122	...	42302	Dc	vd0.59	vd0.17	vd0.42	v0.46	E0.97↑	0.84	9 Mo Sep	v0.34	v0.71	21
22	....	None Paid			...	Nil	....	9.32	42.6	15.0	9-30-99	....	...	30839	Je	d0.04	d0.15	v0.02	v0.03	vd0.52	d0.65	3 Mo Sep	v0.02	vd0.11	22
23◆	1995	Q0.14	1-31-00	1-13	0.56	0.56	0.54	4.94	225	87.4	9-30-99	3.04	...	29633	Dc	1.53	v1.69	v1.95	v□2.15	....	1.75	9 Mo Sep	v□1.75	v1.35	23
24◆	....	None Since Public			...	Nil	....	120	244	70.2	9-30-99	4.21	...	36563	Dc	v0.61	v0.83	vd0.56	vd0.40	....	d0.19	9 Mo Sep	v0.37	v0.58	24
25	....	None Since Public			...	Nil	....	204	397	135	10-31-99	126	...	±34130	Jl	d0.13	□d0.85	vd0.18	□vd0.21	v□d0.60	0.04	3 Mo Oct	v0.17	v0.81	25
26	....	None Since Public			...	Nil	....	73.9	201	62.1	9-30-99	....	...	27780	Dc	vp0.63	v0.64	v0.30	v1.11	....	0.28	9 Mo Sep	v0.48	vd0.35	26
27	1995	Q0.492	12-31-99	12-28	1.969	1.969	1.969	Co option redm fr 12-31-2000 at $25				50.0	...	...	Dc	...	...	...	....	....	....	Mature 12-31-2025			27
28◆	....	Q0.033	12-5-97	11-19	...	Nil	....	4.95	77.4	44.3	9-30-99	62.2	...	8232	Mr	0.27	0.56	v[62]0.79	v[63]d0.70	....	0.90	6 Mo Sep	vd0.58	v1.02	28
29	....	None Since Public			...	Nil	....	22.5	30.5	9.29	9-30-99	33.7	25	15417	Mr	d0.52	vd0.66	vd0.82	vd1.00	....	d1.27	6 Mo Sep	vd0.48	vd0.75	29
30◆	....	h[64]....	12-12-95	12-13	...	Nil	....	1.05	17.1	26.3	9-30-99	0.21	...	9610	Dc	vd0.28	vd0.01	vd0.15	vd0.32	....	d0.16	9 Mo Sep	vd0.24	vd0.08	30
31	....	None Since Public			...	Nil	....	....	3.70	3.74	6-30-99	p0.83	p...	★19325	Dc	...	...	...	vd0.36	....	d0.84	6 Mo Jun	vd0.17	vd0.65	31
32◆	....	None Since Public			...	Nil	....	10.2	47.2	45.7	9-30-99	198	...	20111	Dc	v0.85	v0.98	v1.08	v1.30	....	1.51	9 Mo Sep	v0.92	v1.13	32
33◆	1965	Q0.04	12-10-99	11-18	0.16	0.16	0.16	152	2385	1912	6-30-99	2016	...	149124	Sp	1.67	v1.47	v□0.92	vd0.76	vP0.67	0.67				33
34◆	1933	Q0.18	10-23-99	9-28	0.68	0.20	0.51	151	2085	1353	9-30-99	1212	...	p300477	Dc	v1.63	v1.95	v2.33	v2.67	E3.05	2.91	9 Mo Sep	v1.94	v2.18	34
35	1991	Q0.31	11-1-99	10-6	1.24	1.24	1.24	55.0	672	1191	9-30-99	2119	[66]240	69939	Dc	v1.96	v2.51	v□1.41	vd19.30	....	d18.60	12 Mo Sep	v□d0.45	vd18.60	35
36	....	None Since Public			...	Nil	....	11.3	43.9	26.8	6-30-99	p12.7	...	★29252	Dc	...	...	...	v0.22	....	0.87	9 Mo Sep	v0.61	v1.26	36
37◆	....	None Paid			...	Nil	....	Total Assets $56.54M			9-30-99	25.6	306	4001	Dc	v0.24	v0.37	v0.59	vNil	....	d0.01	9 Mo Sep	v0.15	v0.14	37
38	....	None Since Public			...	Nil	....	Total Assets $56.75M			9-30-99	16.5	...	16457	Mr	0.49	v□0.07	vd0.71	v0.12	....	0.07	6 Mo Sep	vd0.04	vd0.09	38
39	....	None Since Public			...	Nil	....	3.37	3.64	0.79	9-30-99	....	4	41282	Dc	0.01	vd1.37	v∆d0.94	vd0.48	....	d0.58	9 Mo Sep	vd0.06	vd0.16	39
40	....	None Since Public			...	Nil	....	12.1	16.5	10.2	6-30-99	0.89	p...	★21448	Dc	...	...	...	vpd0.21	....	....	6 Mo Jun	n/a	vpd0.12	40
41◆	1912	gQ0.20	12-31-99	11-29	g0.80	0.80	g0.68	....	1848	1160	j9-30-99	1727	[67]135	432959	Dc	v0.46	v1.28	v1.70	v1.67	....	j1.96	9 Mo Sep	v1.19	v1.48	41
42	....	None Since Public			...	Nil	....	167	775	369	9-30-99	1.20	...	36453	Dc	pvd2.02	vd0.49	vd4.54	v1.45	....	1.72	9 Mo Sep	v0.51	v0.78	42
43	....	None Since Public			...	Nil	....	7.26	25.1	10.9	9-30-99	0.13	...	97741	Dc	vd0.04	vd0.18	vd0.15	vd0.18	....	d0.12	9 Mo Sep	vd0.13	vd0.07	43
44◆	....	None Since Public			...	Nil	....	110	206	74.0	9-30-99	300	...	29645	Dc	v0.11	v0.50	v0.68	v□0.09	....	d0.24	9 Mo Sep	v0.57	v0.24	44
45◆	1995	Q0.08	12-31-99	12-13	0.32	0.32	0.32	64.7	1047	453	9-30-99	2535	...	114480	Dc	v□2.34	□v1.39	□v0.93	vd0.11	E1.35↓	d0.52	9 Mo Sep	v□1.58	v□1.17	45
46	....	Terms&trad. basis should			be checked in detail			Wrrts expire 12-22-2000				....	...	8010	Dc	...	...	...	....	....	....				46
47	1995	Q0.06	12-31-99	12-8	0.24	0.24	0.21	2.80	192	100	9-30-99	195	...	16549	Dc	v1.05	v0.55	v□1.06	v1.17	....	1.28	9 Mo Sep	v0.87	v0.98	47
48	....	None Paid			...	Nil	....	1.77	2.73	0.33	9-30-99	0.44	...	2445	Dc	v0.01	vd0.03	v0.10	vd0.04	....	0.12	9 Mo Sep	vNil	v0.16	48
49	....	None Since Public			...	Nil	....	22.2	23.3	8.39	9-30-99	1.30	...	25926	Dc	vd1.19	vd1.19	vd1.53	vd0.78	....	d0.79	9 Mo Sep	vd0.52	vd0.53	49
50◆	....	None Since Public			...	Nil	....	677	768	126	9-30-99	450	...	164265	Dc	vd0.07	vd0.34	vd0.10	v0.01	E0.25↓	0.26	9 Mo Sep	vd0.09	v0.16	50

◆**Stock Splits & Divs By Line Reference Index** [2]3-for-1,'97. [9]2-for-1,'98. [11]2-for-1,'96. [16]2-for-1,'98. [19]2-for-1,'95. [21]2-for-1,'99. [23]3-for-2,'95,'97. [24]2-for-1,'95. [28]3-for-2,'97. [30]No adj for stk dstr Novavax Inc. [32]2-for-1,'99. [33]2-for-1,'95:No adj for stk dstr Unisource Worldwide. [34]2-for-1,'97. [37]1-for-5 REVERSE,'98. [41]2-for-1,'98. [44]2-for-1,'97. [45]2-for-1,'95. [50]2-for-1,'99(twice).

¶ S&P 500
# MidCap 400
✣ SmallCap 600
• Options

Index	Ticker	Name of Issue (Call Price of Pfd. Stocks)	Market	Com. Rank. & Pfd. Rating	Inst. Hold Cos	Inst. Hold Shs. (000)	Principal Business	Price Range 1971-97 High	1971-97 Low	1998 High	1998 Low	1999 High	1999 Low	Dec. Sales in 100s	December, 1999 Last Sale Or Bid High	Low	Last	%Div Yield	P-E Ratio	EPS 5 Yr Growth	% Annualized Total Return 12 Mo	36 Mo	60 Mo
1	IMPX	IMP Inc	NSC	B–	5	16	Mfr integrated circuits	235	4⅜	16 9/16	1 9/16	7 13/16	1 1/16	14766	6⅛	2 7/16	3 3/16	...	d	Neg	5.4	–43.7	–25.5
2	ICH	✓IMPAC Commercial Hldgs[51]	AS	NR	11	1434	Real estate investment trust	20¾	15	19¾	1⅞	7¼	4⅝	12321	6	4 11/16	5¼	...	d	...	4.1	...	...
3	IMH	✓IMPAC Mtge Hldgs	AS,Ch,Ph	NR	21	3080	Real estate investment trust	18 13/16	8	18¼	2¾	6 3/16	3 7/16	25264	4 7/16	3 7/16	4⅛	e12.6	14	40	7.3	–28.1	...
4	IMCO	✓IMPCO Technologies	NNM	B–	25	1629	Mfr electr auto fuel mgmt sys	21¾	2¼	17¾	10¼	16 11/16	7	10752	16 11/16	12 11/16	13 15/16	...	18	4	6.2	16.8	10.4
5•[1]	IMP	✓Imperial Bancorp	NY,Ch	B–	110	15059	Commercial bkg,California	31¼	⅜	30¾	9⅜	27	14⅜	33805	25 3/16	21¼	24⅛	s...	16	42	69.3	27.6	47.7
6•[2]	ICI	✓Imperial Chem Ind ADR[54]	NY,B,P	B–	131	34858	Leading int'l chemical co	108⅛	10¾	80½	30⅜	52⅝	31	21526	45⅜	36⅜	42 9/16	4.9	19	–10	28.6	–1.9	2.9
7•[3]	ICII	✓Imperial Credit	NNM	NR	77	22105	Mortgage banking operations	29¼	2	27⅜	3⅝	10 3/16	3⅞	24562	6½	5	6¼	...	d	Neg	–25.4	–33.2	21.0
8	ICMI	✓Imperial Credit Comm'l Mtg[55]	NNM	NR	78	19905	Real estate investment trust	19⅛	14¼	16¾	6½	11 9/16	8 5/16	34623	11 9/16	11	11⅜	10.1	14	...	36.1	...	...
9•[4]	IMO	✓Imperial Oil Ltd	AS,To,B,Mo,Ph,P	B+	120	40140	Canadian oil:Exxon owns 70%	21¾	5 3/16	21⅜	13⅜	24 7/16	14½	12899	24 5/16	20⅞	21⅝	◆2.5	13	13	40.1	16.1	19.8
10	IHK	✓Imperial Sugar	AS	↓C	70	10457	Ref beet/cane sugar:sweet'nrs	58¾	5¼	12⅛	5⅞	9¾	2 15/16	18584	4⅜	2 15/16	3 5/16	...	d	1	–58.7	–39.1	–16.7
11	ITY	✓Imperial Tobacco Grp ADS[59]	NY	NR	46	17216	Mfr cigarettes/tobacco prd	....	....	22 9/16	20¼	24⅞	15½	6509	21 1/16	15½	15 13/16	5.6	9	...	–21.9	...	...
12	IMX	✓Implant Sciences	AS	NR	..	...	Mfr radiaion therapy implants	....	....	....	....	7¾	3⅝	3663	7¾	5½	5⅞	...	d	...	...	...	...
13	WS	Wrrt (Pur 1 com at $9)	AS	....	1	23		....	....	....	....	1⅛	¼	1203	1⅛	¼	13/16	...	..	...	...	...	...
14•[5]	IMRS	✓IMRglobal Corp	NNM	NR	130	15111	Application softwr outsourcing	25 5/16	5	42 3/16	16⅝	32⅝	7	69603	14 7/16	10⅝	12 9/16	...	21	...	–57.3	10.6	...
¶15•[6]	RX	✓IMS Health	NY	NR	730	251194	Healthcare information svcs	22¾	14	38 7/16	21 5/16	39 3/16	21½	258900	27¼	22½	27 3/16	0.3	32	...	...	...	...
16•[2]	INFS	✓In Focus Systems	NNM	B	99	14445	Mfr LCD project'n panel prod	29⅛	2¾	21½	3½	25½	6 5/16	78911	24 7/16	19½	23 3/16	...	31	–33	161	29.3	12.4
17	IHHI	✓In Home Health	NNM	↑B–	6	1277	Home health/nursing services	21⅜	1⅞	4½	1 1/16	4¼	1 1/16	2662	3	1⅞	2⅛	...	7	12	17.3	24.9	15.8
✣18•[7]	ICO	✓InaCom Corp	NY	B	170	21503	Franchise/oper computer str	40⅝	6¼	37¼	13½	17¾	3⅞	213479	10⅜	5 7/16	7 5/16	...	..	...	–50.8	–43.2	0.9
¶19•[8]	N	✓Inco Ltd	NY,To,B,C,Ch,Mo,Ph,P	B–	332	91687	Producer of nickel & copper	46¾	7⅞	20 11/16	8¼	24 15/16	10⅜	124823	23 9/16	18 1/16	23½	...	d	Neg	125	–9.0	–2.9
20	Pr E	5.50%Red Sr'E'Cv Pfd([62]51.375)	NY	B+	10	580		56½	47⅛	48 13/16	32 13/16	43	33 7/16	244	42¼	39⅜	40⅜B	6.8	..	...	...	...	...
21	NVB	✓ CI VBN[63] Shrs	NY	NR	29	5970		31¾	10⅝	14⅝	3½	9⅞	5	2027	9	7 13/16	8 11/16	...	..	...	71.6	–28.2	...
22	IOT	✓Income Opportunity Rlty	AS	NR	1	2	Real estate investment trust	39	⅞	12⅛	6⅛	8	4¾	135	5⅝	5¼	5⅜B	11.2	13	NM	–7.2	–16.3	–7.5
✣23•[1]	INCY	✓INCYTE Pharmaceuticals	NNM,Ch,Ph	NR	175	16640	Bio-pharmaceutical R&D	45¼	3 5/16	51	17⅜	73⅛	16 7/16	160860	73⅛	28¼	60	...	d	NM	60.5	32.6	54.0
24	IBCP	✓Independent Bank	NNM	A+	42	1854	Commercial banking,Michigan	24½	1 15/16	28¾	17⅛	20⅛	12¾	6374	17 5/16	12¾	14⅝	s3.8	14	7	–17.8	11.6	19.4
25	IBK	✓Independent Bankshares	AS,Ph	B	8	185	Bank holding, Texas	33 11/16	1⅛	19⅝	10¼	15⅞	10 3/16	262	15¼	12⅞	13⅞	1.4	13	26	22.7	5.5	26.5
#26	IEI	✓Indiana Energy[65]	NY,Ch,Ph	↑A–	127	7629	Hldg co:gas service, Indiana	25 11/16	1¾	26⅜	19⅝	24⅝	17⅝	12958	21 1/16	17⅝	17¾	5.5	13	2	–24.6	3.4	7.7
27	IMK	Indiana Mich Pwr7.60%JrSubDebs	NY	....[66]	1	20	Electric power utility	....	....	26 9/16	24¾	25 15/16	18⅞	2674	22	18⅞	19 15/16	9.5	..	...	–15.1	...	...
28	IMJ	Indiana Mich Pwr 8%JrSubDebs[68]	NY	....[69]	3	21	Electric power utility	26	23½	26 5/16	25 1/16	26 5/16	20⅜	617	23⅝	20⅜	20⅜	9.8	..	...	–13.7	1.8	...
29	INDG	Indigo N.V.	NNM	NR	16	1505	Mfr offset color printing sys	64¾	3¼	7⅝	1½	5 11/16	2 9/16	37662	3 5/16	2 11/16	3 3/16	...	d	37	–19.7	–13.2	–28.1
30•[9]	IMIC	✓Industri-Matematik Intl	NNM	NR	31	4134	Dvp client/server software	31⅜	5⅝	33⅜	3	7 1/16	1 9/16	101948	7 1/16	2¾	6⅛	...	d	...	22.5	–22.4	...
31	IDS	✓Industrial Data Systems	AS	NR	1	28	Dgn ruggedized PCs	11	5/16	9⅜	3	10¾	¾	7255	1	13/16	⅞	...	d	...	–89.2	...	...
32	IDG	✓Industrial Distribution Grp	NY	NR	21	1123	Mfr/dstr industrial products	23¼	14 9/16	21 5/16	4¾	8½	2¼	4352	3 15/16	2 11/16	3¼	...	9	...	–57.4	...	...
33	IDSA	Industrial Svcs America	NSC	B–	1	1	Waste mgmt svc/eqp	14	4⅛	7	1¾	5⅞	1¼	1552	2½	1¾	1¾B	...	d	Neg	–30.5	–45.9	...
34	IBA	Industrias Bachoco ADS[70]Unit[71]	NY	NR	4	944	Mex prd:poultry/eggs/swine	20⅞	14⅜	19⅜	6 13/16	11 5/16	6½	3568	11¼	8	10¾	3.3	6	...	...	...	...
35	NTZ	✓Industrie Natuzzi ADS[72]	NY,Ch,Ph,P	NR	43	21037	Mfr contemporary furniture	29 5/16	6½	29¼	14	24¾	12 7/16	10719	15⅞	12 7/16	13¼	4.6	..	...	–44.1	–14.3	–2.9
36	NDE	✓IndyMac Mortgage Hldgs	NY,Ch,P	NR	133	36078	Real estate investment trust	26⅛	3⅛	27 3/16	7⅜	17 7/16	9 13/16	90942	13½	10	12¾	11.9	d	Neg	38.9	–6.5	19.4
37	INTI	✓Inet Technologies	NNM	NR	73	33170	Computer software/svcs	....	....	....	....	74⅞	15¼	19581	74⅞	53½	69⅞	...	..	88	...	...	...
38•[2]	INF	✓Infinity Broadcasting'A'	NY,Ph	NR	422	153465	Radio stations,outdoor ads	....	....	27⅝	20½	41½	23½	209209	41½	35⅛	36 3/16	...	80	...	32.2	...	...
39	INCX	✓INFOCURE Corp	NNM	NR	88	13206	Medical practice mgmt softwr	4⅞	1 15/16	16 7/16	3 15/16	33½	10½	243884	33½	13 15/16	31 3/16	...	..	...	94.9	...	...
40	IN	Infonet Services'B'	NY	NR	..	...	Data communication svcs	....	....	....	....	30	21 3/16	547185	30	21 3/16	26¼	...	d	...	...	...	...
41	IHI	✓Information Holdings	NY	NR	29	4726	Information publishing	....	....	16¾	8½	29½	13⅛	2588	29½	20½	29 1/16	...	75	...	84.5	...	...
✣42•[4]	IRIC	✓Information Resources	NNM	B–	110	21957	Data base prod mktg info svc	44¾	7 11/16	19½	6⅞	12⅛	6¼	15292	10½	7¾	9¼	...	..	NM	–9.2	–12.9	–7.6
#43•[6]	IFMX	✓Informix Corp	NNM	B–	212	61806	Mkts database mgmt softw	36¾	5/16	10 7/16	3½	14	6	1169819	12	8¾	11 7/16	...	29	Neg	15.8	–17.5	–5.9
44	INFY	✓Infosys Technologies ADS[79]	NNM	NR	32	1366	Software development svcs	....	....	....	....	360	34	15695	360	204⅛	330	0.0	..	45	...	...	...
45•[2]	ING	✓ING Groep ADS[80]	NY,Ph	NR	126	23901	Insurance/invest bkg svcs	53	38⅞	76¾	36 1/16	70	47 7/16	10674	61 11/16	56⅜	61	1.9	12	18	0.5	...	...
¶46•[10]	IR	✓Ingersoll-Rand	NY,B,Ch,P,Ph	A–	852	133466	Std mchny,eqp:bear'gs,tools	46¼	4¾	54	34	73 13/16	44⅝	182744	55¼	44⅞	55 1/16	1.2	16	21	17.9	24.5	23.2
47•[11]	IM	✓Ingram Micro'A'	NY	NR	140	31755	Dstr microcomputer prod	34¾	18	54⅝	26⅝	36 5/16	10	105541	13 11/16	12⅜	13⅛	...	11	20	–62.9	–17.1	...
48•[6]	INHL	✓Inhale Therapeutic Sys	NNM	NR	117	10935	Dvlp stge:drug delivery sys	37¼	5⅛	36½	20⅛	50¾	22⅞	65606	50¾	29½	42 9/16	...	d	–10	29.0	41.2	35.7
49•[12]	INKT	✓Inktomi Corp	NNM	NR	308	48674	Internet software svcs	....	....	39⅝	4½	104	26	907725	104	57 7/16	88¾	...	d	...	178	...	...
50	IMN	✓Inmet Mining	To	C	3	2683	Gold,silver,copper mining	17½	5 3/16	6 5/16	2½	3 13/16	1½	11486	2¾	2 5/16	2 11/16	...	7	NM	–11.0	–26.2	–26.0

Uniform Footnote Explanations-See Page 4. Other: [1]Ph:Cycle 3. [2]CBOE:Cycle 1. [3]CBOE,P:Cycle 2. [4]CBOE:Cycle 2. [5]ASE,CBOE,P:Cycle 2. [6]ASE:Cycle 2. [7]ASE,Ph:Cycle 1. [8]ASE:Cycle 1,To:Cycle 2. [9]CBOE,Ph:Cycle 2. [10]CBOE:Cycle 3. [11]ASE,CBOE,Ph:Cycle 3. [12]Ph:Cycle 1. [51]AMRESCO Capital plan acq,0.661 com. [52]To be determined. [53]Incl current amts. [54]ADR equals 4 ord shrs,1'. [55]Imperial Credit Ind plan acq,$11.57. [56]5 Mo Dec'97. [57]Fiscal Mar'97 & prior. [58]12 Mos Sep'97. [59]Ea ADS rep 2 ord,10P. [60]if com exceeds $10.50 for 20 con trad days. [61]Stk dstr of Gartner Group Inc. [62]Fr 8-21-2001,mand 8-21-2006 at $50. [63]Hldr opt Cv upon 'Sig Sale Event' re-spec cond. [64]Fr 5-29-2006 or anytime upon'Sig Sale Event'. [65]Plan comb w/SIGCORP Inc, 1 new. [66]Rated 'BBB' by S&P. [67]Or earlier for'Tax Event're-spec cond. [68]Jr Sub Deferrable Int Debs Sr'A'. [69]Rated'BBB'by S&P. [70]Ea ADS rep 6 units,no par. [71]Ea unit rep 1 Ser'B' & 1 Ser'L'shr. [72]Ea ADS rep 1 ord shr Lit.250. [73]Approx. [74]Fiscal Jan'97 & prior. [75]11 Mo Dec'97. [76]Stk dstr of VideOcart Inc. [77]As restated by Co. [78]As restated by co.. [79]Ea ADS rep 0.5 Equity Shr,par Rs.10. [80]Ea ADS rep 1 ord,NLG 1.00. [81]In cash or stk.

Index	Cash Divs. Ea. Yr. Since	Dividends: Latest Payment Period $	Date	Ex. Div.	Total $ So Far 1999	Ind. Rate	Paid 1998	Financial Position Mil-$ Cash& Equiv.	Curr. Assets	Curr. Liab.	Balance Sheet Date	Capitalization Lg Trm Debt Mil-$	Shs. 000 Pfd.	Com.	Earnings $ Per Shr. Years End	1995	1996	1997	1998	1999	Last 12 Mos.	Interim Earnings Period	$ per Shr. 1998	1999	Index
1◆	....	None Since Public			...	Nil	....	0.80	11.7	16.1	9-26-99	0.40	...	3367	Mr	v2.00	vd4.40	vd1.40	vd2.73	....	d1.31	6 Mo Sep	vd2.34	vd0.92	1
2	1997	0.12½	10-22-99	10-6	0.35	[52]....	1.68	Total Assets $387M			9-30-99	276	480	8418	Dc	...	n/a	v1.61	vd1.26	....	d0.89	9 Mo Sep	vd0.96	vd0.59	2
3◆	1996	Q0.13	1-17-00	12-30	†0.974	0.52	1.43	Total Assets $1437.2M			9-30-99	1182	1200	22730	Dc	pv0.05	v1.32	vd0.99	vd0.25	....	0.29	9 Mo Sep	v0.09	v0.63	3
4	....	None Since Public			...	Nil	....	2.90	61.0	17.0	10-31-99	[53]18.0	...	8483	Ap	v0.64	0.65	v0.43	v0.60	v0.71	0.76	6 Mo Oct	v0.30	v0.35	4
5◆	....	8%Stk	3-5-99	2-17	8%Stk	Stk	....	Total Deposits $5656.78M			9-30-99	180	...	41542	Dc	0.57	v1.28	v1.26	v0.93	....	1.47	9 Mo Sep	v0.60	v1.14	5
6◆	1927	0.825	10-12-99	8-18	2.075	2.08	2.147	822	4395	4386	j12-31-98	3009	...	728000	Dc	□4.76	2.52	v2.36	v1.76	E2.25	1.36	3 Mo Mar	v0.77	v0.37	6
7◆	....	5%Stk	12-28-92	12-14	...	Nil	....	Total Deposits $1571.73M			9-30-99	260	1200	33143	Dc	v0.40	v1.95	□v2.20	vd1.93	....	d0.28	9 Mo Sep	vd2.07	vΔd0.42	7
8	1998	0.33	1-14-00	12-29	1.15	1.15	0.98	Total Assets $688M			9-30-99	272	...	28500	Dc	...	...	v[56]0.06	v0.68	....	0.79	9 Mo Sep	v0.57	v0.68	8
9◆	1891	gQ0.19½	1-1-00	11-29	g0.74	0.78	g0.737	463	2037	1938	j12-31-98	1312	...	431000	Dc	0.89	v1.49	v1.83	v1.26	....	j1.15	9 Mo Sep	v0.95	v0.84	9
10	1997	Div Postponed 10-29-99			0.09	Nil	0.12	81.0	452	244	6-30-99	547	...	33520	Sp	Δd0.31	[57]0.92	pv[58]0.92	v□d0.24	Pvd0.57	d0.57				10
11	1998	0.599	2-18-00	12-8	0.827	0.88	0.755	214	929	1566	j9-30-98	1144	...	247191	Sp	...	...	v1.39	v1.51	....	1.68	3 Mo Mar	v0.65	v0.82	11
12	....	None Since Public			...	Nil	....	6.15	7.04	1.71	6-30-99	0.63	...	5069	Je	...	...	...	vd0.02	vd0.07	d0.13	3 Mo Sep	v0.01	vd0.05	12
13	....	Terms&trad. basis should be checked in detail						Wrrts expire 6-23-2002				....	...	1138	Je	...	...	...	...	....	....	Callable at 20¢[60]			13
14◆	....	....			...	Nil	....	75.3	158	63.5	9-30-99	1.63	...	38556	Dc	p0.05	vp0.14	v0.52	v0.50	....	0.61	9 Mo Sep	v0.33	v0.44	14
15◆	1997	Q0.02	12-10-99	10-29	h[61]0.08	0.08	0.06	230	684	623	9-30-99	....	...	307927	Dc	p0.26	v0.58	v0.93	v0.66	E0.85	0.92	9 Mo Sep	v0.32	v0.58	15
16◆	....	None Since Public			...	Nil	....	61.0	177	43.3	9-30-99	....	...	22521	Dc	v0.99	v0.58	v0.90	vd0.03	....	0.75	9 Mo Sep	vd0.13	v0.65	16
17◆	....	None Since Public			...	Nil	....	21.4	35.0	21.3	9-30-99	0.04	200	5521	Sp	0.30	vd0.64	vd4.19	v0.15	v0.30	0.30				17
18	....	None Since Public			...	Nil	....	...	...	0.02	9-30-99	530	...	45631	Dc	v1.16	v1.66	v2.17	v2.26	....	....	9 Mo Sep	n/a	vd2.98	18
19	1934	Div Omitted 2-10-99			...	Nil	t0.10	82.0	874	560	12-31-98	1457	9427	191961	Dc	pv1.82	v1.09	v0.25	vd0.63	Ed0.15	d0.30	9 Mo Sep	vd0.50	vd0.17	19
20	1996	Q0.68¾	12-1-99	11-1	2.75	2.75	2.75	Cv into 1.19474 com, $41.85				....	9427	...	Dc	...	...	...	...	....	....				20
21	1996	Div Omitted 2-10-99			...	Nil	0.08	Co opt to cv into com[64]				....	...	25899	Dc	...	...	...	...	....	....				21
22◆	1985	Q0.15	12-31-99	12-13	0.60	0.60	0.60	Total Assets $87.74M			9-30-99	60.2	...	1529	Dc	vd0.57	vd0.37	v2.18	vd0.44	....	0.43	9 Mo Sep	vd0.34	v0.53	22
23◆	....	None Since Public			...	Nil	....	82.0	98.9	43.7	9-30-99	0.24	...	28455	Dc	vd0.59	d0.33	v0.43	v0.12	....	d0.68	9 Mo Sep	v0.07	vd0.73	23
24◆	1974	sQ0.14	1-31-00	1-3	s0.524	0.56	s0.466	Total Deposits $1292.97M			9-30-99	17.3	★600	11485	Dc	v0.91	v1.05	v1.17	v1.31	....	1.04	9 Mo Sep	v0.76	v0.49	24
25◆	1994	Q0.05	11-30-99	11-10	0.20	0.20	0.20	Total Deposits $317.86M			9-30-99	13.0	5	2171	Dc	v0.67	v0.84	v1.03	v1.02	....	1.11	9 Mo Sep	v0.74	v0.83	25
26◆	1946	Q0.24¼	12-1-99	11-9	0.95	0.97	0.90¾	0.02	52.8	132	6-30-99	183	...	29788	Sp	1.10	1.40	v0.68	v1.33	Pv1.40	1.40				26
27	1998	Q0.47½	12-31-99	12-28	1.90	1.90	1.23	Co option fr 5-7-2003 at $25[67]				★125	...	...	Dc	...	...	...	...	....	....	Mature 6-30-2038			27
28	1996	Q0.50	12-31-99	12-28	2.00	2.00	2.00	Co option redm fr 3-26-2001 at $25				40.0	...	...	Dc	...	...	...	...	....	....	Mature 3-31-2026			28
29	....	None Since Public			...	Nil	....	42.3	98.2	72.8	12-31-97	....	...	53846	Dc	d0.78	vd1.48	vd0.88	Pvd0.22	....	d0.16	9 Mo Sep	vd0.16	vd0.10	29
30	....	None Since Public			...	Nil	....	41.5	63.3	22.7	10-31-99	0.02	...	31604	Ap	...	p0.07	pv0.25	v0.30	vd1.09	d1.09	6 Mo Oct	vd0.45	vd0.45	30
31	....	None Paid			...	Nil	....	1.18	4.87	1.47	9-30-99	0.40	...	13074	Dc	0.04	v0.04	v0.03	v0.03	....	d0.04	9 Mo Sep	v0.05	vd0.02	31
32	....	None Since Public			...	Nil	....	1.03	144	57.1	9-30-99	45.6	...	8590	Dc	v0.79	pv1.14	v0.91	v0.75	....	0.37	9 Mo Sep	v0.58	v0.20	32
33	....	None Since Public			...	Nil	....	1.05	11.5	12.0	9-30-99	2.26	...	1930	Dc	v0.40	v0.24	v0.07	vd0.26	....	d0.23	9 Mo Sep	v0.15	v0.18	33
34	1998	0.114	10-18-99	10-4	0.346	0.35	0.376	72.5	204	34.7	12-31-98	27.8	...	300000	Dc	...	1.40	v2.32	v1.85	....	1.85				34
35◆	1994	0.611	7-16-99	5-14	0.611	0.61	†0.60	138	346	95.3	12-31-97	2.26	...	56879	Dc	1.06	v1.34	v1.04	n/a	....	....	6 Mo Jun	v0.69	v0.77	35
36	1985	[73]0.60	12-6-99	10-28	[73]1.74	1.52	1.89	Total Assets $3497.55M			9-30-99	150	...	76618	Dc	v1.25	v1.51	v0.43	v0.48	....	d0.03	9 Mo Sep	v1.57	v1.06	36
37	....	None Since Public			...	Nil	....	122	146	30.8	9-30-99	....	...	45295	Dc	v0.04	v0.22	v0.30	v0.40	....	0.59	9 Mo Sep	v0.28	v0.47	37
38	....	None Since Public			...	Nil	....	129	732	325	9-30-99	248	...	p±1070715	Dc	...	...	pv0.23	v0.33	E0.45	0.39	9 Mo Sep	v0.24	v0.30	38
39◆	....	None Since Public			...	Nil	....	23.6	70.9	26.6	9-30-99	30.2	...	29133	Dc	p0.08	pv[74]0.10	v[75]d0.98	vd0.19	....	0.09	9 Mo Sep	v0.18	v□0.46	39
40	....	None Since Public			...	Nil	....	40.2	117	81.2	9-30-99	93.5	...	★±469496	Mr	...	...	...	v±0.01	....	d0.01	6 Mo Sep	v±d0.01	v±d0.03	40
41	....	None Since Public			...	Nil	....	2.89	29.8	27.6	9-30-99	2.48	...	16948	Dc	...	...	pvd0.48	v0.28	....	0.39	9 Mo Sep	v0.09	v0.20	41
42	....	h[76]....	10-31-90	10-15	...	Nil	....	13.3	110	115	9-30-99	3.06	...	28174	Dc	vd0.43	vd0.27	v0.26	v0.13	....	0.06	9 Mo Sep	v0.13	v0.06	42
43◆	....	None Since Public			...	Nil	....	213	428	316	9-30-99	....	...	201346	Dc	v[77]0.26	v[78]d0.49	vd2.36	v0.30	E0.39	d0.12	9 Mo Sep	v0.17	vd0.25	43
44◆	1999	0.03	12-15-99	11-8	0.032	0.075	....	98.9	125	14.0	3-31-99	....	...	33069	Mr	v0.12	v0.15	v0.20	v0.29	....	0.53	6 Mo Sep	v0.18	v0.42	44
45	1993	[81]0.558	9-14-99	8-30	[81]1.141	1.14	1.111	Equity per shr $35.89			12-31-98	282678	87000	946000	Dc	2.39	2.43	v2.59	v3.27	....	5.17	9 Mo Sep	v2.38	v4.28	45
46◆	1910	Q0.17	12-1-99	11-12	0.64	0.68	0.60	63.6	2444	1529	9-30-99	2116	...	163576	Dc	v1.69	v2.21	v2.31	v3.08	E3.55	3.47	9 Mo Sep	v2.17	v2.56	46
47	....	None Since Public			...	Nil	....	134	5960	3778	10-02-99	1472	...	±144149	Dc	±v0.74	v±0.88	±v1.32	±v1.64	....	1.19	9 Mo Sep	v±1.15	vΔ±0.70	47
48	....	None Since Public			...	Nil	....	58.3	64.4	16.0	9-30-99	4.90	...	17037	Dc	vd0.78	vd0.88	vd0.72	vd1.17	....	d1.48	9 Mo Sep	vd0.77	vd1.08	48
49◆	....	None Since Public			...	Nil	....	112	128	27.6	6-30-99	8.09	...	100636	Sp	...	...	pd0.18	vd0.28	Pvd0.24	d0.24				49
50	....	None Paid			...	Nil	....	87.3	147	43.6	j9-30-99	58.2	...	38337	Dc	vd0.39	vd2.39	vd2.00	v0.25	....	j0.40	9 Mo Sep	v0.67	v0.82	50

◆**Stock Splits & Divs By Line Reference Index** [1]1-for-10 REVERSE,'99. [3]3-for-2,'97. [5]Adj for 8%,'99:10%,'97:3-for-2,'96,'98. [6]No adj for stk dstr of Zeneca Group plc,'93. [7]3-for-2,'95:10%,'96:2-for-1,'96. [9]3-for-1,'98. [14]3-for-2,'97,'98. [15]2-for-1,'99:No adj for spin-off,'98. [16]2-for-1,'98. [17]1-for-3 REVERSE,'98. [22]2-for-1,'96. [23]2-for-1,'97. [24]3-for-2,'97,'98:Adj for 5%,'99. [25]4-for-3,'95:5-for-4,'97. [26]4-for-3,'98. [35]2-for-1,'96. [39]2-for-1,'99. [43]2-for-1,'95. [44]To split 2-for-1,hldrs Feb 11,'00. [46]3-for-2,'97. [49]2-for-1,'99(twice).

¶ S&P 500 · # MidCap 400 · ✣ SmallCap 600 · • Options

Index	Ticker	Name of Issue (Call Price of Pfd. Stocks)	Market	Com. Rank. & Pfd. Rating	Inst. Hold Cos	Inst. Hold Shs. (000)	Principal Business	Price Range 1971-97 High	1971-97 Low	1998 High	1998 Low	1999 High	1999 Low	December, 1999 Dec. Sales in 100s	Last Sale Or Bid High	Low	Last	%Div Yield	P-E Ratio	EPS 5 Yr Growth	% Annualized Total Return 12 Mo	36 Mo	60 Mo
1	IDYN	✓InnerDyne Inc	NNM	C	18	2679	Surgical access products	18½	1⅛	3¾	⅞	4¼	1⅛	13676	4¼	3⅜	3½	...	70	NM	155	2.5	−1.4
2	KPA	✓Innkeepers USA Trust	NY,Ch,Ph	NR	127	17806	Real Estate Invest Trust	17⅝	7	16⅞	8 7/16	12	7⅝	48333	8½	7⅝	8 3/16	13.7	10	12	−22.3	−8.4	12.1
3	Pr A	8.625% cm Cv Pfd([51]25)	NY	NR	18	3076		....	....	....	....	19⅝	16¼	537	17⅞	17	17⅝	12.2	..	...	...	...	...
✣4•[1]	INVX	✓Innovex Inc	NNM	B	106	5925	Thin-film disk drive pd	42⅞	1/64	28⅛	9	21	7½	33312	10¼	8 9/16	9⅝	1.7	21	15	−30.8	−29.1	13.2
5	IHT	✓Innsuites Hospitality SBI	AS,Ch	NR	3	36	Real estate investment trust	23½	4¼	5½	2 15/16	3 11/16	1⅝	1490	2½	1⅝	2½	0.4	d	−40	−32.0	−19.9	−18.4
6•[2]	INPR	✓Inprise Corp	NNM,Ch	C	63	18777	Dsgn/mkt PC softwr dvlp tools	86¾	4¾	11⅞	4 13/16	20	2 11/16	1244822	20	8½	11 1/16	...	13	NM	101	26.7	12.6
✣7•[3]	IO	✓Input/Output Inc	NY,Ph,P	B	169	32342	Mfr seismic data acquis'n sys	40½	1⅜	29 11/16	5⅞	9	4¼	88029	5⅞	4¼	5 1/16	...	d	Neg	−30.8	−35.1	−15.6
8	ICCI	✓Insight Communications	NNM	NR	127	22490	Own/oper cable TV stations	....	....	....	....	33⅞	19⅝	54879	29⅞	23⅝	29⅝	...	d	...	...	...	...
✣9•[4]	NSIT	✓Insight Enterprises	NNM	NR	232	20737	Mkt computer products	20⅛	2 11/16	36 13/16	12	41¾	18⅝	57391	41¾	32¾	40⅝	...	36	45	22.8	71.5	...
10	IFS	✓Insignia Financial Group	NY	NR	61	11855	Real estate management svcs	....	....	14½	8 13/16	15½	7¼	9255	8 13/16	7¾	8 11/16	...	40	...	−28.4	...	...
11	ISV	✓InSite Vision	AS	NR	11	2110	Dvlp ophthalmic pharma'l prd	11¾	1½	4 9/16	¾	3⅛	¾	17515	2¾	2 1/16	2¾	...	d	40	120	−22.9	−10.4
✣12•[5]	INSUA	✓Insituform Technol'A'	NNM	B−	168	14880	Mkts sewer/PL repair process	26½	1⅛	15¾	7¾	32 7/16	14	21172	32 7/16	24 9/16	28¼	...	32	74	94.8	56.5	19.4
13	INSO	✓INSO Corp	NNM	NR	66	7543	Mkt/dvp textual info software	68	7½	29	10⅝	39	4½	106333	39	22⅛	32¼	...	d	Neg	29.0	−6.7	13.0
14	NSPR	✓INSpire Insurance Solutions	NNM	NR	87	11155	Insurance ind out sourcing svcs	14⅛	8	35⅝	13 1/16	23⅛	3 9/16	51756	6½	3 11/16	4⅝	...	d	...	−75.0	...	...
✣15	III	✓Insteel Industries Inc	NY	†B	56	3767	Mfrs wire & wire products	12¾	2 15/16	8 7/16	3⅞	9⅞	4⅞	1845	9⅝	8 5/16	9 1/16	2.6	8	−23	92.4	4.1	8.5
16	INSW	✓InsWeb Corp	NNM	NR	36	8294	Online insurance marketplace	....	....	....	....	44	....	43294	35 11/16	22¼	25 9/16	...	..	...	...	...	...
17	IGR	✓Integra Inc	AS	NR	24	1883	Outpatient mental hlth svcs	22¾	1 11/16	2⅞	1⅛	2⅞	1	11317	1¾	1 7/16	1 11/16	...	6	31	35.0	−23.4	−37.4
18	IART	✓Integra LifeSciences Holdings	NNM	NR	15	2465	Human tissue regeneration R&D	27	5	10¾	3 1/16	10⅜	3	5438	6½	5⅜	5⅞	...	d	−5	75.0	−12.5	...
19	INVI	✓Integral Vision	NNM	C	21	1838	Quality control equip	16¾	1⅜	5½	⅞	3¼	1	14006	2¼	1⅜	2⅛	...	5	7	88.9	−27.7	−31.2
#20•[6]	IDTI	✓Integrated Device Tech	NNM	C	205	56033	Mfrs integrated circuits	33½	1 9/16	16½	4⅛	30	5	420121	30	23 1/16	29	...	27	Neg	374	28.6	14.4
21	IEE	✓Integrated Electrical Svcs	NY	NR	70	7858	Electrical contracting svcs	....	....	24¼	12⅜	23 5/16	8⅛	19790	10 15/16	8⅛	10 1/16	...	7	...	−54.8	...	...
22	IOI	✓Integrated Orthopaedics	AS,Ch	C	3	86	Out-patient diagnostic ctrs	12	¼	8⅛	2 7/16	3 3/16	½	6456	2⅞	1¼	2	...	d	Neg	−27.3	−26.3	−6.6
23	ITR	✓Integrated Trans Ntwk Grp[60]	AS	NR	..	...	Auto rental/repair svcs	....	....	....	....	6⅞	½	....	....	....	....	...	..	...	...	...	...
¶24•[7]	INTC	✓Intel Corp	NNM	A−	2537	1770174	Semiconductor memory circts	51	1/64	63 1/16	32 13/16	89½	50⅛	4206742	85½	70 9/16	82 5/16	0.1	36	25	39.3	36.3	59.9
25	ICOMC	✓Intelect Communications	NSC	C	21	7136	Mfr telecommun systems	16	⅛	8⅛	1 5/16	2⅝	½	632517	2 5/16	⅝	1⅜	...	d	Neg	−8.3	−32.6	−8.2
26	FILM	INTELEFILM Corp	NNM	NR	9	1194	Dvlp childrens radio prgms	16½	2	4⅜	2¾	6½	1¼	62833	6½	2¼	4 13/16	...	1	NM	63.8	1.3	−5.7
27	IDN	Intelli-Check Inc	AS	NR	..	...	Mfr document varification sys	....	....	....	....	13½	7½	8356	13½	9	11⅛	...	d	...	...	...	...
28	ICL	✓Intellicall Inc	AS,Ph,P	C	14	1615	Mfr/mkt pay telephones	18½	2⅞	6 3/16	1⅜	3½	½	16642	1⅜	½	1⅛	...	d	22	−48.6	−42.4	−21.4
29	ITC.EC	Intelligent Controls	ECM	NR	1	5	Mfr ind'l monitoring,ctrl eqp	6½	1⅝	3⅛	1¾	3 5/16	2¼	176	2¾	2¼	2¼	...	8	51	−5.3	6.3	...
30	IXP	✓Intelligent Polymers	AS	NR	..	...	Dvp controlled release drug pd	....	....	....	....	33¾	29	494	33¾	31⅝	33½	...	..	...	...	...	...
31	INS	✓Intelligent Systems	AS,P	C	14	1273	Personal computer enhanc'mt	32¾	⅞	5⅛	1⅜	4¼	1 9/16	1775	4¼	2½	4	...	d	−26	137	10.1	13.5
32	IPAR	✓Inter Parfums	NNM	B	18	824	Mkts imported fragrances	18	¾	9¼	4¾	11⅝	5½	305	9¾	8⅞	9⅜B	...	16	−8	53.1	13.0	4.6
✣33	INTL	✓Inter-Tel Inc	NNM	B	151	13127	Mfr electronic telecommun eqp	32⅜	5/16	28½	9½	28⅛	11½	42304	26⅜	19⅛	25	0.2	26	19	7.2	38.3	47.3
34	ININ	✓Interactive Intelligence	NNM	NR	10	480	Communic/interact'n software	....	....	....	....	40	13	15830	28½	20¼	26⅝	...	d	...	...	...	...
35	IPIX	✓Interactive Pictures	NNM	NR	40	3729	Internet photo & imaging sys	....	....	....	....	26⅞	14	29067	26 7/16	20¼	23 5/16	...	..	...	...	...	...
36	ICPT	✓InterCept Group	NNM	NR	27	1671	Computer software/svcs	....	....	8 15/16	4½	31¼	7 1/16	28334	31¼	15⅜	29 11/16	...	61	...	310	...	...
37	IFC	✓Interchange Finl Svcs	AS	A	22	1387	Commercial banking,New Jersey	21 13/16	13/16	23¼	14 1/16	19⅝	15½	1133	18⅛	16⅛	16⅜	2.9	12	10	3.5	20.2	27.4
38•[5]	IDC	✓Interdigital Communications	AS,Ph,P	C	59	14412	Wireless digital communic prd	20⅝	2	7 7/16	2 9/16	82	4	647655	82	9¼	75	...	85	NM	1544	133	59.0
39	IREP	✓Interep Natl Radio Sales'A'	NNM	NR	..	...	Natl sport radio represent'n	....	....	....	....	16	12	119307	16	12	13⅜	...	d	...	...	...	...
✣40•[8]	IFSIA	✓Interface Inc'A'	NNM	B+	165	36324	Mfr carpet/tile	15 13/16	1⅝	22⅞	8¼	11¾	4	83633	5 15/16	4	5¾	3.1	29	−8	−36.4	−15.2	0.5
41	INTF	Interface Systems	NNM	C	11	343	Printers,computer communic prd	20	⅝	6½	1½	26⅞	1⅝	12399	26⅞	12 9/16	24¾	...	d	Neg	692	79.9	28.5
42•[9]	INGR	✓Intergraph Corp	NNM	C	75	17673	Computer graphics systems	40½	3⅞	10 9/16	4 11/16	10¼	3 3/16	60568	5	3 13/16	4 11/16	...	d	4	−18.5	−23.0	−10.4
✣43•	IS	✓Interim Services	NY,Ph	NR	264	41467	Temporary help services	31⅛	10	34¼	13¼	24 13/16	13¾	58596	24 13/16	18 1/16	24¾	...	20	17	5.9	11.8	15.0
44	INIT	✓Interliant Inc	NNM	NR	30	1191	Provide web site svcs	....	....	....	....	35⅝	9¼	134568	35⅝	20¼	26	...	..	...	...	...	...
45	ILI	✓Interlott Technologies	AS,Ch,Ph	NR	6	81	Mfr instant lottery machines	13⅝	5¾	14	6 1/16	7	4	691	5¼	4	5⅛	...	14	NM	−21.2	−9.9	−10.1
✣46•[10]	IMG	✓Intermagnetics Genl	AS,P	B−	50	1878	Mfr superconductive mtls	25 9/16	2 1/16	11⅝	5¼	12 15/16	5¼	17798	9¼	5⅞	8¾	...	d	Neg	42.9	−7.6	−3.6
47	ICIX	✓Intermedia Communications	NNM	NR	277	44331	Local telephone svc-Florida	30 15/16	2⅞	45⅝	12¾	42⅞	13 1/16	293633	42⅞	27⅝	38 13/16	...	d	Neg	125	44.5	45.9
✣48•[8]	INMT	✓Intermet Corp	NNM	B	164	18660	Iron foundry-auto indus	19⅞	3⅝	23¾	8½	15¾	8¼	29652	11 13/16	9	11⅝	1.4	7	NM	−9.5	−9.3	12.4
49	ICM	✓Internacional De Ceramica ADS[63]	NY,P	NR	2	154	Mfr glazed ceramic tile-Mexico	21¾	4¼	8¾	2 7/16	6¾	2 11/16	1075	6¾	5¼	6⅜B	...	d	Neg	70.0	5.9	−20.8
50	INAP	✓InterNAP Network	NNM	NR	68	3342	Internet connectivity svc	....	....	....	....	185 15/16	20	69600	185 15/16	88	173	...	..	...	...	...	...

Uniform Footnote Explanations-See Page 4. Other: [1]ASE,CBOE,Ph:Cycle 2. [2]CBOE:Cycle 1. [3]CBOE:Cycle 2. [4]ASE,P,Ph:Cycle 2. [5]P:Cycle 3. [6]CBOE,Ph:Cycle 2. [7]ASE,CBOE,P,Ph:Cycle 1. [8]ASE:Cycle 2. [9]ASE:Cycle 1. [10]ASE,CBOE:Cycle 1. [51]Fr 5-19-2003. [52]Pfd in $M. [53]Fiscal Mar'97 & prior. [54]12 Mo Dec'97:Mar'97 earned d$2.96. [55]Incl current amts. [56]Fiscal Jun'96 & prior. [57]12 Mo Dec '97:Fiscal Jun'97 earned $0.99. [58]Fiscal Dec'98 & prior. [59]Incl 2.7M restricted shs. [60]ASE trading halted 8-24-99. [61]Excl spcl shrs. [62]11 Mo Jun,'98. [63]Ea ADS rep 5 Ltd Vtg Units(rep 1'D'&1'L'shr).

Splits ◆ Index	Cash Divs. Ea. Yr. Since	Dividends: Latest Payment Period $	Date	Ex. Div.	Total $ So Far 1999	Ind. Rate	Paid 1998	Financial Position Mil-$ Cash& Equiv.	Curr. Assets	Curr. Liab.	Balance Sheet Date	Capitalization Lg Trm Debt Mil-$	Shs. 000 Pfd.	Com.	Earnings $ Per Shr. Years End	1995	1996	1997	1998	1999	Last 12 Mos.	Interim Earnings Period	$ per Shr. 1998	1999	Index
1	....	None Since Public			...	Nil	....	6.60	11.5	2.27	9-30-99	0.30	...	22045	Dc	vd0.32	vd0.23	vd0.04	v0.02	....	0.05	9 Mo Sep	v0.01	v0.04	1
2	1995	Q0.28	1-25-00	12-29	1.12	1.12	1.10	Total Assets $771.66M			9-30-99	242	4630	34677	Dc	v0.57	v0.66	v0.85	v□0.89	....	0.80	9 Mo Sep	v□0.73	v0.64	2
3	1998	Q0.539	1-25-00	12-29	2.156	2.156	0.958	Cv into 1.4811 com				....	4630	...	Dc	...	...	...	...	....	....				3
4◆	1993	Q0.04	11-24-99	11-8	0.16	0.16	0.14	25.5	76.3	45.3	9-30-99	26.4	...	14822	Sp	0.70	v0.91	v2.31	v1.05	v0.44	0.44				4
5	1971	0.01	10-31-99	10-14	0.01	0.01	0.10	Total Assets $67.85M			10-31-99	35.1	...	2562	Ja	vd7.40	vd0.87	vd0.56	vd0.10	....	d0.08	9 Mo Oct	v0.07	v0.09	5
6	....	None Paid			...	Nil	....	179	226	80.7	9-30-99	18.4	[52]3	57928	Dc	0.45	[53]d2.96	v[54]d1.06	v0.14	E0.86	1.21	9 Mo Sep	vd0.08	v0.99	6
7◆	....	None Since Public			...	Nil	....	86.2	255	34.0	8-31-99	8.67	...	50669	My	v0.66	v0.95	v0.38	v1.28	vd2.17	d2.63	6 Mo Nov	v0.13	vd0.33	7
8	....	None Since Public			...	Nil	....	Total Assets $1127M			9-30-99	[55]574	1200	±59383	Dc	...	...	...	vpd1.36	....	d4.52	9 Mo Sep	vNil	vd3.16	8
9◆	....	None Since Public			...	Nil	....	28.7	260	140	9-30-99	8.91	...	25858	Dc	p0.26	[56]0.32	v[57]0.55	v0.81	....	1.14	9 Mo Sep	v0.57	v0.90	9
10	....	None Since Public			...	Nil	....	Total Assets $752.3M			9-30-99	158	...	20855	Dc	...	...	pv0.67	pv0.50	....	0.22	9 Mo Sep	v0.43	v0.15	10
11	....	None Since Public			...	Nil	....	3.00	3.41	1.30	9-30-99	....	1	20276	Dc	vd1.38	vd0.72	vd0.85	vd0.60	....	d0.24	9 Mo Sep	vd0.51	vd0.15	11
12	....	None Since Public			...	Nil	....	79.8	175	54.0	9-30-99	116	...	25127	Dc	vd0.04	v0.17	v□0.36	v0.66	....	0.89	9 Mo Sep	v0.48	v0.71	12
13◆	....	None Since Public			...	Nil	....	20.2	52.4	38.7	10-31-99	0.22	...	15825	Ja	v0.49	vd1.61	vd0.03	v[58]d1.30	....	d4.82	9 Mo Oct	v0.19	vd3.33	13
14◆	....	None Since Public			...	Nil	....	29.6	71.9	25.8	9-30-99	....	...	18998	Dc	...	pvd0.05	v0.13	v0.58	....	d0.58	9 Mo Sep	v0.42	vd0.74	14
15	1986	Q0.06	1-4-00	12-15	0.24	0.24	0.24	0.83	71.3	35.6	10-02-99	46.2	...	8457	Sp	0.76	0.50	vd0.04	v□0.04	v1.18	1.18				15
16	....	None Since Public			...	Nil	....	104	112	5.09	9-30-99	1.40	...	34669	Dc	...	...	...	vpd0.92	....	....	9 Mo Sep	n/a	vpd0.85	16
17	....	None Since Public			...	Nil	....	2.30	4.36	8.49	9-30-99	....	...	10139	Dc	vd0.26	vd1.39	vd6.17	vd0.09	....	0.29	9 Mo Sep	vd0.12	v0.26	17
18◆	....	None Since Public			...	Nil	....	20.8	40.1	11.0	9-30-99	8.25	...	16143	Dc	vd2.42	vd0.54	vd1.14	vd0.76	....	d0.51	9 Mo Sep	vd0.59	vd0.34	18
19	....	None Since Public			...	Nil	....	0.40	10.9	10.5	9-30-99	....	...	9025	Dc	vd1.33	vd0.22	vd0.02	vd1.24	....	0.40	9 Mo Sep	vd1.21	v□0.43	19
20◆	....	None Since Public			...	Nil	....	321	474	168	9-26-99	180	...	91057	Mr	Δ1.44	vd0.54	v0.10	vd3.45	E1.06↑	0.39	6 Mo Sep	vd3.33	v0.51	20
21	....	None Since Public			...	Nil	....	2.93	335	159	9-30-99	227	...	[59]38652	Sp	...	...	pv1.08	pv1.11	v1.39	1.39				21
22	....	None Since Public			...	Nil	....	3.30	11.0	3.08	9-30-99	1.74	300	6497	Dc	v0.10	v0.12	vd2.43	vd1.16	....	d1.33	9 Mo Sep	vd0.57	vd0.74	22
23	....	None Since Public			...	Nil	....	Total Assets $68.7M			3-31-99	4.72	...	12595	Dc	...	v0.76	v0.97	□v1.17	....	0.97	3 Mo Mar	v0.33	v0.13	23
24◆	1992	Q0.03	12-1-99	11-3	0.14	0.12	0.06½	11891	17916	6389	9-25-99	884	...	3341000	Dc	v1.01	1.45	v1.93	v1.72	E2.30	2.09	9 Mo Sep	v1.13	v1.50	24
25	....	0.10	2-3-86	1-13	...	Nil	....	0.20	14.4	25.5	9-30-99	0.04	3719	60937	Dc	0.87	vd3.33	vd1.01	vd1.78	....	d1.12	9 Mo Sep	vd0.89	vd0.23	25
26◆	....	None Since Public			...	Nil	....	2.52	26.2	16.2	9-30-99	0.73	6	6132	Dc	d2.22	vd1.99	vd2.33	v1.03	....	4.07	9 Mo Sep	vd1.83	v1.21	26
27	....	None Since Public			...	Nil	....	0.17	0.43	0.16	6-30-99	0.01	p...	★6271	Dc	...	...	...	vd0.35	....	d0.36	6 Mo Jun	vd0.14	vd0.15	27
28	....	None Since Public			...	Nil	....	0.02	6.09	3.59	9-30-99	9.24	...	12080	Dc	vd0.80	vd0.62	vd1.20	vd0.19	....	d0.96	9 Mo Sep	v0.17	vd0.60	28
29	....	None Since Public			...	Nil	....	4.81	8.22	1.25	9-25-99	0.05	...	4819	Dc	0.05	vd0.13	v0.13	v0.15	....	0.30	9 Mo Sep	v0.01	v0.16	29
30	....	None Since Public			...	Nil	....	21.7	51.7	1.08	6-30-98	....	...	[61]3738	Je	...	...	vd3.42	[62]....	....	....				30
31	....	0.10	9-19-89	8-25	...	Nil	....	0.81	3.59	4.34	9-30-99	0.20	...	5104	Dc	v0.03	v0.80	vd1.41	vd0.30	....	d0.11	9 Mo Sep	vd0.32	vd0.13	31
32	....	None Since Public			...	Nil	....	18.0	70.1	25.5	9-30-99	0.06	...	7556	Dc	v0.87	v0.57	v0.48	v0.52	....	0.57	9 Mo Sep	v0.38	v0.43	32
33◆	1998	Q0.01	1-15-00	12-29	0.04	0.04	0.04	63.5	150	54.4	9-30-99	....	...	25908	Dc	v0.36	v0.34	v0.57	v0.32	....	0.95	9 Mo Sep	v0.09	v0.72	33
34	....	None Since Public			...	Nil	....	24.5	29.1	7.75	9-30-99	0.49	...	13809	Dc	...	...	...	vd0.84	....	d0.79	9 Mo Sep	vd0.63	d0.58	34
35	....	None Since Public			...	Nil	....	68.2	74.4	2.80	9-30-99	0.02	...	16563	Dc	...	...	...	vpd1.65	....	....	9 Mo Sep	n/a	vd1.27	35
36	....	None Since Public			...	Nil	....	1.16	13.9	42.7	9-30-99	0.20	...	10116	Dc	...	...	n/a	v0.30	....	0.49	9 Mo Sep	v0.20	v0.39	36
37◆	1981	Q0.12	1-14-00	12-15	0.46	0.48	0.39	Total Deposits $602.50M			9-30-99	....	...	6890	Dc	v0.97	v1.00	v1.17	v1.19	....	1.41	9 Mo Sep	v0.82	v1.04	37
38	....	None Since Public			...	Nil	....	80.3	93.1	12.6	9-30-99	2.67	102	48174	Dc	v0.78	vd0.26	vd0.72	v0.75	....	0.88	9 Mo Sep	v0.39	v0.52	38
39	....	None Since Public			...	Nil	....	15.2	84.5	38.7	9-30-99	100	...	★±10341	Dc	...	...	...	vd0.03	....	d1.17	9 Mo Sep	vd0.47	vd1.61	39
40◆	1977	Q0.04½	11-24-99	11-9	0.18	0.18	0.16½	10.9	452	198	10-03-99	427	...	±52631	Dc	v□±0.50	v±0.60	v±0.76	v±0.56	....	0.20	9 Mo Sep	v±0.69	v±0.33	40
41	....	0.04	11-20-95	10-12	...	Nil	....	1.62	6.48	2.55	6-30-99	0.08	...	4489	Sp	0.04	d0.44	d2.47	vd0.48	Pvd0.06	d0.06				41
42	....	None Since Public			...	Nil	....	53.0	406	262	9-30-99	57.2	...	49059	Dc	vd0.98	vd1.46	vd1.46	vd0.41	Ed1.94	d1.98	9 Mo Sep	v0.03	vd1.54	42
43◆	....	None Since Public			...	Nil	....	48.6	747	595	9-24-99	660	...	63517	Dc	v0.76	v0.69	v1.05	□v1.29	....	1.27	9 Mo Sep	v□0.93	v0.91	43
44	....	None Since Public			...	Nil	....	52.6	62.2	15.0	9-30-99	1.66	...	43676	Dc	...	...	...	vpd2.47	....	....	9 Mo Sep	n/a	vd1.13	44
45	....	None Since Public			...	Nil	....	0.06	8.91	17.4	9-30-99	0.29	1335	3210	Dc	v0.62	v0.41	v0.45	v0.50	....	0.37	9 Mo Sep	v0.36	vΔ0.23	45
46◆	....	2%Stk	9-17-98	8-25	...	Nil	2%Stk	7.52	59.6	23.4	8-29-99	26.6	70	12384	My	0.33	0.33	v0.21	v0.21	vd0.57	d0.55	3 Mo Aug	v0.07	v0.09	46
47◆	....	None Since Public			...	Nil	....	482	761	190	9-30-99	2882	581	51591	Dc	□vd0.96	vd2.04	v□d7.23	vd13.23	Ed11.75	d11.61	9 Mo Sep	vd10.45	vd8.83	47
48	1996	Q0.04	12-30-99	11-29	0.16	0.16	0.16	....	0.24	0.14	9-30-99	25.5	...	25356	Dc	v1.02	v1.69	v1.55	v1.58	....	1.72	9 Mo Sep	v1.27	v1.41	48
49	....	None Since Public			...	Nil	....	10.3	92.1	44.2	12-31-97	131	...	108895	Dc	d2.70	Δ0.35	vΔd0.04	....	....	d0.04				49
50◆	....	None Since Public			...	Nil	....	13.3	15.1	6.78	6-30-99	6.78	p...	★62201	Dc	...	...	...	vpd0.31	....	....	6 Mo Jun	n/a	vpd0.34	50

◆Stock Splits & Divs By Line Reference Index [4]3-for-2,'95:2-for-1,'96. [7]2-for-1,'94,'96. [9]3-for-2,'97,'98,'99. [13]2-for-1,'95. [14]3-for-2,'98. [18]1-for-2 REVERSE,'98. [20]2-for-1,'95. [24]2-for-1,'95,'97,'99. [26]1-for-2 REVERSE,'96. [33]2-for-1,'97. [37]3-for-2,'97,'98. [40]2-for-1,'98. [43]2-for-1,'97. [46]5-for-4,'94:Adj for 2%,'98. [47]2-for-1,'98. [50]To split 2-for-1,ex Jan 10,'00.

¶ S&P 500 # MidCap 400 ✣ SmallCap 600 • Options

Index	Ticker	Name of Issue (Call Price of Pfd. Stocks)	Market	Com. Rank. & Pfd. Rating	Inst. Hold Cos	Inst. Hold Shs. (000)	Principal Business	1971-97 High	1971-97 Low	1998 High	1998 Low	1999 High	1999 Low	Dec. Sales in 100s	December, 1999 Last Sale Or Bid High	Low	Last	%Div Yield	P-E Ratio	EPS 5 Yr Growth	% Annualized Total Return 12 Mo	36 Mo	60 Mo
1	YLF	✓Intl Airline Support Grp	AS	B–	8	745	Sell used&new aircraft parts	232⅞	1 11/16	11	3¼	5½	3⅜	1014	3⅞	3⅜	3¾	...	5	NM	–18.9	7.7	12.3
2	IAL	✓Intl Aluminum	NY,B,Ch,P	B–	34	1518	Mfr & sale aluminum prod	36¾	1	36	26 11/16	30⅝	23⅜	394	24¾	23⅜	23½	5.1	11	–1	–17.0	1.2	–1.1
¶3•[1]	IBM	✓Intl Bus. Machines	NY,To,B,C,Ch,P,Ph,Mo	B	2393	924528	Lgst mfr business machines	56¾	9 7/16	94 15/16	47 13/16	139 3/16	80⅞	1585531	122⅛	102¼	107⅞	0.4	29	26	17.5	42.9	43.8
¶4•[2]	IFF	✓Intl Flavors/Fragr	NY,B,C,Ch,P,Ph	A	469	71702	Dvlp,mfr flavor&frag prod	55⅞	5 9/16	51⅞	32 1/16	48½	33⅝	55472	38⅜	34¼	37⅝	4.0	24	–5	–11.6	–2.4	–0.9
#5•[3]	IGT	✓Intl Game Technology	NY,Ch,Ph,P	B+	221	55914	Coin oper video/reel games	41⅜	7/16	28 11/16	16⅛	24⅛	14⅛	48336	20 11/16	17⅜	20 5/16	...	31	–1	–16.3	4.1	5.8
6•[4]	IHF	✓Intl Home Foods	NY,Ph	NR	118	20600	Mfr self-stable food prod	28⅜	20	35	10⅛	21⅜	13 11/16	120992	17 15/16	15	17⅜	...	14	...	3.0	...	...
#7•[5]	IMC	✓Intl Multifoods	NY,Ch,P	B–	155	12250	Diversified food prod/svcs	32 7/16	3¾	31 7/16	15⅛	27¼	11⅝	25303	14 3/16	11⅝	13¼	6.0	66	Neg	–46.9	–6.8	–2.6
¶8•[1]	IP	✓Intl Paper	NY,B,C,Ch,P,Ph,Mo	B–	895	330011	Mfr paper,pulp&wood prod	61	7⅛	55¼	35½	59½	39½	463198	57 11/16	50 9/16	56 7/16	1.8	70	–42	28.4	14.1	11.0
9	IPP	Intl Paper Cap Tr 7.875% Sub Debs[51]	NY	BBB–[52]	9	281	Subsid of Intl Paper	....	....	25 15/16	25	26	20½	22180	22½	20½	21 3/16	9.3	..	...	–10.6	...	...
✣10•[6]	IRF	✓Intl Rectifier	NY,B,Ch,P	B–	171	31698	Power semiconductors	27	½	14¾	4¼	26	6¼	64855	26	20⅝	26	...	53	5	167	19.5	17.0
11	IRI	✓Intl Remote Imaging	AS	C	7	33	Mfr urinalysis workstation	50	⅝	4⅞	¾	1⅝	½	6853	1⅛	9/16	13/16	...	d	Neg	0.0	–40.9	–31.2
12	IRD.A	✓Intl Road Dynamics 'A'	To	NR	..	...	Mfr traffic mgmt,monitor'g sys	3	⅝	2¼	11/16	1 5/16	5/16	5290	9/16	5/16	½	...	d	–31	–48.4	–31.1	...
13	ISH	✓Intl Shipholding	NY	B	38	3072	Ocean freight transportation	21 13/16	1½	17 5/16	14½	16 5/16	9 15/16	652	13 5/16	11⅜	11⅝	2.2	4	–8	–24.5	–12.9	–4.1
14•[7]	ISP	✓Intl Specialty Products	NY,Ph,P	NR	79	11040	Mfr specl derivative chemicals	18	5⅜	20½	9 9/16	13 13/16	7	11414	9 3/16	7	9 3/16	...	29	–20	–32.3	–9.1	5.3
#15	ISCA	✓Intl Speedway 'A'	NNM	NR	130	10014	Own/oper 3 super speedways	24⅞	17	41¾	23	71⅛	34	50714	65 15/16	49⅞	50⅜	0.1	38	26	24.5	35.2	...
16	INB	Intl Thunderbird Gaming	To,Vc	NR	1	196	Mfr slot machines, gaming prd	6⅜	3/16	1⅞	3/16	1 7/16	7/16	8694	⅞	⅝	13/16	...	d	Neg	33.6	–32.7	–15.4
17•[8]	ICGE	Internet Capital Group	NNM	NR	105	16235	Business to business net svc	....	....	....	....	212	6	986822	212	79¼	170	...	..	...	...	...	...
18	INCC	Internet Communications	NSC	C	2	40	Telecommunication equip,svcs	16	2	8¾	1¾	10	1⅜	113210	10	1 13/16	3 9/16	...	d	...	–11.0	–14.8	–2.9
19	HHH	Internet HOLDRs Trust	AS	NR	4	13	Internet companies invest trust	....	....	....	....	185	101	257492	185	136 7/16	169 1/16	...	..	...	...	...	...
20	IPIC	✓Interneuron Pharmaceuticals	NNM	C	33	1905	Pharmaceuticals res & dvlp	44½	1⅜	15½	2½	8¾	1⅛	192167	8¾	3¼	5¾	...	d	–9	74.3	–39.6	3.2
21	IPX	✓Interpool, Inc	NY	NR	71	9474	Leases dry cargo containers	17¾	7 11/16	18 15/16	9⅞	16⅞	6⅞	6914	8⅞	6⅞	7 7/16	2.0	7	3	–55.0	–20.9	–4.5
¶22•[9]	IPG	✓Interpublic Grp Cos	NY,To,Ch,P	A+	746	217381	Worldwide advertis'g agencies	26½	⅛	40 5/16	22 9/16	58⅜	34⅜	224855	58⅜	46½	57 11/16	0.6	44	21	45.9	55.4	41.8
#23•[9]	IBC	✓Interstate Bakeries	NY,Ph,P	NR	212	35489	Largest independent U.S.baker	37½	5 13/16	38	23⅜	27	16 3/16	88084	18 11/16	16 3/16	18⅛	1.5	11	37	–30.6	–6.7	24.7
24	IGC	✓Interstate Genl L.P.'A'	AS,P	NR	6	159	Homebuild'g/real estate dvlp	67½	9 11/16	27½	2⅜	8	3⅛	420	8	7⅛	8	...	d	Neg	...	...	...
25	II	✓Intersystems Inc	AS,Ch	B–	6	110	Mkts thermoplastic resins	11	9/16	2½	11/16	1⅛	7/16	8026	13/16	7/16	9/16	...	56	NM	–43.8	–19.1	–16.4
26	WS	Wrrt(Pur 1 com at $2)	AS	....	1	8		1½	⅛	⅝	1/64	¼	1/32	646	3/16	1/16	3/16	...	..	...	...	...	...
27	ITN	✓InterTan Inc	NY,Ch,Ph,P	C	103	13747	Retails consumer electronics	62¾	3¼	7⅝	3⅜	29 3/16	5 15/16	61128	29 3/16	21	26⅛	...	d	Neg	350	75.0	26.3
28	ITP	✓Intertape Polymer Group	NY	B+	46	8375	Mfr plastic packag'g prod	25	3⅞	25⅞	16⅛	33⅜	23 9/16	2340	28¼	24⅛	28 3/16	◆0.4	15	18	11.2	7.6	30.4
29	ITRU	✓InterTrust Technologies	NNM	NR	..	...	Dvlp digital rights mgmt sys	....	....	....	....	187¼	18	72889	187¼	104 9/16	117⅝	...	..	...	...	...	...
✣30•[9]	INTV	✓InterVoice-Brite Inc	NNM	B	185	16901	Mfr phone voice response sys	15 9/16	3/16	18⅛	3¾	25⅛	8 15/16	133799	25⅛	14⅛	23¼	...	d	Neg	34.9	56.0	27.6
31•[6]	ITVU	✓InterVU Inc	NNM	NR	82	4879	Internet video delivery sys	10¼	8⅛	32⅜	5⅛	124	12¾	93935	124	60⅜	105	...	d	...	724	...	...
32	IWOV	✓Interwoven Inc	NNM	NR	..	...	Dvlp website mgmt softwr	....	....	....	....	177⅞	17	29030	177⅞	111	121⅝	...	..	...	...	...	...
33•[3]	IBI	✓Intimate Brands 'A'	NY,Ph,P	NR	..	...	Intimate apparel/pers care pd	23 13/16	12¾	30⅜	17⅛	52⅜	27 5/16	61889	43¾	39¼	43⅛	s1.3	24	14	61.2	43.3	...
34	IDR	✓Intrawest Corp	NY,Ch,Ph,To,Mo,Vc	NR	42	15101	Dvlp,oper mountain resorts, NA	19⅛	13½	29	10 3/16	19⅜	14 9/16	7081	17 11/16	15 3/16	17 5/16	0.9	8	21	3.6	...	...
35	INET	✓Intrenet Inc	NSC	B–	5	9688	Genl/spcl trucking services	6	½	4¾	2	4¼	2	6177	2 15/16	2 5/16	2⅜	...	d	–35	–28.7	0.4	–11.8
#36•[9]	INTU	✓Intuit Inc	NNM	B–	478	157414	Dvlp financial softwr prd	29¾	3 5/16	24 7/16	11 5/16	64	22½	613340	64	49⅝	59 15/16	...	31	NM	148	78.8	40.1
✣37•[6]	IVC	✓Invacare Corp	NY	B+	173	18752	Home healthcare medical eqp	33¼	13/16	28¾	19⅛	26 15/16	17 7/16	20356	21 7/16	17 7/16	20 1/16	0.2	13	2	–16.2	–9.8	3.5
#38	ITG	✓Investment Tech Group	NY	NR	182	16873	Securities executn/analysis sv	32¾	4¾	64⅞	18	74	17 13/16	51019	29	22	28¾	...	14	NM	–50.5	16.9	35.4
39	IGI	✓Investors Group	To	A	15	1780	Financial planning svcs,prd	24¼	1½	28⅛	17½	26½	17	11595	20 15/16	17½	20⅝	2.5	20	22	–20.2	17.6	21.5
40	ITIC	✓Investors Title Co	NNM	A–	23	600	Land title/mortgage insur	24¼	11/16	28½	16½	23	13¾	477	18½	16½	17¼B	0.7	9	14	–17.3	3.7	22.4
41	IOX	✓Iomed Inc	AS	NR	2	47	Drug delivery system R & D	....	....	8¼	1	4⅜	1¾	2989	4	3⅛	3½	...	..	44	60.0	...	...
42•[2]	IOM	✓Iomega Corp	NY	B–	82	21332	Mfr computer disk drives	27 9/16	1/16	13¾	2 15/16	10 3/16	2⅞	677696	4 7/16	3¼	3⅜	...	d	Neg	–53.8	–26.9	66.5
43•[10]	IONA	✓IONA Technologies ADR[65]	NNM	NR	28	3002	Prov computer software pds	27	11⅜	41	14⅞	55¼	12⅛	48936	55¼	31	54½	...	..	56	43.4	...	...
✣44•[11]	ION	✓Ionics Inc	NY,Ch,Ph,P	B+	154	9334	Water purify equip:wtr & chem	53	¾	45⅞	22½	36 15/16	24⅞	11003	29⅛	25½	28⅛	...	23	2	–6.1	–16.3	–2.0
#45•[12]	IPL	✓IPALCO Enterprises	NY,B,C,Ch,Ph,P	B+	218	29470	Hldg:electr sv,Indianapolis	21⅛	2	27 13/16	19⅞	28 9/16	15⅝	51332	18⅛	15⅝	17 1/16	3.5	12	12	–36.7	11.0	16.9
46	IPI	✓IPC Communications	AS	NR	32	925	Telecommunication svcs/eqp	....	....	13½	4¾	77½	4 15/16	2130	77½	53¾	71	...	d	...	1376	...	...
47	IPCR	✓IPC Holdings	NNM	NR	66	21104	Casualty reinsurance	32⅞	19	33¼	19	23 3/16	14¼	14515	18¾	14¼	14⅞	4.3	12	–7	–32.0	–5.4	...
48	IPS	IPSCO Inc[67]	NY,To,Ch	B+	30	14078	Mfr steel/steel products	32 11/16	3⅜	33	16¼	24⅛	15⅝	173	20 5/16	18¼	19½	◆1.8	8	12	15.1	3.7	13.8
49	IIR	✓IRI International	NY	NR	48	8883	Mfr land-base drilling rigs	21⅛	12¾	14 15/16	2½	6 3/16	2⅞	30399	4½	2 15/16	4	...	d	...	0.0	...	...
50•[13]	IRIDQ	✓Iridium World Communications'A'	OTC	D	32	325	Dvp stage:global communic sys	54⅝	17	72 3/16	26¾	44½	2¾	....	....	....	....	...	..	Neg	...	...	...

Uniform Footnote Explanations-See Page 4. Other: [1]ASE,CBOE,P,Ph:Cycle 1. [2]CBOE:Cycle 2. [3]ASE,CBOE:Cycle 1. [4]ASE,Ph:Cycle 3. [5]Ph:Cycle 1. [6]CBOE:Cycle 3. [7]Ph:Cycle 3. [8]ASE,CBOE,Ph:Cycle 3. [9]CBOE:Cycle 1. [10]ASE,CBOE:Cycle 3. [11]ASE,P:Cycle 1. [12]P:Cycle 1. [13]ASE,CBOE,P,Ph:Cycle 3. [51]Jr Sub Deferrable Int Debs. [52]Rated BBB by S&P. [53]Fiscal Aug'95 & prior. [54]12 Mo Nov'96:Fiscal Aug'96 earned $0.57. [55]Fiscal Jan'97 & prior. [56]11 Mo Dec'97. [57]To be determined. [58]Stk dstr of American Cmnty Pptys. [59]Dstr of 0.25 wrrt,'91. [60]If com exceeds $5 for 30 con trad days. [61]Dec'98 & prior in $Cdn. [62]Non-Resort Preferred Shr. [63]9 Mo Jun'95. [64]Spl div. [65]Ea ADR rep 1 ord, IR.002. [66]Subsid pfd in $M. [67]Amts. prior to 1999 $Cdn.

Splits ◆ Index	Cash Divs. Ea. Yr. Since	Dividends: Latest Payment Period $	Date	Ex. Div.	Total $ So Far 1999	Ind. Rate	Paid 1998	Financial Position Mil-$ Cash& Equiv.	Curr. Assets	Curr. Liab.	Balance Sheet Date	Capitalization Lg Trm Debt Mil-$	Shs. 000 Pfd.	Com.	Earnings $ Per Shr. Years End	1995	1996	1997	1998	1999	Last 12 Mos.	Interim Earnings Period	$ per Shr. 1998	1999	Index
1	....	None Since Public			...	Nil	....	1.51	18.1	6.09	8-31-99	14.6	...	2187	My	vd12.69	15.27	v□1.25	v2.03	v0.72	0.81	3 Mo Aug	v0.16	v0.25	1
2	1966	Q0.30	1-10-00	12-16	1.20	1.20	1.20	2.51	91.0	23.1	9-30-99	....	...	4292	Je	3.18	1.78	v1.39	v2.82	v2.41	2.08	3 Mo Sep	v0.79	v0.46	2
3◆	1916	Q0.12	12-10-99	11-8	0.47	0.48	0.43	7470	42877	37778	9-30-99	13807	2546	1802604	Dc	v1.77	v2.51	v3.01	v3.28	E3.67	4.22	9 Mo Sep	v2.05	v2.99	3
4◆	1956	Q0.38	1-11-00	12-20	1.52	1.52	1.48	92.1	870	341	9-30-99	3.92	...	105105	Dc	v2.22	v1.70	v1.99	v1.90	E1.57	1.51	9 Mo Sep	v1.57	v1.18	4
5	1993	Div Omitted 4-22-99			0.03	Nil	0.12	445	975	213	9-30-99	990	...	87355	Sp	0.71	0.93	v1.13	v1.33	v□0.65	0.65				5
6	....	None Since Public			...	Nil	....	16.6	546	414	9-30-99	1024	...	73754	Dc	...	pv1.34	□v0.36	v0.21	....	1.25	9 Mo Sep	vd0.11	v0.93	6
7	1923	Q0.20	1-17-00	12-23	0.80	0.80	0.80	6.57	369	295	8-31-99	121	...	18739	Fb	v1.32	v0.15	v1.08	vd6.98	....	0.20	9 Mo Nov	vd7.27	vd0.09	7
8◆	1946	Q0.25	12-15-99	11-17	1.00	1.00	1.00	353	7202	4395	9-30-99	7584	...	414079	Dc	v4.41	1.04	vd0.50	v0.77	E0.81	0.57	9 Mo Sep	v0.49	v□0.29	8
9	1998	Q0.492	12-1-99	11-12	1.969	1.969	0.366	Co option redm fr 12-1-2003,$25				★700	...	...	Dc	...	...	...	....	....	....	Mature 12-1-2038			9
10◆	....	0.053	10-1-81	9-4	...	Nil	....	30.5	302	135	10-03-99	156	...	52013	Je	0.84	v1.29	vd0.84	v0.32	v□0.39	0.49	3 Mo Sep	vNil	v0.10	10
11	....	None Since Public			...	Nil	....	1.07	11.8	9.02	9-30-99	7.00	3	9173	Dc	v0.34	vd1.21	vd0.16	vd0.06	....	d1.15	9 Mo Sep	vd0.02	vd1.11	11
12	....	None Since Public			...	Nil	....	....	11.1	6.27	j5-31-99	0.82	...	12768	Nv	0.01	0.10	v0.04	vd0.24	....	jd0.15	6 Mo May	vd0.11	vd0.02	12
13◆	1988	Q0.06¼	12-17-99	12-1	0.25	0.25	0.25	33.3	110	78.9	9-30-99	402	...	6377	Dc	v3.14	v□1.29	v0.32	v□1.09	....	2.74	9 Mo Sep	v□0.67	v2.32	13
14	....	0.02½	1-17-95	12-27	...	Nil	....	407	705	313	10-03-99	785	...	68743	Dc	v0.68	v0.82	v0.96	v0.08	....	0.32	9 Mo Sep	v0.77	v1.01	14
15	1997	A0.06	6-30-99	5-26	0.06	0.06	0.06	59.7	106	149	8-31-99	283	...	±53125	Nv	±[53]0.53	±[54]0.55	v±0.77	v±1.00	....	1.34	9 Mo Aug	v±0.62	v±0.96	15
16	....	None Paid			...	Nil	....	1.38	4.37	8.45	j9-30-99	1.81	...	31021	Dc	0.27	v0.25	vd0.70	vd0.49	....	jd0.03	9 Mo Sep	vd0.43	v0.03	16
17◆	....	None Since Public			...	Nil	....	209	225	24.2	9-30-99	1.63	...	★261450	Dc	...	...	...	pv0.08	....	....	9 Mo Sep	n/a	vd0.03	17
18	....	None Since Public			...	Nil	....	0.17	8.31	7.04	9-30-99	0.04	...	5711	Dc	d0.41	v[55]d0.33	[56]n/a	vd1.36	....	d0.77	9 Mo Sep	vd0.98	vd0.39	18
19	....	Plan qtly div			...	[57]....	....	....	...	...		....	...	★6500	Dc	...	...	...	....	....	....				19
20	....	None Since Public			...	Nil	....	36.2	38.3	27.1	6-30-99	1.16	5239	41930	Sp	d0.59	d0.76	vd1.35	vd1.69	Pvd0.90	d0.90				20
21◆	1996	Q0.03¾	1-15-00	12-30	0.15	0.15	0.15	Total Assets $1346.7M			9-30-99	880	...	27580	Dc	vΔ1.10	v1.16	□v0.89	v1.31	....	1.09	9 Mo Sep	v0.96	v0.74	21
22◆	1971	Q0.08½	3-15-00	2-24	0.33	0.34	0.30	809	5237	4901	9-30-99	855	...	280652	Dc	v0.56	v0.85	v0.95	v1.10	E1.30	1.24	9 Mo Sep	v0.72	v0.86	22
23◆	1991	Q0.07	2-1-00	1-12	0.28	0.28	0.28	....	359	371	11-13-99	352	...	68355	My	0.53	v0.35	v1.28	v1.71	v1.74	1.70	24 Wk Nov	v0.91	v0.87	23
24◆	1998	Div Omitted 8-13-98			...	Nil	h[58]0.10	Total Assets $41.7M			9-30-99	4.61	...	2056	Dc	vd1.45	v□5.20	vd1.75	v0.25	....	d1.89	9 Mo Sep	v0.94	vd1.20	24
25	....	[59]Wrrt	10-15-91	10-16	...	Nil	....	0.33	7.04	6.29	9-30-99	22.7	...	7926	Dc	d0.16	vd0.37	v0.08	v0.05	....	0.01	9 Mo Sep	v0.06	v0.02	25
26	....	Terms&trad. basis should	be checked in detail					Wrrts expire 12-31-2001				....	...	680	Dc	...	...	...	....	....	....	Expiration date can be shortened[60]			26
27◆	....	None Since Public			...	Nil	....	26.4	174	73.1	9-30-99	....	...	20001	Je	0.81	d0.21	vd1.45	vd1.05	vd1.76	d1.53	3 Mo Sep	vd0.02	v0.21	27
28◆	1993	gA0.16	4-5-99	3-17	g0.16	0.16	g0.13	....	260	277	j12-31-98	321	...	25194	Dc	v0.97	v1.13	v0.53	v[61]1.68	....	1.87	9 Mo Sep	0.80	v0.99	28
29	....	None Since Public			...	Nil	....	15.3	16.0	4.03	6-30-99	p....	...	★37751	Dc	...	...	...	vpd0.91	....	....	6 Mo Jun	n/a	vpd0.43	29
30◆	....	None Paid			...	Nil	....	29.9	170	65.4	8-31-99	135	...	32038	Fb	v0.53	v0.39	vd0.16	v0.68	....	d0.52	9 Mo Nov	v0.44	vd0.76	30
31	....	None Since Public			...	Nil	....	100	104	5.34	9-30-99	....	★1280	15113	Dc	...	pvd0.66	vd0.90	vd1.73	....	d1.53	9 Mo Sep	vd1.49	vd1.29	31
32	....	None Since Public			...	Nil	....	25.2	27.5	4.83	6-30-99	1.00	p...	★21792	Dc	...	...	...	vpd0.74	....	....	6 Mo Jun	n/a	vpd0.44	32
33◆	1995	Q0.14	12-14-99	12-1	s0.547	0.56	0.533	21.0	936	859	10-30-99	250	...	±249128	Ja	pv0.88	v0.97	v1.09	±v1.51	E1.80	1.60	9 Mo Oct	v±0.58	v±0.67	33
34	1991	S0.08	1-26-00	1-10	0.16	0.16	0.16	121	576	456	j6-30-99	838	[62]16727	43254	Je	‡[63]0.51	0.82	v1.05	v1.25	v1.45	j1.45				34
35	....	None Paid			...	Nil	....	0.92	47.8	30.5	9-30-99	25.6	...	13724	Dc	vd0.02	vd0.26	v0.10	v0.21	....	d0.15	9 Mo Sep	v0.19	vd0.17	35
36◆	....	None Since Public			...	Nil	....	1241	1564	754	10-31-99	38.6	...	p195323	Jl	d0.37	vd0.15	v0.48	vd0.08	vP1.97	1.92	3 Mo Oct	vd0.28	vd0.33	36
37◆	1994	Q0.01¼	1-17-00	12-30	0.05	0.05	0.05	17.6	409	158	9-30-99	457	...	±29977	Dc	v±1.07	v±1.28	v±0.05	v1.50	....	1.60	9 Mo Sep	v1.03	v1.13	37
38◆	1999	[64]4.00	4-21-99	4-22	[64]4.00	Nil	....	Total Assets $187.71M			9-24-99	....	...	31021	Dc	v0.81	v1.26	v1.42	v2.25	....	2.09	9 Mo Sep	v1.02	v0.86	38
39◆	1987	gQ0.13	2-1-00	12-29	g0.46½	0.52	g0.36	Total Assets $1746.3M			j9-30-99	172	...	210799	Dc	v0.46	v0.56	v0.70	v0.89	....	j1.05	9 Mo Sep	v0.64	v0.80	39
40	1983	Q0.03	12-30-99	12-21	0.12	0.12	0.12	Total Assets $55.6M			9-30-99	....	...	2771	Dc	v1.15	v1.37	v1.60	v1.92	....	1.93	9 Mo Sep	v1.40	v1.41	40
41	....	None Since Public			...	Nil	....	17.0	19.1	1.06	9-30-99	p....	p...	6508	Je	Δd0.47	Δ0.42	Δvd4.51	vd0.29	v0.02	Nil	3 Mo Sep	v0.01	vd0.01	41
42◆	....	None Since Public			...	Nil	....	132	498	350	9-26-99	49.2	...	269784	Dc	v0.03	v0.21	v0.42	vd0.20	Ed0.41	d0.38	9 Mo Sep	vd0.28	vd0.46	42
43	....	None Since Public			...	Nil	....	53.3	77.0	14.8	12-31-97	0.09	...	19071	Dc	0.14	v0.10	v0.25	Pv0.37	....	0.31	9 Mo Sep	v0.14	v0.08	43
44◆	....	None Paid			...	Nil	....	11.9	181	94.9	9-30-99	1.76	...	16171	Dc	v1.37	v1.65	v1.73	v1.31	E1.25	1.27	9 Mo Sep	v0.97	v0.93	44
45◆	1934	Q0.15	1-15-00	12-15	0.58¾	0.60	0.53¾	36.9	183	221	9-30-99	870	[66]59	85728	Dc	v0.87	v1.00	Δv0.99	v1.42	E1.45	1.38	12 Mo Sep	v1.25	v1.38	45
46◆	....	None Since Public			...	Nil	....	11.1	152	142	6-30-99	239	...	8355	Sp	...	...	pd1.10	v0.14	vPd3.97	d3.97				46
47◆	1996	Q0.16	12-16-99	11-26	1.11¼	0.64	†2.07	Equity per shr $22.61			12-31-98	....	...	25034	Dc	v2.90	v3.55	v3.79	v2.55	....	1.21	9 Mo Sep	v2.33	v0.99	47
48◆	1988	gQ0.12½	12-31-99	12-8	g0.50	0.50	g0.45½	....	0.04	0.25	j2-28-99	439	6000	40703	Dc	v1.98	v2.00	v3.14	v2.63	....	2.33	9 Mo Sep	v1.39	v1.09	48
49	....	None Since Public			...	Nil	....	39.8	172	17.1	9-30-99	....	...	39900	Dc	...	pv0.37	□pv0.40	v0.31	....	d0.23	9 Mo Sep	v0.32	vd0.22	49
50	....	None Since Public			...	Nil	....	File bankruptcy Chapt 11			3-31-99	....	...	±19750	Dc	vd0.27	vd0.64	vd2.25	vd8.91	....	d10.90	3 Mo Mar	vd1.45	vd3.44	50

◆Stock Splits & Divs By Line Reference Index [3]2-for-1,'97,'99. [4]3-for-1,'94. [8]2-for-1,'95. [10]2-for-1,'95. [13]5-for-4,'95. [17]2-for-1,'99. [21]3-for-2,'97. [22]3-for-2,'97:2-for-1,'99. [23]2-for-1,'97. [24]No adj for stk dstr,'95,'98:1-for-5 REVERSE,'98. [27]To split 3-for-2,ex Jan 14,'00. [28]2-for-1,'96. [30]2-for-1,'99. [33]Adj for 5%,'99. [36]2-for-1,'95:3-for-1,'99. [37]2-for-1,'95. [38]No adj for stk dstr,'99. [39]2-for-1,'98. [42]5-for-4,'94:3-for-1,'96:2-for-1,'96,'97. [44]2-for-1,'95. [45]3-for-2,'96:2-for-1,'99. [46]2-for-1,'98. [47]2-for-1,'99. [48]3-for-2,'98.

¶ S&P 500
\# MidCap 400
✣ SmallCap 600
• Options

Index	Ticker	Name of Issue (Call Price of Pfd. Stocks)	Market	Com. Rank. & Pfd. Rating	Inst. Hold Cos	Inst. Hold Shs. (000)	Principal Business	Price Range 1971-97 High	1971-97 Low	1998 High	1998 Low	1999 High	1999 Low	December, 1999 Dec. Sales in 100s	Last Sale Or Bid High	Low	Last	%Div Yield	P-E Ratio	EPS 5 Yr Growth	% Annualized Total Return 12 Mo	36 Mo	60 Mo
1	IRM	✓Iron Mountain	NY	NR	165	23740	Records mgmt co	26½	9 3/16	36¼	20 15/16	39½	25⅛	27713	39½	29⅛	39 5/16	...	d	−43	9.0	25.1	...
2	IRS	✓IRSA Inversiones y Rep GDS[51]	NY,Ch	NR	49	4298	Real estate dvlp - Argentina	46	14½	40 13/16	18	34⅝	20½	1609	32 11/16	31¾	31⅞B	s1.9	13	6	19.7	3.0	7.3
3	IRT	✓IRT Property	NY,Ch,P	NR	105	8320	Real estate investment trust	16 5/16	1 3/16	12 5/16	8⅜	10 1/16	7¼	26592	7⅞	7¼	7 13/16	12.0	10	16	−13.4	−3.9	3.6
4	IRSN	✓Irvine Sensors	NSC	C	5	345	Mfr infrared sensors/elec pd	12	⅛	4⅜	1 1/16	2 9/16	1⅛	63531	2½	1¾	2⅛	...	d	−9	47.9	31.4	−18.1
5•[1]	ISIP	✓Isis Pharmaceuticals	NNM	C	72	3668	Antisense drug research/dvlp	24¾	3¼	16¼	7	17⅜	3⅞	273319	16½	3⅞	6¼	...	d	−14	−51.7	−29.7	9.3
6	OREX	Isolyser Co	NNM	NR	34	5992	Mfr disposable medical prod	23	1⅞	3 15/16	1	5	1 1/16	35991	3½	2 5/16	3	...	d	−36	180	−24.9	−19.9
7	IST	✓ISPAT Intl 'A'	NY	NR	55	14483	Mini-mills:steel/steel prod	30	17¾	30¼	4¾	16⅛	6⅞	19595	16⅛	13⅞	16⅛	...	29	−26	111	...	...
8•[2]	ISSX	✓ISS Group	NNM	NR	139	21716	Network Security software	....	....	30 5/16	8½	71⅛	20	117381	71⅛	44⅜	71⅛	...	d	...	159	...	...
9	ITX	✓IT Group	NY,B,Ch,Ph,P	C	89	15339	Waste mgmt services	109½	6⅜	11½	5	17⅜	7¼	22032	10 7/16	8⅜	9⅛	...	4	NM	−18.0	2.9	−5.7
10	Pr	7% cm Cv Dep[56]Ex[57]Pfd([58]25.70)	NY	NR	8	576		25⅛	15½	21⅞	17⅜	23½	17 5/16	456	19½	17 5/16	18⅜	9.5	..	...	...	...	...
11	ITCD	✓ITC DeltaCom	NNM	NR	162	19093	Long-distance telephone svs	10 11/16	6 15/16	25½	8 5/16	40¾	12½	122020	28⅜	22½	27⅝	...	d	...	81.1	...	...
12	ITII	✓ITI Technologies	NNM	NR	78	4697	Mfr wireless security sys	36¾	9¼	34⅛	19⅞	37¼	19½	4909	31	27⅞	30	...	19	17	−3.2	25.6	5.7
13	ITLA	✓ITLA Capital	NNM	NR	60	6403	Special'd lend'g&deposit svcs	21¼	10	24	8½	20	11¾	4980	14¾	11¾	12 9/16	...	6	NM	−16.9	−5.7	...
✣14•[3]	ITRI	✓Itron Inc	NNM	NR	72	7885	Mfr wireless communications pd	60	13½	22	4¼	9 15/16	3⅞	26739	6½	4½	6⅛	...	d	Neg	−14.8	−29.9	−21.3
15	ESI	✓ITT Educational Svcs	NY,Ch	NR	..	...	Oper technical skill schools	27	4¼	36⅛	21⅜	40⅜	14¾	74189	17⅝	14¾	15 7/16	...	17	19	−54.6	−12.6	28.1
¶16•[4]	IIN	✓ITT Industries	NY,P	NR	391	64420	Dsgn,mfr engineered prd & sys	33 11/16	21¼	40⅞	28⅛	41½	30½	48403	35⅝	32	33 7/16	1.8	13	−12	−14.5	13.0	...
17	TURF	✓iTurf Inc'A'	NNM	NR	29	1393	Internet community/mktg svc	....	....	....	....	66	9 7/16	119171	20 1/16	11 9/16	12 7/16	...	d	...	...	...	...
18	ITXC	✓ITXC Corp	NNM	NR	24	2710	Internet based voice/fax svcs	....	....	....	....	52⅛	12	36257	49½	30	33⅝	...	..	...	...	...	...
#19•[4]	IVX	✓IVAX Corp	AS,Ch,Ph,P	C	173	36819	Pharm,personal care prod	41⅜	15/16	12 9/16	6 3/16	25 13/16	11 1/16	79993	25 13/16	17⅞	25¾	...	44	−7	107	35.9	6.4
20	IVCO	IVC Industries	NSC	NR	3	5	Dvlp,mfr vitamin products	44	9	21	4	13½	2¾	1837	4⅞	4¾	4 13/16	...	d	Neg	−13.4	−20.3	−24.4
21	IXX	✓Ivex Packaging	NY	NR	128	17291	Integrated specialty packaging	24	10	29½	13½	20⅛	6⅞	10710	10½	8¾	10	...	7	...	57.0	...	...
22	IVIL	✓iVillage Inc	NNM	NR	61	4963	Online womens network	....	....	....	....	130	19½	175497	29¾	19½	20¼	...	..	...	...	...	...
23	IWRK	Iwerks Entertainment	NNM	C	22	4922	Prod movie-based spcl theaters	37	1⅞	3½	9/16	1½	⅝	8480	13/16	⅝	¾	...	d	−36	−32.3	−47.6	−31.5
24•[5]	IIXL	✓iXL Enterprises	NNM	NR	58	11318	Internet strategy consult'g sv	....	....	....	....	58	12	117628	58	36¼	55½	...	..	...	...	...	...
25	EXNT	✓IXnet Inc	NNM	NR	26	5325	On-line/telecommunic svcs	....	....	....	....	36¼	13½	46797	36¼	16½	30⅛	...	d	...	...	...	...
26	JAX	✓J. Alexander's Corp	NY,Ch	B−	15	916	Fast food restaurant:Franch'g	18 13/16	3/16	6 1/16	2 3/16	4 9/16	1 15/16	3856	3¼	2 11/16	3⅛	...	d	Neg	−21.9	−27.6	−12.2
✣27	JJSF	✓J & J Snack Foods	NNM	↑B+	94	5376	Mfrs frozen snack foods	20¾	3⅝	23	12½	25	15½	5619	21⅞	15½	20½	...	14	17	−8.4	14.9	12.0
#28•[6]	JBL	✓Jabil Circuit	NY	B	354	58423	Mfr circuit board assemblies	36	⅞	37 7/16	11½	77 15/16	28½	124217	77 15/16	63 15/16	73	...	62	54	96.3	94.1	136
✣29•[4]	JBX	✓Jack in the Box	NY,Ph,P	NR	252	30196	Oper Jack-in-Box,Chi-Chi rstr	21	3¼	22 7/16	12 9/16	29 7/16	18 3/16	46705	21¾	18 3/16	20 11/16	...	11	NM	−6.2	32.6	37.2
30•[4]	J	✓Jackpot Enterprises	NY,P	B	34	2673	Slot mach in Nev retail strs	23 5/16	1	13 15/16	9⅛	10¼	7 1/16	8229	8½	7¾	8 5/16	...	7	7	−11.9	−5.2	3.0
31	JLN	✓Jaclyn, Inc	AS,Ch	C	7	200	Popular priced handbags	15¼	1 7/16	5⅞	3⅛	4	1 13/16	857	3 1/16	1 13/16	2¾	...	d	−49	−26.7	−20.6	−12.5
32	JACO	✓Jaco Electronics	NNM	B−	16	1777	Dstr electronic components	18½	½	7⅝	2¼	6 9/16	2½	4354	6	3 11/16	5 3/16	...	d	Neg	29.7	−15.2	2.6
#33•[3]	JEC	✓Jacobs Engr Group	NY,Ph,P	B+	227	18193	Full-service engr organiz'n	36½	½	40¾	24¾	42¾	29¼	14961	32½	29¼	32½	...	13	24	−20.2	11.2	11.9
34	JCBS	✓Jacobson Stores	NNM	B−	26	1961	Specialty department stores	43½	⅞	15¾	6½	9	4	2364	8 3/16	5 11/16	5⅞	...	10	NM	−16.1	−14.0	−8.3
35•[7]	JAKK	✓JAKKS Pacific	NNM	NR	107	9749	Dvlp toys/electronic pds	7 7/16	3	8 15/16	4 11/16	29 5/16	7	129020	27⅜	16⅛	18 11/16	...	19	...	162	52.1	...
✣36•[1]	JBM	✓Jan Bell Marketing	AS,Ch,Ph,P	B−	72	10274	Design,mfr fine jewelry	34	1¾	7 15/16	2⅜	7½	2 1/16	35483	2 15/16	2½	2⅞	...	6	NM	−55.3	11.7	−6.4
37•[8]	JANNF	Jannock Ltd[63]	NNM,To,Mo	B−	23	13948	Brick, vinyl prod, steel prd	25¾	1 1/16	15½	8	12½	9 1/16	1725	12½	11⅛	11⅞	◆2.9	2	33	32.5	−1.7	6.7
38	JAZZ	Jazztel plc ADS[64]	NNM	NR	..	...	Telecommunic svcs,Spain	....	....	....	....	72⅝	17	186672	72⅝	17	65⅛	...	d	...	...	...	...
39	JBOH	✓JB Oxford Holdings	NSC	B−	17	257	Securities broker dealer	5⅞	5/16	4½	⅜	25¾	1⅜	151400	10⅜	7 7/16	7 11/16	...	14	NM	324	77.5	50.4
40	JAZ	✓JCC Holding 'A'	AS	NR	17	2114	Own/oper casinos	....	....	4⅜	3¼	10	2 11/16	5616	5½	2 11/16	2 13/16	...	..	...	−16.7	...	...
41	JDEC	✓J D Edwards	NNM	NR	153	18538	Resource planning software	40⅝	23	49½	22⅞	33¼	10⅞	333793	33¼	24¾	29⅞	...	d	Neg	5.3	...	...
42	JDAS	✓JDA Software Group	NNM	NR	114	15535	Dgn retail business softwr	30 9/16	7½	39 7/16	7	19⅜	5¾	72927	19⅜	13⅝	16⅜	...	d	...	69.0	−4.8	...
43	JDN	✓JDN Realty	NY,Ch	NR	130	14680	Real estate investment trust	23 5/16	11 15/16	23⅛	18½	23⅜	14⅞	39484	17	14⅞	16⅛	9.8	11	18	−18.9	2.7	12.6
44•[9]	JDSU	✓JDS Uniphase Corp	NNM	C	613	178308	Mfr communic ind prod	11⅞	7/16	17⅞	7 13/16	177½	14 13/16	1633911	177½	104 13/16	161 5/16	...	d	Neg	831	191	182
✣45	JEF	✓Jefferies Group	NY,Ch,Ph,P	A−	152	9841	Equity securities broker	48	1 15/16	59½	16 9/16	65	18½	17892	22⅞	18½	22	0.9	8	30	...	...	...
¶46•[10]	JP	✓Jefferson-Pilot	NY,B,C,Ch,P,Ph	A+	536	54267	Insurance hldg co, life	57 13/16	1¾	78⅜	48 11/16	79⅝	61 3/16	52213	69⅛	61 3/16	68¼	1.9	18	15	−7.3	24.4	27.5
47	NBX	Jefferson-Pilot 7.25% 'ACES'	NY	NR	18	742	Automatic Com Exch Securities	122 7/16	71¾	148	80⅜	127¼	79¾	867	97½	79¾	83¾	6.3	..	...	−15.6	2.2	...
48	JS	✓Jefferson Smurfit Grp ADS[67]	NY,Ph	NR	36	6747	Produce paper&board/pkg prd	35 5/16	23½	39½	13¼	31¼	16½	3418	30½	27¼	29	2.3	16	6	68.3	5.1	...
49	JC	✓Jenny Craig	NY,Ph,P	B−	23	3726	Weight loss centers/svcs	33⅞	4⅜	7⅝	4¼	6 7/16	2	44602	4½	2	3¾	...	d	Neg	−37.5	−25.3	−12.9
50	JET	✓Jetronic Indus	AS	B−	1	395	Mfr electr eq:furniture strs	10	⅛	3 3/16	15/16	1 7/16	9/16	4333	1⅜	9/16	15/16	...	d	NM	−6.3	−10.6	4.6

Uniform Footnote Explanations-See Page 4. Other: [1]ASE,CBOE:Cycle 1. [2]CBOE:Cycl3 1. [3]Ph:Cycle 1. [4]CBOE:Cycle 3. [5]ASE,CBOE,Ph:Cycle 1. [6]CBOE,P,Ph:Cycle 3. [7]P,Ph:Cycle 3. [8]Mo:Cycle 3. [9]ASE,CBOE,P:Cycle 3. [10]ASE:Cycle 1. [51]Ea GDS rep 10 com,P$1 par. [52]Accum on Pfd. [53]To be determined. [54]Fiscal Mar'98 & prior. [55]9 Mo Dec'98. [56]Dep for 0.01 shr 7% cm Cv Exch Pfd. [57]Co opt exch for $25 amt 7% Cv 2008. [58]To 9-30-99,scale to $25 in 2003. [59]83.3% owned by ITT Corp. [60]Subsid Pfd in $M. [61]86.9% owned by IPC Communications. [62]®$1.26,'96. [63]Jun'94 & prior prices in Canadian $. [64]Ea ADS rep 1 ord. [65]2 Mo Dec'98. [66]Stk dstr of Jefferies Group,'99. [67]Ea ADS rep 10 Nominal Value, IR 25p.

Splits ◆ Index	Cash Divs. Ea. Yr. Since	Dividends: Latest Payment Period $	Date	Ex. Div.	Total $ So Far 1999	Ind. Rate	Paid 1998	Financial Position Mil-$ Cash& Equiv.	Curr. Assets	Curr. Liab.	Balance Sheet Date	Capitalization Lg Trm Debt Mil-$	Shs. 000 Pfd.	Com.	Earnings $ Per Shr. Years End	1995	1996	1997	1998	1999	Last 12 Mos.	Interim Earnings Period	$ per Shr. 1998	1999	Index
1◆	....	None Since Public			...	Nil	....	3.47	144	116	9-30-99	598	...	35416	Dc	pvd0.16	v□±...	vd0.26	vd0.11	....	d0.47	9 Mo Sep	vd0.06	vd0.42	1
2◆	1999	1.6%Stk	11-26-99	11-12	s1.36	0.60	....	44.4	153	149	6-30-99	96.3	...	188476	Je	2.19	1.87	2.70	v1.93	v2.40	2.40				2
3	1978	Q0.23½	12-1-99	11-17	0.93	0.94	0.91½	Total Assets $569M			9-30-99	286	...	33234	Dc	□v0.61	□v0.65	v0.82	v□0.78	....	0.82	9 Mo Sep	v0.60	v0.64	3
4	....	None Paid			...	[52]Nil	....	2.76	8.90	3.63	6-27-99	0.50	14	34911	Sp	d0.20	vd0.94	vd0.73	vΔd0.24	....	d0.34	9 Mo Jun	vΔd0.08	vd0.18	4
5	....	None Since Public			...	Nil	....	43.8	48.5	17.6	9-30-99	85.8	...	★32245	Dc	vd1.10	vd1.04	vd1.17	vd1.60	....	d2.11	9 Mo Sep	vd0.98	vd1.49	5
6◆	....	None Since Public			...	Nil	....	18.5	62.4	14.9	9-30-99	3.68	...	40732	Dc	vd0.02	□vd0.52	□vd2.37	Δvd0.49	....	d0.12	9 Mo Sep	vd0.32	v0.05	6
7	1998	0.11¼	6-4-99	5-14	0.11¼	[53]....	0.11¼	525	2298	1334	12-31-98	2400	...	±120000	Dc	5.01	5.52	v2.46	v1.93	....	0.55	9 Mo Sep	v1.75	v0.37	7
8◆	....	None Since Public			...	Nil	....	134	160	25.5	9-30-99	0.52	...	40627	Dc	...	...	pvd0.15	vd0.14	....	d0.02	9 Mo Sep	vd0.11	v0.01	8
9◆	....	None Since Public			...	Nil	....	21.5	539	315	10-01-99	664	70	22764	Dc	d0.40	vd1.48	v[54]d1.79	v[55]d0.63	....	2.18	9 Mo Sep	v□d1.83	v0.98	9
10	1993	Q0.43¾	12-31-99	12-8	1.75	1.75	1.75	Cv into 1.0703 com,$23.36				....	2056	...	Mr	...	...	...	....	....	....				10
11◆	....	None Since Public			...	Nil	....	289	365	68.5	9-30-99	516	1481	59432	Dc	vd0.02	pvd0.10	vd0.25	v□d0.51	....	d0.90	9 Mo Sep	v□d0.32	vd0.71	11
12	....	None Since Public			...	Nil	....	3.88	58.5	11.4	9-30-99	....	...	8530	Dc	v1.26	v1.63	v0.87	v1.61	....	1.57	9 Mo Sep	v1.11	v1.07	12
13	....	None Since Public			...	Nil	....	Total Deposits $909M			9-30-99	34.3	...	7206	Dc	vd0.52	v1.36	v1.57	v1.89	....	2.14	9 Mo Sep	v1.38	v1.63	13
14	....	None Since Public			...	Nil	....	2.84	83.9	37.7	9-30-99	63.4	...	14955	Dc	v0.81	vd0.11	v0.07	vd0.42	....	d0.47	9 Mo Sep	vd0.47	vΔd0.52	14
15◆	....	None Since Public			...	Nil	....	55.6	81.2	62.8	9-30-99	....	...	[59]24720	Dc	v0.42	v0.55	v0.71	v0.51	....	0.92	9 Mo Sep	v0.32	v□0.73	15
16	1996	Q0.15	1-1-00	11-22	0.60	0.60	0.60	218	1735	1882	9-30-99	478	...	87915	Dc	□v8.93	v1.85	□v0.94	v13.55	E2.50	1.03	9 Mo Sep	v14.25	v1.73	16
17	....	None Since Public			...	Nil	....	68.2	72.9	3.73	10-30-99	....	...	±18918	Ja	...	vNil	vNil	v0.03	....	d0.48	9 Mo Oct	vNil	vd0.51	17
18	....	None Since Public			...	Nil	....	10.0	13.0	5.53	6-30-99	p0.12	p...	★34840	Dc	...	...	...	vpd0.45	....	....	9 Mo Sep	n/a	vpd1.56	18
19	....	0.05	6-3-96	5-8	...	Nil	....	68.0	338	206	9-30-99	45.7	...	105521	Dc	vΔ0.96	v□d1.31	□vd1.88	v□0.62	....	0.58	9 Mo Sep	v□0.41	v0.37	19
20◆	....	None Paid			...	Nil	....	1.13	45.9	23.5	10-31-99	28.2	...	2088	Jl	0.48	0.16	v0.64	v0.56	vd3.28	d0.98	3 Mo Oct	v0.08	v2.38	20
21	....	None Since Public			...	Nil	....	4.06	199	127	9-30-99	436	...	20947	Dc	□v2.14	pv0.84	□vd0.75	v1.35	....	1.38	9 Mo Sep	v1.02	v1.05	21
22	....	None Since Public			...	Nil	....	56.1	71.5	34.1	9-30-99	....	...	29534	Dc	...	...	...	vpd2.59	....	....	9 Mo Sep	n/a	vd4.74	22
23	....	None Since Public			...	Nil	....	3.43	18.1	16.3	9-30-99	0.67	...	12391	Je	d1.32	v0.26	vd0.84	vd0.95	vd0.39	d0.44	3 Mo Sep	vd0.08	vd0.13	23
24	....	None Since Public			...	Nil	....	104	186	38.7	9-30-99	1.32	[60]48	64636	Dc	...	...	...	vpd1.10	....	....	9 Mo Sep	n/a	vd1.85	24
25	....	None Since Public			...	Nil	....	4.06	21.8	36.7	3-31-99	46.5	...	[61]★50575	Sp	...	...	...	vpd0.83	Pvd1.35	d1.35				25
26	....	None Paid			...	Nil	....	0.79	2.09	7.95	10-03-99	18.1	...	6772	Dc	v0.92	v[62]1.26	□vd0.95	vd0.27	....	d0.04	9 Mo Sep	vd0.34	vd0.11	26
27	....	None Since Public			...	Nil	....	6.67	60.7	44.2	6-26-99	45.9	...	8973	Sp	0.61	v0.65	v0.91	v1.26	Pv1.50	1.50				27
28◆	....	None Since Public			...	Nil	....	141	588	331	8-31-99	33.3	...	p87674	Au	0.12	v0.34	v0.69	v0.74	v1.12	1.17	3 Mo Nov	v0.24	v0.29	28
29	....	None Since Public			...	Nil	....	10.9	97.2	2.29	9-30-99	303	...	38276	Sp	d1.77	0.51	□v0.89	v□1.77	v1.95	1.95				29
30	....	0.08	11-29-96	11-13	...	Nil	....	67.6	71.2	7.34	9-30-99	....	...	8617	Je	v0.71	v0.62	v0.84	v0.79	v0.53	1.25	3 Mo Sep	v0.13	v0.85	30
31	....	0.12½	2-15-95	1-9	...	Nil	....	2.04	21.3	6.11	9-30-99	....	...	2711	Je	vd0.86	v0.25	v0.28	v0.02	vd0.66	d0.66	3 Mo Sep	v0.03	v0.03	31
32◆	....	None Since Public			...	Nil	....	1.75	62.6	20.4	9-30-99	18.6	...	3654	Je	0.78	v1.08	v0.53	v0.30	vd0.31	d0.19	3 Mo Sep	vd0.06	v0.06	32
33	....	0.028	12-15-83	11-15	...	Nil	....	53.8	811	637	6-30-99	168	...	25924	Sp	1.27	1.56	v1.80	v2.08	Pv2.47	2.47				33
34	....	0.12½	10-10-96	9-11	...	Nil	....	0.62	138	58.3	10-30-99	109	...	5788	Ja	vd0.73	vd1.98	v0.21	v0.28	....	0.62	9 Mo Oct	vd0.93	vd0.59	34
35◆	....	None Since Public			...	Nil	....	73.4	119	45.3	9-30-99	....	...	★18882	Dc	p0.15	v0.23	v0.35	v0.59	....	1.00	9 Mo Sep	v0.45	v0.86	35
36	....	None Since Public			...	Nil	....	0.24	110	53.5	10-30-99	50.0	...	22501	Ja	vd0.13	v0.03	v0.39	v0.60	....	0.46	9 Mo Oct	vd0.14	vd0.28	36
37	1945	gQ0.12½	1-1-00	12-13	g0.50	0.50	g0.50	16.1	419	215	j12-31-98	272	1379	34473	Dc	0.61	v1.65	v1.44	v1.30	....	j4.13	9 Mo Sep	v0.67	v3.50	37
38	....	None Since Public			...	Nil	....	76.6	131	55.8	9-30-99	225	...	★52546	Dc	...	...	...	vd0.47	....	d6.25	9 Mo Sep	vd0.31	vd6.09	38
39	....	None Paid			...	Nil	....	Total Assets $431.97M			9-30-99	0.04	...	14384	Dc	v0.40	v0.23	v0.09	vd0.13	....	0.55	9 Mo Sep	vd0.25	vΔ0.43	39
40	....	None Paid			...	Nil	....	10.3	11.2	25.6	9-30-99	320	...	±10079	Dc	...	...	vpd3.61	v[65]d0.37	....	....	9 Mo Sep	n/a	vd2.06	40
41	....	None Since Public			...	Nil	....	130	424	315	7-31-99	....	...	106772	Oc	0.22	0.30	0.39	v0.68	vPd0.37	d0.37				41
42◆	....	None Since Public			...	Nil	....	81.9	126	23.2	9-30-99	....	...	23916	Dc	pv0.28	v0.43	v0.63	vd0.11	....	d0.18	9 Mo Sep	v0.06	vd0.01	42
43◆	1994	Q0.39½	12-23-99	12-7	1.54½	1.58	1.413	Total Assets $1103.44M			9-30-99	550	2000	33850	Dc	□v0.85	v1.00	□v1.16	v1.28	....	1.50	9 Mo Sep	v0.96	v1.18	43
44◆	....	None Since Public			...	Nil	....	960	1219	149	9-30-99	....	...	321846	Je	...	0.03	vd0.14	vd0.59	vd1.08	d1.47	3 Mo Sep	0.05	vd0.34	44
45◆	1988	0.05	12-21-99	11-18	h[66]0.20	0.20	0.20	Total Assets $3615M			6-25-99	149	...	23943	Dc	v1.19	v1.84	v2.80	v2.96	....	2.71	9 Mo Sep	v2.18	v1.93	45
46◆	1913	Q0.33	3-5-00	2-9	1.28½	1.32	1.152	Total Assets $24159.00M			9-30-99	894	...	104726	Dc	v2.53	v2.71	v3.47	v3.91	E3.75	4.28	9 Mo Sep	v3.01	v3.38	46
47	1995	Q1.314	12-22-99	12-1	5.256	5.256	5.256	Exch for com NationsBank(or cash)re-spec cond				....	...	★1650	Dc	...	...	...	....	....	....	Mature 1-21-2000			47
48◆	1995	0.256	11-1-99	9-29	0.664	0.66	0.694	1040	2466	1404	12-31-98	2060	...	1107047	Dc	4.48	2.09	v1.49	v1.77	....	1.77				48
49	....	0.15	4-8-94	3-25	...	Nil	....	38.9	77.7	51.2	9-30-99	7.39	...	20689	Je	0.46	v0.93	v□0.40	v0.10	vd0.03	d0.33	3 Mo Sep	v0.12	vd0.18	49
50	....	None Paid			...	Nil	....	0.06	16.5	8.64	10-31-99	5.39	...	3702	Ja	vd0.62	vd0.36	v0.33	v0.16	....	d0.01	9 Mo Oct	v0.22	v0.05	50

◆**Stock Splits & Divs By Line Reference Index** [1]3-for-2,'98. [2]Adj for 2.8%,'95. [6]2-for-1,'95. [8]2-for-1,'99. [9]1-for-4 REVERSE,'96. [11]2-for-1,'98. [15]3-for-2,'96(twice). [20]1-for-8 REVERSE,'99. [28]2-for-1,'99. [32]10%,'95:4-for-3,'95. [35]3-for-2,'99. [42]3-for-2,'98. [43]3-for-2,'98. [44]2-for-1,'96,'97,'99(twice). [45]2-for-1,'96,'97:No adj for stk dstr,'99. [46]3-for-2,'95,'98. [48]2-for-1,'95.

¶ S&P 500
\# MidCap 400
✣ SmallCap 600
• Options

Index	Ticker	Name of Issue (Call Price of Pfd. Stocks)	Market	Com. Rank. & Pfd. Rating	Inst. Hold Cos	Inst. Hold Shs. (000)	Principal Business	Price Range 1971-97 High	1971-97 Low	1998 High	1998 Low	1999 High	1999 Low	December, 1999 Dec. Sales in 100s	Last Sale Or Bid High	Low	Last	%Div Yield	P-E Ratio	EPS 5 Yr Growth	% Annualized Total Return 12 Mo	36 Mo	60 Mo
1	JCTCF	✔Jewett-Cameron Trading	NSC	NR	2	2	Lumber & building pds	6⅛	3	6¾	4⅝	5½	4⅜	542	5⅛	5	5	...	10	53	2.6	8.9	...
2	JFAX	✔JFAX.COM Inc	NNM	NR	20	3793	Net based message,commun sv	...	...	...	...	10 5/16	3 13/16	108581	8⅝	4¼	6¾	...	..	...	...	...	...
3	JCC	✔Jilin Chemical Ind ADS[51]	NY,Ph	NR	3	70	Chemical pd-Republic of China	40½	10⅝	14	3⅜	14	4 1/16	2562	9	7⅛	7⅛	1.7	..	...	51.4	−18.7	...
4	JST	✔Jinpan Intl	AS	NR	4	151	Mfr cast resin transformers	...	...	8¾	2	6	1½	1775	2¾	2	2¼	...	4	...	−21.7	...	...
✣5•[1]	JLG	✔JLG Indus	NY,Ph	B+	210	28613	Mobile aerial lifts:cranes	29½	5/16	20¾	13	22	11⅜	37047	17⅛	13¾	15 15/16	0.3	12	19	2.1	0.0	39.6
6	JLK	✔JLK Direct Distribution'A'	NY	NR	38	2919	Direct metal pds	32 15/16	20	39½	9¼	13½	7	3376	10 7/16	7⅞	10 9/16	...	12	...	1.2	...	...
7	JHPC	✔JLM Couture	NSC	B−	4	185	Design/mfr bridal apparel	7½	⅜	5¼	2	3½	1⅜	1191	1⅞	1 7/16	1⅝	...	6	NM	−46.9	−31.2	3.5
8	JMAR	✔JMAR Technologies	NNM	B−	14	645	Precision mfg & meas equip	13½	7/16	3½	1 5/16	4⅝	1 7/16	83828	4⅝	1½	4 9/16	...	d	53	115	24.3	53.7
9	JNIC	✔JNI Corp	NNM	NR	..	...	Fibre channel hardwr/softwr pd	...	...	...	...	114¾	19	119237	82 15/16	52½	66	...	..	...	...	...	...
✣10	JAS.A	✔Jo-Ann Stores'A'	NY,Ch,Ph	B	79	4509	Fabric/housewares retail strs	27 13/16	9/16	31⅞	14 15/16	17¼	9⅝	2900	13	9⅜	11¼	...	8	10	−30.2	−11.3	4.9
11	JAS.B	Cl'B'(non-vtg)	NY	B	28	5750		24⅜	9¾	27½	13½	14	9½	995	12⅛	9½	10 1/16	...	7	10	−27.5	−13.2	...
12•[2]	JNC	✔John Nuveen 'A'	NY,Ph,P	NR	102	3744	Mkt,manage tax-free invest pd	41⅝	15⅛	41¾	31 9/16	43 11/16	34 5/16	3758	37⅜	34 5/16	36 1/16	3.2	13	12	0.1	13.9	12.7
13•[1]	JM	✔Johns Manville Corp	NY,P	B	112	24961	Bldg,constrn,filtration prd	15¼	4	18⅛	9⅝	19½	10	37031	14	11½	13 15/16	1.7	9	26	−13.8	11.1	22.4
¶14•[3]	JCI	✔Johnson Controls	NY,B,Ch,P,Ph,NSC	↑A+	562	54597	Auto interior sys/bldg ctrls	51	⅞	61⅞	40½	76 11/16	49	70129	57½	49	56⅞	2.0	13	18	−2.1	14.0	21.4
¶15•[4]	JNJ	✔Johnson & Johnson	NY,To,B,C,Ch,P,Ph	A+	2085	780196	Health care products	67 5/16	2⅜	89¾	63⅜	106⅞	77	711054	103 7/16	90⅛	93¼	1.2	31	9	12.5	24.9	29.6
16	JII	✔Johnston Industries	NY,Ch	C	17	1255	Mfrs ind'l/apparel textiles	13¾	¼	6⅛	2 13/16	3 5/16	1 7/16	6047	1 15/16	1 9/16	1 11/16	...	d	Neg	−46.0	−37.9	−29.3
#17•[5]	JNY	✔Jones Apparel Group	NY,Ch,Ph,P	B+	424	91885	Design,dstr womens apparel	28 11/16	3 7/16	37¾	15⅞	35⅞	21½	104434	28¾	24 13/16	27⅛	...	16	29	22.9	13.3	33.5
18	JOIN	✔Jones Intercable	NNM	C	26	1187	Cable television systems	20⅞	⅛	35 7/16	13⅞	77⅞	33¼	9222	77⅞	52	69½	...	d	−34	97.9	87.0	42.4
19	JOINA	✔ Class A (1/10 vtg)	NNM	C	155	15862		20⅞	2⅞	35⅞	14⅜	78	33¼	113933	78	55	69 5/16	...	d	−5	94.6	88.3	41.4
20	JLL	✔Jones Lang LaSalle	NY	NR	61	4146	Real estate products/svcs	38 9/16	23	48	21 15/16	36½	9 3/16	6748	12 7/16	9 3/16	11⅞	...	d	...	−59.7	...	...
✣21•[5]	JMED	✔JONES PHARMA	NNM	B+	275	27702	Mfr brand/generic drug prod	33 11/16	⅜	27¼	13 11/16	46¼	17 9/16	72782	46¼	34¼	43 7/16	0.2	42	40	80.5	21.9	87.4
¶22•[5]	JOS	✔Jostens Inc	NY,B,Ch,Ph,P	B−	258	24588	School class rings,yearbook	38⅝	⅞	26 9/16	18¾	27⅛	17¼	73336	24⅜	17¼	24 5/16	3.6	16	NM	−3.1	9.0	9.6
23	JOL	✔Joule Inc	AS	B	9	232	Office/engineering temp help	13	11/16	5¾	1⅞	4⅝	1½	1043	2 1/16	1 9/16	1¾	...	9	−3	−12.5	−20.6	−0.7
24	JRC	✔Journal Register	NY,Ph	NR	72	8573	Newspaper publisher U.S.	21 1/16	14	23⅞	12⅛	23	11⅜	12752	15⅞	11⅞	15 7/16	...	15	...	2.9	...	...
25	JPR	✔JP Realty	NY,Ph	NR	96	9240	Real estate investment trust	27¾	17⅜	26	18½	21 5/16	15 5/16	16257	17 1/16	15 5/16	15⅝	12.3	10	7	−11.8	−8.1	2.2
✣26	JSB	✔JSB Financial[58]	NY	NR	128	3752	Savings bank, New York	50⅝	10⅝	60	44¾	63 3/16	47⅜	3298	59¾	50⅛	51⅞	3.5	16	16	−1.5	14.5	20.8
27	JSI	✔JumboSports Inc	NY,Ch,Ph,P	D	4	256	Oper sporting equip superstrs	29½	1¼	2 1/16	⅛	¼	....	32191	.02	....	....	...	d	Neg	−96.0	−91.4	−81.9
28	JNPR	✔Juniper Networks	NNM	NR	177	10538	Communication eqp	...	...	...	...	384⅜	34	178373	384⅜	272⅛	340	...	..	...	...	...	...
29	JUNO	Juno Lighting	NNM	A−	..	...	Mfrs recessed/track light'g	21	1⅝	25	15¾	24 9/16	9¼	3654	12 9/16	9¼	10⅝	3.9	8	4	−55.2	−12.1	−8.6
30•[6]	JWEB	✔Juno Online Svcs	NNM	NR	44	1975	Internet access services	...	...	...	...	87	8⅞	1061097	87	14 9/16	35½	...	..	...	...	...	...
31	JPTR	✔Jupiter Communications	NNM	NR	..	...	Internet research svcs	...	...	...	...	...	21	18979	37	28¾	30¼	...	..	...	...	...	...
32•[5]	FEETQ	✔Just For Feet	NNM	D	99	8492	Athletic/outdoor footwear	38¼	3 3/16	29⅛	11⅛	19¾	1 3/16	...	...	...	...	...	..	Neg	...	...	...
✣33	JSTN	✔Justin Indus	NNM	A−	108	9541	Bldg mtl:leather gds,towers	25⅝	5/16	17	10⅜	16	9 11/16	10318	15⅝	14¼	14⅞	1.3	18	−5	15.1	10.5	6.1
34	JWG	✔JWGenesis Financial	AS	B	22	612	Investment bkg/sec brokerage	15⅞	1/32	13¾	5¼	29¾	5 15/16	14157	29¾	15½	29⅝	...	8	39	395	57.4	62.1
¶35•[5]	KM	✔K mart	NY,B,C,Ch,P,Ph	B+	579	365628	Operates discount dept strs	28⅛	5 1/16	20⅞	10½	18⅝	9 1/16	1746637	12¼	9 7/16	10 1/16	...	8	NM	−34.3	−1.0	−4.0
✣36•[7]	KTO	✔K2 Inc	NY,B,Ch,P,Ph	B+	95	8328	Snow skis,fish tackle,ind prod	32 15/16	7/16	23 11/16	7¾	11⅝	6 15/16	11579	8	7¼	7⅝	...	8	−12	−24.3	−33.4	−12.0
✣37	KSWS	✔K Swiss Inc 'A'	NNM	B	..	...	Dvlp/mkt athletic footwear	15⅛	3⅞	15⅝	8	59 13/16	10 13/16	48313	19 11/16	12 9/16	18 9/16	0.3	7	44	39.3	56.4	14.2
38	KTEL	K-Tel International	NNM	C	13	690	Produce music/video products	5⅝	3/16	39 7/16	3 3/16	14	4½	141669	10¼	5½	5⅞	...	d	−39	−44.0	15.6	22.6
39	KTII	✔K-Tron Intl	NNM	B−	32	1927	Digital process ctr feeders	20¾	2¾	21¼	15¼	18⅝	12⅝	966	14 1/16	12⅝	13½	...	6	NM	−26.0	9.6	4.7
40	KV.B	✔K-V Pharmaceutical Cl'B'[60]	NY,Ph	B−	31	784	Mfr drugs for major firms	15 11/16	⅛	23 7/16	12 13/16	21½	13	1175	21 7/16	17⅝	21 7/16	...	17	NM	3.6	41.8	41.4
41	KV.A	✔ Cl'A' 1/20 vtg	NY,Ph	C	46	2649		15 15/16	2 15/16	23 7/16	12 15/16	21 15/16	12¾	3719	21 15/16	17⅝	21 15/16	...	17	NM	6.0	41.4	42.6
42	KS	✔Kafus Industries	AS	NR	9	620	Prod wood panel/newsprint pds	6⅜	3¼	6 3/16	3	11½	4	14804	9	6 3/16	8 15/16	...	d	...	120	...	...
43•[8]	KLU	✔Kaiser Aluminum[62]	NY,Ch,Ph,P	NR	75	22573	Aluminum mfr/fabricated prd	21	6⅜	11⅝	4⅝	10⅛	4¾	17498	7 15/16	5⅞	7 11/16	...	d	−19	57.7	−12.9	−6.7
44	KSR	✔Kaiser Group Intl[63]	NY,Ch	C	20	3399	Environmental consult'g svcs	18½	1¾	3 3/16	1 1/16	1½	¼	29548	¾	⅜	⅜	...	d	Neg	−73.9	−41.5	−34.6
45	KRSC	✔Kaiser Ventures	NNM	B	26	3035	Waste management services	20¼	2	14⅝	8	19⅜	8	3051	19⅜	12	16	...	6	38	86.7	21.1	20.7
46	KANA	✔Kana Communications	NNM	NR	35	1763	e-business software prd	...	...	...	...	245	15	35311	245	138⅜	205	...	..	...	...	...	...
47	KPP	✔Kaneb Pipe Line Ptnrs L.P.	NY	NR	37	751	Pipeline & terminaling svcs	36 11/16	13¾	37⅞	29⅝	34 7/16	22	11846	25¼	22	24 11/16	11.3	9	6	−18.1	1.9	13.0
48	KAB	✔Kaneb Services	NY,B,Ch,P,Ph	B−	59	14036	Ind svcs, pipelines & terminals	40⅛	1¼	6 7/16	3½	5⅛	3 13/16	14476	4 7/16	4⅛	4⅜	...	6	−3	9.4	10.4	15.5
49	KNK	✔Kankakee Bancorp	AS	NR	10	248	Savings bank, Illinois	37¾	13½	37½	24	29	19½	279	23½	19½	19¾	2.4	17	1	−21.8	−5.6	6.3
#50•[9]	KLT	✔Kansas City Pwr & Lt[65]	NY,B,CS,Ch,Ph,P	B+	184	19764	Supplies elec to K.C. suburbs	29 15/16	5 5/16	31 13/16	28	29⅝	20 13/16	29276	23	20 13/16	22 1/16	7.5	15	−4	−20.3	−2.6	5.0

Uniform Footnote Explanations-See Page 4. Other: [1]CBOE:Cycle 1. [2]ASE:Cycle 1. [3]Ph:Cycle 1. [4]ASE,CBOE,P,Ph:Cycle 1. [5]CBOE:Cycle 3. [6]ASE,CBOE:Cycle 1. [7]Ph:Cycle 2. [8]P,Ph:Cycle 1. [9]P:Cycle 1. [51]Ea ADS rep 100 Cl'H' ord shrs,RMB 1.00. [52]12 Mo Dec:Fiscal Jun'95 earn $0.74. [53]12 Mo Dec: May '95 earned d$0.16. [54]12 Mo Dec:May'95 earned d$0.16. [55]Fiscal Jun'95 & prior. [56]12 Mo Dec'96:Fiscal Jun'96 earned $1.28. [57]Incl $0.047925 return of capital,'97. [58]North Fork Bancorp plan acq,3 com. [59]Incl liabs subj to compromise. [60]Conv into Cl'A'shr for shr. [61]Accum on Pfd. [62]0.10 vtg. [63]Formerly ICF Kaiser Intl. [64]10 Mo Dec'95. [65]Western Resource plan acq,stk.

Index	Cash Divs. Ea.Yr. Since	Dividends Latest Payment Period $	Date	Ex. Div.	Total $ So Far 1999	Ind. Rate	Paid 1998	Financial Position Mil-$ Cash& Equiv.	Curr. Assets	Curr. Liab.	Balance Sheet Date	Capitalization Lg Trm Debt Mil-$	Shs. 000 Pfd.	Com.	Earnings $ Per Shr. Years End	1995	1996	1997	1998	1999	Last 12 Mos.	Interim Earnings Period	$ per Shr. 1998	1999	Index
1	....	None Paid			...	Nil	....	0.22	5.41	1.23	8-31-99	....	...	1095	Au	0.07	0.29	v0.39	v0.08	v0.52	0.52				1
2	....	None Since Public			...	Nil	....	25.0	50.8	4.70	9-30-99	1.91	p...	32855	Dc	...	...	...	vpd0.52	....	....	9 Mo Sep	n/a	v□d0.38	2
3	1996	0.116	8-20-99	5-12	0.116	0.12	0.314	27.8	371	399	12-31-98	769	...	3411078	Dc	2.99	v1.08	v0.36	v0.20	....	....	6 Mo Jun	n/a	v0.16	3
4	....	None Since Public			...	Nil	....	1.19	6.81	2.87	12-31-97	....	...	2998	Dc	p0.17	p0.78	n/a	Pv0.53	....	0.53				4
5◆	1993	Q0.01	1-3-00	12-13	0.02	0.04	0.02	7.32	388	130	10-31-99	237	...	44321	Jl	0.49	0.95	v1.04	v1.05	v1.36	1.36	3 Mo Oct	v0.23	v0.23	5
6	....	None Since Public			...	Nil	....	3.88	195	63.1	9-30-99	....	...	±24510	Je	...	pbv0.72	vp0.92	±v1.07	Pv±0.83	0.85	3 Mo Sep	v0.15	v0.17	6
7◆	....	None Since Public			...	Nil	....	0.15	7.70	3.44	7-31-99	....	...	2060	Oc	0.05	0.30	v0.41	v0.28	....	0.26	9 Mo Jul	v0.40	v0.38	7
8	....	None Since Public			...	Nil	....	3.54	16.2	8.51	9-30-99	0.59	...	18045	Dc	v0.01	v0.05	v0.10	v0.04	....	d0.06	9 Mo Sep	v0.03	vd0.07	8
9	....	None Since Public			...	Nil	....	n/a	8.91	9.29	6-30-99	....	p...	★21783	Dc	...	...	...	pv0.03	....	....	6 Mo Jun	n/a	vp0.09	9
10◆	....	....	8-16-95	8-17	...	Nil	....	27.9	634	255	10-30-99	329	...	±17833	Ja	v±0.90	v±1.26	±v□1.60	v±0.69	....	1.36	9 Mo Oct	v±d0.40	v±0.27	10
11	....	None Since Public			...	Nil	....	....	....	...		....	...	8941	Ja	v±0.90	±v1.26	±v□1.60	v±0.69	....	1.36	9 Mo Oct	v±d0.40	v±0.27	11
12	1992	Q0.29	12-15-99	11-29	1.13	1.16	0.98	Total Assets $501.82M			9-30-99	....	1800	±31154	Dc	v1.87	v1.98	v2.13	v2.43	....	2.77	9 Mo Sep	v1.75	v2.09	12
13	1996	Q0.06	1-7-00	12-21	0.24	0.24	0.18	29.1	544	371	9-30-99	558	...	147283	Dc	v0.73	□v2.27	v0.92	Δv□1.15	....	1.49	9 Mo Sep	vΔ□0.87	v□1.21	13
14◆	1901	Q0.28	1-5-00	12-13	1.00	1.12	0.92	248	3647	4060	6-30-99	1294	.3	85325	Sp	2.27	2.69	v3.12	v3.63	vP4.48	4.48				14
15◆	1944	Q0.28	12-7-99	11-12	1.09	1.12	0.97	3593	12857	6980	10-03-99	1992	...	1390556	Dc	v1.82	v2.12	v2.41	v2.23	E3.05	2.52	9 Mo Sep	v2.17	v2.46	15
16◆	....	Div Omitted 8-13-97			...	Nil	....	1.39	95.9	142	10-02-99	1.22	...	10722	Dc	[52]d0.24	□v0.31	vd0.81	vd0.06	....	d0.52	9 Mo Sep	vd0.13	vd0.59	16
17◆	....	None Since Public			...	Nil	....	36.4	1361	892	10-03-99	839	...	p122505	Dc	v0.60	v0.76	v1.13	v1.47	....	1.70	9 Mo Sep	v1.17	v1.40	17
18	....	5%Stk	5-7-85	4-1	...	Nil	....	20.8	82.2	152	9-30-99	1643	...	±42050	Dc	v±□[53]d0.67	v±d2.00	v±d1.11	v±d1.96	....	d5.11	9 Mo Sep	vd1.66	vd4.81	18
19	....	5%Stk	5-7-85	4-1	...	Nil	....	....	....	...		....	...	36143	Dc	±v□[54]d2.67	v±d2.00	v±d1.11	v±d1.96	....	d1.96				19
20	....	None Since Public			...	Nil	....	21.6	308	219	9-30-99	324	...	30189	Dc	...	pv1.10	vp1.27	v1.25	....	d4.26	9 Mo Sep	v0.53	vd4.98	20
21◆	1989	Q0.02½	1-3-00	12-13	0.088	0.10	0.073	162	189	14.3	9-30-99	....	...	43353	Dc	v0.33	v0.43	v0.73	v0.96	E1.04	0.97	9 Mo Sep	v0.75	v0.76	21
22	1960	Q0.22	12-1-99	11-10	0.88	0.88	0.88	11.6	248	319	10-02-99	....	...	33365	Dc	□[55]1.12	v[56]0.94	v1.47	v1.14	E1.50	1.21	9 Mo Sep	v1.10	v1.17	22
23	....	None Since Public			...	Nil	....	0.24	12.1	9.72	6-30-99	....	...	3674	Sp	0.26	0.28	v0.29	v0.19	Pv0.20	0.20				23
24	....	None Since Public			...	Nil	....	6.16	86.9	66.5	9-30-99	736	...	46524	Dc	...	pv0.74	v0.51	v□0.94	....	1.00	9 Mo Sep	v□0.65	v0.71	24
25	1994	[57]Q0.48	12-28-99	12-10	1.87½	1.92	1.81½	Total Assets $758M			9-30-99	393	...	17351	Dc	v1.26	v1.45	□v1.56	v1.58	....	1.51	9 Mo Sep	v1.13	v□1.06	25
26	1990	Q0.45	11-17-99	11-1	1.80	1.80	1.60	Total Deposits $1092.04M			9-30-99	50.0	...	9346	Dc	v2.01	v2.56	v3.64	v4.41	....	3.31	9 Mo Sep	v3.37	v2.27	26
27◆	....	None Since Public			...	Nil	....	File bankruptcy Chapt 11			1-29-99	[59]324	...	20420	Ja	v0.35	vd1.53	vd5.47	vd4.58	....	d4.58				27
28◆	....	None Since Public			...	Nil	....	84.6	102	34.4	9-30-99	....	p...	51787	Dc	...	...	...	vpd0.84	....	....	9 Mo Sep	n/a	vpd0.29	28
29◆	1987	0.10	4-15-99	3-11	0.20	0.40	0.36	5.44	66.3	22.0	8-31-99	212	...	2412	Nv	1.08	v1.08	v1.10	v1.43	....	1.37	9 Mo Aug	v1.06	v1.00	29
30	....	None Since Public			...	Nil	....	108	126	41.7	9-30-99	0.66	...	34640	Dc	...	...	...	vpd1.85	....	....	9 Mo Sep	n/a	vpd1.39	30
31	....	None Since Public			...	Nil	....	47.0	57.2	16.8	p6-30-99	....	...	★14160	Dc	...	...	...	pvd0.21	....	....	9 Mo Sep	n/a	v0.05	31
32◆	....	None Since Public			...	Nil	....	File bankruptcy Chapt 11				372	...	31211	Ja	v0.38	v□0.55	v0.70	v0.84	....	d0.28	6 Mo Jul	v0.44	v□d0.68	32
33	1984	Q0.05	1-4-00	12-22	0.20	0.20	0.20	4.96	237	65.4	9-30-99	60.4	...	25481	Dc	v0.94	v0.87	v0.99	v1.00	....	0.85	9 Mo Sep	v0.78	v0.63	33
34◆	....	None Paid			...	Nil	....	Total Assets $103M			9-30-99	....	...	5953	Dc	v0.64	v1.26	v1.50	v1.25	....	3.55	9 Mo Sep	v0.72	v3.02	34
35	....	0.12	12-11-95	11-7	...	Nil	....	345	9696	4769	10-27-99	4746	...	486895	Ja	□d1.14	vd0.45	v0.51	v1.01	E1.20	0.70	9 Mo Oct	v0.34	v0.03	35
36◆	1978	Div Discontinued 5-6-99			0.22	Nil	0.44	9.86	307	111	9-30-99	93.7	...	17900	Dc	v1.03	v1.51	v1.31	v0.29	....	1.00	9 Mo Sep	v0.17	v0.88	36
37◆	1994	0.01½	1-14-00	12-29	0.05½	0.06	0.04	55.7	136	19.9	9-30-99	....	...	±10791	Dc	v0.14	v0.06	v0.35	v1.10	....	2.88	9 Mo Sep	v0.77	v2.55	37
38◆	....	None Since Public			...	Nil	....	7.63	35.9	34.7	9-30-99	4.00	...	9775	Je	d0.34	d0.10	v0.41	vd0.31	vd1.25	d0.59	3 Mo Sep	vd0.37	v0.29	38
39	....	None Since Public			...	Nil	....	1.75	36.0	21.8	10-02-99	8.92	...	2966	Dc	vd3.00	v1.28	v1.69	v2.03	....	2.19	9 Mo Sep	v1.44	v1.60	39
40◆	....	0.003	12-18-80	12-5	...	[61]Nil	....	3.60	59.4	24.6	9-30-99	22.3	241	±18762	Mr	±0.21	±v0.47	v±0.58	v±1.17	....	1.27	6 Mo Sep	v0.28	v0.38	40
41◆	....	None Since Public			...	Nil	....	....	....	...		....	...	12185	Mr	v±0.21	v±0.47	v±0.58	±v1.17	....	1.27	6 Mo Sep	v0.28	v0.38	41
42	....	None Paid			...	Nil	....	0.49	2.27	42.9	9-30-98	216	16	24513	Sp	...	vd0.21	vd0.29	vd0.60	....	d0.60				42
43	....	0.05	12-15-92	11-23	...	Nil	....	8.60	972	564	9-30-99	970	...	79405	Dc	v0.69	vNil	v0.57	v0.01	Ed1.30↓	d1.66	9 Mo Sep	v0.50	vd1.17	43
44◆	....	None Since Public			...	Nil	....	55.7	304	242	9-30-99	138	...	23823	Dc	‡v[64]0.02	v0.17	vd0.22	v□d3.87	....	d0.32	9 Mo Sep	v□d2.80	v□0.75	44
45	....	None Paid			...	Nil	....	56.7	58.6	14.2	9-30-99	16.8	...	10699	Dc	v0.13	v0.24	v0.08	v0.11	....	2.79	9 Mo Sep	v0.03	v2.71	45
46	....	None Since Public			...	Nil	....	18.2	20.4	5.36	6-30-99	0.64	p...	★27546	Dc	...	...	...	vpd0.59	....	....	6 Mo Jun	n/a	vpd0.56	46
47	1990	0.70	11-12-99	10-27	2.75	2.80	2.60	5.93	29.7	33.4	9-30-99	156	...	18310	Dc	v2.20	v±2.46	v±2.55	v2.67	....	2.88	9 Mo Sep	v1.93	v2.14	47
48	....	0.02	7-1-86	6-10	...	Nil	....	22.8	106	64.0	9-30-99	208	569	31501	Dc	vΔ1.59	v0.19	v0.30	v0.40	....	0.78	9 Mo Sep	v0.28	v0.66	48
49	1995	Q0.12	12-1-99	11-9	0.48	0.48	0.48	Total Deposits $348.00M			9-30-99	....	...	1252	Dc	v1.18	v1.18	v2.00	v1.56	....	1.14	9 Mo Sep	v1.32	v0.90	49
50	1921	Q0.41½	12-20-99	11-24	1.66	1.66	1.64	36.8	256	521	9-30-99	847	797	61898	Dc	v1.92	v1.69	v1.18	v1.89	E1.46	1.29	12 Mo Sep	v1.90	v1.29	50

◆Stock Splits & Divs By Line Reference Index [5]2-for-1,'95(twice):3-for-1,'96. [7]1-for-3 REVERSE,'95. [10]2-for-1 in Cl'B','95. [14]2-for-1,'97. [15]2-for-1,'96. [16]3-for-2,'94. [17]2-for-1,'96,'98. [21]3-for-2,'96(twice),'99. [27]3-for-2,'94. [28]To split 3-for-1,ex Jan 18,'00. [29]No adj for reclassification,'99. [32]3-for-2,'95,'96. [34]3-for-2,'97. [36]Adj to 5%,'94. [37]2-for-1,'99. [38]2-for-1,'98. [40]3-for-2,'98. [41]3-for-2,'98. [44]Propose 1-for-4.77 REVERSE split.

¶ S&P 500
# MidCap 400
✣ SmallCap 600
• Options

Index	Ticker	Name of Issue (Call Price of Pfd. Stocks)	Market	Com. Rank. & Pfd. Rating	Inst. Hold Cos	Inst. Hold Shs. (000)	Principal Business	Price Range 1971-97 High	1971-97 Low	1998 High	1998 Low	1999 High	1999 Low	December, 1999 Dec. Sales in 100s	Last Sale Or Bid High	Low	Last	%Div Yield	P-E Ratio	EPS 5 Yr Growth	% Annualized Total Return 12 Mo	36 Mo	60 Mo
¶1•1	KSU	✓Kansas City So. Ind	NY,B,Ch,P,Ph	B+	522	82348	RR fin'l svcs,mutual funds,RE	35⅛	⅛	57 7/16	23	75	37½	143409	75	56⅛	74⅝	0.2	28	–6	52.2	71.9	49.7
2	KT	✓Katy Indus	NY,B,Ch,Ph,P	B–	45	3563	Indus machin'y&components	45	2	21 7/16	13¾	18 9/16	7⅝	2590	10¾	7⅝	8 11/16	3.5	7	NM	–49.4	–14.1	2.6
¶3•2	KBH	✓Kaufman & Broad Home	NY,Ph	B–	312	33032	Single-family home builder	25½	5⅜	35	17⅛	30¼	16¾	45368	24¼	21	24 3/16	1.2	7	66	–14.7	25.2	15.4
#4•3	KDN	✓Kaydon Corp	NY,Ch,Ph	A	209	23152	Mfrs bear'gs/filtration prod	34 15/16	15/16	45 15/16	22 13/16	41 1/16	23	21884	27 15/16	25½	26 13/16	1.6	14	18	–32.2	5.7	19.0
5	KBK	✓KBK Capital	AS,P	NR	16	535	Non-bank commercial financ'g	13⅛	3¾	14⅝	8⅜	9⅜	3⅜	559	5¼	3⅜	3⅜	...	18	–12	–63.3	–8.3	–11.6
6	KCS	✓KCS Energy Inc	NY	C	44	10155	Oil & gas explor,prod'n,mkt	30 9/16	7/16	21	2 15/16	3½	3/16	35013	15/16	½	13/16	...	d	Neg	–72.6	–63.9	–36.3
#7•4	KEA	✓Keane Inc	AS,P,Ph	B+	308	34398	Computer software services	41½	1/64	60 15/16	24¾	43⅝	17¼	101040	35	25 1/16	32⅛	...	26	45	–19.6	26.7	40.5
8•5	KBL	✓Keebler Foods	NY,Ph	NR	235	31352	Mfr cookies & crackers	....	....	37 13/16	23⅞	40½	25 11/16	49246	28¾	25 11/16	28⅛	...	32	...	–25.2	...	...
9	KEI	✓Keithley Instruments	NY	↑B	28	1972	Mfr electronic test instr/sys	19⅝	1¼	9½	3¾	22⅝	6½	6678	20⅝	16⅝	20⅝	0.8	11	74	127	32.1	34.2
¶10•6	K	✓Kellogg Co	NY,B,C,Ch,P,Ph	A–	527	316078	Convenience food products	50½	1 5/16	50 3/16	28½	42¼	30	142467	34 3/16	30	30 13/16	3.2	21	–10	–7.2	0.5	3.7
11•7	KELL	✓Kellstrom Industries	NNM	NR	88	5494	Renovat'n jet engines,parts	27½	4¾	34¼	9⅛	28¾	7½	39435	9⅝	7 11/16	9⅛	...	6	...	–68.3	2.9	...
✣12•5	KWD	✓Kellwood Co	NY,B,Ch,Ph	B+	206	21860	Mfrs & mkts apparel	38 9/16	1 7/16	36 11/16	22½	28⅞	16¼	11401	20½	18 1/16	19 7/16	3.3	97	–32	–20.0	1.4	1.2
#13•5	KELYA	✓Kelly Services'A'[51]	NNM	A	132	26891	Temporary help services	38¾	5/16	38½	23¾	32½	22⅞	14308	26½	22⅞	25⅛	3.8	11	8	–18.0	0.7	1.2
✣14•8	KEM	✓KEMET Corp	NY	NR	194	31938	Mfr tantalum/ceramic capacitrs	36⅛	5	22 1/16	8¾	45⅜	9⅞	84982	45⅜	34⅜	45 1/16	...	48	–24	301	24.7	24.9
#15•3	KMT	✓Kennametal, Inc	NY,B,Ch,P	B+	195	24371	Tungsten-base carbide prod	55 11/16	2½	54¾	15⅝	33⅞	16⅜	26819	33⅞	29¼	33⅝	2.0	24	–14	62.3	–2.8	8.7
16	KCP	✓Kenneth Cole Productions'A'	NY,Ch,Ph,P	NR	99	6190	Design,mkt footwear/handbags	22¾	5 3/16	26¾	12 15/16	49½	18 5/16	7641	49½	42⅝	45¾	...	31	19	144	43.4	34.4
✣17•8	KNT	✓Kent Electronics	NY,Ch,Ph,P	B+	150	17068	Dstr variety wiring products	43¾	1 5/16	28¾	7 9/16	24 7/16	8⅛	28989	24	21½	22¾	...	..	–44	78.4	–4.0	11.5
18	KYF	✓Kentucky First Bancorp	AS,Ph	NR	9	91	Savings bank, Kentucky	15¼	10	16	12⅛	12 15/16	10	155	10½	10¼	10¼	4.9	13	...	–16.9	2.1	...
19	KPC	Kentucky Pwr 8.72% Sr'A'Debs[52]	NY	....[53]	1	2	Subsid of Amer Elec Pwr	26⅞	24¼	26½	25 9/16	26 5/16	23	291	24¾	23	23	9.5	..	...	–3.0	5.3	...
¶20•9	KMG	✓Kerr-McGee	NY,To,B,C,Ch,P,Ph	B–	521	65224	Petroleum, chemicals,coal	75	15 13/16	73 3/16	36 3/16	62	28½	104142	62	53⅛	62	2.9	21	Neg	69.1	–1.6	9.4
21	KMD	Kerr-McGee 5.50% 'DECS'2004	NY	....[54]	13	2812	Exch Notes For Com Stock	....	....	....	....	43¼	30 13/16	4644	35⅝	30 13/16	32⅜B	5.6			...	...	...
22	KEQU	✓Kewaunee Scientific	NNM	B	15	326	Furniture & eqp for labs	15¾	1¼	14½	9	12	9	220	10¾	9⅞	9⅞B	2.8	7	NM	–9.0	22.3	38.8
23	KEG	✓Key Energy Services	NY,Ch,Ph	NR	105	49704	Provides oil field services	38⅜	2	22	3 5/16	5⅞	2 15/16	95013	5¼	4⅛	5 3/16	...	d	Neg	10.7	–23.9	1.5
24	KP	✓Key Production	NY	B	41	5008	Oil & gas expl,dvlp,prd	14⅝	1¾	12⅝	5	11	5⅛	8320	8¼	6¾	7½	...	23	3	42.9	–16.2	10.2
¶25•3	KEY	✓KeyCorp	NY,P	A+	688	216880	Commercial bkg,Ohio,Nthn US	36 9/16	1 1/16	44⅞	23⅜	38⅛	21	300403	26 13/16	21	22⅛	4.7	9	9	–28.3	–1.3	16.1
#26•10	KSE	✓KeySpan Corp	NY,B,C,Ch,P,Ph	B+	302	56503	Elec & gas service in N.Y.	30½	3¾	34 3/16	25⅜	31 5/16	22½	81808	26 1/16	22½	23 3/16	7.7	15	Neg	–20.3	8.7	18.0
27	KES	✓Keystone Consol Ind	NY,Ch	B–	33	1204	Mfr steel & wire products	25¾	1 11/16	13⅛	6 9/16	9¾	3¾	5035	6⅛	3 13/16	5 15/16	...	d	Neg	–26.9	–10.4	–15.3
#28•8	KSTN	✓Keystone Financial	NNM	A–	124	11408	General banking, Pennsylvania	42¼	5¾	42⅛	25¼	37½	19¾	26276	24	19¾	21 1/16	5.5	13	4	–40.8	–2.1	5.8
29	KTR	✓Keystone Property Trust	AS	NR	13	3369	Real estate investment trust	19¼	6⅜	20	11⅞	17	12½	832	15¾	14½	15½	7.6	19	76	5.5	30.3	28.7
30	KFX	✓KFX Inc	AS,Ch	NR	16	825	Licenses coal efficiency tech	8½	2 7/16	3⅞	1⅛	2 3/16	⅞	8534	1¾	1	1 11/16	...	d	–8	12.5	–32.6	–19.1
31	KRC	✓Kilroy Realty	NY,Ch	NR	159	19834	Real estate investment trust	29½	22	30	18½	26½	18	25096	22⅜	18 11/16	22⅜	7.5	15	...	5.0	...	...
32	KBALB	✓Kimball Intl Cl'B'	NNM	A–	106	9792	Furniture,pianos,organs	23 7/16	1¼	24 15/16	14⅞	21	14 9/16	10843	16⅞	15⅜	16½	3.9	11	8	–9.9	–3.9	8.6
¶33•11	KMB	✓Kimberly-Clark	NY,B,C,Ch,P,Ph	A–	1312	391453	Tissue,pers. care,hlthcare pd	56⅞	1 3/16	59 7/16	35⅞	69 9/16	44 13/16	317539	67 13/16	60⅞	65 7/16	1.6	21	45	22.4	13.4	...
34	KIM	✓Kimco Realty	NY,Ph	NR	230	32897	Real estate investment trust	36 3/16	12 13/16	41⅝	33 7/16	40¾	30⅞	56442	34⅝	30⅞	33⅞	7.8	15	15	–9.1	4.8	12.2
35	Pr D	7.50%Sr'D'cm[61]Dep Pfd([62]NC)	NY	BBB+	8	93		....	....	27 15/16	23¼	26⅛	20⅝	3168	22⅜	20⅝	21 5/16	8.8	..	...	...	...	...
36	KGCPrB	Kinam Gld $3.75'B'CvPfd([64]51.875)	NY	BB	8	882	Gold & silver mining,explor	66⅝	34	49	35½	36¾	25	937	28 11/16	25	26⅜	14.2	..	...	...	...	...
37	KIN	✓Kinark Corp	AS,B,P	B–	13	766	Chemical packag'g/dstr:mfg	10⅞	½	3¾	2⅛	3⅜	1	1236	1½	1⅛	1½	...	14	65	–31.4	–26.7	–14.3
#38•12	KMI	✓Kinder Morgan	NY,Ch	B+	243	43899	Nat'l gas,mineral resources	36	4 7/16	40 5/16	22 5/16	24 11/16	12 3/16	68903	21⅝	17⅛	20 3/16	1.0	d	Neg	–12.6	–5.3	8.3
39•7	KMP	✓Kinder Morgan Egy Ptnrs L.P.	NY	NR	148	13630	Liquid natl gas pipeline sys	41¼	11½	38⅛	28 9/16	45⅝	33	14338	44	39½	41 7/16	7.0	16	25	22.6	53.9	37.8
40	KPG	✓King Power Intl	AS	NR	1	.2	Sells duty free merchandise	17	2	9¾	1 3/16	2⅞	15/16	1591	1 13/16	1	1 1/16	...	d	...	–57.5	...	...
41	KINN	✓Kinnard Investments	NNM,Ch	B–	9	378	Securities broker/dealer	8¼	¾	7	2⅝	8¼	3⅝	5822	8¼	5⅜	7 7/16	...	..	–20	56.6	9.0	32.0
42	KGC	✓Kinross Gold	NY,To,Ch,Ph,Vc	C	99	36173	Acquis/dev of precious metals	10⅝	¼	5⅛	1¾	3¾	1½	68974	2 1/16	1 11/16	1⅞	...	d	Neg	–18.9	–35.9	–18.2
✣43•5	KEX	✓Kirby Corp	NY,B,Ch,Ph,P	B	92	13023	Tows freight by barge:insur	45¾	⅞	25 11/16	17¼	22⅜	16½	5453	20 11/16	17 13/16	20½	...	19	12	2.8	1.3	0.7
44	KIT	✓Kit Mfg	AS	C	9	144	Mobile hms:recr'l vehicles	23⅜	1	8⅛	4⅝	7½	3⅞	442	5⅛	4½	4½	...	13	Neg	–2.7	–26.3	–17.3
45	KTTY	✓Kitty Hawk	NNM	NR	40	5590	Air freight charter svcs	23¾	8	25½	8⅛	14⅛	6 1/16	6501	8⅜	6 5/16	6⅞	...	5	19	–37.5	–11.7	...
¶46•13	KLAC	✓KLA-Tencor Corp	NNM,Ch	B–	551	73799	Electro-optical test sys	76⅞	1 3/16	48	20¾	113⅛	42⅜	431059	113⅛	82 5/16	111⅜	...	..	–19	157	46.4	35.4
47•7	KLM	✓KLM Royal Dutch Air	NY,B,Ch,P,Ph	NR	67	20678	Worldwide air transport	39⅜	2½	49 11/16	23	34⅛	24⅛	14944	27⅝	24⅛	24 15/16	e2.5	18	–9	37.1	15.8	13.6
48	KDX	Klondex Mines Ltd	Vc	NR	1	81	Acq,explore natural res prop	2⅞	5/16	11/16	3/16	⅝	1/16	713	3/16	1/16	1/16	...	d	6	–80.0	–54.6	...
49	KM Pr	Kmart Fin I 7.75% Tr Cv Pfd[68]	NY	B	122	11532	Subsid of K mart Corp	61¼	46¼	74¼	47½	65⅝	42 9/16	17383	48⅜	43 5/16	43¾	8.9	..	...	...	...	...
50	KNP	K N Energy 8.25% PEPS Unit[71]	NY	....[72]	14	1128	Premium Eq Partic Sec Units	....	....	44½	35	39 5/16	23⅜	7276	34	27	32½	10.9	..	...	–4.1	...	...

Uniform Footnote Explanations-See Page 4. Other: [1]P:Cycle 3. [2]Ph:Cycle 1. [3]Ph:Cycle 3. [4]ASE,Ph:Cycle 2. [5]CBOE:Cycle 2. [6]ASE:Cycle 3. [7]CBOE:Cycle 3. [8]CBOE:Cycle 1. [9]CBOE,Ph:Cycle 1. [10]CBOE,Ph:Cycle 2. [11]ASE,CBOE,P:Cycle 1. [12]P:Cycle 2. [13]CBOE,Ph:Cycle 3. [51]Non-vtg. [52]Jr Sub Deferrable Int Debs. [53]Rated BBB by S&P. [54]Rated'BBB'by S&P. [55]Cash or stk re-spec cond. [56]Pfd in $Mil. [57]Fiscal Dec'96 & prior. [58]9 Mo Dec'98:post merger. [59]Stk dstr of Keycon Indus Inc. [60]Excl subsid pfd. [61]Dep for 0.10 shr Sr'D'cm Pfd. [62]Co Redm opt for cash fr 6-19-2001,re-spec cond. [63]If com exceeds $48.30 for 20 of 30 trad days. [64]Thru 8-15-2000,scale to $50 in 2004. [65]Into Kinross Gold Corp Com. [66]Redemption of stk purch rt. [67]Fiscal Aug'96 & prior. [68]Red thru 6-16-2000 at $52.7125,scale to $50 in 2006. [69]In Kmart com to 6-15-2016. [70]or earlier upon 'Tax Event're-spec cond. [71]Ea unit consists of stk pur contr&U.S. Tres Nte. [72]Rated'BB+' by S&P.

Index	Cash Divs. Ea. Yr. Since	Dividends: Latest Payment Period $	Date	Ex. Div.	Total $ So Far 1999	Ind. Rate	Paid 1998	Financial Position Mil-$ Cash & Equiv.	Curr. Assets	Curr. Liab.	Balance Sheet Date	Capitalization Lg Trm Debt Mil-$	Shs. 000 Pfd.	Com.	Earnings $ Per Shr. Years End	1995	1996	1997	1998	1999	Last 12 Mos.	Interim Earnings Period	$ per Shr. 1998	1999	Index
1◆	1978	Q0.04	1-3-00	12-13	0.16	0.16	0.16	322	655	357	9-30-99	781	650	110524	Dc	v1.80	v1.31	vd0.13	v1.66	E2.70	2.26	9 Mo Sep	v1.41	v2.01	1
2	1991	Q0.07½	1-24-00	12-22	0.30	0.30	0.30	11.4	253	114	9-30-99	158	...	8370	Dc	v3.18	v1.64	v1.38	v1.55	....	1.26	9 Mo Sep	v1.00	v0.71	2
3	1986	Q0.07½	2-24-00	12-8	0.30	0.30	0.30	Total Assets $2818.94M			8-31-99	1552	...	47689	Nv	0.73	d1.54	v1.50	v2.32	E3.25	2.75	9 Mo Aug	v1.30	v1.73	3
4◆	1986	Q0.11	1-3-00	12-10	0.40	0.44	0.36	100	230	62.4	10-02-99	....	...	30787	Dc	v1.14	v1.53	v1.86	v2.17	....	1.92	9 Mo Sep	v1.66	v1.41	4
5	....	None Since Public			...	Nil	....	Total Assets $105M			9-30-99	49.0	...	3162	Dc	0.51	v0.45	v0.60	v0.64	....	0.19	9 Mo Sep	v0.57	v0.12	5
6◆	1992	Div Omitted 3-31-99			0.02	Nil	0.08	0.02	0.05	0.44	9-30-99	....	...	29268	Dc	v0.91	v0.84	vd3.19	vd10.08	....	d8.54	9 Mo Sep	vd1.44	v0.10	6
7◆	....	0.001	5-27-86	5-6	...	Nil	....	88.0	368	100	9-30-99	1.76	...	±71680	Dc	v±0.29	v±0.38	v±0.68	v±1.33	E1.22	1.37	9 Mo Sep	v±1.01	v±1.05	7
8	....	None Since Public			...	Nil	....	13.8	306	410	4-24-99	507	...	83789	Dc	...	p0.03	□vp0.77	v□1.10	....	0.89	9 Mo Sep	v□0.71	v0.50	8
9◆	1964	Q0.041	12-31-99	12-15	0.148	0.164	0.127	13.5	42.9	20.4	6-30-99	3.00	...	±7177	Sp	0.66	d0.70	v0.10	v0.62	Pv1.79	1.79				9
10◆	1923	Q0.24½	12-15-99	11-26	0.96	0.98	0.92	150	1686	1640	9-30-99	1611	...	405404	Dc	v1.12	v1.25	□v1.36	v1.23	E1.48	0.70	9 Mo Sep	v1.12	v0.59	10
11	....	None Paid			...	Nil	....	7.21	357	42.1	9-30-99	333	...	11911	Dc	vp0.10	v0.56	v0.95	v1.53	....	1.64	9 Mo Sep	v1.06	v1.17	11
12◆	1962	Q0.16	12-17-99	12-1	0.64	0.64	0.64	111	868	240	10-31-99	370	...	27846	Ap	0.53	1.32	v1.75	v1.85	v0.07	0.20	6 Mo Oct	v1.14	v1.27	12
13	1962	Q0.24	12-10-99	11-24	0.95	0.96	0.91	60.6	748	468	10-03-99	....	...	±35892	Dc	v±1.83	v±1.91	v±2.12	v±2.23	E2.36	2.34	9 Mo Sep	v±1.58	v±1.69	13
14◆	....	None Since Public			...	Nil	....	6.92	218	138	9-30-99	120	...	±39757	Mr	±1.67	v±0.95	v±1.25	v±0.16	E0.94↓	0.46	6 Mo Sep	v0.05	v0.35	14
15◆	1944	Q0.17	11-24-99	11-8	0.68	0.68	0.68	32.5	752	369	9-30-99	703	...	30179	Je	2.58	2.62	v2.69	v2.58	v1.31	1.39	3 Mo Sep	v0.25	v0.33	15
16◆	....	None Since Public			...	Nil	....	36.6	123	25.5	9-30-99	....	...	±14012	Dc	±v0.73	±v0.90	±v0.91	v±1.20	....	1.48	9 Mo Sep	v±0.90	v±1.18	16
17◆	....	None Since Public			...	Nil	....	103	439	118	10-02-99	207	...	28072	Mr	1.22	v1.00	v1.26	v0.01	....	0.19	6 Mo Sep	v0.02	v0.20	17
18	1996	Q0.12½	10-30-99	10-14	0.50	0.50	0.50	Total Deposits $55.2M			9-30-99	7.03	...	1137	Je	...	vp0.65	v0.59	v0.75	v0.75	0.77	3 Mo Sep	v0.19	v0.21	18
19	1995	Q0.545	12-31-99	12-28	2.18	2.18	2.18	Co option redm fr 4-20-2000 at $25				40.0	...	...	Dc	...	...	...	....	....	....	Mature 6-30-2025			19
20	1941	Q0.45	1-3-00	12-1	1.80	1.80	1.80	184	1096	826	9-30-99	2476	...	86466	Dc	vd0.60	v4.43	v4.04	v1.06	E3.01	d1.47	9 Mo Sep	v2.95	v□0.42	20
21	1999	Q0.456	2-1-00	1-12	0.45⅛	1.825	....	Amt pay maturity based on Devon Corp Stk[55]				....	...	★8656	Dc	...	...	...	...	....	....	Due 8-2-2004			21
22	1996	Q0.07	12-15-99	11-29	0.25	0.28	0.21	0.01	21.9	11.3	10-31-99	....	...	2466	Ap	vd0.46	v0.15	v0.95	v1.06	v1.38	1.48	6 Mo Oct	v0.56	v0.66	22
23	....	None Since Public			...	Nil	....	12.3	144	78.0	9-30-99	694	...	82740	Je	0.33	v0.45	v0.66	v1.23	vd1.94	d1.93	3 Mo Sep	v0.10	v0.11	23
24	....	0.15	4-30-92	3-25	...	Nil	....	3.91	15.2	12.3	9-30-99	65.0	...	11556	Dc	v0.32	v0.69	v0.80	v0.38	....	0.32	9 Mo Sep	v0.32	v0.26	24
25◆	1963	Q0.26	12-15-99	12-1	1.04	1.04	0.94	Total Deposits $43466.00M			9-30-99	17058	...	447306	Dc	vΔ1.65	v1.67	v2.07	v2.23	E2.45	2.44	9 Mo Sep	v1.65	v1.86	25
26◆	1989	Q0.44½	2-1-00	1-10	1.78	1.78	1.187	130	993	1028	9-30-99	1663	[56]84	133866	Dc	2.10	v[57]2.24	pv1.00	‡[58]d1.34	E1.60	d1.03	9 Mo Sep	v0.75	v1.06	26
27	....	h[59]....	3-2-84	3-5	...	Nil	....	....	118	124	9-30-99	101	...	9927	Dc	v0.86	v0.38	v1.28	v0.40	....	d0.37	9 Mo Sep	v0.57	vd0.20	27
28◆	1985	Q0.29	1-20-00	1-5	1.16	1.16	1.40	Total Deposits $4913.75M			9-30-99	808	...	48707	Dc	v1.59	v1.71	v1.68	v1.92	....	1.60	9 Mo Sep	v1.44	v1.12	28
29	1994	Q0.29½	10-29-99	10-12	1.12	1.18	0.97	Total Assets $814.9M			9-30-99	489	1100	8293	Dc	d0.03	v1.00	v0.88	□v1.75	....	0.81	9 Mo Sep	v1.61	v0.67	29
30	....	None Paid			...	Nil	....	1.27	2.48	2.10	9-30-99	17.7	...	24482	Dc	vΔd0.47	vd0.25	vd0.21	vd0.28	....	d0.36	9 Mo Sep	vd0.18	vd0.26	30
31	1997	Q0.42	1-10-00	12-29	1.66½	1.68	1.60¼	Total Assets $1244.92M			9-30-99	527	[60]...	27894	Dc	p1.02	pv1.02	vp1.25	v1.43	....	1.50	9 Mo Sep	v1.07	v1.14	31
32◆	1954	Q0.16	1-14-00	12-21	0.64	0.64	0.62	128	400	178	9-30-99	1.39	...	±40385	Je	v±0.99	v±1.08	v±1.38	v±1.32	v±1.47	1.45	3 Mo Sep	v0.31	v0.29	32
33◆	1935	Q0.26	1-4-00	12-8	1.03	1.04	0.99	194	3419	3951	9-30-99	1996	...	544347	Dc	0.06	2.49	v□1.58	v□2.13	E3.09	2.92	9 Mo Sep	v□1.52	v2.31	33
34◆	1992	Q0.66	1-18-00	12-30	2.37	2.64	†1.97	Total Assets $2913.66M			9-30-99	1141	1329	60731	Dc	v1.32	v1.59	v1.78	v□2.02	....	2.29	9 Mo Sep	v1.50	v1.77	34
35	1998	0.46⅞	1-18-00	12-30	1.87½	1.875	0.604	Cv into 0.621 com				....	4292	...	Dc	...	...	...	....	....	....	Redm opt for com fr 6-19-2001[63]			35
36	1994	Q0.93¾	11-15-99	11-3	3.75	3.75	3.75	Cv into 4.8512[65]				....	1840	...	Dc	...	...	...	....	....	....				36
37	....	[66]0.01	11-1-90	10-9	...	Nil	....	0.13	13.0	6.25	9-30-99	9.31	...	6712	Dc	vd0.50	v0.21	v0.09	v0.09	....	0.11	9 Mo Sep	v0.11	v0.13	37
38◆	1937	Q0.05	12-30-99	12-13	0.65	0.20	0.76	22.4	960	1472	9-30-99	3575	70	112560	Dc	v1.22	v1.43	v1.63	v0.92	....	d0.23	9 Mo Sep	v1.00	vd0.15	38
39◆	1992	Q0.72½	11-15-99	10-27	2.77½	2.90	2.388	29.7	101	75.6	9-30-99	765	...	49327	Dc	v0.85	v0.90	v1.02	□v2.09	....	2.56	9 Mo Sep	v□1.53	v□2.00	39
40	....	None Paid			...	Nil	....	2.28	33.8	29.0	9-30-99	0.24	...	20250	Dc	...	pv0.09	v0.40	vd0.21	....	d0.31	9 Mo Sep	v0.18	v0.08	40
41	....	0.02½	1-31-95	1-9	...	Nil	....	Total Assets $34.66M			9-30-99	....	...	4895	Dc	v0.54	v1.92	v0.05	vd0.58	....	0.01	9 Mo Sep	vd0.53	v0.06	41
42	....	None Since Public			...	Nil	....	120	224	71.8	6-30-99	122	385	p303726	Dc	v0.12	v0.08	vd0.71	vd1.08	....	d1.14	9 Mo Sep	vd0.08	vd0.14	42
43	....	0.10	9-5-89	8-8	...	Nil	....	21.9	93.3	61.4	9-30-99	106	...	p24543	Dc	v0.34	v1.06	v0.88	v0.46	....	1.09	9 Mo Sep	v0.23	v0.86	43
44	....	None Paid			...	Nil	....	4.27	12.9	5.56	7-31-99	....	...	1111	Oc	1.21	v1.20	vd2.08	vd0.32	Pv0.34	0.34				44
45	....	None Since Public			...	Nil	....	0.99	190	164	9-30-99	463	...	17057	Dc	0.55	[67]0.52	v1.60	v0.99	....	1.27	9 Mo Sep	v0.30	v0.58	45
46◆	....	None Since Public			...	Nil	....	753	1084	373	9-30-99	....	...	89949	Je	1.20	v2.34	v1.24	v1.52	v0.43	0.74	3 Mo Sep	v0.11	v0.42	46
47◆	1995	†7.548	10-14-99		†8.163	0.62	1.268	1678	5043	4405	j3-31-99	7719	21150	46114	Mr	3.55	v1.60	Δv3.89	v3.59	....	1.42	6 Mo Sep	v4.55	v2.38	47
48	....	None Paid			...	Nil	....	0.23	0.24	0.02	j9-30-99	....	...	5265	Dc	d0.04	vd0.04	vd0.04	vd0.02	....	jd0.03	9 Mo Sep	vd0.02	vd0.03	48
49	1996	Q0.96⅞	12-15-99	12-10	3.875	3.875	3.87½	Cv into 3.33 com, $15[69]				....	3000	...	Ja	...	...	...	....	....	....	Mand Red 6-15-2016[70]			49
50	1999	1.774	11-30-99	11-26	3.596	3.547	....	....	...	...		....	...	★8000	Dc	...	...	...	....	....	....	Mature 11-30-2001			50

◆Stock Splits & Divs By Line Reference Index [1]3-for-1,'97. [4]2-for-1,'97. [6]2-for-1,'97. [7]3-for-2,'94:2-for-1,'96,'97. [9]2-for-1,'95. [10]2-for-1,'97. [12]3-for-2,'94. [14]2-for-1,'95. [15]2-for-1,'94. [16]2-for-1,'95. [17]3-for-2,'95:2-for-1,'96. [25]2-for-1,'98. [26]No adj for mgr w/KeySpan(Bklyn Union). [28]3-for-2,'96. [32]2-for-1,'97. [33]2-for-1,'97. [34]3-for-2,'95. [38]3-for-2,'99. [39]2-for-1,'97. [46]2-for-1,'95:To split 2-for-1,ex Jan 19,'00. [47]3-for-4 REVERSE,'99.

¶ S&P 500
\# MidCap 400
✣ SmallCap 600
• Options

Index	Ticker	Name of Issue (Call Price of Pfd. Stocks)	Market	Com. Rank. & Pfd. Rating	Inst. Hold Cos	Inst. Hold Shs. (000)	Principal Business	1971-97 High	1971-97 Low	1998 High	1998 Low	1999 High	1999 Low	Dec. Sales in 100s	Dec. 1999 Last Sale Or Bid High	Low	Last	%Div Yield	P-E Ratio	EPS 5 Yr Growth	Total Return 12 Mo	36 Mo	60 Mo
1	KNAP	✔Knape & Vogt Mfg	NNM	B	18	375	Mfr home furnishing items	22¾	1 9/16	24¾	16½	18	12	511	15⅝	13 13/16	13 13/16	4.8	11	12	-14.1	-2.3	-3.1
¶2•[1]	KRI	✔Knight-Ridder Inc	NY,B,Ch,P	A-	510	71199	Newspapers:business info svs	57⅛	1 11/16	59⅝	40½	65	46	111269	59 13/16	54⅜	59 9/16	1.5	18	20	18.5	17.8	21.1
3	KNGT	✔Knight Transportation	NNM	NR	66	6215	Trucking-gen'l commodities	21 5/16	7⅝	28½	12⅞	25	10¾	8305	18⅞	14	17⅛	...	18	25	-35.8	10.8	12.6
4	VLCCF	✔Knightsbridge Tankers	NNM	NR	..	...	Sale/leaseback shipp'g vessels	33⅜	20	30¾	18½	21⅞	11½	40970	14⅞	11½	13½	13.3	13	...	-28.2	...	...
5	NITE	✔Knight/Trimark Grp'A'	NNM	NR	171	21424	Investment mgmt svcs	...	...	13⅜	2¼	81⅝	10	776790	57½	41⅛	46	...	41	...	284	...	...
6	KE	✔Koger Equity	AS,Ch,P	B-	93	25210	Real estate investment trust	23⅜	3¼	23½	15¼	18⅝	12⅜	6236	16⅞	15 5/16	16⅞	8.3	13	26	6.8	1.7	22.2
¶7•[2]	KSS	✔Kohl's Corp	NY,Ph,P	NR	605	132596	Oper family oriented dept strs	37 11/16	3 5/16	61½	32⅜	81¼	57¼	148565	73 1/16	62 15/16	72 3/16	...	48	27	17.5	54.5	48.7
8•[3]	KOL	✔Kollmorgen Corp	NY,Ch,Ph	B-	41	6689	Motor/ctrls,elec optic instr	36¾	1 3/16	24¼	13⅜	17¼	8⅞	9060	12 5/16	8⅞	12 5/16	0.6	34	30	-18.7	4.4	17.2
✣9•[3]	KMAG	✔Komag Inc	NNM,Ch	B-	109	23847	Mfr thin film computer disks	37 7/16	3	16	2	15⅝	1 9/16	215310	4¾	2¼	3⅛	...	d	Neg	-69.9	-51.3	-24.2
10•[2]	PHG	✔Koninklijke Philips Electron NV	NY,Ch,P,Ph	NR	400	62970	World-wide mfr operations	88⅞	6	102⅞	42	136½	66⅝	81975	136½	120 5/16	135	0.7	28	46	102	52.3	38.2
11	KPT	✔Konover Property	NY,Ph,P	NR	35	1933	Real estate investment trust	29½	5⅛	10	5¾	9 3/16	4¾	8043	6 5/16	5 5/16	6 5/16	7.9	15	75	-3.5	1.0	-17.0
12	KOR	✔Koor Indus Ltd ADS[51]	NY,Ph,P	NR	39	2559	Telecommun,electr,chem,food	23¾	15	26 9/16	12½	25⅜	16	7508	21¾	18⅝	20	1.2	..	-32	17.3	8.0	...
13	KEP	✔Korea Electric Power ADS[54]	NY,Ch,Ph	NR	118	49248	Electric utility-Korea	28¼	7 7/16	22¼	6 7/16	21¾	12 1/16	121359	20 1/16	14 9/16	16¾	1.3	20	-7	8.4	-4.8	-3.5
14	KTC	✔Korea Telecom ADS[55]	NY	NR	151	54635	Telecommunications svcs, Korea	...	...	...	...	77½	27 9/16	60034	77½	50	74⅜	...	..	...	...	...	...
15	KOREA	Korea Thrunet'A'	NNM	NR	..	..	Internet services,Korea	...	...	...	...	84	18	332895	84	48½	67⅞	...	..	...	...	...	...
16•[4]	KFY	✔Korn/Ferry Intl	NY	NR	61	10343	Executive placement svcs	...	...	...	...	36⅝	11	24300	36⅝	22 13/16	36⅜	...	d	Neg	...	...	...
17	KQIP	KPNQuest N.V.'C'	NNM	NR	..	...	Fiber optic internet svcs	...	...	...	...	72⅜	20 13/16	87242	72⅜	36⅜	63¾	...	..	...	...	...	...
18	KRT	✔Kranzco Realty Trust	NY,Ph,P	NR	31	1475	Real estate investment trust	27	14	19¾	13⅜	15 5/16	7½	17563	9 1/16	7 9/16	8 13/16	14.8	44	-26	-32.1	-9.3	-3.6
19	Pr	9.75%cm Cv B-1 Pfd([59]25)	NY	NR	2	.3		26¾	18	27⅝	22 1/16	22½	15 7/16	54	17¾	15 7/16	29⅜B	8.3	..	...	...	...	...
20	KFI	✔Krause's Furniture	AS	NR	17	8651	Mfr/retail custom-crafted furn	12	½	4 7/16	11/16	3½	¾	8317	2 15/16	1¼	2⅞	...	d	Neg	70.4	30.9	-3.6
¶21•[5]	KR	✔Kroger Co	NY,B,C,Ch,Ph,P	B+	951	588570	Supermkt/convenience stores	18⅝	⅞	30⅜	17	34⅞	14⅞	1821842	22 3/16	14⅞	18⅞	...	23	12	-36.9	18.0	25.9
✣22	KRON	✔Kronos Inc	NNM	B+	177	7821	Mfr data collection systems	24 11/16	5¼	30	16 11/16	64	22¼	15775	64	48½	60	...	35	28	104	41.3	39.2
23	KRG	✔KRUG International	AS	B-	13	724	Aerospace/marine/housewares	13⅞	⅛	6½	1 9/16	2⅜	1⅛	771	1 15/16	1 5/16	1¾	...	d	Neg	7.7	-28.6	-12.1
24	KUB	✔Kubota Corp ADR[64]	NY,B,Ch,Ph	NR	9	153	Agricul mchy,pipe,Japan	195	5½	67 1/16	34¾	86½	46	305	86¼	77⅛	77½	1.2	34	-10	36.2	-5.3	-9.7
✣25•[2]	KLIC	✔Kulicke & Soffa Ind	NNM	↓C	184	14502	Equip to mfr semiconductors	58⅝	1/16	29⅝	9⅜	45¼	17⅝	160370	45¼	31½	42 9/16	...	d	Neg	140	30.8	32.3
26	KYO	✔Kyocera Corp[65] ADR	NY,B,Ch,P	NR	54	9955	Ceramic products,elec/other	92	5/16	58	39 13/16	280 15/16	44⅝	18060	280 15/16	112	262	0.2	..	-11	408	63.9	29.6
27	LLL	✔L-3 Communications Hldgs	NY,Ph	NR	171	16744	Communication systems/pds	...	...	49½	22	54¼	34¼	35501	45½	36⅜	41⅝	...	27	...	-10.6	...	...
✣28•[6]	LZB	✔La-Z Boy	NY,Ch,P,Ph	A	189	27208	Mfr of reclining chairs	14 15/16	⅜	22⅝	14 1/16	24⅝	15⅝	23814	19⅝	15 7/16	16 13/16	1.9	12	18	-4.1	22.0	12.1
29	LB	✔LaBarge Inc	AS,Ch,P	B	13	2082	Mfr electronic devices/cable	10⅞	⅜	5¾	2 9/16	3½	1	16591	2 7/16	1 1/16	2 3/16	...	d	Neg	-18.6	-28.1	13.0
30	LABS	✔LabOne Inc	NNM	B-	47	5775	Insurance/hlth testing labs	32 9/16	2⅜	16 11/16	9 5/16	12¾	5⅞	6012	7⅞	5⅞	6⅞	10.5	19	NM	-34.4	...	...
31	LAB	✔LaBranche & Co	NY	NR	30	7522	Invest/finance svcs NYSE	...	...	...	...	14⅞	9 1/16	19261	13 5/16	9 1/16	12¾	...	..	...	...	...	...
✣32	LRW	✔Labor Ready	NY	NR	167	13296	Temp workers construction	11 7/16	1 15/16	27	6¾	28 7/16	9 5/16	76906	14 15/16	11 11/16	12⅛	...	18	86	-6.2	45.7	...
33	LBC	✔Laboratorio Chile ADS[66]	NY,Ch,Ph,P	NR	32	1551	Mfr,dstr pharmaceutical prod	32⅛	11	23	8½	19⅞	11	9723	18½	16¾	17⅝B	4.8	..	...	30.2	7.1	-0.6
34	LH	✔Laboratory Corp Amer Hldgs	NY,Ch,Ph,P	C	74	22544	Clinical lab svcs in U.S.	30⅞	1 5/16	2¾	1⅛	3⅞	1¼	70024	3¾	3 1/16	3 11/16	...	53	40	168	8.6	-22.5
35	PrA	8.50%cmCv[67]Ex Pfd([68]52.83)	NY	B+	41	3225		59¼	42	58½	40	70	41¼	2935	70	60	69	6.2	..	...	...	...	...
36	PrB	8.50%cmCv[69]'PIK'Pfd([70]52.83)	NY	B+	4	188		60½	44	57	40	70	41	60	70	62¾	67⅛B	6.3	..	...	...	...	...
37	LG	✔Laclede Gas	NY,Ch,Ph	B	104	5746	Distr nat gas in St. Louis	28⅝	2 15/16	27 15/16	22⅜	27	20	6435	23	20	21⅝	6.2	15	2	-14.4	1.9	7.7
38	LDSH	✔Ladish Co	NNM	NR	39	8037	Produce jet engine components	...	...	16⅛	5⅜	8 15/16	5 13/16	7804	7	5⅞	6⅜	...	10	...	-23.9	...	...
39•[6]	LAF	✔Lafarge Corp	NY,B,Ch,Mo,Ph,P	B+	218	31048	Major cement producer	34 9/16	6¾	42⅛	23¾	40¾	25 11/16	33450	27¾	25 11/16	27⅝	2.2	8	24	-30.4	13.0	11.2
40•[7]	LDW	✔Laidlaw Inc	NY,Ch,Ph	B	251	130934	Waste mgmt/transport'n svc	24⅝	2 1/16	16⅝	8⅝	10½	5 1/16	404349	5 13/16	5 1/16	5¼	◆3.7	d	Neg	-45.6	-20.9	-5.6
41	UXL	Laidlaw One 5.75% Ex Nts 2000	NY	...[73]	2	137	Subsid of Laidlaw Inc	54 9/16	21¼	45 1/16	20	38 9/16	29 7/16	2	36½	35½	34½B	3.5	..	...	35.2	-2.3	...
42	LHP	✔Lakehead Pipe Line Ptnrs L.P.	NY,Ch,Ph,P	NR	71	3080	Own/oper oil&gas pipeline sys	47⅞	20⅞	54	43	48¾	32¼	23810	37 7/16	32¼	34 13/16	10.1	13	7	-22.1	8.1	14.6
43•[3]	LRCX	✔Lam Research	NNM,Ch	C	261	33249	Mfrs plasma etching equip	73⅜	2	33	8⅜	112½	18 1/16	263204	112½	78⅛	111 9/16	...	d	Neg	526	58.3	24.5
44	LAMR	✔Lamar Advertising 'A'	NNM	NR	253	37896	Outdoor advertising	28 5/16	10 11/16	41½	19¼	64½	27¾	42310	64½	56¼	60 9/16	...	d	Neg	62.6	55.6	...
45	LMS	✔Lamson & Sessions	NY,Ch,Ph,P	B-	44	6805	Mfr PVC electr prod/other	21¼	1¾	7⅞	3⅞	6 15/16	4 5/16	4787	5⅜	4 5/16	4⅞	...	7	NM	-4.9	-12.4	-4.1
46	LFL	✔Lan Chile ADS[76]	NY	NR	15	1910	Domestic,Int'l air svc, Chile	14⅛	12	14 11/16	2½	8 11/16	3½	5802	7 9/16	6 11/16	7 9/16	e1.2	12	...	63.5	...	...
#47•[8]	LANC	✔Lancaster Colony	NNM	A+	199	17571	Mfr food/auto prod	38½	5/16	45⅜	24 1/16	37	24 11/16	28432	35	29½	33⅛	1.9	14	9	5.1	4.4	13.0
#48	LNCE	✔Lance, Inc	NNM	B-	100	10857	Snack foods:vending	28¼	1⅝	26⅞	18	20½	9	27342	10 13/16	9	10	9.6	13	91	-46.3	-13.3	-6.2
49	LAN	✔Lancer Corp	AS	B+	29	1778	Mfr beverage dispensing sys	17⅝	1 1/16	18¼	8⅞	12 15/16	4	7012	5⅞	4	4⅝	...	d	Neg	-58.0	-30.1	-2.4
50•[9]	LFG	✔Landamerica Financial Grp	NY	NR	133	10008	Title insurance svcs	33 11/16	5 5/16	65	31	58 15/16	15⅝	10846	19¾	15 5/16	18⅜	1.1	5	33	-66.8	-1.5	12.8

Uniform Footnote Explanations-See Page 4. Other: [1]Ph:Cycle 1. [2]CBOE:Cycle 1. [3]P:Cycle 3. [4]P:Cycle 2. [5]ASE,CBOE,P:Cycle 1. [6]Ph:Cycle 2. [7]ASE:Cycle 3. [8]CBOE:Cycle 3. [9]ASE,P:Cycle 3. [51]Ea ADS rep 0.20 Ord Shrs, NIS 0.001. [52]Approx. [53]Excl $14.3M Deferred shrs. [54]Ea ADS rep 0.5 com,5,000 Won. [55]Ea ADS rep 0.5 shr,W5,000. [56]To be determined. [57]Incl $0.21218 return of cap,'98. [58]Incl current amts. [59]Fr 6-3-2002 re-spec cond. [60]1.338 to 6-3-2000:1.374 to 6-3-2001:then 1.41. [61]Fr 6-4-98 thru 6-3-99 (or earlier Re-spec cond). [62]Special dstr. [63]Fiscal Dec'98 & prior. [64]ADR's equal 20 com shrs,par 50 Yen. [65]ADR's equal to 1 com par 50 yen. [66]Ea ADS rep 20 com no par. [67]Co opt fr 6-30-2000exch for$50amt8.5%Cv2012. [68]Fr 7-7-2000,scale to $50 in 2006. [69]Pay In Kind. [70]Fr 6-30-2000,scale to $50 in 2006. [71]Payable in Pfd stk to 6-30-2003. [72]Fr 6-30-2000. [73]Rated BBB+r by S&P. [74]Exchangeable Notes. [75]Fiscal Oct'96 & prior. [76]Ea ADS rep 5 com shrs,no par.

Index	Cash Divs. Ea.Yr. Since	Latest Payment Period $	Date	Ex. Div.	Total $ So Far 1999	Ind. Rate	Paid 1998	Cash& Equiv.	Curr. Assets	Curr. Liab.	Balance Sheet Date	Lg Trm Debt Mil-$	Shs. 000 Pfd.	Com.	End	1995	1996	1997	1998	1999	Last 12 Mos.	Interim Period	1998	1999	Index
1	1934	Q0.16½	12-3-99	11-9	0.66	0.66	0.66	1.80	36.2	19.2	10-02-99	21.1	...	±4272	Je	±1.40	±0.01	v±1.33	±vd1.64	v±1.24	1.30	3 Mo Sep	v±0.42	v±0.48	1
2◆	1941	Q0.23	11-22-99	11-8	0.89	0.92	0.80	31.7	512	571	9-26-99	1173	1374	83937	Dc	□v1.67	v2.75	v4.08	v3.73	E3.31	3.14	9 Mo Sep	v2.90	v2.31	2
3◆	....	None Since Public			...	Nil	....	0.52	28.5	30.4	9-30-99	6.51	...	15115	Dc	v0.43	v0.52	v0.67	v0.87	....	0.97	9 Mo Sep	v0.64	v0.74	3
4	1997	0.45	11-10-99	10-22	1.80	1.80	2.36	0.31	17.3	9.03	12-31-98	127	...	17100	Dc	...	...	n/a	v1.02	....	1.02				4
5◆	....	None Since Public			...	Nil	....	Total Assets $534M			9-30-99	....	...	111435	Dc	...	...	pv0.34	vp0.53	....	1.12	9 Mo Sep	v0.36	v0.95	5
6	1997	Q0.35	2-3-00	12-29	1.30	1.40	1.10	Total Assets $840.62M			9-30-99	306	...	26758	Dc	v1.61	□v0.54	v□0.96	v1.10	....	1.32	9 Mo Sep	v0.83	v1.05	6
7◆	....	None Since Public			...	Nil	....	36.0	1367	643	10-30-99	495	...	163025	Ja	v0.49	v0.68	v0.91	v1.18	E1.51↑	1.40	9 Mo Oct	v0.60	v0.82	7
8	1943	Q0.02	12-1-99	11-16	0.08	0.08	0.08	6.60	102	77.7	9-30-99	50.9	...	10308	Dc	v0.26	v0.86	v1.90	v□1.40	....	0.36	9 Mo Sep	v1.04	vNil	8
9◆	....	None Since Public			...	Nil	....	83.8	163	358	10-03-99	2.12	...	65449	Dc	v2.14	v2.07	vd0.42	vd6.89	Ed1.30	d5.05	9 Mo Sep	vd6.56	vd4.72	9
10	1994	0.924	4-14-99	3-26	0.924	0.92	0.826	14441	35852	19626	j12-31-98	6140	...	368495	Dc	□4.91	v□1.21	vΔ4.65	vΔ18.07	E4.90	17.00	9 Mo Sep	v4.48	v3.41	10
11	1999	0.12½	12-30-99	12-13	0.50	0.50	....	Total Assets $688.27M			9-30-99	316	792	30869	Dc	vd1.11	□vd0.54	□vd0.04	v0.14	....	0.41	9 Mo Sep	vd0.05	v0.22	11
12	1996	[52]0.096	1-24-00	12-22	0.33	0.23	0.452	513	2226	1443	12-31-97	540	...	[53]15897	Dc	2.24	v2.35	v1.75	Pv0.15	....	0.15				12
13	1995	[52]0.223		12-28	0.202	0.22	0.139	406	2425	5966	12-31-98	16731	...	628220	Dc	1.11	0.65	v0.21	v0.82	....	0.82				13
14	....	[52]0.198		12-29	...	[56]...	....	804	2507	2850	12-31-98	p3048	...	★312200	Dc	...	...	...	v0.28	....	0.28				14
15	....	None Since Public			...	Nil	....	53.9	63.6	58.4	6-30-99	185	...	★65917	Dc	...	...	...	vd0.13	....	....	6 Mo Jun	n/a	vd0.26	15
16	....	None Since Public			...	Nil	....	125	224	101	10-31-99	3.53	...	36047	Ap	v0.27	v0.36	v0.40	v0.23	vd2.37	d2.09	6 Mo Oct	v0.05	v0.33	16
17	....	None Since Public			...	Nil	....	48.6	247	84.7	p3-31-99	★804	...	±★444000	Dc	...	...	...	vpd0.14		....	3 Mo Mar	n/a	vpd0.03	17
18	1993	Q0.32½	1-21-00	12-23	1.76½	1.30	[57]1.92	Total Assets $539M			9-30-99	[58]353	3083	10563	Dc	v0.91	v□0.75	v□0.73	v0.37	....	0.20	9 Mo Sep	v0.52	v0.35	18
19	1997	0.609	1-20-00	12-23	2.438	2.438	2.438	Cv into[60]1.304 com[61]				....	310			...	...	...	....	....	....				19
20	....	None Paid			...	Nil	....	0.08	26.9	25.4	10-31-99	20.9	...	22050	Ja	vd2.21	vd1.28	vd0.39	vd0.24	....	d0.25	9 Mo Oct	vd0.22	vd0.23	20
21◆	....	†[62]10.00	12-2-88	12-5	...	Nil	....	283	5597	6299	11-06-99	7863	...	834337	Ja	v□0.64	v□0.68	v□0.85	v□[63]0.85	E0.84↓	1.04	9 Mo Oct	v□0.27	v□0.46	21
22◆	....	None Since Public			...	Nil	....	41.0	125	104	9-30-99	....	...	12443	Sp	0.69	0.91	0.89	v1.15	v1.71	1.71				22
23◆	....	Wrrt	1-31-95	2-1	...	Nil	....	4.45	15.1	12.1	9-30-99	2.09	...	4976	Mr	v0.23	v0.40	v0.05	vd1.71	....	d1.30	6 Mo Sep	vd0.56	vd0.15	23
24	1949	0.489	12-17-99	9-27	0.909	0.91	0.79	893	6226	4265	3-31-99	2200	...	1409655	Mr	3.17	v3.04	v2.16	v1.68	....	2.30	6 Mo Sep	v0.34	v0.96	24
25◆	....	0.02	7-8-85	6-10	...	Nil	....	39.3	261	94.0	9-30-99	....	...	23569	Sp	2.38	0.60	v1.79	vd0.23	vd0.72	d0.72				25
26◆	1960	0.247	12-15-99	9-28	0.455	0.46	0.39½	1748	5203	2129	3-31-99	306	...	190318	Mr	4.10	v1.96	v1.86	v1.26	....	1.26				26
27	....	None Since Public			...	Nil	....	70.8	582	311	9-30-99	605	...	32769	Dc	...	...	pv0.43	v1.26	....	1.57	9 Mo Sep	v0.75	v1.06	27
28◆	1963	Q0.08	12-10-99	11-17	0.32	0.32	0.30	12.7	448	141	10-23-99	121	...	52143	Ap	v0.67	v0.71	v0.83	v0.93	v1.24	1.45	6 Mo Oct	v0.48	v0.69	28
29	....	0.03	11-2-84	10-1	...	Nil	....	0.94	28.9	16.3	10-03-99	19.4	...	14741	Je	v0.09	v0.23	v0.49	v0.30	vd0.20	d0.36	3 Mo Sep	v0.07	vd0.09	29
30◆	1924	Q0.18	12-7-99	11-26	0.76	0.72	0.80	1.56	31.0	11.6	9-30-99	25.2	...	11533	Dc	vd0.76	vd0.51	vd1.05	v0.52	....	0.37	9 Mo Sep	v0.38	v0.23	30
31	....	None Since Public			...	Nil	....	Total Assets $465M			9-30-99	186	...	45875	Dc	...	...	...	pv0.69	....	....	9 Mo Sep	n/a	vp0.35	31
32◆	....	None Paid			...	Nil	....	14.4	148	50.4	10-01-99	6.62	6486	42786	Dc	v0.07	v□0.05	v0.17	v0.46	....	0.68	9 Mo Sep	v0.28	v□0.50	32
33	1994	0.282	12-13-99	11-23	0.839	0.84	0.739	10.2	103	86.4	12-31-97	52.5	...	316000	Dc	0.25	0.76	v0.81	n/a	....	....	3 Mo Mar	v0.24	v0.36	33
34	....	Wrrt	4-28-95		...	Nil	....	19.7	501	260	9-30-99	511	11190	128780	Dc	v□d0.03	vd1.25	vd1.06	v0.20	E0.07	0.31	9 Mo Sep	vNil	v0.11	34
35	1997	Q1.06¼	12-31-99	12-15	4.25	4.25	4.25	Cv into 18.1818 com				....	4363	...	Dc	...	...	...	....	....	....	Mand redm 6-30-2012 $50			35
36	1997	Q1.06¼	12-31-99	12-15	4.25	[71]4.25	4.25	Cv into 18.1818 com[72]				....	6410	...	Dc	...	...	...	....	....	....	Mand redm 6-30-2012 $50			36
37◆	1946	Q0.33½	1-3-00	12-8	1.34	1.34	1.32	11.5	113	108	6-30-99	204	78	18878	Sp	1.27	1.87	v1.84	v1.58	Pv1.43	1.43				37
38	....	None Since Public			...	Nil	....	1.55	79.4	40.2	3-31-99	8.51	...	13906	Dc	...	...	pv1.39	v1.55	....	0.66	9 Mo Sep	v1.33	v0.44	38
39	1983	Q0.15	12-1-99	11-9	0.60	0.60	0.51	222	1148	565	9-30-99	737	4900	68446	Dc	v1.82	v1.95	v2.54	v3.24	....	3.63	9 Mo Sep	v2.33	v2.72	39
40	1969	gQ0.07	11-15-99	10-28	g0.28	0.28	g0.28	265	564	459	8-31-99	3113	547	330210	Au	±0.48	v±0.55	v±1.92	v±1.05	v±d3.39	d3.39				40
41	1996	Q0.306	12-1-99	11-10	1.222	1.22	1.222	Exch for com U.S.Filter(or cash)re-spec cond				....	...	[74]★2966	Au	...	...	...	....	....	....	Mature 12-31-2000			41
42	1992	Q0.87½	11-12-99	10-27	3.48½	3.50	3.36	53.8	108	49.9	9-30-99	775	...	±28903	Dc	v1.60	v2.11	v3.02	v3.07	....	2.70	9 Mo Sep	v2.43	v2.06	42
43	....	None Since Public			...	Nil	....	314	793	266	9-26-99	327	...	39441	Je	3.27	vd3.95	vd0.83	vd3.80	vd2.93	d1.65	3 Mo Sep	vd0.70	v0.58	43
44◆	....	None Since Public			...	Nil	....	10.7	135	98.3	9-30-99	1594	...	±87851	Dc	v0.21	v[75]0.25	v0.05	vd0.24	....	d0.45	9 Mo Sep	vd0.09	v□d0.30	44
45	....	0.05	12-10-85	11-18	...	Nil	....	1.12	99.0	58.9	10-02-99	43.4	...	13453	Dc	v0.90	v0.02	□vd0.35	v0.50	....	0.69	9 Mo Sep	v0.42	v0.61	45
46	1998	0.093	5-26-99	5-7	†0.132	0.09	0.229	25.2	250	235	12-31-97	109	...	318909	Dc	0.09	0.13	n/a	Pv0.49	....	0.64	9 Mo Sep	v0.31	v0.46	46
47◆	1963	Q0.16	12-31-99	12-8	0.61	0.64	0.57	5.07	352	141	9-30-99	3.28	...	40025	Je	1.57	v1.71	v2.01	v2.22	v2.28	2.36	3 Mo Sep	v0.48	v0.56	47
48	1945	Q0.24	11-15-99	11-3	0.96	0.96	0.96	4.15	88.8	38.6	9-25-99	63.3	...	29958	Dc	vd0.23	v0.82	v1.00	v0.92	....	0.80	9 Mo Sep	v0.75	v0.63	48
49◆	....	None Since Public			...	Nil	....	0.60	60.5	37.5	9-30-99	16.0	...	9125	Dc	v0.46	v0.63	v0.65	v0.63	....	d0.49	9 Mo Sep	v0.66	vd0.46	49
50	1993	Q0.05	12-15-99	11-29	0.20	0.20	0.20	Total Assets $1662.18M			9-30-99	208	2200	13986	Dc	v1.89	v4.01	v2.84	v5.05	....	3.52	9 Mo Sep	v3.61	v2.08	50

◆**Stock Splits & Divs By Line Reference Index** [2]2-for-1,'96. [3]3-for-2,'98. [5]2-for-1,'99. [7]2-for-1,'96,'98. [9]2-for-1,'96. [21]2-for-1,'97,'99. [22]3-for-2,'96,'99. [23]10%,'94. [25]2-for-1,'95. [26]2-for-1,'98. [28]3-for-1,'98. [30]No adj for stk dstr SLH Corp'97:3-for-2,'99. [32]3-for-2,'96,'97,'98,'99. [37]2-for-1,'94. [44]3-for-2,'98. [47]4-for-3,'94:3-for-2,'98. [49]3-for-2,'95,'96,'97.

¶ S&P 500 # MidCap 400 ✤ SmallCap 600 • Options

Index	Ticker	Name of Issue (Call Price of Pfd. Stocks)	Market	Com. Rank. & Pfd. Rating	Inst. Hold Cos	Inst. Hold Shs. (000)	Principal Business	Price Range 1971-97 High	1971-97 Low	1998 High	1998 Low	1999 High	1999 Low	Dec. Sales in 100s	December, 1999 Last Sale Or Bid High	Low	Last	%Div Yield	P-E Ratio	% Annualized EPS 5 Yr Growth	Total Return 12 Mo	36 Mo	60 Mo
1	LDR	✓Landauer Inc	AS,Ch	B+	80	4955	Provides radiation monitor svc	28⅜	4 9/16	32⅜	23¾	32¾	20 9/16	3868	24 15/16	20 9/16	21⅞	6.4	20	3	−28.9	1.2	11.2
✤2•[1]	LNY	✓Landry's Seafood Restaurants	NY	NR	109	11201	Oper seafood restaurants	34⅝	6	31 11/16	5 3/16	10⅞	4⅝	25196	9½	7 15/16	8 11/16	...	d	Neg	15.8	−25.9	−9.2
#3•[2]	LE	✓Lands' End	NY,Ch,Ph,P	B	187	8558	Mkts men/women's apparel	38½	4 7/16	44¼	15⅝	83½	23¾	86064	62⅜	33¾	34¾	...	24	7	29.0	9.5	20.4
✤4•[3]	LSTR	✓Landstar System	NNM	NR	177	9049	Transport'n svcs/trucking	37¾	12¼	45⅝	21 1/16	47⅝	31 11/16	11302	47⅝	33 1/16	42 13/16	...	11	7	5.1	22.6	5.5
5	LR	✓Lanier Worldwide	NY	NR	..	...	Mkt office equip/supplies	....	....	....	....	6½	2⅝	426852	4⅜	2⅝	3⅞	...	8	...	...	...	...
6	LNOP	LanOptics Ltd	NNM	NR	4	315	Mfr local area netwk products	24¼	3 11/16	4 11/16	1	8¼	1 7/16	8999	7⅛	5½	5 13/16	...	d	Neg	221	−7.6	−6.5
7	LHO	✓LaSalle Hotel Properties	NY,Ph	NR	73	7125	Real-estate investment trust	....	....	18 9/16	7½	16⅛	10½	12768	12⅜	10 13/16	11 11/16	13.0	11	...	26.3	...	...
8	LSH	✓LaSalle Re Holdings	NY	NR	60	10570	Prop & casualty reinsurance	36⅛	19¼	42 15/16	19½	22½	10⅞	24412	16¾	12	16½	...	d	...	−18.9	−10.1	...
9	LMM	✓Laser Mortgage Mgmt	NY	NR	15	7319	Real estate investment trust	15	13 9/16	17⅝	3½	5¾	3⅛	5570	4 1/16	3⅝	4 1/16	...	d	...	15.2	...	...
10	LSR	Laser Technology	AS,Ch	B−	5	337	Mfr laser speed/distance instr	8½	2⅜	5 15/16	2⅞	2 7/16	1⅛	4997	1½	1 3/16	1⅜	...	d	−34	−57.7	−29.2	−14.4
✤11•[2]	LVCI	✓Laser Vision Centers	NNM	C	134	14872	Laser equip/advertising	8 7/16	1¾	11 7/16	3¼	37 13/16	7 13/16	200757	15⅛	9 9/16	10 9/16	...	22	NM	−4.2	58.1	21.9
12	LSCP	✓Laserscope	NNM	C	16	3224	Mfr surgical laser systems	31½	1⅜	5⅜	15/16	2¾	⅝	38024	1⅝	11/16	1	...	d	−26	−44.6	−46.3	−23.2
13	LASE	✓Lasersight Inc	NNM	NR	37	2982	Dgn/dvlp laser systems	18	2⅜	8	1 9/16	20⅜	3⅞	70880	15⅜	7 3/16	10	...	d	Neg	105	15.4	−4.2
14	LSO	✓LASMO plc ADS[52]	NY,P	NR	9	903	Oil & gas explor,dvlp,prod'n	14⅝	4⅝	14½	4⅞	8 9/16	4½	2905	6⅜	5½	6¼	1.8	d	26	18.5	−18.6	−0.2
✤15	LSON	✓Lason Inc	NNM	NR	236	18085	Records/document mgmt svcs	30⅛	14	64⅝	25⅛	68¼	9¾	416335	25 7/16	9¾	11	...	15	...	−81.1	−18.7	...
✤16•[2]	LSCC	✓Lattice Semiconductor	NNM	B+	277	42662	Mkt program'ble logic devices	37¼	1⅝	28½	9 7/16	54⅜	18⅞	139383	54⅜	42⅛	47⅛	...	d	Neg	107	27.3	41.5
17•[1]	EL	✓Lauder (Estee) Co	NY	NR	303	67312	Mfr,mkt skin care,fragrance pd	28 3/16	13	43¼	23 5/16	56½	37¼	92362	51 7/16	40¼	50 7/16	0.4	47	20	20.2	27.0	...
18	ECT	Laud(Est)Co 6.25%'TRACES'2001	NY	NR	13	618	Trust Auto Com Exch Secur	....	....	78¼	49 15/16	96½	68½	1484	87⅝	71⅛	86 9/16	4.4	..	...	17.2	...	...
19	ECJ	Laud(Est)Co 6.25%'TRACES'2002	NY	NR	12	601	Trust Automatic Com Exch Secs	....	....	....	....	103	74½	906	96	78 9/16	94¾	5.7	..	...	...	...	...
20	LAUN	✓Launch Media	NNM	NR	30	2608	Internet-based music svcs	....	....	....	....	36 1/16	7⅞	34557	21⅜	16⅜	18 15/16	...	..	...	...	...	...
21	LD	✓Laurentian Bank, Canada	To	BI	5	750	General banking, Quebec	32	9 1/16	38	22⅝	29¾	17⅛	10449	19½	17⅛	17¾	5.2	9	33	36.4	0.3	7.4
✤22	LAWS	✓Lawson Products	NNM	B+	88	3783	Dstr fasteners, maint parts	35¼	11/16	31⅞	20¼	28⅛	20⅝	5230	23¾	22¼	23⅛	2.6	12	4	3.0	4.1	−0.2
23	LKI	✓Lazare Kaplan Intl	AS	B−	38	2444	Cutter/merchant diamonds	27	2¾	13⅝	6½	11¼	6⅞	1479	8⅛	7⅛	8⅛	...	d	Neg	16.1	−22.0	−3.1
#24•[4]	LEA	✓Lear Corp	NY,Ph,P	NR	380	62346	Mfr auto/light truck seat sys	51 11/16	15½	57¾	29 13/16	53 15/16	28¾	71007	33⅝	28¾	32	...	9	8	−16.9	−2.1	10.1
25	LTRE	✓Learning Tree Intl	NNM	NR	78	9237	Provides educat'n/train'g svcs	48⅝	8	29¾	7 9/16	32⅝	6	27600	32⅝	22⅜	28	...	49	NM	209	−1.7	...
26	LTWO	✓Learn2.com Inc	NNM	NR	42	3089	Dvp entertainment/educ softwr	22⅝	1⅜	12⅝	1¼	10	2¼	614779	5¾	3	3¼	...	d	−1	23.5	−4.4	−9.0
27	TLF	✓Leather Factory	AS	NR	1	33	Mfr,dstr leather products	7⅝	½	⅝	⅛	1⅛	¼	1334	1	13/16	13/16	...	27	−31	225	0.0	−28.2
28	LECT	LecTec Corp	NNM	C	12	374	Mfr medical electrodes/tapes	16	2 9/16	5¾	2⅛	4¾	1 3/16	3074	2 5/16	1 3/16	1⅝	...	d	Neg	−38.1	−39.3	−25.9
#29	LEE	✓Lee Enterprises	NY,Ch	A−	178	21749	Newspaper publish:radio,TV	30½	9/16	33⅞	21 13/16	32¼	26⅛	9095	32¼	27 11/16	31 15/16	2.0	21	7	3.5	13.4	15.5
#30•[2]	LGTO	✓Legato Systems	NNM	NR	383	64346	Network storage mgmt sftwr	12	2⅜	33⅞	9¼	82½	15 1/16	336182	82½	65½	68 13/16	...	..	56	109	104	...
#31•[5]	LM	✓Legg Mason Inc	NY,B,Ph	A	241	34015	Regional securities broker	28⅛	1 15/16	32¼	17 5/16	42⅞	26 7/16	29089	36¼	32 15/16	36¼	0.9	21	35	15.8	37.2	37.1
¶32•[4]	LEG	✓Leggett & Platt	NY,Ch,P,Ph	A	383	107821	Mfr springs,etc for furn,bed	23⅞	⅛	28¾	16⅞	28 9/16	18⅝	79882	22	19 15/16	21 7/16	1.7	15	16	−1.0	9.1	21.7
33	SXT	Lehman Br Gl Tel'SUNS' 2000	AS	NR	..	...	Stock Upside Note Sec	28½	20½	29¾	22⅛	29	23¼	221	29	25½	28⅜	3.5	..	...	14.5	23.0	20.3
¶34•[6]	LEH	✓Lehman Br Holdings	NY,P	NR	604	71472	Investment banking svcs	56½	13¾	85	22⅜	85 9/16	43 13/16	132802	85 9/16	76⅜	84 11/16	0.4	11	49	93.4	40.1	42.8
35	LEQ	Lehman Br Hldg 8.30%'QUICS'	NY	....[54]	4	7	Qtly Income Capital Securities	26¾	23⅞	26⅝	22	25⅞	21⅝	4904	24 9/16	21⅝	22¼	9.3	..	...	−4.4	4.4	...
36	YCS	Lehman Br Hldg 5.0%'YEELDS'	AS	NR	4	21	Yld Enhanced Eq Link Debt Sec	....	....	86	61¼	94⅛	81½	263	94⅛	92¼	93¾	3.5	..	...	14.2	...	...
37	LPHL	✓Leisureplanet Holdings	NNM	NR	3	31	Internet travel/leisure svcs	9	2⅞	8	¾	16½	15/16	96171	16½	6½	12½	...	d	Neg	1234	47.8	...
38•[7]	LEN	✓Lennar Corp	NY,B,Ch,P,Ph	A−	223	29423	Bldr residential communities	44 11/16	¼	36 3/16	14⅞	27⅞	13 1/16	66136	17 3/16	15⅝	16¼	0.3	6	8	−35.5	...	...
39	LII	✓Lennox Intl	NY	NR	25	7294	Mfr climate control sys	....	....	....	....	19⅞	8⅞	50085	11 7/16	8⅞	9 3/16	3.7	6	...	...	...	...
40•[8]	LHSP	✓Lernout & Hauspie Speech Pds	NNM	NR	83	8484	Computer software svcs	29 7/16	5½	68	21 9/16	49 3/16	25¾	139947	49 3/16	37	46¼	...	63	NM	41.8	76.8	...
41	LUK	✓Leucadia National	NY,Ch,P,Ph	B	144	19830	Consumer finance,life insur	36⅝	1/16	41⅛	26¼	33⅜	20⅛	26003	23⅜	20½	23⅛	e6.8	6	18	...	...	...
42•[9]	LVLT	✓Level 3 Communications	NNM	NR	250	58249	Telecom/informat'n svcs	....	....	44	22⅜	100⅛	38	322069	85 3/16	65 5/16	81⅞	...	d	...	89.9	...	...
43	LXP	✓Lexington Corporate Prop Tr	NY	NR	57	3406	Real estate investment trust	16 13/16	8¼	16⅜	10 13/16	12⅞	8 13/16	10993	10⅜	8 13/16	9 3/16	13.1	9	16	−18.7	−8.1	9.0
¶44•[10]	LXK	✓Lexmark Intl Group'A'	NY,P	NR	697	114434	Mfr laser & inkjet printers	19	6 11/16	51	17½	104	42 1/16	257414	95⅛	71⅜	90½	...	40	NM	80.3	87.2	...
#45•[9]	LGE	✓LG&E Energy	NY,B,Ch,P,Ph	B	260	31408	Hldg co:Gas & Elec	25⅞	4 13/16	29 9/16	22½	28¾	17⅜	58801	20 9/16	17⅜	17 7/16	7.3	11	Neg	−35.0	−6.9	1.4
46•[10]	LHSG	✓LHS Group	NNM	NR	56	10910	Computer software/svcs	32⅞	8	76½	25½	59⅛	21	35500	29¼	23⅝	24 9/16	...	41	70	−52.4	...	...
✤47	LBY	✓Libbey Inc	NY,P	NR	149	14846	Produce glass tableware	42¼	11⅞	39½	28¼	33¾	24	7459	29	26 1/16	28¾	1.0	11	−6	0.3	2.0	11.6
48	LBRT	✓Liberate Technologies	NNM	NR	61	4771	Internet delivery software pd	....	....	....	....	297	14⅝	93383	297	116½	257	...	...	...	...	...	...
49	LBI	✓Liberte Investors	NY,B,Ch,P,Ph	NR	21	2100	Invest in first mtg/cons'tr nts	35 13/16	⅜	4¼	2⅝	3⅞	3	10928	3 7/16	3	3 7/16	e...	43	NM	3.6	−7.8	15.0
50	LC	✓Liberty Corp	NY,Ch,P,Ph	B+	90	7695	Insurance hldg: TV: S&L	47 5/16	1 13/16	52 15/16	36¼	54 9/16	39 13/16	3986	45¾	39 13/16	42 3/16	2.1	12	7	−12.8	4.3	12.9

Uniform Footnote Explanations-See Page 4. Other: [1]CBOE:Cycle 1. [2]CBOE:Cycle 3. [3]Ph:Cycle 1. [4]ASE:Cycle 3. [5]CBOE:Cycle 2. [6]ASE,CBOE,P:Cycle 1. [7]ASE:Cycle 2. [8]ASE,CBOE,P,Ph:Cycle 3. [9]Ph:Cycle 3. [10]CBOE,Ph:Cycle 1. [51]To be determined. [52]Ea ADS rep 3 ord,25p. [53]Re-spec cond. [54]Rated BBB+ by S&P. [55]Incl curr amts. [56]Stk dstr of HomeFed Corp. [57]Incl current amts. [58]Subsid Pfd. [59]Spl div.

Index	Cash Divs. Ea. Yr. Since	Dividends: Latest Payment Period $	Date	Ex. Div.	Total $ So Far 1999	Ind. Rate	Paid 1998	Financial Position Mil-$: Cash& Equiv.	Curr. Assets	Curr. Liab.	Balance Sheet Date	Capitalization: Lg Trm Debt Mil-$	Shs. 000 Pfd.	Com.	Earnings $ Per Shr. Years End	1995	1996	1997	1998	1999	Last 12 Mos.	Interim Earnings Period	$ per Shr. 1998	1999	Index
1	1990	Q0.35	1-14-00	12-21	1.40	1.40	1.30	3.62	16.9	18.0	6-30-99	....	...	8658	Sp	1.19	v1.26	v1.39	v1.47	Pv1.09	1.09				1
2◆	....	None Since Public			...	Nil	....	26.4	60.0	101	9-30-99	....	...	24824	Dc	0.55	v0.06	v1.03	v□0.10	....	d0.28	9 Mo Sep	v□0.88	v0.50	2
3◆	....	0.10	12-29-93	11-30	...	Nil	....	8.09	317	200	10-29-99	....	...	30149	Ja	v0.89	v1.53	v2.00	v1.01	....	1.47	9 Mo Oct	v0.18	v0.64	3
4	....	None Since Public			...	Nil	....	30.0	237	162	9-25-99	35.6	...	9530	Dc	v1.94	v1.47	v1.96	v1.07	E4.05	3.97	9 Mo Sep	v0.05	v2.95	4
5	....	Plan qtly div			...	[51]....	....	18.2	590	434	p7-02-99	546	...	79150	Je	...	...	...	....	pv0.50	0.50				5
6	....	None Since Public			...	Nil	....	7.88	16.5	5.19	12-31-98	....	...	5697	Dc	0.70	vd0.62	vd0.76	vd2.35	....	d1.82	9 Mo Sep	vd1.56	vd1.03	6
7	1998	Q0.38	1-14-00	12-29	1.51	1.52	0.63½	Total Assets $534M			9-30-99	248	...	15421	Dc	...	...	pv0.90	vp1.15	....	1.05	9 Mo Sep	vp1.01	v0.91	7
8	1996	Div Omitted 9-30-99			1.12½	Nil	3.00	Equity per shr $23.39			9-30-98	....	3000	15179	Sp	n/a	5.40	v5.14	v2.80	Pvd0.61	d0.61				8
9	1998	Div Omitted 6-23-99			†2.00	Nil	†2.32	Total Assets $208.7M			9-30-99	....	...	14861	Dc	...	...	n/a	vd4.16	....	d2.33	9 Mo Sep	vd2.68	vd0.85	9
10	....	None Paid			...	Nil	....	1.05	8.52	1.16	6-30-99	0.15	...	4995	Sp	0.14	v0.15	v0.10	v0.15	....	d0.17	9 Mo Jun	v0.15	vd0.17	10
11◆	....	None Paid			...	Nil	....	61.2	81.3	18.2	10-31-99	7.26	3	25205	Ap	d0.41	d0.88	vd0.73	vd0.20	v0.27	0.49	6 Mo Oct	v0.06	v0.28	11
12	....	None Since Public			...	Nil	....	0.89	24.0	15.6	9-30-99	2.31	...	12612	Dc	vd0.51	vd0.18	vd0.07	vd0.79	....	d1.02	9 Mo Sep	vd0.24	vd0.47	12
13	....	None Paid			...	Nil	....	14.6	33.8	9.06	9-30-99	154	4000	17804	Dc	v0.64	vd0.69	vd0.80	vd1.26	....	d1.09	9 Mo Sep	vd0.79	vd0.62	13
14	1995	0.111	4-12-99	3-10	0.111	0.11	0.114	459	905	532	j12-31-98	1239	10000	965966	Dc	0.07	0.26	v0.18	vd2.19	....	d2.19				14
15	....	None Since Public			...	Nil	....	10.4	202	94.4	9-30-99	143	...	18897	Dc	pv0.33	v0.55	v0.90	v1.35	....	0.72	9 Mo Sep	v1.03	v0.40	15
16◆	....	None Since Public			...	Nil	....	135	234	171	10-02-99	171	...	47926	Mr	1.00	v0.98	v1.19	v0.88	....	d0.71	6 Mo Sep	v0.41	vd1.18	16
17◆	1996	Q0.05	1-7-00	12-14	0.18½	0.20	0.17	250	1648	968	9-30-99	425	3600	±236962	Je	±p0.45	p±0.59	v±0.74	v±0.89	v±1.03	1.08	3 Mo Sep	v±0.27	v±0.32	17
18	1998	0.951	12-6-99	11-17	3.805	3.80	1.902	6-3-2001 exch for 0.833-1 Lauder(Estee)com[53]				....	...	4077	Je	...	...	...	...	....	....				18
19	1999	1.352	11-23-99	11-18	4.055	5.40	....	2-18-2002 exch for 0.8-1 Estee Lauder Cl'A'[53]				....	...	★1734	Je	...	...	...	...	....	....				19
20	....	None Since Public			...	Nil	....	71.5	78.6	9.91	9-30-99	1.00	...	12785	Dc	...	...	...	vpd2.80	....	....	9 Mo Sep	n/a	vd2.92	20
21	1871	gQ0.23	2-1-00	12-30	g0.92	0.92	g0.92	Total Deposits $10537M			j7-31-99	285	6404	20154	Oc	1.58	2.23	v2.55	v2.83	Pv2.10	j2.10				21
22	1973	Q0.15	1-19-00	1-3	0.56	0.60	0.56	25.8	126	33.1	9-30-99	23.5	...	10349	Dc	v1.75	v1.73	v1.91	v1.76	....	2.01	9 Mo Sep	v1.30	v1.55	22
23	....	0.12½	11-12-81	10-23	...	Nil	....	5.85	141	36.7	8-31-99	38.1	...	8251	My	d0.18	1.12	v1.54	v0.31	vd0.74	d0.56	3 Mo Aug	vd0.06	v□0.12	23
24	....	None Paid			...	Nil	....	71.0	3436	3361	10-02-99	3757	...	67100	Dc	v□1.79	v2.38	□v3.05	v1.70	E3.71	2.15	9 Mo Sep	v1.97	v2.42	24
25◆	....	None Since Public			...	Nil	....	81.8	104	58.1	6-30-99	....	...	21646	Sp	0.38	0.49	v0.47	v0.48	Pv0.57	0.57				25
26	....	None Since Public			...	Nil	....	11.5	21.5	8.42	9-30-99	....	...	50993	Dc	vd1.33	vd1.80	vd1.64	vd1.03	....	d1.09	9 Mo Sep	vd0.52	vd0.58	26
27	....	None Since Public			...	Nil	....	0.56	12.0	9.41	9-30-99	0.15	...	9853	Dc	v0.12	vd0.10	v0.01	vNil	....	0.03	9 Mo Sep	vd0.01	v0.02	27
28◆	....	5%Stk	7-29-94	7-11	...	Nil	....	0.54	5.48	2.50	9-30-99	....	...	3876	Je	0.04	vd0.17	vd0.59	vd0.10	vd0.43	d0.55	3 Mo Sep	vd0.04	vd0.16	28
29◆	1960	Q0.16	1-3-00	11-29	0.60	0.64	0.56	27.9	108	78.1	6-30-99	186	...	±44398	Sp	±1.24	±0.95	v±1.33	v±1.37	Pv±1.52	1.52				29
30◆	....	None Since Public			...	Nil	....	144	225	53.4	9-30-99	....	...	84981	Dc	v0.10	v0.12	v0.21	v0.34	E0.41	0.36	9 Mo Sep	v0.16	v0.18	30
31◆	1983	Q0.08	1-10-00	12-13	0.275	0.32	0.23	Total Assets $3716M			9-30-99	99.7	...	57186	Mr	v0.74	v1.03	v1.31	v1.55	....	1.77	6 Mo Sep	v0.78	v1.00	31
32◆	1939	Q0.09	1-3-00	11-23	0.35	0.36	0.308	21.8	1239	447	9-30-99	745	...	196285	Dc	v0.75	v□0.84	v1.08	v1.24	E1.43	1.39	9 Mo Sep	v0.93	v1.08	32
33	1996	0.976	4-10-99	3-24	0.976	0.98	7.554	Int fr 4-10-95,re-specified cond.				....	...	★1300	Dc	...	...	...	...	....	....	Mature 4-10-2000			33
34	1994	Q0.09	11-30-99	11-10	0.36	0.36	0.30	Total Assets $202149M			8-31-99	29857	21013	120014	Nv	1.76	v3.24	v4.72	v5.19	E7.85	6.38	9 Mo Aug	v4.67	v5.86	34
35	1996	Q0.519	12-31-99	12-13	2.075	2.075	2.075	Co option redm fr 3-31-2001 at $25				★200	...	...	Nv	...	...	...	...	....	....	Mature 12-31-2035			35
36	1998	Q0.83⅛	11-26-99	11-8	3.32½	3.325	0.83⅛	At maturity Cisco Sys com or cash[53]				★66.5	...	...	Nv	...	...	...	...	....	....	Mature 2-26-2001			36
37	....	None Since Public			...	Nil	....	20.8	48.7	20.4	6-30-99	33.6	...	±6415	Je	p0.41	pd1.34	v1.22	v0.63	vd1.48	d1.77	3 Mo Sep	vd0.15	vd0.44	37
38◆	1978	Q0.01¼	11-15-99	11-3	0.05	0.05	0.05	Total Assets $2204M			8-31-99	[55]712	...	±58358	Nv	±1.95	±2.43	v±2.23	v±2.49	E2.80	2.92	9 Mo Aug	v±1.37	v±1.80	38
39	1999	0.09½	12-28-99	12-15	0.18	0.34	....	41.1	931	599	9-30-99	309	...	45041	Dc	...	v1.59	vd0.99	v1.47	....	1.55	9 Mo Sep	v1.40	v1.48	39
40◆	....	None Since Public			...	Nil	....	128	163	33.0	12-31-97	30.8	...	46098	Dc	d0.84	vd0.26	vd0.97	Pvd1.05		0.73	9 Mo Sep	vd1.25	v0.53	40
41◆	1999	1.58	12-27-99	12-15	†13.58	1.58h[56]	....	Total Assets $3053M			9-30-99	[57]581	...	56804	Dc	v1.81	□v0.92	v□10.67	v0.86	....	3.94	9 Mo Sep	v0.40	v□3.48	41
42◆	....	None Since Public			...	Nil	....	4746	5070	939	9-30-99	3977	...	341076	Dc	...	...	p0.99	v2.66	Ed1.65	d1.04	9 Mo Sep	v2.81	vd0.89	42
43	1994	Q0.30	11-15-99	10-28	1.50	1.20	1.17	Total Assets $656M			9-30-99	373	2000	17219	Dc	□v0.35	v0.56	□v0.59	v0.78	....	0.99	9 Mo Sep	v0.58	v0.79	43
44◆	....	None Since Public			...	Nil	....	122	1101	700	9-30-99	149	...	127725	Dc	±v□0.33	v±P0.85	v□±1.09	v±1.70	E2.25	2.15	9 Mo Sep	v1.13	v1.58	44
45◆	1913	Q0.31¾	1-14-00	12-29	1.24	1.27	1.20	104	786	1075	9-30-99	1600	[58]1913	129677	Dc	v1.25	v1.57	v1.47	□vd0.67	....	1.66	12 Mo Sep	v□d0.47	v1.66	45
46◆	....	None Since Public			...	Nil	....	134	238	79.7	9-30-99	....	...	57950	Dc	v0.01	v0.09	v0.23	v0.32	....	0.60	9 Mo Sep	v0.16	v0.44	46
47	1993	Q0.07½	12-2-99	11-8	0.30	0.30	0.30	2.54	183	97.7	9-30-99	176	...	16018	Dc	v1.97	v2.12	v2.27	v1.42	E2.53	1.42	9 Mo Sep	v1.89	v1.89	47
48◆	....	None Since Public			...	Nil	....	146	155	48.2	8-31-99	....	...	41784	My	...	...	...	....	vpd1.17	....	6 Mo Nov	vpd0.51	vd1.21	48
49	1998	†0.06	6-30-99	6-17	†0.06	Nil	[59]0.031	Total Assets $58.67M			9-30-99	....	...	20256	Je	d0.23	0.07	v0.07	v0.07	v0.09	0.08	3 Mo Sep	v0.03	v0.02	49
50	1941	Q0.22	1-4-00	12-13	0.88	0.88	0.84	Total Assets $2393.97M			9-30-99	251	503	19434	Dc	v2.72	v1.66	v3.34	v0.80	....	3.64	9 Mo Sep	vd1.19	v1.65	50

◆Stock Splits & Divs By Line Reference Index [2]2-for-1,'95. [3]2-for-1,'94. [11]2-for-1,'99. [16]2-for-1,'99. [17]2-for-1,'99. [25]3-for-2,'96. [28]Adj to 5%,'94. [29]2-for-1,'95. [30]2-for-1,'96,'98,'99. [31]4-for-3,'97:2-for-1,'98. [32]2-for-1,'95,'98. [38]3-for-2,'94:No adj for stk dstr,'97. [40]2-for-1,'98. [41]2-for-1,'95. [42]2-for-1,'98. [44]2-for-1,'99. [45]2-for-1,'96. [46]2-for-1,'98. [48]To split 2-for-1,ex Jan 18,'00.

¶ S&P 500
# MidCap 400
✣ SmallCap 600
• Options

Index	Ticker	Name of Issue (Call Price of Pfd. Stocks)	Market	Com. Rank. & Pfd. Rating	Inst. Hold Cos	Inst. Hold Shs. (000)	Principal Business	Price Range 1971-97 High	1971-97 Low	1998 High	1998 Low	1999 High	1999 Low	Dec. Sales in 100s	December, 1999 Last Sale Or Bid High	Low	Last	%Div Yield	P-E Ratio	EPS 5 Yr Growth	% Annualized Total Return 12 Mo	36 Mo	60 Mo
1•[1]	LDIG	✔Liberty Digital 'A'	NNM	NR	66	4925	Programing/distrib music svcs	7 13/16	6 3/4	9 15/16	2 3/8	75 3/4	4 1/16	51221	75 3/4	48 3/8	74 1/4	...	d	...	1484	...	...
2	L	✔Liberty Financial Cos	NY,Ch	NR	111	8980	Asset management svcs	38 1/4	15 15/16	40 5/8	20 1/8	29 11/16	20 1/8	7069	24 1/16	21 3/8	22 15/16	1.7	10	10	-13.6	-2.6	...
3	LRY	✔Liberty Property Trust	NY,Ch,Ph,P	NR	249	52303	Real estate investment trust	29 3/8	17 3/8	28 3/4	20 1/8	25 15/16	20 1/4	50675	24 7/8	22 1/8	24 3/4	8.4	13	6	9.0	5.9	12.8
4	LIFC	✔LifeCell Corp	NNM	C	26	2383	Dvlp stge:human cell prod	16 1/4	1 3/8	8 3/8	3 1/4	7 1/2	3 1/8	10207	5 1/2	4 3/8	5 1/8	...	d	6	17.1	17.9	20.7
5	LFMN	✔LifeMinders.com Inc	NNM	NR	..	...	Online direct marketing	....	....	....	....	62 1/2	14	56760	62 1/2	18 1/8	57 3/4	...	..	...	...	...	...
6	LCUT	✔Lifetime Hoan	NNM	B+	35	4234	Mfr household cutlery/prod	12 1/4	4 1/4	12 9/16	8	10 7/8	4 3/4	18147	6 1/8	4 3/4	5 1/4	4.8	9	4	-44.4	-16.9	-5.7
7	LTBG	✔Lightbridge Inc	NNM	NR	35	7163	Computer software/svcs	19 1/2	5 3/4	20 1/4	3 1/8	34 5/8	4 5/16	47673	34 5/8	20	27 3/4	...	d	...	405	48.0	...
8	LIHRY	✔Lihir Gold ADS[53]	NNM	NR	7	413	Gold mining,exploration	40 3/4	18 1/2	36 1/2	17 3/4	24 1/16	11 1/2	205	15 3/8	13 1/2	14B	...	d	...	-36.7	-28.4	...
✣9	LVC	✔Lillian Vernon	AS	B	55	4131	Direct mail catalog sales	22 5/8	4 1/16	19 1/4	12 5/8	16 3/8	11	2866	12 1/4	11	11 1/8	2.9	29	-19	-30.9	-1.1	-4.2
¶10•[2]	LLY	✔Lilly (Eli)	NY,B,C,Ch,P,Ph	A-	1513	674290	Ethical drugs:agri chemicals	70 7/16	2 1/16	91 5/16	57 11/16	97 3/4	60 9/16	529349	73 7/8	63 5/8	66 1/2	1.6	29	-13	-24.2	23.7	34.8
✣11	LI	✔Lilly Industries'A'	NY,Ch,Ph	B+	129	11530	Dvlp & mfr indus'l coatings	24 5/8	1/4	24 5/8	14 3/8	20 3/16	12 7/8	6947	14 7/16	12 7/8	13 7/16	2.4	10	10	-31.3	-8.1	1.1
¶12•[3]	LTD	✔Limited Inc	NY,B,Ch,P,Ph	A-	483	143487	Women's apparel stores	32 7/8	1/32	36 1/2	20 1/2	50 5/8	27 1/2	151999	44 1/16	39 3/16	43 5/16	1.4	25	13	...	...	...
#13•[4]	LNCR	✔Lincare Holdings	NNM	NR	309	51937	In-home respiratory svcs	29 1/2	3 3/16	44 3/8	26 7/8	40 5/8	17 1/4	117905	35 1/8	28 3/8	34 11/16	...	20	19	-14.5	19.2	19.1
14	LECO	✔Lincoln Electric Hldgs	NNM	B	124	16196	Mfr arc welding products	42 3/8	21	49 3/4	16 5/8	23 3/4	17 5/8	14722	20 7/8	18 7/8	20 5/8	2.7	13	-7	-5.2	-12.6	...
¶15•[2]	LNC	✔Lincoln Natl Corp	NY,B,C,Ch,P,Ph	A-	655	146335	Multiline insurance hldg co	39 1/16	2 3/8	49 7/16	33 1/2	57 1/2	36	128362	42 5/8	36 9/16	40	2.9	14	10	0.2	18.2	21.9
16	Pr	$3.00 cm Cv A Pfd (80)vtg	NY,Ch	NR	5	2	life,accid,health,prop/cas	580	38 1/2	740	590	795	725	....	....	....	640B	0.5	..	...	...	...	...
17	LNDL	✔Lindal Cedar Homes	NSC	C	10	653	Pre-cut home packages	7 1/2	1/8	3 7/8	1 7/16	3 1/8	1	3045	3 1/8	2	2 1/4	...	10	Neg	38.5	-19.9	-7.1
18	LIND	✔Lindberg Corp	NNM	B	44	1974	Heat treating of metals	17 1/8	9/16	25	8 3/8	13 3/8	7 5/8	5913	9 1/4	7 5/8	7 3/4	4.1	5	1	-12.1	-5.6	7.5
✣19	LNN	✔Lindsay Mfg	NY	B+	92	6770	Mfr elec pwr irrigation sys	33 1/2	1 5/16	32 9/16	11 1/4	22 3/8	13 1/2	6990	18 1/4	16 1/8	18 1/4	0.8	18	4	24.2	-3.5	16.0
#20•[5]	LLTC	✔Linear Technology Corp	NNM	A-	554	135849	Mfrs integrated circuits	37 1/2	3/4	45 1/4	19 9/16	83 3/16	41 3/4	374880	83 3/16	64	71 9/16	0.2	55	17	60.3	48.8	42.6
✣21•[2]	LIN	✔Linens'n Things	NY,Ch,Ph	NR	..	...	Retail home accessories	22 1/4	7 3/4	40 5/8	16 5/8	52 1/16	22 7/16	109448	34 1/8	22 7/16	29 5/8	...	24	71	-25.2	44.6	...
22	LGF	✔Lions Gate Entertainment	AS,To	NR	12	4302	Entertain,TV film,animat'n	....	....	3 3/4	2 5/8	4	1 1/2	21090	2 1/2	2 1/16	2 3/8	...	d	...	-25.5	...	...
✣23•[4]	LIPO	✔Liposome Co	NNM,Ch	C	148	10899	Lipid/liposome drug tech	29 1/2	7/8	16 7/8	3 3/8	28 1/2	6 3/8	104121	14	8 3/8	12 3/16	...	39	NM	-20.9	-13.9	7.8
24	LIQB	✔Liqui-Box Corp	NNM	A-	44	1195	Plastic packaging & pkg sys	40 1/2	3/4	60	35 1/4	55 1/2	44 15/16	785	55 1/4	44 15/16	49 1/2	1.6	13	15	-3.4	16.7	9.8
25	LQID	✔Liquid Audio	NNM	NR	45	5429	Internet music delivery sys	....	....	....	....	49 1/4	15	69512	37 3/4	25	26 1/4	...	..	...	...	...	...
26	LAD	✔Lithia Motors'A'	NY	NR	62	4456	Retail new/used vehicles	19	9 1/2	18 1/4	9 1/4	23 3/4	15	2982	19	15 3/4	17 7/8	...	12	...	8.3	17.1	...
#27•[6]	LIT	✔Litton Indus	NY,B,C,Ch,P,Ph	B	260	38612	Defense & marine systems	74 3/4	1 3/16	68	47 7/16	74 5/8	42 7/16	29726	50 5/16	43 3/4	49 7/8	...	19	-2	-23.6	1.6	...
¶28•[7]	LIZ	✔Liz Claiborne	NY,Ph,P	B+	410	47887	Designer womens apparel	57 15/16	13/16	54 7/8	25	40 11/16	30 7/8	61333	39 1/2	37 1/4	37 5/8	1.2	13	18	20.7	0.3	18.8
29	LRT	✔LL&E Royalty Tr UBI	NY,B,P	NR	20	222	Royalties of oil & gas prop	17 1/8	1 3/8	5 1/4	2 1/8	2 7/8	1	18815	1 9/16	1 3/16	1 7/16	6.3	13	-18	-38.2	-26.8	-9.7
30	LNR	✔LNR Property	NY	NR	117	18379	Real estate investment/mgmt	27 1/8	21 1/8	30	11 7/8	24	16 1/2	33161	20 1/4	16 1/2	19 7/8	0.3	8	...	-0.1	...	...
31	L	✔Loblaw Cos	To,Mo,Vc	A+	14	15228	Food retailer & wholesaler	27 3/16	7/16	38	24	43	32	63124	37	33	35 1/4	0.7	29	20	-5.2	36.4	35.8
32	LFIN	✔Local Financial	NNM	NR	64	8524	General banking, Oklahoma	....	....	13 3/4	6 15/16	11	8	11580	10 9/16	9 3/8	10 3/8	...	10	...	15.3	...	...
¶33•[8]	LMT	✔Lockheed Martin[59]	NY,P	NR	763	382656	Aerospace/defense systems	56 11/16	25	58 15/16	41	46	16 3/8	521493	22	19	21 7/8	4.0	15	-4	-47.1	-20.3	...
34•[9]	LOD	✔Lodgian Inc	NY,Ph,P	NR	48	8976	Own/oper hotels in U.S.	20 1/2	2 3/8	22 1/2	2 1/4	7 1/8	3 3/8	21455	5 5/8	4 3/4	5	...	10	-39	2.6	-32.3	-12.9
35•[7]	LWN	✔Loewen Group	NY,Ch,Ph,To	D	43	2801	Oper funeral homes/svcs	43	8 3/16	28 7/8	7	8 11/16	1/4	148220	5/8	3/8	7/16	...	d	Neg	-94.8	-77.5	-55.8
36•[7]	LCP	✔Loews Cineplex Entertain't	NY,To	NR	57	9984	Motion picture exhibiter	....	....	20	7 1/4	12 15/16	5 3/4	31333	6 5/8	5 3/4	5 7/8	...	d	...	-42.0	...	...
¶37•[6]	LTR	✔Loews Corp	NY,B,Ch,P,Ph	B-	508	57987	Insurance sub:tobacco:hotels	115 5/8	3/4	108 1/4	78	104 1/2	58 1/2	67518	66	58 1/2	60 11/16	1.6	6	-5	-37.4	-12.7	8.1
38•[6]	LOJN	✔LoJack Corp	NNM	B-	71	9559	Mfr stolen vehicle track'g svs	18 7/8	1 1/4	15 5/8	8	12 3/4	6 1/4	20773	8	6 1/4	6 3/4	...	13	19	-43.2	-12.3	3.9
39	LDP	✔London Pacific Grp ADS[60]	NY	NR	20	2094	Capital investment mgmt	27 3/8	12	17 7/16	10 5/8	46 7/16	12 5/16	37182	46 7/16	25 1/4	36	2.5	10	-10	198	45.3	15.7
#40•[6]	STAR	✔Lone Star Steakhouse/Saloon	NNM	NR	155	21640	Own/oper full svc restaurants	45	3 3/8	23 7/16	6	11 3/4	6 5/8	88249	10 1/8	7 1/16	8 15/16	...	26	-15	-2.9	-30.7	-14.9
41•[9]	LSS	✔Lone Star Technologies	NY	B-	92	13501	Provides oilfield prd/svcs	59 3/16	2 1/4	33 7/16	8 5/8	29 3/16	10 1/4	13319	29 3/16	24 1/8	27 1/2	...	d	Neg	172	17.4	31.5
¶42•[10]	LDG	✔Longs Drug Stores	NY,Ch,Ph,P	B+	278	17458	Self-service drug store chain	32 3/4	3 13/16	44 1/2	26	39 1/2	22 1/4	18603	25 15/16	22 1/4	25 13/16	2.2	14	9	-30.0	3.9	12.9
#43•[6]	LFB	✔Longview Fibre	NY,Ph,P	B-	164	23849	Logs,board,paper & cv prod	23 5/8	1 5/8	17 7/16	9 7/16	17 7/16	10 5/16	37788	16 1/4	11 15/16	14 1/4	†2.2	37	Neg	25.8	-5.2	1.1
44•[11]	LOOK	✔LookSmart Ltd	NNM	NR	25	16267	Internet directory svcs	....	....	....	....	45	12	71705	38 1/4	26 3/8	27	...	..	...	...	...	...
45•	LOR	✔Loral Space & Communications	NY	NR	264	137123	Satellite based telecommun eqp	24 1/4	11 1/8	33 15/16	10 3/4	24 3/4	13 1/2	457174	24 3/4	15 3/4	24 5/16	...	d	Neg	36.5	9.8	...
46	LD	✔Louis Dreyfus Natural Gas	NY,Ch	NR	161	19512	Oil&gas acq'n dvlp, prod'n	24 7/8	10 3/8	20 5/8	10 1/2	23 5/16	11 1/16	13770	18 1/2	16	18 1/8	...	d	Neg	27.2	1.9	7.3
¶47•[12]	LPX	✔Louisiana Pacific	NY,B,Ch,P,Ph	B-	391	68424	Lumber,plywood & pulp	48	1 5/8	24 3/16	16 3/8	24 7/8	11 3/8	216016	14 11/16	12 3/8	14 1/16	4.0	7	40	-20.7	-10.1	-10.0
¶48•[13]	LOW	✔Lowe's Cos	NY,B,Ch,P	A	952	261870	Dstr bldg mtls: consum'r gds	24 9/16	5/8	52 3/16	21 9/16	66 7/16	43	371972	60	47 15/16	59 3/4	0.2	36	21	17.0	50.3	28.6
49	LYTS	✔LSI Industries	NNM	B	79	6290	Mfrs outdoor lighting sys	22	2 1/16	24	15 3/4	25 1/2	15 7/8	5528	25 1/2	19 3/8	21 5/8	e1.5	12	21	-2.0	19.4	28.7
¶50•[7]	LSI	✔LSI Logic	NY,Ch,P	B-	560	106519	Mfr integrated circuits(ASICs)	62 1/2	2 7/16	29 3/8	10 1/2	71 3/8	16 1/8	459042	71 3/8	50	67 1/2	...	79	Neg	319	36.1	27.4

Uniform Footnote Explanations-See Page4. Other: [1]CBOE,P:Cycle 2. [2]ASE:Cycle 1. [3]ASE,CBOE:Cycle 2. [4]CBOE:Cycle 2. [5]P:Cycle 2. [6]CBOE:Cycle 3. [7]CBOE:Cycle 1. [8]P,Ph:Cycle 3. [9]Ph:Cycle 2. [10]Ph:Cycle 3. [11]ASE,CBOE,Ph:Cycle 1. [12]ASE:Cycle 2. [13]Ph:Cycle 1. [51]6 Mo Dec'97. [52]Fiscal Sep'95. [53]Ea ADS rep 20 ord, no par. [54]Stk dstr of Too Inc. [55]Stk dstr of Abercrombie & Fitch. [56]Stk dstr of Lincoln Elec Hldgs,'98. [57]Stk dstr of Western Atlas Inc. [58]Fiscal Jun'97 & prior. [59]Instl. hldgs over 90%. [60]Ea ADS rep 4 ord, 5¢. [61]Incl current amts. [62]Fiscal Mar'96 & prior. [63]12 Mo Dec'96.

Index	Cash Divs. Ea.Yr. Since	Dividends: Latest Payment Period $	Date	Ex. Div.	Total $ So Far 1999	Ind. Rate	Paid 1998	Financial Position Mil-$: Cash& Equiv.	Curr. Assets	Curr. Liab.	Balance Sheet Date	Capitalization: Lg Trm Debt Mil-$	Shs. 000 Pfd.	Com.	Earnings $ Per Shr. Years End	1995	1996	1997	1998	1999	Last 12 Mos.	Interim Earnings $ per Shr. Period	1998	1999	Index
1	....	None Since Public			...	Nil	....	24.8	87.2	144	9-30-99	97.5	...	±197133	Dc	....	pd0.54	v[51]d0.01	vd0.38	....	d2.32	6 Mo Jun	vd0.14	vd2.08	1
2◆	1995	Q0.10	12-8-99	11-22	0.40	0.40	0.40	Total Assets $17847.00M			9-30-99	526	325	47279	Dc	v1.76	v2.24	v2.77	v□2.63	....	2.20	9 Mo Sep	v2.00	v1.57	2
3	1994	Q0.52	1-15-00	12-29	1.87	2.08	1.71	Total Assets $3087M			9-30-99	1463	5000	67004	Dc	v0.89	v1.14	v1.39	v1.59	....	1.89	9 Mo Sep	v1.19	v1.49	3
4	....	None Since Public			...	Nil	....	4.10	9.48	3.24	9-30-99	....	119	11909	Dc	vd1.10	vd1.14	vd1.04	vd0.72	....	d0.79	9 Mo Sep	vd0.46	vd0.53	4
5	....	None Since Public			...	Nil	....	11.3	22.4	4.50	9-30-99	0.09	p...	★19631	Dc	...	...	...	vpd0.40	....	....	9 Mo Sep	n/a	vpd1.50	5
6◆	1997	Q0.06¼	11-19-99	11-3	0.25	0.25	0.25	0.24	79.3	20.4	9-30-99	....	...	12600	Dc	v0.54	v0.74	v0.75	v0.98	....	0.62	9 Mo Sep	v0.62	v0.26	6
7	....	None Since Public			...	Nil	....	25.7	48.3	16.1	9-30-99	0.31	...	16465	Dc	p[52]d0.19	pv0.16	vd0.80	vd0.44	....	d0.08	9 Mo Sep	vd0.04	v0.32	7
8	....	None Since Public			...	Nil	....	82.5	125	74.1	12-31-98	274	...	942000	Dc	d0.01	d0.40	v0.01	vd0.01		d0.01				8
9	1992	Q0.08	3-1-00	2-11	0.32	0.32	0.32	14.2	85.9	23.5	8-28-99	....	...	9152	Fb	v0.57	v0.55	v0.93	v0.34	....	0.38	6 Mo Aug	vd0.50	vd0.46	9
10◆	1885	Q0.26	3-10-00	2-11	0.92	1.04	0.80	3358	6595	3187	9-30-99	2816	...	1090521	Dc	v1.99	v1.36	vd0.35	v□1.88	E2.31	2.26	9 Mo Sep	v□1.37	v1.75	10
11◆	1957	Q0.08	1-3-00	12-8	0.32	0.32	0.32	6.73	162	110	8-31-99	211	...	±23233	Nv	±0.88	v±0.81	±v1.20	v±1.35	....	1.41	9 Mo Aug	v±0.96	v±1.02	11
12	1970	h[54]Q0.15	12-14-99	12-1	h[54]0.60	0.60	h[55]0.52	173	2001	1249	10-30-99	650	...	214814	Ja	2.68	v1.54	v0.79	v8.32	E1.71↑	1.68	9 Mo Oct	v▲7.18	v0.54	12
13◆	....	None Since Public			...	Nil	....	12.3	116	53.1	9-30-99	155	...	54041	Dc	v0.90	v1.16	v1.36	v1.44	E1.75	1.66	9 Mo Sep	v1.04	v1.26	13
14◆	1915	0.14	1-14-00	12-29	0.48	0.56	[56]0.70	34.0	447	246	9-30-99	45.2	...	45129	Dc	±2.63	v±2.99	v±3.45	v1.91	....	1.56	9 Mo Sep	v1.46	v1.11	14
15◆	1920	Q0.29	2-1-00	1-6	1.10	1.16	1.30	Total Assets $96501M			9-30-99	1457	33	195473	Dc	v2.30	v2.44	v4.49	v2.51	E2.95	2.73	9 Mo Sep	v1.89	v2.11	15
16	1965	Q0.75	3-5-00	2-11	3.00	3.00	3.00	Cv into 16 common				....	33	...	Dc	b8.72	...	...	....	....	....				16
17	....	0.018	6-20-80	6-2	...	Nil	....	8.10	19.3	8.94	10-03-99	4.56	...	4131	Dc	v0.33	v0.37	vd0.60	vd0.23	....	0.23	9 Mo Sep	vd0.23	v0.23	17
18	1956	Q0.08	12-1-99	11-8	0.32	0.32	0.32	0.16	22.4	12.5	9-30-99	39.6	...	5925	Dc	v1.18	v1.03	v0.05	v1.74	....	1.43	9 Mo Sep	v1.41	v1.10	18
19◆	1996	Q0.035	11-30-99	11-10	0.14	0.14	0.137	32.5	56.9	16.8	8-31-99	....	...	12409	Au	0.73	v1.08	v1.34	v1.61	v0.96	0.99	3 Mo Nov	v0.10	v0.13	19
20◆	1992	Q0.04	11-10-99	10-20	0.15½	0.16	0.13	861	986	143	9-26-99	....	...	154312	Je	0.56	0.86	v0.86	v1.13	v1.22	1.30	3 Mo Sep	v0.28	v0.36	20
21◆	....	None Since Public			...	Nil	....	18.4	430	276	10-02-99	....	...	39450	Dc	□vNil	v0.39	v0.65	v0.94	E1.25	1.13	9 Mo Sep	v0.38	v0.57	21
22◆	....	None Since Public			...	Nil	....	Total Assets $327M			j3-31-99	53.3	...	30551	Mr	...	...	vd0.04	vd0.58	....	jd0.73	3 Mo Jun	vNil	vd0.15	22
23	....	None Since Public			...	Nil	....	62.3	75.1	14.2	10-03-99	2.82	...	39157	Dc	vd1.50	vd0.57	vd0.71	vd0.12	E0.31	0.25	9 Mo Sep	vd0.16	v0.21	23
24	1977	Q0.20	1-12-00	12-31	0.74	0.80	0.61	5.51	45.9	20.6	10-02-99	....	...	4509	Dc	v1.92	v2.41	v2.72	v3.45	....	3.90	9 Mo Sep	v2.92	v3.37	24
25	....	None Since Public			...	Nil	....	70.5	72.6	6.50	9-30-99	1.54	...	★21365	Dc	...	...	...	vpd0.85	....	....	9 Mo Sep	n/a	vpd2.07	25
26	....	None Since Public			...	Nil	....	26.2	276	200	9-30-99	62.3	10	±11729	Dc	pv0.60	pv0.88	v0.82	v1.14	....	1.49	9 Mo Sep	v0.81	v1.16	26
27◆	....	h[57]....	3-17-94	3-18	...	Nil	....	68.4	2170	1924	10-31-99	1300	411	45530	Jl	2.84	3.15	v3.40	v3.82	v2.58	2.70	3 Mo Oct	v1.01	v□1.13	27
28	1984	Q0.11¼	12-3-99	11-9	0.45	0.45	0.45	11.2	1040	500	10-02-99	....	...	59117	Dc	v1.90	v2.14	v2.63	v2.57	E3.02	2.72	9 Mo Sep	v2.11	v2.26	28
29	1983	0.028	1-14-00	1-3	0.092	0.09	0.493	Total Assets $2.34M			9-30-99	....	...	18991	Dc	v0.35	v0.83	v0.67	v0.49	....	0.11	9 Mo Sep	v0.45	v0.07	29
30	1997	0.01¼	11-15-99	11-3	0.05	0.05	0.05	Total Assets $2082.54M			8-31-99	1220	...	±35700	Nv	...	p1.37	vp±1.55	v±2.02	....	2.63	9 Mo Aug	v1.44	v2.05	30
31◆	1956	gQ0.06	12-30-99	12-13	g0.22	0.24	g0.20	n/a	2288	2527	j6-19-99	1982	...	274546	Dc	v0.60	v0.72	v0.88	v1.06	....	j1.22	9 Mo Sep	v0.68	v0.84	31
32	....	None Paid			...	Nil	....	Total Deposits $1724.69M			9-30-99	380	...	20537	Dc	0.73	0.69	[58]d1.53	v0.89	....	1.03	9 Mo Sep	v0.66	v□0.80	32
33◆	1995	Q0.22	12-31-99	11-29	0.88	0.88	0.82	....	10129	9734	9-30-99	10463	...	395953	Dc	v1.55	v3.05	v3.04	v2.63	E1.50	1.49	9 Mo Sep	v2.30	v□1.16	33
34	....	None Since Public			...	Nil	....	23.4	118	91.0	9-30-99	884	...	27887	Dc	v0.42	v□0.77	□v0.80	v□d0.16	....	0.49	9 Mo Sep	v□d0.17	v□0.48	34
35	1991	Div Omitted 12-22-98			...	Nil	g0.20	File bankruptcy Chapt 11			9-30-99	2344	8800	74145	Dc	vd1.69	v0.97	v0.49	vd8.22	....	d9.58	9 Mo Sep	v0.01	vd1.35	35
36	....	None Since Public			...	Nil	....	28.2	59.8	194	8-31-99	780	...	±58623	Fb	...	vd0.01	pvd0.01	vd0.12	....	d0.42	6 Mo Aug	v±0.20	v±d0.10	36
37◆	1967	Q0.25	12-1-99	10-28	1.00	1.00	1.00	Total Assets $72611.10M			9-30-99	5699	...	106050	Dc	v14.98	v11.91	v6.90	v4.06	E10.00	3.92	9 Mo Sep	v6.79	v□6.65	37
38	....	None Paid			...	Nil	....	7.90	25.7	8.22	8-31-99	1.01	...	16370	Fb	v0.51	v0.36	v0.48	v0.57	....	0.51	6 Mo Aug	v0.32	v0.26	38
39	1993	0.332	8-30-99	8-11	0.888	0.89	0.888	160	197	23.4	12-31-98	....	...	64424	Dc	9.53	v1.64	v1.64	v1.85	....	3.79	6 Mo Jun	v1.02	v2.96	39
40	....	None Since Public			...	Nil	....	71.3	88.2	38.8	9-07-99	....	...	33093	Dc	v1.27	v1.49	v1.65	v□0.81	....	0.35	9 Mo Sep	□v0.72	v0.26	40
41	....	None Paid			...	Nil	....	34.0	161	70.0	9-30-99	[61]37.0	...	22586	Dc	v0.46	v1.19	v□2.40	v∆d1.43	....	d1.70	9 Mo Sep	vd0.15	vd0.42	41
42◆	1961	Q0.14	1-10-00	11-26	0.56	0.56	0.56	29.2	572	379	10-28-99	151	...	39346	Ja	1.14	v1.48	v1.47	v1.64	E1.83	1.76	9 Mo Oct	v1.03	v1.15	42
43	1937	0.12	1-10-00	12-21	†0.28	0.32	0.54	....	169	94.9	7-31-99	521	...	51677	Oc	1.47	v1.09	v0.25	vd0.13	Pv0.39	0.39				43
44	....	None Since Public			...	Nil	....	117	134	26.9	9-30-99	0.30	p...	85550	Dc	...	...	...	vpd0.43	....	....	9 Mo Sep	n/a	vd1.36	44
45	....	None Since Public			...	Nil	....	265	1179	693	9-30-99	1987	60806	244869	Dc	[62]d0.08	[63]0.05	v0.06	vd0.68	Ed1.05	d0.66	9 Mo Sep	vd0.45	vd0.43	45
46	....	None Since Public			...	Nil	....	6.06	113	76.6	9-30-99	604	...	40226	Dc	v0.40	v0.76	vd0.53	v∆d1.10	....	d0.33	9 Mo Sep	vd0.45	v0.32	46
47	1973	Q0.14	12-1-99	11-15	0.56	0.56	0.56	168	818	589	9-30-99	653	...	106447	Dc	vd0.48	vd1.87	vd0.94	v0.02	E2.07	1.85	9 Mo Sep	vd0.13	v1.70	47
48◆	1961	Q0.035	1-28-00	1-12	0.12	0.14	0.11½	705	3877	2391	10-29-99	1733	...	382322	Ja	v0.68	v0.86	v1.02	v1.36	E1.65	1.65	9 Mo Oct	v1.08	v1.37	48
49◆	1988	Q0.08	11-16-99	11-5	†0.36¼	0.32	†0.31¾	11.8	81.7	29.3	9-30-99	1.67	...	10177	Je	0.79	0.80	v0.97	v1.29	v1.70	1.82	3 Mo Sep	v0.40	v0.52	49
50◆	....	None Since Public			...	Nil	....	456	1151	531	9-30-99	811	...	148725	Dc	v1.75	v1.07	v□1.12	vd0.93	E0.85	0.54	9 Mo Sep	vd1.04	□v0.43	50

◆Stock Splits & Divs By Line Reference Index [2]3-for-2,'97. [6]10%,'94,'95,'97. [10]2-for-1,'95,'97. [11]3-for-2,'94. [13]2-for-1,'98. [14]No adj for stk dstr,'98. [15]2-for-1,'99. [19]3-for-2,'96,'97,'98. [20]2-for-1,'95,'99. [21]2-for-1,'98. [22]1-for-2 REVERSE,'98. [27]No adj for stk dstr Western Atlas,'94. [31]3-for-1,'96. [33]2-for-1,'99. [37]2-for-1,'95. [42]2-for-1,'97. [48]2-for-1,'94,'98. [49]Adj for 5%,'94:3-for-2,'95. [50]2-for-1,'95.

¶ S&P 500
# MidCap 400
✣ SmallCap 600
• Options

Index	Ticker	Name of Issue (Call Price of Pfd. Stocks)	Market	Com. Rank. & Pfd. Rating	Inst. Hold Cos	Inst. Hold Shs. (000)	Principal Business	Price Range 1971-97 High	1971-97 Low	1998 High	1998 Low	1999 High	1999 Low	Dec. Sales in 100s	December, 1999 Last Sale Or Bid High	Low	Last	%Div Yield	P-E Ratio	EPS 5 Yr Growth	% Annualized Total Return 12 Mo	36 Mo	60 Mo
1	LTC	✓LTC Properties	NY,P	NR	82	10078	Real estate investment trust	21½	9¾	21 15/16	15 9/16	17⅛	7¾	44043	9⅝	7¾	8 7/16	18.5	7	5	...	...	...
2•[1]	LTV	✓LTV Corp	NY,P	B–	156	63553	Steel prod'n/energy prd	21¼	9⅜	14 9/16	5	8	3 1/16	170046	4 3/16	3⅜	4⅛	2.9	d	Neg	–26.5	–28.5	–23.3
#3•[2]	LZ	✓Lubrizol Corp	NY,B,Ch,Ph,P	B	242	40370	Dvlp specialty chemicals	46 15/16	6 15/16	40 3/16	22⅜	31⅜	18	45000	31⅜	26⅜	30⅞	3.4	15	–14	25.2	3.3	1.4
✣4	LUB	✓Luby's Inc	NY,Ch,P	A–	137	9203	Cafeteria style restaurants	25⅞	⅜	19½	13⅜	18⅝	9 11/16	33058	11 13/16	9 11/16	11⅜	7.0	9	–9	–22.4	–13.0	–9.1
¶5•[3]	LU	✓Lucent Technologies	NY,Ch,P	NR	2069	127281[7]	Mfr telecommun sys,softwr,prd	22 11/16	6¾	56 15/16	18⅜	84 3/16	47	2337327	84 3/16	72 13/16	75	0.1	68	...	36.7	87.0	...
6	LUMT	✓Luminant Worldwide	NNM	NR	45	3308	Internet/electr commerce sv	....	....	....	....	52	18	48935	48	30	45½	...	d	...	...	...	...
7•[4]	LUX	✓Luxottica Group ADS[54]	NY,Ch,Ph,P	NR	87	25101	Design/mfr eyeglass frames	16 7/16	1 9/16	19½	7½	21⅜	9¾	22980	19⅝	15¾	17 9/16	0.6	24	15	47.7	20.1	22.0
8	LXU.EC	Luxtec Corp	ECM	C	3	75	Mfr fiber optic surgical instr	16¼	5/16	6⅜	2	4	1½	686	4	1 9/16	2¾	...	d	–15	4.8	1.6	–5.4
9	LVMHY	✓LVMH Moet Henn Lou Vttn ADS[55]	NNM	NR	34	1528	Prod's wine,spirits,luxury prd	51 15/16	3 7/16	42½	23 3/16	91½	37½	2553	91½	65½	91	0.7	..	–12	173	27.3	30.5
10•[5]	LCOS	✓Lycos Inc	NNM	NR	252	34648	Dvp internet online guides	10½	1 7/16	34⅜	7½	93⅝	25 9/16	696560	93⅝	55 11/16	79 9/16	...	d	Neg	187	212	...
✣11	LDL	✓Lydall, Inc	NY,Ph	B	116	12109	Engineered fiber materials	28½	¼	20 13/16	9 1/16	12⅞	5⅛	25975	8⅞	5⅛	6⅝	...	22	–25	–44.2	–33.5	–16.4
12	LGL	✓Lynch Corp	AS	B	16	496	Transport'n & fin'l svcs: commun	109¾	¾	113	69½	87	18⅞	356	26	21⅜	25 13/16	...	d	Neg	...	...	...
13	LIC	✓Lynch Interactive	AS	NR	13	487	Telephone svc/TV stations	....	....	....	....	120	42	386	120	64	99⅞	...	..	...	...	...	...
#14•[6]	LYO	✓Lyondell Chemical	NY,Ch,Ph,P	B–	256	104797	Petrochemical refin'g/mktg	33½	13⅛	38⅛	15	22½	11¼	141808	14	11¼	12¾	7.1	d	Neg	–24.7	–12.8	–9.4
15	MFW	✓M&F[59]Worldwide	NY	NR	58	9875	Mfr licorice & flavorings	10 9/16	4¾	11⅛	8	10⅛	4⅜	17902	5⅝	4⅜	5 1/16	...	4	27	–49.7	...	...
16	MTB	✓M&T Bank	NY	A+	216	5021	Comm'l bkg,Buffalo,New York	468	2¾	582	400	582½	406	2533	470	406	414¼	1.2	13	15	–19.2	13.9	26.2
17	MHMY	✓M.H.Meyerson & Co	NNM	NR	13	658	Broker/dealer, underwriter	6½	⅞	4⅝	⅝	21⅞	2⅛	29612	6¼	4	5¼	...	9	87	144	17.3	30.7
18	TUC	✓Mac-Gray Corp	NY	NR	28	4256	Coin/card oper laundry svcs	16⅝	11	20½	7⅝	11½	3¼	3977	4 3/16	3¼	3 13/16	...	10	...	–66.5	...	...
✣19•[7]	MRD	✓MacDermid, Inc	NY	A	160	14375	Indust'l metal finish'g chems	34	¼	42⅜	23 5/16	46¾	28⅞	9504	41 7/16	36½	41 1/16	0.2	27	34	5.2	65.7	59.9
20	MAC	✓Macerich Co	NY,Ch,P	NR	168	27978	Real estate investment trust	29 11/16	18⅛	30⅜	22¼	27¼	17 5/16	23356	20⅞	17 5/16	20 13/16	9.8	17	10	–11.6	–0.3	7.3
21	CLI	✓Mack-Cali Realty	NY,Ch,P	NR	268	49767	Real estate investment trust	43	14⅞	41⅜	26⅛	33⅝	23⅛	45287	26 13/16	23⅛	26 1/16	8.9	13	5	–8.8	0.7	18.4
✣22•[8]	MACR	✓Macromedia Inc	NNM,Ch	NR	307	31786	Dvlp software authoring tools	63¾	3¾	35¼	7⅞	88 11/16	26⅜	158900	88 11/16	61 9/16	73⅛	...	..	15	117	59.6	41.8
23	MXICY	Macronix Intl ADR[62]	NNM	NR	8	626	Mfr integrated circuits	21	5½	14⅝	5¼	19⅛	6½	2463	19⅛	13	19⅛	...	d	Neg	194	40.1	...
24	SHOO	✓Madden (Steven) Ltd	NNM	NR	63	5966	Mkt fashion footwear for women	10⅛	1½	11⅞	3 9/16	20⅛	6¾	59397	20⅛	12¾	19 1/16	...	25	NM	124	54.9	32.7
25	MAD	✓Madeco S.A. ADS[63]	NY,P	NR	36	4622	Mfr copper/aluminum prd-Chile	41¼	15	17⅝	4	12¼	6⅜	7373	11⅞	9⅝	11⅛	3.2	9	1	40.3	–19.6	–13.0
26•[1]	MADGF	✓Madge Networks N.V.	NNM	NR	14	625	Dvlp,mfr computer products	48⅝	3¾	7¾	1¾	10¼	1 7/16	234009	10¼	2⅝	7 5/16	...	19	Neg	125	–9.5	–9.1
27	MDSN	✓Madison Gas & Elec	NNM	B+	67	2424	Util:elec & gas in Wisconsin	27½	4¾	23¾	20⅝	23⅞	16⅜	5980	21 1/16	18⅛	20⅛	6.5	14	2	–5.8	6.1	4.5
✣28	MAFB	✓MAF Bancorp	NNM	NR	132	10674	Savings bank, Illinois	24 7/16	1 3/16	29¼	18¾	27½	18⅞	17576	22½	20	20 15/16	1.7	11	15	–19.9	12.1	25.3
✣29•[2]	MGL	✓Magellan Health Svcs	NY,P	NR	111	22059	Operates hospitals	34½	4⅝	28 7/16	6⅜	11⅛	3 9/16	13910	6⅞	5 5/16	6 5/16	...	42	NM	–24.6	–34.4	–21.7
30	MPET	✓Magellan Petroleum	NSC,P,B	B–	15	270	Oil:gas int:Australia,Canada	16¾	⅜	3⅛	1⅛	2 13/16	1⅛	25940	1½	1⅛	1¼	...	21	8	–7.0	–28.0	13.8
31•[9]	MGA	✓Magna Intl Cl'A'	NY,To,P	B	162	29937	Mfrs automotive parts	73⅞	1 11/16	79½	53⅞	64 15/16	40 1/16	26284	44¼	40 1/16	42⅜	2.4	9	...	–30.1	–6.8	4.3
#32•[10]	MAG	✓MagneTek Inc	NY,Ch,Ph,P	B–	..	...	Mfrs diverse group elec prod	25½	6¾	20 11/16	8 15/16	12 13/16	6⅛	60621	8 7/16	6½	7 11/16	...	3	NM	–33.5	–15.8	–10.7
33	MHR	✓Magnum Hunter Resources	AS	NR	22	4308	Oil & gas explor'n dvlp,prod	8 7/16	2	7 15/16	2¾	4⅜	2⅜	17357	3 1/16	2⅜	2⅞	...	d	–40	–2.6	–13.0	–7.5
34	WS	Wrrt(Pur1com at $6.50)	AS	....	12	812		....	....	....	....	1⅜	3/16	2107	⅞	3/16	3/16	...	..	...	...	...	...
35	MTA	✓Magyar Tavkozlesi ADS[71]	NY	NR	133	17436	Telecommunicat'n svcs,Hungary	26⅝	18⅝	33½	18¾	36½	24 15/16	14382	36½	30 3/16	36	0.4	27	...	21.5	...	...
36	NOW	✓MAI Systems	AS	NR	16	2369	Installs,supports info sys	12¼	2½	5⅜	1¼	4	7/16	16722	1¼	½	13/16	...	d	Neg	–69.8	–50.2	...
37•[10]	MWL	✓Mail-Well Inc	NY,Ph	NR	161	30870	U.S.lrgst envlp mfr/printer	20½	2⅜	24 15/16	5¾	17 13/16	11⅛	42401	13¾	11⅛	13½	...	18	28	18.0	35.6	...
38	MAP	✓Maine Public Service	AS	B	22	430	Electric pwr northern Maine	31¼	4 3/16	17 3/16	11¾	19⅛	12⅞	364	19	17 1/16	17⅜	6.9	8	–22	21.6	6.1	4.5
39	MAL	✓Malan Realty Investors	NY,Ch,Ph	NR	20	1503	Real estate investment trust	19 9/16	11⅜	18 5/16	14½	15⅞	12	2464	14⅛	12	13⅜	12.7	12	5	–5.2	4.1	11.8
40	MBE	✓Malibu Entmt Intl	AS,Ch	NR	4	38	Own, oper family fun attract'ns	12	1 15/16	4 7/16	15/16	1 15/16	⅛	10863	½	⅛	⅛	...	d	Neg	–86.9	–64.1	–53.6
¶41•[11]	MKG	✓Mallinckrodt Inc	NY,B,C,Ch,P,Ph	B	411	58348	Hlth care prd/spcl chem	46⅝	2¼	40 1/16	19¾	37 9/16	25 9/16	45177	33¼	29	31 13/16	2.1	13	–27	5.5	–8.5	3.2
42	MLRC	✓Mallon Resources	NNM	C	32	3448	O&G mineral explor,dvl,prod	34	⅝	12⅞	6⅜	9 7/16	4	14805	6¼	4	5 15/16	...	d	–20	–13.6	–12.9	–4.9
43	TMNG	✓Management Network Grp	NNM	NR	..	...	Management consulting svcs	....	....	....	....	35⅛	17	56726	35⅛	24⅞	32⅝	...	..	...	...	...	...
#44•[12]	MBG	✓Mandalay Resort Group	NY,B,Ch,P	B	257	54010	Casino-hotels,Las Vegas,Reno	49¾	2¼	26½	7⅛	26 5/16	11 9/16	123647	24½	19 15/16	20⅛	...	29	–10	77.9	–16.3	–2.7
✣45	MTW	✓Manitowoc Company	NY,Ph	B	253	16500	Mfr heavy-lift cranes:shipyd	27⅛	9/16	31 5/16	16 5/16	43¾	24 3/16	16685	34	26½	34	0.9	14	97	16.9	25.5	42.7
¶46•[2]	HCR	✓Manor Care	NY	NR	326	70010	Long-term care/rehab svcs	....	....	35	23½	33½	12¾	121368	20	12¾	16	...	13	...	–45.5	...	...
#47•[6]	MAN	✓Manpower Inc	NY,P	NR	271	60225	Worldwide employment svcs	50⅜	11⅛	45¾	18¼	39½	20¼	70739	39½	35¼	37⅝	0.5	20	–5	50.4	5.6	6.6
48	MHC	✓Manufactured Home Communities	NY	NR	145	19826	Real estate investment trust	27¾	12⅞	27¼	22	27	21 13/16	16139	24½	23 11/16	24 5/16	6.4	22	11	1.8	7.5	10.8
49•[11]	MANU	✓Manugistics Group	NNM	C	84	9972	Dvp business oper plan'g softr	49¾	3	66⅜	6⅛	35⅞	5¼	276753	35⅞	17	32 5/16	...	d	Neg	159	17.7	51.9
50	MFC	Manulife Financial	NY,To	NR	20	1729	Life&hlth insur/fin'l svcs	....	....	....	....	14⅜	10 9/16	57207	12 15/16	12	12 11/16	...	..	...	...	...	...

Uniform Footnote Explanations-See Page 4. Other: [1]ASE,CBOE:Cycle 2. [2]Ph:Cycle 2. [3]CBOE,Ph:Cycle 1. [4]Ph:Cycle 3. [5]ASE,CBOE,P:Cycle 3. [6]CBOE:Cycle 3. [7]P:Cycle 2. [8]P:Cycle 1. [9]CBOE:Cycle 2. [10]P:Cycle 3. [11]CBOE:Cycle 1. [12]ASE:Cycle 3. [51]Stk dstr of LTC Healthcare. [52]Fiscal Dec 95 & prior. [53]9 Mo Sep 96. [54]Each ADS rep 1 ord,1000 lire. [55]Ea ADS rep 0.2 ord. [56]2 Mo Jul'95. [57]Stk dstr of Corcap Inc. [58]Stk dstr of Lynch Interactive Corp. [59]Parker Hannifin plan acq. [60]Right dstr of Mafco Cons Group,'96. [61]Incl current amts. [62]Ea ADS rep 10 ord shs NT 10. [63]Ea ADS rep 10 ord, no par. [64]Jun'95 & prior. [65]12 Mo Dec'96:Fiscal Jun'96 earn $2.84. [66]Jan'99 & prior in $Cdn. [67]®$7.74,'97. [68]Fiscal Jul'97 & prior. [69]5 Mo Dec'98:Fiscal Jul'98 earned $6.22. [70]5 mo Dec'98:Fiscal Jul'98 earn $1.72. [71]Ea ADS rep 5 ord shrs,HUF 100. [72]12 Mo Dec '95:Fiscal Sep '95 earn d$0.34. [73]Incl redemption of stk purch rt. [74]To be determined. [75]Excl susbid pfd.

Index	Splits ◆ Cash Divs. Ea. Yr. Since	Dividends: Latest Payment Period $	Date	Ex. Div.	Total $ So Far 1999	Ind. Rate	Paid 1998	Financial Position Mil-$: Cash& Equiv.	Curr. Assets	Curr. Liab.	Balance Sheet Date	Capitalization: Lg Trm Debt Mil-$	Shs. 000 Pfd.	Com.	Earnings $ Per Shr. Years End	1995	1996	1997	1998	1999	Last 12 Mos.	Interim Earnings Period	$ per Shr. 1998	1999	Index
1	1992	Q0.39	12-31-99	12-13	1.56	1.56	h[51]1.53½	Total Assets $720.65M			9-30-99	245	7080	27368	Dc	v1.01	v1.44	v1.25	v1.39	....	1.26	9 Mo Sep	v1.08	v0.95	1
2	1996	Q0.03	12-7-99	11-10	0.12	0.12	0.12	167	1521	871	9-30-99	402	500	99961	Dc	1.71	v1.01	□v0.37	vd0.29	Ed1.90	d2.08	9 Mo Sep	v0.33	vd1.46	2
3	1935	Q0.26	3-10-00	2-8	1.04	1.04	1.04	163	763	277	9-30-99	390	...	54610	Dc	v2.37	v2.79	v2.66	v1.27	E2.04	1.38	9 Mo Sep	v1.53	v1.64	3
4	1965	Q0.20	1-3-00	12-16	0.80	0.80	0.80	0.29	10.1	49.8	8-31-99	78.0	...	22420	Au	1.55	1.66	v1.22	v0.22	v1.26	1.29	3 Mo Nov	v0.25	v0.28	4
5◆	1996	Q0.02	3-1-00	1-27	0.08	0.08	0.07⅞	1495	20810	11956	6-30-99	3712	...	p3133093	Sp	p[52]d0.34	p[53]0.09	v0.21	v0.36	vP□1.10	1.10				5
6	....	None Since Public			...	Nil	....	29.3	53.2	24.2	9-30-99	4.62	...	24213	Dc	...	...	...	vpd4.56	....	d4.80	9 Mo Sep	vpd3.72	vpd3.96	6
7◆	1990	0.11	7-16-99	7-1	0.11	0.11	0.091	41.6	633	737	12-31-98	323	...	224648	Dc	0.46	0.60	v0.63	v0.69	....	0.72	3 Mo Mar	v0.19	v0.22	7
8	....	None Paid			...	Nil	....	0.06	5.13	3.71	7-31-99	0.46	10	2876	Oc	d4.19	d0.22	vd0.13	v0.06	Pvd0.34	d0.34				8
9◆	1988	0.17	12-22-99	11-29	0.598	0.60	0.582	5725	37383	41510	j12-31-98	9342	...	97881	Dc	1.71	1.47	v1.71	v0.72	....	0.72				9
10◆	....	None Since Public			...	Nil	....	163	282	110	10-31-99	2.06	...	101588	Jl	[56]...	d0.11	vd0.12	vd1.57	vd0.60	d0.85	3 Mo Oct	vd0.04	vd0.29	10
11◆	....	h[57]....	7-11-88	7-13	...	Nil	....	3.27	96.7	58.5	9-30-99	43.7	...	15681	Dc	v1.23	v1.38	v1.27	v0.26	....	0.30	9 Mo Sep	v0.65	v0.69	11
12◆	....	h[58]....	9-1-99	9-2	h[58]...	Nil	....	78.6	145	65.1	9-30-99	122	...	1412	Dc	v3.66	v□2.88	vd2.03	v2.37	....	d1.71	9 Mo Sep	v2.14	v□d1.94	12
13	....	None Since Public			...	Nil	....	17.4	49.2	46.6	3-31-99	118	...	1418	Dc	...	...	...	n/a	....	....	9 Mo Sep	n/a	v□d5.15	13
14	1989	Q0.22½	12-15-99	11-22	0.90	0.90	0.90	258	1375	748	9-30-99	6256	...	117594	Dc	v4.86	v1.58	v3.58	v0.67	Ed0.20	d0.55	9 Mo Sep	v1.00	v□d0.22	14
15	....	h[60]....	12-30-96	12-31	...	Nil	....	1.50	64.7	19.3	10-03-99	37.0	20	20663	Dc	p□v0.59	v8.07	v0.96	v1.71	....	1.32	9 Mo Sep	v0.95	v0.56	15
16	1979	Q1.25	12-30-99	11-29	4.50	5.00	3.80	Total Deposits $15.42M			9-30-99	1775	...	7794	Dc	v17.98	21.31	v25.26	v26.16	E33.00	31.78	9 Mo Sep	v19.01	v24.63	16
17	....	0.03	5-13-94	4-7	...	Nil	....	5.06	26.0	7.89	10-31-99	2.00	...	6443	Ja	0.13	v0.33	vd0.34	v0.04	....	0.60	9 Mo Oct	vd0.34	v0.22	17
18	....	None Since Public			...	Nil	....	8.88	32.3	26.3	9-30-99	91.0	...	12628	Dc	...	v0.55	pv0.63	v0.54	....	0.38	9 Mo Sep	v0.36	v0.20	18
19◆	1946	Q0.02	1-10-00	12-13	0.08	0.08	0.077	13.3	211	141	9-30-99	230	...	25157	Mr	v0.50	v0.85	v1.20	v1.43	....	1.52	6 Mo Sep	v0.66	v0.75	19
20	1994	Q0.51	12-7-99	11-17	1.96½	2.04	1.86½	Total Assets $2486.24M			9-30-99	1718	9115	34070	Dc	□0.78	□v0.93	□v0.85	v□1.11	....	1.24	9 Mo Sep	v□0.68	v□0.81	20
21	1994	Q0.58	1-21-00	12-31	2.23	2.32	2.05	Total Assets $3598.13M			9-30-99	[61]1579	...	58395	Dc	v1.22	v□1.73	□v0.12	v□2.11	....	1.96	9 Mo Sep	v□1.57	v1.42	21
22◆	....	None Since Public			...	Nil	....	127	162	46.3	9-30-99	....	...	p49690	Mr	v0.59	vd0.16	vd0.16	v0.44	E0.71	0.59	6 Mo Sep	v0.08	v0.23	22
23◆	1996	20.72%Stk	9-30-98	8-4	...	Nil	0.034	261	475	147	12-31-98	580	...	1946776	Dc	1.13	v0.82	v0.41	vd0.25	....	d0.25				23
24	....	None Paid			...	Nil	....	18.4	51.7	11.0	9-30-99	0.22	...	11507	Dc	0.45	v0.13	v0.30	v0.50	....	0.76	9 Mo Sep	v0.33	v0.59	24
25	1994	0.19	5-20-99	4-30	0.363	0.36	0.599	20.7	402	284	12-31-97	166	...	371000	Dc	1.38	0.64	v1.24	....	....	1.24				25
26	....	None Since Public			...	Nil	....	130	195	108	12-31-98	0.90	...	41690	Dc	0.01	vd0.47	vd1.69	v□0.92	E0.38	d0.66	9 Mo Sep	v0.72	vd0.86	26
27◆	1909	Q0.328	12-15-99	11-29	1.308	1.313	1.298	5.55	64.6	34.9	9-30-99	160	...	16080	Dc	v1.49	v0.40	v1.40	v1.38	....	1.44	12 Mo Sep	v1.43	v1.44	27
28◆	1994	Q0.09	1-4-00	12-13	0.32	0.36	0.233	Total Deposits $2693.49M			9-30-99	1294	...	24056	Dc	[64]1.13	□[65]0.99	v1.59	v□1.67	....	1.95	9 Mo Sep	v1.23	v1.51	28
29	....	None Since Public			...	Nil	....	40.3	333	486	6-30-99	1102	...	31803	Sp	d1.54	v1.04	v□0.16	v□0.44	vP0.15	0.15				29
30	....	None Paid			...	Nil	....	12.2	14.7	1.80	9-30-99	....	...	25108	Je	0.03	v0.06	v0.03	v0.04	v0.04	0.06	3 Mo Sep	vd0.01	v0.01	30
31	1992	t0.25	12-15-99	11-26	[66]1.22	1.00	g1.32	513	2736	2293	6-30-99	245	...	±78355	Dc	5.20	4.97	v[67][68]7.74	v[69][70]1.55	E4.77	....	6 Mo Jun	n/a	v2.52	31
32	....	None Since Public			...	Nil	....	17.0	305	176	9-30-99	15.0	...	24101	Je	□0.29	d3.78	v□1.04	v1.20	v1.24	2.24	3 Mo Sep	v0.29	v1.29	32
33	....	Wrrt	7-16-99	7-19	Wrrt	Nil	....	3.32	16.6	15.2	9-30-99	230	1080	20184	Dc	d0.28	v0.01	vd0.21	vd2.26	....	d2.46	9 Mo Sep	vd0.31	vd0.51	33
34	....	Terms&trad. basis should			be checked in detail			Wrrts expire 7-1-2002				....	...	10512	Dc	...	...	...	....	....	....	Callable at 1¢			34
35	1998	0.134	6-8-99	5-21	0.134	0.13	0.128	22.0	295	476	12-31-98	699	...	1037282	Dc	Δd0.04	0.69	n/a	v1.30	....	1.35	3 Mo Mar	v0.30	v0.35	35
36	....	None Since Public			...	Nil	....	3.24	17.3	39.7	9-30-99	0.34	...	10842	Dc	vΔ1.12	vd1.85	vd1.08	vd0.23	....	d0.39	9 Mo Sep	vd0.34	vd0.50	36
37◆	....	None Since Public			...	Nil	....	98.0	367	259	9-30-99	673	...	49194	Dc	v□0.46	v0.48	v□0.75	v□0.53	....	0.74	9 Mo Sep	v0.67	v0.88	37
38	1944	Q0.30	1-1-00	12-13	1.05	1.20	1.00	23.7	43.4	21.9	9-30-99	44.6	...	1617	Dc	v□0.57	v1.31	vd1.35	v1.39	....	2.13	12 Mo Sep	v0.33	v2.13	38
39	1994	Q0.42½	1-20-00	12-29	1.70	1.70	1.70	Total Assets $255.81M			9-30-99	197	...	5172	Dc	v0.49	v0.17	v0.15	v□0.45	....	1.12	9 Mo Sep	v□0.21	v□0.88	39
40	....	None Since Public			...	Nil	....	1.10	5.97	12.4	9-30-99	19.4	1	52509	Dc	□[72]d0.64	v□d2.87	vd1.41	vd0.71	....	d0.60	9 Mo Sep	vd0.37	vd0.26	40
41	1971	Q0.16½	12-31-99	12-6	[73]0.66	0.66	0.66	26.0	1171	1140	9-30-99	742	98	69579	Je	2.32	2.77	v2.53	vd3.90	v2.72	2.51	3 Mo Sep	v0.74	v0.53	41
42◆	....	None Paid			...	Nil	....	1.37	3.60	3.54	9-30-99	32.9	555	7833	Dc	□vd1.05	□vd0.88	vd0.92	vd2.61	....	d2.77	9 Mo Sep	vd0.06	vd0.22	42
43	....	None Since Public			...	Nil	....	50.1	62.7	4.30	10-02-99	p....	...	★27261	Dc	...	...	...	pv0.18	....	0.21	9 Mo Sep	v0.13	v0.16	43
44	....	None Since Public			...	Nil	....	103	249	216	10-31-99	2459	...	90679	Ja	v1.30	v0.97	v0.94	v0.90	E0.69	0.92	9 Mo Oct	v0.74	v□0.76	44
45◆	1945	Q0.07½	12-10-99	11-29	0.30	0.30	0.30	12.3	189	200	9-30-99	79.8	...	25983	Dc	0.56	v0.99	v1.39	v1.97	....	2.45	9 Mo Sep	v1.53	v2.01	45
46	....	None Since Public			...	Nil	....	91.7	519	460	9-30-99	696	...	103043	Dc	pv1.06	pv1.02	pv1.40	v□0.19	E1.27↓	1.22	9 Mo Sep	v□d0.05	vΔ0.98	46
47	1994	S0.10	12-14-99	12-1	0.20	0.20	0.19	138	2198	1424	9-30-99	521	...	75856	Dc	v1.59	v1.94	v1.97	v0.93	E1.86	1.11	9 Mo Sep	v1.11	v1.29	47
48◆	1993	0.38¾	1-14-00	12-29	1.163	1.55	1.45	Total Assets $1193M			9-30-99	654	...	24062	Dc	v0.74	v0.98	□v1.16	v1.12	....	1.11	9 Mo Sep	v0.85	v0.84	48
49◆	....	None Since Public			...	Nil	....	46.3	99.4	65.7	8-31-99	....	...	27500	Fb	v0.21	v0.19	vd0.57	vd3.64	....	d2.98	9 Mo Nov	vd0.95	vd0.29	49
50	....	Plan annual div			...	[74]....	....	Total Assets $55167M			6-30-99	pj627	[75]...	p486585	Dc	...	...	...	pv1.47	....	....	6 Mo Jun	n/a	vp0.82	50

◆Stock Splits & Divs By Line Reference Index [5]2-for-1,'98,'99. [7]5-for-1,'98. [9]10%,'99. [10]2-for-1,'98,'99. [11]2-for-1,'95. [12]No adj for stk dstr,'99. [19]3-for-1,'96,'98. [22]2-for-1,'95. [23]7-for-5,'96:29%,'97:21.1762%,'98:10%,'99. [27]3-for-2,'96. [28]10%,'95:3-for-2,'97,'98. [37]3-for-2,'97:2-for-1,'98. [42]1-for-4 REVERSE,'96. [45]3-for-2,'96,'99. [48]2-for-1,'94. [49]2-for-1,'97.

¶ S&P 500
\# MidCap 400
✣ SmallCap 600
• Options

Index	Ticker	Name of Issue (Call Price of Pfd. Stocks)	Market	Com. Rank. & Pfd. Rating	Inst. Hold Cos	Inst. Hold Shs. (000)	Principal Business	Price Range 1971-97 High	1971-97 Low	1998 High	1998 Low	1999 High	1999 Low	December, 1999 Dec. Sales in 100s	Last Sale Or Bid High	Low	Last	%Div Yield	P-E Ratio	EPS 5 Yr Growth	% Annualized Total Return 12 Mo	36 Mo	60 Mo
1•[1]	MQST	✓MapQuest.com Inc	NNM	NR	47	3247	Provide online mapping info	....	....	....	....	32½	8¾	96067	32½	22 9/16	22 9/16	...	d	...	...	...	...
✣2	MCS	✓Marcus Corp	NY,Ph	A–	100	12197	Hotels:restaurants:theatres	20 15/16	5/16	19 1/16	12 7/16	16 5/16	10½	3067	14 3/16	12 3/16	13 7/16	1.6	18	–7	–15.9	–0.2	2.9
3•[2]	MRBA	✓Marimba Inc	NNM	NR	73	2502	Internet-based softwr solut'n	....	....	....	....	74⅜	20	126005	48⅛	24 5/16	46 1/16	...	..	...	...	...	...
4•[3]	MRL	✓Marine Drilling	NY,Ph	B–	210	43315	Contract drill'g o & g wells	246⅞	¾	26 11/16	7	22½	5 15/16	113247	22½	16⅛	22 7/16	...	d	9	197	4.5	49.5
5	MARPS	✓Marine Petrol Tr[51]	NSC	NR	6	112	Oil & gas royalties-Gulf Oil	45	5	19½	12⅛	19	12⅜	323	15 1/16	13⅞	15 1/16	10.7	9	6	31.6	8.7	13.9
6	HZO	✓MarineMax Inc	NY	NR	16	1026	Recreational boat dealer/svcs	....	....	14 3/16	7 5/16	13	7⅞	3596	10	8 7/16	9½	...	8	...	20.6	...	...
7	TUG	✓Maritrans Inc.	NY	B–	30	6111	U.S.coast marine transporter	10¼	1¾	11⅝	6 5/16	6⅞	4¾	5420	5 9/16	4¾	5⅜	7.4	90	...	–11.8	1.0	4.1
#8•[3]	IV	✓Mark IV Industries	NY,Ch,P	B+	196	29720	Power transfer eqp/audio prod	28	1/32	24⅛	12⅛	21⅞	12 13/16	36951	18⅞	16½	17 11/16	1.2	11	2	37.9	–3.9	4.4
9	MKL	✓Markel Corp	NY	B+	112	2163	Insurance broker/underwriter	161⅛	7½	187	132	193	143¼	3772	157¼	143¼	155	...	17	21	–14.4	19.9	30.2
10	MSGI	✓Marketing Services Group	NNM	C	28	1375	Provide telemarketing svcs	28¾	⅝	5 9/16	2	60⅛	3⅛	125641	20¼	14 7/16	16¾	...	d	Neg	379	63.8	25.0
11	MKSP	✓Marketing Specialists	NNM	NR	24	3349	Sales & marketing services	....	....	15⅝	15	15½	2	13451	4 7/16	2½	3¾	...	..	...	–75.2	...	...
12	MKTW	✓MarketWatch.com	NNM	NR	55	2148	Internet financial news svcs	....	....	....	....	130	26⅛	17795	47 1/16	36	36½	...	d	...	...	...	...
13	NRG	✓MarkWest Hydrocarbon	AS	NR	15	2757	Natural gas processing svcs	25	10	22½	7	11⅜	4¾	1282	6⅞	4¾	6½	...	81	...	–27.8	–25.1	...
14	MTY	✓Marlton Technologies	AS	B–	10	471	Mfr custom trade show exhibits	29	⅜	7⅝	2¾	5¼	1½	2523	3 3/16	1 9/16	2 13/16	...	10	12	–31.8	–10.1	26.3
¶15•[4]	MAR	✓Marriott Intl 'A'	NY	NR	457	125316	Hotel mgmt/franchising	....	....	37 15/16	19⅜	44½	29	113136	34¼	29 9/16	31 9/16	0.7	20	23	9.5	...	...
¶16•[5]	MMC	✓Marsh & McLennan	NY,B,Ch,P	A	950	186058	Insur brokerage & agency serv	53 5/16	2 9/16	64 5/16	43⅜	96¾	57⅛	196290	96¾	77¾	95 11/16	1.9	28	13	67.5	44.1	33.3
17	MARSA	✓Marsh Supermkts'A'	NNM	A	22	1723	Food chain, Indiana & Ohio	23½	1	18¼	13	18	11	640	14½	13 9/16	13⅞	3.2	11	24	–16.5	3.6	9.2
#18•[6]	MI	✓Marshall & Ilsley	NY	A–	262	35750	Commercial bkg,Wisconsin	62¼	1⅜	62¼	39⅜	72¾	54⅜	32016	68 3/16	59 9/16	62 13/16	1.5	20	22	9.1	24.0	29.6
19	MSO	✓Martha Stewart Living'A'	NY	NR	..	...	Homeowners'how to'prd/svcs	....	....	....	....	50	18	40061	31	20 1/16	24	...	..	...	...	...	...
#20	MLM	✓Martin Marietta Materials	NY,Ch,Ph,P	NR	321	42774	Aggregates/bldg materials	38½	16½	62 3/16	35 13/16	68⅛	35¼	54886	42⅝	35⅜	41	1.3	16	16	–33.4	22.4	20.0
21	MVL	✓Marvel Enterprises	NY,Ch,Ph	NR	48	13259	Design,mkt,dstr spcl toys	26¼	7 9/16	11 5/16	4 5/16	9¾	4 11/16	17846	7⅞	5⅝	5½	...	d	Neg	–11.1	–34.4	...
¶22•[7]	MAS	✓Masco Corp	NY,B,Ch,P	B+	718	283990	Bldg & home improv't prod	26⅞	1 3/16	33	20¾	33 11/16	22½	339934	26 9/16	22½	25⅜	1.9	20	NM	–10.4	14.1	20.0
✣23•[8]	MSX	✓MascoTech, Inc	NY,Ch,P	B	149	14568	Mfr powertrain,chassis,auto pd	28⅛	1½	26 7/16	15¼	17¾	10⅝	23863	14	10⅝	12 11/16	2.5	7	NM	–24.4	–6.8	0.9
24	MYS	✓Masisa S.A.[56]ADS	NY,P	NR	22	2004	Mfr particle board, Chile	34¾	8 11/16	11½	4½	13	5⅜	1530	13	11⅞	12⅞	2.1	14	...	110	0.6	–10.4
25•[9]	MTZ	✓MasTec Inc	NY,Ch,Ph	B	111	7781	Telephone/elec sv	55¾	1 1/16	34 3/16	12⅜	44½	19⅝	18987	44½	38⅛	44½	...	48	3	112	8.0	45.5
26	MAST	✓Mastech Corp	NNM	NR	141	14536	Info technology services	18 3/16	5 11/16	30 7/16	15½	30¾	10⅜	122897	25¾	18 7/16	24¾	...	31	37	–13.5	38.0	...
27	MATVY	✓Matav-Cable Sys ADS[59]	NNM	NR	16	1230	Cable TV services	20¾	12⅞	27 13/16	14¾	65	19⅞	4890	65	48 15/16	58	...	..	...	199	62.0	...
28	MXC	✓MATEC Corp	AS	B–	7	148	Steel cable:electr:instr	8⅞	9/16	6	3¼	6¼	3 5/16	257	6¼	5⅛	6¼	...	22	NM	78.6	40.6	15.8
✣29•[10]	MSC	✓Material Sciences	NY,Ch,Ph	B	96	10053	Steel coil protective coat'gs	22⅜	3⅞	13 3/16	6½	16	6⅜	8090	12 11/16	9⅞	10 3/16	...	9	–1	19.8	–17.3	–8.5
30	MLK	✓Matlack Systems	NY,Ch,Ph	C	25	3458	Bulk commodities trucking	12¼	2 1/16	12¼	6⅝	7⅝	3 3/16	2324	3 15/16	3 3/16	3 3/16	...	d	Neg	–58.9	–22.6	–20.4
31	MC	✓Matsushita El Ind[62] ADR	NY,B,Ch,P,Ph	NR	94	4662	Japan mfr consumer elec eq	219 1/16	6 3/16	182¼	128	299⅝	157½	1505	299⅝	245	279	0.4	89	57	60.8	20.3	12.1
¶32•[7]	MAT	✓Mattel, Inc	NY,B,Ch,P,Ph	A–	792	340919	Design,mfg,market toys	42¼	1 5/16	46 9/16	21¼	30 5/16	11 11/16	696489	15½	12	13⅛	2.7	18	–5	–43.3	–21.2	–2.9
33	MLP	✓Maui Land & Pineapple	AS	NR	9	213	Land devel/pineapple business	....	....	21⅝	8 13/16	30¾	9	319	18⅞	17⅜	17⅜	...	17	...	94.3	...	...
34	MAVK	✓Maverick Tube	NNM,Ch	B–	85	7174	Mfr welded tube for o&g ind	51¼	2 3/16	26⅞	5	26¾	5⅜	43699	26½	20	24 11/16	...	d	–15	344	57.1	39.8
35	MAV	✓Mavesa, S.A. ADS[63]	NY,Ch	NR	31	12782	Mfr,dstr food/soap products	10⅞	5¼	6¼	2⅜	5	2¼	20494	3 3/16	2 9/16	3 1/16	2.6	9	...	–16.1	...	...
36	MAXC	✓Maxco Inc	NNM	B–	13	368	Distrib construction supplies	12½	7/16	11½	6	9⅞	4½	683	9⅞	7¾	9⅞	...	17	55	46.3	9.6	3.0
37•[11]	MAXI	✓Maxicare Health Plans	NNM	NR	34	10190	Multi-state HMO services	31⅛	6⅜	13⅛	2⅝	7	2 5/16	10267	3⅝	2 5/16	2⅞	...	d	Neg	–46.5	–49.4	–28.3
38	MXG	✓Maxim Group	NY	NR	40	8141	Franchisor floor cover'g ctrs	17⅞	5¼	24 9/16	14 1/16	25⅝	4	19046	6⅞	5	5⅜	...	d	Neg	–77.6	–32.5	–15.7
#39•[12]	MXIM	✓Maxim Integrated Prod	NNM	B+	482	250179	Mfr,mkt integrated circuits	19⅛	5/16	22¾	11⅛	48 5/16	19 15/16	596968	48 5/16	38 15/16	47 3/16	...	71	29	117	63.6	64.3
40	MMP	✓Maxim Pharmaceuticals	AS	NR	14	556	Dvlp therapeutics & vaccines	19¼	6¾	23	11⅝	20⅛	7½	9995	20⅛	13⅛	20	...	d	...	30.1	41.9	...
41	WS	Wrrt(Pur 1 com at$10.50)	AS	....	1	10		9½	1¼	12	2¼	9⅝	1 15/16	2102	9⅝	4¼	9⅝	...	..	...	...	...	...
✣42	MMS	✓MAXIMUS Inc	NY	NR	143	10448	Consult'g svs to gvt agencies	32⅞	16	37	20 7/16	41½	20¾	10514	36 15/16	27¾	33 15/16	...	26	...	–8.3	...	...
43•[4]	MXTR	✓Maxtor Corp	NNM	NR	71	40177	Hard disk storage pred	....	....	16¼	6¾	21¼	4¼	350458	7 5/16	5	7¼	...	..	...	–48.2	...	...
44	MXWL	✓Maxwell Technologies	NNM	B–	63	2699	Defense/comm'l electr sys	39⅜	2 9/16	42¼	16⅜	40⅝	6¾	19886	11⅜	8⅜	10	...	15	NM	–75.2	–23.1	22.3
45	MMX	✓Maxx Petroleum[66]	AS,To	NR	12	4262	Oil & gas acq,dvlp,prodn, Cdn	12 9/16	13/16	5¾	1⅞	4 7/16	1 13/16	1587	2 15/16	1⅞	2¾	...	d	Neg	46.7	–27.8	–15.8
#46	MXM	✓MAXXAM Inc	AS,B,Ch,P,Ph	B–	98	2311	Alum'n/forest prod:RE mgmt	67⅝	2⅛	65¼	41½	64¾	41⅜	1827	47¼	41⅜	42⅞	...	12	NM	–25.3	–3.4	6.8
47	MAXY	Maxygen Inc	NNM	NR	..	...	Molecular evolution gene R&D	....	....	....	....	82	16	131703	82	16	71	...	..	...	...	...	...
¶48•[8]	MAY	✓May Dept Stores	NY,B,C,Ch,P,Ph	A+	821	258519	Large department store chain	38 1/16	1 3/16	47¼	33 3/16	45⅜	29 3/16	239323	34⅜	29 3/16	32¼	2.8	12	5	–17.7	...	...
¶49•[13]	MYG	✓Maytag Corp	NY,B,Ch,P	B	581	47037	Mfrs major home appliances	37 9/16	4	64½	35⅜	74 13/16	31¼	97824	50¼	44¾	48	1.5	13	NM	–21.8	36.7	28.9
50	MAZL	✓Mazel Stores	NNM	NR	18	1859	'Close-out'/mdse strs/whlsale	29¼	11	20⅝	8⅜	16¼	8	10995	9 13/16	8⅞	9¼	...	18	...	–28.2	–25.6	...

Uniform Footnote Explanations-See Page 4. Other: [1]Ph:Cycle 3. [2]ASE,P,Ph:Cycle 3. [3]CBOE:Cycle 2. [4]Ph:Cycle 1. [5]P:Cycle 1. [6]ASE,Ph:Cycle 3. [7]ASE:Cycle 1. [8]CBOE:Cycle 3. [9]CBOE,Ph:Cycle 1. [10]Ph:Cycle 2. [11]ASE:Cycle 3. [12]P:Cycle 2. [13]CBOE:Cycle 1. [51]Units of int. [52]9 Mo Sep'97. [53]®$0.84,'96. [54]Stk dstr of Jackpot Enterprises. [55]2 Mo Dec'97. [56]Ea ADS rep 30 ord, no par. [57]Approx. [58]Stk dstr of National Beverage Corp,'91. [59]Ea ADS rep 2 ord NIS 1. [60]To be determined. [61]Restated fr $0.78,'96. [62]Each ADR equal 10 com yen 50 par. [63]Ea ADS rep 60 com,nominal val Bs.10. [64]10 Mo Jan'96. [65]If com exceeds $12 for 20 of 30 con trad days. [66]Sep'97 & prior pricing in $Cdn. [67]Excl ESOP Shs.

Index	Splits ◆	Cash Divs. Ea. Yr. Since	Dividends: Latest Payment Period $	Date	Ex. Div.	Total $ So Far 1999	Ind. Rate	Paid 1998	Financial Position Mil-$ Cash& Equiv.	Curr. Assets	Curr. Liab.	Balance Sheet Date	Capitalization Lg Trm Debt Mil-$	Shs. 000 Pfd.	Com.	Earnings $ Per Shr. Years End	1995	1996	1997	1998	1999	Last 12 Mos.	Interim Earnings Period	$ per Shr. 1998	1999	Index
1		....	None Since Public			...	Nil	....	47.6	61.2	9.49	9-30-99	....	...	33573	Dc	...	...	...	vpd0.11	....	d0.39	9 Mo Sep	pvd0.07	vpd0.35	1
2	◆	1983	Q0.05½	11-15-99	10-21	0.22	0.22	0.22	4.32	22.3	61.0	8-26-99	252	...	±29908	My	0.82	v1.42	v1.04	v0.94	v0.77	0.74	6 Mo Nov	v0.66	v0.63	2
3		....	None Since Public			...	Nil	....	58.3	68.6	14.3	9-30-99	0.05	...	23077	Dc	...	...	...	vpd0.37	....	....	9 Mo Sep	n/a	vd0.21	3
4		....	None Since Public			...	Nil	....	8.32	32.3	32.0	9-30-99	....	...	57183	Dc	vd0.09	v0.45	v1.11	v1.15	....	d0.03	9 Mo Sep	v1.02	vd0.16	4
5		1966	0.517	12-28-99	11-26	1.61	1.61	1.552	1.61	2.16	0.13	9-30-99	....	...	2000	Je	1.07	v1.59	v1.96	v1.49	v1.54	1.74	3 Mo Sep	v0.34	v0.54	5
6		....	None Since Public			...	Nil	....	21.1	179	158	6-30-99	3.42	...	15238	Sp	...	...	‡pv[52]0.96	vp1.14	Pv1.21	1.21				6
7		1994	Q0.10	12-8-99	11-22	0.40	0.40	0.37	18.5	53.0	33.6	9-30-99	71.5	...	11828	Dc	v0.41	v...	v0.94	v0.26	....	0.06	9 Mo Sep	v0.21	v0.01	7
8	◆	1990	Q0.05½	1-3-00	12-15	0.21½	0.22	0.19	2.20	1002	576	8-31-99	794	...	46568	Fb	1.39	v[53]0.84	v□1.66	v□0.89	E1.65↓	1.63	9 Mo Nov	v□0.58	v□1.32	8
9		....	None Since Public			...	Nil	....	Total Assets $2507.34M			9-30-99	389	...	5599	Dc	v6.15	v8.30	v8.92	v10.17	....	9.37	9 Mo Sep	v7.07	v6.27	9
10	◆	....	h[54]....	7-31-90	7-12	...	Nil	....	14.6	45.4	38.6	9-30-99	1.04	50	25844	Je	0.06	d0.36	vd2.85	vd0.37	vd1.39	d1.45	3 Mo Sep	vd0.06	vd0.12	10
11		....	None Since Public			...	Nil	....	4.44	76.2	75.9	9-30-99	246	...	13838	Dc	...	...	pv0.01	Pvp1.01	....	....	9 Mo Sep	n/a	vd2.12	11
12		....	None Since Public			...	Nil	....	19.7	29.3	5.62	9-30-99	....	...	13853	Dc	...	...	v‡[55]d0.01	vd1.38	....	d3.54	9 Mo Sep	vd0.91	vd3.07	12
13		....	None Since Public			...	Nil	....	2.01	26.5	18.5	9-30-99	32.1	...	8456	Dc	p0.63	vp1.15	v0.91	vd0.14	....	0.08	9 Mo Sep	vd0.13	v0.09	13
14		....	0.15	11-13-79	10-30	...	Nil	....	0.59	32.2	16.6	9-30-99	14.3	...	7329	Dc	v0.32	v0.45	v0.36	v0.35	....	0.28	9 Mo Sep	v0.25	v0.18	14
15		1998	Q0.05½	1-14-00	12-29	0.21	0.22	0.145	240	1239	1421	6-18-99	1178	...	248783	Dc	±p0.83	±p1.00	v2.46	v1.46	E1.60	1.60	9 Mo Sep	v1.02	v1.16	15
16	◆	1923	Q0.45	2-14-00	1-6	1.70	1.80	1.466	641	3403	3559	9-30-99	2591	...	266795	Dc	v1.82	v2.08	v1.59	v2.98	E3.45	3.17	9 Mo Sep	v2.28	v2.47	16
17		1960	Q0.11	11-1-99	10-13	0.44	0.44	0.44	24.3	178	123	6-19-99	232	...	±8521	Mr	±1.07	v±d0.03	±□v1.07	v±1.28	....	1.32	6 Mo Sep	±v0.61	±v0.65	17
18		1938	Q0.24	12-14-99	11-26	0.94	0.96	0.86	Total Deposits $15638.25M			9-30-99	569	336	106507	Dc	v1.90	v2.03	v2.42	v2.61	E3.12	3.05	9 Mo Sep	v1.89	v2.33	18
19		....	None Since Public			...	Nil	....	22.3	59.4	55.6	6-30-99	p....	...	★±48526	Dc	...	...	...	pv0.27	....	0.20	9 Mo Sep	vp0.30	vp0.23	19
20		1994	Q0.13	12-31-99	11-29	0.52	0.52	0.50	0.60	429	219	9-30-99	603	...	46710	Dc	v1.47	v1.71	v2.13	v2.48	E2.62	2.64	9 Mo Sep	v1.82	v1.98	20
21		....	None Since Public			...	Nil	....	79.1	196	94.2	9-30-99	250	17	33532	Dc	v1.05	v0.61	vd1.06	vd1.23	....	d2.14	9 Mo Sep	v0.15	v□d0.76	21
22	◆	1944	Q0.12	2-7-00	1-5	0.57	0.48	0.43	145	2160	970	9-30-99	2420	...	p447000	Dc	vd0.63	v0.91	v1.17	v1.39	E1.27	1.32	9 Mo Sep	v0.95	v0.88	22
23		1993	Q0.08	11-15-99	10-13	0.30	0.32	0.26	12.3	467	244	9-30-99	1374	...	44572	Dc	v0.81	Δv0.50	v2.12	v1.83	....	1.75	9 Mo Sep	v1.47	v1.39	23
24		1993	[57]0.274	5-24-99	5-7	[57]0.274	0.27	0.224	52.3	160	41.7	12-31-98	11.4	...	841000	Dc	0.85	0.65	v0.87	v0.95	....	0.95				24
25	◆	....	h[58]....	9-9-91	9-10	...	Nil	....	28.7	411	168	9-30-99	290	...	28157	Dc	pvd0.11	v1.25	v1.44	vd0.51	....	0.93	9 Mo Sep	vd0.38	v1.06	25
26	◆	....	None Since Public			...	Nil	....	116	230	49.9	9-30-99	30.0	...	50459	Dc	pv0.30	pv0.10	v0.35	v0.67	....	0.81	9 Mo Sep	v0.45	v0.59	26
27		1998	1.024	12-14-98	11-16	...	[60]....	2.084	0.28	13.4	52.7	12-31-98	45.3	...	27232	Dc	p0.60	v1.13	v1.54	v1.16	....	0.23	3 Mo Mar	v0.48	vd0.45	27
28		1998	†1.75	5-15-98	5-18	...	Nil	†1.75	2.60	9.27	2.99	10-03-99	....	...	2651	Dc	v0.11	vd0.03	v0.18	v0.32	....	0.29	9 Mo Sep	v0.25	v0.22	28
29	◆	....	None Since Public			...	Nil	....	1.96	121	78.0	8-31-99	128	...	15605	Fb	v[61]0.55	v1.04	v0.42	v□0.66	....	1.10	9 Mo Nov	v□0.41	v0.85	29
30	◆	....	None Since Public			...	Nil	....	2.27	45.7	19.8	6-30-99	50.3	...	8814	Sp	0.74	d0.17	v0.21	vd0.23	....	d0.91	9 Mo Jun	v0.20	vd0.48	30
31		1950	0.509	12-17-99	9-27	1.052	1.05	0.823	15312	37027	22784	3-31-99	5185	...	2112318	Mr	d2.60	v4.90	v3.10	v3.12	....	3.12				31
32	◆	1990	Q0.09	1-4-00	12-8	0.34	0.36	0.30	92.7	3307	2486	9-30-99	1084	...	p420777	Dc	v1.11	v1.23	v□0.94	v1.10	E0.72	0.66	9 Mo Sep	v0.27	vd0.17	32
33	◆	1999	0.12½	3-24-99	3-4	0.12½	[60]....	....	1.27	42.6	19.6	9-30-99	30.9	...	7189	Dc	vd0.22	vd0.10	v0.12	v□0.60	....	1.03	9 Mo Sep	v0.03	v0.46	33
34	◆	....	None Since Public			...	Nil	....	1.63	82.9	38.6	9-30-99	38.5	...	14440	Sp	d0.16	v0.50	v0.97	v0.73	vd0.68	d0.68				34
35		1993	0.019	12-6-99	11-17	0.079	0.08	0.087	19.1	95.6	71.7	j10-31-97	8.72	...	2460000	Oc	0.33	v0.67	v0.48	n/a	Pv0.35	0.35				35
36		....	None Paid			...	Nil	....	1.36	43.2	28.6	9-30-99	40.0	68	3151	Mr	vd0.68	v5.46	v0.30	v0.12	....	0.60	6 Mo Sep	v0.46	v0.94	36
37		....	None Paid			...	Nil	....	66.2	103	74.1	9-30-99	....	...	17925	Dc	v1.15	v1.05	vd1.96	vd1.54	....	d0.62	9 Mo Sep	vd1.22	vd0.30	37
38		....	None Since Public			...	Nil	....	64.9	216	252	11-06-99	7.50	...	19038	Ja	‡[64]d1.02	v0.15	□v0.96	vd1.08	....	d0.60	9 Mo Oct	v□d1.02	v□d0.54	38
39	◆	....	None Since Public			...	Nil	....	579	794	147	9-25-99	....	...	273358	Je	v0.15	v0.44	v0.47	v0.59	v0.65	0.67	3 Mo Sep	v0.17	v0.19	39
40		....	None Paid			...	Nil	....	5.83	8.05	10.5	6-30-99	1.03	...	10204	Sp	pd0.87	vd0.20	vd1.03	vd2.37	Pvd3.94	d3.94				40
41		....	Terms&trad. basis should			be checked in detail			Wrrts expire 7-10-2001				....	...	2500	Sp	...	...	...	....	....	....	Callable at 1¢[65]			41
42		....	None Since Public			...	Nil	....	87.7	180	37.7	6-30-99	1.48	...	20984	Sp	...	p0.58	p0.54	v0.82	Pv1.32	1.32				42
43		....	None Since Public			...	Nil	....	285	645	499	10-02-99	113	...	113232	Dc	...	...	vpd3.62	v0.47	....	....	9 Mo Sep	n/a	vd0.53	43
44	◆	....	5%Stk	1-21-94	12-27	...	Nil	....	8.99	88.1	25.5	10-31-99	0.21	...	9564	Jl	0.06	□d2.29	v0.60	vd0.10	v1.12	0.68	3 Mo Oct	v0.25	vd0.19	44
45	◆	....	None Paid			...	Nil	....	....	9.47	14.5	j6-30-99	48.0	...	14858	Dc	0.32	v0.68	v0.48	vd3.03	....	jd2.82	6 Mo Jun	vd0.11	v0.10	45
46		....	5%Stk	11-17-75	9-24	...	Nil	....	209	1272	683	9-30-99	1978	669	7001	Dc	v6.08	v2.42	v7.14	vd2.10	....	3.55	9 Mo Sep	v□1.58	v7.23	46
47		....	None Since Public			...	Nil	....	36.1	38.3	5.48	9-30-99	1.16	p...	★28911	Dc	...	...	...	vpd0.40	....	....	9 Mo Sep	n/a	vpd0.36	47
48	◆	1911	0.22¼	12-15-99	11-29	0.89	0.89	0.847	34.0	5303	2775	10-30-99	3567	[67]...	330858	Ja	v□1.88	v□1.91	v□2.07	v2.30	E2.60	2.46	9 Mo Oct	v0.99	v1.15	48
49		1946	Q0.18	12-15-99	11-29	0.72	0.72	0.70	27.4	1103	939	9-30-99	415	...	84427	Dc	□vd0.14	v□1.35	v1.87	v□3.05	E3.57↑	3.59	9 Mo Sep	v□2.30	v2.84	49
50		....	None Since Public			...	Nil	....	2.68	111	33.3	10-30-99	46.1	...	9142	Ja	p0.70	p0.93	v0.92	v0.57	....	0.51	9 Mo Oct	v0.20	v0.14	50

◆**Stock Splits & Divs By Line Reference Index** [2]3-for-2,'95,'97. [8]Adj to 5%,'97. [10]1-for-4 REVERSE,'95. [16]2-for-1,'97:3-for-2,'98. [22]2-for-1,'98. [25]3-for-2,'97. [26]2-for-1,'98. [29]3-for-2,'94. [30]3-for-2,'94. [32]5-for-4,'94,'95,'96. [33]4-for-1,'98. [34]2-for-1,'97. [39]2-for-1,'95,'97,'99. [44]2-for-1,'96. [45]1-for-4 REVERSE,'98. [48]3-for-2,'99.

¶ S&P 500 · # MidCap 400 · ✣ SmallCap 600 · • Options

Index	Ticker	Name of Issue (Call Price of Pfd. Stocks)	Market	Com. Rank. & Pfd. Rating	Inst. Hold Cos	Inst. Hold Shs. (000)	Principal Business	1971-97 High	1971-97 Low	1998 High	1998 Low	1999 High	1999 Low	Dec. Sales in 100s	December, 1999 Last Sale Or Bid High	Low	Last	%Div Yield	P-E Ratio	EPS 5 Yr Growth	Total Return 12 Mo	36 Mo	60 Mo
¶1•[1]	MBI	✓MBIA Inc	NY,Ch,Ph,P	A+	668	89817	Insurance for muni bonds	67⅝	5 5/16	80 15/16	46 1/16	71⅞	45⅛	87884	52⅞	45 7/16	52 13/16	1.6	11	2	−18.3	2.8	15.3
2	MBD	MBIA Inc 6.95%'QUIDS'	NY	....[51]	1	.8	Qtly Income Debt Sec	....	....	25 13/16	25 1/16	25 7/16	19⅝	1526	22⅝	19⅝	19¾	8.8	..	...	−16.9	...	...
¶3•[2]	KRB	✓MBNA Corp	NY,Ch,Ph,P	A	805	566870	Bank hldg/credit card svc'g	20⅝	1½	25⅞	13½	33¼	20 13/16	336000	27 11/16	22⅝	27¼	1.0	23	27	11.0	32.1	45.2
4	MCX	✓MC Shipping	AS,Ph,P	C	5	107	Inv/owns 2nd hand cargo ships	15⅝	2⅛	3 11/16	⅝	1 7/16	11/16	2528	1 9/16	⅞	1	...	d	−27	53.0	−35.1	−19.3
5	MCAF	McAfee.com Corp'A'	NNM	NR	..	...	Online PC security svcs	....	....	....	....	63¾	12	338177	63¾	12	45	...	...	...	...	...	...
6	MCB	MCB Financial	AS	NR	1	35	General banking,Calif	....	....	....	....	11½	10¾	96	11½	10¾	11	...	11	...	...	...	...
7	MCCL	✓McClain Industries	NNM	B	8	276	Solid waste handling svcs	11 7/16	1/16	6 9/16	3	7⅛	3⅞	846	5 11/16	3⅞	5B	...	6	−16	−13.0	−0.4	−6.8
8	MNI	✓McClatchy Co 'A'	NY,Ch,P,Ph	B+	140	12986	Publish newsp CA,WA,Alaska	35 9/16	10⅝	39 9/16	24 15/16	43¾	29	7514	43¾	35⅞	43¼	0.9	25	10	23.6	17.0	21.9
#9•[3]	MKC	✓McCormick[54] & Co	NY,Ph	A−	266	41806	Spices, flavoring, tea, mixes	30¼	1 5/16	36 7/16	27 1/16	34⅝	26⅝	28763	32⅞	28¼	29¾	2.6	18	13	−10.1	10.5	12.8
¶10•[1]	MDR	✓McDermott Intl	NY,B,C,Ch,P,Ph	B−	308	51006	Offshore oil & gas constr	46⅝	7⅜	43 15/16	19¼	32½	7¼	213358	9 5/16	7¼	9 1/16	2.2	8	NM	−63.0	−18.1	−16.3
¶11•[4]	MCD	✓McDonald's Corp	NY,To,B,C,Ch,P,Ph	A+	1548	883241	Fast food restaurant:franch'g	27 7/16	⅜	39¾	22 5/16	49 9/16	35 15/16	792299	46¾	39 9/16	40 5/16	0.5	29	8	5.6	21.9	23.3
12	MCW	McDonald's Cp 7.50% Sub Deb'36	NY	....[55]	7	69	Sub Deferrable Int Debs	26 5/16	24¼	26⅞	24⅝	26 5/16	21⅝	2841	24⅝	21⅝	22¼	8.4	..	...	−6.5	4.0	...
13	MCJ	McDonald's Cp 7.50% Sub Deb'37	NY	....[55]	6	84	Sub Deferrable Int Debs	26⅝	24⅛	26¾	25 3/16	26⅜	21¾	2027	24¾	21¾	22½	8.3	..	...	−6.2	...	...
14	MGRC	✓McGrath RentCorp	NNM	B+	69	6026	Rents/sells modular offices	28½	1⅜	24¾	13⅞	22½	15⅞	2163	18½	16½	17½	2.7	10	20	−18.4	13.1	18.3
¶15•[1]	MHP	✓McGraw-Hill Companies	NY,B,Ch,P,Ph	[58]	713	149491	Books:educ/info svs:publ:TV	37 11/16	11/16	51⅝	34¼	63⅛	47⅛	102677	63⅛	56⅛	61⅝	1.4	32	11	23.8	41.8	33.1
¶16•[5]	WCOM	✓MCI WorldCom	NNM	B	2281	1775576	Telecommun'ns network	26 9/16	....	50½	18 11/16	64½	44 1/16	5095702	56 1/16	49 5/16	53 1/16	...	40	NM	11.4	45.3	52.4
¶17•[6]	MCK	✓McKesson HBOC	NY,P	NR	708	180438	Dstr drugs, toiletries/hm pd	56⅞	15 1/16	96¼	47⅞	89¾	18 9/16	331660	23 9/16	20	22½	1.1	17	−38	−71.4	−6.1	8.2
18•[7]	MCLD	✓McLeodUSA Inc'A'	NNM	NR	248	86040	Local,L-D telecommun svcs	20⅞	8 3/16	24⅛	7⅝	63⅜	15 3/16	179093	63⅜	42⅜	58⅞	...	d	−33	278	66.6	...
19•[8]	MMR	✓McMoRan Exploration	NY,Ph	NR	61	3736	Oil&gas expl,dev/sulfur mining	....	....	16 1/16	12¼	25	12	4437	22	18⅞	21⅛	...	d	...	50.9	...	...
#20•[6]	MCN	✓MCN Energy Gp	NY	B+	285	40654	Natural gas dstr,Michigan	40½	8 7/16	39⅞	16 7/16	25⅝	15 15/16	83136	25⅝	23 9/16	23¾	4.3	..	Neg	31.2	−2.5	10.0
21	MRI.A	✓McRae Indus'A'[59]	AS	↓B	13	445	Mfr combat boots/elect sys	10¾	1⅝	8¾	5¾	6¼	4½	505	5⅝	5 1/16	5⅝	6.4	13	−16	−5.6	−13.3	0.1
22	MRI.B	Cl'B' Cv[60]	AS	↓B	2	102		10½	1/16	8	6	6	4⅝	10	5⅛	5⅛	5⅛B	...	18	−16	−8.9	−19.6	−5.0
✣23	MWT	✓McWhorter Technologies	NY	NR	66	4951	Produce ind'l resin products	27 7/16	12⅞	28⅝	18⅞	22¾	12 7/16	4609	16⅛	12¾	16	...	14	8	−30.1	−11.2	1.5
24	MDCA	MDC Corp Cl'A'[61]	NNM,Ch,To	C	35	6559	Advertising/mktg svcs	12¾	4⅞	14⅛	6¼	14½	7⅜	11679	9	7½	8⅜	...	6	−4	−9.0	−4.9	...
✣25	MDC	✓M.D.C. Hldgs	NY,Ch,P	B	160	14522	Home bldg,mtge banking	22½	⅛	24	13	22	13⅜	9196	16	13 15/16	15 11/16	1.3	5	32	−25.8	23.4	27.4
26	MDS.B	✓MDS Inc 'B'[54]	To	B+	5	765	Own/oper medical laboratories	35¾	4¼	34½	24	34⅞	26¼	11660	29¾	27⅛	29½	0.5	26	13	0.5	8.2	...
27•[3]	MDU	✓MDU Resources Group	NY,Ch,P	B+	188	15006	Gas & elec utility:coal,o&g	22 9/16	2 7/16	28⅞	18 13/16	27 3/16	18 13/16	21381	22⅝	18 13/16	20	4.2	19	...	−21.4	13.8	15.8
¶28•[7]	MEA	✓Mead Corp	NY,B,C,Ch,P,Ph	B−	493	74128	Mfr paper,lumber,wood prod	37 11/16	1 15/16	37 5/16	25 13/16	46 5/16	28 9/16	84328	43⅝	35 1/16	43 7/16	1.6	29	−25	50.9	16.6	14.6
29	MEAD	✓Meade Instruments	NNM	NR	58	2890	Dgn telescopes & accessor's	10¾	6¼	13⅜	8⅝	30⅝	10½	16757	30 9/16	24	28½	...	18	...	134	...	...
30	MIG	✓Meadowbrook Insurance Grp	NY,P	NR	20	2249	Alternat'e Mkt risk mgmt ins	34⅛	15¼	35	14 15/16	17 7/16	4¾	5700	6 15/16	4¾	6 9/16	1.8	d	Neg	−59.7	−31.8	...
31	MSS	✓Measurement Specialties	AS	B−	22	531	Mfr temp,distance,pressure eq	7	1	4 7/16	2¼	23⅞	4¼	9022	21¼	16	20⅞	...	19	48	377	96.5	42.9
32	MECH	✓MECH Financial	NNM	NR	34	855	General bkg,Connecticut	28⅝	10	33	20¼	39⅝	27¾	17891	37 15/16	32 3/16	34 9/16	2.3	14	...	27.2	31.6	...
33	MEDX	✓Medarex Inc	NNM	C	39	3994	Dvlp stage:AIDS,cancer R & D	17¼	2½	8¼	2¾	41½	2⅞	200641	41½	11⅜	37¼	...	d	1	1129	74.6	66.9
34•[9]	MRE	✓Medco Research	NY,Ch,Ph,P	B−	83	5616	R&D pharmaceutical/med prod	33⅝	9/16	26⅝	13 9/16	30¾	20½	20812	30¾	26 5/16	30 1/16	...	24	NM	15.6	42.0	21.5
35	MDV	✓Medeva ADR	NY,Ch,P	NR	22	1592	Pharmaceut'ls U.K. & abroad	22⅛	5⅝	12¾	5 9/16	12¼	6¼	9473	12¼	10½	10¾	3.4	17	−2	40.3	−10.6	4.6
36	MDBK	✓Medford Bancorp	NNM	A	43	2811	General Banking, Mass	21⅛	1⅝	22½	11½	19½	14 7/16	2761	17½	16	16⅝	e2.6	12	10	2.3	12.2	22.0
37	MDA	✓Media Arts Group	NY,Ph	NR	31	1542	Mfr,mkt gift & art products	17⅝	1 5/16	25¾	7	14 11/16	3 1/16	12906	4	3 1/16	3 7/16	...	3	NM	−75.6	10.3	−9.0
#38	MEG.A	✓Media General Cl'A'	AS,Ch,P,Ph	B	187	16672	Newspaper:newsprint:TV	50½	1 13/16	53½	33⅞	59½	44 5/16	12201	53	46¾	52	1.2	17	−4	−0.7	21.4	14.4
39	MMXI	✓Media Metrix	NNM	NR	74	3968	Internet audience measur't sv	....	....	....	....	74	17	68819	44½	31⅜	35¾	...	..	...	...	...	...
40	MBAY	✓MediaBay Inc	NNM	NR	11	1559	Mkt,sell audio books	11⅛	4	20⅞	3⅜	19 15/16	7¼	21206	13	10 15/16	11 3/16	...	d	...	−3.8	...	...
¶41•[9]	UMG	✓MediaOne Group[62]	NY,P	NR	1185	353038	Cable/telecommunic svcs	29⅛	14⅜	50⅛	27	83	46⅛	418190	81 5/16	75 11/16	76 13/16	...	d	...	63.4	61.1	...
42	UMX	MediaOne Grp 6.25% 'PIES'	NY	BBB−	38	3982	Premium Income Exch Sec	....	....	68	44	114⅛	61	6375	113½	102	108	3.4	..	...	69.3	...	...
43	XVF	MediaOne Grp 7.00% 'PIES'	NY	NR	..	...	Premium Income Exch Sec	....	....	....	....	50⅝	41¾	25740	49½	45 1/16	48	6.3	..	...	...	...	...
44	MPLX	✓Mediaplex Inc	NNM	NR	..	...	e-commerce business solutions	....	....	....	....	78⅛	20¾	61378	78⅛	30¾	62¾	...	..	...	...	...	...
45	DOC	✓Medical Advisory Systems	AS	NR	1	7	Medical assistance pds/svcs	....	....	....	....	29⅞	6⅛	3724	13½	9 9/16	13	...	62	...	...	...	...
46	MAI	✓Medical Assurance	NY	NR	109	7930	Professional liability insur	26 7/16	4 5/16	33⅛	21¾	33⅛	20	13932	22 11/16	20	21 3/16	s...	10	15	−29.5	22.0	21.2
47•[10]	MMGR	✓Medical Manager	NNM	B−	132	11578	Hlth care ind mgmt sys/softwr	55⅞	5¼	65¼	30¼	112¾	37½	61770	87	60½	84¼	...	..	−33	91.5	20.2	34.5
48	MDCL	MedicalControl Inc	NSC	NR	9	130	Healthcare cost mgmt svcs	10½	3¼	8⅝	3¾	9⅝	5¾	3804	8¾	5¾	8⅝	...	d	Neg	6.2	19.9	−1.4
49	MDLI	MedicalLogic Inc	NNM	NR	..	...	Internet based medical svcs	....	....	....	....	29⅝	17	142621	29 9/16	17	21	...	..	...	...	...	...
✣50•[11]	MRX	✓Medicis Pharmaceutical 'A'	NY,Ph	B−	211	23961	Dvlp dermatology medicines	37 5/16	¾	43 3/16	20	47¾	20¼	28018	43¾	34⅞	42 9/16	...	29	23	6.6	29.6	97.3

Uniform Footnote Explanations-See Page 4. Other: [1]Ph:Cycle 2. [2]ASE,CBOE:Cycle 3. [3]Ph:Cycle 3. [4]CBOE:Cycle 3. [5]ASE,CBOE,P,Ph:Cycle 3. [6]P:Cycle 2. [7]CBOE:Cycle 1. [8]CBOE:Cycle 2. [9]ASE:Cycle 1. [10]ASE,Ph:Cycle 3. [11]ASE,CBOE:Cycle 1. [51]Rated 'AA' by S&P. [52]Or earlier upon'Tax Event're-spec cond. [53]To be determined. [54]Non-vtg. [55]Rated AA- by S&P. [56]or earlier for 'Tax Event' re-spec cond. [57]or earlier for'Tax Event' re-spec cond. [58]S&P is a division of the McGraw-Hill Companies; common not ranked, pfd not rated. [59]1/10 vtg. [60]Cv into 1 Cl'A'. [61]Subordinate vtg shrs. [62]AT&T plan acq,0.95 com&$30.85 cash. [63]Pfd in $M. [64]Re-spec cond.

Index	Cash Divs. Ea. Yr. Since	Dividends: Latest Payment Period $	Date	Ex. Div.	Total $ So Far 1999	Ind. Rate	Paid 1998	Financial Position Mil-$ Cash& Equiv.	Curr. Assets	Curr. Liab.	Balance Sheet Date	Capitalization Lg Trm Debt Mil-$	Shs. 000 Pfd.	Com.	Earnings $ Per Shr. Years End	1995	1996	1997	1998	1999	Last 12 Mos.	Interim Earnings Period	$ per Shr. 1998	1999	Index
1◆	1987	Q0.204	1-14-00	12-16	0.80	0.82	0.78½	Total Assets $11774.76M			9-30-99	689	...	99578	Dc	v3.21	v3.72	v4.22	v4.32	E4.75	2.96	9 Mo Sep	v3.29	v1.93	1
2	1999	Q0.434	11-1-99	10-27	1.699	1.738	....	Co opt to redm fr 11-1-2003 at $25[52]				★50.0	...	...	Dc	...	...	...	....	....	....	Mature 11-1-2038			2
3◆	1991	Q0.07	1-1-00	12-13	0.27	0.28	0.233	Total Deposits $17624M			9-30-99	6096	8574	801781	Dc	v0.45	0.59	v0.77	v0.97	E1.20	1.13	9 Mo Sep	v0.67	v0.83	3
4	1995	Div Omitted 9-7-99			0.05	Nil	0.05	19.8	30.3	24.5	12-31-98	118	...	8134	Dc	vd0.32	v0.42	Δvd0.27	vΔd0.20	....	d0.20				4
5	....	None Since Public			...	Nil	....	2.41	6.53	27.1	9-30-99	....	...	★±42250	Dc	...	...	...	vpd0.06	....	....	9 Mo Sep	n/a	vpd0.61	5
6◆	1999	0.01	12-17-99	12-1	0.02	[53]....	....	Total Deposits $155M			9-30-99	0.36	...	2060	Dc	...	...	v0.64	v0.74	....	1.03	9 Mo Sep	v0.50	v0.79	6
7◆	....	None Paid			...	Nil	....	2.86	87.3	39.4	6-30-99	48.5	...	4653	Sp	0.53	v0.90	vd0.36	v0.72	Pv0.90	0.90				7
8◆	1930	Q0.09½	1-3-00	12-14	0.38	0.384	0.38	6.94	215	221	9-26-99	927	...	±44948	Dc	v±0.90	v±1.18	±v1.80	±v1.41	....	1.73	9 Mo Sep	v±0.93	v±1.25	8
9	1929	Q0.19	1-24-00	12-29	0.68	0.76	0.64	13.8	506	533	8-31-99	242	...	±70791	Nv	1.20	±□v0.62	v±1.30	v±1.41	E1.63	1.36	9 Mo Aug	v±0.73	v±0.68	9
10	1955	Q0.05	1-1-00	12-13	0.20	0.20	0.20	224	1405	1251	9-30-99	323	...	59543	Mr	0.23	vd3.95	v3.48	v□3.16	E1.15	0.80	6 Mo Sep	v2.76	v0.40	10
11◆	1976	Q0.04⅞	12-15-99	11-29	0.19½	0.20	0.17⅝	425	1394	2355	9-30-99	6289	...	1354019	Dc	v0.97	v1.08	v1.14	v1.10	E1.40	1.29	9 Mo Sep	v0.85	v1.04	11
12	1996	Q0.46⅞	12-31-99	12-13	1.87½	1.88	1.87½	Co option redm fr 12-31-2001 at $25[56]				200	...	...	Dc	...	...	...	....	....	....	Mature 9-30-2036			12
13	1997	Q0.46⅞	12-31-99	12-13	1.87½	1.87	1.87½	Co option redm fr 12-31-2001 at $25[57]				★150	...	...	Dc	...	...	...	....	....	....	Mature 1-2-2037			13
14◆	1990	Q0.12	10-29-99	10-13	0.46	0.48	0.38	Total Assets $292.89M			9-30-99	109	...	12695	Dc	v0.86	v1.01	v1.58	v1.67	....	1.74	9 Mo Sep	v1.25	v1.32	14
15◆	1937	Q0.21½	12-10-99	11-23	0.86	0.86	†0.78¼	15.4	1774	1695	9-30-99	407	1	196100	Dc	v1.14	v2.48	v1.45	v□1.71	....	1.90	9 Mo Sep	v□1.34	v1.53	15
16◆	....	None Paid			...	Nil	....	307	9707	15553	9-30-99	13245	11190	p2838345	Dc	v0.43	□vd3.67	v0.27	v□d1.34	E1.33	1.42	9 Mo Sep	v□d1.84	v0.92	16
17◆	1995	Q0.06	1-3-00	11-29	0.30½	0.24	0.50	207	6797	5105	9-30-99	1126	195	281592	Mr	1.45	v1.51	pv0.89	v0.31	E1.35	0.43	6 Mo Sep	v0.34	v0.46	17
18◆	....	None Since Public			...	Nil	....	1463	1752	272	9-30-99	1801	★1000	155298	Dc	pvd0.20	vd0.28	vd0.73	vd1.00	....	d1.43	9 Mo Sep	vd0.74	vd1.18	18
19	....	None Since Public			...	Nil	....	4.47	57.5	41.7	9-30-99	....	...	12805	Dc	...	...	vpd0.74	vd1.96	....	d0.04	9 Mo Sep	vd1.86	v0.06	19
20◆	1989	Q0.25½	11-24-99	11-8	1.02	1.02	1.02	30.3	687	957	9-30-99	1864	...	85655	Dc	v1.48	v2.23	v1.91	vd3.54	E0.10	0.06	9 Mo Sep	vd3.95	v□d0.35	20
21	1985	Q0.09	12-31-99	12-8	0.36	0.36	0.36	5.42	27.5	5.85	10-30-99	5.21	...	±2769	Jl	±0.80	v±0.84	v±0.85	v±0.82	±v0.28	0.45	3 Mo Oct	v0.03	v0.20	21
22	....	0.02½	7-22-83	7-5	...	Nil	....	....	...	....		....	...	911	Jl	±0.80	±0.84	v±0.85	v±0.82	Pv0.28	0.28				22
23	....	None Since Public			...	Nil	....	5.44	143	8.50	7-31-99	131	...	10052	Oc	1.02	v1.32	v1.48	v1.24	Pv1.17	1.17				23
24◆	....	None Paid			...	Nil	....	30.5	252	153	j6-30-99	453	...	±17848	Dc	±v0.27	±v0.58	±vd1.82	v±0.88	....	j1.05	9 Mo Sep	v0.62	v0.79	24
25	1994	Q0.05	11-23-99	11-4	0.20	0.20	0.15	Total Assets $871.47M			9-30-99	207	...	22315	Dc	0.86	□v0.98	□v1.18	v□2.32	....	3.50	9 Mo Sep	v□1.59	v2.77	25
26◆	1981	gS0.071	10-1-99	9-22	g0.143	0.14	g0.12¾	111	428	224	j4-30-99	213	...	±56394	Oc	±0.67	±0.93	P±v1.15	v±1.02	....	j1.12	6 Mo Apr	v±0.63	v±0.73	26
27◆	1937	Q0.21	1-1-00	12-7	0.81	0.84	0.77½	38.8	333	218	9-30-99	488	167	57012	Dc	v0.95	v1.05	v1.24	v0.66	....	1.07	9 Mo Sep	v0.68	v1.09	27
28◆	1940	Q0.17	12-1-99	11-8	0.65	0.68	0.64	139	1179	686	10-03-99	1333	...	102644	Dc	v3.17	v1.84	v1.41	v1.14	E1.48	1.50	9 Mo Sep	v0.77	v1.13	28
29	....	None Since Public			...	Nil	....	1.39	52.0	27.3	8-31-99	5.58	...	7924	Fb	v0.34	vd0.76	v0.52	v0.80	....	1.55	9 Mo Nov	v0.74	v1.49	29
30	1996	Q0.03	1-7-00	12-15	0.12	0.12	0.09	Total Assets $537.92M			9-30-99	58.0	...	8512	Dc	vp1.32	v0.95	v1.42	v0.65	....	d0.17	9 Mo Sep	v0.39	v□d0.43	30
31	....	None Paid			...	Nil	....	3.13	18.6	10.7	9-30-99	2.90	...	3788	Mr	v0.27	v0.33	v0.21	v0.46	....	1.09	6 Mo Sep	v0.01	v0.64	31
32	1998	Q0.20	11-12-99	10-28	0.75	0.80	0.45	Total Deposits $665M			9-30-99	330	...	4996	Dc	pvd2.76	v0.22	v2.49	v1.63	....	2.44	9 Mo Sep	v□1.40	v□2.21	32
33	....	None Since Public			...	Nil	....	20.2	22.2	3.21	9-30-99	0.03	...	31707	Dc	vd0.69	vd0.45	vd2.93	vd0.89	....	d0.55	9 Mo Sep	vd0.67	vd0.33	33
34	....	None Since Public			...	Nil	....	22.9	34.6	5.28	9-30-99	....	...	10473	Dc	vd0.32	v0.40	v0.96	v1.50	....	1.27	9 Mo Sep	v1.11	v0.88	34
35	1991	0.133	10-28-99	8-4	0.373	0.37	0.367	10.6	259	188	12-31-98	155	...	338930	Dc	1.05	v0.21	v1.39	v0.74	....	0.64	6 Mo Jun	v0.48	v0.38	35
36◆	1988	†0.18	1-14-00	12-13	†0.53	0.44	†0.48	Total Deposits $902M			9-30-99	134	...	8378	Dc	v1.01	v1.11	v1.19	v1.31	....	1.43	9 Mo Sep	v0.99	v1.11	36
37	....	None Since Public			...	Nil	....	0.57	56.9	18.1	9-30-99	1.20	...	12940	Mr	d0.07	vd1.09	□v1.04	v1.34	....	1.01	6 Mo Sep	v0.58	v0.25	37
38	1923	Q0.15	12-15-99	11-26	0.60	0.60	0.56	9.80	173	166	9-26-99	798	...	±26599	Dc	v2.01	v±2.65	v□1.97	v±2.63	....	2.98	9 Mo Sep	v±1.81	v±2.16	38
39	....	None Since Public			...	Nil	....	45.8	49.4	8.57	9-30-99	0.22	...	19659	Dc	...	...	...	vpd1.49	....	....	9 Mo Sep	n/a	vd0.50	39
40	....	None Since Public			...	Nil	....	0.97	21.5	13.8	9-30-99	39.3	...	9158	Dc	...	pvd1.29	vd1.95	vd1.13	....	d1.05	9 Mo Sep	vd0.65	vd0.57	40
41	....	None Since Public			...	Nil	....	1182	2373	2765	9-30-99	8501	[63]1028	611981	Dc	p□0.30	vpd0.90	vd0.88	v□Δ2.34	Ed1.10	....	9 Mo Sep	n/a	vΔd0.32	41
42	1998	Q0.908	11-15-99	10-27	3.633	3.633	1.01	Mand Exch 8-15-2001,com of AirTouch Commun[64]				....	...	★26000	Dc	...	...	...	....	....	....	Mature 8-15-2001			42
43	....	Plan qtly div			...	3.04	....	Mand Exch 11-15-2002,com of Vodafone Air Touch ADRs re-spec cond				....	...	★26000	Dc	...	...	...	....	....	....	Mature 11-15-2002			43
44	....	None Since Public			...	Nil	....	16.5	22.2	7.47	9-30-99	0.26	p...	★30717	Dc	...	...	...	vpd0.25	....	....	9 Mo Sep	n/a	vpd1.56	44
45	....	None Paid			...	Nil	....	1.24	1.76	0.31	7-31-99	0.13	...	4411	Oc	...	v0.06	v0.09	v0.14	....	0.21	9 Mo Jul	v0.05	v0.12	45
46◆	....	5%Stk	2-15-00	1-5	...	Stk	5%Stk	Total Assets $1117M			9-30-99	....	...	22402	Dc	v1.29	v1.35	v1.58	v□2.06	....	2.08	9 Mo Sep	v□1.47	v1.49	46
47	....	None Since Public			...	Nil	....	73.6	236	78.5	p9-30-99	168	...	35010	Je	0.93	0.48	vd1.60	v0.46	vp0.48	Nil	3 Mo Sep	vp0.19	vd0.29	47
48	....	None Since Public			...	Nil	....	0.75	3.85	3.07	9-30-99	0.37	...	4579	Dc	d0.08	v0.13	v0.07	vd0.30	....	d0.36	9 Mo Sep	vd0.18	vd0.24	48
49	....	None Since Public			...	Nil	....	45.1	51.7	8.56	9-30-99	1.66	p...	★30475	Dc	...	...	...	vpd0.42	....	....	9 Mo Sep	n/a	vpd0.66	49
50◆	....	None Since Public			...	Nil	....	275	329	46.4	9-30-99	....	...	±28823	Je	±0.12	v±0.48	v±0.83	±vd0.51	v±1.41	1.46	3 Mo Sep	v0.28	v0.33	50

◆Stock Splits & Divs By Line Reference Index [1]2-for-1,'97. [3]3-for-2,'94,'96,'97(twice),'98. [6]3-for-2,'98:4-for-3,'98. [7]4-for-3,'95. [8]5-for-4,'97. [11]2-for-1,'94,'99. [14]2-for-1,'97. [15]2-for-1,'96,'99. [16]2-for-1,'96:3-for-2,'99. [17]2-for-1,'98. [18]2-for-1,'99. [20]2-for-1,'94. [24]1-for-6 REVERSE,'96. [26]2-for-1,'96. [27]3-for-2,'95,'98. [28]2-for-1,'97. [36]2-for-1,'94,'98. [46]2-for-1,'97:10%,'98. [50]1-for-14 REVERSE,'95:3-for-2,'96,'97,'99.

¶ S&P 500
# MidCap 400
✣ SmallCap 600
• Options

Index	Ticker	Name of Issue (Call Price of Pfd. Stocks)	Market	Com. Rank. & Pfd. Rating	Inst. Hold Cos	Inst. Hold Shs. (000)	Principal Business	Price Range 1971-97 High	1971-97 Low	1998 High	1998 Low	1999 High	1999 Low	Dec. Sales in 100s	December, 1999 Last Sale Or Bid High	Low	Last	%Div Yield	P-E Ratio	EPS 5 Yr Growth	% Annualized Total Return 12 Mo	36 Mo	60 Mo
#1•[1]	MEDI	✓MedImmune Inc	NNM	NR	507	56165	Drug R&D-infectious diseases	27½	1 11/16	50 11/16	19 7/16	175 13/16	43	221375	175 13/16	117	165⅞	...	..	NM	234	169	149
2	MT	✓Meditrust Corp[51](Unit)	NY,Ch,Ph,P	NR	221	54367	REIT:health care facilities	45 1/16	11 11/16	36¾	11 13/16	16½	5¼	210488	6 13/16	5¼	5½	...	3	Neg	−55.7	−41.8	−21.1
3	MDX	MedPartners 6.50% 'TAPS'	NY	NR	15	2313	Threshold Apprec Price Sec	26⅛	20⅝	22⅛	5	11¾	5	13269	8	6⅝	7 15/16	...	..	...	22.4	...	...
✣4	MEDQ	✓MedQuist Inc	NNM,Ch,Ph	B	324	31255	Mgmt & info svcs to hospitals	17 9/16	1 5/16	40	15	45¾	21½	135098	33	22¾	25 13/16	...	25	74	−34.7	46.6	60.8
5	MSCP	✓Medscape Inc	NNM	NR	29	2746	Internet based hlth care svcs	...	...	...	...	17 1/16	8	65260	12 13/16	9⅛	10	...	..	...	...	...	...
6	MEDS	✓Medstone Intl	NNM	B–	24	1776	Mkts kidney stone treat't eq	42	⅞	11½	5¼	8⅝	4⅜	3944	5 15/16	4⅜	4¾	...	8	15	−27.6	...	...
7	TOX	✓Medtox Scientific	AS,Ch	C	10	86	Mfr diagnostic screen'g tests	1032½	5	8¾	3¾	10½	2⅛	2001	9¼	7	8⅞	...	d	NM	753	50.6	−10.7
¶8•[2]	MDT	✓Medtronic, Inc	NY,B,Ch,P,Ph	A	1400	754934	Cardiac pacemakers:med.serv	26⅜	⅛	38⅜	22 11/16	44⅝	29 15/16	768161	40 9/16	32 13/16	36 7/16	0.4	71	6	−1.4	29.6	40.0
9	MEGO	✓Mego Financial	NNM	B–	10	246	Consumer financial svcs	66¾	15/16	33¾	4⅛	9	3 9/16	2357	4½	3⅝	4⅛	...	14	Neg	−14.2	...	...
¶10•[3]	MEL	✓Mellon Financial	NY,B,Ch,P	A–	1030	341412	Fin'l services,comm'l bkg	32⅜	2 7/16	40 3/16	22½	40 3/16	31	315494	38¼	32⅜	34 1/16	2.3	19	22	1.6	27.6	39.3
11	MBRS	✓MemberWorks Inc	NNM	NR	91	10591	Membership svcs programs	22⅝	10½	40¼	12⅛	52½	20	38088	33⅞	22 11/16	33 3/16	...	64	...	12.5	29.6	...
12•[4]	WFR	✓MEMC Electronic Materials	NY,Ch,Ph,P	NR	78	12665	Produce silicon wafers	55	14 7/16	19	2 15/16	21⅝	5⅜	41352	13 1/16	9 15/16	12¼	...	d	Neg	44.1	−18.3	...
✣13•[5]	SUIT	✓Men's Wearhouse	NNM	B+	282	27061	Retail off-price men's attire	27½	2½	36⅞	14	34 15/16	19½	66660	31	23⅞	29⅜	...	20	24	−7.5	21.6	24.1
✣14•[6]	MNTR	✓Mentor Corp	NNM	B	188	19291	Medical devices/hlth care pr	41	1/16	37¼	9⅜	29	12⅜	20204	29	22⅞	25 13/16	0.4	23	−2	10.7	−3.9	25.0
#15•[6]	MENT	✓Mentor Graphics	NNM	C	167	52165	Elec dsgn automat'n softwr sys	26	5¼	11 13/16	5 7/16	15 1/16	7½	154845	13½	8¾	13 3/16	...	60	Neg	55.1	10.6	−2.9
16•[7]	MRNT	✓MERANT plc ADS[56]	NNM	NR	29	819	Design computer compilers/eqp	46	8¼	60⅝	7½	37⅝	8⅛	8611	37⅝	30½	31	...	78	NM	229	26.7	19.9
#17•[2]	MRBK	✓Mercantile Bankshares	NNM	A	247	26092	Comm'l bkg,Baltimore, MD	40¼	⅞	40¼	25¼	39 15/16	30	30092	35½	30	31 15/16	3.0	14	12	−14.9	17.9	23.6
18•[7]	MERCS	✓Mercer Intl SBI	NNM	B	28	9242	Paper,pulp manufacturing	27¾	2⅜	12 1/16	5 9/16	8¼	3½	16538	4 15/16	4⅛	4⅝	1.1	d	Neg	−31.6	...	...
19	MGP	✓Merchants Group	AS	B–	31	1165	Property & casualty insurance	21¼	6½	27⅜	18½	24⅜	19¼	571	22¾	19¼	19½	2.1	8	NM	−1.6	3.0	6.4
20	MBNY	✓Merchants NY Bancorp	NNM	A–	35	804	Commercial Bank,New York	24⅜	1⅛	24	15⅜	20¾	15⅞	3906	17½	16½	17⅛	2.9	17	14	−2.3	31.9	26.3
¶21•[8]	MRK	✓Merck & Co	NY,B,C,Ch,P,Ph	A+	2211	1253340	Ethical drugs/specialty chem	54 1/16	1 5/16	80⅞	50 11/16	87⅜	60 15/16	1105405	78⅛	66 1/16	67 3/16	1.7	27	16	−7.5	21.0	31.2
22	MAX	✓Mercury Air Group	AS,B,P	B	17	1071	Airport ancillary svs:electr	8 5/16	1/16	9	5 13/16	8¾	5⅝	2987	8¼	7½	8⅛	...	10	7	1.6	12.8	15.6
23•[9]	MCY	✓Mercury General	NY,Ph	A	131	18331	Underwrites auto ins,Calif	55½	2 11/16	70	33	45½	20 15/16	28456	23 7/16	20 15/16	22¼	3.8	9	18	−47.7	−3.3	11.5
✣24•[7]	MERQ	✓Mercury Interactive	NNM	NR	354	36345	Mfr software testing prod	14½	3½	31⅝	10 9/16	110¼	21	88318	110¼	79 3/16	107 15/16	...	..	NM	242	155	74.8
¶25•[9]	MDP	✓Meredith Corp	NY,Ch,P,Ph	B+	383	31248	Magazines, broadcasting,RE	36 15/16	5/16	48½	26 11/16	42	30⅝	17451	42	37 3/16	41 11/16	0.7	25	18	11.0	17.7	30.4
26	KITS	✓Meridian Diagnostics	NNM	B+	35	3342	Immunodiagnostic test kits	15½	¾	15¼	4 7/16	8¾	5¾	7821	7⅝	5 15/16	7¼	2.8	45	−1	10.3	−15.7	13.4
27	MDG	✓Meridian Gold	NY,Ch,Ph	C	79	30890	Gold/silver min'g,process'g	17⅝	1⅞	6¼	1⅞	9 3/16	3 13/16	11521	6⅞	5⅝	6 13/16	...	d	Neg	19.8	18.2	15.7
28	MTEC	✓Meridian Medical Tech	NNM	C	16	865	Medical injection technology	67	3	15¼	4⅜	8	3½	3218	6¾	5	5⅝	...	d	Neg	21.6	−13.3	−6.8
29	TMR	✓Meridian Resource	NY,Ch,P	C	84	14969	Oil & gas explor,dev,prod'n	38¾	5/16	9 9/16	2	6 7/16	2	43968	4	2 9/16	3 1/16	...	d	Neg	−3.9	−43.7	−20.7
30•[9]	MHX	✓MeriStar Hospitality	NY,Ch,Ph	NR	165	36372	Real estate investment trust	38 5/16	16¼	36⅞	12¼	24 5/16	14 7/16	55028	17	14 7/16	16	12.6	11	...	...	...	...
31	MMH	✓Meristar Hotels & Resorts	NY,Ph	NR	56	13942	Own/oper hotels	...	...	4	1 13/16	4 9/16	2⅛	10963	3⅝	3	3 3/16	...	17	...	35.7	...	...
32	MMSI	✓Merit Medical Systems	NNM	B	16	1131	Mfr disposable medical prod	21½	2 13/16	9⅛	5	8 11/16	4½	6781	7⅝	6 9/16	7¼	...	18	14	9.4	−5.2	10.6
33	MTH	✓Meritage Corp	NY,Ph	B–	19	926	Single-Family homebuilding	32¼	2 7/16	20⅜	9⅝	15 13/16	9¾	2646	11 7/16	9⅞	10⅞	...	4	NM	−10.8	14.0	30.9
34	MHG	✓Meritage Hospitality Grp	AS	NR	..	...	Oper Wendy's restaurants	...	...	...	...	2⅞	2	1174	2⅞	2	2⅞	...	36	...	...	...	...
#35•[2]	MRA	✓Meritor Automotive	NY	NR	262	35782	Mfr automotive components	27⅝	20 11/16	28⅜	14⅛	26½	14 3/16	65060	19 13/16	16¾	19⅜	2.2	7	...	−5.9	...	...
¶36•[10]	MER	✓Merrill Lynch	NY,B,C,Ch,P,Ph	A–	964	203006	Investment,finance,insurance	78 3/16	13/16	109⅛	35¾	102½	62	484387	85⅛	76 9/16	83 5/16	1.3	15	13	26.5	28.7	38.2
37	BNX	Mer Lyn Bond Index Notes'2002'	AS	NR	..	...	Unsecured Debt Sec	...	...	...	...	20⅛	19⅞	2378	20⅛	19⅞	19⅞	...	..	...	...	...	...
38	MIX	Merrill Lynch & Co'MITTS'2001	NY	NR	1	1	Mkt Index Target-Term Secs	15⅛	9⅝	19 15/16	14	23 13/16	19¾	1454	23 13/16	22 7/16	23 13/16	...	..	...	20.6	27.9	...
39	MIM	Merrill Lynch & Co'MITTS'2002	NY	NR	1	10	Mkt Index Target-Term Sec	11½	9⅜	15¼	10⅝	17 9/16	14 13/16	1426	17 9/16	16 11/16	17½B	...	..	...	16.2	...	...
40	RUM	Merrill Lynch & Co'MITTS'2004	AS	NR	1	3	Mkt Index Target-Term Sec	10⅛	8¼	10⅛	8	10⅜	8½	8935	10⅜	9 5/16	10⅜	...	..	...	13.7	...	...
41	MLF	Merrill Lynch & Co'MITTS'2005(Jl)	AS	NR	1	10	Mkt Index Target-Term Secs	...	...	10⅝	9⅛	11 11/16	10 3/16	6212	11 11/16	11⅛	11 11/16	...	..	...	12.6	...	...
42	MIJ	Merrill Lynch & Co'MITTS'2005(Sp)	NY	NR	..	...	Mkt Index Target-Term Secs	...	...	10⅝	9⅝	11 11/16	10⅛	3625	11 11/16	11 5/16	11 11/16	...	..	...	11.3	...	...
43	EFM	Merrill Lynch & Co'MITTS'2006(Fb)	AS	NR	..	...	Mkt Index Target-Term Sec	...	...	10⅝	9⅛	11	9½	1960	10⅝	9⅞	10 7/16	...	..	...	0.6	...	...
44	FML	Merrill Lynch & Co'MITTS'2006(Mr)	AS	....	..	...	Mkt Index Target-Term Secs	...	...	...	...	10 7/16	8¾	2798	9¾	9⅜	9⅝	...	..	...	...	...	...
45	MDJ	Merrill Lynch & Co'MITTS'2006(Je)	AS	NR	..	...	Mkt Index Target-Term Secs	...	...	...	...	10⅛	8 13/16	4563	9 7/16	8⅞	9 5/16	...	..	...	...	...	...
46	IEM	Merrill Lynch & Co'MITTS'2007	NY	NR	..	...	Mtk Index Target-Term Secs	10	8¼	9½	8⅛	10⅝	9	428	10 9/16	10⅜	10 7/16B	...	..	...	12.1	...	...
47	CSM	Mer Lyn Consum Staples'MITTS'	AS	NR	..	...	Mkt Index Target-Term Sec	...	...	...	...	10⅛	7¾	10053	8⅜	7¾	7 13/16	...	..	...	...	...	...
48	RNS	Merrill Lyn Depositor 8.54%'STEERS'	[11]	NR	..	...	1999 REN-CI Trust Ctfs	...	...	...	...	21½	18	740	21½	18	19¼	11.1	..	...	...	...	...
49	LTS	Merrill Lyn 5.75%'STRIDES'	AS	NR	4	1530	Stock Return Inc Debt Secs	...	...	10¾	9¾	12 11/16	10	1711	12⅝	12⅜	12 7/16B	4.6	..	...	23.0	...	...
50	NML	Merrill Lyn 5.25%'STRIDES'	AS	NR	..	...	Stock Return Inc Debt Secs	...	...	...	...	12¼	....	661	12¼	11 13/16	12¼	4.3	..	...	...	...	...

Uniform Footnote Explanations-See Page 4. Other: [1]ASE,CBOE,P:Cycle 3. [2]CBOE:Cycle 2. [3]CBOE:Cycle 3. [4]ASE,CBOE:Cycle 1. [5]Ph:Cycle 2. [6]ASE,P:Cycle 1. [7]CBOE:Cycle 1. [8]ASE,CBOE,P,Ph:Cycle 1. [9]Ph:Cycle 3. [10]ASE,CBOE,P,Ph:Cycle 3. [11]NY [51]Trades with 1 shr Meditrust Oper Co. [52]To be determined. [53]Incl 8.5M paired series com. [54]Stk dstr of UroGen Corp. [55]Stk dstr of Mego Mtg Corp,'97. [56]Ea ADS rep 1 ord, par 10p. [57]Fiscal Jun'97 & prior. [58]Fiscal Jan'98 & prior. [59]Stk dstr of MeriStar Hotels & Resorts. [60]Incl 4M Exch shs. [61]Re-spec cond. [62]Total Issue Amt. [63]As defined. [64]Or anytime upon'Tax Event're-spec cond. [65]Issue amt.

Index	Splits ◆ Cash Divs. Ea.Yr. Since	Dividends Latest Payment Period $	Date	Ex. Div.	Total $ So Far 1999	Ind. Rate	Paid 1998	Financial Position Mil-$ Cash& Equiv.	Curr. Assets	Curr. Liab.	Balance Sheet Date	Capitalization Lg Trm Debt Mil-$	Shs. 000 Pfd.	Com.	Earnings $ Per Shr. Years End	1995	1996	1997	1998	1999	Last 12 Mos.	Interim Earnings Period	$ per Shr. 1998	1999	Index
1◆	....	None Since Public			...	Nil	....	159	225	39.5	9-30-99	17.5	...	p67419	Dc	vd0.71	vd0.71	vd0.79	v0.91	E1.05↑	1.59	9 Mo Sep	vd0.31	v0.37	1
2◆	1986	Q0.46	11-15-99	10-27	1.84	[52]....	†4.222	Total Assets $5686M			9-30-99	2708	700	[53]142320	Dc	□v2.09	v2.20	v2.12	vd1.29	E2.00	0.40	9 Mo Sep	vd0.86	v0.83	2
3	1998	S0.721	8-31-99	8-26	1.443	[52]....	1.37	At 8-31-2000 pur MedPtnrs com re-spec cond				....	...	★17000	Dc	...	...	...	...	....	....	Final settlement date 8-31-2000			3
4◆	....	None Since Public			...	Nil	....	68.3	148	58.1	9-30-99	0.11	...	35907	Dc	v□d0.15	v0.20	v0.34	v0.09	E1.03	0.49	9 Mo Sep	v0.34	v0.74	4
5	....	None Since Public			...	Nil	....	60.9	77.7	11.1	9-30-99	....	...	44844	Dc	...	...	...	vpd0.61	....	....	9 Mo Sep	n/a	vd1.19	5
6	....	h[54]....	1-15-96	12-27	...	Nil	....	12.7	23.0	2.79	9-30-99	....	...	4822	Dc	v0.70	vd0.04	v0.72	v0.82	....	0.62	9 Mo Sep	v0.65	v0.45	6
7◆	....	None Paid			...	Nil	....	0.29	9.62	11.0	9-30-99	2.18	...	2904	Dc	vd15.40	vd11.80	vNil	vd0.79	....	d0.43	9 Mo Sep	v0.06	v0.42	7
8◆	1977	Q0.04	1-28-00	1-5	0.145	0.16	0.12	217	2524	1104	10-29-99	18.1	...	1194386	Ap	0.32	v0.45	v0.55	v0.48	v0.40	0.51	6 Mo Oct	v0.30	v0.42	8
9◆	....	h[55]....	9-2-97	9-3	...	Nil	....	Total Assets $159M			8-31-99	4.48	...	3501	Au	0.48	1.44	5.94	vd0.90	v0.30	0.30				9
10◆	1895	Q0.20	11-15-99	10-27	0.78	0.80	0.70½	Total Deposits $32029.00M			9-30-99	4356	...	508650	Dc	1.13	v1.29	v1.44	v1.63	E1.80	1.86	9 Mo Sep	v1.20	v□1.43	10
11	....	None Since Public			...	Nil	....	38.1	138	190	9-30-99	....	...	15471	Je	...	pvd0.49	vd0.35	v0.19	□v0.46	0.52	3 Mo Sep	v□0.07	v0.13	11
12	....	None Since Public			...	Nil	....	20.6	273	213	9-30-99	834	...	69556	Dc	pv2.78	v2.45	vd0.16	vd7.80	....	d3.85	9 Mo Sep	vd6.01	vd2.06	12
13◆	....	None Since Public			...	Nil	....	14.7	406	139	10-30-99	57.3	...	±41916	Ja	0.55	v0.67	v0.87	v□1.17	E1.50	1.11	9 Mo Oct	vp0.66	v□0.60	13
14◆	1987	Q0.02½	1-20-00	12-27	0.10	0.10	0.10	58.6	158	31.9	10-01-99	....	...	24370	Mr	0.92	v1.06	v0.91	v0.55	E1.12	0.84	6 Mo Sep	v0.52	v0.81	14
15	....	0.06	8-12-93	7-26	...	Nil	....	110	265	127	9-30-99	....	...	64200	Dc	v78.00	vd0.08	vd0.48	vd0.01	E0.22↑	d0.07	9 Mo Sep	v0.02	vd0.04	15
16	....	None Since Public			...	Nil	....	121	246	29.9	4-30-99	....	...	p28626	Ap	d0.69	[57]d0.72	v1.06	v[58]1.07	vd1.00	0.40	6 Mo Oct	vd1.23	v0.17	16
17◆	1909	Q0.24	12-31-99	12-21	0.94	0.96	0.86	Total Deposits $5910.56M			9-30-99	82.7	...	68929	Dc	v1.46	v1.64	v1.84	v2.04	E2.26	2.19	9 Mo Sep	v1.51	v1.66	17
18	1997	A0.05	5-10-99	4-28	0.05	0.05	0.04	10.3	111	101	9-30-99	192	...	16635	Dc	v5.03	Pv1.15	vd2.18	v0.59	....	d0.99	9 Mo Sep	v0.98	vd0.60	18
19	1993	Q0.10	12-2-99	11-15	0.35	0.40	0.20	Total Assets $272.34M			9-30-99	....	...	2617	Dc	vd1.19	vd0.36	v1.41	v2.04	....	2.40	9 Mo Sep	v1.49	v1.85	19
20◆	1932	Q0.12½	12-28-99	12-14	0.45	0.50	0.40	Total Deposits $898.03M			9-30-99	130	...	19231	Dc	v0.57	v0.63	v0.73	v0.80	....	1.03	9 Mo Sep	v1.28	v1.51	20
21◆	1935	Q0.29	1-3-00	12-1	1.10	1.16	0.94½	3780	11015	7670	9-30-99	3214	...	2337423	Dc	v1.32	v1.56	v1.87	v2.15	E2.45	2.37	9 Mo Sep	v1.57	v1.79	21
22◆	....	0.01¼	8-1-97	7-11	...	Nil	....	4.91	63.5	3.60	9-30-99	63.2	...	6685	Je	v0.55	v0.56	v0.49	v0.38	v□0.73	0.80	3 Mo Sep	v□0.18	v□0.25	22
23◆	1986	Q0.21	12-30-99	12-13	0.84	0.84	0.70	Total Assets $1919.18M			9-30-99	78.0	...	54655	Dc	1.66	v1.92	v2.82	v3.21	....	2.47	9 Mo Sep	v2.58	v1.84	23
24◆	....	None Since Public			...	Nil	....	173	203	75.5	9-30-99	....	...	38360	Dc	vd0.19	v0.14	v0.20	v0.56	E0.80↑	0.77	9 Mo Sep	v0.32	v0.53	24
25◆	1930	Q0.07½	12-15-99	11-26	0.30	0.30	0.28	11.2	284	353	9-30-99	485	...	±51620	Je	±□0.72	v±0.96	v±1.72	v±1.46	v±1.67	1.66	3 Mo Sep	v0.35	v0.34	25
26◆	1990	Q0.05	12-7-99	11-22	0.20	0.20	0.20	7.23	30.9	13.0	6-30-99	21.6	...	14384	Sp	0.29	v0.36	v0.41	v0.34	Pv0.16	0.16				26
27	....	0.05	12-31-95	12-5	...	Nil	....	34.1	110	13.5	12-31-98	....	10	73641	Dc	v0.03	vd0.22	vd0.94	vd0.53	....	d0.51	6 Mo Jun	vd0.14	vd0.12	27
28	....	None Since Public			...	Nil	....	0.43	21.4	16.5	10-31-99	17.4	...	2995	Jl	0.15	0.41	vd2.16	□v0.03	vd0.58	d0.55	3 Mo Oct	v0.08	v0.11	28
29	....	1.60	3-5-86	1-27	...	Nil	....	6.93	43.4	46.1	9-30-99	270	3983	46185	Dc	v0.23	v0.47	vd0.85	vd5.80	....	d0.90	9 Mo Sep	vd4.85	v0.05	29
30	1998	Q0.50½	1-31-00	12-29	2.02	2.02	h[59]0.318	Total Assets $3099M			9-30-99	1662	...	47726	Dc	p0.29	□pv0.31	□v1.27	□v1.40	....	1.49	9 Mo Sep	v1.40	v□1.49	30
31	....	Plan qtly div			...	....	....	3.58	93.8	121	9-30-99	56.8	...	29532	Dc	...	...	pv0.12	pv0.13	....	0.21	9 Mo Sep	v0.15	v0.23	31
32	....	None Since Public			...	Nil	....	0.73	39.5	10.8	9-30-99	24.2	...	7572	Dc	v0.18	v0.31	v0.11	v0.33	....	0.40	9 Mo Sep	v0.23	v0.30	32
33◆	....	0.06	1-16-97	12-26	...	Nil	....	Total Assets $225M			9-30-99	95.7	...	5465	Dc	v0.34	v□0.09	v2.68	v3.92	....	3.04	9 Mo Sep	v2.68	v1.80	33
34	....	None Paid			...	Nil	....	1.54	2.50	3.18	8-31-99	13.9	45	5753	Nv	...	...	v□d0.50	□v0.36	Pv0.08	0.08				34
35	1997	Q0.10½	12-13-99	11-18	0.42	0.42	0.42	45.0	1389	1115	6-30-99	878	...	69118	Sp	...	p1.41	pv1.44	v2.13	vP2.81	2.81				35
36◆	1961	Q0.27	11-24-99	11-3	1.05	1.08	0.92	Total Assets $312936M			9-24-99	55400	43	[60]370670	Dc	v2.71	v4.11	v4.83	v3.00	E5.65	5.22	9 Mo Sep	v2.14	v4.36	36
37	....	Plan semi-annual div			...	[52]....	....	Amt pay mat based in U.S. Dom Master Index[61]				[62]★30.0	...	...	Dc	...	...	...	...	....	....	Due 12-23-2002			37
38	....	....			...	....	....	Int based on S&P 500,as defined				....	...	★11000	Dc	...	...	...	...	....	....	Due 5-10-2001			38
39	....	....			...	....	....	Int based on S&P 500,as defined				....	...	★17500	Dc	...	...	...	...	....	....	Due 9-16-2002			39
40	....	....			...	....	....	Int based on Russell 2000,as defined				....	...	★16750	Dc	...	...	...	...	....	....	Due 9-30-2004			40
41	....	....			...	....	....	Int based on S&P 500,as defined				....	...	★28500	Dc	...	...	...	...	....	....	Due 7-1-2005			41
42	....	....			...	....	....	Int based on S&P 500,as defined				....	...	★8200	Dc	...	...	...	...	....	....	Due 9-28-2005			42
43	....	....			...	....	....	Int based on Merrill Lyn EuroFund Index,as defined				....	...	6700	Dc	...	...	...	...	....	....	Due 2-8-2006			43
44	....	....			...	....	....	Int based on S&P 500,as defined				....	...	★7000	Dc	...	...	...	...	....	....	Due 3-27-2006			44
45	....	....			...	....	....	Int based on Dow Jones Ind'l Average[63]				....	...	★5200	Dc	...	...	...	...	....	....	Due 6-26-2006			45
46	....	....			...	....	....	Int based on S&P 500,as defined				....	...	★1650	Dc	...	...	...	...	....	....	Due 9-24-2007			46
47	....	None Since Public			...	Nil	....	Int based on S&P Consum Staples'SPDR'Fund as defined				....	...	★7200	Dc	...	...	...	...	....	....	Due 4-19-2006			47
48	....	Plan semi-annual div			...	2.13	....	Co opt to redm fr 3-1-2007 $25[64]				[65]25.0	...	...	Dc	...	...	...	...	....	....	Mature 3-1-2027			48
49	1999	S0.288	12-1-99	11-10	0.575	0.575	....	At maturity Lucent Technologies com or cash[61]				....	...	★6600	Dc	...	...	...	...	....	....	Mature 6-1-2000			49
50	1999	S0.26¼	8-23-99	8-4	0.26¼	0.53	....	Amt pd mat(8-23-2000)based on NASDAQ-100 Index[61]				★18.0	...	...	Dc	...	...	...	...	....	....	Mature 8-23-2000			50

◆**Stock Splits & Divs By Line Reference Index** [1]2-for-1,'99. [2]No adj for recap,'97. [4]3-for-2,'97:2-for-1,'98:Vote Dec 30 on 1-for-5 REVERSE. [7]1-for-20 REVERSE,'99. [8]2-for-1,'95,'97,'99. [9]No adj for stk dstr Mego Mtg,'97:1-for-6 REVERSE,'99. [10]2-for-1,'97,'99. [13]3-for-2,'95,'98. [14]2-for-1,'95. [17]3-for-2,'97. [20]2-for-1,'95,'97,'99. [21]2-for-1,'99. [22]10%,'95,'96:5-for-4,'97. [23]2-for-1,'97. [24]2-for-1,'99. [25]2-for-1,'95,'97. [26]3-for-2,'95:Adj for 3%,'94. [33]1-for-3 REVERSE,'97. [36]2-for-1,'97.

¶ S&P 500
# MidCap 400
✢ SmallCap 600
• Options

Index	Ticker	Name of Issue (Call Price of Pfd. Stocks)	Market	Com. Rank. & Pfd. Rating	Inst. Hold Cos	Inst. Hold Shs. (000)	Principal Business	Price Range 1971-97 High	1971-97 Low	1998 High	1998 Low	1999 High	1999 Low	December, 1999 Dec. Sales in 100s	Last Sale Or Bid High	Low	Last	%Div Yield	P-E Ratio	EPS 5 Yr Growth	% Annualized Total Return 12 Mo	36 Mo	60 Mo
1	IML	Merrill Lyn 6.25%'STRYPES'	NY	NR	14	1475	Struct Yld Prd Exch For Stk	44⅝	32½	39 11/16	21	28	15½	5888	19	16	17⅞	13.4	..	...	−15.6	−16.8	...
2	BOB	Merrill Lyn 7.875%'STRYPES'	NY	NR	2	93	Struct Yld Pfd Exch For Stk	...	...	73	36½	56½	36½	2823	54½	46¼	52⅝	8.1	..	...	5.1	...	...
3	ESM	Mer Lyn Energy Sel'MITTS'2006	AS	NR	1	120	Mkt Index Target-Term Secs	...	...	...	...	11 9/16	9½	2164	11	10½	10 11/16	...	..	...	...	...	...
4	ESY	Mer Lyn En Sel SPDR'MITTS'2006	AS	NR	..	...	Mkt Index Target-Term Sec	...	...	...	...	10	8 3/16	7583	9⅛	8 3/16	8 5/16	...	..	...	...	...	...
5	MLH	Merrill Lyn Hlt/Bio'MITTS'2001	AS	NR	..	...	Mkt Index Target-Term Secs	11	9 7/16	11¾	9	10¾	9⅝	628	10½	10	10½	...	..	...	3.7	3.2	...
6	DJM	Merr Lyn Dow Jones'MITTS'2002	NY	NR	1	.3	Mkt Index Target-Term Sec	10	9⅝	11 7/16	8¾	13 1/16	10⅞	1525	12 15/16	12½	12 15/16	...	..	...	17.6	...	...
7	GMM	Merr Lyn Global Ind'MITTS'2004	AS	....	..	...	Mkt Index Target-Term Sec	...	...	...	...	10⅛	9⅞	5187	10⅛	9⅞	10 1/16	...	..	...	...	...	...
8	MEM	Mer Lyn Maj8 Eur Ind'MITTS'2002	AS	NR	..	...	Mkt Index Target-Term Secs	10	8¼	12⅞	9 9/16	15⅝	12	455	15⅝	14⅛	15⅝	...	..	...	23.0	...	...
9	EEM	Mer Lyn Maj 11 Intl'MITTS'2002	AS	NR	..	...	Mkt Index Target-Term Sec	10 3/16	9 9/16	12⅜	9¼	14 11/16	11⅝	351	14 11/16	13⅝	14½B	...	..	...	22.1	...	...
10	EUM	Mer Lyn Maj 11 Intl'MITTS'2006	AS	NR	..	...	Mkt Index Target-Term Sec	...	...	...	...	10	8¼	2711	9⅞	8¼	9⅞	...	..	...	...	...	...
11	JEM	Merrill Lyn Nikkei'MITTS'2002(Je)	NY	NR	1	10	Mkt Index Target-Term Sec	10¾	8 3/16	9⅜	8⅛	10 3/16	8⅝	6333	9 13/16	9 5/16	9⅝	...	..	...	10.8	...	...
12	MNN	Merrill Lyn Nikkei'MITTS'2002(AU)	AS	NR	1	300	Mkt Index Target-Term Sec	...	...	...	...	10 1/16	9⅜	4311	9 13/16	9 7/16	9 13/16	...	..	...	...	...	...
13	MLN	Merrill Lyn Nikkei'MITTS'2005	AS	NR	1	65	Mkt Index Target-Term Secs	...	...	10	9⅞	11 1/16	9 13/16	3037	10 13/16	10 5/16	10 11/16	...	..	...	6.9	...	...
14	NKM	Mer Lyn Nikkei'MITTS'2006	AS	NR	..	...	Mkt Index Target-Term Sec	...	...	...	...	10	8½	9569	9⅝	8½	9½	...	..	...	...	...	...
15	OPG	Mer Lyn Oracle'ProGros'2003	AS	NR	..	...	Protected Growth Sec	...	...	11	8 1/16	13	10	1461	13	12½	12 13/16	...	..	...	19.2	...	...
16	RSM	Mer Lyn Russell 2000'MITTS'2006	AS	NR	..	...	Mkt Index Target-Term Sec	...	...	...	...	10	8⅜	6410	9⅜	8 9/16	9⅜	...	..	...	...	...	...
17	RSY WS	Mer Lyn Russell 2000 Wrrt[54]	AS	....	1	260	Index Call Warrants	...	...	...	...	5½	3⅝	990	5½	4⅛	5½	...	..	...	...	...	...
18	MPF	Mer Lyn S&P'MITTS'2006	AS	NR	..	...	Mkt Index Target-Term Sec	...	...	...	...	10 1/16	8¾	6227	9 11/16	8¾	9⅜	...	..	...	...	...	...
19	GWM	Mer Lyn Sel Sect SPDR 'MITTS' 2006	AS	NR	..	...	Mkt Index Target-Term Sec	...	...	...	...	10⅛	8⅝	5089	9 9/16	8⅞	9½	...	..	...	...	...	...
20	TKM	Merrill Lynch Tech'MITTS' 2001	NY	NR	1	10	Mkt Index Target-Term Secs	12 9/16	9⅛	15 7/16	10¾	17⅝	15⅛	629	17⅝	17 3/16	17⅝	...	..	...	15.1	19.8	...
21	PGT	Mer Lyn Telebras'ProGroS'2005	AS	NR	1	18	Protected Growth Sec	...	...	10⅞	7⅜	9⅝	7 11/16	529	9⅝	8⅜	9⅝B	...	..	...	15.4	...	...
22	MTT	Mer Lyn Top Ten Yld'MITTS'2006	AS	NR	1	1	Mkt Index Target-Term Sec	12¾	9 9/16	15⅛	11 15/16	16¾	13½	1213	14½	13½	13 15/16B	...	..	...	−2.2	11.7	...
23	MRM	✓Merrimac Industries	AS	B−	16	388	Mfr/design signal components	18 1/16	3 5/16	15 15/16	6⅜	10¼	4⅝	773	7⅞	6¼	6⅝	...	d	Neg	−5.4	−11.6	2.4
✢24•[1]	MESA	✓Mesa Air Group	NNM	C	118	20294	Western U.S. commuter airline	24	¾	9 13/16	3⅞	9⅝	4¼	68715	5 3/16	4¼	4¾	...	d	Neg	−39.2	−11.1	−12.2
25	MTR	✓Mesa Royalty Tr UBI	NY,B,Ch,Ph	NR	9	1155	Royalty interests,oil & gas	49	17	46¼	41½	49¼	43	75	47½	47	47½	5.5	18	−4	12.7	9.1	10.5
26	MSB	✓Mesabi Tr Ctfs SBI	NY,B,Ch	NR	14	814	Royalties from Res. Mining	18¼	1	4½	2 15/16	3 7/16	2 9/16	8138	3 3/16	2¼	3 1/16	11.4	7	17	13.2	0.7	12.1
27	MCC	✓Mestek Inc	NY,B,Ch,Ph	B	41	2208	Climate control eqp:engin'g	31½	2¼	22⅝	17⅝	23	18¼	824	20¼	18½	20¼	...	11	13	1.3	7.1	15.7
28	MPR	✓Met-Pro Corp	NY,Ph	B+	40	2085	Pollution control,fluid hdlg	18½	⅛	16½	10⅝	14	9⅝	1886	10½	9⅝	10	3.2	9	15	−16.2	−6.9	9.6
29	METG	✓META Group	NNM	NR	65	4938	Computer eqp research svcs	23	10 5/16	33¾	14 15/16	32	8	19106	19¼	13¾	19	...	26	2	−36.1	2.1	...
30	MCRE	✓MetaCreations Corp	NNM	NR	35	4333	Dgn computer graphic sys	41	6½	12¾	2 15/16	10¼	4 9/16	185729	10¼	5 11/16	8⅝	...	d	−26	59.9	−9.9	...
31	MTLC	Metalclad Corp	NSC	C	6	14	Insulation contracting svcs	65⅝	9⅜	20	2 13/16	6⅞	1¼	8015	6⅝	5¼	5 11/16	...	d	45	124	−20.5	−20.6
32	MUI	✓Metals USA	NY,Ph	NR	68	12092	Steel processor/svcs	16½	10	20⅛	6 9/16	13½	7 7/16	15890	9¾	7 13/16	8½	...	9	...	−12.8	...	...
33	MMWW	✓Metamor Worldwide	NNM	NR	151	17126	Information technology svcs	35¼	10¼	39⅝	17⅞	41⅝	12 9/16	329053	41⅝	26	29⅛	...	18	86	16.5	7.1	...
34	MSLV	✓MetaSolv Software	NNM	NR	..	...	Telecommunic software prd	...	...	...	...	97	19	51669	97	58	81¾	...	..	...	...	...	...
35•[2]	MEOH	✓Methanex Corp	NNM	NR	47	37177	Prod Methanol, synthetic gas	18⅞	5½	9¼	4¾	5⅝	2¼	12818	2 13/16	2¼	2⅝	...	d	Neg	−48.1	−33.7	−27.4
✢36	METHA	✓Methode Electronics'A'	NNM	B+	171	24177	Electronic component devices	27⅛	¾	18½	10⅝	36	10	94270	36	26⅞	32⅛	0.6	38	2	108	18.1	24.7
37	MKA	✓Metrika Systems	AS	NR	21	1144	Dvlp process optimization sys	18½	13⅞	18	8	9¾	5 1/16	1860	6⅛	5 1/16	6	...	11	10	−30.4	...	...
38•[2]	MXT	✓Metris Cos	NY,Ph	NR	297	37488	Market consumer credit pds	24½	8	40⅜	7¾	47½	18⅝	42904	39½	30 5/16	35 11/16	0.1	d	...	42.2	44.0	...
39•[1]	MGM	✓Metro-Goldwyn-Mayer	NY	NR	68	14724	Motion picture, TV production	22 3/16	19	27	7⅛	25½	10¼	29433	24 13/16	21⅞	23 9/16	...	d	...	78.7	...	...
40	MISI	✓Metro Information Svcs	NNM	NR	65	3390	Custom softwr dvlp svcs	29¼	12½	41¾	18⅜	37	12	16205	26¼	14 7/16	24	...	22	...	−20.0	...	...
41	MGS	✓MetroGas S.A. Cl'B'ADS[59]	NY,Ch,Ph	NR	2	40	Gas distribution-Argentina	11 13/16	6½	10⅛	6¼	10⅛	7 9/16	309	8 15/16	8⅜	8¼B	6.7	10	...	6.3	9.0	6.7
42•[1]	MFNX	✓Metromedia Fiber Network'A'	NNM	NR	260	89588	Fiber optic communicat'n svcs	3⅛	1¾	19 1/16	1 15/16	49⅞	16⅞	594971	49⅞	35⅜	47 15/16	...	d	−22	188	...	...
43•	MMG	✓Metromedia Intl Grp	AS,B,Ch,P,Ph	C	129	29831	Telecommunic/home prds	38⅜	11/16	18 7/16	2¼	8¾	2⅞	83940	5¼	3⅞	4¾	...	d	58	−12.6	−21.6	−12.2
44	Pr	7.25%cmCv[61]Pfd(52.5375)	AS	NR	29	1719		57¾	42½	68	18	37	21¼	2340	30	24¼	30	12.1	..	...	...	...	...
45	MX	Metso Corp ADS[62]	NY	NR	1		Dsgn/mfr pulp machinery	38	26¾	36 5/16	18⅞	26⅞	10⅛	1137	13¾	10¾	13½	7.8	4	33	−46.0	−23.8	...
46•[2]	MTD	✓Mettler-Toledo Intl	NY	NR	189	27645	Mfr weighing instruments	18¾	14	28 15/16	16¼	39½	19⅝	16144	39½	34	38 3/16	...	30	...	36.1	...	...
47	MFRI	✓MFRI, Inc	NNM	B	23	1921	Mfr air pollut'n filter bags	11	3⅝	9⅜	4½	5¾	2¾	881	4 11/16	4⅛	4 5/16	...	25	−22	−13.8	−18.4	−4.8
48•[3]	MOGN	✓MGI PHARMA, Inc	NNM	C	30	2497	Develop,mkt pharmaceuticals	25¼	2¾	24	3 11/16	14¾	7	15470	12 13/16	9¾	11 15/16	...	75	NM	22.4	41.1	13.8
49	MGI	✓MGI Properties[63]	NY,Ph,P	NR	76	3093	Real estate investment trust	25⅝	2⅞	30⅝	22¾	28 13/16	5⅛	7904	5⅞	5⅛	5¼	...	1	40	1.1	12.2	20.1
¶50•[4]	MTG	✓MGIC Investment	NY,Ch,Ph,P	A	557	101729	Provides private mtge insur	66 15/16	6 13/16	74½	24¼	62¾	30⅛	114286	62¾	56	60 9/16	0.2	15	24	51.5	16.8	29.8

Uniform Footnote Explanations-See Page 4. Other: [1]CBOE:Cycle 2. [2]CBOE:Cycle 1. [3]ASE,CBOE:Cycle 1. [4]ASE:Cycle 3. [51]re-spec cond. [52]Then ea April (re-spec cond). [53]Re-spec cond. [54]Exercise price based on Russell 200 Index as defined. [55]Dstr of 1 wrrt. [56]Fiscal May'95 & prior. [57]12 Mo Dec'96:May'96 earn. d$0.30. [58]Incl current amts. [59]Ea ADS rep 10 Cl'B'shrs, 1 peso. [60]Pfd in $M. [61]Fr 9-15-2000. [62]Ea ADS rep 1 shr,FIM 10. [63]Plan liquidation of co. [64]Liq div.

Splits ◆ Index	Cash Divs. Ea. Yr. Since	Dividends: Latest Payment Period $	Date	Ex. Div.	Total $ So Far 1999	Ind. Rate	Paid 1998	Financial Position Mil-$ Cash& Equiv.	Curr. Assets	Curr. Liab.	Balance Sheet Date	Capitalization Lg Trm Debt Mil-$	Shs. 000 Pfd.	Com.	Earnings $ Per Shr. Years End	1995	1996	1997	1998	1999	Last 12 Mos.	Interim Earnings Period	$ per Shr. 1998	1999	Index
1	1996	Q0.598	1-3-00	12-15	2.391	2.39	2.391	At maturity IMC Global Com or Cash[51]				....	...	★5661	Dc	...	...	...	....	....	....	Mature 7-1-2001			1
2	1998	Q1.066	2-1-00	1-12	4.262	4.262	3.209	At maturity CIBER Inc Com or Cash re-spec cond				....	...	1750	Je	...	...	...	....	....	....	Mature 2-1-2001			2
3	....	None Since Public			...	Nil	....	Int based on S&P Energy Sel'SPDR'Fund,as defined				....	...	★5100	Dc	...	...	...	....	....	....	Due 2-21-2006			3
4	....	....			...	....	....	Int based on Select Sector SPDR Fd Index,as defined				....	...	★4400	Dc	...	...	...	....	....	....	Due 9-20-2006			4
5	....	....			...	....	....	Int based on Hlthcr/Biotech Portfolio,as defined				....	...	★1500	Dc	...	...	...	....	....	....	Due 10-31-2001			5
6	....	....			...	....	....	Int based on Dow Jones Ind Avg,as defined				....	...	★9000	Dc	...	...	...	....	....	....	Due 1-14-2003			6
7	....	....			...	....	....	Int based on global Mkt Index,as defined				....	...	★4700	Dc	...	...	...	....	....	....	Due 12-22-2004			7
8	....	....			...	....	....	Int based in Maj 8 European Index,as defined				....	...	★7200	Dc	...	...	...	....	....	....	Due 8-30-2002			8
9	....	....			...	....	....	Int based on Maj 11 Intl Mkt Index,as defined				....	...	★2750	Dc	...	...	...	....	....	....	Due 12-6-2002			9
10	....	....			...	....	....	Int based on Maj 11 Intl Mkt Index,as defined				....	...	★25000	Dc	...	...	...	....	....	....	Due 5-26-2006			10
11	....	....			...	....	....	Int based on Nikkei 225,as defined				....	...	★2500	Dc	...	...	...	....	....	....	Due 6-14-2002			11
12	....	....			...	....	....	Int based on Nikkei 225,as defined				....	...	★4700	Dc	...	...	...	....	....	....	Due 9-20-2002			12
13	....	....			...	....	....	Int based on Nikkei 225,as defined				....	...	★2500	Dc	...	...	...	....	....	....	Due 9-21-2005			13
14	....	....			...	....	....	Int based in Nikkei 225 as defined				....	...	★2500	Dc	...	...	...	....	....	....	Due 8-4-2006			14
15	....	Callable fr 4-1-99[52]			...	....	....	At maturity apprec based on oracle cp com[53]				....	...	★3100	My	...	...	...	....	....	....	Mature 3-31-2003			15
16	....	....			...	....	....	Int based on Russell 200 Index as defined				....	...	★3500	Dc	...	...	...	....	....	....	Due 7-21-2006			16
17	....	Terms&trad. basis should be checked in detail						Wrrts expire 5-25-2001				....	...	★1200	Dc	...	...	...	....	....	....				17
18	....	....			...	....	....	Int based on S&P 500 as defined				....	...	★2500	Dc	...	...	...	....	....	....	Due 8-4-2006			18
19	....	....			...	....	....	Int based on Select Sector SPDR Fd Index, as defined				....	...	★7000	Dc	...	...	...	....	....	....	Due 5-25-2006			19
20	....	....			...	....	....	Int based on CBOE Tech Index, as defined				....	...	★2500	Dc	...	...	...	....	....	....	Due 8-15-2001			20
21	....	Callable fr 6-1 to 6-30-2004[53]			...	....	....	At maturity apprec based on Telebras com[53]				....	...	★1450	Dc	...	...	...	....	....	....	Mature 5-19-2005			21
22	....	....			...	....	....	Int based on DJIA Top Ten Yld com,as defined				....	...	★3500	Dc	...	...	...	....	....	....	Due 8-15-2006			22
23◆	....	0.091	9-19-97	9-3	...	Nil	....	0.77	10.2	3.84	10-02-99	3.37	...	1739	Dc	v0.86	vd0.17	v0.79	v0.19	....	d0.17	9 Mo Sep	v0.59	v0.23	23
24	....	None Since Public			...	Nil	....	56.1	122	106	6-30-99	235	...	33840	Sp	0.42	v1.00	vd1.72	vd1.89	Pvd0.39	d0.39				24
25	1980	0.327	1-31-00	12-29	2.593	2.59	3.938	Total Assets $14.19M			9-30-99	....	...	1864	Dc	3.20	v4.13	v5.02	v3.35	....	2.60	6 Mo Jun	v2.05	v1.30	25
26	1990	0.11½	11-20-99	10-27	0.35	0.35	0.54	....	...	...		....	...	13120	Ja	0.28	v0.43	v0.50	v0.43	....	0.43				26
27	....	[55]....	9-22-86	8-25	...	Nil	....	2.03	126	89.2	9-30-99	0.34	...	8829	Dc	v1.21	v1.49	v1.61	v1.80	....	1.88	9 Mo Sep	v1.18	v1.26	27
28◆	1992	Q0.08	3-10-00	2-23	0.48	0.32	0.30	5.19	34.2	13.1	10-31-99	10.4	...	6392	Ja	0.69	v0.86	v1.00	v1.03	....	1.09	9 Mo Oct	v0.76	v0.82	28
29◆	....	None Paid			...	Nil	....	11.8	58.8	38.3	9-30-99	....	...	10104	Dc	v0.45	v0.31	v0.48	v0.70	....	0.72	9 Mo Sep	v0.48	v0.50	29
30	....	None Since Public			...	Nil	....	40.8	70.5	9.54	9-30-99	....	...	24771	Dc	vd0.15	vd0.37	vd0.36	vd0.83	....	d0.17	9 Mo Sep	vd0.68	vd0.02	30
31◆	....	None Paid			...	Nil	....	0.94	4.21	1.81	9-30-99	3.10	...	4544	Dc	[56]d11.30	[57]d2.40	vd1.60	vd1.60	....	d1.43	9 Mo Sep	vd0.89	vd0.72	31
32	....	None Since Public			...	Nil	....	8.00	492	169	9-30-99	443	...	38143	Dc	...	pv0.53	vp0.53	v1.07	....	0.98	9 Mo Sep	v0.85	v0.76	32
33◆	....	None Since Public			...	Nil	....	10.3	217	124	9-30-99	267	...	34273	Dc	±v0.29	v□±0.57	±v0.82	v±1.88	....	1.61	9 Mo Sep	v±1.39	v±1.12	33
34	....	None Since Public			...	Nil	....	12.4	31.4	20.9	9-30-99	....	p...	★33278	Dc	...	...	...	vd0.02	....	0.17	9 Mo Sep	vd0.15	v0.04	34
35	....	None Paid			...	Nil	....	182	467	132	6-30-99	399	...	173137	Dc	1.05	vd0.04	v1.10	vd0.39	....	d0.54	9 Mo Sep	vd0.27	vd0.42	35
36◆	1983	Q0.05	1-31-00	1-12	0.20	0.20	0.20	35.0	177	57.1	10-31-99	....	...	±35990	Ap	±0.75	v±0.92	v±1.06	v±1.00	v±0.93	0.84	6 Mo Oct	v±0.48	v±0.39	36
37	....	None Since Public			...	Nil	....	2.40	69.3	40.3	10-02-99	....	...	7418	Dc	v0.57	v0.76	v0.82	v0.77	....	0.53	9 Mo Sep	v0.57	v0.33	37
38◆	1997	0.01	11-22-99	11-9	0.02½	0.04	†0.02½	Total Deposits $588.30M			9-30-99	345	866	38598	Dc	pv0.14	v0.59	v0.94	v1.41	....	d0.58	9 Mo Sep	v1.02	v□d0.97	38
39	....	None Since Public			...	Nil	....	Total Assets $3292.48M			9-30-99	[58]1317	...	151593	Dc	...	pvd0.01	vpd4.47	vd2.08	....	d3.96	9 Mo Sep	vd1.73	vd3.61	39
40	....	None Since Public			...	Nil	....	4.01	66.9	24.5	9-30-99	78.3	...	14971	Dc	pv0.24	vp0.42	v0.66	v0.97	....	1.09	9 Mo Sep	v0.70	v0.82	40
41◆	1995	0.499	12-3-99	11-19	0.55	0.55	0.638	7.39	137	140	12-31-97	269	...	569170	Dc	0.72	0.67	v0.81	....	....	0.81				41
42◆	....	None Since Public			...	Nil	....	383	559	166	9-30-99	689	...	±190062	Dc	vd0.09	vd0.15	vd0.28	v0.01	....	d0.23	9 Mo Sep	v0.01	vd0.23	42
43	....	0.09	1-3-94	12-10	...	Nil	....	62.0	178	134	9-30-99	210	[60]207	p93283	Dc	v□d15.51	v□d2.04	v□1.48	vd2.01	....	d2.41	9 Mo Sep	vd1.02	vd1.42	43
44	1997	Q0.90⅝	12-15-99	11-18	3.625	3.625	3.62½	Cv into 3.3333 com				....	4140	...	Dc	...	...	...	....	....	....				44
45	1997	1.05	4-23-99	4-5	1.05	1.05	1.074	301	1135	696	12-31-98	360	...	p135726	Dc	3.09	2.23	v3.70	v3.39	....	3.39				45
46	....	None Since Public			...	Nil	....	14.9	369	300	9-30-99	284	...	38554	Dc	...	pn/a	□vd0.76	v0.92	....	1.26	9 Mo Sep	v0.51	v0.85	46
47	....	None Since Public			...	Nil	....	1.55	60.0	24.4	10-31-99	40.1	...	4922	Ja	v0.52	0.70	v0.54	v0.07	....	0.17	9 Mo Oct	v0.36	v0.46	47
48	....	None Paid			...	Nil	....	19.2	23.5	3.45	9-30-99	....	...	14939	Dc	vd0.21	vd0.50	vd0.13	v0.03	....	0.16	9 Mo Sep	v0.01	v0.14	48
49	1972	[64]4.50	11-23-99	11-24	[64]24.16	Nil	1.22	Total Assets $172M			8-31-99	[58]34.6	...	13774	Nv	1.25	2.11	v□1.53	v2.12	....	10.17	9 Mo Aug	v1.65	v□9.70	49
50◆	1991	Q0.02½	12-1-99	11-4	0.10	0.10	0.10	Total Assets $3072.82M			9-30-99	411	...	105708	Dc	v1.75	2.16	v2.75	v3.39	E4.16	3.96	9 Mo Sep	v2.49	v3.06	50

◆Stock Splits & Divs By Line Reference Index [23]10%,'98. [28]3-for-2,'95,'96. [29]3-for-2,'98. [31]1-for-10 REVERSE,'99. [33]3-for-2(twice),'96. [36]3-for-2,'95. [38]2-for-1,'99. [41]11.05%,'97. [42]2-for-1,'98(twice),'99. [50]2-for-1,'97.

¶ S&P 500
# MidCap 400
✤ SmallCap 600
• Options

Index	Ticker	Name of Issue (Call Price of Pfd. Stocks)	Market	Com. Rank. & Pfd. Rating	Inst. Hold Cos	Inst. Hold Shs. (000)	Principal Business	Price Range 1971-97 High	1971-97 Low	1998 High	1998 Low	1999 High	1999 Low	Dec. Sales in 100s	December, 1999 Last Sale Or Bid High	Low	Last	%Div Yield	P-E Ratio	EPS 5 Yr Growth	% Annualized Total Return 12 Mo	36 Mo	60 Mo
1•[1]	MGG	✔**MGM Grand**	NY,P	B–	157	11982	Hotel/casino & airline oper	49¾	8¾	39⅞	22 9/16	54 9/16	27⅛	41493	52	45¾	50 5/16	1.6	33	1	85.5	13.0	15.8
2	MHO	✔**M/I Schottenstein Homes**	NY,Ch,Ph	NR	66	4553	Single family homebuilder	19½	6⅝	26 13/16	16¾	22¼	13⅛	10434	15¾	13⅛	15 9/16	1.3	4	31	–28.5	12.7	17.6
3	MAJ	✔**Michael Anthony Jewelers**	AS,Ch,Ph	B	20	1776	Mfr handcrafted gold jewelry	16	2¼	3⅜	2	4 15/16	2¾	900	3⅛	2¾	2 15/16	...	8	–7	–9.6	–1.4	–15.3
✤4•[2]	MIKE	✔**Michaels Stores**	NNM	B–	188	23979	Specialty retail stores	46½	2½	39 15/16	15½	35⅞	16	38997	32⅛	25⅜	28½	...	16	NM	57.5	33.4	–3.9
✤5•[3]	MCRL	✔**Micrel Inc**	NNM	B	229	26337	Mfr,mkt integrated circuits	23 7/16	2¼	28 1/16	11⅜	58 11/16	22	54245	58⅝	43	56 15/16	...	..	38	128	99.7	77.0
#6•[4]	MWHS	✔**Micro Warehouse**	NNM	NR	170	23991	Direct mkt computer products	56⅞	9	36⅜	10¼	47	11 5/16	271341	18⅞	11¾	18½	...	13	–17	–45.3	16.3	–12.0
✤7•[3]	MICA	✔**MicroAge Inc**	NNM	B	76	3980	Franchises computer stores	32½	2 3/16	18¾	8¼	18⅝	2	447385	9¼	3	3½	...	d	Neg	–77.2	–44.1	–21.5
8	MICT	✔**Microcell Telecomm'B'**	NNM,To	NR	57	8384	Dvp stg:wireless comm svcs	12½	5¾	10	4 7/16	32⅞	5⅞	67032	32⅞	25 3/16	32⅞	...	d	–44	454	...	...
#9•[5]	MCHP	✔**Microchip Technology**	NNM	NR	340	44932	Mfr microcontrollers/spcl prd	49⅜	2 1/16	41	17	77	25 7/16	162422	77	59¾	68 7/16	...	39	10	85.0	26.4	30.2
10	MCDE	✔**Microcide Pharmaceuticals**	NNM	NR	22	3649	Dvp stg:biopharmaceu'l R&D	20½	8½	10⅞	3½	9⅜	3¾	11435	9⅜	6⅛	8⅞	...	d	...	129	–3.9	...
11	MFI	✔**MicroFinancial Inc**	NY	NR	50	2869	Financial svcs	....	....	....	....	19⅞	8 15/16	1893	11 15/16	10¾	11 11/16	1.4	..	...	...	...	...
12•[5]	MUSE	✔**Micromuse Inc**	NNM	NR	184	14705	Dvp computer software	....	....	41½	8	182½	20¼	54368	182½	113½	170	...	..	...	772	...	...
13•[5]	MUEI	✔**Micron Electronics**	NNM,Ch	B–	93	10666	Mfr IBM compatible products	29⅞	7/16	24¾	8 7/16	19⅜	9	233256	12 11/16	9 13/16	11⅛	...	27	–11	–35.7	–17.0	5.8
¶14•[6]	MU	✔**Micron Technology**	NY,Ch,Ph,P	B–	626	155266	Mfr microcomputer parts	94¾	11/16	55⅝	20 1/16	85	34¼	1250787	85	58½	77¾	...	69	Neg	53.8	38.7	28.8
15	NOIZ	**Micronetics Wireless**	NSC	NR	1	2	Mfr noise test'g/microwave prd	4¾	5/16	3	1¼	8⅞	1¼	54069	8⅜	4⅜	7 9/16	...	95	33	303	71.5	37.1
✤16•[1]	MCRS	✔**MICROS Systems**	NNM	B+	179	14498	Mfr point-of-sale computer sys	27¾	⅜	39½	21½	76¼	26⅝	22730	76¼	50 5/16	74	...	44	39	125	68.8	31.4
17•[7]	MSCC	✔**Microsemi Corp**	NNM	B–	39	7136	Mfr silicon semiconductors	18⅜	1/16	22⅛	6⅛	13⅛	6¼	8073	9	7⅜	8⅞	...	68	NM	–19.3	–14.6	11.6
¶18•[6]	MSFT	✔**Microsoft Corp**	NNM,Ch	A–	2424	2115772	Software for microcomputers	37 11/16	⅛	72	31⅛	119 15/16	68	6624836	119 15/16	90⅞	116¾	...	77	41	68.4	78.2	72.6
19	MSTR	✔**MicroStrategy Inc'A'**	NNM	NR	75	6654	Computer software & svcs	....	....	46	12	234⅝	14 11/16	64271	234⅝	115⅝	210	...	..	...	567	...	...
20	MTST	✔**Microtest Inc**	NNM	C	20	1584	Local area netwk cabling prd	26	3⅜	7	2 3/16	13	2	122548	13	5⅝	9	...	d	–38	227	–2.6	–17.6
21	MAA	✔**Mid-Amer Apart Communities**	NY,Ch,P	NR	83	7066	Real estate investment trust	30½	19¾	29⅞	22⅝	25	20⅞	11485	22 13/16	21½	22⅝	10.2	28	–3	10.2	0.5	5.2
22	MAB	✔**Mid-America Bancorp**	AS,Ch,Ph	A–	41	1384	Commercial banking, Kentucky	33 11/16	1⅝	33¼	21 3/16	36¼	22 3/16	6185	36¼	25 9/16	28½	s3.0	14	16	15.1	25.1	21.5
23•[1]	MME	✔**Mid Atlantic Medical Svcs**	NY,Ch,Ph,P	B	108	29478	Health care mgmt services	30¼	¼	14	4 7/16	13⅛	5⅛	14686	9 11/16	7⅝	8 5/16	...	14	–11	–15.3	–14.7	–18.3
24	MRR	✔**Mid-Atlantic Realty Trust SBI**	NY,Ph	NR	49	5623	Real estate investment trust	15	7⅜	15	11	12⅝	8⅞	6305	10⅛	9 9/16	10 1/16	10.7	12	15	–9.8	4.9	13.8
25	MBP	✔**Mid Penn Bancorp**	AS	NR	1	.4	General banking, Penn	29 15/16	28¼	29	20⅝	25 15/16	22¼	86	24½	22⅝	22¼B	se3.4	18	...	11.2	...	...
#26•[2]	MEC	✔**MidAmerican Energy Hldg**	NY,P	B+	270	47812	Electric & gas utility	42	1 5/16	35	22½	36 1/16	26 7/16	91894	33 13/16	33¼	33 11/16	...	12	20	–2.9	0.1	16.6
27	MDS	✔**Midas Inc**	NY	NR	136	12333	Automotive repair svcs	....	....	32⅝	14¾	35⅝	18	6454	23	20¼	21⅞	0.4	12	...	–29.5	...	...
28	MRS	✔**Midcoast Energy Resources**	AS,Ph	NR	53	5720	Gas pipeline operations/svcs	20⅜	6 9/16	19	13 5/16	21	15	14074	18¾	15¾	16¾	1.7	12	65	0.1	36.1	...
29	MLAN	✔**Midland Co**	NNM	B+	49	1856	Insurance,transpt'n,sportswr	21 11/16	7/16	32 13/16	19¼	29 5/16	19¼	1173	23½	19⅞	20¾	1.3	7	39	–13.0	19.0	9.1
30	MSL	✔**MidSouth Bancorp**	AS	B	4	21	General banking, Louisiana	14 7/16	2⅞	15 11/16	10⅞	11 11/16	9	199	9¾	9	8¾B	2.3	10	12	–19.8	12.8	20.7
31	Pr	**6.07%[52]Adj[53]Rt'A'cmCvPfd([54]14**	AS	NR	1	1		40½	13⅜	46½	32½	35	28	6	28½	28	26⅞B	3.2	..	...	...	...	...
✤32	MWY	✔**Midway Games**	NY,Ch	NR	128	17022	Dstr entertainment softwr	26 13/16	15	25 11/16	9	24⅞	7⅝	41187	24 7/16	20⅛	23 15/16	...	..	...	118	5.7	...
✤33	MEH	✔**Midwest Express Holdings**	NY,P	NR	133	9669	Passenger jet airline	26 7/16	8	38 7/16	21 9/16	34 13/16	24	9112	33	28 13/16	31⅞	...	12	46	21.1	25.9	...
34	MIHL	**MIH Limited'A'**	NNM	NR	30	4693	Pay television/media svcs	....	....	....	....	75	18	25719	72⅞	48 9/16	59	...	..	...	...	...	...
35	MHU	✔**MIIX Group**	NY	NR	44	3233	Medical liability insurance	....	....	....	....	18 9/16	11 11/16	8718	14¾	11 11/16	14⅝	1.4	9	...	...	...	...
36	MKS	✔**Mikasa Inc**	NY,Ch	B	54	3207	Dvlp, mkt tableware/gift prd	17⅝	9	15⅛	10¼	13¾	7⅜	1159	10⅞	9 11/16	10 1/16	2.0	10	–2	–19.6	0.9	–8.4
37	MIKN	✔**Mikohn Gaming**	NNM	NR	17	1643	Mfr progressive jackpot sys	18	3⅜	9	3	6 1/16	2¾	13301	5 7/16	4 3/16	5⅛	...	14	–3	32.3	–0.8	–9.4
¶38•[8]	MZ	✔**Milacron Inc**	NY,B,C,Ch,P	B	308	24747	Machine tools: plastics mchy	46¾	2¼	33¾	14½	24½	13½	31732	15½	13½	15⅜	3.1	8	–1	–18.0	–9.1	–6.5
39	MS	✔**Milestone Scientific**	AS,Mo	NR	11	1574	Dvp/mfr healthcare pds	30⅛	4 7/16	24½	13/16	3	11/16	9868	15/16	11/16	13/16	...	d	–24	–27.8	–45.4	...
40•[9]	MCH	✔**Millennium Chemicals**	NY,Ch	NR	184	54527	Mfr Industrial chemicals	26⅜	16⅝	37⅛	18¼	28⅜	16 9/16	39746	21¾	17 13/16	19¾	3.0	26	...	2.3	6.5	...
#41	MLNM	✔**Millennium Pharmaceuticals**	NNM	NR	253	21751	Pharmaceutical R&D	24⅝	10½	26½	9⅝	144	24¾	105994	144	94¾	122	...	d	...	372	91.5	...
#42•[3]	MLHR	✔**Miller (Herman)**	NNM	B+	267	43721	Office furniture & systems	29⅛	⅛	36¼	18 3/16	27⅛	15⅝	98942	24½	20⅝	23	0.7	14	37	–13.9	18.5	30.1
43•[8]	MLR	✔**Miller Industries**	NY,Ch,P	NR	63	17520	Mfr towing & recovery equip	22⅞	2 5/16	12	3¾	7	1¾	32031	3⅜	2 1/16	2⅞	...	d	Neg	–36.1	–41.6	3.0
44•[5]	MICC	✔**Millicom Intl Cellular S.A.**	NNM	NR	61	18416	Cellular telephone ntwrk	57½	18¾	53⅞	12⅜	68¼	21¾	28907	68¼	46⅞	62⅜	...	d	–33	78.9	24.8	15.7
¶45•[10]	MIL	✔**Millipore Corp**	NY,Ch,Ph,P	B	388	38600	Separations technology sys	52	2¾	38 7/16	17¼	42⅛	23 7/16	62066	40	32⅝	38⅝	1.1	30	–40	38.2	–1.0	11.1
46	MLS	✔**Mills Corp**	NY,Ch,P	NR	106	8088	Real estate investment trust	28⅞	15⅛	27½	17¾	22⅝	15 9/16	27124	18⅛	15 9/16	17⅞	11.2	14	40	–0.4	–1.2	9.3
47	MIMS	✔**MIM Corp**	NNM	NR	19	838	Pharmacy mgmt organization	17½	3⅜	6½	2¼	4⅝	1½	86570	4⅝	2¼	2 7/16	...	d	NM	–27.8	–21.3	...
48•[11]	MSPG	✔**MindSpring Enterprises[57]**	NNM	NR	147	8558	Internet access provider	5¾	⅞	39½	4⅝	66½	23	455420	40 7/16	26⅛	26⅜	...	d	...	–12.9	197	...
49	MNES	✔**Mine Safety Appl**	NNM	B	59	1457	Safety & health protect'n eq	73½	2¼	87	57¼	81	50½	488	65	56¾	64	2.1	22	3	–7.9	8.5	9.6
#50•[2]	MTX	✔**Minerals Technologies**	NY,Ph,P	B+	210	20032	Mkts specialty minerals & prd	46⅛	16	55 9/16	35⅞	57	36¾	15912	40 13/16	36¾	40 1/16	e0.2	15	13	–1.9	–0.5	6.8

Uniform Footnote Explanations-See Page 4. Other: [1]ASE:Cycle 3. [2]P:Cycle 3. [3]CBOE:Cycle 2. [4]ASE,Ph:Cycle 2. [5]CBOE:Cycle 1. [6]ASE,CBOE,P,Ph:Cycle 1. [7]Ph:Cycle 3. [8]Ph:Cycle 2. [9]CBOE:Cycle 3. [10]ASE:Cycle 1. [11]ASE,CBOE,Ph:Cycle 3. [51]Excl subsid pfd shs. [52]Rate adjusted annually:min 6%,max 10%. [53]Rate set at 10% after 8-1-2005. [54]Fr 8-1-2000. [55]87% owned by WMS Indus. [56]Incl current amts. [57]Plan comb/w Earthlink Network,1 new. [58]Redemption of stk purch rt. [59]Incl redemption of stk purch rt.

Index	Cash Divs. Ea. Yr. Since	Latest Payment Period $	Date	Ex. Div.	Total $ So Far 1999	Ind. Rate	Paid 1998	Cash& Equiv.	Curr. Assets	Curr. Liab.	Balance Sheet Date	Lg Trm Debt Mil-$	Shs. 000 Pfd.	Com.	End	1995	1996	1997	1998	1999	Last 12 Mos.	Period	1998	1999	Index
1◆	2000	Q0.20	3-10-00	2-11	...	0.80	....	108	262	249	9-30-99	1349	...	56885	Dc	v0.96	v□1.38	v□1.96	v1.22	E1.55	1.29	9 Mo Sep	v0.83	v□0.90	1
2	1998	Q0.05	1-21-00	12-30	0.20	0.20	0.15	Total Assets $530M			9-30-99	210	...	8747	Dc	v1.12	□v1.60	v2.15	v3.26	....	4.36	9 Mo Sep	v2.32	v3.42	2
3	....	None Since Public			...	Nil	....	0.25	64.7	29.1	10-30-99	13.1	...	6358	Ja	v0.09	v0.22	vd0.34	v□0.33	....	0.36	9 Mo Oct	v0.17	v0.20	3
4	....	None Since Public			...	Nil	....	21.6	727	341	10-30-99	222	...	30914	Ja	vd0.96	vd1.35	v1.05	v1.43	E1.75	1.52	9 Mo Oct	v0.43	v0.52	4
5◆	....	None Since Public			...	Nil	....	10.2	108	33.4	9-30-99	11.2	...	41238	Dc	v0.19	v0.23	v0.40	v0.40	....	0.52	9 Mo Sep	v0.44	v0.56	5
6◆	....	None Since Public			...	Nil	....	199	568	237	9-30-99	....	...	35781	Dc	v1.05	v□0.49	vd1.06	v0.85	E1.38	1.41	9 Mo Sep	v0.47	v1.03	6
7◆	....	None Since Public			...	Nil	....	57.3	818	763	5-02-99	16.8	...	20497	Oc	0.02	0.89	v1.43	vd0.42	....	d7.05	9 Mo Jul	vd0.61	vd7.24	7
8	....	None Since Public			...	Nil	....	84.4	160	122	j12-31-98	966	...	±52898	Dc	d0.18	vd1.46	vd6.50	vd7.39	....	jd7.64	9 Mo Sep	vd5.15	vd5.40	8
9◆	....	None Since Public			...	Nil	....	43.9	218	134	9-30-99	16.0	...	50935	Mr	v0.80	v0.94	v1.14	v0.94	E1.76	1.18	6 Mo Sep	v0.56	v0.80	9
10	....	None Since Public			...	Nil	....	23.6	25.3	3.60	9-30-99	1.93	...	11138	Dc	pvd0.53	pvd0.07	vd0.43	vd0.89	....	d1.08	9 Mo Sep	vd0.68	vd0.87	10
11	1999	0.04	1-14-00	12-29	0.11½	0.16	....	Total Assets $261M			9-30-99	144	...	12856	Dc	v0.27	v0.52	v0.76	v1.19	....	....	9 Mo Sep	n/a	v1.69	11
12	....	None Since Public			...	Nil	....	64.7	78.1	17.2	6-30-99	....	...	16043	Sp	...	...	pd0.73	vd0.18	....	0.44	9 Mo Jun	vd0.29	v0.33	12
13	....	None Since Public			...	Nil	....	338	544	247	9-02-99	5.00	...	96282	Au	v0.74	v0.48	v0.92	v0.50	v0.38	0.41	3 Mo Nov	v0.12	v0.15	13
14◆	....	0.05	5-31-96	5-7	...	Nil	....	1614	2830	922	9-02-99	1528	...	±269439	Au	3.95	2.76	v1.55	vd1.10	vd0.26	1.12	3 Mo Nov	vd0.19	v1.19	14
15	....	None Since Public			...	Nil	....	0.91	4.16	0.77	9-30-99	0.85	...	3763	Mr	0.10	Δv0.10	v0.13	v0.08	....	0.08	6 Mo Sep	v0.07	v0.07	15
16◆	....	None Since Public			...	Nil	....	33.2	170	85.7	9-30-99	5.88	...	16420	Je	v0.73	v0.15	v1.01	v□1.20	v1.60	1.69	3 Mo Sep	v0.21	v0.30	16
17	....	0.06	1-16-87	12-19	...	Nil	....	7.41	111	62.7	7-04-99	33.2	...	10914	Sp	0.74	0.98	v1.03	v0.98	Pv0.13	0.13				17
18◆	....	None Since Public			...	Nil	....	18902	21963	8332	9-30-99	....	p...	p5174116	Je	0.29	0.43	v0.66	v0.83	v1.42	1.51	3 Mo Sep	v0.31	v0.40	18
19	....	None Since Public			...	Nil	....	43.8	103	31.5	9-30-99	....	...	±38560	Dc	...	...	pvNil	v0.16	....	0.28	9 Mo Sep	v0.09	v0.21	19
20	....	None Since Public			...	Nil	....	6.47	25.0	6.31	9-25-99	....	...	8312	Dc	v0.64	vd1.43	v0.04	vd0.10	....	d0.72	9 Mo Sep	v0.02□	vd0.60	20
21	1994	Q0.575	10-29-99	10-20	2.30	2.30	2.20	Total Assets $1315.77M			9-30-99	719	6939	18424	Dc	v1.00	v1.21	v□1.05	v□0.87	....	0.82	9 Mo Sep	v□0.69	v□0.64	21
22◆	1950	3%Stk	12-17-99	12-1	s0.854	0.85	s0.792	Total Deposits $960.16M			9-30-99	70.6	...	10628	Dc	v0.78	1.44	v1.70	v1.88	....	1.99	9 Mo Sep	v1.48	v1.59	22
23◆	....	None Since Public			...	Nil	....	200	311	194	9-30-99	....	...	49886	Dc	□v1.28	vd0.06	v0.31	v0.20	E0.59	0.54	9 Mo Sep	v0.08	v0.42	23
24	1993	Q0.27	12-15-99	11-29	1.05	1.08	1.01	Total Assets $327.87M			9-30-99	175	...	14185	Dc	Δ0.51	v0.56	□v0.72	□v0.84	....	0.87	9 Mo Sep	v0.62	v0.65	24
25◆	1997	sQ0.19	11-22-99	11-8	s†2.181	0.76	s0.689	Total Deposits $219M			9-30-99	15.4	...	2893	Dc	v1.04	v1.16	v1.40	v1.28	....	1.24	9 Mo Sep	v1.03	v0.99	25
26	....	4%Stk	1-17-91	12-11	...	Nil	....	Total Assets $11010M			9-30-99	6298	[51]...	59868	Dc	v1.22	v1.54	□v0.75	v□2.15	....	2.77	9 Mo Sep	v1.67	v□2.29	26
27	1998	Q0.02	1-1-00	12-13	0.08	0.08	0.04	28.8	166	70.1	9-25-99	111	...	16268	Dc	...	p1.83	vpd1.21	v1.63	....	1.80	9 Mo Sep	v1.65	v1.82	27
28◆	1996	Q0.07	12-1-99	11-17	0.274	0.28	0.25	1.47	51.4	49.8	9-30-99	63.4	...	★12722	Dc	v1.08	v0.73	v1.10	v1.25	....	1.41	9 Mo Sep	v0.82	v0.98	28
29◆	1961	Q0.068	1-6-00	12-20	0.26½	0.27	0.246	Total Assets $871.98M			9-30-99	45.9	...	9530	Dc	v1.04	v0.12	v1.89	v2.86	....	3.21	9 Mo Sep	v1.80	v2.15	29
30◆	1995	Q0.05	1-3-00	12-13	0.20	0.20	0.17	Total Deposits $240.21M			9-30-99	3.39	153	2474	Dc	0.55	v0.45	v0.61	v0.83	....	0.87	9 Mo Sep	v0.63	v0.67	30
31	1996	0.21⅜	1-3-00	12-13	0.877	0.85	0.939	Cv into 2.998 com				....	157	...	Dc	...	...	...	...	...	...				31
32	....	None Since Public			...	Nil	....	36.2	181	50.2	9-30-99	....	...	[55]37985	Je	...	pv0.76	vΔ1.06	v1.10	v0.16	0.19	3 Mo Sep	v0.26	v0.29	32
33◆	....	None Since Public			...	Nil	....	29.3	52.5	90.5	9-30-99	3.11	...	14131	Dc	pv1.23	v1.51	v1.74	v2.51	....	2.77	9 Mo Sep	v1.93	v2.19	33
34	....	None Since Public			...	Nil	....	87.5	260	300	9-30-98	85.3	...	±★49891	Mr	...	...	vpd1.52	....	....	....	6 Mo SepΔ	n/a	vp±0.02	34
35	1999	0.05	1-19-00	12-29	0.05	0.20	....	Total Assets $1788M			9-30-99	19.5	...	15453	Dc	...	...	...	pv2.47	....	1.60	9 Mo Sep	v1.95	v1.08	35
36	1997	Q0.05	1-11-00	12-28	0.20	0.20	0.20	0.55	222	60.8	9-30-99	90.0	...	17483	Dc	v1.34	v0.91	v1.18	v0.78	....	1.01	9 Mo Sep	v0.01	v0.24	36
37	....	None Since Public			...	Nil	....	2.21	70.0	25.4	9-30-99	85.9	...	10764	Dc	vd0.68	v0.06	v0.24	v□d0.60	....	0.37	9 Mo Sep	v□d0.66	v0.31	37
38	1923	Q0.12	12-12-99	11-19	0.48	0.48	0.48	41.2	708	554	9-30-99	320	60	37013	Dc	v3.07	v1.74	v2.01	v1.05	E1.90	1.88	9 Mo Sep	v0.45	v1.28	38
39	....	None Since Public			...	Nil	....	1.40	3.58	0.94	9-30-99	2.25	...	8765	Dc	pd0.62	vd0.43	vd1.21	vd1.22	....	d1.14	9 Mo Sep	vd0.62	vd0.54	39
40	1997	Q0.15	12-17-99	12-1	0.60	0.60	0.60	78.0	781	380	9-30-99	993	...	68231	Dc	p5.10	vp1.89	v2.47	v2.17	E0.75↓	1.96	9 Mo Sep	v1.65	v1.44	40
41	....	None Since Public			...	Nil	....	225	241	38.1	9-30-99	26.0	...	p43395	Dc	pv0.07	vpd0.40	vd2.87	v0.33	Ed0.02↓	0.73	9 Mo Sep	vd0.44	vd0.04	41
42◆	1945	Q0.036	1-14-00	12-1	0.145	0.15	0.145	78.2	392	380	9-04-99	95.5	...	80024	My	v0.46	v0.46	v0.77	v1.39	v1.67	1.67	6 Mo Nov	v0.84	v0.84	42
43◆	....	None Since Public			...	Nil	....	9.88	192	76.2	10-31-99	128	...	46698	Ap	Δv0.25	v0.26	v0.35	v0.27	v0.05	d0.06	6 Mo Oct	v0.12	v0.01	43
44	....	None Since Public			...	Nil	....	53.1	454	354	12-31-98	931	...	48627	Dc	d0.63	d0.38	vd2.30	v1.11	....	d0.98	9 Mo Sep	vd0.52	vd2.61	44
45◆	1966	Q0.11	1-25-00	12-22	0.44	0.44	0.42	52.4	354	290	9-30-99	308	...	45264	Dc	v1.86	v0.98	vd0.89	v0.09	E1.28	1.13	9 Mo Sep	vd0.09	v0.95	45
46	1994	Q0.503	1-25-00	1-6	1.99½	2.01	1.93½	Total Assets $1032.45M			9-30-99	[56]872	...	23943	Dc	v□0.46	□v0.64	□v0.97	v□1.10	....	1.28	9 Mo Sep	v□0.71	v□0.89	46
47	....	None Since Public			...	Nil	....	20.4	94.8	80.5	9-30-99	2.85	...	18729	Dc	vd1.43	vd3.32	vd1.07	v0.26	....	d0.01	9 Mo Sep	v0.37	v0.10	47
48◆	....	None Since Public			...	Nil	....	386	403	59.1	9-30-99	181	...	63615	Dc	pvd0.10	vd0.24	vd0.09	v0.20	Ed0.60	d0.28	9 Mo Sep	v0.13	vd0.35	48
49	1918	Q0.34	12-10-99	11-17	1.36	1.36	1.33	19.0	230	130	9-30-99	11.9	22	4872	Dc	v3.32	v4.74	v4.80	v4.10	....	2.86	9 Mo Sep	v2.99	v1.75	49
50	1993	†[58]Q0.02½	12-17-99	11-1	†[59]0.11	0.10	0.10	16.4	217	115	9-26-99	74.8	...	21150	Dc	v1.72	v1.86	v2.18	v2.50	....	2.67	9 Mo Sep	v1.86	v2.03	50

◆Stock Splits & Divs By Line Reference Index [1]To split 2-for-1,ex Feb 28,'00. [5]2-for-1,'97,'99. [6]2-for-1,'94. [7]3-for-2,'94. [9]3-for-2,'94(twice),'97. [14]5-for-2,'94:2-for-1,'95. [16]2-for-1,'98. [18]2-for-1,'94,'96,'98,'99. [22]Adj for 3%,'99. [23]2-for-1,'94. [25]2-for-1,'97:Adj for 5%,'99. [28]10%,'98:5-for-4,'99. [29]3-for-1,'98. [30]4-for-3,'95,'96:12.5%,'97:3-for-2,'98. [33]3-for-2,'97,'98. [42]2-for-1,'97,'98. [43]2-for-1,'96:3-for-2,(twice),'96. [45]2-for-1,'95. [48]3-for-1,'98:2-for-1,'99.

¶ S&P 500
# MidCap 400
✢ SmallCap 600
• Options

Index	Ticker	Name of Issue (Call Price of Pfd. Stocks)	Market	Com. Rank. & Pfd. Rating	Inst. Hold Cos	Inst. Hold Shs. (000)	Principal Business	Price Range 1971-97 High	1971-97 Low	1998 High	1998 Low	1999 High	1999 Low	December, 1999 Dec. Sales in 100s	Last Sale Or Bid High	Last Sale Or Bid Low	Last Sale Or Bid Last	%Div Yield	P-E Ratio	EPS 5 Yr Growth	% Annualized Total Return 12 Mo	36 Mo	60 Mo
#1•[1]	MNMD	✓MiniMed Inc	NNM	NR	278	18170	Mfr medication infusion systems	22¼	3⅞	59	16	108¼	38½	156336	77½	50⅛	73¼	...	..	NM	40.5	65.9	...
¶2•[2]	MMM	✓Minnesota Min'g/Mfg	NY,B,C,Ch,P,Ph	A	1186	277647	Scotch tapes: coated abrasives	105½	10¾	97⅞	65⅝	103⅜	69 5/16	235773	100 13/16	91⅞	97⅞	2.3	25	6	41.1	...	...
#3•[3]	MPL	✓Minnesota Power	NY,B,C,Ch,P,Ph	B+	196	17184	Electric utility	22	3 3/16	23⅛	19	22 1/16	16	32223	17 7/16	16	16 15/16	6.3	15	3	−18.4	13.4	13.0
4	MNTX	✓Minntech Corp	NNM	B	32	4034	Mfrs dialysis eqp & supplies	23⅝	⅞	17¾	8⅞	16 15/16	8½	9105	10⅛	8½	9⅝	1.0	10	34	−37.3	−4.8	−8.6
5•[4]	MIPS	✓MIPS Technologies'A'	NNM	NR	91	9604	Dgn/dvp microprocessors	....	....	32	9⅝	69	24½	76037	66	43 13/16	52	...	84	NM	62.5	...	...
¶6•[5]	MIR	✓Mirage Resorts	NY,B,Ch,P	B	438	115221	Hotel-casino complex	30⅜	1/32	26¾	13 3/16	26⅜	11½	321484	15 15/16	12¾	15⅛	...	21	−16	1.3	−11.2	8.9
7	MRVT	✓Miravant Medical Technologies	NNM	NR	33	894	Dvlp,mfr medical devices	74¼	10 11/16	40⅝	4 11/16	16¼	6 5/16	26132	14½	9	9 5/16	...	d	−9	−27.7	−30.7	...
8	MCSW	✓Mission Critical Software	NNM	NR	51	5642	Sys adminstr/oper mgt softw	....	....	....	....	77⅝	16	32165	77⅝	54¼	70	...	..	...	...	...	...
9	MSW	✓Mission West Prop	AS,B,P	NR	41	5507	Real estate business trust	55 5/16	15	11	6½	9 1/16	6 7/16	7543	8 3/16	6⅞	7¾	7.7	..	...	20.8	−51.2	−28.1
✢10	GRO	✓Mississippi Chemical	NY,Ch,Ph	NR	120	13727	Prod/supp nitrogen fertilizers	27¼	14¾	20 3/16	11	15⅛	4 9/16	22747	6⅞	4 9/16	6 3/16	1.9	d	Neg	−54.1	−34.6	−16.8
11	MND.A	✓Mitchell Energy/Dev'A'	NY,B,P,Ph	B−	73	4056	Oil & gas:pipeline:real estate	45 11/16	1	29¼	9⅝	25¼	10½	3719	24⅛	21¼	22 1/16	2.2	82	Neg	98.8	2.4	9.3
12	MND.B	✓ Cl'B' non-vtg	NY	B−	66	8285		29½	13	29⅛	9⅞	24 13/16	11	7241	23 7/16	21	21 9/16	2.5	67	Neg	91.6	2.2	6.0
13	MLT	✓Mitel Corp	NY,To,B,Ch,Mo,P,Ph	B	46	13600	Telecommunications eq	41	⅝	16½	6½	14	5	10826	14	10	13¾	...	..	−34	88.0	30.1	31.5
14	MITY	✓Mity-Lite Inc	NNM	NR	13	278	Mfr folding leg tables	14 3/16	3½	13½	8 1/16	20¾	8 11/16	1390	18⅜	14¾	15 9/16	...	19	20	66.7	23.9	24.7
15	MKSI	✓MKS Instruments	NNM	NR	66	6618	Semiconductor mfg equip	....	....	....	....	36½	11⅞	8970	36½	23¾	36⅛	...	68	−3	...	...	...
16	NUT	✓ML Macadamia[53]Orchards'A'	NY,Ch,P,Ph	B	7	129	Owns macadamia nut orchards	11½	2¼	4 3/16	3	3 15/16	3	2946	3⅞	3 11/16	3¾	10.7	13	30	30.3	12.8	17.4
17•[6]	MMCN	✓MMC Networks	NNM	NR	151	15436	Mfr network processors	28¼	11	34¼	7¾	57	11¾	154339	35	19½	34⅜	...	76	...	159	...	...
18	MMI	✓MMI Companies	NY,Ph	B	85	11438	Insurance/risk mgmt svcs	33⅜	12⅛	26	13¾	17 11/16	3 5/16	43281	8 15/16	3 5/16	8⅝	4.2	d	Neg	−47.1	−34.5	−10.2
19	MOCO	✓MOCON Inc	NNM	B+	29	2313	Mfr specialized test instr	15	5/16	11⅝	4 1/16	8½	4⅜	3006	7	5½	6	3.3	13	8	8.0	4.0	14.1
20	MMPT	✓Modem Media.Poppe Tyson'A'	NNM	NR	36	1997	Interactive marketing svcs	....	....	....	....	79	16	32379	71¼	52¼	70⅜	...	..	...	...	...	...
21	MODM	✓Modern Medl Modalities	NSC	NR	1	7	Leases'MRI','CT Scan'equip	18	1 15/16	5 7/16	1/16	4⅜	⅛	6838	3	1½	2 1/16	...	d	Neg	3558	−2.4	−22.3
#22•[7]	MODI	✓Modine Mfg	NNM	A	132	13512	Auto parts: heating: air-cond	40½	⅝	38⅝	26⅝	38	23	16853	29⅝	25	25	3.7	11	2	−28.9	0.4	−0.3
#23•[2]	MPS	✓Modis Professional Svcs	NY	NR	278	76535	Temporary personnel service	38	1¾	38 1/16	9 15/16	17½	7	162314	14 13/16	9½	14¼	...	17	66	−2.6	−12.3	44.2
#24•[1]	MHK	✓Mohawk Industries	NY	B	239	36324	Mfr resident'l/commer'l carpet	24 5/16	4 13/16	42 7/16	20½	42	18⅜	31465	26 13/16	23¼	26⅜	...	12	52	−37.3	21.7	25.5
25	MB	✓Molecular Biosystems	NY,Ch,Ph,P	C	56	6038	Organic & biochemical R&D	40⅞	½	10 13/16	2⅜	4	¾	21785	1⅜	¾	1	...	d	3	−66.0	−46.4	−37.8
¶26•[8]	MOLX	✓Molex Inc	NNM	A	313	33161	Terminals,connectors,switch	38⅜	⅛	39	23	57	25½	186293	57	50	56 11/16	0.2	48	8	49.0	31.8	27.0
27•[2]	MOLXA	✓ Cl'A'(non-vtg)	NNM	A	237	58502		35½	5 5/16	34⅞	21¾	46⅝	22½	80279	46⅝	40½	45¼	0.2	38	8	42.3	26.2	23.7
28•[9]	MOL.A	✓Molson Inc 'A'	To,Mo	B	21	7924	Brewer:chem specialities	36	3 15/16	28	19¾	28 3/16	19⅞	6402	27	25	26¾	2.7	..	NM	25.3	10.9	9.5
29	MOL.B	Class'B' (vtg)	To,Mo	B	1	435	retail lumber & bldg mat'ls	36	4	28¼	20¼	28	19⅞	32	27	25⅜	27	2.7	..	77	26.5	11.7	9.9
✢30	MNC	✓Monaco Coach	NY	NR	164	11826	Mfr motor coaches	7 15/16	2⅜	17 11/16	7⅛	30 15/16	15⅛	13804	25¾	19 15/16	25 9/16	...	12	44	44.8	80.3	44.3
31•[1]	MOND	✓Mondavi(Robert)'A'	NNM	B+	111	5444	Produces premium wines	56¾	6¼	50¼	20⅛	41⅜	29	12310	40	33¼	34¾	...	17	15	−15.0	−1.6	24.8
32	WVQ	Monongahela Pwr 8% 'QUIDS'	NY	....[57]	1	24	Qtly Income Debt Securities	26⅜	24¼	26⅜	24¾	25⅞	23 3/16	509	24⅝	23 3/16	23B	8.7	..	...	−1.1	5.6	...
33	MNRO	✓Monro Muffler Brake	NNM	B	30	3388	Provides auto repair services	19¾	7 13/16	16⅞	5⅝	9 3/16	5¾	2401	7⅞	6¾	7½	...	15	−14	3.4	−17.6	−8.7
¶34•[2]	MTC	✓Monsanto Co	NY,B,C,Ch,P,Ph	B	1012	438449	Life sci:agri,food & pharm	52 5/16	1⅝	63 15/16	33¾	50 13/16	32¾	793537	45⅝	34⅞	35 7/16	0.3	42	Neg	−25.2	...	...
35	MCT	Monsanto Co 6.50%'ACES'[58]	NY	NR	93	10594	Automotive Com Exch Securities	....	....	49⅜	40	51	31⅞	39280	40½	31⅞	33⅛	7.8	..	...	−28.1	...	...
#36•[10]	MTP	✓Montana Power	NY,B,C,Ch,P,Ph	B+	374	48666	Utility: electric & gas	16⅛	4 3/16	28 9/16	14½	42⅝	24 9/16	96191	37 7/16	30 11/16	36 1/16	2.2	26	16	31.1	57.2	33.0
37	MNT	✓Montedison S p A ADS[59]	NY,Ch,P,Ph	NR	4	538	Int'l chemical concern	75¼	1 5/16	29⅜	16 11/16	27⅝	14 3/16	736	16¾	15⅛	16¼	2.2	13	NM	−32.8	12.1	−0.8
38•[3]	MNY	✓MONY Group	NY,Ph	NR	156	13905	Life insurance/annuities	....	....	32¾	23½	33 13/16	23¼	12384	30 15/16	26⅜	29 3/16	1.4	8	...	−5.4	...	...
39	MOG.B	✓Moog, Inc Cl'B'	AS	B	9	58	Mfr electrohydraulic ctrl sys	40	13/16	45¼	32½	41¼	35⅜	8	40½	40½	39⅞B	...	16	54	3.6	16.8	22.2
40	MOG.A	✓ Class'A'(Ltd-vtg)	AS,B	B	99	5519		40¼	1 13/16	47⅛	24 3/16	38 15/16	20 13/16	3506	27	21	27	...	10	55	−31.0	4.9	23.9
41•[11]	MCL	✓Moore Corp Ltd	NY,To,B,Ch,Mo,P	B−	91	23652	Produces business forms	33¾	7 13/16	17 11/16	9 7/16	12⅜	5 13/16	16971	7 1/16	5 13/16	6 1/16	3.3	14	Neg	−43.8	−31.0	−17.0
42	MMD	✓Moore Medical Corp	AS,Ch,Ph	C	26	1150	Dstr drugs,med'l/beauty prod	33¼	5/16	15¼	10⅛	14⅞	7	2026	9¾	7 11/16	9¾	...	12	−9	−27.8	−1.7	−5.8
43	MG	✓Morgan Group	AS	B−	6	242	Transport svcs-mfg homes,RVS	10⅝	6¾	11¾	6½	10	5⅜	265	6⅜	5⅜	5¾	1.4	27	−6	−21.2	−7.6	−3.2
¶44•[12]	JPM	✓Morgan (J.P.)	NY,B,C,Ch,P,Ph	B+	1093	109759	Comm'l&wholesale bkg,NY	125¾	7 11/16	148¾	72⅛	147 13/16	97¼	220468	139⅛	122¼	126⅝	3.2	13	2	24.6	12.7	22.0
45	JPW	Morgan J.P. Index Fd'ComPS'	AS	NR	1	1935	Commodity-Indexed Pfd Sec	....	....	....	....	27	12 5/16	141	26½	25½	26⅜	...	..	...	...	...	...
46	JPO	Morgan J.P. Index Fd 2.50%'ComPS'	AS	NR	..	...	Commodity-Indexed Pfd Sec	25	19	19	11¼	19⅞	9⅝	289	19⅞	18¼	19⅜	3.2	..	...	73.1	...	...
47	MOR	✓Morgan Keegan Inc	NY,Ch,Ph	B+	72	5517	Hldg:regional brokerage	26⅝	13/16	28 9/16	14⅞	20	15⅞	11965	18¼	16½	16¾	1.9	12	12	−9.2	15.5	29.3
¶48•[13]	MWD	✓Morgan Stan Dean Witter	NY,Ch	NR	1354	300111	Provides financial svcs/prod	59½	13½	97½	36½	142⅞	70 13/16	373968	142⅞	119¼	142¾	1.1	17	31	103	65.0	55.3
49	BGS	Morgan StanDW 2003'BRIDGES'[62]	NY	NR	..	...	BRoadInDex Guarded Eq-link Secs	....	....	11¼	9¼	13 1/16	11	918	13 1/16	12 5/16	13 1/16	...	..	...	16.1	...	...
50	BDJ	Mor StaDW DJ 2004'BRIDGES'[62]	NY	NR	..	...	BRoadInDex Guarded Eq-link Sec	....	....	10½	8⅛	11⅝	9 7/16	1003	11⅝	10 15/16	11⅝	...	..	...	17.7	...	...

Uniform Footnote Explanations-See Page 4. Other: [1]P:Cycle 2. [2]CBOE:Cycle 1. [3]Ph:Cycle 2. [4]ASE,CBOE,P,PH:Cycle 1. [5]ASE:Cycle 2. [6]CBOE,Ph:Cycle 1. [7]P:Cycle 1. [8]ASE,CBOE,Ph:Cycle 2. [9]Vc:Cycle 1. [10]Ph:Cycle 1. [11]CBOE:Cycle 1,To:Cycle 2. [12]Ph:Cycle 3. [13]ASE,CBOE,P,Ph:Cycle 1. [51]Excl subsid pfd. [52]Fiscal Nov'97 & prior. [53]L.P. Dep Unit. [54]Excl 1.5M Cl B units. [55]®$1.95,'96. [56]Incl 5.6M equiv 'B' shrs. [57]Rated 'A' by S&P. [58]Monsanto Cp Pur contract & Jr Sub Defr Deb. [59]ADS's represent'g 10 ord shrs par 1000 lire. [60]Fiscal Dec'95 & prior. [61]12 Mo Nov,'96. [62]Medium-Term Notes Series'C'.

Index	Splits ◆ Cash Divs. Ea. Yr. Since	Dividends Latest Payment Period $	Date	Ex. Div.	Total $ So Far 1999	Ind. Rate	Paid 1998	Financial Position Mil-$ Cash& Equiv.	Curr. Assets	Curr. Liab.	Balance Sheet Date	Capitalization Lg Trm Debt Mil-$	Shs. 000 Pfd.	Com.	Earnings $ Per Shr. Years End	1995	1996	1997	1998	1999	Last 12 Mos.	Interim Earnings Period	$ per Shr. 1998	1999	Index
1◆	....	None Since Public			...	Nil	....	168	267	19.9	10-01-99	1.00	...	31105	Dc	v0.11	v0.13	v0.24	v0.46	E0.70	0.64	9 Mo Sep	v0.29	v0.47	1
2◆	1916	Q0.56	12-12-99	11-17	2.24	2.24	2.20	490	6583	3865	9-30-99	1550	...	401334	Dc	v2.31	v3.62	v5.06	v□2.97	E4.00	3.86	9 Mo Sep	v2.36	v3.25	2
3◆	1945	Q0.26¾	12-1-99	11-10	1.07	1.07	1.02	312	698	551	9-30-99	790	[51]200	73461	Dc	1.08	v1.14	v1.23	v1.34	....	1.13	12 Mo Sep	v1.35	v1.13	3
4	1994	A0.10	9-24-99	9-8	0.10	0.10	0.10	8.92	41.9	7.04	9-30-99	....	...	6914	Mr	0.62	vd0.51	v0.69	v1.05	....	0.97	6 Mo Sep	v0.42	v0.34	4
5	....	None Since Public			...	Nil	....	53.7	61.2	17.2	9-30-99	....	...	±37443	Je	vd0.77	vd0.78	vd1.13	v0.01	v0.58	0.62	3 Mo Sep	v0.09	v0.13	5
6◆	....	0.003	7-10-78	6-27	...	Nil	....	101	428	299	9-30-99	2117	...	193195	Dc	v□0.88	v1.05	v1.09	v□0.45	E0.73	0.28	9 Mo Sep	v□0.55	v□0.38	6
7◆	....	None Paid			...	Nil	....	14.9	24.9	3.66	9-30-99	7.69	...	18016	Dc	vd1.19	vd1.37	vd2.36	vd1.94	....	d1.35	9 Mo Sep	vd1.51	vd0.92	7
8	....	None Since Public			...	Nil	....	62.2	65.8	13.6	9-30-99	....	...	14011	Je	...	...	...	....	pv0.03	0.16	3 Mo Sep	vd0.07	v0.06	8
9◆	1999	Q0.15	1-10-00	12-28	0.60	0.60	....	Total Assets $714.26M			9-30-99	165	...	16960	Dc	v1.06	v0.72	v[52]18.48	vd0.13	....	....	9 Mo Sep	n/a	v0.37	9
10	1995	Q0.03	11-24-99	11-8	0.33	0.12	0.40	1.72	157	59.8	9-30-99	323	...	26132	Je	2.34	v2.46	v2.29	v0.84	Pvd0.14	d0.51	3 Mo Sep	v0.16	vd0.21	10
11	1976	Q0.12	1-12-00	12-27	0.48	0.48	0.48	20.6	76.1	150	10-31-99	394	...	±49118	Ja	v±0.69	v±1.96	□vd0.41	vd1.04	....	0.27	9 Mo Oct	v±d0.07	v±1.24	11
12	1992	Q0.13¼	1-12-00	12-27	0.53	0.53	0.53	....	...	...		....	...	26796	Ja	v±0.74	±v2.01	□vd0.45	v±d0.99	....	0.32	9 Mo Oct	v±d0.03	v±1.28	12
13	....	None Since Public			...	Nil	....	138	633	305	j6-25-99	261	1616	115524	Mr	0.45	v0.32	v0.80	v0.20	....	j0.02	3 Mo Jun	v0.13	vd0.05	13
14◆	....	None Since Public			...	Nil	....	6.66	15.9	3.88	9-30-99	....	...	4814	Mr	v0.40	v0.51	v0.63	v0.78	....	0.82	6 Mo Sep	v0.40	v0.44	14
15	....	None Since Public			...	Nil	....	58.4	124	35.9	9-30-99	11.8	...	24576	Dc	v0.77	v0.46	v0.76	v0.24	....	0.53	9 Mo Sep	v0.21	v0.50	15
16	1986	Q0.10	2-15-00	12-29	0.37½	0.40	0.30	5.01	9.94	4.20	9-30-99	....	...	[54]7500	Dc	v0.16	v0.40	v2.06	v0.13	....	0.30	9 Mo Sep	vd0.03	v0.14	16
17	....	None Since Public			...	Nil	....	69.9	88.3	10.5	9-30-99	....	...	31703	Dc	...	pv0.03	v0.04	v0.25	....	0.45	9 Mo Sep	v0.16	v0.36	17
18	1993	Q0.09	1-14-00	12-30	0.35	0.36	0.31	Total Assets $1987.72M			9-30-99	119	...	19173	Dc	□v2.54	v[55]2.22	□v1.81	v0.59	....	d2.86	9 Mo Sep	v0.22	vd3.23	18
19◆	1984	Q0.05	2-18-00	2-2	0.20	0.20	0.20	6.34	11.4	2.68	9-30-99	....	...	6288	Dc	v0.38	v0.47	v0.57	v0.36	....	0.45	9 Mo Sep	v0.25	v0.34	19
20	....	None Since Public			...	Nil	....	43.7	64.7	27.5	9-30-99	....	...	[56]±11371	Dc	...	...	vpd0.48	vpd0.38	E0.19	0.04	9 Mo Sep	vd0.29	v0.13	20
21◆	....	None Since Public			...	Nil	....	0.74	3.91	4.93	9-30-99	2.53	...	2506	Dc	vd0.46	v0.16	v0.08	vd1.34	....	d0.76	9 Mo Sep	vd0.61	vd0.03	21
22	1959	Q0.23	12-2-99	11-18	0.90	0.92	0.82	57.0	470	242	9-26-99	178	...	29515	Mr	v2.03	v2.10	v2.39	v2.46	....	2.32	6 Mo Sep	v1.30	v1.16	22
23◆	....	....			...	Nil	....	24.9	441	152	9-30-99	245	...	96041	Dc	pv0.38	vp0.36	v0.93	v□2.84	E0.83	1.03	9 Mo Sep	v2.64	v0.83	23
24◆	....	None Since Public			...	Nil	....	....	988	598	10-02-99	363	...	60625	Dc	0.13	v0.95	v1.30	v1.86	....	2.29	9 Mo Sep	v1.48	v1.91	24
25	....	None Paid			...	Nil	....	13.0	16.9	8.34	9-30-99	4.16	...	18727	Mr	d1.62	vd0.78	vd1.19	vd1.14	....	d0.92	6 Mo Sep	vd0.34	vd0.12	25
26◆	1976	Q0.02½	1-25-00	12-29	0.07	0.10	0.06	260	932	344	9-30-99	24.3	...	±156771	Je	±0.79	v±0.92	±v1.05	v±1.15	v±1.14	1.18	3 Mo Sep	v0.25	v0.29	26
27◆	1990	Q0.02½	1-25-00	12-29	0.07	0.10	0.06	....	...	...		....	...	78302	Je	±0.79	±0.93	±1.06	±v1.15	±v1.14	1.18	3 Mo Sep	v±0.25	v±0.29	27
28	1950	gQ0.18	1-1-00	12-9	g0.72	0.72	g0.72	39.3	543	700	j9-30-99	1165	...	±59209	Mr	±d5.27	v±0.57	±v1.89	v±2.82	....	j0.12	6 Mo Sep	v±3.14	v±0.44	28
29	1944	gQ0.18	1-1-00	12-9	g0.72	0.72	g0.72	....	...	...		....	...	12094	Mr	±d5.27	±0.57	±v1.89	±v2.82	....	j0.05	6 Mo Sep	v±3.22	v±0.45	29
30◆	....	None Since Public			...	Nil	....	....	133	105	10-02-99	....	...	18862	Dc	v0.32	v0.38	v0.71	v1.19	....	2.08	9 Mo Sep	v0.79	v1.68	30
31	....	None Since Public			...	Nil	....	....	364	89.6	9-30-99	231	...	±15478	Je	1.39	bv0.72	v±1.80	±v1.83	v±1.94	2.01	3 Mo Sep	v0.51	v0.58	31
32	1995	Q0.50	12-31-99	12-28	2.00	2.00	2.00	Co opt redm fr 6-19-2000 at $25				40.0	...	...	Dc	...	...	...	...	....	....				32
33◆	....	5%Stk	6-18-98	6-4	...	Nil	5%Stk	3.07	52.5	38.7	9-30-99	71.5	92	8322	Mr	0.86	v1.13	v1.10	v0.53	....	0.49	6 Mo Sep	v0.70	v0.66	33
34◆	1925	Q0.03	12-10-99	11-10	0.12	0.12	0.12	84.0	5635	3555	9-30-99	5961	...	634608	Dc	v1.27	v0.65	v0.77	vd0.41	E0.85	d0.16	9 Mo Sep	v0.56	v0.81	34
35	1999	0.65	11-30-99	11-24	2.60	2.60	....	11-30-2003 exch for Monsanto Co com re-spec						17500	Dc	...	...	...	...	....	...				35
36◆	1935	Q0.20	2-1-00	1-5	0.80	0.80	0.80	Total Assets $3049.21M			9-30-99	650	581	110201	Dc	v0.46	v1.02	v1.14	v1.48	....	1.41	9 Mo Sep	v0.84	v0.78	36
37◆	1997	0.372	6-10-99	5-20	0.372	0.365	0.289	Equity per shr $8.26			12-31-98	4540	...	2977315	Dc	Δ0.21	0.73	v1.19	v1.29	....	1.29				37
38	1999	Q0.10	12-24-99	12-1	0.40	0.40	....	Total Assets $24301M			9-30-99	258	...	47238	Dc	...	...	pv□2.72	v□3.99	....	3.60	9 Mo Sep	v□3.22	v2.83	38
39	....	0.05	10-5-88	9-2	...	Nil	....	8.92	398	170	6-30-99	357	100	±8913	Sp	±1.00	v□±1.47	v±1.88	v±2.26	....	2.58	9 Mo Jun	v±1.66	v±1.98	39
40	....	0.07	10-5-88	9-2	...	Nil	....	....	...	...		....	...	7327	Sp	±1.00	v□±1.47	v±1.88	v±2.26	Pv±2.70	2.70				40
41	1934	tQ0.05	1-7-00	12-1	t0.20	0.20	t0.57	99.5	815	629	6-30-99	204	...	88457	Dc	v2.61	v1.50	v0.59	vd6.19	E0.45	0.40	9 Mo Sep	vd6.36	v0.23	41
42	....	None Paid			...	Nil	....	....	36.1	14.5	10-02-99	....	...	2941	Dc	v0.80	vd0.19	vd1.00	v0.95	....	0.79	9 Mo Sep	v0.74	v0.58	42
43	1994	Q0.02	1-22-00	1-5	0.08	0.08	0.08	2.08	18.8	15.1	9-30-99	0.29	...	±2447	Dc	v±0.79	v±d0.76	v0.09	v0.35	....	0.21	9 Mo Sep	v0.27	v0.13	43
44	1892	Q1.00	1-14-00	12-16	3.96	4.00	3.80	Total Deposits $48823.00M			9-30-99	25402	3094	173145	Dc	v6.42	v7.63	v7.17	v4.71	E9.90	8.19	9 Mo Sep	v4.28	v7.76	44
45	....	None Since Public			...	Nil	....	At mat pymt based on JPMC I Crude Oil Index				....	...	★5400	Dc	...	...	...	...	....	....	Mature 3-4-2002			45
46	1997	Q0.15⅝	12-31-99	12-28	0.62½	0.625	0.62½	At mat pymt based on JPMCI Crude Oil Index				....	...	★2000	Dc	...	...	...	...	....	....				46
47◆	1984	Q0.08	1-14-00	12-14	0.29	0.32	0.25	Total Assets $1600.07M			10-31-99	....	...	29362	Jl	0.78	1.10	v1.10	v1.47	v1.41	1.36	3 Mo Oct	v0.30	v0.25	47
48◆	1993	Q0.40	1-20-00	1-10	0.96	1.60	0.80	Total Assets $340870M			8-31-99	29038	6238	556962	Nv	[60]2.44	p[61]3.22	vp4.16	v□5.52	vP8.20	8.20				48
49	....	None Since Public			...	Nil	....	Int based on Final Index Value S&P 500 as defined				★25.0	...	...	Nv	...	...	...	...	....	....	Due 12-31-2003			49
50	....	None Since Public			...	Nil	....	Int based on Dow Jones Ind Avg as defined				★25.0	...	...	Nv	...	...	...	...	....	....	Due 4-30-2004			50

◆Stock Splits & Divs By Line Reference Index [1]2-for-1,'99. [2]2-for-1,'94. [3]2-for-1,'99. [6]2-for-1,'96. [7]3-for-2,'95. [9]1-for-30 REVERSE,'97. [14]3-for-2,'99. [19]3-for-2,'97. [21]1-for-2 REVERSE,'99. [23]2-for-1,'95:3-for-1,'96. [24]3-for-2,'93,'97. [26]5-for-4 in Cl'A','97:5-for-4,'95,'97. [27]5-for-4,'94,'95,'97(twice). [30]3-for-2,'987(twice),'99. [33]Adj for 5%,'98. [34]5-for-1,'96:No adj for dstr of Solutia,'97. [36]2-for-1,'99. [37]0.74-for-1 REVERSE,'96:1-for-1.92 REVERSE,'99. [47]3-for-2,'95,'97. [48]2-for-1,'97:To split 2-for-1,ex Jan 27,'00.

¶ S&P 500
# MidCap 400
✣ SmallCap 600
• Options

Index	Ticker	Name of Issue (Call Price of Pfd. Stocks)	Market	Com. Rank. & Pfd. Rating	Inst. Hold Cos	Inst. Hold Shs. (000)	Principal Business	Price Range 1971-97 High	1971-97 Low	1998 High	1998 Low	1999 High	1999 Low	December, 1999 Dec. Sales in 100s	Last Sale Or Bid High	Low	Last	%Div Yield	P-E Ratio	EPS 5 Yr Growth	% Annualized Total Return 12 Mo	36 Mo	60 Mo
1	BRX	Mor StaDW DJ Euro 2004'BRIDGES'[51]	NY	NR	..	...	BRoadInDex Guarded Eq-link Sec	....	....	10½	7⅞	11 5/16	8 11/16	1646	11 5/16	9⅞	11B	...	..	...	12.8	...	...
2	RBT	Mor StaDW Hi Tec 2005'BRIDGES'[51]	NY	NR	..	...	BRoadInDex Guarded Eq-link Sec	....	....	....	....	10⅜	8⅝	3857	10⅜	9⅝	10	...	..	...	...	...	...
3	MCP	Mor StaDW 3%Canon'CPS'2000	AS	NR	1	7	Currency Protected Sec	....	....	....	....	103¼	91	....	....	....	....	...	..	...	...	...	...
4	SPS	Morgan StanDW 3%'CPS'2000	AS	NR	1	7	Currency Protected Sec	....	....	194⅞	124⅝	278 3/16	141⅜	....	....	....	....	...	..	...	...	...	...
5	MWN	Morgan StanDW 7.25%'C'Nts	NY	NR	..	...	Medium-Term Notes	....	....	....	....	25 9/16	21¼	1366	22 11/16	21¼	21⅝	8.4	..	...	...	...	...
6	MPQ	Morgan StanDW'PEEQS'	AS	NR	..	...	Protected Exch Equity-Link Sec	98	62¼	123 3/16	93	143	121	19	143	138	143B	...	..	...	16.2	24.2	...
7	APP	MorganStanDW 6%Appl Mat'PERQS'[56]	AS	NR	3	322	Applied Materials 'PERQS'	....	....	42¼	23½	69⅜	40⅜	359	69⅜	62⅞	69⅜	3.4	..	...	76.0	...	...
8	RCP	MorganStanDW 6% Cisco'PERQS'[57]	AS	NR	2	172	cisco systems Inc'PERQS'	....	....	....	....	8¾	6¼	60922	8 9/16	7	7⅜	5.3	..	...	...	...	...
9	RPW	MorganStanDW 6% MCI'PERQS'[57]	AS	NR	6	1147	MCI WorldCom Inc'PERQS'	....	....	....	....	9⅝	7¼	3999	8¼	7¼	8	6.4	..	...	...	...	...
10	ORP	MorganStanDW 6.00% Oracle'PERQS'[58]	AS	NR	..	...	Oracle Corp Reset 'PERQS'	....	....	....	....	28½	21⅜	8715	28½	25⅛	28⅜	5.0	..	...	...	...	...
11	RPS	MorganStanDW 6% Sun Micro'PERQS'[60]	AS	NR	5	488	Sun Microsystems Reset'PERQS'	....	....	....	....	8½	6¼	11993	8¼	7¾	8	...	..	...	...	...	...
12	MSP	Morgan Stan Fin 8.20% Cp Uts[62]	NY	NR	23	238	Deb & Pur contract equity unit	26⅜	23¾	26½	25	26 1/16	22¼	2331	24⅞	22¼	23⅛	8.9	..	...	−2.7	5.4	...
13	MSE	Morgan Stan Fin 8.40% Cp Uts[63]	NY	NR	22	421	Deb & Pur contract equity unit	26½	24⅜	26½	25⅛	26 3/16	22⅜	2386	25	22⅜	23⅛	9.1	..	...	−2.0	5.0	...
14	MSV	Morgan Stan Fin 9% Cp Uts[64]	NY	NR	17	201	Deb & Pur contract equity unit	27⅜	24¾	27	25 3/16	26 5/16	24 13/16	1870	25¼	24 13/16	24 15/16	9.0	..	...	5.2	7.3	...
15	MR	✓Morgan's Foods	AS,Ch	C	5	232	Ky Fried Chicken franchise	81 1/16	1⅝	3⅝	2	5½	2¼	1399	3 11/16	2⅝	2⅝	...	d	−36	20.0	0.4	−19.5
✣16	MK	✓Morrison Knudsen	NY,P	B−	157	21452	Heavy contstr in west'n U.S.	15½	3½	15¼	8⅛	11 7/16	7 3/16	37177	8 13/16	7 3/16	7 13/16	...	9	NM	−19.9	−4.6	11.7
17	WS	Wrrt(Pur 1 com at $12)	NY,Ch,Ph	....	20	90		7½	2⅝	7¾	2⅝	5	1⅞	2619	3	1⅞	2 5/16	...	..	...	...	...	...
18	MHI	✓Morrison Management Specialists	NY,Ch,P	NR	73	7361	Hlth care food/nutrit'n svcs	20 3/16	10¾	22⅞	16	25¾	17½	2929	21¾	19	21 9/16	0.7	19	...	14.0	16.8	...
19	MRG	✓Morton's Restaurant Group	NY,Ch	NR	..	...	Own/oper full svc restaurants	25 1/16	7	25⅛	12⅝	20 11/16	13	2929	16⅛	14 15/16	15½	...	d	14	−17.9	−2.8	5.3
20	MGX	✓Mossimo Inc	NY,Ch,Ph,P	NR	20	871	Dsgn,mkt men's activewear	50⅛	3	16	1	13¼	6⅜	11735	9¼	6⅜	8 1/16	...	d	Neg	−19.9	−13.3	...
21	MTHR	MotherNature.com Inc	NNM	NR	..	...	Online retail hlth care prd	....	....	....	....	14 9/16	7 3/16	163396	14 9/16	7 3/16	7 5/16	...	..	...	...	...	...
22	MOTO	✓Moto Photo	NSC	B−	6	805	One-hour photo processing	6⅜	7/16	3	⅞	2 7/16	½	6840	1⅛	½	⅞	...	5	NM	−28.9	−23.4	−18.7
¶23•[1]	MOT	✓Motorola, Inc	NY,B,Ch,P,Ph	A	1569	408054	Semiconductors:communic eq	90½	2⅛	65⅞	38⅜	149½	62 9/16	736716	149½	114¼	147¼	0.3	72	Neg	143	34.9	21.4
24	MOVA	✓Movado Group	NNM	NR	90	8024	Mfr, dstr quality watches	23½	5⅝	31⅞	14¾	28⅛	17¾	17728	23 13/16	17¾	21 13/16	0.5	10	15	−17.7	16.1	24.8
25	MSI	✓Movie Star Inc	AS	B−	8	261	Mfr women's apparel	3 9/16	3/16	1¾	⅜	2 13/16	13/16	6261	1⅛	13/16	15/16	...	7	NM	−42.3	18.6	−5.6
26	HEAR	✓Mpath Interactive	NNM	NR	45	3298	Internet'live community'svcs	....	....	....	....	51¼	9¼	112509	37½	15⅛	26⅝	...	d	...	...	...	...
27	MPPP	✓MP3.com Inc	NNM	NR	61	5836	On-line music services	....	....	....	....	105	23 5/16	182481	44	25	31 11/16	...	..	...	...	...	...
28	MPWG	✓MPW Industrial Svcs	NNM	NR	30	4309	Industrial/facility svcs	9 7/16	9	15¾	6¾	13	6⅛	2419	8⅞	7 9/16	7 15/16	...	13	...	−29.4	...	...
29•[2]	MRVC	✓MRV Communications	NNM	NR	79	8053	Mfr computer networking prd	40¼	1 3/16	29¾	5 1/16	71⅝	5¾	327252	71⅝	31⅞	62⅞	...	d	−47	916	42.5	73.2
✣30	MSCA	✓M.S. Carriers	NNM	B+	139	8355	Motor carrier,gen'l freight	28½	4	35⅝	15¾	35	22 3/16	11285	28	22 3/16	23⅞	...	10	16	−27.5	14.3	1.9
31•[3]	MSM	✓MSC Industrial Direct'A'	NY,P,Ph	NR	..	...	Mkt industrial prd to indl co	23 1/16	9½	33½	12¼	26¼	7½	58190	14⅜	8⅞	13¼	...	18	...	−41.4	−10.5	...
32	MNS	✓MSC.Software Corp	NY,Ch	B−	49	7332	Softw for computer-aid-eng'g	23	4¼	12⅜	5 3/16	10 5/16	4⅞	19872	10 5/16	7¼	10⅛	...	d	Neg	44.6	8.7	1.1
33•[4]	MTSC	✓MTS Systems	NNM	B+	90	11206	Mfr testing systems: services	20	3/16	19¼	10⅞	14⅝	7½	14006	9 15/16	7½	7¾	3.1	13	11	−41.4	−5.0	10.1
✣34•[5]	MLI	✓Mueller Industries	NY,Ch,Ph,P	NR	224	19903	Mfr fabricated steel prod	29 11/16	1¾	40	14⅞	36 15/16	19 7/16	25604	36 15/16	31⅜	36¼	...	16	24	78.5	23.5	37.2
35	MTI	✓Multigraphics Inc	AS,Ch,Ph	NR	9	1818	Sell, svc graphic arts prod	30⅝	1½	10	2⅜	3⅝	1 1/16	1595	1¼	1⅛	1⅛	...	d	−49	−62.5	−43.8	−38.7
36	MZON	✓Multiple Zones Intl	NNM	NR	19	1295	Direct mkt computer products	28¾	3½	59	2½	24½	5	80921	10 5/16	5½	7 3/16	...	d	...	−59.2	−9.7	...
37	MMA	✓Muni Mtge & Equity L.L.C.[68]	NY	NR	20	458	Invest co:tax-exempt mtge bonds	21	13⅝	22⅜	15⅜	21⅛	16⅞	4560	19 7/16	18 3/16	18½	8.8	11	...	19.7	14.8	...
#38•[6]	MUR	✓Murphy Oil	NY,B,Ch,P,Ph	B	268	30190	International integrated oil	64	4⅛	54 7/16	34½	61⅝	32⅞	42120	57 13/16	51 7/16	57⅜	2.4	26	Neg	43.4	...	...
39•[3]	MLG	✓Musicland Stores	NY,Ph,P	NR	131	19826	Sell pre-recrd music,video prd	23⅜	11/16	18	6½	15¼	6¾	41541	8¾	6¾	8 7/16	...	6	NM	−45.1	77.8	−1.3
40•[7]	HITS	✓musicmaker.com Inc	NNM	NR	30	3943	Net based customized music CD	....	....	....	....	28⅛	5½	77036	8	5½	5⅞	...	d	...	...	...	...
✣41•[8]	MM	✓Mutual Risk Management	NY,Ph	A	201	34110	Provides risk mgmt services	29 15/16	4¼	39 15/16	25⅜	43¼	9 13/16	46842	16 15/16	13 3/16	16 13/16	1.7	13	16	−56.6	−2.2	12.5
✣42	MYE	✓Myers Indus	AS,Ch	A	150	10303	Tire svc eqp:plastic prod	17 9/16	⅛	26 1/16	14⅞	27½	12¾	7375	16⅜	14⅜	15¾	1.5	10	14	−32.8	11.9	15.5
#43•[1]	MYL	✓Mylan Labs	NY,B,Ch,P	A−	428	77831	Pharmaceutical products	25 5/16	1/64	35 15/16	17 1/16	32	17 1/16	119293	25⅝	20⅜	25 3/16	0.6	21	...	−19.5	15.7	8.0
44	MYR	✓MYR Group	NY,Ch,Ph	B+	36	3195	Transmiss'n sys for elec util	17 11/16	½	17 3/16	10⅛	29½	10 1/16	4799	29½	18¼	29⅜	0.5	17	33	158	58.0	45.7
45	MYGN	✓Myriad Genetics	NNM	NR	53	3432	R&D human gene products	46	16½	25⅝	5¾	50¾	8½	29916	50¾	30½	46	...	d	...	360	22.1	...
46	NAR Pr	NAB Exch Pfd Tr[71]	NY	A	5	96	Closed-end mgmt inv co	....	....	26	24¼	25⅞	20	9331	23¼	20	21 11/16	9.3	..	...	−8.8	...	...
47	NABI	✓Nabi	NNM	C	52	13531	Blood plasma prod/med R&D	14¾	⅜	4⅞	1	6	2⅜	39516	5¼	3 13/16	4⅝	...	d	−17	72.1	−19.1	−9.2
¶48•[9]	NGH	✓Nabisco Group Holdings	NY,Ch,Ph,P	B−	487	240022	Packaged food products	65	21⅞	38 1/16	21 5/16	33 9/16	9¾	318793	12	10	10⅝	4.6	13	Neg	...	...	...
49•[10]	NA	✓Nabisco Holdings'A'	NY,Ch,Ph	NR	..	...	Mfr,dstr packaged foods	48½	24½	54¼	31¾	45 13/16	31 3/16	86832	36⅞	31 3/16	31½	2.4	24	−25	−22.7	−5.1	...
#50•[11]	NBR	✓Nabors Industries	AS,To,Ch,Ph,P	B	373	89005	Contract drill'g & services	46 13/16	⅜	31 9/16	11¾	31¼	10¾	183733	31¼	23⅝	30 15/16	...	..	80	129	17.1	36.6

Uniform Footnote Explanations-See Page 4. Other: [1]ASE:Cycle 1. [2]ASE,CBOE,P:Cycle 1. [3]CBOE:Cycle 1. [4]ASE,CBOE,P:Cycle 2. [5]Ph:Cycle 3. [6]P:Cycle 2. [7]CBOE,Ph:Cycle 3. [8]Ph:Cycle 2. [9]ASE,CBOE,Ph:Cycle 3. [10]ASE,CBOE:Cycle 3. [11]CBOE:Cycle 3. [51]Medium-Term Notes Series'C'. [52]Call:Fr $16 - $18(5/30/02 - 11/30/04). [53]To be determined.. [54]To be determined. [55]To 4-20-2001 re-spec cond. [56]Performance Equity-Linked Red Qtly-Pay Sec. [57]Performance Equity-Linked Red Qtly Pay Sec. [58]Reset Perform Equity-Linked Qtly Pay Sec. [59]Adj reset yearly & maturiry. [60]Reset Perform Equity-Linked Qtrly Pay Sec. [61]Adj reset yearly + maturity. [62]Ea rep $25 amt 8.20%Sub Deb 11-30-2015&Pur cont. [63]Ea rep$25 amt 8.40% Sub Deb 8-30-2015 &Pur cont. [64]Ea rep $25 amt 9% Sub Deb 2-28-2015&Pur cont. [65]9 Mo Dec'98. [66]Fiscal Jan'98 & prior. [67]Return of capital. [68]Growth Shares. [69]Incl 12M Cap Distr Shrs. [70]Excl 0.94M shrs subject to redemption. [71]Trust Units Exch for Pref Shs. [72]Or earlier re-spec cond. [73]Stk dstr of R J Reynolds Tobacco Hldgs. [74]Fiscal Sep'96 & prior. [75]12 Mo Dec'97. [76]Fiscal Sep'97 & prior.

Splits ◆	Dividends							Financial Position				Capitalization			Earnings $ Per Shr.							Interim Earnings			
	Cash Divs. Ea. Yr.	Latest Payment			Total $			Mil-$			Balance	Lg Trm	Shs. 000		Years						Last 12	$ per Shr.			
Index	Since	Period $	Date	Ex. Div.	So Far 1999	Ind. Rate	Paid 1998	Cash& Equiv.	Curr. Assets	Curr. Liab.	Sheet Date	Debt Mil-$	Pfd.	Com.	End	1995	1996	1997	1998	1999	Mos.	Period	1998	1999	Index
1	....	None Since Public			...	Nil	....	Int based on Dow Jones Euro STOXX 50 as defined				★25.0	...	...	Nv	...	...	...	...	....	....	Due 7-30-2004			1
2	....	....			...	....	....	Int based on Morg Stan Hi Tech 35 Index as defined[52]				....	...	★4500	Nv	...	...	...	...	....	....				2
3	....	Plan semi-annual div			...	[53]....	....	At maturity apprec based on Canon Cp M-T Nts				★10.3	...	...	Dc	...	...	...	...	....	....	Mature 8-8-2000			3
4	....	Plan semi-annual div			...	[54]....	....	At maturity apprec based on Sony Cp M-T Nts'C'				★105	...	...	Mr	...	...	...	...	....	....	Mature 5-17-2000			4
5	1999	Q0.453	12-17-99	11-30	0.906	1.813	....	Co opt to redm fr 6-17-2004 at $25				★65.0	...	...	Nv	...	...	...	...	....	....	Due 6-17-2029			5
6	....	At maturity pymt based on par or S&P 500 Index			...	....	....	Exch in U.S.$ based on 10% S&P 500[55]				★69.6	...	...	Dc	...	...	...	...	....	....	Due 5-1-2001			6
7	1998	Q0.59¼	11-15-99	10-27	2.37	2.37	1.178	Int based on Applied Materials as defined				....	...	★1450	Dc	...	...	...	...	....	....	Mature 5-15-2000			7
8	....	Plan qtly div			...	0.39	....	Int based on Cisco sys as defined				....	...	★3828	Jl	...	...	...	...	....	....	Mature 8-1-2001			8
9	1999	Q0.128	12-15-99	11-26	0.403	0.51	....	Int based on MCI WorldCom as defined				....	...	★14100	Dc	...	...	...	...	....	....	Mature 3-15-2001			9
10	1999	0.225	12-15-99	11-26	0.225	1.42	....	Int based on Oracle Corp com as defined[59]				....	...	★3794	My	...	...	...	...	....	....	Mature 12-15-2001			10
11	1999	0.098	11-30-99	11-10	0.21	[54]....	....	Int based on Sun Microsystems com as defined[61]				....	...	★14573	Je	...	...	...	...	....	....	Mature 5-30-2001			11
12	1995	Q0.513	11-30-99	11-10	2.05	2.05	2.05	Pur cont:pur0.125 8.20% cm Pfd 5-30-2015,$25				....	...	★6000	Dc	...	...	...	...	....	....	Red fr 11-30-2000 Debs$25:pur cont $0.025			12
13	1995	Q0.52½	11-30-99	11-10	2.10	2.10	2.10	Pur cont:pur0.125 8.40% cm Pfd 2-28-2015,$25				....	...	★7000	Dc	...	...	...	...	....	....	Red fr8-30-2000 Debs$25:pur cont $0.025			13
14	1995	Q0.56¼	11-30-99	11-10	2.25	2.25	2.25	Pur cont:pur 0.125 9% cm Pfd 8-30-2014,$25				....	...	★5350	Dc	...	...	...	...	....	....	Red fr 2-28-2000 Debs $25:Pur cont $0.025			14
15◆	....	0.24	6-21-74	5-24	...	Nil	....	6.28	10.2	14.0	11-07-99	49.6	...	2911	Fb	v0.38	vd1.37	vd0.31	v□d0.25	....	d0.07	36 Wk Nov	vd0.02	v0.16	15
16	....	0.05	2-15-94	1-25	...	Nil	....	38.4	526	372	8-27-99	100	...	52350	Nv	0.28	vd0.14	v0.59	v0.69	....	0.86	9 Mo Aug	v0.49	v0.66	16
17	....	Terms&trad. basis should			be checked in detail			Wrrts expire 3-11-2003				....	...	2765	Nv	...	...	...	...	....	....				17
18	1996	Q0.04	10-29-99	10-6	0.16	0.16	0.49	3.53	44.7	25.8	8-31-99	47.5	...	12125	My	...	p0.70	v0.87	v0.95	v1.12	1.16	3 Mo Aug	v0.26	v0.30	18
19	....	None Since Public			...	Nil	....	2.63	18.1	22.6	10-03-99	58.0	...	5618	Dc	vd2.18	v0.26	v1.00	vd0.28	....	d0.09	9 Mo Sep	v0.84	v□1.03	19
20	....	None Since Public			...	Nil	....	0.05	17.4	11.6	9-30-99	....	...	15058	Dc	pv1.47	vp0.73	vd1.25	vd0.92	....	d0.57	9 Mo Sep	vd0.75	vd0.40	20
21	....	None Since Public			...	Nil	....	27.6	30.4	12.4	9-30-99	12.3	p...	★15074	Dc	...	...	...	vpd2.83	....	....	9 Mo Sep	n/a	vpd4.50	21
22	....	None Paid			...	Nil	....	1.28	9.28	6.80	9-30-99	8.38	1000	7773	Dc	vd0.69	v0.10	v0.18	v0.18	....	0.18	9 Mo Sep	v0.07	v0.07	22
23◆	1942	Q0.12	1-14-00	12-13	0.48	0.48	0.48	3527	16015	11898	10-02-99	3598	...	609094	Dc	v3.37	1.90	v1.94	vd1.61	E2.05	1.01	9 Mo Sep	vd1.87	v0.75	23
24◆	1994	Q0.02½	10-29-99	10-14	0.09½	0.10	0.08	15.3	272	81.5	10-31-99	50.0	...	±13003	Ja	v±0.86	v±1.02	v±1.29	v±1.58	....	2.14	9 Mo Oct	v±1.17	v±1.73	24
25	....	0.027	4-30-72	4-7	...	Nil	....	0.67	31.9	11.2	9-30-99	17.9	...	14880	Je	d0.36	vd0.38	v0.04	v0.08	v0.17	0.14	3 Mo Sep	v0.08	v0.05	25
26	....	None Since Public			...	Nil	....	76.2	81.3	5.58	9-30-99	0.18	...	23919	Dc	...	...	...	vpd0.95	....	d1.04	9 Mo Sep	vpd0.75	vpd0.84	26
27	....	None Since Public			...	Nil	....	447	456	40.4	9-30-99	....	...	68529	Dc	...	...	...	v‡[65]d0.01	....	....	9 Mo Sep	n/a	vpd0.19	27
28	....	None Since Public			...	Nil	....	0.33	53.6	20.8	9-30-99	77.2	...	10879	Je	...	...	pv0.29	pv0.37	v0.60	0.63	3 Mo Sep	v0.14	v0.17	28
29◆	....	None Paid			...	Nil	....	46.2	165	47.9	9-30-99	91.9	...	27152	Dc	vd0.07	vd0.49	v0.88	Δvd0.86	....	d0.08	9 Mo Sep	vd0.77	v0.01	29
30	....	None Since Public			...	Nil	....	0.35	91.9	75.4	9-30-99	180	...	12302	Dc	v1.01	v1.02	v1.54	v1.99	....	2.31	9 Mo Sep	v1.45	v1.77	30
31◆	....	None Since Public			...	Nil	....	2.73	328	80.8	8-28-99	69.5	...	±68053	Au	±p0.29	p±0.34	v±0.53	v±0.69	v±0.72	0.72				31
32	....	0.06	9-4-96	8-14	...	Nil	....	22.0	67.5	61.9	9-30-99	70.3	...	13842	Dc	v0.99	v0.70	v[66]0.83	vd0.95	....	d1.43	9 Mo Sep	v0.41	vd0.07	32
33◆	1967	Q0.06	1-3-00	12-15	0.24	0.24	0.24	17.5	209	90.3	6-30-99	60.1	...	20864	Sp	0.58	0.74	v1.10	v1.08	Pv0.59	0.59				33
34◆	....	None Since Public			...	Nil	....	156	443	173	9-25-99	131	...	34971	Dc	v1.17	v1.57	v1.78	v1.90	....	2.30	9 Mo Sep	v1.45	v1.85	34
35◆	....	[67]5.00	5-27-97		...	Nil	....	1.26	23.9	35.3	10-30-99	0.52	...	2848	Jl	1.65	vd16.23	v0.04	v0.37	vd0.05	d0.36	3 Mo Oct	v0.06	vd0.25	35
36	....	None Since Public			...	Nil	....	13.2	73.3	48.9	9-30-99	1.10	...	13335	Dc	pv0.32	v0.91	vd0.42	vd0.64	....	d0.26	9 Mo Sep	vd0.68	vd0.30	36
37	1997	Q0.40½	11-1-99	10-14	1.59	1.62	1.51	Total Assets $514M			9-30-99	67.0	[69]33	17401	Dc	...	v0.55	v1.50	v1.60	....	1.63	9 Mo Sep	v1.21	v1.24	37
38◆	1961	Q0.35	12-1-99	11-9	1.40	1.40	1.40	43.9	546	453	9-30-99	427	...	44974	Dc	vd2.65	v3.07	v2.94	vd0.32	E2.17	d0.02	9 Mo Sep	v1.04	v1.34	38
39	....	None Since Public			...	Nil	....	65.9	515	383	9-30-99	259	...	36168	Dc	vd4.00	vd5.80	v0.41	v1.04	....	1.49	9 Mo Sep	vd0.35	v0.10	39
40	....	None Since Public			...	Nil	....	67.7	68.8	1.96	9-30-99	0.17	...	★32994	Dc	...	...	...	vpd1.98	....	d2.20	9 Mo Sep	vd0.67	vd0.89	40
41◆	1991	Q0.07	11-19-99	11-3	0.25	0.28	0.21	Total Assets $3605M			9-30-99	116	...	[70]43705	Dc	v0.81	v0.95	v1.16	v1.43	....	1.30	9 Mo Sep	v1.06	v0.93	41
42◆	1966	Q0.06	1-3-00	12-8	0.224	0.24	0.191	7.91	208	88.6	9-30-99	293	...	19992	Dc	v0.78	v1.03	v1.10	v1.43	....	1.52	9 Mo Sep	v0.97	v1.06	42
43◆	1983	Q0.04	1-14-00	12-29	0.16	0.16	0.16	294	640	87.4	9-30-99	24.8	...	129230	Mr	v0.85	v0.51	v0.82	v0.91	E1.18	0.86	6 Mo Sep	v0.58	v0.53	43
44◆	1989	Q0.03¾	12-15-99	11-29	0.15	0.15	0.14	0.67	103	67.0	9-30-99	3.84	...	6049	Dc	v0.55	v0.54	v0.96	v1.20	....	1.76	9 Mo Sep	v0.82	v1.38	44
45	....	None Since Public			...	Nil	....	24.4	31.6	14.3	9-30-99	....	...	10116	Je	pd1.19	d0.78	vd1.03	vd1.05	vd1.06	d1.00	3 Mo Sep	vd0.29	vd0.23	45
46	1998	0.50	12-31-99	12-13	2.011	2.02	0.506	Exch for NAB Pref Shs or cash re-spec cond				....	16000	...	Dc	...	...	...	...	....	....	Mand exch 12-31-2047[72]			46
47	....	None Paid			...	Nil	....	0.59	70.0	45.5	9-30-99	100	...	34960	Dc	vd0.52	□v0.40	vd0.32	vd0.62	....	d0.38	9 Mo Sep	vd0.18	v0.06	47
48◆	1995	Q0.12¼	1-4-00	12-16	h[73]1.66	0.49	2.56¼	215	1858	1668	9-30-99	3851	205	326147	Dc	□v1.58	v1.74	□v1.09	vd1.91	E0.85	7.80	9 Mo Sep	vd0.08	v□9.63	48
49	1995	Q0.18¾	1-4-00	12-16	0.73¾	0.75	0.70	76.0	1671	1626	9-30-99	3692	...	±264621	Dc	v□1.20	v0.06	v□1.61	vd0.27	E1.30	9.44	9 Mo Sep	v±d0.08	v±9.63	49
50	....	0.06	7-19-82	6-24	...	Nil	....	175	354	151	9-30-99	325	...	p138774	Dc	±0.58	±[74]0.76	±[75][76]1.29	v1.16	E0.28	0.37	9 Mo Sep	v0.96	v0.17	50

◆**Stock Splits & Divs By Line Reference Index** [15]1-for-6 REVERSE,'97. [23]2-for-1,'94. [24]5-for-4,'97:3-for-2,'97. [29]3-for-2,'96:2-for-1,'96. [31]2-for-1,'98. [33]2-for-1,'96,'98. [34]2-for-1,'95,'98. [35]1-for-2.5 REVERSE,'97. [38]No adj for stk dstr Deltic Timber. [41]4-for-3,'96:2-for-1,'97. [42]10%,'95,'97,'99. [43]3-for-2,'95. [44]4-for-3,'95:5-for-3,'97. [48]1-for-5 REVERSE,'95:No adj for stk dstr,'99.

¶ S&P 500
# MidCap 400
✣ SmallCap 600
• Options

Index	Ticker	Name of Issue (Call Price of Pfd. Stocks)	Market	Com. Rank. & Pfd. Rating	Inst. Hold Cos	Inst. Hold Shs. (000)	Principal Business	Price Range 1971-97 High	1971-97 Low	1998 High	1998 Low	1999 High	1999 Low	December, 1999 Dec. Sales in 100s	Last Sale Or Bid High	Low	Last	%Div Yield	P-E Ratio	EPS 5 Yr Growth	% Annualized Total Return 12 Mo	36 Mo	60 Mo
¶1	NC	✓NACCO Indus Cl'A'	NY,B,Ch,Ph,P	B+	219	3305	Forklifts,sm applncs/Coal mng	127	2 5/16	177	76 1/4	97	44 1/2	6711	56	46	55 9/16	1.5	7	13	−38.8	2.3	4.0
2•[1]	NTAI	✓Nam Tai Electronics	NNM	B+	17	1231	Mfr electronic products	32 1/4	1/2	18	9 1/8	19 1/2	7 3/4	12162	14 3/8	11 9/16	13 7/8	2.3	d	Neg	26.4	23.3	7.1
3	QQQ	Nasdaq -100 Trust Ser 1	AS	NR	81	3309	Long-term unit invest trust	...	...	...	...	187 1/2	97	2326710	187 1/2	147 1/2	182 3/4	...	...	...	...	...	...
✣4	NAFC	✓Nash Finch Co	NNM	B	80	4561	Dstr food & non-food prod	27 1/2	2	20	12 13/16	14 1/2	5 7/8	14771	7 7/16	5 7/8	6 3/8	5.6	d	Neg	−53.3	−30.2	−13.8
✣5•[2]	NSH	✓Nashua Corp	NY,To,B,Ch,Ph,P	C	71	4302	Office copy & computer prod	44 7/8	4 1/4	17 1/2	11 9/16	15 13/16	6 1/2	5243	7 11/16	6 1/2	7 1/2	...	58	−36	−43.7	−14.5	−17.6
6	NAB	✓Natl Australia Bk ADR[52]	NY,Ch,P	NR	64	3727	Commercial banking,Australia	81 1/4	12 1/8	77	56 7/8	97 3/4	70 1/16	2979	76 3/8	71 13/16	76 1/4	4.7	13	1	7.4	15.2	20.6
7	NAU	Natl[53]Austr Bk7.875%ExCaps	NY	NR	..	...	Capital Sec & Pur contract	30 3/8	24 1/2	30	24 3/4	34 1/4	26 1/8	39289	27 11/16	26 1/8	27 5/8	7.1	..	...	6.0	...	...
8	NBT	✓Natl Bancshares Texas	AS	NR	7	33	Commercial banking, Laredo	22	7 1/4	22 15/16	15	16 5/8	13 15/16	753	15	14 1/4	14 1/2B	...	15	−5	−12.8	6.5	...
9•[3]	NA	✓Natl Bk of Canada	To,Mo	B+	22	9752	General Bkg,Canada	25 1/8	2	32	19	25 9/16	16 15/16	135213	18 13/16	17	18 1/2	3.9	8	13	−22.8	13.6	18.3
10	NBG	Natl Bank of Greece ADS[54]	NY	NR	..	...	International banking svc	...	...	...	...	15 1/8	12 1/4	8844	14 3/4	13 3/8	14 1/16	...	23	...	...	...	...
11	FIZ	✓Natl Beverage	AS,P	B−	20	1110	Mfr,bottle softdrinks	12 7/8	1 7/8	12 1/16	8 13/16	9 3/4	7 3/8	1264	8 1/4	7 3/8	8 1/4	...	12	7	−12.0	−2.9	22.6
¶12•[2]	NCC	✓Natl City Corp	NY,Ch,Ph,P	A−	704	302321	Comml bkg,Ohio,midwest	33 3/4	1 1/4	38 3/4	28 7/16	37 13/16	22 1/8	280220	26 7/16	22 1/8	23 11/16	4.8	11	7	−32.4	5.1	17.0
#13•[4]	NCBC	✓Natl Commerce Bancorp	NNM	A	174	44889	Commercial bkg,Tennessee	17 7/8	1/8	27 3/8	13 3/8	26 1/2	17 1/2	58340	26 1/8	22 1/8	22 11/16	1.9	24	17	22.6	36.2	35.0
✣14•[4]	NLCS	✓Natl Computer Sys	NNM	B+	269	23077	Optical mark/read process eq	19 3/4	1/16	37 13/16	15 1/2	41 3/4	23	41767	40 9/16	35 1/4	37 5/8	0.5	32	27	2.3	44.8	39.0
✣15•[5]	NDC	✓Natl Data	NY,Ch,P	B	274	26910	Telep/computer svs: billing	47 1/2	15/16	49	26 3/16	55 1/4	21 3/4	74865	43	31 1/16	33 15/16	0.9	29	71	−29.8	−7.2	15.9
16•[6]	NDB	✓Natl Discount Brokers Grp	NY,Ch,Ph	B−	54	1825	Hldg co:securities brokerage	18 1/2	3/8	33 1/2	8 1/8	93	16	124714	36 7/16	26 1/16	26 1/4	...	10	14	31.3	36.3	37.3
17	NSV	✓Natl Equipment Svcs	NY	NR	46	5390	Equipment rental svcs	...	...	16 1/2	4 1/8	12 7/8	5 3/8	27932	9 15/16	5 3/8	6 1/4	...	8	...	−45.7	...	...
#18	NFG	✓Natl Fuel Gas	NY,B,Ch,P	B+	259	15282	Natural gas utility hldg co	48 15/16	3 11/16	49 5/8	39 5/8	52 15/16	37 1/2	15072	50 3/4	46 3/16	46 1/2	4.0	16	−3	7.1	8.2	17.9
19•[5]	TEE	✓Natl Golf Properties	NY,Ch,P	NR	81	5382	Real estate investment trust	35	17	33 1/8	22 7/8	29 5/8	18 3/8	15133	21 1/8	18 3/8	19 3/4	9.1	17	1	−26.5	−9.4	4.0
20	NGG	✓Natl Grid Group ADS[56]	NY	NR	2	213	Electric svc UK & U.S.	...	...	...	...	41	36	111	41	36	37 7/8B	2.8	17	...	...	...	...
21	NHI	✓Natl Health Investors	NY,Ph,P	NR	93	9420	Real estate Investment trust	44 3/4	20	42 1/4	24 1/4	28 1/4	14 1/8	29002	17 1/4	14 1/4	14 7/8	19.9	6	2	−30.8	−18.9	−1.7
22	Pr	8.50%cm Cv Pfd(NC)	NY	NR	5	363		39 1/4	22 1/4	38 1/4	23 1/8	25 3/8	13 1/2	438	15 1/2	13 1/2	14 3/8	14.8	..	...	...	...	...
23	NHR	✓Natl Health Realty	AS,Ph	NR	20	2113	Real estate investment trust	...	...	21 5/16	11 1/8	12 1/2	7 7/8	1708	9 5/8	7 7/8	8 1/4	16.1	9	...	−18.8	...	...
24	NHC	✓Natl Healthcare	AS,Ph	NR	16	2395	Health care ctrs/home care	61 7/8	7 3/8	55 7/8	14	17 1/4	3 3/8	2099	5 7/8	4	5 1/4	...	d	Neg	...	...	...
25	NHHC	Natl Home Health Care	NNM	B−	17	815	Home health care services	7 1/8	7/16	5 1/8	3 7/8	5	2 1/4	863	4 1/4	3 3/4	3 13/16	...	10	−5	−19.7	−10.7	6.9
26	EGOV	✓Natl Information Consortium	NNM	NR	77	12168	Government internet use svc	...	...	...	...	44 1/8	11 1/4	64499	44 1/8	25 3/4	32	...	d	...	...	...	...
✣27	NATI	✓Natl Instruments	NNM	NR	191	19261	Dvp instrument'n softwr/hardwr	22 5/16	6 7/16	24 5/16	11 11/16	39 1/8	17 3/16	32534	39 1/8	28 7/8	38 1/4	...	47	23	68.3	39.2	..
28•[7]	NOI	✓Natl-Oilwell Inc	NY	NR	126	22178	Oil & gas ind equip/repair svc	44 7/16	8 1/2	40 7/16	7 5/8	18 1/2	8 1/2	33012	15 11/16	12 1/2	15 11/16	...	..	NM	40.2	0.7	..
29	NP	✓Natl Power PLC ADS[60]	NY,Ph	NR	31	18045	Elec generation&sale U.K.	40	23 3/4	46 3/4	31 1/8	36 11/16	20	12371	28 7/8	20	21 1/2	1.5	9	...	−37.4	−9.0	..
✣30	NPK	✓Natl Presto Indus	NY,B,Ch,Ph	B	110	3171	Mfr,distr small appliances	83	3 9/16	43 1/2	36 1/16	42 7/8	34 1/8	5662	36	34 1/8	35 1/2	5.6	13	...	−12.2	3.4	1.9
31	NAP	✓Natl Processing	NY,Ph	NR	53	5387	Transaction processing svcs	20 7/8	6 3/4	13 1/4	5 1/8	10 9/16	4	1629	8 7/8	7 13/16	8 7/8	...	d	Neg	61.4	−17.8	..
32	NLP	✓Natl Realty L.P.	AS	NR	7	7	Real estate investments	32 1/2	2 7/16	24 1/8	18 1/2	23 3/4	17 3/8	760	19 5/8	17 3/8	17 3/8	2.9	1	NM	−21.9	14.7	18.6
33	NRX	Natl Rural Util Co-Op 7.375%'QUICS'	NY	....[61]	4	68	Quarterly Income Capital Sec	...	...	26	24 15/16	26 1/16	20 9/16	5029	22 1/2	20 9/16	20 15/16	8.8	..	...	−11.4	...	..
34	NRV	Natl Rural Util Co-Op 7.65%'QUICS'	NY	....[61]	3	75	Quarterly Income Capital Sec	25 7/8	24 3/4	26 1/16	25	26	21	1805	23 5/16	21	21 11/16	8.8	..	...	−8.8	...	..
35	NRU	Natl Rural Util Co-Op 8%'QUICS'	NY	....[61]	3	162	Quarterly Income Capital Sec	26 3/8	24 1/4	26 5/8	25 3/8	26 5/16	21 1/2	1831	24 1/4	21 1/2	22 1/16	9.1	..	...	−7.0	3.7	..
36•[4]	NVH	✓Natl R.V.Holdings	NY	NR	119	6710	Design,mfr motorhomes	22 3/4	2 11/16	33 11/16	13 1/8	29 1/2	16 1/4	9062	20 11/16	17	19 1/4	...	7	61	−25.2	26.2	42.3
¶37•[7]	NSM	✓Natl Semiconductor	NY,B,C,Ch,P,Ph	C	465	124830	Integ circuits & transistors	42 7/8	11/16	28 1/4	7 7/16	51 7/8	8 7/8	563550	51 7/8	40 9/16	42 13/16	...	d	Neg	217	20.4	17.0
¶38•[8]	NSI	✓Natl Service Indus	NY,B,Ch,P	A	323	23316	Lighting eq:textile rental	52 1/4	1 1/2	60 3/4	30 1/8	41 7/16	26 7/8	43848	30 3/16	26 7/8	29 1/2	4.3	10	10	−19.5	−4.8	6.2
39	NSD	✓Natl-Standard	AS,B,Ch	C	13	746	Mfr steel wire prod:machinery	48 1/4	1	7	2 1/2	6 7/16	2 3/8	909	4 1/16	3	3 1/8	...	3	17	8.7	−25.3	−23.1
40•[7]	NS	✓Natl Steel 'B'	NY,Ph,P	NR	79	11183	Mfg flat rolled carbon steel	22 7/8	7 1/2	21 3/4	5 1/16	10 5/8	5 5/8	21512	7 5/8	5 11/16	7 7/16	3.8	37	Neg	8.4	−4.9	−11.6
41	NTSC	✓Natl Technical Sys	NNM	B	17	1198	Testing/engineering services	11	1/8	9 11/16	3 7/8	7	2 3/4	28090	7	2 3/4	3 7/8	e1.0	11	35	−20.1	21.4	8.5
42•[7]	TEAM	✓Natl TechTeam Inc	NNM	C	23	1741	Business mgmt services/sys	30 1/8	3/8	12	5 5/16	7 13/16	3 5/8	27759	6 7/8	3 5/8	4 13/16	...	d	Neg	−26.0	−37.8	−1.7
43	NW	✓Natl Westminster ADS[63]	NY,B,Ch,Ph,P	NR	55	932	Genl bkg,U.K. & worldwide	106 1/2	20 7/8	122 1/2	69 1/2	150 15/16	101	1035	139	121 3/4	129 1/4	2.8	14	8	12.3	27.7	27.1
44	NRI	✓Nationsrent Inc	NY	NR	21	1678	Equipment rental svcs	...	...	9 9/16	4	8 5/8	5 3/8	9202	6 11/16	5 7/16	5 5/8	...	12	...	−2.2	...	..
45•[4]	NFS	✓Nationwide Finl Svcs'A'	NY,Ch,Ph	NR	259	21067	Annuity/life insurance pd	38 1/4	23 3/8	55 7/8	28 1/4	54 1/8	26 3/4	48398	35 9/16	26 3/4	27 15/16	1.4	10	...	−45.5	...	..
46	NHP	✓Nationwide Health Prop	NY,Ch,Ph	NR	162	28495	REIT:health care facilities	25 7/8	4 7/8	26 15/16	19 3/8	22 1/4	11 3/4	48868	14 13/16	11 3/4	13 3/4	13.1	11	1	−29.1	−10.2	2.6
47•[9]	NMSS	✓Natural Microsystems	NNM	NR	49	4027	Mfr call processing software	53 1/2	3 7/8	47 1/16	6	48 3/4	2 15/16	42876	48 3/4	35 3/4	46 13/16	...	d	Neg	543	14.1	48.2
✣48	NATR	✓Nature's Sunshine Prod	NNM	A	90	6606	Direct sale health rel'd pr	30 1/2	3/16	28 5/8	13 5/8	15 7/8	6 15/16	8213	8 11/16	7 1/8	8	1.7	7	22	−46.9	−23.0	2.8
✣49•[4]	NAUT	✓Nautica Enterprises	NNM	B+	179	24136	Mfr men's robes,sportswear	37	1/16	32 1/2	13 1/4	17 5/16	10 1/2	46601	13 3/8	10 1/2	11 5/16	...	9	19	−24.6	−23.5	2.4
50•[1]	NAVR	✓Navarre Corp	NNM	NR	33	1882	Dstr pre recorded music/softwr	18 5/16	1 11/16	27	2	21 15/16	5 1/2	166880	8 1/2	5 1/2	5 3/4	...	d	Neg	−42.9	24.2	27.4

Uniform Footnote Explanations-See Page 4. Other: [1]CBOE:Cycle 3. [2]ASE:Cycle 1. [3]Mo:Cycle 2. [4]CBOE:Cycle 1. [5]Ph:Cycle 2. [6]Ph:Cycle 1. [7]CBOE:Cycle 2. [8]Ph:Cycle 3. [9]P,Ph:Cycle 2.
[51]To be determined. [52]ADS's represent 5 Ord par A$1. [53]Ea rep $25 amt 7.875% Cap Sec&Pur Cont. [54]Ea ADS rep 0.2 ord shrs. [55]Pfd in $M. [56]Ea ADS rep 5 shrs,11.76 Pence par. [57]Approx.
[58]If com exceeds $27.625 for 20 of 30 con trad days. [59]Stk dstr of National Health Rlty,'98. [60]Ea ADS rep four ord shrs. [61]Rated A+ by S&P. [62]12 Mo Dec'95. [63]ADS's representing 6 Ord shrs.
[64]Incl current amts.

Splits ◆ Index	Cash Divs. Ea. Yr. Since	Dividends: Latest Payment Period $	Date	Ex. Div.	Total $ So Far 1999	Ind. Rate	Paid 1998	Financial Position Mil-$ Cash& Equiv.	Curr. Assets	Curr. Liab.	Balance Sheet Date	Capitalization Lg Trm Debt Mil-$	Shs. 000 Pfd.	Com.	Earnings $ Per Shr. Years End	1995	1996	1997	1998	1999	Last 12 Mos.	Interim Earnings Period	$ per Shr. 1998	1999	Index
1	1947	Q0.21½	12-15-99	11-29	0.85	0.86	0.81	41.0	778	633	9-30-99	297	...	±8156	Dc	□Δv7.30	v5.67	v7.55	v12.53	E8.25↓	8.32	9 Mo Sep	v±8.66	v±□4.45	1
2	1994	Q0.08	1-17-00	12-29	0.31	0.32	0.21	71.7	97.0	19.5	12-31-98	....	...	9813	Dc	v1.40	v1.16	v3.68	v0.34	....	d0.59	9 Mo Sep	v1.07	v0.14	2
3	....	Plan qtly div			...	....	....	Int based on Nasdaq-100,as defined				....	...	[51]...	Dc	...	...	...	...	....	....	Mand termination 3-10-2119			3
4	1926	Q0.09	12-10-99	11-23	0.36	0.36	0.72	1.30	486	360	10-09-99	348	...	11344	Dc	v1.60	v1.82	vd0.11	□vd4.96	....	d4.80	9 Mo Sep	v□0.85	v1.01	4
5	....	0.18	10-3-95	9-8	...	Nil	...	25.8	80.1	36.7	10-01-99	0.64	...	5892	Dc	vd2.31	v□3.98	vd1.38	vd2.04	....	0.13	9 Mo Sep	vd1.93	v0.24	5
6	1985	1.846	12-27-99	11-22	3.581	3.58	3.149	Total Deposits $104239M			6-30-99	9187	...	1486435	Sp	5.33	5.75	v5.45	v4.09	Pv6.11	6.11				6
7	1997	Q0.492	12-31-99	12-13	1.477	1.969	1.969	Hldrs Pur cont opt ex1.6365Bk OrdShs(or cash)				....	...	★35000	Sp	...	...	...	....	....	....	Red fr 3-19-2007(or earlier)re-spec cond			7
8	....	None Since Public			...	Nil	....	Total Deposits $487.32M			9-30-99	2.25	...	4141	Dc	vΔ1.33	v1.23	v1.60	v1.14	....	1.00	9 Mo Sep	v0.85	v0.71	8
9	1983	gQ0.18	2-1-00	12-24	g0.70	0.72	g0.66	Total Deposits $52532M			j7-31-99	1125	12680	172320	Oc	1.26	1.76	v1.84	v1.67	Pv2.21	j2.21				9
10	....	Plan annual div			...	[51]....	....	....	...	...		526	...	33069	Dc	...	...	...	v0.60	....	0.60				10
11◆	....	None Paid			...	Nil	....	33.2	101	40.2	10-30-99	41.3	...	18283	Ap	0.41	v0.83	v0.56	v0.68	v0.68	0.69	6 Mo Oct	v0.48	v0.49	11
12◆	1936	Q0.285	2-1-00	1-6	1.06	1.14	0.94	Total Deposits $50395.45M			9-30-99	14805	722	616565	Dc	1.52	1.65	v1.83	v1.61	E2.20	2.10	9 Mo Sep	v1.18	v1.67	12
13◆	1939	Q0.10½	1-3-00	12-8	0.36	0.42	0.29	Total Deposits $4396.32M			9-30-99	774	...	108238	Dc	v0.49	v0.58	v0.69	v0.83	....	0.95	9 Mo Sep	v0.61	v0.73	13
14◆	1976	Q0.05	1-5-00	12-16	0.25	0.20	0.19½	33.0	203	156	10-30-99	5.18	...	32005	Ja	v0.53	v0.44	v0.80	v1.00	....	1.19	9 Mo Oct	v0.70	v0.89	14
15◆	1977	Q0.07½	11-30-99	11-12	0.30	0.30	0.30	3.67	230	166	8-31-99	169	...	33903	My	0.76	d0.31	v0.91	vd1.90	v2.02	1.19	6 Mo Nov	v0.92	v□0.09	15
16	....	None Since Public			...	Nil	....	Total Assets $327.51M			8-31-99	....	...	16985	My	1.07	1.52	v0.72	v0.89	v1.49	2.67	6 Mo Nov	v0.32	v1.50	16
17	....	None Since Public			...	Nil	....	Total Assets $1119M			9-30-99	748	[55]95	23781	Dc	...	...	pv0.33	v□0.68	....	0.76	9 Mo Sep	v□0.48	v0.56	17
18	1903	Q0.46½	1-14-00	12-29	1.83	1.86	1.77	35.8	258	703	6-30-99	726	...	38798	Sp	2.03	v2.77	v2.98	v□0.84	Pv2.95	2.95				18
19	1993	Q0.45	11-15-99	10-27	1.77	1.80	1.73	Total Assets $777.98M			9-30-99	442	...	12421	Dc	v1.25	v1.17	v1.25	v1.32	....	1.15	9 Mo Sep	v0.82	v0.65	19
20	1999	[57]0.453	1-27-00	12-8	1.04	1.06	....	68.6	255	955	j9-30-98	1328	...	1474400	Mr	...	...	v2.15	....	....	2.28	6 Mo SepΔ	0.76	0.89	20
21	1992	Q0.74	1-31-00	12-28	2.96	2.96	2.96	Total Assets $806.47M			9-30-99	360	769	24365	Dc	v2.48	v2.81	v2.92	v2.69	....	2.55	9 Mo Sep	v2.05	v1.91	21
22	1994	Q0.53⅛	12-31-99	12-16	2.12½	2.125	2.12½	Cv into 0.905 com, $27.625				....	769	...	Dc	...	...	...	...	....	....	Redm for 0.905 com[58]			22
23◆	1998	Q0.33¼	1-14-00	12-29	1.33	1.33	0.99¾	Total Assets $253.76M			9-30-99	105	...	9589	Dc	...	p1.23	n/a	v0.87	....	0.95	9 Mo Sep	v0.64	v0.72	23
24	1984	0.60	2-16-98	11-26	...	Nil	h[59]0.60	38.3	109	88.9	9-30-99	62.8	...	11430	Dc	v2.32	v2.97	v3.58	vd0.58	....	d0.77	9 Mo Sep	v0.74	v0.55	24
25◆	....	3%Stk	12-8-97	11-4	...	Nil	....	8.65	20.1	1.44	10-31-99	....	...	5049	Jl	0.27	v0.64	v0.35	v0.23	v0.22	0.39	3 Mo Oct	v0.04	v0.21	25
26	....	None Since Public			...	Nil	....	94.7	101	6.10	9-30-99	0.30	...	53115	Dc	...	...	...	vpd0.22	....	d0.27	9 Mo Sep	vpd0.11	vpd0.16	26
27◆	....	None Since Public			...	Nil	....	121	210	55.9	9-30-99	3.71	...	50007	Dc	v0.37	v0.51	v0.67	v0.73	....	0.82	9 Mo Sep	v0.52	v□0.61	27
28◆	....	None Since Public			...	Nil	....	15.5	437	140	9-30-99	195	...	p58259	Dc	pv0.68	□v0.25	□v0.99	v1.30	....	0.07	9 Mo Sep	v1.21	vd0.02	28
29◆	1992	[57]0.324	1-24-00	12-1	1.814	0.324	1.854	341	1949	1324	j3-31-99	2559	...	1239000	Mr	v...	v3.15	v1.80	v2.46	....	2.46				29
30	1994	2.00	3-11-99	2-25	2.00	2.00	2.00	223	264	37.1	10-03-99	....	...	7345	Dc	v2.61	v2.00	v2.31	v2.68	....	2.80	9 Mo Sep	v1.26	v1.38	30
31	....	None Since Public			...	Nil	....	138	248	107	9-30-99	2.16	...	50773	Dc	v0.60	v0.68	v0.42	v0.30	....	d0.83	9 Mo Sep	v0.19	vd0.94	31
32◆	1993	Q0.12½	1-5-00	12-13	0.50	0.50	†1.97½	Total Assets $356.15M			9-30-99	298	...	6322	Dc	v0.58	vd0.06	v1.35	v7.36	....	16.14	9 Mo Sep	v4.08	v12.86	32
33	1998	Q0.461	12-15-99	12-10	1.383	1.844	0.538	Co option redm fr 9-15-2003 at $25				★200	...	...	My	...	...	...	....	....	....	Mature 9-15-2047			33
34	1997	Q0.478	12-15-99	12-10	1.912	1.913	1.91¼	Co option redm fr 9-15-2002				★75.0	...	...	My	...	...	...	....	....	....	Mature 9-15-2046			34
35	1996	Q0.50	12-31-99	12-28	2.00	2.00	2.00	Co option redm fr 12-31-2001 at $25				125	...	...	My	...	...	...	....	....	....	Mature 12-31-2045			35
36◆	....	None Since Public			...	Nil	....	31.4	120	34.5	9-30-99	0.09	...	10499	Dc	□v[62]0.50	v0.84	v1.39	v2.11	....	2.79	9 Mo Sep	v1.52	v2.20	36
37	....	None Paid			...	Nil	....	537	1044	599	8-29-99	393	...	171519	My	v1.97	v1.30	v0.01	vd0.60	vd6.04	d4.06	6 Mo Nov	vd1.20	v□0.78	37
38	1937	Q0.32	11-1-99	10-20	1.28	1.28	1.24	2.25	680	424	8-31-99	435	...	40691	Au	1.93	2.11	v2.36	v2.53	v3.03	3.01	3 Mo Nov	v0.62	v0.60	38
39	....	0.10	4-2-87	2-27	...	Nil	....	2.73	39.1	55.5	7-04-99	11.1	...	5729	Sp	1.37	1.65	d1.71	vd1.27	Pv0.93	0.93				39
40	1998	0.07	12-9-99	11-22	0.28	0.28	0.28	148	1040	542	9-30-99	561	...	±41288	Dc	±Δv2.22	Δ±v0.74	□v±4.76	v±1.94	E0.20	d0.44	9 Mo Sep	v±1.50	v±d0.88	40
41	1993	†0.05	8-4-99	7-13	†0.07	0.04	†0.07	2.50	28.5	11.0	10-31-99	16.0	...	8353	Ja	0.14	v0.20	v0.42	v□0.37	....	0.36	9 Mo Oct	v□0.23	v0.22	41
42	....	None Paid			...	Nil	....	14.1	44.2	19.2	9-30-99	5.57	...	13234	Dc	v0.23	v0.23	vd0.12	vd0.24	....	d0.17	9 Mo Sep	v0.03	v0.10	42
43	1920	1.292	10-15-99	8-11	3.626	3.63	3.564	Book Value $43.13			12-31-98	12226	472000	1705000	Dc	6.29	2.36	v3.59	v8.98	....	8.98				43
44	....	None Since Public			...	Nil	....	Total Assets $1427.02M			9-30-99	[64]923	...	56454	Dc	...	...	pv0.38	v0.37	....	0.48	9 Mo Sep	v0.23	v0.34	44
45	1997	Q0.10	1-17-00	12-30	0.36	0.40	0.28	Total Assets $82677.00M			9-30-99	598	...	±128529	Dc	pv1.43	pv1.54	pv1.98	v2.58	....	2.86	9 Mo Sep	v1.92	v2.20	45
46◆	1986	Q0.45	12-10-99	11-9	1.80	1.80	1.68	Total Assets $1424.33M			9-30-99	778	1000	46216	Dc	v1.33	v1.36	v1.47	v1.39	....	1.25	9 Mo Sep	v1.15	v1.01	46
47◆	....	None Since Public			...	Nil	....	20.1	43.4	13.4	9-30-99	0.03	...	11197	Dc	v0.18	v0.17	v0.34	vd0.49	....	d1.32	9 Mo Sep	v0.06	vd0.77	47
48◆	1988	Q0.033	11-19-99	11-8	0.133	0.133	0.133	22.4	66.3	31.8	9-30-99	....	...	17172	Dc	v0.63	v0.86	v1.06	v1.25	....	1.12	9 Mo Sep	v0.91	v0.78	48
49◆	....	None Paid			...	Nil	....	39.5	254	94.4	8-28-99	....	...	34617	Fb	0.75	v1.02	v1.35	v1.45	E1.30	1.26	6 Mo Aug	v0.69	v0.50	49
50◆	....	None Since Public			...	Nil	....	1.94	95.0	72.8	9-30-99	0.11	...	23513	Mr	0.20	vd0.92	vd0.14	vd4.41	....	d0.65	6 Mo Sep	vd4.01	vd0.25	50

◆**Stock Splits & Divs By Line Reference Index** [11]2-for-1,'96. [12]2-for-1,'99. [13]2-for-1,'97,'98. [14]2-for-1,'98. [15]3-for-2,'95. [23]2-for-1,'95,'97,'99. [25]Adj to 3%,'97. [27]3-for-2,'97,'99. [28]2-for-1,'97. [29]5-for-2,'95. [32]3-for-1,'96. [36]3-for-2,'96,'98. [46]2-for-1,'96. [47]2-for-1,'96. [48]10%,'95:3-for-2,'96. [49]2-for-1,'96. [50]2-for-1,'96.

¶ S&P 500
# MidCap 400
✣ SmallCap 600
• Options

Index	Ticker	Name of Issue (Call Price of Pfd. Stocks)	Market	Com. Rank. & Pfd. Rating	Inst. Hold Cos	Inst. Hold Shs. (000)	Principal Business	Price Range 1971-97 High	1971-97 Low	1998 High	1998 Low	1999 High	1999 Low	December, 1999 Dec. Sales in 100s	Last Sale Or Bid High	Last Sale Or Bid Low	Last Sale Or Bid Last	%Div Yield	P-E Ratio	EPS 5 Yr Growth	% Annualized Total Return 12 Mo	36 Mo	60 Mo
#1•[1]	NCI	✔Navigant Consulting	NY	NR	354	35360	Consulting services	27 11/16	10 11/16	49	24	54¼	8 11/16	204219	11¾	8 11/16	10⅞	...	11	...	−77.7	−19.9	...
2	FLYR	✔Navigant Intl	NNM	NR	44	4710	Travel management svcs	...	...	10¼	3 11/16	12⅛	4¾	38151	12⅛	8⅞	11 11/16	...	14	...	52.0	...	...
3	NAVG	✔Navigators Group	NNM	B−	39	2262	Marine prop/casualty insur	48¼	8 5/16	20¾	13¼	16⅛	9⅛	2051	12	9⅛	9¾B	...	61	NM	−37.1	−18.9	−7.6
4	NAVI	✔NaviSite Inc	NNM	NR	..	...	Web side hosting,mgmt svcs	...	...	...	...	113½	14	60829	113½	49 15/16	100	...	d	...	...	...	...
¶5•[2]	NAV	✔Navistar Intl	NY,B,C,Ch,P,Ph	B−	421	48978	Heavy & medium duty trucks	455	8⅜	35⅞	17	56¼	27⅛	114965	47⅝	37	47	...	6	57	64.9	72.7	25.5
6	Pr D	Cv Jr D[53]Pref(25)	NY	NR	1	179		36¾	4	20	14½	18	14¼	1	15	15	14¾B	...	..	...	...	...	...
7	NBCI	✔NBC Internet 'A'	NNM	NR	..	...	Internet portal svcs	...	...	...	...	95	59	125846	95	59	77¼	...	..	...	...	...	...
✣8•[3]	NBTY	✔NBTY Inc	NNM	B	131	19814	Mfr vitamins,food supplem'ts	11½	1/64	24⅜	4⅜	12½	4 7/16	110130	12½	9⅜	11 9/16	...	30	40	62.3	22.2	44.9
#9	NCH	✔NCH Corp	NY,Ch,Ph	B+	90	1805	Cleaning & other chemicals	78¼	12⅛	73⅞	51 15/16	65⅞	44¼	782	46 11/16	44¼	44 9/16	3.1	11	−2	−22.9	−7.4	−5.0
10	NCS	✔NCI Building Systems	NY	B+	129	11262	Design,mfr metal build'g sys	20	2 11/16	32 5/16	14½	28 3/16	14½	15042	18½	14½	18½	...	8	23	−34.2	2.4	16.5
11	NRW	✔NCL Holdings ADS[54]	NY	NR	3	170	Oper passenger cruise line	...	...	...	...	17¾	9⅝	9730	17¾	11⅝	16 13/16	...	..	...	...	...	...
#12•[4]	NCOG	✔NCO Group	NNM	NR	222	20566	Financial svcs	29¼	8 11/16	45	16 15/16	54⅞	24⅜	178694	49	24⅜	30⅛	...	28	...	−33.1	38.9	...
#13•[5]	NCR	✔NCR[55]Corp[56]	NY,Ch	NR	380	68216	Dvlp services info tech prod	41⅜	25⅞	41⅞	23½	55¾	26 11/16	125261	38⅝	31	37⅞	...	24	...	−9.3	4.0	...
✣14•[6]	NCSS	✔NCS Healthcare 'A'	NSC	NR	92	6654	Hlthcare facil/pharmacy svcs	35¼	16½	34	11⅞	24¾	1½	120692	3	1½	2⅜	...	d	Neg	−89.9	−56.4	...
15	NFF	✔Neff Corp'A'	NY	NR	19	1877	Equipment/tool rentals	...	...	14 7/16	5	18 7/16	5 7/16	20078	8⅞	6 1/16	6⅜	...	15	...	2.0	...	...
#16•[2]	NMG.A	✔Neiman-Marcus Group'A'	NY,Ph,P	B−	3	1312	Operates dept/specialty strs	45½	10⅛	43 7/16	15	32	21⅛	33331	28 11/16	25 5/16	27 15/16	...	13	23	12.0	3.1	15.7
17	NMG.B	Cl'B'	NY	B−	2	11		...	...	...	...	27 7/16	20½	28091	27 7/16	23 9/16	26 15/16	...	14	40	...	...	...
18	NMN	Nematron Corp	AS	NR	4	1510	Industr'l automat'n hdrwr/sftwr	10¾	4	7	9/16	5⅛	1	2826	4⅛	2¼	2¾	...	69	5	42.0	−18.7	...
19•[2]	NMGC	✔NeoMagic Corp	NNM	NR	85	7656	Dvlp multimedia accel pds	26⅛	11⅛	23¾	10½	22¼	7⅛	105289	11⅝	9 1/16	10 15/16	...	15	...	−50.6	...	...
20	NEO	✔Neopharm Inc	AS,Ph	NR	25	1900	Dvp stg:Pharmaceutical R&D	14½	2¼	13¼	2	21⅝	10	5361	21 9/16	16 11/16	21 9/16	...	53	NM	77.8	39.2	...
21	NTEC	✔Neose Technologies	NNM	NR	22	2888	Dvlp stge:Biomedical R&D	24	11¼	18¼	7⅝	17⅝	8 9/10	10143	17	9 15/16	14⅜	...	d	...	2.2	−7.2	...
22	NERAY	Nera AS ADS	NNM	NR	1	2	Wireless telecomm eqp/svcs	10½	5¼	5½	1	5⅜	1⅜	2381	5	3 1/16	4¾	...	30	...	246	−14.7	...
23•[6]	NTBK	✔Net.Bank Inc	NNM	NR	77	4016	Internet banking svcs	4 7/16	2⅞	12⅛	3 9/16	83	8 11/16	204602	26 11/16	17	18½	...	..	...	102	...	...
24•[7]	NETP	✔Net Perceptions	NNM	NR	36	1996	Internet retail softwr prd	...	...	...	...	43⅛	9¾	133826	43⅛	27⅝	42	...	d	...	...	...	...
25	NCNT	✔Netcentives Inc	NNM	NR	..	...	On-line marketing svcs	...	...	...	...	96	10¼	95831	96	26⅝	62 5/16	...	..	...	...	...	...
26	NTIA	Netia Holdings ADS[60]	NNM	NR	13	2815	Local/long dist telephone svcs	...	...	...	...	22⅝	13⅛	22134	19½	14½	17⅝	...	..	...	...	...	...
27	NETM	NetManage Inc	NNM	NR	53	14854	Dvlp,mkt networking softwr pd	34	2⅛	5 1/16	⅞	7⅛	1⅞	191316	7⅛	4½	4 15/16	...	27	−9	168	−6.3	−24.6
28	NETO	✔NetObjects Inc	NNM	NR	16	917	Internet software solutions	...	...	...	...	20⅝	5	84097	19	12½	16½	...	..	...	...	...	...
29•[2]	NTPA	✔Netopia Inc	NNM	NR	94	8954	Internet connectivity softwr	19	3½	11½	3⅝	63⅞	5¼	72154	62⅛	42 15/16	54 5/16	...	d	...	697	104	...
30	NTRT	NetRatings Inc	NNM	NR	..	...	Internet audience measur't sv	...	...	...	...	53¾	17	117767	53¾	17	48⅛	...	d	...	...	...	...
31	NTSL	✔NetSolve Inc	NNM	NR	25	1123	Computer network mgmt/sec svcs	...	...	...	...	37	13	29524	35⅞	21¼	31½	...	..	...	...	...	...
32	NSPK	✔NetSpeak Corp	NNM	NR	13	654	Dvp/mkt computer softwr	27¾	7 3/16	33⅛	4 7/16	22	8⅝	64399	22	15¾	21¼	...	d	...	88.9	...	...
33•[5]	NTOP	✔Net2Phone	NNM	NR	48	3007	Internet telephone svcs	...	...	...	...	92⅝	15	379852	70⅜	45½	45 15/16	...	d	...	...	...	...
34	NASC	✔Network Access Solutions	NNM	NR	32	5357	Digital subscriber line svcs	...	...	...	...	39	8 3/16	50457	39	19½	33	...	d	...	...	...	...
¶35	NTAP	✔Network Appliance	NNM	NR	432	104151	Network data storage devices	9	1 11/16	24	6½	91⅞	19 1/16	522579	91⅞	59 11/16	83 1/16	...	..	NM	271	136	...
#36•[8]	NETA	✔Networks Associates	NNM,Ch	NR	373	59125	Dvlp network,security softwr	52 5/16	⅞	67 11/16	25½	67½	10 1/16	1177854	28¼	20⅜	26 11/16	...	d	Neg	−59.7	−3.1	46.3
37•[8]	NCDI	✔Network Computing Devices	NNM	NR	22	4126	Computer network systems	19	2⅞	13¾	4⅜	9	3⅞	49290	9	5⅝	7⅞	...	d	5	12.5	−8.0	13.1
✣38•[8]	NWK	✔Network Equip Tech	NY,Ch,Ph,P	B	94	15385	Mfr,mkt communic products	42	4	20⅝	8	14 13/16	7 5/16	51319	14 13/16	10⅜	11 13/16	...	d	Neg	15.2	−10.5	−13.2
39	NETS	✔Network Event Theater	NNM	NR	46	4630	Dvlp stg:entertainm't network	7⅛	1⅞	19 5/16	2½	32	11½	78515	32	23⅝	29¾	...	d	−8	130	81.2	...
40	NPLS	✔Network Plus	NNM	NR	53	4162	Telecommunications svcs	...	...	...	...	30 9/16	10	100693	21½	12½	21	...	d	Neg	...	...	...
41•[9]	NSOL	✔Network Solutions	NNM	NR	176	12266	Internet consulting svcs	13⅜	5⅞	86⅛	6¼	287¾	49	194252	287¾	149⅛	217 9/16	...	..	NM	233	...	...
42	NETN	✔Networks North	NSC	NR	2	136	Dstr two-way interactive TV	11 11/16	9/16	5⅜	1⅛	4 7/16	1⅜	4320	2	1⅜	1⅞	...	d	...	−33.3	−28.5	−17.6
43	NZRO	✔NetZero Inc	NNM	NR	43	3859	Internet access service	...	...	...	...	40	16	279160	40	20	26 15/16	...	..	...	...	...	...
44	NEU	✔Neuberger Berman	NY	NR	..	...	Investment advisory svcs	...	...	...	...	32¼	23⅝	15160	27 15/16	23⅝	24⅞	1.6	..	...	...	...	...
45	NAH	✔New Amer Healthcare	NY	NR	8	1598	Oper acute care hospitals	...	...	13 1/16	8¾	11 3/16	1/32	58552	½	1/32	¼	...	d	...	−97.8	...	...
¶46•[4]	NCE	✔New Century Energies[63]	NY,Ph	NR	440	50175	Elec & nat'l gas utilities	49⅝	39	52¼	41⅝	49 1/16	30 5/16	54113	32 5/16	30 5/16	30⅜	7.6	10	4	−33.5	...	...
47	NCEN	✔New Century Fin'l	NNM	NR	42	5329	Orig/svc subprime mtg loans	20⅛	9⅝	13⅝	2¾	20½	10 11/16	8983	16¾	14½	15¾	...	7	...	17.8	...	...
✣48	NEB	✔New England Bus Svc	NY,Ch	B+	117	11265	Standardized business forms	34¼	1 13/16	39⅛	26 15/16	39 9/16	18	8987	24 7/16	18	24 7/16	3.3	13	17	−35.7	7.3	9.0
#49•[4]	NES	✔New England El Sys[64]	NY,B,Ch,P,Ph	A−	239	20587	Hldg co: electric service	43⅜	6	49⅛	38 15/16	53¾	47¾	43672	53¾	51⅛	51¾	4.6	20	−3	12.7	20.5	16.8
50	NEON	✔New Era of Networks	NNM	NR	154	13363	Integration software/svcs	8¾	5⅜	46¾	4⅝	78⅜	12 3/16	216115	60⅜	43½	47⅝	...	d	...	8.2	...	...

Uniform Footnote Explanations-See Page 4. Other: [1]CBOE:Cycle 2. [2]CBOE:Cycle 1. [3]P:Cycle 3. [4]Ph:Cycle 3. [5]ASE,CBOE:Cycle 1. [6]Ph:Cycle 1. [7]ASE,CBOE,Ph:Cycle 2. [8]CBOE:Cycle 3. [9]CBOE,Ph:Cycle 1. [51]Fiscal Apr'97 & prior. [52]12 Mo Dec'98. [53]Divds cm at 120% of cash declared on com stk. [54]Ea ADS rep 4 Ord Shares,NOK2.30. [55]Plan Midcap 400 delisting: eff Jan 4. [56]Plan S&P 500 listing: eff Jan 4. [57]Fiscal Sep'97 & prior. [58]12 Mo Dec'98:Fiscal Sep'98 earn d$1.69. [59]10 Mo Dec'96. [60]Ea ADS rep 1 ord. [61]Fiscal Dec'95 & prior. [62]12 Mo Jun'96. [63]Northern States plan acq,1.55 com. [64]Natl Grid Grp plc plan acq,$53.75. [65]Subsid Pfd in $M.

Splits ◆ Index	Cash Divs. Ea. Yr. Since	Dividends: Latest Payment Period $	Date	Ex. Div.	Total $ So Far 1999	Ind. Rate	Paid 1998	Financial Position Mil-$ Cash& Equiv.	Curr. Assets	Curr. Liab.	Balance Sheet Date	Capitalization Lg Trm Debt Mil-$	Shs. 000 Pfd.	Com.	Earnings $ Per Shr. Years End	1995	1996	1997	1998	1999	Last 12 Mos.	Interim Earnings Period	$ per Shr. 1998	1999	Index
1◆	....	None Since Public			...	Nil	....	83.3	211	82.4	9-30-99	.....	...	41642	Dc	pv0.10	vp0.15	pv0.47	v0.43	....	1.02	9 Mo Sep	v0.41	v1.00	1
2	....	None Since Public			...	Nil	....	4.39	46.7	32.8	9-26-99	84.0	...	12645	Dc	...	...	pv[51]0.49	v[52]0.18	....	0.86	9 Mo Sep	v0.23	v0.91	2
3	....	None Since Public			...	Nil	....	Total Assets $629.00M			9-30-99	25.0	...	8407	Dc	v1.53	v2.02	v1.50	v1.36	....	0.16	9 Mo Sep	v1.11	vd0.09	3
4	....	None Since Public			...	Nil	....	69.6	75.7	14.9	10-31-99	0.14	...	28049	Jl	...	...	...	....	pvd1.51	d4.44	3 Mo Oct	vd0.56	vd3.49	4
5	....	3.00	1-15-81	12-22	...	Nil	....	Total Assets $6093M			7-31-99	2060	177	63584	Oc	1.83	v±0.49	±v1.65	v±4.11	vP8.20	8.20				5
6	....	None Paid			...	Nil	....	Cv into 0.3125 com				....	172	...	Oc	...	...	...	....	....	....				6
7	....	None Since Public			...	Nil	....	190	284	53.0	p6-30-99	0.43	...	±50956	Dc	...	...	...	vpd7.22	....	....	6 Mo Jun	n/a	vpd3.68	7
8◆	....	None Paid			...	Nil	....	23.5	200	101	6-30-99	199	...	67023	Sp	0.09	0.22	v0.42	v0.56	Pv0.39	0.39				8
9	1965	Q0.35	12-15-99	11-29	1.40	1.40	1.40	40.1	304	97.9	10-31-99	0.95	...	5408	Ap	4.29	v4.51	v4.73	v4.97	v4.25	3.95	6 Mo Oct	v2.18	v1.88	9
10◆	....	None Since Public			...	Nil	....	5.30	201	146	7-31-99	411	...	18511	Oc	1.26	v1.51	v1.64	v2.05	Pv□2.46	2.46				10
11	....	None Since Public			...	Nil	....	378	697	2977	j12-31-98	6070	...	238250	Dc	...	...	vd0.01	v0.02	....	0.02				11
12◆	....	None Since Public			...	Nil	....	48.8	146	80.1	9-30-99	324	...	p25374	Dc	p0.24	pv0.34	v0.57	v0.89	....	1.09	9 Mo Sep	v0.61	v0.81	12
13	....	None Since Public			...	Nil	....	595	2435	1638	9-30-99	32.0	...	96562	Dc	pvd22.49	vd1.07	v0.07	v1.20	E1.60	1.49	9 Mo Sep	v0.71	v1.00	13
14	....	None Since Public			...	Nil	....	20.3	274	84.4	9-30-99	102	...	±20388	Je	p±v0.28	v±0.26	v±0.69	±v0.58	vd0.67	d0.83	3 Mo Sep	v□0.24	v0.08	14
15	....	None Since Public			...	Nil	....	Total Assets $665.61M			9-30-99	226	...	±21165	Dc	...	...	vpd0.21	v□d0.23	....	0.42	9 Mo Sep	v□d0.41	v0.24	15
16	....	0.05	1-31-95	1-6	...	Nil	....	214	1037	486	10-30-99	340	...	±49174	Jl	0.70	1.26	v1.32	v2.13	Pv1.90	2.14	3 Mo Oct	v0.52	v0.76	16
17	....	None Since Public			...	Nil	....	....	....	....		....	...	21347	Jl	±v0.70	±v1.26	±v1.32	±v2.13	Pv±1.90	1.90				17
18	....	None Paid			...	Nil	....	1.71	8.87	7.44	9-30-99	1.65	...	12605	Dc	0.14	0.13	v[57]d2.33	v[58]d1.53	....	0.04	9 Mo Sep	vd1.43	v0.14	18
19	....	None Since Public			...	Nil	....	88.4	133	37.8	10-31-99	.....	...	25280	Ja	...	pvd0.07	vp0.82	v1.19	....	0.72	9 Mo Oct	v0.85	v0.38	19
20◆	....	None Since Public			...	Nil	....	25.5	25.6	1.69	9-30-99	.....	...	10997	Dc	pvd0.36	vd0.24	vd0.25	vd0.19	....	0.41	9 Mo Sep	vd0.22	v0.38	20
21	....	None Since Public			...	Nil	....	35.8	37.9	3.11	9-30-99	7.30	...	11429	Dc	d1.05	vd0.82	vd0.96	vd1.25	....	d1.30	9 Mo Sep	vd0.90	vd0.95	21
22◆	1996	0.002	10-1-98	9-22	...	Nil	0.016	16.9	267	143	12-31-97	78.1	...	66005	Dc	0.30	v0.24	v0.16	....	....	0.16				22
23◆	....	None Since Public			...	Nil	....	Total Deposits $486M			9-30-99	112	...	★29394	Dc	...	N[59]d1.44	vd0.55	v0.23	....	0.13	9 Mo Sep	v0.19	v0.09	23
24	....	None Since Public			...	Nil	....	0.97	4.50	4.03	12-31-98	0.54	2168	★21322	Dc	...	...	...	vpd0.35	....	d0.08	9 Mo Sep	vd0.95	vd0.68	24
25	....	None Since Public			...	Nil	....	36.2	38.6	11.0	6-30-99	0.97	p...	★31793	Dc	...	...	...	pvd1.05	....	....	6 Mo Jun	n/a	pvd0.78	25
26	....	None Since Public			...	Nil	....	.....	2036	229	p3-31-99	728	...	★26494	Dc	...	...	...	vpd5.14	....	....	3 Mo Mar	n/a	vpd4.89	26
27◆	....	None Since Public			...	Nil	....	84.0	108	31.3	9-30-99	.....	...	63428	Dc	vd0.52	vd0.13	vd0.78	vd0.19	....	0.18	9 Mo Sep	vd0.39	vd0.02	27
28	....	None Since Public			...	Nil	....	39.0	44.5	6.68	6-30-99	0.14	...	24646	Sp	...	...	...	...	...	....	9 Mo Jun	n/a	vd3.31	28
29	....	None Since Public			...	Nil	....	32.2	45.4	13.3	6-30-99	.....	...	13093	Sp	0.25	0.33	vd0.05	vd0.90	Pvd0.60	d0.60				29
30	....	None Since Public			...	Nil	....	28.7	30.0	5.75	9-30-99	0.32	p...	★14872	Dc	...	...	...	vpd1.67	....	d2.94	9 Mo Sep	vpd1.04	vpd2.31	30
31	....	None Since Public			...	Nil	....	6.58	12.7	6.03	6-30-99	0.76	p...	★13409	Mr	...	...	...	pv0.08	....	....	3 Mo Jun	n/a	pv0.07	31
32	....	None Since Public			...	Nil	....	35.1	38.2	2.93	9-30-99	.....	...	12952	Dc	vd0.15	vd0.41	vd0.54	vd0.98	....	d1.02	9 Mo Sep	vd0.72	vd0.76	32
33	....	None Since Public			...	Nil	....	84.8	98.6	16.2	10-31-99	.....	...	±51597	Jl	...	...	v±d0.06	v±d0.12	Pv±d1.63	d1.76	3 Mo Oct	vd0.04	vd0.17	33
34	....	None Paid			...	Nil	....	63.5	67.5	11.9	9-30-99	17.6	...	45140	Dc	...	...	...	vpd0.08	....	d0.67	9 Mo Sep	vd0.04	vd0.63	34
35◆	....	None Since Public			...	Nil	....	272	395	68.6	10-29-99	0.05	...	149338	Ap	pd0.05	0.05	v...	v0.15	v0.23	0.31	6 Mo Oct	v0.10	v0.18	35
36◆	....	None Since Public			...	Nil	....	300	609	328	9-30-99	380	...	139216	Dc	v0.41	v0.59	vd0.27	v0.26	Ed0.63	d0.81	9 Mo Sep	vd0.15	vd1.22	36
37	....	None Since Public			...	Nil	....	15.8	58.5	24.6	9-30-99	.....	...	16226	Dc	vd0.25	vd0.32	v0.15	vd0.56	....	d1.04	9 Mo Sep	vd0.21	vd0.69	37
38	....	None Since Public			...	Nil	....	147	232	55.3	9-26-99	24.7	...	21421	Mr	v1.50	v∆1.08	v0.65	v∆d0.33	....	d0.59	6 Mo Sep	v0.29	v0.03	38
39	....	None Since Public			...	Nil	....	28.3	34.7	5.20	9-30-99	6.43	...	17339	Je	[61]d0.41	[62]d0.43	vd0.71	vd0.34	vd0.72	d0.62	3 Mo Sep	vd0.13	vd0.03	39
40	....	None Since Public			...	Nil	....	60.0	93.5	40.5	9-30-99	30.0	...	9220	Dc	pv0.05	pv0.02	vpd0.05	vpd0.12	....	d0.75	9 Mo Sep	vd0.05	vd0.68	40
41◆	....	None Since Public			...	Nil	....	197	339	257	9-30-99	.....	...	33419	Dc	vd0.14	pvd0.07	v0.15	v0.33	....	0.61	9 Mo Sep	v0.23	v0.51	41
42◆	....	None Paid			...	Nil	....	2.28	5.61	1.87	j8-31-99	2.08	900	2857	Au	0.17	0.23	0.23	v0.22	vd0.36	jd0.36				42
43	....	None Since Public			...	Nil	....	24.0	27.0	10.9	6-30-99	3.53	p...	★102905	Je	...	...	...	....	pvd0.44	....	3 Mo Sep	n/a	vd1.04	43
44	2000	Q0.10	1-25-00	1-7	...	0.40	....	Equity per shr $5.00			6-30-99	p35.0	...	★50022	Dc	...	...	...	pv2.92	....	....	9 Mo Sep	n/a	p2.00	44
45	....	None Since Public			...	Nil	....	5.15	51.7	30.3	9-30-99	101	...	17442	Mr	...	...	pv0.20	□vNil		d3.22	6 Mo Sep	v0.03	vd3.19	45
46	1997	Q0.58	2-15-00	1-26	2.32	2.32	2.32	40.5	887	1584	9-30-99	2566	...	115549	Dc	pv2.77	pv2.64	v□2.50	v3.05	E3.00	3.11	12 Mo Sep	v2.90	v3.11	46
47	....	None Since Public			...	Nil	....	Total Assets $733.47M			9-30-99	356	...	14665	Dc	...	pv0.20	v1.40	v2.03	....	2.32	9 Mo Sep	v1.48	v1.77	47
48	1965	Q0.20	11-19-99	11-3	0.80	0.80	0.80	4.07	103	46.7	9-25-99	130	...	13855	Je	1.07	0.81	v1.38	v1.77	v1.81	1.86	3 Mo Sep	v0.37	v0.42	48
49	1947	Q0.59	1-3-00	12-8	2.36	2.36	2.36	201	622	484	9-30-99	1010	[65]19	59117	Dc	v3.15	v3.22	v3.39	v3.04	E2.60	2.50	12 Mo Sep	v3.39	v2.50	49
50◆	....	None Since Public			...	Nil	....	52.9	121	36.5	9-30-99	.....	...	33713	Dc	...	pvd0.49	vd0.32	vd0.38	....	d1.05	9 Mo Sep	vd0.63	vd1.30	50

◆Stock Splits & Divs By Line Reference Index [1]3-for-2,'98. [8]2-for-1,'98:3-for-1,'98. [10]2-for-1,'98. [12]3-for-2,'97. [20]2-for-1,'96. [22]5-for-1,'97. [23]3-for-1,'99. [27]2-for-1,'94,'95. [35]2-for-1,'97,'98,'99. [36]3-for-2,'95(twice),'96,'98. [41]2-for-1,'99:Propose 2-for-1 stk split. [42]3-for-2,'96. [50]2-for-1,'98.

¶ S&P 500
# MidCap 400
✣ SmallCap 600
• Options

Index	Ticker	Name of Issue (Call Price of Pfd. Stocks)	Market	Com. Rank. & Pfd. Rating	Inst. Hold Cos	Inst. Hold Shs. (000)	Principal Business	Price Range 1971-97 High	1971-97 Low	1998 High	1998 Low	1999 High	1999 Low	Dec. Sales in 100s	December, 1999 Last Sale Or Bid High	Low	Last	%Div Yield	P-E Ratio	EPS 5 Yr Growth	% Annualized Total Return 12 Mo	36 Mo	60 Mo
1	NJP	N.J. Eco Dvl Auth 7.6% Bonds	NY	NR	5	39	Qtly Income Debt Securities	26¼	25¼	26¾	25	26⅜	23	5058	24⅛	23	23 3/16	8.2	..	...	−4.8	...	...
✣2	NJR	✓New Jersey Resources	NY,Ch,Ph	A−	178	6564	Supplies gas in New Jersey	42 1/16	4⅜	40¼	31½	41⅛	33⅝	6075	40½	38⅞	39 1/16	4.4	16	9	3.3	15.3	17.4
3	NZ	✓New Mexico/Ariz Land	AS	B−	19	1096	Real estate,mineral explor'n	19⅞	1⅜	11	7⅛	9 13/16	4 7/16	1025	5¼	4¾	5	...	7	−6	−40.7	4.3	17.4
4•[1]	NXL	✓New Plan Excel Realty Tr	NY,Ch,P	NR	226	26832	Real estate investment trust	26⅜	½	26⅛	19¼	22 9/16	14¾	177607	16 7/16	14¾	15 13/16	10.3	7	6	−22.4	−8.4	2.6
5	Pr A	8.50% cm Cv Sr'A'[53]Pfd([54]25)	NY	NR	13	1105		31⅜	24⅞	33½	23	28⅛	21	617	22¾	21	21¼	10.0	..	...	...	...	...
¶6•[2]	NYT	✓New York Times Cl'A'	NY,B,Ch,P,Ph	B	595	97368	Newspapers,mag's,TV,CATV	33¼	9/16	40 11/16	20½	49 15/16	26½	119124	49 15/16	38 1/16	49⅛	0.9	29	17	43.2	38.8	36.7
7•[3]	NN	✓Newbridge Networks	NY,To,Ph,P	B	240	48748	Mfr digital networking prod	69⅜	¾	39 3/16	15 7/16	39⅞	14	282306	25½	21 1/16	22 9/16	...	7	−10	−25.7	−7.1	3.5
8	NER	✓Newcor Inc	AS	B−	18	1318	Specialized ind'l mchy	19½	⅝	9⅞	2⅝	5¾	1 5/16	2303	3¼	2¼	2 7/16	...	d	−29	−37.1	−28.7	−17.2
¶9•[4]	NWL	✓Newell Rubbermaid	NY,Ch,Ph,P	A+	837	214914	Mfr,mkt consumer products	43 13/16	3/16	55 3/16	35 11/16	52	25¼	196138	34	28	29	2.8	35	2	−28.2	−1.0	8.6
✣10•[5]	NFX	✓Newfield Exploration	NY,Ch	NR	281	39124	Oil&gas explor,devlp, prod'n	33	7⅞	27 11/16	15 7/16	35	14⅞	46018	27 5/16	21	26¾	...	d	Neg	28.1	1.0	21.7
11	Pr A	6.50% Newfld Fin I cm[57]'QUIPS'([58]52.27)	NY	B	21	2092		...	...	...	...	56 13/16	43⅛	3125	47 5/16	43⅛	46¾	7.0	..	...	...	...	...
12	NHL	✓Newhall Land/Farming[60]	NY,Ch,P	B	54	12680	Agriculture,real estate	35¾	⅞	34¾	20¼	28	22 3/16	10552	27	23⅜	27	e1.5	25	24	6.5	19.6	20.2
¶13•[6]	NEM	✓Newmont Mining	NY,B,Ch,P,Ph	B−	507	123064	Gold min'g:explor,dev,prod	81 15/16	6 3/16	34⅞	13¼	30 1/16	16⅜	217718	25 7/16	21¼	24½	0.5	d	Neg	35.1	−17.6	−6.6
14	NR	✓Newpark Resources	NY,Ch,Ph	B	200	49093	Oil & gas ind enviro svcs	22½	9/16	25½	5 5/16	11 7/16	4⅞	80565	6¼	5 1/16	6⅛	...	d	Neg	−10.1	−13.0	1.7
15•[7]	NEWP	✓Newport Corp	NNM	B	49	4969	Mfr laser/electro-optic eqp	33	⅛	22⅞	8⅞	46 1/16	11 9/16	57354	46 1/16	24⅞	45¾	0.1	54	21	172	73.3	43.1
#16•[1]	NNS	✓Newport News Shipbuilding	NY,Ch,Ph	NR	204	21556	Shipbuilding constr'n U S	26⅜	13	33 7/16	22½	34¼	24¾	40564	32⅞	24¾	27½	0.6	11	...	−17.3	23.2	...
17•[8]	NWS	✓News Corp Ltd ADS[61]	NY,B,Ch,Ph,P	NR	277	95472	TV broadcstg,movies,newspapers	31⅝	2 11/16	33½	20 3/16	41	24 11/16	126212	41	35 9/16	38¼	0.2	44	−9	45.0	22.8	...
18•[9]	NXTV	✓Next Level Communic	NNM	NR	..	...	Dsgn broad band communic eq	...	...	...	...	75 1/16	20	127407	75 1/16	53½	74⅞	...	..	...	...	...	...
19	NXCD	✓NextCard Inc	NNM	NR	74	6690	Computer software/svcs	...	...	...	...	53⅛	19⅛	196671	37¼	24⅞	28⅞	...	..	...	...	...	...
¶20•[10]	NXTL	✓NEXTEL Communic'ns'A'	NNM	C	665	166851	Provides mobile commun svcs	54⅞	9	34⅛	15⅝	117⅜	25	881014	110⅜	85⅝	103⅛	...	d	−25	337	99.1	48.3
21	MNX	Nextel $1.015 STRYPES Trust	AS	NR	11	296	Struct Yld Prd Exch For Stk	28½	13⅛	29 15/16	14¾	94¾	21	751	91¾	73½	90	1.1	..	...	351	...	...
22	NXRA	✓Nextera Enterprises'A'	NNM	NR	36	5736	Corporate consulting svcs	...	...	...	...	13 3/16	3½	125526	13 3/16	7⅜	12⅞	...	..	...	...	...	...
23	NXLK	✓NEXTLINK Communications'A'	NNM	NR	263	58481	Telecommunication svcs	14½	9 11/16	20 13/16	5¼	91½	12¾	302783	91½	50¼	83 1/16	...	d	...	486	...	...
24	NFC	✓NFC plc[64]ADS	AS,Ph	NR	3	91	Road freight/distribution:RE	33 13/16	10	21 11/16	8¼	22¼	8½	582	22¼	16¼	19⅝B	⊙4.4	20	11	103	16.7	14.8
✣25•[6]	NFO	✓NFO Worldwide	NY	NR	115	10949	Custom market research svcs	21⅝	4 5/16	22	5½	22⅞	8½	31894	22⅞	11	22⅜	...	30	13	94.6	15.2	28.5
¶26•[5]	NMK	✓Niagara Mohawk Holdings	NY,B,C,Ch,P,Ph	B	388	113614	Hldg co:Electric & gas N.Y.	25½	6½	16 13/16	10⅛	16 7/16	13 1/16	81739	15¼	13⅜	13 15/16	...	..	Neg	−13.6	12.2	1.3
27•[11]	NICE	✓NICE-Systems[67] ADR	NNM	NR	36	2794	Dvp/dgn voice logging sys	59⅛	9 15/16	49¼	11⅝	50⅞	20⅝	55827	50⅞	40	49 9/16	...	39	−18	128	39.8	...
¶28•[2]	GAS	✓NICOR Inc	NY,B,C,Ch,P,Ph	A−	369	24096	Utility hldg: natural gas	42 15/16	7½	44 7/16	37⅛	42 15/16	31 3/16	26565	34 15/16	31 3/16	32½	4.8	12	4	−19.9	0.6	12.0
¶29•[12]	NKE	✓NIKE, Inc Cl'B'[68]	NY,Ch,P,Ph	A	638	124534	Athletic footwear	76⅜	13/16	52 11/16	31	66 15/16	38¾	294730	55⅞	39 13/16	49 9/16	1.0	27	1	23.3	−5.3	22.8
✣30	NDN	✓99(Cents) Only Stores	NY,Ph,P	NR	147	11826	Oper deep-discount retail strs	25 1/16	8 5/16	49⅜	21 3/16	52½	25	37637	38½	28⅜	38¼	...	31	...	−22.1	54.2	...
31	NTT	✓Nippon Tel & Tel ADS[69]	NY,Ch,Ph,P	NR	112	11424	Telecommunications svcs, Japan	52½	33¾	49½	31	92½	36	29325	88⅞	80	86⅛	0.4	60	33	131	30.5	16.0
32	NIC	NIPSCO Cap Mkt 7.75% Debt Sec	NY	....[70]	1	1	Qtly Debt Capital Securities	25½	23	26⅛	25	25¾	20	904	23	20	20 13/16	9.3	..	...	−11.5	3.0	...
#33•[2]	NI	✓NiSource Inc	NY,CS	A+	354	57029	Util hldg co:Elec/nat'l gas	24 15/16	4	33¾	24⅝	30 15/16	16⅜	84756	19 3/16	16⅜	17⅞	6.0	11	5	−38.8	0.6	8.2
34•[13]	NL	✓NL Industries, Inc	NY,B,C,Ch,P,Ph	B−	75	6465	Mfr commodity chemicals	486¼	3⅜	27 1/16	12¾	15 7/16	8¾	7806	15 7/16	13 5/16	15 1/16	0.9	5	NM	7.5	12.1	4.5
35	NMTI	✓NMT Medical	NNM	NR	18	2135	Dgn/dvp medical devices	17¼	7¾	11⅛	2½	7½	1¾	12841	3	1¾	2⅞	...	d	Neg	−23.3	−38.7	...
36	NNBR	✓NN Ball & Roller	NNM	NR	42	9798	Mfr steel balls/rollers	26¾	6¼	13	5¾	7⅝	4¾	4379	7¼	5⅞	7¼	4.4	15	−9	30.1	−18.8	0.0
#37•[1]	NBL	✓Noble Affiliates	NY,B,Ch,P,Ph	B−	293	43627	Oil & gas explor'n,prod'n	50	1 3/16	46 3/16	21 15/16	35	19⅛	82620	22½	19⅛	21 7/16	0.7	26	Neg	−12.4	−23.1	−2.3
#38•[14]	NE	✓Noble Drilling Corp	NY,Ch,P	B−	376	104035	Contr drill'g oil/gas wells	38 3/16	1⅝	34 11/16	10¾	32⅞	12	286625	32⅞	25⅛	32¾	...	44	NM	153	18.1	41.0
39	NOBL	✓Noble International	NNM	NR	17	1003	Component supplier to auto ind	9¼	6⅞	12½	6¼	20⅛	9	14358	15 7/16	13¼	14⅜	...	13	...	57.5	...	...
40•[15]	NOK	✓Nokia Corp [72]ADS[73]	NY,Ph	NR	828	289518	Telecommun sys & equipment	25⅝	5 3/16	62 11/16	16⅝	196	62 5/16	815925	196	138	191 1/16	0.2	88	...	220	139	85.3
41	NOLD	Noland Co	NNM	B	18	292	Distr plumb'g: heat'g, elect'l	27¼	2½	28 15/16	20	28⅞	16½	136	18¼	17¾	17⅞	1.8	11	1	−24.3	−5.3	0.5
42	NAEPrT	NorAm Fin I 6.25% Cv'[74]TOPrS'[75]	NY	BB+	1	.3	Subsid of Reliant Energy Inc	74¾	50	84	73	82⅛	71 1/16	1	71 1/16	71 1/16	69B	4.5	..	...	...	...	...
43•[16]	NOR	✓Noranda Inc	To,Mo,Vc	B	34	12878	Metal mining/mfg:forest pr	38	6 9/16	30⅛	13⅞	22 5/16	15	98747	19⅝	17⅛	19⅜	4.1	57	−18	37.7	−9.4	−1.6
44	NAT	✓Nordic Amer Tanker Shipping	AS	NR	12	2749	Charter Shipping vessels	19⅜	16 5/16	16½	10⅝	12¾	9⅝	3331	11	9⅞	10⅝	12.7	..	...	3.9	...	...
#45	NDSN	✓Nordson Corp	NNM	A−	125	4472	Industrial application eqp	65	3 3/16	52⅜	42¼	65 15/16	43	6005	52	46⅞	48¼	2.2	17	−5	−4.4	−7.3	−2.8
¶46•[17]	JWN	✓Nordstrom, Inc	NY,Ch	A−	395	68544	Dept stores:upscale apparel	34 1/16	3/16	40⅜	21 7/16	44 13/16	21 11/16	109114	27⅞	23 9/16	26 5/16	1.2	18	6	−23.3	15.5	5.9
¶47•[14]	NSC	✓Norfolk Southern	NY,B,C,Ch,Ph,P	A	721	243156	RR hldg co:motor carrier	38⅛	1⅞	41¾	27 7/16	36 7/16	19⅝	236068	23	19⅝	20½	3.9	26	−7	−33.4	−8.9	3.0
48	NHY	✓Norsk Hydro A.S. ADS[79]	NY,B,Ch,Ph,P	NR	87	15454	Fertilizers:oil,gas:metals	61¼	8 7/16	51¾	30 9/16	46⅝	32¾	14422	42¾	38 1/16	42¾	1.8	11	−14	28.0	−5.3	3.8
49	NRRD	✓Norstan, Inc	NNM	B	45	5876	Digital commun,info proc sys	25½	3/16	29	13⅛	18 3/16	5⅜	28445	7 7/16	5⅜	6⅜	...	d	Neg	−64.1	−29.2	−6.0
50	NTK	✓Nortek Inc	NY,B,Ch,P,Ph	B	127	7943	Mfr comm'l,resid'l bldg prd	27½	15/16	36¼	19¾	41	22¼	7624	28	22¼	28	...	6	32	1.4	11.9	18.7

Uniform Footnote Explanations-See Page 4. Other: [1]ASE:Cycle 2. [2]P:Cycle 1. [3]P:Cycle 3. [4]CBOE,P:Cycle 3. [5]ASE:Cycle 3. [6]Ph:Cycle 3. [7]P:Cycle 2. [8]CBOE,Ph:Cycle 1. [9]ASE,CBOE,Ph:Cycle 3. [10]CBOE:Cycle 2. [11]CBOE:Cycle 1. [12]ASE,CBOE,P,Ph:Cycle 1. [13]Ph:Cycle 2. [14]CBOE:Cycle 3. [15]ASE,CBOE:Cycle 1. [16]Mo:Cycle 2. [17]ASE:Cycle 1. [51]Subsid pfd in $M. [52]Fiscal July'97 & prior. [53]Fr 2-5-2002(or for com stk re-spec cond). [54]Co opt to redm anytime to preserve'REIT'atatus. [55]Oct'97 & prior. [56]12 Mo Dec'98. [57]Qtly Income Cv Pfd Sec. [58]Fr 8-15-2002,scale to $50 in 2009. [59]Of Newfield Exploration to 8-15-2029. [60]Ltd Ptnrshp(Dep Rect). [61]Each ADS represents 4 Ord. [62]Pfd in M$. [63]Incl 1777M ltd vtg ord shs. [64]Ea ADS rep 5 Var Vtg Ord shr,6⅔. [65]Approx. [66]©$0.0373,'99. [67]Ea ADR rep 1 ord shr NIS 1.00. [68]Ltd vtg. [69]Ea ADS rep .005 com, par y50,000. [70]Rated BBB+ by S&P. [71]Excl subsid pfd. [72]Ea ADS rep 1 'A' sh,FIM 20. [73]Redesignated as Com from Pfd Apr'95. [74]Trust Originated Preferred Securities. [75]Red fr 6-30-2000,if com exceeds 125%Cv pr 20 con days. [76]of Relianat Energy Inc. [77]or anytime for 'Tax'Event're spec cond. [78]Stk dstr of Canadian Hunter Expl & Nexfor Inc,'99. [79]Ea ADR rep 1 ord,Nok20.

Index	Splits ◆ Cash Divs. Ea.Yr. Since	Dividends: Latest Payment Period $	Date	Ex. Div.	Total $ So Far 1999	Ind. Rate	Paid 1998	Financial Position Mil-$ Cash& Equiv.	Curr. Assets	Curr. Liab.	Balance Sheet Date	Capitalization Lg Trm Debt Mil-$	Shs. 000 Pfd.	Com.	Earnings $ Per Shr. Years End	1995	1996	1997	1998	1999	Last 12 Mos.	Interim Earnings Period	$ per Shr. 1998	1999	Index
1	1997	Q0.47½	11-15-99	10-27	1.90	1.90	1.90	Co option redm fr 6-30-2002 at $25				★375	...	...	Dc	...	...	...	....	....	....	Mature 2-15-2029			1
2	1951	Q0.43	1-3-00	12-13	1.68	1.72	1.64	6.22	136	164	6-30-99	286	[51]21	17821	Sp	1.41	2.06	v2.21	v2.33	Pv2.49	2.49				2
3◆	....	5%Stk	11-1-84	10-9	...	Nil	....	Total Assets $90.2M			9-30-99	24.2	...	6926	Dc	0.93	v0.81	v0.38	v0.53	....	0.71	9 Mo Sep	v0.31	v0.49	3
4	1942	Q0.40¾	10-15-99	9-19	1.61½	1.63	1.48½	Total Assets $2954M			9-30-99	968	2287	88514	Dc	1.19	1.25	v[52]1.30	vp1.47	E2.20	1.36	9 Mo Sep	v1.10	v0.99	4
5	1997	Q0.53⅛	10-15-99	9-29	2.12½	2.12	2.12½	Cv into 1.24384 com				....	2124	...	Dc	...	...	...	....	....	....				5
6◆	1958	Q0.10½	12-17-99	11-29	0.41	0.42	0.37	43.5	529	851	9-26-99	598	...	±171256	Dc	v±0.70	v±0.43	v±1.33	v□1.49	E1.70	1.59	9 Mo Sep	v±□1.04	v±1.14	6
7◆	....	None Since Public			...	Nil	....	832	1905	762	j10-31-99	430	...	181266	Ap	1.16	1.22	v0.91	vd0.10	v1.01	j2.34	6 Mo Oct	v0.50	v1.83	7
8◆	1991	Div Omitted 3-5-98			...	Nil	0.05	4.48	64.1	40.8	9-30-99	136	...	4921	Dc	0.18	d0.23	v[55]0.79	v[56]d0.19	....	d0.66	9 Mo Sep	v0.07	vd0.40	8
9◆	1946	Q0.20	12-3-99	11-10	0.80	0.80	0.72	33.9	2539	1414	9-30-99	1362	...	282038	Dc	v1.40	v1.61	v1.82	v2.38	E0.83	0.99	9 Mo Sep	v1.47	v0.08	9
10◆	....	None Since Public			...	Nil	....	30.4	85.5	55.6	9-30-99	269	...	41606	Dc	v0.45	v1.03	v1.07	vd1.55	....	d1.45	9 Mo Sep	v0.29	v0.39	10
11	1999	0.831	11-15-99	10-27	0.831	3.25	....	Cv into 1.3646 com[59]				....	2875	...	Dc	...	...	...	....	....	....	Mand Cv 8-15-2029			11
12	1936	Q0.10	12-13-99	12-1	†0.62	0.40	†0.52	Total Assets $507.50M			9-30-99	230	...	30926	Dc	v0.75	v1.18	v1.28	v1.86	....	1.10	9 Mo Sep	v1.79	v1.03	12
13◆	1934	Q0.03	12-15-99	11-29	0.12	0.12	0.12	31.4	490	193	9-30-99	1073	...	167607	Dc	v0.95	v0.63	v0.44	v□d2.27	Ed0.08↓	d2.79	9 Mo Sep	v□0.39	vd0.13	13
14◆	....	5%Stk	12-31-95	11-28	...	Nil	....	2.95	110	41.2	9-30-99	207	...	69004	Dc	v0.27	v0.35	v0.58	vd0.93	....	d0.95	9 Mo Sep	v□d0.17	vΔd0.19	14
15	1978	S0.02	1-7-00	12-8	0.04	0.04	0.04	4.86	73.5	21.8	9-30-99	15.4	...	9150	Dc	v0.45	v0.52	v0.77	v0.96	....	0.85	9 Mo Sep	v0.68	v0.57	15
16	1997	Q0.04	11-8-99	10-21	0.16	0.16	0.16	3.00	589	444	9-19-99	522	...	32972	Dc	p1.55	pv1.60	vd1.36	v1.85	....	2.53	9 Mo Sep	v1.35	v2.03	16
17◆	1984	0.033	11-10-99	10-5	0.066	0.07	0.065	4314	11179	8376	j6-30-98	14009	[62]608	[63]3754185	Je	Δ1.36	□1.27	□v1.18	v1.04	vΔP0.92	0.88	3 Mo Sep	v0.20	v0.16	17
18	....	None Since Public			...	Nil	....	12.5	58.9	41.6	9-30-99	0.45	...	★78467	Dc	...	...	...	vpd1.08	....	....	9 Mo Sep	n/a	vpd0.79	18
19	....	None Since Public			...	Nil	....	Total Assets $389M			9-30-99	229	...	46327	Dc	...	...	...	n/a	....	....	9 Mo Sep	n/a	vpd1.28	19
20	....	None Since Public			...	Nil	....	1379	2069	1542	9-30-99	8991	7988	±p364426	Dc	vd2.31	vd2.50	v□d6.41	v□d5.98	Ed4.50	d5.20	9 Mo Sep	v□d4.56	vd3.78	20
21	1997	Q0.254	11-15-99	10-28	1.015	1.015	1.015	At maturity NEXTEL'A'Com or Cash re-spec cond				....	...	★7169	Dc	...	...	...	....	....	....	Mature 5-15-2000			21
22	....	None Since Public			...	Nil	....	5.29	55.8	50.8	9-30-99	34.1	...	±33406	Dc	...	...	...	vpd0.61	....	....	9 Mo Sep	n/a	vd0.01	22
23◆	....	None Since Public			...	Nil	....	1644	1738	202	9-30-99	3057	12043	±133081	Dc	...	pvd0.91	vpd1.96	vd3.13	....	d4.45	9 Mo Sep	vd2.09	vd3.41	23
24◆	1990	[65]0.268	3-1-00	2-2	[66]0.877	0.86	5.617	77.2	690	51.0	j9-30-98	251	...	523800	Sp	0.21	0.93	0.67	v0.95	Pv1.00	1.00				24
25◆	....	None Since Public			...	Nil	....	13.6	153	101	9-30-99	193	...	22342	Dc	v0.48	v0.51	v0.60	v0.67	....	0.75	9 Mo Sep	v0.44	v0.52	25
26	....	0.28	11-30-95	11-2	...	Nil	....	146	871	815	9-30-99	5383	13752	187285	Dc	v1.44	□v0.97	v0.16	vd0.95	E0.10	d0.10	12 Mo Sep	vd0.85	v□d0.10	26
27	....	None Since Public			...	Nil	....	103	147	14.8	12-31-97	....	...	★13233	Dc	v0.06	v0.70	vd0.35	Pv0.37	....	1.26	9 Mo Sep	v0.20	v1.09	27
28	1954	Q0.39	2-1-00	12-28	1.54	1.56	1.46	51.6	343	578	9-30-99	437	125	47047	Dc	v1.96	v2.71	v2.61	v2.42	E2.65	2.44	12 Mo Sep	v2.58	v2.44	28
29◆	1984	Q0.12	1-5-00	12-16	0.48	0.48	0.48	226	3457	1808	8-31-99	462	300	±280041	My	±1.36	±1.80	v±2.68	±v1.35	v±1.57	1.86	6 Mo Nov	v±0.80	v±1.09	29
30◆	....	None Since Public			...	Nil	....	50.2	147	16.6	9-30-99	6.72	...	25053	Dc	p0.48	pv0.62	v0.81	v1.09	....	1.25	9 Mo Sep	v0.68	v0.84	30
31◆	1995	0.102	12-20-99	9-27	0.363	0.36	0.164	13692	32378	30942	3-31-99	40797	...	15912	Mr	0.81	0.64	v0.51	v1.44	....	1.44				31
32	1996	Q0.484	12-31-99	12-28	1.937	1.938	1.93¾	Co option redm fr 3-31-2001 at $25				★75.0	...	...	Dc	...	...	...	....	....	....	Mature 3-31-2026			32
33◆	1987	Q0.27	2-18-00	1-27	1.02	1.08	0.96	23.7	678	1279	9-30-99	2187	[51]140	125056	Dc	v1.35	v1.43	v1.53	v1.59	E1.65	1.52	12 Mo Sep	v1.53	v1.52	33
34	1998	Q0.035	12-30-99	12-14	0.14	0.14	0.09	181	542	312	9-30-99	244	...	51661	Dc	v1.66	v0.21	vd0.19	v□7.25	....	3.11	9 Mo Sep	v□6.89	v2.75	34
35	....	None Since Public			...	Nil	....	1.26	27.4	11.0	9-30-99	1.92	...	10783	Dc	v0.15	vd0.21	vd0.19	vd0.36	....	d0.23	9 Mo Sep	vd0.40	v□d0.27	35
36◆	1994	Q0.08	11-24-99	11-10	0.32	0.32	0.32	1.89	37.3	13.3	9-30-99	....	...	15244	Dc	v0.79	v0.83	v0.57	v0.52	....	0.48	9 Mo Sep	v0.41	v0.37	36
37	1975	Q0.04	11-22-99	11-4	0.16	0.16	0.16	65.5	193	135	9-30-99	670	...	57046	Dc	v0.08	v1.55	v1.73	vd2.88	E0.84	d2.40	9 Mo Sep	v0.01	v0.49	37
38	....	None Since Public			...	Nil	....	153	329	249	9-30-99	748	...	131439	Dc	vd0.08	□v0.67	v1.98	v1.23	E0.75	0.84	9 Mo Sep	v0.98	v□0.59	38
39	....	None Since Public			...	Nil	....	2.32	52.7	27.5	9-30-99	116	[71]...	7208	Dc	...	pv0.16	vp0.40	vΔ0.60	....	1.13	9 Mo Sep	v0.29	v0.82	39
40◆	1995	0.44	4-7-99	3-18	0.44	0.44	0.283	17188	46460	26476	j12-31-98	1530	221165	1146872	Dc	Δ0.62	0.57	v0.99	vΔ1.68	E2.18	1.15	9 Mo Sep	v1.46	v0.93	40
41	1934	Q0.08	10-21-99	10-6	0.32	0.32	0.32	4.08	126	62.3	9-30-99	28.3	...	3701	Dc	v1.34	v1.58	v1.50	v1.59	....	1.64	9 Mo Sep	v1.05	v1.10	41
42	1996	Q0.78⅛	12-31-99	12-28	3.12½	3.125	3.12½	Cv into 33.62 cash & 1.55[76]				....	3000	...	Dc	...	...	...	....	....	....	Mand redm 6-30-2026(co can extend)[77]			42
43	1930	gQ0.20	12-15-99	11-24	g[78]0.80	0.80	g1.00	834	3701	1783	j9-30-99	2931	12000	246169	Dc	2.26	v1.02	v1.00	v2.66	....	j0.34	9 Mo Sep	v2.66	v0.34	43
44	1997	0.36	11-12-99	10-25	1.35	1.35	1.43	3.64	3.81	0.72	12-31-98	30.0	...	9707	Dc	...	...	...	n/a	....	....	EPS Not Meaningful			44
45	1969	Q0.26	1-4-00	12-15	0.96	1.04	0.88	19.4	340	242	8-01-99	72.8	...	16464	Oc	v2.84	v2.92	v2.85	v1.25	Pv2.84	2.84				45
46◆	1971	Q0.08	12-15-99	11-26	0.32	0.32	0.30	40.0	1732	984	10-31-99	747	...	134598	Ja	v1.01	v0.91	v1.20	v1.41	E1.50	1.43	9 Mo Oct	v0.95	v0.97	46
47◆	1901	Q0.20	12-10-99	11-3	0.80	0.80	0.80	56.0	1316	2054	9-30-99	7329	...	380628	Dc	v1.77	v2.01	v1.90	v1.93	E0.80	0.97	9 Mo Sep	v1.51	v0.55	47
48	1985	[65]0.76½	6-2-99	4-20	[65]0.76½	0.77	0.847	4429	45311	26627	j12-31-98	24105	...	229073	Dc	□4.90	v4.18	v3.22	v2.15	E3.90	1.61	9 Mo Sep	v1.95	v1.41	48
49◆	....	0.017	7-3-78	6-12	...	Nil	....	0.30	183	99.9	10-30-99	76.9	...	10922	Ap	0.80	v0.94	v1.08	v0.39	v0.56	d1.11	6 Mo Oct	v0.61	vd1.06	49
50	....	0.02½	2-1-91	12-21	...	Nil	....	97.0	713	381	10-02-99	1021	...	±11593	Dc	v1.19	v2.07	v2.15	v□3.17	....	4.64	9 Mo Sep	v2.18	v3.65	50

◆Stock Splits & Divs By Line Reference Index [3]10%,'95,'96,'97:6-for-5,'98:3-for-2,'99. [6]2-for-1,'98. [7]2-for-1,'96. [8]Adj to 5%,'97. [9]2-for-1,'94. [10]2-for-1,'96. [13]1.2481-for-1,'94. [14]2-for-1,'97(twice). [17]2-for-1,'94:No adj for dstr Spons ADR,'94. [23]2-for-1,'99. [24]3-for-4 REVERSE,'98. [25]3-for-2,'94,'96,'97. [29]2-for-1,'95,'96. [30]5-for-4,'97,'98. [31]Adj for 2%,'95. [33]2-for-1,'98. [36]3-for-2,'95(twice). [40]2-for-1,'95,'98,'99. [46]2-for-1,'98. [47]3-for-1,'97. [49]2-for-1,'96.

¶ S&P 500
\# MidCap 400
✣ SmallCap 600
• Options

Index	Ticker	Name of Issue (Call Price of Pfd. Stocks)	Market	Com. Rank. & Pfd. Rating	Inst. Hold Cos	Inst. Hold Shs. (000)	Principal Business	Price Range 1971-97 High	1971-97 Low	1998 High	1998 Low	1999 High	1999 Low	December, 1999 Dec. Sales in 100s	Last Sale Or Bid High	Low	Last	%Div Yield	P-E Ratio	EPS 5 Yr Growth	% Annualized Total Return 12 Mo	36 Mo	60 Mo
1	NRT	Nortel Inversora 10%[51]'MEDS'[52]	NY	NR	4	268	Mandatorily Exch Debt Sec	63 7/16	37¼	68 7/16	38	63½	41¼	1880	61⅛	52	61⅛	6.9	..	...	28.2	24.4	...
¶2•[1]	NT	✔Nortel Networks	NY,To,B,Ch,P,Ph,Mo,Vc	B	918	388116	Telecommunication equip	28½	⅝	34⅝	13⅜	110	25 1/16	1031689	110	73⅜	101	0.1	88	Neg	306	91.7	67.8
✣3•[2]	NVX	✔North American Vaccine	AS,Ch,Ph,P	C	64	7333	Dvlp immunobiological prod	30¼	1	25	6¼	9⅛	3 13/16	32496	5⅞	3⅞	4½	...	d	−44	−49.3	−43.1	−11.7
4	NET	✔North Europn Oil Rty Tr	NY,B,Ch	NR	26	897	Oil,gas royalty,W Germany	30 3/16	5¼	16 11/16	12¾	16	13	2034	14¾	13	14¾	8.3	12	4	17.0	14.1	12.3
5•[3]	TNFI	✔North Face	NNM	NR	44	4599	Outdoor apparel/eqp	33	13½	29	9⅛	16 11/16	3 15/16	59559	5½	3 15/16	4 1/16	...	d	...	−68.8	−40.5	...
#6•[4]	NFB	✔North Fork Bancorp	NY,Ph	B	347	72089	Comm'l bkg,Long Island,NY	22½	¾	27 9/16	14⅛	26¾	17⅛	128735	20 5/16	17⅛	17⅜	e4.1	11	24	−25.0	17.1	34.4
7	NBN	✔Northeast Bancorp	AS,Ph	B+	11	158	Savings & loan, Maine	19½	3 1/16	19½	8	11½	7	1368	8⅞	7	8⅛	2.6	9	9	−18.5	0.5	6.1
8	NEP	✔Northeast Pennsylvania Finl	AS,Ph	NR	10	1040	Savings & loan,Penn	....	....	16	8⅝	13	9 5/16	3941	10¼	9 5/16	10	2.4	13	...	−12.3	...	...
#9•[5]	NU	✔Northeast Utilities	NY,B,C,Ch,P,Ph	B	218	80023	Utility hldg co:Conn, Mass	28⅞	5½	17¼	11 11/16	22	13 9/16	105359	21 9/16	20½	20 9/16	...	32	Neg	29.1	18.3	3.1
10	NBP	✔Northern Border Ptnrs L.P.	NY,Ch,P	NR	64	2488	Natural gas pipeline transpt'n	35	20½	36⅛	31⅛	35½	21⅝	24582	25 7/16	21⅝	23	10.6	9	6	−23.3	1.9	10.6
¶11•[6]	NSP	✔Northern States Pwr[58]	NY,B,C,Ch,P,Ph	A−	407	58203	Elec & gas util:WI,MN,ND,SD	29 7/16	3 13/16	30 13/16	25 11/16	27 15/16	19 5/16	82471	20⅞	19 5/16	19½	7.4	12	−1	−25.3	0.2	3.3
12	NTI	✔Northern Technol Intl	AS,Ch	B+	11	530	Mfr corrosion inhibiting prd	12¾	1	10¾	5	8⅜	5¼	954	7⅝	6⅛	7¼B	2.2	11	16	16.3	10.8	12.3
¶13•[7]	NTRS	✔Northern Trust	NNM	A	602	141441	Comm'l bkg,Chicago, Ill.	35¾	9/16	44 15/16	27⅞	54⅝	40⅛	161677	54⅝	46 9/16	53	1.0	31	17	22.8	44.9	46.1
14•[8]	NFLD	✔Northfield Laboratories	NNM,Ch	NR	39	1641	Dvp stge:alternative blood prd	26⅝	5⅝	18⅛	8½	16⅜	10⅛	15194	13	10⅛	11 1/16	...	d	1	−10.6	1.0	1.5
15•[9]	CBRYA	✔Northland Cranberries'A'	NNM	B+	47	10565	Grows & sells cranberries	27½	2⅛	19⅛	7¾	10 7/16	5	34651	6⅛	5	6	2.7	21	77	−32.1	−35.2	0.6
16	NPNT	✔NorthPoint Communic Grp	NNM	NR	99	9618	Provide local data ntwk svcs	....	....	....	....	48¾	17⅝	267345	31⅜	23⅝	24	...	d	...	...	...	...
17	NRIM	✔Northrim Bank	NNM	NR	28	1223	General banking, Alaska	13⅛	3⅝	19 1/16	10⅜	15	8 15/16	5146	10¾	8 15/16	9 15/16	s2.0	10	20	−23.2	14.0	22.2
¶18•[9]	NOC	✔Northrop Grumman	NY,B,Ch,P,Ph	B	456	57777	Aerospace: aircraft:missile	127⅞	1 9/16	139	59 5/16	75 15/16	47	91729	58½	47	54 1/16	3.0	8	27	−24.1	−11.4	7.6
19•[2]	NWAC	✔Northwest Airlines	NNM	NR	149	44591	Domestic, int'l air service	55⅞	11½	65 5/16	18⅝	35½	21½	157191	24¼	21½	22¼	...	7	Neg	−13.0	−17.2	7.2
20	NWB	Northwest Airlines 9.50% 'QUIBS'	NY	....[61]	..	...	Qtly Interest Bonds	....	....	....	....	24⅞	19⅜	6284	23	19⅜	19¾	12.0	..	...	...	...	...
✣21•[5]	NWNG	✔Northwest Natural Gas	NNM	B+	164	8433	Gas utility, Oreg. & Wash.	31⅜	3 13/16	30¾	24¼	27⅞	19½	12538	25⅛	21⅛	21 15/16	e5.6	16	−6	−10.9	1.8	7.8
✣22	NOR	✔NorthWestern Corp	NY,Ch,Ph	A	135	7851	Elec & nat gas in Neb, S.D.	23½	3 3/16	27⅜	20¼	27⅛	20⅝	10079	23	21 1/16	22	5.0	13	10	−13.1	13.6	16.3
23	NCX	NOVA Chemicals	NY	NR	77	22286	Mfr commodity chemicals	....	....	21 7/16	11	24 1/16	13	7837	22 3/16	18 9/16	19 5/16	◆1.4	23	...	50.9	...	...
#24•[9]	NIS	✔NOVA Corp	NY,Ch	NR	277	62395	Bankcard transactn process svc	39⅞	12⅞	37⅞	22	34 15/16	17⅞	39936	32	29⅜	31 9/16	...	..	...	−9.0	12.6	...
25	NFI	✔NovaStar Financial	NY	NR	12	2833	Real estate investment trust	18 13/16	14½	21⅛	3	7¼	2⅝	5627	3¾	3	3⅛	...	d	...	−46.4	...	...
26	NOX	✔Novavax Inc	AS,P	NR	21	1237	Pharma'l delivery sys R&D	8¼	2⅝	6⅛	1¼	6 3/16	1⅞	6461	6 3/16	4⅝	5⅝	...	d	12	190	17.8	...
¶27•[10]	NOVL	✔Novell Inc	NNM,Ch	B	587	197261	Dvlp networking software	35¼	3/16	19	6 13/16	41 3/16	16 1/16	1612017	41 3/16	19	39 15/16	...	73	−25	120	61.6	18.5
#28•[11]	NVLS	✔Novellus Systems	NNM,Ch	B	419	33510	Mfr of semiconductor equip	66⅜	1⅜	59 5/16	20⅞	128⅜	44⅞	464386	128⅜	71⅝	122½	...	65	−31	148	65.5	37.5
29	NVO	✔Novo-Nordisk A/S ADR[65]	NY,B,Ch,P,Ph	NR	59	4373	Ind'l enzymes: insulin	73	1 11/16	84⅞	53⅞	70⅛	47½	1751	68¾	63 1/16	64⅝	0.6	27	9	−1.9	12.2	23.0
30•[12]	NPCI	NPC Intl	NNM	B	80	6702	Pizza Hut franchise	15½	1⅞	14⅝	8⅞	18⅜	7½	66653	12 9/16	7½	7⅞	...	9	NM	−34.7	−1.5	9.8
31	NSS	✔NS Group	NY,Ch	↓C	73	9656	Mfrs specialty steel prod	41⅜	1⅞	18	4	13 11/16	3⅝	30074	10 13/16	6½	7⅝	...	d	−44	71.9	19.2	13.1
32	NSH	✔NS Power Holdings	To	NR	13	6607	Electric utility, Canada	17½	10⅜	20⅛	14¾	19 5/16	13	18086	15⅝	13	14⅜	5.8	13	...	−16.9	5.2	11.3
#33•[4]	NST	✔NSTAR	NY	NR	146	20467	Hldg co:electric & gas	....	....	....	....	43 5/16	36⅝	43075	41 11/16	38¼	40½	4.9	14	...	...	...	...
34	NSO	✔nSTOR Technologies	AS	NR	6	232	Dvp/mfr disk array pds	3⅛	1½	2⅞	5/16	5	1½	103693	5	1⅝	2 3/16	...	d	Neg	−14.6	...	...
35•[13]	NTLI	✔NTL Inc	NNM	NR	326	85202	Telecommunications svcs	27 5/16	1 13/16	52	21⅜	127⅞	42 1/16	251009	127⅞	89 5/16	124¾	...	d	−41	177	83.6	49.6
36	NTN	✔NTN Communications	AS,P	C	19	3391	Viewer response TV network	75	⅛	2⅝	5/16	5 3/16	9/16	111940	5 3/16	3 1/16	3 11/16	...	d	−36	556	−1.1	−9.3
37	WS	Wrrt(Pur 1com at$0.96)	AS	....	5	14		....	....	2	½	3 13/16	1⅜	379	3 13/16	3	2⅞B	...	..	...	...	...	...
38•[14]	NUS	✔Nu Skin Enterprises'A'	NY,Ph	NR	59	7340	Dstr/sell personal care prd	30⅞	16	28 11/16	10 3/16	25¼	8½	20511	13½	8½	9 1/16	...	8	...	−61.6	−33.5	...
¶39•[7]	NUE	✔Nucor Corp	NY,B,Ch,P,Ph	A−	490	56162	Steel joists,angles,rounds	72	¼	60⅝	35¼	61 13/16	41⅝	83521	57 7/16	49¼	54 13/16	0.9	22	−1	28.0	3.3	0.6
40	NEV	✔Nuevo Energy	NY,Ch,Ph	C	128	15764	Oil & gas explor,dev,prod'n	58⅛	7	40 9/16	9 15/16	19½	6⅛	23769	19½	14 7/16	18¾	...	d	Neg	63.0	−28.8	0.8
41	Pr T	Nuevo Finl$2.875[69]([70]52.01)	NY	NR	10	1999		58⅜	45	50½	31¼	34	25⅝	692	27 11/16	25⅝	27¼	10.6	..	...	...	...	...
42	CEL	Nuevo Grupo Iusacell ADS	NY	NR	42	9288	Wireless telecommun svc,Mexico	....	....	....	....	18 11/16	9	53454	18 11/16	12	14 15/16	...	..	...	...	...	...
43	NUI	✔NUI Corp	NY,Ch,Ph	B	115	6246	Hldg:gas sv in N.J.,Florida	29¾	5¼	29 7/16	20 5/16	28 3/16	20⅜	5213	28 3/16	24¾	26⅜	3.7	14	15	2.3	9.5	18.2
44	NMC	✔Numac Energy	AS,To,B,Ph,Mo	C	16	6642	Canada oil/gas:field constr	23	1 11/16	4 3/16	1 15/16	4 3/16	1½	1961	3 9/16	2 13/16	3½	...	14	−5	55.6	−4.4	−9.5
45	NEW	✔Nvest L.P.	NY,Ch	NR	40	1241	Provides invest't mgmt svcs	31	6¾	36⅞	21 1/16	27 11/16	15 3/16	5873	20⅛	15 3/16	15⅞	15.9	8	10	−36.4	−4.5	10.0
46	NVR	✔NVR Inc	AS,P	NR	129	5600	Single-family home builder	29¼	5⅛	50¼	21⅝	58	38	5457	49 13/16	42½	47¾	...	6	68	0.1	54.3	54.1
47	NYE	Nycomed Amersham ADS[72]	NY	NR	10	729	Medl/pharmaceutical R&D	39 1/16	33⅝	40½	27½	43½	29⅛	520	32 7/16	29⅜	29 7/16	1.5	..	...	−10.7	...	...
48•[14]	NYF	✔NYFIX Inc	AS,Ch,P	NR	22	579	Mfr securities account'g sys	6⅝	1 5/16	6 5/16	3 9/16	31¾	4¼	18423	31¾	24⅛	28⅜	...	..	−5	376	112	78.4
49	NYM	✔NYMAGIC, Inc	NY	B	47	4992	Marine/liab ins underwriter	39¾	3 11/16	34¼	19¾	20 11/16	12	878	14½	12 5/16	13 3/16	3.0	8	12	−34.7	−8.0	−4.4
✣50•[14]	OAK	✔Oak Indus	NY,B,Ch,P,Ph	B−	172	16760	Mfr electr controls/circuits	192½	1 9/16	41¼	21 13/16	106⅛	26	77703	106⅛	74 7/16	106⅛	...	61	NM	203	66.5	35.9

Uniform Footnote Explanations-See Page 4. Other: [1]ASE,CBOE,P:Cycle 3,To:Cycle 1. [2]ASE,CBOE:Cycle 3. [3]CBOE:Cycle 3. [4]Ph:Cycle 2. [5]Ph:Cycle 3. [6]ASE,CBOE,P:Cycle 3. [7]CBOE:Cycle 1. [8]CBOE,Ph:Cycle 2. [9]CBOE:Cycle 2. [10]ASE:Cycle 2. [11]CBOE,P:Cycle 3. [12]P:Cycle 3. [13]CBOE,Ph:Cycle 3. [14]ASE:Cycle 3. [51]Co opt red fr 4-16-2000 re spec cond. [52]Co can red earlier due to "Tax Event". [53]For Argentina,France-ADS(rep 10 Cl'B'Ord P$1). [54]To be determined. [55]Susid pfd in $M. [56]Excl 6.1M ESOP shrs. [57]Incl 6.4M sub units. [58]Plan mgr,name chge,Xcel Energy. [59]5 Mo Aug'95. [60]Pfd in $M. [61]Rated'BB'by S&P. [62]or earlier upon 'Tax Event' re-spec cond. [63]Total issue amt. [64]10 Mo Dec'95. [65]Ea ADR rep 0.50 'B'shr,DKR 10 par. [66]Spl div. [67]Fiscal Oct'96 & prior. [68]Re-spec cond. [69]'TECONS'-Term Cv Shrs Sr'A'. [70]Fr 12-15-99,scale to $50 in 2006. [71]Into Nuevo Energy com. [72]Ea ADS rep 5 ord shr,25p. [73]Fiscal Mar'97 & prior. [74]9 Mo Dec'97.

Index (Splits ◆)	Cash Divs. Ea. Yr. Since	Dividends: Latest Payment Period $	Date	Ex. Div.	Total $ So Far 1999	Ind. Rate	Paid 1998	Financial Position Mil-$: Cash& Equiv.	Curr. Assets	Curr. Liab.	Balance Sheet Date	Capitalization: Lg Trm Debt Mil-$	Shs. 000 Pfd.	Com.	Earnings $ Per Shr. Years End	1995	1996	1997	1998	1999	Last 12 Mos.	Interim Earnings Period	$ per Shr. 1998	1999	Index
1	1996	S2.10	10-15-99	9-29	4.20	4.20	4.20	Hldr opt exch for 0.8696 ADS(or Cl'B' shrs)[53]				....	...	★5952	Sp	...	...	...	....	....	....	For Argentina,France-ADS(rep 10 Cl'B'Ord P$1)			1
2◆	1965	tQ0.03¾	12-31-99	12-1	t0.15	0.15	t0.15	2281	10317	5983	12-31-98	1648	30000	p1335477	Dc	0.46	v0.60	v0.78	vd0.49	E1.15	0.16	9 Mo Sep	vd1.04	vd0.39	2
3	....	None Since Public			...	Nil	....	1.92	8.91	18.7	9-30-99	101	2000	32870	Dc	vd0.17	vd0.63	vd1.39	vd1.76	....	d1.78	9 Mo Sep	vd1.03	vd1.05	3
4	1976	0.25	8-25-99	8-11	0.91	1.22	1.54	....	2.26	2.17	7-31-99	....	...	8697	Oc	1.43	1.05	v1.51	v1.54	....	1.22	9 Mo Jul	v1.23	v0.91	4
5	....	None Since Public			...	Nil	....	10.1	175	149	9-30-99	1.28	...	12741	Dc	pv0.47	v□0.62	v0.96	v0.29	....	d1.89	9 Mo Sep	v0.31	vd1.87	5
6◆	1994	Q0.18	2-15-00	1-12	†0.72½	0.72	0.47½	Total Deposits $6570.9M			9-30-99	1494	...	130403	Dc	v0.70	v0.65	v1.20	v1.18	E1.63	1.32	9 Mo Sep	v1.06	v1.20	6
7◆	1988	Q0.053	11-19-99	10-27	0.212	0.21	0.212	Total Deposits $225.27M			9-30-99	116	...	2771	Je	0.73	0.55	v0.56	v0.96	v0.86	0.92	3 Mo Sep	v0.23	v0.29	7
8	1999	Q0.06	12-1-99	11-10	0.22	0.24	....	Total Deposits $364M			6-30-99	143	...	5801	Sp	...	...	pn/a	p0.01	Pv0.80	0.80				8
9	1999	0.10	12-30-99	11-29	0.10	[54]....	....	402	1177	1444	9-30-99	2947	[55]277	[56]131566	Dc	v2.24	v0.01	vd1.05	vd1.12	E0.65	d0.63	12 Mo Sep	vd0.52	vd0.63	9
10	1994	Q0.61	11-12-99	10-27	2.44	2.44	2.30	32.8	67.2	133	9-30-99	939	...	[57]29327	Dc	v1.94	v1.88	v1.97	v2.27	....	2.68	9 Mo Sep	v1.65	v2.06	10
11◆	1910	Q0.36¼	1-20-00	12-31	1.44	1.45	1.42	86.7	892	1919	9-30-99	2593	1050	154799	Dc	v1.96	v1.91	v1.61	v1.84	E1.70	1.70	9 Mo Sep	v1.26	v1.12	11
12	1989	Q0.16	12-17-99	12-1	0.16	0.16	0.15	2.75	6.15	0.68	8-31-99	....	...	3865	Au	0.42	0.49	v0.61	v0.63	v0.64	0.64				12
13◆	1896	Q0.135	1-3-00	12-8	0.48	0.54	0.42	Total Deposits $19061.25M			9-30-99	1313	1200	222594	Dc	v0.93	v1.11	v1.33	v1.52	E1.72	1.68	9 Mo Sep	v1.12	v1.28	13
14	....	None Since Public			...	Nil	....	45.1	45.7	1.49	8-31-99	....	...	14240	My	d0.76	vd0.37	vd0.30	vd0.42	vd0.53	d0.55	3 Mo Aug	d0.12	d0.14	14
15◆	1988	Q0.04	11-12-99	10-27	0.16	0.16	0.16	0.77	141	30.9	8-31-99	148	...	±20338	Au	†[59]d0.28	±0.50	v±0.16	v±0.19	v±0.28	0.28				15
16	....	None Since Public			...	Nil	....	303	322	33.6	9-30-99	52.3	...	123016	Dc	...	...	...	vpd0.46	Ed1.95	d1.30	9 Mo Sep	vd0.53	vd1.37	16
17◆	1995	Q0.05	10-29-99	10-15	s0.198	0.20	s0.188	Book Value $8.40			12-31-98	....	...	p4947	Dc	0.57	v0.63	v1.04	v1.05	....	1.05	9 Mo Sep	v0.77	v0.77	17
18	1951	Q0.40	12-11-99	11-24	1.60	1.60	1.60	37.0	2876	2443	9-30-99	2300	...	69489	Dc	v4.71	v4.15	v5.98	v2.79	E6.60	4.93	9 Mo Sep	v□2.83	v□4.97	18
19	....	None Since Public			...	Nil	....	757	2284	3822	9-30-99	4728	[60]246	84470	Dc	vΔ2.90	v4.52	v□5.29	vd3.48	E3.20	0.72	9 Mo Sep	vd1.25	v2.95	19
20	1999	0.51½	11-15-99	10-27	0.51½	2.37	....	Co opt redm fr 8-27-2004 at $25[62]				[63]★125	...	...	Dc	...	...	...	....	....	....	Mature 8-15-2039			20
21◆	1952	†0.00½	12-15-99	11-26	†1.225	1.22	1.22	18.0	122	197	9-30-99	386	374	25049	Dc	v1.60	v1.94	v1.76	v1.02	....	1.39	9 Mo Sep	v0.80	v1.17	21
22◆	1947	Q0.278	12-1-99	11-10	1.05	1.11	1.24¼	38.5	355	270	9-30-99	286	37	23109	Dc	v1.11	v1.28	v1.31	v1.44	....	1.67	9 Mo Sep	v0.86	v1.09	22
23	1998	g0.10	2-15-00	1-27	g0.40	0.40	g0.10	37.0	665	490	12-31-98	1280	...	p92153	Dc	...	...	pv1.85	v0.17	....	0.86	9 Mo Sep	v0.17	v0.86	23
24	....	None Since Public			...	Nil	....	44.1	223	132	9-30-99	168	...	73625	Dc	p†[64]0.24	v0.25	v0.58	vd0.18	....	0.21	9 Mo Sep	v0.40	v0.79	24
25	1998	0.35	4-15-99	9-28	0.35	[54]....	0.75	Total Assets $771.15M			9-30-99	657	...	7585	Dc	...	pd0.07	vd0.26	vd2.71	....	d3.24	9 Mo Sep	v0.64	v0.11	25
26	....	None Since Public			...	Nil	....	1.05	1.14	0.95	9-30-99	....	...	15008	Dc	vpd0.85	vd0.54	vd0.39	vd0.57	....	d0.40	9 Mo Sep	vd0.42	vd0.25	26
27	....	None Since Public			...	Nil	....	992	1371	401	7-31-99	....	...	333066	Oc	0.90	v0.35	vd0.22	v0.29	vP0.55	0.55				27
28◆	....	None Since Public			...	Nil	....	354	661	132	9-25-99	....	...	39106	Dc	v2.41	v2.85	vd2.88	v1.51	E1.88†	1.33	9 Mo Sep	v1.28	v1.10	28
29◆	1982	0.418	4-6-99	3-25	0.418	0.42	0.305	435	2090	558	12-31-98	294	...	±74189	Dc	1.87	v1.86	v2.16	v2.55	....	2.36	9 Mo Sep	v1.94	v1.75	29
30	....	[66]0.422	8-30-95	8-9	...	Nil	....	2.89	13.7	42.2	9-28-99	156	...	24469	Mr	v0.09	v0.72	v0.41	v1.92	....	0.89	6 Mo Sep	v1.51	v□0.48	30
31	....	0.03	3-27-92	2-28	...	Nil	....	30.8	147	50.3	6-26-99	72.7	...	21420	Sp	□d0.36	d0.76	v□0.92	vΔ0.18	Pv□d2.04	d2.04				31
32	1992	gQ0.20¾	11-15-99	10-27	g0.83	0.83	g0.82	n/a	170	435	j9-30-99	1286	...	86912	Dc	1.11	1.05	n/a	v0.99	....	1.13	9 Mo Sep	v0.69	v0.83	32
33	1999	Q0.50	2-1-00	1-6	0.48½	2.00	....	81.9	814	1009	9-30-99	1627	93	60142	Dc	...	...	...	pv2.36	E2.90†	2.65	12 Mo Sep	v2.70	v2.65	33
34	....	None Since Public			...	Nil	....	0.76	19.1	15.0	9-30-99	19.9	...	p26579	Dc	vNil	Δv[67]0.73	vd0.42	vd0.63	....	d0.59	9 Mo Sep	vd0.47	vd0.43	34
35◆	....	None Since Public			...	Nil	....	1568	1969	1030	9-30-99	7483	758	105356	Dc	vd2.41	vd6.56	□vd8.48	v□d10.15	....	d12.64	9 Mo Sep	v□d7.34	vd9.83	35
36	....	None Paid			...	Nil	....	3.96	7.39	5.64	9-30-99	6.10	161	28930	Dc	vd0.19	vd1.02	vd0.55	vd0.10	....	d0.12	9 Mo Sep	vd0.01	vd0.03	36
37	....	Terms&trad. basis should be checked in detail						Wrrts expire 2-18-2001				....	...	565	Dc	...	...	...	....	....	....	Callable fr 2-18-2000 at $3.25[68]			37
38	....	None Since Public			...	Nil	....	108	295	195	9-30-99	87.8	...	±87284	Dc	pv0.50	v1.01	v1.10	v1.19	....	1.09	9 Mo Sep	v0.94	v0.84	38
39	1973	Q0.13	2-11-00	12-29	0.51	0.52	0.46	598	1441	583	10-02-99	390	...	87213	Dc	v3.14	v2.83	v3.35	v3.00	E2.55	2.38	9 Mo Sep	v2.30	v1.68	39
40	....	None Since Public			...	Nil	....	2.19	75.7	42.0	9-30-99	361	...	18471	Dc	v0.68	v1.97	v□1.06	vd4.76	....	d2.82	9 Mo Sep	vd1.29	v0.65	40
41	1997	Q0.71⅞	12-15-99	12-10	2.875	2.875	2.875	Cv into 0.8421 com $59.375[71]				...	2300	...	Dc	...	...	...	....	....	....	Mand redm 12-15-2026			41
42	....	None Since Public			...	Nil	....					375	...	±1325936	Dc	...	...	...	vpd1.10	....	....	3 Mo Mar	n/a	vp0.30	42
43	1923	Q0.24½	12-15-99	11-29	0.98	0.98	0.98	Total Assets $844.23M			9-30-99	272	...	12750	Sp	0.60	1.52	v1.75	v□1.40	v1.93	1.93				43
44	....	....			...	Nil	....	21.5	52.8	47.3	j6-30-99	195	...	95511	Dc	d1.91	v0.18	v0.13	vd1.38	....	j0.17	9 Mo Sep	vd1.33	v0.22	44
45	1987	0.63	2-15-00	12-29	2.52	2.52	†2.66	....	4.87	4.72	9-30-99	....	...	6204	Dc	v1.73	v1.85	v2.21	v2.00	....	1.95	9 Mo Sep	v1.49	v1.44	45
46	....	None Since Public			...	Nil	....	Total Assets $814.86M			9-30-99	190	...	9365	Dc	vΔ1.06	v1.70	v2.18	v□4.97	....	7.96	9 Mo Sep	v□3.83	v6.82	46
47◆	1998	0.16	11-9-99	10-4	0.44	0.44	s0.426	190	1049	468	6-30-99	669	...	630000	Dc	...	±p[73]0.75	v[74]d1.28	n/a	....	....	6 Mo Jun	v0.75	v0.55	47
48◆	....	None Since Public			...	Nil	....	3.58	12.5	5.73	9-30-99	2.25	...	15767	Dc	...	vd0.04	vd0.21	vd0.17	....	0.02	9 Mo Sep	vd0.16	v0.03	48
49	1989	Q0.10	1-11-00	12-28	0.40	0.40	0.40	Total Assets $708.48M			9-30-99	13.7	...	9686	Dc	v1.77	v2.15	v2.67	v1.91	....	1.70	9 Mo Sep	v1.40	v1.19	49
50	....	0.30	3-10-83	2-17	...	Nil	....	8.18	163	51.3	9-30-99	208	...	17282	Dc	v□d2.88	v□2.29	v1.20	v1.46	E1.73†	1.57	9 Mo Sep	v1.15	v1.26	50

◆Stock Splits & Divs By Line Reference Index [2]2-for-1,'98,'99. [6]2-for-1,'97:3-for-2,'98. [7]2-for-1,'95:3-for-2,'97. [11]2-for-1,'98. [13]2-for-1,'96,'99. [15]2-for-1,'96. [17]Adj for 5%,'99. [21]3-for-2,'96. [22]2-for-1,'97. [28]2-for-1,'97:To split 3-for-1,ex Jan 18,'00. [29]4-for-1,'94. [35]4-for-3,'95:5-for-4,'99. [47]Adj for 3.4%,'98. [48]3-for-2,'99.

¶ S&P 500
# MidCap 400
✣ SmallCap 600
• Options

Index	Ticker	Name of Issue (Call Price of Pfd. Stocks)	Market	Com. Rank. & Pfd. Rating	Inst. Hold Cos	Inst. Hold Shs. (000)	Principal Business	Price Range 1971-97 High	1971-97 Low	1998 High	1998 Low	1999 High	1999 Low	December, 1999 Dec. Sales in 100s	Last Sale Or Bid High	Low	Last	%Div Yield	P-E Ratio	EPS 5 Yr Growth	% Annualized Total Return 12 Mo	36 Mo	60 Mo
1	OAKT	✓Oak Technology	NNM	C	62	16495	Mfr hi performance CD-ROM prod	30¾	5⅝	7¼	1⅝	11	2 13/16	99347	11	6	9 7/16	...	d	Neg	170	–5.7	...
2•[1]	OO	✓Oakley Inc	NY,P	NR	90	15980	Mfr sport sunglasses & goggles	27 3/16	8⅜	15	8¼	9⅞	5 9/16	55909	7 1/16	5 5/16	5 9/16	...	15	–8	–41.5	–20.3	...
✣3•[2]	OH	✓Oakwood Homes	NY,Ch,Ph,P	↓A–	140	29424	Mobile home mfr/retailer/prk	33⅝	⅛	42¼	10⅞	20⅝	1 3/16	75881	3 5/16	2 9/16	3 3/16	1.3	d	Neg	–78.9	–48.0	–23.3
4•[3]	OSII	✓Objective Sys Integrators	NNM	NR	26	3280	Dvlp client/server softwr prd	56¼	3⅜	14⅝	3⅛	8 15/16	2 1/16	102200	8 15/16	3⅞	6⅝	...	d	Neg	43.2	–34.8	...
¶5•[4]	OXY	✓Occidental Petrol'm	NY,To,B,C,Ch,P,Ph	B	522	259749	Major diversified energy co	39⅝	7⅜	30 7/16	16⅝	24 9/16	14⅝	198072	22⅜	19 7/16	21⅝	4.6	37	74	34.8	1.7	6.9
#6•[2]	OEI	✓Ocean Energy	NY,Mo,Ph	NR	318	107513	Oil&gas explor,dev,prod'n	70 9/16	8¾	57½	5 1/16	11 13/16	3 13/16	170821	8¼	6 5/16	7¾	...	d	Neg	21.6	–47.4	–5.9
✣7•[5]	OII	✓Oceaneering Intl	NY,Ph,P	B–	179	18350	Offshore oil/gas field serv	27 5/16	⅞	24	8¾	23⅝	9½	31043	15	12⅛	14 15/16	...	17	30	–0.4	–2.0	7.8
8	OCFC	✓OceanFirst Financial	NNM	NR	76	6638	Savings bank,New Jersey	19⅜	9 11/16	20½	10⅝	19⅜	12⅞	7834	18¾	16⅞	17 5/16	3.5	14	...	7.7	13.6	...
9	CHUX	✓O'Charley's Inc	NNM	B	72	12419	Franch:Full svc restaurants	12 15/16	1 5/16	15 3/16	7⅛	18	10	26274	14	10	13⅛	...	14	34	–7.1	14.9	12.4
10•[6]	OTL	✓Octel Corp	NY	NR	105	10657	Specialty chem:fuel additives	....	....	34¼	11 7/16	15 7/16	9 9/16	6641	10⅝	9 11/16	10⅜	...	3	...	–25.2	...	...
11•[7]	OCLR	✓Ocular Sciences	NNM	NR	127	13431	Mfr soft contact lenses	28⅛	16½	35⅛	16	35¼	13½	36905	20¾	17½	18⅞	...	13	42	–29.4	...	...
12	OCN	✓Ocwen Financial	NY	NR	73	19793	Financial svcs co	28 13/16	7½	30¾	5 11/16	11⅞	5 9/16	51324	6¾	5 9/16	6¼	...	48	–46	–49.2	–22.2	...
13	ODETA	✓Odetics,Inc'A'[54]	NNM	B–	9	236	Mfr sys that automate storage	23¼	3¾	17⅛	4	15½	7 1/16	15791	15½	12 3/16	13½	...	d	Neg	72.8	...	...
14	ODSI	✓ODS Networks	NNM	B–	19	1326	Mfr computer network'g prd	43¼	4	9 11/16	2⅛	14 5/16	2½	52218	14 5/16	7 15/16	9 1/16	...	d	Neg	202	–8.9	–9.1
15•[8]	OEA	✓OEA Inc	NY,Ch,Ph,P	B	63	7991	Auto airbag initiators	50⅝	3/16	29 9/16	7¾	15 7/16	4 5/16	25588	5 7/16	4 5/16	4⅞	...	d	Neg	–58.7	–52.3	–27.1
16	OOC	✓OEC Compression	AS	C	7	85	Oil & gas prod'n & equip	3⅞	⅜	2¾	1 1/16	1⅞	9/16	2302	15/16	9/16	9/16	...	d	–14	–50.0	–26.9	2.4
¶17•[9]	ODP	✓Office Depot	NY,Ph,P	B+	608	279808	Office supply strs/rental eqp	21 7/16	1	24 13/16	10 9/16	26	9	559890	11¼	9 13/16	11	...	17	6	–55.4	–2.5	–6.8
#18•[10]	OMX	✓OfficeMax Inc	NY,Ch,P	NR	252	55907	Oper office prod superstores	19¼	9⅝	19⅝	6⅝	12½	4 7/16	255643	6¼	5 1/16	5 7/16	...	91	Neg	–55.6	–20.3	–14.2
19	OPAY	Official Payments[56]	NNM	NR	..	...	Electronic pymt svc to gvt	....	....	....	....	57⅜	17¼	50114	57⅜	29	52	...	d	...	...	...	...
✣20•[11]	OLOG	✓Offshore Logistics	NNM	B–	136	13262	Transp'n svc to oil/gas indus	34	½	25 13/16	8¾	14⅜	7 15/16	25817	10	7 15/16	9⅜	...	26	–12	–21.1	–21.5	–6.3
#21•[4]	OG	✓Ogden Corp	NY,B,Ch,Ph,P	B+	199	29985	Support services	44⅝	3 13/16	32½	23	28	8 7/16	42121	13	11⅜	11 15/16	...	12	16	–50.6	–10.3	–3.8
22	Pr	$1.875 cm Cv Pfd(50)1/2vtg	NY	NR	2		aviation,environ'l svc	243	22⅛	180	145	160	68	16	68	68	71⅜B	†4.7	..	...	...	...	...
#23•[2]	OGE	✓OGE Energy	NY,B,C,Ch,P,Ph	A–	240	23249	Utility:el sv-OK,Westn AR	27⅜	5¾	30	25⅝	29 1/16	18 7/16	39570	21 11/16	18 7/16	19	7.0	10	6	–30.7	2.4	9.3
24	OAR	✓Ohio Art[59]	AS	C	8	53	Mfr toys:plastic prod	31¼	1 3/16	41½	12½	26¾	9¾	1137	26¾	19½	22¾	...	d	Neg	22.5	10.5	9.9
#25•[12]	OCAS	✓Ohio Casualty	NNM	B+	178	36905	Hldg: full multiple insur line	25½	1	25⅞	16⅞	21 11/16	14⅞	42784	17⅜	15	16 1/16	5.7	46	7	–16.1	1.7	7.6
26	OJA	Ohio Power 7.92% Jr Sub Debs[61]	NY	NR	2	44	Contr by Amer Elec Pwr	25⅞	23⅜	26⅜	25	26 1/16	21⅜	1227	23 7/16	21⅜	21 9/16	9.2	..	...	–8.5	...	...
27	OPJ	Ohio Power 8.16% Jr Sub Debs[62]	NY	....[63]	4	52	Contr by Amer Elec Pwr	26¼	23¾	26¼	25¼	25⅞	22¼	949	24	22¼	22¼	9.2	..	...	–5.4	4.4	...
28	OJB	Ohio Power 7.375% Sr Notes	NY	....[64]	3	97	Contr by Amer Elec Pwr	....	....	26	24½	26⅛	20	2372	22 1/16	20	20¾	8.9	..	...	–12.2	...	...
29	ODC	✓Oil Dri Amer Cl'A'	NY,Ch	B+	43	3536	Absorbent minerals,cat bx,etc	25	⅞	17⅛	10 13/16	16⅜	9¾	1698	15⅝	13⅜	14⅜	2.5	12	7	–1.8	0.8	–1.6
¶30•[3]	OK	✓Old Kent Finl	NY,Ph	A+	281	34036	Commercial bkg,Michigan	38 3/16	15/16	44 5/16	27½	46⅞	33 9/16	138312	42¼	33 9/16	35⅜	s2.5	16	9	–14.4	27.1	31.8
31	OLDB	✓Old Natl Bancorp(Ind)	NNM	A	72	8544	Commercial bkg,Indiana	30 7/16	4⅜	38 3/16	28 9/16	36 13/16	27⅛	12169	33¾	31	32 7/16	s2.1	21	8	–1.6	19.5	17.6
#32•[12]	ORI	✓Old Republic Intl	NY,Ch,Ph,P	A	289	88284	Insur:life,disab,prop,casual	26 13/16	⅜	32¼	17 15/16	22¾	12 1/16	75612	14	12 1/16	13⅝	3.8	7	14	–37.6	–6.4	10.1
33	OLCMF	✓Olicom A/S	NNM	NR	4	37	Mfr computer softwr & hardwr	34⅝	6¾	31⅜	4⅞	8⅜	7/16	63585	2¼	⅝	15/16	...	1	Neg	–83.7	–63.2	–38.0
#34•[11]	OLN	✓Olin Corp	NY,B,C,Ch,P,Ph	B	187	23783	Mfg metal & ammunition pds	51⅜	3¼	49 5/16	23⅞	29¼	9½	50866	19⅞	17⅝	19 13/16	4.0	57	–24	...	...	...
#35•[11]	OLS	✓Olsten Corp	NY,P	B	186	43235	Provide temp work forces	33⅝	1/32	17⅝	4½	11½	5 3/16	102728	11½	10⅛	11 5/16	...	54	–40	55.3	–7.2	–10.5
✣36	OMP	✓OM Group	NY	NR	..	...	Produce specialty chemicals	42 1/16	9 5/16	46	25	42½	26½	14481	35 5/16	31½	34 7/16	1.2	15	15	–4.6	9.6	17.9
37	OHI	✓Omega Healthcare Investors	NY,P	NR	92	5207	Real estate investment trust	38¾	18⅝	40⅛	26	30½	12⅜	34906	16 9/16	12⅜	12 11/16	...	7	7	–52.3	–20.3	–3.5
38	OME	✓Omega Protein	NY,Ph	NR	27	5981	Fishing&fish processing svcs	....	....	19½	3¾	11½	2¼	14999	3⅜	2¼	3⅛	...	d	...	–69.1	...	...
39	OMM	✓OMI Corp	NY	NR	57	18300	Intl shipping svcs	....	....	8⅜	2 9/16	3 7/16	1 5/16	79011	2 1/16	1½	2 1/16	...	d	...	–36.6	...	...
#40•[13]	OCR	✓Omnicare, Inc	NY,B,Ch,Ph,P	A–	291	72919	Long-term care pharmacy svcs	34 9/16	1 5/16	41 9/16	25	36 3/16	6⅞	100083	13 9/16	11¼	12	0.8	11	12	–65.2	–27.7	2.4
¶41•[5]	OMC	✓Omnicom Group	NY,Ch,Ph,P	A+	788	144103	Major int'l advertising co	42⅜	1⅜	58½	37	107½	55 15/16	163664	107½	87⅛	100	0.7	50	21	73.9	65.7	53.2
42•[14]	OMPT	✓Omnipoint Corp	NNM	NR	179	26848	Personal communic svcs	35½	6⅞	30	4⅝	120⅝	9½	169933	120⅝	76⅜	120⅝	...	d	Neg	1195	84.4	...
✣43	OMN	✓Omnova Solutions	NY	NR	2	146	Mfr emulsion polymers/bldg pd	....	....	....	....	11⅛	5 13/16	35668	7 15/16	5 13/16	7¾	...	..	...	...	...	...
44•[15]	ASGN	✓On Assignment	NNM	B+	..	...	Provides temporary lab svcs	29⅝	3½	39½	20⅝	39¼	21 5/16	8130	30⅜	27	29⅞	...	25	31	–13.4	26.6	30.2
45	ONDS	OnDisplay Inc	NNM	NR	..	...	e-commerce software	....	....	....	....	116⅝	28	80146	116⅝	28	90⅞	...	..	...	...	...	...
46	ONHN	✓OnHealth Network	NNM	NR	48	12248	Elec'nic pub medl,hlth info	30	1⅛	11⅜	2 3/16	22¾	4⅝	79957	14	8½	8 15/16	...	d	16	78.7	41.0	–4.9
47	FLWS	✓1-800-FLOWERS.com'A'	NNM	NR	34	6735	e-commerce floral/gift prd	....	....	....	....	23 3/16	10¼	78121	16¼	10¼	10 11/16	...	d	...	...	...	...
48	OLP	✓One Liberty Properties	AS	NR	4	3	Real estate investment trust	18⅛	5⅞	14¾	11⅞	15¼	12 1/16	128	13 5/16	12¾	13	9.2	8	14	17.7	10.3	14.6
49	Pr	$1.60 cm Cv Pfd([70]16.50)	AS	NR	5	23		17⅞	10	17¾	16 5/16	17⅜	15 7/16	80	16¾	15 7/16	15½B	10.3	..	...	...	...	...
50	OV	✓One Valley Bancorp	NY,Ph	A+	117	9749	Commercial banking,W.Va.	41⅛	6⅜	40¼	28⅛	40⅛	29⅛	6871	34 9/16	29⅛	30⅝	3.4	13	6	–4.3	3.8	14.4

Uniform Footnote Explanations-See Page 4. Other: [1]CBOE,Ph:Cycle 2. [2]Ph:Cycle 3. [3]Ph:Cycle 1. [4]CBOE:Cycle 2. [5]P:Cycle 1. [6]CBOE:Cycle 3. [7]CBOE:Cycle 1. [8]ASE:Cycle 1. [9]ASE,CBOE,P,Ph:Cycle 3. [10]ASE,CBOE,P:Cycle 3. [11]ASE:Cycle 2. [12]Ph:Cycle 2. [13]P,Ph:Cycle 3. [14]ASE,CBOE,Ph:Cycle 2. [15]P,Ph:Cycle 2. [51]Pfd in $M. [52]®$1.05,'96. [53]6 Mo Dec'96. [54]0.10 vtg. [55]Stk dstr of ATL Products Inc. [56]dba US Audio Tex. [57]12 Mo Mar'97:Fiscal Jun'96 earned $0.77. [58]Addl ptc 150% of amt qtly com div exceeds $0.667. [59]ASE trading halted 5-5-99. [60]Fiscal Dec'97 & prior. [61]Jr Sub Deferrable Int Deb Sr'B'. [62]Jr Sub Deferrable Int Deb Sr'A'. [63]Rated BBB+ by S&P. [64]Rated'BBB+'by S&P. [65]Stk dstr of Arch Chemicals,'99. [66]To be determined. [67]Stk dstr of Omega Worldwide Inc. [68]Fiscal Sep'97 & prior. [69]12 Mo Dec,'98. [70]Hldrs opt $16.50 for 90 days.

Index	Splits ◆ Cash Divs. Ea. Yr. Since	Dividends Latest Payment Period $	Date	Ex. Div.	Total $ So Far 1999	Ind. Rate	Paid 1998	Financial Position Mil-$ Cash& Equiv.	Curr. Assets	Curr. Liab.	Balance Sheet Date	Capitalization Lg Trm Debt Mil-$	Shs. 000 Pfd.	Com.	Earnings $ Per Shr. Years End	1995	1996	1997	1998	1999	Last 12 Mos.	Interim Earnings Period	$ per Shr. 1998	1999	Index
1◆	....	None Since Public			...	Nil	....	127	151	11.6	9-30-99	....	...	40860	Je	0.67	v0.87	v0.55	v0.14	vd1.24	d1.19	3 Mo Sep	vd0.35	vd0.30	1
2◆	....	None Since Public			...	Nil	....	10.5	105	35.9	9-30-99	18.2	...	70678	Dc	p0.58	v0.64	v0.28	v0.34	....	0.37	9 Mo Sep	v0.29	v0.32	2
3◆	1976	Q0.01	11-24-99	11-5	0.04	0.04	0.04	Total Assets $1392.82M			6-30-99	356	...	47126	Sp	p0.98	1.47	v1.75	v1.17	vPd0.67	d0.67				3
4	....	None Since Public			...	Nil	....	31.4	45.2	20.3	9-30-99	....	...	35877	Je	0.23	v0.29	vd0.58	vd0.36	vd0.97	d1.10	3 Mo Sep	vNil	vd0.13	4
5	1975	Q0.25	1-15-00	12-8	1.00	1.00	1.00	151	1491	1577	9-30-99	5144	[51]238	367578	Dc	1.31	□v1.81	vd1.43	v0.99	E0.58	0.12	9 Mo Sep	v1.09	v□0.22	5
6◆	....	None Since Public			...	Nil	....	53.9	252	288	9-30-99	1539	50	166873	Dc	v0.66	v[52]1.09	v□1.79	vd4.04	....	d2.64	9 Mo Sep	vd1.76	vd0.36	6
7	....	0.05	12-31-77	11-28	...	Nil	....	8.18	141	82.9	9-30-99	112	...	23328	Mr	v0.53	v0.81	v0.93	v1.12	....	0.90	6 Mo Sep	v0.62	v0.40	7
8◆	1997	0.15	11-15-99	10-28	0.57	0.60	0.46	Total Deposits $1045M			9-30-99	30.0	...	13157	Dc	...	v[53]d0.39	v1.77	v0.95	....	1.21	9 Mo Sep	v0.72	v0.98	8
9◆	....	None Since Public			...	Nil	....	0.69	16.5	33.9	10-03-99	70.6	...	15639	Dc	v0.85	vd0.10	v0.66	v0.79	....	0.92	9 Mo Sep	v□0.59	v□0.72	9
10	....	None Since Public			...	Nil	....	25.8	247	206	9-30-99	194	...	13641	Dc	...	...	v6.90	v4.85	....	3.72	9 Mo Sep	v3.59	v2.46	10
11	....	None Since Public			...	Nil	....	43.2	101	31.5	9-30-99	1.96	...	22916	Dc	v0.46	pv0.52	v0.98	v1.31	....	1.49	9 Mo Sep	v0.95	v1.13	11
12◆	....	None Since Public			...	Nil	....	Total Deposits $1776.65M			9-30-99	222	...	p71451	Dc	v0.46	v0.94	v1.39	vd0.02	....	0.13	9 Mo Sep	v0.15	v0.30	12
13◆	....	h[55]....	10-31-97	11-3	...	Nil	....	1.91	47.6	30.0	9-30-99	29.4	...	±9120	Mr	±v0.40	v±0.59	v±d0.95	v±d2.57	....	d2.27	6 Mo Sep	vd1.30	vd1.00	13
14◆	....	None Since Public			...	Nil	....	69.1	83.8	27.7	9-30-99	0.01	...	18596	Dc	v0.81	v0.66	vd0.30	vd1.50	....	d1.30	9 Mo Sep	vd0.52	vd0.32	14
15	1990	Div Omitted 3-8-99			...	Nil	0.08¼	0.88	97.4	36.6	10-31-99	91.0	...	20617	Jl	1.04	1.25	v1.73	v□d0.45	vPd0.12	d0.12	3 Mo Oct	vd0.13	vd0.13	15
16	....	None Paid			...	Nil	....	0.40	8.62	9.49	9-30-99	57.6	...	28987	Dc	vd0.11	vd0.01	vd0.07	vNil	....	d0.01	9 Mo Sep	v0.02	v0.01	16
17◆	....	None Since Public			...	Nil	....	575	2722	1784	9-25-99	533	...	329179	Dc	v0.55	v0.53	v0.65	v0.61	E0.66↓	0.63	9 Mo Sep	v0.43	v0.45	17
18◆	....	None Since Public			...	Nil	....	70.4	1434	977	10-23-99	15.5	...	125216	Ja	v1.04	v0.55	v0.72	v0.39	E0.06	d0.17	9 Mo Oct	v0.45	vd0.11	18
19	....	None Since Public			...	Nil	....	0.51	1.28	2.33	9-30-99	p0.11	...	★20000	Dc	...	...	...	vd0.02	....	d0.10	9 Mo Sep	vd0.02	vd0.10	19
20	....	0.12	12-15-84	11-25	...	Nil	....	34.4	219	106	9-30-99	230	...	21103	Mr	0.96	v[57]1.03	v1.36	v0.97	....	0.36	6 Mo Sep	v0.71	v0.10	20
21	1972	Div Omitted 9-17-99			0.93¾	Nil	1.25	119	1178	466	9-30-99	1850	40	49466	Dc	v0.15	v1.28	v1.49	v1.70	....	0.99	9 Mo Sep	v1.27	v□0.56	21
22	1968	†0.838	12-29-99	12-10	†3.35	[58]3.35	3.35	Cv into 5.97626 common				....	41	...	Dc	...	...	...	....	....	....				22
23◆	1908	Q0.33¼	1-28-00	1-6	1.33	1.33	1.33	16.7	589	1256	9-30-99	1051	...	77801	Dc	1.53	v1.63	v1.62	v2.04	E1.92	1.90	12 Mo Sep	v2.06	v1.90	23
24◆	1930	Div Omitted 5-21-99			0.04	Nil	0.16	2.34	21.9	26.5	10-31-99	0.98	...	887	Ja	v2.04	vd1.86	v[60]d5.68	vd2.10	....	d0.42	9 Mo Oct	v0.41	v2.09	24
25◆	1923	Q0.23	12-10-99	11-29	0.92	0.92	0.88	Total Assets $4536M			9-30-99	242	...	60083	Dc	v1.34	v1.46	v2.03	v1.29	E0.35	2.01	9 Mo Sep	v0.97	v□1.69	25
26	1997	Q0.49½	12-31-99	12-28	1.98	1.98	1.98	Co option redm fr 3-18-2002 at $25				★50.0	...	...	Dc	...	...	...	....	....	....	Mature 3-31-2027			26
27	1995	Q0.51	12-31-99	12-28	2.04	2.04	2.04	Co option redm fr 10-18-2000 at $25				★85.0	...	...	Dc	...	...	...	....	....	....	Mature 9-30-2025			27
28	1998	Q0.461	12-31-99	12-28	1.844	1.844	1.234	Co option redm fr 4-29-2003 at $25				★140	...	...	Dc	...	...	...	....	....	....	Mature 6-30-2038			28
29	1970	Q0.09	3-17-00	2-9	0.36	0.36	0.40	2.12	51.8	13.4	10-31-99	38.2	...	±5720	Jl	1.15	0.50	v1.03	v0.77	v1.20	1.16	3 Mo Oct	v0.34	v0.30	29
30◆	1937	Q0.22	12-15-99	11-8	s0.801	0.88	s0.688	Total Deposits $13571.45M			9-30-99	200	...	117722	Dc	v1.28	v1.46	v1.70	v1.75	E2.26	1.82	9 Mo Sep	v1.44	v1.51	30
31◆	1984	5%Stk	1-28-00	1-15	0.663	0.68	s0.584	Total Deposits $5025.33M			9-30-99	....	...	45600	Dc	v1.12	v1.30	v1.35	v1.39	....	1.54	9 Mo Sep	v1.18	v1.33	31
32◆	1942	Q0.13	12-15-99	12-1	0.49	0.52	0.387	Total Assets $6904.00M			9-30-99	150	271	126233	Dc	v1.52	□v1.62	v2.11	v2.33	....	1.99	9 Mo Sep	v1.69	v1.35	32
33	....	None Since Public			...	Nil	....	22.2	111	39.1	12-31-98	....	...	18523	Dc	v0.87	v0.50	vd1.15	vd1.28	E1.49	d7.16	6 Mo Jun	v0.54	vd5.34	33
34◆	1926	Q0.20	12-10-99	11-8	h[65]0.90	0.80	1.20	56.4	509	261	9-30-99	229	...	45051	Dc	v2.67	v5.27	v3.00	v1.63	E0.35	0.42	9 Mo Sep	v1.46	v0.25	34
35◆	1977	Div Postponed 7-30-99			0.08	Nil	0.22	13.8	1337	530	10-03-99	774	...	±81308	Dc	±v1.19	v±0.71	±v1.15	v±0.05	....	0.21	9 Mo Sep	vd0.10	v0.06	35
36◆	1994	Q0.10	11-30-99	11-17	0.40	0.40	0.36	9.24	497	123	9-30-99	385	...	23782	Dc	v1.36	v1.56	v1.79	v2.05	....	2.23	9 Mo Sep	v1.52	v1.70	36
37	1992	Q0.70	11-15-99	10-27	2.80	[66]....	[67]2.68	Total Assets $1085.06M			9-30-99	587	4300	19887	Dc	v□1.83	v2.01	v2.16	v3.39	....	1.82	9 Mo Sep	v3.13	v1.56	37
38	....	None Since Public			...	Nil	....	12.5	94.2	26.2	9-30-99	10.7	...	23875	Dc	...	...	pv[68]0.54	v[69]0.95	....	d0.23	9 Mo Sep	v0.83	vd0.35	38
39	....	None Since Public			...	Nil	....	14.7	43.5	45.1	9-30-99	248	...	41647	Dc	...	...	pv0.26	v1.00	....	d1.07	9 Mo Sep	v1.10	v∆d0.97	39
40◆	1989	Q0.02¼	12-10-99	11-22	0.09	0.09	0.08	93.6	743	334	9-30-99	737	...	91296	Dc	v0.43	v0.61	v0.69	v0.90	E1.10	0.80	9 Mo Sep	v0.61	v0.51	40
41◆	1986	Q0.17½	1-6-00	12-16	0.60	0.70	0.50	337	4235	4903	9-30-99	1154	...	177446	Dc	v0.93	v1.12	v1.37	v1.68	E2.02	1.94	9 Mo Sep	v1.09	v1.35	41
42	....	None Since Public			...	Nil	....	369	498	418	9-30-99	2710	...	53938	Dc	pd0.96	vd2.74	□vd6.10	v□d12.40	....	d13.10	9 Mo Sep	vd8.58	vd9.28	42
43	1999	0.05	11-30-99	11-17	0.05	[66]....	....	6.00	196	102	p8-31-99	p200	...	41798	Nv	...	...	...	pv1.09	....	....	9 Mo Aug	n/a	vp0.78	43
44◆	....	None Since Public			...	Nil	....	39.3	61.8	8.85	9-30-99	....	...	10823	Dc	v0.41	v0.51	v0.75	v1.00	....	1.21	9 Mo Sep	v0.71	v0.92	44
45	....	None Since Public			...	Nil	....	15.9	20.6	5.42	9-30-99	2.30	p...	★19198	Dc	...	...	...	vpd0.75		....	9 Mo Sep	n/a	vpd0.70	45
46	....	None Since Public			...	Nil	....	4.97	14.8	5.13	9-30-99	....	...	20313	Dc	vd1.90	vd1.36	vd1.73	vd1.12	....	d2.19	9 Mo Sep	vd0.70	vd1.77	46
47	....	None Since Public			...	Nil	....	174	199	48.4	9-26-99	10.5	...	±61622	Je	...	...	...	pv0.04	vd0.27	d0.53	3 Mo Sep	vd0.05	vd0.31	47
48	1992	Q0.30	12-30-99	12-17	1.50	1.20	1.20	Total Assets $87.28M			9-30-99	35.9	658	2972	Dc	v1.16	v0.50	v1.00	v2.16	....	1.57	9 Mo Sep	v1.57	v0.98	48
49	1990	Q0.40	12-30-99	12-17	2.00	1.60	1.60	Cv into 0.825 com,$20				....	799	...	Dc	...	...	...	....	....	....				49
50◆	1981	Q0.26	1-14-00	12-29	0.98	1.04	0.87	Total Deposits $4587M			9-30-99	430	...	33387	Dc	v1.82	v1.91	v2.07	v2.15	....	2.33	9 Mo Sep	v1.60	v1.78	50

◆Stock Splits & Divs By Line Reference Index [1]2-for-1,'96. [2]2-for-1,'96. [3]2-for-1,'96. [6]No adj for stk dstr,'98. [8]2-for-1,'98. [9]3-for-2,'94,'98. [12]2-for-1,'97. [13]No adj for stk dstr,'97. [14]2-for-1,'95. [17]3-for-2,'94,'99. [18]3-for-2,'95,'96. [23]2-for-1,'98. [24]2-for-1,'96. [25]2-for-1,'99. [30]2-for-1,'97:Adj for 5%,'99. [31]3-for-2,'99. [32]3-for-2,'96,'98. [34]2-for-1,'96:No adj for stk dstr,'99. [35]3-for-2,'93,'96. [36]3-for-2,'96. [40]2-for-1,'95,'96. [41]2-for-1,'95,'97. [44]2-for-1,'97. [50]5-for-4,'96,'97.

¶ S&P 500
# MidCap 400
✣ SmallCap 600
• Options

Index	Ticker	Name of Issue (Call Price of Pfd. Stocks)	Market	Com. Rank. & Pfd. Rating	Inst. Hold Cos	Inst. Hold Shs. (000)	Principal Business	Price Range 1971-97 High	1971-97 Low	1998 High	1998 Low	1999 High	1999 Low	December, 1999 Dec. Sales in 100s	Last Sale Or Bid High	Last Sale Or Bid Low	Last Sale Or Bid Last	%Div Yield	P-E Ratio	EPS 5 Yr Growth	% Annualized Total Return 12 Mo	36 Mo	60 Mo
1	OCQ	✓Oneida Ltd	NY,B,Ch	B+	89	8693	Table&cookware:indus.wire	27⅛	¾	32 3/16	12 13/16	33 1/16	13 1/16	3603	23½	21	21¾	1.8	d	Neg	49.6	29.6	26.2
2	ONEM	✓OneMain.com Inc	NNM	NR	50	3561	Internet access svcs	...	...	...	...	46¾	14 9/16	121250	19½	14 7/16	15	...	d	...	...	...	...
¶3•[1]	OKE	✓ONEOK Inc	NY,B,Ch,P	A–	270	11905	Natural gas dstr: oil & gas	40 11/16	4 13/16	44¼	29¾	37 3/16	24½	19518	29¼	25	25⅛	4.9	12	10	–27.5	–2.1	11.6
4	ONX	✓Onix Systems	AS	NR	15	729	Dgn measurem'nt instruments	...	...	16	5⅛	7⅞	4½	2984	6⅛	4⅞	6⅛	...	20	...	–3.9	...	...
5	ONDI	✓Ontrack Data Intl	NNM	NR	22	1265	Provide data recovery svcs	28	10¾	24½	6	13¾	3⅜	16403	13¾	10½	12 1/16	...	27	...	89.2	–7.0	...
6	ONT	✓ON2.com Inc	AS	NR	5	854	Video compression tech	...	...	...	...	40¾	7 1/16	80378	40¾	17	29	...	..	...	...	...	...
7•[2]	VIP	✓Open-Joint/Vimpel Commun ADS[51]	NY,Ph	NR	44	4425	Telecommunic svcs Russia	44⅞	22⅞	59 7/16	4 9/16	45⅞	12 3/16	54373	45⅞	18	44⅝	...	d	Neg	245	23.6	...
8•[3]	OMKT	✓Open Market	NNM	NR	81	10943	Dvlp software products	42¼	6½	29⅛	4¼	49⅞	11 3/16	324975	49⅞	32¾	45⅛	...	d	...	286	49.5	...
9	OTEX	✓Open Text	NNM,To	NR	55	5543	Develops network software	26½	4⅛	26⅜	10	42½	9½	45343	20	14⅛	18	...	21	NM	–26.0	37.8	...
10	OPTV	OpenTV Corp 'A'	NNM	NR	..	...	Dvlp interactive TV software	...	...	...	...	94⅛	20	105450	94⅛	55½	80¼	...	..	...	...	...	...
11	OPI	✓Opinion Research	AS	NR	20	1767	Market research info svcs	8¾	3⅛	9⅜	4⅛	9⅞	3¼	2080	9⅞	6	9	...	64	24	63.6	38.7	12.3
12	OCCF	✓Optical Cable	NNM	NR	24	533	Mfr fiber optic cables	34	2⅜	17	6½	24¾	8½	7927	22	16 7/16	20	...	..	...	64.9	20.3	...
13	OPT	✓OptiCare Health Sys	AS	NR	4		Operates eyecare centers	...	...	...	...	12½	2¾	3463	4	2¾	3½	...	..	...	...	...	...
14	OPTO	Optio Software	NNM	NR	..	...	e-business software svc	...	...	...	...	29¼	10	237587	29¼	10	23½	...	..	...	...	...	...
¶15•[4]	ORCL	✓Oracle Corp	NNM,Ch	B+	1300	671061	Mkts database mgmt softwr	28 1/16	3/16	29 15/16	11 13/16	113⅜	21	3037474	113⅜	67½	112 1/16	...	..	26	290	82.5	67.1
16	ORNGY	✓Orange PLC ADR[52]	NNM	NR	29	7695	Cellular telecommun svcs	22¼	13⅜	65¾	19¾	174⅛	62⅛	6851	174⅛	152	165½	...	..	...	187	118	...
17	ORBT	Orbit International	NSC	B–	6	76	Apparel,electronic equipment	39¾	3/16	13½	4½	6 9/16	1	3933	1⅞	1⅛	1⅜	...	13	NM	169	23.6	18.7
18	OE	✓Orbital Engine ADS[53]	NY,Ph,P	NR	8	132	Two-stroke engine technology	30½	3 5/16	7⅛	2½	5¼	1⅞	19942	5⅛	4⅛	4 5/16	...	d	–38	50.0	–7.8	–11.6
✣19•[5]	ORB	✓Orbital Sciences Corp	NY,Ph	B–	161	17219	Dvlp/mfr aerospace products	30¾	9¼	50	17⅜	45 5/16	10⅝	146578	19¼	10⅝	18 9/16	...	d	...	–57.8	2.5	–0.7
20	ORBK	✓Orbotech Ltd Ord	NNM	NR	96	12465	Mfr/svc electro-optical sys	41 1/16	1¾	31 13/16	14	81½	26 3/16	32132	81½	60	77½	...	42	29	146	101	70.3
21	ORCT	✓Orckit Communications	NNM	NR	62	6653	Digital subscriber line sys	22½	8⅝	24¼	9⅛	40½	13¾	44889	36¾	27⅛	34 5/16	...	d	–39	112	52.1	...
#22•[1]	OS	✓Oregon Steel Mills	NY,Ch,Ph,P	B–	146	18131	Mfr steel plate,steel pipe	38⅝	7 5/16	26½	9 7/16	17	6¼	41048	8¼	6¼	7 15/16	7.1	12	91	–29.4	–18.9	–9.2
✣23•[1]	ORLY	✓O'Reilly Automotive	NNM	B+	217	32157	Oper automotive parts stores	14	4⅜	24 3/16	12 5/16	27 5/16	17⅞	43596	24	19 7/16	21½	...	24	23	–8.8	39.2	28.4
✣24•[2]	ORG	✓Organogenesis Inc	AS,Ch,Ph,P	C	85	9104	Dvlp living organ equivalent	25 3/16	1¾	37 13/16	7¾	16 3/16	6 9/16	53255	12 5/16	8 1/16	8 11/16	...	d	–10	–15.2	–6.9	3.0
25	OFG	✓Oriental Finl Group	NY	B+	45	1023	Savings bank, Puerto Rico	23⅝	¾	35	22 1/16	32⅞	19 11/16	2890	22½	19 11/16	22 1/16	2.7	11	20	–28.0	23.4	35.4
26	OHC.A	✓Oriole Homes[54]Cv'A'	AS,B,Ph	C	5	145	Homes & condominium apts	19½	1 9/16	5 7/16	2⅛	2¾	1½	294	2⅜	1½	1⅝	...	8	14	–31.6	–38.9	–24.1
27	OHC.B	Class 'B'(1/10 vtg)	AS	C	11	945	in south Florida area	17½	4	5¼	2⅛	2 13/16	⅞	1623	1 3/16	1	1⅛	...	5	14	–52.6	–45.3	–29.7
28	IX	ORIX Corp ADS[56]	NY	NR	10	677	Provide financial svcs	...	...	38⅜	31⅜	123¾	29⅞	544	123¾	82½	113 7/16	...	83	...	199	...	...
29	OHB	✓Orleans Homebuilders	AS	B–	7	268	Community devel:leisure sv	14	1/16	3	15/16	2 9/16	1¼	873	1¾	1¼	1¾	...	5	31	–24.3	20.5	5.9
30	OLS	Orleans Resources	Mo	NR	..	...	Wollastonite mining	2⅞	...	2⅜	1/16	⅜	.02	10645	⅛	.02	1/16E	...	d	–48	–43.2	...	...
31	OROA	✓OroAmerica Inc	NNM	NR	19	895	Mfr,dstr 14 karat gold jewelry	18	3½	13⅝	4½	15	5½	2677	7	5¾	6¼	...	d	–38	–36.7	7.7	–4.8
32	ORTC	✓Ortec Intl	NSC	NR	8	1883	Dvp stg:replacement skin R&D	15⅛	4¾	23	5¾	14	5⅛	3383	10	6¼	7½	...	d	–5	–42.9	–10.3	...
✣33•[6]	OCA	✓Orthodontic Centers of Amer	NY,Ph	NR	233	37130	Manage orthodontic centers	22⅝	2¾	24 1/16	11¾	20⅛	10 13/16	51401	13¼	11	11 15/16	...	12	50	–38.6	–9.3	30.9
34	OLGC	✓OrthoLogic Corp	NNM	C	50	12599	Magnetic healing prod	26¾	1⅜	7¾	2¼	4 3/16	2¼	45310	3 1/16	2¼	2 9/16	...	d	–10	–23.4	–23.1	7.4
35	ORYX	Oryx Technology	NSC	NR	4	67	Designs/mfr specl components	4 1/16	¾	1½	⅜	2 9/16	1	11990	2 5/16	1⅝	1 15/16	...	d	68	47.6	–12.3	15.6
36	OSE	✓Osage Systems Group	AS	NR	3	70	Computer systems & svcs	130	.01	7½	4½	8¼	7/16	19461	1 13/16	1	1¼	...	d	...	–77.8	132	–19.7
37	OSH	✓Oshman's Sporting Gds	AS	C	11	581	Retails sporting goods	26	1⅝	9⅜	3	3⅝	1⅜	2525	2	1⅜	1 9/16	...	d	Neg	–51.9	–32.7	–28.7
38	OSIP	✓OSI Pharmaceuticals	NNM	C	22	5576	Human cancer research	12½	1 1/16	9¼	2¼	8 7/16	2 11/16	46506	8 7/16	4 1/16	7 15/16	...	d	–9	149	7.6	24.8
39	OSM	✓Osmonics, Inc	NY	B	39	5025	Reverse osmosis/ultrafiltrtn	24⅞	1/16	17½	7¾	12¼	7½	3176	9 3/16	7⅞	9 3/16	...	21	–47	8.9	–25.3	–9.2
✣40•[1]	OSTE	✓Osteotech Inc	NNM	B–	111	7357	Process transplant'n bonetissue	21 13/16	2 3/16	31 5/16	8¾	41⅛	11¾	44522	17 7/16	12⅝	13⅜	...	15	57	–56.9	42.0	35.6
41	OTR	✓OTR Express	AS	B–	7	155	Trucking-gen'l commodities	10¼	2½	8	2¾	5¼	1½	1025	2	1½	1 9/16	...	13	57	–68.8	–23.6	–29.5
42	OTTR	✓Otter Tail Power	NNM	A–	85	1899	Electric sv: Minn/Dakotas	41¼	7 1/16	42¾	30⅛	45 9/16	34	2714	41¼	37½	37½	5.3	13	4	–1.3	10.9	8.4
#43•[7]	OSSI	✓Outback Steakhouse	NNM	B+	338	51081	Oper full-svc restaurants	27 3/16	2¼	28 1/16	15 9/16	40⅛	19 13/16	184198	27½	21¾	25 15/16	...	16	19	–2.3	13.3	10.6
44	OUTL	✓Outlook Group	NNM	C	17	1539	Printing,graphic,pack'g svcs	24½	3⅞	6⅞	3⅛	5	1⅞	1686	4¾	3⅝	4¼	...	12	NM	0.0	–3.6	–18.1
#45	OSG	✓Overseas Shiphldg	NY,B,Ch,P,Ph	B–	97	10322	Major internat'l shipowner	27⅜	2 3/16	22⅞	13 1/16	17½	10½	4550	15⅛	13⅜	14 13/16	4.1	d	–27	–3.5	–0.9	–5.2
¶46•[8]	OWC	✓Owens-Corning	NY,B,Ch,P,Ph	B–	337	44991	Glass fiber/polyester resins	82½	8⅞	46⅝	25⅝	43¾	14 1/16	122778	19⅝	14 1/16	19 5/16	1.6	4	Neg	–45.0	–22.5	...
¶47•[9]	OI	✓Owens-Illinois	NY,P	NR	397	118987	Mfr glass/plastic packag'g prd	38⅜	7⅞	49	23¾	33 7/16	19 5/16	88128	25 7/16	23 1/16	25 1/16	...	13	–17	–18.2	3.3	17.9
48	Pr A	$2.375 cm Cv Pfd ([59]51.6625)	NY	B+	68	8005		...	...	55⅝	34½	44⅞	29½	5315	32 1/16	29½	31¼	7.6	..	...	...	...	...
✣49•[10]	OMI	✓Owens & Minor	NY,Ch,Ph,P	B	165	26278	Hospital supply:drug distr	18 3/16	3/16	19⅞	10	17	7 9/16	25411	9½	8	8 15/16	3.4	11	NM	–42.1	–2.9	–7.5
#50•[11]	OXHP	✓Oxford Health Plans	NNM	B–	225	43153	Hlth benefit svcs N.Y. area	89	1¾	22	5 13/16	24¼	9¾	444705	16½	10⅝	12 11/16	...	..	Neg	–14.7	–39.9	–8.3

Uniform Footnote Explanations-See Page 4. Other: [1]Ph:Cycle 2. [2]CBOE:Cycle 1. [3]ASE,CBOE:Cycle 2. [4]CBOE:Cycle3. [5]ASE,CBOE:Cycle 3. [6]ASE:Cycle 3. [7]ASE,CBOE,P:Cycle 2. [8]Ph:Cycle 3. [9]CBOE:Cycle 2. [10]P:Cycle 1. [11]CBOE,P,Ph:Cycle 2. [51]Ea ADS rep 0.75 com,5 rubles. [52]Ea ADR rep 5 ord shs Par0.20p. [53]Ea ADS rep 8 ord, A$0.50. [54]Cv into 1 Cl'B' shr. [55]Incl current amts. [56]Ea ADS rep 0.5 ord,50Yen. [57]To be determined. [58]Pfd in $M. [59]Fr 5-15-2001 scale to $50 in 2008.

Index	Cash Divs. Ea. Yr. Since	Dividends: Latest Payment Period $	Date	Ex. Div.	Total $ So Far 1999	Ind. Rate	Paid 1998	Financial Position Mil-$ Cash & Equiv.	Curr. Assets	Curr. Liab.	Balance Sheet Date	Capitalization Lg Trm Debt Mil-$	Shs. 000 Pfd.	Com.	Earnings $ Per Shr. Years End	1995	1996	1997	1998	1999	Last 12 Mos.	Interim Earnings Period	$ per Shr. 1998	1999	Index
1◆	1936	Q0.10	12-30-99	12-8	0.40	0.40	†0.50	4.26	311	156	10-30-99	111	87	16620	Ja	v1.09	v1.00	v1.71	v1.16	....	d0.16	9 Mo Oct	v0.96	vd0.36	1
2	....	None Since Public			...	Nil	....	72.4	80.2	55.3	9-30-99	4.00	...	23449	Dc	...	...	...	vpd3.57	....	d3.97	9 Mo Sep	vpd2.65	vpd3.05	2
3	1939	Q0.31	11-15-99	10-27	1.24	1.24	1.21	4.40	439	544	8-31-99	810	19946	30884	Au	1.58	v1.93	v2.13	v2.23	v2.06	2.06				3
4	....	None Since Public			...	Nil	....	5.74	106	29.1	10-02-99	....	...	14358	Dc	v0.34	v0.46	v0.79	v0.55	....	0.31	9 Mo Sep	v0.45	v0.21	4
5	....	None Since Public			...	Nil	....	27.1	35.1	5.71	9-30-99	....	...	9960	Dc	pv0.28	v0.38	v0.56	v0.52	....	0.45	9 Mo Sep	v0.43	v0.36	5
6	....	None Since Public			...	Nil	....	10.0	10.6	1.30	9-30-99	....	2000	23178	Dc	...	...	...	vpd0.14	....	....	9 Mo Sep	n/a	vd0.27	6
7	....	None Since Public			...	Nil	....	16.6	72.4	119	12-31-98	164	...	p14143	Dc	1.19	v1.90	v2.38	vd0.18	....	d0.11	9 Mo Sep	vd0.53	vd0.46	7
8	....	None Since Public			...	Nil	....	33.1	63.3	30.1	9-30-99	2.72	...	43859	Dc	pvd1.49	vpd0.96	vd1.87	vd0.91	....	d0.36	9 Mo Sep	vd0.72	vd0.17	8
9	....	None Since Public			...	Nil	....	130	183	27.3	9-30-99	....	...	24153	Je	pd1.29	d3.59	vd0.78	vd1.33	v0.85	0.87	3 Mo Sep	v0.08	v0.10	9
10	....	None Since Public			...	Nil	....	33.6	37.9	8.25	p9-30-99	....	p...	★±43762	Dc	...	...	...	....	....	....	9 Mo Sep	n/a	vpd0.26	10
11	....	None Since Public			...	Nil	....	0.31	36.6	17.9	9-30-99	46.9	...	4244	Dc	d0.39	v0.19	v0.28	v□Nil	....	0.14	9 Mo Sep	v□0.29	v□0.43	11
12◆	....	None Since Public			...	Nil	....	5.01	23.6	3.68	7-31-99	....	...	37508	Oc	p0.14	p0.19	0.20	v0.19	....	0.19	9 Mo Jul	v0.14	v0.14	12
13	....	None Since Public			...	Nil	....	3.20	25.4	25.3	9-30-99	38.5	...	8862	Dc	...	...	...	vpd0.19	....	....	9 Mo Sep	n/a	vd0.21	13
14	....	None Since Public			...	Nil	....	1.60	9.55	10.4	10-31-99	p0.05	...	★16919	Ja	...	...	...	v0.02	....	0.05	9 Mo Oct	v0.04	v0.07	14
15◆	....	None Since Public			...	Nil	....	2721	4788	2549	8-31-99	301	...	1423672	My	0.30	v0.40	v0.54	v0.54	v0.87	0.96	6 Mo Nov	v0.32	v0.41	15
16	....	None Since Public			...	Nil	....	99.2	865	768	6-30-99	3015	...	1198036	Dc	pd1.40	d1.80	vd0.98	n/a	....	....	6 Mo Jun	n/a	vd0.08	16
17◆	....	h....	5-14-71	3-25	...	Nil	....	3.14	11.7	3.43	9-30-99	3.80	...	2026	Dc	d11.34	vd2.67	v0.90	v0.81	....	0.11	9 Mo Sep	v0.79	v0.09	17
18	....	1.33%Stk	10-30-92	9-23	...	Nil	....	32.2	47.8	20.4	j6-30-99	19.6	...	323941	Je	d0.14	d1.37	vd2.68	vd2.19	vd1.44	d1.44				18
19	....	None Since Public			...	Nil	....	39.2	386	376	9-30-99	314	...	37417	Dc	□vd0.03	v0.55	v0.69	vd0.18	Ed1.00	....	9 Mo Sep	n/a	vd1.92	19
20◆	....	t0.66	1-25-93	10-20	...	Nil	....	94.7	195	51.0	9-30-98	2.69	...	20175	Dc	0.78	v1.44	v1.68	Pv1.53	....	1.85	9 Mo Sep	v1.46	v1.78	20
21	....	None Since Public			...	Nil	....	41.8	69.7	15.5	12-31-98	....	...	16828	Dc	d0.19	vd0.25	vd0.01	vd0.99	....	d1.32	9 Mo Sep	vd0.63	vd0.96	21
22	1988	Q0.14	11-30-99	11-9	0.56	0.56	0.56	0.68	240	130	9-30-99	303	...	25777	Dc	v0.62	v1.02	v0.45	v0.45	....	0.66	9 Mo Sep	v0.62	v0.83	22
23◆	....	None Since Public			...	Nil	....	3.23	350	140	9-30-99	51.7	...	50678	Dc	v0.40	v0.45	v0.55	v0.71	....	0.91	9 Mo Sep	v0.50	v0.70	23
24◆	....	None Since Public			...	Nil	....	14.0	15.6	3.58	9-30-99	17.9	...	30466	Dc	vd0.52	vd0.27	vd0.70	vd0.48	Ed0.85	d0.86	9 Mo Sep	vd0.28	vd0.66	24
25◆	1992	tQ0.15	1-15-00	12-28	t0.565	0.60	t0.469	Total Deposits $657M			9-30-99	153	1340	12776	Je	0.89	v1.06	v1.21	v1.57	v1.97	2.08	3 Mo Sep	v0.45	v0.56	25
26	....	0.20	1-12-95	12-23	...	Nil	....	Total Assets $107M			6-30-99	[55]47.8	...	±4625	Dc	v±d2.54	v±0.02	±vd4.51	v±0.02	....	0.21	9 Mo Sep	v±d0.18	v±0.01	26
27	....	0.22½	1-12-95	12-23	...	Nil		....	....	...		....	...	2761	Dc	v±d2.54	v±0.02	±vd4.51	v±0.02	....	0.21	9 Mo Sep	v±d0.18	v±0.01	27
28	1999	0.05¼	7-16-99	3-29	0.05¼ [57]	....	....	Book Value $18.15			3-31-98	15339	...	64870	Mr	v1.12	v1.18	v1.37	....	....	1.37				28
29	....	0.067	3-8-82	2-5	...	Nil	....	Total Assets $146M			9-30-99	83.0	100	11358	Je	0.10	Δ0.10	Δv0.45	v0.14	v0.36	0.38	3 Mo Sep	v0.08	v0.10	29
30◆	....	None Paid			...	Nil	....	0.84	1.58	0.35	j9-30-99	5.60	...	p220761	Mr	d0.01	vd0.02	vd0.05	vd0.50	....	jd0.15	6 Mo Sep	vd0.36	vd0.01	30
31	....	None Since Public			...	Nil	....	12.7	74.2	28.1	10-29-99	....	...	5858	Ja	v0.06	v0.35	v1.06	v1.02	....	d0.03	9 Mo Oct	v0.64	vd0.41	31
32	....	None Since Public			...	Nil	....	5.81	5.81	1.17	9-30-99	1.06	...	6563	Dc	vd4.44	vd0.64	vd1.01	vd1.43	....	d1.65	9 Mo Sep	vd0.94	vd1.16	32
33◆	....	None Since Public			...	Nil	....	5.38	111	23.0	9-30-99	42.9	...	48126	Dc	0.23	v0.33	v0.50	v0.70	E0.96	0.89	9 Mo Sep	v0.50	v□0.69	33
34◆	....	None Since Public			...	Nil	....	5.54	48.9	9.24	9-30-99	....	[58]11	27280	Dc	vd0.09	v0.11	vd0.71	vd0.71	....	d0.05	9 Mo Sep	vd0.69	vd0.03	34
35	....	None Paid			...	Nil	....	5.04	5.24	0.93	8-31-99	....	4	15522	Fb	Δd0.73	d0.19	vd0.54	vd0.05	....	d0.11	6 Mo Aug	vd0.02	vd0.08	35
36	....	None Paid			...	Nil	....	1.35	22.6	28.7	9-30-99	0.63	3	10645	Dc	...	...	vpd0.18	vd0.40	....	d1.08	9 Mo Sep	vd0.09	vd0.77	36
37	....	0.05	1-11-91	12-21	...	Nil	....	0.42	123	67.7	10-30-99	48.5	...	5827	Ja	v0.32	vd4.67	v□1.07	vd0.23	....	d1.16	9 Mo Oct	v0.05	vd0.88	37
38	....	None Since Public			...	Nil	....	21.0	24.6	4.75	6-30-99	0.32	...	21503	Sp	d0.25	d0.50	vd0.44	vd0.48	Pvd0.46	d0.46				38
39◆	....	None Since Public			...	Nil	....	17.8	87.8	54.6	9-30-99	33.0	...	14233	Dc	v0.83	v0.93	v0.68	vd0.08	....	0.43	9 Mo Sep	vd0.15	v0.36	39
40◆	....	None Since Public			...	Nil	....	21.2	45.1	11.9	9-30-99	3.62	...	14185	Dc	v0.38	vd0.03	v0.43	v0.73	....	0.89	9 Mo Sep	v0.51	v0.67	40
41	....	None Since Public			...	Nil	....	0.36	11.8	18.9	9-30-99	36.8	...	1783	Dc	vd0.09	vd0.20	v0.28	v0.48	....	0.12	9 Mo Sep	v0.38	v0.02	41
42	1938	Q0.49½	12-10-99	11-10	1.98	1.98	1.92	12.7	102	68.2	9-30-99	190	388	11925	Dc	v2.38	v2.46	v2.58	Δv2.41	....	2.97	9 Mo Sep	v□1.54	v2.10	42
43◆	....	None Since Public			...	Nil	....	70.3	112	86.8	9-30-99	0.72	...	74994	Dc	v0.79	v0.97	v0.85	v□1.29	E1.60	1.50	9 Mo Sep	v□0.95	v1.16	43
44	....	None Since Public			...	Nil	....	3.21	22.1	8.16	8-28-99	3.97	...	4556	My	0.26	d1.19	vd0.32	vd0.04	v0.30	0.36	6 Mo Nov	v0.18	v0.24	44
45	1973	Q0.15	11-23-99	10-29	0.60	0.60	0.60	48.2	97.8	52.5	9-30-99	795	...	33672	Dc	vd0.24	v0.07	v0.52	v□d0.66	....	d1.28	9 Mo Sep	v0.99	vΔ0.37	45
46	1996	Q0.07½	1-15-00	12-29	0.30	0.30	0.30	99.0	1532	2021	9-30-99	2189	...	54812	Dc	v4.41	vd5.54	v□1.17	v□d12.44	E4.75	d12.35	9 Mo Sep	v□3.53	v3.62	46
47	....	None Since Public			...	Nil	....	235	2168	1316	9-30-99	5505	9050	150125	Dc	v1.37	v1.55	□v2.01	v□0.71	E1.90	0.25	9 Mo Sep	v□2.00	v1.54	47
48	1998	Q0.59⅜	11-15-99	10-28	2.37½	2.375	1.155	Cv into 0.9491 com				....	9050	...	Dc	...	...	...	....	....	....				48
49◆	1926	Q0.07½	1-15-00	12-29	0.23	0.30	0.20	0.58	518	327	9-30-99	150	...	32709	Dc	vd0.53	v0.25	v0.60	v0.56	E0.82	0.77	9 Mo Sep	v0.36	v0.57	49
50◆	....	None Since Public			...	Nil	....	1067	1220	901	9-30-99	358	[58]321	81520	Dc	v0.71	v1.25	vd3.70	vd7.79	....	Nil	9 Mo Sep	vd7.57	v0.22	50

◆**Stock Splits & Divs By Line Reference Index** [1]3-for-2,'97. [12]2-for-1(twice),'96. [15]3-for-2,'95,'96,'97,'99:To split 2-for-1,ex Jan 19,'00. [17]1-for-3 REVERSE,'99. [20]3-for-2,'99. [23]2-for-1,'97,'99. [24]5-for-4,'95,'97(twice),'98. [25]6-for-5,'96:5-for-4,'97:4-for-3,'94,'98. [30]3-for-2,'96. [33]2-for-1(twice),'96. [34]2-for-1,'96. [39]3-for-2,'94. [40]3-for-2,'99. [43]3-for-2,'94,'99. [49]3-for-2,'94. [50]2-for-1,'95,'96.

¶ S&P 500 # MidCap 400 ✣ SmallCap 600 • Options

Index	Ticker	Name of Issue (Call Price of Pfd. Stocks)	Market	Com. Rank. & Pfd. Rating	Inst. Hold Cos	Inst. Hold Shs. (000)	Principal Business	Price Range 1971-97 High	1971-97 Low	1998 High	1998 Low	1999 High	1999 Low	Dec. Sales in 100s	December, 1999 Last Sale Or Bid High	Low	Last	%Div Yield	P-E Ratio	EPS 5 Yr Growth	% Annualized Total Return 12 Mo	36 Mo	60 Mo
✣1	OXM	✓Oxford Indus	NY,Ch	B+	89	4149	Mfr wearing apparel	38¾	1¾	37 11/16	22½	29¾	19	1610	21 5/16	19	19 13/16	4.2	7	42	-27.3	-3.3	1.6
2	OTF	✓Oxford Tax Exempt Fund II LP	AS	NR	13	18	Investment/finance svcs	27⅝	20	28⅞	22½	26	22 7/16	2766	24⅞	22 7/16	22⅝	9.5	8	...	4.6	...	...
✣3•[1]	PCMS	✓P-COM Inc	NNM	NR	137	27211	Wireless telecommun svcs	29⅜	3¾	21¼	2 5/16	10⅜	3 5/16	388420	10	5½	8⅞	...	13	Neg	122	-15.8	...
4	PAB	✓PAB Bankshares	AS,Ph	NR	4	68	General banking Valdosta, GA	12 1/16	7½	27⅜	11 11/16	19⅝	13	319	15⅛	13¼	13 5/16	3.1	16	-3	-26.9	9.1	...
5	PACW	✓Pac-West Telecommun	NNM,Sg	NR	..	...	Communic svc-western U.S.	....	....	....	....	30	10	61553	27	20½	26½	...	..	...	...	...	...
¶6•[2]	PCAR	✓PACCAR Inc	NNM	B+	400	36058	Mfr trucks,ind'l/oilfield eq	59½	1⅜	66¾	37	63	39½	197972	46⅝	40¾	44 5/16	e2.7	7	21	13.6	14.2	21.6
7	PCTH	✓Pacific Aerospace & Elect	NNM	NR	8	462	Electronics/aluminum parts	7	1 15/16	7	1 7/16	3	⅝	54221	1½	¾	1¼	...	d	-14	-45.9	-24.8	...
#8•[3]	BOH	✓Pacific Century Finl	NY,Ch,Ph,P	A-	234	52264	Commercial bkg,Hawaii	28 1/16	15/16	25⅞	14¾	24 15/16	17⅜	40706	20 7/16	17⅜	18 11/16	3.6	10	2	-20.7	-0.9	11.4
9	PGEX	✓Pacific Gateway Exchange	NNM	NR	120	12740	Telecommunications svcs	55½	12	62	21⅛	48½	13⅛	127149	18⅝	15	17 1/16	...	23	85	-64.5	-22.4	...
10	PGP	✓Pacific Gateway Prop	AS	B-	8	383	Real estate investments	20½	2⅛	11⅞	4¼	10	6	298	10	9¼	10	4.8	..	-46	66.3	49.6	22.2
11	PAG	✓Pacific Gulf Properties	NY,Ch,P	NR	132	12690	Real estate investment trust	24⅝	12¾	23 15/16	16¼	23 7/16	17½	15116	21	19⅜	20¼	8.7	7	52	9.8	9.6	15.7
✣12•[4]	PSUN	✓Pacific Sunwear of Calif	NNM	NR	..	...	Casual clothing retail chain	15 5/16	1 1/16	26¼	8	36¾	9 15/16	120479	36¾	29⅞	31⅞	...	33	60	207	64.6	62.0
#13•[2]	PHSY	✓PacifiCare Health Sys	NNM	B	210	34638	Health maintenance svcs	98¾	1 5/16	88⅞	46¾	98⅛	31⅛	102141	55	44¾	53	...	9	-15	-27.1	-13.3	-4.0
14	PCQ	PacifiCorp 8.375% 'QUIDS'[54]	NY	....[55]	2	11	Qtly Income Debt Securities	26¾	24¼	26 7/16	25⅛	26 1/16	21½	1396	24¼	21½	22½	9.3	..	...	-3.7	4.3	...
15	PCX	PacifiCorp 8.55%'QUIDS'[54]	NY	NR	6	50	Qtly Income Debt Securities	26¼	24¼	25¾	24 15/16	25⅝	23	272	24¾	23	23⅛B	9.2	..	...	-8.6	-0.5	...
16	ICED	✓Packaged Ice	NNM	NR	37	7386	Mfr/dstr packaged ice pds	....	....	....	....	8⅝	2⅜	24786	3 13/16	3	3¼	...	..	...	...	...	...
17	PKTR	✓Packeteer Inc	NNM	NR	71	3691	Network software prod	....	....	....	....	77½	15	34822	77½	50¼	71	...	..	...	...	...	...
¶18•[5]	PTV	✓Pactiv Corp	NY	NR	..	...	Specialty packaging prd	....	....	....	....	14½	9 5/16	143538	11⅛	9 5/16	10⅝	...	..	...	...	...	...
19•[4]	PAGE	✓Paging Network	NNM,Ch	C	116	49041	Provides paging svcs in U.S.	29¼	5 5/16	16⅝	3 9/16	7	⅝	1285055	1¾	⅝	13/16	...	d	-38	-82.7	-62.4	-45.5
¶20•[6]	PWJ	✓Paine Webber Group	NY,B,Ch,P,Ph	B+	395	86899	Major securities broker	37⅜	5/16	53⅜	20⅜	49¾	31¾	104578	40	35⅞	38 13/16	1.1	10	72	1.6	29.4	33.7
21	SIS	Paine Webber Gp Stk Index Sec	AS	NR	3	1241	Stock Index Return Securities	20 13/16	8½	23⅝	17	28½	21¾	621	28⅛	26⅛	28½	...	..		20.6	25.3	26.6
22•[6]	PAIR	✓PairGain Technologies	NNM	NR	167	32522	Mfr telecommunications prd	43¼	1¾	24⅜	6	18 9/16	7 13/16	293330	17¼	13	14 3/16	...	..	18	84.6	-22.5	32.0
23	PTN	Palatin Technologies	AS	NR	9	567	Dvp stg: Medical imaging sys	10¾	5¼	9 1/16	1⅜	7⅛	2¼	16394	3¾	2¼	2½	...	d	...	-39.4	...	...
¶24•[7]	PLL	✓Pall Corp	NY,B,P	B+	452	93999	Fine filters,fluid contr eq	29⅜	⅛	26⅝	19⅜	26 3/16	15¾	55407	24¼	19⅞	21 9/16	3.0	44	-17	-12.1	-2.9	5.4
25	PCN	✓Pameco Corp'A'	NY,Ph	NR	24	2449	Distr heat,cooling,refrig sys	22¾	14	24	8½	11¾	3 5/16	3299	4⅜	3 5/16	4	...	d	Neg	-65.4	...	...
26	PNP	✓Pan Pacific Retail Prop	NY,Ph	NR	100	7630	Real estate investment trust	22	19½	22¾	16½	20⅝	15⅛	7937	17	15⅛	16 5/16	9.8	11	...	-11.0	...	...
27	PANA	✓PANACO Inc	BB	C	4	6524	Oil & gas explor,dev,prod'n	6⅜	1	4¾	¾	1⅜	5/16	35677	7/16	5/16	⅜	...	d	Neg	-62.0	-58.7	-38.8
28•[8]	PB	✓Panamerican Beverages'A'	NY,Ch	NR	142	57273	Soft drink bottler Latin Amer	40	7½	41 15/16	14 13/16	27⅞	14 9/16	40944	23½	18	20 9/16	1.2	..	Neg	-4.5	-3.1	6.6
29	SPOT	✓PanAmSat Corp	NNM	NR	108	12329	Satellite communic svcs	46¼	28	66⅛	26½	65½	26⅜	120365	65½	41⅝	59⅜	...	70	...	52.5	...	...
30	PVI	✓Panavision Inc	NY,Ch,Ph	NR	16	208	Mfr hi-quality film camera sy	28¼	16	28	11⅞	12 13/16	4⅛	961	4¾	4⅛	4 11/16	...	d	Neg	-62.1	-39.1	...
31	PCP	✓PanCanadian Petroleum	To,Mo,Vc	B+	6	2418	Crude oil & natural gas	30 11/16	⅞	24	16	25¾	15	12197	23 11/16	20 9/16	23	1.7	23	-6	35.6	-3.6	4.4
32	PAMX	✓Pancho's Mexican Buffet	NSC	C	7	151	Cafeteria-style restaurants	47⅝	1⅛	7⅛	1 11/16	4¾	1 15/16	1421	3⅛	2 11/16	2⅞	...	2	-14	62.3	-24.4	-30.4
33	PTRY	✓Pantry Inc	NNM	NR	29	7281	Oper convenience stores	....	....	....	....	18 11/16	7⅛	22829	15⅛	7⅛	14⅛	...	20	...	...	...	...
#34•[6]	PZZA	✓Papa John's Intl	NNM	NR	266	24066	Franchises pizza restaurants	39½	5¾	45⅞	26¼	47⅜	21¼	327037	37⅝	21¼	26 1/16	...	17	40	-40.9	-8.3	15.9
35	PTC	✓PAR Technology	NY,Ch,Ph	B	19	1184	Retail/defense computer sys	29½	2⅜	9½	5⅛	9¾	4⅛	5179	5⅛	4 7/16	4¾	...	9	-29	-20.8	-30.0	-6.4
36	PLS	Paracelsus Healthcare	NY,Ph	NR	24	7749	Own,oper hlthcare facilities	10½	2 13/16	5⅛	1¼	1⅝	¼	23008	¾	¼	7/16	...	d	Neg	-72.0	-50.6	...
37•[9]	PDYN	✓Paradyne Networks	NNM	NR	73	14166	Communic hardware/software	....	....	....	....	58	17	135980	33¼	25	27¼	...	..	...	...	...	...
38	PLLL	✓Parallel Petroleum	NNM	C	13	913	Oil & gas:acq,dvlp,drilling	8⅛	1/32	7 1/16	1⅜	3	1	13849	2⅛	1⅜	1 11/16	...	d	Neg	17.4	-28.9	-10.1
¶39•[10]	PMTC	✓Parametric Technology	NNM,Ph	B+	475	214262	Mechanical design softwr prd	32⅛	½	36 5/16	8½	35 15/16	11 11/16	1145583	35 15/16	21¾	27 1/16	...	63	7	66.5	1.9	25.9
✣40•[11]	PRXL	✓PAREXEL Intl	NNM	NR	148	15628	Pharmaceutical R&D	44¾	9⅜	45½	20¼	29⅜	7⅝	36503	12 9/16	10⅞	11 13/16	...	20	NM	-52.8	-22.9	...
✣41•[4]	PKE	✓Park Electrochemical	NY,Ch,Ph,P	B	145	6869	Printed circuit materials	37⅞	¼	32½	10 15/16	38 9/16	23⅛	15872	35 15/16	23⅝	26 9/16	1.2	13	1	-6.2	6.6	13.8
42	PRK	✓Park National Corp	AS,Ch	A	45	2139	General banking, Ohio	93⅞	12⅝	102⅝	80 15/16	116	86 11/16	503	116	94	96	s2.7	21	13	5.3	28.9	23.1
#43•[6]	PPE	✓Park Place Entertainment	NY	NR	270	161655	Own/operate casinos	....	....	7 7/16	6	14	6 1/16	255999	12 15/16	11	12½	...	26	...	96.1	...	...
44•[9]	PKD	✓Parker Drilling	NY,B,Ch,Ph,P	B-	99	14547	Land contract drilling sv	36¾	1 5/16	13 3/16	2 13/16	5⅝	2¼	117327	4	3	3 3/16	...	..	...	0.0	-30.8	-7.7
¶45•[1]	PH	✓Parker-Hannifin	NY,B,Ch,P,Ph	B+	478	85069	Fluid pwr systems & comp	51¼	1 11/16	52⅝	26 9/16	51 7/16	29½	81250	51 7/16	44⅞	51 5/16	1.3	18	8	59.1	27.8	22.7
46	PRKR	✓ParkerVision Inc	NNM	NR	32	683	Dvlp video camera control sys	32⅛	2½	27¼	10 13/16	39 1/16	18½	13853	31	22	30¾	...	d	-7	30.9	31.6	52.3
47	PKY	✓Parkway Properties	NY	NR	110	6998	Real estate investment trust	34 15/16	3 3/16	35	25 13/16	34 11/16	26⅜	8623	29⅝	26¾	28 13/16	6.9	15	8	-1.9	8.9	33.3
48	PRLX	✓Parlex Corp	NNM	B-	25	1218	Mfrs electronic components	31¼	1 5/16	21½	8	28 11/16	9¼	9037	28 11/16	18 11/16	26 5/16	...	30	23	163	54.5	25.5
49	PRE	✓PartnerRe Ltd	NY,Ph	NR	138	31216	Prop catastrophe re-insur	46⅜	18½	52½	33⅝	46 3/16	28 9/16	23764	32½	29 5/16	32 7/16	3.1	12	1	-27.1	0.6	11.6
50	PGNS	✓PathoGenesis Corp	NNM	NR	95	6067	Dvp stage:drug R&D	40¾	9¼	61½	22	59	10 1/16	28924	23	17¼	21 7/16	...	d	NM	-63.0	-0.5	...

Uniform Footnote Explanations-See Page 4. Other: [1]Ph:Cycle 2. [2]CBOE:Cycle 2. [3]ASE,P:Cycle 2. [4]Ph:Cycle 3. [5]ASE,Ph:Cycle 2. [6]CBOE:Cycle 1. [7]CBOE:Cycle 3. [8]ASE,CBOE:Cycle 1. [9]CBOE,Ph:Cycle 1. [10]CBOE,P,Ph:Cycle 2. [11]ASE,Ph:Cycle 3. [51]Incl current amts. [52]Fiscal Sep'95 & prior. [53]12 Mo Dec'96:Sep'96 earn $2.27. [54]Junior Subordinated Deferrable Interest Debs. [55]Rated A-by S&P. [56]Pfd in $M. [57]To be determined. [58]10 Mo Jun'96. [59]Fiscal Sep'95. [60]Fiscal Aug'98 & prior. [61]®$4.50,'96.

Splits ◆ Index	Cash Divs. Ea. Yr. Since	Dividends: Latest Payment Period $	Date	Ex. Div.	Total $ So Far 1999	Ind. Rate	Paid 1998	Financial Position Mil-$ Cash& Equiv.	Curr. Assets	Curr. Liab.	Balance Sheet Date	Capitalization Lg Trm Debt Mil-$	Shs. 000 Pfd.	Com.	Earnings $ Per Shr. Years End	1995	1996	1997	1998	1999	Last 12 Mos.	Interim Earnings Period	$ per Shr. 1998	1999	Index
1	1960	Q0.21	11-27-99	11-10	0.84	0.84	0.80	9.95	280	130	8-27-99	40.7	...	7721	My	1.22	v0.25	v2.23	v2.75	v3.11	2.98	6 Mo Nov	v1.61	v1.48	1
2	1997	Q0.54	2-14-00	12-29	2.06	2.16	2.01	Total Assets $318.4M			9-30-99	52.6	...	7337	Dc	...	1.95	v2.18	v2.56	....	2.72	9 Mo Sep	v1.82	v1.98	2
3◆	....	None Since Public			...	Nil	....	14.0	122	84.3	9-30-99	64.2	...	64474	Dc	v0.11	v0.22	v0.43	vΔd1.44	E0.66	d2.34	9 Mo Sep	vd1.22	□d2.12	3
4◆	1996	Q0.10¼	1-14-00	12-29	0.36½	0.41	0.24¼	Total Deposits $414M			9-30-99	49.4	...	8290	Dc	1.07	v0.60	v0.72	v0.78	....	0.82	9 Mo Sep	v0.60	v0.64	4
5	....	None Since Public			...	Nil	....	38.9	68.2	23.6	6-30-99	150	p...	★33410	Dc	...	...	...	vpd0.04	....	....	6 Mo Jun	n/a	vp0.04	5
6◆	1943	Q0.30	3-3-00	2-16	†2.40	1.20	†2.10	Total Assets $7655M			9-30-99	3387	...	78323	Dc	v3.25	v2.59	v4.41	v5.30	E6.20	6.58	9 Mo Sep	v3.84	v5.12	6
7	....	None Paid			...	Nil	....	2.61	56.5	22.2	8-31-99	81.8	...	19695	My	vd0.41	vd0.16	v0.17	v0.27	vd0.74	d0.53	3 Mo Aug	vd0.29	vd0.08	7
8◆	1899	Q0.17	12-14-99	11-16	0.68	0.68	0.65¾	Total Deposits $9290.39M			9-30-99	795	...	80243	Dc	v1.45	v1.62	v1.72	v1.32	E1.81	1.61	9 Mo Sep	v0.89	v1.18	8
9	....	None Since Public			...	Nil	....	15.0	166	182	9-30-99	....	...	19488	Dc	pv0.12	v0.34	v0.64	v0.97	....	0.74	9 Mo Sep	v0.75	v0.52	9
10	1998	0.15	12-30-99	12-8	0.48	0.48	0.05	Total Assets $62.5M			9-30-99	44.8	300	3934	Dc	□vd0.64	vΔ2.58	vd0.44	v0.14	....	0.01	9 Mo Sep	v0.10	vd0.03	10
11	1994	Q0.44	1-14-00	12-29	1.72	1.76	1.68	Total Assets $881M			9-30-99	[51]413	2763	20460	Dc	v1.68	vd0.02	v1.47	v2.76	....	2.78	9 Mo Sep	v1.24	v1.26	11
12◆	....	None Since Public			...	Nil	....	12.1	90.8	31.6	10-31-99	....	...	31346	Ja	v0.10	v0.26	v0.53	v0.73	....	0.98	9 Mo Oct	v0.49	v0.74	12
13	....	None Since Public			...	Nil	....	1200	1656	1206	9-30-99	625	...	43571	Dc	±[52]3.62	v±[53]2.39	±vd0.75	v±4.40	E6.10	5.92	9 Mo Sep	v±3.12	v4.64	13
14	1995	Q0.523	12-31-99	12-28	2.094	2.094	2.094	Co option redm fr 5-31-2000 at $25				110	...	...	Dc	...	...	...	....	....	....	Mature 6-30-2035			14
15	1997	Q0.534	12-31-99	12-13	1.603	2.138	1.603	Co option redm at $25				55.8	...	...	Dc	...	...	...	....	....	....	Mature 12-31-2025			15
16	....	None Since Public			...	Nil	....	2.40	41.9	34.6	9-30-99	316	[56]28	19286	Dc	...	...	vpd0.85	Pvd2.35	....	....	9 Mo Sep	n/a	v0.10	16
17	....	None Since Public			...	Nil	....	57.8	62.3	8.75	9-30-99	0.94	p...	★26790	Dc	...	...	...	vpd0.49	....	....	6 Mo Jun	n/a	vd0.72	17
18	....	Plan qtly div			...	[57]....	....	18.0	1031	1703	p6-30-99	1186	...	171356	Dc	...	...	...	pv0.39	....	....	6 Mo Jun	n/a	vp0.28	18
19◆	....	None Since Public			...	Nil	....	102	203	233	9-30-99	1999	...	103960	Dc	vd0.43	vd1.02	□vd1.38	vd1.57	Ed1.20	d2.26	9 Mo Sep	vd1.20	v□d1.89	19
20◆	1975	Q0.11	1-5-00	12-1	0.44	0.44	0.44	Total Assets $56344.13M			9-30-99	5362	[56]190	142717	Dc	v0.35	v2.24	v2.56	v2.72	E3.80	3.50	9 Mo Sep	v2.10	v2.88	20
21	....	....			...	....	....	Based on S&P Midcap 400 as defined				....	...	2800	Dc	...	...	...	....	....	....	Due 6-2-2000			21
22◆	....	None Since Public			...	Nil	....	199	287	29.2	9-30-99	1.74	...	71184	Dc	v0.02	v0.47	v0.63	v0.53	ENil	0.06	9 Mo Sep	v0.48	v0.01	22
23	....	None Since Public			...	Nil	....	11.5	12.9	2.61	9-30-99	....	752	7244	Je	...	‡[58]d1.82	vd2.80	vd3.15	Pvd2.02	d1.56	3 Mo Sep	vd0.66	vd0.20	23
24	1974	Q0.16	11-15-99	10-25	0.64	0.64	0.62	110	695	522	10-30-99	102	...	124003	Jl	□1.04	1.21	v0.53	v0.75	v0.41	0.49	3 Mo Oct	v□0.12	v0.20	24
25	....	None Since Public			...	Nil	....	0.14	165	86.9	8-31-99	77.2	...	±9209	Fb	v0.83	pv1.71	±v1.08	v±d0.02	....	d1.35	6 Mo Aug	v±1.11	v±d0.22	25
26	1997	Q0.40	1-21-00	12-20	1.58	1.60	1.50¼	Total Assets $762.38M			9-30-99	238	...	21253	Dc	...	pn/a	v□0.55	v1.35	....	1.48	9 Mo Sep	v1.00	v1.13	26
27	....	0.03	4-15-91	4-16	...	Nil	....	5.69	15.5	23.3	9-30-99	131	...	23986	Dc	vd0.81	vd0.16	□v0.05	vd1.96	....	d2.11	9 Mo Sep	vd0.71	v□d0.86	27
28◆	1993	Q0.06	12-30-99	12-21	0.24	0.24	0.24	131	485	679	12-31-98	771	...	129645	Dc	v±0.87	v±1.21	v±1.43	v±0.92	E0.08	d0.22	9 Mo Sep	v±0.74	v±d0.40	28
29	....	None Paid			...	Nil	....	6.83	442	107	9-30-99	2802	...	149289	Dc	...	pv0.37	v□p0.80	v0.83	....	0.85	9 Mo Sep	v0.62	v0.64	29
30	....	None Since Public			...	Nil	....	5.72	58.3	41.6	9-30-99	472	...	8056	Dc	pv0.36	v0.84	v1.03	vd4.35	....	d2.48	9 Mo Sep	vd3.85	vd1.98	30
31◆	1960	gQ0.10	12-31-99	12-6	g0.40	0.40	g0.40	38.6	631	447	j9-30-99	1118	...	251735	Dc	0.91	v1.38	v1.31	v0.59	....	j1.01	9 Mo Sep	v0.38	v0.80	31
32◆	....	Div Omitted 4-27-98			...	Nil	....	1.24	2.16	4.99	9-30-99	0.22	...	1464	Sp	d3.66	d0.27	vd3.21	vd8.55	v1.29	1.29				32
33	....	None Since Public			...	Nil	....	61.2	155	153	6-24-99	425	...	★18111	Sp	...	...	...	pv0.26	Pv□0.72	0.72				33
34◆	....	None Since Public			...	Nil	....	45.5	79.5	55.0	9-26-99	0.93	...	30444	Dc	v0.44	v0.65	v0.91	v□1.25	E1.50	1.59	9 Mo Sep	v□0.82	v1.16	34
35	....	None Since Public			...	Nil	....	1.03	79.7	27.9	9-30-99	....	...	8223	Dc	v0.58	v0.69	vd0.99	v0.14	....	0.55	9 Mo Sep	vd0.10	v0.31	35
36	....	None Since Public			...	Nil	....	5.54	112	88.2	9-30-99	556	...	57668	Dc	pv[59]0.12	v□d5.75	vd0.12	v□d0.09	....	d0.39	9 Mo Sep	vΔ0.06	vd0.24	36
37	....	None Since Public			...	Nil	....	61.1	109	28.1	9-30-99	0.29	...	30816	Dc	...	...	v0.81	vd0.14	....	0.09	9 Mo Sep	vd0.11	v0.12	37
38	....	None Since Public			...	Nil	....	1.18	7.61	6.81	9-30-99	18.0	975	18332	Dc	v0.01	v0.28	v0.15	vd0.73	....	d0.72	9 Mo Sep	vNil	v0.01	38
39◆	....	None Since Public			...	Nil	....	326	617	415	7-03-99	....	...	269257	Sp	0.30	0.52	v0.32	v□0.38	vP0.43	0.43				39
40◆	....	None Since Public			...	Nil	....	98.3	293	157	9-30-99	....	...	25265	Je	d6.31	v0.39	v0.56	v0.38	v0.62	0.58	3 Mo Sep	v0.22	v0.18	40
41◆	1985	Q0.08	2-1-00	12-31	0.32	0.32	0.32	136	240	65.8	8-29-99	100	...	10436	Fb	v2.11	v1.58	v2.07	v1.38	....	2.04	9 Mo Nov	v0.89	v1.55	41
42◆	1986	Q0.65	1-3-00	12-21	s2.286	2.60	1.829	Total Deposits $1978.46M			9-30-99	0.08	...	9734	Dc	v2.81	v3.22	v3.81	v4.22	....	4.56	9 Mo Sep	v3.28	v3.62	42
43	....	None Paid			...	Nil	....	215	532	423	9-30-99	2521	...	304879	Dc	...	...	Pv0.26	vp0.42	E0.49	0.36	9 Mo Sep	vp0.45	v□0.39	43
44	....	0.01	2-17-87	1-28	...	Nil	....	20.8	135	78.0	9-30-99	629	...	77273	Dc	0.07	0.07	v0.23	v[60]0.36	....	....	9 Mo Sep	n/a	vd0.32	44
45◆	1949	Q0.17	12-3-99	11-19	0.68	0.68	0.60	64.4	1811	741	9-30-99	718	...	111994	Je	1.97	v2.14	v2.44	v□2.88	v2.83	2.79	3 Mo Sep	v0.71	v0.67	45
46	....	None Since Public			...	Nil	....	15.1	21.5	2.51	9-30-99	....	...	11779	Dc	vd0.43	vd0.17	vd0.28	vd0.41	....	d0.65	9 Mo Sep	vd0.29	vd0.53	46
47◆	1986	Q0.50	12-28-99	12-10	1.90	2.00	1.60	Total Assets $640.08M			9-30-99	294	2650	10101	Dc	v4.16	v3.81	v2.01	v2.21	....	1.94	9 Mo Sep	v1.72	v1.45	47
48◆	....	None Since Public			...	Nil	....	2.01	32.1	11.8	9-26-99	2.28	...	4807	Je	0.41	v0.21	v0.57	v0.71	v0.63	0.87	3 Mo Sep	v0.04	v0.28	48
49	1994	Q0.25	12-1-99	11-17	1.00	1.00	0.86	Equity per shr $36.74			12-31-97	....	10000	53842	Dc	4.07	v[61]4.58	v4.69	Pv4.34	....	2.73	9 Mo Sep	v3.29	v1.68	49
50	....	None Since Public			...	Nil	....	40.1	64.7	12.0	9-30-99	....	...	16447	Dc	vd2.20	vd1.66	vd2.10	v0.11	Ed0.44↓	d0.32	9 Mo Sep	vd0.06	vd0.49	50

◆**Stock Splits & Divs By Line Reference Index** [3]2-for-1,'95,'97. [4]2-for-1,'98. [6]15%,'94:2-for-1,'97. [8]3-for-2,'94:2-for-1,'97. [12]3-for-2,'96,'97,'98,'99. [19]2-for-1,'95. [20]3-for-2,'94,'97. [22]2-for-1(twice),'96. [28]2-for-1,'97. [31]2-for-1,'97. [32]1-for-3 REVERSE,'99. [34]3-for-2,'96(twice). [39]2-for-1,'96,'98. [40]2-for-1,'97. [41]2-for-1,'95. [42]Adj for 5%,'99. [45]3-for-2,'95,'97. [47]3-for-2,'96. [48]3-for-2,'97.

¶ S&P 500
# MidCap 400
✣ SmallCap 600
• Options

Index	Ticker	Name of Issue (Call Price of Pfd. Stocks)	Market	Com. Rank. & Pfd. Rating	Inst. Hold Cos	Inst. Hold Shs. (000)	Principal Business	Price Range 1971-97 High	1971-97 Low	1998 High	1998 Low	1999 High	1999 Low	December, 1999 Dec. Sales in 100s	Last Sale Or Bid High	Low	Last	%Div Yield	P-E Ratio	EPS 5 Yr Growth	% Annualized Total Return 12 Mo	36 Mo	60 Mo
1	POG	✓Patina Oil & Gas	NY,Ch,Ph,P	NR	41	8480	Oil & gas explor,dvlp,prod'n	10⅝	6⅛	8	2¼	9⅛	2 11/16	11184	8⅝	7¼	8⅝	0.9	d	Neg	196	−1.8	...
2	Pr	7.125% cm Cv Pfd([51]26.247)	NY,Ch	CALL	10	581		33	22¼	29⅝	17	28½	15½	656	26⅛	25½	25⅞B	...	..	...	...	...	...
3	WS	Wrrt(Pur 1com at$12.50)	NY	....	6	265		3	15/16	1⅝	¼	1 9/16	¼	674	¾	½	⅝	...	..	...	...	...	...
4	PATK	✓Patrick Indus	NNM	B	51	2861	Dstr wall/ceiling panels:mfg	20⅛	⅛	17	13¼	16⅛	7 5/16	7830	14⅛	8¾	9¼	1.7	6	−1	−39.2	−14.2	4.0
✣5•[1]	PDCO	✓Patterson Dental	NNM	B+	284	20868	Dstr dental supplies & equip	30½	7	46⅜	28⅛	50⅛	33⅛	38814	47½	39⅜	42⅝	...	25	19	−2.0	31.4	25.3
6•[2]	PTEN	✓Patterson Energy	NNM	NR	108	15775	Oil&gas contract drilling	32⅝	1½	20	3 7/16	16¾	2⅝	147255	14 1/16	9⅞	13	...	d	Neg	220	27.0	50.8
7•[3]	PAUH	✓Paul Harris Stores	NNM	NR	40	4089	Retail womens apparel	30⅝	1	16	5⅛	8½	2 7/16	34506	3⅜	2 9/16	2¾	...	8	16	−66.2	−46.3	−1.7
✣8•[4]	PXR	✓Paxar Corp	NY	B+	128	23184	Mfr/mkts product ID systems	21 1/16	⅛	15½	7 13/16	11½	6¾	23666	9 5/16	8	8 7/16	...	13	7	−5.6	−15.1	10.8
9•[1]	PAX	✓Paxson Communications 'A'	AS,Ch	NR	88	13133	Radio/TV broadcstg,programs	22⅛	6⅝	13 13/16	5 3/16	17 7/16	7⅝	30871	12	10½	11 15/16	...	d	−13	29.9	15.5	...
¶10•[5]	PAYX	✓Paychex Inc	NNM	A+	600	142725	Computer payroll acctg svcs	23	3/16	36 11/16	20 1/16	44⅞	23 9/16	246550	43 13/16	38⅛	40	0.9	61	32	18.0	39.4	51.1
#11•[1]	PSS	✓Payless ShoeSource	NY,P	NR	278	22568	Footwear retailer U.S.	67⅞	20	77	37	59 13/16	40	31737	47¾	40	47	...	11	...	−0.8	7.8	...
12	PBOC	✓PBOC Holdings	NNM	NR	46	6055	Savings bank, California	....	....	14¾	7¾	11⅛	7⅝	21692	9½	7⅞	9 7/16	...	5	...	−7.9	...	...
13	PCTI	✓PC-Tel Inc	NNM	NR	..	...	Dvlp data communic solutions	....	....	....	....	54	17	41927	54	34⅝	52½	...	..	...	...	...	...
14	PCOR	✓pcOrder.com Inc'A'	NNM	NR	45	1543	Online retail computer pds	....	....	....	....	94	21	79779	74¾	39⅞	51	...	d	...	...	...	...
15	PDSF	✓PDS Financial	NNM	NR	7	323	Finance gaming eqp.furniture	8½	1	10½	2	5	1	4833	1 13/16	1	1 11/16	...	d	−36	−46.0	−1.2	−21.9
16	CRA	✓PE Corp-Celera Genomics Grp	NY	NR	153	18840	Sale & support genomic info	....	....	....	....	192 13/16	14 3/16	132565	192 13/16	59¾	149	...	d	...	...	...	...
¶17•[6]	PEB	✓PE Corp-PE Biosystems Grp	NY,B,Ch,P,Ph	B	497	90759	Biotechnology R&D/software svcs	43 1/16	3⅝	50 5/16	27¼	125⅞	43 15/16	109820	125⅞	81⅜	120 5/16	0.3	53	42	...	...	...
18	PAE	✓Peace Arch Entertainment'B'	AS,To	NR	3	61	Dvlp,mkt TV programming	....	....	....	....	5 3/16	2¾	2241	5⅛	2¾	5	...	6	...	...	...	...
19	PTT	Peak Trends Tr'TrENDS'2001	AS	NR	5	1474	Trust Enhanced Dividend Sec	....	....	15¾	7⅞	11½	3⅞	2887	9⅜	7⅝	8⅝	...	..	...	6.8	...	...
20	PY	✓Pechiney[54]ADS[55]	NY,Ch,Ph,P	NR	22	4741	Aluminum production/products	26⅛	16½	25¼	14⅛	36 7/16	15 11/16	4987	36 7/16	29¼	36 5/16	1.0	16	...	129	24.6	...
¶21•[7]	PE	✓PECO Energy	NY,B,C,Ch,P,Ph	B	587	95906	Elec & gas:Phila/S.E. Penna	33½	9	42 3/16	18⅞	50½	30¾	139851	35⅛	31⅞	34¾	2.9	12	1	−14.6	16.5	13.1
✣22	PDX	✓Pediatrix Medical Group	NY,Ch	NR	151	14970	Physician mgmt svs-NICU	64¾	18½	60⅞	32 3/16	65 9/16	6	59988	9¾	6 9/16	7	...	4	34	−88.3	−42.6	...
23	PMFG	✓Peerless Mfg	NNM	B	17	296	Mfr industrial filters	25	1 7/16	15⅜	9	14½	8¾	582	13	9¼	13	3.8	10	20	22.1	5.8	8.1
24•[2]	PRLS	✓Peerless Systems	NNM	NR	52	6498	Digital document pd softwr	23	8½	24⅜	2 13/16	15½	5⅞	45682	10¼	7 11/16	7¾	...	24	...	−8.8	−23.0	...
25	PGTV	✓Pegasus Communications'A'	NNM	NR	118	9786	Broadcast/satellite/cable T.V.	25½	8⅛	26⅝	10⅝	102¾	21 3/16	35616	102¾	65⅜	97¾	...	d	...	290	92.3	...
26	PEGA	✓Pegasystems Inc	NNM	NR	39	3358	Customer svc mgmt softwr	40	10	31⅞	3 7/16	13½	3⅝	60398	13½	7¼	11¼	...	d	Neg	171	−28.0	...
27	PFI	Pelican Financial	AS	NR	..	...	Finance & banking services	....	....	....	....	7½	3⅝	2095	7	3⅝	3¾	...	2	...	...	...	...
28	PDR	✓Pendaries Petroleum	AS,To	NR	8	617	Oil & gas explor, dvlp	24	9⅝	12½	5/16	3⅞	⅜	11457	3⅞	1⅞	3⅜	...	d	...	672	−34.0	...
29	PNG	✓Penn-America Group	NY	NR	40	4320	Insur: commercial prop/liab'y	21¾	4 5/16	23	8⅛	11 7/16	7	1398	8 1/16	7	7¾	2.7	23	−6	−12.6	−8.8	11.1
30	PNN.A	✓Penn Engr & Mfg'A'	NY,Ch	B+	24	798	Captive fasteners: DC motors	27¼	1 1/16	26⅛	16¼	22⅞	17½	209	22¼	21⅛	20⅞B	2.3	10	3	8.2	2.3	17.2
31	PNN	✓ Com(non-vtg)	NY	B+	53	4996		27⅞	15	28½	17 3/16	25⅞	17¼	820	25½	22 13/16	23⅛B	2.1	12	3	5.6	6.2	...
32	PTA	✓Penn Treaty American	NY	B	86	5997	Accident & health insurance	35½	3	32¾	18	29⅝	13 15/16	7940	16	13 15/16	15¾	...	7	11	−41.5	−15.4	8.6
33	PVA	✓Penn Virginia	NY,Ph	B	71	5165	Nat'l resources:O&G:Inv'mnt	34½	4⅜	30	18⅛	23 3/16	16 1/16	3525	18¾	16 1/16	16¾	5.4	15	−5	−4.5	−6.9	5.9
34	PN	✓Pennaco Energy	AS	NR	23	5332	Oil & gas expl,dev	....	....	5⅛	3½	12⅞	2⅞	28536	9⅞	6⅞	8	...	..	...	121	...	...
35	PFG	PennCorp Financial Group	NY,Ph	NR	41	2642	Accident,sickness,life insur	40⅜	12¼	36⅜	7/16	1½	¼	46337	11/16	⅜	7/16	...	d	Neg	−56.3	−76.9	−49.2
36	Pr	$3.375 cm Cv Pfd([58]52.03)	NY	BB−	2	84		91½	50½	79¾	7½	14⅞	8 15/16	411	13¼	10⅞	12	...	..	...	...	...	...
¶37•[8]	JCP	✓Penney (J.C.)	NY,B,C,Ch,Ph,P	B	693	206169	Dept stores,disc:mail order	68¼	4 15/16	78¾	42⅝	54 7/16	17 11/16	339204	23 5/16	17 11/16	19 15/16	5.8	10	−14	−54.9	−22.4	−11.1
38	KTP	Penney(J.C.) 7.625% CortTS Tr Debs	NY	....[60]	1	10	Corporate-Backed Trust Sec	....	....	....	....	25⅛	16½	4825	19 13/16	16½	18⅜	10.4	..	...	...	...	...
39	PEI	✓Pennsylvania RE Inv Tr SBI	NY,Ph	NR	87	2872	Real estate investment trust	30⅜	2	25¼	18⅝	21 11/16	14	13814	17 5/16	14	14 9/16	12.9	9	−3	−17.0	−7.8	4.1
#40•[9]	PZL	✓Pennzoil-Quaker State	NY	NR	188	47139	Motor oil/refin pd/auto svcs	....	....	18	13⅜	16½	8½	69336	10 11/16	8½	10 3/16	7.4	d	...	−26.5	...	...
41	PSO	✓Penobscot Shoe[63]	AS	B	7	83	Mfr casual sport footwear	10 3/16	⅜	8⅜	5⅜	12¾	6⅞	35	11⅝	11½	11⅜B	1.8	8	36	57.3	30.2	25.9
42	JIT	✓Pentacon Inc	NY	NR	14	1028	Dist hardware/fasteners	....	....	14 11/16	3⅛	6 3/16	2 1/16	12689	3⅛	2⅛	3⅛	...	16	...	−27.5	...	...
#43•[4]	PNR	✓Pentair, Inc.	NY,Ch,Ph	A	305	31695	Mfr indl eqp/specialty prod	39⅞	⅛	46¼	26¾	49 7/16	29⅞	46658	38⅝	31¾	38½	1.7	17	11	−1.8	7.7	14.4
44	PNTK	Pentech International	NNM	C	10	1275	Mkts writing/drawing prod	9⅞	⅜	3	9/16	2⅛	⅝	12887	⅞	⅝	11/16	...	d	−46	−24.2	−16.7	−29.7
45	PEN	✓Pentegra Dental Group	AS	NR	5	946	Dental practice mgmt svcs	....	....	9	1¾	3	1	10100	1 5/16	1	1 3/16	...	5	...	−52.5	...	...
46•[9]	PME	✓Penton Media	NY	NR	114	20790	Publishing/information svcs	....	....	20¼	12½	29⅝	12⅝	14725	24¾	18⅞	24	0.5	..	...	19.2	...	...
47•[9]	PBCT	✓People's Bank	NNM	B	94	11474	Savings bank,Bridgeport,CT	39⅛	1	41½	18 13/16	32¼	19¼	24614	22⅛	19¼	21⅛	5.3	14	5	−20.6	6.3	25.7
¶48•[6]	PGL	✓Peoples Energy	NY,B,C,Ch,P,Ph	B+	323	16581	Gas utility in Chicago	62⅞	7	40⅛	32⅛	40¼	31¾	13597	38	33¼	33½	5.9	13	5	−11.4	4.9	11.2
49•[2]	PHBK	✓Peoples Heritage Finl Gr	NNM	B	319	59234	Svgs bank,Portland,Maine	23 13/16	15/16	26¾	12 13/16	20¼	14 5/16	83280	17 7/16	14 5/16	15 1/16	3.2	12	11	−22.7	5.0	23.5
50	PHC	✓Peoples Holding	AS	A−	24	207	Commercial banking,Mississippi	37 5/16	10 1/16	46	31	37	27	378	30¾	27⅝	28⅞	2.9	12	10	−8.4	7.1	13.5

Uniform Footnote Explanations-See Page 4. Other: [1]CBOE:Cycle 3. [2]CBOE:Cycle 2. [3]Ph:Cycle 1. [4]Ph:Cycle 2. [5]Ph:Cycle 3. [6]P:Cycle 3. [7]P:Cycle 1. [8]ASE:Cycle 2. [9]CBOE:Cycle 1.
[51]Thru 5-1-2000,scale to $25 in 2006. [52]Stk dstr of Celera Genomics Grp,'99. [53]To be determined. [54]Ea ADS rep 0.5 Ord'A'shr,EC15.24. [55]Alcan Alum plan acq,0.8908 ADS. [56]Fiscal Dec'95. [57]11 Mo Dec'98.
[58]Thru 7-15-2000,scale to $50 in 2005. [59]Incl redemption stk pur rt,'99. [60]Rate'A'by S&P. [61]Fiscal Aug'96 & prior. [62]12 Mo Dec'97:Fiscal Aug'97 earn $1.18. [63]Reidman Corp(81.8%)plan mgr,$11.75.
[64]Fiscal Sep'97 & prior. [65]Fiscal Sep'98 earn $0.54.

Index	Splits ◆ Cash Divs. Ea. Yr. Since	Dividends: Latest Payment Period $	Date	Ex. Div.	Total $ So Far 1999	Ind. Rate	Paid 1998	Financial Position Mil-$ Cash& Equiv.	Curr. Assets	Curr. Liab.	Balance Sheet Date	Capitalization Lg Trm Debt Mil-$	Shs. 000 Pfd.	Com.	Earnings $ Per Shr. Years End	1995	1996	1997	1998	1999	Last 12 Mos.	Interim Earnings Period	$ per Shr. 1998	1999	Index
1	1997	Q0.02	12-31-99	12-13	0.05	0.08	0.04	2.35	17.9	18.1	9-30-99	130	3057	16538	Dc	pvd0.15	v0.08	vd1.11	vd0.68	....	d0.21	9 Mo Sep	vd0.46	v0.01	1
2	1996	0.322	1-21-00		1.781	Call	1.781	Cv into 2.9036 com				....	p624	...	Dc	...	...	...	....	....	....	Called Jan 21 at $26.069			2
3	....	Terms&trad. basis should			be checked in detail			Wrrts expire 5-2-2001				....	...	3000	Dc	...	...	...	....	....	....				3
4◆	1995	Q0.04	1-5-00	12-13	0.16	0.16	0.16	0.30	80.9	32.7	9-30-99	23.2	...	5696	Dc	v1.70	v1.81	v1.40	v1.57	....	1.46	9 Mo Sep	v1.19	v1.08	4
5◆	....	None Since Public			...	Nil	....	90.8	318	104	10-30-99	1.45	...	33689	Ap	v0.75	v0.86	v1.00	v1.23	v1.49	1.70	6 Mo Oct	v0.66	v0.87	5
6◆	....	None Since Public			...	Nil	....	10.6	51.4	30.1	9-30-99	40.7	...	32681	Dc	v0.18	v0.21	v0.75	vd0.01	....	d0.48	9 Mo Sep	v0.18	vd0.29	6
7	....	None Since Public			...	Nil	....	1.69	67.3	51.4	10-30-99	....	...	10901	Ja	v0.16	v0.85	v0.86	v0.75	....	0.34	9 Mo Oct	v0.33	vd0.08	7
8◆	....	None Paid			...	Nil	....	31.3	259	154	9-30-99	178	...	46709	Dc	v0.52	v0.68	□v0.49	v0.68	....	0.64	9 Mo Sep	v0.51	v0.47	8
9◆	....	None Since Public			...	Nil	....	435	535	167	9-30-99	498	501	±61981	Dc	v□d1.05	vd1.10	v3.50	vd2.29	....	d5.14	9 Mo Sep	vd1.02	vd3.87	9
10◆	1988	Q0.09	11-15-99	10-28	0.27	0.36	0.18	1830	1942	1526	11-30-99	....	...	247137	My	0.17	v0.23	v0.31	v0.41	v0.56	0.66	6 Mo Nov	v0.26	v0.36	10
11	....	None Since Public			...	Nil	....	211	606	218	10-30-99	126	...	30296	Ja	pv1.34	v2.67	v3.31	v3.78	E4.37	4.29	9 Mo Oct	v3.31	v3.82	11
12	....	None Since Public			...	Nil	....	Total Deposits $1691M			9-30-99	1245	...	20424	Dc	...	...	n/a	v0.59	....	1.79	9 Mo Sep	vd0.14	v1.06	12
13	....	None Since Public			...	Nil	....	23.5	35.4	19.0	6-30-99	p....	p...	★15602	Dc	...	...	...	v0.04	....	0.19	6 Mo Jun	v0.06	v0.21	13
14	....	None Since Public			...	Nil	....	63.1	74.3	41.2	9-30-99	....	...	±15989	Dc	v0.03	vd0.02	vd0.09	vd0.75	....	d0.75	9 Mo Sep	vd0.43	vd0.43	14
15	....	None Since Public			...	Nil	....	Total Assets $120.89M			9-30-99	95.8	...	3707	Dc	d1.50	v0.10	v0.28	v0.09	....	d0.24	9 Mo Sep	v0.21	vd0.12	15
16	....	None Since Public			...	Nil	....	80.1	252	76.7	9-30-99	....	...	25972	Je	...	...	...	vpd0.34	vd1.79	d2.39	3 Mo Sep	vd0.15	vd0.75	16
17◆	1971	0.08½	1-3-00	11-29	h[52]0.34	0.34	0.34	163	893	608	9-30-99	35.7	...	103074	Je	0.79	0.16	v1.32	v0.56	v2.21	2.29	3 Mo Sep	v0.20	v0.28	17
18	....	None Since Public			...	Nil	....	Total Assets $45.6M			j5-31-99	15.1	...	±★5036	Au	...	...	...	±v0.63	Pv±0.58	j0.58				18
19	1998	Q0.354	11-16-99	10-28	1.416	[53]....	0.638	Exch for 0.8696-1 shr Peak Int Ltd 5-15-2001				....	...	★6000	Mr	...	...	...	....	....	....				19
20	1996	0.35	7-22-99	6-28	0.35	0.35	0.279	1206	4203	4345	12-31-98	1526	1091	79486	Dc	2.70	vd3.72	v1.91	v2.22	....	2.22				20
21	1902	Q0.25	12-20-99	11-10	1.00	1.00	1.00	642	1525	1178	9-30-99	6051	2302	185786	Dc	v2.64	v2.24	□v1.44	v□2.32	E3.00↓	2.24	9 Mo Sep	v2.36	v□2.28	21
22	....	....			...	Nil	....	0.44	83.4	51.4	9-30-99	2.20	...	15575	Dc	pv0.57	v0.90	v1.33	v1.82	....	1.78	9 Mo Sep	v1.31	v1.27	22
23	1954	Q0.12½	11-19-99	11-3	0.50	0.50	0.50	0.70	22.0	10.6	9-30-99	....	...	1456	Je	0.85	v0.55	v0.37	v1.68	v1.27	1.33	3 Mo Sep	v0.14	v0.20	23
24	....	None Since Public			...	Nil	....	22.6	43.5	5.40	10-31-99	....	...	13781	Ja	pv[56]d0.24	v0.46	v0.42	v0.39	....	0.32	6 Mo Jul	v0.18	v0.11	24
25	....	None Since Public			...	Nil	....	22.7	69.8	86.4	9-30-99	611	127	±19740	Dc	pΔvd1.59	v□d1.56	v□d3.02	vd6.64	....	d11.11	9 Mo Sep	vd3.66	vd8.13	25
26	....	None Since Public			...	Nil	....	28.4	57.7	21.1	9-30-99	0.14	...	28897	Dc	v0.12	v0.28	v0.04	vd0.46	....	d0.53	9 Mo Sep	vd0.04	vd0.11	26
27	....	None Since Public			...	Nil	....	Total Deposits $48.4M			6-30-99	p....	...	★4233	Dc	...	....	...	v1.28	....	1.96	6 Mo Jun	v0.41	v□1.09	27
28	....	None Since Public			...	Nil	....	6.73	7.13	0.08	6-30-99	....	...	8879	Dc	v0.05	vd0.08	vd0.10	vd0.31	....	d0.23	6 Mo Jun	vd0.15	vd0.07	28
29◆	1995	Q0.05¼	12-8-99	11-22	0.20¾	0.21	0.20	Total Assets $221.82M			9-30-99	1.86	...	8131	Dc	v0.78	v1.04	v1.17	v0.90	....	0.34	9 Mo Sep	v0.69	v0.13	29
30◆	1967	Q0.12	12-15-99	11-29	0.48	0.48	0.45	14.9	102	25.3	9-30-99	....	...	±8660	Dc	±v2.02	v±1.79	±v1.67	±v1.91	....	2.00	9 Mo Sep	v1.39	v1.48	30
31	1996	Q0.12	12-15-99	11-29	0.48	0.48	0.45	....	....	...		....	...	6958	Dc	±v2.02	v±1.79	±v1.67	v±1.91	....	2.00	9 Mo Sep	v1.39	v1.48	31
32◆	....	None Paid			...	Nil	....	Total Assets $662.94M			9-30-99	82.9	...	7809	Dc	v1.51	v1.66	v0.98	v2.64	....	2.39	9 Mo Sep	v1.96	v1.71	32
33◆	1984	Q0.22½	12-14-99	11-22	0.90	0.90	0.90	....	7.82	7.51	9-30-99	78.5	...	8922	Dc	v1.18	v1.50	v1.88	v1.13	....	1.10	9 Mo Sep	v1.21	v1.18	33
34	....	None Paid			...	Nil	....	1.11	7.08	7.17	9-30-99	12.4	...	18361	Dc	...	...	...	v[57]d0.34	....	....	9 Mo Sep	n/a	v0.31	34
35	1993	Div Omitted 8-26-98			...	Nil	0.10	Total Assets $3444M			9-30-99	280	5175	29215	Dc	v2.12	v□2.49	v1.07	v□d15.17	....	d7.19	9 Mo Sep	v□d11.47	vd3.49	35
36	1995	Div Omitted 8-26-98			...	Nil	2.53⅛	Cv into 2.212 com,$22.60				....	2300	...	Dc	...	...	...	....	....	....	Arrears $4.21875 to 10-15-99			36
37	1922	0.288	2-1-00	1-6	[59]2.18½	1.15	2.17	853	12430	7787	10-30-99	6504	800	260442	Ja	3.48	2.25	v2.10	v2.19	E2.05↓	2.01	9 Mo Oct	v1.42	v1.24	37
38	1999	0.529	9-1-99	8-27	0.529	1.91	....	Co option to redm at $25				....	...	★4000	Ja	...	...	...	....	....	....	Due 3-1-2097			38
39	1962	Q0.47	12-15-99	11-26	1.88	1.88	1.88	Total Assets $531.68M			9-30-99	351	...	13328	Dc	1.29	[61]1.27	□v[62]1.31	v□1.76	....	1.61	9 Mo Sep	v1.34	v1.19	39
40	1999	0.18¾	12-15-99	11-26	0.75	0.75	....	19.1	769	422	9-30-99	1060	...	77973	Dc	....	...	vNil	vd0.96	....	d1.14	9 Mo Sep	v0.15	vd0.03	40
41	1976	Q0.05	10-25-99	10-12	0.20	0.20	0.20	4.34	15.8	2.61	8-27-99	....	...	1388	Nv	0.30	v0.58	0.32	v1.07	....	1.51	9 Mo Aug	v0.72	v1.16	41
42	....	None Since Public			...	Nil	....	0.31	175	45.9	9-30-99	162	...	16668	Dc	...	...	p[64]0.41	v[65]0.56	....	0.20	9 Mo Sep	v0.46	v0.10	42
43◆	1976	Q0.16	11-12-99	10-27	0.64	0.64	0.60	30.2	1096	778	9-25-99	1045	...	★48177	Dc	v1.81	v1.73	v2.11	v2.46	E2.29	2.16	9 Mo Sep	v1.70	v1.40	43
44	....	None Since Public			...	Nil	....	0.90	40.2	27.1	7-18-99	1.60	...	12570	Sp	d0.10	d0.51	0.05	vd0.28	Pvd0.03	d0.03				44
45	....	None Since Public			...	Nil	....	0.07	7.05	12.4	9-30-99	6.65	...	10806	Mr	...	...	n/a	v0.29	....	0.23	6 Mo Sep	v0.13	v0.07	45
46	1998	Q0.03	1-3-00	12-19	0.12	0.12	0.03	9.98	84.6	91.0	9-30-99	213	...	31314	Dc	...	...	pv0.66	v0.50	....	0.14	9 Mo Sep	v0.38	v□0.02	46
47◆	1993	Q0.28	11-15-99	10-28	1.03	1.12	0.84	Total Assets $9918.70M			12-31-98	1234	...	p62252	Dc	1.21	v1.31	v1.51	v1.44	....	1.53	9 Mo Sep	v1.28	v1.37	47
48	1937	Q0.49	1-14-00	12-20	1.95	1.96	1.91	67.4	363	357	6-30-99	522	...	35489	Sp	v1.78	v2.96	v2.81	v2.25	vP2.61	2.61				48
49◆	1994	Q0.12	11-16-99	11-3	0.47	0.48	0.44	Total Deposits $8102.44M			9-30-99	4206	...	102102	Dc	v0.89	v1.03	v1.29	v1.12	....	1.29	9 Mo Sep	v0.76	v0.93	49
50◆	1987	Q0.21	1-3-00	12-22	0.82	0.84	0.672	Total Deposits $986.85M			9-30-99	34.1	...	6232	Dc	v1.57	v1.62	v1.82	v1.94	....	2.39	9 Mo Sep	v1.41	v1.86	50

◆Stock Splits & Divs By Line Reference Index [4]2-for-1,'94. [5]3-for-2,'94,'98. [6]2-for-1,'97,'98. [8]5-for-4,'94,'95,'96,'97. [9]3-for-2,'95. [10]3-for-2,'95,'96,'97,'98,'99. [17]No adj for stk dstr,'99:2-for-1,'99. [29]3-for-2,'97. [30]4-for-1,'96. [32]3-for-2,'95. [33]2-for-1,'97. [43]2-for-1,'96. [47]3-for-2,'97. [49]2-for-1,'98. [50]4%,'94:3-for-2,'96,'98.

¶ S&P 500
# MidCap 400
✣ SmallCap 600
• Options

Index	Ticker	Name of Issue (Call Price of Pfd. Stocks)	Market	Com. Rank. & Pfd. Rating	Inst. Hold Cos	Inst. Hold Shs. (000)	Principal Business	1971-97 High	1971-97 Low	1998 High	1998 Low	1999 High	1999 Low	Dec. Sales in 100s	December, 1999 Last Sale Or Bid High	Low	Last	%Div Yield	P-E Ratio	EPS 5 Yr Growth	% Annualized Total Return 12 Mo	36 Mo	60 Mo
¶1•1	PSFT	✔PeopleSoft Inc	NNM,Ch	B+	374	96736	Mfr human resource mgmt softwr	39½	1 1/16	57 7/16	16½	26⅜	11½	845676	24 7/16	18¼	21 5/16	...	d	-49	...	...	...
¶2•2	PBY	✔Pep Boys-Man,Mo,Ja	NY,B,Ch,P,Ph	A-	272	34190	Retail chain: auto parts, etc.	38¼	3/16	26 11/16	12⅜	21⅝	8 1/16	76771	10 1/16	8 1/16	8 15/16	3.0	10	-33	-42.0	-32.9	-21.2
3•3	PBG	✔Pepsi Bottling Group	NY,Ph	NR	214	83954	Mfr,dstr Pepsi-Cola beverages	...	...	...	...	25¼	15½	151794	18½	15½	16 9/16	0.5	31	...	...	...	...
4•4	GEM	✔Pepsi-Gemex [52]S.A.	NY,Ch,Ph,P	NR	23	6920	Soft drink bottler, Mexico	31⅛	5⅝	14 9/16	5⅝	11 1/16	4½	17070	6 15/16	5⅝	6 7/16	...	22	NM	-17.6	-7.7	-14.5
5	PAS	✔PepsiAmericas Inc 'B'	NY,Ch,Ph,P	NR	21	5225	Bottle/dstr soft drink prod	14¼	3⅞	9 1/16	4 7/16	7¼	3⅜	5622	5	3⅝	3¾	...	d	Neg	...	...	...
¶6•2	PEP	✔PepsiCo Inc	NY,B,C,Ch,P,Ph	A	1661	852796	Soft drink:snack foods	41 5/16	9/16	44 13/16	27 9/16	42 9/16	30⅛	939877	37¾	33 13/16	35¼	1.5	29	6	-12.5	...	...
7•5	PSTI	✔Per-Se Technologies	NNM,Ch	NR	94	12303	Hospital/Dr. acc rec mgmt svcs	159¾	10½	37½	7⅞	18	6	86049	8 13/16	6	8⅜	...	14	Neg	-7.9	-35.4	-33.5
8	PRCP	✔Perceptron Inc	NNM	B-	39	5192	Laser-based sensor/image sys	39¼	3½	24½	4¼	9⅞	3	9995	4 9/16	3 7/16	4	...	d	Neg	-39.6	-51.1	-23.4
9•6	PRGN	✔Peregrine Systems	NNM	NR	258	36701	Dvp computer software	10¼	4	23 9/16	6	96¾	16⅞	158107	96¾	65 11/16	84 3/16	...	d	...	264	...	...
✣10	PFGC	✔Performance Food Group	NNM	B+	143	9461	Market,dstr food products	26¼	6½	29⅛	15⅝	30½	20¾	9959	25 9/16	20¾	24⅝	...	19	20	-13.3	16.3	24.2
11	PF	✔perfumania.com inc	AS	NR	1	127	On-line fragrance sales	...	...	...	...	22¼	5¾	11528	22¼	10¾	22¼	...	..	...	...	...	...
12	PCR	✔Perini Corp	AS,B,Ch	B-	41	2331	Construction:R.E. develop	44	3	11¼	4¼	7½	2⅝	6201	4 11/16	3¼	3⅞	...	d	90	-24.4	-20.8	-16.2
13	Pr	$2.125[58]Dep Cv[59]Ex Pfd(25)	AS	NR	4	103		28⅛	11½	20	15¼	21¼	14	133	18	16	18	...	..	...	...	...	...
¶14•7	PKI	✔PerkinElmer Inc	NY,B,Ch,Ph,P	B+	334	33585	Scientific equip,sys & svcs	26¾	⅞	33¾	18⅞	45	25½	35060	43⅝	37 13/16	41 11/16	1.3	25	NM	52.5	30.3	27.3
15	PERL	✔Perle Systems	NSC	C	4	742	Computer systems/services	9¼	¾	2¾	1⅜	31⅝	1 13/16	864458	31⅝	3⅜	8⅝	...	34	92	272	47.2	15.9
16	PBT	✔Permian Basin Rty Tr[60]	NY,B,Ch,P,Ph	NR	14	3590	Royalty oil interests,Texas	25	3	5 9/16	3½	6⅛	3 5/16	12409	5¾	4 15/16	5 11/16	3.5	28	-8	55.3	16.9	15.5
17•7	PER	✔Perot Systems'A'	NY,Ph	NR	49	3389	Computer software & svcs	...	...	...	...	85¾	15 5/16	64329	20⅝	18	18⅞	...	32	...	...	...	...
#18•8	PRGO	✔Perrigo Co	NNM	NR	135	51350	Mfr store brand pharmac'l prd	34⅞	8	14¼	7 3/16	9⅞	7	77862	8 13/16	7 9/16	8	...	24	-45	-9.2	-4.3	-8.5
19	PGA	✔Personnel Group of America	NY,Ch,Ph,P	NR	137	21087	Personnel staffing services	19⅝	5½	24	8¼	18 9/16	4 15/16	32319	11 11/16	7½	10¼	...	10	33	-41.4	-5.3	...
20•9	IIT	✔Perusahaan PT IndoSat ADS[61]	NY,Ch,Ph,P	NR	64	7664	Intl telecommun svc Indonesia	41⅝	16 5/16	19	4⅝	25 11/16	9⅞	38488	22⅛	13⅞	21⅝	2.5	19	-1	82.4	-5.6	-7.7
21•10	PETC	✔Petco Animal Supplies	NNM	NR	98	15077	Pet food/supplies stores	33	7 9/16	26¼	5⅝	18 7/16	6	41016	15⅛	12⅛	14⅞	...	14	34	47.8	-10.5	9.1
22	PCZ	✔Petro-Canada Variable Vtg	NY,Ch,Ph	NR	92	61476	Oil&gas explor,intl,integted	21 5/16	10⅛	18 13/16	9½	16 15/16	10⅜	4944	14 13/16	13¼	14⅜	◆1.9	14	-12	38.8	3.0	...
23	PEX	✔PetroCorp Inc	AS	NR	21	2393	Oil & gas explor'n,dvlp,prod'n	12¼	5¾	9½	5	7½	4¼	607	6⅛	5½	5 13/16	...	d	Neg	1.1	-14.3	-11.8
24	PETD	✔Petroleum Development	NNM	B-	25	3351	Oil&gas explor,dev,prod'n	12⅛	⅛	6⅝	2 15/16	5 9/16	2⅞	11898	4 9/16	3⅝	3 13/16	...	8	45	24.5	-3.1	26.3
25•11	PGO	✔Petroleum Geo-Svcs A/S ADS[62]	NY,Ph	NR	170	29760	Marine seismic data svcs	38 7/16	4¾	38 3/16	11¾	24⅝	10⅝	56692	18¼	15	17 13/16	...	59	-9	13.1	-2.9	13.9
26	PSJ	✔Petsec Energy ADS[63]	NY	NR	8	1047	Oil & gas explor, prod'n	27⅝	12⅞	22⅜	1⅛	2 3/16	½	4039	11/16	½	½	...	d	-23	-70.4	-72.0	...
27•12	PETM	✔PETsMART Inc	NNM,Ch	B-	156	55244	Pet food/supplies superstores	29⅞	6	13⅛	4¾	11⅛	2⅝	396841	5 15/16	4¼	5¾	...	23	-26	-47.7	-35.9	-12.8
28	PV	✔Pfeiffer Vacuum Technol ADS[65]	NY	NR	10	1118	Turbomolecular vacuum pumps	24	8 1/16	65⅞	17 11/16	51¼	23	736	27¾	23	23⅛	...	18	...	-39.2	23.1	...
¶29•13	PFE	✔Pfizer, Inc	NY,B,C,Ch,P,Ph	A	1986	1934105	Health care,csmr prd,sp chem	26 11/16	7/16	43	23 11/16	50 1/16	31 9/16	2567517	36½	32 9/16	32 7/16	1.1	40	19	-21.4	34.2	40.1
30	PFSW	PFSweb Inc	NNM	NR	..	...	Transaction management svcs	...	...	...	...	52 11/16	17	262517	52 11/16	17	37½	...	..	...	...	...	...
¶31•14	PCG	✔PG&E Corp	NY,B,C,Ch,P,Ph,Vc	B	580	180941	Elec & gas util:North'n Calif	36¾	8½	35 1/16	29 1/16	34	20¼	208879	22 11/16	20¼	20½	5.9	11	-6	-32.2	3.6	2.2
✣32•15	PPDI	✔Pharmaceutical Product Devlpmt	NNM	NR	174	14175	Product development svcs	47¾	12¼	30 11/16	13	38½	8 9/16	63108	13¾	9⅞	11⅞	...	11	NM	-60.5	-22.2	...
33	PRX	✔Pharmaceutical Resources	NY,Ch,P,Ph	C	35	2643	Mfr prescript'n generic drugs	27¼	1	6 11/16	1⅜	8 11/16	3⅞	12134	6	4½	4 15/16	...	62	-44	3.9	12.1	-11.8
¶34•2	PNU	✔Pharmacia & Upjohn	NY,P	NR	1075	373598	R&D pharmaceutical/hlth prd	44⅝	27½	57¼	33¾	66⅝	43½	561065	55⅛	43½	45	2.4	26	-4	-18.9	7.0	...
35•12	PCOP	✔Pharmacopeia Inc	NNM	NR	47	6714	Pharmaceutical R&D	31½	12⅛	22⅝	7⅝	23¼	5 7/16	42287	23¼	16¼	22⅝	...	d	NM	138	5.3	...
36	PARS	✔Pharmos Corp	NSC	C	16	913	Drug delivery system R&D	52	½	3 9/16	1 7/16	2 7/16	1 1/16	121708	2 7/16	1¼	2⅛	...	d	51	35.3	13.6	9.9
¶37•16	PD	✔Phelps Dodge	NY,B,C,Ch,P,Ph	B	454	47778	Largest US copper prod'r	89⅝	6 7/16	71¾	43⅞	70⅝	41⅞	115757	67⅜	50 15/16	67⅛	3.0	d	Neg	37.3	3.3	5.0
✣38	PSC	✔Phila Suburban	NY,B,Ch,Ph	A-	142	7987	Water svc in suburban Phila	22 9/16	2 11/16	30 1/16	18⅞	29¾	19¾	10004	23 3/16	20 3/16	20 11/16	3.5	19	5	-27.8	15.5	23.6
¶39•14	MO	✔Philip Morris Cos	NY,B,C,Ch,P,Ph	A	1937	1495467	Cigarettes,food prod,brew'g	48⅛	½	59½	34¾	55 9/16	21¼	2710319	27⅜	21⅝	23	8.3	7	5	-55.0	-11.3	8.5
40•2	PHI	✔Philippine Long D Tel ADS[72]	NY,B,Ch,P	NR	117	25183	Tel service in Philippines	42⅝	¼	28⅞	15 5/16	33½	18 9/16	32437	27⅝	20⅛	25⅞	0.4	d	Neg	0.2	1.7	-0.4
41	Pr A	Global Dep[75] Cv Pfd(NC)	NY	BB	30	5450		68⅝	44⅛	52½	35¼	57½	38 7/16	3914	48½	40⅛	47⅝	7.3	..	...	...	...	...
42	PHR	✔Philips Intl Realty	NY,Ph	NR	48	5550	Real estate investment trust	...	...	17¾	13⅞	17	13 1/16	2362	16⅝	16	16 7/16	9.2	..	...	17.3	...	...
¶43•17	P	✔Phillips Petroleum	NY,To,B,C,Ch,P,Ph	B+	660	155711	Domestic integ oil: chems	52¼	4⅜	53¼	40⅝	57¼	37 11/16	127610	49 15/16	44⅞	47	2.9	22	-20	13.5	5.1	10.8
✣44•5	PVH	✔Phillips-Van Heusen	NY,B,Ch,Ph,P	B+	114	15948	Apparel mfr & retailer	39	⅜	15⅛	6½	10⅝	5⅝	8129	8 7/16	7 3/16	8 5/16	1.8	14	-4	17.7	-15.5	-10.2
45	PXP	✔Phoenix Investment Partners	NY,Ph	NR	74	13093	Invest mgmt/finl advisory svcs	22⅞	5½	10⅛	6 9/16	10¼	6 15/16	9393	8⅝	7 9/16	8⅛	3.0	11	6	-0.9	7.6	...
46	PRG	✔Phoenix Restaurant Group	AS,Ph	NR	12	4747	Oper family style restaurants	6	1⅝	3¾	⅞	1 5/16	7/16	2722	11/16	½	⅝	...	d	Neg	-47.3	-41.5	-29.6
47•7	PTEC	✔Phoenix Technologies	NNM	↑B	75	10588	Mfr PC system software	20⅝	1¼	14¾	5	18 3/16	7¼	37612	18⅛	13⅜	15 13/16	...	..	-41	83.3	-0.7	16.1
48	PHCM	✔Phone.com Inc	NNM	NR	108	9404	Dvp softwr for wireless phones	...	...	...	...	175	8	441589	170	98	115 15/16	...	d	...	...	...	...
49•14	PLP	✔Phosphate Res Ptnrs LP	NY,B,Ch,P,Ph	NR	35	28956	Prod phosphate fertilizer	31¼	8	10 13/16	5 7/16	12⅛	9	16154	10⅝	9½	9 15/16	...	41	-46	8.9	...	...
50	PHX	Photoelectron Corp	AS	NR	8	210	Dvlp stge:Radosurgery Sys	11⅛	4⅛	9⅞	2¼	6⅝	1	6141	3⅜	2⅛	2½	...	d	29	-42.9	...	...

Uniform Footnote Explanations-See Page 4. Other: [1]ASE,CBOE,P:Cycle 1. [2]CBOE:Cycle 1. [3]ASE,CBOE,P:Cycle 3. [4]ASE,CBOE:Cycle 1. [5]CBOE:Cycle 3. [6]CBOE,Ph:Cycle 1. [7]Ph:Cycle 3. [8]ASE,CBOE:Cycle 3. [9]CBOE:Cycle 2. [10]P:Cycle 3. [11]ASE,CBOE:Cycle 2. [12]Ph:Cycle 2. [13]ASE,CBOE,P,Ph:Cycle 3. [14]ASE:Cycle 3. [15]Ph:Cycle 1. [16]ASE:Cycle 1. [17]ASE:Cycle 2.
[51]Stk dstr of Momentum Business Applications,'99. [52]Global Dep shrs,rep 6ord Ptd Ctf rep1B,1L&1Dshr. [53]Stk dstr of Buenos Aires Embotelladora S.A.. [54]Fiscal Sep'98 & prior. [55]Fiscal Dec'98 & prior. [56]12 Mo Jun'99. [57]1 Mo Jan'99. [58]Dep for1/10 shr $21.25 cm Cv Exch Pfd. [59]Co opt to exch for $25amt 8½%Cv2012. [60]Unit Benef. Int. [61]Ea ADS rep 10'B'shr,par 500 Rupiah. [62]Ea ADS rep 1 ord shr, NOK 5. [63]Ea ADS rep 5 ord shrs,p0.20A. [64]Fiscal Jun'96 & prior. [65]Ea ADS rep 1 ord shr,DM50. [66]To be determined. [67]Subsid. Pfd in $M. [68]Fiscal Sept'97 & prior. [69]3 Mo Dec'98:Fiscal Sept'98 earned d$0.45. [70]Redempt'n of Stk Pur Rt. [71]Pfd in $M. [72]Ea ADS rep 1 com,par P5. [73]Approx. [74]®$3.57,'96. [75]Ea GDS rep 1 Sr III Cv Pfd. [76]®$0.49,'96. [77]Fiscal Sep'95 & prior. [78]Freeport-McMoRan Inc owns 51%.

Splits ◆ Index	Cash Divs. Ea. Yr. Since	Dividends: Latest Payment Period $	Date	Ex. Div.	Total $ So Far 1999	Ind. Rate	Paid 1998	Financial Position Mil-$ Cash& Equiv.	Curr. Assets	Curr. Liab.	Balance Sheet Date	Capitalization Lg Trm Debt Mil-$	Shs. 000 Pfd.	Com.	Earnings $ Per Shr. Years End	1995	1996	1997	1998	1999	Last 12 Mos.	Interim Earnings Period	$ per Shr. 1998	1999	Index
1◆	....	h[51]....	1-15-99	1-19	h[51]...	Nil	....	487	957	630	9-30-99	.....	...	245624	Dc	v0.12	v0.15	v0.44	v0.55	Ed0.61	d0.58	9 Mo Sep	v0.45	vd0.68	1
2	1950	Q0.068	1-24-00	1-6	0.26¾	0.27	0.25½	46.8	677	507	10-30-99	773	...	53152	Ja	1.34	v1.62	v0.80	v0.08	E0.94	0.48	9 Mo Oct	v0.39	v0.79	2
3	1999	0.02	1-3-00	12-8	0.04	0.08	....	164	1717	1087	9-04-99	3272	...	±155006	Dc	...	...	...	pvd0.77	E0.54	d0.47	9 Mo Sep	v0.40	v0.70	3
4	1997	0.145	7-2-98	6-18	...	Nil	0.145	32.1	151	17.0	12-31-98	185	...	1343595	Dc	±d0.23	0.65	v0.78	v0.30	....	0.30				4
5	....	h[53]....	6-17-98		...	Nil	h[53]....	0.55	27.0	10.5	9-30-99	33.2	...	±p86760	Dc	0.83	d3.46	vd0.91	v[54]d0.45	....	d0.25	9 Mo Sep	vd0.40	vd0.20	5
6◆	1952	Q0.135	1-3-00	12-8	0.53	0.54	0.51	550	3597	3402	9-04-99	2641	...	1455698	Dc	v1.00	v0.72	v1.36	v1.31	E1.22	1.28	9 Mo Sep	v1.07	v1.04	6
7◆	....	None Since Public			...	Nil	....	38.1	140	75.5	9-30-99	175	...	28007	Dc	p0.03	vpd5.73	Δvd3.84	v□d21.51	E0.60	d2.01	9 Mo Sep	v□d21.63	vd2.13	7
8◆	....	None Since Public			...	Nil	....	5.53	51.9	10.6	9-30-99	7.34	...	8169	Je	v1.07	v0.86	v1.28	v[55]d0.41	v[56]d0.56	d0.47	3 Mo Sep	v0.05	v0.14	8
9◆	....	None Since Public			...	Nil	....	24.9	93.3	58.2	9-30-99	0.69	...	50956	Mr	pd0.26	pv0.09	vd0.74	vd0.54	....	d0.21	6 Mo Sep	vd0.46	vd0.13	9
10◆	....	None Since Public			...	Nil	....	7.07	238	164	10-02-99	94.7	...	14112	Dc	v0.82	v0.94	v1.06	v1.24	....	1.28	9 Mo Sep	v0.90	v0.94	10
11	....	None Since Public			...	Nil	....	11.2	12.7	0.27	10-31-99	.....	...	7500	Ja	...	...	...	□v[57]d0.05	....	....	9 Mo Oct	n/a	pvd0.43	11
12	....	0.20	12-18-90	11-20	...	Nil	....	33.6	280	207	9-30-99	77.4	281	5682	Dc	vd6.38	vd15.13	v0.01	v1.08	....	d16.45	9 Mo Sep	v0.88	vd16.65	12
13	....	0.53⅛	12-15-95	11-20	...	Nil	....	Cv into 0.662 com,$37.75				.....	1000	...	Dc	...	...	...	.....	.....	....	Arrears to 12-15-99			13
14	1965	Q0.14	2-10-00	1-19	0.56	0.56	0.56	88.4	731	848	10-03-99	115	...	46172	Dc	v1.32	v1.27	v0.74	v2.22	E1.66	3.13	9 Mo Sep	v1.77	v2.68	14
15◆	....	None Paid			...	Nil	....	1.73	28.9	25.5	j5-31-99	9.83	...	7731	My	0.50	d0.58	vd0.68	v0.30	v0.17	j0.17	6 Mo Nov	v0.11	v0.11	15
16	1981	0.052	1-14-00	12-29	0.356	0.20	0.249	Southland Royalty (prop)				.....	...	46609	Dc	v0.25	v0.42	v0.48	v0.22	....	0.20	6 Mo Jun	v0.14	v0.12	16
17	....	None Since Public			...	Nil	....	263	496	229	9-30-99	0.26	...	91879	Dc	v0.16	v0.24	v0.12	v0.42	....	0.60	9 Mo Sep	v0.29	v0.47	17
18	....	None Since Public			...	Nil	....	1.26	377	136	10-02-99	115	...	73346	Je	v0.58	v0.52	v0.58	vd0.69	v0.02	0.33	3 Mo Sep	vd0.17	v0.14	18
19◆	....	None Since Public			...	Nil	....	1.10	150	64.5	10-03-99	270	...	25772	Dc	pv0.44	v0.57	v0.80	v0.96	....	1.03	9 Mo Sep	v0.69	v0.76	19
20	1995	0.539	7-15-99	6-4	0.539	0.54	0.094	152	250	94.1	12-31-98	2.54	...	1035500	Dc	1.92	v2.13	v1.41	v1.14	....	1.14				20
21◆	....	None Since Public			...	Nil	....	5.50	152	101	10-30-99	107	...	21107	Ja	vd0.63	vd0.63	vd0.64	vd0.11	E1.10	0.96	9 Mo Oct	vd0.48	v0.59	21
22	1991	gQ0.10	1-1-00	12-7	g0.32	0.40	g0.32	69.0	1354	1056	j6-30-99	1743	...	271159	Dc	0.79	v0.94	v1.13	v0.35	....	j0.69	9 Mo Sep	v0.28	v0.62	22
23	....	None Since Public			...	Nil	....	12.2	16.8	14.3	9-30-99	45.1	...	8656	Dc	vd1.11	v0.49	v0.22	vd2.82	....	d2.66	9 Mo Sep	vd0.28	vd0.12	23
24	....	None Paid			...	Nil	....	9.59	23.0	22.0	9-30-99	.....	...	15738	Dc	v0.13	v0.31	v0.61	v0.41	....	0.48	9 Mo Sep	v0.31	v0.38	24
25◆	....	None Since Public			...	Nil	....	53.3	432	415	12-31-98	1422	...	★100087	Dc	v0.68	v0.89	□v1.09	v1.32	....	0.30	9 Mo Sep	v0.99	v□d0.03	25
26	....	None Since Public			...	Nil	....	13.5	95.3	81.0	12-31-98	107	...	107601	Dc	d0.02	□v[64]0.85	v0.70	vd4.32	....	d4.32				26
27◆	....	None Since Public			...	Nil	....	38.6	542	339	10-31-99	270	...	111689	Ja	d0.03	v0.17	vd0.28	v0.20	E0.25	d0.06	9 Mo Oct	v0.03	v□d0.23	27
28◆	1999	0.217	6-25-99	6-14	0.217	[66]....	....	36.9	87.9	32.6	12-31-97	1.59	...	8800	Dc	0.35	0.90	v1.32	....	....	1.32				28
29◆	1901	Q0.09	3-9-00	2-16	0.307	0.36	0.253	4908	11484	9092	10-03-99	525	...	3871259	Dc	v0.42	v0.50	v0.57	v0.85	E0.82	0.73	9 Mo Sep	v0.69	v0.57	29
30	....	None Since Public			...	Nil	....	2.41	51.0	30.2	6-30-99	.....	...	★17405	Mr	...	...	...	pv0.17	....	....	3 Mo Jun	n/a	p0.02	30
31	1919	Q0.30	1-15-00	12-13	1.20	1.20	1.20	306	4213	6850	9-30-99	9253	[67]480	383980	Dc	v2.99	v1.75	v1.75	v1.88	E1.85	1.91	9 Mo Sep	v1.37	v1.40	31
32	....	None Since Public			...	Nil	....	41.3	177	78.7	9-30-99	0.15	...	24629	Dc	□pvd0.24	vd0.17	v0.42	v0.85	....	1.09	9 Mo Sep	v0.56	v0.80	32
33	....	0.02	7-5-89	5-26	...	Nil	....	0.15	38.3	17.3	10-02-99	1.09	...	29541	Dc	0.04	d0.45	v[68]d0.48	v□[69]d0.23	....	0.08	9 Mo Sep	vd0.34	vd0.03	33
34	1996	Q0.27	2-1-00	1-5	1.08	1.08	1.08	1382	4696	3246	9-30-99	339	7	518499	Dc	vp1.41	v1.07	v0.61	v1.31	E1.76	1.45	9 Mo Sep	v0.95	v1.09	34
35	....	None Since Public			...	Nil	....	63.9	89.6	42.0	9-30-99	0.04	...	19960	Dc	vd2.77	vd0.77	vd0.58	vd0.54	....	d0.03	9 Mo Sep	vd0.60	vd0.09	35
36	....	None Paid			...	Nil	....	3.09	6.23	3.95	9-30-99	.....	...	44361	Dc	vd0.37	vd0.28	vΔd0.32	vd0.15	....	d0.11	9 Mo Sep	vd0.12	vd0.08	36
37	1987	Q0.50	12-10-99	11-17	2.00	2.00	[70]2.00½	165	1013	754	9-30-99	807	...	p80967	Dc	v10.66	v6.98	v6.63	v3.26	Ed0.35	d1.43	9 Mo Sep	v3.97	v□d0.72	37
38◆	1939	Q0.18	12-1-99	11-9	0.70	0.72	0.66½	6.45	55.5	122	9-30-99	412	[71]176	40962	Dc	v0.77	v0.82	v0.88	v1.03	E1.10	0.79	9 Mo Sep	v0.89	v0.65	38
39◆	1928	Q0.48	1-10-00	12-13	1.80	1.92	1.64	5876	21893	18023	9-30-99	12160	...	2366139	Dc	□v2.16	v2.54	v2.58	v2.20	E3.18	2.52	9 Mo Sep	v2.09	v2.41	39
40◆	1953	[73]0.025	1-14-00	12-22	0.105	0.11	0.097	5321	35832	40925	j12-31-98	117918	293907	121134	Dc	1.61	[74]1.82	v1.40	vNil	....	d0.28	3 Mo Mar	v0.44	v0.16	40
41	1995	0.87½	1-14-00	12-22	3.50	3.50	3.50	Cv into 1.713 com				.....	4616	...	Dc	...	...	...	.....	.....	....	Co opt to convert re-spec cond			41
42	1998	Q0.37¾	1-18-00	12-29	1.47	1.51	0.519	Total Assets $307M			9-30-99	180	...	★9806	Dc	...	...	pv1.00	vp0.45	....	....	9 Mo Sep	n/a	v0.82	42
43	1934	Q0.34	12-1-99	10-28	1.36	1.36	1.36	180	2779	2590	9-30-99	5093	...	253284	Dc	v1.78	v4.91	v3.61	v0.91	E2.12	0.61	9 Mo Sep	v1.71	v1.41	43
44	1970	Q0.03¾	12-10-99	11-17	0.15	0.15	0.15	41.3	417	117	10-31-99	249	...	27290	Ja	v0.01	v0.68	vd2.46	v□0.47	....	0.58	9 Mo Oct	v0.41	v0.52	44
45◆	1993	Q0.06	12-9-99	11-23	0.24	0.24	0.24	51.9	93.5	63.7	9-30-99	331	...	43726	Dc	v0.40	v[76]0.50	v0.44	v0.68	....	0.71	9 Mo Sep	v0.33	v0.36	45
46	....	None Since Public			...	Nil	....	1.70	51.7	46.3	9-29-99	72.5	...	13485	Dc	□[77]0.30	v□0.14	vd1.56	vΔd0.45	....	d1.90	9 Mo Sep	vΔd0.17	□vd1.62	46
47	....	None Since Public			...	Nil	....	55.6	94.5	41.5	9-30-99	1.55	...	24036	Sp	0.58	0.73	v0.74	v0.03	v0.07	0.07				47
48◆	....	None Since Public			...	Nil	....	118	129	48.8	9-30-99	0.39	p...	★62584	Je	...	vd0.27	vd0.84	vd1.02	Pvd1.49	d1.22	3 Mo Sep	vd0.35	vd0.08	48
49	1986	Div Omitted 10-28-99			0.43	Nil	0.22	3.00	159	56.7	9-30-99	542	...	[78]103500	Dc	v1.56	v1.71	v□d3.29	v0.31	....	0.24	9 Mo Sep	v0.61	v□0.54	49
50	....	None Since Public			...	Nil	....	0.59	2.93	1.79	10-02-99	.....	...	7762	Dc	vd3.72	vd3.12	vd0.87	vd1.02	....	d0.95	9 Mo Sep	vd0.77	vd0.70	50

◆**Stock Splits & Divs By Line Reference Index** [1]2-for-1,'94,'95,'96,'97. [6]2-for-1,'96:No adj for stk dstr,'97. [7]2-for-1,'95:1-for-3 REVERSE,'99. [8]3-for-2,'95. [9]2-for-1,'99. [10]3-for-2,'96. [15]2-for-1,'94. [19]2-for-1,'98. [21]3-for-2,'96. [25]2-for-1,'94,'98. [27]3-for-2,'95:2-for-1,'96. [28]42.8571%,'98. [29]2-for-1,'95,'97:3-for-1,'99. [38]3-for-2,'96:4-for-3,'98. [39]3-for-1,'97. [40]2-for-1,'97. [45]3-for-2,'93:No adj for stk dstr Duff & Phelps CR Ratings'94. [48]2-for-1,'99.

¶ S&P 500
# MidCap 400
✣ SmallCap 600
• Options

Index	Ticker	Name of Issue (Call Price of Pfd. Stocks)	Market	Com. Rank. & Pfd. Rating	Inst. Hold Cos	Inst. Hold Shs. (000)	Principal Business	Price Range 1971-97 High	1971-97 Low	1998 High	1998 Low	1999 High	1999 Low	December, 1999 Dec. Sales in 100s	Last Sale Or Bid High	Last Sale Or Bid Low	Last Sale Or Bid Last	%Div Yield	P-E Ratio	EPS 5 Yr Growth	% Annualized Total Return 12 Mo	36 Mo	60 Mo
✣1	PLAB	✔Photronics, Inc	NNM	↓B	171	15429	Manufacture,mkt'photo masks'	32¹⁄₁₆	⁵⁄₁₆	37⅞	9½	30⅜	17½	119568	30⅜	23	28⅝	...	64	−1	19.4	28.3	23.8
2•[1]	PHYC	✔PhyCor Inc	NNM	NR	149	36887	Oper mult-special medl clinics	41¾	2¼	28½	3¹⁵⁄₁₆	8⅜	1	282094	2⅛	1	1⅞	...	4	Neg	−72.5	−59.6	−28.1
3	PIC	✔Piccadilly Cafeterias	NY	B–	47	3656	Cafeterias in south & so'west	26¼	4⁵⁄₁₆	14	9⅝	11½	3	4268	5	3¹¹⁄₁₆	4	12.0	80	−10	−59.8	−20.8	−8.6
✣4•[2]	PCTL	✔PictureTel Corp	NNM	B	96	14946	Mfr visual communications sys	44¾	1⁹⁄₁₆	11¹⁵⁄₁₆	4¾	11	3¼	116704	6½	3¾	4⁵⁄₁₆	...	d	Neg	−34.9	−45.1	−18.5
5	PDB	✔Piedmont Bancorp	AS	NR	5	173	Svgs bank, North Carolina	19⅞	9⅛	11¾	8⅞	11⁵⁄₁₆	7	756	11⁵⁄₁₆	7	11⁵⁄₁₆	4.2	28	13	32.8	7.2	...
✣6	PNY	✔Piedmont Natural Gas	NY,Ch,Ph,P	A–	191	8511	Natural gas dstr, Carolinas	36⁷⁄₁₆	1¹⁵⁄₁₆	36⅛	27⅞	36⅝	28⅝	28165	32⅞	28¹⁵⁄₁₆	30⅛	4.6	16	8	−12.7	13.6	15.0
✣7•[3]	PIR	✔Pier 1 Imports	NY,Ch,P,Ph	B+	235	67738	Import specialty stores	15¹⁵⁄₁₆	⅛	20¾	6¹⁄₁₆	12⅜	5¼	227024	7¹⁄₁₆	5⅞	6⅜	1.9	10	36	−33.2	−5.3	12.2
8	PLH	✔Pierce Leahy	NY,Ph	NR	50	6466	Archive records mgmt svcs	31⅝	14¹³⁄₁₆	28⅞	16¾	43¼	20¹⁄₁₆	10795	43¼	31¾	43¼	...	..	...	69.6	...	...
9•[4]	CHX	✔Pilgrim's Pride'B'	NY,Ch,Ph	B	115	7226	Produces,mkts chicken prd	11⁵⁄₁₆	2⁷⁄₁₆	16⅞	7⅛	20	6¹⁄₁₆	12637	8¹³⁄₁₆	6¹⁵⁄₁₆	8⁵⁄₁₆	0.7	5	NM	−36.8	13.7	5.7
10	CHX.A	Cl'A'	NY	B	44	2674		....	....	....	....	16¼	4⁹⁄₁₆	6325	6½	5	6⁷⁄₁₆	0.9	4	58	...	...	...
✣11•[5]	PTX	✔Pillowtex Corp	NY,Ph	NR	108	5777	Mfr bedroom textile products	35¼	8	52	23⅛	28⅜	2¾	46221	6⁷⁄₁₆	3¾	6³⁄₁₆	3.9	30	−11	−76.4	−29.2	−7.7
12	PA	✔PIMCO Advisors Hldgs L.P.	NY	NR	120	7596	Mutual fd mgmt/advisory svc	34¹³⁄₁₆	15⅝	35¹⁵⁄₁₆	24¼	38³⁄₁₆	26½	27315	38³⁄₁₆	37	37¹¹⁄₁₆	6.4	25	...	30.5	26.9	22.4
13	PLE	✔Pinnacle Bancshares	AS	B	12	253	General banking Jasper, AL	18¾	2	18⅝	8⅞	12	8	329	9	8	8B	5.0	8	7	−28.8	0.8	7.3
14	BIGT	✔Pinnacle Holdings	NNM	NR	179	31660	Real estate investment trust	....	....	....	....	44	13⅜	48265	44	28¼	42⅜	...	d	...	...	...	...
¶15•[6]	PNW	✔Pinnacle West Capital	NY,B,C,Ch,P,Ph	B	345	61424	Hldg:Arizona Pub Svc	42¾	5	49¼	39⅜	43⅜	30³⁄₁₆	76152	34	30³⁄₁₆	30⁹⁄₁₆	4.6	10	9	−25.3	2.0	13.1
16	PIO	✔Pioneer Corp ADR[55]	NY,B,Ch,Ph	NR	11	327	High fi stereo audio/Japan	43⅜	⅞	20⁹⁄₁₆	14⅞	29¾	16	1125	29¾	21⁵⁄₁₆	27⅜	0.3	d	69	67.8	12.9	2.8
✣17	PIOG	✔Pioneer Group	NNM	B	118	16160	Mutual fund underwrtr,gold mng	33⅞	¼	33⅞	9⁹⁄₁₆	21¼	10	9675	18½	14½	15¾	...	d	Neg	−20.3	−12.2	−5.5
#18•[7]	PXD	✔Pioneer Natural Res	NY,Ch,Ph,P,To	C	160	66942	Oil & gas explor,dev,prod'n	44⅜	5¼	30	7¾	13³⁄₁₆	5	57313	9⅜	7⅝	8¹⁵⁄₁₆	...	d	Neg	2.1	−37.4	−15.0
19	PRRR	✔Pioneer Railcorp	NSC,Ch	B	1	1	Railroad shipping transport'n	4½	⅞	2¼	1	2¼	1⅛	1054	1⁹⁄₁₆	1⅛	1⁵⁄₁₆	1.5	..	−25	6.7	−18.6	−10.5
✣20•[8]	PIOS	✔Pioneer Std Electr	NNM	B+	168	22314	Dstr electronic components	19¼	³⁄₁₆	16⅞	5⅝	15⅜	6¼	43072	15⅜	11¹⁵⁄₁₆	14⁷⁄₁₆	0.8	12	1	55.8	4.3	7.7
¶21•[9]	PBI	✔Pitney Bowes	NY,B,Ch,P,Ph	A+	896	204578	Postage meters: mailing sys	45¾	⁷⁄₁₆	66⅜	42³⁄₁₆	73⁵⁄₁₆	40⅞	221530	49	40⅞	48⁵⁄₁₆	2.1	21	11	−25.6	23.4	27.9
22	Pr	$2.12 cm Cv Pref(28)vtg	NY,Ch	NR	2	2	copying & dictating sys	650	23⅛	850	680	847	847	....	....	....	773B	0.3	..	...	...	...	...
23	PDM	✔Pitt-DesMoines Inc	AS	B+	40	2452	Steel fabricating, contract'g	20	1¼	32⅜	15	62½	19	1136	24¾	19½	24⅝	2.8	8	13	5.6	24.6	22.4
24	PW	✔Pitts & W Va RR SBI	AS	NR	8	32	Real estate investment trust	8⅜	4	8¼	7	8⁷⁄₁₆	6⁹⁄₁₆	470	7¼	6⁹⁄₁₆	7¹⁄₁₆	7.8	13	...	−4.1	7.3	8.1
✣25	PZX	✔Pittston BAX Group	NY,Ch,P	NR	113	15674	Global freight transportation	31	17	25⅞	5⁵⁄₁₆	11⅝	6	10567	11³⁄₁₆	9⅜	10⅝	2.3	11	Neg	−2.0	−17.5	...
#26•[4]	PZB	✔Pittston Brinks Grp	NY,B,C,Ch,P,Ph	B+	185	31325	Security svcs/home security	47¹⁄₁₆	8½	42⅞	28	31¹³⁄₁₆	18⅛	44239	22⅞	18³⁄₁₆	22	0.5	10	4	−30.7	...	...
27	PZM	✔Pittston Minerals Group	NY,P	NR	20	963	Coal & minerals mining	30½	6⅝	9¾	1¹⁵⁄₁₆	2¼	1	14014	1¾	1⅛	1⅝	...	d	−47	−26.5	−50.9	−39.9
28	PRY	Pittway Corp[58]	NY,Ph	B	31	5394	Alarms,security prod	34½	6³⁄₁₆	42½	19⅞	45¹⁄₁₆	21½	9564	45¹⁄₁₆	25½	45¹⁄₁₆	0.2	16	14	...	...	...
29	PRY.A	✔ Class'A'(1/10 vtg)	NY	B	150	26118		35	5³⁄₁₆	39⁹⁄₁₆	17⅞	45	21¼	39475	45	28⅞	44¹³⁄₁₆	0.3	46	7	...	...	...
30•[10]	PIXR	✔Pixar	NNM	NR	118	9929	Digital animation studio/films	49½	12¼	66	20¼	50⅝	33	85799	44⅞	34¾	35⅜	...	45	NM	1.1	39.6	...
31	PZZI	✔Pizza Inn	NNM	NR	20	739	Oper/franchises pizza restr	6	³⁄₁₆	6⅝	4¼	4¹¹⁄₁₆	2⅞	4494	4⅛	3¼	4⅛	5.8	16	1	−0.8	0.2	10.1
¶32•[11]	PDG	✔Placer Dome Inc	NY,To,Mo,P	B–	429	129361	Mining:gold,silver,copper	33⅛	2⁹⁄₁₆	17⅞	7⅞	17½	9³⁄₁₆	289832	11⁷⁄₁₆	10³⁄₁₆	10¾	0.9	72	...	−5.7	−19.9	−12.1
33	PAA	✔Plains All Amer Pipeline	NY	NR	29	2109	Crude oil pipeline svcs	....	....	20³⁄₁₆	16¼	20¼	9⅝	57508	13⅝	9⅝	13	14.8	..	...	−18.3	...	...
✣34•[12]	PLX	✔Plains Resources	AS,Ph,P	C	121	14283	Oil & gas expl,devel,prod'n	30¾	2½	21	13⁷⁄₁₆	20³⁄₁₆	8⅛	22619	13	9¹⁄₁₆	12½	...	d	Neg	−11.1	−7.2	18.4
35	POLY	Planet Polymer Technologies	NSC	NR	7	426	Dvlp stg:specialty chemical	16	1	2⅝	⅝	3½	1⅛	8345	3⅛	2	2¹³⁄₁₆	...	d	5	32.3	−11.1	...
36	PLRX	✔PlanetRx.com Inc	NNM	NR	..	...	Online healthcare services	....	....	....	....	36½	14	69066	20¾	14	14½	...	d	...	...	...	...
✣37•[13]	PLT	✔Plantronics Inc	NY	NR	205	15087	Mfr telephone headsets	41⁷⁄₁₆	7¼	87	39¼	87½	43⅛	15285	71⁹⁄₁₆	60¹¹⁄₁₆	71⁹⁄₁₆	...	20	24	−16.8	47.2	36.8
38	PTIS	✔Plasma Therm	NNM	B–	15	2577	Mfr semiconductor prod	12³⁄₁₆	¼	9¼	2⅜	12½	2¹⁄₁₆	58198	12½	7¾	12¼	...	d	Neg	211	43.7	12.2
39	PSU	Plastic Surgery	AS	NR	..	...	Dv stg: plastic surgeon net sv	....	....	....	....	8⅜	6¼	6510	8⅜	6¼	6½	...	..	...	...	...	...
40	PLAA	✔Playboy Enterprises'A'(vtg)	NY,B,Ch,P	B–	21	397	Magazine,clubs,cable prog'g	16⅜	1	20¼	11	32	16⅛	753	21³⁄₁₆	17⁵⁄₁₆	20½	...	68	NM	7.2	26.5	16.6
41•[14]	PLA	✔ Cl 'B' non-vtg	NY,P	B–	77	10715		16¹¹⁄₁₆	3⅜	22⁷⁄₁₆	11⅞	36⅛	17¹⁵⁄₁₆	11944	25⁵⁄₁₆	21¹⁄₁₆	24⁵⁄₁₆	...	..	NM	16.1	35.6	18.3
42	PCO	✔Playcore Inc	AS	NR	22	909	Mfr wooden playground equip	17¾	2½	5¼	3⅜	10¾	4¼	3014	10¾	6⅜	8⅛	...	12	3	78.1	35.7	−0.9
43•[9]	PYX	✔Playtex Products	NY,Ch,P	NR	109	35714	Mfr personal care products	13⅛	6⅜	17⅛	9⁷⁄₁₆	17⅛	11½	17153	15½	13⅛	15⅜	...	22	13	−4.3	24.3	16.6
44•[15]	PLC	✔PLC Systems	AS,P,Ph	C	18	330	Heart laser technology	34⅞	3¹⁄₁₆	22	2¾	7⁷⁄₁₆	1¹³⁄₁₆	47446	2⁷⁄₁₆	1¹³⁄₁₆	2	...	d	Neg	−48.4	−55.4	−16.5
45	PLM	✔PLM International	AS	B–	23	1034	Fin'l svcs/leasing	11⅜	1½	9¼	5¹⁄₁₆	7	4⅜	4200	6⅛	5⅝	5⅞	...	13	NM	−11.3	23.2	17.0
46	PLUG	✔Plug Power	NNM	NR	..	...	Dv stg:residential fuel cells	....	....	....	....	34½	15	77102	34½	18⅞	28¼	...	d	...	...	...	...
47•[13]	PCL	✔Plum Creek Timber	NY,Ch,Ph,P	NR	116	5818	Paper & forest pds	36	6⁵⁄₁₆	34⅞	23⁷⁄₁₆	32⅛	23⅛	28975	25⅝	23⅛	25	9.1	16	−15	4.3	6.4	12.8
48	PLR.A	✔Plymouth Rubber'A'vtg	AS	B–	4	2	Plastic & rubber specialties:	11⁷⁄₁₆	⅝	8⅛	5⅜	9	6¹⁄₁₆	220	8⅜	7⅞	8⅛	...	5	2	30.0	4.2	3.2
49	PLR.B	Class B Com, non-vtg	AS	B–	4	133	tapes,films,rubber bands	11⁹⁄₁₆	⁷⁄₁₆	7¼	4½	7⅞	5¾	133	6¹⁵⁄₁₆	6⅜	6¹³⁄₁₆	...	5	2	11.2	−0.6	1.6
50	PMC	✔PMC Capital	AS	NR	12	319	Loans to small businesses	17⅜	3	15	8	10⅛	7¾	4996	8¾	8	8¼	e12.1	7	3	8.2	−7.0	0.0

Uniform Footnote Explanations-See Page 4. Other: [1]P,Ph:Cycle 3. [2]Ph:Cycle 1. [3]CBOE:Cycle 3. [4]Ph:Cycle 2. [5]CBOE:Cycle 2. [6]P:Cycle 1. [7]ASE:Cycle 3. [8]ASE,CBOE,P:Cycle 1. [9]ASE:Cycle 1. [10]ASE,CBOE,Ph:Cycle 1. [11]ASE,CBOE,P,Ph,To:Cycle 3. [12]ASE,CBOE:Cycle 1. [13]ASE:Cycle 2. [14]Ph:Cycle 3. [15]CBOE:Cycle 1. [51]Pfd in $M. [52]Fiscal Jun'95 & prior. [53]12 Mo Dec'96. [54]Subsid pfd in $M. [55]ADR representing 1 shr,par 50 yen. [56]Excl 4.1M Trust shs. [57]®$1.08,'96. [58]Honeywell Intl plan acq,$45.50. [59]Stk dstr of of Penton Media. [60]Stk dstr of Penton Media. [61]Fiscal Jun'96 & prior. [62]12 Mo Dec'97. [63]Redemption of stk purch rt. [64]Incl current amts. [65]Excl $7M subsid pfd.

Splits ◆ Index	Cash Divs. Ea. Yr. Since	Dividends: Latest Payment Period $	Date	Ex. Div.	Total $ So Far 1999	Ind. Rate	Paid 1998	Financial Position Mil-$ Cash& Equiv.	Curr. Assets	Curr. Liab.	Balance Sheet Date	Capitalization Lg Trm Debt Mil-$	Shs. 000 Pfd.	Com.	Earnings $ Per Shr. Years End	1995	1996	1997	1998	1999	Last 12 Mos.	Interim Earnings Period	$ per Shr. 1998	1999	Index
1◆	....	None Since Public			...	Nil	....	14.7	70.0	64.4	5-02-99	104	...	23805	Oc	0.83	0.87	v1.03	v0.84	vP0.45	0.45				1
2◆	....	None Since Public			...	Nil	....	85.9	557	567	9-30-99	314	...	73444	Dc	v0.41	v0.60	v0.05	vd1.55	E0.43	d6.64	9 Mo Sep	vd0.61	vΔd5.70	2
3	1947	Q0.12	1-4-00	12-1	0.48	0.48	0.48	....	30.5	126	9-30-99	....	...	10528	Je	0.40	v0.04	v0.89	v0.75	v0.38	0.05	3 Mo Sep	v0.18	vd0.15	3
4◆	....	None Since Public			...	Nil	....	73.0	192	97.0	10-03-99	55.1	4479	40526	Dc	v0.57	v0.81	vd1.04	vd1.45	....	d3.18	9 Mo Sep	vd0.11	vd1.83	4
5	1996	Q0.12	1-17-00	12-29	0.48	0.48	0.44	Total Deposits $103M			9-30-99	16.8	...	2532	Je	p0.71	0.45	vd0.20	v0.61	v0.46	0.41	3 Mo Sep	v0.15	v0.10	5
6	1956	Q0.34½	1-4-00	12-21	1.36	1.38	1.28	49.4	152	229	7-31-99	333	...	31181	Oc	1.45	v1.66	v1.79	v1.96	Pv1.86	1.86				6
7◆	1986	Q0.03	2-16-00	1-31	0.12	0.12	0.11	27.3	371	123	8-28-99	85.1	...	96681	Fb	v0.11	v□0.47	v0.72	v0.77	E0.66↑	0.68	9 Mo Nov	v0.50	v0.41	7
8◆	....	None Since Public			...	Nil	....	2.03	66.8	86.1	9-30-99	564	[51]5	17075	Dc	...	pd0.56	pvd0.24	vd0.65	....	0.36	9 Mo Sep	vd0.60	v0.41	8
9◆	1987	Q0.01½	12-30-99	12-8	0.04½	0.06	0.04	15.7	278	124	9-30-99	184	...	±41384	Sp	d0.19	□d0.11	v0.99	v1.20	v1.58	1.58				9
10	1999	Q0.01½	12-30-99	12-8	0.03	0.06	....	....	...	...		....	...	13794	Sp	v0.19	v□d0.11	v0.99	v1.21	....	1.52	6 Mo Mar	v0.43	v0.74	10
11	1995	Q0.06	9-30-99	9-15	0.18	0.24	0.24	7.67	822	948	10-02-99	400	65	14320	Dc	v1.08	v□1.39	□v0.74	v2.52	....	0.21	9 Mo Sep	v1.63	vd0.68	11
12	1995	Q0.60	1-31-00	12-29	2.33	2.40	2.19	....	34.2	32.4	9-30-99	....	...	49553	Dc	...	vp0.98	pv1.39	v1.52	....	1.49	9 Mo Sep	v1.11	v1.08	12
13◆	1987	Q0.10	12-17-99	12-2	0.40	0.40	0.40	Total Deposits $193M			9-30-99	9.39	...	1792	Dc	v[52]0.83	v[53]0.55	v1.15	v0.83	....	0.95	9 Mo Sep	v0.60	v0.72	13
14	....	Plan annual div			...	....	....	5.06	9.91	24.8	6-30-99	442	...	★40676	Dc	...	...	...	vpd1.71	....	d0.56	9 Mo Sep	vd2.46	vd1.31	14
15	1993	Q0.35	12-1-99	10-28	1.32½	1.40	1.225	24.0	618	851	9-30-99	1977	[54]...	84738	Dc	v□2.27	v□2.41	v2.74	v2.85	E3.05	3.51	12 Mo Sep	v2.66	v□3.51	15
16	1989	0.041	12-31-99	9-27	0.076	0.08	0.066	828	2922	1317	6-30-99	942	...	179573	Mr	d0.52	v0.11	v0.26	v0.05	....	d0.06	3 Mo Jun	v0.01	vd0.10	16
17◆	1979	Div Omitted 8-5-98			...	Nil	0.20	46.6	114	121	9-30-99	64.6	...	26504	Dc	v0.90	v0.74	v1.17	vd1.32	....	d3.31	9 Mo Sep	vd0.92	v□d2.91	17
18	1987	Div Omitted 2-2-99			...	Nil	0.10	33.2	165	187	9-30-99	1714	...	100306	Dc	Δvd2.96	v3.47	□vd16.88	vd7.46	Ed0.22	d6.73	9 Mo Sep	vd1.04	vd0.31	18
19◆	1998	0.02¼	6-30-99	4-28	0.02¼	0.02	0.02	0.26	3.73	5.57	9-30-99	13.7	...	4611	Dc	0.11	v0.02	v0.08	v0.09	....	0.01	9 Mo Sep	v0.14	v0.06	19
20◆	1965	Q0.03	2-1-00	1-4	0.12	0.12	0.12	39.1	767	267	9-30-99	333	...	[56]27090	Mr	1.09	v1.00	v1.14	v1.03	....	1.19	6 Mo Sep	v0.42	v0.58	20
21◆	1934	Q0.25½	12-12-99	11-23	1.02	1.02	0.90	152	2630	2745	9-30-99	1899	p88	265256	Dc	v1.91	v1.56	v1.80	v2.06	E2.33	2.27	9 Mo Sep	v1.47	v1.68	21
22	1979	Q0.53	1-1-00	12-15	2.12	2.12	2.12	Cv into 16 com				....	75	...	Dc	...	...	...	....	....	....				22
23◆	1988	Q0.17	12-10-99	11-23	0.68	0.68	0.60	22.4	204	90.5	9-30-99	....	...	7286	Dc	v1.86	v1.78	v2.02	v2.72	....	3.07	9 Mo Sep	v1.82	v2.17	23
24	1964	0.14	12-29-99	12-1	0.55	0.55	0.55	0.04	9.19	0.02	9-30-99	....	...	1510	Dc	v0.55	v0.54	v0.55	v0.55	....	0.55	9 Mo Sep	v0.41	v0.41	24
25	1996	Q0.06	12-1-99	11-10	0.24	0.24	0.24	31.8	371	347	9-30-99	122	...	20825	Dc	v1.68	v1.72	v1.62	vd0.68	E1.00	1.17	9 Mo Sep	vd1.22	v0.63	25
26	1990	Q0.02½	12-1-99	11-10	0.10	0.10	0.10	44.4	355	316	9-30-99	62.5	...	40861	Dc	v1.33	v1.54	v1.90	v2.02	E2.11	2.04	9 Mo Sep	v1.47	v1.49	26
27	1993	Div Omitted 5-7-99			0.02½	Nil	0.23¾	2.71	127	136	9-30-99	167	113	10086	Dc	1.45	v[57]1.08	v0.09	vd0.42	....	d1.97	9 Mo Sep	vd0.32	vd1.87	27
28◆	1990	Q0.022	1-4-00	12-15	0.087	0.087	h[59]0.122	75.8	749	428	9-30-99	103	...	±42755	Dc	±v0.96	v±1.73	±v1.30	v±0.97	....	2.85	9 Mo Sep	v±0.65	v±2.53	28
29◆	1990	Q0.03	1-4-00	12-15	0.12	0.12	h[60]0.155	....	...	...		....	...	34842	Dc	±v0.96	v±1.73	±v1.30	±v0.97	....	0.97				29
30	....	None Since Public			...	Nil	....	Total Assets $328.02M			10-02-99	....	...	46473	Dc	pv0.05	v0.54	v0.46	v0.15	....	0.79	9 Mo Sep	v0.13	v0.77	30
31	1997	Q0.06	1-21-00	1-5	0.24	0.24	0.24	0.40	10.1	4.40	9-26-99	7.61	...	11704	Je	v0.22	v0.28	v0.33	v0.36	v0.23	0.26	3 Mo Sep	v0.04	v0.07	31
32	1987	tS0.05	9-20-99	8-18	t0.10	0.10	t0.10	347	627	278	6-30-99	915	...	325611	Dc	v0.31	vd0.27	vd1.06	v0.36	E0.15↓	....	9 Mo Sep	n/a	v0.09	32
33	1999	Q0.48⅛	11-12-99	10-28	1.587	1.925	....	3.19	522	507	9-30-99	323	...	±34386	Dc	...	...	vpd0.36	n/a	....	....	9 Mo Sep	v0.38	v1.13	33
34	....	None Since Public			...	Nil	....	3.87	539	528	9-30-99	653	47	17917	Dc	v0.16	v□1.23	v0.77	vd3.77	....	d3.62	9 Mo Sep	v0.22	v0.37	34
35	....	None Since Public			...	Nil	....	0.38	0.97	0.27	9-30-99	0.02	500	6371	Dc	d0.46	vd0.54	vd0.18	vd0.31	....	d0.20	9 Mo Sep	vd0.22	vd0.11	35
36	....	None Since Public			...	Nil	....	62.7	76.5	4.64	6-30-99	1.60	p...	★50849	Dc	...	...	...	vpd1.00	....	d2.89	9 Mo Sep	vd0.25	vpd2.14	36
37◆	....	None Since Public			...	Nil	....	47.1	123	42.1	9-25-99	....	...	16560	Mr	v1.42	v1.67	v2.15	v□3.02	E3.57	3.28	6 Mo Sep	v1.43	v1.69	37
38	....	None Paid			...	Nil	....	6.51	31.6	12.8	8-31-99	3.48	...	11220	Nv	0.10	0.28	v0.42	v0.12	....	d0.33	9 Mo Aug	v0.30	vd0.15	38
39	....	None Since Public			...	Nil	....	2.64	2.69	1.08	p6-30-99	3.33	...	★5515	Dc	...	...	...	....	....	....	Pro forma EPS not reported			39
40	....	0.03	7-16-82	6-28	...	Nil	....	26.1	182	101	9-30-99	88.0	...	±23618	Dc	±0.03	±[61]0.21	±v[62]0.96	v±0.21	....	0.30	9 Mo Sep	v±d0.03	v±0.06	40
41	....	None Since Public			...	Nil	....	....	...	...		....	...	17916	Dc	±0.03	±[61]0.21	v±[62]0.96	±v0.21	....	0.16	3 Mo Mar	v±Nil	v±d0.05	41
42	....	None Since Public			...	Nil	....	0.72	56.7	57.2	9-30-99	49.3	...	7941	Dc	v0.67	v0.26	v□0.28	v0.51	....	0.69	9 Mo Sep	v0.59	v0.77	42
43	....	None Since Public			...	Nil	....	7.50	207	139	9-25-99	1039	...	60547	Dc	v□0.07	v0.36	v□0.37	v0.57	E0.70	0.64	9 Mo Sep	v0.47	v0.54	43
44	....	None Since Public			...	Nil	....	5.61	9.95	4.20	9-30-99	1.62	...	21223	Dc	v0.12	vd0.09	vd0.84	vd0.86	....	d0.42	9 Mo Sep	vd0.70	vd0.26	44
45	....	[63]0.01	7-24-97	6-20	...	Nil	....	Total Assets $150.82M			9-30-99	73.2	...	7983	Dc	v0.51	v0.40	v0.50	v0.57	....	0.45	9 Mo Sep	v0.41	v0.29	45
46	....	None Since Public			...	Nil	....	17.2	18.3	4.77	6-30-99	0.16	...	★42208	Dc	...	...	...	vd0.71	....	d1.00	6 Mo Jun	vd0.40	vd0.69	46
47	1989	Q0.57	11-24-99	11-9	2.28	2.28	2.26	127	142	75.9	9-30-99	[64]785	...	69207	Dc	v2.17	v4.71	v1.72	v0.90	....	1.61	9 Mo Sep	v0.61	v1.32	47
48◆	....	5%Stk	8-19-96	6-20	...	Nil	....	0.34	29.3	25.1	8-27-99	12.1	...	±2059	Nv	±1.41	v±0.84	v±0.58	±v0.84	....	1.51	9 Mo Aug	v±0.47	v±1.14	48
49◆	....	5%Stk	8-19-96	6-20	...	Nil	....	....	...	...		....	...	1248	Nv	±1.41	±v0.84	v±0.58	±v0.84	....	1.51	9 Mo Aug	v±0.47	v±1.14	49
50	1984	†0.26½	1-10-00	12-29	1.00	1.00	†1.31½	Total Assets $166M			9-30-99	74.6	[65]...	11829	Dc	v1.03	v1.18	v1.35	v1.16	....	1.21	9 Mo Sep	v0.84	v0.89	50

◆**Stock Splits & Divs By Line Reference Index** [1]3-for-2,'95:2-for-1,'97. [2]3-for-2,'94,'95,'96. [4]2-for-1,'95. [7]3-for-2,'97,'98. [8]Vote 10% stk div,ex Jan 5,'00. [9]3-for-2 in Cl'A','99. [13]2-for-1,'97. [17]2-for-1,'94. [19]2-for-1,'95. [20]3-for-2,'94,'95. [21]2-for-1,'98. [23]3-for-2,'97:2-for-1,'98. [28]3-for-2,'96:2-for-1,'98:No adj for stk dstr of Penton Media,'98. [29]No adj for stk dstr of Penton Media,'98:3-for-2,'96:2-for-1,'98. [37]2-for-1,'97. [48]10% in Cl'B','95:Adj for 5% in Cl'B','96. [49]10%,'95:Adj for 5%,'96.

¶ S&P 500
# MidCap 400
✣ SmallCap 600
• Options

Index	Ticker	Name of Issue (Call Price of Pfd. Stocks)	Market	Com. Rank. & Pfd. Rating	Inst. Hold Cos	Inst. Hold Shs. (000)	Principal Business	Price Range 1971-97 High	1971-97 Low	1998 High	1998 Low	1999 High	1999 Low	December, 1999 Dec. Sales in 100s	Last Sale Or Bid High	Low	Last	%Div Yield	P-E Ratio	EPS 5 Yr Growth	% Annualized Total Return 12 Mo	36 Mo	60 Mo
1	PCC	✔PMC Commercial Tr	AS	NR	18	784	Real estate investment trust	20¾	11¼	20¾	13 1/16	16 11/16	9¾	8156	12 7/16	9¾	10⅛	18.2	6	10	−31.1	−8.1	7.1
2•[1]	PMCS	✔PMC-Sierra Inc	NNM	C	407	51945	Supplies integrated circuits	17 9/16	1⅝	32 13/16	11 7/16	161⅛	31 5/16	299829	161⅛	101⅛	160 5/16	...	..	NM	408	178	111
3	PFC	✔PMCC Financial	AS	NR	1	15	Consumer financial svcs	....	....	9⅜	5⅜	9¼	3¾	1830	5⅜	3¾	3¾	...	9	...	−53.8	...	...
#4•[2]	PMA	✔PMI Group	NY,Ch,P	NR	261		Private mortgage insurer	49 5/16	22 11/16	57	22	55½	26 11/16	53457	50 15/16	47½	48 13/16	0.3	11	16	49.3	10.2	...
¶5•[3]	PNC	✔PNC Bank Corp	NY,Ch,P	A−	812	162215	Comml bkg,Penn,mid Atlantic	58¾	2¼	66¾	38¾	62	43	289065	56½	43	44½	4.0	11	18	−15.0	9.2	20.7
6	Pr C	$1.60cm Cv C Pfd(20)vtg	NY	BBB	2	3		96⅞	14	105	68¼	99	72⅝	20	92	72⅝	74¼B	2.2	..	...	...	...	...
7	Pr D	$1.80cm Cv D Pfd(20)vtg	NY	NR	3	2		96¼	15½	106	72	101¼	73¼	12	93¼	73¼	74¼B	2.4	..	...	...	...	...
✣8•[4]	PPP	✔Pogo Producing	NY,B,Ch,P,Ph	B	162	33840	Oil&gas explor,dev,prod'n	49⅞	2½	34 11/16	9 13/16	23 7/16	8 15/16	40393	20½	15⅝	20⅜	0.6	46	Neg	58.0	−24.0	3.3
9	Pr Q	6.50%[53]Pogo Trl Cv[54]QUIPS(52.275)	NY	B	29	1992		....	....	....	....	57⅜	43¼	4544	49¼	43¼	49¼	6.6	..	...	...	...	...
10•[5]	PKX	✔Pohang Iron & Steel ADS[56]	NY,Ch,Ph,P	NR	179	51613	Steel production, Korea	37⅞	14⅛	25 3/16	10	42 3/16	13 13/16	85882	39 3/16	32⅞	35	0.7	17	9	110	21.2	4.6
✣11•[6]	PII	✔Polaris Industries	NY,Ch,P,Ph	A−	164	10454	Mfrs snowmobiles & ATV's	36¼	4 11/16	39⅜	24	45 11/16	27	12425	39	34	36¼	2.2	12	1	−5.4	17.7	6.2
¶12•[7]	PRD	✔Polaroid Corp	NY,B,C,Ch,P,Ph	B−	266	36366	Photographic equip & film	74¾	7 1/16	49 15/16	17 7/16	30⅝	16½	154276	19½	16½	18 13/16	3.2	16	Neg	3.3	−22.8	−8.8
#13•[8]	PMS	✔Policy Mgmt Systems	NY,Ch,Ph,P	B−	198	33095	Computer softw for insur co's	43⅝	4	57¾	28 13/16	54 15/16	16⅝	35479	26 3/16	19 11/16	25 9/16	...	d	7	−49.4	3.5	4.0
14•[9]	RL	✔Polo Ralph Lauren'A'	NY,Ph	NR	125	23709	Retail apparel/home prd	33	21¾	31⅜	15⅞	25⅜	16 1/16	40280	18	16⅛	17 1/16	...	17	...	−11.1	...	...
15	PPK	Polyair Inter Pack[58]	AS,To	NR	4	405	Mfr plastic pds	6½	3 13/16	5 5/16	3¾	5¼	3½	193	4⅞	4¼	4½	...	8	...	15.4	1.5	...
#16	PLCM	✔Polycom Inc	NNM	NR	221	22139	Dvlp audio conferencing prd	10¾	2⅝	23⅛	5	67¼	11 15/16	112605	67¼	47	63 11/16	...	75	...	186	136	...
17	PLMD	✔PolyMedica Corp	NNM,P	NR	69	6457	Mfr polyurethane-based medl pd	16 11/16	3⅛	13½	7¼	30 15/16	5	77678	24½	14 11/16	23⅛	...	25	32	152	...	...
18	PGI	✔Polymer Group	NY,Ph	NR	82	13248	Mfr,mkt polyolefin products	20⅝	9	13 15/16	7⅜	20½	8¾	19097	19 1/16	16¾	18¼	0.4	18	...	83.9	9.6	...
19	PLY	✔Polyphase Corp	AS,Ph,P	C	4	92	Food/elec/forestry eq,comput's	10⅝	⅛	1 3/16	¼	⅞	5/16	11021	11/16	⅜	½	...	d	−22	60.3	−54.3	−33.2
20	PLI	✔PolyVision Corp	AS	C	7	422	Mfr visual display products	116¼	¼	2⅜	11/16	3⅝	1 9/16	5676	2½	1 11/16	2 7/16	...	1	NM	18.2	48.1	−23.6
✣21	POP	✔Pope & Talbot	NY,B,Ch,P	B−	88	7143	Tissue:diapers:pulp:lumber	32⅝	2	16⅞	7⅝	16¼	6 1/16	18627	16¼	10⅞	16	2.8	..	−5	101	5.8	5.5
22	BPOP	✔Popular Inc	NNM	A	90	21804	General banking,Puerto Rico	28½	7/16	37½	23	37⅞	24 15/16	19473	29 1/16	24 15/16	27 15/16	2.3	15	15	−16.3	20.4	34.9
23	PSI	✔Porta Systems	AS,B,Ch,P	C	12	489	Mfr telecommunications eq	130	¾	5⅜	1¼	2½	⅝	5531	1	⅝	¾	...	d	NM	−63.6	−22.7	−48.2
24•[10]	PRSF	✔Portal Software	NNM	NR	70	12727	Customer mgmt,bill'g softwr	....	....	....	....	126	14	163173	121	91	102⅞	...	d	...	...	...	...
25	PGB	Portland Genl Elec 8.25% 'QUIDS'[62]	NY	....[63]	1	.5	Quarterly Income Debt Sec	27	24⅛	26½	25⅛	26 1/16	22 3/16	571	24⅝	22 3/16	22½	9.2	..	...	−5.2	4.1	...
26	PT	✔Portugal Telecom ADS[65]	NY,Ch,Ph,P	NR	82	46785	Telecommun svcs, Portugal	9 9/16	3 9/16	12½	6 7/16	11½	7 11/16	64922	11½	9⅝	10⅞	1.7	23	24	25.2	27.1	...
27	PPS	✔Post Properties	NY,Ph,P	NR	208	28162	Real estate investment trust	43½	27¼	42	35 13/16	42⅛	35	96566	38 11/16	36	38¼	7.3	16	12	6.9	4.9	10.8
28•[11]	POT	✔Potash Corp Saskatchewan	NY,To,Ch,Mo,P	A−	168	17416	Mine & produce potash	89⅞	10¾	97 3/16	48⅜	74 3/16	42 9/16	26337	49¾	43⅝	48 3/16	◆1.4	d	Neg	−22.7	−15.5	9.6
¶29•[2]	PCH	✔Potlatch Corp	NY,B,Ch,P,Ph	B−	247	14720	Lumber, plywood, papers	52¾	4⅞	48⅜	31	45½	32½	14610	44 11/16	40	44⅝	3.9	31	−14	26.5	5.6	8.0
30	PEQ	Potomac Edison 8.00% 'QUIDS'	NY	A−[68]	..	...	Qtly Income Debt Securities	27⅛	24	26½	24⅞	26	22⅞	698	24½	22⅞	23⅛B	8.6	..	...	−1.8	5.4	...
#31•[3]	POM	✔Potomac Electric Pwr	NY,B,Ch,P,Ph	B	293	47891	Utility: el sv DC,MD,VA	29⅝	4 3/16	27 13/16	23 1/16	31¾	21¼	80504	24⅞	21¼	22 15/16	7.2	12	10	−7.1	2.7	11.4
32	POW	✔Power Corp of [69]Canada[70]	To	A−	9	4973	Financial svcs/insurance	26	1 7/16	37½	21¾	35⅜	21 11/16	29330	28	23⅞	24¾	2.0	11	27	−24.2	24.0	23.5
33	PWF	✔Power Financial	To	A	19	16020	Financial svcs/insurance,Cdn	25⅛	2 1/16	37½	22⅛	35⅝	20 13/16	18878	28¼	23⅛	24	2.8	11	27	−27.9	31.4	33.6
34	POWI	✔Power Integrations	NNM	NR	143	23320	Dgn integrated circuits	4¾	4	13⅝	3⅞	57¾	10⅜	76356	53⅞	40	47 15/16	...	62	...	296	...	...
35	PWG	✔PowerGen PLC ADS[71]	NY	NR	46	7681	Elec generation&sale,U.K.	55	28⅞	61¾	48	59⅛	27½	8492	35 9/16	27½	31⅝	5.1	13	Neg	−38.3	−2.4	...
✣36	PWAV	✔Powerwave Technologies	NNM	NR	232	16416	Dgn/mfr wireless communic eqp	49	11	22 15/16	5⅝	80 1/16	16 13/16	98118	72⅝	48¼	58⅜	...	..	...	213	58.6	...
¶37•[3]	PPL	✔PP&L Resources	NY,B,C,Ch,Ph,P	B+	376	51537	Hldg co:Penn Pwr & Lt	31	6½	28 15/16	20⅞	32	20⅜	102661	23 7/16	20⅜	22⅞	4.4	10	11	−14.9	5.9	10.8
¶38•[3]	PPG	✔PPG Indus	NY,B,Ch,P,Ph	A−	646	92289	Coatings&chem/flat glass	67½	1 11/16	76⅝	49⅛	70¾	47 15/16	72008	63	55½	62 9/16	2.4	20	6	10.3	6.2	13.8
¶39•[12]	PX	✔Praxair Inc	NY,P	NR	628	126521	Ind'l gases/spcl coatings	58	13⅝	53⅞	30 11/16	58⅛	32	115424	51¾	43 15/16	50 5/16	1.1	18	14	44.6	4.1	21.0
✣40	PPD	✔Pre-Paid Legal Svcs	NY,Ch,Ph,P	B	193	13574	Sells legal svc contracts	34⅝	¼	44 3/16	13½	39 15/16	19⅞	25679	24⅝	21½	24	...	14	50	−27.3	9.6	64.4
#41•[8]	PCP	✔Precision Castparts	NY,Ch,Ph,P	A−	218	18600	Castings for aircraft engines	67 11/16	3/16	64¼	32⅝	47¼	23 7/16	31264	28 7/16	23 7/16	26¼	0.9	7	24	−40.3	−18.7	5.9
42	PDS	✔Precision Drilling	NY,To,Ch,Ph	NR	150	21062	Oilfield & industrial svcs	37 3/16	15 3/16	25¾	10	27⅞	8 13/16	28469	25¾	20⅛	25 11/16	...	61	...	127	13.9	...
43	PRRC	✔Precision Response	NNM	NR	31	6646	Telemarketing/customer svc	46½	6⅛	11	3¾	29⅜	3⅛	42607	29⅜	20 11/16	24¼	...	78	...	218	−11.6	...
44	PCSN	Precision Standard	NSC	B−	9	714	Aircraft maintenance/systems	24½	1½	6¼	1⅛	12 7/16	3⅜	1820	10	7½	9⅞	...	5	NM	172	79.0	31.6
45	PRDS	✔Predictive Systems	NNM	NR	..	...	Computer ntwk consult'g svc	....	....	....	....	68	18	24531	68	40⅜	65½	...	..	...	...	...	...
46	PI	Premdor Inc	NY,Ph,To,Mo	B−	31	14382	Mfr,dstr wood doors	14⅜	6¾	11¾	6 7/16	12⅛	8⅛	451	9 3/16	8⅛	8⅞	...	10	...	−5.3	0.5	4.5
47	PPA	Premier Bancorp	AS	NR	..	...	General banking,Penn	....	....	....	....	12¾	12½	6	12¾	12½	12¾	...	16	...	...	...	...
✣48	PMB	✔Premier Bancshares	NY	NR	68	2187	General banking, Georgia	17 15/16	4 13/16	30	15¼	26½	13⅛	11416	17⅜	13⅛	13⅝	2.6	22	26	−47.0	24.2	...
49	PFP	✔Premier Farnell PLC ADS[74]	NY	NR	24	3094	Dstr electronic components	25¼	13	14¼	4¾	14¾	4⅞	5339	14¾	11⅛	13⅞	2.1	30	...	189	−14.4	...
50	Pr	$1.35 cm Cv[75]Pref[76]ADS[77](NC)	NY	NR	25	1663		29	19	22⅞	15½	21	15 1/16	273	20⅜	19¼	19¼	7.2	..	...	...	...	...

Uniform Footnote Explanations-See Page 4. Other: [1]P,Ph:Cycle 2. [2]CBOE:Cycle 3. [3]Ph:Cycle 2. [4]CBOE,P:Cycle 2. [5]CBOE,Ph:Cycle 2. [6]ASE:Cycle 3. [7]CBOE:Cycle 1. [8]ASE:Cycle 2. [9]CBOE,Ph:Cycle 1. [10]CBOE,P,Ph:Cycle 1. [11]CBOE,To:Cycle 3. [12]ASE:Cycle 1. [51]®$2.87,'96. [52]®$0.96,'96. [53]Quarterly Income Preferred Securities. [54]Fr 6-1-2002,scale to 50 in 2009. [55]Of Pogo Producing. [56]Ea ADS rep 0.25 com, par 5000 won. [57]Approx. [58]Sep'99 & prior pricing in $Cdn. [59]Stk dstr of CardioTech Intl Inc. [60]Fiscal Apr'97 & prior. [61]8 Mo Dec'98:Fiscal Apr'98 earn $d0.06. [62]Jr Sub Deferrable Int Debs. [63]Rated BBB+ by S&P. [64]Payment period can be extended re-spec cond.. [65]Ea ADS rep 1 ord shr,par PTE 1,000. [66]Proceeds from sale of rts. [67]Incl proceeds fr sale of rts. [68]Rated A by S&P. [69]Oct'96 & prior pricing in $Cdn. [70]Sub vtg shrs. [71]Ea ADS rep four ord shrs. [72]1996 & prior in Cdn$. [73]Excl subsid pfd. [74]Ea ADS rep 2 ord shrs. [75]Ea Pref ADS rep 1 $1.35 cm Cv Red Pref Shr. [76]Hldrs opt Cv into'Sterling Pref Shrs'. [77]Co opt Cv aft 4-30-2001 if 75% of Pref convtd. [78]To 4-22-2016.

Index	Splits ◆ Cash Divs. Ea. Yr. Since	Dividends: Latest Payment Period $	Date	Ex. Div.	Total $ So Far 1999	Ind. Rate	Paid 1998	Financial Position Mil-$ Cash& Equiv.	Curr. Assets	Curr. Liab.	Balance Sheet Date	Capitalization Lg Trm Debt Mil-$	Shs. 000 Pfd.	Com.	Earnings $ Per Shr. Years End	1995	1996	1997	1998	1999	Last 12 Mos.	Interim Earnings Period	$ per Shr. 1998	1999	Index
1	1994	Q0.46	1-10-00	12-29	1.83½	1.84	1.75½	Total Assets $201M			9-30-99	101	...	6533	Dc	v1.42	v1.51	v1.66	v1.75	....	1.61	9 Mo Sep	v1.32	v1.18	1
2◆	....	None Since Public			...	Nil	....	174	216	79.1	9-26-99	1.63	...	68056	Dc	v0.03	vd0.81	v0.52	vd0.04	....	1.10	9 Mo Sep	vd0.24	v0.90	2
3	....	None Since Public			...	Nil	....	Total Assets $85.6M			9-30-99	67.5	...	3725	Dc	...	pv0.21	vp0.84	vp0.75	....	0.44	9 Mo Sep	vp0.58	v0.27	3
4◆	1995	Q0.04	1-14-00	12-28	0.14	0.16	0.133	Total Assets $2040M			9-30-99	244	...	44670	Dc	v2.57	v3.01	v3.49	v4.03	E4.49	4.23	9 Mo Sep	v3.06	v3.26	4
5	1865	Q0.45	10-24-99	10-13	1.68	1.80	1.58	Total Deposits $45146.00M			9-30-99	10006	6690	294000	Dc	v1.19	v[51]2.88	v3.28	v3.60	E3.90	4.06	9 Mo Sep	v2.68	v3.14	5
6	1984	Q0.40	1-2-00	12-1	1.60	1.60	1.60	Cv into 1.667 com,$12				....	393	...	Dc	...	...	...	....	....	....				6
7	1985	Q0.45	1-2-00	12-1	1.80	1.80	1.80	Cv into 1.667 com,$12				....	501	...	Dc	...	...	...	....	....	....				7
8	1994	Q0.03	11-19-99	11-3	0.12	0.12	0.12	28.4	103	62.8	9-30-99	365	...	40203	Dc	v0.28	v□[52]0.97	v1.06	vd1.14	E0.44	d0.50	9 Mo Sep	vd0.29	v0.35	8
9	1999	Q0.81¼	12-1-99	11-26	1.616	3.25	....	Cv into 2.1053 com[55]				....	3000	...	Dc	...	...	...	....	....	....	Mand redm 6-1-2029			9
10	1995	[57]0.233		12-28	0.214	0.23	0.148	2279	5818	4303	12-31-98	4080	...	94000	Dc	3.25	v1.98	v1.16	v2.10	....	2.10				10
11◆	1987	Q0.20	11-15-99	10-28	0.80	0.80	0.72	3.17	256	261	9-30-99	50.0	...	24398	Dc	v±2.19	v2.24	v2.45	v1.19	....	2.92	9 Mo Sep	v0.32	v2.05	11
12	1952	Q0.15	12-23-99	11-24	0.60	0.60	0.60	88.0	1214	792	9-26-99	573	...	44525	Dc	vd3.09	v□0.33	vd2.81	vd1.15	E1.19	d2.15	9 Mo Sep	v0.55	vd0.45	12
13◆	....	None Since Public			...	Nil	....	29.1	250	110	9-30-99	202	...	35572	Dc	v0.08	v1.22	v1.34	v1.36	Ed0.14	d0.82	9 Mo Sep	v1.01	vd1.17	13
14	....	None Since Public			...	Nil	....	42.4	761	388	10-02-99	80.0	...	±99025	Mr	...	pv0.89	vp1.20	v0.91	....	1.02	6 Mo Sep	v0.73	v□0.84	14
15	....	None Paid			...	Nil	....	5.01	42.8	33.3	j5-01-99	20.1	...	6702	Oc	0.46	0.30	0.28	v0.31	....	j0.37	6 Mo Apr	v0.03	v0.09	15
16	....	None Since Public			...	Nil	....	54.1	117	38.3	9-30-99	....	...	32829	Dc	pd0.10	v0.08	vd0.06	v0.46	....	0.85	9 Mo Sep	v0.26	v0.65	16
17◆	....	h[59]....	6-27-96	6-12	...	Nil	....	11.0	57.9	26.4	9-30-99	19.4	...	★12940	Mr	v0.37	v0.27	v0.79	v0.78	....	0.94	6 Mo Sep	v0.39	v0.55	17
18	1999	Q0.02	12-10-99	11-17	0.02	0.08	....	39.4	318	140	10-02-99	936	...	32000	Dc	pvd1.39	v□0.43	v□0.86	v□0.75	....	0.99	9 Mo Sep	v□0.47	v0.71	18
19	....	None Since Public			...	Nil	....	1.49	63.5	53.6	6-30-99	26.8	66	17812	Sp	0.26	d0.03	vd1.41	□v0.01	Pvd0.10	d0.10				19
20◆	....	None Since Public			...	Nil	....	5.27	58.2	33.6	9-30-99	91.0	357	14121	Dc	vd0.67	vd0.94	v[60]d0.84	□v[61]1.99	....	2.10	9 Mo Sep	v∆0.17	v□0.28	20
21	1948	Q0.11	11-12-99	10-28	0.52	0.44	0.76	114	275	102	9-30-99	199	...	p14981	Dc	vd1.86	v0.29	v0.75	∆vd0.03	....	0.06	9 Mo Sep	v0.49	v0.58	21
22◆	1923	tQ0.16	1-3-00	12-8	0.58	0.64	t0.47	Total Deposits $13770M			9-30-99	1784	4000	135754	Dc	v1.05	v1.34	v1.50	v1.65	....	1.81	9 Mo Sep	v1.21	v1.37	22
23◆	....	None Since Public			...	Nil	....	2.74	24.1	21.6	9-30-99	13.5	...	9489	Dc	∆d22.45	v∆0.23	vd2.26	∆v0.04	....	d1.01	9 Mo Sep	v∆0.13	vd0.92	23
24◆	....	None Since Public			...	Nil	....	202	228	43.2	10-31-99	1.73	p...	79075	Ja	...	...	...	vpd0.30	....	d0.23	9 Mo Oct	vpd0.19	vpd0.12	24
25	1995	Q0.516	12-31-99	12-28	2.06¼	[64]2.063	2.062	Co option redm fr 10-10-2000 at $25				75.0	...	...	Dc	...	...	...	....	....	....	Mature 12-31-2035			25
26◆	1996	[66]0.002	7-22-99	7-8	[67]0.192	0.19	0.161	1489	2546	5798	12-31-98	1195	...	±950000	Dc	0.26	v0.37	v0.40	v0.54	....	0.46	9 Mo Sep	v0.38	v0.30	26
27	1993	Q0.70	1-15-00	12-29	2.75	2.80	2.54½	Total Assets $2257M			9-30-99	893	5000	38776	Dc	□v1.63	v1.94	□v2.09	v2.18	....	2.37	9 Mo Sep	v1.60	v□1.79	27
28	1990	gQ0.25	2-15-00	1-21	g1.33	1.00	g1.44	17.1	681	526	6-30-99	589	...	54250	Dc	v3.68	v4.59	v5.68	v4.82	Ed7.60	d6.79	9 Mo Sep	v3.82	vd7.79	28
29	1939	Q0.43½	12-6-99	11-8	1.74	1.74	1.74	11.3	392	337	9-30-99	702	...	28952	Dc	v3.72	□v2.13	v1.24	v1.28	E1.44↓	1.25	9 Mo Sep	v1.15	v1.12	29
30	1995	Q0.50	12-31-99	12-28	2.00	2.00	2.00	Co option redm fr 6-30-2000 at $25				45.5	...	...	Dc	...	...	...	....	....	....	Mature 9-30-2025			30
31	1904	Q0.41½	12-31-99	12-8	1.66	1.66	1.66	31.2	551	444	9-30-99	2248	3006	118531	Dc	v0.65	v1.82	v1.38	v1.73	E2.00	2.05	12 Mo Sep	v1.49	v2.05	31
32◆	1935	gQ0.12½	1-15-00	12-21	g0.36¼	0.50	g0.43¾	Equity per shr $6.72			j12-31-98	849	25807	196742	Dc	v0.83	v1.22	v1.49	v1.88	....	j2.25	9 Mo Sep	v1.52	v1.89	32
33◆	1957	gQ0.16½	2-1-00	12-29	g0.575	0.66	g0.47½	Equity per shr $5.60			j12-31-98	837	22000	346729	Dc	0.85	v1.05	v1.70	v1.87	....	j2.24	9 Mo Sep	v1.48	v1.85	33
34◆	....	None Since Public			...	Nil	....	60.8	82.1	18.6	9-30-99	1.67	...	26438	Dc	...	pvd0.07	v0.25	v0.48	....	0.77	9 Mo Sep	v0.33	v0.61	34
35◆	1992	0.706	11-8-99	9-29	1.618	1.62	2.721	115	808	969	j3-29-98	690	...	645000	Mr	4.37	4.14	vd1.29	vPd1.29	....	2.48	6 Mo Jun	vd1.43	v2.34	35
36	....	None Since Public			...	Nil	....	71.9	151	45.8	10-03-99	....	...	20158	Dc	pv0.31	pv0.52	v0.92	vd0.17	....	0.16	9 Mo Sep	v0.25	v0.58	36
37	1946	Q0.25	1-1-00	12-8	1.00	1.00	1.50¼	340	1479	1900	9-30-99	3900	4664	143694	Dc	v2.05	v2.05	v1.80	v□2.29	E2.35↑	2.78	9 Mo Sep	v□1.74	v□2.23	37
38◆	1899	Q0.38	12-10-99	11-8	1.52	1.52	1.42	164	3141	2291	9-30-99	1849	...	173796	Dc	v3.78	v3.93	v3.94	v4.48	E3.21	3.22	9 Mo Sep	v3.57	v2.31	38
39	1992	Q0.14	12-15-99	12-3	0.56	0.56	0.50	35.0	1283	1001	9-30-99	2745	750	158950	Dc	v1.82	v1.77	v2.53	v2.60	E2.73	2.68	9 Mo Sep	v1.94	v□2.02	39
40	....	None Paid			...	Nil	....	11.8	62.5	26.5	9-30-99	0.38	21	22547	Dc	v0.34	v0.56	v0.83	v1.26	....	1.71	9 Mo Sep	v0.76	v1.21	40
41◆	1978	Q0.06	1-3-00	12-1	0.24	0.24	0.24	31.6	567	288	9-26-99	342	...	24510	Mr	2.02	v2.57	v3.53	v4.22	E4.00	4.04	6 Mo Sep	v2.03	v1.85	41
42◆	....	None Since Public			...	Nil	....	103	261	170	j4-30-99	215	★4805	42399	Ap	...	p0.99	v1.36	v2.67	v1.22	j0.29	6 Mo Oct	v0.72	vd0.21	42
43	....	None Since Public			...	Nil	....	2.43	53.2	30.6	9-30-99	21.2	...	21634	Dc	pv0.05	vp0.36	vd0.61	vd0.47	....	0.31	9 Mo Sep	vd0.53	v0.25	43
44◆	....	None Paid			...	Nil	....	1.75	42.7	34.1	9-30-99	20.1	...	3978	Dc	d1.24	vd0.32	vd2.30	v2.53	....	1.90	9 Mo Sep	v2.24	v1.61	44
45	....	None Since Public			...	Nil	....	0.36	15.7	3.90	6-30-99	0.40	p...	★22565	Dc	...	...	...	n/a	....	....	6 Mo Jun	n/a	vpd0.01	45
46	....	None Since Public			...	Nil	....	2.64	290	137	6-30-99	174	...	38205	Dc	0.56	[72]0.75	v0.11	v0.77	....	0.92	9 Mo Sep	v0.61	v0.76	46
47	....	None Paid			...	Nil	....	Total Deposits $219M			9-30-99	1.50	[73]...	2921	Dc	...	...	v0.49	v0.60	....	0.79	9 Mo Sep	v0.40	v0.59	47
48◆	1996	Q0.09	11-18-99	11-2	0.36	0.36	0.33	Total Deposits $1309.69M			9-30-99	121	41	p31919	Dc	v0.37	v0.47	v0.73	v0.78	....	0.61	9 Mo Sep	v0.65	v0.48	48
49	1996	0.132	10-15-99	9-22	0.29	0.29	0.395	57.4	566	249	1-31-99	317	27948	271597	Ja	...	v1.17	v0.83	v0.53	....	0.46	9 Mo Oct	v0.25	v0.18	49
50	1996	0.67½	1-26-00	12-15	1.392	1.39	1.434	Cv into 2.06864 Ord shr[78]				....	27900	...	My	...	...	...	....	....	....	Mand Red 4-29-2016, $25			50

◆**Stock Splits & Divs By Line Reference Index** [2]2-for-1,'95,'99. [4]3-for-2,'99. [11]3-for-2,'95. [13]2-for-1,'98. [17]Adj for 5%,'94. [20]1-for-15 REVERSE,'95. [22]2-for-1,'96,'98. [23]1-for-5 REVERSE,'96. [24]To split 2-for-1,ex Jan 20,'00. [26]5-for-1,'99. [32]2-for-1,'98. [33]2-for-1,'97,'98. [34]2-for-1,'99. [35]5-for-2,'95. [38]2-for-1,'94. [41]3-for-2,'94. [42]2-for-1,'97. [44]1-for-4 REVERSE,'98. [48]1.8055-for-1,'97:3-for-2,'98.

¶ S&P 500 # MidCap 400 ✣ SmallCap 600 • Options

Index	Ticker	Name of Issue (Call Price of Pfd. Stocks)	Market	Com. Rank. & Pfd. Rating	Inst. Hold Cos	Inst. Hold Shs. (000)	Principal Business	1971-97 High	1971-97 Low	1998 High	1998 Low	1999 High	1999 Low	Dec. Sales in 100s	December, 1999 Last Sale Or Bid High	Low	Last	%Div Yield	P-E Ratio	EPS 5 Yr Growth	% Annualized Total Return 12 Mo	36 Mo	60 Mo
1	PNB	✔Premier National Bancorp	AS	B	43	2668	General bkg, New York	21⅛	6	22¾	13½	20⅝	15	3817	18 15/16	17¼	18 7/16	3.6	14	17	24.0	10.1	19.3
#2	PKS	✔Premier Parks	NY	NR	256	72884	Own/oper theme parks	21¾	9	33 11/16	14	41⅝	23⅜	85012	30½	23⅝	28⅞	...	d	−8	−4.5	21.6	...
3	Pr A	7.50% Cv Dep[51]'PIES'[52](NC)	NY	CCC+	14	926		....	....	65	34	74	47½	13273	56½	47⅞	54	7.5	..	...	...	...	...
4•[1]	PTEK	✔Premiere Technologies	NNM	NR	80	10047	Telecommunication svcs	50	14½	36⅜	2½	20⅞	4⅜	237413	8⅜	5⅞	7	...	d	Neg	−5.1	−34.6	...
5	WEAR	✔PremiumWear Inc	NNM,Ph	NR	19	770	Intimate apparel:mens wear	18 15/16	¼	8	4 9/16	7 3/16	4¼	444	6	5	5½	...	10	NM	−18.5	12.8	12.2
6•[2]	PP	✔Prentiss Properties Trust	NY,Ch,Ph	NR	195	28369	Real estate investment trust	29¾	20	28¼	18½	24⅜	18⅛	26267	21⅜	18⅝	21⅜	8.2	12	...	3.4	1.5	...
7	PDL.B	✔Presidential Rlty Cl'B'	AS	NR	5	314	Real estate investment trust	14¾	1⅝	8	6 3/16	8⅛	5½	982	6⅞	5½	6⅞	9.3	3	14	−6.0	12.0	4.6
8	PDL.A	Class A	AS	NR	2	1		18⅝	1¾	9¼	6¼	7¾	5⅞	297	6¾	5⅞	6⅝	9.7	3	14	−9.2	10.1	3.7
9	PDC	✔Presley Cos	NY,Ph,P	NR	2	6	Home building/community dvlp	86⅞	2 13/16	6 9/16	2 3/16	6 7/16	1⅞	4264	6 3/16	4 5/16	5½	...	2	NM	135	−0.7	−16.7
10•[3]	PRST	✔Presstek Inc	NNM	B−	50	2273	Dvlp stge:color imaging sys	100	⅞	30¼	5¼	19⅞	5	101662	19⅞	10¾	13⅞	...	d	Neg	104	−27.0	1.9
11	PRVW	Preview Systems	NNM	NR	..	...	Elec prd dstr softwr on net	....	....	....	....	94	21	117862	94	21	64⅞	...	..	...	...	...	...
12•[4]	PTVL	✔Preview Travel	NNM	NR	71	2728	On-line travel svcs	11 15/16	6⅞	44	7½	60¾	14¼	58234	60¾	43	52⅛	...	d	...	183	...	...
13•[5]	PRIA	✔PRI Automation	NNM	NR	205	14583	Mfr semiconductor mfg equip	59	6⅝	37½	9 9/16	68⅛	20¾	89095	68⅛	43½	67⅛	...	d	Neg	158	43.5	52.8
14	PR	✔Price Communications	AS,B,Ch,P	NR	122	36765	Telecommunications/cellular	1¾	....	8	1 9/16	28⅜	7 7/16	40755	28⅜	23¼	27 13/16	s...	d	Neg	285	217	122
15	PCLN	✔priceline.com Inc	NNM	NR	127	36339	Internet based buy/sell svcs	....	....	....	....	165	16	635257	67½	45½	47⅜	...	..	...	...	...	...
✣16	PDE	✔Pride International	NY,Ph	B	211	33587	Oil & gas well svcs in U.S.	37¾	2⅛	27½	6⅛	18 5/16	4 13/16	78059	15 3/16	11⅞	14⅝	...	d	Neg	107	−14.3	23.9
17	PCAG	PrimaCom AG ADS[57]	NNM	NR	14	2896	Own/oper CATV networks	....	....	....	....	36½	15	6502	34¼	22	32⅝	...	..	...	...	...	...
✣18•[4]	PMK	✔Primark Corp	NY,P,Ph	B	128	11625	Fin'l info/hlth care svcs	42	4¾	44½	22½	29 3/16	18⅞	7342	27 15/16	24¾	27 13/16	...	27	26	2.5	4.0	16.2
19	PMCP	Prime Capital	NSC	C	4	853	Specialty financial svcs	7½	4	6¼	1 5/16	3¾	⅜	7118	2	13/16	⅞	...	d	−37	−68.2	−45.0	...
20	PGE	✔Prime Group Realty Tr	NY,Ph	NR	68	12741	Real estate investment trust	20 9/16	19 3/16	22¼	13	17 13/16	12⅝	16644	15½	12¾	15 3/16	8.9	5	...	9.6	...	...
✣21•[6]	PDQ	✔Prime Hospitality	NY,P	NR	176	38181	Own,manage hotel chain	23 3/16	1½	21¼	4	12 15/16	7 9/16	34829	9⅛	8 3/16	8 13/16	...	12	9	−16.6	−18.2	3.3
22•[7]	PRT	✔Prime Retail	NY	NR	109	23456	Real estate investment trust	20½	10⅞	15 9/16	7½	10 3/16	5⅛	41939	6⅜	5⅛	5⅝	...	27	NM	...	...	...
23	Pr B	8.5% Ptc Cv'B'Pfd([61]125)	NY	NR	41	3642		26¼	16¼	24⅞	15¼	17¼	10¼	9007	11 13/16	10¼	11 13/16	18.0	..	...	...	...	...
24•[8]	PRM	✔PRIMEDIA Inc	NY,Ph,P	NR	83	17738	Edu/spcl interest publis'g svc	13 7/16	8½	15	9¼	18 11/16	10¾	32060	16½	12⅛	16½	...	d	−11	38.9	15.4	...
25	PKSI	✔Primus Knowledge Solutions	NNM	NR	34	4667	Problem resolution software	....	....	....	....	58⅛	11	49668	58⅛	41 9/16	45 5/16	...	..	...	...	...	...
26	PRTL	✔Primus Telecomm Grp	NNM	NR	106	11722	Intl & long distance svcs	17	7⅛	31¼	5¼	39	8⅞	73958	39	27	38¼	...	d	−43	132	44.2	...
27	PTNX	✔Printronix Inc	NNM	B−	44	3292	Design,mfr printers	25 13/16	1 9/16	17 11/16	11	24¾	11	5618	23	17	22¾	...	14	16	58.3	19.4	7.0
28•[9]	PZN	✔Prison Realty Trust	NY,Ch,Ph,P	B	184	49854	Real estate investment trust	45 9/16	¾	41½	10½	24⅜	4½	300116	8¼	4½	5 1/16	e...	..	...	−66.7	−42.3	9.7
29	PVTB	✔Private Bancorp Inc	NNM	NR	13	407	Banking/investment svcs, IL	....	....	....	....	35¾	12 7/16	2641	15⅞	12 7/16	13⅜	0.7	18	35	...	...	...
30	PRBZ	✔ProBusiness Services	NNM	NR	110	11693	Employee administrative svcs	15 5/16	7 5/16	47½	14	44¾	18¼	20589	39	25⅝	36	...	d	...	−20.9	...	...
¶31•[10]	PG	✔Procter & Gamble	NY,B,C,Ch,P,Ph	A	1810	682392	Hshld,personal care,food prod	83 7/16	3½	94 13/16	65⅛	115⅝	82	404653	115⅝	103½	109 9/16	1.2	42	7	21.5	28.5	30.8
32	PRGY	✔Prodigy Communications	NNM	NR	42	3511	Internet access svcs	....	....	....	....	50⅝	14	165415	28⅜	19⅛	19⅜	...	d	...	...	...	...
33	MDB	✔Professional Bancorp	AS	B−	19	733	Commercial banking, California	16¾	3 7/16	21 11/16	13⅝	21⅝	7¼	984	9⅛	7¼	7¼	...	d	Neg	−58.5	−9.9	2.7
34	PICM	✔Professionals Group	NNM	NR	39	2758	Hlthcare liability insurance	36¾	5/16	36¾	19 15/16	32¼	20	2954	24⅜	21⅞	23 7/16	...	9	−47	−8.5	15.7	29.8
✣35	PRGX	✔Profit Recovery Grp Intl	NNM	NR	249	26622	Accts pay/audit recovery sys	16 3/16	7 5/16	26 1/16	10 5/16	47½	18¾	149011	38 15/16	23	26 9/16	...	47	...	6.6	35.6	...
36	PGLAF	✔Progen Industries	NSC	NR	1	3	Biotechnology R & D	7¼	4½	7¼	2 5/16	4	2⅜	1265	3⅜	2⅝	2 13/16B	...	d	...	−10.0	...	...
✣37•[11]	PRGS	✔Progress Software	NNM	B	188	13875	Database mgmt sys/softwr	25 5/16	8 1/16	38⅜	14 1/16	61½	19⅞	52581	61½	37⅛	56¾	...	32	...	68.1	62.1	35.2
¶38•[12]	PGR	✔Progressive Corp,Ohio	NY,Ch,Ph,P	B+	452	52948	Insur subsid: hi risk auto	120⅞	1/16	172	94	174¼	68½	89173	81 3/16	68½	73⅛	0.4	18	11	−56.7	3.0	16.3
39	PLD	✔ProLogis Trust	NY,Ch,Ph	NR	242	89654	Real estate investment tr	25½	11½	26½	19¾	22 3/16	16¾	79372	19⅞	16¾	19¼	7.0	25	−5	−0.9	2.2	8.5
40	Pr B	7.00% cm Cv'B'Pfd([63]25)	NY	BBB	45	5750		33¼	22	34⅛	25⅝	28⅝	21⅜	17076	25¼	21⅜	24¾	7.1	..	...	...	...	...
41	PRL	✔Prolong International	AS	NR	2	3	Mfr hi-performance lubricants	6½	1½	3 7/16	1⅜	2	¼	7139	½	5/16	5/16	...	d	...	−78.3	−62.7	...
42•[11]	POI	✔Protection One	NY	NR	53	14981	Security alarm monitoring svc	21¾	4⅜	13⅞	5⅞	9 7/16	1⅜	23710	2⅜	1⅝	1 15/16	...	d	27	−77.4	−32.1	−8.3
#43•[13]	PL	✔Protective Life Corp	NY,Ch	A+	300	42788	Hldg:life,gr accid & health	32¾	½	41¼	28	40¾	27 13/16	37464	32½	28⅞	31 13/16	1.5	15	13	−19.0	18.9	23.7
✣44•[5]	PDLI	✔Protein Design Labs	NNM	C	154	10824	Antibody technology R&D	51½	5⅞	47⅛	16	74 1/16	13⅜	75211	74 1/16	40	70	...	d	−6	203	24.2	34.8
45	PHS	✔ProVantage Health Svcs	NY	NR	32	4000	Health/pharm'l info & svcs	....	....	....	....	22	7¼	17282	10⅜	7¼	8 15/16	...	..	...	...	...	...
46	PZA	✔Provena Foods	AS,Ch,Ph	B	4	17	Process/dstr spec'ty food prd	7⅜	1¾	5½	2 5/16	3¾	2 7/16	795	3	2 7/16	2⅜B	5.1	5	63	−15.9	3.3	4.3
47	PVY	✔Providence Energy	NY	B	51	1398	Natural gas service, R.I.	25 3/16	3 5/16	22¼	19 1/16	38½	18	2797	37 13/16	36½	37⅛	2.9	27	−1	84.5	35.3	25.4
48	PWX	✔Providence & Worcester RR	AS	B+	30	1695	Oper freight railroad sys	22¼	3	18⅞	10¼	14⅝	7⅝	1391	9⅜	7⅝	8	2.0	16	2	−35.1	1.6	4.6
✣49	PBKS	✔Provident Bankshares	NNM	A−	142	9976	Comm'l bkg, Maryland	29 7/16	1 1/16	34 5/16	17⅛	28 9/16	17	23908	19 15/16	17	17 5/16	s3.7	11	18	−21.2	7.4	21.7
50	PCT	Provident Cap Tr II 8.75%'SKIS'	NY	....[67]	3	62	Sub Cap Income Sec	....	....	....	....	25⅝	18 11/16	3502	22½	18 11/16	20	10.9	..	...	...	...	...

Uniform Footnote Explanations-See Page 4. Other: [1]ASE,CBOE:Cycle 2. [2]P:Cycle 2. [3]ASE,CBOE,P,Ph:Cycle 1. [4]CBOE,Ph:Cycle 1. [5]CBOE:Cycle 2. [6]Ph:Cycle 1. [7]P:Cycle 3. [8]Ph:Cycle 3. [9]ASE,CBOE,P:Cycle 1. [10]ASE,CBOE,P,Ph:Cycle 3. [11]CBOE:Cycle 3. [12]Ph:Cycle 2. [13]CBOE:Cycle 1. [51]Dep for .002 % Mand Cv Pfd. [52]Premium Income Equity Secs. [53]Cash or com. [54]re-spec cond. [55]Spl div. [56]®$0.75,'96. [57]Ea ADS rep 0.5 ord. [58]Stk dstr of Mich Consol Gas. [59]To be determined. [60]Stk dstr of Horizon Group Pptys. [61]Co opt red re spec cond. [62]Pfd in $M. [63]Fr 2-21-2001,or earlier to preserve'REIT'status. [64]Fiscal Sep'96 & prior. [65]12 Mo Dec'97. [66]Subsid Pfd. [67]Rated'BB'by S&P. [68]Or earlier upon'Tax Event're-spec cond.

Splits ◆ Index	Cash Divs. Ea.Yr. Since	Dividends: Latest Payment Period $	Date	Ex. Div.	Total $ So Far 1999	Ind. Rate	Paid 1998	Financial Position Mil-$ Cash& Equiv.	Curr. Assets	Curr. Liab.	Balance Sheet Date	Capitalization Lg Trm Debt Mil-$	Shs. 000 Pfd.	Com.	Earnings $ Per Shr. Years End	1995	1996	1997	1998	1999	Last 12 Mos.	Interim Earnings Period	$ per Shr. 1998	1999	Index
1◆	1986	Q0.16½	1-14-00	1-3	0.56	0.66	0.473	Total Deposits $1360.34M			9-30-99	75.0	...	14990	Dc	v0.89	v1.08	v1.13	v0.82	....	1.29	9 Mo Sep	v0.50	v0.97	1
2◆	....	None Since Public			...	Nil	....	171	513	374	9-30-99	1888	5000	78249	Dc	pv□d0.20	v0.07	v0.38	v□0.26	....	d0.54	9 Mo Sep	v1.48	v□0.68	2
3	1998	Q1.01¼	1-3-00	12-13	4.05	[53]4.05	2.02½	Cv into 1.6616 com				....	5000	...	Dc	...	...	...	....	....	....	Mand conv 4-1-2001[54]			3
4	....	None Since Public			...	Nil	....	10.7	108	266	9-30-99	176	...	46941	Dc	pv0.17	v□pd0.11	vd0.78	vd1.67	....	d2.65	9 Mo Sep	vd1.03	vd2.01	4
5	....	[55]5.39	3-5-97	3-6	...	Nil	....	0.90	19.3	5.55	10-02-99	....	...	2545	Dc	vd0.13	v3.37	v0.36	v0.60	....	0.54	9 Mo Sep	v0.42	v0.36	5
6	1997	Q0.44	1-14-00	12-29	1.68	1.76	1.60	Total Assets $1940M			9-30-99	855	3774	37608	Dc	p1.46	pn/a	□v1.49	v□1.89	....	1.72	9 Mo Sep	v□1.38	v1.21	6
7	1980	Q0.16	12-30-99	9-8	0.64	0.64	0.63	Total Assets $65.3M			9-30-99	39.5	...	±3626	Dc	±v0.55	v±0.73	v±0.77	v±0.77	....	2.63	9 Mo Sep	v±0.65	v±2.51	7
8	1980	Q0.16	12-30-99	12-8	0.64	0.64	0.63	....	...	...		....	...	479	Dc	v±0.55	v±0.73	v±0.77	v±0.77	....	2.63	9 Mo Sep	v±0.65	v±2.51	8
9◆	....	None Since Public			...	Nil	....	Total Assets $236M			p9-30-99	155	...	10439	Dc	vΔ±d3.80	±vNil	±vd8.60	vΔ0.70	....	2.91	9 Mo Sep	vΔ±0.07	v±Δ2.28	9
10◆	....	None Paid			...	Nil	....	18.9	37.4	12.7	10-02-99	9.44	...	32343	Dc	v0.09	v0.21	v0.44	vd0.08	....	d0.75	9 Mo Sep	v0.09	vd0.58	10
11	....	None Since Public			...	Nil	....	20.6	23.5	3.64	9-30-99	0.35	...	★15768	Dc	...	...	...	vpd5.51	....	....	9 Mo Sep	n/a	pd3.95	11
12	....	None Since Public			...	Nil	....	23.7	34.7	12.2	9-30-99	1.07	...	13939	Dc	...	pd0.65	n/a	vd2.11	....	d2.72	9 Mo Sep	vd1.15	vd1.76	12
13◆	....	None Since Public			...	Nil	....	60.0	121	42.9	6-27-99	0.53	...	22000	Sp	0.59	0.90	v1.32	vd1.22	vPd1.67	d1.67				13
14◆	....	5%Stk	8-25-99	8-10	5%Stk	Stk	....	206	237	57.9	9-30-99	700	...	56960	Dc	v0.17	v1.16	vd0.22	v□d0.40	....	d0.04	9 Mo Sep	□d0.33	v0.03	14
15	....	None Since Public			...	Nil	....	192	234	43.7	9-30-99	0.01	...	146427	Dc	...	...	...	vd1.41	....	....	9 Mo Sep	n/a	vd1.02	15
16	....	None Since Public			...	Nil	....	195	428	263	9-30-99	1189	...	60415	Dc	v0.61	v[56]0.77	v2.16	v1.39	Ed1.03	d0.80	9 Mo Sep	v1.19	vΔd1.00	16
17	....	None Since Public			...	Nil	....	Equity per shr $3.32			9-30-98	p211	...	★19729	Dc	...	...	vpd0.45	....	....	....	9 Mo SepΔ	n/a	vpd0.49	17
18	....	h[58]0.34½	5-13-88	6-1	...	Nil	....	14.9	150	319	9-30-99	151	...	19987	Dc	□v0.84	v□1.38	v□0.78	v□6.66	....	1.02	9 Mo Sep	v□6.19	v□0.55	18
19	....	None Since Public			...	Nil	....	Total Assets $49.5M			9-30-99	23.8	25	4468	Dc	vd0.43	v0.85	vd0.66	vd1.14	....	d1.21	9 Mo Sep	vd0.07	vd0.14	19
20	1998	Q0.33¾	1-20-00	12-29	1.35	1.35	1.179	Total Assets $1236.31M			9-30-99	604	6000	15136	Dc	...	pv0.48	pv0.60	v□0.91	....	2.98	9 Mo Sep	v□0.65	v2.72	20
21	....	None Since Public			...	Nil	....	32.8	78.2	70.3	9-30-99	566	...	48865	Dc	v0.54	Δv0.68	v0.54	v1.00	....	0.75	9 Mo Sep	v0.80	v□0.55	21
22	1994	Q0.29½	11-15-99	11-3	1.18	[59]....	h†[60]1.68	Total Assets $2001.83M			9-30-99	1291	11192	p43368	Dc	vd0.96	v□d0.63	□vd0.25	vd0.20	....	0.21	9 Mo Sep	vd0.31	v□0.10	22
23	1994	0.53⅛	11-15-99	11-3	2.12½	2.13	h[60]2.125	Cv into 1.196 com, $20.90				....	2982	...	Dc	...	...	...	....	....	....				23
24	....	None Since Public			...	Nil	....	30.0	498	557	9-30-99	2099	p5750	145252	Dc	vd0.92	v□d0.20	v□d1.72	vd0.71	....	d0.91	9 Mo Sep	vd0.54	vd0.74	24
25	....	None Since Public			...	Nil	....	12.6	55.7	13.6	9-30-99	p0.03	p...	★14319	Dc	...	...	...	vpd1.32	....	....	9 Mo Sep	n/a	vd0.43	25
26	....	None Since Public			...	Nil	....	84.5	307	271	9-30-99	648	...	36792	Dc	pvd0.48	vd0.75	vd1.99	vd2.61	....	d3.41	9 Mo Sep	vd1.99	vd2.79	26
27◆	....	None Since Public			...	Nil	....	9.05	46.7	24.2	9-24-99	....	...	6330	Mr	v0.82	v1.40	v1.83	v1.71	....	1.58	6 Mo Sep	v0.80	v0.67	27
28◆	1999	†0.60	9-30-99	9-15	†1.80	[59]....	....	Total Assets $2784M			9-30-99	1016	4300	118382	Dc	v0.18	v0.36	v0.61	v□0.34	....	....	9 Mo Sep	n/a	v0.69	28
29	1999	Q0.02½	12-31-99	12-15	0.05	0.10	....	Total Deposits $386M			9-30-99	....	...	★4584	Dc	v0.38	v0.47	v0.75	v0.86	....	0.73	9 Mo Sep	v0.61	v0.48	29
30◆	....	None Since Public			...	Nil	....	61.4	781	739	9-30-99	0.51	...	23257	Je	...	...	pvd0.59	pvd0.41	vd0.77	d0.80	3 Mo Sep	vd0.24	vd0.27	30
31◆	1891	Q0.32	11-15-99	10-20	1.21	1.28	1.07½	2471	11826	12675	9-30-99	7212	[62]1781	1314171	Je	1.86	2.14	v2.28	v2.56	v2.59	2.59	3 Mo Sep	v0.80	v0.80	31
32	....	None Since Public			...	Nil	....	10.4	71.3	133	9-30-99	....	...	p64099	Dc	vd0.37	vd8.76	vd7.66	vd1.60	....	d1.17	9 Mo Sep	vd1.30	vd0.87	32
33◆	1998	0.05	6-15-99	5-27	0.05	[59]....	0.10	Total Deposits $244M			9-30-99	0.75	...	2025	Dc	v1.28	vd2.78	v0.97	v0.74	....	d0.92	9 Mo Sep	v0.52	vd1.14	33
34◆	....	None Paid			...	Nil	....	Total Assets $1105.18M			9-30-99	17.5	...	9061	Dc	v□1.91	v2.27	v2.59	vd0.35	....	2.70	9 Mo Sep	vd1.10	vΔ1.95	34
35◆	....	None Since Public			...	Nil	....	40.4	124	59.6	9-30-99	71.9	...	48662	Dc	pv0.14	vp0.26	v0.34	v0.53	....	0.56	9 Mo Sep	v0.23	v□0.26	35
36	....	None Since Public			...	Nil	....	3.07	4.01	0.83	6-30-99	0.03	...	18842	Je	d0.34	d0.21	d0.21	vd0.26	vd0.28	d0.28				36
37◆	....	None Since Public			...	Nil	....	130	187	100	8-31-99	....	...	17465	Nv	0.81	v0.28	vd0.09	v1.18	Pv1.78	1.78				37
38	1965	Q0.06½	12-31-99	12-8	0.26	0.26	0.25	Total Assets $9744.20M			9-30-99	1041	...	73112	Dc	v3.26	v4.11	v5.31	v6.11	E4.10↓	4.99	9 Mo Sep	v5.02	v3.90	38
39	1994	Q0.33½	2-23-00	2-7	1.30	1.34	1.24	Total Assets $5949.07M			9-30-99	2484	25197	161628	Dc	v0.61	v0.63	v0.04	v0.51	....	0.76	9 Mo Sep	v0.35	v□0.60	39
40	1996	Q0.43¾	12-31-99	12-9	1.75	1.75	1.75	Cv into 1.282 com $19.50				....	7538	...	Dc	...	...	...	....	....	....				40
41	....	None Since Public			...	Nil	....	1.23	13.7	7.90	9-30-99	2.35	...	28446	Dc	vd0.02	v0.03	v0.08	v0.02	....	d0.14	9 Mo Sep	v0.09	vd0.07	41
42	....	[55]7.00	11-24-97	11-25	...	Nil	....	28.7	218	238	9-30-99	1075	...	126944	Dc	□d0.87	v[64]d0.01	v[65]d0.70	vΔd0.04	....	d0.47	9 Mo Sep	vΔ0.01	vd0.42	42
43◆	1926	Q0.12	11-29-99	11-9	0.47	0.48	0.43	Total Assets $12507.12M			9-30-99	426	...	64502	Dc	v1.33	v1.46	v1.78	v2.04	....	2.20	9 Mo Sep	v1.51	v1.67	43
44	....	None Since Public			...	Nil	....	20.9	23.8	7.39	9-30-99	9.81	...	18723	Dc	vd0.54	vd0.76	vd1.35	vd0.51	....	d0.52	9 Mo Sep	vd0.23	vd0.24	44
45	....	None Since Public			...	Nil	....	14.2	135	77.2	10-30-99	....	...	18150	Ja	...	...	...	pv0.57	....	....	9 Mo Oct	n/a	vp0.50	45
46	1988	Q0.03	12-31-99	12-8	0.12	0.12	0.12	0.74	6.29	5.51	9-30-99	5.79	...	2959	Dc	v0.03	v0.20	v0.44	v0.77	....	0.44	9 Mo Sep	v0.32	vd0.01	46
47	1849	Q0.27	11-15-99	11-1	1.08	1.08	1.08	3.10	34.9	61.6	6-30-99	92.7	[66]48	6086	Sp	1.09	1.57	v1.35	v1.09	Pv1.40	1.40				47
48	1989	Q0.04	11-25-99	11-8	0.15	0.16	0.12	5.07	11.0	3.18	9-30-99	....	.6	4278	Dc	v0.43	v0.54	v0.82	□v1.16	....	0.51	9 Mo Sep	v□1.19	v0.54	48
49◆	1988	sQ0.16	11-12-99	10-28	s0.596	0.64	s0.493	Total Deposits $3656.32M			9-30-99	663	...	25519	Dc	v0.88	v1.02	v0.95	v1.47	....	1.63	9 Mo Sep	v1.08	v1.24	49
50	1999	Q0.547	12-31-99	12-28	1.106	2.188	....	Co option to redeem fr 6-30-2004[68]				★125	...	...	Dc	...	...	...	....	....	....	Mature 6-30-2029			50

◆Stock Splits & Divs By Line Reference Index [1]3-for-2,'97:10%,'96(twice),'99:Vote 10% stk div,ex Jan 3,'00. [2]2-for-1,'98. [9]1-for-5 REVERSE,'99. [10]5-for-4,'94:2-for-1,'95,'97. [13]2-for-1,'97. [14]2-for-1,'98:5-for-4,'95,'97,'98(twice):5-for-4,'99(twice):Adj for 5%,'99. [27]3-for-2,'94,'96. [28]2-for-1,'95,'96. [30]3-for-2,'98. [31]2-for-1,'97. [33]Adj to 5%,'96. [34]10%,'96,'98,'99. [35]3-for-2,'99. [37]3-for-2,'98:To split 2-for-1,ex Jan 24,'00. [43]2-for-1,'95,'98. [49]2-for-1,'98:5%,'99.

¶ S&P 500
# MidCap 400
✣ SmallCap 600
• Options

Index	Ticker	Name of Issue (Call Price of Pfd. Stocks)	Market	Com. Rank. & Pfd. Rating	Inst. Hold Cos	Inst. Hold Shs. (000)	Principal Business	Price Range 1971-97 High	1971-97 Low	1998 High	1998 Low	1999 High	1999 Low	December, 1999 Dec. Sales in 100s	Last Sale Or Bid High	Low	Last	%Div Yield	P-E Ratio	EPS 5 Yr Growth	% Annualized Total Return 12 Mo	36 Mo	60 Mo
#1•[1]	PFGI	✔Provident Financial Group	NNM,C,P,Ph	A–	130	12923	Commercial banking,Ohio	54¼	1⅜	56⅛	26½	45 15/16	33 1/16	23747	41 3/16	33 1/16	35⅞	2.5	11	14	–2.9	3.7	21.4
2	PROV	✔Provident Finl Hldg	NNM	NR	20	1954	Savings bank,MA	22¼	10	24½	13½	20 9/16	15½	6419	18 11/16	16¼	16½	...	6	...	–3.3	5.6	...
¶3•[2]	PVN	✔Providian Financial	NY	NR	798	104309	Consumer loans/svcs	31 3/16	19 7/16	75 11/16	28⅜	138	69½	173260	91⅛	77 7/16	91 1/16	0.2	24	...	21.7	...	...
✣4•[2]	PROX	✔Proxim Inc	NNM	NR	152	9555	Wireless networking prds	51¼	3⅝	28⅝	10⅞	118	20¾	50860	118	55⅜	110	...	..	10	312	68.5	91.7
5	PTS	✔Prudential Steel	To	B	11	2598	Mfr tubing & pipe products	26⅝	2 11/16	17⅞	5½	14¾	4 11/16	16698	14	10 5/16	13	1.5	..	–20	93.0	25.3	28.4
6	PSB	✔PS Business Parks	AS,Ch	B+	65	11553	Real estate investment trust	23½	8⅜	26⅝	18	26⅜	20¼	4292	22¾	21¼	22¾	4.4	15	1	–0.7	10.0	15.7
7	PSG	✔PS Group Holdings	NY,B,Ch,P,Ph	B–	31	1924	Aircraft leas'g/fuel dstr	72¼	2 11/16	13¾	10⅜	11⅝	8	991	11⅜	10½	11¼	...	7	–18	27.2	18.0	18.4
8•[3]	PSIX	✔PSINet Inc	NNM	NR	218	37939	Leading Internet svc provider	29	4¼	25 1/16	5	73¾	21	335817	70½	50⅛	61¾	...	d	–37	196	78.4	...
#9	PSSI	✔PSS World Medical	NNM	NR	202	46120	Dstr med'l supplies/equip	33¾	3 11/16	24½	12	23⅛	6	129767	11	8⅞	9 7/16	...	14	71	–59.0	–13.1	12.3
10	PMD	✔Psychemedics Corp	AS,P,Ph	B–	17	1300	Laboratory testing, svcs	10 7/16	⅜	6	4	5⅜	4	4537	5	4⅛	5	3.2	42	8	1.1	–3.7	11.0
11	PSNRY	✔PT Pasifik Sat Nusantara ADS[51]	NNM	NR	9	3247	Satellite based comm sv,Asia	20½	9⅜	16¼	2¾	17	3¾	7351	17	7¾	15	...	..	...	332	7.7	...
12•[4]	TLK	✔P.T. Telekomunikasi ADS[52]	NY,P	NR	72	14432	Telecommun svcs, Indonesia	34⅛	7 5/16	9⅞	2⅜	13¾	5 3/16	83484	11⅛	8 11/16	11	s0.6	23	–17	98.1	–27.3	...
13	TPI	PT. Tri Polyta Indonesia ADS[53]	NY	NR	4	143	Polyproplene resins, plastics	30¾	9/16	2⅞	¼	1½	⅜	5440	1 3/16	⅞	15/16	...	d	Neg	131	–46.9	–47.2
¶14•[5]	PEG	✔Public Svc Enterpr	NY,B,C,Ch,P,Ph	B+	573	94589	Hldg co:Public Svc Elec&Gas	36⅛	7	42¾	30 5/16	42⅝	32	156555	35½	32	34 13/16	6.2	11	3	–8.1	15.9	13.3
#15•[6]	PNM	✔Public Svc New Mexico	NY,B,Ch,P	B	219	29578	Utility:electric,gas,water	39¼	7⅝	24¾	17⅜	21½	14⅞	26477	17¼	15 9/16	16¼	4.9	8	3	–16.9	–2.5	7.5
✣16	PGS	✔Public Svc No Car[55]	NY,P	B+	129	5993	Natural gas: Raleigh-Durham	24⅜	1 13/16	26 1/16	19⅛	33¼	22 5/16	23808	33¼	31⅝	32 5/16	3.1	27	1	28.5	26.1	22.8
17•[7]	PSA	✔Public Storage	NY,Ch,Ph	NR	263	60134	R.E.invest tr:mini-warehouse	31⅜	6¼	33⅝	22⅝	29⅜	20 13/16	60170	23⅛	20 13/16	22 11/16	3.9	15	7	–13.3	–7.3	13.8
18	CARD	✔PubliCARD Inc	NNM,B,Ch	NR	30	1262	Computer software & svcs	11¾	⅝	14⅜	1¼	15½	5⅝	7598	9	5⅝	6 9/16	...	d	...	–53.1	65.9	22.5
19	PRN	✔Puerto Rican Cement	NY,Ch	B+	43	1749	Lgst mfr of cement in P.R.	50¾	13/16	54½	33⅜	38⅝	30⅜	472	35¼	33½	34	2.2	14	–4	–0.5	5.0	6.1
#20•[8]	PSD	✔Puget Sound Energy	NY,B,Ch,P	B	191	26443	Electricity in west'n Wash	30 3/16	9 1/16	30¼	24 1/16	28⅜	18⅝	44477	20 11/16	18⅝	19⅜	9.5	10	9	–24.8	0.1	7.0
21	PLFC	✔Pulaski Furniture	NNM	†B+	29	1299	Mfr,sells wooden furniture	27	¾	27	17¾	23¾	14	2037	17¾	14	15½	4.4	6	–8	–33.1	0.5	3.0
22	PTZ	✔Pulitzer Inc	NY,Ch,Ph	A–	115	6944	Newspaper publishing	63 11/16	9⅛	92⅛	57 7/16	88⅞	36¼	9919	41	38⅛	40 5/16	1.5	66	–11	...	...	...
¶23•[6]	PHM	✔Pulte Corp	NY,B,Ch,P,Ph	B+	322	27188	Homebuilding/fin'l services	21¼	1/32	36 3/16	19 15/16	31¼	16¾	27720	22½	19 7/16	22½	0.7	6	5	–18.5	28.2	23.5
24	PPRO	✔PurchasePro.com	NNM	NR	19	1665	Business-business e-commerce svc	....	....	....	....	175	8	184680	175	90 5/16	137½	...	d	...	...	...	...
25	PXT	✔PXRE Group	NY	B	93	10227	Reinsurance:prop,casualty	38¼	5	35¼	20⅝	26¼	9 15/16	18519	13⅛	10	13	1.8	d	Neg	–46.2	–16.5	–11.6
26	PYR	PYR Energy	AS	NR	3	920	Oil & gas exploration svc	....	....	....	....	4⅝	3 7/16	4633	4⅝	3 7/16	4½	...	d	...	...	...	...
27	OPC	✔Q C Optics	AS	NR	..	...	Elec ind defect detection sys	6½	2⅜	5⅛	1 3/16	2¼	¾	2797	1½	1	1 1/16	...	d	Neg	–32.0	–39.3	...
28	WS	Wrrt(Pur 1com at$7.80)	AS	....	..	...		1⅝	⅛	1	⅛	9/16	1/32	670	1/16	1/32	1/32B	...	..	...	...	...	...
29	QADI	✔QAD Inc	NNM	NR	21	684	Provide ERO software	23¼	11⅛	17⅜	2⅞	18	2 13/16	85710	18	4	13 15/16	...	d	Neg	291	...	...
30	QGENF	✔QIAGEN N V	NNM	NR	30	1271	Separate/purify nucleic acids	30⅛	6	39⅛	20⅝	84	31¾	8019	84	66½	75½	...	..	56	151	80.5	...
#31•[6]	QLGC	✔QLogic Corp	NNM	NR	330	28704	Mkt sys level integ circuits	11⅜	13/16	33 11/16	6	167½	23¼	165018	167½	110	159⅞	...	..	90	390	192	149
32•[7]	QLTI	QLT Phototherapeutics	NNM,To	C	154	43284	Biopharmaceutical R&D	14 5/16	1 11/16	13 13/16	5⅜	64⅛	11¼	113897	64⅛	40 13/16	58¾	...	d	–9	423	80.8	84.1
33	AQM	✔QMS Inc	NY,Ch,P	C	23	710	Mfr printers, graphic prod	26¾	2¼	5	2 9/16	6	2½	5504	3 3/16	2½	2⅞	...	d	Neg	–9.8	–18.2	–19.5
✣34	QRSI	✔QRS Corp	NNM	NR	..	...	Merchandise mgmt database svc	28	6 3/16	36 9/16	13 13/16	115	26 15/16	58395	115	58⅞	105	...	98	15	228	76.8	65.7
35	QSND	QSound Labs	NSC	C	5	293	License/mkt 3-D sound tech	23⅝	⅝	3⅝	1⅛	4½	1⅞	99394	3 7/16	1⅞	2	...	d	37	–10.0	5.3	–7.7
36	QMDC	✔QuadraMed Corp	NNM	NR	80	9102	Financial mgmt softwr/svcs	27½	6½	36½	12⅞	30⅛	3⅞	67901	9	6½	8¾	...	d	...	–57.5	–8.8	...
✣37	KWR	✔Quaker Chemical Corporation	NY	B–	72	3599	Specialty chemical prod	26	13/16	21	13	18⅜	13½	2131	15¾	13⅞	14¼	5.5	11	41	–17.0	–0.2	–1.0
38	QFAB	✔Quaker Fabric	NNM	NR	46	5239	Mfr woven upholstery fabrics	16 5/16	3 13/16	21 9/16	3⅞	6⅝	3	24955	5	3⅛	4¼	...	43	–25	–32.0	–23.0	–12.9
¶39•[6]	OAT	✔Quaker Oats	NY,To,B,Ch,P,Ph	B	676	88734	Human & pet food processor	55⅛	1⅜	65 9/16	48½	71	50⅞	65832	67⅛	61 9/16	65⅝	1.7	24	–25	12.3	22.5	19.5
¶40•[9]	QCOM	✔QUALCOMM Inc	NNM	B	678	351823	Mfr digital wireless commun pd	9	13/16	8 7/16	4¾	185 1/16	6 9/16	5217679	185 1/16	88¾	176⅛	...	..	55	...	...	...
✣41•[10]	NX	✔Quanex Corp	NY,Ch,Ph,P	B	167	11674	Mfr steel bars, alum sheet	36½	2⅛	33 13/16	15⅝	29	15⅜	14572	25 9/16	19 1/16	25½	2.5	10	6	16.4	–0.1	4.7
42	PWR	✔Quanta Services	NY	NR	126	12162	Telecomm/electric svcs	....	....	23	11	44⅜	20⅛	30552	32	24⅛	28¼	...	26	...	28.0	...	...
#43•[11]	DSS	✔Quantum Corp (DSSG)	NY	NR	175	118478	Dgn/dvp DLT tape drives	....	....	....	....	22¼	10⅝	188174	16⅝	13 7/16	15⅛	...	12	...	...	...	...
44	HDD	✔Quantum Corp(HDDG)	NY	NR	114	53356	Dgn/dvp hard disk drives	....	....	....	....	9 3/16	5½	158597	7½	5⅝	6 15/16	...	d	...	...	...	...
45•[12]	QBR.A	✔Quebecor[66]Cl'A'[67]	To,B,Mo	B+	9	1971	Print'g,publish'g,forest prod	22⅜	7/16	21⅝	16½	39½	34 5/16	990	39½	34⅞	38¼	1.3	6	23	...	34.3	27.6
46	QBR.B	Cl'B'[68]	To	B+	11	3102		32⅜	4 11/16	33	23⅝	39	31	10943	39	34½	38½	1.2	6	23	18.6	20.6	18.6
47	PRW	✔Quebecor Printing[69]	NY	NR	47	26104	Commercial printing svcs	19⅞	14¼	21⅞	15⅜	25 1/16	20 9/16	10493	22 15/16	21 3/16	22¼	1.3	16	9	3.9	9.8	...
✣48	QCSB	✔Queens County Bancorp	NNM	NR	143	6857	Savings bank, Queens,N.Y.	27	3 11/16	31 11/16	22¾	36⅛	25¾	12773	30¼	25¾	27⅛	3.7	16	20	–5.8	27.9	38.8
49	PASA	✔quepasa.com inc	NNM	NR	9	436	Spanish-language internet svc	....	....	....	....	26⅞	6	194529	16	9	12 11/16	...	d	...	...	...	...
50•[11]	DGX	✔Quest Diagnostics	NY,Ch,Ph	NR	189	25038	Clinical laboratory test svcs	20⅞	13¼	23 1/16	14½	32 15/16	17¾	17408	32 15/16	28⅞	30 9/16	...	53	...	71.6	26.4	...

Uniform Footnote Explanations-See Page 4. Other: [1]CBOE:Cycle 1. [2]CBOE:Cycle 3. [3]ASE,CBOE,Ph:Cycle 1. [4]ASE,P:Cycle 1. [5]ASE:Cycle 3. [6]Ph:Cycle 1. [7]Ph:Cycle 3. [8]ASE,CBOE,Ph:Cycle 3. [9]ASE,CBOE,P,Ph:Cycle 1. [10]P:Cycle 1. [11]CBOE:Cycle 2. [12]Mo:Cycle 2. [51]Ea ADS rep 3 com, 250 rupiah. [52]Ea ADS rep 20 Sr'B',500 Rupiah. [53]Ea ADS rep 10 com, 1,000 Rupiah. [54]Subsid pfd in $M. [55]SCANA Corp plan acq,$33 in cash or stk. [56]Cash equiv $0.65. [57]Pfd in $M. [58]Stk dstr of Pulitzer Inc,'99. [59]8 Mo Aug'97. [60]If com exceeds $10.80 for 20 con trad days. [61]Fiscal Dec'95 & prior. [62]Fiscal Sep'97 & prior. [63]12 mo Dec'98:Sep'98 earn $0.17. [64]12 Mo Dec'95:fiscal Jun'95 earned $6.00. [65]Stk dstr of Leap. [66]Multiple vtg shrs. [67]Nov'98 & prior in $US. [68]Sub vtg shrs. [69]Sub Vtg Shrs.

Index	Cash Divs. Ea. Yr. Since	Dividends: Latest Payment Period $	Date	Ex. Div.	Total $ So Far 1999	Ind. Rate	Paid 1998	Financial Position Mil-$ Cash& Equiv.	Curr. Assets	Curr. Liab.	Balance Sheet Date	Capitalization Lg Trm Debt Mil-$	Shs. 000 Pfd.	Com.	Earnings $ Per Shr. Years End	1995	1996	1997	1998	1999	Last 12 Mos.	Interim Earnings Period	$ per Shr. 1998	1999	Index
1◆	1985	Q0.22	11-26-99	11-9	0.88	0.88	0.80	Total Deposits $6330.93M			9-30-99	1015	70	p44031	Dc	v1.75	v1.94	v2.63	v2.56	E3.28	2.83	9 Mo Sep	v2.13	v2.40	1
2	....	None Since Public			...	Nil	....	Total Deposits $686M			9-30-99	....	...	4179	Je	...	n/a	0.41	v1.11	v2.53	2.57	3 Mo Sep	v0.37	v0.41	2
3◆	1997	Q0.05	12-15-99	11-29	0.20	0.20	0.15	Total Deposits $7353.6M			9-30-99	1189	...	141971	Dc	pv0.89	pv1.08	vp1.33	v2.04	E3.75	3.34	9 Mo Sep	v1.39	v2.69	3
4	....	None Since Public			...	Nil	....	89.4	115	10.6	9-30-99	....	...	11736	Dc	v0.35	v0.71	v0.01	v0.42	....	0.42	9 Mo Sep	v0.34	v0.34	4
5◆	1994	gQ0.05	12-31-99	12-13	g0.20	0.20	g0.20	....	106	37.6	j9-30-99	....	...	30236	Dc	v0.32	v0.70	v1.39	v0.42	....	j0.11	9 Mo Sep	v0.33	v0.02	5
6	1991	Q0.25	12-31-99	12-13	1.00	1.00	1.43	Total Assets $906.39M			9-30-99	45.8	2	23645	Dc	1.37	1.59	v1.00	v1.51	....	1.53	9 Mo Sep	v1.17	v1.19	6
7	1995	†3.00	12-31-98	1-4	...	Nil	†3.00	26.2	46.9	16.3	9-30-99	28.1	...	6068	Dc	v0.50	v1.58	vd0.43	v0.52	....	1.73	9 Mo Sep	vd0.67	v0.54	7
8	....	None Since Public			...	Nil	....	1543	1830	340	9-30-99	2403	...	65004	Dc	vpd2.01	vd1.40	vd1.14	vd5.32	....	d6.10	9 Mo Sep	vd2.70	vd3.48	8
9◆	....	None Since Public			...	Nil	....	45.3	575	198	9-30-99	186	...	70922	Mr	0.01	v0.23	v0.26	v0.61	....	0.68	6 Mo Sep	v0.31	v0.38	9
10◆	1997	Q0.04	12-22-99	12-6	0.16	0.16	0.11	6.23	11.7	2.24	9-30-99	....	...	21585	Dc	v0.07	v0.11	v0.11	v0.11	....	0.12	9 Mo Sep	v0.09	v0.10	10
11	....	None Since Public			...	Nil	....	6.25	6.25	136	12-31-97	....	...	78786	Dc	pd0.21	vd0.03	v0.09	n/a	....	....	3 Mo Mar	vd0.06	vNil	11
12◆	1996	0.089	7-12-99	5-27	s0.089	0.065	0.034	283	416	287	12-31-98	927	...	10080000	Dc	0.85	v1.26	v0.49	v0.30	....	0.47	3 Mo Mar	vd0.09	v0.08	12
13	....	0.32½	6-14-96	5-14	...	Nil	....	32.8	116	74.5	12-31-97	197	...	257500	Dc	1.00	v0.43	vd3.45	....	....	d3.45				13
14	1907	Q0.54	12-31-99	12-8	2.16	2.16	2.16	84.0	1950	3610	9-30-99	5749	[54]170	218591	Dc	v2.71	v2.52	v2.41	v2.79	E3.30	3.34	12 Mo Sep	v2.78	v□3.34	14
15	1996	Q0.20	2-18-00	1-28	0.80	0.80	0.77	88.6	354	199	9-30-99	977	128	40774	Dc	v1.72	v1.71	v1.91	v1.95	....	1.95	12 Mo Sep	v2.00	v1.95	15
16	1958	Q0.24¾	1-1-00	12-8	0.97½	0.99	0.94	23.1	86.6	150	6-30-99	157	...	20578	Sp	1.16	1.26	v1.34	v1.23	Pv1.18	1.18				16
17	1981	[56]....	1-14-00	12-13	0.88	0.88	0.88	Total Assets $4206.14M			9-30-99	172	11141	±136354	Dc	v0.95	v1.10	v0.91	v1.30	....	1.48	9 Mo Sep	v0.95	v1.13	17
18	....	5%Stk	9-30-77	8-25	...	Nil	....	5.89	16.0	8.88	9-30-99	0.88	...	21747	Dc	d0.02	...	vd0.12	vd0.44	....	d1.14	9 Mo Sep	vd0.13	vd0.83	18
19	1986	tQ0.19	2-11-00	1-6	t0.76	0.76	t0.76	17.7	95.1	29.8	9-30-99	82.9	...	5186	Dc	v2.90	v2.66	v2.91	v2.11	....	2.43	9 Mo Sep	v1.73	v2.05	19
20	1943	Q0.46	11-15-99	10-14	1.84	1.84	1.84	72.2	410	79.0	9-30-99	1790	[57]168	84561	Dc	v0.94	pv1.70	v1.25	v1.85	E1.97	2.08	12 Mo Sep	v1.67	v2.08	20
21	1977	Q0.17	1-5-00	12-15	0.68	0.68	0.68	1.03	84.1	25.4	7-11-99	39.5	...	2830	Oc	1.56	1.51	vd0.87	v2.25	Pv2.76	2.76				21
22◆	1918	0.15	11-1-99	10-6	h[58]0.60	0.60	0.60	574	648	38.9	9-30-99	....	...	±22510	Dc	v±2.23	v±2.58	±v2.94	v3.35	....	0.61	9 Mo Sep	v2.29	vd0.45	22
23◆	1977	Q0.04	1-3-00	12-8	0.16	0.16	0.14	Total Assets $2619.10M			9-30-99	518	...	43250	Dc	v1.07	v3.57	v1.20	v2.33	E3.60	3.35	9 Mo Sep	v1.45	v2.47	23
24◆	....	None Since Public			...	Nil	....	48.5	50.6	3.62	9-30-99	....	...	28026	Dc	...	...	vd0.24	vd0.52	....	d1.96	9 Mo Sep	vd0.35	vd1.79	24
25	1989	0.06	12-2-99	11-9	0.64	0.24	1.01	Total Assets $666.50M			9-30-99	150	...	11751	Dc	v4.52	v3.69	□v3.39	v□0.26	....	d0.50	9 Mo Sep	v□0.48	vd0.28	25
26	....	None Since Public			...	Nil	....	6.52	6.64	0.14	5-31-99	....	25	14069	Au	...	...	v[59]d0.01	vd0.01	....	d0.09	9 Mo Aug	v0.01	vd0.07	26
27	....	None Since Public			...	Nil	....	3.96	8.36	0.97	9-30-99	....	...	3243	Dc	0.42	vd0.09	v0.08	v0.06	....	d0.34	9 Mo Sep	v0.17	vd0.23	27
28	....	Terms&trad. basis should be checked in detail						Wrrts expire 10-23-2001				....	...	950	Dc	...	...	...	...	....	....	Callable at 20¢[60]			28
29	....	None Since Public			...	Nil	....	13.3	106	88.6	10-31-99	17.2	...	30328	Ja	[61]d0.03	v0.04	v0.38	vd1.22	....	d0.77	9 Mo Oct	vd1.06	vd0.61	29
30◆	....	None Since Public			...	Nil	....	30.1	58.5	19.8	12-31-97	5.01	...	33554	Dc	0.09	v0.18	v0.26	Pv0.36	....	0.46	9 Mo Sep	v0.25	v0.35	30
31◆	....	None Paid			...	Nil	....	116	154	20.5	9-26-99	....	...	36547	Mr	v0.03	v0.24	v0.42	v0.69	....	1.07	6 Mo Sep	v0.27	v0.65	31
32◆	....	None Paid			...	Nil	....	271	289	10.6	j6-30-99	....	368	63492	Dc	d0.39	vd0.10	vd0.32	vd0.45	....	jd0.50	9 Mo Sep	vd0.31	vd0.36	32
33	....	None Since Public			...	Nil	....	5.19	110	107	10-01-99	17.6	...	13255	Dc	d4.15	0.40	v[62]d2.44	v[63]0.14	....	d1.54	9 Mo Sep	v0.13	v□d1.55	33
34◆	....	None Since Public			...	Nil	....	43.5	63.4	11.8	9-30-99	....	...	13521	Dc	v0.19	v0.51	v0.67	v0.91	....	1.07	9 Mo Sep	v0.64	v0.80	34
35	....	None Since Public			...	Nil	....	1.60	3.54	0.34	6-30-99	....	...	24134	Dc	d0.27	vd0.21	vd0.03	vd0.05	....	jd0.10	9 Mo Sep	vd0.04	vd0.09	35
36	....	None Since Public			...	Nil	....	21.7	100	38.1	9-30-99	115	...	25142	Dc	pvd8.10	vd0.26	vd4.91	vd0.98	....	d0.34	9 Mo Sep	vd1.23	vd0.59	36
37	1954	Q0.19½	1-31-00	1-12	0.76½	0.78	0.73	11.6	105	55.1	9-30-99	25.1	...	8929	Dc	v0.76	vd0.88	v1.45	v1.20	....	1.32	9 Mo Sep	v1.12	v1.24	37
38◆	....	None Since Public			...	Nil	....	0.46	89.2	28.4	10-02-99	60.2	...	15682	Dc	v0.45	v0.69	v0.85	v0.40	....	0.10	9 Mo Sep	v0.38	v0.08	38
39◆	1906	Q0.285	1-14-00	12-15	1.14	1.14	1.14	431	1222	1071	9-30-99	715	979	133791	Dc	v[64]5.23	v1.78	vd6.80	v1.97	E2.77	3.31	9 Mo Sep	v1.47	v2.81	39
40◆	....	h[65]....	9-23-98	9-24	...	Nil	h[65]....	1614	2978	876	9-30-99	660	...	659832	Sp	0.07	v0.04	v0.16	v0.18	v0.31	0.31				40
41	1988	Q0.16	12-31-99	12-20	0.64	0.64	0.64	41.8	216	135	7-31-99	194	...	14267	Oc	□v2.20	v□2.20	v4.38	v0.65	vP2.56	2.56				41
42	....	None Since Public			...	Nil	....	12.6	298	164	9-30-99	147	...	±36469	Dc	...	pv0.18	vp0.60	v0.84	....	1.11	9 Mo Sep	v0.58	v0.85	42
43	....	None Since Public			...	Nil	....	683	1085	615	p6-27-99	338	...	p164767	Mr	...	...	...	pv0.73	E1.30	0.56	6 Mo Sep	v0.59	v0.42	43
44	....	None Since Public			...	Nil	....	421	1129	528	9-26-99	112	...	83574	Mr	...	...	...	vpd1.90	Ed1.75	d2.46	6 Mo Sep	vd0.97	vd1.53	44
45	1976	g0.12	6-11-99	5-13	g0.24	0.48	g0.44	7.80	2982	2298	j9-30-99	6299	...	±64686	Dc	±2.83	v±2.23	v±2.18	v±2.64	....	j6.09	9 Mo Sep	v±1.73	v±5.18	45
46	1986	gQ0.12	12-7-99	11-9	g0.48	0.48	g0.44	....	...	...		....	...	40042	Dc	±2.83	±2.23	±v2.18	±v2.64	....	j6.09	9 Mo Sep	v±1.73	v±5.18	46
47	1992	Q0.07	12-1-99	11-8	0.28	0.28	0.24	0.31	954	710	12-31-98	1199	...	±p140107	Dc	v±1.05	v±1.09	±v1.12	v±1.29	....	1.44	9 Mo Sep	v0.85	v1.00	47
48◆	1994	Q0.25	11-15-99	10-28	1.00	1.00	0.667	Total Deposits $1133.38M			9-30-99	699	...	21185	Dc	v0.77	v0.85	v1.07	v1.34	....	1.65	9 Mo Sep	v0.97	v1.28	48
49	....	None Since Public			...	Nil	....	39.3	40.6	3.81	9-30-99	2.25	...	★14653	Dc	...	...	...	vd0.72	....	d2.03	9 Mo Sep	vd0.59	vd1.90	49
50	....	None Since Public			...	Nil	....	36.8	875	638	9-30-99	1230	...	43196	Dc	pd0.78	pn/a	vd0.77	v0.89	....	0.58	9 Mo Sep	v0.71	v0.40	50

◆Stock Splits & Divs By Line Reference Index [1]3-for-2,'96. [3]3-for-2,'98. [5]3-for-1,'97. [9]3-for-1,'95. [10]Adj for 3%,'96. [12]Adj for 8%,'99. [22]5-for-4,'95:4-for-3,'96:No adj for stk dstr,'99. [23]2-for-1,'98. [24]3-for-2,'99. [30]2-for-1,'99. [31]2-for-1,'99(twice). [32]2-for-1,'99. [34]3-for-2,'99. [38]3-for-2,'98. [39]2-for-1,'94. [40]2-for-1,'99:4-for-1,'99. [48]4-for-3,'96:3-for-2,'97(twice),'98.

¶ S&P 500 # MidCap 400 ✤ SmallCap 600 • Options Index	Ticker	Name of Issue (Call Price of Pfd. Stocks)	Market	Com. Rank. & Pfd. Rating	Inst. Hold Cos	Inst. Hold Shs. (000)	Principal Business	Price Range 1971-97 High	1971-97 Low	1998 High	1998 Low	1999 High	1999 Low	December, 1999 Dec. Sales in 100s	Last Sale Or Bid High	Low	Last	%Div Yield	P-E Ratio	EPS 5 Yr Growth	% Annualized Total Return 12 Mo	36 Mo	60 Mo
1	QSFT	✓Quest Software	NNM	NR	59	4670	Application & info softwr	....	....	....	....	120	14	17338	120	74 9/16	102	...	..	...	...	...	...
#2•[1]	STR	✓Questar Corp	NY,Ch,Ph,P	A−	271	53728	Nat'l gas dstr:oil/gas:mfg	22⅜	1 15/16	22⅜	15 13/16	19 15/16	14¾	56571	17¼	14¾	15	4.5	18	−4	−19.6	−2.9	5.6
3	QSC	✓Questcor Pharmaceuticals	AS	NR	18	3708	Dvlp stge: pharmaceutical prd	9½	⅝	5½	2⅛	3½	1 1/16	17910	1½	1⅛	1¼	...	d	−8	−61.5	−31.8	−25.0
✤4•[1]	ZQK	✓Quiksilver, Inc	NY,Ph	†B+	194	20055	Designs/dstr casual clothing	15 13/16	1⅛	20 13/16	8 9/16	30 13/16	12 15/16	40329	19	13¾	15½	...	14	24	−22.4	29.7	25.1
5	KWK	✓Quicksilver Resources	AS	NR	5	2720	Oil & gas explor,dev prod'n	....	....	....	....	7 13/16	3 5/16	10363	4⅝	3 5/16	4⅜	...	49	...	...	...	...
6	LQU	✓Quilmes Ind(Quinsa) ADS[51]	NY,Ph,P	NR	66	20823	Beer producer Argentina	15⅞	8⅝	14	6⅜	12¾	7½	14232	12½	11½	11 15/16	2.1	15	3	31.2	11.5	...
7	LQ	✓Quinenco S.A. ADS[53]	NY	NR	41	9440	Diversified industrial/finl svcs	19⅜	9⅜	13¼	4	12	6	12939	11⅝	9	11⅛	1.1	6	2	41.1	...	...
8	QTEL	✓Quintel Communications	NNM	NR	17	880	Dvlp mkt tel entertainm't svc	17	3 13/16	7	1 1/16	12	¾	123333	12	4 3/16	9	...	d	Neg	380	−1.4	...
¶9•[2]	QTRN	✓Quintiles Transnational	NNM,Ch	B+	354	80213	Contract pharma'l/biotech resh	43 11/16	4 1/16	56⅞	33⅜	53⅜	16	299316	23½	17	18 11/16	...	13	55	−65.0	−17.3	20.8
10	QNTS	✓Quintus Corp	NNM	NR	..	...	e-customer relations mgmt svc	....	....	....	....	59¼	18	70723	58 11/16	39½	45⅞	...	..	...	...	...	...
11	QUIX	✓Quixote Corp	NNM	B	43	4964	Mfr highway safety products	22¾	⅛	16⅛	8	16⅛	11¼	2010	16⅛	15¼	15¼	1.8	16	NM	26.6	19.6	9.5
#12•[3]	QHGI	✓Quorum Health Group	NNM	NR	175	55262	Own,oper acute care hospitals	28¼	10	33 13/16	9½	13½	6	92397	9 7/16	7⅜	9 5/16	...	28	−16	−28.0	−22.3	−6.0
13•[4]	QWST	✓Qwest Communications	NNM	NR	608	137651	Telecommunication svcs	17¼	5½	25⅝	11	52⅜	25	2054315	44 5/16	34	43	...	..	26	72.1	...	...
14	QXLC	✓QXL.com ADS[54]	NNM	NR	..	...	Online trading svcs	....	....	....	....	151	14	12488	151	31⅞	118½	...	..	...	...	...	...
15•[1]	FLC	✓R&B Falcon	NY,Ch,Ph	NR	280	90950	Contract drilling:oil/gas	42 13/16	4½	35⅜	6¾	16 1/16	5 3/16	397598	14 1/16	10 11/16	13¼	...	d	−3	75.2	−12.3	...
16	RBIN	✓R & B Inc	NNM	B	29	2289	Mkt replacement auto parts	12	4	13⅞	6⅛	10¾	4⅜	2544	6⅜	4⅝	4⅝	...	6	16	−43.5	−15.4	−5.8
17	RGFC	✓R & G Financial 'B'	NNM	NR	26	2013	Mortgage banking, Puerto Rico	11¾	4	22	9¼	21½	9⅞	9266	12⅝	9⅞	11½	1.4	9	36	−44.7	21.5	...
✤18	RDN	✓Radian Group	NY,Ph,P	B+	354	35629	Private mortgage insurance	61⅞	9	70	25⅜	55 15/16	33 5/16	37108	48 15/16	44⅞	47¾	0.3	12	17	4.2	9.4	27.5
19	RADA	✓Radica Games	NNM	B	6	904	Dvp/mfr casino theme games	19	¾	22¼	9¾	16 5/16	7	9929	8¼	7	7⅜	...	5	NM	−46.8	63.5	8.6
20	ROIA	✓Radio One'A'	NNM	NR	96	7846	Own,operate radio stations	....	....	....	....	97½	24	28865	97½	62 11/16	92	...	d	...	...	...	...
21	UNCA	✓Radio Unica Communic	NNM	NR	..	...	Own/oper radio stations	....	....	....	....	33⅛	16	22034	29 9/16	21	28⅞	...	31	...	...	...	...
22	RSYS	✓RadiSys Corp	NNM	NR	95	10583	Dgn embedded computer solut'ns	49 11/16	6	25¾	7 9/16	54⅞	13 15/16	26583	54⅞	38	51	...	57	30	156	16.3	...
23	RDWR	Radware Ltd	NNM	NR	26	697	Internet traffic mgmt prd	....	....	....	....	87	18	58298	55½	37⅝	43⅛	...	..	...	...	...	...
24	RMG	✓Ragen Mackenzie Grp	NY	NR	19	1113	Provides financial svcs/pds	....	....	15½	8 13/16	21⅜	9¾	3766	21¼	18	18	...	15	12	50.8	...	...
25	RAIL	✓RailAmerica Inc	NNM	B	35	5743	Operates short-line railroads	7⅜	1⅜	8¾	5	10⅞	7 1/16	23782	9 15/16	7⅞	8 9/16	...	13	41	0.7	20.7	24.1
26•[5]	RAIN	✓Rainforest Cafe	NNM	NR	68	9073	Own/operate restaurant	25 7/16	2⅛	22	5⅜	7 7/16	3⅛	105371	4¾	3⅛	4	...	8	NM	−34.5	−36.6	...
✤27•[6]	RAH	✓Ralcorp Holdings	NY,P	NR	188	22378	Mfr cereals,snacks,pkg foods	28⅝	9⅜	21 11/16	13	20⅞	15¾	13197	20 1/16	18½	19 15/16	...	17	43	9.2	−0.8	−1.6
¶28•[6]	RAL	✓Ralston-Purina Group	NY,B,C,Ch,P,Ph	B+	605	172164	Pet food,batteries	32 5/16	1⅜	39 1/16	26	33	25½	194730	29⅝	25½	27⅞	1.4	17	26	...	...	...
29	IBX	Ralston Purina 7.0% SAILS[57]	NY	NR	22	1450	Stk Apprec Inc Linked Sec	70¾	59¼	70⅜	49	53¾	33¾	9162	37 11/16	33¾	36 9/16	11.9	..	...	−23.2	...	...
30	RMBS	✓Rambus Inc	NNM	NR	155	10455	Dgn/dvp computer chips	86¾	12	105⅞	35½	117½	51½	244615	74 7/16	65½	67 7/16	...	..	NM	−29.9	...	...
31	RCO	✓Ramco Energy ADS[59]	AS	NR	2	43	Oil & gas expl,prd'n,Russia	20⅛	12⅞	13 5/16	3⅜	7	3⅝	505	6¼	4⅞	6¼	...	d	Neg	78.6	...	...
32	RPT	✓Ramco-Gershenson Prop Tr	NY,Ch,Ph	NR	32	1819	Real estate investment trust	30	12½	21⅝	14	17	11¾	3884	13¼	11¾	12⅝	13.3	12	2	−2.7	...	...
33	RAC	✓Rampart Capital	AS	NR	..	...	Financial svcs/real estate	....	....	....	....	9	3⅝	3826	8 7/16	3⅝	4	...	7	...	...	...	...
34	WS	Wrrt(Pur1com at$10.64)	AS	....	..	...		....	....	....	....	1¾	5/16	806	1¾	5/16	9/16	...	..	...	...	...	...
35	RGI	✓Randers Killam Group	AS	B−	1	23	Engineer'g/constr'n mgmt svcs	12 3/16	1¼	4⅜	1 9/16	4 7/16	1⅞	174	4⅜	4¼	4¼	...	d	−12	94.5	24.8	14.2
36	RRC	✓Range Resources	NY,Ch,Ph	↓C	67	14282	Oil & gas production	23⅝	15/16	17½	2⅞	7⅛	1 9/16	62038	3 7/16	2 7/16	3 3/16	...	d	Neg	−5.8	−42.3	−13.6
37•[7]	RGO	✓Ranger Oil Ltd	NY,To,B,Ch,Ph,Mo,P	C	77	43861	Oil & gas explor & prod'n	20⅞	⅞	7½	3 15/16	5½	2⅝	32129	3⅜	2¾	3⅛	...	d	Neg	−29.6	−31.7	−11.3
38	RRRR	✓Rare Medium Group	NNM	C	49	6006	Internet business svcs	25	¼	7½	1⅝	44 11/16	3⅝	428496	44 11/16	25½	34⅛	...	d	2	727	84.5	36.1
#39•[2]	RATL	✓Rational Software	NNM	C	324	70722	Dvlp softwr develop't tools	44¼	1⅛	27⅜	10½	53 11/16	21⅞	159222	53 11/16	44¼	49⅛	...	62	NM	85.4	7.5	70.0
✤40•[8]	RJF	✓Raymond James Finl	NY,Ch,Ph	A−	183	21399	Invest firm & brokerage	26⅝	11/16	36½	16¾	25 3/16	16 11/16	32769	19 11/16	17¼	18⅝	1.6	11	18	−10.6	20.6	31.4
#41•[6]	RYN	✓Rayonier Inc	NY,Ph,P	NR	208	21991	Mfg/logs,timber&wood prods	53	26¾	52½	36⅝	52⅞	36¼	16112	48 9/16	43 7/16	48 5/16	3.0	22	29	8.2	11.1	12.7
42	ROV	✓Rayovac Corp	NY,Ph	NR	104	24379	Mfr gen'l/spec'l batteries	19⅝	14	28	13¼	31 5/16	16⅞	33042	24 15/16	16⅞	18⅞	...	23	...	−29.3	...	...
43	RAY	✓Raytech Corp	NY,Ch	D	21	1102	Energy absorb'g & transm'n pr	33 11/16	½	5¾	2 13/16	7 9/16	2 9/16	1558	3 15/16	3 3/16	3⅜	...	1	10	17.4	−8.3	−5.1
¶44•[5]	RTN.B	✓Raytheon Co'B'	NY,B,C,Ch,P,Ph	A	763	167437	Defense&comm'l electr:constr	60 9/16	1¼	60¾	40 11/16	76 9/16	22 3/16	304026	31⅜	25¼	26 9/16	3.0	19	−4	−49.3	−16.7	−1.9
45	RTN.A	Cl'A'	NY,Ph	A	399	76497		57	48	59⅝	39⅞	75⅜	21¼	190384	29¾	23 13/16	24 13/16	3.2	12	...	−51.2	...	...
46•[9]	RAZF	✓Razorfish Inc'A'	NNM	NR	52	3303	Digital communic solutions	....	....	....	....	99	16	118498	99	66	95⅛	...	d	...	...	...	...
47•[10]	RCNC	✓RCN Corp	NNM	NR	208	25598	Telecommunication svcs	21⅝	12 7/16	30⅝	8¾	54½	17¾	99951	49⅝	40 11/16	48½	...	d	...	174	...	...
48	RDO	✓RDO Equipment'A'	NY,Ch,Ph	NR	25	2777	Sell,svc John Deere equip	25¼	14⅞	19¾	7⅛	10⅜	5½	2728	6½	5½	5⅞	...	8	...	−21.7	...	...
✤49•[2]	RDRT	✓Read-Rite Corp	NNM	C	123	19072	Supply thinfilm record'g heads	49½	8⅝	18⅜	5 7/16	20 9/16	3 5/16	181197	5⅝	3⅞	4¾	...	d	Neg	−67.9	−42.7	−23.9
#50•[11]	RDA	✓Reader's Digest Assn'A'	NY,Ch,Ph,P	B	252	42758	Magazine/book publishing	56⅜	20⅞	29 3/16	16¼	42½	24¾	75950	30⅛	27⅜	29¼	0.7	21	−9	16.9	−7.5	−6.9

Uniform Footnote Explanations-See Page 4: Other: [1]Ph:Cycle 2. [2]CBOE:Cycle 1. [3]ASE,Ph:Cycle 1. [4]ASE,CBOE,P,Ph:Cycle 1. [5]CBOE:Cycle 2. [6]CBOE:Cycle 3. [7]To:Cycle 1. [8]ASE:Cycle 3. [9]Ph:Cycle 1. [10]P:Cycle 3. [11]ASE,CBOE:Cycle 1. [51]Ea ADS rep 1 non-vtg Preferred Stock,no par. [52]Inc 68.4M Vtg Shrs. [53]Ea ADS rep 10 ord,no par. [54]Ea ADS rep 5 ord shs,0.05p. [55]Redemption stk purch rt. [56]Stk dstr of Agribrands Intl Inc. [57]Stock Appreciation Income Linked Securities. [58]Re-spec cond. [59]Ea ADS rep 1 ord shr,10 pence. [60]Pfd in $M. [61]If com exceeds $14.25 for 10 con trad days. [62]Fiscal Dec'96 & prior.

Index	Splits ◆ Cash Divs. Ea. Yr. Since	Dividends: Latest Payment Period $	Date	Ex. Div.	Total $ So Far 1999	Ind. Rate	Paid 1998	Financial Position Mil-$ Cash& Equiv.	Curr. Assets	Curr. Liab.	Balance Sheet Date	Capitalization Lg Trm Debt Mil-$	Shs. 000 Pfd.	Com.	Earnings $ Per Shr. Years End	1995	1996	1997	1998	1999	Last 12 Mos.	Interim Earnings Period	$ per Shr. 1998	1999	Index
1	....	None Since Public			...	Nil	....	52.6	67.6	24.1	9-30-99	....	...	38811	Dc	...	...	...	pv0.05	....	0.05	9 Mo Sep	pv0.03	vp0.03	1
2◆	1935	Q0.17	12-13-99	11-17	0.67	0.68	0.65¼	....	178	275	9-30-99	692	...	82441	Dc	v1.03	v1.19	v1.26	v0.93	....	0.84	9 Mo Sep	v1.21	v1.12	2
3◆	1998	0.502	5-15-98	4-29	...	Nil	1.004	2.97	3.61	1.32	10-31-99	0.12	p2134	24361	Jl	d0.32	d0.27	vd0.54	vd0.37	Pvd0.43	d0.48	3 Mo Oct	vd0.10	vd0.15	3
4◆	....	None Since Public			...	Nil	....	2.28	179	77.7	7-31-99	25.7	...	22698	Oc	v0.48	v0.54	v0.60	v0.82	vP1.14	1.14				4
5	....	None Since Public			...	Nil	....	3.17	15.4	12.2	9-30-99	117	...	★17878	Dc	...	...	p0.61	v0.42	....	0.09	9 Mo Sep	v0.39	v0.06	5
6	1996	0.255	7-14-99	7-8	0.255	0.25	0.222	123	371	276	12-31-98	37.0	...	[52]±106569	Dc	0.59	v0.57	v0.68	v0.89	....	0.81	9 Mo Sep	v0.57	v0.49	6
7	1998	0.11½	5-25-99	5-4	0.11½	0.12	0.437	136	785	641	12-31-97	693	...	1029240	Dc	2.30	0.70	v1.80	....	....	1.80				7
8	....	None Since Public			...	Nil	....	39.9	53.5	17.7	8-31-99	....	...	15380	Nv	p0.64	v0.76	v0.76	vd1.00	....	d0.25	9 Mo Aug	vd0.60	v0.15	8
9◆	....	None Since Public			...	Nil	....	186	728	565	9-30-99	16.1	...	114952	Dc	v0.24	v0.10	v0.75	v1.06	E1.40	1.14	9 Mo Sep	v0.57	v0.65	9
10	....	None Since Public			...	Nil	....	7.71	21.0	18.1	9-30-99	1.33	p...	★31125	Mr	...	...	...	vpd0.55	....	....	9 Mo Sep	n/a	vpd0.08	10
11	1993	S0.14	1-11-00	12-6	0.28	0.28	0.26	0.47	26.8	8.94	9-30-99	8.63	...	8103	Je	v0.76	vd1.26	vd0.48	vNil	v0.95	0.98	3 Mo Sep	v0.20	v0.23	11
12◆	....	None Since Public			...	Nil	....	16.5	442	211	9-30-99	844	...	70658	Je	v0.76	v0.93	v□1.11	v1.12	v0.52	0.33	3 Mo Sep	v0.33	v0.14	12
13◆	....	None Since Public			...	Nil	....	860	1909	955	9-30-99	2352	...	748000	Dc	vd0.08	vd0.02	v0.04	vd1.51	E0.10	0.10	9 Mo Sep	vd1.58	v0.03	13
14	....	None Since Public			...	Nil	....	39.3	42.7	6.00	6-30-99	....	p...	★113774	Mr	...	...	...	vpd0.07	....	....	6 Mo Sep	n/a	vd4.35	14
15◆	....	None Since Public			...	Nil	....	678	1000	276	9-30-99	2943	300	193629	Dc	Δv0.15	v0.67	vd0.04	v□0.75	Ed0.38	d0.19	9 Mo Sep	v□0.66	v□d0.28	15
16	....	None Since Public			...	Nil	....	1.94	147	34.5	9-25-99	91.9	...	8206	Dc	v0.56	v0.71	v0.83	v0.90	....	0.82	9 Mo Sep	v0.72	v0.64	16
17◆	1996	Q0.042	11-26-99	11-16	0.14⅞	0.166	0.111	Total Deposits $1270.21M			9-30-99	415	2000	±28659	Dc	v0.56	v0.60	v0.81	v1.12	....	1.33	9 Mo Sep	v0.82	v1.03	17
18◆	1993	Q0.03	12-2-99	11-2	0.12	0.12	0.12	Total Assets $1663M			9-30-99	....	800	p37153	Dc	v2.09	v2.55	v3.06	v3.72	E4.00	3.59	9 Mo Sep	v2.71	v2.58	18
19	....	None Since Public			...	Nil	....	44.3	82.7	17.3	3-31-99	....	...	18732	Dc	□d0.91	0.07	v1.37	v2.41	....	1.57	9 Mo Sep	v1.58	v0.74	19
20	....	None Since Public			...	Nil	....	4.43	25.7	10.4	9-30-99	108	...	★±22803	Dc	...	...	...	vpd0.35	....	d0.27	9 Mo Sep	vd0.30	vd0.22	20
21	....	None Since Public			...	Nil	....	88.8	96.5	4.98	p6-30-99	111	p...	★20897	Dc	...	...	...	vpd2.78	....	0.94	6 Mo Jun	n/a	vpd0.99	21
22◆	....	None Since Public			...	Nil	....	24.2	124	52.1	9-30-99	....	...	16389	Dc	v0.23	v0.87	v1.29	v0.45	....	0.90	9 Mo Sep	v0.34	v0.79	22
23	....	None Since Public			...	Nil	....	10.7	14.1	2.71	6-30-99	....	p...	★14604	Dc	...	...	...	vpd0.16	....	....	9 Mo Sep	n/a	vpd0.02	23
24	....	None Since Public			...	Nil	....	Total Assets $699.12M			6-25-99	....	...	12902	Sp	v0.68	v1.04	v1.44	v1.01	Pv1.20	1.20				24
25	....	None Since Public			...	Nil	....	13.9	69.9	45.9	9-30-99	275	464	11646	Dc	v0.04	v0.10	v0.22	v0.44	....	0.65	9 Mo Sep	v0.34	v0.55	25
26◆	....	None Since Public			...	Nil	....	15.8	45.6	17.6	10-03-99	....	...	23902	Dc	p□v0.10	v0.27	v0.46	v□0.57	....	0.52	9 Mo Sep	v□0.46	v0.41	26
27◆	....	[55]0.32	2-13-97		...	Nil	....	2.00	132	67.0	6-30-99	4.08	...	30630	Sp	1.00	vd1.42	v16.01	v1.32	Pv1.15	1.15				27
28◆	1934	Q0.10	12-13-99	11-18	0.40	0.40	h[56]0.40	85.0	1473	1913	9-30-99	1252	...	305042	Sp	p□0.92	v□1.08	v1.27	v3.38	v1.60	1.60				28
29	1997	1.08½	2-1-00	1-12	4.34	4.34	4.34	Exch for Interstate Bakeries com 8-1-2000[58]				★420	...	...	Sp	...	...	...	...	...	...				29
30	....	None Since Public			...	Nil	....	83.3	93.4	28.5	6-30-99	....	...	23549	Sp	d1.24	d0.73	v0.09	v0.28	Pv0.35	0.35				30
31	....	0.018	7-14-97	6-4	...	Nil	....	32.1	35.9	4.66	j12-31-98	....	...	25748	Dc	0.04	0.05	v0.03	vd0.05	....	d0.09	6 Mo Jun	v0.02	vd0.02	31
32◆	1989	Q0.42	1-18-00	12-29	1.68	1.68	1.68	Total Assets $546.20M			9-30-99	333	[60]34	7218	Dc	0.48	vp0.13	v1.25	v0.98	....	1.02	9 Mo Sep	v0.72	v0.76	32
33	....	None Since Public			...	Nil	....	Equity per shr $3.50			6-30-99	0.65	...	★3250	Dc	...	...	vd0.03	v0.92	....	0.61	9 Mo Sep	v0.81	v0.50	33
34	....	Terms&trad. basis should			be checked in detail			Wrrts expire 3-20-2001				....	...	400	Dc	...	...	...	....	....	....	Callable at 5¢[61]			34
35◆	....	None Paid			...	Nil	....	1.38	44.2	14.9	10-02-99	0.72	...	25435	Mr	0.05	v[62]0.15	v0.15	v0.12	....	d0.43	6 Mo Sep	v0.06	vd0.49	35
36	1995	Div Postponed 12-8-99			0.03	Nil	0.12	14.5	80.9	51.2	9-30-99	672	1150	37636	Dc	v0.31	v0.69	vd1.31	vd6.82	....	d3.90	9 Mo Sep	vd2.92	vNil	36
37	....	Div Omitted 3-6-98			...	Nil	....	32.9	179	176	6-30-99	331	...	126002	Dc	0.20	vd0.57	v0.09	vd0.84	....	d0.37	9 Mo Sep	vd0.65	vd0.18	37
38	....	Wrrt	6-29-90	6-18	...	Nil	....	59.3	72.4	13.6	9-30-99	3.00	[60]35	41704	Dc	vd0.47	vd0.35	vd0.63	vd0.02	....	d2.11	9 Mo Sep	v0.28	vd1.81	38
39◆	....	None Since Public			...	Nil	....	266	405	168	9-30-99	....	...	87333	Mr	d0.13	vd0.62	vd0.44	v0.65	....	0.79	6 Mo Sep	v0.22	v0.36	39
40◆	1985	Q0.07½	1-10-00	12-10	0.28	0.30	0.24	Total Assets $4997M			6-25-99	....	...	47335	Sp	0.99	1.39	v2.04	v1.86	Pv1.76	1.76				40
41	1994	Q0.36	12-31-99	12-8	1.29	1.44	1.24	3.67	275	182	9-30-99	433	...	27464	Dc	v4.75	vd3.28	v2.97	v2.22	E2.25	2.25	9 Mo Sep	v1.72	v1.75	41
42	....	None Since Public			...	Nil	....	11.1	257	152	9-30-99	307	...	27490	Sp	...	...	p0.38	v□0.58	v0.83	0.83				42
43	....	0.05	3-17-88	2-22	...	Nil	....	9.77	83.1	69.1	10-03-99	20.5	...	3481	Dc	v4.26	v4.65	v4.41	v4.61	....	4.66	9 Mo Sep	v3.71	v3.76	43
44◆	1998	Q0.20	1-31-00	12-30	0.80	0.80	0.80	113	9220	7890	10-03-99	7296	...	±338425	Dc	v3.23	pv3.17	v2.18	v±2.53	E1.40	2.15	9 Mo Sep	v±1.45	v±□1.07	44
45	1998	Q0.20	1-31-00	12-30	0.80	0.80	0.80	....	...	...		....	...	100805	Dc	v3.23	±pv3.17	v2.18	±v2.53	....	2.15	9 Mo Sep	v±1.45	v±□1.07	45
46	....	None Since Public			...	Nil	....	58.2	81.4	16.0	9-30-99	0.32	...	p±41817	Dc	...	...	...	vpd0.19	....	d0.09	9 Mo Sep	pvd0.01	v0.09	46
47◆	....	None Since Public			...	Nil	....	1592	1704	192	9-30-99	1743	259	76324	Dc	...	pvd0.11	□vd0.89	v□d3.35	....	d4.29	9 Mo Sep	vd2.34	v□d3.28	47
48	....	None Since Public			...	Nil	....	3.71	309	259	10-31-99	30.4	...	±13181	Ja	p0.63	±pv0.68	±v1.00	v±0.13	....	0.78	9 Mo Oct	v±d0.02	v±0.63	48
49	....	None Since Public			...	Nil	....	224	354	184	6-30-99	451	...	49676	Sp	2.60	d0.92	v1.56	vd6.59	vPd3.16	d3.16				49
50	1990	Q0.05	11-2-99	10-19	0.20	0.20	0.72½	431	1233	970	9-30-99	....	[60]22	±106470	Je	±2.35	±v0.73	v±1.24	v±0.16	vΔ±1.15	1.39	3 Mo Sep	vΔ±0.02	v±0.26	50

◆Stock Splits & Divs By Line Reference Index [2]2-for-1,'98. [3]2.5-for-1,'95. [4]2-for-1,'98:3-for-2,'99. [9]2-for-1,'95,'97. [12]3-for-2,'97. [13]2-for-1,'98,'99. [15]2-for-1,'97. [17]9-for-5,'97:2-for-1,'98. [18]2-for-1,'96. [22]3-for-2,'99. [26]3-for-2,'96,'98. [27]No adj for spin-off,'97. [28]Stk dstr Ralcorp Hldgs,'94:3-for-1,'98. [32]1-for-4 REVERSE,'96. [35]1-for-5 REVERSE,'99. [39]1-for-3 REVERSE,'95:2-for-1,'96. [40]3-for-2,'97,'98. [44]2-for-1,'95. [47]2-for-1,'98.

¶ S&P 500
# MidCap 400
✣ SmallCap 600
• Options

Index	Ticker	Name of Issue (Call Price of Pfd. Stocks)	Market	Com. Rank. & Pfd. Rating	Inst. Hold Cos	Inst. Hold Shs. (000)	Principal Business	Price Range 1971-97 High	1971-97 Low	1998 High	1998 Low	1999 High	1999 Low	December, 1999 Dec. Sales in 100s	Last Sale Or Bid High	Last Sale Or Bid Low	Last Sale Or Bid Last	%Div Yield	P-E Ratio	EPS 5 Yr Growth	% Annualized Total Return 12 Mo	36 Mo	60 Mo
		Reader's Digest Assn'A' (Cont.)																					
1	RDB	Cl 'B'(vtg)	NY,Ph,P	B	34	5061		54	21⅝	29¼	16	39⅛	23¾	1700	27 9/16	25	26½	0.8	19	−9	10.6	−7.3	−6.8
2	RDT	Reader's Digest $1.93'TRACES'	NY	NR	18	1470	Trust Automatic Com Exch Secs	....	....	28 3/16	17⅞	38⅝	25½	7717	27⅞	25⅞	27⅛	7.1	..	...	11.5	...	...
3•[1]	RNWK	✔RealNetworks Inc	NNM	NR	243	22381	Computer software/svcs	9 11/16	6¼	24⅞	6¾	186	18	378093	186	119⅛	120 5/16	...	..	...	572	...	...
4	O	✔Realty Income	NY,Ph,P	NR	66	2902	Real estate investment trust	27 13/16	15¼	27⅜	23 7/16	25	20	11253	21⅞	20	20⅝	10.5	13	12	−9.2	3.2	13.2
5	OUI	Realty Income 8.25% Sr Notes	NY	....[51]	1	3	Real estate investment trust	....	....	25 11/16	24¼	25⅜	21⅛	4362	22⅛	21⅛	22	9.4	..	...	−3.9	...	...
6	RA	✔Reckson Associates Realty	NY	NR	192	38210	Real estate investment trust	29⅛	12	26 13/16	19	26¾	18	30641	20 13/16	18⅛	20½	7.3	18	18	−1.3	5.4	...
7	RA.B	Cl'B'[52]Exch Common	NY	NR	63	7594		....	....	....	....	27¾	18⅞	8429	23	18⅞	22¾	9.8	22	17	...	...	...
8	Pr A	7.625cm Cv'A'Pfd([54]25.953)	NY	NR	60	6711		....	....	25 1/16	18 15/16	24 11/16	18	6203	19⅞	18	19⅞	9.6	..	...	...	...	...
9•[2]	RCOT	✔Recoton Corp	NNM	B	49	4622	Mfr consumer electronic prod	29	1/32	39 7/16	13⅛	21¾	5 7/16	25004	9¼	7¼	9	...	d	Neg	−49.8	−15.5	−13.7
10	RHAT	✔Red Hat Inc	NNM	NR	83	5175	Computer software & svcs	....	....	....	....	302⅝	14	287416	302⅝	196	211¼	...	d	...	...	...	...
11•[3]	RBAK	✔Redback Networks	NNM	NR	158	11988	Provide internet access sys	....	....	....	....	187	11½	214995	187	134	177½	...	d	...	...	...	...
12	REBC	✔Redwood Empire Bancorp	NNM,Ch	B	18	537	Savings bank, California	18¼	5⅝	21⅞	13	29	17	2786	23½	17¾	19⅛	1.3	15	NM	13.1	19.0	22.2
13	RWT	✔Redwood Trust	NY	NR	53	6249	Real estate investment trust	57½	15½	26	10⅜	17⅞	11¼	8681	13¾	11 5/16	12½	...	17	...	−9.6	−28.2	...
14	Pr B	9.74%'B'cm Cv Pfd ([55]31)	NY	NR	8	68		56¾	29½	34	24	31⅜	25½	343	27¾	25¾	27⅛	11.1	..	...	...	...	...
¶15•[4]	RBK	✔Reebok Intl	NY,B,Ch,P,Ph	B	276	41132	Markets athletic footwear	52⅞	2 13/16	33 3/16	12 9/16	22¾	7 13/16	78189	9 3/16	7 13/16	8 3/16	...	15	−36	−45.0	−42.0	−26.7
16	RUK	✔Reed Intl P.L.C.[56] ADS[57]	NY,Ph	NR	15	4503	Publishing/information svcs	43	22¾	48¼	28½	40½	22 9/16	2714	30⅛	24	29⅞	3.2	26	10	−1.5	−4.4	7.4
17	RJI	✔Reeds Jewelers	AS	B	15	403	Retail jewelry store chain	6⅛	1¼	5¾	3	4⅜	2⅝	525	3⅛	2⅝	3	...	6	2	−22.6	−0.6	−2.4
18	REF	✔REFAC	AS,Ch,Ph	B	24	796	Int'l transfer of technology	16⅛	¼	15½	6½	8 13/16	3½	3561	5	3½	4	...	4	20	−44.3	−9.6	−5.2
✣19	RBC	✔Regal Beloit	AS,Ch,P	A−	163	13868	Cutting tools:pwr transm'ns	32¾	7/16	33¼	17½	25⅝	15 9/16	9548	21⅞	20⅜	20⅝	2.3	11	10	−8.3	3.7	11.0
20	REG	✔Regency Realty	NY	NR	111	16821	Real estate investment trust	28¼	15⅛	27 13/16	20¼	23⅛	18¾	19102	20 13/16	18 13/16	20	9.2	13	19	1.9	1.6	12.2
✣21•[5]	REGN	✔Regeneron Pharmaceuticals	NNM	NR	81	6078	Drug R&D:neurological diseases	24⅞	3	11	5¾	13	5⅜	28429	13	7 9/16	12¾	...	d	28	72.9	−7.5	33.6
¶22•[6]	RGBK	✔Regions Financial	NNM	A	389	55169	Commercial bkg,Alabama	45	1⅛	45⅝	28⅞	41⅝	23 3/16	137568	28 13/16	23 3/16	25⅛	4.0	11	7	−35.9	1.6	13.3
✣23•[7]	RGIS	✔Regis Corp	NNM	B	200	26448	Operate hair salons in malls	23	2⅝	26 13/16	15	28 9/16	16 11/16	41102	21¾	18¼	18⅞	0.6	23	20	−28.7	20.9	23.7
24	RHB	✔RehabCare Group	NY,Ph	B+	63	3987	Dvlp rehabilitation programs	31⅛	4 5/16	31¾	11	22 11/16	13 13/16	4329	21⅜	18 7/16	21¼	...	10	27	13.7	16.7	19.7
25	RGA	✔Reinsurance Group of Amer	NY	B+	147	18062	Mkts life reinsurance	31⅛	9¾	47 1/16	25 1/16	49 3/16	22⅛	28984	31⅛	23¾	27¾	0.9	40	−4	−40.2	10.5	21.3
26•[8]	REL	✔Reliance Group Hldgs	NY,B,Ch,Ph,P	B	132	30266	Hldg co:Ins,investments R.E.	15⅛	3½	19 13/16	10¾	13 11/16	2 13/16	258123	7¾	4	6⅝	4.8	d	Neg	−46.1	−7.2	9.0
✣27	RS	✔Reliance Steel & Aluminum	NY,Ch	NR	155	12160	Process,dstr metal products	21 13/16	4 11/16	27½	16 1/16	26¾	16 13/16	8074	25	19⅛	23 7/16	0.9	12	20	28.3	15.6	34.2
¶28•[9]	REI	✔Reliant Energy	NY,B,C,Ch,P,Ph	B	588	139067	Elec utility hldg co:Texas	27¼	5½	33⅜	25	32½	22¾	129934	25 1/16	22¾	22⅞	6.6	4	Neg	−24.6	6.3	12.0
#29•[10]	RLR	✔ReliaStar Financial	NY,Ch,Ph,P	A	398	57332	Insurance/financial services	41 9/16	1	52 7/16	29	49 13/16	31 11/16	64510	45	37¾	39 3/16	2.1	16	9	−13.5	13.2	24.9
✣30•[9]	RMDY	✔Remedy Corp	NNM	NR	147	17983	Dvlp client/server softwr prd	55¾	7 11/16	25½	7 9/16	50¼	10½	102334	50¼	34¾	47⅜	...	62	40	240	−4.1	...
31	REMX	✔RemedyTemp Inc 'A'	NNM	NR	55	4284	Temporary personnel svcs	28⅛	13	36¼	11⅛	20⅛	9 13/16	8740	20⅛	14¼	19	...	11	...	25.6	3.3	...
32	RES	✔Renaissance Energy	To	B+	29	14468	Oil & gas explor,dvlp,prod'n	51	15/16	31 11/16	15½	25⅜	12½	100323	16 7/16	13⅞	14½	...	..	Neg	−16.9	−32.3	−11.8
33•[11]	REGI	✔Renaissance Worldwide	NNM	NR	79	19095	Information technology svcs	28½	12¼	31¾	5⅛	8⅜	2 11/16	92521	7¾	4⅝	7⅜	...	d	...	20.4	−31.6	...
34	RNR	✔RenaissanceRe Holdings	NY	NR	108	10920	Prop catastrophe reinsurance	50	19½	50¾	34½	43 3/16	30	12032	42½	37 1/16	40⅞	3.4	12	−9	15.9	10.7	...
✣35•[12]	RCGI	✔Renal Care Group	NNM	NR	268	32696	Provide nephrology svcs	24 5/16	8	30 5/16	18	34⅜	14¼	78771	24	20	23⅜	...	24	...	−18.9	18.8	...
36•[7]	RCII	✔Rent-A-Center	NNM	NR	142	18113	Rent/sell household prds	28¾	3 5/16	32½	18	34¼	15¼	21685	21¾	16¾	19 13/16	...	16	29	−37.6	11.0	...
37•[2]	RWY	✔Rent-Way Inc	NY	NR	144	15236	Rent household prod	21¾	4	34¾	17⅛	30	13 15/16	18553	19 13/16	15¼	18 11/16	...	28	69	−23.1	24.8	22.6
38	RENT	✔Rentrak Corp	NNM	B−	16	822	Dstr prerecd video cassettes	11⅛	⅞	10⅜	2	7⅜	2½	15498	7⅜	5	7 1/16	...	15	NM	157	...	...
39•[9]	REP	✔Repsol S.A.[67] ADS[68]	NY,Ch,Ph,P	NR	178	83241	Integrated oil co in Spain	15 3/16	5 7/16	19 3/16	13 9/16	24¼	15 7/16	77386	24¼	21½	23¼	1.5	20	10	31.0	25.7	24.6
✣40•[13]	RGC	✔Republic Group	NY,Ch	B	88	3551	Mfr recycle paper board/gypsum	22	1/16	22⅜	13	21¼	12⅞	2565	16 5/16	14 15/16	15⅛	2.4	10	6	−22.9	7.6	14.7
¶41•[14]	RNB	✔Republic New[69]York[70]	NY,B,Ch,Ph,P	A−	390	47475	Comm'l bkg,NY & worldwide	59 15/16	1 1/16	73¼	36 3/16	72	36 9/16	175021	72	70⅜	72	1.4	18	3	61.1	23.1	28.8
42•[15]	RSG	✔Republic Services	NY	NR	278	149999	Waste management svcs	....	....	27 7/16	13⅜	25½	8⅞	179323	14 7/16	11¼	14¼	...	12	...	−22.7	...	...
43	REFR	✔Research Frontiers	NNM	C	11	259	Light flow control devices	16⅞	13/16	11⅛	5 7/16	15 7/16	6¾	20954	15 7/16	9 5/16	14 13/16	...	d	5	41.1	24.1	18.8
✣44•[16]	RMD	✔ResMed Inc	NY	B	171	11392	Mfr sleep disorder eqp	15½	4⅞	48¼	13⅞	52⅛	19 3/16	18046	47¾	39 1/16	41¾	...	37	34	−8.0	56.1	...
45	RZT	✔ResortQuest Intl	NY	NR	43	4894	Prov vacat'n condo/home rentals	....	....	18¾	6½	22 15/16	3⅝	29710	6¼	3⅝	4⅛	...	12	...	−71.8	...	...
46	REXI	✔Resource America'A'[71]	NNM	B	75	11183	Oil & gas expl,prod'n,drill	18 13/16	7/16	37½	7 9/16	18½	6½	47510	9	6 13/16	7⅞	1.7	6	46	−12.0	9.8	44.3
47	RAS	✔Resource Asset Invstmt	AS	NR	22	2587	Real estate investment trust	....	....	19½	8⅝	13 7/16	9 15/16	6120	11 1/16	9 15/16	10 13/16	18.9	5	...	23.3	...	...
48•[14]	RBMG	✔Resource Bancshares Mtg Gp	NNM	NR	102	12054	Mortgage banking services	19 1/16	5 5/16	23¼	9½	17	4 7/16	31117	5¼	4 7/16	4½	9.7	4	9	−70.9	−27.4	−3.2
49	RBV	✔Resource Bankshares	AS	NR	4	258	General banking, VA	22½	5⅝	25	16½	22⅝	8¼	533	11¾	8¼	8⅝	4.6	d	Neg	−53.7	1.8	...

Uniform Footnote Explanations-See Page 4. Other: [1]CBOE,Ph:Cycle 2. [2]ASE:Cycle 2. [3]ASE,CBOE:Cycle 1. [4]ASE:Cycle 1. [5]ASE,Ph:Cycle 2. [6]Ph:Cycle 1. [7]Ph:Cycle 3. [8]ASE,Ph:Cycle 1. [9]CBOE:Cycle 3. [10]ASE,Cycle 1. [11]CBOE:Cycle 2. [12]ASE:Cycle 3. [13]P:Cycle 1. [14]Ph:Cycle 2. [15]CBOE:Cycle 1. [16]ASE,P:Cycle 3. [51]Rated BBB- by S&P. [52]Exch for com stk fr 10/2003. [53]To be determined. [54]Fr 4-13-2003,or earlier to preserve'REIT'status. [55]Or for 1 com based on cv price re-spec cond. [56]Ea ADS rep 2 ord, 25p. [57]Own 50% interest in Reed Elsevier plc. [58]Proportionate shr of Reed Elsevier. [59]Fiscal Feb'96 & prior. [60]12 Mo Dec'96. [61]Steinberg Gp owns 50% com. [62]Subsid Pfd in $M. [63]Incl 11M ESOP shs. [64]Fiscal Jun'96 & prior. [65]12 Mo Dec'97:Fiscal Jun'97 earn $0.71. [66]Stk dstr of BlowOut Entmt Inc. [67]Each ADS rep 1 ord, 500 Ptas. [68]Instituto Nacional de Hidrocarburos owns 70.5%. [69]HSBC Holdings plan acq,$72. [70]Plan S&P 500 delisting: eff Jan 3. [71]Radcliffe,Mitchell prop acq,$15.

Common and Convertible Preferred Stocks

Splits ◆ Index	Cash Divs. Ea. Yr. Since	Dividends: Latest Payment Period $	Date	Ex. Div.	Total $ So Far 1999	Ind. Rate	Paid 1998	Financial Position Mil-$ Cash& Equiv.	Curr. Assets	Curr. Liab.	Balance Sheet Date	Capitalization Lg Trm Debt Mil-$	Shs. 000 Pfd.	Com.	Earnings $ Per Shr. Years End	1995	1996	1997	1998	1999	Last 12 Mos.	Interim Earnings Period	$ per Shr. 1998	1999	Index
1	1992	Q0.05	11-2-99	10-19	0.20	0.20	0.72½	....	...	...		....	...	12433	Je	±2.35	v±0.73	v±1.24	v±0.16	Δv±1.15	1.39	3 Mo Sep	v±Δ0.02	v±0.26	1
2	1998	Q0.483	11-15-99	10-28	1.934	1.93	1.461	2-15-2001ex for Read Digest com re-spec cond				....	...	★11854	Je	...	...	...	....	....	....	Due 2-15-2001			2
3◆	....	None Since Public			...	Nil	....	326	336	64.2	9-30-99	....	...	74403	Dc	...	pvd0.07	pvd0.20	vd0.25	....	0.04	9 Mo Sep	vd0.28	v0.01	3
4	1994	M0.18	1-17-00	12-30	2.08½	2.16	1.96½	Total Assets $890.34M			9-30-99	230	4140	26822	Dc	v1.27	v1.40	v1.48	v□1.56	....	1.54	9 Mo Sep	v1.16	v1.14	4
5	1998	M0.172	1-15-00	12-30	2.063	2.063	0.269	Co option redm fr 11-15-2008 at $25				★100	...	...	Dc	...	...	...	....	....	....	Mature 11-15-2008			5
6◆	1995	0.37⅛	1-14-00	12-30	1.41¾	1.49	0.98¾	Total Assets $2681M			9-30-99	1238	15192	±50854	Dc	p□v0.51	v□0.92	□v1.10	v□0.99	....	1.14	9 Mo Sep	v□0.74	v0.89	6
7	1999	Q0.56	1-31-00	1-12	0.983	2.24	....	....	...	...		....	...	[53]...	Dc	□v0.51	v□0.92	v□1.10	v□0.99	....	1.02	3 Mo Mar	v0.25	v0.28	7
8	1998	Q0.477	1-31-00	1-12	1.906	1.906	1.049	Cv into .8738 com				....	9192	...	Dc	...	...	...	....	....	....				8
9◆	....	None Since Public			...	Nil	....	14.2	378	112	9-30-99	234	...	11733	Dc	v1.34	v0.73	v1.18	v0.36	....	d2.82	9 Mo Sep	v0.86	vd2.32	9
10◆	....	None Since Public			...	Nil	....	14.0	19.9	6.64	5-31-99	p....	p...	★66580	Fb	...	...	...	pvNil	....	d0.21	9 Mo Nov	vNil	vd0.21	10
11◆	....	None Since Public			...	Nil	....	65.5	82.4	24.9	9-30-99	1.21	...	43563	Dc	...	...	...	vpd0.39	....	d0.38	9 Mo Sep	pvd0.28	pvd0.27	11
12	1998	Q0.06	10-15-99	9-28	0.18	0.24	0.08	Total Deposits $368M			9-30-99	....	...	3370	Dc	v1.04	vd0.71	v1.02	v1.47	....	1.25	9 Mo Sep	v1.05	v□0.83	12
13	1995	0.25	1-21-00	12-29	0.15	[53]....	0.63	Total Assets $2081.47M			9-30-99	994	910	8780	Dc	v0.85	v1.32	v1.81	v□d2.28	....	0.75	9 Mo Sep	v□d2.58	v0.45	13
14	1996	Q0.75½	1-21-00	12-29	3.02	3.02	3.02	Cv into 1 com				....	910	...	Dc	...	...	...	....	....	....				14
15	....	0.07½	10-2-96	9-9	...	Nil	....	143	1304	665	9-30-99	400	...	56265	Dc	v2.07	v2.03	v2.32	v0.42	E0.56	0.33	9 Mo Sep	v0.54	v0.45	15
16	1995	0.303	10-8-99	8-16	0.969	0.97	1.047	2.00	226	129	[58]j12-31-98	36.0	4068	1144499	Dc	1.52	3.64	v2.59	v1.16	....	1.16				16
17◆	....	None Since Public			...	Nil	....	0.90	94.4	12.5	8-31-99	60.1	...	8476	Fb	v□0.41	v0.48	□v0.33	v0.50	....	0.54	9 Mo Nov	v0.02	v0.06	17
18	....	Div Omitted 11-26-97			...	Nil	....	5.48	8.26	1.71	9-30-99	....	...	3795	Dc	0.44	v0.88	v1.36	v1.21	....	0.99	9 Mo Sep	v0.94	v0.72	18
19◆	1961	Q0.12	1-14-00	12-29	0.48	0.48	0.48	5.04	200	72.3	9-30-99	160	...	20973	Dc	v1.57	v1.53	v1.83	v2.02	....	1.83	9 Mo Sep	v1.53	v1.34	19
20	1994	Q0.46	11-24-99	11-8	1.84	1.84	1.76	Total Assets $2608M			9-30-99	775	1503	±59264	Dc	±v0.75	±v0.82	±v1.23	v±1.75	....	1.49	9 Mo Sep	v1.42	v1.16	20
21	....	None Since Public			...	Nil	....	64.0	74.2	8.87	9-30-99	2.15	...	±31325	Dc	±d1.19	v±d1.33	vd0.40	vd0.28	....	d0.87	9 Mo Sep	vd0.10	vd0.69	21
22◆	1968	Q0.25	1-3-00	12-14	0.98	1.00	0.89	Total Assets $41229.16M			9-30-99	388	...	218650	Dc	v1.58	v1.81	v2.15	v1.88	E2.40	2.32	9 Mo Sep	v1.32	v1.76	22
23◆	1995	0.03	11-30-99	11-10	0.12	0.12	0.073	12.1	117	99.3	9-30-99	160	...	38714	Je	0.57	v0.28	v0.19	v0.85	v0.76	0.84	3 Mo Sep	v0.22	v0.30	23
24◆	....	None Since Public			...	Nil	....	4.53	63.5	44.1	9-30-99	45.8	...	6658	Dc	[59]0.84	v[60]0.93	v1.47	v□1.82	E2.12	2.15	9 Mo Sep	v□1.23	v1.56	24
25◆	1993	Q0.06	11-24-99	11-1	0.22	0.24	0.173	Total Assets $5180M			9-30-99	184	...	45130	Dc	v1.25	v1.45	v1.42	v1.48	....	0.69	9 Mo Sep	v1.35	v0.56	25
26	1986	Q0.08	1-1-00	12-13	0.32	0.32	0.32	Total Assets $14486.89M			9-30-99	456	...	[61]114835	Dc	□0.79	v0.41	□v1.94	v□2.78	....	d0.85	9 Mo Sep	v□2.50	v□d1.13	26
27◆	1995	Q0.05	1-5-00	12-15	0.17	0.20	0.143	10.7	418	140	9-30-99	343	...	27787	Dc	v0.97	v1.27	v1.43	v1.69	....	1.94	9 Mo Sep	v1.27	v1.52	27
28◆	1922	Q0.37½	3-10-00	2-14	1.50	1.50	1.50	3833	5863	8064	9-30-99	4768	[62]10	[63]295672	Dc	v4.46	v1.66	v1.66	vd0.50	E5.70	4.01	9 Mo Sep	v0.92	v5.43	28
29◆	1936	Q0.20½	11-12-99	10-21	0.80	0.82	0.71	Total Assets $23441.1M			9-30-99	909	...	p88751	Dc	v1.99	v2.37	v2.55	v2.56	....	2.43	9 Mo Sep	v2.18	v2.05	29
30◆	....	None Since Public			...	Nil	....	138	201	60.2	9-30-99	0.06	...	29018	Dc	v0.27	v0.56	v0.89	v0.63	....	0.77	9 Mo Sep	v0.45	v0.59	30
31	....	None Since Public			...	Nil	....	2.63	86.1	38.0	6-27-99	....	...	±8850	Sp	p0.52	p0.89	v1.13	v1.50	Pv1.71	1.71				31
32	....	None Since Public			...	Nil	....	4.15	132	134	j9-30-99	1407	...	142815	Dc	v0.66	v1.61	v0.98	vd0.08	....	j0.10	9 Mo Sep	v0.01	v0.19	32
33◆	....	None Since Public			...	Nil	....	14.4	224	125	9-25-99	53.2	...	56508	Dc	p...	p[64]0.15	vp[65]0.14	vd0.57	....	d0.63	9 Mo Sep	v0.18	vΔ0.12	33
34	1995	Q0.35	12-2-99	11-16	1.40	1.40	1.20	Total Assets $1599.57M			9-30-99	94.1	...	20484	Dc	6.75	v6.01	v6.06	v3.33	....	3.33	9 Mo Sep	v3.74	v3.74	34
35◆	....	None Paid			...	Nil	....	26.7	143	74.6	9-30-99	82.6	...	44660	Dc	...	0.37	v0.56	v0.83	....	0.97	9 Mo Sep	v0.60	v0.74	35
36◆	....	None Since Public			...	Nil	....	Total Assets $1486.16M			9-30-99	783	260	25293	Dc	v0.52	v0.72	v1.03	v0.83	....	1.27	9 Mo Sep	v0.78	v1.22	36
37◆	....	None Paid			...	Nil	....	Total Assets $495M			6-30-99	198	...	21631	Sp	0.22	v0.46	□v0.78	v1.08	P□v0.68	0.68				37
38	....	h[66]....	11-25-96	11-14	...	Nil	....	3.20	42.5	33.1	9-30-99	....	...	10482	Mr	d2.68	v0.52	v0.41	v0.18	....	0.46	6 Mo Sep	v0.12	v0.40	38
39◆	1990	0.19	7-9-99	6-29	0.358	0.36	0.326	1243	5947	6791	12-31-98	2663	...	900000	Dc	1.05	1.02	v0.92	v1.13	E1.15	1.13				39
40◆	1992	Q0.09	12-15-99	11-26	0.36	0.36	0.36	3.80	39.3	26.3	9-30-99	154	...	11818	Je	1.00	1.27	v1.67	v1.51	v1.29	1.54	3 Mo Sep	v0.28	v0.53	40
41◆	1975	Q0.26	1-1-00	12-13	1.03	1.04	0.98	Total Deposits $31856.22M			9-30-99	4140	7501	104740	Dc	v2.33	v3.54	v3.94	v2.07	E4.00	3.76	9 Mo Sep	v1.15	v2.84	41
42	....	None Since Public			...	Nil	....	9.80	322	421	9-30-99	1154	...	175448	Dc	...	...	pv0.74	vp1.01	E1.20	1.15	9 Mo Sep	vp0.74	vp0.88	42
43◆	....	None Since Public			...	Nil	....	7.90	8.03	0.20	9-30-99	....	...	11336	Dc	vd0.32	vd0.25	vd0.32	vd0.24	....	d0.27	9 Mo Sep	vd0.18	vd0.21	43
44◆	....	None Since Public			...	Nil	....	17.5	56.2	20.3	9-30-99	....	...	14876	Je	v0.32	v0.32	v0.51	v0.70	v1.04	1.14	3 Mo Sep	v0.21	v0.31	44
45	....	None Since Public			...	Nil	....	26.3	37.9	41.5	9-30-99	63.2	...	18519	Dc	...	...	pv0.45	v0.41	....	0.35	9 Mo Sep	vp0.64	vp0.58	45
46◆	1995	Q0.033	11-30-99	11-12	0.133	0.133	0.133	Total Assets $821.33M			6-30-99	524	...	22074	Sp	0.41	0.63	v0.84	vΔ1.59	....	1.30	9 Mo Jun	v1.16	vΔ0.87	46
47	1998	0.51	12-30-99	12-15	2.04	2.04	1.77	Total Assets $229.05M			9-30-99	116	...	6178	Dc	...	...	n/a	v1.81	....	1.99	9 Mo Sep	v1.30	v1.48	47
48◆	1996	Q0.11	12-14-99	11-12	0.43	0.44	0.29	Total Assets $1108M			9-30-99	6.29	...	20026	Dc	v0.86	v1.00	v1.05	v2.07	....	1.14	9 Mo Sep	v1.53	v0.60	48
49◆	1996	Q0.10	1-21-00	1-5	0.36	0.40	0.18	Total Deposits $240M			9-30-99	23.9	...	2536	Dc	0.53	v0.76	v0.84	v1.13	....	d0.19	9 Mo Sep	v0.85	vd0.47	49

◆Stock Splits & Divs By Line Reference Index [3]2-for-1,'99. [6]2-for-1,'97. [9]3-for-2,'94. [10]To split 2-for-1,ex Jan 10,'00. [11]2-for-1,'99. [17]10%,'94,'95:2-for-1,'98. [19]2-for-1,'94. [22]2-for-1,'97. [23]3-for-2,'96,'99. [24]3-for-2,'97. [25]3-for-2,'97,'99. [27]3-for-2,'97,'99. [28]2-for-1,'95. [29]2-for-1,'97. [30]3-for-2,'96:2-for-1,'96. [33]2-for-1,'98. [35]3-for-2,'97,'98. [36]3-for-2,'95:2-for-1,'95. [37]3-for-2,'95. [39]3-for-1,'99. [40]10%,'97. [41]2-for-1,'98. [43]5-for-4,'94. [44]2-for-1,'98. [46]3-for-1,'98:1-for-10 REVERSE,'95:Adj to 6%,'96:5-for-2,'96. [48]10%,'95:Adj for 5%,'97. [49]2-for-1,'98.

¶ S&P 500 # MidCap 400 ✤ SmallCap 600 • Options

Index	Ticker	Name of Issue (Call Price of Pfd. Stocks)	Market	Com. Rank. & Pfd. Rating	Inst. Hold Cos	Inst. Hold Shs. (000)	Principal Business	1971-97 High	1971-97 Low	1998 High	1998 Low	1999 High	1999 Low	Dec. Sales in 100s	Last Sale Or Bid High	Low	Last	%Div Yield	P-E Ratio	EPS 5 Yr Growth	Total Return 12 Mo	36 Mo	60 Mo
✤1•[1]	RESP	✓Respironics Inc	NNM	B	136	17668	Home med'l respiratory prod	30⅝	1 3/16	29⅝	9⅞	21⅜	7½	42777	8⅝	7½	8	...	21	–23	–60.2	–22.9	–7.5
2	RETK	✓Retek Inc	NNM	NR			e-commerce software solutions	....	....	....	....	122 13/16	15	333984	122 13/16	50¼	75¼	...	..	...	...	...	...
3•[2]	RTRSY	✓Reuters Group[51] ADS	NNM,Ch	NR	235	15674	International news agency	76⅞	4⅛	74¾	42⅛	100	50¼	29054	86	64⅞	80 13/16	1.7	31	6	29.9	4.8	15.9
4	RPCLF	✓Revenue Properties Ltd	NNM,To	NR	10	12746	Real estate development	3¼	1⅜	2⅝	1¼	1⅞	1 5/16	142	1 9/16	1 5/16	1 5/16	◆5.8	d	–48	–10.2	–4.5	–1.8
5•[3]	REV	✓Revlon Inc'A'	NY,Ch,Ph,P	NR	62	3271	Cosmetics/personal care prod	55½	22½	56⅝	12	32¼	7¼	60330	10 9/16	7¼	7 15/16	...	d	–17	–51.5	–35.7	...
6	RSC	✓Rex Stores	NY,B,Ch,P,Ph	B+	88	7902	Retails consumer electronics	24	2⅜	15¾	9 9/16	42⅝	11	22735	41¼	30 7/16	35	...	17	6	159	62.7	16.6
7•[4]	RXSD	✓Rexall Sundown	NNM	NR	121	13053	Mkt vitamins/supplements	31¾	2 5/16	39	11	22⅞	9½	149016	11⅝	9½	10 5/16	...	12	58	–26.3	–8.7	26.0
8	REX	✓Rexx Environmental	AS	C	3	56	Environmental services	236	1	5⅜	1¾	4 3/16	7/16	7193	4 3/16	1⅛	2⅞	...	d	–46	21.1	20.9	–8.1
¶9•[5]	RLM	✓Reynolds Metals[53]	NY,B,C,Ch,P,Ph	B–	462	51124	Aluminum mfg,finished pr	79¾	6	68⅛	46⅞	77¾	38¾	144201	77¾	62 7/16	76⅝	1.8	43	15	49.2	13.4	12.0
#10•[6]	REY	✓Reynolds & Reynolds'A'	NY,Ch,Ph,P	↑A	303	60581	Mfr business forms: EDP sys	30⅝	⅜	24	12⅝	25 5/16	17 5/16	54000	22 15/16	19⅝	22½	2.0	15	12	0.0	–3.0	14.3
11•[7]	RFMD	✓RF Micro Devices	NNM	NR	261	45047	Dvlp integrated circuits	5 15/16	2 9/16	12 11/16	2 7/16	83	11 3/16	515883	74	61½	68 7/16	...	..	NM	493	...	...
12•[4]	RFS	✓RFS Hotel Investors	NY,Ph	NR	105	12805	Real estate investment trust	21¼	10¼	21½	9½	14½	10⅛	23564	11⅛	10⅛	10 7/16	14.8	8	5	–3.4	–10.8	2.5
13•[8]	RGS	✓RGS Energy Group	NY,B,Ch,P	B+	164	11817	Hldg co: electric & gas	34½	7⅞	33¼	28⅝	31 9/16	20	41622	22 5/16	20	20 9/16	8.8	10	5	–29.6	9.9	7.6
14	RHD	✓R.H. Donnelley	NY	NR	204	26793	Bus info: publish: mkt: TV	....	....	15⅛	10	20¼	14⅜	20994	19 3/16	17½	18⅞	...	12	...	29.6	...	...
15•[6]	RHA	✓Rhodia ADS[55]	NY	NR	3	37	Produce specialty chemicals	....	....	30 7/16	11 13/16	23⅝	12⅛	1611	23⅝	18½	23⅝	...	22	...	59.0	...	...
16	RTHM	✓Rhythms NetConnections	NNM	NR	139	12683	Hi-speed internet access svcs	....	....	....	....	111½	26 1/16	378341	37½	26 9/16	31	...	..	...	...	...	...
17	RCF	✓Rica Foods	AS	NR	1	31	Integrated poultry business	13⅞	⅜	8	2 13/16	12	6	670	12	10⅝	12	...	31	NM	52.4	21.2	66.6
18	RELL	✓Richardson Electronics	NNM	B	49	7323	Mfr electron tube,semicond'r	22¼	3¾	14½	6 7/16	10	4⅞	10169	8¼	6 5/16	7½	2.1	12	53	–20.2	–1.2	1.2
19	RIC	✓Richmont Mines[60]	AS,To,Ph	B–	8	3897	Gold mining, Canada	9	½	3¼	2 1/16	3⅛	1⅜	1149	1 9/16	1⅜	1 9/16	...	d	Neg	–34.2	–35.2	–15.8
20	RHT	✓Richton Intl	AS	B–	11	53	Distr sprinkler irrigation sys	27½	7/16	11⅛	5⅝	17 5/16	8⅝	347	15⅞	14 3/16	14⅜	...	7	40	66.7	47.3	32.2
21	RDL	✓Riddell Sports	AS	NR	22	1392	Mfr football helmets/equip	16	1¾	6⅝	2⅝	7⅞	2¾	3796	3 1/16	2⅛	3 1/16	...	d	Neg	–38.9	–9.4	11.4
✤22•[5]	RIGS	✓Riggs Natl Corp	NNM	B–	126	9167	Comm'l bkg,Washington,D.C.	41½	3¾	31½	18¾	22	11⅞	26401	14½	11⅞	13 9/16	1.5	14	–3	–34.5	–7.7	10.4
23	RIT	✓RightCHOICE Managed Care'A'[61]	NY,Ch	NR	25	2670	Manage hlth care,Missouri	18⅞	8⅞	13⅛	8⅜	13	9½	878	11½	10⅝	11½	...	14	–24	0.0	2.7	–3.9
24	ROM	✓Rio Algom Ltd	AS,To,B,Ph,Mo	B–	50	16327	Mng:uran'm,copper,molybdenum	27⅛	4 3/16	20½	10⅝	16¾	9⅝	572	14⅝	11⅜	14 9/16	◆1.3	d	Neg	41.0	–11.0	–1.8
25	RTP	✓Rio Tinto[62]plc ADS	NY,Ch,Ph	NR	59	10679	Hldg co:mining,metals,energy	73⅛	2⅝	60¾	37 7/16	95⅛	46⅛	9106	95⅛	79¼	94¾	2.2	50	–14	117	18.1	16.4
26	RCHI	✓Risk Capital Holdings	NNM	NR	61	9418	Reinsurance:prop,casualty	23⅜	15⅞	25½	18 13/16	22⅝	11	10632	13¼	11¼	12⅝	...	d	...	–42.0	–13.3	...
27	RBA	✓Ritchie Bros Auctioneers	NY	NR	43	3352	Auctioneer industrial eqp	....	....	29¾	17	39½	26 7/16	2596	30¾	27½	27¾	...	18	...	3.0	...	...
¶28•[9]	RAD	✓Rite Aid	NY,B,Ch,P,Ph	B+	598	191533	Discount drug stores	34 3/16	3/16	50⅝	29 3/16	51⅛	4½	1389738	13¼	7 9/16	11⅛	4.1	53	–5	–77.1	–16.0	1.2
29	RVFD	✓Riviana Foods	NNM	B+	60	4031	Process/mkt rice products	21⅞	11⅝	25¾	18¾	24½	17	1711	19¼	17	17¾	3.2	11	11	–26.4	3.2	...
30	RIV	✓Riviera Holdings	AS,Ph	NR	5	3032	Oper hotel & casino Las Vegas	17¾	11	15⅛	3⅞	7⅜	3⅞	2975	6⅝	5	6⅝	...	d	Neg	45.7	–23.5	...
31	RTC	✓Riviera Tool	AS	NR	18	1439	Mfr metal stamping die sys	11¼	4 5/16	10 1/16	4 3/16	5¼	3	1110	3 15/16	3 5/16	3⅞	s...	5	...	–14.3	...	...
#32•[10]	RJR	✓R.J. Reynolds Tobacco	NY	NR	250	60107	Mfr,dstr tobacco prod	....	....	....	....	34	16	117895	22⅜	16	17⅝	17.6	1	...	...	...	...
33	RLI	✓RLI Corp	NY	B+	99	5879	Property/contact lens insur	40 5/16	5/16	45⅝	30 11/16	38 13/16	27⅞	6776	34⅝	33	34	1.6	11	NM	4.0	10.0	23.2
34•[4]	RMII	✓RMI.Net	NNM	NR	15	581	Internet access svcs	3¾	1	29	1⅞	20	5⅞	70292	10	7⅝	8 5/16	...	d	Neg	–34.2	82.2	...
35•[8]	ROAD	✓Roadway Express	NNM	NR	108	7290	Long-Haul freight svcs	29⅞	10¼	26¾	9⅝	23⅜	13½	16654	22¾	16⅝	21⅝	0.9	11	NM	51.3	4.8	...
36	RESC	Roanoke Electric Steel	NNM	B+	50	3281	Mfr merchant steel products	17 15/16	1 11/16	22¾	9⅞	17¾	10¾	2403	17	15½	16¼	2.5	8	17	13.5	16.2	22.0
✤37	RBN	✓Robbins & Myers	NY	A–	96	5825	Electric motors, fans, pumps	40½	13/16	39¾	17⅝	25⅞	15	5434	23 3/16	19⅝	22⅝	1.0	23	–6	3.4	–2.5	21.4
#38•[8]	RHI	✓Robert Half Intl	NY,Ch,Ph,P	B	240	60704	Personnel placement services	43 1/16	....	60¼	29	48⅝	20 7/16	49739	29½	26⅞	28 9/16	...	19	39	–35.8	7.9	29.1
39	RPI	✓Roberts Realty Investors	AS	NR	3	62	Real estate investment trust	9½	8⅛	9½	7 1/16	8½	7⅛	1188	7¾	7 5/16	7¾	e7.0	35	...	21.4	...	...
40	RHH	✓Robertson-Ceco Corp	NY,Ch,Ph	B–	33	2855	Mfr,dstr construction prod	800 9/16	2¼	11 1/16	7¼	11⅛	7	4900	10 1/16	7¾	9⅞	...	5	NM	27.4	7.8	24.9
41	ROBV	✓Robotic Vision Sys	NNM	C	41	4345	3-D sensor-based robotic sys	27¾	7/16	14⅜	2	10 1/16	1	98558	10 1/16	5 13/16	9¼	...	d	Neg	229	–8.0	8.2
42	ROAC	✓Rock of Ages'A'	NNM	NR	30	2314	Integrated granite quarrier	21¾	15	18¼	9⅛	14 15/16	4¼	8043	6	4¼	4 9/16	...	13	...	–68.0	...	...
43	RKT	✓Rock-Tenn 'A'	NY,Ch	NR	83	9647	Mfr recycled paperb'rd/contain	24	12¼	21 13/16	10	19	12 9/16	5052	15⅝	14	14¾	2.0	13	–3	–11.1	–7.5	1.7
¶44•[6]	ROK	✓Rockwell Intl	NY,To,B,C,Ch,P	B+	576	93756	Electronics,auto,aerospace pd	70⅝	2¼	61⅝	32⅛	64 15/16	39 15/16	80539	52 1/16	44	47⅞	2.1	17	Neg	...	...	...
45	RMCF	Rocky Mtn Choc Factory	NNM	B–	13	297	Mfr gourmet chocolate prod	19	1⅝	7¾	4	6 11/16	3	2318	5⅞	4¾	5¼	...	66	–16	0.0	–3.0	–17.2
46	RSTI	✓Rofin-Sinar Technologies	NNM	NR	24	2489	Dgn/dvp laser products	19⅝	9½	25⅝	7	12⅞	5⅛	3541	8	6½	7⅛	...	22	...	–24.0	–15.4	...
47	RCN	Rogers Cantel MobComm'B'	NY,Ch,To,Mo	C	44	13366	Cellular telephone svc Canada	31⅞	9	14⅛	6½	37 9/16	12½	19633	37 9/16	31¼	36⅜	...	d	Neg	199	23.4	4.5
48•[11]	RG	Rogers Commun[67]Cl'B'[68]	NY,Ch	C	124	54015	CATV in Can.,U.S.,Ireland	24⅞	9/16	13⅞	3 7/16	38¾	8 9/16	52591	36⅝	22⅜	24¾	...	4	NM	179	34.8	5.7
49	RCI.A	✓ Cl'A'Cv	To,Mo	C	1	589	provid'g entnmt,info svcs	25⅝	¼	14¾	5⅜	39½	13⅞	358	37⅝	33⅝	36⅞	...	9	NM	159	50.4	12.6
50	ROG	✓Rogers Corp	AS,B,P	B–	72	5346	Polymeric mtls: eng'd comp	46½	1¼	46 13/16	20½	41⅛	23½	2298	41⅛	37⅛	38¼	...	17	7	28.0	12.1	9.0

Uniform Footnote Explanations-See Page 4. Other: [1]CBOE:Cycle 3. [2]ASE,CBOE:Cycle 2. [3]ASE,CBOE,Ph:Cycle 1. [4]Ph:Cycle 2. [5]P:Cycle 2. [6]CBOE:Cycle 1. [7]CBOE:Cycle 2. [8]Ph:Cycle 3. [9]Ph:Cycle 1. [10]ASE,CBOE,P:Cycle 2. [11]ASE,CBOE,P,Ph,To:Cycle 1. [51]Each ADS represents 6 ord shrs par 2.5p. [52]Approx. [53]Alcoa Inc plan acq,1.06 com. [54]Excl 20M Cl'B' privately held. [55]Ea ADS rep 1 ord,100 FF. [56]To be determined. [57]Pfd in $M. [58]Fiscal Jun'95 & prior. [59]3 Mo Sep'96:Fiscal Jun'96 earned d$0.21. [60]Feb'96 & prior prices in $Cdn. [61]dba Alliance Blue Cross Blue Shield. [62]Ea ADS rep 4 ord,10p. [63]8 Mo Dec'97:Apr'97 earn $1.00. [64]Stk dstr of BF Enterpr. [65]Stk dstr of Conexant Systems,'98. [66]Accum on pfd. [67]Non-vtg. [68]1995 & prior prices in Cdn$. [69]Excl shrs hld by subsid.

Index	Splits ◆ Cash Divs. Ea. Yr. Since	Dividends Latest Payment Period $	Date	Ex. Div.	Total $ So Far 1999	Ind. Rate	Paid 1998	Financial Position Mil-$ Cash& Equiv.	Curr. Assets	Curr. Liab.	Balance Sheet Date	Capitalization Lg Trm Debt Mil-$	Shs. 000 Pfd.	Com.	Earnings $ Per Shr. Years End	1995	1996	1997	1998	1999	Last 12 Mos.	Interim Earnings $ per Shr. Period	1998	1999	Index
1◆	....	None Since Public			...	Nil	....	18.4	193	4.59	9-30-99	99.4	...	29870	Je	0.67	v0.71	v0.82	vd0.06	v0.72	0.38	3 Mo Sep	v0.19	vd0.15	1
2	....	None Since Public			...	Nil	....	0.50	36.8	19.0	9-30-99	....	...	★45500	Dc	...	...	...	pv0.09	....	....	9 Mo Sep	n/a	vd0.12	2
3◆	1984	0.35	9-13-99	8-4	[52]1.40¾	1.41	1.408	1006	1607	2250	j12-31-98	16.0	...	p1421601	Dc	2.40	v2.78	v2.89	v2.77	E2.60	2.87	6 Mo Jun	v1.26	v1.36	3
4	1994	g0.06	10-12-99	9-29	g0.11	0.11	g0.09	Total Assets $1323M			j6-30-99	794	...	69773	Dc	0.09	v0.05	vd0.35	vNil	....	jd0.03	9 Mo Sep	v0.04	v0.01	4
5	....	None Since Public			...	Nil	....	97.7	907	601	9-30-99	1688	1	±51243	Dc	p±vd0.97	v±□0.50	±□v1.14	v□d1.79	Ed6.36	d5.32	9 Mo Sep	v□d0.43	vd3.96	5
6	....	None Since Public			...	Nil	....	4.92	191	85.6	10-31-99	42.8	...	9185	Ja	v1.56	v0.80	v0.91	v1.43	....	2.11	9 Mo Oct	v0.42	v□1.10	6
7◆	....	None Since Public			...	Nil	....	2.12	212	63.7	8-31-99	....	...	64419	Au	0.08	0.33	pv0.53	vp0.94	v0.88	0.90	3 Mo Nov	v0.16	v0.18	7
8	....	None Since Public			...	Nil	....	0.17	5.49	4.79	9-30-99	0.66	...	2468	Dc	vd3.32	vd0.64	vd0.08	vd0.20	....	d0.58	9 Mo Sep	v0.22	vd0.16	8
9	1942	Q0.35	1-3-00	11-29	1.40	1.40	1.40	62.0	1368	1258	9-30-99	1009	...	63227	Dc	v5.25	v□1.06	v1.84	v□2.18	E1.80	5.89	9 Mo Sep	v□d2.76	v0.95	9
10◆	1953	Q0.11	1-13-00	12-15	0.40	0.44	0.36	123	459	227	6-30-99	382	...	[54]77239	Sp	0.92	v1.10	v0.70	v1.27	vP1.53	1.53				10
11◆	....	None Since Public			...	Nil	....	43.1	159	25.3	9-25-99	10.5	...	79370	Mr	pd0.12	pv0.04	vd0.01	v0.26	....	0.47	6 Mo Sep	v0.06	v0.27	11
12	1993	Q0.38½	11-15-99	11-4	1.54	1.54	1.51	Total Assets $689.5M			9-30-99	185	974	24990	Dc	v1.26	v1.37	v1.35	v1.31	....	1.29	9 Mo Sep	v1.15	v1.13	12
13	1944	Q0.45	1-25-00	12-31	1.80	1.80	1.80	4.55	199	223	9-30-99	720	820	36254	Dc	v1.69	v2.32	v2.30	v2.31	....	2.15	12 Mo Sep	v2.20	v2.15	13
14◆	1998	Div Omitted 3-16-99			...	Nil	0.17½	3.52	98.9	91.1	9-30-99	438	...	33477	Dc	...	...	pv1.75	v1.78	....	1.54	9 Mo Sep	v1.63	v1.39	14
15	1999	0.18	7-28-99	7-29	0.18	[56]....	....	114	4400	4682	12-31-98	526	...	174741	Dc	...	...	vpd6.48	v0.78	....	1.06	9 Mo Sep	v0.85	v1.13	15
16	....	None Since Public			...	Nil	....	449	493	56.7	9-30-99	500	...	77142	Dc	...	...	...	pvd0.58	....	....	6 Mo Sep	n/a	vpd2.80	16
17◆	....	None Paid			...	Nil	....	3.80	27.4	21.2	6-30-99	21.6	[57]4	7419	Sp	[58]d0.45	‡pv[59]0.28	v0.11	v0.16	....	0.39	9 Mo Jun	v0.13	v0.36	17
18	1988	Q0.04	12-1-99	11-8	0.16	0.16	0.16	15.5	203	35.9	8-31-99	117	...	±12632	My	Δ0.11	0.68	v□d0.08	v0.77	v0.60	0.64	3 Mo Aug	v0.17	v0.21	18
19	....	None Paid			...	Nil	....	10.4	16.0	3.27	j6-30-99	....	...	15296	Dc	v0.20	v0.20	v0.16	v0.25	....	jd0.05	9 Mo Sep	v0.25	vd0.05	19
20	....	0.11	10-30-79	10-17	...	Nil	....	0.08	80.1	69.2	9-30-99	5.33	...	3021	Dc	v0.43	v0.54	v0.68	v1.06	....	1.95	9 Mo Sep	v1.06	v1.95	20
21	....	None Since Public			...	Nil	....	0.37	93.1	28.0	9-30-99	145	...	9264	Dc	v□0.29	v0.33	vd0.07	vd0.78	....	d0.37	9 Mo Sep	v0.37	v0.78	21
22	1996	Q0.05	11-1-99	10-20	0.20	0.20	0.20	Total Deposits $4089.00M			9-30-99	416	4000	28312	Dc	v2.54	v1.79	v1.27	v1.21	....	0.98	9 Mo Sep	v1.24	v□1.01	22
23	....	None Since Public			...	Nil	....	232	366	298	9-30-99	28.1	...	±18673	Dc	v±1.26	v±d0.11	±vd1.29	v±0.30	....	0.83	9 Mo Sep	v±0.14	v±0.67	23
24	1961	gQ0.07	12-31-99	12-1	g0.28	0.28	g0.49	48.0	786	434	j6-30-99	258	[57]223	60623	Dc	2.55	v1.82	v1.20	v0.31	....	jd3.53	9 Mo Sep	v0.29	vd3.55	24
25	1988	0.594	9-1-99	8-11	2.08	2.08	2.08	1316	4519	4784	12-31-98	1678	10870	1369630	Dc	3.69	3.13	v3.48	v1.90	....	1.88	6 Mo Jun	v0.39	v0.37	25
26	....	None Since Public			...	Nil	....	Total Assets $870.98M			9-30-99	....	...	17090	Dc	pv0.06	v0.24	v0.12	v0.17	....	d0.47	9 Mo Sep	vd0.11	vd0.75	26
27	....	Plan annual div			...	....	....	94.5	143	108	9-30-99	39.3	...	16549	Dc	...	...	p‡[63]0.10	v1.54	....	1.51	9 Mo Sep	v0.87	v0.84	27
28◆	1968	Q0.11½	10-25-99	10-14	0.46	0.46	0.43	98.5	4002	2297	8-28-99	5413	...	258927	Fb	v0.92	□v0.85	v1.22	v0.54	E0.21	0.73	6 Mo Aug	vd0.08	v0.11	28
29	1995	Q0.14	1-11-00	12-3	0.50	0.56	0.55	15.7	107	56.2	9-26-99	1.49	...	14583	Je	v0.96	v1.15	v1.26	v1.42	v1.60	1.63	3 Mo Sep	v0.28	v0.31	29
30	....	None Since Public			...	Nil	....	72.9	85.0	31.4	9-30-99	223	...	4523	Dc	v1.25	v1.63	v0.40	v□d0.21	....	d0.56	9 Mo Sep	v□d0.21	vd0.56	30
31◆	....	5%Stk	2-1-00	12-27	...	Stk	5%Stk	0.11	15.3	4.32	8-31-99	9.24	...	3380	Au	...	p0.31	v0.44	v0.71	v0.72	0.72				31
32	1999	0.77½	1-3-00	12-8	0.77½	3.10	....	2503	3477	3771	9-30-99	1983	...	109630	Dc	...	...	...	vpd2.75	....	20.71	9 Mo Sep	vp0.44	vp□23.90	32
33◆	1976	Q0.14	1-14-00	12-29	0.54	0.56	0.50	Total Assets $1186.30M			9-30-99	....	...	9924	Dc	0.81	v2.28	v2.66	v2.65	....	3.10	9 Mo Sep	v1.89	v2.34	33
34	....	None Since Public			...	Nil	....	6.21	12.2	10.7	9-30-99	2.74	2	18118	Dc	d0.04	vd0.64	vd0.76	vd1.39	....	d1.49	9 Mo Sep	vd0.99	vd1.09	34
35	1996	Q0.05	12-1-99	11-9	0.20	0.20	0.20	92.5	402	361	9-11-99	....	...	19377	Dc	vd0.62	v1.07	v1.80	v1.31	E1.95↑	1.82	36 Wk Sep	v0.81	v1.32	35
36◆	1978	Q0.10	11-24-99	11-3	0.39	0.40	0.372	43.0	156	46.2	7-31-99	128	...	11005	Oc	1.67	v1.30	v1.49	v1.77	Pv2.03	2.03				36
37◆	1989	Q0.05½	1-31-00	1-12	0.22	0.22	0.22	8.90	156	83.0	8-31-99	191	...	10939	Au	Δ1.09	Δ1.84	v2.29	v2.43	v1.06	0.99	3 Mo Nov	v0.34	v0.27	37
38◆	....	h[64]....	8-3-87	6-22	...	Nil	....	182	502	182	9-30-99	2.61	...	89706	Dc	v0.46	v0.67	v1.00	v1.39	....	1.50	9 Mo Sep	v1.01	v1.12	38
39	1997	0.135	1-14-00	12-28	†1.09½	0.54	0.57¼	Total Assets $125M			9-30-99	85.1	...	4818	Dc	□d0.08	□d0.02	vd0.62	v□0.26	....	0.22	9 Mo Sep	□v0.16	□v0.12	39
40	....	6.601	9-16-85	8-26	...	Nil	....	38.3	107	45.3	9-30-99	....	...	16112	Dc	vd0.22	v□3.26	Δv1.17	v1.40	....	1.93	9 Mo Sep	v1.02	v1.55	40
41	....	None Paid			...	Nil	....	3.48	66.0	69.4	6-30-99	2.93	...	27337	Sp	0.63	0.60	v0.03	vd1.65	Pvd0.38	d0.38				41
42	....	None Since Public			...	Nil	....	5.77	50.1	31.7	9-30-99	12.8	...	±7443	Dc	v0.35	±v0.45	v0.53	v0.91	....	0.34	9 Mo Sep	v0.64	□v0.07	42
43◆	1994	Q0.07½	11-22-99	11-4	0.30	0.30	0.30	3.12	236	146	6-30-99	476	...	±34957	Sp	±1.21	v±1.50	v±0.47	v±1.20	Pv±1.13	1.13				43
44◆	1948	Q0.25½	12-6-99	11-10	1.02	1.02	h[65]1.02	356	3582	2108	9-30-99	911	...	190222	Sp	3.42	3.34	v2.97	v□d2.07	v2.90	2.90				44
45	....	None Since Public			...	[66]Nil	....	0.31	6.10	4.11	8-31-99	4.31	...	2600	Fb	0.42	vd0.47	v0.08	v0.16	....	0.08	6 Mo Aug	v0.25	v0.17	45
46	....	None Since Public			...	Nil	....	35.8	112	41.6	6-30-99	6.86	...	11527	Sp	p0.37	p0.84	v0.77	v0.58	Pv0.32	0.32				46
47	....	None Since Public			...	Nil	....	Equity per shr Neg			j12-31-98	1950	...	±92958	Dc	±d0.46	v±d0.72	v±d4.05	±vd0.85	....	jd1.41	9 Mo Sep	vd0.49	vd1.05	47
48	....	0.009	7-30-82	7-12	...	Nil	....	Equity per shr Neg			j12-31-98	5254	15058[69]	±289035	Dc	±d1.78	v±d1.72	±vd3.17	v±2.92	....	j3.96	9 Mo Sep	v2.83	v±3.87	48
49	....	g†0.007	8-4-80	7-18	...	Nil	....	Cv into Cl'B'shr for shr				....	...	56240	Dc	±d1.78	±vd1.72	vd3.17	±v2.92	....	j3.96	9 Mo Sep	v±2.83	±3.87	49
50◆	....	0.01½	2-12-92	1-9	...	Nil	....	18.1	79.4	38.4	10-03-99	12.2	...	7529	Dc	v1.69	v1.83	v2.10	v1.74	....	2.24	9 Mo Sep	v1.23	v1.73	50

◆Stock Splits & Divs By Line Reference Index [1]2-for-1,'95. [3]2-for-1,'94. [7]3-for-2,'96:2-for-1,'97. [10]2-for-1,'94,'96. [11]2-for-1,'99(twice). [14]1-for-5 REVERSE,'98. [17]1-for-3 REVERSE,'98. [28]2-for-1,'98. [31]Adj for 5%,'99. [33]5-for-4,'95,'98. [36]3-for-2,'95,'98. [37]2-for-1,'96. [38]2-for-1,94,'96:3-for-2,'97. [43]10%,'96. [44]No adj for stk dstr Meritor Automotive,'97:No adj for stk dstr,'99. [50]2-for-1,'95.

¶ S&P 500
# MidCap 400
✣ SmallCap 600
• Options

Index	Ticker	Name of Issue (Call Price of Pfd. Stocks)	Market	Com. Rank. & Pfd. Rating	Inst. Hold Cos	Inst. Hold Shs. (000)	Principal Business	Price Range 1971-97 High	1971-97 Low	1998 High	1998 Low	1999 High	1999 Low	December, 1999 Dec. Sales in 100s	Last Sale Or Bid High	Last Sale Or Bid Low	Last Sale Or Bid Last	%Div Yield	P-E Ratio	EPS 5 Yr Growth	% Annualized Total Return 12 Mo	36 Mo	60 Mo
¶1•[1]	ROH	✔Rohm & Haas	NY,B,Ch,P,Ph	A	586	164790	Mfr specialty chem & plastics	33¾	1 9/16	38⅞	26	49¼	28⅛	110310	41⅞	36 1/16	40 11/16	1.9	33	6	37.8	16.7	19.1
2	ROHN	✔ROHN Industries	NNM,Ch	B	53	11308	Telecom equip/metal fab	15⅞	13/16	6¼	1¾	4 5/16	1 1/16	39330	3⅞	2⅜	2⅞	...	24	−28	−16.4	−21.2	−1.1
#3•[2]	ROL	✔Rollins Inc	NY,B,Ch,P,Ph	B	90	11202	Pest controls/protective svcs	30¾	2⅛	21 9/16	15¼	17¾	14¾	5169	16 3/16	14¾	15	1.3	46	−35	−13.2	−7.1	−6.1
✣4•[3]	RLC	✔Rollins Truck Leasing	NY,B,Ch,P,Ph	A	166	33201	Truck, trailer leasing	12¼	3/16	15¼	8⅞	14½	9 1/16	14760	11 15/16	11	11 15/16	1.8	12	12	−17.5	14.2	10.3
5	ROMC	✔Romac Intl	NNM	NR	109	27334	Personnel placement service	25⅛	3⅛	32⅛	11¾	24¼	5⅞	62211	15⅝	11	13 7/16	...	35	NM	−39.6	7.3	...
✣6•[4]	ROP	✔Roper Industries	NY	B+	187	23691	Mfr fluid handl'g/ctrl prd	34⅞	2⅞	34 1/16	13 5/16	38 9/16	19⅝	17833	38⅜	33¼	37 13/16	0.7	25	17	87.3	25.9	25.7
7	RSLN	✔Roslyn Bancorp	NNM	NR	159	28910	Savings bank,New York	25	14⅞	30⅞	12¾	22 7/16	16	78977	20¼	16 11/16	18½	3.0	50	...	−11.4	...	...
#8•[5]	ROST	✔Ross Stores	NNM	B+	393	80117	Apparel,shoes,linen retailer	21 3/16	15/16	25	11⅝	26⅛	17	220005	20⅜	17	17 15/16	0.7	11	38	−8.1	13.6	46.3
9	ROS	✔Rostelecom Telecommun ADS[52]	NY	NR	50	8069	Telecomm svc,Russia	....	....	23⅛	1 9/16	17	3 11/16	54140	17	6⅞	17	...	d	...	306	...	...
10	RMI	✔Rotonics Manufacturing	AS,Ch	B−	5	288	Mfr,mkt plastic containers	10⅛	3/16	1 9/16	9/16	1 11/16	¾	3907	1⅝	1¼	1 9/16	2.6	13	−13	62.4	4.8	5.0
11	RH	✔Rottlund Co	AS	NR	15	896	Dgn/build single family homes	10⅝	3⅛	4⅞	2¾	5¾	2⅜	976	2¾	2⅜	2⅝	...	3	−10	−34.4	−19.0	−12.9
12•[6]	ROU	✔Rouge Industries 'A'	NY,Ph,P	NR	44	7112	Integrated domestic steel mfr	34¼	11 15/16	16⅛	6¼	14	5⅝	13466	8⅛	6	7⅞	1.5	d	Neg	−8.8	−27.2	−22.3
13•[7]	RSE	✔Rouse Co	NY,Ph	B−	189	54826	Real estate investment trust	33	7/16	35 11/16	23⅛	27¾	19¾	39292	22⅜	19¾	21¼	5.6	17	NM	−18.6	−8.8	6.1
14	Pr B	6.00% cm Cv'B'Pfd([53])	NY	BB+	40	3166		50½	44¾	53	42	44	30⅞	5707	34	30⅞	32⅝	9.2	..	...	...	...	...
¶15•[1]	RDC	✔Rowan Cos	NY,B,Ch,P	B−	339	49933	Contract drilling:aircraft sv	43 15/16	1/16	32½	9	21 11/16	8½	203114	21 11/16	16 9/16	21 11/16	...	d	NM	120	−1.4	28.3
16	ROW	✔Rowe Cos	NY,Ph	B+	29	1882	Mfr living room furniture	11 11/16	3/16	10 9/16	6⅛	12¾	7⅝	2049	9 13/16	8¼	8 7/16	1.7	9	16	−6.0	9.9	17.0
17	ROWE	✔RoweCom Inc	NNM	NR	34	2181	Business e-commerce solutions	....	....	....	....	53 9/16	13⅛	45818	53 9/16	40 15/16	45⅜	...	d	...	...	...	...
✣18	RAM	✔Royal Appliance Mfg	NY,Ph,P	NR	53	4021	Assemble,mkt vacuum cleaners	31	2½	7⅛	2¼	7⅛	3	6377	6 1/16	4 9/16	4⅞	...	7	NM	32.2	−10.8	6.9
19•[8]	RY	✔Royal Bank Canada[54]	NY,Mo,To,Vc,P	B+	136	70256	Banking:Canada&worldwide	57 15/16	12 7/16	64⅜	37	56	40	4021	46⅝	42⅝	44⅛	◆3.4	6	11	−8.2	11.9	13.9
20•[9]	RCL	✔Royal Caribbean Cruises	NY	B+	294	60138	Operates passenger cruise line	26 13/16	7 13/16	45½	17	58⅞	31⅜	129788	54	45 5/16	49 5/16	0.9	25	13	34.5	63.5	30.2
21	Pr	$3.625 Cv'A'Pfd([55]52.5375)	NY	↑BB+	38	2498		85⅜	50	139	60 1/16	172 5/16	98 11/16	618	165¼	141¾	151½B	2.4	..	...	...	...	...
¶22•[1]	RD	✔Royal Dutch Petrol	NY,B,C,Ch,P,Ph	A−	1431	598899	Owns 64% Royal Dutch/Shell	59 7/16	1⅜	60⅜	39¾	67⅜	39 9/16	497680	63⅝	55⅝	60 9/16	2.2	31	−32	30.0	16.2	21.9
23	RGLD	✔Royal Gold Inc	NNM,To	C	16	2229	Gold mining,U.S.	18¼	1/32	7⅛	3 1/16	6⅛	3 5/16	6644	4⅛	3 5/16	3⅝	...	d	Neg	0.0	−35.3	−14.9
24	RYG	Royal Group Tech[58]	NY,Ch	NR	49	11631	Produce PVC building products	31⅜	13¾	34⅛	14½	30 3/16	16⅞	8019	23 13/16	20¼	21 3/16	...	9	20	−5.0	4.4	...
25	ROCLF	✔Royal Olympic Cruise Line	NNM	NR	8	2359	Operates passenger cruise line	....	....	16⅞	2⅝	5⅛	1½	3610	4⅞	3¾	4⅞	...	..	...	44.4	...	...
26	KPN	✔Royal PTT Nederland ADS[59]	NY,Ph,P	NR	49	7805	Telecom sv, Netherlands	42⅝	34⅛	65¼	29½	98⅜	38 11/16	12848	98⅜	55½	96	1.0	57	−1	...	...	...
27	RES	✔RPC Inc	NY,B	B	52	7289	Svc oil&gas eqp/mfr boats	16¼	⅞	14¼	7	9 13/16	5 11/16	4133	6 15/16	5 11/16	5¾	2.4	29	−1	−20.5	−6.7	9.8
#28•[10]	RPM	✔RPM, Inc	NY	A+	265	51786	Protective coatings: fabrics	16 13/16	3/16	18	12¾	16½	9 15/16	91313	11⅞	9 15/16	10 3/16	4.8	16	1	−34.1	−6.3	−0.1
✣29	RSAS	✔RSA Security	NNM	NR	196	24230	Dvlp,mkt computer security pds	54½	3½	42¾	5 7/16	80	14¼	218765	80	36¼	77½	...	21	80	237	35.0	75.6
30	RSLC	✔RSL Communications 'A'	NNM	NR	73	9898	Telecommunication svcs	35¼	21⅛	44½	15 1/16	42	12⅛	157770	23	15 11/16	17⅛	...	d	...	−41.9	...	...
✣31•[11]	RTI	✔RTI Intl Metals	NY,Ch,P	B−	108	12136	Produce titanium metal prod	130	2	24 11/16	10⅝	16	5 7/16	33509	8	5 7/16	7½	...	19	NM	−46.4	−35.6	6.4
32	RTO	RTO Enterprises	To	NR	2	436	Sell/rent furniture,hsld prd	5⅝	1⅛	2½	1	2⅛	15/16	10376	1 11/16	15/16	1 9/16	...	8	20	24.9	−33.4	2.0
✣33•[10]	RI	✔Ruby Tuesday	NY,P	A−	216	21971	Oper specialty restaurants	29¾	11/16	21¼	12 1/16	22 1/16	16 5/16	21889	20	16 5/16	18 3/16	0.5	16	69	−14.0	25.2	−5.0
#34	RDK	✔Ruddick Corp	NY,Ch	A	141	28387	Food supermkts/thread,yarn	21⅜	⅛	23	15	22¾	15⅛	15123	18	15⅛	15½	2.3	14	9	−31.4	5.4	12.4
35	RTEC	✔Rudolph Technologies	NNM	NR	..	...	Semiconductor mfg sys	....	....	....	....	36¾	16	31995	36¾	25	33½	...	d	...	...	...	...
✣36	RURL	✔Rural/Metro Corp	NNM	B−	75	5255	Emergency ambulance/fire svcs	39¾	12½	35½	6⅛	12	3 15/16	31625	6 7/16	3 15/16	4¼	...	4	−1	−60.9	−50.8	−25.6
✣37•[12]	RUS	✔Russ Berrie & Co	NY,Ch	B+	122	8835	Mkts variety of gift items	31 9/16	8 11/16	30½	15¾	27½	18 15/16	8587	26¼	23½	26¼	3.0	13	49	15.3	16.9	17.7
¶38•[1]	RML	✔Russell Corp	NY,Ch,P,Ph	B−	231	15603	Athletic wear, knit gds, cloth	40⅜	5/16	33⅞	18	25⅛	12⅛	17989	17⅛	12⅞	16¾	3.3	..	Neg	−15.0	−15.5	−10.0
✣39•[10]	RYAN	✔Ryan's Family Stk Hse	NNM	B+	183	26400	Cafeteria-style restaurants	16	5/16	13⅜	7 3/16	14 1/16	8¼	33159	10⅛	8¼	8½	...	8	17	−31.3	7.3	2.5
40	RYAAY	✔Ryanair Holdings ADS[63]	NNM	NR	83	9255	Oper low fare airline	30¼	21⅛	43½	22	57¼	30	8966	56¼	49	55⅛	...	43	...	46.0	...	...
¶41•[5]	R	✔Ryder System	NY,B,Ch,P,Ph	B	368	59366	Equip leasing/transp'n svcs	43	13/16	40 9/16	19 7/16	28¾	18 13/16	96583	24 15/16	20⅛	24 7/16	2.5	22	56	−3.7	−2.5	4.4
#42•[4]	RT	✔Ryerson Tull	NY,B,C,Ch,P,Ph	B−	192	20787	Steel producer/distrib/process	58⅝	14½	30½	14⅛	25 1/16	14	13142	20 11/16	18	19 7/16	1.0	9	32	16.4	0.0	−10.4
✣43•[4]	RYL	✔Ryland Group	NY,B,Ch,P,Ph	B	186	13420	Constr single family homes	33	13/16	31⅝	19 7/16	30 7/16	19¾	12777	23 7/16	19 15/16	23 1/16	0.7	6	NM	−19.6	20.9	11.7
44	SPY	S&P Dep Receipts	AS	NR	276	27768	SPDRS Stock Price Index Secs	99	42 13/16	124¾	90⅞	147 9/16	120⅜	1215288	147 9/16	139	146⅞	1.0	..	...	20.5	27.5	28.5
45	MDY	S&P MidCap Dep Receipts	AS	NR	100	10274	SPDRS Stock Price Index secs	66½	37	73¾	51¼	82¼	66⅛	166508	82¼	76⅝	81⅛	⊙0.8	..	...	14.8	21.0	...
46	XLB	S&P Sel Basic Ind SPDR Fund	AS	NR	..	...	SPDRS Sock Price Index Secs	....	....	22	20¾	28½	20⅞	41321	26 11/16	23 13/16	26 9/16	...	..	...	22.3	...	...
47	XLV	S&P Sel Consumer Svcs SPDR Fund	AS	NR	4	309	SPDRS Stock Price Index Secs	....	....	26	24 13/16	30⅞	25 5/16	28529	30⅞	28⅜	30⅞	...	..	...	18.8	...	...
48	XLP	S&P Sel Consum Staples SPDR Fund	[13]	NR	14	785	SPDRS Stock Price Index Secs	....	....	27⅝	25⅞	27 15/16	22¼	81631	25⅜	22⅜	23	...	..	...	−14.5	...	...
49	XLY	S&P Sel Cyclical/Transp'n SPDR Fund	AS	NR	5	476	SPDRS Stock Price Index Secs	....	....	26⅜	25 5/16	31⅛	25⅛	48126	31⅛	28¼	31 1/16	...	..	...	19.3	...	...
50	XLE	S&P Sel Energy SPDR Fund	AS	NR	12	897	SPDRS Stock Price Index Secs	....	....	23 13/16	23 3/16	30 5/16	21⅛	62574	28	26⅛	27⅛	...	..	...	17.6	...	...

Uniform Footnote Explanations-See Page 4. Other: [1]ASE:Cycle 1. [2]Ph:Cycle 2. [3]P:Cycle 1. [4]Ph:Cycle 3. [5]P:Cycle 2. [6]P:Cycle 3. [7]Ph:Cycle 1. [8]To:Cycle 1. [9]ASE,P:Cycle 3. [10]CBOE:Cycle 1. [11]ASE,Ph:Cycle 3. [12]CBOE:Cycle 3. [13]AS [51]®$1.57,'96. [52]Ea ADS rep 6 ord par 0.0025 roubles. [53]Fr 4-1-2000 for 1.311 com only,re-spec cond. [54]Sep'95 & prior prices in Cdn$. [55]Fr 2-17-2000 or earlier upon Liab tax law chge. [56]Approx. [57]Proportionate shr of group B/S. [58]Sub vtg shrs. [59]Ea ADS rep 1 ord,NLG 10. [60]Stk dstr of TNT Post Group NV. [61]Fiscal Jul'96 & prior. [62]5 Mo Dec'97:Jul'97 earn d$0.53. [63]Ea ADS rep 5 ord,4 IR pence. [64]8 Mo Mar'96. [65]©$1.50,'99. [66]©$0.6428,'98. [67]To be determined.

Splits ◆ Index	Cash Divs. Ea.Yr. Since	Dividends: Latest Payment Period $	Date	Ex. Div.	Total $ So Far 1999	Ind. Rate	Paid 1998	Financial Position Mil-$ Cash& Equiv.	Curr. Assets	Curr. Liab.	Balance Sheet Date	Capitalization Lg Trm Debt Mil-$	Shs. 000 Pfd.	Com.	Earnings $ Per Shr. Years End	1995	1996	1997	1998	1999	Last 12 Mos.	Interim Earnings Period	$ per Shr. 1998	1999	Index
1◆	1927	Q0.19	12-1-99	11-3	0.74	0.76	0.693	83.0	2427	2189	9-30-99	3242	...	218884	Dc	v1.40	v1.79	v2.13	v□2.52	E1.24↓	1.31	9 Mo Sep	v□2.05	v0.84	1
2	....	†0.10	12-29-97	12-11	...	Nil	....	27.6	82.4	24.7	9-30-99	9.42	...	52752	Dc	v0.57	v0.89	v0.36	v0.27	....	0.12	9 Mo Sep	v0.22	v0.07	2
3	1961	Q0.05	12-10-99	11-8	0.20	0.20	0.50	69.9	163	119	9-30-99	3.59	...	30076	Dc	v1.10	v0.64	v0.04	v0.21	....	0.33	9 Mo Sep	v0.19	v0.31	3
4◆	1976	Q0.05½	12-15-99	11-10	0.20½	0.22	0.167	34.3	150	80.0	9-30-99	802	...	57215	Sp	0.61	0.52	v0.68	v0.85	v0.97	0.97				4
5◆	....	None Since Public			...	Nil	....	22.8	180	57.0	9-30-99	....	...	46500	Dc	v0.18	v0.26	v0.44	v0.33	....	0.38	9 Mo Sep	v0.18	v0.23	5
6◆	1992	Q0.07	1-28-00	1-12	0.26	0.28	0.24	3.50	146	60.1	7-31-99	126	...	30306	Oc	0.77	0.93	v1.16	v1.24	vP1.53	1.53				6
7	1997	Q0.14	12-10-99	12-1	0.51½	0.56	0.37½	Total Deposits $4102M			9-30-99	200	...	73554	Dc	...	n/a	v0.83	v1.36	....	0.37	9 Mo Sep	v0.96	v□d0.03	7
8◆	1994	Q0.03¼	1-3-00	12-1	0.12½	0.13	0.10½	31.6	635	456	10-30-99	24.0	...	88543	Ja	v0.44	v[51]0.79	v1.18	v1.40	E1.69↑	1.64	9 Mo Oct	v0.92	v1.16	8
9	1998	0.022	11-20-98	5-28	...	Nil	0.022	82.4	301	319	1-01-99	348	233438	700313	Dc	3.46	2.47	v0.35	vd4.58	....	d4.58				9
10	1996	A0.04	1-29-99	1-14	0.04	0.04	0.04	....	15.9	6.07	9-30-99	4.85	...	14979	Je	0.24	v0.10	v0.10	v0.03	v0.09	0.12	3 Mo Sep	v0.02	v0.05	10
11	....	None Since Public			...	Nil	....	Total Assets $102M			9-30-99	49.3	...	5804	Mr	v0.74	v0.22	vd0.10	v0.90	....	0.86	6 Mo Sep	v0.29	v0.25	11
12	1994	Q0.03	1-21-00	1-5	0.12	0.12	0.12	9.14	538	295	9-30-99	87.0	...	±22131	Dc	±v4.37	±v1.07	v±1.02	v±1.06	Ed1.30	d1.35	9 Mo Sep	v±0.72	v±d1.69	12
13	1978	Q0.30	12-21-99	12-13	0.90	1.20	1.12	Total Assets $4461.16M			9-30-99	3505	4050	71966	Dc	v□d0.19	□v0.12	□v2.59	Δv1.34	....	1.25	9 Mo Sep	v1.11	v1.02	13
14	1997	Q0.75	1-3-00	12-13	2.25	3.00	3.00	Cv into 1.311 com, $38.125				....	4050	...	Dc	...	...	...	....	....	....				14
15	....	0.01	9-5-86	8-8	...	Nil	....	60.0	292	81.5	9-30-99	368	...	83268	Dc	vd0.22	0.70	□v1.76	v1.43	Ed0.19	d0.07	9 Mo Sep	v1.36	vd0.14	15
16◆	1954	Q0.035	1-10-00	12-15	0.127	0.14	0.109	4.71	79.6	44.1	8-29-99	58.7	...	13390	Nv	0.48	0.48	v0.43	v0.79	....	0.92	9 Mo Aug	v0.51	v0.64	16
17	....	None Since Public			...	Nil	....	47.2	53.2	8.14	9-30-99	....	...	10108	Dc	...	...	...	vpd1.87	....	d0.68	9 Mo Sep	vpd2.65	vpd1.46	17
18	....	None Since Public			...	Nil	....	0.33	98.0	63.6	9-30-99	28.0	...	17270	Dc	vd0.57	v0.39	v0.52	v0.12	....	0.72	9 Mo Sep	vd0.12	v0.48	18
19	1870	gQ0.54	2-24-00	1-21	g1.88	2.16	g1.76	Total Deposits $190460M			j7-31-99	4678	59500	313791	Oc	3.49	4.09	v4.91	v5.30	....	j4.87	9 Mo Jul	v4.05	v3.62	19
20◆	1993	Q0.11	12-29-99	12-1	0.40	0.44	0.33	172	286	890	12-31-98	2341	3450	★179573	Dc	1.18	v1.18	P□v1.20	v1.83	....	2.01	9 Mo Sep	v1.70	v1.88	20
21	1997	Q0.90⅝	2-15-00	1-26	3.62½	3.625	3.62½	Cv into 3.0864 com				....	3450	...	Dc	...	...	...	....	....	....				21
22◆	1947	[56]0.59½	9-29-99	8-6	[56]1.35	1.35	1.369	1642	13559	18684	[57]12-31-98	3619	2	2144296	Dc	2.04	v2.65	v2.30	v0.13	E1.95	0.67	9 Mo Sep	v1.14	v1.68	22
23	....	None Since Public			...	Nil	....	4.18	6.29	2.93	9-30-99	....	...	17565	Je	d0.14	v0.04	v0.26	vd0.21	vd0.51	d0.39	3 Mo Sep	v□d0.07	v0.05	23
24	....	None Since Public			...	Nil	....	....	563	348	j6-30-99	568	...	±86095	Sp	±0.74	±0.98	v±1.19	v±1.43	Pv±1.72	j1.72				24
25	....	None Since Public			...	Nil	....	3.75	48.5	49.5	5-31-98	19.2	...	13998	Nv	...	d0.10	v1.00	....	....	....	6 Mo MayΔ	n/a	vd0.42	25
26◆	1996	0.318	10-5-99	8-31	0.928	0.93	h[60]1.195	509	3192	3954	12-31-98	448	...	476534	Dc	3.05	2.88	v2.82	v1.70	....	1.70				26
27◆	1997	0.035	12-10-99	11-8	0.14	0.14	0.14	15.4	76.2	36.8	9-30-99	1.54	...	28564	Dc	v0.37	v0.46	v0.75	v0.55	....	0.20	9 Mo Sep	v0.54	v0.19	27
28◆	1969	Q0.12¼	10-29-99	10-14	0.47½	0.49	0.571	34.4	772	350	8-31-99	866	...	108020	My	0.69	0.72	v0.76	v0.84	v0.86	0.64	3 Mo Aug	v0.29	v0.07	28
29◆	....	None Since Public			...	Nil	....	668	722	210	9-30-99	....	...	38555	Dc	v0.22	v0.34	v0.41	v0.69	....	3.73	9 Mo Sep	v0.40	v3.44	29
30	....	None Since Public			...	Nil	....	467	726	471	12-31-98	1090	...	±52970	Dc	...	pd11.92	vd5.27	v□d4.52	....	d5.98	9 Mo Sep	v□d3.17	vd4.63	30
31◆	....	0.25	9-1-91	7-26	...	Nil	....	1.06	236	42.1	9-30-99	29.7	...	20848	Dc	vd0.30	v1.70	v2.92	v3.29	....	0.39	9 Mo Sep	v2.97	v0.07	31
32	....	None Paid			...	Nil	....	Total Assets $71.6M			j6-30-99	18.4	...	20671	Dc	0.17	[61]0.41	‡v[62]0.10	v0.24	....	0.19	9 Mo Sep	v0.18	v0.13	32
33◆	1998	S0.04½	7-30-99	7-14	0.09	0.09	0.09	9.87	55.7	89.9	9-05-99	76.7	...	31058	My	1.73	d0.08	v0.70	v0.84	v1.08	1.16	3 Mo Aug	v0.23	v0.31	33
34◆	1976	Q0.09	1-1-00	12-8	0.33	0.36	0.32	13.4	345	222	6-27-99	210	...	46438	Sp	0.84	v0.92	v1.02	v1.00	Pv1.08	1.08				34
35	....	None Since Public			...	Nil	....	0.29	18.5	19.3	9-30-99	p....	p...	★13943	Dc	...	...	...	vpd2.23	....	d0.77	9 Mo Sep	vpd1.49	vpd0.03	35
36	....	None Since Public			...	Nil	....	4.72	230	81.3	9-30-99	274	...	14577	Je	□v0.92	v1.14	v1.04	v0.54	v1.06	1.02	3 Mo Sep	v0.21	v□0.17	36
37	1986	Q0.20	12-3-99	11-17	0.80	0.80	0.76	184	321	42.9	9-30-99	....	...	20548	Dc	v0.77	v1.45	v3.69	v1.81	....	2.06	9 Mo Sep	v1.35	v1.60	37
38	1963	Q0.14	2-21-00	2-3	0.56	0.56	0.56	11.4	697	304	10-03-99	307	...	33058	Dc	v1.38	v2.11	v1.47	vd0.29	....	0.08	9 Mo Sep	vd0.16	v0.21	38
39	....	None Since Public			...	Nil	....	0.69	13.5	158	9-29-99	63.9	...	36167	Dc	0.57	v0.55	v0.82	v0.94	....	1.07	9 Mo Sep	v0.71	v0.84	39
40	....	None Since Public			...	Nil	....	51.0	69.6	56.2	j3-31-98	1.13	...	158334	Mr	...	pd[64]95.45	v1.29	....	....	1.29				40
41	1976	Q0.15	12-20-99	11-16	0.60	0.60	0.60	315	1353	1806	9-30-99	1875	...	64223	Dc	v□1.96	v□d0.39	v2.25	v2.16	E1.10↓	6.70	9 Mo Sep	v1.33	v5.87	41
42	1995	Q0.05	2-1-00	1-4	0.20	0.20	0.20	....	846	252	9-30-99	259	78	24774	Dc	v2.55	v□1.17	v2.13	v□13.55	E2.20↓	4.17	9 Mo Sep	v□11.30	v1.92	42
43	1975	Q0.04	1-30-00	1-12	0.16	0.16	0.16	Total Assets $1286.05M			9-30-99	368	364	14260	Dc	vd0.31	v0.87	v1.32	v□2.79	....	4.04	9 Mo Sep	v□1.67	v2.92	43
44	1993	0.372	10-29-99	9-17	1.489	1.49	1.403	Int based on S&P 500,as defined				....	...	72465	Dc	§61.61	§74.08	...	...	....	....	Mand termination 1-22-2018			44
45	1995	0.17	10-29-99	9-17	[65]2.182	0.68	[66]1.235	Int based on S&P MidCap 400,as defined				....	...	10484	Dc	...	...	...	...	....	....	Mand termination 4-27-2020			45
46	1999	0.075	10-29-99	9-17	0.233	[67]....	....	Net Asset Val $21.63			12-30-98	....	...	500	Dc	...	...	...	...	....	....	Int based on S&P 500:Callable re-spec cond			46
47	1999	Q4.00	7-30-99	6-18	4.00	[67]....	....	Net Asset Val $25.92			12-30-98	....	...	1550	Dc	...	...	...	...	....	....	Int based on S&P 500:Callable re-spec cond			47
48	1999	0.055	10-29-99	9-17	0.205	[67]....	....	Net Asset Val $27.47			12-30-98	....	...	2800	Dc	...	...	...	...	....	....	Int based on S&P 500:Callable re-spec cond			48
49	1999	0.037	10-29-99	9-17	0.107	[67]....	....	Net Asset Val $25.80			12-30-98	....	...	700	Dc	...	...	...	...	....	....	Int based on S&P 500:Callable re-spec cond			49
50	1999	0.13	10-29-99	9-17	0.366	[67]....	....	Net Asset Val $23.71			12-30-98	....	...	2100	Dc	...	...	...	...	....	....	Int based on S&P 500:Callable re-spec cond			50

◆**Stock Splits & Divs By Line Reference Index** [1]3-for-1,'98. [4]3-for-2,'94,'98. [5]2-for-1,'96,'97. [6]2-for-1,'97. [8]2-for-1,'97,'99. [16]105,'99. [20]2-for-1,'98. [22]4-for-1,'97. [26]No adj for stk dstr,'98. [27]2-for-1,'97. [28]5-for-4,'95,'97. [29]2-for-1,'95,'96. [31]1-for-10 REVERSE,'94. [33]1-for-2 REVERSE,'96:2-for-1,'98:No adj for spinoff,'96. [34]2-for-1,'95.

¶ S&P 500
# MidCap 400
✣ SmallCap 600
• Options

Index	Ticker	Name of Issue (Call Price of Pfd. Stocks)	Market	Com. Rank. & Pfd. Rating	Inst. Hold Cos	Inst. Hold Shs. (000)	Principal Business	Price Range 1971-97 High	1971-97 Low	1998 High	1998 Low	1999 High	1999 Low	December, 1999 Dec. Sales in 100s	Last Sale Or Bid High	Low	Last	%Div Yield	P-E Ratio	EPS 5 Yr Growth	% Annualized Total Return 12 Mo	36 Mo	60 Mo
1	XLF	S&P Sel Financial SPDR Fund	AS	NR	10	1322	SPDRS Stock Price Index Secs	...	...	23 13/16	23¼	29¼	20⅞	147153	25⅝	22¾	23¾	...	..	...	2.3	...	...
2	XLI	S&P Sel Industrial SPDR Fund	AS	NR	..	...	SPDRS Stock Price Index Secs	...	...	24 9/16	23¼	30⅝	23½	41955	29⅝	27⅛	29⅝	...	..	...	21.3	...	...
3	XLK	S&P Sel Technology SPDR Fund	AS	NR	28	3999	SPDRS Stock Price Index Secs	...	...	33 3/16	31¾	55	32	129576	55	46½	53⅞	...	..	...	65.1	...	...
4	XLU	S&P Sel Utilities SPDR Fund	AS	NR	2	457	SPDRS Stock Price Index Secs	...	...	30 13/16	29⅝	31½	26 11/16	26341	29⅞	27 13/16	28⅛	...	..	...	−5.1	...	...
5•[1]	SONE	✓S1 Corp	NNM	NR	121	11025	Internet banking svcs	22½	2⅝	18⅞	3 3/16	89	14½	215447	89	47	78⅛	...	d	...	412	148	...
✣6•[1]	SIII	✓S3 Inc	NNM	NR	143	29528	Mfr accelerators/software prd	23¾	3¼	9¼	1½	12⅞	6	391097	12½	8 7/16	11 9/16	...	d	Neg	57.1	−10.7	8.7
7	SSA	✓Saatchi & Saatchi ADS[53]	NY	NR	12	3117	Int'l advertising services	9 7/16	8¾	14 13/16	7⅞	31½	10⅛	11605	31½	24	30⅜	0.4	33	...	156	...	...
8	SBR	✓Sabine Royalty Tr UBI	NY,Ph	NR	26	728	Royalties of oil & gas prop	27½	7¾	16⅞	11⅝	15⅜	12 1/16	3351	14¾	13 1/16	13 7/16	10.5	10	6	18.6	15.4	18.9
9•[2]	TSG	✓SABRE Holdings'A'	NY,Ch,Ph	NR	172	19998	Travel reservation & info sys	37	23¼	44⅞	23	72	38¼	42967	56⅛	43⅞	51¼	...	26	...	15.2	22.5	...
¶10•[3]	SAFC	✓SAFECO Corp	NNM	B+	436	92187	Hldg co: fire & casualty ins	55⅜	1½	56	38¼	46¾	21 13/16	213814	25¼	21 13/16	24⅞	5.9	17	−4	−39.7	−11.4	2.5
11•[4]	SFE	✓Safeguard Scientifics	NY,B,Ch,Ph,P	B	206	9504	Computer products & services	47 7/16	¼	45⅜	17⅛	185 7/16	27½	168880	185 7/16	111	163	...	66	46	494	72.5	95.3
✣12•[1]	SFSK	✓Safeskin Corp	NNM	B	156	11271	Mfr disposable latex gloves	29	2 9/16	47⅛	17⅜	26¼	7⅛	137751	12 11/16	11 7/16	12⅛	...	26	10	−49.7	1.8	29.3
13	ABAGE	✓Safety Components Intl	NNM	NR	17	1675	Mfr auto airbags/ordnance prd	22½	8½	19	9⅜	15⅞	⅝	19350	1 9/16	⅝	⅞	...	d	Neg	−94.5	−54.0	−47.2
14•[5]	SK	✓Safety-Kleen Corp	NY,B,Ch,P,Ph	↑B–	183	41579	Industrial waste disposal	82 13/16	2⅝	19½	7½	19⅜	9 1/16	55325	12½	9 1/16	11 5/16	...	11	NM	−19.9	23.8	−7.9
¶15•[6]	SWY	✓Safeway Inc	NY,Ch,Ph,P	B+	1069	370759	Food supermarket chain	31 11/16	2 7/16	61⅜	30½	62 7/16	29 5/16	799396	37½	29 5/16	35¾	...	19	30	−41.3	18.7	35.1
16	SGA	✓Saga Communications'A'	AS	NR	55	12822	Own,oper radio & T.V. stations	16	3⅝	16⅝	11 3/16	22⅛	13 11/16	6682	22	18 5/16	20¼	...	45	27	23.9	28.0	35.1
17•[7]	AGS	✓Saga Systems	NY,Ph	NR	86	9538	Computer software & svcs	14½	10	33	11⅛	24⅞	4¾	21453	24⅞	18¾	19 15/16	...	27	...	10.0	...	...
18	JOE	✓St. Joe Co	NY,Ph	B–	143	19801	Real estate dvlp,RR,forest pd	38½	8½	37	18½	28 9/16	20 1/16	21087	25¼	22¼	24 5/16	0.3	19	1	3.8	9.1	9.4
19	SAJ	✓St. Joseph Lt & Pwr[58]	NY,Ch	B+	48	1279	Utility:elec,natural gas in Mo	18 15/16	2¾	19⅜	17¼	21¼	15½	3206	21 1/16	20¼	20½	4.9	25	−8	20.2	16.2	13.9
¶20•[1]	STJ	✓St. Jude Medical	NY,Ch,Ph	B	410	53195	Heart valve:electro med dev	46	1/16	39 11/16	19 3/16	40¾	22 15/16	115776	31 7/16	26	30 11/16	...	27	−19	10.1	−10.2	3.0
21	SLW	St. Laurent Paperboard[59]	NY	NR	28	8004	Mfr paper pds	25	11⅜	19 11/16	8⅝	18¾	9½	515	13⅛	11⅜	13⅛	...	24	Neg	22.1	−16.1	−5.5
✣22	MARY	✓St. Mary Land Exploration	NNM	NR	122	7071	Oil & gas explor,dvlp,prod'n	46	10⅞	39⅝	15	29 13/16	14⅞	8411	27	20¼	24¾	0.8	..	Neg	35.1	0.7	14.4
¶23•[1]	SPC	✓St. Paul Cos	NY,P	B+	595	180205	General line of insurance	42¾	1 15/16	47 3/16	28 1/16	37 1/16	25⅜	116959	34 3/16	30 3/16	33 11/16	3.1	13	−12	0.1	7.9	11.8
24	SPCPrM	6.00%[60] Cv[61]'MIPS'([62]50)	NY	A–	31	2385		75	50	81 3/16	56¼	64½	51	2196	60	56	59B	5.1	..	...	...	...	...
#25•[4]	SKS	✓Saks Inc	NY	B	350	87551	Oper specialty dept stores	32 7/16	2⅜	44 7/16	16⅜	39½	14⅝	179883	18⅞	15⅛	15 9/16	...	9	91	−50.7	−5.2	7.1
26	SALM	✓Salem Communications'A'	NNM	NR	78	8714	Own,operate radio stations	...	...	...	...	31⅛	16⅛	25607	23½	16⅝	22⅝	...	d	...	...	...	...
27	STCIA	✓Salient 3 Communic[65]'A'	NNM	B	30	2587	Voice, data commun'ns eqp	31	2⅝	12¼	6	9⅜	5 1/16	3977	8	6	7	...	15	70	−23.3	−19.1	−10.7
28	SAL	✓Salisbury Bancorp	AS	NR	6	104	General banking,Connecticut	...	...	23	17½	22¼	18⅞	31	19½	19	18¾B	e2.6	12	...	−7.9	...	...
29	CXB	Salomon SB 6.25%'DECS'2001	NY	NR	7	599	Exch Notes For Com Stock	65½	50½	69½	43	108	62½	1867	108	93	108	3.2	..	...	71.3	28.3	...
30	XSB	Salomon SB Hldg Eq Nts 2001	NY	NR	1	1	S&P 500 Equity Link Notes	21¾	15	28½	20⅞	34	27⅝	472	34	31⅜	34	...	..	...	19.3	27.3	...
31	ASB	Salomon SB Hldg Eq Nts 2005	AS	NR	1	2	S&P 500 Equity Link Notes	...	...	15⅛	13¾	17⅛	14 15/16	901	17⅛	16½	17B	...	..	...	14.3	...	...
32	SSB	Salomon SB Hldg Eq Nts 2006	AS	NR	1	79	The Street.com Equity Link Nts	...	...	...	...	11⅞	9	3089	11⅞	10⅞	11 11/16	...	..	...	...	...	...
33	NXS	Salomon SB Nikkei'MITTS'2002	NY	NR	3	167	MKT Index Target-Term Sec	10 3/16	8⅝	9⅞	8	11	8 9/16	4010	10½	9 11/16	9⅞B	...	..	...	13.7	...	...
34	SFP	✓Salton Inc	NY	NR	97	6620	Mfr kitchen/beauty appliances	8½	½	17 3/16	5 5/16	39 7/16	14	66333	39 7/16	24¾	33 7/16	...	13	NM	100	94.2	76.4
35	BIN	✓Sames Corp	AS,Ch	C	22	1313	Mfr coatings application eq	48⅛	5⅜	50	11¼	24¼	13	1250	17¼	13	15⅛B	...	d	Neg	−8.3	−27.6	−3.1
36•[8]	SAMC	Samsonite Corp	NNM	NR	31	4205	Luggage,wtr treatmt eq,apparel	53⅛	9¼	37⅞	4⅛	8 3/16	4⅞	7251	6 3/16	5⅜	5 13/16	...	d	26	4.5	−46.7	...
37	SJT	✓San Juan Basin Rty Tr	NY,Ch,P	NR	51	19912	Royalty gas interest,N.M.	19¾	4¾	9⅜	5⅛	10⅜	5¼	25634	10⅜	9 3/16	10⅜	5.2	19	10	108	19.1	20.7
38	SCAI	✓Sanchez Computer Assoc	NNM	NR	100	6120	Dgn/dvp financial svcs softwr	14 15/16	1¾	17 5/16	6⅞	52¾	9½	38697	51⅜	32⅜	41 3/16	...	..	22	184	119	...
39	SNDT	Sand Technology Sys Intl'A'	NNM	C	1	38	Mkt/svc computer peripheral pr	15⅜	⅛	13⅛	3¼	8¼	2⅝	4543	7 1/16	4 11/16	6⅛	...	d	Neg	9.5	−6.8	49.8
40	SNDK	✓SanDisk Corp	NNM	NR	163	16000	Dgn flash mem storage pd	40	8¾	26¼	5⅛	100⅝	13¼	152025	100⅝	62⅜	96¼	...	..	NM	581	115	...
41	SNDS	✓Sands Regent	NSC	C	8	632	Casino-hotel Reno Nevada	22¼	1⅝	2⅝	¾	2 9/16	⅞	2285	2	1½	1⅝	...	d	−11	55.9	−16.8	−24.3
42•[5]	SANG	✓SangStat Medical	NNM	NR	100	12024	Mfr therapeutic/monitor'g prd	41⅜	4¼	40⅜	15⅛	32⅞	10 15/16	35671	32	22½	29¾	...	d	−21	40.0	3.9	45.1
#43•[1]	SANM	✓Sanmina Corp	NNM	NR	483	56063	Mfr electronic circuit boards	45⅜	2½	62½	19⅝	109¼	49½	150532	109¼	92½	99⅞	...	66	NM	59.8	53.0	71.7
44	IMI	✓Sanpaolo IMI[67]ADS	NY	NR	44	7761	Banking/finance svcs, Italy	...	...	35¾	28¾	39¾	24 5/16	6396	27¾	24½	27⅜	...	18	...	...	...	...
45	SCOC	✓Santa Cruz Operation	NNM	NR	59	9312	Provides open sys software	15	3⅛	6½	2⅜	35⅞	3¾	570333	35⅞	14¼	30⅜	...	66	−5	585	63.1	26.5
46	SFF	Santa Fe Energy[69]Tr 'SPERs'	NY	NR	17	129	Secure Principal Ener Receipt	23⅝	14¼	21 1/16	17⅛	18 7/16	16 1/16	2694	17¾	17 3/16	17⅝	9.1	..	...	12.3	5.7	12.6
47•[9]	SDC	✓Santa Fe Intl	NY,Ph	NR	205	30480	Contract drilling svcs	57	28½	42 15/16	11 3/16	27	12 13/16	66755	26	20 13/16	25⅞	0.5	20	...	79.6	...	...
#48•[10]	SFS	✓Santa Fe Snyder	NY,P	C	331	133522	Oil & gas explor,dev,prod'n	22⅜	7	11 11/16	5⅜	10⅞	4¾	213329	8 5/16	6¾	8	...	d	Neg	10.3	...	...
49	ISA	✓Santa Isabel ADS[73]	NY,Ch,Ph,P	NR	29	3446	Supermarket chain Chile & Peru	32¼	15⅜	19⅝	4¾	12⅞	5⅜	1732	10¼	9	9¾	...	d	Neg	47.2	−24.0	...
50•[11]	SAP	✓SAP Aktiengesellschaft ADS[74]	NY	NR	164	28044	Computer software & svcs	...	...	60⅛	29 11/16	55	23¾	266320	55	32⅝	52 1/16	0.2	..	...	45.0	...	...

Uniform Footnote Explanations-See Page 4. Other: [1]CBOE:Cycle 1. [2]ASE,CBOE:Cycle 2. [3]CBOE:Cycle 2. [4]Ph:Cycle 2. [5]CBOE,Ph:Cycle 1. [6]ASE,CBOE,P:Cycle 3. [7]Ph:Cycle 1. [8]CBOE:Cycle 3. [9]ASE,CBOE,P,Ph:Cycle 1. [10]ASE:Cycle 1. [11]Ph:Cycle 3. [51]To be determined. [52]Pfd in $M. [53]Ea ADS rep 5 ord shrs,10p. [54]Stk of Safeguard Bus.Sys. [55]®$0.42,'96. [56]Fiscal Sep'96 & prior. [57]68%owned-Alfred I. duPont testamentary trust. [58]UtiliCorp United plan acq,$23 in stk. [59]May'99 & prior pricing in $Cdn. [60]Issued by subsid St. Paul Cos L.L.C.. [61]Monthly Income Preferred Shrs. [62]Fr 6-1-1999,If less then 5% shrs outstanding. [63]Co opt conv right expire 5-31-99 re-spec cond. [64]Or prior based on re-pymt Cv Debs re-spec cond. [65]Non-vtg. [66]Stk dstr of Culligan Water Technologies. [67]Ea ADS rep 2 com,LIT5000. [68]Stk dstr of Beni Stabili SPA. [69]Dep Unit int Santa Fe EnTr&$20U.S.Gvt Obl(2008). [70]Fiscal June'96. [71]Fiscal Jun'97 & prior:6 Mo Dec earned $1.12v. [72]Stk dstr of Monterey Res,'97. [73]Ea ADS rep 15 com, no par. [74]ADS rep 0.083 non-voting Pref sh. [75]Incl 61M Ord Shs.

Index	Cash Divs. Ea. Yr. Since	Dividends: Latest Payment Period $	Date	Ex. Div.	Total $ So Far 1999	Ind. Rate	Paid 1998	Financial Position Mil-$ Cash& Equiv.	Curr. Assets	Curr. Liab.	Balance Sheet Date	Capitalization Lg Trm Debt Mil-$	Shs. 000 Pfd.	Com.	Earnings $ Per Shr. Years End	1995	1996	1997	1998	1999	Last 12 Mos.	Interim Earnings Period	$ per Shr. 1998	1999	Index
1	1999	0.075	10-29-99	9-17	0.215 [51]....	....		Net Asset Val $23.42			12-30-98	....	...	2650	Dc	...	...	...	....	....	....	Int based on S&P 500:Callable re-spec cond			1
2	1999	0.054	10-29-99	9-17	0.186 [51]....	....		Net Asset Val $24.04			12-30-98	....	...	700	Dc	...	...	...	....	....	....	Int based on S&P 500:Callable re-spec cond			2
3	1999	Q4.00	7-30-99	6-18	4.00 [51]....	....		Net Asset Val $32.83			12-30-98	....	...	...	Dc	...	...	...	....	....	....	Int based on S&P 500:Callable re-spec cond			3
4	1999	0.223	10-29-99	9-17	0.598 [51]....	....		Net Asset Val $30.72			12-30-98	....	...	...	Dc	...	...	...	....	....	....	Int based on S&P 500:Callable re-spec cond			4
5◆	....	None Since Public			...	Nil	....	45.2	74.9	26.5	9-30-99	....	[52]23	p37551	Dc	pd0.15	vd1.88	vd1.57	vd1.40	....	d0.63	9 Mo Sep	vd1.08	vd0.31	5
6◆	....	None Since Public			...	Nil	....	147	364	250	9-30-99	104	...	p76109	Dc	v0.75	v0.81	v0.17	vd2.22	....	d1.83	9 Mo Sep	vd0.84	vd0.45	6
7	1998	0.049	10-4-99	8-18	0.276	0.11	0.104	31.0	293	330	j12-31-98	95.7	...	222947	Dc	...	p0.35	v29.29	v0.91	....	0.91				7
8	1983	0.094	12-29-99	12-13	1.407	1.41	1.654	Total Assets $4.61M			9-30-99	....	...	14579	Dc	v1.02	v1.44	v1.68	v1.57	....	1.37	9 Mo Sep	v1.27	v1.07	8
9	....	None Since Public			...	Nil	....	412	852	480	9-30-99	....	...	±129481	Dc	p±1.20	±pv1.44	±v1.53	v±1.78	....	1.95	9 Mo Sep	v±1.62	v±1.79	9
10◆	1933	Q0.37	1-24-00	1-5	1.44	1.48	1.34	Total Assets $30284.00M			9-30-99	1313	...	130012	Dc	v3.16	v3.47	v3.31	v2.51	E1.50	2.25	9 Mo Sep	v1.81	v1.55	10
11◆	....	h[54]....	3-4-80	3-5	...	Nil	....	71.5	591	304	9-30-99	365	...	34825	Dc	v0.53	v0.61	v0.66	v3.22	....	2.47	9 Mo Sep	v2.04	v1.29	11
12◆	....	None Since Public			...	Nil	....	6.83	92.8	35.5	9-30-99	107	...	57516	Dc	v0.29	v[55]0.43	v0.70	v0.70	E0.46	0.30	9 Mo Sep	v0.71	v0.31	12
13	....	None Since Public			...	Nil	....	9.48	75.7	41.6	9-25-99	146	...	5136	Mr	0.99	v□0.77	v1.17	vd2.52	....	d2.94	6 Mo Sep	v0.27	vd0.15	13
14◆	....	0.02½	9-20-93	8-16	...	Nil	....	9.17	588	422	8-31-99	1882	...	100638	Au	d1.20	[56]d2.00	vd5.32	□v0.20	v□1.03	1.03				14
15◆	....	None Since Public			...	Nil	....	83.3	2754	3209	9-11-99	5950	...	508800	Dc	v□0.68	v0.97	□v1.25	v1.59	E1.87	1.80	36 Wk Sep	v1.09	v1.30	15
16◆	....	None Since Public			...	Nil	....	8.33	29.3	11.2	9-30-99	85.4	...	±16479	Dc	±v0.17	v±0.24	±v0.28	v±0.39	....	0.45	9 Mo Sep	v0.29	v0.35	16
17	....	None Since Public			...	Nil	....	47.3	143	78.5	9-30-99	0.33	...	28614	Dc	...	n/a	v0.25	v0.87	....	0.75	9 Mo Sep	v0.58	v0.46	17
18◆	1990	0.02	3-31-99	3-15	0.02	0.08	0.08	169	231	154	9-30-99	4.81	...	[57]87074	Dc	v0.81	v1.92	v0.38	v0.31	....	1.25	9 Mo Sep	v0.27	v1.21	18
19◆	1949	Q0.25	11-18-99	11-1	1.00	1.00	0.98	0.56	32.6	38.3	9-30-99	75.4	...	8252	Dc	v1.41	v1.32	v1.36	v1.31	....	0.81	9 Mo Sep	v1.18	v0.68	19
20◆	....	0.067	8-24-94	8-4	...	Nil	....	89.4	695	252	9-30-99	530	...	84152	Dc	v1.30	v0.66	v□0.59	v1.50	E1.16	0.22	9 Mo Sep	v1.14	vd0.14	20
21	....	None Paid			...	Nil	....	12.3	225	89.2	j3-31-99	356	...	49292	Dc	3.30	Nil	vd0.98	vd0.47	....	j0.38	9 Mo Sep	vd0.26	v0.59	21
22	1993	Q0.05	11-15-99	11-3	0.20	0.20	0.20	6.59	22.6	11.0	9-30-99	13.6	...	11098	Dc	v0.20	v1.17	v2.15	vd0.81	....	Nil	9 Mo Sep	vd0.37	v0.44	22
23◆	1872	Q0.26	1-17-00	12-29	1.03	1.04	0.98½	Total Assets $39203.00M			9-30-99	1793	...	227255	Dc	v2.85	v2.47	v3.83	v0.32	E2.60	3.37	9 Mo Sep	vd0.09	v□2.96	23
24	1995	0.25	12-31-99	12-28	3.00	3.00	3.00	Cv into 0.8475 St. Paul com,$59[63]				....	4140	...	Dc	...	...	...	....	....	....	Mand redemption 5-31-2025[64]			24
25◆	....	....			...	Nil	....	20.9	2219	1101	10-30-99	2090	...	143816	Ja	□vd0.81	v0.78	□v0.81	v□0.17	E1.80	1.23	9 Mo Oct	v□d0.53	v□0.53	25
26	....	None Since Public			...	Nil	....	37.3	60.8	8.84	9-30-99	100	...	★±23456	Dc	...	...	...	vd0.09	....	d0.28	9 Mo Sep	vd0.07	v□d0.26	26
27	1943	Div Omitted 4-28-98			...	Nil	0.10	0.88	55.6	22.2	10-01-99	13.8	...	±6135	Dc	v±2.57	v±d0.30	±v0.42	vd2.65	....	0.47	9 Mo Sep	vd3.02	v0.10	27
28	1998	†0.34	1-28-00	12-29	†0.63	0.48	0.11	Total Deposits $155M			9-30-99	42.0	...	1506	Dc	...	...	v1.40	v1.47	....	1.62	9 Mo Sep	v1.13	v1.28	28
29	1997	Q0.871	2-1-00	1-12	3.484	3.484	3.484	Amt pay maturity based on Cinn Bell com stk				....	...	★3500	Dc	...	...	...	....	....	....	Due 2-1-2001			29
30	....	....			...	....	....	Amt pay at mat based on S&P 500 re-spec cond				....	...	★2671	Dc	...	...	...	....	....	....	Due 8-13-2001			30
31	....	....			...	....	....	Amt pay at mat based on S&P 500 re-spec cond				....	...	★3400	Dc	...	...	...	....	....	....	Due 8-1-2005			31
32	....	....			...	....	....	Amt pay of mat based on TheStreet.com Internet Set Index re-spec cond				....	...	★6500	Dc	...	...	...	....	....	....	Due 5-30-2006			32
33	....	....			...	....	....	Int based on Nikkei 225,as defined				....	...	★6500	Dc	...	...	...	....	....	....	Due 8-20-2002			33
34◆	....	None Since Public			...	Nil	....	8.34	335	155	9-25-99	182	...	10332	Je	v0.07	v0.46	v0.23	v0.99	v2.37	2.64	3 Mo Sep	v0.68	v0.95	34
35	....	Div Omitted 4-28-98			...	Nil	....	7.58	72.0	47.3	8-31-99	4.77	...	2967	Nv	1.39	d3.60	vd12.92	vd4.60	....	d0.57	9 Mo Aug	vd4.66	vd0.63	35
36	....	h[66]....	9-12-95	9-13	...	Nil	....	40.0	326	163	10-31-99	464	201	p19712	Ja	d3.38	vd0.71	□v2.70	v□d6.79	....	d6.87	9 Mo Oct	□vd2.40	vd2.48	36
37	1981	0.083	1-14-00	12-29	0.657	0.54	0.68¾	Total Assets $49.5M			9-30-99	....	...	46609	Dc	v0.30	v0.81	v1.04	v0.64	....	0.56	9 Mo Sep	v0.52	v0.44	37
38◆	....	None Since Public			...	Nil	....	22.9	43.0	12.6	9-30-99	....	...	24325	Dc	v0.09	v0.06	v0.14	v0.28	....	0.28	9 Mo Sep	v0.19	v0.19	38
39◆	....	None Since Public			...	Nil	....	4.77	6.26	0.26	j7-31-98	....	...	8520	Jl	0.08	0.08	vd0.06	vd0.11	Pvd0.58	jd0.23	3 Mo Oct	vd0.15	v0.20	39
40	....	None Since Public			...	Nil	....	139	223	77.5	9-30-99	....	...	★32006	Dc	pv0.45	v0.60	v0.79	v0.43	....	0.68	9 Mo Sep	v0.30	v0.55	40
41	....	0.05	3-18-96	2-21	...	Nil	....	8.20	10.8	14.3	9-30-99	0.42	...	4496	Je	vd2.54	v0.45	vd0.17	vd0.27	vd0.31	d0.07	3 Mo Sep	vd0.11	v0.13	41
42	....	None Since Public			...	Nil	....	34.3	96.8	27.1	9-30-99	40.0	...	17325	Dc	vd0.92	vd1.03	vd1.36	vd2.39	....	d2.13	9 Mo Sep	vd1.82	vd1.56	42
43◆	....	None Since Public			...	Nil	....	455	885	217	10-02-99	355	...	58892	Sp	0.51	v0.84	v0.68	v1.43	v1.52	1.52				43
44	1999	h[68]....	10-31-99	11-3	h[68]0.694 [51]....	....		Book Value $18.29			12-31-98	56770	...	841311	Dc	...	...	pv0.26	v1.52	....	1.52				44
45	....	None Since Public			...	Nil	....	53.8	93.3	58.7	6-30-99	....	...	33569	Sp	d0.20	d0.62	vd0.41	vd0.41	Pv0.46	0.46				45
46	1993	0.467	11-30-99	11-10	1.667	1.60	1.724	Liq date 2-15-2008				....	...	6300	Dc	...	...	...	....	....	....				46
47	1997	Q0.03¼	1-17-00	12-29	0.13	0.13	0.13	124	352	182	12-31-98	....	...	114762	Dc	...	p[70]0.54	pv[71]1.96	v2.50	E1.31	1.87	9 Mo Sep	v1.79	v1.16	47
48◆	....	h[72]....	7-25-97	7-28	...	Nil	....	30.7	183	156	9-30-99	688	...	184415	Dc	v0.13	v□d0.05	v0.43	vd0.96	Ed0.91	d1.77	9 Mo Sep	vd0.17	v□d0.98	48
49	1996	0.073	6-8-98	5-20	...	Nil	0.073	31.4	141	139	12-31-97	114	...	330000	Dc	0.88	1.10	v0.32	Pvd2.54	....	d2.54				49
50	1999	0.104	5-17-99	5-4	0.104	0.10	....	0.79	2704	n/a	12-31-98	2.06	...	[75]±104564	Dc	±v0.30	±v0.30	±v0.41	v0.50	....	0.50				50

◆**Stock Splits & Divs By Line Reference Index** [5]2-for-1,'99. [6]2-for-1,'95. [10]2-for-1,'95. [11]3-for-2,'95:2-for-1,'94,'96. [12]2-for-1,'97,'98. [14]1-for-4 REVERSE,'98. [15]2-for-1,'96,'98. [16]5-for-4,'95,'96,'97,'98,'99. [18]3-for-1,'98. [19]2-for-1,'96. [20]3-for-2,'95. [23]2-for-1,'94,'98. [25]2-for-1,'97. [34]3-for-2,'99. [38]2-for-1,'99. [39]2-for-1,'97. [43]2-for-1,'96,'98. [48]No adj for stk dstr,'97.

¶ S&P 500
# MidCap 400
✣ SmallCap 600
• Options

Index	Ticker	Name of Issue (Call Price of Pfd. Stocks)	Market	Com. Rank. & Pfd. Rating	Inst. Hold Cos	Inst. Hold Shs. (000)	Principal Business	Price Range 1971-97 High	1971-97 Low	1998 High	1998 Low	1999 High	1999 Low	December, 1999 Dec. Sales in 100s	Last Sale Or Bid High	Last Sale Or Bid Low	Last Sale Or Bid Last	%Div Yield	P-E Ratio	EPS 5 Yr Growth	% Annualized Total Return 12 Mo	36 Mo	60 Mo
1•[1]	SAPE	✓Sapient Corp	NNM	NR	220	27205	Dgn/dvp info tech softwr	15 11/16	5¼	34½	12⅛	141¼	23⅞	138996	141¼	73¼	140 15/16	...	..	59	421	140	...
2	SPP	Sappi Ltd ADS[51]	NY	NR	9	2638	Paper & paper products	....	....	4¾	3 9/16	11 5/16	3 9/16	51025	11 5/16	8 13/16	9⅝	2.0	18	...	156	...	...
¶3•[2]	SLE	✓Sara Lee Corp	NY,C,B,Ch,P,Ph	A−	1002	495421	Processed foods:consumer pr	28⅞	5/16	31 13/16	22⅛	28¾	21 1/16	331836	25 1/16	21 1/16	22 1/16	2.4	19	−15	−20.1	8.0	14.3
4	SIFY	Satyam Infoway ADS[54]	NNM	NR	..	...	Internet access svc,India	....	....	....	....	175	18	88496	175	105½	155	...	...	...	...	...	...
5	SCNYA	✓Saucony Inc'A'	NNM	B−	17	358	Athletic/recreat'l footwear	14½	1/16	8	3⅝	26	5	5857	15½	11 13/16	14¾	...	10	2	107	45.9	24.8
6	SCNYB	Cl'B'[55]	NNM	B−	33	2872		12¾	3 5/16	8½	3¾	28½	4⅝	7324	14 9/16	10¾	13⅞	...	25	Neg	122	39.4	23.9
7	SHS	✓Sauer Inc	NY	NR	40	2557	Dgn mfr hydraulic sys	....	....	18⅝	6 1/16	17⅛	5¼	11407	13 13/16	8 15/16	9 1/16	3.1	11	...	23.4	...	...
8	BFS	✓Saul Centers	NY,Ch,P	NR	49	1901	Real estate investment trust	20¼	12⅝	19 1/16	15	17⅞	13 15/16	3951	15⅛	13 15/16	14 1/16	11.1	16	2	0.6	5.7	9.4
9•[3]	VAI	✓Savia SA de CV ADS[56]	NY,Ch,Ph	NR	8	5114	Agrobiotech products	37⅛	7⅞	27⅛	18	25⅝	20 3/16	3214	22	20¾	22	...	d	Neg	−6.9	3.7	5.9
10	SVTG	✓Savoir Technology Grp	NNM	B−	42	4416	Dstr semiconductor parts	14½	1⅞	13 7/16	4 5/16	12½	4 9/16	26127	7⅝	5¼	7⅛	...	26	NM	−18.0	−16.5	2.2
11•[4]	SAWS	✓Sawtek Inc[57]	NNM	NR	201	28928	Dvlp elec signal components	24 15/16	8¼	16¼	5⅛	67¼	8¾	142532	67¼	39¾	66 9/16	...	92	88	661	49.8	...
12	SBAC	✓SBA Communications'A'	NNM	NR	28	9795	Wireless communic infrastruct	....	....	....	....	18¾	7¾	64122	18¾	11 1/16	18¾	...	..	...	...	...	...
¶13•[5]	SBC	✓SBC Communications	NY,B,Ch,P,Ph	A−	1861	924251	Tel svc:Ark,Kan,Mo,Okl,Tex	38 1/16	4 9/16	54⅞	35	59 15/16	44 1/16	1035371	55½	47⅜	48¾	2.0	24	1	−7.5	26.5	22.7
14	XTS	SBC Commun 7.75%'DECS' 2001	NY	NR	16	3634	Exch Notes For Com Stock	52¾	38¾	53¼	33¼	96 13/16	37¾	149	96 13/16	81 7/16	95⅝B	3.2	..	...	125	...	...
15	SBTV	✓SBS Broadcasting	NNM	NR	..	...	TV broadcast'g Scandinavia	29½	12	34⅛	18¼	51⅛	24¾	12600	51⅛	41	48 11/16	...	d	−24	80.3	41.0	18.9
16	SBSE	✓SBS Technologies	NNM	B−	39	3210	Mfr avionic/computer I/O equip	39¾	3¾	33¾	8½	40	15¾	13928	40	31 3/16	36½	...	18	NM	97.3	−0.5	52.8
#17•[6]	SCG	✓SCANA Corp	NY,B,C,Ch,P,Ph	A−	271	45587	Hldg co: electric & gas	29 15/16	4⅜	37¼	27⅞	32 9/16	21⅛	65127	28 5/16	25¼	26⅞	4.1	16	5	−11.9	5.7	11.3
18	SCV.A	Scania AB'A'ADS[60]	NY,Ch,Ph	NR	..	...	Mfr heavy trucks & buses	30¾	22	28⅞	17	38¼	19	1	35½	35½	35⅛B	1.9	25	...	102	16.5	...
19	SCV.B	✓ Cl'B'ADS	NY,Ch,Ph	NR	1	50		31	22¼	28	17 11/16	38 1/16	19	6	37	36	35⅜B	1.9	25	...	101	16.7	...
20	SGK	✓Schawk Inc'A'	NY,Ch	B−	45	9015	Digital imaging prepress svcs	20½	5	17⅜	9⅜	14⅛	7⅛	4129	8¾	7 15/16	8½	1.5	12	47	−37.5	1.2	−2.1
21	ESH	✓Scheib (Earl)	AS	B−	23	2442	Chain-auto paint shops	24 7/16	1⅛	9⅝	4¾	6½	2¾	3420	4 3/16	2¾	2 15/16	...	d	4	−46.6	−25.1	−12.9
22•[3]	HSIC	✓Schein (Henry)	NNM	NR	175	27324	Market healthcare pds	43½	16	51⅛	24¾	46⅞	10⅜	92573	13 15/16	10¾	13 5/16	...	15	−12	−70.3	−27.1	...
23	SHP	✓Schein Pharmaceutical	NY	NR	47	2788	Mfr/dev generic drug pds	....	....	32¾	5 1/16	17⅜	8 3/16	4593	12¾	8¾	12⅛	...	35	−5	−16.7	...	...
24	SCHR	✓Scherer Healthcare	NNM	B−	9	429	Health care products/services	38	1½	5⅜	2⅛	4¾	2⅜	727	3 3/16	2⅜	3⅛	...	7	NM	−26.5	11.6	−31.1
¶25•[7]	SGP	✓Schering-Plough	NY,B,C,Ch,P,Ph	A+	1827	979535	Pharmaceut'l/consumer prod	32	¾	57¾	30 5/16	60 13/16	40¼	860419	51¾	40¼	42⅜	1.2	30	20	−22.6	40.7	38.7
¶26•[8]	SLB	✓Schlumberger Ltd	NY,B,C,Ch,P,Ph	B+	1531	330530	Oilfield svs: electronics	94 7/16	1 15/16	86 7/16	40 1/16	70 11/16	45 7/16	619568	62½	52 11/16	56⅛	1.3	52	4	...	...	...
27	SCHN	✓Schnitzer Steel Ind'A'	NNM	B−	52	3380	Recycles steel/mfr steel prd	38½	17⅜	29⅜	11⅛	23	9	3192	20 9/16	17¾	19	1.1	56	−26	33.8	−8.6	−1.8
#28•[3]	SCHL	✓Scholastic Corp	NNM	B	170	11015	Publish child'ns books,edu mtl	78¾	20¾	57	28⅞	64⅛	39	30200	64⅛	53 15/16	62 3/16	...	26	14	16.0	−2.6	4.0
29	SHF	✓Schuff Steel	AS	NR	14	1028	Fabricate structural steel	12	7½	15⅝	3¼	7⅝	3½	3059	4⅛	3½	4	...	5	...	−27.3	...	...
30	SHLR	✓Schuler Homes	NNM	B−	32	8070	Residential homebldg,Hawaii	30¼	4⅞	10⅛	5⅞	9	5¾	1014	6 13/16	6	6½	...	6	25	−8.8	1.3	−14.5
#31•[9]	SHLM	✓Schulman (A.)	NNM	A	204	21077	Plastic mfr/merchant resins	32¾	¼	26½	13 7/16	22¾	13	28761	16¾	14½	16 5/16	3.1	11	4	−26.0	−10.6	−8.1
32	SAVO	✓Schultz Sav-O Stores	NNM	A−	53	3254	Food wholesaler/supermkts	17¼	¼	17¾	15	17⅜	11¼	1202	13	11¼	12¾	2.8	10	14	−21.0	13.3	16.9
¶33•[4]	SCH	✓Schwab(Charles)Corp	NY,Ch,P,Ph	A	827	362357	Discount brokerage/svcs	14¾	3/16	34¼	9¼	77½	25 7/16	882521	41	32	38¼	0.2	56	28	37.4	76.6	72.9
✣34	SWM	✓Schweitzer-Mauduit Intl	NY,P	NR	142	10146	Mfr tobacco-related paper	44½	20⅜	38⅝	13	17½	11½	7548	13⅞	11 13/16	13 7/16	4.5	8	1	−9.1	−22.7	...
#35•[3]	SCI	✓SCI Systems	NY,Ch,Ph	B	327	62647	Electronic prod/systems	53⅜	1/32	57 15/16	20¾	86 5/16	25¼	115966	86 5/16	68⅛	82 3/16	...	39	19	42.3	54.6	55.8
¶36•[10]	SFA	✓Scientific-Atlanta	NY,B,C,Ch,Ph,P	B+	458	52760	Electronic instr & commun eq	24 15/16	3/16	27 15/16	11¾	66½	22⅛	189283	66½	51½	55⅞	0.1	39	97	145	55.4	22.0
37•[11]	SG	✓Scientific Games Hldgs	NY	NR	71	9789	Mfr instant lottery tickets	43	7	24	15¾	21 3/16	14½	12527	17 11/16	14¾	16 9/16	...	9	3	−12.3	−14.8	−7.9
38	STIZ	✓Scientific Technologies	NNM	B+	9	370	Mfr electr equip/software	24	15/16	20	4⅝	7 9/16	3 7/16	1261	7	5 5/16	5 7/16	3.5	12	...	18.5	−7.9	7.2
39	SQST	✓SciQuest.com Inc	NNM	NR	..	...	Sells scientific prod on web	....	....	....	....	91⅝	16	153274	91⅝	31¼	79½	...	..	...	...	...	...
40•[12]	SCIX	✓Scitex Corp, Ord	NNM	NR	41	7956	Imaging, comput graphics	44⅜	⅞	14 11/16	5¾	16 1/16	8 7/16	70673	16 1/16	12 15/16	14 9/16	...	26	−6	23.9	15.3	−1.3
41	SCMM	✓SCM Microsystems	NNM	NR	62	2337	Dgn/dvp data security pds	31½	13	89	23	104⅛	37¼	14975	67¼	55	63 15/16	...	d	82	−10.0	...	...
42	SCP	✓Scope Indus	AS,P	B−	19	112	Waste mat recycl'g, o & g	67	11/16	77	59½	71	43¾	173	55	43¾	44⅛B	2.3	d	Neg	−32.1	−1.9	15.7
43	SCO	✓SCOR ADS[63]	NY	NR	19	1258	Prop-casualty,life reinsurance	52⅛	34	73	46	68½	42 15/16	660	46⅜	42 15/16	44¼	3.4	9	13	−31.5	12.5	...
✣44	SCTT	✓Scott Technologies	NNM	C	104	13087	Life support respiratory prd	27½	4⅝	16¾	10	21⅝	15⅜	9157	21 3/16	18¼	18⅞	...	8	NM	14.2	16.3	25.2
45	SCOT	✓Scottish Annuity & Life Hldgs	NNM	NR	45	9275	Life/health ins,invest pds	....	....	16⅛	11⅜	14⅜	7¾	23366	8⅞	7¾	8 3/16	2.4	..	...	−39.5	...	...
46	SPI	✓Scottish Power ADS[65]	NY,Ph	NR	20	2217	Electric utility, U.K.	35¼	27⅛	44 13/16	33	44½	27¾	119980	35½	27¾	28	5.5	10	...	−28.9	...	...
✣47•[5]	SMG	✓Scotts Co 'A'	NY,P	NR	192	14201	Mfr lawn,golf turf care prd	31¾	13½	41⅝	26	48	31 15/16	10685	40½	36¾	40¼	...	18	43	4.7	26.5	20.5
48	POOL	✓SCP Pool	NNM	NR	87	10419	Dstr swimming pools/prod	16	4 5/16	16 15/16	9	29⅛	12⅜	12681	29⅛	23⅛	25 15/16	...	14	38	71.5	41.6	...
49	SKP	✓SCPIE Holdings	NY	NR	81	4345	Provide medl malpractice insur	32⅛	18¼	38⅜	26⅝	36 1/16	23 11/16	2596	34 15/16	32	32⅛	1.0	10	7	7.3	...	...
50•[13]	SSP	✓Scripps(E.W.)'A'	NY,Ch	A−	182	26423	Newspapers:TV/radio	52⅜	13	58½	38½	53	40½	33283	47 7/16	41½	44 13/16	1.2	25	2	−8.8	9.9	9.7

Uniform Footnote Explanations-See Page 4. Other: [1]CBOE,Ph:Cycle 1. [2]ASE,CBOE,P:Cycle 1. [3]CBOE:Cycle 1. [4]CBOE:Cycle 3. [5]P:Cycle 1. [6]P,Ph:Cycle 1. [7]P:Cycle 2. [8]ASE,CBOE,P,Ph:Cycle 2. [9]P,Cycle 3. [10]CBOE,P,Ph:Cycle 3. [11]CBOE:Cycle 2. [12]ASE:Cycle 1. [13]ASE,CBOE:Cycle 2. [51]Ea ADS rep 1 ord,R 1. [52]Approx. [53]Pfd in $M. [54]Ea ADS rep 1 equity shr,Rs.10. [55]Formerly Hyde Athletic Indus'B'. [56]Ea ADS rep 4 ptc ctf ea rep Cl 1'A'com. [57]Plan Midcap 400 listing: eff Jan 4. [58]Stock or cash re-spec cond. [59]Subsid pfd in $M. [60]Ea ADS rep 1 vtg'A'shr,SEK10. [61]Stk dstr of Sedco Forex Hldgs Ltd. [62]®$1.67,'97. [63]Ea ADS rep 1 ord shr, FRF25 par. [64]33 Wk Dec'98. [65]Ea ADS rep 4 ord shrs, 50p. [66]Restated by co from $1.11.

Splits ◆	Cash Divs.	Dividends						Financial Position				Capitalization			Earnings $ Per Shr.							Interim Earnings			
		Latest Payment			Total $			Mil-$				Lg Trm Debt	Shs. 000		Years						Last 12		$ per Shr.		
Index	Ea. Yr. Since	Period $	Date	Ex. Div.	So Far 1999	Ind. Rate	Paid 1998	Cash& Equiv.	Curr. Assets	Curr. Liab.	Balance Sheet Date	Mil-$	Pfd.	Com.	End	1995	1996	1997	1998	1999	Mos.	Period	1998	1999	Index
1◆	....	None Since Public			...	Nil	....	99.9	188	28.7	9-30-99	....	...	56134	Dc	v0.07	v0.14	v0.24	v0.24	E0.55	0.43	9 Mo Sep	v0.14	v0.33	1
2◆	1999	[52]0.186	2-7-00	12-15	0.165	0.19	....	2966	9116	8946	j9-30-98	11998	...	223750	Sp	...	...	0.16	v0.26	Pv0.54	0.54				2
3◆	1946	Q0.135	1-3-00	11-29	0.50	0.54	0.46	169	5250	5904	10-02-99	2140	[53]258	p908697	Je	0.81	v0.89	v0.99	vd0.57	v1.26	1.19	3 Mo Sep	v0.35	v0.28	3
4◆	....	None Since Public			...	Nil	....	0.24	3.63	8.19	6-30-99	p0.01	...	★21156	Mr	...	...	...	vd0.40	....	....	3 Mo Jun	n/a	vd0.08	4
5	....	None Since Public			...	Nil	....	4.85	71.5	21.9	10-01-99	0.36	...	±6353	Dc	v±0.26	v±0.24	±vd0.76	v±0.56	....	1.50	9 Mo Sep	v±0.38	v±1.32	5
6	....	None Since Public			...	Nil	....	....	...	...		....	...	3573	Dc	v±0.26	v±0.24	±vd0.76	Pv±0.55	....	0.55				6
7	1998	Q0.07	1-14-00	12-29	0.28	0.28	0.14	5.93	167	109	10-03-99	95.1	...	27410	Dc	...	...	pv1.10	v1.01	....	0.83	9 Mo Sep	v0.90	v0.72	7
8	1993	Q0.39	1-31-00	1-12	1.56	1.56	1.56	Total Assets $291.26M			9-30-99	303	...	13334	Dc	v□0.60	v□0.53	□v0.40	vΔ0.77	....	0.91	9 Mo Sep	v□0.57	v0.71	8
9	....	0.135	5-30-96	5-15	...	Nil	....	573	1185	330	12-31-98	491	...	460228	Dc	Δ0.74	v0.92	v10.52	vd0.67	....	d0.55	6 Mo Jun	vd0.08	v0.04	9
10	....	None Since Public			...	Nil	....	7.17	193	188	9-30-99	4.45	...	13102	Dc	vd1.36	v0.52	v0.55	v□0.34	....	0.27	9 Mo Sep	vNil	vd0.07	10
11◆	....	None Since Public			...	Nil	....	115	145	9.94	9-30-99	1.79	...	42250	Sp	0.17	v...	v0.49	v0.61	v0.72	0.72				11
12	....	None Since Public			...	Nil	....	2.70	32.3	40.7	9-30-99	256	...	±28746	Dc	...	...	...	vpd0.76	....	....	9 Mo Sep	n/a	vpd1.42	12
13◆	1984	Q0.24⅜	2-1-00	1-6	0.96½	0.975	0.92½	267	7533	11243	9-30-99	11266	...	3411380	Dc	v□1.60	Δv1.72	v0.80	v□2.05	E2.05	1.67	9 Mo Sep	vΔ1.78	vΔ1.40	13
14	1997	0.768	12-15-99	11-26	3.071	3.07	3.071	Amt pay maturity based on Tel de Mexico'L'ADS[58]				....	...	9000	Dc	...	...	...	....	....	....	Due 3-15-2001			14
15	....	None Since Public			...	Nil	....	109	254	118	12-31-98	281	...	14886	Dc	d4.23	vd4.96	vd3.18	vd2.30	....	d2.34	6 Mo Jun	vd0.97	vd1.01	15
16	....	None Paid			...	Nil	....	2.24	45.1	11.4	9-30-99	....	...	5881	Je	vd0.65	v0.97	v0.09	v1.64	v1.99	2.06	3 Mo Sep	v0.43	v0.50	16
17◆	1946	Q0.275	1-1-00	12-8	1.43	1.10	1.53¼	57.0	516	824	9-30-99	1610	[59]117	103573	Dc	v1.70	v2.05	v2.06	v2.12	E1.73	1.54	9 Mo Sep	v1.81	v1.23	17
18	1996	0.66	5-17-99	4-29	0.66	0.66	0.609	219	2435	1561	12-31-98	816	...	±200000	Dc	p±2.47	±1.44	v1.25	v1.39	....	1.39				18
19	1996	0.66	5-17-99	4-29	0.66	0.66	0.609	....	...	...		....	...	100000	Dc	p±2.47	±1.44	v1.25	v1.39	....	1.39				19
20	1977	tQ0.03¼	12-31-99	12-14	t0.22¾	0.13	t0.26	4.74	61.4	33.7	9-30-99	71.3	...	21202	Dc	v±0.29	v±d1.34	v±0.55	v±1.06	....	0.74	9 Mo Sep	v0.84	v0.52	20
21	....	0.04½	10-15-93	9-29	...	Nil	....	2.03	6.80	7.36	10-31-99	....	...	4359	Ap	vd1.22	v0.19	v0.23	v0.22	v0.01	d0.16	6 Mo Oct	v0.35	v0.18	21
22	....	None Since Public			...	Nil	....	39.0	768	358	9-25-99	294	...	40701	Dc	p0.70	v0.97	vd0.03	v0.39	....	0.90	9 Mo Sep	v0.33	v0.84	22
23	....	None Since Public			...	Nil	....	0.99	198	200	9-25-99	101	...	32693	Dc	vd0.52	v0.05	v0.39	v□d3.72	....	0.35	9 Mo Sep	v□d3.72	v0.35	23
24	....	None Paid			...	Nil	....	2.08	7.01	3.18	9-30-99	0.29	22	4336	Mr	0.40	vd0.06	v1.33	v0.51	....	0.43	6 Mo Sep	v0.31	v0.23	24
25◆	1952	Q0.12½	11-30-99	11-3	0.48½	0.50	0.42½	1665	4790	3310	9-30-99	1010	...	1469075	Dc	v0.59	v0.82	v0.97	v1.18	E1.42	1.36	9 Mo Sep	v0.90	v1.08	25
26◆	1957	Q0.18¾	1-7-00	12-23	h[61]0.75	0.75	0.75	4021	8638	3716	9-30-99	3563	...	549844	Dc	v1.32	v1.70	v2.52	v1.81	E1.08	1.14	9 Mo Sep	v1.31	v0.64	26
27	1994	Q0.05	11-19-99	11-2	0.20	0.20	0.20	6.17	128	35.6	8-31-99	120	...	±9726	Au	2.82	2.24	v2.05	v0.93	v0.34	0.34				27
28	....	None Since Public			...	Nil	....	2.87	551	274	8-31-99	329	...	±16540	My	±2.38	±1.97	v±0.02	v±1.45	v±2.20	2.39	6 Mo Nov	v±0.86	v±1.05	28
29	....	None Since Public			...	Nil	....	12.8	91.8	36.8	9-30-99	102	...	7065	Dc	...	pv1.02	pv1.10	v0.60	....	0.86	9 Mo Sep	v0.34	v0.60	29
30	....	None Since Public			...	Nil	....	Total Assets $488.60M			9-30-99	245	...	20081	Dc	v0.35	vd0.55	v0.29	v0.63	....	1.12	9 Mo Sep	v0.42	v0.91	30
31◆	1968	Q0.12½	11-3-99	10-21	0.50	0.50	0.46	56.8	408	118	10-31-99	65.0	11	31130	Au	1.43	1.12	v1.37	v□1.48	v1.51	1.51				31
32◆	1960	Q0.09	11-26-99	11-9	0.34	0.36	0.30	27.9	71.7	42.1	10-09-99	12.1	...	6041	Dc	v0.79	v0.92	v1.06	v1.23	....	1.25	40 Wk Oct	v0.82	v0.84	32
33◆	1989	Q0.014	11-26-99	11-9	0.056	0.06	0.054	Total Assets $25088.02M			9-30-99	465	...	819969	Dc	v0.21	0.29	v0.33	v0.42	E0.68	0.62	9 Mo Sep	v0.30	v0.50	33
34	1996	Q0.15	12-13-99	11-4	0.60	0.60	0.60	5.60	155	111	9-30-99	105	...	15703	Dc	p1.81	v2.38	v2.77	v1.92	....	1.63	9 Mo Sep	v1.79	v1.50	34
35◆	....	None Since Public			...	Nil	....	147	1776	1074	9-26-99	139	...	72095	Je	0.82	1.35	v[62]1.69	v2.13	v2.01	2.12	3 Mo Sep	v0.45	v0.56	35
36◆	1976	Q0.01½	12-15-99	11-29	0.06	0.06	0.06	318	861	254	10-01-99	0.38	...	78561	Je	v0.83	vd0.08	v0.82	v1.02	vP1.30	1.42	3 Mo Sep	v0.19	v0.31	36
37◆	....	None Since Public			...	Nil	....	13.6	82.8	49.8	9-30-99	....	...	11914	Dc	v1.64	v1.41	v0.72	v1.58	E1.95	1.78	9 Mo Sep	v1.12	v1.32	37
38	1988	Q0.04¾	12-8-99	11-19	0.19	0.19	0.18	11.4	28.9	6.38	9-30-99	....	...	9634	Dc	v0.66	v0.53	v0.62	v0.46	....	0.46	9 Mo Sep	v0.36	v0.36	38
39	....	None Since Public			...	Nil	....	4.91	18.7	3.78	9-30-99	1.03	p...	★25549	Dc	...	...	...	vpd0.61	....	....	9 Mo Sep	n/a	vpd1.08	39
40	....	t0.13	12-12-96	11-21	...	Nil	....	83.4	405	160	12-31-98	1.28	...	43039	Dc	d0.81	vd4.16	v0.01	vd2.58	....	0.56	9 Mo Sep	vd2.73	v0.41	40
41	....	None Since Public			...	Nil	....	123	170	28.1	9-30-99	....	...	14115	Dc	vd2.39	pvd1.09	pv0.06	vd0.38	....	d0.24	9 Mo Sep	v0.06	v0.20	41
42	1976	A1.00	1-5-00	11-23	1.00	1.00	†1.25	17.7	25.7	8.38	9-30-99	....	...	1115	Je	1.15	3.23	v15.94	v13.98	vd0.75	d1.41	3 Mo Sep	vNil	vd0.66	42
43	1997	1.49	6-23-99	5-28	1.49	1.49	1.423	Book Value $46.28			12-31-98	16.4	...	34243	Dc	5.46	vP4.10	v4.34	v4.66	....	4.76	6 Mo Jun	v2.01	v2.11	43
44	....	0.06	12-15-93	11-24	...	Nil	....	25.0	93.4	67.3	9-30-99	28.5	...	17869	Dc	v±d0.89	v±1.24	v□d0.10	□vd0.38	....	2.51	9 Mo Sep	v□d0.26	v□2.63	44
45	1999	0.05	12-22-99	12-1	0.15	0.20	....	Total Assets $254M			12-31-98	....	...	18568	Dc	...	...	...	‡v[64]0.12	....	....	9 Mo Sep	n/a	v0.33	45
46◆	1993	†0.519		11-30	1.503	1.54	1.452	116	791	2432	j3-31-98	1032	...	p1837000	Mr	2.02	2.49	n/a	Pv2.70	....	2.70				46
47	....	None Since Public			...	Nil	....	34.2	693	391	7-03-99	856	177	p28600	Sp	[66]0.99	d0.65	v1.35	v1.22	vP□2.27	2.27				47
48◆	....	None Since Public			...	Nil	....	0.62	133	54.1	9-30-99	34.0	...	11394	Dc	vp□0.50	v0.47	v0.71	v1.15	....	1.80	9 Mo Sep	v1.42	v□2.07	48
49	1997	Q0.08	12-30-99	12-10	0.32	0.32	0.24	Total Assets $852.35M			9-30-99	....	...	12068	Dc	pv2.44	vp3.02	vp2.66	v3.06	....	3.11	9 Mo Sep	v2.21	v2.26	49
50	1922	Q0.14	12-10-99	11-26	0.56	0.56	0.54	14.8	444	553	9-30-99	502	...	±78109	Dc	v±1.66	±v1.95	v1.93	v1.62	....	1.82	9 Mo Sep	v1.08	v1.28	50

◆**Stock Splits & Divs By Line Reference Index** [1]2-for-1,'98,'99. [2]10-for-1,'99. [3]2-for-1,'98. [4]To split 4-for-1,ex Jan 10,'00. [11]2-for-1,'99. [13]2-for-1,'98. [17]2-for-1,'95. [25]2-for-1,'95,'97,'98. [26]2-for-1,'97. [31]5-for-4,'94. [32]2-for-1,'95:3-for-2,'97. [33]3-for-2,'95,'97,'98:2-for-1,'95,'99. [35]2-for-1,'97. [36]2-for-1,'94. [37]2-for-1,'95. [46]5-for-2,'97. [48]3-for-2,'97,'98.

¶ S&P 500 · # MidCap 400 · ✣ SmallCap 600 · • Options

Index	Ticker	Name of Issue (Call Price of Pfd. Stocks)	Market	Com. Rank. & Pfd. Rating	Inst. Hold Cos	Inst. Hold Shs. (000)	Principal Business	Price Range 1971-97 High	1971-97 Low	1998 High	1998 Low	1999 High	1999 Low	December, 1999 Dec. Sales in 100s	Last Sale Or Bid High	Low	Last	%Div Yield	P-E Ratio	EPS 5 Yr Growth	% Annualized Total Return 12 Mo	36 Mo	60 Mo
1	SLJ	Scripps Financial	AS	NR	1	49	Commercial bank, California	...	...	...	...	16½	13⅜	856	15½	13⅜	13½	0.9	16	...	...	...	...
2•1	SDLI	✓SDL Inc.	NNM	NR	248	30017	Mfr fiber optic prd	16 3/16	4	22 1/16	4 1/16	250	19⅛	154080	250	154¼	218	...	..	74	1008	156	...
3	SCRA	✓Sea Containers Ltd Cl'A'[51]	NY	B	86	10338	Ferry/rail svcs/ship container	32½	11¾	44¾	19	39	20¾	14962	31⅞	23¾	26⅝	4.5	8	7	-7.7	23.4	19.4
4	SCR B	Cl'B'	NY,Ch,Ph	B	13	223		37⅛	6	44½	20¾	38¾	22¼	658	31⅝	24¼	26 7/16	4.1	8	7	-7.2	22.7	18.2
5	SEB	✓Seaboard Corp	AS[10]	B	42	222	Food prodn:poultry,pork:bank'g	457	4⅝	445	256	461	185	141	252	185	194¼	0.5	8	17	-53.8	-9.6	4.2
6	SEAC	✓SeaChange Intl	NNM	NR	30	4734	Digital video pds software	26 5/16	4¼	9 9/16	3 9/16	40	3⅞	58976	40	17¼	35⅝	...	d	-48	766	27.7	...
7	SBCFA	✓Seacoast Banking FL'A'	NNM	B+	42	1188	Commercial bkg,Florida	39½	5½	40	22¾	35⅝	26⅛	1384	30⅛	28¼	28⅝	3.6	13	8	4.3	6.7	14.5
8	SCFS	✓Seacoast Finl Svcs	NNM	NR	72	10944	General banking,Mass	...	...	10⅝	9½	12 9/16	9½	23932	10¾	9 13/16	10 9/16	2.0	..	...	0.3	...	...
✣9	CKH	✓SEACOR SMIT	NY	NR	131	8396	Oper fleet o&g svc vessels	73⅝	13	61 15/16	31¼	57⅞	38½	9892	54	47	51¾	...	14	41	4.7	-6.3	21.6
¶10•2	SEG	✓Seagate Technology	NY,Ch,Ph,P	B	598	157716	Computer magnetic disc drives	56¼	2	34½	16⅛	48 13/16	25⅛	449359	48 13/16	36½	46 9/16	...	10	-4	53.9	5.6	31.2
¶11•3	VO	✓Seagram Co Ltd	NY,To,B,Ch,Ph,Mo,P	B	515	129723	Beverages/film&music entmt	42¾	1⅝	46 11/16	25⅛	65	36⅝	156752	46 7/16	41 5/16	44¾	1.5	d	Neg	19.4	6.7	10.5
12	VOY	Seagram Co Ltd 7.50% Cv Eq Sec[56]	NY	NR	59	15585	Adj conv-rate Equity Sec	...	...	...	...	55 3/16	40	15155	46⅞	43 3/16	45	8.4	..	...	...	...	...
13	VOS	Seagram(Jos)&Sons 8.0%'QUIDS'	NY	....[57]	8	244	Qtly Income Debt Sec	...	...	25½	25⅛	26	20 11/16	12014	23⅜	20 11/16	21⅜	9.4	..	...	-8.8	...	...
¶14•4	SEE	✓Sealed Air	NY	NR	484	68151	Protective packaging mtl	...	...	68	27⅜	68 7/16	44½	117387	51 15/16	44½	51 13/16	...	32	...	1.5	...	...
15	Pr A	$2.00 Cv Pfd'A'([58]51.40)	NY	BB	190	21694		...	...	65½	31⅞	65	44 11/16	61505	50½	44 11/16	50½	4.0	..	...	...	...	...
16	SCC	Sears Canada	To,Mo,P	B	13	5913	Mail order/dept stores	25¾	4¼	29	15¼	40½	17 13/16	18001	40½	35⅝	40	0.6	24	59	124	58.9	41.6
¶17•5	S	✓Sears,Roebuck	NY,B,C,Ch,P,Ph	B	779	267239	Large retailer gen mdse:credit	65¼	14⅝	65	39 1/16	53 3/16	26 1/16	510159	35½	28¾	30⅝	3.0	9	-4	-26.9	-11.2	...
18	SRH	Sears Roebuck Accept 6.95% Notes	NY	....[61]	3	34	Redeemable Notes	...	...	25 7/16	24½	25 7/16	18 11/16	7132	20 13/16	18 11/16	19⅝	8.9	..	...	-16.8	...	...
19	SRF	Sears Roebuck Accept 7.0% Notes	NY	....[61]	6	163	Redeemable Notes	...	...	25¾	24¼	25½	18¾	7998	20 13/16	18¾	19⅞	8.8	..	...	-15.4	...	...
20•6	FOTO	✓Seattle FilmWorks	NNM	↓B	37	5665	Mail order:film proc'g/eqp	15	⅛	13 3/16	2 11/16	5 15/16	2¼	24360	3⅝	2 11/16	2¾	...	d	Neg	-39.9	-40.7	-10.3
21	SEWY	✓Seaway Food Town	NNM	↑A-	24	596	Food supermkts Ohio, Mich	17 7/16	⅞	21	12½	30	11	8270	22⅝	15⅝	16¼	1.1	15	23	-0.6	11.2	91.3
22	SECM	✓Secom General	NSC	C	..	...	Mfr custom tooling	206⅝	4⅝	12½	5/16	5¼	1¼	1089	5¼	2½	2½	...	2	Neg	38.5	-34.8	-23.4
23	SECD	✓Second Bancorp	NNM	A-	28	806	General banking,Ohio	28	3⅜	38¼	19¾	30¾	19 1/16	2045	24½	22⅜	22⅜	2.5	28	-11	2.9	15.4	18.9
24•7	SCUR	✓Secure Computing	NNM	NR	27	3042	Computer security sys	64½	4¾	22¼	6⅜	29	2¼	195048	14⅜	7¾	12 9/16	...	d	Neg	-34.1	11.2	...
25	SAI	✓Security Assoc Intl	AS	NR	3	49	Security alarm monitor'g svcs	...	...	8½	3 15/16	5	1½	3371	3 15/16	1½	3⅞	...	d	...	10.7	...	...
26	SCC	✓Security Capital Corp'A'	AS	NR	4	1774	Dgn craft kits/franchise daycare ctr	...	...	...	...	9 7/16	3 15/16	149	6 13/16	5⅞	5⅞	...	19	NM	...	...	...
27	SCZ	✓Security Capital Grp'B'[64]	NY	NR	118	33845	Investment co	35½	29½	32½	11⅞	16	11⅝	33333	13 3/16	11⅞	12½	...	d	...	-7.8	...	...
28	SCZ.A	Cl'A' Vtg[65]	NY	NR	29	768		1750	1500	1600	600	765	594	11	625	601	620	...	d	...	-6.1	...	...
29	RTY	Security Cap U.S. Rlty ADS[66]	NY	NR	15	3914	Real estate investment U.S.	...	...	...	...	19¼	13⅝	11098	14¾	13⅜	14 1/16	...	..	...	...	...	...
30	SPN	✓Security of Pennsylvania Finl	AS	NR	6	230	Savings & loan,Pennsylvania	...	...	...	10	11	9	583	10⅛	9	9½	2.1	..	...	-6.4	...	...
31	SECX	✓SED Intl Holdings	NNM	C	16	2949	Dstr computers/eqp so'estn US	20½	⅞	14⅜	3 5/16	5½	1½	22718	2 5/16	1½	2 5/16	...	d	Neg	-47.2	-43.0	-15.1
32	SDNA	✓Sedona Corp	NSC	C	10	894	Dvlp imaging prod & software	9⅝	¼	3½	1	3½	1⅛	84514	3½	1½	3 7/16	...	d	-24	44.7	-2.0	48.9
33	SEGU	✓Segue Software	NNM	NR	30	2435	Dvp software testing prd	40½	7½	25¾	9⅞	26¼	4	27945	26¼	17⅞	25	...	d	Neg	23.5	11.1	...
✣34•2	SEIC	✓SEI Investments	NNM	A-	204	7262	Diversified investment services	44½	2⅛	100½	37	129	77⅝	10482	129	99	119	0.3	35	34	20.2	76.1	48.3
✣35•8	SEI	✓Seitel Inc	NY,Ph,P	B	153	14880	Acquires,mkts seismic data	25⅞	⅜	19⅝	8 11/16	18⅛	5½	50133	7 1/16	5⅞	6¾	...	12	8	...	...	...
36	SLS	✓Selas Corp of Amer	AS,B,Ch,Ph	B-	23	1491	Heat processing equipment	13½	15/16	12⅝	6 7/16	8⅜	4¼	1982	6 1/16	4 13/16	6 1/16	2.7	d	Neg	-16.5	-14.1	2.8
✣37•9	SIGI	✓Selective Insurance Gr	NNM	B+	156	12146	Property/casualty insurance	28⅝	⅝	29¼	16 11/16	22½	16½	21785	17⅞	16½	17 3/16	3.5	9	6	-11.8	-0.1	10.0
38	SLF	✓Selfcare Inc	AS	NR	11	760	Mfr selftest med diagnostic pd	18	6⅞	11⅞	1¼	5 15/16	2	7899	4 5/16	3	3 5/16	...	d	...	59.4	-36.8	...
39	SMGS	✓SEMCO Energy	NNM	B+	53	2181	Integrated natural gas sys	20 3/16	1⅞	18⅜	13⅛	17½	10 15/16	13521	13⅞	10 15/16	11 13/16	e6.9	14	28	-23.2	-3.4	3.4
40	SMNS	✓Seminis Inc'A'	NNM	NR	26	8607	Dvp mkt vegetable seeds	...	...	...	...	15 5/16	5	121218	7⅛	5	6 5/16	...	..	...	...	...	...
¶41•10	SRE	✓Sempra Energy	NY,Ph	NR	411	105609	Electric utility,Cal	...	...	29 9/16	23¾	26	17⅛	263363	18 13/16	17⅛	17⅜	9.0	10	-2	-26.5	...	...
42	SMTC	✓Semtech Corp	NNM	B-	182	27660	Mfr silicon rectifiers	18 3/16	¼	18	4 13/16	57½	12¼	99278	55	40⅜	52⅛	...	77	46	191	130	140
43	SNTKY	Senetek Plc ADS[70]	NSC	NR	16	3144	Dvlp stge:biotechnology R&D	10¼	¼	5	1½	3¼	15/16	53842	2	1¼	1⅜	...	d	-30	-13.5	4.0	-5.4
44	SNH	Senior Housing Prop Trust	NY	NR	..	...	Real estate investment trust	...	...	...	...	16 15/16	10⅞	21728	13⅛	11⅛	12⅜	19.4	6	...	...	...	...
#45•10	SRM	✓Sensormatic Elect	NY,Ch,Ph,P	C	200	60145	Electronic article surveil sys	39¼	⅛	20	3⅛	17 15/16	7	67210	17 7/16	13½	17 7/16	...	37	82	151	1.6	-13.0
46	VCR	✓Sensory Science	AS,Ch,P	C	15	1476	Dvlp, mkt consumer electrs prd	24⅛	½	4 11/16	1¾	4	1½	22212	2	1 9/16	1¾	...	d	-8	-40.4	13.8	-2.6
47	SKV	✓Sentry Technology	AS,Ch,Ph	NR	8	1044	Mfr,mkt surveillance equip	4¼	1 5/16	2	½	¾	1/16	11673	¼	1/16	⅛	...	d	...	-85.0	...	...
#48•11	SEPR	✓Sepracor Inc	NNM	NR	303	23674	Pharmaceut'l prd/drug R&D	42¾	3¾	95¼	33	140⅞	58¾	75478	106 15/16	90½	99 3/16	...	d	-22	12.6	81.4	88.9
#49	SQA.A	✓Sequa Corp Cl'A'	NY	B-	100	3355	Mfr jet engine components	88⅜	17⅝	75⅞	45¾	72¾	44	1659	59⅞	51	53 15/16	...	10	NM	-9.9	11.2	15.7
50	SQA.B	Class B (10 votes)	NY	B-	22	1446	specialty instr & chemicals	91½	8⅞	85¾	68	77½	54¼	326	62¾	54¼	60	...	11	NM	-18.4	6.3	17.6

Uniform Footnote Explanations-See Page 4. Other: [1]ASE,CBOE:Cycle 3. [2]ASE:Cycle 3. [3]P:Cycle 2,To:Cycle 1. [4]ASE,Ph:Cycle 1. [5]ASE,CBOE,P,Ph:Cycle 1. [6]P:Cycle 3. [7]ASE:Cycle 2. [8]CBOE:Cycle 2. [9]Ph:Cycle 3. [10]ASE:Cycle 1. [11]CBOE:Cycle 1. [51]0.10 vtg. [52]Incl current amts. [53]2 Mo Dec'98. [54]Fiscal Jan '96 & prior. [55]12 Mos Jun'96. [56]Seagram Co Ltd Pur Contract & 7.50% Sub Note. [57]Rated'BBB'by S&P. [58]Fr 3-31-2001,scale to $50 in 2008. [59]Mand redemption 3-31-2018. [60]Com exceed $70.6563 20(out 30)trad days. [61]Rated 'A-' by S&P. [62]®$1.26,'96. [63]Fiscal Sep'96 & prior. [64]0.005 vtg. [65]Cv into 50 Cl'B' fr 1-1-98. [66]Ea ADS rep 1 ord,$2 Par. [67]Incl curr amts. [68]Stk dstr of Eagle Geophysical Inc. [69]Excl subsid pfd. [70]Ea ADS rep 1 ord,5p. [71]One wrrt for ea 10 com held.

Index (Splits ◆)	Cash Divs. Ea. Yr. Since	Dividends: Latest Payment Period $	Date	Ex. Div.	Total $ So Far 1999	Ind. Rate	Paid 1998	Financial Position Mil-$ Cash& Equiv.	Curr. Assets	Curr. Liab.	Balance Sheet Date	Capitalization Lg Trm Debt Mil-$	Shs. 000 Pfd.	Com.	Earnings $ Per Shr. Years End	1995	1996	1997	1998	1999	Last 12 Mos.	Interim Earnings Period	$ per Shr. 1998	1999	Index
1	1999	S0.06	1-21-00	1-5	0.12	0.12	....	Book Value $6.55			6-30-99	....	...	6895	Dc	...	...	...	v0.84	....	0.87	9 Mo Sep	0.62	0.65	1
2◆	....	None Since Public			...	Nil	....	292	368	30.2	9-30-99	0.46	...	35367	Dc	vd0.16	v0.27	vd0.92	v0.44	....	0.67	9 Mo Sep	v0.16	v0.40	2
3	1992	Q0.30	11-22-99	11-3	1.10	1.20	0.88½	Equity per shr $25.11			12-31-98	[52]1056	150	±18303	Dc	v±6.54	v±1.20	±v2.07	v±3.11	....	3.43	6 Mo Jun	v±1.13	v□±1.45	3
4	1978	Q0.27	11-22-99	11-3	0.995	1.08	0.805	....	...	...		....	...	2382	Dc	v±6.54	v±1.20	±v2.07	v±3.11	....	3.43	6 Mo Jun	v±1.13	v□±1.45	4
5	1959	Q0.25	12-31-99	12-17	1.00	1.00	1.00	107	584	391	9-30-99	310	...	1488	Dc	v13.58	Δv1.91	v20.55	v35.20	....	24.68	9 Mo Sep	v10.63	v0.11	5
6◆	....	None Since Public			...	Nil	....	9.33	46.2	23.6	9-30-99	1.49	...	20928	Dc	v0.07	v0.24	vd0.16	vd0.25	....	d0.01	9 Mo Sep	vd0.21	v0.03	6
7	1940	Q0.26	1-3-00	12-14	0.96	1.04	0.88	Total Assets $883M			9-30-99	25.0	...	±4829	Dc	v±1.51	v±1.71	v1.42	v1.84	....	2.28	9 Mo Sep	v1.34	v1.78	7
8	1999	Q0.05	11-19-99	11-3	0.10	0.20	....	Total Deposits $1530.5M			9-30-99	186	...	26432	Dc	...	...	...	v‡[53]d0.15	....	....	9 Mo Sep	n/a	v0.72	8
9	....	None Since Public			...	Nil	....	171	279	74.5	9-30-99	465	...	11281	Dc	v1.37	v□2.80	□v7.50	vΔ8.17	....	3.82	9 Mo Sep	v6.25	vΔ1.90	9
10◆	....	None Since Public			...	Nil	....	1415	3031	1565	10-01-99	703	...	208304	Je	1.76	v0.97	v2.62	vd2.17	v4.53	4.66	3 Mo Sep	vd0.12	v0.01	10
11	1937	tQ0.16½	12-15-99	11-29	t0.66	0.66	t0.66	1420	8965	7877	9-30-99	7561	...	433506	Je	[54]9.13	[55]0.37	v1.35	v2.68	v1.81	d1.61	3 Mo Sep	v3.33	v□d0.09	11
12	1999	0.94	12-21-99	12-16	1.88	3.76	....	On 6-21-2004 Cv into Seagram Co Ltd Com re-spec cond				....	...	★18500	Je	...	...	...	....	....	....				12
13	1998	Q0.50	12-31-99	12-28	2.00	2.00	0.228	Co opt to redm fr 11-20-2003 at $25				★500	...	...	Je	...	...	...	....	....	....	Mature 12-31-2038			13
14	....	None Since Public			...	Nil	....	74.4	873	678	9-30-99	701	35759	83517	Dc	...	p0.19	n/a	vp0.12	E1.60	0.65	9 Mo Sep	n/a	v1.17	14
15	1998	Q0.50	1-3-00	12-8	2.00	2.00	1.00	Cv into 0.8845644 com[59]				....	35759		Dc	...	...	...	....	....	....	Red restr'n 3-31-2001 to 3-30-2003[60]			15
16	1961	gQ0.06	12-15-99	11-10	g0.24	0.24	g0.24	190	2149	1250	j1-02-99	681	...	p106048	Dc	v0.12	v0.09	v1.10	v1.38	....	j1.67	9 Mo Sep	v0.58	v0.87	16
17◆	1935	Q0.23	1-3-00	11-23	0.92	0.92	0.92	281	27434	12492	10-02-99	13245	...	377954	Dc	v4.50	v3.12	v2.99	v□2.74	E3.40	3.24	9 Mo Sep	v1.36	v1.86	17
18	1999	Q0.434	1-24-00	1-5	1.737	1.738	....	Co option redm fr 10-23-2003 at $25				★250	...	...	Dc	...	...	...	....	....	....	Mature 10-23-2038			18
19	1998	Q0.43¾	12-1-99	11-12	1.75	1.75	0.865	Co option redm fr 3-1-2003 at $25				★250	...	...	Dc	...	...	...	....	....	....	Mature 3-1-2038			19
20◆	....	None Since Public			...	Nil	....	13.8	29.1	9.07	6-26-99	0.57	...	16301	Sp	0.33	0.45	v0.57	v0.43	Pvd0.62	d0.62				20
21◆	1964	0.04½	11-19-99	11-5	0.18	0.18	0.16½	9.76	79.4	62.7	8-28-99	49.2	...	6674	Au	0.68	0.83	v0.97	v1.05	v1.12	1.12				21
22◆	....	None Paid			...	Nil	....	0.07	8.87	12.0	6-30-99	....	...	1061	Sp	1.40	v0.05	v0.30	vd5.55	Pv1.37	1.37				22
23◆	1940	Q0.14	1-31-00	1-12	0.55	0.56	0.51	Total Deposits $1106.35M			9-30-99	187	...	10517	Dc	v1.13	v[62]1.27	v1.32	v0.52	....	0.80	9 Mo Sep	v0.92	v1.20	23
24	....	None Since Public			...	Nil	....	5.65	16.0	10.5	9-30-99	....	...	21738	Dc	pvd0.08	vd1.76	vd0.27	vd0.20	....	d1.96	9 Mo Sep	vd0.27	vd2.03	24
25	....	None Paid			...	Nil	....	1.69	4.41	6.86	9-30-99	7.05	566	7114	Dc	...	...	pvd1.24	vd1.06	....	d0.49	9 Mo Sep	vd0.88	vd0.31	25
26◆	....	None Paid			...	Nil	....	0.57	30.1	23.7	9-30-99	18.2	...	±6443	Dc	±d0.08	±v[63]0.14	±v0.66	±v0.41	....	0.31	9 Mo Sep	v±0.44	v±0.34	26
27	....	None Since Public			...	Nil	....	Total Assets $4095.23M			9-30-99	1585	258	±56340	Dc	...	p1.39	v1.28	v±d1.10	....	d0.98	9 Mo Sep	□±d1.11	□±d0.99	27
28	....	None Since Public			...	Nil	....	....	...	...		....	...	1343	Dc	...	...	±v1.28	v±d1.10	....	d1.78	3 Mo Mar	v±0.03	□±d0.65	28
29	....	None Since Public			...	Nil	....	Net Asset Val $12.86			12-31-98	[67]632	...	173124	Dc	...	...	...	§12.86	....	....				29
30	1999	Q0.05	11-22-99	11-4	0.10	0.20	....	Total Deposits $98.0M			9-30-99	....	...	1508	Je	...	...	...	pv0.61	v0.04	....	3 Mo Sep	n/a	v0.22	30
31	....	None Paid			...	Nil	....	5.59	150	104	9-30-99	....	...	7014	Je	v0.74	v0.76	v1.04	vd0.03	vd4.36	d4.30	3 Mo Sep	v0.03	v0.09	31
32	....	None Since Public			...	Nil	....	1.79	2.04	0.69	9-30-99	0.01	5	23896	Dc	vd0.14	vd0.39	□vd0.47	vd0.36	....	d0.36	9 Mo Sep	vd0.27	vd0.27	32
33	....	None Since Public			...	Nil	....	21.1	34.0	15.9	9-30-99	0.88	...	9086	Dc	pvd0.20	v0.09	vd1.31	vd0.34	....	d1.72	9 Mo Sep	v0.02	vd1.36	33
34	1988	S0.20	1-28-00	1-5	0.36	0.40	0.30	53.4	125	119	9-30-99	29.0	...	17728	Dc	v0.98	v0.35	v1.40	v2.29	....	3.37	9 Mo Sep	v1.50	v2.58	34
35◆	....	h[68]....	6-10-99	5-14	h[68]...	Nil	....	Total Assets $541M			9-30-99	222	...	24286	Dc	v0.42	v0.74	v1.43	v1.05	....	0.55	9 Mo Sep	v0.76	v0.26	35
36◆	1990	Q0.04½	3-31-00	3-13	0.18	0.18	0.18	3.49	49.8	35.8	9-30-99	4.21	...	5141	Dc	v0.44	v0.78	v0.82	v0.68	....	d0.09	9 Mo Sep	v0.61	vd0.16	36
37◆	1929	Q0.15	12-1-99	11-10	0.59	0.60	0.56	Total Assets $2563.22M			9-30-99	88.8	...	27483	Dc	v1.81	v1.83	v2.27	v1.74	....	1.88	9 Mo Sep	v1.37	v1.51	37
38	....	None Since Public			...	Nil	....	7.31	40.7	47.3	9-30-99	41.6	[69]6	17980	Dc	pvd2.61	vd6.00	□vd3.29	vd1.55	....	d1.74	9 Mo Sep	vd0.45	vd0.64	38
39◆	1956	†Q0.20½	2-15-00	2-2	†0.86½	0.82	s0.781	3.51	100	107	9-30-99	170	[69]6	17878	Dc	v0.83	vd0.93	v1.08	Δv□0.55	....	0.84	12 Mo Sep	v0.79	v0.84	39
40	....	None Since Public			...	Nil	....	23.0	501	144	6-30-99	486	28	±59824	Sp	...	...	...	pv0.01	....	....	9 Mo Jun	n/a	v□d0.14	40
41	1998	Q0.39	1-15-00	12-17	1.56	1.56	0.39	474	2962	3197	9-30-99	2934	...	240351	Dc	p1.67	v1.77	v1.82	v1.24	E1.70	1.58	9 Mo Sep	v0.88	v1.22	41
42◆	....	3%Stk	4-22-83	3-14	...	Nil	....	53.0	111	22.3	10-31-99	....	...	31886	Ja	0.30	v0.30	v0.47	v0.41	....	0.68	9 Mo Oct	v0.28	v0.56	42
43	....	None Paid			...	Nil	....	1.60	4.93	8.68	9-30-99	7.12	...	58134	Dc	d0.08	vd0.10	vd0.32	vd0.41	....	d0.31	9 Mo Sep	vd0.23	v□d0.13	43
44	1999	Q0.60	11-22-99	10-18	0.60	2.40	....	Equity per shr $17.21			6-30-99	[52]200	...	26000	Dc	...	...	...	v2.01	....	2.00	9 Mo Sep	v1.40	v1.39	44
45	....	Div Suspended 8-14-97			...	Nil	....	205	760	389	9-30-99	426	700	76082	Je	1.02	vd1.33	vd0.29	vd0.50	v0.35	0.47	3 Mo Sep	vd0.06	v0.06	45
46	....	[71]Wrrt	3-19-90	3-20	...	Nil	....	0.34	34.7	26.9	9-30-99	....	...	13891	Mr	vd0.25	v0.16	v0.23	v0.08	....	d0.06	6 Mo Sep	v0.11	vd0.03	46
47	....	None Since Public			...	Nil	....	1.18	17.1	6.32	9-30-99	2.93	5079	9751	Dc	pd0.23	v0.23	vd2.08	vd0.59	....	d0.67	9 Mo Sep	vd0.40	vd0.48	47
48	....	None Since Public			...	Nil	....	377	391	54.7	9-30-99	492	...	33135	Dc	vd1.54	vd2.25	vd0.97	vd3.23	Ed4.90↓	d4.86	9 Mo Sep	vd2.10	vd3.73	48
49	....	0.15	7-1-93	6-9	...	Nil	....	400	1080	666	9-30-99	500	413	±10370	Dc	±v0.57	v□±0.65	±v1.66	v±5.87	....	5.47	9 Mo Sep	v±2.50	v±□2.10	49
50	....	0.12½	7-1-93	6-9	...	Nil	....	Cv into 1 Cl'A'				....	...	3330	Dc	v±0.57	v□±0.65	±v1.66	v±5.87	....	5.47	9 Mo Sep	v±2.50	v±2.10	50

◆Stock Splits & Divs By Line Reference Index [2]3-for-2,'96:2-for-1,'99:Vote Feb 28 on 2-for-1. [6]3-for-2,'99. [10]2-for-1,'96. [17]No adj for stk dstr Allstate Corp,'95. [20]2-for-1,'94:3-for-2,'95,'96,'97. [21]2-for-1,'97:3-for-2,'98. [22]1-for-5 REVERSE,'99. [23]3-for-2,'95:2-for-1,'97. [26]1-for-8 REVERSE,'96. [35]2-for-1,'97. [36]3-for-2,'97. [37]2-for-1,'97. [39]Adj for 5%,'98. [42]2-for-1,'98,'99.

¶ S&P 500
# MidCap 400
✣ SmallCap 600
• Options

Index	Ticker	Name of Issue (Call Price of Pfd. Stocks)	Market	Com. Rank. & Pfd. Rating	Inst. Hold Cos	Inst. Hold Shs. (000)	Principal Business	Price Range 1971-97 High	1971-97 Low	1998 High	1998 Low	1999 High	1999 Low	Dec. Sales in 100s	December, 1999 Last Sale Or Bid High	Low	Last	%Div Yield	P-E Ratio	EPS 5 Yr Growth	% Annualized Total Return 12 Mo	36 Mo	60 Mo
		Sequa Corp Cl'A' (Cont.)																					
1	Pr	$5 cm Cv Pfd(100)vtg	NY	NR	10	289		115½	51	109¼	83	101	86	48	93¾	89 9/16	89½B	5.6	..	...	...	...	...
2	SRK	✔SeraCare Inc	AS	NR	9	183	Whole blood collection/distrib	....	....	8 15/16	4	6⅝	2½	3941	3¾	2½	3½	...	14	...	-37.8	...	...
3	SERO	✔Serologicals Corp	NNM	NR	99	15917	Biomedical pr:human antibodies	17 9/16	4 11/16	30⅜	15 7/16	30¾	3¼	29915	7¼	5⅜	6	...	27	7	-80.0	-27.3	...
¶4•[1]	SRV	✔Service Corp Intl	NY,B,Ch,P	A	545	185048	Funeral service:cemetery	38	⅛	47⅛	29½	38⅞	6 3/16	381843	7 9/16	6 3/16	6 15/16	...	9	6	-81.3	-36.3	-11.8
✣5•[1]	SVE	✔Service Experts	NY,Ph	NR	101	7067	Install,svc-climate ctrl sys	30⅜	13	38	20	29¾	5⅛	41639	6 5/16	5¼	5 13/16	...	5	...	-80.1	-39.3	...
6•[2]	SVM	✔ServiceMaster Co	NY,B,Ch,Ph,P	A+	344	95449	Health care sv: cleaning svs	19 11/16	1/16	25½	16	22	10⅛	181683	13	10⅛	12 5/16	2.9	17	...	-43.0	4.1	14.2
7	SVT	✔Servotronics, Inc	AS,B	B-	7	66	Mfr advanced electr products	13 3/16	1/16	13⅜	6⅝	7⅜	4¼	111	5¼	4⅞	5 1/16	...	13	16	-22.1	-2.7	11.3
8	SVEV	✔7-Eleven Inc	NNM	B-	57	16532	Oper 7-Eleven convenience strs	7 11/16	½	3	1 9/16	2¾	1⅝	68640	2	1⅝	1¾	...	11	-14	-6.6	-15.7	-16.9
9•[3]	SEV	✔Seven Seas Petroleum	AS,To	NR	30	5566	Dvp stg:oil&gas acq/exp/dvp	....	....	31¼	4⅝	9¼	1½	42426	2⅝	1½	1¾	...	d	...	-73.8	...	...
10•[4]	SFX	✔SFX Entertainment'A'	NY	NR	250	49869	Prod live entertain't events	....	....	37 9/16	13½	51 11/16	25	231395	37¼	25	36 3/16	...	d	...	-0.8	...	...
11	SGG	✔SGL Carbon AG ADS[52]	NY	NR	4	167	mfr carbon/graphite prod	52⅝	33⅞	44⅛	19¼	28¾	13¼	1995	23¼	17⅝	21¼	...	d	-37	7.6	-19.7	...
12	SH	✔Shandong Huaneng Pwr ADS[53]	NY,Ch,Ph	NR	38	16574	Electric generating, China	14½	6	8⅞	3 7/16	6⅞	3⅜	10464	5 1/16	4 1/16	4 5/16	11.1	5	...	4.6	-18.7	-10.0
13•[5]	SHI	✔Shanghai Petrochemical ADS[54]	NY,P	NR	14	273	Integrated petroleum process'g	49¼	15	17 7/16	5 5/16	25½	7	4480	18⅜	15	15 1/16	2.4	38	-27	80.0	-16.6	-8.1
¶14•[6]	SMS	✔Shared Medical Sys	NY,Ph	A	326	23345	Fin'l/admin hosp computer sv	72⅛	2 7/16	86½	40 1/16	73½	35½	35491	55⅛	43 9/16	50 15/16	1.6	18	14	3.7	2.7	11.1
15	SHRP	✔Sharper Image	NNM	B-	43	3598	Catalog mdsr/retail stores	11	15/16	22⅜	2½	25	8	65533	23½	12	12 11/16	...	14	62	6.8	49.3	13.9
16	SJR	✔Shaw Communications	NY,To	NR	70	29375	Cable T.V. svcs,Canada	16¼	1½	29⅛	14¾	46½	23 15/16	9544	34⅜	30¼	33⅛	0.2	..	...	...	...	...
17	SGR	✔Shaw Group	NY,Ch	B+	80	6455	Fabricator of piping systems	37	2¾	27 15/16	6⅜	25½	8 3/16	10057	25½	20¼	25 5/16	...	17	34	216	2.7	41.3
#18•[7]	SHX	✔Shaw Indus	NY,Ch,P	B-	318	67153	Carpet manufacturer	25½	⅛	24¼	10 13/16	24 5/16	13¼	151202	16	13¼	15½	1.3	9	-2	-35.7	10.6	2.4
19	SHM	✔Sheffield Pharmaceuticals	AS,Ph,P	NR	5	518	Dvlp stge: biomedical R&D	9⅞	1⅛	2½	⅝	5¼	2	22872	5¼	2½	5	...	d	34	111	10.1	7.4
20•[8]	SHC	✔Shell Canada'A'vtg	To,Mo	B	10	4049	Canad'n integrated oil unit	29¼	3¼	27 3/16	20½	34	21	11598	30½	27½	29 5/16	2.5	21	5	29.2	22.2	19.7
21•[7]	SC	✔Shell Transp/Trad ADR[56]	NY,B,Ch,P,Ph	A-	234	43382	Owns 36% Royal Dutch/Shell	47 5/16	15/16	46½	31	53¼	30⅛	55195	50⅝	43	49	2.7	28	-36	36.4	16.9	22.3
¶22•[5]	SHW	✔Sherwin-Williams	NY,B,Ch,Ph,P	A+	547	108512	Large paint & varnish mfr	33⅜	⅝	37⅞	19 7/16	32⅞	18¾	172363	21 15/16	18¾	21	2.3	12	10	-27.1	-7.6	6.4
23	SHD	✔Sherwood Brands 'A'	AS	NR	2	410	Mfr candy,cookies & foods pds	....	....	5 15/16	2	4⅜	1⅜	3400	3½	2⅛	2⅞B	...	d	...	-8.0	...	...
24	WS	Wrrt(Pur1com'A'$7.50)	AS	....	1	12		....	....	⅞	¼	¾	3/16	662	9/16	⅜	¼B	...	..	...	...	...	...
25	SHN	✔Shoney's Inc	NY,Ch,Ph,P	C	41	9158	Restaurant chain	33⅝	½	5⅞	1 5/16	3⅝	1	59287	1 7/16	1	1⅜	...	d	Neg	0.0	-41.9	-35.9
26•[1]	SATH	✔Shop at Home	NNM	NR	51	4549	Retail merchandise via TV	5¼	2	10 11/16	1⅞	30⅛	6⅝	159948	13½	9	9 15/16	...	d	-3	34.7	55.9	...
✣27•[9]	SKO	✔Shopko Stores	NY,Ph,P	NR	250	27947	Genl merchandise discount strs	29 15/16	8⅝	37	21⅜	40¾	18½	52302	23	18½	23	...	7	23	-30.8	15.3	20.9
28	SPNW	✔ShopNow.com Inc	NNM	NR	20	2929	Online marketplace svcs	....	....	....	....	25⅛	10 15/16	67707	25⅛	16⅜	18 15/16	...	..	...	...	...	...
✣29•[10]	SWD	✔Shorewood Packaging[62]	NY	B	129	19030	Print/mfr paperboard packag'g	18 9/16	1 15/16	20½	12⅛	20⅝	11¾	20246	19¼	15 11/16	18 15/16	...	14	13	-7.6	13.5	7.0
30	SHO	✔Showpower Inc[64]	AS	NR	4	390	Temp power/temp control eqp	....	....	17	7	10⅞	3½	7112	7	4⅜	6⅞	...	d	...	-19.1	...	...
31	SHU	✔Shurgard Storage Centers	NY,P	NR	129	9294	Real estate investment trust	30	17¾	29 9/16	23 9/16	27⅞	20 5/16	15682	23 9/16	20 5/16	23 3/16	8.6	16	3	-2.7	-0.8	10.1
#32•[11]	SEBL	✔Siebel Systems	NNM	NR	418	109851	Mkting info softwr sys	12⅜	2⅛	18½	7 9/16	92	15¾	577255	92	67	84	...	..	...	395	132	...
33	SIEB	Siebert Finl	NNM	NR	18	401	Investment co	3⅛	1 5/16	19	2¼	70⅝	8½	25371	18⅜	13¾	14¾	1.1	82	...	58.7	85.7	...
✣34•[9]	SIE	✔Sierra Health Services	NY,Ch,Ph,P	B	144	19802	Owns/operates HMO in Nev	27¾	7/16	27 9/16	15⅞	22⅛	4⅝	68391	9 5/16	4⅝	6 11/16	...	3	-6	-68.3	-25.4	-20.2
#35	SRP	✔Sierra Pacific Resources(New)	NY,B,Ch,P	B+	126	28657	Utility hldg:elec gas,water	27⅝	3 3/16	26 15/16	22 3/16	27	16⅞	74570	18 15/16	16⅞	17⅜	5.8	10	-2	-30.4	0.3	3.5
36	SIF	✔SIFCO Indus	AS	B	28	1368	Precision forg'gs:mach'd parts	24	1	27 3/16	11⅜	14⅞	6 9/16	3155	7 11/16	6⅝	7⅛	2.8	10	NM	-41.4	-10.5	13.8
37	SIG	✔SIGCORP, Inc[66]	NY,Ch,Ph	A	115	6610	Utility:elec/gas,Evansville	30⅛	2¾	36⅞	26⅞	36⅛	22 5/16	9320	26½	22 5/16	22¾	5.5	11	5	-33.2	3.9	10.2
¶38•[12]	SIAL	✔Sigma-Aldrich	NNM	A+	476	71869	Specialty chem prod	41⅛	½	42¾	25¾	35¼	24½	153304	32 3/16	27⅜	30 1/16	1.0	17	9	3.3	-0.3	13.8
39	SIGM	Sigma Designs	NNM	C	19	1265	Encod'g/decod'g add-on cards	22¼	2	4½	⅞	13 3/16	2⅞	108327	13 3/16	6 9/16	11	...	d	79	283	1.6	13.9
40	SGMA	✔Sigmatron International	NNM	NR	12	332	Mfr electronic components	25⅜	5½	12	15/16	8¾	2⅛	2576	8½	6½	6½	...	8	-6	117	-29.4	-3.1
41	SIA	✔Signal Apparel	NY,Ch,P	C	8	1096	Hosiery,knitwear,apparel	24⅜	13/16	3¼	¾	1⅞	¼	19624	1¼	¼	15/16	...	d	39	-31.9	-32.2	-34.7
42	STZ	✔Signal Technology	AS	C	20	2142	Mfr electronic components/sys	10	2 13/16	7	2¼	9⅝	2 9/16	5154	9⅝	4¼	7¼	...	18	-30	170	-1.7	10.6
43	SIGYY	✔Signet Group ADR[67]	NNM	NR	11	2957	Retail jewelry in U.K.&U.S.	148¾	3¾	25⅛	12⅜	32¼	15⅛	680	32¼	28	31¾	1.9	..	...	110	31.3	25.1
44	SLGN	✔Silgan Holdings	NNM	NR	50	9856	Mfr steel/plastic containers	41½	20	36⅝	19⅛	27⅞	11¼	5680	16½	11¼	13⅜	...	8	NM	-51.9	...	...
¶45•[13]	SGI	✔Silicon Graphics	NY,Ch,Ph,P	C	328	84528	Mfr/svc CAE workstations	45⅝	2 11/16	16½	7⅜	20⅞	6⅞	920409	12 13/16	8⅞	9 11/16	...	d	Neg	-24.8	-27.6	-20.8
46	SIMG	✔Silicon Image	NNM	NR	..	...	Dvlp,mkt semiconductors	....	....	....	....	83⅛	12	31596	83⅛	36⅛	70 1/16	...	..	...	...	...	...
47	SSTI	✔Silicon Storage Tech	NNM	NR	40	5882	Flash memory components	20½	2⅝	6½	1¼	46½	2¼	126291	46½	24½	41¼	...	d	Neg	1593	104	...
✣48	SIVB	✔Silicon Valley Bancshrs	NNM	B	142	12374	Commercial bkg,California	29⅞	1	39	10 5/16	55¼	15	48752	55¼	36	49½	...	33	20	191	45.7	49.2
✣49•[5]	SVGI	✔Silicon Valley Group	NNM	↓C	123	20753	Mfr equip for semicond'r ind	49⅜	4	27⅞	6⅝	20⅛	9⅜	60166	20⅛	12 11/16	17¾	...	d	Neg	39.2	-4.1	-3.0

Uniform Footnote Explanations-See Page 4. Other: [1]Ph:Cycle 2. [2]Ph:Cycle 1. [3]ASE:Cycle 3. [4]ASE,CBOE,Ph:Cycle 1. [5]CBOE:Cycle 3. [6]P:Cycle 1. [7]CBOE:Cycle 2. [8]To:Cycle 2. [9]Ph:Cycle 3. [10]P:Cycle 3. [11]ASE,CBOE:Cycle 2. [12]CBOE:Cycle 1. [13]ASE:Cycle 2. [51]®$1.07,'96. [52]Ea ADS rep 0.33 Ord Shr, DM 5. [53]Ea ADS rep 50 Ord'N' shrs,par RMB 1.00. [54]Ea ADS rep 100 Cl'H' shrs,RMB 1 par. [55]Stk dstr of Corus Entmt Inc. [56]Each N.Y. shr rep 6 ord shrs. [57]Proportionate shr of group B/S. [58]If com'A'exceeds $10.05 for 20 trad dasy. [59]Special $4 deb dstr. [60]Fiscal Feb'97 & prior. [61]49 Wks Jan'98. [62]Chesapeake Corp plan acq,$17.25. [63]Spec divd. [64]GE Energy Services plan acq,$7. [65]Pfd in $M. [66]Plan comb w/Indiana Energy,1.33 new. [67]Ea Spons ADR rep 30 ord,10p.

Index (Splits ◆)	Cash Divs. Ea. Yr. Since	Dividends: Latest Payment Period $	Date	Ex. Div.	Total $ So Far 1999	Ind. Rate	Paid 1998	Financial Position Mil-$ Cash& Equiv.	Curr. Assets	Curr. Liab.	Balance Sheet Date	Capitalization Lg Trm Debt Mil-$	Shs. 000 Pfd.	Com.	Earnings $ Per Shr. Years End	1995	1996	1997	1998	1999	Last 12 Mos.	Interim Earnings Period	$ per Shr. 1998	1999	Index
1	1987	Q1.25	2-1-00	1-10	5.00	5.00	5.00	Cv into 1.3219 com,$75.65				....	413	...	Dc	b1.10	...	...	....	....	....				1
2	....	None Since Public			...	Nil	....	0.53	35.1	24.7	8-31-99	22.0	1	7644	Fb	...	vd0.20	v0.08	v0.24	....	0.25	6 Mo Aug	v0.08	v□0.09	2
3◆	....	None Since Public			...	Nil	....	1.49	56.7	24.9	9-26-99	15.6	...	22305	Dc	v□0.26	v0.39	v0.51	v0.63	....	0.22	9 Mo Sep	v0.47	v0.06	3
4◆	1973	Div Postponed 10-6-99			0.36	Nil	0.34½	206	1092	788	9-30-99	4111	...	272061	Dc	□v0.86	v[51]1.08	v□1.47	v1.31	E0.79	0.78	9 Mo Sep	v1.08	v∆0.55	4
5	....	None Since Public			...	Nil	....	16.4	141	41.8	9-30-99	157	...	18183	Dc	pvd0.08	v0.74	v1.06	v1.37	E1.08	0.83	9 Mo Sep	v1.07	v0.53	5
6◆	1962	Q0.09	1-31-00	1-12	0.36	0.36	0.33	76.9	927	766	9-30-99	1688	...	310498	Dc	vp0.39	vp0.46	pv0.55	v0.64	E0.71	0.54	9 Mo Sep	v0.48	v0.38	6
7◆	....	8%Stk	7-1-96	5-29	...	Nil	....	0.82	15.3	2.68	9-30-99	6.77	...	2405	Dc	0.12	v0.52	v0.36	v0.48	....	0.38	9 Mo Sep	v0.27	v□0.17	7
8	....	None Since Public			...	Nil	....	4.09	411	729	9-30-99	2205	...	409978	Dc	v∆0.40	v0.20	v0.16	∆v0.12	....	0.16	9 Mo Sep	v∆0.11	v∆0.15	8
9	....	None Since Public			...	Nil	....	24.2	44.7	6.93	9-30-99	110	...	37833	Dc	vd0.23	vd0.17	vd0.24	vd2.49	....	d2.55	9 Mo Sep	vd0.10	vd0.16	9
10◆	....	None Since Public			...	Nil	....	549	772	358	9-30-99	1391	...	±66383	Dc	...	...	vpd0.55	vd1.83	....	d0.72	9 Mo Sep	v±d1.38	v±d0.27	10
11	1997	0.321	5-4-98	4-21	...	Nil	0.321	43.7	685	414	12-31-98	....	...	21095	Dc	1.80	v1.95	v1.84	vd2.51	....	d2.51				11
12	1995	0.181	9-24-99	9-1	0.483	0.48	0.362	188	429	97.8	12-31-98	77.2	...	±4304716	Dc	0.92	v1.02	v0.96	v0.81	....	0.81				12
13	1994	0.362	7-6-99	5-11	0.362	0.36	0.724	316	862	709	12-31-98	434	...	±7200000	Dc	3.90	v1.80	v1.20	v0.40	....	0.40				13
14	1977	Q0.21	1-17-00	12-29	0.84	0.84	0.84	65.5	466	230	9-30-99	178	...	26899	Dc	v1.64	v1.93	v2.37	v2.62	E2.85	2.89	9 Mo Sep	v1.93	v2.20	14
15	....	None Since Public			...	Nil	....	7.33	85.7	42.4	10-31-99	2.40	...	12009	Ja	0.05	vd0.53	v0.07	v0.51	....	0.91	9 Mo Oct	vd0.57	vd0.17	15
16	1984	gS0.04	12-1-99	10-29	gh[55]0.08	0.08	g0.08	....	97.0	316	j8-31-99	1337	12700	±89804	Au	...	0.91	v0.24	vd0.01	v0.23	j0.23				16
17	....	None Since Public			...	Nil	....	3.74	251	121	8-31-99	91.7	...	★14736	Au	0.50	0.94	v1.18	v1.49	v1.47	1.47				17
18	1972	0.05	11-26-99	11-10	0.10	0.20	0.07½	25.9	1144	588	10-02-99	769	...	133785	Dc	v□0.47	v0.25	v0.22	v0.16	E1.70	1.48	9 Mo Sep	vd0.05	v1.27	18
19	....	None Since Public			...	Nil	....	0.99	1.30	1.62	9-30-99	2.00	13	27296	Dc	d0.90	vd0.65	vd0.80	vd0.85	....	d0.12	9 Mo Sep	vd0.88	vd0.15	19
20◆	1965	gQ0.18	12-15-99	11-26	g0.72	0.72	g0.72	d50.0	1324	731	j6-30-99	433	.1	289368	Dc	1.55	v1.77	v1.69	v1.49	....	j1.38	9 Mo Sep	v1.09	v0.98	20
21◆	1898	0.542	11-5-99	9-29	1.337	1.34	1.31¼	1094	9040	12456	[57]12-31-98	2413	12000	9943510	Dc	1.49	v1.99	v1.74	v0.05	E1.75	0.51	9 Mo Sep	v0.99	v1.45	21
22◆	1979	Q0.12	11-15-99	10-28	0.48	0.48	0.45	5.01	1665	1309	9-30-99	624	...	165876	Dc	v1.17	v1.33	v1.50	v1.57	E1.78	1.74	9 Mo Sep	v1.29	v1.46	22
23	....	None Since Public			...	Nil	....	1.08	19.7	11.6	10-31-99	1.30	...	±3700	Jl	...	...	p0.12	v0.28	vd0.34	d0.60	3 Mo Oct	v0.33	v0.07	23
24	....	Terms&trad. basis should be checked in detail						Wrrts expire 5-6-2003				....	...	891	Jl	...	...	...	....	....	....	Callable at 10¢[58]			24
25	....	[59]. . .	8-3-88	8-4	...	Nil	....	15.3	86.2	127	8-01-99	375	...	49480	Oc	0.60	v1.14	vd0.74	v□d2.18	....	d0.83	40 Wk Jul	v□d1.93	vd0.58	25
26	....	None Since Public			...	Nil	....	22.5	49.0	29.0	9-30-99	75.8	138	30397	Je	vd0.14	vd0.14	v0.12	v0.09	vd0.14	d0.16	3 Mo Sep	vd0.01	vd0.03	26
27	....	0.11	9-15-96	8-28	...	Nil	....	34.0	1006	942	10-30-99	444	...	30396	Ja	1.20	[60]1.40	‡v[61]1.71	v2.10	....	3.53	9 Mo Oct	v0.57	v□2.00	27
28	....	None Since Public			...	Nil	....	6.47	11.2	20.0	6-30-99	6.17	p...	★33255	Dc	...	...	...	pvd1.71	....	....	6 Mo Jun	n/a	pvd1.14	28
29◆	....	[63]2.167	7-2-91	7-3	...	Nil	....	7.73	153	102	10-30-99	262	...	27367	Ap	0.78	v□0.74	v□0.84	v0.95	v□1.25	1.32	6 Mo Oct	v□0.62	v0.69	29
30	....	None Since Public			...	Nil	....	3.27	7.64	4.71	9-30-99	2.29	...	3422	Dc	...	...	pv0.34	vpd0.18	....	d0.21	9 Mo Sep	vp0.05	v0.02	30
31	1994	Q0.50	11-22-99	11-4	1.99	2.00	1.95	Total Assets $1263M			9-30-99	547	4000	±29175	Dc	±v1.43	v±1.39	±v1.40	±v1.39	....	1.43	9 Mo Sep	v±1.05	v□±1.09	31
32◆	....	None Since Public			...	Nil	....	671	917	209	9-30-99	300	...	p192762	Dc	pvNil	v0.04	vd0.02	v0.22	E0.51	0.45	9 Mo Sep	v0.11	v0.35	32
33◆	1998	Q0.04	10-29-99	10-19	0.16	0.16	0.10½	Total Assets $30.25M			9-30-99	....	...	22883	Dc	p0.11	vp0.13	v0.12	v0.20	....	0.18	9 Mo Sep	v0.15	v0.13	33
34◆	....	None Since Public			...	Nil	....	111	332	353	9-30-99	281	...	26876	Dc	v0.80	v1.15	v0.89	v1.43	E2.17	0.71	9 Mo Sep	v1.34	v0.62	34
35	1951	Q0.25	2-1-00	1-12	1.00	1.00	1.45	28.8	475	1087	9-30-99	1670	[65]p240	78414	Dc	v1.58	v1.56	v1.65	v1.64	E1.70	1.49	9 Mo Sep	v1.56	v1.41	35
36	1996	Q0.05	11-11-99	10-26	0.20	0.20	0.20	1.49	49.3	19.1	9-30-99	13.0	...	5194	Sp	0.55	1.09	v1.36	v1.78	v0.72	0.72				36
37◆	1944	Q0.31	12-20-99	11-17	1.24	1.24	1.21	11.6	152	221	9-30-99	285	194	23631	Dc	v∆1.63	v1.83	v1.95	v2.12	....	2.03	12 Mo Sep	v2.11	v2.03	37
38◆	1970	Q0.07¾	1-3-00	12-13	0.29	0.31	0.28	90.8	858	137	9-30-99	0.36	...	100894	Dc	v1.30	v1.45	v1.62	v1.64	E1.76	1.71	9 Mo Sep	v1.25	v1.32	38
39	....	None Since Public			...	Nil	....	21.8	42.9	17.2	10-31-99	0.35	[65]1	15929	Ja	d1.81	v0.14	vd0.50	vd0.21	....	d0.02	9 Mo Oct	vd0.10	v0.09	39
40	....	None Since Public			...	Nil	....	0.15	40.6	16.7	10-31-99	23.3	...	2881	Ap	0.69	v0.86	v1.11	v0.18	v0.59	0.78	6 Mo Oct	v0.15	v0.34	40
41	....	0.03	1-4-88	12-15	...	Nil	....	0.44	11.5	100	10-02-99	27.9	[65]53	44869	Dc	vd3.80	vd2.91	vd2.39	vd1.22	....	d1.44	9 Mo Sep	vd0.50	vd0.72	41
42	....	None Since Public			...	Nil	....	5.67	33.9	13.9	9-30-99	5.73	...	7672	Dc	vd0.04	v0.29	v0.04	vd0.97	....	0.41	9 Mo Sep	vd1.02	v0.36	42
43◆	1999	0.121	11-22-99	10-13	0.599	0.60	....	25.9	557	152	j1-31-98	185	12323	1686966	Ja	d3.90	13.60	v0.72	n/a	....	....	9 Mo Oct	v0.30	v0.59	43
44	....	None Since Public			...	Nil	....	6.31	583	446	9-30-99	894	...	17552	Dc	p□vd0.82	p□v1.49	□v2.40	v2.30	....	1.65	9 Mo Sep	v1.92	v1.27	44
45	....	None Since Public			...	Nil	....	538	1527	1055	9-30-99	388	18	183803	Je	1.28	v0.65	v0.43	vd2.47	v0.28	d0.65	3 Mo Sep	vd0.24	vd1.17	45
46	....	None Since Public			...	Nil	....	12.6	14.8	6.09	6-30-99	0.77	p...	★25137	Dc	...	...	...	pvd0.46	....	....	6 Mo Jun	n/a	pvd0.23	46
47	....	None Since Public			...	Nil	....	4.27	57.1	37.6	9-30-99	....	...	24724	Dc	v0.32	v0.49	vd0.30	vd0.77	....	d0.71	9 Mo Sep	vd0.47	vd0.41	47
48◆	....	5%Stk	5-25-92	5-12	...	Nil	....	Total Deposits $3404.80M			9-30-99	38.5	...	★22327	Dc	v0.99	v1.11	v1.36	v1.38	....	1.52	9 Mo Sep	v1.16	v1.30	48
49	....	None Since Public			...	Nil	....	151	504	131	6-30-99	5.29	...	33065	Sp	1.57	2.07	v0.08	vd0.42	vPd0.77	d0.77				49

◆Stock Splits & Divs By Line Reference Index [3]3-for-2,'97,'98. [4]2-for-1,'96. [6]3-for-2,'96,'97,'98. [7]Adj to 8%,'96. [10]3-for-2,'99. [20]3-for-1,'97. [21]3-for-1,'97. [22]2-for-1,'97. [29]3-for-2,'98. [32]2-for-1,'96,'98,'99. [33]1-for-7 REVERSE,'96:4-for-1,'98. [34]3-for-2,'98. [37]3-for-2,'97. [38]2-for-1,'97. [43]1-for-10 REVERSE,'97. [48]2-for-1,'98.

¶ S&P 500
# MidCap 400
✣ SmallCap 600
• Options

Index	Ticker	Name of Issue (Call Price of Pfd. Stocks)	Market	Com. Rank. & Pfd. Rating	Inst. Hold Cos	Inst. Hold Shs. (000)	Principal Business	Price Range 1971-97 High	1971-97 Low	1998 High	1998 Low	1999 High	1999 Low	December, 1999 Dec. Sales in 100s	Last Sale Or Bid High	Low	Last	%Div Yield	P-E Ratio	EPS 5 Yr Growth	% Annualized Total Return 12 Mo	36 Mo	60 Mo
1	SSRI	✓Silver Standard Resources	NSC	NR	5	374	Silver exploration/dvlp'mt	6¼	2⅝	5 9/16	⅝	2 1/16	¾	10616	1⅜	1 1/16	1 5/16	...	d	Neg	68.0	-32.4	...
2	SVR	✓Silverleaf Resorts	NY	NR	25	1665	Dvlp/market timeshare resorts	26¼	14⅝	29⅛	6 13/16	10⅝	5 9/16	6977	7 5/16	6 11/16	7⅛	...	5	90	-23.5	...	...
3	SSSW	✓SilverStream Software	NNM	NR	35	1958	Dvlp internet mgmt software	....	....	....	....	123	16	23261	123	79	119	...	..	...	...	...	...
4•[1]	SPG	✓Simon Property Group[53]	NY,Ph,P	NR	325	113648	Real estate investment trust	34⅝	21⅛	34⅞	25 13/16	30 15/16	20 7/16	74320	24⅜	20 7/16	22 15/16	8.8	22	5	-13.1	-3.1	5.7
5	Pr B	6.50%'B' cm Cv Pfd(105[54])	NY	↑BBB	13	3279		....	....	87½	79	84	60½	337	70	60½	60½	10.7	..	...	...	...	...
✣6•[2]	SMPS	✓Simpson Indus	NNM	B+	106	9663	Machined metal auto parts	15 11/16	9/16	15⅜	8¾	12⅝	8½	12773	12⅛	9 11/16	11¼	3.6	11	1	20.6	4.9	8.1
✣7	SSD	✓Simpson Manufacturing	NY	NR	137	5236	Building:hardware,materials	42	9⅝	43	25¼	54 15/16	32¾	2528	44½	40½	43¾	...	15	38	16.9	23.9	32.4
8	SMU	✓Simula Inc	NY,Ch,P	NR	14	729	Mfr occupant safety systems	25¼	2¾	18½	5	8¼	4 7/16	15059	7⅜	5 9/16	5 7/16	...	d	Neg	-25.0	-26.2	-18.3
9•[3]	SBGI	✓Sinclair Broadcast Group'A'	NNM	NR	155	39216	Own/oper T.V. stations	24⅛	8	31⅛	6¾	21½	7 15/16	160088	12 9/16	9⅞	12 3/16	...	d	Neg	-37.6	-2.0	...
10	SEW	✓Singer Co N.V.	NY,Ch,Ph,P	D	29	261	Mfr sewing machines/electr prd	39¼	8	11 3/16	3⅝	5⅞	½	73003	13/16	½	½	...	d	Neg	-87.3	-71.7	-55.5
11•[4]	SIPX	✓SIPEX Corp	NNM	NR	118	17318	Mfrs integrated circuits	40⅛	4¾	42	16⅜	36¼	8 15/16	82186	27	12 11/16	24 9/16	...	36	NM	-30.1	15.1	...
12	CDRD	✓Sirius Satellite Radio	NNM	NR	87	7942	Dvlp stge:oper radio sys	25¼	2⅝	44	11½	48½	19½	80282	48½	24¼	44½	...	d	-48	29.9	121	...
13	SWW	✓SITEL Corp	NY	NR	72	20195	Telemarketing Services	25⅝	3⅜	13 9/16	1¾	7 11/16	2	61874	7 11/16	5 9/16	7	...	d	-29	187	-21.1	...
14	SIZ	✓Sizeler Property Inv	NY,Ch,Ph,P	NR	21	1642	Real estate investment trust	22	7⅜	11⅜	8	9 7/16	7¾	2345	8½	8	8⅛	10.8	25	-7	2.9	3.7	4.8
15	SZ	✓Sizzler International	NY,P	NR	44	9496	Chicken/steak franch'd restr	18⅞	2	4	1½	3 3/16	1 11/16	16594	2⅞	2 7/16	2½	...	9	NM	11.1	-4.6	-15.6
16	SJW	✓SJW Corp	AS	A–	39	302	Water service in California	60½	6¾	71	48½	121	57¼	767	121	118½	120¼	2.0	25	9	111	42.1	36.3
17•[5]	SKM	✓SK Telecom [59]ADS	NY,Ch	NR	..	...	Wireless telecommun svc, Korea	17 5/16	4 7/16	11½	4 15/16	40⅛	8 15/16	167157	40⅛	21⅝	38⅜	s0.0	..	-5	300	49.8	...
18	SKX	✓Skechers U.S.A. Cl'A'	NY	NR	17	1527	Dgn/mkt footwear	....	....	....	....	12⅜	3 5/16	22018	4⅜	3 3/16	3 13/16	...	10	NM	...	...	...
19	NZSKY	Sky Network Television ADS[61]	NNM	NR	7	384	Pay TV operator,New Zealand	17	14⅝	16¼	9⅞	19⅛	13⅝	37	16	14⅝	16B	...	..	...	14.3	...	...
✣20•[6]	SKY	✓Skyline Corp	NY,B,Ch,P,Ph	A	100	5093	Mobile homes,recreatn'l veh	74	8½	34⅞	24 3/16	32½	21⅛	4046	25¼	21⅛	23½	3.1	10	12	-25.8	0.6	7.1
21	SKYM	✓SkyMall Inc	NNM	NR	15	534	In-flight sales catalog	10¾	4⅛	48	1⅞	31¼	4½	52168	11	7	7⅜	...	d	...	-64.7	-6.0	...
✣22•[7]	SKYW	✓SkyWest Inc	NNM	B	223	14664	Regional airline service	20½	1⅛	34¼	13⅜	40 9/16	19⅝	50230	29½	21⅛	28	0.4	14	44	-14.0	60.5	36.4
23	SLG	✓SL Green Realty	NY	NR	138	21286	Real estate investment trust	27	22½	28	17⅛	22 5/16	17½	27414	22	20	21¾	6.7	16	...	7.7	...	...
24	PrA	8.00% Cv[62]'PIERS'[63]([64]25.889)	NY	NR	12	1704		....	....	26⅝	21⅛	24	19¾	4935	23⅞	21⅞	23¾	8.4	..	...	...	...	...
25	SL	✓SL Industries	NY,B,Ph	B	32	2286	Specialty ind'l prod & svs	16¼	7/16	15⅜	9½	15½	11⅜	1178	12½	11½	11⅝	0.9	21	1	-8.1	15.3	21.8
✣26	SLI	✓SLI Inc	NY	NR	173	16707	Mfr miniature light prd	29 13/16	5 9/16	41⅞	9¼	35	8 5/16	73666	13 9/16	10	13 9/16	...	11	50	-51.1	-20.9	...
¶27•[8]	SLM	✓SLM Holding	NY,B,Ch,P	A	521	144211	Student loan fin'g program	47 3/16	2⅜	51⅜	27½	53 15/16	39½	94361	50 7/16	41 11/16	42¼	1.5	14	18	-10.8	18.5	38.1
28	SWLDY	✓Smallworldwide ADS[67]	NNM	NR	13	2050	Dvp client/server softr	29¼	10⅝	36½	5¾	20⅞	5¼	8321	11¼	7¾	8¼	...	d	Neg	-34.0	-11.4	...
29	SMF	✓Smart & Final Inc	NY,Ch,Ph,P	B	50	9657	Oper food svc warehouse strs	26	10 3/16	20¼	7⅛	12⅝	6	6805	7¼	6	7¼	...	d	Neg	-24.2	-29.7	-11.4
30	SMDK	✓SmartDisk Corp	NNM	NR	..	...	Digital data transfer pds	....	....	....	....	63 11/16	13	25399	39¼	25¾	32¾	...	d	...	...	...	...
31	SMV.A	✓Smedvig Cl'A'ADS[69]	NY,Ch	NR	3	364	Offshore drilling & oil svcs	34	21⅝	25½	7⅛	13⅛	7½	170	12	11 1/16	11⅞B	3.5	13	...	45.8	-16.1	...
32	SMV.B	✓ Cl'B' ADS[70]	NY,Ch	NR	1	19	Offshore drilling & oil svcs	34¾	18¾	23¼	5¾	11¾	6¼	121	10½	9 1/16	10½	3.9	11	...	47.5	-17.2	...
✣33	AOS	✓Smith (A.O.)	NY,Ph	B+	171	10247	Mfr elec mtrs/heat'g&fluid sys	28 15/16	1 1/16	35⅞	15 13/16	32	18 13/16	11192	22¼	18 13/16	21⅞	2.2	11	4	-9.1	5.2	8.3
34	SMC.A	Cl'A'[71]	AS,Ch	B+	16	284		28¾	1⅜	35 11/16	16⅜	31½	19 3/16	28	22	19 3/16	20⅝B	2.3	10	4	-10.9	3.9	8.4
35	SRW	✓Smith(Charles E.)Res Rlty	NY,Ch,Ph	NR	121	14136	Real estate investment trust	35¾	21¾	35¾	28 5/16	35⅞	28⅛	7010	35⅝	31¼	35⅝	6.2	12	24	17.5	13.9	14.9
#36•[9]	SII	✓Smith Intl	NY,B,Ch,P,Ph	B–	333	37226	Varied line drill,boring eq	87⅞	1¼	64½	17¼	52 1/16	23 3/16	132880	50⅛	36¼	49 11/16	...	..	-7	97.3	3.5	32.1
37	SNN	Smith & Nephew plc ADS[73]	NY	NR	..	...	Mfr medical/healthcare prd	....	....	....	....	34⅝	32¾	138	34⅝	32¾	33½B	...	23	...	...	...	...
✣38•[9]	SFD	✓Smithfield Foods	NY	B	244	20436	Fresh pork,processed meats	35⅝	1/32	36⅜	14 11/16	34 1/16	20	31083	26	23 3/16	24	...	9	38	-29.2	8.1	8.5
39•[7]	SBH	✓SmithKline Beecham ADS[74]	NY,Ch,P	NR	513	106271	Ethical drugs:healthcare prod	53⅝	9¼	71⅞	48 1/16	76⅜	56 1/16	87945	72 3/16	58⅞	64⅛	1.5	34	34	-6.3	25.9	32.6
40	SMTI	SMTEK Intl	NSC,P,Ph	C	5	6	Mfrs printed circuit boards	261⅝	6⅜	18¾	6⅞	12	3	3272	5¼	3	3⅞	...	d	31	-34.4	-34.1	-29.3
#41	SJM.A	✓Smucker (J.M.) Cl'A'	NY,Ch,Ph	A–	107	5240	Preserves: jellies & fillings	39	½	28 3/16	20⅝	25¾	18⅜	3685	20 5/16	18⅜	19½	3.1	15	3	-19.1	6.0	-1.6
42	SJM.B	✓ Cl'B' non-vtg	NY	A–	63	7778		35⅛	15¼	27¾	20 1/16	24	15 9/16	3806	17	15 9/16	16¼	3.7	12	3	-24.2	3.3	-3.2
43•[6]	SSCC	✓Smurfit-Stone Container	NNM,Ch	NR	290	120098	Produce paperboard & pkg prd	23⅛	9	22	9¾	25¾	14 13/16	381022	25⅝	19⅜	24½	...	d	Neg	54.9	15.1	7.6
¶44•[3]	SNA	✓Snap-On Inc	NY,B,Ch,P,Ph	B+	333	42666	Hand tools: auto/ind'l maint	46 5/16	2 7/16	46 7/16	25½	37 13/16	26 7/16	58692	31⅛	26 7/16	26 9/16	3.5	11	-45	-21.5	-7.1	6.3
✣45	SNC	✓Snyder Communications(SNC)	NY,Ch,Ph	NR	205	39394	Provides marketing svcs	38 15/16	17	54 3/16	26⅝	41	11¾	113048	21 3/16	12 1/16	19¼	...	..	...	...	...	...
46	STX	Snyder Comm $1.68 'STRYPES'	NY	NR	2	177	Struct Yld Prd Exch For Stk	35¼	26	47⅛	25½	36	14¾	4759	26	17 13/16	23¾	7.1	..	...	-17.8	...	...
47	SQM	✓Sociedad Quimica Y Minera ADS[78]	NY,Ch,P	NR	85	3253	Produce natural nitrates	67¾	23	47	20	42⅜	27¼	9907	31¾	28 1/16	31 9/16	3.2	12	24	-3.3	-14.0	4.0
48	SQM.A	Cl'A' ADS[79]	NY	NR	14	176		....	....	....	....	40½	26	322	32	28	31½	3.2	12	24	...	...	...
49	SDH	✓Sodexho Marriott Svcs	NY,Ph	NR	122	15176	Food svc/facilities mgmt	....	....	33⅜	24	28⅜	12⅞	23802	16 1/16	12⅞	13	...	16	NM	-52.8	...	...
50•[10]	SOFN	✓Softnet Systems	NNM	C	72	5799	Electronic info/mgmt sys	16⅜	¾	21	5 9/16	69½	14½	117433	30½	23½	25⅛	...	d	-29	44.6	76.6	26.9

Uniform Footnote Explanations-See Page 4. Other: [1]ASE:Cycle 2. [2]P:Cycle 2. [3]ASE:Cycle 3. [4]CBOE,Ph:Cycle 3. [5]CBOE:Cycle 3. [6]CBOE:Cycle 2. [7]CBOE:Cycle 1. [8]ASE,CBOE:Cycle 1. [9]Ph:Cycle 1. [10]CBOE,P,Ph:Cycle 2. [51]Fiscal Sep'95 & prior. [52]15 Mo Dec'96. [53]Trades w/1sh SPG Realty Consultants. [54]Fr 9-24-2003. [55]®$1.67,'96. [56]50% owned by Semi-Tech Ltd. [57]7 Mo Dec'96:Fiscal May'96 earn $.21. [58]Incl redemption of stk purch rt. [59]Ea ADS rep 0.011 com, 5,000 won. [60]Approx. [61]Ea ADS rep 10 Ord Shrs. [62]Preferred Inc Equity Red Shs. [63]Anytime to preserve'REIT'status. [64]Fr 7-15-2003,in com re-spec cond. [65]Fiscal Nov'96 & prior. [66]12 Mo Dec'97:Fiscal Nov'97 earned $0.73. [67]Ea ADS rep 1 Ord, par .01p. [68]12 Mo Jun'96. [69]Ea ADS rep 1 Cl'A'Ord,NOK 3. [70]Ea ADS rep 1 Cl'B'Ord,NOK3(nonvtg re-spec cond). [71]Cv into common shr for shr. [72]Incl current amts. [73]Ea ADS rep 10 Ord,10 pence. [74]Each ADS rep 5 Ord,25p. [75]Stk dstr of Circle.com. [76]Stk dstr of Ventiv Health Inc & Circle.com. [77]Re-spec cond. [78]Ea ADS rep 10 Sr'B'shrs,no-par. [79]Ea ADS rep 10 Sr'A'shrs. [80]To be determined. [81]Fiscal Dec'96 & prior. [82]22 Wk Aug'98.

Splits ◆ Index	Cash Divs. Ea. Yr. Since	Dividends: Latest Payment Period $	Date	Ex. Div.	Total $ So Far 1999	Ind. Rate	Paid 1998	Financial Position Mil-$ Cash& Equiv.	Curr. Assets	Curr. Liab.	Balance Sheet Date	Capitalization Lg Trm Debt Mil-$	Shs. 000 Pfd.	Com.	Earnings $ Per Shr. Years End	1995	1996	1997	1998	1999	Last 12 Mos.	Interim Earnings Period	$ per Shr. 1998	1999	Index
1	....	None Since Public			...	Nil	....	1.03	1.18	0.20	j6-30-99	....	...	p19532	Dc	[51]d0.19	[52]d0.24	vd0.22	vd0.74	....	d0.47	6 Mo Jun	vd0.31	vd0.04	1
2	....	None Since Public			...	Nil	....	Total Assets $438M			9-30-99	229	...	12889	Dc	v0.01	pv0.64	v1.21	v1.45	....	1.53	9 Mo Sep	v1.14	v1.22	2
3	....	None Since Public			...	Nil	....	56.4	63.1	7.93	p9-30-99	0.62	...	★17562	Dc	...	...	...	vpd1.33	....	....	6 Mo Jun	n/a	vpd0.83	3
4	1994	Q0.50½	11-19-99	11-3	2.02	2.02	2.02	Total Assets $13708.7M			9-30-99	8544	4904	±173481	Dc	□±v1.08	v□±1.01	v±1.08	vΔ1.02	....	1.03	9 Mo Sep	vΔ0.67	v□0.68	4
5	1998	Q1.62½	12-31-99	12-15	6.50	6.50	1.751	Cv into 2.586 com				....	★4844	...	Dc	...	...	...	....	....	....				5
6◆	1972	Q0.10	12-16-99	11-30	0.40	0.40	0.40	5.72	122	87.1	9-30-99	106	...	18009	Dc	v0.85	v0.97	v0.55	v0.80	....	1.03	9 Mo Sep	v0.63	v0.86	6
7	....	None Since Public			...	Nil	....	44.1	169	35.8	9-30-99	2.58	...	12016	Dc	v1.23	v[55]1.68	v2.17	v2.58	....	3.01	9 Mo Sep	v1.93	v2.36	7
8◆	....	None Since Public			...	Nil	....	3.67	71.9	51.6	9-30-99	45.5	...	10376	Dc	v0.31	v□d0.76	vd0.38	vd2.80	....	d1.95	9 Mo Sep	vd0.65	v0.20	8
9◆	....	None Since Public			...	Nil	....	8.36	1043	295	9-30-99	2339	3450	±96986	Dc	v□±0.08	v±0.02	□vd0.10	v□d0.17	....	d0.34	9 Mo Sep	v□d0.03	vd0.20	9
10	1992	Div postponed 3-20-98			...	Nil	0.05	File bankruptcy Chapt 11			1-03-98	278	75	[56]51053	Dc	v1.64	v0.56	vd4.67	Pvd4.17	....	d4.71	6 Mo Jun	vd0.40	vd0.94	10
11◆	....	None Since Public			...	Nil	....	16.3	54.0	10.0	10-02-99	....	...	18103	Dc	vd0.19	v0.29	v0.71	v1.06	....	0.69	9 Mo Sep	v0.74	v0.37	11
12	....	None Paid			...	Nil	....	474	474	139	9-30-99	★471	2816	★26820	Dc	vd0.23	vd0.29	vd5.08	vd4.79	....	d4.07	9 Mo Sep	vd3.51	vd2.79	12
13◆	....	None Since Public			...	Nil	....	12.1	192	111	9-30-99	146	...	67650	Dc	vd0.29	‡v[57]0.16	v0.04	v□d0.01	....	d0.07	9 Mo Sep	v□d0.03	vd0.09	13
14	1987	Q0.22	12-2-99	11-23	0.88	0.88	†[58]0.89	Total Assets $285.90M			9-30-99	294	...	7887	Dc	0.31	v□0.27	v0.30	v0.33	....	0.32	9 Mo Sep	v0.24	v0.23	14
15	....	0.04	10-12-95	9-26	...	Nil	....	21.0	30.0	24.7	10-17-99	24.8	...	28776	Ap	0.24	vd4.99	v0.02	v0.19	v0.26	0.29	24 Wk Oct	v0.13	v0.16	15
16	1932	Q0.60	12-1-99	11-4	2.40	2.40	2.34	1.67	20.2	19.2	9-30-99	90.0	...	3045	Dc	3.55	v5.75	v4.80	v5.05	....	4.78	12 Mo Sep	v4.87	v4.78	16
17◆	1997	[60]0.007		12-29	s0.004	0.01	0.004	654	1196	1020	12-31-98	984	...	6426	Dc	0.44	0.43	v0.12	v0.22	....	0.22				17
18	....	None Since Public			...	Nil	....	4.53	139	75.4	9-30-99	2.99	...	±34814	Dc	vΔpd0.04	pv±0.04	pv±0.24	pv±0.50	....	0.40	9 Mo Sep	pv±0.62	pv±0.52	18
19	....	None Since Public			...	Nil	....	1.12	41.1	78.5	j12-31-97	81.6	...	365621	Dc	d0.19	d0.50	vNil	....	....	Nil	No Recent Reporting			19
20	1960	Q0.18	1-3-00	12-15	0.72	0.72	0.60	112	173	48.6	8-31-99	....	...	9000	My	1.38	1.84	v2.07	v2.10	v2.80	2.38	6 Mo Nov	v1.49	v1.07	20
21	....	None Since Public			...	Nil	....	0.95	11.8	20.7	9-30-99	....	...	10423	Dc	pv0.14	pv0.38	v0.30	v0.30	....	d1.00	9 Mo Sep	v0.08	vd1.22	21
22◆	1987	Q0.03	1-14-00	12-29	0.12	0.12	0.11	183	233	83.5	9-30-99	56.4	...	24557	Mr	v0.21	v0.50	v1.04	v1.69	....	1.96	6 Mo Sep	v0.91	v1.18	22
23	1997	Q0.36¼	1-14-00	12-29	1.40	1.45	1.40	Total Assets $1031.6M			6-30-99	329	4600	24192	Dc	...	pv0.72	pv1.02	v□1.22	....	1.33	9 Mo Sep	v□0.94	v□1.05	23
24	1998	Q0.50	1-14-00	12-29	2.00	2.00	0.244	Cv into 1.0215 com				....	4600	...	Dc	...	...	...	....	....	....	Mand Red 4-15-2008 $25			24
25	1973	S0.05	11-23-99	10-28	0.10	0.10	0.08	....	59.0	31.0	10-31-99	35.5	...	5610	Jl	0.62	0.59	v1.30	v0.90	v0.92	0.56	3 Mo Oct	v0.21	vd0.15	25
26◆	....	None Since Public			...	Nil	....	10.3	392	238	10-03-99	144	...	35812	Dc	0.41	[65]0.55	[66]0.69	v1.10	....	1.22	9 Mo Sep	v0.77	v0.89	26
27◆	1983	Q0.16	12-17-99	12-1	0.61	0.64	0.57	Total Assets $43807M			9-30-99	5675	...	159083	Dc	Δ□v1.51	□2.12	v□2.80	v2.95	E3.00	2.85	9 Mo Sep	v2.29	v2.19	27
28	....	None Since Public			...	Nil	....	No Recent Finls				0.52	p...	★7063	Je	0.24	p[68]0.39	Pv0.19	Pv0.51	Pvd0.78	d0.85	3 Mo Sep	vd0.17	vd0.24	28
29	1991	Div Postponed 2-17-99			0.05	Nil	0.20	26.3	256	131	10-10-99	141	...	29137	Dc	v0.88	v1.15	v0.29	□vd0.33	....	d0.47	40 Wk Oct	v□0.27	v□0.13	29
30	....	None Since Public			...	Nil	....	1.34	12.6	11.5	6-30-99	....	...	★15524	Dc	...	...	...	vd0.68	....	d0.57	6 Mo Jun	vd0.35	vd0.24	30
31	1995	0.215	10-6-99	9-20	0.406	0.41	0.254	116	269	101	12-31-98	506	...	±41214	Dc	p±0.68	±v0.94	v1.94	v±0.68	....	0.92	3 Mo Mar	v±0.28	v±0.52	31
32	1997	0.215	10-6-99	9-20	0.406	0.41	0.254	....	...	...		....	...	13864	Dc	p±0.68	±v0.94	v1.94	±v0.68	....	0.92	3 Mo Mar	v±0.28	v±0.52	32
33◆	1983	Q0.12	11-15-99	10-27	0.48	0.48	0.347	10.0	416	203	9-30-99	344	...	±23394	Dc	v±1.94	v±2.06	±v5.46	±v1.84	....	2.04	9 Mo Sep	v1.39	v1.59	33
34◆	1940	Q0.12	11-15-99	10-27	0.48	0.48	0.347	....	...	...		....	...	±23221	Dc	v±1.94	v±2.06	±v5.46	±v1.84	....	2.04	9 Mo Sep	v1.39	v1.59	34
35	1994	Q0.55	11-15-99	11-5	2.155	2.20	2.095	Total Assets $1489M			9-30-99	[72]896	5526	19760	Dc	v0.81	v1.11	v1.86	□v2.39	....	2.90	9 Mo Sep	v□1.31	v□1.82	35
36	....	0.08	2-21-86	2-10	...	Nil	....	28.2	1009	426	9-30-99	331	...	48914	Dc	v1.16	v1.62	v2.55	v0.70	E0.21	0.69	9 Mo Sep	v1.04	v1.03	36
37	....	None Since Public			...	Nil	....	292	571	376	j12-31-98	13.0	450	1114270	Dc	...	...	...	v1.32	....	1.45	6 Mo Jun	v0.71	v0.84	37
38◆	....	None Paid			...	Nil	....	26.8	963	556	10-31-99	965	...	44137	Ap	0.80	v0.42	v1.17	v1.34	v2.32	2.61	6 Mo Oct	v0.33	v0.62	38
39◆	1990	0.225	1-14-00	11-3	0.727	0.94	0.887	333	3636	3639	j12-31-98	2079	...	5588000	Dc	1.40	v1.47	v1.62	v0.91	E1.87	1.06	9 Mo Sep	v1.18	v1.33	39
40◆	....	1.20	4-4-89	3-13	...	Nil	....	4.05	28.4	23.2	9-30-99	7.23	...	2267	Je	Δd3.00	Δd0.80	vd0.60	v0.40	vd1.41	d1.49	3 Mo Sep	v0.14	v0.06	40
41	1949	Q0.15	12-1-99	11-15	0.59	0.60	0.55	25.0	250	79.8	10-31-99	75.0	...	±28984	Ap	±1.25	±1.01	v±1.06	±v□1.24	±v1.29	1.32	6 Mo Oct	v±0.67	v±0.70	41
42	1991	Q0.15	12-1-99	11-15	0.59	0.60	0.55	....	...	...		....	...	14727	Ap	±1.25	±1.01	v±1.06	±v□1.24	±v1.29	1.32	6 Mo Oct	v±0.67	v±0.70	42
43	....	None Since Public			...	Nil	....	86.0	1910	1613	9-30-99	5631	...	217665	Dc	v□2.21	□v1.04	v0.01	v□d1.48	Ed0.40	d2.34	9 Mo Sep	v□0.27	v□d0.59	43
44◆	1939	Q0.23	12-10-99	11-17	0.90	0.92	0.86	42.6	1265	504	10-02-99	670	...	p58514	Dc	v1.83	v2.13	v2.44	vd0.08	E2.39	1.90	9 Mo Sep	vd0.29	v1.69	44
45	....	h[75]....	10-28-99	10-29	h[76]...	Nil	....	40.6	335	313	9-30-99	148	...	71547	Dc	pv0.34	vp□0.30	pvd0.17	v0.32	....	0.16	9 Mo Sep	v0.24	v0.08	45
46	1997	0.419	11-15-99	10-28	1.678	1.68	1.678	At maturity Snyder Commun com&cash or cash[77]				....	...	★4500	Dc	...	...	...	....	....	....	Mature 11-15-2000			46
47	1994	1.003	5-17-99	4-28	1.003	1.00	0.976	60.7	511	142	12-31-98	410	...	±249336	Dc	1.97	2.92	v2.58	v2.75	....	2.75				47
48	1999	1.003	5-17-99	4-28	1.003	1.00	....	....	...	...		....	...	128960	Dc	1.97	2.92	v2.58	v2.75	....	2.75				48
49	1999	0.08	12-10-99	11-18	0.08	[80]....	....	48.0	642	718	8-31-99	1010	...	62247	Au	pd0.08	p[81]0.16	vpd0.04	vp[82]0.08	v0.81	0.81				49
50	....	None Paid			...	Nil	....	151	159	17.9	6-30-99	20.7	...	15880	Sp	d2.21	□d0.01	v□d0.33	□vd2.30	Pvd4.09	d4.09				50

◆**Stock Splits & Divs By Line Reference Index** [6]3-for-2,'94. [8]3-for-2,'95. [9]2-for-1,'98. [11]2-for-1,'97. [13]2-for-1,'96(twice). [17]Adj for 3%,'98. [22]2-for-1,'98. [26]3-for-2,'96,'98. [27]7-for-2,'98. [33]3-for-2,'98. [34]3-for-2,'98. [38]2-for-1,'97. [39]2-for-1,'97. [40]1-for-20 REVERSE,'99. [44]3-for-2,'96.

¶ S&P 500
\# MidCap 400
✣ SmallCap 600
• Options

Index	Ticker	Name of Issue (Call Price of Pfd. Stocks)	Market	Com. Rank. & Pfd. Rating	Inst. Hold Cos	Inst. Hold Shs. (000)	Principal Business	Price Range 1971-97 High	1971-97 Low	1998 High	1998 Low	1999 High	1999 Low	December, 1999 Dec. Sales in 100s	Last Sale Or Bid High	Last Sale Or Bid Low	Last Sale Or Bid Last	%Div Yield	P-E Ratio	EPS 5 Yr Growth	% Annualized Total Return 12 Mo	36 Mo	60 Mo
1	SSPE	✓Software Spectrum	NNM	B	39	2779	Reseller of business software	33½	9¼	24¼	10¾	21 7/16	7	67009	21 7/16	10 15/16	17 11/16	...	13	18	11.4	−15.4	3.4
2	SWCM	✓Software.com Inc	NNM	NR	74	5444	Internet communic software	....	....	....	....	119⅛	15	116023	118	85	96	...	d	...	...	...	...
✣3•[1]	SOL	✓Sola International	NY,Ch,P	NR	180	18230	Mfr plastic eyeglass lenses	39	16⅜	43¾	13	19 7/16	9⅛	17082	14 9/16	11	13⅞	...	60	−26	−19.6	−28.5	...
¶4•[2]	SLR	✓Solectron Corp	NY,Ph,P	B+	794	245574	Mfr computer prod/subsys	23 11/16	⅜	46¾	17 11/16	98	37¼	352837	98	80⅛	95⅛	...	77	23	105	92.5	69.1
#5•[2]	SOI	✓Solutia Inc	NY	NR	372	65466	Mfr chemical based materials	27¾	18 11/16	32	18 11/16	26 5/16	13½	167898	16⅛	13½	15 7/16	0.3	8	...	−30.8	...	...
6	SMRA	✓Somera Communications	NNM	NR	..	...	Telecommun infrastructure eq	....	....	....	....	20	12	147216	19⅝	12 1/16	12 7/16	...	21	...	...	...	...
7	SOMR	✓Somerset Group	NNM	B	14	212	Construction prd/sv,banking	22¼	3 3/16	26½	15¾	23	14⅝	163	19⅝	17⅞	19B	1.1	16	...	17.3	15.8	20.6
8	SNRA	Sonera Corp ADS[52]	NNM	NR	..	...	Telecommunic svc,Finland	....	....	....	....	73⅛	25 3/16	105297	73⅛	41¼	69¼	...	35	...	...	...	...
9	SAH	✓Sonic Automotive'A'	NY	NR	94	15706	Own/oper auto dealerships	6 3/16	4 11/16	18 7/16	4 13/16	18 15/16	7 11/16	45794	10¾	7 11/16	9¾	...	9	...	−43.0	...	...
✣10•[3]	SONC	✓Sonic Corp	NNM	↑B+	173	14804	Oper fast food drive-in restr	20 5/16	5 7/16	25⅞	10¾	33⅞	21⅞	23767	28 13/16	23¾	28½	...	20	24	14.6	18.9	26.3
11	SFO	✓Sonic Foundry	AS	NR	9	282	Computer software pds	....	....	14⅞	5⅜	25½	6 11/16	26842	25½	10 15/16	23 11/16	...	d	...	143	...	...
12	WS	Wrrt(Pur1com at$11.25)	AS	....	1	38		....	....	5⅛	1	13⅝	1 13/16	5721	13⅝	3⅝	12	...	..	...	...	...	...
13	SNWL	✓SonicWALL Inc	NNM	NR	..	...	Design internet security prd	....	....	....	....	45⅝	14	56144	45⅝	32⅞	40¼	...	d	...	...	...	...
#14•[4]	SON	✓Sonoco Products	NY,Ch,Ph,P	B+	254	41172	Mfr paper packaging products	32¼	½	40	22⅛	30½	20 11/16	61465	23⅜	20 11/16	22¾	3.3	13	−8	−20.9	4.7	9.3
15	SSN	✓Sonus Corp	AS	NR	5	1047	Own/oper hearing care clinics	....	....	9⅞	3 3/16	5¾	2¾	2883	3¾	2¾	3	...	d	...	−20.0	...	...
16•[5]	SNE	✓Sony Corp[55] ADR	NY,To,B,C,Ch,P,Ph,Mo	NR	238	23412	Color TV sets,tape rec,radio	103 11/16	2 11/16	97 3/16	60¼	295⅞	65½	61474	295⅞	177⅜	284¾	0.1	87	NM	297	63.9	39.2
#17•[6]	BID	✓Sotheby's Hldgs Cl'A'	NY,Ch,P	B−	144	34610	Worlds largest art auctioneer	37	7 11/16	41⅜	15	47	25	49322	32⅝	26 7/16	30	1.3	46	12	−5.1	19.4	23.4
18	SRCM	✓Source Media	NNM	NR	36	1707	Provide info via on line svcs	14½	3⅜	38	3 15/16	25¼	5⅝	137883	20⅜	13⅝	18½	...	d	−10	2.4	39.1	...
19	SJI	✓South Jersey Indus	NY,B,Ch,Ph	B+	76	2827	Hldg co: gas, fuel oil, sand	30½	4½	30¾	22	30¾	21½	4986	29½	28	28 7/16	5.1	16	...	14.9	11.4	16.3
#20•[7]	SDW	✓Southdown, Inc	NY,Ch,Ph,P	B−	362	26786	Cement:concrete:environ'l svc	59¾	1⅜	74	36 7/16	69 15/16	45 5/16	25381	52	45⅞	51⅝	1.2	9	NM	−11.7	19.5	30.1
21	SRN	✓Southern Banc(AL)	AS,Ph	NR	8	220	Savings & loan Gadsen, AL	18	10	19⅝	12 1/16	12⅞	8	250	9¾	8¼	8¼	4.2	14	...	−29.3	−11.4	...
22	SCE.Q	So Cal Edison 8.375%'QUIDS'	AS	....[57]	1	1	Qtly Income Debt Securities	26⅞	24⅛	26⅜	25⅛	25 15/16	21¾	953	24 13/16	21¾	23	9.1	..	...	−1.9	5.9	...
¶23•[1]	SO	✓Southern Co	NY,B,C,Ch,P,Ph	A−	741	240622	Elec util hldg:Southeast	26¼	3 15/16	31 9/16	23 15/16	29⅝	22 1/16	322684	24 3/16	22 1/16	23½	5.7	12	−2	−14.9	6.8	9.0
24	KTS	South Co Cap Tr I 8.19%[59]Ex'CorTS'[60]	NY	....[61]	..	...	Corporate-Backed Trust Sec	....	....	....	....	25⅛	24¼	68	25	24⅜	24¼B	8.5	..	...	...	...	...
✣25	SEHI	✓Southern Energy Homes	NNM	NR	55	6937	Producer of manufactured homes	18⅛	5 9/16	13⅜	5⅜	7	1⅞	8462	2 9/16	1⅞	2⅜	...	17	−22	−61.7	−41.1	−16.9
26	PCU	✓Southern Peru Copper	NY,P	NR	59	2670	Copper mining,southern Peru	21⅛	12½	16 11/16	8 11/16	18 3/16	8 7/16	6273	15 7/16	13¾	15 7/16	1.0	53	−30	65.5	6.2	...
✣27•[7]	SUG	✓Southern Union	NY,B,Ch,P	B	68	8670	Natural gas dstr: oil & gas	15⅝	3	23 5/16	13 13/16	23 3/16	16 9/16	14624	19 15/16	17 7/16	19⅛	s...	55	−13	−13.5	21.2	29.8
28	SZB	✓SouthFirst Bancshares	AS	NR	4	90	Savings & loan, Alabama	22¾	10	22⅝	14⅞	16⅛	9⅜	90	11⅛	9⅜	9⅜B	6.4	7	28	−37.6	−7.5	...
¶29•[8]	SOTR	✓SouthTrust Corp	NNM	A+	466	79425	Commercial bkg,Alabama	42 13/16	9/16	45⅜	24⅞	42⅞	32¾	116016	40 7/16	32¾	37 13/16	2.3	15	12	4.8	20.6	29.4
30	SWTX	✓Southwall Technologies	NNM	C	12	842	Produces thin film coatings	12	2⅛	8¾	3⅝	5½	2½	9474	5	4 1/16	4⅝	...	d	−45	2.8	−9.5	11.0
¶31•[9]	LUV	✓Southwest Airlines	NY,B,Ch,P,Ph	A	661	302774	Airline svc mid-so'west U.S.	11 11/16	1/64	15 13/16	10 3/16	23 9/16	14⅜	429019	17 3/16	15 5/16	16⅛	0.1	18	23	7.5	36.0	27.1
32	OKSB	✓Southwest Bancorp(OK)	NNM	B+	22	1017	Commercial banking,Oklahoma	28½	11	32¾	19¾	27	19½	2030	22⅛	19½	20	2.0	9	9	−23.6	0.7	10.7
✣33	SWX	✓Southwest Gas[66]	NY,B,Ch,P,Ph	B	167	14708	Natural gas,banking,R.E. dvlp	26¾	6⅛	26⅞	17 5/16	29½	20⅜	14385	23⅝	20⅜	23	3.6	19	NM	−10.9	10.2	15.0
34	SGB	✓Southwest Georgia Finl	AS	NR	1	.3	Commercial bank, Georgia	20½	15½	26 9/16	18¼	24⅛	14½	81	16⅝	14½	14½	4.3	10	6	−39.0	−4.7	...
35•[10]	SWS	✓Southwest Securities Grp	NY,Ph	B+	101	3616	Securities/brokerage svcs	24⅛	4 7/16	26⅛	14 3/16	87 1/16	18 3/16	31956	32 15/16	26 1/16	27⅛	1.2	13	27	64.7	43.7	48.4
36	SWWC	✓Southwest Water Co	NNM	B	21	798	Water utility:serves CA,NM,TX	10 1/16	1	11 5/16	7	18⅝	7⅜	1872	16⅞	14½	15	1.4	18	35	50.1	36.6	42.2
37	DSW	Southwest'n Bell Tel 6.78% Debs	NY	....[67]	4	31	Telecommunication svcs	....	....	26¼	24⅛	26	19 9/16	5372	21 11/16	19 9/16	20 13/16	8.3	..	...	−13.5	...	...
✣38	SWN	✓Southwestern Energy	NY,Ch,Ph	B+	135	16586	Hldg gas utility,Ark: o & g	21⅞	⅝	12 15/16	5½	11	5 3/16	8216	7⅜	5⅝	6 9/16	3.7	18	Neg	−9.6	−22.4	−13.2
#39•[4]	SVRN	✓Sovereign Bancorp	NNM	A−	273	72219	Savings bank,Wyomissing, PA	18 7/16	¾	22¾	8¾	26¼	7	569555	9⅛	7	7 7/16	1.3	6	11	−47.2	0.1	15.3
40	SSS	✓Sovran Self Storage	NY,Ph,P	NR	77	3327	Real estate investment trust	33	22⅜	32⅝	21¼	27 1/16	17½	13528	20	17½	18⅝	12.2	9	10	−18.7	−8.9	...
41	SBSA	✓Spanish Broadcasting Sys'A'	NNM	NR	..	...	Spanish radio broadcstg U.S.	....	....	....	....	42	20	56818	42	30⅝	40¼	...	d	...	...	...	...
42	SEH	✓Spartech Corp	NY,Ch,Ph,P	B	162	12890	PVC compounds,plastic sheet	22 11/16	11/16	23⅛	14¾	33⅝	20	17694	33⅝	27	32¼	1.1	22	11	48.2	44.5	48.0
43	SPA	✓Sparton Corp	NY,Ch,Ph	B−	28	1705	Sonobuoys: conveyors,auto eq	24	1	10⅜	5½	7 7/16	4½	1875	5 5/16	4⅝	5 5/16	...	d	45	−10.5	−11.8	4.0
44	STY	✓Spatial Technology	AS	NR	10	2432	Dvlp 3-D modeling software	6⅛	1⅛	3 9/16	1¼	5⅞	2 9/16	8037	5⅞	3⅞	4¾	...	d	−6	33.4	−3.3	...
45	CHM	✓Specialty Chemical Res	AS,Ph	NR	3	156	Dvlp/pkg auto,ind'l chem prd	12⅛	1	1 7/16	3/16	15/16	3/16	2017	¼	3/16	3/16	...	d	−13	−50.1	−50.0	−42.6
✣46	SEC	✓Specialty Equipment	NY	NR	86	10301	Mfr food service equipment	17½	4½	27⅛	16⅜	34⅛	20 7/16	4946	24⅜	21 9/16	23 15/16	...	11	NM	−11.5	24.2	18.8
47	SPTR	✓SpecTran Corp[68]	NNM,Ch	B	7	546	Mfrs optical fibers	28⅝	¼	11 7/16	2⅞	12⅞	3¼	5426	8 15/16	8¾	8⅞	...	d	−13	115	−25.8	12.7
48•[1]	SPCT	✓Spectrian Corp	NNM	NR	52	8214	Supply linear pwr amplifiers	66⅜	7	20½	8	36⅝	8⅛	45835	29	21¼	28¼	...	d	Neg	119	53.9	0.1
✣49•[11]	SFAM	✓SpeedFam-IPEC Inc	NNM	NR	123	15601	Mfr semiconductor mfg eq	60⅞	9½	31¼	8⅞	21¾	8⅝	112397	14⅛	10	12 15/16	...	d	Neg	−24.5	−23.1	...
50•[3]	TRK	✓Speedway Motorsports	NY,Ch,Ph	NR	126	10925	Own,oper motor speedways	31	8 13/16	30 1/16	14¾	47½	24¼	32210	30	25¼	27 13/16	...	27	31	−2.4	9.8	...

Uniform Footnote Explanations-See Page 4. Other: [1]CBOE:Cycle 2. [2]CBOE:Cycle 1. [3]ASE:Cycle 3. [4]Ph:Cycle 1. [5]ASE,P,Ph:Cycle 1. [6]ASE:Cycle 1. [7]Ph:Cycle 3. [8]P:Cycle 3. [9]CBOE:Cycle 3. [10]CBOE,P:Cycle 3. [11]CBOE,Ph:Cycle 1. [51]Fiscal Mar'96 & prior. [52]Ea ADS rep 1 ord shr. [53]To be determined. [54]If com exceeds $20 for 20 of 30 con trad days. [55]ADR equal 1 ord shr, 50y. [56]9 Mo Jun,'96. [57]Rated A by S&P. [58]Subsid. Pfd in $M. [59]Exch for portion'Deposited Assets're-spec cond. [60]Due 2-1-2037. [61]Rated'BBB+'by S&P. [62]Or earlier upon'Tax Event're-spec cond. [63]Tota Issue Amt. [64]Total issue amt. [65]Re-spec cond. [66]Oneok Inc plan acq,$30. [67]Rated'AA'by S&P. [68]Lucent Technologies plan acq,$9.

Splits ◆ Index	Cash Divs. Ea. Yr. Since	Dividends: Latest Payment Period $	Date	Ex. Div.	Total $ So Far 1999	Ind. Rate	Paid 1998	Financial Position Mil-$ Cash& Equiv.	Curr. Assets	Curr. Liab.	Balance Sheet Date	Capitalization Lg Trm Debt Mil-$	Shs. 000 Pfd.	Com.	Earnings $ Per Shr. Years End	1995	1996	1997	1998	1999	Last 12 Mos.	Interim Earnings Period	$ per Shr. 1998	1999	Index
1	....	None Since Public			...	Nil	....	6.34	160	129	10-31-99	24.4	...	3853	Ap	[51]1.73	v1.73	vd0.20	v1.03	v1.43	1.35	6 Mo Oct	v0.60	v0.52	1
2	....	None Since Public			...	Nil	....	71.3	86.7	13.6	9-30-99	....	...	41229	Dc	...	...	...	vpd0.23	....	d0.23	9 Mo Sep	vd0.21	vd0.21	2
3	....	None Since Public			...	Nil	....	22.8	354	143	9-30-99	206	...	24868	Mr	□1.51	v1.24	□v2.00	v0.49	....	0.23	6 Mo Sep	v0.78	v0.52	3
4◆	....	None Since Public			...	Nil	....	1688	3994	1113	8-31-99	923	...	p292954	Au	0.46	0.55	v0.69	v0.82	v1.13	1.23	3 Mo Nov	v0.26	v□0.36	4
5	1997	A0.04	12-10-99	11-10	0.04	0.04	0.04	7.00	1020	899	9-30-99	597	...	110143	Dc	...	pv0.14	pv1.27	v2.03	E1.86	1.81	9 Mo Sep	v1.56	v1.34	5
6	....	None Since Public			...	Nil	....	0.19	27.2	19.7	9-30-99	p0.58	...	★46563	Dc	...	...	...	v0.50	....	0.59	9 Mo Sep	v0.35	v0.44	6
7◆	1994	S0.10	9-10-99	8-25	0.20	0.20	0.18	0.44	3.94	0.83	9-30-99	....	...	2909	Dc	v1.29	v0.78	v0.93	v0.97	....	1.19	9 Mo Sep	v0.74	v□0.96	7
8	....	Plan annual div			...	[53]....	....	72.0	447	309	6-30-99	963	...	★722000	Dc	...	...	...	v1.97	....	2.01	6 Mo Jun	v0.19	v0.23	8
9◆	....	None Since Public			...	Nil	....	69.8	499	344	9-30-99	214	22	±36070	Dc	...	p0.37	vp0.43	v±0.74	....	1.12	9 Mo Sep	v±0.50	v±0.88	9
10◆	....	None Since Public			...	Nil	....	1.61	12.6	20.3	8-31-99	79.6	...	18582	Au	0.70	0.56	v0.95	□v1.03	v1.41	1.41				10
11	....	None Since Public			...	Nil	....	5.89	11.6	2.73	9-30-99	5.24	...	6497	Sp	p0.07	p0.08	...	vd0.43	vd2.11	d2.11				11
12	....	Terms&trad. basis should	be checked in detail					Wrrts expire 4-22-2003				....	...	1000	Dc	...	...	...	...	...	....	Callable fr 10-22-1999 at 10¢[54]			12
13	....	None Since Public			...	Nil	....	8.77	13.3	6.97	9-30-99	....	p...	★23601	Dc	...	...	...	vd0.13	....	d0.02	9 Mo Sep	vd0.11	vNil	13
14◆	1925	Q0.19	12-10-99	11-17	0.75	0.76	0.72	52.1	721	454	9-26-99	791	...	101969	Dc	v1.49	v1.57	vNil	v□1.84	E1.78↓	1.64	9 Mo Sep	v□1.53	v1.33	14
15	....	None Since Public			...	Nil	....	0.50	5.35	9.98	7-31-99	2.59	13333	6109	Jl	...	...	pvd0.42	vd0.89	vd0.80	d0.66	3 Mo Oct	vd0.24	vd0.10	15
16	1947	0.204	12-6-99	9-27	0.378	0.38	0.38	6171	25793	16324	3-31-99	8718	...	409933	Mr	1.26	2.49	v3.66	v3.29	....	3.26	6 Mo Sep	v1.39	v1.36	16
17	1988	Q0.10	12-3-99	11-9	0.40	0.40	0.40	3.82	441	297	9-30-99	100	...	±58789	Dc	v±0.58	v±0.73	±v0.72	v±0.79	....	0.65	9 Mo Sep	v±0.11	v±d0.03	17
18	....	None Since Public			...	Nil	....	5.77	14.7	13.9	9-30-99	100	855	13666	Dc	vd1.65	vd1.39	□vd2.59	vd5.21	....	d3.02	9 Mo Sep	vd4.51	vd2.32	18
19	1952	Q0.36	9-30-99	9-8	1.44	1.44	1.44	3.06	84.3	169	9-30-99	186	1421	11150	Dc	v1.65	v2.84	v1.47	v1.02	....	1.79	12 Mo Sep	v1.02	v1.79	19
20	1996	Q0.15	11-30-99	11-10	0.60	0.60	0.45	35.3	345	153	9-30-99	167	...	35900	Dc	v2.03	v□2.97	v3.98	v3.18	....	5.62	9 Mo Sep	v1.65	v4.09	20
21	1995	Q0.08¾	12-20-99	11-17	0.35	0.35	0.35	Total Deposits $80.7M			9-30-99	....	...	1055	Je	...	♪v[56]0.34	v0.12	v0.49	v0.57	0.60	3 Mo Sep	v0.14	v0.17	21
22	1995	Q0.523	12-31-99	12-28	2.094	2.09	2.094	Co option redm fr 5-25-2000 at $25				100	...	...	Dc	...	...	...	...	...	....	Mature 6-30-2044			22
23◆	1948	Q0.33½	12-6-99	10-28	1.34	1.34	1.34	768	3968	6452	9-30-99	13939	[58]369	673093	Dc	v1.66	v1.68	v1.42	v1.34	E1.90	1.59	12 Mo Sep	v1.76	v1.59	23
24	....	Plan semi-annual div			...	2.05	....	Co redm opt fr 2-1-2007 $25[62]				[63]★29.0	...	[64]...	Dc	...	...	...	...	...	....	Red premium 2-1-07 to 2-1-17[65]			24
25◆	....	None Since Public			...	Nil	....	3.90	70.9	51.6	10-01-99	3.30	...	12133	Dc	v0.78	v1.00	v0.75	v□0.72	....	0.14	9 Mo Sep	v0.63	v0.05	25
26	1996	0.07½	12-6-99	11-17	0.152	0.15	0.51	102	327	112	9-30-99	210	...	±79920	Dc	±v3.31	v±2.25	v±2.32	v0.68	....	0.29	9 Mo Sep	v0.64	v0.25	26
27◆	....	5%Stk	8-6-99	7-21	5%Stk	Stk	5%Stk	0.60	84.7	165	6-30-99	490	...	p48499	Je	0.55	0.69	v0.62	v0.39	v0.32	0.35	12 Mo Sep	v0.32	v0.35	27
28	1995	Q0.15	11-15-99	10-28	0.60	0.60	0.60	Total Deposits $116M			6-30-99	....	...	929	Sp	0.74	d0.02	v0.62	v0.67	Pv1.44	1.44				28
29◆	1944	Q0.22	1-1-00	11-23	0.85	0.88	0.737	Total Deposits $27497.18M			9-30-99	4606	...	167803	Dc	v1.57	1.79	v2.03	v2.25	E2.60	2.53	9 Mo Sep	v1.66	v1.94	29
30	....	None Since Public			...	Nil	....	0.30	19.9	21.0	10-03-99	0.08	...	7476	Dc	v0.10	v0.35	v0.29	vd1.03	....	d0.70	9 Mo Sep	vd0.41	vd0.08	30
31◆	1976	Q0.006	1-4-00	12-6	0.021	0.02	0.018	266	488	1001	9-30-99	617	...	504436	Dc	v0.36	v0.41	v0.62	v0.82	E0.90	0.90	9 Mo Sep	v0.63	v0.71	31
32	1981	Q0.10	1-3-00	12-16	0.39	0.40	0.35	Total Deposits $826.11M			9-30-99	25.0	...	3959	Dc	v1.43	v1.56	v0.88	v1.89	....	2.34	9 Mo Sep	v1.32	v1.77	32
33	1956	Q0.20½	12-1-99	11-12	0.82	0.82	0.82	5.83	124	214	9-30-99	820	...	30869	Dc	vd0.66	v0.25	v0.61	v1.65	....	1.19	9 Mo Sep	v0.80	v0.34	33
34	1997	Q0.13	1-31-00	12-29	0.48	0.62	0.44	Total Deposits $179M			9-30-99	8.00	...	2319	Dc	v1.16	v1.21	v1.34	v1.41	....	1.41	9 Mo Sep	v1.09	v1.09	34
35◆	1991	Q0.08	1-3-00	12-13	0.271	0.32	s0.219	Total Assets $3796.59M			9-24-99	57.5	...	11803	Je	0.54	v1.25	v1.51	v1.75	v2.21	2.02	3 Mo Sep	v0.40	v0.21	35
36◆	1960	Q0.053	10-20-99	9-28	0.213	0.21	s0.197	0.24	18.8	15.9	9-30-99	33.3	10	6439	Dc	v0.23	v0.30	v0.41	v0.51	....	0.85	9 Mo Sep	v0.39	v0.73	36
37	1998	Q0.43	12-31-99	12-13	1.289	1.719	0.955	Co option redm fr 3-31-2003 at $25[62]				★200	...	...	Dc	...	...	...	...	....	....	Mature 3-31-2048			37
38	1939	Q0.06	11-5-99	10-18	0.24	0.24	0.24	1.56	69.8	56.4	9-30-99	283	...	24944	Dc	v□0.46	v0.78	v0.76	vd1.23	....	0.37	12 Mo Sep	vd1.07	v0.37	38
39◆	1987	Q0.02½	2-15-00	1-27	0.09½	0.10	0.073	Total Deposits $11883.10M			9-30-99	4382	...	★219286	Dc	v0.69	v0.58	v0.63	v0.85	....	1.16	9 Mo Sep	v0.58	v0.89	39
40	1995	Q0.57	1-21-00	1-4	2.25	2.28	2.18	Total Assets $529M			9-30-99	194	1200	12464	Dc	0.91	pv1.87	v1.96	v□1.94	....	2.01	9 Mo Sep	v□1.47	v1.54	40
41	....	None Since Public			...	Nil	....	20.9	44.1	24.8	6-27-99	★241	p...	★±56949	Sp	...	...	...	v□d0.33	....	d0.95	9 Mo Jun	v□d0.06	vd0.68	41
42	1995	Q0.08½	1-19-00	1-3	0.28	0.34	0.24	8.25	192	115	7-31-99	206	...	27291	Oc	0.80	v0.74	v0.92	v1.18	Pv1.48	1.48				42
43	....	0.13	1-15-90	12-11	...	Nil	....	17.3	87.9	18.7	9-30-99	....	...	7828	Je	vd0.83	vd0.52	v4.31	v0.38	vd0.10	d0.10	3 Mo Sep	v0.01	v0.01	43
44	....	None Since Public			...	Nil	....	2.71	8.10	4.08	9-30-99	....	...	9405	Dc	p0.07	vd0.03	vd0.24	v0.02	....	d0.11	9 Mo Sep	v0.02	vd0.11	44
45	....	None Since Public			...	Nil	....	....	12.4	14.5	9-30-99	8.46	...	4257	Dc	vd0.51	vd0.45	vd5.43	vd0.63	....	d0.61	9 Mo Sep	vd0.26	vd0.24	45
46	....	None Since Public			...	Nil	....	8.24	173	123	10-31-99	138	...	19186	Ja	□0.42	□v1.70	v1.86	v□2.18	....	2.22	9 Mo Oct	v□1.48	v1.52	46
47	....	None Since Public			...	Nil	....	3.74	30.9	47.1	9-30-99	1.70	...	7194	Dc	v0.10	v0.61	v0.68	v0.07	....	d0.20	9 Mo Sep	Nil	vd0.27	47
48	....	None Since Public			...	Nil	....	49.7	103	26.4	9-26-99	4.59	...	11449	Mr	v0.66	vd0.49	v0.83	vd3.50	....	d2.90	6 Mo Sep	vd0.78	vd0.18	48
49	....	None Since Public			...	Nil	....	132	301	63.8	8-31-99	116	...	29436	My	p0.18	p1.16	v1.67	v0.83	vd4.84	d4.54	6 Mo Nov	vd0.83	vd0.53	49
50◆	....	None Since Public			...	Nil	....	27.4	74.7	100	9-30-99	459	...	41620	Dc	□v0.52	v0.64	v0.89	v1.00	....	1.02	9 Mo Sep	v0.79	v0.81	50

◆Stock Splits & Divs By Line Reference Index [4]2-for-1,'95,'99. [7]5-for-4,'96,'97. [9]2-for-1,'99. [10]3-for-2,'95,'98. [14]10%,'98. [23]2-for-1,'94. [25]5-for-4,'95:3-for-2,'96. [27]4-for-3,'96:3-for-2,'98:Adj for 5%,'99. [29]3-for-2,'98. [31]3-for-2,'97,'98,'99. [35]10%,'97,'99. [36]6-for-5,'96:5-for-4,'98:3-for-2,'99. [39]10%,'94:6-for-5,'98. [50]2-for-1,'96.

¶ S&P 500 · # MidCap 400 · ✣ SmallCap 600 · • Options

Index	Ticker	Name of Issue (Call Price of Pfd. Stocks)	Market	Com. Rank. & Pfd. Rating	Inst. Hold Cos	Inst. Hold Shs. (000)	Principal Business	Price Range 1971-97 High	1971-97 Low	1998 High	1998 Low	1999 High	1999 Low	Dec. Sales in 100s	December, 1999 Last Sale Or Bid High	Low	Last	%Div Yield	P-E Ratio	EPS 5 Yr Growth	% Annualized Total Return 12 Mo	36 Mo	60 Mo
1	SPZN	Speizman Ind	NNM	B–	20	894	Sells knitting/hosiery mach's	20	2½	7½	3 5/16	6	2⅞	795	5¼	4	4¾	...	53	–15	8.6	–7.2	4.8
2•[1]	SPGLA	✓Spiegel Cl'A'[51]	NNM	C	78	7542	Catalog:apparel,gen'l mdse	26¾	3⅛	10⅞	2⅜	15⅛	5	74754	9⅞	6	7	...	17	41	22.3	–0.1	–6.7
3	SPK	✓Spieker Properties	NY	NR	275	51968	Real estate investment trust	43	18½	43 15/16	31	41 9/16	32¼	52479	37 9/16	32¼	36 7/16	6.7	11	96	12.2	6.3	19.5
4	SPNX	✓Spinnaker Exploration	NNM	NR	14	3414	Oil & gas expl,dev,prod	....	....	....	....	16¾	12 9/16	21996	16¼	13	14⅛	...	..	...	...	...	...
5	SKK.A	Spinnaker Industries'A'	AS	C	2	.2	Mfr adhesive tape prd	74	½	25	18	17¾	12	27	13⅛	12	11⅝B	...	8	24	–35.4	–41.5	32.9
6	SKK	✓ Com(1/10 vtg)	AS	C	6	142		54	17	24	17¾	17½	11¾	38	13⅛	11¾	11⅞	...	8	12	–30.7	–31.5	...
7•[2]	SPLH	✓Splash Technology Hldgs	NNM	NR	48	6536	Dvp color servers for copiers	48¼	10⅜	26⅛	6¼	10⅝	5⅝	69803	9 5/16	7	8 13/16	...	22	...	18.5	–25.7	...
8	SPLT	✓Splitrock Services	NNM	NR	26	4059	Data communication svcs	....	....	....	....	25	8 15/16	82525	25	14 13/16	19⅞	...	d	...	...	...	...
9	GYM	✓Sport Supply Group	NY,Ch,Ph	B–	30	2899	Mfr/dstr sports equipment	18	4⅜	10¼	5⅞	11⅞	5 11/16	6442	7 1/16	5 11/16	6⅞	...	12	26	–25.7	7.7	–7.5
✣10•[2]	TSA	✓Sports Authority	NY,Ch,Ph,P	NR	84	6235	Sporting goods superstores	29	10 13/16	18¾	3 13/16	8½	1⅝	106224	2 7/16	1⅝	2	...	d	Neg	–61.9	–54.9	–32.1
11	SCY	✓Sports Club	AS	NR	13	2720	Dvp/oper sports&fitness clubs	9½	2⅛	9¼	3¾	6⅛	3⅛	1703	4½	3⅛	3⅞	...	22	3	–1.6	10.5	–10.5
12•[3]	SPLN	✓SportsLine.com Inc	NNM	NR	123	12241	Internet base sport media info	11½	7	39⅝	6⅜	83¼	15¾	97607	83¼	41⅛	50⅛	...	d	...	222	...	...
¶13•[4]	SMI	✓Springs Industries'A'	NY,Ch,Ph,P	B+	269	7341	Finished fabrics:hm furn'gs	54¾	4⅛	61	31¾	44½	27 1/16	7933	40 13/16	37 5/16	39 15/16	3.3	11	–7	0.0	0.6	4.7
¶14•[5]	FON	✓Sprint Corp(FON Group)	NY,B,C,Ch,P,Ph	B	1185	432002	Diversified telecommun svs	30 5/16	2 11/16	42⅝	27⅝	75 15/16	36⅞	534633	71½	63 7/16	67 5/16	0.7	36	...	61.7	...	...
15	Pr	$1.50 cm Cv Ser 1 Pfd(42 1/2)vtg	NY	A–	5	5		170	16	225	190	560	290	.....	....	....	530B	0.3	..	...	...	...	...
16	Pr A	$1.50 cm Cv Ser 2 Pfd(50)vtg	NY	A–	7	9		176	14	290	180¾	595	288¼	42	579	559	545B	0.3	..	...	...	...	...
¶17•[6]	PCS	✓Sprint Corp(PCS Grp)	NY	NR	745	156752	Wireless telecomm svcs	....	....	23⅜	12¾	113⅝	20⅞	505410	113⅝	88⅜	102½	...	d	...	343	...	...
18	FXN	Sprint Corp 8.25%'DECS' 2000	NY	....[59]	34	3005	Exch Notes For Com Stock	44¾	32⅝	83	43½	91½	67¾	5713	84	73 5/16	74¼	3.5	..	...	–7.0	34.0	...
✣19•[5]	ST	✓SPS Technologies	NY,B,Ch,Ph	B	160	7395	Ind'l fasteners:mtls hldg	50 9/16	1 13/16	65	37	57	28⅜	7190	32 11/16	29 13/16	31 15/16	...	8	58	–43.6	–0.1	20.3
20	SPSS	✓SPSS Inc	NNM	NR	79	6911	Dvlp statistical software prd	35½	6⅝	27	16⅛	29½	13⅝	9270	26½	20¾	25¼	...	25	16	33.8	–3.2	14.4
#21•[7]	SPW	✓SPX Corp	NY,Ch,P	C	325	24614	Engine parts: piston rings	70⅝	2 9/16	79¼	38⅝	94	40¾	28014	81¾	74⅛	80 13/16	...	16	...	20.6	27.9	38.4
22•[8]	SPYG	✓Spyglass Inc	NNM	NR	52	2605	Internet connectivity provider	61	4 1/16	32¼	4¼	44 1/16	8⅝	150785	44 1/16	20¾	37 15/16	...	d	Neg	72.4	44.8	...
✣23•[9]	STAF	✓StaffMark Inc	NNM	NR	90	7901	Provide staffing svcs	40½	9¾	44⅞	12¾	24⅝	5¾	46372	8⅛	6¾	7 9/16	...	17	...	–66.2	–15.4	...
24•[10]	SGE	✓Stage Stores	NY	NR	73	22592	Own/oper family apparel stores	44⅝	16¼	53¾	8½	10⅛	2⅛	27015	3½	2⅛	2 5/16	...	d	...	–75.3	–49.8	...
25	SA	✓Stage II Apparel	AS	C	4	151	Mkts sports/casual apparel	10⅝	½	2 1/16	½	3 15/16	⅞	1056	1 9/16	1⅛	1⅛	...	d	10	12.5	–17.5	–22.9
26	SFG	✓StanCorp Financial Group	NY	NR	115	14004	Life & disability insurance	....	....	....	....	30	20 15/16	19531	28 7/16	24¼	25 3/16	1.0	10	...	...	...	...
27	AJX	✓Standard Automotive	AS	NR	6	246	Mfr trailer chassis/containers	....	....	12¾	4⅝	19½	7⅜	2947	9¼	7⅜	9	...	8	...	5.9	...	...
28	Pr	8.50% Sr Cv Pfd([61]12)	AS	NR	5	175		....	....	14⅛	6⅜	19⅝	8¾	2381	10½	9¼	10	10.2	..	...	...	...	...
29	STW	✓Standard Commercial	NY,Ph	B–	52	9244	Leaf tobacco,world mkt	31¼	⅛	17½	6⅜	9¼	2¾	4525	3 15/16	3⅛	3 9/16	5.6	8	NM	–56.5	–42.1	–17.5
✣30•[11]	SMSC	✓Standard Microsystems	NNM	C	55	8488	MOS/VLSI integrated circuits	31⅝	1/16	11⅞	4⅝	13⅝	6	13919	12 15/16	10 7/16	10 15/16	...	d	Neg	38.4	4.4	–18.5
✣31	SMP	✓Standard Motor Prod	NY,Ch	B–	100	7602	Ignition & fuel sys parts	26⅞	13/16	26½	16 5/16	29⅝	15¾	4837	18⅞	15¾	16⅛	2.2	8	–22	–31.9	6.6	–2.3
✣32•[12]	SPF	✓Standard Pacific	NY,B,Ch,P,Ph	NR	160	16103	Single family home builder	19⅞	⅛	21	7⅞	15 3/16	8⅞	21433	11 9/16	10	11	1.8	5	NM	–20.8	24.2	13.3
#33	SR	✓Standard Register	NY	A	144	14683	Business forms & handl'g eq	36 5/16	13/16	40	24½	33¼	18⅞	9986	21⅛	18 15/16	19⅝	4.5	7	11	–35.2	–13.5	5.1
✣34	SXI	✓Standex Intl	NY,B,Ch,Ph	A–	108	7275	Diversified manufacturing	37	15/16	35⅞	19	29	19½	5728	21¾	19⅝	20 15/16	3.8	8	–1	–17.5	–9.4	–5.3
¶35•[13]	SWK	✓Stanley Works	NY,B,Ch,P,Ph	B	329	51275	Mfr full line hardware prod	47⅝	1⅜	57¼	23½	35	22	42202	32½	28⅝	30⅛	2.9	18	–15	12.1	6.3	14.0
¶36•[14]	SPLS	✓Staples Inc	NNM,Ph	B+	850	340353	Office product superstores	13⅝	13/16	30 13/16	10 9/16	35 15/16	16 7/16	939404	24¼	18½	20¾	...	31	32	–28.7	37.3	33.8
37	STY	✓Star Data Systems	To	C	1	50	Online,real-time finl svcs	9 7/16	3	8 9/16	4 5/16	6½	2½	5981	3 5/16	2 13/16	3¼	...	33	Neg	–46.7	–5.5	...
38	SGU	✓Star Gas Ptnrs L.P.	NY	NR	22	616	Retail dstr propane gas	24¾	19	24¾	13⅞	20¼	12¼	13546	14 15/16	12¼	13⅛	17.5	d	...	–0.1	–6.5	...
39	SGH	Sr Sub Units L.P.	NY	NR	7	273		....	....	....	....	9⅝	4¾	1416	8	4¾	5 1/16	...	d	...	...	...	...
40	KAP	✓Star Struck Ltd	AS	C	1	4	Watch batteries/catalog sales	20¾	¾	5¼	2 15/16	8¾	3	30	4½	4⅜	4¼B	...	d	Neg	21.4	8.7	–18.1
41•[15]	STRX	✓STAR Telecommunications	NNM	NR	54	4922	Long distance telecom svcs	17 11/16	4⅜	37⅞	7⅛	16½	4½	338870	9½	6¾	7⅞	...	d	Neg	–35.1	...	...
#42•[16]	SBUX	✓Starbucks Corp	NNM	NR	375	69423	Retails high-quality coffees	22⅝	2⅛	29 15/16	14⅝	41	19⅞	431579	29⅛	23¾	24¼	...	45	39	–13.5	19.3	28.9
43	STRM	✓StarMedia Network	NNM	NR	89	22336	Ethnic specific internet svcs	....	....	....	....	70	15	288675	49½	27½	40 1/16	...	d	...	...	...	...
44	STMT	✓Starmet Corp	NNM	C	9	433	Mfr depleted uranium parts	31	2⅝	38	3	10½	1½	4803	8 1/16	4⅛	6½	...	d	–9	–23.5	–11.8	–2.1
45	SCX	✓Starrett (L.S.)'A'	NY,B,Ch	B+	63	2165	Mechanics' measuring tools	40	3⅜	41⅛	29 13/16	34 7/16	21	1202	23⅞	21	22 7/16	3.6	10	3	–32.7	–5.2	2.8
46	STGC	✓Startec Global Communic	NNM	NR	31	1728	Long distance telecom svcs	23	12	29⅛	3⅜	23¾	4⅝	9524	23¾	16¾	21⅜	...	d	...	122	...	...
47	SRT	✓StarTek Inc	NY,Ph	NR	48	3266	Outsourced svcs	16⅜	10⅝	13⅛	8 1/16	69	9 15/16	37682	42⅜	23 9/16	36¼	...	43	...	193	...	...
48	SFI	✓Starwood Financial'A'SBI	NY,Ch	NR	32	1078	Real estate investment trust	120 3/16	2⅝	80¼	24¾	82	16½	50945	18 1/16	16½	16⅞	s10.4	10	NM	–69.7	24.8	43.4
49•[1]	HOT	✓Starwood Hotels&Res[65]Worldwide	NY,Ch,P	NR	415	141206	Own/oper hotels&gaming facilities	101 1/16	1¾	57⅞	18¾	37¾	19½	143859	23 13/16	19 15/16	23½	2.6	16	–20	6.0	–10.5	18.3
50	STB	✓State Bancorp	AS	A	7	123	Commercial bkg, New York	24 15/16	3 15/16	23 15/16	14⅝	17 13/16	14⅛	800	15⅞	14⅛	14 9/16	se3.6	10	15	–0.9	22.7	26.9

Uniform Footnote Explanations-See Page 4. Other: [1]CBOE:Cycle 2. [2]ASE,CBOE:Cycle 1. [3]ASE,CBOE,P,Ph:Cycle 1. [4]P:Cycle 2. [5]Ph:Cycle 2. [6]CBOE,Ph:Cycle 2. [7]CBOE:Cycle 3. [8]ASE,CBOE,Ph:Cycle 1. [9]P,Ph:Cycle 1. [10]CBOE,P,Ph:Cycle 1. [11]ASE:Cycle 2. [12]Ph:Cycle 3. [13]P:Cycle 1. [14]ASE,CBOE,P,Ph:Cycle 3. [15]ASE,CBOE,P:Cycle 2. [16]CBOE:Cycle 1. [51]Non-vtg. [52]8 Mo Sep'96. [53]Fiscal Sep'97 & prior. [54]10 Mo Oct'95. [55]Fiscal Oct '96. [56]11 Mo Sep,'97. [57]Stk dstr of Sprint Corp(PCS). [58]Pfd in $M. [59]Rated BBBr by S&P. [60]Stock or cash re-specified cond.. [61]Fr 7-22-2000 if com exceeds$18/on 20 of 30 trad days. [62]Subject to chge,min $9 per shr re-spec cond. [63]Incl. 3.15M sub Uts. [64]To be determined. [65]Trades w/1 sh Starwood Hotels&Resorts Worldwide Corp.

Splits ◆ Index	Cash Divs. Ea.Yr. Since	Dividends: Latest Payment Period $	Date	Ex. Div.	Total $ So Far 1999	Ind. Rate	Paid 1998	Financial Position Mil-$ Cash& Equiv.	Curr. Assets	Curr. Liab.	Balance Sheet Date	Capitalization Lg Trm Debt Mil-$	Shs. 000 Pfd.	Com.	Earnings $ Per Shr. Years End	1995	1996	1997	1998	1999	Last 12 Mos.	Interim Earnings Period	$ per Shr. 1998	1999	Index
1	....	None Paid			...	Nil	....	0.74	45.9	29.6	10-02-99	5.20	...	3229	Je	0.40	d0.17	v0.80	v0.56	vd0.08	0.09	3 Mo Sep	vd0.05	v0.12	1
2	....	0.05	11-7-95	10-27	...	Nil	....	58.0	1545	715	10-02-99	522	...	±131805	Dc	v±d0.09	v±d0.12	±vd0.28	v±0.03	....	0.41	9 Mo Sep	v±d0.30	v±0.08	2
3	1994	Q0.61	2-4-00	12-29	2.40	2.44	2.28	Total Assets $4202.85M			9-30-99	1966	15250	64917	Dc	□v0.46	v□0.84	v2.04	v2.07	E3.37	2.25	9 Mo Sep	v1.58	v1.76	3
4	....	None Since Public			...	Nil	....	Equity per shr $8.58			6-30-99	p....	p...	★20420	Dc	...	...	...	vpd0.45	....	....	6 Mo Jun	n/a	vpd0.13	4
5◆	....	1.73¾	8-16-96	8-19	...	Nil	....	77.1	124	49.8	9-30-99	126	...	±7342	Dc	v0.08	±□vd0.11	vd0.28	v±d0.92	....	1.43	9 Mo Sep	v±d0.47	v±1.88	5
6	....	1.73¾	8-16-96	8-19	...	Nil	....	....	...	...		....	...	3776	Dc	0.08	±□vd0.11	vd0.28	±vd0.92	....	1.43	9 Mo Sep	v±d0.47	v±Δ1.88	6
7	....	None Since Public			...	Nil	....	64.7	85.4	23.5	9-30-99	....	...	14081	Dc	...	‡[52]d0.93	[53]0.41	v0.94	....	0.41	9 Mo Sep	v0.81	v0.28	7
8	....	None Since Public			...	Nil	....	91.5	160	42.1	9-30-99	261	...	★56831	Dc	...	...	...	vd1.30	....	d2.15	9 Mo Sep	vd0.74	vd1.59	8
9◆	....	0.03	11-27-95	11-16	...	Nil	....	1.21	41.8	14.0	7-02-99	16.1	...	7253	Sp	‡[54]0.20	[55]d2.77	‡[56]Nil	v0.60	Pv0.60	0.60				9
10◆	....	None Since Public			...	Nil	....	18.1	479	399	10-24-99	126	...	32022	Ja	v0.71	v0.94	v0.70	vd2.01	Ed0.05	d0.28	9 Mo Oct	vd2.04	vΔd0.31	10
11	....	None Since Public			...	Nil	....	55.3	60.1	25.6	9-30-99	104	...	17704	Dc	v0.14	v0.15	v0.12	v□0.33	....	0.18	9 Mo Sep	v□0.25	v□0.10	11
12	....	None Since Public			...	Nil	....	98.3	140	12.9	9-30-99	90.0	...	23591	Dc	vd1.42	vd1.92	vd2.54	vd1.94	....	d2.26	9 Mo Sep	vd1.42	v□d1.74	12
13	1898	Q0.33	1-3-00	12-16	1.32	1.32	1.32	0.48	807	286	10-02-99	278	...	±17891	Dc	±v3.69	±v□4.29	v3.34	v±1.97	E3.60	3.27	9 Mo Sep	v1.26	v2.56	13
14◆	1939	Q0.12½	12-29-99	12-6	0.50	0.50	[57]0.50	426	5589	6318	9-30-99	12822	...	±871441	Dc	□1.37	v□1.39	v1.09	v□1.77	E1.85	1.79	9 Mo Sep	v□p1.29	v1.31	14
15	1967	Q0.37½	12-29-99	12-6	1.50	1.50	1.50	Cv into 6 FON Grp & 1.5 PCS Grp com				....	43	...	Dc	...	...	...	...	....	....				15
16	1969	Q0.37½	12-29-99	12-6	1.50	1.50	1.50	Cv into 6.18 FON Grp & 1.54 PCS Grp com				....	257	...	Dc	...	...	...	....	....	....				16
17◆	....	None Paid			...	Nil	....	16.0	1333	2802	9-30-99	9630	[58]247	p430943	Dc	...	...	vpd2.86	□pd4.42	Ed4.10	d5.35	9 Mo Sep	pd2.99	□d3.92	17
18	1995	Q0.657	12-31-99	11-26	2.629	2.63	2.629	Amt pay maturity based on SBC Communic stk[60]				....	...	3900	Dc	...	...	...	....	....	....	Due 3-31-2000			18
19◆	....	0.16	10-4-93	9-14	...	Nil	....	10.8	305	140	9-30-99	182	...	12596	Dc	v1.25	v1.77	v2.54	v3.42	E3.95	3.80	9 Mo Sep	v2.59	v2.97	19
20	....	None Since Public			...	Nil	....	12.1	58.0	37.1	9-30-99	....	...	9070	Dc	v0.35	v0.66	v0.37	v0.87	....	1.00	9 Mo Sep	v1.00	v1.13	20
21	....	0.10	3-10-97	2-19	...	Nil	....	42.9	925	665	9-30-99	1273	...	31182	Dc	□vd0.32	v□d4.04	□vd0.27	vd1.94	E5.17	....	9 Mo Sep	n/a	v3.75	21
22◆	....	None Since Public			...	Nil	....	30.1	41.1	5.91	6-30-99	....	...	16525	Sp	0.23	0.27	vd0.81	vd0.60	Pvd0.12	d0.12				22
23	....	None Since Public			...	Nil	....	0.78	214	85.5	9-30-99	298	...	29391	Dc	p0.37	pv0.67	v1.00	v0.63	....	0.45	9 Mo Sep	v1.03	v0.85	23
24	....	None Since Public			...	Nil	....	7.53	527	197	10-30-99	445	...	±28085	Ja	p0.91	□±v0.88	±□v1.30	v±0.13	....	d0.71	9 Mo Oct	v±0.23	□vd0.61	24
25	....	0.03	12-23-94	12-9	...	Nil	....	0.84	3.07	2.81	9-30-99	....	...	4109	Dc	vd0.78	vd1.66	vd2.24	vd0.59	....	d0.12	9 Mo Sep	vd0.46	v0.01	25
26	1999	0.06	12-3-99	11-9	0.12	0.24	....	Total Assets $5645M			9-30-99	....	...	33720	Dc	...	...	...	pv2.32	....	2.51	6 Mo Jun	vp0.91	vp1.10	26
27	....	None Since Public			...	Nil	....	5.56	41.8	30.0	9-30-99	59.2	1133	3698	Mr	...	p0.03	pv0.21	v0.69	....	1.13	6 Mo Sep	v0.14	v0.58	27
28	1998	Q0.25½	12-31-99	12-16	1.02	1.02	0.92½	Cv into 1 com,$12[62]				....	1150	...	Mr	...	...	...	....	....	....				28
29◆	1998	0.05	12-15-99	11-26	0.20	0.20	0.10	37.3	655	466	9-30-99	203	...	12957	Mr	0.01	v1.64	v2.05	v0.66	....	0.46	6 Mo Sep	v0.47	v0.27	29
30◆	....	None Since Public			...	Nil	....	70.7	127	24.9	8-31-99	2.56	...	15680	Fb	0.86	vd1.54	vd1.22	vd0.79	....	d0.75	9 Mo Nov	v0.12	v0.16	30
31	1960	Q0.09	12-1-99	11-10	0.34	0.36	0.16	32.8	420	179	9-30-99	179	...	12996	Dc	v1.23	v1.12	vd2.63	v1.69	....	1.97	9 Mo Sep	v1.58	v1.86	31
32	1976	Q0.05	11-23-99	11-5	0.20	0.20	0.17	Total Assets $871M			9-30-99	418	...	29494	Dc	vd0.90	v0.28	v0.92	□v1.57	....	2.24	9 Mo Sep	v□0.87	vΔ1.54	32
33	1927	Q0.22	12-3-99	11-17	0.88	0.88	0.84	63.6	488	122	10-03-99	204	...	±27853	Dc	v±1.67	v±2.20	±v2.33	v±2.08	....	2.74	9 Mo Sep	v1.37	v2.03	33
34	1964	Q0.20	11-24-99	11-3	0.77	0.80	0.76	4.01	233	84.2	9-30-99	147	...	12851	Je	2.64	2.21	v2.00	v1.52	v2.41	2.54	3 Mo Sep	v0.61	v0.74	34
35◆	1877	Q0.22	12-27-99	11-23	0.87	0.88	0.83	131	1149	735	10-02-99	299	...	89425	Dc	v0.66	v1.08	vd0.47	v1.53	E1.72	1.47	9 Mo Sep	v1.24	v1.18	35
36◆	....	None Since Public			...	Nil	....	91.3	2173	1496	10-30-99	493	...	469805	Ja	v0.21	v0.29	v0.34	v0.41	E0.68	0.56	9 Mo Oct	v0.26	v0.41	36
37	....	None Paid			...	Nil	....	6.31	16.0	16.1	j5-31-99	13.2	...	16885	My	0.69	0.38	v0.44	vd1.25	v0.05	j0.10	3 Mo Aug	v0.01	v0.06	37
38	1996	0.575	11-15-99	11-3	2.27½	2.30	2.20	4.49	86.9	106	9-30-99	277	...	[63]17525	Sp	pd0.58	p0.58	v0.37	vd0.16	vd2.53	d2.53				38
39	....	Plan qtly div			...	[64]....	....	....	...	...		....	...	2492	Sp	vpd0.58	pv0.58	v0.37	v±d0.16	....	d0.62	3 Mo DecΔ	v±0.66	v±0.20	39
40	....	s0.097	3-22-83	2-22	...	Nil	....	....	5.47	2.39	9-30-99	0.63	...	2026	Dc	d0.35	vd1.05	vd0.23	vd0.18	....	d0.16	9 Mo Sep	vd0.20	vd0.18	40
41◆	....	None Since Public			...	Nil	....	17.0	227	404	9-30-99	42.7	...	58617	Dc	pv0.13	pvd0.23	vp0.17	v0.32	....	d0.60	9 Mo Sep	v0.14	vd0.78	41
42◆	....	None Since Public			...	Nil	....	149	386	224	6-27-99	....	...	182189	Sp	0.18	0.28	v0.33	v0.37	vP0.54	0.54				42
43	....	None Since Public			...	Nil	....	133	141	16.7	6-30-99	2.80	...	64006	Dc	...	...	...	vpd1.09	....	d1.48	9 Mo Sep	vpd0.84	vpd1.23	43
44◆	....	0.10	3-5-93	2-12	...	Nil	....	0.03	6.76	20.3	7-04-99	2.65	...	4791	Sp	Δd0.02	vd0.50	v0.10	vd3.97	Pvd0.51	d0.51				44
45	1934	Q0.20	1-5-00	12-15	0.80	0.80	0.78	15.8	136	23.1	9-25-99	3.30	...	±6697	Je	±1.91	±2.45	v±2.84	v3.33	v2.44	2.30	3 Mo Sep	v0.57	v0.43	45
46	....	None Since Public			...	Nil	....	43.9	104	87.8	9-30-99	177	...	9445	Dc	...	pvd0.52	v0.25	v□d2.02	....	d5.13	9 Mo Sep	vd0.87	vd3.98	46
47	....	None Since Public			...	Nil	....	46.6	69.5	33.9	9-30-99	2.54	...	13986	Dc	...	pv0.34	pv0.47	v0.62	....	0.84	9 Mo Sep	v0.34	v0.56	47
48◆	1998	Q0.57	1-28-00	12-29	s1.70	1.76	0.73	Total Assets $2108M			9-30-99	1816	p11700	±p85919	Dc	v±d0.30	v±d1.32	v±0.06	v±1.36	....	1.73	9 Mo Sep	v0.94	v1.31	48
49◆	1995	Q0.15	1-21-00	12-29	0.60	0.60	2.04	195	871	1435	9-30-99	5925	[58]148	p188359	Dc	□v0.95	Δv0.86	□vd1.94	v6.63	vE1.50	d3.26	9 Mo Sep	v5.87	v□d4.02	49
50◆	1987	sQ0.13	1-14-00	12-15	s0.479	0.52	s0.482	Total Deposits $678.98M			9-30-99	....	...	6988	Dc	v0.83	v0.88	v1.04	v1.17	....	1.46	9 Mo Sep	v0.78	v1.07	50

◆Stock Splits & Divs By Line Reference Index [5]3-for-2,'94,'96:2-for-1,'96. [9]5-for-4,'94. [10]3-for-2,'96. [14]No adj for stk dstr,'96,'98:2-for-1,'99. [17]To split 2-for-1,ex Feb 7,'00. [19]2-for-1,'97. [22]2-for-1,'95. [29]Adj to 1%,May'97. [30]Adj to 5%,'96. [35]2-for-1,'96. [36]3-for-2,'94,'95,'96,'98,'99. [41]2.05-for-1,'98. [42]2-for-1,'95,'99. [44]2-for-1,'97. [48]1-for-6 REVERSE,'98. [49]1-for-6 REVERSE,'95:3-for-2,'97. [50]10%,'95:6-for-5,'97:Adj for 6%,'99.

¶ S&P 500
# MidCap 400
✣ SmallCap 600
• Options

Index	Ticker	Name of Issue (Call Price of Pfd. Stocks)	Market	Com. Rank. & Pfd. Rating	Inst. Hold Cos	Inst. Hold Shs. (000)	Principal Business	Price Range 1971-97 High	1971-97 Low	1998 High	1998 Low	1999 High	1999 Low	Dec. Sales in 100s	December, 1999 Last Sale Or Bid High	Low	Last	%Div Yield	P-E Ratio	EPS 5 Yr Growth	% Annualized Total Return 12 Mo	36 Mo	60 Mo
¶1•[1]	STT	✔State Street Corp	NY,Ch,Ph,P	A+	773	113026	Banking/financial svcs	63 11/16	¼	74 5/16	47⅞	95¼	55½	91388	75	67 1/16	73 1/16	0.9	24	19	5.0	32.5	40.3
2•[2]	SIB	✔Staten Island Bancorp	NY,Ph	NR	113	15181	Savings & loan, New York	21⅛	12	23 13/16	13½	20⅜	15⅞	16957	20⅜	17½	18	2.4	14	...	−7.7	...	...
3	STNV	Statia Terminals Grp	NNM	NR	3	75	Marine terminating svcs	....	....	....	....	20	5¼	51211	9½	5¼	5⅜	...	..	...	...	...	...
4•[3]	STN	✔Station Casinos	NY,Ph	NR	134	24295	Own/oper gaming enterprises	24½	6⅛	16⅝	4	27⅜	7 15/16	117069	24 1/16	16½	22 7/16	...	31	29	174	30.4	11.5
5	SES	✔Stav Electrical Sys	AS	NR	1	40	Electric/commun engineer'g svcs	....	....	6⅛	4⅜	5¼	1 5/16	1961	3	2 1/16	2⅞	...	2	...	−30.5	...	...
6	SIZL	Steakhouse Partners	NSC	NR	2	390	Oper full-svc restaurants	....	....	7⅝	2½	10	3¾	4525	6 1/16	4½	6 1/16	...	d	...	−6.7	...	...
7	STLD	✔Steel Dynamics	NNM	NR	113	19439	Oper steel minimill	28¾	15¾	23¾	9⅜	21¼	11¾	42788	18	13 9/16	15 15/16	...	23	NM	35.6	−5.9	...
8•[4]	SCS	✔Steelcase Inc'A'	NY,Ph	NR	75	7293	Mfr office furniture	....	....	38⅜	12¾	20¾	11	32884	13⅛	11	12	3.7	10	...	−22.9	...	...
✣9	SMRT	✔Stein Mart	NNM	B+	128	20939	Off-price retail store chain	17 1/16	3 11/16	19 7/16	6	12	4⅞	50237	6 1/16	4⅞	5 11/16	...	12	5	−18.4	−17.4	−2.2
10•[5]	STNR	✔Steiner Leisure	NNM	NR	123	12950	Spa svcs/skin&hair care pds	21 13/16	5¾	35 11/16	14⅜	35⅞	12¾	43360	18	14⅞	16 11/16	...	14	NM	−47.9	23.3	...
11	LVB	✔Steinway Musical Instruments	NY,Ph	NR	64	5708	Mfr musical instruments	25	15¼	35	16 5/16	27	15⅞	4494	20¼	17¾	20¼	...	13	...	−22.1	5.2	...
12•[6]	STE.A	Stelco Inc'A'	To,Mo	B−	17	15865	Leader in Canadian steel	41	⅞	14⅝	6⅞	12 3/16	7½	32072	11⅛	8¾	10 13/16	1.1	11	−1	36.6	9.8	6.8
13	SCL	✔Stepan Co	NY,Ch	A−	56	2764	Basic/intermediate chemicals	32⅜	1¼	32¼	23⅛	26 11/16	22 3/16	1499	23⅞	22 3/16	23⅜	2.8	13	9	−9.9	7.1	11.9
14	Pr	5.50% cm Cv Pfd([55]25.41)	NY	NR	..	...		34	22½	35	30	30	27	8	28⅜	27½	27¼B	5.0	..	...	...	...	...
15	TSC	✔Stephan Co	AS,B	B+	22	1148	Mfr hair & skin care prod	22	1/32	14½	9 5/16	11⅝	3⅜	3890	4¼	3⅜	3¾	2.1	14	−30	−63.0	−33.2	−21.2
#16•[5]	STE	✔STERIS Corp	NY	B−	275	38395	Mfr sterile processing sys	25⅛	1¾	35 15/16	18½	35 1/16	9 7/16	140820	13⅞	9 7/16	10¼	...	13	77	−64.0	−22.2	1.8
17•[5]	STL	✔Sterling Bancorp	NY,Ch	B+	44	2227	Commercial bkg,New York	23¼	4½	28	15 15/16	21⅞	15 9/16	1465	17 13/16	15 13/16	16	s3.5	10	22	−20.8	8.3	25.0
#18•[7]	SE	✔Sterling Commerce	NY,Ch,Ph,P	NR	360	63722	Dvp elec data interchge softr	45	24	50¼	20⅛	46 7/16	17 15/16	198414	36½	25½	34	...	26	...	−24.4	−1.2	...
#19•[2]	SSW	✔Sterling Software	NY,B,Ch,P,Ph	↓C	321	65424	Mkts sys,applications sftwr pd	40 11/16	2½	32 13/16	17¾	32	18⅛	105932	32	26 1/16	31½	...	d	Neg	16.4	...	...
20	STHLY	Stet Hellas Telecomm ADS[57]	NNM	NR	64	6772	Mobile telecommun-svc,Greece	....	....	49⅛	19⅝	51½	15	41602	31	19 15/16	30½	...	..	...	−5.8	...	...
#21•[8]	SSSS	✔Stewart & Stevenson	NNM	B	123	19863	Diesel/turbine eng pwr sys	53¾	1 3/16	26⅜	8¼	15 9/16	6¾	29024	12⅞	10 9/16	11⅞	2.9	17	Neg	25.4	−24.3	−17.8
#22•[5]	STEI	✔Stewart Enterprises'A'	NNM	B+	219	59198	Funeral/cemetery services	24¼	3 9/16	29	15⅞	23¾	3 13/16	256677	5¼	4	4¾	1.7	6	13	−78.5	−34.3	−9.9
23	STC	✔Stewart Information Sv	NY	B+	109	10586	Title insurance	14⅝	½	33⅞	14¼	31½	10⅛	12252	14⅜	10⅛	13 5/16	1.2	5	40	−53.2	10.1	13.0
24	SF	✔Stifel Financial	NY,Ch,Ph	B−	34	3256	Securities broker/fin'l svcs	15 7/16	2⅜	18 3/16	8 11/16	12	8⅞	1307	10⅝	9⅝	9⅞	s1.2	11	NM	5.6	15.8	23.1
✣25	SWC	✔Stillwater Mining	AS,Ph	NR	259	30098	Platinum/palladium mining	19¾	8 11/16	27 5/16	10 9/16	34½	19⅜	47381	32⅜	22¾	31⅞	...	43	76	21.3	38.8	28.9
26•[7]	STM	✔STMicroelectronics N.V.	NY,Ch,Ph,P	NR	233	36562	Mfr,dstr semiconductors	49½	10 13/16	45⅞	17 15/16	154	40¼	157094	154	123	151 7/16	...	86	−3	289	63.0	67.9
27•[9]	SCSWF	✔Stolt Comex Seaway	NNM	NR	62	12318	O&G engineering,constr'n svcs	22 13/16	1 15/16	25	6 1/16	15⅛	6	24578	12½	10	11 1/16	...	24	NM	63.9	25.6	37.1
28	STOPrE	Stone Container CvExPfd[59]($25.52)	NY,Ch	D	18	1235	Paperboard packaging prod	26¾	8¾	22⅞	14⅛	23⅝	17¼	2444	23½	20¾	23½	...	..	...	...	...	...
✣29	SGY	✔Stone Energy	NY	NR	196	13559	Oil & gas explor dvlp prod'n	37 3/16	9⅞	40¼	19⅝	56⅛	22 1/16	29328	41¾	33½	35⅝	...	d	Neg	23.9	6.0	13.1
✣30	SW	✔Stone & Webster	NY,B,Ch,P,Ph	↓C	113	5186	Engineer'g,constr,consulting	55⅛	7⅞	50 9/16	28⅜	34⅜	13½	13930	19¼	15 7/16	16 13/16	...	d	Neg	−48.6	−17.6	−11.3
31	SRI	✔Stoneridge Inc	NY	NR	77	5266	Mfr auto electronic parts	20 13/16	14	23 1/16	13⅞	23	12	3187	16⅜	12	15 7/16	...	9	...	−32.1	...	...
32	SOS	✔Storage Computer	AS	NR	13	418	Mfr data storage systems	19⅞	5	9⅝	1	8½	¾	28021	8½	1	5	...	d	Neg	51.0	−27.5	...
#33•[5]	STK	✔Storage Technology	NY,B,Ch,Ph,P	B−	225	80217	Data storage equipment	201⅞	4⅝	51⅛	20⅛	41⅝	14¼	97917	20½	16 1/16	18 7/16	...	..	75	−48.3	−6.6	6.1
34	SUS	✔Storage USA	NY,Ch,Ph,P	NR	130	9376	Real estate investment trust	41¾	21¾	41¼	28¼	35⅝	26	18538	30 9/16	26½	30¼	8.9	14	7	2.3	−0.5	9.0
35	SAA	✔Strategia Corp	AS	NR	4	115	Computer systems svcs	15¾	7½	9⅞	½	2⅜	7/16	4285	1 3/16	⅝	1	...	6	...	33.3	...	...
36	SDIX	✔Strategic Diagnostics	NNM	B−	28	3525	Diagnostic kits comml applic	10½	1	4¾	1½	10 3/16	1 11/16	50924	8½	4 15/16	6 9/16	...	d	NM	228	48.6	10.4
37	STRD	✔Strategic Distribution	NNM	C	32	11365	Outsources indust supply svcs	9⅛	¼	7½	1 13/16	3¼	1⅛	13678	1 15/16	1¼	1 7/16	...	d	Neg	−41.0	−43.3	−21.5
38	SFT	✔Stratesec Inc	AS	NR	4	175	Provide security systems svcs	13¼	7⅞	9¾	13/16	2⅜	⅞	2485	1 11/16	1 3/16	1 7/16	...	21	NM	−4.2	...	...
39	STRA	✔Strayer Education	NNM	NR	96	8028	College education institution	36 11/16	6 11/16	41¼	24⅜	39⅝	12⅞	16791	23	17 9/16	19¾	1.2	17	...	−43.5	9.6	...
40	FUEL	✔Streicher Mobile Fueling	NSC,Ch	NR	3	.5	Vehicle mobile fueling svcs	11	2¾	5¼	1¾	9½	2	1679	8¼	6½	6⅞	...	76	−1	182	−7.3	...
✣41•[10]	SRR	✔Stride Rite	NY,Ch,Ph,P	B+	192	31047	Mfr/retail children's shoes	31⅞	⅜	15¾	6⅝	13 7/16	5 3/16	71223	6 9/16	5 3/16	6½	3.1	15	90	−23.9	−11.7	−8.2
#42•[1]	SDRC	✔Structural Dynamics Res	NNM	B−	152	28157	Mechanical design software	37⅜	1⅜	29	7½	23 7/16	8 13/16	113459	13¾	10	12¾	...	17	NM	−35.8	−13.9	18.9
43	RSB	Struct Prd Sr S&P 1999[61]'TIERS'[62]	AS	NR	..	...	Trust Ser 1999-2	....	....	....	....	10¼	9⅞	1538	10¼	9⅞	10⅛	...	..	...	...	...	...
#44•[11]	SYK	✔Stryker Corp	NY,Ph	A−	309	37394	Specialty medical devices	45 5/16	5/16	55¾	31	73¼	44 7/16	55552	73¼	56 9/16	69⅝	0.2	42	Neg	26.8	33.0	30.9
45	STU	✔Student Loan Corp	NY	NR	66	18573	Orignates,svcs student loans	54¼	14¼	51 1/16	40	50½	37⅜	1623	50½	49	49⅞	4.8	11	8	16.2	12.8	24.4
✣46•[5]	RGR	✔Sturm Ruger	NY,Ch,P	B+	108	8565	Pistols, revolvers & rifles	27	5/16	21¼	10 9/16	12 15/16	8¼	19162	9 15/16	8¼	8⅞	9.0	9	−4	−19.4	−18.2	−4.0
47	IBUY	✔Styleclick.com Inc	NNM	NR	16	956	Fashion e-commerce website	25⅝	3¾	24⅞	6	22¼	6¼	33382	14¾	10¾	11 15/16	...	d	...	−29.8	27.1	...
48	SLAM	✔Suburban Lodges America	NNM	NR	24	4725	Own/manage lodging facilities	30¼	10½	19⅜	6¼	9¾	4¾	11035	6 3/16	4⅞	5 3/16	...	8	...	−36.6	−31.3	...
49	SPH	✔Suburban Propane Ptnrs L.P.	NY,Ch,Ph	NR	36	1407	Retail marketer of propane	21⅞	15⅜	20	17⅛	20¾	16 7/16	16618	19⅛	16 7/16	17⅜	e11.5	21	...	2.9	8.3	...
#50•[11]	SZA	✔Suiza Foods	NY,Ph	NR	297	24843	Mfr/distr milk prds	62½	14	67	25 11/16	50¼	29⅝	43637	39¾	35¼	39⅝	...	13	35	−22.2	25.1	...

Uniform Footnote Explanations-See Page 4. Other: [1]Ph:Cycle 2. [2]CBOE,Ph:Cycle 1. [3]ASE:Cycle 1. [4]ASE,CBOE,Ph:Cycle 1. [5]CBOE:Cycle 3. [6]To:Cycle 2. [7]CBOE:Cycle 1. [8]P:Cycle 3. [9]CBOE,Ph:Cycle 3. [10]P:Cycle 1. [11]Ph:Cycle 3. [51]To be determined. [52]Incl 3.8M sub shrs. [53]Fiscal Mar'98 & prior. [54]Spl div. [55]Thru 8-31-2000,scale to $25 in 2002. [56]Stk dstr of Sterling Commerce Inc. [57]Ea ADR rep 1 ord,Drs.500. [58]Approx. [59]Co opt exch for$25amt 7%Cv2007 on div pmt dates. [60]Incl current amts. [61]Principal-Protected Asset Backed Trust Ctf. [62]Callable in 2002,re-spec cond. [63]82% owned by Citibank.

Index	Cash Divs. Ea. Yr. Since	Dividends: Latest Payment Period $	Date	Ex. Div.	Total $ So Far 1999	Ind. Rate	Paid 1998	Financial Position Mil-$ Cash& Equiv.	Curr. Assets	Curr. Liab.	Balance Sheet Date	Capitalization Lg Trm Debt Mil-$	Shs. 000 Pfd.	Com.	Earnings $ Per Shr. Years End	1995	1996	1997	1998	1999	Last 12 Mos.	Interim Earnings Period	$ per Shr. 1998	1999	Index
1◆	1910	Q0.16	1-18-00	12-30	0.58	0.64	0.50	Total Deposits $31953.00M			9-30-99	922	...	159977	Dc	v1.47	v1.78	v2.32	v2.66	E3.00	2.94	9 Mo Sep	v1.98	v2.26	1
2	1998	Q0.11	11-12-99	10-25	0.41	0.44	0.23	Total Deposits $1810.42M			9-30-99	1881	...	39615	Dc	...	p0.75	pvd0.29	v1.06	....	1.30	9 Mo Sep	v0.78	v1.02	2
3	1999	Q0.45	11-12-99	10-27	0.767	[51]....	....	17.5	30.6	21.7	6-30-99	101	...	[52]±11400	Dc	...	...	...	pv±0.85	....	....	9 Mo Sep	n/a	vp±0.52	3
4	....	None Since Public			...	Nil	....	53.7	100	125	9-30-99	887	...	42123	Dc	v0.75	v0.39	v[53]d0.09	vd0.28	....	0.72	9 Mo Sep	v□Nil	□v1.00	4
5	1999	[54]0.26	9-25-99	8-9	[54]0.26	Nil	....	....	2.71	4.24	6-30-98	0.08	...	★1414	Dc	...	...	v1.40	Pv1.57	....	1.57				5
6	....	None Since Public			...	Nil	....	1.95	14.9	46.3	9-07-99	14.1	...	3332	Dc	...	pd1.70	vd1.36	v□d1.26	....	d2.38	9 Mo Sep	vd0.59	vd1.71	6
7	....	None Since Public			...	Nil	....	7.06	233	64.7	9-30-99	509	...	47953	Dc	pvd0.62	□pvd0.07	□v1.06	v0.65	....	0.70	9 Mo Sep	v0.48	v0.53	7
8	1998	Q0.11	1-14-00	12-29	0.44	0.44	0.30	23.4	1003	917	8-27-99	54.9	...	±152484	Fb	...	pd2.25	vP1.40	v1.44	....	1.23	9 Mo Nov	v1.13	v0.92	8
9◆	....	None Since Public			...	Nil	....	12.7	290	126	10-02-99	58.0	...	44495	Dc	v0.39	v0.56	v0.73	v0.44	....	0.49	9 Mo Sep	v0.10	v0.15	9
10◆	....	None Since Public			...	Nil	....	35.6	54.8	13.4	9-30-99	0.04	...	16617	Dc	vd0.04	v0.17	v0.73	v1.04	....	1.24	9 Mo Sep	v0.75	v0.95	10
11	....	None Since Public			...	Nil	....	3.93	194	49.1	10-02-99	145	...	±9255	Dc	p□b1.36	□±v1.00	±v1.45	v±1.75	....	1.59	9 Mo Sep	v±1.42	v±1.26	11
12	1997	gQ0.03	2-1-00	1-14	g0.12	0.12	g0.12	255	1449	641	j9-30-99	578	2700	±105374	Dc	±1.35	v±0.63	v±1.14	±v1.03	....	j0.96	9 Mo Sep	v±0.88	v±0.81	12
13◆	1967	Q0.16¼	12-15-99	11-26	0.613	0.65	0.70	4.64	174	105	9-30-99	112	784	9514	Dc	v1.46	v1.71	v1.86	v2.12	....	1.82	9 Mo Sep	v1.62	v1.32	13
14	1995	Q0.34⅜	3-1-00	2-11	1.37½	1.375	1.37½	Cv into 1.14175 com				....	651	...	Dc	...	...	...	....	....	....				14
15	1995	Q0.02	11-18-99	10-28	0.08	0.08	0.08	10.9	30.6	5.40	9-30-99	10.6	...	4666	Dc	v1.06	v1.13	v1.20	v0.15	....	0.26	9 Mo Sep	v0.31	v0.42	15
16◆	....	None Since Public			...	Nil	....	32.3	414	146	9-30-99	266	...	67498	Mr	0.33	vd0.46	v0.93	v1.20	E0.82↓	1.08	6 Mo Sep	v0.47	v0.35	16
17◆	1946	Q0.14	12-31-99	12-13	s0.483	0.56	0.40	Total Deposits $779M			9-30-99	31.1	244	8401	Dc	v0.73	v0.96	v1.21	v1.40	....	1.56	9 Mo Sep	v1.04	v1.20	17
18	....	None Since Public			...	Nil	....	262	492	198	9-30-99	....	...	79969	Sp	p0.59	0.77	v0.64	vd0.67	v1.31	1.31				18
19◆	....	h[56]....	10-7-96	10-8	...	Nil	....	647	908	258	6-30-99	....	...	84247	Sp	0.20	3.49	vd1.66	v0.89	vPd0.13	d0.13				19
20	....	None Since Public			...	Nil	....	8.79	79.4	105	12-31-97	174	...	72600	Dc	vd0.49	v0.06	v0.28	....	....	0.28				20
21	1988	Q0.08½	2-11-00	1-27	0.34	0.34	0.34	19.9	450	197	10-30-99	78.4	...	27992	Ja	1.87	v0.51	v1.57	vd2.51	E0.70	d2.38	9 Mo Oct	v0.32	v0.45	21
22◆	1992	Q0.02	1-28-00	1-12	0.08	0.08	0.06	69.9	334	117	7-31-99	921	...	±108600	Oc	0.36	0.62	□0.78	v0.43	Pv□0.84	0.84				22
23◆	1967	Q0.04	1-31-00	12-29	0.15½	0.16	0.14	Total Assets $523.76M			9-30-99	19.1	...	±14633	Dc	v±0.55	v±1.07	±v1.11	v±3.32	....	2.80	9 Mo Sep	v2.40	v1.88	23
24◆	1992	0.03	11-24-99	11-8	s0.12	0.12	s0.114	Total Assets $365.92M			9-30-99	35.0	...	6712	Dc	v0.12	v0.59	v0.88	v0.73	....	0.91	9 Mo Sep	v0.59	v0.77	24
25◆	....	None Since Public			...	Nil	....	10.6	49.4	37.2	9-30-99	50.0	...	37882	Dc	vNil	v∆d0.09	vd0.18	v0.38	....	0.75	9 Mo Sep	v0.25	v0.62	25
26◆	1999	[58]0.06	6-15-99	5-27	[58]0.06	[51]....	....	1101	3034	1429	12-31-98	756	...	★288299	Dc	2.02	v2.25	v1.46	v1.45	E1.77	1.66	9 Mo Sep	v1.02	v1.24	26
27◆	....	Stk	6-25-98	6-26	...	Nil	s....	9.38	303	235	11-30-98	219	...	±76045	Nv	v0.07	vd0.49	0.82	±∆v0.91	....	0.47	9 Mo Aug	v±∆0.74	v±0.30	27
28	....	0.43¾	2-17-97	2-5	...	Nil	....	Cv into 0.729 com,$34.28,com of Smurfit Stone Container				....	4600	...	Dc	...	...	...	....	....	....	Arrears $4.8125 to 11-15-99			28
29	....	None Since Public			...	Nil	....	41.8	72.3	44.9	9-30-99	100	...	18331	Dc	v0.49	v0.90	v0.78	vd3.43	....	d2.86	9 Mo Sep	v0.38	v0.95	29
30	1939	Div Omitted 10-27-99			0.45	Nil	0.60	35.1	422	590	9-30-99	19.9	...	13065	Dc	v1.04	∆vd1.32	v2.59	vd3.83	....	d9.18	9 Mo Sep	v0.81	vd4.54	30
31	....	None Since Public			...	Nil	....	4.64	190	125	9-30-99	315	...	22397	Dc	...	pv0.66	vp1.36	v1.49	....	1.73	9 Mo Sep	v1.13	v1.37	31
32	....	None Since Public			...	Nil	....	1.53	11.9	10.6	9-30-99	1.06	...	11418	Dc	v0.21	v0.43	v0.33	vd0.97	....	d0.96	9 Mo Sep	vd0.31	vd0.30	32
33◆	....	None Paid			...	Nil	....	233	1465	998	6-25-99	20.5	...	100179	Dc	vd1.46	∆□v1.43	v1.89	v1.86	....	0.02	9 Mo Sep	v1.35	vd0.49	33
34	1994	Q0.67	1-10-00	12-21	2.65	2.68	1.92	Total Assets $1761M			9-30-99	[60]800	...	28042	Dc	v1.86	v2.07	v2.31	v2.17	....	2.24	9 Mo Sep	v1.64	v1.71	34
35	....	None Since Public			...	Nil	....	1.99	9.09	4.63	9-30-99	0.88	...	4668	Dc	Nil	vd0.29	vd0.75	vd0.52	....	0.17	9 Mo Sep	vd0.38	v0.31	35
36	....	None Since Public			...	Nil	....	1.15	13.9	3.66	9-30-99	6.75	2164	16380	Dc	vd0.46	vd2.12	v0.11	v0.05	....	d0.18	9 Mo Sep	v0.08	vd0.15	36
37◆	....	3%Stk	12-29-95	12-14	...	Nil	....	1.15	96.9	41.2	9-30-99	21.4	...	30992	Dc	v0.05	vd0.34	vd0.52	vd0.03	....	d0.07	9 Mo Sep	vd0.02	vd0.06	37
38	....	None Since Public			...	Nil	....	0.02	3.27	2.58	9-30-99	0.12	...	5867	Dc	d0.43	vd0.58	vd0.85	vd0.58	....	0.07	9 Mo Sep	vd0.79	vd0.14	38
39◆	1996	Q0.06	1-24-00	1-6	0.21	0.24	0.18	20.2	38.4	23.1	9-30-99	....	...	15413	Dc	p0.72	pv0.83	v0.93	v1.12	....	1.19	9 Mo Sep	v0.76	v0.83	39
40	....	None Since Public			...	Nil	....	0.37	10.2	11.9	10-31-99	4.52	...	2690	Ja	0.07	vd0.26	vd0.18	vd0.42	....	0.09	9 Mo Oct	vd0.22	v0.29	40
41	1955	Q0.05	12-15-99	11-23	0.20	0.20	0.20	44.5	258	77.9	8-27-99	....	...	46000	Nv	d0.17	0.05	v0.40	v0.44	....	0.44	9 Mo Aug	v0.56	v0.56	41
42	....	None Since Public			...	Nil	....	134	237	129	9-30-99	....	...	35726	Dc	vd0.09	v1.05	v0.81	v0.93	E0.75	0.88	9 Mo Sep	v0.67	v0.62	42
43	....	Plan semi-annaul div			...	[51]....	....	At mat amt pay based on S&P 500,as defined				....	...	★2700	Dc	...	...	...	....	....	....	Due 12-8-2006			43
44◆	1992	Q0.13	1-31-00	12-29	0.12	0.13	0.11	102	1193	674	9-30-99	1348	...	96980	Dc	v0.88	1.08	v1.28	v0.40	E1.65	d0.93	9 Mo Sep	v1.08	vd0.25	44
45	1993	Q0.60	12-1-99	11-10	1.95	2.40	0.60	Total Assets $10368M			9-30-99	57.0	...	[63]20000	Dc	v3.03	v3.25	v2.58	v3.67	....	4.43	9 Mo Sep	v2.51	v3.27	45
46◆	1955	Q0.20	12-15-99	11-29	0.80	0.80	0.80	76.8	151	38.1	9-30-99	....	...	26911	Dc	v0.97	v1.28	v1.03	v0.87	....	1.05	9 Mo Sep	v0.67	v0.85	46
47	....	None Since Public			...	Nil	....	4.49	12.6	1.77	9-30-99	....	...	7405	Dc	p0.12	v0.20	v0.06	vd1.41	....	d2.29	9 Mo Sep	vd0.56	vd1.44	47
48	....	None Since Public			...	Nil	....	19.0	27.2	10.8	9-30-99	97.5	...	14205	Dc	p0.14	pv0.31	v0.53	v0.17	....	0.62	9 Mo Sep	vNil	v0.45	48
49	1996	†0.513	11-9-99	10-27	†2.02½	2.00	2.00	19.6	88.7	88.7	6-26-99	428	...	22236	Sp	p0.79	p0.92	v0.46	v1.30	Pv0.83	0.83				49
50	....	None Since Public			...	Nil	....	62.2	735	604	9-30-99	1256	...	31201	Dc	p□v0.65	□v2.00	□v1.27	v∆2.82	....	3.07	9 Mo Sep	v∆2.07	v2.32	50

◆Stock Splits & Divs By Line Reference Index [1]2-for-1,'97. [9]2-for-1,'98. [10]3-for-2,'97,'98. [13]2-for-1,'94. [16]2-for-1,'95,'98. [17]Adj for 5%,'99. [19]No Adj for stk dstr,'96:2-for-1,'98. [22]3-for-2,'96:2-for-1,'98. [23]2-for-1,'99. [24]Adj for 5%,'99. [25]3-for-2,'99. [26]2-for-1,'99. [27]2-for-1,'98:3-for-2,'98. [33]2-for-1,'98. [37]Adj for 3%,'95. [39]3-for-2,'97. [44]2-for-1,'96. [46]2-for-1,'96.

¶ S&P 500
# MidCap 400
✣ SmallCap 600
• Options

Index	Ticker	Name of Issue (Call Price of Pfd. Stocks)	Market	Com. Rank. & Pfd. Rating	Inst. Hold Cos	Inst. Hold Shs. (000)	Principal Business	Price Range 1971-97 High	1971-97 Low	1998 High	1998 Low	1999 High	1999 Low	December, 1999 Dec. Sales in 100s	Last Sale Or Bid High	Low	Last	%Div Yield	P-E Ratio	EPS 5 Yr Growth	% Annualized Total Return 12 Mo	36 Mo	60 Mo
1	SM	✓Sulzer Medica ADS[51]	NY	NR	2	69	Dgn/mfr implantable medical pd	30½	20 5/16	28⅞	15 15/16	21 13/16	16	926	19⅞	17⅞	18⅝	1.3	19	...	−1.7	...	...
2	SUMX	✓Summa Industries	NNM	↑B	21	557	Mfrs ind'l plastic components	16⅝	¼	15	7	16⅝	8¼	3029	13⅛	10⅜	11 9/16	...	8	48	27.6	22.8	14.0
¶3•[1]	SUB	✓Summit Bancorp	NY,B,Ch,P	A−	480	76454	Comm'l bks,New Jersey,Penn	53⅜	2 7/16	53⅞	30¾	44½	28½	91989	33¾	28½	30⅝	4.3	12	11	−27.6	4.7	17.5
4•[2]	SMMT	✓Summit Design	NNM	NR	38	4033	Graphical design softwr	18¾	5¼	17⅛	4¾	9⅝	2⅛	54672	4 3/16	2⅞	3½	...	4	46	−62.4	−30.1	...
5	SMT	✓Summit Properties	NY,Ch,Ph	NR	112	13421	Real estate investment trust	22½	15½	22	16½	20⅝	16	28034	19	16½	17⅞	9.3	8	32	13.1	1.2	7.0
✣6•[3]	BEAM	✓Summit Technology	NNM	B−	132	12365	Dvlp medl laser surgery prod	38¾	¼	7½	3	29⅜	4 5/16	372530	21⅝	10¼	11 11/16	...	d	NM	167	...	...
7	SUI	✓Sun Communities	NY,Ch,Ph,P	NR	140	13258	Real estate investment trust	38	19¾	36¼	29⅞	37⅛	29¾	7801	32 5/16	29¾	32 3/16	6.3	22	7	−1.8	3.5	14.5
8	SNHY	✓Sun Hydraulics	NNM	NR	29	1544	Dgn/mfr hydraulic systems	13	9½	18¼	8	9¾	5¾	5463	6⅞	5¾	6½	2.5	22	...	−20.2	...	...
9•[4]	SIH	✓Sun Intl Hotels Ord	NY,Ch,Ph	NR	59	11642	Oper resort & casino hotels	54¼	29⅛	51¼	30 3/16	47 15/16	17 1/16	23031	19¾	17 1/16	19⅝	...	11	...	−57.4	−19.0	...
¶10•[5]	SUNW	✓Sun Microsystems	NNM,Ch,Ph	B+	1621	936519	Mkt networked workstations	13 5/16	⅜	22⅛	9 7/16	83	21 13/16	4110735	83	64 3/16	77 7/16	...	..	26	263	130	104
11	SNR	✓Sunair Electronics	AS	B−	7	528	Mfr communications equip	14⅞	⅝	3⅜	1⅞	3 1/16	2	784	2 11/16	2⅛	2¼	...	23	38	−14.3	1.9	4.4
12•[6]	SOC	✓Sunbeam Corp	NY,P	NR	101	34518	Consumer prd:outdoor,househld	50 7/16	11	53	4⅝	9⅛	3⅞	153196	5	3⅞	4 3/16	...	d	Neg	−39.1	−45.2	−30.4
13	SNB	✓Sunburst Hospitality	NY	NR	37	6733	Own/oper hotels	11⅝	8⅝	9 15/16	3	6¾	3¾	38209	5⅝	4⅞	5⅝	...	13	...	32.4	...	...
14	SU	✓Suncor Energy	NY,To	B+	120	51784	Integrated oil & gas oper,Cdn	39¾	10 3/16	38¾	27 13/16	42⅞	26 5/16	3790	42	36 5/16	41¾	◆1.1	21	6	42.2	29.4	33.9
#15•[7]	SDS	✓SunGard Data Systems	NY	B+	452	85235	Provides data process'g svcs	31 7/16	2⅜	40	21 11/16	41 15/16	16⅞	125231	24¾	22	23¾	...	18	13	−40.2	6.4	19.8
16•[2]	RAYS	✓Sunglass Hut Intl	NNM	NR	124	37763	Sell nonprescript'n sunglasses	36 15/16	5	13	3⅜	17½	6⅝	42765	14	11¼	11¼	...	20	−7	60.7	15.8	−0.3
¶17•[8]	SUN	✓Sunoco Inc	NY,B,Ch,Ph,P	B	416	64440	Petroleum refining&mktg	73⅛	12¾	44 5/16	29½	39 7/16	22⅞	66435	25 13/16	23 1/16	23½	4.3	34	46	−32.6	1.8	−0.5
18	SUNQ	✓Sunquest Information Sys	NNM	NR	46	2703	Healthcare info systems	19¾	6½	15	6¾	17¾	9⅜	3270	14½	12	13½	...	15	27	−4.4	−1.8	...
19•[1]	SNRZ	✓Sunrise Assisted Living	NNM	NR	205	19807	Own/oper assisted living facil	43¼	20	53⅛	22½	52½	9¼	70862	14 3/16	10⅞	13¾	...	12	...	−73.5	−21.0	...
✣20•[9]	SMD	✓Sunrise Medical	NY,P	B−	100	14772	Mfrs home health care prod	36¾	1 13/16	16¼	6 9/16	12½	4 7/16	8219	7⅛	5¾	6 3/16	...	56	19	−50.3	−27.0	−25.9
21	SSC	✓Sunshine Mining & Refining	NY,B,Ch,Ph,Vc,P	C	36	654	Silver & gold mining	210	1	13½	4	6	1¼	45256	1⅜	1¼	1⅜	...	d	−16	14.8	−15.1	−18.8
22	SDP	✓SunSource Inc	NY,Ph	NR	25	2084	Industrial pds & svcs	26	23 5/16	29 11/16	13⅝	19	3 7/16	9209	6⅝	3 11/16	4¼	...	d	...	−77.1	...	...
23•[1]	OWN	✓Sunterra Corp	NY,Ph	NR	115	25635	Dvlp,oper timeshare resorts	32 3/16	9 1/16	26⅜	3⅜	16 1/16	8 3/16	25279	13½	10 5/16	11½	...	8	...	−23.3	−21.2	...
¶24•[10]	STI	✓SunTrust Banks	NY,B,Ph,P	A+	634	162869	Comm'l bkg,Georgia,FL,Tenn	75¼	2 5/16	87¾	54	79 13/16	60 7/16	216129	72 15/16	67¼	68 13/16	2.0	21	8	−8.2	13.7	26.0
25	SAE	✓Super-Sol Ltd ADS[57]	NY	NR	7	1023	Supermarket chain,Israel	15¾	12¼	18¼	10 5/16	17	11 9/16	1425	17	14⅞	17	1.0	26	...	40.8	...	...
26•[7]	SUPG	✓SuperGen Inc	NNM	NR	57	2948	Dvp stg:pharmaceutical R&D	19	4⅛	18 1/16	5⅛	34 15/16	8¼	94603	34¾	24	29⅝	...	d	−27	218	33.8	...
27	SUPC	✓Superior Consultant Hlds	NNM	NR	78	5568	Healthcare industry mgmt svcs	37¼	14¾	48¼	27 11/16	47¼	10	17132	15¼	13	14¼	...	51	...	−67.2	−16.8	...
#28•[4]	SUP	✓Superior Indus Intl	NY,Ph,P	A	195	14084	Custom auto accessories	49⅜	⅛	33⅞	20 1/16	29⅜	22¾	11253	27¼	24½	26 13/16	1.3	11	6	−2.4	6.2	1.1
29	SUT	✓Superior Telecom	NY,Ch,Ph	NR	100	7357	Mfr copper wire/cable prd	26¼	10¼	40 11/16	22⅛	39¾	11⅛	42099	16 7/16	13	15 7/16	1.6	..	...	−58.7	6.4	...
30	Pr A	8.50% Superior Tr I cmCvPfd([62]52.55)	[11]	CCC+	25	982		...	...	...	...	51⅛	31¾	382	35½	32	33½	12.7	..	...	...	...	...
31	SGC	✓Superior Uniform Group	AS,Ch,Ph	B+	40	3278	Hospital & ind'l uniforms, etc	22¾	⅜	18⅝	11⅝	15¾	8	5614	9¾	8	9	6.0	8	6	−35.0	−9.3	−3.0
32	UNR	✓Supermercados Unimarc ADS[65]	NY	NR	11	1035	Oper supermarket chain,Chile	19⅛	12	12⅜	1⅞	4¾	2⅛	2543	3	2 9/16	2 13/16	2.8	..	...	−31.0	...	...
¶33•[12]	SVU	✓Supervalu Inc	NY,B,Ch,P,Ph	B+	509	107550	Large food wholesaler:retail	21⅛	⅜	28 15/16	20 3/16	28⅞	16 13/16	133321	20⅛	16 13/16	20	2.7	11	30	−26.7	15.2	13.7
34	STS	✓Supreme Industries'A'	AS	B−	30	3222	Mfrs specialized truck bodies	8 13/16	5/16	13 1/16	6 9/16	9⅞	5¾	3535	7⅝	5¾	6 3/16	s...	7	14	−22.0	23.7	16.2
35	SRY	✓Surety Capital[66]	AS	C	10	1490	Banking svcs/loans	22½	1 9/16	7 1/16	1 15/16	3⅜	7/16	...	...	...	...	...	..	Neg	...	...	...
36	SLTI	Surgical Laser Tech	NSC	C	8	12	Dvlp,mfr laser surgery sys	108¾	5	9½	1¼	4½	1	3447	2 5/16	1⅜	1⅝	...	d	Neg	28.6	−34.3	−26.9
✣37	SUSQ	✓Susquehanna Bancshares	NNM	A−	116	8887	Comm'l bkg,Pennsylvania	25 15/16	1 15/16	26¾	15½	21¼	14⅞	17712	17⅜	15	15⅞	4.3	11	11	−19.7	4.5	14.1
38	SBB	✓Sussex Bancorp	AS	NR	1	16	Commercial bank, New Jersey	...	...	13	8⅝	12⅜	8⅝	54	9¾	8⅝	8¾	1.4	17	5	−12.5	...	...
39	SVI	✓SVI Holdings[67]	AS	NR	16	618	Provide computer svcs	...	...	8½	5⅝	15⅜	7¼	38645	14⅛	10⅞	12	...	86	...	64.1	...	...
40	SNKI	✓Swank Inc	NSC	B−	6	124	Leather goods:jewelry	3½	5/16	2¾	⅞	1 13/16	¾	7187	1	¾	15/16	...	6	70	−48.3	16.4	−2.5
41•[1]	SFY	✓Swift Energy	NY,Ch,P	B−	104	14002	Oil & gas explor,dev,prod'n	34 3/16	15/16	21	6 15/16	14	5 1/16	29636	11½	9 13/16	11½	...	14	74	55.9	−22.5	7.4
✣42	SABI	✓Swiss Army Brands	NNM	C	48	2243	Dstr Swiss Army Knife prod	18¼	2⅜	12¾	8⅛	11½	6⅝	2181	8¼	6⅝	7⅛	...	d	Neg	−26.0	−18.7	−10.6
43	SCM	✓Swisscom AG ADS[69]	NY	NR	35	8354	Telecom/internet access svcs	...	...	43½	27⅛	46⅛	29⅜	7617	41¾	33⅝	40½	1.5	25	...	−3.0	...	...
44	SYI	✓S Y Bancorp	AS	A−	9	632	General banking,Kentucky	25¼	5 1/16	29	19¼	27½	21⅜	481	23⅛	21¾	21⅞	1.6	16	24	−5.7	16.6	27.3
45•[13]	SYBS	✓Sybase Inc	NNM	C	166	54623	Dvlp database mgmt software	57	6¾	11¼	4½	19 13/16	5 9/16	225459	19 13/16	15 1/16	17	...	27	−30	130	0.6	−20.0
46	SYC	✓Sybron Chemicals	AS	NR	30	4358	Enviro & textile dye'g chem'ls	34½	10	37	11¼	20½	11	739	13⅞	11	11¾	...	8	5	−13.0	−9.8	−5.4
#47•[8]	SYB	✓Sybron Intl	NY,Ph	NR	335	81915	Mfr orthodontic/dental lab prd	24¼	3½	29⅛	16⅜	30 13/16	20 11/16	57829	24 15/16	21½	24 11/16	...	21	18	−9.2	14.4	23.4
48	SCMR	✓Sycamore Networks	NNM	NR	..	...	High speed data transport pd	...	...	...	...	328	38	70981	328	213¼	308	...	d	...	...	...	...
#49•[14]	SYKE	✓Sykes Enterprises	NNM	NR	187	21302	Info technology svcs	35 7/16	8	30½	12 9/16	51½	20 7/16	87170	51½	39½	43⅞	...	93	82	43.9	20.8	...
#50•[15]	SLVN	✓Sylvan Learning Systems	NNM	NR	238	34836	Tutorial educational services	30 13/16	4¾	36⅞	17⅛	34⅝	10 11/16	174817	14 11/16	10 15/16	13	...	24	42	−57.4	−11.8	8.3

Uniform Footnote Explanations-See Page 4. Other: [1]CBOE:Cycle 1. [2]CBOE:Cycle 3. [3]ASE,CBOE,P:Cycle 3. [4]CBOE:Cycle 2. [5]ASE,CBOE,P,Ph:Cycle 1. [6]ASE,CBOE:Cycle 1. [7]P,Ph:Cycle 1. [8]Ph:Cycle 2. [9]P:Cycle 2. [10]P:Cycle 1. [11]NY [12]Ph:Cycle 1. [13]Ph:Cycle 3. [14]ASE:Cycle 3. [15]ASE:Cycle 2. [51]Ea ADS rep 0.10 ord, P30CHF. [52]Stk dstr of LCA-Vision,'97. [53]7 Mo Dec'97. [54]Pfd in $M. [55]Revised by Co from $1.63. [56]Accum on Pfd. [57]Ea ADS rep 5 ord shs,NIS0.10. [58]Approx. [59]12 Mo Dec'95. [60]Fiscal Apr'97 & prior. [61]8 Mo Dec'98:Fiscal Apr'98 earned$1.97. [62]Fr 3-31-2003. [63]Of Superior Telecom. [64]Fr 3-31-2002 to 3-30-2003 re-spec cond. [65]Ea ADS rep 50 ord,no par. [66]ASE trading halted 11-8-99. [67]Plan name chge,SVI Systems. [68]12 Mo Mar'98. [69]Ea ADS rep 0.10 ord,25CHF.

Splits ◆ Index	Cash Divs. Ea.Yr. Since	Dividends: Latest Payment Period $	Date	Ex. Div.	Total $ So Far 1999	Ind. Rate	Paid 1998	Financial Position Mil-$ Cash& Equiv.	Curr. Assets	Curr. Liab.	Balance Sheet Date	Capitalization Lg Trm Debt Mil-$	Shs. 000 Pfd.	Com.	Earnings $ Per Shr. Years End	1995	1996	1997	1998	1999	Last 12 Mos.	Interim Earnings Period	$ per Shr. 1998	1999	Index
1	1998	0.25	5-27-99	4-16	0.25	0.25	0.197	119	737	499	12-31-98	212	...	10000	Dc	...	p0.70	v1.19	v0.98	....	0.98				1
2	....	0.32	11-30-84	7-11	...	Nil	....	0.92	30.5	18.8	11-30-99	29.0	...	4322	Au	v0.25	v0.35	v0.64	v1.10	v1.46	1.49	3 Mo Nov	v0.32	v0.35	2
3◆	1935	Q0.33	2-1-00	1-4	1.26	1.32	1.14	Total Deposits $24351.17M			9-30-99	3971	...	174766	Dc	v1.87	v1.67	v2.09	v2.63	E2.66	2.58	9 Mo Sep	v1.96	v1.91	3
4	....	None Since Public			...	Nil	....	27.0	35.0	11.2	9-30-99	....	...	15801	Dc	pvd0.33	v0.10	vd0.42	v0.32	E0.83	d0.31	9 Mo Sep	v0.28	vd0.35	4
5	1994	Q0.41¾	2-15-00	1-10	1.66	1.67	1.62	Total Assets $1196.60M			9-30-99	620	...	28712	Dc	v□0.83	v□0.92	v1.17	v□2.28	....	2.31	9 Mo Sep	v1.06	v1.09	5
6◆	....	h[52]....	12-29-97	12-16	...	Nil	....	84.5	128	25.8	9-30-99	0.16	...	46746	Dc	vd0.11	vd1.19	v0.28	□v1.20	....	d0.44	9 Mo Sep	v□1.06	vd0.58	6
7	1994	Q0.51	10-19-99	10-6	2.02	2.04	1.94	Total Assets $897.56M			9-30-99	388	...	17433	Dc	v1.19	v□1.35	v1.37	v1.53	....	1.44	9 Mo Sep	v1.30	v1.21	7
8	1997	Q0.04	1-15-00	12-29	0.16	0.16	0.19½	1.09	15.8	7.37	9-30-99	10.8	...	6385	Dc	p1.10	vp0.40	v0.73	v0.87	....	0.30	9 Mo Sep	v0.74	v0.17	8
9	....	None Since Public			...	Nil	....	61.2	121	167	12-31-98	566	...	33577	Dc	0.79	v1.58	□v2.53	v1.70	....	1.75	3 Mo Mar	v0.87	v0.92	9
10◆	....	None Since Public			...	Nil	....	4113	7662	3128	9-26-99	★1500	...	1562118	Je	0.23	v0.30	v0.49	v0.48	v0.63	0.72	3 Mo Sep	v0.07	v0.16	10
11	....	†1.75	6-20-88	5-10	...	Nil	....	1.68	9.34	0.54	6-30-99	....	...	3718	Sp	0.04	d0.26	v0.02	v0.01	....	0.10	9 Mo Jun	v0.01	v0.10	11
12	1992	Div Discontd 8-24-98			...	Nil	0.02	29.0	1050	1997	9-30-99	817	...	100902	Dc	v0.61	vd2.75	v1.25	v□d7.99	Ed1.90	d4.57	9 Mo Sep	v□d4.96	vd1.54	12
13	....	None Since Public			...	Nil	....	Total Assets $414.47M			9-30-99	269	...	18757	Dc	...	...	v[53]0.81	v□0.18	....	0.43	9 Mo Sep	v□0.19	□v0.44	13
14◆	1990	gQ0.17	12-24-99	12-13	g0.68	0.68	g0.68	19.0	436	390	j6-30-99	1041	[54]★507	110493	Dc	v1.38	v1.71	v2.04	v1.70	....	j1.39	9 Mo Sep	v1.31	v1.00	14
15◆	....	None Since Public			...	Nil	....	388	769	333	9-30-99	5.29	...	128237	Dc	v0.61	v0.41	v0.87	v1.10	E1.33	0.79	9 Mo Sep	v0.71	vΔ0.40	15
16◆	....	None Since Public			...	Nil	....	6.34	152	81.7	10-30-99	138	...	45323	Ja	p0.38	vNil	□vd1.25	v0.38	E0.57↑	0.56	9 Mo Oct	v0.34	v0.52	16
17	1904	Q0.25	12-10-99	11-8	1.00	1.00	1.00	84.0	1424	1642	9-30-99	872	...	90227	Dc	□v2.24	vd2.17	v2.70	v2.95	E0.70	1.21	9 Mo Sep	v2.39	v0.65	17
18	....	None Since Public			...	Nil	....	45.5	90.4	28.6	9-30-99	3.38	...	15541	Dc	pv0.18	vp0.29	v0.18	v0.54	....	0.93	9 Mo Sep	v0.33	v0.72	18
19	....	None Since Public			...	Nil	....	36.7	145	42.6	9-30-99	625	...	21938	Dc	pd1.15	pvd0.40	v0.20	v1.11	....	1.14	9 Mo Sep	v0.73	v0.76	19
20	....	None Since Public			...	Nil	....	2.26	261	152	10-01-99	175	...	22234	Je	v[55]0.93	vd1.89	v0.55	vd0.55	v0.20	0.11	3 Mo Sep	v0.16	v0.07	20
21◆	....	0.80	9-29-81	9-9	...	[56]Nil	....	1.42	13.5	34.1	9-30-99	14.6	...	37690	Dc	vd1.04	v0.40	vd0.64	vd2.00	....	d0.31	9 Mo Sep	vd1.90	vd0.21	21
22	1998	Div Omitted 7-23-99			0.20	Nil	0.40	3.95	225	86.4	9-30-99	124	...	6749	Dc	...	pv1.35	pv1.88	v2.00	....	d0.84	9 Mo Sep	v1.55	vd1.29	22
23◆	....	None Since Public			...	Nil	....	Total Assets $1100M			9-30-99	636	...	35972	Dc	pv0.89	vp0.40	v□0.56	□v1.20	....	1.44	9 Mo Sep	v□0.85	v1.09	23
24◆	1985	Q0.34½	12-15-99	11-29	1.38	1.38	1.00	Total Deposits $58644.06M			9-30-99	6325	...	319965	Dc	v2.47	2.76	v3.13	v3.04	....	3.24	9 Mo Sep	v2.58	v2.78	24
25	1997	[58]0.172	12-22-99	11-26	[58]0.172	0.17	0.149	35.6	285	863	12-31-98	96.3	...	209251	Dc	...	p0.85	v8.56	v0.72	....	0.66	9 Mo Sep	v0.56	v0.50	25
26	....	None Since Public			...	Nil	....	32.8	37.9	3.23	9-30-99	....	...	24953	Dc	[59]d0.32	vd0.55	vd0.85	vd0.77	....	d1.51	9 Mo Sep	vd0.55	vd1.29	26
27	....	None Since Public			...	Nil	....	36.0	85.6	14.1	9-30-99	....	...	10469	Dc	p0.36	vp0.38	v0.53	v0.91	....	0.28	9 Mo Sep	v0.65	v0.02	27
28	1985	Q0.09	1-24-00	1-6	0.34	0.36	0.30	107	264	89.8	9-30-99	0.45	...	26651	Dc	v1.78	v1.63	v1.96	v1.88	E2.49	2.52	9 Mo Sep	v1.17	v1.81	28
29◆	1998	Q0.06¼	11-5-99	10-27	0.25	0.25	0.20	15.5	653	488	9-30-99	1179	p17712	19565	Dc	...	p0.56	vp[60]1.45	v[61]1.10	....	....	9 Mo Sep	v1.75	v□1.76	29
30	1999	Q1.06¼	12-15-99	11-29	2.12½	4.25	....	Cv into 1.1161 com[63]				....	3332	...	Dc	...	...	...	....	....	....	Co'Spcl'Redm opt at $52.975[64]			30
31	1977	Q0.135	11-26-99	11-10	0.54	0.54	0.51	4.09	83.4	19.9	9-30-99	20.4	...	7728	Dc	v0.45	v1.07	v1.14	v1.00	....	1.10	9 Mo Sep	v0.69	v0.79	31
32	1998	0.079	6-3-99	5-14	0.079	0.08	0.228	26.0	102	104	12-31-97	18.7	...	1261844	Dc	...	1.17	v1.11	....	....	....	6 Mo JunΔ	n/a	0.38	32
33◆	1936	Q0.135	3-15-00	2-28	0.53½	0.54	0.52½	11.3	1975	2203	9-11-99	1851	6	139604	Fb	v1.22	v1.30	v1.82	v1.57	E1.83↑	1.56	9 Mo Nov	v1.35	v1.34	33
34◆	....	5%Stk	12-6-99	11-24	10%Stk	Stk	5%Stk	0.24	66.1	27.5	9-30-99	30.6	...	±10839	Dc	v±0.60	v±0.40	±v0.68	±v□0.81	....	0.91	9 Mo Sep	v±0.60	v±0.70	34
35	....	None Paid			...	Nil	....	Total Deposits $96.55M			6-30-99	4.35	...	5760	Dc	v0.26	v0.31	vd0.60	vd0.32	....	d0.14	6 Mo Jun	vd0.08	v0.10	35
36◆	....	None Since Public			...	Nil	....	3.78	6.71	1.28	10-03-99	0.03	...	1978	Dc	vd0.05	vd2.30	vd0.20	vd1.29	....	d1.50	9 Mo Sep	vd0.77	vd0.98	36
37◆	1982	Q0.17	11-22-99	10-28	0.62	0.68	0.57	Total Deposits $3153.37M			9-30-99	404	...	36977	Dc	v0.95	v0.95	v1.20	v1.26	....	1.39	9 Mo Sep	v0.92	v1.05	37
38◆	1998	Q0.03	1-25-00	1-5	0.12	0.12	0.26½	Total Deposits $138M			9-30-99	....	...	1421	Dc	v0.37	v0.38	v0.51	v0.50	....	0.51	9 Mo Sep	v0.37	v0.38	38
39	....	None Since Public			...	Nil	....	0.71	30.4	25.5	9-30-99	1.20	...	32493	Mr	...	...	v[68]0.46	v0.17	....	0.14	6 Mo Sep	v0.14	v0.11	39
40	....	0.006	7-21-86	6-30	...	Nil	....	0.02	74.2	45.1	9-30-99	9.57	...	16569	Dc	vd0.55	v0.08	v0.29	v0.22	....	0.15	9 Mo Sep	v0.07	vNil	40
41◆	....	None Since Public			...	Nil	....	42.1	69.1	32.4	9-30-99	239	...	21682	Dc	v0.49	v1.25	v1.26	vd2.93	....	0.85	9 Mo Sep	vd3.11	v0.67	41
42	....	None Paid			...	Nil	....	....	74.3	34.3	9-30-99	....	...	7854	Dc	v0.38	vd0.64	vd0.49	v0.18	....	d0.14	9 Mo Sep	v0.10	vd0.22	42
43	1999	0.603	7-6-99	6-1	0.603	0.60	....	1265	3237	3124	12-31-98	3370	...	73550	Dc	...	...	vpd0.42	v1.62	....	1.62				43
44◆	1993	Q0.09	1-3-00	12-16	0.23½	0.36	0.26½	Total Deposits $555M			9-30-99	2.10	...	6669	Dc	v0.61	v0.77	v0.96	v1.21	....	1.37	9 Mo Sep	v0.90	v1.06	44
45	....	None Since Public			...	Nil	....	275	476	364	9-30-99	....	...	81530	Dc	vd0.27	vd1.05	vd0.70	vd1.15	E0.64	0.25	9 Mo Sep	vd0.97	v0.43	45
46	....	None Since Public			...	Nil	....	18.6	109	57.1	9-30-99	124	...	5731	Dc	v1.12	v1.50	v1.84	v□1.49	....	1.51	9 Mo Sep	v□1.26	v1.28	46
47◆	....	None Since Public			...	Nil	....	18.5	492	192	9-30-99	926	...	103803	Sp	□0.55	0.60	□v0.82	v0.68	v1.18	1.18				47
48	....	None Since Public			...	Nil	....	22.0	52.2	11.7	7-31-99	p....	p...	★78031	Jl	...	...	...	....	vpd0.51	d0.51				48
49◆	....	None Since Public			...	Nil	....	31.7	217	112	9-30-99	79.7	...	42365	Dc	pv0.09	pv0.29	v0.14	v0.20	....	0.47	9 Mo Sep	v0.56	v0.83	49
50◆	....	None Since Public			...	Nil	....	32.2	177	150	9-30-99	125	...	50955	Dc	v0.14	v0.40	v0.69	v0.70	....	0.55	9 Mo Sep	v0.31	v□0.16	50

◆Stock Splits & Divs By Line Reference Index [3]3-for-2,'97. [6]3-for-2,'95. [10]2-for-1,'95,'96,'99(twice). [14]2-for-1,'97. [15]2-for-1,'95,'97. [16]2-for-1,'94,'95. [21]1-for-8 REVERSE,'99. [23]3-for-2,'97. [24]2-for-1,'96. [29]5-for-4,'98,'99. [33]2-for-1,'98. [34]10%,'95:Adj for 5%,'99(twice). [36]1-for-5 REVERSE,'99. [37]3-for-2,'97,'98. [38]2-for-1,'98. [41]10%,'94,'97. [44]10%,'94:2-for-1,'96,'99. [47]2-for-1,'97,'98. [49]3-for-2,'96,'97. [50]3-for-2,'96,'98.

¶ S&P 500
# MidCap 400
✤ SmallCap 600
• Options

Index	Ticker	Name of Issue (Call Price of Pfd. Stocks)	Market	Com. Rank. & Pfd. Rating	Inst. Hold Cos	Inst. Hold Shs. (000)	Principal Business	1971-97 High	1971-97 Low	1998 High	1998 Low	1999 High	1999 Low	Dec. Sales in 100s	December, 1999 Last Sale Or Bid High	Low	Last	%Div Yield	P-E Ratio	EPS 5 Yr Growth	% Annualized Total Return 12 Mo	36 Mo	60 Mo
#1•[1]	SYMC	✓Symantec Corp	NNM	B−	333	45261	PC applications,sys softwr pd	51	5¼	32⅝	8 11/16	69 5/16	12½	274047	69 5/16	43⅜	58⅝	...	31	NM	170	59.3	27.4
#2•[2]	SBL	✓Symbol Technologies	NY,Ch,Ph,P	B+	322	71648	Bar code laser scanners	20	½	42 15/16	16 5/16	65	26	79760	65	47⅛	63 9/16	0.0	52	24	49.6	69.8	47.7
✤3•[3]	SYMM	✓Symmetricom Inc	NNM	B	61	3811	Electronic parts mfr	26⅝	1/16	12¾	4	12⅞	5⅞	38478	12⅞	7⅛	9 15/16	...	d	Neg	48.6	−20.6	−5.8
4	SIGC	Symons Intl Group	NNM	NR	11	1092	Property & Casualty insurance	24	12⅜	21⅞	5	9¾	1	13319	1¾	1	1 7/16	...	d	...	−80.2	−55.9	...
5	SYM	✓Syms Corp	NY,B,Ch	B	61	6534	Off-price apparel stores	18⅝	6⅜	15 15/16	8⅛	9	4¾	3084	6 3/16	4¾	5	...	10	5	−44.4	−16.2	−5.1
6	SMMX	✓Symyx Technologies	NNM	NR	..	...	New mfg materials R&D	....	....	....	....	35 13/16	14	34148	33¼	24⅞	30	...	..	...	...	...	...
7	SBIO	✓Synbiotics Corp	NNM	B−	23	2683	Dvlp/mfr biological products	15¾	1½	4	2	5⅜	2	6795	2½	2 1/16	2⅜	...	60	−4	−6.1	−8.9	4.4
#8•[4]	SNPS	✓Synopsys Inc	NNM	B	434	65603	Dvlp elec sys design softwr	50½	9	54½	24½	75⅝	37⅛	270204	75⅝	58	66¾	...	30	35	23.0	13.0	25.0
¶9•[5]	SNV	✓Synovus Financial	NY,Ch,Ph	A+	284	84079	Commercial bkg,Georgia	22 7/16	¼	25 15/16	17¼	25⅛	17¼	64107	21½	18½	19⅞	1.8	25	17	−15.8	13.8	32.8
10	SYBB	✓SYNSORB Biotech[51]	NNM,To	NR	7	1148	Pharmaceutical R&D	12⅝	1⅞	11 15/16	1 11/16	2 15/16	1⅛	5394	2 1/16	1½	1⅞	...	d	−35	−21.1	−45.5	...
11	SYNT	✓Syntel Inc	NNM	NR	49	2178	Info technology staffing svcs	12 3/16	5 11/16	39¾	8¾	19⅝	7	23245	19⅝	12⅜	16 3/16	...	29	63	43.1	...	...
12•[6]	NZYM	✓Synthetech Inc	NNM	B−	21	2858	Produce pharmaceutical prod	13⅞	¼	8	3⅜	6½	3¼	14043	3⅞	3¼	3¾	...	10	22	−26.8	−33.3	15.7
13	SYQTQ	SyQuest Technology	OTC,Ch	D	9	172	Mfr Winchester disk cartridges	28½	1 11/16	3½	⅛	....	....	....	....	....	....	...	..	Neg	...	...	...
¶14•[6]	SYY	✓Sysco Corp	NY,B,Ch,P	A+	724	219033	Food distr & service systems	23⅝	⅛	28 11/16	19 15/16	41⅛	24 15/16	128101	39⅝	35 11/16	39 9/16	1.2	35	11	46.1	36.4	27.1
15•[3]	SSAX	✓System Software	BB,Ch	C	59	4936	Business application softwr pd	122	3 13/16	40½	13¾	28¼	1	42779	2¼	1	2	...	d	Neg	−92.8	−63.8	−45.4
16	SYX	✓Systemax Inc	NY,Ch,Ph	NR	71	6176	Direct mkt computer pds/svcs	53	13⅛	25¼	9¼	23 13/16	7 3/16	15106	9¾	7¾	8½	...	8	8	−63.6	−42.0	...
17•[7]	SCTC	✓Systems & Computer Tech	NNM	B−	120	17524	Comput'g sys/softw for educ	26¼	⅞	30⅞	8½	19½	7 13/16	77929	19¼	11⅝	16¼	...	28	23	18.2	26.9	9.4
✤18•[8]	TJCO	✓T J International[52]	NNM	B	134	6065	Prefab joists for constrn	33	⅝	34½	16½	42	21¼	13370	42	41 9/16	42	0.5	24	NM	64.8	22.9	20.0
19	TBP	✓Tab Products	AS,B,P	B	26	1869	Office/computer access eq	20⅝	7/16	15 7/16	5	8	4⅝	3186	7¾	5 7/16	6½	3.1	5	−4	14.2	−7.7	1.5
20	THW	✓Tag Heuer International ADS[53]	NY,Ch,Ph	NR	10	705	Mfr Swiss sports watches	20½	8	13	5¼	14 9/16	6⅞	623	13¼	11⅜	11⅜	0.9	16	...	61.7	−10.3	...
21	TAG	✓Tag-It Pacific	AS	NR	4	4	Mfr brand identity pds	....	....	4⅜	¾	9⅛	4	4488	6	4 5/16	5⅝	...	27	...	28.6	...	...
22•[9]	TSM	✓Taiwan Semiconductor Mfg ADS[55]	NY,Ph	NR	165	65699	Contracted semiconductor mfg	18 9/16	8¾	17	7½	45¾	11	130115	45¾	35 13/16	45	...	..	...	363	...	...
23•[3]	TLB	✓Talbots Inc	NY,Ph,P	NR	145	11969	Retail women's apparel	43	16¾	31 9/16	13½	53 15/16	22 9/16	18854	51⅜	44	44⅝	1.1	27	−10	44.1	17.6	8.8
24	TLM	✓Talisman Energy[56]	NY,To,Ph	B−	139	29313	Oil & gas explor,dvlp,prod Cdn	49 15/16	10¼	32 3/16	14⅝	33 5/16	14 9/16	10300	27	22 11/16	25¾	...	d	Neg	47.1	−17.3	1.8
✤25•[10]	TALK	✓Talk.com Inc	NNM	NR	140	36953	Computer software/svcs	26 1/16	4	30	4¾	22⅞	7½	367866	22⅞	14⅜	17¾	...	d	Neg	6.0	7.1	...
¶26•[11]	TAN	✓Tandy Corp	NY,B,Ch,C,P	B−	675	142259	Retails consumer electronics	23	⅛	31 15/16	15 3/16	79½	20 9/16	698991	79½	41⅜	49 3/16	0.4	35	22	141	66.6	33.3
27	TAC	✓Tandycrafts, Inc	NY,B,Ch	C	26	2674	Leather crafts,picture frames	27⅝	15/16	5½	2⅝	3¾	1⅞	10032	3½	2⅞	3 1/16	...	d	−15	−17.0	−20.1	−22.4
28	SKT	✓Tanger Factory Outlet Ctrs	NY	NR	75	2833	Real estate investment trust	34¾	20¼	31⅞	18 13/16	26¾	18 11/16	8503	22	18 15/16	20¾	11.7	17	−1	8.9	−0.1	6.3
29	Pr A	Cm Cv[58]Dep Pfd(25)	NY	BB−	5	672		30⅞	18¾	28½	18¾	25 1/16	19 1/16	168	20¼	19 3/16	19¾B	11.0	..	...	...	...	...
30	TARO	✓Taro Pharmaceutical Ind	NNM	NR	23	1209	Hldg co: pharmaceutical prod	12¾	⅝	7¼	3¾	19	4⅞	23223	14⅞	10½	14½	...	30	6	186	31.5	14.5
31	TARR	Tarragon Realty Investors[59]	NNM	NR	12	109	Real estate investment trust	57¼	2 13/16	28½	11	16½	9⅞	1766	11⅛	10	10¼	4.1	26	NM	−3.4	2.9	14.3
32	TBC	✓Tasty Baking	NY,B,Ph	B	43	3451	Snack cake,pies,cookies,donuts	21⅝	2 1/16	22⅝	13 13/16	15 11/16	8⅛	5177	9¾	8⅛	8 7/16	5.7	15	−5	−42.1	−5.4	−0.7
33	TCO	✓Taubman Centers	NY,Ph	NR	118	37644	Real estate investment trust	15½	8⅞	14¾	12⅛	14⅛	10½	22406	11⅜	10½	10¾	9.1	49	−10	−15.7	1.1	10.2
34	TBW	✓T B Wood's	NY,P	NR	25	2275	Elec/mech ind pwr transmisn pd	21 7/16	7⅜	24½	11¾	12¾	8¼	788	9 13/16	8¼	8½	4.2	9	2	−27.1	−5.2	...
35	TCLPZ	✓TC Pipelines L.P.	NNM	NR	15	4002	Natural gas pipeline system	....	....	....	....	21	13⅞	50451	16¾	13⅞	14⅛	...	..	...	...	...	...
✤36	TBY	✓TCBY Enterprises	NY,Ph,P	B−	64	4002	Franchises frozen yogurt strs	29	¼	10¼	5⅛	7 7/16	3½	16261	4 1/16	3½	3 13/16	5.2	12	NM	−43.6	1.7	−4.0
#37•[12]	TCB	✓TCF Financial	NY,Ch,Ph,P	A−	273	62999	Commercial banking,MN,IL,WI,MI	34⅜	1⅜	37¼	15 13/16	30 11/16	21 11/16	76117	29⅝	23¾	24⅞	3.0	13	19	5.6	7.0	22.1
38	TCII	TCI Intl	NNM	C	8	248	High freq antenna,reconn sys	25 7/16	1⅞	6	1⅜	9¾	1 15/16	15611	9¾	4	9 7/16	...	d	Neg	372	10.5	18.0
39	TCSI	✓TCSI Corp	NNM	NR	42	8455	Dvlp telecomm software	29¾	1 5/16	8 15/16	1⅜	4¼	1¼	394571	4¼	1½	3 3/16	...	d	Neg	52.2	−20.1	−14.1
40	TWE	✓TD Waterhouse Group	NY,To	NR	62	11349	Discount brokerage svcs	....	....	....	....	27¼	11 7/16	141065	18 3/16	15	16½	...	59	...	...	...	...
41	TDK	✓TDK Corp[62] ADS	NY,B,Ch	NR	26	411	Ferrite, ceramics, mag tapes	95	2½	90¼	58	143½	67	1040	143½	107 1/16	135 5/16	0.4	48	49	50.7	28.0	23.8
42	TMI	✓Team, Inc	AS,Ch	B−	17	1155	Environmental services	35¾	1¼	5⅞	2⅞	4⅞	1 11/16	2710	2⅜	1 11/16	1 15/16	...	..	NM	−46.6	7.4	0.7
#43•[13]	TECD	✓Tech Data Corp	NNM	B+	247	37837	Dstr computer hardware prod	51¾	1	53⅛	33¾	44 11/16	14½	169642	27¼	20	27⅛	...	12	31	−32.6	−0.3	9.8
44	TO	✓Tech/Ops Sevcon	AS	B+	17	570	Mfr vehicle speed controllers	22⅞	1 5/16	17¾	10 13/16	18½	9⅝	999	10¼	9⅝	10¼	7.0	10	14	−22.5	−2.6	12.6
45	TSY	✓Tech-Sym	NY,Ch,P,Ph	B	50	3910	Electronic components/sys	40	⅜	31⅞	20½	30	16¼	4847	20⅞	16¼	20⅝	...	d	Neg	−7.3	−11.5	−2.6
46	TSH	✓Teche Holding	AS	NR	10	373	Savings & loan, Louisiana	24	10	22⅞	13	17½	13	425	14⅜	13	13¼	3.8	10	9	−11.7	0.2	...
47	TCPI	Technical Chemicals & Products	NNM	NR	13	942	Dvlp medical diagnostic eqp	22⅜	2	13¾	1⅜	2¼	¼	133817	1¾	⅜	½	...	d	Neg	−66.0	−62.0	...
48	TCLN	Techniclone Corp	NSC	NR	20	737	R&D monoclonal antibodies	9	⅛	2⅝	½	2	¼	469587	1	¼	½	...	d	10	−51.5	−51.0	...
✤49•[2]	TNL	✓Technitrol Inc	NY,Ch,Ph	B+	150	7641	Electronic/mechanical prod	43⅛	1/16	44⅜	16⅞	46¼	19⅞	7386	46	41 3/16	44½	0.6	18	37	40.8	33.4	47.4
✤50•[4]	TSCC	✓Technology Solutions	NNM	B	161	35121	Computer sys consult'g/svcs	25	1 7/16	23 11/16	6⅛	39¼	6⅜	133570	39¼	27¼	32¾	...	d	−38	206	21.1	71.1

Uniform Footnote Explanations-See Page 4. Other: [1]P:Cycle 1. [2]ASE:Cycle 1. [3]P:Cycle 2. [4]CBOE:Cycle 3. [5]CBOE,Ph:Cycle 2. [6]CBOE:Cycle 2. [7]ASE:Cycle 2. [8]Ph:Cycle 3. [9]ASE,CBOE,P:Cycle 1. [10]CBOE,Ph:Cycle 1. [11]ASE,CBOE:Cycle 1. [12]CBOE:Cycle 1. [13]P:Cycle 3. [51]Jan'98 & prior pricing in $Cdn. [52]Plan SmallCap 600 delisting: eff Jan 6. [53]Ea ADS rep 0.1 Ord shrs SFr 10. [54]4 Mo Dec'97. [55]Ea ADS rep 5 ord,par NT $10. [56]Sep'97&prior pricing in $Cdn. [57]Stk of Color Tile. [58]Dep for 0.10 shr Sr'A'cm Cv Redm Pfd. [59]Reflects reverse mgr w/Natl Inc Rlty Tr. [60]To be determined. [61]Incl 3.2M Sub Units. [62]ADS equal to 1 com shr,par 50 yen. [63]Fiscal May'97 & prior. [64]7 Mo Dec'98:Fiscal May'98 earned $0.49.

Index	Cash Divs. Ea.Yr. Since	Dividends: Latest Payment Period $	Date	Ex. Div.	Total $ So Far 1999	Ind. Rate	Paid 1998	Financial Position Mil-$ Cash& Equiv.	Curr. Assets	Curr. Liab.	Balance Sheet Date	Capitalization Lg Trm Debt Mil-$	Shs. 000 Pfd.	Com.	Earnings $ Per Shr. Years End	1995	1996	1997	1998	1999	Last 12 Mos.	Interim Earnings Period	$ per Shr. 1998	1999	Index
1	....	None Since Public			...	Nil	....	210	337	206	10-01-99	0.91	...	58143	Mr	vd0.76	v0.47	v1.42	v0.86	E1.88	1.54	6 Mo Sep	v0.16	v0.84	1
2◆	1997	S0.01½	10-8-99	9-15	0.028	0.03	0.022	25.5	511	199	9-30-99	69.3	...	88481	Dc	v0.51	v0.55	v0.76	v0.99	E1.23	1.14	9 Mo Sep	v0.73	v0.88	2
3	....	None Since Public			...	Nil	....	62.3	87.6	18.1	9-30-99	7.98	...	15152	Je	0.66	0.47	v0.83	vd0.10	vd0.08	d0.04	3 Mo Sep	v0.02	v0.06	3
4	....	None Since Public			...	Nil	....	Total Assets $735.22M			9-30-99	143	...	10385	Dc	pv0.69	v1.76	□v1.59	vd1.39	....	d4.01	9 Mo Sep	vd0.26	vd2.88	4
5	....	0.05	8-1-94	6-27	...	Nil	....	3.04	153	66.7	8-28-99	....	...	16463	Fb	v0.59	v1.08	v1.29	v1.00	....	0.48	6 Mo Aug	v0.36	vd0.16	5
6	....	None Since Public			...	Nil	....	15.1	18.4	15.2	9-30-99	7.01	p...	★28684	Dc	...	...	...	vpd0.46	....	....	9 Mo Sep	n/a	vpd0.03	6
7	....	None Since Public			...	Nil	....	6.90	17.6	5.66	9-30-99	6.12	...	9189	Dc	v0.09	v1.46	v0.02	vd0.23	....	0.04	9 Mo Sep	vd0.21	vΔ0.06	7
8◆	....	None Since Public			...	Nil	....	645	851	240	7-03-99	11.4	...	70845	Sp	0.75	v0.27	v1.25	vΔ0.93	vP2.20	2.20				8
9◆	1930	Q0.09	1-3-00	12-21	0.343	0.36	0.28	Total Deposits $9275.35M			9-30-99	229	...	p279806	Dc	v0.44	0.53	v0.62	v0.70	E0.80	0.76	9 Mo Sep	v0.51	v0.57	9
10	....	None Paid			...	Nil	....	16.7	17.4	4.34	j6-30-99	9.96	...	31277	Dc	d0.21	vd0.07	vd0.51	vd0.67	....	jd0.74	9 Mo Sep	vd0.48	vd0.55	10
11◆	....	None Since Public			...	Nil	....	58.9	93.6	35.5	9-30-99	....	...	38228	Dc	p0.11	pv0.11	pv0.26	v0.63	....	0.55	9 Mo Sep	v0.49	v0.41	11
12	....	None Paid			...	Nil	....	7.57	13.7	0.75	9-30-99	0.15	...	14255	Mr	v0.19	v0.29	v0.09	v0.38	....	0.36	6 Mo Sep	v0.14	v0.12	12
13	....	None Since Public			...	Nil	....	File bankruptcy Chapt 11			6-30-98	2.32	...	128492	Sp	d1.07	d12.38	d2.25	....	....	d1.51	9 Mo JunΔ	vd2.14	vd1.40	13
14◆	1970	Q0.12	1-28-00	1-5	0.40	0.48	0.35½	143	2575	1673	10-02-99	1055	...	329380	Je	0.69	0.76	v0.85	v0.95	v1.08	1.13	3 Mo Sep	□0.26	v□0.31	14
15◆	....	0.40	1-10-96	12-26	...	Nil	....	18.0	168	130	7-31-99	138	10	11991	Oc	3.24	d3.04	vd0.12	vd11.20	vPd7.46	d7.46				15
16	....	None Since Public			...	Nil	....	42.6	408	218	9-30-99	1.99	...	35555	Dc	pv0.93	v1.15	v1.02	v1.11	....	1.02	9 Mo Sep	v0.80	v0.71	16
17◆	....	None Since Public			...	Nil	....	7.31	189	61.5	6-30-99	78.1	...	31906	Sp	0.11	0.31	v0.69	v0.59	vP0.58	0.58				17
18	1977	Q0.05½	1-12-00	12-23	0.22	0.22	0.22	112	314	88.6	10-02-99	142	1125	15513	Dc	vd1.80	v0.82	v1.44	v1.57	....	1.78	9 Mo Sep	v1.23	v1.44	18
19	1971	Q0.05	12-15-99	11-22	0.20	0.20	0.20	14.8	56.9	23.1	8-31-99	3.90	...	5025	My	0.25	0.57	v0.75	v0.46	v0.03	1.20	6 Mo Nov	v0.02	v1.19	19
20	1998	0.098	7-6-99	6-7	0.098	0.10	0.075	71.2	282	140	j12-31-98	140	...	5384	Dc	p0.98	p0.62	□v0.60	v0.73	....	0.73				20
21	....	None Since Public			...	Nil	....	0.03	16.7	10.5	9-30-99	....	...	6728	Dc	...	...	‡v[54]0.03	v0.11	....	0.21	9 Mo Sep	v0.07	v0.17	21
22◆	....	Plan annual div			...	Nil	....	545	1046	468	12-31-97	610	...	7278999	Dc	p0.38	p0.48	v0.37	n/a	....	....	9 Mo Sep	v0.25	v0.23	22
23	1994	Q0.12	12-20-99	12-2	0.46	0.48	0.44	11.6	387	146	10-30-99	100	...	31489	Ja	v1.82	v1.91	v0.18	v1.15	....	1.63	9 Mo Oct	v0.89	v1.37	23
24	....	g0.09½	10-15-91	9-19	...	Nil	....	24.6	456	452	j6-30-99	1953	...	119083	Dc	0.42	v0.91	v0.70	vd2.31	....	jd1.34	9 Mo Sep	vd0.33	v0.64	24
25◆	....	None Since Public			...	Nil	....	43.6	113	62.8	9-30-99	85.0	...	64670	Dc	vp0.32	v0.35	vd0.33	vΔd5.20	....	d0.86	9 Mo Sep	vΔd3.69	vΔ0.65	25
26◆	1987	Q0.05½	1-19-00	12-30	0.15	0.22	0.20	54.3	1379	880	9-30-99	325	74	193315	Dc	v0.79	vd0.41	v0.82	v0.27	E1.42	1.08	9 Mo Sep	v0.04	v0.85	26
27	....	h[57]....	4-9-79	4-10	...	Nil	....	0.82	72.1	29.1	9-30-99	39.3	...	12011	Je	vd0.89	vd0.15	vd0.15	v0.37	vd1.96	d2.05	3 Mo Sep	v0.08	vd0.01	27
28	1993	Q0.60½	11-15-99	10-27	2.41½	2.42	2.35	Total Assets $467.75M			9-30-99	307	88	7850	Dc	v1.36	v□1.46	v1.54	v□1.28	....	1.26	9 Mo Sep	v□1.11	v□1.09	28
29	1994	Q0.545	11-15-99	10-27	2.176	2.18	2.117	Cv into 0.901 com, $27.75				....	883	...	Dc	b1.93	...	...	...	....	....				29
30	....	None Since Public			...	Nil	....	1.11	39.7	27.8	12-31-98	16.3	...	±10051	Dc	±0.19	v±0.21	v±0.14	v±0.23	....	0.48	9 Mo Sep	v0.11	v0.36	30
31◆	1979	Q0.10½	11-15-99	10-28	0.42	0.42	0.80	Total Assets $368.72M			9-30-99	276	...	8082	Dc	ΔvEd0.01	v1.21	vΔ1.43	v□d0.02	....	0.39	9 Mo Sep	v□0.13	v□0.54	31
32◆	1915	Q0.12	12-1-99	11-3	0.48	0.48	0.48	0.03	30.3	16.0	9-25-99	21.1	...	7822	Dc	v0.73	v0.82	v0.77	v0.72	....	0.56	9 Mo Sep	v0.50	v□0.34	32
33	1993	Q0.24½	1-20-00	12-29	0.96	0.98	0.93½	Total Assets $1554.41M			9-30-99	868	8000	53278	Dc	vΔ0.44	□v0.47	v0.48	v□0.32	....	0.22	9 Mo Sep	v□0.22	v□0.12	33
34	1996	Q0.09	10-29-99	10-13	0.36	0.36	0.35	3.07	56.5	23.8	10-01-99	33.0	...	p5480	Dc	vp1.21	v□1.06	v1.47	v1.33	....	0.92	9 Mo Sep	v1.08	v0.67	34
35	1999	0.45	11-12-99	10-27	0.618	[60]...	....	Total Assets $250.7M			9-30-99	....	...	[61]±17500	Dc	...	...	v...	vp1.62	....	....	9 Mo Sep	n/a	vp0.64	35
36	1988	Q0.05	1-11-00	12-23	0.20	0.20	0.20	18.3	50.7	11.7	8-29-99	1.27	...	22887	Nv	d0.83	v0.26	v0.36	v0.43	....	0.31	9 Mo Aug	v0.41	v0.29	36
37◆	1988	Q0.18¾	11-30-99	11-3	0.72½	0.75	0.613	Total Deposits $6633.74M			9-30-99	1767	...	82950	Dc	v□0.87	v1.20	v1.69	v1.76	E1.95	1.91	9 Mo Sep	v1.30	v1.45	37
38	....	None Since Public			...	Nil	....	8.36	21.8	8.99	6-30-99	....	...	3205	Sp	0.39	0.31	d1.75	vd1.17	Pvd0.37	d0.37				38
39◆	....	None Since Public			...	Nil	....	34.9	55.7	6.98	9-30-99	....	...	22686	Dc	v0.42	v0.01	vd0.12	vd0.20	....	d0.59	9 Mo Sep	vd0.02	vd0.41	39
40	....	None Since Public			...	Nil	....	Equity per shr $3.97			4-30-99	....	...	★375000	Oc	...	...	...	pv0.15	Pv0.28	0.28				40
41	1976	0.246	12-27-99	9-27	0.49	0.49	0.385	1693	3809	1067	3-31-99	14.8	...	133190	Mr	1.97	3.65	v3.32	v2.85	....	2.85				41
42	....	0.02	3-1-93	2-3	...	Nil	....	0.56	22.1	5.00	8-31-99	21.3	...	8235	My	vd0.22	vd1.80	v0.15	v0.23	v0.04	0.01	3 Mo Aug	v0.04	v0.01	42
43◆	....	None Since Public			...	Nil	....	4.21	3488	2711	10-31-99	308	227	52142	Ja	v0.56	v1.35	v1.92	Δv2.47	....	2.35	9 Mo Oct	v1.79	v1.67	43
44◆	1990	Q0.18	1-7-00	12-16	0.72	0.72	0.63	3.57	13.9	7.06	7-03-99	....	...	3111	Sp	0.81	0.97	v0.61	v1.04	Pv1.00	1.00				44
45	....	5%Stk	12-18-59		...	Nil	....	3.77	158	50.0	9-30-99	1.64	...	6036	Dc	v1.95	v□3.60	v1.21	v0.83	....	d4.80	9 Mo Sep	v1.69	vd3.94	45
46	1995	Q0.12½	12-31-99	12-15	0.50	0.50	0.50	Total Deposits $298.55M			6-30-99	75.3	...	2803	Sp	0.80	v0.70	v1.23	v1.17	Pv1.29	1.29				46
47	....	None Since Public			...	Nil	....	5.68	10.7	1.52	9-30-99	....	13	11978	Dc	□vd0.18	vd0.27	vd0.45	vd1.09	....	d1.17	9 Mo Sep	vd0.73	vd0.81	47
48	....	None Paid			...	Nil	....	0.64	1.07	6.31	10-31-99	3.45	...	81215	Ap	d0.44	vd0.30	vd1.57	vd0.49	vd0.30	d0.29	6 Mo Oct	vd0.12	vd0.11	48
49◆	1975	Q0.068	1-28-00	1-5	0.25½	0.27	0.23¼	64.4	224	94.4	10-01-99	50.8	...	16235	Dc	v0.71	v1.27	v2.53	v2.06	....	2.42	9 Mo Sep	v1.56	v1.92	49
50◆	....	None Since Public			...	Nil	....	108	215	61.4	9-30-99	....	...	42893	Dc	0.10	0.13	v[63]0.38	v‡[64]0.10	....	d0.33	9 Mo Sep	v0.44	v0.01	50

◆Stock Splits & Divs By Line Reference Index [2]3-for-2,'97,'98,'99. [8]2-for-1,'95. [9]3-for-2,'96,'97,'98. [11]3-for-2,'98. [14]2-for-1,'98. [15]3-for-2,'95:1-for-4 REVERSE,'99. [17]2-for-1,'98. [22]45% stk div,'98:23% stk div,'99. [25]3-for-2,'96:2-for-1,'97. [26]2-for-1,'97,'99. [31]10%,'94,'95,'96,'97. [32]5-for-4,'97. [37]2-for-1,'95,'97. [39]3-for-2,'96. [43]2-for-1,'94. [44]2-for-1,'95. [49]3-for-1,'94:2-for-1,'97. [50]3-for-2,'96,'97,'98.

¶ S&P 500
# MidCap 400
✚ SmallCap 600
• Options

Index	Ticker	Name of Issue (Call Price of Pfd. Stocks)	Market	Com. Rank. & Pfd. Rating	Inst. Hold Cos	Inst. Hold Shs. (000)	Principal Business	Price Range 1971-97 High	1971-97 Low	1998 High	1998 Low	1999 High	1999 Low	Dec. Sales in 100s	December, 1999 Last Sale Or Bid High	Low	Last	%Div Yield	P-E Ratio	EPS 5 Yr Growth	% Annualized Total Return 12 Mo	36 Mo	60 Mo
1•[1]	TEK.A	Teck Corp Cl'A'	To,Mo	B–	1	741	Mining & petroleum	34	7/16	23	9½	16 1/16	10 5/16	139	15	12⅝	13B	1.5	d	Neg	22.5	–23.4	–11.1
2	TEK.B	✓ Cl'B'	To	B–	22	7431		35⅝	2 5/10	22½	8½	17 5/10	9 11/10	51297	15	12 3/10	13⅝	1.5	d	Neg	23.5	–23.8	–10.9
3•[2]	TCNO	✓Tecnomatix Technologies Ltd	NNM	NR	33	3155	Computer-aided prod'n softwr	41	3⅝	39	7⅛	33	11½	23252	33	26 15/16	28¾	...	61	NM	64.3	2.8	41.2
#4•[3]	TE	✓TECO Energy	NY,B,C,Ch,P,Ph	A	353	55088	Hldg co:Tampa Electric	28 3/16	2 3/16	30⅝	24¾	28	18⅜	78526	20	18⅜	18 9/16	7.0	13	–1	–30.1	–3.6	3.2
#5•[4]	TECUA	✓Tecumseh Products Cl'A'	NNM	B+	216	10292	Refrigeration prod:motors	60¼	24	58	42⅜	67¾	41½	14575	48 7/16	44⅛	47 3/16	2.7	7	–4	3.6	–4.1	3.6
6	TECUB	Cl'B'	NNM	B+	59	4404		62¾	4⅜	59¼	43¼	61½	37½	4073	44⅛	40	41¾	3.1	8	–4	–5.3	–7.6	1.0
7	TK	✓Teekay Shipping	NY,Ch	NR	69	9916	Transp'n svc to oil industry	38	22⅝	33¾	15⅜	19¼	13 5/16	18435	16¼	13¾	15 15/16	5.4	d	–35	–10.7	–18.2	...
8	TFR	Tefron Ltd	NY	NR	8	1689	Mfr intimate apparel	23⅛	17	27 3/16	5	13⅞	6½	7044	13⅞	10 3/16	12½	...	25	...	90.5	...	...
9	TRC	✓Tejon Ranch	NY,Ch,P	B	51	5992	Seed:cattle:farm'g:oil:land	63¼	1 5/16	32¾	18¼	33 13/16	16⅛	3346	25 1/16	19 13/16	23¾	0.2	88	37	19.7	18.5	14.9
10	TKLC	✓Tekelec	NNM	B	157	27591	Telecommun'ns test eqp	24 11/16	⅜	25⅞	10 1/16	24⅞	6½	173046	24⅞	16¼	22½	...	..	40	35.9	79.1	40.7
¶11•[5]	TEK	✓Tektronix Inc	NY,B,Ch,P,Ph	B	318	38821	Mfrs electronic equipment	46 7/16	3	48 3/16	13 11/16	40	17 9/16	92157	40	33⅛	38⅞	1.2	41	Neg	31.6	6.0	12.9
12•[6]	TBFC	✓Telebanc Financial[51]	NNM	NR	118	11949	Savings & loan, Virginia	....	....	18 3/16	3 15/16	75⅞	15	193033	31⅝	23¼	26	...	..	...	53.5	...	...
13•[7]	TEO	✓Tel Argentina-France Tel'B'ADS[52]	NY,Ch,P	NR	113	34439	Telecommun svcs - Argentina	36 1/16	12⅞	38 7/16	20	36⅛	20½	44658	35 3/16	29¼	34¼	4.3	22	...	30.6	25.7	10.8
14•[8]	TLD	✓Tele Danmark A/S ADS[53]	NY,Ph,P	NR	77	14750	Domestic/intl phone sv Denmark	16 5/16	11⅛	35⅜	15 7/16	38⅞	24	4126	38⅞	31⅝	37¾	1.3	29	7	14.4	45.2	29.3
15•[5]	NZT	✓Telecom Corp New Zealand ADS[54]	NY,Ph,P	NR	125	14399	Provides telecommun svcs	44½	10 9/16	41⅛	28¾	42½	31¼	9361	38¾	33 9/16	38½	5.0	18	11	14.2	4.8	15.6
16	TI	✓Telecom Italia SpA Ord ADS[55]	NY,P	NR	..	...	Telecommunication svcs,Italy	68 9/16	25⅝	90⅞	53	143⅝	82½	8235	143⅝	107¾	140	0.8	45	18	63.4	48.8	...
17•[9]	TI.A	Savings ADS[56]	NY	NR	1	8		42	18⅝	64	39	75	48¼	37	62	53½	60½	2.4	20	...	–2.0	29.9	...
18•[10]	TBH	✓Tele Brasil-Telebras Hldrs ADS[57]	NY	NR	290	35252	Telecommun svcs, Brasil	....	....	127 15/16	51⅝	135⅜	50⅛	291626	135⅜	89⅝	128¾	...	11	...	80.5	...	...
19	RTB	Tele Brasil-Teleb Portfolio ADS[59]	NY	NR	5	171	Telecommun svcs,Brasil	....	....	101	68⅞	133½	53	174	133½	96	129¾	...	..	...	77.1	...	...
20	TSU	✓Tele Celular Sul Partici ADS[60]	NY	NR	61	6628	Celular telecomm svcs	....	....	30¼	12¾	35	15⅝	19570	35	19½	31¾	...	..	...	87.9	...	...
21	TRO	✓Tele Centro Oeste Partici ADS[62]	NY	NR	55	34162	Celular telecomm svcs	....	....	7½	2	7¼	2 3/16	51605	7¼	3 15/16	6½	...	..	...	143	...	...
22	TCS	✓Tele Centro Sul Partici ADS[63]	NY	NR	125	8523	Telecommunications svcs	....	....	61⅞	40½	93	27⅜	25292	93	66⅞	90¾	...	..	...	121	...	...
23	TBE	✓Tele Leste Celular Part ADS[64]	NY	NR	36	834	Celular telecom svcs	....	....	50¾	20¼	47	17¼	2419	47	29⅞	42½	...	..	...	57.7	...	...
24	TND	✓Tele Nordeste Cel Partici ADS[65]	NY	NR	56	2350	Celular telecommun svcs	....	....	33	10½	53¼	11¾	5565	53¼	25⅝	50½	...	..	...	183	...	...
25	TCN	✓Tele Norte Celular Part ADS[64]	NY	NR	40	615	Celular telecommun svcs	....	....	47 15/16	11¼	45	16¼	3526	45	29⅞	42 15/16	...	..	...	92.6	...	...
26	TNE	✓Tele Norte Leste Partici ADS[66]	NY	NR	143	24557	Telecommunication svcs	....	....	20	11¾	26 13/16	8 9/16	163490	26 13/16	17½	25½	...	..	...	110	...	...
27	TSD	✓Tele Sudeste Celular Part ADS[63]	NY	NR	91	9919	Cellular telecomm svcs	....	....	32⅝	16	41½	12¾	57512	41½	20½	38 13/16	...	..	...	90.8	...	...
28	TLCP	TeleCorp PCS 'A'	NNM	NR	..	...	Wireless communic svcs	....	....	....	....	42⅞	20	95586	42⅞	34⅜	38	...	..	...	...	...	...
✚29	TDY	✓Teledyne Technologies	NY	NR	..	...	Electronic,communic,aerospace	....	....	....	....	10 11/16	7 13/16	86538	10½	7 13/16	9 7/16	...	..	...	...	...	...
#30•[3]	TFX	✓Teleflex Inc	NY,B,Ch,Ph,P	A+	287	23662	Auto,med'l,aerospace,marine prd	39¾	⅛	46⅜	29½	50 7/16	28⅞	37201	34½	28⅞	31 5/16	1.7	13	16	–30.5	7.8	13.6
31•[7]	TAR	✓Telefonica De Argentina ADS[68]	NY,Ch,Ph,P	NR	176	58221	Telecommun svcs Argentina	41¼	14⅝	39⅜	19	39⅞	20½	110552	31¼	25 15/16	30⅞	4.5	11	10	16.0	11.2	8.0
32•[7]	TDP	✓Telefonica del Peru ADS[69]	NY,Ch,Ph	NR	126	57456	Telecommunication svcs,Peru	27 9/16	16¾	23 1/16	10¼	16⅜	10½	51543	13⅜	12 1/16	13⅜	2.8	15	44	8.7	–8.4	...
33•[4]	TEF	✓Telefonica S.A. ADS[70]	NY,P,Ph	NR	276	35360	Domestic/intl tel sv in Spain	30	5	49 11/16	27½	79⅞	39⅝	39781	79⅞	63	78 13/16	s...	40	15	91.6	57.4	52.7
34	TFONY	✓Telefonos de Mex'A'ADR[71]	NSC	NR	26	7331	Telephone service in Mexico	4	1/16	2⅞	1⅝	5¾	1⅞	28907	5¾	4⅝	5½	1.1	26	–1	141	55.1	25.8
35•[11]	TMX	✓Telefonos de Mex'L'ADS[72]	NY,Ch,Ph,P	NR	430	142267	Telephone service in Mexico	76⅛	23	58 7/16	32¾	113⅞	39⅞	253800	113⅞	92	112½	1.4	25	–1	138	54.4	25.7
36•[12]	TGO	✓Teleglobe Inc[74]	NY,To,Ph	B	100	39650	Telecommunications svcs	22 3/16	2¼	36⅝	14¼	40 15/16	14 13/16	31811	26 1/16	19½	22 11/16	1.5	d	Neg	–36.1	5.3	21.0
37	TMB	✓Telemig Celular Partici ADS[65]	NY	NR	48	3270	Celular telecomm svcs	....	....	39	18	49	14	8878	49	32¾	46⅜	...	..	...	121	...	...
#38•[13]	TDS	✓Telephone & Data Sys	AS,Ch,P	A–	289	40305	Telecommunications 29 states	57	1 9/16	50⅛	30⅝	137	44⅛	60008	137	116⅛	126	0.4	34	–11	183	52.9	23.4
39	TCP	✓Telesp Celular Partici ADS[75]	NY	NR	104	19486	Celular telecommun svcs	....	....	31⅞	16 3/16	45⅞	12 13/16	94016	45⅞	28⅜	42⅜	...	..	...	146	...	...
40	TSP	✓Telesp Participacoes ADS[66]	NY	NR	143	44688	Telecommunication svcs	....	....	31¾	21	27½	13 7/16	191267	24 15/16	17 13/16	24 7/16	...	18	...	12.3	...	...
41•[14]	TLSP	✓TeleSpectrum Worldwide	NNM	NR	60	13029	Telemktg/mkt research svcs	22⅛	2 15/16	11½	2 11/16	12	3⅞	106031	8¼	5¼	7⅛	...	22	...	–27.4	–23.4	...
42	TIWI	Telesystem Intl Wireless	NNM,To	NR	42	17006	Dvp stg:telecomm svcs	....	....	22⅛	7⅞	37 5/16	12½	7126	37 5/16	23½	37¼	...	d	–15	201	...	...
43•[8]	TTEC	✓TeleTech Holdings	NNM	NR	83	17222	Provide client/customer svcs	40⅜	9⅞	18⅛	6 3/16	34⅜	5 9/16	100953	34⅜	20 9/16	33 11/16	...	78	76	229	9.0	...
44	TLL	✓Teletouch Communications	AS	NR	4	696	Mobile communications svcs	9	2 1/16	5 7/16	2⅛	2½	⅜	2989	1 1/16	⅝	¾	...	d	2	–64.7	–32.6	...
45	TWSTY	✓Telewest Commun plc ADS[76]	NNM	NR	40	2018	Cable TV/telephone svcs	30¾	10⅜	34⅜	11½	60	28⅞	5227	60	46¾	55¼	...	d	...	95.6	38.6	15.8
46•[15]	TGNT	✓Teligent Inc 'A'	NNM	NR	119	4514	Telecommunications svcs	27¼	21½	35⅜	18¼	75⅝	28⅞	47569	67½	54 11/16	61¾	...	d	...	115	...	...
¶47•[16]	TLAB	✓Tellabs, Inc	NNM	B	991	256770	Voice,data commun'ns eqp	32½	5/16	46 9/16	15 11/16	77¼	32⅜	998202	70⅛	60⅛	64 3/16	...	49	47	88.2	50.8	56.2
48	TLS	Telstra Corp ADS[77]	NY	NR	20	2496	Telecommun svc,Australia	....	....	23¾	19 5/16	29 11/16	23¼	1481	28⅞	26⅛	27¼	1.6	38	...	23.4	...	...
49	TLS.PP	1st[78]Installm't[79]ADS[80]	NY	....	..	...		....	....	....	....	19 1/16	15 1/16	5693	19 1/16	16 11/16	17 3/16	2.6	..	...	...	...	...
50	TLTN	✓Teltrend Inc	NNM	NR	41	3823	Dgn/dvp network svcs tel equip	58¼	13¾	24⅜	11	32 3/16	14⅛	42380	32 3/16	19¼	30¼	...	25	–8	58.2	2.9	...

Uniform Footnote Explanations-See Page 4. Other: [1]Vc:Cycle 2. [2]CBOE:Cycle 2. [3]Ph:Cycle 2. [4]ASE:Cycle 3. [5]ASE,P:Cycle 3. [6]Ph:Cycle 1. [7]ASE,CBOE,P:Cycle 1. [8]CBOE:Cycle 1. [9]ASE,CBOE:Cycle 3. [10]CBOE,Ph:Cycle 1. [11]ASE,CBOE,P,Ph:Cycle 2. [12]ASE,CBOE:Cycle 2. [13]P:Cycle 2. [14]CBOE:Cycle 3. [15]CBOE,P,Ph:Cycle 2. [16]P:Cycle 3. [51]E Trade plan acq,2.1 com. [52]Ea ADS rep 5 Cl'B'Ord,Ps1.00. [53]Ea ADS rep 0.5 com DKK10. [54]Ea ADS rep 8 ord, NZ$1.00. [55]Ea ADS rep 10 ord shrs,Lit 1,000. [56]Ea ADS rep 10 svgs shrs,Lit 1,000. [57]Ea ADS rep 1 ord. [58]To be determined. [59]Ea ADS rep 1000 RCTB 40 portfolio ctfs. [60]Ea ADS rep 10000 Pfd shrs,no par. [61]Approx. [62]Ea ADS rep 3000 Pfd shrs,no par. [63]Ea ADS rep 5000 Pfd shrs,no par. [64]Ea ADS rep 50000 Pfd shrs,no par. [65]Ea ADS rep 20000 Pfd shrs,no par. [66]Ea ADS rep 1000 Pfd shrs,no par. [67]Pfd in $M. [68]Ea ADS rep 10'B'ord shrs, p$1.00. [69]Ea ADS rep 10 com shrs, S/1.00. [70]Each ADS rep 3 shrs par 500 pesetas. [71]Each ADR rep 1 'A' ord. [72]Each ADS rep 20 'L' ord. [73]Fr1-1-2001,prv'd'A'&'AA'shr less than51%outstg. [74]May'97 & prior pricing in $Cdn. [75]Ea ADS rep 2500 Pfd shrs,no par. [76]Ea ADS rep 10 com, L.1 par. [77]Ea ADS rep 5 ord,A$0.50. [78]Full pay't ADS rep 5 ord A$0.50. [79]2nd pay't(39%)paid 11-2-2000. [80]1st Installm't ADS (61% paid).

Index	Splits ◆ Cash Divs. Ea.Yr. Since	Dividends Latest Payment Period $	Date	Ex. Div.	Total $ So Far 1999	Ind. Rate	Paid 1998	Financial Position Mil-$ Cash& Equiv.	Curr. Assets	Curr. Liab.	Balance Sheet Date	Capitalization Lg Trm Debt Mil-$	Shs. 000 Pfd.	Com.	Earnings $ Per Shr. Years End	1995	1996	1997	1998	1999	Last 12 Mos.	Interim Earnings Period	$ per Shr. 1998	1999	Index
1	1977	gS0.10	12-31-99	12-13	g0.20	0.20	g0.20	263	422	89.3	j9-30-99	686	...	±107580	Dc	v±0.97	v±2.65	vd1.81	±vd0.51	....	jd0.47	9 Mo Sep	v±0.06	v±0.10	1
2	1994	gS0.10	12-31-99	12-13	g0.20	0.20	g0.20	....	...	...		....	...	102915	Dc	±0.97	±v2.65	vd1.81	±vd0.51	....	jd0.47	9 Mo Sep	v±0.06	v±0.10	2
3	1998	....			...	Nil	....	86.5	115	20.0	12-31-97	97.8	...	9972	Dc	0.55	v0.82	v0.30	PvΔ0.52	....	0.47	9 Mo Sep	vΔ0.27	v0.22	3
4	1900	Q0.32½	11-15-99	10-28	1.28½	1.30	1.225	9.90	446	868	9-30-99	1269	...	129448	Dc	v1.55	v1.67	v1.54	v1.57	E1.45↓	1.28	9 Mo Sep	v1.37	v1.08	4
5	1992	Q0.32	12-17-99	12-1	1.22	1.28	1.20	297	899	284	9-30-99	15.4	...	±19955	Dc	v±5.45	v±5.15	v±4.59	v±3.47	E6.45	5.35	9 Mo Sep	v±3.63	v±5.51	5
6	1940	Q0.32	12-17-99	12-1	1.22	1.28	1.20	....	...	...		....	...	5470	Dc	v±5.45	v±5.15	±v4.59	v±3.47	....	5.35	9 Mo Sep	v±3.63	v±5.51	6
7	1995	0.21½	10-29-99	10-13	0.86	0.86	0.86	127	166	72.2	3-31-99	603	...	31648	Mr	v1.17	v1.50	v2.44	v□1.70	....	d0.01	6 Mo Sep	v□1.50	vd0.21	7
8	....	None Since Public			...	Nil	....	34.6	59.7	18.2	12-31-97	....	...	±13415	Dc	...	pv1.29	v1.06	Pv0.90	....	0.51	9 Mo Sep	v0.78	v0.39	8
9	1982	S0.02½	12-10-99	11-17	0.05	0.05	0.05	10.8	45.4	41.0	9-30-99	6.52	...	12696	Dc	v0.03	v0.13	v0.24	Δv0.24	....	0.27	9 Mo Sep	v0.02	v0.05	9
10◆	....	None Since Public			...	Nil	....	50.9	166	168	9-30-99	....	...	55330	Dc	v0.13	vd0.06	v0.51	v0.67	....	0.15	9 Mo Sep	v0.43	vd0.09	10
11◆	1972	Q0.12	1-31-00	1-12	0.48	0.48	0.48	43.0	732	517	8-28-99	151	...	47249	My	1.75	v1.95	v2.29	v1.60	vd1.07	0.94	6 Mo Nov	vd1.87	v0.14	11
12◆	....	None Since Public			...	Nil	....	Total Deposits $2163M			9-30-99	477	...	33641	Dc	...	...	pv0.45	vd0.04	....	0.18	9 Mo Sep	vd0.11	v□0.11	12
13◆	1995	0.685	12-28-99	12-16	1.459	1.46	1.949	No Recent Finls				1158	...	±984381	Sp	1.55	...	...	...	...	1.55				13
14◆	1995	0.506	5-10-99	4-26	0.506	0.50	0.493	114	1881	2374	12-31-98	929	...	216460	Dc	1.20	v1.00	v0.44	v1.37	E1.33	1.37	6 Mo Jun	v0.58	v0.58	14
15◆	1992	0.452	12-27-99	11-30	1.912	1.91	†1.904	370	795	1188	3-31-99	594	...	1752802	Mr	2.06	1.72	v2.03	v2.01	E2.10	2.01				15
16	1995	1.11	8-4-99	7-14	1.11	1.11	0.705	2283	13147	18465	12-31-98	5983	...	±7421	Dc	±1.71	±1.92	v1.96	v3.09	....	3.09				16
17	1996	1.426	8-4-99	7-14	1.426	1.43	1.009	....	...	...		....	...	2166	Dc	±1.71	...	...	v3.09	....	3.09				17
18	1999	0.402		1-4	1.116	[58]....	....	No Recent Finls				....	...	...	Dc	...	...	...	E11.00	E12.00	....				18
19	1999	0.014		12-30	0.951	[58]....	....	No Recent Finls				....	...	...	Dc	...	...	...	....	....	....				19
20	1999	[61]0.197		12-29	0.094	[58]....	....	....	...	...		....	...	p11549	Dc	...	...	...	....	....	....				20
21	1999	0.018	7-14-99	6-25	0.337	[58]....	....	....	...	...		....	...	p38497	Dc	...	...	...	....	....	....				21
22	1999	[61]1.07		12-29	0.871	[58]....	....	....	...	...		....	...	p23098	Dc	...	...	...	....	....	....				22
23	1999	1.152	12-23-99	1-4	2.922	[58]....	....	....	...	...		....	...	p2310	Dc	...	...	...	n/a	....	....	3 Mo Mar	vNil	vNil	23
24	1999	[61]0.275		12-28	0.852	[58]....	....	....	...	...		....	...	p5775	Dc	...	...	...	....	....	....				24
25	1999	0.15	6-10-99	4-21	0.422	[58]....	....	....	...	...		....	...	p2310	Dc	...	...	...	....	....	....				25
26	1999	0.388	7-15-99	4-28	0.388	[58]....	....	....	...	...		....	...	p115491	Dc	...	...	...	n/a	....	....	3 Mo Mar	v0.37	v0.38	26
27	1999	0.055	12-29-99	3-15	0.833	[58]....	....	....	...	...		....	...	...	Dc	...	...	...	....	....	....				27
28	....	None Since Public			...	Nil	....	80.4	113	72.2	9-30-99	628	[67]268	★85024	Dc	...	...	...	vpd1.30	....	....	9 Mo Sep	n/a	vpd2.45	28
29	....	None Since Public			...	Nil	....	....	195	102	p9-30-99	100	...	27009	Dc	...	...	...	pv1.41	....	....	9 Mo Sep	n/a	vp1.06	29
30◆	1977	Q0.13	12-15-99	11-22	0.50½	0.52	0.44½	46.2	628	316	9-26-99	280	...	37971	Dc	v1.37	v1.58	v1.86	v2.15	....	2.42	9 Mo Sep	v1.49	v1.76	30
31◆	1994	0.699	12-14-99	12-2	0.699	1.40	1.398	11.1	965	1302	9-30-98	1879	...	±2140854	Sp	1.94	v1.63	v2.01	v2.24	E2.85	2.24				31
32	1996	[61]0.112	3-6-00	1-27	0.38	0.37	0.51	109	2160	3124	j12-31-98	1622	...	±2338442	Dc	1.35	1.49	v1.71	v0.89	....	0.89				32
33◆	1947	2%Stk	12-15-99	11-2	6%Stk	Stk	s0.471	Equity per shr $5.03			12-31-98	15224	...	3136500	Dc	1.10	0.92	v1.23	v1.47	E1.95	1.47				33
34	1951	0.016	12-30-99	12-20	0.061	0.06	0.06	1823	3485	2192	12-31-98	1872	...	±7724000	Dc	0.12	0.16	v0.19	v0.21	....	0.21				34
35	1991	0.394	12-30-99	12-20	1.517	1.58	1.50	Exch for'AA'shrs[73]				....	...	7724000	Dc	2.40	v3.33	E3.70	v4.20	E4.55	4.20				35
36◆	1991	Q0.08½	12-31-99	12-13	0.34	0.34	0.33	28.1	913	767	6-30-99	1159	5000	252953	Dc	0.71	v0.84	v1.02	v0.04	....	d0.58	9 Mo Sep	v0.78	v0.16	36
37	1999	0.321	6-16-99	4-21	0.321	[58]....	....	72.6	146	158	12-31-98	33.4	210030	124369	Dc	...	...	...	v0.02	....	0.02				37
38	1974	Q0.11½	12-31-99	12-13	0.46	0.46	0.44	86.5	447	484	9-30-99	1281	260	±61756	Dc	v1.74	v2.07	vd0.19	v1.03	E3.75	3.45	9 Mo Sep	v1.05	v3.47	38
39	1999	0.378	7-9-99	1-13	0.378	[58]....	....	179	351	279	12-31-97	579	...	p46196	Dc	...	...	n/a	n/a	....	....				39
40	1999	0.32	12-24-99	1-4	0.32	[58]....	....	688	1963	2059	12-31-98	....	210030	124369	Dc	...	...	...	v1.36	....	1.36				40
41	....	None Since Public			...	Nil	....	....	78.1	58.1	9-30-99	110	...	32593	Dc	p0.12	pv0.32	vd6.36	vd0.25	....	0.32	9 Mo Sep	vd0.39	v0.18	41
42	....	None Since Public			...	Nil	....	295	474	486	12-31-98	1081	...	73316	Dc	vpd0.50	vpd0.73	vpd1.41	vd2.45	....	d2.52	9 Mo Sep	vd1.42	vd1.49	42
43	....	None Since Public			...	Nil	....	57.6	143	62.6	9-30-99	24.0	...	61380	Dc	pv0.08	v0.24	v0.34	v0.31	....	0.43	9 Mo Sep	v0.22	v0.34	43
44◆	....	None Paid			...	Nil	....	5.09	17.0	7.63	8-31-99	76.4	102	4235	My	pd3.21	d1.73	v□d2.72	vd1.66	vd2.52	d2.52	3 Mo Aug	vd0.53	vd0.53	44
45	....	None Since Public			...	Nil	....	Equity per shr Neg			12-31-98	4262	...	2139501	Dc	d2.50	d4.90	vd5.90	vd2.99	....	d2.99				45
46	....	None Since Public			...	Nil	....	227	291	198	9-30-99	800	...	±54111	Dc	...	...	vd2.94	vd5.35	Ed9.50	d9.06	9 Mo Sep	vd3.35	vd7.06	46
47◆	....	None Since Public			...	Nil	....	924	1610	262	10-01-99	3.32	...	402276	Dc	v0.32	v0.32	v0.71	v1.03	E1.32	1.25	9 Mo Sep	v0.68	v0.90	47
48◆	1999	0.753	11-8-99	9-7	0.984	0.435	....	592	2800	5305	6-30-98	2972	...	2866600	Je	...	0.54	0.48	v0.73	....	0.73				48
49	....	Plan semi-annual div			...	0.44	....	....	...	...		....	...	55574	Je	...	...	...	....	....	....				49
50	....	None Since Public			...	Nil	....	27.8	57.3	15.7	10-30-99	....	...	5780	Jl	p1.19	1.86	v1.45	v0.34	v1.18	1.19	3 Mo Oct	v0.41	v0.42	50

◆**Stock Splits & Divs By Line Reference Index** [10]2-for-1,'95,'97,'98. [11]3-for-2,'97. [12]2-for-1,'99. [13]2-for-1,'97. [14]2-for-1,'99. [15]2-for-1,'97. [30]2-for-1,'97. [31]2-for-1,'95. [33]3-for-1,'99:Adj for 2%,'99. [36]2-for-1,'98. [44]2-for-3 REVERSE,'98. [47]2-for-1,'95,'96,'99. [48]4-for-1,'99.

¶ S&P 500
# MidCap 400
✣ SmallCap 600
• Options

Index	Ticker	Name of Issue (Call Price of Pfd. Stocks)	Market	Com. Rank. & Pfd. Rating	Inst. Hold Cos	Inst. Hold Shs. (000)	Principal Business	Price Range 1971-97 High	1971-97 Low	1998 High	1998 Low	1999 High	1999 Low	December, 1999 Dec. Sales in 100s	Last Sale Or Bid High	Last Sale Or Bid Low	Last Sale Or Bid Last	%Div Yield	P-E Ratio	EPS 5 Yr Growth	% Annualized Total Return 12 Mo	36 Mo	60 Mo
1	TELT	Teltronics Inc	NSC	C	3	32	Mfr telecommunications eq	39 1/16	1 7/16	9	1 1/2	7	1 1/2	8931	3 15/16	3	3 5/16	...	37	NM	96.3	–1.8	0.8
✣2•[1]	TLXN	✔Telxon Corp	NNM	B–	85	6242	Hand-held microcomputer sys	29 3/4	3 9/16	38 5/8	11	20 1/2	5 3/4	45361	20 1/2	14 3/4	16	0.1	d	Neg	15.4	9.4	3.1
¶3•[2]	TIN	✔Temple-Inland	NY,B,P	B	437	43343	Containers,paper,finl svcs	69 7/16	10 1/8	67 1/4	42 11/16	77 1/2	53 5/8	59349	66 1/16	56 9/16	65 15/16	1.9	22	–33	13.3	9.1	10.4
4	TNR	✔TENERA Inc	AS	NR	1	2	Svcs/softw to utility&mfg	39 1/2	7/16	2 3/4	1/2	2	3/4	3129	15/16	3/4	13/16	...	6	NM	–50.0	5.7	3.4
¶5•[2]	THC	✔Tenet Healthcare	NY,B,Ch,P,Ph	B–	548	273003	Specialty & gen'l hospitals	34 7/8	3/16	40 15/16	23 3/4	27 3/16	15 3/8	240673	24 7/8	20 3/4	23 1/2	...	31	15	–10.5	2.4	10.7
6	TENF	✔TenFold Corp	NNM	NR	53	3551	Design,dvlp software prod	....	....	....	....	44 1/8	17	44467	44 1/8	25 1/16	39 15/16	...	..	...	...	...	...
7	TGC	Tengasco Inc	AS	NR	3	202	Dvp stg:dvp oil/gas leases	18 1/2	1/4	13 1/2	3 1/2	14 3/8	4 1/2	15008	14 3/8	5 11/16	10 5/8	...	d	Neg	82.8	...	...
8	TANT	✔Tennant Co	NNM	A–	76	3909	Ind'l floor maintenance eq	39 5/8	2 9/16	45 3/4	33	45	31 7/16	2827	35 1/4	32 1/4	32 3/4	2.3	14	8	–16.7	8.3	8.8
✣9•[2]	TEN	✔Tenneco Automotive	NY,B,C,Ch,P,Ph	B	5	1057	Auto parts/emission ctrl prd	71	16 3/4	47 1/2	29 1/2	37 1/4	7	75393	9 1/2	7 1/4	9 5/16	12.9	4	...	...	...	...
10	TVC	Tenn Val Auth'PARRS' 'D'	NY	....[53]	16	508	Putable Automatic Reset Sec	....	....	26 1/2	24 7/8	26 3/8	20 7/8	12510	22 15/16	20 7/8	21 5/8	7.8	..	...	–11.8	...	...
11	TVE	Tenn Val Auth'PARRS'2029	NY	NR	6	89	Putable Automatic Reset Sec	....	....	....	....	24 7/8	20 1/16	16520	21 3/4	20 1/16	20 3/4	7.8	..	...	...	...	...
12	TVB	Tenn Val Auth 7.50%'QUIDS'	NY	NR	7	78	Qtly Income Debt Securities	26 7/16	23 3/4	26 11/16	25 3/16	26 1/16	22 1/8	5012	24 11/16	22 1/8	23	8.2	..	...	–4.1	4.7	...
13	TVA	Tenn Val Auth 8.00%'QUIDS'	NY,P	NR	6	53	Qtly Income Debt Securities	27 1/4	24	27 1/8	25 1/2	26 1/4	24 3/8	5589	25 3/8	24 3/8	24 3/4	8.1	..	...	2.2	6.2	...
14	TPP	✔Teppco Ptnrs L.P.	NY,Ch,P	NR	72	4746	Refined petrol prod pipeline	28 1/4	7 7/8	30 11/16	23 1/4	28 1/4	17 1/8	20086	20 3/8	17 1/8	19 5/16	9.8	11	2	–15.3	4.3	16.9
¶15•[3]	TER	✔Teradyne Inc	NY,B,Ch,P	B–	586	151839	Mfr electronic sys/software	29 9/16	5/16	24 3/16	7 1/2	66	20 5/8	323763	66	41 5/8	66	...	64	3	212	75.6	51.0
16•[4]	TEX	✔Terex Corp	NY,Ch,Ph	B–	220	21998	Mfr truck trailers, heavy eqp	27 1/4	3/8	31 1/2	13 3/8	35 1/2	22 1/8	27169	28 11/16	25 1/16	27 3/4	...	7	NM	–2.8	39.9	31.7
17•[5]	TRA	✔Terra Industries	NY,To,B,Ch,Mo,P,Ph	B	68	17670	Produce fertilizers/agric svcs	33 13/16	2 1/2	13 1/8	3 7/8	7 1/2	15/16	30288	2 3/16	1 1/4	1 9/16	...	d	Neg	–74.4	–51.8	–30.5
18	TRRA	Terra Networks ADS[56]	NNM	NR	..	...	Internet access svc	....	....	....	....	57 3/8	13 7/16	267943	57 3/8	33 1/8	54 3/4	...	..	...	...	...	...
19	TNH	Terra Nitrogen Com L.P. Uts	NY	NR	12	69	Produce nitrogen fertilizers	43 7/8	23 1/4	31 3/8	9 3/8	12 3/8	3	9639	3 15/16	3	3 3/4	...	d	Neg	–63.6	...	...
20	TNA	✔Terra Nova (Bermuda)Hldg[57]	NY,Ph	NR	68	17300	Prop,casualty,marine insurance	30	14 1/8	35	23	32 5/8	21 1/4	36727	30	28 1/2	30	0.8	11	...	19.9	12.7	...
21•[6]	TSO	✔Tesoro Petroleum	NY,B,Ch,P,Ph	B–	162	27792	Integrated oil company	32 1/4	2 1/2	21 3/8	9 9/16	18 13/16	7 7/16	37916	12 1/4	9 3/4	11 9/16	...	d	Neg	–4.6	–6.2	4.6
22	Pr A	7.25% cm Cv Dep[59]'PIES'[60](NC)	NY	BB–	38	7214		....	....	19 3/4	11 1/8	17 13/16	9 11/16	9045	12 13/16	10 11/16	12	9.6	..	...	...	...	...
✣23•[7]	TTI	✔TETRA Technologies	NY	B	88	10323	Mfr,mkt specialty chemicals	30	5 3/4	25 1/2	7 5/8	11 13/16	6 1/16	11491	7 7/8	6 1/16	7 1/4	...	5	16	–33.7	–34.0	–9.4
24•[1]	TEVA	✔Teva Pharm Indus ADR[62]	NNM	NR	219	29225	Pharmac'ls,veterinary prod	69 1/4	1/2	50 7/8	31 5/8	72 1/2	39 3/8	106221	72 1/2	53 7/8	71 11/16	0.3	34	1	77.2	13.3	25.1
¶25•[8]	TX	✔Texaco Inc	NY,To,B,C,Ch,P,Ph	B	1412	350749	Major international oil co	63 7/16	10	65	49 1/16	70 1/16	44 9/16	425053	61 1/8	52 3/8	54 5/16	3.3	23	–5	5.6	6.7	16.7
26	FTF	✔Texarkana First Financial	AS	NR	10	447	Savings & loan, Arkansas	27 1/8	10	30 5/8	19 7/8	24 1/2	19	200	19 1/2	19 1/4	19 1/4	3.5	9	...	–14.3	10.0	...
27	TXB	✔Texas Biotechnology	AS,Ch,P	NR	25	6486	Dvlp stge:biotechnology R&D	7 1/4	1 1/8	9 1/2	2 7/16	7 15/16	3 1/2	35800	7 15/16	4 1/8	7 15/16	...	d	22	60.8	22.0	40.7
28	WS	Wrrt(Pur 1 com at$8.44)	AS	....	1	.9		2 3/8	1/8	2 3/4	1/16	2	1/4	5517	2	3/8	1 15/16	...	..	...	...	...	...
✣29•[9]	TXI	✔Texas Indus	NY,B,Ch,Ph	B	224	13868	Cement,aggregate,concrete pd	52	1 1/8	68 1/4	19 9/16	42 9/16	21 5/8	17221	42 9/16	36	42 9/16	0.7	14	8	59.5	20.0	20.3
30	Pr S	TXI Cap Tr I 5.50%[64]'SpuRS'([65]50)	NY	B+	14	640		....	....	50 5/8	28 1/4	39 11/16	31	942	38 7/8	36	38 1/2	7.1	..	...	...	...	...
¶31•[10]	TXN	✔Texas Instruments	NY,B,C,Ch,P	B	1445	596167	Semiconductors:el'tronic eqp	35 5/8	1 11/16	45 3/16	20 1/8	111 1/2	43	849524	111 1/2	92 5/8	96 5/8	0.2	57	7	126	83.4	60.8
32	TPL	✔Texas Pac Ld Tr[67]	NY,B,Ch,Ph	B+	23	294	Holds surface rights:royalties	71	2 7/16	54 5/8	35 3/4	59 1/2	37 3/4	1756	42	37 3/4	38 5/16	1.0	24	8	–28.3	13.2	17.4
¶33•[3]	TXU	✔Texas Utilities[68]	NY,B,C,Ch,P,Ph	B	831	162340	Electric utility holding co.	49 3/4	14 7/8	48 1/16	38 3/8	47 3/16	32 3/4	280834	36 15/16	32 3/4	35 9/16	6.7	11	NM	–19.6	0.9	8.5
¶34•[7]	TXT	✔Textron, Inc	NY,B,C,Ch,P,Ph	A	658	97372	Aerospace/coml prod/finl svcs	70 3/4	2 7/8	80 15/16	52 1/16	98	65 7/8	94227	77 3/16	69	76 11/16	1.7	19	35	2.6	19.7	27.5
35	Pr A	$2.08 cm Cv A Pfd(50)vtg	NY,B	BBB+	7	6	Mfrs commercial products	292	19	351	233 1/4	422	304 1/8	20	324 1/2	316 3/4	337 1/2B	0.6	..	...	...	...	...
36	Pr B	$1.40 cm Cv B Pfd(45)vtg	NY,B	BBB+	2	.6	Financial & insurance svcs	250 1/4	14	286	185 1/2	350	262	1	262	262	276 1/8B	0.5	..	...	...	...	...
37	THK	✔Thackeray Corp	AS,Ch,Ph	NR	9	1615	Builder's hardware:Real est	22 5/8	1/2	4 1/16	2 7/8	4 3/4	3	57	3 3/4	3 3/8	3 1/4B	...	d	–17	–3.7	5.7	–6.8
38•[6]	TGLO	✔theglobe.com	NNM	NR	42	4466	On-line internet svcs	....	....	48 1/2	4 1/2	42 3/4	8 3/16	149299	12	8 3/16	8 3/8	...	..	...	–48.1	...	...
✣39•[1]	TGX	✔Theragenics Corp	NY	B	85	8227	Dvlp/mfr medical devices	27	1/8	35 3/8	9 5/16	17 3/4	5	44790	9 5/8	7 5/8	9 1/16	...	19	79	–44.4	–6.9	50.4
40	TDX	✔Thermedics Detection	AS,Ch,Ph	NR	10	473	Mfr detection/measurement sys	13 1/4	8 3/4	11 11/16	6	10 7/8	6 3/4	1959	9 1/2	6 3/4	6 3/4	...	26	4	–12.2	...	...
41•[2]	TMD	✔Thermedics Inc	AS,Ch,P,Ph	B	55	5122	Mfrs biomedical prod & sys	31 7/8	2	17 15/16	6 5/8	11 3/8	4 3/4	10555	5 7/8	5	5 7/16	...	d	Neg	–49.7	–33.1	–15.7
42	TBA	✔Thermo BioAnalysis	AS	NR	43	1390	Mfr biotech instr/info mgmt sys	20	9	22 3/4	8 1/2	21	12 7/16	1066	18 3/4	17 3/8	18 3/8	...	20	...	38.7	10.8	...
43	TCA	✔Thermo Cardiosystems	AS,Ph,P	B–	75	8803	Heart ventricle assist device	55 3/8	1 5/16	28	7 1/2	12 3/8	5 3/8	23620	7	5 3/8	6 9/16	...	29	4	–37.1	–39.7	–9.2
44	TCK	✔Thermo Ecotek	AS,P	B–	43	1122	Oper non-utility elec pwr fac	18 1/2	7 5/16	19 3/4	10 1/16	11 1/8	5 1/16	2827	7 1/2	5 1/16	5 5/16	...	d	Neg	–49.7	–29.6	...
¶45•[1]	TMO	✔Thermo Electron	NY,B,Ch,Ph,P	B+	411	110623	Eng'd ind'l pr: environ instr	44 1/2	3/8	44 1/4	13 9/16	20 1/4	12 1/2	131288	16 1/8	13 11/16	15	...	14	Neg	–11.4	–28.6	–5.5
46	TFG	✔Thermo Fibergen	AS,Ch	NR	14	2556	Dvlp pulp residue recovery sys	11 3/4	7 1/2	9 7/8	7 1/4	12 3/16	8 1/2	811	12 3/16	10 7/8	12 3/16	...	..	...	38.3	5.1	...
47•[7]	TFT	✔Thermo Fibertek	AS,Ph,P	B+	40	2827	Mfr paper produc'g/recycl'g eq	20 5/16	3 9/16	14 1/4	4 15/16	7 15/16	6 1/8	2743	7 1/4	6 1/4	7 1/8	...	25	5	0.0	–8.5	1.1
48•[11]	THI	✔Thermo Instrument Sys	AS,Ch,Ph,P	B+	82	8464	Mfrs analytical instruments	34 11/16	1 1/16	35 7/16	7 7/8	17 7/16	8 1/8	6106	12 3/4	10 3/8	11 1/8	...	18	5	–26.1	–25.1	–2.2
49	TOC	✔Thermo Optek	AS,Ch,Ph	NR	39	1910	Dvlp,mfr analytical instr	19 5/8	10 1/2	18 5/16	7 3/16	12 3/4	7 5/8	1684	12 3/8	9 5/8	11 3/8	...	15	20	30.9	...	...
50	TSR	✔Thermo Sentron	AS	NR	9	754	Mfr weighing & inspection eqp	17	8 9/16	12 5/8	8 1/8	15 5/8	9 5/8	374	15	14 3/8	14 1/2	...	23	...	47.8	2.4	...

Uniform Footnote Explanations-See Page 4. Other: [1]CBOE:Cycle 3. [2]ASE:Cycle 2. [3]P:Cycle 1. [4]ASE,Ph:Cycle 1. [5]CBOE:Cycle 1. [6]Ph:Cycle 2. [7]Ph:Cycle 3. [8]ASE:Cycle 1. [9]ASE,CBOE,P:Cycle 1. [10]ASE,CBOE,P,Ph:Cycle 1. [11]ASE:Cycle 3. [51]Subsid. pfd. in $M. [52]Stk dstr of Pactiv Corp. [53]Rate'AAA'by S&P. [54]Put option on int reset date re-spec cond. [55]Put optn on int reset date re-spec cond. [56]Ea ADS rep 1 ord. [57]Markel Corp plan acq,$34 in cash or stk. [58]Accum on pfd. [59]Dep for 7.25% Mand Cv Pfd. [60]Premium Income Equity Secs. [61]re-spec cond. [62]Ea ADR rep 1 Ord,NIS.10. [63]If com exceeds $11.81 for 30 con trad days. [64]Fr 6-30-2001. [65]Shared Preferrence Redeemable Securities. [66]Texas Indus Com. [67]Sub-share ctfs. [68]d/b/a TXU Corp. [69]Excl subsid pfd. [70]Redemption of stk purch rt. [71]Incl 4.7M com subject to redemption. [72]Stk dstr of Thermo Vision Corp.

Splits ◆ Index	Cash Divs. Ea.Yr. Since	Dividends: Latest Payment Period $	Date	Ex. Div.	Total $ So Far 1999	Ind. Rate	Paid 1998	Financial Position Mil-$: Cash& Equiv.	Curr. Assets	Curr. Liab.	Balance Sheet Date	Capitalization: Lg Trm Debt Mil-$	Shs. 000 Pfd.	Com.	Earnings $ Per Shr. Years End	1995	1996	1997	1998	1999	Last 12 Mos.	Interim Earnings Period	$ per Shr. 1998	1999	Index
1◆	....	None Since Public			...	Nil	....	0.80	11.0	10.5	9-30-99	1.63	125	4055	Dc	0.09	vd1.05	vd0.74	v0.04	....	0.09	9 Mo Sep	v0.16	v0.21	1
2	1988	A0.01	3-25-99	3-11	0.01	0.01	0.01	12.1	189	159	9-30-99	108	...	16277	Mr	v1.00	vd0.44	□v1.01	vd8.50	....	d8.21	6 Mo Sep	vd0.40	vd0.11	2
3	1984	Q0.32	12-15-99	11-29	1.28	1.28	1.28	Total Assets $17001M			9-30-99	4564	[51]225	55852	Dc	v5.01	v2.39	v0.90	v□1.21	E3.05	0.40	9 Mo Sep	v□1.53	v0.72	3
4	....	0.10	7-10-91	7-1	...	Nil	....	3.26	11.3	6.06	9-30-99	....	...	9951	Dc	vp0.07	vd0.11	vd0.19	v0.16	....	0.14	9 Mo Sep	v0.13	v0.11	4
5	....	0.12	9-10-93	8-16	...	Nil	....	143	3951	1767	8-31-99	6525	...	311380	My	□1.04	□1.78	v□d0.68	v1.22	v0.79	0.76	3 Mo Aug	v0.44	v0.41	5
6	....	None Since Public			...	Nil	....	54.8	70.5	20.1	9-30-99	3.10	...	34631	Dc	...	Nil	vd0.04	v0.03	....	0.18	9 Mo Sep	vd0.03	v0.12	6
7	....	None Since Public			...	Nil	....	0.60	0.83	2.28	9-30-99	3.33	20	8452	Dc	d0.11	vd0.32	vd0.67	vd0.42	....	d0.50	9 Mo Sep	vd0.23	vd0.31	7
8◆	1933	Q0.19	12-31-99	12-14	0.76	0.76	0.74	12.7	151	52.3	9-30-99	24.4	...	9042	Dc	v1.98	v2.09	v2.41	v2.67	....	2.29	9 Mo Sep	v1.91	v1.53	8
9◆	1948	h[52]....	11-4-99		h[52]0.90	1.20	1.20	42.0	1216	888	9-30-99	796	...	p33675	Dc	v4.17	v□3.72	v□2.11	v1.51	E2.37	....	9 Mo Sep	n/a	v□d0.58	9
10	1998	Q0.422	12-1-99	11-26	1.687	1.688	0.806	Co option reset int rate fr 6-1-2003[54]				★500	...	...	Sp	...	...	...	....	....	....	Mature 6-1-2028			10
11	1999	Q0.40⅝	11-1-99	10-27	0.79	1.625	....	Co option reset int rate fr 5-1-2004[55]				★450	...	...	Sp	...	...	...	....	....	....				11
12	1996	Q0.46⅞	12-31-99	12-28	1.87½	1.875	1.87½	Co opt redm fr 3-31-2001 at $25				★500	...	...	Sp	...	...	...	....	....	....	Mature 3-31-2046			12
13	1995	Q0.50	12-31-99	12-28	2.00	2.00	2.00	Co option redm fr 3-30-2000 at $25				600	...	...	Sp	...	...	...	....	....	....	Mature 3-31-2045			13
14◆	1990	Q0.47½	11-5-99	10-27	1.85	1.90	1.75	35.4	240	215	9-30-99	456	...	32917	Dc	v1.54	v1.89	v1.95	v□1.61	....	1.76	9 Mo Sep	v□1.19	v1.34	14
15◆	....	None Paid			...	Nil	....	223	904	366	10-03-99	8.84	...	170998	Dc	v0.95	v0.55	v0.74	v0.59	E1.04	0.71	9 Mo Sep	v0.53	v0.65	15
16	....	0.06	6-5-91	5-14	...	Nil	....	154	1338	611	9-30-99	1066	...	27500	Dc	v□d3.37	v1.86	v□1.44	v□3.25	....	4.30	9 Mo Sep	v□2.44	v3.49	16
17	1993	Div Omitted 8-4-99			0.07	Nil	0.20	5.56	345	154	9-30-99	478	...	75308	Dc	v□2.01	v1.72	v2.80	vd0.35	....	d1.31	9 Mo Sep	v0.15	v□d0.81	17
18	....	None Since Public			...	Nil	....	137	155	45.8	p6-30-99	9.74	...	★275500	Dc	...	...	...	vpd0.68	....	....	6 Mo Jun	n/a	vpd0.37	18
19	1997	Div Omitted 10-22-98			...	Nil	2.89	0.01	65.2	64.5	9-30-99	5.71	...	18502	Dc	v6.55	v6.35	v4.17	v1.60	....	d0.40	9 Mo Sep	v1.65	vd0.35	19
20	1996	0.06	12-27-99	12-1	0.24	0.24	0.23	Equity per shr $21.98			12-31-98	175	...	25969	Dc	v2.63	v2.69	v2.82	v□3.22	....	2.81	6 Mo Jun	v□1.73	v1.32	20
21	....	0.10	8-25-86	8-5	...	[58]Nil	....	15.6	468	306	9-30-99	491	104	32411	Dc	□2.29	v□2.90	v1.14	v□d0.71	....	d0.12	9 Mo Sep	v□0.76	v1.35	21
22	1998	Q0.289	1-1-00	12-13	1.156	1.156	0.289	Cv into 0.8455 com				....	9000	...	Dc	...	...	...	....	....	....	Mand conv 7-1-2001[61]			22
23	....	None Since Public			...	Nil	....	4.85	125	48.3	9-30-99	80.4	...	13529	Dc	v0.72	v0.97	v0.98	v0.64	....	1.46	9 Mo Sep	v0.57	v□1.39	23
24	1984	0.053	11-30-99	11-4	0.215	0.21	0.24	49.2	776	538	12-31-98	202	...	62277	Dc	v1.15	v1.20	v1.65	v1.15	E2.13	1.30	9 Mo Sep	v1.09	v1.24	24
25◆	1903	Q0.45	12-10-99	11-3	1.80	1.80	1.80	219	5973	5194	9-30-99	6626	650	553060	Dc	v□1.28	v3.68	v4.87	v□1.04	E2.40	1.17	9 Mo Sep	v□1.43	v1.56	25
26	1996	Q0.17	10-22-99	10-6	0.65	0.68	0.58	Total Deposits $153M			6-30-99	15.0	...	1561	Sp	...	1.31	1.68	v1.94	....	2.08	9 Mo Jun	v1.40	v1.54	26
27	....	None Since Public			...	Nil	....	12.9	15.4	2.67	9-30-99	....	...	34240	Dc	vd0.83	vd0.87	vd0.24	vd0.43	....	d0.45	9 Mo Sep	vd0.31	vd0.33	27
28	....	Terms&trad. basis should			be checked in detail			Wrrts expire 12-31-2000				....	...	3550	Dc	...	...	...	....	....	....	Callable at 5¢[63]			28
29◆	1962	Q0.07½	11-30-99	11-1	0.30	0.30	0.30	7.97	301	152	8-31-99	691	...	21030	My	1.94	3.52	v3.42	v4.69	v3.92	3.00	6 Mo Nov	v2.18	v1.26	29
30	1998	Q0.68¾	12-31-99	12-28	2.75	2.75	1.564	Cv into 0.72218 com[66]				....	4000	...	My	...	...	...	....	....	....				30
31◆	1962	Q0.04¼	11-22-99	10-28	0.17	0.17	0.17	2015	5488	2438	9-30-99	1159	...	p801995	Dc	v1.41	v0.09	v□2.30	v0.51	E1.71	1.41	9 Mo Sep	v0.27	v1.17	31
32	1956	A0.40	3-15-99	3-4	0.40	0.40	0.40	Total Assets $16.6M			9-30-99	....	...	2640	Dc	v1.09	v1.46	v2.39	v2.22	....	1.60	9 Mo Sep	v1.38	v0.76	32
33	1917	Q0.60	1-3-00	12-7	2.30	2.40	2.20	849	4524	7837	9-30-99	18532[69]	...	276407	Dc	vd0.61	v3.35	v2.85	v2.79	E3.15	3.14	12 Mo Sep	v2.34	v3.14	33
34◆	1942	Q0.32½	1-1-00	12-8	1.26	1.30	1.108	Total Assets $15098M			10-02-99	5181	264	148741	Dc	v2.77	v1.47	v3.29	v3.68	E4.00	14.37	9 Mo Sep	v2.68	□v13.37	34
35	1968	Q0.52	1-1-00	12-8	2.08	2.08	2.08	Cv into 4.4 common				....	178	...	Dc	...	...	...	....	....	....				35
36	1968	Q0.35	1-1-00	12-8	1.40	1.40	1.40	Cv into 3.6 common				....	86		Dc	...	...	...	....	....	....				36
37	....	0.30	6-5-74	5-6	...	Nil	....	Total Assets $11.47M			9-30-99	....	...	5107	Dc	d0.38	v0.12	v0.15	vd0.04	....	d0.05	9 Mo Sep	vd0.03	vd0.04	37
38◆	....	None Since Public			...	Nil	....	69.9	73.6	8.60	9-30-99	5.14	...	26619	Dc	...	...	vpd0.46	vd3.37	....	....	9 Mo Sep	n/a	vd1.39	38
39◆	....	None Paid			...	Nil	....	34.4	43.1	2.62	9-30-99	....	...	29510	Dc	v0.07	v0.14	v0.33	v0.46	....	0.49	9 Mo Sep	v0.35	v0.38	39
40	....	None Since Public			...	Nil	....	10.0	74.5	12.4	10-02-99	....	...	19317	Dc	v0.15	v0.04	v0.48	v0.45	....	0.26	9 Mo Sep	v0.36	v0.17	40
41	....	None Since Public			...	Nil	....	116	343	134	10-02-99	121	...	41938	Dc	v0.48	v0.75	v1.07	Δv0.44	....	d0.50	9 Mo Sep	vΔ0.46	vd0.48	41
42	....	None Since Public			...	Nil	....	29.6	166	90.1	10-02-99	50.0	...	20628	Dc	pv0.33	vd0.05	v0.70	v0.70	....	0.90	9 Mo Sep	v0.42	v0.62	42
43◆	....	None Since Public			...	Nil	....	80.4	133	15.3	10-02-99	70.0	...	38467	Dc	v0.27	v0.25	v0.23	v0.20	....	0.23	9 Mo Sep	v0.14	v0.17	43
44◆	....	None Since Public			...	Nil	....	13.4	131	98.4	7-03-99	61.3	...	35949	Sp	0.57	0.70	v0.64	v0.86	vPd1.65	d1.65				44
45◆	....	[70]0.006	2-12-96	1-25	...	Nil	....	1134	3016	1415	10-02-99	1908	...	158237	Dc	v0.95	v1.17	v1.41	vΔ1.04	E1.05	d0.83	9 Mo Sep	v□Δ0.78	vd1.09	45
46	....	None Since Public			...	Nil	....	46.2	56.0	62.2	10-02-99	....	...	[71]14243	Dc	pvd0.06	vd0.03	v0.07	v0.02	....	0.06	9 Mo Sep	v0.01	v0.05	46
47◆	....	None Since Public			...	Nil	....	86.9	260	105	10-02-99	154	...	61183	Dc	v0.32	v0.31	v0.26	v0.29	....	0.28	9 Mo Sep	v0.22	0.21	47
48◆	....	None Since Public			...	Nil	....	199	1353	1026	10-02-99	537	...	119241	Dc	v0.64	v1.01	v1.09	Δv0.78	....	0.61	9 Mo Sep	v0.60	v0.43	48
49	....	h[72]....	12-15-97	12-16	...	Nil	....	52.1	263	133	10-02-99	69.0	...	51092	Dc	pv0.36	v0.55	v0.75	vΔ0.65	....	0.74	9 Mo Sep	v0.42	v0.51	49
50	....	None Since Public			...	Nil	....	10.5	57.2	43.1	10-02-99	....	...	9436	Dc	pv0.55	v0.56	v0.66	v0.59	....	0.63	9 Mo Sep	v0.45	v0.49	50

◆Stock Splits & Divs By Line Reference Index [1]1-for-25 REVERSE,'94. [8]2-for-1,'95. [9]No adj for spinoff,'96,'99. [14]2-for-1,'98. [15]2-for-1,'95,'99. [25]2-for-1,'97. [29]2-for-1,'97. [31]2-for-1,'95,'97,'99. [34]2-for-1,'97. [38]2-for-1,'99. [39]2-for-1,'98. [43]3-for-2,'96. [44]3-for-2,'96. [45]3-for-2,'95,'96. [47]3-for-2,'95,'96. [48]5-for-4,'96,'97.

¶ S&P 500
# MidCap 400
✤ SmallCap 600
• Options

Index	Ticker	Name of Issue (Call Price of Pfd. Stocks)	Market	Com. Rank. & Pfd. Rating	Inst. Hold Cos	Inst. Hold Shs. (000)	Principal Business	Price Range 1971-97 High	1971-97 Low	1998 High	1998 Low	1999 High	1999 Low	December, 1999 Dec. Sales in 100s	Last Sale Or Bid High	Low	Last	%Div Yield	P-E Ratio	EPS 5 Yr Growth	% Annualized Total Return 12 Mo	36 Mo	60 Mo
1	TTRIF	Thermo Tech Technologies	BB	NR	3	381	Liquid waste mgmt svcs	4 1/16	5/16	2¼	⅛	13/16	1/32	574907	3/16	1/32	1/32	...	d	...	–87.2	–67.6	...
2	TTT	✓Thermo Terratech	AS,Ch	B	15	1281	Thermal process furnace sys	17¼	1 1/16	8⅜	3¾	6⅞	3⅞	231	6⅞	6⅝	6⅝B	...	d	Neg	51.4	–12.5	–3.4
3	VIZ	✓Thermo Vision	AS	NR	12	768	Mfr/dgn photonics pds	8⅛	7½	8 1/16	2 1/16	7	2¾	382	7	6¾	6 15/16	...	..	...	122	...	...
4	TLZ	✓ThermoLase Corp	AS,Ch,Ph,P	NR	33	2118	Dvlp hair removal system	36½	3 9/16	11¼	4¼	4⅞	1 5/16	7786	2⅜	1⅞	1 15/16	...	d	Neg	–57.5	–50.3	–12.9
5	TLZ.U	Units[51]	AS	....	4	31		18⅞	16⅜	17 3/16	15⅛	17¾	15 13/16	271	17½	17⅛	17B	...	..	...	5.4	...	...
6	TMQ	✓ThermoQuest Corp	AS,Ph,P	NR	65	4511	Mfr spcl analytical instr	20⅝	11½	19 15/16	6 7/16	14½	9⅜	1641	11¼	9⅜	10 5/16	...	12	16	–20.3	–7.1	...
7	THN	✓ThermoRetec Corp	AS	NR	14	2265	Oper soil-remediation centers	17⅜	5½	7½	1¾	6¾	1⅞	584	6¾	6⅝	6⅝	3.0	d	Neg	275	–4.8	–5.9
8	TKN	✓ThermoTrex Corp	AS,Ch,Ph,P	B–	33	1614	Optics,electro-optic sys R&D	59⅛	7 9/16	23¼	8⅛	9¼	5¼	8144	9¼	7	7⅞	...	d	Neg	–8.0	–34.0	–10.2
9	THV	ThermoView Industries	AS	NR	..	...	Mfr vinyl replacement windows	....	....	....	....	7⅛	2	21441	6¾	2	3⅞	...	..	...	...	...	...
10	THM	✓Thermwood Corp	AS,B,P	B–	6	20	Mfr,svcs ind'l robots & sys	16¼	1⅞	10¾	5 11/16	7⅜	4½	792	6⅜	5⅜	5⅝	...	9	–21	–2.2	–10.7	1.7
11•[1]	TSCM	✓TheStreet.com Inc	NNM	NR	53	4987	Web-based financial info	....	....	....	....	71¼	14	126479	22	14 3/16	19 3/16	...	d	...	...	...	...
¶12•[2]	TNB	✓Thomas & Betts	NY,B,Ch,P	B+	409	50568	Elec connectors,components	59¼	4 7/16	64	33 5/16	53 11/16	27 9/16	117617	43⅜	27 9/16	31⅞	3.5	11	10	–24.6	–8.3	1.7
13	TGIS	✓Thomas Group	NNM	NR	19	839	Provides management svcs	20	5	13	7	11 7/16	6 5/16	7817	11 7/16	6 5/16	11¼	...	14	–14	9.8	7.7	12.5
✤14	TII	✓Thomas Indus	NY,Ch	B	131	11225	Light'g/compressors,vac pumps	22 5/16	1 3/16	26 13/16	16 15/16	22 7/16	15 15/16	4528	20 7/16	16	20 7/16	1.5	13	19	5.7	15.4	18.5
✤15	TNM	✓Thomas Nelson	NY,Ch,P	B+	73	6804	Book publ:prod'r,mktr-Bible	26½	3/16	15 11/16	10½	13½	8 1/16	5902	10⅜	8½	9¼	1.7	15	91	–30.5	–13.5	–12.1
16	TNM.B	Cl'B'	NY	B+	3	57		26	2½	16½	11¼	13½	8⅞	156	10	8⅞	9⅜B	1.7	16	90	–29.5	–21.7	–12.0
17•[3]	TOC	✓Thomson Corp[52]	To,Mo	B+	26	7251	Publishing:info,travel svcs	40½	2 3/16	46	29 1/16	51	35½	73255	41 15/16	37⅛	38	1.8	46	9	7.5	9.7	19.5
18	TMS	THOMSON Multimedia ADS[53]	NY	NR	..	...	Mfr consumer electronic prd	....	....	....	....	54⅝	22 9/16	2976	54⅝	42½	53⅜	...	..	...	...	...	...
✤19	THO	✓Thor Industries	NY,Ph	A–	103	4930	Mfr travel trailers,mtr hms	23 1/16	2¼	29 11/16	20	32	22¼	2439	30½	27 1/16	30 7/16	0.3	11	23	19.7	22.5	19.2
20	TMA	✓Thornburg Mortgage Asset	NY,P	NR	57	2615	Real estate investment trust	24 9/16	6¾	18½	5⅝	11⅜	7 7/16	19197	8 9/16	7 15/16	8¼	11.2	15	–9	19.4	–19.7	12.1
21	Pr A	9.68% cm Cv Sr'A'Pfd([55])	NY,Ch	NR	6	74		27½	24⅝	26¾	17¾	25 5/16	19 9/16	2509	20¼	19 3/16	19½	12.4	..	...	...	...	...
22	TRV	✓Thousand Trails	AS	NR	6	1541	Oper campgrounds & cabins	6	13/16	5 13/16	3½	5¼	4 3/16	415	5	4⅝	5	...	8	NM	21.2	51.5	...
✤23	THQI	✓THQ Inc	NNM	NR	131	15071	Mkt toys & games/software	57½	11/16	20 15/16	6 5/16	39¼	10 15/16	128374	38¾	22	23 3/16	...	14	NM	24.3	77.5	41.1
¶24•[4]	COMS	✓3Com Corp	NNM	B–	646	138735	Mfr computer commun'n sys	81⅜	1⅜	51⅛	22 15/16	53¾	20	2201270	53¾	39⅜	47	...	35	–1	4.9	–13.8	12.9
25	TDDD	✓3D Labs	NNM	NR	3	227	Supply 3D semiconductors	50	11	32⅞	2¼	8 15/16	2¾	102130	8 15/16	3 11/16	5⅞	...	d	...	67.9	–36.6	...
26	THD	✓3Dshopping.com	AS	NR	..	...	Web site svcs	....	....	....	....	15	5⅞	18186	15	7⅝	14	...	d	...	...	...	...
27	WS	Wrrt(Pur 1 com at $18)	AS	....	..	...		....	....	....	....	3⅛	1⅛	5055	3⅛	1⅞	3⅛	...	..	...	...	...	...
28	TDSC	✓3D Systems	NNM	B–	13	1739	Eqpmt:prod'n plastic models	49½	1½	12½	5⅛	8¾	4	17958	8¾	7	8½	...	d	Neg	13.3	–12.6	–3.1
29•[5]	TDFX	✓3Dfx Interactive	NNM	NR	69	6838	Dvp 3D computer software	23	8⅞	35¼	8	23	7½	108562	10½	8⅜	9 13/16	...	..	...	–22.3	...	...
✤30	TFS	✓Three-Five Systems	NY,Ch,P	B–	65	5559	Mfr opto-electr components	37½	5/16	17 5/16	4 13/16	41½	5 15/16	31301	41½	30¾	41	...	..	–6	303	62.4	8.7
31	THR	✓Three Rivers Finl	AS,Ph	NR	4	114	Savings & loan, Michigan	19¾	9 1/16	21 11/16	12⅝	16½	10¾	251	15⅞	14⅞	15 9/16	3.0	18	...	19.3	13.4	...
32	TIBX	✓TIBCO Software	NNM	NR	52	4013	Network software solutions	....	....	....	....	195	15	73690	195	87⅜	153	...	d	...	...	...	...
33•[6]	TMCS	✓Ticketmaster OnlineCitySrch'B'	NNM	NR	101	8849	Internet entertain't guide svcs	....	....	80½	14	75⅛	17⅞	190407	47⅜	29⅜	38 7/16	...	d	...	–31.4	...	...
34	TIXX	✓Tickets.com Inc	NNM	NR	..	...	Entertainment ticket source	....	....	....	....	32	12½	79932	21 15/16	14	14 5/16	...	..	...	...	...	...
#35•[6]	TDW	✓Tidewater Inc	NY,B,Ch,P,Ph	B	336	35553	Offshore service vessels	70½	3	55 3/16	17 1/16	36½	18 5/16	112767	36	28 9/16	36	1.7	31	31	58.6	–5.6	16.3
#36•[7]	TIF	✓Tiffany & Co.	NY,P,Ph	B+	388	61781	Retailer:jewelry,gift items	24 5/16	2 7/16	26	13½	90	25¼	94721	90	75¾	89¼	0.3	51	27	246	70.7	56.9
✤37•[8]	TBL	✓Timberland Co Cl'A'	NY,Ch,P	B	165	8362	Mfrs men/women footwear	42 11/16	2½	43⅞	14	54⅛	20¾	19764	54⅛	45½	52⅞	...	18	NM	133	40.9	37.2
38	TMBS	✓Timberline Software	NNM	B+	47	5198	Dvlp account'g,info mgt sftwr	11⅛	¼	15½	6 1/16	15 11/16	8¼	14645	14¼	11 11/16	13 7/16	1.2	18	53	32.0	52.2	52.5
¶39•[9]	TWX	✓Time Warner Inc	NY,B,Ch,P,Ph	B–	1478	778290	Publish'g,entertainment,video	31	¾	63⅛	29 1/16	78⅝	57 3/16	593914	72 13/16	60⅛	72 5/16	0.2	94	NM	16.8	58.5	34.0
40•[9]	TWTC	✓Time Warner Telecom 'A'	NNM	NR	147	14053	Local telephone service	....	....	....	....	51⅝	14	75449	51⅝	28¼	49 15/16	...	d	...	...	...	...
¶41•[10]	TMC	✓Times Mirror 'A'	NY,B,Ch,P	B	354	25913	Newspaper:books info svc	61¾	2 3/16	65 13/16	48 15/16	72⅝	53 5/16	38932	68⅝	63¾	67	1.2	20	29	21.2	11.7	17.9
42	TME	Times Mirror 4.25%'PEPS'2001	NY	....[60]	6	117	Prem Equity Ptcp Sec	58¼	24	62½	18¾	147 15/16	50	315	147 15/16	119 1/16	123¾B	1.3	..	...	126	40.2	...
¶43•[10]	TKR	✓Timken Co.	NY,B,Ch,Ph,P	B	324	36126	Bearings, alloy steels	41½	6 1/16	41 15/16	13⅝	25 13/16	15⅝	40889	20 9/16	17⅞	20 7/16	3.5	23	–3	12.5	–0.8	6.0
44	TPY	✓Tipperary Corp	AS	C	18	2692	Oil & gas explor,dev,prod'n	7[54] 13/16	3/16	4⅝	⅞	1 15/16	9/16	7808	1½	1	1⅜	...	d	–20	29.5	–33.3	–18.4
45•[5]	TTN	✓Titan Corp	NY,B,Ch,P,Ph	C	96	15529	Information systems/svcs	17½	1	8¼	3 13/16	48⅜	4¾	217920	48⅜	27 1/16	47 5/16	...	..	...	760	141	49.3
46	Pr	$1 cm Cv Pfd(20)vtg 1/3	NY,B,Ch,P	NR	1	.4		15½	4⅛	14⅜	11	32	10⅝	966	32	19 5/16	31½	3.2	..	...	...	...	...
47•[11]	TEXP	✓Titan Exploration	NNM	NR	83	27058	Oil&gas explor, dvlp, prod'n	14¾	6¾	9⅝	5⅜	7 3/16	3	71960	5 7/16	3⅛	5 7/16	...	d	...	–17.1	–23.2	...
✤48•[2]	TWI	✓Titan Intl	NY,Ph,P	NR	86	12118	Mfr off-highway eqp wheels	24	6 11/16	20⅜	8 9/16	14½	4 13/16	10632	7 13/16	4 13/16	6½	0.9	d	Neg	–31.1	–19.7	–11.5
49	TTP	✓Titan Pharmaceuticals	AS	NR	40	7313	Biopharmaceutical R&D	13	2⅛	6⅛	1⅞	19½	2¾	55788	19½	13⅝	19	...	d	45	398	31.4	...
50•[12]	TIE	✓Titanium Metals	NY	NR	72	12170	Prod titanium sponge&mill prd	38⅜	22½	33	7⅛	13¼	3 9/16	46880	5⅜	3 9/16	4½	...	d	...	–46.2	–48.0	...

Uniform Footnote Explanations-See Page 4. Other: [1]CBOE,P,Ph:Cycle 3. [2]ASE:Cycle 3. [3]To:Cycle 2. [4]P:Cycle 1. [5]ASE,CBOE,P,Ph:Cycle 3. [6]CBOE,Ph:Cycle 1. [7]Ph:Cycle 2. [8]ASE,P,Ph:Cycle 2. [9]Ph:Cycle 3. [10]CBOE:Cycle 3. [11]ASE,CBOE,P,Ph:Cycle 1. [12]P,Ph:Cycle 1. [51]1 com shr & 1 Redemption Right. [52]All divd,finl pos'n and earnings amts in $U.S.. [53]Ea ADS rep 1 ord. [54]Incl current amts. [55]Fr 12-1-99 into 1 com re-spec cond. [56]11 Mo Jun'97. [57]If com exceeds $24 for 10 con trad days. [58]Fiscal Dec'98 & prior. [59]Incl curr amts. [60]Rated A+r by S&P. [61]Co opt to redeem from 3-15-2000 re-spec cond. [62]Co can extend to 3-21-2001. [63]Pfd in $M.

Index	Cash Divs. Ea. Yr. Since	Latest Payment Period $	Date	Ex. Div.	Total $ So Far 1999	Ind. Rate	Paid 1998	Cash& Equiv. (Mil-$)	Curr. Assets	Curr. Liab.	Balance Sheet Date	Lg Trm Debt Mil-$	Shs. 000 Pfd.	Com.	End	1995	1996	1997	1998	1999	Last 12 Mos.	Interim Period	1998	1999	Index
1	....	None Since Public			...	Nil	....	1.06	3.18	24.3	j4-30-99	2.45	...	198077	Ap	...	d1.20	vd0.50	vd0.26	vd0.21	jd0.21				1
2	....	None Since Public			...	Nil	....	3.89	144	120	10-02-99	119	...	19072	Mr	v0.18	vd0.01	v0.17	vd0.07	....	d2.23	6 Mo Sep	vd0.14	vd2.30	2
3	....	None Since Public			...	Nil	....	0.34	21.6	15.5	10-02-99	....	...	8059	Dc	v0.02	pv0.21	v0.34	v0.03	....	0.01	9 Mo Sep	v0.03	v0.01	3
4◆	....	None Since Public			...	Nil	....	1.80	42.4	36.5	7-03-99	115	...	39348	Sp	d0.04	d0.03	vd0.31	vd1.07	vPd2.37	d2.37				4
5	....	None Paid			...	Nil	....	....	...	...		....	...	★2000	Sp	...	...	...	....	....	....				5
6	....	None Since Public			...	Nil	....	42.7	329	167	10-02-99	....	...	50563	Dc	v0.47	v0.57	v0.80	vΔ0.71	....	0.83	9 Mo Sep	v0.50	v0.62	6
7◆	1994	S0.10	9-30-99	9-16	0.20	0.20	0.20	0.06	71.4	68.3	10-02-99	2.65	...	13608	Mr	v0.42	vd0.21	v0.02	vd0.29	....	d0.19	6 Mo Sep	vd0.37	vd0.27	7
8	....	None Since Public			...	Nil	....	62.5	328	123	7-03-99	204	...	22369	Sp	1.94	2.16	v0.43	vΔd0.30	....	d7.17	9 Mo Jun	v0.73	vd6.14	8
9◆	....	None Since Public			...	Nil	....	0.70	13.5	11.0	9-30-99	p20.8	p6	★7174	Dc	...	...	...	vpd3.28	....	....	9 Mo Sep	n/a	vpd0.93	9
10◆	....	None Paid			...	Nil	....	0.05	9.69	6.34	10-31-99	2.92	...	985	Jl	1.90	1.55	v0.69	v0.86	v□0.52	0.66	3 Mo Oct	v0.15	v0.29	10
11	....	None Since Public			...	Nil	....	137	141	9.33	9-30-99	....	...	24522	Dc	...	...	vpd0.95	vpd1.65	....	d1.32	9 Mo Sep	vd1.57	vd1.24	11
12◆	1934	Q0.28	1-4-00	12-13	1.12	1.12	1.12	85.7	1142	595	10-03-99	837	...	57818	Dc	v1.68	v1.12	v2.81	v1.54	E2.85↓	2.99	9 Mo Sep	v0.73	v2.18	12
13	....	None Since Public			...	Nil	....	10.1	27.4	8.56	9-30-99	4.02	...	±4837	Dc	v±1.08	v±0.29	v±0.38	v±d0.80	....	0.78	9 Mo Sep	v±d1.26	v±0.32	13
14◆	1955	Q0.07½	1-1-00	12-1	0.30	0.30	0.30	14.2	62.0	30.9	9-30-99	40.5	...	15823	Dc	v0.83	v1.09	v1.38	v1.50	....	1.57	9 Mo Sep	v1.16	v1.23	14
15◆	1989	Q0.04	2-14-00	1-27	0.16	0.16	0.16	2.86	170	39.8	9-30-99	90.1	...	±14231	Mr	v±d0.70	v±1.37	±v0.73	v±0.58	....	0.63	6 Mo Sep	v0.35	v0.40	15
16◆	1989	Q0.04	2-14-00	1-27	0.16	0.16	0.16	....	...	...		....	...	1104	Mr	±vd0.70	±v1.37	±v0.73	±v0.58	....	0.60	3 Mo Jun	±v0.08	±v0.10	16
17	1980	tQ0.17	12-15-99	11-16	t0.65¾	0.68	t0.628	307	2092	2073	12-31-98	2408	24000	618493	Dc	1.34	v0.95	v0.91	v2.97	....	0.83	9 Mo Sep	v2.52	v0.38	17
18	....	None Since Public			...	Nil	....	261	2979	1414	6-30-99	[54]p26.0	...	★124354	Dc	...	...	...	pv3.15	....	....	6 Mo Jun	n/a	v0.70	18
19◆	1987	Q0.02	1-4-00	12-21	0.08	0.08	0.08	54.0	203	74.6	10-31-99	....	...	12142	Jl	1.03	1.21	v1.31	v1.58	v2.52	2.75	3 Mo Oct	v0.57	v0.80	19
20	1993	Q0.23	11-17-99	10-27	0.92	0.92	1.40½	Total Assets $4532M			9-30-99	924	2760	21490	Dc	v0.88	v1.73	v1.94	v0.75	....	0.57	9 Mo Sep	v0.82	v0.64	20
21	1997	Q0.60½	1-10-00	12-29	2.42	2.42	2.42	Cv into 1 com				....	2400	...	Dc	...	...	...	....	....	....				21
22	....	None Paid			...	Nil	....	1.30	7.95	25.5	9-30-99	9.62	...	7978	Je	d3.22	vΔd0.08	v0.88	v2.96	v0.66	0.64	3 Mo Sep	v0.17	v0.15	22
23◆	....	None Since Public			...	Nil	....	26.7	99.3	30.4	9-30-99	....	...	18474	Dc	v0.08	v0.17	v0.60	v0.92	....	1.64	9 Mo Sep	v0.23	v0.95	23
24◆	....	None Since Public			...	Nil	....	1705	3502	1219	8-27-99	19.4	...	345029	My	0.87	v1.02	v1.42	v0.08	v1.09	1.36	6 Mo Nov	v0.62	v0.89	24
25	....	None Since Public			...	Nil	....	13.2	23.4	14.3	12-31-98	0.48	...	17081	Dc	pd0.11	v0.19	v1.01	vd1.98	....	d0.49	9 Mo Sep	vd1.68	vd0.19	25
26	....	None Since Public			...	Nil	....	8.96	9.51	0.53	9-30-99	0.01	...	4786	Je	...	...	v[56]d0.59	vd0.28	vd1.09	d1.35	3 Mo Sep	vd0.05	vd0.31	26
27	....	Terms&trad. basis should be checked in detail						Wrrts expire 7-20-2004				....	...	1100	Je	...	...	...	...	....	....	Callable fr 12-20-99 at 25¢[57]			27
28◆	....	None Paid			...	Nil	....	10.7	55.9	23.2	10-01-99	4.50	...	11639	Dc	v0.87	v0.41	vd0.40	v0.18	....	d0.55	9 Mo Sep	v0.12	vd0.61	28
29	....	None Since Public			...	Nil	....	74.1	208	92.1	10-31-99	....	...	24573	Ja	...	pvd1.74	vd0.16	v[58]1.33	....	....	9 Mo Oct	n/a	vd1.48	29
30◆	....	None Paid			...	Nil	....	7.47	89.4	33.1	9-30-99	6.23	...	12068	Dc	v0.78	vd0.37	v0.49	v0.25	....	0.35	9 Mo Sep	v0.16	v0.26	30
31◆	1996	Q0.11½	1-3-00	12-13	0.46	0.46	s0.391	Total Deposits $64.7M			9-30-99	[59]22.6	...	703	Je	...	v0.72	v0.61	v0.97	v0.83	0.89	3 Mo Sep	v0.18	v0.24	31
32	....	None Since Public			...	Nil	....	3.29	29.9	16.2	3-31-99	....	p...	★57982	Nv	...	...	...	vpd0.28	Pvd0.12	d0.12				32
33	....	None Since Public			...	Nil	....	67.9	75.7	14.9	9-30-99	0.53	...	±83077	Dc	...	...	vpd1.44	vd1.16	Ed1.55	d1.23	9 Mo Sep	vd0.92	vd0.99	33
34	....	None Since Public			...	Nil	....	20.1	29.7	30.3	6-30-99	p1.25	p...	★60775	Dc	...	...	...	vpd1.10	....	....	6 Mo Jun	n/a	vpd0.40	34
35	1992	Q0.15	12-2-99	11-18	0.60	0.60	0.60	137	340	70.7	9-30-99	....	...	55621	Mr	v1.23	v2.35	v5.18	v3.68	E1.15	2.29	6 Mo Sep	v2.03	v0.64	35
36◆	1988	Q0.06	1-10-00	12-16	0.21	0.24	0.16	155	903	274	10-31-99	252	...	72358	Ja	v0.61	v0.83	v1.01	v1.25	E1.74	1.56	9 Mo Oct	v0.51	v0.82	36
37◆	....	None Since Public			...	Nil	....	67.5	426	141	9-24-99	100	...	±20909	Dc	v±d0.53	v±0.91	±v2.02	±v2.52	....	2.92	9 Mo Sep	v±1.62	v±2.03	37
38◆	1994	Q0.04	11-19-99	10-27	0.13	0.16	0.097	17.1	23.8	18.2	9-30-99	....	...	12797	Dc	v0.14	v0.17	v0.36	v0.56	....	0.74	9 Mo Sep	v0.35	v0.53	38
39◆	1930	Q0.04½	12-15-99	11-29	0.18	0.18	0.18	645	8600	8576	9-30-99	18387	19400	±1286521	Dc	□vd0.23	v□d0.48	□vd0.03	vd0.31	E0.77	0.64	9 Mo Sep	vd0.13	v□0.82	39
40	....	None Since Public			...	Nil	....	272	311	124	9-30-99	403	...	±104538	Dc	...	...	...	pvd1.02	....	d1.12	9 Mo Sep	vd0.84	vd0.94	40
41	1892	Q0.20	12-10-99	11-22	0.80	0.80	0.72	180	817	938	9-30-99	1493	1450	±59988	Dc	v±□10.02	v±1.53	v2.29	v±16.06	E3.37↓	5.47	9 Mo Sep	v±12.96	v±2.37	41
42	1996	Q0.417	12-15-99	11-26	1.668	1.668	1.668	Amt pay maturity based America Online stk[61]				....	...	1305	Dc	...	...	...	....	....	....	Due 3-15-2001[62]			42
43◆	1922	Q0.18	12-6-99	11-17	0.72	0.72	0.72	18.3	839	507	9-30-99	328	...	61930	Dc	v1.78	v2.19	v2.69	v1.82	E0.90	0.87	9 Mo Sep	v1.61	v0.66	43
44	....	5%Stk	3-12-84	2-6	...	Nil	....	0.91	2.81	2.20	6-30-99	19.2	...	15152	Sp	d0.11	d0.07	v0.04	vd0.49	Pvd0.63	d0.63				44
45	....	None Paid			...	Nil	....	4.21	163	71.6	9-30-99	118	695	45308	Dc	vd0.33	vd0.27	v0.25	vd0.03	....	0.27	9 Mo Sep	v□d0.01	v0.29	45
46	1973	Q0.25	3-10-00	2-2	1.00	1.00	1.00	Cv into 0.666 common				....	695	...	Dc	bd1.44	...	...	....	....	....				46
47	....	None Since Public			...	Nil	....	1.75	28.1	14.7	9-30-99	75.0	...	36731	Dc	p0.18	vpd0.07	vd0.99	vd1.22	....	d1.56	9 Mo Sep	vd0.40	vd0.74	47
48◆	1993	Q0.01½	1-14-00	12-29	0.06	0.06	0.06	12.8	289	142	9-30-99	250	...	20672	Dc	v1.50	v1.50	v1.10	v0.38	....	d0.50	9 Mo Sep	v0.62	vd0.26	48
49	....	None Since Public			...	Nil	....	9.15	9.28	1.16	9-30-99	....	[63]5	15620	Dc	pvd1.74	vd1.67	v0.04	vd0.81	....	d0.80	9 Mo Sep	vd0.56	vd0.55	49
50	1998	Div Postponed 11-2-99			0.12	Nil	0.12	6.79	334	104	9-30-99	295	...	31371	Dc	pvd0.27	v1.72	v2.49	v1.46	....	d0.47	9 Mo Sep	v1.49	vd0.44	50

◆Stock Splits & Divs By Line Reference Index [4]2-for-1,'95. [7]3-for-2,'95. [9]1-for-3 REVERSE,'99. [10]1-for-5 REVERSE,'98. [12]2-for-1,'96. [14]3-for-2,'97. [15]5-for-4,'95. [16]5-for-4,'95. [19]3-for-2,'98. [23]1-for-15 REVERSE,'95:3-for-2,'98,'99. [24]2-for-1,'94,'95. [28]1-for-3 REVERSE,'95. [30]4-for-3,'99. [31]10%,'98. [36]2-for-1,'96,'99. [37]2-for-1,'99. [38]3-for-2,'95,'96:5-for-4,'97:4-for-3,'98,'99. [39]2-for-1,'98. [43]2-for-1,'97. [48]3-for-2,'95(twice).

¶ S&P 500 # MidCap 400 ✣ SmallCap 600 • Options

Index	Ticker	Name of Issue (Call Price of Pfd. Stocks)	Market	Com. Rank. & Pfd. Rating	Inst. Hold Cos	Inst. Hold Shs. (000)	Principal Business	Price Range 1971-97 High	1971-97 Low	1998 High	1998 Low	1999 High	1999 Low	December, 1999 Dec. Sales in 100s	Last Sale Or Bid High	Low	Last	%Div Yield	P-E Ratio	EPS 5 Yr Growth	% Annualized Total Return 12 Mo	36 Mo	60 Mo
1	TIVO	✔Tivo Inc	NNM	NR	48	1607	Personal TV viewing svc	....	....	....	....	59⅜	16	131902	48⅞	24⅝	33¾	...	..	...	...	...	...
¶2•[1]	TJX	✔TJX Companies	NY,B,Ch,P,Ph	B	899	292497	Off-price specialty stores	19¼	1/16	30	15½	37	16½	809447	25 13/16	16½	20 7/16	0.7	12	66	-29.2	21.5	41.7
3•[2]	TLCV	✔TLC Laser Eye Centers	NNM,To	NR	45	6813	Oper vision disorder centers	9⅜	7¼	22⅝	9 1/16	53½	10½	94220	19⅛	10½	13 1/16	...	..	71	-36.3	22.3	...
4	TMPW	✔TMP Worldwide	NNM	NR	197	18706	Advertising/marketing svcs	28¾	12½	42⅝	15½	161	37	108290	161	93⅜	142	...	d	4	238	123	...
✣5	TNP	✔TNP Enterprises[51]	NY,Ch,Ph	B	186	8650	Electric sv:Texas & New Mex	33¾	6¾	38 11/16	29	42⅛	28	6503	41 7/16	40 9/16	41¼	2.8	20	NM	12.3	18.8	27.4
6	TP	✔TNT Post Group ADS[52]	NY	NR	10	646	Mail,express & logistics svcs	....	....	33	18⅞	40	22⅞	3263	29 15/16	25½	28⅝	1.1	..	...	-10.7	...	...
7	TOD	✔Todd Shipyards	NY,Ch	C	27	1699	Major shipbldg & repair co	41¾	1⅝	7½	4 1/16	9 9/16	4	2043	8 15/16	7⅜	7 13/16	...	4	97	64.5	6.3	6.3
8	THT	✔Todhunter Intl	AS	B	24	1534	Distr/bottle alcoholic bev'ges	16¾	5¾	10½	6¾	10⅜	6¾	394	9¼	9⅛	9⅛	...	10	NM	12.3	1.9	-10.1
9	TOF	✔Tofutti Brands	AS,Ph	B–	3	13	Non-dairy frozen desserts	18	3/16	2	⅞	3¾	⅞	2892	2 1/16	1 9/16	1 11/16	...	15	59	92.8	44.3	11.0
10•[3]	TOK	✔Tokheim Corp	NY,B,Ch,Ph	C	46	6823	Design/mfr gas station equip	35¼	⅞	23	5⅛	12 9/16	2½	33413	5¼	3⅛	3⅝	...	d	Neg	-61.8	-23.6	-17.5
✣11•[4]	TOL	✔Toll Brothers	NY,Ch,Ph,P	B+	184	19665	Luxury single family homes	27½	2¼	31⅝	17⅜	24⅜	15 9/16	28345	18 11/16	16⅛	18⅝	...	7	19	-17.4	-1.5	13.2
12	TKS	✔Tomkins plc ADS[53]	NY,P	NR	47	16316	Industrial & consumer pd/mgmt co	23½	7 3/16	26⅝	14⅝	19½	12⅛	8735	15	12⅛	14 11/16	6.8	10	9	-21.3	-2.5	6.2
13•[2]	TOM	✔Tommy Hilfiger	NY,Ph	NR	338	65898	Design,mkt men's sportswear	30 9/16	3¾	35 3/16	17⅛	41 1/16	22⅛	241723	27¼	22⅛	23⅜	...	9	32	-21.6	-0.7	16.0
14	TMP	✔Tompkins Trustco	AS	A+	17	1764	Comm'l banking,Tompkins Cty,NY	28 13/16	5⅝	40¾	28½	35⅞	27⅞	408	30⅜	27⅞	28⅞	3.7	12	11	-13.9	14.2	10.2
15•[5]	TOO	✔Too Inc	NY	NR	129	18717	Women's apparel stores	....	....	....	....	19⅞	13 9/16	31204	18⅝	15¾	17¼	...	35	...	...	...	...
16	TLXAF	Toolex Intl NV	NNM	NR	10	3867	Compact disc eqp/svcs	28	7¼	21¼	7¼	17½	10⅛	4790	17½	14¾	17	...	23	...	51.1	17.0	...
17	TR	✔Tootsie Roll Indus	NY,Ch,Ph	A+	158	10197	'Tootsie' line of candies	30 13/16	3/16	46½	27 7/16	46 15/16	29⅜	14307	33 1/16	29½	32 15/16	s0.8	23	16	-10.2	25.1	22.7
18	TPC	✔Top Air Mfg	AS	NR	1	18	Mfr agricultural sprayers	3¼	⅜	2⅞	1	2⅛	9/16	923	13/16	9/16	¾	...	d	Neg	-25.0	-15.7	2.7
19	TRU	✔Torch Energy Royalty Trust	NY,Ch,Ph,P	NR	12	245	Royalty interest o&g prop	24	5½	9⅛	4¼	6¼	3¾	12795	4 9/16	3¾	4 1/16	...	4	-19	14.5	-10.5	-6.8
¶20•[6]	TMK	✔Torchmark Corp	NY,B,Ch,P	A	453	80048	Insurance:fin'l services	42 13/16	1¼	49 13/16	31 13/16	38	24 9/16	75458	32⅞	26 9/16	29 1/16	1.2	11	6	...	...	...
21	TRGL	Toreador Royalty	NNM	NR	9	1055	Oil & gas explor & devel	14¾	9/16	4½	2	4¾	2¼	941	4½	3 9/16	4⅜	...	..	-13	40.0	20.5	3.1
✣22•[7]	TTC	✔Toro Co	NY,Ch,Ph	↑B+	154	7329	Power mowers, sprinklers, etc	46 5/16	2 5/16	42¾	16½	39½	28¾	12270	38	31⅞	37 5/16	1.3	14	6	32.8	2.2	6.9
23•[8]	TD	✔Toronto-Dominion Bk[58]	NY,Ch,Ph,P,Vc	↑A–	136	120382	General Banking,Canada	19⅝	13/16	26⅛	12 1/16	30½	16⅜	24708	27 9/16	23⅝	27	◆2.2	4	29	59.5	33.3	25.3
24	TS.B	✔Torstar Corp'B'	To	NR	17	4204	Newspaper/book publishing	25¼	1 13/16	27 1/16	14	18⅝	13⅞	13926	16	14	15¾	3.7	23	-35	-9.7	1.5	9.9
¶25•[9]	TOS	✔Tosco Corp	NY,B,Ch,P,Ph	B	422	126292	Refining & dstr petroleum prod	75 3/16	1 11/16	37⅞	19¾	30⅜	18 13/16	161105	29¼	24¾	27 3/16	1.0	15	...	6.2	3.0	25.0
26•[10]	TOT	✔Total Fina'B' [59]ADS	NY,P	NR	245	43357	Intl o&g explor,dev,prod'n	59 7/16	19½	67⅛	46 11/16	72⅝	49⅞	68797	70⅝	63 5/16	69¼	1.2	24	17	41.4	21.9	21.1
27	WS	Wrrt(Pur1ADS at $46.94)	NY	....	9	732		....	....	....	....	29	18½	780	29	22⅛	28½	...	...	...	...	...	...
#28	TRL	✔Total Renal Care Hldgs	NY,Ph,P	NR	250	61735	Provides dialysis services	34⅜	10 7/16	36⅛	18⅞	29⅝	5 11/16	105630	7 11/16	6	6 11/16	...	32	...	-77.4	-32.5	...
29•[11]	TSS	✔Total System Svcs	NY,Ch,Ph	A+	52	5077	Bankcard data process'g svc	23 1/16	¼	24 3/16	14 7/16	26¼	14⅛	8070	17⅜	15	16 5/16	0.2	48	25	-30.4	-2.0	24.4
✣30•[6]	TWR	✔Tower Automotive	NY,Ph	NR	289	45932	Engineered metal stampings	24 5/16	3 11/16	27½	15½	28¼	13⅜	68569	15¾	13⅜	15 7/16	...	8	37	-38.1	-0.4	28.0
31•[12]	TSEMF	✔Tower Semiconductor	NNM	NR	12	1078	Mfr integrated circuits	36	5⅛	13	5⅝	13¾	6⅛	15888	11 7/16	8⅞	10 15/16	...	d	Neg	15.1	3.0	4.5
32	TCT	✔Town & Country Trust	NY,Ch	NR	63	2750	Real estate investment trust	23⅛	12	17 15/16	13¼	19¼	14¾	5649	18 15/16	16½	17 15/16	9.1	35	6	22.9	18.1	16.3
33	TPN	✔TownPagesNet.com[63]ADS	AS	NR	6	295	Internet-based U.K. local info	....	....	....	....	13½	4	8318	6⅜	4	5⅛	...	..	...	...	...	...
34•[13]	TM	✔Toyota Motor ADS[64]	NY	NR	46	3100	Autos,forklifts,prefab homes	65	13/16	59⅝	40 15/16	97⅜	45 15/16	6297	97⅜	67¼	97⅜	0.4	48	22	84.2	20.0	19.3
¶35•[14]	TOY	✔Toys R Us	NY,B,Ch,P,Ph	B	554	196286	Disc toy supermarts:dept str	42⅞	5/16	32¾	15⅝	24¾	13⅛	447312	17 15/16	13½	14 5/16	...	9	Neg	-15.5	-21.8	-14.1
36	TCC	✔Trammell Crow	NY,Ph	NR	95	12163	Commercial real estate svcs	25¾	17½	37 9/16	15	28	10½	18408	12¼	10½	11⅝	...	9	...	-58.5	...	...
37	TRNI	Trans-Industries Inc	NNM	B–	5	87	Electronic info display sys	13¼	11/16	17	6⅞	9	4¼	1862	6⅛	4¼	5½	...	13	NM	-36.2	5.2	40.8
38	TLX	✔Trans-Lux	AS,B,Ph	B	15	373	Electronic displays/theatres	16¾	13/16	16	5½	11⅛	5⅞	544	8¼	7 1/16	7 1/16	2.0	10	-3	-21.2	-12.5	-3.4
39•[1]	TWA	✔Trans World Airlines	AS,P	NR	63	6491	Domestic,intl air service	23¾	4	15⅛	3 11/16	7¾	2¾	172136	4	2¾	2¾	...	d	...	-43.6	-25.2	...
40	WS	Wrrt(Pur 1com at$14.40)	AS	....	9	.5		15½	1 15/16	9⅞	2	4¾	⅝	1971	1⅛	⅝	¾	...	...	...	...	...	...
41•[15]	TWMC	✔Trans World Entertainment	NNM	B–	132	29189	Retails records,tapes,video	13 5/16	9/16	30 3/16	10 13/16	18¾	9	70403	11 7/16	9	10½	...	10	NM	-44.9	67.8	34.2
#42•[7]	TSAI	✔Transaction Sys Architects'A'	NNM	NR	258	29840	Dvlp financial software	45¾	7½	50½	27 1/16	51	20¼	197780	36⅝	20¼	28	...	20	NM	-44.0	-5.6	...
43	TA	✔TransAlta Corp	To,Mo	B+	16	9466	Electric service in Alberta	22⅞	2 11/16	25⅜	18 3/16	25⅛	12¼	183900	16	12¼	14⅛	7.1	11	2	-34.4	-1.7	5.2
44	TFD	Transamerica Fin 7.10%'QUIBS'	NY	....[66]	8	106	Qtly Interest Bonds	....	....	25½	24¾	25⅝	19 9/16	8627	21 9/16	19 9/16	20	8.9	..	...	-15.1	...	...
45	TRH	✔Transatlantic Holdings	NY,Ch,Ph,P	A	149	34021	Reinsur: property/casualty	76 9/16	12 9/16	94½	68¾	80½	69 1/16	2407	78⅝	74 11/16	78 1/16	0.6	16	19	4.0	14.1	16.7
46•[16]	TRP	✔TransCanada P.L.	NY,To,Mo,Ch,Ph,P	A–	149	97561	Nat gas pipeline/o&g explr	29	3¾	27⅝	13⅜	15⅜	7 13/16	38993	11⅛	7 13/16	8¾	◆8.8	d	-14	...	...	...
47	TCI	✔Transcontinental Rlty	NY,Ch	NR	7	51	Real estate investment trust	54	1 11/16	18¼	11½	16⅜	10⅞	2447	13⅛	12	12⅝	4.8	4	NM	2.3	10.6	9.3
48	TFH	✔Transfinancial Holdings	AS	NR	11	693	Motor freight transport'n	11⅞	1	10½	4⅛	6½	2¾	1124	5½	5	5¼	...	d	Neg	16.7	-10.1	-11.2
49	TRGP	✔Transit Group	NSC	C	9	1122	Pick-up/shipping/delivery svc	9	1⅝	8½	2¾	6⅞	2¾	4672	4⅛	2¾	3 1/16	...	7	NM	-41.7	3.6	-9.3
50	TKTX	✔Transkaryotic Therapies	NNM	NR	102	9982	Dvp stg:Biotechnology R&D	44¾	12¾	39¾	15	53½	22¾	66403	48⅞	32⅞	38½	...	d	...	51.7	27.7	...

Uniform Footnote Explanations-See Page 4. Other: [1]CBOE:Cycle 1. [2]CBOE:Cycle 2. [3]P,Ph:Cycle 3. [4]ASE:Cycle 3. [5]CBOE,Ph:Cycle 2. [6]ASE:Cycle 2. [7]Ph:Cycle 3. [8]To:Cycle 3,ASE:Cycle 1. [9]ASE:Cycle 1. [10]ASE,CBOE,P:Cycle 1. [11]Ph:Cycle 2. [12]P,Ph:Cycle 1. [13]CBOE,P:Cycle 1. [14]CBOE,P:Cycle 3. [15]ASE,CBOE:Cycle 3. [16]CBOE:Cycle 3,Vc:Cycle 2. [51]Investor Group plan acq,$44. [52]Ea ADS rep 1 ord, NLG 1. [53]Each ADS rep 4 ord, 5p. [54]To be determined. [55]Stk dstr of Waddell & Reed Fin'l Inc. [56]Stk of Southland Royalty. [57]Fiscal Jul'95 earn $2.81. [58]Aug'96 & prior pricing in Cdn$. [59]Each ADS rep 0.50 ord'B'FF50. [60]Excl subsid pfd. [61]12 Mo Dec,'95:yr May'95 earned $0.22. [62]Spl div. [63]Ea ADS rep 1 ord,1 pence. [64]Each ADR rep 2 ord, y50. [65]4 Mo Dec'95. [66]Rated'A'by S&P. [67]Stk dstr of Nova Corp Alta(New). [68]Incl curr amts.

Index	Cash Divs. Ea.Yr. Since	Dividends Latest Payment Period $	Date	Ex. Div.	Total $ So Far 1999	Ind. Rate	Paid 1998	Financial Position Mil-$ Cash& Equiv.	Curr. Assets	Curr. Liab.	Balance Sheet Date	Capitalization Lg Trm Debt Mil-$	Shs. 000 Pfd.	Com.	Earnings $ Per Shr. Years End	1995	1996	1997	1998	1999	Last 12 Mos.	Interim Earnings Period	$ per Shr. 1998	1999	Index
1	....	None Since Public			...	Nil	....	12.0	22.4	4.14	6-30-99	0.56	p...	★35809	Dc	...	...	...	vpd0.90	....	....	6 Mo Jun	n/a	vpd0.64	1
2◆	1980	Q0.035	3-2-00	2-8	0.135	0.14	0.11½	24.5	1852	1628	10-30-99	120	...	310081	Ja	v□0.07	v□1.05	v0.87	v1.27	E1.67	1.63	9 Mo Oct	v0.88	v1.24	2
3	....	None Paid			...	Nil	....	152	174	26.9	5-31-99	11.0	...	37394	My	d0.08	vd0.16	vd0.47	vd0.34	vd0.11	0.04	3 Mo Aug	v0.01	v0.16	3
4	....	None Since Public			...	Nil	....	59.5	518	495	9-30-99	133	...	±40225	Dc	pv0.15	pvd2.72	±v0.38	v±0.14	....	d0.63	9 Mo Sep	v±0.57	v±d0.20	4
5	1936	Q0.29	12-15-99	11-22	1.41	1.16	1.10	19.3	30.2	185	9-30-99	341	31	13417	Dc	vΔ2.98	v2.00	v2.26	v1.46	....	2.06	9 Mo Sep	v1.69	v2.29	5
6	1998	0.12	10-6-99	9-2	0.322	0.32	0.135	563	5122	5108	j1-01-98	317	...	p467715	Dc	...	p0.73	0.75	n/a	....	....	6 Mo Jun	v0.38	v0.39	6
7	....	0.33	2-1-87	1-9	...	Nil	....	51.0	76.8	16.9	10-03-99	....	...	9701	Mr	v0.42	vd2.14	v0.82	v1.75	....	2.19	27 Wk Sep	v0.01	v0.45	7
8	....	None Paid			...	Nil	....	6.49	54.4	13.7	6-30-99	37.6	...	5501	Sp	□d2.20	v0.92	v0.94	v0.95	Pv0.91	0.91				8
9	....	None Since Public			...	Nil	....	1.41	3.55	0.69	10-02-99	0.01	...	6300	Dc	0.01	v0.02	v0.08	v0.08	....	0.11	9 Mo Sep	v0.07	v0.10	9
10	....	0.14	8-30-91	8-5	...	Nil	....	20.9	293	267	8-31-99	398	765	12671	Nv	0.16	vd0.45	□v0.31	v□d0.46	....	d2.37	9 Mo Aug	v□d0.12	v□d2.03	10
11	....	None Paid			...	Nil	....	Total Assets $1.62M			7-31-99	707	...	36451	Oc	1.47	v1.50	□v1.86	v□2.25	vP□2.75	2.75				11
12	1988	0.736	10-21-99	8-18	0.997	1.00	0.902	409	1922	1995	j5-01-99	172	22789	948989	Ap	1.15	1.19	v1.37	v1.52	v1.42	1.42				12
13◆	....	None Since Public			...	Nil	....	242	700	257	3-31-99	609	...	94324	Mr	0.83	v1.14	v1.49	v1.86	E2.50	2.29	6 Mo Sep	v0.76	v1.19	13
14◆	1935	Q0.27	12-15-99	11-29	1.03	1.08	0.913	Total Deposits $535.75M			9-30-99	40.1	...	4768	Dc	v1.63	v1.75	v2.00	v2.27	....	2.45	9 Mo Sep	v1.70	v1.88	14
15	....	None Since Public			...	Nil	....	24.9	81.7	66.6	10-30-99	50.0	...	30674	Ja	...	...	...	pv0.43	....	0.49	9 Mo Oct	vp0.15	vp0.21	15
16	....	None Since Public			...	Nil	....	3.10	87.2	51.1	12-31-97	....	...	27300	Dc	p0.82	0.60	0.73	....	....	0.73				16
17◆	1943	Q0.06¼	1-7-00	12-16	s0.227	0.25	s0.18	109	227	75.1	10-02-99	7.50	...	±48735	Dc	v0.80	v0.94	v1.21	v1.37	....	1.46	9 Mo Sep	v1.06	v1.15	17
18	....	None Paid			...	Nil	....	0.01	16.2	8.23	8-31-99	7.64	...	4976	My	0.12	0.17	v0.19	v0.19	vd0.25	d0.31	3 Mo Aug	vd0.04	vd0.10	18
19	1994	Q0.332	12-10-99	11-26	1.107	[54]....	1.502	Total Assets $50.84M			9-30-99	....	...	8600	Dc	v2.53	v1.95	v1.69	v1.50	....	1.06	9 Mo Sep	v1.21	v0.77	19
20◆	1933	Q0.09	2-1-00	1-5	0.36	0.36	h[55]0.58	Total Assets $11382.56M			9-30-99	372	...	131537	Dc	v0.99	v2.17	v2.39	v□1.77	E2.60	1.93	9 Mo Sep	v□1.24	vΔ1.40	20
21	....	h[56]....	11-16-81	10-8	...	Nil	....	1.03	1.86	0.32	9-30-99	10.4	...	5177	Dc	vd0.08	v0.14	vd0.01	vd0.05	....	0.01	9 Mo Sep	vd0.01	v0.05	21
22	1984	Q0.12	1-12-00	12-16	0.48	0.48	0.48	1.92	583	351	7-30-99	196	...	12674	Oc	v[57]0.32	v2.90	□v2.93	v0.31	Pv2.64	2.64				22
23◆	1857	gQ0.21	1-31-00	12-14	g0.72	0.84	g0.66	Total Deposits $143656M			j7-31-99	3490	16000	620317	Oc	1.26	v1.48	v1.77	v1.81	Pv4.90	j4.90				23
24◆	1958	gQ0.145	12-31-99	12-14	g0.58	0.58	g0.565	n/a	447	269	j6-30-99	632	...	±74638	Dc	±0.48	±0.81	v±3.27	v±d0.07	....	j0.68	9 Mo Sep	v±0.05	v±0.80	24
25◆	1989	Q0.07	1-3-00	12-21	0.26	0.28	0.24	83.2	1625	1583	9-30-99	1560	...	143934	Dc	v0.69	v1.16	v1.37	v0.67	E1.83	0.76	9 Mo Sep	v1.36	v1.45	25
26	1992	0.865	8-10-99	7-15	0.865	0.86	0.92¼	14079	57815	42270	j12-31-98	25325[60]	...	p616735	Dc	1.61	2.24	v2.57	v2.12	E2.84	2.12				26
27	....	Terms&trad. basis should be checked in detail						Wrrts expire 8-5-2003				....	...	3606	Dc	...	...	...	...	....	....				27
28◆	....	None Since Public			...	Nil	....	70.7	657	240	9-30-99	1434	...	81189	Dc	p□v[61]0.32	v□0.55	v0.82	v□0.19	....	0.21	9 Mo Sep	v□d0.01	v0.01	28
29◆	1990	Q0.01	1-3-00	12-21	0.04	0.04	0.035	35.4	173	88.1	9-30-99	0.20	...	194918	Dc	v0.14	0.21	v0.25	v0.28	....	0.34	9 Mo Sep	v0.19	v0.25	29
30◆	....	None Since Public			...	Nil	....	1.07	575	410	9-30-99	933	...	46879	Dc	v0.53	v0.78	□v1.14	v1.68	....	2.02	9 Mo Sep	v1.18	v1.52	30
31	....	[62]1.00	10-20-97	9-24	...	Nil	....	64.4	85.3	19.2	12-31-98	12.1	...	12084	Dc	1.76	v0.76	v1.38	vd1.18	....	d1.71	9 Mo Sep	vd0.86	vd1.39	31
32	1993	Q0.41	12-10-99	11-17	1.64	1.64	1.60	Total Assets $452M			9-30-99	418	...	15788	Dc	v0.36	0.36	v□0.42	v0.40	....	0.51	9 Mo Sep	v0.28	v0.39	32
33	....	None Since Public			...	Nil	....	0.06	2.51	4.74	12-31-98	....	850	★7000	Dc	...	...	...	vd0.29	....	....	6 Mo Jun	n/a	v0.13	33
34	1970	0.18	12-9-99	9-27	0.351	0.35	0.587	16661	47953	43102	3-31-99	25223	...	3760650	Mr	1.24	1.62	v1.78	v2.01	....	2.01				34
35	....	None since reorg.			...	Nil	....	297	3700	3969	10-30-99	1240	...	239948	Ja	v0.53	v1.54	v1.70	vd0.50	E1.55	1.32	9 Mo Oct	vd1.64	v0.18	35
36	....	None Since Public			...	Nil	....	56.8	350	221	9-30-99	62.8	...	35565	Dc	...	pv0.57	vpd0.42	v1.28	....	1.29	9 Mo Sep	v0.87	v0.88	36
37	1998	[62]0.10	5-22-98	5-14	...	Nil	[62]0.10	0.02	23.5	13.9	9-30-99	4.05	...	3140	Dc	v0.26	v0.56	v0.86	v1.28	....	0.43	9 Mo Sep	v0.90	v0.05	37
38	1986	Q0.035	1-19-00	12-31	0.14	0.14	0.14	5.89	21.8	10.1	9-30-99	60.7	...	±1267	Dc	v±0.79	±v0.89	v±0.80	v±0.85	....	0.73	9 Mo Sep	v0.60	v0.48	38
39	....	None Since Public			...	Nil	....	239	675	1125	9-30-99	674	12002	59933	Dc	Δ[65]d1.15	v□d6.60	v□d1.98	□vd2.14	Ed1.30	d2.81	9 Mo Sep	v□d0.80	vd1.47	39
40	....	Terms&trad. basis should be checked in detail						Wrrts expire 8-23-2002				....	...	1967	Dc	...	...	...	...	....	....				40
41◆	....	None Since Public			...	Nil	....	86.7	605	345	10-30-99	19.7	...	53040	Ja	d0.87	v0.24	v0.66	v1.20	....	1.11	9 Mo Oct	v0.18	v0.09	41
42◆	....	None Since Public			...	Nil	....	72.1	179	89.4	6-30-99	1.86	...	32551	Sp	□0.28	0.47	±v0.81	v1.02	Pv1.38	1.38				42
43	1956	gQ0.25	1-1-00	11-29	g1.00	1.00	g0.98	Total Assets $6015M			j9-30-99	1684	7000	168996	Dc	1.14	v1.14	v1.14	v1.29	....	j1.27	9 Mo Sep	v0.89	v0.87	43
44	1999	Q0.44⅜	2-1-00	1-12	1.765	1.775	....	Co opt redm fr 11-3-2003 at $25				★200	...	...	Dc	...	...	...	...	....	....	Mature 11-1-2028			44
45◆	1990	Q0.12½	3-17-00	3-1	0.47	0.50	0.42	Total Assets $5413.79M			9-30-99	....	...	34716	Dc	v3.82	v4.48	v5.34	v7.10	E5.00	6.49	9 Mo Sep	v5.48	v4.87	45
46	1964	gQ0.28	1-31-00	12-28	g0.84	1.12	gh[67]1.21	350	2672	3566	j12-31-98	13917	10253	464000	Dc	1.75	v1.85	v1.85	v0.78	Ed0.14	j0.89	9 Mo Sep	v0.94	v1.05	46
47◆	1995	Q0.15	12-31-99	12-13	0.60	0.60	†1.60	Total Assets $424M			9-30-99	[68]309	6	p8637	Dc	vΔd1.29	Δvd2.02	v3.22	v1.78	....	3.06	9 Mo Sep	v2.07	v3.35	47
48	....	....			...	Nil	....	1.53	38.3	32.8	9-30-99	....	...	3252	Dc	v0.85	v0.12	v0.18	vd0.39	....	d0.45	9 Mo Sep	vd0.38	vd0.44	48
49	....	None Paid			...	Nil	....	3.25	78.3	70.8	9-30-99	86.0	...	31926	Dc	d0.85	vd1.48	vd1.08	v0.49	....	0.47	9 Mo Sep	v0.14	v0.12	49
50	....	None Since Public			...	Nil	....	80.8	82.4	11.0	9-30-99	10.6	...	22584	Dc	p0.14	pvd0.81	vd0.74	vd1.05	....	d2.25	9 Mo Sep	vd0.62	vd1.82	50

◆**Stock Splits & Divs By Line Reference Index** [2]2-for-1,'97,'98:No adj for dstr of Waban, Inc,'89. [13]2-for-1,'95,'99. [14]10%,'95:3-for-2,'98. [17]2-for-1,'95,'98:Adj for 3%,'99. [20]2-for-1,'97. [23]2-for-1,'99. [24]2-for-1,'98. [25]3-for-1,'97. [28]5-for-3,'97. [29]2-for-1,'94,'95,'96:3-for-2,'98. [30]2-for-1,'98. [41]2-for-1,'97:3-for-2,'98. [42]2-for-1,'96. [45]3-for-2,'97. [47]3-for-2,'96.

¶ S&P 500 # MidCap 400 ✣ SmallCap 600 • Options

Index	Ticker	Name of Issue (Call Price of Pfd. Stocks)	Market	Com. Rank. & Pfd. Rating	Inst. Hold Cos	Inst. Hold Shs. (000)	Principal Business	1971-97 High	1971-97 Low	1998 High	1998 Low	1999 High	1999 Low	Dec. Sales in 100s	Dec. 1999 Last Sale Or Bid High	Low	Last	%Div Yield	P-E Ratio	EPS 5 Yr Growth	% Annualized Total Return 12 Mo	36 Mo	60 Mo
1	TMN	✓Transmedia Network	NY,Ch,Ph,P	↓C	26	3601	Restaurant charge cards	16 5/16	3/16	8 3/4	1 13/16	6 1/8	1 13/16	6063	2 3/4	2 1/8	2 1/2	...	d	Neg	17.6	−19.7	−22.9
2	TMG	✓TransMontaigne Inc	AS	NR	66	11978	Transport,store,mkt petrol prd	20 3/8	9 11/16	17 1/16	9 7/8	16 1/4	4 1/2	17853	7 1/8	4 1/2	7	...	..	...	−53.7	−19.7	...
3	TFN	✓Transnational Finl Network	AS	NR	1	6	Originates,svcs mtge loans	....	....	9	3 3/8	7 1/4	15/16	2901	1 5/8	15/16	1 3/8	...	d	...	−67.6	...	...
¶4•[1]	RIG	✓Transocean Sedco Forex[52]	NY,P	NR	472	76474	Offshore oil&gas drilling svcs	60 1/2	7 5/8	59 15/16	23	36 1/2	19 5/8	461509	34 3/8	23 7/8	33 11/16	0.4	16	63	26.2	3.0	31.3
5•[2]	TMM	✓Transportacion Maritima ADS[53]	NY,Ph,P	NR	12	6954	Maritime Shipping, Mexico	12 7/8	3 5/8	8 3/16	3	7 5/16	2 3/8	20554	5	3 1/8	4 11/16	...	d	...	−12.8	−3.7	−8.4
6•[3]	TMM.A	CPO ADS[54]	NY,Ph	NR	8	5380		11 5/8	2 7/8	7 1/4	2 1/2	6 3/4	2	7536	4 3/4	3	4 1/4	...	6	−25	−5.6	−2.8	−6.8
7	TGS	✓Transportadora De Gas ADS[56]	NY,Ch,P	NR	39	11894	Natural gas transp'n-Argentina	14	6 1/2	12 1/2	7	10 1/2	7 1/2	15868	9 3/8	8 3/16	9 3/16	10.9	9	...	1.1	−0.6	8.7
8	TUI	✓Transportation Components	NY	NR	7	1326	Distrib truck parts/supplies	....	....	11 3/4	3	5 1/2	2 1/8	13199	3	2 1/4	2 7/8	...	..	...	−37.8	...	...
9	TPR	✓TransPro Inc	NY,Ch,P	NR	44	3865	Auto/truck radiator,metal pd	17 3/4	5 1/2	8 15/16	4 3/8	7 7/8	4 5/16	1510	6 3/4	5 15/16	6 7/16	3.1	7	−20	36.9	−8.4	...
10	TT	✓TransTechnology	NY,B,Ch,P	B	46	3201	Ind fastener/aerospace defense	30 7/8	7/8	30 5/8	18 9/16	21 1/4	8	6890	12 5/8	8 1/2	11 1/16	2.4	6	25	−45.7	−16.3	0.8
11•[1]	TXCC	✓TranSwitch Corp	NNM	NR	288	25188	Mfr eqp for semicond'r ind	14 7/16	2 7/16	30 3/16	5	72 5/8	19 13/16	103761	72 5/8	44	72 9/16	...	96	NM	182	176	...
12	TWH	✓Transworld HealthCare	AS	C	17	1457	Home infusion/nursing svc	19 3/4	2 5/8	7 13/16	2 1/8	5	1 1/2	4911	2 5/8	1 1/2	1 7/8	...	d	Neg	−60.0	−44.6	−33.0
13	TNZR	✓Tranz Rail Hlds ADS[58]	NNM	NR	17	7750	Freight transport railroad	18 7/8	11	11 5/8	3 13/16	8 3/8	4 3/8	1367	5 7/8	5 1/8	5 3/8B	3.7	6	−6	−16.6	−30.1	...
14•[4]	TAP	✓Travelers Prop Casualty 'A'	NY,Ch,P	NR	287	56801	Property & casualty insurance	45	23 1/8	46 1/16	24 1/8	41 7/8	27 11/16	61129	35 1/4	30 7/8	34 1/4	1.5	10	...	12.0	0.0	...
15	TRR	✓TRC Cos	NY,Ch,P	B−	19	1981	Environment consult/research	17	1/32	5 11/16	3 3/4	8 3/16	4 1/2	1305	8 3/16	6 5/16	7 11/16	...	18	90	39.8	19.5	−0.8
✣16	TG	✓Tredegar Corp	NY,P	B+	121	9029	Plastics, aluminum & energy	25	1 7/16	31 1/4	16 1/8	32 15/16	16 1/16	11850	20 3/4	16 1/16	20 11/16	0.8	15	19	−7.4	16.4	42.5
17	TRE	✓Tremont Corp	NY,Ph,P	B−	33	1367	Titanium prd/bentonite min'g	58 1/2	5 3/4	60 5/8	31 1/2	33 5/8	13 11/16	1390	16 1/2	13 11/16	15	1.9	4	NM	−54.2	−24.9	5.4
✣18	TWK	✓Trenwick Group	NY	A−	123	8757	Reinsurance:prop,casualty	39 5/8	5 15/16	41 3/4	26 3/4	35 1/4	14 3/8	22955	20 1/2	14 3/8	16 15/16	6.1	94	−28	−45.8	−15.2	−7.0
19	TWP	Trex Co	NY	NR	36	5717	Mfr non-wood decking prd	....	....	....	....	32 1/2	10	3589	27 3/8	23 3/4	26 3/4	...	..	...	...	...	..
20•[5]	TXM	✓Trex Medical	AS	NR	37	2747	Mfr mammography equipment	26	11	19 11/16	5 1/2	8 3/4	2 3/16	15676	2 13/16	2 3/16	2 13/16	...	d	...	−66.9	−40.0	..
21	TGIC	✓Triad Guaranty	NNM	B	67	4042	Mortgage Insurance coverage	57 3/4	3 13/16	43 3/8	10 1/2	23 11/16	11 1/2	8519	23 11/16	20 1/8	22 3/4	...	11	39	3.1	16.9	40.5
22	TGL	✓Triangle Bancorp[62]	NY	NR	52	2604	General banking, N. Carolina	24 1/2	5 11/16	23 1/2	14 13/16	23 1/2	15 1/8	6229	21 7/16	17 11/16	19 3/8	2.1	18	18	25.2	23.6	26.1
23•[6]	VIRS	✓Triangle Pharmaceuticals	NNM	NR	90	14819	Dvp stg:Pharmaceutical R&D	26 7/8	10	21 1/8	8 3/8	23 5/8	10 1/4	47561	19 5/8	10 5/16	12 13/16	...	d	...	−6.0	−17.6	..
✣24•[7]	TRY	✓Triarc Cos Cl'A'	NY,B,Ch,P,Ph	C	87	8430	Beverages,restaurants,LP gas	33	3/8	28 1/4	12 3/8	22 1/8	14 3/4	6547	19 1/2	17 1/4	18 3/8	...	29	NM	15.7	16.9	9.4
¶25•[8]	TRB	✓Tribune Co.	NY,B,Ch,P	A	649	134003	Newspaper pub,brdcg,CATV	31 5/16	3	37 1/2	22 3/8	60 7/8	30 1/8	179723	58 15/16	47 1/4	55 1/16	0.7	10	37	68.5	42.5	34.0
26	TXA	Tribune Co Exch[65]AOL 'PHONES'[66]	NY	....[67]	15	3230	Exch Sub Debs	....	....	....	....	190	150	15974	190	150	159	2.0	..	...	...	...	..
27	TRD	Tribune Co 6.25%'DECS' 2001	NY	NR	11	399	Exch Notes for Com Stock	....	....	29 1/2	17 3/4	30 3/4	16 1/16	9736	18 5/8	16 7/16	17 5/8	9.9	..	...	−23.0	...	..
28•[9]	TMAR	✓Trico Marine Svcs	NNM	NR	67	7103	Oil & gas industry svcs	45 1/2	8	30 1/2	4 3/8	9 13/16	4 1/4	56592	8	6 1/2	7 1/16	...	d	...	44.9	−33.5	..
29	TDR	✓TRICOM SA ADR[70]	NY	NR	9	918	Telecommunication svcs	....	....	13	3 7/16	22 5/8	6	18341	22 5/8	12 5/8	22	...	26	9	214	...	..
¶30•[10]	YUM	✓Tricon Global Restaurants	NY	NR	606	103454	Oper family style restaurants	36 1/4	27 7/8	50 7/8	25 1/16	73 7/8	35	153760	41 3/8	37 9/16	38 5/8	...	11	...	−22.9	...	..
31	TRID	✓Trident Microsystems	NNM	C	22	3172	Dvlp computer graphics prod	37 3/4	4 1/2	10 7/8	2 1/2	12	4	20464	11 1/2	8 3/4	10 1/4	...	d	Neg	149	−15.3	−1.8
32	TGN	✓Trigen Energy	NY,Ch,Ph	NR	36	3045	Oper community energy sys	32 1/4	15 3/4	19 15/16	9 3/4	24 3/16	11 3/8	2454	18 1/8	16 1/8	17 3/8	0.8	12	−1	53.2	−14.8	−1.6
#33	TGH	✓Trigon Healthcare	NY,Ph	NR	256	27175	Manage hlth care svcs,Virginia	27 1/4	15 3/8	38 3/8	23 1/2	39	21 1/2	36698	30 7/8	25 13/16	29 1/2	...	15	...	−20.9	...	..
✣34•[11]	TRMB	✓Trimble Navigation Ltd	NNM	B−	85	7753	Mfr electr navigat'n instr	35 3/8	5 3/4	24 3/8	7	23 1/8	7 1/4	44864	23 1/8	15 1/2	21 5/8	...	d	Neg	198	23.4	5.6
#35•[7]	TRN	✓Trinity Indus	NY,B,Ch,P	B+	288	29294	Railcars: containers, steel	54 3/8	3/4	55 11/16	27 9/16	39 7/8	26 1/4	31935	29 11/16	26 5/8	28 7/16	2.5	7	13	−24.5	...	..
36	TRT	✓Trio-Tech Intl	AS	B−	5	50	Dsgn/mfr envmtl test eqp	11 11/16	2 3/16	6 1/2	2 1/8	4 7/8	2 5/8	754	3 7/8	3 3/8	3 11/16	...	74	−34	22.9	−3.3	..
37•[8]	TQNT	✓TriQuint Semiconductor	NNM	NR	158	14259	Mfr,mkt integrated circuits	30 5/16	3	18 5/16	7 5/16	113 3/4	10 5/16	77813	113 3/4	83	111 1/4	...	..	NM	772	85.3	91.6
38	TTEL	Tritel Inc'A'	NNM	NR	..	...	Dvp stage:wireless commun svc	....	....	....	....	35 1/8	18	209601	35 1/8	18	31 11/16	...	..	...	...	...	..
39•[12]	OIL	✓Triton Energy	NY,B	C	63	8448	Oil & gas explor'n,devel't	60 1/4	1 1/8	43 3/8	7 1/8	27 1/2	5 3/16	82543	24 1/8	18 1/2	20 5/8	...	d	Neg	160	−24.8	−9.5
40	TPCS	✓Triton PCS Holdings'A'	NNM	NR	..	...	Wireless communic svcs	....	....	....	....	47 1/4	18	42063	47 3/16	37 1/4	45 1/2	...	d	...	...	...	..
41	TGI	✓Triumph Group	NY,Ph	NR	88	5653	Mfr,repair aircraft components	37 1/4	19	50 7/8	24	35 1/8	22 1/2	3919	24 1/2	23 3/16	24 3/16	...	9	...	−24.4	0.4	..
42•[2]	TZH	✓TrizecHahn Corp[72]	NY,Ch,Ph,P	B	141	71851	Real estate/oil&gas/gold min'g	27 9/16	5 7/8	25 1/8	16 1/8	22 13/16	15 1/2	40184	17 5/16	15 1/2	16 7/8	2.1	9	19	−16.2	−7.1	6.9
¶43•[10]	TROW	✓T.Rowe Price Assoc	NNM	A	331	54984	Advisor to mutual funds,dstr	36 7/8	1 1/8	42 7/8	20 7/8	43 1/4	25 7/8	72221	39 1/8	32 5/8	36 15/16	1.4	21	28	9.1	20.7	39.4
✣44•[13]	TNO	✓True North Communicns	NY,B,Ch,Ph	B	226	29440	Int'l advertising agency	27 3/4	1 5/16	34	18 13/16	47	22 1/2	47120	47	39 11/16	44 11/16	1.3	d	Neg	69.7	29.9	18.8
45	DJT	✓Trump Hotels & Casino Res	NY,Ch,Ph	NR	39	10791	Own,operate gaming operations	35 1/2	6 1/4	12	2 3/4	6 13/16	3 1/4	37342	3 15/16	3 1/4	3 3/8	...	d	−26	−10.0	−34.5	..
46	TCNJ	✓Trust Co of New Jersey	NNM	B+	51	1266	Commercial bkg,New Jersey	25 1/2	5/16	30 1/4	18 1/2	25	20 3/8	2724	23	21	22 7/8	2.3	16	46	−4.5	20.4	14.1
¶47•[7]	TRW	✓TRW Inc	NY,B,Ch,P,Ph	B+	502	74552	Car & truck:elec/space:ind'l	61 5/16	2 9/16	58	42 11/16	59 7/8	41 3/16	66080	55 1/4	50 5/16	51 15/16	2.5	15	−21	−4.9	4.1	12.3
48	Pr B	$4.40 cm Cv II Pref (104)vtg	NY,B	A	5	1	& energy: computer svs	495	36	495	420	505	402	1	452	452	457 1/8B	1.0	..	...	...	...	..
49	Pr D	$4.50cmCv II Pref 3 (100)	NY,B	A	4	.8	spacecraft,tools,pumps	423 1/4	37 3/8	405	379	418	330	5	375	375	386 7/8B	1.2	..	...	...	...	..
50	TSII	✓TSI Inc	NNM	B+	34	2597	Flow measurement instr	12 1/2	1/64	10 3/8	6 5/8	14 15/16	7 1/2	4918	12	10 3/8	11 3/4	1.0	14	17	35.8	2.0	25.0

Uniform Footnote Explanations-See Page 4. Other: [1]Ph:Cycle 2. [2]CBOE,Ph:Cycle 1. [3]Ph:Cycle 1. [4]Ph:Cycle 3. [5]ASE:Cycle 3. [6]P,Ph:Cycle 3. [7]ASE:Cycle 1. [8]CBOE:Cycle 2. [9]ASE,CBOE:Cycle 2. [10]CBOE:Cycle 1. [11]P:Cycle 3. [12]ASE,CBOE,Ph:Cycle 1. [13]CBOE:Cycle 3. [51]Fiscal Apr'98 & prior. [52]Formerly Transocean Offshore. [53]Ea ADS rep 1 'L'shr,no par. [54]Ea ADS rep 1 ord Part'n ctf(rep 1ser'A'shr int). [55]Approx. [56]Ea ADS rep 5 Cl'B'shrs, Ps1. [57]11 Mo Sep,'97. [58]Ea ADS rep 3 ord shs. [59]82.7% owned by Travelers Group. [60]®$2.83,'96. [61]9 Mo Sep'95. [62]Centura Banks plan acq,0.45 com. [63]6 Mo Dec'95. [64]Pfd in $M. [65]Partic Hybrid Optional Nts Exch Sec. [66]Due 5-15-2029. [67]Rated'A-r'by S&P. [68]Based on Value of Amer Online Stk,re-spec cond. [69]Based on Amer Online Stk value,re-spec cond. [70]Ea ADS rep 1 Cl'A',RD$10. [71]Spl div. [72]Sub vtg shrs. [73]6 Mo Dec '95.

Splits ◆ Index	Cash Divs. Ea.Yr. Since	Dividends: Latest Payment Period $	Date	Ex. Div.	Total $ So Far 1999	Ind. Rate	Paid 1998	Financial Position Mil-$ Cash& Equiv.	Curr. Assets	Curr. Liab.	Balance Sheet Date	Capitalization Lg Trm Debt Mil-$	Shs. 000 Pfd.	Com.	Earnings $ Per Shr. Years End	1995	1996	1997	1998	1999	Last 12 Mos.	Interim Earnings Period	$ per Shr. 1998	1999	Index
1◆	....	0.02	11-3-97	10-16	...	Nil	....	3.23	97.4	53.3	6-30-99	33.0	...	13353	Sp	0.46	v0.25	vd0.04	vd0.67	Pvd0.79	d0.79				1
2	....	None Since Public			...	Nil	....	3.52	453	189	9-30-99	427	...	30592	Je	pvd1.32	v0.30	v0.41	v[51]0.29	n/a	....	3 Mo Sep	v0.02	vd0.24	2
3	....	None Since Public			...	Nil	....	Total Assets $30.1M			9-30-99	19.0	...	4279	Dc	...	pv0.10	pv0.20	pv0.34	....	d0.20	9 Mo Sep	v0.25	vd0.29	3
4◆	1993	Q0.03	12-17-99	12-1	0.12	0.12	0.12	90.4	568	499	p6-30-99	824	...	p209000	Dc	v0.82	v1.07	v1.38	v3.41	E2.17	2.90	9 Mo Sep	v2.38	v1.87	4
5	....	0.174	11-29-96	11-20	...	Nil	....	99.3	321	338	12-31-98	573	...	56598	Dc	0.94	0.75	n/a	vd0.18	....	d0.18				5
6	....	[55]0.174	11-29-96	11-20	...	Nil	....	....	...	...		....	...	42432	Dc	0.94	0.75	...	....	....	0.75				6
7	1995	0.499	8-5-99	7-26	[55]0.999	1.00	1.00	80.7	145	379	12-31-97	424	...	794495	Dc	±1.14	±1.03	v1.06	....	....	1.06				7
8	....	None Since Public			...	Nil	....	5.11	121	46.3	9-30-99	61.5	...	17626	Dc	...	...	pv0.45	vp0.46	....	....	9 Mo Sep	n/a	v0.25	8
9	1996	Q0.05	1-10-00	12-16	0.20	0.20	0.20	0.91	130	38.3	9-30-99	60.8	30	6597	Dc	vp1.39	v1.28	v1.20	v0.24	....	0.88	9 Mo Sep	v0.36	v1.00	9
10	1992	Q0.06½	12-1-99	11-10	0.26	0.26	0.26	1.60	131	127	9-26-99	204	...	6137	Mr	v1.44	v1.69	v1.95	v□2.30	....	1.76	6 Mo Sep	v□0.84	v□0.30	10
11◆	....	None Since Public			...	Nil	....	85.8	105	11.5	9-30-99	....	...	25997	Dc	vd0.12	vd0.57	vd0.10	v0.27	....	0.76	9 Mo Sep	v0.16	v0.65	11
12	....	None Since Public			...	Nil	....	6.57	53.0	80.2	6-30-99	0.01	...	17551	Sp	0.13	□0.26	‡v[57]d2.56	v0.07	....	d0.24	9 Mo Jun	vNil	vd0.31	12
13	1997	0.099	10-1-99	9-7	0.203	0.20	0.206	5.45	54.0	77.2	6-30-99	112	...	120772	Je	1.29	1.02	v0.99	v0.68	v0.90	0.94	3 Mo Sep	v0.03	v0.07	13
14	1996	Q0.12½	11-24-99	10-28	0.50	0.50	0.40	Total Assets $51173.00M			9-30-99	2326	...	[59]±389241	Dc	±pv1.28	±v1.02	v3.12	v3.42	....	3.52	9 Mo Sep	v2.48	v□2.58	14
15	....	None Since Public			...	Nil	....	0.83	36.2	18.7	9-30-99	0.30	...	6800	Je	0.61	d0.19	vd0.07	v0.16	v0.36	0.42	3 Mo Sep	v0.07	v0.13	15
16◆	1989	Q0.04	1-1-00	12-15	0.16	0.16	0.15	19.4	195	104	9-30-99	250	...	37262	Dc	0.60	v1.15	v1.48	v1.78	....	1.42	9 Mo Sep	v1.33	v0.97	16
17	1998	Q0.07	12-30-99	12-13	0.28	0.28	0.21	3.05	12.1	18.5	9-30-99	....	...	6387	Dc	v0.70	v3.90	v1.76	v□11.18	....	3.41	9 Mo Sep	v□9.69	v1.92	17
18◆	1988	Q0.26	12-31-99	12-13	1.04	1.04	1.00	Total Assets $1432M			9-30-99	185	...	p18586	Dc	v2.59	v[60]2.85	□v3.01	v2.95	....	0.18	9 Mo Sep	v1.95	vd0.82	18
19	....	None Since Public			...	Nil	....	0.31	8.13	8.21	9-30-99	10.9	...	14121	Dc	...	...	...	vp0.50	....	....	9 Mo Sep	n/a	v□0.94	19
20	....	None Since Public			...	Nil	....	5.88	155	66.5	7-03-99	8.50	...	32003	Sp	‡p[61]0.02	v0.39	v0.50	v0.56	Pvd0.87	d0.87				20
21◆	....	None Since Public			...	Nil	....	Total Assets $252.31M			9-30-99	34.5	...	13302	Dc	v0.58	v0.83	v1.26	v1.76	....	2.08	9 Mo Sep	v1.29	v1.61	21
22◆	1994	Q0.10	12-31-99	12-13	0.38	0.40	0.347	Total Deposits $1742.78M			9-30-99	144	...	25256	Dc	v0.48	v0.68	v0.83	v0.84	....	1.06	9 Mo Sep	v0.58	v0.80	22
23	....	None Since Public			...	Nil	....	161	166	25.5	9-30-99	0.04	...	37577	Dc	p[63]d0.07	pvd1.89	vd2.00	vd2.93	....	d3.21	9 Mo Sep	vd2.06	vd2.34	23
24	....	5%Stk	4-25-86	3-25	...	Nil	....	291	496	246	10-03-99	847	...	±23660	Dc	vd1.24	v□d0.28	□v0.01	v0.46	....	0.63	9 Mo Sep	v0.45	v□0.62	24
25◆	1902	Q0.09	12-9-99	11-23	0.36	0.36	0.34	1173	2186	850	9-26-99	2275	[64]281	237632	Dc	v0.92	v1.32	v1.41	v1.50	E5.46	5.56	9 Mo Sep	v1.08	v□5.14	25
26	....	Plan qtly div			...	3.14	....	Co redm opt anytime[68]				....	...	★7000	Dc	...	...	...	....	....	....	Hldrs exch opt for cash[69]			26
27	1998	Q0.437	11-15-99	10-28	1.746	1.746	0.485	Amt pay mat based on The Learning Co com stk				....	...	4600	Dc	...	...	...	....	....	....	Due 8-15-2001			27
28◆	....	None Since Public			...	Nil	....	9.47	41.5	37.8	9-30-99	394	...	28386	Dc	pvd0.21	v□0.88	v2.11	v1.20	....	d0.96	9 Mo Sep	v1.15	v□d1.01	28
29	....	None Since Public			...	Nil	....	7.52	47.6	136	6-30-99	200	...	±24845	Dc	v0.32	v0.41	□v0.17	v0.78	....	0.86	9 Mo Sep	v0.55	v0.63	29
30	....	None Since Public			...	Nil	....	214	666	1359	3-20-99	3333	...	153534	Dc	...	p0.85	pvd0.77	v2.84	E3.65	3.94	36 Wk Sep	v1.89	v2.99	30
31	....	None Since Public			...	Nil	....	31.8	53.7	17.3	9-30-99	0.07	...	13206	Je	v0.61	v1.26	v1.09	vd0.39	vd0.94	d0.88	3 Mo Sep	vd0.21	vd0.15	31
32	1994	0.035	1-11-00	12-29	0.14	0.14	0.14	21.5	44.4	77.7	9-30-99	397	...	12407	Dc	v0.93	v□1.20	v0.41	v□0.55	....	1.45	9 Mo Sep	v□0.30	v□1.20	32
33	....	None Since Public			...	Nil	....	1792	2251	1061	9-30-99	249	...	39266	Dc	p0.86	□pvd2.73	pv2.23	v2.88	E2.03	0.96	9 Mo Sep	v1.75	vd0.17	33
34	....	None Since Public			...	Nil	....	96.8	160	55.8	10-01-99	34.0	...	22557	Dc	v0.53	vd0.51	v0.40	vd2.38	....	d0.12	9 Mo Sep	vd1.56	v0.70	34
35◆	1964	Q0.18	1-31-00	1-12	0.71	0.72	0.68	Total Assets $1654M			9-30-99	99.1	...	39458	Mr	v2.72	v3.21	v2.36	v4.25	E4.20	4.18	6 Mo Sep	v2.33	v2.26	35
36◆	....	None Paid			...	Nil	....	5.77	13.3	6.73	9-24-99	0.87	...	2747	Je	0.28	v0.42	v0.51	v0.33	v0.07	0.05	3 Mo Sep	v0.04	v0.02	36
37◆	....	None Since Public			...	Nil	....	183	240	28.0	9-30-99	5.72	...	★18500	Dc	v0.28	v0.48	v0.50	vd0.28	....	1.09	9 Mo Sep	vd0.53	v0.84	37
38	....	None Since Public			...	Nil	....	486	495	54.6	9-30-99	552	p46	★101904	Dc	...	...	...	n/a	....	....	9 Mo Sep	n/a	vd0.38	38
39	....	[71]0.01	6-16-95	5-26	...	Nil	....	213	255	73.2	6-30-99	409	5210	35750	Dc	v0.05	□v0.62	□v0.14	vd5.21	....	d3.27	9 Mo Sep	vd1.65	v0.29	39
40	....	None Since Public			...	Nil	....	46.3	85.9	45.3	6-30-99	484	p1330	±★60411	Dc	...	...	...	vpd1.04	....	d2.08	6 Mo Jun	d0.33	vpd1.37	40
41	....	None Since Public			...	Nil	....	7.18	206	93.0	9-30-99	118	...	±11662	Mr	p1.18	□±v1.27	±vΔ2.14	v±2.62	....	2.71	6 Mo Sep	v1.23	v1.32	41
42	1993	S0.17½	9-17-99	9-1	0.35	0.35	0.30	Equity per shr $13.37			12-31-98	4862	...	±152700	Dc	0.52	vp0.18	v0.32	v3.11	E1.90↓	1.82	9 Mo Sep	v1.86	v0.57	42
43◆	1986	Q0.13	1-12-00	12-23	0.40	0.52	0.34	Total Assets $953.93M			9-30-99	17.1	...	119652	Dc	□v0.62	v0.79	v1.12	v1.34	E1.80	1.66	9 Mo Sep	v0.99	v1.31	43
44◆	1963	Q0.15	1-3-00	12-15	0.60	0.60	0.60	144	1254	1421	9-30-99	39.8	...	48202	Dc	0.87	v0.81	vd1.17	v0.78	....	d0.02	9 Mo Sep	v0.73	vd0.07	44
45	....	None Since Public			...	Nil	....	179	289	239	9-30-99	1847	...	22195	Dc	‡[73]d0.19	v□d0.25	vd1.85	vd1.79	....	d5.05	9 Mo Sep	vd1.05	v□d4.31	45
46	1983	Q0.13	12-1-99	11-3	0.52	0.52	0.48	Book Value $9.84			12-31-98	....	...	19241	Dc	0.62	v1.04	v1.33	v1.39	....	1.44	9 Mo Sep	v0.91	v0.96	46
47◆	1936	Q0.33	3-15-00	2-9	1.32	1.32	1.26	294	5199	7452	9-30-99	5530	...	121605	Dc	v3.32	v3.62	vd0.40	v3.83	E3.41	2.94	9 Mo Sep	v2.88	v1.99	47
48	1968	Q1.10	3-15-00	2-9	4.40	4.40	4.40	Cv into 8.80 common				....	40	...	Dc	...	...	...	....	....	....				48
49	1968	Q1.12½	3-15-00	2-9	4.50	4.50	4.50	Cv into 7.448 common				....	69		Dc	...	...	...	....	....	....				49
50◆	1975	Q0.03	11-23-99	11-5	0.12	0.12	0.12	3.44	49.7	27.8	9-30-99	2.00	...	11339	Mr	v0.49	v0.62	v0.58	v0.68	....	0.82	6 Mo Sep	v0.30	v0.44	50

◆**Stock Splits & Divs By Line Reference Index** [1]3-for-2,'94. [4]2-for-1,'97. [11]3-for-2,'99:To split 3-for-2,ex Jan 11,'00. [16]3-for-2,'96:3-for-1,'98. [18]3-for-2,'97. [21]3-for-2,'96:2-for-1,'97. [22]3-for-2,'98. [25]2-for-1,'97,'99. [28]2-for-1,'97. [35]No adj for stk dstr,'97. [36]3-for-2,'97. [37]3-for-2,'99:Vote Jan 31 on 2-for-1,hldrs Feb 1. [43]2-for-1,'98. [44]2-for-1,'95. [47]2-for-1,'96. [50]2-for-1,'96.

¶ S&P 500
# MidCap 400
✤ SmallCap 600
• Options

Index	Ticker	Name of Issue (Call Price of Pfd. Stocks)	Market	Com. Rank. & Pfd. Rating	Inst. Hold Cos	Inst. Hold Shs. (000)	Principal Business	1971-97 High	1971-97 Low	1998 High	1998 Low	1999 High	1999 Low	Dec. Sales in 100s	December, 1999 Last Sale Or Bid High	Low	Last	%Div Yield	P-E Ratio	EPS 5 Yr Growth	% Annualized Total Return 12 Mo	36 Mo	60 Mo
1•[1]	TSFW	✔TSI Intl Software	NNM	NR	147	19308	Computer software svcs	7 9/16	4½	25½	4¾	66¾	13¼	97046	66¾	39⅝	56⅝	...	d	...	137	...	...
✤2•[2]	TBI	✔Tuboscope Inc	NY,Ph	B–	148	14708	Oil & gas ind services/prod	36	4½	26½	6 5/16	16⅞	5	22676	15⅞	10 15/16	15⅞	...	..	–9	95.4	0.8	21.5
3•[3]	TAM	✔TubosDeAceroMex ADR[51]	AS,B,Ch,P,Ph	NR	86	16379	Mfr seamless steel pipe, tub'g	30	11/16	21½	4⅛	14 11/16	5 13/16	31979	14¼	12 7/16	13 9/16	2.9	38	NM	120	–2.8	25.5
4	TUES	✔Tuesday Morning	NNM	NR	68	7420	Deep discount retail stores	....	....	....	....	26¾	15	31747	26	16	18 7/16	...	32	...	...	...	...
5	TLRK	Tularik Inc	NNM	NR	..	...	Pharmaceutical R&D	....	....	....	....	39 1/16	14	98416	39 1/16	14	32⅝	...	..	...	...	...	...
¶6•[4]	TUP	✔Tupperware Corp	NY,P	NR	371	43082	Mfr home/personal care prd	55½	22½	29	11 7/16	25½	15 1/16	62136	20 3/16	15⅞	16 15/16	5.2	12	...	8.0	–29.3	...
7	TUTS	✔Tut Systems	NNM	NR	53	2980	Dgn,dev telecomm eqp	....	....	....	....	86¼	18	73583	60⅞	37⅝	53⅝	...	d	...	...	...	...
8	TZA	✔TV Azteca,S.A. ADS[52]	NY	NR	47	18917	Television broadcasting-Mexico	23 3/16	16	23 1/16	4¼	9 13/16	3¾	259321	9 13/16	5½	9	0.2	32	...	35.4	...	...
9	TVGIA	✔TV Guide'A'	NNM	NR	151	33499	Satellite deliver'd prgm svc	7⅞	1 5/16	13⅜	5⅛	48½	10 15/16	140789	48½	30 11/16	43	...	..	...	264	115	71.1
10	TVX	✔TVX Gold	NY,To,Ch,Ph,Mo,P	NR	71	37842	Acq,dvlp precious metals prop	11⅜	1¾	4½	1 1/16	2 1/16	11/16	131575	⅞	¾	¾	...	d	Neg	–57.1	–54.1	–35.6
11•[3]	TW	✔20th Century Indus	NY,Ch,Ph,P	B	77	64482	Ins hldg:auto/homeowners,Cal	34	1/16	30⅜	20 15/16	23 9/16	16	11629	19¾	18⅞	19 5/16	3.3	13	NM	–13.8	7.0	14.6
12	TDI	✔Twin Disc	NY,Ch	B+	29	1073	Indust'l pwr transmission eqp	35	6	33⅜	20¼	22 9/16	11	1345	14	11	11⅞	5.9	d	Neg	–40.0	–15.4	–5.1
13	TWLB	✔Twinlab Corp	NNM	NR	78	9050	Mfr nutritional supplements	27⅛	10¾	47⅞	11½	15⅝	6½	35932	9¾	7¾	7 15/16	...	17	...	–39.5	–13.2	...
14	IIVI	✔II-VI Inc	NNM	B–	22	1122	Mfr optical laser components	31¾	13/16	24	5⅞	23 7/16	7	6990	23 7/16	17¼	20⅛	...	20	13	156	–7.9	38.6
¶15•[5]	TYC	✔Tyco International	NY,B,Ch,P,Ph	B+	1828	1430992	Fire prot'n sys:cable:solar	22¾	1/16	39 9/16	20⅛	53⅞	22½	5005146	41 9/16	22½	39	0.1	26	33	3.6	43.8	46.6
16	TYL	✔Tyler Technologies	NY,B,Ch,Ph	C	65	7621	Info mgmt/sell auto pd/finl svc	18⅛	1⅜	11⅜	5	6⅞	3⅜	38061	6⅝	3⅜	5½	...	d	21	–10.2	43.1	11.1
#17•[6]	TSN	✔Tyson Foods Cl'A'	NY,Ph	B+	232	67264	Integrated poultry business	24¼	1/32	26	16 5/16	23¾	14⅞	54253	17¾	15⅞	16¼	1.0	16	63	–23.0	–10.1	3.4
18•[7]	UAL	✔UAL Corp	NY,B,C,Ch,P,Ph	B–	262	38585	Holding:United Airlines	147	6½	97½	55¼	87⅜	57 9/16	126145	78¾	68	77 9/16	...	8	81	29.9	7.5	28.9
#19•[7]	UCR	✔UCAR International	NY	NR	..	...	Mfr graphite/carbon electrodes	50½	23¾	41½	12 1/16	28 7/16	13 9/16	67073	22⅜	15¾	17 13/16	...	10	Neg	0.0	–22.1	...
20•[3]	UGI	✔UGI Corp	NY,Ph,B,Ch,P	↑B+	138	14549	Holding co:natural gas,Pa	30⅛	4 9/16	29¾	20½	24 11/16	15	14649	22⅛	19 5/16	20 7/16	7.3	12	20	–7.6	3.2	6.6
21•[8]	UGLY	✔Ugly Duckling	NNM	NR	33	6177	Used car sales/financing	25¾	6¾	13	4	9⅝	4⅛	7370	8¼	6½	6⅞	...	53	NM	40.6	–29.4	...
22	UCI	✔UICI	NY,Ph	B+	116	18520	Hldg:accident,hlth,life ins	36¼	⅞	36¾	11⅝	29	9⅜	72441	25	9⅜	10 9/16	...	6	10	–56.9	–31.2	4.5
#23•[9]	UDS	✔Ultramar Diamond Shamrock	NY,Ph,P	NR	313	69543	Refiner/mkt petroleum prod	34¾	14⅞	36¼	21 13/16	28	17⅞	51314	25 3/16	21⅜	22 11/16	4.8	11	–46	–1.9	–6.9	1.7
24	UGP	Ultrapar Participacoes SA ADS[58]	NY	NR	..	...	Liquid petrol gas/chem-Brazil	....	....	....	....	13 9/16	8½	20011	13½	10 9/16	11½	...	..	...	...	...	...
✤25•[7]	UTEK	✔Ultratech Stepper	NNM	NR	96	5861	Mfg photolithography eq	47½	6¼	26⅝	12¾	21 3/16	12 7/16	52947	19⅜	15¼	16⅛	...	d	Neg	0.8	–12.1	–3.2
26	UPX	✔Unapix Entertainment	AS	NR	17	1027	Licensor films,TV programs	5 11/16	1 11/16	6 1/16	1¾	3½	1½	8793	2 5/16	1½	1⅞	...	d	Neg	–14.3	–23.1	–9.0
27	UNI	✔Uni-Marts Inc	AS	C	10	698	Operates convenience stores	9⅝	2¼	5¼	2⅝	3	11/16	2316	1⅛	11/16	13/16	...	d	Neg	–70.5	–47.5	–31.5
28	UBB	✔Unibanco Banc/Unibanco Hld[62]GDS[63]	NY,Ph	NR	..	...	Commercial banking, Brazil	43 3/16	18 15/16	42½	7¼	31 15/16	9 13/16	47912	31 15/16	23 3/16	30⅛	3.3	11	...	124	...	...
29	UCP	✔UniCapital Corp	NY	NR	64	18194	Equip lease financing	....	....	19⅝	3⅞	8½	1 9/16	85932	4 5/16	2 3/16	3 11/16	...	8	...	–50.0	...	...
30	UNAM	✔Unico American	NNM	B+	27	2302	Ins co & ins agcy hldg co	14⅛	⅝	18⅛	8⅞	13¾	6⅜	3341	7⅜	6½	7	3.6	7	11	–37.6	–12.6	11.1
¶31•[7]	UCM	✔Unicom Corp	NY,B,C,Ch,P,Ph	B	590	142889	Hldg co:Commonwealth Ed	43⅞	16¼	41 3/16	30	42 13/16	30 15/16	172053	34⅞	31	33½	4.8	13	–22	–9.4	13.0	12.8
32	UDG	✔Unidigital Inc	AS	NR	9	431	Digital prepress svcs	10⅛	4⅛	10⅜	3⅞	6⅞	2⅝	2344	4¼	2⅝	4 1/16	...	d	...	–20.7	–6.7	...
#33•[8]	UFI	✔Unifi, Inc	NY,Ch,Ph,P	B+	166	44961	Texturizing polyester yarns	43⅝	1/32	42 3/16	11½	21¼	10 9/16	28463	13½	11⅞	12 5/16	...	18	–13	–37.1	–26.8	–12.6
34	UNF	✔UniFirst Corp	NY	A	85	6962	Operates garment rental svcs	28¼	3¼	30⅝	20	24 3/16	10 3/16	5411	15⅛	11	12⅝	1.2	11	8	–44.2	–15.4	1.4
35	UGS	✔Unigraphics Solutions'A'	NY	NR	46	3789	Computer software/svcs	....	....	16	6½	36 7/16	13⅜	3801	27	21 5/16	27	...	27	...	86.2	...	...
36	UL	✔Unilever ADR[68]	NY,B,Ch,P,Ph	NR	65	12158	Sister co to Unilver NV	34 15/16	11/16	46⅜	30 5/16	46 13/16	25 13/16	35051	30½	25 13/16	30¼	e2.5	18	9	–22.5	14.4	16.2
¶37•[10]	UN	✔Unilever N.V.[69]	NY,B,Ch,Ph,P	A–	634	119813	Controls vast int'l enterprise	62⅞	1 5/16	86 1/16	55⅝	88¼	48⅞	197088	55⅜	48⅞	54 7/16	e1.9	19	8	–26.2	13.2	18.2
¶38•[11]	UK	✔Union Carbide[71]	NY,B,C,Ch,P,Ph	NR	475	88812	Chemicals & plastics	56 13/16	9¾	55¾	36¾	67¾	37⅛	149625	67¾	58	66¾	1.3	33	–6	59.8	19.9	20.1
¶39•[12]	UNP	✔Union Pacific	NY,B,C,Ch,P,Ph	B	884	178131	RR,oil/gas,truck'g,RE,min'g	74½	5 13/16	63¾	37 5/16	67⅞	39	188971	47 3/16	39	43 11/16	1.8	15	Neg	–1.5	...	...
¶40•[3]	UPR	✔Union Pacific Resources Group	NY,Ch,Ph,P	NR	596	182843	Oil&gas explor,dvlp,prod'n	31⅝	21	25¼	8¼	19⅜	7 11/16	223620	13½	10 15/16	12¾	1.6	29	Neg	43.0	–23.1	...
¶41•[12]	UPC	✔Union Planters	NY,Ch,Ph,P	B+	378	40148	Comml bkg,Memphis, Tenn	68⅝	2½	67 15/16	40⅛	49⅝	38¼	70451	44 11/16	38¼	39 7/16	5.1	13	5	–9.0	4.2	17.7
42	UB	✔UnionBanCal Corp	NY	B+	248	150866	Comm'l bkg,affil Bk of Tokyo	35 13/16	1 15/16	38 5/16	23⅝	46 7/16	30⅛	107734	45 9/16	35½	39 7/16	2.5	14	27	19.6	34.0	38.4
43	UBT	UnionBanCal Fin Tr I 7.375% Notes	NY	BBB[74]	5	64	Comm'l bkg,affil Bk of Tokyo	....	....	....	....	25 11/16	18 15/16	8204	21 7/16	18 15/16	20	9.2	..	...	...	...	...
44	UQM	✔Unique Mobility	AS	C	14	1061	R&D electric motor tech	9⅞	2⅝	8 15/16	4	6¾	3⅛	12671	4⅝	3¼	4⅛	...	d	–7	–21.4	4.4	–6.4
45	UTCI	✔Uniroyal Technology	NNM	NR	26	2293	Dvlp plastic/chemical prod	6⅝	2	10⅞	5⅜	26⅜	7¼	20536	26⅜	16½	25½	...	61	94	152	106	47.7
46•[13]	UNS	✔Unisource Energy	NY,B,Ch,P,Ph	B–	113	18057	Electric service, Arizona	325	5	18 15/16	12¼	13 15/16	10⅜	29546	12 11/16	11	11 3/16	...	7	6	–17.1	–12.1	–3.9
¶47•[11]	UIS	✔Unisys Corp	NY,B,C,Ch,P,Ph	C	701	218938	Mfrs business info systems	48⅜	1¾	35⅜	13 5/16	49 11/16	20 15/16	513328	34⅞	27⅞	31 15/16	...	21	NM	–7.3	67.9	29.9
48	UNT	✔Unit Corp	NY,Ch	B–	75	16267	Onshore contract drilling,o&g	34	1	9⅞	3⅝	9	3½	30443	7 11/16	4⅞	7 11/16	...	d	Neg	83.6	–8.0	20.7
49	UAH	✔United Amer Healthcare	NY,Ch,Ph,P	C	12	656	Manage HMO's Michigan & Ohio	29½	1 9/16	2⅞	¾	1 15/16	¾	6518	1⅜	1	1 1/16	...	9	16	–10.5	–43.1	–46.8
50•[14]	UAM	✔United Asset Mgmt	NY,Ch,P	A	120	35289	Hldg co:instit'l inv mgmt svc	30¼	4 7/16	29⅝	19¾	26	17⅜	37817	19 9/16	17½	18 9/16	4.3	18	–15	–25.9	–8.4	3.4

Uniform Footnote Explanations-See Page 4. Other: [1]ASE,CBOE,Ph:Cycle 1. [2]ASE,CBOE:Cycle 2. [3]CBOE:Cycle 1. [4]CBOE,Ph:Cycle 1. [5]ASE,CBPOE,P,Ph:Cycle 1. [6]P:Cycle 1. [7]CBOE:Cycle 2. [8]CBOE:Cycle 3. [9]CBOE,Ph:Cycle 3. [10]ASE:Cycle 2. [11]ASE:Cycle 1. [12]Ph:Cycle 2. [13]ASE,P:Cycle 2. [14]P:Cycle 2. [51]ADR equal 1 ord shr. [52]Ea ADS rep 16 OrdPtcCtf(1'A'shr,1'D-A'shr&1'D-L'). [53]Jun'95 & Prior. [54]12 Mo Dec'96:Fiscal Jun'96 earned $1.01. [55]Incl 102.645M equiv'B'shrs. [56]Spl dstr & 1-for-2 REVERSE in recap,'94. [57]Subsid Pfd in $M. [58]Ea ADS rep 1000 Pfd Stk,no par. [59]To be determined. [60]15015.9M Pfd shrs&2.7M com shrs. [61]Incl current amts. [62]Ea GDS rep 500 UTS no par. [63]Unit rep 1 Unibnc de Brasil pfd&1Unibnc Hld pfd. [64]Shs in millions. [65]Fiscal Mar'96 & prior. [66]12 Mo Dec'96. [67]Pfd in $M. [68]Ea Amer shr rep 4 ord,1.25 P. [69]NY Shrs. [70]Approx. [71]Dow Chemical plan acq,0.537 com. [72]®$3.90,'96. [73]83% owned by Union Pacific Corp. [74]Rated 'BBB' by S&P. [75]Total issue amt in $M. [76]12 Mo Mar'97:Fiscal Oct'96 earned d$0.26.

Index (Splits ♦)	Cash Divs. Ea. Yr. Since	Dividends: Latest Payment Period $	Date	Ex. Div.	Total $ So Far 1999	Ind. Rate	Paid 1998	Financial Position Mil-$: Cash& Equiv.	Curr. Assets	Curr. Liab.	Balance Sheet Date	Capitalization: Lg Trm Debt Mil-$	Shs. 000 Pfd.	Com.	Earnings $ Per Shr. Years End	1995	1996	1997	1998	1999	Last 12 Mos.	Interim Earnings Period	$ per Shr. 1998	1999	Index
1♦	....	None Since Public			...	Nil	....	16.4	54.9	26.4	9-30-99	....	...	25625	Dc	v0.08	v0.10	v0.14	v0.30	....	d0.19	9 Mo Sep	v0.16	vd0.33	1
2	....	None Since Public			...	Nil	....	6.30	200	104	9-30-99	204	...	44336	Dc	v0.44	v□d1.17	v1.14	v0.89	....	0.02	9 Mo Sep	v0.81	vd0.06	2
3	1998	0.404	5-24-99	5-12	0.404	0.40	0.42½	65.7	402	198	12-31-98	49.8	...	68235	Dc	Δ0.16	2.27	Δv1.89	Δv1.51	....	0.36	6 Mo Jun	v1.16	v0.01	3
4	....	None Since Public			...	Nil	....	11.4	209	118	9-30-99	185	...	38810	Dc	...	...	...	pv0.39	....	0.57	9 Mo Sep	vp0.02	vp0.20	4
5	....	None Since Public			...	Nil	....	104	107	22.5	9-30-99	10.3	p...	★42221	Dc	...	...	...	vpd0.31	....	....	9 Mo Sep	n/a	vpd0.55	5
6	1996	Q0.22	1-14-00	12-14	0.88	0.88	0.88	29.8	391	308	9-25-99	296	...	57658	Dc	p2.57	pv2.71	v1.32	v1.18	E1.40	1.26	9 Mo Sep	v0.54	v0.62	6
7	....	None Since Public			...	Nil	....	40.4	55.3	7.40	9-30-99	....	...	11699	Dc	...	...	...	vpd1.63	....	d1.05	9 Mo Sep	vpd1.26	vpd0.68	7
8	1998	0.02	10-14-99	10-5	0.02	0.02	0.031	103	561	161	12-31-98	527	...	±9300000	Dc	...	pΔv0.50	pv0.74	v0.05	....	0.28	9 Mo Sep	vd0.08	v0.15	8
9♦	....	None Since Public			...	Nil	....	102	443	494	9-30-99	625	...	±304438	Dc	v±0.16	v±0.21	±v0.31	v±0.44	....	....	9 Mo Sep	n/a	v±0.09	9
10	....	None Paid			...	Nil	....	18.3	251	78.8	6-30-99	50.9	...	161783	Dc	v0.06	vd0.53	vd0.36	vd0.48	....	d0.43	6 Mo Jun	vd0.02	v0.03	10
11	1996	Q0.16	12-22-99	12-10	0.64	0.64	0.58	Total Assets $1.43M			9-30-99	78.8	...	86802	Dc	v0.90	v0.92	v1.37	v1.19	E1.45	0.84	9 Mo Sep	v1.27	v0.92	11
12	1934	Q0.17½	12-1-99	11-9	0.73½	0.70	0.80	5.65	100	41.4	9-30-99	35.1	...	2835	Je	v2.02	v2.34	v2.75	v3.24	vd0.36	d0.89	3 Mo Sep	v0.21	vd0.32	12
13	....	None Since Public			...	Nil	....	13.7	141	38.9	9-30-99	47.4	...	30979	Dc	pv0.42	v□p0.15	v0.84	v□1.10	....	0.47	9 Mo Sep	v□0.83	v0.20	13
14♦	....	None Paid			...	Nil	....	6.90	30.5	12.8	9-30-99	2.78	...	6352	Je	0.47	0.70	v1.08	v1.02	v0.84	1.01	3 Mo Sep	v0.10	v0.27	14
15♦	1975	Q0.01¼	2-1-00	12-30	0.05	0.05	0.05	1625	10522	8421	6-30-99	8293	...	p1688708	Sp	□[53]0.36	p[54]d0.38	□d0.67	v□1.01	vP1.53	1.53				15
16	....	0.02	2-20-90	1-31	...	Nil	....	1.68	38.9	37.7	9-30-99	54.4	...	42806	Dc	vd0.85	vd3.09	vd0.16	vd0.24	....	d0.24	9 Mo Sep	v0.07	v0.07	16
17♦	1976	Q0.04	3-15-00	2-28	0.13	0.16	0.10	30.0	1727	987	9-30-99	1515	...	[55]±229585	Sp	±1.01	±0.40	±v0.85	v±0.11	v±1.00	1.00				17
18♦	....	[56]41.90½	7-11-94	7-12	...	Nil	....	1398	3775	5950	9-30-99	5067	10	53524	Dc	v□5.23	v□5.85	v9.04	v6.83	E10.05	9.48	9 Mo Sep	v6.57	v□9.22	18
19	....	None Since Public			...	Nil	....	19.0	467	311	9-30-99	651	...	45088	Dc	p□v1.87	Δv3.00	vd3.49	v□d0.66	E1.75	1.57	9 Mo Sep	vd1.05	v1.18	19
20	1885	Q0.37½	1-1-00	11-26	1.47	1.50	1.45	157	356	315	6-30-99	894	[57]20	p27241	Sp	□0.24	v1.19	v1.57	v1.22	Pv1.74	1.74				20
21	....	None Since Public			...	Nil	....	Total Assets $522.63M			9-30-99	318	...	14880	Dc	pvd0.72	v0.60	v0.52	vd0.31	....	0.13	9 Mo Sep	vd0.05	v0.39	21
22♦	....	None Since Public			...	Nil	....	Total Assets $3487M			9-30-99	1118	...	46404	Dc	v1.41	v1.66	v1.91	v1.26	....	1.93	9 Mo Sep	v0.78	v1.45	22
23	1992	Q0.275	3-2-00	2-15	1.10	1.10	1.10	136	1304	1217	9-30-99	1492	...	86658	Dc	Δv1.30	vd0.54	□v1.94	vd0.89	E2.09	0.95	9 Mo Sep	vd0.13	v1.71	23
24	....	Plan semi-annual div			...	[59]....	....	40.9	103	48.2	6-30-99	p163	...	[60]★15018688	Dc	...	...	...	v0.50	....	....	6 Mo Jun	n/a	v0.40	24
25♦	....	None Since Public			...	Nil	....	143	197	30.9	9-30-99	....	...	21383	Dc	v1.20	v1.66	v0.81	vd2.76	Ed0.13↓	d0.85	9 Mo Sep	vd2.06	vd0.15	25
26♦	....	5%Stk	5-6-96	4-18	...	Nil	....	Total Assets $78.27M			9-30-99	[61]31.0	502	10214	Dc	0.22	v0.08	v0.19	vd0.01	....	d0.08	9 Mo Sep	vd0.03	v□d0.10	26
27	....	0.03	4-16-97	3-24	...	Nil	....	1.53	21.1	20.5	7-01-99	33.8	...	6910	Sp	±0.66	v±0.44	□vd0.69	v□d0.02	Pvd0.32	d0.32				27
28	1998	0.577	8-6-99	7-20	0.976	0.98	1.511	....	....	...	12-31-97	4188	...	[64]±26758	Dc	...	pv2.86	v2.77	....	....	2.77				28
29	....	None Since Public			...	Nil	....	Total Assets $3791M			9-30-99	2677	...	53326	Dc	...	pv0.46	p0.46	v1.08	....	0.48	9 Mo Sep	v0.71	v0.11	29
30	1991	A0.25	7-15-99	6-29	0.25	0.25	0.07	Total Assets $120.58M			9-30-99	....	...	6305	Dc	[65]0.97	v[66]1.10	v1.20	v1.36	....	1.05	9 Mo Sep	v1.02	v0.71	30
31	1890	Q0.40	2-1-00	12-29	1.60	1.60	1.60	688	3203	2952	9-30-99	7759	[67]2	217517	Dc	□v3.07	v3.09	□vd1.10	v2.34	E2.60	2.79	12 Mo Sep	v□d0.69	v□2.79	31
32	....	None Since Public			...	Nil	....	0.73	26.0	22.5	8-31-99	79.2	...	5987	Au	p0.54	p0.44	v0.41	v□0.34	v□d1.75	d1.75				32
33	1990	Div Discontinued 7-16-98			...	Nil	0.28	42.6	378	139	9-26-99	487	...	59205	Je	1.67	□1.18	v1.81	v□2.08	v□0.97	0.69	3 Mo Sep	v□0.34	v0.06	33
34♦	1979	Q0.03¾	1-3-00	12-9	0.143	0.15	0.12	2.91	138	76.3	8-31-99	111	...	±19888	Au	1.01	1.20	v1.40	v1.62	v1.18	1.18				34
35	....	None Since Public			...	Nil	....	15.3	144	119	9-30-99	....	...	±36299	Dc	...	...	pv0.31	v0.18	....	1.00	9 Mo Sep	vd0.12	v0.70	35
36♦	1937	0.252	12-27-99	11-17	†5.008	0.76	0.599	7329	15435	12688	j12-31-98	1609	...	2911335	Dc	1.24	v1.34	v2.97	v1.75	....	1.67	9 Mo Sep	v1.33	v1.25	36
37♦	1955	[70]0.353	12-17-99	11-10	†[70]0.953	1.05	1.003	22881	48191	39614	j12-31-98	5023	940	571575	Dc	2.07	v2.23	v4.80	v2.85	E2.88	2.72	9 Mo Sep	v2.22	v2.09	37
38	1918	Q0.22½	12-1-99	11-15	0.90	0.90	0.90	36.0	2013	1624	9-30-99	1868	...	133858	Dc	v5.85	v[72]3.90	v□4.53	v2.91	E2.03↑	2.09	9 Mo Sep	v2.41	v□1.59	38
39♦	1900	Q0.20	1-3-00	12-6	0.80	0.80	1.03	198	1380	2889	9-30-99	8708	...	248568	Dc	v4.60	v4.14	v1.74	vd2.57	E2.95	1.50	9 Mo Sep	vd1.80	v2.27	39
40	1996	Q0.05	1-2-00	12-16	0.20	0.20	0.20	137	565	733	9-30-99	2966	...	[73]252050	Dc	p1.25	v1.28	v1.33	vd3.63	E0.44	d2.77	9 Mo Sep	vd0.01	v0.85	40
41	1987	Q0.50	11-15-99	10-28	2.00	2.00	2.00	Total Deposits $24391.45M			9-30-99	1133	[67]22	141031	Dc	v2.66	v2.05	v2.45	v1.58	E3.09	2.35	9 Mo Sep	v1.39	v2.16	41
42♦	1957	Q0.25	1-7-00	12-1	0.76	1.00	0.56	Total Deposits $25175.92M			9-30-99	744	...	164634	Dc	v1.73	v1.37	v2.30	v2.65	E2.86	2.46	9 Mo Sep	v2.01	v1.82	42
43	1999	Q0.461	11-15-99	11-9	1.362	1.844	....	Co option redm fr 2-18-2004 at $25				....	...	[75]★350	Dc	...	...	...	...	....	....	Mature 5-15-2029			43
44♦	....	None Since Public			...	Nil	....	1.16	7.93	6.18	9-30-99	3.92	...	16575	Mr	d0.13	[76]d0.25	vd0.23	vd0.24	....	d0.42	6 Mo Sep	vd0.15	vd0.33	44
45	....	None Paid			...	Nil	....	1.08	68.8	50.7	6-27-99	109	...	12084	Sp	Δd0.02	d1.09	v0.03	v□0.55	Pv0.42	0.42				45
46♦	....	0.08	3-10-00	2-11	...	[59]....	....	132	347	229	9-30-99	1988	...	32340	Dc	v1.70	v3.75	v2.59	v0.87	....	1.55	12 Mo Sep	v0.82	v1.55	46
47	....	0.25	8-7-90	6-18	...	Nil	....	374	2631	2507	9-30-99	951	...	p309905	Dc	vd4.35	v□d0.34	vd5.30	v1.06	E1.55	1.63	9 Mo Sep	v0.60	v□1.17	47
48	....	None Since Public			...	Nil	....	1.86	20.1	19.0	9-30-99	62.1	...	★33816	Dc	v0.19	v0.37	v0.45	v0.09	....	d0.07	9 Mo Sep	v0.10	vd0.06	48
49	....	None Since Public			...	Nil	....	19.9	29.4	31.2	9-30-99	0.25	...	6779	Je	1.01	vd0.42	vd0.52	vd3.88	v0.09	0.12	3 Mo Sep	v0.02	v0.05	49
50♦	1986	Q0.20	1-14-00	12-29	0.80	0.80	0.80	121	294	204	9-30-99	878	...	58656	Dc	v0.95	v1.36	vd0.06	v1.15	E1.05	1.02	9 Mo Sep	v0.89	v0.76	50

♦**Stock Splits & Divs By Line Reference Index** [1]2-for-1,'99. [9]2-for-1,'96,'99. [14]2-for-1,'95. [15]2-for-1,'95,'97,'99. [17]3-for-2,'97. [18]1-for-2 REVERSE,'94:4-for-1,'96:No adj for cash dstr:$167.62,'94. [22]4-for-1,'95. [25]2-for-1,'95. [26]Adj for 5%,'96. [34]2-for-1,'94. [36]4-for-1,'97. [37]4-for-1,'97. [39]No Adj for stk dstr Union Pac Res Gr,'96. [42]3-for-1,'98. [44]12 Mo Mar'97:Fiscal Oct'96 earned d$0.26. [46]1-for-5 REVERSE,'96. [50]2-for-1,'96.

¶ S&P 500
# MidCap 400
✜ SmallCap 600
• Options

Index	Ticker	Name of Issue (Call Price of Pfd. Stocks)	Market	Com. Rank. & Pfd. Rating	Inst. Hold Cos	Inst. Hold Shs. (000)	Principal Business	Price Range 1971-97 High	1971-97 Low	1998 High	1998 Low	1999 High	1999 Low	December, 1999 Dec. Sales in 100s	Last Sale Or Bid High	Low	Last	%Div Yield	P-E Ratio	EPS 5 Yr Growth	% Annualized Total Return 12 Mo	36 Mo	60 Mo
1•[1]	UAG	✔United Auto Group	NY	NR	53	11075	Franchised auto dealerships	35¼	13¾	26 5/16	8⅞	13¼	5¾	12089	9¼	7⅛	8 15/16	...	d	...	-2.7	-29.7	...
2	AFP	✔United Capital Corp	AS	B	15	320	Antenna sys/wire prd/R.E.	29	1¼	26½	14	19½	13	286	19½	18⅝	18⅝	...	8	NM	9.6	28.6	17.0
3	UCFC	✔United Community Finl	NNM	NR	31	2865	Savings & loan, Ohio	....	....	18⅛	10	15½	9⅜	17832	10 13/16	9 9/16	9 15/16	e3.0	..	...	10.4	...	...
4•[2]	UDI	✔United Dominion Indus	NY,To,B,Mo	B+	104	16118	Ind'l engin'g,mfg & constr	115⅜	6 13/16	35	16⅛	27⅝	18⅝	7506	21 1/16	18⅞	19 15/16	1.8	8	12	-0.5	-4.1	2.0
5	UDR	✔United Dominion Rlty Tr	NY,Ch,P	NR	181	26781	Real estate investment trust	16⅞	1 7/16	14 13/16	10 1/16	12 1/16	9 1/16	63260	10⅞	9⅛	9⅞	10.7	20	3	5.5	-6.6	0.0
6	UDM	United Domin Rlty Tr 8.50% Nts	NY	....[53]	..	...	Monthly Income Notes	....	....	26	25	26¾	22 7/16	651	25⅛	23⅝	23⅝	9.0	..	...	-0.6	...	...
7	UFCS	United Fire & Casualty	NNM	B+	48	3412	Fire/casualty insur:life	47	⅝	45¾	32	35½	19¼	1597	22⅞	19¼	22⅝	3.0	16	-6	-31.0	-12.1	6.8
8	UG	✔United-Guardian Inc	AS,Ch	B	10	419	Fine chem:pharmac'tls:R&D	14⅞	1¼	6 11/16	3½	4⅞	2¾	923	3⅞	3	3½	2.3	13	54	-20.9	28.5	15.4
¶9•[3]	UNH	✔United Healthcare	NY,Ph,P	B+	726	146648	Manages health maint svcs	69	11/16	73 15/16	29 9/16	70	39⅜	145261	56⅜	48 15/16	53⅛	0.1	17	Neg	23.4	5.7	3.4
✜10	UIL	✔United Illuminating	NY,B,Ch,P,Ph	B	153	4348	Elec serv to parts of Conn	46	9	54 3/16	41 11/16	53⅝	38⅞	6495	53⅝	49 13/16	51⅜	5.6	14	...	6.1	26.5	20.4
11	UIC	✔United Industrial	NY,B,Ch	B–	50	3779	Defense:energy sys:plastic pd	24⅞	½	14	8⅛	12½	7⅜	8685	9¾	8⅛	9 3/16	4.4	10	44	-2.3	20.6	18.0
12	UMH	✔United Mobile Homes	AS,Ch,Ph	B+	12	274	Real estate investment trust	14	1	12½	9⅜	10 15/16	7⅞	1958	8½	7⅞	8¼	9.1	14	9	-15.8	-3.6	9.1
✜13	UNFI	✔United Natural Foods	NNM	NR	95	8562	Distributor natural foods/pd	27⅛	12½	33⅜	19	29¾	7	55802	13⅛	7	12	...	29	9	-50.3	-11.0	...
14	UPFC	✔United PanAm Finl	NNM	NR	21	3370	Consumer finance	....	....	14 1/16	3	5⅛	1 3/16	6820	2¼	1¼	1 15/16	...	d	...	-53.7	...	...
15	UPCOY	United Pan-Euro Commun'A'ADS[56]	NNM	NR	51	2670	Own/oper CATV system	....	....	....	....	140½	31⅛	19959	140½	93	127½	...	..	...	...	...	...
16	UPS	✔United Parcel'B'	NY	NR	..	...	Express carrier/pkg delivery	....	....	....	....	76 15/16	50	309553	69 11/16	63¼	69	...	99	...	...	...	...
17	UPK	✔United Park City Mns	NY,B,Ch,P	C	9	179	Real estate development	140	3¾	37	24⅝	37 5/16	24⅜	253	29 5/16	27¾	27¾	...	d	-30	8.3	36.1	36.3
18•[4]	URI	✔United Rentals	NY,Ph	NR	215	37273	Equipment rental svcs	19 5/16	13½	48 1/16	10 9/16	35 11/16	14 5/16	84009	19 15/16	15¾	17⅛	...	13	...	-48.3	...	...
19	AGA	✔U.S. Aggregates	NY	NR	27	3648	Produce,dstr aggregates	....	....	....	....	15½	9½	10287	12¾	11⅛	12	1.0	11	...	...	...	...
¶20•[5]	USB	✔U.S. Bancorp	NY,B,Ch,P,Ph	B+	858	379858	Comml bkg,MN,upper midwest	38⅞	2 1/16	47 5/16	25⅝	38 1/16	21⅞	902457	35½	21⅞	23 13/16	3.3	11	20	-31.1	3.9	19.6
21	USC	✔U.S. Can	NY,Ch,Ph	NR	77	10214	Mfr steel packaging containers	23¼	11	18¼	12 13/16	26⅜	13½	3787	19⅞	17¾	19⅞	...	12	Neg	11.2	5.6	0.9
22•[6]	USM	✔U.S. Cellular	AS,Ch,Ph,P	B–	166	17302	Oper cellular telephone sys	41⅜	12¾	41	27 11/16	125¾	37	65265	119⅛	95½	100 15/16	...	30	55	166	53.6	25.2
23	USEG	U.S. Energy Corp	NNM	C	16	779	Mining & svs: retailer	36 13/16	⅛	8⅞	13/16	6¾	1⅞	5506	4	2¾	3½	...	d	Neg	75.0	-30.1	-2.6
24	USEY	✔U.S. Energy Systems	NSC	NR	8	305	Cogeneration/ind energy sys	5⅝	1¾	3⅛	¾	4¼	1⅞	17595	4¼	2 11/16	3 15/16	...	d	...	28.6	-0.5	...
25	UXP	✔U.S. Exploration	AS	NR	2	1284	Natl gas gathering,O&G prop	8¼	½	4	1¼	2 3/16	11/16	2903	1	11/16	¾	...	d	-40	-52.0	-43.3	0.0
#26•[7]	UFS	✔U.S. Foodservice	NY,Ch,Ph	NR	368	89184	Dstr to food service industry	18 9/16	4⅝	24⅝	15⅝	26½	14½	118753	19	14½	16¾	...	17	41	-30.0	7.2	30.0
27	USFS	✔U.S. Franchise Systems'A'	NNM	NR	35	5268	Franchise lodging facilities	16	5	14⅜	4	23¼	4⅛	26484	4 15/16	4⅛	4½	...	16	...	-54.4	-23.7	...
✜28	UH	✔U.S. Home	NY,P	NR	152	11822	Builder-developer	39⅜	14	47⅞	25½	39¼	24⅛	9069	26 1/16	24⅛	25 9/16	...	5	16	-23.1	-0.6	9.7
29•[8]	USI	✔U.S. Industries	NY,P	NR	203	71644	Mfr consumer/industrial prd	30 9/16	8 7/16	30¾	11 3/16	20 3/16	13 1/16	51093	15¼	13 1/16	14	1.4	9	17	-22.9	-14.5	...
30	USLM	✔U.S. Lime & Minerals	NNM	B	17	370	Mine,sell limestone/lime prd	14¾	1 7/16	9⅛	6	11	5⅝	975	8	6¼	7	1.4	10	2	-2.1	-5.9	4.4
31	USL	✔U S Liquids	AS	NR	45	3674	Non-hazarardous waste mgmt svcs	19⅜	9½	25¼	14	26⅜	5⅝	12264	8½	6½	8⅜	...	15	...	-62.8	...	...
32•[7]	OFIS	✔U.S Office Products	NNM	NR	68	10222	Office products supplier	121 5/16	26 11/16	85½	3⅞	7 9/16	2⅜	46016	4 3/16	3⅛	3⅛	...	d	Neg	...	...	...
33	USV	✔U.S. Restaurant Properties	NY,B,Ch	NR	59	2904	Real estate investment trust	25 11/16	6¾	30⅛	21 13/16	24⅝	14 1/16	16052	15¼	14 1/16	14¼	13.1	..	Neg	-35.0	-0.7	16.8
34	Pr A	$1.93 cm Cv Sr'A'Pfd([63]25)	NY	NR	19	1586		26 11/16	25	28 15/16	22 3/16	23⅜	13 9/16	4805	14⅞	13 9/16	13⅞	13.9	..	...	...	...	...
✜35	UTC	✔U.S. Trust[64]	NY	B+	222	7181	Banking/financial svcs	65¾	2⅜	84⅛	46¾	96½	69¾	11783	81 9/16	75½	80 3/16	1.1	22	NM	6.6	28.0	...
¶36•[9]	USW	✔U S West[65]	NY,B,Ch,P,Ph	B+	1060	285788	Tel svc:Mtn St,NW,Pac NW	50¾	13 13/16	65 7/16	44⅝	73	51½	405127	73	61 9/16	72	e3.0	27	2	16.5	37.1	...
✜37•[10]	USTR	✔United Stationers	NNM	B–	193	26518	Wholesaler of office prod	24⅝	1	36 9/16	19⅞	29⅛	13	67210	29⅛	22¼	28 9/16	...	13	64	9.9	43.2	54.4
¶38•[7]	UTX	✔United Technologies	NY,B,C,Ch,P,Ph	B+	1357	364873	Aerospace,climate ctrl sys	44 7/16	1 5/16	56¼	33½	75 15/16	51⅝	297702	65	55	65	1.2	22	25	21.4	27.2	35.3
39	UTS	✔UTS Energy	To	NR	2	3600	Oil&gas explor,dvlp,prod'n	6⅜	⅛	1 3/16	¼	¾	3/16	6910	½	⅜	7/16	...	d	-44	10.8	-42.2	-17.3
40	UU	United Utilities ADS[67]	NY,Ph	NR	1	185	Utility:water & electric	....	....	32⅜	25⅞	29¼	16¾	72	20	16¾	19½B	7.5	98	...	-24.7	...	...
✜41	UWR	✔United Water Res[69]	NY,Ch,Ph,P	B	140	7654	Hldg co:water util in N.J.	23	2⅜	25	15¾	34½	18 7/16	8733	34½	33⅜	34 3/16	e2.8	35	6	48.5	36.4	28.9
42	UWZ	✔United Wisconsin Svcs	NY,Ph	NR	39	5967	Managed care svcs,Wisconsin	....	....	9⅜	4 13/16	9¾	3 13/16	3718	6	3 13/16	4¼	1.2	39	...	-50.5	...	...
43	UCOMA	✔UnitedGlobalCom Inc'A'	NNM	NR	179	55355	Intl multi-channel TV svcs	10⅜	3⅞	10¼	3⅞	72½	9⅜	305531	72½	48¼	70⅝	...	28	NM	635	126	51.9
44	UTL	✔UNITIL Corp	AS	A–	36	691	Hldg co: elec utility in N.H.	24¾	5 15/16	28 13/16	21⅛	38 9/16	21¾	1733	38 9/16	28⅜	35¾	3.9	20	-1	48.3	28.5	24.4
#45•[2]	UNIT	✔Unitrin Inc	NNM	B+	157	15248	Ins hldg:life,accid&hlth,prop	34¼	12¼	37 1/16	27¾	42⅜	30½	25498	39	36	37⅝	3.7	15	20	9.1	15.0	16.5
#46•[7]	UVV	✔Univl Corp	NY,B,Ch,Ph,P	B+	243	21935	Leaf tobacco/building prod	41 11/16	1⅜	49½	31½	35¾	19 7/16	25657	25 11/16	21¼	22 13/16	5.4	6	35	-32.2	-7.6	6.8
47	PANL	✔Univl Display	NSC,Ph	NR	8	347	Dvp stg:electronics R&D	10½	3⅝	6¾	3 9/16	19⅜	3	72832	19⅜	5	16¾	...	d	...	326	43.1	...
#48•[11]	UFC	✔Univl Foods	NY,Ch,P	A–	250	35249	Flavor/color/dehy.prod/yeast	21 7/16	11/16	27¾	19 7/16	27⅜	18¼	26759	21¾	19⅛	20⅜	2.6	13	9	-23.9	7.8	11.2
✜49	UFPI	✔Univl Forest Products	NNM	NR	111	6594	Mfr,dstr lumber products	18	5⅞	20½	12¼	24⅛	11 15/16	7628	15½	13	14¾	0.5	10	18	-26.1	4.1	18.5
50	UHT	✔Univl Health Realty	NY,Ch	NR	36	1381	Real estate investment trust	22⅜	8¼	22½	17 15/16	20¾	14¼	5209	16⅞	14¼	14⅝	12.4	10	...	-18.2	-2.5	6.5

Uniform Footnote Explanations-See Page 4. Other: [1]CBOE,P:Cycle 2. [2]Ph:Cycle 2. [3]ASE,CBOE,Ph:Cycle 1. [4]ASE,Ph:Cycle 1. [5]ASE,CBOE:Cycle 1. [6]ASE,Ph:Cycle 2. [7]CBOE:Cycle 2. [8]CBOE:Cycle 1. [9]ASE,CBOE,P,Ph:Cycle 3. [10]CBOE:Cycle 3. [11]Ph:Cycle 3. [51]Incl 0.6M non-vtg common stk. [52]6 Mo Dec'98. [53]Rated'BBB'by S&P. [54]Fiscal Oct'95 & prior. [55]12 Mo Jul'96. [56]Ea ADS rep 1 ord,No Par. [57]To be determined. [58]Telephone Data Sys own 80.8% of com. [59]Fiscal Mar'97 & prior. [60]9 Mo Dec'97. [61]Stk dstr,Aztec Tech,Navigant Intl,School Specialty,& Workflow Mgmt. [62]Incl current amts. [63]Fr 11-15-2002(or for Com Stk re-spec cond). [64]No adj for stk dstr of Chase Manhattan Bk. [65]Qwest Commun plan acq,$69 in stk. [66]Sr A ESOP Cv Pfd. [67]Ea par L ADS rep 2 Ord. [68]Approx. [69]Suez Lyonnaise plan acq,$35. [70]Pfd in $M. [71]Fiscal Feb'98 7 prior. [72]10 Mo Dec'98. [73]Excl subsid pfd.

Index	Cash Divs. Ea. Yr. Since	Latest Payment Period $	Date	Ex. Div.	Total $ So Far 1999	Ind. Rate	Paid 1998	Cash& Equiv. (Mil-$)	Curr. Assets	Curr. Liab.	Balance Sheet Date	Lg Trm Debt Mil-$	Shs. 000 Pfd.	Shs. 000 Com.	End	1995	1996	1997	1998	1999	Last 12 Mos.	Period	1998	1999	Index
1	....	None Since Public			...	Nil	....	44.1	618	525	9-30-99	214	...	[51]21999	Dc	p0.51	vp1.22	vd0.54	v□0.02	....	d0.06	9 Mo Sep	v□0.92	v□0.84	1
2	....	None Paid			...	Nil	....	42.0	53.2	25.8	9-30-99	31.5	...	4736	Dc	vd0.32	v1.06	v1.59	v2.92	....	2.34	9 Mo Sep	v2.37	v1.79	2
3	1998	0.07½	12-15-99	11-26	†6.30	0.30	0.07½	Total Deposits $778M			9-30-99	3.50	...	35324	Dc	...	...	pv0.62	‡v[52]0.08	....	....	9 Mo Sep	n/a	v0.25	3
4	1987	tQ0.09	12-31-99	12-1	t0.36	0.36	t0.36	123	921	477	12-31-98	545	...	40087	Dc	v1.91	v2.13	v3.10	v2.45	....	2.66	9 Mo Sep	v1.53	v1.74	4
5	1973	Q0.26½	1-31-00	1-12	1.058	1.06	1.04	Total Assets $3763M			9-30-99	2177	18200	102997	Dc	v0.50	v□0.49	v0.60	v0.49	....	0.49	9 Mo Sep	v0.50	v0.50	5
6	1998	0.177	1-15-00	12-29	2.125	2.12	0.165	Co option redm fr 11-15-2008,$25				★57.5	...	...	Dc	...	...	...	....	....	....	Mature 11-15-2008			6
7♦	1968	Q0.17	1-5-00	12-13	0.68	0.68	0.66	Total Assets $1468.84M			9-30-99	....	...	10074	Dc	v2.66	v2.04	v2.68	v2.28	....	1.40	9 Mo Sep	v1.86	v0.98	7
8	1997	A0.08	1-7-00	12-13	0.07	0.08	0.06	2.93	5.61	0.37	9-30-99	0.01	...	4889	Dc	0.06	v0.11	v0.17	v0.21	....	0.27	9 Mo Sep	v0.17	v0.23	8
9♦	1990	A0.03	4-15-99	3-30	0.03	0.03	0.03	1174	3623	5469	9-30-99	250	...	169753	Dc	v1.57	v1.76	v2.26	vd1.12	E3.12	2.84	9 Mo Sep	vd1.67	v2.29	9
10	1900	Q0.72	1-1-00	12-7	2.88	2.88	2.88	18.0	227	249	9-30-99	622	43	14335	Dc	v3.63	v2.87	v3.26	v3.00	....	3.58	9 Mo Sep	v2.89	v3.47	10
11	1968	Q0.10	11-30-99	11-9	0.40	0.40	0.40	8.96	111	53.3	9-30-99	....	...	12294	Dc	v0.07	v0.52	v1.19	v1.03	....	0.95	9 Mo Sep	v0.55	v0.47	11
12	1990	Q0.18¾	12-15-99	11-10	0.75	0.75	0.73¾	Total Assets $55.8M			9-30-99	30.6	...	7271	Dc	v0.44	v0.61	v0.63	v0.60	....	0.61	9 Mo Sep	v0.44	v0.45	12
13	....	None Since Public			...	Nil	....	4.80	193	120	10-31-99	25.2	...	18260	Jl	v[54]0.37	v[55]0.32	v□0.63	v0.74	v0.73	0.41	3 Mo Oct	v0.26	vd0.06	13
14	....	None Since Public			...	Nil	....	Total Deposits $298M			9-30-99	159	...	16594	Dc	v0.04	v0.09	v0.53	v0.42	....	d0.28	9 Mo Sep	v0.67	vd0.03	14
15	....	None Since Public			...	Nil	....	46.9	231	1471	p9-30-98	p644	...	★130201	Dc	...	...	vpd0.88	n/a	....	....	3 Mo Mar	n/a	d0.64	15
16	2000	0.30	1-7-00	11-24	...	[57]....	....	2643	6919	6098	9-30-99	1817	...	★±1203232	Dc	...	...	...	pv±1.55	E0.70	....	9 Mo Sep	n/a	vp±0.19	16
17♦	....	None Paid			...	Nil	....	Total Assets $20.5M			9-30-99	....	...	3249	Dc	0.28	vd0.22	vd0.84	v0.20	....	d1.54	9 Mo Sep	vd0.49	vd2.23	17
18	....	None Since Public			...	Nil	....	Total Assets $4526M			9-30-99	2215	...	72050	Dc	...	p0.20	n/a	v□0.48	....	1.31	9 Mo Sep	v□0.23	v1.06	18
19	2000	Q0.03	1-10-00	12-22	...	0.12	....	3.77	104	52.0	9-30-99	165	...	14901	Dc	...	...	...	pv0.66	....	1.09	9 Mo Sep	vp0.50	vp0.93	19
20♦	1930	Q0.19½	12-15-99	11-29	0.78	0.78	0.70	Total Deposits $47978.00M			9-30-99	16155	...	p727650	Dc	v1.16	pv1.57	v1.11	v1.78	E2.15↓	2.03	9 Mo Sep	v1.31	v1.56	20
21	....	None Since Public			...	Nil	....	32.1	230	161	10-04-99	280	...	13447	Dc	v0.48	v□1.30	vd2.45	vd1.21	....	1.60	9 Mo Sep	vd1.43	v□1.38	21
22	....	None Since Public			...	Nil	....	184	421	267	9-30-99	540	...	[58]±87469	Dc	v1.19	v1.51	v1.29	v2.48	....	3.34	9 Mo Sep	v2.17	v3.03	22
23	....	None Since Public			...	Nil	....	8.63	11.3	5.41	8-31-99	0.76	...	8771	My	d0.42	v0.04	vd0.58	vd0.15	vd1.63	d1.60	3 Mo Aug	vd0.18	vd0.15	23
24	....	None Since Public			...	Nil	....	0.20	1.36	1.64	10-31-99	1.70	250	5153	Ja	p0.17	v□d2.56	vd0.23	vd0.14	....	d0.42	9 Mo Oct	vd0.10	vΔd0.38	24
25	....	None Paid			...	Nil	....	1.57	3.78	34.5	9-30-99	....	443	15592	Dc	d0.19	[59]d0.13	‡v[60]d1.06	vd1.67	....	d1.51	9 Mo Sep	vd0.33	vd0.17	25
26♦	....	None Since Public			...	Nil	....	59.5	1036	546	10-02-99	559	...	101518	Je	□0.30	vNil	pv0.44	□vd0.42	□v0.91	0.96	3 Mo Sep	v0.18	v0.23	26
27	....	None Since Public			...	Nil	....	5.23	20.5	10.2	9-30-99	....	...	±19899	Dc	...	vd0.75	vd0.71	vd0.16	....	0.28	9 Mo Sep	vd0.18	v0.26	27
28	....	None Since Public			...	Nil	....	Total Assets $1612.63M			9-30-99	723	...	13677	Dc	v2.78	v3.28	□v3.50	v□4.68	E5.20	4.96	9 Mo Sep	v□3.48	v3.76	28
29♦	1997	Q0.05	1-21-00	12-29	0.20	0.20	0.20	146	1574	745	6-30-99	1070	...	89759	Sp	pd1.23	□2.01	□v2.66	vd0.40	vP1.51	1.51				29
30	1995	Q0.02½	12-15-99	11-29	0.10	0.10	0.10	13.9	23.4	5.81	9-30-99	38.3	...	3982	Dc	v1.11	v0.66	v0.78	v0.74	....	0.71	9 Mo Sep	v0.54	v0.51	30
31	....	None Since Public			...	Nil	....	0.47	55.0	45.2	9-30-99	92.6	...	15731	Dc	...	pv0.38	vp0.59	v0.93	....	0.55	9 Mo Sep	v0.64	v0.26	31
32♦	....	h[61]....	6-12-98	6-10	...	Nil	h[61]....	29.3	675	370	10-23-99	1165	...	36802	Ap	p0.91	p0.83	v□2.56	v2.20	vd5.48	d4.49	6 Mo Oct	v□d2.48	vd1.49	32
33♦	1986	Q0.46½	3-15-00	2-28	1.79	1.86	1.57¼	Equity per shr $7.44			12-31-98	[62]342	3680	★15364	Dc	v0.73	v0.80	vd0.88	v□d0.08	....	0.03	9 Mo Sep	v□0.27	v0.38	33
34	1998	Q0.48¼	3-15-00	2-28	1.93	1.93	2.086	Cv into 0.9384 com				....	3200	...	Dc	...	...	...	....	....	....				34
35♦	1854	Q0.22	1-25-00	1-6	0.84	0.88	0.69	Total Deposits $3646.11M			9-30-99	[62]215	...	18655	Dc	vd2.62	v1.95	v2.39	v2.96	E3.59	3.52	9 Mo Sep	v2.19	v2.75	35
36	1984	Q0.53½	2-1-00	1-6	†2.35½	2.14	2.14	55.0	2651	6962	9-30-99	9754	...	505306	Dc	p□v2.48	vΔ2.51	v□2.42	vp2.84	E2.65	2.61	9 Mo Sep	vp2.11	v1.88	36
37♦	....	0.02½	3-28-95	3-9	...	Nil	....	12.6	840	501	9-30-99	295	...	33990	Dc	v□0.17	v±1.02	v□0.21	v□1.76	....	2.21	9 Mo Sep	v□1.19	v1.64	37
38♦	1936	Q0.20	12-10-99	11-17	0.76	0.80	0.69½	1115	10316	8141	9-30-99	2110	[66]13042	p478741	Dc	1.43	v1.74	v2.11	v2.52	E2.90	3.50	9 Mo Sep	v1.94	v2.92	38
39	....	None Paid			...	Nil	....	5.52	5.58	0.31	j9-30-99	....	...	46101	Dc	d0.04	v0.02	vd0.27	vd0.07	....	jd0.02	9 Mo Sep	vd0.07	vd0.02	39
40	1999	[68]0.477	2-24-00	12-21	2.402	1.46	....	543	1288	3676	3-31-98	2450	...	p544800	Mr	...	1.47	v0.20	....	....	0.20				40
41	1886	†0.30	12-1-99	11-10	†1.02	0.96	0.93	4.17	127	202	9-30-99	664	[70]57	38865	Dc	v0.54	v1.00	v0.83	v1.17	....	0.99	12 Mo Sep	v1.11	v0.99	41
42	1998	A0.05	12-29-99	12-30	0.05	0.05	0.05	145	232	129	9-30-99	....	...	16845	Dc	...	...	pv0.95	vp0.96	....	0.11	6 Mo Jun	vp0.53	vd0.32	42
43♦	....	None Since Public			...	Nil	....	811	1127	694	9-30-99	3545	171	±82870	Dc	±vd1.35	±d1.78	v□[71]d3.38	‡v[72]d6.86	....	2.49	6 Mo Jun	□±d3.03	v±6.32	43
44	1908	Q0.34½	11-15-99	10-28	1.38	1.38	1.36	3.15	27.4	25.9	9-30-99	85.0	[73]...	4706	Dc	v1.85	v1.89	v1.76	v1.72	....	1.77	12 Mo Sep	v1.68	v1.77	44
45♦	1990	Q0.35	12-2-99	11-12	1.40	1.40	1.30	Total Assets $6098.90M			9-30-99	78.9	...	72343	Dc	v1.85	v1.74	v1.55	v6.51	....	2.50	9 Mo Sep	v5.92	v1.91	45
46	1927	Q0.31	2-14-00	1-6	1.20	1.24	1.12	82.8	1276	1029	9-30-99	202	...	30982	Je	0.73	Δ2.04	v2.89	v3.99	v3.80	3.95	3 Mo Sep	v0.78	v0.93	46
47	....	None Since Public			...	Nil	....	6.93	7.55	0.29	9-30-99	....	200	13212	Dc	d0.38	vd0.21	vd0.64	vd0.27	....	d0.38	9 Mo Sep	vd0.16	vd0.27	47
48♦	1934	Q0.13¼	12-1-99	11-3	0.53	0.53	0.53	7.53	396	202	6-30-99	392	...	50278	Sp	1.27	v0.85	v1.26	v1.40	vP1.57	1.57				48
49	1993	S0.04	12-15-99	11-29	0.07½	0.08	0.07	9.73	227	98.9	9-25-99	148	...	20287	Dc	v0.80	v0.98	v0.93	v1.28	....	1.44	9 Mo Sep	v1.14	v1.30	49
50	1987	Q0.45½	12-31-99	12-14	1.81	1.82	1.75½	Total Assets $161.88M			9-30-99	60.2	...	8965	Dc	v1.52	v1.58	v1.56	v1.60	....	1.53	9 Mo Sep	v1.18	v1.11	50

♦**Stock Splits & Divs By Line Reference Index** [7]3-for-2,'95,'96. [9]2-for-1,'94. [17]1-for-20 REVERSE,'95. [20]3-for-1,'98. [26]2-for-1,'99. [29]3-for-2,'97. [32]3-for-2,'97:1-for-4 REVERSE,'98. [33]3-for-2,'97. [35]No adj for stk dstr of Chase Manhattan Bk:2-for-1,'97. [37]2-for-1,'95,'98. [38]2-for-1,'96,'99. [43]2-for-1,'99. [45]2-for-1,'99. [48]2-for-1,'98.

¶ S&P 500
\# MidCap 400
✤ SmallCap 600
• Options

Index	Ticker	Name of Issue (Call Price of Pfd. Stocks)	Market	Com. Rank. & Pfd. Rating	Inst. Hold Cos	Inst. Hold Shs. (000)	Principal Business	Price Range 1971-97 High	1971-97 Low	1998 High	1998 Low	1999 High	1999 Low	December, 1999 Dec. Sales in 100s	Last Sale Or Bid High	Low	Last	%Div Yield	P-E Ratio	EPS 5 Yr Growth	% Annualized Total Return 12 Mo	36 Mo	60 Mo
✤1•[1]	UHS	✔Univl Health Svs Cl'B'[51]	NY,Ph	B+	254	27682	Acute care hospitals	50 13/16	1½	59¾	38 7/16	55⅛	23⅛	25665	36 15/16	32 5/16	36	...	15	22	-30.6	7.9	24.1
#2•[2]	UVN	✔Univision Communic 'A'	NY,Ch,Ph	NR	393	61359	Spanish-language TV brodcg US	35 11/16	11½	42	21 1/16	103 3/16	34⅛	63904	103 3/16	86 11/16	102 3/16	...	..	...	184	77.1	...
3	UNO	✔Uno Restaurant Corp	NY	B	28	2470	Operates pizza restaurants	12¼	2 15/16	7 3/16	5¼	13 7/16	6¼	2747	11⅛	9⅝	11⅛	...	13	11	70.9	26.7	6.7
¶4•[3]	UCL	✔Unocal Corp	NY,B,C,Ch,P,Ph	B	737	183961	Oil & gas explor,dvlp,prod'n	45⅞	3 7/16	42⅛	28 5/16	46⅝	27½	176748	35⅝	32 1/16	33 9/16	2.4	56	-11	17.5	-4.3	6.7
5	UNA	✔UNOVA Inc	NY	NR	136	49242	Indl automation systems	20 5/16	14⅛	24	12⅜	20	11⅞	10925	14¼	12 3/16	13	...	13	...	-28.3	...	...
¶6•[4]	UNM	✔UnumProvident Corp	NY	B	646	159637	Disablilty/life/hlth insur	39 1/16	1 13/16	42 7/16	26⅛	56⅞	26	206996	32 15/16	26¼	32 1/16	1.8	12	Neg	-21.7	11.3	26.3
7	UND	UNUMProvident Corp 8.80%'MIDS'	NY	...[53]	5	19	Monthly Income Debt Sec	27¾	25	26⅝	25¾	26⅛	22⅜	3299	24 1/16	22⅜	22⅝	9.7	..	...	-4.3	3.6	...
8	UPM	✔UPM-Kymmene Corp ADS[54]	NY	NR	21	776	Mfr paper/forest pds	....	....	....	....	42¾	29¼	1227	42¾	34 3/16	42¾	1.9	15	...	...	...	...
9	URBN	✔Urban Outfitters	NNM	B+	74	7435	Retail/wholesale apparel,gifts	27⅜	9	24¾	11	31 1/16	12⅛	13452	29⅝	19	29⅛	...	28	10	72.6	30.9	16.7
10	URB	✔Urban Shopping Centers	NY,Ch	NR	106	12502	Real estate investment trust	35⅛	18¾	36	30⅛	33 3/16	24	12450	27¼	24	27⅛	8.3	21	-1	-10.7	4.6	14.7
✤11	URS	✔URS Corp	NY,B,Ch,P,Ph	B	141	11688	Engin'g & architectural svcs	230	2¼	23 11/16	11 5/16	29 9/16	15½	13350	21 15/16	17	21 11/16	...	11	28	-7.2	34.1	32.2
12	UBP	✔Urstadt Biddle Properties	NY,Ch,Ph	NR	20	634	RE inv tr: purch/lease back	13⅞	4½	10⅛	7 1/16	8⅝	6 11/16	725	7 7/16	7⅛	7 5/16	9.6	14	26	-1.1	1.6	10.1
13	UBP.A	Cl'A'	NY	NR	15	495		....	....	9 11/16	7⅜	8 11/16	7⅛	1042	7¾	7⅛	7 11/16	10.1	16	25	2.3	...	...
¶14•[5]	U	✔US Airways Group	NY,B,C,Ch,Ph,P	B–	300	27740	Hldg:major airline carrier	65¾	3¼	83¼	34¾	64	24⅛	107569	33	26 9/16	32 1/16	...	7	NM	-38.3	11.1	49.8
15	USDL	✔US Diagnostic Inc	NSC	NR	17	1352	Acquire & own med facilities	14¾	3	5¼	¾	2 3/16	¾	39551	1⅛	¾	1 1/16	...	d	-37	25.8	-51.4	...
16	CLEC	✔US LEC Corp'A'	NNM	NR	75	3011	Telecommunication svcs	....	....	28 5/16	6	33 9/16	12⅞	14589	32¼	25 1/16	32¼	...	41	...	118	...	...
✤17•[6]	USON	✔US Oncology	NNM	NR	200	45486	Provides managed oncology svcs	26⅞	5⅝	17⅝	7 13/16	15 9/16	3 13/16	184637	5¼	4⅜	4 15/16	...	11	29	-66.1	-21.6	...
✤18•[1]	USAD	✔USA Detergents	NNM	NR	50	3416	Mfr laundry/hshld cleaning prd	48	7⅜	18⅜	5⅝	8	2¼	37072	4 7/16	2¼	2¾	...	15	-34	-62.1	-59.6	...
19•[7]	USAI	✔USA Networks	NNM	NR	334	85730	Oper low-pwr TV'sales'stations	25⅞	1 5/16	37⅝	13 13/16	56⅞	31⅛	319782	56⅞	39 15/16	55¼	...	..	NM	66.8	67.8	59.9
20	USAK	✔USA Truck	NNM	B	30	2469	General commodities truck'g	20¼	6¼	17⅞	9¼	13⅝	7 9/16	1784	9	7 9/16	7⅞	...	8	11	-32.3	-0.5	-12.1
21	USNA	✔USANA Inc	NNM	NR	20	1003	Mfr nutritional/hlth prd	14⅝	4⅝	24⅛	8	18	3 13/16	8248	6¼	3 13/16	5	...	11	66	-50.6	-17.2	...
22	UBH	✔U.S.B. Holding	NY	NR	25	657	Commercial bkg,New York	26 13/16	2⅜	24	11¼	16 13/16	13 3/16	1327	15 15/16	14⅞	15 15/16	1.8	17	11	-3.9	...	...
23•[8]	USU	✔USEC Inc	NY,Ph	NR	151	64078	Uranium fuel enrichment svcs	....	....	16 5/16	13	15 3/16	6⅝	134462	8⅜	6⅝	7	15.7	7	...	-43.9	...	...
✤24	USFC	✔USFreightways Corp	NNM	B+	301	25426	Trucking-gen'l commodities	36¾	9 5/16	40⅜	17⅜	52	26⅜	58190	51 15/16	39⅛	47⅞	0.8	13	20	66.1	21.9	15.0
#25•[9]	USG	✔USG Corp	NY,P	NR	293	36284	Gypsum base bldg products	51½	9⅝	58¾	35½	65	41⅛	47710	49⅞	43 11/16	47⅛	1.3	6	NM	-6.6	12.1	19.6
26•[10]	USIX	✔USinternetworking, Inc.	NNM	NR	96	7804	Pkged softwr application svcs	....	....	....	....	69⅞	9 9/16	175620	69⅞	37¼	69⅞	...	..	...	...	...	...
✤27	USTB	✔UST Corp[60]	NNM	B	186	20838	Comm'l bkg,Massachusetts	29⅝	2¼	30⅜	16⅜	31⅞	20 1/16	26806	31⅞	31 7/16	31¾	1.9	19	32	37.9	17.9	27.4
¶28•[9]	UST	✔UST Inc	NY,B,Ch,P	A+	521	131021	Snuff,tobacco,wine,spirits	36 15/16	7/16	36⅞	24 9/16	34 15/16	24 1/16	98549	27¾	24 1/16	25 3/16	7.0	9	5	-23.4	-2.9	3.0
29	UAX	✔USURF America	AS	NR	..	...	Dvlp stg:wireless internet sv	....	....	5½	½	13¾	2½	23984	5⅞	2 11/16	4¼	...	d	...	15.3	...	...
30	USWB	✔USWeb Corp	NNM	NR	297	44411	Internet consulting svcs	14⅝	7 1/16	38¾	7¾	58½	17	845154	58½	35¼	44 7/16	...	d	...	68.5	...	...
¶31•[11]	MRO	✔USX-Marathon Grp	NY,B,C,Ch,P,Ph,Mo	NR	800	233478	Oil&gas explor,devel,prod'n	50	14½	40½	25	33⅞	19⅝	285849	28	23⅝	24 11/16	3.4	17	NM	-15.6	3.9	11.8
¶32•[11]	X	✔USX-U.S. Steel Group	NY,Ch,Ph,P	NR	453	62784	Integrated steel producer	46	20	43 1/16	20 7/16	34¼	21¾	200156	33	24⅝	33	3.0	83	-10	48.9	5.3	1.9
33	Pr A	6.50% cm Cv Pfd([63]51.30)	NY	BB	27	737		61½	41⅜	52 11/16	42½	50⅞	41 15/16	1117	44	42¼	43½	7.5	..	...	...	...	...
34	Pr Z	USX Cpl 6.75%[65]Cv[66]'QUIPS'([67]51.625)	[12]	BB+	5	99		50 9/16	44⅝	52¾	41½	48 7/16	39	2297	43 1/16	39¾	42¾	7.9	..	...	...	...	...
35•[11]	UM	✔Utah Medical Products	NY,Ch	B+	25	1576	Mfr medical devices/supplies	23½	⅝	8⅞	5	8 3/16	5 9/16	3060	6⅞	6⅛	6¾	...	10	-4	2.9	-20.4	-4.5
36•[13]	UTI	✔UTI Energy	AS,Ch,Ph	NR	114	10949	Contract drilling/o&g svcs	48⅝	1	26 7/16	5¾	24	5⅛	21324	23⅜	17½	23 1/16	...	d	-35	218	25.1	83.7
#37•[1]	UCU	✔UtiliCorp United	NY,B,Ch,P,Ph	B+	283	33283	Utility: electric & gas	26 1/16	1 15/16	26⅝	22½	26	18 9/16	51408	20⅜	18 9/16	19 7/16	6.2	11	7	-14.9	8.8	8.3
38	Pr W	9.75% UGU Cap Tr I'PEPS'Unit	NY	NR	4	258		....	....	....	....	25 13/16	22 5/16	5976	23⅞	22 5/16	22⅝	10.8	..	...	...	...	...
39	LNUX	VA Linux Systems	NNM	NR	..	...	Linux-based solutions	....	....	....	....	320	30	217453	320	30	206⅝	...	..	...	...	...	...
40•[14]	MTN	✔Vail Resorts	NY,Ch,Ph	NR	80	26490	Operates premier resort area	28⅞	17⅜	31⅞	15½	23¾	14⅛	19354	22½	15¾	17 15/16	...	56	...	-18.5	...	...
✤41•[7]	VCI	✔Valassis Communications	NY,Ph,P	NR	438	54971	Prints consumer promotion prd	25¼	6¼	34½	19 7/16	46½	29 1/16	55377	44¼	37⅛	42¼	...	23	NM	23.4	44.5	33.5
#42•[2]	VLO	✔Valero Energy	NY	NR	246	47482	Oil&gas refining/mkt	35⅛	26 15/16	36½	17⅝	25 5/16	16 11/16	32580	21⅜	19	19⅞	1.6	d	Neg	-5.0	...	...
43	VHI	✔Valhi Inc	NY,Ph,P	B	51	3140	Multi-industrial mgmt co	22¾	1	14⅛	9 1/16	14	10 3/16	1508	11¼	10 3/16	10½	1.9	15	48	-6.0	20.6	...
44•[15]	VLY	✔Valley Natl Bancorp	NY,Ph	A	86	5720	Commercial bkg,New Jersey	30¾	½	34 5/16	22⅝	29½	23 5/16	19290	28	23 15/16	28	s3.7	16	9	13.7	22.2	17.2
45	VLG	✔Valley Natl Gases	AS	NR	14	1259	Indust'l gases/welding eqp	11¼	8	12⅛	5	6	2 13/16	683	3½	3 1/16	3 3/16	...	11	21	-43.3	...	...
46	VR	✔Valley Resources	AS,B	B+	13	677	Supplies gas serv in R.I.	18 15/16	1 1/16	13⅝	11	23⅛	10½	3092	23⅛	22	22¼	3.4	27	...	88.5	33.4	20.6
✤47•[5]	VALM	✔Valmont Indus	NNM	B	91	6571	Self prop irrig sys:steel tubg	23⅞	3/16	25	12¼	18¼	11¼	4775	17 7/16	13⅛	16 1/16	1.6	16	8	17.7	-6.5	15.3
48•[16]	VAL	✔Valspar Corp	NY,Ch,Ph,P	A+	148	17904	Mfr paints & coatings	33 1/16	3/16	42⅛	25¾	41⅞	29¼	14383	41⅞	38 15/16	41⅞	1.2	22	13	13.7	15.5	...
49•[10]	VUSA	✔Value America	NNM	NR	53	3580	Internet shopping svcs	....	....	....	....	74¼	4¾	186329	13 1/16	4¾	5 1/16	...	d	...	...	...	...
50	VCD	✔Value City Dept Stores	NY,Ph	NR	80	8688	Oper off-price dept str chain	25	5¾	22⅜	7⅝	19½	8 3/16	8427	19½	13⅞	15⅛	...	17	-4	8.5	12.9	11.6

Uniform Footnote Explanations-See Page 4. Other: [1]Ph:Cycle 2. [2]ASE:Cycle 3. [3]P:Cycle 1. [4]ASE,Ph:Cycle 3. [5]P:Cycle 3. [6]ASE,CBOE:Cycle 3. [7]CBOE:Cycle 1. [8]ASE,CBOE:Cycle 1. [9]CBOE:Cycle 2. [10]ASE,CBOE,Ph:Cycle 3. [11]ASE:Cycle 1. [12]NY [13]ASE,Ph:Cycle 1. [14]CBOE,P:Cycle 3. [15]Ph:Cycle 3. [16]P:Cycle 2. [51]Ltd vtg. [52]Excl subsid pfd. [53]Rated 'A' by S&P. [54]Ea ADS rep 1 ord shr FIM10. [55]Excl 0.4M Unit vtg stk. [56]Pfd in $M. [57]Incl 173M exch sub equiv. [58]12 Mo Dec'95:Aug'95 earn $0.01. [59]Incl redemption of Stk Pur Rt. [60]Citizens Finl plan acq,$32. [61]Subsid pfd in $M. [62]Pfd in $M,incl subsid pfd. [63]Thru 3-31-2000,scale to $50 in 2003. [64]Cv into 1.084 com,$46.125. [65]Quarterly Income Preferred Securities. [66]To 4-1-99(at$50 for'Tax Event're-spec cond). [67]Subsid USX Corp. [68]Into USX-U.S. Steel Grp com to 3-31-2037. [69]Pfd mature 11-16-2004. [70]Fiscal Sep'97 & prior. [71]Fiscal Jul'97 & prior. [72]12 Mo Jan'99:Fiscal Jul'98 earn $0.63.

Index (◆ Splits)	Cash Divs. Ea.Yr. Since	Latest Payment Period $	Date	Ex. Div.	Total $ So Far 1999	Ind. Rate	Paid 1998	Mil-$ Cash& Equiv.	Curr. Assets	Curr. Liab.	Balance Sheet Date	Lg Trm Debt Mil-$	Shs. 000 Pfd.	Com.	Years End	1995	1996	1997	1998	1999	Last 12 Mos.	Interim Period	$ per Shr. 1998	1999	Index
1◆	....	0.10	10-20-89	9-26	...	Nil	....	7.09	371	205	9-30-99	400	...	±30660	Dc	v±1.26	v±1.65	v2.03	v±2.39	E2.40	2.58	9 Mo Sep	v1.78	v1.97	1
2◆	....	None Since Public			...	Nil	....	15.9	169	156	9-30-99	277	9	±101935	Dc	±p0.07	□±p0.31	v±0.71	v±0.09	E0.65	0.51	9 Mo Sep	v±0.02	v□±0.44	2
3◆	....	None Since Public			...	Nil	....	1.31	5.85	24.4	6-27-99	39.5	...	11190	Sp	0.53	v0.12	v0.20	v□0.50	Pv0.85	0.85				3
4	1916	Q0.20	2-10-00	1-6	0.80	0.80	0.80	209	1360	1346	9-30-99	3356	[52]...	242418	Dc	0.91	vd0.07	□v2.46	v0.54	E0.60	0.05	9 Mo Sep	v0.66	v0.17	4
5	....	None Since Public			...	Nil	....	3.24	1124	717	9-30-99	366	...	55293	Dc	...	pv0.78	vd3.17	v1.27	....	1.01	9 Mo Sep	v0.55	v0.29	5
6◆	1925	Q0.14¾	11-19-99	11-3	0.34¾	0.59	0.40	Total Assets $38071.10M			9-30-99	1516	...	240028	Dc	v1.13	v1.44	v1.84	v1.82	E2.80	d1.67	9 Mo Sep	v2.15	vd1.34	6
7	1995	M0.183	12-31-99	12-28	2.20	2.20	2.20	Co option redm fr 5-11-2000 at $25				150	...	...	Dc	...	...	...	....	....	....	Mature 5-31-2025			7
8	1998	0.83	4-8-99	3-19	0.83	0.83	0.68	8809	17085	17641	j12-31-97	17420	...	270389	Dc	...	...	v2.78	....	....	2.78				8
9◆	....	None Since Public			...	Nil	....	15.6	72.6	33.6	10-31-99	....	...	17619	Ja	v0.70	v0.75	v0.78	v0.88	....	1.03	9 Mo Oct	v0.59	v0.74	9
10	1994	Q0.56	12-3-99	11-15	2.24	2.24	2.10	Total Assets $1752M			9-30-99	1031	3773	[55]17931	Dc	v□1.35	v1.42	v□1.27	v1.27	....	1.29	9 Mo Sep	v0.75	v□0.77	10
11	....	5%Stk	9-11-87	8-26	...	Nil	....	19.7	680	293	7-31-99	667	[56]100	15653	Oc	0.67	v0.81	v1.08	v1.43	Pv1.98	1.98				11
12◆	1970	Q0.17½	1-21-00	1-5	0.68	0.70	0.65	Total Assets $176M			7-31-99	47.3	350	±10713	Oc	0.36	v0.90	v0.79	v0.52	Pv0.54	0.54				12
13	1999	Q0.19½	1-21-00	1-5	0.76	0.78	....	....	...	...		....	...	5179	Oc	0.36	v0.99	v0.86	v0.57	....	0.48	9 Mo Jul	v0.42	v0.33	13
14	....	0.03	7-31-90	7-10	...	Nil	....	1029	2179	2746	9-30-99	1904	...	71459	Dc	v0.55	v2.35	v9.87	v5.60	E4.75	4.85	9 Mo Sep	v4.40	v3.65	14
15	....	None Paid			...	Nil	....	7.62	58.8	57.8	9-30-99	129	...	22636	Dc	vΔ0.64	vd0.48	vd5.26	vΔd0.02	....	d0.42	9 Mo Sep	v0.12	vΔd0.28	15
16	....	None Since Public			...	Nil	....	8.06	170	82.6	9-30-99	40.0	...	±27436	Dc	...	...	vd0.25	v0.52	....	0.79	9 Mo Sep	v0.34	v0.61	16
17◆	....	None Since Public			...	Nil	....	2.07	394	154	9-30-99	331	...	85879	Dc	v0.30	v0.37	v0.48	v0.61	....	0.47	9 Mo Sep	v0.44	v0.30	17
18◆	....	None Since Public			...	Nil	....	4.36	52.5	43.6	9-30-99	36.7	...	13826	Dc	vp0.43	v0.27	vd1.53	□v0.08	....	0.18	9 Mo Sep	vΔNil	v0.10	18
19◆	....	None Since Public			...	Nil	....	386	1306	995	9-30-99	856	...	[57]±348598	Dc	[58]d0.19	pd0.04	v0.12	v0.43	....	0.23	9 Mo Sep	v0.14	vd0.06	19
20	....	None Since Public			...	Nil	....	1.01	24.2	22.9	9-30-99	15.1	...	9298	Dc	v0.60	v0.35	v0.83	v1.11	....	0.96	9 Mo Sep	v0.84	v0.69	20
21◆	....	None Since Public			...	Nil	....	1.52	17.7	20.1	10-02-99	8.00	...	10165	Dc	v0.20	v0.38	v0.50	v0.68	....	0.47	9 Mo Sep	v0.49	v0.28	21
22◆	1996	Q0.07	1-14-00	12-29	0.26	0.28	0.205	Total Deposits $1152.83M			9-30-99	27.6	...	15884	Dc	v0.65	v0.64	v0.70	v0.72	....	0.93	9 Mo Sep	v0.51	v0.72	22
23	1998	Q0.275	12-15-99	11-23	1.10	1.10	0.275	37.7	1192	373	9-30-99	500	...	90600	Je	...	...	1.33	n/a	v1.52	1.05	3 Mo Sep	v0.63	v0.16	23
24	1992	Q0.093	1-7-00	12-21	0.28	0.373	0.373	6.28	352	387	10-02-99	103	...	26481	Dc	v1.51	v1.40	v2.19	v2.70	E3.65†	3.44	9 Mo Sep	v1.94	v2.68	24
25	1998	Q0.15	12-15-99	11-23	0.45	0.60	[59]0.11	273	972	476	9-30-99	577	...	49441	Dc	d0.71	v0.31	v3.03	v6.61	E8.53	7.92	9 Mo Sep	v4.78	v6.09	25
26◆	....	None Since Public			...	Nil	....	29.1	84.4	37.6	9-30-99	34.6	...	60953	Dc	...	...	...	n/a	....	....	9 Mo Sep	n/a	vd2.49	26
27	1995	Q0.15	1-20-00	12-21	0.60	0.60	0.52	Total Deposits $4263.09M			9-30-99	33.4	...	42821	Dc	v0.92	v1.53	v1.08	v1.28	....	1.65	9 Mo Sep	v0.88	v1.25	27
28	1912	Q0.44	3-15-00	3-1	1.68	1.76	1.62	13.0	389	286	9-30-99	240	...	171093	Dc	v2.17	v2.44	v2.37	v2.44	E2.68	2.55	9 Mo Sep	v1.87	v1.98	28
29	....	....			...	Nil	....	0.09	0.37	0.56	9-30-99	....	...	12371	Dc	...	d0.04	d0.10	vd0.14	....	d0.53	9 Mo Sep	vd0.12	vd0.51	29
30	....	None Since Public			...	Nil	....	116	357	246	9-30-99	2.63	...	85803	Dc	...	pvd2.46	vd4.78	vd3.07	....	d2.82	9 Mo Sep	vd1.81	vd1.56	30
31	1991	Q0.21	12-10-99	11-15	0.84	0.84	0.84	87.0	4002	2803	9-30-99	3497	[61]184	310719	Dc	v□d0.31	v□2.31	v1.58	v1.05	E1.48	1.25	9 Mo Sep	v1.36	v1.56	31
32	1991	Q0.25	12-10-99	11-15	1.00	1.00	1.00	6.00	1437	1166	9-30-99	543	[62]69	88394	Dc	v□3.43	v□2.97	v4.88	v3.92	E0.40	0.96	9 Mo Sep	v3.11	v□0.15	32
33	1993	Q0.81¼	12-31-99	11-29	3.25	3.25	3.25	Cv USX-U.S.Steel Gp[64]				....	6900	...	Dc	...	...	...	....	....	....				33
34	1997	0.84⅜	12-31-99	12-28	3.37½	3.375	3.37½	Cv into 1.081 com,$46.25[68]				....	6700	...	Dc	...	...	...	....	....	....	Mand redm 3-31-2037			34
35	....	0.02	8-30-93	8-25	...	Nil	....	0.57	9.00	2.37	9-30-99	1.75	...	6453	Dc	0.83	v0.93	v0.51	v0.59	....	0.70	9 Mo Sep	v0.43	v0.54	35
36◆	....	None Since Public			...	Nil	....	12.7	52.4	28.4	9-30-99	32.1	...	17813	Dc	v0.01	v0.42	v0.83	v0.47	....	d0.22	9 Mo Sep	v0.48	vd0.21	36
37◆	1939	Q0.30	12-13-99	11-18	1.20	1.20	1.20	181	3302	3510	9-30-99	2234	[52]...	92921	Dc	v1.14	v1.46	□v1.65	v1.63	E1.78	1.75	9 Mo Sep	v1.18	v1.30	37
38	1999	0.32½	11-16-99	11-10	0.32½	2.44	....	Pur contract to 11-16-2002 re-spec[69]				....	...	9000		...	...	...	....	....	....				38
39	....	None Since Public			...	Nil	....	14.7	24.4	10.5	10-29-99	0.67	p...	★39702	Jl	...	...	...	....	vpd1.01	....	3 Mo Oct	n/a	vpd0.56	39
40	....	None Since Public			...	Nil	....	18.9	91.9	122	10-31-99	424	...	±34618	Jl	...	p0.39	vp[70]0.72	vp0.87	v0.37	0.32	3 Mo Oct	vd0.59	vd0.64	40
41	....	0.093	4-26-93	3-30	...	Nil	....	7.70	147	160	9-30-99	304	...	56248	Dc	v0.15	v0.67	v1.13	□v1.42	....	1.88	9 Mo Sep	v1.06	v1.52	41
42	1997	Q0.08	12-7-99	11-5	0.32	0.32	0.32	7.82	862	702	9-30-99	846	...	55754	Dc	v1.17	pv1.42	v1.74	vd0.84	....	d1.55	9 Mo Sep	v0.67	vd0.04	42
43	1987	Q0.05	12-31-99	12-8	0.20	0.20	0.20	205	665	359	9-30-99	629	...	114571	Dc	v0.60	v0.37	□v0.53	v□1.94	....	0.72	9 Mo Sep	v□1.86	v0.64	43
44◆	1936	Q0.26	1-3-00	12-1	s0.996	1.04	0.895	Total Deposits $496M			9-30-99	365	...	60427	Dc	v1.18	v1.26	v1.52	v1.67	....	1.73	9 Mo Sep	v1.23	v1.29	44
45	....	None Since Public			...	Nil	....	0.38	25.7	14.7	9-30-99	55.8	...	9348	Je	pv0.29	pv0.34	vpd0.27	v0.31	v0.32	0.30	3 Mo Sep	v0.09	v0.07	45
46	1962	Q0.18¾	1-15-00	12-29	0.75	0.75	0.74¾	0.75	18.6	14.6	8-31-99	32.6	...	4993	Au	0.61	0.94	v0.86	v0.73	v0.84	0.84				46
47◆	1980	Q0.06½	1-14-00	12-29	0.26	0.26	0.24¼	12.8	214	130	9-25-99	84.8	...	23476	Dc	v0.90	v0.76	v1.33	v1.02	....	0.98	9 Mo Sep	v0.79	v0.75	47
48◆	1964	Q0.13	1-14-00	12-29	0.46	0.52	0.42	26.2	539	359	7-30-99	339	...	43235	Oc	1.08	v1.26	v1.49	v1.63	Pv1.87	1.87				48
49	....	None Since Public			...	Nil	....	121	136	46.6	9-30-99	....	...	44754	Dc	...	...	vd0.09	vd2.80	....	d4.79	9 Mo Sep	vd1.53	vd3.52	49
50	....	None Since Public			...	Nil	....	27.0	503	292	10-30-99	141	...	32850	Ja	0.43	0.68	[71]0.12	v[72]0.75	....	0.89	9 Mo Oct	v0.26	v0.40	50

◆Stock Splits & Divs By Line Reference Index [1]2-for-1,'96. [2]2-for-1,'98. [3]5-for-4,'95:10%,'99. [6]2-for-1,'97:No adj for mgr,'99. [9]2-for-1,'96. [12]2-for-1 in Cl'A',98. [17]2-for-1,'96. [18]3-for-2,'96. [19]2-for-1,'98. [21]2-for-1,'98. [22]10%,2-for-1,'96,'97:10%,'98. [26]3-for-2,'99. [36]3-for-1,'97. [37]3-for-2,'99. [44]5-for-4,'98:Adj for 5%,'99. [47]2-for-1,'97. [48]2-for-1,'97.

¶ S&P 500 · # MidCap 400 · ✣ SmallCap 600 · • Options

Index	Ticker	Name of Issue (Call Price of Pfd. Stocks)	Market	Com. Rank. & Pfd. Rating	Inst. Hold Cos	Inst. Hold Shs. (000)	Principal Business	1971-97 High	1971-97 Low	1998 High	1998 Low	1999 High	1999 Low	Dec. Sales in 100s	Last Sale Or Bid High	Low	Last	%Div Yield	P-E Ratio	EPS 5 Yr Growth	Total Return 12 Mo	36 Mo	60 Mo
1	VALU	✔Value Line	NNM	B+	50	1138	Investment advisory services	51	12½	49⅞	33	42	33	1133	36⅝	34¼	36	2.8	13	−1	−6.1	9.1	14.3
2•[1]	VVTV	✔ValueVision Intl'A'	NNM	NR	111	29448	Oper TV home shopping ntwrk	15⅝	½	15¼	3	62	6½	87040	62	38¾	57 5/16	...	86	NM	715	120	64.6
3•[2]	VANS	✔Vans Inc	NNM	NR	58	8969	Mfr,mkt casual shoes	25¾	3⅛	15⅜	5 1/16	13⅝	5⅝	15298	13⅜	11 1/16	12¼	...	17	NM	78.2	−0.7	9.2
4•[3]	VNTV	✔Vantive Corp	NNM	NR	137	18272	Customer interaction software	42¾	6	39¾	5	19⅞	6	85436	19⅞	15	18⅛	...	d	Neg	127	−16.6	...
#5•[4]	VRC	✔Varco Int'l	NY,Ch,P	B	228	44912	Oil & gas drill'g tools	33 15/16	15/16	32 3/16	5 7/16	14¼	6 15/16	92897	11 7/16	9 3/16	10 3/16	...	15	39	31.4	−1.4	28.8
✣6•[5]	VAR	✔Varian Medical Systems	NY,B,Ch,P,Ph	B+	193	24402	Prov integrated oncology svcs	67	1⅜	58⅜	31 3/16	43	16¼	23110	30	26 1/16	29 13/16	...	d	Neg	...	...	...
7	MEW	Vasogen Inc	AS,To	NR	1	86	Biotechnology R&D	3 11/16	13/16	1 9/16	13/16	6¼	1 5/16	3498	4¾	3⅛	4⅝	...	d	...	195	38.3	...
8•[4]	VRI	✔Vastar Resources	NY,Ch,Ph,P	NR	172	15996	Oil&gas explor,dvlp,prod'n	44 9/16	21⅞	48 15/16	31¾	70½	37⅞	21047	59 13/16	51 15/16	59	0.5	37	3	37.4	16.6	19.8
9	VDC	✔VDC Communications	AS	NR	2	128	Wireless telecomm svcs	250	2½	8⅝	3⅛	6⅛	¾	26057	2 5/16	¾	2¼	...	d	...	−48.6	−24.6	−16.7
10	VEB	✔Veba Corp ADS[52]	NY	NR	22	1253	Elec,chem,trad/transp sv,tele	69	51⅛	72⅝	47¼	66 5/16	41½	2502	51½	41½	50 1/16	1.6	..	...	−14.8	...	...
11•[6]	VECO	✔Veeco Instruments	NNM	NR	115	10427	Microelectronic prod mfg eqp	73⅝	7¾	55¼	19⅝	64½	24 7/16	37745	50	40¼	46 13/16	...	35	47	−11.9	28.6	35.8
12	VELCF	✔Velcro Indus NV	NSC,Mo	B+	32	4664	Mfr fastening tapes:other	9⅞	7/16	21	9 3/16	17½	10	9736	13¼	10½	12 1/16	1.8	11	16	−18.0	27.3	15.0
13•[7]	Z	✔Venator Group	NY,B,C,Ch,P,Ph	B−	169	107015	Variety,discount,shoe stores	36⅝	2	27¼	5 13/16	12	3 3/16	105056	7 11/16	6¼	7	...	d	Neg	7.7	−31.7	−14.0
14	VTR	✔Ventas Inc	NY	NR	115	40259	Real estate investment trust	....	....	28⅝	9½	13¾	3 3/16	38317	4⅞	3 11/16	4 3/16	...	..	...	−63.8	...	...
15	VENT	Venturian Corp	NNM	C	7	68	Computer sys,softwr/defense pd	15 15/16	2 7/16	10⅛	5 5/16	8⅝	4 5/16	1069	7½	4⅝	6	...	14	NM	−2.3	10.7	13.9
16	VERA	✔Veramark Technologies	NNM	C	14	982	Telecommun's mgmt sys	17⅛	1¼	8 7/16	3	15	5⅝	9561	12¾	10⅞	12¼	...	38	NM	113	15.9	7.7
17•[8]	VRLK	✔Verilink Corp	NNM	NR	9	2403	Telecommun ntwk access prod	37¾	5¼	11 3/16	2⅞	5 7/16	1 13/16	40038	5 7/16	3⅛	4 5/16	...	d	Neg	17.0	−49.4	...
18	VRIO	✔Verio Inc	NNM	NR	209	44128	Internet service provider	....	....	15 15/16	6½	55⅝	10½	400768	55⅝	35⅞	46 3/16	...	d	...	313	...	...
19•[3]	VRSN	✔VeriSign Inc	NNM	NR	336	79462	Digital certificate svcs	....	....	19⅜	3½	212	13½	506316	212	88 3/16	190 15/16	...	d	...	1193	...	...
20•[7]	VTS	✔Veritas DGC	NY,Ch,Ph	NR	162	15963	Seismic data services	50⅛	12¾	60⅞	10⅝	23⅞	8¾	40115	15 13/16	13⅛	14	...	54	24	7.7	−8.9	...
#21•[9]	VRTS	✔VERITAS Software	NNM	NR	505	143138	Dvlp storage mgmt software	12	1/16	21 11/16	7 15/16	147⅞	19 5/16	647008	147⅞	89⅞	143⅛	...	d	−9	617	170	179
✣22•[10]	VRTY	✔Verity Inc	NNM	NR	170	25337	Mfr,mkt software tools	28⅜	2 3/16	14⅜	2⅛	61½	12⅞	667620	60 3/16	24⅞	42 9/16	...	85	NM	222	77.0	...
23	VPS	✔Vermont Pure Hldgs Ltd	AS	NR	9	188	Bottles natural spring water	8¼	1	5⅝	2 11/16	5	2⅜	2821	3¼	2⅜	2¾	...	8	NM	−41.3	7.9	−0.9
24	VSR	✔Versar Inc	AS	B−	13	357	Technical environmental svcs	18	1⅞	6⅞	1½	3 1/16	1⅝	2317	2 7/16	1 13/16	2⅛	...	8	−6	9.7	−11.5	...
25	VRSA	VersaTel Telecom	NNM	NR	21	2071	Telecommunication svcs	....	....	....	....	45 1/16	10¼	26844	45 1/16	27¾	34 15/16	...	..	...	...	...	...
26•[3]	VRTL	✔Vertel Corp	NNM	C	18	3272	Dvlp,mfr netwrk softwr/sys	19¾	1 13/16	6½	⅞	14	1 1/16	605540	14	1⅞	5 7/16	...	d	NM	222	−7.0	6.3
27	VTX	✔Vertex Communic'ns[56]	NY	B	42	2721	Mfr earth station antennas	27½	1¾	26¾	13	21 5/16	10¾	4998	21	18 15/16	20½	...	d	Neg	29.1	4.2	10.6
✣28•[11]	VRTX	✔Vertex Pharmaceuticals	NNM	NR	148	14020	Immunology,antiviral drug R&D	52¾	6½	40⅜	14½	37¼	19⅜	45859	37¼	25¾	35	...	d	−7	17.6	−4.6	18.5
29	VERT	✔VerticalNet Inc	NNM	NR	127	11708	Internet access svcs	....	....	....	....	181⅞	8	262359	181⅞	86⅜	164	...	d	...	...	...	...
30•[7]	VTA	✔Vesta Insurance Group	NY,Ch,Ph	B	40	7472	Property & casualty insurance	64½	13 1/16	64¾	5	8⅜	3⅜	17545	4 3/16	3¾	3⅞	...	..	...	−35.1	−49.9	−26.8
31•[12]	VCAI	✔Veterinary Ctrs of Amer	NNM	NR	121	12441	Own/oper veterinary hospitals	32¾	2⅞	21	12⅜	20⅛	9	31980	13¾	9⅞	12⅞	...	15	NM	−35.4	5.4	9.0
¶32•[13]	VFC	✔VF Corp	NY,B,P	A	492	103208	Apparel mfr:intimate,leisure	48¼	9/16	54 11/16	33 7/16	55	27 7/16	68815	31⅞	27 7/16	30	2.9	9	15	−34.4	−1.8	6.7
¶33•[3]	VIA.B	✔Viacom Inc Cl'B'[57]	NY,Ph	B−	705	386264	Diverse entmt/commun'ns co	30⅝	7 1/16	37⅛	20¼	60 7/16	35⅝	249848	60 7/16	49 1/16	60 7/16	...	..	−4	63.8	51.5	24.4
34•[14]	VIA	✔ Cl'A'	NY,B,P	B−	175	33894		33¾	2½	36⅞	19 15/16	60 7/16	35 5/16	31457	60 7/16	49 7/16	60 7/16	...	..	−20	64.4	51.9	23.8
#35•[15]	VVI	✔Viad Corp	NY,B,C,Ch,P,Ph	B	301	61752	Travel & leisure svcs	33¼	4⅞	30 9/16	18 3/16	33⅞	24	49213	29⅞	26⅛	27⅞	1.3	22	NM	−7.2	21.1	8.2
36	VX	✔VIALOG Corp	AS	NR	11	197	Telecommunications svcs	....	....	....	....	8	2⅜	16509	4 1/16	2 9/16	3⅛	...	d	...	...	...	...
37•[16]	VIAS	✔VIASOFT Inc[58]	NNM	C	52	5992	Dvlp/svcs system software	65¼	3⅞	43⅞	2¾	8 13/16	3⅛	46217	6¾	5¼	5 11/16	...	d	Neg	−18.8	−50.6	...
38•[17]	VYTL	✔Viatel Inc	NNM	NR	206	24390	Long dist telecomm svcs	12¼	4⅛	23½	5	58⅜	15⅞	88172	56¼	41⅝	53⅝	...	d	−26	134	81.3	...
39	VII	✔Vicon Indus	AS	B−	24	758	Closed circ TV security sys	12⅝	1/16	13 15/16	4⅝	10⅜	5	5282	6	5	6	...	6	NM	−18.6	44.2	28.9
✣40•[17]	VICR	✔Vicor Corp	NNM	B+	110	10105	Mfr modular pwr converters	36¼	1¼	29¾	5 9/16	45¼	8 13/16	34020	45¼	28 1/16	40½	...	..	−9	350	34.4	26.0
41	VS	✔Video Services	AS	NR	10	4983	Post TV production svcs	12	2¾	4⅜	1⅞	4½	1⅝	829	4½	2 13/16	4½	...	d	Neg	28.6	−0.9	−1.1
42	VDO	Videotron Group Ltd[61]	To	NR	12	6033	Broadcast'g/telecommun svcs	17	3¾	23½	12⅜	32½	20	24927	24⅞	20¾	24½	0.2	d	Neg	7.2	29.1	13.6
43	VIDIE	Vidikron Technologies Group	BB	C	5	15	Dvlp stge:projection TV R&D	670	30	62½	1¼	5	1/16	4091	9/16	⅛	⅛	...	d	6	−91.0	−87.1	−73.6
44	VIGN	✔Vignette Corp	NNM	NR	152	29941	Internet softw'r pds/svcs	....	....	....	....	168⅝	9½	283756	168⅝	98	163	...	d				
45	VCO	✔Viña Concha y Toro ADS	NY,Ph	NR	48	1587	Chilean wine producer/exporter	34⅝	14½	35⅞	18½	40⅜	23⅝	2154	39⅜	37 13/16	37⅝B	1.1	25	19	48.1	19.1	20.5
✣46•[7]	VPI	✔Vintage Petroleum	NY,Ph	B	186	37288	Oil & gas explor,dev,prod'n	25⅞	2¾	23⅛	7¼	15⅛	4 1/16	64850	12 1/16	9 1/16	12 1/16	...	d	Neg	40.2	−10.9	7.9
47	VRTA	✔Virata Corp	NNM	NR	..	...	Provide communic processors	....	....	....	....	41	14	120807	41	23 3/16	29⅞	...	..	...	...	...	...
48	VIR	✔Virco Mfg	AS	A	43	2489	Chairs,tables,contract seating	23⅛	⅛	26⅛	14 9/16	17 13/16	12	1666	13⅜	12	13	0.6	10	30	−13.4	26.3	33.3
49	VPA	Virginia El & Pwr 6.70% Sr Notes	NY	NR	4	33	Electric utility, Virginia	....	....	....	....	24¾	22⅝	3681	23 15/16	22 3/16	22¾	7.4	..	...	...	...	...
50	VEA	Virginia El & Pwr 7.15% Sr Notes	NY	NR	5	37	Electric utility, Virginia	....	....	26⅛	24⅝	25⅞	19 15/16	3109	21 11/16	19 15/16	20 9/16	8.7	..	...	−12.4	...	...

Uniform Footnote Explanations-See Page 4. Other: [1]ASE,CBOE,P:Cycle 3. [2]ASE,CBOE:Cycle 1. [3]CBOE:Cycle 3. [4]Ph:Cycle 3. [5]ASE:Cycle 2. [6]ASE,CBOE,P:Cycle 1. [7]Ph:Cycle 2. [8]ASE,P:Cycle 1. [9]ASE,CBOE,P:Cycle 2. [10]ASE,CBOE:Cycle 3. [11]Ph:Cycle 1. [12]ASE,P:Cycle 3. [13]CBOE:Cycle 2. [14]CBOE:Cycle 3,Ph:Cycle 2. [15]ASE:Cycle 1. [16]ASE,CBOE:Cycle 2. [17]CBOE:Cycle 1.
[51]Stk dstr of Varian Inc&Varian Semicon Equip'99. [52]Ea ADS rep 1 ord,DM5. [53]Incl curr amt. [54]To be determined. [55]Stk dstr of Sarnia Corp,'94. [56]TriPoint Global Communications plan acq,$22. [57]Non-vtg. [58]Compuware Corp plan acq,$9. [59]1 Stk purch rt. [60]Fiscal Jul 31 & prior. [61]Sub vtg shrs. [62]Approx.

Index	Splits ◆ Cash Divs. Ea. Yr. Since	Dividends Latest Payment Period $	Date	Ex. Div.	Total $ So Far 1999	Ind. Rate	Paid 1998	Financial Position Mil-$ Cash& Equiv.	Curr. Assets	Curr. Liab.	Balance Sheet Date	Capitalization Lg Trm Debt Mil-$	Shs. 000 Pfd.	Com.	Earnings $ Per Shr. Years End	1995	1996	1997	1998	1999	Last 12 Mos.	Interim Earnings Period	$ per Shr. 1998	1999	Index
1	1983	Q0.25	11-12-99	10-27	1.00	1.00	1.00	53.9	62.8	8.98	10-31-99	....	...	9979	Ap	v2.32	v4.18	v4.56	v3.53	v2.72	2.85	6 Mo Oct	v1.20	v1.33	1
2	....	None Since Public			...	Nil	....	315	389	60.2	10-31-99	....	5340	37374	Ja	v0.38	v0.56	v0.57	v0.18	....	0.67	9 Mo Oct	v0.16	v0.65	2
3	....	None Since Public			...	Nil	....	12.4	116	52.0	8-28-99	10.0	...	13525	My	d3.86	□0.40	v0.76	vd0.20	v0.64	0.71	6 Mo Nov	v0.53	v0.60	3
4◆	....	None Since Public			...	Nil	....	88.5	156	46.1	9-30-99	69.0	...	27680	Dc	v0.09	v0.42	vd0.28	vd0.09	....	d0.30	9 Mo Sep	vd0.13	vd0.34	4
5◆	....	0.03	8-13-82	7-26	...	Nil	....	38.7	314	108	9-30-99	....	...	65273	Dc	v0.23	v0.38	v0.76	v0.92	....	0.67	9 Mo Sep	v0.76	v0.51	5
6◆	1973	Div postponed 5-10-99			h[51]0.10	Nil	0.39	26.2	371	268	7-02-99	58.5	...	30534	Sp	3.96	v3.81	v3.67	v2.43	vPd0.79	d0.79				6
7	....	None Paid			...	Nil	....	12.4	12.7	0.72	j2-28-99	....	...	26574	Nv	d0.25	d0.30	d0.37	vd0.29	....	jd0.27	6 Mo May	vd0.14	vd0.12	7
8	1994	Q0.07½	12-1-99	11-3	0.30	0.30	0.30	10.5	323	268	9-30-99	1068	...	97644	Dc	v1.05	v2.26	v2.46	v1.39	....	1.58	9 Mo Sep	v1.21	v1.40	8
9	....	None Paid			...	Nil	....	0.79	2.39	2.59	6-30-99	....	...	18311	Je	d6.20	...	pd0.44	vd0.76	vd2.72	d1.76	3 Mo Sep	vd1.01	vd0.05	9
10	1998	0.815	6-4-99	5-25	0.815	0.81	0.867	...	...	...		2034	...	±34760	Dc	...	n/a	...	...	...	....				10
11	....	None Since Public			...	Nil	....	80.9	198	52.3	9-30-99	8.77	...	17517	Dc	v1.09	v1.22	v1.32	v0.85	....	1.35	9 Mo Sep	v0.55	v1.05	11
12◆	1992	A0.22	1-5-00	12-2	0.20	0.22	0.20	4.09	74.0	58.7	9-30-98	53.8	...	30040	Sp	0.47	0.54	v0.65	v0.91	Pv1.12	1.12				12
13	....	0.15	3-1-95	1-26	...	Nil	....	63.0	1364	1186	10-30-99	313	...	137502	Ja	d1.23	v1.26	vd0.07	vd1.00	Ed0.04↓	0.01	9 Mo Oct	vd1.27	v±d0.26	13
14	1999	Div Omitted 5-14-99			0.39	Nil	Stk	Total Assets $1052.00M			9-30-99	[53]975	...	67959	Dc	...	...	pv1.28	pv□0.82	....	....	9 Mo Sep	n/a	v0.79	14
15◆	1999	0.04½	12-31-99	12-16	0.09	[54]....	....	1.31	13.9	5.24	9-30-99	4.21	...	1340	Dc	vd0.13	v0.06	vd1.87	v1.36	....	0.42	9 Mo Sep	v1.00	v0.06	15
16	....	0.02	1-29-96	1-10	...	Nil	....	5.95	9.91	4.72	9-30-99	....	...	7633	Dc	v0.13	vd0.86	vd0.69	v0.13	....	0.32	9 Mo Sep	v0.07	v0.26	16
17	....	None Since Public			...	Nil	....	14.0	36.7	20.6	10-01-99	....	...	14022	Je	0.04	0.24	v0.29	vd0.08	vd0.98	d1.70	3 Mo Sep	v0.05	vd0.67	17
18◆	....	None Since Public			...	Nil	....	493	571	179	9-30-99	684	...	77128	Dc	...	...	vpd1.45	v□d2.62	....	d2.22	9 Mo Sep	v□d2.24	vd1.84	18
19◆	....	None Since Public			...	Nil	....	160	184	36.0	9-30-99	....	...	102510	Dc	...	pvd0.19	pvd0.28	vd0.24	....	d0.04	9 Mo Sep	vd0.20	vd0.01	19
20	....	None Since Public			...	Nil	....	35.3	174	78.0	10-31-99	130	...	22111	Jl	p0.31	p0.07	v1.30	v2.87	v0.88	0.26	3 Mo Oct	v0.60	v□d0.02	20
21◆	....	None Since Public			...	Nil	....	643	751	200	9-30-99	448	...	259175	Dc	v0.02	v0.09	v0.15	v0.33	Evd0.01	d1.58	9 Mo Sep	v0.20	vd1.71	21
22◆	....	None Since Public			...	Nil	....	107	126	20.3	8-31-99	....	...	29926	My	pvd1.09	vd0.06	vd0.83	vd0.74	v0.44	0.50	6 Mo Nov	v0.14	v0.20	22
23	....	None Paid			...	Nil	....	1.51	8.77	4.33	7-31-99	14.6	...	10290	Oc	d0.30	vd0.13	v0.11	v0.26	....	0.33	9 Mo Jul	v0.07	v0.14	23
24	....	h[55]....	6-27-94	6-28	...	Nil	....	0.06	16.8	7.58	9-30-99	....	...	6402	Je	0.10	v0.19	v0.24	vd1.50	v0.29	0.26	3 Mo Sep	v0.06	v0.03	24
25	....	None Since Public			...	Nil	....	460	530	69.0	p3-31-99	★676	...	★59060	Dc	...	...	...	vpd1.56	....	....	3 Mo Mar	n/a	vpd0.81	25
26	....	None Since Public			...	Nil	....	10.2	16.8	7.51	9-30-99	....	...	25484	Dc	d1.78	d0.19	vd0.52	v0.29	....	d0.01	9 Mo Sep	v0.05	vd0.25	26
27	....	None Since Public			...	Nil	....	13.5	74.6	19.1	7-02-99	0.05	...	5088	Sp	1.12	1.32	v1.47	v1.90	....	d0.55	9 Mo Jun	v1.39	vd1.06	27
28	....	None Since Public			...	Nil	....	188	194	13.0	9-30-99	5.26	...	25644	Dc	vd1.25	vd2.13	vd0.82	vd1.31	....	d2.18	9 Mo Sep	vd0.81	vd1.68	28
29◆	....	None Since Public			...	Nil	....	114	124	17.1	9-30-99	102	...	35606	Dc	...	...	vpd0.47	Pvd0.64	....	d1.41	9 Mo Sep	vpd0.41	vpd1.18	29
30◆	1994	Div Postponed 3-31-99			0.03¾	Nil	0.15	Total Assets $1007.19M			9-30-99	98.3	...	18676	Dc	v2.25	v2.62	v3.18	vd7.61	....	....	9 Mo Sep	n/a	v0.96	30
31	....	None Since Public			...	Nil	....	26.0	53.2	46.2	9-30-99	140	...	21580	Dc	vd0.13	vd0.92	v0.53	v0.74	E0.87	0.95	9 Mo Sep	v0.61	v0.82	31
32◆	1941	Q0.22	12-20-99	12-8	0.85	0.88	0.81	81.7	2071	1283	10-02-99	523	1693	118118	Dc	v1.19	v2.28	v2.70	v3.10	E3.30	3.03	9 Mo Sep	v2.26	v2.19	32
33◆	....	None Since Public			...	Nil	....	674	4982	4185	9-30-99	6142	...	±696987	Dc	v±0.22	v±0.15	±v1.03	v±d0.11	E0.57	0.47	9 Mo Sep	v±d0.26	v□±0.32	33
34◆	....	None Since Public			...	Nil	....	....	...	...		....	...	138341	Dc	±0.22	v±1.62	v±1.03	v□d0.11	....	0.47	9 Mo Sep	v±d0.26	v□±0.32	34
35◆	1936	Q0.09	1-3-00	12-1	0.34	0.36	0.32	185	854	3859	9-30-99	377	358	94970	Dc	□vd0.04	v0.30	v□1.03	v1.52	E1.26	3.52	9 Mo Sep	v1.14	v3.14	35
36	....	None Since Public			...	Nil	....	2.53	13.9	17.0	9-30-99	74.0	...	9054	Dc	...	...	vpd1.83	Pvd1.13	....	d1.50	9 Mo Sep	vpd0.86	vd1.23	36
37◆	....	None Since Public			...	Nil	....	78.3	103	33.4	9-30-99	....	...	18025	Je	0.36	0.36	vd0.90	v0.40	vd0.46	d0.07	3 Mo Sep	vd0.37	v0.02	37
38	....	None Since Public			...	Nil	....	507	620	336	9-30-99	1291	...	p46755	Dc	pd2.04	vd2.47	vd1.90	v□d4.44	....	d6.33	9 Mo Sep	v□d2.96	vd4.85	38
39	....	[59]....	12-5-86	12-29	...	Nil	....	2.53	39.4	9.14	6-30-99	6.38	...	4561	Sp	d0.49	v0.11	v0.52	v1.50	Pv1.01	1.01				39
40◆	....	None Since Public			...	Nil	....	55.2	120	29.2	9-30-99	....	...	±41244	Dc	v±0.68	±v0.60	±v0.60	±v0.37	....	0.40	9 Mo Sep	v±0.29	v±0.32	40
41	....	None Since Public			...	Nil	....	0.33	20.2	21.2	9-30-99	42.4	...	13286	Je	0.26	0.13	vp[60]d0.01	vpd0.01	vd0.14	d0.14	3 Mo Sep	vd0.02	vd0.02	41
42◆	1987	gQ0.01½	12-21-99	11-29	g0.06	0.06	g0.06	Total Assets $3060M			j8-31-99	970	...	±115759	Au	v0.10	vd0.34	v2.15	v□d0.37	vd1.80	jd1.80				42
43◆	....	None Since Public			...	Nil	....	0.14	7.37	7.94	3-31-99	0.25	252	1050	Dc	vd20.80	vd39.60	vd25.60	vd17.04	....	d15.02	3 Mo Mar	vd3.76	vd1.74	43
44◆	....	None Since Public			...	Nil	....	73.7	99.6	47.7	9-30-99	0.01	...	56176	Dc	...	...	...	vpd0.73	....	d0.98	9 Mo Sep	vpd0.51	vpd0.76	44
45	1995	[62]0.084	1-7-00	12-21	0.432	0.42	0.386	2.25	118	64.6	12-31-98	13.6	...	719171	Dc	0.53	1.07	v1.31	v1.49	....	1.49				45
46◆	1992	Div Omitted 2-15-99			0.02½	Nil	0.08½	5.94	110	100	9-30-99	652	...	62408	Dc	v0.27	v0.85	v1.39	vd1.69	....	d1.03	9 Mo Sep	vd0.41	v0.25	46
47	....	None Since Public			...	Nil	....	4.14	7.41	5.69	10-03-99	0.99	p...	★19472	Mr	...	...	...	vpd1.42	....	....	6 Mo Sep	n/a	vpd0.60	47
48◆	1975	Q0.02	1-31-00	12-29	0.075	0.08	0.068	2.54	98.4	40.4	10-31-99	44.2	...	10919	Ja	0.48	v0.86	v1.25	v1.60	....	1.32	9 Mo Oct	v1.31	v1.03	48
49	1999	Q0.41⅞	12-31-99	12-14	0.931	1.675	....	Co option redm fr 6-30-2002 at $25				★150	...	...	Dc	...	...	...	....	....	....	Mature 6-30-2009			49
50	1998	Q0.447	12-31-99	12-14	1.787	1.788	0.894	Co option redm fr 6-30-2003 at $25				★150	...	...	Dc	...	...	...	....	....	....	Mature 6-30-2038			50

◆Stock Splits & Divs By Line Reference Index [4]2-for-1,'96. [5]2-for-1,'97. [6]2-for-1,'94:No adj for stk dstr,'99. [12]10-for-1,'99. [15]3-for-2,'98:10%,'99. [18]2-for-1,'99. [19]2-for-1,'99(twice). [21]2-for-1,'95,'99:3-for-2,'96,'97,'98,'99. [22]2-for-1,'99. [29]2-for-1,'99. [30]3-for-2,'96. [32]2-for-1,'97. [33]2-for-1,'99. [34]2-for-1,'99. [35]2-for-1,'94:No adj for restruct'g,'96. [37]2-for-1,'96. [40]2-for-1,'95. [42]2-for-1,'94. [43]1-for-40 REVERSE,'99. [44]2-for-1,'99. [46]2-for-1,'97. [48]10%,'95,96,'98,'99.

¶ S&P 500
\# MidCap 400
✣ SmallCap 600
• Options

Index	Ticker	Name of Issue (Call Price of Pfd. Stocks)	Market	Com. Rank. & Pfd. Rating	Inst. Hold Cos	Inst. Hold Shs. (000)	Principal Business	Price Range 1971-97 High	1971-97 Low	1998 High	1998 Low	1999 High	1999 Low	December, 1999 Dec. Sales in 100s	Last Sale Or Bid High	Low	Last	%Div Yield	P-E Ratio	EPS 5 Yr Growth	% Annualized Total Return 12 Mo	36 Mo	60 Mo
#1•[1]	VSH	✓Vishay Intertechnology	NY,B,Ch,Ph,P	B	279	60193	Electronic resistive systems	30 11/16	1/16	18¾	7⅜	32	8⅞	107718	32	25 11/16	31⅝	...	36	−39	173	26.6	17.5
✣2•[2]	VSIO	✓Visio Corp	NNM	NR	174	18076	Dvlp drawing/diagramm'g softwr	42⅝	8	50⅞	14	48 11/16	21⅞	112791	48 11/16	35¾	47½	...	39	...	29.9	24.3	...
3	VEI	✓Vista Energy Resources	AS	NR	2	2	Oil & gas explor,dev,prod'n	....	....	3⅜	1⅝	2¾	1⅛	1578	2	1½	2	...	d	...	−5.9	...	...
4	WS	Wrrt(Pur at com at $4)	AS	....	1			4⅛	¼	2⅛	½	1 1/16	⅛	131	½	⅛	½	...	..	...	...	...	...
5	VGZ	✓Vista Gold	AS,To,Ph	C	6	4674	Gold/mineral explor'n,devel	14¾	3/16	1	⅛	¼	⅛	51858	⅛	⅛	⅛	...	d	Neg	−39.7	−59.1	−44.3
6	VDAT	✓Visual Data	NNM	NR	15	377	Produce visual on-line info	6½	2⅜	7 5/16	1 3/16	46½	6¼	104461	17 11/16	9¾	11½	...	d	−30	67.3	...	...
7	VNWK	✓Visual Networks	NNM	NR	173	16545	Mfr computer systems	....	....	39¾	16⅝	81½	25½	73354	81½	57¾	79¼	...	..	...	111	...	...
#8•[3]	VISX	✓VISX Inc	NNM,Ch	B−	439	40915	Mfr vision correct'n sys	10 1/16	1 1/16	22	4⅞	103⅞	21½	1082225	90⅛	48 15/16	51¾	...	38	NM	141	112	82.1
9	VSF	✓Vita Food Products	AS	NR	1	15	Produce/mkt specialty food pds	4	1¼	2⅜	¼	3¾	⅞	763	2¼	1 11/16	1⅞	...	d	...	114	...	...
10	WS	Wrrt(Pur 1 com at $9)	AS	....	2	5		⅝	⅛	5/16	1/32	¼	1/16	212	1/16	1/16	1/16B	...	..	...	...	...	...
11	VTCH	✓Vitech America	NNM	NR	17	4713	Mfr/distr computer eqp	20 15/16	7⅜	21¼	7½	15½	6	14708	8¾	6	8	...	d	Neg	−48.1	−2.1	...
#12•[4]	VTSS	✓Vitesse Semiconductor	NNM	B−	546	123155	Dvlp,mfr integrated circuits	14⅛	½	24 11/16	8 9/16	55⅜	20⅜	392976	53 13/16	44⅛	52 7/16	...	..	NM	130	91.1	128
13	VTNA	Vitran Corp	NNM,To	NR	11	1398	Freight services	7	2⅜	6½	1⅝	6¾	4¾	199	5 9/16	4⅞	5⅜	1.3	4	...	6.2	31.2	...
14	VITR	✓Vitria Technology	NNM	NR	28	913	Dvlp e-business software	....	....	....	....	310	16	42860	310	103	234	...	..	...	...	...	...
15•[5]	VTO	✓Vitro,Sociedad Anonima ADS[54]	NY,Ph,P	NR	42	13922	Mfr flat glass/glass products	26⅞	4⅜	13⅜	3¼	7½	3½	46044	5⅞	4¾	5½	4.7	d	−46	26.2	2.5	−11.4
16•[2]	VVUS	✓Vivus Inc	NNM	NR	51	5795	Dvlp stge:pharmac'l R&D	41⅞	5⅝	15½	2 1/16	6	1 15/16	556561	6	1 15/16	3⅛	...	18	NM	21.7	−44.1	−16.1
17	VIXL	✓Vixel Corp	NNM	NR	..	...	Computer software & systems	....	....	....	....	53½	17	145491	44	17	17 1/16	...	..	...	...	...	...
#18•[5]	VL	✓Vlasic Foods Intl	NY	NR	139	10791	Mfr/dvlp specialty foods	....	....	27	13 11/16	23 7/16	4 15/16	39789	8 5/16	4 15/16	5 11/16	...	d	...	−76.1	...	...
19	VOCL	✓VocalTec Commun Ltd	NNM	NR	11	343	Voice/audio communic softwr	33¼	3⅞	24⅝	5 9/16	19¾	8	51157	19¾	13	16¾	...	d	−41	48.9	41.8	...
20•[6]	VOD	✓Vodafone AirTouch ADR[55]	NY,Ch,Ph,P	NR	1167	546658	Mobile telecom svcs in U.K.	15 1/16	1 15/16	33⅜	13 11/16	53⅝	33⅛	616148	53¼	47	49½	0.4	52	8	54.6	83.7	51.3
21	VTEK	✓Vodavi Technology	NNM	NR	1	3	Dgn/dvp telephone sys & prd	8⅛	2⅛	5⅜	1¾	3¾	1⅛	3303	3¼	2⅝	3 1/16	...	9	14	11.3	−4.9	...
✣22	VOL	✓Volt Info Sciences	NY	B	90	5262	Tech svs: mfr typesetters	70¼	1/16	58¼	15 5/16	27 7/16	15½	5016	27 7/16	19⅞	23⅞	...	13	16	5.8	−6.4	20.4
23•[7]	VOLVY	✓Volvo AB 'B' ADR[57]	NNM	NR	38	4659	Swedish auto,truck,bus mfg	30⅝	4 11/16	35½	19¼	32¼	23¾	19134	25⅞	23¾	25¼	2.4	14	8	11.3	...	...
24	VOO	✓Vornado Operating	AS	NR	46	1094	Real estate investments	....	....	8½	5¾	10	5⅜	2430	6 15/16	5⅜	6	...	..	...	−25.6	...	...
25	VNO	✓Vornado Realty Trust	NY,B,Ch,Ph	NR	221	57304	Real estate investment trust	47⅜	3/16	49 13/16	26	40	29 11/16	57072	33 15/16	29 11/16	32½	e5.9	11	13	...	...	...
26	Pr A	$3.25 Cv'A'Pfd([60]NC)	NY	BBB−	45	4628		68¾	48¾	70½	39¼	56	43	13730	47⅝	43	46⅝	7.0	..	...	...	...	...
27•[5]	VOYN	✓Voyager.net	NNM	NR	29	3473	Dial-up internet svc provider	....	....	....	....	20½	6 3/16	74832	11 9/16	7⅜	9 3/16	...	..	...	...	...	...
28	VSEC	VSE Corp	NNM	B+	5	25	Engin'g,dev,test,mgmt svc	17 3/16	⅝	13	5½	12¼	6⅜	100	9	7⅛	7¾	1.8	11	−23	−28.4	−11.7	10.8
29	VIS	✓VSI Holdings	AS	NR	4	309	Mktg svcs/Entmt/Retail	17	⅛	8⅛	3 3/16	7¼	3	4902	4¾	3	4 7/16	...	49	NM	−15.5	55.2	51.2
30•[8]	VTEL	✓Vtel Corp	NNM	C	34	5423	Mfr multimedia conferenc'g sys	26	3½	7 11/16	2½	9¼	2	52900	3 15/16	3	3¼	...	d	Neg	28.1	−31.0	−17.7
31	VUL	✓Vulcan Int'l Corp	AS,Ch	B	13	141	Shoe lasts,heels:bowl pins	40	1½	41¼	30	38⅛	26¾	288	31½	30½	31½	2.5	35	82	−4.8	3.1	15.6
¶32•[9]	VMC	✓Vulcan Materials	NY,B,Ch,Ph	A	355	63178	Constr'n materials/chemicals	34⅝	⅞	44 11/16	31 5/16	51¼	34 5/16	38859	41	36¾	39 15/16	2.0	18	20	−7.5	27.7	21.5
33	VYSI	✓Vysis Inc	NNM	NR	7	1167	Cancer product R & D	....	....	12⅜	3	6 13/16	2 7/16	10143	3 15/16	2 7/16	3⅝	...	d	...	−32.6	...	...
✣34	WDFC	✓W D-40 Co	NNM	B+	138	5298	Aerosol lubricant/rust prev	32⅞	⅝	33	20	29⅛	17⅝	14185	24	17⅝	22⅛	5.8	16	1	−18.7	−0.2	5.1
✣35•[5]	WNC	✓Wabash National	NY,Ph,P	NR	147	16537	Mfr/mkt truck trailers	43½	8 11/16	31¾	10¼	22½	10⅞	18780	15⅜	13 1/16	15	1.1	13	...	−25.5	−5.9	−16.9
¶36•[1]	WB	✓Wachovia Corp	NY,B,Ph,P	A−	628	102786	Comml bkg, N.&S.Carolina, GA	83 15/16	2 1/16	96 13/16	72¾	92 5/16	65 7/16	96982	80 1/16	65 7/16	68	3.2	14	8	−20.3	9.0	19.4
37	WAK	✓Wackenhut Corp Cl'A'	NY,Ch	B	69	1860	Investigative/security sv/sys	31	13/16	26	18	29¾	12⅜	6832	14 15/16	12⅜	14 15/16	...	12	21	−40.9	−3.6	17.3
38	WAK B	✓ Cl'B'	NY,Ch	B	41	6915		27⅞	6	23	14 13/16	24	8¼	14667	10 13/16	8¼	10 5/16	...	8	21	−52.6	−11.1	11.6
39•[4]	WHC	✓Wackenhut Corrections	NY,Ch,Ph	NR	77	6199	Oper correctional facilities	45	4½	30⅞	15	28 9/16	9⅝	21666	12 5/16	9⅝	11 11/16	...	13	43	−59.2	−16.4	7.0
40•[2]	WDR	✓Waddell & Reed Fin'l 'A'	NY,Ph	NR	271	24487	Investment mgmt svcs	....	....	28	16 7/16	28	18 9/16	12491	27 3/16	24⅝	27⅛	2.0	19	...	17.2	...	...
41	WDR.B	Cl'B'	NY	NR	133	16924		....	....	24⅛	18⅝	27⅝	18¼	8853	25⅛	23⅛	25⅛	2.1	18	...	10.6	...	...
¶42•[10]	WMT	✓Wal-Mart Stores	NY,B,Ch,P	A+	1897	1580519	Operates discount stores	20 15/16	1/64	41⅜	18¾	70¼	38 11/16	1370434	70¼	57	69⅛	0.3	55	16	70.5	83.6	46.5
43	WDN	✓Walden Residential Prop	NY,Ch	NR	113	8918	Real estate investment trust	26⅞	16¼	27⅛	19¼	21 15/16	16	24563	21⅝	20 7/16	21⅝	8.9	41	−6	17.0	4.2	13.5
44	Pr B	9.16% Sr'B'Cv Pfd([67]25)	NY	NR	16	1151		30½	23	30½	22⅝	25⅛	20 1/16	231	24⅛	23	24¾B	9.3	..	...	...	...	...
¶45•[11]	WAG	✓Walgreen Co	NY,B,Ch,P	A+	964	509151	Major retail drug chain	16 13/16	1/16	30 3/16	14¾	33 15/16	22 11/16	419706	32⅞	27¼	29¼	0.5	47	17	6.4	46.6	43.0
46	WSDI	✓Wall Street Deli	NNM	C	13	402	Operates fast food restaurants	14½	1⅛	5¼	3	5⅛	1	2674	1⅝	1	1⅛	...	d	−28	−67.3	−40.2	−35.1
#47•[2]	WCS	✓Wallace Computer Svc	NY,Ch,Ph,P	A	218	32210	Business forms:comm'l print	40⅜	⅞	40	15 7/16	27¼	14 15/16	67209	20⅝	14 15/16	16⅝	4.0	9	7	−34.9	−19.6	5.1
48•[12]	WLT	✓Walter Industries	NY	NR	97	31880	Homebuilding Prd & svcs	22	11 13/16	22⅝	10¾	16 7/16	7 15/16	18567	11½	7 15/16	10 13/16	...	14	NM	−29.2	−8.4	...
#49•[3]	WAC	✓Warnaco Group'A'	NY,Ph,P	B−	242	45348	Mfr women's intimate apparel	35 9/16	10½	44 7/16	18½	30⅝	10⅛	193937	13 7/16	10⅛	12 5/16	2.9	6	1	−50.5	−24.4	−5.5
¶50•[11]	WLA	✓Warner-Lambert	NY,B,C,Ch,P,Ph	A−	1654	559969	Drugs:toiletries:food:gum	50⅞	1 7/16	85 15/16	39⅜	93 15/16	60 13/16	569181	90	79⅜	81 15/16	1.0	43	...	10.2	50.3	47.5

Uniform Footnote Explanations-See Page 4. Other: [1]P:Cycle 1. [2]Ph:Cycle 3. [3]ASE:Cycle 3. [4]CBOE:Cycle 1. [5]CBOE:Cycle 2. [6]ASE,CBOE,P:Cycle 3. [7]CBOE,Ph:Cycle 1. [8]CBOE:Cycle 3. [9]P:Cycle 2. [10]ASE,CBOE,P,Ph:Cycle 3. [11]ASE:Cycle 1. [12]Ph:Cycle 1. [51]If com exceeds $6 for 90 con days. [52]Fiscal Dec'95 & prior in Cdn Funds. [53]If com exceeds $11.40 for 20 of 30 con trad days. [54]Ea ADS rep 3 ord. [55]Each ADR rep 10 ord shr,5p. [56]Approx. [57]Each ADR rep 1 Cl'B' shr 25 SEK. [58]11 Wk Dec'98. [59]Stk dstr of Vornado Oper Co. [60]Fr 4-1-2001 into 0.68728 com,re-spec cond. [61]Re-spec cond. [62]'Spcl Redm'fr 4-1-2001 into 1.38465 com,re-spec cond. [63]8 Mo Sep'95. [64]Fiscal Dec'95 & prior. [65]12 Mo Jul'96. [66]®$3.80,'96. [67]Fr 4-30-2006,or earlier to preserve'REIT'status. [68]To be determined.

Splits ◆ Index	Cash Divs. Ea.Yr. Since	Dividends Latest Payment Period $	Date	Ex. Div.	Total $ So Far 1999	Ind. Rate	Paid 1998	Financial Position Mil-$ Cash& Equiv.	Curr. Assets	Curr. Liab.	Balance Sheet Date	Capitalization Lg Trm Debt Mil-$	Shs. 000 Pfd.	Com.	Earnings $ Per Shr. Years End	1995	1996	1997	1998	1999	Last 12 Mos.	Interim Earnings Period	$ per Shr. 1998	1999	Index
1◆	....	5%Stk	6-11-98	5-28	...	Nil	5%Stk	102	960	328	9-30-99	724	...	±84657	Dc	v±1.18	±v0.62	±v0.63	v±0.10	E0.88↑	0.11	9 Mo Sep	v0.54	v0.55	1
2◆	....	None Since Public			...	Nil	....	112	153	42.0	6-30-99	....	...	30166	Sp	p0.10	0.38	v0.44	v0.89	Pv1.23	1.23				2
3	....	None Since Public			...	Nil	....	0.02	4.62	4.84	9-30-99	52.6	...	16367	Dc	...	...	vpd0.03	vd1.95	....	d1.89	9 Mo Sep	vd0.05	v0.01	3
4	....	Terms&trad. basis should			be checked in detail			Wrrts expire 11-1-2002				....	...	4739	Dc	...	...	...	...	....	....	Callable at 8¢[51]			4
5	....	None Paid			...	Nil	....	3.92	14.5	6.05	6-30-99	14.2	...	90715	Dc	[52]0.07	vd0.21	vd0.61	vd0.02	....	d0.13	6 Mo Jun	v0.03	vd0.08	5
6	....	None Since Public			...	Nil	....	5.70	7.71	1.86	6-30-99	0.91	...	8234	Sp	d0.43	d1.35	vd1.42	vd1.06	Pvd1.20	d1.20				6
7	....	None Since Public			...	Nil	....	54.9	73.3	32.1	9-30-99	0.87	...	24761	Dc	...	...	vpd0.01	v0.02	....	0.37	9 Mo Sep	vd0.40	vd0.05	7
8◆	....	None Since Public			...	Nil	....	225	310	50.5	9-30-99	....	...	64313	Dc	vd0.30	v0.27	v0.23	v0.39	E1.36	1.23	9 Mo Sep	v0.13	v0.97	8
9	....	None Since Public			...	Nil	....	0.08	7.18	3.95	9-30-99	4.03	...	3707	Dc	p0.07	v0.28	vd0.25	vd0.16	....	d0.01	9 Mo Sep	vd0.18	vd0.03	9
10	....	Terms&trad. basis should			be checked in detail			Wrrts expire 1-16-2002				....	...	750	Dc	...	...	...	....	....	....	Callable at 1¢[53]			10
11◆	....	Wrrt	3-22-99		Wrrt	Nil	....	9.59	89.8	50.2	9-30-99	52.2	...	15196	Dc	v0.76	v0.85	v1.06	v1.34	....	d1.06	9 Mo Sep	v0.92	vd1.48	11
12◆	....	None Since Public			...	Nil	....	198	320	27.0	6-30-99	....	...	153470	Sp	0.02	0.11	v0.22	v0.34	Pv0.42	0.42				12
13	1995	gS0.035	12-31-99	12-13	g0.07	0.07	g0.07	n/a	62.6	64.7	j6-30-99	62.0	...	9888	Dc	v0.32	v0.05	v0.54	v0.83	....	j0.97	9 Mo Sep	v0.63	v0.77	13
14◆	....	None Since Public			...	Nil	....	65.9	75.2	17.7	6-30-99	....	...	30959	Dc	...	...	...	vpd0.48	....	....	9 Mo Sep	n/a	vpd0.49	14
15◆	1992	0.26¼	4-14-99	3-31	0.26¼	0.26	0.246	78.0	729	606	12-31-98	1298	...	314000	Dc	0.59	Δd4.53	Δv1.05	vΔd0.73	....	d0.73				15
16◆	....	None Since Public			...	Nil	....	42.2	49.4	33.0	9-30-99	....	...	32156	Dc	vd0.85	vd0.55	v1.03	vd2.52	....	0.18	9 Mo Sep	vd2.55	v0.15	16
17	....	None Since Public			...	Nil	....	Equity per shr $1.18			7-04-99	p10.2	p...	★21629	Dc	...	...	...	pvd1.42	....	....	6 Mo Jun	n/a	pvd0.61	17
18	....	None Since Public			...	Nil	....	0.26	298	143	10-31-99	499	...	45502	Jl	...	...	pv1.10	vpd0.52	vd2.78	d2.79	3 Mo Oct	v0.10	v0.09	18
19	....	None Since Public			...	Nil	....	36.4	50.4	7.85	12-31-98	....	...	11413	Dc	d0.23	vd0.86	vd0.89	vd2.08	....	d2.40	9 Mo Sep	vd1.71	vd2.03	19
20◆	1989	[56]0.106	2-21-00	11-23	0.211	0.21	0.19	6.10	792	1530	j3-31-99	1700	...	p29921400	Mr	0.31	v0.39	v0.46	v0.68	E0.95	0.26	6 Mo Sep	v0.37	vd0.05	20
21	....	None Since Public			...	Nil	....	2.38	21.6	5.96	9-30-99	9.74	...	4342	Dc	v0.17	vd1.02	v0.05	v0.23	....	0.33	9 Mo Sep	v0.15	v0.25	21
22◆	....	0.003	11-15-67	10-10	...	Nil	....	24.9	437	284	7-30-99	56.2	...	15030	Oc	□1.13	□1.51	v2.62	v1.37	Pv1.91	1.91				22
23◆	1984	0.606	5-17-99	4-29	0.606	0.61	0.554	20224	105046	81375	j12-31-98	26012	...	±442000	Dc	3.03	3.94	v2.98	v2.35	E1.80	8.86	6 Mo Jun	v1.27	v7.78	23
24	....	None Since Public			...	Nil	....	Total Assets $23.6M			9-30-99	4.59	...	4068	Dc	...	...	...	v‡[58]d0.22	....	....	9 Mo Sep	n/a	vd1.18	24
25◆	1990	†Q0.48	11-16-99	11-4	†1.807	1.92	h[59]1.64	Total Assets $5.31M			9-30-99	2073	13789	85948	Dc	v1.12	v1.25	v0.79	v1.59	E3.10	1.91	9 Mo Sep	v1.19	v1.51	25
26	1997	Q0.81¼	1-3-00	12-20	3.25	3.25	3.25	Cv into 1.38465 com				....	5789	...	Dc	...	...	...	....	....	....	'REIT status'redm provision anytime[61][62]			26
27	....	None Since Public			...	Nil	....	17.7	22.0	15.4	9-30-99	1.84	...	p31650	Dc	...	...	...	vpd1.05	....	....	9 Mo Sep	n/a	vpd0.45	27
28◆	1973	Q0.036	2-22-00	1-28	0.144	0.14	0.144	0.29	25.6	13.2	9-30-99	6.34	...	2115	Dc	v0.76	v0.79	vd0.68	v0.75	....	0.69	9 Mo Sep	v0.49	v0.43	28
29	....	None Since Public			...	Nil	....	0.64	61.6	56.9	6-30-99	19.3	...	32611	Sp	‡[63]d0.03	d0.80	vp0.18	v0.27	....	0.09	9 Mo Jun	v0.20	v0.02	29
30	....	None Since Public			...	Nil	....	12.7	60.4	48.8	10-31-99	0.25	...	24534	Jl	[64]0.30	p[65]d0.57	vd2.45	v0.12	vd0.66	d0.56	3 Mo Oct	vd0.32	vd0.22	30
31	1976	Q0.20	12-15-99	12-1	0.80	0.80	0.80	47.8	50.8	18.2	9-30-99	....	...	1094	Dc	vd0.07	v1.63	v1.44	v1.23	....	0.91	6 Mo Jun	v0.69	v0.37	31
32◆	1934	Q0.19½	12-10-99	11-22	0.78	0.78	0.693	84.6	703	494	9-30-99	688	...	100049	Dc	v1.54	v1.79	v2.03	v2.50	E2.26	2.29	9 Mo Sep	v1.92	v1.71	32
33	....	None Since Public			...	Nil	....	9.98	18.7	9.10	9-30-99	0.14	...	9926	Dc	...	pd2.98	vd15.89	vd1.91	....	d1.40	9 Mo Sep	vd1.35	vd0.84	33
34◆	1973	Q0.32	1-28-00	1-5	1.28	1.28	1.28	9.94	52.1	20.4	8-31-99	14.1	...	15603	Au	1.33	v1.38	v1.37	v1.40	v1.41	1.37	3 Mo Nov	v0.24	v0.20	34
35◆	1993	Q0.04	1-27-00	1-11	0.15	0.16	0.14	32.4	443	180	9-30-99	162	482	22979	Dc	v1.34	v0.19	v0.74	v0.99	....	1.17	9 Mo Sep	v0.92	v1.10	35
36	1936	Q0.54	12-1-99	11-2	2.06	2.16	1.86	Total Deposits $39708.85M			9-30-99	8576	...	202743	Dc	v3.36	v[66]3.65	v2.94	v4.18	E4.95	4.79	9 Mo Sep	v3.01	v3.62	36
37◆	1966	Div Discontinued 5-7-99			0.15	Nil	0.29	Total Assets $465.00M			10-03-99	8.40	...	±14967	Dc	v±0.60	v±0.65	±v0.01	v□1.03	....	1.23	9 Mo Sep	v□±0.72	v±0.92	37
38◆	1993	Div Discontinued 5-7-99			0.15	Nil	0.29	....	...	...		....	...	11111	Dc	±0.60	±0.66	±v0.01	□v±1.03	....	1.23	9 Mo Sep	v±□0.72	v±0.92	38
39◆	....	None Since Public			...	Nil	....	22.7	107	36.7	10-03-99	....	...	22387	Dc	v0.25	v0.37	v0.52	v□0.74	....	0.91	9 Mo Sep	v□0.55	v0.72	39
40	1998	Q0.13¼	2-1-00	1-7	0.53	0.53	0.39¾	146	184	225	9-30-99	....	...	±57885	Dc	...	...	pv1.10	v1.27	....	1.45	9 Mo Sep	v0.94	v1.12	40
41	1999	Q0.13¼	2-1-00	1-7	0.53	0.53	....	....	...	...		....	...	31912	Dc	...	...	pv±1.10	v1.27	....	1.37	3 Mo Mar	0.25	v±0.35	41
42◆	1973	Q0.05	1-10-00	12-15	0.18⅞	0.20	0.15	1435	26955	28992	10-31-99	16559	...	4453743	Ja	v0.60	v0.67	v0.78	v0.99	E1.25	1.17	9 Mo Oct	v0.64	v0.82	42
43	1994	Q0.48¼	12-1-99	11-16	1.93	1.93	1.93	Total Assets $1497.44M			9-30-99	768	6993	25465	Dc	v□0.80	□v1.02	v□0.55	v□0.60	....	0.53	9 Mo Sep	v□0.64	v□0.57	43
44	1996	Q0.57¼	12-1-99	11-16	2.29	2.29	2.29	Cv into 1.1406 com				....	1709	...	Dc	...	...	...	....	....	....				44
45◆	1933	Q0.034	12-11-99	11-10	0.13⅛	0.135	0.12⅝	142	3222	1924	8-31-99	....	...	1004000	Au	0.33	v0.38	v0.44	v0.54	v0.62	0.62				45
46	....	None Since Public			...	Nil	....	1.22	4.68	6.88	10-02-99	....	...	2896	Je	vd0.27	vd0.72	v0.02	vd1.24	vd0.79	d0.87	3 Mo Sep	v0.01	vd0.07	46
47◆	1933	Q0.16½	3-20-00	2-28	0.64½	0.66	0.62½	13.3	458	214	10-31-99	406	...	41887	Jl	1.23	1.60	v1.86	v1.71	v1.80	1.84	3 Mo Oct	v0.40	v0.44	47
48	1999	0.03	11-30-99	11-8	0.03	[68]....	....	Total Assets $3366.73M			8-31-99	2335	...	50036	My	pd0.75	□d1.56	v0.67	v□1.08	v0.69	0.76	3 Mo Aug	v0.17	v0.24	48
49◆	1995	Q0.09	1-6-00	12-3	0.36	0.36	0.36	13.8	1045	740	10-02-99	847	...	55635	Dc	v□1.10	vd0.16	v0.42	v□0.22	E1.92↓	1.15	9 Mo Sep	v□0.72	v1.65	49
50◆	1926	Q0.20	12-10-99	11-3	0.80	0.80	0.64	1600	5049	3378	9-30-99	1281	...	858661	Dc	v0.90	v0.95	v1.04	v1.48	E1.92	....	9 Mo Sep	n/a	v1.41	50

◆**Stock Splits & Divs By Line Reference Index** [1]2-for-1,'95:5-for-4,'99. [2]2-for-1,'97. [8]2-for-1,'99(twice). [11]10%,'98. [12]3-for-2,'97:2-for-1,'98,'99. [14]To split 2-for-1,ex Jan 19,'00. [15]6-for-5,'95. [16]2-for-1,'97. [20]5-for-1,'99. [22]2-for-1,'95:3-for-2,'97. [23]5-for-1,'94:No adj for stk dstr of Swedish Match,'96. [25]2-for-1,'97. [28]2-for-1,'96:5-for-4,'98. [32]3-for-1,'99. [34]2-for-1,'97. [35]3-for-2,'94. [37]5-for-4 in Cl'B','95,'96. [38]5-for-4,'95,'96. [39]2-for-1,'96. [42]2-for-1,'99. [45]2-for-1,'95,'97,'99. [47]2-for-1,'96. [49]2-for-1,'94. [50]2-for-1,'96:3-for-1,'98.

¶ S&P 500
# MidCap 400
✣ SmallCap 600
• Options

Index	Ticker	Name of Issue (Call Price of Pfd. Stocks)	Market	Com. Rank. & Pfd. Rating	Inst. Hold Cos	Inst. Hold Shs. (000)	Principal Business	Price Range 1971-97 High	1971-97 Low	1998 High	1998 Low	1999 High	1999 Low	Dec. Sales in 100s	December, 1999 Last Sale Or Bid High	Low	Last	%Div Yield	P-E Ratio	EPS 5 Yr Growth	% Annualized Total Return 12 Mo	36 Mo	60 Mo
1	WARP	**Warp 10 Technologies[51]**	NSC	NR	2	11	Dvp stg:pub/graphic art sys	17½	⅜	5	¼	3 11/16	1	99711	3 11/16	1⅛	2 9/16	...	d	...	78.3	5.4	...
2•[1]	WFSL	**✓Washington Federal**	NNM	A	189	25395	Svgs & ln,Wash,Oregon,Idaho	28 3/16	⅝	27 15/16	20¼	25⅞	17⅝	66129	20 13/16	17⅝	19¾	4.9	10	8	−6.9	12.7	22.9
#3•[2]	WGL	**✓Washington Gas Lt**	NY,B,Ch,Ph,P	↓A–	238	16159	Natural gas:D.C.,Md,Va	31⅜	2½	30¾	23 1/16	29 7/16	21	22758	29¼	27 1/16	27½	4.4	19	1	6.8	11.9	16.5
4	WHI	**✓Washington Homes**	NY	NR	21	2238	Builds single-family homes	10⅜	3¼	6¼	3½	8⅜	4 11/16	3459	5 7/16	4 11/16	5B	...	3	59	−14.9	3.6	8.2
¶5•[3]	WM	**✓Washington Mutual**	NY,Ph	B+	976	457721	Savings bank, Pacific,NW	48 7/16	1	51 11/16	26¾	45¾	24 11/16	597948	29⅝	24 11/16	25⅞	4.0	8	19	−30.8	−1.5	21.1
#6	WPO	**✓Washington Post'B'**	NY,B,P,Ph	A–	278	5441	Newspaper, magazine, TV	491 11/16	3 11/16	605½	462	594½	490⅛	3107	574 1/16	540	555⅞	0.9	24	15	−2.9	19.6	19.5
7•[3]	WRE	**✓Washington REIT SBI**	NY,Ch,Ph,P	NR	116	6495	Real estate investm't trust	24¾	1	18¾	15 1/16	18¾	13 13/16	22770	15 9/16	13 13/16	15	7.8	12	8	−13.3	1.5	5.2
8	WSB	**✓Washington Savings Bank**	AS	B	12	156	Savings bank,Waldorf, Maryland	9⅞	¼	9⅛	3¾	4¾	3⅛	416	3⅝	3⅛	3⅛	3.2	14	−16	−28.7	−12.1	−2.3
¶9•[4]	WMI	**✓Waste Management**	NY,Ch,Ph,P	B–	1007	502865	Waste mgmt svcs	44⅛	1⅜	58 3/16	34 7/16	60	14	742000	17 7/16	14⅛	17 3/16	0.1	9	Neg	−63.1	−18.6	8.6
10	WSII	**✓Waste Systems Intl**	NNM	NR	17	8994	Dvp stage:enviro mgt svc	25	15/16	10½	2½	8⅜	2⅝	5882	5⅞	2⅝	4¾	...	d	−29	−13.6	17.1	...
11	PIK	**✓Water Pik Technologies**	NY	NR	..	...	Mfr personal hlth care prd	....	....	....	....	10½	6¾	41261	9¾	6¾	9 9/16	...	..	...	...	...	...
12	WLK	**✓Waterlink Inc**	NY,Ph	NR	30	3496	Water purify/treatm't sys	20⅝	11	18¾	2⅜	5 7/16	2¼	6421	3 3/16	2¼	2½	...	d	...	−31.0	...	...
#13•[5]	WAT	**✓Waters Corp**	NY,P	NR	399	54345	Mfr liquid chromatography inst	24 3/16	6⅝	43¾	18¼	67 11/16	36¼	75341	53	42⅞	53	...	31	26	21.5	51.7	...
✣14•[3]	WJ	**✓Watkins-Johnson**	NY,B,Ch,P,Ph	B–	92	3930	Semiconductor mfg equip	57	3 13/16	29½	16⅜	40¼	20⅛	7657	40¼	38⅛	40	...	12	Neg	100	20.0	7.9
✣15•[5]	WSO	**✓Watsco, Inc[54]**	NY,Ch	A–	157	17007	Dstrb air cond/heat'g pd	22 15/16	7/16	24 7/16	11¾	19⅞	9¾	13414	11 9/16	9⅞	11 9/16	0.9	11	22	−30.5	−14.8	20.6
16	WSO.B	**Cl'B'[56]**	AS	A–	5	49		22 11/16	3/16	23 7/16	12	19¾	9¾	306	11¼	9¾	11⅜B	0.9	13	20	−28.9	−12.7	21.4
¶17•[6]	WPI	**✓Watson Pharmaceuticals**	NY,Ph	B+	549	57291	Mfr off-patent medications	34⅛	6	63	30½	62 15/16	26½	151319	43 5/16	34	35 13/16	...	21	28	−43.0	16.9	22.3
✣18•[7]	WTS	**✓Watts Industries'A'**	NY,Ph	A–	146	14000	Mkts water & steam valves	29	6¼	31⅜	14 15/16	22¼	12 1/16	12331	14¾	12½	14¾	2.4	12	NM	...	...	...
#19•[5]	WMO	**✓Wausau-Mosinee Paper**	NY	A–	164	30268	Print,write,specialty papers	26	⅛	24⅛	12⅛	18 7/16	10⅝	17284	14⅛	11 7/16	11 11/16	2.7	14	−6	−32.8	−12.8	−5.7
20	WAVX	**✓Wave Systems 'A'**	NNM	NR	48	3094	Dvlp stage: computer sys	7 11/16	½	5⅝	11/16	29	3¾	147456	16½	10⅛	11 15/16	...	d	−5	221	76.1	31.8
21•[5]	WAVO	**✓WAVO Corp**	NNM	NR	35	2417	Dvlp stge:data broadcasting	20½	5	19⅛	3¼	10⅞	3½	164098	6	3 13/16	3⅞	...	d	−9	−51.7	−17.4	−8.4
22	WPK	**WBK 10%'STRYPES' Trust**	NY	NR	23	5574	Struct Yld Prd Exch For Stk	34¼	26½	36⅜	24½	36 9/16	28½	7242	32 9/16	31 5/16	32 1/16	9.8	..	...	12.0	...	...
#23•[8]	WFT	**✓Weatherford Intl**	NY,Ch	B–	388	77604	Oil & gas ind services/equip	73	¼	58 7/16	15	42⅛	16¾	136627	39 15/16	31 9/16	39 15/16	...	d	Neg	106	16.3	45.8
24•[5]	WBB	**✓Webb (Del) Corp**	NY,B,Ch,P,Ph	B+	129	13344	Real estate development	38	2	34⅞	17 1/16	29	19 9/16	8654	24 15/16	21½	24⅞	...	7	NM	−9.7	15.6	8.0
25	WEBB	**✓WEBB Interactive Svcs**	NSC	NR	6	47	Dvlp,mkt World Wide Websites	12⅝	1¼	16	3¼	23¼	7½	80751	23¼	14¼	22¾	...	d	...	73.3	78.5	...
26	WEB	**✓Webco Industries**	AS,P	NR	30	1392	Mfr steel tubing/pipe	17¼	4 13/16	10 3/16	5½	6 15/16	2½	4846	3½	2½	3 5/16	...	33	80	−50.0	−14.2	−17.7
27	WLNK	**✓WebLink Wireless'A'[63]**	NNM	NR	49	26358	Wireless messaging svcs	13¼	4⅜	10⅞	5	18⅝	3¾	98092	18⅝	7 11/16	15½	...	d	...	179	32.8	...
28	EWA	**WEBS,Australia Index Series**	AS	NR	17	266	World Equity Benchmark Shrs	11⅞	8 9/16	10⅝	7⅜	11⅝	9 9/16	1797	11 1/16	10 3/16	11 1/16	2.3	..	...	19.4	3.5	...
29	EWO	**WEBS,Austria Index Series**	AS	NR	4	991	World Equity Benchmark Shrs	11¾	9⅞	14	8¾	10⅜	8⅛	2075	8 13/16	8⅛	8 5/16	7.9	..	...	−14.3	−5.1	...
30	EWK	**WEBS,Belgium Index Series**	AS	NR	4	343	World Equity Benchmark Shrs	18⅜	14 9/16	25 11/16	16⅛	22½	15	1319	16½	15	16⅛	13.1	..	...	−14.2	13.6	...
31	EWC	**WEBS,Canada Index Series**	AS	NR	5	165	World Equity Benchmark Shrs	14¾	10¼	15⅝	9¾	16¾	11½	1066	16¾	14 11/16	16½	3.5	..	...	48.8	15.3	...
32	EWQ	**WEBS,France Index Series**	AS	NR	20	1124	World Equity Benchmark Shrs	16 9/16	12½	23¼	14⅝	27⅝	20 5/16	6776	27⅝	25	27⅝	0.9	..	...	31.8	27.1	...
33	EWG	**WEBS,Germany Index Series**	AS	NR	26	1699	World Equity Benchmark Shrs	18 7/16	12 13/16	25⅞	16½	26 11/16	19 5/16	15741	26 11/16	22½	26 11/16	3.1	..	...	22.6	24.8	...
34	EWH	**WEBS,Hong Kong Index Series**	AS	NR	17	1446	World Equity Benchmark Shrs	18 3/16	9⅞	11 7/16	5 5/16	14½	8 1/16	12348	14½	13 3/16	14¼	2.7	..	...	56.7	2.5	...
35	EWI	**WEBS,Italy Index Series**	AS	NR	16	742	World Equity Benchmark Shrs	20 1/16	13	30¾	19 13/16	30⅜	20⅝	4322	25	21 15/16	25	9.3	..	...	0.8	27.2	...
36	EWJ	**WEBS,Japan Index Series**	AS	NR	65	15633	World Equity Benchmark Shrs	16 9/16	9 9/16	11¾	7⅝	16 5/16	9 11/16	106082	16 5/16	14⅞	16 5/16	1.0	..	...	60.8	8.1	...
37	EWM	**WEBS,Malaysia(Free)Index Series**	AS	NR	20	2472	World Equity Benchmark Shrs	16⅛	4 11/16	6¾	1⅝	7 3/16	2⅞	35358	7 3/16	5⅛	7 1/16	2.8	..	...	106	−19.6	...
38	EWW	**WEBS,Mexico(Free)Index Series**	AS	NR	..	...	World Equity Benchmark Shrs	17¾	10⅛	16½	6 13/16	18⅛	7 11/16	6559	18⅛	15½	18 1/16	2.3	..	...	77.4	19.4	...
39	EWN	**WEBS,Netherlands Index Series**	AS	NR	12	415	World Equity Benchmark Shrs	24¾	16 5/16	30 5/16	20 1/16	27 9/16	22⅛	1357	25 5/16	22 11/16	25 5/16	8.6	..	...	5.8	16.4	...
40	EWS	**WEBS,Singapore(Free)Index Series**	AS	NR	24	1608	World Equity Benchmark Shrs	12 15/16	6½	7 7/16	3 1/16	9 7/16	5¼	18950	9 7/16	8 5/16	9 3/16	1.6	..	...	52.6	−6.9	...
41	EWP	**WEBS,Spain Index Series**	AS	NR	13	439	World Equity Benchmark Shrs	22¼	13⅜	32⅜	20 7/16	33 13/16	24¼	2344	28¾	26⅞	28¼	4.0	..	...	−1.4	22.7	...
42	EWD	**WEBS,Sweden Index Series**	AS	NR	3	131	World Equity Benchmark Shrs	21 5/16	13 5/16	24 15/16	13 15/16	30 1/16	18¾	1138	30 1/16	26	29½	5.7	..	...	62.8	26.5	...
43	EWL	**WEBS,Switzerland Index Series**	AS	NR	16	409	World Equity Benchmark Shrs	16 11/16	11½	20 11/16	12 9/16	18 7/16	14 13/16	6204	16¼	15 7/16	16	7.8	..	...	−3.5	15.5	...
44	EWU	**WEBS,U.K. Index Series**	AS	NR	24	1122	World Equity Benchmark Shrs	18½	12	22 5/16	16¼	22⅞	19⅜	11083	21⅝	20⅝	21 7/16	6.4	..	...	12.0	16.8	...
45	WEBT	**✓WebTrends Corp**	NNM	NR	99	4787	Internet access software	....	....	....	....	100	13	59860	100	55	81	...	..	...	...	...	...
46	WGNR	**✓Wegener Corp**	NSC	B–	8	259	Provides cable TV prod/svcs	16⅛	5/16	3¾	1 5/16	4	1⅜	23506	3⅜	2⅛	2 5/16	...	..	−21	29.8	−16.3	−2.5
47	WNI	**✓Weider Nutrition Intl'A'**	NY	NR	31	3428	Mfr nutritional supplements	19¾	10⅜	17½	3 13/16	7 9/16	3	14344	4 9/16	3⅛	3 11/16	4.1	d	...	−39.1	...	...
48	WRI	**✓Weingarten Rlty SBI**	NY,Ch,Ph,P	NR	136	8795	Real estate investment trust	45⅝	¼	46⅞	35 15/16	45⅝	37	9980	39⅜	37	38 15/16	7.3	10	5	−6.4	5.1	7.2
49•[7]	WS	**✓Weirton Steel**	NY,Ch,Ph	C	29	7916	Major integrated steelmaker	15⅜	2	4 9/16	1 7/16	8	1 7/16	104494	8	3	6 13/16	...	d	Neg	336	24.9	−5.4
50	WMK	**✓Weis Markets**	NY,B,Ch,Ph	A–	72	17106	Food supermkts,PA,MD,NY,WV,VA	41⅝	1⅝	38⅞	33¼	44 5/16	32⅞	4837	44 5/16	38 5/16	43½	2.4	22	2	15.1	14.1	15.7

Uniform Footnote Explanations-See Page 4. Other: [1]P:Cycle 2. [2]P:Cycle 1. [3]ASE:Cycle 1. [4]ASE,CBOE,Ph:Cycle 1. [5]Ph:Cycle 2. [6]ASE,CBOE:Cycle 2. [7]Ph:Cycle 3. [8]CBOE:Cycle 2.
[51]Results prior to'97 in Cdn$. [52]Reflects Dec'98 East Enviro Svcs acquis. [53]Pfd in $M. [54]Ltd vtg. [55]Incl current amts. [56]Cv into 1 Cl'A'. [57]Stk dstr of Circo Intl Inc. [58]Excl subsidiary pfd stk.
[59]Fiscal Aug'96 & prior. [60]12 Mo Dec'97:Aug'97 earn $1.34. [61]Re-spec cond. [62]Final div. [63]Formerly PageMart Wireless'A'. [64]Incl $0.1763 return of cap,'98.

Index	Splits ♦ Cash Divs. Ea.Yr. Since	Dividends: Latest Payment Period $	Date	Ex. Div.	Total $ So Far 1999	Ind. Rate	Paid 1998	Financial Position Mil-$ Cash& Equiv.	Curr. Assets	Curr. Liab.	Balance Sheet Date	Capitalization Lg Trm Debt Mil-$	Shs. 000 Pfd.	Com.	Earnings $ Per Shr. Years End	1995	1996	1997	1998	1999	Last 12 Mos.	Interim Earnings Period	$ per Shr. 1998	1999	Index
1	....	None Paid			...	Nil	....	0.83	0.88	0.09	7-31-99	.....	...	25685	Jl	...	d0.18	vd0.24	vd0.07	vd0.09	d0.11	3 Mo Oct	vd0.01	vd0.03	1
2♦	1983	Q0.24	1-28-00	1-5	0.898	0.96	0.816	Total Assets $5739M			6-30-99	955	...	54659	Sp	1.34	1.41	v1.83	v1.93	vP2.05	2.05				2
3♦	1852	Q0.30½	2-1-00	1-6	1.215	1.22	1.19½	26.9	250	285	9-30-99	506	283	46474	Sp	1.45	v1.85	v1.85	v1.54	v1.47	1.47				3
4	....	0.05	10-7-94	9-20	...	Nil	....	Total Assets $179.45M			10-31-99	76.4	...	7929	Jl	±0.64	±0.47	v±□d1.62	±v0.48	±v1.30	1.46	3 Mo Oct	v±0.16	v±0.32	4
5♦	1986	Q0.26	11-15-99	10-27	0.98	1.04	0.82	Total Deposits $81624.49M			9-30-99	52532	...	577304	Dc	v1.44	v0.54	v1.24	v2.56	E3.25	2.64	9 Mo Sep	v2.29	v2.37	5
6	1956	Q1.30	11-5-99	10-20	5.20	5.20	5.00	47.4	379	416	10-03-99	398	12	±p9378	Dc	v±17.15	v±20.05	v±26.15	v±41.10	E23.21	22.49	9 Mo Sep	v±34.79	v±16.18	6
7	1962	Q0.29¼	12-30-99	12-9	1.15¾	1.17	1.11	Total Assets $602M			9-30-99	326	...	35721	Dc	v0.88	v0.88	v0.90	v1.15	....	1.23	9 Mo Sep	v0.87	v0.95	7
8	1993	S0.05	9-17-99	9-1	0.10	0.10	0.10	Book Value $5.43			10-31-98	0.33	...	4424	Jl	0.50	0.52	v0.24	v0.39	Pv0.23	0.22	3 Mo Oct	v0.05	v0.04	8
9	1998	0.01	10-19-99	9-28	0.02	0.02	0.01	222	4797	5883	9-30-99	8713	...	619630	Dc	v0.54	v0.37	v□1.26	v□[52]d1.31	E1.90	d0.33	9 Mo Sep	vd1.44	vd0.46	9
10♦	....	None Since Public			...	Nil	....	2.46	14.7	21.6	9-30-99	172	...	20331	Dc	vd4.08	vd4.90	v□d1.51	v□d0.97	....	d1.72	9 Mo Sep	v□d0.64	v□d1.39	10
11	....	None Since Public			...	Nil	....	....	68.2	41.4	p9-30-99	40.9	...	9453	Dc	...	...	...	pv1.01	....	....	9 Mo Sep	n/a	vp0.51	11
12	....	None Since Public			...	Nil	....	1.73	87.4	52.5	9-30-99	78.4	...	12636	Sp	...	p0.28	v□0.10	vd1.46	vd0.33	d0.33				12
13♦	....	None Since Public			...	Nil	....	4.31	253	178	9-30-99	123	[53]9	62190	Dc	p□v0.27	v□0.30	vd0.16	v1.13	....	1.69	9 Mo Sep	v0.65	v1.21	13
14	1974	Div Deferred 11-22-99			0.48	Nil	0.48	110	183	49.9	9-24-99	5.87	...	6627	Dc	v3.58	v0.37	v3.99	vd6.36	....	3.26	9 Mo Sep	vd6.16	v3.46	14
15♦	1984	Q0.02½	10-29-99	10-13	0.10	0.10	0.072	7.26	430	101	9-30-99	[55]176	...	±29134	Dc	v±0.46	v±0.61	v±0.68	v±0.89	....	1.02	9 Mo Sep	v±0.74	v±0.87	15
16♦	1975	Q0.02½	10-29-99	10-13	0.10	0.10	0.072	....	...	...		....	...	3194	Dc	v±0.46	v±0.61	±v0.68	v±0.89	....	0.91	3 Mo Mar	v±0.06	v±0.08	16
17♦	....	None Since Public			...	Nil	....	113	373	91.9	9-30-99	150	...	95980	Dc	v0.56	v0.89	v1.01	v1.32	E1.75	1.48	9 Mo Sep	v0.92	v1.08	17
18♦	1986	Q0.08¾	12-10-99	11-23	h[57]0.35	0.35	0.35	5.04	379	106	9-30-99	117	...	±26474	Je	±1.54	±d1.70	±v1.89	v1.95	v±1.34	1.19	3 Mo Sep	v0.46	v0.31	18
19♦	1960	Q0.08	2-14-00	1-27	0.31	0.32	0.273	2.54	259	110	9-30-99	228	[58]...	51417	Dc	0.85	[59]1.12	v[60]1.12	v0.73	....	0.83	9 Mo Sep	v0.56	v0.66	19
20	....	None Since Public			...	Nil	....	13.1	14.7	4.29	9-30-99	....	.4	±40249	Dc	±d0.50	±d0.64	±d0.78	v±d0.44	....	d0.59	9 Mo Sep	±vd0.35	±vd0.50	20
21	....	None Since Public			...	Nil	....	2.74	9.54	7.94	9-30-99	0.06	502	28924	Dc	vd1.57	vd0.76	vd1.29	vd1.38	....	d1.07	9 Mo Sep	vd0.91	vd0.60	21
22	1997	Q0.78⅜	11-15-99	10-28	3.13½	3.14	3.13½	At maturity Westpac Banking com or cash[61]				....	...	32840	Dc	...	...	...	....	....	....	Mature 11-15-2000			22
23♦	....	0.01	4-23-84	4-24	...	Nil	....	21.2	852	608	9-30-99	628	...	108088	Dc	v0.38	□v2.39	□v1.77	v0.66	....	d0.35	9 Mo Sep	v0.91	vd0.10	23
24	1990	[62]0.05	9-11-98	8-12	...	Nil	[62]0.15	Total Assets $1982.04M			9-30-99	1108	...	18223	Je	1.87	d0.44	□v2.22	v2.30	v3.11	3.40	3 Mo Sep	v0.45	v0.74	24
25	....	None Since Public			...	Nil	....	6.45	6.92	2.44	9-30-99	2.67	85	7741	Dc	d0.19	vd0.55	vd1.05	vd4.35	....	d4.38	9 Mo Sep	vd2.38	vd2.41	25
26	....	None Since Public			...	Nil	....	0.23	56.0	19.9	10-31-99	45.9	...	7074	Jl	d0.07	0.37	v0.55	v0.86	v0.26	0.10	3 Mo Oct	v0.17	v0.01	26
27	....	None Since Public			...	Nil	....	6.21	70.0	109	9-30-99	523	...	±40608	Dc	pd1.44	vd1.30	vd1.10	□vd1.03	....	d2.21	9 Mo Sep	v□d0.67	vd1.85	27
28	1996	0.017	12-30-99	12-21	0.252	0.25	0.183	Net Asset Val $9.99			8-31-99	0.99	...	5400	Au	...	§10.15	§10.35	§7.75	§9.99	....	Book-Entry Form			28
29	1998	0.102	8-31-99	8-25	0.102	0.66	0.664	Net Asset Val $9.13			8-31-99	0.08	...	1400	Au	...	§10.40	§10.51	§10.11	§9.13	....	Book-Entry Form			29
30	1996	2.113	8-31-99	8-25	2.113	2.11	3.57	Net Asset Val $16.07			8-31-99	1.66	...	840	Au	...	§14.99	§15.64	§18.40	§16.07	....	Book-Entry Form			30
31	1996	0.004	12-30-99	12-21	0.57	0.57	0.697	Net Asset Val $13.22			8-31-99	0.37	...	700	Au	...	§10.60	§13.43	§9.90	§13.22	....	Book-Entry Form			31
32	1996	0.248	8-31-99	8-25	0.248	0.25	0.404	Net Asset Val $22.90			8-31-99	....	...	3401	Au	...	§12.73	§14.50	§19.13	§22.90	....	Book-Entry Form			32
33	1996	0.566	12-30-99	12-21	0.814	0.82	0.312	Net Asset Val $21.17			8-31-99	1.21	...	4801	Au	...	§13.64	§16.31	§20.25	§21.17	....	Book-Entry Form			33
34	1996	0.132	12-30-99	12-21	0.383	0.38	0.409	Net Asset Val $11.83			8-31-99	1.37	...	6526	Au	...	§13.05	§14.73	§6.41	§11.83	....	Book-Entry Form			34
35	1996	2.084	8-31-99	8-25	2.084	2.33	2.332	Net Asset Val $21.56			8-31-99	4.73	...	2700	Au	...	§13.79	§16.66	§22.89	§21.56	....	Book-Entry Form			35
36	1997	0.11	12-30-99	12-21	0.159	0.16	0.011	Net Asset Val $13.22			8-31-99	0.46	...	54001	Au	...	§14.33	§12.61	§8.39	§13.22	....	Book-Entry Form			36
37	1996	0.017	8-31-99	8-25	0.017	0.20	[64]0.24½	Net Asset Val $5.59			8-31-99	....	...	17025	Au	...	§13.80	§8.23	§2.11	§5.59	....	Book-Entry Form			37
38	1996	0.088	8-31-99	8-25	0.088	0.42	0.42	Net Asset Val $13.39			8-31-99	0.07	...	1600	Au	...	§11.52	§15.11	§8.11	§13.39	....	Book-Entry Form			38
39	1996	1.774	8-31-99	8-25	1.774	2.18	1.971	Net Asset Val $23.45			8-31-99	2.38	...	1351	Au	...	§17.36	§21.42	§23.50	§23.45	....	Book-Entry Form			39
40	1996	0.093	12-30-99	12-21	0.152	0.15	0.12	Net Asset Val $7.93			8-31-99	0.06	...	14300	Au	...	§11.38	§8.66	§3.30	§7.93	....	Book-Entry Form			40
41	1996	1.086	8-31-99	8-25	1.086	1.12	1.121	Net Asset Val $25.59			8-31-99	1.34	...	1425	Au	...	§14.09	§18.49	§23.84	§25.59	....	Book-Entry Form			41
42	1996	1.01	12-30-99	12-21	1.69	1.69	1.007	Net Asset Val $22.26			8-31-99	0.58	...	900	Au	...	§14.67	§18.32	§18.39	§22.26	....	Book-Entry Form			42
43	1996	0.391	8-31-99	8-25	0.391	1.25	1.247	Net Asset Val $15.39			8-31-99	0.90	...	2501	Au	...	§12.29	§13.79	§15.55	§15.39	....	Book-Entry Form			43
44	1996	0.396	12-30-99	12-21	1.373	1.37	0.589	Net Asset Val $20.25			8-31-99	5.01	...	5601	Au	...	§13.15	§16.50	§18.48	§20.25	....	Book-Entry Form			44
45	....	None Since Public			...	Nil	....	77.5	82.2	6.99	9-30-99	.....	...	12747	Dc	...	...	v0.04	v0.02	....	0.14	9 Mo Sep	v0.01	v0.13	45
46	....	None Since Public			...	Nil	....	8.86	19.6	5.60	9-03-99	0.90	...	11683	Au	0.05	0.16	vd0.19	v0.23	v0.02	Nil	3 Mo Nov	v0.02	vNil	46
47	1997	Q0.03¾	12-20-99	12-8	0.15	0.15	0.15	2.25	126	145	8-31-99	4.70	...	±25042	My	...	p0.69	p0.17	v0.56	vd0.35	d0.41	3 Mo Aug	v0.07	v0.01	47
48	1958	Q0.71	12-15-99	11-29	2.84	2.84	2.68	Total Assets $1250.14M			9-30-99	564	8900	26692	Dc	v1.69	v2.03	v2.05	v□2.08	E3.90	2.11	9 Mo Sep	v□1.55	v□1.58	48
49	....	0.16	12-15-90	11-26	...	Nil	....	75.3	425	256	9-30-99	305	[53]23	41580	Dc	v□1.26	v□d1.05	vd0.42	vd0.15	....	d1.53	9 Mo Sep	v0.16	vd1.22	49
50	1940	Q0.26	11-19-99	11-3	1.02	1.04	0.98	408	582	104	9-25-99	....	...	41690	Dc	v1.84	v1.87	v1.87	v2.00	....	1.95	9 Mo Sep	v1.48	v1.43	50

♦**Stock Splits & Divs By Line Reference Index** [2]10%,'94,'95,'96,'97,'98,'99. [3]2-for-1,'95. [5]3-for-2,'98. [10]1-for-5 REVERSE,'98. [13]2-for-1,'99. [15]3-for-2,'95,'96,'98. [16]3-for-2,'95,'96,'98. [17]2-for-1,'97. [18]2-for-1,'94:No adj for stk dstr,'99. [19]4-for-3,'94:10%,'94:5-for-4,'96. [23]2-for-1,'97.

¶ S&P 500
\# MidCap 400
✣ SmallCap 600
• Options

Index	Ticker	Name of Issue (Call Price of Pfd. Stocks)	Market	Com. Rank. & Pfd. Rating	Inst. Hold Cos	Inst. Hold Shs. (000)	Principal Business	Price Range 1971-97 High	1971-97 Low	1998 High	1998 Low	1999 High	1999 Low	December, 1999 Dec. Sales in 100s	Last Sale Or Bid High	Low	Last	%Div Yield	P-E Ratio	EPS 5 Yr Growth	% Annualized Total Return 12 Mo	36 Mo	60 Mo
1	WLC	✔Wellco Enterprises	AS	B–	5	65	Footwear mfr: shoe mchy	20⅞	⅜	14¼	9⅜	10⅛	5¼	127	7⅞	7	6⅝B	3.0	d	Neg	–26.7	–12.3	9.4
2	RPP	Wellington Properties Trust	AS	NR	1	1	Real estate investment trust	6 13/16	3 13/16	10 9/16	3 13/16	7	¾	747	2¾	2⅛	2½	s17.6	d	–24	–33.3	–10.6	...
#3•[1]	WLM	✔Wellman Inc	NY,P	B	163	26070	Mfr/recycles textile fibers	43	6	26 7/16	9	19	8¼	35447	19	15½	18⅝	1.9	d	Neg	87.8	5.2	–6.4
¶4•[2]	WLP	✔Wellpoint Hlth Networks	NY,Ch,P	B+	498	58672	Hlth care svcs,California	61⅛	23	87⅞	42 1/16	97	48¼	62232	67⅝	58	65 15/16	...	15	6	–24.2	24.2	25.5
¶5•[3]	WFC	✔Wells Fargo	NY,B,C,Ch,P,Ph	A	1573	1053028	Comm'l banking,Minneapolis	39½	1	43⅞	27½	49 15/16	32 3/16	847331	48⅝	38½	40 7/16	2.0	18	3	3.2	29.0	33.5
6	WRP	✔Wellsford Real Properties	AS	NR	67	16379	Land dvlp/investments	17¼	10½	15⅝	6¾	12¼	7⅝	15123	8⅞	7 11/16	8½	...	18	...	–17.6	...	...
7	WGA	✔Wells-Gardner Electr	AS	B–	16	900	Video monitors:TV receivers	20 1/16	¼	6 7/16	2¼	4 1/16	1⅞	1423	3 5/16	2¾	3⅛	s...	45	NM	28.2	–7.7	5.1
8	WMD	✔Wendt-Bristol Health Svcs	AS	B–	1	18	Nursing homes/medical svcs	7 13/16	5/16	1⅝	1	1 11/16	⅝	1042	13/16	⅝	⅝	...	d	–48	–52.4	–25.3	7.4
9	WENPrT	Wendy's Fin $2.50 'TECONS'([52]51.50)	[4]	BBB–	55	3027	Subsid Wendy's Intl	62⅛	49	56⅝	46 13/16	64¼	46 11/16	9669	51¾	46 11/16	47⅞	5.2	..	...	...	...	...
¶10•[5]	WEN	✔Wendy's Intl	NY,B,Ch,Ph,P	A–	417	75195	Fast food restaurant:franch'g	27 15/16	1 1/16	25 3/16	18⅛	31 11/16	19 11/16	102137	22½	19 11/16	20 13/16	1.2	16	2	–3.7	1.6	8.9
✣11•[6]	WERN	✔Werner Enterprises	NNM	A+	179	25787	Motor carrier,gen'l freight	21 5/16	2¾	22⅜	11¼	22¼	12¼	51899	15⅝	12¼	14 1/16	0.7	11	13	–20.1	–0.5	2.7
12	WCSTF	✔Wescast Industries 'A'	NNM	NR	27	2143	Mfr exhaust manifolds	37½	7½	31 11/16	21	34	20 11/16	890	24	20 15/16	21¼	1.5	3	26	–26.2	–2.4	19.1
13	WSC	✔Wesco Financial	AS([10]),B,P	B+	68	6414	Prop & casualty insur/metal sv	339⅞	2 1/16	395	280	354	241½	384	277	241½	245	0.5	45	22	–30.7	9.8	16.9
14	WCC	✔WESCO International	NY	NR	72	13551	Dstr elect prod & supplies	....	....	....	....	22⅞	5½	27935	8⅞	6 5/16	8⅞	...	d	...	...	...	...
✣15	WJCO	✔Wesley Jessen VisionCare	NNM	NR	154	15302	Mfr soft contact lenses	39⅝	13	40¼	16⅛	40 15/16	20¼	25595	40 15/16	28 7/16	37⅞	...	21	...	36.5	...	...
16•[7]	WMAR	✔West Marine	NNM	NR	72	4871	Oper retail boat'g supply strs	41½	6¾	30⅛	6⅜	15¼	7½	14848	8¾	7¾	8¼	...	41	–27	–16.5	–33.7	–2.9
17	WQP	West Penn Pwr 8.00% 'QUIDS'	NY	....[54]	1	.2	Qtly Income Debt Securities	26 13/16	24	26⅜	25⅛	25⅞	22⅞	831	24½	22⅞	23B	8.7	..	...	–1.9	5.2	...
18	WST	✔West Pharmaceutical Services	NY,Ph	B	111	8878	Pharmaceutical packaging	35 1/16	1 5/16	35 11/16	25¾	40 7/16	30⅞	1626	35	30⅞	30 15/16	2.2	12	–4	–11.7	5.1	4.4
19	WTSC	✔West TeleServices	NNM	NR	67	5187	Telecommunication svcs	25½	10⅛	18¼	8⅜	25⅛	7¼	14314	25⅛	16⅞	24 7/16	...	32	18	151	2.4	...
20	WSTF	✔Westaff Inc	NNM	NR	28	2054	Temp staffing services	12 1/16	4½	21 11/16	5 13/16	9 13/16	4½	10717	9	5⅜	8¼	...	18	–5	32.0	13.3	...
#21	WABC	✔Westamerica Bancorporation	NNM,Ch	A	171	14665	Commercial bkg,California	35	1¼	37¼	23⅜	37½	26⅜	31238	32⅛	26⅜	27 15/16	2.6	15	15	–22.5	15.2	25.3
22	WE	✔Westcoast Energy	NY,To,B,Ch,P,Ph,Mo,Vc	B+	92	21122	Gas pipeline oper, Canada	23½	5	25 7/16	17⅜	20 13/16	15 3/16	5197	16 9/16	15 3/16	16 1/16	◆5.5	5	...	–13.7	4.9	6.5
23	WES	✔Westcorp, Inc	NY,Ph	B	46	3978	Svgs&loan,California	23⅞	3½	20 5/16	5½	16⅝	6⅜	3849	16	14	14½	1.4	11	–49	113	–11.0	16.5
24•[1]	WSTL	✔Westell Technologies'A'	NNM	NR	51	4398	Dvlp telecommunication prd	56	6½	15¼	2¾	13	3 13/16	205764	13	8⅞	10¾	...	d	Neg	121	–22.3	...
25•[7]	WDC	✔Western Digital	NY,B,Ch,P,Ph	C	108	23615	Mfr computer hard disk drives	54¾	⅛	22 1/16	7⅛	21 7/16	2¾	521115	4½	3½	4 3/16	...	d	Neg	–72.2	–47.1	–12.9
26	WGR	✔Western Gas Resources	NY	B–	111	15250	Oper nat'l gas process'g ctrs	45⅛	8⅝	22⅛	5 5/16	20	3⅞	15803	13¾	10⅞	13 3/16	1.5	d	Neg	135	–10.4	–5.9
27	Pr A	$2.625 cm Cv Pfd([55]51.313)	NY	B+	25	2104		51	30	42¾	32⅛	36 13/16	26 11/16	942	29½	26 11/16	26¾	9.8	..	...	...	...	...
28	WIR	✔Western Properties Tr SBI	AS,Ch,P	NR	48	2808	Real estate investment trust	21	9 15/16	15 5/16	10⅞	12 11/16	9⅜	14218	10	9⅜	9 9/16	11.7	9	5	–10.4	–1.3	3.2
29•[1]	WR	✔Western Resources	NY,B,Ch,P,Ph	B+	200	24890	Electric & gas utility	43 7/16	7¼	44 3/16	32 9/16	33⅞	16 13/16	148117	19 9/16	16 13/16	16 15/16	12.6	10	Neg	–44.7	–12.6	–3.9
30	WSH	✔Western Star Trucks Hldg	AS	NR	10	1998	Dsgn,builds heavy duty trucks	33¼	19 7/16	22½	9⅞	19½	12¾	614	18¼	16¼	16¼	◆1.7	6	–39	32.2	–11.4	...
31•[8]	WWCA	✔Western Wireless'A'	NNM	NR	273	43427	Wireless communic svcs	25½	10	24⅝	14½	75¼	19¾	221606	68	46¾	66¾	...	d	–29	...	...	...
32	WEA	✔Westfield America	NY	NR	75	4441	Real estate investment trust	17 13/16	14¼	18¾	15 11/16	18¼	12	12442	13¾	12	12 5/16	11.8	68	...	–21.7	...	...
33	WAB	✔Westinghouse Air Brake	NY,Ch,Ph,P	NR	85	21814	Mfr train air brakes	28 15/16	8⅝	29 13/16	17⅛	25 15/16	16 3/16	26194	18⅜	16 3/16	17¾	0.2	9	14	–27.2	12.3	...
34	WI	✔Westminster Capital	AS	NR	2	63	Buy'g/phone svc,sak display	....	....	....	....	3⅝	2½	529	3¼	2½	3¼	...	17	NM	...	...	...
35	WLB	✔Westmoreland Coal	AS	C	8	1590	Coal mining/electric svc	65¼	½	4⅝	⅛	4 15/16	2⅝	2452	3⅝	2 11/16	3¼	...	d	Neg	–14.7	48.1	–13.6
36	Pr	Ser'A'cm[57]Cv[58]ExPfd([59]25.638)	AS	C	6	198		29	6	18	4½	20⅜	15⅝	185	18	15⅝	15½B	...	..	...	...	...	...
37	WN	✔Weston (George) Ltd	To,Mo,Vc	A–	13	1271	Food prd,dstr,retail: paper	41 3/16	⅞	60	37 5/16	65¾	46⅞	13638	57 5/16	49½	55¼	0.9	5	64	–4.9	36.6	33.0
38	WSTNA	✔Weston(Roy F)'A'	NNM	C	29	3804	Environmental consult'g svcs	23	2⅛	4⅜	2¼	3½	1⅞	7751	2 7/16	1⅞	2 1/16	...	21	91	–25.0	–16.2	–18.5
39	WBK	✔Westpac Banking ADS[60]	NY,Ch,Ph,P	NR	30	2223	Commercial banking,Australia	32 15/16	8⅜	37¼	25¾	38⅞	29⅜	1114	35	33⅜	34⅜	4.1	14	10	7.4	11.1	20.4
#40•[9]	WXS	✔Westpoint Stevens	NY	NR	180	27596	Hshld prod,apparel,txtls	24 1/16	5⅝	37⅞	21¾	37 9/16	15 3/16	80783	21⅛	15 3/16	17½	0.5	10	NM	–44.4	5.6	19.6
¶41•[10]	W	✔Westvaco Corp	NY,B,Ch,P,Ph	B	372	78557	Printing & converting paper	37½	1 15/16	34⅛	21	33½	20 13/16	38154	33½	29⅜	32⅝	2.7	29	–6	25.9	7.6	7.7
#42•[11]	WON	✔Westwood One	NY,Ph	B–	212	31792	Produces nat'l radio prog'ms	38	1⅛	36½	15½	76	22 13/16	53966	76	53	76	...	..	NM	149	66.0	50.8
✣43•[12]	WTSLA	✔Wet Seal Cl'A'	NNM	B–	124	7460	Retail:womens casual apparel	41⅛	2¼	38¼	13⅜	47	11½	35892	13 11/16	11½	12¼	...	7	NM	–59.4	–16.9	22.9
¶44•[12]	WY	✔Weyerhaeuser Co	NY,B,C,Ch,P,Ph	B+	770	152393	Timber products: cartons	63 15/16	13 11/16	62	36¾	73 15/16	49 9/16	207820	72 15/16	59⅝	71 13/16	2.2	23	–11	45.2	18.4	17.6
45	WFSI	✔WFS Financial	NNM	NR	42	3308	Auto loan financing svcs	24¾	8⅜	14⅞	4¼	23 15/16	5	2179	22⅝	20⅛	21⅛	...	15	Neg	238	2.1	...
¶46•[9]	WHR	✔Whirlpool Corp	NY,B,C,Ch,P,Ph	B	495	65298	Major household appliances	73½	5½	75¼	43 11/16	78¼	40 15/16	67687	65 13/16	56¾	65 1/16	2.1	14	–10	20.3	14.5	7.9
47	WHT	✔White Electronic Designs	AS	NR	13	3153	Dsgn/mfr memory circuit prd	44⅞	¼	2 15/16	¾	5½	15/16	27075	5½	3⅜	4¾	...	40	NM	262	41.2	10.1
48	Pr	$3.00 cm Cv Sr vtg Pfd(25)	AS	NR	1	20		72	25	39½	19½	71	24½	111	71	45⅛	61½	4.9	..	...	...	...	...
49	WTM	✔White Mountains Insurance Grp	NY,B,Ch,P,Ph	B	70	2258	Property & casualty insur	124	24⅛	153¼	117	150	115	3263	121	115	120½	1.3	7	NM	–12.9	9.1	11.7
50	WHJI	✔Whitehall Jewellers	NNM	NR	85	7368	Operate spcl jewelry stores	28¼	8	20½	9½	38	12 5/16	11145	38	30⅜	36⅞	...	24	...	105	46.9	...

Uniform Footnote Explanations-See Page 4. Other: [1]CBOE:Cycle 2. [2]ASE,CBOE:Cycle 1. [3]ASE,CBOE,P,Ph:Cycle 1. [4]NY [5]P:Cycle 3. [6]Ph:Cycle 3. [7]ASE:Cycle 1. [8]Ph:Cycle 2. [9]CBOE:Cycle 3. [10]P:Cycle 1. [11]Ph:Cycle 1. [12]CBOE:Cycle 1. [51]Spl div. [52]Term Cv Shrs Sr 'A'. [53]Into Wendy's Intl com to 9-15-2026. [54]Rated'A' by S&P. [55]Thru 2-15-2000,scale to $50 in 2004. [56]Stk dstr of Voice Stream Wireless Corp,'99. [57]Dep for 0.25 shr Ser'A'Cv Exch Pfd. [58]Co opt exch for $100 amt 8.50%Cv 2012. [59]Thru 6-30-2000,scale to $25 in 2002. [60]Each ADS rep 5 Ord shrs,A$1.00. [61]Approx. [62]®$2.61,'97.

Splits ◆ Index	Cash Divs. Ea. Yr. Since	Dividends: Latest Payment: Period $	Date	Ex. Div.	Total $: So Far 1999	Ind. Rate	Paid 1998	Financial Position Mil-$: Cash& Equiv.	Curr. Assets	Curr. Liab.	Balance Sheet Date	Capitalization: Lg Trm Debt Mil-$	Shs. 000: Pfd.	Com.	Earnings $ Per Shr.: Years: End	1995	1996	1997	1998	1999	Last 12 Mos.	Interim Earnings: Period	$ per Shr.: 1998	1999	Index
1◆	1986	S0.10	1-7-00	12-15	0.20	0.20	0.20	0.06	8.65	5.13	10-02-99	0.31	...	1163	Je	0.37	0.53	v0.66	vd0.29	vd0.72	d0.75	3 Mo Sep	vd0.13	vd0.16	1
2◆	1996	Q0.11	1-17-00	12-31	s0.444	0.44	0.442	Total Assets $51.43M			9-30-99	32.6	★700	1372	Dc	d0.71	vd0.67	vd0.24	vd0.80	....	d1.74	9 Mo Sep	vd0.20	vd1.14	2
3	1988	Q0.09	12-15-99	11-29	0.36	0.36	0.36	....	251	142	9-30-99	376	...	33933	Dc	2.20	v0.81	v0.97	v0.37	Ed0.35↓	d1.15	9 Mo Sep	v1.11	v□d0.41	3
4◆	....	[51]10.00	5-16-96	5-17	...	Nil	....	3209	3885	2462	9-30-99	502	...	63638	Dc	v±2.71	v±3.04	v3.27	v±3.29	E4.30	4.17	9 Mo Sep	v2.31	v□3.19	4
5◆	1939	Q0.20	12-1-99	11-3	0.78½	0.80	0.70	Total Deposits $131557M			9-30-99	25696	6578	1642295	Dc	v1.36	v1.54	v1.75	v1.17	E2.25	1.53	9 Mo Sep	v1.29	v1.65	5
6	....	None Since Public			...	Nil	....	Total Assets $385M			9-30-99	120	...	±20692	Dc	...	p0.31	±v0.18	v±0.46	....	0.48	9 Mo Sep	v0.33	v0.35	6
7◆	....	5%Stk	4-22-99	4-9	5%Stk	Stk	....	0.10	16.7	3.31	9-30-99	5.33	...	4533	Dc	vd0.25	v0.10	v0.17	v0.21	....	0.07	9 Mo Sep	v0.18	v0.04	7
8	....	None Since Public			...	Nil	....	0.14	3.39	5.36	9-30-99	13.6	...	6069	Dc	v0.04	vd0.04	v0.26	vd0.04	....	d0.16	9 Mo Sep	vd0.01	□vd0.13	8
9	1996	Q0.62½	12-15-99	12-10	2.50	2.50	2.50	Cv into 1.8932 com,$26.41[53]				....	4000	...	Dc	...	...	...	....	....	....	Mand Red 9-15-2026			9
10	1976	Q0.06	11-30-99	11-10	0.24	0.24	0.24	238	358	217	10-03-99	447	...	119570	Dc	v0.88	v1.19	v0.97	v0.95	E1.30	1.09	9 Mo Sep	v0.85	v0.99	10
11◆	1987	Q0.02½	1-25-00	1-6	0.10	0.10	0.088	18.3	185	119	9-30-99	120	...	47506	Dc	v0.77	v0.86	v1.01	v1.19	E1.25	1.31	9 Mo Sep	v0.87	v0.99	11
12	1996	gQ0.08	11-12-99	10-27	g0.32	0.32	g0.32	86.3	164	41.0	j6-27-99	5.01	...	p±13127	Dc	±1.65	v±2.53	±v2.91	v±3.53	....	j4.31	9 Mo Sep	v±2.40	v±3.18	12
13	1973	Q0.29½	12-8-99	11-1	1.18	1.18	1.14	Total Assets $2695.56M			9-30-99	33.6	...	7120	Dc	v4.85	v4.30	v14.30	v10.08	....	5.46	9 Mo Sep	v9.21	v4.59	13
14	....	None Since Public			...	Nil	....	31.8	674	487	9-30-99	421	...	±47843	Dc	...	...	...	vpd0.05	....	d0.32	9 Mo Sep	vpd0.35	□pd0.62	14
15	....	None Since Public			...	Nil	....	9.61	146	64.6	10-02-99	54.0	...	17495	Dc	pvd1.37	p□vd0.07	v0.44	v1.57	....	1.83	9 Mo Sep	v1.10	v1.36	15
16◆	....	None Since Public			...	Nil	....	4.54	181	56.5	10-02-99	67.9	...	17165	Dc	v0.61	v0.68	v0.86	v0.06	....	0.20	9 Mo Sep	v0.48	v0.62	16
17	1995	Q0.50	12-31-99	12-28	2.00	2.00	2.00	Co option redm fr 6-12-2000 at $25				70.0	...	...	Dc	...	...	...	....	....	....	Mature 6-30-2025			17
18	1950	Q0.17	2-2-00	1-14	0.65	0.68	0.61	37.5	176	83.6	9-30-99	155	...	14912	Dc	v1.71	v0.99	v2.68	v0.40	....	2.49	9 Mo Sep	vd0.20	v1.89	18
19	....	None Since Public			...	Nil	....	35.7	167	73.3	9-30-99	30.8	...	63330	Dc	pv0.42	vp0.52	vp0.59	v0.73	....	0.76	9 Mo Sep	v0.55	v0.58	19
20◆	....	....			...	Nil	....	4.20	123	66.0	7-10-99	42.6	...	15870	Oc	p0.56	p0.61	v0.62	v0.25	Pv0.47	0.47				20
21◆	1935	Q0.18	11-19-99	11-3	0.66	0.72	0.52	Total Deposits $3080.56M			9-30-99	46.5	...	37605	Dc	v0.98	v1.08	v1.10	v1.73	....	1.89	9 Mo Sep	v1.27	v1.43	21
22	1967	gQ0.32	12-31-99	12-8	g1.28	1.28	g1.26	107	1596	1935	j12-31-98	5297	28631	112671	Dc	2.01	v1.96	v1.99	v1.53	....	j2.16	9 Mo Sep	v0.94	v1.57	22
23◆	1989	Q0.05	1-28-00	1-12	0.20	0.20	0.25	Total Deposits $2253.95M			9-30-99	509	...	26555	Dc	v1.29	v1.21	v1.40	vd0.56	....	1.36	9 Mo Sep	vd0.59	vΔ1.33	23
24◆	....	None Since Public			...	Nil	....	13.6	44.7	17.8	9-30-99	1.96	...	±36615	Mr	v±d0.07	v±d0.41	v±d0.38	v±d0.96	....	d0.68	6 Mo Sep	vd0.46	vd0.18	24
25◆	....	None Since Public			...	Nil	....	185	525	574	10-02-99	371	...	112324	Je	1.28	1.00	v2.86	vd3.32	vd5.51	d5.36	3 Mo Sep	d2.20	vΔd2.05	25
26	1991	Q0.05	2-14-00	12-29	0.20	0.20	0.20	5.47	266	275	9-30-99	369	4160	32153	Dc	vd0.84	v0.66	vd0.28	vd2.42	....	d3.07	9 Mo Sep	vd0.06	v□d0.71	26
27	1994	Q0.65⅝	2-14-00	12-29	2.62½	2.625	2.62½	Cv into 1.2579 com,$39.75				....	2400	...	Dc	...	...	...	....	....	....				27
28	1965	Q0.28	12-15-99	11-23	1.12	1.12	1.12	Total Assets $415.55M			9-30-99	212	...	17231	Dc	v0.61	v0.72	□v0.85	v0.78	....	1.10	9 Mo Sep	v0.45	v0.77	28
29	1924	Q0.53½	1-3-00	12-7	2.14	2.14	2.13	208	635	1173	9-30-99	3366	249	68092	Dc	v2.71	v2.41	v7.51	vΔ0.65	E1.75	0.02	9 Mo Sep	vΔ1.94	v1.31	29
30	1994	gQ0.10	12-31-99	12-10	g0.40	0.40	g0.40	3.28	554	334	j6-30-99	168	...	14327	Je	3.73	v2.89	v2.26	v0.02	v1.99	j1.99				30
31	....	h[56]....	5-3-99	5-3	h[56]...	Nil	....	8.86	107	83.3	9-30-99	1195	...	±p77064	Dc	□vd0.87	vd2.00	vd3.76	vd2.95	....	d2.68	9 Mo Sep	vd2.20	vd1.93	31
32	1997	Q0.36¼	1-31-00	12-29	1.44¼	1.45	1.41½	Total Assets $3573.40M			9-30-99	2349	2738	73347	Dc	...	pv0.42	v0.54	v1.20	....	0.18	9 Mo Sep	v1.13	v0.11	32
33	1995	Q0.01	11-30-99	11-15	0.04	0.04	0.04	7.49	267	150	9-30-99	414	...	p51651	Dc	v□1.32	v1.15	v1.42	v□1.75	....	1.92	9 Mo Sep	v□1.30	v□1.47	33
34	....	None Paid			...	Nil	....	Total Assets $46.08M			9-30-99	0.30	...	7835	Dc	v0.17	v0.20	v0.17	v0.73	....	0.19	9 Mo Sep	v0.73	v0.19	34
35	....	0.08	12-10-92	11-12	...	Nil	....	31.9	38.7	25.3	9-30-99	1.33	575	7060	Dc	d13.11	Δv2.74	v3.34	v□d0.22	....	d6.21	9 Mo Sep	v□6.44	v0.45	35
36	....	a0.531	7-1-95	6-16	...	Nil	....	Cv into 1.708 com,$14.64				....	2300	...	Dc	...	...	...	....	....	....	Arrears $11.15625 to 1-1-00			36
37◆	1930	gQ0.12	1-1-00	12-13	g0.42	0.48	g0.283	n/a	3160	3158	j10-09-99	2593	...	130943	Dc	v1.34	v1.73	v1.82	v5.82	....	j11.01	40 Wk Sep	v1.16	v6.35	37
38	....	None Paid			...	Nil	....	1.09	87.8	45.8	9-30-99	9.73	...	±9957	Dc	v±0.16	v±d1.74	±vd1.18	v0.09	....	0.10	9 Mo Sep	v0.05	v0.06	38
39	1817	[61]0.643	1-11-00		1.427	1.40	1.283	Book Value $10.68			9-30-98	1502	...	1898994	Sp	1.88	2.33	v[62]2.61	v1.93	Pv2.49	2.49				39
40◆	1999	0.02	12-1-99	11-10	0.06	0.08	....	0.16	567	382	9-30-99	1275	...	53390	Dc	vd1.99	v0.91	v1.25	v□1.51	....	1.77	9 Mo Sep	v□1.02	v1.28	40
41◆	1892	Q0.22	1-3-00	12-1	0.88	0.88	0.88	109	738	425	10-31-99	1502	...	100293	Oc	□2.80	2.09	v1.58	v1.30	v1.11	1.11				41
42	....	5%Stk	7-22-85	7-3	...	Nil	....	10.5	143	118	p9-30-99	160	3825	±55462	Dc	±Pv0.28	v±0.51	±v0.74	v±0.39	....	0.44	9 Mo Sep	v±0.24	v±0.29	42
43	....	None Since Public			...	Nil	....	33.6	87.4	64.6	10-30-99	0.26	...	±13803	Ja	0.47	v±1.13	±v1.53	v±1.91	....	1.75	9 Mo Oct	v±1.00	v±0.84	43
44	1933	Q0.40	11-29-99	10-27	1.60	1.60	1.60	Total Assets $12949M			9-26-99	4243	...	p234849	Dc	v3.91	v2.33	v1.71	v1.47	E3.10	2.36	9 Mo Sep	v1.32	v□2.21	44
45◆	....	....			...	....	....	Total Assets $1914.23M			9-30-99	1018	...	25759	Dc	v1.33	v1.50	v1.22	vd0.64	....	1.43	9 Mo Sep	vd0.66	v1.41	45
46	1929	Q0.34	12-31-99	11-29	1.36	1.36	1.36	230	3389	3130	9-30-99	772	...	74428	Dc	v2.78	v2.08	vd0.20	v4.25	E4.54	4.15	9 Mo Sep	v3.16	v3.06	46
47	....	None Paid			...	Nil	....	....	23.8	14.1	7-03-99	2.38	120	15910	Sp	pd1.00	v0.14	v0.02	vd0.02	....	0.12	9 Mo Jun	vd0.27	vd0.13	47
48	1992	Q0.75	12-30-99	12-14	3.00	3.00	3.00	Cv into 13.33 com, $1.875				....	120	...	Sp	...	...	...	....	....	....				48
49◆	1995	Q0.40	12-22-99	12-9	1.60	1.60	1.60	Total Assets $1905M			9-30-99	137	...	6091	Dc	□v9.41	v0.60	□v6.22	v11.94	....	18.34	9 Mo Sep	v10.61	v17.01	49
50◆	....	None Since Public			...	Nil	....	....	174	154	10-31-99	16.1	...	9641	Ja	p0.62	vΔ0.89	v□1.10	v1.38	....	1.54	9 Mo Oct	v0.29	v0.45	50

◆**Stock Splits & Divs By Line Reference Index** [1]3-for-1,'97. [2]58.33%,'99. [4]No adj for recap&mgr w/Blue Cross Cal,'96. [5]2-for-1,'97. [7]Adj for 5%,'99. [11]3-for-2,'96:5-for-4,'98. [16]2-for-1,'96. [20]3-for-2,'98. [21]3-for-1,'98. [23]Adj to 5%,'96. [24]2-for-1,'96. [25]2-for-1,'97. [37]3-for-1,'98. [40]2-for-1,'98. [41]3-for-2,'95. [45]10%,'96. [49]No adj for stk dstr,'93. [50]To split 3-for-2,ex Jan 5,'00.

¶ S&P 500
# MidCap 400
✣ SmallCap 600
• Options

Index	Ticker	Name of Issue (Call Price of Pfd. Stocks)	Market	Com. Rank. & Pfd. Rating	Inst. Hold Cos	Inst. Hold Shs. (000)	Principal Business	Price Range 1971-97 High	1971-97 Low	1998 High	1998 Low	1999 High	1999 Low	December, 1999 Dec. Sales in 100s	Last Sale Or Bid High	Low	Last	%Div Yield	P-E Ratio	EPS 5 Yr Growth	% Annualized Total Return 12 Mo	36 Mo	60 Mo
#1•[1]	WH	✓Whitman Corp	NY,B,Ch,P,Ph	B	240	64536	Prod/distr Pepsi	41 1/4	2 9/16	26 5/8	14 7/8	24 15/16	12 3/16	80971	13 7/8	12 3/16	13 7/16	0.3	24	−37	...	...	...
2	WIX	✓Whitman Education Group	AS	C	15	1925	Oper spcl medl training school	14 7/8	5/8	6 7/8	2 5/8	6 1/8	1 5/8	14419	2 3/4	1 5/8	2 3/4	...	16	NM	−17.0	−27.6	−4.8
✣3	WHIT	✓Whittman-Hart Inc	NNM	NR	257	37692	Info technology services	17 1/2	4	28 1/4	13	81 1/8	17	504370	81 1/8	46 5/8	53 5/8	...	..	...	94.1	62.0	...
✣4•[2]	WFMI	✓Whole Foods Market	NNM	B	288	20867	Natural food supermkt chain	51 3/8	7 1/4	70 1/8	32	49 5/8	28 1/4	64887	48	37 5/8	46 5/8	...	30	60	−4.1	27.3	35.2
✣5•[1]	WHX	✓WHX Corp	NY,P	NR	92	8654	Large U.S. steel producer	40 1/8	2 3/8	17 3/8	9 1/2	11 3/4	6 3/8	23363	9 5/16	8 1/8	9	...	d	Neg	−10.6	0.5	−7.4
6	Pr	Sr'A'cm Cv Pfd([52]51.30)	NY,Ch	B	17	1355		77 3/4	30 5/8	57	37 1/2	42 3/4	29	4242	34 3/8	30 1/4	32 7/16	10.0	..	...	...	...	...
7	Pr B	Sr'B'cm Cv Pfd([53]51.875)	NY	B−	19	1190		51 1/4	30 1/2	50 1/2	33 3/4	39 3/8	25 1/16	2364	28 15/16	25 1/16	25 13/16	14.5	..	...	...	...	...
✣8	WIC	✓WICOR, Inc[54]	NY,Ch	B+	192	14074	Util hldg:Wisconsin Gas	23 15/16	3 7/8	25 1/2	19 5/8	30 5/16	18 3/4	20494	30	28 13/16	29 3/16	3.1	22	5	38.5	22.3	20.7
9•[3]	OATS	✓Wild Oats Markets	NNM	NR	133	16958	Natural foods supermarket	19 5/16	5 3/4	25 1/2	11 11/16	28 1/2	14 11/16	72126	24 5/8	17 7/16	22 3/16	...	58	...	6.2	39.7	...
10	JW.A	✓Wiley(John)Sons 'A'[55]	NY,Ch	A−	134	35939	College text,reference books	14 1/4	1 3/16	24 1/8	12 1/4	24 7/8	14 15/16	14005	18 1/2	15 1/16	16 3/4	0.9	23	21	−29.7	29.1	26.3
11	JW.B	Cl 'B'[56]	NY,Ch	A−	17	1852		14 1/8	1/8	23 15/16	12 3/16	24 7/8	14 7/8	330	18 3/8	15	16 5/8	0.8	23	21	−29.7	29.0	26.1
¶12•[4]	WLL	✓Willamette Indus	NY,Ch,Ph	B+	448	78177	Mfr wood and paper products	43 1/2	1 1/4	40 1/2	23	52 1/8	31 1/2	49388	46 5/8	40 1/16	46 7/16	1.6	21	−16	40.9	12.2	16.6
13	WG	✓Willbros Group	NY,Ch	NR	36	4730	Oil & gas indus services	24 7/16	8 7/8	19 13/16	5 1/8	9	4 1/2	7940	5 1/4	4 5/8	4 5/8	...	d	Neg	−16.8	−22.0	...
14	WTU	✓Williams Coal Seam Gas Rlty[57]	NY,Ch	NR	9	126	Natural gas royalty interests	29 1/4	13 7/16	17 1/8	8 3/8	11 1/8	5 7/8	11454	6 3/4	5 7/8	6 1/4	19.4	5	−12	−22.2	−20.6	−7.6
15•[5]	WCG	✓Williams Communic Grp	NY	NR	..	...	Voice/data communic svcs&eq	...	...	...	...	35 7/16	23 1/4	174469	29 13/16	23 1/4	28 15/16	...	d	...	...	...	...
¶16•[4]	WMB	✓Williams Cos	NY,B,Ch,P,Ph	B	924	287925	Gas PL,petrol prod,telecomm	28 11/16	2 1/8	36 15/16	20	53 3/4	28	448702	34 3/4	28	30 9/16	2.0	87	−41	−0.5	20.5	32.9
17	WMCO	Williams Controls	NNM	NR	14	2392	Mfr electr/transportation pd	4	1/4	3 3/8	2	3 3/8	1 15/16	12057	2 1/4	2	2 1/4	...	d	Neg	−6.6	3.5	−8.7
#18•[6]	WSM	✓Williams-Sonoma	NY,Ph	B	309	39781	Retails cook'g/serv'g equip	25	9/16	40 3/4	17 7/16	60 5/16	25 1/4	83538	60 5/16	41 3/4	46	...	37	52	14.1	36.7	25.3
19	WLFC	✓Willis Lease Finance	NNM	NR	53	4087	Lease aircraft engines	24 1/8	8	25 3/4	13 1/2	19 3/4	3 1/4	9779	6 7/8	4 5/8	6 7/16	...	12	8	−59.1	−20.6	...
20	WLMR	✓Wilmar Industries	NNM	NR	70	9617	Distribute repair/maint pds	30 1/4	11	28 1/4	15	23 3/4	10	13807	17 3/4	12 1/8	17 3/8	...	17	NM	−14.5	−14.4	...
#21•[7]	WL	✓Wilmington Trust Corp	NY,Ph	A+	205	12294	Commercial bkg,Delaware	66	1 1/16	68 1/2	46 3/8	63 1/2	44 3/4	14756	52	44 3/4	48 1/4	3.5	13	9	−19.4	9.9	20.1
22	WOC	✓Wilshire Oil Texas	NY,To,B,Ch,Ph,Vc	B−	20	1427	Oil & gas expl & prod'n	12 9/16	2 9/16	6 5/8	4 1/16	5 1/4	3 5/16	4307	4 1/16	3 5/16	3 3/4	...	d	Neg	−16.7	−8.6	−9.5
23•[8]	WIND	✓Wind River Systems	NNM	B	147	18625	Dvlp software development sys	31 13/16	1 5/16	34 7/16	18 11/16	45	11 1/4	203598	45	31 3/4	36 5/8	...	68	45	17.1	20.8	70.8
24•[9]	WND	✓Windmere-Durable Hldgs	NY,Ch,Ph,P	B−	80	9172	Mfr small electr appliances	29	1/16	37 3/8	4 1/16	17 1/4	4 11/16	19082	17 1/4	14	17	...	d	−33	119	10.0	18.1
25	WCAP	Winfield Capital	NNM	NR	13	294	Investment co	11 1/4	5/8	13 1/8	7/8	65 1/16	6 1/4	109586	56	26 1/8	37 1/2	...	14	...	494	197	...
26	WNMLA	✓Winmill & Co'A'	NSC	B−	1	1	Invest mgmt,brokerage svcs	22 3/16	5/16	3 1/2	1 5/8	15 5/8	1 7/8	2152	2 3/16	1 7/8	1 15/16	...	1	NM	−35.4	−13.6	5.2
¶27•[10]	WIN	✓Winn-Dixie Stores	NY,B,Ch,Ph,P	A−	274	35834	Food supermarkets in south	44	2 9/16	62 13/16	28 5/8	46 11/16	22 5/16	64418	26 7/8	22 5/16	23 15/16	4.3	19	−5	−45.1	−6.4	1.3
✣28•[10]	WGO	✓Winnebago Indus	NY,B,Ch,P,Ph	↑B	137	7593	Mfr mtr homes: recr vehicles	48 1/4	1 3/4	16 3/8	8 1/4	28 3/4	12 7/8	14438	21 1/8	18 5/8	20 1/16	1.0	10	24	34.1	43.1	18.8
29•[11]	WCII	✓WinStar Communications	NNM	NR	331	42395	Telecommun,informat'n svcs	32 1/2	7/8	48 1/8	10 1/4	81 1/2	28 1/2	248529	81 1/2	50 1/2	75 1/4	...	d	Neg	92.9	53.0	52.8
30	WXH	✓Winston Hotels	NY	NR	52	3528	Real estate investment trust	15 1/8	8 3/4	14	6 3/4	10 1/2	7 3/4	12732	8 5/8	7 3/4	8 1/8	13.8	13	−5	12.6	−7.0	5.4
31	WFI	✓Winton Financial	AS	B	9	197	Savings & loan, Ohio	10 5/16	4 3/4	20 5/8	9 3/4	15 1/2	10 3/8	436	14 11/16	12 3/4	13 1/8	2.4	21	10	5.4	35.2	22.6
32	WFII	✓Wireless Facilities	NNM	NR	..	...	Wireless communic ntwk svcs	...	...	...	...	74 3/8	15	63551	59 1/2	38	43 5/8	...	..	...	...	...	...
33	WTT	✓Wireless Telecom	AS,Ch,Ph,P	B	16	2895	Mfr communic sys test'g eqp	16 3/4	5/16	9 5/8	1 7/16	4 5/16	1 1/2	49607	3 15/16	2 1/4	3 3/16	...	9	1	70.0	−31.5	−1.5
#34•[10]	WCLX	✓Wisconsin Central Trans	NNM	NR	168	37110	Oper regional railroad sys	44	2 3/4	30 3/4	12 9/16	22 3/8	12 3/8	43697	15 1/4	12 15/16	13 7/16	...	10	14	−21.8	−30.3	−0.4
#35•[10]	WEC	✓Wisconsin Energy Corp	NY,B,C,Ch,P,Ph	B+	295	60228	Hdlg:El & gas utility	32	3 9/16	34	27	31 9/16	19 1/16	72231	20 1/16	19 1/16	19 1/4	8.1	10	−4	−34.7	−5.1	−0.3
36	WZR	✓Wiser Oil	NY,Ch,Ph	C	33	1540	Oil/gas explor,devel,prod'n	33 3/16	2	14 1/4	1 5/8	4 15/16	1 7/16	7059	3	2 1/4	2 1/2	...	d	Neg	17.6	−49.3	−28.4
37	WLRF	✓WLR Foods Inc	NNM	C	40	2568	Major turkey/chicken producer	21 11/16	5 3/4	9 3/4	5	10	5 1/4	11253	6 1/4	5 1/4	5 3/4	...	6	NM	−36.1	−21.0	−18.4
38	WMC	WMC Ltd [60]ADS	NY,P	NR	18	2669	Expl/dvlp mineral&petro prod	31 1/4	10 1/4	15	9 5/8	22	11 1/2	1033	22	18 1/8	21 7/8	0.7	59	4	83.9	−2.9	0.7
39•[12]	WMS	✓WMS Industries	NY,B,Ch,Ph,P	B−	75	12014	Coin-op games:casino hotels	34	1	33 3/4	2 1/2	17	6 15/16	32743	13 11/16	10 1/4	13 1/8	...	..	−45	...	...	...
40	WLHN	✓Wolohan Lumber	NNM	B	31	1564	Building supply centers	25 1/4	7/8	14	8 3/8	13 3/4	10 3/4	1349	13 1/8	11 15/16	12 1/8	2.3	9	3	−4.7	1.2	−1.9
✣41•[13]	WLV	✓Wolverine Tube	NY,Ch,Ph	NR	113	10497	Mfr copper,copper-alloy tube	43 1/2	15 1/2	42 1/2	18 11/16	26 3/4	13 3/8	8492	15 3/8	13 1/2	14 1/8	...	..	−34	−32.7	−26.3	−9.9
✣42•[14]	WWW	✓Wolverine World Wide	NY,B,Ch,Ph,P	B+	187	24413	Mfr branded footwear	31 1/8	3/16	30 15/16	8 1/16	14 1/4	8 7/8	44470	11 1/4	9	10 15/16	1.1	17	10	−16.6	−16.6	8.4
43	WOMN	✓Women.com Networks	NNM	NR	..	...	Internet netwk for women	...	...	...	...	23 3/8	10	31805	18 1/2	12 1/4	14 1/4	...	..	...	...	...	...
44	WDHD	✓Woodhead Indus	NNM	B+	63	7361	Electrical specialty prod	21 1/2	13/16	20	8 1/8	15 3/8	8 5/16	5649	13 5/8	11 1/8	11 5/8	3.1	12	−2	−7.8	−3.1	4.0
45•[15]	WAXS	World Access	NNM	C	101	8223	Mfg wireline/wireless switch	34 1/8	1	40	12	22 3/4	6 3/8	180686	22 1/8	14 1/2	19 1/4	...	d	Neg	−9.9	34.0	...
46	INT	✓World Fuel Services	NY,Ch,Ph,P	B+	61	6672	Aviat'n fuel'g svc/oil recy'g	21	3/4	23 13/16	9 1/8	15 7/8	7	10282	8 5/8	7	7 1/2	2.7	10	4	−29.0	−19.1	3.7
47	WWFE	✓World Wrestling Fed Entr'A'	NNM	NR	..	...	Pro wrestling entertainment	...	...	...	...	34	14 1/16	85154	20 5/8	14 1/16	17 1/4	...	..	...	...	...	...
48•[16]	WGAT	✓WorldGate Communic'A'	NNM	NR	63	3523	TV based internet access svc	...	...	...	...	55 3/4	19 1/8	134071	50	28 3/4	47 9/16	...	..	...	...	...	...
49	WTX	✓Worldtex Inc	NY,P	NR	36	10522	Mfr covered elastic yarn	10 1/4	3 1/2	8 1/8	3	4 1/4	1	20714	1 7/8	1	1 9/16	...	d	Neg	−55.4	−44.0	−15.5
50	WRO	✓Woronoco Bancorp	AS	NR	10	1004	Savings & loan, Mass	...	...	...	...	10 7/8	8 1/2	1479	10	9 7/16	9 11/16	1.8	..	...	...	...	...

Uniform Footnote Explanations-See Page 4. Other: [1]CBOE:Cycle 3. [2]ASE:Cycle 2. [3]ASE,CBOE:Cycle 3. [4]CBOE:Cycle 2. [5]CBOE,Ph:Cycle 2. [6]ASE,CBOE,P:Cycle 2. [7]P:Cycle 2. [8]ASE,P:Cycle 2. [9]P:Cycle 3. [10]CBOE:Cycle 1. [11]ASE,CBOE:Cycle 1. [12]Ph:Cycle 1. [13]ASE:Cycle 3. [14]Ph:Cycle 3. [15]ASE,CBOE,Ph:Cycle 1. [16]ASE,CBOE,Ph:Cycle 3. [51]Stk dstr of Hussman Intl Inc & Midas Group Inc. [52]Thru 6-30-2000,scale to $50 in 2003. [53]Thru 9-30-2000,scale to $50 in 2004. [54]Wisconsin Energy plan acq,$31.50 cash or stk. [55]1/10 vtg. [56]Cv into 1 Cl 'A'. [57]Trust Units. [58]12 Mo Dec'95. [59]Subsid pfd. [60]Each ADS rep 4 ord shr,$A0.50. [61]Fiscal Jun'97 & prior. [62]Stk dstr of Midway Games Inc.

Index (Splits ◆)	Cash Divs. Ea.Yr. Since	Dividends: Latest Payment Period $	Date	Ex. Div.	Total $ So Far 1999	Ind. Rate	Paid 1998	Financial Position Mil-$: Cash& Equiv.	Curr. Assets	Curr. Liab.	Balance Sheet Date	Capitalization: Lg Trm Debt Mil-$	Shs. 000 Pfd.	Com.	Earnings $ Per Shr. Years End	1995	1996	1997	1998	1999	Last 12 Mos.	Interim Earnings Period	$ per Shr. 1998	1999	Index
1◆	1950	Q0.01	1-3-00	12-8	0.13	0.04	h[51]0.26½	117	516	707	10-02-99	803	...	141157	Dc	v1.26	v1.32	v0.04	v□0.60	E0.55	0.12	9 Mo Sep	v□0.49	v0.01	1
2◆	....	None Paid			...	Nil	....	1.56	33.7	28.5	9-30-99	10.2	...	13450	Mr	d0.01	vd0.38	v0.01	v0.22	....	0.17	6 Mo Sep	vd0.03	vd0.08	2
3◆	....	None Since Public			...	Nil	....	138	227	45.6	9-30-99	....	...	56596	Dc	pv0.04	v0.15	v0.22	v0.35	....	0.46	9 Mo Sep	v0.24	v0.35	3
4	....	None Since Public			...	Nil	....	9.02	141	121	9-26-99	209	...	26378	Sp	0.58	vd0.54	v1.06	v1.64	v1.54	1.54				4
5	....	None Paid			...	Nil	....	196	855	528	9-30-99	864	5883	14391	Dc	v□1.79	vd0.83	□vd8.83	Δv0.99	....	d1.59	9 Mo Sep	vΔ□1.03	vΔd1.55	5
6	1993	Q0.81¼	1-3-00	12-13	3.25	3.25	3.25	Cv into 3.1686 com, $15.78				....	2700	...	Dc	...	...	...	....	....	....				6
7	1995	Q0.93¾	1-3-00	12-13	3.75	3.75	3.75	Cv into 2.451 com, $20.40				....	3500	...	Dc	...	...	...	....	....	...				7
8◆	1960	Q0.22½	11-30-99	11-8	0.89	0.90	0.87	0.39	296	202	9-30-99	192	...	37630	Dc	1.16	v1.27	v1.33	v1.21	....	1.36	9 Mo Sep	v0.79	v0.94	8
9◆	....	None Since Public			...	Nil	....	20.3	70.1	68.5	10-02-99	88.0	...	22061	Dc	p0.02	vpd0.90	v0.43	v0.58	....	0.38	9 Mo Sep	v0.51	v□0.31	9
10◆	1982	Q0.036	1-18-00	12-21	0.135	0.143	0.12	2.42	140	226	10-31-99	95.0	...	±61921	Ap	±0.28	±0.37	±v0.31	v±0.55	v±0.60	0.72	6 Mo Oct	v±0.30	v±0.42	10
11◆	1904	Q0.032	1-18-00	12-21	0.12	0.128	0.10⅝	....	...	...		....	...	12134	Ap	±0.28	±0.37	±v0.31	v±0.55	v±0.60	0.72	6 Mo Oct	v±0.30	v±0.42	11
12◆	1962	Q0.18	12-14-99	11-24	0.70	0.72	0.64	20.1	881	447	9-30-99	1681	...	111561	Dc	v4.65	v1.73	v0.65	v0.80	E2.21	1.65	9 Mo Sep	v0.73	v1.58	12
13	....	None Since Public			...	Nil	....	6.42	66.0	59.2	9-30-99	....	...	12941	Dc	v0.94	v0.09	v0.96	vd0.30	....	d1.59	9 Mo Sep	vd0.31	vd1.60	13
14	1993	0.272	11-29-99	11-10	1.207	1.21	1.633	Total Assets $40.71M			9-30-99	....	...	9700	Dc	v2.69	v2.25	v1.91	v1.65	....	1.27	9 Mo Sep	v1.31	v0.93	14
15	....	None Since Public			...	Nil	....	119	1178	622	9-30-99	1915	...	★±463599	Dc	...	pvd0.01	p±vd0.07	p±vd0.87	....	d1.32	9 Mo Sep	±d0.27	±d0.72	15
16◆	1974	Q0.15	12-27-99	12-8	0.60	0.60	0.60	287	4256	5301	9-30-99	7773	p...	434734	Dc	v4.17	v1.07	□v1.04	v□0.29	E0.35	0.10	9 Mo Sep	v□0.38	v□0.19	16
17	....	None Paid			...	Nil	....	1.41	30.1	10.5	6-30-99	22.5	79	19879	Sp	0.26	vd0.03	vd0.12	vNil	Pvd0.54	d0.54				17
18◆	....	None Since Public			...	Nil	....	4.79	378	240	10-31-99	40.2	...	56414	Ja	v0.05	v0.43	v0.75	v0.96	E1.23↓	1.09	9 Mo Oct	v0.20	v0.33	18
19	....	None Since Public			...	Nil	....	Total Assets $416.29M			9-30-99	303	...	7398	Dc	pv1.03	v0.74	vΔ0.94	v□1.27	....	0.55	9 Mo Sep	v□0.88	v0.16	19
20	....	None Since Public			...	Nil	....	25.8	93.2	23.1	9-24-99	....	...	12408	Dc	pvd0.36	v0.51	v0.69	v0.92	....	1.01	9 Mo Sep	v0.70	v0.79	20
21	1914	Q0.42	11-15-99	10-28	1.65	1.68	1.53	Total Deposits $5065.45M			9-30-99	168	...	32565	Dc	v2.53	v2.79	v3.08	v3.34	E3.66	3.55	9 Mo Sep	v2.47	v2.68	21
22◆	....	3%Stk	2-20-98	1-14	...	Nil	3%Stk	2.51	11.3	6.88	9-30-99	47.8	...	8797	Dc	v0.43	v0.48	v0.58	v0.11	....	d0.05	9 Mo Sep	v0.21	v0.05	22
23◆	....	None Since Public			...	Nil	....	73.8	119	56.5	10-31-99	140	...	42106	Ja	0.15	v0.29	v0.11	v0.61	....	0.54	9 Mo Oct	v0.40	v0.33	23
24	....	0.05	6-17-97	5-30	...	Nil	....	5.53	440	148	9-30-99	290	...	22592	Dc	vd0.11	v□0.23	v1.00	v1.33	....	d0.15	9 Mo Sep	v1.34	vd0.14	24
25	....	None Paid			...	Nil	....	Total Assets $50.19M			9-30-99	18.6	...	5346	Mr	...	v0.07	vd0.40	v4.54	....	2.60	6 Mo Sep	v1.45	vd0.49	25
26	....	None since 1968			...	Nil	....	6.60	7.02	2.17	9-30-99	....	...	±1655	Dc	v±0.10	v±d0.23	v±0.43	v±0.35	....	1.54	9 Mo Sep	v±0.15	v±1.34	26
27◆	1934	M0.08½	1-3-00	12-13	0.76½	1.02	1.02	56.2	1669	1416	9-22-99	37.9	...	148629	Je	v1.55	v1.68	v1.36	v1.33	v1.23	1.28	12 Wk Sep	v0.10	v0.15	27
28	1995	S0.10	1-10-00	12-8	0.20	0.20	0.20	48.2	204	80.0	8-31-99	....	...	22299	Au	1.10	0.49	v0.90	v1.00	v1.96	2.08	3 Mo Nov	v0.43	v0.55	28
29	....	None Paid			...	Nil	....	476	707	399	9-30-99	2079	8164	54935	Dc	v[58]d0.70	vd3.00	vd7.68	vd12.61	....	d14.32	9 Mo Sep	vd8.76	vd10.47	29
30	1994	Q0.28	1-17-00	12-29	1.12	1.12	1.08	Total Assets $414M			9-30-99	70.2	3000	16814	Dc	v0.96	v1.00	v0.91	v0.77	....	0.63	9 Mo Sep	v0.68	v0.54	30
31◆	1991	Q0.08	1-10-00	12-29	0.30	0.32	0.25	Total Deposits $319.31M			6-30-99	103	...	4399	Sp	0.53	v0.30	v0.80	v0.96	Pv0.64	0.64				31
32	....	None Since Public			...	Nil	....	4.03	42.9	20.0	6-30-99	0.87	p...	★39028	Dc	...	...	...	pv0.17	....	0.17	9 Mo Sep	p0.14	vp0.14	32
33◆	1992	Div Discontd 5-15-98			...	Nil	0.10	23.6	26.0	2.88	9-30-99	....	...	17140	Dc	0.29	v0.42	v0.45	v0.07	....	0.34	9 Mo Sep	v0.04	v0.31	33
34◆	....	None Since Public			...	Nil	....	3.62	118	142	9-30-99	331	...	51250	Dc	□v0.88	v□0.98	v1.51	v1.49	E1.30↓	1.29	9 Mo Sep	v1.15	v0.95	34
35	1939	Q0.39	12-1-99	11-9	1.56	1.56	1.55½	40.1	640	793	9-30-99	2189	[59]305	117878	Dc	v2.13	v1.97	v0.54	v1.65	E2.00	1.93	9 Mo Sep	v1.19	v1.47	35
36	1941	Div Omitted 12-10-98			...	Nil	0.12	22.9	35.7	14.4	9-30-99	125	...	8952	Dc	v2.50	v0.72	v0.37	vd2.73	....	d2.11	9 Mo Sep	vd1.83	vd1.21	36
37◆	....	0.06	8-1-97	7-9	...	Nil	....	0.26	177	81.6	10-02-99	53.9	...	16564	Je	0.90	d0.27	vd1.85	vd1.55	v□2.44	1.03	3 Mo Sep	v□1.56	v0.15	37
38	1990	0.078	11-1-99	9-28	0.155	0.16	0.304	107	1384	792	j12-31-98	2286	...	1145049	Dc	Δ0.82	1.11	[61]0.80	v0.37	....	0.37				38
39◆	....	h[62]....	4-6-98	4-7	...	Nil	h[62]....	66.8	194	80.6	9-30-99	....	...	30619	Je	0.80	v0.19	v1.67	vd0.84	v0.18	0.09	3 Mo Sep	vd0.06	vd0.15	39
40	1983	Q0.07	1-3-00	12-2	0.28	0.28	0.28	0.12	94.5	41.7	9-25-99	12.7	...	5106	Dc	v0.52	v0.88	v0.62	v1.03	....	1.38	9 Mo Sep	v0.74	v1.09	40
41	....	None Since Public			...	Nil	....	14.1	217	68.2	10-02-99	176	20	12725	Dc	v2.26	v2.77	□v2.13	v1.72	....	0.12	9 Mo Sep	v1.48	v□d0.12	41
42◆	1988	Q0.03	2-1-00	12-30	0.11¾	0.12	0.104	7.64	389	53.5	9-11-99	197	...	41297	Dc	v0.62	v0.76	v0.96	v0.97	....	0.66	36 Wk Sep	v0.61	v0.30	42
43	....	None Since Public			...	Nil	....	40.5	54.1	13.3	9-30-99	....	p...	★45654	Dc	...	...	...	vpd1.71	....	....	9 Mo Sep	n/a	vpd2.23	43
44◆	1961	Q0.09	11-22-99	11-4	0.36	0.36	0.36	0.49	59.9	24.7	7-03-99	50.3	...	11122	Sp	0.85	0.98	v1.10	v0.35	Pv0.96	0.96				44
45	....	5%Stk	4-24-92	3-18	...	Nil	....	108	326	137	9-30-99	141	...	45265	Dc	v0.12	v0.46	v0.70	vd5.45	....	d4.22	9 Mo Sep	vd1.02	v0.21	45
46◆	1994	Q0.05	1-7-00	12-15	0.20	0.20	0.20	10.6	168	96.1	9-30-99	18.8	...	12175	Mr	v0.90	v1.08	v1.27	v1.21	....	0.77	6 Mo Sep	v0.60	v0.16	46
47	....	None Since Public			...	Nil	....	226	289	89.7	10-31-99	10.9	...	±68167	Ap	...	...	...	v....	pv0.59	....	6 Mo Oct	n/a	vp0.34	47
48	....	None Since Public			...	Nil	....	100	107	6.76	6-30-99	0.33	...	21441	Dc	...	...	...	vpd2.24	....	....	6 Mo Jun	n/a	v□d1.18	48
49	....	None Since Public			...	Nil	....	9.69	122	47.7	9-30-99	198	...	14271	Dc	v0.36	v0.75	v□0.44	vd0.41	....	d0.44	9 Mo Sep	v0.13	v0.10	49
50	1999	Q0.04¼	10-12-99	9-23	0.04¼	0.17	....	Total Deposits $272M			9-30-99	130	...	5999	Dc	...	...	pv0.68	....	....	....				50

◆**Stock Splits & Divs By Line Reference Index** [1]No adj for stk dstr,'98. [2]2-for-1,'96. [3]2-for-1,'96,'98. [8]2-for-1,'98. [9]3-for-2,'98,'99. [10]2-for-1,'95,'98,'99. [11]2-for-1,'95,'98,'99. [12]2-for-1,'97. [16]3-for-2,'96:2-for-1,'97. [18]3-for-2,'94(twice):2-for-1,'98. [22]Adj for 3%,'98. [23]3-for-2,'96,'97,'99. [27]2-for-1,'95. [31]2-for-1,'94,'98. [33]3-for-2,'95:2-for-1,'94,'96. [34]2-for-1,'94:3-for-1,'96. [37]3-for-2,'95. [39]No adj for stk dstr WHG Resorts & Casinos'97:No adj for stk dstr,'98. [42]3-for-2,'94,'95,'96,'97. [44]3-for-2,'95. [46]3-for-2,'95,'97.

¶ S&P 500
\# MidCap 400
✣ SmallCap 600
• Options

Index	Ticker	Name of Issue (Call Price of Pfd. Stocks)	Market	Com. Rank. & Pfd. Rating	Inst. Hold Cos	Inst. Hold Shs. (000)	Principal Business	Price Range 1971-97 High	1971-97 Low	1998 High	1998 Low	1999 High	1999 Low	December, 1999 Dec. Sales in 100s	Last Sale Or Bid High	Low	Last	%Div Yield	P-E Ratio	EPS 5 Yr Growth	% Annualized Total Return 12 Mo	36 Mo	60 Mo
¶1•[1]	WTHG	✓Worthington Indus	NNM,Ph	A–	318	40469	Steel process'g, plastics	23½	1/16	19 9/16	10⅜	17 11/16	11 1/16	122469	16¾	14½	16 9/16	3.6	20	–10	38.1	0.6	–0.7
2	WPPGY	✓WPP Group ADS[51]	NNM	NR	74	9377	Intl mktg/advertising svcs	65 5/16	2½	38⅝	17⅜	83⅛	29	15336	83⅛	70	83⅛	0.3	50	23	171	58.2	62.6
3	WPS	✓WPS Resources	NY,B,Ch,P	B+	128	7538	Electric & natural gas	36½	5⅜	37½	29 15/16	35¾	24 7/16	12313	26½	24 7/16	25⅛	8.0	13	–3	–23.6	2.2	5.2
¶4•[2]	WWY	✓Wrigley, (Wm) Jr	NY,Ch,Ph,P	A+	464	39235	Major chewing gum producer	82 1/16	1 1/16	104 5/16	70 15/16	100⅝	66½	51257	83¾	77¼	82 15/16	†1.7	31	7	–5.9	15.6	13.0
5	WYN	✓Wyndham Intl 'A'	NY	NR	110	39829	Own,manage hotels	....	....	....	....	4⅞	2 7/16	285865	2 15/16	2 7/16	2 15/16	...	..	...	...	...	...
✣6	WN	✓Wynn's Intl	NY,Ch,Ph	A–	107	13899	Automotive parts:petrochem	24 3/16	⅝	25¾	15 1/16	22 3/16	12 11/16	6944	15⅛	12 11/16	14⅛	2.0	10	21	–35.2	2.2	19.0
✣7	XRIT	✓X-Rite Inc	NNM	B+	69	5979	Quality control instruments	24	⅞	19	6½	8⅞	5¾	12351	7 7/16	6	6¼	1.6	11	–3	–18.2	–27.0	–19.9
8	XLA	✓Xcelera.com Inc	AS,Ch	↑B–	1	.2	Investment co	3 9/16	1/16	1½	15/16	191 9/16	1⅛	48617	191 9/16	36	139½	...	..	–12	11083	477	220
9	XCL	✓XCL Ltd	AS,Ch,P	C	19	689	Oil & gas explor'n,prod'n	69⅜	1⅞	6½	1 13/16	2⅛	¼	26649	½	¼	¼	...	d	39	–86.7	–18.1	–33.9
10•[3]	XEIK	✓Xeikon N.V. ADR[53]	NNM	NR	16	929	Dvp digital color print sys	27⅜	5⅜	28	13⅝	32⅛	15 1/16	54574	19⅛	15 1/16	18	...	34	...	–23.4	33.9	...
¶11•[4]	XRX	✓Xerox Corp	NY,B,C,Ch,P,Ph	B	1369	531587	Copiers & duplicators: svs	44	4½	60 13/16	33 1/16	63 15/16	19	2157274	27	19	22 11/16	3.5	10	NM	–60.9	–3.1	8.8
12	KTX	Xerox Cap Tr I 8%'CorTS'[54]	NY	....[55]	..	...	Corporate-Backed Trust Sec	....	....	....	....	25	21¾	108	24⅝	21¾	21¾	9.2	..	...	...	...	...
13•[5]	XICO	✓Xicor Inc	NNM	C	24	2572	Dev-reprogrammable semicon	29	⅝	3¾	¾	16 9/16	1⅛	155726	16 9/16	8 15/16	13 11/16	...	d	Neg	874	10.1	41.9
¶14•[6]	XLNX	✓Xilinx Inc	NNM	B+	692	264309	Supplier of semiconductors	14⅝	13/16	16¾	7 7/16	48 9/16	15 5/16	1665621	48 9/16	38	45½	...	64	19	181	70.6	56.1
✣15•[5]	XIRC	✓Xircom Inc	NNM	B	257	17937	Mfr computer network'g prd	31⅛	7	36⅛	9¼	75 15/16	15¾	156050	75 15/16	46¾	75	...	44	NM	121	51.1	33.4
16•[7]	XL	✓XL Capital Ltd'A'	NY,Ph	B+	405	108116	Provides excess liability insur	65 3/16	12¾	84	59⅛	75¾	41 15/16	110715	52⅝	46½	51⅞	3.4	11	27	–28.7	14.1	24.7
17	XMSR	✓XM Satellite Radio'A'	NNM	NR	..	...	Dv stg:audio enter/progamming	....	....	....	....	44¾	11⅝	25684	44¾	23	38⅛	...	d	...	...	...	...
18•[8]	XPDR	Xpedior Inc	NNM	NR	..	...	e-business solutions	....	....	....	....	33 15/16	19	269483	33 15/16	19	28¾	...	..	...	...	...	...
19•[2]	XTR	✓XTRA Corp	NY,B,Ch,P	B+	119	9761	Leases transportation equip	60	1 11/16	66 1/16	37½	47 13/16	37½	3543	42⅞	40 3/16	42⅝	...	17	–3	3.0	0.3	–0.2
¶20•[9]	YHOO	✓Yahoo Inc	NNM	NR	538	58159	Internet navigational svc	17¾	2 3/16	143	14 7/16	448	110	2492150	448	224 15/16	432 11/16	...	..	...	265	474	...
21	YCC	✓Yankee Candle Inc	NY	NR	64	9764	Mfr,mkt scented candles	....	....	....	....	24¾	14 3/16	22719	18¼	15¼	16 5/16	...	..	...	...	...	...
22	YES	✓Yankee Energy System	NY	B+	72	3641	Hldg co: gas utility,Conn	29¼	11 15/16	31 7/16	22½	44⅛	22 7/16	11211	44⅛	42½	43 15/16	3.2	35	–7	57.1	33.6	21.3
23	YZC	Yanzhou Coal Mining ADS[61]	NY	NR	10	1519	Coal mining, China	....	....	16 13/16	4⅞	22½	6¾	261	15⅞	13⅜	14⅛	...	7	...	90.6	...	...
✣24•[10]	YELL	✓Yellow Corp	NNM	C	160	19377	Hldg:motor freight carrier	42½	3⅞	29⅞	9 11/16	19⅝	14⅜	18496	18⅛	14 7/16	16 13/16	...	9	NM	–12.1	5.4	–6.3
25	YOCM	YOCREAM Intl	NSC	B–	1	10	Mfg/sells frozen yogurt	9⅛	1	7	2¾	6	3¾	2691	4 15/16	3¾	4B	...	10	69	–23.8	23.5	4.2
26	YFED	York Financial	NNM	B+	21	1196	Savings & loan,Pennsylvania	26 3/16	1⅛	24 1/16	13¼	15 11/16	10⅝	2441	12 15/16	10⅝	11¼	s4.4	12	1	–18.7	5.3	12.0
#27•[11]	YRK	✓York International[63]	NY,Ch,Ph,P	NR	271	36088	Mfr climate control systems	57	22⅝	52¾	27½	47½	21	66279	28¼	22⅛	27 7/16	2.2	9	NM	–31.6	–20.0	–4.7
28	YORK	✓York Research	NNM	B–	26	1937	Energy svs/project dvlp	22½	1¼	8⅝	3	7½	3¼	20438	3⅞	3¼	3¾	...	d	Neg	11.1	–26.6	–1.3
29	YNR	✓Young & Rubicam[64]	NY	NR	296	42636	Marketing/communication svcs	....	....	35⅞	19¾	71⅞	31¼	94375	71⅞	50 9/16	70¾	0.1	35	...	119	...	...
30•[12]	YBTVA	✓Young Broadcasting'A'	NNM	NR	142	10160	Own/oper T.V. stations	42	13½	70⅛	21⅛	65¼	36⅝	21722	51½	37 13/16	51	...	d	2	21.8	20.4	23.5
31•[13]	YPF	✓YPF Sociedad Anonima ADS[65]	NY,P	NR	117	10604	O&G expl,dvlp,prd-Argentina	38⅛	14⅜	36½	18 11/16	44¾	26½	8539	42¼	36 9/16	36 15/16	2.4	18	...	35.4	16.7	15.2
32	ZTEL	Z-Tel Technologies	NNM	NR	..	...	Telecommon/internet access svcs	....	....	....	....	46⅝	30	141178	46⅝	30	40⅜	...	..	...	...	...	...
✣33•[11]	ZLC	✓Zale Corp	NY,Ch	NR	376	32926	Operate jewelry stores	28 3/16	8	34⅛	19½	51¾	30 5/16	54874	50⅞	43½	48⅜	...	21	22	50.0	36.0	32.2
34•[11]	ZAP	✓Zapata Corp	NY,To,B,Ch,P	B	51	3589	Fish protein prd/food pkg svcs	198⅛	1 9/16	24 15/16	6⅛	16	4½	28228	6⅛	4½	4⅝	...	d	20	...	...	...
35	IZAP	✓ZapMe Corp	NNM	NR	..	...	Dv stg:interact'e school ntwk	....	....	....	....	13¾	5 5/16	51959	11⅛	8¼	8⅝	...	..	...	...	...	...
✣36•[6]	ZBRA	✓Zebra Technologies'A'	NNM	NR	258	19730	Mfr bar code labeling sys	38¼	7¼	44⅝	25	64½	22⅞	35614	60½	51½	58½	...	25	13	104	35.8	24.9
37	ZMX	✓Zemex Corp	NY,To	B–	28	2639	Ind'l min'ls,metal powders	21¼	2½	10¼	5⅞	9¾	5	1110	9¾	8	9⅛	...	13	–8	46.0	12.1	4.3
✣38	ZNT	✓Zenith Natl Insurance	NY,Ch	B–	87	11853	Workmen's compens'n insur	30 7/16	⅛	30½	22⅞	26 11/16	19¼	3059	21 1/16	19¼	20⅝	4.8	6	20	–6.7	–5.3	2.1
39	ZCO	✓Ziegler Cos	AS,Ch	B–	12	245	Investment banking,financ'g	26	1¾	25¼	17½	20⅝	14⅛	61	15	14½	14⅝B	3.6	d	Neg	–19.6	–2.1	3.7
40•[12]	ZD	✓Ziff-Davis ZD	NY	NR	87	16811	Magazine/electronic publish	....	....	23 15/16	3⅝	29	11	61787	18 9/16	14 5/16	15 13/16	...	d	...	0.0	...	...
41	ZDZ	✓Ziff-Davis ZDNet[69]	NY,Ph	NR	61	5314	Internet based info svcs	....	....	....	....	55½	13⅜	77448	23⅞	18 9/16	21	...	d	...	...	...	...
42	ZILA	✓Zila Inc	NNM	C	41	1795	Mkt non-prescription medl prod	10¼	⅛	10 7/16	3⅞	12 1/16	2⅝	92395	3½	2⅝	2 15/16	...	d	–11	–70.3	–23.8	–2.0
#43•[7]	ZION	✓Zions Bancorp	NNM	A	345	38953	Commercial bkg,Utah	46	½	62½	37⅞	75⅞	48¼	141964	71	58⅜	59 3/16	...	22	15	–3.7	33.3	48.4
44•[5]	ZITL	✓Zitel Corp	NSC	C	17	1073	Mfr semicond'r memory sys	72⅞	⅝	17⅛	2⅛	7	⅝	710258	7	1	2 7/16	...	d	Neg	–42.7	–62.0	–17.5
✣45•[14]	ZIXI	✓Zixit Corp	NNM	C	78	3425	Computer software svcs	33¾	3 11/16	12 5/16	3¼	90	6 11/16	193540	71 5/16	32⅝	39⅝	...	d	–28	271	81.7	32.8
46•[13]	ZOLT	✓Zoltek Co	NNM	↓B–	36	1977	Mfr carbon fibers	65¾	1⅛	42¼	8¼	13 3/16	6⅝	26349	12	8 9/16	8⅝	...	d	–46	–6.1	–38.1	19.6
47•[14]	ZONA	✓Zonagen Inc	NNM	C	54	2683	Dvlp stge: Fertility research	45¾	3⅜	40¼	12	35¾	2 5/16	43013	7⅜	3¾	4⅜	...	d	–3	–77.1	–22.4	–9.6
48•[15]	ZRAN	✓Zoran Corp	NNM	NR	67	5538	Dvp integrated circuits	40¼	10⅛	19 3/16	4⅞	56 11/16	8½	78115	56 11/16	39⅝	55¾	...	..	NM	219	45.8	...
49	ZIGO	✓Zygo Corp	NNM	B–	31	5102	Mfrs measur'g instr/sys	40	1¼	22 7/16	5	25 1/16	7¼	15229	25 1/16	18⅞	20⅛	...	d	Neg	133	–8.2	53.9

Uniform Footnote Explanations-See Page 4. Other: [1]Ph:Cycle 3. [2]ASE:Cycle 3. [3]ASE,P,Ph:Cycle 2. [4]CBOE,P:Cycle 1. [5]CBOE:Cycle 3. [6]CBOE,P:Cycle 3. [7]Ph:Cycle 1. [8]CBOE,Ph:Cycle 3. [9]ASE,CBOE,P,Ph:Cycle 2. [10]ASE,P:Cycle 1. [11]CBOE:Cycle 2. [12]CBOE:Cycle 1. [13]ASE,CBOE:Cycle 1. [14]ASE,CBOE:Cycle 2. [15]Ph:Cycle 2. [51]Ea ADS rep 5 ord,10p. [52]Subsid pfd. [53]Ea ADS rep 1 ord shr. [54]Due 2-1-2027. [55]Rated'BBB+'by S&P. [56]Or earlier upon'Tax Event're-spec cond. [57]Total Issue Amt. [58]Fiscal Nov'97 & prior. [59]Fiscal Nov'98 & prior. [60]10 Mo Dec'95. [61]Ea ADS rep 50'H'shs,RMB 1. [62]To be determined. [63]Instl. hldgs over 90%. [64]Plan S&P 500 listing: eff Jan 6. [65]Ea ADS rep 1 Cl'D' shr PS.1. [66]Stk dstr of Zap.Com. [67]Fiscal Sep'97 & prior. [68]12 Mo Dec'98:Fiscal Sep'98 earn $2.94. [69]Exch for Ziff-Davis com,re-spec cond.

Index	Cash Divs. Ea. Yr. Since	Dividends: Latest Payment Period $	Date	Ex. Div.	Total $ So Far 1999	Ind. Rate	Paid 1998	Financial Position Mil-$ Cash& Equiv.	Curr. Assets	Curr. Liab.	Balance Sheet Date	Capitalization Lg Trm Debt Mil-$	Shs. 000 Pfd.	Com.	Earnings $ Per Shr. Years End	1995	1996	1997	1998	1999	Last 12 Mos.	Interim Earnings Period	$ per Shr. 1998	1999	Index
1	1968	Q0.15	12-29-99	12-13	0.59	0.60	0.55	7.05	605	441	8-31-99	364	...	89113	My	1.29	v1.04	v0.96	v1.03	v□0.67	0.81	6 Mo Nov	v□0.41	v0.55	1
2◆	1993	0.008	11-30-99	10-20	0.21%	0.21	0.19	424	1510	1777	j12-31-98	194	...	766500	Dc	0.75	1.05	v1.26	v1.56	....	1.66	9 Mo Sep	v0.69	v0.79	2
3	1940	Q0.50½	12-20-99	11-16	2.00	2.02	1.96	6.62	214	220	9-30-99	415	[52]512	26831	Dc	v2.32	v2.00	v2.25	v1.76	....	2.00	12 Mo Sep	v1.99	v2.00	3
4	1913	Q0.35	2-1-00	1-12	1.33	1.40	†1.30	457	1002	281	9-30-99	....	...	±115767	Dc	±1.93	v±1.99	±v2.34	v±2.63	E2.69	2.63	9 Mo Sep	v±2.02	v±2.02	4
5	....	None Since Public			...	Nil	....	114	462	405	9-30-99	3418	10171	p167662	Dc	...	...	...	vpd1.26	....	....	9 Mo Sep	n/a	v□d6.13	5
6◆	1975	Q0.07	1-4-00	12-13	0.27	0.28	0.233	61.8	184	83.8	9-30-99	....	...	18656	Dc	v0.75	v0.97	v1.29	v1.39	....	1.49	9 Mo Sep	v1.05	v1.15	6
7◆	1986	Q0.02½	11-15-99	10-14	0.10	0.10	0.10	25.5	63.4	6.23	10-02-99	....	...	21235	Dc	v0.47	v0.73	v0.85	v0.32	....	0.58	9 Mo Sep	v0.17	v0.43	7
8◆	....	0.077	4-24-89		...	Nil	....	Total Assets $26.5M			1-31-99	....	...	13206	Ja	v0.27	v0.06	v0.13	v0.22	....	0.22				8
9◆	....	None Since Public			...	Nil	....	0.60	1.35	101	9-30-99	....	1283	23378	Dc	vd5.77	vd0.98	vd1.36	vd0.87	....	d0.92	9 Mo Sep	vd0.46	vd0.51	9
10	....	None Since Public			...	Nil	....	33.7	84.1	19.7	12-31-97	....	...	28473	Dc	p0.03	pv0.07	vd0.02	Pv0.56	....	0.53	9 Mo Sep	v0.34	v0.31	10
11◆	1930	Q0.20	1-1-00	12-1	0.78	0.80	0.70	106	12576	7690	9-30-99	11616	8785	664262	Dc	vd0.66	v1.66	v2.02	v0.52	E2.22	2.46	9 Mo Sep	vd0.39	v1.55	11
12	....	Plan semi-annual div			...	2.00	....	Co red opt fr 2-1-07 at $25[56]				[57]★27.0	...	...	Dc	...	...	...	....	....	....	Red premium 2-1-07 to 2-1-17 re-spec cond			12
13	....	None Since Public			...	Nil	....	14.4	39.1	33.1	10-03-99	9.64	...	20404	Dc	v0.53	v0.70	vd0.13	vd1.53	....	d0.77	9 Mo Sep	vd1.02	vd0.26	13
14◆	....	None Since Public			...	Nil	....	428	781	190	10-02-99	....	...	318852	Mr	0.32	v0.35	v0.40	v□0.42	E0.71	0.56	6 Mo Sep	v□0.18	v0.32	14
15	....	None Since Public			...	Nil	....	134	217	71.5	9-30-99	....	...	★28959	Sp	d3.44	0.30	vd0.46	v0.78	v1.69	1.69				15
16◆	1992	Q0.44	10-8-99	9-22	1.76	1.76	2.08	Total Assets $14097.84M			9-30-99	411	...	±127603	Dc	3.21	5.39	[58]7.84	v[59]5.86	E4.60	4.55	9 Mo Sep	v±4.45	v±3.14	16
17	....	None Since Public			...	Nil	....	236	236	32.3	6-30-99	p0.35	★10499	★±43863	Dc	...	...	...	pvd0.76	....	d1.07	9 Mo Sep	vpd0.27	vpd0.58	17
18	....	None Since Public			...	Nil	....	1.44	38.4	118	p3-31-99	9.10	...	★50000	Dc	...	...	...	vpd0.73	....	....	7 Mo Jul	n/a	vp0.01	18
19	....	Div Postponed 6-19-98			...	Nil	0.44	Total Assets $1576.00M			6-30-99	866	...	13187	Sp	3.39	v2.56	v2.78	v3.88	Pv2.49	2.49				19
20◆	....	None Since Public			...	Nil	....	676	734	157	9-30-99	....	...	p263240	Dc	‡v[60]...	vd0.03	vd0.13	v0.11	E0.24	0.25	9 Mo Sep	vd0.08	v0.06	20
21	....	None Since Public			...	Nil	....	6.26	59.1	59.2	10-02-99	195	...	54499	Dc	...	...	...	pv0.33	....	....	9 Mo Sep	n/a	□v0.24	21
22	1989	Q0.35½	12-30-99	12-16	1.41	1.42	1.37	5.44	63.8	60.4	6-30-99	164	...	10635	Sp	1.20	2.10	v1.62	v1.04	Pv1.26	1.26				22
23	1998	0.344	7-12-99	4-28	0.344	[62]....	0.174	35.1	176	179	12-31-98	13.9	...	2600000	Dc	...	p1.90	pv3.04	v2.11	....	2.11				23
24	....	0.23½	5-15-95	4-25	...	Nil	....	22.4	317	454	9-30-99	275	...	24879	Dc	vd1.07	vd0.97	v1.83	vd1.06	E1.85	1.63	9 Mo Sep	vd1.36	v1.33	24
25	....	None Since Public			...	Nil	....	0.17	4.39	1.96	7-31-99	0.22	...	2305	Oc	0.14	Nil	v0.19	v0.30	....	0.41	9 Mo Jul	v0.21	v0.32	25
26◆	1984	sQ0.124	11-15-99	11-3	s0.495	0.50	s0.472	Total Deposits $1106.82M			9-30-99	302	...	10025	Je	0.83	1.07	v0.72	v0.96	v0.92	0.91	3 Mo Sep	v0.23	v0.22	26
27	1991	Q0.15	12-30-99	12-17	0.60	0.60	0.48	34.3	1473	968	9-30-99	921	...	38971	Dc	vd2.38	v3.37	v1.10	v3.36	E2.96	2.33	9 Mo Sep	v□2.57	v1.54	27
28	....	0.20	3-22-78	2-23	...	Nil	....	10.1	131	136	8-31-99	150	...	14916	Fb	v0.35	v0.52	Δv0.17	vd0.40	....	d0.35	6 Mo Aug	vd0.31	vd0.26	28
29	1999	0.02½	12-15-99	11-29	0.07½	0.10	....	93.3	1259	1370	9-30-99	299	...	69607	Dc	...	...	vpd0.37	v□d1.34	....	2.00	9 Mo Sep	v□d1.84	v1.50	29
30	....	None Since Public			...	Nil	....	2.40	84.3	56.9	9-30-99	644	...	±13494	Dc	v□±0.23	v±0.08	□vd0.08	v0.27	....	d1.48	9 Mo Sep	vd0.21	vd1.96	30
31	1993	0.22	11-30-99	11-23	0.88	0.88	0.88	116	1555	2422	j12-31-98	2578	...	353000	Dc	2.25	v2.31	v2.48	v1.64	E2.05	1.80	9 Mo Sep	v1.32	v1.48	31
32	....	None Since Public			...	Nil	....	1.52	2.90	12.2	p9-30-99	12.7	p...	★30454	Dc	...	...	...	vpd1.19	....	....	9 Mo Sep	n/a	vpd1.09	32
33	....	None Since Public			...	Nil	....	46.8	1276	752	10-31-99	99.6	...	35983	Jl	v0.88	v□1.23	v1.38	v1.84	v2.21	2.30	3 Mo Oct	v0.06	v0.15	33
34	1997	Div Omitted 11-3-98			h[66]...	Nil	0.21	115	198	30.2	9-30-99	10.7	11	23887	Dc	0.14	vΔ0.22	v[67]0.56	v[68]2.56	....	d0.54	9 Mo Sep	v2.70	vd0.40	34
35	....	None Since Public			...	Nil	....	19.9	22.1	6.49	6-30-99	4.61	p...	★42476	Dc	...	...	...	vpd0.32	....	....	6 Mo Jun	n/a	vpd0.36	35
36◆	....	None Since Public			...	Nil	....	216	332	45.1	10-02-99	0.06	...	±31339	Dc	v0.93	v1.19	v1.65	v1.29	E2.30	1.57	9 Mo Sep	v1.30	v1.58	36
37◆	....	2%Stk	11-2-98	10-15	...	Nil	2%Stk	0.71	43.0	17.6	9-30-99	50.6	...	8847	Dc	v1.01	v0.31	v0.69	v0.60	....	0.69	9 Mo Sep	v0.47	v0.56	37
38	1978	Q0.25	2-15-00	1-27	1.00	1.00	1.00	Total Assets $1628.99M			9-30-99	148	...	17201	Dc	v0.36	v2.12	v1.57	v1.11	....	3.78	9 Mo Sep	v1.04	v▲3.71	38
39	1954	Q0.13	11-12-99	10-28	0.52	0.52	†0.82	Total Assets $135.65M			9-30-99	5.25	...	2436	Dc	v1.68	v1.51	v0.14	vd1.20	....	d0.76	9 Mo Sep	vd0.49	vd0.05	39
40	....	None Since Public			...	Nil	....	29.8	326	392	9-30-99	1265	...	103339	Dc	...	...	vpd0.09	vd0.78	....	d0.47	9 Mo Sep	vd0.86	vd0.55	40
41	....	None Since Public			...	Nil	....	0.49	38.6	18.1	9-30-99	....	...	13707	Dc	...	...	...	vpd0.13	....	d0.01	9 Mo Sep	pvd0.12	Nil	41
42	....	None Paid			...	Nil	....	3.49	32.4	8.49	10-31-99	9.55	29	41019	Jl	Δd0.04	d0.03	vd0.20	vd0.15	vd0.05	d0.07	3 Mo Oct	v0.02	vNil	42
43◆	1966	Div Omitted 12-20-99			0.86	Nil	0.52	Total Deposits $13008.77M			9-30-99	570	...	p85503	Dc	v1.37	v1.68	v1.89	v1.91	E2.70	2.37	9 Mo Sep	v1.50	v1.96	43
44◆	....	None Paid			...	Nil	....	3.27	10.6	6.13	6-30-99	4.92	...	21946	Sp	0.56	0.26	vd1.15	vd2.48	Pvd0.59	d0.59				44
45	....	0.366	3-28-95	3-1	...	Nil	....	38.7	39.4	8.46	9-30-99	....	...	15309	Dc	vd0.29	vd0.04	vd1.17	v1.66	....	d0.16	9 Mo Sep	v0.11	vd1.71	45
46◆	....	....			...	Nil	....	15.9	59.4	12.6	6-30-99	5.44	...	16201	Sp	0.21	v0.45	v0.78	v0.58	Pvd0.16	d0.16				46
47	....	None Paid			...	Nil	....	22.6	26.2	2.93	9-30-99	....	...	11266	Dc	vd1.11	vd1.92	vd1.46	vd1.09	....	d1.39	9 Mo Sep	vd0.56	vd0.86	47
48	....	None Since Public			...	Nil	....	18.4	49.5	12.1	9-30-99	....	...	★13396	Dc	v0.11	v0.22	v0.38	v0.08	....	0.35	9 Mo Sep	v0.01	v0.28	48
49◆	....	None Since Public			...	Nil	....	17.9	55.7	11.1	9-30-99	....	...	11467	Je	0.33	v0.72	v0.24	v0.58	vd0.36	d0.21	3 Mo Sep	vd0.10	v0.05	49

◆Stock Splits & Divs By Line Reference Index [2]1-for-5 REVERSE,'95:2-for-1,'99. [6]3-for-2,'93,'96,'97,'98. [7]2-for-1,'94. [8]3-for-2,'99:2-for-1,'99:To split 2-for-1,ex Jan 10,'00. [9]1-for-15 REVERSE,'97. [11]3-for-1,'96:2-for-1,'99. [14]3-for-1,'95:2-for-1,'99(twice). [16]2-for-1,'96. [20]3-for-2,'97:2-for-1,'98,'99. [26]10%,'95,'96:5-for-4,'97:Adj for 5%,'99. [36]2-for-1,'95. [37]Adj for 2%,'98. [43]4-for-1,'97. [44]2-for-1,'96. [46]3-for-2,'95:2-for-1,'96. [49]3-for-2,'95:2-for-1,'97.

STANDARD & POOR'S

PREFERRED STOCK SUMMARY

Exchange / Ticker	Cm Divd	Issue	Rating	Reg. Call Price (Begins) Thru [see footnotes for Sink'g Fd]	Dividends Latest Payments Period $	Date	Ex Div.	Ind. Rate	Last Sale or Bid(B)	% Div. Yld.
N SEPPr		AB Svensk Exp Exch[1]7.375%	AA−	25(8/31/03)	Q0.46	12-1-99	11-10	1.84	21½	8.6
N SEPPrA		AB Svensk Exp Exch[2] 7.20% 'B'	NR	25(11/30/02)	Q0.45	12-1-99	11-10	1.80	21⅛	8.5
N ABNPrB	*	ABN AMRO Cap Fd II 7.125%	A+	[3]25(3/31/04)	Q0.45	12-31-99	12-28	1.78	19⅞	9.0
N EKPPr		A/S Eksportfinans 8.70%	AA	25(3/19/03)	Q0.54	12-20-99	12-01	2.17	25	8.7
N ANBPrA		Abbey National Sr'A'ADS[4]	A+	[5]25.875(11/15/01)	0.49	1-6-00	12-08	1.97	24⅜	8.1
N SUA	*	Abbey Nat'l 7% Cap Sec	NR	[6]25(4/28/04)	Q0.44	1-18-00	12-30	1.75	19¾	8.9
N SUD	*	Abbey Natl 7.25% Cap Sec	NR	[7]25(7/14/01)	Q0.45	12-15-99	11-26	1.81	20½	8.8
N AGUPr	*	Agrium Inc 8.00%'COPrS'	BB+	[8]25(4/21/03)	Q0.50	12-31-99	12-13	2.00	16⅜	12.2
N AIFPrT	*	AICI Cap Tr 9%	B+	[7]25(9/29/02)	Q0.56	12-31-99	12-13	2.25	13⅞	16.2
N ALPPrO	*	Alabama Power 5.83%'A'	A−	25(8/18/08)	Q0.36	1-1-00	12-15	1.46	23B	6.3
N ALPPrQ	*	Ala Pwr Cap I 7.375% Tr Sec	A−	[9]25(3/30/01)	Q0.46	12-31-99	12-14	1.84	20½	9.0
N ALPPrR	*	Ala Pwr Cap II 7.60%[10]'TOPrS'	A−	[11]25(2/15/02)	Q0.47	12-31-99	12-14	1.90	21¼	9.0
N AOGPrA		Alberta Energy 9.50%	NR	[6]25(9/29/04)	0.63	12-31-99	12-13	2.37	23¾	10.0
A AAPr	*	Alcoa Inc $3.75	A−	100	Q0.94	1-1-00	12-08	3.75	56	6.7
N AREPrA	*	Alexandria Re Eq 9.50%	NR	25(6/10/04)	Q0.59	1-14-00	12-31	2.38	19⅞	11.9
N ALLPrA	*	Allstate Fin I 7.95%[12]'QUIPS'	A−	[7]25(11/24/01)	Q0.50	12-31-99	12-28	1.99	22¼	8.9
N AOPrA	*	AMERCO 8.50% Sr'A'	BB+	25(11/30/00)	Q0.53	12-1-99	11-08	2.13	25½	8.3
N AAGPrT	*	Amer Annu Cap Tr I 9.25%'TOPrS'	BBB	[13]25(11/6/01)	Q0.58	1-15-00	1-12	2.31	23	10.1
A ACMPrA	*	Amer Coin Merch Tr I 10.50%	NR	[6]10(9/14/01)	Q0.26	12-15-99	12-10	[14]....	4⅞	....
N AFGPrT	*	Amer Finl Cap Tr 9.125%[10]'TOPrS'	BBB−	[11]25(10/21/01)	Q0.57	1-15-00	1-12	2.28	23	9.9
N AGCPrM	*	Amer Genl 8.45%'A'[15]'MIPS'	A	25(6/4/00)	M0.18	12-31-99	12-28	2.11	22⅝	9.3
N AGCPrA	*	Amer Gen Cap I 7.875%[10]'TOPrS'	A	[3]25(9/7/04)	Q0.49	12-31-99	12-28	1.97	21⅞	9.0
N ALLPrI		AmerHer8.5%[19]FELINE[20]'PRIDES'[2]	BBB+	[22]NC	Q1.06	12-31-99	12-28	4.25	86¾	4.9
N ARNPrA	*	Amer Re Cap 8.50%[12] 'QUIPS'	A+	25(9/29/00)	Q0.53	12-31-99	12-28	2.13	24	8.9
N ACPPr	*	Amer R.E.Ptnrs 5%[23]'PIK'	NR	[24]10(3/30/00)	[25]Stk	3-31-99	3-11	0.50	7⅞B	6.4
N AWKPrA	*	Amer Water Wks 5% Pref	NR	25	Q0.31	12-1-99	11-09	1.25	17½B	7.1
N ANJPr		ANZ[28]Exch Pfd II 8.08%[29]'TrUEPrS'	A−	[30]NC	0.51	1-18-00	12-29	2.02	21⅜	9.5
N AIVPrG	*	Apartm't Inv&Mgmt9.375% 'G'	B+	[31]25(7/14/08)	Q0.59	1-17-00	12-29	2.34	16⅞	13.9
N ASNPrB	*	Archstone Commun'ts 9% Sr'B'[32]	BBB	[33]25(5/23/00)	Q0.56	12-31-99	12-09	2.25	20⅝	10.9
N ASNDPrD	*	Archstone Commun'ts 8.625%'C'[34]	BBB	[35]25(8/19/02)	Q0.54	12-31-99	12-09	2.16	19¾	10.9

Exchange / Ticker	Cm Divd	Issue	Rating	Reg. Call Price (Begins) Thru [see footnotes for Sink'g Fd]	Dividends Latest Payments Period $	Date	Ex Div.	Ind. Rate	Last Sale or Bid(B)	% Div Yld
N AGRPrA		Argentaria Pfd Cap 7.80%'A'	BBB+	25(6/29/02)	Q0.49	12-31-99	12-13	1.96	21⅝	9.
A ATPPr	*	Argo Capital 11% Cap Sec	NR	[36]10(11/5/03)	Q0.28	1-17-00	12-13	1.10	8¼B	13.
N AECPrA	*	Assoc Estates Rlty 9.75%[37]Dep	B+	25(7/24/00)	Q0.61	12-15-99	11-29	2.44	15	16.
N CIVPrB	*	Atlantic Cap I 8.25%[12]'QUIPS'	BBB	[6]25(9/30/01)	Q0.52	12-31-99	12-28	2.06	21¼	9.
N CIVPrC	*	Atlantic Cap II 7.375%	BBB	[6]25(11/3/03)	Q0.46	12-31-99	12-14	1.84	20¼	9.
N ANZPr	*	Austr&N.Zealand Bk 9.125%	A	25(2/24/03)	Q0.57	12-31-99	12-13	2.28	25	9.
N AVBPrH	*	AvalonBay 8.70% Sr 'H'	BBB	25(10/14/08)	Q0.54	3-15-00	2-28	2.17	19	11.
N AVAPrA	*	Avista Capital I 7.875%[10]'TOPrS'	BBB−	[11]25(2/14/02)	Q0.49	12-31-99	12-28	1.97	20½	9
N AVAPrL	*	Avista Corp[38]Dep'RECONS'[39]	NR	[40]	Q0.31	12-15-99	11-19	1.24	15¼	8.
N BGAPr	*	Banco Ganadero Cl'C'[41]	NR	NC	[42]0.23		12-27	[43]0.99	7⅞	12.
N ONEPrC	*	Bank One Adj[44]Div'C'	A−	100	Q1.63	11-30-99	11-03	6.50	97	6.
N ONEPrT	*	Bank One Capital I 8.00%	A−	[6]25(9/19/04)	0.31	11-15-99	11-09	2.00	23	8.
N BKUPrB		Bank United 9.60%	BB+	26.25(9/29/00)	Q0.60	12-31-99	12-13	2.40	26½	9.
N BACPrZ	*	BankAmer Cap I 7.75%[10]'TOPrS'	A−	[45]25(12/19/01)	Q0.48	12-31-99	12-28	1.94	22	8.
N BTPrS	*	Bankers Tr 7.75% Dep'S'[46]	BBB	25(5/31/00)	Q0.48	12-1-99	11-10	1.94	26	7.
N BUFPrC	*	BankUnited Cap III 9.00%	NR	[45]25(3/30/03)	Q0.56	12-31-99	12-13	2.25	15¼	14.
N BCBPr	*	Barclays Bk[47]E1/E2[48]Unit ADS[49]	A+	25(4/29/03)	0.50	12-1-99	11-22	2.00	22⅜	9.
N CTHPrB		BCH Capital 9.43%'B'	BBB+	[50]25(7/11/05)	Q0.59	12-31-99	12-14	2.36	24⅝	9.
N CTHPr		BCH Capital 10.50% 'A'	BBB+	[52]26.3125 11/21/00	Q0.66	12-31-99	12-14	2.63	25½	10
N HPNPr		BCH Intl-P.R. 9.875%'A''MIPS'[15]	BBB−	[51]26.25 11/21/00	0.21	12-31-99	12-27	2.47	25½B	9.
N BPCPrA		BCP Intl 8%Exch Pref'A'	NR	[53]50(6/29/03)	Q1.00	12-31-99	12-14	4.00	103B	3.
N BSCPrE	*	Bear Stearns 6.15% Sr'E'Dep[54]	BBB	50(1/14/08)	Q0.77	1-15-00	12-29	3.08	42	7.
N BSCPrY	*	Bear Stearns Cap II 7.12%	BBB	[6]25(12/14/03)	Q0.47	1-17-00	12-29	1.88	21	8.
N BBCPrA	*	Bergen Cap Tr I 7.80%[10]'TOPrS'	NR	[3]25(5/25/04)	Q0.49	12-31-99	12-28	1.95	12¾	15
N GRPrA	*	BFGoodrich Cap 8.30%[55]'QUIPS'	BBB	[56]25(7/5/00)	Q0.52	12-31-99	12-28	2.08	21⅞	9.
N BGEPrA	*	BGE Cap Tr 7.16%[10]'TOPrS'	A−	[6]25(6/14/03)	Q0.45	12-31-99	12-28	1.79	20½	8.
N BKPrC	*	BNY Cap II 7.80%	NR	[6]25(8/31/02)	Q0.49	12-1-99	11-12	1.95	22	8.
N BKPrD	*	BNY Cap III 7.05%	A−	[6]25(3/23/03)	Q0.44	12-1-99	11-12	1.76	19¾	8.
N BREPrA	*	BRE Properties 8.50%	BBB−	25(1/28/04)	Q0.53	12-31-99	12-13	2.13	18⅝	11.
N BSFPrC		BSCH Finance Sr'C'	BBB+	26.02(12/30/00)	Q0.51	12-31-99	12-14	2.03	21½	9.

Footnotes and Sinking Fund: [1] Co opt exch for 7.375% non-cm Pfd. [2] Co opt exch for 7.20% non-cm Pfd. [3] Or earlier upon'Spcl Event're-spec cond. [4] Ea ADS rep 1 non-cm $-denominated Pref. [5] Re-spec cond (amt incl Relevant Red Prem). [6] Or earlier upon'Tax Event're-spec cond. [7] or earlier upon 'Tax Event' re-spec cond. [8] Or earlier uopn'Tax Event're-spec cond. [9] or anytime upon 'Special Event're-spec cond. [10] Trust Originated Preferred Securities. [11] or anytime upon'Tax Event're-spec cond. [12] Quarterly Income Preferred Securities. [13] or earlier for 'Tax Event're-spec cond. [14] To be determined. [15] Monthly Income Preferred Shrs. [16] Pfd Redeemable Increased Div Equity Sec. [17] Ea Sec consists of stk pur contr & 6.75% Tr Pfd. [18] Pur cont for Amer Herit Life com fr 6-16-2000re-spec cond. [19] Pfd Redeemable Increased Div Equity Sec. [20] Ea Sec consists of stk pur contr & 6.75% Tr Pfd. [21] Pur cont for Amer Herit Life com fr 6-16-2000re-spec cond. [22] Mand 8-16-2002:Cv to Jr Debs on'Tax Ev're-spec cond. [23] Pay in kind. [24] Pay in cash or Dep Units. [25] Cash equiv $0.50. [26] Trust Units Exch for Pref Shs. [27] Exch for cash or ANZ pref shrs re-spec cond. [28] Trust Units Exch for Pref Shs. [29] Exch for cash or ANZ pref shrs re-spec cond. [30] Mand 1-15-2048. [31] or earlier under'REIT'reclass'n re-spec cond. [32] Formerly Security Cap Pac Tr Sr'B'Pfd. [33] Fr 5-24- 2000,or earlier to preserve'REIT'status. [34] Formerly Security Cap Atl 8.625%'A'Pfd. [35] Fr 8-20-2002,or earlier to preserve'REIT'status. [36] Or earlier for'Spcl Event're-spec cond. [37] Dep for 0.10 shr 9.75% Cl'A'cm Red Pfd. [38] Mand conv into 1 com 11-1-2001. [39] Dep for 0.10 shr $12.40 Sr'L'Cv Pfd. [40] Fr 12-15-98 to 11-1-2001 re-spec cond. [41] Ea ADS rep 100 Cl 'C' Cm Ptcp Pref,Ps.10. [42] Approx. [43] Subject to minimum div based on'B'shrs. [44] Rate adjusted qtrly:min 6.5%,max 12.50%. [45] or earlier upon'Tax Event're-spec cond. [46] Dep for 0.01 shr 7.75% cm Pfd Sr'S'. [47] Ea El ADS rep 1 8% note $20 amt. [48] Ea E2 ADS rep 1 8% note $5 amt. [49] Ea E1 note cv into El pref, E2 into E2 pref. [50] Red fr 7-12-2000 at $25 re spec cond. [51] Red fr 11-22-99 at $25 re-spec cond. [52] Red fr 11-22-99 at $25 re-spec cond. [53] or after 6-21-2001 'Tax Event' re-spec cond. [54] Dep for 0.25 shr 6.15% Sr'E'cm Pfd. [55] Qtly Income Pfd Securities. [56] Mand redem repymt of 8.30% Jr Debs.

Exchange Ticker	Cm Divd	Issue	Rating	Reg. Call Price (Begins) Thru [see footnotes for Sink'g Fd]	Dividends Latest Payments Period $	Date	Ex Div.	Ind. Rate	Last Sale or Bid(B)	% Div. Yld.
BSFPrD		BSCH Finance 8.74%'D'	BBB+	26.09(9/29/01)	Q0.55	12-31-99	12-14	2.19	24¼B	9.0
BSFPrF		BSCH Finance 8.125%'F'	BBB+	26.0156(2/14/02)	Q0.51	12-31-99	12-14	2.03	22⅛	9.2
BSFPrG		BSCH Finance 8.125%'G'	BBB+	26.0156(5/8/02)	Q0.51	12-31-99	12-14	2.03	22	9.2
BSFPrH		BSCH Finance 7.79%'H'	BBB+	25(6/16/02)	Q0.49	12-31-99	12-14	1.95	20¾	9.4
BSFPrJ		BSCH Finance 7.35%'J'	BBB+	25(12/30/02)	Q0.46	12-31-99	12-14	1.84	19⅞	9.2
BTPrA	*	BT Preferred Cp Tr I 8.125%	BBB	[1]25(1/31/02)	Q0.51	12-31-99	12-14	2.03	23	8.9
CSDPrA	*	Cadbury Sch LP 8.625%[2]'QUIPS'	BBB+	25(4/11/02)	Q0.54	12-15-99	12-10	2.16	23⅝	9.2
CGGPrT	*	Canadian Genl Cp 9.125%'TOPrS'	BBB+	[3]25(3/30/01)	Q0.57	12-31-99	12-28	2.28	23⅝	9.7
CZXPr	*	Canadian Occ Pet 9.75%	BB+	[4]25(10/29/03)	Q0.61	12-31-99	12-13	2.44	23¼	10.5
KREPrL	*	Capital Re LLC 7.65%'MIPS'[5]	BBB+	25	M0.16	12-31-99	12-28	1.91	21½	8.9
CPLPr	*	Carol P&L $5 Vtg	BBB+	110	Q1.25	4-1-00	3-13	5.00	72⅜B	6.9
CREPrB	*	CarrAmerica Realty 8.57%	BBB	25(8/11/02)	0.54	11-30-99	11-17	2.14	16⅛	13.3
CREPrC	*	CarrAmerica Realty 8.55%[6]Dep'C'	BBB−	25(11/5/02)	Q0.53	11-30-99	11-17	2.14	16	13.4
CBLPrA	*	CBL & Assoc Prop 9.00%	NR	25(6/30/03)	Q0.56	12-30-99	12-13	2.25	18¾	12.0
CNTPrA	*	Centerpoint Prop Tr 8.48%'A'	BBB−	25(10/29/02)	Q0.53	1-31-00	1-12	2.12	18½	11.5
CERPr	*	Central Ill Lt 4.50% Vtg	A	100	Q1.13	1-3-00	12-08	4.50	61⅝B	7.3
CFBPr	*	CFC Preferred 9.375% Tr Sec	B+	[7]25(5/14/02)	Q0.59	12-31-99	12-28	2.34	22½	10.4
CMV	*	Chase Cap IV 7.34% Cap Sec'D'	BBB+	[4]25(12/4/02)	Q0.46	12-31-99	12-28	1.83	21⅛	8.7
CBO	*	Chase Cap VII 7.00% Cap Sec'G'	A−	[4]25(5/27/04)	Q0.44	1-31-00	1-26	1.75	20⅜	8.6
CMBPrN	*	Chase Mhtn Adj[8]Rt'N'	A−	25	0.32	12-31-99	12-13	1.13	23½	4.8
CMBPr	*	Chase Preferred Cap 8.10%	A	[9]25(9/17/01)	Q0.51	12-31-99	12-13	2.02	23½	8.6
CCPPrA		Chevy Chase10.375%[10]ExCap'A'	B	[11]52.594(1/14/07)	Q1.30	1-15-00	12-29	5.19	48⅝B	10.7
CCNPrA	*	Chris-Craft Ind $1 Vtg	NR	25	Q0.25	12-29-99	12-13	1.00	14½B	6.9
CPrG	*	Citigroup 6.213% Sr'G'Dep[12]	A	50(7/10/07)	Q0.78	12-1-99	11-10	3.11	43B	7.2
CPrE	*	Citigroup Cap I 8.00% Tr Sec	NR	[13]25(10/6/01)	Q0.50	12-31-99	12-28	2.00	23⅜	8.6
CPrN	*	Citigroup Cap IV 6.85% 'TRuPs'[14]	A	[13]25(1/21/03)	Q0.43	12-31-99	12-28	1.71	19⅝	8.8
CPrW	*	Citigroup Cap V 7.0%[14]'TruPS'	NR	[15]25(11/14/03)	Q0.44	1-18-00	1-12	1.75	20⅛	8.7
CPrX	*	Citigroup Cap VI 7.0%[14]'TruPS'	NR	[4]25(3/14/04)	Q0.43	11-15-99	11-09	1.72	20⅛	8.6
CVXPrT	*	Cleveland El III'93'A'[16]Dep	BB−	25	Q0.53	11-1-99	10-13	2.12	25⅜	8.4
CPMPrA		CL&P Capital L.P.9.30%[17]'MIPS'	B	25	M0.19	12-31-99	12-28	2.32	24⅜	9.5
CGPPrT	*	Coastal Fin I 8.375%[18]'TOPrS'	BB+	[4]25(5/12/03)	Q0.52	12-31-99	12-28	2.09	23	9.1
N CLPr	*	Colgate-Palmolive$4.25Vtg	BBB+	100	Q1.06	12-31-99	12-13	4.25	86B	4.9
N CLPPrA	*	Colonial Prop Tr 8.75% Sr'A'	BB+	25(11/5/02)	Q0.55	12-31-99	12-13	2.19	17¾	12.4
N CWEPrT	*	ComEd Fin 1 8.48%[18]'TOPrS'	BBB−	[1]25(9/29/00)	Q0.53	12-31-99	12-28	2.12	24	8.9
N CBHPrT		Commerce Cap Tr I 8.75%	NR	[4]25(6/29/00)	Q0.55	12-31-99	11-10	2.19	23½	9.3
N CQPrA	*	COMSAT Cap I 8.125%[19]'MIPS'	BBB	[20]25(7/17/00)	M0.17	12-31-99	12-28	2.03	20¼	10.1
N CAGPrB	*	ConAgra Cap L.C.Adj[21]Rt'B'	BBB−	25	0.12	12-31-99	12-28	1.26	17½	7.2
N CNCPrF	*	Conseco 7%[22]FELINE[23]'PRIDES'[24]	BBB−	[25]NC	Q0.88	11-16-99	11-10	3.50	23⅜	15.0
N CNCPrT	*	Conseco Fin Tr I 9.16%[26]'TOPrS'	BB+	[27]25(11/18/01)	Q0.57	12-31-99	12-28	2.29	21⅛	10.8
N CNCPrV	*	Conseco Fin Tr V 8.70%'TOPrS'[18]	BBB−	[4]25(9/29/03)	Q0.54	12-31-99	12-28	2.17	20⅛	10.8
N CNCPrH	*	Conseco Fin Tr VII 9.44%'TOPrS'[28]	BBB−	[29]25(8/31/04)	Q0.59	12-31-99	12-28	2.36	22¼	10.6
N EDPrA	*	Consol Ed N.Y. $5 Vtg	A−	105	Q1.25	11-1-99	10-08	5.00	67⅜	7.4
N CMSPrJ	*	Consum Egy Fin I 8.36%[18]'TOPrS'	BB+	[30]25(12/30/00)	Q0.52	12-31-99	12-28	2.09	21½	9.7
N CMSPrK		Consum Egy Fin II 8.20%[18]'TOPrS'	BB	[3]25(9/29/02)	Q0.51	12-31-99	12-28	2.05	20⅝	9.9
N CMSPrL	*	Consum Eqy Fin III 9.25%[28]'TOPrS'	BB	[29]25(11/3/04)	0.37	12-31-99	12-28	2.31	22½	10.3
N OCEPrB	*	Corporate Off Pr Tr 10%'B'Pfd	NR	[31]25(7/14/04)	Q0.63	1-14-00	12-29	2.50	17¼	14.5
N CPZPrA	*	CPL Cap I 8%[2]'QUIPS'	BBB+	[32]25(4/29/02)	Q0.50	12-31-99	12-28	2.00	21⅝	9.3
N CWNPrA	*	Crown Amer Rlty Tr 11%	NR	[33]52.50(7/30/07)	Q1.38	12-17-99	12-01	5.50	35⅜	15.5
N CIVPrD	*	Delmarva Pwr Fin I Cp Sec 8.125%	BBB+	[3]25(9/29/01)	Q0.51	12-31-99	12-28	2.03	21½	9.4
N DDRPrC	*	Develp Div Rlty 8.375%[34]Dep	BBB−	25(7/6/03)	Q0.52	12-15-99	12-01	2.09	17⅛	12.2
N DDRPrD		Develp Div Rlty 8.68%[35]Dep	NR	25(8/19/03)	Q0.54	12-15-99	12-01	2.17	18¼	11.9
N DLJPr T	*	DLJ Cap Trust I 8.42%	BBB	[1]25(8/30/01)	0.18	12-31-99	12-28	2.10	22⅛	9.5
N DLJPrB	*	Donald,Luf,Jen Fixed/Adj[36]5.30%	BBB	[37]50(1/14/03)	0.66	1-14-00	12-29	2.65	48	5.5
N DFT	*	Downey Fin'l Cap Tr I 10% Sec	BB	[29]25(7/22/04)	Q0.63	12-15-99	11-26	2.50	21¼	11.8
N DUKPrT	*	Duke Cap Fin 7.375%[18]'TOPrS'	A−	[4]25(6/29/03)	Q0.46	12-31-99	12-14	1.84	21½	8.6
N DUKPrU	*	Duke Cap FinII 7.375%[2]'QUIPS'	A−	[4]25(9/30/03)	Q0.46	12-31-99	12-14	1.84	21⅜	8.6
N DUKPrW	*	Duke Cap Fin Tr III 8.375%	NR	[4]25(8/30/04)	0.59	11-30-99	11-10	2.09	24⅜	8.6
N DUKPrA	*	Duke Energy 6.375%'A'	A−	25.80(12/15/03)	Q0.40	12-16-99	11-09	1.59	24	6.6
N DUKPrQ	*	Duke En CapTr I 7.20%[2]'QUIPS'	A−	[3]25(12/30/02)	Q0.45	12-31-99	12-14	1.80	20⅞	8.6
N DREPrF	*	Duke-Weeks Rlty 8%'F'	BBB	25(10/9/02)	Q0.50	1-31-00	1-12	2.00	18¼	11.0
N DQPrA	*	Duquesne Cap L.P.8.375%[38]'MIPS'	BBB−	25(5/30/01)	M0.17	12-31-99	12-28	2.09	22⅛	9.5
N DDPrB	*	du Pont(E.I.) $4.50	A	120	Q1.13	1-25-00	1-06	4.50	71¾	6.3

ootnotes and Sinking Fund: [1] or anytime upon'Tax Event're-spec cond. [2] Quarterly Income Preferred Securities. [3] or earlier upon'Tax Event're-spec cond. [4] Or earlier upon'Tax Event're-spec cond. [5] Monthly income referred shrs. [6] Dep for 0.10 shr 8.55%Sr'C'cm Pfd. [7] or earlier upon 'Tax Event're-spec cond. [8] Rate adjusted qtrly:min 4.50%,max 10.50%. [9] Or earlier upon 'Tax Event' re-spec cond. [10] Mand Ex for'B'Pfd Chevy Chase Bk -spec cond. [11] or earlier at $50 for'Tax Event're-spec cond. [12] Dep for 0.20 shr 6.213%Sr'G'cmPfd. [13] or earlier upon'Tax Event' re-spec cond. [14] Trust Preferred Securities. [15] Or earlier upon'Tax Event re-spec cond. [16] Dep r 0.05 shr Serial Pfd,$42.40 Sr T. [17] Monthly Income Preferred Shrs. [18] Trust Originated Preferred Securities. [19] Monthly Income Preferred Shs. [20] Or earlier re spec cond. [21] Rate adjusted qtrly:min 5.0%,max 10.50%. [22] Pfd edeemable Increased Div Equity Sec. [23] Ea Sec consists of stk pur contr &6.75% Tr Pfd. [24] Pur cont for Conseco Inc com. [25] Mand 2-16-2001:Cv to Jr Debs on'Tax Event're-spec cond. [26] Fr 11-19-2001. [27] or earlier upon ax Event' re-spec cond. [28] Trust Originated Preferred Securities. [29] Or earlier upon'Spcl Event're-spec cond. [30] or anytime upon'Special Event're-spec cond. [31] Or earlier to preserve'REIT'status re-spec cond. [32] or earlier on'Special Event're-spec cond. [33] or earlier re-spec event. [34] Dep for 0.10 shr 8.375%Sr'C'cmRedPfd. [35] Dep for 0.10 shr 8.68% Sr'D'cm Red Pfd. [36] 4/15/98-1/15/2003,adj aft(5.70%min,11.30%max). [37] Or earlier For'Special vent're-spec cond. [38] Monthly Income Preferred Shrs.

Exchange	Ticker	Cm Divd	Issue	Rating	Reg. Call Price (Begins) Thru [see footnotes for Sink'g Fd]	Dividends Latest Payments Period $	Date	Ex Div.	Ind. Rate	Last Sale or Bid(B)	% Div. Yld.
N	EGPPrA	*	Eastgroup Prop 9.00%'A'	NR	5 6/18/03	Q0.56	1-14-00	12-28	2.25	19	11.8
A	EBTPrA	*	EBH Capital Tr I 9.40%	NR	[1]8(12/14/04)	0.10	12-15-99	12-10	0.75	7½B	10.0
A	EBSPr	*	EBI Cap Tr I 8.50%	NR	[1]25(9/29/03)	Q0.53	12-31-99	12-13	2.13	18¼	11.6
N	ELOPrA	*	EDF Lond Cap 8.625%[2]'QUIPS'	BB+	[1]25(11/18/02)	Q0.54	12-31-99	12-28	2.16	23	9.4
N	EIXPrA	*	EIX Trust I 7,875%'QUIPS'[3]	BBB+	[1]25(7/25/04)	Q0.49	11-30-99	11-24	1.97	21⅝	9.1
N	EIXPrB	*	EIX Tr II 8.60% 'B'[3]'QUIPS'	BBB+	[1]25(10/28/04)	0.19	11-30-99	11-24	2.15	25	8.6
N	EPGPr	*	El Paso Tenn 8.25% Jr 'A'[4]	BB+	[5]50(12/30/01)	Q1.03	12-31-99	12-14	4.13	52½	7.9
N	ENEPrC	*	Enron Cap LLC 8% 'MIPS'[6]	BBB−	25	M0.17	12-31-99	12-28	2.00	23⅜	8.6
N	ENEPrA	*	Enron Cap Res L.P.9%'A'	BBB−	25	M0.19	12-31-99	12-28	2.25	24½	9.2
N	ENEPrT	*	Enron Cap Tr I 8.30% [7]'TOPrS'	BBB−	[8]25(12/30/01)	Q0.52	12-31-99	12-28	2.08	21⅞	9.5
N	ENEPrR	*	Enron Cap Tr II 8.125%[7]'TOPrS'	BBB−	[9]25(3/30/02)	Q0.51	12-31-99	12-28	2.03	21½	9.5
N	EAIPrA	*	Entergy Ark Cap I 8.50% [2]'QUIPS'	BB+	[10]25(8/13/01)	Q0.53	12-31-99	12-28	2.13	20¼	10.5
N	GSUPrD	*	Entergy Gulf States[11]Dep[12]Adj'B'	BB+	50[13]	0.88	12-15-99	11-23	3.50	49B	7.1
N	EGSPrA	*	EnterGulfStCp I 8.75%[2]'QUIPS'	BB	[14]25(2/27/02)	Q0.55	12-31-99	12-28	2.19	20⅞	10.5
N	LPLPrB	*	Entergy Louis Cp I 9%[2]QUIPS'	BB+	[8]25(7/15/01)	Q0.56	12-31-99	12-28	2.25	22⅛	10.2
N	PEGPrS	*	Enterprise Cap Tr I 7.44%[16]'TOPrS'	BB+	[1]25(3/30/03)	Q0.47	12-31-99	12-28	1.86	18⅝	10.0
N	PEGPrR	*	Enterprise CapTr III 7.25%[17]'TOPrS'	BB+	[8]25(6/29/03)	Q0.45	12-31-99	12-28	1.81	18⅜	9.9
N	ERE	*	Equitable Res Cap Tr 7.35%	BBB+	[1]25(4/14/13)	Q0.46	1-18-00	12-30	1.84	19⅛	9.6
N	ENNPrA	*	Equity Inns 9.50%	B	25(6/24/03)	Q0.59	1-31-00	12-29	2.38	15⅜	15.4
N	EOPPrC	*	Equity Office Prop 8.625%	BBB	25(12/7/03)	Q0.54	12-15-99	11-29	2.16	20½	10.5
N	EQRPrD	*	Equity Res Pr Tr 8.60%,'D'Dep[18]	BBB	25(7/14/07)	Q0.54	1-18-00	12-16	2.15	19¾	10.9
N	EQRPrL	*	Equity Res Prop Tr 7.625%'L'	BBB	25(2/12/03)	Q0.48	12-31-99	12-16	1.91	18⅞	10.1
N	ESBPrA		Espirito Santo Overseas 8.50%'A'	BBB+	25(11/30/03)	Q0.53	12-31-99	12-13	2.13	21½	9.9
N	ESBPrB		Espirito Santo Overseas 8.50%'B'	BBB+	25(8/31/04)	0.57	12-1-99	11-19	2.13	21½	9.9
A	FWTPrA	*	F W Capital 9.375%	BB+	[1]10(2/15/04)	0.23	10-15-99	10-12	0.94	7¾	12.1
N	FWCPrA	*	F W Preferred Cap Tr 9.00%	BBB−	[1]25(1/14/04)	Q0.56	1-18-00	1-12	2.25	14⅝	15.4
N	FIGPrA	*	Farmers Grp Cap 8.45%[2]'QUIPS'	AA−	25(9/26/00)	Q0.53	12-31-99	12-28	2.11	22½	9.4
N	FIGPrB	*	Farmers Gp Cp II 8.25[2]'QUIPS'	A+	25(9/26/00)	Q0.52	12-31-99	12-28	2.06	22⅛	9.3
N	FREPrB		Fed'l Home Loan Mtg Var Rt[19]	NR	50(6/29/01)	0.65	12-31-99	12-09	2.34	43¾B	5.4
N	FREPrF		Fed'l Home Loan Mtg 5%	AA−	50(3/30/03)	Q0.63	12-31-99	12-09	2.50	37B	6.8
N	FREPrL		Fed'l Home Loan Mtg'L'	A−	[20]50	0.46	12-31-99	12-09	[21]2.98	48B	6.2

Exchange	Ticker	Cm Divd	Issue	Rating	Reg. Call Price (Begins) Thru [see footnotes for Sink'g Fd]	Dividends Latest Payments Period $	Date	Ex Div.	Ind. Rate	Last Sale or Bid(B)	% Div Yld
N	FNMPrA		Federal Natl Mtge 6.41%'A'	NR	50(2/28/01)	Q0.80	12-31-99	12-15	3.21	49	6.
N	FNMPrB		Federal Natl Mtge 6.50%'B'	NR	50(4/11/01)	Q0.81	12-31-99	12-15	3.25	49¼B	6.
N	FRTPrA	*	Fed'l Rlty Inv Tr 7.95%	BBB	25(10/5/02)	0.50	1-31-00	1-12	1.99	17¼	11.
N	FCHPrB	*	FelCor Lodging Tr 9% Dep 1	BB−	25(5/6/03)	Q0.56	1-31-00	12-28	2.25	15⅝	14.
N	FIAPr		Fiat SpA Pref ADR[22]	NR	NC	0.48	8-4-99	7-14	0.48	14B	3.
N	FBAPrT	*	First America Cap Tr 8.50%	NR	[1]25(6/29/03)	Q0.53	12-31-99	12-13	2.13	21½B	9.
N	FBPPrA		First Bancorp 7.125%'A'	NR	25.50(4/29/04)	M0.15	12-31-99	12-27	1.78	21⅝B	8.
N	FRPrA	*	First Indl Rlty Tr 9.50%	BBB−	25(11/16/00)	Q0.59	12-31-99	12-13	2.38	22¾	10.
N	FBFPrH	*	Fleet Cap Tr I 8.00%[7]'TOPrS'	NR	[23]25(4/14/01)	Q0.50	12-31-99	12-13	2.00	22	9.
N	FBFPrI	*	Fleet Cap Tr III 7.05%[7]'TOPrS'	NR	[24]25(3/30/03)	Q0.44	12-31-99	12-28	1.76	19⅜	9.
N	FBFPrJ	*	Fleet Cap Tr IV 7.17%'TOPrS'	NR	[1]25(3/30/03)	0.45	12-31-99	12-28	1.79	20	9
N	FBFPrF	*	FleetBoston Finl 7.25% Dep[25]	BBB	25(4/14/01)	Q0.45	1-15-00	12-29	1.81	26	7.
N	FPrB	*	Ford Motor[26]Dep'B'	A	25(11/30/02)	Q0.52	12-1-99	10-28	2.06	26½	7.
N	FPrT	*	Ford Mtr Cap Tr I 9.00%[7]'TOPrS'	BBB+	[27]25(11/30/02)	Q0.56	12-31-99	12-14	2.25	25⅛	9.
N	FPCPrA	*	FPC Cap I 7.10%[2]'QUIPS'	BBB+	[28]25(4/12/04)	Q0.44	11-15-99	11-09	1.77	20⅞	8.
N	FCXPrB	*	Freept-McMo Cp/Gld'B'[29]Dep[30]	B−	[31]NC	Q0.24	11-1-99	10-13	[32]....	19¾	..
N	FCXPrD		Freept-McMo Cp Silver'D'[33]Dep[34]	BB−	[31]NC	Q†0.19	11-1-99	10-13	[35]....	12⅝	e..
N	FMTPr	*	Fremont Genl Fin I 9%[7]'TOPrS'	BB+	[9]25(3/30/01)	Q0.56	12-31-99	12-28	2.25	14¾	15.
N	GLRPrB		G&L Realty 9.80%	NR	25(12/31/01)	M0.20	1-15-00	12-29	2.45	14½	17.
N	GCVPr	*	Gabelli Conv Sec Fd 8%	AAA	[36]25(4/14/02)	Q0.50	12-27-99	12-16	2.00	23¼B	8.
N	GABPr	*	Gabelli Eq Tr 7.25% Tax Adv	NR	25(6/8/03)	Q0.45	12-27-99	12-16	1.81	21⅞	8.
N	GGTPr	*	Gabelli Global Multimedia 7.92%	NR	[37]25(5/31/02)	Q0.49	12-27-99	12-16	1.98	22⅞	8.
N	GBPPrA		Gables Residential Tr 8.30%	BBB−	25(7/23/02)	Q0.52	12-15-99	11-29	2.08	18⅜	11.
N	GAMPr		Genl Amer Inv Tax-Adv 7.20%	NR	25(6/22/03)	Q0.45	12-23-99	12-02	1.80	21¾	8.
N	GMPrX	*	GenMtr Cap TrSr'D'8.67%[7]'TOPrS'	BBB+	[8]25	Q0.54	2-1-00	1-12	2.17	25	8.
N	GMPrY	*	GenMtr Cap TrSr'G'9.87%[7]'TOPrS'	BBB+	[1]25(1/31/00)	Q0.62	2-1-00	1-12	2.47	26	9.
N	GPEPrT	*	Georgia Pwr Cap Tr I 7.75%	A−	[1]25(9/29/01)	Q0.48	12-31-99	12-14	1.94	21⅞	8
N	GPEPrU	*	Georgia Pwr Cap Tr II 7.60%	A−	[8]25(1/15/02)	Q0.47	12-31-99	12-14	1.90	21½	8
N	GPEPrV	*	Geo Pwr CapTr III 7.75%[2]'QUIPS'	A−	[38]25(6/10/02)	Q0.48	12-31-99	12-14	1.94	22	8
N	GPEPrA	*	Georgia Pwr Cap Tr IV 6.85%	A−	[1]25(2/24/04)	Q0.43	12-31-99	12-14	1.71	20¾	8.
A	HOOPrA	*	Glacier Water Tr 9.0625%	NR	25(1/30/03)	M0.19	12-15-99	12-10	2.27	14¼	15

Footnotes and Sinking Fund: [1] Or earlier upon'Tax Event're-spec cond. [2] Quarterly Income Preferred Securities. [3] Qtly Income Preferred Securities. [4] Formerly Tenneco Inc. [5] or earlier re-spec cond. [6] Monthly income preferred shrs. [7] Trust Originated Preferred Securities. [8] or earlier upon'Tax Event're-spec cond. [9] or anytime upon'Tax Event're-spec cond. [10] or earlier upon 'Tax Event're-spec cond. [11] Dep for 1/2'B'. [12] Rate adjusted qtrly:min 7%,max 13.50%. [13] SF 50. [14] or earlier upon 'Tax Event' re-spec cond. [15] Trust Orginated Preferred Securities. [16] Trust Orginated Preferred Securities. [17] Trust Originated Preferred Securities. [18] Dep for 0.10 shr 8.60% cm Pfd. [19] Rate adjusted qtrly:max 9.00%. [20] On 12-31-2004 & 0n Dec 31 every 5 yrs aft. [21] Reset every 5 yrs beg 1-1-2005,max 11%. [22] Each ADR rep 5 preference shrs, lit.1000. [23] or anytime upon'Tax Event' re-spec cond. [24] or anytime uopn'Tax-Event're-spec cond. [25] Dep for 0.10 shr 7.25% Ser V Perpetual Pfd. [26] Dep for .0005 shr Series'B'cm Pfd. [27] or anytime upon'Spcl Event're-spec cond. [28] Or earlier upon'Spcl Event're-spec cond. [29] Dep for 0.05 shr Gold Denominated Pfd. [30] Mand red 8-1-2003 for value 0.10 once gold. [31] Re-specified cond. [32] Based on curr val of.000875 oz gold on div date. [33] Dep for 0.025 shr Silver-Denominated Pfd. [34] Redeem Pfd with value 0.05 in slvr. [35] Based on Dollar Equivalent value of oz silver. [36] Or earlier re spec-cond. [37] Or earlier re-spec cond. [38] or earlier upon 'Tax Event're-sec cond.

Exchange	Ticker	Cm Divd	Issue	Rating	Reg. Call Price (Begins) Thru [see footnotes for Sink'g Fd]	Dividends Latest Payments Period $	Date	Ex Div.	Ind. Rate	Last Sale or Bid(B)	% Div. Yld.
N	GRTPrB	*	Glimcher Realty Tr 9.25% 'B'	B	25(11/14/02)	Q0.58	1-14-00	12-29	2.31	15¼	15.2
N	GRMPrA	*	Grand Met Del L.P. 9.42%	A–	25(11/15/04)	Q0.59	11-1-99	10-27	2.35	26⅛	9.0
N	GLPrA	*	Great Lakes REIT 9.75%	NR	25(12/15/03)	Q0.61	12-1-99	11-17	2.44	19½	12.5
N	GWFPrT	*	Great Westn Finl I 8.25%[1]'TOPrS'	BBB–	[2]25(12/30/00)	Q0.52	12-31-99	12-28	2.06	22⅜	9.2
N	GTEPrY	*	GTE Delaware 8.75%'B'[3]'MIPS'	BBB+	25(3/5/00)	M0.18	12-31-99	12-28	2.19	24¾	8.8
N	GOUPrA	*	Gulf Cda Res[4]AdjSer1 Pref	NR	5	Mg0.02	1-12-00	12-29	0.25	2⅛	11.8
N	GUPPrA	*	Gulf Pwr Cap Tr I 7.625%'QUIPS'	A–	[5]25(1/30/02)	Q0.48	12-31-99	12-14	1.91	21⅜	8.9
N	GUPPrB		Gulf Pwr Cap Tr II 7.00%'QUIPS'	A–	[6]25(1/19/03)	Q0.44	12-31-99	12-14	1.75	19⅜	9.0
N	HBCPr		Harris Pfd Cap 7.375%[7]Exch'A'	A	[8]25(3/29/03)	Q0.46	12-30-99	12-13	1.84	20⅜	9.1
N	HIGPrQ	*	Hartford Cap I 7.70%[9]'QUIPS'	BBB+	[10]25(2/27/01)	Q0.48	12-31-99	12-28	1.93	21⅛	9.1
N	HIGPrB	*	Hartford Cap II 8.35%[9]'QUIPS'	BBB+	[11]25(10/29/01)	Q0.52	12-31-99	12-28	2.09	23⅛	9.0
N	HLIPrA	*	Hartford Life Cap 7.20%[12]'TruPS'	BBB+	[6]25(6/29/03)	Q0.45	1-18-00	1-12	1.80	21	8.6
N	HEPrS	*	Hawaii El Cp Tr I 8.36%[1]'TOPrS'	BB+	[8]25(2/3/02)	Q0.52	12-31-99	12-28	2.09	21⅛	9.9
N	HCPPrC	*	Health Care Prop 8.60%Sr'C'Dep[13]	BB+	25(10/26/02)	0.18	12-31-99	12-13	2.15	14⅝	14.7
N	HCNPrB	*	HealthCare REIT 8.875%	BB+	25(4/30/03)	Q0.55	1-18-00	12-28	2.22	14⅜	15.4
N	HRPrA	*	Healthcare Realty Tr 8.875%'A'	NR	25(9/29/02)	Q0.55	11-26-99	11-03	2.22	15¼	14.5
A	HFTPr	*	Heartland Finl Cap Tr I 9.60%	NR	[6]25(9/29/04)	0.47	12-31-99	12-28	2.40	26B	9.2
N	HEPrQ	*	HECO Cap I 8.05%[9]'QUIPS'	BBB–	[14]25(3/26/02)	Q0.50	12-31-99	12-28	2.01	21	9.6
N	HEPrT	*	HECO Cap II 7.30%[9]'QUIPS'	BBB–	[6]25(12/14/03)	Q0.46	12-31-99	12-28	1.82	19⅜	9.4
N	HFPrA	*	Heller Finl 8.125% Ser'A'	BBB	25(9/14/00)	Q0.51	11-15-99	10-28	2.03	26	7.8
N	HPCPrA	*	Hercules Tr I 9.42%[1]'TOPrS'	BB	[14]25(3/16/04)	Q0.59	12-31-99	12-28	2.35	20⅞	11.3
N	HIWPrD	*	Highwoods Prop 8.00% 'D'Dep[15]	BBB	25(4/23/03)	Q0.50	1-31-00	12-30	2.00	17	11.8
N	REIPrA	*	HL&P Cap Tr I 8.125%	BBB	[5]25(2/3/02)	Q0.51	12-31-99	12-28	2.03	21¾	9.4
N	HPTPrA	*	Hospitality Prop Tr 9.50%'A'	BB+	[16]25(4/11/04)	Q0.59	12-31-99	12-13	2.38	17¼	13.8
N	HMTPrA	*	Host Marriott 10%'A'	B	[17]25(8/2/04)	Q0.63	1-14-00	12-29	2.50	18½	13.5
N	HMTPrB	*	Host Marriott 10%'B'	B	[16]25 4/28/05	0.33	1-14-00	12-29	2.50	18½	13.5
N	HIPrP	*	Househld Cap Tr 7.25%	A–	[18]25(3/18/03)	Q0.45	12-31-99	12-28	1.81	19⅝	9.2
N	HIPrT	*	Househld Cap Tr 8.25%'TOPrS'	BBB+	25(6/29/00)	Q0.52	12-31-99	12-28	2.06	21¾	9.5
N	HIPrY	*	Househld Cap Tr 8.70%	BBB+	[19]25(6/29/01)	Q0.54	12-31-99	12-28	2.18	22⅝	9.6
N	HBBPrA		HSBC Bank[20]A1/A2[21]Unit[22]ADS	NR	[22]25.888 10/4/00	0.50	12-15-99	11-23	1.91	21⅝	8.8
N	IACPrA	*	IAC Cap Tr 8.25%'TOPrS'	BBB–	[23]25(12/30/02)	Q0.52	12-31-99	12-28	2.06	18½	11.1
N	IPCPrM	*	IllinoisPwrCap9.45%'A'[3]'MIPS'	BB+	25	M0.20	12-31-99	12-28	2.36	24⅛	9.8
N	IPCPrT	*	Illinois PwrFin I 8%[1] 'TOPrS'	BB+	[24]25(1/30/01)	Q0.50	12-31-99	12-28	2.00	20	10.0
A	IBKPr	*	Independent Cap Tr 8.50%	NR	[25]10(9/21/03)	Q0.21	12-31-99	12-13	0.85	6⅞	12.4
N	INGPrA		ING Cap Fdg Tr I 7.70%	A	[26]25(6/24/04)	Q0.48	12-31-99	12-28	1.93	21⅛	9.1
N	IRPrG	*	Ing-Rand GthFELINE[27]PRIDES[28]	NR	[29]NC	0.05	11-16-99	11-10	[30]0.20	23½B	0.8
N	IRPrI	*	Ing-Rand6.75%[31]FELINE[32]PRIDES	NR	[29]NC	0.42	11-16-99	11-10	[33]1.69	25½	6.6
N	IBMPrA	*	Int Bus Mach 7 1/2% [34]Dep	A–	25(6/30/01)	Q0.47	1-4-00	12-16	1.88	25½	7.4
A	IKTPrA	*	INTRUST Cap Tr 8.24%	NR	[19]25(12/30/02)	Q0.52	12-31-99	12-13	2.06	24¾	8.3
N	JYPPrZ	*	JCP&L Cap L.P.8.56%'MIPS'[3]	BBB+	25(5/17/00)	M0.18	12-31-99	12-28	2.14	24⅛	8.9
N	JDNPrA	*	JDN Realty 9.375%	BB+	25(9/14/03)	Q0.59	12-31-99	12-13	2.34	17⅝	13.3
N	KABPrA	*	Kaneb Svcs Adj Rt'A'[35]	NR	10.80 6/30/00	0.21	12-31-99	12-09	0.84	10¼B	8.2
N	KSUPr		Kansas City So.Ind 4% Vtg	NR	NC	Q0.25	1-3-00	12-13	1.00	14¾B	6.8
N	KLTPrA	*	Kansas City P&L 3.80%	BBB+	103.70	Q0.95	3-1-00	2-04	3.80	65B	5.8
A	KBKPr	*	KBK Capital 9.50%	NR	[6]10(11/29/01)	Q0.24	11-30-99	11-10	0.95	6⅝	14.3
N	KLTPrT	*	KCPL Financing I 8.3%[1]'TOPrS'	BBB+	[5]25(3/30/02)	Q0.52	12-31-99	12-28	2.08	22⅝	9.2
N	KSEPrA	*	KeySpan Corp 7.95% AA	BBB	25(5/31/00)	Q0.50	12-1-99	11-08	1.99	25½	7.8
N	KIMPrC	*	Kimco Rlty 8.375% Sr'C'Dep[36]	BBB+	25(4/14/01)	Q0.52	1-18-00	12-30	2.09	19⅛	10.9
N	KRTPrD	*	Kranzco Rlty Tr 9.50% 'D'	NR	25(12/10/02)	Q0.59	1-20-00	12-23	2.38	13¾	17.3
N	LSHPrA	*	LaSalle Re Hldg 8.75%	BB+	25(3/26/07)	Q0.55	12-1-99	10-28	2.19	18	12.2
N	LSOPrA	*	LASMO plc Sr'A'ADS[37]	BB+	[38]25(6/15/00)	0.56	1-18-00	12-27	2.25	25⅜	8.9
N	LEHPrC	*	Lehman Br Hldg 5.94%Sr'C'Dep[39]	NR	50(5/30/08)	Q0.74	11-30-99	11-10	2.97	41	7.2
N	LEHPrI	*	Lehman Br Hldg 8.0% Sr'I'	BBB+	[6]25(3/30/04)	0.50	12-31-99	12-28	2.00	21⅜	9.4
N	LEHPrJ	*	Leh Br Hldg Cap Tr II 7.875%	BBB+	[40]25(6/29/04)	Q0.49	12-31-99	12-28	1.97	20⅜	9.7
N	LRYPrA	*	Liberty Property Tr 8.80%	BB+	[41]25(7/29/02)	Q0.55	1-30-00	1-12	2.20	19½	11.3
N	LNCPrX	*	Lincoln Natl Cp I 8.75%'QUIPS'[9]	BBB	[42]25(7/1/01)	Q0.55	12-31-99	12-28	2.19	24¼	9.0
N	LNCPrY		Lincoln Natl Cp II 8.35%[1]'TOPrS'	BBB	[43]25(8/20/01)	Q0.52	12-31-99	12-28	2.09	22⅜	9.3
N	LITPrB	*	Litton Indus $2 B Vtg	BBB+	80	Q0.50	1-1-00	12-15	2.00	25½B	7.9
N	LWNPr	*	Loewen Grp Cap 9.45%'A'[3]'MIPS'	BB–	25(8/30/04)	0.20	3-1-99	2-24	Nil	¾	....
N	LTCPrB	*	LTC Properties 9.0% Sr'B'	NR	[44]25(12/31/01)	M0.19	1-15-00	12-29	2.25	12⅞	17.5
N	MKGPr	*	Mallinckrodt Inc 4% Vtg	BBB+	110	Q1.00	12-31-99	12-06	4.00	60B	6.7
A	MFGPrA		MB Capital I 8.75%	NR	[5]10(2/8/03)	Q0.22	10-15-99	10-12	0.88	9B	9.7

ootnotes and Sinking Fund: [1] Trust Originated Preferred Securities. [2] or anytime upon 'Tax Event're-spec cond. [3] Monthly Income Preferred Shrs. [4] Adj mthly, 80% Cdn Prime. [5] or earlier upon'Tax Event're-spec cond. Or earlier upon'Tax Event're-spec cond. [7] Exch by co for 1 new Pfd re-spec cond. [8] or anytime upon'Tax Event're-spec cond. [9] Quarterly Income Preferred Securities. [10] Or earlier upon'Special Event're-spec cond. [11] or earlier pon'Special Event're-spec cond. [12] Trust Preferred Securities. [13] Dep for 0.01 shr 8.60% Sr'B'cm Pfd. [14] or earlier upon 'Tax Event' re-spec cond. [15] Dep for 0.10 shr 8.00% Sr'D'cm Pfd. [16] Or earlier to preserve'REIT'status e-spec cond. [17] Or earlier to preserve'REIT'status. [18] Or anytime upon'Tax Event' re-spec cond. [19] Or anytime upon'Tax Event're-spec cond. [20] Ea A1 ADS rep 1 non-cm $-denominated Pref. [21] Ea A2 ADS rep 1 non-cm $-enominated Pref. [22] Pref redeem:Ser A1$20,Ser A2$5. [23] or earlier upon'Tax Event're spec-cond. [24] Or anytime upon'Special Event're-spec cond. [25] Or earlier re-spec cond. [26] Or earlier upon'Spec Event're-spec cond. [27] Ea ec consist of stk pur contract&1/40 int US Tr Sec. [28] Pur cont for Ingersoll-Rand com to 5-16-2001 re-spec cond. [29] Mand 5-16-2003:Cv on'Tax Event're-spec cond. [30] Contractual Adj Payment. [31] Pfd Redeemable Increased iv Equity Sec. [32] Ea Sec consists of stk pur contr&6.22% Tr Pfd. [33] $1.555 & $0.1325 contract adj pymt. [34] Dep for 0.25 shr Ser'A' 7 1/2% Pfd stk. [35] Rate adjusted qtrly:min 7.50%,max 14%. [36] Dep for 0.10 shr 8.375% r'C'cm Red Pfd. [37] Ea ADS rep 1 cm Dollar Pref shr Series'A'. [38] Plus $1.00 special div. [39] Dep for 0.10 shr 5.94% Sr'C' cm Pfd. [40] Or earlier upon'Spcl Event're-spec cond. [41] or earlier for Tax status chge re-spec cond. [42] or arlier upon 'Tax Event're-spec cond. [43] Or earlier upon 'Tax Event' re spec cond. [44] or earlier for chge in 'Tax Status're-spec cond.

Exchange	Ticker	Cm Divd	Issue	Rating	Reg. Call Price (Begins) Thru [see footnotes for Sink'g Fd]	Dividends Latest Payments Period $	Date	Ex Div.	Ind. Rate	Last Sale or Bid(B)	% Div. Yld.
N	KRBPrA	*	MBNA Corp 7.50% Sr'A'	NR	25(1/14/01)	Q0.47	1-15-00	12-28	1.88	25	7.5
N	KRBPrC	*	MBNA Capital C 8.25%[1]'TOPrS'	NR	[2]25(2/14/02)	Q0.52	1-15-00	12-28	2.06	19¼	10.7
A	MSTPr	*	MBNK Cap Tr I 9.625%	NR	[3]10(12/30/04)	0.06	12-31-99	12-13	....	10	....
N	MCNPrI	*	MCN Egy 8%[4]FELINE[5]'PRIDES'	NR	[6]NC	Q1.00	12-31-99	12-28	4.00	40⅝	9.8
N	MCNPrA	*	MCN Financing I 8.625%[1]'TOPrS'	BBB–	[3]25(7/29/01)	Q0.54	12-31-99	12-28	2.16	21	10.3
N	MCNPrT	*	MCN Mich L.P. 9.375%	BBB–	25	M0.20	12-31-99	12-28	2.34	24	9.8
N	UMGPrX	*	MediaOne Fin'A' 7.96%[1]'TOPrS'	BBB+	[7]25(9/10/00)	Q0.50	12-31-99	12-28	1.99	23⅜B	8.5
N	UMGPrY	*	MediaOne Fin'B' 8.25%[1]'TOPrS'	BBB+	[8]25(10/28/01)	Q0.52	12-31-99	12-28	2.06	23½B	8.8
N	UMGPrA	*	MediaOne Fin I 9.30%[1]'TOPrS'	BB+	[3]25(9/10/00)	Q0.58	12-31-99	12-28	2.33	25⅛	9.3
N	UMPrB	*	MediaOne Fin II 9.30%[1]'TOPrS'	BB+	[3]25(10/28/01)	Q0.59	12-31-99	12-28	2.38	25⅛	9.5
N	UMGPrC	*	MediaOne Fin III 9.04% [1]'TOPrS'	BB+	[3]25(10/27/03)	Q0.56	12-31-99	12-28	2.26	25¼	9.0
N	MTPr	*	Meditrust Corp 9.00%Sr'A'Dep[9]	NR	25(6/16/03)	Q0.56	12-31-99	12-13	2.25	12	18.8
N	MUKPrA	*	MEPC Intl Cap 9.125%[10]'QUIPS'	NR	25(9/20/05)	Q0.57	12-31-99	12-28	2.28	21	10.9
N	MERPrA	*	Merrill Lynch 9%'A'[11]Dep	A	25(12/29/04)	Q0.56	12-30-99	12-13	2.25	29⅞	7.5
N	MERPrB	*	Merr Lyn Cap Tr I 7.75%[1]'TOPrS'	A	[8]25(12/29/06)	Q0.48	12-30-99	12-27	1.94	21⅝	9.0
N	MERPrC	*	Mer Lyn Pref CpTr II 8%[1]'TOPrS'	A	[2]25(3/29/07)	Q0.50	12-30-99	12-27	2.00	22½	8.9
N	MERPrD	*	Mer LynPrefCpTrIII 7%[1]'TOPrS'	A	[3]25(3/29/08)	Q0.44	12-30-99	12-27	1.75	19⅞	8.8
N	MERPrE	*	Mer LynPrefCpTrIV7.12%[1]'TOPrS'	A	[3]25(6/29/08)	Q0.45	12-30-99	12-27	1.78	19⅞	9.0
N	MTTPrX	*	Met-Ed Cap Tr 7.35% Pfd Secs	NR	[12]25(5/27/04)	Q0.46	12-1-99	11-26	1.84	20¼	9.1
N	MAAPrC	*	Mid-Am Apt Comm'ties 9.375%	B+	25(6/29/03)	Q0.59	1-15-00	12-29	2.34	16⅛	14.5
N	MECPrA	*	MidAmer En Fin I 7.98%[13]'QUIPS'	A–	[8]25(12/17/01)	Q0.50	12-31-99	12-28	2.00	21⅞	9.1
N	MEPrA	*	Mission Capital 9.875%[14]'MIPS'	BBB	25	M0.21	12-31-99	12-28	2.47	24⅞	9.9
N	MEPrB	*	Mission Capital 8.50%[14]'MIPS'	NR	25(8/7/00)	M0.18	12-31-99	12-28	2.13	25¼	8.4
N	MPPrD	*	Miss Pwr Cp Tr I 7.75%[1]'TOPrS'	A–	[15]25(2/25/02)	Q0.48	12-31-99	12-13	1.94	21¼B	9.1
A	MPNPrC	*	Monongahela Pwr 4.50% C	A–	103.50	Q1.13	2-1-00	1-12	4.50	73B	6.2
N	MTPPrA	*	Montana Pwr Cap I 8.45%'QUIPS'	BBB–	[16]25(11/5/01)	Q0.53	12-31-99	12-28	2.11	24⅜	8.7
N	JPMPrH	*	Morgan(JP)6.625%'H'Dep[17]	A+	50(3/30/06)	Q0.83	12-31-99	12-16	3.31	48½B	6.8
N	MWDPrF	*	MorSt DeanWt[18]5.91% Fx/Ad Dp[19]	NR	[20]50(11/29/01)	Q0.74	11-30-99	10-28	[19]2.96	50B	5.9
N	MPLPr	*	MP&L Cap I 8.05%[13]'QUIPS'	BBB–	[21]25(3/19/01)	Q0.50	12-31-99	12-28	2.01	21¾	9.3
N	MWC	*	MSDW CapTr I 7.10%Cap Sec	A–	[8]25(3/11/03)	Q0.44	11-30-99	11-10	1.77	20⅛	8.8
N	NGHPrU	*	Nabisco Grp Hldgs 9.50%'TOPrS'	BB	[3]25(9/29/03)	Q0.59	12-30-99	12-27	2.38	25¼	9.4
N	NWPrC		Natl Westminster Pref'C'ADS	A+	26.50(4/8/02)	0.54	1-18-00	12-08	1.92	21¼	9.1
N	NFSPrA	*	Nat Finl Sv Cp II 7.10%'TruPS'	A–	[3]25(10/18/03)	Q0.44	11-1-99	10-27	1.77	19⅞	9.0
N	NBD		NB Capital 8.35% Sr'A'Dep[22]	A–	[8]26.044(9/2/07)	Q0.52	12-30-99	12-16	2.09	21½	9.7
N	NBPrA		NB Capital Tr I 7.84%[1]'TOPrS'	A–	[8]25(12/30/01)	Q0.49	12-31-99	12-28	1.96	21⅞	9.0
A	NBNPr	*	NBN Cap Tr 9.60%	NR	[3]7(12/30/04)	0.07	12-31-99	12-13	0.67	5⅞B	11.4
N	NXLPrB	*	New Plan Ex Rlty 8.625%'B'Dep[23]	A–	25(1/12/03)	Q0.54	10-15-99	9-29	2.16	19⅜	11.2
A	NBSPrA	*	New South Cap Tr 8.50%	NR	[3]10(6/29/03)	Q0.21	12-31-99	12-13	0.85	7⅝	11.1
N	NWS.A		News Corp Ltd Vtg ADS[24]	BB+	NC	0.08	11-10-99	10-05	0.17	33½	0.5
N	NOPPrA	*	Newscorp Overseas[25]8.625%	BB	25	Q0.54	12-31-99	12-14	2.16	21½	10.0
N	NOPPrB	*	Newscorp Overseas[25]Adj Rt[26]'B'	BB	25	0.41	12-31-99	12-14	1.55	16¾	9.3
N	NMKPrN	*	Niagara Moh Pw Fixed/Adj'D'	BB+	50(12/30/04)	0.30	12-31-99	12-15	[27]3.45	51⅜	6.7
N	NIPrB	*	NiSource 7.75%[28]'PIES'	NR	[3]50(2/18/03)	Q†0.97	11-19-99	11-16	3.88	36⅛	10.7
N	NSRPr	*	Norfolk So'n Ry $2.60 A Vtg	NR	50	Q0.65	12-15-99	11-03	2.60	37½B	6.9
N	NTL		Nortel Inversora Sr'B'Pfd ADS[29]	NR	[30]NC	0.09	12-30-99	12-20	0.49	19⅜	2.5
N	NIPrA	*	No'n Ind Pub Sv Adj[31]Rt	A–	50	Q0.75	1-14-00	12-14	3.00	48B	6.3
N	NORPrB	*	NorthWestern Cap Fin 7.20%	A–	25 11/17/03	0.45	12-31-99	12-28	1.80	20⅜	8.8
N	NCXPrA	*	Nova Chemicals 9.04%	BBB–	[3]25(1/25/04)	Q0.56	12-31-99	12-14	2.26	20⅛	11.2
N	NSPPrT	*	NSP Financing I 7.875%[1]'TOPrS'	A	[8]25(1/30/02)	Q0.49	12-31-99	12-28	1.97	21¾	9.1
N	NVPPr	*	NVP Cap I 8.20%[13]'QUIPS'	BB+	[3]25(4/1/02)	Q0.51	12-31-99	12-28	2.05	21¾	9.4
N	NVPPrB	*	NVP Cap III 7.75%	BB+	[3]25(10/5/03)	Q0.48	12-31-99	12-28	1.94	20¼	9.6
N	NORPrA	*	NWPS Cap Fin 8.125% Tr Sec 1	A–	25(9/29/00)	Q0.51	12-31-99	12-28	2.03	22¼	9.1
N	OGEPr	*	OGE Energy Cap Tr I 8.375%	A–	[12]25(10/14/04)	Plan qtly div			2.09	25⅝	8.2
N	OECPrM	*	Ohio Ed 7.75%'A'	B+	25	Q0.48	1-1-00	12-13	1.94	25⅜	7.6
N	OECPrT	*	Ohio Ed Fin Tr 9.00%CapSec	B+	25(12/30/00)	Q0.56	12-31-99	12-28	2.25	22	10.2
N	OHIPrB	*	Omega Healthcare 8.625%'B'	BB+	25(6/30/03)	Q0.54	11-15-99	10-27	2.16	11¼	19.3
N	OFGPrA		Oriental Finl Grp 7.125%[32]'MIPS'	NR	25.50(5/29/04)	M0.15	1-31-00	1-12	1.78	24⅛B	7.4
A	PETPrB	*	Pac Ent $4.40	A–	101.50	Q1.10	1-15-00	12-17	4.40	64⅜B	6.8
A	PCGPrU	*	Pac G&E 7.04% Red 1st Vtg	A–	25.88(1/30/03)	Q0.44	11-15-99	10-13	1.76	24⅝	7.1
N	PACPrT	*	Pac Telesis Fin I 7.56%'TOPrS'	A	[2]25(1/8/01)	Q0.47	12-31-99	12-28	1.89	22	8.6
N	PACPrU	*	Pac Telesis Fin II 8.50%[1]'TOPrS'	A	[2]25(6/18/01)	Q0.53	12-31-99	12-28	2.13	24⅝	8.7
N	PPWPrA	*	PacifiCorp Cap I 8.25%'QUIPS'[13]	BBB+	[33]25(6/10/01)	Q0.52	12-31-99	12-28	2.06	22¼	9.3

Footnotes and Sinking Fund: [1] Trust Originated Preferred Securities. [2] or anytime upon'Tax Event're-spec cond. [3] Or earlier upon'Tax Event're-spec cond. [4] Ea Sec consists of Stk Pur Contr & 7.25%Tr Pfd Sec. [5] Pur cont for MCN com fr 5-2000 re-spec cond. [6] Mat 5-16-2002:Cv to JrDebs on 'Tax Ev're-spec cond. [7] or earlier upon 'Tax Event' re-spec cond. [8] or earlier upon'Tax Event're-spec cond. [9] Dep for 0.10 shr 9.00% Sr'A'cm Pfd. [10] Qtly Income Pfd Securities. [11] Dep for .0025 shr 9% Sr'A'cm Pfd. [12] Or earlier upon'Spcl Event're-spec cond. [13] Quarterly Income Preferred Securities. [14] Monthly Income Preferred Shrs. [15] or anytime upon 'Tax Event' re-spec cond. [16] or earlier upon 'Tax Event're-spec cond. [17] Dep for 0.01 shr 6.625%cm Sr'H'Pfd. [18] Dep for 0.25 shr'A'Fixed/Adj Pfd. [19] 2/28/97-11/30/01,adj aft(min6.41%,max12.41%). [20] Or earlier re-spec cond. [21] or earlier upon'Tax Event'. [22] Dep for 0.025 shr 8.35% Sr'A'Pfd. [23] Dep for 0.10 shr 8.625%Sr'B'cm Pfd. [24] Ea ADS rep 4 Pfd Ltd Vtg Ord Shrs. [25] Gtd by News Corp Ltd. [26] Rate adjusted qtrly:min 5.75%,max 11%. [27] To 12-31-2004 then rate adj min 7.655%,max 13.655%. [28] Premium Income Equity Securities. [29] Ea ADS rep 0.05 Sr'B'Pfd. [30] Redm for chg in control re-spec cond. [31] Rate adjusted qtrly:min 6%,max 12.50%. [32] Monthly Income Preferred Stock. [33] or earlier upon'Special Event're-spec cond.

Ticker	Cm Divd	Issue	Rating	Reg. Call Price (Begins) Thru [see footnotes for Sink'g Fd]	Dividends Latest Payments Period $	Date	Ex Div.	Ind. Rate	Last Sale or Bid(B)	% Div. Yld.
PPWPrB	*	PacifiCorp Cap II 7.70%	BBB+	[1]25(8/3/02)	Q0.48	12-31-99	12-28	1.93	20¾	9.3
PKYPrA	*	Parkway Properties 8.75%'A'	NR	25(4/22/03)	Q0.55	1-15-00	12-29	2.19	18	12.2
PREPrA		PartnerRe Ltd 8%	A–	25(7/9/02)	Q0.50	12-1-99	10-28	2.00	21⅞	9.2
PEPrX	*	Peco En Cap TrII 8.00%[2]'QUIPS'	BBB–	[3]25(6/5/02)	M0.17	1-31-00	1-12	2.00	23¾	8.4
PECPrX	*	Penelec Cap Tr 7.34%[4]'TOPrS'	NR	[5]25(8/31/04)	Q0.46	12-1-99	11-26	1.83	20¼	9.1
PCGPrCA	*	PG&E Cap I 7.90%[2]'QUIPS'	A–	[6]25(11/27/00)	Q0.49	12-31-99	12-28	1.98	22¼	8.9
PGOPrA	*	PGS Tr I 9.625%	BB+	[7]25(6/29/04)	Q0.60	12-31-99	12-28	2.41	23⅛	10.4
PPrC	*	Phillips 66 Cap I 8.24%[4]'TOPrS'	BBB	[8]25(5/28/01)	Q0.52	12-31-99	12-28	2.06	22	9.4
PDGPrA	*	Placer Dome 8.625%Sr'A'[9]'COPrS'	BB+	[8]25(12/16/01)	Q0.54	12-31-99	12-28	2.16	17½	12.3
PLPrT	*	PLC Cap 8.25%[4]'TOPrS'	BBB+	[8]25(4/28/02)	Q0.52	12-31-99	12-28	2.06	22	9.4
PPSPrB	*	Post Properties 7.625% Sr'B'	BBB	25(10/27/07)	Q0.48	12-31-99	12-13	1.91	16½	11.6
POMPrT	*	Potomac El Pwr 7.375%[4]'TOPrS'	BBB+	[10]25(5/31/03)	Q0.46	12-1-99	11-26	1.84	21⅜	8.6
PPLPrA	*	PP&L Inc 4.40%	BBB+	102	Q1.10	1-1-00	12-08	4.40	62⅜B	7.1
PPLPrC		PP&L Cap 8.20%[4]TOPrS'	BBB	[8]25(3/30/02)	Q0.51	1-1-00	12-29	2.05	21¼	9.7
PPLPrD	*	PP&L Cap 8.10%[4]'TOPrS'	BBB	[1]25(6/30/02)	Q0.51	1-1-00	12-29	2.02	22	9.2
PMBPr	*	Premier Cap Tr I 9.00%	NR	[11]25(12/30/07)	Q0.56	12-31-99	12-13	2.25	24	9.4
PGEPrB	*	Prime Grp Realty 9.00%'B'	NR	25(6/4/03)	Q0.56	1-31-00	12-29	2.25	14⅞	15.1
PRTPrA	*	Prime Retail 10.50%'A'	NR	25	Q0.66	11-15-99	11-03	2.63	14¾	17.9
PZNPrA	*	Prison Realty Tr 8.0%	NR	25(1/29/03)	Q0.50	1-15-00	12-29	2.00	13⅛	15.2
PLDPrD	*	ProLogis Trust 9.00% 'D'	BBB	25(4/12/03)	Q0.49	12-31-99	12-09	1.98	18¼	10.8
PLPrP		Prot Life[15]6.5%[16]FELINE[17]'PRIDES'	A–	[18]NC	Q0.81	12-31-99	12-28	3.25	52⅞	6.1
PSBPrA	*	PS Business Parks 9.25%'A' Dep[19]	BB+	[20]25(4/29/04)	Q0.58	12-31-99	12-13	2.31	19¾	11.7
PSRPrC	*	PSCO Cap Tr 7.60%[4]'TOPrS'	BBB	[10]25(5/10/03)	Q0.47	12-31-99	12-28	1.90	21	9.0
PEGPrU	*	PSE&G Cap Tr I 8.625%[2]'QUIPS'	BBB	[8]25(6/25/01)	Q0.54	12-31-99	12-28	2.16	23⅜	9.2
PEGPrT	*	PSE&G Cap Tr II 8.125%[2]'QUIPS'	BBB	[8]25(2/6/02)	Q0.51	12-31-99	12-28	2.03	21⅞	9.3
PSTPrA	*	PSO Cap 8.00%[4]'TOPrS'	A–	[21]25(4/29/02)	Q0.50	12-31-99	12-28	2.00	21⅛	9.5
PEGPrX	*	Pub Sv E&G Cap 8.00%'MIPS'	BBB+	25(9/14/00)	M0.17	12-31-99	12-28	2.00	21⅝	9.3
PSAPrK	*	Public Storage 8.25% 'K' Dep[22]	BBB+	[23]25(1/18/04)	Q0.52	12-31-99	12-13	2.06	20	10.3
PSAPrL	*	Public Storage 8.25% 'L' Dep[24]	NR	[25]25(3/9/04)	Q0.52	12-31-99	12-13	2.06	19¾	10.4
PWJPrA	*	PWG Cap Tr I 8.30%	NR	[26]25(11/30/01)	M0.17	1-3-00	12-29	2.07	22¼	9.4
PWJPrB	*	PWG Cap Tr II 8.08%	NR	[27]25(2/27/02)	M0.17	1-3-00	12-29	2.02	21⅞	9.3

Exchange	Ticker	Cm Divd	Issue	Rating	Reg. Call Price (Begins) Thru [see footnotes for Sink'g Fd]	Dividends Latest Payments Period $	Date	Ex Div.	Ind. Rate	Last Sale or Bid(B)	% Div. Yld.
A	CQPPrA	*	Quad City Hld Tr I 9.20% Cap Sec	NR	[10]10(6/29/04)	Q0.23	12-31-99	12-28	0.92	9¾B	9.4
N	OPrB	*	Realty Income 9.375%	BB+	[10]25(5/24/04)	Q0.59	12-31-99	12-13	2.34	17⅜	13.5
N	REIPrC	*	REI Tr I 7.20%'C'[4]'TOPrS'	BBB	[10]25(2/25/04)	Q0.45	12-31-99	12-28	1.80	19½	9.2
N	RLRPrA	*	ReliaStar Fin I 8.20%[4]'TOPrS'	BBB+	[8]25(3/28/01)	Q0.51	12-31-99	12-28	2.05	21½	9.5
N	RLRPrB		ReliaStar Fin II 8.10%[4]'TOPrS'	BBB+	[1]25(6/2/02)	Q0.51	12-31-99	12-28	2.02	21	9.7
N	REPPrA		Repsol Intl Cap Ltd 7.45%	BBB	25(10/20/02)	Q0.47	12-31-99	12-14	1.86	20⅝	9.0
N	RNBPrD	*	Republic NY Adj [28]Rt Dep	NR	25	0.31	1-1-00	12-13	1.13	23½B	4.8
N	RNBPrF	*	Republic NY $2.8575	A+	50(9/30/07)	Q0.71	1-1-00	12-13	2.86	43½B	6.6
N	RPOPrA	*	Rhone-Poul Overseas 8.125%	BB	25(7/7/03)	Q0.51	12-31-99	12-13	2.03	20⅞	9.7
N	RSEPrZ	*	Rouse Cap 9.25%[29]'QUIPS'	BB+	[30]25(11/26/99)	Q0.58	12-31-99	12-28	2.31	18⅛	12.8
N	RBSPrG		Royal Bk Scotland Ser'G'ADS[31]	NR	25(3/30/03)	0.46	12-30-99	12-14	1.88	19⅞	9.5
N	RBSPrH		Royal Bk Scotland Ser'H'ADS[32]	A–	25(3/30/04)	0.45	12-30-99	12-14	1.81	18⅝	9.8
N	RBSPrI		Royal Bk Scotland Ser'I' ADS[33]	NR	25(9/29/04)	0.50	12-30-99	12-14	2.00	20½	9.8
N	RBSPrJ		Royal Bk Scotland Ser'J'ADS[34]	A–	25(12/30/04)	0.53	12-30-99	12-14	2.12	22	9.6
A	RGLPr	*	Royce Focus Tr 7.45%	NR	25(11/30/02)	Q0.47	12-23-99	12-02	1.86	20¾	9.0
A	ROYPr		Royce Micro-Cap Tr 7.75%	NR	[35]25(6/30/02)	Q0.48	12-23-99	12-02	1.94	22	8.8
N	RVTPrA	*	Royce Value Trust 7.30%	NR	[36]25(6/21/03)	Q0.46	12-23-99	12-02	1.82	20½	8.9
A	SDOPrH	*	San Diego G&E $1.82	A	26	Q0.46	1-15-00	12-17	1.82	24	7.6
N	SACPrT	*	SCE&G Trust I 7.55%	A–	[26]25(9/29/02)	Q0.47	12-31-99	12-28	1.89	20⅞	9.1
A	SKVPrA		Sentry Technology [37]5%'A'	NR	[38]	5.00>...2-12-99		1-27	[39]Stk	¼	....
N	SJRPrA	*	Shaw Communic 8.45%[9]'A'COPrS	BB+	[40]25(9/29/02)	Q0.53	12-31-99	12-13	2.11	19¼	11.0
N	SHUPrC	*	Shurgard Storage 8.70% 'C'	BBB–	25(12/7/03)	Q0.54	12-31-99	11-29	2.17	20⅛	10.8
N	SBPrG	*	SI Fin Tr I 9.50%[41]'TRUPS'Uts[42]	BB+	[8]25(6/30/01)	Q0.59	12-31-99	12-14	2.38	25½B	9.3
N	SRPPrT	*	Sierra Pac Pwr Cp 8.60%[4]'TOPrS'	BBB	[10]25(7/29/01)	Q0.54	12-31-99	12-28	2.15	23⅝	9.1
N	SJIPrT	*	SJG Cap Tr 8.35%	BBB–	[43]25(4/29/02)	Q0.52	12-31-99	12-28	2.09	18½	11.3
N	SLMPrA	*	SLM Holdings 6.87%'A'	A–	50(11/15/09)	Plan qtly div			3.48	48B	7.3
N	SORPr	*	Source Capital $2.40 Vtg	NR	27.50	Q0.60	12-15-99	11-23	2.40	28	8.6
N	SACPr	*	So.Carolina E&G 5%	A–	52.50	Q0.63	1-1-00	12-08	2.50	35⅜B	7.1
N	SWXPrA	*	So.W.Gas Cp I 9.125%'TOPrS'	BB	[44]25(12/30/00)	Q0.57	12-31-99	12-28	2.28	24	9.5
P	SOUPr	*	South'n Cal Gas 6% A	A	NC	Q0.38	1-15-00	12-17	1.50	19½B	7.7
A	SBNPrA	*	Southern Cap Tr 8.25%	BBB+	[8]10(6/29/03)	Q0.21	12-31-99	12-13	0.82	8⅝	9.6

ootnotes and Sinking Fund: [1] or anytime upon'Tax Event're-spec cond. [2] Quarterly Income Preferred Securities. [3] Or earlier uopn'Tax Event' re-spec cond. [4] Trust Originated Preferred Securities. [5] Or earlier upon'Special vent're-spec cond. [6] or earlier upon'Special Event'. [7] Or earlier upon'Spcl Event're-spec cond. [8] or earlier upon'Tax Event're-spec cond. [9] Canadian Originated Preferred Securities. [10] Or earlier upon'Tax Event're-spec cond. or anytime upon 'Tax Event' re spec cond. [12] Pfd Redeemable Increased Div Equity Sec. [13] Ea Sec consists of stk pur contr & 6.5%Tr Pfd. [14] Pur cont Protect Life Com fr 2-16-2001,re-spec cond. Pfd Redeemable Increased Div Equity Sec. [16] Ea Sec consists of stk pur contr & 6.5%Tr Pfd. [17] Pur cont Protect Life Com fr 2-16-2001,re-spec cond. [18] Mand 2-16-2003:Cv to Jr Debs on'Tax Event're-spe cond. [19] Dep for 01 shr 9.25% cm Sr'A' Pfd. [20] or earlier to preserve 'REIT' status re-spec cond. [21] Or earlier for'Tax Event're-spec cond. [22] Dep for .001 shr 8.25% cm Sr'K'Pfd. [23] Or earlier preserve'REIT'statues re-spec cond. [24] Dep for 01 shr 8.25% cm Sr'L'Pfd. [25] Or earlier to preserve'REIT'status re-spec cond. [26] or earlier upon 'Tax Event're-spec cond. [27] or earlier upon'Tax Event' re-spec cond. [28] Rate adjusted qtrly:min 4.50%,max 10.50%. [29] Mand 12-1-2025. [30] or earlier upon 'Tax Event'. [31] Ea ADS rep 1 non-cm Dollar Pref Series'G'. [32] Ea ADS rep 1 non-cm Dollar Pref Ser'H'. [33] Ea ADS rep 1 non-cm Dollar Pref Ser'I'. [34] Ea ADS rep 1 non-cm Dollar Pref Ser'J'. [35] or arlier re-spec cond. [36] Or earlier re-spec cond. [37] Mand redm 2-13-2001at'DeemedValue'(cash/6%nts). [38] At 'Deemed Value' re-spec cond. [39] Payable in ComStk to'99/semi-annual div fr 2000. [40] or earlier upon 'Tax Event' re-pec cond. [41] Trust & Preferred stk & Pwr Contract Unit. [42] Pur cont 6-30-2021 1 shr 9.50%'F'Dep Pfd at $25. [43] Or anytime upon'Tax Event're-spec cond. [44] Or anytime upon 'Tax Event' re-spec cond.

Exchange Ticker	Cm Divd	Issue	Rating	Reg. Call Price (Begins) Thru [see footnotes for Sink'g Fd]	Dividends Latest Payments Period $	Date	Ex Div.	Ind. Rate	Last Sale or Bid(B)	% Div. Yld.
N SOPrA	*	South'nCo Cap TrIII 7.75%[2]'QUIPS'	BBB+	[3]25(6/5/02)	Q0.48	12-31-99	12-14	1.94	21⅞	8.9
N SOPrB	*	South'nCo CapTrV 7.125%[5]'TOPrS'	NR	[6]25(6/29/03)	Q0.45	12-31-99	12-14	1.78	20⅛	8.9
N SOPrC	*	South'nCo Cap Tr V 6.875%'QUIPS'	BBB+	[7]25(12/22/03)	Q0.43	12-31-99	12-14	1.72	19¼	8.9
N SUGPrA	*	So Union Financ'g 9.48%[4]'TOPrS'	BBB–	25(5/16/00)	Q0.59	12-31-99	12-28	2.37	24⅝	9.6
N SSSPrB	*	Sovran Self Storage 9.85%	NR	[6]25(7/29/04)	Q0.62	12-31-99	12-15	2.46	19½	12.6
N SPSPrT	*	Sowest Pub Sv Cap 7.85%[5]'TOPrS'	BBB+	[3]25(10/20/01)	Q0.49	12-1-99	11-26	1.96	21⅜	9.2
N SGVPrB	*	SPG Properties 8.75% 'B'	NR	25(9/28/06)	Q0.55	12-31-99	12-15	2.19	20¼	10.8
N SPKPrC	*	Spieker Prop $1.97 Sr'C'	BBB–	25(10/9/02)	Q0.49	1-31-00	1-19	1.97	18	11.0
N SSR	*	SSBH Cap I 7.20%[8]'TruPS'	BBB+	[9]25(1/27/03)	Q0.45	12-31-99	12-28	1.80	20¼	8.9
N SFIPrD	*	Starwood Financial 8.00%'D'	BB+	25(10/7/02)	Q0.50	12-15-99	11-26	2.00	13⅛	15.3
N SVCPr		Stokely-Van Camp 5% Pref	BBB–	NC	Q0.25	1-3-00	12-15	1.00	16⅜	6.1
N SLMPr	*	Student Ln Mktg Adj[10]Rt A	NR	51.50	Q0.63	12-31-99	12-15	2.50	41B	6.1
N SAIPrV	*	SunAmer Cap II 8.35%[4]'TOPrS'	AA	[11]25(9/29/00)	Q0.52	12-30-99	12-27	2.09	24⅜	8.6
N SAIPrW	*	SunAmer Cap III 8.30% [4]'TOPrS'	AA	[12]25(11/12/01)	Q0.52	12-30-99	12-27	2.07	24¼	8.5
N SUPrA	*	Suncor Energy 9.125%	NR	[6]25(3/14/04)	Q0.57	12-31-99	12-13	2.28	21¼	10.7
N SDPPr	*	SunSource Cap 11.60%	NR	[7]25(9/30/02)	M0.24	1-3-00	12-21	[13]....	12⅛	....
N SWOPrA	*	SWEPCO Cap 7.875% Trust'A'	A–	[11]25(4/29/02)	Q0.49	12-31-99	12-28	1.97	22⅛	8.9
N TLMPrB		Talisman Engy 8.90% Pfd Secs	BBB–	[6]25(6/14/04)	Q0.56	11-15-99	10-28	2.23	21½	10.4
N TCOPrA	*	Taubman Centers 8.30%'A'	BBB–	25(10/2/02)	Q0.52	12-31-99	12-17	2.08	15⅛	13.7
N TFIPr	*	TCI Commun Fin I 8.72%[4]TOPrS'	A	[14]25(1/30/01)	Q0.55	12-31-99	12-28	2.18	25¼	8.6
N TFIPrA	*	TCI Comm Fin II 10% Tr Sec	A	[11]25(5/30/01)	Q0.63	12-31-99	12-28	2.50	25⅞	9.7
N TFIPrB	*	TCI Comm Fin IV 9.72% Tr Sec	A	[15]25(3/30/02)	Q0.61	12-31-99	12-28	2.43	26⅛	9.3
A TDSPrA	*	TDS Capital I 8.50%[4]'TOPrS'	BB+	[7]25(11/17/02)	Q0.53	12-31-99	12-28	2.13	21¼	10.0
A TDSPrB	*	TDS Capital II 8.04% [4]'TOPrS'	BB+	[6]25(3/30/03)	Q0.50	12-31-99	12-28	2.01	19⅞	10.1
N TXCPrA	*	Texaco Cap LLC 6.875%'MIPS'[16]	A+	25	M0.14	12-31-99	12-28	1.72	20	8.6
N TXTPrT	*	Textron Cap I 7.92% Tr Sec	BBB+	[11]25(2/8/01)	Q0.49	12-31-99	12-28	1.98	21½	9.2
N TWXPrT	*	Time Warn Cp I 8.78% Tr Sec	BB+	[17]25(12/30/00)	Q0.55	12-31-99	12-28	2.22	24⅞	8.9
N TEDPrK	*	Toledo Ed Adj[18]Sr'A'	B+	25	0.44	12-1-99	11-10	1.75	24¾B	7.1
N TMKPrM	*	Torchmark Cap 9.18%[19]'MIPS'	BBB+	25	M0.19	12-31-99	12-28	2.29	24⅛	9.5
N BTAPrA		Totta & Acores Fin 8.875%'A'	BBB	[20]25(10/10/06)	0.55	12-30-99	12-14	2.22	23⅛	9.6
N TCLPr	*	TransCanada Cap 8.75% '[4]TOPrS'	BBB	[3]25(7/22/01)	Q0.55	12-31-99	12-28	2.19	22⅝	9.7

Exchange Ticker	Cm Divd	Issue	Rating	Reg. Call Price (Begins) Thru [see footnotes for Sink'g Fd]	Dividends Latest Payments Period $	Date	Ex Div.	Ind. Rate	Last Sale or Bid(B)	% Div. Yld.
N TRPPr	*	TransCanada P.L. 8.25%	BBB	[6]25(10/7/03)	Q0.52	12-31-99	12-13	2.06	21⅜	9.
N TRPPrC	*	TransCanada P.L. 8.50% [22]'COPrS'	BBB	[23]25(11/6/01)	Q0.53	12-31-99	12-28	2.13	22½	9.4
N TAPPrA	*	Travelers P&C Cap I 8.08%	A–	[7]25(4/29/01)	Q0.51	12-31-99	12-28	2.02	22⅝	8.
N TAPPrB	*	Travelers P&C Cap II 8.00%	NR	[7]25(5/14/01)	Q0.50	12-31-99	12-28	2.00	22⅜	8.
N TYPr	*	Tri-Continental $2.50 Vtg	NR	55	Q0.63	1-3-00	12-08	2.50	34½B	7.
N TXUPrA	*	TXU Cap I 7.25%	BBB–	[6]25(12/29/03)	Q0.45	12-31-99	12-28	1.81	19½	9.
N TUEPrM	*	TXU Elec Cap I 8.25%'TOPrS'	BBB–	[24]25(10/31/01)	0.52	12-31-99	12-14	2.06	21¾	9.
N TUEPrO	*	TXU Elec Cap III 8.00%'QUIPS'	BBB–	[25]25(12/31/00)	Q0.50	12-31-99	12-14	2.00	21¼	9.
N UALPrB	*	UAL Corp 12.25%[26]Dep'B'	B+	25(7/11/04)	Q0.77	2-1-00	1-12	3.06	29⅞	10.
N UALPrT	*	UAL Cp Cap Tr I 13.25%[4]'TOPrS'	B+	[23]25(7/11/04)	Q0.83	12-31-99	12-14	3.31	27⅝	12.
N UDSPrA	*	UDS Cap I 8.32%[4]'TOPrS'	BB+	[3]25(6/29/02)	Q0.52	12-31-99	12-28	2.08	18⅞	11.
N UILPrA	*	Utd Cap Fd L.P.9.625%CapSec'A'	BB	25(4/29/00)	M0.20	12-31-99	12-28	2.41	24⅝	9.
N UDRPrB	*	Utd Dominion Rlty 8.60%'B'	BBB	25(5/28/07)	Q0.54	11-30-99	11-10	2.15	17⅞	12.
A UHGPrA	*	U.S. Home&Garden Tr 9.40%	NR	[6]25(4/14/03)	0.20	12-15-99	12-10	2.35	14	16.
N USBPrA	*	USB Cap II 7.20%[4]'TOPrS'	BBB+	[6]25(3/31/03)	[27]0.45	1-3-00	12-29	1.80	19¾	9.
N XLCPr	*	USX Capital LLC 8.75%[28]'MIPS'	BB	25	M0.18	12-31-99	12-28	2.19	23⅞	9.
N UCUPrC	*	UtiliCorp Capital 8.875%[19]'MIPS'	BB+	25(6/11/00)	M0.18	12-31-99	12-28	2.22	22¾	9.
N VVIPr	*	Viad Corp $4.75	BB+	101[29]	Q1.19	1-15-00	12-15	4.75	51½	9.
N VELPrT	*	Va Pwr Cap Tr 1 [30]8.05%	BBB+	[31]25(8/29/00)	Q0.50	12-31-99	12-14	2.01	21⅝	9.
N VNOPrB	*	Vornado Rlty Tr 8.50%'B'	BBB–	[6]25(3/16/04)	Q0.53	1-3-00	12-20	2.13	19⅛	11.
N VNOPrC		Vornado Rlty Tr 8.50%'C'	BBB–	[6]25(5/16/04)	Q0.53	1-3-00	12-20	2.13	19	11.
N WDNPrD	*	Walden Res Prop 9.00%	NR	25(12/31/07)	Q0.56	12-1-99	11-16	2.25	15⅛B	14.
N WECPrA	*	WEC Cap Tr I 6.85%[8]'TruPS'	NR	[32]25(3/24/04)	Q0.43	12-31-99	12-28	1.71	19½	8.
N WRIPrC	*	Weingarten Realty 7.0% 'C'	A–	50(3/14/04)	Q0.88	12-15-99	11-29	3.50	36⅝	9.
N WGRPr	*	Western Gas Res $2.28	B+	25	Q0.57	2-14-00	12-29	2.28	23	9.
N WRPrA	*	Western Res Cap 7.875%[1]'QUIPS'	BBB–	[7]25(12/10/00)	Q0.49	12-31-99	12-28	1.97	20⅛	9.
N WRPrB	*	Western Res CapII 8.50%[1]'QUIPS'	BBB–	[6]25(7/30/01)	Q0.53	12-31-99	12-28	2.13	22½	9.
N WBKPrA		Westpac Cap Tr I 8%[33]'TOPrS'	NR	[34]25(7/15/04)	Q0.50	12-31-99	12-28	2.00	21⅝	9.
N WXHPrA	*	Winston Hotels 9.25%'A'	NR	25(9/27/01)	Q0.58	1-17-00	12-29	2.31	14¾	15.
A WISPr	*	Wis P&L 4.50 Vtg	A	107	Q1.13	12-15-99	11-26	4.50	66⅝B	6.
N YCT	*	Yorkshire Cap Tr I 8.08%	NR	[6]25(6/8/03)	Q0.51	12-31-99	12-28	2.02	18⅝	10.

Footnotes and Sinking Fund: [1] Quarterly Income Preferred Securities. [2] Quarterly Income Preferred Securities. [3] or earlier upon 'Tax Event' re-spec cond. [4] Trust Originated Preferred Securities. [5] Trust Originated Preferred Securities. [6] Or earlier upon'Tax Event're-spec cond. [7] or earlier upon'Tax Event're-spec cond. [8] Trust Preferred Securities. [9] or earlier upon'Tax Event' re spec cond. [10] Rate adjusted qtrly:min 5%,max 14%. [11] or anytime upon'Tax Event're-spec cond. [12] or earlier for 'Tax Event're-spec cond. [13] To be determined. [14] or anytime upon'Special Event' re-spec cond. [15] or anytime upon'Tax Event' re-spec cond. [16] Monthly Income Preferred shrs. [17] Or anytime upon'Special Event're-spec cond. [18] Rate adjusted qtrly:min 7%,max 14%. [19] Monthly Income Preferred Shrs. [20] Or fr 10-11-2001 re-spec cond. [21] Canadian Originated Preferred Securities. [22] Canadian Originated Preferred Securities. [23] or earlier upon 'Tax Event're-spec cond. [24] or anytime upon 'Tax Event're-spec cond. [25] or earlier upon 'Tax Event'. [26] Dep for 0.001 shr 12.25% Sr'B'Pfd. [27] Approx. [28] Monthly income preferred shrs. [29] SF 100. [30] Trust Preferred Sec. [31] or earlier for 'Special Event'. [32] Or earlier upon'Tax event're-spec cond. [33] Trust Originated Preferred Sec. [34] Or earlier upon'Spcl Event're-spec cond.

STANDARD & POOR'S

CLOSED–END FUND SUMMARY

EXPLANATION OF ABBREVIATIONS

D	Bond Fund–Corporate	FT	Finite Trust	GVT	Long Term Govt., GNMA	MU	Tax Free Income, General
:	Common Stock	GB	Global Bond–Long Term	ICA	Income & Capital Appreciation	MUS	Tax Free Income–State Specific
A	Capital Appreciation	GE	Global Equity	ICF	Income–Global Corp. & Govt.	P	Income From Preferred Stock
V	Convertible Bond & Pfd Stk	GEA	Global Equity–Asia	INTL	International	PM	Precious Metals
G	Emerging Growth Com Stk	GEC	Global Equity–Country Specific	IRE	Income–Real Estate	SB	Small Business Investments
L	Flexible–Short selling, hedge, etc	GSB	Global Short–Term Bond	MI	Income from Mortgages	ST	Short Term Investments

otnoted amounts for cash or stock refer to Investment Income & Capital Gain for the calendar year stated.
et Asset Values (NAV) are reported on a weekly basis. The premium or discount at which an issue trades (price percentage over or under the current NAV) a tool used to compare and evaluate current market trends.

Ticker Symbol	Fund	Rating	Exc.	Type	Dividends: Latest Payment Period $	Latest Payment Date	Latest Payment Ex. Div.	So Far 1999 Invest. Income	So Far 1999 Cap. Gain	Ind. Rate	Div. Yld. %	1998 Invest. Income	1998 Cap. Gain	Price Range 1998 - 1999 High	1998 - 1999 Low	December, 1999 Last Sale or Bid High	Last Sale or Bid Low	Last Sale or Bid Last	Net Assets % NAV Prem. Disc.	Latest NAV	Latest Date	Com. Shs. 000
ACG	ACM Gvt Income Fund	NR	NY	GVT	0.075	1-21-00	1-5	0.90	....	0.90	14.0	0.921	0.343	11½	6 5/16	7½	6 5/16	6 7/16	-15.4	7.61	12-23-99	58511
AOF	ACM Gvt Opportunity Fd	NR	NY	GVT	0.06	1-21-00	1-5	0.638	0.022	0.72	⊙9.9	0.63	....	8¾	6¼	7¼	6¼	7¼	-7.2	7.81	12-23-99	13072
GSF	ACM Gvt Securities	NR	NY	GVT	0.075	1-21-00	1-5	0.90	....	0.90	14.1	[1]0.90	....	10 13/16	6 3/16	6 9/16	6 3/16	6⅜	-16.2	7.61	12-23-99	78072
SI	ACM Gvt Spectrum Fund	NR	NY	GVT	0.05	1-21-00	1-5	0.545	....	0.60	11.0	0.547	....	6⅞	5⅜	5 11/16	5 7/16	5 7/16	-17.1	6.56	12-23-99	37028
ADF	ACM Managed Dollar Income	NR	NY	ICA	0.113	1-21-00	12-28	†1.38	....	1.35	e16.1	†1.449	1.21	14 9/16	7¾	9⅝	8¼	8⅜	-7.9	9.09	12-23-99	22003
AMF	ACM Managed Income Fund	NR	NY	ICA	0.085	1-21-00	12-28	1.00	0.423	1.02	⊙17.4	†0.94	0.021	10 9/16	5⅝	7 3/16	5⅝	5⅞	2.2	5.75	12-23-99	22818
AMU	ACM Muni Securities Income	NR	NY	MU	0.073	1-21-00	1-5	0.87	....	0.87	8.2	0.88	....	15⅛	10⅛	11 1/16	10⅛	10⅝	-6.1	11.32	12-23-99	10789
ADX	Adams Express	NR	NY	ICA	2.09	12-27-99	11-18	2.39	0.06	0.36	⊙1.1	[2]0.45	1.65	33 15/16	21 13/16	33 15/16	30¼	33 9/16	-15.9	39.91	12-23-99	51877
AAT	All-American Term Trust	NR	NY	BD	0.07	12-31-99	12-23	0.89	....	0.84	7.1	0.995	....	14⅜	11⅛	11 15/16	11 3/16	11 13/16	-9.2	13.01	12-23-99	13707
AMO	Alliance All-Mkt Adv Fd	NR	NY	CA	3.823	1-7-00	12-29	4.263	....	4.21	10.3	5.158	....	50¾	27⅞	44½	40½	41	-19.4	50.85	12-23-99	2508
AWG	Alliance World Dollar Gvt Fd	NR	NY	GB	0.11	1-21-00	1-5	1.425	0.739	1.32	⊙15.0	†1.65	2.062	16⅛	8 11/16	9 7/16	8 11/16	8 13/16	-13.5	10.19	12-23-99	8653
AWF	Alliance World Dollar Gvt Fd II	NR	NY	GB	0.103	1-21-00	1-5	1.275	....	1.23	14.8	1.354	1.527	14 7/16	7 1/16	8⅞	8⅛	8 5/16	-17.0	10.01	12-23-99	74491
ALM	Allmerica Sec Tr	NR	NY	BD	©0.04	1-7-00	12-21	0.76	0.04	0.80	⊙9.1	0.83	....	11⅜	8 13/16	9¼	8 13/16	8 13/16	-31.8	12.93	12-23-99	8592
XAA	Amer Muni Income Portfolio	Af	NY	MU	0.066	1-12-00	12-29	[3]0.769	....	0.79	6.8	†0.754	....	14 9/16	11⅛	11 15/16	11⅛	11 11/16	-12.7	13.38	12-22-99	5756
AXT	Amer Muni Term Trust	AAf	NY	MU	0.054	1-12-00	12-29	†0.733	0.003	0.65	⊙e6.3	0.65	0.083	11¾	10⅛	10 7/16	10¼	10¼	-4.7	10.76	12-22-99	8455
BXT	Amer Muni Term Trust II	AAf	NY	MU	0.052	1-12-00	12-29	†0.718	0.001	0.62	⊙e6.1	0.62	0.038	11¾	10 1/16	10 5/16	10⅛	10⅛	-6.9	10.87	12-22-99	7356
CXT	Amer Muni Term Trust III	AAf	NY	MU	0.048	1-12-00	12-29	0.57	0.003	0.57	⊙5.7	0.57	0.061	11½	9¾	10 1/16	9¾	9 15/16	-7.8	10.78	12-22-99	5300
SLA	Amer Select Portfolio	BBBf	NY	C	0.088	1-12-00	12-29	1.05	....	1.05	9.0	1.032	....	12½	11 1/16	11 11/16	11 1/16	11 11/16	-7.2	12.59	12-22-99	11877
ASP	Amer Strategic Inc Portfolio	Af	NY	MI	0.085	1-12-00	12-29	1.015	....	1.02	9.1	0.973	....	12¼	10 15/16	11⅜	10 15/16	11¼	-8.2	12.25	12-22-99	4703
BSP	Amer Strategic Inc Portfolio II	Af	NY	MI	0.088	1-12-00	12-29	†1.047	....	1.05	e9.2	1.002	0.006	12⅛	10 15/16	11½	10 15/16	11⅜	-8.4	12.42	12-22-99	17791
CSP	Amer Strategic Inc Portfol III	Af	NY	MI	0.088	1-12-00	12-29	1.034	....	1.05	9.4	1.002	....	12	10⅝	11¼	10⅞	11 3/16	-5.5	11.84	12-22-99	23837
APX	Apex Muni Fund	NR	NY	MU	0.059	12-30-99	12-21	0.656	....	0.71	8.2	0.637	....	10⅞	8 9/16	9⅞	8 9/16	8 11/16	-9.6	9.61	12-23-99	19597

form Footnote Explanations-See page 4. Other: [1] Includes partial div. [2] Incl $1.74 in cash or stk,'98. [3] Incl $0.0026 taxable net invt income.

Ticker Symbol	Fund	Rating	Exc.	Type	Dividends: Latest Payment Period $	Date	Ex. Div.	So Far 1999 Invest. Income	So Far 1999 Cap. Gain	Ind. Rate	Div. Yld. %	1998 Invest. Income	1998 Cap. Gain	Price Range 1998 - 1999 High	1998 - 1999 Low	December, 1999 Last Sale or Bid High	Low	Last	Net Assets % NAV Prem. Disc.	Latest NAV	Latest Date	Com. Shs. 000
AF	Argentina Fund	NR	NY	GEC	0.70	1-13-00	12-28	0.45	....	0.31	⊙2.6	0.25	....	13 5/16	6 1/2	12 1/2	11 3/8	11 7/8	-20.1	16.74	12-23-99	9284
ASA	ASA Ltd	NR	NY	PM	Q0.15	11-26-99	11-17	0.60	....	0.60	3.2	0.80	....	26 5/8	13 5/8	19 3/4	18 5/16	18 15/16	-19.2	23.44	12-22-99	9600
APB	Asia Pacific Fund	NR	NY	GEA	0.14	1-14-00	12-29	0.043	....	0.14	1.2	0.19	0.06	12	4 3/8	11 5/16	9 15/16	11 1/4	-19.7	14.01	12-23-99	18930
GRR	Asia Tigers Fund	NR	NY	GEA	A0.072	1-14-00	12-21	0.01	....	0.07	0.7	....	....	10 1/4	4 3/8	10 1/4	9 5/16	10 1/4	-22.5	13.23	12-23-99	20515
OST	Austria Fund	NR	NY	GEC	Q0.288	10-8-99	9-24	1.229	0.697	1.15	⊙9.0	1.385	0.365	14 1/16	8 7/16	13 1/16	9 1/8	12 13/16	-12.8	14.69	12-23-99	11703
RTR	Auto Com ExSecTrII6.5%'TRACES'	NR	NY	ICA	Q0.388	11-15-99	10-28	1.552	....	1.55	16.2	1.552	....	28 1/4	8 3/4	10 1/2	8 3/4	9 9/16	-61.1	24.56	12-23-99	9934
BKF	Baker,Fentress & Co	NR	NY	CA	[1]12.30	1-7-00	-28	[2]h1.12	3.18	0.26	⊙1.8	[3]0.26	3.51	21 3/16	13 11/16	14 3/16	13 11/16	14 1/8	-4.0	14.72	12-23-99	35983
BCV	Bancroft Convertible Fd	NR	AS	CV	3.08	12-28-99	11-22	1.396	2.284	0.80	3.9	0.873	2.942	30 3/8	19 7/8	20 3/4	19 7/8	20 3/8	-22.3	26.23	12-23-99	3795
BEM	Bergstrom Capital	NR	AS	ICA	13.50	6-7-99	5-18	0.12	13.38	0.12	⊙0.1	0.161	10.589	240 1/2	131	240 1/2	219 1/2	236	-13.5	272.93	12-23-99	1000
BXL	Bexil Corp	NR	AS	ICA	0.30	12-31-99	12-17	1.20	....	1.20	12.6	1.20	....	14 1/2	9	9 7/8	9	9 1/2	-24.5	12.59	12-23-99	762
BAT	BlackRock Advantage Term	AAAf	NY	MI	0.05	1-31-00	12-27	0.604	....	0.60	6.6	0.625	....	10 1/8	8 7/8	9 1/4	8 15/16	9 1/16	-10.3	10.10	12-22-99	9511
BCT	BlackRock Broad Inv Gr 2009	NR	AS	FT	0.069	1-31-00	12-8	0.838	....	0.83	7.3	0.90	....	14	11	11 1/2	11	11 3/8	-14.3	13.28	12-22-99	2957
BFC	BlackRock CA Ins Muni 2008 Tr	AAAf	NY	MUS	0.064	1-3-00	12-13	0.708	....	0.77	5.5	0.772	....	16 1/2	13 1/2	14 9/16	13 7/8	13 7/8	-13.9	16.11	12-23-99	10407
RAA	BlackRock CA Inv Qual Muni	NR	AS	MUS	0.073	1-3-00	11-10	0.804	....	0.88	6.0	0.877	....	16 3/4	14 3/8	15	14 7/8	14 3/4	4.2	14.16	12-23-99	1007
BRF	BlackRock Fl Ins Muni 2008 Tr	AAAf	NY	MUS	0.072	1-3-00	12-13	0.791	....	0.86	6.1	0.863	....	17	13 1/2	14 1/2	13 5/8	14 1/8	-9.3	15.57	12-23-99	8707
RFA	BlackRock Fl Inv Qual Muni	NR	AS	MUS	0.066	1-3-00	11-10	0.729	....	0.80	6.5	0.758	....	16	12 5/16	12 13/16	12 5/16	12 5/16	-13.1	14.16	12-23-99	1127
BHY	BlackRock High Yield Trust	NR	NY	CA	0.134	1-31-00	12-8	1.439	....	1.62	13.9	....	....	15 3/16	11 3/16	12 7/16	11 3/16	11 11/16	-15.4	13.81	12-23-99	6307
BKT	BlackRock Income Trust	NR	NY	GVT	0.047	1-31-00	12-27	0.516	....	0.56	9.7	0.563	....	7 1/4	5 5/8	6 1/16	5 5/8	5 3/4	-20.0	7.19	12-22-99	62850
BRM	BlackRock Ins Muni 2008 Tr	AAAf	NY	MU	0.066	1-3-00	12-13	0.729	....	0.80	5.8	0.795	0.005	16 7/16	13 7/16	14 1/16	13 7/16	13 3/4	-14.0	15.99	12-23-99	27207
BMT	BlackRock Ins Muni Term	AAAf	NY	MU	0.052	1-3-00	12-13	0.573	....	0.62	6.6	0.625	....	11 15/16	9	10	9	9 7/16	-11.0	10.60	12-23-99	25886
BKN	BlackRock Inv Qual Muni Tr	NR	NY	MU	0.072	1-3-00	12-13	0.791	....	0.86	6.7	0.825	0.15	16 1/16	11 3/4	13 3/16	11 3/4	12 7/8	-6.5	13.77	12-23-99	16707
BQT	BlackRock Inv Qual Term Tr	NR	NY	BD	0.038	12-20-99	12-8	0.504	....	0.45	5.7	0.55	....	9 1/16	7 13/16	8 1/16	7 13/16	7 7/8	-10.7	8.82	12-22-99	36811
BMN	BlackRock Muni Target Term	AAAf	NY	MUS	0.051	1-3-00	12-13	0.615	....	0.62	6.3	0.615	....	11 3/4	9 1/4	10 1/16	9 1/4	9 13/16	-7.4	10.60	12-23-99	45411
RNJ	BlackRock NJ Inv Qual Muni	NR	AS	MUS	0.061	1-3-00	12-13	0.67	....	0.73	6.0	0.712	....	15 3/8	11 3/8	12 7/16	11 3/8	12 1/8	-9.4	13.39	12-23-99	1007
BLN	BlackRock NY Ins Muni 2008 Tr	AAAf	NY	MUS	0.071	1-3-00	12-13	0.784	....	0.855	5.8	0.855	....	17 3/16	14	14 15/16	14	14 11/16	-6.0	15.63	12-23-99	11257
RNY	BlackRock NY Inv Qual Muni	NR	AS	MUS	0.068	1-3-00	12-13	0.749	....	0.82	6.6	0.818	....	16	11 1/4	13 3/8	11 1/4	12 3/8	-11.3	13.95	12-23-99	1307
BNA	BlackRock No Amer Gvt Inc	NR	NY	GVT	0.07	12-31-99	12-13	0.84	....	0.84	9.2	0.84	....	10 13/16	9	9 5/8	9	9 1/8	-18.9	11.25	12-22-99	36207
BPS	BlackRock Penn Strat Muni Tr	NR	AS	MUS	0.077	1-3-00	12-13	0.153	....	0.92	6.9	....	....	16	13 1/8	15 1/4	13 1/8	13 3/8	-1.4	13.57	12-23-99	1757
BSD	BlackRock Strategic Muni Tr	NR	NY	MU	M0.078	1-3-00	12-13	0.156	....	0.94	7.5	....	....	15 1/16	11 15/16	13 3/16	11 15/16	12 1/2	-7.1	13.45	12-23-99	6700
BGT	BlackRock Strategic Term	AAAf	NY	FT	0.04	1-31-00	12-27	0.475	....	0.47	5.3	0.475	....	9 5/16	8 7/16	8 7/8	8 11/16	8 13/16	-6.4	9.41	12-22-99	57511
BTT	BlackRock Target Term	AAAf	NY	MI	0.039	1-31-00	12-27	0.503	....	0.47	4.9	0.537	....	9 13/16	9 3/16	9 11/16	9 1/2	9 5/8	-1.9	9.81	12-22-99	95461
BTM	BlackRock 2001 Term Trust	AAAf	NY	MI	0.025	1-31-00	12-27	†0.391	....	0.30	e3.4	0.40	....	9 1/4	8 9/16	8 15/16	8 13/16	8 13/16	-5.0	9.28	12-22-99	142011
BLU	Blue Chip Value Fund	NR	NY	ICA	0.92	1-14-00	12-29	0.525	0.605	[4]0.88	⊙10.1	0.79	0.80	12 1/16	7 5/8	9 3/4	8 5/16	8 11/16	-11.0	9.76	12-23-99	16740
BTF	Boulder Total Return Fund	NR	NY	P	0.077	12-30-99	12-21	0.924	....	0.92	9.5	1.182	0.529	16 5/16	9 3/8	10 5/16	9 3/8	9 11/16	-24.7	12.86	12-23-99	9417
BZF	Brazil Fund	NR	NY	GEC	0.30	1-30-00	12-28	0.79	2.27	0.30	⊙1.6	0.555	2.32	23 1/2	8 15/16	18 5/8	15 3/16	18 1/2	-18.4	22.66	12-23-99	16429
BZL	Brazilian Equity Fund	NR	NY	GEC	0.12	1-15-99	12-29	0.12	....	0.10	1.7	....	4.97	9 1/8	3	6	4 9/16	5 13/16	-18.0	7.09	12-23-99	6227
CVF	Castle Convert Fund	NR	AS	CV	0.63	12-28-99	12-22	1.32	0.30	1.32	e⊙6.1	†1.46	0.05	27 1/8	20 1/4	22	20 1/4	21 13/16	-17.0	26.27	12-23-99	2236
CEE	Central European Eq Fd	NR	NY	GEC	0.14	11-27-98	11-12	....	....	Nil	....	1.67	5.04	20 15/16	9 3/4	14 1/2	12 7/16	14 7/16	-22.2	18.55	12-23-99	10398
CRF	Central European Value Fd	NR	NY	GEC	0.998	12-31-98	12-22	....	....	Nil	....	0.47	0.665	13 3/16	7 13/16	11 7/8	9 11/16	11 7/8	-11.6	13.44	12-23-99	5878
CEF	Central Fund,Cda'A'	NR	AS	PM	gA0.01	11-12-99	10-27	g0.01	....	0.01	◆0.2	g0.01	....	5 7/16	3 3/8	4 5/16	3 7/8	4 3/16	8.2	3.87	12-23-99	19115
CET	Central Securities	NR	AS	CA	[5]2.40	12-22-99	11-9	[6]0.26	2.34	0.26	⊙1.0	[7]0.31	1.63	31 3/8	18 7/8	27 7/16	25 1/2	27 1/4	-19.2	33.74	12-23-99	14861
CWF	Chartwell Div & Inc Fund	NR	NY	CA	0.103	12-30-99	12-13	1.24	....	1.24	12.1	0.516	....	15 5/8	9 13/16	10 1/2	9 13/16	10 1/4	-19.7	12.77	12-22-99	15537
CH	Chile Fund Inc	NR	NY	GEC	0.63	12-29-99	12-13	0.39	0.96	0.28	⊙2.5	....	4.96	17 7/8	7 1/8	11 9/16	10 3/8	11 1/4	-25.4	15.08	12-23-99	14328
CHN	China Fund	NR	NY	GEC	0.111	1-17-00	12-28	0.078	....	0.11	1.0	....	0.50	12 1/2	4 15/16	11 3/16	10	10 5/8	-24.5	14.07	12-23-99	10073
HIS	CIGNA High Income Shs	NR	NY	BD	†0.078	1-10-00	12-23	†0.882	....	0.81	e15.1	†0.864	....	8 11/16	5 1/4	6 5/16	5 1/4	5 3/8	-9.4	5.93	12-23-99	51226

Uniform Footnote Explanations-See page 4. Other: [1] Incl $9.06 return of cap,'00. [2] Stk dstr of Consolidated Tomaka Land Co. [3] Incl $1.75 in cash or stk'98. [4] Plan cash payment of 10% of NAV. [5] In cash or stk. [6] Incl $2.40 in cash or stk,'99. [7] Incl $1.74 in cash or stk,'98.

Ticker Symbol	Fund	Rating	Exc.	Type	Dividends: Latest Payment: Period $	Date	Ex. Div.	So Far 1999: Invest. Income	So Far 1999: Cap. Gain	Ind. Rate	Div. Yld. %	1998: Invest. Income	1998: Cap. Gain	Price Range: 1998 - 1999 High	1998 - 1999 Low	December, 1999 Last Sale or Bid: High	Low	Last	Net Assets: % NAV Prem. Disc.	Latest NAV	Latest Date	Com. Shs. 000
IIS	**CIGNA Investment Securities**	**NR**	**NY**	**BD**	0.065	1-10-00	12-23	1.12	0.086	1.12	⊙7.9	1.20	....	18 3/8	14	14 1/2	14 1/16	14 3/16	-20.2	17.77	12-23-99	4792
CIM	**CIM High Yield Sec**	**NR**	**AS**	**BD**	†0.02	12-30-99	12-20	†0.71	....	0.69	e13.1	†0.833	....	8 15/16	5 1/16	5 1/2	5 1/16	5 1/4	-19.2	6.50	12-23-99	5868
CLM	**Clemente Strategic Value Fd**	**NR**	**NY**	**GE**	©....	1-31-00	12-27	....	....	Nil	⊙....	....	0.884	17	8 3/8	17	13 1/8	14 1/4	-22.4	18.37	12-23-99	4980
CNN	**CNA Income Shares**	**NR**	**NY**	**BD**	Q0.24	1-17-00	12-29	0.96	....	0.96	13.5	0.96	....	12 7/16	6 7/8	7 3/4	6 7/8	7 1/8	-19.1	8.81	12-22-99	9002
RIF	**Cohen & Steers Rlty Inc Fd**	**NR**	**AS**	**IRE**	Q0.13	1-14-00	12-17	0.70	1.31	0.52	⊙8.0	†1.96	....	12 3/4	6	7 5/16	6	6 1/2	5.0	6.19	12-23-99	2999
RFI	**Cohen & Steers Total Rt Rty Fd**	**NR**	**NY**	**IRE**	†0.03	1-14-00	12-17	†1.17	1.80	0.96	e9.0	†2.84	....	19 7/8	10	11 3/8	10	10 5/8	3.7	10.25	12-23-99	7399
CCA	**Colonial Calif Insured Muni Fd**	**NR**	**AS**	**MU**	0.078	1-4-00	12-14	....	....	[1]....	....	....	....	15 1/8	12 1/2	15 1/16	12 1/2	12 1/2	-9.9	13.88	12-23-99	2000
CXE	**Colonial High Income Muni**	**NR**	**NY**	**MU**	0.04	1-7-00	12-29	0.496	....	0.48	7.5	0.526	....	9 1/16	6 1/16	6 11/16	6 1/16	6 3/8	-13.1	7.34	12-23-99	31069
CFX	**Colonial Insured Muni Fd**	**NR**	**AS**	**MU**	0.082	1-4-00	12-14	....	....	[1]....	....	....	....	15 1/8	12 1/8	15 1/8	12 1/8	12 3/4	-7.6	13.80	12-23-99	2000
CIF	**Colonial Interm Hi Income**	**NR**	**NY**	**BD**	0.08	1-7-00	12-29	0.705	....	0.70	⊙13.5	0.684	0.008	8 1/4	4 15/16	5 11/16	4 15/16	5 3/16	-14.5	6.07	12-23-99	20155
CMK	**Colonial InterMkt Inc Tr I**	**NR**	**NY**	**ICF**	0.074	1-3-00	12-13	0.904	....	0.89	11.0	0.923	0.091	11 1/8	7 7/8	8 7/16	7 7/8	8 1/8	-20.4	10.21	12-23-99	11009
CXH	**Colonial Inv Grade Muni**	**NR**	**NY**	**MU**	0.049	1-3-00	12-3	0.574	....	0.58	6.9	0.61	....	11 13/16	8 3/8	9 1/8	8 3/8	8 7/16	-16.4	10.09	12-23-99	11509
CMU	**Colonial Muni Inc Tr[2]**	**NR**	**NY**	**MU**	0.037	1-7-00	12-29	0.458	....	0.44	8.0	0.492	....	8 7/16	5 3/8	5 7/8	5 3/8	5 1/2	-13.9	6.39	12-23-99	27645
CNM	**Colonial NY Insured Muni Fd**	**NR**	**AS**	**MUS**	0.084	1-21-00	1-5	....	....	[1]....	....	....	....	15 1/16	11 7/8	15	11 7/8	12 3/8	-10.6	13.84	9-30-99	1600
CFD	**Conseco Strategic Inc Fund**	**NR**	**NY**	**CA**	0.101	1-7-00	12-29	1.465	....	1.44	14.1	0.431	....	15 1/16	10	10 15/16	10	10 3/16	-19.0	12.57	12-23-99	6735
COY	**Corporate High Yield Fund**	**NR**	**NY**	**BD**	0.108	1-7-00	12-29	1.353	0.114	1.30	⊙13.6	1.462	....	15 3/16	9	10 1/16	9	9 9/16	-16.3	11.43	12-23-99	23956
KYT	**Corporate High Yield Fd II**	**NR**	**NY**	**BD**	0.129	1-7-00	12-29	1.307	....	1.55	16.2	1.353	....	13 3/4	8 11/16	9 3/4	8 3/4	9 9/16	-8.3	10.43	12-23-99	8865
CYE	**Corporate High Yield Fd III**	**NR**	**NY**	**CA**	0.132	1-7-00	12-29	1.50	0.03	1.59	⊙15.9	1.124	....	15 1/2	9 1/2	10 1/2	9 1/2	10	-16.9	12.03	12-23-99	35070
CIK	**Credit Suisse Mgt Income**	**NR**	**NY**	**SB**	M0.06	12-15-99	12-2	0.72	....	0.72	11.9	0.72	....	8 7/8	5 9/16	6 3/16	5 9/16	6 1/16	-17.1	7.31	12-23-99	34612
CGF	**Credit Suisse Mgt Strat Global**	**NR**	**NY**	**ICF**	0.073	12-15-99	12-2	0.922	....	0.87	13.1	0.948	....	10 7/8	6 1/2	6 7/8	6 1/2	6 5/8	-21.1	8.40	12-23-99	8454
CUR	**Current Inc Shares**	**NR**	**NY**	**C**	0.22	12-15-99	11-23	0.82	....	0.88	8.8	0.83	....	12 7/8	10	10 5/16	10	10	-18.1	12.21	12-23-99	3673
DBS	**Debt Strategies Fund**	**NR**	**NY**	**ICA**	0.08	1-7-00	12-29	0.849	....	0.96	15.8	0.957	....	11 1/8	5 15/16	6 7/16	5 15/16	6 1/16	-18.6	7.45	12-23-99	31425
DSU	**Debt Strategies Fund II**	**NR**	**NY**	**ICA**	0.084	1-7-00	12-29	0.929	....	1.01	14.4	0.554	....	10 7/16	6 13/16	7 1/4	6 13/16	7	-19.5	8.70	12-23-99	62610
DBU	**Debt Strategies Fund III**	**NR**	**NY**	**CA**	0.093	1-7-00	12-29	0.985	....	1.11	13.4	0.253	....	10 1/8	7 13/16	9	7 7/8	8 5/16	-13.4	9.60	12-23-99	11010
DDF	**Delaware Grp Dividend Income**	**NR**	**NY**	**ICA**	0.125	12-31-99	12-15	1.392	0.108	1.50	⊙12.5	1.375	1.288	19 15/16	10	12 1/16	10	12	-5.7	12.73	12-23-99	14307
DGF	**Delaware Grp Global Div & Inc**	**NR**	**NY**	**ICF**	0.125	12-31-99	12-15	1.328	0.172	1.50	⊙12.9	†1.465	0.459	18 3/4	10 7/8	12 1/4	10 7/8	11 5/8	-16.9	13.99	12-23-99	6651
DHY	**DLJ High Yield Bond Fund**	**NR**	**NY**	**ICA**	0.083	12-21-99	12-13	0.983	....	0.99	14.7	0.395	....	10 1/8	6 11/16	7 9/16	6 11/16	6 3/4	-16.3	8.06	12-22-99	44007
DSF	**Dresdner RCN Global Strategic Inc**	**NR**	**NY**	**GB**	0.18	1-18-00	12-23	0.42	0.211	0.60	⊙10.3	0.565	0.113	8 1/8	5 3/4	6 3/16	5 3/4	5 13/16	-22.4	7.49	12-23-99	11955
DCM	**Dreyfus Cal Muni Income**	**NR**	**AS**	**MUS**	0.047	12-28-99	12-10	0.564	....	0.56	6.9	0.567	....	10 13/16	7 9/16	8 3/8	7 9/16	8 1/16	-6.3	8.60	12-23-99	4555
DHF	**Dreyfus High Yield Strategies**	**NR**	**NY**	**CA**	0.128	1-14-00	12-21	1.478	....	1.53	15.4	0.84	....	15 3/8	9 1/2	10 9/16	9 1/2	9 15/16	-3.9	10.34	12-23-99	62815
DMF	**Dreyfus Muni Income**	**NR**	**AS**	**MU**	0.044	12-28-99	12-10	0.532	....	0.53	7.5	0.582	....	10 15/16	6 15/16	7 1/2	6 15/16	7 1/16	-15.8	8.39	12-23-99	20344
DNM	**Dreyfus N.Y. Muni Income**	**NR**	**AS**	**MUS**	0.064	12-28-99	12-10	0.514	0.023	0.49	⊙6.3	0.567	0.027	11 1/4	7 7/16	7 13/16	7 1/2	7 3/4	-13.1	8.92	12-23-99	3817
DSI	**Dreyfus Strategic Gvts**	**NR**	**NY**	**GVT**	0.063	1-5-00	12-13	0.688	....	0.75	9.6	0.75	....	9 13/16	7 1/2	8 9/16	7 1/2	7 13/16	-19.3	9.68	12-23-99	14641
DSM	**Dreyfus Strategic Muni Bd Fd**	**NR**	**NY**	**MU**	0.047	12-28-99	12-10	0.578	....	0.56	7.6	0.616	....	11 1/8	7 1/8	7 11/16	7 1/8	7 3/8	-11.6	8.34	12-23-99	47784
LEO	**Dreyfus Strategic Municipals**	**NR**	**NY**	**MU**	0.061	12-28-99	12-10	0.557	0.015	0.55	⊙7.3	0.618	....	11 3/16	7 3/8	8 1/16	7 3/8	7 1/2	-16.6	8.99	12-23-99	58549
DUC	**Duff/Phelps Util & Cp Bd Tr**	**NR**	**NY**	**BD**	0.098	12-31-99	12-13	1.176	....	1.18	10.2	1.176	....	15 3/4	11	12 7/8	11	11 9/16	-7.7	12.52	12-23-99	26015
DNP	**Duff/Phelps Util Income**	**NR**	**NY**	**ICA**	0.065	2-10-00	1-27	0.78	....	0.78	e9.4	0.78	....	11 1/2	8 1/4	9 1/4	8 1/4	8 5/16	-5.9	8.83	12-23-99	205714
DTF	**Duff/Phelps Util Tax-Free Inc**	**NR**	**NY**	**MU**	0.078	12-31-99	12-13	0.95	....	0.93	7.4	0.96	....	17 1/2	12 1/4	13 1/4	12 1/4	12 9/16	-14.8	14.74	12-23-99	8480
CEV	**Eaton Vance Calif Muni Inc Tr**	**NR**	**AS**	**MUS**	0.064	12-17-99	12-18	0.574	....	0.77	7.0	....	....	15 3/8	10 7/16	11 7/16	10 7/16	11	-0.6	11.07	12-23-99	7038
FEV	**Eaton Vance Fla Muni Income Tr**	**NR**	**AS**	**MUS**	M0.063	12-17-99	12-8	0.565	....	0.75	7.0	....	....	15 7/8	10 1/4	10 7/8	10 1/4	10 11/16	-4.6	11.20	12-23-99	4212
MMV	**Eaton Vance Mass Muni Inc Tr**	**NR**	**AS**	**MUS**	0.064	12-17-99	12-8	0.574	....	0.77	7.2	....	....	15 3/8	10 7/16	11 11/16	10 7/16	10 3/4	-0.7	10.83	12-23-99	2544
EMI	**Eaton Vance Mich Muni Inc Tr**	**NR**	**AS**	**MUS**	0.063	12-17-99	12-8	0.563	....	0.75	7.4	....	....	15 3/4	9 15/16	10 7/8	9 15/16	10 3/16	-9.4	11.24	12-23-99	2080
EVN	**Eaton Vance Muni Income Tr**	**NR**	**NY**	**MU**	0.069	12-17-99	12-8	0.619	....	0.83	7.1	....	....	15 3/8	10 3/4	12 1/4	11	11 5/8	4.4	11.13	12-23-99	16134
EVJ	**Eaton Vance N.J. Muni Income Tr**	**NR**	**AS**	**MUS**	0.063	12-17-99	12-8	0.563	....	0.75	7.1	....	....	15 1/2	10 3/16	11 3/8	10 3/16	10 1/2	-5.1	11.06	12-23-99	4464
EVY	**Eaton Vance N.Y. Muni Income Tr**	**NR**	**AS**	**MUS**	0.064	12-17-99	12-8	0.574	....	0.77	7.0	....	....	15 5/16	9 7/8	11 3/8	9 7/8	10 15/16	-2.9	11.26	12-23-99	5257

Uniform Footnote Explanations-See page 4. Other: [1] To be determined. [2] Unit Benef. Int.

Ticker Symbol	Fund	Rating	Exc.	Type	Dividends: Latest Payment Period $	Date	Ex. Div.	So Far 1999 Invest. Income	So Far 1999 Cap. Gain	Ind. Rate	Div. Yld. %	1998 Invest. Income	1998 Cap. Gain	Price Range 1998 - 1999 High	1998 - 1999 Low	December, 1999 Last Sale or Bid High	Low	Last	Net Assets % NAV Prem. Disc.	Latest NAV	Latest Date	Com. Shs. 000
EVO	Eaton Vance Ohio Muni Income Tr	NR	AS	MUS	0.063	12-17-99	12-8	0.565	....	0.75	7.1	....	....	15¾	9 13/16	11⅛	9 10/16	10½	-7.0	11.29	12-23-99	2770
EVP	Eaton Vance Penn Muni Income Tr	NR	AS	MUS	0.063	12-17-99	12-8	0.565	....	0.75	7.5	....	....	15⅝	10	10 15/16	10	10 1/16	-10.4	11.23	12-23-99	2655
EVF	Eaton Vance Sr Income Tr	NR	NY	BD	0.074	1-14-00	12-27	†0.891	....	0.89	e9.5	....	....	10⅛	9⅛	9⅞	9 3/16	9⅜	-5.7	9.94	12-23-99	35660
BDF	1838 Bond-Deb Trad'g	NR	NY	BD	0.363	1-25-00	12-28	†1.57	....	1.45	e9.0	1.52	....	22¼	16 1/16	16 11/16	16 1/16	16 3/16	-20.0	20.23	12-23-99	3673
ECF	Ellsworth Cv Growth/Income	NR	AS	CV	[1]1.29	11-29-99	10-27	[1]0.584	0.976	0.36	⊙4.3	[2]0.348	1.362	12¼	8⅛	8 13/16	8 3/16	8 7/16	-22.7	10.92	12-23-99	8551
EFL	Emerging Mkts Fltg Rt Fd	NR	NY	P	0.133	12-23-99	12-10	1.59	....	1.59	14.7	1.59	0.279	17	8⅝	11 7/16	10⅛	10 13/16	-8.1	11.76	12-23-99	4227
EMD	Emerging Mkts Income Fund	NR	NY	GE	0.413	12-23-99	12-10	1.65	....	1.65	14.5	†2.433	....	18 7/16	9 3/16	13¼	10 13/16	11⅜	-9.4	12.55	12-23-99	3768
EDF	Emerging Mkts Income Fund II	NR	NY	GB	0.413	12-23-99	12-10	1.65	....	1.65	16.3	1.804	0.876	16 7/16	8	11 11/16	9½	10⅛	-6.4	10.82	12-23-99	23166
EMG	Emerging Mkts Infrastructure	NR	NY	GE	[3]0.16	9-24-99	9-8	[3]0.16	....	0.16	1.4	....	0.862	12½	5⅜	11 5/16	9½	11¼	1.3	11.11	12-23-99	15059
ETF	Emerging Mkts Telecommun Fd	NR	NY	GE	A1.961	1-15-99	12-29	0.011	1.95	Nil	⊙....	0.01	3.70	16⅜	7½	16⅜	12⅞	16⅜	-16.5	19.62	12-23-99	7758
EGX	Engex Inc	NR	AS	CA	1.36	12-27-89	11-28	....	....	Nil	....	....	....	18⅞	6¾	18⅞	13¼	18⅞	15.6	16.33	12-23-99	977
EQS	Equus II Inc	NR	NY	CA	[4]4.25	12-31-99	11-10	....	4.25	0.04	0.4	[4]1.15	....	28⅞	10⅛	10⅞	10⅛	10 5/16	-32.6	15.31	12-23-99	4954
EF	Europe Fund	NR	NY	GE	2.716	12-31-99	12-16	0.134	2.582	0.13	⊙0.7	0.13	3.36	23 11/16	14⅝	19¾	16¾	18⅞	-6.5	20.18	12-23-99	10066
EWF	European Warrant Fund	NR	NY	GE	[5]©3.35	12-30-99	12-9	[5]....	3.35	Nil	⊙....	[6]....	3.00	24⅝	11	18¾	15⅜	18 9/16	-15.8	22.04	12-22-99	11966
EIS	Excelsior Inc Shares	NR	NY	BD	0.26	1-28-00	12-21	1.02	....	1.04	7.3	1.13	....	17 5/16	14¼	15 1/16	14¼	14¼	-19.4	17.68	12-22-99	2186
FAK	Fidelity Advisor Korea Fund	NR	NY	CA	Plan annual div			....	....	....	....	....	....	11⅞	3 1/16	11⅞	10⅝	11½	-24.2	15.18	12-23-99	6243
IAF	First Australia Fund	NR	AS	GEC	0.21	1-14-00	12-29	0.298	0.507	0.80	⊙10.5	[7]0.465	0.421	8½	5⅛	8	7⅝	7⅝	-19.3	9.45	12-23-99	17190
FAX	First Australia Prime	NR	AS	GB	0.06	1-14-00	12-29	0.72	....	0.72	14.2	0.72	....	8 1/16	4 15/16	5½	4 15/16	5 1/16	-19.0	6.25	12-23-99	266736
FCO	First Commonwealth Fund	NR	NY	GB	0.078	1-14-00	12-29	†0.635	0.31	0.93	e10.1	0.945	....	12½	9⅛	9 13/16	9⅛	9 5/16	-23.6	12.03	12-23-99	9266
FF	First Financial Fund	NR	NY	ICA	0.08	12-10-99	11-26	0.13	3.04	0.05	⊙0.7	0.14	3.31	23⅞	7	8⅜	7 5/16	7 11/16	-13.1	8.85	12-23-99	25065
ISL	First Israel Fund	NR	NY	GEC	1.87	12-29-99	12-13	0.71	2.57	0.50	⊙2.9	....	0.47	17¾	9¾	17¾	15½	17	-10.1	18.90	12-23-99	4463
FPF	First Philippine Fund	NR	NY	GEC	©1.50	1-15-97	12-23	....	....	Nil	....	....	....	9 1/16	3¼	6⅜	5 7/16	6⅜	-16.0	7.59	12-23-99	11225
EME	Foreign/Colon'l Emg MidEast Fd	NR	NY	CA	1.642	1-12-00	12-29	....	0.548	0.01	⊙0.1	1.27	....	18½	12	18½	14	16⅝	-21.5	21.17	12-22-99	2807
FTD	Fort Dearborn Inc Sec	NR	NY	BD	0.267	12-10-99	11-18	1.04	0.007	1.04	⊙8.5	1.04	0.50	16½	12	12 13/16	12	12¼	-17.6	14.86	12-23-99	8789
FOR	Fortis Securities	NR	NY	BD	0.057	1-11-00	12-22	0.702	....	0.68	9.9	0.729	....	9 15/16	6¾	7 1/16	6¾	6⅞	-18.0	8.38	12-23-99	12642
FRF	France Growth Fund	NR	NY	GEC	©1.70	1-14-00	12-28	0.781	2.417	0.78	⊙5.1	0.394	2.037	16½	9 9/16	16½	14 11/16	15 5/16	-20.5	19.27	12-23-99	15345
FKL	Franklin Capital	NR	AS	CA	†1.765	10-20-97	-28	....	....	Nil	....	....	....	11⅛	4⅝	11⅛	8½	10¼	15.2	8.90	12-23-99	760
FMI	Franklin Multi-Income Tr	NR	NY	ICA	0.056	1-14-00	12-29	0.736	0.241	0.67	⊙9.1	0.768	0.231	11 3/16	7	7½	7	7⅜	-20.2	9.24	12-23-99	5858
FT	Franklin Universal Tr	NR	NY	C	0.067	1-31-00	1-12	0.804	0.057	0.80	e11.7	†0.844	....	10 5/16	6⅝	7 15/16	6⅝	6 13/16	-18.9	8.40	12-23-99	26865
GCV	Gabelli Conv Securities Fd	NR	NY	CA	©0.43	12-27-99	12-15	0.60	0.43	0.92	8.7	0.92	....	11⅞	8 15/16	10 9/16	8 15/16	10 9/16	-7.4	11.41	12-23-99	7917
GAB	Gabelli Equity Trust	NR	NY	CA	0.36	12-27-99	12-15	[8]h1.53	....	[9]....	....	1.165	....	12 11/16	9½	12 11/16	11½	12 9/16	0.7	12.47	12-23-99	106479
GGT	Gabelli Global Multimedia Tr	NR	NY	CA	©3.12	12-27-99	12-15	....	3.62	0.12	⊙0.6	0.55	0.25	19¾	8	19¾	15	18¾	-2.8	19.29	12-23-99	10834
GUT	Gabelli Utility Trust	NR	NY	CA	0.05	2-25-00	2-14	0.15	....	0.60	7.9	....	....	10 3/16	7 7/16	8 1/16	7½	7⅝	0.6	7.58	12-23-99	10468
GAM	Genl Amer Investors	NR	NY	CA	[4]©3.13	12-21-99	11-10	[4]0.43	4.06	0.47	⊙1.3	[10]0.477	3.243	37 3/16	24½	37 3/16	33¾	37 3/16	-8.7	40.72	12-23-99	24917
GER	Germany Fund	NR	NY	GEC	1.19	11-29-99	11-17	0.85	0.90	1.51	⊙10.0	2.13	4.56	20½	12 3/16	15⅜	12¾	15⅛	-9.4	16.70	12-23-99	14485
GHI	Global High Inc Dollar Fd	NR	NY	GB	0.106	12-31-99	12-23	1.212	....	1.27	11.2	1.086	0.414	14½	9¼	11⅜	10 13/16	11 5/16	-21.1	14.34	12-23-99	21765
GIF	Global Income Fund	NR	AS	ICA	0.05	12-31-99	12-17	0.62	....	0.60	13.5	0.78	....	8⅝	4⅛	4 11/16	4⅛	4 7/16	-23.1	5.77	12-23-99	4939
GDF	Global Partners Income Fd	NR	NY	GB	0.119	12-23-99	12-10	1.425	....	1.43	14.8	†1.673	....	15 7/16	8⅜	10 9/16	9 11/16	9 11/16	-18.3	11.85	12-23-99	14674
GSG	Global Small Cap Fund	NR	AS	GE	©0.749	12-31-99	12-23	....	0.749	Nil	⊙....	....	0.684	26⅜	10½	26⅜	19¼	26⅜	-1.0	26.64	12-23-99	3802
GCH	Greater China Fund	NR	NY	CA	Div Omitted 12-21-98			....	....	Nil	....	0.053	4.367	12⅛	3½	8 11/16	7 9/16	8⅜	-24.2	11.05	12-23-99	12593
GCM	Greenwich Street CA Muni Fd	NR	AS	GVT	0.049	12-30-99	12-27	0.588	....	0.59	5.6	0.648	0.023	14⅛	10⅜	11⅜	10⅜	10⅝	-18.1	12.97	12-23-99	3658
GSI	Greenwich Street Muni Fund	NR	NY	MU	0.047	2-25-00	2-17	0.569	....	0.56	5.7	0.592	....	11 13/16	9 11/16	10⅛	9 11/16	9¾	-5.0	10.26	12-23-99	19882
HQH	H&Q Healthcare Inv	NR	NY	CA	©1.33	12-30-99	11-16	[5]....	1.33	Nil	⊙....	[6]....	0.36	22	11	22	15¾	21½	-15.5	25.45	12-23-99	9453
HQL	H&Q Life Sciences Investors	NR	NY	CA	©1.17	12-30-99	11-16	[5]....	1.17	Nil	⊙....	[6]....	0.28	20 5/16	9	20 5/16	13 5/16	20	-4.4	20.93	12-23-99	7295
HAT	Hatteras Income Sec	NR	NY	BD	†0.182	12-31-99	12-9	†1.117	....	1.08	e9.1	1.105	....	15 11/16	11⅝	12¾	11⅝	11⅞	-18.9	14.65	12-23-99	3364

Uniform Footnote Explanations-See page 4. Other: [1] Incl $0.314 in cash or stk,'99. [2] Incl $1.41 in cash or stkm'98. [3] Approx. [4] In cash or stk. [5] In cash or stk,'99. [6] In cash or stk,'98. [7] Incl $0.358 in cash or stk,'98. [8] Stk dstr of Gabelli Utilities Tr. [9] Co plans 2.5% of NAV quarterly. [10] Incl $3.51 in cash or stk,'98.

Ticker Symbol	Fund	Rating	Exc.	Type	Dividends: Latest Payment: Period $	Date	Ex. Div.	So Far 1999: Invest. Income	So Far 1999: Cap. Gain	Ind. Rate	Div. Yld. %	1998: Invest. Income	1998: Cap. Gain	Price Range: 1998 - 1999 High	1998 - 1999 Low	December, 1999 Last Sale or Bid: High	Low	Last	Net Assets: % NAV Prem. Disc.	Latest NAV	Latest Date	Com. Shs. 000
HHGP	Harris & Harris Group	NR	NNM	CA	[1]0.35	3-25-99	3-17	[1]0.35	....	Nil	....	[2]0.75	....	19⅜	1	19⅜	4⅞	11½	508.5	1.89	12-23-99	10591
HTI	Heartland Technology[3]	NR	AS	IRE	None Since Public			....	....	Nil	....	....	....	17½	2⅛	3³⁄₁₆	2⅛	3	-34.2	4.56	9-30-99	1671
HIO	High Income Opp Fd	NR	NY	BD	0.084	3-31-00	3-24	1.02	....	1.01	11.9	†1.117	....	12¹³⁄₁₆	8¼	8¹¹⁄₁₆	8¼	8½	-19.0	10.49	12-23-99	72230
HYI	High Yield Income Fd	NR	NY	BD	0.06	12-31-99	12-13	0.72	....	0.72	13.4	0.72	....	8⅛	5⅛	5¾	5⅛	5⅜	-16.9	6.47	12-23-99	11240
HYP	High Yield Plus Fund	NR	NY	BD	†0.088	1-7-00	12-28	†0.895	....	0.87	e14.2	0.848	....	10	5¹⁵⁄₁₆	6⅝	5¹⁵⁄₁₆	6⅛	-12.2	6.98	12-23-99	15209
HTR	Hyperion Total Return Fd	NR	NY	MI	0.07	1-27-00	12-29	0.745	....	0.84	11.3	0.75	....	9¹¹⁄₁₆	7⅛	7¹¹⁄₁₆	7⅜	7⁷⁄₁₆	-21.6	9.48	12-22-99	22994
HTB	Hyperion 2002 Term Trust	AAAf	NY	BD	0.035	12-31-99	12-20	0.45	....	0.43	5.3	0.475	....	8⁹⁄₁₆	7¹⁵⁄₁₆	8⁵⁄₁₆	8⅛	8⅛	-8.1	8.84	12-22-99	30447
HTO	Hyperion 2005 Inv Grd Oppt Tr	AAf	NY	MI	0.044	1-27-00	12-29	0.745	....	0.53	6.7	0.55	....	9⅛	7⁷⁄₁₆	8¹⁄₁₆	7⅞	7¹⁵⁄₁₆	-12.6	9.08	12-22-99	17047
IFT	Income Opportunities Fd 2000	NR	NY	GVT	0.065	1-17-00	12-29	0.542	....	0.78	8.3	†0.638	....	9¹⁵⁄₁₆	9⁷⁄₁₆	9¹⁵⁄₁₆	9¹¹⁄₁₆	9⅜	-6.3	10.01	12-23-99	11058
IFN	India Fund	NR	NY	GEC	0.01	1-10-97	12-24	....	....	Nil	....	....	....	16¹³⁄₁₆	5³⁄₁₆	16¹³⁄₁₆	13⅞	16¾	-24.7	22.24	12-23-99	33636
IGF	India Growth Fund	NR	NY	GEC	0.08	1-15-97	12-27	....	....	Nil	....	....	....	15⅜	6⅛	15⅜	12½	15¼	-30.3	21.89	12-23-99	9831
IF	Indonesia Fund	NR	NY	GEC	0.045	9-24-99	9-8	0.045	....	[4]....	....	....	....	7¼	2¼	5¾	5	5⁷⁄₁₆	23.8	4.39	12-23-99	4609
PIF	Insured Muni Income Fd	NR	NY	MU	0.064	12-31-99	12-16	0.768	....	0.77	6.7	0.768	....	14⅞	11⁵⁄₁₆	12⁵⁄₁₆	11⁵⁄₁₆	11⁹⁄₁₆	-18.7	14.23	12-23-99	20628
GHS	Invesco Global Health Sci	NR	NY	CA	0.94	12-17-99	11-19	0.07	2.324	[5]....	⊙....	[6]1.066	2.642	21¼	13⁵⁄₁₆	15³⁄₁₆	13⁵⁄₁₆	14¾	-16.8	17.72	12-23-99	30156
PPM	Investment Grade Muni Inc	NR	NY	MU	0.09	12-31-99	12-16	0.90	0.015	0.90	⊙7.0	0.90	....	16⁵⁄₁₆	12¹¹⁄₁₆	13⁵⁄₁₆	12¹¹⁄₁₆	12¹³⁄₁₆	-17.7	15.57	12-23-99	10357
IRL	Irish Investment Fund	NR	NY	GEC	1.731	12-20-99	12-9	0.127	1.604	0.13	⊙0.8	....	1.142	24¹⁵⁄₁₆	14⁵⁄₁₆	16⅝	14½	15⁵⁄₁₆	-22.4	19.72	12-23-99	5009
ITA	Italy Fund	NR	NY	GEC	2.182	12-30-99	12-22	1.246	1.937	0.21	⊙1.2	0.21	0.247	17⅜	10½	17⅜	14⁷⁄₁₆	17	-10.7	19.03	12-23-99	8769
JGF	Jakarta Growth Fund	NR	NY	GEC	0.02	12-22-97	11-20	....	....	Nil	....	....	....	4¾	1⁷⁄₁₆	3¼	2¹³⁄₁₆	3³⁄₁₆	6.2	3.00	12-23-99	5018
JEQ	Japan Equity Fund	NR	NY	GEC	Div Omitted 12-4-97			....	....	Nil	....	....	....	11³⁄₁₆	5¼	10¹⁄₁₆	9⅛	9¹¹⁄₁₆	-6.0	10.31	12-23-99	10816
JOF	Japan OTC Equity Fund	NR	NY	GEC	0.005	12-21-98	11-19	....	....	0.08	0.7	0.005	....	14¹⁵⁄₁₆	3⅝	12⅛	10½	11¹³⁄₁₆	-19.5	14.67	12-23-99	11388
JFC	Jardine Fleming China Reg Fd	NR	NY	GEA	0.04	12-30-99	12-15	0.04	....	Nil	....	....	....	10½	3½	8⁷⁄₁₆	7¹¹⁄₁₆	8⁷⁄₁₆	-26.3	11.45	12-23-99	9101
JFI	Jardine Fleming India Fund	NR	NY	GEC	©0.012	9-14-95	8-22	....	....	Nil	....	....	....	11⅞	4½	11⅞	9⅜	11⅞	-30.4	17.07	12-22-99	11307
BTO	John Hancock Bk/Thrift Opp	NR	NY	CA	0.70	12-30-99	12-17	0.147	0.553	0.15	⊙1.8	0.143	1.169	14¹⁵⁄₁₆	7⅜	8⅞	7⅜	8⁷⁄₁₆	-6.2	8.99	12-23-99	86425
JHS	John Hancock Inc Sec[7]	NR	NY	P	0.278	12-30-99	12-16	1.103	....	1.11	8.7	1.135	....	17⅛	12⁷⁄₁₆	13³⁄₁₆	12⁷⁄₁₆	12¹¹⁄₁₆	-17.4	15.36	12-23-99	10627
JHI	John Hancock Inv Tr[7]	NR	NY	BD	0.368	12-30-99	12-16	1.468	....	1.47	8.9	1.515	....	22⅞	16⅛	17¹⁄₁₆	16⅛	16⁹⁄₁₆	-17.6	20.10	12-23-99	7783
PGD	John Hancock Patr Gl Div Fd	NR	NY	P	0.081	1-31-00	1-5	1.011	....	0.97	10.1	1.05	....	13¹⁵⁄₁₆	9⅛	10³⁄₁₆	9⅛	9⁹⁄₁₆	-22.9	12.41	12-23-99	8345
PPF	John Hancock Patr Pfd Div Fd	NR	NY	P	0.072	1-31-00	1-6	0.864	....	0.86	8.7	1.155	....	15¹⁄₁₆	9½	10⁷⁄₁₆	9½	9⅞	-16.0	11.75	12-23-99	7257
PDF	John Hancock Patr Prem Dv Fd	NR	NY	P	0.054	12-31-99	12-15	0.674	....	0.65	8.4	0.70	....	10⅜	7¹⁄₁₆	8½	7¹⁄₁₆	7¾	-15.9	9.21	12-23-99	14980
PDT	John Hancock Patr Prem Dv II	NR	NY	P	0.065	1-14-00	-15	0.84	....	0.78	8.9	0.90	....	12¾	8⅜	10	8⅜	8¹³⁄₁₆	-21.0	11.16	12-23-99	15003
DIV	John Hancock Patr Sel Div Tr	NR	NY	P	0.09	1-31-00	1-6	1.159	....	1.08	9.3	1.237	....	16⅜	11¼	12¹³⁄₁₆	11¼	11⅝	-18.2	14.22	12-23-99	9885
KHI	Kemper High Income	NR	NY	BD	0.081	1-13-00	12-31	0.93	....	0.97	12.6	0.90	....	10½	7⁷⁄₁₆	8¹¹⁄₁₆	7⁷⁄₁₆	7¹¹⁄₁₆	-2.9	7.92	12-23-99	23919
KGT	Kemper Interm Gvt Tr	NR	NY	GVT	0.045	12-31-99	12-13	[8]0.575	....	0.54	8.4	0.60	....	8³⁄₁₆	6³⁄₁₆	6¹¹⁄₁₆	6⁷⁄₁₆	6⁷⁄₁₆	-11.6	7.28	12-23-99	33996
KMM	Kemper Multi-Mkt Income	NR	NY	ICF	0.18	1-15-00	12-31	0.868	....	0.93	11.7	0.81	....	10½	7¹¹⁄₁₆	8⁷⁄₁₆	7¹¹⁄₁₆	7¹⁵⁄₁₆	-19.3	9.83	12-23-99	20090
KTF	Kemper Muni Income	NR	NY	MU	0.069	12-31-99	12-13	0.822	....	0.82	8.3	0.87	....	14¹⁵⁄₁₆	9⁷⁄₁₆	10⅝	9⁷⁄₁₆	9¹⁵⁄₁₆	-7.7	10.77	12-23-99	38542
KST	Kemper Strategic Income Tr	NR	AS	BD	0.15	1-13-00	12-31	1.80	....	1.80	14.8	1.80	....	20⁵⁄₁₆	12⅛	15⅛	12⅛	12³⁄₁₆	-7.7	13.21	12-23-99	3462
KSM	Kemper Strategic Muni Tr	NR	NY	MU	©0.05	1-13-00	12-31	0.75	0.01	0.75	⊙7.8	0.761	....	13½	9½	10⁷⁄₁₆	9½	9⁹⁄₁₆	-13.9	11.10	12-23-99	10704
KEF	Korea Equity Fund	NR	NY	GEC	0.02	12-29-95	12-21	....	....	Nil	....	....	....	5¹⁵⁄₁₆	1⅞	5¹⁄₁₆	4¹¹⁄₁₆	4⅞	-26.1	6.60	12-23-99	8409
KF	Korea Fund	NR	NY	GEC	©0.60	9-30-96	9-12	....	....	Nil	....	....	....	17	5½	17	14⅝	17	-26.1	22.99	12-23-99	50000
KIF	Korean Investment Fund	NR	NY	GEC	0.293	1-12-96	12-27	....	....	Nil	....	....	....	9⅛	1¹⁵⁄₁₆	8¹¹⁄₁₆	7¹¹⁄₁₆	8¹¹⁄₁₆	-25.4	11.65	12-23-99	8451
LAQ	Latin America Equity Fd	NR	NY	GEC	0.11	1-15-99	12-29	0.11	....	0.11	0.9	[9]....	1.50	14³⁄₁₆	5½	12¹¹⁄₁₆	10¾	12⅝	-23.1	16.42	12-23-99	8614
LAM	Latin America Inv Fd	NR	NY	GEC	0.50	12-29-99	12-13	0.92	....	0.50	3.8	....	2.42	15⅛	5⅞	13¼	11¾	13¹⁄₁₆	-22.8	16.91	12-23-99	7925
LDF	Latin American Discovery Fd	NR	NY	GEC	0.056	1-14-00	12-10	0.034	....	0.03	0.3	....	6.666	18½	4¼	11	9¼	10¹¹⁄₁₆	-21.4	13.60	12-23-99	12193
FND	LCM Internet Growth Fund	NR	AS	C	Plan annual div			....	....	[4]....	....	....	....	14	9½	14	10⅛	13	-2.7	13.36	12-23-99	4600
USA	Liberty ALL-STAR Eqty[7]	NR	NY	CA	0.34	1-3-00	11-17	1.39	....	[10]....	....	1.40	....	14¹¹⁄₁₆	10	11⁹⁄₁₆	10¾	11¹⁄₁₆	-20.0	13.83	12-23-99	94998
ASG	Liberty ALL-STAR Growth Fd	NR	NY	CA	0.31	1-3-00	11-17	[11]1.23	....	1.24	11.5	1.36	....	14¼	8⅝	10¹⁵⁄₁₆	9⅞	10¹³⁄₁₆	-14.7	12.68	12-23-99	12938

Uniform Footnote Explanations-See page 4. Other: [1] Contingent upon transact with NBX Corp&3Com Corp. [2] Spl div. [3] Dec'98 & prior,co reported as an invest co. [4] To be determined. [5] Plan cash payment of 10% of NAV. [6] Incl $2.1034 in cash or stk,'98. [7] Shrs Ben Int. [8] Incl $0.01 return of cap,'99. [9] In cash or stk. [10] Co plans 2.5% of NAV quarterly. [11] Incl $0.32 return of cap,'99.

Ticker Symbol	Fund	Rating	Exc.	Type	Dividends: Latest Payment Period $	Date	Ex. Div.	So Far 1999 Invest. Income	So Far 1999 Cap. Gain	Ind. Rate	Div. Yld. %	1998 Invest. Income	1998 Cap. Gain	Price Range 1998 - 1999 High	1998 - 1999 Low	December, 1999 Last Sale or Bid High	Low	Last	Net Assets % NAV Prem. Disc.	Latest NAV	Latest Date	Com. Shs. 000
LNV	**Lincoln Natl Cv Sec**	**NR**	**NY**	**CV**	0.20	1-14-00	12-29	0.90	....	0.88	5.5	†1.00	1.76	19 3/16	12 3/4	16 1/16	14 3/16	16	-24.0	21.05	12-22-99	6372
LND	**Lincoln Natl Income Fd**	**NR**	**NY**	**C**	†0.27	1-14-00	12-29	0.98	0.06	0.96	⊙9.9	†1.17	0.31	14 5/8	9 5/8	11 1/8	9 5/8	9 11/16	-22.1	12.43	12-22-99	7105
MF	**Malaysia Fund**	**NR**	**NY**	**GEC**	Div Omitted 12-18-98			....	....	Nil	....	0.034	....	9 15/16	2 15/16	7 3/16	5 11/16	7 1/16	36.6	5.17	12-23-99	9738
MHY	**Managed High Inc Portfolio**	**NR**	**NY**	**BD**	0.081	2-25-00	2-17	0.99	....	0.97	11.9	1.04	....	12 1/2	8	8 7/16	8	8 1/8	-19.8	10.13	12-23-99	44236
PHT	**Managed High Yield Fd**	**NR**	**NY**	**BD**	0.105	12-31-99	12-16	1.26	....	1.26	12.6	1.26	....	14 13/16	9	10 1/4	9	10	-13.1	11.51	12-23-99	6032
HYF	**Managed High Yield Plus Fd**	**NR**	**NY**	**CA**	0.125	1-14-00	12-27	1.50	....	1.50	13.7	0.613	....	15 1/8	10 1/16	11 3/8	10 1/16	10 15/16	-9.6	12.10	12-23-99	31489
MMU	**Managed Muni Portfolio**	**NR**	**NY**	**MU**	0.05	12-30-99	12-22	0.595	....	0.60	6.6	0.555	0.118	12 7/16	9	9 7/16	9	9 1/16	-16.9	10.90	12-23-99	34607
MTU	**Managed Muni Portfolio II**	**NR**	**NY**	**MU**	0.05	12-30-99	12-22	0.595	....	0.60	6.6	0.555	0.177	12 1/2	8 15/16	9 7/16	8 15/16	9 1/16	-16.9	10.91	12-23-99	11235
MHE	**Mass Hlth & Edu Tax-Exempt Tr**	**NR**	**AS**	**MU**	0.064	3-31-00	3-13	0.749	....	0.76	6.6	0.682	....	15 3/8	10 15/16	12 1/2	10 15/16	11 1/2	-7.6	12.44	12-23-99	2313
MCI	**MassMutual Corp Inv**	**NR**	**NY**	**ICA**	†1.46	1-19-00	12-29	†1.98	....	1.72	e8.0	†2.00	0.05	28 1/2	19 3/8	23 3/4	19 3/8	21 3/8	-5.6	22.65	12-23-99	8587
MPV	**MassMutual Part'n Inv**	**NR**	**NY**	**ICA**	†0.65	1-19-00	12-29	†1.14	....	0.96	e9.4	†1.091	0.019	13 1/4	9 3/4	10 5/8	10	10 1/4	-11.0	11.52	12-23-99	9333
MRF	**Mentor Income Fund**	**NR**	**NY**	**MI**	0.06	1-3-00	12-13	0.72	....	0.72	10.1	0.69	....	9 15/16	7 1/16	7 5/8	7 1/16	7 1/8	-22.5	9.19	12-23-99	11818
MXE	**Mexico Eqty & Income Fd**	**NR**	**NY**	**GEC**	[1]0.121	1-14-00	12-21	0.93	....	Nil	⊙....	....	3.56	11 1/16	4 1/4	9	8	8 15/16	-17.6	10.85	12-22-99	11825
MXF	**Mexico Fund**	**NR**	**NY**	**GEC**	0.015	1-28-00	12-22	[2]0.444	....	0.44	2.5	[2]†0.826	....	20 3/4	7 9/16	17 13/16	16 1/8	17 3/8	-27.5	23.97	12-22-99	50507
MCR	**MFS Charter Income Tr**	**NR**	**NY**	**BD**	0.06	12-31-99	12-13	0.742	....	0.72	8.9	0.822	....	10 5/16	7 3/4	8 3/16	7 3/4	8 1/16	-16.9	9.70	12-23-99	67139
MGF	**MFS Gvt Mkts Income Tr**	**NR**	**NY**	**ICF**	0.04	12-31-99	12-13	0.458	....	0.48	8.4	0.468	....	6 7/8	5 5/8	6	5 5/8	5 11/16	-17.2	6.87	12-23-99	66611
MIN	**MFS Interm Income SBI**	**NR**	**NY**	**ICF**	0.045	12-31-99	12-13	0.505	....	0.54	8.9	0.509	....	7 1/2	5 15/16	6 1/4	5 15/16	6 1/16	-15.0	7.13	12-23-99	138848
MMT	**MFS Multimkt Income**	**NR**	**NY**	**BD**	0.045	12-31-99	12-13	0.562	....	0.54	9.8	0.584	....	7 15/16	5 1/2	5 13/16	5 1/2	5 1/2	-22.0	7.05	12-23-99	92880
MFM	**MFS Municipal Inc Tr**	**NR**	**NY**	**MU**	M0.044	12-31-99	12-13	0.528	....	0.528	8.1	0.572	....	9 5/8	6 3/8	7 3/8	6 3/8	6 1/2	-17.1	7.84	12-23-99	39225
MFV	**MFS Special Value Trust**	**NR**	**NY**	**ICA**	0.638	12-31-99	12-13	1.56	0.59	1.65	⊙11.2	1.679	0.639	20 11/16	13 3/4	16 1/8	13 3/4	14 3/4	8.6	13.58	12-23-99	6354
MXA	**Minnesota Muni Inc Portfolio**	**Af**	**AS**	**MUS**	M0.066	1-12-00	12-29	0.862	....	0.795	6.7	†0.765	....	15 3/4	11 1/2	12 9/16	11 1/2	11 15/16	-10.2	13.30	12-22-99	4147
MNA	**Minnesota Muni Term Trust**	**Af**	**NY**	**MUS**	0.051	1-12-00	12-29	[3]†0.72	0.004	0.61	⊙e6.2	†0.658	0.105	11 5/8	9 3/4	10	9 3/4	9 13/16	-5.8	10.42	12-22-99	5733
MNB	**Minnesota Muni Term Tr-II**	**Af**	**AS**	**MUS**	0.049	1-12-00	12-1	[4]0.596	0.025	0.59	⊙6.2	†0.593	0.083	11 9/16	9 9/16	10	9 9/16	9 9/16	-6.3	10.20	12-22-99	3460
MTS	**Montgomery St Inc Sec**	**NR**	**NY**	**BD**	0.34	12-30-99	12-17	1.36	....	1.36	8.8	1.37	0.02	20 1/2	15	15 15/16	15	15 1/2	-15.6	18.36	12-23-99	10273
MGC	**Morgan Grenfell Smallcap**	**NR**	**NY**	**CA**	0.21	9-21-98	8-14	....	....	Nil	⊙....	....	2.45	14 3/8	6 15/16	14 3/8	12	14 3/16	-7.2	15.28	12-23-99	9802
AFF	**Morgan StanDW Africa Inv Fd**	**NR**	**NY**	**GEC**	0.246	1-14-00	12-17	0.87	....	0.87	8.4	0.35	1.847	14 3/4	8 1/16	10 11/16	9 9/16	10 3/8	-25.9	14.00	12-23-99	14346
APF	**Morgan StanDW Asia-Pac Fund**	**NR**	**NY**	**GEA**	Div Omitted 12-18-98			....	....	Nil	....	0.033	....	11 13/16	5 1/4	11 13/16	10 3/8	11 13/16	-18.8	14.54	12-23-99	67275
IIC	**Morgan StanDW Cal Ins Muni Inc**	**NR**	**NY**	**MUS**	0.065	3-17-00	3-1	0.757	....	0.78	6.7	0.75	....	15 3/8	11 1/2	12 1/2	11 1/2	11 5/8	-13.3	13.41	12-23-99	12816
IQC	**Morgan StanDW Cal Qual Muni**	**NR**	**NY**	**MUS**	0.065	3-17-00	3-1	0.757	....	0.78	7.1	0.728	....	14 5/8	11	12 1/4	11	11	-13.7	12.74	12-23-99	11042
RNE	**Morgan StanDW Eastern Europe**	**NR**	**NY**	**CA**	Div Omitted 12-18-98			....	....	Nil	....	....	4.272	26 1/2	6 7/8	17 1/8	12 1/8	16 7/8	-7.3	18.20	12-23-99	4467
MSF	**Morgan StanDW Emerging Mkt**	**NR**	**NY**	**GE**	Div Omitted 12-18-98			....	....	Nil	....	0.114	2.179	16 5/16	6 3/16	16 5/16	13 1/16	16 5/16	-19.9	20.37	12-23-99	21455
MSD	**Morgan StanDW Emer'g Mkt Debt**	**NR**	**NY**	**GB**	0.286	1-14-00	12-17	0.802	....	1.04	15.3	1.089	2.944	15 9/16	5 15/16	7 1/2	6 5/8	6 13/16	-17.4	8.25	12-23-99	21851
MGB	**Morgan StanDW Global Opt Bd Fd**	**NR**	**NY**	**GB**	0.27	1-14-00	12-17	1.057	....	1.06	12.7	1.176	2.186	14 15/16	7 1/4	9 1/8	8 1/8	8 3/8	-20.1	10.48	12-23-99	4178
GVT	**Morgan StanDW Gvt Income SBI**	**NR**	**NY**	**GVT**	0.045	3-17-00	3-1	0.552	....	0.54	6.7	0.591	....	9 1/8	7 15/16	8 1/4	8 1/16	8 1/16	-10.2	8.98	12-23-99	42604
YLD	**Morgan StanDW High Income Adv**	**NR**	**NY**	**BD**	0.045	1-21-00	12-28	0.585	....	0.54	e16.6	†0.606	....	6 5/16	3 1/16	3 1/2	3 1/16	3 1/4	-1.8	3.31	12-23-99	30017
YLT	**Morgan StanDW High Inc Adv II**	**NR**	**NY**	**BD**	0.048	1-21-00	12-28	†0.644	....	0.57	e16.6	0.63	0.048	6 5/8	3 1/8	3 3/4	3 1/8	3 7/16	-8.1	3.74	12-23-99	35611
YLH	**Morgan StanDW High Inc Adv III**	**NR**	**NY**	**BD**	0.055	1-21-00	12-28	0.705	....	0.66	17.0	0.72	....	7 1/2	3 11/16	4 1/8	3 11/16	3 7/8	-4.8	4.07	12-23-99	12877
MSY	**Morgan StanDW Hi Yld Fd**	**NR**	**NY**	**BD**	0.115	1-14-00	12-17	1.463	0.789	1.23	⊙11.1	1.392	0.521	16 5/8	11	11 9/16	11	11 1/16	-12.8	12.69	12-23-99	8803
ICB	**Morgan StanDW Income Sec**	**NR**	**NY**	**P**	0.11	3-17-00	3-1	†1.343	....	1.32	e9.1	1.32	....	18 15/16	14 1/4	16	14 1/4	14 9/16	-14.3	16.99	12-23-99	11809
IIF	**Morgan StanDW India Inv Fd**	**NR**	**NY**	**GEC**	0.167	1-10-95	12-23	....	....	Nil	....	....	....	16 1/2	5 5/8	16 1/2	13 1/2	16 1/2	-23.9	21.68	12-23-99	34237
ICS	**Morgan StanDW Ins Cal Muni Sec**	**NR**	**NY**	**MUS**	0.063	3-17-00	3-1	0.75	....	0.75	6.0	0.773	0.157	15 3/4	12 1/2	13 1/8	12 1/2	12 9/16	-12.2	14.31	12-23-99	4199
IMB	**Morgan StanDW Ins Muni Bd Tr**	**NR**	**NY**	**MU**	0.073	3-17-00	3-1	0.195	....	0.87	7.3	0.975	....	16 11/16	11 11/16	12 7/16	11 11/16	11 15/16	-14.6	13.97	12-23-99	5138
IIM	**Morgan StanDW Ins Muni Income**	**NR**	**NY**	**MU**	0.073	3-17-00	3-1	0.848	....	0.87	6.9	0.795	....	15 3/8	12 5/16	13 3/16	12 5/16	12 9/16	-7.2	13.54	12-23-99	28433
IMS	**Morgan StanDW Insured Muni Sec**	**NR**	**NY**	**MU**	†0.075	3-17-00	3-1	†0.79	....	0.78	e6.5	0.803	0.186	15 1/2	11 7/8	12 13/16	11 7/8	12	-17.1	14.47	12-23-99	8810
IMT	**Morgan StanDW Insured Muni Tr**	**NR**	**NY**	**MU**	0.078	3-17-00	3-1	0.907	....	0.93	7.3	0.945	0.104	16 5/16	12 1/2	13 5/16	12 1/2	12 11/16	-14.2	14.79	12-23-99	22413

Uniform Footnote Explanations-See page 4. Other: [1] Approx. [2] In cash or stk. [3] Incl $0.0026 taxable net invt income. [4] Incl $0.008 taxable net invt income.

Ticker Symbol	Fund	Rating	Exc.	Type	Dividends – Latest Payment: Period $	Date	Ex. Div.	So Far 1999: Invest. Income	Cap. Gain	Ind. Rate	Div. Yld. %	1998: Invest. Income	Cap. Gain	Price Range 1998 - 1999: High	Low	December, 1999 Last Sale or Bid: High	Low	Last	Net Assets: % NAV Prem. Disc.	Latest NAV	Latest Date	Com. Shs. 000
OIA	**Morgan StanDW Muni Inc Opp**	**NR**	**NY**	**MU**	0.053	3-17-00	3-1	0.608	....	0.63	8.1	0.578	....	9 15/16	7 9/16	8 3/16	7 9/16	7 3/4	-4.4	8.11	12-23-99	21090
OIB	**Morgan StanDW Muni Inc Opp II**	**NR**	**NY**	**MU**	0.043	3-17-00	3-1	0.51	....	0.51	7.2	0.532	....	9 3/16	7	7 5/8	7	7 1/8	-15.1	8.39	12-23-99	19972
OIC	**Morgan StanDW Muni Inc Opp III**	**NR**	**NY**	**MU**	0.045	3-17-00	3-1	0.54	0.01	0.54	⊙6.8	0.608	....	10 3/4	7	8 1/16	7	8	-14.3	9.33	12-23-99	10523
TFA	**Morgan StanDW Muni Income Tr**	**NR**	**NY**	**MU**	0.043	3-17-00	3-1	0.465	0.011	0.51	⊙6.6	0.517	0.063	9 7/8	7 11/16	8 1/8	7 11/16	7 3/4	-16.5	9.28	12-23-99	29465
TFB	**Morgan StanDW Muni Inc Tr II**	**NR**	**NY**	**MU**	0.043	3-17-00	3-1	0.487	0.03	0.51	⊙6.3	0.525	0.185	10	7 13/16	8 5/16	7 13/16	8 1/16	-14.2	9.40	12-23-99	25852
TFC	**Morgan StanDW Muni Inc Tr III**	**NR**	**NY**	**MU**	0.038	3-17-00	3-1	0.45	0.027	0.45	⊙6.0	0.495	0.063	9 11/16	7 7/16	7 3/4	7 7/16	7 1/2	-18.5	9.20	12-23-99	6331
PIA	**Morgan StanDW Muni Prem Inc**	**NR**	**NY**	**MU**	0.045	3-17-00	3-1	[1]0.518	0.071	0.54	⊙7.2	0.578	0.261	10 5/16	7 3/8	8 1/8	7 3/8	7 1/2	-17.2	9.06	12-23-99	23585
IQN	**Morgan StanDW N.Y. Qual Muni**	**NR**	**NY**	**MUS**	0.065	3-17-00	3-1	0.757	....	0.78	6.7	0.705	....	14 3/8	11 7/16	12 5/16	11 7/16	11 5/8	-9.7	12.87	12-23-99	5079
IQI	**Morgan StanDW Qual Muni Inc**	**NR**	**NY**	**MU**	0.078	3-17-00	3-1	0.93	....	0.93	7.5	0.93	0.047	16 1/4	12 5/16	13	12 5/16	12 7/16	-15.7	14.75	12-23-99	33362
IQT	**Morgan StanDW Qual Muni Inv**	**NR**	**NY**	**MU**	0.078	3-17-00	3-1	0.907	....	0.93	7.6	0.945	0.112	16 1/16	12 1/16	13 1/4	12 1/16	12 3/16	-14.4	14.23	12-23-99	18047
IQM	**Morgan StanDW Qual Muni Sec**	**NR**	**NY**	**MU**	0.068	3-17-00	3-1	0.787	....	0.81	7.0	0.757	....	14 1/2	11 5/16	12	11 5/16	11 1/2	-13.5	13.29	12-23-99	18132
MUA	**MuniAssets Fund**	**NR**	**NY**	**MU**	0.065	12-30-99	12-21	0.807	....	0.78	7.1	0.838	....	14 15/16	10 3/4	11 5/8	10 3/4	11	-15.8	13.07	12-23-99	10432
MAF	**Municipal Advantage Fund**	**NR**	**NY**	**MU**	0.067	12-31-99	12-14	0.798	....	0.80	6.9	0.798	....	14 1/2	11 5/16	12	11 5/16	11 9/16	-11.0	12.99	12-23-99	7257
MHF	**Municipal High Income Fd**	**NR**	**NY**	**MU**	0.049	2-25-00	2-17	0.582	....	0.582	7.8	0.615	....	10 7/16	7 1/16	7 15/16	7 1/16	7 7/16	-16.0	8.85	12-23-99	20406
MNP	**Municipal Partners Fund**	**NR**	**NY**	**MU**	0.067	12-23-99	12-10	0.798	....	0.80	7.3	0.798	....	14 1/4	10 9/16	11 3/8	10 9/16	10 15/16	-16.4	13.08	12-23-99	5757
MPT	**Municipal Partners Fund II**	**NR**	**NY**	**MU**	0.063	12-23-99	12-10	0.75	....	0.75	6.7	0.75	....	13 5/8	10 3/4	11 9/16	10 15/16	11 3/16	-12.5	12.78	12-23-99	6007
MEN	**MuniEnhanced Fund**	**NR**	**NY**	**MU**	0.053	12-30-99	12-21	0.642	....	0.64	7.1	0.67	0.50	12 9/16	8 3/4	9 3/4	8 3/4	9 1/16	-11.7	10.26	12-23-99	20319
CLH	**MuniHoldings Cal Insured Fund**	**NR**	**NY**	**MUS**	0.068	12-30-99	12-21	0.844	....	0.82	6.9	0.869	0.075	16 5/8	11 7/16	12 7/8	11 7/16	11 13/16	-8.5	12.91	12-23-99	8327
MUC	**MuniHoldings Cal Insured Fund II**	**NR**	**NY**	**MUS**	0.07	12-30-99	12-21	0.816	....	0.84	7.1	0.62	0.028	16 1/16	11 5/16	12 1/2	11 5/16	11 13/16	-5.0	12.43	12-23-99	9807
MCF	**MuniHoldings Cal Insured Fund III**	**NR**	**NY**	**MUS**	0.067	12-30-99	12-21	0.80	....	0.80	7.1	0.147	....	16 3/16	10 1/2	12	10 1/2	11 1/4	-5.8	11.94	12-23-99	7522
CIL	**MuniHoldings Cal Insured Fund IV**	**NR**	**NY**	**MU**	0.067	12-30-99	12-21	0.675	....	0.80	7.2	....	....	15 5/8	10 7/16	12	10 7/16	11 1/8	-6.5	11.90	12-23-99	9867
CAF	**MuniHoldings Cal Insured Fund V**	**NR**	**NY**	**MU**	0.069	12-30-99	12-21	0.283	....	0.83	6.8	....	....	15 5/16	11 5/16	13 1/4	11 3/8	12 1/4	-8.3	13.36	12-23-99	4907
MFL	**MuniHoldings Fla Insured Fund**	**NR**	**NY**	**MUS**	0.069	12-30-99	12-21	0.828	....	0.82	6.8	0.858	0.339	17	11	12 5/8	11	12 1/8	-3.5	12.57	12-23-99	10798
MUF	**MuniHoldings Fla Insured Fund II**	**NR**	**NY**	**MUS**	0.064	12-30-99	12-21	0.795	....	0.77	6.8	0.621	0.025	16	10 5/8	11 11/16	10 5/8	11 1/4	-8.2	12.25	12-23-99	8841
MFD	**MuniHoldings Fla Insured Fund III**	**NR**	**NY**	**MUS**	0.061	12-30-99	12-21	0.768	....	0.73	6.8	0.133	....	15 3/4	10 1/16	11 1/2	10 1/16	10 3/4	-9.3	11.85	12-23-99	6181
MFR	**MuniHoldings Fla Insured Fund IV**	**NR**	**NY**	**MU**	0.065	12-30-99	12-21	0.671	....	0.78	7.1	....	....	15 5/8	10 1/2	12 1/8	10 1/2	11	-6.6	11.78	12-23-99	9117
FDM	**MuniHoldings Fla Insured Fund V**	**NR**	**AS**	**MUS**	0.069	12-30-99	12-21	0.296	....	0.83	6.7	....	....	15 1/4	11 1/8	12 3/4	11 1/4	12 3/8	-7.0	13.30	12-23-99	3507
MHD	**MuniHoldings Fund**	**NR**	**NY**	**MU**	0.25	12-30-99	12-21	0.942	0.169	0.97	⊙7.5	0.961	0.322	17 7/16	12 1/16	13	12 1/8	12 15/16	-2.2	13.23	12-23-99	13777
MUH	**MuniHoldings Fund II**	**NR**	**NY**	**MU**	0.087	12-30-99	12-21	0.841	0.015	0.86	7.6	0.634	....	16 3/4	10 5/8	12 1/4	10 5/8	11 1/4	-6.4	12.02	12-23-99	11073
MUS	**MuniHoldings Insured Fund**	**NR**	**NY**	**MU**	0.159	12-30-99	12-21	0.865	0.089	0.84	⊙7.1	0.524	0.233	16 7/16	11 1/16	11 7/8	11 1/16	11 3/4	-1.0	11.87	12-23-99	12833
MUE	**MuniHoldings Insured Fund II**	**NR**	**NY**	**MU**	0.065	12-30-99	12-21	0.629	....	0.78	7.5	....	....	15 3/8	9 7/8	11 13/16	9 7/8	10 3/8	-11.6	11.74	12-23-99	10607
MSR	**MuniHoldings Insured Fund III**	**NR**	**NY**	**MU**	0.067	12-30-99	12-21	0.447	....	0.84	7.3	....	....	15 9/16	10 11/16	12 1/4	10 11/16	11 1/2	-5.6	12.18	12-23-99	6807
MOU	**MuniHoldings Insured Fund IV**	**NR**	**AS**	**MU**	0.077	12-30-99	12-21	0.157	....	0.92	7.4	....	....	15 5/16	11 1/8	13 3/8	11 1/8	12 1/2	-13.3	14.42	12-23-99	1266
MCG	**MuniHoldings Mich Insured Fund**	**NR**	**NY**	**MU**	0.064	12-30-99	12-21	0.645	....	0.77	7.2	....	....	16	10 1/4	11 1/4	10 1/4	10 11/16	-11.3	12.05	12-23-99	4453
MDH	**MuniHoldings Mich Insured Fd II**	**NR**	**AS**	**MU**	0.075	12-30-99	12-21	0.182	....	0.90	7.2	....	....	15 13/16	11	14 3/4	11	12 1/2	-11.3	14.10	12-23-99	3407
MUJ	**MuniHoldings N.J. Insured Fund**	**NR**	**NY**	**MUS**	0.068	12-30-99	12-21	0.817	....	0.81	7.0	0.603	0.043	16 1/4	10 7/8	12 1/16	10 7/8	11 1/2	-7.0	12.37	12-23-99	7000
MWJ	**MuniHoldings N.J. Insured Fund II**	**NR**	**NY**	**MUS**	0.059	12-30-99	12-21	0.765	....	0.71	6.8	0.147	....	16 1/4	9 11/16	10 15/16	9 11/16	10 3/8	-8.8	11.37	12-23-99	6152
MNJ	**MuniHoldings N.J. Insured Fund III**	**NR**	**NY**	**MU**	0.063	12-30-99	12-21	0.661	....	0.75	7.1	....	....	15 5/8	10	11 7/8	10	10 5/8	-9.5	11.74	12-23-99	5298
MHJ	**MuniHoldings N.J. Insured Fund IV**	**NR**	**AS**	**MUS**	0.067	12-30-99	12-21	0.293	....	0.80	6.7	....	....	15 3/8	11	12 1/2	11	11 7/8	-10.6	13.28	12-23-99	2807
MUN	**MuniHoldings N.Y. Fund**	**NR**	**NY**	**MUS**	0.064	12-30-99	12-21	0.812	....	0.77	6.9	0.631	0.051	15 15/16	10 3/8	12	10 3/8	11 1/8	-8.0	12.09	12-23-99	7581
MHN	**MuniHoldings N.Y. Insured Fund**	**NR**	**NY**	**MUS**	0.069	12-30-99	12-21	0.852	....	0.83	6.8	0.866	0.135	16 1/2	11 9/16	12 3/8	11 9/16	12 1/8	-5.2	12.79	12-23-99	9787
MNU	**MuniHoldings N.Y. Insured Fund II**	**NR**	**NY**	**MUS**	0.062	12-30-99	12-21	0.783	....	0.74	6.9	0.136	....	15 3/4	10	11 1/2	10	10 11/16	-5.6	11.32	12-23-99	5591
MNK	**MuniHoldings N.Y. Insured Fund III**	**NR**	**NY**	**MU**	0.062	12-30-99	12-21	0.677	....	0.74	7.0	....	....	15 3/16	10 1/4	11 1/2	10 1/4	10 5/8	-6.4	11.35	12-23-99	5007
MNW	**MuniHoldings N.Y. Insured Fund IV**	**NR**	**AS**	**MUS**	0.069	12-30-99	12-21	0.293	....	0.83	6.9	....	....	15 1/4	11 1/4	13	11 1/4	12	-8.2	13.07	12-23-99	3907
MPI	**MuniHoldings Penn Insured Fd**	**NR**	**AS**	**MUS**	0.062	12-30-99	12-21	0.587	....	0.74	7.0	....	....	16 7/8	10 3/16	10 13/16	10 3/16	10 5/8	-12.8	12.19	12-23-99	2082

Uniform Footnote Explanations-See page 4. Other: [1] Approx.

Ticker Symbol	Fund	Rating	Exc.	Type	Dividends: Latest Payment Period $	Date	Ex. Div.	So Far 1999 Invest. Income	So Far 1999 Cap. Gain	Ind. Rate	Div. Yld. %	1998 Invest. Income	1998 Cap. Gain	Price Range 1998 - 1999 High	1998 - 1999 Low	December, 1999 Last Sale or Bid High	Low	Last	Net Assets % NAV Prem. Disc.	Latest NAV	Latest Date	Com. Shs. 000
MIF	MuniInsured Fund	NR	AS	MU	0.057	12-30-99	12-21	0.463	0.02	0.45	⊙6.1	0.498	0.186	10 3/16	7 1/8	7 7/8	7 5/16	7 7/16	-17.0	8.96	12-23-99	8079
MVS	MuniVest Florida Fund	NR	NY	MUS	0.056	12-30-99	12-21	0.714	....	0.67	6.5	0.762	....	14 1/2	9 15/16	10 1/2	9 15/16	10 1/4	-15.8	12.17	12-23-99	5989
MVF	MuniVest Fund	NR	AS	MU	0.047	12-30-99	12-21	0.571	....	0.56	7.1	0.59	0.029	10 5/8	7 5/16	7 15/16	7 5/16	7 7/8	-8.0	8.56	12-23-99	61123
MVT	MuniVest Fund II	NR	NY	MU	0.068	12-30-99	12-21	0.822	....	0.82	7.3	0.833	....	15 1/16	10 7/8	11 3/4	10 7/8	11 1/4	-10.9	12.62	12-23-99	19907
MVM	MuniVest MI Insured Fund	NR	NY	MUS	0.062	12-30-99	12-21	0.741	....	0.74	6.9	0.749	....	15 1/16	10 1/4	10 7/8	10 1/4	10 3/4	-14.1	12.52	12-23-99	7388
MVJ	MuniVest NJ Fund	NR	NY	MUS	0.062	12-30-99	12-21	0.778	....	0.74	6.9	0.773	....	15 5/16	10 9/16	11 3/8	10 9/16	10 3/4	-12.4	12.27	12-23-99	5520
MVP	MuniVest PA Insured Fund	NR	NY	MUS	0.06	12-30-99	12-21	0.716	....	0.72	6.9	0.718	....	14 1/4	9 7/8	10 11/16	9 7/8	10 1/2	-10.3	11.70	12-23-99	4037
MZA	MuniYield Arizona Fund	NR	AS	MUS	0.057	12-30-99	12-21	0.72	....	0.68	6.4	0.73	....	14 9/16	10 1/4	11 3/8	10 1/4	10 5/8	-14.1	12.37	12-23-99	4444
MYC	MuniYield California Fund	NR	NY	MUS	0.069	12-30-99	12-21	0.856	....	0.83	6.9	0.921	0.579	17	11 5/16	12 3/8	11 5/16	12	-9.0	13.19	12-23-99	21184
MIC	MuniYield CA Insured Fund	NR	NY	MUS	0.065	12-30-99	12-21	0.826	....	0.78	6.9	0.829	0.597	16 7/8	11 1/16	12 9/16	11 1/16	11 5/16	-10.1	12.58	12-23-99	16549
MCA	MuniYield CA Insured Fund II	NR	NY	MUS	0.066	12-30-99	12-21	0.845	....	0.79	7.0	0.875	0.638	17 3/8	11 1/8	12 5/8	11 1/8	11 1/4	-13.4	12.99	12-23-99	18328
MYF	MuniYield Florida Fund	NR	NY	MUS	M0.063	12-30-99	12-21	0.814	....	0.76	6.8	0.864	0.43	16 3/4	10 13/16	11 1/2	10 13/16	11 1/4	-13.7	13.04	12-23-99	7994
MFT	MuniYield FL Insured Fund	NR	NY	MUS	0.063	12-30-99	12-21	0.835	....	0.76	6.5	0.845	0.423	16 11/16	11 1/16	11 15/16	11 1/16	11 5/8	-11.3	13.11	12-23-99	8378
MYD	MuniYield Fund	NR	NY	MU	0.075	12-30-99	12-21	0.924	....	0.90	7.7	0.983	0.646	17 3/8	11 1/8	12 9/16	11 1/8	11 5/8	-9.5	12.85	12-23-99	38317
MYI	MuniYield Insured Fund	NR	NY	MU	0.072	12-30-99	12-21	0.876	....	0.86	7.3	0.894	0.446	17 1/16	11 1/2	12 3/4	11 1/2	11 13/16	-11.9	13.41	12-23-99	61946
MYM	MuniYield Michigan Fund	NR	NY	MUS	0.066	12-30-99	12-21	0.851	....	0.79	7.2	0.902	0.435	16 3/4	10 15/16	11 7/8	10 15/16	11	-16.2	13.12	12-23-99	7768
MIY	MuniYield MI Insured Fund	NR	NY	MU	0.069	12-30-99	12-21	0.834	....	0.83	7.0	0.851	0.21	16 15/16	11 1/2	12 1/4	11 1/2	11 15/16	-12.7	13.68	12-23-99	7432
MYJ	MuniYield New Jersey Fund	NR	NY	MUS	0.067	12-30-99	12-21	0.858	....	0.80	7.0	0.896	0.31	17 1/8	11 1/16	12 5/16	11 1/16	11 3/8	-14.0	13.22	12-23-99	910
MJI	MuniYield NJ Insured Fund	NR	NY	MUS	0.067	12-30-99	12-21	0.855	....	0.80	6.6	0.886	0.217	17 3/8	11 5/16	12 5/8	11 5/16	12 1/16	-9.1	13.27	12-23-99	858
MYN	MuniYield NY Insured Fund	NR	NY	MUS	0.069	12-30-99	12-21	0.875	....	0.83	7.0	0.903	0.651	17 3/8	11 1/2	12 5/8	11 1/2	11 13/16	-8.1	12.86	12-23-99	1256
MYT	MuniYield NY Insured Fund II	NR	NY	MUS	0.068	12-31-99	12-21	0.815	0.003	0.78	⊙6.8	0.844	0.113	16 3/16	10 3/4	12 1/8	10 3/4	11 1/2	-11.7	13.03	12-23-99	2666
MPA	MuniYield Pennsylvania Fund	NR	NY	MUS	0.067	12-30-99	12-21	0.844	....	0.80	6.8	0.892	0.454	17 1/8	11	12	11	11 11/16	-12.5	13.35	12-23-99	574
MQY	MuniYield Quality Fund	NR	NY	MU	0.069	12-30-99	12-21	0.85	....	0.82	7.2	0.881	....	15 7/8	11	12	11	11 5/16	-15.3	13.35	12-23-99	3042
MQT	MuniYield Quality Fund II	NR	NY	MU	0.069	12-31-99	12-21	0.841	....	0.82	7.6	0.889	0.487	16 1/4	10 1/2	11 9/16	10 1/2	10 13/16	-10.2	12.04	12-23-99	2236
NBM	Nations Bal Target Mat Fd	NR	NY	GVT	0.11	12-30-99	12-9	0.395	....	0.44	5.3	0.39	0.228	10 1/8	8 3/16	8 11/16	8 3/16	8 3/8	-13.8	9.72	12-23-99	523
NGI	Nations Gvt Inc Term Tr 2003	AAAf	NY	GVT	0.047	12-30-99	12-9	0.558	....	0.56	6.3	0.572	....	9 1/2	8 5/8	8 15/16	8 13/16	8 15/16	-6.4	9.55	12-23-99	1476
NGF	Nations Gvt Inc Term Tr 2004	NR	NY	GVT	0.049	12-30-99	12-9	0.593	....	0.59	6.6	0.601	....	9 3/4	8 9/16	9	8 13/16	8 7/8	-7.2	9.56	12-23-99	1225
HYB	New Amer Hi Income Fd	NR	NY	ICA	†0.035	1-31-00	12-29	†0.537	....	0.51	e16.3	†0.552	....	5 11/16	3	3 5/8	3	3 1/8	-19.3	3.87	12-23-99	6576
GF	New Germany Fund	NR	NY	GEC	1.07	11-27-99	11-17	0.05	1.02	1.01	⊙8.2	2.07	3.57	19 3/16	11 1/16	12 5/8	11 1/16	12 1/4	-16.9	14.75	12-23-99	3054
NAZ	Nuveen AZ Prem Inc Muni Fd	NR	NY	MUS	0.084	12-23-99	12-13	0.845	0.013	0.85	6.1	0.828	....	17 3/4	13 5/8	15 1/8	13 5/8	13 7/8	0.1	13.86	12-23-99	434
NAC	Nuveen CA Divd Adv Muni Fd	NR	NY	MUS	0.072	12-23-99	12-13	0.432	....	0.86	7.3	....	....	15 1/4	11 9/16	12 15/16	11 9/16	11 13/16	-2.8	12.15	12-23-99	2030
NQC	Nuveen CA Inv Qual Muni	NR	NY	MUS	0.077	12-23-99	12-13	0.951	....	0.92	7.2	0.975	0.029	18 1/4	12 5/8	14 1/2	12 5/8	12 13/16	-8.9	14.06	12-23-99	1329
NCO	Nuveen CA Muni Mkt Oppt	NR	NY	MUS	0.082	12-23-99	12-13	1.011	....	0.98	7.2	1.014	0.118	18 7/8	13	15 1/4	13	13 9/16	-4.8	14.24	12-23-99	797
NCA	Nuveen CA Muni Val Fd	NR	NY	MUS	0.058	12-23-99	12-13	0.512	0.002	0.50	⊙6.3	0.516	0.049	10 7/8	7 7/16	8 1/2	7 7/16	7 7/8	-15.6	9.33	12-23-99	2522
NCP	Nuveen CA Perf Plus Muni	NR	NY	MUS	0.08	12-23-99	12-13	0.993	....	0.96	7.3	1.026	0.048	18 3/4	12 3/4	14 15/16	12 3/4	13 3/16	-6.5	14.11	12-23-99	1265
NCU	Nuveen CA Prem Inc Muni	NR	AS	MUS	0.067	12-23-99	12-13	0.783	....	0.80	6.2	†0.745	....	15 1/8	11 3/4	13 3/16	11 3/4	12 7/8	3.6	12.43	12-23-99	574
NUC	Nuveen CA Qual Income Muni	NR	NY	MUS	0.082	12-23-99	12-13	0.978	....	0.98	7.4	0.978	0.018	18 3/8	13 1/16	15 7/16	13 1/16	13 5/16	-8.7	14.58	12-23-99	2155
NVC	Nuveen CA Select Qual Muni	NR	NY	MUS	0.079	12-23-99	12-13	0.948	....	0.95	7.2	0.96	0.107	17 3/4	12 7/16	14 1/2	12 7/16	13 1/8	-6.7	14.07	12-23-99	2264
NTC	Nuveen CT Prem Inc Muni	NR	NY	MUS	0.068	12-23-99	12-13	0.81	....	0.82	5.5	0.798	....	17	14 3/4	15 1/4	14 3/4	14 13/16	14.6	12.92	12-23-99	520
NAD	Nuveen Dividend Adv Muni Fd	NR	NY	MU	0.074	12-23-99	12-13	0.444	....	0.89	7.3	....	....	15 1/8	11 11/16	12 7/8	11 11/16	12 1/8	-3.0	12.50	12-23-99	3430
NQF	Nuveen FL Inv Qual Muni	NR	NY	MUS	0.107	12-23-99	12-13	0.948	0.028	0.95	⊙7.2	†0.978	0.025	18 1/2	12 13/16	14 1/4	12 13/16	13 1/8	-6.0	13.96	12-23-99	1634
NUF	Nuveen FL Qual Income Muni	NR	NY	MUS	0.076	12-23-99	12-13	0.906	....	0.91	7.0	0.911	....	17 3/8	12 13/16	13 5/8	12 13/16	12 15/16	-10.2	14.40	12-23-99	1414
NPG	Nuveen GA Prem Inc Muni	NR	AS	MUS	0.067	12-23-99	12-13	0.804	....	0.80	6.3	0.797	....	17 3/16	12 7/16	13 13/16	12 7/16	12 11/16	-1.0	12.81	12-23-99	374
NPC	Nuveen Ins CA Prem Inc Muni	NR	NY	MUS	0.037	12-23-99	12-13	0.877	....	0.84	6.3	0.815	....	16 15/16	12 15/16	14	12 15/16	13 3/8	-3.4	13.84	12-23-99	640
NCL	Nuveen Ins CA Prem Inc Muni 2	NR	NY	MUS	0.148	12-23-99	12-13	0.859	0.008	0.80	e6.8	†0.759	....	15 11/16	11 5/8	12 13/16	11 5/8	11 11/16	-9.6	12.93	12-23-99	1257

Uniform Footnote Explanations-See page 4.

					Dividends									Price Range					Net Assets			
					Latest Payment			So Far 1999				1998				December, 1999			% NAV			Com.
Ticker Symbol	Fund	Rating	Exc.	Type	Period $	Date	Ex. Div.	Invest. Income	Cap. Gain	Ind. Rate	Div. Yld. %	Invest. Income	Cap. Gain	1998 - 1999 High	1998 - 1999 Low	Last Sale or Bid High	Last Sale or Bid Low	Last Sale or Bid Last	Prem. Disc.	Latest NAV	Latest Date	Shs. 000
NXC	Nuveen Ins CA Sel Tax-Free Inc	NR	NY	MUS	0.066	12-23-99	12-13	0.792	....	0.79	6.2	0.794	....	16 1/16	11	13⅜	12 11/16	12 13/16	-11.2	14.43	12-23-99	6257
NFL	Nuveen Ins FL Prem Inc Muni	NR	NY	MUS	0.067	12-23-99	12-13	0.788	....	0.80	6.3	0.76	....	15 15/16	12⅜	13⅜	12⅜	12¾	-7.0	13.71	12-23-99	14291
NIO	Nuveen Ins Muni Oppt Fd	NR	NY	MU	0.075	12-23-99	12-13	0.933	....	0.89	7.3	0.96	0.041	17⅛	11½	13 1/16	11½	12 3/16	-13.1	14.02	12-23-99	80588
NNF	Nuveen Ins NY Prem Inc Muni	NR	NY	MUS	0.07	12-23-99	12-13	0.833	....	0.83	6.6	0.822	....	16½	12½	13¼	12½	12 9/16	-7.6	13.60	12-23-99	8249
NXN	Nuveen Ins NY Sel Tax-Free Inc	NR	NY	MUS	0.065	12-23-99	12-13	0.78	....	0.78	6.2	0.78	....	15⅞	12¼	12⅞	12¼	12½	-12.5	14.29	12-23-99	3907
NPX	Nuveen Ins Prem Inc Muni 2	NR	NY	MU	0.061	12-23-99	12-13	0.726	....	0.73	7.1	0.726	....	14	10⅛	11	10⅛	10¼	-16.4	12.26	12-23-99	37239
NQI	Nuveen Ins Quality Muni	NR	NY	MU	0.077	12-23-99	12-13	0.918	....	0.92	e7.0	†0.93	0.126	16¾	11 13/16	13 5/16	11 13/16	13 3/16	-4.0	13.73	12-23-99	37657
NQM	Nuveen Inv Quality Muni	NR	NY	MU	0.081	12-23-99	12-13	0.957	0.004	0.92	⊙7.9	0.978	....	16¾	11½	12⅝	11½	11 11/16	-15.4	13.81	12-23-99	35639
NMY	Nuveen MD Prem Inc Muni Fd	NR	NY	MUS	0.065	12-23-99	12-13	0.779	....	0.78	6.4	0.768	....	16½	11 13/16	13 1/16	11 13/16	12⅛	-6.2	12.93	12-23-99	10438
NMT	Nuveen MA Prem Inc Muni Fd	NR	NY	MUS	0.071	12-23-99	12-13	0.846	....	0.85	6.1	†0.851	....	17½	14	14 15/16	14	14	5.6	13.26	12-23-99	4640
NMP	Nuveen MI Prem Inc Muni	NR	NY	MUS	0.069	12-23-99	12-13	0.827	....	0.83	7.0	0.816	....	16	11 11/16	12 15/16	11 11/16	11 15/16	-12.2	13.60	12-23-99	7678
NUM	Nuveen MI Qual Income Muni	NR	NY	MUS	0.156	12-23-99	12-13	0.922	0.076	0.92	⊙7.3	0.939	0.061	17⅝	12½	14⅛	12½	12 11/16	-10.0	14.10	12-23-99	11489
NOM	Nuveen MO Prem Inc Muni	NR	AS	MUS	0.065	12-23-99	12-13	0.768	....	0.77	5.6	†0.758	....	15 9/16	12 11/16	13 13/16	12⅞	13 13/16	7.3	12.87	12-23-99	2154
NMA	Nuveen Muni Advantage Fd	NR	NY	MU	0.08	12-23-99	12-13	0.993	....	0.96	8.0	0.996	....	16 11/16	11 15/16	12⅞	11 15/16	12	-12.9	13.77	12-23-99	42621
NMI	Nuveen Muni Income Fd	NR	NY	MU	0.116	12-23-99	12-13	0.691	0.058	0.69	⊙6.6	0.708	0.075	12 13/16	9⅞	10 11/16	9⅞	10½	-6.4	11.22	12-23-99	7954
NMO	Nuveen Muni Mkt Oppt	NR	NY	MU	0.081	12-23-99	12-13	1.005	....	0.97	7.9	1.008	0.015	16 13/16	11 15/16	13	11 15/16	12¼	-11.6	13.86	12-23-99	45195
NUV	Nuveen Muni Value Fd	NR	NY	MU	0.043	12-23-99	12-13	0.51	0.001	0.51	⊙6.5	0.528	0.093	10⅛	7 11/16	8 3/16	7 11/16	7⅞	-16.0	9.37	12-23-99	194960
NQJ	Nuveen NJ Inv Qual Muni	NR	NY	MUS	0.114	12-23-99	12-13	0.918	0.038	0.92	⊙7.3	0.948	0.025	18½	12 3/16	13⅝	12 3/16	12⅝	-11.4	14.25	12-23-99	19902
NNJ	Nuveen NJ Prem Inc Muni	NR	NY	MUS	0.072	12-23-99	12-13	0.864	....	0.86	7.0	†0.868	....	17	11¾	13 5/16	11¾	12 5/16	-11.3	13.88	12-23-99	11981
NAN	Nuveen NY Divd Adv Muni Fd	NR	NY	MUS	0.072	12-23-99	12-13	0.429	....	0.86	7.0	....	....	15⅛	11 13/16	12 11/16	11 13/16	12 5/16	-0.3	12.35	12-23-99	8250
NQN	Nuveen NY Inv Qual Muni	NR	NY	MUS	0.08	12-23-99	12-13	0.984	....	0.96	7.4	1.05	0.086	18 5/16	12⅜	13½	12⅜	12 15/16	-6.7	13.87	12-23-99	17517
NNY	Nuveen NY Muni Val Fd	NR	NY	MUS	0.042	12-23-99	12-13	0.504	....	0.50	6.4	0.536	0.097	10 13/16	7½	8 5/16	7½	7 13/16	-15.5	9.25	12-23-99	15120
NNP	Nuveen NY Perform Plus Muni	NR	NY	MUS	0.144	12-23-99	12-13	1.019	0.062	0.98	⊙7.5	1.071	....	19 1/16	12 5/16	14	12 5/16	13	-6.7	13.93	12-23-99	14802
NUN	Nuveen NY Qual Income Muni	NR	NY	MUS	0.076	12-23-99	12-13	0.934	....	0.91	7.2	0.936	0.033	17	12	13⅝	12	12⅝	-10.1	14.05	12-23-99	23817
NVN	Nuveen NY Select Qual Muni	NR	NY	MUS	0.08	12-23-99	12-13	0.987	....	0.95	7.3	0.99	0.043	17½	12 3/16	13 11/16	12 3/16	13	-8.5	14.20	12-23-99	23111
NNC	Nuveen NC Prem Inc Muni	NR	NY	MUS	0.068	12-23-99	12-13	0.799	....	0.81	6.0	0.792	....	16¾	13 1/16	14 3/16	13 1/16	13½	7.1	12.60	12-23-99	6261
NUO	Nuveen OH Qual Income Muni	NR	NY	MUS	0.082	12-23-99	12-13	0.984	....	0.98	6.5	0.977	....	19 15/16	15⅛	15 11/16	15⅛	15⅛	-0.4	15.18	12-23-99	9419
NQP	Nuveen PA Inv Qual Muni	NR	NY	MUS	0.154	12-23-99	12-13	1.005	0.073	0.97	⊙7.3	1.008	0.005	18⅜	12¾	14⅜	12¾	13¼	-7.0	14.24	12-23-99	16014
NPY	Nuveen PA Prem Inc Muni 2	NR	NY	MUS	0.083	12-23-99	12-13	0.797	0.015	0.81	⊙6.8	0.756	....	14⅝	11 5/16	12⅝	11 5/16	12	-8.5	13.11	12-23-99	15747
NPP	Nuveen Perform Plus Muni	NR	NY	MU	0.072	12-23-99	12-13	0.899	....	0.86	⊙7.4	†0.947	0.012	16⅛	11 3/16	12 5/16	11 3/16	11⅝	-13.6	13.46	12-23-99	59573
NPI	Nuveen Prem Income Muni	NR	NY	MU	0.069	12-23-99	12-13	0.85	....	0.83	7.0	0.873	0.068	15 7/16	11¼	12 5/16	11¼	11 15/16	-9.9	13.25	12-23-99	63785
NPM	Nuveen Prem Income Muni 2	NR	NY	MU	0.097	12-23-99	12-13	0.943	0.017	0.95	⊙6.9	0.93	0.045	17½	13⅛	14 5/16	13⅛	13¾	-4.1	14.34	12-23-99	40868
NPT	Nuveen Prem Income Muni 4	NR	NY	MU	0.07	12-23-99	12-13	0.825	0.007	0.83	⊙6.8	0.816	....	15⅛	11 7/16	12 11/16	11 7/16	12⅛	-9.0	13.32	12-23-99	43203
NIF	Nuveen Prem Insured Muni Inc	NR	NY	MU	0.075	12-23-99	12-13	0.90	....	0.90	6.9	0.918	0.04	17	12⅛	13½	12⅛	13⅛	-6.9	14.10	12-23-99	19262
NPF	Nuveen Prem Muni Income	NR	NY	MU	0.081	12-23-99	12-13	0.966	....	0.97	7.7	0.987	0.002	17 7/16	12¼	13⅞	12¼	12 9/16	-10.4	14.02	12-23-99	19928
NQU	Nuveen Qual Income Muni Fd	NR	NY	MUS	0.083	12-23-99	12-13	1.023	....	0.99	8.1	1.026	....	17⅜	12 1/16	13 5/16	12 1/16	12 3/16	-13.6	14.11	12-23-99	53777
NIM	Nuveen Select Maturities Muni	NR	NY	MU	0.155	12-23-99	12-13	0.617	0.103	0.62	⊙e6.5	†0.61	0.042	12¼	9 5/16	10⅛	9 5/16	9½	-15.7	11.27	12-23-99	12381
NQS	Nuveen Select Qual Muni	NR	NY	MU	0.086	12-23-99	12-13	0.958	0.002	0.95	⊙7.9	†0.969	....	16 11/16	11 11/16	12⅞	11 11/16	12 1/16	-12.8	13.83	12-23-99	33781
NXP	Nuveen Select Tax-Free Inc	NR	NY	MU	0.075	12-23-99	12-13	0.90	....	0.90	6.8	0.90	....	17	13	14⅜	13⅛	13 5/16	-10.7	14.90	12-23-99	16378
NXQ	Nuveen Select Tax-Free Inc 2	NR	NY	MU	0.073	12-23-99	12-13	0.87	....	0.87	6.7	0.873	....	16 11/16	12⅜	13⅝	12⅜	13	-12.0	14.78	12-23-99	17607
NXR	Nuveen Select Tax-Free Inc 3	NR	NY	MU	0.068	12-23-99	12-13	0.816	....	0.816	6.6	0.826	....	16	12⅛	12⅞	12⅛	12⅜	-13.3	14.28	12-23-99	12964
NSL	Nuveen Senior Income Fd	NR	NY	ICF	0.076	12-23-99	12-13	0.076	....	[1]....	....	....	....	10 1/16	8 13/16	10 1/16	8 13/16	9½	-0.4	9.54	12-23-99	32000
NTX	Nuveen TX Qual Income Muni	NR	NY	MUS	0.169	12-23-99	12-13	0.908	0.093	0.91	⊙7.6	0.912	0.075	16⅞	11½	12 13/16	11½	11 15/16	-14.1	13.89	12-23-99	9437
NPV	Nuveen VA Prem Inc Muni Fd	NR	NY	MUS	0.07	12-23-99	12-13	0.765	....	0.84	6.7	0.822	....	17½	12½	14⅜	12½	12⅝	-5.6	13.37	12-23-99	8619
OMS	Oppenheimer Multi-Sector[2]	NR	NY	BD	0.07	12-27-99	12-8	0.815	....	0.84	11.0	0.818	....	10¾	7 5/16	7⅞	7 5/16	7⅝	-19.9	9.52	12-23-99	29116

Uniform Footnote Explanations-See page 4. Other: [1] To be determined. [2] Shrs Beneficial Int.

Ticker Symbol	Fund	Rating	Exc.	Type	Dividends: Latest Payment: Period $	Date	Ex. Div.	So Far 1999: Invest. Income	So Far 1999: Cap. Gain	Ind. Rate	Div. Yld. %	1998: Invest. Income	1998: Cap. Gain	Price Range: 1998 - 1999: High	1998 - 1999: Low	December, 1999 Last Sale or Bid: High	Low	Last	Net Assets: % NAV Prem. Disc.	Latest: NAV	Latest: Date	Com. Shs. 000
PHF	**Pacholder High Yield Fund**	NR	AS	BD	M0.14	12-31-99	12-21	1.68	....	1.68	14.5	1.70	....	18 7/8	11 5/16	12 7/16	11 5/16	11 5/8	-14.0	13.52	12-22-99	9503
PAI	**Pacific Am'n Inc Shrs**	NR	NY	ICA	0.285	12-15-99	11-10	1.05	0.035	1.00	⊙8.4	1.18	0.35	17	11 11/16	12 5/16	11 11/16	11 7/8	-18.2	14.51	12-23-99	9389
PKF	**Pakistan Investment Fd**	NR	NY	GEC	0.055	1-14-00	12-17	0.163	....	0.11	4.5	0.022	....	5 5/16	1 7/16	2 5/8	2 1/4	2 7/16	-28.1	3.39	12-23-99	11605
PEO	**Petroleum & Resources**	NR	NY	ICA	1.73	12-27-99	11-18	0.72	1.61	0.88	⊙2.7	0.78	1.51	40 1/8	27 3/4	32 3/4	30 1/16	32 1/4	-17.2	38.97	12-23-99	13841
PPR	**Pilgrim Prime Rate Tr**	NR	NY	BD	0.067	1-13-00	12-28	0.784	....	0.80	10.0	†0.849	....	10 1/2	7 3/4	9 11/16	7 3/4	8	-10.9	8.98	12-23-99	130619
PCM	**PIMCO Comml Mtg Sec Tr**	NR	NY	ICA	†0.144	1-13-00	12-29	†1.225	....	1.13	e9.4	†1.131	....	14 3/8	11 5/16	12	11 5/16	12	-7.7	13.00	12-22-99	11007
MUO	**Pioneer Interest Shs**	NR	NY	BD	0.24	12-31-99	12-14	0.95	....	0.96	9.4	1.04	....	15 1/16	9 15/16	10 1/2	9 15/16	10 1/4	-17.3	12.39	12-23-99	7395
PGF	**Portugal Fund**	NR	NY	GEC	©1.23	12-29-99	12-13	0.16	6.90	0.84	⊙6.4	4.93	....	24 1/8	11 3/4	13 5/8	12 1/16	13 1/16	-14.8	15.33	12-23-99	5328
PFD	**Preferred Income Fund**	NR	NY	P	0.56	12-30-99	12-21	1.096	0.364	1.01	⊙8.2	1.186	0.465	16 5/8	11 1/4	12 15/16	11 1/4	12 1/4	-10.8	13.73	12-23-99	9839
PFO	**Preferred Income Oppt Fd**	NR	NY	P	0.58	12-30-99	12-21	†0.999	0.335	0.85	⊙e8.1	1.083	0.048	13 5/8	9 5/16	10 5/8	9 5/16	10 7/16	-3.5	10.81	12-23-99	11151
PHY	**Prospect Street Hi Income**	NR	NY	BD	0.095	12-31-99	12-17	1.25	....	1.14	18.4	0.98	....	13 1/8	6	7 5/16	6	6 3/16	-11.4	6.98	12-23-99	26545
PCA	**Putnam Cal Inv Grade Muni**	NR	AS	MUS	0.078	1-3-00	12-16	0.87	0.051	0.87	⊙7.1	0.885	....	16 5/8	12 1/8	13 3/16	12 1/8	12 1/4	-14.8	14.37	12-23-99	4607
PCV	**Putnam Cv Opp Inc Tr**	NR	NY	CA	0.386	1-3-00	12-16	†1.872	0.939	1.86	⊙10.3	1.86	....	27 1/2	17 7/8	18 3/4	17 7/8	18 1/8	-23.1	23.56	12-23-99	3713
PDI	**Putnam Dividend Income**	NR	NY	P	0.056	1-3-00	12-16	†0.681	....	0.67	e7.3	†0.701	....	11 3/16	8 5/8	10 1/16	8 5/8	9 1/8	-17.2	11.02	12-23-99	10825
PCF	**Putnam Hi Income Cv/Bd Fd**	NR	NY	CV	0.071	1-3-00	12-16	0.852	0.14	0.85	⊙12.6	0.852	0.383	11 5/8	6 3/8	7 5/8	6 3/8	6 3/4	-18.7	8.30	12-23-99	13516
PYM	**Putnam Hi Yield Muni**	NR	NY	MU	0.048	1-3-00	12-16	0.661	....	0.58	8.2	0.69	....	11 11/16	6 7/8	7 11/16	6 7/8	7 1/16	-16.5	8.46	12-23-99	22063
PGM	**Putnam Inv Grade Muni Tr**	NR	NY	MU	0.08	1-3-00	12-16	0.96	....	0.96	8.7	0.96	....	15 5/8	10 7/16	12	10 7/16	11 1/16	3.1	10.73	12-23-99	20928
PMG	**Putnam Inv Grade Muni Tr II**	NR	NY	MU	†0.067	1-3-00	12-16	0.918	....	0.79	e7.5	0.96	....	15 5/8	10 1/4	11 3/16	10 1/4	10 1/2	-17.5	12.72	12-23-99	13357
PML	**Putnam Inv Grade Muni Tr III**	NR	AS	MU	0.062	1-3-00	12-16	0.785	....	0.74	7.3	0.80	....	14	10	10 5/8	10	10 1/8	-17.5	12.28	12-23-99	4007
PTM	**Putnam Managed Hi Yield Tr**	NR	NY	BD	0.104	1-3-00	12-16	1.352	0.164	1.24	⊙12.5	1.382	....	16	9 1/2	11 1/2	9 1/2	9 15/16	-15.8	11.80	12-23-99	7507
PMM	**Putnam Managed Muni Income**	NR	NY	MU	†0.064	1-3-00	12-16	0.762	....	0.76	9.4	0.762	....	13 3/4	8	8 13/16	8	8 1/8	-7.5	8.78	12-23-99	46399
PMT	**Putnam Master Income Tr**	NR	NY	ICF	0.058	6-1-99	5-18	0.358	....	0.70	10.8	0.746	....	9 1/16	6 1/16	6 1/2	6 1/16	6 1/2	-17.1	7.84	12-23-99	53096
PIM	**Putnam Master Interm Income**	NR	NY	BD	0.055	1-3-00	12-16	0.67	....	0.66	11.1	0.70	....	8 1/2	5 7/8	6 5/16	5 7/8	5 15/16	-22.1	7.62	12-23-99	100015
PMO	**Putnam Muni Opport Tr**	NR	NY	MU	0.076	1-3-00	12-16	†0.909	....	0.91	e8.3	0.91	....	15 7/8	10 13/16	11 3/4	10 13/16	11	-13.9	12.78	12-23-99	16157
PMN	**Putnam NY Inv Grade Muni**	NR	AS	MUS	0.068	1-3-00	12-16	†0.811	....	0.81	e7.1	0.81	....	15 1/4	10 7/8	12 1/16	10 7/8	11 3/8	-12.7	13.03	12-23-99	2847
PPT	**Putnam Premier Income Tr**	NR	NY	BD	0.06	10-1-99	9-16	0.606	....	0.72	11.9	0.741	....	8 7/8	5 5/16	6 5/16	5 5/16	6 1/16	-19.5	7.53	12-23-99	140249
PMH	**Putnam Tax-Free Hlth Care Fd**	NR	NY	MU	†0.081	1-3-00	12-16	0.90	0.046	0.90	⊙e8.1	0.90	0.048	16 3/8	11	12	11	11 1/8	-18.8	13.70	12-23-99	13807
RCS	**RCM Strategic Global Gvt Fund**	NR	NY	GB	†0.144	1-25-00	12-29	†0.948	....	0.89	e9.9	†0.936	....	11 3/16	8 1/2	9 1/16	8 11/16	9	-17.7	10.93	12-23-99	30516
ROC	**R.O.C. Taiwan Fund SBI**	NR	NY	GEC	0.29	10-23-98	9-28	....	....	Nil	....	2.43	....	10 1/4	5	8 3/4	7 13/16	8 7/16	-12.4	9.63	12-23-99	32699
FUND	**Royce Focus Trust**	NR	NNM	GE	[1]0.145	12-23-99	12-2	[1]0.048	0.097	[2]....	⊙....	....	....	6 1/8	3 11/16	5	4 5/8	4 3/4	-17.9	5.75	12-23-99	8423
OTCM	**Royce Micro-Cap Tr**	NR	NNM	CA	[1]0.27	12-23-99	12-2	[1]0.27	....	0.27	3.0	0.29	....	11 3/8	7 1/4	9 3/16	8 3/8	9	-14.9	10.57	12-23-99	13465
RVT	**Royce Value Trust**	NR	NY	CA	[3]0.33	12-23-99	12-2	[3]1.37	....	1.37	10.5	[4]1.16	....	17 1/2	11	13 3/16	12 1/2	13 1/16	-14.3	15.25	12-23-99	32880
PEFX	**S&P 500 Protected Equity Fd**	NR	NNM	CA	Plan annual div			....	....	....	....	....	....	10 1/16	9 15/16	10	10	10	....	....	....	31510
PBA	**SAL Trust Preferred Fund I**	NR	AS	ICA	0.61	12-31-99	12-16	0.609	....	....	....	....	....	26 1/8	24 3/8	25 5/8	24 3/8	24 5/8	....	....	....	946
SBF	**Salomon Bros Fund**	NR	NY	CA	2.794	12-23-99	12-10	0.167	3.633	0.17	⊙0.8	0.269	3.19	21 11/16	14 1/2	21 11/16	18 1/4	20 3/8	6.6	19.12	12-23-99	89907
HIF	**Salomon Bros High Income Fd**	NR	NY	ICF	0.125	12-23-99	12-10	1.50	....	1.50	13.1	1.50	0.112	17 1/4	10 1/16	11 15/16	10 1/16	11 7/16	-4.6	11.99	12-23-99	4869
HIX	**Salomon Bros High Income Fd II**	NR	NY	ICF	†0.028	1-5-00	12-28	1.38	....	1.38	e13.1	†0.757	....	15 1/2	9 15/16	11	9 15/16	10 1/2	-16.7	12.60	12-23-99	66742
SBG	**Salomon Bros 2008 WW Dlr Gvt**	NR	NY	GVT	†0.061	12-23-99	12-10	†0.937	....	0.88	e11.1	0.876	....	10 1/4	7 5/8	8 13/16	7 5/8	7 15/16	-16.2	9.47	12-23-99	34511
SBW	**Salomon Bros W W Income Fd**	NR	NY	C	†0.241	12-23-99	12-10	†1.666	....	1.43	e13.9	†1.817	....	15 3/4	7	11 9/16	10	10 5/16	-17.4	12.48	12-23-99	12732
LBF	**Scudder Global Hi Inc Fd**	NR	NY	GE	0.15	1-13-00	12-28	0.60	....	0.60	12.8	1.50	....	15 1/4	4 1/2	4 15/16	4 5/8	4 11/16	-24.5	6.21	12-23-99	9180
SAF	**Scudder New Asia Fd**	NR	NY	GEA	0.44	1-13-98	12-29	....	....	Nil	....	0.15	0.29	19 7/8	6 9/16	19 7/8	16 7/8	19 13/16	-13.7	22.97	12-23-99	8805
SQF	**Seligman Quality Muni Fd**	NR	NY	MU	0.35	12-23-99	12-13	0.774	0.285	0.77	⊙7.0	0.90	0.314	16 1/8	10 13/16	11 3/4	10 13/16	10 15/16	-16.3	13.06	12-23-99	4652
SEL	**Seligman Select Muni Fund**	NR	NY	MU	0.12	12-23-99	12-13	0.648	0.066	0.65	⊙7.3	0.768	0.108	14 3/16	8 3/4	9 9/16	8 3/4	8 15/16	-15.8	10.61	12-23-99	13279
ARK	**Senior High Income Portfolio**	NR	NY	BD	0.076	1-7-00	12-29	0.864	....	0.91	14.1	0.906	....	10 7/16	6 1/4	6 13/16	6 1/4	6 7/16	-16.9	7.75	12-23-99	53870
SGF	**Singapore Fund**	NR	NY	GEC	Div Omitted 12-3-99			....	....	Nil	....	0.105	....	10 9/16	4 1/8	9 1/4	8 9/16	9 1/16	-17.1	10.93	12-22-99	9201

Uniform Footnote Explanations-See page 4. Other: [1] In cash or stk. [2] To be determined. [3] In cash or stk,'99. [4] In cash or stk,'98.

					Dividends									Price Range					Net Assets			
					Latest Payment			So Far 1999				1998				December, 1999			% NAV			
Ticker Symbol	Fund	Rating	Exc.	Type	Period $	Date	Ex. Div.	Invest. Income	Cap. Gain	Ind. Rate	Div. Yld. %	Invest. Income	Cap. Gain	1998 - 1999 High	Low	Last Sale or Bid High	Low	Last	Prem. Disc.	Latest NAV	Date	Com. Shs. 000
SBI	Smith Barney Inter Muni Fd	NR	AS	MU	0.044	3-31-00	3-24	0.528	0.006	0.53	⊙6.3	0.549	0.036	11¼	8 5/16	8⅞	8 5/16	8⅜	-15.2	9.88	12-23-99	8364
SBT	Smith Barney Muni Fund	NR	AS	MU	0.063	3-31-00	3-24	0.756	....	0.756	6.1	0.807	0.032	15½	11⅞	12 7/16	12⅛	12 7/16	-14.9	14.62	12-23-99	4021
SOR	Source Capital[1]	NR	NY	CA	†4.66	12-15-99	11-23	†7.86	....	4.40	e9.1	†4.62	....	57	41½	49⅛	46¼	48⅜	-0.8	48.76	12-23-99	7575
SOA	Southern Africa Fund	NR	NY	GEC	©0.49	1-7-00	12-29	....	0.383	0.49	⊙3.3	0.419	2.59	17½	7	15¼	13 3/16	14¾	-22.0	18.92	12-23-99	6007
SNF	Spain Fund	NR	NY	GEC	3.111	1-7-00	12-29	1.911	4.361	1.91	⊙13.6	1.922	1.948	22 5/16	13¼	18⅜	13⅜	14	-26.4	19.01	12-23-99	8561
SPR	Sterling Capital	NR	AS	CA	0.50	1-21-00	12-28	0.085	....	0.09	1.4	0.90	....	8⅛	5⅝	7⅛	6½	6⅝	-19.4	8.22	12-23-99	2500
SGL	Strategic Global Income Fd	NR	NY	ICF	0.084	12-31-99	12-23	1.037	....	1.01	10.1	1.079	....	12⅝	9½	10 5/16	9½	10	-20.8	12.62	12-23-99	21407
SWZ	Swiss Helvetia Fund	NR	NY	GEC	0.135	3-15-00	2-28	0.03	0.025	0.14	⊙1.0	0.067	0.939	17⅜	12 1/16	14⅞	13¼	13 13/16	-20.3	17.33	12-23-99	24642
TYW	Taiwan Equity Fd	NR	NY	GEC	Div Omitted 12-2-99			©....	0.775	Nil	....	....	....	16 13/16	7½	16 13/16	14 15/16	16¾	-5.7	17.77	12-22-99	4507
TWN	Taiwan Fund	NR	NY	GEC	Div Omitted 12-23-99			1.01	....	Nil	⊙....	....	4.61	21¾	10¾	20¾	18⅛	20⅜	-7.6	22.04	12-22-99	16366
CVT	TCW Conv Sec Fund	NR	NY	ICA	†0.92	1-14-00	12-29	†1.03	....	0.84	e8.8	†0.87	....	11	7⅝	10¾	9½	9 9/16	-21.3	12.15	12-23-99	41990
TDT	TCW/DW Term Trust 2000	AAAf	NY	GVT	0.031	1-21-00	1-5	0.521	....	0.38	4.0	0.558	....	9 13/16	9⅛	9 11/16	9 7/16	9 9/16	-2.1	9.77	12-23-99	45284
TRM	TCW/DW Term Trust 2002	AAAf	NY	BD	M0.055	1-21-00	1-5	0.66	....	0.66	7.3	0.66	0.028	9 15/16	8 13/16	9 7/16	8 13/16	9 1/16	-6.4	9.68	12-23-99	40884
TMT	TCW/DW Term Trust 2003	AAAf	NY	BD	0.053	1-21-00	12-28	†0.641	....	0.63	e7.0	0.63	....	9¾	8⅞	9 3/16	8 15/16	9	-8.0	9.78	12-23-99	87468
TCH	Templeton China World Fd	NR	NY	GEC	0.152	1-13-00	12-28	0.091	....	0.09	1.1	0.29	0.08	9⅛	4¼	8	7¼	8	-23.8	10.50	12-22-99	19320
TDF	Templeton Dragon Fd	NR	NY	GEA	0.297	12-29-99	12-16	1.137	....	0.79	8.1	0.892	0.66	12	5¼	9 15/16	8⅝	9 13/16	-19.9	12.25	12-23-99	52860
EMF	Templeton Emerg Mkts	NR	NY	GE	0.01	1-13-00	12-28	0.093	0.051	0.10	⊙0.7	0.29	4.68	19 15/16	8⅝	13 9/16	10 15/16	13 9/16	0.8	13.45	12-23-99	17651
TEA	Templeton Emerg Mkts Apprec	NR	NY	GE	0.345	1-13-00	12-28	0.598	....	0.55	4.7	0.565	0.95	13¼	6¾	11 15/16	10½	11⅝	-21.8	14.86	12-22-99	4385
TEI	Templeton Emerg Mkts Income	NR	NY	GE	0.31	1-13-00	12-28	1.24	....	1.24	13.3	1.24	....	13 9/16	7⅞	9¾	9 3/16	9 5/16	-24.1	12.27	12-23-99	47606
TGG	Templeton Global Gvts	NR	NY	GB	0.05	1-14-00	12-29	0.60	....	0.60	©10.4	0.579	0.021	7 11/16	5⅝	6 3/16	5⅝	5¾	-18.2	7.03	12-23-99	22643
GIM	Templeton Global Income	NR	NY	ICF	0.05	12-31-99	12-14	0.60	....	0.60	10.2	0.60	0.005	7 11/16	5¾	6 3/16	5¾	5⅞	-20.8	7.42	12-23-99	116283
TRF	Templeton Russia Fund	NR	NY	CA	0.122	1-13-00	12-28	0.28	....	0.38	1.9	....	4.36	40 15/16	6 1/16	21¼	11⅛	19 15/16	57.1	12.69	12-22-99	5409
TVF	Templeton Vietnam&SE Asia Fd	NR	NY	GEC	0.11	1-14-98	12-29	....	....	Nil	....	0.11	....	11¼	4	9⅜	8¾	9 5/16	-22.7	12.05	12-23-99	4681
TC	Thai Capital Fund	NR	NY	GEC	Div Omitted 12-4-98			....	....	Nil	....	....	....	6 15/16	2 1/16	5⅛	4½	4⅞	56.8	3.11	12-23-99	6279
TTF	Thai Fund	NR	NY	GEC	Div Omitted 12-18-98			....	....	Nil	....	0.235	....	10⅞	3¾	8	7	7 13/16	40.8	5.55	12-23-99	13268
TMF	Thermo Opportunity Fd	NR	AS	CA	0.06	12-31-96	12-24	....	....	Nil	....	....	....	11⅞	5 9/16	7⅞	7 1/16	7 11/16	-15.0	9.04	12-23-99	1760
TAI	Transamerica Inc Shrs	NR	NY	P	†0.178	1-15-00	12-29	1.89	0.013	1.92	e9.1	†1.937	0.085	27 13/16	20¾	22⅜	20¾	21	-11.4	23.69	12-23-99	6319
TLI	Travelers Corporate Loan Fund	NR	NY	BD	0.096	2-25-00	2-17	0.933	0.269	1.15	8.2	0.071	....	15 1/16	12⅞	14 5/16	12⅞	14 1/16	-7.9	15.27	12-23-99	9782
TY	Tri-Continental	NR	NY	ICA	3.244	12-17-99	12-8	0.48	3.794	0.48	⊙1.7	0.52	4.275	32½	23	32½	27¼	27⅞	-14.9	32.75	12-23-99	117378
TKF	Turkish Investment Fund	NR	NY	GEC	0.03	1-14-00	12-17	0.118	....	0.03	0.2	0.138	....	17 15/16	3 13/16	17 15/16	10 11/16	17¾	-8.7	19.44	12-23-99	6634
TUX	Tuxis Corp	NR	AS	MU	0.40	12-31-99	12-17	1.60	....	1.60	13.9	1.34	....	16¾	11⅜	12	11⅜	11½	-26.3	15.61	12-23-99	725
TTR	2002 Target Term Trust	AAAf	NY	ICA	0.072	12-31-99	12-16	0.862	....	0.86	6.3	0.862	....	14½	13¼	13⅝	13⅜	13 9/16	-5.7	14.38	12-22-99	7803
UIF	USLIFE Income Fund	NR	NY	BD	Q0.19	12-1-99	11-17	0.76	....	0.76	9.6	0.76	....	10½	7 15/16	9 7/16	7 15/16	7 15/16	-15.4	9.38	12-23-99	5644
VKA	Van Kampen Adv Muni	NR	NY	MU	0.075	12-31-99	12-13	0.90	....	0.90	7.1	0.907	....	16 11/16	12 1/16	13 1/16	12 1/16	12¾	-13.0	14.66	12-23-99	19107
VKI	Van Kampen Adv Mun II	NR	AS	MU	0.065	12-31-99	12-13	0.75	....	0.78	7.2	0.744	....	14¼	10 9/16	11 13/16	10 9/16	10⅞	-14.4	12.71	12-23-99	8168
VAP	Van Kampen Adv PA Mun	NR	NY	MUS	0.08	12-31-99	12-13	0.96	....	0.96	7.0	0.96	....	18 3/16	12⅞	14⅝	12⅞	13⅝	-14.4	15.92	12-23-99	4362
VBF	Van Kampen Bd	NR	NY	BD	Q0.349	12-31-99	12-13	1.408	....	1.40	8.9	1.45	....	21 7/16	15 9/16	16 5/16	15 9/16	15 11/16	-17.3	18.96	12-23-99	11362
VKC	Van Kampen CA Muni	NR	AS	MUS	0.185	12-31-99	12-13	0.575	0.143	0.51	⊙6.7	0.664	0.325	12 11/16	7¼	8 3/16	7¼	7 9/16	-14.7	8.87	12-23-99	3256
VQC	Van Kampen CA Qual Mun	NR	NY	MUS	0.083	12-31-99	12-13	0.99	....	0.99	7.4	0.99	0.199	18 13/16	13¼	14 7/16	13¼	13 7/16	-13.6	15.55	12-23-99	9671
VCV	Van Kampen CA Val Mun	NR	NY	MUS	0.07	12-31-99	12-13	0.82	....	0.84	6.1	0.743	....	16 9/16	12¾	13 13/16	12¾	13 11/16	-6.8	14.69	12-23-99	6030
VXS	Van Kampen Cv Sec	NR	NY	ICA	1.004	12-31-99	12-13	0.84	0.794	0.84	⊙3.2	0.88	0.943	25⅞	17⅜	25⅞	24¼	25⅞	-21.5	32.96	12-23-99	3242
VOF	Van Kampen FL Mun Op	NR	AS	MUS	0.061	12-31-99	12-13	0.732	....	0.73	6.3	0.732	....	15⅛	10¾	12⅛	10¾	11⅝	-11.1	13.08	12-23-99	1683
VFM	Van Kampen FL Qual Mun	NR	NY	MUS	0.079	12-31-99	12-13	0.948	....	0.95	7.0	1.027	....	18	13⅛	13⅞	13⅛	13 9/16	-11.8	15.37	12-23-99	6506
VIT	Van Kampen Hi Inc	NR	NY	FT	0.054	12-31-99	12-13	0.668	....	0.65	14.4	0.702	....	7⅝	4¼	5	4¼	4½	-11.6	5.09	12-23-99	13711
VLT	Van Kampen Hi Inc II	NR	NY	BD	0.072	12-31-99	12-13	0.899	....	0.86	15.0	0.967	....	10½	5 11/16	7 3/16	5 11/16	5¾	-12.2	6.55	12-23-99	8109

Uniform Footnote Explanations-See page 4. Other: [1] Co plan offer for pfd .66 com.

Ticker Symbol	Fund	Rating	Exc.	Type	Dividends: Latest Payment Period $	Date	Ex. Div.	So Far 1999 Invest. Income	So Far 1999 Cap. Gain	Ind. Rate	Div. Yld. %	1998 Invest. Income	1998 Cap. Gain	Price Range 1998 - 1999 High	1998 - 1999 Low	December, 1999 Last Sale or Bid High	Low	Last	Net Assets % NAV Prem. Disc.	Latest NAV	Latest Date	Com. Shs. 000
VIN	**Van Kampen Inc Tr**	**NR**	**NY**	**BD**	0.05	12-31-99	12-13	0.60	....	0.60	10.6	0.645	....	8 5/16	5 5/8	6 3/16	5 5/8	5 11/16	-21.5	7.24	12-23-99	15308
VIM	**Van Kampen Ins Muni**	**NR**	**NY**	**MU**	0.083	12-31-99	12-13	0.99	....	0.99	7.2	0.99	0.164	17 7/8	13 9/16	14 3/16	13 9/16	13 11/16	-9.4	15.11	12-23-99	9734
VIG	**Van Kampen Inv Grade**	**NR**	**NY**	**MU**	M0.052	12-31-99	12-13	0.654	....	0.624	7.7	0.684	....	11 1/2	7 3/4	8 1/2	7 3/4	8 1/8	-11.9	9.22	12-23-99	4839
VIC	**Van Kampen Inv Gr CA Mun**	**NR**	**NY**	**MUS**	0.083	12-31-99	12-13	0.99	....	0.99	6.9	0.99	0.339	18 1/2	13 1/8	14 3/8	13 1/8	14 1/4	-4.2	14.88	12-23-99	4645
VTF	**Van Kampen Inv Gr FL Mun**	**NR**	**NY**	**MUS**	0.083	12-31-99	12-13	0.99	....	0.99	7.1	0.99	0.056	19	13 13/16	14 3/8	13 13/16	13 7/8	-12.0	15.77	12-23-99	4148
VGM	**Van Kampen Inv Gr Mun**	**NR**	**NY**	**MU**	0.083	12-31-99	12-13	0.99	....	0.99	7.6	0.997	0.073	17 9/16	12 9/16	13 5/8	12 9/16	13	-15.6	15.40	12-23-99	27013
VTJ	**Van Kampen Inv Gr NJ Mun**	**NR**	**NY**	**MUS**	0.079	12-31-99	12-13	0.948	....	0.95	6.8	0.948	0.066	18 3/8	13 3/4	15 5/8	13 3/4	13 15/16	-12.5	15.93	12-23-99	3931
VTN	**Van Kampen Inv Gr NY Mun**	**NR**	**NY**	**MUS**	0.083	12-31-99	12-13	0.964	....	1.00	7.1	0.948	0.005	18	13 1/2	14 15/16	13 1/2	14 1/8	-12.6	16.17	12-23-99	6204
VTP	**Van Kampen Inv Gr PA Mun**	**NR**	**NY**	**MUS**	0.098	12-31-99	12-13	0.972	0.017	0.97	⊙7.2	0.972	0.009	18 1/16	13 5/16	14 15/16	13 5/16	13 1/2	-17.0	16.26	12-23-99	7421
VMV	**Van Kampen MA Val Mun**	**NR**	**AS**	**MUS**	0.069	12-31-99	12-13	0.788	....	0.83	5.9	0.78	....	16 5/16	12 7/8	14 1/8	13 1/8	14 1/16	-1.3	14.24	12-23-99	2661
VMT	**Van Kampen Mun Inc**	**NR**	**NY**	**MU**	M0.05	12-31-99	12-13	0.63	....	0.60	7.9	0.67	....	11 1/2	7 3/8	8	7 3/8	7 5/8	-13.2	8.78	12-23-99	28685
VMO	**Van Kampen Muni Opp**	**NR**	**NY**	**MU**	0.075	12-31-99	12-13	0.90	....	0.90	6.9	0.90	....	16 7/8	12 3/4	13 11/16	12 3/4	13 1/8	-15.2	15.47	12-23-99	15353
VOT	**Van Kampen Mun Opp II**	**NR**	**NY**	**MU**	0.065	12-31-99	12-13	0.78	....	0.78	6.7	0.78	....	14 3/4	10 13/16	11 15/16	10 13/16	11 11/16	-10.5	13.06	12-23-99	11681
VKQ	**Van Kampen Mun Tr**	**NR**	**NY**	**MU**	0.08	12-31-99	12-13	0.96	....	0.96	7.5	0.96	0.426	17 3/8	12 1/8	13 1/4	12 1/8	12 3/4	-11.3	14.37	12-23-99	36365
VJV	**Van Kampen NJ Val Mun**	**NR**	**AS**	**MUS**	0.068	12-31-99	12-13	0.77	....	0.81	6.5	0.75	....	15 3/16	11 13/16	12 3/4	11 13/16	12 1/2	-9.6	13.83	12-23-99	2500
VNM	**Van Kampen NY Qual Mun**	**NR**	**NY**	**MU**	0.075	12-31-99	12-13	0.90	....	0.90	6.9	0.92	0.048	17 1/8	12 11/16	13 3/4	12 11/16	13 1/16	-15.8	15.52	12-23-99	5656
VNV	**Van Kampen NY Val Mun**	**NR**	**NY**	**MUS**	0.068	12-31-99	12-13	0.79	....	0.81	6.3	0.78	....	15 5/8	12 1/16	12 7/8	12 1/16	12 13/16	-9.3	14.13	12-23-99	4291
VOQ	**Van Kampen OH Qual Mun**	**NR**	**NY**	**MUS**	0.084	12-31-99	12-13	1.008	....	1.01	6.8	1.008	0.015	19 1/2	14 1/2	15 15/16	14 1/2	14 3/4	-6.4	15.76	12-23-99	4248
VOV	**Van Kampen OH Val Mun**	**NR**	**AS**	**MUS**	0.061	12-31-99	12-13	0.712	....	0.73	6.0	0.702	....	14 3/4	11 5/8	12 5/16	11 5/8	12 1/8	-12.2	13.81	12-23-99	1681
VPQ	**Van Kampen PA Qual Mun**	**NR**	**NY**	**MUS**	0.088	12-31-99	12-13	1.02	0.003	1.02	⊙7.2	1.097	....	18 7/16	13 13/16	14 15/16	14	14 1/4	-9.9	15.81	12-23-99	8193
VPV	**Van Kampen PA Val Mun**	**NR**	**NY**	**MUS**	0.065	12-31-99	12-13	0.78	....	0.78	6.6	0.77	....	15 1/8	11 11/16	12 1/4	11 11/16	11 7/8	-16.4	14.20	12-23-99	4469
VKL	**Van Kampen Sel Sec Mun**	**NR**	**AS**	**MU**	0.06	12-31-99	12-13	0.72	....	0.72	7.0	0.72	....	13 9/16	10 1/16	10 3/4	10 1/16	10 5/16	-16.2	12.30	12-23-99	4682
VVR	**Van Kampen Sr Income**	**NR**	**NY**	**MU**	0.067	1-31-00	12-28	0.774	0.009	0.80	⊙9.8	0.317	0.002	10 7/16	7 15/16	9 1/8	7 15/16	8 1/8	-18.4	9.96	12-23-99	180010
VKS	**Van Kampen Str Sec Mun**	**NR**	**NY**	**MU**	0.065	12-31-99	12-13	0.78	....	0.78	6.7	0.78	....	14 7/8	10 13/16	11 11/16	10 13/16	11 11/16	-9.9	12.97	12-23-99	10807
VKV	**Van Kampen Value Muni**	**NR**	**NY**	**MU**	0.068	12-31-99	12-13	0.81	....	0.81	6.8	0.81	....	15 3/16	11 1/16	12 1/8	11 1/16	12	-11.8	13.60	12-23-99	23555
VES	**Vestaur Securities**	**NR**	**NY**	**BD**	Q0.26	1-14-00	12-29	1.04	....	1.04	8.8	1.04	0.03	15 3/16	11 7/8	12 13/16	11 7/8	11 7/8	-14.1	13.83	12-22-99	6722
VAZ	**Voyageur Arizona Muni Income**	**NR**	**AS**	**MUS**	0.064	12-31-99	12-15	0.772	....	0.77	6.1	0.772	....	15 7/8	12 1/8	13 1/8	12 1/8	12 9/16	-7.7	13.61	12-23-99	2982
VCF	**Voyageur CO Ins Muni Income**	**NR**	**AS**	**MUS**	0.061	12-31-99	12-15	0.735	....	0.74	6.1	0.735	....	15 3/16	11 13/16	12 1/2	11 15/16	12 1/8	-8.7	13.28	12-23-99	4837
VFL	**Voyageur FL Insured Muni Inc**	**NR**	**AS**	**MUS**	0.063	12-31-99	12-15	0.757	....	0.76	6.3	0.757	....	15 5/16	11 7/16	12 3/16	11 7/16	12 1/16	-13.7	13.97	12-23-99	2422
VMN	**Voyageur Minn Muni Income**	**NR**	**AS**	**MUS**	0.123	12-31-99	12-15	0.925	0.051	0.87	6.4	0.93	....	17	12 7/8	14 7/16	12 7/8	13 11/16	-0.8	13.80	12-23-99	2595
VMM	**Voyageur Minn Muni Income II**	**NR**	**AS**	**MUS**	0.068	12-31-99	12-15	0.818	....	0.82	6.7	0.818	....	15 1/2	11 1/2	12 1/2	11 1/2	12 1/4	-7.6	13.26	12-23-99	7252
VYM	**Voyageur Minn Muni Income III**	**NR**	**AS**	**MUS**	0.063	12-31-99	12-15	0.757	....	0.76	6.7	0.757	....	14 9/16	10 3/4	12 1/8	10 3/4	11 3/8	-6.9	12.22	12-23-99	1837
WDV	**Worldwide Dollarvest Fund**	**NR**	**NY**	**GB**	M0.053	1-7-00	12-29	0.556	....	0.639	12.8	1.53	1.906	13 3/4	4 3/4	5	4 3/4	5	-22.0	6.41	12-23-99	6494
ZSEV	**Z Seven Fund**	**NR**	**NNM**	**GE**	[1]0.05	12-30-99	12-17	[1]0.05	....	0.05	0.7	0.174	....	10 1/2	6 1/16	7 11/16	6 5/8	7 11/16	3.6	7.42	12-23-99	2545
ZIF	**Zenix Income Fund**	**NR**	**NY**	**BD**	0.054	2-25-00	2-17	0.662	....	0.65	13.9	†0.764	....	8 9/16	4 7/16	5	4 7/16	4 11/16	-13.5	5.42	12-23-99	15808
ZF	**Zweig Fund**	**NR**	**NY**	**CA**	Q0.29	10-26-99	10-6	1.19	....	[2]....	....	1.22	....	14 5/16	8 7/8	10 3/8	9 13/16	10 1/16	-16.2	12.01	12-23-99	60136
ZTR	**Zweig Total Return Fd**	**NR**	**NY**	**ICA**	0.06	12-27-99	12-9	0.82	....	0.72	11.1	0.84	....	9 13/16	6 1/4	7	6 1/4	6 1/2	-17.0	7.83	12-23-99	89771

Uniform Footnote Explanations-See page 4. Other: [1] Approx. [2] Co plans 2.5% of NAV quarterly.

STANDARD & POOR'S

MUTUAL FUND SUMMARY

PERFORMANCE OF S&P SUPER COMPOSITE 1500, S&P 500, S&P MIDCAP 400 AND THE SMALLCAP 600

	% Change From Previous Dec. 31 — At Dec. 31						Dividends		$10,000 Invested	1999 Range		
	1994	1995	1996	1997	1998	Dec 31 1999	paid 1998	paid 1999	12-31-93 Now Worth	High	Low	Close 12-31-99
S&P 500	+1.32	+37.58	+22.96	+33.36	28.58	21.04	16.20	16.69	35,112	1473.13	1211.89	1469.25
MIDCAP 400	–3.58	+30.95	+19.20	+32.25	19.11	14.72	4.17	4.75	28,209	445.10	352.35	444.67
SMALLCAP 600	–4.77	+29.96	+21.32	+25.58	-1.31	12.41	1.40	1.39	21,966	197.79	154.14	197.79
S&P SUPER COMP 1500	....	+36.52	+22.41	+32.93	26.35	20.26	3.31	3.44	....	309.46	254.39	308.89

EXPLANATION OF COLUMN HEADINGS AND FOOTNOTES

Fund-Year Formed: Title of fund and year originated or * initially offered to public.

Principal Objective: CA—Capital Appreciation; E—Objectives treated equally; EG—Emerging Growth; G—Growth; I—Income; P—Preservation of Capital; R—Return on Capital; S—Stability; VA—Value Oriented; in order of importance.

Type: B—Balanced; BD—Bond; C—Com; CV—Cv Bond & Pfd; FL—Flexible; GB—Lg term gov't, GNMA, etc; GL—Global (may incl. U.S. secs.); H—Hedge; INTL—Int'l; L—Leverage; P—Pfd; PM—Precious Metals; O—Options; SP—Specialized; TF—Tax Free; ST—Short term invests.

Total Net Assets: Total assets at market value less current liabilities (includes cash/equiv.).

Cash & Equivalent: Cash and receivables plus U.S. Govt securs., short term commercial paper and short-term municipal and corporate bonds and notes, less current liabilities.

IRA & Keogh: All funds have plans available except where noted as follows: ʃ—No IRA plan available †—No Keogh plan available.

Net Assets per share % Change: Represents NAV (net asset value) at end of period plus capital gains and dividends distributed during the period, less NAV at beginning of period; divided by NAV at beginning of period, all on a per share basis & excl. sales charge.

Minimum Unit: Minimum initial purchase of shares (exclusive of contractual plans); usually lower for retirement plans.

Maximum Sales Charge %: A charge, covering costs and commissions added to net asset value in computing the offering price. Represents a percentage of the offering price (E.R.F.—Early Redemption Fee).

Distributions: Dividends from net investment income and distributions from security profits to record holders in year indicated.

$10,000 Invested 12-31-93 Now Worth: Shows the results of a $10,000 investment assuming that all dividends and capital gains are reinvested at year end. Calculations are based on NAV and exclude any sales charge. Mutual funds formed during 1994 are included from the date of offering.

Price Record: Ranges are based on net asset value per share.

% Yield From Investment Income: Dividends from investment income in 1998 divided by current offering price.

§—Fund not presently offered. ★—Rated AAAf by S&P n/a: Not available

#—1999 prices and NAV % change at end of month or latest available.

Ticker Symbol	Fund	Year Offered	Prin. Obj.	Type	Sept. 30, 1999 Total Net Assets (MIL.$)	Cash & Equiv (MIL.$)	See Foot-notes	Net Assets per Share % Change from Previous Dec. 31 At: Dec. 31 1995	1996	1997	1998	Dec. 31, 1999	Min. Unit	Max. Sales Chg. %	Distributions Per Share from Invest. Income 1998	1999	Security Profits 1998	1999	$10,000 Invested 12-31-93 Now Worth	PRICE RECORD NAV Per Sh 1999 High	Low	#12-31-99 NAV Per Shr.	Offer Price	% Yield From Inv. Inc.
AGNMX	AARP GNMA & U.S.Treasury	*'84	I	GB	4204.8	n/a	....	+12.5	+4.2	+7.7	+6.1	−5.0	$500	None	0.904	0.077	....	...	12,522	15.25	14.31	14.40	14.40	6.3
AGIFX	AARP Growth & Income Fund	*'84	GI	C	6108.8	n/a	....	+31.4	+21.4	+30.6	−5.0	+2.7	$500	None	0.91	0.83	....	...	20,936	56.17	47.32	49.99	49.99	1.8
ACRNX	Acorn Fund	'70	G	C	3288.5	n/a	[1]	+21.5	+22.9	+24.7	+5.6	+11.3	$1,000	None	0.03	0.029	1.06	0.189	20,135	20.54	15.64	18.53	18.53	0.2
ACINX	Acorn International Fund	*'92	G	INTL	1934.4	n/a	....	+8.9	+20.6	+1.6	+15.5	+70.4	$1,000	None	0.15	0.15	0.27	...	25,264	35.33	20.44	35.33	35.33	0.4
AAGFX	AIM Aggressive Growth Fund	*'84	G	C	2702.3	n/a	....	+41.4	+14.2	+12.0	+4.9	+43.5	$500	5.5	....	....	0.392	6.441	31,907	64.49	41.82	62.58	66.22	....
AMBLX	AIM Balanced Fund Cl.A	'78	GI	FL	1498.6	n/a	....	+34.6	+19.0	+24.1	+11.1	+17.8	$500	4.75	0.345	0.569	0.065	...	24,454	32.69	27.58	32.69	34.32	1.0
CHTRX	AIM Charter Cl.A	'67	GI	C	4671.5	n/a	....	+35.3	+19.2	+24.4	+25.9	+24.1	$500	5.5	0.072	0.01	0.522	0.01	29,999	18.52	14.59	18.48	19.56	0.4
CSTGX	AIM Constellation Cl.A	'66	G	C	13454.9	n/a	....	+35.3	+16.1	+12.6	+18.5	+43.5	$500	5.5	....	....	0.731	3.28	30,438	40.71	28.57	40.51	42.87	....
AUTLX	AIM Global Utilities Cl.A	*'88	IG	C	193.7	n/a	[2]	+27.1	+13.6	+23.3	+15.2	+25.5	$500	5.5	0.40	0.287	0.783	...	22,804	26.49	20.23	26.08	27.60	1.4
AMHYX	AIM High Yield Fund Cl.A	*'78	I	BD	1410.1	n/a	[3]	+16.2	+14.7	+11.8	−6.3	+1.2	$500	4.75	0.74	0.814	0.015	...	13,918	8.88	7.94	8.06	8.46	8.7
AMIFX	AIM Income Cl.A	*'68	I	BD	399.2	n/a	[4]	+21.9	+8.1	+11.5	+3.2	−3.4	$500	4.75	0.414	0.506	0.053	...	13,549	8.47	7.58	7.59	7.97	5.2
AGOVX	AIM Intermed. Govt. Fund Cl.A	*'87	IP	GB	247.4	n/a	[5]★	+15.7	+2.2	+8.7	+4.6	−2.4	$500	4.75	0.315	0.554	....	...	12,676	9.58	8.80	8.80	9.24	3.4
AIIEX	AIM Intl. Equity Cl.A	*'92	GP	INTL	1903.2	n/a	....	+16.3	+18.9	+5.7	+13.3	+54.4	$500	5.5	0.106	....	0.209	0.93	24,700	27.81	17.53	27.81	29.43	0.4
SHTIX	AIM Limited Maturity Treas. Shs.	*'87	I	GB	382.6	n/a	★	+9.2	+4.6	+5.8	+2.6	+2.6	$500	1.0	0.176	0.461	....	...	12,887	10.17	9.96	9.96	10.06	1.7
AMBDX	AIM Municipal Bond Cl.A	*'77	I	TF	317.4	n/a	[6]∫†	+12.8	+3.7	+7.1	+3.9	−2.3	$500	4.75	0.315	0.415	....	...	12,247	8.41	7.74	7.74	8.13	3.9
AGWFX	AIM Select Growth Cl.A	*'67	G	C	351.3	n/a	[7]	+34.1	+18.5	+19.1	+26.8	+41.0	$500	5.5	....	....	0.523	1.062	32,112	26.23	18.76	26.23	27.76	....
AVLFX	AIM Value Cl.A	*'84	GI	C	10609.2	n/a	....	+34.7	+14.3	+23.8	+32.3	+29.6	$500	5.5	0.088	....	2.61	3.25	33,727	50.62	39.41	48.83	51.67	0.2
WEINX	AIM Weingarten Cl.A	*'66	G	C	7780.5	n/a		+34.4	+17.3	+25.6	+32.2	+34.2	$500	5.5	0.014	....	1.458	3.19	34,954	31.55	24.37	30.11	31.86	....
ALSCX	Alger Small Cap. Portfolio Cl. B	*'86	G	C	405.8	n/a	[8]	+48.8	+4.0	+8.9	+8.6	+31.0	None	ERF	....	....	1.02	1.807	22,873	11.86	8.81	10.40	10.40	....
AGBBX	Alliance Growth Fund Cl.B	*'87	G	C	4944.6	n/a	[9]	+28.6	+22.3	+26.3	+26.5	+23.8	$250	ERF	....	....	3.711	7.44	30,518	48.33	39.38	42.73	42.73	....
CABDX	Alliance Growth & Income:Cl A	'32	IG	C	1381.6	n/a		+37.4	+23.9	+28.3	+20.4	+5.2	$250	4.25	0.04	0.03	0.351	...	26,503	4.04	3.34	3.60	3.76	1.1
AHHBX	Alliance High Yield Cl.B	*'97	IG	BD	523.3	n/a	[10]	....	....	+23.2	−1.9	−3.2	$250	ERF	0.994	0.91	0.151	...	.....	10.24	8.95	8.95	8.95	11.1
ALIFX	Alliance International Cl.A	*'81	G	INTL	78.1	n/a	....	+10.0	+7.0	+1.6	+9.4	+33.5	$250	4.25	0.475	....	1.043	1.192	18,426	20.25	15.02	20.25	21.15	2.2
AGSAX	Alliance Global Strategic Income Trust Cl.A.	*'96	I	GL	34.2	n/a	....	....	....	....	+2.0	+6.4	$250	4.25	1.025	0.90	....	...	.....	10.61	9.81	10.09	10.54	9.7
ALCAX	Alliance Muni Income:Cal.Cl.A	*'86	I	TF	691.4	n/a	∫†	+23.6	+3.0	+10.6	+6.2	−3.6	$250	4.25	0.584	0.51	....	...	12,988	11.35	10.38	10.38	10.84	5.4
BUICX	Alliance Muni Income:Insur.Cal.Cl.A	*'86	I	TF	113.3	n/a	∫†	+23.8	+1.6	+9.7	+6.0	−4.8	$250	4.25	0.661	0.60	....	...	12,420	14.28	12.95	12.95	13.52	4.9
ALNYX	Alliance Muni Income:N.Y.Cl.A	*'86	I	TF	227.7	n/a	∫†	+20.9	+2.9	+10.9	+5.7	−4.2	$250	4.25	0.528	0.50	....	...	12,587	10.33	9.36	9.36	9.78	5.4
CABTX	Alliance Muni Bond:Insur.Natl.Cl.A	*'77	I	TF	170.6	n/a	∫†	+22.1	+2.1	+9.3	+5.5	−6.9	$250	4.25	0.48	0.391	0.223	...	12,165	10.36	9.18	9.19	9.60	5.0
ALTHX	Alliance Muni Bond:Natl. Cl.A	*'86	I	TF	411.1	n/a	∫†	+21.9	+3.0	+9.7	+5.6	−10.5	$250	4.25	0.579	0.031	0.097	...	11,781	11.04	9.80	9.80	10.23	5.7
ANEAX	Alliance New Europe Fund Inc.	*'90	G	GL	125.5	n/a	....	+18.5	+20.1	+16.6	+24.5	+25.5	$250	4.25	....	....	2.555	0.909	27,121	22.25	17.82	22.25	23.24	....
ANABX	Alliance North Amer. Govt. Inc. Cl.B	*'92	IP	GL	1106.2	n/a	[11]	+27.0	+21.5	+13.1	+5.3	+2.8	$250	ERF	0.873	0.564	0.027	...	13,451	7.91	7.02	7.26	7.26	12.0
APGBX	Alliance Premier Growth Cl.B	*'92	G	C	6976.9	n/a	[10]	+36.5	+23.1	+31.6	+47.9	+27.6	$250	ERF	....	....	0.61	2.38	39,103	35.29	28.82	34.54	34.54	....
QUABX	Alliance Quasar Fund Cl.B	*'90	G	C	588.5	n/a	....	+45.3	+30.9	+16.4	−5.8	+12.0	$250	4.25	....	....	1.01	...	21,279	25.21	19.72	25.21	25.21	....
AREBX	Alliance Real Estate Invest. Cl.B	*'96	I	SP	153.9	n/a	[10]	....	....	+21.7	−20.7	−8.5	$250	ERF	0.457	0.393	0.095	...	.....	11.35	8.47	9.28	9.28	4.9
ATEBX	Alliance Technology Cl.B	*'93	CA	SP	2996.6	n/a	....	+44.7	+18.6	+3.9	...	+71.2	$250	None	....	....	5.17	4.04	38,768	121.57	72.73	121.57	121.57	....
AWPAX	Alliance Worldwide Fund Cl.A	*'94	G	GL	333.1	n/a	[12]	+4.9	+22.5	+12.8	+8.4	+54.4	$250	4.25	0.122	....	1.639	1.057	.....	14.91	9.63	14.91	15.57	0.8
BCHYX	Amer. Century Cal. High Yield Muni Fund	*'87	I	TF	338.3	n/a	∫†	+17.8	+5.6	+10.1	+5.1	−3.7	$1,000	None	0.466	0.442	....	...	13,141	9.88	9.01	9.01	9.01	5.2
BCINX	Amer. Century Cal. Insured Tax-Free	*'87	I	TF	211.2	n/a	∫†★	+18.6	+3.5	+9.0	+5.0	−4.8	$1,000	None	0.468	0.446	....	...	12,519	10.64	9.57	9.59	9.59	4.9
BCITX	Amer. Century Intermed.-Term Tax Free	*'83	I	TF	459.7	n/a	∫†	+13.3	+3.0	+7.2	+4.1	−1.5	$1,000	None	0.474	0.437	....	...	12,366	11.39	10.64	10.67	10.67	4.4
BCLTX	Amer. Century Cal. Long Term Tax Free	*'83	I	TF	328.6	n/a	∫†	+19.2	+2.3	+9.4	+5.0	−9.1	$1,000	None	0.535	0.094	....	...	11,931	11.72	10.46	10.47	10.47	5.1
BGNMX	Amer. Century GNMA Fund	*'85	I	GB	1353.9	n/a	★	+15.4	+4.9	+8.5	+5.7	+0.3	$1,000	None	0.597	0.58	....	...	13,716	10.71	10.08	10.14	10.14	5.9
TWCGX	Amer. Century Growth Fund	'58	G	C	7827.2	n/a	[13]	+20.1	+15.1	+28.8	+35.6	+34.1	$2,500	None	....	....	5.389	4.14	31,826	35.16	26.63	32.28	32.28	....
TWTIX	Amer. Century Intermed.-Term Tax Free	*'84	I	TF	164.6	n/a	∫†	+12.5	+3.7	+2.6	+1.1	−0.7	$1,000	None	....	0.469	0.077	0.05	11,608	10.67	9.98	9.99	9.99	....
TWTLX	Amer. Century Long-Term Tax Free	*'84	I	TF	109.7	n/a	∫†	+17.2	+2.1	+0.3	+0.9	−4.9	$1,000	None	....	0.517	0.177	...	10,826	10.86	9.69	9.71	9.71	....

Uniform Footnote Explanations-See page 235. **Stock Splits & Divs.** (figures adjusted): [1] 2% redemption under 60 days. [2] Was Utilities Fund(5/95). [3] Rated Bf. [4] Rated BBBf. [5] Was Govt. Secs.(3/97). [6] Rated Af. [7] Was Aim Growth (9/98). [8] 5% E.R.F.reducing 1% per yr.over 6 yrs.. 3-for-1 split, Sept.'95. [9] 4% E.R.F. reducing 1% per year.. [10] 4% ERF reducing over 4 yrs. [11] 3% ERF reducing over 3 yrs.. [12] Was WW Privatization Fund(12/97). [13] Was 20th Cent. Growth(9/97).

Ticker Symbol	Fund	Year Offered	Prin. Obj.	Type	Sept. 30, 1999 Total Net Assets (MIL.$)	Sept. 30, 1999 Cash & Equiv (MIL.$)	See Foot-notes	Net Assets per Share % Change from Previous Dec. 31 At: Dec. 31 1995	1996	1997	1998	Dec. 31, 1999	Min. Unit	Max. Sales Chg. %	Distributions Per Share from Invest. Income 1998	Invest. Income 1999	Security Profits 1998	Security Profits 1999	$10,000 Invested 12-31-93 Now Worth	PRICE RECORD 1999 High	1999 Low	NAV Per Sh #12-31-99 NAV Per Shr.	Offer Price	% Yield From Inv. Inc.
TWCIX	Amer. Century Select Fund	*'58	G	C	6889.9	n/a	1	+ 22.5	+ 19.4	+ 31.6	+ 34.6	+ 21.9	$2,500	None	....	....	9.95	5.09	29,024	56.42	46.76	52.68	52.68	....
TWUSX	Amer. Century Short Term Govt.	*'82	I	GB	804.6	n/a	2	+ 10.3	+ 4.0	+ 5.8	+ 5.5	+ 1.2	$2,500	None	0.463	0.435	....	...	12,893	9.54	9.19	9.22	9.22	5.0
BTMTX	Amer. Century Target 2000 Fund	*'85	R	SP	202.0	n/a	★	+ 20.7	+ 2.0	+ 7.0	+ 15.2	+ 2.9	$1,000	None	5.57	....	1.322	...	14,538	96.98	93.95	96.98	96.98	5.7
BTFIX	Amer. Century Target 2005 Fund	*'85	R	SP	490.5	n/a	★	+ 32.6	− 1.2	+ 11.6	+ 19.5	− 5.8	$1,000	None	3.393	....	1.069	...	14,993	76.44	71.00	71.63	71.63	4.7
BTTNX	Amer. Century Target 2010 Fund	*'85	R	SP	241.0	n/a	★	+ 42.1	− 3.5	+ 16.7	+ 23.2	− 11.8	$1,000	None	2.78	....	1.489	...	15,372	61.19	53.32	53.56	53.56	5.2
BTFTX	Amer. Century Target 2015 Fund	*'86	R	SP	218.4	n/a	★	+ 52.7	− 6.0	+ 22.9	+ 19.7	− 14.6	$1,000	None	2.096	....	0.082	...	15,490	49.39	41.42	41.64	41.64	5.0
BTTTX	Amer. Century Target 2020 Fund	*'90	R	SP,BD	318.4	n/a	★	+ 61.3	− 8.4	+ 28.6	+ 40.0	− 18.4	$1,000	None	2.061	....	5.203	...	17,864	36.58	29.15	29.41	29.41	7.0
TWCUX	Amer. Century Ultra Fund	*'81	G	C	33051.6	n/a	3	+ 37.4	+ 14.0	+ 22.4	+ 33.8	+ 37.0	$2,500	None	....	....	3.122	...	33,844	45.78	32.83	45.78	45.78	....
	Amer.Funds Group:																							
AMCPX	AMCAP	*'67	G	C	6278.2	1018.3	....	+ 28.3	+ 14.0	+ 28.7	+ 28.6	+ 16.0	$1,000	5.75	0.13	0.10	2.29	1.66	27,997	19.74	17.10	18.78	19.93	0.7
ABALX	Amer.Balanced	'32	IS	B	6095.9	854.1	....	+ 26.5	+ 12.8	+ 20.5	+ 10.8	+ 1.2	$500	5.75	0.56	0.42	1.05	1.11	19,338	16.85	14.06	14.42	15.30	3.7
AHITX	Amer.High-Income Trust	*'88	I	BD	2777.4	185.6	....	+ 20.0	+ 12.4	+ 12.4	+ 1.6	− 1.2	$1,000	4.75	1.27	0.125	0.045	...	14,473	14.57	13.44	13.84	14.53	8.7
AMRMX	Amer. Mutual	'49	ISG	C	10192.8	2631.2	....	+ 30.9	+ 15.9	+ 26.1	+ 14.3	− 0.7	$250	5.75	0.80	0.555	2.93	5.05	21,757	32.33	23.34	23.83	25.28	3.2
ABNDX	Bond Fund of Amer.	*'74	I	BD	9514.2	632.5	....	+ 17.7	+ 6.4	+ 9.5	+ 5.0	+ 0.5	$1,000	4.75	0.949	0.698	0.141	...	13,762	13.68	12.88	12.98	13.63	7.0
CAIBX	Capital Income Builder	*'87	IG	C,BD	8735.3	2528.2	....	+ 24.5	+ 17.1	+ 22.8	+ 11.4	− 3.8	$1,000	5.75	1.95	1.455	2.81	1.54	18,726	48.32	41.69	42.67	45.27	4.3
CWBFX	Capital World Bond	*'87	I	BD,GL	553.8	25.9	....	+ 20.9	+ 6.1	− 0.4	+ 9.9	− 4.0	$1,000	4.75	0.80	0.50	0.323	0.068	13,277	16.36	14.90	14.96	15.71	5.1
CWGIX	Capital World Growth & Inc.	*'93	GI	GL	9442.2	585.7	....	+ 21.1	+ 22.3	+ 17.6	+ 15.7	+ 26.5	$1,000	5.75	0.56	0.505	2.37	1.81	25,798	30.05	25.32	29.83	31.65	1.8
AEPGX	Europacific Growth	*'84	G	INTL	25954.1	1962.0	....	+ 12.8	+ 18.3	+ 9.1	+ 15.4	+ 56.1	$250	5.75	0.36	0.29	1.26	1.39	26,514	42.66	28.28	42.66	45.26	0.8
ANCFX	Fundamental Investors	'32	GI	C	14559.7	1040.5	....	+ 33.5	+ 19.8	+ 26.1	+ 16.5	+ 23.7	$250	5.75	0.40	0.40	2.59	2.79	29,441	33.99	28.60	32.59	34.58	1.2
AGTHX	Growth Fund of Amer.	'58	G	C	20791.6	2699.6	4	+ 29.7	+ 14.9	+ 26.6	+ 31.5	+ 44.5	$1,000	5.75	0.09	0.045	2.21	3.19	35,850	30.31	22.32	29.14	30.92	0.3
AMECX	Income Fund Amer.	'70	I	FL	21891.3	1953.7	....	+ 28.5	+ 14.9	+ 21.5	+ 9.2	+ 0.5	$1,000	5.75	0.88	0.87	1.19	0.81	19,195	18.17	15.46	15.74	16.70	5.3
AIBAX	Intermed.Bond Fund of Amer.	*'88	IP	BD	1535.7	62.4	....	+ 13.5	+ 4.0	+ 6.8	+ 6.5	+ 1.6	$1,000	4.75	0.81	0.82	....	...	13,245	13.55	12.93	12.93	13.57	6.0
AIVSX	Investment Co. Amer.	'33	GI	C	51071.7	7113.1	....	+ 30.3	+ 19.2	+ 29.4	+ 22.2	+ 15.9	$250	5.75	0.51	0.52	2.94	3.04	28,522	35.07	30.84	32.46	34.44	1.5
ANEFX	New Economy Fund	*'83	G	C	8168.0	997.4	....	+ 24.2	+ 12.8	+ 28.5	+ 28.3	+ 40.9	$1,000	5.75	0.14	0.18	2.54	2.34	29,875	31.18	22.94	29.82	31.64	0.4
ANWPX	New Perspective	*'73	G	GL	25752.3	3311.7	....	+ 20.3	+ 17.1	+ 14.9	+ 27.9	+ 39.2	$250	5.75	0.26	0.17	1.57	2.34	29,653	30.34	23.18	29.44	31.24	0.8
SMCWX	SMALLCAP World Fund	*'90	G	C	8982.5	464.2	....	+ 22.3	+ 19.5	+ 11.6	+ 0.1	+ 61.4	$1,000	5.75	0.09	0.015	1.29	0.605	25,560	39.14	23.55	39.14	41.53	0.2
AFTEX	Tax-Exempt Fund of Amer.	*'79	I	TF	1908.5	69.4	....	+ 16.9	+ 4.7	+ 9.2	+ 5.9	− 3.8	$1,000	4.75	0.613	0.442	0.186	...	13,044	12.48	11.50	11.50	12.07	5.1
TAFTX	Tax Exempt Fund of Calif.	*'86	I	TF	380.1	10.0	∫†	+ 17.2	+ 3.3	+ 8.7	+ 6.0	− 3.2	$1,000	4.75	0.783	0.552	0.226	...	12,828	16.49	15.31	15.32	16.08	4.9
TMMDX	Tax Exempt Fund of Maryland	*'86	I	TF	106.6	2.0	∫†	+ 16.1	+ 3.6	+ 8.7	+ 5.6	− 3.0	$1,000	4.75	0.765	0.618	0.095	...	12,763	16.20	14.99	15.00	15.75	4.9
TFVAX	Tax Exempt Fund of Virginia	*'86	I	TF	118.7	2.1	∫†	+ 15.5	+ 3.3	+ 7.6	+ 5.6	− 3.6	$1,000	4.75	0.754	0.548	0.179	...	12,455	16.50	15.25	15.26	16.02	4.7
AMUSX	U.S.Govt.Securities	*'85	IP	GB	1310.0	34.0	....	+ 14.9	+ 1.5	+ 8.1	+ 7.6	− 2.5	$1,000	4.75	0.81	0.625	....	...	12,618	13.41	12.45	12.46	13.08	6.2
AWSHX	Washington Mutual Investors	'52	IG	C	53537.3	1125.5	....	+ 40.6	+ 20.0	+ 32.9	+ 19.0	+ 1.0	$250	5.75	0.61	0.58	2.595	3.11	27,085	36.55	28.73	29.56	31.36	1.9
AMRGX	Amer. Growth Fund	'58	G	C,CV	70.2	n/a	....	+ 25.4	+ 11.9	+ 13.3	+ 4.9	+ 9.9	None	5.75	....	0.10	....	0.60	17,596	10.63	9.19	10.29	10.92	....
CAAPX	Ariel Appreciation Fund	*'90	G	C	352.8	n/a		+ 24.1	+ 23.6	+ 38.1	+ 8.7	− 4.3	$1,000	None	0.036	0.042	3.46	3.15	20,185	38.85	29.36	30.97	30.97	0.1
ARGFX	Ariel Growth Fund	*'86	GR	C	215.1	n/a	....	+ 18.4	+ 23.3	+ 36.6	+ 0.2	− 6.9	$1,000	None	0.081	0.076	0.124	6.03	17,822	41.50	29.02	31.11	31.11	0.3
BSPAX	Bear Stearns S&P STARS Ptfl Cl.A	*'95	G	C	284.0	n/a	....	....	+ 27.5	+ 17.8	+ 39.0	+ 37.6	$1,000	4.75	....	....	0.923	0.281	.....	31.33	22.26	31.33	33.15	....
BEONX	Berger One Hundred	*'66	G	C	1334.5	n/a	....	+ 21.3	+ 13.8	+ 14.4	+ 15.8	+ 51.5	$250	None	....	....	0.975	3.583	25,848	21.50	14.50	18.53	18.53	....
BRWIX	Brandywine Fund	*'85	G	C	4199.2	n/a	....	+ 35.9	+ 24.8	+ 12.5	− 0.9	+ 47.0	$25,000	None	0.264	....	0.073	1.643	27,823	43.95	29.15	42.88	42.88	0.6
BURHX	Burnham Fund Cl.A	'61	GI	C	160.5	n/a	....	+ 26.8	+ 22.1	+ 23.4	+ 27.7	+ 25.5	$1,000	3.0	0.26	....	1.63	1.29	31,200	42.10	31.85	41.71	43.91	0.6
CSIEX	Calvert Social Inv.Equity Ptfl	*'87	GR	C	166.4	n/a	....	+ 20.3	+ 21.8	+ 18.8	+ 10.9	+ 15.8	$1,000	4.75	....	....	0.014	...	19,672	30.76	25.25	29.88	31.37	....
CSIFX	Calvert Social Inv.Mgd.Growth	*'82	GI	B	708.6	n/a	....	+ 25.3	+ 9.4	+ 17.4	+ 5.9	− 1.6	$1,000	4.75	0.553	....	....	...	15,982	34.66	31.26	32.33	33.94	1.6
CTFLX	Calvert TF Reserve Ltd.Term Ptfl	*'81	I	TF	577.9	n/a	∫†	+ 5.4	+ 3.5	+ 4.0	+ 3.8	− 0.3	$2,000	2.0	0.396	0.033	0.001	...	12,023	10.74	10.63	10.64	10.75	3.7
CGVIX	Capstone:Govt.Income Fund	*'68	IP	GB	10.2	n/a	5	+ 5.5	+ 3.9	+ 4.4	+ 4.4	+ 0.2	$10,000	None	0.82	....	....	...	12,127	25.20	24.54	24.58	24.58	3.3
TRDFX	Capstone:Growth Fund	*'52	G	C	81.4	n/a	....	+ 27.5	+ 17.7	+ 28.7	+ 23.0	+ 22.5	$200	None	0.123	0.02	0.661	1.29	26,860	19.31	16.05	18.63	18.63	0.7

Uniform Footnote Explanations-See page 235. **Stock Splits & Divs.** (figures adjusted): [1] Was 20th Cent.Select(9/97). [2] Was 20th Cent. US Govts(9/97). [3] 0.5% redempt.fee. Was 20th Cent. Ultra(9/97). [4] 2-for-1 split.Dec.'96. [5] 5-for-1 reverse stock split(1/97).

Ticker Symbol	Fund	Year Offered	Prin. Obj.	Type	Sept. 30, 1999 Total Net Assets (MIL.$)	Sept. 30, 1999 Cash & Equiv (MIL.$)	See Foot-notes	Net Assets per Share % Change from Previous Dec. 31 At: Dec. 31 1995	1996	1997	1998	Dec. 31, 1999	Min. Unit	Max. Sales Chg. %	Distributions Per Share from Invest. Income 1998	Invest. Income 1999	Security Profits 1998	Security Profits 1999	$10,000 Invested 12-31-93 Now Worth	PRICE RECORD 1999 High	1999 Low	#12-31-99 NAV Per Shr.	Offer Price	% Yield From Inv. Inc.
CNJFX	Capstone: Japan Fund	*'89	G	C,SP	4.8	n/a	....	– 3.2	– 16.1	– 24.6	+ 6.7	+ 58.6	$200	None	....	....	....	...	12,881	7.85	4.60	7.85	7.85	....
CLMBX	Columbia Growth	'67	G	C	1860.4	n/a	....	+ 32.9	+ 20.9	+ 26.3	+ 29.7	+ 9.8	$1,000	None	....	....	....	...	28,727	53.24	41.88	48.91	48.91	....
DRCVX	Comstock Partners Capital Value Cl.A	*'85	RI	L	62.8	n/a	1	– 3.2	– 5.7	– 27.2	– 22.1	– 21.1	$2,500	4.5	0.31	0.31	....	...	3,925	4.21	2.93	2.94	3.08	10.1
CSGWX	Concert Growth Fund Cl.A	*'87	G	C	4164.2	n/a	2	+ 32.8	+ 17.8	+ 27.1	+ 17.8	+ 21.0	$250	8.5	....	....	....	...	27,689	26.20	20.86	25.82	28.22	....
COIGX	Cowen Income + Growth Cl.A	*'86	IG	C	35.6	0.5	3	+ 36.0	+ 12.4	+ 21.9	+ 0.4	– 9.0	$1,000	4.75	0.269	0.193	0.717	...	16,003	12.78	10.03	10.34	10.86	2.5
CWNOX	Cowen Opportunity Cl.A	*'88	G	C	22.1	0.9	....	+ 15.4	+ 24.6	+ 10.4	– 25.4	+ 29.1	$1,000	4.75	....	....	....	...	15,869	13.63	8.86	12.83	13.47	....
RPFCX	Davis Convertible Fund Cl. A		G	CV	119.1	n/a	....	....	....	+ 35.2	– 4.5	+ 11.9	$1,000	4.75	0.60	0.60	....	0.77	.....	26.83	23.10	25.21	26.47	2.3
RPFGX	Davis Financial Fund Cl. A	*'91	G	C	410.1	n/a	....	....	....	+ 45.5	+ 13.4	– 0.9	$1,000	4.75	....	....	....	...	.....	33.00	26.75	29.07	30.52	....
DGIAX	Davis Growth & Income Fund Cl. A	*'98	GI	C	51.8	n/a	....	....	....	....	....	+ 6.8	$1,000	4.75	0.032	0.178	....	...	.....	11.44	9.69	10.78	11.32	0.3
NYVTX	Davis New York Venture Cl.A	*'69	G	C	7169.7	n/a	4	+ 40.5	+ 26.6	+ 33.7	+ 14.6	+ 17.5	$1,000	4.75	0.105	0.003	0.48	0.62	31,383	29.61	24.32	28.76	30.19	0.3
RPFRX	Davis Real Estate Fund Cl. A	*'94	G	SP	162.7	n/a	....	....	....	+ 25.9	– 16.1	– 9.1	$1,000	4.75	0.60	0.57	....	...	.....	21.99	17.01	18.27	19.18	3.1
DELDX	Delaware:Delaware Equity Inc. Cl.A	*'57	GI	C	1688.2	18.6		+ 32.2	+ 20.0	+ 25.8	– 7.0	– 6.4	$1,000	5.75	0.44	0.44	....	...	17,233	19.74	16.30	16.68	17.70	2.5
DEDTX	Delaware:Delaware Growth & Income Cl.A	*'86	GI	C	894.8	13.4	....	+ 36.1	+ 19.8	+ 28.9	– 2.6	– 8.5	$1,000	5.75	0.18	0.10	....	...	18,637	18.69	15.09	15.52	16.47	1.1
DELFX	Delaware:Delaware Balanced Cl.A	*'38	GI	C	560.4	9.5	....	+ 25.5	+ 13.7	+ 23.9	+ 11.6	– 19.8	$1,000	5.75	0.36	0.24	....	...	15,602	23.93	18.39	18.83	19.98	1.8
DFCIX	Delaware:Delcap Fund Cl.A	*'86	G	C	649.5	26.6	....	+ 29.8	+ 14.1	+ 14.4	+ 16.0	+ 62.7	$1,000	5.75	....	....	3.93	5.02	30,282	35.90	22.45	33.53	35.58	....
DEGIX	Delaware:Intl.Equity Fund Cl.A	*'91	I	INTL	101.5	2.5	....	+ 11.5	+ 22.8	+ 11.8	+ 7.8	+ 11.3	$1,000	5.75	0.06	0.24	....	...	18,716	16.90	14.86	16.83	17.86	0.3
DMFIX	Delaware:Tax Free Insur.Fund Cl.A	*'85	I	TF	66.9	n/a	....	+ 13.6	+ 2.2	+ 8.3	+ 4.3	– 7.8	$1,000	4.75	0.475	0.088	0.123	...	11,849	11.07	10.04	10.04	10.43	4.6
DMTFX	Delaware:Tax Free USA Fund Cl.A	*'84	I	TF	478.3	n/a	5	+ 13.3	+ 0.7	+ 8.0	+ 4.3	– 5.5	$1,000	4.75	0.546	0.54	0.024	...	11,756	11.77	10.53	10.53	10.94	5.0
DMUSX	Delaware:Tax Free USA Intermed.Fund	*'93	I	TF	25.5	n/a	....	+ 11.9	+ 4.4	+ 6.3	+ 5.3	– 1.7	$1,000	3.0	0.456	0.424	....	...	12,520	10.80	10.10	10.11	10.40	4.4
DTRIX	Delaware:Limited-Term Govt.Cl.A	*'85	I	GB	282.1	5.9	6	+ 8.5	+ 3.0	+ 5.1	+ 6.7	+ 0.5	$1,000	3.0	0.497	0.474	....	...	12,356	8.71	8.27	8.27	8.50	5.8
DELTX	Delaware:Trend Fund Cl.A	'68	G	C	515.8	43.3	7	+ 42.0	+ 9.9	+ 19.0	+ 11.7	+ 66.4	$1,000	5.75	....	....	2.60	2.97	31,066	24.13	15.38	24.13	25.60	....
DEVLX	Delaware:Small Cap Value Fund Cl.A	*'87	G	C	222.2	4.9	....	+ 23.5	+ 21.6	+ 32.7	– 5.7	– 6.6	$1,000	5.75	....	0.163	....	...	16,499	28.07	23.33	24.69	26.20	....
DODGX	Dodge & Cox Stock	'64	G	C	4346.9	n/a	....	+ 33.0	+ 22.0	+ 24.5	+ 5.4	+ 13.4	$2,500	None	1.56	1.06	7.42	1.29	25,401	110.53	88.18	100.52	100.52	1.6
DREVX	Dreyfus Fund	'47	GI	C	2461.4	n/a	....	+ 23.3	+ 5.1	– 6.1	+ 17.1	+ 15.5	$2,500	None	0.105	0.03	....	...	15,767	13.31	11.32	13.28	13.28	0.8
DRGMX	Dreyfus GNMA	'85	I	GB	993.3	n/a	....	+ 14.7	+ 3.7	+ 8.5	+ 4.1	– 0.3	$2,500	None	0.919	0.672	....	...	13,033	14.65	13.85	13.85	13.85	6.6
DREQX	Dreyfus Growth Opport.	*'72	GIS	C	438.5	n/a	....	+ 26.7	+ 21.8	+ 8.5	+ 15.9	+ 19.7	$2,500	None	0.073	....	0.462	0.981	21,882	11.70	9.80	11.70	11.70	0.6
DCVIX	Dreyfus/Laurel Core Value Inv.	'47	GI	C	539.5	n/a	....	+ 35.6	+ 21.0	+ 23.7	+ 7.1	+ 6.9	$1,000	None	0.168	0.06	2.82	0.379	23,330	34.73	28.74	30.83	32.71	0.5
DRTAX	Dreyfus Municipal Bond	'76	IS	TF	2793.1	n/a	ʃ†	+ 15.3	+ 3.1	+ 4.9	+ 5.1	– 6.2	$2,500	None	0.579	0.564	0.224	...	11,445	12.63	11.21	11.22	11.22	5.2
DRLEX	Dreyfus Premier Aggressive Growth	'68	G	L	120.6	n/a	8	+ 13.0	– 2.4	– 13.0	– 30.8	+ 36.9	$2,500	3.0	....	....	....	...	8,454	11.88	7.91	11.88	12.60	....
EVCAX	EV Calif. Municipals Cl.B	'85	I	TF	252.8	n/a	9 ʃ†	+ 18.0	+ 1.7	+ 10.2	+ 5.2	– 7.0	$1,000	ERF	0.444	0.423	....	...	11,787	10.35	9.13	9.14	9.14	4.9
EVFLX	EV Florida Municipals Cl.B	*'90	I	TF	332.6	n/a	10 ʃ†	+ 18.1	+ 0.7	+ 7.1	+ 5.4	– 6.5	$1,000	ERF	0.467	0.418	....	0.125	11,448	11.35	9.99	10.00	10.00	4.7
EVHMX	EV National Municipals Cl.B	*'85	I	TF	1765.7	n/a	11 ʃ†	+ 19.3	+ 3.4	+ 12.1	+ 4.7	– 8.6	$1,000	ERF	0.538	0.466	....	...	12,188	10.77	9.32	9.32	9.32	5.8
EVNYX	EV N.Y. Municipals Cl.B	*'90	I	TF	388.1	n/a	10 ʃ†	+ 17.5	+ 1.7	+ 8.7	+ 5.6	– 6.6	$1,000	ERF	0.502	0.439	0.151	...	11,646	11.56	10.28	10.28	10.28	4.9
EVSGX	EV Strategic Income Cl.B	*'90	I	GL	154.0	n/a	....	+ 12.3	+ 9.2	+ 7.4	+ 1.4	+ 4.6	$1,000	ERF	0.683	0.671	....	...	13,243	9.03	8.55	8.67	8.67	7.9
EVGOX	EV Government Obligs. Cl.A	*'84	I	GB	219.9	n/a	....	+ 13.5	+ 3.0	+ 7.0	+ 5.6	– 0.2	$1,000	3.75	0.79	0.695	....	...	12,919	10.40	9.70	9.70	10.18	7.8
EVTMX	EV Utilities Fund Cl. A	*'81	R	C	433.0	n/a		+ 26.6	+ 7.3	+ 14.0	+ 23.2	+ 15.8	$1,000	4.75	0.235	0.103	0.037	...	19,420	13.48	10.12	11.65	12.36	1.9
ETHSX	EV Worlwide Health Sciences Cl.A	*'85	G	GL	87.8	n/a	12	+ 58.9	+ 18.1	+ 10.6	+ 23.2	+ 22.7	$200	None	....	....	0.672	1.423	29,398	20.03	15.54	20.03	21.25	....
EKBBX	Evergreen Balanced Cl. B	'35	IS	B	404.1	n/a	13	+ 26.6	+ 16.0	+ 18.7	+ 9.3	+ 10.6	$1,000	ERF	0.302	0.197	2.034	1.454	20,103	12.05	10.39	10.74	10.74	2.8
EKPBX	Evergreen Cap. Preserv. & Income Cl.B	*'91	IS	BD	15.3	n/a	14	+ 7.4	+ 5.6	+ 5.1	+ 3.5	+ 2.8	$1,000	ERF	0.473	0.406	....	...	12,771	9.68	9.53	9.53	9.53	5.0
EKDMX	Evergreen Diversified Bond Cl. B	'35	I	BD	38.5	n/a	15	+ 15.1	+ 5.9	+ 10.6	+ 5.8	– 4.4	$1,000	ERF	0.938	0.785	....	...	12,708	15.96	14.43	14.43	14.43	6.5
EFONX	Evergreen Foundation Cl.Y	*'90	GI	C	1185.4	n/a	....	+ 29.2	+ 9.5	+ 24.9	+ 12.1	+ 13.0	$1,000	None	0.489	0.357	0.151	0.585	22,137	22.77	20.44	22.75	22.75	2.1
EVGRX	Evergreen Fund Cl.Y	'71	GR	C	1085.6	n/a	....	+ 37.1	+ 16.8	+ 30.2	+ 7.2	+ 15.9	$1,000	None	0.054	....	0.068	1.075	26,008	27.51	23.59	27.25	27.25	0.2
EKGAX	Evergreen Global Opport. Cl.A	*'88	G	GL	49.7	n/a	16	+ 23.7	+ 3.5	+ 1.1	– 1.8	+ 71.7	$1,000	5.75	....	....	1.217	4.901	22,414	29.83	19.36	29.74	31.22	....
EVVTX	Evergreen Growth & Income Cl.Y	*'86	G	C	578.0	n/a	....	+ 32.8	+ 23.8	+ 30.7	+ 5.1	+ 14.4	$1,000	None	0.199	0.005	0.778	0.601	26,301	32.38	27.15	32.38	32.38	0.6

Uniform Footnote Explanations-See page 235. **Stock Splits & Divs.** (figures adjusted): [1] Was Dreyfus Cap. Value(7/96). [2] Was Common Sense Growth(1/98). [3] ERF removed.. [4] Was NY Venture (9/95). [5] Long Term Bond. [6] Was Treasury Res.Intermed.(8/95). [7] Was Delta Trend. [8] Was Capital Growth(9/96). [9] 6% E.R.F.reducing 1% per yr.over 6 yrs. [10] 6%E.R.F.reducing 1% per yr. [11] 6%E.R.F.reducing 1% per yr. Was Hi Yld Muni. [12] Was Capstone Medical Research(9/96). two-for-one split, 9/96. [13] Was Keystone Balanced(1/98). [14] 3% ERF reducing over 4 yrs.. Was Keystone America(11/97). [15] Was Keystone Diversified Bond Cl. B. Incl.Keystone Quality Bond(1/98). [16] Was Keystone America(11/97).

Ticker Symbol	Fund	Year Offered	Prin. Obj.	Type	Sept. 30, 1999 Total Net Assets (MIL.$)	Sept. 30, 1999 Cash & Equiv (MIL.$)	See Foot-notes	Net Assets per Share % Change from Previous Dec. 31 At: Dec. 31 1995	1996	1997	1998	Dec. 31, 1999	Min. Unit	Max. Sales Chg. %	Distributions Per Share from Invest. Income 1998	Invest. Income 1999	Security Profits 1998	Security Profits 1999	$10,000 Invested 12-31-93 Now Worth	PRICE RECORD 1999 High	1999 Low	NAV Per Sh #12-31-99 NAV Per Shr.	Offer Price	% Yield From Inv. Inc.
EKHBX	Evergreen High Yield Cl. B	'35	I	BD	44.1	n/a	[1]	+ 8.8	+ 10.1	+ 12.2	− 2.9	− 1.3	$1,000	ERF	0.309	0.026	....	...	11,387	4.06	3.82	3.93	3.93	7.9
EVTRX	Evergreen Income & Growth Cl.Y	*'78	IG	C	800.2	n/a	....	+ 23.4	+ 12.6	+ 19.6	− 0.8	+ 15.9	$1,000	None	1.015	1.08	2.125	0.395	17,884	23.30	19.88	22.38	22.38	4.5
EKIAX	Evergreen Intermed.Term Bond Cl.A	*'87	I	BD	97.0	n/a	[2]	+ 14.0	+ 4.7	+ 8.1	+ 6.5	− 3.4	$1,000	4.75	0.607	0.479	....	...	12,916	9.14	8.33	8.33	8.61	7.0
EKZBX	Evergreen Intl. Growth Cl.B	'54	G	GL	63.2	n/a	[3]	+ 11.4	+ 13.7	+ 10.8	+ 14.8	+ 26.5	$1,000	ERF	....	....	....	0.411	19,137	9.61	7.52	9.61	9.61	....
EKLAX	Evergreen Latin America Cl.A	*'93	GI	GL	4.9	n/a	[4]	+ 9.5	+ 18.1	+ 24.2	− 38.1	+ 61.1	$1,000	5.75	....	....	....	...	14,623	11.42	5.79	11.42	11.99	....
EKOAX	Evergreen Omega Fund Cl.A	*'68	C	C	371.4	n/a	[2]	+ 35.9	+ 10.7	+ 19.3	+ 26.0	+ 43.9	$1,000	5.75	....	....	2.609	0.993	30,719	33.55	23.66	33.55	35.22	....
EKWBX	Evergreen Precious Metals Cl.B	*'74	GI	PM	16.7	n/a	[5]	− 0.4	+ 2.6	− 39.3	− 11.6	+ 2.9	$1,000	ERF	....	....	....	...	4,836	14.10	9.66	11.55	11.55	....
EMUNX	Evergreen Short-Intermed.Munic.Cl.Y	*'91	IP	TF	149.2	n/a	....	+ 6.4	+ 2.6	+ 3.6	+ 3.8	− 2.0	$1,000	None	0.324	0.118	0.077	0.054	11,390	10.24	9.81	9.82	9.82	3.3
EKABX	Evergreen Small Co. Growth Cl. B	'35	G	C	106.6	n/a	[6]	+ 46.6	+ 0.9	+ 12.8	− 18.2	+ 74.7	$1,000	ERF	....	....	1.184	...	23,606	9.40	5.00	9.40	9.40	....
EKJBX	Evergreen Strategic Growth Cl. B	'35	G	C	103.2	n/a	[7]	+ 27.0	+ 12.0	+ 31.6	+ 23.8	+ 34.8	$1,000	ERF	....	....	1.34	1.803	30,364	12.89	10.00	11.91	11.91	....
EKEBX	Evergreen Municipal Bond Cl. B	*'78	IP	TF	87.4	n/a	[8]∫†	+ 16.3	+ 3.0	+ 7.9	+ 2.7	− 9.6	$1,000	ERF	0.30	0.049	0.111	0.039	11,136	7.68	6.80	6.80	6.80	4.4
EKSAX	Evergreen Strategic Income Cl.A	*'87	IG	BD	151.7	n/a	[2]	+ 10.4	+ 10.6	+ 8.5	+ 3.2	− 5.4	$1,000	4.75	0.478	0.05	....	...	11,834	6.90	6.35	6.46	6.78	7.1
FAIMX	Fairmont Fund	*'81	G	C	14.9	n/a	....	+ 27.9	+ 11.2	+ 16.0	− 3.1	− 17.4	$1,000	None	....	....	....	...	14,169	26.58	20.92	22.15	22.15	....
FALDX	Federated American Leaders Cl.A	'68	IG	C	1640.2	n/a	[9]	+ 33.3	+ 19.1	+ 30.6	+ 10.4	+ 6.6	$500	4.5	0.104	0.142	1.587	0.522	24,401	27.80	22.97	25.34	26.81	0.4
LEIFX	Federated Equity Income Cl.A	*'86	IR	CV	943.1	n/a	[10]	+ 30.5	+ 18.9	+ 21.8	+ 15.1	+ 17.3	$500	4.5	0.562	0.26	0.907	0.001	24,444	22.12	18.56	22.12	23.41	2.4
FGMAX	Federated GNMA Trust	*'82	I	GB	892.8	n/a	★	+ 15.6	+ 4.7	+ 7.4	+ 6.0	− 4.3	$25,000	None	0.642	0.115	....	...	12,857	11.39	10.67	10.77	10.77	6.0
FGOIX	Federated Govt. Income	'86	I	GB	1064.8	n/a	[11]★	+ 13.7	+ 3.8	+ 8.6	+ 7.4	− 1.8	$1,500	1.0	0.536	0.516	....	...	13,261	9.01	8.27	8.28	8.36	6.4
FICMX	Federated Income Trust	*'82	I	GB	695.7	n/a	★	+ 14.9	+ 4.5	+ 7.5	+ 5.8	− 3.9	$25,000	None	0.565	0.111	....	...	12,914	10.41	9.79	9.87	9.87	5.7
FHTFX	Federated Municipal Opport.	*'87	I	TF	261.2	n/a	[12]∫†	+ 15.4	+ 1.8	+ 9.5	+ 4.9	− 7.4	$1,500	1%+ERF	0.507	0.416	....	...	11,733	10.99	9.73	9.73	9.83	5.2
LMSFX	Federated Municipal Securities Cl.A	'76	I	TF	501.0	n/a	∫†	+ 6.2	+ 0.3	+ 7.9	+ 5.0	− 10.4	$500	4.5	0.471	0.091	....	...	10,402	11.08	9.76	9.77	10.23	4.6
FUSGX	Federated Fund for U.S.Govt. Secs. Cl.A	'69	I	BD	975.3	n/a	★	+ 13.4	+ 3.5	+ 7.6	+ 6.1	+ 0.4	$500	4.5	0.486	0.48	....	...	13,197	7.97	7.42	7.47	7.82	6.2
LBUTX	Federated Utility Cl.A	*'87	IG	C	735.0	24.9	†	+ 24.9	+ 7.8	+ 11.9	+ 12.7	− 8.0	$500	4.5	0.375	0.298	2.314	...	14,403	13.47	11.65	11.88	12.57	3.0
FEUTX	Federated Utility Fund Cl.F	*'87	IG	SP	512.2	17.4	[13]†	+ 24.9	− 5.5	+ 14.6	+ 12.8	− 7.9	$1,500	1%+ERF	0.378	0.299	2.314	...	13,069	13.47	11.64	11.88	12.00	3.2
FIGTX	Federated US Govt.Secs. 2-5 yrs.	*'83	I	GB	661.7	n/a	[14]★	+ 8.4	− 1.9	+ 6.5	+ 7.5	− 1.0	$25,000	None	0.515	0.456	....	...	11,824	10.93	10.35	10.35	10.35	5.0
FSGVX	Federated US Govt.Secs. 1-3 yrs.	*'84	I	GB	491.9	n/a	[15]★	+ 4.3	− 0.8	+ 5.3	+ 5.9	+ 2.1	$25,000	None	0.481	0.43	....	...	11,851	10.54	10.32	10.32	10.32	4.7
FAEGX	Fidelity Advisor Equity Growth Cl.T	*'92	G	C	6950.4	n/a	....	+ 39.1	+ 13.0	+ 23.5	+ 37.7	+ 35.5	$2,500	3.5	....	....	6.61	5.70	32,960	72.66	57.08	71.61	74.21	....
FAGNX	Fidelity Advisor:Natural Resources Cl.T	*'87	GP	SP	281.6	n/a	[16]	+ 28.6	+ 30.5	+ 0.2	− 16.3	+ 34.2	$2,500	3.5	....	0.01	0.71	...	18,454	24.28	15.06	22.58	23.40	....
FAGVX	Fidelity Advisor:Govt.Invest.Cl.T	*'87	I	GB	231.7	n/a	[17]	+ 17.2	+ 2.0	+ 8.2	+ 2.5	− 3.0	$2,500	3.5	....	0.487	....	...	12,462	9.95	9.15	9.15	9.48	....
FAGOX	Fidelity Advisor:Growth Opport.Cl.T	*'87	G	C	24122.2	n/a	[17]	+ 33.0	+ 17.8	+ 28.4	+ 23.5	− 6.3	$2,500	3.5	0.35	0.37	1.87	0.03	23,931	55.01	45.07	46.66	48.35	0.7
FAHIX	Fidelity Advisor:Municipal Income Cl.T	*'87	I	TF	334.8	n/a	[18]	+ 16.3	+ 2.7	+ 9.6	+ 5.8	− 2.7	$2,500	3.5	0.521	0.55	....	...	12,425	12.61	11.63	11.63	12.05	4.3
FAHYX	Fidelity Advisor:High Yield Cl.T	*'87	IR	CV	2344.8	n/a	[19]	+ 18.1	+ 17.8	+ 13.8	− 4.1	+ 1.1	$2,500	3.5	0.608	0.082	0.13	...	15,135	12.21	11.11	11.37	11.78	5.2
FAIGX	Fidelity Advisor:Growth & Inc. Cl. T	*'87	IG	CV,C	2778.6	n/a	[17]	+ 13.9	+ 8.2	+ 22.1	+ 15.0	− 0.2	$2,500	3.5	0.51	0.349	1.73	0.05	16,407	19.74	17.74	18.25	18.91	2.7
FAERX	Fidelity Advisor:Overseas Cl.T	*'90	G	INTL	1407.9	n/a	[20]	+ 8.6	+ 12.3	+ 11.3	+ 11.3	+ 35.0	$2,500	3.5	0.04	....	0.14	...	20,803	23.76	16.91	23.76	24.62	0.2
FASFX	Fidelity Advisor:Short Fxd.-Inc. Cl.T	*'87	IS	ST	308.7	n/a	[17]	+ 9.6	+ 2.9	+ 5.5	+ 5.8	− 2.5	$2,500	1.5	0.54	....	....	...	11,868	9.35	9.11	9.11	9.25	5.8
FASPX	Fidelity Advisor:Strategic Opport. Cl.T	*'83	G	C	406.4	n/a		+ 38.0	− 7.2	+ 24.8	+ 0.8	− 4.3	$2,500	3.5	....	....	0.65	0.68	14,323	28.63	21.84	23.07	23.91	....
FASMX	Fidelity Asset Manager	*'88	GI	SP	12240.2	n/a	....	+ 17.9	+ 6.2	+ 21.9	+ 15.1	+ 8.6	$2,500	None	0.60	0.476	3.15	...	17,839	18.76	16.92	18.38	18.38	3.3
FASGX	Fidelity Asset Manager Growth	*'91	GI	C	5064.2	n/a	....	+ 19.9	+ 7.8	+ 26.2	+ 17.5	+ 5.3	$2,500	None	0.35	....	2.68	...	18,689	20.55	18.50	19.67	19.67	1.8
FBALX	Fidelity Balanced	*'86	IG	B	5889.6	n/a	....	+ 14.6	+ 8.9	+ 22.8	+ 18.5	− 4.9	$2,500	None	0.46	0.21	1.27	...	16,373	18.22	14.55	15.36	15.36	3.0
FBGRX	Fidelity Blue Chip Growth	*'87	G	C	23298.0	n/a	....	+ 28.6	+ 14.1	+ 26.9	+ 33.0	+ 23.8	$2,500	3.0	0.10	0.14	2.06	2.07	33,664	60.11	49.12	60.11	60.11	0.2
FAGIX	Fidelity Capital & Income	'77	IR	BD	2641.4	n/a	[21]	+ 16.3	+ 9.7	+ 14.1	+ 3.2	+ 5.6	$2,500	None	0.789	0.123	0.26	0.39	15,277	10.34	9.23	9.29	9.29	8.5
FTHRX	Fidelity Intermed. Bond	*'75	IS	BD	3238.3	n/a		+ 12.4	+ 2.8	+ 7.3	+ 7.2	+ 0.4	$1,000	None	0.628	0.552	....	...	13,077	10.29	9.76	9.76	9.76	6.4
FCNTX	Fidelity Contrafund	'67	G	C	41035.1	n/a	[22]	+ 36.2	+ 16.1	+ 22.3	+ 30.7	+ 14.7	$2,500	3.0	0.35	0.30	3.92	4.67	28,673	67.33	56.12	60.02	61.88	0.6
FDESX	Fidelity Destiny Plan I	'69	G	C	6979.3	n/a	[23]	+ 36.8	+ 18.5	+ 30.5	+ 24.9	+ 4.8	$3,000	8.67	0.42	0.44	2.17	3.44	26,666	29.65	23.53	24.33	24.33	1.7
FDETX	Fidelity Destiny Plan II	*'85	G	C	5226.8	n/a	[24]	+ 35.8	+ 17.9	+ 29.3	+ 26.1	+ 24.9	$3,000	8.67	0.12	0.11	3.04	1.43	33,975	16.76	13.89	16.24	16.24	0.7

Uniform Footnote Explanations-See page 235. Stock Splits & Divs. (figures adjusted): [1] Was Keystone High Income(1/98). [2] Was Keystone America(11/97). [3] Was Keystone Intl(1/98). [4] Was Keystone Fund of Americas(7/97). [5] Was Keystone Precious Metals(1/98). [6] Was Small Co. Growth Cl. B. [7] Was Strategic Growth (1/98). [8] Was Keystone Tax Free(1/98). [9] Was under Liberty Funds. [10] Was Convert.Secs. & Inc.. [11] 1% E.R.F.reducing over 4 yrs. Was Fortress Group(4/96). [12] Was Fortress Group(4/96). 1% E.R.F.reducing over 4 yrs. [13] 1% E.R.F. reducing over 4 yrs. Was Fortress Utility(6/96). [14] Was Intermed.Govt.Trust(5/95). [15] Was Short-Intermed Govt(5/95). [16] Was Plymouth Series. Was Global Res.Cl.A(9/96). [17] Was Plymouth Series. [18] Was Plymouth Series. Was High Inc. Muni(12/97). [19] Was Plymouth Aggressive Inc.Ptfl. [20] Was European Invmt. [21] Closed to new investors. Was High Inc. [22] Was Contrafund. Sales charges waived for retirement accts. [23] Contractual Plan. [24] Contractual Plan. 3-for-1 split,June '96.

Ticker Symbol	Fund	Year Offered	Prin. Obj.	Type	Sept. 30, 1999 Total Net Assets (MIL.$)	Cash & Equiv (MIL.$)	See Foot-notes	Net Assets per Share % Change from Previous Dec. 31 At: Dec. 31 1995	1996	1997	1998	Dec. 31, 1999	Min. Unit	Max. Sales Chg. %	Distributions Per Share from Invest. Income 1998	1999	Security Profits 1998	1999	$10,000 Invested 12-31-93 Now Worth	PRICE RECORD NAV Per Sh — 1999 — High	Low	#12-31-99 NAV Per Shr.	Offer Price	% Yield From Inv. Inc.
FEMKX	Fidelity Emerging Markets	*'90	G	INTL	393.9	n/a	....	– 3.2	+ 10.0	– 40.9	– 26.6	+ 70.5	$2,500	3.0	....	....	....	...	6,466	12.02	6.60	12.02	12.39	....
FEQIX	Fidelity Equity Income	'66	IG	C	22848.3	n/a	1	+ 31.1	+ 20.5	+ 29.4	+ 12.1	+ 7.1	$2,500	None	0.85	0.82	2.39	5.13	24,763	63.00	51.81	53.48	53.48	1.6
FFIDX	Fidelity Fund	'30	GI	C	13270.7	n/a	....	+ 32.2	+ 18.9	+ 31.5	+ 29.8	+ 22.9	$2,500	None	0.24	0.21	1.81	2.21	33,798	42.61	34.25	42.61	42.61	0.6
FGOVX	Fidelity Govt. Inc.	'79	IS	GB	1588.8	n/a	....	+ 17.5	+ 1.6	+ 8.5	+ 8.0	– 5.8	$2,500	None	0.561	0.20	....	...	12,506	10.16	9.35	9.35	9.35	6.0
FGRIX	Fidelity Growth & Income	*'85	GI	C,CV	45985.1	n/a	1	+ 34.8	+ 18.1	+ 29.8	+ 27.0	+ 8.9	$2,500	3.0	0.39	0.28	2.16	2.44	29,236	50.18	41.90	47.16	47.16	0.8
FLPSX	Fidelity Low Priced Stock	*'89	G	C	6947.5	n/a	....	+ 24.8	+ 25.7	+ 25.5	+ 0.2	+ 4.9	$2,500	3.0	0.20	0.15	1.94	1.19	21,708	25.04	20.79	22.64	23.34	0.9
FMAGX	Fidelity Magellan Fund	'65	G	C	92187.0	n/a	2	+ 36.6	+ 9.4	+ 26.1	+ 32.5	+ 23.5	$2,500	3.0	0.67	0.73	5.15	11.39	30,282	136.63	118.82	136.63	140.86	0.5
FOCPX	Fidelity O-T-C	*'84	G	C	7411.2	n/a	1	+ 38.2	+ 13.0	+ 10.0	+ 37.5	+ 65.3	$2,500	3.0	....	....	2.38	4.16	37,990	67.97	43.62	67.97	67.97	....
FOSFX	Fidelity Overseas	*'84	G	GL	4235.1	n/a	1	+ 9.0	+ 13.0	+ 10.6	+ 12.8	+ 42.0	$2,500	3.0	0.20	0.44	0.51	2.64	22,082	48.01	34.57	48.01	48.01	0.4
FPURX	Fidelity Puritan	'47	IP	FL	24419.1	n/a	....	+ 21.1	+ 14.1	+ 17.9	+ 15.0	+ 1.4	$2,500	None	0.67	0.50	1.56	0.81	19,377	21.12	18.07	19.03	19.03	3.5
FDFFX	Fidelity Retirement Growth	*'83	IG	C	5389.9	n/a	....	+ 23.9	+ 7.8	+ 17.9	+ 35.2	+ 29.0	$2,500	None	0.14	....	2.13	0.61	27,464	26.10	19.87	25.85	25.85	0.5
FBIOX	Fidelity Select Ptfl:Biotechnology	*'85	G	C	1074.9	n/a	....	+ 49.1	+ 5.1	+ 14.6	+ 28.6	+ 75.9	$2,500	3.0	....	....	2.09	2.82	33,230	68.54	37.53	67.13	69.21	....
FDCPX	Fidelity Select Ptfl:Computers	*'85	G	C	2237.5	n/a	....	+ 52.1	+ 31.2	– 1.7	+ 95.5	+ 77.2	$2,500	3.0	....	....	....	14.92	81,887	106.67	66.88	104.51	107.74	....
FSELX	Fidelity Select Ptfl:Electronics	*'85	G	C	4270.9	n/a	....	+ 67.6	+ 41.7	+ 12.4	+ 51.1	+ 105.1	$2,500	3.0	....	....	....	6.62	96,954	90.91	46.37	88.88	91.63	....
FSPHX	Fidelity Select Ptfl:Health Care	*'81	G	C	2536.3	n/a	....	+ 44.9	+ 14.8	+ 28.8	+ 40.5	– 2.9	$2,500	3.0	0.19	0.08	6.17	7.85	35,455	145.25	117.34	124.82	128.68	0.1
FSTCX	Fidelity Select Ptfl:Telecommunications	*'85	CA	C	1010.9	n/a	....	+ 24.0	+ 5.1	+ 25.3	+ 40.3	+ 64.3	$2,500	3.0	....	....	2.96	10.48	39,185	91.16	71.50	88.70	91.44	....
FHIGX	Fidelity Spartan Muni Income	'77	I	TF,BD	4374.5	n/a	3∫†	+ 15.3	+ 1.6	+ 8.1	+ 5.9	– 6.7	$2,500	None	0.607	0.051	0.007	0.006	11,599	12.92	11.91	11.91	11.91	5.1
FTRNX	Fidelity Trend	'58	G	C	1217.2	n/a	....	+ 21.9	+ 9.4	+ 8.0	+ 15.7	+ 29.0	$2,500	None	0.05	....	6.95	...	20,035	74.61	55.44	71.72	71.72	0.1
FIUIX	Fidelity Utilities Fund	*'87	I	C	2488.6	n/a	....	+ 30.0	+ 11.0	+ 18.9	+ 27.5	+ 11.5	$2,500	None	0.35	0.08	1.29	...	23,147	26.93	22.46	25.77	25.77	1.4
FDVLX	Fidelity Value	*'78	G	C	4056.7	n/a	....	+ 27.1	+ 16.8	+ 21.2	...	+ 8.2	$2,500	None	0.55	0.73	7.15	5.62	20,928	57.32	41.38	43.81	43.81	1.3
FIFIX	First Investors Fund for Income	'70	I	BD	388.6	n/a	....	+ 17.8	+ 11.9	+ 12.2	+ 4.0	+ 2.4	$1,000	6.25	0.416	0.352	....	...	15,861	4.25	3.89	3.94	4.20	9.9
FIISX	First Investors Global Fund	'81	G	C	316.5	n/a		+ 17.8	+ 4.5	+ 10.8	+ 16.7	+ 28.9	$1,000	6.25	....	....	0.078	0.822	19,738	8.72	7.33	8.72	9.30	....
FITAX	First Investors Insured Tax Exempt	'76	IS	TF	994.4	n/a	∫†★	+ 15.7	+ 2.7	+ 8.0	+ 5.9	– 3.9	$1,000	6.25	0.516	0.43	....	...	12,525	10.67	9.68	9.71	10.36	5.0
FICAX	First Investors MSITF Calif.Cl.A	'87	I	TF	14.1	n/a	∫†★	+ 18.0	+ 3.9	+ 8.4	+ 5.2	– 3.7	$1,000	6.25	0.556	0.469	....	...	12,845	12.34	11.27	11.28	12.03	4.6
FIMAX	First Investors MSITF Mass. Cl.A	'86	I	TF	20.8	n/a	∫†★	+ 16.7	+ 2.2	+ 7.3	+ 3.3	– 2.7	$1,000	6.25	0.582	0.527	....	...	12,335	12.15	11.15	11.17	11.91	4.9
FTMIX	First Investors MSITF Michigan Cl.A	'86	I	TF	35.5	n/a	∫†★	+ 17.2	+ 3.1	+ 8.7	+ 4.8	– 3.3	$1,000	6.25	0.591	0.501	....	...	12,552	13.24	12.15	12.16	12.97	4.6
FINJX	First Investors MSITF New Jersey Cl.A	*'88	I	TF	54.0	n/a	∫†★	+ 16.2	+ 3.2	+ 7.4	+ 4.8	– 2.4	$1,000	6.25	0.628	0.54	....	...	12,488	13.45	12.41	12.45	13.28	4.7
FIOHX	First Investors MSITF Ohio Cl.A	'86	I	TF	18.9	n/a	∫†★	+ 16.9	+ 3.9	+ 7.4	+ 4.4	– 2.1	$1,000	6.25	0.572	0.554	....	...	12,666	12.83	11.88	11.88	12.67	4.5
FTPAX	First Investors MSITF Penn. Cl.A	*'90	I	TF	37.9	n/a	∫†★	+ 17.9	+ 2.9	+ 7.8	+ 5.2	– 3.7	$1,000	6.25	0.709	0.41	....	...	12,573	13.42	12.35	12.36	13.18	5.4
FNYFX	First Investors N.Y.Insured Tax Free	'83	I	TF	169.8	n/a	∫†★	+ 15.1	+ 2.2	+ 7.8	+ 4.5	– 4.3	$1,000	6.25	0.68	0.553	....	...	12,174	15.03	13.64	13.66	14.57	4.7
FLEGX	Flag Investors Emerging Growth Cl.A	*'88	G	C	66.5	n/a	4	+ 37.2	+ 18.5	+ 14.9	+ 6.6	+ 48.6	$2,000	4.5	....	....	....	0.76	31,071	33.54	18.89	33.54	35.12	....
FLINX	Flag Investors Intermed. Term Inc. Cl.A	*'91	IS	GB	45.1	n/a	....	+ 15.1	+ 3.4	+ 6.9	+ 6.6	– 1.7	$2,000	1.5	0.60	0.35	....	...	12,958	10.53	9.95	9.95	10.10	5.9
FLMMX	Flag Investors Managed Munic.	*'90	I	TF	35.2	n/a	∫†	+ 17.4	+ 2.1	+ 7.9	+ 5.5	– 5.7	$2,000	4.5	0.495	0.28	....	...	12,005	11.07	10.03	10.04	10.51	4.7
TISHX	Flag Investors Communications Cl. A	*'84	IG	C	1644.3	n/a	5	+ 31.6	+ 7.1	+ 36.3	+ 79.5	+ 44.7	$2,000	4.5	0.125	0.19	1.08	4.72	46,903	45.81	33.14	43.65	45.71	0.3
FLTSX	Flag Invest.Total Return US Treas. Cl.A	*'88	I	GB	116.8	n/a	....	+ 20.5	– 1.6	+ 5.6	+ 7.6	– 8.1	$2,000	4.45	0.583	0.368	....	...	11,961	10.35	9.13	9.13	9.56	6.1
FLVBX	Flag Investors Value Builder Cl.A	*'92	GI	C	650.5	n/a	....	+ 32.4	+ 24.4	+ 22.4	+ 17.5	+ 13.3	$2,000	4.5	0.565	0.365	0.33	0.57	26,731	25.70	22.16	24.75	25.92	2.2
FECLX	Fortis Equity:Capital Fund Cl.A	'49	GI	C	545.3	n/a	....	+ 21.5	+ 18.7	+ 23.2	+ 23.7	+ 30.9	$500	4.75	....	....	6.26	5.35	29,461	25.22	19.80	22.91	24.05	....
FGRWX	Fortis Growth Fund Cl.A	'59	G	C	738.3	n/a	....	+ 25.3	+ 17.3	+ 13.3	+ 16.9	+ 48.4	$500	4.75	....	0.049	9.57	6.845	26,491	36.07	27.33	36.07	37.87	....
FIUGX	Fortis Inc:U.S.Govt.Secs.Cl.E	*'73	I	GB	216.8	n/a	....	+ 15.5	+ 3.1	+ 8.5	+ 8.3	– 2.5	$500	4.5	0.507	0.445	....	...	12,892	9.49	8.81	8.81	9.23	5.5
FRGRX	Founders Growth	'61	G	C	2566.6	n/a	....	+ 45.5	+ 16.4	+ 26.2	+ 24.7	+ 37.6	$1,000	None	0.01	....	1.13	4.18	35,427	26.26	20.02	23.90	23.90	....
FPPTX	FPA Capital Fund	*'68	G	C	530.0	5.5	....	+ 37.7	+ 46.0	+ 16.3	– 4.5	+ 3.1	$1,500	6.5	0.25	0.16	1.59	0.83	25,231	36.71	29.03	31.02	33.18	0.8
FPNIX	FPA New Income	*'69	I	BD	534.4	2.5	....	+ 13.8	+ 9.8	+ 7.9	+ 1.8	– 0.7	$1,500	4.5	0.49	0.36	0.02	...	13,643	10.94	10.26	10.30	10.79	4.5
FPRAX	FPA Paramount Fund	*'58	G	C	171.2	33.9	6	+ 11.6	+ 36.8	– 1.5	– 7.7	+ 1.3	$1,500	6.5	0.20	0.04	1.90	...	15,241	10.10	8.10	9.19	9.83	2.0
FPPFX	FPA Perennial Fund	*'84	GI	C	39.4	0.9	....	+ 14.9	+ 39.6	+ 20.6	+ 2.2	+ 4.1	$1,500	6.5	0.15	....	2.02	0.52	20,560	24.11	17.50	20.45	21.87	0.7

Uniform Footnote Explanations-See page 235. Stock Splits & Divs. (figures adjusted): [1] Sales charges waived for retirement accts. [2] Closed to new investors(9/30/97). [3] Was Court St. Hi Yld TF(10/97). [4] Min.invmt.for Flag investors is $500. [5] Was Tel. Income (9/98). [6] Closed to new investors.

Ticker Symbol	Fund	Year Offered	Prin. Obj.	Type	Sept. 30, 1999 Total Net Assets (MIL.$)	Sept. 30, 1999 Cash & Equiv (MIL.$)	See Foot-notes	Net Assets per Share % Change from Previous Dec. 31 — At: Dec. 31 1995	1996	1997	1998	Dec. 31, 1999	Min. Unit	Max. Sales Chg. %	Distributions Per Share from Invest. Income 1998	Invest. Income 1999	Security Profits 1998	Security Profits 1999	$10,000 Invested 12-31-93 Now Worth	PRICE RECORD — 1999 — High	1999 Low	NAV Per Sh #12-31-99 NAV Per Shr.	Offer Price	% Yield From Inv. Inc.
	Franklin Funds:																							
FISAX	**Adjust.U.S.Govt.Secs.**	*'87	I	SP	288.7	n/a	[1]★	+ 8.9	+ 4.6	+ 6.8	+ 3.8	+ 3.9	$1,000	2.25	0.498	0.409	....	...	12,871	9.37	9.26	9.27	9.48	5.3
AGEFX	**AGE High Income Cl.I**	*'69	I	BD	2892.7	n/a	....	+ 17.8	+ 11.8	+ 11.3	+ 1.5	− 0.3	$1,000	4.25	0.264	0.242	....	...	14,596	2.78	2.48	2.51	2.62	10.1
FKTFX	**Calif. Tax-Free Income Cl.I**	*'77	I	TF	13927.1	n/a	....	+ 14.6	+ 4.6	+ 8.5	+ 6.1	− 4.6	$1,000	4.25	0.40	0.332	0.007	0.005	12,730	7.45	6.73	6.73	7.03	5.7
FKDNX	**Dynatech Series**	'67	G	C	499.3	n/a	....	+ 26.2	+ 28.9	+ 14.9	+ 25.8	+ 37.0	$1,000	4.5	....	0.37	....	...	33,888	27.85	20.69	27.77	29.46	....
FKREX	**Equity Fund**	*'33	G	C	669.2	n/a	....	+ 32.6	+ 22.7	+ 26.8	+ 12.8	+ 51.4	$1,000	4.5	0.017	0.055	0.576	0.564	34,704	15.11	10.25	15.11	16.03	0.1
FISEX	**Equity Income**	*'88	IR	SP	389.5	n/a	....	+ 25.1	+ 12.3	+ 26.6	+ 6.5	− 6.1	$1,000	4.5	0.638	0.527	1.07	...	17,733	21.04	17.25	17.66	18.74	3.4
FKTIX	**Federal Tax Free Income**	*'83	I	TF	6915.5	n/a	....	+ 14.6	+ 4.0	+ 8.7	+ 5.8	− 3.1	$1,000	4.25	0.672	0.608	....	0.007	12,658	12.44	11.39	11.39	11.90	5.6
FRGUX	**Global Utilities**	*'92	GI	C,GL	198.9	n/a	....	+ 27.0	+ 14.6	+ 26.1	+ 6.1	+ 49.4	$1,000	4.5	0.188	0.35	0.775	2.96	26,532	22.11	14.95	20.35	21.59	0.9
FKGRX	**Growth Series**	*'48	G	C	2127.8	n/a	....	+ 38.4	+ 16.7	+ 18.6	+ 18.5	+ 12.1	$1,000	4.5	0.439	0.454	0.209	0.264	26,184	35.26	31.00	34.54	36.65	1.2
FKINX	**Income Series**	*'48	I	C,BD	6782.3	n/a	....	+ 20.3	+ 9.9	+ 16.7	+ 0.4	− 1.3	$1,000	4.25	0.18	0.165	....	0.014	14,341	2.37	2.13	2.15	2.25	8.0
FRDPX	**Mgd.Tr-Rising Divds.**	*'87	I	C	364.0	n/a	....	+ 30.0	+ 23.1	+ 32.1	+ 5.7	− 10.2	$1,000	4.5	0.112	0.171	1.986	1.66	19,022	24.55	18.65	19.30	20.48	0.5
FRHIX	**Tax Free:Hi Yld.TF Inc**	*'86	I	TF	5654.1	n/a	∫†	+ 15.9	+ 5.3	+ 10.3	+ 4.7	− 3.5	$1,000	4.25	0.679	0.59	....	0.003	13,261	11.55	10.51	10.51	10.98	6.2
FTFIX	**Tax Free:Insur.TF Inc.**	*'85	I	TF	1585.3	n/a	∫†★	+ 13.3	+ 3.5	+ 7.9	+ 5.9	− 3.7	$1,000	4.25	0.693	0.56	0.052	0.02	12,452	12.36	11.26	11.26	11.76	5.9
FRALX	**Tax Free:Alabama TF Inc**	*'87	I	TF	224.2	n/a	∫†	+ 14.9	+ 3.8	+ 8.8	+ 3.3	− 4.0	$1,000	4.25	0.631	0.55	0.047	0.007	12,315	11.76	10.69	10.69	11.16	5.7
FTAZX	**Tax Free:Arizona TF Inc**	*'87	I	TF	824.5	n/a	∫†	+ 14.2	+ 2.9	+ 8.0	+ 5.3	− 4.4	$1,000	4.25	0.631	0.523	0.015	...	12,265	11.47	10.37	10.37	10.83	5.8
FRCIX	**Tax Free:Cal.Insur.TF Inc.**	*'85	I	TF	1708.5	n/a	∫†★	+ 16.0	+ 4.0	+ 8.0	+ 6.3	− 3.9	$1,000	4.25	0.634	0.56	0.067	...	12,618	12.60	11.49	11.50	12.01	5.3
FRCOX	**Tax Free:Colo. TF Inc**	*'87	I	TF	286.5	n/a	∫†	+ 15.7	+ 3.6	+ 8.6	+ 5.6	− 4.7	$1,000	4.25	0.61	0.545	0.076	0.012	12,406	12.15	10.96	10.96	11.45	5.3
FXCTX	**Tax Free:Connecticut TF Inc.**	*'88	I	TF	236.0	n/a	....	+ 14.0	+ 3.8	+ 8.2	+ 5.8	− 5.1	$1,000	4.25	0.583	0.514	....	...	12,174	11.35	10.19	10.19	10.64	5.5
FRFLX	**Tax Free:Florida TF Inc. Cl.I**	*'87	I	TF	1639.9	n/a	∫†	+ 14.3	+ 3.7	+ 7.8	+ 6.2	− 3.7	$1,000	4.25	0.625	0.553	0.008	...	12,649	11.98	10.94	10.95	11.44	5.5
FMDTX	**Tax Free:Maryland TF Inc.**	*'88	I	TF	245.0	n/a	....	+ 16.9	+ 3.3	+ 8.3	+ 5.7	− 4.1	$1,000	4.25	0.586	0.508	0.043	0.03	12,594	11.74	10.67	10.67	11.14	5.3
FMISX	**Tax Free:Mass.Insur.TF Inc.**	*'85	I	TF	329.6	n/a	∫†★	+ 13.8	+ 3.3	+ 9.0	+ 5.3	− 4.0	$1,000	4.25	0.59	0.525	0.068	...	12,487	11.78	10.72	10.73	11.21	5.3
FTTMX	**Tax Free:Michigan Insur.TF Inc.**	*'85	I	TF	1143.5	n/a	∫†★	+ 13.5	+ 3.6	+ 7.9	+ 6.3	− 2.6	$1,000	4.25	0.613	0.545	0.055	0.001	12,637	12.34	11.41	11.41	11.92	5.1
FMINX	**Tax Free:Minn.Insur.TF Inc.**	*'85	I	TF	484.9	n/a	∫†★	+ 13.0	+ 2.4	+ 6.7	+ 5.6	− 6.5	$1,000	4.25	0.624	0.244	0.024	0.024	11,800	12.23	11.13	11.13	11.62	5.4
FRMOX	**Tax Free:Missouri TF Inc**	*'87	I	TF	380.2	n/a	∫†	+ 15.3	+ 3.3	+ 8.6	+ 5.6	− 4.6	$1,000	4.25	0.623	0.552	0.032	0.01	12,379	12.28	11.09	11.09	11.58	5.4
FRNJX	**Tax Free:N.J. TF Inc**	*'88	I	TF	672.0	n/a	∫†	+ 15.2	+ 3.4	+ 8.1	+ 6.0	− 3.7	$1,000	4.25	0.62	0.552	....	...	12,474	12.06	11.01	11.01	11.50	5.4
FNYTX	**Tax Free:N.Y. TF Inc**	*'82	I	TF	4608.6	n/a	....	+ 13.2	+ 2.8	+ 8.2	+ 5.7	− 3.2	$1,000	4.25	0.655	0.578	....	...	12,497	12.12	11.09	11.10	11.59	5.7
FRNYX	**Tax Free:N.Y.Insur. TF Inc.**	*'91	I	TF	246.7	n/a	★	+ 18.1	+ 3.7	+ 8.5	+ 5.8	− 3.7	$1,000	4.25	0.57	0.508	0.057	0.004	12,455	11.77	10.77	10.77	11.25	5.1
FXNCX	**Tax Free:N.C. TF Inc.**	*'87	I	TF	344.1	n/a	∫†	+ 15.8	+ 3.5	+ 8.7	+ 5.8	− 4.5	$1,000	4.25	0.613	0.545	....	...	12,426	12.26	11.10	11.10	11.59	5.3
FTOIX	**Tax Free:Ohio Insur.TF Inc.**	*'85	I	TF	751.2	n/a	∫†★	+ 14.0	+ 3.4	+ 7.4	+ 5.8	− 4.5	$1,000	4.25	0.622	0.405	0.03	0.017	12,229	12.57	11.53	11.53	12.04	5.2
FRORX	**Tax Free:Oregon TF Inc**	*'87	I	TF	465.2	n/a	∫†	+ 14.8	+ 3.7	+ 8.0	+ 5.3	− 4.2	$1,000	4.25	0.619	0.534	....	...	12,347	11.92	10.83	10.83	11.31	5.5
FRPAX	**Tax Free:Penn.TF Inc**	*'86	I	TF	699.7	n/a	∫†	+ 14.0	+ 3.8	+ 9.2	+ 5.4	− 4.4	$1,000	4.25	0.561	0.486	0.014	...	12,604	10.59	9.59	9.59	10.02	5.6
FPRTX	**Tax Free:P.R. TF Inc.**	*'85	I	TF	210.1	n/a	∫†	+ 14.1	+ 3.1	+ 8.5	+ 5.6	− 2.6	$1,000	4.25	0.607	0.53	0.038	0.02	12,577	11.95	11.02	11.02	11.51	5.3
FRVAX	**Tax Free:Virginia TF Inc**	*'87	I	TF	361.6	n/a	∫†	+ 15.1	+ 3.0	+ 8.2	+ 5.7	− 4.4	$1,000	4.25	0.609	0.535	0.026	...	12,379	11.97	10.85	10.85	11.33	5.4
FKUSX	**U.S. Govt. Securities Cl.I**	*'70	I	BD	7907.0	n/a	★	+ 16.2	+ 4.3	+ 9.1	+ 6.4	− 0.8	$1,000	4.25	0.452	0.325	....	...	13,579	6.92	6.46	6.53	6.82	6.6
FKUTX	**Utilities Series**	*'48	GI	C	1597.6	n/a	....	+ 29.7	+ 1.8	+ 23.7	+ 7.2	− 12.0	$1,000	4.25	0.524	0.792	0.331	0.364	13,605	11.07	8.47	8.59	8.97	5.8
FEFPX	**Frontier Funds:Equity Ptfl.**	'92	G	C	0.5	n/a	....	− 1.3	− 17.7	− 39.5	− 28.5	+ 48.9	$1,000	8.0	....	....	....	...	4,515	3.56	2.13	3.32	3.61	....
GABVX	**Gabelli Value Fund**	*'89	G	C	1047.6	n/a	†	+ 22.5	+ 8.7	+ 47.7	+ 22.9	+ 31.7	$1,000	5.5	....	....	1.49	1.72	31,865	20.85	15.98	19.45	20.58	....
GSCGX	**Goldman Sachs Capital Growth Cl.A**	'90	G	C	1957.5	n/a	....	+ 24.7	+ 26.9	+ 34.7	+ 33.3	+ 26.8	$1,500	5.5	....	....	0.722	2.19	36,353	28.42	22.78	27.47	29.07	....
GSIFX	**Goldman Sachs Intl. Equity Cl.A**	*'92	G	INTL	952.7	n/a	....	+ 18.8	+ 18.7	+ 4.3	+ 17.7	+ 30.0	$1,500	5.5	....	0.338	1.114	2.57	20,952	26.98	20.78	25.12	26.58	....
GSGRX	**Goldman Sachs Growth & Income Cl.A**	*'93	GI	C	794.9	n/a	....	+ 33.3	+ 23.9	+ 27.5	− 5.7	+ 5.6	$1,500	5.5	0.135	0.228	....	1.33	22,207	27.34	22.50	23.93	25.32	0.5
GSSQX	**Goldman Sachs Core U.S. Equity Cl.A**	*'91	G	C	602.6	n/a	....	+ 35.2	+ 21.5	+ 31.5	+ 20.5	+ 22.3	$1,500	5.5	0.043	0.001	0.479	3.54	32,248	37.31	30.95	34.82	36.85	0.1
GPAFX	**Guardian Park Ave. Cl.A**	*'72	GR	FL	2811.2	n/a	....	+ 34.2	+ 26.0	+ 34.3	+ 15.0	+ 17.0	$1,000	4.5	0.167	0.068	0.998	1.228	30,127	62.39	50.63	59.42	62.22	0.3
TACAX	**Hancock(J) Cal.Tax Free Inc.Cl.A**	*'89	I	TF	304.5	n/a	[2]∫†	+ 21.4	+ 4.3	+ 9.8	+ 6.0	− 2.7	$1,000	4.75	0.506	0.566	....	...	13,034	11.27	10.33	10.33	10.82	4.7

Uniform Footnote Explanations-See page 235. **Stock Splits & Divs.** (figures adjusted): [1] Was Adjust.Rate Mtge. [2] Formerly Transamerica Group.

Ticker Symbol	Fund	Year Offered	Prin. Obj.	Type	Sept. 30, 1999 Total Net Assets (MIL.$)	Cash & Equiv (MIL.$)	See Foot-notes	Net Assets per Share % Change from Previous Dec. 31 At: Dec. 31 1995	1996	1997	1998	Dec. 31, 1999	Min. Unit	Max. Sales Chg. %	Distributions Per Share from Invest. Income 1998	1999	Security Profits 1998	1999	$10,000 Invested 12-31-93 Now Worth	PRICE RECORD NAV Per Sh — 1999 — High	Low	#12-31-99 NAV Per Shr.	Offer Price	% Yield From Inv. Inc.
TSEGX	Hancock(J) Small Cap. Growth Cl. B	*'87	G	C	451.1	n/a	[1]	+ 42.1	+ 12.9	+ 14.9	+ 8.5	+ 59.8	$1,000	ERF	....	....	....	1.508	31,481	13.83	8.94	13.83	13.83	....
NTTFX	Hancock(J) Global Technology	*'83	GI	C	462.5	n/a	[2]	+ 46.6	+ 12.5	+ 6.3	+ 47.9	+ 130.2	$1,000	5.0	....	....	....	3.03	65,359	84.23	37.89	84.23	88.66	....
TSGIX	Hancock(J) Govt.Inc. Cl.B	*'88	IP	GB	173.0	n/a	[3]	+ 17.2	+ 0.6	+ 8.4	+ 7.3	− 3.6	$1,000	ERF	0.481	0.445	....	...	12,533	9.43	8.65	8.65	8.65	5.6
TAGRX	Hancock(J) Growth & Inc.Cl.A	*'49	GI	FL	445.6	n/a	[4]	+ 36.5	+ 22.2	+ 36.4	+ 15.6	+ 27.3	$1,000	5.75	0.141	0.046	0.934	...	30,669	27.49	20.38	27.02	28.44	0.5
TSHYX	Hancock(J) High Yld. Bond Cl.B	*'87	I	BD	814.7	n/a	[5]	+ 13.9	+ 13.6	+ 16.2	− 11.7	+ 8.2	$1,000	ERF	0.659	0.56	....	0.098	13,560	6.82	6.24	6.31	6.31	10.4
TSHTX	Hancock(J) High Yld.Tax Free Cl.B	*'86	I	TF	111.2	n/a	[5]∫†	+ 18.4	....	+ 8.5	+ 4.2	− 5.0	$1,000	ERF	0.429	0.428	....	...	12,005	9.59	8.66	8.66	8.66	5.0
FRBFX	Hancock(J)Inv. II Regional Bank Cl. B	*'85	G	SP	3341.9	n/a	[6]	+ 47.3	+ 28.2	+ 52.6	− 2.3	− 24.9	$1,000	ERF	0.225	0.093	....	...	21,101	54.72	38.28	39.13	39.13	0.6
JHNBX	Hancock (J) Bond Cl. A	*'73	I	BD	1235.0	n/a	[7]	+ 18.8	+ 3.8	+ 9.3	+ 6.7	− 6.5	$1,000	4.5	0.911	0.161	....	...	13,070	15.38	14.17	14.17	14.84	6.1
SOVIX	Hancock(J.)Sovereign Investors Cl.A	'36	GI	FL	1746.4	n/a	[8]	+ 28.9	+ 17.5	+ 28.9	+ 15.3	+ 2.2	$1,000	5.0	0.31	0.26	1.29	...	22,568	26.07	23.30	24.51	25.80	1.2
TAMBX	Hancock(J) Tax Free Bond Cl.A	*'90	I	TF	558.6	n/a	[4]∫†	+ 19.7	+ 4.0	+ 9.5	+ 4.9	− 3.8	$1,000	4.75	0.508	0.51	....	...	12,504	11.03	10.01	10.02	10.49	4.8
HULAX	Hawaiian Tax Free Trust	*'85	I	TF	605.2	n/a	∫†	+ 15.1	+ 3.7	+ 6.9	+ 3.1	− 3.1	$1,000	4.0	0.327	0.562	....	...	12,161	11.79	10.80	10.81	11.26	2.9
HRTVX	Heartland Value Fund	*'84	G	C	1117.1	n/a	[9]	+ 29.7	+ 20.9	+ 22.9	− 13.5	+ 24.6	$1,000	None	....	....	....	...	21,103	36.50	26.53	36.50	36.50	....
HRCPX	Heritage Capital Apprec. Trust Cl.A	*'85	G	C	172.4	n/a	....	+ 20.1	+ 18.5	+ 42.4	+ 33.7	+ 39.7	$1,000	4.75	....	....	1.319	2.62	36,907	33.26	24.28	32.33	33.94	....
HRCVX	Heritage Income-Growth Trust Cl.A	*'86	IG	FL	60.4	n/a	....	+ 27.5	+ 21.9	+ 26.5	+ 3.5	+ 1.3	$1,000	4.75	0.333	0.255	0.621	...	20,428	16.65	14.66	15.30	16.06	2.1
HRSCX	Heritage Small Cap Stock Cl.A	*'93	G	C	130.9	n/a	....	+ 36.9	+ 27.1	+ 29.1	− 12.2	+ 7.1	$1,000	4.75	....	....	....	...	21,123	27.52	21.52	26.88	28.22	....
HSTVX	Heritage Value Equity Cl.A	*'94	G	C	14.9	n/a	....	+ 36.5	+ 13.1	+ 25.2	− 0.7	− 2.9	$1,000	4.75	0.164	....	0.119	...	18,637	21.52	17.37	18.79	19.73	0.8
TWRSX	Hibernia Capital Apprec.	*'88	G	C	345.1	n/a	[10]	+ 37.4	+ 23.3	+ 31.3	+ 25.4	+ 18.2	$1,000	4.5	0.024	....	2.78	3.15	31,982	27.73	24.05	25.75	26.96	0.1
TLMIX	Hibernia La. Munic. Income	*'88	I	TF	91.1	n/a	[11]∫†	+ 15.6	+ 4.0	+ 8.2	+ 4.5	− 3.4	$1,000	4.5	0.379	0.495	0.112	0.095	12,475	11.48	10.41	10.43	10.75	3.5
TWRGX	Hibernia U.S. Govt. Income	*'88	I	GB	84.3	n/a	[12]	+ 15.1	+ 3.5	+ 7.9	+ 5.8	− 1.4	$1,000	4.5	0.388	0.516	....	...	12,967	10.38	9.69	9.69	9.99	3.9
IDITX	IDEX II:Flexible Income Ptfl.Cl.A	*'87	I	FL	14.5	n/a	....	+ 18.2	+ 3.3	+ 11.1	+ 7.6	+ 0.4	$500	4.75	0.583	0.496	....	...	14,054	10.00	9.37	9.48	9.95	5.9
IGLBX	IDEX II:Global Ptfl.Cl.A	*'92	G	GL	435.4	n/a	....	+ 19.9	+ 26.7	+ 20.1	+ 24.9	+ 58.8	$500	5.5	....	....	....	...	35,825	43.71	27.40	43.71	46.25	....
IDETX	IDEX II:Growth Ptfl.Cl.A	*'86	G	C	1331.6	n/a	....	+ 47.1	+ 16.8	+ 16.4	+ 63.9	+ 34.1	$500	5.5	....	....	0.386	...	40,307	54.00	35.54	48.06	50.86	....
IHIYX	IDEX II:Income Plus Cl.A	*'85	I	BD	60.5	n/a	....	+ 18.0	+ 9.0	+ 11.1	+ 4.2	− 6.1	$500	4.75	0.673	0.108	0.197	...	13,422	10.39	9.56	9.56	10.04	6.7
IGTEX	IDEX II:Tax Exempt Ptfl.Cl.A	*'85	I	TF	21.2	n/a	....	+ 12.6	+ 1.8	+ 9.9	+ 4.5	− 7.5	$500	4.75	0.492	0.372	0.197	...	11,897	11.76	10.35	10.38	10.90	4.5
INBNX	IDS Bond Cl.A	*'74	IS	BD	2570.7	n/a	[13]	+ 21.3	+ 2.9	+ 8.5	+ 5.3	− 0.8	$2,000	5.0	0.344	0.307	0.045	...	13,552	5.13	4.74	4.76	5.01	6.9
INVPX	IDS Equity Select Cl.A	'57	G	C	1157.5	n/a	[14]	+ 27.9	+ 24.5	+ 29.3	+ 18.7	+ 24.1	$2,000	5.0	0.03	....	1.511	...	27,933	18.46	14.00	18.23	19.19	0.2
INIDX	IDS Growth Cl.A	*'72	G	C	4535.8	n/a	[15]§	+ 41.1	+ 24.5	+ 20.5	+ 22.5	+ 37.4	$2,000	5.0	....	....	1.701	...	36,698	50.96	37.12	50.96	53.64	....
INHYX	IDS High Yield Tax Exempt Cl.A	'78	I	TF	5246.9	n/a	∫†	+ 16.9	+ 1.2	+ 9.0	+ 5.3	− 7.6	$2,000	5.0	0.257	0.024	....	...	11,919	4.69	4.29	4.29	4.52	5.7
INMUX	IDS Mutual Cl.A	'40	GIS	B	3101.2	n/a	....	+ 24.6	+ 13.4	+ 17.3	+ 9.1	− 0.5	$2,000	5.0	0.451	0.26	1.508	...	17,470	14.15	12.48	12.69	13.36	3.4
INNDX	IDS New Dimensions Cl.A	'68	G	C	13570.7	n/a	....	+ 35.6	+ 24.5	+ 24.4	+ 28.2	+ 24.1	$2,000	5.0	0.059	....	1.689	...	32,410	36.55	28.25	35.78	37.66	0.2
INSEX	IDS Selective Cl.A	'45	IS	BD	1113.0	n/a	....	+ 20.6	+ 2.3	+ 6.7	+ 7.9	− 3.4	$2,000	5.0	0.562	0.482	0.073	...	13,131	9.31	8.47	8.47	8.92	6.3
INSTX	IDS Stock Cl.A	'45	IS	C	3104.8	n/a	....	+ 25.4	+ 19.3	+ 24.8	+ 18.9	+ 4.3	$2,000	5.0	0.309	0.154	2.036	...	22,505	29.92	25.47	27.63	29.08	1.1
INTAX	IDS Tax Exempt Bond Cl.A	'76	I	TF	892.9	n/a	∫†	+ 18.4	+ 0.6	+ 9.1	+ 5.4	− 4.8	$2,000	5.0	0.204	0.188	....	...	12,087	4.20	3.78	3.78	3.98	5.1
FIIIX	Invesco Industrial Income	'60	IG	C	4614.8	n/a	....	+ 27.0	+ 16.4	+ 25.9	+ 15.8	+ 2.5	$1,000	None	0.696	0.188	1.511	...	21,252	17.09	14.77	15.25	15.25	4.6
FLRFX	Invesco Bluechip Growth	'35	GI	C	1223.6	n/a	....	+ 29.3	+ 20.9	+ 26.6	+ 40.8	+ 37.3	$1,000	None	0.02	....	0.506	0.761	34,892	8.42	6.37	8.11	8.11	0.2
INREX	Investors Research	*'59	G	L	20.1	n/a	....	+ 16.8	− 2.0	+ 21.4	+ 3.8	+ 13.2	None	5.75	....	....	....	...	16,426	4.30	3.55	4.30	4.47	....
TRUSX	ISI Total Return U.S.Treas.	*'88	I	GB	153.5	n/a	....	+ 21.0	....	+ 10.1	+ 7.6	− 7.6	$5,000	4.45	0.583	0.424	....	...	12,729	10.35	9.13	9.13	9.56	6.1
MCFIX	Ivy Bond Fund Cl.A	*'85	I	BD	77.9	n/a	[16]	+ 16.0	+ 7.7	+ 11.5	....	− 7.6	$1,000	4.75	0.684	0.521	....	...	12,356	9.53	8.29	8.29	8.70	7.9
MCGLX	Ivy Global Fund Cl.A	*'91	G	GL	11.2	0.7	....	+ 11.3	+ 16.2	− 8.7	+ 8.6	+ 26.4	$1,000	5.75	0.01	....	0.545	0.885	15,398	13.92	10.82	13.42	14.24	0.1
IVYFX	Ivy Growth Cl.A	'60	G	C	305.7	12.2	[17]	+ 26.1	+ 17.2	+ 11.3	+ 14.0	+ 31.6	$1,000	5.75	0.017	....	0.397	4.02	23,863	25.73	19.00	22.15	23.50	0.1
IVYIX	Ivy Growth with Income Cl.A	*'84	G	C	60.6	1.8	....	+ 22.8	+ 4.2	+ 11.4	+ 9.8	+ 10.7	$1,000	5.75	0.099	....	0.182	1.48	16,442	15.36	12.90	13.51	14.33	0.7
IVINX	Ivy International Cl.A	*'86	G	INTL	1488.4	74.4	....	+ 11.6	+ 19.7	+ 10.3	+ 5.6	+ 20.9	$1,000	5.75	....	0.237	....	2.485	19,432	48.41	39.93	47.09	49.96	....
JANSX	Janus Fund	*'70	G	C	32695.2	1929.0	....	+ 29.4	+ 19.7	+ 22.2	+ 35.1	+ 46.4	$1,000	None	....	0.34	....	4.89	37,025	47.15	33.55	44.05	44.05	....
JAVLX	Janus Twenty Fund	*'85	G	C	26170.5	4161.1	....	+ 36.2	+ 28.4	+ 29.4	+ 72.0	+ 64.5	$1,000	None	....	0.19	....	4.08	59,738	83.43	53.41	83.43	83.43	....

Uniform Footnote Explanations-See page 235. Stock Splits & Divs. (figures adjusted): [1] Formerly Transamerica Group. 5% E.R.F.. 4-for-1 split 5/98. [2] Was under AFA Group.. Was Natl.Tele.& Tech. [3] Formerly Transamerica Group. Incl. Govt. Secs. Tr.(9/95). 5% E.R.F.. [4] Formerly Transamerica Group. [5] 5% ERF reducing over 6 yrs. Formerly Transamerica Group. [6] 5% E.R.F.reducing 1% p.a.. [7] Incl. Invest. Quality Bond(9/95). [8] Was Sovereign Investors. [9] 3% E.R.F.. [10] Was Tower Cap. Apprec.(11/98). [11] Was Tower La. Muni. Inc. (11/98). [12] Was Tower U.S. Govt. Income (11/98). [13] $2.50 redemption charge. [14] Was IDS Variable Pymt. Was Equity Plus (3/95). [15] Also custodian fee. [16] Incl.ret.of cap.. [17] Incl. Amer. Fund(4/95). Was Ivy Fund.

Ticker Symbol	Fund	Year Offered	Prin. Obj.	Type	Sept. 30, 1999 Total Net Assets (MIL.$)	Sept. 30, 1999 Cash & Equiv (MIL.$)	See Foot-notes	Net Assets per Share % Change from Previous Dec. 31 At: Dec. 31 1995	1996	1997	1998	Dec. 31, 1999	Min. Unit	Max. Sales Chg. %	Distributions Per Share from Invest. Income 1998	Invest. Income 1999	Security Profits 1998	Security Profits 1999	$10,000 Invested 12-31-93 Now Worth	PRICE RECORD 1999 High	1999 Low	NAV Per Sh #12-31-99 NAV Per Shr.	Offer Price	% Yield From Inv. Inc.
JAVTX	Janus Venture Fund	*'85	G	C	1556.4	104.3	....	+ 26.4	+ 7.8	+ 12.4	+ 13.7	+ 137.9	$1,000	None	....	5.72	....	8.54	43,706	124.49	54.23	121.67	121.67	....
KAUFX	Kaufmann Fund	*'86	G	C	2904.5	n/a	1	+ 36.8	+ 20.8	+ 12.6	– 0.4	+ 22.1	$1,500	None	....	....	0.667	0.986	24,666	5.95	4.86	5.95	5.95	....
KGRAX	Kemper Growth Cl.A	'66	G	C	2054.3	n/a	....	+ 31.6	+ 16.2	+ 16.3	+ 14.2	+ 36.5	$1,000	5.75	....	....	0.06	1.76	26,087	19.43	14.84	18.56	19.69	....
KGRBX	Kemper Growth Cl.B	*'94	G	C	480.7	n/a	2	+ 16.9	+ 15.1	+ 15.1	+ 13.0	+ 35.0	$1,000	ERF	....	....	0.06	1.76	23,058	18.04	13.90	17.10	17.10	....
KHYAX	Kemper High Yield Cl.A	*'78	I	BD	2951.5	n/a	....	+ 15.9	+ 13.7	+ 11.0	+ 1.3	+ 1.4	$1,000	4.5	0.771	0.699	....	...	14,875	7.92	7.13	7.18	7.52	10.3
KHYBX	Kemper High Yield Cl.B	*'94	IG	BD	1146.1	n/a	2	+ 14.9	+ 12.7	+ 10.8	+ 0.5	+ 0.7	$1,000	ERF	0.699	0.642	....	...	14,549	7.91	7.12	7.17	7.17	9.7
KICAX	Kemper Inc. Cap. Pres. Cl.A	'72	I	BD	385.7	n/a	....	+ 20.6	+ 1.8	+ 8.3	+ 7.6	– 3.3	$1,000	4.5	0.535	0.44	....	...	13,378	8.73	7.95	7.96	8.34	6.4
KMBAX	Kemper Municipal Bond Cl.A	*'76	ISG	TF	2724.1	n/a	∫†	+ 17.9	+ 3.1	+ 6.9	+ 5.2	– 7.1	$1,000	4.5	0.465	0.118	0.245	...	12,001	10.33	9.39	9.40	9.84	4.7
KSCAX	Kemper Small Cap.Equity Cl.A	'69	G	C	562.2	n/a	3	+ 30.1	+ 14.0	+ 19.8	– 3.6	+ 33.2	$1,000	5.75	....	....	0.41	0.36	22,016	7.70	5.13	7.70	8.17	....
KCTAX	Kemper State TF Inc.Ser:Cal.Cl.A	*'83	I	TF	844.1	n/a	∫†	+ 18.9	+ 2.8	+ 8.3	+ 5.4	– 7.2	$1,000	4.5	0.327	0.06	0.135	...	12,261	7.57	6.87	6.91	7.24	4.5
KTCAX	Kemper Technology Cl.A	'48	GI	C	1955.4	n/a	....	+ 40.9	+ 20.8	+ 6.6	+ 43.3	+ 113.8	$1,000	5.75	....	....	1.07	1.94	61,648	28.33	14.31	28.33	30.06	....
KTRAX	Kemper Total Return Cl.A	*'64	B	C	2714.0	n/a	....	+ 25.5	+ 15.9	+ 18.8	+ 15.6	+ 7.8	$1,000	5.75	0.298	0.075	0.68	...	19,488	11.79	10.63	11.46	12.16	2.5
KTRBX	Kemper Total Return Cl.B	*'94	GI	C,FL	729.0	n/a	2	+ 24.3	+ 15.0	+ 17.6	+ 14.5	+ 7.3	$1,000	ERF	0.189	....	0.68	...	20,818	11.77	10.61	11.46	11.46	1.6
KUSAX	Kemper U.S.Govt. Secs. Cl.A	*'77	IP	BD	2857.2	n/a	★	+ 17.5	+ 3.2	+ 8.9	+ 7.4	– 5.0	$1,000	4.5	0.63	0.10	....	...	13,069	8.80	8.23	8.25	8.64	7.3
KUMBX	Kemper U.S.Mtge Cl.B	*'94	I	GB	142.6	n/a	2	+ 14.7	+ 1.1	+ 7.8	+ 5.7	– 4.6	$1,000	ERF	0.393	0.064	....	...	12,807	7.06	6.61	6.66	6.66	5.9
LMVTX	Legg Mason Value Trust	*'82	G	C	10332.6	n/a	....	+ 39.7	+ 37.4	+ 36.7	+ 46.4	+ 23.2	$1,000	None	....	0.627	0.986	...	47,989	77.74	60.60	75.27	75.27	....
	Liberty - Colonial:																							
COLFX	The Colonial Fund Cl. A	*'54	GI	B	906.5	n/a	....	+ 28.3	+ 16.4	+ 24.1	+ 12.8	+ 7.3	$1,000	5.75	0.26	0.11	0.438	1.19	21,961	11.26	9.80	10.11	10.73	2.4
COEAX	Global Equity Cl. A	*'92	G	GL	49.7	n/a	....	+ 15.3	+ 18.7	+ 14.7	+ 14.2	+ 15.7	$1,000	5.75	0.353	0.037	0.136	0.315	20,389	16.52	13.96	16.52	17.53	2.0
CFSAX	Federal Securities Cl. A	*'84	I	GB	683.4	n/a	....	+ 19.8	+ 0.7	+ 9.0	+ 8.4	– 4.7	$1,000	4.75	0.604	0.634	....	...	12,837	11.12	9.96	9.96	10.46	5.8
COLGX	Select Value Cl. A	'49	G	C	386.1	n/a	4	+ 37.9	+ 20.6	+ 33.2	+ 14.2	+ 8.6	$1,000	5.75	....	....	0.72	2.27	26,704	23.63	19.83	21.53	22.84	....
CHYBX	High Yield Municipal Cl. A	*'94	I	TF	67.4	n/a	....	+ 16.4	+ 3.8	+ 9.2	+ 6.0	– 11.1	$1,000	4.75	0.518	....	....	...	12,433	10.58	9.41	9.41	9.88	5.2
COLHX	High Yield Secs. Cl. A	'71	I	BD	543.8	n/a	....	+ 16.9	+ 11.4	+ 12.6	+ 1.3	+ 3.1	$1,000	4.75	0.571	0.412	....	...	15,269	6.94	6.49	6.55	6.88	8.3
COLTX	Tax Exempt Fund Cl. A	'78	I	TF	2142.4	n/a	5∫†	+ 17.2	+ 2.4	+ 8.9	+ 6.1	– 8.5	$1,000	4.75	0.895	0.163	....	...	11,812	13.94	12.52	12.53	13.15	6.8
CFGAX	U.S. Growth & Income Cl. A	*'92	GI	C	326.5	n/a	6	+ 29.6	+ 19.8	+ 35.3	+ 19.9	+ 11.1	$1,000	5.75	....	....	0.87	1.50	27,955	22.64	19.54	20.75	22.02	....
CVLAX	Value Fund Cl. A	*'98	G	C	12.2	n/a	....	....	....	+ 31.0	+ 7.6	+ 0.4	$1,000	5.75	0.19	0.029	1.94	...	.....	13.61	10.83	11.42	12.12	1.6
CSMIX	Small Cap Value Cl. A	*'86	G	C	221.6	n/a	7	+ 37.6	+ 18.4	+ 24.0	– 6.2	+ 4.1	$1,000	5.75	....	....	....	...	20,989	31.24	24.77	31.24	33.15	....
COSIX	Strategic Income Fund Cl. A	'77	I	BD	695.5	n/a		+ 19.4	+ 9.8	+ 8.2	+ 5.0	– 2.2	$1,000	4.75	0.576	0.336	....	...	14,028	7.14	6.58	6.62	6.95	8.3
CUTLX	Utilities Fund Cl. A	*'81	GI	C	346.1	n/a		+ 33.9	+ 5.8	+ 27.7	+ 21.4	+ 4.7	$1,000	4.75	0.494	0.314	0.658	...	20,649	23.47	20.53	22.54	23.66	2.1
	Liberty - Crabbe Huson:																							
CHREX	Real Estate Invstmt. Cl. A	*'94	GI	C	8.7	n/a	....	+ 9.1	+ 35.0	+ 18.0	– 23.3	– 9.0	$1,000	5.75	0.417	0.35	0.175	...	.....	12.95	8.69	9.21	9.67	4.3
	Liberty - Newport:																							
NJOAX	Japan Opport. Cl. A	*'96	G	INTL	16.8	n/a	8	....	....	– 0.1	+ 15.4	+ 147.6	$1,000	5.75	....	....	....	...	.....	25.78	9.98	25.78	27.35	....
CNTAX	Tiger Cl. A	*'89	G	INTL	276.9	n/a	9	+ 16.2	+ 10.9	– 34.1	– 12.1	+ 73.5	$1,000	5.75	0.151	....	....	...	11,397	13.50	6.76	13.50	14.32	1.1
	Liberty - Stein Roe Advisor:																							
SRSAX	Growth Stock Cl. A	*'97	G	C	87.6	n/a	....	....	....	....	+ 24.5	+ 35.9	$1,000	5.75	....	....	....	...	.....	19.97	14.64	19.97	21.19	....
STMAX	Tax Managed Growth Cl. A	*'96	G	C	89.1	n/a	....	....	....	+ 24.4	+ 21.5	+ 28.1	$2,500	5.75	....	....	....	...	.....	19.43	14.70	19.43	20.62	....
SAIAX	Young investor Cl. A	*'98	G	C	93.5	n/a	....	....	....	....	....	+ 30.8	$1,000	None	....	....	....	...	.....	17.90	13.51	17.90	17.90	....
	Liberty Funds:																							
FTITX	F.T.Series:Intl.Equity Cl.A	*'84	GR	INTL	268.2	n/a	†	+ 6.3	+ 5.7	+ 7.1	+ 24.1	+ 58.7	$500	4.5	....	....	1.481	...	23,795	31.10	19.52	30.97	32.77	....
LDDVX	Lindner Dividend	*'76	IG	C	671.4	n/a	10	+ 21.1	+ 11.3	+ 13.3	– 9.3	+ 9.3	$2,000	ERF	0.46	1.67	0.502	...	14,655	24.35	22.00	24.06	24.06	1.9
LDNRX	Lindner Growth Fund	'54	GI	C	382.2	n/a	10†	+ 19.9	+ 20.9	+ 8.4	– 17.3	+ 11.1	$2,000	ERF	....	0.23	2.74	0.873	14,351	17.51	14.15	16.84	16.84	....
LAFFX	Lord Abbett:Affiliated Cl.A	'34	GI	C	8926.4	253.0	....	+ 30.9	+ 20.0	+ 24.4	+ 14.0	+ 16.1	$250	5.75	0.24	0.15	0.95	1.76	26,768	16.95	14.51	15.20	16.13	1.5
LBNDX	Lord Abbett:Bond Debenture Cl.A	*'71	IR	BD,CV	2322.7	141.9	....	+ 15.9	+ 10.6	+ 12.2	+ 4.6	+ 2.4	$1,000	4.75	0.76	0.625	....	...	14,850	9.51	8.82	9.05	9.50	8.0

Uniform Footnote Explanations-See page 235. Stock Splits & Divs. (figures adjusted): [1] exit fee 0.2%. [2] 4% E.R.F.. [3] Was Summit. [4] Was Growth Shares(4/97). [5] Incl.Liberty Fin'l Tax Free Bond(3/95). [6] Was Colonial U.S. Stk. Fund (9/98). [7] Was Small Stock(4/97). [8] Was Newport Japan Fund(12/97). [9] Prior to 3/95 was Newport Tiger. [10] 2% E.R.F..

Ticker Symbol	Fund	Year Offered	Prin. Obj.	Type	Sept. 30, 1999 Total Net Assets (MIL.$)	Sept. 30, 1999 Cash & Equiv (MIL.$)	See Foot-notes	Net Assets per Share % Change from Previous Dec. 31 At: Dec. 31 1995	1996	1997	1998	Dec. 31, 1999	Min. Unit	Max. Sales Chg. %	Distributions Per Share from Invest. Income 1998	Invest. Income 1999	Security Profits 1998	Security Profits 1999	$10,000 Invested 12-31-93 Now Worth	PRICE RECORD 1999 High	1999 Low	NAV Per Sh #12-31-99 NAV Per Shr.	Offer Price	% Yield From Inv. Inc.
LCFIX	Lord Abbett: Cal. Tax-Free Inc. Cl.A	*'85	I	TF	207.0	n/a	∫†	+17.1	+3.2	+8.6	+6.2	−7.0	$1,000	4.75	0.544	0.43	....	...	11,627	11.07	9.80	9.81	10.14	5.4
LAGWX	Lord Abbett:Developing Growth Cl.A	'73	G	C,SP	1274.9	109.6	....	+45.1	+21.5	+30.2	+8.3	+34.9	$1,000	5.75	0.048	....	....	0.36	35,614	20.56	14.44	20.56	21.81	0.2
LAGIX	Lord Abbett:Global Income Cl.A	*'88	IR	GL	96.1	2.9	....	+16.6	+5.7	+4.0	+10.9	−10.3	$1,000	4.75	0.531	0.41	....	...	12,330	8.50	7.16	7.16	7.52	7.1
LAGEX	Lord Abbett:Global Equity Cl.A	*'88	G	GL	59.2	n/a	....	+8.2	+8.5	+7.7	+9.0	+12.4	$1,000	5.75	0.03	....	0.85	...	15,475	13.81	10.92	13.81	13.81	0.2
LAVLX	Lord Abbett Mid-Cap Value Cl.A	'83	G	C	354.6	26.4	1	+22.6	+19.0	+27.8	−0.4	−0.5	$1,000	5.75	....	....	....	...	17,960	14.25	11.54	13.24	14.05	....
LRLCX	Lord Abbett Research:Large Cap	*'92	GI	C	153.1	5.3	....	+34.8	+20.0	+23.3	+15.9	+17.4	$1,000	5.75	0.07	0.09	0.17	1.31	28,821	26.31	22.18	25.00	26.53	0.3
LRSCX	Lord Abbett Research:Small Cap	*'96	G	C	211.8	3.2	....	....	....	+36.6	−7.4	+8.2	$1,000	5.75	....	....	....	...	.....	17.11	13.14	16.50	17.51	....
LANSX	Lord Abbett:Tax Free Inc.:National Cl.A	*'84	IP	TF	542.9	n/a	∫†	+15.5	+3.8	+9.7	+6.4	−6.2	$1,000	4.75	0.594	0.466	0.19	...	12,063	11.73	10.45	10.47	10.82	5.5
LANYX	Lord Abbett:Tax Free Inc:N.Y. Cl.A	*'84	I	TF	248.5	n/a	....	+14.3	+3.5	+8.2	+6.2	−5.3	$1,000	4.75	0.592	0.466	....	...	11,702	11.37	10.21	10.22	10.56	5.6
LATIX	Lord Abbett:Tax Free Inc:Texas Cl.A	*'87	I	TF	84.5	n/a	∫†	+16.2	+3.8	+9.3	+5.1	−11.5	$1,000	4.75	0.556	....	0.02	...	11,428	10.50	9.24	9.24	9.55	5.8
LAGVX	Lord Abbett:U.S.Govt. Secs. Cl.A	'32	IS	BD	1400.5	n/a	2	+13.1	+1.4	+8.7	+8.0	+8.6	$500	4.75	0.178	0.426	....	...	14,007	2.64	2.27	2.43	2.55	7.0
LUBIX	Lutheran Bro Income	*'72	I	BD	686.2	n/a	....	+17.1	+2.0	+8.1	+8.6	−3.2	$500	5.0	0.53	0.44	....	...	12,922	8.85	8.08	8.09	8.43	6.3
MCSGX	Mainstay Government Fund	*'86	I	GB	515.5	n/a	3	+13.9	+0.4	+8.3	+6.9	−8.4	$500	ERF	0.382	....	....	...	11,788	8.48	7.73	7.73	7.73	4.9
	Mass.Finl.Services:																							
MFBFX	MFS Bond Fund Cl.A	'74	I	BD	820.5	n/a	....	+20.7	+3.6	+9.9	+4.3	−1.9	$1,000	4.75	0.882	0.854	0.04	...	13,442	13.35	12.15	12.18	12.79	6.9
MCGBX	MFS Capital Growth Cl.B	*'86	G	C	452.2	n/a	4	+39.3	+16.0	+22.8	+30.4	+23.5	$1,000	ERF	....	....	1.795	...	31,668	21.39	16.97	21.22	21.22	....
MFEGX	MFS Emerging Growth Fund Cl.A	*'93	GR	C	5850.6	n/a	....	+41.2	+14.8	+20.6	+24.4	+49.3	$1,000	5.75	....	....	0.406	...	38,051	66.59	40.84	66.59	70.65	....
MEGBX	MFS Emerging Growth Cl.B	*'86	G	C	7428.5	n/a	....	+40.1	+13.8	+19.7	+23.5	+48.1	$1,000	ERF	....	....	0.406	...	36,302	64.45	39.78	64.45	64.45	....
MGMTX	MFS Govt.Mortgage Fund Cl.A	'86	I	GB	587.2	n/a		+15.4	+3.0	+8.2	+5.9	−0.5	$1,000	4.75	0.419	0.349	....	...	13,253	6.71	6.25	6.32	6.64	6.3
MGTBX	MFS Govt.Mortgage Fund Cl.B	*'93	I	GB	91.4	n/a		+15.2	+2.2	+7.6	+5.1	−1.0	$1,000	ERF	0.362	0.30	....	...	12,812	6.72	6.27	6.34	6.34	5.7
MFGSX	MFS Govt.Securities Cl.A	'84	I	GB	350.5	n/a	....	+18.9	+0.6	+8.9	+8.1	−4.0	$1,000	4.75	0.582	0.361	....	...	13,085	9.91	9.12	9.13	9.59	6.1
MGOFX	MFS Growth Opportunities Cl.A	*'71	G	C	1051.0	n/a	....	+34.3	+21.8	+22.6	+28.1	+31.1	$1,000	5.75	....	....	1.888	1.84	32,299	19.07	15.12	19.07	20.23	....
MHITX	MFS High Income Fund Cl.A	*'78	I	BD	740.7	n/a	....	+16.6	+12.0	+12.4	+0.4	+2.9	$1,000	4.75	0.433	0.28	....	...	14,861	5.33	4.93	4.99	5.24	8.3
MHIBX	MFS High Income Fund Cl.B	*'93	I	BD	508.0	n/a	....	+15.0	+11.2	+11.6	−0.2	−0.4	$1,000	ERF	0.398	0.111	....	...	13,718	5.33	4.93	4.99	4.99	8.0
MMNSX	MFS Managed Sectors Fund Cl.A	*'93	G	SP	330.3	n/a	....	+33.0	+17.2	+24.4	+10.3	+81.6	$1,000	5.75	....	....	1.74	2.123	37,404	21.48	12.83	21.48	22.79	....
MSEBX	MFS Managed Sectors Fund Cl.B	*'86	G	SP	126.7	n/a	....	+32.0	+16.3	+24.4	+9.7	+65.1	$1,000	ERF	....	....	1.61	...	33,378	21.68	12.96	21.68	21.68	....
MMBFX	MFS Municipal Bond Fund Cl.A	'76	I	TF	1363.4	n/a	∫†	+16.5	+1.4	+8.5	+4.4	−8.1	$1,000	4.75	0.492	0.176	0.103	...	11,510	11.06	9.90	9.90	10.39	4.7
MMIBX	MFS Municipal Income Fund Cl.B	*'86	I	TF	121.9	n/a	....	+13.5	+3.1	+8.5	+3.8	−5.3	$1,000	ERF	0.373	0.306	....	...	11,832	9.06	8.22	8.22	8.22	4.5
MFRFX	MFS Research Fund Cl.A	'74	GI	C,BD	3036.6	n/a	....	+38.5	+24.5	+20.3	+22.6	+23.3	$1,000	5.75	....	....	0.952	2.14	31,483	29.40	24.48	28.86	30.62	....
MSFRX	MFS Total Return Cl.A	'70	IG	C,BD	3732.2	n/a	5	+25.4	+14.3	+20.2	+11.1	−4.3	$1,000	4.75	0.546	0.438	2.07	...	17,787	15.78	13.61	13.88	14.57	3.7
MCOFX	MFS Capital Opport. Fund Cl. A	*'83	G	C	1449.8	n/a	....	+44.1	+16.5	+26.0	+26.7	+45.8	$1,000	5.75	....	....	0.923	3.31	38,098	22.50	16.58	21.01	22.29	....
MWEBX	MFS World Equity Fund Cl.B	*'86	G	GL	284.6	n/a	....	+17.5	+19.4	+15.3	+16.2	+11.4	$1,000	ERF	....	....	0.994	...	20,165	24.40	20.56	24.04	24.04	....
MWGTX	MFS World Govts.Fund Cl.A	*'81	PI	BD,INTL	102.0	n/a	6	+15.4	+5.4	+0.4	+4.1	−3.5	$1,000	4.75	....	0.78	0.726	...	11,482	10.63	9.40	9.41	9.88	....
MIGFX	Mass.Invest.Growth Stock Cl.A	'32	G	C	5787.5	n/a	....	+28.2	+23.5	+47.2	+39.3	+27.8	$1,000	5.75	0.006	....	1.386	...	38,669	20.33	15.67	20.33	21.57	....
MITTX	Mass.Invest.Trust Cl.A	'24	IR	C	8014.5	n/a	....	+38.9	+25.4	+31.1	+22.5	+4.3	$1,000	5.75	0.159	0.075	1.052	0.101	28,884	21.87	18.70	20.95	22.23	0.7
MABAX	Merrill Lynch:Basic Value Cl.A	*'77	GI	C	5131.3	n/a	....	+32.6	+17.3	+29.3	+11.2	+10.1	$1,000	6.5	0.80	0.72	2.42	2.99	25,115	45.02	36.63	38.15	40.26	2.0
MLCPX	Merrill Lynch:Capital Fund Cl.A	*'73	GI	B	3217.3	n/a	....	+32.3	+12.1	+21.1	+6.2	+4.6	$1,000	6.5	1.08	0.938	1.17	2.99	20,111	37.83	31.24	32.07	33.85	3.2
MLHIX	Merrill Lynch:Corp.Bond:Hi Inc.Cl.A	*'78	I	BD	807.9	n/a	7	+16.2	+10.6	+10.9	−5.8	+7.8	$1,000	4.0	0.669	0.704	....	0.149	14,111	7.16	6.52	6.65	6.93	9.7
MAFSX	Merrill Lynch:Federal Secs.Trust Cl.A	'84	I	GB	209.1	n/a	....	+14.8	+4.0	+8.4	+5.8	+0.9	$1,000	4.0	0.523	0.559	....	...	13,305	9.80	9.28	9.32	9.71	5.4
MLHYX	Merrill Lynch:Muni Bond National Cl.A	*'79	I	TF	808.8	n/a	8∫†	+17.4	+4.1	+9.0	+4.6	−10.0	$1,000	4.0	0.518	0.043	....	...	11,738	10.70	9.53	9.53	9.93	5.2
MLMBX	Merrill Lynch:Muni Bond:Insured Cl.A	*'77	I	TF	1133.6	n/a	∫†	+17.0	+2.7	+8.4	+2.8	−10.5	$1,000	4.0	0.381	0.061	....	...	11,181	8.22	7.22	7.23	7.53	5.1
MLNYX	Merrill Lynch:N.Y.Muni Bond Cl.B	*'85	I	TF	179.6	n/a	9∫†	+15.3	+2.2	+9.2	+1.8	−11.4	$1,000	ERF	0.444	0.035	....	...	10,562	11.58	10.07	10.12	10.12	4.4
MBPCX	Merrill Lynch:Pacific Fund Cl.B	*'88	G	INTL	629.0	n/a	10	+7.1	+3.3	−7.4	+7.1	+85.9	$1,000	ERF	0.52	....	....	...	20,764	31.12	16.18	31.12	31.12	1.7
EMGSX	Midas Fund	*'86	G	PM	88.7	n/a	11	+36.7	+21.2	−59.0	−28.4	−9.9	$500	None	....	....	....	...	3,628	1.68	1.20	1.36	1.36	....

Uniform Footnote Explanations-See page 235. Stock Splits & Divs. (figures adjusted): [1] Was Value Apprec.(5/96). [2] Was Lord Abbett Inc. [3] 5% E.R.F.reducing over 7 yrs. Was Mackay-Shields Govt.Plus. [4] All Cl.B funds have 4% ERF reducing over 6 years. [5] Was Mass.Inc.Dvlpmt. [6] Was Mass.Fin'l Intl.Tr.Bond. [7] Rated "BBB" or lower. [8] Was High Yld.. [9] 4% E.R.F.reducing over 5 yrs. [10] 4% ERF reducing 1% p.a.. [11] 1% charge if redeemed within 30 days.

Ticker Symbol	Fund	Year Offered	Prin. Obj.	Type	Sept. 30, 1999 Total Net Assets (MIL.$)	Sept. 30, 1999 Cash & Equiv (MIL.$)	See Foot-notes	Net Assets per Share % Change from Previous Dec. 31 — At: Dec. 31 1995	1996	1997	1998	Dec. 31, 1999	Min. Unit	Max. Sales Chg. %	Distributions Per Share from Invest. Income 1998	Invest. Income 1999	Security Profits 1998	Security Profits 1999	$10,000 Invested 12-31-93 Now Worth	PRICE RECORD NAV Per Sh — 1999 — High	1999 Low	#12-31-99 NAV Per Shr.	Offer Price	% Yield From Inv. Inc.
AMOBX	Mgn. Stanley D. Witter Amer. Opport. Fund .	'79	G	C	7463.5	n/a	1	+ 42.0	+ 10.2	+ 31.5	+ 29.3	+ 33.0	$1,000	ERF	....	....	5.292	1.06	32,981	43.31	32.78	42.63	42.63	....
CLFBX	Mgn. Stanley D. Witter Cal. TF Inc. Cl. B ..	*'84	I	TF	805.5	n/a	∫†	+ 14.7	+ 2.9	+ 6.0	+ 3.3	− 8.1	$1,000	ERF	0.525	0.043	0.008	...	11,188	12.92	11.72	11.73	11.73	4.5
CAPBX	Mgn. Stanley D. Witter Cap. Growth Secs. Cl.B..	*'90	G	C	450.0	n/a	....	+ 31.3	+ 10.5	+ 24.4	+ 15.2	− 1.3	$1,000	ERF	....	....	1.713	...	19,906	18.45	13.97	14.94	14.94	....
CNSBX	Mgn. Stanley D. Witter Convert. Secs. Cl.B .	*'85	RI	CV	231.6	n/a	....	+ 20.3	+ 16.7	+ 16.2	− 4.8	+ 24.6	$1,000	ERF	0.672	0.42	....	...	18,809	16.03	12.99	16.03	16.03	4.2
DGRBX	Mgn. Stanley D. Witter Develop. Growth ..	*'83	G	C	767.8	n/a	....	+ 47.4	+ 12.0	+ 12.9	+ 7.6	+ 69.9	$1,000	ERF	....	....	0.37	...	32,506	44.47	24.27	42.01	42.01	....
DINBX	Mgn. Stanley D. Witter Diversified Inc. Cl. B..	*'92	I	BD	892.2	n/a	2	+ 12.2	+ 8.0	+ 5.8	+ 3.1	− 10.0	$1,000	ERF	0.717	....	....	...	11,741	8.99	8.03	8.06	8.42	8.5
DIVBX	Mgn. Stanley D. Witter Dividend Growth Cl. B .	*'81	IGE	C	17512.4	n/a	....	+ 34.6	+ 19.2	+ 25.5	+ 17.6	− 3.8	$1,000	ERF	0.764	0.47	1.775	0.80	22,119	68.17	55.74	57.74	57.74	1.3
EUGBX	Mgn. Stanley D. Witter European Growth Cl. B ..	*'90	G	GL	2034.6	n/a	....	+ 24.4	+ 28.7	+ 14.3	+ 23.4	+ 13.0	$1,000	ERF	....	....	1.883	...	27,253	24.03	18.88	21.94	23.16	....
FDLBX	Mgn. Stanley D. Witter Fed. Secs. Tr. Cl. B .	*'87	I	GB	550.3	n/a	★	+ 18.1	+ 0.7	+ 7.8	+ 8.3	− 5.0	$1,000	ERF	0.518	0.505	....	...	12,531	9.67	8.67	8.67	8.67	6.0
GLBBX	Mgn. Stanley D. Witter Global Divd. Growth..	*'93	G	GL	3378.2	n/a	2	+ 19.6	+ 16.5	+ 11.5	+ 11.3	+ 4.2	$1,000	ERF	0.095	0.071	1.218	0.485	19,297	14.67	12.56	13.20	13.20	0.7
GRTBX	Mgn.Stanley D. Witter Growth Cl. B ..	*'92	G	C	929.6	n/a	3	+ 24.5	+ 18.7	+ 13.0	+ 19.9	+ 32.7	$1,000	ERF	....	....	3.507	1.045	24,497	20.10	15.76	20.10	20.10	....
GUTBX	Mgn. Stanley D. Witter Global Utilities Cl. B ..	*'94	GI	GL	766.9	n/a	2	+ 14.2	+ 13.1	+ 18.5	+ 37.3	+ 15.3	$1,000	ERF	0.10	0.06	1.957	0.446	24,230	20.04	16.87	19.11	19.11	0.5
HCRBX	Mgn. Stanley D. Witter Health Sciences Cl. B ..	*'92	G	C	277.9	n/a	2	+ 62.0	+ 1.0	+ 5.1	+ 17.4	+ 6.4	$1,000	ERF	....	....	3.409	...	20,084	14.56	12.02	14.41	14.41	....
HYLBX	Mgn. Stanley D. Witter High Yield Secs. Cl. B .	*'79	IG	BD	1867.8	n/a	4	+ 16.4	+ 12.6	+ 11.4	− 3.2	− 3.5	$1,000	5.5	0.703	0.383	....	...	12,725	5.90	5.22	5.27	5.27	13.3
IISBX	Mgn. Stanley D. Witter Inter. Inc. Secs. Cl.B..	*'89	I	FL	120.1	n/a	....	+ 13.3	+ 2.9	+ 6.1	+ 6.3	− 6.0	$1,000	ERF	0.446	0.072	....	...	11,989	9.85	9.15	9.15	9.15	4.9
ISMBX	Mgn. Stanley D. Witter Intl. SmallCap Cl.B ..	*'94	G	INTL	66.2	n/a	5	+ 2.9	+ 1.0	− 17.0	+ 4.0	+ 64.4	$1,000	ERF	....	....	....	...	14,749	12.71	7.62	12.71	12.71	....
LATBX	Mgn. Stanley D. Witter Latin America Growth..	*'92	G	GL	113.4	n/a	2	− 20.3	+ 22.0	+ 30.6	− 39.0	+ 53.1	$1,000	ERF	....	....	....	...	9,061	12.77	6.47	12.77	12.77	....
DWLTX	Mgn.Stanley D. Witter Limited Municipal ..	*'93	I	TF	50.2	n/a	....	+ 16.4	+ 3.1	+ 6.3	+ 4.6	− 1.4	$1,000	None	0.355	0.346	....	...	12,131	10.47	9.88	9.90	9.90	3.6
DWAZX	Mgn.Stanley D. Witter MSMS Arizona..	*'91	I	TF	38.0	n/a	....	+ 16.9	+ 2.8	+ 7.3	+ 3.5	− 3.5	$1,000	4.0	0.461	0.442	....	0.014	12,042	10.72	9.79	9.81	10.22	4.5
DWCAX	Mgn. Stanley D. Witter MSMS California...	*'91	I	TF	98.4	n/a	....	+ 18.8	+ 4.5	+ 8.2	+ 3.7	− 4.1	$1,000	4.0	0.487	0.465	....	...	12,236	11.06	10.02	10.06	10.48	4.6
DWFLX	Mgn. Stanley D. Witter MSMS Florida..	*'91	I	TF	55.0	n/a	....	+ 16.9	+ 3.0	+ 8.1	+ 2.6	− 3.6	$1,000	4.0	0.487	0.503	....	...	12,088	10.98	9.97	10.00	10.42	4.7
DWNJX	Mgn. Stanley D. Witter MSMS New Jersey ..	*'91	I	TF	39.2	n/a	....	+ 16.7	+ 3.2	+ 8.8	+ 4.4	− 5.5	$1,000	4.0	0.474	0.253	....	0.067	12,022	11.08	10.08	10.09	10.51	4.5
DWOHX	Mgn. Stanley D. Witter MSMS Ohio...	*'91	I	TF	16.4	n/a	....	+ 18.0	+ 3.6	+ 7.9	+ 3.7	− 3.4	$1,000	4.0	0.469	0.455	....	...	12,262	11.06	10.15	10.15	10.57	4.4
DWPAX	Mgn. Stanley D. Witter MSMS Pennsylvania..	*'91	I	TF	50.5	n/a	....	+ 17.2	+ 3.4	+ 8.2	+ 3.5	− 4.7	$1,000	4.0	0.473	0.427	....	0.018	12,054	11.08	10.03	10.04	10.46	4.5
NREBX	Mgn.Stanley D. Witter Natural Resources Cl. B..	*'81	G	C	184.3	n/a	....	+ 22.7	+ 26.7	+ 13.3	− 21.6	+ 26.4	$1,000	ERF	0.141	....	....	...	17,315	14.05	9.91	13.47	13.47	1.0
NGTVX	Mgn. Stanley D. Witter North Amer. Govt. Inc..	*'92	I	GL,B	126.4	n/a	....	+ 15.4	+ 3.8	+ 7.7	+ 6.6	+ 1.2	$1,000	None	0.463	0.30	....	...	11,941	8.69	8.41	8.43	8.43	5.5
NYFBX	Mgn. Stanley D. Witter N.Y. Tax Free Cl. B...	'85	I	TF	139.0	n/a	∫†	+ 15.5	+ 2.4	+ 8.2	+ 1.8	− 7.5	$1,000	ERF	0.456	0.116	....	...	11,134	12.02	10.88	10.91	10.91	4.2
TGRBX	Mgn.Stanley D. Witter Pacific Growth Cl. B.	*'90	G	GL	609.8	n/a	2	+ 3.9	+ 4.8	− 38.8	− 10.5	+ 68.1	$1,000	ERF	....	....	....	...	8,271	17.45	9.94	17.45	17.45	....
METBX	Mgn. Stanley D. Witter Precious Metals & Min.	*'90	G	PM	31.4	n/a	2	+ 5.0	+ 1.7	+ 26.9	− 14.4	+ 2.7	$1,000	ERF	....	....	....	...	10,531	5.78	4.21	4.95	4.95	....
SHORT	Mgn. Stanley D. Witter Short Term Bond Fund ..	*'94	I	BD	159.2	n/a	....	+ 11.5	+ 4.4	+ 6.2	+ 6.2	+ 0.4	$1,000	None	0.538	0.287	....	...	12,957	9.55	9.29	9.29	9.29	5.8
DWSHX	Mgn. Stanley D. Witter Short-Term U.S. Treas .	*'91	I	ST	306.9	n/a	....	+ 9.6	+ 3.8	+ 5.9	+ 6.2	+ 0.8	$1,000	None	0.472	0.455	....	...	12,742	10.12	9.74	9.74	9.74	4.8
SMPBX	Mgn. Stanley D. Witter Small Cap. Growth Cl.B .	*'93	G	C	402.1	n/a	2	+ 60.2	+ 13.7	+ 10.6	+ 19.4	+ 115.8	$1,000	ERF	....	....	....	...	49,520	50.36	22.34	50.36	50.36	....
SRTBX	Mgn. Stanley D. Witter Strategist Cl. B ..	*'88	GI	FL	1825.4	n/a	6	+ 24.1	+ 15.2	+ 15.7	+ 14.9	+ 11.6	$1,000	ERF	0.258	0.079	1.528	...	20,807	21.51	18.42	20.75	20.75	1.2
TAXDX	Mgn. Stanley D. Witter Tax Exempt Secs. Cl. D..	*'80	IP	TF	898.4	n/a	∫†	+ 16.9	+ 3.4	+ 8.0	+ 4.4	− 3.1	$1,000	4.0	0.559	0.538	0.045	0.032	12,467	12.11	11.06	11.07	11.07	5.0
TRFBX	Mgn. Stanley D. Witter Total Return Cl. B ...	*'94	GI	C	199.6	n/a	....	+ 27.5	+ 20.4	+ 26.9	+ 16.9	+ 24.6	$1,000	None	....	....	0.889	...	28,375	21.61	17.13	21.41	21.41	....
USGBX	Mgn. Stanley D. Witter U.S. Govt. Secs Cl. B.	*'84	I	GB	4393.9	n/a	★	+ 16.3	+ 3.0	+ 8.2	+ 6.5	− 6.6	$1,000	ERF	0.491	....	....	...	12,441	9.20	8.59	8.59	8.59	5.7
UTLBX	Mgn. Stanley D. Witter Utilities Cl. B...	*'88	I	C	2599.3	n/a	....	+ 27.9	+ 4.8	+ 24.8	+ 21.4	+ 9.8	$1,000	ERF	0.418	0.356	1.01	1.09	20,113	20.56	18.41	19.70	19.70	2.1
VADBX	Mgn. Stanley D. Witter Val. Added Mkt. Equity ..	*'87	G	C	1330.6	n/a	....	+ 28.9	+ 17.1	+ 26.6	+ 10.8	− 1.1	$1,000	ERF	0.107	....	2.607	...	20,961	41.10	33.58	35.31	35.31	0.3
WWIBX	Mgn. Stanley D. Witter Worldwide Tr. Cl. B .	*'89	I	GL	69.1	n/a	....	+ 17.7	+ 11.7	+ 3.1	+ 9.3	− 9.5	$1,000	ERF	0.608	0.439	....	...	12,818	9.11	7.73	7.73	7.73	7.9
BEGRX	Mutual Beacon Fund..........................	*'62	GI	C	3133.1	n/a	7	+ 25.7	+ 20.8	+ 22.7	+ 2.3	+ 7.8	$5,000	None	0.45	0.042	0.87	0.267	21,697	15.35	13.02	13.84	13.84	3.3
MQIFX	Mutual Qualified Fund........................	*'80	GI	C,BD	3104.8	n/a	8	+ 26.2	+ 12.5	+ 24.5	+ 0.3	+ 6.2	$1,000	None	0.45	0.048	1.33	0.519	19,901	19.15	15.99	16.91	16.91	2.7
MUTHX	Mutual Shares Fund............................	'49	G	SP	5391.8	n/a	9	+ 28.6	+ 10.9	+ 26.1	+ 0.3	+ 6.7	$5,000	None	0.53	0.054	1.29	0.362	20,113	22.79	19.40	20.43	20.43	2.6
MUIFX	Nationwide Fund..................................	'33	I	C	2310.0	n/a	10	+ 36.2	+ 17.6	+ 39.4	+ 24.8	− 6.9	$250	4.5	0.156	0.183	0.486	...	26,072	35.31	28.97	30.00	31.41	0.5
NBSSX	Neub. & Berman Focus Fund..............	'52	G	SP	1276.5	n/a	11	+ 36.2	+ 16.3	+ 23.5	+ 13.2	+ 25.7	$1,000	None	0.09	0.10	1.97	5.31	28,086	43.10	34.19	39.10	39.10	0.2

Uniform Footnote Explanations-See page 235. **Stock Splits & Divs.** (figures adjusted): [1] All DW Funds listed"ERF". have 5% ERF reducing over 6 yrs. [2] 5% ERF reducing over 6 yrs. [3] 5% ERF reducing over 6 yrs. Was DW TCW Core Equity(3/98). [4] Rated'BBB' or lower. Incl. DW High Income Secs.(11/97). [5] 5%ERF reducing over 6 yrs. [6] Includes Managed Assets(1/96). [7] 3-for-1 split, Feb.'97. [8] Closed to new investors. 2-for-1 split, Feb. '97.. [9] Closed to new investors. 5-for-1 split, Feb.'97.. [10] Was MIF Nat'wide Fund. [11] Was Selected Sectors(3/95).

Ticker Symbol	Fund	Year Offered	Prin. Obj.	Type	Sept. 30, 1999 Total Net Assets (MIL.$)	Cash & Equiv (MIL.$)	See Foot-notes	Net Assets per Share % Change from Previous Dec. 31 At: Dec. 31 1995	1996	1997	1998	Dec. 31, 1999	Min. Unit	Max. Sales Chg. %	Distributions Per Share from Invest. Income 1998	Invest. Income 1999	Security Profits 1998	Security Profits 1999	$10,000 Invested 12-31-93 Now Worth	PRICE RECORD NAV Per Sh 1999 High	1999 Low	#12-31-99 NAV Per Shr.	Offer Price	% Yield From Inv. Inc.
NGUAX	Neub. & Berman Guardian Fund	'50	G	FL	3209.4	n/a	....	+ 32.0	+ 17.8	+ 17.4	+ 2.1	– 17.0	$1,000	None	0.125	0.119	3.91	...	15,563	25.98	17.86	18.50	18.50	0.7
NLMBX	Neub.& Berman Ltd. Maturity Bond Fund	*'86	I	BD	231.3	n/a	....	+ 10.3	+ 3.3	+ 6.6	+ 1.1	+ 1.1	$2,000	None	0.249	0.547	....	...	12,365	9.89	9.20	9.43	9.43	2.6
NMANX	Neub. & Berman Manhattan Fund	*'79	G	C	560.4	n/a	....	+ 31.0	+ 9.9	+ 27.1	+ 16.1	+ 49.7	$1,000	None	....	....	0.83	1.20	30,658	16.69	10.95	16.69	16.69	....
NBMUX	Neub. & Berman Munic. Secs. Trust	*'87	I	TF	34.9	n/a	....	+ 7.9	+ 2.7	+ 7.2	+ 5.5	– 2.9	$2,000	None	0.42	0.264	....	...	11,695	11.44	10.72	10.74	10.74	3.9
NPRTX	Neub. & Berman Partners Fund	*'75	G	FL	2692.3	n/a	....	+ 35.2	+ 26.6	+ 28.3	+ 6.1	+ 7.4	$1,000	None	....	0.29	2.41	3.10	24,549	29.33	22.98	24.00	24.00	....
NEFGX	New England Growth	'68	G	C	1653.1	n/a	....	+ 37.8	+ 17.1	+ 24.0	+ 29.6	+ 14.0	$2,500	6.5	0.009	....	2.12	1.952	27,493	12.52	10.09	11.00	11.67	0.1
NICSX	Nicholas Fund	'69	G	C	4782.8	n/a	....	+ 34.7	+ 19.4	+ 36.4	+ 5.5	+ 0.1	$500	None	0.134	0.052	2.472	4.74	22,472	92.92	72.62	81.15	81.15	0.2
NCTWX	Nicholas II Fund	*'83	GR	C	874.1	n/a	....	+ 28.4	+ 7.9	+ 36.3	+ 8.7	– 0.2	$1,000	None	0.137	....	4.00	...	20,670	37.84	30.50	35.96	35.96	0.4
NTHEX	Northeast Investors Tr	'50	IG	FL	2062.6	n/a	....	+ 16.8	+ 19.3	+ 13.4	+ 0.1	+ 3.4	$1,000	None	1.00	1.06	0.177	...	16,731	10.93	9.66	9.77	9.77	10.2
	Nuveen Funds:																							
FLAAX	All-Amer. Muni. Cl. A	*'88	I	TF	291.8	n/a	....	+ 7.6	+ 7.8	+ 8.9	+ 8.4	– 7.0	$3,000	4.2	0.548	0.376	0.045	...	12,696	11.56	10.31	10.32	10.77	5.1
NMSAX	Balanced Muni. & Stock Fund Cl. A	*'96	IG	B	114.4	n/a	....	....	....	+ 16.2	+ 10.2	+ 3.0	$3,000	5.25	0.66	0.48	0.68	...	.....	25.82	23.83	24.69	26.20	2.5
NSBAX	Balanced Stock & Bond Cl. A	*'96	G	B	62.0	n/a	....	....	....	+ 19.3	+ 13.5	+ 8.3	$3,000	5.25	0.646	0.594	1.15	0.954	.....	27.71	24.84	25.72	27.29	2.4
NCAIX	CA Insur. Muni. Bond Cl.A	*'94	I	TF	48.2	n/a	....	+ 8.2	+ 7.0	+ 6.6	+ 8.1	– 4.9	$3,000	4.2	0.531	0.392	0.008	...	12,523	11.16	10.15	10.17	10.62	5.0
NCAAX	CA Muni. Bond Cl. A	'94	I	TF	45.0	n/a	....	+ 6.8	+ 7.3	+ 7.6	+ 7.7	– 5.6	$3,000	4.2	0.537	0.27	0.048	...	12,424	10.95	10.03	10.04	10.48	5.1
NONE	European Value Cl. A	*'98	GI	INTL	3.2	n/a	....	....	....	....	....	+ 23.1	$3,000	5.75	0.023	....	....	...	.....	23.85	18.61	23.85	25.31	0.1
NONE	Nuveen High Muni. Bond Fund Cl. A	*'99	IR	TF	3.2	0.1	....	....	....	....	....	....	$3,000	4.25	....	0.189	....	...	.....	20.17	18.59	18.62	19.44	....
FGATX	GA Muni. Bond Cl. A	*'86	I	TF	118.1	n/a	....	+ 7.6	+ 6.2	+ 9.0	+ 9.3	– 6.7	$3,000	4.2	0.552	0.397	....	...	12,714	11.31	10.08	10.09	10.53	5.2
FINTX	Inter. Muni. Bond Cl. A	*'92	I	TF	50.6	n/a	....	+ 7.0	+ 6.8	+ 7.4	+ 8.6	– 4.4	$3,000	3.0	0.473	0.448	0.078	...	12,908	11.18	10.14	10.16	10.47	4.5
FKYTX	KY Muni. Bond Cl. A	*'87	I	TF	439.0	n/a	....	+ 8.5	+ 7.0	+ 7.6	+ 7.3	– 5.6	$3,000	4.2	0.522	0.406	0.069	...	12,678	11.44	10.34	10.36	10.81	4.8
FLTDX	Ltd. Muni. Bond Cl. A	*'87	I	TF	427.3	n/a	....	+ 5.2	+ 5.3	+ 5.7	+ 2.8	– 1.3	$3,000	2.5	0.128	0.362	....	...	12,154	10.99	10.43	10.44	10.71	1.2
FMOTX	MO Muni. Bond Cl. A	*'87	I	TF	226.5	n/a	....	+ 7.4	+ 6.2	+ 7.4	+ 8.5	– 6.3	$3,000	4.2	0.554	0.319	....	...	12,479	11.36	10.26	10.28	10.73	5.2
NNYAX	NY Muni. Bond Cl. A	*'94	I	TF	82.6	n/a	....	+ 7.3	+ 7.3	+ 7.2	+ 5.0	– 4.9	$3,000	4.2	0.143	0.358	....	...	12,349	11.10	10.14	10.15	10.59	1.4
FOHTX	OH Muni. Bond Cl. A	*'85	I	TF	445.4	n/a	....	+ 7.4	+ 5.8	+ 6.9	+ 7.6	– 5.9	$3,000	4.2	0.585	0.379	0.045	...	12,373	11.82	10.67	10.69	11.16	5.2
NRGAX	Growth Cl.A	*'97	G	C	100.7	n/a	....	....	....	....	+ 25.0	+ 14.0	$3,000	5.25	....	....	....	...	.....	28.68	23.80	28.50	30.24	....
NONE	Income Fund Cl. A	*'98	P	BD	1.4	n/a	....	....	....	....	....	....	$3,000	4.75	....	0.297	....	...	.....	20.04	18.72	18.78	19.72	....
FTNTX	TN Muni. Bond Cl. A	*'87	I	TF	264.8	n/a	....	+ 7.3	+ 6.2	+ 7.0	+ 8.1	– 5.3	$3,000	4.2	0.561	0.502	....	...	12,457	11.60	10.40	10.42	10.88	5.2
NNGAX	Growth & Income Stock Fund Cl. A	*'96	GI	C	716.6	n/a	....	....	....	+ 23.3	+ 8.9	+ 8.6	$3,000	5.25	0.204	....	2.223	...	.....	27.71	23.14	25.25	26.79	0.8
NMBIX	Insur. Muni. Bond Cl. A	'94	I	TF	111.6	n/a	....	+ 8.9	+ 5.3	+ 6.6	+ 8.1	– 5.6	$3,000	4.2	0.565	0.315	0.001	...	12,387	11.28	10.26	10.28	10.73	5.3
NMBAX	Muni Bond Cl. A	*'95	I	TF	121.4	n/a	....	+ 7.5	+ 6.4	+ 7.1	+ 8.2	– 3.8	$3,000	4.2	0.45	0.413	0.026	...	12,891	9.67	8.83	8.85	9.24	4.9
NNYIX	NY Insur. Muni Bond Cl. A	*'94	I	TF	56.7	n/a	....	+ 8.0	+ 6.1	+ 6.0	+ 7.2	– 3.1	$3,000	4.2	0.522	0.468	0.029	0.004	12,567	10.80	9.92	9.94	10.38	5.0
OAKMX	Oakmark Fund	*'91	G	C	4787.3	445.2	....	+ 34.4	+ 16.2	+ 32.2	– 6.3	– 10.1	$2,500	None	0.44	0.263	1.60	4.73	17,931	40.25	26.14	27.20	27.20	1.6
OAKIX	Oakmark International Fund	*'92	G	INTL	811.0	25.1	....	+ 8.2	+ 28.0	+ 3.8	– 4.3	+ 34.7	$2,500	None	0.296	....	1.072	...	16,882	15.17	10.90	14.70	14.70	2.0
PGSGX	One Group:Small Cap. Cl.A	*'91	G	C	27.3	n/a	1	+ 22.0	+ 13.3	+ 27.9	– 4.5	+ 17.0	$1,000	4.5	....	....	1.194	...	18,094	11.33	8.75	11.27	11.89	....
PGLAX	One Group:Louisiana Municipal Cl.A	*'90	I	TF	70.5	n/a	2∫†	+ 11.2	+ 0.9	+ 6.9	– 4.8	– 2.7	$1,000	4.5	0.425	0.413	0.023	...	11,839	10.43	9.64	9.66	10.12	4.2
PAVGX	One Group:Value Growth Cl.A	*'90	G	C	307.0	n/a	2	+ 28.3	– 5.3	+ 34.2	+ 27.7	+ 7.0	$1,000	4.5	0.036	0.016	0.928	...	20,430	15.65	13.49	14.72	15.54	0.2
RCVGX	Oppenheimer Bond Fund for Growth	*'86	GI	CV	214.9	n/a	3	+ 25.1	+ 6.4	+ 18.2	– 0.2	+ 13.3	$2,000	3.25	0.442	0.468	....	...	17,416	17.30	14.69	16.35	16.90	2.6
OPOCX	Oppenheimer Discovery	*'85	G	C	750.1	n/a	....	+ 36.3	+ 14.6	+ 10.2	– 2.3	+ 44.0	$1,000	5.75	....	....	1.424	...	21,480	65.62	37.97	65.62	69.62	....
OPPEX	Oppenheimer Equity Inc.Cl.A	'68	I	B	2791.4	n/a		+ 27.4	+ 19.6	+ 29.2	+ 10.1	– 14.6	$1,000	5.75	0.491	0.359	1.165	...	18,010	14.79	11.46	11.81	12.53	3.9
OPPAX	Oppenheimer Global Cl.A	'69	G	GL	3772.0	n/a	....	+ 16.4	+ 17.3	+ 21.9	+ 12.1	+ 56.5	$1,000	5.75	0.388	....	2.989	4.12	28,265	62.55	41.70	62.55	66.37	0.6
OPGSX	Oppenheimer Gold & Spl.Minerals	*'83	G	PM	90.9	n/a	....	– 1.5	+ 5.9	– 31.9	– 1.3	+ 13.1	$1,000	5.75	0.018	....	....	...	7,454	12.30	8.94	10.46	11.10	0.2
OPPSX	Oppenheimer Growth Cl.A	'72	G	SP	1713.8	n/a	....	+ 34.9	+ 23.6	+ 17.9	+ 10.5	+ 54.4	$1,000	5.75	0.478	....	3.078	5.91	34,344	48.40	34.95	48.40	51.35	0.9
OPPHX	Oppenheimer High Yield Cl.A	'78	I	BD	1136.6	n/a	....	+ 14.4	+ 8.2	+ 11.4	– 0.5	+ 3.3	$1,000	4.75	1.128	1.142	....	...	13,861	13.57	12.35	12.45	13.07	8.6
MSIGX	Oppenheimer Main Street Inc. & Growth	*'88	GI	C	7579.4	n/a	....	+ 30.6	+ 15.7	+ 25.2	+ 24.8	+ 5.3	$1,000	5.75	0.249	0.029	1.501	...	24,464	45.29	38.92	42.00	44.56	0.6

Uniform Footnote Explanations-See page 235. Stock Splits & Divs. (figures adjusted): [1] Was Gulf South(11/97). Was Paragon Group(4/96). [2] Was Paragon Group(4/96). [3] Was Rochester Bond for Growth(3/96).

Ticker Symbol	Fund	Year Offered	Prin. Obj.	Type	Sept. 30, 1999 Total Net Assets (MIL.$)	Cash & Equiv (MIL.$)	See Foot-notes	Net Assets per Share % Change from Previous Dec. 31 At: Dec. 31 1995	1996	1997	1998	Dec. 31, 1999	Min. Unit	Max. Sales Chg. %	Distributions Per Share from Invest. Income 1998	1999	Security Profits 1998	1999	$10,000 Invested 12-31-93 Now Worth	PRICE RECORD NAV Per Sh — 1999 — High	Low	#12-31-99 NAV Per Shr.	Offer Price	% Yield From Inv. Inc.
OPSIX	Oppenheimer Strategic Inc.Cl.A	*'88	I	CV,GB	3580.0	n/a	....	+ 14.6	+ 12.0	+ 7.9	+ 1.0	+ 3.1	$1,000	4.75	0.369	0.36	....	...	13,801	4.59	4.30	4.36	4.58	8.1
OPTAX	Oppenheimer Municipal Bond Cl.A	'76	IS	TF	555.8	n/a	[1]∫†	+ 17.9	+ 3.6	+ 9.1	+ 5.9	− 7.3	$1,000	4.75	0.517	0.317	....	...	11,892	10.48	9.32	9.32	9.78	5.3
OPTRX	Oppenheimer Total Return Cl.A	'44	GI	B	2731.0	n/a	....	+ 29.8	+ 19.6	+ 27.1	+ 20.5	+ 9.1	$1,000	5.75	0.154	0.089	0.869	...	23,916	13.74	11.97	13.25	14.06	1.1
PGBBX	PaineWebber Global Income Cl.B	*'87	IG	GL	13.5	n/a	[2]†	+ 12.1	+ 6.1	+ 2.9	+ 12.7	− 5.2	$1,000	ERF	0.85	0.435	....	...	12,448	10.59	9.53	9.56	9.56	8.9
PAXWX	Pax World Fund	*'71	IGE	B	967.5	n/a	....	+ 28.9	+ 10.2	+ 24.8	+ 24.1	+ 9.1	$250	None	0.47	0.20	0.88	...	24,602	24.42	21.52	23.40	23.40	2.0
PBHGX	PBHG Growth Fund	*'85	G	C	2681.1	n/a	[3]	+ 50.3	+ 9.8	− 3.3	+ 0.6	+ 85.5	$1,000	None	....	....	....	...	31,180	47.38	22.06	47.38	47.38	....
PENNX	Pennsylvania Mutual	'62	G	C	409.3	n/a	[4]	+ 18.6	+ 12.3	+ 24.9	+ 3.7	− 1.0	$2,000	ERF	0.05	....	0.71	...	16,959	7.83	6.39	7.28	7.28	0.7
NWWOX	Phoenix Aberdeen Worldwide Opportunities	'56	G	C	172.9	n/a		+ 14.8	+ 14.8	+ 13.7	+ 30.4	+ 14.5	$250	4.75	....	....	2.378	1.37	22,396	11.21	9.04	10.58	11.11	....
PHSKX	Phoenix Aggressive Growth Cl.A	*'81	G	C	337.6	n/a	[5]	+ 50.1	+ 10.9	+ 18.4	+ 29.6	+ 68.6	$500	4.75	....	....	0.003	...	41,386	32.79	18.14	30.73	32.26	....
PHBLX	Phoenix Balanced	*'70	IG	C,BD	1520.8	n/a	....	+ 23.0	+ 8.6	+ 17.8	+ 18.1	+ 3.4	$500	4.75	0.409	0.25	0.678	...	18,351	18.62	16.89	17.65	18.53	2.2
CTESX	Phoenix Cal.Tax Exempt Bonds	*'84	I	TF	85.7	n/a	∫†	+ 18.7	+ 2.1	+ 7.6	+ 5.0	− 5.5	$500	4.75	0.636	0.509	0.062	...	12,279	13.35	11.97	12.00	12.60	5.0
NASTX	Phoenix Equity Opportunities Cl.A	'44	IGE	C	202.1	n/a	....	+ 32.9	+ 11.6	+ 8.1	+ 24.5	+ 31.7	$500	4.75	....	....	0.63	1.355	24,948	10.19	8.01	9.52	9.52	....
PHGRX	Phoenix Growth	'58	G	C	2625.7	n/a	[6]	+ 33.7	+ 14.9	+ 22.4	+ 28.9	+ 15.1	$500	4.75	....	....	2.435	...	27,451	33.93	26.16	30.96	32.50	....
PHCHX	Phoenix High Yield	*'80	IR	BD	392.0	n/a	....	+ 16.8	+ 16.4	+ 13.1	− 6.2	+ 9.3	$500	4.75	0.808	0.628	....	...	14,566	8.06	7.49	7.89	8.28	9.8
NAINX	Phoenix Inc.& Growth Cl.A	'40	I	FL	510.5	n/a	[7]	+ 23.0	+ 12.4	+ 16.6	+ 10.6	+ 5.5	$500	4.75	0.375	0.253	0.79	...	17,662	9.79	9.13	9.78	10.27	3.7
NAMFX	Phoenix Multi Sector Fxd.Inc.Cl.A	*'89	IP	INTL,BD	127.9	n/a	....	+ 19.1	+ 13.0	+ 5.5	− 6.4	+ 6.4	$2,500	4.75	1.072	0.828	....	...	13,221	11.56	10.78	11.22	11.78	9.1
PTRFX	Phoenix Strategic Allocation Cl.A	*'82	GI	FL	293.0	n/a	[8]	+ 18.0	+ 8.8	+ 20.0	+ 19.6	+ 4.5	$500	4.75	0.24	0.119	1.211	0.10	18,812	18.37	16.55	17.56	18.44	1.3
PHTBX	Phoenix Tax Exempt Bond	*'88	IP	TF	92.4	n/a	∫†	+ 17.8	+ 3.8	+ 7.9	+ 3.1	− 3.5	$500	4.75	0.576	0.511	....	...	12,168	11.18	10.16	10.16	10.67	5.4
PABRX	Phoenix-Engemann Balanced Return Cl.A	*'87	GI	B	102.5	n/a	[9]	+ 27.2	+ 17.8	+ 18.8	+ 29.0	+ 11.4	$1,500	5.5	0.398	....	2.25	...	24,456	40.74	34.15	38.80	40.73	1.0
PASGX	Phoenix-Engemann Growth Cl.A	*'86	G	C	481.0	n/a	[9]	+ 27.1	+ 22.5	+ 15.2	+ 42.2	+ 24.6	$1,000	5.5	....	....	2.391	...	30,572	39.25	26.36	33.24	34.90	....
PANFX	Phoenix-Engemann Nifty Fifty Cl.A	*'91	G	C	265.9	n/a	[9]	+ 28.2	+ 26.5	+ 19.0	+ 35.1	+ 19.0	$1,000	5.5	....	....	0.661	...	31,367	50.52	38.37	46.16	48.46	....
ZAPAX	Phoenix-Zweig Appreciation Cl. A	*'91	GS	C	146.9	n/a	....	+ 23.7	+ 15.2	+ 23.7	− 1.4	− 26.0	$1,000	5.5	0.072	....	1.74	...	12,617	16.34	11.64	11.99	12.69	0.6
ZAPCX	Phoenix-Zweig Appreciation Cl. C	*'92	GS	C	116.0	n/a	[10]	+ 23.1	+ 14.4	+ 22.9	− 2.0	− 26.3	$1,000	ERF	....	....	1.74	...	12,176	16.09	11.37	11.79	11.79	....
ZGVAX	Phoenix-Zweig Govt. Fund Cl. A	*'85	IP	GB	23.8	n/a	....	+ 13.4	− 0.5	+ 8.2	+ 8.7	− 3.3	$1,000	4.75	0.527	0.379	....	...	12,473	10.44	9.71	9.72	10.20	5.2
ZMAAX	Phoenix-Zweig Managed Assets Cl. A	*'93	G	C	105.0	n/a	....	+ 15.9	+ 9.7	+ 15.3	+ 14.8	+ 0.1	$1,000	5.5	0.384	0.16	0.04	...	16,357	15.00	13.83	14.04	14.86	2.6
ZMACX	Phoenix-Zweig Managed Assets Cl. C	*'93	GS	GL	385.9	n/a	[10]	+ 15.1	+ 9.0	+ 14.5	+ 14.0	− 0.3	$1,000	ERF	0.287	0.105	0.04	...	15,756	14.84	13.68	13.92	13.92	2.1
ZSTAX	Phoenix-Zweig Strategy Fund Cl. A	*'89	GS	C	260.0	n/a	....	+ 24.8	+ 12.9	+ 18.0	− 2.0	+ 0.8	$1,000	5.5	0.18	0.105	0.48	3.569	16,605	15.52	10.98	11.24	11.89	1.5
ZSTCX	Phoenix-Zweig Strategy Fund Cl.C	*'92	GS	C	226.2	n/a	[10]	+ 25.3	+ 12.1	+ 17.3	− 2.8	+ 0.4	$1,000	ERF	0.035	0.045	0.48	3.569	16,143	15.55	11.05	11.31	11.31	0.3
PGWCX	PIMCO:Growth Cl.C	*'84	G	C	1890.3	n/a	....	+ 27.6	+ 17.9	+ 21.9	+ 37.5	+ 38.0	$1,000	ERF	....	....	3.91	5.66	34,554	36.82	28.07	34.29	34.29	....
PILCX	PIMCO:International Cl.C	*'86	G	INTL	93.1	n/a	....	+ 5.8	+ 1.9	+ 2.4	+ 7.7	+ 25.8	$1,000	ERF	....	....	1.14	1.74	13,746	12.89	10.44	12.08	12.08	....
POPCX	PIMCO:Opportunity Cl.C	*'84	G	C	293.0	n/a	....	+ 42.4	+ 11.0	− 4.6	− 0.2	+ 59.5	$1,000	ERF	....	....	4.62	7.88	22,851	31.32	19.82	26.68	26.68	....
PPMCX	PIMCO:Precious Metals Cl.C	*'88	G	C	12.1	n/a	....	− 4.2	− 2.5	− 48.3	− 11.3	− 8.1	$1,000	ERF	....	....	....	...	3,555	5.62	3.98	4.53	4.53	....
PQNCX	PIMCO:Renaissance Cl.C	*'88	G	CV	384.4	n/a	[11]	+ 27.4	+ 24.4	+ 34.4	+ 9.2	− 13.9	$1,000	ERF	....	....	2.26	...	19,026	18.49	12.71	13.93	13.93	....
PTACX	PIMCO:Target Cl.C	*'92	G	C	865.4	n/a	[12]	+ 30.4	+ 15.7	+ 16.4	+ 22.1	+ 63.3	$1,000	ERF	....	....	0.94	1.80	35,961	22.70	14.24	22.70	22.70	....
PCGRX	Pioneer Capital Growth Cl.A	*'90	G	C	1069.3	52.4	....	+ 30.5	+ 11.6	+ 17.2	− 5.1	+ 12.1	$1,000	5.75	0.02	....	0.89	2.64	20,846	22.46	17.75	18.68	19.82	0.1
PEQIX	Pioneer Equity-Income Cl.A	*'90	IR	C	639.7	4.8	....	+ 31.6	+ 11.8	+ 30.9	+ 17.3	+ 0.2	$1,000	5.75	0.465	0.339	0.73	1.759	22,365	31.58	26.56	27.26	28.92	1.6
PEURX	Pioneer Europe Cl.A	*'91	G	INTL	254.1	8.2	....	+ 21.3	+ 26.6	+ 21.4	+ 20.9	+ 24.5	$1,000	5.75	0.10	....	0.76	1.11	29,717	37.97	29.25	37.97	40.29	0.2
PIODX	Pioneer Fund Cl.A	'28	GI	C	5866.0	53.3	....	+ 26.3	+ 19.0	+ 38.2	+ 28.5	+ 15.0	$50	5.75	0.215	0.11	1.31	2.22	30,510	49.57	42.16	47.60	50.50	0.4
PIOTX	Pioneer II Cl.A	*'69	GI	C	5127.3	46.7	....	+ 27.0	+ 21.8	+ 23.3	− 7.9	+ 1.0	$50	5.75	0.18	0.10	0.15	0.513	17,422	22.29	19.53	20.51	21.76	0.8
PRFDX	Price T.Rowe:Equity Income	*'85	I	C	12782.4	n/a	....	+ 32.7	+ 20.1	+ 28.1	+ 9.0	+ 4.3	$2,500	None	0.61	0.68	1.49	1.97	24,231	29.56	24.18	24.81	24.81	2.5
PRGFX	Price T.Rowe:Growth Stock	'50	G	C	4871.5	n/a	....	+ 30.9	+ 21.8	+ 26.3	+ 26.2	+ 21.0	$2,500	None	0.25	0.10	4.27	5.42	30,995	37.34	30.92	33.27	33.27	0.8
PRGIX	Price T.Rowe:Growth & Income	*'82	GIE	C	3453.0	n/a	....	+ 30.3	+ 25.3	+ 23.2	+ 9.9	+ 4.2	$2,500	None	0.53	0.65	2.13	2.25	22,988	29.71	23.67	24.44	24.44	2.2
PRHYX	Price T.Rowe:High Yield	'84	I	BD	1657.2	n/a	....	+ 14.0	+ 11.0	+ 13.8	+ 3.6	− 4.2	$2,500	None	0.693	0.066	....	...	13,177	8.55	7.83	7.94	7.94	8.7
PRITX	Price T.Rowe:Intl.Stock	*'80	G	INTL	10272.1	n/a	....	+ 11.4	+ 15.9	+ 2.7	+ 15.9	+ 33.9	$2,500	None	0.22	0.13	0.35	0.91	20,413	19.03	14.17	19.03	19.03	1.2

Uniform Footnote Explanations-See page 235. **Stock Splits & Divs.** (figures adjusted): [1] Was Tax Free Bond(10/96). [2] 5% E.R.F.reducing over 6 yrs. [3] Was Capstone PBHG. [4] 1% E.R.F.. [5] Was Stock(6/96). [6] Was Chase Fd. of Boston. [7] Incl.Convert. Fd. (10/23/98). [8] Was Total Return(11/96). [9] Was Pasadena Group(10/97). [10] 1.25% ERF within 12 mos.. [11] Was Equity Inc.(2/97). [12] ERF 1% within 1 yr.

Ticker Symbol	Fund	Year Offered	Prin. Obj.	Type	Sept. 30, 1999 Total Net Assets (MIL.$)	Cash & Equiv (MIL.$)	See Foot-notes	Net Assets per Share % Change from Previous Dec. 31 — At: Dec. 31 1995	1996	1997	1998	Dec. 31, 1999	Min. Unit	Max. Sales Chg. %	Distributions Per Share from Invest. Income 1998	1999	Security Profits 1998	1999	$10,000 Invested 12-31-93 Now Worth	PRICE RECORD NAV Per Sh — 1999 — High	Low	#12-31-99 NAV Per Shr.	Offer Price	% Yield From Inv. Inc.
PRNEX	Price T.Rowe:New Era	'69	G	C	1117.7	n/a	. . . .	+ 20.7	+ 24.3	+ 10.7	− 10.0	+ 20.9	$2,500	None	0.40	0.30	3.17	1.82	19,011	25.01	18.41	21.80	21.80	1.8
PRNHX	Price T.Rowe:New Horizons	'60	G	C	4779.8	n/a	. . . .	+ 55.2	+ 16.9	+ 9.7	+ 5.6	+ 30.9	$2,500	None	. . . .	. . . .	1.27	3.02	27,567	27.99	20.18	27.53	27.53	. . . .
PRCIX	Price T.Rowe:New Income	*'73	IP	BD	1885.9	n/a	. . . .	+ 17.8	+ 2.2	+ 9.0	+ 4.4	− 2.1	$2,500	None	0.515	0.467	0.14	. . .	13,117	8.83	8.16	8.16	8.16	6.3
OTCFX	Price T.Rowe:Small-Cap Stock	*'56	G	C	1494.5	n/a	1	+ 33.7	+ 21.0	+ 28.7	− 3.6	+ 14.3	$2,500	None	0.10	0.08	0.50	0.89	22,941	22.80	18.29	22.80	22.80	0.4
PRTAX	Price T.Rowe:Tax-Free Income	'76	I	TF	1384.7	n/a	∫†	+ 17.3	+ 3.1	+ 9.1	+ 5.4	− 4.2	$2,500	None	0.463	0.449	0.04	0.01	12,603	10.05	9.09	9.09	9.09	5.1
PRMGX	Principal Balanced Fund Cl.A	*'88	R	BD	110.8	n/a	2	+ 23.0	+ 13.4	+ 17.1	+ 10.3	− 0.1	$300	4.75	0.29	0.319	0.454	0.641	17,260	16.24	14.25	14.44	15.16	1.9
PRBDX	Principal Bond Fund Cl.A	*'88	I	BD	147.4	n/a	3	+ 21.6	+ 2.6	+ 10.6	+ 7.0	− 5.1	$1,000	4.75	0.708	0.455	0.033	. . .	13,381	11.63	10.49	10.51	11.03	6.4
PCACX	Principal Capital Value Cl.A	'69	GI	C	541.5	n/a	4	+ 31.6	+ 23.5	+ 28.4	+ 11.2	− 15.8	$300	4.75	0.26	0.252	1.951	. . .	19,383	33.27	24.92	25.32	26.58	1.0
PEMGX	Principal Midcap Fund Cl.A	*'88	G	C	302.4	n/a	5	+ 34.2	+ 20.6	+ 22.9	− 0.2	+ 11.3	$300	4.75	. . . .	. . . .	. . . .	2.03	22,757	47.35	38.46	46.71	49.04	. . . .
PRGVX	Principal Govt. Secs. Income Cl.A	*'85	I	GB	238.7	n/a	2	+ 18.7	+ 3.6	+ 9.4	+ 7.0	− 1.9	$1,000	4.75	0.706	0.465	. . . .	. . .	13,430	11.66	10.83	10.93	11.48	6.1
PRGWX	Principal Growth Fund Cl.A	*'69	G	C	465.4	n/a	6	+ 33.3	+ 12.2	+ 24.8	+ 20.3	+ 12.0	$300	4.75	0.336	0.119	. . . .	. . .	25,828	70.05	60.13	69.16	72.61	0.5
PTBDX	Principal Tax Exempt Bond Cl.A	*'86	I	TF	191.3	n/a	2 ∫†	+ 20.3	+ 4.4	+ 8.9	+ 5.0	− 4.3	$1,000	4.75	0.611	0.543	0.005	. . .	12,465	12.59	11.45	11.46	12.03	5.1
PRWLX	Principal International Fund Cl.A	*'82	G	GL	335.0	n/a	7 †	+ 11.4	+ 23.7	+ 12.2	+ 7.0	+ 8.9	$300	4.75	. . . .	0.114	0.456	. . .	16,989	10.78	9.10	9.87	10.36	. . . .
PBQAX	Prudential:Equity Cl.A	*'90	G	C	2118.2	n/a	. . . .	+ 31.3	+ 17.4	+ 17.1	+ 8.5	+ 0.5	$1,000	5.0	0.278	0.16	1.49	0.415	20,116	22.81	18.19	19.29	20.31	1.4
PBQFX	Prudential:Equity Cl.B	*'82	G	C	2360.5	n/a	8	+ 30.4	+ 16.6	+ 22.9	+ 7.6	+ 0.1	$1,000	ERF	0.115	0.08	1.49	0.415	20,429	22.70	18.17	19.26	19.26	0.6
PRGLX	Prudential:Global Cl.B	*'84	G	GL	294.6	n/a	9	+ 14.1	+ 27.1	+ 4.0	+ 22.1	+ 46.8	$1,000	ERF	0.02	0.051	0.61	1.81	25,547	23.24	16.35	22.90	22.90	0.1
PBGPX	Prudential:Govt.Income Cl.B	*'85	I	GB	243.1	n/a	10	+ 18.0	+ 0.5	+ 8.3	+ 7.7	− 5.9	$1,000	ERF	0.486	0.283	. . . .	. . .	12,417	9.26	8.43	8.43	8.43	5.8
PBHYX	Prudential:High Yield Cl.B	'79	R	BD	1951.3	n/a	11	+ 16.1	+ 11.2	+ 11.6	− 0.6	− 1.0	$1,000	ERF	0.72	0.42	. . . .	. . .	13,781	8.00	7.29	7.36	7.36	9.8
PBHMX	Prudential:Natl.Muni.Cl.B	'80	I	TF	103.8	n/a	12 ∫†	+ 15.7	+ 2.2	+ 9.1	+ 4.9	− 4.3	$1,000	ERF	0.726	0.664	0.122	. . .	12,135	16.22	14.74	14.75	14.75	4.9
PRUAX	Prudential:Utility Cl.A	*'90	IG	C	2724.0	n/a	. . . .	+ 25.3	+ 21.5	+ 26.4	+ 8.0	− 5.3	$1,000	5.0	0.324	0.162	0.94	0.199	18,166	12.83	10.71	11.05	11.63	2.8
PRUTX	Prudential:Utility Cl.B	*'81	I	C	1467.4	n/a	13	+ 24.4	+ 20.7	+ 25.6	+ 7.2	− 5.6	$1,000	ERF	0.228	0.114	0.94	0.199	17,482	12.80	10.71	11.05	11.05	2.1
PAGVX	Putnam Amer. Govt. Income Cl.A	'85	I	GB	1564.0	n/a	★	+ 17.7	+ 2.0	+ 8.9	+ 8.3	− 3.4	$500	4.75	0.528	0.451	. . . .	. . .	13,281	9.00	8.22	8.23	8.64	6.1
PAPAX	Putnam Asia Pacific Cl. A	'91	G	INTL	244.8	n/a	. . . .	+ 2.7	+ 5.9	− 15.0	− 9.6	+ 107.5	$500	5.75	1.12	0.13	. . . .	. . .	16,699	19.00	8.73	19.00	20.16	5.6
PCAPX	Putnam Capital Appreciation Cl. A	'93	G	C	1067.4	n/a	. . . .	+ 34.4	+ 30.0	+ 29.7	+ 8.5	+ 15.4	$500	5.75	0.144	. . . .	0.502	. . .	30,190	26.14	20.96	26.14	27.73	0.5
PDETX	Putnam Global Equity Fund Cl. A	'94	G	C	385.7	n/a	. . . .	+ 28.7	+ 16.6	+ 22.8	+ 17.8	+ 44.0	$500	5.75	. . . .	0.693	1.237	. . .	. . . . .	20.10	13.33	18.41	19.53	. . . .
PDINX	Putnam Diversified Income Cl. A	'88	I	BD	1508.7	n/a	. . . .	+ 18.1	+ 8.4	+ 7.8	− 1.7	− 0.1	$500	4.75	0.86	0.72	. . . .	. . .	12,821	11.55	10.63	10.77	11.31	7.6
PMEAX	Putnam Emerging Markets Cl. A	'95	G	INTL	58.3	n/a	. . . .	− 7.1	+ 23.6	− 7.1	− 24.5	+ 77.7	$500	5.75	0.066	. . . .	. . . .	. . .	. . . . .	12.51	6.63	12.51	13.27	0.5
PEUGX	Putnam Europe Growth Cl. A	'90	G	INTL	855.2	n/a	. . . .	+ 21.2	+ 22.5	+ 21.7	+ 23.4	+ 22.1	$500	5.75	0.212	. . . .	0.994	. . .	28,967	26.59	21.14	26.55	28.17	0.8
PEYAX	Putnam Equity Income Cl.A	'88	GI	BD	1150.4	n/a	. . . .	+ 26.2	+ 21.1	+ 26.1	+ 12.3	− 9.3	$500	5.75	0.28	0.21	1.534	. . .	19,885	17.61	13.61	13.94	14.79	1.9
PGEOX	Putnam(George) Cl.A	'37	GIS	B	3671.7	n/a	. . . .	+ 29.4	+ 15.9	+ 20.6	+ 10.3	+ 0.4	$500	5.75	0.60	0.60	1.199	1.225	19,950	19.46	16.01	16.28	17.27	3.5
PUTIX	Putnam Global Growth & Income Cl. A	'95	GI	INTL	36.0	n/a	. . . .	. . . .	+ 19.8	+ 21.4	. . . .	+ 4.7	$500	5.75	0.09	0.03	0.29	. . .	. . . . .	14.96	12.70	13.60	14.43	0.6
PEQUX	Putnam Global Growth Cl.A	'67	G	GL	3872.5	n/a		+ 14.7	+ 16.5	+ 12.6	+ 28.7	+ 49.3	$500	5.75	0.048	. . . .	0.323	. . .	28,651	19.29	12.16	18.59	19.72	0.2
PXGIX	Putnam Growth & Income II	'95	GI	C	1261.6	n/a	. . . .	. . . .	+ 20.9	+ 24.6	+ 12.1	− 10.2	$500	5.75	0.24	0.15	1.135	. . .	. . . . .	15.86	12.08	12.38	13.14	1.8
POGAX	Putnam Growth Opportunities Cl. A	'95	G	C	1443.5	n/a	. . . .	. . . .	. . . .	+ 30.0	+ 47.4	+ 51.4	$500	5.75	. . . .	. . . .	. . . .	. . .	. . . . .	29.85	19.31	29.85	31.67	. . . .
PGRWX	Putnam Growth & Income Cl.A	'57	GI	C	20886.1	n/a	. . . .	+ 36.1	+ 21.5	+ 24.2	+ 14.9	− 7.0	$500	5.75	0.46	0.315	1.506	. . .	21,880	23.07	18.28	18.75	19.89	2.3
PHSTX	Putnam Health Sciences Cl.A	*'82	G	C	2706.7	n/a	. . . .	+ 46.8	+ 12.5	+ 32.0	+ 26.5	− 4.4	$500	5.75	. . . .	. . . .	5.011	. . .	30,344	64.12	54.63	61.20	64.93	. . . .
PHIGX	Putnam High Yield Cl.A	*'78	I	BD	2427.3	n/a	. . . .	+ 17.2	+ 12.0	+ 14.0	− 7.4	+ 3.5	$500	4.75	1.253	0.852	. . . .	. . .	13,711	11.13	10.15	10.35	10.87	11.5
PHYIX	Putnam High Yield Advantage Cl.A	*'86	I	BD	980.9	n/a	. . . .	+ 17.9	+ 10.0	+ 12.7	− 8.8	− 3.8	$500	4.75	0.941	0.077	. . . .	. . .	12,208	8.45	7.64	7.79	8.18	11.5
PINCX	Putnam Income Cl.A	'54	IS	B	1182.8	n/a	. . . .	+ 19.1	+ 3.7	+ 8.0	+ 3.6	− 3.5	$500	4.75	0.444	0.317	. . . .	. . .	12,909	6.95	6.34	6.36	6.68	6.6
POVSX	Putnam Intl. Growth Cl. A	'91	G	INTL	3256.0	n/a	. . . .	+ 13.9	+ 16.0	+ 17.9	+ 18.8	+ 54.3	$500	5.75	0.211	. . . .	0.36	. . .	28,612	29.68	19.03	29.68	31.49	0.7
PNGAX	Putnam Intl. Growth & Income Cl. A	'96	GI	INTL	490.0	n/a	. . . .	. . . .	. . . .	+ 19.8	+ 11.4	+ 10.2	$500	5.75	0.248	0.044	0.496	. . .	. . . . .	13.74	10.72	12.17	12.91	1.9
PINOX	Putnam Intl. New Opportunities Cl. A		G	INTL	895.0	n/a	. . . .	. . . .	+ 16.9	+ 1.4	+ 15.9	+ 92.3	$500	5.75	. . . .	. . . .	. . . .	. . .	. . . . .	24.83	12.97	24.83	26.34	. . . .
PNVAX	Putnam Intl. Voyager Cl. A	'95	G	INTL	240.4	n/a	. . . .	. . . .	+ 20.0	+ 16.4	+ 27.0	+ 87.7	$500	5.75	0.135	. . . .	0.271	. . .	. . . . .	25.71	13.51	25.70	27.27	0.5
PINVX	Putnam Investors Cl.A	'25	GIS	C	6000.0	n/a	. . . .	+ 37.5	+ 21.2	+ 34.2	+ 35.2	+ 30.1	$500	5.75	. . . .	0.128	0.382	. . .	37,961	19.15	14.37	19.15	20.32	. . . .

Uniform Footnote Explanations-See page 235. Stock Splits & Divs. (figures adjusted): [1] Was OTC Fund(4/97). [2] Was Princor Series(12/97). [3] Was Princor Bond(12/97). [4] Was Princor Cap. Accum.(12/97). [5] Was Princor Emerging Growth(12/97). [6] WAs Princor Series(12/97). [7] Was Princor World(12/97). [8] 5%E.R.F.reducing 1% per yr. [9] 5% E.R.F.reducing 1% per yr. [10] 5%E.R.F.,reducing 1% per yr. [11] 5% E.R.F.,reducing 1% per yr. [12] 4% E.R.F.,reducing over 5 yrs. [13] 5% E.R.F.reducing over 5yrs.

Ticker Symbol	Fund	Year Offered	Prin. Obj.	Type	Sept. 30, 1999 Total Net Assets (MIL.$)	Cash & Equiv (MIL.$)	See Foot-notes	Net Assets per Share % Change from Previous Dec. 31 At: Dec. 31 1995	1996	1997	1998	Dec. 31, 1999	Min. Unit	Max. Sales Chg. %	Distributions Per Share from Invest. Income 1998	Invest. Income 1999	Security Profits 1998	Security Profits 1999	$10,000 Invested 12-31-93 Now Worth	PRICE RECORD 1999 High	1999 Low	NAV #12-31-99 Per Shr.	Offer Price	% Yield From Inv. Inc.
PTFHX	Putnam Municipal Income Cl.A	*'89	I	TF	768.8	n/a	ʃ†	+ 18.3	+ 3.0	+ 9.2	+ 5.0	− 5.6	$500	4.75	0.456	0.286	....	...	12,358	9.39	8.50	8.51	8.93	5.1
PNOPX	Putnam New Opportunities Cl.A	*'90	G	C	11838.4	n/a	....	+ 46.3	+ 10.8	+ 22.4	+ 24.0	+ 68.2	$500	5.75	....	....	1.875	7.30	42,706	90.96	56.70	90.96	96.51	....
POEGX	Putnam OTC Emerging Growth Cl.A	*'82	G	C	3030.2	n/a	....	+ 54.9	+ 4.5	+ 10.2	+ 10.6	+ 114.6	$500	5.75	....	....	0.563	...	43,100	37.01	15.87	37.01	39.27	....
PTAEX	Putnam Tax Exempt Inc.Cl.A	'76	I	TF	1736.9	n/a	ʃ†	+ 17.1	+ 2.4	+ 9.3	+ 4.1	− 8.3	$500	4.75	0.416	0.042	0.027	...	11,548	9.26	8.37	8.38	8.80	4.7
PANVX	Putnam New Value Cl. A	'95	GI	C	377.3	n/a	....	....	+ 24.5	+ 18.8	+ 5.3	− 0.3	$500	5.75	0.131	0.164	1.316	1.39	.....	15.73	11.48	11.86	12.58	1.0
PTHYX	Putnam Tax Free High Yield Cl.B	*'85	I	TF	655.9	n/a	[1]ʃ†	+ 15.6	+ 2.3	+ 8.2	+ 4.2	− 3.7	$500	ERF	0.657	0.678	....	...	12,095	14.75	13.43	13.43	13.43	4.9
PDVAX	Putnam Strategic Income Cl. A	'96	I	BD	80.5	n/a	....	....	....	+ 9.5	− 2.6	+ 1.5	$500	4.75	0.613	0.624	....	...	.....	7.79	7.15	7.26	7.62	8.0
PVISX	Putnam Vista Cl.A	*'68	G	C	3641.1	n/a	....	+ 38.7	+ 22.2	+ 22.7	+ 18.8	+ 51.1	$500	5.75	....	....	1.028	2.29	35,913	18.13	12.57	17.46	18.53	....
PVOYX	Putnam Voyager Cl.A	*'69	G	C	17095.8	n/a	....	+ 39.8	+ 12.8	+ 25.7	+ 23.5	+ 54.8	$500	5.75	0.023	....	1.585	2.98	38,009	31.06	21.44	30.96	32.85	0.1
PVIIX	Putnam Voyager II Cl. A	'93	G	C	959.8	n/a	....	+ 49.9	+ 6.3	+ 23.4	+ 23.1	+ 78.9	$500	None	....	....	0.832	2.16	43,433	38.45	22.00	38.45	40.80	....
RMUNX	Rochester Fund Municipals	*'86	IP	TF	3569.2	n/a	ʃ†	+ 18.1	+ 5.1	+ 9.0	+ 6.3	− 5.7	$2,000	4.0	0.967	0.951	0.002	...	12,450	18.89	16.77	16.78	17.62	5.5
LTNYX	Rochester Limited Term N.Y.Municipal	*'91	I	TF	1087.2	n/a	ʃ†	+ 14.3	+ 4.6	+ 7.8	+ 5.4	− 1.2	$5,000	2.0	0.151	0.139	....	...	13,354	3.38	3.19	3.19	3.31	4.6
SACPX	Salomon Bros.Capital Fund	*'76	GI	C	197.3	n/a	....	+ 34.6	+ 26.0	+ 26.1	+ 21.8	+ 19.6	$1,000	None	0.041	....	2.838	2.061	26,854	27.37	21.93	25.43	25.43	0.2
SAIFX	Salomon Bros. Investors Cl.O	'58	GI	C	641.2	n/a		+ 40.1	+ 29.2	+ 25.7	+ 14.6	+ 5.3	$500	None	0.169	0.16	2.00	2.37	27,100	26.07	20.10	20.69	20.69	0.8
SCDGX	Scudder Fds:Growth & Inc	'29	GI	C	6809.9	n/a		+ 31.5	+ 17.1	+ 20.1	+ 6.1	+ 3.3	$1,000	None	0.605	0.41	2.09	0.08	20,796	29.59	24.86	26.69	26.69	2.3
SCDUX	Scudder Fds: Large Co. Value	'56	G	C	2346.8	n/a	[2]	+ 31.6	+ 19.7	+ 32.4	+ 9.6	− 2.1	$1,000	None	0.18	....	2.10	...	20,163	31.80	26.39	26.91	26.91	0.7
SCINX	Scudder Fds:International	'53	G	INTL	3735.0	n/a	....	+ 12.2	+ 9.9	+ 8.0	+ 18.6	+ 50.7	$1,000	None	....	....	5.56	2.65	23,088	70.94	46.53	70.74	70.74	....
SCMBX	Scudder Fds:Man.Mun.Bds	'76	IR	TF	737.0	n/a	ʃ†	+ 16.7	+ 4.0	+ 8.5	+ 5.7	− 6.0	$1,000	None	0.416	0.113	0.05	...	12,312	9.25	8.51	8.52	8.52	4.9
SUSIX	Security Capital U.S. Real Estate Cl.I	*'97	GI	SP	52.7	n/a	....	....	....	....	− 15.4	− 0.9	$250,000	None	....	0.364	0.29	...	.....	11.04	8.61	9.37	9.37	....
SUSRX	Security Capital U.S. Real Estate Cl.R	*'97	GI	SP	2.7	n/a	....	....	....	....	− 14.2	− 5.0	$2,500	None	0.10	....	0.29	...	.....	11.03	8.61	9.37	9.37	1.1
SECEX	Security Equity Cl.A	'62	G	C	917.2	n/a	....	+ 38.3	+ 22.7	+ 29.1	+ 26.3	+ 7.2	$100	5.75	0.035	....	0.681	...	28,890	10.95	9.61	10.70	11.35	0.3
SBDFX	Security Inc.Corp.Bond	*'70	IP	GB	49.4	n/a	....	+ 17.6	− 0.6	+ 9.3	+ 6.7	− 4.2	$100	4.75	0.384	0.373	....	...	11,989	7.18	6.47	6.47	6.79	5.7
SECIX	Security Growth & Income Cl.A	'44	IG	FL	74.8	n/a	....	+ 27.4	+ 19.2	+ 30.5	− 16.7	− 1.0	$100	5.75	0.115	....	....	...	15,068	8.02	6.64	6.89	7.31	1.6
SECUX	Security Ultra	'69	G	C	96.2	n/a	....	+ 19.0	+ 18.0	+ 17.6	+ 15.4	+ 53.6	$100	5.75	....	....	1.907	...	27,339	12.12	7.42	12.12	12.86	....
SLASX	Selected Amer. Shares	'33	GI	B	3155.7	n/a	....	+ 37.4	+ 22.3	+ 36.6	+ 16.2	+ 19.3	$1,000	None	0.15	0.10	0.26	1.26	30,802	36.87	30.36	35.80	35.80	0.4
SCFIX	Seligman Capital Cl.A	'69	G	C,L	278.9	n/a	....	+ 35.8	+ 17.0	+ 21.6	+ 18.6	+ 48.5	$1,000	4.75	....	....	0.676	2.772	31,509	27.01	18.60	27.01	28.36	....
SCSFX	Seligman Com.Stock Cl.A	'29	IG	C,FL	676.0	n/a	....	+ 27.8	+ 16.3	+ 21.6	+ 16.3	+ 2.6	$1,000	4.75	0.282	0.23	2.468	1.027	21,156	17.19	14.44	14.93	15.67	1.8
SLMCX	Seligman Communic. & Info.Cl.A	*'83	GR	C,SP	4436.8	n/a	....	+ 43.6	+ 11.5	+ 24.4	+ 33.7	+ 71.8	$1,000	4.75	....	....	0.345	5.553	61,673	47.25	28.43	47.25	49.61	....
SGRFX	Seligman Growth Cl.A	'37	G	C	973.9	n/a	[3]	+ 28.4	+ 22.3	+ 16.4	+ 34.2	+ 29.1	$1,000	4.75	0.01	....	0.73	0.96	30,401	8.87	7.25	8.62	9.05	0.1
SINFX	Seligman Income Cl.A	'47	I	B	211.0	n/a	....	+ 20.2	+ 8.3	+ 13.1	+ 7.1	− 2.6	$1,000	4.75	0.65	0.409	0.856	...	14,544	14.58	13.11	13.57	14.25	4.6
SENCX	Sentinel Group:Com.Stk	*'33	GI	C	1496.7	n/a	....	+ 34.0	+ 20.8	+ 27.4	+ 13.9	− 5.0	$500	5.0	0.421	0.273	3.805	...	22,047	45.98	38.51	39.66	41.75	1.0
SEQUX	Sequoia Fund	'69	G	C	3921.5	n/a	§†	+ 41.3	+ 21.5	+ 43.2	+ 34.6	− 17.6	$1,000	None	0.37	0.025	8.02	5.08	27,730	160.40	123.30	127.27	127.27	0.3
SHAPX	SMBS Appreciation Cl.A	'70	G	C	3031.7	n/a	....	+ 28.9	+ 17.6	+ 26.1	+ 18.8	+ 13.7	$1,000	5.0	0.05	1.674	1.183	...	25,639	17.14	15.02	15.73	16.56	0.3
SHRCX	SMBS Calif.Munic.Cl.A	*'84	IP	TF	707.0	n/a	?ʃ	+ 21.5	+ 5.5	+ 10.7	+ 5.3	− 6.4	$1,000	4.0	0.807	0.632	0.098	...	13,077	17.11	15.18	15.24	15.88	5.1
SLDSX	SMBS Diversified Strategic Inc.Cl.B	*'89	I	FL	1717.2	n/a	....	+ 14.5	+ 9.5	+ 6.7	+ 5.1	− 1.2	$1,000	ERF	0.552	0.434	....	...	13,405	7.94	7.34	7.34	7.34	7.5
HGVSX	SMBS Govt.Securities Cl.B	*'84	I	GB	73.8	n/a	[4]	+ 12.4	− 0.4	+ 10.4	+ 7.2	− 5.6	$1,000	ERF	0.528	0.413	....	...	12,120	10.01	9.00	9.00	9.00	5.9
HBDIX	SMBS Investment Grade Bond Cl.B	*'82	I	BD	207.9	n/a	....	+ 33.0	− 2.8	+ 7.8	+ 7.5	− 9.7	$1,000	ERF	0.729	0.616	0.364	...	12,216	13.21	11.19	11.21	11.21	6.5
SHMGX	SMBS Managed Govt.Cl.A	*'84	I	GB	314.4	n/a	....	+ 12.9	+ 3.3	+ 9.1	+ 5.1	− 5.7	$1,000	4.5	0.712	0.058	....	...	12,384	12.79	11.90	11.97	12.53	5.7
SHMMX	SMBS Managed Municipals Cl.A	*'81	I	TF	2128.5	n/a	....	+ 19.8	+ 3.9	+ 10.4	+ 4.5	− 7.7	$1,000	4.0	0.802	0.614	0.113	...	12,671	16.14	14.11	14.15	14.74	5.4
SOPTX	SMBS Premium Total Return Cl.B	*'85	GI	C	1992.6	n/a	....	+ 21.1	+ 18.8	+ 23.9	− 0.3	− 15.0	$1,000	ERF	0.30	0.14	0.547	...	15,408	22.89	17.43	17.94	17.94	1.7
SXMTX	SMBS Tax Exempt Cl.B	*'85	I	TF	322.2	n/a	?ʃ	+ 15.0	+ 3.7	+ 8.8	+ 3.3	− 5.6	$1,000	ERF	0.603	0.813	0.429	...	11,843	17.69	15.80	15.80	15.80	3.8
SLSUX	SMBS Utilities Fund Cl.B		IG	C	518.7	n/a	....	+ 30.0	+ 0.5	+ 19.4	+ 10.4	+ 10.3	$1,000	ERF	0.11	0.253	4.57	0.078	17,096	14.61	13.12	14.61	14.61	0.8
SBCIX	Smith Barney Equity Income Cl.A	*'66	IG	C	759.1	n/a	[5]	+ 22.3	+ 16.1	+ 27.7	+ 8.6	− 6.8	$1,000	5.0	0.274	0.044	0.001	...	17,398	20.30	16.81	17.00	17.89	1.5
SGENX	SoGen Intl.Fund	'70	G	GL	1920.6	n/a	†	+ 15.2	+ 13.6	+ 8.3	− 7.4	+ 7.0	$1,000	3.75	....	....	0.52	...	14,394	26.77	22.13	24.65	25.61	....

Uniform Footnote Explanations-See page 235. Stock Splits & Divs. (figures adjusted): [1] 5% ERF reducing over 7 yrs. [2] Incl.Scudder Special:. Each Special hldr.rec'd 4.5785 Cap.Growth shs. [3] Was Natl. Investors. [4] Was Hutton Govt.Secs. [5] Was Inc. & Growth(4/96).

Ticker Symbol	Fund	Year Offered	Prin. Obj.	Type	Sept. 30, 1999 Total Net Assets (MIL.$)	Cash & Equiv (MIL.$)	See Foot-notes	Net Assets per Share % Change from Previous Dec. 31 At: Dec. 31 1995	1996	1997	1998	Dec. 31, 1999	Min. Unit	Max. Sales Chg. %	Distributions Per Share from Invest. Income 1998	Invest. Income 1999	Security Profits 1998	Security Profits 1999	$10,000 Invested 12-31-93 Now Worth	PRICE RECORD 1999 High	1999 Low	NAV Per Sh #12-31-99 NAV Per Shr.	Offer Price	% Yield From Inv. Inc.
SSEAX	State St. Research Alpha Cl.A	*'86	IG	C	97.7	n/a	[1]	+ 28.4	+ 8.2	+ 26.8	+ 1.1	− 5.9	$2,500	4.5	0.28	0.14	....	...	15,971	16.32	13.34	13.98	14.83	1.9
SSAVX	State St. Research Argo Cl.A	*'86	G	C	65.1	n/a	....	+ 33.6	+ 13.3	+ 26.6	+ 13.8	− 3.1	$2,500	4.5	0.055	0.07	1.531	3.61	20,096	22.06	14.18	14.86	15.77	0.3
SSGRX	State St.Research Global Resources Cl.A	*'90	G	SP	72.3	n/a	[2]	+ 22.6	+ 64.5	+ 6.2	− 48.6	+ 15.5	$2,500	4.5	....	....	0.748	...	12,156	14.20	7.73	11.41	12.11	....
SSHAX	State St. Research High Income Cl.A	*'86	I	BD	583.9	n/a	....	+ 12.0	+ 16.3	+ 13.8	− 1.2	− 1.6	$2,500	4.5	0.522	0.308	0.172	...	14,180	5.79	5.25	5.26	5.51	9.5
SSAMX	State St. Research Managed Assets Cl.A	*'88	G	FL	287.6	n/a	....	+ 22.5	+ 19.6	+ 15.3	+ 8.1	+ 10.4	$2,500	4.5	0.22	0.15	0.879	0.037	18,991	11.27	9.92	11.27	11.80	1.9
SSGIX	State St. Research Govt. Income Cl.A	*'87	I	GB	486.8	n/a	[3]	+ 17.1	+ 3.5	+ 8.8	+ 8.2	− 2.5	$2,500	4.5	0.703	0.671	....	...	13,508	13.05	12.01	12.01	12.58	5.6
SSATX	State St. Research Tax Exempt Cl.A	*'86	I	TF	191.6	n/a	....	+ 16.2	+ 3.2	+ 9.9	+ 5.3	− 6.1	$2,500	4.5	0.377	0.228	0.042	...	12,145	8.62	7.79	7.79	8.16	4.6
STSTX	State St. Research Invest.Trust Cl.S	'24	GI	C	1005.1	n/a		+ 32.9	+ 21.4	+ 29.2	+ 28.8	+ 14.8	$2,500	None	0.09	0.03	0.952	0.134	29,743	14.21	12.24	14.10	14.10	0.6
SRFBX	SteinRoe Balanced Fund	'49	GI	FL	254.3	n/a	[4]	+ 22.1	+ 16.7	+ 17.2	+ 9.3	+ 11.8	$2,500	None	0.18	0.919	2.07	2.30	19,570	34.13	31.56	32.54	32.54	0.6
SRFCX	SteinRoe Capital Opport.	*'69	G	C	439.3	n/a	[5]	+ 51.1	+ 24.7	+ 6.2	− 1.6	+ 38.1	$2,500	None	....	....	....	3.99	27,165	36.56	26.67	36.56	36.56	....
SRFSX	SteinRoe Growth Stock	'58	G	C	831.2	n/a	....	+ 35.4	+ 20.6	+ 31.4	+ 25.5	+ 35.8	$2,500	None	....	....	....	3.44	35,179	55.39	43.14	55.39	55.39	....
SRGNX	SteinRoe Growth & Income	*'87	G	C	375.9	n/a	[6]	+ 29.8	+ 21.6	+ 25.6	+ 18.4	+ 10.9	$2,500	None	0.05	0.197	0.37	1.16	26,004	29.19	25.36	27.44	27.44	0.2
SRDSX	SteinRoe Disciplined Stk. Fund	*'68	G	C	604.2	n/a	....	+ 18.5	+ 18.5	+ 25.6	− 27.8	+ 9.3	$2,500	None	....	0.11	....	5.00	13,445	24.68	17.58	18.06	18.06	....
STRFX	Strong Total Return	*'81	GI	FL	1166.6	n/a	....	+ 26.8	− 3.2	+ 23.6	+ 30.6	+ 36.6	$250	None	0.073	....	....	...	26,686	53.41	33.87	47.10	47.10	0.2
SBABX	SunAmerica Balanced Assets Cl.B	*'85	GI	C,BD,P	177.3	n/a	....	+ 26.7	+ 8.2	+ 23.1	+ 12.7	+ 20.3	$500	ERF	0.102	0.124	....	1.98	22,285	22.30	19.10	20.97	20.97	0.5
SEGAX	Sunamerica Small Co. Growth Cl.A	*'86	G	C	147.0	n/a	....	+ 49.5	+ 14.8	+ 3.0	+ 11.8	+ 81.4	$500	5.75	....	....	1.399	4.97	37,536	39.19	23.60	38.16	40.49	....
SGTBX	SunAmerica U.S.Govt.Secs.Cl.B	*'86	IP	GB	82.4	n/a	[7]	+ 14.4	+ 2.2	+ 7.0	+ 5.8	− 2.3	$2,500	ERF	0.372	0.316	....	...	12,763	8.84	8.31	8.31	8.31	4.5
TEDMX	Templeton Developing Markets	*'91	G	INTL	2428.7	n/a	....	− 0.3	+ 18.8	− 9.5	− 18.5	+ 51.6	$100	5.75	0.19	....	0.05	...	12,118	15.61	9.49	15.61	16.56	1.1
TEMFX	Templeton Foreign	'82	G	INTL	11644.3	n/a	....	+ 11.0	+ 17.8	+ 7.3	− 5.4	+ 37.3	$100	5.75	0.26	0.268	0.765	0.035	18,333	11.22	8.10	11.22	11.90	2.2
TEGOX	Templeton Global Opportunities	*'90	G	INTL	586.6	n/a	....	+ 11.6	+ 16.3	+ 14.2	− 4.5	+ 20.1	$100	5.75	....	0.085	....	0.363	16,371	17.12	13.59	17.12	18.16	....
TEPLX	Templeton Growth	'54	G	GL	12952.0	n/a	[8]	+ 19.5	+ 20.1	+ 16.8	− 3.0	+ 28.4	$100	5.75	0.405	0.458	2.035	0.601	21,108	20.12	16.02	19.96	21.18	1.9
TEMGX	Templeton Smaller Cos.Growth	*'81	G	GL	1011.5	n/a	[9]	+ 17.5	+ 21.6	+ 7.5	− 11.7	+ 8.7	$100	5.75	0.11	0.154	0.175	0.359	14,064	7.60	6.46	7.12	7.55	1.5
TEMWX	Templeton World	'77	G	GL	8865.9	n/a	....	+ 21.1	+ 20.9	+ 20.0	+ 5.1	+ 26.3	$100	5.75	0.36	0.336	1.385	1.09	23,601	18.81	15.29	18.69	19.83	1.8
THIMX	Thornburg Intermed. Muni Cl.A	*'88	I	TF	362.9	n/a	[10]∫†	+ 14.9	+ 3.0	+ 9.2	+ 5.0	− 4.2	$1,000	4.75	0.574	0.31	....	...	12,350	13.75	12.77	12.79	13.05	4.4
THNYX	Thornburg Intermed. N.Y.Muni Cl.A	*'88	I	TF	25.0	n/a	[11]∫†	+ 14.5	+ 3.1	+ 4.5	+ 3.2	− 2.3	$1,000	4.75	0.319	0.37	....	...	11,953	12.86	12.10	12.11	12.36	2.6
LTCAX	Thornburg Ltd.Term Muni-Cal.Cl.A	*'88	I	TF	112.1	n/a	[12]∫†	+ 15.5	+ 3.4	+ 4.1	+ 4.5	− 1.2	$1,000	4.75	0.497	0.31	....	...	12,258	13.06	12.52	12.53	12.72	3.9
LTMFX	Thornburg Ltd. Term Munic:Natl. Cl.A	*'84	I	TF	785.1	n/a	[13]	+ 9.4	+ 3.9	+ 5.4	+ 4.3	− 1.8	$5,000	2.5	0.547	0.293	....	...	12,087	13.65	13.05	13.05	13.25	4.1
UNACX	United Accumalative Cl.A	'40	G	C	1849.8	n/a	....	+ 33.8	+ 12.0	+ 28.9	+ 21.8	+ 10.6	$500	5.75	0.105	0.015	1.08	...	25,995	9.78	7.92	9.14	9.70	1.1
UNHIX	United High Inc.	*'79	IG	B	921.2	n/a	....	+ 17.1	+ 11.3	+ 13.7	+ 3.8	+ 2.1	$1,000	5.75	0.802	0.736	....	...	15,155	9.54	8.77	8.88	9.42	8.5
UNCMX	United Income	'40	IS	C	7416.7	n/a	[14]	+ 29.5	+ 20.2	+ 27.1	+ 22.8	+ 15.8	$500	5.75	0.06	0.059	1.74	0.52	27,627	8.45	7.32	8.13	8.63	0.7
UNMBX	United Munic.Bond	'76	IS	TF	869.8	n/a	∫†	+ 19.7	+ 3.9	+ 9.9	+ 5.1	− 6.7	$500	4.25	0.37	0.334	0.111	...	12,464	7.48	6.58	6.58	6.87	5.4
UNVGX	United Vanguard Cl.A	'69	G	C	1936.8	n/a	....	+ 24.6	+ 7.5	+ 19.2	+ 31.1	+ 43.1	$500	5.75	0.01	....	0.115	0.871	31,780	12.31	9.00	12.31	13.06	0.1
USTEX	USAA Tax Exempt Long Term Fund	*'82	I	TF,BD	2058.2	n/a	∫†	+ 18.1	+ 4.2	+ 10.1	+ 5.4	− 5.3	$3,000	None	0.703	0.698	....	...	12,469	14.09	12.60	12.60	12.60	5.6
INIVX	Van Eck Funds:Intl.Investors	*'55	G	PM	178.1	n/a	....	− 8.9	− 9.3	− 35.9	− 11.8	− 12.6	$1,000	5.75	0.06	0.03	....	...	4,042	7.37	5.37	5.73	6.08	1.0
ACSTX	Van Kampen Comstock Cl. A	'68	G	FL	1730.9	n/a	[15]	+ 35.2	+ 21.2	+ 28.7	+ 19.4	− 6.0	$1,000	5.75	0.283	0.187	2.67	0.421	22,841	17.92	14.29	14.80	15.70	1.8
ACEGX	Van Kampen Emerging Growth Cl. A	*'70	G	FL	4170.8	n/a		+ 44.1	+ 17.8	+ 20.7	+ 33.9	+ 100.6	$1,000	5.75	....	....	2.309	9.302	51,071	87.65	47.72	87.37	92.70	....
ACENX	Van Kampen Enterprise Cl. A	'53	G	FL	2085.8	n/a	....	+ 33.4	+ 22.1	+ 27.8	+ 23.1	+ 12.0	$1,000	5.75	0.044	0.004	0.776	0.317	28,614	24.19	20.03	22.79	24.18	0.2
ACEIX	Van Kampen Equity Income Cl. A	*'60	IP	C	961.7	n/a	....	+ 32.5	+ 15.1	+ 23.6	+ 16.7	+ 0.1	$1,000	5.75	0.175	0.105	0.451	0.082	21,668	8.40	7.43	7.64	8.11	2.2
ACFMX	Van Kampen Ltd. Mat. Govt. Cl. A		IP	GB	37.6	n/a	....	+ 9.7	+ 3.2	+ 5.8	+ 5.2	+ 1.7	$1,000	2.25	0.66	0.587	....	...	12,828	12.16	11.78	11.78	12.05	5.5
ACGVX	Van Kampen Govt. Secs. Cl. A	*'84	I	GB	1689.3	n/a	....	+ 16.2	+ 1.7	+ 8.8	+ 8.0	− 3.5	$1,000	4.75	0.645	0.568	....	...	12,824	10.44	9.51	9.51	9.98	6.5
ACGIX	Van Kampen Growth & Inc. Cl. A	'46	GS	C	933.5	n/a	[16]	+ 35.3	+ 17.7	+ 24.1	+ 18.2	− 2.4	$1,000	5.75	0.199	0.142	1.109	...	22,480	20.75	17.03	17.74	18.82	1.1
ACHBX	Van Kampen Harbor Cl. A	'56	ISG	CV,BD	391.2	n/a	....	+ 22.8	+ 11.6	+ 16.3	+ 7.2	+ 45.0	$1,000	5.75	0.537	0.391	0.753	0.914	23,263	20.23	14.74	20.23	21.46	2.5
ACPAX	Van Kampen Pace Cl. A	*'69	G	FL	3493.3	n/a		+ 32.6	+ 20.2	+ 29.7	+ 21.4	+ 12.4	$1,000	5.75	0.106	....	1.254	2.29	27,108	16.03	13.36	13.82	14.66	0.7
VKCIX	Van Kampen Cal. Ins. TF Cl. A	*'85	IP	TF	161.7	n/a	∫†★	+ 17.8	+ 4.0	+ 8.7	+ 6.2	− 7.3	$1,000	3.0	0.882	0.414	....	...	11,996	18.67	16.70	16.77	17.33	5.1

Uniform Footnote Explanations-See page 235. Stock Splits & Divs. (figures adjusted): [1] Was Equity Income(3/98). [2] Was Global Energy('97). [3] Was Metlife State St.Govt Inc.. [4] Was Stein Roe Balanced. Was Total Return(4/96). [5] 2-for-1 split, Aug. '95. [6] Was Prime Equities(2/96). [7] 4% E.R.F.. [8] In Can. Curr.. Spun-off Can.assets. [9] Now incls.Global II assts.. Was Global. [10] Incl.ret.of cap. Incl. Mackenzie Natl. Muni (9/97). [11] Incl.ret.of cap. Incl.Mackenzie NY Muni(9/97). [12] Incl.ret.of cap.. Incl. Mackenzie Cal.Muni(9/97). [13] Incl. Mackenzie Ltd Term Muni(9/97). [14] Adjtd. for 5-for-1 stk. split 6/98. [15] Formerly Amer. Cap. Group(10/95). [16] Incl.Van Kamp.Growth & Inc.(10/95).

Ticker Symbol	Fund	Year Offered	Prin. Obj.	Type	Sept. 30, 1999 Total Net Assets (MIL.$)	Sept. 30, 1999 Cash & Equiv (MIL.$)	See Footnotes	Net Assets per Share % Change from Previous Dec. 31 — At: Dec. 31 1995	1996	1997	1998	Dec. 31, 1999	Min. Unit	Max. Sales Chg. %	Distributions Per Share from Invest. Income 1998	Invest. Income 1999	Security Profits 1998	Security Profits 1999	$10,000 Invested 12-31-93 Now Worth	PRICE RECORD NAV Per Sh — 1999 — High	1999 Low	#12-31-99 NAV Per Shr.	#12-31-99 Offer Price	% Yield From Inv. Inc.
VKHYX	Van Kampen Hi Yld. Cl. A	*'86	I	SP	246.0	n/a	....	+ 16.8	+ 11.9	+ 10.5	– 1.3	+ 4.5	$1,000	4.65	0.84	0.70	....	...	14,419	9.19	8.56	8.68	9.11	9.2
VKMTX	Van Kampen Ins. TF Cl. A	*'84	I	TF	1174.1	n/a	∫†★	+ 17.1	+ 3.5	+ 7.9	+ 4.3	– 6.1	$1,000	4.65	0.952	0.676	0.036	...	12,014	19.63	17.60	17.63	18.51	5.1
VKMPX	Van Kampen Penn. TF Inc. Cl. A	*'87	I	TF	204.9	n/a	∫†	+ 16.2	+ 3.7	+ 8.3	+ 5.2	– 6.5	$1,000	4.65	0.93	0.543	....	...	12,117	18.14	16.32	16.33	17.14	5.4
VKMHX	Van Kampen TF High Inc. Cl. A	*'85	I	TF	744.6	n/a	∫†	+ 15.2	+ 2.9	+ 8.8	+ 5.8	– 4.8	$1,000	4.65	0.836	0.67	....	...	12,367	14.93	13.48	13.48	14.15	5.9
VKMGX	Van Kampen U.S. Govt Cl. A	'84	I	GB	1902.6	n/a	★	+ 17.1	+ 3.8	+ 8.2	+ 5.6	– 1.2	$1,000	4.65	0.979	0.766	....	...	13,035	14.47	13.48	13.52	14.19	6.9
VFIIX	Vanguard FIS:GNMA	*'80	I	G	12590.1	n/a	....	+ 16.6	+ 5.0	+ 9.1	+ 7.0	– 4.6	$3,000	None	0.695	0.11	0.02	...	13,498	10.47	9.77	9.86	9.86	7.0
VWEHX	Vanguard FIS:High Yield Corp. Ptfl.	*'78	I	BD	5714.2	n/a	[1]	+ 18.5	+ 9.0	+ 11.4	+ 5.2	+ 1.5	$3,000	None	0.668	0.554	....	...	15,641	7.90	7.30	7.39	7.39	9.0
VWESX	Vanguard FIS:Long-Term Corp.	*'73	I	BD	3870.9	n/a	[2]	+ 25.5	+ 1.7	+ 13.1	+ 7.6	– 6.6	$3,000	None	0.589	0.513	0.082	0.055	13,767	9.38	8.11	8.11	8.11	7.3
VWAHX	Vanguard High Yield Muni Bond	*'79	I	TF	2959.1	n/a	∫†	+ 19.5	+ 4.3	+ 8.9	+ 6.1	– 5.0	$3,000	None	0.631	0.378	....	...	12,997	11.05	10.04	10.04	10.04	6.3
VFINX	Vanguard Index Trust:500 Ptfl.	'76	GI	SP	89364.2	n/a	....	+ 37.2	+ 22.7	+ 33.0	+ 27.9	+ 20.0	$3,000	None	0.862	1.00	0.42	0.455	34,776	135.33	112.44	135.33	135.33	0.6
VWIGX	Vanguard Intl.Growth Ptfl.	'85	G	INTL	7937.7	n/a		+ 14.9	+ 14.5	+ 4.0	+ 16.8	+ 19.8	$3,000	None	0.22	....	0.16	...	19,279	22.60	17.92	22.49	22.49	1.0
VMRGX	Vanguard Morgan Growth	'68	G	C	4028.4	n/a	....	+ 35.6	+ 22.8	+ 29.4	+ 21.6	+ 22.3	$3,000	None	0.18	0.60	1.43	0.60	31,500	24.30	19.36	22.92	22.92	0.8
VWSTX	Vanguard Mun.Short Term	'76	I	TF	1865.6	n/a	[3]∫†	+ 5.9	+ 3.6	+ 4.0	+ 4.2	+ 2.3	$3,000	None	0.607	0.534	....	...	12,406	15.65	15.44	15.45	15.45	3.9
VWITX	Vanguard Mun.Intermed	'76	I	TF	8305.3	n/a	[4]∫†	+ 14.7	+ 4.0	+ 6.9	+ 5.4	– 2.5	$3,000	None	0.659	0.375	....	...	12,960	13.59	12.74	12.77	12.77	5.2
VWLTX	Vanguard Mun.Long Term	'76	I	TF	1549.3	n/a	[5]∫†	+ 19.9	+ 4.2	+ 9.0	+ 4.9	– 3.3	$3,000	None	0.579	0.574	....	...	13,344	11.34	10.27	10.31	10.31	5.6
VTRIX	Vanguard:Trustees'Equity:Intl.Ptfl.	*'83	G	INTL	970.0	n/a	....	+ 1.4	+ 9.7	– 7.1	+ 12.7	+ 16.1	$10,000	None	0.01	0.01	0.42	...	14,224	29.68	23.65	29.12	29.12	....
VWINX	Vanguard:Wellesley Income	'68	I	FL	7519.5	n/a	....	+ 24.8	+ 9.0	+ 19.5	+ 11.6	– 10.2	$3,000	None	1.13	0.84	1.14	0.175	15,591	22.28	18.73	18.85	18.85	6.0
VWELX	Vanguard:Wellington Fund	'28	GIR	B	25701.5	n/a	....	+ 32.4	+ 15.9	+ 22.9	+ 11.8	+ 2.9	$3,000	None	1.13	0.75	2.44	1.50	21,609	31.98	27.33	27.96	27.96	4.0
VWNDX	Vanguard:Windsor Fund	'58	GI	C	16365.3	n/a	[6]	+ 30.0	+ 26.2	+ 21.6	+ 0.4	+ 10.3	$3,000	None	0.25	0.109	1.23	1.90	22,070	18.99	14.64	15.17	15.17	1.6
VWNFX	Vanguard:Windsor II Fund	*'85	GI	C	30315.6	n/a	....	+ 38.6	+ 24.0	+ 32.1	+ 15.9	– 5.7	$3,000	None	0.64	0.68	2.67	2.50	24,540	33.60	24.22	24.97	24.97	2.6
VCAGX	Vista Capital Growth	*'87	G	C	567.5	n/a	....	+ 22.2	+ 24.2	+ 22.9	+ 5.0	+ 0.2	$2,500	4.75	....	....	3.92	...	19,311	46.05	38.28	41.93	44.49	....
VGRIX	Vista Growth & Income	*'87	GI	C	1344.5	n/a	....	+ 27.4	+ 19.6	+ 28.6	+ 13.7	– 7.3	$2,500	4.75	0.182	0.147	4.75	...	19,951	46.85	37.87	39.39	41.79	0.4
VEEDX	Vontobel Eastern European Debt	*'97	R	BD	10.7	n/a	....	....	....	– 0.6	+ 24.3	– 9.0	$1,000	None	1.64	....	0.21	...	.....	10.39	9.17	9.29	9.29	17.7
VEEEX	Vontobel Eastern European Equity	*'96	R	INTL	26.9	n/a	....	....	....	+ 8.6	– 46.6	+ 14.5	$1,000	None	....	....	....	...	.....	9.32	6.92	9.32	9.32	....
VNEPX	Vontobel Intl. Equity	*'84	G	INTL	151.5	n/a	[7]	+ 10.9	+ 16.8	+ 9.4	+ 16.5	+ 43.6	$1,000	None	....	0.96	0.96	...	22,545	28.01	19.18	28.01	28.01	....
VUSVX	Vontobel U.S. Value	*'90	GI	C	100.0	n/a	....	+ 40.4	+ 21.3	+ 34.2	+ 13.8	– 14.0	$1,000	None	0.16	0.112	1.90	...	22,457	17.37	13.78	14.27	14.27	1.1
SFAAX	Wells Fargo Asset Allocation Fund	*'92	SG	FL	1306.0	n/a	....	+ 28.9	+ 11.4	+ 21.6	+ 24.7	+ 9.1	$250	4.5	0.362	0.43	2.308	3.89	23,067	27.81	22.84	23.76	25.21	1.4
OEVGX	Wells Fargo Variable Rate Govt.		I	GB	101.2	n/a	[8]	....	....	+ 5.6	– 1.6	+ 2.2	None	None	....	0.378	....	...	.....	9.11	8.87	8.91	9.33	....
SHPMX	World Funds:Sand Hill Manager	*'95	G	C	14.2	n/a	....	....	+ 19.4	+ 17.9	+ 1.6	+ 18.9	$25,000	None	....	....	....	...	.....	17.62	14.48	17.59	17.59	....

Uniform Footnote Explanations-See page 235. **Stock Splits & Divs.** (figures adjusted): [1] 1% exit fee. [2] Was Westminster Bd. Inv. Gr.. [3] Was Warwick Municipal. [4] Was Warwick Intermediate. [5] Was Warwick Long Term. [6] Closed to new investors. [7] Was Europacific(3/97). [8] Was Overland Express Var. Rate Govt.(12/97).

STANDARD & POOR'S

VARIABLE ANNUITY/LIFE INVESTMENT SUMMARY

EXPLANATION OF ABBREVIATIONS

AG	Aggr. Growth	GB	Global Bond	HYB	High Yield Bond	MI	Mortgage Income
B	Balanced	GE	Global Equity	IB	Income—Bond	MM	Money Market
CA	Capital Appreciation	GM	Global Mixed	IE	Income—Equity	NR	Natural Resources
CB	Corporate Bond	G+I	Growth and Income	IM	Income—Mixed	PM	Precious Metals
FP	Flexible Portfolio	GNMA	Ginnie Mae	IX	Index	RE	Real Estate
G	Growth	GV	Government	INT	International	SC	Small Capitalization

PERFORMANCE OF THE S&P 500[1]

% Change from Previous Dec. 31			
At Dec. 31			
1996	1997	1998	Dec. 28, 1999
+23.0	+33.4	+28.6	+20.1

Company Name (Contract Name)	Investment Vehicle	Investment Manager/ Sub Manager	Inv. Obj.	Date First Offered	3/31/97 Tot. Assets ($ Mil)	Fees & Expenses: % Sep. Acct.	% Fund Chge.	Admin./ Surrender/ Sales Charge	% Change in Unit Value from Previous Dec. 31: 1996	1997	1998	YTD	Unit Value Dec. 28 1999
AEtna Life Ins. & Annuity	AEtna Growth & Income VP	AEtna Life Ins. & Annuity	G+I	8/91	7,140.2	1.50	0.30	ADMIN: $20 annual contract fee.	+22.9	+28.3	+14.2	+13.7	28.820
(Var.Annuity Acct.C-Qual)	AEtna Money Market VP	AEtna Life Ins. & Annuity	MM	8/91	643.9	1.50	0.36	SUR: 5% yrs. 1-5, scale to 0%	+4.1	+4.2	+5.2	+2.7	12.910
1-800-525-4225	AEtna Bond VP	AEtna Life Ins. & Annuity	IB	8/91	620.4	1.50	0.31	through yr. 10.	+2.3	+7.0	+7.9	-2.9	13.860
	AEtna Balanced VP	AEtna Life Ins. & Annuity	FP	8/91	1,360.9	1.50	0.33		+13.7	+21.0	+16.6	+10.0	24.140
Allianz Life Ins. Co.	High Income	Franklin Advisers Inc.	IM	1/89	433.3	1.40	0.64	ADMIN: $30 annual contract fee.	+12.3	+10.0	-0.5	-1.5	20.889
(Franklin ValuemarkII-VA)	U.S. Gov't Securities	Franklin Advisers Inc.	GV	3/89	790.3	1.40	0.54	*Note: 5% yrs. 1&2, 4% yr. 3,	+2.2	+7.8	+5.9	-2.3	18.572
1-800-782-VALU	Global Income	Franklin Advisers Inc.	GM	1/89	204.3	1.40	0.73	3% yr. 4, 1.5% yr. 5.	+8.1	+1.0	+5.6	-7.2	16.624
	Growth & Income	Franklin Advisers Inc.	G	1/89	1,103.9	1.40	0.58	3% yr. 4, 1.5% yr. 5 in NY.	+12.6	+26.0	+6.8	-1.2	25.915
	Natural Resources	Franklin Advisers Inc.	PM	1/89	91.3	1.40	0.68		+2.5	-20.1	-26.4	+27.1	10.808
	Real Estate Securities	Franklin Advisers Inc.	RE	1/89	354.1	1.40	0.67		+31.0	+19.0	-18.0	-9.3	20.958
	Income Securities	Franklin Advisers Inc.	IM	1/89	1,313.7	1.40	0.56		+9.7	+15.5	+0.2	-3.6	24.226
	Global Communications	Franklin Advisers Inc.	G	1/89	1,043.0	1.40	0.51		+5.6	+25.0	+9.6	+35.1	38.232
	Rising Dividends	Franklin Advisers Inc.	G+I	1/92	602.7	1.40	0.79		+22.4	+31.2	+5.4	-12.5	18.516
	International Equity	FAI/Templeton Inv. Coun'l	INT	1/92	1,140.6	1.40	1.12		+21.2	+10.1	+4.1	+21.8	22.461
	Pacific Growth	FAI/Templeton Inv. Coun'l	INT	1/92	306.2	1.40	1.14		+9.6	-36.8	-14.3	+35.0	10.905
	Developing Mkt. Portfolio	FAI/Templeton Inv. Coun'l	INT	3/94	337.1	1.40	1.75		+19.9	-10.0	-22.7	+49.0	11.910
	Global Growth	FAI/Templeton Inv. Coun'l	GE	3/94	641.0	1.40	1.25		+19.6	+11.9	+7.5	+17.5	19.156

DEFINITION: **Unit Value** is the value of a separate account after deducting all investment charges and mortality and expense fees.

[1]Assumes daily reinvestment of dividends. VA–Variable Annuity.

Company Name (Contract Name)	Investment Vehicle	Investment Manager/ Sub Manager	Inv. Obj.	Date First Offered	3/31/97 Tot. Assets ($ Mil)	% Sep. Acct.	% Fund Chge.	Fees & Expenses: Admin./ Surrender/ Sales Charge	% Change in Unit Value from Previous Dec. 31: 1996	1997	1998	YTD	Unit Value Dec. 28 1999
Anchor Nat'l Life Ins.	Cash Management	Capital Research & Mgt.	MM	2/84	95.8	1.30	0.64	ADMIN: $30 annual contract fee.	+3.6	+3.7	+3.6	+3.2	19.860
(American Pathway II-VA)	High Yield Bond	Capital Research & Mgt.	HYB	2/84	118.9	1.30	0.69	SUR: 5% yrs. 1 through 5.	+12.2	+11.4	+0.7	-2.9	44.180
1-800-445-7862	Growth-Income	Capital Research & Mgt.	G+I	2/84	868.9	1.30	0.59		+17.6	+26.4	+16.3	+6.2	87.270
	Growth	Capital Research & Mgt.	G	2/84	731.7	1.30	0.62		+13.1	+26.5	+34.6	+43.6	153.98
	U.S. Government	Capital Research & Mgt.	IB	11/85	92.0	1.30	0.66		+1.7	+6.8	+6.7	-1.4	23.980
	Asset Allocation	Capital Research & Mgt.	FP	4/89	146.0	1.30	0.77		+14.3	+19.1	+8.6	+7.2	30.970
	International	Capital Research & Mgt.	INT	8/90	238.4	1.30	1.40		+19.8	+10.7	+17.6	+57.1	36.030
Anchor Nat'l Life Ins.	Strat. Multi Asset	Wellington	FP	3/87	54.9	1.40	1.30	ADMIN: $30 annual contract fee.	+13.2	+12.7	+13.6	+24.0	33.020
(ICAP II-VA)	Growth	Wellington	G	9/84	359.2	1.40	0.90	SUR: 5% yr. 1, scale down 1% per	+23.3	+28.6	+27.2	+23.1	84.600
1-800-445-7862	Capital Appreciation	Wellington	AG	3/87	543.2	1.40	1.00	yr. through yr. 5.	+23.4	+23.7	+20.5	+60.8	84.810
	Growth & Income	Wellington	G+I	3/87	35.2	1.40	1.10		+18.6	+27.0	+28.3	+13.9	42.130
	Gov't & Qual. Bd.	Wellington	IB	9/84	216.7	1.40	0.80		+1.6	+8.0	+7.6	-3.0	30.440
	High Yield	Wellington	HYB	12/85	38.6	1.40	1.00		+10.1	+9.7	-5.8	+4.3	24.970
	Natural Resources	Wellington	NR	12/87	46.6	1.40	1.20		+12.5	-9.8	-18.5	+35.8	19.570
	Multi Asset	Wellington	FP	3/87	144.6	1.40	1.20		+12.3	+19.5	+22.7	+10.3	36.670
	Money Market	Wellington	MM	9/84	83.8	1.40	0.70		+3.5	+3.7	+3.7	+3.3	19.270
Fidelity Invt. Life Ins.	Fidelity VIP-Money Mkt.	Fidelity Mgt. & Research	MM	1/88	1,258.5	1.00	0.38	ADMIN: $30 annual contract fee.	+4.3	+4.5	+4.6	+4.3	17.430
(Fid. Retirement Res-VA)	Fidelity VIP-Invt. Grade	Fidelity Mgt. & Research	IB	12/88	244.9	1.00	0.80	SUR: 5% yr. 1, scale down 1% per	+2.1	+8.0	+8.0	-1.8	19.870
1-800-544-6666	Fidelity VIP-High Income	Fidelity Mgt. & Research	HYB	2/88	1,664.7	1.00	0.97	yr. through yr. 5.	+12.9	+16.5	-5.1	+6.9	29.430
(Ext. 2327)	Fidelity VIP-Eq. Income	Fidelity Mgt. & Research	G+I	2/94	7,190.8	1.00	0.74		+13.1	+26.9	+10.7	+4.3	45.490
	Fidelity VIP-Growth	Fidelity Mgt. & Research	G	2/88	5,897.6	1.00	0.84		+13.6	+22.3	+38.4	+34.6	79.650
	Fidelity VIP-Overseas	Fidelity Mgt. & Research	GE	2/88	1,743.9	1.00	1.26		+12.1	+10.5	+11.9	+37.5	36.180
	Fidelity VIP-Asset Mgr.	Fidelity Mgt. & Research	FP	8/89	3,622.2	1.00	1.08		+13.4	+19.5	+14.1	+9.5	31.000
Fortis Benefits Ins. Co.	Divers. Income Port.	Fortis Investors	IB	5/88	100.8	1.35	0.75	ADMIN: $35 annual contract fee.	+2.8	+8.9	+4.9	-3.0	1.997
(Opportunity-VA)	Growth Stock Port.	Fortis Investors	G	5/88	596.0	1.35	0.82	SUR: 5% yrs. 1 through 5.	+14.9	+10.9	+17.4	+47.8	5.720
1-800-800-AMEV	Asset Alloc. Port.	Fortis Investors	FP	5/88	386.0	1.35	0.70		+11.0	+18.6	+18.4	+16.1	3.862
	Money Market Port.	Fortis Investors	MM	5/88	72.0	1.35	0.55		+3.8	+3.9	+3.9	+3.5	1.586
	U.S. Gov't Port.	Fortis Investors	GV	5/89	148.0	1.35	0.64		+0.8	+7.6	+7.4	-3.2	17.824
Fortis Benefits Ins. Co.	Divers. Income Port.	Fortis Investors	IB	1/90	4.1	0.90	0.75	ADMIN: No annual contract fee.	+3.0	+9.2	+5.1	-2.8	17.969
(Wall St. Ser. 220-VUL)	Growth Stock Port.	Fortis Investors	G	1/90	107.7	0.90	0.81	SUR: varies	+13.8	+11.1	+17.6	+48.1	42.941
1-800-800-AMEV	Asset Alloc. Port.	Fortis Investors	FP	1/90	23.2	0.90	0.70	SALES: 9.8% prem. tax&sales chrg.	+11.0	+18.8	+18.6	+16.3	31.627
	Money Market Port.	Fortis Investors	MM	1/90	5.6	0.90	0.55		+3.9	+4.1	+4.1	+3.7	14.572
	U.S. Gov't Port.	Fortis Investors	GV	1/90	5.5	0.90	0.64		+1.1	+7.8	+7.6	-3.1	16.904
General American Life	S&P 500 Index	Conning Asset Mgt.	IX	5/88	360.6	1.00	0.30	ADMIN: No annual contract fee.	+20.0	+31.5	+26.9	+18.4	65.543
(Var. Annuity Contract)	Money Market	Conning Asset Mgt.	MM	5/88	74.7	1.00	0.21	SUR: 9% yr. 1, scale down 1% per	+4.4	+4.7	+4.6	+4.1	17.252
1-800-449-6447	Bond Index	Conning Asset Mgt.	IB	5/88	34.7	1.00	0.43	yr. through yr. 9	+2.0	+8.2	+7.5	-3.9	20.149
	Managed Equity	Conning Asset Mgt.	G	5/88	49.8	1.00	0.60		+19.7	+22.1	+13.1	+0.8	43.060
	Asset Allocation	Conning Asset Mgt.	FP	5/88	90.9	1.00	0.60		+14.5	+17.6	+16.7	+21.5	40.236

DEFINITION: **Unit Value** is the value of a separate account after deducting all investment charges and mortality and expense fees.

VA–Variable Annuity.

Company Name (Contract Name)	Investment Vehicle	Investment Manager/ Sub Manager	Inv. Obj.	Date First Offered	3/31/97 Tot. Assets ($ Mil)	% Sep. Acct.	% Fund Chge.	Fees & Expenses Admin./ Surrender/ Sales Charge	–% Change in Unit Value– from Previous Dec. 31 1996	1997	1998	YTD	Unit Value Dec. 28 1999
G.T. Global/Gen. Amer. Life	Global Income	G.T. Global Mgt.	GM	2/93	37.4	1.40	1.25	ADMIN: $30 annual contract fee.	+14.7	+14.6	+17.9	-2.7	22.964
(GT Global Allocator-VA)	Gov't Sec. Fund	G.T. Global Mgt.	GV	2/93	4.9	1.40	1.00	SUR: 6% yr. 1, scale down 1% per	+0.8	+6.8	+7.5	-4.3	14.609
1-800-548-9994	Diversified Income	G.T. Global Mgt.	GB	2/93	9.6	1.40	1.00	yr. through yr. 6.	NA	NA	NA	-3.5	17.437
	Capital Appreciation	G.T. Global Mgt.	SC	2/93	33.2	1.40	1.00		+16.9	+13.3	+6.6	+48.0	41.148
	Telecommunications	G.T. Global Mgt.	GE	10/93	60.1	1.40	1.25		+17.7	+13.0	+20.4	+97.7	53.165
	Money Market	G.T. Global Mgt.	MM	2/93	28.5	1.40	0.75		+3.3	+3.4	+3.4	+3.0	14.638
	International Equity	G.T. Global Mgt.	INT	7/94	5.5	1.40	1.25		NA	NA	NA	+44.3	17.468
Guardian Ins. & Annuity	Value LineStrat.AssetMgt.	Value Line, Inc.	G+I	10/87	1,072.6	1.15	0.58	ADMIN: $35 annual contract fee.	+14.5	+14.3	+26.0	+21.4	43.470
(Guardian Investor-VA)	Value Line Centurion	Value Line, Inc.	G	11/83	603.9	1.15	0.53	SUR: Sin. prem.: 6% yr. 1 & 2, scale	+16.0	+20.0	+26.0	+24.0	52.670
1-800-221-3253	Guardian Stock Fund	Guardian Investor Svs.	G	4/83	2,303.0	1.15	0.56	down 1% per yr. through yr. 7.	+25.4	+34.0	+18.5	+27.9	55.480
	Guardian Bond Fund	Guardian Investor Svs.	IB	5/83	337.4	1.15	0.57	Flex: Lessor of: 6% prem. paid	+1.7	+7.7	+6.8	-1.9	18.030
	Guardian Cash Fund	Guardian Investor Svs.	MM	11/81	396.7	1.15	0.55	past 7 yrs. or 6% withdrawl.	+3.8	+3.9	+3.9	+3.6	14.300
	Baillie Gifford Int'l Fund	Guardian/Baillie Gifford	INT	2/91	455.6	1.15	1.67		+14.0	+10.6	+19.8	+34.7	28.590
	Baillie Gifford Emer.Mkt.Fd.	Guardian/Baillie Gifford	INT	10/94	87.9	1.15	1.90		+23.1	+0.8	-27.6	+65.5	12.830
	Gabelli Capital Asset Fund	Gabelli Funds, Inc.	G	6/95	52.3	1.15	1.20		+9.7	+41.0	+10.4	+16.5	21.390
Hartford Life Ins.	Bond Fund	Hartford Investment Mgt.	IB	8/77	409.8	1.25	0.57	ADMIN: $30 annual contract fee.	+2.2	+9.9	+6.8	-3.2	2.185
(The Director II-VA)	Stock Fund	Hartford/Wellington	G	8/77	2,229.0	1.25	0.53	SUR: 6% yr. 1, scale down 1% per	+22.8	+29.8	+31.8	+17.1	7.100
1-800-862-6668	Money Market	Hartford Investment Mgt.	MM	6/80	590.9	1.25	0.48	yr. through yr. 7.	+3.9	+4.0	+4.0	+3.6	1.777
	Advisers	Hartford/Wellington	FP	3/83	6,185.0	1.25	0.70		+15.1	+23.0	+23.1	+8.5	4.771
	Int'l Opportunities	Hartford/Wellington	INT	7/90	1,026.0	1.25	1.00		+11.5	-0.9	+11.8	+35.4	2.222
	Capital Appreciation	Hartford/Wellington	AG	4/84	3,361.0	1.25	0.76		+19.2	+20.8	+14.1	+32.2	7.307
	Mortgage Securities	Hartford Investment Mgt.	GNMA	1/85	315.7	1.25	0.50		+3.8	+7.6	+5.4	+0.2	2.216
	Index	Hartford Investment Mgt.	IX	5/87	701.0	1.25	0.49		+20.6	+31.0	+26.5	+18.1	5.563
	Dividend and Growth	Hartford/Wellington	G+I	2/94	1,068.0	1.25	1.00		+21.4	+30.2	+15.0	+3.2	2.551
Keyport Life Ins.	Stein Roe Money Market	Stein Roe & Farnham	MM	5/85	64.8	1.40	0.62	ADMIN: $36 annual contract fee.	+3.6	+3.7	+3.7	+3.3	14.752
(Preferred Advisor-VA)	Stein Roe Mtg. Sec. Fd.	Stein Roe & Farnham	MI	10/86	72.7	1.40	0.70	SUR: 7% yr. 1, scale down 1% per	+3.4	+7.5	+5.3	-0.3	18.764
1-800-437-4466	Stein Roe Balanced Fund	Stein Roe & Farnham	FP	5/85	293.0	1.40	0.68	yr. through yr. 7.	+14.5	+15.2	+11.0	+10.1	29.946
	Stein Roe Growth Stock	Stein Roe & Farnham	G	5/87	164.8	1.40	0.77		+20.0	+30.5	+26.1	+33.2	59.701
	Stein Roe Small Co. Growth	Stein Roe & Farnham	AG	5/85	178.6	1.40	0.80		+26.4	+6.3	-18.4	+42.0	36.001
	Stein Roe Global Utilities	Stein Roe & Farnham	G+I	7/93	45.5	1.40	0.86		+5.2	+27.0	+16.7	+24.1	22.249
	Colonial Growth & Income	Colonial-Keyport	G+I	7/93	74.3	1.40	0.87		+16.7	+27.2	+9.1	+3.3	21.814
	Colonial Strategic Income	Colonial-Keyport	IB	7/94	54.6	1.40	0.80		+8.5	+7.7	+4.6	+0.2	14.265
	Colonial U.S. Growth & Inc.	Colonial-Keyport	G	7/94	64.8	1.40	1.00		+20.1	+30.4	+18.5	+21.6	29.939
	Colonial Int'l Fund for Growth	Colonial-Keyport	INT	5/94	28.4	1.40	1.74		+3.6	-4.1	+11.4	+36.7	14.707
	Newport Tiger Fund	Newport	AG	5/95	33.5	1.40	1.35		+9.7	-32.1	-7.7	+65.1	12.987
Lincoln National Life Ins.	Growth Fund	Capital Research & Mgt.	G	8/89	3,741.0	1.35	0.56	ADMIN: $35 annual contract fee.	+11.9	+28.4	+33.7	+52.4	5.994
(Ameri Legacy II-VA)	Growth-Income Fund	Capital Research & Mgt.	G+I	8/89	5,291.0	1.35	0.56	SUR: 6% yr. 1, scale down 1% per	+17.2	+24.2	+16.8	+8.3	3.449
1-800-443-8137	Asset Allocation Fund	Capital Research & Mgt.	FP	8/89	1,162.0	1.35	0.59	yr. through yr. 7.	+14.2	+18.9	+11.6	+4.4	2.784
(cont'd)	High Yield Bond Fund	Capital Research & Mgt.	HYB	8/89	679.0	1.35	0.63		+11.7	+10.9	-0.9	+4.4	2.330

DEFINITION: **Unit Value** is the value of a separate account after deducting all investment charges and mortality and expense fees.

VA–Variable Annuity. VUL–Variable Universal Life.

Company Name (Contract Name)	Investment Vehicle	Investment Manager/ Sub Manager	Inv. Obj.	Date First Offered	3/31/97 Tot. Assets ($ Mil)	% Sep. Acct.	% Fund Chge.	Fees & Expenses Admin./ Surrender/ Sales Charge	–% Change in Unit Value– from Previous Dec. 31 1996	1997	1998	YTD	Unit Value Dec. 28 1999
Lincoln National Life Ins.	U.S. Gov't/AAA Bd. Fd.	Capital Research & Mgt.	GV	8/89	467.0	1.35	0.58		+1.7	+7.0	+6.7	-1.9	1.778
(Ameri Legacy II-VA)	Cash Management Fund	Capital Research & Mgt.	MM	8/89	254.0	1.35	0.58		+3.7	+3.8	+3.7	+3.3	1.448
1-800-443-8137	International	Capital Research & Mgt.	INT	5/90	2,537.0	1.35	0.96		+16.0	+7.6	+19.6	+69.8	3.835
MFS/Sun Life (U.S.)	Money Market	MFS	MM	12/84	14.1	1.30	0.59	ADMIN: $30 annual contract fee.	-3.1	+3.7	+3.7	+3.3	17.786
(Compass 2-NY-VA)	High Yield	MFS	HYB	12/84	11.5	1.30	1.05	SUR: 5% yrs. 1 through 5.	-0.7	+7.9	+2.9	+5.4	30.395
1-800-343-2829	Capital Appreciation	MFS	AG	12/84	53.1	1.30	0.85		+29.1	+21.5	+27.1	+27.2	95.600
(Ext. 3052)	Government Securities	MFS	GV	12/84	25.3	1.30	0.64		+0.3	+7.3	+7.3	-3.2	25.108
	Global Government	MFS	GB	5/88	8.1	1.30	1.12		+2.2	-2.0	+14.0	-6.3	19.360
	Total Return	MFS	B	5/88	37.8	1.30	0.85		+8.9	+20.4	+10.3	+0.8	32.455
	Managed Sectors	MFS	AG	5/88	9.8	1.30	1.03		+6.9	+24.0	+10.8	+72.0	79.295
MFS/Sun Life (U.S.)	Capital Appreciation	MFS	G	11/91	729.5	1.40	0.83	ADMIN: $30 annual contract fee.	+19.8	+18.3	+30.3	+27.0	44.190
(Regatta Gold-VA)	Mass Investors Trust	MFS	G+I	11/91	592.0	1.40	0.66	SUR: 6% yrs. 1&2, 5% yrs. 3&4, 4%	+23.7	+27.3	+24.9	+4.8	33.247
1-800-343-2829	Managed Sectors	MFS	AG	11/91	166.9	1.40	0.84	yrs. 5&6, 3% yr. 7.	+16.0	+20.8	+13.6	+71.8	43.718
	Global Growth	MFS	GE	11/93	190.3	1.40	1.22		+11.5	+11.4	+15.3	+58.3	27.963
	Total Return	MFS	B	11/91	1,029.0	1.40	0.78		+12.5	+19.2	+11.2	+0.7	22.291
	Utilities	MFS	G+I	11/93	71.6	1.40	0.70		+18.7	+29.3	+17.4	+28.1	28.247
	Government Securities	MFS	GV	11/91	257.0	1.40	0.63		+0.2	+7.2	+7.3	-3.3	14.601
	Global Government	MFS	GB	11/91	93.0	1.40	0.95		+3.2	-1.7	+13.3	-6.4	14.261
	High Yield	MFS	HYB	11/91	130.9	1.40	0.88		+10.6	+11.6	-0.7	+5.3	18.979
	Money Market	MFS	MM	11/91	349.9	1.40	0.58		+3.5	+3.6	+3.6	+3.2	12.619
Nationwide Life Ins.	Money Market	AmeriCapital Asset Mgt.	MM	5/88	21.0	1.30	0.60	ADMIN: $30 annual contract fee.	+3.5	+3.7	+3.6	+3.3	15.771
(American Cap. Inv.-VA)	Enterprise	AmeriCapital Asset Mgt.	G	5/88	84.8	1.30	0.60	SUR: 7% yr. 1, scale down 1% per	+23.2	+29.0	+23.4	+22.1	61.693
1-800-421-5666	Asset Allocation	AmeriCapital Asset Mgt.	FP	5/88	64.0	1.30	0.60	yr. through yr. 7.	+12.4	+20.2	+14.2	+3.3	33.910
	Domestic Income	AmeriCapital Asset Mgt.	HYB	5/88	19.8	1.30	0.60		+5.3	+10.5	+5.5	-3.4	18.805
	Government	AmeriCapital Asset Mgt.	GV	1/90	57.3	1.30	0.60		+0.8	+8.2	+7.1	-4.6	16.530
North American Sec. Life	Mid Cap Blend	Fidelity Mgt.	G	6/85	1,227.0	1.40	0.89	ADMIN: $30 annual contract fee.	+18.5	+16.6	+8.8	+21.8	38.110
(Venture-VA)	U.S. Gov't Securities	Salomon Bros.	GV	3/88	198.0	1.40	0.87	SUR: 6% yrs. 1&2, 5% yr. 3, 4%	+1.9	+6.7	+6.2	-1.5	18.300
1-800-334-4437	Money Market	Wellington Mgt.	MM	6/85	393.0	1.40	0.60	yr. 4, 3% yr. 5, 2% yr. 6.	+3.6	+3.7	+3.6	+3.1	16.290
	Global Equity	Oechsle Int'l	GE	3/88	729.0	1.40	1.23		+11.0	+18.7	+11.1	+1.4	24.440
	Global Bond	Fidelity Mgt.	GB	3/88	232.0	1.40	1.14		+11.4	+1.6	+6.0	-7.8	19.670
	Conser. Asset Allocat'n	Fidelity Mgt.	FB	4/87	198.0	1.40	0.88		+5.5	+9.7	+9.3	-15.1	15.380
	Moderate Asset Allocat'n	Fidelity Mgt.	FB	4/87	580.0	1.40	0.86		+8.4	+14.0	+13.8	-22.7	16.030
	Large Cap Growth	Fidelity Mgt.	FB	4/87	217.0	1.40	0.88		+11.4	+17.3	+17.6	+22.9	28.320
Northbrook Life Ins.	Money Market	Dean Witter InterCapital	MM	10/90	359.7	1.35	0.59	ADMIN: $30 annual contract fee.	+3.6	+3.7	+4.1	+3.3	13.450
(Dean Witter VA-II)	High Yield	Dean Witter InterCapital	HYB	10/90	278.9	1.35	0.74	SUR: 6% yr. 1, scale down 1% per	+10.3	+10.4	-7.3	-2.8	23.970
1-800-869-3863	Stock Equity	Dean Witter InterCapital	G	10/90	536.6	1.35	0.62	yr. through yr. 6.	+10.7	+35.4	+29.1	+52.1	76.100
	Quality Income Plus	Dean Witter InterCapital	IB	10/90	448.1	1.35	0.58		+0.0	+9.5	+7.5	-5.7	18.180
(cont'd)	Strategist	Dean Witter InterCapital	FP	10/90	430.9	1.35	0.58		+13.3	+12.1	+25.2	+14.4	30.760

DEFINITION: **Unit Value** is the value of a separate account after deducting all investment charges and mortality and expense fees.

VA–Variable Annuity. VUL–Variable Universal Life.

Company Name (Contract Name)	Investment Vehicle	Investment Manager/ Sub Manager	Inv. Obj.	Date First Offered	3/31/97 Tot. Assets ($ Mil)	% Sep. Acct.	% Fund Chge.	Fees & Expenses Admin./ Surrender/ Sales Charge	–% Change in Unit Value– from Previous Dec. 31 1996	1997	1998	YTD	Unit Value Dec.28 1999
Northbrook Life Ins.	Dividend Growth	Dean Witter InterCapital	IE	10/90	1,345.5	1.35	0.69		+22.1	+23.8	+13.1	-5.0	34.890
(Dean Witter VA-II)	Utilities	Dean Witter InterCapital	IM	10/90	405.0	1.35	0.73		+7.0	+25.3	+22.4	+10.3	32.600
1-800-869-3863	European Growth	Dean Witter InterCapital	INT	3/91	328.1	1.35	1.73		+28.0	+14.4	+22.7	+25.1	42.630
	Capital Growth	Dean Witter InterCapital	G	3/91	89.0	1.35	0.86		+9.9	+22.7	+18.4	+28.9	30.700
	Global Dividend Growth	Dean Witter InterCapital	GE	2/94	359.0	1.35	0.90		+15.9	+10.4	+11.3	+10.8	18.820
	Pacific Growth	Dean Witter InterCapital	INT	2/94	129.4	1.35	1.33		+2.3	-38.6	-11.3	+60.0	8.570
Phoenix Mutual Life	MultiSector Fixed Income	Phoenix Invest. Counsel	HYB	1/83	100.5	1.25	0.65	ADMIN: $35 annual contract fee.	+11.0	+9.7	-5.3	+4.1	3.970
(Big Edge Plus -VA)	Money Market Series	Phoenix Invest. Counsel	MM	1/83	84.3	1.25	0.55	SUR: 6% yr. 1, scale down 1% per	+3.7	+3.9	+3.8	+3.5	2.314
1-800-243-4840	Growth Series	Phoenix Invest. Counsel	G	1/83	878.5	1.25	0.79	yr. through yr. 6.	+11.2	+19.6	+28.4	+26.9	17.538
	Strategic Allocation	Phoenix Invest. Counsel	FP	1/83	354.9	1.25	0.74		+7.7	+19.2	+19.3	+9.2	5.763
Phoenix Mutual Life	MultiSector Fixed Income	Phoenix Invest. Counsel	HYB	9/88	12.5	0.80	0.65	ADMIN: $60 annual contract fee.	+11.5	+10.2	-4.9	+4.6	2.288
(Flex Edge-VUL)	Money Market Series	Phoenix Invest. Counsel	MM	9/88	16.0	0.80	0.55	SUR: Varies yrs. 1 through 10.	+4.2	+4.3	+4.3	+3.9	1.562
1-800-243-4840	Growth Series	Phoenix Invest. Counsel	G	9/88	173.9	0.80	0.79		+11.7	+20.1	+29.0	+27.5	6.910
	Strategic Allocation	Phoenix Invest. Counsel	FP	9/88	26.8	0.80	0.74		+8.2	+19.8	+19.8	+9.7	3.659
Putnam/Hartford Life Ins.	VT Asia Pacific	Putnam Mgt. Co.	INT	1/95	110.4	1.40	1.07	ADMIN: $25 annual contract fee.	+7.6	-15.8	-6.8	+98.3	16.960
(Putnam Capital Mgr-VA)	VT Diversified Income	Putnam Mgt. Co.	IB	1/93	637.7	1.40	0.80	SUR: 6% yr. 1, scale down 1% per	+7.3	+5.9	-2.7	+0.2	12.508
1-800-862-6668	VT Int'l Growth	Putnam Mgt. Co.	INT	1/97	200.0	1.40	1.20	yr. through yr. 6.	NA	NA	+17.0	+53.6	20.590
	VT Int'l Growth & Income	Putnam Mgt. Co.	INT	1/97	260.0	1.40	1.12		NA	NA	+9.7	+21.9	15.753
	VT Int'l New Opportunities	Putnam Mgt. Co.	INT	1/97	127.9	1.40	1.60		NA	NA	+14.0	+96.0	21.998
	VT New Opportunities	Putnam Mgt. Co.	AG	1/94	3,080.9	1.40	0.63		+8.6	+21.6	+22.7	+61.3	40.021
	VT New Value	Putnam Mgt. Co.	G+I	1/97	233.6	1.40	0.85		NA	NA	+4.8	-2.7	11.023
	VT Utilities Growth & Income	Putnam Mgt. Co.	G+I	1/92	891.9	1.40	0.74		+14.2	+25.3	+13.3	-2.2	22.323
	VT Vista	Putnam Mgt. Co.	G	1/97	218.6	1.40	0.87		NA	NA	+17.8	+45.2	20.786
Security Benefit Life	Growth Series	Security Management	G	6/84	726.0	1.20	0.87	ADMIN: $30 annual contract fee.	+21.2	+27.2	+23.9	+6.2	76.570
(Variflex Qualified-VA)	Income/Growth Series	Security Management	G+I	6/84	962.0	1.20	0.86	SUR: 8% yr. 1, scale down 1% per	+16.8	+25.0	+6.3	-0.7	61.400
1-800-888-2461	Money Market Series	Security Management	MM	6/84	126.0	1.20	0.61	yr. through yr. 8	+3.8	+3.9	+3.9	+3.3	20.360
	High Grade Series	Security Management	IB	5/85	120.0	1.20	0.86		-1.9	+8.5	+6.9	-4.9	23.920
Union Central Life	Equity Portfolio	Carillon Advisers	G	6/85	114.2	1.45	0.75	ADMIN: $30 annual contract fee.	+22.7	+18.8	-16.4	-0.4	41.228
(Carillon Account-VA)	Bond Portfolio	Carillon Advisers	IB	6/85	17.6	1.45	0.73	SUR: 7% yrs. 1&2, scale down 1%	+5.6	+9.4	+5.1	-2.3	28.333
1-800-999-1840	Money Market	Scudder	MM	6/85	8.7	1.45	0.69	per yr. through yr. 8.	+3.6	+3.7	+3.9	+3.7	17.911
	Scudder Cap. Growth	Scudder	G	5/92	28.9	1.45	0.71		+18.4	+33.8	+21.6	+32.0	36.612
	Scudder Int'l	Scudder	INT	5/92	26.4	1.45	1.39		+13.1	+7.5	+16.9	+49.9	30.242
Zurich Kemper Life Ins.	Money Market I	Kemper Financial Services	MM	4/82	26.0	1.25	0.56	ADMIN: $30 annual contract fee.	+3.4	+4.0	+3.9	+3.5	1.289
(Passport-VA)	Total Return	Kemper Financial Services	FP	4/82	109.1	1.25	0.61	SUR: 4% yr. 1, 3% yrs. 2&3,	+15.3	+18.5	+13.8	+12.5	2.156
1-800-621-5001	High Yield	Kemper Financial Services	HYB	4/82	92.8	1.25	0.67	2% yrs. 4&5, 1% yr. 6.	+12.6	+10.3	+0.2	+0.8	1.902
	Growth	Kemper Financial Services	CA	12/83	99.3	1.25	0.67		+20.1	+19.8	+13.7	+33.6	3.138
	Gov't Securities	Kemper Financial Services	GV	11/89	26.9	1.25	0.63		+1.3	+7.6	+5.8	-0.7	1.426
	International	Kemper Financial Services	INT	1/92	44.4	1.25	1.00		+15.0	+8.2	+8.7	+41.2	2.605

DEFINITION: **Unit Value** is the value of a separate account after deducting all investment charges and mortality and expense fees.

VA–Variable Annuity. VUL–Variable Universal Life.

THE BOND GUIDE

HOW TO USE STANDARD & POOR'S BOND GUIDE

The Bond Guide in a one-page format employs two sets of column headings in the corporate bond section.

1—One set of headings, in italics explained below, relates to the company title, industry code, fixed charge coverage, balance sheet figures, long-term debt outstanding, capitalization and total debt-to-capital ratio.

2—The second set of headings, in lightface type, explained on page 259, ralates to the individual issues of the debtor companies, ie., the exchange where traded, description of issue, interest dates, recent rating history (present rating, prior rating and date of change), redemption provisions, and additional statistics.

It is necessary to read these instructions along with those on pages 260 and 261 to correctly interpret data and abbreviations used in the Bond Guide.

EXPLANATION OF COLUMN HEADINGS RELATING TO DEBTOR COMPANIES

Title-Industry Code & Co. Finances (in italics)	Industry	Fixed Charge Coverage 19– 19– 19–	Year End	Millions $ Cash & Equiv. / Curr. Assets / Curr. Liabs. / Balance Sheet Date	L. Term Debt (Mil. $)	Capitalization (Mil. $)	Total Debt % Capital
The name of the issuer. Pertinent information as to control; name change; subsidiary, etc., footnoted to reference on respective pages. For explanation of standard abbreviations see page 261.	Industry code — Company's principal business is indicated by numerical reference to directory.	Represents number of times available earnings *(before income taxes and extraordinary charges or credits)* cover fixed charges. Charges include interest on funded debt, other interest, amortization of debt discount and expense and similar charges.	Represents month fiscal year ends. For fiscal years ending March 31 or earlier, figures are shown under columns of preceding calendar year.	Figures are reported in millions of dollars (000,000 omitted) as: 1275—$1,275,200,000); 17.5—$17,500,000. Data is updated from annual and interim reports, date of which is shown. Utilities with a reasonable debt to property ratio may often report current liabilities in excess of current assets. In many instances this is of no real significance as utilities have constant tax deferrals, high current debt maturity and the ability to forecast revenues.	Debts and certain obligations due after one year, including bonds, debentures, mortgages, and capitalized lease obligations. Increased debt resulting from new financing and offered subsequent to latest balance sheet data is indicated by symbol ★.	The sum of the stated values of common shareholders' equity, preferred and preference stock, total debt, and minority interest.	Total debt (including short-term debt) of company dividend by total capital. Provides a measurement of company's degree of leverage.

HOW TO USE STANDARD & POOR'S BOND GUIDE (continued)

EXPLANATION OF COLUMN HEADINGS RELATING TO INDIVIDUAL ISSUES

Column Heading	Explanation
Exchange	Traded: ● New York Stock Exchange; ◆ American Stock Exchange
Individual Issue Statistics	Description of individual issues—For abbreviations see page 261.
Interest Dates	Interest dates are indicated by first letter of alternate six month in which interest is payable. (An) or (Q) precededs dates on which interest is payable either annually or quarterly. Unless otherwise noted, dates are the first day of the month. Month of maturity is indicated by a capital letter. Symbols following interest dates note foreign issues payable in U.S. funds or currency of issuing country, and issues in default. See page 260 for explanation.
S&P Rating	Standard & Poor's Rating definitions appear in the front section of the Bond Guide. Please see the Table of Contents for specific location each month.
Eligibility	Eligible for bank purchase. See page 260.
Bond Form	BE – Book-Entry; C – Coupon; CR – Coupon or Registered; R – Registered
Redemption Provisions — Regular (Begins) Price Thru	Regular call price with beginning or ending date. See page 260 for additional information.
Redemption Provisions — Sinking Fund (Begins) Price Thru	Sinking fund, if any, is reported together with applicable price and data.
Redemption Provisions — Refund/Other Restrictions (Begins) Price Thru	Refund restrictions are denoted by the symbol ®, giving date at which restriction expires. Redemption provision may include the symbol NC, which means non-callable, and others (‡, Z, *), which are explained on page 260.
Outst'g (Mil. $)	Amount of issue outstanding, in millions of dollars, as of the latest available complete balance sheet.
Underwriting Firm Year	Indicates by key to Directory of Underwriters (see Table of Contents), the original underwriter, usually the head of the syndicate, and the year the issue was originally offered.
Price Range 19xx High Low	Price ranges for current calendar year to date. An explanation of pricing methodology for listed and over-the-counter bonds appears on page 260.
Mo. End Price Sale(s) or Bid	Last sale price is shown for listed issues, and latest bid price or S&P valuation for over-the-counter issues or listed issues not traded last day of the month. "Flat" indicates issue is traded "without accrued interest". A—Ask price.
Curr. Yield—Yield to Mat.	Yields both current and to maturity, are computed on month-end price shown in preceding column.

UNIFORM FOOTNOTE EXPLANATIONS

To provide for consistency, eliminate repetition, and allow space for situations requiring further explanation, items recurring frequently that demand footnote explanation have been designated with specific symbols, which are explained on this page. Additional explanations appear at the bottom of respective pages.

ISSUE DESCRIPTION & YIELD—See how to use explanation on pages 258-259.
Other situations require uniform footnotes, as follows:

● —Listed on New York Stock Exch.
◆ —Listed on American Stock Exch.
$ —Prin. & int. pay. in U.S. funds; tax status not determined.
§ — Int. and/or prin. in default
A — Ask price.
© — Prin. & int. pay. in Canadian funds.
‡ – Price in Canadian funds

BOND FORM—BE—Book-Entry; C—Coupon; R—Registered; CR—Coupon & Registered.

EARNINGS—Explanation of earnings per share for the company into which bonds are convertible, see page 452.

ELIGIBILITY—Under regulations of the Comptroller of the Currency, only certain bonds are eligible for bank investment as indicated by the following symbols:

X — Issues eligible as bank investments on the basis of confirmatory ratings.
Y — Issues ineligible on the basis of confirmatory ratings, but not in default.
Z — Bonds with default status.
Q — Foreign bonds, eligibility not determined by rating agencies.

OTHER FOOTNOTES:

★— Giving effect to new financing.
c — Company only.
d — Deficit.
p — Pro-forma.
△— Times Earned 1996, 1997, 1998
: — Currency of country of origin

REDEMPTION PROVISIONS

Regular Call Price—The Bond Guide reports the present call price and, if not currently callable, designates the date when a company may normally redeem bonds. Bonds may be called by a company in whole or in part at the regular call price usually on a sliding scale to par at maturity.

Special Redemptions—Some indentures contain special redemption provisions with requirements for retirement under terms of sinking, improvement, maintenance and replacement funds, etc. Details should be checked carefully.

Sinking Fund Call Price—A sinking fund makes possible the retirement of a substantial portion of the issue prior to maturity. Included in the indenture are terms covering amounts to be called, years of call and a sliding scale of call prices. Bonds to be retired are determined by lot, or provision is often made for purchase of bonds in the open market or by tender if cost is below the sinking fund call price. Also reported is the date when sinking fund starts, if not currently in operation.

Applicable footnotes are:

✲ — On interest dates.
‡ — On interest dates; price decline within 12 mos.
± — Price decline within 12 mos.
□ — Debt retirement & improve fund.
■ — In whole only.
Z — Callable re specified conditions.
▲ — Through application of trust moneys or proceeds of eminent domain.

Refund/Other Restrictions—Some indentures include a restrictive clause for a period of five to ten years after issue, to assure holders that their investment is not disturbed during that period. Reported is the earliest call price preceded by symbol ® and date when company may normally call bonds for refunding purposes. Column is also used to denote special call features.

PRICING METHODOLOGY

Listed Bonds—Ranges represent actual high and low trades as recorded on an exchange; they do not include bid prices or valuations. However, for the period between date of offering and date of listing, they include high and low over-the-counter bid prices.

Over-the-Counter Bonds—Ranges are based on best available information as to high and low bid prices during the period. Due to lack of complete data from an official centralized source, they should be viewed as reasonable approximations. Ranges for over-the-counter utility bonds on which quotations are unavailable, or unrealistic, are based on valuations made by Standard & Poor's. Included in the various factors used are: prevailing yields; market conditions; S&P Debt Ratings; call features; etc. Subscribers are alerted to the fact that these valuations may differ somewhat from actual trading prices.

ABBREVIATIONS USED

Accr — Accrue(s)
adj — Adjustment
Asmd — Assumed
Astd — Assented
C/D — Ctfs of Deposit
Chge — Change
CT— Collateral Trust
Coll — Collateral
Con — Consolidated
Ctfs — Certificates
Ctrl — Control
Curr — Current
Cv — Convertible
Deb — Debenture
Def — Default
Dev — Development
Dfrd — Deferred
Disc — Discount
Excl — Excludes
Ext — External
Extd — Extended
1st — First Mortgage
F/R — Floating Rate
Fdg — Funding
Fr — From
Fxd — Fixed
Gen — General
Gtd — Guaranteed
HRO— Holder's repayment option
Imp — Improvement
Inc — Income
Incl — Includes
IPO —Initial Public Offering
Ln — Lien
Lshld — Leasehold
Mand — Mandatory
M–T—Medium Term
Mtg — Mortgage
NC — Non - Callable
non-cm — Non - Cumulative
NR — Not Rated
Nts — Notes
OID — Original Issue Discount
PF — Purchase Fund
PIK — Pay - In - Kind
Perp — Perpetual
Pr — Prior
Pr Ln — Prior Lien
Ptc — Participating
RE — Real Estate
Rdj — Readjustment
Red— Redemption
Ref — Refunding
Reg — Registered
Rest'n — Restriction
s — Sale
SF — Sinking Fund
Sec — Secured
Ser — Serial; Series
Spl — Special
Sr — Senior
Stpd — Stamped
Sub — Subordinated
Subj — Subject
Tr — Trustees or Trustee
Unif— Unified
V/R — Variable Rate
Var — Various; variable
vtg — Voting
ws — With stock
ww — With warrants
xs — Without stock
xw — Without warrants

DIRECTORY OF UNDERWRITERS

Security underwriters listed below are keyed by the symbols to the column in the Corporate and Foreign bond sections headed Underwriting, which shows the principal underwriter and year in which bonds were offered originally. Home offices only are shown, plus telephone number for that office; many of the firms have extensive branch operations in other cities.

Symbols		Telephone
0	Out of Business	
A1	Advest Inc., Hartford, Conn.	(860) 509-1000
A2	Allen & Co., Inc., N.Y.	(212) 832-8000
A3	ABM AMRO Chicago Corp, Chicago.	(312) 855-7600
A4	Asiel & Co., N.Y.	(212) 747-1000
B1	Bache Halsey Stuart Shields, Inc (Now Prudential Securities)	
B2	BancAmer Robertson Stephens, San Fran.	(415) 781-9700
B3	Baird (Robert W.), Milwaukee	(414) 765-3500
B4	BT Alex Brown, Baltimore	(410) 727-1700
B5	Bank of America, San Fran.	(415) 622-2201
B6	Bankers Trust Co., N.Y.	(212) 250-2500
B7	Bear, Stearns & Co., N.Y.	(212) 272-2000
B8	Blyth Eastman Dillon, N.Y. (Mgr w/PaineWebber Inc)	
B9	Bradford (J. C.), Nashville	(615) 748-9000
B10	Brown (Alex.) & Sons (Now BT Alex Brown)	
B11	BT Securities, N.Y. (Now BT Alex Brown)	
C1	Chase Securities, N.Y.	(212) 834-5158
C2	Chemical Securities, N.Y.	(212) 834-4500
C3	Chicago Corp. (Now ABN AMR Chicago)	
C4	Citicorp Securities Inc. N.Y.	(212) 559-1000
C5	CS First Boston (Now Credit Suisse First Boston)	
C6	Credit Suisse First Boston, N.Y.	(212) 325-2000
D1	Dain Bosworth, Minneapolis	(612) 371-2811
D2	Daiwa Securities Amer., N.Y.	(212) 945-0100
D3	Dean Witter Capital Mkts (Now Morgan Stanley Dean Witter)	
D4	Dillon, Read & Co. (Now SBC Warburg Dillon Read)	
D5	Deutsche Morgan Grenfell, N.Y.	(212) 469-5000
D6	Donaldson, Lufkin & Jennrette, N.Y.	(212) 504-3000
D7	Drexel, Burnham, Lambert, N.Y.	(ob)
D8	duPont, Walston, Inc., N.Y.	(ob)
E1	Eastman Dillon, Union Securities (Mgr w/Blyth Eastman,Paine Webber)	
E2	Edwards (A. G.) & Sons, St. Louis	(314) 955-3000
E3	Equitable Secur., Nashville, TN.	(615) 780-9300
E4	Ernst & Co., N.Y.	(212) 898-6200
F1	First Boston Corp., N.Y. (Now CS First Boston)	
F2	First Chicago Capital Mkts, Chi	(312) 732-5600
F3	Freeman Secur., Jersey City, N.J.	(201) 434-7400
F4	Furman Selz Inc., N.Y.	(212) 309-8200
G1	Goldman, Sachs Inc., N.Y.	(212) 902-1000
H1	Halsey, Stuart Colk Inc., Chicago (Now Prudential Securities)	
H2	Hambrecht & Quist, San Fran.	(415) 576-3300
H3	Herzig (P. R.) & Co., N.Y.	(212) 797-2900
H4	Hutton (E. F.) & Co., N.Y. (Now Lehman Bros)	
I1	Interstate/Johnson Lane, Charlotte, N.C.	(704) 379-9000
J1	Jeffries & Co., Los Angeles	(310) 445-1199
J2	Jones (Edward D.) & Co., St. Louis	(314) 515-2000
K1	Kemper Securities Inc., Chi.	(312) 574-6000
K2	Kidder, Peabody & Co., N.Y.	(212) 510-3000
K3	Kuhn, Loeb & Co., N.Y. (Now Lehman Bros)	
L1	Lazard Freres & Co., N.Y.	(212) 632-6000
L2	Legg Mason Wood Walker, Balt.	(410) 539-0000
L3	Lehman Bros., N.Y.	(212) 526-2001
M1	McDonald & Co. Secur., Cleve.	(216) 443-2300
M2	Merrill Lynch Capital Mkts, N.Y.	(212) 449-1000
M3	Montgomery Secur. (Now Nations Banc Montgomery Secur.)	
M4	Morgan, Keegan & Co., Memphis	(901) 524-4100
M5	Morgan (J. P.) Securities, N.Y.	(212) 483-2323
M6	Morgan Stanley & Co. (Now Morgan Stanley Dean Witter)	
M7	Morgan Stanley Dean Witter, N.Y.	(212) 761-4000
M8	Moseley Int'l., Inc., N.Y.	(ob)
N1	NatWest Secur. Ltd, N.Y.	(212) 602-4800
N2	NationsBanc Montgomery Secur., San Fran.	(415) 627-2000
N3	Nomura Securities Int'l., N.Y.	(212) 667-9300
O1	Offerman & Co., Minneapolis	(612) 541-8999
O2	Ohio (The) Co., Columbus	(614) 464-6811
O3	Oppenheimer & Co., N.Y.	(212) 667-7000
P1	PaineWebber Inc., N.Y.	(212) 713-2000
P2	Piper Jaffray Inc., Minneapolis	(612) 342-6000
P3	Principal Fin'l Secur., Dallas	(214) 880-9000
P4	Prudential Securities, N.Y.	(212) 214-1000
R1	Raymond, James & Assoc. St. Petersburg, Fla.	(813) 573-3800
R2	RBC Dominion Sec., Toronto	(416) 842-2000
R3	Robertson, Stephens (Now BancAmer Robertson Stephens)	
R4	Robinson-Humphrey, Atlanta	(404) 266-6000
R5	Rothschild Inc., N.Y.	(212) 403-3500
R6	Rothschild (L.F.) & Co., Inc., N.Y.	(ob)
S1	Salomon Bros. Inc. (Now Salomon Smith Barney)	
S2	Schroder Wertheim, N.Y.	(212) 492-6000
S3	ScotiaMcLeod Inc., Toronto	(416) 863-7411
S4	Salomon Smith Barney, N.Y.	(212) 7837000
S5	Shearson Lehman Hutton, N.Y. (Now Lehman Bros)	
S6	SBC Warburg Dillon Read, N.Y.	(212) 906-7000
S7	Smith Barney (Now Salomon Smith Barney)	
S8	Smithers (F. S.) Inc., N.Y.	(ob)
S9	Stephens Inc, Little Rock, AR	(501) 374-4361
S10	Stern Bros. & Co., Kansas City, MO	(816) 471-6460
S11	Stifel, Nicolaus & Co., St. Louis	(314) 342-2000
S12	Stone & Webster Securities, N.Y.	(ob)
U1	UBS Securities Inc., N.Y.	(212) 821-3000
W1	Warburg Paribas Becker, N.Y. (Acq by Merrill Lynch)	
W2	Wedbush Morgan Sec., L.A.	(213) 688-8000
W3	Wertheim Schroder, N.Y. (Now Schroder Wertheim)	
W4	Wheat First Butcher & Singer, Richmond VA.	(804) 649-2311
W5	White, Weld & Co. Inc., N.Y. (Acq by Merrill Lynch)	
W6	Wood, Gundy & Co., N.Y.	(212) 856-6777

ob—Out of business.

INDUSTRY CODE CLASSIFICATIONS

0– Not specific
1– Advertising/Communications
2– Aerospace
a– Major Contractor
b– Subsystems/components
c– Research/develop.
3– Aircraft manufacturing/components
a– Services
4– Air Transport
a– Cargo/charter
5– Aluminum
6– Arms/Ammunition
7– Auto rental/service
8– Auto parts/equipment
9– Auto/Truck mfrs.
a– Trucks, trailers
b– Motor homes
10– Banking
a– Savings Banks
b– Savings and Loan
11– Beverages
a– Beer and Ale
b– Distillers
c– Wines and Liquors
e– Soft drink syrup
f– Bottlers
12– Broadcasting
a– CATV
b– Radio
c– TV
d– Equipment
e– Programming/Entertainment
13– Building
a– Brick, cement
b– Climate controls
c– Contracting, engineering, construction
d– Forest products
e– Hardware/hand tool
f– Plumbing
g– Roofing, Wallboard
h– Homebuilding
14– Chemicals
a– Agricultural
b– Industrial gases
c– Sulphur
15– Coatings, paint, varnishes
16– Containers
a– Glass
b– Metal
c– Paper
d– Plastic
17– Conglomerate/Diversified
a– Diversified
18– Cosmetics/Toiletries
19– Cosmetics– Toiletries– Drugs
20– Data Processing
a– Leasing/distributor
b– Computer systems
c– Computer services
d– Software
e– Peripherals
f– Components
21– Drugs– Generic and OTC
a– Ethical
b– Biotechnology
c– Research
d– Drug Wholesalers
22– Education
23– Electronics/Electric
a– Industry leaders
b– Component, controls
c– Motors
d– Household appliances
e– Information svcs, communication sys
f– Radio, TV, tape
g– Electronic equipment
h– Semiconductors
i– Defense electronics
24– Filmed Entertainment
a– Distributor
b– Theaters
c– Services/technology/equipment
25– Finance
a– Consumer loan
b– Agency
c– Leasing
d– Receivables
e– Services
f– S.B.I.C.
g– Diversified/Misc.
h– Mortgage Banking/Brokers
i– Pawnshops
26– Food
a– Bakery, mill, sugar
b– Canned
c– Corn refiners
d– Dairy products
e– Meat/poultry
f– Pkgd./snacks
g– Distributors
h– Candy, gum
i– Seafood
j– Frozen
27– Food serving
a– Food Servicing
b– Fast foods
c– Restaurants
28– Glass/products
29– Graphic Arts
a– Printing
b– Supplies, equipment
30– Health Care Centers
a– Health Care Services
31– Home Furnishings
a– Carpets, floor cov.
b– Furniture
32– Hotels/Motels/Inns
33– Household Products
34– Housewares
35– Insurance
a– Life/Health
b– Broker/agency
c– Property/Casualty
d– Multiline
36– Investment
37– Jewelry, silverware, time pieces, china
38– Land dev./Real Estate
39– Leather/Shoes
a– Shoe producer
b– Shoe mfr./dstr.
d– Leather
40– Leisure/Amusement
a– Boating
b– Bowling/billiard
c– Musical instr.
d– Photo equipment/finishing
e– Records/homevideo
f– Sports/Outdoor equipment
g– Tourism/resorts
h– Toys, games
i– Casinos/gaming
j– Gambling/Amusement equipment
k– Sports collectibles
l– Racetracks
m–Misc.
41– Machinery
a– Agriculture
b– Construction material handling
c– Industrial
d– Machine tools
e– Specialties
f– Steam generator
g– Components (General Industrial)
h– Flow Control Filtration Components
i– Bearings
42– Manufacturing/Distr
a– Consumer
b– Industrial
43– Medical equipment/supply
a– Laboratory/research
44– Metal
a– Precious fabricating
d– Other fabricating
45– Mining/Diversified
a– Coal
b– Copper
c– Lead, Zinc
d– Uranium
e– Gold
f– South African Gold
g– Silver
h– Exploration/development
i– Industrial Minerals
j– Junior Gold
46– Mobile/Modular Homes
a– Components
47– Mutual Fund
48– Office Equipment
a– Furniture
b– Forms, supplies
49– Oil and Gas
a– Crude producer
b– Domestic
c– International
d– Retailer
e– Well supply, service, drilling
f– Canadian
g– Refiner
h– Foreign
50– Paper/Products
51– Pet and Supplies
52– Plastic/Products
53– Pollution Control
54– Publishing
a– Books
b– Periodicals
c– Newspapers
d– Textbooks
e– Electronic
55– Railroads
56– Rail Equipment
a– Car leasing
b– Parts, accessories
57– Real Estate Investment Trust
58– Rendering
59– Retail Stores
a– Apparel
b– Convenience foods
c– Food supermarkets
d– Variety
e– Drugs
f– Department
g– Discount
h– Mail order/catalogs
i– Showroom/catalog
j– Furniture
k– Fabric
l– Specialty
m–Warehouse clubs
60– Retail merchandiser
61– Rubber
a– Fabricating
62– Securities
63– Services
64– Shipping/Shipbuilding
65– Specialty instruments
66– Steel– Iron
a– Major integrated
b– Other integrated
c– Stainless
d– Other specialties
e– Ore producer
f– Steel mill machinery
g– Steel Converter/Processor
h– Steel Minimill
67– Telecommunications
a– Local
b– Long Distance
c– Foreign
d– Telegraph
e– Satellite
f– Equipment/Services
g– Mobile, cellular
68– Textiles
a– Producer
b– Synthetic fibers
c– Apparel manufacturer
69– Tobacco
a– Cigarettes
c– Leaf/snuff
70– Transportation
a– Bus
b– Freight forwarding
71– Trucking
72– Utilities– Electric
a– Operating
b– Holding
73– Utilities– Gas
a– Pipeline cos.
b– Distributors
c– Producer, gatherer
d– LP gas
e– Integrated
74– Utilities– Water
75– Util.– Diversified

Title-Industry Code & Co. Finances (In Italics) / Exchange ↓ Individual Issue Statistics	Ind / Interest Dates	Fixed Charge Coverage 1996 / S&P Rating	1997 / Date of Last Rating Change	1998 / Prior Rating	Eligible ↓	Year End / Bond Form	Million $ Cash & Equiv. / Redemption Provisions Regular Price	Million $ Curr. Assets / Regular (Begins) Thru	Million $ Curr. Liab. / Sinking Fund Price	Balance Sheet Date / Sinking Fund (Begins) Thru	L. Term Debt (Mil $) / Refund/Other Restriction Price	Refund/Other Restriction (Begins) Thru	Capital-ization (Mil $) / Outst'g (Mil $)	Total Debt % Capital / Underwriting Firm	Underwriting Year	Price Range 1999 High	Price Range 1999 Low	Mo. End Price Sale(s) or Bid	Curr. Yield	Yield to Mat.
AAF-McQuay Inc	***42b***	***2.40***	***1.54***	***1.36***		***Je***	***9.85***	***368.0***	***330.0***	***3-31-99***	***138.0***		***472.0***	***56.7***						
Sr Nts[1] 8⅞s 2003	Fa15	B+			Y	R	NC	....	....	....	....	....	125	C4	'96	98	65	88⅛	10.07	10.07
AAi.FosterGrant, Inc	***37***	***n/a***	***n/a***	***n/a***		***Dc***	***2.94***	***82.00***	***58.70***	***10-2-99***	***75.30***		***97.80***	***102.0***						
Sr Nts[2] 'B' 10¾s 2006	jJ15	CCC	8/99	B+	Y	BE	105.375	(7-15-02)	....	....	[3]Z110.75	7-15-01	75.0	Exch.	'98	95	33	33	....	....
Aames Financial	***25h***	***△2.01***	***△2.65***	***△d4.47***		***Je***				***9-30-99***	***281.0***		***421.0***	***65.3***						
• Sr Nts 10½s 2002	[4]Feb	NR				R	■100	(2-1-00)	100	....	....	....	23.0	P2	'95	97	71	72	14.58	14.57
Sr Nts[2] 9⅛s 2003	mN	CCC+	11/98	B	Y	BE	104.562	(11-1-00)	....	....	....	....	150	B7	'96	75⅝	63	63⅛	14.46	14.45
AAR Corp	***3a***	***△4.06***	***△4.53***	***△4.22***		***My***	***1.44***	***497.6***	***156.5***	***8-31-99***	***181.0***		***507.0***	***35.7***						
Nts[5] 9½s 2001	mN	BBB	7/97	BBB–	X	R	NC	....	....	....	....	....	65.0	G1	'89	108½	103	103	9.22	9.22
Nts 7¼s 2003	aO15	BBB	7/97	BBB–	X	R	NC	....	....	....	....	....	50.0	G1	'93	104¼	97⅞	97⅞	7.41	7.41
Nts 6⅞s 2007	jD15	BBB			X	BE	NC	....	....	....	....	....	60.0	G1	'97	104⅛	93	93	7.39	7.39
[6]Abbey Healthcare Group	***30a***	***2.06***	***d0.18***	***d1.27***		***Dc***	***26.60***	***206.0***	***159.0***	***9-30-99***	***399.0***		***346.0***	***122.0***						
Sr[1]Sub Nts 9½s 2002	mN	B	11/98	B+	Y	R	102.375	10-31-00	....	....	....	....	200	D6	'93	101½	94	98⅛	9.68	9.68
Abbott Laboratories	***21a***	***29.11***	***22.84***	***21.26***		***Dc***	***630.3***	***5878***	***4329***	***9-30-99***	***1336***		***8879***	***24.9***						
Nts 5.60s 2003	aO	AAA			X	BE	NC	....	....	....	....	....	200	G1	'93	102⅛	96	96	5.83	5.83
Nts 6.80s 2005	Mn15	AAA			X	BE	NC	....	....	....	....	....	150	G1	'95	108⅝	99⅛	99⅛	6.86	6.86
Nts 6.40s 2006	jD	AAA			X	BE	NC	....	....	....	....	....	250	G1	'96	107½	95⅞	95⅞	6.68	6.67
Nts 5.40s 2008	mS15	AAA			X	BE	NC	....	....	....	....	....	200	G1	'98	100¾	89	89	6.07	6.07
Accuride Corp	***8***	***n/a***	***n/a***	***1.40***		***Dc***	***18.60***	***156.0***	***79.80***	***9-30-99***	***455.0***		***429.0***	***108.0***						
Sr Sub[2]Nts[7] 'B' 9¼s 2008	Fa	B–			Y	BE	104.625	(2-1-03)	....	....	[8]Z109.25	2-1-03	200	Exch.	'98	102¼	90	91	10.16	10.16
[9]ACME Television/Finance	***12c***	***n/a***	***n/a***	***n/a***		***Dc***	***0.76***	***26.50***	***28.00***	***9-30-99***	***202.0***		***268.0***	***75.7***						
Sr[10]Disc Nts[11] 'B' 10⅞s 2004	mS30	B–			Y	BE	105.438	(9-30-01)	....	....	[12]Z110.875	9-30-00	175	Exch.	'98	90½	79¾	90	....	Flat
Adams Outdoor Advertising	***1***	***n/a***	***n/a***	***n/a***		***Dc***	***6.11***	***20.20***	***4.97***	***9-30-99***	***126.0***		***60.20***	***209.0***						
Sr Nts[2] 10¾s 2006	Ms15	B			Y	BE	105.375	(3-15-01)	....	....	....	....	105	Exch.	'96	110	101	104	10.34	10.33
Adelphia Communications	***12a***	***0.50***	***0.49***	***0.38***		***Mr***				***9-30-99***	***3968***		***4584***	***86.6***						
Sr Deb[13]'B' 9⅞s 2005	Ms	B+	9/98	B	Y	BE	NC	....	....	....	....	....	130	D6	'93	111½	101¼	101½	9.73	9.73
Sr Nts[14] 'B' 10¼s 2000	jJ15	B+	9/98	B	Y	R	NC	....	....	....	....	....	100	Exch.	'94	104½	100¼	100⅝	10.19	10.18
Sr Nts[14] 'B' 9¼s 2002	aO	B+	9/98	B	Y	BE	NC	....	....	....	....	....	325	Exch.	'97	106½	99⅜	99½	9.30	9.30
Sr Nts[14] 7½s 2004	Jj15	B+			Y	BE	NC	....	....	....	....	....	100	Exch.	'99	102¾	92½	94	7.98	7.98
Sr([15]PIK)Nts[14]'B' 9½s 2004	Fa15	B+	9/98	B	Y	R	103.56	2-14-00	....	....	....	....	[16]31.8	Exch.	'94	107⅛	100	100	9.50	9.50
Sr Nts[14] 'B' 10½s 2004	jJ15	B+	11/98	NR	Y	BE	NC	....	....	....	....	....	150	Exch.	'97	114	103	103¾	10.12	10.12
Sr Nts 'B' 9⅞s 2007	Ms	B+	9/98	B	Y	BE	NC	....	....	....	....	....	350	Exch.	'97	112½	101¼	101½	9.73	9.73
Sr Nts[14] 7¾s 2009	Jj15	B+			Y	BE	NC	....	....	....	....	....	300	Exch.	'99	102¼	88¼	89½	8.66	8.66
Sr Nts[14] 7⅞s 2009	Mn	B+			Y	BE	NC	....	....	....	....	....	350	C1	'99	100	88	89¾	8.77	8.77
Sr Nts[14] 9⅜s 2009	mN15	B+			Y	BE	NC	....	....	....	....	....	500	C6	'99	100⅝	98	98	9.57	9.56
Sr Nts[2] 'B' 8⅜s 2008	Fa	B+	9/98	B	Y	BE	NC	....	....	....	....	....	150	Exch.	'98	105	92¾	92¾	9.03	9.03
ADT Operations	***63***	***Merged into Tyco Intl, see***																		
Sr Nts[2] 8¼s 2000	fA	A–	7/97	BBB–	X	R	NC	....	....	....	....	....	9.50	M2	'93	104	100⅞	100⅞	8.18	8.18
Advanced Accessory Sys	***42b***	***n/a***	***n/a***	***n/a***		***Dc***	***11.20***	***106.0***	***66.90***	***9-30-99***	***170.0***		***198.0***	***90.9***						
Sr Sub Nts[2] 'B' 9¾s 2007	aO	B–			Y	BE	104.875	(10-1-02)	....	....	[17]Z109.75	10-1-00	125	Exch.	'98	102	89¼	90¼	10.80	10.80
Advanced Micro Dev.	***23h***	***d13.07***	***d1.23***	***d1.19***		***Dc***	***377.0***	***1160***	***753.4***	***9-26-99***	***1441***		***3595***	***47.9***						
Sr Sec Nts[2] 11s 2003	fA	B	4/98	BB–	Y	BE	105.50	(8-1-01)	....	....	....	....	400	D6	'96	106½	90¼	99¾	11.03	11.02
Advanced Radio Telecom	***67f***	***n/a***	***n/a***	***d1.53***		***Dc***	***197.3***	***206.8***	***17.12***	***9-30-99***	***109.0***		***378.0***	***28.8***						
Sr Nts[2] 14s 2007	Fa15	CCC	6/98	CCC+	Y	R	107	(2-15-02)	....	....	[18]Z114	2-14-00	135	M2	'97	93	66	92¾	15.09	15.09
[19]Advanstar Communications	***63***	***n/a***	***n/a***	***n/a***		***Dc***	***9.06***	***54.80***	***94.60***	***9-30-99***	***524.0***		***687.0***	***78.5***						
Sr Sub Nts[20] 9¼s 2008	Mn	B–		B–	Y	BE	104.625	(5-1-03)	....	....	[21]Z109.75	5-1-01	150	Exch.	'98	104¼	92½	94⅛	9.83	9.83

Uniform Footnote Explanations-See Page 260. Other: [1] Co must offer repurch at 101 on Chge of Ctrl. [2] (HRO)On Chge of Ctrl at 101. [3] Max $26.25M red w/proceeds of Equity Off'g. [4] Int pd monthly. [5] (HRO)For Trigger Event at 100. [6] Now Apria Healthcare Group. [7] Co may repurch at 100&prem for Ctrl Chge. [8] Max $80M red w/proceeds of Eq Off'g. [9] Data of ACME Tel LLC. [10] (HRO)On Chge of Ctrl(Accreted Val). [11] Int accrues at 9-30-00. [12] Accreted:Max $61.3M red w/proceeds Eq Off'g. [13] Co must offer repurch at 100 on Chge of Ctrl. [14] (HRO)On Chge of Ctrl at 100. [15] Co may pay int in add'l nts to 2-15-99. [16] Incl disc. [17] Max $44M red w/proceeds of Pub Eq Off'g. [18] Max $33.8M red w/proceeds of Pub Eq Off'g. [19] Subsid & data of Advanstar Inc. [20] (HRO)On Chge of Ctrl at 100,to 5-01-03,101 aft. [21] Max $52M red w/proceeds of Equity Off'g.

Exchange / Individual Issue Statistics (Title-Industry Code & Co. Finances (In Italics))	Interest Dates (Ind)	S&P Rating (FCC 1996)	Date of Last Rating Change (FCC 1997)	Prior Rating (FCC 1998)	Eligible	Bond Form (Year End)	Regular Price (Cash & Equiv., Million $)	Regular (Begins) Thru (Curr. Assets)	Sinking Fund Price (Curr. Liab.)	Sinking Fund (Begins) Thru (Balance Sheet Date)	Refund/Other Restriction Price (L. Term Debt (Mil $))	Refund/Other Restriction (Begins) Thru	Outst'g (Mil $) (Capital-ization (Mil $))	Underwriting Firm (Total Debt % Capital)	Underwriting Year	Price Range 1999 High	Price Range 1999 Low	Mo. End Price Sale(s) or Bid	Curr. Yield	Yield to Mat.
ADVANTA Corp	***25e***	***2.45***	***0.88***	***d0.28***		***Dc***				***9-30-99***	***950.0***		***1527***	***62.2***						
M-T Nts[1]'C' 7⅜s 2000	aO16	BB–	2/98	BB	Y	BE	NC	....	....	....	....	....	25.0	B7	'97	97⅜	95⅛	96¾	7.62	7.62
M-T Nts 'D' 7½s 2000	fA28	BB–	2/98	BB	Y	BE	NC	....	....	....	....	....	50.0	M2	'97	97¾	95¾	97½	7.69	7.69
Nts 7s 2001	Mn	BB–	2/98	BB	Y	BE	NC	....	....	....	....	....	200	S1	'96	95⅞	92⅜	94	7.45	7.45
Advantica Restaurant Grp	***27c***	***n/a***	***n/a***	***d0.60***		***Dc***	***87.20***	***239.4***	***452.6***	***9-29-99***	***980.0***		***1263***	***93.0***						
Sr Nts[2] 11¼s 2008	Jj15	B	4/98	NR	Y	BE	105.625	(1-15-03)	....	....	[3]Z110	1-15-01	592	Exch.	'98	103¾	74	74	15.20	15.19
AEP Industries	***52***	***1.38***	***1.44***	***1.16***		***Oc***	***3.18***	***210.5***	***153.7***	***7-31-99***	***287.0***		***390.0***	***81.0***						
Sr Sub Nts[2] 9⅞s 2007	mN15	B			Y	BE	104.938	(11-15-02)	....	....	[4]109.875	11-15-02	200	Exch.	'98	104½	94½	96¼	10.26	10.26
Aeroquip-Vickers Inc	***41h***	***Merged into Eaton Corp,see***																		
M-T Nts 6.61s 2002	[5]mn	A	3/99	BBB+	X	BE	NC	....	....	....	....	....	25.0	M6	'97	101⅛	97⅜	97¾	6.76	6.76
M-T Nts 7.58s 2012	[6]mn	A	3/99	BBB+	X	BE	NC	....	....	....	....	....	10.0	M6	'97	107⅞	94⅜	94¾	8.00	8.00
M-T Nts 7.09s 2018	[7]mn	A	3/99	BBB+	X	BE	NC	....	....	....	....	....	25.0	M6	'97	96⅞	84⅞	86⅜	8.21	8.21
AES Corp	***63***	***2.24***	***1.72***	***1.69***		***Dc***	***751.0***	***1866***	***1878***	***9-30-99***	***7387***		***10821***	***77.2***						
Sr Nts 8s 2008	QDec31	BB			Y	BE	100	(12-9-00)	....	....	....	....	200	G1	'98	100	90¼	91½	8.74	8.74
Sr Nts 9½s 2009	Jd	BB			Y	BE	[8]Z100	....	....	....	....	....	750	S4	'99	104½	99½	100⅞	9.42	9.42
Sr Sub Exch Nts[2] 8⅜s 2007	fA15	B+			Y	BE	104.188	(10-15-02)	....	....	Z108.375	8-15-00	325	Exch.	'97	102	90	92¾	9.03	9.03
Sr Sub Nts[2] 10¼s 2006	jJ15	B+			Y	BE	105.125	(1-15-01)	....	....	....	....	250	M5	'96	108¼	99¾	101½	10.10	10.10
Sr Sub Nts[2] 8½s 2007	mN	B+			Y	BE	104.25	(11-1-02)	....	....	[9]Z108.50	11-1-00	375	Exch.	'98	102½	90½	93½	9.09	9.09
Aetna Services Inc[10]	***35d***	***3.01***	***6.48***	***6.61***		***Dc***	***3482***			***9-30-99***	***2958***		***14264***	***20.7***						
Deb 6¾s 2013	mS15	A	7/97	A–	X	BE	NC	....	....	....	....	....	200	G1	'93	101⅜	86	86	7.85	7.85
Deb 8s 2017	Jj15	A	7/97	A–	X	R	102.80	1-14-01	100	....	....	....	200	M2	'87	104¼	95⅞	95⅞	8.34	8.34
Deb 7¼s 2023	fA15	A	7/97	A–	X	BE	NC	....	....	....	....	....	200	G1	'93	100¾	86⅜	86½	8.38	8.38
Deb[11] 7⅝s 2026	fA15	A	7/97	A–	X	BE	NC	....	....	....	....	....	450	M2	'96	105¼	89⅜	89½	8.52	8.52
[12]Deb[11] 6.97s 2036	fA15	A	7/97	A–	X	BE	NC	....	....	....	....	....	300	M2	'96	106⅛	93⅞	97⅜	7.16	7.16
Nts 6¾s 2001	fA15	A	7/97	A–	X	BE	NC	....	....	....	....	....	300	M2	'96	101⅞	99⅛	99⅛	6.81	6.81
• Nts 6⅜s 2003	fA15	A	7/97	A–	X	BE	NC	....	....	....	....	....	200	G1	'93	101⅞	96⅛	95⅛	6.70	6.70
Nts[11] 7⅛s 2006	fA15	A	7/97	A–	X	BE	NC	....	....	....	....	....	350	M2	'96	105⅛	95¾	96	7.42	7.42
AFC Enterprises	***27b***	***n/a***	***n/a***	***n/a***		***Dc***	***14.30***	***56.90***	***95.20***	***9-5-99***	***326.0***		***449.0***	***78.8***						
Sr Sub Nts[2] 10¼s 2007	Mn15	B			Y	BE	105.125	(5-15-02)	....	....	[4]Z110.25	5-15-00	175	Exch.	'97	106½	97½	100⅝	10.19	10.18
Affinity Group	***23e***	***1.68***	***2.36***	***1.21***		***Dc***	***4.16***	***79.50***	***128.0***	***9-30-99***	***287.0***		***218.0***	***135.0***						
Sr[2]Nts 11s 2007	Ao	B			Y	BE	105.50	(4-1-02)	....	....	[13]Z110	3-31-00	130	Exch.	'97	103½	92	95	11.58	11.58
AGCO Corp	***41a***	***n/a***	***5.59***	***2.69***		***Dc***	***18.00***	***1619***	***680.0***	***9-30-99***	***851.0***		***1719***	***49.5***						
Sr Sub Nts[14] 8½s 2006	Ms15	BB+			Y	BE	104.25	(3-15-01)	....	....	....	....	250	M5	'96	97	90	91⅛	9.33	9.33
[15]Agricultural Min & Chem	***14a***	***5.01***	***1.49***	***0.73***		***Dc***	***5.56***	***345.5***	***154.2***	***9-30-99***	***478.0***		***1663***	***31.9***						
Sr Nts[2] 10¾s 2003	mS30	BB–	4/97	B+	Y	R	102.688	9-29-00	....	....	....	....	159	M6	'93	104	47	70	15.36	15.35
Ahmanson (C.H.)& Co	***10b***	***Merged w/Washington Mutual,see***																		
Nts 8¼s 2002	aO	BBB+			X	R	[16]Z100	....	....	....	....	....	250	G1	'92	108⅛	101⅞	101⅞	8.10	8.10
Sub Nts[1] 7⅞s 2004	mS	BBB			X	BE	NC	....	....	....	....	....	125	L3	'94	109¾	100½	100½	7.84	7.83
Air Products & Chemicals	***14b***	***Δ4.91***	***Δ4.64***	***Δ4.04***		***Sp***	***61.60***	***1782***	***1858***	***9-30-99***	***1462***		***5396***	***45.1***						
Deb 8½s 2006	Ao	A	4/96	A+	X	R	100	(4-1-04)	....	....	....	....	100	G1	'86	109⅝	101⅛	102	8.33	8.33
• Deb 8¾s 2021	Ao15	A	4/96	A+	X	R	NC	....	....	....	....	....	100	S5	'91	No Sale		102⅛	8.57	8.57
Deb[17] 7.34s 2026	Jd15	A			X	BE	NC	....	....	....	....	....	100	G1	'96	116¼	97⅞	98⅛	7.48	7.48
Deb 7.80s 2026	Jd15	A			X	BE	NC	....	....	....	....	....	100	G1	'96	117⅝	93¼	93¼	8.36	8.36
Nts 8⅞s 2001	fA	A	4/96	A+	X	R	NC	....	....	....	....	....	100	S5	'89	107⅝	102⅛	102⅛	8.69	8.69
Nts 8.35s 2002	Jj15	A	4/96	A+	X	BE	NC	....	....	....	....	....	100	G1	'95	107⅛	101½	101½	8.23	8.22
Nts 6¼s 2003	Jd15	A	4/96	A+	X	R	NC	....	....	....	....	....	100	L3	'93	101⅜	95¾	95¾	6.53	6.53

Uniform Footnote Explanations-See Page 260. Other: [1] Issued in min denom $100T. [2] (HRO)On Chge of Ctrl at 101. [3] Max $207M red w/proceeds of Pub Eq Off'g. [4] Max $70M red w/proceeds of Pub Eq Off'g. [5] Due 7-30-02. [6] Due 6-6-12. [7] Due 1-5-18. [8] Plus Make-Whole Amt. [9] Max $125M red w/proceeds of Eq Off'g. [10] Was Aetna Life & Casualty,now Aetna Inc. [11] Gtd by Aetna Inc. [12] (HRO)On 8-15-04 at 100. [13] Max $39M red w/proceeds of Pub Eq Off'g. [14] Co must offer repurch at 101 on Chge of Ctrl. [15] Now Terra Indus Inc. [16] Plus Make-Whole Premium. [17] (HRO)On 6-15-08 at 100.

Title-Industry Code & Co. Finances (In Italics)	*Ind*	*Fixed Charge Coverage 1996*	*1997*	*1998*		*Year End*	*Million $ Cash & Equiv.*	*Curr. Assets*	*Curr. Liab.*	*Balance Sheet Date*	*L. Term Debt (Mil $)*		*Capital-ization (Mil $)*	*Total Debt % Capital*						
Individual Issue Statistics / Exchange	Interest Dates	S&P Rating	Date of Last Rating Change	Prior Rating	Eligible	Bond Form	Redemption Provisions: Regular Price	Regular (Begins) Thru	Sinking Fund Price	Sinking Fund (Begins) Thru	Refund/Other Restriction Price	Refund/Other Restriction (Begins) Thru	Outst'g (Mil $)	Underwriting Firm	Underwriting Year	Price Range 1999 High	Price Range 1999 Low	Mo. End Price Sale(s) or Bid	Curr. Yield	Yield to Mat.
***Air Products & Chemicals** (Cont.)*																				
Nts 7⅜s 2005	Mn	**A**	4/96	A+	X	BE	NC	....	....	....	....	....	150	L3	'95	107½	98	98	7.53	7.53
M-T Nts[1] 'D' 7¼s 2016	Ao15	**A**			X	BE	NC	....	....	....	....	....	125		'96	110	90½	90½	8.01	8.01
Airborne Freight	***4a***	***2.37***	***7.59***	***12.52***		***Dc***	***20.65***	***451.5***	***294.7***	***9-30-99***	***299.0***		***1141***	***26.2***						
Nts 8⅞s 2002	jD15	**BBB+**	4/98	BBB	X	R	NC	....	....	....	....	....	100	G1	'92	108¾	102½	102½	8.66	8.66
Nts 7.35s 2005	mS15	**BBB+**	4/98	BBB	X	BE	NC	....	....	....	....	....	100	G1	'95	104⅞	95⅞	96	7.66	7.66
***AirTouch Communications**[2]*	***67g***	***4.37***	***7.02***	***5.75***		***Dc***	***876.3***	***892.2***	***15.95***	***6-25-99***	***2743***		***14072***	***19.5***						
Nts 7⅛s 2001	jJ15	**A**	6/99	BBB+	X	BE	[3]Z100	....	....	....	....	....	250	L3	'96	104⅛	100¼	100¼	7.11	7.11
Nts 7s 2003	aO	**A**	6/99	BBB+	X	BE	[3]Z100	....	....	....	....	....	250	L3	'96	106¼	99¼	99¼	7.05	7.05
Nts 6.35s 2005	Jd	**A**	6/99	BBB+	X	BE	[4]Z100	....	....	....	....	....	200	M7	'98	104⅜	95⅝	95⅝	6.66	6.66
Nts 7½s 2006	jJ15	**A**	6/99	BBB+	X	BE	[3]Z100	....	....	....	....	....	400	L3	'96	111⅜	99½	99⅝	7.53	7.53
Nts 6.65s 2008	Mn	**A**	6/99	BBB+	X	BE	[4]Z100	....	....	....	....	....	500	M7	'98	106⅞	94¼	94¼	7.06	7.06
*[5]**AK Steel Corp***	***66a***	***6.67***	***3.27***	***6.95***		***Dc***	***203.0***	***1568***	***1112***	***9-30-99***	***1304***		***2837***	***55.4***						
Sr[6]Nts[7] 9⅛s 2006	jD15	**BB**	10/99	BB–	Y	BE	104.56	(12-15-01)	....	....	....	....	550	Exch.	'96	107¼	98½	101¾	8.97	8.97
SR[8]Nts[7] 7⅞s 2009	Fa15	**BB**	10/99	BB–	Y	BE	103.938	(2-15-04)	....	....	[9]Z107.875	2-15-02	450	Exch.	'99	101¼	90¾	94½	8.33	8.33
AKI Holding Corp	***19***	*∆n/a*	*∆n/a*	*∆0.67*		***Je***	***0.47***	***33.90***	***16.50***	***9-30-99***	***161.0***		***214.0***	***75.7***						
Sr[10]Disc Nts[11] 13½s 2009	jJ	**B–**			Y	BE	106.75	(7-1-03)	....	....	[12]Z113.50	7-1-01	[13]50.0	Exch.	'99	47¼	32½	47¼	....	Flat
AKI Inc	***19***	***Subsid of AKI Holding,see***																		
Sr Nts[7] 10½s 2008	jJ	**B+**			Y	BE	105.25	(7-1-01)	....	....	[14]Z110.50	7-1-01	112	Exch.	'98	98½	86½	89	11.80	11.79
***Alabama Gas Corp**[15]*	***73b***	***3.68***	***3.69***	***4.09***		***Sp***	***4.45***	***13.00***	***259.0***	***6-30-99***	***372.0***		***746.0***	***50.1***						
M-T Nts 'A' 6.70s 2005	[16]mn	**A+**			X	BE	NC	....	....	....	....	....	10.0	S1	'95	105¾	96⅜	96⅜	6.95	6.95
M-T Nts 'A' 7.20s 2014	[17]mn	**A+**			X	BE	103.60	(1-13-05)	....	....	....	....	10.0	S1	'94	107⅝	94⅛	94⅛	7.65	7.65
M-T Nts 'A' 7.70s 2025	[18]mn	**A+**			X	BE	103.85	(6-20-05)	....	....	....	....	10.0	S1	'95	109½	94¼	94⅜	8.16	8.16
M-T Nts 'A' 7.97s 2026	[19]mn	**A+**			X	BE	103.99	(9-23-06)	....	....	....	....	10.0	S7	'96	112	96⅜	96½	8.26	8.26
***Alabama Power Co.**[20]*	***72a***	***3.62***	***3.74***	***2.92***		***Dc***	***15.70***	***943.0***	***1116***	***6-30-99***	***3089***		***6486***	***57.7***						
1st 6s 2000	Ms	**A+**	3/95	A	X	R	NC	....	....	....	....	....	100	M5	'93	100¾	99⅞	100	6.00	6.00
1st 7¾s 2023	Fa	**A+**	3/95	A	X	R	104.38	1-31-00	Z100	....	....	....	100	S1	'93	103	94	95⅜	8.13	8.12
1st 7.45s 2023	jJ	**A+**	3/95	A	X	R	104.34	6-30-00	Z100	....	....	....	150	L3	'93	103⅛	92¼	92⅜	8.06	8.06
1st 7.30s 2023	mN	**A+**	3/95	A	X	R	104.25	10-31-00	Z100	....	....	....	100	P1	'93	102⅛	90⅛	90¼	8.09	8.09
1st 9s 2024	jD	**A+**	3/95	A	X	R	106.32	11-30-00	Z100	....	....	....	150	D6	'94	108⅛	101½	103½	8.70	8.69
Sr Nts 'G' 5⅜s 2008	aO	**A**			X	BE	[4]Z100	....	....	....	....	....	160	C1	'98	99	86¼	86½	6.21	6.22
Sr Nts 'H' 5.49s 2005	mN	**A**			X	BE	[4]Z100	....	....	....	....	....	225	C1	'98	100⅛	91⅛	91⅛	6.02	6.03
Sr Nts 'I' 5.35s 2003	mN15	**A**			X	BE	NC	....	....	....	....	....	156	G1	'98	99⅝	94	94⅛	5.68	5.68
Sr Nts 'K' 7⅛s 2004	fA15	**A**			X	BE	NC	....	....	....	....	....	250	L3	'99	101¼	99⅜	99⅜	7.17	7.17
Sr Nts 'L' 7⅛s 2007	aO	**A**			X	BE	[4]100	....	....	....	....	....	200	C1	'99	101⅝	98⅞	98⅞	7.21	7.21
***Aladdin Gaming/Capital**[21]*	***40i***	*n/a*	*n/a*	*n/a*		***Dc***	***2.46***	***9.85***	***29.00***	***9-30-99***	***403.0***		***414.0***	***97.3***						
Sr[22]Disc[23]Nts[24] 'B' 13½s 2010	Ms	**CCC–**	5/99	CC	Y	BE	106.75	(3-1-03)	....	....	[25]Z113.50	3-1-01	[13]221	M2	'98	44⅝	22½	40	....	Flat
Alaris Medical	***43***	*n/a*	*n/a*	***0.58***		***Dc***	***22.28***	***209.3***	***78.55***	***9-30-99***	***527.0***		***536.0***	***101.0***						
Sr Sub Nts 9¾s 2006	jD	**B–**	5/98	B	Y	BE	104.875	(12-1-01)	....	....	....	....	200	Exch.	'97	103¼	79	86½	11.27	11.27
Albertson's, Inc	***59c***	***12.11***	***9.89***	***8.85***		***Ja***	***219.1***	***4665***	***4163***	***10-28-99***	***4961***		***10858***	***49.7***						
Deb 7¾s 2026	Jd15	**A**	6/99	A+	X	BE	NC	....	....	....	....	....	200	G1	'96	116¼	98⅜	98⅞	7.84	7.84
Nts 6⅜s 2000	Jd	**A**	6/99	A+	X	BE	NC	....	....	....	....	....	200	G1	'95	101½	100	100⅛	6.37	6.37
Sr Nts 6.55s 2004	fA	**A**			X	BE	[4]Z100	....	....	....	....	....	300	G1	'99	100	97¼	97⅜	6.73	6.73
Sr Nts 6.95s 2009	fA	**A**			X	BE	[4]Z100	....	....	....	....	....	350	G1	'99	100¼	96	96	7.24	7.24
Sr Deb 7.45s 2029	fA	**A**			X	BE	[4]Z100	....	....	....	....	....	650	G1	'99	101⅛	95	95	7.84	7.84
M-T Nts 'B' 6.77s 2009	[26]jd	**A**	6/99	A+	X	BE	NC	....	....	....	....	....	60.0	G1	'97	108¾	96	96	7.05	7.05

Uniform Footnote Explanations-See Page 260. Other: [1] Issued in min denom $100T. [2] Now Vodafone AirTouch. [3] Greater of 100 or amt based on formula. [4] Red at greater of 100 or amt based on formula. [5] Gtd by & data of AK Steel Holding. [6] Gtd by AK Steel Holding. [7] (HRO)On Chge of Ctrl at 101. [8] Gtd by AK Steel Hldgs. [9] Max $157.5M red w/proceeds of Equity Off'g. [10] Int accrues at 13.5% fr 7-1-03. [11] (HRO)On Chge of Ctrl at 101(Accreted Amt). [12] Accreted Amt:Max $17.5M red w/proceeds Equity Off'g. [13] Incl disc. [14] Max $40.3M red w/proceeds of Equity Off'g. [15] Subsid of Energen Corp. [16] Due 7-15-05. [17] Due 1-13-14. [18] Due 6-20-25. [19] Due 9-23-26. [20] Subsid of Southern Co. [21] Gtd by & data of Aladdin Gaming Hld. [22] Int accrues at 13.5% fr 3-1-03. [23] (HRO)On Chge of Ctrl at 101(Accreted Val). [24] State gaming laws may req hldr's sale/co red. [25] Accreted Val:Max $78M red w/proceeds Pub Eq Off'g. [26] Due 7-21-09.

Title-Industry Code & *Co. Finances (In Italics)*	Ind	*Fixed Charge Coverage 1996*	*1997*	*1998*		*Year End*	*Million $ Cash & Equiv.*	*Curr. Assets*	*Curr. Liab.*	*Balance Sheet Date*	*L. Term Debt (Mil $)*	*Capital-ization (Mil $)*	*Total Debt % Capital*							
Individual Issue Statistics Exchange ↓	Interest Dates	S&P Rating	Date of Last Rating Change	Prior Rating	Eligible ↓	Bond Form	Redemption Provisions: Regular Price	Regular (Begins) Thru	Sinking Fund Price	Sinking Fund (Begins) Thru	Refund/Other Restriction Price	Refund/Other Restriction (Begins) Thru	Outst'g (Mil $)	Underwriting Firm	Underwriting Year	Price Range 1999 High	Price Range 1999 Low	Mo. End Price Sale(s) or Bid	Curr. Yield	Yield to Mat.
***Albertson's, Inc** (Cont.)*																				
M-T Nts 'B' 6.56s 2027	[1]jd	**A**	6/99	A+	X	BE	NC	....	....	....	....	....	30.0	G1	'97	109½	96¼	96¼	6.82	6.81
M-T Nts 'C' 6.57s 2028	[2]jd	**A**	6/99	A+	X	BE	NC	....	....	....	....	....	43.5	G1	'98	101⅜	85¾	85⅞	7.65	7.65
M-T Nts 'C' 6⅝s 2028	Jd	**A**	6/99	A+	X	BE	NC	....	....	....	....	....	150	G1	'98	101½	85⅞	86	7.70	7.70
Alco Capital Resources	***25***	***Now IKON Capital Inc,see***																		
M-T Nts 'A' 6.99s 2000	[3]jd15	**BBB+**	8/98	A–	X	BE	NC	....	....	....	....	....	20.0	M2	'95	101½	99¾	100	6.99	6.99
M-T Nts 'A' 6¾s 2000	[4]jd15	**BBB+**	8/98	A–	X	BE	NC	....	....	....	....	....	25.0	L3	'95	101⅜	99⅜	99¾	6.77	6.77
M-T Nts 'A' 6.73s 2000	jd15	**BBB+**	8/98	A–	X	BE	NC	....	....	....	....	....	12.5	C1	'95	101¼	99⅜	99¾	6.75	6.75
M-T Nts 'B' 6.19s 2000	[5]jd15	**BBB+**	8/98	A–	X	BE	NC	....	....	....	....	....	10.0	C1	'95	100⅝	98⅛	98⅜	6.29	6.29
M-T Nts 'B' 6.20s 2000	[6]jd15	**BBB+**	8/98	A–	X	BE	NC	....	....	....	....	....	22.0	L3	'95	100⅝	98⅛	98⅜	6.30	6.30
Alco Standard	***50***	***Now IKON Office Solutions,see***																		
Nts 8⅞s 2001	Ao15	**BBB+**	8/98	A–	X	R	NC	....	....	....	....	....	43.3	G1	'91	107½	102⅜	102⅜	8.67	8.67
Aliant Communications	***67a***	***Acq by ALLTEL Corp,see***																		
Nts 6¾s 2028	Ao	**NR**				BE	[7]Z100	....	....	....	....	....	100	M2	'98	101⅞	84⅜	84½	7.99	7.99
Allbritton Communications Co	***12c***	***1.42***	***1.04***	***1.26***		***Sp***	***8.81***	***57.80***	***30.30***	***6-30-99***	***428.0***	***223.0***	***193.0***							
Sr Sub Deb[8]'B' 9¾s 2007	mN30	**B–**			Y	BE	103.90	(11-30-02)	....	....	....	....	271	Exch.	'96	108¼	99	100¼	9.73	9.72
Sr Sub Nts[8] 8⅞s 2008	Fa	**B–**			Y	BE	104.438	(2-1-03)	....	....	[9]Z108.875	2-1-01	150	Exch.	'98	104	94½	96	9.24	9.24
Allegheny Generating[10]	***72***	***3.48***	***3.83***	***3.41***		***Dc***	***0.05***	***6.01***	***70.20***	***6-30-99***	***149.0***	***368.0***	***56.8***							
Deb 5⅝s 2003	mS	**A**			X	R	NC	....	[11]Z100	....	....	....	50.0	P4	'93	100⅜	94½	94½	5.95	5.95
Deb 6⅞s 2023	mS	**A**			X	R	103.28	(9-1-03)	[11]Z100	....	....	....	100	G1	'93	102⅛	85¾	85⅞	8.01	8.00
[12]***Allegheny Ludlum***	***66c***	***13.74***	***25.82***	***24.78***		***Dc***	***49.00***	***1290***	***637.0***	***9-30-99***	***257.0***	***1748***	***18.9***							
Deb 6.95s 2025	jD15	**A**			X	BE	NC	....	....	....	....	....	150	G1	'95	106⅜	89	89⅛	7.80	7.80
Allegiance Corp	***30a***	***Merged into Cardinal Health,see***																		
Deb 7.80s 2016	aO15	**A**	2/99	BBB	X	BE	NC	....	....	....	....	....	150	G1	'96	108¾	98¼	99	7.88	7.88
Deb[13] 7s 2026	aO15	**A**	2/99	BBB	X	BE	NC	....	....	....	....	....	200	G1	'96	102¼	99½	99½	7.04	7.04
Nts 7.30s 2006	aO15	**A**	2/99	BBB	X	BE	NC	....	....	....	....	....	200	G1	'96	106⅜	98¼	98⅜	7.42	7.42
Allegiance Telecom	***67f***	***n/a***	***n/a***	***n/a***		***Dc***	***609.6***	***665.5***	***91.96***	***9-30-99***	***506.0***	***1038***	***47.3***							
Sr Nts 12⅞s 2008	Mn15	**NR**				BE	106.438	(5-15-03)	....	....	[14]Z112.875	5-15-01	205	M7	'98	113½	97	111⅛	11.59	11.58
Sr Disc[15]Nts[16] 11¾s 2008	Fa15	**NR**				BE	105.875	(2-15-03)	....	....	[17]Z111.75	2-15-01	445	Exch.	'98	72½	48	71½	....	Flat
Allergan, Inc	***43***	***n/a***	***n/a***	***n/a***		***Dc***	***264.9***	***767.9***	***427.7***	***9-24-99***	***248.0***	***957.0***	***25.9***							
M-T Nts 6.83s 2001	Jd15	**A**			X	BE	NC	....	....	....	....	....	14.0	M2	'95	103¼	99⅞	99⅞	6.84	6.84
M-T Nts 6.92s 2002	[18]jd15	**A**			X	BE	NC	....	....	....	....	....	20.0	M2	'95	104⅜	99⅝	99⅝	6.95	6.95
Alliance Gaming Corp	***40i***	***△1.55***	***△1.30***	***△0.81***		***Je***	***22.19***	***179.8***	***54.66***	***9-30-99***	***317.0***	***284.0***	***112.0***							
Sr Sub[8]Nts[19] 'B' 10s 2007	fA	**CCC+**	2/99	B–	Y	R	105	(5-1-02)	....	....	[20]Z110	8-4-00	150	Exch.	'98	92	56	58	17.24	17.23
Allied Holdings	***71***	***n/a***	***n/a***	***1.57***		***Dc***	***51.16***	***219.8***	***120.8***	***9-30-99***	***349.0***	***411.0***	***84.9***							
Sr Nts 8⅝s 2007	aO	**B+**	11/99	BB–	Y	BE	[21]100	9-30-02	....	....	[22]Z108.625	10-1-00	150	Exch.	'97	103	85¼	88	9.80	9.80
Allied Waste Industries	***53***	***d5.55***	***1.96***	***3.98***		***Dc***	***101.6***	***2850***	***3221***	***9-30-99***	***9242***	***11281***	***94.5***							
Sr[23]Disc Nts[24] 11.30s 2007	Jd	**BB–**	11/98	B+	Y	BE	107	(6-1-01)	....	....	[25]Z111.30	6-1-01	[26]418	Exch.	'97	86	85⅜	86	....	Flat
AlliedSignal Inc	***17***	***Now Honeywell Intl,see***																		
Deb 9.065s 2033	jD	**A**			X	BE	NC	....	....	....	....	....	51.2	Exch.	'98	131	113⅜	113½	7.99	7.99
Nts 6¾s 2000	fA15	**A**			X	BE	NC	....	....	....	....	....	100	G1	'95	101¾	100⅛	100⅛	6.74	6.74
Nts 6⅛s 2005	jJ	**A**			X	BE	NC	....	....	....	....	....	117	Exch.	'98	101¾	95	95	6.45	6.45
Nts 6.20s 2008	Fa	**A**			X	BE	[27]Z100	....	....	....	....	....	200	G1	'98	102¼	92½	92½	6.70	6.70
Allmerica Financial Corp	***35c***	***11.30***	***17.84***	***15.91***		***Dc***				***9-30-99***	***500.0***	***2748***	***19.8***							
• Sr Deb 7⅝s 2025	aO15	**A–**			X	BE	NC	....	....	....	....	....	200	M2	'95	No Sale		95⅞	7.95	7.95
Allstate Corp	***35***	***39.82***	***44.72***	***30.42***		***Dc***				***9-30-99***	***2106***	***19322***	***7.0***							
Deb 7½s 2013	Jd15	**A+**	11/97	A	X	BE	NC	....	....	....	....	....	250	G1	'93	114⅜	97¼	97¼	7.71	7.71

Uniform Footnote Explanations-See Page 260. Other: [1] Due 7-26-27. [2] Due 2-23-28. [3] Due 5-18-00. [4] Due 7-25-00. [5] Due 12-4-00. [6] Due 12-1-00. [7] Red at greater of 100 or amt based on formula. [8] (HRO)On Chge of Ctrl at 101. [9] Max $52M red w/proceeds of Pub Eq Off'g. [10] Affil with Allegheny Pwr Sys. [11] Conditional SF. [12] Now Allegheny Technologies. [13] (HRO)On 10-15-03 at 100. [14] Max $71.8M red w/proceeds of Equity Off'g. [15] Int accrues at 11.75% fr 2-15-03. [16] (HRO)On Chge of Ctrl at 101(Accreted Val). [17] Accr Val:Max $156M red w/proceeds of Eq Off'g. [18] Due 6-14-02. [19] State gaming laws may req hldr's sale/Co red. [20] Max $50M red w/proceeds Pub Eq Off'g. [21] Plus Make-Whole Amt. [22] Max $52.5M red w/proceeds of Pub Eq Off'g. [23] Int accrues at 11.3% fr 6-1-01. [24] (HRO)On Chge of Ctrl at 101(Accreted). [25] Max $139M red w/proceeds of Equity Off'g. [26] Incl disc. [27] Red at greater of 100 or amt based on forumla.

Title-Industry Code & Co. Finances (In Italics) / Exchange, Individual Issue Statistics	Ind / Interest Dates	S&P Rating	Fixed Charge Coverage 1996 / Date of Last Rating Change	1997 / Prior Rating	1998 / Eligible	Year End / Bond Form	Million $ Cash & Equiv. / Redemption Provisions: Regular Price	Curr. Assets / Regular (Begins) Thru	Curr. Liab. / Sinking Fund Price	Balance Sheet Date / Sinking Fund (Begins) Thru	L. Term Debt (Mil $) / Refund/Other Restriction Price	Refund/Other Restriction (Begins) Thru	Capital-ization (Mil $) / Outst'g (Mil $)	Total Debt % Capital / Underwriting Firm	Year	Price Range 1999 High	Low	Mo. End Price Sale(s) or Bid	Curr. Yield	Yield to Mat.
Allstate Corp (Cont.)																				
Sr Deb 6¾s 2018	Mn15	A+			X	BE	NC	....	....	....	....	....	250	G1	'98	105⅛	87⅜	89⅝	7.55	7.55
Sr Deb 6.90s 2038	Mn15	A+			X	BE	NC	....	....	....	....	....	250	G1	'98	105¼	84¼	88	7.84	7.84
Nts 6¾s 2003	Jd15	A+	11/97	A	X	BE	NC	....	....	....	....	....	300	G1	'93	104¼	97⅝	97⅝	6.91	6.91
ALLTEL Corp[1]	***67a***		***3.52***	***5.47***	***4.57***	***Dc***	***37.00***	***1170***	***1179***	***9-30-99***	***3813***		***7901***	***49.2***						
Deb 7¼s 2004	Ao	A–	5/98	A+	X	R	NC	....	....	....	....	....	250	S9	'94	107⅝	99⅞	99⅞	7.26	7.26
Deb 6¾s 2005	mS15	A–	5/98	A+	X	BE	NC	....	....	....	....	....	200	S9	'95	106¼	96¾	96¾	6.98	6.98
Deb 6½s 2013	mN	A–	5/98	A+	X	R	NC	....	....	....	....	....	200	S9	'93	105¼	88¼	88¼	7.37	7.37
Deb 7s 2016	Ms15	A–	5/98	A+	X	BE	[2]Z100	....	....	....	....	....	300	S9	'96	108	91½	92½	7.57	7.57
Deb 6.80s 2029	Mn	A–			X	BE	[3]Z100	....	....	....	....	....	300	S9	'99	100¾	85⅞	87	7.82	7.82
[4]Aluminum Co. of Amer	***5***		***10.18***	***10.98***	***8.55***	***Dc***	***297.0***	***4754***	***3176***	***9-30-99***	***2669***		***10693***	***31.1***						
Bonds 'B' 6½s 2005	Jd15	A+			X	BE	[3]Z100	....	....	....	....	....	200	Exch.	'98	101⅝	95⅝	95⅝	6.80	6.80
Bonds 6¾s 2028	Jj15	A+			X	BE	[3]Z100	....	....	....	....	....	300	M5	'98	104½	88⅝	88⅝	7.62	7.62
Nts 5¾s 2001	Fa	A+			X	BE	NC	....	....	....	....	....	250	C5	'94	101¼	99⅛	99⅛	5.80	5.80
Amax, Inc	***5***	***See Cyprus Amax Minerals***																		
• Nts 9⅞s 2001	Jd13	BBB–			X	R	NC	....	....	....	....	....	91.0	M2	'91	No Sale		103½	9.54	9.54
Amazon.com	***59l***		***n/a***	***n/a***	***n/a***	***Dc***	***905.6***	***1080***	***357.6***	***9-30-99***	***1462***		***1895***	***77.8***						
Sr[5]Disc Nts[6] 10s 2008	mN	B			Y	BE	[7]Z100	4-30-03	....	....	[8]Z110	5-1-03	[9]530	Exch.	'98	72½	63	63½	....	Flat
AMB Property	***57***		***n/a***	***5.98***	***2.78***	***Dc***				***9-30-99***	***1278***		***3612***	***39.3***						
Nts 7.10s 2008	Jd30	BBB			X	BE	[3]Z100	....	....	....	....	....	175	M7	'98	100⅜	90⅝	90⅝	7.83	7.83
Ambac Financial Group[10]	***35c***		***16.95***	***14.40***	***11.04***	***Dc***				***9-30-99***	***424.0***		***2451***	***17.3***						
Deb 9⅜s 2011	fA	AA	8/95	AA+	X	R	NC	....	....	....	....	....	150	S1	'91	129½	118⅝	114¼	8.21	8.20
Deb 7½s 2023	Mn	AA	8/95	AA+	X	R	NC	....	....	....	....	....	75.0	M6	'93	109⅛	94⅛	95	7.89	7.89
AMC Entertainment	***24b***		***2.45***	***d0.26***	***0.25***	***Mr***	***10.40***	***102.0***	***194.0***	***9-30-99***	***700.0***		***804.0***	***87.6***						
Sr Sub[5]Nts 9½s 2009	Ms15	B–	2/99	B	Y	BE	104.75	(3-15-02)	....	....	....	....	200	Exch.	'97	102¼	81½	89	10.67	10.67
Amerada Hess	***49b***		***6.13***	***0.93***	***d3.36***	***Dc***	***25.59***	***2053***	***1866***	***9-30-99***	***2336***		***5329***	***45.1***						
Nts 7⅜s 2009	aO	BBB			X	BE	[3]Z100	....	....	....	....	....	300	M5	'99	100⅝	97⅝	97¾	7.54	7.54
Nts 7⅞s 2029	aO	BBB			X	BE	[3]Z100	....	....	....	....	....	700	M5	'99	101⅜	96½	97¾	8.06	8.06
AMERCO	***7***		***2.14***	***2.19***	***2.33***	***Mr***				***9-30-99***	***1087***		***1751***	***62.1***						
Sr Nts[5] 7.20s 2002	Ao	BBB			X	BE	[3]Z100	....	....	....	....	....	150	N2	'99	103	97⅝	97⅝	7.38	7.38
Sr Nts[5] 7.85s 2003	Mn15	BBB			X	BE	NC	....	....	....	....	....	175	S1	'96	104¾	98	98	8.01	8.01
M-T Nts[11] 7.47s 2027	Jj15	BBB			X	BE	NC	....	....	....	....	....	40.0		'97	106⅞	94¾	94¾	7.88	7.88
[12]America West Airlines	***4***		***3.10***	***5.34***	***7.33***	***Dc***	***247.0***	***481.0***	***661.0***	***9-30-99***	***156.0***		***973.0***	***27.2***						
Sr Nts[5] 10¾s 2005	mS	B			Y	R	105.375	(9-1-00)	....	....	....	....	50.0	Exch.	'95	107	96¾	97⅛	11.07	11.07
Amer Architectural Prod	***42b***		***n/a***	***n/a***	***0.53***	***Dc***	***0.19***	***72.45***	***72.93***	***9-30-99***	***128.0***		***147.0***	***106.0***						
Sr Nts 11¾s 2007	jD	CCC+	9/99	B–	Y	BE	105	(12-1-02)	....	....	[13]Z111.75	11-1-00	125	Exch.	'98	87	28	28¼	....	....
Amer Bldrs & Contractors	***13g***		***n/a***	***n/a***	***n/a***	***Dc***	***3.02***	***346.0***	***179.0***	***9-30-99***	***262.0***		***294.0***	***90.5***						
Sr Sub Nts[5] 10⅝s 2007	Mn15	B			Y	BE	105.3125	(5-15-02)	....	....	[14]Z110.625	5-15-00	100	Exch.	'97	104	87¾	93	11.42	11.42
Amer Express	***25e***		***3.39***	***3.98***	***3.93***	***Dc***				***9-30-99***	***6720***		***41147***	***76.3***						
Nts 8½s 2001	fA15	A+	3/93	AA–	X	R	NC	....	....	....	....	....	300	L3	'91	107	102⅝	102⅝	8.28	8.28
Nts[15] 6¾s 2004	Jd23	A+			X	BE	NC	....	....	....	....	....	500	L3	'97	105¾	98¼	98¼	6.87	6.87
Deb 8⅝s 2022	Mn15	A+	3/93	AA–	X	R	103.861	(5-15-02)	....	....	....	....	132	S1	'92	109	101⅜	102⅝	8.40	8.40
Amer Express Credit	***25d***		***1.30***	***1.29***	***1.31***	***Dc***	***2586***			***6-30-99***	***2778***		***23504***	***91.0***						
• Sr Nts 6⅛s 2000	Jd15	A+			X	R	NC	....	....	....	....	....	300	L3	'93	101⅜	99⅛	99⅝	6.15	6.15
Sr Nts 6½s 2000	fA	A+			X	BE	NC	....	....	....	....	....	250	L3	'95	101¾	100	100⅛	6.49	6.49
Sr Nts 6¾s 2001	Jd	A+			X	BE	NC	....	....	....	....	....	250	G1	'95	103	99¾	99¾	6.77	6.77

Uniform Footnote Explanations-See Page 260. Other: [1] See Aliant Commun,Mid-Penn Tel,360(Degrees). [2] Greater of 100 or amt based on formula. [3] Red at greater of 100 or amt based on formula. [4] Now Alcoa Inc. [5] (HRO)On Chge of Ctrl at 101. [6] Int accrues at 10% fr 5-1-03. [7] Plus Accreted Val. [8] Max $186M red w/proceeds of Equity Off'g. [9] Incl disc. [10] Was AMBAC Inc. [11] (HRO)On 1-15-07('12&'17)at 100. [12] Now America West Holdings. [13] Max $43.8M red w/proceeds Eq Off'g. [14] Max $35M red w/proceeds of Pub Eq Off'g. [15] Co may red in whole,at 100,for tax law chge.

Title-Industry Code & Co. Finances (In Italics)	Ind	Fixed Charge Coverage 1996	1997		1998	Year End	Million $ Cash & Equiv.	Curr. Assets	Curr. Liab.	Balance Sheet Date	L. Term Debt (Mil $)		Capital-ization (Mil $)	Total Debt % Capital						
Individual Issue Statistics Exchange ↓	Interest Dates	S&P Rating	Date of Last Rating Change	Prior Rating	Eligible ↓	Bond Form	Redemption Provisions: Regular Price	Regular (Begins) Thru	Sinking Fund Price	Sinking Fund (Begins) Thru	Refund/Other Restriction Price	Refund/Other Restriction (Begins) Thru	Outst'g (Mil $)	Underwriting Firm	Underwriting Year	Price Range 1999 High	Price Range 1999 Low	Mo. End Price Sale(s) or Bid	Curr. Yield	Yield to Mat.
***Amer Express Credit** (Cont.)*																				
Sr Nts 6⅛s 2001	mN15	**A+**			X	BE	NC	....	....	....	....	....	300	G1	'95	101⅞	98⅝	98⅝	6.21	6.21
Step-Up(Reset)[1]Sr Nts 6¼s 2005	fA10	**A+**			X	R	100	(8-10-00)	....	....	....	....	100	L3	'93	101¾	97¾	97¾	6.39	....
Amer Fin'l Group	***35c***	***5.65***	***7.11***		***9.22***	***Dc***				***9-30-99***	***738.0***		***2665***	***27.7***						
• Sr Deb 7⅛s 2007	jD15	**BBB+**	10/98	BBB	X	BE	[2]Z100	....	....	....	....	....	100	C5	'97	103	99⅛	91⅞	7.76	7.75
• Sr Deb 7⅛s 2009	Ao15	**BBB+**			X	BE	[2]Z100	....	....	....	....	....	350	D6	'99	99⅝	96⅞	90¾	7.85	7.85
Amer & Foreign Pwr	***13d***	***Now Boise Cascade Corp,see***																		
• Deb 5s 2030	Ms	**BB+**	9/98	BBB–	Y	CR	107.50	2-28-10	....	....	....	....	32.8	D4	'30	69⅞	58	57⅝	8.68	8.68
Amer Gen'l[3]Corp[4]	***25g***	***2.72***	***2.73***		***3.06***	***Dc***				***9-30-99***	***8717***		***21530***	***64.8***						
Nts 9⅝s 2000	jJ15	**AA–**	11/94	AA	X	R	NC	....	....	....	....	....	200	M2	'88	105⅞	101⅝	101¾	9.46	9.46
Nts 6¼s 2003	Ms15	**AA–**	11/94	AA	X	R	NC	....	....	....	....	....	100	F1	'93	102¼	97⅛	97⅛	6.44	6.43
Nts 7¾s 2005	Ao	**AA–**			X	R	NC	....	....	....	....	....	150	S1	'95	110⅜	101½	101½	7.64	7.64
Nts 6¾s 2005	Jd15	**AA–**			X	BE	NC	....	....	....	....	....	150	M2	'95	105⅜	97	97	6.96	6.96
Nts 7½s 2025	jJ15	**AA–**			X	BE	NC	....	....	....	....	....	150	M5	'95	111⅝	94¼	95⅝	7.84	7.84
Nts 6⅝s 2029	Fa15	**AA–**			X	BE	NC	....	....	....	....	....	150	D6	'99	100¼	83¾	85¼	7.77	7.77
American Gen'l[5]Finance[6]	***25a***	***1.17***	***1.48***		***1.61***	***Dc***	***99.30***			***6-30-99***	***5433***		***10564***	***85.1***						
Sr Nts 6⅞s 2000	Jj15	**A+**			X	R	NC	....	....	....	....	....	150	M5	'93	101⅜	100	100	6.88	6.87
Sr Nts 8s 2000	Fa15	**A+**			X	BE	NC	....	....	....	....	....	200	L3	'95	102⅝	100¼	100¼	7.98	7.98
Sr Nts 7¼s 2000	Ao15	**A+**			X	BE	NC	....	....	....	....	....	200	G1	'95	102⅛	100¼	100¼	7.23	7.23
Sr Nts 5⅞s 2000	jJ	**A+**			X	BE	NC	....	....	....	....	....	150	M5	'93	100⅝	99¾	99¾	5.89	5.89
Sr Nts 6⅛s 2000	mS15	**A+**			X	BE	NC	....	....	....	....	....	200	M6	'97	101⅛	99⅝	99¾	6.14	6.14
Sr Nts 6s 2001	Jd	**A+**			X	BE	NC	....	....	....	....	....	200	L3	'98	101¼	98⅝	98¾	6.08	6.08
Sr Nts 5.80s 2002	Ms15	**A+**			X	BE	NC	....	....	....	....	....	200	M7	'99	100	97¼	97¼	5.96	5.96
Sr Nts 7.45s 2002	jJ	**A+**			X	R	NC	....	....	....	....	....	150	G1	'92	106⅛	100⅞	100⅞	7.39	7.38
Sr Nts 5.90s 2003	Jj15	**A+**			X	BE	NC	....	....	....	....	....	200	G1	'88	101¼	96⅜	96⅜	6.12	6.12
• Sr Nts 6⅜s 2003	Ms	**A+**			X	BE	NC	....	....	....	....	....	150	S1	'93	100⅝	96⅝	96¼	6.62	6.62
Sr Nts 6.20s 2003	Ms15	**A+**			X	BE	NC	....	....	....	....	....	200	C1	'98	102⅜	97	97	6.39	6.39
Sr Nts 5¾s 2003	mN	**A+**			X	BE	NC	....	....	....	....	....	400	D6	'98	100⅜	94⅞	94⅞	6.06	6.06
Sr Nts 6¾s 2004	mN15	**A+**			X	BE	NC	....	....	....	....	....	200	D6	'99	99¼	97½	97½	6.92	6.92
Sr Nts 7¼s 2005	Mn15	**A+**			X	BE	NC	....	....	....	....	....	200	C1	'95	107½	99¼	99¼	7.30	7.30
Sr Nts 5⅞s 2005	jD15	**A+**			X	BE	NC	....	....	....	....	....	200	M2	'98	101⅝	92¼	92⅜	6.36	6.36
Sr Nts 8⅛s 2009	fA15	**A+**			X	R	NC	....	....	....	....	....	150	S1	'89	117⅛	102⅛	102⅛	7.96	7.95
• Sr Nts 8.45s 2009	aO15	**A+**			X	R	NC	....	....	....	....	....	150	B7	'89	No Sale		101	8.37	8.37
M-T Nts 'C'[7] 6¾s 2000	[8]ao	**A+**			X	BE	NC	....	....	....	....	....	5.00	G1	'93	101¼	100	100⅛	6.74	6.74
M-T Nts 'C'[7] 5.48s 2000	[9]ao	**A+**			X	BE	NC	....	....	....	....	....	5.00	G1	'93	100	99	99⅛	5.53	5.53
M-T Nts 'C'[7] 6.45s 2003	[10]ao	**A+**			X	BE	NC	....	....	....	....	....	5.00	G1	'93	102¾	98	98	6.58	6.58
M-T Nts 'D' 7.23s 2000	[11]ms15	**A+**			X	BE	NC	....	....	....	....	....	10.0		'95	102⅛	100⅜	100⅜	7.20	7.20
M-T Nts 'D' 6.37s 2000	[12]ms15	**A+**			X	BE	NC	....	....	....	....	....	10.0		'95	101¼	100	100	6.37	6.37
M-T Nts 'D' 6.76s 2000	[13]ms15	**A+**			X	BE	NC	....	....	....	....	....	11.0		'95	102	100⅛	100⅛	6.75	6.75
M-T Nts 'D' 6.65s 2000	[14]ms15	**A+**			X	BE	NC	....	....	....	....	....	29.0		'95	101¾	100	100	6.65	6.65
M-T Nts 'D' 6.89s 2002	[15]ms15	**A+**			X	BE	NC	....	....	....	....	....	25.0		'95	104	99½	99½	6.92	6.92
M-T Nts 'D' 6.796s 2005	[16]ms15	**A+**			X	BE	NC	....	....	....	....	....	10.0		'95	105	96⅞	96⅞	7.02	7.01
M-T Nts 'E' 5.84s 2001	[17]fa	**A+**			X	BE	NC	....	....	....	....	....	35.0	M2	'98	100¾	98⅞	98⅞	5.91	5.91
M-T Nts 'E' 5¾s 2001	[18]fa	**A+**			X	BE	NC	....	....	....	....	....	46.0	M2	'98	100⅝	97¾	97¾	5.88	5.88
M-T Nts 'E' 6¼s 2002	[19]fa	**A+**			X	BE	NC	....	....	....	....	....	100	L3	'97	102	97⅝	97⅝	6.40	6.40
American Greetings	***29***	***9.27***	***12.76***		***11.08***	***Fb***	***28.53***	***1103***	***550.4***	***8-31-99***	***455.0***		***1695***	***20.6***						
Nts[20] 6.10s 2028	fA	**A**			X	BE	NC	....	....	....	....	....	300	G1	'98	102⅞	89⅜	89⅜	6.83	6.82

Uniform Footnote Explanations-See Page 1. Other: [1] Int 6.25% to 8-9-00,7.45% aft. [2] Plus Make-Whole Amt. [3] Was Amer Gen'l Insur. [4] See USLIFE Corp,Western Natl. [5] Sub Credithrift Fin'l Inc(Amer Gen'l). [6] Was Credithrift Fin'l Corp. [7] Issued in min denom $100T. [8] Due 1-31-00. [9] Due 10-4-00. [10] Due 3-3-03. [11] Due 4-27-00. [12] Due 6-30-00. [13] Due 8-17-00. [14] Due 8-30-00. [15] Due 7-31-02. [16] Due 7-20-05. [17] Due 1-29-01. [18] Due 11-20-01. [19] Due 12-18-02. [20] (HRO)On 8-1-09 at 100.

Company rows (italics): Title-Industry Code & Co. Finances (In Italics) | Ind | Fixed Charge Coverage 1996, 1997, 1998, Year End | Million $: Cash & Equiv., Curr. Assets, Curr. Liab. | Balance Sheet Date | L. Term Debt (Mil $) | Capital-ization (Mil $) | Total Debt % Capital

Exchange / Individual Issue Statistics	Interest Dates	S&P Rating	Date of Last Rating Change	Prior Rating	Eligible	Bond Form	Redemption Provisions: Regular Price	Regular (Begins) Thru	Sinking Fund Price	Sinking Fund (Begins) Thru	Refund/Other Restriction Price	Refund/Other Restriction (Begins) Thru	Outst'g (Mil $)	Underwriting Firm	Underwriting Year	Price Range 1999 High	Price Range 1999 Low	Mo. End Price Sale(s) or Bid	Curr. Yield	Yield to Mat.
Amer Health Prop	***57***	***Merged into Health Care Prop,see***																		
Nts 7.05s 2002	Jj15	BBB–			X	BE	[1]100	....	....	....	....	....	100	G1	'97	98¾	95½	96¾	7.29	7.29
Nts 7½s 2007	Jj15	BBB–			X	BE	[1]100	....	....	....	....	....	120	G1	'97	97⅜	87⅞	90¼	8.31	8.31
Amer Home Products	***21a***		***5.69***	***8.59***	***9.83***	***Dc***	***2583***	***9596***	***7549***	***9-30-99***	***3622***		***11460***	***48.6***						
Deb 7¼s 2023	Ms	A	7/97	A–	X	BE	NC	....	....	....	....	....	250	F1	'93	112⅝	92¾	93¾	7.73	7.73
Nts 7.70s 2000	Fa15	A	7/97	A–	X	BE	NC	....	....	....	....	....	1000	G1	'95	102¾	100⅛	100⅛	7.69	7.69
Nts 6½s 2002	aO15	A	7/97	A–	X	BE	NC	....	....	....	....	....	250	F1	'92	104⅛	98¾	98¾	6.58	6.58
Nts 7.90s 2005	Fa15	A	7/97	A–	X	BE	NC	....	....	....	....	....	1000	G1	'95	113¼	102⅜	102⅝	7.70	7.70
Amer Pad & Paper	***48b***		***1.75***	***0.90***	***0.04***	***Dc***	***1.55***	***158.0***	***348.0***	***9-30-99***	***138.0***		***392.0***	***97.7***						
Sr Sub Nts[2] 13s 2005	§mN15	D	12/99	CCC–	Z	BE			Default 11-15-99 int				130	Exch.	'96	65¼	9¼	11	....	Flat
Amer Radio Systems	***12b***	***Acquired by CBS Corp,see***																		
Sr Sub Nts[3] 9s 2006	Fa	BB+	12/98	BB–	Y	R	104.50	(2-1-01)	....	....	....	....	175	C5	'96	109¼	104½	105½	8.53	8.53
Amer Safety Razor	***18***		***2.84***	***3.01***	***2.16***	***Dc***	***7.57***	***121.1***	***45.76***	***9-30-99***	***120.0***		***188.0***	***67.0***						
Sr Nts[2] 'B' 9⅞s 2005	fA	B+	4/99	BB–	Y	R	104.389	(8-1-00)	....	....	....	....	100	D6	'95	101¼	97	97⅝	10.12	10.11
Amer Skiing	***32***		***Δ0.61***	***Δ0.91***	***Δd0.09***	***Jl***	***7.83***	***48.70***	***140.1***	***10-24-99***	***414.0***		***783.0***	***64.1***						
Sr Sub Nts[2] 'B' 12s 2006	jJ15	CCC	7/99	CCC+	Y	BE	106.25	(7-15-01)	....	....	....	....	120	Exch.	'97	104	76	91¼	13.15	13.14
American Standard[4]	***13b***		***2.62***	***2.78***	***2.86***	***Dc***	***45.00***	***1880***	***2343***	***9-30-99***	***1944***		***2243***	***110.0***						
SF Deb 9¼s 2016	jD	BB–	9/95	B+	Y	R	103.238	11-30-00	100	....	....	....	150	F1	'86	102⅝	98¼	98¾	9.37	9.37
Sr Nts 7⅛s 2003	Fa15	BB–			Y	BE	NC	....	....	....	....	....	125	G1	'98	100½	93½	95½	7.46	7.46
Sr Nts 7⅜s 2005	Ao15	BB–			Y	BE	NC	....	....	....	....	....	250	G1	'98	101⅛	91½	94⅝	7.79	7.79
Sr Nts[5] 7⅜s 2008	Fa	BB–			Y	BE	NC	....	....	....	....	....	350	G1	'98	101	88½	91¾	8.04	8.04
Sr Nts 7⅝s 2010	Fa15	BB–			Y	BE	NC	....	....	....	....	....	275	G1	'98	101⅝	88½	91¼	8.36	8.35
American Stores	***59c***	***Merged into Albertson's Inc,see***																		
Deb 7.40s 2005	Mn15	A	6/99	BBB+	X	R	NC	....	....	....	....	....	200	M5	'95	108⅜	100⅝	100⅝	7.35	7.35
Deb 7.90s 2017	Mn	A	6/99	BBB+	X	BE	NC	....	....	....	....	....	100	M5	'97	114⅛	100¾	100⅞	7.83	7.83
Deb 8s 2026	Jd	A	6/99	BBB+	X	BE	NC	....	....	....	....	....	350	M5	'96	115⅞	101⅛	101¼	7.90	7.90
Deb[6] 7½s 2037	Mn	A	6/99	BBB+	X	BE	NC	....	....	....	....	....	200	M5	'97	112½	100⅞	100⅞	7.43	7.43
Nts 9⅛s 2002	Ao	A	6/99	BBB+	X	R	NC	....	....	....	....	....	250	L3	'92	110¼	105¼	105¼	8.67	8.67
AmeriKing, Inc	***27b***		***n/a***	***0.82***	***1.30***	***Dc***	***9.81***	***16.90***	***30.20***	***6-28-99***	***221.0***		***211.0***	***105.0***						
Sr Nts[2] 10¾s 2006	jD	B–			Y	R	105.375	(12-1-01)	....	....	....	....	100	D6	'96	106½	87½	92	11.68	11.68
AmeriSteel Corp	***66h***		***1.78***	***3.56***	***3.64***	***Mr***	***6.96***	***227.0***	***94.00***	***9-30-99***	***191.0***		***419.0***	***46.5***						
Sr Nts[2] 'B' 8¾s 2008	Ao15	BB–	8/99	B+	Y	BE	104.375	(4-15-03)	....	....	[7]Z108.75	4-15-01	130	Exch.	'98	102½	96	100½	8.71	8.71
[8]Ameritech Capital Funding	***25***		***7.45***	***8.30***	***7.87***	***Dc***	***292.0***	***4719***	***9456***	***6-30-99***	***6157***		***19034***	***43.3***						
[9]Gtd Deb 7½s 2005	Ao	AA+			X	BE	NC	....	....	....	....	....	192	L3	'95	111⅞	101	101	7.43	7.43
[9]Gtd([10]Amort[11])Deb 8.85s 2005	Jd	AA+	7/91	AAA	X	BE	NC	....	....	....	....	....	53.7	G1	'91	119⅛	106⅞	106⅞	8.28	....
[9]Gtd([12]Amort) Deb 9.10s 2016	Jd	AA+	7/91	AAA	X	BE	NC	....	....	....	....	....	96.3	G1	'91	132½	112¾	112¾	8.07	....
[9]Gtd Deb 6.45s 2018	Jj15	AA+			X	BE	NC	....	....	....	....	....	300	G1	'98	105¼	87⅝	88	7.33	7.33
[9]Gtd Deb 6⅞s 2027	aO15	AA+			X	BE	NC	....	....	....	....	....	200	G1	'97	110½	90¼	90½	7.60	7.60
[9]Gtd Deb 6.55s 2028	Jj15	AA+			X	BE	NC	....	....	....	....	....	400	G1	'98	106⅜	86⅜	86¾	7.55	7.55
[9]Gtd Deb[13] 5.95s 2038	Jj15	AA+			X	BE	NC	....	....	....	....	....	250	G1	'98	103⅝	95¾	95¾	6.21	6.21
[9]Gtd Nts 5.65s 2001	Jj15	AA+			X	BE	NC	....	....	....	....	....	400	G1	'98	101¼	99	99	5.71	5.71
[9]Gtd Nts 6⅛s 2001	aO15	AA+			X	BE	NC	....	....	....	....	....	250	G1	'97	102⅞	98⅞	98⅞	6.19	6.19
[9]Gtd Nts 6.30s 2004	aO15	AA+			X	BE	NC	....	....	....	....	....	250	G1	'97	105⅜	96¾	96¾	6.51	6.51
[9]Gtd Nts 6.15s 2008	Jj15	AA+			X	BE	NC	....	....	....	....	....	400	G1	'98	105¾	92⅜	92⅝	6.64	6.64
Ames Department Stores	***59g***		***2.41***	***5.62***	***4.45***	***Ja***	***42.38***	***1287***	***816.3***	***10-30-99***	***800.0***		***924.0***	***49.8***						
Sr Nts[2] 10s 2006	Ao15	B+			Y	BE	105	(4-15-03)	....	....	[14]Z110	4-15-02	200	Exch.	'99	99½	96¾	98	10.20	10.20

Uniform Footnote Explanations-See Page 260. Other: [1] Plus Make-Whole Amt. [2] (HRO)On Chge of Ctrl at 101. [3] Co must offer repurch at 101 on Chge of Ctrl. [4] Subsid & data of Amer Stand Cos Inc. [5] Gtd by Amer Standard Cos. Inc. [6] (HRO)On 5-1-09 at 100. [7] Max $45.5M red w/proceeds Equity Off'g. [8] Gtd by & data of Ameritech Corp(acq by SBC Commun). [9] Gtd by Ameritech Corp. [10] Prin pyts due ea 6-1:97-8,$74.49,99-01,$102.42. [11] Prin pyts due ea 6-1:02-05,$135.94. [12] Prin pyts due ea 6-1:06-15,$75.80,16,$242.00. [13] (HRO)On 1-15-05 at 100. [14] Max $70M red w/proceeds of Pub Eq Off'g.

Exchange / Individual Issue Statistics	Interest Dates	S&P Rating	Date of Last Rating Change	Prior Rating	Eligible	Bond Form	Redemption Provisions: Regular Price	Regular (Begins) Thru	Sinking Fund Price	Sinking Fund (Begins) Thru	Refund/Other Restriction Price	Refund/Other Restriction (Begins) Thru	Outst'g (Mil $)	Underwriting Firm	Underwriting Year	Price Range 1999 High	Price Range 1999 Low	Mo. End Price Sale(s) or Bid	Curr. Yield	Yield to Mat.
Title-Industry Code & Co. Finances (In Italics)	*Ind*	*Fixed Charge Coverage 1996*	*1997*	*1998*		*Year End*	*Million $ Cash & Equiv.*	*Curr. Assets*	*Curr. Liab.*	*Balance Sheet Date*	*L. Term Debt (Mil $)*		*Capital-ization (Mil $)*	*Total Debt % Capital*						
AMF Bowling Worldwide[1]	***40b***	***n/a***	***0.79***	***0.10***		***Dc***	***14.80***	***198.0***	***137.0***	***6-30-99***	***1024***		***1808***	***58.5***						
• Sr Sub Nts[2]'B' 10⅞s 2006	Ms15	CCC+	11/98	B	Y	BE	105.438	(3-15-01)	....	....	....	....	250	G1	'96	89	64½	42⅛	....	....
• Sr Sub[3]Disc Nts[4]'B'[1] 12¼s 2006	Ms15	CCC+	11/98	B	Y	BE	106.125	(3-15-01)	....	....	....	....	[5]452	G1	'96	65	50	30	....	....
Amgen Inc	***21b***	***n/a***	***n/a***	***43.12***		***Dc***	***1524***	***2126***	***818.0***	***9-30-99***	***223.0***		***2791***	***8.2***						
Deb[6] 8⅛s 2097	Ao	A			X	BE	[7]Z100	....	....	....	....	....	100	M2	'97	122⅜	99⅝	99¾	8.15	8.15
Nts 6½s 2007	jD	A			X	BE	[8]Z100	....	....	....	....	....	100	G1	'97	105¾	94¾	94¾	6.86	6.86
[9]Amoco Co[10]	***49c***	***n/a***	***n/a***	***3.66***		***Dc***	***875.0***	***17226***	***18166***	***12-31-98***	***10918***		***56613***	***24.3***						
Gtd[11]Nts 6¼s 2004	aO15	AA+	1/99	AAA	X	BE	NC	....	....	....	....	....	200	M6	'97	105⅝	97½	97½	6.41	6.41
Gtd[11]Nts 6½s 2007	fA	AA+	1/99	AAA	X	BE	NC	....	....	....	....	....	300	M6	'97	108	96⅜	96⅜	6.74	6.74
Amphenol Corp	***23b***	***5.61***	***2.34***	***1.80***		***Dc***	***8.97***	***340.7***	***147.6***	***9-30-99***	***938.0***		***675.0***	***139.0***						
Sr Sub Nts 9⅞s 2007	Mn15	B–			Y	BE	104.938	(5-15-02)	....	....	[12]109.875	5-15-00	240	D6	'97	104½	99¾	104	9.50	9.49
AMR Corp	***4***	***3.83***	***5.22***	***6.61***		***Dc***	***1965***	***5112***	***6509***	***9-30-99***	***[13]5217***		***12190***	***46.7***						
SF Deb 8⅝s 2017	Ms	BBB–	6/97	BB+	X	R	103.45	2-28-00	100	....	....	....	93.5	S1	'87	103⅛	95¾	96½	8.94	8.94
Deb 9s 2012	fA	BBB–	6/97	BB+	X	R	NC	....	....	....	....	....	350	G1	'92	121⅛	104⅝	104⅝	8.60	8.60
• Deb 9s 2016	mS15	BBB–	6/97	BB+	X	R	NC	....	....	....	....	....	100	D7	'86	123½	103¾	s105¼	8.55	8.55
Deb[14] 10.20s 2020	Ms15	BBB–	6/97	BB+	X	R	NC	....	....	....	....	....	125	M6	'90	129⅝	114⅜	114½	8.91	8.91
Deb[15] 9.88s 2020	Jd15	BBB–	6/97	BB+	X	R	NC	....	....	....	....	....	100	M6	'90	126⅝	111⅝	111¾	8.84	8.84
Deb 10s 2021	Ao15	BBB–	6/97	BB+	X	R	NC	....	....	....	....	....	350	G1	'91	127¾	112⅜	112½	8.89	8.89
Deb 9¾s 2021	fA15	BBB–	6/97	BB+	X	R	NC	....	....	....	....	....	200	M2	'91	125½	110	110⅛	8.85	8.85
Deb 9.80s 2021	aO	BBB–	6/97	BB+	X	R	NC	....	....	....	....	....	100	G1	'91	126⅛	110½	110⅝	8.86	8.86
Nts[16] 9¾s 2000	Ms15	BBB–	6/97	BB+	X	R	NC	....	....	....	....	....	200	M6	'90	104	100⅝	100⅝	9.69	9.69
Nts 10s 2001	Fa	BBB–	6/97	BB+	X	R	NC	....	....	....	....	....	100	M6	'91	107¼	102½	102½	9.76	9.75
Nts 9½s 2001	Mn15	BBB–	6/97	BB+	X	R	NC	....	....	....	....	....	200	S1	'91	107⅛	102½	102½	9.27	9.27
M-T Nts 'D'[17] 8.47s 2002	[18]mn15	BBB–	6/97	BB+	X	BE	NC	....	....	....	....	....	28.0	M6	'92	106⅞	101⅞	101⅞	8.31	8.31
M-T Nts 'D'[17] 8.60s 2002	[19]mn15	BBB–	6/97	BB+	X	BE	NC	....	....	....	....	....	10.0	M2	'92	107⅜	102⅛	102⅛	8.42	8.42
AMRESCO INC.	***25g***	***2.37***	***1.90***	***0.56***		***Dc***				***9-30-99***	***1881***		***2501***	***75.2***						
• Sr Sub Nts[20] 10s 2003	[21]Jan15	NR				R	100	(1-15-01)	....	....	....	....	50.0	P2	'96	92	42	s60	16.67	16.65
• Sr Sub Nts '97A 10s 2004	Ms15	CCC–	11/99	CCC+	Y	BE	NC	....	....	....	....	....	192	P2	'97	90	43⅛	s57⅛	17.51	17.50
Sr Sub Nts 9⅞s 2005	Ms15	CCC–	11/99	CCC+	Y	R	104.938	(3-15-02)	....	....	....	....	290	M6	'98	86½	45	63	15.67	15.67
AmSouth Bancorp[22]	***10***	***2.52***	***2.60***	***2.53***		***Dc***				***9-30-99***	***4239***		***5711***	***74.2***						
Sub Deb[23] 6¾s 2025	mN	BBB+			X	BE	NC	....	....	....	....	....	150	M6	'95	105	96	96	7.03	7.03
Sub Nts 7¾s 2004	Mn15	BBB+	6/95	A–	X	BE	NC	....	....	....	....	....	150	S1	'94	109	100	100	7.75	7.75
Sub Nts 6⅛s 2009	Ms	BBB+			X	BE	[8]Z100	....	....	....	....	....	175	D6	'99	99⅛	88¼	88¼	6.94	6.94
Amtran, Inc	***4***	***d7.86***	***1.64***	***6.25***		***Dc***	***109.1***	***208.2***	***232.8***	***9-30-99***	***282.0***		***433.0***	***65.6***						
Sr Nts[2] 9⅝s 2005	jD15	B+			Y	BE	104.813	(6-15-03)	....	....	[24]Z109.625	6-15-01	125	M7	'98	104½	93¾	96	10.03	10.02
Anadarko Petroleum Corp[25]	***49***	***3.27***	***3.31***	***0.76***		***Dc***	***14.80***	***259.9***	***232.5***	***9-30-99***	***1405***		***2913***	***48.2***						
Deb[26] 7¼s 2025	Ms15	BBB+			X	BE	NC	....	....	....	....	....	100	M5	'95	106¼	96¼	100⅛	7.24	7.24
Deb 7s 2027	mN15	BBB+			X	BE	NC	....	....	....	....	....	100	M5	'97	105⅛	88⅛	88½	7.91	7.91
Deb 6⅝s 2028	Jj15	BBB+			X	BE	NC	....	....	....	....	....	100	C6	'98	96⅜	83¾	84¼	7.86	7.86
Deb 7.20s 2029	Ms15	BBB+			X	BE	NC	....	....	....	....	....	200	G1	'99	100⅜	90	90⅜	7.97	7.97
Deb[27] 7.73s 2096	mS15	BBB+			X	BE	NC	....	....	....	....	....	100	M2	'96	112	96⅝	96⅝	8.00	8.00
Deb[28] 7¼s 2096	mN15	BBB+			X	BE	NC	....	....	....	....	....	100	C5	'96	105	85¾	86⅛	8.42	8.42
Nts 8¼s 2001	mN15	BBB+	1/92	A–	X	R	NC	....	....	....	....	....	100	M5	'91	107⅛	101¾	101¾	8.11	8.11
Nts 6¾s 2003	Ms15	BBB+			X	R	NC	....	....	....	....	....	100	K2	'93	104¼	98	98	6.89	6.89
Nts 5⅞s 2003	aO15	BBB+			X	R	NC	....	....	....	....	....	100	K2	'93	101⅜	94¾	94¾	6.20	6.20
Analog Devices	***23h***	***21.44***	***19.86***	***17.01***		***Oc***	***637.1***	***1249***	***357.7***	***7-31-99***	***99.80***		***1636***	***7.2***						
Nts 6⅝s 2000	Ms	BBB+	11/95	BBB	X	R	NC	....	....	....	....	....	80.0	G1	'93	101	100	100	6.63	6.62

Uniform Footnote Explanations-See Page 260. Other: [1] Was AMF Group Inc. [2] (HRO)On Chge of Ctrl at 101. [3] Int accrues at 12.25% fr 3-15-01. [4] (HRO)On Chge of Ctrl at 101(Accreted Val). [5] Incl disc. [6] Co may red in whole,at 100,for Tax Event. [7] Greater of 100 or amt based on formula. [8] Red at greater of 100 or amt based on formula. [9] Gtd by & data of BP Amoco. [10] Was Standard Oil(Ind). [11] Gtd by Amoco Corp. [12] Max $96M red w/proceeds of Pub Eq Off'g. [13] Issue debt only. [14] Int may be adj for Designated Event&Rat'g Chge. [15] Int sub to adj for Designated Event&Rat'g Chge. [16] Int subj to adj for Designated Event&Rat'g Chge. [17] Issued in min denom $100T. [18] Due 2-20-02. [19] Due 3-4-02. [20] Death red benefits,ltd,as defined. [21] Int pd monthly. [22] Was Alabama Bancorporation. [23] (HRO)On 11-1-05 at 100. [24] Max $43.8M red w/proceeds of Pub Eq Off'g. [25] Was Anadarko Production. [26] (HRO)On 3-15-00 at 100. [27] (HRO)On 9-15-26 at 100. [28] Co may shorten mty for Tax Event.

Title-Industry Code & Co. Finances (In Italics) / Individual Issue Statistics (Exchange)	Ind / Interest Dates	Fixed Charge Coverage 1996 / S&P Rating	1997 / Date of Last Rating Change	1998 / Prior Rating	Eligible	Year End / Bond Form	Million $ Cash & Equiv. / Redemption Provisions: Regular Price	Million $ Curr. Assets / Regular (Begins) Thru	Million $ Curr. Liab. / Sinking Fund Price	Balance Sheet Date / Sinking Fund (Begins) Thru	L. Term Debt (Mil $) / Refund/Other Restriction Price	Refund/Other Restriction (Begins) Thru	Capital-ization (Mil $) / Outst'g (Mil $)	Total Debt % Capital / Underwriting Firm	Underwriting Year	Price Range 1999 High	Price Range 1999 Low	Mo. End Price Sale(s) or Bid	Curr. Yield	Yield to Mat.
Anheuser-Busch	*11a*	*8.73*	*7.86*	*7.28*		*Dc*	*132.0*	*1684*	*1822*	*9-30-99*	*4835*		*8980*	*53.8*						
[1]Deb[2] 9s 2009	jD	A+	5/97	AA–	X	R	NC	....	....	....	....	....	350	D4	'89	128⅝	111¾	111¾	8.05	8.05
Deb 7¼s 2015	mS15	A+	5/97	AA–	X	BE	103.57	(9-15-05)	....	....	....	....	150	D4	'95	108¾	96⅛	96⅜	7.52	7.52
Deb 7⅛s 2017	jJ	A+			X	BE	103.026	(7-1-07)	....	....	....	....	250	D4	'97	108	94⅞	95⅛	7.49	7.49
Deb 7⅜s 2023	jJ	A+	5/97	AA–	X	R	103.28	(7-1-03)	....	....	....	....	200	D4	'93	105¾	92	92⅛	8.01	8.00
Deb 7s 2025	jD	A+	5/97	AA–	X	BE	103.34	(12-1-05)	....	....	....	....	200	D4	'95	104	89½	89⅝	7.81	7.81
Deb 6¾s 2027	jD15	A+			X	BE	[3]Z100	....	....	....	....	....	100	M5	'97	108¼	88¾	88¾	7.61	7.60
Deb 6½s 2028	Jj	A+			X	BE	[3]Z100	....	....	....	....	....	100	S6	'98	103¾	86⅛	86⅛	7.55	7.55
Nts 6.90s 2002	aO	A+	5/97	AA–	X	R	100	....	....	....	....	....	200	D4	'92	101¼	99⅛	99¾	6.92	6.92
Nts 6¾s 2003	fA	A+	5/97	AA–	X	BE	NC	....	....	....	....	....	200	D4	'96	106	99⅜	99⅜	6.79	6.79
Nts 6¾s 2005	Jd	A+	5/97	AA–	X	BE	100	(6-1-02)	....	....	....	....	200	D4	'95	104⅛	98	98	6.89	6.89
Nts 7s 2005	mS	A+	5/97	AA–	X	BE	100	(9-1-02)	....	....	....	....	100	D4	'95	104½	98⅞	98⅞	7.08	7.08
Nts 6¾s 2006	mN	A+	5/97	AA–	X	BE	100	(11-1-03)	....	....	....	....	250	D4	'96	104¾	96½	97	6.96	6.96
Nts 7.10s 2007	Jd15	A+			X	BE	100	(6-15-04)	....	....	....	....	250	M5	'97	107⅛	98⅞	98⅞	7.18	7.18
Nts 5⅜s 2008	mS15	A+			X	BE	NC	....	....	....	....	....	100		'98	100⅜	87⅞	87⅞	6.12	6.12
Nts 5⅛s 2008	aO	A+			X	BE	NC	....	....	....	....	....	100		'98	98⅝	86⅜	86⅜	5.93	5.94
Nts 5¾s 2010	Ao	A+			X	BE	[3]Z100	....	....	....	....	....	150	G1	'99	99½	88½	88½	6.50	6.50
Nts 5¾s 2011	J15	A+			X	BE	100	(1-15-06)	....	....	....	....	150	G1	'99	100	86⅞	86⅞	6.62	6.62
Anixter Inc[4]	*67f*	*3.17*	*3.31*	*3.41*		*Dc*	*14.30*	*1009*	*434.0*	*7-2-99*	*476.0*		*874.0*	*54.5*						
[5]Nts 8s 2003	mS15	BBB–			X	BE	NC	....	....	....	....	....	100	M2	'96	107⅞	97¾	97¾	8.18	8.18
ANR [6]Pipeline[7]	*73a*	*4.76*	*5.24*	*7.48*		*Dc*	*5.60*	*266.0*	*185.0*	*6-30-99*	*498.0*		*1216*	*41.0*						
• Deb 9⅝s 2021	mN	BBB+	4/99	BBB	X	R	NC	....	....	....	....	....	300	L3	'91	No Sale		115⅛	8.36	8.36
• Deb 7⅜s 2024	Fa15	BBB+	4/99	BBB	X	BE	NC	....	....	....	....	....	125	C4	'94	No Sale		85⅛	8.66	8.66
• Deb[8] 7s 2025	Jd	BBB+	4/99	BBB	X	BE	NC	....	....	....	....	....	75.0		'95	99⅛	92½	91⅛	7.68	7.68
Aon Corp	*35d*	*12.11*	*10.46*	*11.70*		*Dc*				*9-30-99*	*1617*		*5952*	*46.1*						
• Nts 7.40s 2002	aO	AA–	2/97	AA	X	R	NC	....	....	....	....	....	100	M2	'92	No Sale		98⅛	7.54	7.54
Nts 6.70s 2003	Jd15	AA–	2/97	AA	X	R	NC	....	....	....	....	....	150	M6	'93	104½	98⅛	98⅛	6.83	6.83
Nts 6.30s 2004	Jj15	AA–	2/97	AA	X	R	NC	....	....	....	....	....	100	M6	'94	103¼	96¼	96¼	6.55	6.54
AP Holdings	*63*	*n/a*	*n/a*	*n/a*		*Dc*	*6.89*	*45.60*	*42.70*	*9-30-99*	*216.0*		*152.0*	*143.0*						
Sr[9]Disc[10]Nts 11¼s 2008	Ms15	B–			Y	BE	105.625	(3-15-03)	....	....	[11]Z111.125	3-15-01	[12]70.0	Exch.	'98	58¼	40	40	....	Flat
Apache Corp[13]	*49a*	*3.23*	*3.01*	*d0.91*		*Dc*	*16.67*	*355.1*	*342.6*	*9-30-99*	*1422*		*4012*	*36.0*						
Deb[14] 7⅜s 2047	fA15	BBB+			X	BE	NC	....	....	....	....	....	150	G1	'97	100⅛	89½	90	8.19	8.19
Deb 7⅝s 2096	mN	BBB+	1/97	BBB	X	BE	NC	....	....	....	....	....	150	G1	'96	102¼	89¾	90⅛	8.46	8.46
• Nts 9¼s 2002	Jd	BBB+	1/97	BBB	X	R	NC	....	....	....	....	....	100	G1	'92	110	103¼	103	8.98	8.98
Sr Nts[15] 7s 2018	Fa	BBB+			X	BE	NC	....	....	....	....	....	50.0	M2	'98	100	90¼	90¾	7.71	7.71
Sr Nts 7⅝s 2019	jJ	BBB+			X	BE	NC	....	....	....	....	....	150	B7	'99	101¾	96	96⅞	7.87	7.87
Nts 7.70s 2026	Ms15	BBB+	1/97	BBB	X	BE	NC	....	....	....	....	....	100	F2	'96	106¾	95¾	96¼	8.00	8.00
Nts 7.95s 2026	Ao15	BBB+	1/97	BBB	X	BE	NC	....	....	....	....	....	180	G1	'96	110	98⅝	99⅛	8.02	8.02
Appalachian Power[16]	*72a*	*2.87*	*2.51*	*2.98*		*Dc*	*30.10*	*541.0*	*742.0*	*6-30-99*	*1449*		*2874*	*56.5*						
1st 6⅜s 2001	Ms	A	10/97	A–	X	BE	[17]Z100	....	Z100	....	....	....	100	L3	'96	102⅛	99⅛	99⅛	6.43	6.43
1st 6.80s 2006	Ms	A	10/97	A–	X	BE	[17]Z100	....	Z100	....	....	....	100	L3	'96	107⅛	95⅞	95⅞	7.09	7.09
Sec M-T Nts 6.71s 2000	[18]ao	A	10/97	A–	X	BE	NC	....	....	....	....	....	48.0	S1	'97	101⅝	100	100⅛	6.70	6.70
Sec M-T Nts 7.38s 2002	[19]jd	A	10/97	A–	X	BE	100	....	Z100	....	....	....	50.0	S1	'92	101¼	99⅝	99⅝	7.41	7.41
Sec M-T Nts 7.40s 2002	jD	A	10/97	A–	X	BE	NC	....	....	....	....	....	30.0	S1	'92	106¼	100¼	100¼	7.38	7.38
Sec M-T Nts 6.65s 2003	Mn	A	10/97	A–	X	BE	100.95	4-30-00	Z100	....	....	....	40.0	S1	'93	101⅛	97¾	97¾	6.80	6.80
Sec M-T Nts 6.85s 2003	Jd	A	10/97	A–	X	BE	100.98	5-31-00	Z100	....	....	....	30.0	S1	'93	101⅜	98⅛	98⅛	6.98	6.98

Uniform Footnote Explanations-See Page 260. Other: [1] (HRO)At 100 for Rat'g Decline. [2] Co may red at 100 if 80% outstg put. [3] Red at greater of 100 or amt based on formula. [4] Subsid & data of Anixter Intl. [5] Gtd by Anixter Intl. [6] Subsid of Amer Natural Resources(Coastal Corp). [7] Was Mich Wisc PL. [8] (HRO)On 6-1-05 at 100. [9] Int accr 11.25% fr 3-15-03. [10] (HRO)On Chge of Ctrl at 101(Accreted Amt). [11] Accreted Amts:Red w/proceeds of Pub Eq Off'g. [12] Ind disc. [13] See DEKALB Energy. [14] Co may advance mty for Tax Event. [15] (HRO)On Chge of Ctrl at 100. [16] Subsid of Amer Elec Pwr. [17] Greater of 100 or amt based on formula. [18] Due 6-1-00. [19] Due 8-15-02.

Title-Industry Code & Co. Finances (In Italics) / Exchange ↓ Individual Issue Statistics	Ind / Interest Dates	Fixed Charge Coverage 1996 / S&P Rating	1997 / Date of Last Rating Change	1998 / Prior Rating	Eligible ↓	Year End / Bond Form	Cash & Equiv. (Million $) / Redemption Provisions: Regular Price	Curr. Assets (Million $) / Regular (Begins) Thru	Curr. Liab. (Million $) / Sinking Fund Price	Balance Sheet Date / Sinking Fund (Begins) Thru	L. Term Debt (Mil $) / Refund/Other Restriction Price	Refund/Other Restriction (Begins) Thru	Capital-ization (Mil $) / Outst'g (Mil $)	Total Debt % Capital / Underwriting Firm	Underwriting Year	Price Range 1999 High	Price Range 1999 Low	Mo. End Price Sale(s) or Bid	Curr. Yield	Yield to Mat.
Appalachian Power (Cont.)																				
Sec M-T Nts 6s 2003	mN	**A**	10/97	A–	X	BE	100.86	10-31-00	Z100	....	....	....	30.0	S1	'93	101⅝	95⅜	95⅜	6.29	6.29
Sec M-T Nts 8s 2005	Mn	**A**	10/97	A–	X	BE	NC	....	....	....	....	....	50.0	S1	'95	112⅛	102⅛	102⅛	7.83	7.83
Sec M-T Nts 6.89s 2005	[1]ms	**A**	10/97	A–	X	BE	NC	....	....	....	....	....	30.0	S1	'95	106⅜	97⅛	97⅛	7.09	7.09
Sec M-T Nts 8½s 2022	jD	**A**	10/97	A–	X	BE	104.25	(12-4-02)	Z100	(12-4-02)	....	....	70.0	S1	'92	112½	101	101	8.42	8.41
Sec M-T Nts 7.80s 2023	Mn	**A**	10/97	A–	X	BE	105.46	4-30-00	Z100	....	....	....	40.0	S1	'93	104¾	95½	95½	8.17	8.17
Sec M-T Nts 7.15s 2023	mN	**A**	10/97	A–	X	BE	105.01	10-31-00	Z100	....	....	....	30.0	S1	'93	101⅜	88⅞	89	8.03	8.03
Sec M-T Nts 7⅛s 2024	Mn	**A**	10/97	A–	X	BE	103.57	(5-1-04)	Z100	(5-1-04)	....	....	50.0	S1	'93	103⅜	88½	88⅝	8.04	8.04
Sr Nts 'C' 6.60s 2009	Mn	**BBB+**			X	BE	[2]Z100	....	....	....	....	....	150	M2	'99	100	91¼	91⅜	7.22	7.22
Apple Computer Inc	***20b***	***Δd4.32***	***Δ6.31***	***Δ11.06***		***Sp***	***3226***	***4285***	***1549***	***9-30-99***	***300.0***		***2877***	***33.2***						
Nts 6½s 2004	Fa15	**BB–**	8/99	B+	Y	BE	[3]Z100	....	....	....	....	....	300	G1	'94	95½	90½	92⅝	7.02	7.02
Apple South	***27c***	***Now Avado Brands,see***																		
Sr Nts 9¾s 2006	Jd	**B+**	12/97	BB–	Y	BE	NC	....	....	....	....	....	125	M5	'96	100½	83	91	10.71	10.71
Applied Extrusion Tech	***52***	***1.80***	***1.40***	***1.11***		***Sp***	***5.97***	***81.12***	***45.74***	***6-30-99***	***187.0***		***286.0***	***65.0***						
Sr Nts[4] 11½s 2002	Ao	**B**	5/95	B–	Y	R	105	3-31-00	....	....	....	....	150	M2	'94	104¼	101½	102½	11.22	11.22
Applied Materials	***23g***	***46.70***	***39.59***	***10.66***		***Oc***	***2259***	***4404***	***1402***	***8-1-99***	***612.0***		***4287***	***14.4***						
Sr Nts 8s 2004	mS	**A–**	12/99	BBB+	X	BE	NC	....	....	....	....	....	100	M6	'94	109½	102⅛	102⅛	7.83	7.83
Sr Nts 6¾s 2007	aO15	**A–**	12/99	BBB+	X	BE	[5]Z100	....	....	....	....	....	200	M6	'97	103⅝	94¾	94¾	7.12	7.12
Sr Nts 7⅛s 2017	aO15	**A–**	12/99	BBB+	X	BE	[5]Z100	....	....	....	....	....	200	M6	'97	101⅛	91¼	91⅜	7.80	7.80
Applied Power	***41e***	***n/a***	***n/a***	***n/a***		***Au***	***22.30***	***409.0***	***324.0***	***8-31-99***	***808.0***		***1240***	***68.2***						
Sr Sub Nts[4] 8¾s 2009	Ao	**B+**			Y	BE	104.35	3-31-04	....	....	[6]Z108.75	4-1-02	2000	G1	'99	102½	92½	97⅞	8.94	8.94
ARA Services	***27a***	***Gtd by ARAMARK Corp,see ARAMARK Services***																		
Gtd[7]Nts[8] 10⅝s 2000	fA	**BBB–**	7/94	BB	X	R	NC	....	100	....	....	....	100	G1	'91	106¾	101¼	101¼	10.49	10.49
[9]ARAMARK Services, Inc[10]	***27a***	***2.54***	***2.86***	***2.84***		***Sp***	***26.60***	***978.0***	***902.0***	***7-2-99***	***1598***		***1699***	***95.5***						
Gtd[11]Nts 6¾s 2004	fA	**BBB–**			X	BE	[5]Z100	....	....	....	....	....	300	M5	'98	102⅛	95½	95½	7.07	7.07
Gtd[11]Nts 8.15s 2005	Mn	**BBB–**			X	BE	NC	....	....	....	....	....	150	G1	'95	108⅞	100⅝	100⅝	8.10	8.10
Gtd[11]Nts 7s 2006	jJ15	**BBB–**			X	BE	[5]Z100	....	....	....	....	....	300	G1	'98	103⅛	94⅛	94⅜	7.42	7.42
Gtd[11]Nts 7.10s 2006	jD	**BBB–**			X	BE	NC	....	....	....	....	....	125	M5	'96	104	94⅜	94½	7.51	7.51
Arcadia Financial Ltd[12]	***25a***	***4.81***	***d0.48***	***d0.79***		***Dc***	***10.80***			***9-30-99***	***453.0***		***668.0***	***65.9***						
Sr Nts 11½s 2007	Ms15	**B–**	8/99	B	Y	BE	105.75	(3-15-02)	....	....	....	....	75.0	D6	'97	103½	62	103	11.17	11.16
Arch Communications Group[13]	***67g***	***d1.10***	***d1.03***	***d0.74***		***Dc***	***21.50***	***99.20***	***170.0***	***9-30-99***	***1358***		***1180***	***115.0***						
◆Sr Disc[14]Nts 10⅞s 2008	Ms15	**CCC+**	2/99	CCC	Y	R	104.078	(3-15-01)	....	....	....	....	[15]275	P4	'96	59⅞	30	43	....	Flat
Archer-Daniels-Midland	***26c***	***Δ3.39***	***Δ2.68***	***Δ2.13***		***Je***	***1110***	***6304***	***4481***	***9-30-99***	***3200***		***10981***	***43.2***						
Deb Zero Cpn 2002	[16]	**AA–**	10/89	A	X	R	100	....	....	....	....	....	[15]400	G1	'82	85¾	83⅛	85⅜	....	0.16
Deb 10¼s 2006	Jj15	**AA–**	10/89	A	X	R	NC	....	....	....	....	....	100	G1	'86	127½	113	113	9.07	9.07
Deb 8⅞s 2011	Ao15	**AA–**			X	BE	NC	....	....	....	....	....	300	S1	'91	129⅜	109⅜	109⅜	8.11	8.11
Deb 8⅛s 2012	Jd	**AA–**			X	BE	NC	....	....	....	....	....	300	S9	'92	123⅞	103⅛	103⅛	7.88	7.88
Deb 7⅛s 2013	Ms	**AA–**			X	BE	NC	....	....	....	....	....	250	S1	'93	114	95¼	95¼	7.48	7.48
Deb 8⅜s 2017	Ao15	**AA–**			X	BE	NC	....	....	....	....	....	300	S1	'92	125¾	105¾	105¾	7.92	7.92
Deb 7½s 2027	Ms	**AA–**			X	BE	NC	....	....	....	....	....	350	S1	'97	119⅜	95¾	95¾	7.83	7.83
Deb 6¾s 2027	jD15	**AA–**			X	BE	NC	....	....	....	....	....	200	S1	'97	109½	87⅜	87⅜	7.73	7.72
Deb 6⅝s 2029	Mn	**AA–**			X	BE	NC	....	....	....	....	....	300	M2	'99	99⅝	85¾	85¾	7.73	7.73
Deb 6.95s 2097	jD15	**AA–**			X	BE	[5]Z100	....	....	....	....	....	250	S1	'97	110⅛	87½	87½	7.94	7.94
Nts 6¼s 2003	Mn15	**AA–**			X	BE	NC	....	....	....	....	....	250	S9	'93	103⅝	97⅝	97⅝	6.40	6.40
Archstone Communities Tr	***57***	***n/a***	***n/a***	***2.01***		***Dc***				***9-30-99***	***2440***		***5125***	***47.6***						
Nts 7.20s 2003	Ao15	**BBB+**			X	BE	[2]Z100	....	....	....	....	....	120	M5	'98	101¾	97⅞	97⅞	7.36	7.36

Uniform Footnote Explanations-See Page 260. Other: [1] Due 6-22-05. [2] Plus Make-Whole Amt. [3] Plus Make-Whole Premium. [4] (HRO)On Chge of Ctrl at 101. [5] Red at greater of 100 or amt based on formula. [6] Max $70M red w/proceeds of Equity Off'g. [7] Gtd by ARA Group Inc. [8] (HRO)Under certain conditions. [9] Gtd by & data of ARAMARK Corp. [10] See ARA Services. [11] Gtd by ARAMARK Corp. [12] See Olympic Fin'l. [13] See USA Mobile Communications II. [14] Int accrues at 10.875% fr 3-15-01. [15] Incl disc. [16] Due May 1.

Title-Industry Code & Co. Finances (In Italics) / Exchange — Individual Issue Statistics	Ind / Interest Dates	Fixed Charge Coverage 1996 / S&P Rating	1997 / Date of Last Rating Change	1998 / Prior Rating	Eligible	Year End / Bond Form	Million $ Cash & Equiv. / Redemption Provisions: Regular Price	Curr. Assets / Regular (Begins) Thru	Curr. Liab. / Sinking Fund Price	Balance Sheet Date / Sinking Fund (Begins) Thru	L. Term Debt (Mil $) / Refund/Other Restriction Price	Refund/Other Restriction (Begins) Thru	Capital-ization (Mil $) / Outst'g (Mil $)	Total Debt % Capital / Underwriting Firm	Underwriting Year	Price Range 1999 High	Price Range 1999 Low	Mo. End Price Sale(s) or Bid	Curr. Yield	Yield to Mat.
***Archstone Communities Tr** (Cont.)*																				
M-T Nts 'B' 6.17s 2000	aO15	BBB+			X	BE	[1]Z100	....	....	....	....	....	25.0	G1	'98	99⅝	98¼	99	6.23	6.23
ARCO Chemical	***14***	***Acquired by Lyondell Petrochemical, see***																		
Deb 9.90s 2000	mN	BB	4/99	BBB+	Y	R	NC	....	....	....	....	....	200	M2	'90	102⅞	100½	101⅛	9.79	9.79
Deb 9⅜s 2005	jD15	BB	4/99	BBB+	Y	R	NC	....	....	....	....	....	100	S1	'90	106⅞	97⅛	101½	9.24	9.23
Deb 10¼s 2010	mN	BB	4/99	BBB+	Y	R	NC	....	....	....	....	....	100	M2	'90	113⅜	101⅛	105¾	9.69	9.69
Deb 9.80s 2020	Fa	BB	4/99	BBB+	Y	R	NC	....	....	....	....	....	224	M2	'90	102⅞	93⅛	100	9.80	9.80
Argosy Gaming	***40i***	***d0.05***	***0.51***	***1.59***		***Dc***	***37.70***	***72.97***	***106.2***	***9-30-99***	***346.0***		***452.0***	***86.5***						
• 1st 13¼s 2004	Jd	BB–	12/99	B+	Y	BE	106.625	(6-1-00)	....	....	....	....	235	B7	'96	114¾	105	106½	12.44	12.44
Aristar Inc[2]	***25a***	***1.82***	***1.59***	***1.66***		***Dc***	***41.50***			***6-30-99***	***1881***		***2526***	***82.4***						
Sr Nts[3] 6.30s 2000	jJ15	A–			X	BE	NC	....	....	....	....	....	100	G1	'95	101⅛	99¾	99⅞	6.31	6.31
Sr Nts[3] 6⅛s 2000	jD	A–			X	BE	NC	....	....	....	....	....	150	M2	'96	100¾	99¼	99¼	6.17	6.17
• Sr Nts[3] 7¾s 2001	Jd15	A–			X	BE	NC	....	....	....	....	....	150	M2	'94	No Sale		95	8.16	8.16
Sr Nts[3] 7¼s 2001	Jd15	A–			X	BE	NC	....	....	....	....	....	100	L3	'96	103½	100⅛	100⅛	7.24	7.24
Sr Nts[3] 6s 2001	fA	A–			X	BE	NC	....	....	....	....	....	200	C1	'98	100⅝	98⅛	98⅜	6.10	6.10
Sr Nts 6s 2002	Mn15	A–			X	BE	NC	....	....	....	....	....	150	N2	'99	99¾	97	97	6.19	6.19
Sr[3]Nts 6¾s 2001	fA15	A–			X	BE	NC	....	....	....	....	....	100	G1	'96	102½	100⅝	99½	6.78	6.78
Sr Nts[3] 6.30s 2002	aO	A–			X	BE	NC	....	....	....	....	....	150	L3	'97	101½	97⅝	97⅝	6.45	6.45
Sr Nts[3] 6½s 2003	mN15	A			X	BE	NC	....	....	....	....	....	150	G1	'97	102½	97	97	6.70	6.70
Sr Nts 5.85s 2004	Jj27	A–			X	BE	NC	....	....	....	....	....	200	M2	'99	99⅞	94⅛	94¼	6.21	6.21
Sr Nts 7⅜s 2004	mS	A–			X	BE	NC	....	....	....	....	....	300		'99	101⅜	99½	99½	7.41	7.41
Sr Nts 7¼s 2006	Jd15	A–			X	BE	NC	....	....	....	....	....	250	C6	'99	102⅛	98	98	7.40	7.40
Arizona Public Service[4]	***75***	***3.17***	***3.46***	***3.70***		***Dc***	***11.70***	***428.0***	***670.0***	***6-30-99***	***1955***		***3921***	***50.2***						
1st 5¾s 2000	mS15	A–	10/97	BBB+	X	R	NC	....	....	....	[5]Z100.80	9-14-00	100	S1	'93	100¾	99¼	99¼	5.79	5.79
1st 8⅛s 2002	Ms15	A–	10/97	BBB+	X	R	NC	....	....	....	[5]Z102.25	3-14-00	125	S1	'92	107¾	101¾	101¾	7.99	7.98
1st 6⅝s 2004	Ms	A–	10/97	BBB+	X	R	NC	....	....	....	[5]Z103.08	2-29-00	100	S1	'94	105⅛	97	97	6.83	6.83
1st 10¼s 2020	Mn15	A–	10/97	BBB+	X	R	104.63	(5-15-00)	Z100	....	[5]Z105.09	5-14-00	124	S1	'90	110	105½	105½	9.72	9.71
1st 9½s 2021	Ao15	A–	10/97	BBB+	X	R	103.78	(4-15-01)	Z100	....	[5]Z104.53	4-14-00	100	F1	'91	110⅜	101¼	101¼	9.38	9.38
1st 9s 2021	jD15	A–	10/97	BBB+	X	R	103.94	(12-15-01)	Z100	....	[5]Z104.73	12-14-00	150	S1	'91	110⅞	101¼	101½	8.87	8.87
1st 7¼s 2023	fA	A–	10/97	BBB+	X	R	102.72	(8-1-03)	....	....	[5]Z103.81	7-31-00	100	F1	'93	104¼	88	89⅜	8.11	8.11
1st 8¾s 2024	Jj15	A–	10/97	BBB+	X	R	104.31	(1-15-02)	....	....	[5]Z105.02	1-14-01	175	F1	'92	111¼	100	101½	8.62	8.62
1st 8s 2025	Fa	A–	10/97	BBB+	X	R	103.38	(2-1-03)	Z100	(2-1-03)	[5]Z104.73	1-31-00	88.5	S1	'93	109⅝	94⅞	95	8.42	8.42
Sr(Sec)Nts 6¾s 2006	mN15	A–	10/97	BBB+	X	BE	[6]Z100	....	....	....	....	....	100	C5	'96	106	94½	94½	7.14	7.14
Nts 6¼s 2005	Jj15	BBB			X	BE	[6]Z100	....	....	....	....	....	100	C6	'98	102½	94⅜	94⅜	6.62	6.62
Arkansas Power & Light[7]	***72a***	***Now Entergy Arkansas, see***																		
1st 6s 2003	aO	BBB+	10/97	BBB	X	BE	101.19	9-30-00	Z100	....	....	....	155	K2	'93	99⅝	95⅛	95⅛	6.31	6.31
1st 6.65s 2005	fA	BBB+	10/97	BBB	X	BE	102.04	7-31-00	Z100	....	....	....	115	K2	'93	102⅝	96	96	6.93	6.93
1st 7½s 2007	fA	BBB+	10/97	BBB	X	R	103.13	7-31-00	Z100	....	....	....	100	B7	'92	103¾	98⅞	98⅞	7.59	7.58
1st 7s 2023	aO	BBB+	10/97	BBB	X	BE	103.95	9-30-00	Z100	....	....	....	175	G1	'93	98½	84⅝	84⅝	8.27	8.27
1st 8¾s 2026	Ms	BBB+	10/97	BBB	X	BE	106.563	(3-1-01)	Z100	(3-1-01)	....	....	85.0	B7	'96	111½	101⅜	101½	8.62	8.62
Arkla Inc	***73e***	***Now NorAm Energy, see***																		
Deb 8.90s 2006	jD15	BBB	10/96	BBB–	X	R	NC	....	....	....	....	....	145	F1	'86	118⅞	106	106	8.40	8.39
Armco Inc.	***66a***	***Acquired by AK Steel Hldgs, see AK Steel***																		
Sr Nts[8] 9s 2007	mS15	BB	10/99	BB–	Y	BE	104.50	(9-15-02)	....	....	[9]Z109	9-15-00	150	Exch.	'97	105	99½	101⅛	8.90	8.90
Armstrong World Indus	***31a***	***12.85***	***12.64***	***6.05***		***Dc***	***63.10***	***429.0***	***848.0***	***9-30-99***	***1586***		***2587***	***66.3***						
• Deb 9¾s 2008	Ao15	A–	7/98	A	X	R	NC	....	....	....	....	....	125	S7	'88	108⅛	108⅛	108⅛	9.02	9.02

Uniform Footnote Explanations-See Page 260. Other: [1] Plus Make-Wole Amt. [2] Subsid of Great Western Fin'l. [3] Issued in min denom $100T. [4] Subsid of Pinnacle West Capital Corp. [5] In whole. [6] Plus Make-Whole Amt. [7] Subsid of Entergy Corp,now Entergy Arkansas. [8] (HRO)On Chge of Ctrl at 101. [9] Max $50M red w/proceeds of Pub Eq Off'g.

Exchange / Individual Issue Statistics	Interest Dates	S&P Rating	Date of Last Rating Change	Prior Rating	Eligible	Bond Form	Redemption Provisions: Regular Price	Regular (Begins) Thru	Sinking Fund Price	Sinking Fund (Begins) Thru	Refund/Other Restriction Price	Refund/Other Restriction (Begins) Thru	Outst'g (Mil $)	Underwriting Firm	Underwriting Year	Price Range 1999 High	Price Range 1999 Low	Mo. End Price Sale(s) or Bid	Curr. Yield	Yield to Mat.
Title-Industry Code & Co. Finances (In Italics)	*Ind*	*Fixed Charge Coverage 1996*	*1997*	*1998*		*Year End*	*Million $ Cash & Equiv.*	*Curr. Assets*	*Curr. Liab.*	*Balance Sheet Date*	*L. Term Debt (Mil $)*		*Capital-ization (Mil $)*	*Total Debt % Capital*						
***Armstrong World Indus** (Cont.)*																				
Sr Nts 6.35s 2003	fA15	A−			X	BE	NC	....	....	....	....	....	200	C1	'98	101⅝	96⅜	96⅜	6.59	6.59
Sr Nts 6½s 2005	fA15	A−			X	BE	NC	....	....	....	....	....	150	M6	'98	102¾	94½	94½	6.88	6.88
Sr Nts 7.45s 2029	Mn15	A−			X	BE	NC	....	....	....	....	....	200	M5	'99	100⅝	90¼	90⅜	8.24	8.24
Arrow Electronics, Inc	*23*	*10.55*	*6.47*	*4.35*		*Dc*	*49.26*	*3130*	*1340*	*9-30-99*	*1517*		*2455*	*43.1*						
Sr Deb 6⅞s 2018	Jd	BBB+	10/99	A−	X	BE	[1]Z100	....	....	....	....	....	200	M7	'98	98⅞	88¼	88¼	7.79	7.79
Deb 7½s 2027	Jj15	BBB+	10/99	A−	X	BE	NC	....	....	....	....	....	200	M6	'97	105⅛	91¼	91⅜	8.21	8.21
Sr Nts 7s 2007	Jj15	BBB+	10/99	A−	X	BE	NC	....	....	....	....	....	200	M6	'97	106	95⅞	95⅞	7.30	7.30
Arvin Industries	*8*	*2.50*	*3.48*	*3.99*		*Dc*	*45.60*	*859.1*	*734.7*	*10-3-99*	*506.0*		*1331*	*51.2*						
Nts 10s 2000	fA	BBB−			X	BE	NC	....	....	....	....	....	36.0	M2	'90	105¾	101⅜	101⅜	9.86	9.86
Nts 6⅞s 2001	Fa15	BBB−			X	BE	NC	....	....	....	....	....	75.0	M2	'94	101⅝	99⅛	99⅛	6.94	6.93
Nts 7⅛s 2009	Ms15	BBB−			X	BE	[1]Z100	....	....	....	....	....	150	L3	'99	101¾	91⅞	91⅞	7.76	7.75
***ASARCO Inc*[2]**	*45b*	*4.20*	*5.51*	*d0.33*		*Dc*	*152.7*	*981.0*	*642.7*	*9-30-99*	*1081*		*2591*	*43.7*						
Deb 7⅞s 2013	Ao15	B+	11/99	BBB−	Y	R	NC	....	....	....	....	....	100	F1	'93	105⅛	83⅜	83⅜	9.45	9.45
Deb 8½s 2025	Mn	B+	11/99	BBB−	Y	R	NC	....	....	....	....	....	150	C5	'95	103¼	83⅝	83⅝	10.16	10.16
Nts 7s 2001	jD	B+	11/99	BBB−	Y	R	NC	....	....	....	....	....	50.0	C5	'93	100¼	96¼	96¼	7.27	7.27
Nts 7⅜s 2003	Fa	B+	11/99	BBB−	Y	R	NC	....	....	....	....	....	100	F1	'93	101⅛	94⅞	94⅞	7.77	7.77
***Ashland Inc*[3]**	*49d*	*Δ2.88*	*Δ0.91*	*Δ1.95*		*Sp*	*110.0*	*2059*	*1396*	*9-30-99*	*1627*		*4046*	*45.6*						
Sr Nts 6⅝s 2008	Fa15	BBB			X	BE	NC	....	....	....	....	....	150	Exch.	'98	101⅞	91⅞	91⅞	7.21	7.21
M-T Nts 'H' 6.86s 2009	Mn	BBB			X	BE	NC	....	....	....	....	....	150	C6	'99	100	92⅜	92¾	7.40	7.40
Ashland Oil Inc	*49d*	***Now Ashland Inc,see***																		
Deb 8.80s 2012	mN15	BBB			X	BE	NC	....	....	....	....	....	250	S1	'92	122¾	104¾	104¾	8.40	8.40
M-T Nts 'F' 7.91s 2004	[4]jd15	BBB			X	BE	NC	....	....	....	....	....	15.0	C5	'94	108¼	100½	100¾	7.85	7.85
M-T Nts 'F' 7.98s 2004	[4]jd15	BBB			X	BE	NC	....	....	....	....	....	10.0	C4	'94	108½	100¾	101	7.90	7.90
M-T Nts 'F' 7.85s 2004	[5]jd15	BBB			X	BE	NC	....	....	....	....	....	25.0	C5	'94	108¼	100¼	100½	7.81	7.81
M-T Nts 'F' 7.82s 2005	[6]jd15	BBB			X	BE	NC	....	....	....	....	....	30.0	B7	'95	108⅜	99⅞	100¼	7.80	7.80
M-T Nts 'F' 7.90s 2006	[7]jd15	BBB			X	BE	NC	....	....	....	....	....	10.0	C5	'94	110⅛	99¼	99⅝	7.93	7.93
M-T Nts 'F' 7.79s 2006	[8]jd15	BBB			X	BE	NC	....	....	....	....	....	15.0	C5	'94	109½	98¾	99	7.87	7.87
Associated Dry Goods	*59f*	***Subsid of May Dept Stores,see***																		
Deb 8.85s 2006	Ms	A+	7/99	A	X	R	NC	....		....	....	....	100	S5	'86	118⅝	106⅜	106⅜	8.32	8.32
Associated Estates Realty	*57*	*2.23*	*2.02*	*1.61*		*Dc*				*9-30-99*	*552.0*		*775.0*	*65.0*						
Sr Nts 8⅜s 2000	Ao15	B	11/99	BB−	Y	BE	NC	....	....	....	....	....	75.0	D3	'95	102	99	99¼	8.44	8.44
Sr Nts 7.10s 2002	mN15	B	11/99	BB−	Y	BE	NC	....	....	....	....	....	10.0	D3	'95	100½	91½	94¾	7.49	7.49
***Associates Corp of N.A.*[9]**	*25g*	*1.59*	*1.53*	*1.53*		*Dc*	*2827*			*6-30-99*	*35304*		*57286*	*84.1*						
• Sr Deb 6s 2001	Jd15	AA−	6/85	A+	X	R	100	....	....	....	....	....	[10]150	K2	'81	103	96¼	98¼	6.11	6.11
Sr Deb 8.55s 2009	jJ15	AA−			X	R	NC	....	....	....	....	....	200	M6	'89	120½	106⅛	106⅛	8.06	8.05
Sr Deb[11] 6.95s 2018	mN	AA−			X	BE	NC	....	....	....	....	....	1000	B7	'98	107¾	92½	92⅝	7.50	7.50
Sr Nts 6s 2000	Ms15	AA−			X	R	NC	....	....	....	....	....	300	S1	'93	100¾	99⅞	100	6.00	6.00
Sr Nts 5¼s 2000	Ms30	AA−			X	R	NC	....	....	....	....	....	300	S1	'93	100	99½	99¾	5.26	5.26
Sr Nts 9⅛s 2000	Ao	AA−			X	R	NC	....	....	....	....	....	250	S1	'90	104⅜	100⅝	100⅝	9.07	9.07
Sr Nts 6⅜s 2000	Jd15	AA−			X	BE	NC	....	....	....	....	....	500	U1	'97	101⅜	100	100	6.38	6.37
Sr Nts 6s 2000	Jd15	AA−			X	R	NC	....	....	....	....	....	300	M2	'93	100⅞	99¾	99⅞	6.01	6.01
Sr Nts 6⅜s 2000	Fa15	AA−			X	BE	NC	....	....	....	....	....	300	C1	'97	101⅝	99⅞	100	6.38	6.37
Sr Nts 6¼s 2000	mS15	AA−			X	R	NC	....	....	....	....	....	300		'95	101⅜	99⅞	99⅞	6.26	6.26
Sr Nts 6⅝s 2001	Mn15	AA−			X	R	NC	....	....	....	....	....	300	S1	'96	102¾	99⅝	99⅝	6.65	6.65
Sr Nts 5⅞s 2001	Mn16	AA−			X	BE	NC	....	....	....	....	....	300	M2	'98	101⅛	98¾	98¾	5.95	5.95

Uniform Footnote Explanations-See Page 260. Other: [1] Red at greater of 100 or amt based on formula. [2] Acquired by Grupo Mexico. [3] Was Ashland Oil,see. [4] Due 7-21-04. [5] Due 11-30-04. [6] Due 3-21-05. [7] Due 8-5-06. [8] Due 8-9-06. [9] Subsid of Ford Motor Co. [10] Incl disc. [11] Co may red in whole,at 100,for tax law chge.

Title-Industry Code & Co. Finances (In Italics)	Ind	Fixed Charge Coverage 1996	1997	1998	Year End	Million $ Cash & Equiv.	Curr. Assets	Curr. Liab.	Balance Sheet Date	L. Term Debt (Mil $)	Capital-ization (Mil $)	Total Debt % Capital

Exchange ↓ Individual Issue Statistics	Interest Dates	S&P Rating	Date of Last Rating Change	Prior Rating	Eligible ↓	Bond Form	Redemption Provisions: Regular Price	Regular (Begins) Thru	Sinking Fund Price	Sinking Fund (Begins) Thru	Refund/Other Restriction Price	Refund/Other Restriction (Begins) Thru	Outst'g (Mil $)	Underwriting Firm	Underwriting Year	Price Range 1999 High	Price Range 1999 Low	Mo. End Price Sale(s) or Bid	Curr. Yield	Yield to Mat.
***Associates Corp of N.A.** (Cont.)*																				
Sr Nts 5.60s 2001	Jj15	AA–			X	R	NC	....	....	....	....	....	300	S1	'96	100½	98⅞	98⅞	5.66	5.66
Sr Nts 5.85s 2001	Jj15	AA–			X	BE	NC	....	....	....	....	....	500	G1	'98	100⅞	99	99	5.91	5.91
Sr Nts 6¾s 2001	jJ15	AA–			X	R	NC	....	....	....	....	....	350	M6	'96	103¼	99¾	99¾	6.77	6.77
Sr Nts 6¾s 2001	fA	AA–			X	R	NC	....	....	....	....	....	200	C5	'96	103⅜	99¾	99¾	6.77	6.77
Sr Nts 7⅞s 2001	mS30	AA–			X	R	NC	....	....	....	....	....	300	U1	'94	106¼	101½	101½	7.76	7.76
Sr Nts 6.45s 2001	aO15	AA–			X	BE	NC	....	....	....	....	....	325	M6	'97	102¾	99⅛	99⅛	6.51	6.51
Sr Nts 6.70s 2001	Mn29	AA–			X	BE	NC	....	....	....	....	....	300	M5	'97	102⅞	99¾	99¾	6.72	6.72
Sr Nts 5½s 2002	Fa15	AA–			X	BE	NC	....	....	....	....	....	500	B7	'99	100¼	97	97⅛	5.66	5.66
Sr Nts 7½s 2002	Ao15	AA–			X	R	NC	....	....	....	....	....	300	M5	'95	106	100⅞	100⅞	7.43	7.43
Sr Nts 6½s 2002	jJ15	AA–			X	BE	NC	....	....	....	....	....	500	C1	'97	103½	98⅞	98⅞	6.57	6.57
Sr Nts 6⅜s 2002	jJ15	AA–			X	R	NC	....	....	....	....	....	300	C5	'95	102⅞	98⅝	98⅝	6.46	6.46
Sr Nts 5⅞s 2002	jJ15	AA–			X	BE	NC	....	....	....	....	....	300	C6	'98	101⅝	97¼	97⅜	6.03	6.03
Sr Nts 6½s 2002	fA15	AA–			X	BE	NC	....	....	....	....	....	200	C1	'97	103½	98¾	98¾	6.58	6.58
Sr Nts 6⅜s 2002	aO15	AA–			X	R	NC	....	....	....	....	....	300	M6	'95	102⅞	98⅜	98⅜	6.48	6.48
Sr Nts 6½s 2002	aO15	AA–			X	BE	NC	....	....	....	....	....	275	M6	'97	103⅝	98¾	98¾	6.58	6.58
Sr Nts 6s 2002	jD	AA–			X	R	NC	....	....	....	....	....	300	S1	'95	101¾	97¼	97¼	6.17	6.17
Sr Nts 6⅞s 2003	Fa	AA–			X	R	NC	....	....	....	....	....	150	K2	'93	105⅛	99⅛	99⅛	6.94	6.93
Sr Nts 6s 2003	Ao15	AA–			X	BE	NC	....	....	....	....	....	500	C1	'08	102⅛	06½	06⅝	6.21	6.21
Sr Nts 6⅞s 2003	fA	AA–			X	R	NC	....	....	....	....	....	200	C5	'96	105⅝	99	99	6.94	6.94
Sr Nts 5¾s 2003	aO15	AA–			X	R	NC	....	....	....	....	....	300	L3	'93	101⅜	95¼	95¼	6.04	6.04
Sr Nts[1] 5¾s 2003	mN	AA–			X	BE	NC	....	....	....	....	....	2300	B7	'98	101½	95⅛	95¼	6.04	6.04
Sr Nts 5½s 2004	Fa15	AA–			X	BE	NC	....	....	....	....	....	500	B7	'99	99⅝	93⅞	93⅞	5.86	5.86
Sr Nts 6.10s 2005	Jj15	AA–			X	BE	NC	....	....	....	....	....	300	G1	'98	102¾	95	95	6.42	6.42
Sr Nts[2] 7⅜s 2005	Fa15	AA–			X	R	NC	....	....	....	....	....	300	L3	'95	109¼	100⅞	100⅞	7.68	7.68
Sr Nts 6.20s 2005	Mn16	AA–			X	BE	NC	....	....	....	....	....	200	M2	'98	103¼	95⅛	95⅛	6.52	6.52
Sr Nts 6⅝s 2005	Jd15	AA–			X	BE	NC	....	....	....	....	....	300		'95	105	96¾	97⅛	6.82	6.82
Sr Nts 6s 2005	jJ15	AA–			X	BE	NC	....	....	....	....	....	500	C6	'98	102¼	93⅝	93⅝	6.41	6.41
Sr Nts 6⅜s 2005	mN15	AA–			X	R	NC	....	....	....	....	....	200	C5	'95	103⅝	95½	95¾	6.66	6.66
Sr Nts[1] 6¼s 2008	mN	AA–			X	BE	NC	....	....	....	....	....	1500	B7	'98	104¼	92⅛	92⅛	6.78	6.78
M-T Sr Nts 'G'[3] 7.52s 2000	[4]ao	AA–			X	BE	NC	....	....	....	....	....	20.0	M6	'95	102½	100¼	100¼	7.50	7.50
M-T Sr Nts 'G'[3] 7.80s 2000	[5]ao	AA–			X	BE	NC	....	....	....	....	....	20.0	S7	'95	102⅞	100⅜	100⅜	7.77	7.77
M-T Sr Nts 'G'[3] 7.70s 2000	[6]ao	AA–			X	BE	NC	....	....	....	....	....	17.0	L3	'95	102¾	100⅜	100⅜	7.67	7.67
M-T Sr Nts 'G'[3] 7.46s 2000	[7]ao	AA–			X	BE	NC	....	....	....	....	....	25.0	B7	'95	102½	100⅜	100⅜	7.43	7.43
M-T Sr Nts 'G'[3] 7.45s 2000	[8]mn	AA–			X	BE	NC	....	....	....	....	....	32.0	B7	'95	102½	100⅜	100⅜	7.42	7.42
M-T Sr Nts 'G'[3] 7.40s 2000	[9]mn	AA–			X	BE	NC	....	....	....	....	....	20.0	S7	'95	102½	100⅜	100⅜	7.37	7.37
M-T Sr Nts 'G'[3] 7.62s 2002	[10]mn	AA–			X	BE	NC	....	....	....	....	....	25.0	M6	'95	106⅜	101⅜	101⅜	7.52	7.52
M-T Sr Nts 'G'[3] 6.32s 2004	[11]mn	AA–			X	BE	NC	....	....	....	....	....	5.30	M2	'94	103¼	97	97⅛	6.51	6.51
M-T Sr Nts 'G'[3] 6.44s 2004	[12]mn	AA–			X	BE	NC	....	....	....	....	....	26.0	K2	'94	103¾	97⅜	97⅝	6.60	6.60
M-T Sr Nts 'G'[3] 6.20s 2004	[13]mn	AA–			X	BE	NC	....	....	....	....	....	20.0	M6	'94	102¾	96½	96¾	6.41	6.41
M-T Sr Nts 'G'[3] 6.39s 2004	[14]mn	AA–			X	BE	NC	....	....	....	....	....	5.00	F4	'94	103⅝	97⅛	97⅜	6.56	6.56
M-T Sr Nts 'G'[3] 6.41s 2004	[14]mn	AA–			X	BE	NC	....	....	....	....	....	5.00	D4	'94	103¾	97¼	97⅜	6.58	6.58
M-T Sr Nts 'G'[3] 7.08s 2004	[15]mn	AA–			X	BE	NC	....	....	....	....	....	7.00	P1	'94	106¾	99⅝	99¾	7.10	7.10
M-T Sr Nts 'G'[3] 7.64s 2004	[16]mn	AA–			X	BE	NC	....	....	....	....	....	10.0	C5	'94	109½	101¾	101¾	7.51	7.51
M-T Sr Nts 'G'[3] 7.55s 2004	[17]mn	AA–			X	BE	NC	....	....	....	....	....	30.0	M6	'94	109	101⅜	101½	7.44	7.44
M-T Sr Nts 'G'[3] 7⅝s 2004	[18]mn	AA–			X	BE	NC	....	....	....	....	....	10.0	M6	'94	109⅜	101⅝	101¾	7.49	7.49

Uniform Footnote Explanations-See Page 260. Other: [1] Co may red in whole,at 100,for tax law chge. [2] (HRO)On 2-15-00 at 100. [3] Issued in min denom $100T. [4] Due 3-1-00. [5] Due 3-13-00. [6] Due 3-15-00. [7] Due 3-28-00. [8] Due 3-30-00. [9] Due 3-31-00. [10] Due 3-27-02. [11] Due 1-13-04. [12] Due 1-15-04. [13] Due 1-26-04. [14] Due 2-17-04. [15] Due 4-1-04. [16] Due 5-26-04. [17] Due 6-01-04. [18] Due 6-1-04.

Title-Industry Code & Co. Finances (In Italics)	I n d	Fixed Charge Coverage 1996	1997	1998	Year End	Million $ Cash & Equiv.	Curr. Assets	Curr. Liab.	Balance Sheet Date	L. Term Debt (Mil $)	Capital-ization (Mil $)	Total Debt % Capital

Exchange ↓ Individual Issue Statistics	Interest Dates	S&P Rating	Date of Last Rating Change	Prior Rating	Eligible ↓	Bond Form	Redemption Provisions: Regular Price	Regular (Begins) Thru	Sinking Fund Price	Sinking Fund (Begins) Thru	Refund/Other Restriction Price	Refund/Other Restriction (Begins) Thru	Outst'g (Mil $)	Underwriting Firm	Underwriting Year	Price Range 1999 High	Price Range 1999 Low	Mo. End Price Sale(s) or Bid	Curr. Yield	Yield to Mat.
***Associates Corp of N.A.** (Cont.)*																				
M-T Sr Nts 'G'[1] 7.88s 2004	[2]mn	AA–			X	BE	NC	....	....	....	....	....	10.0	U1	'94	110⅝	102⅝	102¾	7.67	7.67
M-T Sr Nts 'G'[1] 7.70s 2004	[3]mn	AA–			X	BE	NC	....	....	....	....	....	10.0	B7	'94	109¾	102	102	7.55	7.55
M-T Sr Nts 'G'[1] 7.81s 2004	[4]mn	AA–			X	BE	NC	....	....	....	....	....	5.00	W3	'94	110⅜	102⅜	102½	7.62	7.62
M-T Sr Nts 'G'[1] 7.92s 2004	[5]mn	AA–			X	BE	NC	....	....	....	....	....	10.0	B7	'94	110⅞	102⅞	102⅞	7.70	7.70
M-T Sr Nts 'G'[1] 7.95s 2004	[5]mn	AA–			X	BE	NC	....	....	....	....	....	10.0	D6	'94	111⅛	103	103	7.72	7.72
M-T Sr Nts 'G'[1] 8.02s 2004	[6]mn	AA–			X	BE	NC	....	....	....	....	....	15.0	D6	'94	111⅜	103¼	103¼	7.77	7.77
M-T Sr Nts 'G'[1] 7.97s 2004	[7]mn	AA–			X	BE	NC	....	....	....	....	....	5.00	P1	'94	111¼	103	103⅛	7.73	7.73
M-T Sr Nts 'G'[1] 7.97s 2005	[8]ao	AA–			X	BE	NC	....	....	....	....	....	17.0	L3	'95	112	102⅞	103⅜	7.71	7.71
M-T Sr Nts 'G'[1] 7.70s 2005	[9]mn	AA–			X	BE	NC	....	....	....	....	....	31.5	S1	'95	110¾	101⅝	102¼	7.53	7.53
M-T Sr Nts 'H'[1] 6.84s 2000	[10]mn	AA–			X	BE	NC	....	....	....	....	....	21.0	M2	'95	101⅞	100¼	100¼	6.82	6.82
M-T Sr Nts 'H'[1] 6.84s 2000	[11]mn	AA–			X	BE	NC	....	....	....	....	....	25.0		'95	102	100¼	100¼	6.82	6.82
M-T Sr Nts 'H'[1] 6¼s 2000	[12]mn	AA–			X	BE	NC	....	....	....	....	....	20.0		'95	101¼	100	100⅛	6.24	6.24
M-T Sr Nts 'H'[1] 6.33s 2000	[13]mn	AA–			X	BE	NC	....	....	....	....	....	50.0		'95	101⅜	100	100⅛	6.32	6.32
M-T Sr Nts 'H'[1] 6.45s 2000	[14]mn	AA–			X	BE	NC	....	....	....	....	....	30.0	M6	'95	101½	100⅛	100⅛	6.44	6.44
M-T Sr Nts 'H'[1] 6.69s 2000	[14]mn	AA–			X	BE	NC	....	....	....	....	....	15.0	B7	'95	101⅞	100¼	100¼	6.67	6.67
M-T Sr Nts 'H'[1] 6.68s 2000	[15]mn	AA–			X	BE	NC	....	....	....	....	....	25.0	B7	'95	102	100⅛	100¼	6.66	6.66
M-T Sr Nts 'H'[1] 6.66s 2000	[16]mn	AA–			X	BE	NC	....	....	....	....	....	15.0	P4	'95	102	100⅛	100⅛	6.65	6.65
M-T Sr Nts 'H'[1] 6.78s 2001	[17]mn	AA–			X	BE	NC	....	....	....	....	....	25.0	L3	'95	103⅜	99⅞	99⅞	6.79	6.79
M-T Sr Nts 'H'[1] 6.81s 2001	[18]mn	AA–			X	BE	NC	....	....	....	....	....	15.0	M2	'95	103½	99⅞	99⅞	6.82	6.82
M-T Sr Nts 'H'[1] 6.93s 2002	[19]mn	AA–			X	BE	NC	....	....	....	....	....	25.0	L3	'95	104⅝	99⅞	99⅞	6.94	6.94
M-T Sr Nts 'H'[1] 6.90s 2002	[20]mn	AA–			X	BE	NC	....	....	....	....	....	22.0	C5	'95	104⅝	99¾	99¾	6.92	6.92
M-T Sr Nts 'H'[1] 6.71s 2002	[21]mn	AA–			X	BE	NC	....	....	....	....	....	21.0	L3	'95	104⅛	99¼	99¼	6.76	6.76
M-T Sr Nts 'H'[1] 6.59s 2002	[22]mn	AA–			X	BE	NC	....	....	....	....	....	20.0	C5	'95	103⅝	98⅞	99	6.66	6.66
M-T Sr Nts 'H'[1] 6.52s 2002	[23]mn	AA–			X	BE	NC	....	....	....	....	....	25.0	U1	'95	103½	98⅝	98¾	6.60	6.60
M-T Sr Nts 'H'[1] 6½s 2002	[24]mn	AA–			X	BE	NC	....	....	....	....	....	20.0	M2	'95	103⅜	98⅝	98¾	6.58	6.58
M-T Sr Nts 'H'[1] 6.01s 2003	[25]mn	AA–			X	BE	NC	....	....	....	....	....	20.0	M2	'96	101¾	97	97¼	6.18	6.18
M-T Sr Nts'H'[1] 6.73s 2003	[26]mn	AA–			X	BE	NC	....	....	....	....	....	25.0	F4	'96	104½	99	99⅛	6.79	6.79
M-T Sr Nts 'H'[1] 6.77s 2003	[27]mn	AA–			X	BE	NC	....	....	....	....	....	17.0	L3	'96	104⅝	99	99⅛	6.83	6.83
M-T Sr Nts 'H'[1] 7s 2003	[28]mn	AA–			X	BE	NC	....	....	....	....	....	16.0	M6	'96	105½	99¾	99¾	7.02	7.02
M-T Sr Nts 'H'[1] 7⅝s 2005	[29]mn	AA–			X	BE	NC	....	....	....	....	....	60.0	D6	'95	110⅜	101¼	101⅞	7.48	7.48
M-T Sr Nts[1]'I' 6.20s 2000	[30]mn	AA–			X	BE	NC	....	....	....	....	....	200	M2	'97	101	100	100	6.20	6.20
Sub Deb 6⅞s 2008	mN15	A+			X	R	NC	....	....	....	....	....	300	S1	'96	108⅛	96	96	7.16	7.16
• Sub Deb 8.15s 2009	fA	A+			X	R	NC	....	....	....	....	....	125	M6	'89	108½	101	100⅝	8.10	8.10
AT&T Capital	***25***	***Gtd by CIT Group Inc,see***																		
Nts[31] 6⅞s 2001	Jj16	A+	11/99	BBB	X	BE	NC	....	....	....	....	....	750	C6	'99	102	99⅝	99⅞	6.88	6.88
Nts[31] 6¾s 2002	Fa4	A+	11/99	BBB	X	BE	NC	....	....	....	....	....	350	C6	'99	102⅝	98½	99	6.82	6.82
M-T Nts '4' 6.57s 2000	[32]fa15	A+	11/99	BBB	X	BE	NC	....	....	....	....	....	50.0	G1	'97	100⅞	99¾	100	6.57	6.57
Nts 6.59s 2000	[33]fa15	A+	11/99	BBB	X	BE	NC	....	....	....	....	....	80.0	M6	'97	101¼	99⅝	100	6.59	6.59
M-T Nts '4' 6.83s 2001	[34]fa15	A+	11/99	BBB	X	BE	NC	....	....	....	....	....	33.0	G1	'97	102	99½	99⅞	6.84	6.84
M-T Nts '4' 6.80s 2001	[35]fa15	A+	11/99	BBB	X	BE	NC	....	....	....	....	....	103	L3	'97	102	99½	99¾	6.82	6.82
M-T Nts '4' 6.70s 2001	Fa15	A+	11/99	BBB	X	BE	NC	....	....	....	....	....	50.0	M2	'97	101¾	99¼	99⅝	6.73	6.72
M-T Nts '4' 6.90s 2002	[36]fa15	A+	11/99	BBB	X	BE	NC	....	....	....	....	....	90.0	M6	'97	102¾	98½	99¼	6.95	6.95
M-T Nts[31] 'F' 7½s 2000	mN15	A+	11/99	BBB	X	BE	NC	....	....	....	....	....	1000	L3	'98	102¾	100½	100½	7.46	7.46
M-T Nts 'F' 6¼s 2001	Mn15	A+	11/99	BBB	X	BE	NC	....	....	....	....	....	750	M5	'98	101⅛	98¼	99	6.31	6.31
M-T Nts 'F' 6.60s 2005	Mn15	A+	11/99	BBB	X	BE	NC	....	....	....	....	....	300	M5	'98	101	92⅞	96⅛	6.87	6.87

Uniform Footnote Explanations-See Page 260. Other: [1] Issued in min denom $100T. [2] Due 6-2-04. [3] Due 6-10-04. [4] Due 7-1-04. [5] Due 7-13-04. [6] Due 7-19-04. [7] Due 7-20-04. [8] Due 3-1-05. [9] Due 4-1-05. [10] Due 4-6-00. [11] Due 5-22-00. [12] Due 6-1-00. [13] Due 6-9-00. [14] Due 6-15-00. [15] Due 7-25-00. [16] Due 8-15-00. [17] Due 7-31-01. [18] Due 8-3-01. [19] Due 7-25-02. [20] Due 7-29-02. [21] Due 9-27-02. [22] Due 10-7-02. [23] Due 10-11-02. [24] Due 10-15-02. [25] Due 2-7-03. [26] Due 3-27-03. [27] Due 4-10-03. [28] Due 4-23-03. [29] Due 4-27-05. [30] Due 2-15-00. [31] Gtd by Newcourt Credit Group. [32] Due 1-21-00. [33] Due 8-4-00. [34] Due 1-30-01. [35] Due 2-1-01. [36] Due 1-30-02.

Exchange / Individual Issue Statistics	Interest Dates	S&P Rating	Date of Last Rating Change	Prior Rating	Eligible	Bond Form	Regular Price	Regular (Begins) Thru	Sinking Fund Price	Sinking Fund (Begins) Thru	Refund/Other Restriction Price	Refund/Other Restriction (Begins) Thru	Outst'g (Mil $)	Underwriting Firm	Underwriting Year	Price Range 1999 High	Price Range 1999 Low	Mo. End Price Sale(s) or Bid	Curr. Yield	Yield to Mat.
Title-Industry Code & Co. Finances (In Italics)	*Ind*	*Fixed Charge Coverage 1996*	*1997*	*1998*		*Year End*	*Million $ Cash & Equiv.*	*Curr. Assets*	*Curr. Liab.*	*Balance Sheet Date*	*L. Term Debt (Mil $)*		*Capital-ization (Mil $)*	*Total Debt % Capital*						
***AT&T Capital** (Cont.)*																				
M-T Nts[1]'G' 7.11s 2001	mS13	A+	11/99	BBB	X	BE	NC	....	....	....	....	....	328	S4	'99	100¾	99⅞	99⅞	7.12	7.12
AT&T[2]Corp[3]	***67b***	***17.49***	***16.32***	***16.69***		***Dc***		***13040***	***23515***	***9-30-99***	***28419***		***111486***	***31.9***						
• Deb 5⅛s 2001	Ao	AA–	10/96	AA	X	R	100	....	....	....	....	....	250	F1	'66	100⅛	97⅜	s97⅝	5.25	5.25
• Deb 8⅛s 2022	Jj15	AA–	10/96	AA	X	BE	103.21	(1-15-02)	....	....	....	....	500	L3	'92	109	99¾	s101	8.04	8.04
• Deb 8⅛s 2024	jJ15	AA–	10/96	AA	X	BE	103.971	(7-15-02)	....	....	....	....	500	M6	'92	109¾	100	s101	8.04	8.04
• Deb 8.35s 2025	Jj15	AA–	10/96	AA	X	BE	103.288	(1-15-05)	....	....	....	....	300	S1	'95	115½	101⅞	103	8.11	8.11
• Nts 6s 2009	Ms15	AA–			X	BE	[4]Z100	....	....	....	....	....	3000	M2	'99	101¼	90⅛	s90⅛	6.66	6.66
• Deb 8⅝s 2031	jD	AA–	10/96	AA	X	BE	105.56	(12-1-01)	....	....	....	....	676	M6	'91	114⅜	103	103¼	8.35	8.35
• Nts 7⅛s 2002	Jj15	AA–	10/96	AA	X	BE	NC	....	....	....	....	....	500	L3	'92	106⅛	100¼	s100⅝	7.08	7.08
• Nts 6½s 2002	mS15	AA–			X	BE	NC	....	....	....	....	....	450		'99	100½	99	s99⅛	6.56	6.56
• Nts 5⅝s 2004	Ms15	AA–			X	BE	[4]Z100	....	....	....	....	....	2000	M2	'99	100½	94⅜	94½	5.95	5.95
• Nts 6¾s 2004	Ao	AA–	10/96	AA	X	BE	NC	....	....	....	....	....	400	S1	'94	106¾	98⅝	99⅛	6.81	6.81
• Nts 7s 2005	Mn15	AA–	10/96	AA	X	BE	NC	....	....	....	....	....	300	M5	'95	109	100	s100¼	6.98	6.98
• Nts 7½s 2006	Jd	AA–	10/96	AA	X	BE	NC	....	....	....	....	....	500	M6	'94	113⅛	101¼	s101⅞	7.36	7.36
• Nts 7¾s 2007	Ms	AA–	10/96	AA	X	BE	NC	....	....	....	....	....	500	L3	'95	115⅜	102¼	102½	7.56	7.56
• Nts 6½s 2029	Ms15	AA–			X	BE	[4]Z100	....	....	....	....	....	3000	M2	'99	100¾	85⅝	85¾	7.58	7.58
• M-T Nts 'A' 8.20s 2005	Fa15	AA–	10/96	AA	X	BE	*100	(2-15-00)	....	....	....	....	100	C1	'95	104¾	100¼	s100⅜	8.17	8.17
M-T Nts 'A' 8s 2025	Mn15	AA–	10/96	AA	X	BE	104.062	(5-15-05)	....	....	....	....	50.0	M6	'95	112¼	99⅛	99⅛	8.07	8.07
M-T Nts 'A' 7¾s 2025	Mn15	AA–	10/96	AA	X	BE	103.713	(5-15-05)	....	....	....	....	25.0	B7	'95	110⅛	96⅞	96⅞	8.00	8.00
[5]Atlanta Gas Light	***73b***	***3.79***	***3.48***	***2.95***		***Sp***	***14.00***	***224.0***	***230.0***	***6-30-99***	***610.0***		***1383***	***47.9***						
M-T Nts 'C' 5.90s 2003	[6]mn	A–			X	BE	NC	....	....	....	....	....	30.0	M2	'93	101¼	95	95	6.21	6.21
M-T Nts 'C' 6.55s 2005	[7]mn	A–			X	BE	100	(12-7-03)	....	....	....	....	42.0	F1	'93	103⅝	94⅝	94⅝	6.92	6.92
M-T Nts 'C' 6s 2006	[8]mn	A–			X	BE	100	(10-23-03)	....	....	....	....	10.0	M2	'93	100⅝	90¾	90¾	6.61	6.61
M-T Nts 'C' 7.05s 2013	[9]mn	A–			X	BE	102.35	(12-1-03)	....	....	....	....	24.5	M2	'93	106⅞	93¼	93¼	7.56	7.56
M-T Nts 'C' 7.20s 2013	[10]mn	A–			X	BE	102.35	(12-7-03)	....	....	....	....	5.25	S1	'93	107½	94⅛	94⅛	7.65	7.65
M-T Nts 'C' 7.20s 2013	[11]mn	A–			X	BE	102.35	(12-15-03)	....	....	....	....	20.0	F1	'93	107½	94⅛	94⅛	7.65	7.65
M-T Nts 'C' 7s 2014	[12]mn	A–			X	BE	102.33	(1-20-04)	....	....	....	....	5.00	M2	'94	106⅝	92½	92½	7.57	7.57
M-T Nts 'C' 7s 2015	[13]mn	A–			X	BE	100	(1-27-07)	....	....	....	....	11.2	M2	'94	105⅛	91⅞	91⅞	7.62	7.62
M-T Nts 'C' 7s 2019	[14]mn	A–			X	BE	103.50	(1-18-19)	....	....	....	....	5.00	M2	'94	103¾	89⅞	89⅞	7.79	7.79
M-T Nts 'C' 7.10s 2019	[14]mn	A–			X	BE	103.55	(1-20-04)	....	....	....	....	38.5	F1	'94	104⅝	90¾	90⅞	7.81	7.81
M-T Nts 'C' 6.85s 2023	[15]mn	A–			X	BE	103.425	(10-26-03)	....	....	....	....	2.00	M2	'93	101⅜	85⅝	85¾	7.99	7.99
M-T Nts 'C' 7.30s 2027	[16]mn	A–			X	BE	NC	....	....	....	....	....	53.5	M2	'97	109⅜	89⅝	89⅝	8.15	8.14
Atlantic City Electric[17]	***72a***	***2.65***	***3.17***	***1.83***		***Dc***	***114.0***	***350.0***	***384.0***	***9-30-99***	***836.0***		***1703***	***54.9***						
1st 7s 2023	mS	A–	10/93	A	X	R	102.88	(9-1-03)	Z100	(9-1-03)	....	....	75.0	K2	'93	103⅛	86½	86⅝	8.08	8.08
1st 6⅝s 2013	fA	A–	10/93	A	X	R	NC	....	....	....	....	....	75.0	G1	'93	105	89⅞	89⅞	7.37	7.37
1st 7s 2028	fA	A–	10/93	A	X	R	104.08	7-31-00	Z100	....	®102.91	7-31-03	75.0	B7	'93	104½	84⅝	84¾	8.26	8.26
Sec M-T Nts 'A' 7.98s 2004	[18]mn	A–	10/93	A	X	BE	100	(5-19-02)	....	....	....	....	19.5	F1	'92	111⅛	102¾	102¾	7.77	7.77
Sec M-T Nts 'A' 7.97s 2004	[19]mn	A–	10/93	A	X	BE	100	(5-19-02)	....	....	....	....	10.5	F1	'92	107⅝	101½	101½	7.85	7.85
Sec M-T Nts 'B' 6.82s 2000	[20]jj	A–	10/93	A	X	BE	NC	....	....	....	....	....	13.0	F1	'93	101⅜	100	100	6.82	6.82
Sec M-T Nts 'B' 6.81s 2000	[20]jj	A–	10/93	A	X	BE	NC	....	....	....	....	....	5.00	F1	'93	101⅜	100	100	6.81	6.81
Sec M-T Nts 'B' 6.81s 2000	[21]jj	A–	10/93	A	X	BE	NC	....	....	....	....	....	5.00	F1	'93	101⅜	100⅛	100⅛	6.80	6.80
Sec M-T Nts 'B' 7.16s 2003	[22]jj	A–	10/93	A	X	BE	NC	....	....	....	....	....	10.0	F1	'93	105⅞	100⅛	100⅛	7.15	7.15
Sec M-T Nts 'B' 7.19s 2003	[22]jj	A–	10/93	A	X	BE	NC	....	....	....	....	....	8.00	F1	'93	106	100⅛	100⅛	7.18	7.18
Sec M-T Nts 'B' 7⅛s 2004	[23]jj	A–	10/93	A	X	BE	100	(2-2-03)	....	....	....	....	28.0	F1	'93	106	99⅝	99⅝	7.15	7.15
Sec M-T Nts 'B' 6.67s 2005	[24]jj	A–	10/93	A	X	BE	NC	....	....	....	....	....	10.0	F1	'93	105⅝	97¼	97¼	6.86	6.86

Uniform Footnote Explanations-See Page 260. Other: [1] Gtd by Newcourt Credit Group. [2] Was American Tel & Tel. [3] See TCI Communications,Vanguard Cellular Sys. [4] Red at greater of 100 or amt based on formula. [5] Subsid & data of AGL Resources. [6] Due 10-6-03. [7] Due 12-7-05. [8] Due 10-23-06. [9] Due 12-2-13. [10] Due 12-9-13. [11] Due 12-13-13. [12] Due 1-21-14. [13] Due 1-27-15. [14] Due 1-18-19. [15] Due 10-26-23. [16] Due 7-15-27. [17] Subsid of Conectiv Inc. [18] Due 5-19-04. [19] Due 5-15-04. [20] Due 1-26-00. [21] Due 1-27-00. [22] Due 1-27-03. [23] Due 2-2-04. [24] Due 3-23-05.

Title-Industry Code & Co. Finances (In Italics) / Individual Issue Statistics (Exchange ↓)	Ind / Interest Dates	Fixed Charge Coverage 1996 / S&P Rating	1997 / Date of Last Rating Change	1998 / Prior Rating	Eligible ↓	Year End / Bond Form	Cash & Equiv. (Million $) / Regular Price	Curr. Assets (Million $) / Regular (Begins) Thru	Curr. Liab. (Million $) / Sinking Fund Price	Balance Sheet Date / Sinking Fund (Begins) Thru	L. Term Debt (Mil $) / Refund/Other Restriction Price	Capital-ization (Mil $) / Refund/Other Restriction (Begins) Thru	Outst'g (Mil $)	Total Debt % Capital / Underwriting Firm	Underwriting Year	Price Range 1999 High	Price Range 1999 Low	Mo. End Price Sale(s) or Bid	Curr. Yield	Yield to Mat.
***Atlantic City Electric** (Cont.)*																				
Sec M-T Nts 'B' 6.40s 2005	[1]jj	**A–**	10/93	A	X	BE	NC	....	....	....	....	....	11.0	F1	'93	103⅝	95¾	95¾	6.68	6.68
Sec M-T Nts 'B' 6.78s 2008	[2]jj	**A–**	10/93	A	X	BE	NC	....	....	....	....	....	10.0	F1	'93	107⅞	96	96	7.06	7.06
Sec M-T Nts 'B' 6¾s 2008	[3]jj	**A–**	10/93	A	X	BE	NC	....	....	....	....	....	10.0	F1	'93	107¾	95¾	95¾	7.05	7.05
Sec M-T Nts 'B' 6¾s 2008	[3]jj	**A–**	10/93	A	X	BE	NC	....	....	....	....	....	11.0	F1	'93	107¾	95¾	95¾	7.05	7.05
Sec M-T Nts 'D' 6.19s 2006	[4]ms	**A–**			X	BE	NC	....	....	....	....	....	50.0	L3	'98	103¼	94	94	6.59	6.58
M-T Nts 6.63s 2003	[5]ms	**BBB+**			X	BE	NC	....	....	....	....	....	30.0	L3	'97	104¼	98⅜	98⅜	6.74	6.74
Atlantic Express Transport'n	***70a***	*n/a*	*n/a*	*n/a*		*Je*	*0.34*	*67.60*	*53.10*	*9-30-99*	*161.0*	*205.0*		*92.2*						
Sr Sec Nts[6] 10¾s 2004	Fa	**B**			Y	BE	105.375	(2-1-01)	....	....	[7]Z110.75	2-1-00	150	Exch.	'97	102⅝	96¼	97	11.08	11.08
Atlantic Richfield[8]	***49b***	*4.93*	*6.22*	*d2.12*		*Dc*	*991.0*	*3146*	*4296*	*9-30-99*	*5691*	*158198*		*47.4*						
• Deb 10⅞s 2005	jJ15	**A**	4/94	A+	X	R	NC	....	....	....	....	....	410	S1	'85	130	116¼	116	9.38	9.37
• Deb 9⅛s 2011	Ms	**A**	4/94	A+	X	R	NC	....	....	....	....	....	253	S1	'86	122⅞	110½	110⅝	8.25	8.25
Deb 8½s 2012	Ao	**A**	4/94	A+	X	BE	NC	....	....	....	....	....	178	G1	'92	125	107¼	107¼	7.93	7.93
• Deb 9⅞s 2016	Ms	**A**	4/94	A+	X	R	NC	....	....	....	....	....	181	S1	'86	126	121⅛	113	8.74	8.74
Deb 9s 2021	Ao	**A**	4/94	A+	X	BE	NC	....	....	....	....	....	209	S1	'91	130½	113½	113½	7.93	7.93
Deb 8¼s 2022	Fa	**A**	4/94	A+	X	BE	NC	....	....	....	....	....	245	S1	'92	121¾	105⅞	105⅞	7.79	7.79
Deb 9s 2031	Mn	**A**	4/94	A+	X	BE	NC	....	....	....	....	....	97.0	S1	'91	134⅛	113¾	113¾	7.91	7.91
Deb 9⅛s 2031	fA	**A**	4/94	A+	X	BE	NC	....	....	....	....	....	155	S1	'91	135⅞	115	115	7.93	7.93
Deb 8¾s 2032	Ms	**A**	4/94	A+	X	BE	NC	....	....	....	....	....	159	G1	'92	130⅞	111⅛	111¾	7.83	7.83
Nts 5.55s 2003	Ao15	**A**			X	BE	[9]Z100	....	....	....	....	....	500	G1	'99	99¾	96¼	96¼	5.77	5.77
Nts 5.90s 2009	Ao15	**A**			X	BE	[9]Z100	....	....	....	....	....	50.0	G1	'99	99¼	90⅝	90⅝	6.51	6.51
[10]Atlantis Group	***52***	*1.99*	*1.12*	*2.02*		*Dc*	*3.63*	*58.80*	*29.90*	*9-30-99*	*81.90*	*130.0*		*66.1*						
Sr Nts[11] 11s 2003	Fa15	**B**	5/95	B–	Y	R	102.75	2-14-00	100	(2-15-01)	....	....	89.5	B7	'93	102⅛	98½	100	11.00	11.00
Atlas Air	***4a***	*n/a*	*n/a*	*n/a*		*Dc*	*448.3*	*518.6*	*185.5*	*9-30-99*	*1322*	*1512*		*80.1*						
Sr Nts[6] 10¾s 2005	fA	**B–**			Y	BE	105.375	(8-1-01)	....	....	[12]Z110.75	8-1-01	150	Exch.	'97	106	98¾	102	10.54	10.54
Auburn Hills Trust	***25c***	***Gtd by Chrysler Corp,see***																		
[13]Gtd[14]Exch[15]Ctfs 12s 2020	[16]Mn	**A+**	10/98	A	X	BE	NC	....	....	....	....	....	550	S1	'90	No Sale		145	....	Flat
Aurora Foods	***26***	*n/a*	*n/a*	*0.67*		*Dc*	*1.42*	*238.0*	*212.0*	*6-30-99*	*689.0*	*1422*		*56.4*						
Sr Sub Nts 'B' 9⅞s 2007	Fa15	**B+**	6/98	B–	Y	BE	104.9375	(2-15-02)	....	....	[17]Z109.875	2-15-00	100	Exch.	'97	109½	99¼	101⅜	9.74	9.74
Sr Sub Nts 'D' 9⅞s 2007	Fa15	**B+**	6/98	B–	Y	BE	104.9375	(2-15-02)	....	....	[18]Z109.875	2-15-00	100	Exch.	'97	109½	99¼	101⅜	9.74	9.74
Sr Sub Nts[19] 'B' 8¾s 2008	jJ	**B+**			Y	BE	104.375	(7-1-03)	....	....	[20]Z108.75	7-1-01	200	Exch.	'98	105½	94¼	95¼	9.19	9.18
Autotote Corp	***40j***	*d1.18*	*d0.14*	*0.01*		*Oc*	*14.50*	*44.70*	*48.10*	*7-31-99*	*154.0*	*108.0*		*144.0*						
Sr Nts[6] 'B' 10⅞s 2004	fA	**B+**			Y	BE	105.438	(8-1-01)	....	....	[21]Z110.875	8-1-00	110	Exch.	'97	106⅛	101⅛	102⅜	10.62	10.62
AutoZone Inc	***59c***	*△29.31*	*△18.66*	*△9.01*		*Au*	*5.92*	*1225*	*1001*	*8-28-99*	*888.0*	*2212*		*40.1*						
Deb 6½s 2008	jJ15	**A–**			X	BE	[9]Z100	....	....	....	....	....	200	M2	'98	102⅜	89¾	89¾	7.24	7.24
Nts 6s 2003	mN	**A–**			X	BE	[9]Z100	....	....	....	....	....	150	M2	'98	100⅛	93⅝	93⅝	6.41	6.41
Avado Brands[22]	***27c***	*4.41*	*3.04*	*2.65*		*Dc*	*3.27*	*31.74*	*84.64*	*10-3-99*	*306.0*	*521.0*		*77.0*						
Sr Sub Nts[6] 11¾s 2009	Jd15	**B–**			Y	BE	105.875	(6-15-04)	....	....	[17]Z111.75	6-15-02	100	Exch.	'99	99	67	75½	15.56	15.55
AvalonBay Communities	***57***	*n/a*	*n/a*	*2.75*		*Dc*				*9-30-99*	*1674*	*4020*		*41.6*						
Sr Nts 6½s 2003	jJ15	**BBB+**			X	BE	[23]Z100	....	....	....	....	....	100	P1	'98	100¼	95⅞	95⅞	6.78	6.78
Sr Nts 6.80s 2006	jJ15	**BBB+**			X	BE	[23]Z100	....	....	....	....	....	150	P1	'98	100½	93	93	7.31	7.31
M-T Nts 7½s 2009	fA	**BBB+**			X	BE	[23]Z100	....	....	....	....	....	150	P1	'99	99½	95⅜	95⅜	7.86	7.86
Avalon Properties	***57***	***Now AvalonBay Communities,see***																		
Nts 7⅜s 2002	mS15	**BBB+**	7/98	BBB	X	BE	[23]Z100	(9-15-00)	....	....	....	....	100	M5	'95	103	98⅞	98⅞	7.46	7.46
Nts 6⅝s 2005	Jj15	**BBB+**	7/98	BBB	X	BE	[23]Z100	....	....	....	....	....	100	P1	'98	99¾	94¼	94¼	7.03	7.03
Nts 6⅞s 2007	jD15	**BBB+**	7/98	BBB	X	BE	[23]Z100	....	....	....	....	....	110	P1	'97	100⅛	92⅛	92⅛	7.46	7.46

Uniform Footnote Explanations-See Page 260. Other: [1] Due 7-18-05. [2] Due 3-26-08. [3] Due 5-12-08. [4] Due 1-7-06. [5] Due 6-2-03. [6] (HRO)On Chge of Ctrl at 101. [7] Max $50M red w/proceeds of Pub Eq Off'g. [8] See Union Texas Petroleum. [9] Red at greater of 100 or amt based on formula. [10] Now Atlantis Plastics. [11] (HRO)On Chge of Ctrl or Fundamental Chge at 101. [12] Max $52.5M red w/proceeds Pub Eq Of'g. [13] Co may exch in whole for Deb'20. [14] Gtd by Chrysler Corp. [15] Int decr fr 14.875 on 10-5-93. [16] Int(11.125%-16.875%)may adj for rat'g chge. [17] Max $35M red w/proceeds of Pub Eq Off'g. [18] Max $35M red/proceeds of Pub Eq Off'g. [19] (HRO)On Chge of Ctrl at 101 fr 7-1-03. [20] Max $70M red w/proceeds of Pub Eq Off'g. [21] Max $38.5M red w/proceeds of Equity Off'g. [22] See Apple South. [23] Plus Make-Whole Amt.

Title-Industry Code & Co. Finances (In Italics) / Individual Issue Statistics (Exchange ↓)	Ind / Interest Dates	Fixed Charge Coverage 1996 / S&P Rating	1997 / Date of Last Rating Change	Prior Rating	1998 / Eligible ↓	Year End / Bond Form	Cash & Equiv. (Million $) / Redemption Provisions: Regular Price	Curr. Assets (Million $) / Regular (Begins) Thru	Curr. Liab. (Million $) / Sinking Fund Price	Balance Sheet Date / Sinking Fund (Begins) Thru	L. Term Debt (Mil $) / Refund/Other Restriction Price	Refund/Other Restriction (Begins) Thru	Capitalization (Mil $) / Outst'g (Mil $)	Total Debt % Capital / Underwriting Firm	Underwriting Year	Price Range 1999 High	Price Range 1999 Low	Mo. End Price Sale(s) or Bid	Curr. Yield	Yield to Mat.
[1]Avco Financial Svcs	***25a***	***n/a***	***n/a***		***1.61***	***Dc***				***9-30-99***	***42879***		***79907***	***88.1***						
Sr Nts 5½s 2000	Ao	**A+**	1/99	A	X	R	NC	....	....	....	....	....	200	M6	'93	100⅛	99⅝	99¾	5.51	5.51
Sr Nts 6.35s 2000	mS15	**A+**	1/99	A	X	R	NC	....	....	....	....	....	200	M6	'95	101½	99⅞	99⅞	6.36	6.36
Sr Nts 7⅜s 2001	fA15	**A+**	1/99	A	X	R	NC	....	....	....	....	....	200	S1	'94	104⅝	100⅜	100⅜	7.35	7.35
Sr Nts 6s 2002	fA15	**A+**	1/99	A	X	R	NC	....	....	....	....	....	200	M2	'95	101⅝	97	97	6.19	6.19
Avery Dennison	***48b***	***7.48***	***9.83***		***9.42***	***Dc***	***5.80***	***963.0***	***786.0***	***10-2-99***	***653.0***		***1472***	***46.2***						
M-T Nts 'B'[2] 7.67s 2004	[3]jj15	**A**			X	BE	NC	....	....	....	....	....	10.0	G1	'94	109⅜	101¼	101¼	7.58	7.57
M-T Nts 'B'[2] 7.67s 2004	[3]jj15	**A**			X	BE	NC	....	....	....	....	....	10.0	G1	'94	109⅜	101¼	101¼	7.58	7.57
M-T Nts 'B'[2] 7.63s 2004	[4]jj15	**A**			X	BE	NC	....	....	....	....	....	8.50	G1	'94	109¼	101⅛	101⅛	7.55	7.54
M-T Nts 'B'[2] 7.57s 2004	[5]jj15	**A**			X	BE	NC	....	....	....	....	....	5.00	G1	'94	109	100⅞	100⅞	7.50	7.50
M-T Nts 'C'[2] 6.98s 2005	[6]jj15	**A**			X	BE	NC	....	....	....	....	....	20.0	G1	'95	107	98	98	7.12	7.12
M-T Nts 'C'[2] 6.98s 2005	[6]jj15	**A**			X	BE	NC	....	....	....	....	....	10.0	G1	'95	107	98	98	7.12	7.12
M-T Nts 'C'[2] 6.99s 2005	[6]jj15	**A**			X	BE	NC	....	....	....	....	....	10.0	G1	'95	107	98	98	7.13	7.13
M-T Nts 'C'[2] 7.56s 2020	[7]jj15	**A**			X	BE	NC	....	....	....	....	....	15.0	M5	'95	112⅜	96	96⅛	7.86	7.86
M-T Nts 'C'[2] 7.56s 2025	[8]jj15	**A**			X	BE	NC	....	....	....	....	....	10.0	G1	'95	113	95¼	95⅜	7.93	7.93
M-T Nts 'C'[2] 7.54s 2025	[9]jj15	**A**			X	BE	NC	....	....	....	....	....	10.0	G1	'95	112¾	95⅛	95¼	7.92	7.91
Avnet, Inc	***23h***	***△13.02***	***△6.84***		***△8.20***	***Je***	***92.90***	***2342***	***805.0***	***10-1-99***	***819.0***		***2240***	***36.6***						
Nts 6.45s 2003	fA15	**A–**	10/99	A	X	BE	NC	....	....	....	....	....	200	M2	'98	104	98⅛	98⅛	6.57	6.57
Nts 6⅞s 2004	Ms15	**A–**	10/99	A	X	BE	NC	....	....	....	....	....	100	D4	'94	106½	99⅛	99⅛	6.94	6.94
Baker Hughes[10]	***49e***	***5.58***	***[11]5.38***		***2.03***	***Dc***	***34.10***	***2315***	***979.4***	***9-30-99***	***2777***		***6128***	***47.0***						
Nts 5.80s 2003	fA15	**A**			X	BE	NC	....	....	....	....	....	100		'99	97¾	95½	95½	6.07	6.07
Nts 8s 2004	Mn15	**A**	7/97	A–	X	R	NC	....	....	....	....	....	100	L3	'92	111⅜	101⅞	101⅞	7.85	7.85
Nts 6¼s 2009	fA15	**A**			X	BE	[12]Z100	....	....	....	....	....	324		'99	94¾	90⅞	90⅞	6.88	6.88
Nts 6s 2009	fA15	**A**			X	BE	[12]Z100	....	....	....	....	....	200		'99	93½	89	89	6.74	6.74
Nts 6⅞s 2029	fA15	**A**			X	BE	[12]Z100	....	....	....	....	....	400		'99	93½	87⅜	87⅝	7.85	7.84
Baker Int'l	***49e***	***Now Baker Hughes, see***																		
Deb 6s 2002	Ms15	**NR**	7/97	A–		R	100	....	....	....	....	....	[13]45.9	G1	'82	110⅛	97⅝	97⅝	6.15	6.15
[14]Baltimore Gas & Elec	***75***	***3.05***	***3.02***		***3.06***	***Dc***	***56.40***	***1653***	***2087***	***9-30-99***	***2588***		***6968***	***53.0***						
1st Ref 5½s 2000	jJ15	**AA–**	10/97	A+	X	R	NC	....	....	....	....	....	125	C4	'93	100⅜	99⅜	99½	5.53	5.53
1st Ref 8⅜s 2001	fA15	**AA–**	10/97	A+	X	R	NC	....	....	....	....	....	125	S1	'91	107⅛	102¼	102¼	8.19	8.19
1st Ref 7¼s 2002	jJ	**AA–**	10/97	A+	X	R	NC	....	....	....	....	....	125	S1	'92	105½	100⅜	100⅜	7.22	7.22
1st Ref 6½s 2003	Fa15	**AA–**	10/97	A+	X	R	NC	....	....	....	....	....	125	G1	'93	104¼	98⅛	98⅛	6.62	6.62
1st Ref 6⅛s 2003	jJ	**AA–**	10/97	A+	X	BE	NC	....	....	....	....	....	125	C4	'93	102¾	96⅞	96⅞	6.32	6.32
1st Ref 5½s 2004	aO15	**AA–**	10/97	A+	X	R	NC	....	....	....	....	....	125	K2	'93	100⅜	93⅞	93⅞	5.86	5.86
1st Ref 7½s 2007	Jj15	**AA–**	10/97	A+	X	R	NC	....	....	....	....	....	125	L3	'92	111⅞	99¾	99¾	7.52	7.52
1st Ref 6⅝s 2008	Ms15	**AA–**	10/97	A+	X	R	NC	....	....	....	....	....	125	M6	'93	107⅛	94¾	94¾	6.99	6.99
1st Ref 7½s 2023	Ms	**AA–**	10/97	A+	X	R	104.65	2-29-00	100	....	....	....	125	F1	'93	102¾	93	93	8.06	8.06
1st Ref 7½s 2023	Ao15	**AA–**	10/97	A+	X	R	104.94	4-14-00	100	....	....	....	100	L3	'93	102⅞	92¾	92⅞	8.08	8.08
M-T Nts 'D'[2] 6.68s 2001	[15]mn	**A**			X	BE	NC	....	....	....	....	....	50.0	L3	'96	102¾	99	99	6.75	6.75
M-T Nts 'D' 6.79s 2004	[16]mn	**A**			X	BE	NC	....	....	....	....	....	20.0	L3	'96	105	97⅛	97⅛	6.99	6.99
M-T Nts 'D' 6.90s 2005	[17]mn	**A**			X	BE	NC	....	....	....	....	....	20.0	L3	'96	105⅝	97½	97½	7.08	7.08
M-T Nts[18] 'E' 6¾s 2012	[19]mn	**A**			X	BE	NC	....	....	....	....	....	30.0	G1	'97	108⅝	98¾	98¾	6.84	6.83
M-T[18]Nts 'E' 6¾s 2012	[19]mn	**A**			X	BE	NC	....	....	....	....	....	30.0	G1	'97	108⅝	98¾	98¾	6.84	6.83
M-T[20]Nts 'E' 6¾s 2012	[21]mn	**A**			X	BE	NC	....	....	....	....	....	25.0	G1	'97	109	97⅝	97⅝	6.91	6.91
M-T[20]Nts 'E' 6.73s 2012	[21]mn	**A**			X	BE	NC	....	....	....	....	....	25.0	G1	'97	109⅜	97⅞	97⅞	6.88	6.88
M-T Nts 'G' 5.78s 2008	[22]mn	**A**			X	BE	NC	....	....	....	....	....	50.0	G1	'98	99¼	88	88	6.57	6.57

Uniform Footnote Explanations-See Page 260. Other: [1] Subsid & data of Associates First Capital. [2] Issued in min denom $100T. [3] Due 5-25-04. [4] Due 6-9-04. [5] Due 6-10-04. [6] Due 6-1-05. [7] Due 6-1-20. [8] Due 5-23-05. [9] Due 5-26-25. [10] See Baker Int'l,Western Atlas. [11] Fiscal Sep'97 & prior. [12] Red at greater of 100 or amt based on formula. [13] Incl disc:defeased,fds deposited w/trustee. [14] Now Constellation Energy Group. [15] Due 10-11-01. [16] Due 11-15-04. [17] Due 2-1-05. [18] (HRO)On 6-5-02 & 07 at 100. [19] Due 6-5-12. [20] (HRO)On 6-12-04(&'07)at 100. [21] Due 6-12-12. [22] Due 10-01-08.

Title-Industry Code & Co. Finances (In Italics) / Individual Issue Statistics, Exchange	Ind / Interest Dates	Fixed Charge Coverage 1996 / S&P Rating	1997 / Date of Last Rating Change	1998 / Prior Rating	Eligible	Year End / Bond Form	Cash & Equiv. / Regular Price	Curr. Assets / Regular (Begins) Thru	Curr. Liab. / Sinking Fund Price	Balance Sheet Date / Sinking Fund (Begins) Thru	L. Term Debt (Mil $) / Refund/Other Restriction Price	Refund/Other Restriction (Begins) Thru	Capitalization (Mil $) / Outst'g (Mil $)	Total Debt % Capital / Underwriting Firm	Underwriting Year	Price Range 1999 High	Price Range 1999 Low	Mo. End Price Sale(s) or Bid	Curr. Yield	Yield to Mat.
Baltimore Gas & Elec *(Cont.)*																				
M-T Nts 'G' 6.20s 2008	[1]mn	A			X	BE	NC	....	....	....	....	....	40.0	L3	'98	102½	91⅛	91⅛	6.80	6.80
Banc One Corp	***10***	***Now Bank One Corp,see***																		
M-T Nts 6.70s 2000	[2]ms25	A+	10/98	AA–	X	BE	NC	....	....	....	....	....	200	G1	'97	101⅜	100⅛	100⅛	6.69	6.69
M-T Nts 6¼s 2000	mS	A+	10/98	AA–	X	BE	NC	....	....	....	....	....	250	G1	'97	101¼	99¾	99¾	6.27	6.27
F/R[3]M-T Nts 2000	[2]Qmar25	A+	10/98	AA–	X	BE	NC	....	....	....	....	....	200	G1	'97	100¼	99⅞	100⅛	....	....
F/R[4]M-T Nts 2001	[5]Qmar25	A+	10/98	AA–	X	BE	NC	....	....	....	....	....	200	G1	'97	100¼	99⅝	100	....	....
M-T Nts 6¼s 2001	aO	A+	10/98	AA–	X	BE	NC	....	....	....	....	....	125	S1	'97	102	98⅝	98⅝	6.34	6.34
M-T Nts 7s 2002	Ms25	A+	10/98	AA–	X	BE	NC	....	....	....	....	....	150	G1	'97	104⅜	99⅝	99⅝	7.03	7.03
M-T Nts[6] 6⅜s 2002	aO	A+	10/98	AA–	X	BE	NC	....	....	....	....	....	75.0	S1	'97	102¾	98	98	6.51	6.51
Sub Deb 7¾s 2025	jJ15	A	10/98	A+	X	BE	NC	....	....	....	....	....	300	S1	'95	117¼	96⅞	97	7.99	7.99
Sub Deb 7⅝s 2026	aO15	A	10/98	A+	X	BE	NC	....	....	....	....	....	500	C5	'96	115⅞	95⅜	95½	7.98	7.98
Sub Deb 8s 2027	Ao29	A	10/98	A+	X	BE	NC	....	....	....	....	....	500	S1	'97	120¾	99½	99⅝	8.03	8.03
Sub Nts 7¼s 2002	fA	A	10/98	A+	X	BE	NC	....	....	....	....	....	350	F1	'92	105½	100⅜	100⅜	7.22	7.22
Sub Nts 8.74s 2003	mS15	A	10/98	A+	X	R	NC	....	....	....	....	....	170	S1	'91	112⅝	104⅞	105	8.32	8.32
Sub Nts 7s 2005	jJ15	A	10/98	A+	X	BE	NC	....	....	....	....	....	300	S1	'95	107¼	98¼	98¼	7.12	7.12
Sub Nts 7.60s 2007	Mn	A	10/98	A+	X	BE	NC	....	....	....	....	....	400	S1	'97	112½	99½	99½	7.64	7.64
Sub Nts 9⅞s 2009	Ms	A	10/98	A+	X	R	NC	....	....	....	....	....	54.2	M2	'89	130⅝	113⅞	113⅞	8.67	8.67
Sub Nts 10s 2010	fA15	A	10/98	A+	X	R	NC	....	....	....	....	....	200	S1	'90	134⅜	115⅞	115⅞	8.63	8.63
Bank of America[7]	***10***	***2.81***	***2.71***	***2.04***		***Dc***				***9-30-99***	***54352***		***105196***	***51.7***						
• Sub Nts[8] 9⅞s 2001	Jd	A	1/98	BBB+	X	BE	NC	....	....	....	....	....	100	F1	'91	109	102¾	101⅝	9.72	9.71
• [8]Sub Nts 8½s 2007	Jj15	A	1/98	BBB+	X	BE	NC	....	....	....	....	....	100	L3	'92	110⅜	104⅛	105	8.10	8.09
Bank of Boston[9]	***10***	***Now BankBoston Corp,see***																		
M-T Nts 6.38s 2000	fA11	A	10/99	A–	X	BE	NC	....	....	....	....	....	50.0	M6	'97	100⅞	99¾	99⅞	6.39	6.39
F/R[10]M-T Nts 2002	QAug12	A	10/99	A–	X	BE	NC	....	....	....	....	....	50.0	M2	'97	99⅝	98½	99⅜	....	....
Sub Nts 6⅞s 2003	jJ15	A–	10/99	BBB+	X	BE	NC	....	....	....	....	....	100	M2	'93	103¾	98½	98½	6.98	6.98
Sub Nts 6⅝s 2004	Fa	A–	10/99	BBB+	X	BE	NC	....	....	....	....	....	300	M2	'94	102⅞	97⅛	97⅛	6.82	6.82
Sub Nts 6⅝s 2005	jD	A–	10/99	BBB+	X	BE	NC	....	....	....	....	....	350	M2	'93	102⅞	95	95½	6.94	6.94
Bank of New York[11]	***10***	***4.52***	***7.17***	***4.26***		***Dc***				***9-30-99***	***2416***		***8995***	***41.0***						
Sub Nts 7⅝s 2002	jJ15	A	5/97	A–	X	BE	NC	....	....	....	....	....	350	L3	'92	106⅞	100⅞	100⅞	7.56	7.56
Sub Nts 7⅞s 2002	mN15	A	5/97	A–	X	BE	NC	....	....	....	....	....	250	S1	'92	108¼	101½	101½	7.76	7.76
Sub Nts 6⅝s 2003	Jd15	A	5/97	A–	X	BE	NC	....	....	....	....	....	300	D6	'93	104⅜	97¾	97¾	6.78	6.78
Sub Nts 6½s 2003	jD	A	5/97	A–	X	BE	NC	....	....	....	....	....	250	G1	'93	104¼	96⅞	96⅞	6.71	6.71
Sub Nts 8½s 2004	jD15	A	5/97	A–	X	BE	NC	....	....	....	....	....	300	U1	'94	114⅝	104	104	8.17	8.17
Sr Sub Nts 7.30s 2009	jD	A			X	BE	NC	....	....	....	....	....	300	M2	'99	100½	98	98	7.45	7.45
Sub M-T Nts 6¾s 2018	Fa12	A			X	BE	*100	(2-12-02)	....	....	....	....	25.0	P1	'98	98¼	88¼	88⅜	7.64	7.64
Bank One Corp[12]	***10***	***3.57***	***2.60***	***2.71***		***Dc***				***9-30-99***	***34735***		***54785***	***63.4***						
Nts[13] 6.40s 2002	fA	A+			X		NC	....	....	....	....	....	1250	M7	'99	100⅜	98¼	98¼	6.51	6.51
Nts[13] 6⅞s 2006	fA	A+			X	BE	NC	....	....	....	....	....	1000	M8	'99	100¼	96⅞	96⅞	7.10	7.10
M-T Nts 'A' 5⅝s 2004	Fa17	A+			X	BE	NC	....	....	....	....	....	500	F2	'99	99⅝	94⅛	94⅛	5.98	5.98
• Sub Deb[14] 7¼s 2004	fA15	A	12/95	A+	X	BE	NC	....	....	....	....	....	200	M6	'92	105	100⅛	97	7.47	7.47
• Sub Nts[14] 8.10s 2002	Ms	A	12/95	A+	X	BE	NC	....	....	....	....	....	200	G1	'92	103¼	100¼	100⅞	8.03	8.03
Bank United	***10***	***n/a***	***n/a***	***1.51***		***Sp***				***6-30-99***	***6387***		***7120***	***89.7***						
Sub Nts 8⅞s 2007	MN	BB+			Y	BE	NC	....	....	....	....	....	220	S7	'97	106⅞	93	93	9.54	9.54
BankAmerica Corp(New)	***10***	***Now Bank of America,see***																		
Nts 6.65s 2001	Mn	A+			X	BE	NC	....	....	....	....	....	250		'96	102¾	99⅝	99⅝	6.68	6.67

Uniform Footnote Explanations-See Page 260. Other: [1] Due 4-8-08. [2] Due 3-24-00. [3] Int adj qtrly(3 Mo LIBOR & 0.07%). [4] Int adj qtrly(3 Mo LIBOR & 0.135%). [5] Due 3-23-01. [6] Issued in min denom of $100T. [7] See BankAmer Corp,NationsBank Corp,Security Pacific. [8] Was Barnett Banks,then NationsBank,then BankAmer. [9] Was First Nat'l Boston. [10] Int adj qtrly(3 Mo LIBOR & 0.10%). [11] See Irving Bank Corp. [12] Was Banc One Corp,see. [13] Co may red in whole, at 100, for tax law chge. [14] Was NBD Bancorp.

Title-Industry Code & Co. Finances (In Italics)	Ind	Fixed Charge Coverage 1996	1997	1998	Year End		Cash & Equiv. (Million $)	Curr. Assets	Curr. Liab.	Balance Sheet Date		L. Term Debt (Mil $)		Capital-ization (Mil $)	Total Debt % Capital					
Exchange ↓ Individual Issue Statistics	**Interest Dates**	**S&P Rating**	**Date of Last Rating Change**	**Prior Rating**	**Eligible ↓**	**Bond Form**	**Redemption Provisions: Regular Price**	**Regular (Begins) Thru**	**Sinking Fund Price**	**Sinking Fund (Begins) Thru**	**Refund/Other Restriction Price**	**Refund/Other Restriction (Begins) Thru**	**Outst'g (Mil $)**	**Underwriting Firm**	**Underwriting Year**	**Price Range 1999 High**	**Price Range 1999 Low**	**Mo. End Price Sale(s) or Bid**	**Curr. Yield**	**Yield to Mat.**
BankAmerica Corp(New) *(Cont.)*																				
Nts 6⅝s 2001	Mn30	A+			X	BE	NC	....	....	....	....	....	300	M2	'96	102¾	99½	99½	6.66	6.66
Sr M-T Nts 'I' 7⅛s 2005	Mn12	A+	10/95	A	X	BE	NC	....	....	....	....	....	150	M2	'95	107⅝	98½	98½	7.23	7.23
Sub Nts 9¾s 2000	jJ	A	10/95	A–	X	R	NC	....	....	....	....	....	100	S1	'90	106⅛	101¾	101¾	9.58	9.58
Sub Nts 9.70s 2000	fA	A	10/95	A–	X	R	NC	....	....	....	....	....	125	M2	'90	106¼	101⅞	102	9.51	9.51
Sub Nts 9⅝s 2001	Fa13	A	10/95	A–	X	R	NC	....	....	....	....	....	125	S1	'91	108⅜	102¾	102¾	9.37	9.37
Sub Nts 9⅜s 2001	Ms	A	10/95	A–	X	BE	NC	....	....	....	....	....	100	L3	'91	108⅛	102⅝	102⅝	9.14	9.13
Sub Nts 9½s 2001	Ao	A	10/95	A–	X	BE	NC	....	....	....	....	....	200	S1	'91	108⅝	103	103	9.22	9.22
Sub Nts 8⅛s 2002	Fa	A	10/95	A–	X	BE	NC	....	....	....	....	....	300	F1	'92	107¾	102⅛	102⅛	7.96	7.95
Sub Nts 8⅜s 2002	Ms15	A	10/95	A–	X	BE	NC	....	....	....	....	....	250	S1	'92	108¾	102⅝	102⅝	8.16	8.16
Sub Nts 7¾s 2002	jJ15	A	10/95	A–	X	BE	NC	....	....	....	....	....	500	S1	'92	107	101½	101½	7.64	7.63
Sub Nts 7.20s 2002	mS15	A	10/95	A–	X	BE	NC	....	....	....	....	....	250	G1	'92	106⅛	100¼	100¼	7.18	7.18
Sub Nts 7½s 2002	aO15	A	10/95	A–	X	BE	NC	....	....	....	....	....	300	S1	'92	107⅛	101	101	7.43	7.43
Sub Nts 7⅞s 2002	jD	A	10/95	A–	X	BE	NC	....	....	....	....	....	250	M2	'92	108⅝	102	102	7.72	7.72
Sub Nts 10s 2003	Fa	A	10/95	A–	X	R	NC	....	....	....	....	....	100	M2	'91	116¼	107⅜	108⅛	9.25	9.25
Sub Nts 6.85s 2003	Ms	A	10/95	A–	X	BE	NC	....	....	....	....	....	250	G1	'93	105¼	99	99	6.92	6.92
Sub Nts 9.20s 2003	Mn15	A	10/95	A–	X	BE	NC	....	....	....	....	....	100	G1	'91	114⅛	105⅞	105⅞	8.69	8.69
Sub Nts 6⅞s 2003	Jd	A	10/95	A–	X	BE	NC	....	....	....	....	....	350	M5	'93	105¼	99	99	6.94	6.94
Sub Nts 7⅝s 2004	Jd15	A	10/95	A–	X	BE	NC	....	....	....	....	....	250	S1	'94	109⅝	101¼	101¼	7.53	7.53
Sub Nts 8⅛s 2004	fA15	A	10/95	A–	X	BE	100	....	....	....	....	....	150	C5	'94	101¾	99¼	99⅞	8.14	8.13
Sub Nts 6¾s 2005	mS15	A	10/95	A–	X	BE	NC	....	....	....	....	....	200	S7	'95	106⅞	97⅛	97⅛	6.95	6.95
Sub Nts 6.20s 2006	Fa15	A			X	BE	NC	....	....	....	....	....	250	G1	'96	103⅜	93⅝	93⅞	6.60	6.60
Sub Nts 7.20s 2006	Ao15	A	10/95	A–	X	BE	NC	....	....	....	....	....	300	L3	'94	108⅞	97⅝	97⅝	7.38	7.38
Sub Nts 7⅛s 2006	Mn	A			X	BE	NC	....	....	....	....	....	250	G1	'96	108⅞	98⅛	98⅛	7.26	7.26
Sub Nts 6⅝s 2007	fA	A			X	BE	NC	....	....	....	....	....	350		'97	106½	94⅝	94⅝	7.00	7.00
Sub Nts 6⅝s 2007	aO15	A			X	BE	NC	....	....	....	....	....	250	C5	'97	106⅝	94½	94½	7.01	7.01
Sub Nts 6¼s 2008	Ao	A			X	BE	NC	....	....	....	....	....	250	B2	'98	104¼	92	92	6.79	6.79
Sub Nts 7⅛s 2009	Ms	A			X	BE	NC	....	....	....	....	....	300		'97	110⅝	97	97	7.35	7.34
Sub Nts 7⅛s 2011	aO15	A			X	BE	NC	....	....	....	....	....	250	U1	'96	111⅛	95½	95½	7.46	7.46
F/R[1]Sub Nts 2003	QAug15	A	10/95	A–	X	BE	NC	....	....	....	....	....	150	F1	'93	99¼	99	99¼	....	....
BankBoston[2]Corp[3]	***10***	***2.50***	***2.40***	***2.08***	***Dc***					***6-30-99***		***5594***	***10668***	***52.4***						
F/R[4]M-T Nts 2000	QMar27	A	10/99	A–	X	BE	NC	....	....	....	....	....	60.0	C6	'98	100	99⅝	100	....	....
F/R[5]M-T Nts 2001	QMar9	A	10/99	A–	X	BE	NC	....	....	....	....	....	80.0	B7	'98	100	98⅜	100	....	....
M-T Nts 6⅛s 2002	Ms15	A	10/99	A–	X	BE	NC	....	....	....	....	....	300		'99	101	97⅝	97⅝	6.27	6.27
Bankers Trust (NY)	***10***	***Merged w/Deutsche Bank***																		
Nts 6¾s 2001	aO3	AA–	5/99	A–	X	BE	NC	....	....	....	....	....	250	U1	'96	102½	99⅜	99⅜	6.79	6.79
•[6]Sr Nts 7⅝s 2005	fA15	AA–	5/99	A–	X	BE	NC	....	....	....	....	....	110	B10	'95	No Sale		85	8.97	8.97
M-T Sr Nts 'A' 6s 2000	fA15	AA–	5/99	A–	X	BE	NC	....	....	....	....	....	25.0	P1	'97	100⅜	99¼	99⅝	6.02	6.02
Sub Deb 9½s 2000	Jd14	A+	5/99	BBB+	X	R	NC	....	....	....	....	....	198	S5	'90	105⅛	101¼	101¼	9.38	9.38
Sub Deb 9.40s 2001	Ms	A+	5/99	BBB+	X	BE	NC	....	....	....	....	....	99.0	M2	'91	107¼	102¼	102½	9.17	9.17
Sub Deb 9s 2001	fA	A+	5/99	BBB+	X	BE	NC	....	....	....	....	....	99.0	L3	'91	107⅝	102⅜	102¾	8.76	8.76
Sub Deb 7½s 2002	Jj15	A+	5/99	BBB+	X	BE	NC	....	....	....	....	....	200	G1	'92	104⅜	100¼	100¼	7.48	7.48
Sub Deb 8⅛s 2002	Mn15	A+	5/99	BBB+	X	BE	NC	....	....	....	....	....	150	L3	'92	106⅝	101½	101½	8.00	8.00
Sub Deb 7⅛s 2002	jJ31	A+	5/99	BBB+	X	BE	NC	....	....	....	....	....	100	M2	'92	103¾	99¼	99¼	7.18	7.18
Sub Deb 7¼s 2003	Jj15	A+	5/99	BBB+	X	BE	NC	....	....	....	....	....	100	L3	'93	104⅜	99½	99½	7.29	7.29
Sub Nts 8⅛s 2002	Ao	A+	5/99	BBB+	X	BE	NC	....	....	....	....	....	150	S7	'95	106⅜	101¾	101¾	7.99	7.98

Uniform Footnote Explanations-See Page 260. Other: [1] Int adj qtrly. [2] Was Bank of Boston,see. [3] Acq by Fleet Finl. [4] Int adj qtrly(3 Mo LIBOR). [5] Int adj qtrly(3 Mo LIBOR & 0.07%). [6] Was Alex. Brown.

Title-Industry Code & Co. Finances (In Italics)	Ind	Fixed Charge Coverage 1996	1997	1998		Year End	Million $ Cash & Equiv.	Curr. Assets	Curr. Liab.	Balance Sheet Date	L. Term Debt (Mil $)		Capitalization (Mil $)	Total Debt % Capital						
Individual Issue Statistics Exchange ↓	Interest Dates	S&P Rating	Date of Last Rating Change	Prior Rating	Eligible ↓	Bond Form	Redemption Provisions: Regular Price	Regular (Begins) Thru	Sinking Fund Price	Sinking Fund (Begins) Thru	Refund/Other Restriction Price	Refund/Other Restriction (Begins) Thru	Outst'g (Mil $)	Underwriting Firm	Underwriting Year	Price Range 1999 High	Price Range 1999 Low	Mo. End Price Sale(s) or Bid	Curr. Yield	Yield to Mat.
***Bankers Trust (NY)** (Cont.)*																				
Sub Nts 8¼s 2005	Mn	A+	5/99	BBB+	X	BE	NC	....	....	....	....	....	150	S7	'95	111¼	102⅝	102⅝	8.04	8.04
Sub Nts 7⅛s 2006	Ms15	A+	5/99	BBB+	X	BE	NC	....	....	....	....	....	150	M6	'96	106¼	96¾	97	7.35	7.34
Sub Nts 7⅜s 2008	Mn	A+	5/99	BBB+	X	BE	NC	....	....	....	....	....	150	S7	'96	108¼	97½	97½	7.56	7.56
Sub Nts 6s 2008	aO15	A+	5/99	BBB+	X	BE	NC	....	....	....	....	....	150	K2	'93	98⅞	89	89¼	6.72	6.72
Sub Nts 7½s 2010	Jd15	A+	5/99	BBB+	X	BE	■100	(6-15-00)	....	....	....	....	75.0	M2	'95	106¾	94⅛	94⅛	7.97	7.97
Sub Nts 7⅛s 2010	[1]Nov22	A+	5/99	BBB+	X	BE	*■100	(11-22-00)	....	....	....	....	50.0	S7	'95	103⅞	92¼	92⅜	7.71	7.71
Sub Nts 7¼s 2011	aO15	A+	5/99	BBB+	X	BE	NC	....	....	....	....	....	150	U1	'96	106⅜	93⅞	93⅞	7.72	7.72
Sub Nts 7¾s 2012	QMay	A+	5/99	BBB+	X	BE	■*100	(5-1-01)	....	....	....	....	50.0	S7	'97	102⅝	97⅞	98⅛	7.90	7.90
Sub Nts 7.15s 2012	fA14	A+	5/99	BBB+	X	BE	[2]■100	8-14-02	....	....	....	....	100	B7	'97	102⅛	93⅝	93⅝	7.64	7.64
Sub Nts 7½s 2015	mN15	A+	5/99	BBB+	X	BE	NC	....	....	....	....	....	150	G1	'95	104¼	96⅛	96¼	7.79	7.79
Sub[3]F/R Nts 2003	QMar19	A+	5/99	BBB+	X	BE	NC	....	....	....	....	....	100	L3	'93	100¼	96⅜	96⅜	....	....
M-T Sub Nts 'A' 6.70s 2007	aO	A+	5/99	BBB+	X	BE	NC	....	....	....	....	....	200	M6	'97	103⅝	93¾	94⅛	7.12	7.12
M-T Sub Nts 'A' 7s 2012	[1]Oct15	A+	5/99	BBB+	X	BE	[4]Z100	(10-15-01)	....	....	....	....	50.0	L3	'97	100	92½	97¾	7.16	7.16
M-T Sub Nts 'A' 7s 2012	[1]Dec4	A+	5/99	BBB+	X	BE	100	(12-4-01)	....	....	....	....	85.0		'97	99¾	92⅝	96	7.29	7.29
BanPonce Corp	*10*	*Now Popular Inc,see*																		
M-T Nts 2 6.488s 2000	[5]jd15	BBB+			X	BE	NC	....	....	....	....	....	25.0	C5	'97	100⅜	99⅞	100⅛	6.48	6.48
M-T Nts 2 6.665s 2001	[6]jd15	BBB+			X	BE	NC	....	....	....	....	....	25.0	C5	'97	101⅛	99⅛	99½	6.70	6.70
Sub Nts 6¾s 2005	jD15	BBB			X	BE	NC	....	....	....	....	....	125	C5	'95	101½	93½	93½	7.22	7.22
Bard (C.R.)	*43*	*6.92*	*5.85*	*5.69*		*Dc*	*59.50*	*509.8*	*344.2*	*9-30-99*	*159.0*		*794.0*	*30.4*						
Deb[7] 6.70s 2026	jD	BBB+			X	BE	NC	....	....	....	....	....	150	M5	'96	103⅛	94¼	94¼	7.11	7.11
Barnett Bks, Inc[8]	*10*	*Merged into NationsBank, see*																		
• Sub Nts 10⅞s 2003	Ms15	A	1/98	BBB+	X	BE	NC	....	....	....	....	....	55.0	F1	'91	118	108⅛	107⅛	10.15	10.15
Sub Nts 6.90s 2005	mS	A	1/98	BBB+	X	BE	NC	....	....	....	....	....	150	M6	'95	106¼	97⅝	97⅝	7.07	7.07
Barrett Resources	*49a*	*13.08*	*4.56*	*d3.49*		*Dc*	*14.60*	*190.0*	*176.0*	*9-30-99*	*306.0*		*652.0*	*46.3*						
Sr Nts 7.55s 2007	Fa	BB+			Y	BE	[9]Z100	....	....	....	....	....	150	G1	'97	98⅝	91⅝	93⅝	8.06	8.06
Baroid Corp	*49e*	*Gtd by Halliburton Co,see*																		
• Sr[10]Nts[11] 8s 2003	Ao15	AA–	10/98	A	X	R	NC	....	....	....	....	....	138	S1	'93	101¼	101¼	100⅝	7.95	7.95
Bausch & Lomb	*43*	*4.84*	*4.76*	*3.10*		*Dc*	*951.0*	*1914*	*811.0*	*9-25-99*	*977.0*		*2479*	*50.0*						
• Deb 7⅛s 2028	fA	BBB			X	BE	[12]Z100	....	....	....	....	....	200	M7	'98	102½	89⅜	88⅜	8.06	8.06
• Nts 6¾s 2004	jD15	BBB			X	BE	[12]Z100	....	....	....	....	....	200	M6	'97	No Sale		96	7.03	7.03
M-T Nts 5.95s 2003	[13]jj15	BBB	12/97	A–	X	BE	NC	....	....	....	....	....	85.0		'93	99⅛	94⅞	94⅞	6.27	6.27
M-T Nts 'B'[14] 6.56s 2026	[15]jj15	BBB	12/97	A–	X	BE	100	(8-13-01)	....	....	....	....	100	M6	'96	102⅜	98	98	6.69	6.69
Baxter Int'l	*43*	*8.74*	*3.50*	*5.79*		*Dc*	*825.0*	*4255*	*2550*	*9-30-99*	*2716*		*6564*	*50.1*						
Nts 8⅛s 2001	mN15	A	10/96	A–	X	R	NC	....	....	....	....	....	150	M2	'91	107⅛	101⅞	101⅞	7.98	7.97
Nts 7⅝s 2002	mN15	A	10/96	A–	X	R	NC	....	....	....	....	....	150	F1	'92	107½	101¼	101¼	7.53	7.53
Nts[16] 9½s 2008	Jd15	A	10/96	A–	X	R	NC	....	....	....	....	....	100	G1	'88	127⅜	111⅜	111⅜	8.53	8.53
Nts 7¼s 2008	Fa15	A	10/96	A–	X	R	NC	....	....	....	....	....	200	F1	'93	110⅝	97⅞	97⅞	7.41	7.41
[17]Bay State Gas	*73b*	*n/a*	*n/a*	*n/a*		*Dc*	*23.70*	*678.0*	*1279*	*9-30-99*	*2187*		*3856*	*61.0*						
M-T Nts[14] 6s 2000	[18]fa	A			X	BE	NC	....	....	....	....	....	10.0	S7	'93	100⅞	99⅝	99¾	6.02	6.01
M-T Nts[14] 6s 2001	[19]fa	A			X	BE	NC	....	....	....	....	....	5.00	S7	'93	101¼	99	99	6.06	6.06
M-T Nts[14] 7.42s 2001	[20]fa	A			X	BE	NC	....	....	....	....	....	10.0	S7	'94	105	100½	100½	7.38	7.38
M-T Nts[14] 7¼s 2002	[21]mn	A			X	BE	NC	....	....	....	....	....	20.0	M2	'92	105¾	100⅛	100⅛	7.24	7.24
M-T Nts[14] 7⅜s 2002	mN	A			X	BE	NC	....	....	....	....	....	7.00	M2	'92	106½	100⅜	100⅜	7.35	7.35
M-T Nts[14] 7.45s 2002	[22]mn	A			X	BE	NC	....	....	....	....	....	5.00	M2	'92	106⅞	100⅝	100⅝	7.40	7.40
M-T Nts[14] 7.37s 2002	[23]mn	A			X	BE	NC	....	....	....	....	....	5.00	M2	'92	106⅝	100⅜	100⅜	7.34	7.34

Uniform Footnote Explanations-See Page 260. Other: [1] Int pd monthly. [2] On 8-14-02. [3] Int(min 6%)adj qtrly. [4] Co may red ea Apr&Oct 15. [5] Due 3-3-00. [6] Due 3-5-01. [7] (HRO)On 12-1-06 at 100. [8] Was Barnett Bks of Fla. [9] Plus Make Whole Amt. [10] (HRO)On Chge of Ctrl at 101. [11] Gtd by Halliburton Co. [12] Red at greater of 100 or amt based on formula. [13] Due 9-8-03. [14] Issued in min denom $100T. [15] Due 8-13-26. [16] (HRO)On 6-15-98 at 100. [17] Acq by & data of NiSource Inc. [18] Due 7-6-00. [19] Due 1-30-01. [20] Due 9-10-01. [21] Due 8-5-02. [22] Due 12-16-02. [23] Due 12-31-02.

Title-Industry Code & Co. Finances (In Italics) / Individual Issue Statistics, Exchange	Ind / Interest Dates	Fixed Charge Coverage 1996 / S&P Rating	1997 / Date of Last Rating Change	1998 / Prior Rating	Eligible	Year End / Bond Form	Cash & Equiv. (Million $) / Regular Price	Curr. Assets (Million $) / Regular (Begins) Thru	Curr. Liab. (Million $) / Sinking Fund Price	Balance Sheet Date / Sinking Fund (Begins) Thru	Refund/Other Restriction Price	L. Term Debt (Mil $) / Refund/Other Restriction (Begins) Thru	Capitalization (Mil $) / Outst'g (Mil $)	Total Debt % Capital / Underwriting Firm	Underwriting Year	Price Range 1999 High	Price Range 1999 Low	Mo. End Price Sale(s) or Bid	Curr. Yield	Yield to Mat.
Bay State Gas (Cont.)																				
M-T Nts[1] 7.38s 2002	[2]mn	**A**			X	BE	NC	....	....	....	....	....	5.00	M2	'92	106¾	100½	100½	7.34	7.34
M-T Nts[1] 6s 2003	[3]fa	**A**			X	BE	NC	....	....	....	....	....	15.0	S7	'93	102	95⅞	95⅞	6.26	6.26
M-T Nts[1] 9.20s 2011	[4]mn	**A**			X	BE	NC	....	....	....	....	....	10.0	M2	'91	130¾	112⅛	112⅛	8.21	8.20
M-T Nts 9.28s 2021	[5]mn	**A**			X	BE	NC	....	....	....	....	....	5.00	M2	'91	133⅞	112¾	112⅞	8.22	8.22
M-T Nts[1] 8.15s 2022	[6]mn	**A**			X	BE	104.075	(5-1-02)	....	....	....	....	12.0	M2	'92	120⅜	101	101⅛	8.06	8.06
BB&T Corp[7]	***10***	***n/a***	***2.91***	***2.73***		***Dc***				***9-30-99***		***6322***	***9416***	***67.1***						
Sub Nts 7¼s 2007	Jd15	**BBB+**			X	BE	NC	....	....	....	....	....	250	B7	'97	108½	96¼	96¾	7.49	7.49
BE Aerospace	***3***	***1.56***	***2.58***	***0.39***		***Fb***	***29.80***	***326.0***	***169.0***	***8-28-99***		***581.0***	***800.0***	***80.3***						
Sr Sub Nts[8]'B' 9⅞s 2006	Fa	**B**			Y	BE	104.94	(2-1-01)	....	....	....	....	99.9	Exch.	'96	106¼	87¼	96½	10.23	10.23
Sr Sub Nts[8]'B' 8s 2008	Ms	**B**			Y	BE	104	(3-1-03)	....	....	[9]Z108	3-1-01	250	Exch.	'98	100	79	87	9.20	9.19
Bear Stearns Cos	***62***	***△1.40***	***△1.29***	***△1.31***		***Je***				***9-24-99***		***15841***	***34491***	***85.5***						
Sr Nts 7⅝s 2000	Ms15	**A**			X	BE	NC	....	....	....	....	....	150	B7	'95	102⅜	100¼	100⅜	7.60	7.60
Sr Nts 6½s 2000	Jd15	**A**			X	BE	NC	....	....	....	....	....	200	B7	'93	101	100	100	6.50	6.50
Sr Nts 6½s 2000	jJ5	**A**			X	BE	NC	....	....	....	....	....	400	B7	'97	101¼	99⅞	100	6.50	6.50
Sr Nts 6¾s 2000	fA15	**A**			X	BE	NC	....	....	....	....	....	200	B7	'95	101⅝	100	100⅛	6.74	6.74
Sr Nts 6¼s 2000	jD	**A**			X	BE	NC	....	....	....	....	....	145	B7	'97	100⅞	99½	99½	6.28	6.28
Sr Nts 5¾s 2001	Fa15	**A**			X	BE	NC	....	....	....	....	....	195	B7	'96	100¼	98½	98⅝	5.83	5.83
Sr Nts 6¾s 2001	Mn	**A**			X	BE	NC	....	....	....	....	....	225	B7	'96	102⅜	99½	99½	6.78	6.78
• Sr Nts[10] 9⅜s 2001	Jd	**A**	4/93	A–	X	BE	NC	....	....	....	....	....	150	B7	'91	No Sale		101	9.28	9.28
Sr Nts 8¼s 2002	Fa	**A**	4/93	A–	X	BE	NC	....	....	....	....	....	150	B7	'92	106⅞	101¾	101⅞	8.10	8.10
Sr Nts 6½s 2002	fA	**A**			X	BE	NC	....	....	....	....	....	250	B7	'97	102⅜	98⅛	98⅛	6.62	6.62
Sr Nts 6⅛s 2003	Fa	**A**			X	BE	NC	....	....	....	....	....	500	B7	'98	100½	96½	96½	6.35	6.35
Sr Nts 6¾s 2003	Ao15	**A**			X	BE	NC	....	....	....	....	....	200	B7	'93	102¾	97⅞	97⅞	6.90	6.90
Sr Nts 6.70s 2003	fA	**A**			X	BE	NC	....	....	....	....	....	200	B7	'93	102¾	97½	97½	6.87	6.87
Sr Nts 6⅝s 2004	Jj15	**A**			X	BE	NC	....	....	....	....	....	250	B7	'94	102½	97	97	6.83	6.83
Sr Nts 8¾s 2004	Ms15	**A**	4/93	A–	X	BE	NC	....	....	....	....	....	150	B7	'92	111¾	104⅜	104⅜	8.38	8.38
Sr Nts 6⅝s 2004	aO	**A**			X	BE	NC	....	....	....	....	....	250	B7	'97	102¾	96½	96½	6.87	6.87
Sr Nts 6.65s 2004	jD	**A**			X	BE	NC	....	....	....	....	....	150	B7	'97	102⅞	96⅝	96⅝	6.88	6.88
Sr Nts 6⅞s 2005	aO	**A**			X	BE	NC	....	....	....	....	....	150	B7	'95	104¼	96¼	96¼	7.14	7.14
Sr Nts 7¼s 2006	aO15	**A**			X	BE	NC	....	....	....	....	....	150	B7	'96	107	97	97	7.47	7.47
Sr Nts 7s 2007	Ms	**A**			X	BE	NC	....	....	....	....	....	350	B7	'97	104¾	95	95	7.37	7.37
Sr Nts 6¾s 2007	jD15	**A**			X	BE	NC	....	....	....	....	....	200	B7	'97	103⅝	93¼	93¼	7.24	7.24
F/R[11]M-T Nts 'B'[1] 2000	QFeb4	**A**			X	BE	NC	....	....	....	....	....	10.0	B7	'94	100	99⅝	100	....	....
F/R[11]M-T Nts 'B'[1] 2000	QMar	**A**			X	BE	NC	....	....	....	....	....	10.0	B7	'94	100	99⅝	99⅞	....	....
F/R[12]M-T Nts 'B' 5.78s 2000	QJun20	**A**			X	BE	NC	....	....	....	....	....	35.0	B7	'97	99⅞	99⅛	99¾	5.79	....
F/R[13]M-T Nts 'B' 5.41s 2000	QJul10	**A**			X	BE	NC	....	....	....	....	....	75.0	B7	'97	99⅞	99¼	99⅞	5.42	....
F/R[11] M-T Nts 'B' 2000	QJul3	**A**			X	BE	NC	....	....	....	....	....	35.0	B7	'97	99⅞	99¼	99⅞	....	....
F/R[11] M-T Nts'B' 2000	QAug25	**A**			X	BE	NC	....	....	....	....	....	100	B7	'97	99⅞	99⅛	99¾	....	....
F/R[14]M-T Nts 'B' 2000	QOct10	**A**			X	BE	NC	....	....	....	....	....	47.3	B7	'97	100¼	99⅝	100	....	....
F/R[15]M-T Nts 'B' 5.80s 2000	QJun12	**A**			X	BE	NC	....	....	....	....	....	75.0	B7	'97	99⅞	99⅛	99¾	5.81	....
M-T Nts 'B' 6.56s 2000	Jd20	**A**			X	BE	NC	....	....	....	....	....	100	B7	'97	101¼	100	100⅛	6.55	6.55
F/R[16]M-T Nts 'B' 2000	[17]Aug29	**A**			X	BE	NC	....	....	....	....	....	50.0	B7	'97	100⅛	99⅝	100	....	....
F/R[18]M-T Nts 'B' 2001	QJan8	**A**			X	BE	NC	....	....	....	....	....	50.0	B7	'97	99¾	99	99¾	....	....
M-T Nts 'B' 7s 2019	Fa26	**A**			X	BE	*■100	(2-26-02)	....	....	....	....	40.0	B7	'99	100¾	85⅞	87½	8.00	8.00
M-T Nts 'B' 8s 2019	jJ15	**A**			X	BE	100	(7-15-01)	....	....	....	....	65.0	B7	'99	101⅞	96¼	99	8.08	8.08

Uniform Footnote Explanations-See Page 260. Other: [1] Issued in min denom $100T. [2] Due 12-31-02. [3] Due 9-29-03. [4] Due 6-6-11. [5] Due 8-12-21. [6] Due 8-26-22. [7] See Southern National. [8] (HRO)On Chge of Ctrl at 101. [9] Max $87M red w/proceeds of Pub Eq Off'g. [10] Issued in min denom $25T. [11] Int adj qtrly. [12] Int to 3-20-98,adj qtrly. [13] Int to 4-13-98,adj qtrly. [14] Int adj qtrly(3 Mo LIBOR & 0.06%). [15] Int to 3-12-98,adj qtrly. [16] Int adj monthly. [17] Int pd monthly. [18] Int adj qtrly(2 yr CMT & 0.20%).

Title-Industry Code & Co. Finances (In Italics) / Individual Issue Statistics (Exchange)	Ind / Interest Dates	Fixed Charge Coverage 1996 / S&P Rating	1997 / Date of Last Rating Change	1998 / Prior Rating	Eligible	Year End / Bond Form	Million $ Cash & Equiv. / Redemption Provisions Regular Price	Curr. Assets / Regular (Begins) Thru	Curr. Liab. / Sinking Fund Price	Balance Sheet Date / Sinking Fund (Begins) Thru	L. Term Debt (Mil $) / Refund/Other Restriction Price	Refund/Other Restriction (Begins) Thru	Capital-ization (Mil $) / Outst'g (Mil $)	Total Debt % Capital / Underwriting Firm	Year	Price Range 1999 High	Low	Mo. End Price Sale(s) or Bid	Curr. Yield	Yield to Mat.
Beazer Homes USA	***13h***	***2.99***	***2.44***	***2.97***		***Sp***				***6-30-99***	***215.0***		***435.0***	***49.4***						
Sr Nts[1] 9s 2004	Ms	B+			Y	R	102.571	2-29-00	....	....	....	....	115	D4	'94	100⅛	94	96⅝	9.31	9.31
[2]***Beckman Instruments***	***43***	***7.16***	***d5.55***	***1.75***		***Dc***	***30.00***	***933.0***	***567.0***	***9-30-99***	***1017***		***1264***	***89.6***						
Deb[3] 7.05s 2026	Jd	NR	9/97	A		BE	Z100	(6-1-06)	....	....	....	....	100	G1	'96	100⅞	93	93⅛	7.57	7.57
Becton,Dickinson	***43***	***△10.08***	***△6.65***	***△6.00***		***Sp***	***64.60***	***1684***	***1329***	***9-30-99***	***954.0***		***3355***	***47.2***						
SF Deb 9¼s 2016	Jd	NR	6/97	A+		R	103.063	5-30-00	100	....	....	....	15.0	G1	'86	104⅛	103⅛	103⅛	8.97	8.97
Deb 8.70s 2025	Jj15	A+			X	BE	103.949	(1-15-05)	....	....	....	....	100	G1	'95	121	103½	105½	8.25	8.24
Deb 7s 2027	fA	A+			X	BE	NC	....	....	....	....	....	200	G1	'97	112⅝	89	90¼	7.76	7.75
Deb 6.70s 2028	fA	A+			X	BE	NC	....	....	....	....	....	200	G1	'98	108	85½	86⅞	7.71	7.71
Nts 8.80s 2001	Ms	A+			X	R	NC	....	....	....	....	....	100	G1	'91	107⅞	102¼	102¼	8.61	8.60
Nts 6.90s 2006	aO	A+			X	BE	NC	....	....	....	....	....	100	G1	'96	110¾	96⅞	96⅞	7.12	7.12
Nts 7.15s 2009	aO	A+			X	BE	[4]Z100	....	....	....	....	....	200	G1	'99	101¼	97⅛	97⅛	7.36	7.36
Bell[5]Atlantic-N.J.[6]	***67a***	***8.80***	***9.07***	***9.60***		***Dc***	***19.20***	***822.0***	***1497***	***6-30-99***	***1130***		***3694***	***48.2***						
Deb 5⅞s 2004	Fa	AA	4/97	AA+	X	BE	NC	....	....	....	....	....	250	M6	'94	103	95⅜	95⅜	6.16	6.16
Bell Atlantic-[6]PA[7]	***67a***	***6.92***	***5.83***	***6.79***		***Dc***	***18.70***	***822.0***	***1404***	***9-30-99***	***1429***		***3481***	***55.0***						
Deb 6s 2028	jD	AA			X	BE	NC	....	....	....	....	....	125	M2	'98	98⅞	79½	79½	7.55	7.55
Bell Tel. of Penna[8]	***67a***	***Now Bell Atlantic-PA,see***																		
Deb 4¾s 2001	Mn	AA	10/87	AA+	X	CR	100	....	....	....	....	....	50.0	F1	'61	98⅞	97⅛	97⅜	4.88	4.88
Deb 6⅝s 2002	mS15	AA			X	BE	NC	....	....	....	....	....	100	S1	'92	104½	99¼	99¼	6.68	6.67
Deb 4⅜s 2003	Fa	AA	10/87	AA+	X	CR	100	....	....	....	....	....	50.0	F1	'63	98	92⅝	92⅝	4.72	4.73
Deb 6⅛s 2003	Ms15	AA			X	BE	NC	....	....	....	....	....	150	S1	'93	103⅝	97½	97½	6.28	6.28
Deb 7⅜s 2007	jJ15	AA			X	BE	NC	....	....	....	....	....	150	F1	'92	113¼	99⅝	99⅝	7.40	7.40
Deb 6¾s 2008	Mn	AA	10/87	AA+	X	R	100.60	4-30-00	....	....	....	....	100	M6	'68	100⅞	96⅜	96⅜	7.00	7.00
• Deb 7⅛s 2012	Jj	AA	10/87	AA+	X	R	101.23	12-31-00	....	....	....	....	75.0	M6	'72	103⅜	94⅛	93¼	7.64	7.64
Deb 7.70s 2023	Jj15	AA			X	BE	103.234	(1-15-03)	....	....	....	....	100	M2	'93	109	95¼	95⅜	8.07	8.07
Deb[9] 8.35s 2030	jD15	AA			X	BE	NC	....	....	....	....	....	175	L3	'90	128¼	105¾	105⅞	7.89	7.89
Deb 8¾s 2031	fA15	AA			X	BE	NC	....	....	....	....	....	125	M2	'91	133⅞	110⅜	110½	7.92	7.92
Deb 7⅜s 2033	Ms15	AA			X	BE	104.28	(3-15-03)	....	....	....	....	225	F1	'93	108	91⅛	91¼	8.08	8.08
BellSouth Capital Funding	***25***	***Issued under support agreement w/BellSouth***																		
Deb[10] 6.04s 2026	mN15	AAA			X	BE	NC	....	....	....	....	....	300	M6	'96	104¾	98¼	98¼	6.15	6.15
• Deb[11] 7.12s 2097	jJ15	AAA			X	BE	[12]Z100	....	....	....	....	....	500	M6	'97	105½	105½	88⅛	8.08	8.08
BellSouth[13]Telecommunications[14]	***67***	***6.75***	***7.92***	***8.39***		***Dc***	***135.0***	***3625***	***6630***	***9-30-99***	***6145***		***17623***	***49.3***						
• Deb 5⅞s 2009	Jj15	AAA			X	R	NC	....	....	....	....	....	350	M6	'93	104¾	90¾	90⅜	6.50	6.50
• Amortizing[15]Deb[16] 6.30s 2015	jD15	AAA			X	BE	NC	....	....	....	....	....	338	S1	'95	No Sale		93⅝	6.73	....
• Deb 7s 2025	aO	AAA			X	BE	NC	....	....	....	....	....	300	M6	'95	113⅞	92⅝	s92⅞	7.54	7.54
• Deb 6⅜s 2028	Jd	AAA			X	BE	[4]Z100	....	....	....	....	....	500	L3	'98	104	84¼	84¼	7.57	7.57
• Deb 8¼s 2032	jJ	AAA			X	R	104.83	(7-1-02)	....	....	....	....	250	G1	'92	115⅞	101⅝	102½	8.05	8.05
• Deb 7⅞s 2032	fA	AAA			X	R	104.29	(8-1-02)	....	....	....	....	300	M6	'92	109⅛	97½	99¼	7.93	7.93
• Deb 7½s 2033	Jd15	AAA			X	R	104.75	(6-15-03)	....	....	....	....	300	G1	'93	109¾	94¼	s94⅜	7.95	7.95
• Deb 6¾s 2033	aO15	AAA			X	R	103.50	(10-15-03)	....	....	....	....	400	M6	'93	103¾	84¾	s85¼	7.92	7.92
• Deb 7⅝s 2035	Mn15	AAA			X	R	103.66	(5-15-05)	....	....	....	....	300	M6	'95	112⅛	94¾	s96½	7.90	7.90
• Deb[17] 5.85s 2045	mN15	AAA			X	BE	NC	....	....	....	....	....	300	M6	'95	No Sale		97	6.03	6.03
• Deb 7s 2095	jD	AAA			X	BE	NC	....	....	....	....	....	500	M6	'95	112	109	87⅝	7.99	7.99
• Nts 6½s 2000	Fa	AAA			X	R	NC	....	....	....	....	....	275	M6	'93	102	99⅝	99⅞	6.51	6.51
• Nts 6¼s 2003	Mn15	AAA			X	R	NC	....	....	....	....	....	450	M6	'93	104¾	97½	97¾	6.39	6.39
• Nts 6⅜s 2004	Jd15	AAA			X	R	NC	....	....	....	....	....	200	G1	'93	105⅛	97⅝	97⅜	6.55	6.55

Uniform Footnote Explanations-See Page 260. Other: [1] (HRO)On Chge of Ctrl at 101. [2] Now Beckman Coulter. [3] (HRO)On 6-1-06 at 100. [4] Red at greater of 100 or amt based on formula. [5] Was New Jersey Bell Tel, see. [6] Subsid of Bell Atlantic Corp. [7] See Bell Tel of Penna. [8] Now Bell Atlantic-Pennsylvania. [9] (HRO)On 12-15-00 & 02 at 100. [10] (HRO)On 11-15-01(06)at 100. [11] Co may red in whole,at 100,for Tax Event. [12] Greater of 100 or amt based on formula. [13] Subsid of BellSouth Corp. [14] See So'n Bell Tel & Tel. [15] Princ pyts due on int dates. [16] Trades as $901.34 princ amt at 6-15-99. [17] (HRO)On 11-15-00 at 100.

Title-Industry Code & Co. Finances (In Italics) / Exchange ↓ Individual Issue Statistics	Ind / Interest Dates	Fixed Charge Coverage 1996 / S&P Rating	1997 / Date of Last Rating Change	1998 / Prior Rating	Eligible ↓	Year End / Bond Form	Million $ Cash & Equiv. / Redemption Provisions Regular Price	Curr. Assets / Regular (Begins) Thru	Curr. Liab. / Sinking Fund Price	Balance Sheet Date / Sinking Fund (Begins) Thru	L. Term Debt (Mil $) / Refund/Other Restriction Price	Refund/Other Restriction (Begins) Thru	Capital-ization (Mil $) / Outst'g (Mil $)	Total Debt % Capital / Underwriting Firm	Underwriting Year	Price Range 1999 High	Price Range 1999 Low	Mo. End Price Sale(s) or Bid	Curr. Yield	Yield to Mat.
BellSouth Telecommunications (Cont.)																				
• Nts 7s 2005	Fa	AAA			X	R	NC	....	....	....	....	....	150	M6	'93	108¾	100	100⅛	6.99	6.99
• Nts 6½s 2005	Jd15	AAA			X	BE	NC	....	....	....	....	....	300	M6	'95	107	96⅛	96⅛	6.76	6.76
Bellwether Exploration	*49b*	*n/a*	*1.95*	*d2.67*		*Dc*	*2.23*	*22.50*	*17.30*	*9-30-99*	*118.0*		*192.0*	*52.1*						
Sr Nts[1] 10⅞s 2007	Ao	B–			Y	BE	105.4375	(4-1-02)	....	....	....	....	100	M5	'97	98	85	88	12.36	12.36
Belo(A.H.)Corp	*54c*	*5.93*	*2.68*	*2.42*		*Dc*	*30.78*	*289.1*	*181.7*	*9-30-99*	*1654*		*2932*	*54.2*						
Sr Deb 7¾s 2027	Jd	BBB–			X	BE	[2]Z100	....	....	....	....	....	200	M6	'97	109⅞	91⅞	94⅛	8.23	8.23
Sr Deb 7¼s 2027	mS15	BBB–			X	BE	[3]Z100	....	....	....	....	....	250	M2	'97	103⅞	86½	88¾	8.17	8.17
Sr Nts 6⅞s 2002	Jd	BBB–			X	BE	[2]Z100	....	....	....	....	....	250	M6	'97	103	98½	98½	6.98	6.98
Sr Nts 7⅛s 2007	Jd	BBB–			X	BE	[2]Z100	....	....	....	....	....	300	M6	'97	105⅝	94⅞	95⅛	7.49	7.49
Bemis Co.	*16d*	*13.50*	*10.26*	*9.52*		*Dc*	*25.00*	*596.9*	*266.0*	*9-30-99*	*367.0*		*1049*	*36.0*						
Nts 6.70s 2005	jJ	A			X	BE	NC	....	....	....	....	....	100	G1	'95	106½	97¼	97¼	6.89	6.89
Beneficial Corp	*25a*	*Merged into Household Intl,see Household Fin*																		
• Deb[4] 8.40s 2008	Mn15	A	1/89	A–	X	R	NC	....	....	....	....	....	47.7	B8	'78	110	106½	101½	8.28	8.27
M-T Nts 'H' 6.80s 2005	[5]jd15	A			X	BE	NC	....	....	....	....	....	25.0	S1	'97	104⅜	97	97	7.01	7.01
M-T Nts 'I' 6.27s 2001	[6]jd15	A			X	BE	NC	....	....	....	....	....	30.0	M5	'97	101¼	99¼	99¼	6.32	6.32
M-T Nts[7] 'I' 6.43s 2002	[8]jd15	A			X	BE	NC	....	....	....	....	....	39.0	S1	'97	101⅞	98⅞	98⅞	6.50	6.50
M-T Nts[7] 'I' 6.55s 2003	[9]jd15	A			X	BE	NC	....	....	....	....	....	32.0	S1	'97	102⅝	97⅞	97⅞	6.69	6.69
M-T Nts[7] 'I' 6.85s 2007	[10]jd15	A			X	BE	NC	....	....	....	....	....	31.0	S1	'97	105½	95⅞	95⅞	7.14	7.14
M-T Nts[7] 'I' 6⅝s 2004	jd15	A			X	BE	NC	....	....	....	....	....	30.0	S1	'97	103¼	97	97	6.83	6.83
Bergen Brunswig	*21d*	*5.20*	*5.68*	*15.40*		*Sp*	*113.0*	*3781*	*2924*	*6-30-99*	*1075*		*2955*	*48.2*						
• Sr Nts 7⅜s 2003	Jj15	BBB–	12/99	BBB+	X	R	NC	....	....	....	....	....	150	M2	'93	104	99¼	96¼	7.66	7.66
Sr Nts 7¼s 2005	Jd	BBB–	12/99	BBB+	X	R	NC	....	....	....	....	....	100	M2	'95	108¼	90¾	92	7.88	7.88
Berkley(W.R.)Corp	*35c*	*4.60*	*3.64*	*2.29*		*Dc*				*9-30-99*	*593.0*		*1282*	*46.3*						
Deb 9⅞s 2008	Mn15	BBB+	5/99	A	X	R	NC	....	....	....	....	....	100	M2	'88	122¼	111	111	8.90	8.89
Deb 8.70s 2022	Jj	BBB+	5/99	A	X	R	NC	....	....	....	....	....	100	M6	'92	117⅜	99	99⅛	8.78	8.77
Nts[11] 6.31s 2000	[12]jd15	BBB+	5/99	A	X	BE	NC	....	....	....	....	....	25.0	M2	'93	100⅞	100	100	6.31	6.31
Nts[11] 6.71s 2003	[13]jd15	BBB+	5/99	A	X	BE	NC	....	....	....	....	....	25.0	M2	'93	103¾	98⅜	98⅜	6.82	6.82
Nts 6¼s 2006	Jj15	BBB+	5/99	A	X	BE	NC	....	....	....	....	....	100	M2	'96	98¾	91½	91⅝	6.82	6.82
Berkshire Hathaway[14]	*35c*	*38.06*	*26.27*	*40.58*		*Dc*				*9-30-99*	*2448*		*59159*	*4.1*						
Deb 9¾s 2018	Jj15	AAA	2/89	AA+	X	R	103.90	1-14-01	100	....	....	....	10.0	S1	'88	108	104½	104½	9.33	9.33
[15]Berry Plastics Corp	*52*	*0.85*	*0.55*	*0.83*		*Dc*	*2.99*	*78.80*	*67.00*	*7-3-99*	*300.0*		*208.0*	*160.0*						
Sr Sub Nts[1] 12¼s 2004	Ao15	B–			Y	R	106.125	4-14-00	....	....	....	....	[16]100	D6	'94	106¼	101	102½	11.95	11.95
Bethlehem Steel Corp[17]	*66a*	*2.37*	*4.51*	*3.70*		*Dc*	*103.0*	*1301*	*1056*	*9-30-99*	*724.0*		*2192*	*39.6*						
• SF Deb 8⅜s 2001	Ms	BB–	6/98	B+	Y	R	100	....	100	....	....	....	41.6	K3	'76	102⅝	96	s98⅜	8.51	8.51
• SF Deb 8.45s 2005	Ms	BB–	6/98	B+	Y	R	100.15	2-28-00	100	....	....	....	90.7	K3	'75	101⅞	92	s94⅜	8.95	8.95
Sr[1]Nts 10⅜s 2003	mS	BB–	6/98	B+	Y	R	NC	....	....	....	....	....	105	S1	'93	109	100	100¾	10.30	10.30
Beverly Enterprises	*30*	*2.38*	*2.31*	*1.46*		*Dc*	*17.50*	*492.0*	*345.0*	*9-30-99*	*776.0*		*1466*	*54.6*						
• Sr Nts[18] 9s 2006	Fa15	B+			Y	R	104.50	(2-15-01)	....	....	....	....	180	D6	'96	106	83	94¼	9.55	9.55
BJ Services[19]	*49e*	*△6.01*	*△8.85*	*△0.83*		*Sp*	*3.92*	*439.0*	*445.0*	*9-30-99*	*423.0*		*1389*	*33.7*						
• Nts 'B' 7s 2006	Fa	BBB+	6/98	BBB	X	BE	NC	....	....	....	....	....	125	Exch.	'96	No Sale		96⅛	7.28	7.28
Black & Decker Corp	*13e*	*2.28*	*3.62*	*4.16*		*Dc*	*142.5*	*2059*	*1649*	*10-3-99*	*1058*		*1734*	*64.4*						
Nts 6⅝s 2000	mN15	BBB	4/99	BBB–	X	R	NC	....	....	....	....	....	250	G1	'93	101⅝	99¾	99¾	6.64	6.64
Nts 7½s 2003	Ao	BBB	4/99	BBB–	X	R	NC	....	....	....	....	....	429	L3	'93	106	100¼	100¼	7.48	7.48
Nts 7s 2006	Fa	BBB	4/99	BBB–	X	R	NC	....	....	....	....	....	207	L3	'94	105½	96⅛	96⅛	7.28	7.28
Black Hills Corp	*72a*	*4.27*	*4.29*	*3.55*		*Dc*	*25.30*	*174.0*	*169.0*	*9-30-99*	*161.0*		*374.0*	*44.7*						
1st 'AB' 8.30s 2024	mS	A+	10/97	A	X	R	104.04	(9-1-04)	....	....	....	....	45.0	M2	'94	113⅞	100½	100⅝	8.25	8.25

Uniform Footnote Explanations-See Page 260. Other: [1] (HRO)On Chge of Ctrl at 101. [2] Greater of 100 or amt based on formula. [3] Red at greater of 100 or amt based on formula. [4] (HRO)On ea Dec 15 to 2008 at 100. [5] Due 7-22-05. [6] Due 7-9-01. [7] Issued in min denom $25T. [8] Due 4-10-02. [9] Due 9-26-03. [10] Due 10-3-07. [11] Issued in min denom $100T. [12] Due 3-6-00. [13] Due 3-4-00. [14] See GEICO Corp. [15] Subsid & data of BPC Holding Corp. [16] Incl disc. [17] See Lukens Inc. [18] (HRO)On Chge of Ctrl at 100. [19] Was Western Co of No Amer.

Title-Industry Code & Co. Finances (In Italics) / Exchange ↓ Individual Issue Statistics	Ind / Interest Dates	Fixed Charge Coverage 1996 / S&P Rating	1997 / Date of Last Rating Change	1998 / Prior Rating	Eligible ↓	Year End / Bond Form	Million $ Cash & Equiv. / Redemption Provisions Regular Price	Curr. Assets / Regular (Begins) Thru	Curr. Liab. / Sinking Fund Price	Balance Sheet Date / Sinking Fund (Begins) Thru	L. Term Debt (Mil $) / Refund/Other Restriction Price	Refund/Other Restriction (Begins) Thru	Capital-ization (Mil $) / Outst'g (Mil $)	Total Debt % Capital / Underwriting Firm	Underwriting Year	Price Range 1999 High	Price Range 1999 Low	Mo. End Price Sale(s) or Bid	Curr. Yield	Yield to Mat.
***Black Hills Corp** (Cont.)*																				
1st[1]'AC' 8.06s 2010	Fa	**A+**	10/97	A	X	R	NC	....	....	....	....	....	30.0	M2	'95	120⅛	103¼	103¼	7.81	7.80
1st 'AD' 6½s 2002	jJ15	**A+**	10/97	A	X	R	NC	....	....	....	....	....	15.0	P1	'95	103⅝	98¾	98¾	6.58	6.58
[2]***Block Fin'l***	***25h***	***△n/a***	***△6.38***	***△6.53***		***Ap***	***212.0***	***1108***	***868.2***	***10-31-99***	***353.0***		***2303***	***64.5***						
• Sr Nts[3] 6¾s 2004	mN	**A**			X	BE	NC	....	....	....	....	....	250	S1	'97	102	95⅛	95¼	7.09	7.09
Blue Bird Body Co[4]	***9a***	***3.37***	***1.32***	***1.96***		***Oc***	***7.31***	***258.0***	***139.0***	***7-31-99***	***316.0***		***302.0***	***114.0***						
Sr[5]Sub[6]Nts 'B' 11¾s 2002	Ao15	**NR**	1/97	B		R	101.469	4-14-00	100	(4-15-00)	....	....	75.0	M2	'92	103⅜	100⅜	100⅜	11.71	11.71
Blyth Industries	***34***	***21.08***	***20.60***	***19.34***		***Ja***	***13.53***	***370.7***	***171.0***	***10-31-99***	***196.0***		***580.0***	***42.1***						
Sr Nts 7.90s 2009	aO	**BBB–**			X	BE	[7]Z100	....	....	....	....	....	150	D6	'99	101¾	95⅜	95⅜	8.28	8.28
Boatmen's Bancshares	***10***	***Merged into NationsBank Corp,see***																		
Sub Nts 9¼s 2001	mN	**A**	12/96	A–	X	R	NC	....	....	....	....	....	150	M6	'89	109⅜	103⅜	103⅜	8.95	8.95
Sub Nts 6¾s 2003	Ms15	**A**	12/96	A–	X	BE	NC	....	....	....	....	....	100	G1	'93	104⅛	98⅜	98⅜	6.86	6.86
Sub Nts 8⅝s 2003	mN15	**A**	12/96	A–	X	R	NC	....	....	....	....	....	50.0	M6	'91	112⅜	104⅛	104⅛	8.28	8.28
Sub Nts 7⅝s 2004	aO	**A**	12/96	A–	X	BE	NC	....	....	....	....	....	100	G1	'92	109	100⅝	100⅝	7.58	7.58
Boeing Capital[8]	***25***	***n/a***	***1.70***	***1.83***		***Dc***	***20.20***			***6-30-99***	***1733***		***2317***	***82.9***						
M-T Nts[9]'X' 6.30s 2001	[10]ms15	**AA–**	11/99	A+	X	BE	NC	....	....	....	....	....	20.0	C1	'97	100¾	98⅞	99⅛	6.36	6.36
M-T Nts[9]'X' 6.325s 2001	[11]ms15	**AA–**	11/99	A+	X	BE	NC	....	....	....	....	....	20.0	C1	'97	100¾	98⅜	98¾	6.41	6.40
M-T Nts[9]'X' 6.35s 2001	[11]ms15	**AA–**	11/99	A+	X	BE	NC	....	....	....	....	....	20.0	P1	'97	100⅞	98⅜	98⅞	6.42	6.42
M-T Nts[9]'X' 6.44s 2004	[12]ms15	**AA–**	11/99	A+	X	BE	NC	....	....	....	....	....	20.0	P1	'97	100¾	94⅜	95⅞	6.72	6.72
Boeing Co[13]	***2a***	***7.43***	***3.06***	***3.91***		***Dc***	***2773***	***16720***	***14171***	***9-30-99***	***5909***		***19583***	***35.3***						
Deb 8.10s 2006	mN15	**AA–**	12/98	AA	X	R	NC	....	....	....	....	....	175	F1	'91	115⅝	102⅜	102⅜	7.91	7.91
Deb 8¾s 2021	fA15	**AA–**	12/98	AA	X	R	NC	....	....	....	....	....	400	F1	'91	127⅛	108½	108⅝	8.06	8.05
Deb[14] 7.95s 2024	fA15	**AA–**	12/98	AA	X	R	NC	....	....	....	....	....	300	F1	'92	117½	103⅞	103⅞	7.65	7.65
Deb 7¼s 2025	Jd15	**AA–**	12/98	AA	X	R	NC	....	....	....	....	....	250	F1	'93	110⅞	93⅜	93½	7.75	7.75
Deb 8¾s 2031	mS15	**AA–**	12/98	AA	X	R	NC	....	....	....	....	....	250	F1	'91	130⅝	109⅛	109¼	8.01	8.01
Deb 8⅝s 2031	Mn15	**AA–**	12/98	AA	X	R	NC	....	....	....	....	....	175	F1	'91	129⅛	107⅝	107¾	8.00	8.00
Deb[15] 7½s 2042	fA15	**AA–**	12/98	AA	X	R	100	(8-15-07)	....	....	....	....	100	Co.	'92	113¼	93	93⅛	8.05	8.05
Deb 7⅞s 2043	Ao15	**AA–**	12/98	AA	X	R	NC	....	....	....	....	....	175	S1	'93	119¾	98⅝	98¾	7.97	7.97
Deb 6⅞s 2043	aO15	**AA–**	12/98	AA	X	R	NC	....	....	....	....	....	125	F1	'93	104¼	85⅜	85⅜	8.05	8.05
Nts 6.35s 2003	Jd15	**AA–**	12/98	AA	X	R	NC	....	....	....	....	....	300	G1	'93	103⅜	97¼	97¼	6.53	6.53
Boise Cascade[16]	***50***	***0.93***	***0.77***	***1.37***		***Dc***	***67.90***	***70.10***	***1204***	***9-30-99***	***1721***		***3372***	***54.2***						
Deb[17] 9.45s 2009	mN	**BB+**	9/98	BBB–	Y	R	NC	....	....	....	....	....	150	G1	'89	115⅛	103⅞	103⅞	9.10	9.10
Deb 7.35s 2016	Fa	**BB+**	9/98	BBB–	Y	BE	NC	....	....	....	....	....	125	S1	'96	95⅜	85½	85½	8.60	8.59
Nts[17] 9.90s 2000	Ms15	**BB+**	9/98	BBB–	Y	R	NC	....	....	....	....	....	100	G1	'90	103¼	100½	100½	9.85	9.85
[17]Nts[18] 9.85s 2002	Jd15	**BB+**	9/98	BBB–	Y	R	NC	....	....	....	....	....	125	F1	'90	108¼	103⅜	103⅜	9.53	9.53
M-T Nts 'A' 7.15s 2001	[19]fa	**BB+**	9/98	BBB–	Y	BE	NC	....	....	....	....	....	25.0	G1	'97	100¼	98½	99	7.22	7.22
M-T Nts 'A' 7.66s 2005	[20]fa	**BB+**	9/98	BBB–	Y	BE	NC	....	....	....	....	....	22.0	G1	'97	100	95¾	96¼	7.96	7.96
M-T Nts 'A' 7.48s 2005	[21]fa	**BB+**	9/98	BBB–	Y	BE	NC	....	....	....	....	....	35.0	G1	'97	99⅛	94⅞	95⅜	7.84	7.84
Boise Cascade Office Products	***48***	***13.08***	***5.95***	***4.70***		***Dc***	***19.56***	***730.4***	***547.5***	***9-30-99***	***281.0***		***937.0***	***36.8***						
Nts 7.05s 2005	Mn15	**BB+**	9/98	BBB–	Y	BE	[22]Z100	....	....	....	....	....	150	G1	'98	98¼	93¼	93¼	7.56	7.56
Borden Chem & Plastic/BCP Fin[23]	***14***	***1.22***	***1.26***	***d0.46***		***Dc***	***6.91***	***132.0***	***77.40***	***9-30-99***	***258.0***		***380.0***	***67.9***						
Nts[24] 9½s 2005	Mn	**B+**	10/98	BB	Y	R	104	(5-1-00)	....	....	....	....	200	C5	'95	100½	69	93	10.22	10.21
Borden (Co.) Inc.	***26***	***1.90***	***1.42***	***1.96***		***Dc***	***0.19***	***0.73***	***0.87***	***9-30-99***	***554.0***		***1108***	***90.7***						
• SF Deb 8⅜s 2016	Ao15	**BB+**	4/96	BBB–	Y	R	100	(4-15-06)	100	(4-15-07)	....	....	78.5	S1	'86	102⅞	67	82⅝	10.14	10.14
SF Deb[17] 9¼s 2019	Jd15	**BB+**	4/96	BBB–	Y	R	103.75	6-14-00	100	(6-15-00)	....	....	48.7	F1	'89	100¾	87⅝	87⅝	10.56	10.55
Deb 9.20s 2021	Ms15	**BB+**	4/96	BBB–	Y	R	NC	....	....	....	....	....	117	F1	'91	101½	90½	90⅝	10.15	10.15

Uniform Footnote Explanations-See Page 260. Other: [1] (HRO)On 2-1-02 at 100. [2] Subsid & data of Block (H & R) Inc. [3] Gtd by Block (H&R) Inc. [4] Gtd by & data of Blue Bird Corp. [5] Gtd on Sr Subord basis by Blue Bird Corp. [6] Co must offer repurch at 101 on Chge in Ctrl. [7] Plus Make-Whole Amt. [8] See McDonnell-Douglas Finance. [9] Issued in min denom $100T. [10] Due 2-26-01. [11] Due 7-26-01. [12] Due 12-20-04. [13] See McDonnell Douglas. [14] (HRO)At 100 on 8-15-2012. [15] (HRO)Fr 8-15-07 at 96. [16] See Amer & Foreign Pwr. [17] (HRO)At 100 for Designated Event&Rat'g Decline. [18] Co may red in whole at 100 if 80% outstg put. [19] Due 5-15-01. [20] Due 5-27-05. [21] Due 6-15-05. [22] Red at greater of 100 or amt based on formula. [23] Gtd by & data of Borden Chem&Plastics LP. [24] (HRO)On Chge of Ctrl at 101.

Title-Industry Code & Co. Finances (In Italics) / Exchange, Individual Issue Statistics	Ind / Interest Dates	Fixed Charge Coverage 1996 / S&P Rating	1997 / Date of Last Rating Change	1998 / Prior Rating	Eligible	Year End / Bond Form	Million $ Cash & Equiv. / Redemption Provisions: Regular Price	Curr. Assets / Regular (Begins) Thru	Curr. Liab. / Sinking Fund Price	Balance Sheet Date / Sinking Fund (Begins) Thru	L. Term Debt (Mil $) / Refund/Other Restriction Price	Refund/Other Restriction (Begins) Thru	Capital-ization (Mil $) / Outst'g (Mil $)	Total Debt % Capital / Underwriting Firm	Underwriting Year	Price Range 1999 High	Low	Mo. End Price Sale(s) or Bid	Curr. Yield	Yield to Mat.
Borden (Co.) Inc. (Cont.)																				
Deb 7⅞s 2023	Fa15	BB+	4/96	BBB–	Y	BE	NC	....	....	....	....	....	250	F1	'93	89¼	78¾	78⅞	9.98	9.98
Borg-Warner Automotive	***8***	***2.95***	***7.13***	***5.99***		***Dc***	***25.20***	***668.4***	***563.5***	***9-30-99***	***777.0***		***1075***	***33.4***						
• Sr Nts 7s 2006	mN	BBB+			X	BE	NC	....	....	....	....	....	150	M2	'96	No Sale		95½	7.33	7.33
Sr Nts 6½s 2009	Fa15	BBB+			X	BE	[1]Z100	....	....	....	....	....	200	M2	'99	100¼	90¾	90¾	7.16	7.16
Sr Nts 8s 2019	aO	BBB+			X	BE	[1]Z100	....	....	....	....	....	150	M2	'99	101	96⅝	96⅝	8.28	8.28
Sr Nts 7⅛s 2029	Fa15	BBB+			X	BE	[1]Z100	....	....	....	....	....	200	M2	'99	99⅝	86¼	86⅝	8.25	8.25
Boston Edison[2]	***72a***	***3.08***	***3.23***	***3.32***		***Dc***	***59.60***	***573.0***	***522.0***	***9-30-99***	***614.0***		***160.0***	***48.7***						
Deb 6.80s 2000	Fa	A–	8/98	BBB	X	R	NC	....	....	....	....	....	65.0	G1	'93	101¼	100	100	6.80	6.80
Deb 6.05s 2000	fA15	A–	8/98	BBB	X	R	NC	....	....	....	....	....	100	G1	'93	100⅞	99½	99⅝	6.07	6.07
Deb 6.80s 2003	Ms15	A–	8/98	BBB	X	R	NC	....	....	....	....	....	150	G1	'93	104¼	98⅜	98⅜	6.91	6.91
Deb 7.80s 2010	Mn15	A–	8/98	BBB	X	R	NC	....	....	....	....	....	125	G1	'95	115⅝	99¼	99⅜	7.85	7.85
Deb 9⅞s 2020	Jd	A–	8/98	BBB	X	R	104.483	(6-1-00)	....	....	....	....	100	G1	'90	109	104¼	105⅛	9.39	9.39
Deb 9⅜s 2021	fA15	A–	8/98	BBB	X	R	104.612	(8-15-01)	....	....	....	....	115	G1	'91	112¼	104½	105	8.93	8.93
Deb 8¼s 2022	mS15	A–	8/98	BBB	X	R	103.78	(9-15-02)	....	....	....	....	60.0	G1	'92	110⅛	95⅝	96⅛	8.58	8.58
Deb 7.80s 2023	Ms15	A–	8/98	BBB	X	R	103.73	(3-16-03)	....	....	....	....	200	G1	'93	106¾	92⅜	93	8.39	8.39
Boston Gas[3]	***73b***	***3.74***	***4.40***	***4.45***		***Dc***	***4.22***	***129.0***	***54.90***	***9-30-99***	***267.0***		***565.0***	***47.4***						
M-T Nts A[4] 9.05s 2021	ao	A			X	BE	NC	....	....	....	....	....	15.0	F1	'91	128⅝	108½	108⅝	8.33	8.33
M-T Nts A[4] 8.33s 2022	[5]ao	A			X	BE	NC	....	....	....	....	....	10.0	F1	'92	120¼	101⅛	101¼	8.23	8.23
M-T Nts A[4] 8.33s 2018	[6]ao	A			X	BE	NC	....	....	....	....	....	10.0	F1	'92	119	101¼	101⅜	8.22	8.22
M-T Nts A[4] 8.33s 2017	[7]ao	A			X	BE	NC	....	....	....	....	....	8.00		'92	118⅝	101⅜	101⅜	8.22	8.22
M-T Nts B[4] 6.93s 2014	[8]ao	A			X	BE	NC	....	....	....	....	....	5.00	F1	'94	109⅝	91⅞	91⅞	7.54	7.54
M-T Nts B[4] 6.93s 2016	[9]ao	A			X	BE	NC	....	....	....	....	....	5.00	F1	'94	103¼	88⅝	88¾	7.81	7.81
M-T Nts B[4] 6.93s 2016	Ao	A			X	BE	NC	....	....	....	....	....	10.0	F1	'94	103¼	88⅛	88⅝	7.82	7.82
M-T Nts B[4] 6.93s 2019	[10]ao	A			X	BE	NC	....	....	....	....	....	10.0	F1	'94	103⅜	87½	87⅝	7.91	7.91
M-T Nts B[4] 6.93s 2024	[11]ao	A			X	BE	NC	....	....	....	....	....	6.00	F1	'94	103⅞	86⅞	86⅞	7.98	7.98
Boston Scientific	***43***	***27.55***	***19.11***	***d3.30***		***Dc***	***72.00***	***1095***	***1042***	***9-30-99***	***761.0***		***3073***	***43.0***						
Nts 6⅝s 2005	Ms15	BBB	9/98	A–	X	BE	NC	....	....	....	....	....	500	L3	'98	97½	92⅛	92⅛	7.19	7.19
Bowater, Inc.	***50***	***5.95***	***2.32***	***2.56***		***Dc***	***70.00***	***648.0***	***378.0***	***9-30-99***	***1494***		***3429***	***44.1***						
Deb[12] 9s 2009	fA	BBB	10/95	BBB–	X	R	NC	....	....	....	[13]Z100	....	250	F1	'89	120½	105⅝	105⅝	8.52	8.52
Deb 9½s 2012	aO15	BBB	10/95	BBB–	X	R	NC	....	....	....	....	....	125	F1	'92	129¼	109	109	8.72	8.72
Deb 9⅜s 2021	jD15	BBB	10/95	BBB–	X	R	NC	....	....	....	....	....	200	F1	'91	127⅝	108½	108⅝	8.63	8.63
Nts 8½s 2001	jD15	BBB	10/95	BBB–	X	R	NC	....	....	....	....	....	18.1	F1	'91	106⅞	101⅝	101⅝	8.36	8.36
Boyd Gaming	***40i***	***[14]1.95***	***1.55***	***1.75***		***Dc***	***63.95***	***125.3***	***114.5***	***9-30-99***	***714.0***		***981.0***	***74.8***						
• Sr Nts 9¼s 2003	aO	BB–	6/99	BB	Y	BE	NC	....	....	....	....	....	200	S1	'96	107¾	98½	102	9.07	9.07
• Sr Sub Nts[15] 9½s 2007	jJ15	B+	6/99	BB–	Y	BE	104.75	(7-15-02)	....	....	....	....	250	Exch.	'97	105¼	96¾	98⅛	9.68	9.68
Boyds Collection	***37***	***n/a***	***n/a***	***n/a***		***Dc***	***8.66***	***61.40***	***12.60***	***6-30-99***	***256.0***		***273.0***	***97.0***						
Sr Sub Nts[15]'B' 9s 2008	Mn15	B–			Y	BE	[16]Z100	5-15-03	....	....	[17]Z109	5-14-01	99.0	Exch.	'99	98¼	87⅞	95	9.47	9.47
Bradley Operating L.P.[18]	***57***	***n/a***	***2.45***	***2.20***		***Dc***				***6-30-99***	***422.0***		***935.0***	***45.1***						
Nts 7s 2004	mN15	BBB–			X	BE	[19]Z100	....	....	....	....	....	100	P1	'97	98⅛	93¼	93¼	7.51	7.51
Nts 7.20s 2008	Jj15	BBB–			X	BE	[1]Z100	....	....	....	....	....	100	P1	'98	97⅛	89⅜	89⅜	8.06	8.05
Briggs & Stratton	***41c***	***Δ11.05***	***Δ6.45***	***Δ10.97***		***Je***	***12.97***	***497.6***	***332.3***	***9-26-99***	***113.0***		***467.0***	***27.4***						
Nts 7¼s 2007	mS15	BBB+			X	BE	[20]Z100	....	....	....	....	....	100	C5	'97	107½	96½	96½	7.51	7.51
Bristol-Myers Squibb	***21a***	***43.99***	***38.98***	***33.91***		***Dc***	***2690***	***8957***	***5401***	***9-30-99***	***1331***		***10284***	***17.9***						
Deb 7.15s 2023	Jd15	AAA			X	BE	NC	....	....	....	....	....	343	S1	'93	115½	95½	97¼	7.35	7.35
Deb 6.80s 2026	mN15	AAA			X	BE	NC	....	....	....	....	....	350	G1	'96	111⅜	91	92¾	7.33	7.33

Uniform Footnote Explanations-See Page 260. Other: [1] Red at greater of 100 or amt based on formula. [2] Subsid of NSTAR. [3] Contr by East'n Gas & Fuel Assoc. [4] Issued in min denom $100T. [5] Due 7-5-22. [6] Due 7-10-18. [7] Due 7-10-17. [8] Due 1-15-14. [9] Due 1-15-16. [10] Due 1-15-19. [11] Due 1-15-24. [12] (HRO)At 100 for Designated Event&Rat'g Decline. [13] Co may red in whole if 90% outstg put. [14] Fiscal Jun'96 & prior. [15] (HRO)On Chge of Ctrl at 101. [16] On Chge of Ctrl. [17] Max $39M red w/proceeds of Pub Eq Off'g. [18] Subsid of Bradley Real Estate. [19] Plus Make-Whole Amt. [20] Greater of 100 or amt based on formula.

Title-Industry Code & Co. Finances (In Italics) / Individual Issue Statistics: Exchange	Ind / Interest Dates	Fixed Charge Coverage 1996 / S&P Rating	1997 / Date of Last Rating Change	1998 / Prior Rating	Year End / Eligible	Bond Form	Million $ Cash & Equiv. / Redemption Provisions: Regular Price	Curr. Assets / Regular (Begins) Thru	Curr. Liab. / Sinking Fund Price	Balance Sheet Date / Sinking Fund (Begins) Thru	L. Term Debt (Mil $) / Refund/Other Restriction Price	Refund/Other Restriction (Begins) Thru	Capital-ization (Mil $) / Outst'g (Mil $)	Total Debt % Capital / Underwriting Firm	Underwriting Year	Price Range 1999 High	Low	Mo. End Price Sale(s) or Bid	Curr. Yield	Yield to Mat.
***Bristol-Myers Squibb** (Cont.)*																				
Deb 6⅞s 2097	fA	**AAA**			X	BE	[1]Z100	....	....	....	....	....	300	G1	'97	111¾	88⅛	90	7.64	7.64
Brown Shoe[2]	***39b***	***2.42***	***0.90***	***2.04***	***Ja***		***47.70***	***522.0***	***255.0***	***10-30-99***	***162.0***		***434.0***	***48.4***						
• Sr Nts[3] 9½s 2006	aO15	**BB**			Y	BE	104.75	(10-15-01)	....	....	....	....	100	S7	'96	107¾	100½	s101¼	9.38	9.38
Browning-Ferris Ind	***53***	***Merged into Allied Waste,see***																		
Deb 9¼s 2021	Mn	**BB–**	7/99	A–	Y	BE	NC	....	....	....	....	....	99.5	S7	'91	120⅛	89⅞	89⅞	10.29	10.29
Deb 7.40s 2035	mS15	**BB–**	7/99	A–	Y	BE	[4]Z100	....	....	....	....	....	360	M6	'95	100⅛	70¾	70¾	10.46	10.46
Sr Nts 6.10s 2003	Jj15	**BB–**	7/99	A–	Y	BE	NC	....	....	....	....	....	200	M5	'96	99⅜	89⅞	90⅝	6.73	6.73
Sr Nts 7⅞s 2005	Ms15	**BB–**	7/99	A–	Y	BE	NC	....	....	....	....	....	300	L3	'95	107⅝	91⅜	91⅝	8.59	8.59
Sr Nts 6⅜s 2008	Jj15	**BB–**	7/99	A–	Y	BE	NC	....	....	....	....	....	161	M5	'96	99	80⅜	80⅜	7.93	7.93
Brunswick Corp	***40a***	***9.69***	***7.52***	***6.48***	***Dc***		***122.9***	***1586***	***1048***	***9-30-99***	***627.0***		***2228***	***35.6***						
Deb 7⅜s 2023	mS	**BBB+**			X	R	NC	....	....	....	....	....	125	M2	'93	102	89⅜	89½	8.24	8.24
Nts 6¾s 2006	jD15	**BBB+**			X	BE	NC	....	....	....	....	....	250	M2	'96	102	93¼	93¼	7.24	7.24
Nts 7⅛s 2027	fA	**BBB+**			X	BE	[1]Z100	....	....	....	....	....	200	M2	'97	98½	86⅝	86¾	8.21	8.21
[5]Buckeye Cellulose	***50***	***△3.80***	***△3.28***	***△2.79***	***Je***		***6.08***	***205.0***	***64.80***	***9-30-99***	***433.0***		***627.0***	***69.1***						
Sr Sub[3]Nts 8½s 2005	jD15	**BB–**			Y	R	104.25	(12-15-00)	....	....	....	....	150	M2	'95	103¾	95⅞	97¼	8.74	8.74
Sr Sub Nts[3] 9¼s 2008	mS15	**BB–**			Y	R	104.625	(9-15-01)	....	....	....	....	100	S1	'96	106½	98¼	100⅞	9.17	9.17
Burlington Industries	***68a***	***△2.80***	***△3.12***	***△1.07***	***Sp***		***35.70***	***634.0***	***202.0***	***10-2-99***	***881.0***		***1510***	***58.3***						
Deb[6] 7¼s 2027	fA	**BB+**	9/99	BBB–	Y	BE	[7]100	....	....	....	....	....	150	M6	'97	102¼	85¼	85¼	8.50	8.50
Nts 7¼s 2005	mS15	**BB+**	9/99	BBB–	Y	BE	NC	....	....	....	....	....	150	M6	'95	106⅝	85⅞	85⅞	8.44	8.44
Burlington Northern	***55***	***Merged into Burlington No'n Santa Fe,see***																		
Deb 8¾s 2022	Fa25	**BBB+**	12/98	BBB	X	BE	NC	....	....	....	....	....	200	M2	'92	125	106½	106⅝	8.21	8.21
Deb 7½s 2023	jJ15	**BBB+**	12/98	BBB	X	BE	103.02	(7-15-03)	....	....	....	....	150	M2	'93	106⅜	91½	91⅝	8.19	8.18
Nts 7s 2002	fA	**BBB+**	12/98	BBB	X	BE	NC	....	....	....	....	....	150	M2	'92	105	100	100	7.00	7.00
Burlington[8]Northern[9]R.R.	***55***	***17.57***	***5.08***	***11.89***	***Dc***		***114.0***	***1199***	***2189***	***6-30-99***	***4892***		***13803***	***36.6***						
• Con Mtg H 9¼s 2006	aO	**BBB+**	12/98	BBB	X	R	NC	....	....	....	....	....	275	M6	'86	118	107	107¾	8.58	8.58
• Con Mtg K 6.55s 2020	Jj	**BBB+**	12/98	BBB	X	R	NC	....	....	....	....	....	3.98	Exch.	'90	100⅞	94¼	82½	7.94	7.94
• Con Mtg L 3.80s 2020	Jj	**BBB+**	12/98	BBB	X	R	NC	....	....	....	....	....	6.20	Exch.	'90	63½	52	50¼	7.56	7.56
• Con Mtg M 3.20s 2045	QJan	**BBB+**	12/98	BBB	X	CR	NC	....	....	....	....	....	13.0	Exch.		53¾	40½	41	7.80	7.80
• Con Mtg N 8.15s 2020	QJan	**BBB+**	12/98	BBB	X	R	NC	....	....	....	....	....	2.51	Exch.	'91	111¾	105	96	8.49	8.49
• Con Mtg O 6.55s 2020	Jj	**BBB+**	12/98	BBB	X	R	NC	....	....	....	....	....	15.4	Exch.	'91	100	82	82½	7.94	7.94
• Con Mtg P 8.15s 2020	Jj	**BBB+**	12/98	BBB	X	R	NC	....	....	....	....	....	5.57	Exch.	'91	111	99	99¼	8.21	8.21
Burlington Northern Santa Fe[10]	***55***	***5.70***	***5.26***	***5.89***	***Dc***		***24.00***	***1115***	***2070***	***9-30-99***	***5619***		***13800***	***41.9***						
Deb 6⅞s 2016	Fa15	**BBB+**	12/98	BBB	X	BE	NC	....	....	....	....	....	175	M6	'96	106⅜	90¼	91⅜	7.52	7.52
Deb 7s 2025	jD15	**BBB+**	12/98	BBB	X	BE	[11]Z100	....	....	....	....	....	350	G1	'95	107⅞	89	90	7.78	7.78
Deb 6⅞s 2027	jD	**BBB+**	12/98	BBB	X	BE	[12]Z100	....	....	....	....	....	200	C1	'97	106⅜	87½	88⅝	7.76	7.76
Deb 6.70s 2008	fA	**BBB+**	12/98	BBB	X	BE	[12]Z100	....	....	....	....	....	200	G1	'98	104	85½	86⅝	7.73	7.73
Deb 6¾s 2029	Ms15	**BBB+**			X	BE	[12]Z100	....	....	....	....	....	200	C1		100⅜	86⅛	87	7.76	7.76
Deb 7.29s 2036	Jd	**BBB+**	12/98	BBB	X	BE	NC	....	....	....	....	....	200	G1	'96	110⅜	98½	98½	7.40	7.40
Deb 7¼s 2097	fA	**BBB+**	12/98	BBB	X	BE	[12]Z100	....	....	....	....	....	200	G1	'97	109⅛	87¼	88½	8.19	8.19
Nts 6⅜s 2005	jD15	**BBB+**	12/98	BBB	X	BE	[7]Z100	....	....	....	....	....	300	G1	'95	104⅜	94⅜	94⅞	6.72	6.72
Nts 6⅛s 2009	Ms15	**BBB+**			X	BE	[12]Z100	....	....	....	....	....	200	C1		100¾	90⅛	90⅛	6.80	6.80
M-T Nts 'A'[13] 6.10s 2027	Fa27	**BBB+**	12/98	BBB	X	BE	NC	....	....	....	....	....	100	S1	'97	103⅞	99⅝	99⅝	6.12	6.12
M-T Nts[14]'A' 6.53s 2037	jJ15	**BBB+**	12/98	BBB	X	BE	NC	....	....	....	....	....	175	M6	'97	107⅝	96⅜	98	6.66	6.66
Burlington Resources[15]	***73e***	***3.72***	***3.89***	***1.64***	***Dc***			***467.0***	***448.0***	***9-30-99***	***1979***		***5189***	***42.3***						
Deb 9⅞s 2010	Jd15	**A–**			X	R	NC	....	....	....	....	....	150	L3	'90	131⅛	115⅞	115⅞	8.52	8.52

Uniform Footnote Explanations-See Page 260. Other: [1] Plus Make-Whole Amt. [2] Was Brown Group. [3] (HRO)On Chge of Ctrl at 101. [4] Red at greater of par & certain int pyts,etc. [5] Now Buckeye Technologies. [6] (HRO)On 8-1-07 at 100. [7] Greater of 100 or amt based on formula. [8] Now Burlington No'n Santa Fe RR. [9] See Gr Nor'n Ry,Nor'n Pac Ry,St Louis-SF Ry. [10] See Burlington No'n, Santa Fe Pacific. [11] Greater of 100 of amt based on formula. [12] Red at greater of 100 or amt based on formula. [13] (HRO)On 2-27-00 ('03&'07) at 100. [14] (HRO)On 7-15-03 at 100. [15] See Louisiana Land/Exp.

Title-Industry Code & Co. Finances (In Italics) / Individual Issue Statistics (Exchange)	Ind / Interest Dates	Fixed Charge Coverage 1996 / S&P Rating	1997 / Date of Last Rating Change	1998 / Prior Rating	Eligible	Year End / Bond Form	Million $ Cash & Equiv. / Regular Price	Curr. Assets / Regular (Begins) Thru	Curr. Liab. / Sinking Fund Price	Balance Sheet Date / Sinking Fund (Begins) Thru	L. Term Debt (Mil $) / Refund/Other Restriction Price	Refund/Other Restriction (Begins) Thru	Capital-ization (Mil $) / Outst'g (Mil $)	Total Debt % Capital / Underwriting Firm	Underwriting Year	Price Range 1999 High	Price Range 1999 Low	Mo. End Price Sale(s) or Bid	Curr. Yield	Yield to Mat.
***Burlington Resources** (Cont.)*																				
Deb 9⅛s 2021	aO	**A–**			X	R	NC	....	....	....	....	....	150	L3	'91	127	110⅞	111⅛	8.21	8.21
Deb 8.20s 2025	Ms15	**A–**			X	R	NC	....	....	....	....	....	150	M6	'95	117⅜	102¼	102½	8.00	8.00
Deb 6⅞s 2026	Fa15	**A–**			X	BE	NC	....	....	....	....	....	150	L3	'96	100½	88	88¼	7.79	7.79
Deb 7⅜s 2029	Ms	**A–**			X	BE	[1]Z100	....	....	....	....	....	450	M7	'99	105¾	93⅜	93⅝	7.88	7.88
Nts 9⅝s 2000	Jd15	**A–**			X	R	NC	....	....	....	....	....	150	L3	'90	105⅝	101⅜	101⅜	9.49	9.49
Nts 8½s 2001	aO	**A–**			X	R	NC	....	....	....	....	....	150	L3	'91	106¾	102¼	102¼	8.31	8.31
Cabot Corp.	***14***	*6.10*	*4.13*	*4.87*		*Sp*	*19.20*	*655.0*	*475.0*	*6-30-99*	*422.0*		*1354*	*50.3*						
M-T Nts 'A' 7.08s 2007	[2]jd15	**BBB+**			X	BE	NC	....	....	....	....	....	30.0	M2	'97	104	97	97	7.30	7.30
M-T Nts 'A' 7.18s 2009	[3]jd15	**BBB+**			X	BE	NC	....	....	....	....	....	30.0	M5	'97	105	97⅛	97⅛	7.39	7.39
M-T Nts 'A 8.34s 2022	[4]jd15	**BBB+**			X	BE	NC	....	....	....	....	....	26.0	G1	'92	112	102¾	102⅞	8.11	8.11
M-T Nts 'A' 8.36s 2022	[5]jd15	**BBB+**			X	BE	NC	....	....	....	....	....	26.0	G1	'92	112¼	103	103	8.12	8.12
M-T Nts[6]'A' 6.57s 2027	[7]jd15	**BBB+**			X	BE	NC	....	....	....	....	....	25.0	M5	'97	102	97¼	97¼	6.76	6.76
M-T Nts 'A' 7.28s 2027	[7]jd15	**BBB+**			X	BE	NC	....	....	....	....	....	25.0	M5	'97	99⅝	90⅞	91	8.00	8.00
[8]Cabot Industrial Prop	***57***	*n/a*	*n/a*	*n/a*		*Dc*				*9-30-99*	*360.0*		*1315*	*27.3*						
• Nts 7⅛s 2004	Mn	**BBB–**			X	BE	[1]Z100	....	....	....	....	....	200	M5	'99	99⅝	98¾	96⅛	7.41	7.41
CAI Wireless Systems	***12a***	*n/a*	*n/a*	*n/a*		*Mr*	*34.30*			*6-30-99*	*369.0*		*433.0*	*101.0*						
Sr[9]Nts 12¼s 2002	§mS15	**D**	7/98	CCC+	Z	R			Default 9-15-98 int				275	S7	'95	23	22	23	....	Flat
[10]CalEnergy Co[11]	***41f***	*1.64*	*1.83*	*1.63*		*Do*				*9-30-99*	*6298*		*7878*	*86.6*						
Sr Nts 6.96s 2003	mS15	**BBB–**	3/99	BB+	X	BE	[12]Z100	....	....	....	....	....	215	C6	'98	104⅛	97¾	98	7.10	7.10
Sr Nts 7.23s 2005	mS15	**BBB–**	3/99	BB+	X	BE	[12]Z100	....	....	....	....	....	260	C6	'98	106½	97⅝	97⅞	7.39	7.39
Sr Nts[9] 9½s 2006	mS15	**BBB–**	3/99	BB+	X	BE	104.75	(9-15-01)	....	....	....	....	225	C5	'96	110¾	106	107½	8.84	8.84
Sr Nts[9] 7.63s 2007	aO15	**BBB–**	3/99	BB+	X	BE	NC	....	....	....	....	....	350	L3	'98	109⅜	98	98	7.79	7.79
Sr Nts[9]'B' 7.52s 2008	mS15	**BBB–**	3/99	BB+	X	BE	[12]Z100	....	....	....	....	....	100	C5	'98	108⅜	97	98⅛	7.66	7.66
Sr Nts 8.48s 2028	mS15	**BBB–**	3/99	BB+	X	BE	[12]Z100	....	....	....	....	....	475	C6	'98	118⅞	101½	103	8.23	8.23
Caliber System	***70b***	***Merged w/Fed'l Express,see***																		
Nts 7.80s 2006	fA	**BBB**	2/98	BBB+	X	BE	NC	....	....	....	....	....	200	G1	'96	107¼	97⅛	97⅝	7.99	7.99
California Energy	***41f***	***Now CalEnergy Co,see***																		
• Ltd Recourse Sr Sec[9]Nts[13] 9⅞s 2003	Jd30	**BBB–**	3/97	BB+	X	BE	104.9375	(6-30-00)	....	....	....	....	200	C5	'95	114	104	105⅜	9.37	9.37
Callon Petroleum	***49***	*n/a*	*n/a*	*n/a*		*Dc*	*7.94*	*18.56*	*15.51*	*9-30-99*	*107.0*		*190.0*	*56.3*						
• Sr Sub Nts[9] 10¼s 2004	QSep15	**NR**				BE	100	(3-15-01)	....	....	....	....	40.0	E2	'99	100	96¾	95½	10.73	10.73
Calpine Corp	***72a***	*0.62*	*1.86*	*1.71*		*Dc*	*173.6*	*333.9*	*162.9*	*9-30-99*	*1667*		*2249*	*74.1*						
Sr Nts[14] 9¼s 2004	Fa	**BB+**	11/99	BB–	Y	BE	104.625	2-29-00	....	....	....	....	105	M6	'94	105	99¾	100¾	9.18	9.18
Sr Nts 7⅝s 2006	ao15	**BB+**	11/99	BB	Y	BE	NC	....	....	....	....	....	250	C6	'99	101½	93¼	95¼	8.01	8.01
Sr Nts 7¾s 2009	Ao15	**BB+**	11/99	BB	Y	BE	NC	....	....	....	....	....	350	C6	'99	101¼	92	94½	8.20	8.20
Camden Property Trust[15]	***57***	*1.80*	*2.42*	*2.14*		*Dc*				*9-30-99*	*[16]1089*		*2163*	*50.3*						
Nts 6⅝s 2001	Fa15	**BBB**	11/98	BBB–	X	BE	[12]Z100	....	....	....	....	....	100	M5	'96	99½	98½	99¼	6.68	6.67
Nts 7s 2004	Ao15	**BBB**			X	BE	[12]Z100	....	....	....	....	....	200	C1	'99	99½	96	96¼	7.27	7.27
Nts 7s 2006	mN15	**BBB**	11/98	BBB–	X	BE	[17]Z100	....	....	....	....	....	75.0	M2	'96	96¼	92⅝	93⅜	7.50	7.50
Campbell Soup	***26***	*Δ9.16*	*Δ6.51*	*Δ8.21*		*Jl*	*34.00*	*1547*	*3373*	*10-31-99*	*1328*		*3552*	*93.4*						
Deb 8⅞s 2021	Mn	**AA–**	9/96	AA	X	BE	NC	....	....	....	....	....	200	G1	'91	135⅛	113	113⅛	7.85	7.84
Nts[18] 8.58s 2001	[19]jd15	**AA–**	9/96	AA	X	BE	NC	....	....	....	....	....	50.0	G1	'91	106¾	102¼	102¼	8.39	8.39
Nts 6.15s 2002	jD	**AA–**			X	BE	[20]Z100	....	....	....	....	....	300	M5	'97	103⅞	98½	98½	6.24	6.24
Nts 5⅝s 2003	mS15	**AA–**	9/96	AA	X	BE	100	(9-15-00)	....	....	....	....	100	G1	'93	100⅝	96⅝	96⅝	5.84	5.84
Nts 4¾s 2003	aO	**AA–**			X	BE	[1]Z100	....	....	....	....	....	300	G1	'98	98¾	93	93	5.11	5.11
Nts 6.90s 2006	aO15	**AA–**			X	BE	[20]Z100	....	....	....	....	....	300	G1	'96	110¼	98¼	98¼	7.02	7.02

Uniform Footnote Explanations-See Page 260. Other: [1] Red at greater of 100 or amt based on formula. [2] Due 2-12-07. [3] Due 2-11-09. [4] Due 8-5-22. [5] Due 12-15-22. [6] (HRO)On 10-21-04 at 100. [7] Due 10-21-27. [8] Subsid & data of Cabot Industrial Trust. [9] (HRO)On Chge of Ctrl at 101. [10] See California Energy. [11] Now MidAmerican Energy Hldg. [12] Plus Make-Whole Amt. [13] Secured by an assignment & pledge of stk in subsid. [14] Co must offer repurch at 101 on Chge of Ctrl. [15] See Oasis Residential. [16] Incl current amts. [17] Plus make-whole amt. [18] Issued in min denom $100T. [19] Due 3-15-01. [20] Greater of 100 or amt based on formula.

Title-Industry Code & Co. Finances (In Italics) / Individual Issue Statistics (Exchange)	Ind / Interest Dates	Fixed Charge Coverage 1996 / S&P Rating	1997 / Date of Last Rating Change	Prior Rating	1998 / Eligible	Year End / Bond Form	Cash & Equiv. (Million $) / Redemption Provisions: Regular Price	Curr. Assets / Regular (Begins) Thru	Curr. Liab. / Sinking Fund Price	Balance Sheet Date / Sinking Fund (Begins) Thru	L. Term Debt (Mil $) / Refund/Other Restriction Price	Refund/Other Restriction (Begins) Thru	Capital-ization (Mil $) / Outst'g (Mil $)	Total Debt % Capital / Underwriting Firm	Underwriting Year	Price Range 1999 High	Price Range 1999 Low	Mo. End Price Sale(s) or Bid	Curr. Yield	Yield to Mat.
***Canandaigua Brands*[1]**	***11c***	***2.40***	***3.64***		***3.58***	***Fb***	***4.34***	***1025***	***499.0***	***8-31-99***	***1274***		***1836***	***71.1***						
Sr Sub Nts[2] 8½s 2009	Ms	B+			Y	BE	104.25	(2-29-04)	....	....	[3]Z108.50	3-1-02	200	C1	'99	103¼	92¼	95¾	8.88	8.88
Canandaigua Wine	***11c***	***Now Canandaigua Brands,see***																		
Sr[2]Sub Nts 8¾s 2003	jD15	B+			Y	R	102.917	12-14-00	....	....	....	....	130	C1	'93	103¼	97	99½	8.79	8.79
Capital Cities/ABC Inc	***12***	***Merged into Disney(Walt)Co,see***																		
Nts 8⅞s 2000	jD15	A	2/96	AA–	X	R	NC	....	....	....	....	....	250	S1	'90	105⅞	101⅝	101⅝	8.73	8.73
Deb 8¾s 2021	fA15	A	2/96	AA–	X	R	NC	....	....	....	....	....	157	S1	'91	123⅜	105	105⅛	8.32	8.32
Capital One Bank	***10***	***Subsid of Capital One Fin'l,see***																		
Sr Nts[4] 7.15s 2006	mS15	BBB–			X	BE	NC	....	....	....	....	....	200	M5	'96	104⅝	94⅛	95	7.53	7.53
***Capital One Financial*[5]**	***10***	***9.72***	***8.82***		***6.01***	***Dc***				***9-30-99***	***4328***		***5765***	***75.1***						
Nts 7¾s 2002	jD	BB+			Y	R	NC	....	....	....	....	....	75.0	D6	'92	101¼	96	97¾	7.93	7.93
Nts 7¼s 2006	Mn	BB+			Y	BE	NC	....	....	....	....	....	225	C1	'99	100¼	94	95¼	7.61	7.61
Capital Re	***35***	***13.02***	***14.79***		***9.06***	***Dc***				***9-30-99***	***100.0***		***677.0***	***14.8***						
Deb 7¾s 2002	mN	A	12/93	A+	X	R	NC	....	....	....	....	....	75.0	G1	'92	107¼	101½	101½	7.64	7.63
CapStar Hotels	***32***	***Now MeriStar Hospitality, see***																		
Sr Sub Nts 8¾s 2007	fA15	B			Y	BE	[6]Z100	8-14-02	....	....	[7]Z108.75	8-15-00	150	Exch.	'97	98½	89¾	92⅛	9.50	9.50
***Cardinal Health*[8]*Inc*[9]**	***21d***	***△14.20***	***△20.99***		***△8.64***	***Je***	***185.0***	***6160***	***3657***	***9-30-99***	***1520***		***5224***	***29.5***						
Nts 6½s 2004	Fa15	A	5/98	A–	X	R	NC	....	....	....	....	....	100	S7	'94	104⅛	96½	96½	6.74	6.74
Nts 6s 2006	Jj15	A	5/98	A–	X	R	NC	....	....	....	....	....	150	B7	'96	102⅛	92½	92½	6.49	6.49
Nts 6¼s 2008	jJ15	A			X	BE	[10]Z100	....	....	....	....	....	150	B7	'98	102⅝	90⅞	90⅞	6.88	6.88
Carlisle Co	***61a***	***11.16***	***8.08***		***7.18***	***Dc***	***10.72***	***538.3***	***253.4***	***9-30-99***	***282.0***		***749.0***	***40.3***						
Nts 7¼s 2007	Jj15	BBB+			X	BE	NC	....	....	....	....	....	150	G1	'97	109⅛	96¼	96¼	7.53	7.53
Sr Nts 6.70s 2008	Mn15	BBB+			X	BE	NC	....	....	....	....	....	100	G1	'98	105½	92¾	92¾	7.22	7.22
***Carnival Corp*[11]**	***40g***	***6.60***	***9.29***		***8.96***	***Nv***	***940.0***	***1222***	***1225***	***8-31-99***	***1184***		***6960***	***17.5***						
• Deb[12] 7.20s 2023	aO	A	2/96	A–	X	BE	NC	....	....	....	....	....	125	G1	'93	No Sale		92⅛	7.82	7.82
Deb[13] 6.65s 2028	Jj15	A			X	BE	NC	....	....	....	....	....	200	B7	'98	100⅜	85⅞	86	7.73	7.73
Nts[14] 5.65s 2000	aO15	A			X	BE	NC	....	....	....	....	....	200	B7	'98	100½	99¼	99⅜	5.69	5.69
• Nts[14] 6.15s 2003	aO	A	2/96	A–	X	BE	NC	....	....	....	....	....	125	G1	'93	98¾	95	94	6.54	6.54
• Nts[12] 7.70s 2004	jJ15	A	2/96	A–	X	BE	NC	....	....	....	....	....	100	G1	'94	No Sale		99	7.78	7.78
Nts[14] 6.15s 2008	Ao15	A			X	BE	NC	....	....	....	....	....	200	B7	'98	102	91⅞	91⅞	6.69	6.69
• Nts[12] 7.05s 2005	Mn15	A	2/96	A–	X	BE	NC	....	....	....	....	....	100	M2	'95	99	99	96	7.34	7.34
Carolina Power & Light	***72a***	***4.42***	***4.52***		***4.66***	***Dc***	***76.70***	***1032***	***903.0***	***9-30-99***	***2800***		***5953***	***49.0***						
1st 6⅛s 2000	Fa	A			X	R	NC	....	....	....	....	....	150	L3	'93	100⅞	100	100	6.13	6.12
1st 6¾s 2002	aO	A			X	R	NC	....	....	....	....	....	100	P4	'92	104⅜	98⅞	98⅞	6.83	6.83
1st 5⅞s 2004	Jj15	A			X	R	NC	....	....	....	....	....	150	P4	'94	102¼	95	95	6.18	6.18
1st 7⅞s 2004	Ao15	A			X	R	NC	....	....	....	....	....	150	P4	'92	110¾	101½	101½	7.76	7.76
1st 6.80s 2007	fA15	A			X	R	[6]Z100	....	....	....	....	....	200	M6	'97	108⅞	96⅛	96⅛	7.07	7.07
1st 8⅝s 2021	mS15	A			X	R	NC	....	....	....	....	....	100	K2	'91	125¾	107	107⅛	8.05	8.05
1st 8.20s 2022	jJ	A			X	R	103.55	(7-1-02)	Z103.55	(7-1-02)	....	....	150	P4	'92	108⅝	97½	98⅛	8.36	8.35
1st 7½s 2023	Ms	A			X	R	103.22	(3-1-03)	Z103.22	(3-1-03)	....	....	150	P4	'93	106¼	92⅛	92¼	8.13	8.13
1st 6⅞s 2023	fA15	A			X	R	102.84	(8-15-03)	Z102.84	(8-15-03)	....	....	100	K2	'93	102	85¾	85⅞	8.01	8.00
Sr Nts[15] 5.95s 2009	Ms	A			X	BE	[10]Z100	....	....	....	....	....	400	S4	'99	100⅛	90⅜	90⅜	6.58	6.58
Carolina Tel. & Tel	***67a***	***Subsid of Sprint Corp,see***																		
Deb 5¾s 2000	fA15	A	4/99	A+	X	BE	NC	....	....	....	....	....	50.0	G1	'93	100⅝	99¼	99½	5.78	5.78
Deb 6⅛s 2003	Mn	A	4/99	A+	X	BE	NC	....	....	....	....	....	50.0	S1	'93	102½	96½	96½	6.35	6.35
Deb 7¼s 2004	jD15	A	4/99	A+	X	R	NC	....	....	....	....	....	50.0	C4	'92	108½	99¼	99¼	7.30	7.30

Uniform Footnote Explanations-See Page 260. Other: [1] See Canandaigua Wine. [2] (HRO)On Chge of Ctrl at 101. [3] Max $70M red w/proceeds of Equity Off'g. [4] (HRO)On 9-15-99 at 100. [5] See Capital One Bank. [6] Plus Make-Whole Amt. [7] Max $52.5M red w/proceeds of Pub Eq Off'g. [8] Was Cardinal Distribution. [9] See Scherer(R.P.)Corp. [10] Red at greater of 100 or amt based on formula. [11] Was Carnival Cruise Lines. [12] Co may red in whole at 100 for certain tax chge. [13] Co may red in whole,at 100,for tax law chge. [14] Co may red in whole,at 100,for tax chge. [15] Secured,as defined.

Title-Industry Code & Co. Finances (In Italics) / Exchange – Individual Issue Statistics	Ind / Interest Dates	Fixed Charge Coverage 1996 / S&P Rating	1997 / Date of Last Rating Change	1998 / Prior Rating	Eligible	Year End / Bond Form	Million $ Cash & Equiv. / Redemption Provisions: Regular Price	Curr. Assets / Regular (Begins) Thru	Curr. Liab. / Sinking Fund Price	Balance Sheet Date / Sinking Fund (Begins) Thru	L. Term Debt (Mil $) / Refund/Other Restriction Price	Capital-ization (Mil $) / Refund/Other Restriction (Begins) Thru	Outst'g (Mil $)	Total Debt % Capital / Underwriting Firm	Underwriting Year	Price Range 1999 High	Price Range 1999 Low	Mo. End Price Sale(s) or Bid	Curr. Yield	Yield to Mat.
***Carolina Tel. & Tel** (Cont.)*																				
Deb 6¾s 2013	fA15	**A**	4/99	A+	X	BE	NC	....	....	....	....	....	50.0	M2	'93	107½	92	92⅛	7.33	7.33
Deb 9s 2016	Mn15	**A**	4/99	A+	X	R	103.36	5-14-00	....	....	....	....	50.0	K2	'86	104¼	102⅜	102½	8.78	8.78
Carpenter Technology	***66c***	***Δ5.34***	***Δ5.33***	***Δ3.39***		***Je***	***5.70***	***424.0***	***319.0***	***9-30-99***	***345.0***	***1143***		***44.6***						
SF Deb 9s 2022	Ms15	**BBB+**	4/99	A–	X	R	104.24	(3-15-02)	100	(3-15-03)	....	....	100	F1	'92	111⅛	105⅜	105⅜	8.54	8.54
M-T Nts 'A'[1] 7.80s 2000	[2]jj15	**BBB+**	4/99	A–	X	BE	NC	....	....	....	....	....	10.0	C5	'94	103⅜	100⅝	100⅝	7.75	7.75
M-T Nts 'A'[1] 7.79s 2001	[3]jj15	**BBB+**	4/99	A–	X	BE	NC	....	....	....	....	....	7.50	M5	'94	105	100⅞	100⅞	7.72	7.72
M-T Nts 'A'[1] 7.80s 2001	[3]jj15	**BBB+**	4/99	A–	X	BE	NC	....	....	....	....	....	7.50	C5	'94	105	100⅞	100⅞	7.73	7.73
CarrAmerica Realty	***57***	***1.99***	***2.57***	***2.89***		***Dc***				***9-30-99***	***1680***	***3580***		***46.7***						
Nts 6⅝s 2000	aO	**BBB**			X	BE	[4]Z100	....	....	....	....	....	150	G1	'98	100⅜	99⅛	99⅜	6.67	6.67
Nts 7.20s 2004	jJ	**BBB**			X	BE	[4]Z100	....	....	....	....	....	150	Exch.	'97	100½	94¼	94¼	7.64	7.64
Nts 6⅝s 2005	Ms	**BBB**			X	BE	[4]Z100	....	....	....	....	....	100	Exch.	'98	97½	90⅞	90⅞	7.29	7.29
Nts 7⅜s 2007	jJ	**BBB**			X	BE	[4]Z100	....	....	....	....	....	125	Exch.	'97	101⅛	91¼	91¼	8.08	8.08
Case Corp[5]	***41***	***4.34***	***4.49***	***1.99***		***Dc***	***184.0***	***4462***	***2316***	***9-30-99***	***3671***	***7060***		***70.5***						
Nts 7¼s 2005	fA	**BBB+**	8/99	A–	X	BE	NC	....	....	....	....	....	298	C5	'95	104⅝	97⅞	97⅞	7.41	7.41
• Nts 7¼s 2016	Jj15	**BBB+**	8/99	A–	X	BE	[6]Z100	....	....	....	....	....	300	C5	'96	No Sale		85	8.53	8.53
Case Credit Corp	***25***	***2.85***	***2.24***	***1.92***		***Dc***	***34.00***			***6-30-99***	***2507***	***3762***		***86.5***						
Gtd[7]Nts 6⅛s 2003	Fa15	**BBB+**	8/99	A–	X	BE	[6]Z100	....	....	....	....	....	200	M2	'96	98⅝	95⅜	95⅜	6.42	6.42
• F/R[8]Nts 2000	QJan21	**BBB+**	8/99	A–	X	BE	NC	....	....	....	....	....	100	C6	'98	No Sale		100	....	....
• Nts 6⅛s 2001	aO15	**BBB+**	8/99	A–	X	BE	NC	....	....	....	....	....	100	C6	'98	No Sale		98¼	6.23	6.23
M-T Nts 'A' 5.84s 2000	[9]ao	**BBB+**	8/99	A–	X	BE	NC	....	....	....	....	....	50.0	C4	'98	100⅛	99½	100	5.84	5.84
M-T Nts 'A' 6s 2001	[10]ao15	**BBB+**	8/99	A–	X	BE	NC	....	....	....	....	....	51.0		'98	100¼	99	99	6.06	6.06
M-T Nts 'A' 5.91s 2001	[11]ao	**BBB+**	8/99	A–	X	BE	NC	....	....	....	....	....	108	C1	'98	100⅛	98¾	98¾	5.98	5.98
M-T Nts 'B' 5.95s 2000	fA	**BBB+**	8/99	A–	X	BE	NC	....	....	....	....	....	100	M5	'98	100¼	99⅜	99⅝	5.97	5.97
M-T Nts 'B' 6.12s 2001	fA	**BBB+**	8/99	A–	X	BE	NC	....	....	....	....	....	125	M5	'98	100⅝	98½	98½	6.21	6.21
Caterpillar Financial Svcs	***25***	***Subsid of Caterpillar Inc,see***																		
Nts[12] 6⅞s 2004	fA	**A+**			X	BE	NC	....	....	....	....	....	500	M2	'99	100⅝	98⅛	98⅛	7.01	7.01
• M-T Nts[1]'D' 9½s 2007	[13]ao	**A+**			X	BE	NC	....	....	....	....	....	10.0		'92	No Sale		111⅜	8.53	8.53
M-T Nts 'E' 6.38s 2001	[14]ao	**A+**			X	BE	NC	....	....	....	....	....	28.0	G1	'97	101⅞	99½	99½	6.41	6.41
M-T Nts 'E' 6.40s 2001	[15]ao	**A+**			X	BE	NC	....	....	....	....	....	25.0	M2	'97	102⅛	99⅛	99¼	6.45	6.45
M-T Nts 'F' 6.28s 2000	[16]ao	**A+**			X	BE	NC	....	....	....	....	....	50.0	G1	'97	101	100	100⅛	6.27	6.27
M-T Nts 'F' 6.32s 2000	[17]ao	**A+**			X	BE	NC	....	....	....	....	....	50.0	G1	'97	101¼	99⅞	99⅞	6.33	6.33
F/R[18]M-T Nts'F' 2001	QFeb5	**A+**			X	BE	NC	....	....	....	....	....	100	M2	'98	100⅜	99⅝	100	....	....
• M-T Nts 'F' 6.40s 2001	[19]ao	**A+**	5/97	A	X	BE	NC	....	....	....	....	....	50.0	L3	'97	No Sale		99½	6.43	6.43
M-T Nts 'F' 6.48s 2001	[20]ao	**A+**			X	BE	NC	....	....	....	....	....	25.0	M2	'97	102½	99⅜	99⅜	6.52	6.52
F/R[21]M-T Nts 'E' 2001	QFeb20	**A+**			X	BE	NC	....	....	....	....	....	25.0	L3	'97	100¼	99⅝	100	....	....
F/R[22] M-T Nts 'F' 2000	QJan20	**A+**			X	BE	NC	....	....	....	....	....	30.0	M2	'97	100⅛	99¾	100	....	....
F/R[23]M-T Nts 'F' 2000	QJul24	**A+**			X	BE	NC	....	....	....	....	....	50.0	L3	'97	100¼	99⅝	100⅛	....	....
F/R[24]M-T Nts 'F' 2000	QSep1	**A+**			X	BE	NC	....	....	....	....	....	50.0	M2	'97	100⅛	99⅝	100	....	....
M-T Nts 'F' 6¾s 2001	[25]ao	**A+**			X	BE	NC	....	....	....	....	....	30.0	G1	'97	102¾	100	100	6.75	6.75
M-T Nts 'F' 6¾s 2001	[26]ao	**A+**			X	BE	NC	....	....	....	....	....	30.0	G1	'97	102⅞	99⅞	99⅞	6.76	6.76
M-T Nts 'F' 6½s 2002	[27]ao	**A+**			X	BE	NC	....	....	....	....	....	35.0	G1	'97	102⅝	99¼	99¼	6.55	6.55
M-T Nts 'F' 6.51s 2002	[28]ao	**A+**			X	BE	NC	....	....	....	....	....	35.0	G1	'97	102⅞	99	99	6.58	6.58
Caterpillar Inc[29]	***41b***	***4.81***	***5.16***	***3.89***		***Dc***	***283.0***	***11977***	***7600***	***9-30-99***	***10106***	***15352***		***65.8***						
• SF Deb 9¾s 2019	Jd	**A+**	5/97	A	X	BE	104.875	5-31-00	100	(6-1-00)	....	....	200	S5	'89	109	104⅛	104½	9.33	9.33
Sr Deb 6⅝s 2028	jJ15	**A+**			X	BE	[30]Z100	....	....	....	....	....	300	G1	'98	103⅝	86¼	86⅜	7.67	7.67

Uniform Footnote Explanations-See Page 260. Other: [1] Issued in min denom $100T. [2] Due 9-28-00. [3] Due 9-19-01. [4] Plus Make-Whole Amt. [5] Acq by New Holland NV. [6] Greater of 100 or amt based on formula. [7] Gtd by Case Corp. [8] Int adj qtrly(3 Mo LIBOR & 0.70%). [9] Due 2-27-00. [10] Due 1-10-01. [11] Due 2-19-01. [12] Co may red in whole, at 100, for tax law chge. [13] Due 2-6-07. [14] Due 5-15-01. [15] Due 8-15-01. [16] Due 5-1-00. [17] Due 9-1-00. [18] Int adj qtrly(3 Mo LIBOR & 0.07%). [19] Due 4-16-01. [20] Due 12-12-01. [21] Int adj qtrly(3 Mo LIBOR&0.10%). [22] Int adj qtrly(3 Mo LIBOR & 0.03%). [23] Int adj qtrly(3 Mo LIBOR & 0.05%). [24] Int adj qtrly(3 Mo LIBOR & 0.055%). [25] Due 6-15-01. [26] Due 7-10-01. [27] Due 2-1-02. [28] Due 6-5-02. [29] Was Caterpillar Tractor. [30] Red at greater of 100 or amt based on formula.

Title-Industry Code & Co. Finances (In Italics) / Individual Issue Statistics (Exchange ↓)	Ind / Interest Dates	1996 / S&P Rating	1997 / Date of Last Rating Change	Prior Rating	1998 / Eligible ↓	Year End / Bond Form	Cash & Equiv. (Million $) / Regular Price	Curr. Assets (Million $) / Regular (Begins) Thru	Curr. Liab. (Million $) / Sinking Fund Price	Balance Sheet Date / Sinking Fund (Begins) Thru	L. Term Debt (Mil $) / Refund/Other Restriction Price	Refund/Other Restriction (Begins) Thru	Capital-ization (Mil $) / Outst'g (Mil $)	Total Debt % Capital / Underwriting Firm	Underwriting Year	Price Range 1999 High	Price Range 1999 Low	Mo. End Price Sale(s) or Bid	Curr. Yield	Yield to Mat.
***Caterpillar Inc** (Cont.)*																				
• Deb 9s 2006	Ao15	**A+**	5/97	A	X	BE	NC	....	....	....	....	....	202	L3	'91	124	106⅛	107	8.41	8.41
• Deb 6s 2007	Mn	**A+**	5/97	A	X	R	100	....	....	....	....	....	[1]250	G1	'82	102½	91½	91¼	6.58	6.58
• Deb 9⅜s 2011	fA15	**A+**	5/97	A	X	BE	NC	....	....	....	....	....	123	G1	'91	No Sale		112⅜	8.34	8.34
• Deb 9⅜s 2021	Ms15	**A+**	5/97	A	X	BE	NC	....	....	....	....	....	236	G1	'91	125	115⅛	112	8.37	8.37
• Deb 8s 2023	Fa15	**A+**	5/97	A	X	BE	NC	....	....	....	....	....	200	L3	'93	112	100	98⅛	8.15	8.15
Deb[2] 7⅜s 2097	Ms	**A+**	5/97	A	X	BE	[3]103.19	(3-1-47)	....	....	....	....	297	M2	'97	111⅛	91⅞	92	8.02	8.02
• Nts 9⅜s 2000	jJ15	**A+**	5/97	A	X	BE	NC	....	....	....	....	....	150	M2	'90	106½	100½	100⅝	9.32	9.31
• Nts 9⅜s 2001	jJ15	**A+**	5/97	A	X	BE	NC	....	....	....	....	....	184	M2	'91	109¾	102¼	102½	9.15	9.14
CBI Indus	***14b***	***Mgr into Praxair, Inc, see***																		
Nts 6¼s 2000	Jd30	**BBB+**	1/96	BBB	X	BE	NC	....	....	....	....	....	75.0	M2	'93	100⅝	99½	99¾	6.27	6.26
Nts 6⅝s 2003	Ms15	**BBB+**	1/96	BBB	X	BE	NC	....	....	....	....	....	75.0	L3	'93	102⅞	97½	97½	6.79	6.79
CBS [4]Corp[5]	***12e***	***0.58***	***1.09***		***1.85***	***Dc***	***185.0***	***2401***	***1809***	***9-30-99***	***2346***		***11885***	***18.4***						
Sr Nts 7.15s 2005	Mn20	**BBB–**	12/98	BB+	X	BE	[6]Z100	....	....	....	....	....	500	Exch.	'98	105¾	98⅛	98½	7.26	7.26
CBS, Inc[7,8]	***12***	***Merged w/Westinghouse El,see CBS Corp***																		
Sr Deb 8⅞s 2022	Jd	**BBB–**	12/98	BB+	X	BE	104.14	(6-1-02)	....	....	....	....	125	S1	'92	110⅜	99⅜	100⅝	8.82	8.82
Sr Nts 7⅝s 2002	Jj	**BBB–**	12/98	BB+	X	BE	NC	....	....	....	....	....	150	S1	'92	104⅝	100¾	100¾	7.57	7.57
Sr Nts 7⅛s 2023	mN	**BBB–**	12/98	BB+	X	BE	NC	....	....	....	....	....	100	B7	'93	101⅞	88⅜	89⅝	7.95	7.95
[9]CenCall Communications	***67g***	***Merged into NEXTEL Communic'ns,see***																		
Sr Redeem[10]Disc Nts[11] 10⅛s 2004	Jj15	**B–**	3/99	CCC+	Y	R	103.20	1-14-01	....	....	....	....	[1]410	M2	'94	104⅝	98	103½	9.78	9.78
Centel Capital	***25***	***Gtd by Sprint Corp,see***																		
Deb[12] 9s 2019	aO15	**BBB+**	4/99	A–	X	R	NC	....	....	....	....	....	150	M6	'89	125⅜	108⅛	108⅞	8.27	8.27
Cendant Corp[13]	***32***	***n/a***	***n/a***		***n/a***	***Dc***	***624.0***	***3489***	***2506***	***9-30-99***	***6138***		***14185***	***55.6***						
Nts 7½s 2000	jD	**BBB**			X	BE	[14]Z100	....	....	....	....	....	400	C1	'98	101⅞	99⅞	100	7.50	7.50
Nts 7¾s 2003	jD	**BBB**			X	BE	[14]Z100	....	....	....	....	....	1150	C1	'98	103¾	99	99⅞	7.76	7.76
CenterPoint Prop Tr	***57***	***2.57***	***3.34***		***3.34***	***Dc***				***9-30-99***	***504.0***		***969.0***	***52.0***						
Sr Nts 6¾s 2005	Ao	**BBB**	1/99	BBB–	X	BE	[6]Z100	....	....	....	....	....	100	L3	'98	98⅝	92¾	92¾	7.28	7.28
M-T Nts 7⅛s 2004	Ms15	**BBB**			X	BE	NC	....	....	....	....	....	100	L3	'99	102⅛	95⅝	95⅝	7.45	7.45
Centex Corp	***13h***	***6.74***	***9.27***		***11.27***	***Mr***				***9-30-99***	***565.0***		***3441***	***59.4***						
Sub Deb 7⅜s 2005	Jd	**BBB–**			X	BE	NC	....	....	....	....	....	100		'95	102⅝	95⅜	96¾	7.62	7.62
Central Bancshrs South	***10***	***Now Compass Bancshares,see***																		
Sub Nts 7s 2003	Mn	**BBB**			X	BE	NC	....	....	....	....	....	75.0	F1	'93	105⅛	99½	99½	7.04	7.03
Central Fidelity Banks	***10***	***Acquired by Wachovia Corp,see***																		
Sub Nts 8.15s 2002	mN15	**A+**	10/98	AA–	X	BE	NC	....	....	....	....	....	150	S1	'92	108⅝	102	102	7.99	7.99
[15]Central Hudson Gas & Elec	***75***	***4.33***	***4.03***		***3.90***	***Dc***	***7.18***	***236.0***	***219.0***	***9-30-99***	***347.0***		***924.0***	***41.9***						
1st 9¼s 2021	Mn	**A**	7/97	A–	X	R	104.08	(5-1-01)	▲100	....	....	....	70.0	K2	'91	111½	104⅛	104¼	8.87	8.87
M-T Nts 'B' 5.93s 2001	[16]jj	**A–**			X	BE	NC	....	....	....	....	....	15.0	C1	'98	100⅞	98	98	6.05	6.05
Central Illinois Light[17]	***75***	***2.87***	***4.47***		***4.05***	***Dc***	***3.00***	***145.0***	***152.0***	***9-30-99***	***238.0***		***700.0***	***46.6***						
1st 6.40s 2000	Fa9	**BBB–**	10/99	AA–	X	BE	NC	....	....	....	....	....	30.0	K2	'93	101⅛	100	100	6.40	6.40
1st 6.82s 2003	Fa10	**BBB–**	10/99	AA–	X	BE	NC	....	....	....	....	....	25.4	K2	'93	104¾	98⅞	98⅞	6.90	6.90
1st 7½s 2007	Jj15	**BBB–**	10/99	AA–	X	BE	NC	....	....	....	....	....	50.0	S7	'92	112⅜	99¾	99¾	7.52	7.52
1st 8.20s 2022	Jj15	**BBB–**	10/99	AA–	X	BE	103.66	(1-15-02)	▲100	(1-15-02)	....	....	65.0	S7	'92	108⅞	98⅜	98½	8.32	8.32
1st 7.80s 2023	Fa9	**BBB–**	10/99	AA–	X	BE	103.90	(2-9-03)	▲100	....	....	....	8.00	K2	'93	115¼	96⅝	96¾	8.06	8.06
1st 7.80s 2023	Fa9	**BBB–**	10/99	AA–	X	BE	103.90	(2-9-03)	▲100	....	....	....	2.00	K2	'93	115¼	96⅝	96¾	8.06	8.06
Central Illinois Pub Serv[18]	***75***	***4.30***	***3.70***		***4.14***	***Dc***	***17.30***	***228.0***	***293.0***	***6-30-99***	***499.0***		***1316***	***50.2***						
1st X 7½s 2007	jJ	**AA–**	12/97	AA+	X	R	100	(7-1-02)	....	....	....	....	50.0	M6	'92	107⅜	99⅜	99⅜	7.55	7.55

Uniform Footnote Explanations-See Page 260. Other: [1] Incl disc. [2] Co may shorten mty for Tax Event. [3] Co may red at make whole & 0.15% to 3-1-47. [4] Was Westinghouse,see. [5] See CBS Inc. [6] Plus Make-Whole Amt. [7] Was Columbia Broadcasting. [8] See Westinghouse Elec. [9] Now OneComm Corp. [10] Int accrues at 10.125% fr 1-15-99. [11] Co must offer 101(Accreted Val),on Chge of Ctrl. [12] (HRO)On 10-15-99 at 100. [13] Was Hospitality Franchise Sys,then HFS Inc. [14] Red at greater of 100 or amt based on formula. [15] Now CH Energy Group. [16] Due 9-10-01. [17] Subsid of CILCORP Inc. [18] Subsid of CIPSCO Inc.

Title-Industry Code & Co. Finances (In Italics) / Individual Issue Statistics (Exchange)	Ind / Interest Dates	S&P Rating	Fixed Charge Coverage 1996 / Date of Last Rating Change	1997 / Prior Rating	1998 / Eligible	Year End / Bond Form	Million $ Cash & Equiv. / Redemption Provisions Regular Price	Curr. Assets / Regular (Begins) Thru	Curr. Liab. / Sinking Fund Price	Balance Sheet Date / Sinking Fund (Begins) Thru	L. Term Debt (Mil $) / Refund/Other Restriction Price	Refund/Other Restriction (Begins) Thru	Capital-ization (Mil $) / Outst'g (Mil $)	Total Debt % Capital / Underwriting Firm	Underwriting Year	Price Range 1999 High	Price Range 1999 Low	Mo. End Price Sale(s) or Bid	Curr. Yield	Yield to Mat.
***Central Illinois Pub Serv** (Cont.)*																				
1st Y 6¾s 2002	mS15	**AA–**	12/97	AA+	X	R	NC	....	....	....	....	....	23.0	M6	'92	104⅞	99¼	99¼	6.80	6.80
1st Z 6s 2000	Ao	**AA–**	12/97	AA+	X	R	NC	....	....	....	....	....	25.0	M6	'93	101	99⅞	100	6.00	6.00
1st Z 6⅜s 2003	Ao	**AA–**	12/97	AA+	X	R	NC	....	....	....	....	....	40.0	M6	'93	104	97⅝	97⅝	6.53	6.53
Sr Nts 6⅛s 2028	jD15	**AA–**			X	BE	[1]Z100	....	....	....	....	....	60.0	L3	'98	99¼	79¾	79⅞	7.67	7.67
[2]Central La Elec.	***72a***		***3.68***	***4.01***	***3.79***	***Dc***	***40.20***	***228.0***	***367.0***	***9-30-99***	***362.0***		***992.0***	***54.1***						
1st X 9½s 2005	Ms15	**A+**	10/97	A	X	R	NC	....	....	....	....	....	60.0	S1	'90	120½	108¾	108¾	8.74	8.73
M-T Nts 7s 2007	[3]ms15	**A+**	10/97	A	X	BE	NC	....	....	....	....	....	25.0	F2	'97	108⅜	95⅞	95⅞	7.30	7.30
Central Power & Light[4]	***72a***		***3.05***	***2.61***	***3.98***	***Dc***	***9.34***	***163.0***	***665.0***	***6-30-99***	***1251***		***2843***	***48.4***						
1st CC 7¼s 2004	aO	**A**			X	R	NC	....	....	....	....	....	100	M2	'92	107¾	99½	99½	7.29	7.29
1st EE 7½s 2002	jD	**A**			X	R	NC	....	....	....	....	....	115	M6	'92	107¼	100⅞	100⅞	7.43	7.43
1st FF 6⅞s 2003	Fa	**A**			X	R	NC	....	....	....	....	....	50.0	M6	'93	105⅛	99⅛	99⅛	6.94	6.93
1st GG 7⅛s 2008	Fa	**A**			X	R	NC	....	....	....	....	....	75.0	M6	'93	110½	97⅝	97¾	7.29	7.29
1st II 7½s 2023	Ao	**A**			X	R	103.32	(4-1-03)	....	....	....	....	100	M6	'93	105⅛	92⅛	92¼	8.13	8.13
1st HH 6s 2000	Ao	**A**			X	R	NC	....	....	....	....	....	100	M6	'93	100⅞	99⅞	99⅞	6.01	6.01
1st KK 6⅝s 2005	jJ	**A**			X	R	NC	....	....	....	....	....	200	M6	'95	105⅝	96½	96½	6.87	6.86
Century Communications[5]	***12a***		***△0.10***	***△0.61***	***△0.69***	***My***	***626.0***	***696.0***	***157.0***	***5-31-99***	***2023***		***1653***	***124.0***						
Sr Nts 9½s 2000	fA15	**BB–**	1/94	B+	Y	R	NC	....	....	....	....	....	150	B11	'92	111½	99¾	100	9.50	9.50
Sr Nts 9¾s 2002	Fa15	**BB–**	1/94	B+	Y	R	NC	....	....	....	....	....	200	D6	'02	109½	100	100½	9.70	9.70
Zero[6]Cpn Sr Disc Nts 2003	[7]	**BB–**	1/94	B+	Y	R	NC	....	....	....	....	....	[8]444	L3	'93	76	69½	71½	....	0.33
Sr Nts 9½s 2005	Ms	**BB–**			Y	R	NC	....	....	....	....	....	250	M2	'95	112	99½	100¼	9.48	9.47
Sr Nts 8¾s 2007	aO	**BB–**			Y	BE	NC	....	....	....	....	....	225	M2	'97	112¾	94⅝	96¼	9.09	9.09
Sr Nts 8⅜s 2007	jD15	**BB–**			Y	BE	NC	....	....	....	....	....	100	D6	'97	110½	92⅜	94	8.91	8.91
Sr Nts 8⅜s 2017	mN15	**BB–**			Y	BE	NC	....	....	....	....	....	[8]100	M5	'97	111½	87	88½	9.46	9.46
[9]Century Telephone Enterprises	***67a***		***5.69***	***8.33***	***2.90***	***Dc***	***37.20***	***285.0***	***316.0***	***9-30-99***	***2042***		***3810***	***55.0***						
Sr Nts 'A' 7¾s 2004	Mn	**BBB+**	12/97	A–	X	R	NC	....	....	....	....	....	50.0	P1	'94	109⅝	100⅜	100⅜	7.72	7.72
Sr Nts 'B' 8¼s 2024	Mn	**BBB+**	12/97	A–	X	R	103.62	(5-1-04)	....	....	....	....	100	P1	'94	112⅜	96⅛	96¼	8.57	8.57
Sr Nts 'C' 6.55s 2005	jD	**BBB+**	12/97	A–	X	R	NC	....	....	....	....	....	50.0	P1	'95	104⅞	93⅞	94	6.97	6.97
Sr Nts 'D' 7.20s 2025	jD	**BBB+**	12/97	A–	X	R	[10]Z100	....	....	....	....	....	100	P1	'95	108¾	87⅞	88	8.18	8.18
Sr Nts 'E' 6.15s 2005	Jj15	**BBB+**			X	BE	[1]Z100	....	....	....	....	....	100	S4	'98	102½	93⅞	93⅞	6.55	6.55
Sr Nts 'F' 6.30s 2008	Jj15	**BBB+**			X	BE	[1]Z100	....	....	....	....	....	240	S4	'98	103⅝	90½	90⅝	6.95	6.95
Deb 'G' 6⅞s 2028	Jj15	**BBB+**			X	BE	[1]Z100	....	....	....	....	....	425	S4	'98	104⅜	83⅞	85⅛	8.08	8.07
Champion Int'l	***50***		***1.92***	***0.98***	***1.31***	***Dc***	***606.0***	***1651***	***1125***	***9-30-99***	***2572***		***6037***	***51.3***						
Deb 7⅝s 2023	mS	**BBB**			X	BE	103.451	(9-1-03)	....	....	....	....	100	G1	'93	103¼	90⅛	90¼	8.45	8.45
Deb 7¾s 2025	mS	**BBB**			X	BE	NC	....	....	....	....	....	150	G1	'95	107	94¾	94⅞	8.17	8.17
Deb 7.35s 2025	mN	**BBB**			X	BE	[10]Z100	....	....	....	....	....	200	S1	'95	102¼	90⅝	90⅝	8.11	8.11
Deb[11] 6.40s 2026	Fa15	**BBB**			X	BE	NC	....	....	....	....	....	200	G1	'96	100½	93¼	93¼	6.86	6.86
Deb[12] 7.20s 2026	mN	**BBB**			X	BE	NC	....	....	....	....	....	200	G1	'96	106¼	94	94	7.66	7.66
Deb 7.15s 2027	jD15	**BBB**			X	BE	NC	....	....	....	....	....	100	G1	'97	99½	87⅞	87⅞	8.14	8.14
Nts 9⅞s 2000	Jd	**BBB**			X	R	NC	....	....	....	....	....	200	G1	'90	105⅜	101¼	101¼	9.75	9.75
Nts 9.70s 2001	Mn	**BBB**			X	R	NC	....	....	....	....	....	200	G1	'91	108¼	103⅛	103⅛	9.41	9.40
Nts 7.10s 2005	mS	**BBB**			X	BE	NC	....	....	....	....	....	150	G1	'95	104½	97	97	7.32	7.32
Nts[13] 6.65s 2037	jD15	**BBB**			X	BE	NC	....	....	....	....	....	100	G1	'97	106¼	93¼	93¼	7.13	7.13
[14]Chancellor Media[15]Corp	***23f***		***0.49***	***1.14***	***1.31***	***Dc***	***86.50***	***680.0***	***444.0***	***9-30-99***	***5646***		***10977***	***51.9***						
Sr Sub Nts[16] 9⅜s 2004	aO	**B**	11/97	B–	Y	R	104.688	(2-1-00)	....	....	....	....	200	B11	'96	109¼	99½	104	9.01	9.01
Chartwell Re[17]Hldgs[18]	***35c***		***4.08***	***4.09***	***4.28***	***Dc***				***6-30-99***	***101.0***		***384.0***	***26.3***						
Sr Nts[19] 10¼s 2004	Ms	**BBB–**	3/96	BB	X	R	103.84	2-29-00	....	....	....	....	75.0	S1	'94	103⅛	98½	103	9.95	9.95

Uniform Footnote Explanations-See Page 260. Other: [1] Red at greater of 100 or amt based on formula. [2] Now Cleco Corp. [3] Due 12-14-07. [4] Subsid of Central & South West. [5] Acq by Adelphia Commun. [6] (HRO)For a Triggering Event at 101. [7] Due 3-15-03. [8] Incl disc. [9] Now CenturyTel Inc. [10] Greater of 100 or amt based on formula. [11] (HRO)On 2-15-06 at 100. [12] (HRO)On 11-1-11 at 100. [13] (HRO)On 12-15-07 at 100. [14] Was Chancellor Broadcasting. [15] Now AMFM Inc. [16] (HRO)On Chge of Ctrl at 101. [17] Was Chartwell Re. [18] Acq by Trenwick Group. [19] (HRO)On Chge of Ctrl & Ratings Decline,at 101.

Title-Industry Code & Co. Finances (In Italics)	Ind	Fixed Charge Coverage 1996		1997	1998	Year End	Million $ Cash & Equiv.	Curr. Assets	Curr. Liab.	Balance Sheet Date	L. Term Debt (Mil $)		Capitalization (Mil $)	Total Debt % Capital						
Exchange ↓ Individual Issue Statistics	**Interest Dates**	**S&P Rating**	**Date of Last Rating Change**	**Prior Rating**	**Eligible ↓**	**Bond Form**	**Redemption Provisions: Regular Price**	**Regular (Begins) Thru**	**Sinking Fund Price**	**Sinking Fund (Begins) Thru**	**Refund/Other Restriction Price**	**Refund/Other Restriction (Begins) Thru**	**Outst'g (Mil $)**	**Underwriting Firm**	**Underwriting Year**	**Price Range 1999 High**	**Price Range 1999 Low**	**Mo. End Price Sale(s) or Bid**	**Curr. Yield**	**Yield to Mat.**
Chase Manhattan Corp[1]	***10***	***2.02***		***1.87***	***1.97***	***Dc***				***9-30-99***	***19182***		***42213***	***43.5***						
F/R[2]M-T Nts 'C' 2000	[3]Jun26	A+	5/98	A	X	BE	NC	....	....	....	....	....	100	C1	'97	100⅛	99¾	100	....	....
Nts 5½s 2001	Fa15	A+	5/98	A	X	BE	NC	....	....	....	....	....	200	C1	'96	100¼	98⅝	98⅝	5.58	5.58
Sr Nts 5¾s 2004	Ao15	A+			X	BE	NC	....	....	....	....	....	500	C1	'99	99⅝	94½	94⅝	6.08	6.08
[4]Sub Deb 8⅝s 2002	Mn	A	5/98	A–	X	R	NC	....	....	....	....	....	150	F1	'92	109	103⅜	103⅜	8.34	8.34
[4]Sub Deb 7⅛s 2005	Ms	A	5/98	A–	X	R	NC	....	....	....	....	....	200	F1	'93	107⅛	99⅛	99⅝	7.15	7.15
[4]Sub Deb 7⅞s 2006	jJ15	A	5/98	A–	X	BE	NC	....	....	....	....	....	150		'94	112⅞	102	102⅛	7.71	7.71
[4]Sub Deb 6½s 2009	Jj15	A	5/98	A–	X	BE	NC	....	....	....	....	....	200	C5	'94	104¾	93¼	93¼	6.97	6.97
Sub Nts 9⅜s 2001	jJ	A	5/98	A–	X	R	NC	....	....	....	....	....	200	M2	'89	109	103⅜	103⅜	9.07	9.07
Sub Nts 9¾s 2001	mN	A	5/98	A–	X	BE	NC	....	....	....	....	....	150	M2	'91	111⅛	104¾	104¾	9.31	9.31
[4]Sub Nts 8½s 2002	Fa15	A	5/98	A–	X	R	NC	....	....	....	....	....	200	M2	'92	108⅛	102⅞	102⅞	8.26	8.26
[4]Sub Nts 8⅛s 2002	Jd15	A	5/98	A–	X	R	NC	....	....	....	....	....	100	G1	'92	107¾	102¼	102¼	7.95	7.94
[4]Sub Nts 7⅝s 2003	Jj15	A	5/98	A–	X	R	NC	....	....	....	....	....	200	L3	'93	107	101⅜	101⅜	7.52	7.52
• Sub Nts 7½s 2003	Fa	A	5/98	A–	X	BE	NC	....	....	....	....	....	200	S1	'93	105½	100⅝	101½	7.39	7.39
• Sub Nts 6½s 2005	fA	A	5/98	A–	X	BE	NC	....	....	....	....	....	200	C1	'93	104⅛	96⅜	95	6.84	6.84
Sub Nts 6s 2005	mN	A			X	BE	NC	....	....	....	....	....	300	C1	'98	101½	93⅛	93⅞	6.39	6.39
• Sub Nts 6¼s 2006	Jj15	A	5/98	A–	X	BE	NC	....	....	....	....	....	200	C1	'96	104	94	s94⅞	6.59	6.59
Sub Nts 7⅛s 2007	Fa	A	5/98	A–	X	BE	NC	....	....	....	....	....	300	C1	'97	108¾	97⅝	97⅝	7.30	7.30
Sub Nts 7¼s 2007	Jd	A	5/98	A–	X	BE	NC	....	....	....	....	....	300	C1	'97	109⅞	98	98	7.40	7.40
Sub Nts 6⅜s 2008	Fa15	A	5/98	A–	X	BE	NC	....	....	....	....	....	200	C1	'98	104	92⅞	92⅞	6.86	6.86
• Sub Nts 6¾s 2008	fA15	A	5/98	A–	X	BE	NC	....	....	....	....	....	200	L3	'93	106	96	94⅝	7.13	7.13
• Sub Nts 6⅛s 2008	aO15	A	5/98	A–	X	BE	NC	....	....	....	....	....	100	C1	'93	102	91	91⅛	6.72	6.72
• Sub Nts 6½s 2009	Jj15	A	5/98	A–	X	BE	NC	....	....	....	....	....	150	G1	'94	105⅜	92¼	92⅞	7.00	7.00
Sub Nts 6s 2009	Fa15	A			X	BE	NC	....	....	....	....	....	350	C1	'99	99¼	90	90	6.67	6.67
Sub Nts 7⅛s 2009	Jd15	A	5/98	A–	X	BE	NC	....	....	....	....	....	250	C1	'97	110⅛	97	97	7.35	7.34
Sub Nts 7s 2009	mN15	A			X	BE	NC	....	....	....	....	....	500	C1	'99	99⅛	96⅛	96⅛	7.28	7.28
[5]Sub[4]Cap Nts 10⅛s 2000	mN	A	5/98	A–	X	R	NC	....	....	....	....	....	150	S1	'88	107⅞	102⅝	102⅝	9.87	9.86
• F/R[6]Sub Nts 2003	QAug	A	5/98	A–	X	BE	NC	....	....	....	....	....	100	S1	'93	93	93	99¼	....	....
• F/R[7]Sub Nts 2003	QJul15	A	5/98	A–	X	BE	NC	....	....	....	....	....	150	B7	'93	No Sale		90	....	....
Sub M-T Nts 'A' 6¾s 2006	mS15	A	5/98	A–	X	BE	NC	....	....	....	....	....	100	C1	'97	105⅞	95¼	95¼	7.09	7.09
Chelsea GCA Realty Ptnr	***57***	***4.56***		***3.28***	***3.06***	***Dc***	***12.20***			***6-30-99***	***395.0***		***711.0***	***55.6***						
Nts[8] 7¾s 2001	Jj26	BBB–	9/97	BB+	X	BE	NC	....	....	....	....	....	100	M2	'96	101¼	98⅜	100⅛	7.74	7.74
Nts 7¼s 2007	aO21	BBB–			X	BE	[9]Z100	....	....	....	....	....	100	M2	'97	98⅛	89	91⅜	7.93	7.93
Chemical Bank	***10***	***Subsid of Chem'l Bkg,see Chase Manhattan***																		
F/R[10]Sub Nts 2003	QJul29	A+	5/98	A	X	BE	NC	....	....	....	....	....	150	B7	'93	100	98⅝	99½	....	....
Sub Nts 7¼s 2002	mS15	A+	5/98	A	X	R	NC	....	....	....	....	....	300	G1	'92	104⅜	99⅝	99⅝	7.28	7.28
Sub Nts 7s 2005	Jd	A+	5/98	A	X	BE	NC	....	....	....	....	....	200	G1	'93	107⅜	98⅜	98⅜	7.12	7.11
Sub Nts 6⅝s 2005	fA15	A+	5/98	A	X	BE	NC	....	....	....	....	....	150	S1	'93	105½	96⅜	96½	6.87	6.86
Sub Nts 6⅛s 2008	mN	A+	5/98	A	X	BE	NC	....	....	....	....	....	150	M2	'93	103½	90⅞	90⅞	6.74	6.74
Sub Nts 6.70s 2008	fA15	A+	5/98	A	X	BE	NC	....	....	....	....	....	150	M6	'93	107⅝	94⅝	94⅝	7.08	7.08
[11]Chesapeake[12]Pot.Tel Md	***67a***	***8.11***		***6.90***	***8.19***	***Dc***	***10.80***	***488.0***	***752.0***	***6-30-99***	***858.0***		***2109***	***51.3***						
Deb 4⅜s 2002	Jj	AA	3/91	AA–	X	CR	100	....	....	....	....	....	50.0	M6	'63	97⅜	95	95	4.61	4.61
Deb 6s 2003	Mn	AA			X	BE	NC	....	....	....	....	....	200	S1	'93	103	96⅞	96⅞	6.19	6.19
Deb 5⅞s 2004	Jd	AA	3/91	AA–	X	R	100	5-31-00	....	....	....	....	60.0	M2	'67	99⅜	94⅞	94⅞	6.19	6.19
Deb 6⅝s 2008	aO	AA	3/91	AA–	X	R	100.65	9-30-00	....	....	....	....	75.0	M6	'68	100⅝	94	94⅛	7.04	7.04
• Deb 7¼s 2012	Fa	AA	3/91	AA–	X	R	101.51	1-31-00	....	....	....	....	50.0	M6	'72	102¼	94	95⅛	7.62	7.62

Uniform Footnote Explanations-See Page 260. Other: [1] See Chem'l Bank,Margaretten Finl. [2] Int adj mthly(1 Mo LIBOR&0.02%). [3] Int pd monthly. [4] Was Chemical Banking. [5] To be exch for Cap Sec when due. [6] Int adj qtrly. [7] Int(min 4.35%)adj qtrly. [8] Gtd by Chelsea GCA Realty Inc. [9] Plus Make-Whole Amt. [10] Int(min 4.20%)adj qtrly. [11] Subsid of Bell Atlantic Corp. [12] Now Bell Atlantic-Maryland.

Title-Industry Code & Co. Finances (In Italics) / Individual Issue Statistics (Exchange)	Ind / Interest Dates	1996 / S&P Rating	1997 / Date of Last Rating Change	1998 / Prior Rating	Eligible	Year End / Bond Form	Cash & Equiv. / Regular Price	Curr. Assets / Regular (Begins) Thru	Curr. Liab. / Sinking Fund Price	Balance Sheet Date / Sinking Fund (Begins) Thru	L. Term Debt (Mil $) / Refund/Other Restriction Price	Refund/Other Restriction (Begins) Thru	Capital-ization (Mil $) / Outst'g (Mil $)	Total Debt % Capital / Underwriting Firm	Underwriting Year	Price Range 1999 High	Price Range 1999 Low	Mo. End Price Sale(s) or Bid	Curr. Yield	Yield to Mat.
***Chesapeake Pot.Tel Md** (Cont.)*																				
Deb 7.15s 2023	Mn	**AA**			X	BE	100	(5-1-13)	....	....	....	....	250	G1	'93	108¾	90⅞	91	7.86	7.86
Deb 8s 2029	a015	**AA**	3/91	AA–	X	R	NC	....	....	....	....	....	50.0	M6	'89	125¼	101⅜	101½	7.88	7.88
Deb 8.30s 2031	fA	**AA**			X	BE	NC	....	....	....	....	....	100	L3	'91	128⅜	104¼	104⅜	7.95	7.95
[1]Chesapeake&Pot.Tel Va[2]	***67a***	*8.94*	*7.85*	*9.02*		*Dc*	*10.40*	*550.0*	*763.0*	*6-30-99*	*844.0*		*2325*	*44.4*						
Deb 7⅛s 2002	Jj15	**AA**	4/97	AA+	X	BE	NC	....	....	....	....	....	100	S1	'92	105⅛	99⅞	99⅞	7.13	7.13
Deb 5¼s 2005	Mn	**AA**	4/97	AA+	X	R	100.19	4-30-00	....	....	....	....	50.0	F1	'66	97⅝	90⅝	90⅝	5.79	5.79
Deb 6⅛s 2005	jJ15	**AA**	4/97	AA+	X	BE	NC	....	....	....	....	....	100	L3	'93	103⅞	94¼	94¼	6.50	6.50
Deb 5⅝s 2007	Ms	**AA**	4/97	AA+	X	R	100.57	2-28-00	....	....	....	....	65.0	F1	'67	98⅜	89⅛	89⅛	6.31	6.31
Deb 6¾s 2008	Mn	**AA**	4/97	AA+	X	R	100.63	4-30-00	....	....	....	....	70.0	M6	'68	100⅞	94½	94⅝	7.13	7.13
• Deb 7¼s 2012	Jd	**AA**	4/97	AA+	X	R	101.40	5-31-00	....	....	....	....	50.0	F1	'72	102⅝	97	98	7.40	7.40
Deb 7⅝s 2012	jD	**AA**	4/97	AA+	X	BE	NC	....	....	....	....	....	100	F1	'92	117⅞	99½	99½	7.66	7.66
Deb 7⅞s 2022	Jj15	**AA**	4/97	AA+	X	BE	NC	....	....	....	....	....	100	S1	'92	120⅝	99⅛	99¼	7.93	7.93
Deb 7¼s 2024	Ao15	**AA**	4/97	AA+	X	BE	103.17	(4-15-03)	....	....	....	....	75.0	L3	'93	104¼	89½	89⅝	8.09	8.09
Deb 7s 2025	jJ15	**AA**	4/97	AA+	X	BE	102.93	(7-15-03)	....	....	....	....	125	C4	'93	101¾	86¼	86⅜	8.10	8.10
Deb 8⅜s 2029	aO	**AA**	4/97	AA+	X	R	NC	....	....	....	....	....	100	M2	'89	132⅝	104⅞	104⅞	7.99	7.99
[1]Chesapeake[3]Pot.TelWashDC	***67a***	*5.30*	*4.99*	*10.80*		*Dc*	*2.23*	*180.0*	*300.0*	*6-30-99*	*164.0*		*676.0*	*41.3*						
Deb 5⅝s 2006	jJ	**AA**	3/83	AAA	X	R	100.35	6-30-00	....	....	....	....	25.0	H1	'66	98	89¾	89¾	6.27	6.27
Deb 7s 2009	Fa	**AA**	3/83	AAA	X	R	100.75	1-31-00	....	....	....	....	50.0	F1	'69	101	95⅞	97⅛	7.21	7.21
Deb 7¾s 2023	Fa	**AA**			X	BE	103.512	(2-1-03)	....	....	....	....	90.0	F1	'93	110⅜	93¾	93⅞	8.26	8.25
[1]Chesapeake&Pot.TelWVa[4]	***67a***	*7.66*	*8.07*	*9.80*		*Dc*	*2.83*	*130.0*	*209.0*	*6-30-99*	*199.0*		*558.0*	*47.5*						
Deb 5s 2000	Ms	**AA**	4/97	AA+	X	CR	100	....	....	....	....	....	25.0	H1	'60	99¾	99¼	99¾	5.01	5.01
Deb 6.05s 2003	Mn15	**AA**	4/97	AA+	X	BE	NC	....	....	....	....	....	50.0	M2	'93	103	96⅝	96⅝	6.26	6.26
Deb 7s 2004	fA15	**AA**	4/97	AA+	X	BE	NC	....	....	....	....	....	50.0	G1	'92	108⅜	98⅞	98⅞	7.08	7.08
• Deb 7¼s 2013	Fa	**AA**	4/97	AA+	X	R	101.70	1-31-00	....	....	....	....	50.0	F1	'73	102½	97	98⅞	7.33	7.33
Chesapeake Corp	***50***	*2.39*	*4.83*	*4.58*		*Dc*	*36.00*	*436.0*	*296.5*	*9-30-99*	*643.0*		*1081*	*58.6*						
Deb[5] 9⅞s 2003	Mn	**BBB**	2/95	BBB–	X	R	NC	....	....	....	....	....	33.6	G1	'91	115	103	103⅛	9.58	9.57
Deb[5] 7.20s 2005	Ms15	**BBB**	2/95	BBB–	X	R	NC	....	....	....	[6]Z100	....	85.0	S1	'93	106¼	92	92⅛	7.82	7.82
Nts[5] 10⅜s 2000	aO	**BBB**	2/95	BBB–	X	R	NC	....	....	....	[6]Z100	....	55.0	S1	'90	107⅝	101½	101⅝	10.21	10.21
Chesapeake Energy	***49a***	*[7]3.64*	*[8]d7.43*	*0.38*		*Dc*	*29.92*	*97.84*	*88.57*	*9-30-99*	*921.0*		*889.4*	*103.3*						
• Sr Nts 'B' 7⅞s 2004	Ms15	**B**	9/98	B+	Y	BE	[9]Z100	....	....	....	....	....	150	D6	'97	90	55⅛	79⅝	9.89	9.89
• Sr Nts[10] 'B' 9⅝s 2005	Mn	**B**			Y	BE	[9]Z100	4-30-02	....	....	[11]Z109.625	5-1-01	500	Exch.	'98	99¾	65	93⅛	10.34	10.33
• Sr Nts[12] 9⅛s 2006	Ao15	**B**	9/98	B+	Y	BE	[13]Z104.5625	(4-15-01)	....	....	....	....	120	B7	'96	95⅛	51¾	s88⅛	10.35	10.35
• Sr Nts 'B' 8½s 2012	Ms15	**B**	9/98	B+	Y	BE	[9]Z100	3-14-04	....	....	....	....	150	D6	'97	87	59	78⅝	10.81	10.81
Chevron Capital U.S.A.	***25***	***Gtd by Chevron Corp,see***																		
Gtd[14]Nts 7.45s 2004	fA15	**AA**			X	BE	100	(8-15-01)	....	....	....	....	350	G1	'94	105½	100¼	100¼	7.43	7.43
Chevron[15]Corp[16]	***49c***	*9.19*	*12.47*	*4.53*		*Dc*	*1465*	*7335*	*9841*	*9-30-99*	*4857*		*25266*	*32.1*						
Nts 6⅝s 2004	aO	**AA**			X	BE	[17]Z100	....	....	....	....	....	500	L3	'99	100⅜	98⅝	98⅝	6.72	6.72
Chiquita Brands Int'l[18]	***26***	*1.13*	*1.08*	*0.91*		*Dc*	*132.9*	*932.8*	*473.7*	*9-30-99*	*1195*		*2087*	*60.2*						
Sr Nts[19] 9⅝s 2004	Jj15	**B+**	3/95	BB–	Y	R	NC	....	....	....	....	....	250	L3	'91	104	70	74	13.01	13.00
Sr Nts[19] 9⅛s 2004	Ms	**B+**	3/95	BB–	Y	R	NC	....	....	....	....	....	175	L3	'94	103	71	73½	12.41	12.41
Sr Nts[19] 10¼s 2006	mN	**B+**			Y	BE	105.125	(11-1-01)	....	....	....	....	150	L3	'96	106	70½	72½	14.14	14.13
• Sr[10]Nts[20] 10s 2009	Jd15	**B+**			Y	BE	[21]Z106	6-14-04	....	....	[22]Z110	6-15-02	200	L3	'99	101	68	s79	12.66	12.65
[23]Chrysler Corp[24]	***9***	*5.53*	*4.64*	*10.20*		*Dc*				*p12-31-98*	*[25]43999*									
Deb 7.45s 2027	Ms	**A+**	10/98	A	X	BE	[26]Z100	....	....	....	....	....	600	S1	'97	117¼	96⅞	97⅛	7.67	7.67
Deb[27] 7.40s 2097	fA	**A+**	10/98	A	X	BE	100	....	....	....	....	....	500	S1	'97	115	92¼	92⅜	8.01	8.01

Uniform Footnote Explanations-See Page 260. Other: [1] Subsid of Bell Atlantic Corp. [2] Now Bell Atlantic-Virginia. [3] Now Bell Atlantic-Washington D.C. [4] Now Bell Atlantic-West Virginia. [5] (HRO)On Chge of Ctrl at 100. [6] In whole,if 80% outstg put. [7] Fiscal Jun'96 & prior. [8] 12 Mo Dec'97. [9] Plus Make-Whole Premium. [10] (HRO)On Chge of Ctrl at 101. [11] Max $167M red w/proceeds Equity Off'g. [12] Co must offer repurch at 101 on Chge of Ctrl. [13] Greater of 104.5625 or amt based on formula. [14] Gtd by Chevron Corp. [15] Was Standard Oil(Calif). [16] See Chevron Capital U.S.A. [17] Red at greater of 100 or amt based on formula. [18] Was United Brands. [19] (HRO)On Chge of Ctrl Triggering Event at 101. [20] Co may red in whole,at 100,for tax law chge. [21] Red at greater or 100 or amt based on formula. [22] Max $70M red w/proceeds of Equity Off'g. [23] See Auburn Hills Trust. [24] Now DaimlerChrysler AG. [25] Incl curr amts. [26] Plus make-whole amt. [27] Red for Tax Event,as defined.

Title-Industry Code & Co. Finances (In Italics) / Exchange, Individual Issue Statistics, Interest Dates	S&P Rating	Date of Last Rating Change	Prior Rating	Eligible	Bond Form	Redemption Provisions: Regular Price	Regular (Begins) Thru	Sinking Fund Price	Sinking Fund (Begins) Thru	Refund/Other Restriction Price	Refund/Other Restriction (Begins) Thru	Outst'g (Mil $)	Underwriting Firm	Underwriting Year	Price Range 1999 High	Price Range 1999 Low	Mo. End Price Sale(s) or Bid	Curr. Yield	Yield to Mat.
Title-Industry Code & Co. Finances (In Italics)		*Fixed Charge Coverage 1996*	*1997*	*1998*	*Year End*	*Million $ Cash & Equiv.*	*Curr. Assets*	*Curr. Liab.*	*Balance Sheet Date*	*L. Term Debt (Mil $)*		*Capital-ization (Mil $)*	*Total Debt % Capital*						
Chrysler Financial Co. L.L.C. 25g	***No Recent Fin'ls***																		
Nts 6⅜s 2000 Jj28	A+	10/98	A	X	BE	NC	....	....	....	....	....	300	M5	'97	101	100	100	6.38	6.37
• Nts 6⅝s 2000 fA15	A+	10/98	A	X	BE	NC	....	....	....	....	....	300	S1	'93	102¼	99⅜	99⅝	6.65	6.65
Nts 5⅞s 2001 Fa7	A+	10/98	A	X	BE	NC	....	....	....	....	....	300	B7	'96	101⅛	99⅛	99⅛	5.93	5.93
Nts 6.95s 2002 Ms25	A+	10/98	A	X	BE	NC	....	....	....	....	....	300	M2	'97	104½	100⅛	100⅛	6.94	6.94
• Put-Ext'd[1]Nts[2] 8½s 2018 [3]Fa	A+	10/98	A	X	R	[4]100	....	....	....	....	....	0.99	M2	'88	101⅞	99	99⅛	8.58	8.57
M-T Nts 'N' 7.96s 2000 [5]ms15	A+	10/98	A	X	BE	NC	....	....	....	....	....	15.0	M2	'95	102⅞	100¼	100¼	7.94	7.94
M-T Nts 'N' 7.73s 2000 [6]ms15	A+	10/98	A	X	BE	NC	....	....	....	....	....	15.0	S1	'95	102⅝	100¼	100¼	7.71	7.71
M-T Nts 'P' 6.17s 2000 [7]ms15	A+	10/98	A	X	BE	NC	....	....	....	....	....	20.0	C2	'95	101½	99⅝	99⅝	6.19	6.19
M-T Nts 'P' 6.20s 2000 [7]ms15	A+	10/98	A	X	BE	NC	....	....	....	....	....	30.0	M2	'95	101⅝	99⅝	99⅝	6.22	6.22
M-T Nts 'P' 6.65s 2002 [8]ms15	A+	10/98	A	X	BE	NC	....	....	....	....	....	20.0	M2	'95	104	99¼	99¼	6.70	6.70
M-T Nts 'Q' 6.61s 2000 [9]fa15	A+	10/98	A	X	BE	NC	....	....	....	....	....	43.0	S1	'97	101¾	100¼	100¼	6.59	6.59
F/R[10]M-T Nts 2000 QJul17	A+	10/98	A	X	BE	NC	....	....	....	....	....	55.0	C1	'97	99⅞	99⅛	99⅞	....	....
F/R[11]M-T Nts 'Q' 2002 [12]Jul17	A+	10/98	A	X	BE	NC	....	....	....	....	....	100		'97	100¼	99½	99⅞	....	....
F/R[13]M-T Nts 'R' 2001 [14]	A+	10/98	A	X	BE	NC	....	....	....	....	....	35.0	S1	'98	100⅛	99½	100	....	....
F/R[13]M-T Nts 'R' 2002 [15]	A+	10/98	A	X	BE	NC	....	....	....	....	....	100	P4	'98	100¼	99⅜	99⅞	....	....
Chubb Capital Corp 25	***Gtd by Chubb Corp,see***																		
Gtd[16]Nts 6⅞s 2003 Fa	AA+			X	R	NC	....	....	....	....	....	100	M5	'93	105½	100⅛	100⅛	6.87	6.87
Chubb Corp[17] 35c		*7.11*	*12.95*	*31.69*	*Dc*				*9-30-99*	*793.0*		*6195*	*9.7*						
Nts 6.15s 2005 fA15	AA+			X	BE	NC	....	....	....	....	....	300	G1	'98	104⅞	95⅞	95⅞	6.41	6.41
Deb 6.60s 2018 fA15	AA+			X	BE	NC	....	....	....	....	....	100	G1	'98	106¼	88⅜	88½	7.46	7.46
CIGNA Corp 35d		*16.70*	*13.99*	*16.95*	*Dc*				*9-30-99*	*1360*		*9273*	*18.5*						
Nts 8¾s 2001 aO	A	10/97	A–	X	BE	NC	....	....	....	....	....	100	F1	'91	107¼	102⅝	102⅝	8.53	8.53
Nts 7.40s 2003 Jj15	A	10/97	A–	X	BE	NC	....	....	....	....	....	100	M2	'93	105⅛	99⅝	99⅝	7.43	7.43
Nts 6⅜s 2006 Jj15	A	10/97	A–	X	BE	NC	....	....	....	....	....	100	C5	'94	101⅝	92⅜	92½	6.89	6.89
Nts 8¼s 2007 Jj	A	10/97	A–	X	BE	NC	....	....	....	....	....	100	G1	'92	113	101¼	101¼	8.15	8.15
Nts 8.30s 2023 Jj15	NR	7/98	A		BE	NC	....	....	....	....	....	16.9	M2	'93	114¾	98	98⅜	8.44	8.44
Nts 7.65s 2023 Ms	A	10/97	A–	X	BE	NC	....	....	....	....	....	100	G1	'93	107¼	91⅜	91⅞	8.33	8.33
[18]Cincinnati Bell 67a		*8.52*	*9.76*	*8.23*	*Dc*	*3.40*	*213.0*	*438.0*	*9-30-99*	*766.0*		*1073*	*92.1*						
[19]Deb[20] 4⅜s 2002 fA	BBB–	11/99	AA–	X	CR	100	....	....	....	....	....	20.0	H1	'62	97½	92⅜	92⅜	4.74	4.74
Nts 9.10s 2000 Jd15	NR	3/97	A–		R	NC	....	....	....	....	....	[21]18.6	M6	'90	104⅞	100⅞	100⅞	9.02	9.02
Nts 7¼s 2023 dJ15	BB+	11/99	A	Y	R	NC	....	....	....	....	....	50.0	M6	'93	111⅝	78	78	9.29	9.29
Cincinnati Financial 35c		*15.05*	*19.95*	*11.96*	*Dc*				*9-30-99*	*546.0*		*5588*	*9.8*						
Deb 6.90s 2028 Mn15	AA–			X	BE	NC	....	....	....	....	....	420	S4	'98	102¼	86¼	87⅜	7.90	7.90
Cincinnati Gas Elec[22] 75		*3.92*	*4.37*	*4.37*	*Dc*	*20.70*	*437.0*	*826.0*	*6-30-99*	*1220*		*3179*	*47.7*						
1st 7¼s 2002 mS	A–	7/95	BBB+	X	R	NC	....	....	....	....	....	100	M6	'92	106	100¼	100¼	7.23	7.23
1st 6.45s 2004 Fa15	A–	7/95	BBB+	X	R	NC	....	....	....	....	....	110	M6	'94	104⅜	96	96	6.72	6.72
1st 7.20s 2023 aO	A–	7/95	BBB+	X	R	103.54	(10-1-03)	Z100	(10-1-03)	....	....	300	M6	'93	103½	88	88⅛	8.17	8.17
Deb 6.40s 2008 Ao	BBB+			X	BE	[23]Z100	....	....	....	....	....	100	M7	'98	102⅞	90½	90⅝	7.06	7.06
Deb[24] 6.90s 2025 Jd	BBB+	7/95	BBB	X	BE	NC	....	....	....	....	....	150	M6	'95	104⅞	97	97	7.11	7.11
[25]Cincinnati Milacron 41d		*3.44*	*4.63*	*4.23*	*Dc*	*41.20*	*709.0*	*555.0*	*9-30-99*	*320.0*		*1032*	*53.2*						
Nts 7⅞s 2000 Mn15	BB+			Y	BE	NC	....	....	....	....	....	100	Exch.		101¼	100	100	7.88	7.87
Nts 8⅜s 2004 Ms15	BB+	10/97	BB	Y	BE	NC	....	....	....	....	....	115	C5		104⅜	98	98	8.55	8.55
Cinemark USA 24b		*1.75*	*1.90*	*1.53*	*Dc*	*7.93*	*40.20*	*91.30*	*6-30-99*	*731.0*		*829.0*	*88.4*						
Sr[26]Nts 12s 2002 Jd	BB–	2/95	B+	Y	R	102	5-31-00	100	(6-1-00)	....	....	1.63	B7	'92	104⅞	100½	100⅝	11.93	11.92
CINergy Corp 72b		*n/a*	*n/a*	*n/a*	*Dc*	*57.50*	*1241*	*1823*	*9-30-99*	*2723*		*6321*	*57.7*						
[26]Deb[27] 6⅛s 2004 Ao15	BBB+			X	BE	[23]Z100	....	....	....	....	....	200		'99	96¼	94	94	6.52	6.52

Uniform Footnote Explanations-See Page 260. Other: [1] Int to 2-1-00,adj aft as defined. [2] (HRO)On 2-1-00 at 100,aft as defined. [3] Due 2-1-18. [4] On 2-1-00,aft as defined. [5] Due 2-28-00. [6] Due 3-2-00. [7] Due 12-6-00. [8] Due 11-12-02. [9] Due 6-16-00. [10] Int adj qtrly, Jan 17, etc. [11] Int adj mthly(1 Mo LIBOR&0.125%). [12] Int pd monthly,ea 3rd Wed. [13] Int adj monthly. [14] Due 1-29-01,int paid monthly,ea 3rd Wed. [15] Due 1-30-02:int pd mthly ea 3rd Wed. [16] Gtd by Chubb Corp. [17] See Chubb Capital. [18] Now BroadWing Inc. [19] Was Cincinnati & Suburban Bell Tel. [20] Oblig of Cinn Bell Tel. [21] Defeased,funds deposited w/trustee. [22] Subsid of CINergy Corp. [23] Red at greater of 100 or amt based on formula. [24] (HRO)On 6-1-05 at 100. [25] Now Milacron Inc. [26] (HRO)On Chge of Ctrl at 101. [27] Issued in min denom $100T.

Title-Industry Code & Co. Finances (In Italics) / Individual Issue Statistics — Exchange	Ind / Interest Dates	Fixed Charge Coverage 1996 / S&P Rating	1997 / Date of Last Rating Change	1998 / Prior Rating	Eligible	Year End / Bond Form	Million $ Cash & Equiv. / Regular Price	Curr. Assets / Regular (Begins) Thru	Curr. Liab. / Sinking Fund Price	Balance Sheet Date / Sinking Fund (Begins) Thru	L. Term Debt (Mil $) / Refund/Other Restriction Price	Capital-ization (Mil $) / Refund/Other Restriction (Begins) Thru	Outst'g (Mil $)	Total Debt % Capital / Underwriting Firm	Underwriting Year	Price Range 1999 High	Price Range 1999 Low	Mo. End Price Sale(s) or Bid	Curr. Yield	Yield to Mat.
***CINergy Corp** (Cont.)*																				
Deb[1] 6.53s 2008	jD16	**BBB+**			X	BE	[2]Z100	....	....	....	....	....	200	Exch.	'98	99⅞	90½	90½	7.22	7.21
[3]Circus Circus Enterpr	***40i***	***3.27***	***2.00***	***1.62***		***Ja***	***104.0***	***249.0***	***216.0***	***10-31-99***	***2459***	***3666***		***67.1***						
Sr Nts 6.45s 2006	Fa	**BBB–**	4/98	BBB	X	BE	NC	....	....	....	....	....	200	M6	'96	92⅛	87¾	87¾	7.35	7.35
Sr Sub Deb[1] 7⅝s 2013	jJ15	**BB+**	4/98	BBB–	Y	R	NC	....	....	....	....	....	150	S1	'93	94	83	87	8.76	8.76
Sr Sub Nts[1] 6¾s 2003	jJ15	**BB+**	4/98	BBB–	Y	R	NC	....	....	....	....	....	150	S1	'93	96¼	90½	94½	7.14	7.14
Sr Sub Nts 9¼s 2005	jD	**BB+**			Y	BE	Z100	....	....	....	[45]Z109.25	12-1-02	275	M2	'98	105½	99	101⅝	9.10	9.10
CIT Group Holding[6]	***25***	***Now CIT Group Inc,see***																		
Nts 6⅜s 2002	Af1	**A+**			X	BE	NC	....	....	....	....	....	200	S1	'97	103	98⅛	98⅜	6.48	6.48
Nts 5½s 2004	Fa15	**A+**			X	BE	NC	....	....	....	....	....	600		'99	99⅝	93⅜	93⅝	5.87	5.88
Nts 6⅝s 2005	Jd15	**A+**			X	BE	NC	....	....	....	....	....	250	U1	'95	104⅞	96⅜	96½	6.87	6.86
Nts 7¼s 2005	fA15	**A+**			X	BE	NC	....	....	....	....	....	350	S4	'99	101¾	99¼	99¼	7.30	7.30
• Nts 5⅞s 2008	aO15	**A+**			X	BE	NC	....	....	....	....	....	200	M6	'93	96⅝	86	85⅝	6.86	6.86
M-T Sr Nts 6.80s 2000	Ao17	**A+**			X	BE	NC	....	....	....	....	....	100	C5	'97	101⅝	100¼	100¼	6.78	6.78
M-T Sr Nts 6.70s 2000	Mn2	**A+**			X	BE	NC	....	....	....	....	....	100	L3	'97	101½	100⅛	100¼	6.68	6.68
M-T Sr Nts 6.70s 2000	Jd2	**A+**			X	BE	NC	....	....	....	....	....	150	M6	'97	101⅝	100⅛	100¼	6.68	6.68
M-T Sr Nts 5s 2000	aO6	**A+**			X	BE	NC	....	....	....	....	....	200	S4	'98	99¼	98⅜	98¾	5.06	5.06
M-T Sr Nts 6.20s 2000	aO20	**A+**			X	BE	NC	....	....	....	....	....	500	M5	'97	101¼	99⅝	99⅝	6.22	6.22
M-T Sr Nts 6⅛s 2000	jD15	**A+**			X	BE	NC	....	....	....	....	....	125	S1	'97	101¼	99⅝	99⅝	6.16	6.16
M-T Sr Nts 5.85s 2001	Fa5	**A+**			X	BE	NC	....	....	....	....	....	75.0	S4	'98	100¾	98⅞	98⅞	5.92	5.92
M-T Sr Nts 6¼s 2001	Ms28	**A+**			X	BE	NC	....	....	....	....	....	100	M5	'96	101⅝	99⅛	99⅛	6.31	6.31
M-T Sr Nts 5.85s 2001	Ao9	**A+**			X	BE	NC	....	....	....	....	....	200	M2	'98	100¾	98⅝	98⅝	5.93	5.93
M-T Sr Nts 6s 2001	Mn8	**A+**			X	BE	NC	....	....	....	....	....	150	G1	'98	101⅛	98¾	98¾	6.08	6.08
M-T Sr Nts 6¾s 2001	Mn14	**A+**			X	BE	NC	....	....	....	....	....	100	U1	'96	102¾	99¾	99¾	6.77	6.77
M-T Sr Nts 6.05s 2001	Jd12	**A+**			X	BE	NC	....	....	....	....	....	150		'98	101¼	98¾	98¾	6.13	6.13
M-T Sr Nts 7⅛s 2002	Jd17	**A+**			X	BE	NC	....	....	....	....	....	150	S7	'96	104⅝	100	100	7.13	7.12
M-T Sr Nts 6⅜s 2002	aO	**A+**			X	BE	NC	....	....	....	....	....	300	L3	'97	102⅜	98	98	6.51	6.51
M-T Sr Nts 6.15s 2002	jD15	**A+**			X	BE	NC	....	....	....	....	....	150	S1	'95	101⅝	97¼	97¼	6.32	6.32
Sr Sub Cap Nts 8⅜s 2001	mN	**A**			X	BE	NC	....	....	....	....	....	100	S1	'91	107½	102⅛	102⅛	8.20	8.20
M-T Sr Sub Cap Nts[1] 9¼s 2001	Ms15	**A**			X	BE	NC	....	....	....	....	....	100	M2	'91	107⅝	102⅝	102⅝	9.01	9.01
CIT[7] Group[8] Inc[9]	***25a***	***1.25***	***1.48***	***1.52***		***Dc***				***9-30-99***	***20293***	***22932***		***87.5***						
Nts 5½s 2001	aO15	**A+**			X	BE	NC	....	....	....	....	....	200	S4	'98	99⅝	97⅜	97⅜	5.65	5.65
Nts 5⅝s 2003	aO15	**A+**			X	BE	NC	....	....	....	....	....	300	S4	'98	99¼	94½	94½	5.95	5.95
Nts[10] 7⅛s 2004	aO15	**A+**			X	BE	NC	....	....	....	....	....	1000	C1	'99	101	99¼	99¼	7.18	7.18
CITGO Petroleum Corp	***49***	***2.56***	***3.25***	***4.46***		***Dc***	***31.70***	***1799***	***1415***	***6-30-99***	***1285***	***3439***		***42.6***						
• Sr Nts 7⅞s 2006	Mn15	**BB**	12/99	BB+	Y	BE	NC	....	....	....	....	....	200	S1	'96	98¼	98¼	93	8.47	8.47
Citicorp	***10***	***Mgr w/Travelers Group,now CitiGroup Inc,see***																		
Sr Nts 5⅝s 2001	Fa15	**AA–**	10/98	A+	X	BE	NC	....	....	....	....	....	300	C4	'96	100⅜	98⅝	98⅝	5.70	5.70
F/R[11]M-T Nts 'C' 2000	QAug15	**AA–**	10/98	A+	X	BE	NC	....	....	....	....	....	80.0	C4	'97	100¼	99¾	100	....	....
F/R[11]M-T Nts 'C' 2000	QSep5	**AA–**	10/98	A+	X	BE	NC	....	....	....	....	....	50.0	C4	'97	100¼	99⅝	100	....	....
F/R[12]M-T Nts 'C' 2001	QJun22	**AA–**	10/98	A+	X	BE	NC	....	....	....	....	....	50.0	G1	'97	100¼	99½	100	....	....
F/R[13]M-T Nts 'C' 2001	QJun25	**AA–**	10/98	A+	X	BE	NC	....	....	....	....	....	50.0	B7	'97	100⅜	99⅝	100	....	....
F/R[14]M-T Nts 'C' 2001	QSep10	**AA–**	10/98	A+	X	BE	NC	....	....	....	....	....	50.0	C5	'97	100¼	99⅜	99⅞	....	....
F/R[15]M-T Nts 'C' 2002	QJun24	**AA–**	10/98	A+	X	BE	NC	....	....	....	....	....	50.0	M2	'97	100⅜	99⅜	100	....	....
F/R[15]M-T Nts 'C' 2002	QSep4	**AA–**	10/98	A+	X	BE	NC	....	....	....	....	....	50.0	M2	'97	100½	99⅜	99¾	....	....
F/R[16] M-T Nts[17]'F' 2000	QNov10	**AA–**	10/98	A+	X	BE	NC	....	....	....	....	....	235	S1	'97	100¼	99⅝	100	....	....

Uniform Footnote Explanations-See Page 260. Other: [1] Issued in min denom $100T. [2] Red at greater of 100 or amt based on formula. [3] Now Mandalay Resort Group. [4] Max $96.2M red w/proceeds of Equity Off'g. [5] Plus Make-Whole premium. [6] Was C.I.T. Financial. [7] Owned by Dai-Ichi Kangyo Bank & Mfrs Hanover. [8] Was CIT Group Hldgs. [9] See AT&T Capital,CIT Group Hldgs. [10] Co may red in whole, at 100, for tax law chge. [11] Int adj qtrly(3 Mo LIBOR & 0.01%). [12] Int adj qtrly(3 Mo LIBOR&0.075%). [13] Int adj qtrly(3 Mo LIBOR & 0.05%). [14] Int adj qtrly(3 Mo LIBOR&0.06%). [15] Int adj qtrly(3 Mo LIBOR&0.08%). [16] Int adj qtrly(3 Mo LIBOR & 0.07%). [17] Issued in min denom $50T.

Title-Industry Code & Co. Finances (In Italics)	Ind	Fixed Charge Coverage 1996	1997		1998	Year End	Million $ Cash & Equiv.	Curr. Assets	Curr. Liab.	Balance Sheet Date	L. Term Debt (Mil $)		Capital-ization (Mil $)	Total Debt % Capital						
Individual Issue Statistics Exchange	Interest Dates	S&P Rating	Date of Last Rating Change	Prior Rating	Eligible	Bond Form	Redemption Provisions: Regular Price	Regular (Begins) Thru	Sinking Fund Price	Sinking Fund (Begins) Thru	Refund/Other Restriction Price	Refund/Other Restriction (Begins) Thru	Outst'g (Mil $)	Underwriting Firm	Underwriting Year	Price Range 1999 High	Price Range 1999 Low	Mo. End Price Sale(s) or Bid	Curr. Yield	Yield to Mat.
***Citicorp** (Cont.)*																				
F/R[1]M-T Nts 'F' 2001	QMay24	**AA–**	10/98	A+	X	BE	NC	....	....	....	....	....	200	G1	'97	100¼	99½	100	....	....
M-T Nts 'F' 6.38s 2002	mN12	**AA–**	10/98	A+	X	BE	NC	....	....	....	....	....	50.0	L3	'97	103	98¼	98¼	6.49	6.49
Sub Nts 7⅛s 2004	Ms15	**A+**	10/98	A	X	BE	NC	....	....	....	....	....	200	S1	'94	106	99⅜	99⅜	7.17	7.17
Sub Nts 7⅝s 2005	Mn	**A+**	10/98	A	X	BE	NC	....	....	....	....	....	150	G1	'95	109⅛	100¾	100¾	7.57	7.57
Sub Nts 6¾s 2005	fA	**A+**	10/98	A	X	BE	NC	....	....	....	....	....	350	G1	'93	105⅛	96⅝	96⅝	6.99	6.99
Sub Nts 7⅛s 2006	Mn15	**A+**	10/98	A	X	BE	NC	....	....	....	....	....	250	G1	'96	107¼	98	98	7.27	7.27
Sub Nts 6⅜s 2006	Jj15	**A+**	10/98	A	X	BE	NC	....	....	....	....	....	250	S1	'96	102¾	94½	94½	6.75	6.75
Sub Nts 7¾s 2006	Jd15	**A+**	10/98	A	X	BE	NC	....	....	....	....	....	250	C4	'94	110⅞	101	101	7.67	7.67
Sub Nts 7.20s 2007	Jd15	**A+**	10/98	A	X	BE	NC	....	....	....	....	....	250	L3	'97	108⅜	97¾	97¾	7.37	7.36
Sub Nts 7¼s 2008	mS	**A+**	10/98	A	X	BE	NC	....	....	....	....	....	200	C4	'96	109⅜	97⅞	97⅞	7.41	7.41
Sub Nts 7¼s 2011	aO15	**A+**	10/98	A	X	BE	NC	....	....	....	....	....	200	B7	'96	110¼	96⅛	96⅛	7.54	7.54
Sub Nts 10¾s 2015	jD15	**A+**	10/98	A	X	R	102.9568	12-14-00	100	....	....	....	150	M2	'85	104¼	103½	103½	10.39	10.38
Sub Securities 9½s 2002	Fa	**A+**	10/98	A	X	BE	NC	....	....	....	....	....	150	G1	'92	110	105	105	9.05	9.05
Sub Securities 8⅝s 2002	jD	**A+**	10/98	A	X	BE	NC	....	....	....	....	....	150	L3	'92	110¼	103⅝	103⅝	8.32	8.32
Sub Securities 8s 2003	Fa	**A+**	10/98	A	X	BE	NC	....	....	....	....	....	400	C4	'93	108⅜	102⅛	102⅛	7.83	7.83
Sub Securities 7⅛s 2003	Jd	**A+**	10/98	A	X	BE	NC	....	....	....	....	....	250	S1	'93	105⅝	99⅝	99⅝	7.15	7.15
Nts 'C' 7s 2007	jJ	**A+**	10/98	A	X	BE	NC	....	....	....	....	....	200	B7	'97	108	96⅞	96⅞	7.23	7.22
M-T Sub Nts 'E' 7½s 2001	Jun15	**A+**	10/98	A	X	BE	100	....	....	....	....	....	10.8	S7	'94	100⅜	100⅛	100⅛	7.49	7.49
M-T Sub Nts 'E' 7.55s 2001	[2]Jul	**A+**	10/98	A	X	BE	100	....	....	....	....	....	10.0	S3	'94	100⅜	100¼	100⅜	7.52	7.52
M-T Sub Nts 'E' 7.85s 2001	[2]Jul15	**A+**	10/98	A	X	BE	100	....	....	....	....	....	7.50	S7	'94	100½	100⅛	100⅜	7.82	7.82
M-T Sub Nts 'E' 7.60s 2001	[2]Aug15	**A+**	10/98	A	X	BE	100	....	....	....	....	....	5.18	S7	'94	100⅜	100⅛	100⅜	7.57	7.57
M-T Sub Nts 'E' 7¾s 2001	[2]Aug15	**A+**	10/98	A	X	BE	100	....	....	....	....	....	8.50	S7	'94	100½	100⅛	100¼	7.73	7.73
M-T Sub Nts 'E' 7⅜s 2012	[2]Jun15	**A+**	10/98	A	X	BE	[3]100	(6-15-01)	....	....	....	....	35.0	M2	'97	103¾	94¾	95½	7.72	7.72
M-T Sub Nts'E' 7½s 2012	[2]Jun17	**A+**	10/98	A	X	BE	[4]100	(6-17-00)	....	....	....	....	25.0	M6	'97	102¾	94⅞	95⅞	7.82	7.82
M-T Sub Nts 'E' 7.08s 2012	[2]Sep15	**A+**	10/98	A	X	BE	■100	(9-15-01)	....	....	....	....	50.0	M2	'97	102¼	92⅞	93½	7.57	7.57
M-T Sub Nts 'F' 6⅜s 2008	Mn15	**A+**			X	BE	NC	....	....	....	....	....	750	S1	'98	103¾	92¼	92¼	6.91	6.91
***CitiGroup Inc**[5]*	***35d***	***2.33***		***1.44***	***1.37***	***Dc***				***9-30-99***	***53462***		***99325***	***54.3***						
Deb[5] 8⅝s 2007	Fa	**AA–**	4/97	A+	X	R	NC	....	....	....	....	....	100	M6	'87	118⅞	106⅛	106⅛	8.13	8.13
Nts 6⅛s 2000	Jd15	**AA–**	4/97	A+	X	BE	NC	....	....	....	....	....	200	M2	'93	101	99¾	99⅞	6.13	6.13
Sr Nts[6] 9½s 2002	Ms	**AA–**	4/97	A+	X	BE	NC	....	....	....	....	....	300	M2	'92	111½	104¾	104¾	9.07	9.07
Nts[7] 5.80s 2004	Ms15	**AA–**			X	BE	NC	....	....	....	....	....	750	S4	'99	99⅞	95⅛	95⅛	6.10	6.10
Nts 6⅝s 2005	mS15	**AA–**	4/97	A+	X	BE	NC	....	....	....	....	....	150	C5	'95	105½	97	97⅛	6.82	6.82
Nts 6¼s 2005	jD	**AA–**	4/97	A+	X	BE	NC	....	....	....	....	....	100	Exch.	'96	103¾	95⅛	95¼	6.56	6.56
Nts[7] 6.20s 2009	Ms15	**AA–**			X	BE	NC	....	....	....	....	....	750	S4	'99	100½	91¾	91¾	6.76	6.76
Nts 7⅞s 2025	Mn15	**AA–**	4/97	A+	X	BE	NC	....	....	....	....	....	200	S7	'95	116⅝	98⅝	100⅜	7.85	7.84
Nts[8] 6⅞s 2025	Jd	**AA–**	4/97	A+	X	BE	NC	....	....	....	....	....	150	S1	'95	105⅞	97⅞	98⅝	6.97	6.97
Nts 6⅝s 2028	Jj15	**AA–**			X	BE	NC	....	....	....	....	....	300	S4	'98	101	85½	86⅛	7.69	7.69
Citizens Utilities	***75***	***3.68***		***1.22***	***1.66***	***Dc***	***35.90***	***291.0***	***472.0***	***9-30-99***	***2080***		***4159***	***55.5***						
Deb 8.45s 2001	mS	**A+**	8/99	AA–	X	BE	NC	....	....	....	....	....	50.0	M6	'91	107¼	102⅛	102⅛	8.27	8.27
Deb 7.45s 2004	Jj15	**A+**	8/99	AA–	X	BE	NC	....	....	....	....	....	100	L3	'92	108¼	100¼	100¼	7.43	7.43
Deb 7.60s 2006	Jd	**A+**	8/99	AA–	X	BE	NC	....	....	....	....	....	175	L3	'94	111⅜	100½	100½	7.56	7.56
Deb 7s 2025	mN	**A+**	8/99	AA–	X	BE	NC	....	....	....	....	....	150	M6	'95	105¼	87⅝	87¾	7.98	7.98
Deb[9] 6.80s 2026	fA15	**A+**	8/99	AA–	X	BE	NC	....	....	....	....	....	100	M6	'96	104⅞	97½	97½	6.97	6.97
Deb[10] 7.68s 2034	aO	**A+**	8/99	AA–	X	BE	NC	....	....	....	....	....	100	M6	'94	121	98	98	7.84	7.84
Deb 7.45s 2035	jJ	**A+**	8/99	AA–	X	BE	NC	....	....	....	....	....	125	M6	'95	111½	91⅜	91½	8.14	8.14

Uniform Footnote Explanations-See Page 260. Other: [1] Int adj qtrly(3 Mo LIBOR & 0.125%). [2] Int pd monthly. [3] Red ea Jun & Dec 15. [4] Red ea Jun & Dec 17. [5] Was Travelers Group. [6] Issued in min denom $250T. [7] Co may red in whole,at 100,for tax law chge. [8] (HRO)On 6-1-05 at 100. [9] (HRO)On 8-15-03 at 100. [10] (HRO)On 10-1-01 at 100.

Title-Industry Code & Co. Finances (In Italics) / Individual Issue Statistics — Exchange	Ind / Interest Dates	Fixed Charge Coverage 1996 / S&P Rating	1997 / Date of Last Rating Change	1998 / Prior Rating	Eligible	Year End / Bond Form	Million $ Cash & Equiv. / Redemption Provisions Regular Price	Curr. Assets / Regular (Begins) Thru	Curr. Liab. / Sinking Fund Price	Balance Sheet Date / Sinking Fund (Begins) Thru	L. Term Debt (Mil $) / Refund/Other Restriction Price	Refund/Other Restriction (Begins) Thru	Capitalization (Mil $) / Outst'g (Mil $)	Total Debt % Capital / Underwriting Firm	Underwriting Year	Price Range 1999 High	Price Range 1999 Low	Mo. End Price Sale(s) or Bid	Curr. Yield	Yield to Mat.
***Citizens Utilities** (Cont.)*																				
Deb 7.05s 2046	aO	**A+**	8/99	AA−	X	BE	NC	....	....	....	....	....	200	L3	'96	106⅜	85½	85⅞	8.21	8.21
Claridge Hotel & Casino	***40i***	*d1.22*	*0.43*	*0.10*		*Dc*	***Bankruptcy Chapt 11***				*85.20*		*63.80*	*140.0*						
• 1st[1]Mtg[2] 11¾s 2002	§Fa	**D**	8/99	CC	Z	R			Default 8-1-99 int				85.0	D6	'94	84	50⅜	53	....	Flat
Clark Equipment Co.	***41b***	***Acquired by Ingersoll-Rand,see***																		
Nts 9¾s 2001	Ms	**A−**	9/97	A	X	R	NC	....	....	....	....	....	100	F1	'91	107½	102½	102½	9.51	9.51
[3]Clark Oil & Refining	***49***	*0.15*	*0.17*	*0.52*		*Dc*	*107.0*	*703.0*	*455.0*	*6-30-99*	*804.0*		*1029*	*78.1*						
• Sr Nts[2] 9½s 2004	mS15	**BB**	2/93	BB+	Y	R	100	....	100	(9-15-03)	....	....	175	G1	'92	102½	55⅝	s75	12.67	12.66
Clean Harbors	***53***	*d0.06*	*0.03*	*0.64*		*Dc*	*3.32*	*55.70*	*40.10*	*9-30-99*	*73.50*		*110.0*	*68.9*						
Sr Nts[2] 12½s 2001	Mn15	**B−**	6/98	B	Y	R	106.25	5-14-00	....	....	....	....	50.0	C5	'94	93	76	78¼	15.97	15.97
Clear Channel Commun	***12b***	*n/a*	*2.39*	*1.93*		*Dc*	*82.70*	*930.0*	*675.0*	*9-30-99*	*4404*		*13722*	*29.3*						
Sr Deb 6⅞s 2018	Jd15	**BBB−**			X	BE	100	....	....	....	....	....	175	S4	'98	99⅞	86⅛	88⅝	7.76	7.76
Deb 7¼s 2027	aO15	**BBB−**			X	BE	[4]Z100	....	....	....	....	....	300	C5	'97	103⅞	87⅝	90¼	8.03	8.03
Sr Nts 6⅝s 2008	Jd15	**BBB−**			X	BE	100	....	....	....	....	....	125	S4	'98	102¾	91¾	92¾	7.14	7.14
Cleveland Elec. Illum[5]	***72a***	*1.75*	*1.80*	*1.70*		*Dc*	*3.87*	*427.0*	*709.0*	*6-30-99*	*2870*		*4502*	*69.7*						
1st 7⅝s 2002	fA	**BB+**	7/97	BB	Y	R	NC	....	....	....	....	....	245	M6	'92	104⅝	99¾	99¾	7.64	7.64
1st 7⅜s 2003	Jd	**BB+**	7/97	BB	Y	R	NC	....	....	....	....	....	100	M6	'93	104⅞	98⅞	98⅞	7.46	7.46
1st B 9½s 2005	Mn15	**BB+**	7/97	BB	Y	BE	100	(5-15-02)	....	....	....	....	300	M6	'95	109	103⅝	103⅝	9.17	9.17
1st ('23E) 9s 2023	jJ	**BB+**	7/97	BB	Y	R	104.13	(7-1-03)	....	....	....	....	150	M6	'93	111¾	100⅜	100⅜	8.97	8.96
Cliffs Drilling	***49e***	*3.31*	*4.75*	*4.80*		*Dc*	*79.30*	*152.4*	*48.60*	*9-30-99*	*203.0*		*449.0*	*45.2*						
Sr Nts 'B'[2] 10¼s 2003	Mn15	**BB−**	3/99	BB+	Y	BE	Z105	(5-15-00)	....	....	....	....	150	J1	'96	105½	92	101	10.15	10.15
Clorox Co	***33***	*△8.23*	*△7.77*	*△7.29*		*Je*	*209.0*	*1154*	*1314*	*9-30-99*	*704.0*		*3013*	*47.9*						
Nts 8.80s 2001	jJ15	**A+**	2/97	AA−	X	R	NC	....	....	....	....	....	200	M5	'91	108⅜	103	103	8.54	8.54
CMI Industries	***68***	*d0.09*	*1.83*	*1.41*		*Dc*	*1.39*	*107.0*	*39.00*	*7-3-99*	*125.0*		*160.0*	*80.0*						
Sr Sub[6]Nts[7] 9½s 2003	aO	**NR**	5/97	B		R	102.375	9-30-00	....	....	[8]Z100	....	125	M2	'93	99	69	69⅛	13.74	13.74
CMS Energy	***75***	*2.32*	*2.28*	*1.75*		*Dc*	*234.0*	*1961*	*1991*	*9-30-99*	*8036*		*10818*	*77.5*						
Sr Nts[2] 8⅞s 2002	mN15	**BB**			Y	BE	NC	....	....	....	....	....	350	M6	'97	103	99½	99½	8.17	8.16
Nts[2] 7⅝s 2004	mN15	**BB**			Y	BE	[9]Z100	....	....	....	....	....	180	M6	'97	103⅛	94⅝	94⅝	8.06	8.06
Gen Term Nts 'A'[10] 7¾s 2002	[11]Nov15	**BB**			Y	BE	100	....	....	....	....	....	4.05		'95	100⅛	99¼	99¼	7.81	7.81
CNA Financial[12]	***35d***	*7.71*	*7.86*	*3.72*		*Dc*				*9-30-99*	*2894*		*11832*	*24.5*						
Deb 7¼s 2023	mN15	**A−**	5/95	A+	X	BE	NC	....	....	....	....	....	250	G1	'93	101⅜	84⅝	84⅝	8.57	8.57
Nts 6¼s 2003	mN15	**A−**	5/95	A+	X	BE	NC	....	....	....	....	....	250	G1	'93	100⅞	95⅛	95⅛	6.57	6.57
Nts 6¾s 2006	mN15	**A−**			X	BE	NC	....	....	....	....	....	250	M2	'96	103	93⅜	93⅜	7.23	7.23
Nts 6.45s 2008	Jj15	**A−**			X	BE	NC	....	....	....	....	....	150	M2	'98	100	90¼	90¼	7.15	7.15
Nts 6½s 2005	Ao15	**A−**			X	BE	NC	....	....	....	....	....	500	L3	'98	101⅛	93¾	93¾	6.93	6.93
Nts 6.95s 2018	Jj15	**A−**			X	BE	NC	....	....	....	....	....	150	M2	'98	99½	83⅞	84	8.27	8.27
Coastal Corp	***73a***	*2.36*	*2.28*	*3.20*		*Dc*	*56.00*	*2560*	*2558*	*9-30-99*	*4945*		*9156*	*58.7*						
• Sr Deb 9¾s 2003	fA	**BBB**	4/99	BBB−	X	R	NC	....	....	....	....	....	101	L3	'91	112	110⅛	104⅜	9.34	9.34
• Sr Deb[13] 10¼s 2004	aO15	**BBB**	4/99	BBB−	X	R	NC	....	....	....	....	....	38.0	D7	'89	115	114	106	9.67	9.67
• Sr Deb 6½s 2008	Jd	**BBB**	4/99	BBB−	X	BE	NC	....	....	....	....	....	200	C1	'98	No Sale		92⅛	7.06	7.06
• Sr Deb 6⅜s 2009	Fa	**BBB**	4/99	BBB−	X	BE	NC	....	....	....	....	....	200	L3	'99	100⅝	97⅝	91	7.01	7.00
• Sr Deb 10¾s 2010	aO	**BBB**	4/99	BBB−	X	R	NC	....	....	....	....	....	57.0	L3	'90	No Sale		119¼	9.01	9.01
• Sr Deb 9⅝s 2012	Mn15	**BBB**	4/99	BBB−	X	R	NC	....	....	....	....	....	150	L3	'92	No Sale		100	9.63	9.62
• Sr Deb[14] 6.70s 2027	Fa15	**BBB**	4/99	BBB−	X	BE	NC	....	....	....	....	....	200	S7	'97	No Sale		101	6.63	6.63
• Sr Deb 6.95s 2028	Jd	**BBB**	4/99	BBB−	X	BE	NC	....	....	....	....	....	200	C1	'98	No Sale		87	7.99	7.99
• Sr Deb 7¾s 2035	aO15	**BBB**	4/99	BBB−	X	BE	NC	....	....	....	....	....	150	L3	'95	No Sale		95¾	8.09	8.09

Uniform Footnote Explanations-See Page 260. Other: [1] Gtd by Claridge, at Park Place Inc. [2] (HRO)On Chge of Ctrl at 101. [3] Now Clark Refining & Marketing. [4] Red at greater of 100 or amt based on formula. [5] Subsid of FirstEnergy Corp. [6] Co must offer repurch at 101 on Chge of Ctrl. [7] Co may red at 100 plus Premium on Chge of Ctrl. [8] On Chge of Ctrl,plus Premium. [9] Plus Make-Whole Amt. [10] Death redemp benefit,ltd,as defined. [11] Int pd monthly. [12] See Continental Corp. [13] On Chge of Ctrl Co may be req to repurch at 100. [14] (HRO)On 2-15-07 at 100.

Title-Industry Code & Co. Finances (In Italics) / Individual Issue Statistics (Exchange ↓)	Ind / Interest Dates	Fixed Charge Coverage 1996 / S&P Rating	1997 / Date of Last Rating Change	1998 / Prior Rating	Eligible ↓	Year End / Bond Form	Million $ Cash & Equiv. / Regular Price	Curr. Assets / Regular (Begins) Thru	Curr. Liab. / Sinking Fund Price	Balance Sheet Date / Sinking Fund (Begins) Thru	L. Term Debt (Mil $) / Refund/Other Restriction Price	Refund/Other Restriction (Begins) Thru	Capital-ization (Mil $) / Outst'g (Mil $)	Total Debt % Capital / Underwriting Firm	Underwriting Year	Price Range 1999 High	Price Range 1999 Low	Mo. End Price Sale(s) or Bid	Curr. Yield	Yield to Mat.
***Coastal Corp** (Cont.)*																				
• Sr Deb 7.42s 2037	Fa15	**BBB**	4/99	BBB−	X	BE	NC	....	....	....	....	....	200	S7	'97	No Sale		91⅞	8.08	8.07
• Sr Nts 10⅜s 2000	aO	**BBB**	4/99	BBB−	X	R	NC	....	....	....	....	....	249	L3	'90	105⅞	103⅜	101½	10.22	10.22
• Sr Nts 10s 2001	Fa	**BBB**	4/99	BBB−	X	R	NC	....	....	....	....	....	299	L3	'91	110⅞	106	102⅝	9.74	9.74
• Sr Nts 8⅛s 2002	mS15	**BBB**	4/99	BBB−	X	R	NC	....	....	....	....	....	250	L3	'92	106⅛	101	100⅝	8.07	8.07
Nts 6.20s 2004	Mn15	**BBB**			X	BE	NC	....	....	....	....	....	200	M7	'99	99⅞	95⅜	95⅜	6.50	6.50
Nts 6½s 2006	Mn15	**BBB**			X	BE	NC	....	....	....	....	....	200	M7	'99	99¾	94	94	6.91	6.91
Coca-Cola Bott Consol	***11f***	***1.85***	***1.65***	***1.58***		***Dc***	***8.38***	***159.3***	***133.3***	***10-3-99***	***734.0***		***550.0***	***96.9***						
Deb 6.85s 2007	mN	**A**	12/99	BBB	X	BE	NC	....	....	....	....	....	100	C4	'95	103	94⅝	94⅝	7.24	7.24
Deb 6⅜s 2009	Mn	**BBB**			X	BE	[1]Z100	....	....	....	....	....	250	S4	'99	99⅜	90⅜	90⅜	7.05	7.05
Deb 7.20s 2009	jJ	**BBB**			X	BE	NC	....	....	....	....	....	100	C4	'97	105¼	95½	95½	7.54	7.54
Coca-Cola Co	***11e***	***14.83***	***22.46***	***19.55***		***Dc***	***1637***	***6124***	***9686***	***9-30-99***	***1108***		***10583***	***10.5***						
Deb 7⅜s 2093	jJ29	**A+**	12/99	AA−	X	R	NC	....	....	....	....	....	116	M2	'93	114⅝	93	93⅛	7.92	7.92
Nts 6⅝s 2002	aO	**A+**	12/99	AA−	X	R	NC	....	....	....	....	....	150	G1	'92	103⅞	98⅞	98⅞	6.70	6.70
Nts 6s 2003	jJ15	**A+**	12/99	AA−	X	R	NC	....	....	....	....	....	150	M2	'93	102	96⅜	96⅜	6.23	6.23
Coca-Cola Enterprises	***11f***	***1.65***	***1.33***	***1.24***		***Dc***	***94.00***	***2483***	***3625***	***10-1-99***	***9762***		***14136***	***79.2***						
Deb 8½s 2012	Fa	**A**	12/99	A	X	BE	NC	....	....	....	....	....	250	S1	'92	125⅝	106⅜	106⅜	7.99	7.99
Deb 7⅛s 2017	fA	**A**			X	BE	NC	....	....	....	....	....	300		'97	110⅛	94	94	7.58	7.58
Deb 8½s 2022	Fa	**A**	12/99	A+	X	BE	NC	....	....	....	....	....	750	S1	'92	126⅞	106¼	106⅜	7.99	7.99
Deb 8s 2022	mS15	**A**	12/99	A+	X	BE	NC	....	....	....	....	....	250	S1	'92	120¾	100½	100⅝	7.95	7.95
Deb 6¾s 2023	mS15	**A**	12/99	A+	X	BE	NC	....	....	....	....	....	250	S1	'93	105⅞	88	88⅛	7.66	7.66
Deb[2] 7s 2026	aO	**A**	12/99	A+	X	BE	NC	....	....	....	....	....	300	L3	'96	109¼	97⅞	97⅞	7.15	7.15
Deb 6.95s 2026	mN15	**A**	12/99	A+	X	BE	NC	....	....	....	....	....	250	U1	'96	108⅜	90¼	90⅝	7.67	7.67
Deb 6.70s 2036	aO15	**A**	12/99	A+	X	BE	NC	....	....	....	....	....	300	S1	'96	104½	98⅛	98½	6.80	6.80
Deb 6¾s 2038	Jj15	**A**	12/99	A+	X	BE	NC	....	....	....	....	....	250	L3	'98	103⅞	85¾	85¾	7.87	7.87
Deb[3] 7s 2098	Mn15	**A**	12/99	A+	X	BE	NC	....	....	....	....	....	250	L3	'98	106¼	85¾	85¾	8.16	8.16
Nts 6⅜s 2001	fA	**A**	12/99	A+	X	BE	NC	....	....	....	....	....	250	L3	'97	102½	99⅜	99⅜	6.42	6.41
Nts 7⅞s 2002	Fa	**A**	12/99	A+	X	BE	NC	....	....	....	....	....	500	S1	'92	107¼	101⅞	101⅞	7.73	7.73
Nts 6⅝s 2004	fA	**A**	12/99	A+	X	BE	NC	....	....	....	....	....	200	L3	'97	105½	97¾	97¾	6.78	6.78
Nts[4] 8s 2005	Jj4	**A**	12/99	A+	X	BE	NC	....	....	....	....	....	250	M2	'92	112¾	103⅞	103⅞	7.70	7.70
Nts 5¾s 2008	mN	**A**	12/99	A+	X	BE	NC	....	....	....	....	....	600	L3	'98	101½	89⅜	89⅜	6.43	6.43
Nts 7⅛s 2009	mS30	**A**	12/99	A+	X	BE	NC	....	....	....	....	....	300		'99	101¼	97⅞	97⅞	7.28	7.28
Cogentrix Energy	***72b***	***1.73***	***1.79***	***2.00***		***Dc***	***44.30***	***180.0***	***133.0***	***6-30-99***	***1137***		***1397***	***87.7***						
Sr Nts[5] 8.10s 2004	Ms15	**BB+**	8/98	BBB−	Y	R	Z100	(3-15-01)	100	(3-15-01)	....	....	100	S1	'94	105⅝	99¼	99¼	8.16	8.16
Coho Energy	***49a***	***2.12***	***1.93***	***0.09***		***Dc***	***Bankruptcy Chapter 11***						***323.0***	***119.0***						
Sr Sub Nts[5] 8⅞s 2007	§aO15	**NR**	9/99	D	Z	R			Default 4-15-99 int				150	M6	'97	85	40	55¼	....	Flat
[6]Coinmach Corp	***63***	***0.53***	***0.55***	***0.84***		***Mr***	***24.00***			***9-30-99***	***692.0***		***747.0***	***93.8***						
Sr Nts'B'[5] 11¾s 2005	mN15	**B**	9/99	B+	Y	R	105.875	(11-15-00)	....	....	....	....	197		'96	110¼	102¼	103	11.41	11.40
Cole Nat'l Group	***59l***	***2.29***	***2.15***	***2.51***		***Ja***	***22.79***	***230.4***	***163.3***	***10-30-99***	***285.0***		***333.0***	***87.1***						
Sr Sub Nts[5] 9⅞s 2006	jD31	**B**	8/99	B+	Y	BE	104.9375	(12-31-01)	....	....	....	....	150	W6	'96	104⅛	74½	74½	13.26	13.25
Colgate-Palmolive Co	***33***	***4.97***	***5.60***	***6.81***		***Dc***	***273.0***	***2431***	***2361***	***9-30-99***	***2187***		***4607***	***61.8***						
M-T Nts 'B' 7.44s 2001	[7]jd	**A**	11/95	A+	X	BE	NC	....	....	....	....	....	10.0	M5	'94	105⅛	100⅞	100⅞	7.38	7.37
M-T Nts 'B' 7.54s 2002	[8]jd	**A**	11/95	A+	X	BE	NC	....	....	....	....	....	10.0	C4	'94	107⅛	101¼	101¼	7.45	7.45
M-T Nts 'B' 7.60s 2004	[9]jd	**A**	11/95	A+	X	BE	NC	....	....	....	....	....	22.0	G1	'94	110¾	101⅞	101⅞	7.46	7.46
M-T Nts 'B' 7.63s 2004	[9]jd	**A**	11/95	A+	X	BE	NC	....	....	....	....	....	5.00	M2	'94	110⅞	102	102	7.48	7.48
M-T Nts 'B' 7.64s 2004	[9]jd	**A**	11/95	A+	X	BE	NC	....	....	....	....	....	20.0	M2	'94	110⅞	102	102	7.49	7.49

Uniform Footnote Explanations-See Page 260. Other: [1] Red at greater of 100 or amt based on formula. [2] (HRO)On 10-01-06 at 100. [3] Co may red in whole for tax event. [4] (HRO)On ea Jan 4 at 100. [5] (HRO)On Chge of Ctrl at 101. [6] Subsid & data of Coinmach Laundry. [7] Due 5-25-01. [8] Due 5-23-02. [9] Due 5-24-04.

Exchange ↓ Individual Issue Statistics	Interest Dates	S&P Rating	Date of Last Rating Change	Prior Rating	Eligible ↓	Bond Form	Redemption Provisions: Regular Price	Regular (Begins) Thru	Sinking Fund Price	Sinking Fund (Begins) Thru	Refund/Other Restriction Price	Refund/Other Restriction (Begins) Thru	Outst'g (Mil $)	Underwriting Firm	Underwriting Year	Price Range 1999 High	Price Range 1999 Low	Mo. End Price Sale(s) or Bid	Curr. Yield	Yield to Mat.
Title-Industry Code & Co. Finances (In Italics)	*Ind*	*Fixed Charge Coverage 1996*	*1997*	*1998*		*Year End*	*Cash & Equiv. (Million $)*	*Curr. Assets*	*Curr. Liab.*	*Balance Sheet Date*	*L. Term Debt (Mil $)*		*Capital-ization (Mil $)*	*Total Debt % Capital*						
Colgate-Palmolive Co *(Cont.)*																				
M-T Nts 'C' 5.58s 2008	[1]jd	**A**			X	BE	NC	....	....	....	....	....	50.0	G1	'98	101¼	88⅞	88⅞	6.28	6.28
M-T Nts 'C' 6.45s 2028	[2]jd	**A**			X	BE	NC	....	....	....	....	....	102	M2	'98	100⅝	83	83⅛	7.76	7.76
Collins & Aikman Products	***8***	***2.31***	***1.04***	***1.06***		***Dc***	***24.40***	***529.0***	***355.0***	***9-25-99***	***917.0***		***799.0***	***118.0***						
Sr[3]Sub[4]Nts[5] 11½s 2006	Ao15	**B**			Y	BE	105.75	(4-15-01)	....	....	....	....	400		'96	107½	94½	98¾	11.65	11.65
Colonial Realty LP	***57***	***2.41***	***2.23***	***2.32***		***Dc***	***3.70***			***6-30-99***	***918.0***		***1780***	***51.6***						
Sr Nts 7½s 2001	jJ15	**BBB−**			X	BE	[6]100	....	....	....	....	....	65.0	L3	'96	101¼	99¼	99¼	7.56	7.56
Sr Nts 8.05s 2006	jJ15	**BBB−**			X	BE	[7]Z100	....	....	....	....	....	65.0	L3	'96	103⅝	95⅝	95⅝	8.42	8.42
Sr Nts 7s 2007	jJ14	**BBB−**			X	BE	[6]Z100	....	....	....	....	....	175	M2	'98	97⅞	89¼	89¼	7.84	7.84
M-T Nts 7.05s 2003	jD15	**BBB−**			X	BE	NC	....	....	....	....	....	50.0	M2	'96	97⅛	94⅛	95½	7.38	7.38
M-T Nts 6.96s 2004	[8]jd15	**BBB−**			X	BE	NC	....	....	....	....	....	75.0	L3	'97	96¼	92⅞	94½	7.37	7.36
M-T Nts 6.98s 2005	[9]jd15	**BBB−**			X	BE	NC	....	....	....	....	....	25.0	U1	'97	95⅜	90¾	92⅝	7.54	7.54
Colorado Interstate Gas[10]	***73c***	***7.54***	***6.13***	***4.26***		***Dc***	***0.45***	***377.0***	***128.0***	***6-30-99***	***280.0***		***824.0***	***34.3***						
• Sr Deb[11] 10s 2005	Jd15	**BBB+**	4/99	BBB	X	R	NC	....	....	....	....	....	180	S5	'90	No Sale		109	9.17	9.17
• Sr Deb 6.85s 2037	Jd15	**BBB+**	4/99	BBB	X	BE	NC	....	....	....	....	....	100	C1	'97	No Sale		96⅛	7.13	7.13
Coltec Industries	***2b***	***Merged into Goodrich (B.F.) Co,see***																		
Nts 9¾s 2000	Ao	**NR**	3/98	BB−	Y	R	NC	....	....	....	....	....	7.56	M6	'92	108⅝	100½	100½	9.70	9.70
[12]***Columbia Gas System***	***73e***	***3.00***	***3.49***	***3.61***		***Dc***	***21.60***	***1158***	***1657***	***9-30-99***	***1951***		***4153***	***51.7***						
Nts 'A' 6.39s 2000	mN28	**BBB+**	4/97	BBB	X	R	NC	....	....	....	....	....	311	Reorg	'95	101⅞	99⅝	99¾	6.41	6.41
Nts 'B' 6.61s 2002	mN28	**BBB+**	4/97	BBB	X	R	NC	....	....	....	....	....	282	Reorg	'95	103⅝	98¾	98¾	6.69	6.69
Nts 'C' 6.80s 2005	mN28	**BBB+**	4/97	BBB	X	R	NC	....	....	....	....	....	286	Reorg	'95	105¾	96½	96½	7.05	7.05
Nts 'D' 7.05s 2007	mN28	**BBB+**	4/97	BBB	X	R	100	(11-28-05)	....	....	....	....	282	Reorg	'95	104⅜	94⅛	94⅛	7.49	7.49
Nts 'E' 7.32s 2010	mN28	**BBB+**	4/97	BBB	X	R	100	(11-28-05)	....	....	....	....	282	Reorg	'95	106¾	95⅝	95⅝	7.65	7.65
Nts 'F' 7.42s 2015	mN28	**BBB+**	4/97	BBB	X	R	102.12	(11-28-05)	....	....	....	....	282	Reorg	'95	104⅛	93	93¼	7.96	7.96
Nts 'G' 7.62s 2025	mN28	**BBB+**	4/97	BBB	X	R	103.61	(11-28-05)	....	....	....	....	282	Reorg	'95	105¼	91⅜	91½	8.33	8.33
Columbia/HCA Healthcare[13]	***30***	***5.99***	***3.27***	***4.34***		***Dc***	***124.0***	***3515***	***3149***	***9-30-99***	***5522***		***12862***	***51.8***						
Deb[14] 8.36s 2024	Ao15	**BB+**	2/99	BBB	Y	R	NC	....	....	....	....	....	150	M6	'94	100⅞	91⅛	91½	9.14	9.14
Deb 7.19s 2015	mN15	**BB+**	2/99	BBB	Y	BE	[15]Z100	....	....	....	....	....	150	M6	'95	91	78	80½	8.93	8.93
Deb 7.05s 2027	jD	**BB+**	2/99	BBB	Y	BE	NC	....	....	....	....	....	150	S1	'95	86½	71¼	73⅝	9.58	9.57
Deb 7¾s 2036	jJ15	**BB+**	2/99	BBB	Y	BE	NC	....	....	....	....	....	100	S1	'96	92½	78¼	81⅝	9.49	9.49
Deb 7½s 2095	mN15	**BB+**	2/99	BBB	Y	BE	NC	....	....	....	....	....	200	M6	'95	87⅛	73⅛	73¼	10.24	10.24
Nts 6.41s 2000	Jd15	**BB+**	2/99	BBB	Y	BE	NC	....	....	....	....	....	196	Exch.	'95	99¼	97⅞	99¼	6.46	6.46
Nts 6⅞s 2001	jJ15	**BB+**	2/99	BBB	Y	BE	NC	....	....	....	....	....	100	S1	'96	99⅝	96⅜	97⅜	7.06	7.06
Nts 7.15s 2004	Ms30	**BB+**	2/99	BBB	Y	BE	NC	....	....	....	....	....	150	S1	'94	99⅞	92½	93¾	7.63	7.63
Nts 7¼s 2008	Mn20	**BB+**	2/99	BBB	Y	BE	NC	....	....	....	....	....	200	M6	'96	99¼	86⅞	88⅝	8.18	8.18
Nts 7.69s 2025	Jd15	**BB+**	2/99	BBB	Y	BE	NC	....	....	....	....	....	291	Exch.	'95	94⅞	77⅜	80⅞	9.51	9.51
M-T Nts 6.87s 2003	mS15	**BB+**	2/99	BBB	Y	BE	NC	....	....	....	....	....	125	L3	'95	98⅞	92¼	93	7.39	7.39
M-T Nts 8.85s 2007	[16]jd15	**BB+**	2/99	BBB	Y	BE	NC	....	....	....	....	....	150	M6	'94	108⅜	95⅞	97¼	9.10	9.10
M-T Nts 9s 2014	jD15	**BB+**	2/99	BBB	Y	BE	NC	....	....	....	....	....	150	L3	'95	108	94⅝	96½	9.33	9.32
M-T Nts 7⅝s 2025	mS15	**BB+**	2/99	BBB	Y	BE	NC	....	....	....	....	....	125	L3	'95	93	78⅛	81½	9.36	9.35
Columbia Healthcare	***30***	***Now Columbia/HCA Healthcare,see***																		
Deb 7½s 2023	jD15	**BB+**	2/99	BBB	Y	R	NC	....	....	....	....	....	150	M6	'93	92	76	80	9.38	9.37
Nts 6⅛s 2000	jD15	**BB+**	2/99	BBB	Y	R	NC	....	....	....	....	....	150	M6	'93	98⅜	96¾	98	6.25	6.25
Columbus Southern Power	***72a***	***3.19***	***3.42***	***3.69***		***Dc***	***7.85***	***386.0***	***413.0***	***6-30-99***	***946.0***		***1873***	***55.0***						
1st 7¼s 2002	aO	**A−**	8/95	BBB+	X	BE	NC	....	....	....	....	....	75.0	L3	'92	105⅛	99½	99½	7.29	7.29
1st 6.60s 2003	[17]mn	**A−**	8/95	BBB+	X	BE	100.95	7-31-00	Z100	....	....	....	40.0	S1	'93	101⅛	97	97	6.80	6.80

Uniform Footnote Explanations-See Page 260. Other: [1] Due 11-06-98. [2] Due 6-16-28. [3] Gtd by Collins & Aikman Corp. [4] Co may red at 100 On Chge of Ctrl. [5] (HRO)On CHge of Ctrl at 101. [6] Plus Make-Whole Amt. [7] Plus make whole Amt. [8] Due 7-24-04. [9] Due 9-26-05. [10] Subsid of Coastal Corp. [11] On Chge of Ctrl Co must offer to repurch at 100. [12] Now Columbia Energy Group. [13] See Columbia Hlthcare,Hosp Corp Amer. [14] (HRO)On Chge of Ctrl at 90.95 on 4-15-04. [15] Greater of 100 & amt based on formula. [16] Due 1-1-07. [17] Due Aug 1.

Title-Industry Code & Co. Finances (In Italics) / Individual Issue Statistics / Exchange	Ind / Interest Dates	Fixed Charge Coverage 1996 / S&P Rating	1997 / Date of Last Rating Change	1998 / Prior Rating	Eligible	Year End / Bond Form	Million $ Cash & Equiv. / Redemption Provisions Regular Price	Curr. Assets / Regular (Begins) Thru	Curr. Liab. / Sinking Fund Price	Balance Sheet Date / Sinking Fund (Begins) Thru	L. Term Debt (Mil $) / Refund/Other Restriction Price	Refund/Other Restriction (Begins) Thru	Capital-ization (Mil $) / Outst'g (Mil $)	Total Debt % Capital / Underwriting Firm	Underwriting Year	Price Range 1999 High	Price Range 1999 Low	Mo. End Price Sale(s) or Bid	Curr. Yield	Yield to Mat.
***Columbus Southern Power** (Cont.)*																				
1st 6.55s 2004	[1]mn	**A–**	8/95	BBB+	X	BE	101.88	2-29-00	....	....	....	....	50.0	S1	'94	101⅛	96¼	96¼	6.81	6.80
1st 8.40s 2022	fA15	**A–**	8/95	BBB+	X	BE	104.20	(8-15-02)	Z100	....	....	....	40.0	L3	'92	110⅝	98½	98½	8.53	8.53
1st 7¾s 2023	[2]mn	**A–**	8/95	BBB+	X	BE	105.43	7-31-00	Z100	....	....	....	40.0	S1	'93	103⅝	92½	92⅝	8.37	8.37
1st 7.45s 2024	[1]mn	**A–**	8/95	BBB+	X	BE	103.73	(3-1-04)	....	....	....	....	50.0	S1	'94	104⅜	89⅜	89½	8.32	8.32
M-T Nts 'A' 6.85s 2005	[3]fa	**BBB+**			X	BE	NC	....	....	....	....	....	48.0	M2	'97	105½	95⅞	95⅞	7.14	7.14
M-T Nts 'A' 6.51s 2008	Fa	**BBB+**			X	BE	[4]Z100	....	....	....	....	....	52.0	M2	'98	103½	91⅞	91⅞	7.09	7.09
Comcast Corp	***12a***	***1.16***	***1.13***	***5.10***		***Dc***	***6236***	***7341***	***4092***	***9-30-99***	***6778***		***15468***	***50.7***						
Sr Sub Deb 10¼s 2001	aO15	**BBB–**	7/99	BB+	X	R	NC	....	....	....	....	....	125	G1	'91	110	103½	104½	9.81	9.81
Sr Sub Deb 9⅜s 2005	Mn15	**BBB–**	7/99	BB+	X	R	104.688	(5-15-00)	....	....	....	....	234	L3	'95	107½	103½	105½	8.89	8.88
Sr Sub Deb 9⅛s 2006	aO15	**BBB–**	7/99	BB+	X	R	104.562	(10-15-00)	....	....	....	....	250	G1	'95	108	103¾	103⅞	8.78	8.78
Sr Sub Deb 9½s 2008	Jj15	**BBB–**	7/99	BB+	X	R	103	1-14-01	....	....	....	....	200	F1	'93	108	102½	103	9.22	9.22
Sr Sub Deb 10⅝s 2012	jJ15	**BBB–**	7/99	BB+	X	R	NC	....	....	....	....	....	300	M2	'92	130½	118⅞	119	8.93	8.93
Comdisco, Inc	***20a***	***△1.71***	***△1.74***	***△1.22***		***Sp***				***9-30-99***	***5056***		***6116***	***82.7***						
Nts 6½s 2000	Jd15	**BBB+**	4/96	BBB	X	BE	NC	....	....	....	....	....	200	M2	'95	100¾	99¾	99¾	6.52	6.52
Nts 5¾s 2001	Fa15	**BBB+**	4/96	BBB	X	BE	NC	....	....	....	....	....	250	S7	'96	99⅞	98⅛	98⅛	5.86	5.86
Nts 5.95s 2002	Ao30	**BBB+**			X	BE	[4]Z100	....	....	....	....	....	350	M2	'99	99⅞	96⅜	96⅜	6.17	6.17
Nts 6⅜s 2002	mN30	**BBB+**			X	BE	NC	....	....	....	....	....	250	S1	'96	101	97¾	97¾	6.52	6.52
Sr Nts 6s 2002	Jj30	**BBB+**			X	BE	NC	....	....	....	....	....	350	S4	'99	101½	96¾	96¾	6.20	6.20
Sr Nts 7¼s 2002	mS	**BBB+**			X	BE	NC	....	....	....	....	....	300	S4	'99	100¼	98⅞	98⅞	7.33	7.33
Nts 6⅛s 2003	Jj15	**BBB+**			X	BE	NC	....	....	....	....	....	250	S4	'98	100¼	95¾	95¾	6.40	6.40
M-T Nts 'F' 6.32s 2000	[5]ms	**BBB+**			X	BE	NC	....	....	....	....	....	25.0	S7	'97	100⅝	99⅛	99¼	6.37	6.37
M-T Nts'H' 6.68s 2001	[6]fa15	**BBB+**			X	BE	NC	....	....	....	....	....	26.0	M2	'99	100⅛	98½	98⅝	6.77	6.77
M-T Nts 'H' 7¼s 2001	[7]fa15	**BBB+**			X	BE	NC	....	....	....	....	....	100		'99	101¼	99⅛	99¼	7.30	7.30
Comerica Inc	***10***	***2.26***	***2.54***	***2.82***		***Dc***				***9-30-99***	***8356***		***12974***	***74.1***						
Sub Nts 7¼s 2007	fA	**A–**			X	BE	NC	....	....	....	....	....	150	L3	'95	107⅛	96¾	96¾	7.49	7.49
Commerce Bancorp	***10***	***13.33***	***7.18***	***7.73***		***Dc***				***9-30-99***	***23.00***		***354.0***	***6.5***						
Sub Nts 8⅜s 2003	jJ15	**NR**				R	102	(7-15-00)	....	....	....	....	23.0	W4	'93	105	101⅛	101⅛	8.28	8.28
Commercial Credit Co[8]	***25a***	***1.34***	***1.39***	***1.63***		***Dc***	***20.30***			***6-30-99***	***6050***		***16406***	***85.5***						
Deb 10s 2009	Mn15	**AA–**	8/99	A+	X	R	NC	....	....	....	....	....	100	S7	'89	131⅛	115¼	116⅜	8.59	8.59
Deb 8.70s 2009	Jd15	**AA–**	8/99	A+	X	R	NC	....	....	....	....	....	150	M6	'89	120⅝	107	107	8.13	8.13
Deb[9] 8.70s 2010	Jd15	**AA–**	8/99	A+	X	R	NC	....	....	....	....	....	100	B7	'90	121¾	107¼	107¼	8.11	8.11
Nts 6⅛s 2000	Ms	**AA–**	8/99	A+	X	R	NC	....	....	....	....	....	100	S1	'93	100¾	99⅞	100	6.13	6.12
Nts 6s 2000	Ao15	**AA–**	8/99	A+	X	BE	NC	....	....	....	....	....	150	S1	'93	100¾	99⅞	99⅞	6.01	6.01
Nts 6¾s 2000	Mn15	**AA–**	8/99	A+	X	BE	NC	....	....	....	....	....	200	C5	'95	101¾	100⅛	100⅛	6.74	6.74
Nts 6s 2000	Jd15	**AA–**	8/99	A+	X	BE	NC	....	....	....	....	....	100	L3	'93	100⅞	99¾	99⅞	6.01	6.01
Nts 5¾s 2000	jJ15	**AA–**	8/99	A+	X	BE	NC	....	....	....	....	....	200	S1	'93	100½	99⅝	99¾	5.76	5.76
Nts 5.55s 2001	Fa15	**AA–**	8/99	A+	X	BE	NC	....	....	....	....	....	200	L3	'96	100⅛	98⅝	98⅝	5.63	5.63
Nts 8¼s 2001	mN	**AA–**	8/99	A+	X	BE	NC	....	....	....	....	....	300	C5	'94	107	102¼	102¼	8.07	8.07
Nts 6.20s 2001	mN15	**AA–**	8/99	A+	X	BE	NC	....	....	....	....	....	200	M5	'96	101⅞	98¾	98¾	6.28	6.28
Nts 7⅜s 2002	Ms15	**AA–**	8/99	A+	X	BE	NC	....	....	....	....	....	200	C5	'95	105⅛	100½	100½	7.34	7.34
Nts 6⅞s 2002	Mn	**AA–**	8/99	A+	X	BE	NC	....	....	....	....	....	200	B7	'95	103¾	99½	99½	6.91	6.91
Nts 6⅜s 2002	Ms15	**AA–**	8/99	A+	X	BE	NC	....	....	....	....	....	200	M5	'95	102½	98⅛	98⅛	6.50	6.50
Nts 6.45s 2002	jJ	**AA–**	8/99	A+	X	BE	NC	....	....	....	....	....	300	S1	'97	102⅝	98½	98½	6.55	6.55
Nts 5⅞s 2003	Jj15	**AA–**	8/99	A+	X	BE	NC	....	....	....	....	....	200	U1	'96	100¾	96½	96½	6.09	6.09
Nts 5.90s 2003	mS	**AA–**	8/99	A+	X	BE	NC	....	....	....	....	....	200	S7	'93	100⅞	95⅝	95⅝	6.17	6.17

Uniform Footnote Explanations-See Page 260. Other: [1] Due Mar 1. [2] Due Aug 1. [3] Due 10-3-05. [4] Red at greater of 100 or amt based on formula. [5] Due 9-25-00. [6] Due 6-29-01. [7] Due 9-20-01. [8] Subsid of Primerica Corp. [9] (HRO)On 6-15-02('05).

Title-Industry Code & Co. Finances (In Italics)	Ind	Fixed Charge Coverage 1996	1997	1998		Year End	Million $ Cash & Equiv.	Curr. Assets	Curr. Liab.	Balance Sheet Date	L. Term Debt (Mil $)		Capital-ization (Mil $)	Total Debt % Capital						
Exchange ↓ Individual Issue Statistics	Interest Dates	S&P Rating	Date of Last Rating Change	Prior Rating	Eligible ↓	Bond Form	Redemption Provisions: Regular Price	Regular (Begins) Thru	Sinking Fund Price	Sinking Fund (Begins) Thru	Refund/Other Restriction Price	Refund/Other Restriction (Begins) Thru	Outst'g (Mil $)	Underwriting Firm	Underwriting Year	Price Range 1999 High	Price Range 1999 Low	Mo. End Price Sale(s) or Bid	Curr. Yield	Yield to Mat.
***Commercial Credit Co** (Cont.)*																				
Nts 7⅞s 2004	jJ15	**AA–**	8/99	A+	X	BE	NC	....	....	....	....	....	200	L3	'94	110	102	102	7.72	7.72
Nts 6½s 2004	fA	**AA–**	8/99	A+	X	BE	NC	....	....	....	....	....	250	S7	'97	103⅝	97	97	6.70	6.70
Nts 7¾s 2005	Ms	**AA–**	8/99	A+	X	BE	NC	....	....	....	....	....	200	M6	'95	110⅛	101½	101½	7.64	7.63
Nts 6½s 2005	Jd	**AA–**	8/99	A+	X	BE	NC	....	....	....	....	....	200	C5	'95	103⅞	96⅛	96⅜	6.74	6.74
Nts 6⅛s 2005	jD	**AA–**	8/99	A+	X	BE	NC	....	....	....	....	....	200	L3	'95	102⅛	94	94	6.52	6.52
Nts 7⅜s 2005	Ao15	**AA–**	8/99	A+	X	BE	NC	....	....	....	....	....	200	S1	'95	108⅜	100	100	7.38	7.37
Nts 6⅝s 2006	mN15	**AA–**	8/99	A+	X	BE	NC	....	....	....	....	....	200	S1	'96	105¼	95¼	96	6.90	6.90
Nts 6¾s 2007	jJ	**AA–**	8/99	A+	X	BE	NC	....	....	....	....	....	300	S1	'97	106¼	95¼	96	7.03	7.03
Nts 6¼s 2008	Jj	**AA–**	8/99	A+	X	BE	NC	....	....	....	....	....	300	S4	'98	103⅛	92⅛	93	6.72	6.72
Nts 10s 2008	jD	**AA–**	8/99	A+	X	R	NC	....	....	....	....	....	150	S7	'88	130½	114⅝	115⅞	8.63	8.63
Nts[1] 6⅝s 2015	Jd	**AA–**	8/99	A+	X	BE	NC	....	....	....	....	....	200	C5	'95	102⅛	98⅝	99¼	6.68	6.67
Nts[2] 7⅞s 2025	Fa	**AA–**	8/99	A+	X	BE	NC	....	....	....	....	....	200	S7	'95	117⅜	101⅜	102⅞	7.65	7.65
Commercial Federal Corp	***10a***	***1.82***	***1.85***	***1.81***		***Je***				***9-30-99***	***424.0***		***5213***	***81.4***						
• Sub Ext'd [3]Nts 7.95s 2006	[4]dec15	**BB–**			Y	R	[5]Z■100	(12-2-01)	....	....	....	....	50.0	B10	'96	101½	89	90	8.83	8.83
Commercial Metals	***66***	***Δ4.90***	***Δ4.23***	***Δ3.82***		***Au***	***44.70***	***662.0***	***372.0***	***11-30-99***	***266.0***		***691.0***	***40.5***						
Nts 7.20s 2005	jJ15	**BBB+**			X	BE	NC	....	....	....	....	....	100	G1	'95	106¾	96⅝	96⅝	7.45	7.45
Nts 6.80s 2007	fA	**BBB+**			X	BE	NC	....	....	....	....	....	50.0	G1	'97	104½	92⅞	93⅛	7.30	7.30
Nts[6] 6¾s 2009	Fa15	**BBB+**			X	BE	[7]Z100	....	....	....	....	....	100	G1	'99	102	91⅝	91⅝	7.37	7.37
Commercial Net Lease Rlty	***57***	***3.74***	***3.58***	***3.28***		***Dc***				***6-30-99***	***265.0***		***720.0***	***45.6***						
Nts 8⅛s 2004	Jd15	**BBB–**			X	BE	[8]Z100	....	....	....	....	....	100	M5	'99	101¾	97⅞	98¼	8.27	8.27
Nts 7⅛s 2008	Ms15	**BBB–**			X	BE	[8]Z100	....	....	....	....	....	100	M5	'98	97⅛	88¼	88¼	8.07	8.07
[9]Commonwealth Edison	***72a***	***3.25***	***2.40***	***2.93***		***Dc***	***645.0***	***3127***	***2790***	***9-30-99***	***7614***		***14357***	***60.7***						
1st Ser 73 9⅜s 2000	Fa15	**BBB+**	6/99	BBB	X	R	NC	....	....	....	....	....	125	S1	'90	104½	100¼	100¼	9.35	9.35
1st Ser 74 9¾s 2020	Fa15	**BBB+**	6/99	BBB	X	R	103.97	(2-15-00)	....	....	....	....	225	S1	'90	109¼	104¼	104¼	9.35	9.35
1st Ser 75 9⅞s 2020	Jd15	**BBB+**	6/99	BBB	X	R	102.27	(6-15-05)	....	....	....	....	260	M6	'90	121⅛	109¼	109⅜	9.03	9.03
1st Ser 76 8¼s 2006	aO	**BBB+**	6/99	BBB	X	R	NC	....	....	....	....	....	100	M6	'91	115⅛	102½	102½	8.05	8.05
1st Ser 78 8⅜s 2006	aO15	**BBB+**	6/99	BBB	X	R	NC	....	....	....	....	....	125	M2	'91	115⅞	103⅛	103⅛	8.12	8.12
1st Ser 81 8⅝s 2022	Fa	**BBB+**	6/99	BBB	X	R	103.84	(2-1-02)	....	....	....	....	200	S1	'92	109¾	99⅝	99⅞	8.64	8.63
1st Ser 83 8s 2008	Mn15	**BBB+**	6/99	BBB	X	R	NC	....	....	....	....	....	140	S1	'92	115⅝	101½	101⅝	7.87	7.87
1st Ser 84 8½s 2022	jJ15	**BBB+**	6/99	BBB	X	R	103.915	(7-15-02)	....	....	....	....	200	M2	'92	109¼	98	98¼	8.65	8.65
1st Ser 85 7⅜s 2002	mS15	**BBB+**	6/99	BBB	X	R	NC	....	....	....	....	....	200	P1	'92	105¾	100⅜	100⅜	7.35	7.35
1st Ser 86 8⅜s 2022	mS15	**BBB+**	6/99	BBB	X	R	103.425	(9-15-02)	....	....	....	....	200	P1	'92	108⅝	97	97¼	8.61	8.61
1st Ser 88 8⅜s 2023	Fa15	**BBB+**	6/99	BBB	X	BE	103.863	(2-15-03)	....	....	....	....	250		'93	109⅝	96¾	97⅛	8.62	8.62
1st Ser 90 6½s 2000	Ao15	**BBB+**	6/99	BBB	X	BE	NC	....	....	....	....	....	230	M2	'93	101⅜	100	100	6.50	6.50
1st Ser 91 8s 2023	Ao15	**BBB+**	6/99	BBB	X	R	103.664	(4-15-03)	....	....	....	....	160	M2	'93	107⅜	93¾	94	8.51	8.51
1st Ser 92 7⅝s 2013	Ao15	**BBB+**	6/99	BBB	X	BE	NC	....	....	....	....	....	220	S1	'93	114⅛	98½	98⅝	7.73	7.73
1st Ser 93 7s 2005	jJ	**BBB+**	6/99	BBB	X	BE	NC	....	....	....	....	....	225	P1	'93	107	98⅛	98⅛	7.13	7.13
1st Ser 94 7½s 2013	jJ	**BBB+**	6/99	BBB	X	BE	NC	....	....	....	....	....	150	P1	'93	112⅜	96⅞	97	7.73	7.73
1st Ser 95 6⅜s 2000	jJ15	**BBB+**	6/99	BBB	X	BE	NC	....	....	....	....	....	100	S1	'93	101½	99⅞	100	6.38	6.37
1st Ser 96 6⅝s 2003	jJ15	**BBB+**	6/99	BBB	X	BE	NC	....	....	....	....	....	100	M2	'93	104⅛	97¾	97¾	6.78	6.78
1st Ser 97 7¾s 2023	jJ15	**BBB+**	6/99	BBB	X	BE	103.765	(7-15-03)	....	....	....	....	150	M2	'93	105⅞	92¼	92⅝	8.37	8.37
• SF Deb 2⅞s 2001	Ao	**BBB**	6/99	BBB–	X	CR	100.18	3-31-00	100.05	....	....	....	6.00	H1	'51	96⅞	93⅜	93⅛	3.09	3.10
SF Deb 3⅛s 2004	aO	**BBB**	6/99	BBB–	X	CR	100.36	3-31-00	100.01	4-1-04	....	....	14.9		'55	87	82⅝	82⅝	3.78	3.80
SF Deb 3⅞s 2008	Jj	**BBB**	6/99	BBB–	X	CR	100.88	6-30-00	100.30	6-30-00	....	....	16.8	F1	'58	93⅛	88¾	88¾	4.37	4.37
SF Deb 4⅝s 2009	Jj	**BBB**	6/99	BBB–	X	CR	101.22	6-30-00	100.53	6-30-00	....	....	7.67	F1	'59	93¾	89⅝	89⅝	5.16	5.16

Uniform Footnote Explanations-See Page 260. Other: [1] (HRO)On 6-1-02 at 100. [2] (HRO)On 2-1-05 at 100. [3] Int to 12-1-01,reset aft. [4] Due 12-1-06:int pd monthly ea 15th. [5] On 12-1-01. [6] Issued in min denom $100T. [7] Red at greater of 100 or amt based on formula. [8] Plus Make-Whole Amt. [9] Subsid of Unicom Corp.

Title-Industry Code & Co. Finances (In Italics) / Individual Issue Statistics (Exchange)	Ind / Interest Dates	S&P Rating	Date of Last Rating Change	Prior Rating	Eligible	Bond Form	Redemption Provisions: Regular Price	Regular (Begins) Thru	Sinking Fund Price	Sinking Fund (Begins) Thru	Refund/Other Restriction Price	Refund/Other Restriction (Begins) Thru	Outst'g (Mil $)	Underwriting Firm	Underwriting Year	Price Range 1999 High	Price Range 1999 Low	Mo. End Price Sale(s) or Bid	Curr. Yield	Yield to Mat.
(Company rows)		*Fixed Charge Coverage 1996*	*1997*	*1998*		*Year End*	*Million $ Cash & Equiv.*	*Curr. Assets*	*Curr. Liab.*	*Balance Sheet Date*	*L. Term Debt (Mil $)*		*Capital-ization (Mil $)*	*Total Debt % Capital*						
***Commonwealth Edison** (Cont.)*																				
SF Deb 4¾s 2011	jD	**BBB**	6/99	BBB–	X	CR	101.56	5-31-00	100.58	5-31-00	....	....	12.8	F1	'61	100	90	99⅝	4.77	4.77
Nts 7⅜s 2004	Jj15	**BBB**	6/99	BBB–	X	BE	NC	....	....	....	....	....	150	S1	'97	106⅝	99½	99½	7.41	7.41
Nts 6.40s 2005	aO15	**BBB**	6/99	BBB–	X	BE	NC	....	....	....	....	....	235	P1	'93	103⅜	94⅝	94⅝	6.76	6.76
Nts 7⅝s 2007	Jj15	**BBB**	6/99	BBB–	X	BE	NC	....	....	....	....	....	150	S1	'97	111⅜	99	99	7.70	7.70
Nts 6.95s 2018	jJ15	**BBB**	6/99	BBB–	X	BE	[1]Z100	....	....	....	....	....	225	P1	'98	105⅛	89¾	90¼	7.70	7.70
***Compass Bancshares**[2]*	*10*	*3.31*	*3.43*	*2.72*		*Dc*				*9-30-99*	*2151*		*3518*	*66.5*						
Sub Nts 8⅜s 2004	mS15	**BBB**			X	BE	NC	....	....	....	....	....	50.0	B7	'94	108⅛	102¼	102⅝	8.16	8.16
Computer Sciences	*20c*	*8.20*	*9.75*	*9.24*		*Mr*	*262.9*	*2555*	*1740*	*10-1-99*	*667.0*		*3375*	*26.0*						
Nts 6¼s 2009	Ms15	**A**			X	BE	[3]Z100	....	....	....	....	....	200	M5	'99	101⅞	91¼	91¼	6.85	6.85
***COMSAT Corp**[4]*	*67e*	*0.86*	*1.54*	*2.06*		*Dc*	*75.03*	*251.1*	*191.2*	*9-30-99*	*379.0*		*1320*	*50.2*						
• Deb 8⅛s 2004	Ao	**A–**	2/96	A	X	R	NC	....	....	....	....	....	70.5	F1	'92	105	104⅛	102¼	7.95	7.95
• Nts 8.95s 2001	Mn15	**A–**	2/96	A	X	R	NC	....	....	....	....	....	75.0	F1	'91	104¼	102½	99½	8.99	8.99
ConAgra Inc	*26*	*△4.03*	*△3.89*	*△4.55*		*My*	*10.70*	*6973*	*6554*	*8-29-99*	*2560*		*9469*	*63.1*						
Sr Nts 5½s 2002	aO15	**BBB+**			X	BE	[3]Z100	....	....	....	....	....	200	M2	'98	100	96⅛	96⅛	5.72	5.72
Sr Nts 9⅞s 2005	mN15	**BBB+**	12/96	BBB	X	BE	NC	....	....	....	....	....	100	M2	'90	122¾	110½	110½	8.94	8.94
Sr Nts 7⅛s 2026	aO	**BBB+**	12/96	BBB	X	BE	NC	....	....	....	....	....	400	S7	'96	107¼	97¾	97¾	7.29	7.29
Sr Nts[5] 6.70s 2027	fA	**BBB+**			X	BE	NC	....	....	....	....	....	300	S7	'97	105⅛	93	93	7.20	7.20
Sr Nts 7s 2028	aO	**BBB+**			X	BE	[3]Z100	....	....	....	....	....	400	M2	'98	104⅝	88⅜	88½	7.91	7.91
Sub Nts 9¾s 2021	Ms	**BBB**	12/96	BBB–	X	BE	NC	....	....	....	....	....	400	M2	'91	135¾	115¾	115⅞	8.41	8.41
Sub Nts 7.40s 2004	mS15	**BBB**	12/96	BBB–	X	BE	NC	....	....	....	....	....	300	F1	'92	108	99¾	99¾	7.42	7.42
Cone Mills	*68a*	*0.87*	*d0.41*	*0.82*		*Dc*	*3.93*	*181.6*	*158.8*	*10-3-99*	*119.0*		*351.0*	*53.3*						
Deb 8⅛s 2005	Ms15	**BB+**	2/98	BBB	Y	BE	NC	....	....	....	....	....	100	M6	'95	110⅞	50	50	16.25	16.24
Conectiv Inc	*75*	*n/a*	*n/a*	*n/a*		*Dc*	*44.40*	*715.0*	*1263*	*6-30-99*	*1961*		*6493*	*42.8*						
M-T Nts'A' 6.73s 2006	Jd	**BBB+**			X	BE	[3]Z100	....	100	(6-1-02)	....	....	250	L3	'99	100	97⅝	97⅝	6.89	6.89
***Connecticut Lt & Pwr**[6]*	*72a*	*0.23*	*d0.58*	*0.08*		*Dc*	*69.10*	*424.0*	*527.0*	*6-30-99*	*1861*		*3312*	*65.1*						
1st & Ref XX 5¾s 2000	jJ	**BBB–**	5/99	BB+	X	R	100	....	Z100	....	....	....	200	M2	'93	99¾	99¼	99⅝	5.77	5.77
1st & Ref YY 7½s 2023	jJ	**BBB–**	5/99	BB+	X	R	104.92	6-30-00	Z100	....	....	....	100	S1	'93	100	87⅜	100	7.50	7.50
1st & Ref ZZ 7⅜s 2025	jD	**BBB–**	5/99	BB+	X	BE	104.17	11-30-00	Z100	....	....	....	125	L3	'93	100	85	100	7.38	7.37
1st & Ref '94B 6⅛s 2004	Fa	**BBB–**	5/99	BB+	X	BE	101.68	1-31-00	Z100	....	....	....	140	S1	'94	100	94⅝	100	6.13	6.12
1st & Ref '94C 8½s 2024	Jd	**BBB–**	5/99	BB+	X	BE	103.87	(6-1-04)	Z100	(6-1-04)	....	....	115	M6	'94	104⅝	97½	97⅝	8.71	8.71
1st & Ref '96A 7⅞s 2001	Jd	**BBB–**	5/99	BB+	X	BE	[7]Z100	....	....	....	....	....	160	M6	'96	102⅞	100⅜	100⅜	7.85	7.84
Conoco Inc	*49b*	*n/a*	*n/a*	*n/a*		*Dc*	*318.0*	*2882*	*3517*	*9-30-99*	*★4717*		*9745*	*52.4*						
Nts 5.90s 2004	Ao15	**A–**			X	BE	[3]Z100	....	....	....	....	....	1350	C6	'99	100	95⅜	95⅜	6.19	6.19
Nts 6.35s 2009	Ao15	**A–**			X	BE	[3]Z100	....	....	....	....	....	750	C6	'99	100¼	92½	92½	6.86	6.87
Nts 6.95s 2029	A015	**A–**			X	BE	[3]Z100	....	....	....	....	....	1900	C6	'99	100½	89⅝	89⅞	7.73	7.73
Conseco Finance**[8]**Corp	*25g*	*8.11*	*4.02*	*1.12*		*Dc*				*9-30-99*	*4486*		*6834*	*65.6*						
• Sr Sub Nts[9] 10¼s 2002	Jd	**BB+**	2/98	BBB	Y	R	NC	....	[10]Z100	....	....	....	267	Exch.	'92	108	102	102¾	9.98	9.97
Conseco Inc	*35a*	*1.62*	*2.27*	*4.96*		*Dc*				*9-30-99*	*6829*		*11087*	*52.0*						
Nts 7⅞s 2000	jD15	**BBB+**	7/99	BBB	X	BE	[3]Z100	....	....	....	....	....	150	M2	'98	101⅝	99	100⅛	7.87	7.86
Nts 8½s 2002	aO15	**BBB+**			X	BE	[3]Z100	....	....	....	....	....	450	C1	'99	101⅜	99¾	101⅛	8.41	8.41
Nts 6.40s 2003	Fa10	**BBB+**	7/99	BBB	X	BE	[3]Z100	....	....	....	....	....	250	M2	'98	97⅝	93⅛	95½	6.70	6.70
Nts 9s 2006	aO15	**BBB+**			X	BE	[3]Z100	....	....	....	....	....	550	C1	'99	104¼	99¼	103⅝	8.69	8.68
• Sr Nts 8⅛s 2003	Fa15	**BBB+**	7/99	BBB	X	BE	NC	....	....	....	....	....	63.5	M2	'93	108¾	96⅞	98⅞	8.22	8.22
• Sr Nts 10½s 2004	jD15	**BBB+**	7/99	BBB	X	BE	NC	....	....	....	....	....	25.0	M6	'94	120	112	105	10.00	10.00
Consolidated Edison	*75*	*4.33*	*4.24*	*4.46*		*Dc*	*189.0*	*1620*	*1757*	*9-30-99*	*4359*		*10551*	*45.4*						
Deb '92A 7⅜s 2000	mS15	**A+**	2/94	AA–	X	R	NC	....	....	....	....	....	150	G1	'92	103½	100⅝	100⅝	7.33	7.33

Uniform Footnote Explanations-See Page 260. Other: [1] Plus Make-Whole Amt. [2] See Central Bancshrs South. [3] Red at greater of 100 or amt based on formula. [4] Was Communications Satellite. [5] (HRO)On 8-1-09 at 100. [6] Contr by Northeast Utilities. [7] Greater of 100 or amt based on formula. [8] Was Green Tree Acceptance,then Green Tree Fin'l. [9] Was Green Tree Finl. [10] Contingent SF.

Title-Industry Code & Co. Finances (In Italics) — Ind	Fixed Charge Coverage 1996	1997	1998	Year End	Million $ Cash & Equiv.	Curr. Assets	Curr. Liab.	Balance Sheet Date	L. Term Debt (Mil $)			Capital-ization (Mil $)	Total Debt % Capital						
Individual Issue Statistics Exchange ↓ — Interest Dates	S&P Rating	Date of Last Rating Change	Prior Rating	Eligible ↓ Bond Form	Redemption Provisions: Regular Price	Regular (Begins) Thru	Sinking Fund Price	Sinking Fund (Begins) Thru	Refund/Other Restriction Price	Refund/Other Restriction (Begins) Thru	Outst'g (Mil $)	Underwriting Firm	Underwriting Year	Price Range 1999 High	Low	Mo. End Price Sale(s) or Bid	Curr. Yield	Yield to Mat.	
***Consolidated Edison** (Cont.)*																			
Deb '92B 7⅝s 2004 ....Ms	A+	2/94	AA–	X R	NC	....	....	....	....	....	150	G1	'92	110	101	101	7.55	7.55	
Deb '92C 7.60s 2000 ....Jj15	A+	2/94	AA–	X R	NC	....	....	....	....	....	125	G1	'92	102⅜	100	100	7.60	7.60	
Deb '93B 6½s 2001 ....Fa	A+	2/94	AA–	X R	NC	....	....	....	....	....	150	L3	'93	102⅝	99⅝	99⅝	6.52	6.52	
Deb '93C 6⅝s 2002 ....Fa	A+	2/94	AA–	X R	NC	....	....	....	....	....	150	L3	'93	104⅛	99¼	99¼	6.68	6.67	
Deb '93D 6⅜s 2003 ....Ao	A+	2/94	AA–	X R	NC	....	....	....	....	....	150	L3	'93	104⅝	98	98	6.51	6.51	
Deb '93G 7½s 2023 ....Jd15	A+	2/94	AA–	X R	103.2725	(6-15-03)	....	....	....	....	380	L3	'93	107	91¾	92⅞	8.08	8.07	
Deb '94A 7⅛s 2029 ....Fa15	A+			X R	103.642	(2-15-04)	....	....	....	....	150	G1	'94	105	86⅝	87¾	8.12	8.12	
Deb '95A 6⅝s 2005 ....jJ	A+			X BE	NC	....	....	....	....	....	100	M2	'95	106⅜	96⅛	96⅛	6.89	6.89	
Deb '96A 7¾s 2026 ....Jd	A+			X BE	102.876	(6-1-06)	....	....	....	....	100	L3	'96	113½	95¼	96⅜	8.04	8.04	
F/R[1]Deb'96 B 2001 ....QDec15	A+			X BE	100	....	....	....	....	....	150	M2	'96	100¼	99½	100	....	....	
F/R[2]Deb '97A 2002 ....QJun15	A+			X BE	*100	....	....	....	....	....	150	G1	'97	100⅜	99¼	99⅞	....	....	
Deb '97B 6.45s 2007 ....jD	A+			X BE	NC	....	....	....	....	....	330	S1	'97	107½	94	94	6.86	6.86	
Deb '98A 6¼s 2008 ....Fa	A+			X BE	NC	....	....	....	....	....	180	S4	'98	105¾	92	92⅜	6.77	6.77	
Deb'98B 7.10s 2028 ....Fa	A+			X BE	103.371	(2-1-08)	....	....	....	....	105	M2	'98	106⅞	87	87⅝	8.10	8.10	
Deb '98C 6.15s 2008 ....jJ	A+			X BE	NC	....	....	....	....	....	100	S4	'98	105⅛	91½	91⅝	6.71	6.71	
Deb '99B 7.15s 2009 ....jD	A+			X BE	NC	....	....	....	....	....	200	M7	'99	99⅝	97¼	97¼	7.35	7.35	
***Consolidated Freightways[3]**.... 71*	*4.70*	*6.61*	*7.44*	*Dc*	*133.2*	*1167*	*945.4*	*9-30-99*	*559.0*			*1460*	*40.6*						
Nts[4] 7.35s 2005 ....Jd	BBB	6/97	BBB–	X R	NC	....	....	....	....	....	100	M2	'95	98⅝	91¼	91¼	8.05	8.05	
***Consolidated Nat Gas**.... 73e*	*5.11*	*4.90*	*4.23*	*Dc*	*114.0*	*944.0*	*1189*	*9-30-99*	*1763*			*4137*	*43.1*						
• SF Deb 8¾s 2019 ....aO	BBB+	12/99	AA–	X R	103.80	9-30-00	100	....	....	....	150	D7	'89	No Sale		101⅛	8.65	8.65	
• Deb 5¾s 2003 ....fA	BBB+	12/99	AA–	X R	NC	....	....	....	....	....	150	S1	'93	101⅝	94¼	95	6.05	6.05	
• Deb 7⅜s 2005 ....Ao	BBB+	12/99	AA–	X BE	NC	....	....	....	....	....	150	M2	'95	105⅝	105⅝	98⅛	7.52	7.52	
• Deb 6s 2010 ....aO15	BBB+	12/99	AA–	X BE	NC	....	....	....	....	....	200	M2	'98	99½	99½	86	6.98	6.98	
• Deb 6⅝s 2013 ....jD	BBB+	12/99	AA–	X R	NC	....	....	....	....	....	150	G1	'93	100½	94	87⅛	7.60	7.60	
• Deb[5] 6⅞s 2026 ....aO15	BBB+	12/99	AA–	X BE	NC	....	....	....	....	....	150	C1	'96	No Sale		98	7.02	7.02	
• Deb 6.80s 2027 ....jD15	BBB+	12/99	AA–	X BE	[6]Z100	....	....	....	....	....	300	C1	'97	93	92	84⅝	8.04	8.03	
Nts 7¼s 2004 ....aO	BBB+	12/99	AA–	X BE	NC	....	....	....	....	....	400	C1	'99	101⅛	98¾	98¾	7.34	7.34	
• Nts 6⅝s 2008 ....jD	BBB+	12/99	AA–	X BE	NC	....	....	....	....	....	150	C1	'96	No Sale		90⅛	7.35	7.35	
***Consolidated Rail**.... 55*	*Now Conrail Inc,merged w/Norfolk So'n,see*																		
Deb 9¾s 2020 ....Jd15	BBB	5/97	A	X BE	NC	....	....	....	....	....	544	M6	'90	132⅞	115⅝	115¾	8.42	8.42	
Deb 7⅞s 2043 ....Mn15	BBB	5/97	A	X BE	NC	....	....	....	....	....	250	M6	'93	113	95⅞	96	8.20	8.20	
Nts 9¾s 2000 ....Jd	BBB	5/97	A	X BE	NC	....	....	....	....	....	250	M6	'90	105½	101⅜	101⅜	9.62	9.62	
***Consumer Portfolio Svcs**.... 25e*	*5.10*	*4.48*	*3.01*	*Dc*				*9-30-99*	*126.0*			*229.0*	*55.0*						
• Partic Eq Nts[7] 10½s 2004 ....[8]Apr15	NR			BE	■100	(4-15-00)	....	....	....	....	20.0	P2	'96	79	16½	s68	15.44	15.44	
• V/R[9]Sub[10]Nts[11] 10½s 2006 ....[8]Jan	NR			BE	100	....	100	....	....	....	20.0		'95	79	16⅛	61	17.21	....	
***Consumers Energy Co[12]**.... 75*	*3.88*	*3.71*	*3.52*	*Dc*	*29.00*	*546.0*	*1067*	*6-30-99*	*2096*			*4753*	*52.8*						
1st 6⅜s 2003 ....mS15	BBB+	10/97	BBB–	X R	101.594	9-14-00	....	....	....	....	300	G1	'93	100⅝	96	96	6.64	6.64	
1st 7⅜s 2023 ....mS15	BBB+	10/97	BBB–	X R	103.688	(9-15-03)	....	....	....	....	300	M6	'93	106	89	89⅛	8.27	8.27	
***Container Corp of Amer**.... 59h*	*Mgr w/Stone Container,see*																		
Sr[13]Nts[14] 9¾s 2003 ....Ao15	B–	11/98	B+	Y R	NC	....	....	....	....	....	500	M6	'93	106	100	100¼	9.73	9.73	
Sr[14]Nts[13]'A' 11¼s 2004 ....Mn	B–	11/98	B+	Y R	105.625	4-30-00	....	....	....	....	300	M6	'94	106⅛	102¾	104½	10.77	10.76	
Sr[14]Nts[13]'B' 10¾s 2002 ....Mn	B–	11/98	B+	Y R	NC	....	....	....	....	....	100	M6	'94	107½	102	103½	10.39	10.39	
***ContiFinancial Corp**.... 25a*	*2.47*	*2.36*	*0.40*	*Mr*				*9-30-99*	*699.0*			*1679*	*72.2*						
Sr Nts[14] 8⅜s 2003 ....fA15	CC	7/99	B–	Y BE	[15]100	....	....	....	....	....	300	B7	'96	95½	9¼	11¼	....	....	
Sr Nts[14] 8⅛s 2008 ....Ao	CC	7/99	B–	Y BE	[6]Z100	....	....	....	....	....	200	C6	'98	95⅛	9¼	11¼	....	....	

Uniform Footnote Explanations-See Page 260. Other: [1] Int adj qtrly(3 Mo LIBOR & 0.10%). [2] Int adj qtrly(3 Mo LIBOR&0.06%). [3] Now CNF Transportation. [4] Issued in min denom $250T. [5] (HRO)On 10-15-06 at 100. [6] Red at greater of 100 or amt based on formula. [7] Hldr may cv 25% into com at $10.15 on mty/red. [8] Int pd monthly. [9] Int thru 12-31-98,incr 0.25% anly aft to 1-1-04. [10] Death red benefit,ltd,as defined. [11] (HRO)For a Special Red Event at 100. [12] Was Consumers Pwr,subsid of CMS Energy. [13] Gtd by JSCE, Inc. [14] (HRO)On Chge of Ctrl at 101. [15] Plus Make-Whole Amt.

Title-Industry Code & Co. Finances (In Italics) / Individual Issue Statistics	Ind / Exchange Interest Dates	Fixed Charge Coverage 1996 / S&P Rating	1997 / Date of Last Rating Change	1998 / Prior Rating	Year End / Eligible	Bond Form	Million $ Cash & Equiv. / Regular Price	Curr. Assets / Regular (Begins) Thru	Curr. Liab. / Sinking Fund Price	Balance Sheet Date / Sinking Fund (Begins) Thru	L. Term Debt (Mil $) / Refund/Other Restriction Price	Refund/Other Restriction (Begins) Thru	Capital-ization (Mil $) / Outst'g (Mil $)	Total Debt % Capital / Underwriting Firm	Underwriting Year	Price Range 1999 High	Low	Mo. End Price Sale(s) or Bid	Curr. Yield	Yield to Mat.
Continental Airlines	**4**	***n/a***	***4.28***	***4.04***	***Dc***		***1299***	***2520***	***2694***	***9-30-99***	***3030***		***3484***	***68.7***						
Sr Nts[1] 9½s 2001	jD15	**BB–**	10/98	B+	Y	BE	[2]Z100	....	....	....	....	....	250	Exch.	'97	105	100	101	9.41	9.40
Sr Nts 8s 2005	jD15	**BB–**			Y	BE	[3]Z100	....	....	....	....	....	200	M7	'98	100½	91	92⅛	8.68	8.68
Continental Bank Corp	**10**	***Subsid of BankAmerica Corp, see***																		
F/R[4]Nts 2000	QMay18	**A+**	10/95	A	X	BE	NC	....	....	....	....	....	150	G1	'93	100⅝	100⅛	100⅛	....	....
Continental Cablevision Inc	**12a**	***Merged into MediaOne Group,see***																		
Sr[5]Deb[6] 8⅞s 2005	mS15	**BBB**	5/98	BBB+	X	R	NC	....	....	....	....	....	275	M6	'93	114¾	106⅝	106⅝	8.34	8.34
Sr Deb[5] 9s 2008	mS	**BBB**	5/98	BBB+	X	R	NC	....	....	....	....	....	300	M6	'93	118¾	107⅜	107⅜	8.38	8.38
Sr[5]Deb[6] 9½s 2013	fA	**BBB**	5/98	BBB+	X	R	104.75	(8-1-05)	....	....	....	....	525	M6	'93	120¾	109¼	109¼	8.70	8.69
Sr[6]Nts[5] 8½s 2001	mS15	**BBB**	5/98	BBB+	X	R	NC	....	....	....	....	....	200	M6	'93	106½	102⅜	102⅜	8.30	8.30
Sr Nts[5] 8⅝s 2003	fA15	**BBB**	5/98	BBB+	X	R	NC	....	....	....	....	....	100	M6	'93	110⅛	104	104	8.29	8.29
Continental Corp	**35c**	***Merged into CNA Fin'l, see***																		
Nts 7¼s 2003	Ms	**BBB–**	10/94	A–	X	R	NC	....	....	....	....	....	150	G1	'93	102½	98⅛	98⅛	7.39	7.39
Nts 8⅜s 2012	fA15	**BBB–**	10/94	A–	X	R	NC	....	....	....	....	....	100	G1	'92	110⅝	98¼	98¼	8.52	8.52
Cooper Indus	**23g**	***4.93***	***7.97***	***6.14***	***Dc***		***11.90***	***1410***	***971.1***	***9-30-99***	***717.0***		***2554***	***35.3***						
M-T Nts 3rd Ser 6⅝s 2008	[7]ms	**A–**			X	BE	NC	....	....	....	....	....	100	C6	'98	104⅜	92⅝	92⅝	6.88	6.88
Cooper Tire & Rubber	**61a**	***n/a***	***13.44***	***12.62***	***Dc***		***40.30***	***644.0***	***216.9***	***9-30-99***	***205.0***		***1133***	***19.0***						
Nts 7¼s 2002	jD16	**BBB+**			X	BE	[8]Z100	....	....	....	....	....	225	M2	'99	99⅞	99¼	99¼	7.30	7.30
Nts 7¾s 2009	Jd15	**BBB+**			X	BE	[8]Z100	....	....	....	....	....	350	M2	'99	99⅜	97⅜	97⅜	7.96	7.96
Nts 8s 2019	jD15	**BBB+**			X	BE	NC	....	....	....	....	....	225	M2	'99	99	95¾	95⅞	8.34	8.34
Nts 7⅝s 2027	Ms15	**BBB+**	11/99	A–	X	BE	NC	....	....	....	....	....	200	M2	'97	116⅝	90⅛	90¼	8.45	8.45
CoreStates Capital[9]	**25**	***Acq by First Union,see***																		
Gtd[10]F/R[11]Sr M-T Nts 2000	[12]	**A**			X	BE	NC	....	....	....	....	....	25.0	C1	'97	100⅛	99⅞	100	....	....
Gtd[10]F/R[13]Sr M-T Nts 2000	[14]	**A**			X	BE	NC	....	....	....	....	....	49.0	D6	'97	100¼	99¾	100	....	....
Gtd[10]Sr M-T Nts 6.186s 2000	[15]ao15	**A**			X	BE	NC	....	....	....	....	....	35.0		'97	100¾	99½	99½	6.22	6.22
F/R[16]Gtd Sr M-T Nts 5.7187s 2000	[17]	**A**			X	BE	NC	....	....	....	....	....	40.0	S7	'97	100¼	99⅝	100	5.72	....
Gtd[10]Sr M-T Nts 5¾s 2001	Jj15	**A**			X	BE	NC	....	....	....	....	....	49.0	M2	'96	100⅛	98⅝	98¾	5.82	5.82
Gtd[10]Sub Nts 9⅝s 2001	Fa15	**A–**			X	R	NC	....	....	....	....	....	150	L3	'91	107¾	103⅛	103⅛	9.33	9.33
Gtd[10]Sub Nts 9⅜s 2003	Ao15	**A–**			X	R	NC	....	....	....	....	....	100	L3	'91	112⅞	106⅛	106⅛	8.83	8.83
• Gtd[18]Sub Nts 5⅞s 2003	aO15	**A–**			X	BE	NC	....	....	....	....	....	200	L3	'93	93	92⅛	90⅛	6.52	6.52
• Gtd[10]Sub Nts 6⅝s 2005	Ms15	**A–**			X	R	NC	....	....	....	....	....	175	M5	'93	99	91½	91	7.28	7.28
Corn Products Intl	**26c**	***1.96***	***2.36***	***5.38***	***Dc***		***51.00***	***493.0***	***313.0***	***9-30-99***	***325.0***		***1584***	***31.3***						
Sr Nts 8.45s 2009	fA15	**BBB+**			X	BE	[3]Z100	....	....	....	....	....	200	L3	'99	101	97¼	97¼	8.69	8.69
Corning Glass Works	**28**	***Now Corning Inc, see***																		
Deb 8¼s 2002	Ms15	**A**	5/96	A+	X	R	NC	....	....	....	....	....	75.0	L1	'87	107⅝	101⅞	101⅞	8.10	8.10
Deb 7s 2007	Ms15	**A**	5/96	A+	X	R	100	....	....	....	....	....	[19]100	L1	'82	106⅝	95⅞	95⅞	7.30	7.30
Deb 8⅞s 2016	Ms15	**A**	5/96	A+	X	R	NC	....	....	....	....	....	75.0	L1	'86	123	107⅝	107¾	8.24	8.24
Corning Inc[20]	**28**	***6.72***	***7.70***	***6.12***	***Dc***		***102.0***	***1632***	***1219***	***9-30-99***	***1287***		***3613***	***45.3***						
Deb 6¾s 2013	mS15	**A**	5/96	A+	X	R	NC	....	....	....	....	....	100	G1	'93	107⅜	91	91	7.42	7.42
Deb 8⅞s 2021	fA15	**A**	5/96	A+	X	R	NC	....	....	....	....	....	75.0	L1	'91	126⅜	109	109⅝	8.10	8.09
Deb[21] 7⅝s 2024	fA	**A**	5/96	A+	X	R	NC	....	....	....	....	....	100	L1	'94	108⅛	101½	101½	7.51	7.51
Deb 6.85s 2029	Ms	**A**			X	BE	NC	....	....	....	....	....	150	G1	'99	101⅜	88⅜	88½	7.74	7.74
Nts 6s 2003	fA15	**A**	5/96	A+	X	R	NC	....	....	....	....	....	100	G1	'93	101⅜	95¾	95¾	6.27	6.27
Nts 6.30s 2009	Ms	**A**			X	BE	NC	....	....	....	....	....	150	G1	'99	101¾	91¾	91¾	6.87	6.87
Costilla Energy	**49**	***1.16***	***0.39***	***d4.12***	***Dc***		***Bankruptcy Chapt 11***				***[22]192.0***		***187.0***	***105.0***						
Sr Nts[1] 10¼s 2006	§aO	**NR**	11/99	D	Z	BE			Default 10-1-99 int				100		'96	72	25	29	....	Flat

Uniform Footnote Explanations-See Page 260. Other: [1] (HRO)On Chge of Ctrl at 101. [2] Plus Make-Whole Premium. [3] Red at greater of 100 or amt based on formula. [4] Int(min 4.50%)adj qtrly. [5] (HRO)For Certain Events at declining prices. [6] Issued in min denom $100T. [7] Due 5-8-98. [8] Plus Make-Whole Amt. [9] See Meridian Bancorp. [10] Gtd by CoreStates Fin'l. [11] Int adj monthly. [12] Due 4-10-00:Int pd mthly ea 8th. [13] Int adj qtrly(3 Mo LIBOR&0.02%). [14] Due 9-15-00:Int pd qtrly ea 3rd Wed,Mar etc. [15] Due 10-2-00. [16] Int adj qtrly(3 Mo LIBOR). [17] Due 10-10-00:Int pd qtrly,ea 3rd Wed,Jan,etc. [18] Gtd by Corestates Fin'l. [19] Incl disc. [20] See Corning Glass Works. [21] (HRO)On 8-1-04 at 100. [22] Liabs subj to compromise.

Title-Industry Code & Co. Finances (In Italics) / Individual Issue Statistics (Exchange)	Ind / Interest Dates	S&P Rating	Date of Last Rating Change	Prior Rating	Eligible	Bond Form	Regular Price	Regular (Begins) Thru	Sinking Fund Price	Sinking Fund (Begins) Thru	Refund/Other Restriction Price	Refund/Other Restriction (Begins) Thru	Outst'g (Mil $)	Underwriting Firm	Underwriting Year	Price Range 1999 High	Price Range 1999 Low	Mo. End Price Sale(s) or Bid	Curr. Yield	Yield to Mat.
Title-Industry Code & Co. Finances	*Ind*	*Fixed Charge Coverage 1996*	*1997*	*1998*		*Year End*	*Million $ Cash & Equiv.*	*Curr. Assets*	*Curr. Liab.*	*Balance Sheet Date*	*L. Term Debt (Mil $)*		*Capital-ization (Mil $)*	*Total Debt % Capital*						
[1]Countrywide Funding	***25h***	***2.33***	***2.33***	***1.64***		***Fb***				***8-31-99***	***11330***		***14666***	***82.1***						
Sub Nts[2] 8¼s 2002	jJ15	A–			X	R	NC	....	....	....	....	....	200	S1	'92	107	101½	101½	8.13	8.13
Countrywide Home Loans	***25h***	***Gtd by Countrywide Credit Indus***																		
Gtd[3]Nts[2] 5.62s 2000	aO16	A			X	BE	NC	....	....	....	....	....	300	L3	'98	99¾	98⅞	99⅛	5.67	5.67
Gtd[4]Nts[2] 6.85s 2004	Jd15	A			X	BE	NC	....	....	....	....	....	750	C1	'99	100¼	97¾	97¾	7.01	7.01
• Gtd[2]M-T Nts[3] 'E' 6.935s 2007	[5]jj15	A			X	BE	NC	....	....	....	....	....	150	L3	'97	No Sale		95¼	7.28	7.28
Gtd[2]M-T Nts[3] 'F' 6.43s 2000	[6]ao15	A			X	BE	NC	....	....	....	....	....	100		'97	101	99⅝	99¾	6.45	6.45
Gtd[2]M-T Nts[3] 'F' 6.38s 2002	[7]jj15	A			X	BE	NC	....	....	....	....	....	150	L3	'97	101⅛	97⅝	97⅝	6.54	6.54
Gtd[2]M-T Nts[3]'F' 6.84s 2004	[8]ao15	A			X	BE	NC	....	....	....	....	....	200	S1	'97	103⅛	97½	97½	7.02	7.02
Gtd[3]M-T Nts[2]'F' 6.51s 2005	[9]jj15	A			X	BE	NC	....	....	....	....	....	163		'98	101½	95⅝	95⅞	6.79	6.79
Gtd[2]M-T Nts[3]'F' 6.70s 2005	Ms10	A			X	BE	NC	....	....	....	....	....	111	L3	'98	102⅜	96⅜	96⅝	6.93	6.93
Gtd[2]M-T Nts 'H' 6¼s 2009	Ao15	A			X	BE	NC	....	....	....	....	....	600	L3	'99	99⅜	89¾	89¾	6.96	6.96
Cox[10]Communications[11]	***54c***	***1.13***	***0.85***	***0.80***		***Dc***	***30.60***			***9-30-99***	***5941***		***11216***	***32.0***						
Deb[10] 7⅛s 2013	Ms	BBB+	8/99	A–	X	R	NC	....	....	....	....	....	8.88	M6	'93	114⅛	94¾	94¾	7.52	7.52
Deb 7¼s 2015	mN15	BBB+	8/99	A–	X	R	[12]Z100	....	....	....	....	....	100	C5	'95	110⅛	93¾	94⅛	7.70	7.70
Deb[10] 7⅜s 2023	jJ	BBB+	8/99	A–	X	R	NC	....	....	....	....	....	1.20	G1	'93	113½	92⅝	92⅝	7.96	7.96
Deb 7⅝s 2025	Jd15	BBB+	8/99	A–	X	R	NC	....	....	....	....	....	150	C5	'95	117	94⅝	94¾	8.05	8.05
Deb 6.80s 2028	fA	BBB+	8/99	A–	X	BE	[13]Z100	....	....	....	....	....	200	M2	'98	106½	85¾	87	7.82	7.81
F/R[14]Nts 2000	QAug15	BBB+			X	BE	100	(2-15-00)	....	....	....	....	525	M2	'99	100	99⅞	100	....	....
Nts[10] 8.55s 2000	Jd	BBB+	8/99	A–	X	R	NC	....	....	....	....	....	6.25	M6	'90	104¼	100¾	100¾	8.49	8.48
Nts 6⅜s 2000	Jd15	BBB+	8/99	A–	X	R	NC	....	....	....	....	....	425	C5	'95	101½	99⅞	100⅛	6.37	6.37
Nts[10] 8⅞s 2001	Ms	BBB+	8/99	A–	X	R	NC	....	....	....	....	....	13.9	G1	'91	107⅛	102	102	8.70	8.70
Nts 7s 2001	fA15	BBB+			X	BE	[13]Z100	....	....	....	....	....	300	M2	'99	100½	99⅜	99¾	7.02	7.02
Nts 6½s 2002	mN15	BBB+	8/99	A–	X	R	[12]Z100	....	....	....	....	....	200	C5	'95	103½	98¼	98¼	6.62	6.62
Nts 7½s 2004	fA15	BBB+			X	BE	[13]Z100	....	....	....	....	....	375	M2	'99	102¼	99⅝	100½	7.46	7.46
Nts 6⅞s 2005	Jd15	BBB+	8/99	A–	X	R	NC	....	....	....	....	....	375	C5	'95	107⅛	96⅞	97¼	7.07	7.07
Nts 7¾s 2006	fA15	BBB+			X	BE	[13]Z100	....	....	....	....	....	400	M2	'99	103½	99¾	100⅞	7.68	7.68
Nts 6.40s 2008	fA	BBB+	8/99	A–	X	BE	[13]Z100	....	....	....	....	....	200	M2	'98	105⅛	91⅝	92⅛	6.95	6.95
Nts 7⅞s 2009	fA15	BBB+			X	BE	[13]Z100	....	....	....	....	....	400	M2	'99	104¾	99⅞	101¼	7.78	7.78
M-T Nts 6.69s 2004	[15]jd15	BBB+	8/99	A–	X	BE	NC	....	....	....	....	....	100		'97	106⅝	97⅝	97⅞	6.84	6.84
M-T Nts 6.85s 2015	Jj15	BBB+	8/99	A–	X	BE	[13]Z100	....	....	....	....	....	100	S4	'98	103⅜	88¾	90	7.61	7.61
M-T Nts 6.95s 2028	Jj15	BBB+	8/99	A–	X	BE	[13]Z100	....	....	....	....	....	100	S4	'98	108¼	87⅜	89	7.81	7.81
CP Ltd Partnership	***57***	***2.24***	***1.95***	***2.10***		***Dc***				***6-30-99***	***452.0***		***933.0***	***48.4***						
Sr Nts 8¾s 2000	Ms2	BBB	11/97	BBB–	X	BE	[16]Z100	....	....	....	....	....	75.0	M2	'95	102⅜	100¼	100¼	8.73	8.73
[17]CPC Int'l	***26***	***5.33***	***6.39***	***6.53***		***Dc***	***127.0***	***2251***	***2159***	***9-30-99***	***1884***		***3644***	***72.4***						
Nts 6.15s 2006	Jj15	A+			X	BE	NC	....	....	....	....	....	300	S1	'96	104¼	94⅜	94⅜	6.52	6.52
Nts 'E' 7¼s 2026	jD15	A+			X	BE	[16]Z100	....	....	....	....	....	300	S1	'96	111⅞	94¼	94⅜	7.68	7.68
M-T Nts 'F' 7s 2017	aO15	A+			X	BE	[16]Z100	....	....	....	....	....	150	S1	'97	105⅛	90⅜	90½	7.73	7.73
Crane Co	***17***	***7.19***	***8.38***	***8.63***		***Dc***	***15.01***	***684.1***	***256.4***	***9-30-99***	***313.0***		***1005***	***31.8***						
Nts 8½s 2004	Ms15	BBB+	3/98	BBB	X	R	NC	....	....	....	....	....	100	M5	'92	113⅛	104⅜	104⅜	8.14	8.14
Nts 6¾s 2006	Ao	BBB+			X	BE	NC	....	....	....	....	....	100	M5	'98	106¼	95⅞	95⅞	7.04	7.04
Crestar Financial	***10***	***Merged into SunTrust Banks,see***																		
Sub Nts[18] 8¼s 2002	jJ15	A	1/99	BBB+	X	BE	NC	....	....	....	....	....	125	M6	'92	108	102⅜	102⅞	8.02	8.02
Sub Nts[18] 8¾s 2004	mN15	A	1/99	BBB+	X	BE	NC	....	....	....	....	....	150	M6	'94	114½	105¼	105¼	8.31	8.31
CRIIMI MAE	***57***	***1.59***	***1.58***	***1.56***		***Dc***	***Bankruptcy Chapt 11***				***1913***		***2171***	***88.1***						
Sr Nts[19] 9⅛s 2002	§jD	D	10/98	B+	Z	BE			Default 12-1-98 int				100	M2	'97	87¾	62	86	....	Flat

Uniform Footnote Explanations-See Page 1. Other: [1] Subsid & data of Countrywide Credit Indus. [2] Gtd by Countrywide Credit Indus. [3] Issued in min denom $100T. [4] Co may red in whole, at 100, for tax law chge. [5] Due 7-16-07. [6] Due 10-23-00. [7] Due 10-8-02. [8] Due 10-22-04. [9] Due 2-11-05. [10] Was Times Mirror(Old). [11] See TCA Cable TV. [12] Greater of 100 & amt based on formula. [13] Red at greater of 100 or amt based on formula. [14] Int adj qtrly(3 Mo LIBOR & 0.60%). [15] Due 9-20-04. [16] Plus Make-Whole Amt. [17] Now Bestfoods. [18] Gtd by SunTrust Banks, Inc. [19] (HRO)Om Chge of Ctrl at 101.

Title-Industry Code & Co. Finances (In Italics) / Individual Issue Statistics — Exchange	Ind / Interest Dates	Fixed Charge Coverage 1996 / S&P Rating	1997 / Date of Last Rating Change	1998 / Prior Rating	Eligible	Year End / Bond Form	Cash & Equiv. (Million $) / Regular Price	Curr. Assets (Million $) / Regular (Begins) Thru	Curr. Liab. / Sinking Fund Price	Balance Sheet Date / Sinking Fund (Begins) Thru	L. Term Debt (Mil $) / Refund/Other Restriction Price	Refund/Other Restriction (Begins) Thru	Capital-ization (Mil $) / Outst'g (Mil $)	Total Debt % Capital / Underwriting Firm	Underwriting Year	Price Range 1999 High	Price Range 1999 Low	Mo. End Price Sale(s) or Bid	Curr. Yield	Yield to Mat.
Crown Castle Intl	***67g***	***0.47***	***d1.16***	***d1.30***		***Dc***	***492.0***	***575.0***	***105.0***	***9-30-99***	***1479***		***3137***	***47.1***						
Sr Nts[1] 9s 2011	Mn15	**B**			Y	BE	104.50	(5-15-04)	....	....	[2]Z109	5-15-02	180	G1	'99	100¼	93	97⅝	9.22	9.22
Sr[3]Disc[1]Nts 10⅜s 2011	[4]Mn15	**B**			Y	BE	105.187	(5-15-04)	....	....	[5]Z110.375	5-15-02	[6]500	G1	'99	63	55¼	62½	....	Flat
Crown Central Petroleum	***49g***	***0.76***	***1.10***	***d1.81***		***Dc***	***10.00***	***192.0***	***216.0***	***9-30-99***	***129.0***		***286.0***	***46.4***						
Sr Nts[1] 10⅞s 2005	Fa	**B**	12/98	BB–	Y	R	105.438	(2-1-00)	....	....	....	....	125	S1	'95	96	71	75½	14.40	14.40
Crown Cork & Seal	***16b***	***2.45***	***2.34***	***1.44***		***Dc***	***219.0***	***3329***	***4290***	***9-30-99***	***3398***		***8965***	***65.4***						
Deb 8s 2023	Ao15	**BBB**	2/98	BBB+	X	BE	103.813	(4-15-03)	....	....	....	....	200	S1	'93	103⅜	90½	90¾	8.82	8.82
• Nts 7⅛s 2002	mS	**BBB**			X	BE	NC	....	....	....	....	....	350	S4	'99	100⅛	99⅜	95	7.50	7.50
Nts 6¾s 2003	Ao15	**BBB**	2/98	BBB+	X	BE	NC	....	....	....	....	....	200	S1	'93	101¼	97¼	97¼	6.94	6.94
Nts 8⅜s 2005	Jj15	**BBB**	2/98	BBB+	X	R	NC	....	....	....	....	....	300	S1	'95	109⅛	101½	101½	8.25	8.25
Crown Paper Co	***50***	***0.47***	***0.31***	***d3.47***		***Dc***	***8.71***	***180.0***	***105.0***	***6-27-99***	***478.0***		***409.0***	***117.0***						
Sr Sub Nts[1] 11s 2005	mS	**CCC+**	4/99	B–	Y	R	105.50	(9-1-00)	....	....	....	....	250	M2	'95	92	60	61	18.03	18.02
CSC Holdings Inc[7]	***12a***	***0.27***	***0.20***	***d0.02***		***Dc***				***6-30-99***	***57.96***		***5058***	***115.0***						
Deb 8⅛s 2009	fA15	**BB+**			Y	BE	NC	....	....	....	....	....	400	B7	'97	111½	97½	99⅞	8.14	8.13
Sr Deb 7⅞s 2018	Fa15	**BB+**			Y	BE	NC	....	....	....	....	....	300	B7	'98	106⅞	91	95¼	8.27	8.27
Sr Deb 7⅝s 2018	jJ15	**BB+**			Y	BE	NC	....	....	....	....	....	500	B7	'98	104½	87⅜	93	8.20	8.20
Sr Nts[8] 7⅞s 2007	jD15	**BB+**			Y	BE	[9]Z100	....	....	....	....	....	500	B7	'97	107⅜	96¼	98½	7.99	7.99
Sr Nts 7¼s 2008	jJ15	**BB+**			Y	BE	NC	....	....	....	....	....	500	B7	'98	105	91⅞	94¾	7.65	7.65
Sr Sub Deb 9⅞s 2013	Fa15	**BB–**	8/97	B	Y	R	104.80	(2-15-03)	....	....	....	....	200	M2	'93	113¾	102¾	104¾	9.43	9.43
Sr Sub Deb 10½s 2016	Mn15	**BB–**	8/97	B	Y	BE	105.25	(5-15-06)	....	....	....	....	250	B7	'96	121½	107¼	111	9.46	9.46
Sr Sub Deb 9⅞s 2023	Ao	**BB–**	8/97	B	Y	BE	104.938	(4-1-03)	....	....	....	....	150	M2	'93	113¾	102½	104½	9.45	9.45
Sr Sub Nts 9¼s 2005	mN	**BB–**	8/97	B	Y	R	104.625	(11-1-00)	....	....	....	....	300	M2	'95	108	100¾	102½	9.02	9.02
Sr Sub Nts 9⅞s 2006	Mn15	**BB–**	8/97	B	Y	BE	104.938	(5-15-01)	....	....	....	....	150		'96	110¼	102¼	105½	9.36	9.36
CSX Corp[10]	***55***	***6.45***	***3.62***	***2.24***		***Dc***	***619.0***	***2527***	***3771***	***10-1-99***	***6096***		***12953***	***55.7***						
Deb 9s 2006	fA15	**BBB**	4/97	BBB+	X	R	NC	....	....	....	....	....	300	F1	'86	118⅜	106¼	106⅜	8.46	8.46
Deb 8⅝s 2022	Mn15	**BBB**	4/97	BBB+	X	BE	NC	....	....	....	....	....	200	L3	'92	123	103½	104⅛	8.28	8.28
Deb 8.10s 2022	mS15	**BBB**	4/97	BBB+	X	BE	NC	....	....	....	....	....	150	F1	'92	117	98¼	98⅞	8.19	8.19
Nts 9½s 2000	fA	**BBB**	4/97	BBB+	X	BE	NC	....	....	....	....	....	250	F1	'90	106	101½	101½	9.36	9.36
Nts 7s 2002	mS15	**BBB**	4/97	BBB+	X	BE	NC	....	....	....	....	....	100	F1	'92	104⅜	99⅛	99¼	7.05	7.05
Nts 6¼s 2008	aO15	**BBB**			X	BE	NC	....	....	....	....	....	400	S4	'98	102⅛	90⅜	90⅜	6.92	6.92
M-T Nts 'C' 6.80s 2028	jD	**BBB**			X	BE	[11]Z100	....	....	....	....	....	200	G1	'98	100½	85¼	85⅝	7.94	7.94
Cummins Engine	***8***	***12.89***	***12.00***	***4.39***		***Dc***	***60.00***	***2242***	***1295***	***9-26-99***	***1166***		***2542***	***45.0***						
Deb 6¾s 2027	Fa15	**BBB+**			X	BE	[12]Z100	(2-15-07)	....	....	....	....	120	G1	'97	101	93⅛	93⅛	7.25	7.25
Cyprus Amax[13]Minerals[14]	***45b***	***1.57***	***1.29***	***1.61***		***Dc***	***845.0***	***1312***	***403.0***	***9-30-99***	***1548***		***3932***	***47.1***						
Nts 7⅜s 2007	Mn15	**BBB–**			X	BE	NC	....	....	....	....	....	250	S7	'95	103⅛	90½	90½	8.15	8.15
Cyprus Minerals	***45b***	***Now Cyprus Amax Minerals,see***																		
Deb 8⅜s 2023	Fa	**BBB–**	11/93	BBB	X	R	103.73	(2-1-03)	....	....	....	....	150	F1	'93	104⅛	92	92⅝	9.04	9.04
Nts[15] 10⅛s 2002	Ao	**BBB–**	11/93	BBB	X	R	NC	....	....	....	[16]Z100	....	150	F1	'90	111¾	103	103	9.83	9.83
Nts 6⅝s 2005	aO15	**BBB–**	11/93	BBB	X	R	NC	....	....	....	....	....	250	K2	'93	102⅝	89⅜	89⅜	7.41	7.41
Cytec Industries	***14***	***n/a***	***n/a***	***n/a***		***Dc***	***14.10***	***480.1***	***360.8***	***9-30-99***	***415.0***		***909.0***	***45.7***						
Nts 6½s 2003	Ms15	**BBB**			X	BE	[11]Z100	....	....	....	....	....	100		'98	101⅜	97⅛	97⅛	6.69	6.69
Dairy Mart Convenience Strs	***59b***	***0.76***	***0.77***	***1.02***		***Ja***	***5.57***	***57.90***	***62.60***	***10-31-99***	***112.0***		***117.0***	***92.3***						
Sr Sub Nts[1] 10¼s 2004	Ms15	**NR**	12/98	B	Y	R	104.75	3-1-00	....	....	....	....	88.5	B7	'94	95	82	82	12.50	12.50
Dan River Inc	***68***	***1.51***	***2.02***	***2.50***		***Dc***	***1.58***	***281.2***	***89.31***	***10-2-99***	***304.0***		***330.0***	***46.1***						
Sr[1]Sub Nts 10⅛s 2003	jD15	**B**			Y	R	103.40	12-14-00	....	....	....	....	120	M2	'93	104¾	97½	100	10.13	10.12

Uniform Footnote Explanations-See Page 260. Other: [1] (HRO)On Chge of Ctrl at 101. [2] Max $63M red w/proceeds of Equity Off'g. [3] Int accrues at 10.375% fr 5-15-04. [4] Fr 5-15-04. [5] Accreted:Max $175M red w/proceeds of Equity Off'g. [6] Incl disc. [7] Was Cablevision Systems Corp. [8] Co may red in whole,at 100,for tax law chge. [9] Greater of 100 or amt based on formula. [10] See Louisville & Nash RR. [11] Red at greater of 100 or amt based on formula. [12] Plus Make Whole Amt. [13] See Amax Inc & Cyprus Minerals. [14] Acq by Phelps Dodge. [15] (HRO)At 100 for Designated Event&Rat'g Decline. [16] Co may red in whole if min 90% amt outstg put.

Title-Industry Code & Co. Finances (In Italics)	Ind	Fixed Charge Coverage 1996		1997	1998	Year End	Million $ Cash & Equiv.	Curr. Assets	Curr. Liab.	Balance Sheet Date	L. Term Debt (Mil $)		Capital-ization (Mil $)	Total Debt % Capital						
Exchange ↓ Individual Issue Statistics	Interest Dates	S&P Rating	Date of Last Rating Change	Prior Rating	Eligible ↓	Bond Form	Redemption Provisions: Regular Price	Regular (Begins) Thru	Sinking Fund Price	Sinking Fund (Begins) Thru	Refund/Other Restriction Price	Refund/Other Restriction (Begins) Thru	Outst'g (Mil $)	Underwriting Firm	Underwriting Year	Price Range 1999 High	Price Range 1999 Low	Mo. End Price Sale(s) or Bid	Curr. Yield	Yield to Mat.
Dana Corp	***8***	***4.09***		***4.34***	***4.53***	***Dc***	***185.0***	***5091***	***4021***	***9-30-99***	***2574***		***6837***	***56.1***						
Nts 6¼s 2004	Ms	A–			X	BE	[1]Z100	....	....	....	....	....	250	M2	'99	101	95¼	95¼	6.56	6.56
Nts 6½s 2008	Ms15	A–			X	BE	[1]Z100	....	....	....	....	....	150	L3	'98	104⅜	92	92	7.07	7.07
Nts 6½s 2009	Ms	A–			X	BE	[1]Z100	....	....	....	....	....	350	M2	'99	101⅛	91	91	7.14	7.14
Nts 7s 2028	Ms	A–			X	BE	[1]Z100	....	....	....	....	....	200	L3	'98	103⅝	87¼	87½	8.00	8.00
Nts 7s 2029	Ms	A–			X	BE	[1]Z100	....	....	....	....	....	400	M2	'99	99¼	87⅛	87¼	8.02	8.02
Danaher Corp	***13e***	***13.81***		***20.37***	***14.71***	***Dc***	***280.1***	***1208***	***801.9***	***10-1-99***	***341.0***		***1849***	***21.6***						
Nts 6s 2008	aO15	A+			X	BE	[2]Z100	....	....	....	....	....	250	S4	'98	99¾	89⅞	89⅞	6.68	6.68
Darden Restaurants	***27c***	***△4.19***		***△8.09***	***△12.48***	***My***	***30.29***	***358.2***	***526.4***	***8-29-99***	***313.0***		***1321***	***24.3***						
• Nts 6⅜s 2006	Fa	BBB+	12/99	BBB	X	BE	[3]Z100	....	....	....	....	....	150	M6	'96	89	89	93⅞	6.79	6.79
Dayton Hudson Corp	***59g***	***3.07***		***4.19***	***4.91***	***Ja***	***246.0***	***7104***	***5970***	***10-30-99***	***5263***		***10849***	***49.9***						
SF Deb 9⅞s 2017	Jd	A–	11/98	BBB+	X	R	103.95	5-31-00	100	....	....	....	150	G1	'87	104½	100	104½	9.45	9.45
SF Deb 9½s 2016	aO15	A–	11/98	BBB+	X	R	102.975	10-14-00	100	....	....	....	87.7	G1	'86	103¼	100⅛	103¼	9.20	9.20
Deb 9¼s 2006	Ms	A–	11/98	BBB+	X	R	100	(3-1-01)	....	....	....	....	100	G1	'86	107⅛	102⅝	102¾	9.00	9.00
Deb 9⅝s 2008	Fa	A–	11/98	BBB+	X	R	NC	....	....	....	....	....	100	G1	'88	127⅛	112½	112½	8.56	8.55
Nts 5⅞s 2008	mN	A–	11/98	BBB+	X	BE	NC	....	....	....	....	....	200	S4	'98	102⅛	89⅝	90¼	6.51	6.51
Deb 9¼s 2011	fA15	A–	11/98	BBB+	X	R	NC	....	....	....	....	....	100	G1	'91	130½	113	113	8.19	8.18
Deb 8.60s 2012	Jj15	A–	11/98	BBB+	X	R	NC	....	....	....	....	....	200	G1	'92	124¾	108⅛	108¼	7.94	7.94
Deb 9⅞s 2020	jJ	A–	11/98	BBB+	X	R	NC	....	....	....	....	....	200	G1	'90	138⅝	119¼	119⅞	8.24	8.24
Deb 9.70s 2021	Jd15	A–	11/98	BBB+	X	R	NC	....	....	....	....	....	200	G1	'91	138	118⅞	119½	8.12	8.12
Deb 9s 2021	aO	A–	11/98	BBB+	X	R	NC	....	....	....	....	....	125	G1	'91	130⅜	111⅞	112½	8.00	8.00
Deb 8⅞s 2022	Ao	A–	11/98	BBB+	X	R	NC	....	....	....	....	....	100	G1	'92	130⅜	110⅝	111⅜	7.97	7.97
Deb 8.80s 2022	Mn15	A–	11/98	BBB+	X	R	NC	....	....	....	....	....	100	G1	'92	129½	109⅞	110⅝	7.95	7.95
Deb 8½s 2022	jD	A–	11/98	BBB+	X	BE	103.75	(12-1-02)	....	....	....	....	200	G1	'92	110	99¼	102	8.33	8.33
Deb 7⅞s 2023	Jd15	A–	11/98	BBB+	X	BE	103.551	(6-15-03)	....	....	....	....	200	G1	'93	108⅞	96¾	98¾	7.97	7.97
Deb 7.65s 2023	fA	A–	11/98	BBB+	X	BE	103.825	(8-1-03)	....	....	....	....	100	G1	'93	109⅛	95¾	96⅜	7.94	7.94
Deb 6¾s 2028	Jj	A–	11/98	BBB+	X	BE	NC	....	....	....	....	....	200	G1	'98	105½	87⅝	88¼	7.65	7.65
Deb 6.65s 2028	fA	A–	11/98	BBB+	X	BE	NC	....	....	....	....	....	200	G1	'98	104¼	86½	87	7.64	7.64
Deb 5.895s 2037	Jd15	A–	11/98	BBB+	X	BE	[4]NC	....	....	....	....	....	100		'97	100½	99¾	99⅞	5.90	5.90
M-T[5]Nts 'H'[6] 5.865s 2027	fA15	A–	11/98	BBB+	X	BE	NC	....	....	....	....	....	75.0		'97	102⅝	99⅛	99½	5.89	5.89
Nts 10s 2000	jD	A–	11/98	BBB+	X	R	NC	....	....	....	....	....	250	G1	'90	108¼	102¾	102¾	9.73	9.73
Nts 9.40s 2001	Fa15	A–	11/98	BBB+	X	R	NC	....	....	....	....	....	100	G1	'91	108	102⅝	102⅝	9.16	9.16
Nts 6.80s 2001	aO	A–	11/98	BBB+	X	BE	NC	....	....	....	....	....	200	G1	'96	103¾	99⅞	99⅞	6.81	6.81
Nts 9¾s 2002	jJ	A–	11/98	BBB+	X	R	NC	....	....	....	....	....	200	G1	'90	113½	105⅝	105¾	9.22	9.22
Nts 6.40s 2003	Fa15	A–	11/98	BBB+	X	BE	NC	....	....	....	....	....	300	G1	'96	103⅜	98¼	98¼	6.51	6.51
Nts 6⅝s 2003	Ms	A–	11/98	BBB+	X	BE	NC	....	....	....	....	....	150	G1	'93	104⅜	98⅞	99	6.69	6.69
Nts 7¼s 2004	mS	A–	11/98	BBB+	X	R	NC	....	....	....	....	....	100	G1	'92	108½	100¾	100⅞	7.19	7.19
Nts 7½s 2006	jJ15	A–	11/98	BBB+	X	BE	NC	....	....	....	....	....	200	M2	'96	111⅞	100¼	100¼	7.48	7.48
Nts 10s 2011	Jj	A–	11/98	BBB+	X	R	NC	....	....	....	....	....	175	G1	'91	135	117½	117½	8.51	8.51
Dayton Power & Light[7]	***75***	***3.95***		***4.16***	***4.19***	***Dc***	***11.10***	***432.0***	***465.0***	***6-30-99***	***661.0***		***2400***	***34.6***						
1st 7⅞s 2024	Fa15	AA–	3/94	A	X	BE	103.765	(2-15-03)	....	....	....	....	220	F1	'93	110⅞	95½	95⅝	8.24	8.23
1st 8.15s 2026	Jj15	AA–	3/94	A	X	BE	104.075	(1-15-03)	Z100	....	....	....	226	M6	'93	111⅛	95⅜	97⅞	8.33	8.33
Dean Foods	***26d***	***△6.75***		***△7.81***	***△3.95***	***My***	***20.80***	***617.0***	***456.4***	***8-29-99***	***658.0***		***1397***	***47.2***						
Sr Nts 6¾s 2005	Jd15	A			X	BE	NC	....	....	....	....	....	100	M6	'95	106¾	97	97	6.96	6.96
Sr Nts 6⅝s 2009	Mn15	A			X	BE	[2]Z100	....	....	....	....	....	200	M2	'99	99⅞	93⅝	93⅝	7.08	7.08
Sr Nts 6.90s 2017	aO15	A			X	BE	NC	....	....	....	....	....	150	G1	'97	106⅞	91⅛	91¼	7.56	7.56

Uniform Footnote Explanations-See Page 260. Other: [1] Plus Make-Whole Amt. [2] Red at greater of 100 or amt based on formula. [3] Greater of 100 or amt based on formula. [4] Co may red in whole,at 100,if amt o/s is less than $10M. [5] Issued in min denom $100T. [6] (HRO)Ea Aug 15 fr 8-15-99 at 100. [7] Subsid of DPL Inc.

Title-Industry Code & Co. Finances (In Italics) / Individual Issue Statistics	Ind / Interest Dates	Fixed Charge Coverage 1996 / S&P Rating	1997 / Date of Last Rating Change	1998 / Prior Rating	Eligible	Year End / Bond Form	Cash & Equiv. (Million $) / Regular Price	Curr. Assets / Regular (Begins) Thru	Curr. Liab. / Sinking Fund Price	Balance Sheet Date / Sinking Fund (Begins) Thru	L. Term Debt (Mil $) / Refund/Other Restriction Price	Refund/Other Restriction (Begins) Thru	Capital-ization (Mil $) / Outst'g (Mil $)	Total Debt % Capital / Underwriting Firm	Underwriting Year	Price Range 1999 High	Price Range 1999 Low	Mo. End Price Sale(s) or Bid	Curr. Yield	Yield to Mat.
Dean Witter, Discover & Co	***25e***	***Now Morgan Stanley Dean Witter,Discover,see***																		
Deb 6¾s 2013	aO15	A+	6/97	A	X	BE	NC	....	....	....	....	....	250	D3	'93	103¼	91⅛	91⅛	7.41	7.41
Deb 6¾s 2016	Jj	A+	6/97	A	X	BE	NC	....	....	....	....	....	150	D3	'96	101¼	87⅞	89	7.58	7.58
LIBOR[1]F/R Nts 2000	QMar	A+	6/97	A	X	BE	NC	....	....	....	....	....	150	D3	'95	100⅝	100	100⅛	....	....
Nts 6¼s 2000	Ms15	A+	6/97	A	X	BE	NC	....	....	....	....	....	400	D3	'93	100¾	99⅞	100	6.25	6.25
Nts 6¾s 2000	fA15	A+	6/97	A	X	BE	NC	....	....	....	....	....	200	D3	'95	101¾	100	100	6.75	6.75
Nts 6⅞s 2003	Ms	A+	6/97	A	X	BE	NC	....	....	....	....	....	750	D3	'93	104⅛	98¾	98¾	6.96	6.96
Nts 6½s 2005	mN	A+	6/97	A	X	BE	NC	....	....	....	....	....	250	D3	'93	103⅝	94¼	94¼	6.90	6.90
M-T Nts 'I' 5.88s 2001	[2]ao	A+	6/97	A	X	BE	NC	....	....	....	....	....	10.0	D3	'94	100¾	99⅛	99⅛	5.93	5.93
M-T Nts 'I' 6s 2001	[3]ao	A+	6/97	A	X	BE	NC	....	....	....	....	....	10.0	D3	'94	100⅞	99¼	99¼	6.05	6.04
M-T Nts 'I' 7¾s 2001	[4]ao	A+	6/97	A	X	BE	NC	....	....	....	....	....	5.00	D3	'94	104¾	101¼	101¼	7.65	7.65
M-T Nts 'I' 7.53s 2001	[5]ao	A+	6/97	A	X	BE	NC	....	....	....	....	....	10.0	D3	'94	104⅜	101	101	7.46	7.45
M-T Nts 'I' 7.58s 2001	[5]ao	A+	6/97	A	X	BE	NC	....	....	....	....	....	50.0	D3	'94	104½	101	101	7.50	7.50
M-T Nts 'I' 7¾s 2001	[6]ao	A+	6/97	A	X	BE	NC	....	....	....	....	....	19.0	D3	'94	105	101¼	101¼	7.65	7.65
M-T Nts 'I' 7.62s 2001	[7]ao	A+	6/97	A	X	BE	NC	....	....	....	....	....	15.0	D3	'94	104¾	101⅛	101⅛	7.54	7.53
M-T Nts 'I' 7.78s 2001	[8]ao	A+	6/97	A	X	BE	NC	....	....	....	....	....	10.0	D3	'94	105⅛	101⅜	101⅜	7.67	7.67
M-T Nts 'I' 7.62s 2002	[9]ao	A+	6/97	A	X	BE	NC	....	....	....	....	....	10.0	D3	'94	105¾	101⅜	101⅜	7.52	7.52
M-T Nts 'I' 8.05s 2004	[10]ao	A+	6/97	A	X	BE	NC	....	....	....	....	....	5.00	D3	'94	110⅜	103	103	7.82	7.81
M-T Nts 'I' 7.81s 2004	[11]ao	A+	6/97	A	X	BE	NC	....	....	....	....	....	10.0	D3	'94	109⅜	102	102	7.66	7.66
M-T Nts 'I' 7.82s 2004	[11]ao	A+	6/97	A	X	BE	NC	....	....	....	....	....	10.0	D3	'94	109⅜	102⅛	102⅛	7.66	7.66
M-T Nts 'I' 7.76s 2004	[12]ao	A+	6/97	A	X	BE	NC	....	....	....	....	....	10.0	D3	'94	109⅛	101⅞	101⅞	7.62	7.62
M-T Nts 'I' 8.02s 2004	[13]ao	A+	6/97	A	X	BE	NC	....	....	....	....	....	10.0	D3	'94	110⅜	102⅞	102⅞	7.80	7.79
M-T Nts 'I' 7.94s 2004	[14]ao	A+	6/97	A	X	BE	NC	....	....	....	....	....	13.0	D3	'94	110	102½	102½	7.75	7.74
M-T Nts 'I' 7.85s 2004	[15]ao	A+	6/97	A	X	BE	NC	....	....	....	....	....	10.0	D3	'94	109⅝	102¼	102¼	7.68	7.68
M-T Nts 'I' 7.97s 2004	[16]ao	A+	6/97	A	X	BE	NC	....	....	....	....	....	10.0	D3	'94	110⅛	102⅝	102⅝	7.77	7.76
M-T Nts 'I' 8.09s 2004	[16]ao	A+	6/97	A	X	BE	NC	....	....	....	....	....	10.0	D3	'94	110¾	103⅛	103⅛	7.84	7.84
M-T Nts 'I' 8.14s 2004	[17]ao	A+	6/97	A	X	BE	NC	....	....	....	....	....	8.00	D3	'94	111	103⅜	103⅜	7.87	7.87
M-T Nts 'I' 8.06s 2004	[18]ao	A+	6/97	A	X	BE	NC	....	....	....	....	....	15.0	D3	'94	110⅝	103	103	7.83	7.82
M-T Nts 'I' 7.86s 2004	[19]ao	A+	6/97	A	X	BE	NC	....	....	....	....	....	5.00	D3	'94	109⅞	102¼	102¼	7.69	7.69
M-T Nts 'I' 7.07s 2014	[20]ao	A+	6/97	A	X	BE	NC	....	....	....	....	....	40.0	D3	'94	107⅜	93½	93½	7.56	7.56
DeepTech International	***49***	***Mgr w/El Paso Energy,see***																		
Sr Sec[21]Nts[22] 12s 2000	jD15	NR	5/97	CCC+		R	100	....	....	....	....	....	82.0	D6	'94	108⅛	103⅝	103⅝	11.58	11.58
Deere & Co.	***41a***	***4.20***	***4.57***	***4.01***		***Oc***				***7-31-99***	***3628***		***13020***	***68.0***						
• Deb[23] 8.95s 2019	Jd15	A+	5/97	A	X	R	100	(6-15-09)	....	....	....	....	200	M2	'89	113⅝	104½	105½	8.48	8.48
• Deb 8½s 2022	Jj9	A+	5/97	A	X	R	NC	....	....	....	....	....	200	M2	'92	119½	104¼	105	8.10	8.09
• Deb 6.55s 2028	aO	A+			X	BE	NC	....	....	....	....	....	200	G1	'98	100⅝	98⅛	86⅜	7.58	7.58
Nts 6.55s 2004	jJ15	A+			X	BE	NC	....	....	....	....	....	250	C1	'99	100⅜	97⅛	97⅛	6.74	6.74
Deere (John) Capital[24]	***25d***	***1.76***	***1.64***	***1.63***		***Oc***				***7-31-99***	***2445***		***7093***	***85.5***						
Nts 5.85s 2001	Jj15	A+			X	BE	NC	....	....	....	....	....	200	M2	'98	100⅜	98⅞	98⅞	5.92	5.92
• Nts 5.35s 2001	aO23	A+			X	BE	NC	....	....	....	....	....	200	M5	'98	99⅜	97	95¼	5.62	5.62
Nts 6s 2009	Fa15	A+			X	BE	NC	....	....	....	....	....	300	C1	'99	99⅜	88½	88½	6.78	6.78
M-T Nts 'C' 6¼s 2000	[25]ms15	A+			X	BE	NC	....	....	....	....	....	25.0		'97	100¾	99¾	99⅞	6.26	6.26
M-T Nts 'C' 6.30s 2002	[26]ms15	A+			X	BE	NC	....	....	....	....	....	25.0	M2	'97	101⅝	97¾	97¾	6.45	6.44
M-T Nts 'C' 6.32s 2002	ms15	A+			X	BE	NC	....	....	....	....	....	25.0	C1	'97	101⅝	97⅝	97⅝	6.47	6.47
M-T Nts 'C' 6.926s 2007	[27]jd30	A+			X	BE	NC	....	....	....	....	....	50.0	C1	'97	105¾	95⅝	95⅝	7.24	7.24
• Sub Deb[28] 8⅝s 2019	fA	A	5/97	A–	X	R	100	(8-1-04)	....	....	....	....	150	G1	'89	105¾	103	103	8.37	8.37

Uniform Footnote Explanations-See Page 260. Other: [1] Int adj qtrly(3 Mo LIBOR & 0.375%). [2] Due 2-7-01. [3] Due 2-8-01. [4] Due 6-1-01. [5] Due 6-11-01. [6] Due 7-9-01. [7] Due 7-23-01. [8] Due 8-1-01. [9] Due 5-15-02. [10] Due 6-8-04. [11] Due 6-10-04. [12] Due 6-22-04. [13] Due 7-6-04. [14] Due 6-28-04. [15] Due 7-1-04. [16] Due 7-8-04. [17] Due 7-20-04. [18] Due 7-21-04. [19] Due 9-8-04. [20] Due 2-10-14. [21] (HRO)On Chge of Ctrl at 101. [22] Gtd by El Paso Energy. [23] (HRO)On 6-15-99 at 100. [24] Was Deere(John)Credit. [25] Due 7-21-00. [26] Due 8-15-02. [27] Due 7-2-07. [28] (HRO)On 8-1-97 at 100.

Title-Industry Code & Co. Finances (In Italics)	*Ind*	*Fixed Charge Coverage 1996*	*1997*	*1998*		*Year End*	*Million $ Cash & Equiv.*	*Curr. Assets*	*Curr. Liab.*	*Balance Sheet Date*	*L. Term Debt (Mil $)*		*Capital-ization (Mil $)*	*Total Debt % Capital*						
Individual Issue Statistics Exchange	Interest Dates	S&P Rating	Date of Last Rating Change	Prior Rating	Eligible	Bond Form	Redemption Provisions: Regular Price	Regular (Begins) Thru	Sinking Fund Price	Sinking Fund (Begins) Thru	Refund/Other Restriction Price	Refund/Other Restriction (Begins) Thru	Outst'g (Mil $)	Underwriting Firm	Underwriting Year	Price Range 1999 High	Price Range 1999 Low	Mo. End Price Sale(s) or Bid	Curr. Yield	Yield to Mat.
***DEKALB Energy*[1]**	***49a***	***Acquired by Apache Corp,see***																		
Nts 9⅞s 2000	jJ15	**BBB+**	1/97	BBB	X	R	NC	....	....	....	....	....	29.2	M2	'90	106½	101⅜	101½	9.73	9.73
Delco Remy Intl	***8***	*Δ1.63*	*Δ1.00*	*Δ1.98*		*Jl*	*11.74*	*470.1*	*206.8*	*10-31-99*	*451.0*		*577.0*	*77.6*						
• Sr Nts[2] 8⅝s 2007	jD15	**B+**			Y	BE	104.313	(12-15-02)	....	....	[3]Z108.625	12-15-00	145	S1	'97	105⅝	91⅛	94½	9.13	9.12
Dell Computer Corp	***20b***	*n/a*	*n/a*	*n/a*		*Ja*	*5857*	*9709*	*5324*	*10-29-99*	*508.0*		*3883*	*13.2*						
Sr Deb 7.10s 2028	Ao15	**BBB+**	10/98	BBB	X	BE	[4]Z100	....	....	....	....	....	300	M7	'98	103⅝	90	90	7.89	7.89
Sr Nts 6.55s 2008	Ao15	**BBB+**	10/98	BBB	X	BE	[4]Z100	....	....	....	....	....	200	M7	'98	103⅞	93⅝	93¾	6.99	6.99
***Delmarva Pwr. & Light*[5]**	***75***	*3.65*	*2.63*	*3.26*		*Dc*	*8.65*	*435.0*	*436.0*	*9-30-99*	*1012*		*1869*	*59.8*						
1st 6.95s 2002	aO	**A**	11/93	A+	X	BE	NC	....	....	....	....	....	30.0	M6	'92	105¼	99½	99½	6.98	6.98
1st 6.40s 2003	jJ	**A**	11/93	A+	X	BE	NC	....	....	....	....	....	90.0	M6	'93	103⅞	97⅝	97⅝	6.56	6.56
1st 8.15s 2015	aO	**A**	11/93	A+	X	BE	104.058	(10-1-02)	Z100	....	....	....	66.0	M6	'92	111	98¾	99¼	8.21	8.21
1st[6] 8½s 2022	Fa	**A**	11/93	A+	X	BE	104.003	(2-1-02)	Z100	....	....	....	50.0	M6	'92	111⅛	100¼	100⅝	8.45	8.45
1st 'I' 7.71s 2025	Jd	**A**			X	BE	103.855	(6-1-05)	....	....	....	....	100	M2	'95	112¼	93¼	93⅝	8.23	8.23
1st([7]Amortizing) 'I' 6.95s 2008	Jd	**A**			X	BE	NC	....	....	....	....	....	25.8	M2	'95	109⅜	96	96¼	7.22	....
M-T Nts 'C' 6.81s 2018	[8]ao	**A–**			X	BE	NC	....	....	....	....	....	33.0		'98	101⅝	87¼	88⅝	7.68	7.68
Delphi Automotive Systems	***8***	*n/a*	*n/a*	*n/a*		*Dc*	*1258*	*8944*	*4764*	*9-30-99*	*1647*		*5520*	*33.2*						
• Deb 7⅛s 2029	Mn	**BBB**			X	BE	[4]Z100	....	....	....	....	....	500	M2	'99	99⅛	89⅛	87¾	8.12	8.12
• Nts 6⅛s 2004	Mn	**BBB**			X	BE	[4]Z100	....	....	....	....	....	500	M2	'99	100⅛	95¾	94¾	6.46	6.46
• Nts 6½s 2009	Mn	**BBB**			X	BE	[4]Z100	....	....	....	....	....	500	M2	'99	99⅝	92⅛	91¼	7.12	7.12
***Delphi Fin'l Group*[9]**	***35a***	*5.45*	*8.84*	*6.37*		*Dc*				*9-30-99*	*422.0*		*917.0*	*46.0*						
Sr Nts[10] 8s 2003	aO	**BBB**	3/97	BBB–	X	R	NC	....	....	....	....	....	85.0	M2	'93	102⅞	96⅞	96⅞	8.26	8.26
Delta Air Lines	***4***	*5.01*	*7.93*	*9.66*		*Je*	*1604*	*3536*	*5373*	*9-30-99*	*★2276*		*7020*	*37.0*						
Eq Tr '92D 8.54s 2007	Jj2	**BBB**	11/96	BBB–	X	R	[11]Z100	....	100	....	....	....	28.5	M2	'92	109¾	101½	101⅝	8.40	8.40
Eq Tr '92E 8.54s 2007	Jj2	**BBB**	11/96	BBB–	X	R	[11]Z100	....	100	....	....	....	28.5	M2	'92	109¾	101½	101⅝	8.40	8.40
Eq Tr '92F 8.54s 2007	Jj2	**BBB**	11/96	BBB–	X	R	[11]Z100	....	100	....	....	....	34.5	M2	'92	111¼	101⅝	101⅝	8.40	8.40
Deb[6] 10⅛s 2010	Mn15	**BBB–**	9/97	BB+	X	R	NC	....	....	....	....	....	113	G1	'90	126⅞	109	110⅜	9.17	9.17
Deb[6] 10⅜s 2011	Fa	**BBB–**	9/97	BB+	X	R	NC	....	....	....	....	....	175	G1	'91	127⅞	112¼	112¼	9.24	9.24
Deb 9s 2016	Mn15	**BBB–**	9/97	BB+	X	R	NC	....	....	....	....	....	101	G1	'86	115½	101¾	101⅞	8.83	8.83
Deb[6] 9¾s 2021	Mn15	**BBB–**	9/97	BB+	X	R	NC	....	....	....	....	....	250	G1	'91	124⅝	110⅛	110⅞	8.79	8.79
Deb[6] 9¼s 2022	Ms15	**BBB–**	9/97	BB+	X	R	NC	....	....	....	....	....	64.0	G1	'92	119⅜	105⅝	106	8.73	8.73
Deb[6] 10⅜s 2022	jD15	**BBB–**	9/97	BB+	X	R	NC	....	....	....	....	....	66.0	G1	'92	131⅜	116⅝	117¼	8.85	8.85
Nts[6] 9⅞s 2000	Mn15	**BBB–**	9/97	BB+	X	R	NC	....	....	....	....	....	142	G1	'90	105	101¼	101¼	9.75	9.75
Nts[6] 8½s 2002	Ms15	**BBB–**	9/97	BB+	X	R	NC	....	....	....	....	....	71.0	G1	'92	107	102⅛	102⅛	8.32	8.32
M-T Nts 6.65s 2004	Ms15	**BBB–**			X	BE	NC	....	....	....	....	....	300	S4	'99	100⅝	95½	95½	6.96	6.96
Delta Financial	***25a***	*n/a*	*3.56*	*1.62*		*Dc*				*9-30-99*	*275.0*		*313.0*	*56.9*						
Sr Nts 9½s 2004	fA	**B**	2/99	B+	Y	R	104.75	(8-1-01)	....	....	....	....	150	D6	'97	87¼	64	65	14.62	14.61
Delta Natural Gas	***73b***	*Δ1.74*	*Δ1.89*	*Δ1.75*		*Je*	*0.18*	*7.31*	*20.10*	*9-30-99*	*51.60*		*89.80*	*66.7*						
Deb[12] 6⅝s 2023	aO	**NR**				BE	104	9-30-00	....	....	....	....	15.0	J2	'93	97⅜	82	82⅛	8.07	8.07
Deb[13] 8.30s 2026	fA	**NR**				BE	105	(8-1-01)	....	....	....	....	15.0	J2	'96	102	97¼	97½	8.51	8.51
Deluxe Corp	***29a***	*12.15*	*14.05*	*30.80*		*Dc*	*113.3*	*418.9*	*376.0*	*9-30-99*	*120.0*		*603.0*	*20.4*						
Nts 8.55s 2001	Fa15	**A+**	3/96	AA–	X	R	NC	....	....	....	....	....	100	G1	'91	106½	101⅞	101⅞	8.39	8.39
Deposit Guaranty	***10***	***Mgr w/First Amer(Tenn),see***																		
Sr Nts 7¼s 2006	Mn	**BBB**			X	BE	NC	....	....	....	....	....	100	C5	'96	108½	98½	98½	7.36	7.36
***Detroit Edison Co*[14]**	***72a***	*3.19*	*3.37*	*3.45*		*Dc*	*23.00*	*990.0*	*1469*	*6-30-99*	*3387*		*7343*	*51.5*						
Sec M-T Nts 'G' 6.56s 2001	Mn	**A–**	10/97	BBB+	X	BE	NC	....	....	....	....	....	100	M6	'93	102⅜	99	99	6.63	6.63
Developers Diversified Rlty	***57***	*2.37*	*2.52*	*2.19*		*Dc*				*9-30-99*	*1111*		*1823*	*53.5*						
Sr Nts 7⅝s 2000	Mn15	**BBB**			X	BE	NC	....	....	....	....	....	100	D3	'95	101¾	100⅛	100⅛	7.62	7.61

Uniform Footnote Explanations-See Page 260. Other: [1] Was DEKALB AgResearch, then DEKALB Corp. [2] (HRO)On Chge of Ctrl at 101. [3] Max $58M red w/proceeds Pub Eq Off'g. [4] Red at greater of 100 or amt based on formula. [5] Merged w/Atlantic Energy to form Conectiv Inc. [6] Issued in min denom $100T. [7] Princ pyts due ea 6/1/97-08. [8] Due 1-9-18. [9] Was Hyponex Corp. [10] (HRO)On Chge of Ctrl & Rat'g Decline at 101. [11] In whole,plus red premium. [12] (HRO)Ea Oct 1 at 100,ltd,as defined. [13] Death red benefit,ltd,as defined. [14] Subsid of DTE Energy.

Title-Industry Code & Co. Finances (In Italics) / Individual Issue Statistics, Exchange, Interest Dates	S&P Rating / Fixed Charge Coverage 1996	Date of Last Rating Change / 1997	Prior Rating / 1998	Eligible / Year End	Bond Form	Regular Price / Cash & Equiv.	Regular (Begins) Thru / Curr. Assets	Sinking Fund Price / Curr. Liab.	Sinking Fund (Begins) Thru / Balance Sheet Date	Refund/Other Restriction Price / L. Term Debt (Mil $)	Refund/Other Restriction (Begins) Thru	Outst'g (Mil $) / Capital-ization (Mil $)	Underwriting Firm / Total Debt % Capital	Underwriting Year	Price Range 1999 High	Price Range 1999 Low	Mo. End Price Sale(s) or Bid	Curr. Yield	Yield to Mat.
***Developers Diversified Rlty** (Cont.)*																			
SF Deb 9¼s 2016 jD15	A			X	R	103.238	12-14-00	100	....	....	....	5.00	G1	'86	104⅜	103⅞	103⅞	8.90	8.90
***[1]DI Industries** 49e*	*n/a*	*3.15*	*2.83*	*Dc*		*20.75*	*51.37*	*29.28*	*9-30-99*	*250.0*		*419.0*	*60.1*						
Sr Nts 8⅞s 2007 jJ	B+			Y	BE	104	(7-1-02)	....	....	[2]Z108.875	7-1-00	175	D6	'97	92½	72½	91¼	9.73	9.72
***Dial Corp(New)** 42a*	*5.46*	*5.74*	*7.87*	*Dc*		*7.92*	*287.0*	*304.0*	*10-2-99*	*239.0*		*666.0*	*35.9*						
Sr Nts 6½s 2008 mS15	BBB+			X	BE	[3]Z100	....	....	....	....	....	200	M2	'98	103½	91⅞	91⅞	7.07	7.07
***[4]Dial Corp[5](OLD)** 28*	*3.17*	*3.88*	*5.30*	*Dc*		*185.0*	*854.0*	*3859*	*9-30-99*	*377.0*		*1148*	*44.4*						
Sr Nts 6⅝s 2003 Jd15	NR	12/99	BBB–		BE	NC	....	....	....	....	....	100	S1	'93	102	96⅝	96¾	6.85	6.85
***Diamond Shamrock** 49g*	***Mgr w/Ultramar Diamond Shamrock,see***																		
Deb 7¼s 2010 Jd15	BBB			X	BE	NC	....	....	....	....	....	25.0		'95	105¼	93	93⅝	7.74	7.74
Deb 8¾s 2015 Jd15	BBB			X	BE	NC	....	....	....	....	....	75.0	L3	'95	115¾	103½	103½	8.45	8.45
Deb 8s 2023 Ao	BBB			X	BE	103.803	(4-1-03)	....	....	....	....	100	L3	'93	94¼	86	89¾	8.91	8.91
Deb[6] 7.65s 2026 jJ	BBB			X	BE	NC	....	....	....	....	....	100	L3	'96	109¼	96⅞	96⅞	7.90	7.90
Nts 9⅝s 2001 Ms	BBB			X	BE	NC	....	....	....	....	....	75.0	M2	'91	106⅝	102	102	9.19	9.19
***[7]Diamond State Telephone[8]** 67a*	*7.66*	*7.30*	*8.22*	*Dc*		*1.44*	*64.60*	*108.0*	*6-30-99*	*91.30*		*328.0*	*39.9*						
Deb 6⅛s 2003 jD	AA	4/97	AA+	X	BE	NC	....	....	....	....	....	20.0	S1	'93	103¾	96½	96½	6.35	6.35
Deb 4⅝s 2005 mS	AA	4/97	AA+	X	R	100.13	8-31-00	....	....	....	....	7.00	D8	'65	97¾	87⅞	87⅞	5.26	5.27
• Deb 7s 2008 jD	AA	4/97	AA+	X	R	100.78	11-30-00	....	....	....	....	10.0	D8	'68	102	98¼	98¼	7.12	7.12
Deb[9] 8⅜s 2019 Ms15	AA	4/97	AA+	X	R	NC	....	....	....	....	....	15.0	S1	'89	128⅜	108½	108½	7.72	7.72
Deb 7s 2023 jD	AA	4/97	AA+	X	BE	100	(12-1-13)	....	....	....	....	20.0	S1	'93	107⅜	89⅛	89¼	7.84	7.84
Deb 8⅝s 2031 aO15	AA	4/97	AA+	X	BE	NC	....	....	....	....	....	15.0	F1	'91	132¼	106⅛	106¼	8.12	8.12
***Dictaphone Corp** 42*	*d0.25*	*d0.56*	*d0.33*	*Dc*		*5.35*	*14.00*	*101.0*	*6-30-99*	*350.0*		*337.0*	*104.0*						
Sr Sub Nts[10] 11¾s 2005 fA	CCC	5/97	B–	Y	R	105.875	(8-1-00)	....	....	....	....	200	M6	'95	76⅝	57	74	15.88	15.87
***Digital Equipment** 20b*	***Acq by Compaq Computer,see***																		
Deb 8⅝s 2012 mN	BB+	9/95	BB–	Y	BE	NC	....	....	....	....	....	250	L3	'92	110⅜	95⅞	101⅜	8.51	8.51
Deb 7¾s 2023 Ao	BB+	9/95	BB–	Y	BE	NC	....	....	....	....	....	250	L3	'93	105½	91	91⅛	8.50	8.50
Nts 7⅛s 2002 aO15	BB+	9/95	BB–	Y	BE	NC	....	....	....	....	....	250	M2	'92	100¾	97⅝	97⅝	7.30	7.30
***Dillard Dept Stores** 59f*	***Now Dillard's Inc,see***																		
Deb 9¼s 2001 aO15	BBB	8/98	A+	X	R	NC	....	....	....	....	....	50.0	G1	'89	109½	103⅜	103⅜	9.19	9.19
Deb 9½s 2009 mS	BBB	8/98	A+	X	R	NC	....	....	....	....	....	50.0	G1	'89	122½	106¼	106¼	8.94	8.94
Deb 7⅞s 2023 Jj	BBB	8/98	A+	X	BE	NC	....	....	....	....	....	100	M6	'93	110⅜	92¼	92⅜	8.53	8.52
Deb 7¾s 2026 jJ15	BBB	8/98	A+	X	BE	NC	....	....	....	....	....	100	C1	'96	109⅝	90⅝	90¾	8.54	8.54
Nts 7.15s 2002 mS	BBB	8/98	A+	X	BE	NC	....	....	....	....	....	100	G1	'92	104¼	98⅞	98⅞	7.23	7.23
Nts 6⅞s 2005 Jd	BBB	8/98	A+	X	BE	NC	....	....	....	....	....	100	M6	'95	103½	95⅛	95⅛	7.23	7.23
Nts 7⅜s 2006 Jd	BBB	8/98	A+	X	BE	NC	....	....	....	....	....	100	M6	'96	106⅝	96	96	7.68	7.68
Nts 9⅛s 2011 fA	BBB	8/98	A+	X	BE	NC	....	....	....	....	....	100	M6	'91	121¼	103⅝	103⅝	8.81	8.80
Nts 7.85s 2012 aO	BBB	8/98	A+	X	BE	NC	....	....	....	....	....	100	G1	'92	111	94¼	95⅛	8.25	8.25
Nts 7¾s 2027 Mn15	BBB	8/98	A+	X	BE	NC	....	....	....	....	....	100	M6	'97	109½	90⅝	90¾	8.54	8.54
***Dillard Investment Co** 25d*	***Subsid of Dillard's Inc,see Dillard Dept Stores***																		
Nts 9¼s 2001 Fa	BBB	8/98	A+	X	BE	NC	....	....	....	....	....	100	M6	'91	107¼	102⅜	102⅜	9.04	9.03
***Dillard's Inc[11]** 59f*	*4.14*	*4.18*	*2.11*	*Ja*		*43.65*	*4002*	*1534*	*10-30-99*	*3554*		*6490*	*54.9*						
Deb 7.13s 2018 fA	BBB	8/98	A+	X	BE	NC	....	....	....	....	....	200	M7	'98	103⅛	86	86	8.29	8.29
Nts 6⅛s 2003 mN	BBB			X	BE	NC	....	....	....	....	....	150	M7	'98	100⅜	94	94	6.52	6.52
Nts 5.79s 2001 mN15	BBB			X	BE	NC	....	....	....	....	....	150	G1	'98	100⅛	96⅞	96⅞	5.98	5.98
Nts 6.43s 2004 fA	BBB	8/98	A+	X	BE	NC	....	....	....	....	....	200	M7	'98	101¾	94	94	6.84	6.84
Nts 6.69s 2007 fA	BBB	8/98	A+	X	BE	NC	....	....	....	....	....	100	M7	'98	103½	90¾	90¾	7.37	7.37

Uniform Footnote Explanations-See Page 260. Other: [1] Now Grey Wolf. [2] Max $52.5M red w/proceeds of Pub Eq Off'g. [3] Red at greater of 100 or amt based on formula. [4] Now Viad Corp. [5] See Greyhound Corp. [6] (HRO)On 7-1-06 at 100. [7] Subsid of Bell Atlantic Corp. [8] Now Bell Atlantic-Delaware. [9] (HRO)On 9-15-99 at 100. [10] (HRO)On Chge of Ctrl at 101. [11] See Mercantile Stores.

Title-Industry Code & Co. Finances (In Italics) / Individual Issue Statistics (Exchange)	Ind / Interest Dates	Fixed Charge Coverage 1996 / S&P Rating	1997 / Date of Last Rating Change	1998 / Prior Rating	Eligible	Year End / Bond Form	Million $ Cash & Equiv. / Redemption Provisions: Regular Price	Curr. Assets / Regular (Begins) Thru	Curr. Liab. / Sinking Fund Price	Balance Sheet Date / Sinking Fund (Begins) Thru	L. Term Debt (Mil $) / Refund/Other Restriction Price	Refund/Other Restriction (Begins) Thru	Capital-ization (Mil $) / Outst'g (Mil $)	Total Debt % Capital / Underwriting Firm	Underwriting Year	Price Range 1999 High	Price Range 1999 Low	Mo. End Price Sale(s) or Bid	Curr. Yield	Yield to Mat.
***Dillard's Inc** (Cont.)*																				
Nts 6.30s 2008	Fa15	**BBB**			X	BE	NC	....	....	....	....	....	100	M7	'98	100⅛	88¾	88¾	7.10	7.10
Nts 6⅝s 2008	mN15	**BBB**			X	BE	NC	....	....	....	....	....	100	C1	'98	102½	89½	89½	7.40	7.40
Nts 6⅝s 2018	Jj15	**BBB**	8/98	A+	X	BE	NC	....	....	....	....	....	100	C1	'98	97⅛	82½	82½	8.03	8.03
Nts 7s 2028	jD	**BBB**			X	BE	NC	....	....	....	....	....	150	M7	'98	100¾	81⅝	81¾	8.56	8.56
Dime Bancorp	***10b***	***1.43***	***1.58***	***2.02***		***Dc***				***9-30-99***	***1365***		***5791***	***74.5***						
Nts 6⅜s 2001	Jj30	**BBB–**			X	BE	NC	....	....	....	....	....	200	M2	'99	100⅛	98½	98½	6.47	6.47
Nts 7s 2001	jJ25	**BBB–**			X	BE	NC	....	....	....	....	....	150	C6	'99	100¼	98⅝	98⅝	7.10	7.10
DiMon Inc	***69c***	***△3.41***	***△1.67***	***△0.60***		***Je***	***21.87***	***1082***	***633.8***	***9-30-99***	***534.0***		***1233***	***67.8***						
Sr Nts[1] 8⅞s 2006	Jd	**BB+**			Y	BE	104.4375	(6-1-01)	....	....	....	....	125		'96	99⅞	89⅜	89⅝	9.90	9.90
Disney (Walt) Co[2]	***40g***	***△4.69***	***△4.66***	***△3.64***		***Sp***	***414.0***	***10200***	***7707***	***9-30-99***	***9278***		***32668***	***35.8***						
Sr Deb[3] 7.55s 2093	jJ15	**A**	2/96	AA–	X	BE	103.02	(7-15-23)	....	....	....	....	300	M6	'93	116⅜	93¼	93⅜	8.09	8.08
Global Nts 5⅛s 2003	jD15	**A**			X	BE	NC	....	....	....	....	....	600	B7	'98	99¾	93½	93½	5.48	5.48
Sr Nts[4] 6⅜s 2001	Ms30	**A**			X	BE	NC	....	....	....	....	....	1300	M2	'96	103	99¾	99¾	6.39	6.39
Sr Nts[4] 6¾s 2006	Ms30	**A**			X	BE	NC	....	....	....	....	....	1300	M2	'96	108½	97¾	97¾	6.91	6.91
M-T Nts 5.624s 2000	Jj13	**A**			X	BE	NC	....	....	....	....	....	200	B7	'98	100½	99⅞	100	5.62	5.62
M-T Nts 5¼s 2003	mN10	**A**			X	BE	NC	....	....	....	....	....	100	B7	'98	100⅞	94½	94½	5.56	5.56
M-T Nts 5¼s 2003	jD	**A**			X	BE	NC	....	....	....	....	....	100	M7	'98	100½	94⅛	94⅛	5.58	5.58
M-T Nts 7s 2012	fA15	**A**			X	BE	100	(8-15-00)	....	....	....	....	25.0	B7	'97	102⅞	94¾	95½	7.33	7.33
F/R[5]M-T Nts[6] 6¾s 2006	QAug15	**A**			X	BE	110	(8-15-17)	....	....	....	....	1300	G1	'96	101	99	99¼	6.80	....
Dole Food Co[7]	***26***	***3.31***	***4.02***	***2.99***		***Dc***	***34.50***	***1134***	***721.8***	***10-9-99***	***1240***		***1947***	***67.7***						
• Deb 7⅞s 2013	jJ15	**BBB–**			X	BE	NC	....	....	....	....	....	175	G1	'93	108	92¼	92⅜	8.53	8.52
• Nts 6¾s 2000	jJ15	**BBB–**			X	BE	NC	....	....	....	....	....	225	G1	'93	102	98½	97½	6.92	6.92
• Nts 7s 2003	Mn15	**BBB–**			X	BE	NC	....	....	....	....	....	300	B11	'93	103⅞	91	94¼	7.43	7.43
Nts 6⅜s 2005	aO	**BBB–**			X	BE	[8]Z100	....	....	....	....	....	300	C1	'98	98⅞	88⅜	88⅜	7.21	7.21
Donaldson,Lufkin&Jenrette	***62***	***1.65***	***1.57***	***1.41***		***Dc***					***4661***		***5017***	***52.2***						
Sr Nts 6s 2001	jD	**A–**			X	BE	NC	....	....	....	....	....	250	D6	'98	100¾	97¾	97¾	6.14	6.14
Sr Nts 5⅞s 2002	Ao	**A–**			X	BE	NC	....	....	....	....	....	650	D6	'99	100¼	97⅛	97⅛	6.05	6.05
Sr Nts 6⅞s 2005	mN	**A–**			X	BE	NC	....	....	....	....	....	500	D6	'95	104⅛	96¼	96¼	7.14	7.14
Sr Nts 6½s 2008	Jd	**A–**			X	BE	NC	....	....	....	....	....	500	D6	'98	101⅞	91⅜	91⅜	7.11	7.11
M-T Nts 6⅜s 2000	[9]jd15	**A–**			X	BE	NC	....	....	....	....	....	75.0	D6	'97	100⅞	100	100	6.38	6.37
M-T Nts 6.11s 2001	Mn15	**A–**			X	BE	NC	....	....	....	....	....	100	D6	'98	100¾	98⅞	98⅞	6.18	6.18
M-T Nts 6.90s 2007	aO	**A–**			X	BE	NC	....	....	....	....	....	150	D6	'97	102⅞	94⅝	94⅝	7.29	7.29
F/R[10]M-T Nts 2007	[11]	**A–**			X	BE	NC	....	....	....	....	....	100	D6	'97	100½	98½	98⅝	....	....
M-T Nts[12] 5⅝s 2016	Fa15	**A–**			X	BE	NC	....	....	....	....	....	250	D6	'96	100⅞	96⅝	98⅞	5.69	5.69
Donnelley(RR) & Sons	***29a***	***4.88***	***4.61***	***6.01***		***Dc***	***66.70***	***1265***	***927.0***	***6-30-99***	***1300***		***2444***	***55.3***						
Deb 8⅞s 2021	Ao15	**A**	9/99	A+	X	R	NC	....	....	....	....	....	150	M2	'91	131⅜	111⅛	111¼	7.98	7.98
Deb 6⅝s 2029	Ao15	**A**	9/99	A+	X	BE	[8]Z100	....	....	....	....	....	200	M5	'99	99	86⅜	86½	7.66	7.66
Nts 9⅛s 2000	jD	**A**	9/99	A+	X	R	NC	....	....	....	....	....	200	L3	'90	107	102⅛	102⅛	8.94	8.93
Nts 7s 2003	Jj	**A**	9/99	A+	X	BE	NC	....	....	....	....	....	110	S1	'93	105¾	100	100	7.00	7.00
Doral Financial	***25h***	***2.57***	***2.91***	***2.43***		***Dc***				***9-30-99***	***888.0***		***1261***	***70.4***						
M-T Nts 'A' 8½s 2004	jJ8	**BBB–**			X	BE	NC	....	....	....	....	....	200	B7	'99	105⅛	98½	98½	8.63	8.63
Dover Corp	***42***	***15.02***	***14.16***	***10.47***		***Dc***	***174.6***	***1618***	***1195***	***9-30-99***	***609.0***		***2956***	***35.3***						
Deb 6.65s 2028	Jd	**A+**			X	BE	NC	....	....	....	....	....	200	G1	'98	106¾	87⅞	88	7.56	7.56
Nts 6.45s 2005	mN15	**A+**			X	BE	NC	....	....	....	....	....	250	G1	'95	106⅜	95⅝	95⅝	6.75	6.74
Nts 6¼s 2008	Jd	**A+**			X	BE	NC	....	....	....	....	....	150	G1	'98	106	92⅝	92⅝	6.75	6.75

Uniform Footnote Explanations-See Page 260. Other: [1] (HRO)On Chge of Ctrl at 101. [2] See Capital Cities/ABC. [3] Issued in min denom $25T. [4] Co may red in whole,at 100,for tax law chge. [5] Int adj qtrly(3 Mo LIBOR less 0.29%). [6] (HRO)On 8-15-07 at 99,'10 at 99.25,'13 at 99.5,'16 at 99.75. [7] Was Castle & Cooke. [8] Red at greater of 100 or amt based on formula. [9] Due 5-26-00. [10] Int adj qtrly(3 Mo LIBOR & 0.375%). [11] Due 10-29-07:Int pd qtrly,3rd Wed,Mar,etc. [12] (HRO)On 2-15-01 at 100.

Title-Industry Code & Co. Finances (In Italics) / Exchange / Individual Issue Statistics	Ind / Interest Dates	Fixed Charge Coverage 1996 / S&P Rating	1997 / Date of Last Rating Change	1998 / Prior Rating	Eligible	Year End / Bond Form	Cash & Equiv. / Regular Price	Curr. Assets / Regular (Begins) Thru	Curr. Liab. / Sinking Fund Price	Balance Sheet Date / Sinking Fund (Begins) Thru	L. Term Debt (Mil $) / Refund/Other Restriction Price	Refund/Other Restriction (Begins) Thru	Capital-ization (Mil $) / Outst'g (Mil $)	Total Debt % Capital / Underwriting Firm	Underwriting Year	Price Range 1999 High	Price Range 1999 Low	Mo. End Price Sale(s) or Bid	Curr. Yield	Yield to Mat.
Dow Capital B.V.	***25***	***Subsid of & gtd by Dow Chemical,see***																		
[1]Gtd[2]Deb 9s 2010	$Mn15	A			Q	R	NC	....	....	....	....	....	91.0	G1	'90	124	107¾	107¾	8.35	8.35
[1]Gtd[2]Deb 9.20s 2010	$Jd	A			Q	R	NC	....	....	....	....	....	181	S1	'90	125⅝	109⅛	109⅛	8.43	8.43
[1]Gtd[2]SF Deb 8.70s 2022	$Mn15	A			Q	R	103.13	(5-15-02)	100	(5-15-03)	....	....	150	M2	'92	110¼	101⅞	103⅛	8.44	8.44
[1]Gtd[2]Nts 7⅜s 2002	$jJ15	A			Q	BE	NC	....	....	....	....	....	150	S1	'92	106⅛	100⅝	100⅝	7.33	7.33
[1]Gtd[2]Nts 7⅛s 2003	$Jj	A			Q	BE	NC	....	....	....	....	....	150	G1	'93	105¾	99⅞	99⅞	7.13	7.13
Dow Chemical Co.	***14***	***6.55***	***6.00***		***4.50***	***Dc***	***1041***	***8167***	***6124***	***9-30-99***	***4130***		***13502***	***39.6***						
Deb 8⅝s 2006	Ao	A	5/88	A–	X	R	NC	....	....	....	....	....	187	S7	'86	114¾	105½	105½	8.18	8.17
Deb 5.97s 2009	Jj15	A			X	BE	NC	....	....	....	....	....	294	Exch.	'99	99¼	89⅞	90¼	6.61	6.61
• Deb 6.85s 2013	fA15	A			X	BE	NC	....	....	....	....	....	138	M2	'93	103¾	94½	85	8.06	8.06
Deb 9s 2021	Ao	A			X	R	NC	....	....	....	....	....	219	M2	'91	125¾	110⅝	111½	8.07	8.07
Deb 8.85s 2021	mS15	A			X	R	NC	....	....	....	....	....	184	L3	'91	124⅛	109⅛	110⅛	8.04	8.04
Deb 7⅜s 2023	Ms	A			X	BE	NC	....	....	....	....	....	150	M2	'93	107¼	93½	94¾	7.78	7.78
Deb 7⅜s 2029	mN	A			X	BE	NC	....	....	....	....	....	1000	M7	'99	99⅝	95⅜	95⅝	7.71	7.71
Nts 9.35s 2002	Ms15	A			X	R	100	(3-15-00)	....	....	....	....	194	M2	'90	103⅞	100¼	100¼	9.33	9.33
Nts 8.55s 2009	aO15	A			X	R	[3]NC	....	....	....	....	....	139	M2	'89	118¾	107	107	7.99	7.99
Dow Corning Corp[4]	***14***	***56.77***	***43.94***		....	***Dc***	***Bankruptcy Chapt 11***				***[5]3560***		***4756***	***75.7***						
Deb 9⅜s 2008	§Fa	NR	6/99	D	Z	R			Default 8-1-95 int				75.0	M6	'88	142⅛	126⅞	141⅞	....	Flat
Deb 8.15s 2029	§aO15	NR	6/99	D	Z	R			Default 10-15-95 int				50.0	M6	'89	138⅛	124½	137⅞	....	Flat
Dow Jones & Co	***54c***	***18.19***	***13.09***		***42.08***	***Dc***	***35.39***	***363.0***	***543.6***	***9-30-99***	***150.0***		***672.0***	***22.3***						
Nts 5¾s 2000	jD	AA–	3/97	AA	X	BE	NC	....	....	....	....	....	150	C2	'95	101¼	99¼	99⅜	5.79	5.79
D.R. Horton	***13h***	***n/a***	***2.11***		***11.53***	***Sp***				***9-30-99***	***1191***		***1407***	***60.8***						
• Sr Nts[6] 8⅜s 2004	Jd15	BB			Y	BE	NC	....	....	....	[7]Z108.375	6-14-00	150	D6	'97	105¼	94⅛	96⅞	8.65	8.64
• Sr[8]Nts[9] 10s 2006	Ao15	BB	6/98	B+	Y	R	105	(4-15-01)	....	....	....	....	149	S7	'96	107½	99½	103½	9.66	9.66
• Sr Nts[6] 8s 2009	Fa	BB			Y	BE	NC	....	....	....	[10]Z108	2-1-02	385	D6	'99	101½	86	86⅛	9.29	9.29
Dresser Industries	***49e***	***Subsid of Halliburton Indus,see***																		
Deb 7.60s 2096	fA15	AA–	10/98	A	X	BE	NC	....	....	....	....	....	300	S1	'96	113⅜	95⅝	95½	7.96	7.96
Nts 6¼s 2000	Jd15	AA–	10/98	A	X	BE	NC	....	....	....	....	....	300	M2	'93	101¼	100	100⅛	6.24	6.24
Dual Drilling Co[11]	***49e***	***d0.56***	***2.00***		***4.11***	***Dc***	***20.07***	***30.89***	***12.74***	***9-30-99***	***168.0***		***461.0***	***36.5***						
Sr Sub Nts[6] 9⅞s 2004	Jj15	NR	6/97	BB–		R	103.29	1-14-01	....	....	....	....	74.0	M2	'94	105	101⅛	103⅛	9.58	9.57
Duane Reade	***59e***	***n/a***	***0.96***		***1.86***	***Dc***	***0.90***	***183.0***	***87.00***	***6-27-99***	***330.0***		***343.0***	***92.7***						
Sr Sub Nts[6] 9¼s 2008	Fa15	B–			Y	BE	109.25	2-15-01	....	....	[12]Z109.25	2-15-01	80.0	D6	'98	104½	97	97⅞	9.45	9.45
Duke Capital[13]	***73a***	***3.83***	***4.08***		***4.80***	***Dc***	***874.0***	***5108***	***4941***	***9-30-99***	***5551***		***12418***	***49.5***						
Sr Nts 'A' 6¼s 2005	jJ16	A			X	BE	[14]Z100	....	....	....	....	....	250	M7	'98	103⅛	94½	94⅝	6.61	6.60
Sr Nts 7¼s 2004	aO	A			X	BE	[14]Z100	....	....	....	....	....	500	M2	'99	101¼	99⅜	99⅜	7.30	7.30
Sr Nts 'B' 6¾s 2018	jJ15	A			X	BE	Z100	....	....	....	Z100	....	150	M7	'98	102½	88¼	89⅛	7.57	7.57
Sr Nts[15] 7½s 2004	aO	A			X	BE	[14]Z100	....	....	....	....	....	500	M2	'99	102	98¾	98¾	7.59	7.59
Sr Nts[15] 8s 2019	aO	A			X	BE	[14]Z100	....	....	....	....	....	500	M2	'99	104½	99¼	100¾	7.94	7.94
Duke Energy[16]	***72a***	***4.86***	***4.47***		***4.98***	***Dc***	***1060***	***6272***	***5966***	***9-30-99***	***[17]8092***		***16823***	***48.2***						
• 1st & Ref 7s 2000	Jd	AA–	10/97	A+	X	R	NC	....	Z100	....	....	....	100	L3	'92	102⅞	99¾	100	7.00	7.00
• 1st & Ref B 7s 2000	jJ	AA–	10/97	A+	X	R	NC	....	Z100	....	....	....	100	G1	'92	103⅜	99¾	100	7.00	7.00
• 1st & Ref 5⅞s 2001	Jd	AA–	10/97	A+	X	R	NC	....	Z100	....	....	....	150	M2	'93	101½	98¼	98¼	5.98	5.98
• 1st & Ref B 6⅝s 2003	Fa	AA–	10/97	A+	X	R	NC	....	Z100	....	....	....	100	G1	'93	105⅞	98⅛	99	6.69	6.69
• 1st & Ref C 5⅞s 2003	Ms	AA–	10/97	A+	X	R	100.259	2-29-00	Z100	....	....	....	75.0	K2	'93	100½	95¾	95¾	6.14	6.14
• 1st & Ref B 6¼s 2004	Mn	AA–	10/97	A+	X	R	101.512	4-30-00	Z100	....	....	....	100	M6	'93	102½	95¾	95¾	6.53	6.53
• 1st & Ref 6⅜s 2008	Ms	AA–	10/97	A+	X	R	101.33	2-29-00	Z100	....	....	....	125	F1	'93	101⅝	94	s94	6.78	6.78

Uniform Footnote Explanations-See Page 260. Other: [1] Gtd by Dow Chemical. [2] Co may red in whole at 100 if add'l pyt due. [3] Red at 100 if $15M or less outstg. [4] Affil. with Dow Chemical. [5] Incl liabs subj to compromise. [6] (HRO)On Chge of Ctrl at 101. [7] Max $52.5M red w/proceeds of Pub Eq Off'g. [8] Co must offer repurch at 101 on Chge of Ctrl. [9] Was Cont'l Homes Hldg. [10] Max $134M red w/proceeds of Equity Off'g. [11] Now Dual Holding,subsid of ENSCO Int'l. [12] Max $28M red w/proceeds of Pub Eq Off'g. [13] Subsid of Duke Energy. [14] Red at greater of 100 or amt based on formula. [15] Co may red in whole, at 100, for tax law chge. [16] See PanEnergy Corp,Panhandle East'n. [17] Total issue amt in $M.

Title-Industry Code & Co. Finances (In Italics)	Ind	Fixed Charge Coverage 1996	1997	1998		Year End	Million $ Cash & Equiv.	Curr. Assets	Curr. Liab.	Balance Sheet Date	L. Term Debt (Mil $)		Capital-ization (Mil $)	Total Debt % Capital						
Individual Issue Statistics Exchange ↓	Interest Dates	S&P Rating	Date of Last Rating Change	Prior Rating	Eligible ↓	Bond Form	Redemption Provisions: Regular Price	Regular (Begins) Thru	Sinking Fund Price	Sinking Fund (Begins) Thru	Refund/Other Restriction Price	Refund/Other Restriction (Begins) Thru	Outst'g (Mil $)	Underwriting Firm	Underwriting Year	Price Range 1999 High	Price Range 1999 Low	Mo. End Price Sale(s) or Bid	Curr. Yield	Yield to Mat.
***Duke Energy** (Cont.)*																				
• 1st & Ref B 6⅞s 2023	fA	**AA–**	10/97	A+	X	R	102.80	7-31-00	Z100	....	....	....	200	K2	'93	102¾	86	s86¾	7.93	7.92
• 1st & Ref 7⅞s 2024	Mn	**AA–**	10/97	A+	X	R	103.592	4-30-00	Z100	....	....	....	150	D6	'94	104⅞	98	98	8.04	8.04
• 1st & Ref 6¾s 2025	fA	**AA–**	10/97	A+	X	R	102.498	7-31-00	Z100	....	....	....	150	S1	'93	102⅛	84	84⅝	7.98	7.97
• 1st & Ref B 7½s 2025	fA	**AA–**	10/97	A+	X	R	103.355	(8-1-00)	Z100	....	....	....	100	D6	'95	104	93	93½	8.02	8.02
• 1st & Ref 7s 2033	jJ	**AA–**	10/97	A+	X	R	102.35	(7-1-03)	Z100	....	....	....	150	L3	'93	104⅝	89⅜	89⅜	7.83	7.83
Sr Nts 'A' 6s 2028	jD	**A+**	3/99	A	X	BE	[1]Z100	....	....	....	....	....	300	S4	'98	98¾	77¾	78¾	7.62	7.62
Sr Nts 'B' 5⅜s 2009	Jj	**A+**	3/99	A	X	BE	[1]Z100	....	....	....	....	....	200	M7	'99	99¼	85⅛	86¼	6.23	6.23
Duke Realty L.P.	***57***	***Now Duke-Weeks Realty,see***																		
Nts 7¼s 2002	mS22	**BBB+**	4/98	BBB	X	BE	NC	....	....	....	....	....	50.0	M2	'95	102⅝	98⅝	98⅝	7.35	7.35
• Nts 7⅜s 2007	fA	**BBB+**	7/99	BBB	X	BE	[2]Z100	....	....	....	....	....	100	G1	'98	No Sale		94⅞	7.77	7.77
Sr Nts 7.30s 2003	Jd30	**BBB+**			X	BE	[2]Z100	....	....	....	....	....	175	M2	'99	101⅝	98⅜	98⅜	7.42	7.42
Nts 7⅜s 2005		**BBB+**	4/98	BBB	X	BE	[2]Z100	(9-22-02)	....	....	....	....	100	M2	'95	103⅝	96⅝	96¾	7.62	7.62
Nts 6¾s 2008	Mn30	**BBB+**			X	BE	[2]Z100	....	....	....	....	....	100	M2	'98	100	91¼	91⅜	7.39	7.39
M-T Nts 7¼s 2028	Jd15	**BBB+**			X	BE	NC	....	....	....	....	....	50.0	M2	'98	85½	74⅜	83⅝	8.67	8.67
Duke-Weeks Realty	***57***	***1.72***	***3.12***	***3.04***		***Dc***				***9-30-99***	***1669***		***4797***	***35.4***						
• Nts 6⅞s 2005	Ms15	**BBB+**	7/99	BBB	X	BE	[2]Z100	....	....	....	....	....	100	G1	'98	No Sale		94⅞	7.25	7.25
Sr Nts 7¾s 2009	mN15	**BBB+**			X	BE	[2]Z100	....	....	....	....	....	150	S4	'99	100¾	97	97	7.99	7.99
du Pont(E.I.) de Nemours	***14***	***7.49***	***8.54***	***8.14***		***Dc***	***2599***	***12107***	***10654***	***9-30-99***	***4622***		***23684***	***35.8***						
Deb 8¼s 2022	Jj15	**AA–**	4/95	AA	X	BE	103.94	(1-15-02)	....	....	....	....	49.0	F1	'92	112	100⅞	102	8.09	8.09
Deb 7.95s 2023	Jj15	**AA–**	4/95	AA	X	BE	103.86	(1-15-03)	....	....	....	....	38.0	F1	'93	109⅛	96⅞	97¾	8.13	8.13
Deb 6½s 2028	Jj15	**AA–**			X	BE	[1]Z100	....	....	....	....	....	300	M5	'98	105¾	86	86⅛	7.55	7.55
Nts[3] 9.15s 2000	Ao15	**AA–**	4/95	AA	X	R	NC	....	....	....	....	....	300	F1	'90	105	100⅞	100⅞	9.07	9.07
Nts 6½s 2002	mS	**AA–**			X	BE	NC	....	....	....	....	....	500	M6	'97	105	99¼	99¼	6.55	6.55
Nts 6¾s 2002	aO15	**AA–**	4/95	AA	X	BE	NC	....	....	....	....	....	300	M6	'92	105¾	99¾	99¾	6.77	6.77
Nts 8½s 2003	Fa15	**AA–**	4/95	AA	X	BE	100	(2-15-01)	....	....	....	....	141	G1	'91	108¾	103⅛	103⅛	8.24	8.24
Nts 8⅛s 2004	Ms15	**AA–**	4/95	AA	X	BE	NC	....	....	....	....	....	331	G1	'92	112¾	103½	103½	7.85	7.85
Nts[4] 6¾s 2004	aO15	**AA–**			X	BE	[1]Z100	....	....	....	....	....	1000	C6	'99	100⅞	98⅝	98⅝	6.84	6.84
Nts 8¼s 2006	mS15	**AA–**	4/95	AA	X	BE	NC	....	....	....	....	....	282	M2	'91	119¼	104½	104½	7.89	7.89
Nts 6¾s 2007	mS	**AA–**			X	BE	NC	....	....	....	....	....	500	M6	'97	109⅞	96⅝	96⅝	6.99	6.99
Nts[4] 6⅞s 2009	aO15	**AA–**			X	BE	[1]Z100	....	....	....	....	....	1000	C6	'99	100⅜	96¾	96¾	7.11	7.11
Duquesne Light Co.[5]	***72a***	***3.36***	***3.18***	***3.41***		***Dc***	***19.50***	***266.0***	***425.0***	***9-30-99***	***1078***		***2304***	***56.0***						
1st CT 6⅝s 2004	Jd15	**BBB+**			X	BE	100.807	6-14-00	....	....	....	....	100	M2	'93	101⅝	96¾	96¾	6.85	6.85
1st CT 7⅝s 2023	Ao15	**BBB+**			X	BE	105.0222	4-14-00	....	....	....	....	100	G1	'93	105½	92½	92⅝	8.23	8.23
1st CT 8⅜s 2024	Mn15	**BBB+**			X	BE	104.764	5-14-00	....	....	....	....	100	G1	'92	105¼	98½	98⅝	8.49	8.49
1st CT 7.55s 2025	Jd15	**BBB+**			X	BE	103.8662	(6-15-00)	....	....	....	....	100	M2	'93	102	91	91⅛	8.29	8.28
• SF Deb 5s 2010	Ms	**BBB**	6/90	BBB–	X	CR	101.31	8-31-00	100.41	8-31-00	....	....	6.04	F1	'60	89	78	77	6.49	6.49
[6]Duty Free Intl.	***59l***	***n/a***	***4.93***	***n/a***		***Mr***	***222.0***	***554.0***	***790.0***	***:3-31-99***	***1981***		***3257***	***53.9***						
Nts 7s 2004	Jj15	**AA–**	8/97	BBB–	X	R	NC	....	....	....	....	....	115	M6	'94	106¼	99⅛	99⅛	7.06	7.06
Dynegy Inc[7]	***73e***	***7.04***	***1.93***	***2.25***		***Dc***	***28.34***	***2743***	***2184***	***9-30-99***	***1416***		***2351***	***54.4***						
Sr Nts 6⅞s 2002	jJ15	**BBB+**			X	BE	NC	....	....	....	....	....	200	L3	'99	100⅝	98⅞	98⅞	6.95	6.95
Sr Nts 7.45s 2006	jJ15	**BBB+**			X	BE	[1]Z100	....	....	....	....	....	200	L3	'99	100⅜	97⅞	97⅞	7.61	7.61
e. spire Communications[8]	***67f***	***[9]d2.38***	***d1.77***	***d0.79***		***Dc***	***92.89***	***217.1***	***215.9***	***9-30-99***	***767.0***		***843.0***	***105.0***						
Sr[10]Disc[11]Nts[12] 12¾s 2006	Ao	**NR**				BE	106.375	(4-1-01)	....	....	....	....	[13]120		'96	73	38	47⅝	....	Flat
Eagle Food Centers, Inc.	***59c***	***1.26***	***1.40***	***0.92***		***Ja***	***12.34***	***101.0***	***179.7***	***10-30-99***	***56.30***		***171.0***	***84.2***						
Sr Nts[10] 8⅝s 2000	Ao15	**B**	12/99	B+	Y	R	101.75	4-14-00	....	....	....	....	100	G1	'93	98½	88	90	9.58	9.58

Uniform Footnote Explanations-See Page 260. Other: [1] Red at greater of 100 or amt based on formula. [2] Plus Make-Whole Amt. [3] Issued in min denom $25T. [4] Co may red in whole, at 100, for tax law chge. [5] Subsid of DQE, Inc. [6] Acquired by & data of BAA plc. [7] Was NGC Corp,see. [8] Was Amer Communications. [9] 6 Mo Dec'96. [10] (HRO)On Chge of Ctrl at 101. [11] Int accrues at 12.75% fr 4-1-01. [12] Was Amer Commun. [13] Incl disc.

Title-Industry Code & Co. Finances (In Italics) / Individual Issue Statistics (Exchange)	Ind / Interest Dates	Fixed Charge Coverage 1996 / S&P Rating	1997 / Date of Last Rating Change	Prior Rating	1998 / Eligible	Year End / Bond Form	Million $ Cash & Equiv. / Redemption Provisions Regular Price	Curr. Assets / Regular (Begins) Thru	Curr. Liab. / Sinking Fund Price	Balance Sheet Date / Sinking Fund (Begins) Thru	L. Term Debt (Mil $) / Refund/Other Restriction Price	Refund/Other Restriction (Begins) Thru	Capital-ization (Mil $) / Outst'g (Mil $)	Total Debt % Capital / Underwriting Firm Year	Price Range 1999 High	Price Range 1999 Low	Mo. End Price Sale(s) or Bid	Curr. Yield	Yield to Mat.
Earthgrains Co	***26a***	*n/a*	*n/a*		*4.07*	*Mr*	*30.60*	*402.0*	*289.0*	*9-14-99*	*382.0*		*1037*	*37.1*					
Nts 6½s 2009	Ao15	**BBB**			X	BE	[1]Z100	....	....	....	....	....	150	M5 '99	100	91	91	7.14	7.14
Eastman Chemical Co	***14a***	*10.06*	*6.84*		*4.75*	*Dc*	*75.00*	*1391*	*940.0*	*9-30-99*	*2090*		*3695*	*50.1*					
Deb 7¼s 2024	Jj15	**BBB+**	9/95	BBB	X	BE	NC	....	....	....	....	....	500	G1 '94	100	89	89⅜	8.11	8.11
Deb[2] 7⅝s 2024	Jd15	**BBB+**	9/95	BBB	X	BE	NC	....	....	....	....	....	200	G1 '94	107	98¾	98¾	7.72	7.72
Deb 7.60s 2027	Fa	**BBB+**			X	BE	NC	....	....	....	....	....	300	M2 '97	103⅞	92⅛	92⅝	8.21	8.20
Nts 6⅜s 2004	Jj15	**BBB+**	9/95	BBB	X	BE	NC	....	....	....	....	....	500	G1 '94	100½	95¼	95⅜	6.68	6.68
Eastman Kodak	***40d***	*33.82*	*16.60*		*20.53*	*Dc*	*604.0*	*6220*	*6570*	*9-30-99*	*920.0*		*6691*	*41.8*					
Deb 9.95s 2018	jJ	**A+**	5/98	AA–	X	R	[3]Z100	....	....	....	....	....	3.10	M6 '88	139⅝	118⅝	118¾	8.38	8.38
Deb 9.20s 2021	Jd	**A+**	5/98	AA–	X	R	NC	....	....	....	....	....	10.3	M2 '91	136¼	112¼	112¼	8.20	8.19
Nts 9⅜s 2003	Ms15	**A+**	5/98	AA–	X	R	NC	....	....	....	....	....	144	G1 '88	114⅞	105⅞	105⅞	8.85	8.85
Nts 9¾s 2004	aO	**A+**	5/98	AA–	X	R	NC	....	....	....	....	....	91.0	F1 '89	121¼	109½	109½	8.90	8.90
Eaton Corp	***8***	*6.13*	*7.71*		*5.10*	*Dc*	*71.00*	*2773*	*2817*	*9-30-99*	*1946*		*5597*	*56.2*					
Deb 8s 2006	fA15	**A**			X	R	NC	....	....	....	....	....	86.0	M2 '86	113¼	101¼	101¼	7.90	7.90
Deb 8.90s 2006	fA15	**A**			X	R	NC	....	....	....	....	....	100	G1 '91	118⅝	105⅞	105⅞	8.41	8.40
Deb[4] 8⅞s 2019	Jd15	**A**			X	R	NC	....	....	....	....	....	38.0	S5 '89	126	108⅛	108⅛	8.21	8.21
Deb 8.10s 2022	fA15	**A**			X	R	NC	....	....	....	....	....	100	G1 '92	118	99⅛	99¼	8.16	8.16
Deb 7⅝s 2024	Ao	**A**			X	R	NC	....	....	....	....	....	100	L3 '94	112¾	94⅜	94½	8.07	8.07
Deb[5] 6½s 2025	Jd	**A**			X	R	NC	....	....	....	....	....	150	L3 '95	103	95	95	6.84	6.84
Deb 7.65s 2029	mN15	**A**			X	BE	NC	....	....	....	....	....	150	G1 '99	99½	95¼	95¼	8.03	8.03
Nts 6.95s 2004	mN15	**A**			X	BE	NC	....	....	....	....	....	250	G1 '99	99¾	97¾	97¾	7.11	7.11
Eaton ETN Offshore Ltd	***8***	*Gtd by & subsid of Eaton Corp,see*																	
Gtd[6]Nts 9s 2001	Fa15	**A**			X	R	NC	....	....	....	[7]Z100	....	100	G1 '91	107½	102⅜	102⅜	8.79	8.79
EchoStar Communications	***67e***	*d1.52*	*d2.00*		*d0.56*	*Dc*	*385.0*	*705.0*	*582.0*	*6-30-99*	*2090*		*2342*	*90.1*					
Sr Sec[8]Disc Nts[9] 12⅞s 2004	Jd	**NR**	1/99	B–	Y	R	104.828	5-31-00	100	(6-1-02)	....	....	[10]624	D6 '94	102¾	101½	101½	....	Flat
Edison Intl	***72b***	*2.74*	*2.63*		*1.71*	*Dc*	*1218*	*3636*	*6182*	*9-30-99*	*11890*		*18906*	*68.8*					
Nts 6⅞s 2004	mS15	**A–**			X	BE	[1]Z100	....	....	....	....	....	750	S4 '99	100¼	97½	97⅞	7.02	7.02
[11]EG&G Inc	***65***	*6.86*	*7.53*		*7.90*	*Dc*	*88.40*	*732.0*	*848.0*	*10-3-99*	*115.0*		*452.0*	*45.7*					
Nts 6.80s 2005	aO15	**BBB+**	5/99	A–	X	R	NC	....	....	....	....	....	115	G1 '95	105¾	94½	94½	7.20	7.20
[12]EKCO Group	***34***	*n/a*	*n/a*		*n/a*	*Dc*	*5.59*	*238.0*	*106.0*	*9-26-99*	*490.0*		*320.0*	*154.0*					
Sr[13]Nts 'B' 9¼s 2006	Ao	**NR**	10/99	B+		BE	104.625	(4-1-01)	....	....	....	....	3.40	Exch. '96	108⅝	92	108⅛	8.55	8.55
El Paso Electric (Texas)	***72a***	*1.40*	*1.82*		*2.03*	*Dc*	*50.10*	*156.0*	*120.0*	*9-30-99*	*815.0*		*1337*	*67.2*					
1st 'B' 7¾s 2001	Mn	**BBB–**	9/99	BB+	X	R	NC	....	....	....	....	....	150	D6 '96	103	100½	100½	7.71	7.71
1st 'C' 8¼s 2003	Fa	**BBB–**	9/99	BB+	X	R	NC	....	....	....	....	....	150	D6 '96	106⅜	101⅜	101⅜	8.14	8.14
1st 'D'[13] 8.90s 2006	Fa	**BBB–**	9/99	BB+	X	R	NC	....	....	....	....	....	236	D6 '96	113¾	103	103	8.64	8.64
1st 'E'[14] 9.40s 2011	Mn	**BBB–**	9/99	BB+	X	R	104.70	(2-1-06)	....	....	[15]....	....	286	D6 '96	117⅛	106⅞	106⅞	8.80	8.79
El Paso[16]Energy[17]	***73a***	*2.48*	*2.43*		*2.41*	*Dc*	*92.00*	*2161*	*2123*	*9-30-99*	*4045*		*7229*	*59.1*					
Sr Nts 'B' 6⅝s 2001	jJ15	**BBB**			X	BE	NC	....	....	....	....	....	600	Exch. '99	99¾	99	99	6.69	6.69
Sr Nts 6¾s 2009	Mn15	**BBB**	9/99	BBB–	X	BE	[18]Z100	....	....	....	....	....	500	D6 '99	99¾	93⅜	93⅜	7.23	7.23
El Paso Natural Gas[19]	***73a***	*1.06*	*2.38*		*2.22*	*Dc*	*10.00*	*1209*	*442.0*	*9-30-99*	*969.0*		*2273*	*51.5*					
Deb 8⅝s 2022	Jj15	**BBB+**	9/99	BBB	X	R	NC	....	....	....	....	....	260	M6 '92	119½	101⅝	101¾	8.48	8.47
Deb 7½s 2026	mN15	**BBB+**	9/99	BBB	X	BE	NC	....	....	....	....	....	200	D6 '96	108½	92	92⅛	8.14	8.14
Nts 7¾s 2002	Jj15	**BBB+**	9/99	BBB	X	R	NC	....	....	....	....	....	215	M6 '92	105⅜	100⅝	100⅝	7.70	7.70
Nts 6¾s 2003	mN15	**BBB+**	9/99	BBB	X	BE	NC	....	....	....	....	....	200	D6 '96	104⅛	97⅜	97⅜	6.93	6.93
Electronic Data Systems	***20c***	*10.26*	*8.75*		*9.62*	*Dc*	*812.0*	*5884*	*4342*	*9-30-99*	*2287*		*8227*	*32.6*					
Nts 6.85s 2004	aO15	**A+**			X	BE	[1]Z100	....	....	....	....	....	500	M2 '99	100⅝	98⅝	98⅝	6.95	6.95

Uniform Footnote Explanations-See Page 260. Other: [1] Red at greater of 100 or amt based on formula. [2] (HRO)On 6-15-06 at 100. [3] Fr7-1-03,greater of 100 or amt based on formula. [4] (HRO)For a Risk Event & on 6-15-04 at 100. [5] (HRO)On 6-1-05 at 100. [6] Gtd by Eaton Corp. [7] Co may red in whole for UK tax law chge. [8] Co to offer 101(Accreted Val)on Chge of Ctrl. [9] Int accr at 12.875% fr 6-1-99. [10] Incl disc. [11] Now PerkinElmer Inc. [12] Acq by & data of CCPC Holding Co. [13] (HRO)On Chge of Ctrl at 101. [14] (HRO)On Chge ot Ctrl at 100. [15] On Chge of Ctrl. [16] Was El Paso Natural Gas. [17] See DeepTech Int'l,Sonat Inc. [18] Plus Make-Whole Amt. [19] Subsid of El Paso Energy.

Title-Industry Code & Co. Finances (In Italics) / Individual Issue Statistics — Exchange	Ind / Interest Dates	1996 / S&P Rating	1997 / Date of Last Rating Change	Prior Rating	1998 / Eligible	Year End / Bond Form	Cash & Equiv. (Million $) / Regular Price	Curr. Assets (Million $) / Regular (Begins) Thru	Curr. Liab. (Million $) / Sinking Fund Price	Balance Sheet Date / Sinking Fund (Begins) Thru	L. Term Debt (Mil $) / Refund/Other Restriction Price	Refund/Other Restriction (Begins) Thru	Capital-ization (Mil $) / Outst'g (Mil $)	Total Debt % Capital / Underwriting Firm	Underwriting Year	Price Range 1999 High	Price Range 1999 Low	Mo. End Price Sale(s) or Bid	Curr. Yield	Yield to Mat.
***Electronic Data Systems** (Cont.)*																				
Nts 7⅛s 2009	aO15	A+			X	BE	[1]Z100	....	....	....	....	....	700	M2	'99	101⅜	97½	97½	7.31	7.31
Nts 7.45s 2029	aO15	A+			X	BE	[1]Z100	....	....	....	....	....	300	M2	'99	102¼	97	97	7.68	7.68
Elizabethtown Water[2]	***74***	*2.40*	*2.92*		*3.33*	*Dc*	*5.49*	*59.60*	*125.0*	*6-30-99*	*268.0*		*503.0*	*53.3*						
Deb 8¾s 2021	aO	A			X	BE	105.08	9-30-00	Z100	....	....	....	27.5		'91	105¾	99½	100¾	8.68	8.68
Deb 8s 2022	mS	A			X	BE	105.20	8-31-00	Z100	....	....	....	15.0	S1	'92	105¾	93⅞	94⅝	8.45	8.45
Deb 7¼s 2028	mN	A			X	BE	105.08	10-31-00	Z100	....	....	....	50.0	S1	'93	102⅛	87⅝	87¾	8.26	8.26
Emerson Electric	***23c***	*13.68*	*15.74*		*13.66*	*Sp*	*266.1*	*5124*	*4590*	*9-30-99*	*1317*		*9684*	*37.5*						
Nts 6.30s 2005	mN	AA+			X	R	NC	....	....	....	....	....	250	G1	'95	106½	95¾	95¾	6.58	6.58
Nts 5½s 2008	mS15	AA+			X	BE	NC	....	....	....	....	....	250	M7	'98	101¾	89	89	6.18	6.18
Nts 5.85s 2009	Ms15	AA+			X	BE	NC	....	....	....	....	....	250	M7	'99	100¾	90¾	90¾	6.45	6.45
Empire District Electric	***72a***	*3.05*	*2.97*		*3.31*	*Dc*	*0.87*	*46.60*	*98.50*	*9-30-99*	*246.0*		*505.0*	*48.7*						
1st 7½s 2002	jJ	A–	5/94	A	X	R	NC	....	....	....	....	....	37.5	S1	'92	106⅝	100½	100½	7.46	7.46
1st 7.60s 2005	Ao	A–			X	R	NC	....	....	....	....	....	10.0	S1	'95	110⅞	100	100	7.60	7.60
1st[3] 8⅛s 2009	mN	A–			X	R	NC	....	....	....	....	....	20.0	S1	'94	114⅛	102⅝	102⅝	7.92	7.92
1st 6½s 2010	Ao	A–			X	BE	NC	....	....	....	....	....	50.0	S4	'98	105⅝	91	91	7.14	7.14
1st 7.20s 2016	jD	A–			X	BE	NC	....	....	....	....	....	25.0	S1	'96	101¼	91¼	91⅜	7.88	7.88
1st 7s 2023	aO	A–	5/94	A	X	R	103.26	(10-1-03)	....	....	....	....	45.0	S1	'93	104⅜	85⅛	85¼	8.21	8.21
1st 7¾s 2025	Jd	A–			X	BE	103.875	(6-1-05)	....	....	....	....	30.0	S1	'95	111½	91⅝	91¾	8.45	8.45
1st[4] 7¼s 2028	Jd	A–	5/94	A	X	R	103.50	5-31-00	....	....	....	....	14.5	J2	'93	104⅜	86⅝	86¾	8.36	8.36
Energen Corp	***73b***	*2.91*	*2.40*		*2.13*	*Sp*	*4.45*	*130.0*	*259.0*	*6-30-99*	*372.0*		*710.0*	*53.2*						
Deb[5] 8s 2007	Fa	A			X	BE	103	1-31-00	....	....	....	....	20.0	J2	'92	103¼	102	102	7.84	7.84
Engle Homes	***13h***	*n/a*	*n/a*		*1.35*	*Oc*				*7-31-99*	*248.0*		*457.0*	*62.1*						
Sr Nts[6] 9¼s 2008	Fa	B			Y	BE	104.625	(2-1-03)	....	....	[7]Z109.25	2-1-01	150	Exch.	'98	101	85	90	10.28	10.27
Engelhard Corp	***44a***	*5.62*	*4.96*		*5.25*	*Dc*	*38.66*	*1211*	*1370*	*9-30-99*	*444.0*		*1724*	*57.9*						
Nts 7s 2001	fA	A–	5/99	A	X	BE	NC	....	....	....	....	....	150	M5	'96	103⅜	99½	99½	7.04	7.03
Nts 7⅜s 2006	fA	A–	5/99	A	X	BE	[8]Z100	....	....	....	....	....	100	M5	'96	109¼	96⅞	96⅞	7.61	7.61
Nts 6.95s 2028	Jd	A–	5/99	A	X	BE	[1]Z100	....	....	....	....	....	120	M5	'98	99⅝	85¼	85⅜	8.14	8.14
Enhance Financial Svcs Grp	***35***	*14.90*	*12.64*		*12.62*	*Dc*				*9-30-99*	*75.00*		*872.0*	*20.8*						
• Deb 6¾s 2003	Ms	A+			X	BE	NC	....	....	....	....	....	75.0	S1	'93	No Sale		98⅞	6.83	6.83
Enron Corp[9]	***73e***	*3.73*	*1.78*		*2.28*	*Dc*	*316.0*	*7567*	*6669*	*9-30-99*	*9593*		*21661*	*41.5*						
Sr Deb 7s 2023	fA15	BBB+	12/95	BBB	X	R	102.575	(8-15-03)	....	....	....	....	100	M2	'93	95⅞	84⅛	84¼	8.31	8.31
Sr Nts 9.65s 2001	Mn15	BBB+	12/95	BBB	X	R	NC	....	....	....	....	....	100	P4	'89	108⅛	103⅛	103⅛	9.36	9.36
[10]Nts[11] 9½s 2001	Jd15	BBB+	12/95	BBB	X	R	NC	....	....	....	....	....	100	B7	'89	108	103⅛	103⅛	9.21	9.21
Nts 6.45s 2001	mN15	BBB+			X	BE	NC	....	....	....	....	....	300	S1	'97	101⅜	98¾	98¾	6.53	6.53
Nts 6½s 2002	fA	BBB+			X	R	[1]Z100	....	....	....	....	....	150	L3	'97	102	98¼	98¼	6.62	6.62
Nts 9⅛s 2003	Ao	BBB+	12/95	BBB	X	R	NC	....	....	....	....	....	200	M6	'91	111	104¾	104¾	8.71	8.71
Nts 9⅞s 2003	Jd15	BBB+	12/95	BBB	X	R	NC	....	....	....	....	....	100	F1	'88	114⅜	107⅛	107⅛	9.22	9.22
Nts 6⅝s 2003	aO15	BBB+			X	BE	[1]Z100	....	....	....	....	....	100	C1	'97	102⅞	97⅝	97⅝	6.79	6.79
Nts 6¾s 2004	mS	BBB+			X	R	NC	....	....	....	....	....	100	N1	'97	103⅝	97⅜	97⅜	6.93	6.93
Nts 7⅝s 2004	mS10	BBB+	12/95	BBB	X	R	NC	....	....	....	....	....	200	M2	'92	107¾	100½	100½	7.59	7.59
Nts 6¾s 2004	mS15	BBB+	12/95	BBB	X	R	NC	....	....	....	....	....	50.0	S1	'95	104	96⅞	96⅞	6.97	6.97
Nts 6⅝s 2005	mN15	BBB+			X	BE	NC	....	....	....	....	....	250	M6	'97	103¼	94¾	95⅛	6.96	6.96
Nts 6.40s 2006	jJ15	BBB+			X	BE	[1]Z100	....	....	....	....	....	250	C1	'98	101¾	92¾	93	6.88	6.88
Nts 7⅛s 2007	Mn15	BBB+	12/95	BBB	X	R	NC	....	....	....	....	....	150	G1	'95	106⅛	96⅝	96⅝	7.37	7.37
Nts 6⅞s 2007	aO15	BBB+	12/95	BBB	X	R	NC	....	....	....	....	....	100	M2	'95	105⅛	94¾	94¾	7.26	7.26

Uniform Footnote Explanations-See Page 260. Other: [1] Red at greater of 100 or amt based on formula. [2] Subsid of E'town Corp. [3] (HRO)On 11-1-01 at 100. [4] Death red benefit,ltd,as defined. [5] (HRO)At 100,ltd as defined. [6] (HRO)On Chge of Ctrl at 101. [7] Max $50M red w/proceeds of Pub Eq Off'g. [8] Greater of 100 or amt based on formula. [9] See InterNorth. [10] Credit Sensitive Nts. [11] Int(9.2%-14%)subj to chge.

Title-Industry Code & Co. Finances (In Italics)	Ind	Fixed Charge Coverage 1996	1997		1998	Year End	Million $ Cash & Equiv.	Curr. Assets	Curr. Liab.	Balance Sheet Date	L. Term Debt (Mil $)		Capital-ization (Mil $)	Total Debt % Capital						
Individual Issue Statistics / Exchange ↓	Interest Dates	S&P Rating	Date of Last Rating Change	Prior Rating	Eligible ↓	Bond Form	Redemption Provisions: Regular Price	Regular (Begins) Thru	Sinking Fund Price	Sinking Fund (Begins) Thru	Refund/Other Restriction Price	Refund/Other Restriction (Begins) Thru	Outst'g (Mil $)	Underwriting Firm	Underwriting Year	Price Range 1999 High	Price Range 1999 Low	Mo. End Price Sale(s) or Bid	Curr. Yield	Yield to Mat.
***Enron Corp** (Cont.)*																				
Nts 6¾s 2009	fA	**BBB+**			X	R	Z100	....	....	....	....	....	200	C5	'97	104¼	93¼	93¼	7.24	7.24
Nts 7⅜s 2019	Mn15	**BBB+**			X	BE	[1]Z100	....	....	....	....	....	500	L3	'99	99⅜	93¾	94	7.85	7.84
Nts(Jul) 6.95s 2028	jJ15	**BBB+**			X	BE	[1]Z100	....	....	....	....	....	250	C1	'98	101¾	87	87⅞	7.91	7.91
Nts(Nov) 6.95s 2028	jJ15	**BBB+**			X	BE	[1]Z100	....	....	....	....	....	250	C6	'98	101¾	87	87⅞	7.91	7.91
Sr Sub Deb 6¾s 2005	jJ	**BBB**	12/95	BBB–	X	R	NC	....	....	....	....	....	200	L3	'93	104⅜	96	96¼	7.01	7.01
Sr Sub Deb 8¼s 2012	mS15	**BBB**	12/95	BBB–	X	R	NC	....	....	....	....	....	150	B7	'92	118⅞	102⅝	102⅝	8.04	8.04
[2]Enron Oil & Gas	***49***	***9.27***	***4.62***		***1.98***	***Dc***	***18.80***	***202.0***	***212.0***	***9-30-99***	***1165***		***2117***	***55.0***						
Nts 6½s 2004	mS15	**A–**			X	BE	NC	....	....	....	....	....	100	S1	'97	103⅛	96¼	96¼	6.75	6.75
Nts 6.70s 2006	mN15	**A–**			X	BE	NC	....	....	....	....	....	150	M5	'96	104⅝	94⅛	94⅛	7.12	7.12
Nts 6½s 2007	jD	**A–**			X	BE	NC	....	....	....	....	....	100	G1	'97	103⅜	92¾	92¾	7.01	7.01
Nts 6s 2008	jD15	**A–**			X	BE	[1]Z100	....	....	....	....	....	175	N2	'98	99½	88⅜	88⅜	6.79	6.79
Nts 6.65s 2028	Ao	**A–**			X	BE	NC	....	....	....	....	....	150	L3	'98	97½	83¼	83⅜	7.98	7.98
ENSCO Intl	***49e***	***7.83***	***18.56***		***15.60***	***Dc***	***194.3***	***298.3***	***124.7***	***9-30-99***	***372.0***		***1609***	***23.1***						
Deb 7.20s 2027	mN15	**BBB**			X	BE	[3]Z100	....	....	....	....	....	150	G1	'97	101⅝	87¼	87¼	8.25	8.25
Nts 6¾s 2007	mN15	**BBB**			X	BE	[3]Z100	....	....	....	....	....	150	G1	'97	101¾	91⅜	91⅜	7.39	7.39
ENSERCH Corp[4]	***73b***	***1.33***	***1.76***		***0.67***	***Dc***	***6.00***	***1250***	***1300***	***6-30-99***	***551.0***		***2134***	***35.4***						
Nts 'A' 6¼s 2003	Jj	**BBB**			X	BE	[1]Z100	....	....	....	....	....	125	M2	'98	102¼	97	97	6.44	6.44
Nts 6⅜s 2004	Fa	**BBB**			X	BE	NC	....	....	....	....	....	150	L3	'94	103⅛	95¾	95¾	6.66	6.66
Nts 7⅛s 2005	Jd15	**BBB**			X	BE	NC	....	....	....	....	....	150	S7	'95	107¼	97½	97½	7.31	7.31
Entergy Louisiana	***72a***	***3.39***	***3.03***		***3.32***	***Dc***	***11.50***	***448.0***	***568.0***	***9-30-99***	***1258***		***2739***	***51.5***						
1st 5.80s 2002	Ms	**BBB**			X	BE	[1]Z100	....	....	....	....	....	75.0	P4	'99	100¼	97⅛	97⅛	5.97	5.97
1st 6½s 2008	Ms	**BBB**			X	BE	[1]Z100	2-28-03	....	....	....	....	115	D6	'98	104½	92¼	92¼	7.05	7.05
Entergy Mississippi[5]	***72a***	***3.46***	***3.04***		***3.19***	***Dc***	***33.60***	***141.0***	***155.0***	***6-30-99***	***463.0***		***966.0***	***51.0***						
Gen & Ref Mtg 6⅞s 2002	Jd	**BBB+**	10/97	BBB	X	BE	[6]Z100	....	....	....	....	....	65.0	B7	'97	100¾	99	99	6.94	6.94
Gen & Ref Mtg 6.20s 2004	Mn	**BBB+**			X	BE	[1]Z100	....	Z100	....	....	....	75.0	S4	'99	100⅜	95	95	6.53	6.53
[7]Envirodyne Industries	***52***	***0.65***	***0.65***		***0.11***	***Dc***	***7.33***	***158.0***	***122.0***	***9-30-99***	***403.0***		***341.0***	***125.0***						
Sr Nts 10¼s 2001	jD	**CCC+**	8/99	B–	Y	R	100	....	....	....	....	....	219	Reorg	'93	81⅛	65⅞	70	14.64	14.64
EnviroSource, Inc.	***44***	***0.72***	***0.76***		***0.79***	***Dc***	***2.74***	***42.89***	***54.32***	***9-30-99***	***279.0***		***278.0***	***101.0***						
Sr[8]Nts 9¾s 2003	Jd15	**B**	5/95	B–	Y	R	103.25	6-14-00	....	....	....	....	220	M6	'93	92	51⅞	63	15.48	15.47
EOP Operating LP	***57***	***n/a***	***n/a***		***n/a***	***Dc***				***9-30-99***	***6110***		***13850***	***44.1***						
Sr Nts 6⅜s 2003	Fa15	**BBB+**	7/99	BBB	X	BE	[9]Z100	....	....	....	....	....	300	Exch.	'98	99⅞	96¼	96¼	6.62	6.62
Sr Nts 6⅝s 2005	Fa15	**BBB+**	7/99	BBB	X	BE	[9]Z100	....	....	....	....	....	400	Exch.	998	100⅜	94	94¼	7.03	7.03
Sr Nts 6¾s 2008	Fa15	**BBB+**	7/99	BBB	X	BE	[9]Z100	....	....	....	....	....	300	Exch.	'98	100	90¾	91¾	7.36	7.36
Sr Nts 7¼s 2018	Fa15	**BBB+**	7/99	BBB	X	BE	[9]Z100	....	....	....	....	....	250	Exch.	'98	99	85⅜	85⅜	8.49	8.49
Nts 6⅜s 2002	Jj15	**BBB+**	7/99	BBB	X	BE	[9]Z100	....	....	....	....	....	200	M2	'99	100⅛	97⅝	97⅝	6.53	6.53
Nts 6½s 2004	Jj15	**BBB+**	7/99	BBB	X	BE	[9]Z100	....	....	....	....	....	300	M2	'99	100¼	95½	95⅝	6.80	6.80
Nts 6.763s 2007	Jd15	**BBB+**	7/99	BBB	X	BE	[9]Z100	....	....	....	....	....	300	Exch.	'98	100¼	91⅞	91⅞	7.36	7.36
Nts 6.80s 2009	Jj15	**BBB+**	7/99	BBB	X	BE	[9]Z100	....	....	....	....	....	500	M2	'99	100¼	91¼	91¼	7.45	7.45
Nts 7½s 2029	Ao19	**BBB+**	7/99	BBB	X	BE	[9]Z100	....	....	....	....	....	200	M2	'99	99⅜	86⅜	87½	8.57	8.57
[10]EOTT Energy Ptnrs/Fin	***49b***	***7.87***	***d2.16***		***d0.40***	***Dc***	***2.03***	***1053***	***1159***	***9-30-99***	***175.0***		***398.0***	***65.1***						
Sr[11]Nts 11s 2009	aO	**BB**			Y	BE	105.50	(10-1-04)	....	....	[12]Z111	9-30-02	235	L3	'99	104½	100	103½	10.63	10.63
Equifax Inc	***63***	***14.18***	***17.74***		***8.66***	***Dc***	***137.1***	***538.7***	***398.8***	***9-30-99***	***939.0***		***1181***	***83.2***						
Deb 6.90s 2028	jJ	**A–**			X	BE	[1]Z100	....	....	....	....	....	150	B7	'98	103½	86⅝	87½	7.89	7.88
Sr Nts[13] 6½s 2003	Jd15	**A–**			X	R	NC	....	....	....	....	....	200	F1	'93	103⅝	97⅛	97⅛	6.69	6.69
Nts[14] 6.30s 2005	jJ	**A–**			X	BE	[1]Z100	....	....	....	....	....	250	B7	'98	103⅜	94¼	94¼	6.68	6.68

Uniform Footnote Explanations-See Page 260. Other: [1] Red at greater of 100 or amt based on formula. [2] Now EOG Resources. [3] Plus Make-Whole Premium. [4] Acquired by Texas Util. [5] Was Mississippi Pwr & Light, see. [6] Greater of 100 or amt based on formula. [7] Now Viskase Cos. [8] Co must offer repurch at 101 on Chge of Ctrl. [9] Plus Make-Whole Amt. [10] Data of EOTT Energy Ptnrs. [11] (HRO)On Chge of Ctrl at 101. [12] Max $82M red w/proceeds of Pub Eq Off'g. [13] (HRO)For a Put Event at 100. [14] Issued in min denom $10T.

Title-Industry Code & Co. Finances (In Italics) / Individual Issue Statistics — Exchange	Ind / Interest Dates	Fixed Charge Coverage 1996 / S&P Rating	1997 / Date of Last Rating Change	Prior Rating	1998 / Eligible	Year End / Bond Form	Million $ Cash & Equiv. / Redemption Provisions: Regular Price	Million $ Curr. Assets / Regular (Begins) Thru	Million $ Curr. Liab. / Sinking Fund Price	Balance Sheet Date / Sinking Fund (Begins) Thru	L. Term Debt (Mil $) / Refund/Other Restriction Price	Refund/Other Restriction (Begins) Thru	Capital-ization (Mil $) / Outst'g (Mil $)	Total Debt % Capital / Underwriting Firm	Underwriting Year	Price Range 1999 High	Price Range 1999 Low	Mo. End Price Sale(s) or Bid	Curr. Yield	Yield to Mat.
Equistar Chemicals L.P.[1]	***49g***	***n/a***	***n/a***		***0.89***	***Dc***	***10.00***	***1211***	***620.0***	***9-30-99***	***2169***		***6004***	***36.8***						
Deb 7.55s 2026	Fa15	**BBB–**			X	BE	NC	....	....	....	....	....	150	S1	'96	91½	80⅝	81⅛	9.31	9.30
Nts 9⅛s 2002	Ms15	**BBB–**			X	BE	NC	....	....	....	....	....	100	L3	'92	106	100¼	101	9.03	9.03
Nts 6½s 2006	Fa1	**BBB–**			X	BE	NC	....	....	....	....	....	150	S1	'96	95¾	88⅛	88¼	7.37	7.36
[2]***Equitable Cos***	***25g***	***1.41***	***1.87***		***2.39***	***Dc***				***9-30-99***	[3]***7805***		***13529***	***57.7***						
Sr Deb 7s 2028	Ao	**A**			X	BE	[4]Z100	....	....	....	....	....	350	D6	'98	105½	87⅝	89½	7.82	7.82
Sr Nts 9s 2004	jD15	**A**	5/97	A+	X	BE	[4]100	....	....	....	....	....	300	D6	'94	114⅛	106⅜	106⅜	8.46	8.46
Sr Nts 6½s 2008	Ao	**A**			X	BE	[4]Z100	....	....	....	....	....	250	D6	'98	104¾	93¼	93¼	6.97	6.97
Equitable of Iowa[5]	***35a***	***n/a***	***3.33***		***3.75***	***Dc***				***12-31-98***	***28267***		***189796***	***88.0***						
Nts 8½s 2005	Fa15	**A+**	8/98	A	X	BE	NC	....	....	....	....	....	100	S1	'95	112⅝	103½	103½	8.21	8.21
Equitable Resources	***73e***	***2.95***	***4.24***		***1.84***	***Dc***	***6.83***	***255.5***	***289.2***	***9-30-99***	***298.0***		***1197***	***34.8***						
Deb 7¾s 2026	jJ15	**A**			X	BE	NC	....	....	....	....	....	115	M5	'96	115¼	94⅞	95	8.16	8.16
ERP Operating L.P.	***57***	***2.37***	***2.53***		***2.02***	***Dc***				***6-30-99***	***4707***		***10480***	***44.9***						
Nts 6.15s 2000	mS15	**BBB+**			X	BE	NC	....	....	....	....	....	145	M5	'98	100½	99¼	99⅜	6.19	6.19
Nts 6.55s 2001	mN15	**BBB+**			X	BE	NC	....	....	....	....	....	150	M2	'97	100¾	98⅜	98⅜	6.66	6.66
Nts 7.95s 2002	Ao15	**BBB+**	8/97	BBB	X	BE	[4]Z100	....	....	....	....	....	125	M2	'95	104¾	100¾	100¾	7.89	7.89
Nts 6.65s 2003	mN15	**BBB+**			X	BE	NC	....	....	....	....	....	50.0	M2	'97	102⅜	96¼	96¼	6.91	6.91
Nts 7.10s 2004	Jd23	**BBB+**			X	BE	[4]Z100	....	....	....	....	....	300	M2	'99	100⅛	97⅜	97⅝	7.27	7.27
Nts 7⅛s 2017	aO15	**BBB+**			X	BE	[6]Z100	....	....	....	....	....	150	M2	'97	97½	85⅝	86	8.28	8.28
[7]***Evans Withycombe Residential***[8]	***57***	***n/a***	***n/a***		***2.12***	***Dc***				***9-30-99***	***4755***		***10442***	***44.8***						
Nts 7½s 2004	Ao15	**BBB+**	12/97	BBB–	X	BE	[4]Z100	....	....	....	....	....	75.0	M2	'97	104½	99½	99⅝	7.53	7.53
Nts 7⅝s 2007	Ao15	**BBB+**	12/97	BBB–	X	BE	[4]Z100	....	....	....	....	....	50.0	M2	'97	105⅜	98⅛	98⅛	7.77	7.77
Evenflo Co	***42a***	***n/a***	***n/a***		***n/a***	***Dc***	***10.40***	***153.0***	***91.00***	***9-30-99***	***120.0***		***184.0***	***65.2***						
Sr Nts[9]'B' 11¾s 2006	fA15	**B+**			Y	BE	105.875	(8-15-02)	....	....	[10]Z111.75	8-15-01	110	Exch.	'99	111¾	95	97⅞	12.01	12.00
Executive Risk	***35c***	***Acq by Chubb Corp***																		
Sr Nts 7⅛s 2007	jD15	**A+**	7/99	BBB+	X	BE	NC	....	....	....	....	....	75.0	C1	'97	107⅞	97⅛	97⅛	7.34	7.33
Excel Realty Trust	***57***	***Now New Plan Excel Realty Tr,see***																		
Sr Nts 6⅞s 2004	aO15	**A**	3/99	BBB–	X	BE	[4]Z100	(10-15-02)	....	....	....	....	75.0	M2	'97	100⅝	95⅛	96	7.16	7.16
[11]***Exxon***[12]***Capital***	***25***	***12.97***	***13.91***		***16.36***	***Dc***	***1190***	***18048***	***21579***	***9-30-99***	***4425***		***53079***	***17.4***						
Gtd[13]Nts 7.45s 2001	jD15	**AAA**			X	R	NC	....	....	....	....	....	245	U1	'91	106	101¼	101¼	7.36	7.36
Gtd[13]Nts 6⅝s 2002	fA15	**AAA**			X	R	NC	....	....	....	....	....	250	U1	'92	104⅜	99⅝	99⅝	6.65	6.65
• Gtd[13]Nts 6s 2005	jJ	**AAA**			X	BE	NC	....	....	....	....	....	250	L3	'93	104½	96⅜	s96¾	6.20	6.20
EZ Communications	***12b***	***Merged into Amer Radio Sys,see***																		
Sr Sub Nts[9] 9¾s 2005	jD	**BB+**	9/99	BBB–	Y	R	104.875	(12-1-00)	....	....	....	....	150	C5	'95	110	104¾	106⅞	9.12	9.12
[14]***Family Restaurants Inc***	***27c***	***d0.21***	***d0.60***		***n/a***	***Dc***	***3.72***	***19.30***	***108.0***	***9-26-99***	***268.0***		***227.0***	***119.0***						
Sr[15]Nts 9¾s 2002	Fa	**CCC**	8/95	CCC+	Y	R	102.786	1-31-00	....	....	....	....	103	D6	'94	62½	44	47	20.74	20.72
Sr Sub[16]Disc Nts[17] 10⅞s 2004	Fa	**CCC–**	8/95	CCC	Y	R	104.078	1-31-00	....	....	....	....	30.6	D6	'94	58	39½	45	....	Flat
[18]***Federal Express***	***70b***	***Δ5.53***	***Δ8.23***		***Δ11.80***	***My***	***380.0***	***3153***	***2678***	***8-31-99***	***1360***		***6182***	***22.0***						
SF Deb[19] 9⅝s 2019	aO15	**BBB**	4/91	BBB+	X	R	103.7805	10-14-00	100	(10-15-00)	....	....	100	K2	'89	105⅞	102⅜	102⅜	9.40	9.40
Nts 9⅞s 2002	Ao	**BBB**			X	BE	NC	....	....	....	....	....	175	M2	'92	109½	105¼	105¼	9.38	9.38
Nts 9.65s 2012	Jd15	**BBB**			X	BE	NC	....	....	....	....	....	300	M2	'92	123½	111⅜	111⅜	8.66	8.66
Fed'l Home Loan Mtg	***25b***	***1.19***	***1.20***		***1.14***	***Dc***				***12-31-98***	***93525***		***298231***	***96.4***						
Nts[20] 6.58s 2002	fA13	**NR**			X	BE	[21]100	....	....	....	....	....	300	G1	'97	100⅞	99¼	99¼	6.63	6.63
Nts[20] 6.65s 2002	mS10	**NR**			X	BE	[21]■100	....	....	....	....	....	200		'97	101	99⅛	99⅛	6.71	6.71
Nts[22] 6¾s 2006	Mn30	**NR**			X	BE	NC	....	....	....	....	....	500		'96	109¼	98⅝	98⅝	6.84	6.84
F/R[23]Deb[20] 2000	QMar10	**NR**			X	BE	NC	....	....	....	....	....	200	M2	'93	100½	99⅛	99¾	....	....

Uniform Footnote Explanations-See Page 260. Other: [1] Was Lyondell Petrochemical Co. [2] Now AXA Financial. [3] Incl curr amts. [4] Plus Make-Whole Amt. [5] Acq by & data of ING Groep NV. [6] Greater of 100 or amt based on formula. [7] Subsid & data of Equity Residential Prop. [8] See Merry Land & Invest. [9] (HRO)On Chge of Ctrl at 101. [10] Max $38.5 red w/proceeds of Pub Eq Off'g. [11] Gtd by & data of Exxon Corp. [12] See Seariver Maritime. [13] Gtd by Exxon Corp. [14] Now Prandium Inc. [15] Co must offer repurch at 101 on Chge of Ctrl. [16] Co must offer repur at 101(Accreted Val)Chge of Ctrl. [17] Int accrues at 10.875% fr 2-1-97. [18] Now FDX Corp. [19] (HRO)At 100 for Restructuring Event,as defined. [20] Issued in min denom $5T. [21] In whole or in part. [22] Issued in min denom $10T. [23] Int(min 5%,max 24%)adj qtrly.

Title-Industry Code & Co. Finances (In Italics)	Ind	Fixed Charge Coverage 1996	1997	1998	Year End	Million $ Cash & Equiv.	Curr. Assets	Curr. Liab.	Balance Sheet Date	L. Term Debt (Mil $)	Capital-ization (Mil $)	Total Debt % Capital

Individual Issue Statistics Exchange ↓	Interest Dates	S&P Rating	Date of Last Rating Change	Prior Rating	Eligible ↓	Bond Form	Redemption Provisions: Regular Price	Regular (Begins) Thru	Sinking Fund Price	Sinking Fund (Begins) Thru	Refund/Other Restriction Price	Refund/Other Restriction (Begins) Thru	Outst'g (Mil $)	Underwriting Firm	Underwriting Year	Price Range 1999 High	Price Range 1999 Low	Mo. End Price Sale(s) or Bid	Curr. Yield	Yield to Mat.
Fed'l Home Loan Mtg *(Cont.)*																				
F/R[1]Deb[2] 2000	QMar18	**NR**			X	BE	NC	....	....	....	....	....	100	M2	'93	100	99	99⅝	....	....
F/R[3]Deb[2] 2003	[4]mn18	**NR**			X	BE	NC	....	....	....	....	....	50.0	M2	'93	99½	94¾	95⅛	....	....
Deb 6.55s 2000	Jj4	**NR**			X	BE	NC	....	....	....	....	....	150	M2	'92	101½	100	100	6.55	Mat.
Deb[2] 6.44s 2000	Jj28	**NR**			X	BE	NC	....	....	....	....	....	150	G1	'93	101½	100	100	6.44	6.44
Deb[2] 5⅞s 2000	Ms22	**NR**			X	BE	NC	....	....	....	....	....	150	L3	'93	101	99⅞	99⅞	5.88	5.88
Deb[2] 6.395s 2000	Mn16	**NR**			X	BE	NC	....	....	....	....	....	175	G1	'95	101¾	100	100	6.39	6.39
Deb[2] 6.54s 2000	Mn19	**NR**			X	BE	NC	....	....	....	....	....	125	G1	'95	102	100⅛	100⅛	6.53	6.53
Deb[2] 5.76s 2000	Jd9	**NR**			X	BE	NC	....	....	....	....	....	100	M6	'95	101	99¾	99¾	5.77	5.77
Deb[2] 5.905s 2000	Jd13	**NR**			X	BE	NC	....	....	....	....	....	150	G1	'95	101¼	99⅞	99⅞	5.91	5.91
Deb[2] 5.97s 2000	mS25	**NR**			X	BE	NC	....	....	....	....	....	160	S1	'97	101½	99¾	99¾	5.98	5.98
Deb[2] 6.04s 2000	mN29	**NR**			X	BE	■100	....	....	....	....	....	100		'97	100⅞	99⅝	99⅝	6.06	6.06
Deb[2] 6⅝s 2001	mN5	**NR**			X	BE	■100	....	....	....	....	....	100	M2	'96	101¼	99½	99½	6.65	6.65
Deb[2] 6.52s 2002	Jj2	**NR**			X	BE	NC	....	....	....	....	....	300	L3	'96	104	99⅞	99⅞	6.53	6.53
Deb[2] 6.63s 2002	Jj24	**NR**			X	BE	■100	....	....	....	....	....	100	M5	'97	101½	99⅜	99⅜	6.67	6.66
Deb[2] 6.34s 2002	mN12	**NR**			X	BE	■100	....	....	....	....	....	125	M5	'97	100⅞	98½	98½	6.43	6.43
Deb 6.22s 2003	Ms24	**NR**			X	BE	NC	....	....	....	....	....	200	M2	'93	104⅛	98½	98½	6.31	6.31
Deb 6.20s 2003	Ao15	**NR**			X	BE	NC	....	....	....	....	....	150	P1	'93	104⅛	98⅝	98⅝	6.28	6.28
Deb[5] 5.035s 2003	Ao28	**NR**			X	BE	NC	....	....	....	....	....	100	M2	'93	100	99⅞	100	5.04	5.03
Deb[2] 5.99s 2003	jD	**NR**			X	BE	NC	....	....	....	....	....	100	L3	'93	103⅜	97	97	6.17	6.17
Deb[2] 6.29s 2004	Fa24	**NR**			X	BE	NC	....	....	....	....	....	100		'97	104¾	97⅞	97⅞	6.42	6.42
Deb[2] 6.313s 2004	Fa26	**NR**			X	BE	NC	....	....	....	....	....	175	M5	'97	104⅞	98	98	6.44	6.44
Deb[2] 6.645s 2004	Ms10	**NR**			X	BE	NC	....	....	....	....	....	200	M5	'97	106⅜	99⅛	99⅛	6.70	6.70
Deb[6] 6.95s 2004	Ao	**NR**			X	BE	NC	....	....	....	....	....	125	M2	'97	107⅞	100¼	100¼	6.93	6.93
Deb[2] 7¼s 2004	Ao28	**NR**			X	BE	NC	....	....	....	....	....	12.0		'94	109⅜	101⅜	101⅜	7.15	7.15
Deb[2] 6.485s 2004	Jd24	**NR**			X	BE	NC	....	....	....	....	....	100	M4	'97	106	98½	98½	6.58	6.58
Deb[2] 8.115s 2005	Jj31	**NR**			X	BE	NC	....	....	....	....	....	100	M6	'95	114⅞	105⅛	105⅛	7.71	7.71
Deb[2] 7.65s 2005	Mn10	**NR**			X	BE	■100	(5-10-00)	....	....	....	....	100	M6	'95	103¼	99⅜	99⅜	7.69	7.69
Deb[2] 7.225s 2005	Mn17	**NR**			X	BE	■100	(5-17-00)	....	....	....	....	125	L3	'95	102⅝	98½	98½	7.33	7.33
Deb[2] 7.09s 2005	Jd	**NR**			X	BE	■100	(6-1-00)	....	....	....	....	100	L3	'95	102½	98¼	98¼	7.21	7.21
Deb[2] 7.05s 2005	Jd8	**NR**			X	BE	■100	(6-8-00)	....	....	....	....	100	B7	'95	102⅜	98⅛	98⅛	7.18	7.18
Deb[2] 6.83s 2005	Jd15	**NR**			X	BE	■100	(6-15-00)	....	....	....	....	45.0		'95	102	97½	97½	7.00	7.00
Deb[2] 6.785s 2005	mS21	**NR**			X	BE	■100	(9-21-00)	....	....	....	....	100		'95	102¼	97⅛	97⅛	6.98	6.98
Deb[2] 6.89s 2005	aO3	**NR**			X	BE	■100	(10-3-00)	....	....	....	....	100	M6	'95	102½	97½	97½	7.07	7.07
Deb[2] 6.97s 2005	aO3	**NR**			X	BE	■100	(10-3-00)	....	....	....	....	100	M6	'95	102¾	97¾	97¾	7.13	7.13
Deb[2] 7.06s 2005	aO4	**NR**			X	BE	■100	(10-4-00)	....	....	....	....	100	M2	'95	102⅞	98	98	7.20	7.20
Deb[2] 6.66s 2005	jD5	**NR**			X	BE	■100	(12-5-00)	....	....	....	....	100	G1	'95	102⅛	96⅝	96⅝	6.89	6.89
Nts[2] 5.95s 2006	Jj19	**NR**			X	BE	NC	....	....	....	....	....	500	G1	'96	104⅜	95	95	6.26	6.26
Deb[2] 6.37s 2006	Jj23	**NR**			X	BE	■100	(1-23-01)	....	....	....	....	100		'95	101½	95½	95½	6.67	6.67
Deb[2] 6¼s 2006	Fa	**NR**			X	BE	■100	(2-1-01)	....	....	....	....	125	B7	'96	101¼	95⅛	95⅛	6.57	6.57
Deb[2] 5.825s 2006	Fa9	**NR**			X	BE	NC	....	....	....	....	....	100	L3	'96	103⅝	94¼	94¼	6.18	6.18
Deb[2] 6.33s 2006	Fa13	**NR**			X	BE	■100	(2-13-02)	....	....	....	....	100	C5	'96	101½	95⅜	95⅜	6.64	6.64
Deb[2] 5.90s 2006	Fa14	**NR**			X	BE	NC	....	....	....	....	....	100	S1	'96	104⅛	94⅝	94⅝	6.23	6.23
Deb[2] 7.12s 2006	Ms27	**NR**			X	BE	■100	(3-27-01)	....	....	....	....	100	G1	'96	103¾	97⅞	97⅞	7.27	7.27
Deb[2] 7.245s 2006	Ao24	**NR**			X	BE	■100	(4-24-01)	....	....	....	....	100		'96	104¼	98¼	98¼	7.37	7.37
Deb[2] 7.20s 2006	jJ18	**NR**			X	BE	NC	....	....	....	....	....	100	M5	'96	112⅛	101	101	7.13	7.13

Uniform Footnote Explanations-See Page 260. Other: [1] Int(min 5%,max 24%)adj qtrly. [2] Issued in min denom $5T. [3] Int(min 5%,max 24%)adj semi-anly. [4] Due 5-19-03. [5] Issued in min denom $10T. [6] Issud in min denom $5T.

Title-Industry Code & Co. Finances (In Italics) / Individual Issue Statistics: Exchange	Ind / Interest Dates	Fixed Charge Coverage 1996 / S&P Rating	Date of Last Rating Change	1997 / Prior Rating	1998 / Eligible	Year End / Bond Form	Million $: Cash & Equiv. / Redemption Provisions: Regular Price	Million $: Curr. Assets / Regular (Begins) Thru	Curr. Liab. / Sinking Fund Price	Balance Sheet Date / Sinking Fund (Begins) Thru	L. Term Debt (Mil $) / Refund/Other Restriction Price	Refund/Other Restriction (Begins) Thru	Capital-ization (Mil $) / Outst'g (Mil $)	Total Debt % Capital / Underwriting Firm	Underwriting Year	Price Range 1999 High	Price Range 1999 Low	Mo. End Price Sale(s) or Bid	Curr. Yield	Yield to Mat.
***Fed'l Home Loan Mtg** (Cont.)*																				
Deb[1] 7.55s 2006	fA23	**NR**			X	BE	■100	....	....	....	....	....	100	G1	'96	101½	98½	98½	7.66	7.66
Deb[1] 7.14s 2006	mS13	**NR**			X	BE	NC	....	....	....	....	....	100	B7	'96	112	100⅝	100⅝	7.09	7.09
Deb[1] 7.44s 2006	mS20	**NR**			X	BE	■100	(9-20-01)	....	....	....	....	100	B7	'96	105⅜	98¾	98¾	7.53	7.53
Deb[1] 7.225s 2006	mN8	**NR**			X	BE	■100	....	....	....	....	....	250	M5	'96	101⅝	97⅝	97⅝	7.40	7.40
Deb[1] 7.09s 2006	mN24	**NR**			X	BE	■100	....	....	....	....	....	500	L3	'96	101½	97⅛	97⅛	7.29	7.29
Deb[1] 6⅞s 2006	mN22	**NR**			X	BE	■100	(11-22-01)	....	....	....	....	150	L3	'96	103⅞	96¾	96¾	7.10	7.10
Deb[1] 6.40s 2006	jD13	**NR**			X	BE	NC	....	....	....	....	....	100	B7	'96	107½	96½	96½	6.63	6.63
Deb[1] 7.14s 2007	Ms12	**NR**			X	BE	■100	(3-12-02)	....	....	....	....	100	B7	'97	105	97⅝	97⅝	7.31	7.31
Deb[1] 6.80s 2007	Ms19	**NR**			X	BE	NC	....	....	....	....	....	100	M2	'97	110¼	98⅝	98⅝	6.89	6.89
Deb[1] 6.943s 2007	Ms21	**NR**			X	BE	NC	....	....	....	....	....	150	M6	'97	111⅛	99⅜	99⅜	6.98	6.98
Deb[1] 7.36s 2007	Jd5	**NR**			X	BE	■100	(6-5-02)	....	....	....	....	100	M5	'97	106⅛	98⅜	98⅜	7.48	7.48
Deb[1] 7.01s 2007	jJ11	**NR**			X	BE	■100	(7-11-02)	....	....	....	....	100	M5	'97	105	97	97	7.23	7.23
Deb[1] 6½s 2008	Fa26	**NR**			X	BE	■100	....	....	....	....	....	300	S4	'98	100	94	94	6.91	6.91
Deb[2] 6.20s 2008	mS8	**NR**			X	BE	■100	....	....	....	....	....	100	M2	'93	99¼	92¼	92¼	6.72	6.72
Deb[1] 6.13s 2008	aO	**NR**			X	BE	■100	....	....	....	....	....	25.0		'93	99	91¾	91¾	6.67	6.67
Deb[1] 6.08s 2008	aO29	**NR**			X	BE	■100	....	....	....	....	....	100	L3	'93	98⅞	91½	91½	6.64	6.64
Deb[1] 6.59s 2008	jD9	**NR**			X	BE	■100	....	....	....	....	....	100	L3	'93	100	93¾	93¾	7.02	7.02
Deb[1] 6.63s 2009	Jj12	**NR**			X	BE	■100	....	....	....	....	....	100	L3	'94	100	93⅞	93⅞	7.06	7.05
Deb[1] 8.02s 2009	fA24	**NR**			X	BE	■100	....	....	....	....	....	100	C5	'94	101¾	98⅜	98⅜	8.15	8.15
Deb[1] 8.29s 2009	mS30	**NR**			X	BE	■100	(9-30-01)	....	....	....	....	25.0	M2	'94	107½	100	100	8.28	8.28
M-T Nts[1] 7.14s 2007	jD15	**NR**			X	BE	NC	....	....	....	....	....	15.0	P4	'92	113	100⅛	100⅛	7.13	7.13
M-T Nts[1] 7.69s 2022	mS15	**NR**			X	BE	NC	....	....	....	....	....	5.50	P4	'92	126½	104¼	104⅜	7.37	7.37
Federal-Mogul	***8***	***0.80***		***4.10***	***2.24***	***Dc***	***65.00***	***2326***	***1771***	***9-30-99***	***3826***		***6056***	***68.8***						
Nts 7½s 2004	jJ	**BB+**			Y	BE	[3]Z100	....	....	....	....	....	250	C1	'98	101	94⅝	94⅝	7.93	7.92
Nts 7¾s 2006	jJ	**BB+**			Y	BE	[3]Z100	....	....	....	....	....	400	C1	'98	102¼	92½	92⅝	8.37	8.37
Nts 7⅞s 2010	jJ	**BB+**			Y	BE	[3]Z100	....	....	....	....	....	350	C1	'98	102⅛	88¾	88⅞	8.86	8.86
Federal Paper Board	***16c***	***Acq by Int'l Paper, see***																		
Deb 8⅛s 2002	jJ	**BBB+**	7/98	A–	X	R	NC	....	....	....	....	....	50.0	M5	'92	106	101⅜	101⅝	8.00	7.99
Deb 10s 2011	Ao15	**BBB+**	7/98	A–	X	R	NC	....	....	....	....	....	200	M5	'91	130	113½	113½	8.81	8.81
Deb 8⅞s 2012	jJ	**BBB+**	7/98	A–	X	R	NC	....	....	....	....	....	125	M5	'92	121½	106⅝	108⅞	8.15	8.15
Federal Realty Inv Tr	***57***	***1.60***		***1.78***	***1.74***	***Dc***				***9-30-99***	***925.0***		***1435***	***64.5***						
Deb 7.48s 2026	fA15	**BBB+**			X	BE	[4]Z100	(8-15-08)	....	....	....	....	50.0	G1	'96	110¾	92¼	92¼	8.11	8.11
Nts 8⅞s 2000	Jj15	**BBB+**			X	BE	NC	....	....	....	....	....	100	G1	'95	103⅛	100	100	8.88	8.87
Nts 6⅝s 2005	jD	**BBB+**			X	BE	NC	....	....	....	....	....	40.0	B10	'95	97¾	89⅞	90¼	7.34	7.34
M-T Nts 6.74s 2004	[5]ms30	**BBB+**			X	BE	NC	....	....	....	....	....	39.5	G1	'98	98⅝	93	94	7.17	7.17
M-T Nts 6.99s 2006	[6]ms30	**BBB+**			X	BE	NC	....	....	....	....	....	40.5		'98	98⅞	90½	91¾	7.62	7.62
M-T Nts[7] 6.82s 2027	fA	**BBB+**			X	BE	NC	....	....	....	....	....	40.0	G1	'97	97½	88½	89½	7.62	7.62
Federated Dept Stores	***59f***	***2.50***		***3.28***	***4.78***	***Ja***	***595.0***	***9498***	***5850***	***10-30-99***	***4658***		***9290***	***38.5***						
• Sr Deb 7s 2028	Fa15	**BBB+**	11/98	BBB–	X	BE	[3]Z100	....	....	....	....	....	300	C6	'98	No Sale		88⅜	7.92	7.92
• Sr Nts[8] 10s 2001	Fa15	**BBB+**	11/98	BBB–	X	BE	NC	....	....	....	....	....	450	G1	'95	108	102¼	102¼	9.78	9.78
• Sr Nts[8] 8⅛s 2002	aO15	**BBB+**	11/98	BBB–	X	BE	NC	....	....	....	....	....	400	G1	'95	108⅜	101¼	102	7.97	7.97
• Sr Nts[8] 8½s 2003	Jd15	**BBB+**	11/98	BBB–	X	BE	NC	....	....	....	....	....	450	G1	'96	110	102⅛	s102⅜	8.30	8.30
Ferro Corp.	***14***	***7.40***		***9.44***	***7.92***	***Dc***	***11.96***	***482.9***	***297.3***	***9-30-99***	***257.0***		***581.0***	***49.5***						
Deb 7⅝s 2013	Mn	**BBB+**			X	R	NC	....	....	....	....	....	25.0	F1	'93	115⅛	93½	95	8.03	8.03
Deb 7⅜s 2015	mN	**BBB+**			X	R	NC	....	....	....	....	....	25.0	C5	'95	109¼	94⅜	95½	7.72	7.72

Uniform Footnote Explanations-See Page 260. Other: [1] Issued in min denom $5T. [2] Issued in min denom $10T. [3] Red at greater of 100 or amt based on formula. [4] Greater of 100 or amt based on formula. [5] Due 3-10-04. [6] Due 3-10-06. [7] (HRO)On 8-1-07 at 100. [8] Co must offer repurch at 101 on Chge of Ctrl.

Company rows (bold italic): Title-Industry Code & Co. Finances (In Italics) | Ind | Fixed Charge Coverage 1996 | 1997 | 1998 | Year End | Million $: Cash & Equiv. | Curr. Assets | Curr. Liab. | Balance Sheet Date | L. Term Debt (Mil $) | Capital-ization (Mil $) | Total Debt % Capital

Exchange / Individual Issue Statistics	Interest Dates	S&P Rating	Date of Last Rating Change	Prior Rating	Eligible	Bond Form	Regular Price	Regular (Begins) Thru	Sinking Fund Price	Sinking Fund (Begins) Thru	Refund/Other Restriction Price	Refund/Other Restriction (Begins) Thru	Outst'g (Mil $)	Underwriting Firm	Underwriting Year	Price Range 1999 High	Price Range 1999 Low	Mo. End Price Sale(s) or Bid	Curr. Yield	Yield to Mat.
[1]Fina Oil & Chemical	***49g***	***n/a***		***n/a***	***6.53***	***Dc***	***245.0***	***3211***	***2825***	***:12-31-98***	***1609***		***6441***	***38.2***						
Gtd[2]Nts 6⅞s 2001	jJ15	A			X	BE	NC	....	....	....	....	....	125	C1	'96	103¾	100⅛	100⅛	6.87	6.87
Finlay Enterprises Inc.	***37***	***1.73***		***1.81***	***1.86***	***Ja***	***4.18***	***399.9***	***265.5***	***10-30-99***	***225.0***		***398.0***	***76.4***						
Sr Deb[3] 9s 2008	Mn	B			Y	R	104.50	(5-1-03)	....	....	[4]Z109	5-1-01	75.0	G1	'98	97⅝	87½	91	9.89	9.89
Finlay Fine Jewelry[5]	***37***	***2.44***		***2.49***	***2.49***	***Ja***	***4.41***	***366.0***	***250.0***	***7-31-99***	***150.0***		***407.0***	***64.6***						
Sr Nts[3] 8⅜s 2008	Mn	B+			Y	R	104.188	(5-1-03)	....	....	108.375	5-1-01	150	G1	'98	99	90	92½	9.05	9.05
FINOVA Capital[6]	***25***	***1.51***		***1.54***	***1.56***	***Dc***				***6-30-99***	***9524***		***11183***	***85.2***						
Nts 8s 2000	Fa	A–	7/96	BBB+	X	BE	NC	....	....	....	....	....	100	S1	'95	102¼	100⅛	100⅛	7.99	7.99
Nts 6.45s 2000	Jd	A–	7/96	BBB+	X	BE	NC	....	....	....	....	....	125	M6	'95	101⅛	99⅞	99⅞	6.46	6.46
Nts 6¼s 2000	fA15	A–			X	BE	NC	....	....	....	....	....	100		'97	101	99⅝	99⅝	6.27	6.27
Nts 6⅝s 2000	aO15	A–	7/96	BBB+	X	BE	NC	....	....	....	....	....	147	L3	'95	101⅜	99⅝	99⅝	6.40	6.40
F/R[7]M-T Nts 'C' 2001	QAug14	A–			X	BE	NC	....	....	....	....	....	100	G1	'98	99¼	99	99¼	....	....
Nts 6⅝s 2001	mS15	A–	7/96	BBB+	X	BE	NC	....	....	....	....	....	100	G1	'95	102¼	98⅞	98⅞	6.70	6.70
Nts 5⅞s 2001	aO15	A–			X	BE	NC	....	....	....	....	....	275		'98	100½	98	98	5.99	6.00
•Nts 9⅛s 2002	Fa27	A–	7/96	BBB+	X	BE	NC	....	....	....	....	....	175	M2	'92	110¼	107⅝	100	9.13	9.12
Nts 7⅛s 2002	Mn	A–			X	BE	NC	....	....	....	....	....	100	C5	'97	104⅛	99⅜	99⅜	7.17	7.17
Nts 6½s 2002	jJ28	A–			X	BE	NC	....	....	....	....	....	100		'97	102⅜	97¾	97¾	6.65	6.65
Nts 6¼s 2002	mN	A–			X	BE	NC	....	....	....	....	....	300	M7	'98	101⅝	97⅛	97⅛	6.44	6.43
Nts 6⅛s 2004	Ms15	A–			X	BE	NC	....	....	....	....	....	200	C1	'99	101	94⅞	95	6.45	6.45
Nts 7⅛s 2004	Mn17	A–			X	BE	NC	....	....	....	....	....	100	L3	'97	105¾	98⅛	98½	7.23	7.23
Nts 6.90s 2004	Jd19	A–			X	BE	NC	....	....	....	....	....	100		'97	104¾	97⅜	97⅜	7.07	7.07
Nts 6⅜s 2005	Mn15	A–			X	BE	NC	....	....	....	....	....	100	C1	'98	102	94	94½	6.75	6.75
Nts 7.40s 2006	Mn6	A–	7/96	BBB+	X	BE	NC	....	....	....	....	....	100		'96	107⅞	97¾	98¼	7.53	7.53
Nts 7.40s 2007	Jd	A–			X	BE	NC	....	....	....	....	....	100	C4	'97	108½	97½	97½	7.59	7.59
M-T Nts 'E' 7.30s 2003	[8]ms15	A–			X	BE	NC	....	....	....	....	....	100	A3	'99	101	99	99	7.37	7.37
[9]Fireman's Fund Mtg	***25***	***1.48***		***2.50***	***2.55***	***Dc***				***3-31-99***	***216.0***		***903.0***	***25.7***						
Nts 8⅞s 2001	aO15	BBB–	6/97	BBB+	X	BE	NC	....	....	....	....	....	138	L3	'91	107½	102½	102½	8.66	8.66
First[10]Amer(Tenn)[11]	***10***	***3.62***		***3.92***	***3.80***	***Dc***				***6-30-99***	***1786***		***3046***	***40.3***						
Sub Nts 6⅞s 2003	Ao15	BBB–			X	R	NC	....	....	....	....	....	50.0	M2	'93	103¼	98⅛	98⅛	7.01	7.01
Sub Nts 6⅝s 2005	jD18	BBB–			X	BE	NC	....	....	....	....	....	50.0	M2	'95	102⅜	94	94	7.05	7.05
First Amer Finl	***35c***	***19.60***		***11.60***	***21.07***	***Dc***				***9-30-99***	***248.0***		***1109***	***22.4***						
Sr Deb 7.55s 2028	Ao	BBB			X	BE	[12]Z100	....	....	....	....	....	100	C1	'98	104⅜	79⅜	79⅜	9.51	9.51
First of America Bank	***10***	***Acq by Nat'l City Corp,see***																		
Sub Nts 8½s 2004	Fa	A–	3/98	BBB+	X	R	NC	....	....	....	....	....	150	M2	'92	112	103¼	103¼	8.23	8.23
Sub Nts 7¾s 2004	jJ15	A–	3/98	BBB+	X	BE	NC	....	....	....	....	....	200	B7	'94	109½	100⅝	100⅝	7.70	7.70
First Bank Nat'l Assn	***10***	***Subsid of 1st Bank Sys,see U.S. Bancorp***																		
Sub[13]Step-Up Nts[14] 6¼s 2005	fA15	A			X	BE	[15]100	8-15-00	....	....	....	....	100	L3	'93	100⅞	97¼	97¼	6.43	6.43
First Bank Systems	***10***	***See U.S Bancorp***																		
F/R[16]M-T Sr Nts 'H' 2000	[17]	A			X	BE	NC	....	....	....	....	....	49.0	M6	'97	100⅛	99⅞	100	....	....
F/R[18]M-T Sr Nts 'H' 2001	[19]	A			X	BE	NC	....	....	....	....	....	25.0	M6	'97	100¼	99¾	100	....	....
F/R[20]M-T Nts[21]'H'[22] 2002	[23]	A			X	BE	NC	....	....	....	....	....	49.0	G1	'98	100⅛	99½	99⅞	....	....
F/R[24]M-T Nts[20]'H'[25] 2002	[23]	A			X	BE	NC	....	....	....	....	....	49.0	G1	'98	100¼	99½	99⅞	....	....
Sub Nts 6⅝s 2003	Mn	A–	8/93	BBB+	X	BE	NC	....	....	....	....	....	100	M6	'93	104⅛	98¾	98¾	6.71	6.71
Sub Nts 8s 2004	jJ2	A–	8/93	BBB+	X	BE	NC	....	....	....	....	....	125	M5	'92	111	103¼	103¼	7.75	7.75
Sub Nts 7⅝s 2005	Mn	A–			X	BE	NC	....	....	....	....	....	150	D6	'95	110⅜	101¾	101¾	7.49	7.49
Sub Nts 6⅞s 2007	mS15	A–			X	BE	NC	....	....	....	....	....	250	M6	'95	107⅜	97¼	97¼	7.07	7.07

Uniform Footnote Explanations-See Page 260. Other: [1] Subsid & data of Petrofina S.A. [2] Gtd by FINA, Inc. [3] (HRO)On Chge of Ctrl at 101. [4] Max $25M red w/proceeds of Pub Eq Off'g. [5] Subsid of Finlay Enterprises, Inc. [6] Was Greyhound Fin'l,see. [7] Int adj qtrly(3 Mo LIBOR & 0.18%). [8] Due 9-22-03. [9] Subsid & data of Fund Amer Enterprises Hldg. [10] See Deposit Guaranty. [11] Acq by AmSouth Bancorp. [12] Plus Make-Whole Amt. [13] Int to 8-14-00, 7.30% aft. [14] Issued in min denom $250T. [15] On 8-15-00. [16] Int adj monthly(1 Mo LIBOR&0.05%). [17] Due 2-16-00:Int pd monthly,3rd Wed. [18] Int adj monthly(1 Mo LIBOR&0.09%). [19] Due 1-17-01:Int pd monthly,3rd Wed. [20] Issued in min denom $100T. [21] Int adj monthly(1 Mo LIBOR & 0.13%). [22] Due 1-16-02. [23] Int pd monthly,ea 3rd Wed. [24] Int adj monthly (1 Mo LIBOR & 0.1%). [25] Due 7-17-02.

Exchange / Individual Issue Statistics (Title-Industry Code & Co. Finances (In Italics))	Interest Dates / Ind	S&P Rating / Fixed Charge Coverage 1996	Date of Last Rating Change / 1997	Prior Rating	Eligible / 1998	Bond Form / Year End	Regular Price / Cash & Equiv. (Million $)	Regular (Begins) Thru / Curr. Assets (Million $)	Sinking Fund Price / Curr. Liab. (Million $)	Sinking Fund (Begins) Thru / Balance Sheet Date	Refund/Other Restriction Price / L. Term Debt (Mil $)	Refund/Other Restriction (Begins) Thru	Outst'g (Mil $) / Capital-ization (Mil $)	Underwriting Firm / Total Debt % Capital	Underwriting Year	Price Range 1999 High	Price Range 1999 Low	Mo. End Price Sale(s) or Bid	Curr. Yield	Yield to Mat.
First Chicago Corp	***10***	***Now First Chicago NBD,see***																		
F/R[1]Sub Nts 2003	QJul28	**A**	12/95	A–	X	BE	NC	....	....	....	....	....	150	F1	'93	100⅝	99	99¾	....	....
Sub Nts 9⅞s 2000	fA15	**A**	12/95	A–	X	BE	NC	....	....	....	....	....	100	S1	'90	106⅝	102⅛	102⅛	9.67	9.67
Sub Nts 11¼s 2001	Fa20	**A**	12/95	A–	X	BE	NC	....	....	....	....	....	100	S1	'91	111¼	104½	104½	10.77	10.76
Sub Nts 10¼s 2001	Mn	**A**	12/95	A–	X	BE	NC	....	....	....	....	....	100	S1	'91	110⅛	104	104	9.86	9.85
Sub Nts 9¼s 2001	mN15	**A**	12/95	A–	X	BE	NC	....	....	....	....	....	100	S1	'91	109⅝	103¾	103¾	8.92	8.91
Sub Nts 8⅞s 2002	Ms15	**A**	12/95	A–	X	BE	NC	....	....	....	....	....	100	S1	'92	109⅝	103½	103½	8.57	8.57
Sub Nts 8¼s 2002	Jd15	**A**	12/95	A–	X	BE	NC	....	....	....	....	....	100	S1	'92	108⅛	102½	102½	8.05	8.05
Sub Nts 7⅝s 2003	Jj15	**A**	12/95	A–	X	BE	NC	....	....	....	....	....	200	S1	'93	107	101⅝	101⅝	7.50	7.50
Sub Nts 6⅞s 2003	Jd15	**A**	12/95	A–	X	BE	NC	....	....	....	....	....	200	S1	'93	104¾	99½	99½	6.91	6.91
Sub Nts 6⅜s 2009	Jj30	**A**	12/95	A–	X	BE	NC	....	....	....	....	....	200	C5	'94	102⅞	92⅛	92⅛	6.92	6.92
First Chicago NBD[2]	***10***	***Merged with Banc One Corp,see***																		
F/R[3]M-T Nts 'G' 2000	QNov13	**A+**			X	BE	NC	....	....	....	....	....	25.0	W2	'97	100¼	99⅝	100	....	....
F/R[3]M-T Nts 'G' 2001	QAug20	**A+**			X	BE	NC	....	....	....	....	....	50.0	C5	'97	100¼	99⅜	99⅞	....	....
F/R[4]M-T Nts 'G' 2002	QJun26	**A+**			X	BE	NC	....	....	....	....	....	50.0	M6	'97	100⅜	99¼	99⅞	....	....
F/R[5]M-T Nts 'G' 2002	QAug12	**A+**			X	BE	NC	....	....	....	....	....	100	F2	'97	100½	99¼	99¾	....	....
Sub Nts 6⅛s 2006	Fa15	**A**			X	BE	NC	....	....	....	....	....	150	F2	'96	101⅞	93¼	93¼	6.57	6.57
First Colony	***35a***	***Merged into Gen'l Elec Corp,see***																		
Sr Nts 6⅝s 2003	fA	**A**	12/96	A–	X	R	NC	....	....	....	....	....	175	F1	'93	104⅝	98¾	98¾	6.71	6.71
First Data	***20c***	***10.35***	***10.23***		***10.91***	***Dc***				***9-30-99***	***2195***		***5612***	***39.1***						
M-T Nts 'D' 6.61s 2000	[6]jj15	**A**			X	BE	NC	....	....	....	....	....	125	L3	'97	101⅝	100⅛	100⅛	6.60	6.60
• Nts[7] 6⅝s 2003	Ao	**A**			X	BE	NC	....	....	....	....	....	200	L3	'93	99	95	94⅞	6.98	6.98
Nts 6¾s 2005	jJ15	**A**			X	BE	NC	....	....	....	....	....	200	L3	'95	106⅛	96⅞	97	6.96	6.96
Nts 6⅜s 2007	jD15	**A**			X	BE	[8]Z100	....	....	....	....	....	250	L3	'97	104½	93⅝	93⅝	6.81	6.81
First Fidelity Bancorp	***10***	***Merged into First Union Corp,see***																		
Sub Nts 6.80s 2003	Jd15	**A–**	1/96	BBB+	X	R	NC	....	....	....	....	....	150	G1	'93	104⅝	98	98	6.94	6.94
[9]First Hawaiian	***10***	***2.65***	***3.05***		***2.67***	***Dc***				***9-30-99***	***7.00***		***2627***	***30.7***						
Sub Nts 6¼s 2000	fA15	**BBB**	2/96	BBB+	X	BE	NC	....	....	....	....	....	100	G1	'93	101	99⅝	99⅝	6.27	6.27
Sub Nts 7⅜s 2006	Mn	**BBB**			X	BE	NC	....	....	....	....	....	50.0	G1	'96	107½	97⅞	97⅞	7.54	7.53
[10]First Industrial,L.P.	***57***	***n/a***	***2.43***		***2.41***	***Dc***				***9-30-99***	***1054***		***2109***	***40.4***						
Nts 7.60s 2007	Mn15	**BBB**			X	BE	[11]Z100	....	....	....	....	....	150	M5	'97	102⅜	92⅞	92⅞	8.18	8.18
Nts 7.15s 2027	Mn15	**BBB**			X	BE	Z100	(5-15-02)	....	....	....	....	100	M5	'97	100⅞	98	98	7.30	7.30
M-T Nts 6.90s 2005	mN21	**BBB**			X	BE	NC	....	....	....	....	....	50.0	M5	'97	103½	91⅜	91⅜	7.55	7.55
M-T Nts 7s 2006	jD	**BBB**			X	BE	NC	....	....	....	....	....	150	M5	'97	102¼	90¼	90¼	7.76	7.76
M-T Nts 7½s 2017	jD	**BBB**			X	BE	[12]Z100	....	....	....	....	....	100	M5	'97	100¼	83¼	84¼	8.90	8.90
First Interstate Bancorp	***10***	***Merged into Wells Fargo,see***																		
Sub Nts 10⅞s 2001	Ao15	**A**	11/98	A–	X	R	NC	....	....	....	....	....	68.0	S1	'91	111	104¼	104½	10.41	10.41
Sub Nts 9.90s 2001	mN15	**A**	11/98	A–	X	R	NC	....	....	....	....	....	150	M6	'91	111⅜	104¾	104¾	9.45	9.45
Sub Nts 9⅛s 2004	Fa	**A**	11/98	A–	X	R	NC	....	....	....	....	....	137	M6	'92	115	106⅛	106⅛	8.60	8.60
First Maryland Bancorp[13]	***10***	***2.88***	***2.73***		***3.38***	***Dc***				***6-30-99***	***896.0***		***2816***	***31.8***						
Sub Nts 8⅜s 2002	Mn15	**A–**			X	BE	NC	....	....	....	....	....	100	L3	'92	108⅛	101¾	101¾	8.23	8.23
Sub Nts 7.20s 2007	jJ	**A–**			X	BE	NC	....	....	....	....	....	200	G1	'97	108¾	95⅞	96⅛	7.49	7.49
Sub Nts 6⅞s 2009	Jd	**A–**			X	BE	NC	....	....	....	....	....	100	S4	'99	101¼	92⅝	93¼	7.37	7.37
First Security	***10***	***2.75***	***2.35***		***2.22***	***Dc***				***9-30-99***	***2582***		***4342***	***59.5***						
Nts 5⅞s 2003	mN	**BBB+**			X	BE	NC	....	....	....	....	....	275	M5	'98	100½	94¼	94⅜	6.23	6.23
Sr Nts 6⅞s 2006	mN15	**BBB+**			X	BE	NC	....	....	....	....	....	150	C5	'96	106¼	94	94¾	7.26	7.26

Uniform Footnote Explanations-See Page 260. Other: [1] Int(min 4.25%)adj qtrly(3 Mo LIBOR & 0.125%). [2] See First Chicago Corp, NBD Bancorp. [3] Int adj qtrly(3 Mo LIBOR & 0.06%). [4] Int adj qtrly(3 Mo LIBOR & 0.10%). [5] Int adj qtrly(3 Mo LIBOR & 0.09%). [6] Due 6-9-00. [7] (HRO)For a Put Event at 100. [8] Red at greater of 100 or amt based on formula. [9] Now BancWest Corp. [10] Now First Indus Realty Trust. [11] Plus Make Whole Amt. [12] Plus Make-Whole Amt. [13] Subsid of Allied Irish Bank plc.

Title-Industry Code & Co. Finances (In Italics) / Individual Issue Statistics — Exchange	Ind / Interest Dates	S&P Rating	Fixed Charge Coverage 1996 / Date of Last Rating Change	1997 / Prior Rating	1998 / Eligible	Year End / Bond Form	Million $ Cash & Equiv. / Redemption Provisions: Regular Price	Curr. Assets / Regular (Begins) Thru	Curr. Liab. / Sinking Fund Price	Balance Sheet Date / Sinking Fund (Begins) Thru	L. Term Debt (Mil $) / Refund/Other Restriction Price	Refund/Other Restriction (Begins) Thru	Capital-ization (Mil $) / Outst'g (Mil $)	Total Debt % Capital / Underwriting Firm	Underwriting Year	Price Range 1999 High	Price Range 1999 Low	Mo. End Price Sale(s) or Bid	Curr. Yield	Yield to Mat.
***First Security** (Cont.)*																				
Sub Nts 7½s 2002	fa15	**BBB**			X	BE	NC	....	....	....	....	....	75.0	F1	'92	106	100	100	7.50	7.50
Sub Nts 7s 2005	jJ15	**BBB**			X	BE	NC	....	....	....	....	....	125	C5	'95	106⅜	96⅛	96⅜	7.26	7.26
First Tenn Nat'l	***10***		***3.16***	***3.15***	***2.63***	***Dc***				***9-30-99***	***477.0***		***3357***	***64.4***						
Sub Nts 6¾s 2005	mN15	**BBB+**			X	BE	NC	....	....	....	....	....	75.0	D6	'95	105½	93⅞	93⅞	7.19	7.19
First Union[1] Corp[2]	***10***		***2.63***	***2.55***	***2.52***	***Dc***				***9-30-99***	***31910***		***47838***	***66.7***						
F/R Ext'd[3]Nts 2000	[4]QJun15	**A**	9/93	A–	X	R	100	....	....	....	....	....	9.00	S5	'85	99¼	99⅛	99¼	....	....
Nts 6⅝s 2004	Jd15	**A**			X	BE	NC	....	....	....	....	....	400		'99	100	97¼	97¼	6.81	6.81
Nts 7.10s 2004	fA15	**A**			X	BE	NC	....	....	....	....	....	350		'99	100⅞	98⅞	98⅞	7.18	7.18
Nts 6.95s 2004	mN	**A**			X	BE	NC	....	....	....	....	....	600		'99	100⅛	98¼	98¼	7.07	7.07
Sub (Reset)[5]Deb[6] 6.824s 2026	fA	**A–**			X	R	NC	....	....	....	....	....	300	C5	'96	107½	96⅞	96⅞	7.04	....
Sub Deb[7] 6.55s 2035	aO15	**A–**			X	R	NC	....	....	....	....	....	250	G1	'95	104⅜	95	95	6.89	6.89
F/R[8]Sub Nts 2003	QJul22	**A–**	9/93	BBB+	X	R	NC	....	....	....	....	....	150	G1	'93	100⅜	99	99¾	....	....
Sub Nts 9.45s 2001	fA15	**A–**	9/93	BBB+	X	R	NC	....	....	....	....	....	150	G1	'91	109⅜	103⅝	103⅝	9.12	9.12
Sub Nts 8⅛s 2002	Jd24	**A–**	9/93	BBB+	X	R	NC	....	....	....	....	....	248	F1	'92	108½	102⅛	102⅛	7.96	7.95
Sub Nts 8s 2002	mN15	**A–**	9/93	BBB+	X	R	NC	....	....	....	....	....	223	G1	'92	108⅝	102	102	7.84	7.84
Sub Nts 7¼s 2003	Fa15	**A–**	9/93	BBB+	X	R	NC	....	....	....	....	....	150	G1	'93	106⅛	100	100	7.25	7.25
Sub Nts 6⅝s 2005	jJ15	**A–**	9/93	BBB+	X	BE	NC	....	....	....	....	....	250	G1	'93	105⅜	95⅞	95⅞	6.91	6.91
Sub Nts 7.05s 2005	fA	**A–**			X	R	NC	....	....	....	....	....	250	G1	'95	107⅞	97⅝	97⅝	7.22	7.22
Sub Nts 6⅞s 2005	mS15	**A–**			X	R	NC	....	....	....	....	....	250		'95	107	96⅞	96⅞	7.10	7.10
Sub Nts 7s 2006	Ms15	**A–**			X	R	NC	....	....	....	....	....	200		'96	107⅞	97⅛	97⅛	7.21	7.21
Sub Nts 7½s 2006	jJ15	**A–**			X	BE	NC	....	....	....	....	....	300	G1	'96	111¼	99½	99½	7.54	7.54
Sub Nts 6.40s 2008	Ao	**A–**			X	BE	NC	....	....	....	....	....	300		'98	105⅝	92¼	92¼	6.94	6.94
Sub Nts 6s 2008	aO30	**A–**			X	R	NC	....	....	....	....	....	200	C1	'93	102⅞	89½	89½	6.70	6.70
Sub Nts 6⅜s 2009	Jj15	**A–**			X	R	NC	....	....	....	....	....	150	G1	'94	104⅝	91⅝	91⅝	6.96	6.96
Sub Nts 8s 2009	fA15	**A–**			X	R	[9]■100	....	....	....	....	....	150	G1	'94	111	99¼	99¼	8.06	8.06
Sub Nts 7.18s 2011	[10]Apr15	**A–**			X	R	Z100	(4-15-00)	....	....	....	....	60.0		'96	103⅞	90⅝	90⅝	7.92	7.92
Sub Nts[11] 7½s 2035	Ao15	**A–**			X	R	NC	....	....	....	....	....	250	G1	'95	115	99	99¼	7.56	7.56
First Union RE Eq SBI	***57***		***1.19***	***1.23***	***0.61***	***Dc***				***9-30-99***	***361.0***		***549.0***	***62.3***						
• Sr[12]Nts 8⅞s 2003	aO	**NR**	9/98	BB–		R	NC	....	....	....	....	....	13.0	S1	'93	101¾	97⅛	98½	9.01	9.01
[13]FirstBank Puerto Rico	***10***		***2.43***	***1.95***	***1.67***	***Dc***				***9-30-99***	***179.0***		***487.0***	***36.8***						
Sub Cap Nts 7⅝s 2005	[14]jd15	**BB+**			Y	BE	NC	....	....	....	....	....	100	J1	'95	99¼	92⅞	92⅞	8.21	8.21
FirstFed Financial	***10b***		***1.16***	***1.36***	***1.68***	***Dc***				***9-30-99***	***1154***		***1383***	***83.4***						
Nts[15] 11¾s 2004	aO	**B+**			Y	BE	105.875	9-30-00	....	....	....	....	50.0	G1	'94	105⅞	100⅛	105⅞	11.10	11.10
Firstar Corp[16]	***10***		***n/a***	***n/a***	***n/a***	***Dc***				***9-30-99***	***5598***		***5282***	***31.6***						
Nts 6.35s 2001	jJ13	**A–**			X	BE	NC	....	....	....	....	....	200	M2	'99	100¼	98⅞	99	6.41	6.41
Nts 6½s 2002	jJ15	**A–**			X	BE	NC	....	....	....	....	....	200	M2	'99	100⅜	98½	98½	6.60	6.60
Fisher Scientific Intl	***43***		***3.49***	***3.03***	***1.55***	***Dc***	***33.90***	***583.0***	***485.0***	***9-30-99***	***1019***		***729.0***	***145.0***						
Sr Nts 7⅛s 2005	jD15	**B+**	12/97	BBB	Y	BE	[17]Z100	....	....	....	....	....	150	C5	'95	96⅜	90⅞	90⅞	7.84	7.84
[18]Fleet Boston Corp[19]	***10***		***3.82***	***4.48***	***3.36***	***Dc***				***9-30-99***	***19789***		***29779***	***66.5***						
Sub Nts 7⅜s 2009	jD	**A–**			X	BE	NC	....	....	....	....	....	500	S4	'99	100	97¾	97¾	7.54	7.54
Fleet Fin'l Group	***10***	***See Fleet Boston Corp***																		
Sr Nts 7⅛s 2000	Mn	**A**	5/98	A–	X	BE	NC	....	....	....	....	....	250	C5	'95	102	100¼	100¼	7.11	7.11
Sub Deb 6⅞s 2028	Jj15	**A–**	5/98	BBB+	X	BE	NC	....	....	....	....	....	500	C6	'98	106¼	86⅝	88	7.81	7.81
Sub Deb 6.70s 2028	jJ15	**A–**			X	BE	NC	....	....	....	....	....	250	M2	'98	104⅛	84⅝	86	7.79	7.79
Sub Nts 6⅞s 2003	Ms	**A–**	5/98	BBB+	X	BE	NC	....	....	....	....	....	150	S1	'93	105	98⅝	98⅝	6.97	6.97

Uniform Footnote Explanations-See Page 260. Other: [1] Was Cameron Fin'l. [2] See First Fid Banc,Signet Banking. [3] Int adj qtrly(3 Mo LIBOR&0.15%). [4] Due 6-15-05. [5] (HRO)On 8-1-06 & 8-1-16 at 100. [6] Int to 8-1-06, 7.574% aft. [7] (HRO)On 10-15-05 at 100. [8] Int(min 4.125%)adj qtrly. [9] On 8-15-04. [10] Int pd mthly Apr 15, etc. [11] (HRO)On Chge of Ctrl at 100. [12] (HRO)For Chge in Ctrl Triggering Event at 101. [13] Now First Bancorp(Puerto Rico). [14] Due 12-20-05. [15] (HRO)On Chge of Ctrl at 101. [16] See Star Banc Corp. [17] Greater of 100 or amt based of formula. [18] D/B/A FleetBoston Finl Corp. [19] See Fleet Finl,Fleet/Norstar Finl,Fleet Mtg,Shawmut Natl.

Title-Industry Code & Co. Finances (In Italics)	Ind	Fixed Charge Coverage 1996	1997	1998		Year End	Million $ Cash & Equiv.	Curr. Assets	Curr. Liab.	Balance Sheet Date	L. Term Debt (Mil $)		Capital-ization (Mil $)	Total Debt % Capital						
Individual Issue Statistics Exchange ↓	Interest Dates	S&P Rating	Date of Last Rating Change	Prior Rating	Eligible ↓	Bond Form	Redemption Provisions: Regular Price	Regular (Begins) Thru	Sinking Fund Price	Sinking Fund (Begins) Thru	Refund/Other Restriction Price	Refund/Other Restriction (Begins) Thru	Outst'g (Mil $)	Underwriting Firm	Underwriting Year	Price Range 1999 High	Price Range 1999 Low	Mo. End Price Sale(s) or Bid	Curr. Yield	Yield to Mat.
***Fleet Fin'l Group** (Cont.)*																				
Sub Nts 8⅛s 2004	jJ	**A–**	5/98	BBB+	X	BE	NC	....	....	....	....	....	250	S1	'92	111⅞	102½	102½	7.93	7.93
Sub Nts 7⅛s 2006	Ao15	**A–**	5/98	BBB+	X	BE	NC	....	....	....	....	....	300	U1	'96	108⅜	97½	97¾	7.29	7.29
Sub Nts 6½s 2008	Ms15	**A–**	5/98	BBB+	X	BE	NC	....	....	....	....	....	250	C1	'98	105½	92⅞	92⅞	7.00	7.00
Sub Nts 6⅜s 2008	Mn15	**A–**			X	BE	NC	....	....	....	....	....	250	L3	'98	104¾	92	92	6.93	6.93
Sub M-T Nts 'K' 7.05s 2012	[1]Aug15	**A–**	5/98	BBB+	X	BE	[2]■100	(8-15-01)	....	....	....	....	25.0	M2	'97	102¼	91⅞	92¾	7.60	7.60
Sub M-T Nts 'K' 7.07s 2012	[1]Aug15	**A–**	5/98	BBB+	X	BE	[2]Z100	(8-15-01)	....	....	....	....	25.0	M2	'97	102⅜	92	92⅞	7.61	7.61
Sub M-T Nts 'K' 7s 2012	[1]Oct15	**A–**	5/98	BBB+	X	BE	[3]Z100	(10-15-01)	....	....	....	....	25.0	M2	'97	102⅛	91½	92⅜	7.58	7.58
Fleet Mortgage Group	***25h***	***Merged into Fleet Fin'l Group,see***																		
Nts 6½s 2000	Jd15	**A+**	5/98	A	X	BE	NC	....	....	....	....	....	200	M5	'95	101⅛	100	100	6.50	6.50
Fleet/Norstar Fin'lGroup	***10***	***Now Fleet Fin'l Group,see***																		
Sub Nts 9.90s 2001	Jd15	**A–**	5/98	BBB+	X	R	NC	....	....	....	....	....	175	M2	'91	109⅝	103¾	103¾	9.54	9.54
Sub Nts 9s 2001	jD	**A–**	5/98	BBB+	X	R	NC	....	....	....	....	....	150	S1	'91	108⅞	103¼	103¼	8.72	8.72
Sub Nts 8⅝s 2007	Jj15	**A–**	5/98	BBB+	X	R	NC	....	....	....	....	....	107	S1	'92	117⅜	104⅝	104⅝	8.24	8.24
Fleming Cos.	***26g***	***1.58***	***1.73***	***1.46***		***Dc***	***39.60***	***1567***	***1249***	***10-2-99***	***1557***		***2113***	***74.1***						
Sr Nts[4] 10⅝s 2001	jD15	**B+**	9/99	BB–	Y	R	103	12-14-00	....	....	....	....	300	M2	'94	103½	93	100½	10.57	10.57
Flores & Rucks	***49a***	***Now Ocean Energy, see***																		
Sr Sub Nts[4] 9¾s 2006	aO	**BB–**	4/98	B–	Y	BE	104.875	(10-1-01)	....	....	....	....	160	M2	'96	110	99¼	109	8.94	8.94
[5]Florida East Coast Ry	***55***	***Coverage not meaningful***																		
• Coll Tr[6] 5s 2001	[7]jj	**NR**	8/93	A	X	R	105	....	*100	....	....	....	[8]12.9	Reorg	'61	98¼	96¼	96⅝	5.17	5.18
Florida Power Corp.[9]	***72a***	***4.73***	***2.74***	***3.74***		***Dc***	***4.50***	***606.0***	***716.0***	***9-30-99***	***1473***		***3577***	***45.4***						
1st 6⅛s 2003	Ms	**AA–**			X	R	NC	....	....	....	[10]Z100	....	70.0	G1	'93	102⅞	97⅜	97⅜	6.29	6.29
1st 6s 2003	jJ	**AA–**			X	R	NC	....	....	....	[10]Z100	....	110	M5	'93	102⅝	96⅝	96⅝	6.21	6.21
1st 6⅞s 2008	Fa	**AA–**			X	R	NC	....	....	....	[10]Z100	....	80.0	M5	'93	108⅞	96⅝	96⅝	7.12	7.11
1st 8s 2022	jD	**AA–**			X	R	103.75	(12-1-02)	100	....	Z100	....	150	S1	'92	110	97¾	97⅞	8.17	8.17
1st 7s 2023	jD	**AA–**			X	R	103.19	(12-1-03)	[10]Z100	....	....	....	100	M5	'93	104¼	87⅞	88	7.95	7.95
Nts 6.33s 2000	jJ	**A+**			X	BE	NC	....	....	....	....	....	75.0	M5	'97	101½	100	100⅛	6.32	6.32
Nts 6.47s 2001	jJ	**A+**			X	BE	NC	....	....	....	....	....	80.0	M5	'97	102⅞	99⅝	99⅝	6.49	6.49
Nts 6.54s 2002	jJ	**A+**			X	BE	NC	....	....	....	....	....	30.0	M5	'97	103⅝	99⅛	99⅛	6.60	6.60
Nts 6.62s 2003	jJ	**A+**			X	BE	NC	....	....	....	....	....	35.0	M5	'97	104½	98¾	98¾	6.70	6.70
Nts 6.69s 2004	jJ	**A+**			X	BE	NC	....	....	....	....	....	40.0	M5	'97	105⅝	98⅝	98⅝	6.78	6.78
Nts 6.72s 2005	jJ	**A+**			X	BE	NC	....	....	....	....	....	45.0	M5	'97	106⅜	98	98	6.86	6.86
Nts 6.77s 2006	jJ	**A+**			X	BE	NC	....	....	....	....	....	45.0	M5	'97	107⅜	97¼	97¼	6.96	6.96
Nts 6.81s 2007	jJ	**A+**			X	BE	NC	....	....	....	....	....	85.0	M5	'97	108⅜	97¼	97¼	7.00	7.00
Nts 6¾s 2028	Fa	**A+**			X	BE	[11]Z100	....	....	....	....	....	150	P1	'98	104¾	88⅝	88¾	7.61	7.60
Florida Power & Light[12]	***72a***	***4.80***	***5.18***	***6.00***		***Dc***	***370.0***	***1618***	***2257***	***9-30-99***	***3091***		***9194***	***39.3***						
1st 5⅝s 2000	Ao	**AA–**	7/95	A+	X	R	NC	....	....	....	....	....	125	M6	'93	100¼	99⅝	99⅞	5.38	5.38
1st 6⅝s 2003	Fa	**AA–**	7/95	A+	X	R	100.64	1-31-00	....	....	....	....	100	M2	'93	101⅜	98½	98½	6.73	6.73
1st[13] 5.79s 2003	[14]jj	**AA–**	7/95	A+	X	BE	NC	....	....	....	....	....	70.0	G1	'93	101⅜	96	96	6.03	6.03
1st 6⅞s 2004	Ao	**AA–**	7/95	A+	X	R	101.58	3-31-00	....	....	....	....	125	S1	'93	102⅜	98¼	98¼	7.00	7.00
1st 6s 2008	Jd	**AA–**			X	R	[15]Z100	....	....	....	....	....	200		'98	103⅛	91⅜	91⅜	6.57	6.57
1st 5⅞s 2009	Ao	**AA–**			X	BE	[11]Z100	....	....	....	....	....	225	N2	'99	100	89⅞	90	6.53	6.53
1st 7.30s 2016	Ao	**AA–**	7/95	A+	X	R	103.43	3-31-00	....	....	....	....	225	L3	'93	103⅞	96⅝	96¾	7.55	7.55
1st 7¾s 2023	Fa	**AA–**	7/95	A+	X	R	104.46	1-31-00	....	....	....	....	150	K2	'93	104⅞	94	94⅛	8.23	8.23
1st 7⅝s 2024	Jd	**AA–**	7/95	A+	X	R	104.11	5-31-00	....	....	....	....	175	K2	'93	104½	92⅞	93	8.20	8.20

Uniform Footnote Explanations-See Page 260. Other: [1] Int pd monthly. [2] Co may red ea Feb & Aug 15. [3] Co may red on Oct 15 only. [4] (HRO)On Chge of Ctrl at 101. [5] Subsid & data of Fla East Coast Indus. [6] Formerly 1st Mtg 'A',5s,2011. [7] Due 11-15-01. [8] Defeased,funds deposited with trustee. [9] Subsid of Florida Progress. [10] In whole. [11] Plus Make-Whole Amt. [12] Subsid of FPL Group. [13] Issued in min denom $100T. [14] Due 9-15-03. [15] Plus Make-Whole Premium.

Exchange ↓ Individual Issue Statistics	Interest Dates	S&P Rating	Date of Last Rating Change	Prior Rating	Eligible ↓	Bond Form	Redemption Provisions: Regular Price	Regular (Begins) Thru	Sinking Fund Price	Sinking Fund (Begins) Thru	Refund/Other Restriction Price	Refund/Other Restriction (Begins) Thru	Outst'g (Mil $)	Underwriting Firm	Underwriting Year	Price Range 1999 High	Price Range 1999 Low	Mo. End Price Sale(s) or Bid	Curr. Yield	Yield to Mat.
Title-Industry Code & Co. Finances (In Italics)	***Ind***	***Fixed Charge Coverage 1996***	***1997***		***1998***	***Year End***	***Million $ Cash & Equiv.***	***Curr. Assets***	***Curr. Liab.***	***Balance Sheet Date***	***L. Term Debt (Mil $)***		***Capital-ization (Mil $)***	***Total Debt % Capital***						
***Florida Power & Light** (Cont.)*																				
1st 7s 2025	mS	AA–	7/95	A+	X	R	103.50	(9-1-03)	....	....	....	....	125	G1	'93	104½	86¾	86¾	8.07	8.07
1st 7.05s 2026	jD	AA–	7/95	A+	X	R	102.73	(12-1-03)	....	....	....	....	135	G1	'93	105⅛	87	87⅛	8.09	8.09
Florsheim Group[1]	*59l*	*1.28*	*1.75*		*0.87*	*Dc*	*4.58*	*133.5*	*56.88*	*10-2-99*	*83.40*		*156.0*	*64.7*						
• [2]Sr[1]Nts 12¾s 2002	mS	B–	5/96	B	Y	R	104.25	8-31-00	....	....	....	....	18.5	S7	'94	108¼	88½	s89½	14.25	14.24
Flowers Indus	*26a*	*n/a*	*n/a*		*4.38*	*Dc*	*23.00*	*704.4*	*714.4*	*10-9-99*	*1116*		*1846*	*59.8*						
• Deb 7.15s 2028	Ao15	BBB–			X	BE	[3]Z100	....	....	....	....	....	200	M7	'98	No Sale		80⅝	8.90	8.90
Fluor Corp	*13c*	*26.81*	*9.30*		*9.04*	*Oc*	*219.8*	*2033*	*2304*	*7-31-99*	*318.0*		*2155*	*31.3*						
Nts 6.95s 2007	Ms	A	3/99	A+	X	BE	[4]Z100	....	....	....	....	....	300	G1	'97	107¼	95⅛	95⅛	7.31	7.31
FMC Corp	*42b*	*4.06*	*2.66*		*3.02*	*Dc*	*76.00*	*1618*	*1392*	*9-30-99*	*1396*		*3289*	*69.7*						
Sr Deb 7¾s 2011	jJ	BBB–	2/98	BBB	X	BE	[4]Z100	....	....	....	....	....	100	M6	'96	106½	95½	95½	8.12	8.11
Sr Nts 6⅝s 2003	mS	BBB–	2/98	BBB	X	BE	NC	....	....	....	....	....	200	M6	'93	98	94¾	94¾	6.73	6.73
M-T Nts 'A' 6¾s 2005	Mn5	BBB–			X	BE	NC	....	....	....	....	....	70.0	M5	'98	97⅝	92⅛	92½	7.30	7.30
M-T Nts 'A' 7s 2008	Mn15	BBB–			X	BE	NC	....	....	....	....	....	100	M5	'98	103⅝	93¼	93¼	7.51	7.51
[5]***Food Lion***	*59c*	*n/a*	*3.45*		*5.51*	*Dc*	*89.80*	*1455*	*1051*	*6-19-99*	*921.0*		*2603*	*37.9*						
Deb 8.05s 2027	Ao15	BBB–	8/99	A–	X	BE	[4]Z100	....	....	....	....	....	150	S1	'97	118	92⅞	92⅞	8.67	8.67
Nts 7.55s 2007	Ao15	BBB–	8/99	A–	X	BE	[4]Z100	....	....	....	....	....	150	S1	'97	111	94¾	94¾	7.97	7.97
Forcenergy Inc	*49*	*2.35*	*d3.79*		*d5.54*	*Dc*	***Bankruptcy Chapt 11***				*689.0*		*591.0*	*117.0*						
Sr Sub[6]Nts[2] 9½s 2006	§mN	NR	4/99	D	Z	BE			Default 5-1-99 int				175	G1	'96	86	35	81⅜	....	Flat
Sr Sub Nts[2] 8½s 2007	§Fa15	NR	4/99	D	Z	BE			Default 8-15-99 int				200	Exch.	'97	86	34	81⅜	....	Flat
Ford Capital B.V.	*25*	***Subsid of & gtd by Ford Motor Co,see***																		
Gtd[7]Deb[8] 9½s 2010	$Jd	A+	12/99	A	Q	BE	NC	....	....	....	....	....	500	M2	'90	125¾	111½	111½	8.52	8.52
Gtd[7]Nts[8] 10⅛s 2000	$mN15	A+	12/99	A	Q	BE	NC	....	....	....	....	....	500	G1	'90	108	102⅞	102⅞	9.84	9.84
Gtd[7]Nts[8] 9⅜s 2001	$Mn15	A+	12/99	A	Q	BE	NC	....	....	....	....	....	250	G1	'91	108¼	103⅛	103⅛	9.09	9.09
Gtd[7]Nts[8] 9½s 2001	$jJ	A+	12/99	A	Q	BE	NC	....	....	....	....	....	300	F1	'91	109	103⅝	103⅝	9.17	9.17
Gtd[7]Nts 9⅞s 2002	$Mn15	A+	12/99	A	Q	BE	NC	....	....	....	....	....	400	F1	'90	112¾	105¾	105¾	9.34	9.34
Ford Holdings, Inc	*25*	***Subsid of & Gtd by Ford Motor Co, see***																		
Gtd Deb 9⅜s 2020	Ms	A+	12/99	A	X	BE	NC	....	....	....	....	....	133	G1	'90	131⅛	113⅞	114	8.22	8.22
Deb[7] 9.30s 2030	Ms	A+	12/99	A	X	BE	NC	....	....	....	....	....	367	Exch.	'98	134⅛	114½	114⅝	8.11	8.11
Gtd Nts 9¼s 2000	Ms	A+	12/99	A	X	BE	NC	....	....	....	....	....	500	G1	'90	104	100½	100½	9.20	9.20
Ford Motor Co	*9*	*1.67*	*2.03*		*2.07*	*Dc*	*20835*			*9-30-99*	*[9]14403*		*170550*	*84.6*						
Deb 9½s 2011	mS15	A+	12/99	A	X	BE	NC	....	....	....	....	....	167	G1	'91	134⅝	115½	115½	8.23	8.22
Deb 6½s 2018	fA	A+	12/99	A	X	BE	NC	....	....	....	....	....	500	G1	'98	104⅛	88¼	88¼	7.37	7.36
Deb 9.215s 2021	mS15	A+	12/99	A	X	BE	NC	....	....	....	....	....	183	Exch.	'98	134¼	113¾	114¾	8.03	8.03
Deb 8⅞s 2022	Jj15	A+	12/99	A	X	BE	NC	....	....	....	....	....	198	B7	'92	128¼	110¼	110⅜	8.04	8.04
Deb 8⅞s 2022	mN15	A+	12/99	A	X	BE	104.153	(11-15-02)	....	....	....	....	250	M5	'92	114⅜	103	107½	8.26	8.25
Deb 7⅛s 2025	mN15	A+	12/99	A	X	BE	NC	....	....	....	....	....	300	L3	'95	110⅛	92⅛	92¼	7.72	7.72
Deb 7½s 2026	fA	A+	12/99	A	X	BE	NC	....	....	....	....	....	250	B7	'96	115⅛	96¼	96⅜	7.78	7.78
Deb[10] 6⅝s 2028	aO	A+	12/99	A	X	BE	NC	....	....	....	....	....	1500	M2	'98	104½	86⅝	87	7.61	7.61
Deb 8.90s 2032	Jj15	A+	12/99	A	X	BE	NC	....	....	....	....	....	502	Exch.	'98	133⅞	111⅛	112⅝	7.92	7.92
Deb[11] 9.95s 2032	Fa15	A+	12/99	A	X	BE	NC	....	....	....	[12]Z100	....	12.0	G1	'92	145⅝	123¼	123½	8.06	8.06
Deb 7⅜s 2043	Jd15	A+	12/99	A	X	BE	NC	....	....	....	....	....	200	G1	'93	118⅛	97⅝	97½	7.95	7.95
Deb 7.40s 2046	mN	A+	12/99	A	X	BE	NC	....	....	....	....	....	500	G1	'96	112¾	93⅛	93¼	7.94	7.94
Deb 9.98s 2047	Fa15	A+	12/99	A	X	BE	NC	....	....	....	....	....	288	Exch.	'98	152⅝	124⅛	124¼	8.03	8.03
[11]Deb[13] 7.70s 2097	Mn15	A+	12/99	A	X	BE	NC	....	....	....	....	....	500	B7	'97	117⅜	95½	95⅝	8.05	8.05

Uniform Footnote Explanations-See Page 260. Other: [1] Was Florsheim Shoe. [2] (HRO)On Chge of Ctrl at 101. [3] Red at greater of 100 or amt based on formula. [4] Greater of 100 or amt based on formula. [5] Now Delhaize America. [6] Co may red at make whole plus 0.5% to 11-1-01. [7] Gtd by Ford Motor Co. [8] Co may red in whole at 100 if certain taxes due. [9] Incl curr amts. [10] Co may red,at 100,for tax law chge. [11] Issued in min denom $5T. [12] Co may red in whole if 95% outstg put. [13] Co may red in whole,at 100,for Tax Event.

Title-Industry Code & Co. Finances (In Italics) / Individual Issue Statistics (Exchange)	Ind / Interest Dates	Fixed Charge Coverage 1996 / S&P Rating	1997 / Date of Last Rating Change	1998 / Prior Rating	Eligible	Year End / Bond Form	Cash & Equiv. (Million $) / Redemption Provisions: Regular Price	Curr. Assets (Million $) / Regular (Begins) Thru	Curr. Liab. (Million $) / Sinking Fund Price	Balance Sheet Date / Sinking Fund (Begins) Thru	L. Term Debt (Mil $) / Refund/Other Restriction Price	Refund/Other Restriction (Begins) Thru	Capitalization (Mil $) / Outst'g (Mil $)	Total Debt % Capital / Underwriting Firm	Underwriting Year	Price Range 1999 High	Price Range 1999 Low	Mo. End Price Sale(s) or Bid	Curr. Yield	Yield to Mat.
***Ford Motor Co** (Cont.)*																				
Nts 9s 2001	mS15	**A+**	12/99	A	X	BE	NC	....	....	....	....	....	350	G1	'91	109	103⅜	103⅜	8.71	8.71
Nts 7¼s 2008	aO	**A+**	12/99	A	X	BE	NC	....	....	....	....	....	500	L3	'96	112⅛	98⅝	98⅝	7.35	7.35
Ford Motor Credit	***25d***	***1.36***	***1.28***	***1.26***		***Dc***	***1515***			***6-30-99***	***69450***		***135852***	***91.6***						
Nts 8⅜s 2000	Jj15	**A+**	12/99	A	X	BE	NC	....	....	....	....	....	500	C5	'95	102⅞	100	100	8.38	8.37
Nts 9½s 2000	Ao15	**A+**	12/99	A	X	BE	NC	....	....	....	....	....	200	G1	'90	105	100⅞	100⅞	9.42	9.42
Nts 6⅜s 2000	Ao15	**A+**	12/99	A	X	BE	NC	....	....	....	....	....	500	G1	'93	101¼	100	100	6.38	6.37
F/R[1]M-T Nts 2000	QAug14	**A+**	12/99	A	X	BE	NC	....	....	....	....	....	200	L3	'97	99¾	99⅛	99¾	....	....
Nts 6.85s 2000	fA15	**A+**	12/99	A	X	BE	NC	....	....	....	....	....	500	G1	'95	102¼	100⅛	100¼	6.83	6.83
Nts 6⅜s 2000	aO6	**A+**	12/99	A	X	BE	NC	....	....	....	....	....	500	S1	'95	101⅝	99¾	99⅞	6.38	6.38
Nts[2] 7½s 2000	mN	**A+**	12/99	A	X	R	NC	....	....	....	....	....	9.20	G1	'85	103⅜	100¾	100¾	7.44	7.44
Nts[3] 6¼s 2000	mN8	**A+**	12/99	A	X	BE	NC	....	....	....	....	....	1000	G1	'95	101½	99⅝	99⅝	6.27	6.27
F/R[4]M-T Nts 2001	QJul13	**A+**	12/99	A	X	BE	NC	....	....	....	....	....	200	L3	'97	99⅞	99⅛	99⅞	....	....
Nts 5¾s 2001	Jj25	**A+**	12/99	A	X	BE	NC	....	....	....	....	....	500	B7	'96	100⅝	99	99	5.81	5.81
Nts 7s 2001	mS25	**A+**	12/99	A	X	BE	NC	....	....	....	....	....	1000	G1	'96	103⅞	100⅛	100⅛	6.99	6.99
Nts[3] 5⅛s 2001	aO15	**A+**	12/99	A	X	BE	NC	....	....	....	....	....	750	M5	'98	99¼	97	97	5.28	5.28
F/R[5]M-T Nts 2001	QDec19	**A+**	12/99	A	X	BE	NC	....	....	....	....	....	160	M2	'97	100⅜	99⅜	100	....	....
Nts 8.20s 2002	Fa15	**A+**	12/99	A	X	BE	NC	....	....	....	....	....	500	G1	'95	107⅜	102¼	102¼	8.02	8.02
Nts[3] 6½s 2002	Fa28	**A+**	12/99	A	X	BE	NC	....	....	....	....	....	1250	G1	'97	102⅝	99	99	6.57	6.57
F/R[6]Nts 7.32s 2002	Mn23	**A+**	12/99	A	X	BE	NC	....	....	....	....	....	300	M2	'97	100⅝	100	100⅛	7.31	....
Nts 8s 2002	Jd15	**A+**	12/99	A	X	BE	NC	....	....	....	....	....	400	M5	'92	107½	102	102	7.84	7.84
Nts[3] 6.55s 2002	mS10	**A+**	12/99	A	X	BE	NC	....	....	....	....	....	1000	G1	'97	103⅛	98⅞	98⅞	6.62	6.62
Nts[3] 5⅝s 2002	aO15	**A+**	12/99	A	X	BE	NC	....	....	....	....	....	150	M5	'98	99¼	95⅞	96	5.60	5.60
Nts 7¾s 2002	mN15	**A+**	12/99	A	X	BE	NC	....	....	....	....	....	400	F1	'92	107⅜	101¾	101¾	7.62	7.62
Nts[3] 6s 2003	Jj14	**A+**	12/99	A	X	BE	NC	....	....	....	....	....	1000	M7	'98	101⅛	96⅞	97	6.19	6.19
Nts 7½s 2003	Jj15	**A+**	12/99	A	X	BE	NC	....	....	....	....	....	500	S1	'93	106½	100⅞	100⅞	7.43	7.43
Nts 6⅛s 2003	Ao28	**A+**	12/99	A	X	BE	NC	....	....	....	....	....	2250	S4	'98	101⅝	97	97	6.31	6.31
Nts 6⅝s 2003	Jd30	**A+**	12/99	A	X	BE	NC	....	....	....	....	....	500	L3	'93	104⅛	98¼	98¼	6.74	6.74
Nts 5¾s 2004	Fa23	**A+**	12/99	A	X	BE	NC	....	....	....	....	....	2000	B7	'99	100	94¾	94¾	6.07	6.07
Nts 7½s 2004	Jd15	**A+**	12/99	A	X	BE	NC	....	....	....	....	....	500	M6	'94	108	100⅞	100⅞	7.43	7.43
Nts 7¾s 2005	Ms15	**A+**	12/99	A	X	BE	NC	....	....	....	....	....	500	M5	'95	110¼	101⅝	101⅝	7.63	7.63
Nts 6¾s 2005	Mn15	**A+**	12/99	A	X	BE	NC	....	....	....	....	....	500	M2	'93	105¾	96¾	97¼	6.94	6.94
Nts 6¼s 2005	jD8	**A+**	12/99	A	X	BE	NC	....	....	....	....	....	500	M2	'95	103¼	94⅝	94⅝	6.61	6.60
Nts 6⅜s 2005	jD15	**A+**	12/99	A	X	BE	NC	....	....	....	....	....	300	L3	'93	103½	95⅛	95⅛	6.70	6.70
Nts 6⅛s 2006	Jj9	**A+**	12/99	A	X	BE	NC	....	....	....	....	....	750	M5	'96	102½	93¼	93⅝	6.54	6.54
Nts 6½s 2006	Fa15	**A+**	12/99	A	X	BE	NC	....	....	....	....	....	300	L3	'94	104	95⅛	95⅛	6.83	6.83
Nts[3] 7.20s 2007	Jd15	**A+**	12/99	A	X	BE	NC	....	....	....	....	....	1000	M2	'97	110⅜	98¼	98¼	7.33	7.33
Nts 6¾s 2008	fA15	**A+**	12/99	A	X	BE	NC	....	....	....	....	....	300	M5	'93	107⅝	94¾	94¾	7.12	7.12
• Nts 6⅜s 2008	mN5	**A+**	12/99	A	X	BE	NC	....	....	....	....	....	300	G1	'93	105⅛	91⅝	92	6.93	6.93
Nts[3] 5.80s 2009	Jj12	**A+**	12/99	A	X	BE	NC	....	....	....	....	....	2300	B7	'99	100⅞	88½	88½	6.55	6.55
Ext'd Nts[7] 5¼s 2000	Ao15	**A+**	12/99	A	X	R	100	....	....	....	....	....	1.72	G1	'85	100	99⅝	99¾	5.26	5.26
M-T Nts 7.35s 2012	[8]May15	**A+**	12/99	A	X	BE	[9]■100	5-14-02	....	....	....	....	60.0	M2	'97	104⅝	95⅞	95⅞	7.67	7.67
M-T Nts 7⅛s 2012	[10]	**A+**	12/99	A	X	BE	[11]■100	7-14-02	....	....	....	....	60.0	M2	'97	104⅞	95½	95½	7.46	7.46
M-T Nts 7s 2012	fA15	**A+**	12/99	A	X	BE	30	....	....	....	....	....	60.0	M2	'97	103½	94½	94½	7.41	7.41
Forest City Enterp	***38***	***1.17***	***1.02***	***1.44***		***Ja***				***10-31-99***	***2717***		***3067***	***88.6***						
Sr Nts[12] 8½s 2008	Ms15	**BB−**			Y	BE	NC	....	....	....	[13]Z108.50	3-14-01	200	G1	'98	101½	92	93	9.14	9.14

Uniform Footnote Explanations-See Page 260. Other: [1] Int adj qtrly(2 Yr CMT & 0.08%). [2] Issued in min denom $5T. [3] Co may red in whole,at 100,for tax law chge. [4] Int adj qtrly. [5] Int adj qtrly(3 Mo LIBOR&0.12%). [6] Int adj qtrly(3 Mo LIBOR&0.1875%). [7] Int adj to maturity. [8] Int pd monthly. [9] On 5-15-02. [10] Due 7-16-12,int pd monthly,ea 15th. [11] On 7-15-02. [12] (HRO)On Chge of Ctrl at 101. [13] Max $66.6M red w/proceeds of Pub Eq Off'g.

Title-Industry Code & Co. Finances (In Italics)	Ind	Fixed Charge Coverage 1996	1997	1998		Year End	Million $ Cash & Equiv.	Curr. Assets	Curr. Liab.	Balance Sheet Date	L. Term Debt (Mil $)		Capital-ization (Mil $)	Total Debt % Capital						
Exchange ↓ Individual Issue Statistics	Interest Dates	S&P Rating	Date of Last Rating Change	Prior Rating	Eligible ↓	Bond Form	Redemption Provisions: Regular Price	Regular (Begins) Thru	Sinking Fund Price	Sinking Fund (Begins) Thru	Refund/Other Restriction Price	Refund/Other Restriction (Begins) Thru	Outst'g (Mil $)	Underwriting Firm	Underwriting Year	Price Range 1999 High	Price Range 1999 Low	Mo. End Price Sale(s) or Bid	Curr. Yield	Yield to Mat.
Forest Oil	***49a***	***1.28***	***1.49***	***0.58***		***Dc***	***3.26***	***70.30***	***64.30***	***9-30-99***	***384.0***		***671.0***	***74.8***						
Sr Sub Nts[1] 10½s 2006	Jj15	B			Y	BE	105.25	(1-15-03)	....	....	[2]Z110.50	2-1-01	100	S4	'99	105½	98⅜	101	10.40	10.39
Fort Howard Corp[3]	***50***	***Merged into James River Corp,see Fort James***																		
Sr Nts 9¼s 2001	Ms15	BBB–	8/97	B+	X	R	NC	....	....	....	....	....	54.9	M6	'93	106⅝	102¼	102¼	9.05	9.05
Sr Nts 8¼s 2002	Fa	BBB–	8/97	B+	X	R	NC	....	....	....	....	....	100	M6	'94	106	101⅝	101⅝	8.12	8.12
Fort James	***50***	***n/a***	***1.72***	***3.88***		***Dc***	***8.00***	***1924***	***1548***	***9-26-99***	***2877***		***4955***	***78.6***						
Sr Nts 6½s 2002	mS15	BBB	8/99	BBB–	X	BE	NC	....	....	....	....	....	100	M2	'97	102⅜	98⅛	98⅛	6.62	6.62
Sr Nts 6⅝s 2004	mS15	BBB	8/99	BBB–	X	BE	[4]Z100	....	....	....	....	....	320	M2	'97	103¼	96½	96½	6.87	6.87
Sr Nts 6⅞s 2007	mS15	BBB	8/99	BBB–	X	BE	[4]Z100	....	....	....	....	....	300	M2	'97	104⅞	94¾	94¾	7.26	7.26
Fortress Group	***13c***	***n/a***	***5.10***	***4.43***		***Dc***				***9-30-99***	***316.0***		***393.0***	***80.2***						
Sr Nts[5] 13¾s 2003	Mn15	NR				BE	NC	....	....	....	....	....	100	B11	'96	105	48⅛	60	22.92	22.89
Fortune Brands[6]	***69a***	***6.10***	***3.98***	***5.91***		***Dc***	***69.30***	***2276***	***2071***	***9-30-99***	***970.0***		***3796***	***27.1***						
• Deb[6] 8⅝s 2021	mN15	A	2/92	A–	X	R	NC	....	....	....	....	....	150	M6	'91	111	104⅜	100	8.63	8.62
• Deb[6] 7⅞s 2023	Jj15	A			X	R	NC	....	....	....	....	....	150	G1	'93	108¼	104	100	7.88	7.87
Deb 6⅝s 2028	jJ15	A			X	BE	[7]Z100	....	....	....	....	....	200	M5	'98	106½	84⅜	84½	7.84	7.84
• Nts[6] 8½s 2003	aO	A	2/92	A–	X	R	NC	....	....	....	....	....	200	M5	'91	108⅜	103½	104⅛	8.16	8.16
Nts 6¼s 2008	Ao	A			X	BE	NC	....	....	....	....	....	200	M7	'98	106⅝	92¼	92¼	6.78	6.78
Foster Wheeler	***13c***	***3.44***	***0.96***	***1.81***		***Dc***	***211.7***	***1726***	***1451***	***9-24-99***	***880.0***		***1485***	***64.2***						
Nts 6¾s 2005	mN15	BBB–	9/99	BBB	X	BE	NC	....	....	....	....	....	200	L3	'95	94	82¼	84	8.04	8.04
[8]FPL Group Capital	***25***	***3.99***	***3.97***	***3.80***		***Dc***	***370.0***	***1618***	***2257***	***9-30-99***	***3091***		***8421***	***36.5***						
Deb[9] 7⅝s 2006	mS15	A+			X	BE	[4]Z100	....	....	....	....	....	600	L3	'99	102¾	99⅝	100⅝	7.58	7.58
Franchise Finance Corp Amer	***57***	***3.23***	***2.84***	***3.43***		***Dc***				***9-30-99***	***501.0***		***1371***	***36.5***						
Sr Nts 7s 2000	mN30	BBB–			X	BE	NC	....	....	....	....	....	150	M2	'95	100¼	99¼	99¼	7.05	7.05
Sr Nts 7⅞s 2005	mN30	BBB–			X	BE	NC	....	....	....	....	....	50.0	M2	'95	102½	96½	96⅝	8.15	8.15
Freep't-McMoRan Copper&Gold	***45b***	***4.56***	***3.83***	***2.39***		***Dc***	***3.36***	***588.1***	***586.3***	***9-30-99***	***2094***		***3127***	***75.5***						
Sr Nts 7½s 2006	mN15	CCC	4/99	CCC+	Y	BE	[10]Z100	....	....	....	....	....	200	U1	'96	74⅞	60⅜	73⅛	10.26	10.25
Sr Nts[11] 7.20s 2026	mN15	CCC	4/99	CCC+	Y	BE	[10]Z100	....	....	....	....	....	250	U1	'96	76	64⅜	75⅜	9.55	9.55
[12]Freeport-McMoRan Res LP	***14a***	***6.26***	***2.24***	***3.16***		***Dc***	***3.00***	***159.8***	***56.70***	***9-30-99***	***542.0***		***412.0***	***130.0***						
Sr Nts 7s 2008	Fa15	BBB	11/98	BBB–	X	BE	[13]Z100	....	....	....	....	....	150	L3	'96	101¼	91¼	91¼	7.67	7.67
Friendly Ice Cream	***27c***	***n/a***	***n/a***	***0.91***		***Dc***	***17.70***	***53.80***	***91.60***	***9-26-99***	***312.0***		***244.0***	***138.0***						
Sr Nts[1] 10½s 2007	jD	B			Y	BE	105.25	(12-1-02)	....	....	[14]Z110.50	12-1-00	200		'97	102	84⅞	85¼	12.32	12.31
Frontier Corp	***67a***	***10.16***	***6.28***	***6.37***		***Dc***	***135.1***	***644.0***	***750.9***	***9-30-99***	***1648***		***1972***	***50.3***						
Nts 7¼s 2004	Mn15	BB	6/99	A	Y	BE	[15]Z100	....	....	....	....	....	300	S1	'97	107¼	96⅛	96⅛	7.54	7.54
Frontier Oil	***49a***	***0.61***	***1.49***	***3.26***		***Dc***	***26.00***	***84.20***	***47.90***	***9-30-99***	***★311.0***		***145.0***	***48.3***						
• Sr Nts[1] 'A' 9⅛s 2006	Fa15	B+	10/99	B	Y	BE	104.563	(2-15-02)	....	....	[16]Z109.125	2-15-01	70.0	Exch.	'98	99⅝	87	86	10.61	10.61
Sr Nts[1] 11¾s 2009	mN15	B+			Y	BE	[4]Z100	11-14-04	....	....	Z111.75	11-15-02	190	B7	'99	99	98½	98½	11.93	11.93
FrontierVision Operating/Capital[17]	***12a***	***d0.06***	***0.02***	***Nil***		***Dc***	***6.07***			***6-30-99***	***881.0***		***1134***	***77.7***						
Sr Sub Nts 11s 2006	aO15	B			Y	BE	105.50	(10-15-01)	....	....	....	....	200	M5	'96	112¾	105	106	10.38	10.38
Fruit of the Loom[18]	***68c***	***2.79***	***d4.33***	***2.47***		***Dc***	***Bankruptcy Chapter 11***				***1121***		***1631***	***68.7***						
◆([19]Sec)Deb 7s 2011	Ms15	D	12/99	CCC–		R	100	....	....	....	....	....	[20]125	G1	'81	97	17¼	s25	....	Flat
Deb 7⅜s 2023	mN	D	12/99	CCC–		R	NC	....	....	....	....	....	150	C5	'93	88¾	35	35½	....	Flat
Nts 6½s 2003	mN15	D	12/99	CCC–		R	NC	....	....	....	....	....	150	C5	'93	95⅝	35	35½	....	Flat
Galaxy Telecom LP/Cap	***12a***	***0.16***	***0.05***	***0.01***		***Dc***	***3.00***			***6-30-99***	***147.0***		***126.0***	***117.0***						
Sr[1]Sub Nts 12⅜s 2005	aO	B–			Y	R	106.15	(10-1-00)	....	....	....	....	120	M2	'95	112	105⅞	106	11.67	11.67
Gannett Co.	***54c***	***9.02***	***13.31***	***22.02***		***Dc***	***54.38***	***982.2***	***916.6***	***9-26-99***	***2497***		***5301***	***18.1***						
• Nts 5.85s 2000	Mn	AA–	2/98	A+	X	BE	NC	....	....	....	....	....	250	G1	'93	100⅝	99	99⅝	5.87	5.87

Uniform Footnote Explanations-See Page 260. Other: [1] (HRO)On Chge of Ctrl at 101. [2] Max $33M red w/proceeds of Equity Off'g. [3] Was Fort Howard Paper. [4] Plus Make-Whole Amt. [5] Co must offer repurch at 101 on Chge of Ctrl. [6] Was Amer Brands. [7] Red at greater of 100 or amt based on formula. [8] Subsid & data of FPL Group,Inc. [9] Gtd by FPL Group Inc. [10] Plus make-whole amt. [11] (HRO)On 11-15-03 at 100. [12] Now Phosphate Res Ptnrs LP. [13] Greater of 100 or amt base on formula. [14] Max $70M red w/proceeds of Pub Eq Off'g. [15] Greater of 100 or amt based on formula. [16] Max $24.5M red w/proceeds of Pub Eq Off'g. [17] Sub & data of FrontierVision Oper L.P. [18] Was Northwest Ind,then Farley/Northwest Ind. [19] Classified Sr Secured Debt. [20] Incl disc.

Title-Industry Code & Co. Finances (In Italics) / Exchange ↓ Individual Issue Statistics	Ind / Interest Dates	Fixed Charge Coverage 1996 / S&P Rating	1997 / Date of Last Rating Change	1998 / Prior Rating	Eligible ↓	Year End / Bond Form	Million $ Cash & Equiv. / Redemption Provisions: Regular Price	Million $ Curr. Assets / Regular (Begins) Thru	Curr. Liab. / Sinking Fund Price	Balance Sheet Date / Sinking Fund (Begins) Thru	L. Term Debt (Mil $) / Refund/Other Restriction Price	Refund/Other Restriction (Begins) Thru	Capital-ization (Mil $) / Outst'g (Mil $)	Total Debt % Capital / Underwriting Firm	Underwriting Year	Price Range 1999 High	Price Range 1999 Low	Mo. End Price Sale(s) or Bid	Curr. Yield	Yield to Mat.
Gap Inc	***59a***	***n/a***	***n/a***	***n/a***		***Ja***	***485.6***	***2617***	***2223***	***10-30-99***	***809.0***		***3364***	***43.0***						
Nts 6.90s 2007	mS15	A			X	BE	[1]Z100	....	....	....	....	....	500	G1	'97	110⅜	96⅝	96⅝	7.14	7.14
GATX Capital	***25c***	***1.91***	***1.93***	***1.57***		***Dc***	***50.20***			***6-30-99***	***1687***		***2116***	***79.7***						
Nts 6½s 2000	mN	BBB+			X	BE	NC	....	....	....	....	....	225	S1	'97	101⅝	99⅝	99¾	6.52	6.52
Nts 6⅞s 2004	mN	BBB+			X	BE	NC	....	....	....	....	....	125	S1	'97	103½	95⅞	95⅞	7.17	7.17
Nts 7¾s 2006	jD	BBB+			X	BE	NC	....	....	....	....	....	350	S4	'99	100¼	98¼	98¼	7.89	7.89
M-T Nts 'D' 6⅞s 2006	jD15	BBB+			X	BE	NC	....	....	....	....	....	200	U1	'96	104⅜	93½	93½	7.35	7.35
Gaylord Container	***16c***	***1.26***	***d0.50***	***d0.13***		***Sp***	***8.70***	***233.5***	***151.2***	***6-30-99***	***925.0***		***843.0***	***111.0***						
Sr Nts 'B' 9¾s 2007	Jd15	B–	8/98	B	Y	BE	104.875	(6-15-02)	....	....	Z109.75	6-15-00	225	Exch.	'97	97¾	86	94¼	10.34	10.34
Sr Sub Nts 9⅞s 2008	Fa15	CCC+	4/98	B–	Y	BE	105.063	(2-15-03)	....	....	....	....	246	Exch.	'98	91	73	86¼	11.45	11.45
GB Property Funding[2]	***25***	***2.00***	***n/a***	....		***Dc***	***Bankruptcy Chapt 11***				***[3]182.0***		***182.0***	***100.0***						
1st[4] 10⅞s 2004	§Jj15	D	1/98	CCC+	Z	R			Default 1-15-98 int				185	S1	'94	73	59⅞	69¾	....	Flat
GBC Bancorp	***10***	***n/a***	***16.90***	***19.05***		***Dc***				***9-30-99***	***89.00***		***217.0***	***41.0***						
• Sub Nts 8⅜s 2007	[5]	NR				BE	102	(8-1-02)	....	....	....	....	40.0	P2	'97	102	94¼	95	8.82	8.81
GE Global Insurance Hldg	***35***	***21.57***	***23.98***	***22.00***		***Dc***				***6-26-99***	***956.0***		***6922***	***13.8***						
• Nts 7s 2026	Fa15	AA			X	BE	NC	....	....	....	....	....	600	M5	'96	No Sale		91	7.69	7.69
GEICO Corp	***35c***	***Merged into Berkshire Hathaway, see***																		
Deb 9.15s 2021	mS15	AAA	4/97	AA	X	R	104.575	(9-15-01)	....	....	....	....	100	S1	'91	113⅜	105¾	106⅞	8.56	8.56
Deb 7.35s 2023	jJ15	AAA	4/97	AA	X	R	NC	....	....	....	....	....	150	S1	'93	110⅜	94⅜	94½	7.78	7.78
Nts 7½s 2005	Ao15	AAA	4/97	AA	X	R	NC	....	....	....	....	....	100	S1	'95	110⅜	101¼	101¼	7.41	7.41
General American Trans[6]	***56a***	***1.90***	***0.36***	***2.23***		***Dc***				***6-30-99***	***1307***		***2360***	***68.8***						
Deb[7] 10⅛s 2002	Ms15	BBB+	5/95	A–	X	BE	NC	....	....	....	....	....	115	S1	'90	112⅛	105¼	105¼	9.62	9.62
Nts 8⅝s 2004	jD	BBB+	5/95	A–	X	BE	NC	....	....	....	....	....	100	M6	'94	112⅞	103⅜	103⅜	8.32	8.32
Nts 6¾s 2006	Ms	BBB+			X	BE	NC	....	....	....	....	....	100	S1	'96	102⅜	94⅛	94⅛	7.17	7.17
Nts 6¾s 2009	Mn	BBB+			X	BE	[1]Z100	....	....	....	....	....	120	S4	'99	102¼	92⅛	92⅛	7.33	7.33
General Electric[8] Capital	***25***	***1.54***	***1.51***	***1.53***		***Dc***				***6-26-99***	***64360***		***200436***	***88.3***						
Deb 5½s 2001	mN	AAA			X	R	100	....	....	....	....	....	[9]500	M6	'81	99½	97⅞	97⅞	5.62	5.62
Nts 8⅜s 2001	Ms	AAA			X	BE	NC	....	....	....	....	....	250	L3	'91	106¼	101⅝	101⅝	8.24	8.24
Nts 8.70s 2003	Fa15	AAA			X	R	NC	....	....	....	....	....	249	S5	'90	112	104⅜	104⅜	8.34	8.33
Nts 7⅞s 2004	mN22	AAA			X	R	NC	....	....	....	....	....	200	S1	'89	112⅛	102⅝	102⅝	7.67	7.67
Nts 8.85s 2005	Ao	AAA			X	BE	NC	....	....	....	....	....	300	G1	'90	117¾	106⅜	106⅜	8.32	8.32
Nts 6½s 2006	mN	AAA			X	BE	NC	....	....	....	....	....	300		'97	107⅛	95¾	95¾	6.79	6.79
Nts 8¾s 2007	Mn21	AAA			X	BE	NC	....	....	....	....	....	250	K2	'90	121⅜	107⅝	107⅝	8.13	8.13
Nts 8⅝s 2008	Jd15	AAA			X	R	NC	....	....	....	....	....	250	K2	'90	122⅜	107⅝	107⅝	8.01	8.01
Nts 8½s 2008	jJ24	AAA			X	R	NC	....	....	....	....	....	250	M2	'90	121⅝	106⅞	106⅞	7.95	7.95
Nts 8.30s 2009	mS20	AAA			X	R	NC	....	....	....	....	....	250	K2	'89	120¼	106⅛	106⅛	7.82	7.82
[10]F/R[11]Nts[12] 2049	mN	AAA			X	R	105	(11-1-19)	....	....	....	....	50.0	K2	'89	99½	99⅜	99½	....	....
[13]F/R[14]Nts[15] 2050	[16]Fa	AAA			X	R	105	(2-1-20)	....	....	....	....	25.0	G1	'90	99½	99⅜	99½	....	....
[17]F/R[18]Nts[13] 2050	[16]Mn	AAA			X	BE	105	(5-1-20)	....	....	....	....	25.0	K2	'90	99½	99⅜	99½	....	....
[13]F/R[19]Nts[20] 2051	[16]Mn	AAA			X	BE	105	(5-31-21)	....	....	....	....	25.0	K2	'91	99½	99⅜	99½	....	....
• Gtd[21]Sub Nts 7⅞s 2006	jD	AAA			X	BE	NC	....	....	....	....	....	250	K2	'91	116⅞	103	103	7.65	7.64
Gtd[21]Sub Nts 8⅛s 2012	Mn15	AAA			X	BE	NC	....	....	....	....	....	450	K2	'92	121⅜	105⅝	105⅝	7.71	7.71
M-T Nts 'A' 5.76s 2000	Ao24	AAA			X	BE	NC	....	....	....	....	....	100	P1	'98	100⅝	99⅞	100	5.76	5.76
M-T Nts 'A' 5.60s 2000	[22]ms15	AAA			X	BE	NC	....	....	....	....	....	255	G1	'98	100⅜	100	100	5.60	5.60
Global M-T Nts 'A' 7.02s 2000	[23]ms15	AAA			X	BE	NC	....	....	....	....	....	25.0	S7	'95	102⅛	100⅜	100⅜	6.99	6.99

Uniform Footnote Explanations-See Page 260. Other: [1] Red at greater of 100 or amt based on formula. [2] Subsid of Pratt Hotel Corp. [3] Liabs subj to compromise. [4] (HRO)On Chge of Ctrl at 101. [5] Due 8-1-07,int pd qtrly ea Jan 15, etc. [6] Subsid of GATX Corp. [7] Int sub to adj for Designated Event&Rat'g Chge. [8] Was General Electric Credit,see First Colony. [9] Incl disc. [10] (HRO)Ea Nov 1:'02,99.6,'05,99.87. [11] (HRO)Ea 3rd Nov 1 fr '08 to maturity at 100. [12] Int adj monthly. [13] Int adj mthly,as defined. [14] (HRO)On Feb 1,2000 at 99.39. [15] (HRO)On Feb 1:2003,99.60,2006,99.87,2009-50,100. [16] Co may pay int monthly or semi-anly. [17] (HRO)On May 1:2003,99.60,2006,99.87,2009-50,100. [18] (HRO)On May 1,2000 at 99.39. [19] (HRO)On May 1,2001 at 99.39. [20] (HRO)On May 1:2004,99.60,2007,99.87,2010-51,100. [21] Gtd by Gen'l Elec Co on Sr Basis. [22] Due 1-14-00. [23] Due 4-25-00.

Title-Industry Code & Co. Finances (In Italics) / Individual Issue Statistics Exchange ↓	Ind / Interest Dates	Fixed Charge Coverage 1996 / S&P Rating	Date of Last Rating Change	1997 / Prior Rating	1998 / Eligible ↓	Year End / Bond Form	Million $ Cash & Equiv. / Redemption Provisions Regular Price	Curr. Assets / Regular (Begins) Thru	Curr. Liab. / Sinking Fund Price	Balance Sheet Date / Sinking Fund (Begins) Thru	L. Term Debt (Mil $) / Refund/Other Restriction Price	Refund/Other Restriction (Begins) Thru	Capital-ization (Mil $) / Outst'g (Mil $)	Total Debt % Capital / Underwriting Firm	Underwriting Year	Price Range 1999 High	Price Range 1999 Low	Mo. End Price Sale(s) or Bid	Curr. Yield	Yield to Mat.
***General Electric Capital** (Cont.)*																				
M-T Nts 'A' 6.12s 2000	[1]ms15	AAA			X	BE	NC	....	....	....	....	....	200	M2	'97	101¼	99⅞	99⅞	6.13	6.13
Global M-T Nts 'A' 5½s 2001	[2]ms15	AAA			X	BE	NC	....	....	....	....	....	15.0	S7	'96	100½	98⅞	98⅞	5.56	5.56
Global M-T Nts 'A' 6.35s 2001	mS15	AAA			X	BE	NC	....	....	....	....	....	250	L3	'97	102⅝	99⅜	99⅜	6.39	6.39
Global M-T Nts 'A' 6.33s 2001	[3]ms15	AAA			X	BE	NC	....	....	....	....	....	500	C1	'99	100⅛	99⅜	99⅜	6.37	6.37
Global M-T Nts 'A' 6.15s 2001	[4]ms15	AAA			X	BE	NC	....	....	....	....	....	200	G1	'97	102⅛	99	99	6.21	6.21
Global M-T Nts 'A' 7.26s 2002	[5]ms15	AAA			X	BE	NC	....	....	....	....	....	15.0	P1	'95	105⅝	100⅞	100⅞	7.20	7.20
M-T Nts 'A' 6.65s 2002	[6]ms15	AAA			X	BE	NC	....	....	....	....	....	500	L3	'99	100⅞	99½	99½	6.68	6.68
M-T Nts 'A' 5.35s 2002	[7]ms15	AAA			X	BE	NC	....	....	....	....	....	200	G1	'98	100	96	96	5.57	5.57
Global M-T Nts 'A' 7s 2009	[8]Jul28	AAA			X	BE	*■100	(7-28-00)	....	....	....	....	100	S4	'99	97⅝	95½	95½	7.33	7.33
M-T Nts 'A' 7½s 2009	mS22	AAA			X	BE	*100	(9-22-00)	....	....	....	....	150	S4	'99	100	97⅝	97⅝	7.68	7.68
Global M-T Nts 'A' 7s 2012	[9]Sep4	AAA			X	BE	*100	....	....	....	....	....	30.0	G1	'97	100⅜	94¼	94¼	7.43	7.43
M-T Nts 'A' 8s 2014	fA20	AAA			X	BE	*100	(8-20-00)	....	....	....	....	225	S4	'99	100¾	98⅜	98⅜	8.13	8.13
M-T Nts 'A' 6.90s 2015	ms15	AAA			X	BE	NC	....	....	....	....	....	250	L3	'98	110⅝	93¾	93¾	7.36	7.36
[10]Gen'l Electric Capital Svcs	***25***	*2.40*		*2.33*	*2.41*	*Dc*				*9-30-99*	*66338*		*231510*	*80.5*						
• Gtd[11]Sub Nts 7½s 2035	fA21	AAA			X	BE	NC	....	....	....	....	....	300	M2	'95	103	102¼	97⅞	7.66	7.66
General Foods Corp	***26f***	*Subsid of Kraft Gen'l Foods, see Philip Morris Cos*																		
Deb 6s 2001	Jd15	A	10/85	AA	X	R	100	....	....	....	....	....	[12]150	G1	'81	101⅛	98⅝	98⅝	6.08	6.08
Deb 7s 2011	Jd15	A	10/85	AA	X	R	100	....	....	....	....	....	[12]200	G1	'81	105⅝	91⅞	91⅞	7.62	7.62
General Mills	***26***	*△7.01*		*△8.11*	*△8.52*	*My*	*46.00*	*1253*	*2018*	*8-29-99*	*1687*		*2784*	*92.2*						
M-T Nts 'E' 5.40s 2008	[13]ms15	A+			X	BE	NC	....	....	....	....	....	40.0	M7	'98	99¼	87½	87½	6.17	6.17
M-T Nts 'E' 5½s 2009	[14]ms15	A+			X	BE	NC	....	....	....	....	....	30.0	B7	'99	100	87½	87½	6.29	6.29
General Motors Acceptance[15]	***25a***	*1.42*		*1.42*	*1.33*	*Dc*				*9-30-99*	*55714*		*125084*	*91.4*						
• Deb 5½s 2001	jD15	A	1/98	A–	X	R	100	....	....	....	....	....	[12]400	M6	'81	101	96¼	s96⅜	5.71	5.71
• Deb 6s 2011	Ao	A	1/98	A–	X	R	100	....	....	....	....	....	[12]400	M6	'81	101	84½	s86⅞	6.91	6.91
• Dfrd Int Deb[16] 2012	[17]	A	1/98	A–	X	R	100	....	....	....	....	....	[12]1214	M6	'82	404¾	354½	s358	....	....
• Dfrd Int Deb[16] 2015	[18]	A	1/98	A–	X	R	100	....	....	....	....	....	[12]1625	M6	'82	333¾	286½	s288¾	....	....
• Nts 7s 2000	Ms	A	1/98	A–	X	BE	NC	....	....	....	....	....	500	M6	'93	102	99¾	s99⅞	7.01	7.01
• Nts 9⅜s 2000	Ao	A	1/98	A–	X	BE	NC	....	....	....	....	....	300	F1	'90	105	100⅜	100½	9.33	9.33
• Nts 9⅝s 2000	Mn15	A	1/98	A–	X	BE	NC	....	....	....	....	....	250	M6	'90	105½	100⅜	100⅞	9.54	9.54
F/R[19]M-T Nts 2000	QOct30	A	1/98	A–	X	BE	NC	....	....	....	....	....	150	M2	'97	100¼	99⅝	100	....	....
• Nts 5⅝s 2001	Fa15	A	1/98	A–	X	BE	NC	....	....	....	....	....	400	G1	'96	101⅛	97	97¾	5.75	5.75
• Nts 7⅛s 2001	Mn	A	1/98	A–	X	BE	NC	....	....	....	....	....	500	L3	'97	104	99⅝	100	7.13	7.12
• Nts 6⅞s 2001	jJ15	A	1/98	A–	X	BE	NC	....	....	....	....	....	500	M6	'96	102⅞	97⅞	98¾	6.96	6.96
M-T Nts 6.40s 2001	[20]ao	A			X	BE	NC	....	....	....	....	....	350	M2	'99	100	99¼	99¼	6.45	6.45
• Nts 6⅜s 2001	jD	A	1/98	A–	X	BE	NC	....	....	....	....	....	500	S1	'97	101½	97¼	98¼	6.49	6.49
F/R[21]M-T Nts[22] 2001	QOct22	A	1/98	A–	X	BE	NC	....	....	....	....	....	50.0	U1	'97	100¼	99¼	99¾	....	....
• Nts 9⅝s 2001	jD15	A	1/98	A–	X	BE	NC	....	....	....	....	....	500	M2	'91	109¾	103⅛	104⅛	9.24	9.24
Nts[23] 5½s 2002	Jj14	A			X	BE	NC	....	....	....	....	....	1000	M5	'99	100⅛	97¼	97¼	5.66	5.66
• Nts 6s 2002	Fa	A			X	BE	NC	....	....	....	....	....	300	B7	'98	101½	98	96⅛	6.24	6.24
• Nts[24] 6¾s 2002	Fa7	A	1/98	A–	X	BE	NC	....	....	....	....	....	1000	M2	'97	104	98½	99⅛	6.81	6.81
• F/R[25]Nts[23] 2002	QApr29	A	1/98	A–	X	BE	NC	....	....	....	....	....	1000		'97	No Sale		99⅜	....	....
• Nts 7s 2002	mS15	A	1/98	A–	X	BE	NC	....	....	....	....	....	500	L3	'92	104¾	99⅝	s100	7.00	7.00
• Nts 6⅝s 2002	aO	A	1/98	A–	X	BE	NC	....	....	....	....	....	500	M6	'95	103¾	98⅛	s98½	6.73	6.73
• Nts 8½s 2003	Jj	A	1/98	A–	X	BE	NC	....	....	....	....	....	500	M2	'93	110⅛	102⅞	102¾	8.27	8.27

Uniform Footnote Explanations-See Page 260. Other: [1] Due 8-15-00. [2] Due 2-9-01. [3] Due 9-17-01. [4] Due 11-5-01. [5] Due 4-29-02. [6] Due 9-3-02. [7] Due 11-18-02. [8] Int pd mthly ea 28th. [9] Int pd monthly. [10] Gtd by & data of Gen'l Elec Co. [11] Gtd on Sr basis by Gen'l Elec Co. [12] Incl disc. [13] Due 12-8-08. [14] Due 1-12-09. [15] See Integon Corp. [16] Pays $10,000 at maturity. [17] Due Dec 1. [18] Due Jun 15. [19] Int adj qtrly(3 Mo LIBOR). [20] Due 9-21-01. [21] Int adj qtrly(3 Mo LIBOR & 0.02%). [22] Issued in min denom $5T. [23] Co may red in whole,at 100,for tax law chge. [24] Co may red in whole, at 100, for tax law chge. [25] Int adj qtrly(3 Mo LIBOR&0.12%).

Title-Industry Code & Co. Finances (In Italics) / Individual Issue Statistics (Exchange)	Ind / Interest Dates	Fixed Charge Coverage 1996 / S&P Rating	1997 / Date of Last Rating Change	Prior Rating	1998 / Eligible	Year End / Bond Form	Cash & Equiv. (Million $) / Redemption Provisions: Regular Price	Curr. Assets / Regular (Begins) Thru	Curr. Liab. / Sinking Fund Price	Balance Sheet Date / Sinking Fund (Begins) Thru	L. Term Debt (Mil $) / Refund/Other Restriction Price	Refund/Other Restriction (Begins) Thru	Capital-ization (Mil $) / Outst'g (Mil $)	Total Debt % Capital / Underwriting Firm	Underwriting Year	Price Range 1999 High	Price Range 1999 Low	Mo. End Price Sale(s) or Bid	Curr. Yield	Yield to Mat.
General Motors Acceptance (Cont.)																				
• Nts[1] 5⅞s 2003	Jj22	A	1/98	A–	X	BE	NC	....	....	....	....	....	1250	B7	'98	102½	95⅛	s95⅝	6.14	6.14
Nts 5.95s 2003	Ms14	A			X	BE	NC	....	....	....	....	....	400	B7	'99	100¾	96½	96½	6.17	6.17
• Nts 6¾s 2003	Ms15	A	1/98	A–	X	BE	NC	....	....	....	....	....	300	U1	'96	102⅞	98⅛	98⅛	6.88	6.88
• Nts 7⅛s 2003	Mn	A	1/98	A–	X	BE	NC	....	....	....	....	....	500	M5	'96	106	98	99	7.20	7.20
Nts[1] 5¾s 2003	mN10	A			X	BE	NC	....	....	....	....	....	1250	M2	'98	100⅞	95⅛	95⅛	6.04	6.04
Nts[2] 6.85s 2004	Jd17	A			X	BE	NC	....	....	....	....	....	1500	M5	'99	100¾	98⅜	98⅜	6.96	6.96
F/R[3]Nts[1] 2004	QApr5	A			X	BE	NC	....	....	....	....	....	1000	B7	'99	99¾	99½	99⅝	....	....
Nts[1] 6¼s 2005	Mn	A			X	BE	NC	....	....	....	....	....	500	B7	'98	103⅝	95¼	95¼	6.56	6.56
• Nts 8¾s 2005	jJ15	A	1/98	A–	X	BE	NC	....	....	....	....	....	200	M2	'90	115	106	104	8.41	8.41
• Nts 6⅝s 2005	aO15	A	1/98	A–	X	BE	NC	....	....	....	....	....	500	M2	'95	105⅝	96	96	6.90	6.90
Nts[1] 6.15s 2007	Ao5	A			X	BE	NC	....	....	....	....	....	1100	B7	'99	100½	92¾	92¾	6.63	6.63
• Nts 6⅛s 2008	Jj22	A			X	BE	NC	....	....	....	....	....	750	B7	'98	103¼	90⅝	s92½	6.62	6.62
Nts[1] 5.85s 2009	Jj14	A			X	BE	NC	....	....	....	....	....	1000	M5	'99	101	88⅞	88⅞	6.58	6.58
Nts[1] 6⅜s 2008	Mn	A			X	BE	NC	....	....	....	....	....	500	B7	'98	105½	93⅜	93⅜	6.83	6.83
• Nts[4] 8⅞s 2010	Jd	A	1/98	A–	X	BE	NC	....	....	....	....	....	500	M2	'90	110	110	106⅝	8.32	8.32
M-T Nts 6.21s 2000	[5]ao	A	1/98	A–	X	BE	NC	....	....	....	....	....	100	M5	'97	101¼	99⅞	99⅞	6.22	6.22
M-T Nts[6] 5.85s 2001	[7]ao	A			X	BE	NC	....	....	....	....	....	200	M2	'98	100½	99⅞	100	5.85	5.85
M-T Nts[6] 5.95s 2001	[7]ao	A			X	BE	NC	....	....	....	....	....	250	L3	'98	101⅛	99	99	6.01	6.01
M-T Nts 5.35s 2001	[8]ao	A			X	BE	NC	....	....	....	....	....	337	B7	'98	99¾	97⅛	97⅛	5.51	5.51
General Motors Corp.	*9*	*2.01*	*1.48*		*1.67*	*Dc*	*158.0*	*3639*	*2596*	*9-30-99*	*[9]1929*		*123840*	*86.1*						
Deb 7.70s 2016	Ao15	A	1/98	A–	X	BE	NC	....	....	....	....	....	500	M5	'96	114⅝	99⅝	100¼	7.68	7.68
Deb 9.40s 2021	jJ15	A	1/98	A–	X	BE	NC	....	....	....	....	....	300	M2	'91	135⅝	114½	116	8.10	8.10
Deb 8.10s 2024	Jd15	A	1/98	A–	X	BE	103.09	(6-15-08)	....	....	....	....	400	L3	'96	112⅛	97¼	97⅝	8.30	8.30
Deb 7.40s 2025	mS	A	1/98	A–	X	BE	NC	....	....	....	....	....	500	S1	'95	112⅝	94¾	95⅝	7.74	7.74
Deb[1] 6¾s 2028	Mn	A			X	BE	NC	....	....	....	....	....	600	B7	'98	105⅞	88¼	88⅝	7.62	7.62
Disc Deb[10] 7¾s 2036	Ms15	A	1/98	A–	X	BE	NC	....	....	....	....	....	[11]377	M6	'96	37	28¼	28¼	....	Flat
Nts 9⅝s 2000	jD	A	1/98	A–	X	BE	NC	....	....	....	....	....	595	S1	'90	107⅝	102½	102½	9.39	9.39
Nts 9⅛s 2001	jJ15	A	1/98	A–	X	BE	NC	....	....	....	....	....	343	M2	'91	108⅝	103	103	8.86	8.86
Nts 8⅞s 2003	Mn15	A	1/98	A–	X	BE	NC	....	....	....	....	....	100	S1	'91	112⅝	105⅛	105⅛	8.44	8.44
Nts 7s 2003	Jd15	A	1/98	A–	X	BE	NC	....	....	....	....	....	255	S1	'93	105⅞	99¼	99¼	7.05	7.05
Nts 7.10s 2006	Ms15	A	1/98	A–	X	BE	NC	....	....	....	....	....	292	M6	'96	109⅛	98⅛	98⅛	7.24	7.24
Nts 8.80s 2021	Ms	A	1/98	A–	X	BE	NC	....	....	....	....	....	524	M2	'91	126	110¼	110¼	7.98	7.98
Genl Physics[12]	*63*	*0.74*	*1.50*		*2.22*	*Dc*	*4.90*	*90.80*	*78.20*	*9-30-99*	*15.20*		*1964*	*51.6*						
• Sr Sub Deb 6s 2004	QJun30	NR				R	NC	....	....	....	....	....	15.0	Mgr	'94	85	53	75	8.00	8.00
General Re Corp[13]	*35c*	***Merged into Berkshire Hathaway, see***																		
Deb 9s 2009	mS12	AAA			X	R	NC	....	....	....	....	....	150	F1	'89	125⅝	111	111	8.11	8.11
Genesis Health Ventures	*30*	*3.33*	*3.31*		*1.78*	*Sp*	*38.87*	*606.6*	*236.6*	*6-30-99*	*1469*		*2371*	*63.4*						
1st[14]A[15] 9¼s 2007	QSep	B	3/99	B+	Y	R	104	8-31-00	....	....	....	....	25.0	B9	'92	94	30	41	22.56	22.54
• Sr Sub Nts[16] 9¾s 2005	Jd15	CCC+	3/99	B–	Y	BE	104.05	(6-15-00)	....	....	....	....	120	M2	'95	99⅝	22	s44⅞	21.73	21.70
Geneva Steel Co.	*66b*	*0.64*	*0.95*		*0.93*	*Sp*	***Bankruptcy Chapt 11***						*440.0*	*86.8*						
Sr[17]Nts[18] 11⅛s 2001	§Ms15	NR	4/99	D	Z	R			Default 3-15-99 int				135	C4	'93	22⅛	12	12	....	Flat
Sr[18]Nts 9½s 2004	§Jj15	NR	4/99	D	Z	R			Default 1-15-99 int				190	C4	'94	23⅛	12	12	....	Flat
Georgia Gulf Corp	*14*	*6.54*	*5.95*		*4.21*	*Dc*	*3.21*	*144.3*	*108.5*	*9-30-99*	*397.0*		*481.0*	*93.6*						
Nts 7⅝s 2005	mN15	BBB–			X	BE	NC	....	....	....	....	....	100	G1	'95	106⅛	90⅜	91¾	8.31	8.31

Uniform Footnote Explanations-See Page 260. Other: [1] Co may red in whole,at 100,for tax law chge. [2] Co may red in whole, at 100, for tax law chge. [3] Int adj qtrly(3 Mo LIBOR & 0.25%). [4] (HRO)On 6-1-00 & '05 at 100. [5] Due 9-19-00. [6] Issued in min denom $5T. [7] Due 4-20-01. [8] Due 12-7-01. [9] Incl curr amts. [10] Int accrues at 7.75% fr 3-15-16. [11] Incl disc. [12] Subsid & data of GP Strategies. [13] See Natl Re. [14] (HRO)For Fundamental Structural Chge at 100. [15] Death Red Benefit,ltd,as defined. [16] (HRO)On Chge of Ctrl at 101. [17] Co must offer 100 for some asset sales. [18] Co must offer repurch at 101 on Chge of Ctrl.

Title-Industry Code & Co. Finances (In Italics) / Individual Issue Statistics / Exchange	Ind / Interest Dates	Fixed Charge Coverage 1996 / S&P Rating	Date of Last Rating Change	1997 / Prior Rating	1998 / Eligible	Year End / Bond Form	Million $ Cash & Equiv. / Redemption Provisions: Regular Price	Million $ Curr. Assets / Regular (Begins) Thru	Million $ Curr. Liab. / Sinking Fund Price	Balance Sheet Date / Sinking Fund (Begins) Thru	L. Term Debt (Mil $) / Refund/Other Restriction Price	Refund/Other Restriction (Begins) Thru	Capitalization (Mil $) / Outst'g (Mil $)	Total Debt % Capital / Underwriting Firm	Underwriting Year	Price Range 1999 High	Price Range 1999 Low	Mo. End Price Sale(s) or Bid	Curr. Yield	Yield to Mat.
Georgia-Pacific Corp	***50***	***1.56***		***1.23***	***1.50***	***Dc***	***64.00***	***4410***	***3953***	***10-2-99***	***5010***		***9516***	***64.2***						
[1]Deb[2] [3]9.95s 2002	Jd15	**BBB–**	11/92	BB+	X	R	NC	....	....	....	....	....	300	B7	'90	110⅜	105⅝	105¾	9.41	9.41
Deb 9½s 2011	jD	**BBB–**	11/92	BB+	X	R	NC	....	....	....	....	....	250	S1	'91	125⅜	110½	110½	8.60	8.60
Deb 7.70s 2015	Jd15	**BBB–**			X	R	NC	....	....	....	....	....	250	G1	'95	106¾	96⅝	97	7.94	7.94
Deb 9⅞s 2021	mN	**BBB–**	11/92	BB+	X	R	104.696	(11-1-01)	....	....	....	....	250	G1	'91	114	107¼	108	9.14	9.14
Deb 9⅝s 2022	Ms15	**BBB–**	11/92	BB+	X	R	104.348	(3-15-02)	....	....	....	....	250	B7	'92	112⅜	104⅞	104⅞	9.18	9.18
Deb 9½s 2022	Mn15	**BBB–**	11/92	BB+	X	R	104.325	(5-15-02)	....	....	....	....	250	G1	'92	115½	104⅝	105¾	8.98	8.98
Deb 9⅛s 2022	jJ	**BBB–**	11/92	BB+	X	R	103.563	(7-1-02)	....	....	....	....	250	S1	'92	110⅛	100¾	100¾	9.06	9.05
Deb 8¼s 2023	Ms	**BBB–**			X	R	103.75	(3-1-03)	....	....	....	....	250	S1	'93	103⅞	95¼	95⅜	8.65	8.65
Deb 8⅛s 2023	Jd15	**BBB–**			X	R	103.376	(6-15-03)	....	....	....	....	250	G1	'93	103⅝	94¾	95	8.55	8.55
Deb 8⅝s 2025	Ao30	**BBB–**			X	R	104.205	(4-30-05)	....	....	....	....	250	S1	'95	107¼	97½	97½	8.85	8.85
Deb 7⅜s 2025	jD	**BBB–**			X	R	NC	....	....	....	....	....	250	S1	'95	103¼	91	91½	8.06	8.06
Deb 7¼s 2028	Jd	**BBB–**			X	R	[4]Z100	....	....	....	....	....	300	M7	'98	101⅜	89¾	90	8.06	8.05
Deb 7¾s 2029	mN15	**BBB–**			X	BE	[4]Z100	....	....	....	....	....	500	M7	'99	98⅞	95¼	95¼	8.14	8.14
Georgia Power Co.[5]	***72a***	***5.24***		***7.00***	***4.58***	***Dc***	***24.60***	***1193***	***1684***	***6-30-99***	***3633***		***7876***	***52.2***						
1st 6s 2000	Ms	**A+**	3/95	A	X	R	NC	....	....	....	....	....	100	M6	'93	100⅞	99⅞	100	6.00	6.00
1st 6⅝s 2003	Ao	**A+**	3/95	A	X	R	100.90	3-31-00	Z100	....	....	....	200	M6	'93	101½	98¼	98¼	6.74	6.74
1st 6.35s 2003	fA	**A+**	3/95	A	X	R	100.73	7-31-00	Z100	....	....	....	75.0	P4	'93	100¾	96⅞	96⅞	6.55	6.55
1st 6⅞s 2008	Ao	**A+**	3/95	A	X	R	103	3-31-00	Z100	....	....	....	50.0	F1	'93	102⅜	95⅝	95⅝	7.19	7.19
1st 7.70s 2025	Mn	**A+**			X	BE	105.19	(5-1-00)	Z100	(5-1-00)	....	....	62.0	M5	'95	107¼	94⅝	94⅝	8.14	8.14
Sr Nts 'C' 5½s 2005	jD	**A**			X	BE	NC	....	....	....	....	....	150	L3	'98	100⅜	91⅜	91⅜	6.02	6.02
Giant Industries	***49g***	***2.47***		***2.34***	***0.84***	***Dc***	***30.61***	***181.6***	***115.5***	***9-30-99***	***258.0***		***393.0***	***65.9***						
Sr[6]Sub Nts 9¾s 2003	mN15	**B+**			Y	R	103.25	11-14-00	....	....	....	....	100	K2	'93	99	95	96	10.16	10.15
Giddings & Lewis	***41d***	***Acquired Thyssen AG***																		
Nts 7½s 2005	aO	**NR**	8/97	BBB		BE	NC	....	....	....	....	....	100	F1	'95	109	97½	97½	7.69	7.69
Gillette Co	***18***	***26.17***		***29.47***	***24.45***	***Dc***	***60.00***	***5445***	***3652***	***9-30-99***	***3270***		***7780***	***53.6***						
Nts 6¼s 2003	fA15	**AA**	6/97	AA–	X	BE	NC	....	....	....	....	....	150	M5	'93	104½	98⅛	98⅛	6.37	6.37
Nts 5¾s 2005	aO15	**AA**	6/97	AA–	X	BE	NC	....	....	....	....	....	200	M5	'93	103¼	94	94	6.12	6.12
Global Marine	***49e***	***4.79***		***7.88***	***6.69***	***Dc***	***35.10***	***173.9***	***113.4***	***9-30-99***	***811.0***		***1869***	***40.6***						
Nts 7s 2028	Jd	**BBB+**			X	BE	[7]Z100	....	....	....	....	....	300	M7	'98	92⅝	85⅝	86¼	8.12	8.11
GlobalStar L.P.	***67e***	***n/a***		***n/a***	***n/a***	***Dc***	***171.0***	***302.0***	***647.0***	***9-30-99***	***1947***		***3067***	***69.0***						
Sr Nts 11⅜s 2004	Fa15	**B**			Y	BE	105.688	(2-15-02)	....	....	....	....	499	Exch.	'97	78	56	69½	16.37	16.36
Sr Nts[6] 11¼s 2004	Jd15	**B**			Y	BE	105.625	(6-15-02)	....	....	....	....	323	Exch.	'97	78	57	68½	16.42	16.41
Sr Nts 10¾s 2004	mN	**B**			Y	BE	105.375	(11-1-02)	....	....	....	....	325	Exch.	'98	75	55	67	16.04	16.04
Golden Books Publishing[8]	***54a***	***[9]d10.87***		***d3.23***	***d5.72***	***Dc***	***Bankruptcy Chapt 11***				***[10]289.0***		***83.00***	***348.0***						
Sr Nts 7.65s 2002	§mS15	**D**	9/98	CCC+	Z	BE			Default 9-15-98 int				150	B7	'92	48	26	41	....	Flat
Golden West Fin'l	***10b***	***1.54***		***1.80***	***2.04***	***Dc***				***9-30-99***	***8922***		***10091***	***68.6***						
Sub Nts[11] 7s 2000	Jj15	**A–**			X	R	NC	....	....	....	....	....	100	G1	'93	101⅝	100	100	7.00	7.00
Sub Nts 10¼s 2000	jD	**A–**			X	R	NC	....	....	....	....	....	115	M2	'88	108¾	103	103	9.95	9.95
Sub Nts[11] 7⅞s 2002	Jj15	**A–**			X	R	NC	....	....	....	....	....	100	L3	'92	106½	101¼	101¼	7.78	7.78
Sub Nts[11] 8⅜s 2002	Ao15	**A–**			X	R	NC	....	....	....	....	....	100	L3	'92	108½	102⅜	102⅜	8.18	8.18
Sub Nts[11] 6.70s 2002	jJ	**A–**			X	BE	NC	....	....	....	....	....	100	G1	'95	103⅝	98⅞	98⅞	6.78	6.78
Sub Nts[11] 7¼s 2002	fA15	**A–**			X	R	NC	....	....	....	....	....	100	G1	'92	105⅝	100⅛	100⅛	7.24	7.24
Sub Nts[11] 6s 2003	aO	**A–**			X	R	NC	....	....	....	....	....	200	G1	'93	101¾	95¾	95¾	6.27	6.27
Goldman Sachs Group	***62***	***n/a***		***n/a***	***n/a***	***Nv***				***8-27-99***	***22745***		***31342***	***72.6***						
Nts[12] 6.65s 2009	Mn15	**A+**			X	BE	NC	....	....	....	....	....	1800	G1	'99	100½	93⅛	93⅛	7.14	7.14

Uniform Footnote Explanations-See Page 260. Other: [1] Credit Sensitive Deb. [2] Int subj to adj for rating chge. [3] Int 10.10% thru 11-2-92. [4] Red at greater of 100 or amt based on formula. [5] Subsid of Southern Co. [6] (HRO)On Chge of Ctrl at 101. [7] Plus Make-Whole Premium. [8] Was West'n Publishing Gr,now Golden Books Fami. [9] 11 Mo Dec'96. [10] Liabs subject to compromise. [11] Issued in min denom $100T. [12] Co may red in whole,at 100,for tax law chge.

Exchange / Individual Issue Statistics	Interest Dates	S&P Rating	Date of Last Rating Change	Prior Rating	Eligible	Bond Form	Redemption Provisions: Regular Price	Regular (Begins) Thru	Sinking Fund Price	Sinking Fund (Begins) Thru	Refund/Other Restriction Price	Refund/Other Restriction (Begins) Thru	Outst'g (Mil $)	Underwriting Firm	Underwriting Year	Price Range 1999 High	Price Range 1999 Low	Mo. End Price Sale(s) or Bid	Curr. Yield	Yield to Mat.
Title-Industry Code & Co. Finances (In Italics)	*Ind*	*Fixed Charge Coverage 1996*	*1997*	*1998*		*Year End*	*Million $ Cash & Equiv.*	*Curr. Assets*	*Curr. Liab.*	*Balance Sheet Date*	*L. Term Debt (Mil $)*		*Capital-ization (Mil $)*	*Total Debt % Capital*						
***Goldman Sachs Group** (Cont.)*																				
• M-T Nts[1]'B' 7.35s 2009	aO	A+			X	BE	NC	....	....	....	....	....	1000	G1	'99	99¾	99¾	80	9.19	9.19
Goodrich (B.F.) Co[2]	***14***	***5.41***	***3.95***	***6.01***		***Dc***	***65.00***	***2145***	***1484***	***9-30-99***	***1527***		***3348***	***54.1***						
Nts 9⅝s 2001	jJ	A–	12/97	BBB+	X	BE	NC	....	....	....	....	....	175	G1	'91	108⅞	103⅜	103⅜	9.31	9.31
Nts 6.45s 2008	Ao15	A–			X	BE	NC	....	....	....	....	....	100	G1	'98	103¼	91½	91½	7.05	7.05
Nts 6.60s 2009	Mn15	A–			X	BE	[3]Z100	....	....	....	....	....	200	M7	'99	99⅞	91⅛	91⅛	7.24	7.24
Nts 7s 2038	Ao15	A–			X	BE	NC	....	....	....	....	....	200	G1	'98	103	84½	84⅝	8.27	8.27
M-T Nts 'A' 6.80s 2018	Fa	A–			X	BE	NC	....	....	....	....	....	130	G1	'98	102⅞	87¼	87⅜	7.78	7.78
M-T Nts 'A' 7.10s 2027	mN15	A–	12/97	BBB+	X	BE	NC	....	....	....	....	....	150	G1	'97	106⅝	87⅞	88	8.07	8.07
Goodyear Tire & Rubber	***61a***	***1.95***	***5.53***	***6.77***		***Dc***	***233.0***	***5628***	***4534***	***9-30-99***	***1673***		***5458***	***31.5***						
Nts 6⅝s 2006	jD	A–	7/98	BBB+	X	BE	[4]Z100	....	....	....	....	....	250	C1	'96	105¼	93½	93½	7.09	7.08
Nts 6⅜s 2008	Ms15	A–	7/98	BBB+	X	BE	[3]Z100	....	....	....	....	....	100	G1	'98	103⅜	91¾	91¾	6.95	6.95
Nts 7s 2028	Ms15	A–			X	BE	[3]Z100	....	....	....	....	....	150	C1	'98	105	87	87⅛	8.03	8.03
[5]Grace(W.R.) & Co-Conn	***14***	***6.00***	***3.10***	***d8.59***		***Dc***	***85.70***	***592.0***	***691.0***	***9-30-99***	***8.10***		***226.0***	***37.6***						
Nts 7.40s 2000	Fa	NR	4/98	BBB		BE	NC	....	....	....	....	....	300	S1	'93	101⅞	100⅛	100⅛	7.39	7.39
• Nts[6] 7¾s 2002	aO	NR	4/98	BBB		BE	NC	....	....	....	....	....	150	S1	'92	100½	100	100¼	7.73	7.73
Nts[6] 8s 2004	fA15	NR	4/98	BBB		BE	NC	....	....	....	....	....	276	M5	'94	109⅞	101½	101½	7.88	7.88
Great Atlantic & Pacific Tea	***59c***	***2.38***	***2.04***	***d2.23***		***Fb***	***144.4***	***1179***	***1123***	***9-11-99***	***885.0***		***1720***	***52.3***						
Sr[7]Nts 7.70s 2004	Jj15	BBB–	4/97	BB+	X	BE	NC	....	....	....	....	....	200	M2	'94	101⅜	95⅝	95⅝	8.07	8.07
Great Lakes Carbon[8]	***14***	***6.64***	***6.52***	***1.37***		***Dc***	***13.00***	***89.70***	***44.70***	***6-30-99***	***283.0***		***394.0***	***74.9***						
Sr Sec Nts[9] 10s 2006	Jj	B+	5/98	BB–	Y	R	105	(1-1-01)	....	....	....	....	65.0	D6	'95	108⅝	108¼	108⅝	9.23	9.22
Great Northern Railway	***55***	***Now Burlington Northern RR,see***																		
• Gen Mtg O 3⅛s 2000	Jj	A	12/98	A–	X	CR	100	....	100	....	....	....	33.5	H1	'45	102	97⅛	98⅛	3.18	Mat.
• Gen Mtg Q 2⅝s 2010	Jj	A	12/98	A–	X	CR	100.25	1-1-01	100	....	....	....	28.8	M6	'46	70⅞	66	67½	3.89	3.92
Great Western Bank,F.S.B.	***10a***	***Subsid of Great West'n Fin'l,see***																		
Sub Nts[10] 9⅞s 2001	Jd15	BBB+	2/93	A–	X	R	NC	....	....	....	....	....	150	F1	'91	109¾	103⅞	103⅞	9.51	9.50
Great West'n Fin'l[11]	***10b***	***Acquired by Washington Mutual,see***																		
Nts[10] 6⅜s 2000	jJ	BBB+			X	R	NC	....	....	....	....	....	225	M2	'93	101¼	99¾	99⅞	6.38	6.38
Nts[10] 8.60s 2002	Fa	BBB+	2/93	A–	X	R	NC	....	....	....	....	....	200	M2	'92	108¼	102¼	102¼	8.41	8.41
Green Tree Financial	***25g***	***Now Conseco Fin'l,see***																		
M-T Nts 6½s 2002	[12]ms	BBB–	2/98	BBB+	X	BE	NC	....	....	....	....	....	220	M2	'97	96¼	92⅝	96¼	6.75	6.75
Greenwich Air Services	***3a***	***Acquired by Gen'l Electric***																		
Sr Nts[9] 10½s 2006	Jd	AAA	9/97	B+	X	BE	105.25	(6-1-01)	....	....	....	....	160	S1	'96	115¼	108¾	108¾	9.66	9.65
Greyhound Corp	***17a***	***Now Dial Corp,see***																		
Sub Deb 10½s 2006	Mn15	BBB–	6/97	BB+	X	R	NC	....	....	....	....	....	150	G1	'86	123⅞	113⅛	113½	9.25	9.25
Greyhound Financial	***25***	***Now FINOVA Capital,see***																		
Nts 7¼s 2001	Ao	A–	7/96	BBB+	X	BE	NC	....	....	....	....	....	100	C4	'94	103⅝	100⅝	100⅝	7.22	7.22
Group 1 Automotive	***59l***	***n/a***	***n/a***	***n/a***		***Dc***	***103.9***	***442.1***	***347.5***	***9-30-99***	***102.0***		***310.0***	***32.2***						
Sr Sub Nts[9] 10⅞s 2009	Ms	B			Y	BE	105.438	(2-29-04)	....	....	[13]Z110.875	3-1-02	100	G1	'99	100¼	93¾	99	10.98	10.98
[14]GS Technologies Oper	***66d***	***1.04***	***1.80***	***0.31***		***Dc***	***8.74***	***251.0***	***136.0***	***6-30-99***	***342.0***		***403.0***	***86.6***						
Sr[15]Nts[16] 12s 2004	mS	B			Y	R	106	8-31-00	....	....	....	....	125	G1	'94	92	47	47	....	....
[15]Sr[16]Nts 12¼s 2005	aO	B			Y	R	106.125	(10-1-00)	....	....	....	....	125	G1	'95	92	45	45	....	....
GTE California	***67a***	***9.56***	***11.14***	***10.60***		***Dc***	***2.90***	***744.0***	***1203***	***6-30-99***	***1691***		***3606***	***51.4***						
Deb 'A' 5⅝s 2001	Fa	AA–	5/95	A+	X	R	NC	....	....	....	....	....	300	M6	'94	101⅛	98⅞	98⅞	5.69	5.69
Deb 'B' 6¾s 2004	Ms15	AA–	5/95	A+	X	R	NC	....	....	....	....	....	250	G1	'94	106½	98⅝	98⅝	6.84	6.84

Uniform Footnote Explanations-See Page 260. Other: [1] Co may red in whole, at 100, for tax law chge. [2] See Coltec Industries. [3] Red at greater of 100 or amt based on formula. [4] Plus Make-Whole Amt. [5] Subsid & data of Grace(W.R.)& Co. [6] Gtd by Grace(W.R.) & Co. [7] Issued in min denom $10T. [8] Subsid of Horsehead Indus. [9] (HRO)On Chge of Ctrl at 101. [10] Issued in min denom $100T. [11] See Great Western Bank. [12] Due 9-26-02. [13] Max $35M red w/proceeds of Equity Off'g. [14] Gtd by & data of GS Technologies Corp. [15] Gtd by GS Technologies Corp. [16] Co must offer repurch at 101 on Chge of Ctrl.

Title-Industry Code & Co. Finances (In Italics) / Individual Issue Statistics / Exchange	Ind / Interest Dates	Fixed Charge Coverage 1996 / S&P Rating	1997 / Date of Last Rating Change	1998 / Prior Rating	Eligible	Year End / Bond Form	Million $ Cash & Equiv. / Regular Price	Curr. Assets / Regular (Begins) Thru	Curr. Liab. / Sinking Fund Price	Balance Sheet Date / Sinking Fund (Begins) Thru	L. Term Debt (Mil $) / Refund/Other Restriction Price	Refund/Other Restriction (Begins) Thru	Capital-ization (Mil $) / Outst'g (Mil $)	Total Debt % Capital / Underwriting Firm	Underwriting Year	Price Range 1999 High	Price Range 1999 Low	Mo. End Price Sale(s) or Bid	Curr. Yield	Yield to Mat.
GTE California (Cont.)																				
Deb 'C' 8.07s 2024	Ao15	**AA–**	5/95	A+	X	R	104.04	(4-15-04)	....	....	....	....	250	S1	'94	112¾	96¼	96½	8.36	8.36
Deb 'D' 7s 2008	Mn	**AA–**			X	BE	NC	....	....	....	....	....	100	G1	'96	111⅛	97⅜	97⅜	7.19	7.19
Deb 'E' 6.70s 2009	mS	**AA–**			X	BE	NC	....	....	....	....	....	300	M2	'97	109⅝	94½	94½	7.09	7.09
Deb 'F' 6¾s 2027	Mn15	**AA–**			X	BE	NC	....	....	....	....	....	200	S4	'98	106⅞	87½	87⅝	7.70	7.70
Deb 'G' 5½s 2009	Jj15	**AA–**			X	BE	NC	....	....	....	....	....	225	M5	'99	100	87¼	87¼	6.30	6.30
GTE Corp	***67a***	***4.76***	***4.33***	***4.43***		***Dc***	***3555***	***11526***	***13662***	***9-30-99***	***14278***		***32306***	***66.2***						
Deb 9⅜s 2000	jD	**A**	3/97	A–	X	R	NC	....	....	....	....	....	500	S1	'90	107⅝	102¼	102¼	9.17	9.17
Deb 9.10s 2003	Jd	**A**	3/97	A–	X	R	NC	....	....	....	....	....	500	P1	'91	115⅛	105¾	105¾	8.61	8.60
Deb 6.36s 2006	Ao15	**A**			X	BE	NC	....	....	....	....	....	450	G1	'98	105½	94¾	94¾	6.71	6.71
Deb 6.46s 2008	Ao15	**A**			X	BE	NC	....	....	....	....	....	250	G1	'98	106⅞	94	94	6.87	6.87
Deb 7.51s 2009	Ao	**A**			X	BE	NC	....	....	....	....	....	500	S1	'97	115⅛	100¼	100⅝	7.46	7.46
Deb 6.84s 2018	Ao15	**A**			X	BE	NC	....	....	....	....	....	600	G1	'98	108	91⅛	91¼	7.50	7.50
Deb 10¼s 2020	mN	**A**	3/97	A–	X	R	104.62	(11-1-00)	....	....	....	....	400	P1	'90	114⅜	106⅞	106⅞	9.59	9.59
Deb 8¾s 2021	mN	**A**	3/97	A–	X	R	NC	....	....	....	....	....	300	M2	'91	130¾	107⅞	108	8.10	8.10
Deb 7.83s 2023	mN	**A**	3/97	A–	X	R	103.92	(5-1-03)	....	....	....	....	500	G1	'93	110	95⅜	95⅜	8.21	8.21
Deb 7.90s 2027	Fa	**A**	3/97	A–	X	BE	103.95	(2-1-07)	....	....	....	....	500	G1	'97	111½	95⅞	96	8.23	8.23
Deb 6.94s 2028	Ao15	**A**			X	BE	NC	....	....	....	....	....	800	G1	'98	109⅝	90¼	90¼	7.69	7.69
M-T Nts 'A' 6.39s 2000	[1]fa	**A**			X	BE	NC	....	....	....	....	....	100	S1	'97	102	100	100	6.39	6.39
M-T Nts 'A' 6.56s 2002	[2]fa	**A**			X	BE	NC	....	....	....	....	....	105	G1	'97	104¼	99⅜	99⅜	6.60	6.60
M-T Nts 'A' 6.60s 2005	[3]fa	**A**			X	BE	NC	....	....	....	....	....	75.0	S1	'97	106½	97	97	6.80	6.80
GTE Florida	***67a***	***6.24***	***6.86***	***5.45***		***Dc***	***108.0***	***1271***	***1381***	***6-30-99***	***889.0***		***2725***	***71.0***						
Deb 'A' 6.31s 2002	jD15	**A+**	3/97	AA–	X	R	NC	....	....	....	....	....	200	M2	'93	103⅝	98⅛	98⅛	6.43	6.43
Deb 'B' 7.41s 2023	jD15	**A+**	3/97	AA–	X	R	103.71	(12-15-03)	....	....	....	....	200	M2	'93	107⅝	91⅞	92	8.05	8.05
Deb 'C' 7¼s 2025	aO15	**A+**	3/97	AA–	X	R	103.23	(10-15-05)	....	....	....	....	100	C5	'95	107⅞	89¾	89⅞	8.07	8.07
Deb 'D' 6¼s 2005	mN15	**A+**	3/97	AA–	X	R	NC	....	....	....	....	....	100	U1	'95	105	95	95	6.58	6.58
Deb 'E' 6.86s 2028	Fa	**A+**			X	BE	NC	....	....	....	....	....	300	B7	'98	108⅞	89⅛	89¾	7.64	7.64
GTE Hawaiian Tel	***67a***	***3.05***	***3.76***	***3.62***		***Dc***	***1.40***	***198.0***	***258.0***	***6-30-99***	***462.0***		***942.0***	***58.7***						
1st BB 6¾s 2005	Fa15	**A**	3/97	BBB+	X	R	NC	....	Z100	....	....	....	125	F1	'93	105½	97⅛	97⅛	6.95	6.95
Deb 'A' 7s 2006	Fa	**A**	3/97	BBB+	X	R	NC	....	....	....	....	....	150	M2	'95	107⅜	96½	96½	7.25	7.25
Deb 7⅜s 2006	mS	**A**	3/97	BBB+	X	BE	NC	....	....	....	....	....	150	G1	'96	110⅜	98	98	7.53	7.52
GTE North Inc	***67a***	***8.66***	***10.48***	***7.20***		***Dc***	***0.40***	***1086***	***1140***	***6-30-99***	***1771***		***3827***	***58.6***						
1st 8½s 2031	jD15	**AA–**	3/97	AA	X	R	104.88	(12-15-01)	....	....	....	....	250	F1	'91	111⅜	100⅛	100¼	8.48	8.48
Deb 'A' 6s 2004	Jj15	**AA–**	3/97	AA	X	R	NC	....	....	....	....	....	250	D4	'94	103⅛	95⅞	95⅞	6.26	6.26
Deb 'C' 7⅝s 2026	Mn15	**AA–**			X	BE	103.25	(5-15-06)	....	....	....	....	200	B7	'96	108¾	91⅜	91½	8.33	8.33
Deb 'D' 6.90s 2008	mN	**AA–**			X	BE	NC	....	....	....	....	....	250	M6	'96	109⅝	96⅛	96¼	7.17	7.17
Deb 'E' 6.40s 2005	Fa15	**AA–**			X	BE	NC	....	....	....	....	....	150	G1	'97	105¼	96½	96½	6.63	6.63
Deb 'F' 6⅜s 2010	Fa15	**AA–**			X	BE	NC	....	....	....	....	....	200	M2	'98	107	92½	92⅝	6.88	6.88
Deb 'G' 6.73s 2028	Fa15	**AA–**			X	BE	NC	....	....	....	....	....	200	M2	'98	107⅜	86½	86½	7.78	7.78
Deb 'H' 5.65s 2008	mN15	**AA–**			X	BE	NC	....	....	....	....	....	250	G1	'98	101⅝	88¾	88¾	6.37	6.37
GTE Northwest	***67a***	***6.53***	***8.17***	***7.53***		***Dc***	***0.10***	***238.0***	***281.0***	***6-30-99***	***766.0***		***1333***	***58.4***						
Deb 'A' 7⅜s 2001	Mn	**AA–**	10/98	A+	X	R	NC	....	....	....	....	....	200	M6	'94	104¾	100½	100½	7.34	7.34
Deb 'B' 7⅞s 2026	Jd	**AA–**	10/98	A+	X	BE	103.23	(6-1-06)	....	....	....	....	175	S7	'96	110⅝	94½	94⅝	8.32	8.32
Deb 'C' 6.30s 2010	Jd	**AA–**	10/98	A+	X	BE	NC	....	....	....	....	....	175	M5	'98	106⅛	91	91	6.92	6.92
Deb 'D' 5.55s 2008	aO15	**AA–**			X	BE	NC	....	....	....	....	....	200	M2	'98	100⅝	87⅜	87⅜	6.35	6.35

Uniform Footnote Explanations-See Page 260. Other: [1] Due 9-11-00. [2] Due 8-14-02. [3] Due 9-22-05.

Title-Industry Code & Co. Finances (In Italics) / Individual Issue Statistics (Exchange)	Ind / Interest Dates	Fixed Charge Coverage 1996 / S&P Rating	Date of Last Rating Change	1997 / Prior Rating	1998 / Eligible	Year End / Bond Form	Cash & Equiv. (Million $) / Redemption Provisions: Regular Price	Curr. Assets (Million $) / Regular (Begins) Thru	Curr. Liab. / Sinking Fund Price	Balance Sheet Date / Sinking Fund (Begins) Thru	L. Term Debt (Mil $) / Refund/Other Restriction Price	Refund/Other Restriction (Begins) Thru	Capitalization (Mil $) / Outst'g (Mil $)	Total Debt % Capital / Underwriting Firm	Underwriting Year	Price Range 1999 High	Price Range 1999 Low	Mo. End Price Sale(s) or Bid	Curr. Yield	Yield to Mat.
GTE South Inc	***67a***	***10.09***		***9.55***	***8.12***	***Dc***	***1.20***	***329.0***	***414.0***	***6-30-99***	***797.0***		***1620***	***56.4***						
Deb 7¼s 2002	fA	AA–	3/97	A+	X	R	NC	....	....	....	....	....	150	S1	'94	105⅞	100⅛	100⅛	7.24	7.24
Deb 'C' 6s 2008	Fa15	AA–	3/97	A+	X	R	NC	....	....	....	....	....	125	G1	'96	103⅜	91⅛	91⅛	6.58	6.58
Deb 'D' 7½s 2026	Ms15	AA–	3/97	A+	X	R	103.10	(3-15-06)	....	....	....	....	250	P1	'96	108⅛	90½	90⅝	8.28	8.28
Deb 'E' 6⅛s 2007	Jd15	AA–			X	BE	NC	....	....	....	....	....	225	B7	'98	104⅜	92¼	92¼	6.64	6.64
GTE Southwest	***67a***	***8.10***		***8.17***	***6.75***	***Dc***	***6.80***	***956.0***	***792.0***	***6-30-99***	***693.0***		***2047***	***53.4***						
1st 8½s 2031	mN15	AA–	3/97	A+	X	R	NC	....	....	....	....	....	100	L3	'91	129	106½	106⅞	7.95	7.95
Deb 'B' 6.54s 2005	jD	AA–	3/97	A+	X	R	NC	....	....	....	....	....	250	P1	'93	106⅛	96⅝	96⅝	6.77	6.77
Deb 'C' 6s 2006	Jj15	AA–	3/97	A+	X	R	NC	....	....	....	....	....	150	B7	'96	103¼	93⅛	93⅛	6.44	6.44
Deb 6.23s 2007	Jj	AA–			X	BE	NC	....	....	....	....	....	150	M2	'98	104⅝	92¾	92¾	6.72	6.72
Guess? Inc	***68***	***6.92***		***3.61***	***4.36***	***Dc***	***44.93***	***209.2***	***82.02***	***9-25-99***	***95.30***		***213.0***	***43.9***						
Sr Sub[1]Nts'B' 9½s 2003	fA15	BB–			Y	R	102.375	8-14-00	....	....	....	....	99.0	M2	'93	101½	96½	101½	9.36	9.36
Guidant Corp	***43***	***n/a***		***n/a***	***n/a***	***Dc***	***26.00***	***873.0***	***781.0***	***9-30-99***	***570.0***		***879.0***	***41.1***						
Nts 6.15s 2006	Fa15	A–			X	BE	NC	....	....	....	....	....	350	M5	'99	99⅞	92¼	92¼	6.67	6.67
Guitar Center Management[2]	***59l***	***n/a***		***n/a***	***3.85***	***Dc***	***0.40***	***167.0***	***105.0***	***9-30-99***	***69.80***		***103.0***	***67.7***						
Sr Nts[3] 11s 2006	jJ	B+			Y	BE	105.50	(7-1-01)	....	....	....	....	66.7	Exch.	'96	106½	97	98	11.22	11.22
Gulf Mobile & Ohio	***55***	***Now Illinois Central Gulf,see***																		
• Inc Deb A 5s 2056	jD	NR	7/94	BBB–		CR	100	....	....	....	....	....	7.60		'58	68⅛	56½	58	....	Flat
Gulf Power Co.[4]	***72a***	***4.30***		***4.08***	***3.03***	***Dc***	***3.30***	***166.0***	***190.0***	***6-30-99***	***402.0***		***930.0***	***55.3***						
1st 6⅛s 2003	jJ	AA–	10/97	A+	X	R	100.66	6-30-00	Z100	....	....	....	30.0	M2	'93	100⅝	96½	96½	6.35	6.35
1st 6½s 2006	mN	AA–	10/97	A+	X	R	[5]Z100	....	....	....	....	....	25.0	C5	'96	106	94⅝	94⅝	6.87	6.87
1st 6⅞s 2026	Jj	AA–	10/97	A+	X	R	102.88	(1-1-06)	Z100	(1-1-06)	....	....	30.0		'96	104	86⅞	86⅞	7.91	7.91
Sr Nts 'B' 7.05s 2004	fA15	A			X	BE	NC	....	....	....	....	....	50.0	B7	'99	101⅜	98	98	7.19	7.19
Gulf States Steel	***66***	***0.97***		***0.39***	***0.89***	***Oc***	***5.10***	***76.00***	***71.00***	***7-31-99***	***[6]228.0***		***192.0***	***119.0***						
1st[3] 13½s 2003	§Ao15	NR	7/99	D	Z	BE			Default 4-15-99 int				190	Exch.	'95	31½	10	10	....	Flat
[7]Gulf States Utilities	***72a***	***2.48***		***1.44***	***1.42***	***Dc***	***79.40***	***612.0***	***437.0***	***6-30-99***	***1752***		***3561***	***51.5***						
1st A 6.41s 2001	fA	BBB–	3/95	BBB	X	R	NC	....	....	....	....	....	170	G1	'93	102¼	98⅝	98⅝	6.50	6.50
1st 8.21s 2002	Jj	BBB–	3/95	BBB	X	R	101.642	12-31-00	Z100	....	®100	12-31-01	150	G1	'92	104	100⅞	101¼	8.11	8.11
1st A 6¾s 2003	Ms	BBB–	3/95	BBB	X	R	NC	....	Z100	....	....	....	50.0	F1	'93	103¾	97½	97½	6.92	6.92
1st A 8¼s 2004	Ao	BBB–	3/95	BBB	X	R	NC	....	....	....	....	....	300	G1	'92	110¾	101¾	101¾	8.11	8.11
1st B 6.77s 2005	fA	BBB–	3/95	BBB	X	R	NC	....	....	....	....	....	120	G1	'93	104½	95	95	7.13	7.13
1st 8.94s 2022	Jj	BBB–	3/95	BBB	X	R	105.364	12-31-00	Z100	....	®104.47	12-31-01	150	G1	'92	105⅞	100⅞	101¼	8.83	8.83
1st 8.70s 2024	Ao	BBB–	3/95	BBB	X	R	103.765	(4-1-02)	Z100	(4-1-02)	....	....	300	G1	'92	110⅞	97⅞	98	8.88	8.88
Halliburton Co.	***49e***	***21.41***		***19.02***	***1.62***	***Dc***	***295.0***	***5761***	***3722***	***9-30-99***	***1059***		***6305***	***32.6***						
Deb 8¾s 2021	Fa15	AA–	10/98	A+	X	R	NC	....	....	....	....	....	200	L3	'91	127⅝	110⅝	110¾	7.90	7.90
Nts 5⅝s 2008	jD	AA–			X	BE	[8]Z100	....	....	....	....	....	150	M2	'98	101⅝	87⅞	87⅞	6.40	6.40
M-T Nts 'A'[9] 6¾s 2027	Fa	AA–	10/98	A+	X	BE	NC	....	....	....	....	....	125	M2	'97	113⅝	95¼	95¼	7.09	7.09
Hallwood Group	***36***	***n/a***		***n/a***	***0.89***	***Dc***				***9-30-99***	***64.20***		***87.90***	***72.7***						
• Coll Sr Sub Deb[10] 7s 2000	QJul31	NR				R	100	....	Z100	....	....	....	14.2	Exch.	'93	99⅛	92½	98	7.14	7.14
• Coll Sub Deb 10s 2005	QJul31	NR				BE	100	....	....	....	....	....	6.81	Exch.	'98	93	77	90	11.11	11.11
Hammons(J.Q.)Hotels LP/Fin.	***32***	***1.49***		***1.20***	***0.86***	***Dc***	***39.80***	***53.40***	***67.80***	***10-1-99***	***809.0***		***865.0***	***95.4***						
1st[3] 8⅞s 2004	Fa15	B+	10/98	BB–	Y	R	104.438	2-14-00	....	....	....	....	300	K2	'94	95¾	90	92	9.65	9.64
Hanna(M.A.)Co[11]	***14***	***6.14***		***5.64***	***2.84***	***Dc***	***47.56***	***697.7***	***417.3***	***9-30-99***	***426.0***		***990.0***	***43.7***						
• Sr Nts 9⅜s 2003	mS15	BBB	5/96	BBB–	X	R	NC	....	....	....	....	....	87.8	S1	'91	No Sale		106⅝	8.81	8.81
Harcourt General[12]	***17a***	***4.49***		***2.09***	***3.84***	***Oc***	***248.0***	***1847***	***1319***	***7-31-99***	***1644***		***2799***	***64.8***						
Sr Deb 8⅞s 2022	Jd	BBB	11/98	BBB+	X	BE	NC	....	....	....	....	....	150	S1	'92	117	102⅝	105	8.45	8.45

Uniform Footnote Explanations-See Page 260. Other: [1] (HRO)On Chge in Ctrl at 101. [2] Now Guitar Center Inc. [3] (HRO)On Chge of Ctrl at 101. [4] Subsid of Southern Co. [5] Greater of 100 or amt based on formula. [6] Liabs subj to compromise. [7] Now Entergy Gulf States,subsid of Entergy Corp. [8] Red at greater of 100 or amt based on formula. [9] (HRO)On 2-1-07 at 100. [10] Issued in min denom $100T. [11] Was Hanna Mining. [12] Was Gen'l Cinema.

Title-Industry Code & Co. Finances (In Italics) / Individual Issue Statistics, Exchange	Ind / Interest Dates	Fixed Charge Coverage 1996 / S&P Rating	1997 / Date of Last Rating Change	1998 / Prior Rating	Eligible	Year End / Bond Form	Cash & Equiv. (Million $) / Redemption Provisions: Regular Price	Curr. Assets (Million $) / Regular (Begins) Thru	Curr. Liab. (Million $) / Sinking Fund Price	Balance Sheet Date / Sinking Fund (Begins) Thru	L. Term Debt (Mil $) / Refund/Other Restriction Price	Refund/Other Restriction (Begins) Thru	Capital-ization (Mil $) / Outst'g (Mil $)	Total Debt % Capital / Underwriting Firm	Underwriting Year	Price Range 1999 High	Price Range 1999 Low	Mo. End Price Sale(s) or Bid	Curr. Yield	Yield to Mat.
***Harcourt General** (Cont.)*																				
Sr Nts 8¼s 2002	Jd	**BBB**	11/98	BBB+	X	BE	NC	....	....	....	....	....	150	S1	'92	105½	101	101	8.17	8.17
Sr Nts 6.70s 2007	fA	**BBB**	11/98	BBB+	X	BE	[1]Z100	....	....	....	....	....	150	S1	'97	100⅜	91⅞	92½	7.24	7.24
Sub Nts 9½s 2000	Ms15	**BBB–**	11/98	BBB	X	R	NC	....	....	....	....	....	125	F1	'88	103½	100½	100½	9.45	9.45
Harleysville Group	***35c***	*5.79*	*11.20*	*13.43*		*Dc*				*9-30-99*	*96.80*		*621.0*	*15.6*						
Nts 6¾s 2003	mN15	**BBB+**			X	R	NC	....	....	....	....	....	75.0	P4	'93	103¼	97½	97½	6.92	6.92
Harman Int'l Indus.	***23f***	*△4.30*	*△4.04*	*△3.18*		*Je*	*11.73*	*669.9*	*262.9*	*9-30-99*	*331.0*		*801.0*	*42.7*						
Sr Nts 7.32s 2007	jJ	**BBB–**			X	BE	NC	....	....	....	....	....	150	C1	'97	104¾	91⅜	91⅜	8.01	8.01
Harnischfeger Indus[2]	***41c***	*4.27*	*4.25*	*d2.60*		*Oc*	*Bankruptcy Chapt 11*				*1047*		*1830*	*61.1*						
Deb 8.90s 2022	§Ms	**NR**	9/99	D	Z	BE			Default 9-1-99 int				75.0	M2	'92	124	37¾	40	....	Flat
Deb 7¼s 2025	§jD15	**NR**	9/99	D	Z	BE			Default 6-15-99 int				150	L3	'95	104⅜	37¾	40	....	Flat
[3]Deb 6⅞s 2027	§Fa15	**NR**	9/99	D	Z	BE			Default 8-15-99 int				150	L3	'97	92¾	37¾	40	....	Flat
[4]***Harrah's Operating Co***	***40i***	*2.69*	*3.05*	*2.64*		*Dc*	*189.9*	*392.4*	*368.3*	*9-30-99*	*2515*		*4077*	*61.8*						
Sr Gtd[5]Nts 7½s 2009	Jj15	**BBB–**			X	BE	[6]Z100	....	....	....	....	....	500	M7	'99	102½	93⅜	93⅜	8.03	8.03
Sr Sub Nts[5] 7⅞s 2005	jD15	**BB+**			Y	BE	[6]Z100	....	....	....	....	....	750	M7	'98	101½	93⅞	96⅝	8.15	8.15
Harris Bankcorp[7]	***10***	*2.12*	*2.02*	*1.34*		*Dc*				*9-30-99*	*1955*		*3546*	*55.1*						
Sub Nts 9⅜s 2001	Jd	**A+**			X	R	NC	....	....	....	....	....	99.4	F1	'89	108½	103⅛	103⅛	9.09	9.09
Harris Corp	***23e***	*△5.40*	*△5.00*	*△11.58*		*Je*	*283.5*	*1213*	*656.9*	*10-1-99*	*415.0*		*2837*	*42.2*						
Deb 7s 2026	Jj15	**BBB**	11/99	A–	X	BE	NC	....	....	....	....	....	100	M6	'96	102¾	86⅜	86½	8.09	8.09
Deb[8] 6.35s 2028	Fa	**BBB**	11/99	A–	X	BE	[6]Z100	(2-2-08)	....	....	....	....	150	M7	'98	103⅜	91	91	6.98	6.98
Nts[9] 6.65s 2006	fA	**BBB**	11/99	A–	X	BE	NC	....	....	....	....	....	100	M5	'96	105¼	99½	99½	6.68	6.68
Harsco Corp.	***17a***	*10.02*	*11.41*	*9.77*		*Dc*	*50.00*	*599.2*	*387.1*	*9-30-99*	*443.0*		*1108*	*42.3*						
Nts 6s 2003	mS15	**A**			X	BE	NC	....	....	....	....	....	150	M5	'93	102⅜	96⅜	96⅜	6.23	6.23
Hartford Electric Lt	***72a***	***Merged into Conn L&P,see***																		
1st 7⅝s 2001	jD	**BBB+**			X	R	100	....	100	....	....	....	30.0	F1	'71	100½	100	100¼	7.61	7.60
1st 7½s 2003	Mn	**BBB+**			X	R	100.31	4-30-00	100.18	4-30-00	....	....	40.0	F1	'73	101	99⅜	99⅜	7.55	7.55
Hartford Finl Svcs Gp[10]	***35d***	*d1.94*	*11.19*	*12.80*		*Dc*				*9-30-99*	*2798*		*9004*	*31.1*						
Sr Nts 6⅜s 2008	mN	**A**			X	BE	[6]Z100	....	....	....	....	....	200	C6	'98	103½	90⅝	91¼	6.99	6.99
Hartford Life	***35a***	*8.69*	*9.19*	*12.81*		*Dc*				*9-30-99*	*900.0*		*3218*	*28.0*						
Nts 7.10s 2007	Jd15	**A**			X	BE	[6]Z100	....	....	....	....	....	200	G1	'97	108¼	96	97	7.32	7.32
Nts 6.90s 2004	Jd15	**A**			X	BE	[6]Z100	....	....	....	....	....	200	G1	'97	105¼	97¼	98⅛	7.03	7.03
Deb 7.65s 2027	Jd15	**A**			X	BE	[6]Z100	....	....	....	....	....	250	G1	'97	114¼	93⅞	96¾	7.91	7.91
Hartmarx Corp	***59a***	*1.39*	*1.95*	*2.27*		*Nv*	*2.05*	*371.5*	*86.13*	*8-31-99*	*202.0*		*410.0*	*51.7*						
Sr Sub Nts[11] 10⅞s 2002	Jj15	**B**	2/98	B–	Y	R	101.554	1-14-01	....	....	....	....	85.1	C5	'94	106	98	99	10.98	10.98
Harveys Casino Resorts	***40i***	*2.57*	*3.56*	*2.69*		*Nv*	*0.03*	*0.04*	*0.04*	*8-31-99*	*150.0*		*351.0*	*42.7*						
Sr[11]Sub Nts[12] 10⅝s 2006	Jd	**B**			Y	BE	105.313	(6-1-01)	....	....	....	....	150	D6	'96	108	101½	103¼	10.29	10.29
Hasbro Inc	***40h***	*10.75*	*12.99*	*9.96*		*Dc*	*108.6*	*2267*	*1839*	*9-26-99*	*408.0*		*2214*	*18.5*						
Deb 6.60s 2028	jJ15	**A**			X	BE	NC	....	....	....	....	....	150	B7	'98	102⅞	85	85	7.76	7.76
Nts 5.60s 2005	mN	**A**			X	BE	NC	....	....	....	....	....	100	B7	'98	99½	89¾	89¾	6.24	6.24
Nts 6.15s 2008	jJ15	**A**			X	BE	NC	....	....	....	....	....	150	B7	'98	104	90⅜	90⅜	6.80	6.80
Hawk Corp	***3***	*0.90*	*1.49*	*2.84*		*Dc*	*2.94*	*64.90*	*33.09*	*9-30-99*	*94.30*		*168.0*	*60.1*						
• Sr Nts[11]'B' 10¼s 2003	jD	**B+**			Y	BE	105.125	(12-1-00)	....	....	....	....	95.6	W3	'96	No Sale		96	10.68	10.67
[13]***Hayes Wheels Int'l***	***8***	*1.30*	*1.66*	*1.97*		*Ja*	*50.60*	*499.9*	*610.0*	*10-31-99*	*1571*		*1817*	*88.3*						
Sr Sub Nts[14] 11s 2006	jJ15	**B**			Y	R	105.50	(7-15-01)	....	....	....	....	250	W6	'96	111½	102¾	104½	10.53	10.52
Haynes Int'l	***44d***	*1.01*	*0.73*	*1.51*		*Sp*	*3.18*	*129.0*	*68.30*	*6-30-99*	*139.0*		*84.60*	*203.0*						
Sr Nts 11⅝s 2004	mS	**B–**			Y	BE	105.813	(9-1-00)	....	....	....	....	140	M2	'96	95⅛	78⅞	86¾	13.40	13.40

Uniform Footnote Explanations-See Page 260. Other: [1] Red at greater of 100 amt based on formula. [2] See Joy Technologies. [3] (HRO)On 2-15-07 at 100. [4] Subsid & data of Harrah's Entertainment. [5] Gtd by Harrah's Entertainment. [6] Red at greater of 100 or amt based on formula. [7] Subsid of Bankmont Fin'l(Bank of Montreal). [8] (HRO)On 2-1-08 at 100. [9] (HRO)On 8-1-01 at 100. [10] Was ITT Hartford Group,see. [11] (HRO)On Chge of Ctrl at 101. [12] State gaming laws may req hldr's sale/co red. [13] Now Hayes Lemmarz Intl,subsid of Varity Corp. [14] Co must offer repurch at 101 on Chge of Ctrl.

Title-Industry Code & Co. Finances (In Italics) / Individual Issue Statistics (Exchange)	Ind / Interest Dates	Fixed Charge Coverage 1996 / S&P Rating	1997 / Date of Last Rating Change	Prior Rating	1998 / Eligible	Year End / Bond Form	Cash & Equiv. (Million $) / Regular Price	Curr. Assets / Regular (Begins) Thru	Curr. Liab. / Sinking Fund Price	Balance Sheet Date / Sinking Fund (Begins) Thru	L. Term Debt (Mil $) / Refund/Other Restriction Price	Refund/Other Restriction (Begins) Thru	Capital-ization (Mil $) / Outst'g (Mil $)	Total Debt % Capital / Underwriting Firm	Underwriting Year	Price Range 1999 High	Price Range 1999 Low	Mo. End Price Sale(s) or Bid	Curr. Yield	Yield to Mat.
Health Care Prop Inv	***57***	***3.30***	***3.32***		***3.14***	***Dc***				***9-30-99***	***813.0***		***1485***	***55.9***						
Sr Nts 6½s 2006	Fa15	**BBB+**			X	BE	NC	....	....	....	....	....	115	M2	'96	95⅛	84¼	84¼	7.72	7.71
Health Care REIT	***57***	***n/a***	***4.02***		***3.12***	***Dc***				***9-30-99***	***529.0***		***1237***	***42.8***						
Nts 7⅝s 2008	Ms15	**BBB–**			X	BE	[1]Z100	....	....	....	....	....	100	B4	'98	100⅞	90⅛	90⅛	8.46	8.46
HEALTHSOUTH Corp[2]	***30***	***5.61***	***6.38***		***6.42***	***Dc***	***161.8***	***1641***	***493.8***	***9-30-99***	***3011***		***6597***	***46.4***						
• Sr Sub Nts[3] 9½s 2001	Ao	**BBB–**	2/98	BB–	X	R	102.375	3-31-00	....	....	....	....	250	S7	'94	104¼	90⅛	s99⅝	9.54	9.54
Hearst-Argyle Television	***12c***	***n/a***	***n/a***		***3.32***	***Dc***	***2.55***	***495.0***	***154.0***	***9-30-99***	***1564***		***2998***	***52.7***						
Deb 7½s 2027	mN15	**BBB–**			X	BE	[4]Z100	....	....	....	....	....	175	C5	'97	107½	90⅞	92¾	8.09	8.09
Sr Nts 7s 2007	mN15	**BBB–**			X	BE	[4]Z100	....	....	....	....	....	125	C5	'97	105	94¾	95⅛	7.36	7.36
Sr Nts 7s 2018	Jj15	**BBB–**			X	BE	[4]Z100	....	....	....	....	....	200	M5	'98	102⅛	88⅛	89¾	7.80	7.80
Hechinger Co[6]	***59l***	***0.38***	***d5.29***		***d0.47***	***Sp***	***Bankruptcy Chapt 11***				***352.0***		***1047***	***84.4***						
Sr Deb 9.45s 2012	§mN15	**NR**	6/99	D	Z	BE			Default 5-15-99 int				100	M6	'92	68	7	12	....	Flat
Sr Nts 6.95s 2003	§aO15	**NR**	6/99	D	Z	BE			Default 10-15-99 int				100	M6	'93	66	7	12	....	Flat
Heinz (H.J.) Co.	***26***	***Δ2.75***	***Δ5.85***		***Δ4.22***	***Ap***	***169.0***	***3107***	***2496***	***10-27-99***	***2825***		***5292***	***62.4***						
Deb 6⅜s 2028	jJ15	**A+**			X	BE	NC	....	....	....	....	....	250	G1	'98	105	85¼	85⅝	7.45	7.44
Nts 6⅞s 2003	Jj15	**A+**	3/95	AA–	X	R	NC	....	....	....	....	....	200	D4	'93	106⅝	99⅞	99⅞	6.88	6.88
Nts 6s 2008	Ms15	**A+**			X	BE	NC	....	....	....	....	....	300	M5	'98	105	92¼	92¼	6.50	6.50
Heller Financial[7]	***25***	***1.31***	***1.38***		***1.44***	***Dc***	***486.0***			***9-30-99***	***8253***		***12838***	***86.0***						
Nts 5⅝s 2000	Ms15	**A–**	7/98	BBB+	X	BE	NC	....	....	....	....	....	200	G1	'93	100¼	99⅜	99⅞	5.63	5.63
Nts 6½s 2000	Mn15	**A–**	7/98	BBB+	X	BE	NC	....	....	....	....	....	200	M2	'93	101⅛	100	100	6.50	6.50
Nts 6¼s 2001	Mn	**A–**	7/98	BBB+	X	BE	NC	....	....	....	....	....	300	M5	'98	101⅜	99	99	6.31	6.31
Nts 6½s 2001	mN	**A–**	7/98	BBB+	X	BE	NC	....	....	....	....	....	200	M5	'96	102⅜	98¾	98¾	6.58	6.58
F/R[8]Nts 2001	QJun25	**A–**			X	BE	NC	....	....	....	....	....	325	C1	'99	100	99⅝	100	....	....
Nts 7s 2002	Mn15	**A–**	7/98	BBB+	X	BE	NC	....	....	....	....	....	150	M5	'95	103¾	99¼	99¼	7.05	7.05
Nts 6.44s 2002	aO6	**A–**	7/98	BBB+	X	BE	NC	....	....	....	....	....	250	M2	'97	102⅜	97⅝	97⅝	6.60	6.60
Hercules, Inc	***14***	***12.02***	***8.74***		***3.68***	***Dc***	***88.00***	***1328***	***1118***	***9-30-99***	***3227***		***4418***	***80.6***						
Nts 6.15s 2000	fA	**BBB–**	10/98	A–	X	BE	NC	....	....	....	....	....	100	M5	'97	101¼	99⅛	99¼	6.20	6.20
Nts 6⅝s 2003	Jd	**BBB–**	10/98	A–	X	BE	NC	....	....	....	....	....	125	M5	'93	104⅝	95⅛	95⅛	6.96	6.96
Nts[9] 6.60s 2027	fA	**BBB–**	10/98	A–	X	BE	NC	....	....	....	....	....	100	M5	'97	98¼	90⅝	90⅝	7.28	7.28
Heritage Media Corp	***12***	***Acquired by News Corp***																		
Sr Sub Nts[3] 8¾s 2006	Fa15	**BB+**	12/97	BBB–	Y	BE	104.375	(2-15-01)	....	....	....	....	175	D6	'96	106½	101	101⅛	8.65	8.65
Hershey Foods	***26h***	***10.59***	***7.81***		***7.08***	***Dc***	***42.90***	***1354***	***859.0***	***10-3-99***	***878.0***		***2258***	***54.3***						
Deb 8.80s 2021	Fa15	**A+**	8/97	AA–	X	R	NC	....	....	....	....	....	100	G1	'91	133⅝	110⅛	110⅛	7.99	7.99
Deb 7.20s 2027	fA15	**A+**			X	BE	NC	....	....	....	....	....	250	G1	1007	115⅝	93	93⅛	7.73	7.73
Nts 6.70s 2005	aO	**A+**	8/97	AA–	X	BE	NC	....	....	....	....	....	200	G1	'95	108	96⅞	96⅞	6.92	6.92
Nts 6.95s 2007	Ms	**A+**	8/97	AA–	X	BE	NC	....	....	....	....	....	150	G1	'97	110⅝	96⅞	96⅞	7.17	7.17
Nts 6.95s 2012	fA15	**A+**			X	BE	NC	....	....	....	....	....	150	G1	'97	114⅜	95⅝	95⅝	7.27	7.27
Hertz Corp[10]	***7***	***1.83***	***2.09***		***2.46***	***Dc***				***9-30-99***	***6566***		***8203***	***80.0***						
Sr Nts 6½s 2000	Ao	**A–**	6/99	BBB+	X	R	NC	....	....	....	....	....	100	M5	'93	101	100	100	6.50	6.50
Sr Nts 6s 2001	Fa	**A–**	6/99	BBB+	X	BE	NC	....	....	....	....	....	150	M5	'94	100⅞	99	99	6.06	6.06
Sr Nts 7s 2001	Ao15	**A–**	6/99	BBB+	X	BE	NC	....	....	....	....	....	150	L3	'94	102⅞	100	100	7.00	7.00
Sr Nts 7⅜s 2001	Jd15	**A–**	6/99	BBB+	X	BE	NC	....	....	....	....	....	100	L3	'94	104	100⅜	100⅜	7.35	7.35
Sr Nts 7s 2002	Mn	**A–**	6/99	BBB+	X	BE	NC	....	....	....	....	....	150	M5	'97	103⅞	99½	99½	7.04	7.03
Sr Nts 6.70s 2002	Jd15	**A–**	6/99	BBB+	X	BE	NC	....	....	....	....	....	150	M5	'95	103⅛	98⅞	98⅞	6.78	6.78
Sr Nts 7⅝s 2002	fA	**A–**	6/99	BBB+	X	R	NC	....	....	....	....	....	100	M2	'92	106	100¾	100¾	7.57	7.57

Uniform Footnote Explanations-See Page 260. Other: [1] Plus Make-Whole Amt. [2] Was HEALTHSOUTH Rehab. [3] (HRO)On Chge of Ctrl at 101. [4] Red at greater of 100 or amt based on formula. [5] Purch offer to Mar 10. [6] Acquired by Leonard Green & Partners. [7] Subsid of Fuji Bank Ltd. [8] Int adj qtrly(3 Mo LIBOR & 0.26%). [9] (HRO)On 8-1-07 at 100. [10] Affil of Ford Motor Co.

Title-Industry Code & Co. Finances (In Italics) / Individual Issue Statistics (Exchange)	Ind / Interest Dates	1996 / S&P Rating	1997 / Date of Last Rating Change	1998 / Prior Rating	Eligible	Year End / Bond Form	Cash & Equiv. (Million $) / Regular Price	Curr. Assets (Million $) / Regular (Begins) Thru	Curr. Liab. (Million $) / Sinking Fund Price	Balance Sheet Date / Sinking Fund (Begins) Thru	L. Term Debt (Mil $) / Refund/Other Restriction Price	Capital-ization (Mil $) / Refund/Other Restriction (Begins) Thru	Outst'g (Mil $)	Total Debt % Capital / Underwriting Firm	Underwriting Year	Price Range 1999 High	Price Range 1999 Low	Mo. End Price Sale(s) or Bid	Curr. Yield	Yield to Mat.
***Hertz Corp** (Cont.)*																				
Sr Nts 6s 2003	Jj15	A–	6/99	BBB+	X	BE	NC	....	....	....	....	....	150	M5	'96	101⅛	96½	96½	6.22	6.22
Sr Nts 7s 2004	jJ	A–	6/99	BBB+	X	BE	NC	....	....	....	....	....	250	M2	'97	105¾	98¾	98¾	7.09	7.09
Sr Nts 6⅜s 2005	aO15	A–	6/99	BBB+	X	R	NC	....	....	....	....	....	100	L3	'93	103	94⅜	94⅜	6.75	6.76
Sr Nts 6½s 2006	Mn15	A–	6/99	BBB+	X	BE	NC	....	....	....	....	....	250	G1	'99	99¾	94⅝	94⅝	6.87	6.87
[1]Sr Nts 6.30s 2006	mN15	A–	6/99	BBB+	X	BE	NC	....	....	....	....	....	150	G1	'96	102¼	97½	97½	6.46	6.46
Sr Nts[2] 7⅝s 2007	fA15	A–			X	BE	NC	....	....	....	....	....	500	M5	'99	102¾	99¼	100½	7.59	7.59
Sr Nts 6⅝s 2008	Mn15	A–	6/99	BBB+	X	BE	NC	....	....	....	....	....	200	M5	'98	104¾	94	94	7.05	7.05
Nts 6¼s 2009	Ms15	A–	6/99	BBB+	X	BE	NC	....	....	....	....	....	300	C1	'99	99½	90½	90½	6.91	6.91
Sr Nts 9s 2009	mN	A–	6/99	BBB+	X	R	[3]NC	....	....	....	....	....	100	M2	'89	123⅝	108⅛	108⅛	8.32	8.32
Sr Nts 7s 2028	Jj15	A–	6/99	BBB+	X	BE	NC	....	....	....	....	....	250	L3	'98	105	88⅞	88⅞	7.88	7.87
• Jr Sub Nts 6⅝s 2000	jJ15	BBB+	6/99	BBB	X	R	NC	....	....	....	....	....	150	M5	'93	101¼	99⅛	99¼	6.68	6.67
• Jr Sub Nts 7s 2003	jJ15	BBB+	6/99	BBB	X	R	NC	....	....	....	....	....	250	M5	'93	104	99	97¼	7.20	7.20
***Highwoods Realty L.P.**[4]*	***57***	*n/a*	*3.03*	*2.61*		*Dc*				*9-30-99*	*1775*	*3966*		*44.8*						
• Nts 6¾s 2003	jD	BBB			X	BE	[5]Z100	....	....	....	....	....	100	G1	'96	No Sale		94⅛	7.17	7.17
Nts 8s 2003	jD	BBB			X	BE	[6]Z100	....	....	....	....	....	150	M7	'98	101¼	95⅛	97⅜	8.22	8.21
• Nts 7s 2006	jD	BBB			X	BE	[5]Z100	....	....	....	....	....	110	G1	'96	No Sale		89¾	7.80	7.80
Hillenbrand Indus	***43***	*11.59*	*13.33*	*14.30*		*Nv*	*198.0*	*767.0*	*332.0*	*8-28-99*	*302.0*	*1280*		*28.0*						
Deb 8½s 2011	jD	A+			X	R	NC	....	....	....	....	....	100	L3	'91	125¾	107⅝	107⅝	7.90	7.90
Deb 7s 2024	Fa15	A+			X	R	NC	....	....	....	....	....	100	L3	'94	107	90⅜	90½	7.73	7.73
Deb 6¾s 2027	jD15	A+			X	BE	[6]Z100	....	....	....	....	....	100	M6	'97	103⅝	87⅛	87⅛	7.75	7.75
Hilton Hotels	***32***	*3.46*	*3.41*	*3.29*		*Dc*	*93.00*	*517.0*	*414.0*	*9-30-99*	*3415*	*3599*		*94.1*						
Nts 7⅜s 2002	Jd	BBB–	12/99	BBB	X	BE	NC	....	....	....	....	....	300	D6	'97	101¾	97¾	98¼	7.51	7.51
Nts 7.70s 2002	jJ15	BBB–	12/99	BBB	X	BE	NC	....	....	....	....	....	300	M2	'92	103⅛	98⅞	99	7.78	7.78
Sr Nts 7s 2004	jJ15	BBB–	12/99	BBB	X	BE	NC	....	....	....	....	....	325	M2	'97	100¼	94⅛	94⅛	7.44	7.44
Sr Nts[7] 7.95s 2007	Ao15	BBB–	12/99	BBB	X	BE	NC	....	....	....	....	....	375	M2	'97	105	94⅛	94⅛	8.45	8.45
Sr Nts[7] 7.20s 2009	jD15	BBB–	12/99	BBB	X	BE	NC	....	....	....	....	....	200	S4	'97	100¼	87½	87½	8.23	8.23
Sr Nts[7] 7½s 2017	jD15	BBB–	12/99	BBB	X	BE	NC	....	....	....	....	....	200	S4	'97	98½	83	83¾	8.96	8.95
***HMH Properties**[8]*	***32***	*n/a*	*n/a*	*1.76*		*Dc*				*6-18-99*	*5782*	*7116*		*81.3*						
Sr Nts[9]'A' 7⅞s 2005	[10]ms15	BB			Y	BE	103.94	(8-1-02)	....	....	....	....	500	D6	'98	99⅜	90	92½	8.51	8.51
Sr Nts[9]'B' 7⅞s 2008	[11]ms15	BB			Y	BE	103.985	(8-1-03)	....	....	....	....	1200	D6	'98	98	87	89⅛	8.84	8.83
Sr Nts 'C' 8.45s 2008	ms15	BB			Y	BE	104.225	(12-1-03)	....	....	....	....	500	D6	'98	101⅛	89½	92½	9.14	9.13
Hoechst Celanese	***14***	**Now HNA Holdings, Inc**																		
Nts 6⅛s 2004	Fa	A+	6/95	AA–	X	BE	NC	....	....	....	....	....	250	C5	'94	101	95⅜	98⅜	6.23	6.23
M-T Nts 'B' 7½s 2004	mN25	A+	6/95	AA–	X	BE	NC	....	....	....	....	....	30.0	C5	'94	106⅛	100⅜	103¼	7.26	7.26
M-T Nts 'B' 7⅛s 2009	Ms15	A+	6/95	AA–	X	BE	NC	....	....	....	....	....	100	C5	'94	105½	96½	101	7.05	7.05
Hollinger Int'l Publishing	***54c***	*1.71*	*3.27*	*5.91*		*Dc*	*61.16*	*405.7*	*444.1*	*9-30-99*	*1488*	*2457*		*61.1*						
• Sr Nts[12] 8⅜s 2005	Ms15	BB	5/99	BB+	Y	BE	NC	....	....	....	....	....	260	M2	'97	107½	97	97½	8.85	8.85
• Sr Sub Nts[9] 9¼s 2006	Fa	BB–			Y	R	104.625	(2-1-01)	....	....	....	....	250	M2	'96	106½	95	98⅛	9.43	9.42
• Sr Sub Nts[12] 9¼s 2007	Ms15	BB–			Y	BE	104.625	(3-15-02)	....	....	....	....	290	M2	'97	108⅞	96⅝	98⅞	9.36	9.35
Home Savings of America	***10a***	***See Washington Mutual***																		
Sub Nts[13] 6s 2000	mN	BBB+			X	BE	NC	....	....	....	....	....	250	L3	'93	100⅝	99⅛	99⅜	6.04	6.04
HomeSide Lending Inc	***25h***	*n/a*	*n/a*	*2.29*		*Sp*				*6-30-99*	*4270*	*5606*		*76.2*						
• Nts 6⅞s 2000	Mn15	A+	3/98	BBB	X	BE	NC	....	....	....	....	....	250	C1	'97	No Sale		98	7.02	7.01
Nts 6.20s 2003	Mn15	A+			X	BE	NC	....	....	....	....	....	225	M5	'98	100⅜	95⅞	96⅝	6.42	6.42

Uniform Footnote Explanations-See Page 260. Other: [1] (HRO)On 11-15-02 at 100. [2] Co may red in whole, at 100, for tax law chge. [3] Red at 100 if $10M or less outstg. [4] Was Highwoods/Forsyth L.P. [5] Plus Make-Whole Amt. [6] Red at greater of 100 or amt based on formula. [7] Int subj to adj for Acq Related Rtg Chge. [8] Gtd by & data of Host Marriott Corp. [9] (HRO)On Chge of Ctrl at 101. [10] Due 8-1-05. [11] Due 8-1-08. [12] Gtd by Hollinger Int'l Inc. [13] Issued in min denom $100T.

Exchange / Individual Issue Statistics	Interest Dates	S&P Rating	Date of Last Rating Change	Prior Rating	Eligible	Bond Form	Regular Price	Regular (Begins) Thru	Sinking Fund Price	Sinking Fund (Begins) Thru	Refund/Other Restriction Price	Refund/Other Restriction (Begins) Thru	Outst'g (Mil $)	Underwriting Firm	Underwriting Year	Price Range 1999 High	Price Range 1999 Low	Mo. End Price Sale(s) or Bid	Curr. Yield	Yield to Mat.
Title-Industry Code & Co. Finances (In Italics)	*Ind*	*Fixed Charge Coverage 1996*	*1997*	*1998*		*Year End*	*Million $ Cash & Equiv.*	*Curr. Assets*	*Curr. Liab.*	*Balance Sheet Date*	*L. Term Debt (Mil $)*		*Capital-ization (Mil $)*	*Total Debt % Capital*						
***HomeSide Lending Inc** (Cont.)*																				
Nts 6¾s 2004	fA	A+	3/98	BBB	X	BE	NC	....	....	....	....	....	200		'97	102¾	96¾	97⅛	6.95	6.95
M-T Nts 6.82s 2001	[1]jd30	A+	3/98	BBB	X	BE	NC	....	....	....	....	....	40.0	M2	'97	102½	98¾	99	6.89	6.89
M-T Nts 6.77s 2001	[2]jd30	A+	3/98	BBB	X	BE	NC	....	....	....	....	....	45.0	C1	'97	102⅛	99⅜	99½	6.80	6.80
M-T Nts 6⅞s 2002	Jd30	A+	3/98	BBB	X	BE	NC	....	....	....	....	....	200	M2	'97	102⅝	98⅞	99⅛	6.94	6.93
Honeywell Inc.	***23***	***8.37***	***8.66***	***8.50***		***Dc***	***152.0***	***3451***	***2233***	***10-3-99***	***1224***		***4264***	***34.7***						
Deb 8⅝s 2006	Ao15	A	5/91	A–	X	R	NC	....	....	....	....	....	100	M6	'86	118⅝	105⅝	105⅝	8.17	8.17
Deb 6⅝s 2028	Jd15	A			X	BE	NC	....	....	....	....	....	250	B7	'98	104⅞	86⅜	86½	7.66	7.66
Nts 6.60s 2001	Ao15	A			X	BE	NC	....	....	....	....	....	100	G1	'96	103	99⅝	99⅝	6.62	6.62
Nts 6¾s 2002	Ms15	A			X	BE	NC	....	....	....	....	....	200	M5	'97	104⅜	99½	99½	6.78	6.78
Nts 7s 2007	Ms15	A			X	BE	NC	....	....	....	....	....	350	M5	'97	109¾	96⅞	96⅞	7.23	7.23
Nts 7⅛s 2008	Ao15	A			X	BE	NC	....	....	....	....	....	200	G1	'96	111¾	97⅞	97⅞	7.28	7.28
Honeywell Intl	***14***	***4.59***	***7.82***	***10.65***		***Dc***	***981.0***	***5867***	***4784***	***9-30-99***	***1287***		***8476***	***36.0***						
• Deb 9⅞s 2002	Jd	A	12/92	A–	X	R	NC	....	....	....	....	....	171	G1	'87	112	100¼	105⅛	9.39	9.39
• Deb 9.20s 2003	Fa15	A	12/92	A–	X	BE	NC	....	....	....	....	....	62.0	G1	'91	No Sale		105¾	8.70	8.70
• Deb 9½s 2016	Jd	A	12/92	A–	X	R	NC	....	....	....	....	....	49.0		'86	No Sale		111½	8.52	8.52
• Bonds Zero Cpn 2001	[3]	NR	8/98	A		CR	100	....	....	....	....	....	[4]28.5	S1	'84	88⅞	85⅝	88⅝	....	0.12
• Bonds Zero Cpn 2003	[3]	NR	8/98	A		CR	100	....	....	....	....	....	[4]28.5	S1	'84	78½	74½	75	....	0.28
• Bonds Zero Cpn 2005	[3]	NR	8/98	A		CR	100	....	....	....	....	....	[4]28.5	S1	'84	68½	64½	64½	....	0.42
• Bonds Zero Cpn 2007	[3]	NR	8/98	A		CR	100	....	....	....	....	....	[4]28.5	S1	'84	59½	55¼	55	....	0.56
• Bonds Zero Cpn 2009	[3]	NR	8/98	A		CR	100	....	....	....	....	....	[4]128	S1	'84	51	47	46⅜	....	0.71
• Nts Zero Cpn 2000	[5]	NR	8/98	A		C	NC	....	....	....	....	....	[4]90.0	S1	'82	96¼	90⅝	s95½	....	0.05
Horace Mann Educators	***35d***	***10.57***	***13.71***	***13.31***		***Dc***				***9-30-99***	***99.70***		***557.0***	***26.8***						
• Sr Nts 6⅝s 2006	Jj15	A–			X	BE	[6]Z100	....	....	....	....	....	100	C5	'96	No Sale		95⅛	6.96	6.96
Hospitality Properties Trust	***57***	***6.31***	***3.43***	***3.65***		***Dc***				***9-30-99***	***415.0***		***1944***	***21.3***						
Sr Nts 7s 2008	Ms	BBB–			X	BE	[7]Z100	....	....	....	....	....	150	D6	'98	93	84¾	85⅝	8.18	8.17
Sr Nts 8½s 2009	[8]Jan15	BBB–			X	BE	100	(12-15-00)	....	....	....	....	150	M2	'98	101⅝	91⅝	91⅝	9.28	9.27
Houghton Mifflin	***54d***	***2.14***	***2.74***	***3.00***		***Dc***	***9.41***	***522.3***	***357.7***	***9-30-99***	***305.0***		***871.0***	***47.5***						
Nts 7⅛s 2004	Ao	BBB+	10/95	A	X	BE	NC	....	....	....	....	....	100	C5	'94	104⅝	97⅝	97⅝	7.30	7.30
Nts 7s 2006	Ms	BBB+			X	BE	NC	....	....	....	....	....	125	M5	'96	104¾	95⅛	95⅛	7.36	7.36
[9]***Household Bank, f.s.b.***	***10b***	***1.54***	***1.68***	***1.62***		***Dc***				***9-30-99***	***34995***		***43578***	***86.5***						
Sub Nts 8.45s 2002	jD10	A–			X	R	NC	....	....	....	....	....	100	M2	'92	109¾	102¼	102¼	8.26	8.26
Sub Nts 6½s 2003	jJ15	A–			X	R	NC	....	....	....	....	....	100	L3	'93	103¼	96⅝	96⅝	6.73	6.73
Household Finance[10]	***25a***	***1.60***	***1.79***	***1.33***		***Dc***				***9-30-99***	***37321***		***43090***	***86.6***						
Nts 6¾s 2000	Jd	A			X	BE	NC	....	....	....	....	....	200	M5	'95	101⅝	100	100⅛	6.74	6.74
Nts 6.45s 2001	Ms15	A			X	BE	NC	....	....	....	....	....	250	C5	'96	102	99⅛	99⅛	6.51	6.51
Nts 8⅜s 2001	mN15	A			X	R	NC	....	....	....	....	....	250	M6	'94	107⅜	102⅛	102⅛	8.20	8.20
F/R[11]M-T Nts 2002	QJun4	A			X	BE	NC	....	....	....	....	....	25.0	P4	'97	100⅜	99⅜	100	....	....
Nts 6.70s 2002	Jd15	A			X	R	NC	....	....	....	....	....	200	M6	'95	103½	98¾	98¾	6.78	6.78
Nts 7⅝s 2003	Jj15	A			X	R	NC	....	....	....	....	....	300	M6	'93	106⅞	100¾	100¾	7.57	7.57
Nts 6⅞s 2003	Ms	A			X	R	NC	....	....	....	....	....	300	M6	'93	104⅜	98⅝	98⅝	6.97	6.97
Nts 7¼s 2003	jJ15	A			X	BE	NC	....	....	....	....	....	250	M5	'96	106⅜	99⅝	99⅝	7.28	7.28
Nts 7s 2003	fA	A			X	BE	NC	....	....	....	....	....	500	C1	'99	101	98⅞	98⅞	7.08	7.08
Nts[12] 6s 2004	Mn	A			X	BE	NC	....	....	....	....	....	1000	M5	'99	100	95	95	6.32	6.32
Nts 8s 2004	fA	A			X	R	NC	....	....	....	....	....	250	M6	'94	110⅝	102⅛	102⅛	7.83	7.83

Uniform Footnote Explanations-See Page 260. Other: [1] Due 7-2-01. [2] Due 9-17-01. [3] Due Aug 1. [4] Incl disc. [5] Due 8-15-00. [6] Greater of 100 or amt based on formula. [7] Plus Make-Whole Amt. [8] Int pd monthly. [9] Subsid & data of Household Int'l. [10] Subsid of Household Int'l. [11] Int adj qtrly(3 Mo LIBOR & 0.2%). [12] Co may red in whole, at 100, for tax law chge.

Title-Industry Code & Co. Finances (In Italics) / Individual Issue Statistics (Exchange)	Ind / Interest Dates	1996 / S&P Rating	1997 / Date of Last Rating Change	1998 / Prior Rating	Eligible	Year End / Bond Form	Cash & Equiv. (Million $) / Regular Price	Curr. Assets (Million $) / Regular (Begins) Thru	Curr. Liab. (Million $) / Sinking Fund Price	Balance Sheet Date / Sinking Fund (Begins) Thru	L. Term Debt (Mil $) / Refund/Other Restriction Price	Refund/Other Restriction (Begins) Thru	Capital-ization (Mil $) / Outst'g (Mil $)	Total Debt % Capital / Underwriting Firm	Underwriting Year	Price Range 1999 High	Price Range 1999 Low	Mo. End Price Sale(s) or Bid	Curr. Yield	Yield to Mat.
Household Finance *(Cont.)*																				
Nts 5⅞s 2004	mS25	A			X	BE	NC	....	....	....	....	....	450	M2	'98	101	93⅞	94	6.25	6.25
Nts 8¼s 2005	Fa15	A			X	R	NC	....	....	....	....	....	200	L3	'95	112⅝	102¾	102¾	8.03	8.03
F/R[1]Nts 2005	QJun17	A			X	BE	NC	....	....	....	....	....	500	M2	'98	100¼	98⅜	99¼	....	....
Nts 7⅛s 2005	mS	A			X	BE	NC	....	....	....	....	....	150	M5	'95	107¼	98⅜	98⅜	7.24	7.24
Nts 7¼s 2006	Mn15	A			X	BE	NC	....	....	....	....	....	250	M6	'96	108⅝	98⅜	98½	7.36	7.36
Nts[2] 7.20s 2006	jJ15	A			X	BE	NC	....	....	....	....	....	1000	C6	'99	101⅜	98¼	98¼	7.33	7.33
Nts 6⅞s 2007	Ms	A			X	BE	NC	....	....	....	....	....	200	L3	'97	106⅞	95½	95½	7.20	7.20
Nts 7.65s 2007	Mn15	A			X	BE	NC	....	....	....	....	....	250	M6	'95	111⅞	99¾	99¾	7.67	7.67
Nts 6.40s 2008	Jd17	A			X	BE	NC	....	....	....	....	....	750	M2	'98	104⅛	92⅛	92⅛	6.95	6.95
Nts[3] 6½s 2008	mN15	A			X	BE	NC	....	....	....	....	....	1000	M7	'98	105	92⅜	92⅜	7.04	7.04
Nts 6.45s 2009	Fa	A			X	R	NC	....	....	....	....	....	200	S1	'94	103¾	91⅞	91⅞	7.02	7.02
Nts 6⅜s 2010	fA	A			X	BE	NC	....	....	....	....	....	500	C6	'98	103⅝	89¾	89¾	7.10	7.10
Nts 7.04s 2012	[4]Aug17	A			X	BE	[5]Z100	(8-17-01)	....	....	....	....	25.0	M2	'97	102⅛	92⅝	92⅝	7.60	7.60
Nts 7.10s 2012	aO24	A			X	BE	*100	(10-24-01)	....	....	....	....	25.0		'97	102¾	93	93	7.63	7.63
M-T Nts 7⅛s 2002	[6]mn15	A			X	BE	NC	....	....	....	....	....	43.5	M2	'97	104½	99½	99½	7.16	7.16
M-T Nts 7.08s 2002	[7]mn15	A			X	BE	NC	....	....	....	....	....	50.0	M6	'97	104⅜	99½	99½	7.12	7.11
F/R[8]M-T Nts 2002	QJul22	A			X	BE	NC	....	....	....	....	....	14.0	U1	'97	100⅜	99¼	99⅞	....	....
M-T Nts 6¼s 2003	[9]mn15	A			X	BE	NC	....	....	....	....	....	110	M2	'98	102	96¼	96¼	6.49	6.49
M-T Nts 7.04s 2012	[4]Jul20	A			X	BE	■100	(7-20-01)	....	....	....	....	25.0	M2	'97	102⅛	92¾	92¾	7.59	7.59
M-T Nts 7.30s 2012	jJ30	A			X	BE	[10]100	7-29-02	....	....	....	....	55.0	M2	'97	104⅝	94⅞	94⅞	7.69	7.69
Sr Sub Nts 9.55s 2000	Ao	A–	4/92	A	X	R	NC	....	....	....	....	....	150	G1	'90	104⅝	100¾	100¾	9.48	9.48
• Sr Sub Nts 9⅝s 2000	jJ15	A–	4/92	A	X	R	NC	....	....	....	....	....	150	L3	'90	105¼	101⅝	100	9.63	9.62
• Sr Sub Nts 9s 2001	mS28	A–	4/92	A	X	R	NC	....	....	....	....	....	100	M6	'89	105½	101⅛	101½	8.87	8.87
Houston Exploration	***49b***	***4.77***	***36.63***	***4.60***		***Dc***	***2.94***	***51.86***	***125.5***	***9-30-99***	***260.0***		***547.0***	***62.2***						
• Sr Sub Nts[11]'B' 8⅝s 2008	Jj	B			Y	BE	104.313	(1-1-03)	....	....	[12]Z108.625	1-1-01	100	Exch.	'98	100	96¾	96½	8.94	8.94
[13]Houston Indus[14]	***72b***	***3.31***	***2.56***	***1.64***		***Dc***	***3833***	***5863***	***8064***	***9-30-99***	***4768***		***14059***	***60.9***						
Deb 9⅜s 2001	Jd	BBB+	10/96	A–	X	R	NC	....	....	....	....	....	250	F1	'91	108¾	103	103	9.10	9.10
Deb 7⅞s 2002	jJ	BBB+	10/96	A–	X	R	NC	....	....	....	....	....	100	F1	'92	106⅞	101	101	7.80	7.80
Houston Lighting & Pwr	***72a***	***See Houston Indus***																		
1st 9.15s 2021	Ms15	A–	10/96	A	X	R	NC	....	....	....	....	....	160	F1	'91	132	110⅜	110½	8.28	8.28
1st 8¾s 2022	Ms	A–	10/96	A	X	R	103.95	(3-1-02)	Z100	....	....	....	100	F1	'92	112¼	102	102	8.58	8.58
1st 7¾s 2023	Ms15	A–	10/96	A	X	R	103.77	(3-15-03)	Z100	....	....	....	250	G1	'93	109⅝	94¼	94¼	8.22	8.22
1st 7½s 2023	jJ	A–	10/96	A	X	R	103.51	(7-1-03)	Z100	....	....	....	200	F1	'93	107⅛	91⅜	91½	8.20	8.20
[15]Hovnanian(K.)Enterprises	***38***	***1.78***	***0.66***	***1.26***		***Oc***				***7-31-99***	***315.0***		***532.0***	***59.2***						
Sub Nts[16] 9¾s 2005	Jd	B			Y	R	104.875	5-31-00	....	....	....	....	100	G1	'93	98⅛	91⅞	95½	10.21	10.21
HRPT Properties Tr[17]	***57***	***3.43***	***3.57***	***3.28***		***Dc***				***9-30-99***	***1430***		***2823***	***34.9***						
Sr Nts 6⅞s 2002	fA26	BBB			X	BE	[18]Z100	....	....	....	....	....	160	M2	'98	100	96	96⅜	7.13	7.13
Sr Nts 6.70s 2005	Fa23	BBB			X	BE	[18]Z100	....	....	....	....	....	100	M2	'98	97⅝	91	91⅝	7.31	7.31
HSBC USA Inc[19]	***10***	***4.27***	***3.15***	***3.44***		***Dc***				***6-30-99***	***1847***		***4089***	***45.2***						
• Sub Nts 7s 2006	mN	A–			X	BE	NC	....	....	....	....	....	300		'96	No Sale		96½	7.25	7.25
Sub Nts 6⅞s 2009	Ms	A–			X	BE	NC	....	....	....	....	....	200		'99	101¾	92⅝	93⅛	7.38	7.38
HS Resources, Inc	***49b***	***1.43***	***1.59***	***0.28***		***Dc***	***3.94***	***77.55***	***89.07***	***9-30-99***	***539.0***		***738.0***	***78.9***						
Sr[11]Sub Nts 9⅞s 2003	jD	B			Y	R	102.50	11-30-00	....	....	....	....	75.0	L3	'93	101¾	97½	99¾	9.90	9.90
Sr[11]Sub Nts 9¼s 2006	mN15	B			Y	BE	104.625	(11-15-01)	....	....	....	....	150		'97	102¼	92	99	9.34	9.34

Uniform Footnote Explanations-See Page 260. Other: [1] Int adj qtrly(3 Mo LIBOR & 0.30%). [2] Co may red in whole, at 100, for tax law chge. [3] Co may red in whole,at 100,for tax law chge. [4] Int pd monthly. [5] Co may red ea Feb & Aug 17. [6] Due 5-30-02. [7] Due 6-3-02. [8] Int adj qtrly(3 Mo LIBOR&0.17%). [9] Due 8-15-03. [10] On 7-30-02. [11] (HRO)On Chge of Ctrl at 101. [12] Max $35M red w/proceeds of Pub Eq Off'g. [13] See Houston Lighting & Power. [14] Now Reliant Energy. [15] Gtd by & data of Hovnanian Enterprises. [16] Gtd by Hovnanian Enterprises. [17] Was Health & Rehabilitation Properties Trust. [18] Plus Make-Whole Amt. [19] Was HSBC Americas,then Marine Midland Banks.

Title-Industry Code & Co. Finances (In Italics) / Individual Issue Statistics (Exchange)	Ind / Interest Dates	Fixed Charge Coverage 1996 / S&P Rating	1997 / Date of Last Rating Change	1998 / Prior Rating	Year End / Eligible	Bond Form	Million $ Cash & Equiv. / Redemption Provisions Regular Price	Curr. Assets / Regular (Begins) Thru	Curr. Liab. / Sinking Fund Price	Balance Sheet Date / Sinking Fund (Begins) Thru	L. Term Debt (Mil $) / Refund/Other Restriction Price	Refund/Other Restriction (Begins) Thru	Capital-ization (Mil $) / Outst'g (Mil $)	Total Debt % Capital / Underwriting Firm	Underwriting Year	Price Range 1999 High	Price Range 1999 Low	Mo. End Price Sale(s) or Bid	Curr. Yield	Yield to Mat.
Hubbell Inc.	***23g***	***24.69***	***32.70***	***24.28***	***Dc***		***35.41***	***601.7***	***380.7***	***9-30-99***	***99.60***		***1122***	***22.7***						
Nts 6⅝s 2005	aO	**AA–**			X	BE	NC	....	....	....	....	....	100	M6	'95	107¼	97⅜	97⅜	6.80	6.80
Hunt (JB) Transport	***71***	***2.44***	***1.75***	***3.59***	***Dc***		***2.82***	***266.8***	***240.6***	***9-30-99***	***417.0***		***834.0***	***52.4***						
Nts 6¼s 2003	mS	**BBB+**	10/96	A–	X	R	NC	....	....	....	....	....	100	M2	'93	99½	94⅝	95¼	6.56	6.56
Sr Nts 7s 2004	mS15	**BBB+**			X	R	NC	....	....	....	....	....	100	M2	'98	102⅝	96⅝	97⅜	7.19	7.19
Huntington Bancshares[1]	***10***	***2.37***	***1.48***	***2.73***	***Dc***					***9-30-99***	***4425***		***6584***	***67.2***						
Sub Nts 7⅞s 2002	mN15	**BBB+**			X	BE	NC	....	....	....	....	....	150	L3	'92	107⅞	100⅞	100⅞	7.81	7.81
Huntington Nat'l Bank	***10***	***Subsid of Huntington Bancshares,see***																		
Sub Nts[2] 7⅝s 2003	Jj15	**A–**			X	BE	NC	....	....	....	....	....	150	L3	'93	107⅜	101⅝	101⅝	7.50	7.50
Sub Nts[2] 6¾s 2003	Jd15	**A–**			X	BE	NC	....	....	....	....	....	100	L3	'93	104⅝	99⅛	99⅛	6.81	6.81
Huntsman Polymers[3]	***14***	***4.05***	***[4]0.40***	***d0.16***	***Dc***			***123.0***	***95.70***	***9-30-99***	***462.0***		***940.0***	***49.1***						
• Sr Nts[5] 11¾s 2004	jD	**BB–**	5/95	B+	Y	R	105.875	11-30-00	....	....	....	....	175	S7	'94	110⅞	96	97⅛	12.10	12.09
Hussmann Intl	***42b***	***n/a***	***n/a***	***6.12***	***Dc***		***43.00***	***514.0***	***239.0***	***9-30-99***	***343.0***		***404.0***	***53.7***						
Sr Nts 6¾s 2008	Jd	**BBB**			X	BE	[6]Z100	....	....	....	....	....	125	B2	'98	103⅜	92⅝	92⅝	7.29	7.29
IBM Credit Corp[7]	***25d***	***1.03***	***1.78***	***1.83***	***Dc***					***6-30-99***	***4434***		***12982***	***84.6***						
M-T Nts 5.05s 2001	Jj22	**A+**			X	BE	NC	....	....	....	....	....	100	P1	'99	99⅞	98⅛	98¼	5.14	5.14
M-T Nts 5.18s 2001	Fa5	**A+**			X	BE	NC	....	....	....	....	....	100	L3	'99	100	98¼	98⅜	5.27	5.27
M-T Nts 5.345s 2001	Ao19	**A+**			X	BE	NC	....	....	....	....	....	75.0	C6	'99	99⅜	98⅛	98⅛	5.45	5.45
• M-T Nts 5.76s 2001	Mn15	**A+**			X	BE	NC	....	....	....	....	....	100	C5	'98	97½	97½	97¾	5.89	5.89
M-T Nts 6.27s 2001	fA6	**A+**			X	BE	NC	....	....	....	....	....	25.0	C1	'99	100	99⅛	99⅛	6.33	6.32
M-T Nts 6.35s 2001	[8]ms	**A+**			X	BE	NC	....	....	....	....	....	100	G1	'99	100⅛	99⅛	99⅛	6.41	6.41
M-T Nts 5½s 2002	Ao15	**A+**			X	BE	NC	....	....	....	....	....	50.0	L3	'99	100	96⅞	96⅞	5.68	5.68
M-T Nts 6.39s 2002	jJ30	**A+**			X	BE	NC	....	....	....	....	....	100	C1	'99	99⅞	98⅝	98⅝	6.48	6.48
M-T Nts 7s 2007	mN5	**A+**	2/98	A	X	BE	*100	....	....	....	....	....	60.0	G1	'96	101⅜	96½	96¾	7.24	7.23
IBP Inc	***26e***	***16.65***	***14.64***	***6.77***	***Dc***		***28.01***	***1507***	***1364***	***9-25-99***	***588.0***		***2630***	***42.1***						
Sr Nts 6⅛s 2006	Fa	**A–**			X	BE	NC	....	....	....	....	....	200	D6	'96	104	94⅛	94⅛	6.51	6.51
Sr Nts 7⅛s 2026	Fa	**A–**			X	BE	103.316	(2-1-06)	....	....	....	....	100	D6	'96	104⅜	89⅝	89¾	7.94	7.94
[9]ICF Kaiser Int'l	***53***	***1.06***	***0.96***	***d3.24***	***Dc***		***55.76***	***304.7***	***242.7***	***9-30-99***	***138.0***		***92.70***	***149.0***						
xwSr[5]Sub Nts 12s 2003	jD31	**NR**	9/99	D		R			Default 6-30-99 int				125	D4	'94	71	49⅝	49¾	24.12	24.08
Idaho Power Co	***72a***	***3.48***	***3.29***	***3.21***	***Dc***		***9.40***	***241.0***	***300.0***	***9-30-99***	***742.0***		***1660***	***50.0***						
1st 8.65s 2000	Jj	**AA–**	10/97	A+	X	R	NC	....	....	....	....	....	80.0	G1	'89	103⅛	100	100	8.65	Mat.
1st 6.40s 2003	Mn	**AA–**	10/97	A+	X	BE	NC	....	....	....	....	....	80.0	S1	'93	103½	97¼	97¼	6.58	6.58
1st 8s 2004	Ms15	**AA–**	10/97	A+	X	R	NC	....	....	....	....	....	50.0	G1	'92	111¼	102⅝	102⅝	7.80	7.79
1st 9½s 2021	Jj	**AA–**	10/97	A+	X	R	104.50	(1-1-01)	....	....	....	....	75.0	G1	'91	110⅝	106⅛	106⅛	8.95	8.95
1st 7½s 2023	Mn	**AA–**	10/97	A+	X	BE	103.366	(5-1-02)	....	....	....	....	80.0	S1	'93	107¼	93¼	93⅜	8.03	8.03
1st 8¾s 2027	Ms15	**AA–**	10/97	A+	X	R	104.188	(3-15-02)	....	....	....	....	50.0	G1	'92	111⅝	100⅞	101	8.66	8.66
Sec M-T Nts 'B' 5.83s 2005	[10]ao	**AA–**			X	BE	NC	....	....	....	....	....	60.0	G1	'98	101⅜	91⅞	91⅞	6.35	6.35
Sec M-T Nts 'B' 7.20s 2009	[11]ao	**AA–**			X	BE	NC	....	....	....	....	....	80.0	G1	'99	100	96⅝	96¾	7.44	7.44
IES Utilities	***75***	***Merged to form Interstate Energy***																		
CT Bonds 7¼s 2006	aO	**A+**	10/97	A	X	BE	▲100	....	....	....	....	....	60.0	C4	'96	108½	96⅞	96⅞	7.48	7.48
CT Bonds[12] 6⅞s 2007	Mn	**A+**	10/97	A	X	BE	▲100	....	....	....	....	....	55.0	C1	'97	109¼	100	100	6.88	6.87
Sr Deb 'A' 6⅝s 2009	fA	**A**	2/98	A–	X	BE	NC	....	....	....	....	....	135	C1	'97	106⅝	92⅜	92⅜	7.17	7.17
[13]IKON Capital Inc[14]	***25***	***1.91***	***1.86***	***2.00***	***Sp***					***6-30-99***	***2161***		***2533***	***85.3***						
M-T Nts 'C' 6.73s 2001	Jd15	**BBB+**	8/98	A–	X	BE	NC	....	....	....	....	....	150	L3	'97	99⅜	97⅛	97⅞	6.88	6.88
M-T Nts 'C 6.42s 2001	[15]jd15	**BBB+**	8/98	A–	X	BE	NC	....	....	....	....	....	25.0	C1	'97	98½	95¾	96½	6.65	6.65

Uniform Footnote Explanations-See Page 260. Other: [1] See Huntington Nat'l Bank. [2] Issued in min denom $250T. [3] Was Rexene Corp. [4] 4 Mos Dec'97. [5] (HRO)On Chge of Ctrl at 101. [6] Red at greater of 100 or amt based on formula. [7] Subsid of Int'l Bus. Mach. [8] Due 8-30-01. [9] Now Kaiser Group Intl. [10] Due 9-9-05. [11] Due 12-1-09. [12] (HRO)On 5-1-02 at 100. [13] See Alco Capital Resources. [14] Now IOS Capital. [15] Due 11-12-01.

Title-Industry Code & Co. Finances (In Italics)	Ind	Fixed Charge Coverage 1996	1997	1998		Year End	Million $ Cash & Equiv.	Curr. Assets	Curr. Liab.	Balance Sheet Date	L. Term Debt (Mil $)		Capital-ization (Mil $)	Total Debt % Capital						
Exchange ↓ Individual Issue Statistics	Interest Dates	S&P Rating	Date of Last Rating Change	Prior Rating	Eligible ↓	Bond Form	Redemption Provisions: Regular Price	Regular (Begins) Thru	Sinking Fund Price	Sinking Fund (Begins) Thru	Refund/Other Restriction Price	Refund/Other Restriction (Begins) Thru	Outst'g (Mil $)	Underwriting Firm	Year	Price Range 1999 High	Low	Mo. End Price Sale(s) or Bid	Curr. Yield	Yield to Mat.
IKON Office Solutions[1]	***50***	***3.60***	***5.49***	***0.73***		***Sp***	***152.0***	***2385***	***1912***	***6-30-99***	***2016***		***4617***	***67.3***						
Nts 6¾s 2004	mN	BBB+	8/98	A–	X	BE	[2]Z100	....	....	....	....	....	125	L3	'97	98⅛	92¼	92⅝	7.29	7.29
Bonds 6¾s 2025	jD	BBB+	8/98	A–	X	BE	[3]Z100	....	....	....	....	....	300	M6	'95	78⅜	73⅝	75¼	8.97	8.97
Nts 7.30s 2027	mN	BBB+	8/98	A–	X	BE	[2]Z100	....	....	....	....	....	125	L3	'97	90¾	78¼	79⅞	9.14	9.14
Illinois Bell Telephone[4]	***67a***	***8.57***	***9.13***	***9.61***		***Dc***	***18.50***	***889.0***	***1830***	***6-30-99***	***565.0***		***2381***	***23.7***						
1st H 4⅜s 2003	jJ	AAA			X	CR	100	....	....	....	....	....	50.0	S1	'63	97⅝	92½	92½	4.73	4.73
Deb 7⅛s 2023	jJ	AAA			X	BE	102.982	(7-1-03)	....	....	....	....	100	L3	'93	103¼	90½	90½	7.87	7.87
Deb 7¼s 2024	Ms15	AAA			X	BE	103.191	(3-15-03)	....	....	....	....	200	G1	'93	105⅛	91⅞	92	7.88	7.88
Deb 6⅝s 2025	Fa	AAA			X	BE	101.904	(2-1-04)	....	....	....	....	100	L3	'94	99⅝	85⅝	85¾	7.73	7.72
Nts 5.80s 2004	Fa	AAA			X	BE	NC	....	....	....	....	....	100	G1	'94	103	96⅛	96⅛	6.03	6.03
Illinois[5] Central[6] RR Co[7]	***55***	***6.68***	***5.72***	***7.92***		***Dc***	***8.90***	***218.0***	***295.0***	***6-30-99***	***528.0***		***1270***	***46.5***						
Nts 6¾s 2003	Mn15	BBB			X	BE	NC	....	....	....	....	....	100	L3	'93	104⅝	98⅞	98⅞	6.83	6.83
Nts 7⅜s 2005	Mn	BBB			X	BE	NC	....	....	....	....	....	100	L3	'95	111	101⅞	101⅞	7.61	7.61
Illinois Power Co[8]	***75***	***3.61***	***2.93***	***0.53***		***Dc***	***34.60***	***462.0***	***926.0***	***9-30-99***	***1943***		***3889***	***64.5***						
• 1st 7.95s 2004	jJ	BBB	4/94	BBB+	X	R	NC	....	....	....	....	....	72.0	M2	'92	101⅜	101⅜	100⅜	7.92	7.92
• New Mtg 6⅛s 2000	Ms15	BBB	4/94	BBB+	X	BE	NC	....	....	....	....	....	40.0	M2	'93	No Sale		99⅝	6.15	6.15
• New Mtg 5⅝s 2000	Ao15	BBB	4/94	BBB+	X	BE	NC	....	....	....	....	....	110	M2	'93	100	97½	99⅜	5.66	5.66
New Mtg 6¼s 2002	jJ15	BBB			X	BE	NC	....	....	....	....	....	100	S4	'98	101⅞	97¼	97⅜	6.42	6.42
• New Mtg 6½s 2003	fA	BBB	4/94	BBB+	X	BE	NC	....	....	....	....	....	100	B7	'93	100⅛	98¼	95½	6.81	6.81
New Mtg 6s 2003	mS15	BBB			X	BE	NC	....	....	....	....	....	100	M5	'98	101½	95¼	95¼	6.30	6.30
• New Mtg 6¾s 2005	Ms15	BBB	4/94	BBB+	X	BE	NC	....	....	....	....	....	70.0	M2	'93	101¼	98	95	7.11	7.10
• New Mtg 7½s 2025	jJ15	BBB	4/94	BBB+	X	R	103.45	(7-15-03)	....	....	....	....	177	M2	'93	102½	90	88⅛	8.51	8.51
Illinois Tool Works	***13e***	***28.99***	***48.73***	***76.04***		***Dc***	***151.0***	***2085***	***1353***	***9-30-99***	***1212***		***5379***	***30.4***						
Nts 5⅞s 2000	Ms	AA–			X	BE	NC	....	....	....	....	....	125	F1	'93	100¾	99⅞	100	5.88	5.87
Nts 5¾s 2009	Ms	AA–			X	BE	[2]Z100	....	....	....	....	....	500	S4	'99	100⅝	89¼	89¼	6.44	6.44
Illinova Corp	***72b***	***3.52***	***2.34***	***0.29***		***Dc***	***55.00***	***672.0***	***1191***	***9-30-99***	***2119***		***3552***	***53.9***						
Sr Nts 7⅛s 2004	Fa	BBB–			X	BE	NC	....	....	....	....	....	100	M2	'97	103¼	97	97	7.35	7.34
M-T Nts 'A' 6.15s 2001	[9]fa	BBB–			X	BE	NC	....	....	....	....	....	30.0	M2	'98	101⅜	98¼	98¼	6.26	6.26
IMC Global Inc[10]	***14a***	***[11]8.30***	***5.78***	***3.00***		***Dc***	***64.70***	***1047***	***453.4***	***9-30-99***	***2535***		***4541***	***56.2***						
Deb 6⅞s 2007	jJ15	BBB			X	BE	NC	....	....	....	....	....	150	M2	'97	100⅛	92⅛	92⅛	7.46	7.46
Sr Deb 9.45s 2011	jD15	NR	8/98	BBB		R	NC	....	....	....	....	....	19.0	M5	'91	119¼	106¼	106¼	8.89	8.89
Deb 7.30s 2028	Jj15	BBB			X	BE	[2]Z100	....	....	....	....	....	150	N2	'98	97⅛	85	86⅛	8.48	8.47
Sr Nts[12] 9¼s 2000	aO	BBB	11/96	BB–	X	R	NC	....	....	....	....	....	15.4	L3	'93	104¼	101⅛	101¼	9.14	9.14
Nts 6⅝s 2001	aO15	BBB			X	BE	NC	....	....	....	....	....	200	M2	'98	102⅛	98	98⅛	6.75	6.75
Nts 7.40s 2002	mN	BBB			X	BE	NC	....	....	....	....	....	300	M2	'98	102⅝	98¾	98¾	7.49	7.49
Nts 6.55s 2005	Jj15	BBB			X	BE	[2]Z100	....	....	....	....	....	150	C1	'98	99	93¾	94	6.97	6.97
Nts 7⅝s 2005	mN	BBB			X	BE	NC	....	....	....	....	....	300	M2	'98	104⅜	97½	97½	7.82	7.82
IMCERA Group	***14***	***Now Mallinckrodt Group,see***																		
Deb 7s 2013	jD15	BBB	9/97	A–	X	BE	NC	....	....	....	....	....	100	G1	'93	115⅛	97	97	7.22	7.22
Nts 6s 2003	aO15	BBB	9/97	A–	X	BE	NC	....	....	....	....	....	100	G1	'93	102½	96⅜	96⅜	6.23	6.23
Imo Industries[13]	***23***	***0.15***	***1.85***	***1.84***		***Dc***	***2.66***	***118.7***	***75.83***	***7-2-99***	***148.0***		***292.0***	***65.8***						
Sr Sub Nts[12] 11¾s 2006	Mn	B–			Y	BE	106	(5-1-01)	....	....	....	....	155	C5	'96	109	101	106¾	11.01	11.01
Indiana Bell Telephone[14]	***67a***	***26.04***	***24.75***	***26.72***		***Dc***	***2.40***	***300.0***	***297.0***	***6-30-99***	***240.0***		***998.0***	***24.0***						
Deb 4⅜s 2003	Jd	AAA			X	CR	100	....	....	....	....	....	20.0	H1	'63	96⅜	91⅞	91⅞	4.76	4.77
Deb 4¾s 2005	aO	AAA			X	R	100.18	9-30-00	....	....	....	....	25.0	M2	'65	99⅜	88	88	5.40	5.40

Uniform Footnote Explanations-See Page 260. Other: [1] See Alco Standard. [2] Red at greater of 100 or amt based on formula. [3] Co may red at greater of 100 or amt based on formula. [4] Subsid of Ameritech Corp. [5] Subsid of Illinois Central Corp. [6] See Gulf,Mobile & Ohio. [7] Acqd by Canadian Natl Rail. [8] Subsid of Illinova Corp. [9] Due 9-10-01. [10] Was IMC Fertilizer Group. [11] Fiscal Jun'96 & prior. [12] (HRO)On Chge of Ctrl at 101. [13] Mgr w/Constellation Capital. [14] Subsid of Ameritech.

Title-Industry Code & Co. Finances (In Italics) / Individual Issue Statistics, Exchange	Ind / Interest Dates	S&P Rating / *Fixed Charge Coverage 1996*	Date of Last Rating Change / *1997*	Prior Rating / *1998*	Eligible	Bond Form / *Year End*	Redemption Provisions: Regular Price / *Million $ Cash & Equiv.*	Regular (Begins) Thru / *Curr. Assets*	Sinking Fund Price / *Curr. Liab.*	Sinking Fund (Begins) Thru / *Balance Sheet Date*	Refund/Other Restriction Price / *L. Term Debt (Mil $)*	Refund/Other Restriction (Begins) Thru	Outst'g (Mil $) / *Capital-ization (Mil $)*	Underwriting Firm / *Total Debt % Capital*	Underwriting Year	Price Range 1999 High	Price Range 1999 Low	Mo. End Price Sale(s) or Bid	Curr. Yield	Yield to Mat.
***Indiana Bell Telephone** (Cont.)*																				
Deb 5½s 2007	Ao	**AAA**			X	R	100.53	3-31-00	....	....	....	....	40.0	S1	'67	97⅞	89⅛	89⅛	6.17	6.17
Deb 7.30s 2026	fA15	**AAA**			X	BE	NC	....	....	....	....	....	150	G1	'96	114⅛	93⅜	93½	7.81	7.81
Indiana Gas[1]	***73b***	***4.84***	***2.21***	***3.93***		***Sp***	***0.51***	***51.30***	***112.0***	***6-30-99***	***182.0***		***457.0***	***43.8***						
Nts A 9⅛s 2021	Fa15	**AA–**			X	R	105.475	(2-15-01)	100	(2-15-02)	....	....	7.00	G1	'91	111⅛	104⅞	104⅞	8.70	8.70
M-T Nts 'F' 6½s 2028	Ms15	**AA–**			X	BE	100	(3-15-03)	....	....	....	....	15.0	J2	'98	98¾	84⅛	84¼	7.72	7.71
M-T Nts[2]'G' 2029	[3]ms15	**AA–**			X	BE	NC	....	....	....	....	....	30.0	M2	'99	101	96¾	96¾	....	....
Indiana Michigan Power	***72a***	***4.56***	***4.38***	***3.16***		***Dc***	***19.80***	***375.0***	***1124***	***9-30-99***	***1124***		***2515***	***57.6***						
Sr Nts 'A' 6⅞s 2004	jJ	**BBB**			X	BE	[4]Z100	....	....	....	....	....	150	M2	'99	100¾	96⅝	96⅝	7.12	7.11
M-T Nts 'A' 6.45s 2008	[5]fn	**BBB**			X	BE	NC	....	....	....	....	....	50.0	M2	'98	101⅞	90	90	7.17	7.17
Indianapolis Pwr & Lt[6]	***72a***	***4.73***	***5.88***	***6.36***		***Dc***	***4.45***	***175.0***	***156.0***	***9-30-99***	***628.0***		***1475***	***44.1***						
1st 6.05s 2004	Fa	**AA–**			X	R	NC	....	▲100	....	....	....	80.0	D4	'94	103¼	95⅞	95⅞	6.31	6.31
1st 8s 2006	aO15	**AA–**	9/93	AA	X	R	NC	....	....	....	....	....	58.8	L3	'91	115⅜	102⅝	102⅝	7.80	7.80
1st 7⅜s 2007	fA	**AA–**	9/93	AA	X	R	NC	....	▲100	....	....	....	80.0	D4	'92	112½	99⅞	99⅞	7.38	7.38
1st 7.05s 2024	Fa	**AA–**			X	R	103.31	(2-1-04)	▲100	....	....	....	100	D4	'94	104⅞	87⅛	87¼	8.08	8.08
Ingersoll-Rand Co.[7]	***41c***	***5.48***	***5.42***	***4.45***		***Dc***	***63.60***	***2444***	***1529***	***9-30-99***	***2116***		***5447***	***45.4***						
Deb 9s 2021	fA15	**A–**	9/97	A	X	BE	NC	....	....	....	....	....	125	S1	'91	126¼	110⅛	110¼	8.16	8.16
Deb[8] 6.48s 2025	Jd	**A–**	9/97	A	X	BE	NC	....	....	....	....	....	150	M2	'95	103½	95⅝	95⅝	6.78	6.78
Deb 7.20s 2025	Jd	**A–**	9/97	A	X	BE	NC	....	100	(6-1-06)	....	....	150	S1	'95	106⅛	91⅜	91⅜	7.88	7.88
Deb[9] 6.391s 2027	mN15	**A–**			X	BE	[4]Z100	(11-15-04)	....	....	....	....	200	M2	'97	104⅛	96	96¼	6.64	6.64
Deb[10] 6.443s 2027	mN15	**A–**			X	BE	[4]Z100	(11-15-07)	....	....	....	....	200	S1	'97	104⅜	93¼	93¼	6.91	6.91
Nts 6.255s 2001	Fa15	**A–**			X	BE	NC	....	....	....	....	....	400	M5	'97	101¼	99¼	99¼	6.30	6.30
Nts 6⅞s 2003	Fa	**A–**	9/97	A	X	BE	NC	....	....	....	....	....	100	S1	'93	104¼	98⅞	98⅞	6.95	6.95
M-T Nts 'A' 6.60s 2000	[11]jj15	**A–**	9/97	A	X	BE	NC	....	....	....	....	....	25.0	S1	'95	101½	100	100	6.60	6.60
M-T Nts 'A' 6.60s 2000	[12]jj15	**A–**	9/97	A	X	BE	NC	....	....	....	....	....	25.0	S1	'95	101½	100	100	6.60	6.60
M-T Nts 'A' 6.53s 2000	[13]jj15	**A–**	9/97	A	X	BE	NC	....	....	....	....	....	15.0	S1	'95	101½	99⅞	100	6.53	6.53
M-T Nts 'A' 6.86s 2002	[14]jj15	**A–**	9/97	A	X	BE	NC	....	....	....	....	....	25.0	S1	'95	104	99¼	99¼	6.91	6.91
M-T Nts 'A' 6.78s 2002	[15]jj15	**A–**	9/97	A	X	BE	NC	....	....	....	....	....	20.0	S1	'95	103¾	99	99	6.85	6.85
M-T Nts 'A' 6.97s 2004	[16]jj15	**A–**	9/97	A	X	BE	NC	....	....	....	....	....	23.0	M2	'95	106	98¼	98¼	7.09	7.09
M-T Nts'B' 6.38s 2001	[17]mn15	**A–**			X	BE	NC	....	....	....	....	....	50.0	S1	'97	102⅛	98¾	98¾	6.46	6.46
M-T Nts 'B' 6.46s 2003	[18]mn15	**A–**			X	BE	NC	....	....	....	....	....	46.2	S1	'97	103⅜	96⅞	96⅞	6.67	6.67
M-T Nts 'B' 6.80s 2005	[19]mn15	**A–**			X	BE	NC	....	....	....	....	....	100	S1	'97	104⅝	95⅛	95⅛	7.15	7.15
M-T Nts[20]'B' 6.13s 2027	[21]mn15	**A–**			X	BE	NC	....	....	....	....	....	60.0	S1	'97	104⅛	98⅝	98⅝	6.22	6.22
M-T Nts[22]'B' 6.23s 2027	[23]mn15	**A–**			X	BE	NC	....	....	....	....	....	50.0	S1	'97	104½	96¼	96¼	6.47	6.47
M-T Nts 'B' 6.015s 2028	Fa15	**A–**			X	BE	[24]100	(2-15-01)	....	....	....	....	100	M5	'97	102⅝	98¾	99	6.08	6.08
Inland Steel Co.[25]	***66a***	***n/a***	***n/a***	***[26]1.41***		***Dc***	***30.80***	***784.0***	***464.0***	***9-30-99***	***958.0***		***1429***	***69.7***						
• 1st R 7.90s 2007	Jj15	**BB**	7/98	BB–	Y	R	100.52	1-14-01	100	....	....	....	61.4	K3	'77	101⅞	89	90	8.78	8.78
Integon Corp	***35c***	***Acquired Gen'l Motors Acceptance,see***																		
Sr Nts 9½s 2001	aO15	**NR**	3/98	B+		R	NC	....	....	....	....	....	75.0	S7	'94	109⅛	103⅞	103⅞	9.15	9.15
Integra Fin'l Corp	***10***	***Merged into National City Corp,see***																		
• Sub Deb 8½s 2002	Mn15	**A–**	5/96	BBB	X	BE	NC	....	....	....	....	....	100	L3	'92	No Sale		100	8.50	8.50
• Sub Nts 6½s 2000	Ao15	**A–**	5/96	BBB	X	R	NC	....	....	....	....	....	100	F1	'93	No Sale		100	6.50	6.50
Integrated Health Svcs	***30***	***2.45***	***2.92***	***1.97***		***Dc***	***71.31***	***755.7***	***3707***	***9-30-99***	***203.0***		***4750***	***72.7***						
Sr[27]Nts[28]'A' 9¼s 2008	Jj15	**NR**	12/99	D		BE	104.65	1-14-03	....	....	....	....	500	Exch.	'97	96	5½	3	....	Flat
Powertel Inc[29]	***67***	***Nil***	***d3.17***	***d1.84***		***Dc***	***436.4***	***503.7***	***85.44***	***9-30-99***	***1248***		***1358***	***78.7***						

Uniform Footnote Explanations-See Page 260. Other: [1] Subsid of Indiana Energy. [2] (HRO)On 10-5-11 at 100. [3] Due 10-5-29. [4] Red at greater of 100 or amt based on formula. [5] Due 11-10-08. [6] Subsid of IPALCO Enterprises. [7] See Clark Equipment. [8] (HRO)On 6-1-05 at 100. [9] (HRO)On ea 11-15 fr 2004 at 100. [10] (HRO)On ea 11-15 fr 2007 at 100. [11] Due 7-28-00. [12] Due 8-1-00. [13] Due 8-11-00. [14] Due 8-5-02. [15] Due 8-12-02. [16] Due 8-11-04. [17] Due 11-19-01. [18] Due 11-19-03. [19] Due 12-5-05. [20] (HRO)On ea 11-19 fr 2001 at 100. [21] Due 11-18-27. [22] (HRO)On ea 11-19 fr 2003 at 100. [23] Due 11-19-27. [24] On any Feb 15. [25] Now Ispat Inland. [26] 6 Mo Dec'98. [27] (HRO)On Chge of Ctrl at 101. [28] May default 1-15-00 int. [29] See InterCel Inc.

Title-Industry Code & Co. Finances (In Italics) / Individual Issue Statistics (Exchange ↓)	Ind / Interest Dates	Fixed Charge Coverage 1996 / S&P Rating	1997 / Date of Last Rating Change	Prior Rating	1998 / Eligible	Year End / Bond Form	Cash & Equiv. (Million $) / Regular Price	Curr. Assets (Million $) / Regular (Begins) Thru	Curr. Liab. (Million $) / Sinking Fund Price	Balance Sheet Date / Sinking Fund (Begins) Thru	L. Term Debt (Mil $) / Refund/Other Restriction Price	Refund/Other Restriction (Begins) Thru	Capital-ization (Mil $) / Outst'g (Mil $)	Total Debt % Capital / Underwriting Firm	Underwriting Year	Price Range 1999 High	Price Range 1999 Low	Mo. End Price Sale(s) or Bid	Curr. Yield	Yield to Mat.
InterCel Inc	***67***	***Now Powertel Inc,see***																		
Sr Disc[1]Nts[2] 12s 2006	Mn	**B**	3/97	B–	Y	R	106	(5-1-01)	....	....	....	....	[3]360	M6	'96	87	72¾	87	....	Flat
Interface Inc	***31a***	***2.32***	***2.75***		***2.95***	***Dc***	***10.94***	***452.6***	***198.8***	***10-3-99***	***427.0***		***851.0***	***52.4***						
Sr Nts 7.30s 2008	Ao	**BB+**			Y	BE	[4]Z100	....	....	....	....	....	150	S4	'98	98⅞	75	76⅞	9.50	9.50
Sr Sub Nts[1] 'B' 9½s 2005	mN15	**BB–**	3/98	B+	Y	BE	104.75	(11-15-00)	....	....	....	....	125	S7	'95	105	88	93⅞	10.12	10.12
Intermedia Communications[5]	***67a***	***d0.62***	***d1.26***		***d1.11***	***Dc***	***482.7***	***761.9***	***190.5***	***9-30-99***	***2882***		***2865***	***82.8***						
Sr Disc[6]Nts[7] 12½s 2006	Mn15	**B**	6/97	B–	Y	R	106.25	(5-15-01)	....	....	....	....	[3]330	B7	'96	88	78	87½	....	Flat
Sr Nts[8]'B' 8⅞s 2007	mN	**B**			Y		104.438	(11-1-02)	....	....	[9]Z108.875	11-1-01	260	Exch.	'98	102⅜	87¾	93	9.54	9.54
Sr Nts'B' 8.60s 2008	Jd	**B**			Y	BE	104.30	(6-1-03)	....	....	[10]Z108.60	6-1-01	500	Exch.	'98	101	85¾	91½	9.40	9.40
Sr Nts[8]'B' 9½s 2009	Ms	**B**			Y	BE	[11]100	2-29-04	....	....	[12]Z109.50	3-1-02	300	Exch.	'99	99½	90	95½	9.95	9.95
Sr Sub[13]Disc Nts[14]'B' 12¼s 2009	Ms	**CCC+**			Y	BE	[15]Z100	2-29-04	....	....	[16]Z112.25	3-1-02	[3]364	Exch.	'99	60½	49½	59⅝	20.55	20.53
Int'l Business Machines	***20b***	***12.45***	***12.84***		***13.16***	***Dc***	***7470***	***42877***	***37778***	***9-30-99***	***13807***		***47971***	***58.2***						
• Deb 7½s 2013	Jd15	**A+**	2/98	A	X	BE	NC	....	....	....	....	....	550	M6	'93	117	100⅝	100¾	7.44	7.44
• Deb 8⅜s 2019	mN	**A+**	2/98	A	X	BE	NC	....	....	....	....	....	750	S1	'89	126½	107⅛	s107⅛	7.82	7.82
• Deb 7s 2025	aO30	**A+**	2/98	A	X	BE	[4]Z100	....	....	....	....	....	600	M2	'95	112½	94⅛	93	7.53	7.53
• Deb[17] 6.22s 2027	fA	**A+**	2/98	A	X	BE	[18]Z100	(8-2-04)	....	....	....	....	500	M6	'97	No Sale		99⅜	6.26	6.26
• Deb 6½s 2028	Jj15	**A+**	2/98	A	X	BE	[4]Z100	....	....	....	....	....	700	M2	'98	106	86	s86	7.56	7.56
• Deb 7s 2045	aO30	**A+**	2/98	A	X	BE	[4]Z100	....	....	....	....	....	150	M2	'95	No Sale		93	7.53	7.53
• Deb 7⅛s 2096	jD	**A+**	2/98	A	X	BE	[11]Z100	....	....	....	....	....	850	S1	'96	No Sale		90¾	7.85	7.85
• Nts 6⅜s 2000	Jd15	**A+**	2/98	A	X	BE	NC	....	....	....	....	....	1250	M6	'93	102	99⅜	s99¾	6.39	6.39
• Nts 7¼s 2002	mN	**A+**	2/98	A	X	BE	NC	....	....	....	....	....	750	F1	'92	107½	100⅞	101	7.18	7.18
• Nts 6.45s 2007	fA	**A+**	2/98	A	X	BE	100	....	....	....	....	....	500	M6	'97	107	95⅝	95¾	6.74	6.74
• Nts 5⅜s 2009	Fa	**A+**			X	BE	[4]Z100	....	....	....	....	....	600	M7	'99	99⅞	87½	86½	6.21	6.21
M-T Nts 5.40s 2009	Jj26	**A+**			X	BE	NC	....	....	....	....	....	100	L3	'99	100⅛	87⅜	87⅜	6.18	6.18
M-T Nts 6.037s 2000	fA7	**A+**	2/98	A	X	BE	NC	....	....	....	....	....	100	C5	'97	101¾	99⅞	99⅞	6.04	6.04
M-T Nts 5.30s 2001	Ms26	**A+**			X	BE	NC	....	....	....	....	....	100	S4	'99	100	98½	98½	5.38	5.38
M-T Nts 5.80s 2001	Mn15	**A+**			X	BE	NC	....	....	....	....	....	100	G1	'98	102⅛	98⅞	98⅞	5.87	5.87
M-T Nts 5.95s 2003	[19]ao	**A+**			X	BE	NC	....	....	....	....	....	100	G1	'98	103¾	97⅛	97⅛	6.13	6.13
M-T Nts 5.37s 2003	mS22	**A+**			X	BE	NC	....	....	....	....	....	185	B7	'98	101⅜	94⅝	94⅝	5.68	5.68
M-T Nts 5.10s 2003	mN10	**A+**			X	BE	NC	....	....	....	....	....	100	P4	'98	100½	93⅝	93⅝	5.45	5.45
M-T Nts 5.40s 2008	aO	**A+**			X	BE	NC	....	....	....	....	....	100	S4	'98	101¾	88	88	6.14	6.14
M-T Nts 5.40s 2008	jD	**A+**			X	BE	NC	....	....	....	....	....	100	B7	'98	101¾	87¾	87¾	6.15	6.15
Intl CableTel Inc	***67***	***Now NTL Inc,see***																		
Sr[7]Dfrd Cpn Nts[20]'B' 11½s 2006	Fa	**B–**	4/97	B	Y	BE	105.75	(2-1-01)	....	....	....	....	[3]1050	Exch.	'96	91	82	90½	12.71	12.70
Int'l Lease Finance	***25c***	***1.69***	***1.82***		***1.88***	***Dc***				***6-30-99***	***12670***		***15651***	***81.0***						
Nts 8¼s 2000	Jj15	**A+**			X	R	NC	....	....	....	....	....	100	S1	'95	102⅝	100	100	8.25	8.25
Nts 6⅜s 2000	Jj18	**A+**			X	BE	NC	....	....	....	....	....	200	G1	'97	100⅞	100	100	6.38	6.37
Nts 6.20s 2000	Mn	**A+**			X	R	NC	....	....	....	....	....	100	M6	'93	100⅞	99⅞	99⅞	6.21	6.21
Nts 7s 2000	Mn15	**A+**			X	R	NC	....	....	....	....	....	100	S1	'95	101⅞	100⅛	100¼	6.98	6.98
Nts 6⅝s 2000	fA15	**A+**			X	BE	NC	....	....	....	....	....	100	M2	'96	101¾	100	100	6.63	6.62
Nts 6¼s 2000	aO15	**A+**			X	BE	NC	....	....	....	....	....	100	S1	'95	101¼	99⅝	99⅝	6.27	6.27
Nts 5⅞s 2001	Jj15	**A+**			X	BE	NC	....	....	....	....	....	200	C1	'98	100⅝	99	99	5.93	5.93
Nts 8⅞s 2001	Ao15	**A+**			X	R	NC	....	....	....	....	....	150	M2	'91	107	102⅜	102⅜	8.67	8.67
Nts 6⅞s 2001	Mn	**A+**			X	BE	NC	....	....	....	....	....	100	S1	'97	102¾	100	100	6.88	6.87
Nts 5.95s 2001	Jd	**A+**			X	BE	NC	....	....	....	....	....	100	M7	'98	100⅞	98¾	98¾	6.03	6.02

Uniform Footnote Explanations-See Page 260. Other: [1] Co must offer repurch at 101 on Chge of Ctrl. [2] Int accrues fr 5-1-01. [3] Incl disc. [4] Red at greater of 100 or amt based on formula. [5] See Shared Tech Fairchild. [6] Int accr at 12.5% fr 5-15-01. [7] (HRO)On Chge of Ctrl at 101(Accreted Val). [8] (HRO)On Chge of Ctrl at 101. [9] Max $65M red w/proceeds of Pub Eq Off'g. [10] Max $125M red w/proceeds of Equity Off'g. [11] Plus Make-Whole Amt. [12] Max $75M red w/proceeds of Pub Eq Off'g. [13] (HRO)On Chge of Ctrl at 101(Accreted Amt). [14] Int accrues at 12.25% fr 3-1-04. [15] Accreted Amt:Plus Make-Whole Amt. [16] Accreted Amt:Max $91M red w/proceeds Pub Eq Off'g. [17] (HRO)On 8-1-04 at 100. [18] Red at greater of 100 or amt based of formula. [19] Due 6-2-03. [20] Int accrues at 11.5% fr 2-1-01.

Title-Industry Code & Co. Finances (In Italics)	Ind	Fixed Charge Coverage 1996	1997		1998	Year End	Million $ Cash & Equiv.	Curr. Assets	Curr. Liab.	Balance Sheet Date	L. Term Debt (Mil $)		Capital-ization (Mil $)	Total Debt % Capital						
Individual Issue Statistics Exchange	Interest Dates	S&P Rating	Date of Last Rating Change	Prior Rating	Eligible	Bond Form	Redemption Provisions: Regular Price	Regular (Begins) Thru	Sinking Fund Price	Sinking Fund (Begins) Thru	Refund/Other Restriction Price	Refund/Other Restriction (Begins) Thru	Outst'g (Mil $)	Underwriting Firm	Underwriting Year	Price Range 1999 High	Price Range 1999 Low	Mo. End Price Sale(s) or Bid	Curr. Yield	Yield to Mat.
***Int'l Lease Finance** (Cont.)*																				
Nts 6½s 2001	jJ	A+			X	BE	NC	....	....	....	....	....	100	M6	'97	102⅛	99⅜	99⅜	6.54	6.54
Nts 6½s 2001	aO15	A+			X	BE	NC	....	....	....	....	....	100	S1	'96	102¼	99¼	99¼	6.55	6.55
Nts 6⅜s 2002	Fa15	A+			X	BE	NC	....	....	....	....	....	100	M6	'97	102⅛	98¾	98¾	6.46	6.46
Nts 5⅝s 2002	Ao15	A+			X	BE	NC	....	....	....	....	....	100	M2	'99	100	97⅛	97⅛	5.79	5.79
Nts 5.90s 2002	Ao15	A+			X	BE	NC	....	....	....	....	....	100	L3	'98	101	97½	97½	6.05	6.05
Nts 5⅝s 2002	Mn	A+			X	BE	NC	....	....	....	....	....	175	L3	'99	100	97⅛	97⅛	5.79	5.79
Nts 6s 2002	Mn15	A+			X	BE	NC	....	....	....	....	....	100	C1	'98	101⅜	97⅝	97⅝	6.15	6.15
Nts 6⅜s 2002	fA	A+			X	BE	NC	....	....	....	....	....	100	C1	'97	102⅝	98⅝	98⅝	6.46	6.46
Nts 5¾s 2003	Jj15	A+			X	BE	NC	....	....	....	....	....	100	B2	'98	100⅝	95⅞	96¼	5.97	5.97
Nts 6s 2003	Jd15	A+			X	BE	NC	....	....	....	....	....	100	G1	1008	101⅛	96⅛	96⅜	6.23	6.23
Nts 8⅜s 2004	jD15	A+			X	R	NC	....	....	....	....	....	100	S1	'94	113⅜	104⅜	104⅝	8.00	8.00
F/R[1]Nts 2001	QFeb	A+			X	BE	NC	....	....	....	....	....	100	L3	'97	100¼	99½	100	....	....
M-T Nts 'G' 8.15s 2004	aO	A+			X	BE	NC	....	....	....	....	....	100	G1	'94	111⅛	103⅝	103⅝	7.86	7.86
M-T Nts 'I' 6.28s 2000	[2]ao15	A+			X	BE	NC	....	....	....	....	....	25.0	S1	'97	100⅞	100	100	6.28	6.28
M-T Nts 'I' 6.31s 2000	[3]ao15	A+			X	BE	NC	....	....	....	....	....	25.0	M6	'97	101	99⅞	99⅞	6.32	6.32
Int'l Minerals & Chem	***14***	***Now IMCERA Group, see***																		
SF Deb 9⅞s 2011	Ms15	BBB	9/97	A–	X	R	100	(3-15-01)	100	(3-15-02)	....	....	134	L1	'86	108	102¾	102¾	9.61	9.61
Intl Paper[4]	***50***	***2.44***	***2.03***		***2.05***	***Dc***	***353.0***	***7202***	***4395***	***9-30-99***	***7584***		***19556***	***47.5***						
• Deb 5⅛s 2012	mN15	BBB+	7/98	A–	X	R	100	....	....	....	....	....	[5]149	G1	'82	88⅜	74⅛	s74⅛	6.91	6.91
Deb[6] 7⅝s 2023	Ms	BBB+	7/98	A–	X	BE	103.43	(3-1-03)	....	....	....	....	200	F1	'93	99¾	90⅛	90¼	8.45	8.45
Deb 6⅞s 2023	mN	BBB+	7/98	A–	X	BE	NC	....	....	....	....	....	200	K2	'93	98¾	87½	87⅝	7.85	7.85
Deb[6] 8⅛s 2024	Jd15	BBB+	7/98	A–	X	BE	103.744	(6-15-04)	....	....	....	....	150	M5	'94	106⅝	97½	97⅝	8.32	8.32
Deb 6⅞s 2029	Ao15	BBB+			X	BE	[7]Z100	....	....	....	....	....	200	M7	'99	98½	86⅝	87⅛	7.89	7.89
Nts[8] 9.70s 2000	Ms15	BBB+	7/98	A–	X	R	NC	....	....	....	....	....	150	F1	'90	104¼	100⅝	100⅝	9.64	9.64
Nts[6] 6⅞s 2000	[2]jj8	BBB+	7/98	A–	X	BE	NC	....	....	....	....	....	175	M2	'96	101⅜	100	100⅛	6.87	6.87
Nts 7s 2001	Jd	BBB+	7/98	A–	X	BE	NC	....	....	....	....	....	250	C5	'96	102⅜	99¾	99¾	7.02	7.02
Nts[8] 9.40s 2002	Jd	BBB+	7/98	A–	X	R	NC	....	....	....	....	....	100	F1	'90	110¼	104¼	104¼	9.02	9.01
Nts[6] 6⅛s 2003	mN	BBB+	7/98	A–	X	BE	NC	....	....	....	....	....	200	C5	'93	100⅛	95⅝	95⅝	6.41	6.41
Nts[6] 7½s 2004	Mn15	BBB+	7/98	A–	X	BE	NC	....	....	....	....	....	150	K2	'94	105⅞	99⅞	99⅞	7.51	7.51
Nts[6] 7⅝s 2004	fA	BBB+	7/98	A–	X	R	NC	....	....	....	....	....	150	M6	'94	106⅞	100⅜	100⅜	7.60	7.60
Nts[6] 7⅞s 2006	fA	BBB+	7/98	A–	X	R	NC	....	....	....	....	....	150	C5	'94	109½	100¼	100¼	7.86	7.85
Nts[8] 7⅝s 2007	Jj15	BBB+	7/98	A–	X	R	NC	....	....	....	....	....	200	K2	'92	108¾	98¾	98¾	7.72	7.72
M-T Nts 'E' 8s 2006	[9]ao	BBB+	7/98	A–	X	BE	NC	....	....	....	....	....	10.0	M6	'94	111⅝	101⅛	101⅛	7.91	7.91
M-T Nts 'E' 8.10s 2009	[10]ao	BBB+	7/98	A–	X	BE	NC	....	....	....	....	....	10.0	M6	'94	114⅝	102⅜	102⅜	7.91	7.91
M-T Nts 'E' 8.10s 2009	[11]ao	BBB+	7/98	A–	X	BE	NC	....	....	....	....	....	7.00	C5	'94	114⅝	102⅜	102⅜	7.91	7.91
M-T Nts 'E' 8.10s 2009	[11]ao	BBB+	7/98	A–	X	BE	NC	....	....	....	....	....	7.00	K2	'94	114⅝	102⅜	102⅜	7.91	7.91
International Shipholding	***64***	***1.49***	***1.14***		***1.66***	***Dc***	***33.30***	***110.0***	***78.90***	***9-30-99***	***402.0***		***590.0***	***69.3***						
• Sr Nts[12] 9s 2003	jJ	BB+	12/97	BB–	Y	R	102.25	6-30-00	....	....	....	....	95.0	B10	'93	103⅜	94¾	96⅝	9.31	9.31
Int'l Telephone & Tel	***17***	***Now ITT Corp,see***																		
Deb 6½s 2001	jJ	BBB	10/95	A+	X	R	100	....	....	....	....	....	[5]150	L3	'81	100⅝	98⅜	98⅜	6.61	6.61
Deb 7½s 2011	jJ	BBB	10/95	A+	X	R	100	....	....	....	....	....	[5]150	L3	'81	101	88¼	93	8.06	8.06
InterNorth,Inc	***73e***	***Now Enron Corp,see***																		
Nts 9⅝s 2006	Ms15	BBB+	12/95	BBB	X	R	NC	....	....	....	....	....	192	G1	'86	119	107¾	107¾	8.93	8.93
[13]Interstate[14]Power[15]	***75***	***3.14***	***2.76***		***2.09***	***Dc***	***64.00***	***419.0***	***672.0***	***9-30-99***	***1597***		***3963***	***47.1***						
1st 8s 2007	Fa15	A+			X	R	NC	....	100	....	....	....	25.0	S1	'92	115⅝	101¾	101¾	7.86	7.86

Uniform Footnote Explanations-See Page 260. Other: [1] Int adj qtrly(3 Mo LIBOR&0.0625%). [2] Due 7-10-00. [3] Due 9-1-00. [4] See Fed'l Paper Board. [5] Incl disc. [6] (HRO)On Chge of Ctrl at 100. [7] Red at greater of 100 or amt based on formula. [8] (HRO)At 100 for certain events. [9] Due 11-15-06. [10] Due 5-20-09. [11] Due 5-18-09. [12] (HRO)On Chge of Ctrl at 101. [13] Now Alliant Energy. [14] See IES Util,Iowa Elec L&P,Iowa So'n Util. [15] See Wisconsin Pwr & Lt.

Title-Industry Code & Co. Finances (In Italics) / Individual Issue Statistics (Exchange)	Ind / Interest Dates	Fixed Charge Coverage 1996 / S&P Rating	Date of Last Rating Change	Fixed Charge Coverage 1997 / Prior Rating	Fixed Charge Coverage 1998 / Eligible	Year End / Bond Form	Cash & Equiv. (Million $) / Regular Price	Curr. Assets (Million $) / Regular (Begins) Thru	Curr. Liab. (Million $) / Sinking Fund Price	Balance Sheet Date / Sinking Fund (Begins) Thru	L. Term Debt (Mil $) / Refund/Other Restriction Price	Refund/Other Restriction (Begins) Thru	Capital-ization (Mil $) / Outst'g (Mil $)	Total Debt % Capital / Underwriting Firm	Underwriting Year	Price Range 1999 High	Price Range 1999 Low	Mo. End Price Sale(s) or Bid	Curr. Yield	Yield to Mat.
***Interstate Power** (Cont.)*																				
1st 8⅝s 2021	mS15	A+			X	R	106.25	9-14-00	100	....	®105.65	9-14-01	25.0	S1	'91	106¾	101⅞	102¼	8.44	8.43
1st 7⅝s 2023	Mn15	A+			X	R	104.03	5-14-00	Z100	....	®104.31	5-14-03	94.0	S1	'93	104½	95¾	95⅞	7.95	7.95
Iowa Elec Lt & Pwr	***75***	***See Interstate Power***																		
1st Y 8⅝s 2001	Mn15	A+	10/97	A	X	R	NC	....	Z100	....	....	....	60.0	M2	'91	107¼	102	102	8.46	8.45
CT Bonds 6s 2008	aO	A+	10/97	A	X	R	NC	....	Z100	....	....	....	50.0	M6	'93	102⅜	89⅝	89⅝	6.69	6.70
CT Bonds 7s 2023	aO	A+	10/97	A	X	R	102.75	(10-1-03)	Z100	....	....	....	50.0	M6	'93	103¾	86⅜	86⅜	8.10	8.10
Iowa-Illinois Gas & Elec	***75***	***Merged into MidAmer Energy,see***																		
1st 6s 2000	Ms15	A+	3/99	AA–	X	R	NC	....	....	....	....	....	35.0	S7	'93	100⅞	99⅞	100	6.00	6.00
1st 7.70s 2004	Mn15	A+	3/99	AA–	X	R	NC	....	....	....	....	....	55.6	S7	'92	110⅛	101⅛	101⅛	7.61	7.61
1st 7.45s 2023	Ms15	A+	3/99	AA–	X	R	103.97	(3-15-03)	Z103.97	(3-15-03)	....	....	6.94	S7	'93	108¾	90⅞	91	8.19	8.19
1st 6.95s 2025	aO15	A+	3/99	AA–	X	R	103.48	(10-15-03)	Z103.48	(10-15-03)	....	....	12.5	S7	'93	103⅝	85¾	85¾	8.10	8.10
Iowa Southern Utilities	***75***	***See Interstate Power***																		
1st 7¼s 2007	mS	A+	10/97	A	X	R	101.70	(9-1-02)	Z100	....	....	....	30.0	G1	'92	107	97¼	97¼	7.46	7.45
Iridium Operating LLC/Capital	***67f***	***n/a***		***n/a***	***n/a***	***Dc***	***Bankruptcy Chapt 11***				***2148***		***3231***	***74.2***						
Sr Nts[1]'D' 10⅞s 2005	§jJ15	D	7/99	CC	Z	BE			Default 7-15-99 int				350	C1	'98	86	4	4	....	Flat
Iron Mountain Inc	***63***	***1.12***		***1.10***	***1.15***	***Dc***	***3.47***	***144.9***	***116.4***	***9-30-99***	***598.0***		***1087***	***55.5***						
Sr Sub Nts[1] 10⅛s 2006	aO	B–			Y	R	105.06	(10-1-01)	....	....	....	....	165	D6	'96	109½	101	101¾	9.95	9.95
IRT Property Co	***57***	***1.85***		***2.39***	***2.25***	***Dc***				***9-30-99***	***286.0***		***554.0***	***51.6***						
Nts 7.45s 2001	Ao	BBB–			X	BE	NC	....	....	....	....	....	50.0	B10	'96	102⅛	99	99	7.53	7.53
Sr Nts 7¼s 2007	fA15	BBB–			X	BE	[2]Z100	....	....	....	....	....	75.0	P1	'97	100⅛	90	90	8.06	8.05
Irving Bank Corp[3]	***10***	***Now Bank of N.Y.,see***																		
SF Deb 8½s 2002	Jd	A+	5/97	A	X	R	100	....	100	....	....	....	16.5	S1	'77	100⅛	100⅛	100⅛	8.49	8.49
ITT Corp(Old)	***17***	***Now ITT Industries***																		
Deb 8¼s 2001	fA	BBB	10/95	A+	X	R	NC	....	....	....	....	....	13.6	M2	'89	101¼	99⅝	101	8.17	8.17
Deb 8⅞s 2008	Fa	BBB	10/95	A+	X	R	NC	....	....	....	....	....	100	M6	'88	111⅜	100⅜	103⅜	8.59	8.58
Deb 9¾s 2021	Fa15	BBB	10/95	A+	X	R	104.875	(2-15-01)	....	....	....	....	250	G1	'91	101⅝	95⅛	101⅝	9.59	9.59
Deb 9½s 2021	Ao15	BBB	10/95	A+	X	R	104.75	(4-15-01)	....	....	....	....	150	S1	'91	99⅜	94½	99¼	9.57	9.57
Deb 7.40s 2025	mN15	BBB			X	BE	[4]Z100	....	....	....	....	....	250	L1	'95	100¼	86¼	89⅝	8.26	8.26
[5]Sr SF Deb 8⅜s 2007	Ms	BBB	10/95	A	X	R	NC	....	100	....	....	....	27.7	M6	'87	102⅝	96	100½	8.33	8.33
[5]Sr Deb 8⅝s 2005	Fa15	BBB	10/95	A	X	R	NC	....	....	....	....	....	90.4	G1	'90	104	98½	102¼	8.44	8.43
[5]Sr Deb[6] 8.55s 2009	Jd15	BBB	10/95	A	X	R	NC	....	....	....	....	....	100	G1	'89	109⅞	99¾	101⅝	8.41	8.41
[5]Sr Deb 6½s 2011	Mn	BBB	10/95	A	X	R	100	....	....	....	....	....	[7]200	L3	'81	98¼	86½	87	7.47	7.47
Sub Deb 8¾s 2006	Ms	BBB–	10/95	A–	X	R	100	(3-1-01)	....	....	....	....	75.0	M6	'86	101¼	96⅝	99¾	8.77	8.77
ITT Corp(New)	***40i***	***Acquired by Starwoods Hotels***																		
Deb[8] 7⅜s 2015	mN15	BB	10/98	BBB	Y	BE	NC	....	....	....	....	....	450	B7	'95	92⅝	77¾	77¾	9.49	9.48
Deb[8] 7¾s 2025	mN15	BB	10/98	BBB	Y	BE	103.186	(11-15-05)	....	....	....	....	150	B7	'95	94	76⅛	76⅛	10.18	10.18
Nts[9] 6¼s 2000	mN15	BB	10/98	BBB	Y	BE	NC	....	....	....	....	....	700	B7	'95	98¾	95½	98⅛	6.37	6.37
Nts[8] 6¾s 2005	mN15	BB	10/98	BBB	Y	BE	NC	....	....	....	....	....	450	B7	'95	95	86⅝	86⅝	7.79	7.79
ITT Hartford Group	***35d***	***Now Hartford Finl Svcs Gp,see***																		
Nts 8.30s 2001	jD	A	9/96	A+	X	R	[10]Z100	....	....	....	....	....	200	G1	'91	105⅞	101⅛	101⅜	8.19	8.19
• Nts[11] 6⅜s 2002	mN	A	9/96	A+	X	R	[10]Z100	....	....	....	....	....	300	G1	'95	101¼	95⅛	96¾	6.59	6.59
ITT Industries[12]	***17***	***3.20***		***4.20***	***2.90***	***Dc***	***218.9***	***1735***	***1882***	***9-30-99***	***478.0***		***3160***	***38.8***						
• [5]Sr Deb 8⅞s 2003	Jd15	BBB	10/95	A	X	R	NC	....	....	....	....	....	110	L3	'78	104⅝	104⅝	102¾	8.64	8.64
[13]ITT Rayonier	***13d***	***5.48***		***5.66***	***3.58***	***Dc***	***3.67***	***275.0***	***182.1***	***9-30-99***	***433.0***		***1107***	***41.7***						
• Nts 7½s 2002	aO15	BBB+	7/96	BBB	X	BE	NC	....	....	....	....	....	110	M6	'92	No Sale		99⅝	7.53	7.53

Uniform Footnote Explanations-See Page 260. Other: [1] (HRO)On Chge of Ctrl at 101. [2] Plus Make-Whole Amt. [3] Was Charter NY Corp. [4] Co may red at greater of 100 or amt based on formula. [5] Was ITT Fin'l. [6] (HRO)On 6-15-98(&'04)at 100. [7] Incl disc. [8] State gaming laws may req hldr's sale/co red. [9] State gaming laws req hldr's sale/co red. [10] Greater:100/Discounted Remaining Fixed Amt Pyts. [11] Was Hartford Finl Serv. [12] See ITT Corp(Old),Int'l Tel & Tel. [13] Now Rayonier Inc.

Title-Industry Code & Co. Finances (In Italics)	Ind	Fixed Charge Coverage 1996	1997	1998		Year End	Million $ Cash & Equiv.	Curr. Assets	Curr. Liab.	Balance Sheet Date	L. Term Debt (Mil $)		Capital-ization (Mil $)	Total Debt % Capital						
Individual Issue Statistics Exchange ↓	Interest Dates	S&P Rating	Date of Last Rating Change	Prior Rating	Eligible ↓	Bond Form	Redemption Provisions: Regular Price	Regular (Begins) Thru	Sinking Fund Price	Sinking Fund (Begins) Thru	Refund/Other Restriction Price	Refund/Other Restriction (Begins) Thru	Outst'g (Mil $)	Underwriting Firm	Underwriting Year	Price Range 1999 High	Price Range 1999 Low	Mo. End Price Sale(s) or Bid	Curr. Yield	Yield to Mat.
James River Corp	***50***	***Merged w/Fort Howard,see Fort James***																		
Deb 9¼s 2021	mN15	BBB	8/99	BBB–	X	R	NC	....	....	....	....	....	200	S1	'91	127½	109½	110¼	8.39	8.39
Deb 7¾s 2023	mN15	BBB	8/99	BBB–	X	R	NC	....	....	....	....	....	150	S1	'93	109⅝	93⅞	94¾	8.18	8.18
Nts 8⅜s 2001	mN15	BBB	8/99	BBB–	X	R	NC	....	....	....	....	....	200	S1	'91	106¾	101¾	101¾	8.23	8.23
Nts 6.70s 2003	mN15	BBB	8/99	BBB–	X	R	NC	....	....	....	....	....	250	S1	'93	103¼	97	97	6.91	6.91
JCAC, Inc	***12b***	***1.47***	***1.02***	***1.17***		***Dc***	***31.55***	***298.1***	***254.4***	***9-30-99***	***1596***		***2834***	***57.6***						
Gtd[1]Sr Sub Nts[2] 10⅛s 2006	Jd15	B+	5/99	B	Y	BE	105.063	(6-15-01)	....	....	....	....	100	D6	'96	111½	105⅜	109	9.29	9.29
JDN Realty	***57***	***n/a***	***5.99***	***2.94***		***Dc***				***9-30-99***	***550.0***		***1030***	***48.8***						
Nts 6.80s 2004	fA	BBB–			X	BE	[3]Z100	....	....	....	....	....	75.0	M2	'97	99	92⅞	92⅞	7.32	7.32
JeffBanks Inc[4]	***10***	***2.62***	***3.21***	***2.05***		***Dc***				***9-30-99***	***191.0***		***349.0***	***54.7***						
Sub Nts 8¾s 2006	Ao	NR				BE	100	(4-1-01)	....	....	....	....	23.0	B10	'96	100¾	89¼	98⅞	8.85	8.85
Jersey Cent'l Pwr.& Lt[5]	***72a***	***3.33***	***4.17***	***4.56***		***Dc***	***1.07***	***470.0***	***536.0***	***9-30-99***	***1134***		***3044***	***41.0***						
• 1st 6⅜s 2003	Mn	A+	1/99	A–	X	R	NC	....	Z100	....	Z100	....	150	L3	'93	103	96⅞	97	6.57	6.57
• 1st 7⅛s 2004	aO	A+	1/99	A–	X	R	100	(10-1-02)	Z100	....	....	....	160	S7	'92	105	98¾	98⅜	7.24	7.24
• 1st 7½s 2023	Mn	A+	1/99	A–	X	R	103.33	(4-27-03)	Z100	....	....	....	125	M2	'93	106	93½	95	7.89	7.89
• 1st 6¾s 2025		A+	1/99	A–	X	R	102.82	(10-27-03)	Z100	....	....	....	150	M6	'93	100⅜	83¾	84	8.04	8.04
Sec M-T Nts 'B'[6] 9s 2002	[7]jj	A+	1/99	A–	X	BE	100	(3-27-01)	Z100	....	....	....	50.0	M2	'91	106⅞	102	102	8.82	8.82
Sec M-T Nts 'B'[6] 8¼s 2006	[8]jj	A+	1/99	A–	X	BE	100	(11-19-01)	Z100	....	....	....	50.0	M2	'91	114⅜	101¾	101¾	8.11	8.11
Sec M-T Nts 'B'[6] 7.90s 2007	[9]jj	A+	1/99	A–	X	BE	100	(1-23-02)	Z100	....	....	....	40.0	M2	'92	106⅛	98¾	98¾	8.00	8.00
Sec M-T Nts 'B'[6] 9.20s 2021	jJ	A+	1/99	A–	X	BE	104.60	(7-1-01)	Z100	....	....	....	50.0	M2	'91	110⅝	102⅛	102⅛	9.01	9.01
Sec M-T Nts 'B'[6] 8.55s 2022	[10]jj	A+	1/99	A–	X	BE	104.28	(1-29-02)	Z100	....	....	....	30.0	M2	'92	120⅜	101½	101⅝	8.41	8.41
Sec M-T Nts 'C'[6] 6.04s 2000	[11]ms	A+	1/99	A–	X	BE	NC	....	Z100	....	....	....	40.0	M2	'93	100⅜	99¾	100	6.04	6.04
Sec M-T Nts 'C'[6] 6.78s 2005	[12]ms	A+	1/99	A–	X	BE	100	(3-29-03)	Z100	....	....	....	50.0	M2	'93	103¼	95⅞	95⅞	7.07	7.07
Sec M-T Nts 'C'[6] 8.82s 2022	[13]ms	A+	1/99	A–	X	BE	104.41	(3-27-02)	Z100	....	....	....	12.0	M2	'92	112⅛	101½	101½	8.69	8.69
Sec M-T Nts 'C'[6] 8.85s 2022	[14]ms	A+	1/99	A–	X	BE	104.43	(3-27-02)	Z100	....	....	....	38.0	M2	'92	123⅞	104⅝	104⅝	8.46	8.46
Sec M-T Nts 'C'[6] 8.32s 2022	[15]ms	A+	1/99	A–	X	BE	104.16	(12-18-02)	Z100	....	....	....	40.0	M2	'92	107½	96⅛	96⅛	8.66	8.65
Sec M-T Nts 'C'[6] 7.98s 2023	[16]ms	A+	1/99	A–	X	BE	103.99	(2-16-03)	Z100	....	....	....	40.0	M2	'93	108	95⅛	95⅛	8.39	8.39
Sec M-T Nts 'D'[6] 8.45s 2025	[17]jd	A+	1/99	A–	X	BE	104.23	(3-23-05)	Z100	....	....	....	50.0	M6	'95	113⅜	99¼	99¼	8.51	8.51
Jitney-Jungle Stores of America	***59c***	[18]***2.92***	[19]***0.59***	***0.83***		***Dc***	***Bankruptcy Chapt 11***				***580.0***		***462.0***	***129.0***						
Sr Nts[2] 12s 2006	§Ms	D	10/99	B+	Z	R			Default 9-1-99 int				200	D6	'96	112¼	24	24	....	Flat
Johnson Controls	***13b***	***6.74***	***4.75***	***4.77***		***Sp***	***248.6***	***3647***	***4060***	***6-30-99***	***1294***		***4026***	***45.1***						
Deb[20] 7.70s 2015	Ms	A–	7/98	A	X	BE	NC	....	....	....	....	....	125	S1	'95	115	101¼	101¼	7.60	7.60
Deb 8.20s 2024	Jd15	A–	7/98	A	X	BE	104.10	(6-15-04)	....	....	....	....	125	S1	'94	111½	98¾	98⅞	8.29	8.29
Deb 6.95s 2045	jD	A–	7/98	A	X	BE	NC	....	....	....	....	....	125	M5	'95	107	85¼	85⅜	8.14	8.14
Nts 6.30s 2008	Fa	A–	7/98	A	X	BE	NC	....	....	....	....	....	175	S4	'98	104	91¾	91¾	6.87	6.87
Nts 7⅛s 2017	jJ15	A–	7/98	A	X	BE	NC	....	....	....	....	....	150	M5	'97	108⅛	92⅝	92¾	7.68	7.68
Johnson & Johnson	***43***	***23.10***	***29.35***	***28.49***		***Dc***	***3593***	***12857***	***6980***	***10-3-99***	***1992***		***18057***	***21.1***						
Deb 6⅝s 2009	mS	AAA			X	BE	NC	....	....	....	....	....	200	C1	'99	100⅜	96¼	96¼	6.88	6.88
Deb 6.73s 2023	mN15	AAA			X	BE	NC	....	....	....	....	....	250	M6	'93	108¾	91⅜	91½	7.36	7.35
Deb 8.72s 2024	mN	AAA			X	BE	104.36	(11-1-04)	....	....	....	....	300	M2	'94	117⅝	107	107⅝	8.10	8.10
Deb 6.95s 2029	mS	AAA			X	BE	NC	....	....	....	....	....	300	C1	'99	99½	94⅜	94½	7.35	7.35
Nts 7⅜s 2002	Jd29	AAA			X	BE	NC	....	....	....	....	....	200	M2	'92	106⅝	101¼	101¼	7.28	7.28
[21]***Johnstown America Indus***	***56***	***0.81***	***1.11***	***2.49***		***Dc***	***13.48***	***144.7***	***91.08***	***9-30-99***	***203.0***		***379.0***	***54.6***						
Sr Sub Nts[2] 11¾s 2005	fA15	B			Y	BE	105.875	(8-15-00)	....	....	....	....	100	C2	'95	108½	101	101¾	11.55	11.54
Jones Intercable	***12a***	***0.05***	***d0.25***	***0.18***		***Dc***	***20.80***	***82.20***	***152.0***	***9-30-99***	***1643***		***1634***	***103.0***						
Sr Nts 9⅝s 2002	Ms15	BBB–	7/99	BB+	X	R	NC	....	....	....	....	....	200	S1	'95	107½	104¼	104⅜	9.22	9.22

Uniform Footnote Explanations-See Page 260. Other: [1] Gtd by Jacor Communications. [2] (HRO)On Chge of Ctrl at 101. [3] Plus Make-Whole Amt. [4] Acq by Hudson United Bancorp. [5] Subsid of Gen'l Pub Utilities. [6] Issued in min denom $100T. [7] Due 3-27-02. [8] Due 11-20-06. [9] Due 1-23-07. [10] Due 1-31-22. [11] Due 3-15-00. [12] Due 3-29-05. [13] Due 3-28-22. [14] Due 3-29-22. [15] Due 12-19-22. [16] Due 2-16-23. [17] Due 3-24-25. [18] Fiscal Apr'96. [19] 35 Wk Dec'97. [20] (HRO)On 3-1-05 at 100. [21] Now Transportation Technologies Ind.

Title-Industry Code & Co. Finances (In Italics) / Individual Issue Statistics (Exchange)	Ind / Interest Dates	Fixed Charge Coverage 1996 / S&P Rating	Date of Last Rating Change	1997 / Prior Rating	1998 / Eligible	Year End / Bond Form	Million $ Cash & Equiv. / Redemption Provisions Regular Price	Curr. Assets / Regular (Begins) Thru	Curr. Liab. / Sinking Fund Price	Balance Sheet Date / Sinking Fund (Begins) Thru	L. Term Debt (Mil $) / Refund/Other Restriction Price	Refund/Other Restriction (Begins) Thru	Capital-ization (Mil $) / Outst'g (Mil $)	Total Debt % Capital / Underwriting Firm	Underwriting Year	Price Range 1999 High	Price Range 1999 Low	Mo. End Price Sale(s) or Bid	Curr. Yield	Yield to Mat.
***Jones Intercable** (Cont.)*																				
Sr Nts 8⅞s 2007	Ao	**BBB–**	7/99	BB+	X	R	101.109	(4-1-04)	....	....	....	....	250	L3	'97	111	101¾	102⅝	8.67	8.67
Sr Nts 7⅝s 2008	Ao15	**BBB–**	7/99	BB+	X	BE	NC	....	....	....	....	....	200	S4	'98	106	97⅝	97⅝	7.81	7.81
Sr Sub Deb 10½s 2008	Ms	**BB+**	8/99	BB	Y	R	105.25	(3-1-00)	....	....	....	....	100	L3	'93	111	105⅝	105⅝	9.94	9.94
JPS Automotive L.P.	***8***	***0.82***		***2.15***	***1.95***	***Dc***	***7.97***	***68.60***	***16.70***	***9-25-99***	***87.60***		***204.0***	***42.9***						
• Sr Nts[1] 11⅛s 2001	Jd15	**B**			Y	R	NC	....	....	....	....	....	117	D6	'94	No Sale		104¼	10.67	10.67
K-III Communications	***54***	***Now PRIMEDIA Inc,see***																		
Sr[1]Nts[2] 10¼s 2004	Jd	**BB–**			Y	R	104.95	5-31-00	....	....	[3]Z101	....	100	M2	'94	106½	100	104	9.86	9.85
Sr Nts[1]'B' 8½s 2006	Fa	**BB–**			Y	BE	104.25	(2-1-01)	....	....	[3]Z101	....	300	Exch.	'96	103	97	98½	8.63	8.63
Kaiser Alum & Chem[4]	***5***	***1.04***		***1.56***	***0.86***	***Dc***	***8.60***	***977.0***	***564.0***	***9-30-99***	***970.0***		***1118***	***86.8***						
Sr Nts[5] 9⅞s 2002	Fa15	**B**	10/96	B+	Y	R	102.75	2-14-00	....	....	....	....	225	M2	'94	102	97	98½	10.03	10.02
Sr Nts[5]'B' 10⅞s 2006	aO15	**B**			Y	BE	105.437	(10-15-01)	....	....	....	....	175		'97	104	97½	100¼	10.85	10.85
Sr[1]Nts 'D' 10⅞s 2006	aO15	**B**			Y	BE	105.437	(10-15-01)	....	....	....	....	50.0	Exch.	'97	104	98	101	10.77	10.77
Sr Sub Nts[5] 12¾s 2003	Fa	**CCC+**	10/96	B–	Y	R	104.25	1-31-00	....	....	....	....	400	M2	'93	102	96	100	12.75	12.74
Kansas City Power & Light	***72a***	***3.26***		***2.07***	***2.11***	***Dc***	***36.80***	***256.0***	***521.0***	***9-30-99***	***847.0***		***2199***	***49.2***						
Sec M-T Nts 7.55s 2000	[6]ao	**A**			X	BE	NC	....	....	....	....	....	15.0	M2	'91	102	100	100	7.55	Mat.
Sec M-T Nts 6.51s 2000	[7]fa	**A**			X	BE	NC	....	....	....	....	....	9.00	M2	'93	101⅛	100	100	6.51	6.51
Sec M-T Nts 6½s 2000	[8]fa	**A**			X	BE	NC	....	....	....	....	....	17.0	M2	'93	101⅛	100	100	6.50	6.50
Sec M-T Nts 6½s 2001	[9]ms	**A**			X	BE	NC	....	....	....	....	....	10.0	M2	'93	102	99½	99½	6.53	6.53
Sec M-T Nts 6.40s 2001	[10]ms	**A**			X	BE	NC	....	....	....	....	....	20.0	M2	'93	102	99¼	99¼	6.45	6.45
Sec M-T Nts 6½s 2003	[11]ms	**A**			X	BE	NC	....	....	....	....	....	9.00	M2	'93	103⅝	97¾	97¾	6.65	6.65
Sec M-T Nts 6½s 2003	[12]ms	**A**			X	BE	NC	....	....	....	....	....	10.0	M2	'93	103⅝	97¾	97¾	6.65	6.65
Sec M-T Nts 7.85s 2004	[13]fa	**A**			X	BE	NC	....	....	....	....	....	14.5	M2	'92	110½	101⅞	101⅞	7.71	7.70
Sec M-T Nts 7.35s 2004	[14]fa	**A**			X	BE	NC	....	....	....	....	....	12.0	M2	'92	108¼	99⅞	99⅞	7.36	7.36
Sec M-T Nts 7.35s 2005	[15]fa	**A**			X	BE	102.21	9-30-00	....	....	....	....	40.0	S7	'92	109⅜	99⅛	99⅛	7.41	7.41
Sec M-T Nts 7½s 2007	[16]fa	**A**			X	BE	103	1-31-00	....	....	....	....	6.00	M2	'93	111½	99	99	7.58	7.57
Sec M-T Nts 6.99s 2007	[17]ms	**A**			X	BE	102.80	3-4-00	....	....	....	....	10.0	M2	'93	108¼	96¼	96¼	7.26	7.26
Sec M-T Nts 6.98s 2007	[17]ms	**A**			X	BE	102.79	3-2-00	....	....	....	....	5.00	M2	'93	108⅛	96¼	96¼	7.25	7.25
Sec M-T Nts 6.98s 2007	[18]ms	**A**			X	BE	102.79	3-8-00	....	....	....	....	6.00	M2	'93	108⅛	96¼	96¼	7.25	7.25
Kansas City So Ind	***55***	***3.81***		***2.24***	***6.46***	***Dc***	***322.8***	***655.1***	***357.7***	***9-30-99***	***781.0***		***1802***	***46.4***						
Deb 8.80s 2022	jJ	**BBB–**	5/97	BBB+	X	BE	104.04	6-30-03	....	....	....	....	100	M2	'92	110	100⅝	103½	8.50	8.50
Deb 7s 2025	jD15	**BBB–**	5/97	BBB+	X	BE	[19]Z100	....	....	....	....	....	100	S1	'95	101⅜	86¾	94¾	7.39	7.39
Nts 7⅞s 2002	jJ	**BBB–**	5/97	BBB+	X	BE	NC	....	....	....	....	....	100	M2	'92	106⅛	101⅜	102⅞	7.65	7.65
Nts 6⅝s 2005	Ms	**BBB–**	5/97	BBB+	X	BE	NC	....	....	....	....	....	100	F1	'93	103⅝	96⅛	98⅞	6.70	6.70
Kansas Gas & Electric[20]	***72a***	***3.25***		***2.38***	***4.01***	***Dc***	***0.04***	***271.0***	***207.0***	***9-30-99***	***684.0***		***1824***	***37.5***						
1st 7.60s 2003	jD15	**BBB+**	1/97	A–	X	R	NC	....	....	....	....	....	135	D4	'92	108	100⅜	100⅜	7.57	7.57
1st 6½s 2005	fA	**BBB+**	1/97	A–	X	R	NC	....	....	....	....	....	65.0	D4	'93	104⅝	95⅜	95⅜	6.82	6.81
1st 6.20s 2006	Jj15	**BBB+**	1/97	A–	X	R	NC	....	....	....	....	....	100	D4	'94	102¾	93⅜	93⅜	6.64	6.64
Kansas Power & Light	***75***	***Now Western Resources,see***																		
1st 8⅞s 2000	Ms	**A–**	10/97	BBB+	X	R	NC	....	....	....	....	....	75.0	D4	'90	103⅝	100¼	100¼	8.85	8.85
Kaufman & Broad Home	***13h***	***1.65***		***2.06***	***2.75***	***Nv***				***8-31-99***	***1552***		***2238***	***69.3***						
• Sr Nts[1] 7¾s 2004	aO15	**BB+**	7/98	BB	Y	R	NC	....	....	....	....	....	175	G1	'97	102⅞	90	s98⅜	7.88	7.88
• Sr Sub Nts[1] 9⅝s 2006	mN15	**BB–**	7/98	B+	Y	R	104.8125	(11-15-01)	....	....	....	....	125	M2	'96	107⅜	99	s107⅜	8.96	8.96
• Sr Sub Nts[1] 9⅜s 2003	Mn	**BB–**	7/98	B+	Y	R	100	(5-1-00)	....	....	....	....	175	M2	'93	103⅞	97⅛	s98⅛	9.55	9.55
KCS Energy Inc	***73e***	***3.44***		***d5.83***	***0.66***	***Dc***	***0.02***	***0.05***	***0.44***	***9-30-99***			***119.0***	***231.0***						
Sr Nts[1]'B' 11s 2003	§Jj15	**D**	8/99	CCC–	Z	BE			Default 7-15-99 int				150	Exch.	'96	96	56	80	....	Flat

Uniform Footnote Explanations-See Page 260. Other: [1] (HRO)On Chge of Ctrl at 101. [2] Red on Chge of Ctrl at 100,plus Applicable Prem. [3] On Chge of Ctrl,plus Premium. [4] Subsid of Kaiser Aluminum Corp. [5] Co must offer repurch at 101 on Chge of Ctrl. [6] Due 1-4-00. [7] Due 2-11-00. [8] Due 2-14-00. [9] Due 1-2-01. [10] Due 3-2-01. [11] Due 4-21-03. [12] Due 5-1-03. [13] Due 7-2-04. [14] Due 8-3-04. [15] Due 10-1-05. [16] Due 1-29-07. [17] Due 3-5-07. [18] Due 3-9-07. [19] Greater of 100 or amt based on formula. [20] Subsid of Western Resources.

Title-Industry Code & Co. Finances (In Italics) / Individual Issue Statistics, Exchange	Ind / Interest Dates	Fixed Charge Coverage 1996 / S&P Rating	1997 / Date of Last Rating Change	1998 / Prior Rating	Eligible	Year End / Bond Form	Cash & Equiv. (Million $) / Regular Price	Curr. Assets (Million $) / Regular (Begins) Thru	Curr. Liab. (Million $) / Sinking Fund Price	Balance Sheet Date / Sinking Fund (Begins) Thru	L. Term Debt (Mil $) / Refund/Other Restriction Price	Refund/Other Restriction (Begins) Thru	Capitalization (Mil $) / Outst'g (Mil $)	Total Debt % Capital / Underwriting Firm	Underwriting Year	Price Range 1999 High	Price Range 1999 Low	Mo. End Price Sale(s) or Bid	Curr. Yield	Yield to Mat.
***KCS Energy Inc** (Cont.)*																				
• Sr Sub Nts[1] 8⅞s 2008	§Jj15	**D**	8/99	C	Z	BE			Default 7-15-99 int				125	S4	'98	66⅜	14½	27¼	....	Flat
Kellogg Co	***26***	***15.17***	***10.15***	***7.66***		***Dc***	***150.8***	***1686***	***1640***	***9-30-99***	***1611***		***2944***	***72.4***						
Nts 4⅞s 2005	aO15	**AA**			X	BE	NC	....	....	....	....	....	200	G1	'98	97⅞	89⅞	89⅞	5.42	5.43
Kellwood Co	***68c***	***△4.01***	***△3.56***	***△4.46***		***Ap***	***111.9***	***868.7***	***240.9***	***10-31-99***	***370.0***		***845.0***	***46.4***						
Deb 7⅝s 2017	aO15	**BBB**			X	BE	[2]Z100	....	....	....	....	....	150	M2	'97	99½	87⅝	87¾	8.69	8.69
Kentucky Power[3]	***72a***	***1.96***	***2.19***	***2.15***		***Dc***	***1.07***	***94.40***	***202.0***	***9-30-99***	***261.0***		***664.0***	***58.3***						
1st 6.65s 2003	Mn	**A**	10/97	BBB+	X	BE	100.95	4-30-00	Z100	....	....	....	15.0	S1	'93	100⅜	97⅛	97⅛	6.85	6.85
1st 6.70s 2003	[4]fa	**A**	10/97	BBB+	X	BE	100.96	5-31-00	Z100	....	....	....	15.0	S1	'93	100½	96⅞	96⅞	6.92	6.92
1st 6.70s 2003	[5]fa	**A**	10/97	BBB+	X	BE	100.96	6-30-00	Z100	....	....	....	15.0	S1	'93	102⅝	97	97	6.91	6.91
1st 7.90s 2023	[4]fa	**A**	10/97	BBB+	X	BE	105.53	5-31-00	Z100	....	....	....	25.0	S1	'93	105⅝	92⅝	95⅛	8.30	8.30
M-T Nts 'A' 6.91s 2007	aO	**BBB**			X	BE	NC	....	....	....	....	....	48.0	M2	'97	104⅞	93¾	93¾	7.37	7.37
M-T Nts 'A' 6.45s 2008	[6]ao	**BBB**			X	BE	NC	....	....	....	....	....	30.0	M2	'98	101⅜	89⅞	89⅞	7.18	7.18
Kentucky Utilities[7]	***72a***	***4.37***	***4.36***	***4.83***		***Dc***	***37.10***	***230.0***	***325.0***	***9-30-99***	***485.0***		***1218***	***44.8***						
1st P 7.92s 2007	Mn15	**AA–**	8/98	AA	X	R	NC	....	....	....	....	....	53.0	G1	'92	115⅜	101½	101½	7.80	7.80
1st P 8.55s 2027	Mn15	**AA–**	8/98	AA	X	R	105.13	(5-15-02)	....	....	....	....	33.0	G1	'92	112⅜	99⅜	99½	8.59	8.59
1st Q 5.95s 2000	Jd15	**AA–**	8/98	AA	X	R	NC	....	....	....	....	....	61.5	G1	'93	101	99¾	99¾	5.96	5.96
1st Q 6.32s 2003	Jd15	**AA–**	8/98	AA	X	R	NC	....	....	....	....	....	62.0	G1	'93	104	97⅜	97⅜	6.49	6.49
1st R 7.55s 2025	Jd	**AA–**	8/98	AA	X	BE	103.775	(6-1-05)	....	....	....	....	50.0	G1	'95	111	92	92⅛	8.20	8.19
1st S 5.99s 2006	Jj15	**AA–**	8/98	AA	X	BE	NC	....	....	....	....	....	36.0	G1	'96	103½	93½	93½	6.41	6.41
Kerr-McGee Corp	***49b***	***6.15***	***5.98***	***0.91***		***Dc***	***184.4***	***1096***	***826.8***	***9-30-99***	***2476***		***3743***	***68.1***						
Deb 7s 2011	mN	**BBB**	3/99	A–	X	R	100	....	....	....	....	....	[8]250	L3	'81	106⅛	92	92½	7.57	7.57
Deb 7⅛s 2027	aO15	**BBB**	3/99	A–	X	BE	[9]Z100	....	....	....	....	....	150	L3	'97	103	86⅝	86¾	8.21	8.21
Nts 6⅝s 2007	aO15	**BBB**	3/99	A–	X	BE	[9]Z100	....	....	....	....	....	150	L3	'97	103¼	91⅝	91⅝	7.23	7.23
Key Plastics, Inc.	***52***	***n/a***	***0.40***	***0.98***		***Dc***	***13.70***	***225.0***	***135.0***	***9-30-99***	***428.0***		***450.0***	***95.1***						
Sr[1]Sub Nts 'B' 10¼s 2007	Ms15	**CCC+**	11/99	B–	Y	BE	105.125	(3-15-02)	....	....	[10]Z109.25	3-15-00	125	Exch.	'97	101¾	38	38	....	....
[11]KeyCorp[12]	***10***	***2.49***	***2.34***	***2.48***		***Dc***				***9-30-99***	***17058***		***32006***	***80.0***						
Sub Nts 8s 2004	jJ	**BBB+**			X	R	NC	....	....	....	....	....	125	M2	'92	110⅜	101⅝	101⅝	7.87	7.87
Sub Nts 6¾s 2006	Ms15	**BBB+**			X	BE	NC	....	....	....	....	....	200	C5	'96	105⅝	95½	95¾	7.05	7.05
Sub Nts 7½s 2006	Jd15	**BBB+**			X	BE	NC	....	....	....	....	....	250	M5	'96	110¼	98⅞	99¼	7.56	7.56
Keystone Finl Mid-Atlantic Fdg	***10***	***n/a***	***4.37***	***4.06***		***Dc***				***9-30-99***	***808.0***		***1130***	***48.3***						
Sr M-T[13]Nts[14] 7.30s 2004	Mn15	**BBB+**	6/98	NR	X	BE	NC	....	....	....	....	....	100	G1	'97	106¼	98¼	98¼	7.43	7.43
Sr M-T[14]Nts[13] 6½s 2008	Mn31	**BBB+**			X	BE	NC	....	....	....	....	....	30.0		'98	102⅝	91⅜	91⅜	7.11	7.11
Kimberly-Clark[15]	***33***	***10.89***	***11.13***	***9.13***		***Dc***	***194.3***	***3419***	***3951***	***9-30-99***	***1996***		***8247***	***35.1***						
Deb 6⅞s 2014	Fa15	**AA**			X	BE	NC	....	....	....	....	....	100	G1	'94	116⅞	94⅝	94⅝	7.27	7.26
Deb 6¼s 2018	jJ15	**AA**			X	BE	[9]Z100	....	....	....	....	....	300	S4	'98	104	88¼	88⅜	7.07	7.07
Deb 7⅞s 2023	Fa	**AA**			X	BE	103.85	(2-1-03)	....	....	....	....	200	G1	'93	111	97⅞	98	8.04	8.03
Deb 6⅜s 2028	Jj	**AA**			X	BE	[9]Z100	....	....	....	....	....	200	S4	'98	105⅛	86⅝	86⅝	7.36	7.36
Nts 9s 2000	fA	**AA**			X	R	NC	....	....	....	....	....	100	G1	'90	106	101⅝	101⅝	8.86	8.85
Nts 8⅝s 2001	Mn	**AA**			X	R	NC	....	....	....	....	....	200	G1	'91	108	102⅝	102⅝	8.40	8.40
Kimco Realty[16]	***57***	***3.56***	***3.56***	***2.98***		***Dc***				***9-30-99***	***1141***		***2746***	***41.6***						
Sr Nts 6½s 2003	aO	**A–**			X	BE	NC	....	....	....	....	....	100	M2	'93	99⅝	95½	95½	6.81	6.81
M-T Nts 7.91s 2005	[17]ao	**A–**			X	BE	NC	....	....	....	....	....	20.0	M2	'95	105¾	99⅝	99⅝	7.94	7.94
Sr Nts 6⅞s 2009	Fa10	**A–**			X	BE	NC	....	....	....	....	....	130	M2	'99	99⅞	91⅜	91⅜	7.52	7.52
M-T Nts 'A' 6.73s 2005	[18]ao	**A–**			X	BE	NC	....	....	....	....	....	100	M2	'98	100	94	94¼	7.14	7.14

Uniform Footnote Explanations-See Page 260. Other: [1] (HRO)On Chge of Ctrl at 101. [2] Plus Make-Whole Amt. [3] Subsid of Amer Elec Pwr. [4] Due Jun 1. [5] Due Jul 1. [6] Due 11-10-08. [7] Subsid of KU Energy. [8] Incl disc. [9] Red at greater of 100 or amt based on formula. [10] Max $44M red w/proceeds of Pub Eq Off'g. [11] Was Key Banks,First Commercial Banks. [12] See Society Corp. [13] Gtd by Keystone Fin'l Inc. [14] Issued in min denom $100T. [15] See Scott Paper Co. [16] See Price REIT. [17] Due 4-26-05. [18] Due 6-30-05.

Title-Industry Code & Co. Finances (In Italics) / Individual Issue Statistics (Exchange)	Ind / Interest Dates	Fixed Charge Coverage 1996 / S&P Rating	1997 / Date of Last Rating Change	1998 / Prior Rating	Eligible	Year End / Bond Form	Million $ Cash & Equiv. / Redemption Provisions: Regular Price	Million $ Curr. Assets / Regular (Begins) Thru	Curr. Liab. / Sinking Fund Price	Balance Sheet Date / Sinking Fund (Begins) Thru	L. Term Debt (Mil $) / Refund/Other Restriction Price	Refund/Other Restriction (Begins) Thru	Capitalization (Mil $) / Outst'g (Mil $)	Total Debt % Capital / Underwriting Firm	Year	Price Range 1999 High	Low	Mo. End Price Sale(s) or Bid	Curr. Yield	Yield to Mat.
Kimco Realty *(Cont.)*																				
M-T Nts 'A' 6.93s 2006	[1]ao	A–			X	BE	NC	....	....	....	....	....	30.0		'98	101⅛	93¼	93¾	7.39	7.39
KinderCare Learning Ctrs	***63***	*△1.09*	*△1.13*	*△1.53*		*My*	*5.75*	*45.60*	*117.0*	*5-28-99*	*414.0*		*478.0*	*89.1*						
Sr Sub Nts[2] 9½s 2009	Fa15	B–			Y	BE	104.75	(2-15-02)	....	....	[3]Z109.50	2-15-00	300	Exch.	'97	105½	91½	97½	9.74	9.74
K mart	***59g***	*1.62*	*2.17*	*3.24*		*Ja*	*345.0*	*9696*	*4769*	*10-27-99*	*4746*		*10746*	*44.9*						
Deb 12½s 2005	Ms	BB+	3/99	BB	Y	R	NC	....	....	....	....	....	100	G1	'85	125¾	112⅛	112⅝	11.10	11.10
Deb 7¾s 2012	aO	BB+	3/99	BB	Y	BE	NC	....	....	....	....	....	200	M6	'92	103½	88	88½	8.76	8.76
Deb[4] 8⅜s 2022	jJ	BB+	3/99	BB	Y	BE	103.913	(7-1-02)	....	....	....	....	100	M6	'92	102⅞	88¾	89⅞	9.32	9.32
Deb 7.95s 2023	Fa	BB+	3/99	BB	Y	BE	NC	....	....	....	....	....	300	G1	'93	103	86⅞	86⅞	9.15	9.15
Nts 8⅜s 2004	jD	BB+			Y	BE	[5]Z100	....	....	....	....	....	300	M7	'99	100¼	98½	98½	8.50	8.50
Nts 8⅛s 2006	jD	BB+	3/99	BB	Y	BE	NC	....	....	....	....	....	200	M6	'91	107½	95¾	96¾	8.40	8.40
Nts 8¼s 2022	Jj	BB+	3/99	BB	Y	BE	NC	....	....	....	....	....	100	M6	'92	103	87⅞	87⅞	9.39	9.39
[6]KN Energy[7]	***73b***	*3.86*	*3.80*	*1.41*		*Dc*	*22.46*	*960.8*	*1472*	*9-30-99*	*3575*		*5516*	*76.3*						
SF Deb 9.95s 2020	Ao	BBB–	2/98	BBB+	X	R	103.58	(4-1-00)	100	(4-1-01)	....	....	20.0	M2	'90	107¾	104⅛	104⅛	9.56	9.56
SF Deb 9⅝s 2021	fA	BBB–	2/98	BBB+	X	R	104.81	(8-1-01)	100	(8-1-02)	....	....	45.0	D4	'91	111¾	106½	106½	9.04	9.04
SF Deb 8.35s 2022	mS15	BBB–	2/98	BBB+	X	BE	104.175	(9-15-02)	100	(9-15-03)	....	....	35.0	M2	'92	109⅝	103⅞	103⅞	8.04	8.04
Deb 6½s 2013	mS	BBB–	2/98	BBB+	X	BE	NC	....	100	(9-1-04)	....	....	50.0	D4	'93	102⅞	89⅝	92	7.07	7.06
Deb[8] 7.85s 2022	mS	BBB–	2/98	BBB+	X	BE	103	8-31-00	....	....	....	....	30.0	J2	'92	109⅝	97⅛	97⅛	8.08	8.08
Deb 8¾s 2024	aO15	BBB–	2/98	BBB+	X	BE	104	(10-15-04)	....	....	....	....	75.0	M2	'94	109⅛	96	100	8.75	8.75
Deb[9] 7.35s 2026	fA	BBB–	2/98	BBB+	X	BE	[10]Z100	(8-1-06)	....	....	....	....	125	M2	'96	105¼	97½	97½	7.54	7.54
Deb[11] 6.67s 2027	mN	BBB–	2/98	BBB+	X	BE	[5]Z100	(11-1-04)	....	....	....	....	150	M2	'97	104	95⅞	95⅞	6.96	6.96
Sr Deb 7¼s 2028	Ms	BBB–			X	BE	[5]Z100	....	....	....	....	....	500	M7	'98	104⅝	88⅜	90⅛	8.04	8.04
Sr Deb 7.45s 2098	Ms	BBB–			X	BE	[5]Z100	....	....	....	....	....	150	M7	'98	103⅞	84¼	87⅝	8.50	8.50
Sr Nts 6.45s 2003	Ms	BBB–			X	BE	NC	....	....	....	....	....	500	M7	'98	101⅝	96½	97	6.65	6.65
Sr Nts 6.65s 2005	Ms	BBB–			X	BE	NC	....	....	....	....	....	500	M7	'98	102	95⅝	95⅞	6.94	6.94
Sr Nts 6.80s 2008	Ms	BBB–			X	BE	[5]Z100	....	....	....	....	....	300	M7	'98	103⅝	93	94⅛	7.22	7.22
Knight-Ridder Inc[12]	***54c***	*7.00*	*7.71*	*5.63*		*Dc*	*31.70*	*512.8*	*571.4*	*9-26-99*	*1173*		*3150*	*42.7*						
Deb 9⅞s 2009	Ao15	A	5/97	AA–	X	R	NC	....	....	....	....	....	200	G1	'89	131⅛	114⅜	114⅜	8.63	8.63
Deb 7.15s 2027	mN	A			X	BE	[5]Z100	....	....	....	....	....	100	G1	'97	109⅛	91	91⅛	7.85	7.85
Amortizing[13]Nts 8½s 2001	mS	A	5/97	AA–	X	R	NC	....	....	....	....	....	120	G1	'91	104½	100⅞	101	8.42	....
Sr Nts 6.30s 2005	jD15	A	5/97	AA–	X	BE	[10]Z100	....	....	....	....	....	100	G1	'95	103¾	94¾	94⅞	6.64	6.64
Kohl's Corp	***59f***	*10.66*	*10.55*	*14.85*		*Ja*	*36.07*	*1367*	*643.7*	*10-30-99*	*495.0*		*2014*	*25.3*						
Nts 6.70s 2006	Fa	BBB+	11/98	BBB	X	BE	NC	....	....	....	....	....	100	M6	'96	104½	95⅝	95⅝	7.02	7.02
Nts 7⅜s 2011	aO15	BBB+	11/98	BBB	X	BE	NC	....	....	....	....	....	100	M6	'96	111¾	96⅞	96⅞	7.61	7.61
Koppers Industries	***14***	*1.66*	*d0.08*	*1.80*		*Dc*	*26.90*	*217.0*	*107.0*	*9-30-99*	*313.0*		*339.0*	*96.8*						
• Sr Nts[2] 8½s 2004	Fa	B–	11/97	BB–	Y	R	104.25	1-31-00	....	....	....	....	11.1	S7	'94	104⅛	70½	72⅝	11.70	11.70
[14]Kraft Inc	***26***	***Subsid of Philip Morris Cos,see***																		
SF Deb 8½s 2017	Fa15	A	11/88	AA	X	R	103	2-14-00	100	....	....	....	175	G1	'87	103⅜	100⅞	102⅜	8.30	8.30
Kroger Co	***59c***	*2.89*	*3.50*	*[15]3.67*		*Ja*	*283.0*	*5597*	*6299*	*11-6-99*	*7863*		*10801*	*77.7*						
Sr Nts 8.15s 2006	jJ15	BBB–	4/97	BB+	X	BE	NC	....	....	....	....	....	222	G1	'96	114⅛	101⅜	102⅛	7.98	7.98
Sr Nts 7.65s 2007	Ao15	BBB–			X	BE	NC	....	....	....	....	....	200	G1	'97	112	98½	98½	7.77	7.77
Sr Nts 6⅜s 2008	Ms	BBB–			X	BE	[16]Z100	....	....	....	....	....	200	M5	'98	103⅞	91	91	7.01	7.01
Sr Nts 7s 2018	Mn	BBB–			X	BE	[5]Z100	....	....	....	....	....	200	G1	'98	105½	88½	89⅛	7.85	7.85
Nts 6.80s 2018	jD15	BBB–			X	BE	[5]Z100	....	....	....	....	....	300	G1	'98	103⅜	86½	87⅛	7.80	7.80
L-3 Communications[17]	***23i***	*n/a*	*n/a*	*2.08*		*Dc*	*70.80*	*582.0*	*311.0*	*9-30-99*	*605.0*		*1152*	*52.5*						
Sr Sub[2]Nts 10⅜s 2007	mN	B	5/98	B–	Y	BE	105.188	(5-1-02)	....	....	[18]Z109.375	5-1-00	225	L3	'97	110¾	103	103¼	10.05	10.05

Uniform Footnote Explanations-See Page 260. Other: [1] Due 7-20-06. [2] (HRO)On Chge of Ctrl at 101. [3] Max $120M red w/proceeds of Pub Eq Off'g. [4] Issued in min denom $100T. [5] Red at greater of 100 or amt based on formula. [6] Was Kansas-Nebraska Natural Gas. [7] Now Kinder Morgan. [8] (HRO)At 100,ltd,as defined. [9] (HRO)On 8-1-06 at 100. [10] Greater of 100 or amt based on formula. [11] (HRO)On 11-1-04 at 100. [12] Was Knight-Ridder Newspapers. [13] Mand amortiz,25% of ea note 9/1/98-01. [14] Now Kraft Gen'l Foods. [15] Dec'98 & prior. [16] Red at greater of 100 or amt based. [17] Subsid of L-3 Communications Hldgs. [18] Max $79M red w/proceeds of Pub Eq Off'g.

Title-Industry Code & Co. Finances (In Italics) / Individual Issue Statistics, Exchange	Ind / Interest Dates	Fixed Charge Coverage 1996 / S&P Rating	1997 / Date of Last Rating Change	1998 / Prior Rating	Eligible	Year End / Bond Form	Million $ Cash & Equiv. / Redemption Provisions Regular Price	Curr. Assets / Regular (Begins) Thru	Curr. Liab. / Sinking Fund Price	Balance Sheet Date / Sinking Fund (Begins) Thru	L. Term Debt (Mil $) / Refund/Other Restriction Price	Refund/Other Restriction (Begins) Thru	Capital-ization (Mil $) / Outst'g (Mil $)	Total Debt % Capital / Underwriting Firm	Underwriting Year	Price Range 1999 High	Price Range 1999 Low	Mo. End Price Sale(s) or Bid	Curr. Yield	Yield to Mat.
***L-3 Communications** (Cont.)*																				
Sr Sub Nts[1] 8½s 2008	Mn15	B			Y	BE	104.25	(5-15-03)	....	....	[2]Z108.50	5-14-01	180	L3	'98	105¼	93⅜	93¾	9.07	9.07
Sr Sub Nts'B' 8s 2008	fA	B			Y	BE	104	(8-1-03)	....	....	[3]Z108	8-1-01	200	Exch.	'98	102	90¾	90¾	8.82	8.81
[4]La Petite Academy	*22*	*1.15*	*1.62*	*0.85*		*Au*	*4.37*	*23.40*	*49.80*	*6-6-99*	*184.0*		*89.20*	*222.0*						
Sr Nts 10s 2008	Mn15	B–			Y	BE	105	(5-5-03)	....	....	[5]Z110	5-15-01	145	Exch.	'98	100½	73½	73½	13.61	13.60
La Quinta Inns	*32*	*Merged into Meditrust Corp,see*																		
Sr Nts 7¼s 2004	Ms15	BB	11/98	BBB–	Y	BE	[6]Z100	....	....	....	....	....	100	M6	'96	92¼	87¾	87¾	8.26	8.26
Sr Nts 7.40s 2005	mS15	BB	11/98	BBB–	Y	BE	NC	....	....	....	....	....	100	M6	'95	91	84⅛	84¼	8.78	8.78
Laclede Gas Co.	*73b*	*3.78*	*3.55*	*3.02*		*Sp*	*11.50*	*113.0*	*108.0*	*6-30-99*	*204.0*		*578.0*	*54.5*						
1st 6¼s 2003	Mn	AA–			X	R	NC	....	Z100	....	....	....	25.0	P1	'93	103⅜	97⅛	97⅛	6.44	6.43
1st 8½s 2004	mN15	AA–	4/91	AA	X	R	NC	....	Z100	....	....	....	25.0	S1	'89	113½	103½	103½	8.21	8.21
1st 8⅝s 2006	Mn15	AA–			X	R	NC	....	Z100	....	....	....	40.0	P4	'91	117¾	104½	104½	8.25	8.25
1st 7½s 2007	mN	AA–			X	R	NC	....	Z100	....	....	....	40.0	P1	'92	113¼	99¾	99¾	7.52	7.52
1st 6½s 2010	mN15	AA–			X	R	NC	....	Z100	....	....	....	25.0	C5	'95	107½	92	92	7.07	7.06
1st 6½s 2012	aO15	AA–			X	R	NC	....	Z100	....	....	....	25.0		'97	107¼	91⅛	91⅛	7.13	7.13
1st 7s 2029	Jd	AA–			X	BE	NC	....	Z100	....	....	....	25.0		'99	100	89¼	89⅜	7.83	7.83
[7]Lady Luck Gaming Finance	*40i*	*1.30*	*0.73*	*1.47*		*Dc*	*40.29*	*43.27*	*17.06*	*9-30-99*	*177.0*		*180.0*	*98.3*						
1st[1] 11⅞s 2001	QMar	B+	4/98	B	Y	BE	101.75	2-29-00	....	....	....	....	156	Exch.	'96	101⅝	99	100¾	11.79	11.78
Lafarge Corp	*13a*	*9.80*	*12.72*	*8.34*		*Dc*	*222.0*	*1148*	*565.0*	*9-30-99*	*737.0*		*2211*	*36.0*						
Sr Nts 6⅜s 2005	[8]jd15	A–			X	BE	[9]Z100	....	....	....	....	....	250	D6	'98	102⅝	94¼	94½	6.75	6.75
Sr Nts 6½s 2008	[10]jd15	A–			X	BE	[9]Z100	....	....	....	....	....	200	D6	'98	104⅛	92	92	7.07	7.06
Sr Nts 6⅞s 2013	[11]jd15	A–			X	BE	[9]Z100	....	....	....	....	....	200	D6	'98	107¾	91¼	91¼	7.53	7.53
Laidlaw Inc.	*53*	*2.33*	*2.90*	*3.37*		*Au*	*265.0*	*564.0*	*459.0*	*8-31-99*	*3113*		*5422*	*41.2*						
Deb 8¾s 2000	$Jj	BBB	3/99	BBB+	Q	BE	NC	....	....	....	....	....	200	G1	'94	101⅞	100	100	8.75	Mat.
Deb 7.70s 2002	$fA15	BBB	3/99	BBB+	Q	BE	NC	....	....	....	....	....	200	G1	'92	103⅜	98¼	98¼	7.84	7.84
Deb 7.05s 2003	$Mn15	BBB	3/99	BBB+	Q	BE	NC	....	....	....	....	....	100	G1	'93	101⅝	95⅝	95⅝	7.39	7.39
Deb 6.65s 2004	$aO	BBB	3/99	BBB+	Q	BE	NC	....	....	....	....	....	225	G1	'97	101½	92	92	7.23	7.23
Deb 7⅞s 2005	$Ao15	BBB	3/99	BBB+	Q	BE	NC	....	....	....	....	....	150	G1	'95	105	95⅛	95⅛	8.28	8.28
Deb 6½s 2005	$Mn	BBB	3/99	BBB+	Q	BE	NC	....	....	....	....	....	200	G1	'98	98⅛	89⅜	89⅜	7.27	7.27
Deb 7.65s 2006	$Mn	BBB			Q	BE	NC	....	....	....	....	....	400	G1	'99	100⅛	92⅞	92⅞	8.24	8.24
Deb 6.70s 2008	$Mn	BBB	3/99	BBB+	Q	BE	NC	....	....	....	....	....	100	G1	'98	100⅜	84⅞	84⅞	7.89	7.89
Deb 8¼s 2023	$Mn15	BBB	3/99	BBB+	Q	BE	NC	....	....	....	....	....	100	G1	'93	103¾	88⅞	88⅞	9.28	9.28
Deb 8¾s 2025	$Ao15	BBB	3/99	BBB+	Q	BE	NC	....	....	....	....	....	150	G1	'95	108⅛	92½	92½	9.46	9.46
Deb[12] 6.72s 2027	$aO	BBB	3/99	BBB+	Q	BE	NC	....	....	....	....	....	200	G1	'97	100⅞	85⅝	86	7.81	7.81
[13]Lakehead Pipe Line Co		*2.21*	*3.05*	*5.09*		*Dc*	*53.80*	*108.4*	*49.90*	*9-30-99*	*775.0*		*1374*	*62.6*						
Sr Nts 7s 2018	aO	NR	8/99	A–		BE	[14]Z100	....	....	....	....	....	100	M2	'98	102⅞	90⅞	91⅜	7.66	7.66
Sr Nts 7⅛s 2028	aO	NR	8/99	A–		BE	[14]Z100	....	....	....	....	....	100	M2	'98	100¾	83⅜	83½	8.53	8.53
Lamar Media Corp[15]	*1*	*[16]2.16*	*1.20*	*0.78*		*Dc*	*10.80*	*135.0*	*95.40*	*9-30-99*	*1594*		*1599*	*53.2*						
• Sr Sub Nts[1] 9⅝s 2006	jD	B			Y	BE	104.813	(12-1-01)	....	....	....	....	255	S7	'96	108½	100⅝	103	9.34	9.34
[1]Sr Sub Nts[17] 9¼s 2007	fA15	B	10/98	B–	Y	BE	104.625	(8-15-02)	....	....	[18]Z109.25	8-15-00	105	C1	'97	109	92¾	94½	9.79	9.79
Sr Sub Nts[1] 8⅝s 2007	mS15	B			Y	BE	104.313	(9-15-02)	....	....	[19]Z108.625	9-15-00	200	Exch.	'97	107⅝	95½	98	8.80	8.80
LaRoche Indus	*14*	*1.07*	*0.33*	*d0.49*		*Fb*	*4.61*	*114.0*	*145.0*	*5-31-99*	*202.0*		*267.0*	*104.0*						
Sr Sub Nts[1]'B' 9½s 2007	mS15	B			Y	BE	104.75	(9-16-02)	....	....	[20]Z109.50	9-15-00	175	Exch.	'98	80	25	27	....	....
LCI Ingternational	*67a*	*Acq by Qwest Communications,see*																		
Sr Nts 7¼s 2007	Jd15	BB+	6/98	BBB	Y	BE	[9]Z100	....	....	....	....	....	350	L3	'97	104⅜	96	96	7.55	7.55

Uniform Footnote Explanations-See Page 260. Other: [1] (HRO)On Chge of Ctrl at 101. [2] Max $63M red w/proceeds of Pub Eq Off'g. [3] Max $70M red w/proceeds of Equity Off'g. [4] Subsid & data of LPA Holdings. [5] Max $51M redw/proceeds of Pub Eq Off'g. [6] Greater of 100 or amt based on formula. [7] Subsid & data of Lady Luck Gaming Corp. [8] Due 7-15-05. [9] Red at greater of 100 or amt based on formula. [10] Due 7-15-08. [11] Due 7-15-13. [12] (HRO)On 10-1-07 at 100. [13] Subsid & data of Lakehead Pipe Line Ptnrs L.P. [14] Plus Make-Whole Amt. [15] Subsid of Lamar Advertising. [16] Fiscal Oct'96 & prior. [17] Was Outdoor Communications. [18] Max $35M red w/proceeds of Pub Eq Off'g. [19] Max $60M red w/proceeds of Pub Eq Off'g. [20] Max $58.3M red w/proceeds of Pub Eq Off'g.

Title-Industry Code & Co. Finances (In Italics) / Individual Issue Statistics (Exchange)	Ind / Interest Dates	Fixed Charge Coverage 1996 / S&P Rating	1997 / Date of Last Rating Change	1998 / Prior Rating	Eligible	Year End / Bond Form	Cash & Equiv. (Million $) / Regular Price	Curr. Assets (Million $) / Regular (Begins) Thru	Curr. Liab. (Million $) / Sinking Fund Price	Balance Sheet Date / Sinking Fund (Begins) Thru	L. Term Debt (Mil $) / Refund/Other Restriction Price	Refund/Other Restriction (Begins) Thru	Capital-ization (Mil $) / Outst'g (Mil $)	Total Debt % Capital / Underwriting Firm	Underwriting Year	Price Range 1999 High	Price Range 1999 Low	Mo. End Price Sale(s) or Bid	Curr. Yield	Yield to Mat.
LDM Technologies	*8*	*2.56*	*1.45*	*0.62*		*Sp*	*5.50*	*153.0*	*154.0*	*6-27-99*	*172.0*		*228.0*	*93.4*						
Sub Nts[1] 10¾s 2007	Jj15	B–			Y	BE	105.375	(1-15-02)	....	....	....	....	109	Exch.	'97	103	86¾	91	11.81	11.81
Lear Corp[2]	*8*	*3.47*	*4.42*	*4.15*		*Dc*	*71.00*	*3436*	*3361*	*10-2-99*	*3757*		*5184*	*72.7*						
Sub Nts[1] 9½s 2006	jJ15	BB–	4/99	BB+	Y	R	104.75	(7-15-01)	....	....	....	....	200	B11	'96	110¾	100⅜	100½	9.45	9.45
Lear Seating	*8*	***Now Lear Corp,see***																		
Sub Nts[3] 8¼s 2002	Fa	BB–	4/99	BB+	Y	R	100	....	....	....	....	....	136	L3	'94	101¼	97	98½	8.38	8.37
Legg Mason Inc	*62*	*3.20*	*2.74*	*2.57*		*Mr*				*9-30-99*	*99.70*		*753.0*	*13.2*						
Sr Nts 6½s 2006	Fa15	BBB			X	BE	NC	....	....	....	....	....	100	L2	'96	103½	94¾	94¾	6.86	6.86
Lehman Bros Hldgs[4]	*62*	*1.07*	*1.07*	*1.07*		*Nv*	*3055*			*8-31-99*	*29857*		*42081*	*84.7*						
Nts 6⅝s 2000	mN15	A			X	BE	NC	....	....	....	....	....	200	L3	'95	101	99¾	99⅞	6.63	6.63
Nts 6.20s 2002	Jj15	A			X	BE	NC	....	....	....	....	....	225	L3	'98	100⅛	97¾	97¾	6.34	6.34
Nts[4] 8⅞s 2002	Ms	A			X	R	NC	....	....	....	....	....	200	L3	'92	106¾	103	103	8.62	8.62
• Nts[4] 8¾s 2002	Mn15	A			X	R	NC	....	....	....	....	....	200	L3	'92	108	100⅛	100½	8.71	8.71
Nts 6½s 2002	aO	A			X	BE	NC	....	....	....	....	....	300	L3	'97	100½	97⅝	97¾	6.65	6.65
Nts 6¼s 2003	Ao	A			X	BE	NC	....	....	....	....	....	500	L3	'98	99⅝	96⅜	96½	6.48	6.48
Nts 6⅛s 2003	jJ15	A			X	BE	NC	....	....	....	....	....	400	L3	'98	99¼	95½	95¾	6.40	6.40
Nts 7⅛s 2003	mS15	A			X	BE	NC	....	....	....	....	....	175	L3	'95	102⅞	98¾	98¾	7.22	7.21
Nts 7¼s 2003	aO15	A			X	BE	NC	....	....	....	....	....	300	L3	'96	103¼	99⅛	99⅛	7.31	7.31
Nts[5] 6⅝s 2004	Ao	A			X	BE	NC	....	....	....	....	....	1250	L3	'99	100⅞	96½	96⅞	6.84	6.84
Nts 7⅜s 2004	Mn15	A			X	BE	NC	....	....	....	....	....	400	L3	'97	103⅞	99⅛	99⅜	7.42	7.42
Nts 8¾s 2005	Ms15	A			X	R	NC	....	....	....	....	....	175	L3	'95	110⅝	104	104	8.41	8.41
Nts 6⅝s 2006	Fa5	A			X	BE	NC	....	....	....	....	....	800	L3	'99	99⅝	94⅛	94¼	7.03	7.03
Nts 8½s 2007	Mn	A			X	BE	NC	....	....	....	....	....	250	L3	'95	112	102⅝	102⅝	8.28	8.28
Nts 7⅜s 2007	Mn15	A			X	BE	NC	....	....	....	....	....	200	L3	'95	105	97½	100⅜	7.35	7.35
Nts 7.20s 2009	fA15	A			X	BE	NC	....	....	....	....	....	250	L3	'97	105	95⅛	95¼	7.56	7.56
Nts 7⅞s 2009	mN	A			X	BE	NC	....	....	....	....	....	400	L3	'99	102¼	99	99¾	7.89	7.89
Nts[6] 8.80s 2015	Ms	A			X	R	NC	....	....	....	....	....	300	L3	'95	115⅛	102⅜	104¾	8.40	8.40
Nts 8½s 2015	fA	A			X	BE	NC	....	....	....	....	....	150	L3	'95	109⅛	101¾	101¾	8.35	8.35
M-T[7]Nts 'E'[8] 8.05s 2019	Jj15	A			X	BE	NC	....	....	....	....	....	50.0	L3	'94	104	87¾	97¼	8.28	8.28
M-T Nts 'E'[8] 8⅞s 2000	Fa15	A			X	BE	NC	....	....	....	....	....	149	L3	'95	102¾	100¼	100¼	8.85	8.85
M-T Nts 'E'[8] 8.36s 2000	[9]fa15	A			X	BE	NC	....	....	....	....	....	20.0	L3	'95	102⅜	100⅜	100⅜	8.33	8.33
F/R[10]M-T Nts 'E' 2000	QJun6	A			X	BE	NC	....	....	....	....	....	50.0	L3	'97	99⅞	98½	99⅞	....	....
M-T Nts 'E' 6.33s 2000	[11]fa15	A			X	BE	NC	....	....	....	....	....	150	L3	'97	100⅜	99⅝	99⅞	6.34	6.34
M-T Nts 'E' 6.40s 2000	[12]fa15	A			X	BE	NC	....	....	....	....	....	230	L3	'97	100½	99⅝	99¾	6.42	6.42
F/R[13]M-T Nts 'E' 2002	QSep19	A			X	BE	NC	....	....	....	....	....	25.0	L3	'97	99½	97¾	99⅜	....	....
M-T Nts 'E' 6⅝s 2002	[14]fa15	A			X	BE	NC	....	....	....	....	....	300	L3	'97	100⅝	97½	97⅞	6.77	6.77
M-T Nts[8] 'E' 7.80s 2005	[15]fa15	A			X	BE	NC	....	....	....	....	....	42.0	L3	'95	103⅜	97½	98¾	7.90	7.90
M-T Nts[8]'F' 7s 2003	Mn15	A			X	BE	NC	....	....	....	....	....	650	L3	'99	100	98⅜	98⅝	7.10	7.10
M-T Nts 'F' 7½s 2006	mS	A			X	BE	NC	....	....	....	....	....	350	L3	'99	101⅛	97⅜	98½	7.61	7.61
Lehman[16]Bros[17]Inc	*62*	*1.03*	*1.05*	*1.06*		*Nv*				*8-31-99*	*4106*		*7612*	*87.8*						
Sr Sub Deb[18] 11⅝s 2005	Mn15	A	5/88	AA–	X	R	NC	....	....	....	....	....	100	S5	'85	127	116⅜	116⅜	9.99	9.99
Sr Sub[8]Nts[18] 9⅞s 2000	aO15	A			X	R	NC	....	....	....	....	....	192	S5	'88	106⅛	102¼	102¼	9.66	9.66
Sr Sub Nts 6⅛s 2001	Fa	A			X	R	NC	....	....	....	....	....	200	L3	'96	100⅛	98¾	98⅞	6.19	6.19
Sr Sub Nts 7⅛s 2002	jJ15	A			X	R	NC	....	....	....	....	....	250	L3	'95	102¾	99⅜	99⅜	7.17	7.17
Sr Sub Nts 7s 2002	aO	A			X	BE	NC	....	....	....	....	....	200	L3	'99	100	99	99	7.07	7.07

Uniform Footnote Explanations-See Page 260. Other: [1] (HRO)On Chge of Ctrl at 101. [2] See Lear Seating. [3] (HRO)On Chge of Ctrl Triggering Event at 101. [4] Was Shearson Lehman Bros Hldgs. [5] Co may red in whole,at 100,for tax law chge. [6] (HRO)On 3-1-02 at 100. [7] (HRO)On 1-15-99 at 98. [8] Issued in min denom $100T. [9] Due 3-8-00. [10] Int adj qtrly(3 Mo LIBOR & 0.29%). [11] Due 8-1-00. [12] Due 8-30-00. [13] Int adj qtrly(3 Mo LIBOR & 0.32%). [14] Due 12-27-02. [15] Due 7-7-05. [16] Was Shearson Lehman Bros Inc,see. [17] Subsid Lehman Bros Hldgs. [18] Was Shearson Lehman Hutton.

Individual Issue Statistics / Exchange	Interest Dates	S&P Rating	Date of Last Rating Change	Prior Rating	Eligible	Bond Form	Redemption Provisions: Regular Price	Regular (Begins) Thru	Sinking Fund Price	Sinking Fund (Begins) Thru	Refund/Other Restriction Price	Refund/Other Restriction (Begins) Thru	Outst'g (Mil $)	Underwriting Firm	Underwriting Year	Price Range 1999 High	Price Range 1999 Low	Mo. End Price Sale(s) or Bid	Curr. Yield	Yield to Mat.
Title-Industry Code & Co. Finances (In Italics)	*Ind*	*Fixed Charge Coverage 1996*	*1997*	*1998*		*Year End*	*Million $ Cash & Equiv.*	*Curr. Assets*	*Curr. Liab.*	*Balance Sheet Date*	*L. Term Debt (Mil $)*		*Capital-ization (Mil $)*	*Total Debt % Capital*						
***Lehman Bros Inc** (Cont.)*																				
Sr Sub Nts 7¼s 2003	Ao15	**A**			X	BE	NC	....	....	....	....	....	275	L3	'96	103⅝	99¼	99¼	7.30	7.30
Sr Sub Nts 7.36s 2003	jD15	**A**			X	R	NC	....	....	....	....	....	200	L3	'93	104⅛	99¼	99¼	7.42	7.41
• Sr Sub Nts 7⅝s 2006	Jd	**A**			X	BE	NC	....	....	....	....	....	300	L3	'96	105⅝	99½	100	7.63	7.62
Sr Sub Nts 7⅜s 2007	Jj15	**A**			X	BE	NC	....	....	....	....	....	300	L3	'97	105⅞	96½	97¼	7.58	7.58
Sr Sub Nts 6⅝s 2008	Fa15	**A**			X	BE	NC	....	....	....	....	....	300	L3	'98	101	92	92½	7.16	7.16
Sr Sub Nts 6½s 2008	Ao15	**A**			X	BE	NC	....	....	....	....	....	300	L3	'98	100	91	91⅝	7.09	7.09
Sr Sub Nts[1] 7½s 2026	fA	**A**			X	BE	NC	....	....	....	....	....	200	L3	'96	102⅜	96⅛	99	7.58	7.57
Leiner Health Products	***19***	*n/a*	*n/a*	*n/a*		*Mr*	*2.34*	*255.0*	*118.0*	*9-30-99*	*294.0*		*274.0*	*109.0*						
Sr Sub Nts[2] 9⅝s 2007	jJ	**B–**			Y	BE	[3]Z■100	6-30-02	....	....	[4]Z109.625	7-1-00	85.0	Exch.	'97	104	70	75	12.83	12.83
Lenfest Communications	***12a***	*0.65*	*0.53*	*0.62*		*Dc*				*9-30-99*	*1436*		*1195*	*120.0*						
Sr Nts 8⅜s 2005	mN	**BB+**			Y	R	NC	....	....	....	....	....	700	S1	'95	109	102½	102½	8.17	8.17
Sub Nts 10½s 2006	Jd15	**BB–**			Y	BE	NC	....	....	....	....	....	300	Exch.	'96	119½	111⅛	112	9.38	9.37
Lennar Corp	***13h***	*n/a*	*n/a*	*n/a*		*Nv*				*8-31-99*	*[5]712.0*		*1515*	*52.7*						
Sr Nts[6] 7⅝s 2009	Ms	**BBB–**			X	BE	[7]Z100	....	....	....	....	....	282	B4	'99	99½	89⅛	89⅛	8.56	8.55
Leslie's Poolmart	***59l***	*n/a*	*n/a*	*n/a*		*Sp*	*0.19*	*90.30*	*66.50*	*7-3-99*	*91.20*		*80.70*	*113.0*						
Sr Nts[2] 10⅜s 2004	jJ15	**B+**			Y	BE	105.188	(7-15-01)	....	....	[8]Z110.375	7-15-00	90.0	Exch.	'97	105	84	85	12.21	12.20
Leucadia Nat'l Corp[9]	***25g***	*2.74*	*0.46*	*1.14*		*Dc*				*9-30-99*	*581.0*		*2748*	*28.4*						
• Sr Nts[2] 7¾s 2013	fA15	**A–**	4/99	BBB+	X	R	NC	....	....	....	....	....	100		'93	101	92¼	93⅛	8.32	8.32
• Sr Sub Nts[2] 8¼s 2005	Jd15	**BBB+**	4/99	BBB	X	R	NC	....	....	....	....	....	100	J1	'95	105	99¼	100	8.25	8.25
• Sr Sub Nts[2] 7⅞s 2006	aO15	**BBB+**	4/99	BBB	X	R	NC	....	....	....	....	....	135	J1	'96	103⅛	99¼	100	7.88	7.87
Levitz Furniture	***59j***	*0.28*	*d0.41*	....		*Mr*	*Bankruptcy Chapt 11*				*362.0*		*273.0*	*189.0*						
Sr Sub Nts[2] 9⅝s 2003	§jJ15	**NR**	4/98	D	Z	R			Default 1-15-98 int				100	D6	'93	61	40	50	....	Flat
[10]Lexmark Intl Inc.	***48***	*n/a*	*n/a*	*34.22*		*Dc*	*122.0*	*1101*	*700.0*	*9-30-99*	*149.0*		*753.0*	*21.2*						
Sr Nts[11] 6¾s 2008	Mn	**BBB–**			X	BE	[12]Z100	....	....	....	....	....	150	M5	'98	101⅝	91¼	91¼	7.40	7.40
Liberty Financial Cos.	***25g***	*n/a*	*n/a*	*10.03*		*Dc*				*9-30-99*	*537.0*		*1824*	*29.4*						
Deb 7⅝s 2008	mN15	**A–**	12/99	A	X	BE	NC	....	....	....	....	....	150	M2	'98	110⅜	88⅝	91¼	8.36	8.36
Nts 6¾s 2008	mN15	**A–**	12/99	A	X	BE	NC	....	....	....	....	....	300	M2	'98	104¼	92⅛	92⅛	7.33	7.33
Liberty Group Oper	***54c***	*1.83*	*2.16*	*0.95*		*Dc*		*23.00*	*117.0*	*9-30-99*	*180.0*		*428.0*	*63.8*						
Sr Sub Nts[2] 9⅜s 2008	Fa	**CCC+**			Y	BE	104.688	(2-1-03)	....	....	[13]Z109.375	2-1-01	180	Exch.	'98	102½	85½	89	10.53	10.53
Liberty Group Publishing	***54***	*1.83*	*2.16*	*0.73*		*Dc*		*23.00*	*118.0*	*9-30-99*	*241.0*		*430.0*	*77.4*						
Sr Disc[14]Deb[2] 11⅝s 2009	Fa	**CCC+**			Y	BE	105.813	(2-1-03)	....	....	....	....	89.0	Exch.	'98	60	47½	55¾	....	Flat
Liberty Nat'l Bank & Trust	***10***	*Subsid of Liberty Nat'l Bancorp,see*																		
Sub Nts[15] 6¾s 2003	Jd	**A+**	10/98	AA–	Y	BE	NC	....	....	....	....	....	55.0		'93	104⅜	98⅝	98⅝	6.84	6.84
[16]Liberty Property L.P.	***57***	*2.00*	*2.23*	*2.48*		*Dc*				*9-30-99*	*1463*		*2900*	*52.2*						
Sr Nts 7.10s 2004	fA15	**BBB–**			X	BE	[7]Z100	....	....	....	....	....	100	L3	'97	98	94¼	95	7.47	7.47
Sr Nts 7¼s 2007	fA15	**BBB–**			X	BE	[7]Z100	....	....	....	....	....	100	L3	'97	96¾	91¼	92⅝	7.83	7.83
Sr Nts 7¾s 2009	Ao15	**BBB–**			X	BE	[7]100	....	....	....	....	....	250	L3	'99	99¼	92⅞	94	8.24	8.24
M-T Nts 6.60s 2002	[17]ms15	**BBB–**			X	BE	NC	....	....	....	....	....	100	L3	'98	98½	96¼	96⅜	6.85	6.85
M-T Nts 6.95s 2006	jD	**BBB–**			X	BE	NC	....	....	....	....	....	100	D6	'97	97¼	90⅛	90⅛	7.71	7.71
M-T Nts 7½s 2018	[18]ms15	**BBB–**			X	BE	[7]Z100	....	....	....	....	....	100	L3	'98	91⅛	83	84¾	8.85	8.85
Lilly (Eli)	***21a***	*7.14*	*10.06*	*15.02*		*Dc*	*3358*	*6595*	*3187*	*9-30-99*	*2816*		*8028*	*39.4*						
• Nts 8⅛s 2001	jD	**AA**			X	BE	NC	....	....	....	....	....	150	M6	'94	107½	101⅛	101⅛	8.03	8.03
Nts 6¼s 2003	Ms15	**AA**	10/94	AAA	X	BE	NC	....	....	....	....	....	200	G1	'93	104¼	98¼	98¼	6.36	6.36
• Nts 8⅜s 2006	jD	**AA**			X	BE	NC	....	....	....	....	....	300	M6	'94	117	108	103	8.13	8.13

Uniform Footnote Explanations-See Page 260. Other: [1] (HRO)On 8-1-03 at 100. [2] (HRO)On Chge of Ctrl at 101. [3] On Chge of Ctrl. [4] Max $25.5M red w/proceeds of Pub Eq Off'g. [5] Incl curr amts. [6] (HRO)On Chge of Ctrl at 100 plus Make Whole Amt. [7] Plus Make-Whole Amt. [8] Max $22.5M red w/proceeds of Pub Eq Off'g. [9] Was Talcott Nat'l. [10] Subsid & data of Lexmark Intl Group. [11] Gtd by Lexmark Intl Group. [12] Red at greater of 100 or amt based on formula. [13] Max $63M red w/proceeds of Pub Eq Off'g. [14] Int accrues at 11.625% fr 2-1-03. [15] Issued in min denom $150T. [16] Data of Liberty Property. [17] Due 6-5-02. [18] Due 1-15-18.

Title-Industry Code & Co. Finances (In Italics) / Exchange ↓ Individual Issue Statistics	Ind / Interest Dates	S&P Rating	1996 (Fixed Charge Coverage) / Date of Last Rating Change	1997 / Prior Rating	1998 / Eligible ↓	Year End / Bond Form	Cash & Equiv. (Million $) / Regular Price	Curr. Assets (Million $) / Regular (Begins) Thru	Curr. Liab. (Million $) / Sinking Fund Price	Balance Sheet Date / Sinking Fund (Begins) Thru	L. Term Debt (Mil $) / Refund/Other Restriction Price	Capital-ization (Mil $) / Refund/Other Restriction (Begins) Thru	Outst'g (Mil $)	Total Debt % Capital / Underwriting Firm	Underwriting Year	Price Range 1999 High	Price Range 1999 Low	Mo. End Price Sale(s) or Bid	Curr. Yield	Yield to Mat.
Lilly (Eli) (Cont.)																				
• Nts 6.57s 2016	Jj	**AA**			X	BE	[1]Z100	....	....	....	....	....	200	M6	'96	100	88½	92	7.14	7.14
• Nts 7⅛s 2025	Jd	**AA**			X	BE	NC	....	....	....	....	....	500	M6	'95	107⅞	97½	96⅝	7.37	7.37
• Nts 6.77s 2036	Jj	**AA**			X	BE	[1]Z100	....	....	....	....	....	300	M6	'96	No Sale		89¾	7.54	7.54
Limited, Inc	***59a***		***9.20***	***10.58***	***10.97***	***Ja***	***173.3***	***2001***	***1249***	***10-30-99***	***650.0***	***3316***		***19.6***						
Deb 7½s 2023	Ms15	**BBB+**	12/95	A	X	BE	103.16	(3-15-03)	....	....	....	....	250	M5	'93	102	89	90	8.33	8.33
Nts 9⅛s 2001	Fa	**BBB+**	12/95	A	X	BE	NC	....	....	....	....	....	150	M6	'91	106⅞	102⅛	102⅛	8.94	8.93
Nts 7.80s 2002	Mn15	**BBB+**	12/95	A	X	BE	NC	....	....	....	....	....	150	G1	'92	106⅜	101⅛	101⅛	7.71	7.71
LIN Holdings	***67g***		***n/a***	***n/a***	***n/a***	***Dc***	***19.70***	***76.20***	***60.00***	***9-30-99***	***780.0***	***1294***		***61.4***						
Sr[2]Disc[3]Nts[4] 10s 2008	Ms	**B–**			Y	BE	105	(3-1-03)	....	....	[5]Z110	3-1-01	325	Exch.	'98	75⅝	64½	67⅜	....	Flat
LIN Television	***67g***	***Subsid of LIN Holdings,see***																		
Sr Sub[6]Nts[7] 8⅜s 2008	Ms	**B–**			Y	BE	[8]Z■100	2-28-03	....	....	[9]Z108.375	3-1-01	300	Exch.	'98	105	93	93	9.01	9.00
Lincoln Nat'l	***35d***		***9.37***	***1.37***	***6.94***	***Dc***				***9-30-99***	***1457***	***6487***		***28.1***						
Deb 7¼s 2005	Mn15	**A–**	5/98	A	X	BE	NC	....	....	....	....	....	200	L3	'95	107⅝	97⅞	97⅞	7.41	7.41
Deb 9⅛s 2024	aO	**A–**	5/98	A	X	BE	104.3325	(10-1-04)	....	....	....	....	200	M6	'94	117⅛	105⅜	106¾	8.55	8.55
Nts 7⅝s 2002	jJ15	**A–**	5/98	A	X	BE	NC	....	....	....	....	....	100	M2	'92	106¾	100⅜	100⅜	7.60	7.60
Nts 6½s 2008	Ms15	**A–**	5/98	A	X	BE	NC	....	....	....	....	....	100	M2	'98	104¾	91¾	92⅛	7.06	7.06
Nts 7s 2018	Ms15	**A–**	5/98	A	X	BE	NC	....	....	....	....	....	200	M2	'98	106⅝	89⅝	89⅞	7.79	7.79
Litchfield Financial[10]	***25h***		***2.19***	***2.01***	***2.01***	***Dc***				***9-30-99***	***160.0***	***288.0***		***70.1***						
[11]Nts[12] 8⅞s 2003	[13]Nov	**NR**				R	100	....	....	....	....	....	15.9	B9	'93	100	91	100	8.88	8.87
[11]Nts[12] 10s 2004	[13]Nov	**NR**				R	102	3-31-00	....	....	....	....	18.3	M1	'95	100⅛	96	100	10.00	10.00
Litton Indus.	***17***		***Δ6.13***	***Δ6.81***	***Δ5.09***	***Jl***	***68.45***	***2170***	***1924***	***10-31-99***	***1300***	***3018***		***55.2***						
Sr Deb 6¾s 2018	Ao15	**BBB**	5/99	BBB+	X	BE	[14]Z100	....	....	....	....	....	200	M2	'98	100⅝	84½	85	7.94	7.94
Deb 7¾s 2026	Ms15	**BBB**	5/99	BBB+	X	BE	[1]Z100	....	....	....	....	....	300	G1	'96	111⅝	91⅞	92½	8.38	8.38
Deb[15] 6.98s 2036	Ms15	**BBB**	5/99	BBB+	X	BE	[1]Z100	(3-15-06)	....	....	....	....	100	G1	'96	106⅜	95⅝	95⅝	7.32	7.32
Sr Nts 6.05s 2003	Ao15	**BBB**	5/99	BBB+	X	BE	NC	....	....	....	....	....	100	M2	'98	101⅝	95⅞	96	6.30	6.30
LNR Property	***38***		***n/a***	***n/a***	***n/a***	***Nv***				***8-31-99***	***1220***	***1839***		***63.1***						
Sr Sub Nts[7] 'B' 9⅜s 2008	Ms15	**B**			Y	BE	104.688	(3-15-03)	....	....	[16]Z109.375	3-15-01	199	Exch.	'98	98	90½	94	9.97	9.97
Lockheed Corp[17]	***2a***	***Now Lockheed Martin, see***																		
Deb 7⅞s 2023	Ms15	**BBB–**	11/99	BBB	X	BE	103.738	(3-15-03)	....	....	....	....	300	F1	'93	108⅞	87¾	87⅞	8.96	8.96
Nts 6¾s 2003	Ms15	**BBB–**	11/99	BBB	X	BE	NC	....	....	....	....	....	300	F1	'93	104⅜	97¼	97¼	6.94	6.94
Lockheed Martin[18]	***2a***		***3.38***	***2.93***	***2.88***	***Dc***		***10129***	***9734***	***9-30-99***	***10463***	***18159***		***66.3***						
Deb[19] 7.65s 2016	Mn	**BBB–**	11/99	BBB	X	BE	NC	....	....	....	....	....	600	G1	'96	113⅜	91¾	93	8.23	8.23
Deb[19] 7¾s 2026	Mn	**BBB–**	11/99	BBB	X	BE	NC	....	....	....	....	....	600	G1	'96	115⅞	90⅝	92⅛	8.41	8.41
Deb 8½s 2029	jD	**BBB–**			X	BE	[14]100	....	....	....	....	....	1250	G1	'99	100	96⅛	100	8.50	8.50
[19]Deb[20] 7.20s 2036	Mn	**BBB–**	11/99	BBB	X	BE	NC	....	....	....	....	....	300	G1	'96	109⅝	93¼	93¼	7.72	7.72
Nts[19] 6.85s 2001	Mn15	**BBB–**	11/99	BBB	X	BE	NC	....	....	....	....	....	750	G1	'96	103¼	98⅞	99	6.92	6.92
Nts[19] 7.45s 2004	Jd15	**BBB–**	11/99	BBB	X	BE	NC	....	....	....	....	....	550	C5	'96	108⅜	98	98⅛	7.59	7.59
Nts 7.95s 2005	jD	**BBB–**			X	BE	NC	....	....	....	....	....	750	G1	'99	100½	98¼	99¼	8.01	8.01
Nts[19] 7¼s 2006	Mn15	**BBB–**	11/99	BBB	X	BE	NC	....	....	....	....	....	750	G1	'96	108⅞	95⅜	95½	7.59	7.59
Nts[19] 7.70s 2008	Jd15	**BBB–**	11/99	BBB	X	BE	NC	....	....	....	....	....	450	C5	'96	113⅛	96¼	96¾	7.96	7.96
Nts 8.20s 2009	jD	**BBB–**			X	BE	NC	....	....	....	....	....	1000	G1	'99	100	97⅞	99⅝	8.23	8.23
Lodester Holdings	***45a***		***n/a***	***n/a***	***n/a***	***Oc***	***2.92***	***61.10***	***52.90***	***7-31-99***	***181.0***	***131.0***		***139.0***						
Sr Nts[7] 11½s 2005	Mn15	**B**			Y	BE	105.75	(5-15-02)	....	....	[21]Z111.50	5-15-01	150	Exch.	'98	84⅝	50	50	23.00	22.98
LodgeNet Entertainment	***24c***		***n/a***	***n/a***	***n/a***	***Dc***	***2.10***	***42.90***	***47.70***	***9-30-99***	***269.0***	***254.0***		***109.0***						
Sr Nts[7] 10¼s 2006	jD15	**B**			Y	BE	105.125	(12-15-01)	....	....	....	....	150	Exch.	'97	102¾	99	100	10.25	10.25

Uniform Footnote Explanations-See Page 260. Other: [1] Greater of 100 or amt based on formula. [2] (HRO)On Chge of Ctrl at 101(Accreted Val). [3] May red in whole,at 100(Accreted)on Ctr Chge. [4] Int accrues at 10% fr 3-1-03. [5] Accreted Val:Max $114M red w/proceeds Eq Off'g. [6] Co may red in whole,at 100,Ctrl Chge to 3-1-03. [7] (HRO)On Chge of Ctrl at 101. [8] On Chge of Ctrl. [9] Max $105M red w/proceeds of Pub Eq Off'g. [10] Acq by Textron Fin'l. [11] Death red benefit,ltd,as defined. [12] (HRO)For Certain Events at 100. [13] Int pd monthly. [14] Red at greater of 100 or amt based on formula. [15] (HRO)On 3-15-06 at 100. [16] Max $70M red w/proceeds of Pub Eq Off'g. [17] See Martin Marietta & Martin Marietta Technol. [18] See Loral Corp. [19] Gtd by Lockheed Martin Tactical Systems, Inc. [20] (HRO)On Chge of Ctrl at 100. [21] Max $52.5M red w/proceeds of Equity Off'g.

Title-Industry Code & Co. Finances (In Italics) / Individual Issue Statistics (Exchange)	Ind / Interest Dates	S&P Rating / Fixed Charge Coverage 1996	Date of Last Rating Change / 1997	Prior Rating / 1998	Eligible	Bond Form / Year End	Redemption Provisions: Regular Price / Cash & Equiv. (Million $)	Regular (Begins) Thru / Curr. Assets (Million $)	Sinking Fund Price / Curr. Liab. (Million $)	Sinking Fund (Begins) Thru / Balance Sheet Date	Refund/Other Restriction Price / L. Term Debt (Mil $)	Refund/Other Restriction (Begins) Thru	Outst'g (Mil $) / Capital-ization (Mil $)	Underwriting Firm / Total Debt % Capital	Underwriting Year	Price Range 1999 High	Price Range 1999 Low	Mo. End Price Sale(s) or Bid	Curr. Yield	Yield to Mat.
Loehmann's Inc	***59a***	***1.87***	***0.22***	....		***Ja***	***Bankruptcy Chapt 11***				***[1]166.0***		***336.0***	***49.4***						
Sr Nts[2] 11⅞s 2003	§Mn15	**NR**	6/99	D	Z	BE			Default 5-15-99 int				95.0	D6	'96	82	14⅞	19	....	Flat
Loews Corp	***35d***	***8.57***	***5.93***	***3.92***		***Dc***				***9-30-99***	***5699***		***16167***	***36.9***						
Deb 8⅞s 2011	Ao15	**AA–**			X	R	NC	....	....	....	....	....	175	S1	'86	124½	105¾	105¾	8.39	8.39
Sr Nts 6¾s 2006	jD15	**AA–**			X	BE	NC	....	....	....	....	....	300	M2	'96	105¾	94½	94½	7.14	7.14
Sr Nts 7⅝s 2023	Jd	**AA–**			X	BE	103.8125	(6-1-03)	....	....	....	....	300	D6	'93	105⅞	90⅞	91	8.38	8.38
Sr Nts 7s 2023	aO15	**AA–**			X	BE	102.387	(10-15-03)	....	....	....	....	400	M5	'93	99¾	84	84⅛	8.32	8.32
[3]Lomak Petroleum	***49a***	***3.60***	***1.87***	***1.86***		***Dc***	***14.51***	***80.90***	***51.26***	***9-30-99***	***672.0***		***732.0***	***82.0***						
Sr Sub Nts[4] 8¾s 2007	Jj15	**B**			Y	BE	104.375	(1-15-02)	....	....	....	....	125	C1	'97	93	60	91¾	9.54	9.53
Long Island Light'g[5]	***75***	***[6]2.16***	***2.41***	***d0.35***		***Dc***		***315.0***	***312.0***	***9-30-99***	***6729***		***6888***	***99.9***						
Deb 6¼s 2001	jJ15	**A–**	6/98	BB+	X	R	NC	....	....	....	....	....	8.46	L3	'93	101⅜	98⅝	98⅝	6.34	6.34
• Deb 7.05s 2003	Ms15	**A–**	6/98	BB+	X	R	NC	....	....	....	....	....	5.89	L3	'93	106	97½	97	7.27	7.27
• Deb 7s 2004	Ms	**A–**	6/98	BB+	X	R	NC	....	....	....	....	....	3.00	L3	'93	103⅝	98⅛	95	7.37	7.37
Deb 7⅛s 2005	Jd	**A–**	6/98	BB+	X	R	NC	....	....	....	....	....	14.3	L3	'93	108⅝	98⅛	98⅛	7.26	7.26
• Deb 9s 2022	mN	**A–**	6/98	BB+	X	R	104.19	(11-1-02)	....	....	....	....	26.9	L3	'92	114⅛	102¼	104	8.65	8.65
• Deb 8.20s 2023	Ms15	**A–**	6/98	BB+	X	R	104	(3-15-03)	....	....	....	....	270	L3	'93	110¼	98	100½	8.16	8.16
Loomis Fargo & Co	***63***	***n/a***	***n/a***	***1.03***		***Dc***	***7.71***	***39.00***	***48.40***	***9-30-99***	***137.0***		***135.0***	***104.0***						
Sr[4]Sub Nts 10s 2004	Jj15	**B**			Y	BE	105	(1-15-01)	....	....	....	....	85.0	Exch.	'97	102	98	99	10.10	10.10
Loral Corp	***23i***	***Merged into Lockheed Martin,see***																		
Sr Deb 9⅛s 2022	Fa	**BBB–**	11/99	BBB	X	R	NC	....	....	....	....	....	100	L3	'92	129½	104½	104⅝	8.72	8.72
Sr Deb 8⅜s 2023	Jj15	**BBB–**	11/99	BBB	X	BE	NC	....	....	....	....	....	100	L3	'93	120⅞	96¼	96¾	8.66	8.65
Sr Deb 7s 2023	mS15	**BBB–**	11/99	BBB	X	BE	NC	....	....	....	....	....	200	L3	'93	104⅜	83¾	83¾	8.36	8.36
Sr Nts 7⅝s 2004	Jd15	**BBB–**	11/99	BBB	X	BE	NC	....	....	....	....	....	250	L3	'94	108⅝	98	98¼	7.76	7.76
Sr Deb 8⅜s 2024	Jd15	**BBB–**	11/99	BBB	X	BE	NC	....	....	....	....	....	400	L3	'94	121⅜	95¼	96¾	8.66	8.65
Sr Deb 7⅝s 2025	Jd15	**BBB–**	11/99	BBB	X	R	NC	....	....	....	....	....	150	B7	'95	112⅜	90	90	8.47	8.47
Loral Space & Communications	***67f***	***n/a***	***4.11***	***0.39***		***Dc***	***265.6***	***1179***	***693.5***	***9-30-99***	***1987***		***4904***	***42.1***						
Sr Nts[4] 9½s 2006	Jj15	**B**			Y	BE	Z104.75	(1-15-03)	....	....	[7]Z109.50	1-15-02	345	Exch.	'99	90⅛	80	90	10.56	10.55
Louis Dreyfus Natural Gas	***73e***	***2.91***	***1.72***	***d0.73***		***Dc***	***6.06***	***113.0***	***76.60***	***9-30-99***	***604.0***		***1116***	***53.4***						
• Sr Sub Nts[2] 9¼s 2004	Jd15	**BB+**			Y	BE	NC	....	....	....	....	....	100	D6	'94	No Sale		100⅛	9.24	9.24
Louisiana Land/Exp	***49a***	***Merged into Burlington Resources,see***																		
Deb 7⅝s 2013	Ao15	**A–**	10/97	BBB	X	R	NC	....	....	....	....	....	100	M5	'93	115⅝	97⅞	97⅞	7.79	7.79
Deb 7.65s 2023	jD	**A–**	10/97	BBB	X	R	NC	....	....	....	....	....	200	M6	'93	108½	94⅛	94⅛	8.13	8.13
• Nts 8¼s 2002	Jd15	**A–**	10/97	BBB	X	R	NC	....	....	....	....	....	100	M6	'92	107½	106½	102⅛	8.08	8.08
Louisiana Power & Light	***72a***	***Now Entergy Louisiana,see***																		
1st 6s 2000	Ms	**BBB**	1/94	BBB+	X	BE	NC	....	Z100	....	....	....	100	K2	'93	100¾	99⅞	99⅞	6.01	6.01
1st 7⅞s 2001	Ao	**BBB**	1/94	BBB+	X	R	100.35	3-31-00	100.32	3-31-00	....	....	18.7	E1	'71	100¾	100¼	100¼	7.86	7.86
1st 7½s 2002	Jj	**BBB**	1/94	BBB+	X	R	100.32	12-31-00	100.23	12-31-00	....	....	23.0	M2	'72	100⅞	99⅞	99⅞	7.51	7.51
1st 7.74s 2002	jJ	**BBB**	1/94	BBB+	X	R	100.97	6-30-00	Z100	....	....	....	179	K2	'92	102⅛	99⅞	99⅞	7.75	7.75
1st 7½s 2002	mN	**BBB**	1/94	BBB+	X	R	100.65	10-31-00	100.40	10-31-00	....	....	15.3	B8	'72	101⅛	99⅝	99⅞	7.51	7.51
1st 8¾s 2006	jD	**BBB**	1/94	BBB+	X	R	102.10	11-30-00	100.67	11-30-00	....	....	21.9	S1	'76	103⅛	102⅛	102⅛	8.57	8.57
1st 8¾s 2026	Ms	**BBB**			X	BE	106.563	(3-1-01)	Z100	....	....	....	115	B7	'96	109⅛	98¾	98⅞	8.85	8.85
Louisville Gas & Electric[8]	***75***	***5.27***	***5.57***	***5.39***		***Dc***	***24.80***	***306.0***	***314.0***	***9-30-99***	***627.0***		***1406***	***44.6***						
• 1st 7½s 2002	jJ	**A+**	8/98	AA–	X	R	100.62	6-30-00	100.22	9-1-00	....	....	20.0	D4	'72	103	100	100	7.50	7.50
1st 6s 2003	fA15	**A+**	8/98	AA–	X	R	NC	....	....	....	....	....	42.6	M6	'93	102⅝	95⅞	95⅞	6.26	6.26
Louisville & Nash RR	***55***	***See CSX Corp***																		
• 1st Ref F 3⅜s 2003	Ao	**A–**	7/98	BBB	X	CR	101.50	4-1-00	101.625	3-31-00	....	....	31.6	H1	'45	90½	88¼	88⅛	3.83	3.84

Uniform Footnote Explanations-See Page 260. Other: [1] Incl liab subj to compromise. [2] Co must offer repurch at 101 on Chge of Ctrl. [3] Now Range Resources. [4] (HRO)On Chge of Ctrl at 101. [5] Subsid of Long Island Power Authority. [6] Yr Dec'96 & prior. [7] Max $123M red w/proceeds of Equity Off'g. [8] Subsid of LG&E Energy.

Title-Industry Code & Co. Finances (In Italics) / Exchange – Individual Issue Statistics	Ind / Interest Dates	Fixed Charge Coverage 1996 / S&P Rating	1997 / Date of Last Rating Change	1998 / Prior Rating	Eligible	Year End / Bond Form	Million $ Cash & Equiv. / Redemption Provisions Regular Price	Million $ Curr. Assets / Regular (Begins) Thru	Million $ Curr. Liab. / Sinking Fund Price	Balance Sheet Date / Sinking Fund (Begins) Thru	L. Term Debt (Mil $) / Refund/Other Restriction Price	Refund/Other Restriction (Begins) Thru	Capital-ization (Mil $) / Outst'g (Mil $)	Total Debt % Capital / Underwriting Firm	Underwriting Year	Price Range 1999 High	Price Range 1999 Low	Mo. End Price Sale(s) or Bid	Curr. Yield	Yield to Mat.
Louisville & Nash RR *(Cont.)*																				
• 1st Ref G 2⅞s 2003	Ao	**A–**	7/98	BBB	X	CR	100.375	4-1-00	100	....	....	....	29.2	M6	'45	90	86⅝	86⅞	3.31	3.33
Lowe's Cos	***59l***	***7.85***	***7.74***	***7.83***		***Ja***	***705.0***	***3877***	***2391***	***10-29-99***	***1733***		***6213***	***30.0***						
Deb 6⅞s 2028	Fa15	**A**			X	BE	NC	....	....	....	....	....	300	M2	'98	107¼	88½	88¾	7.75	7.75
Deb 6½s 2029	Ms15	**A**			X	BE	NC	....	....	....	....	....	400	Exch.	'99	99½	83⅞	84¼	7.72	7.71
Sr Nts 6⅜s 2005	jD15	**A**			X	BE	NC	....	....	....	....	....	100	M2	'95	105¼	94⅝	94⅝	6.74	6.74
M-T Nts 'B' 6.70s 2007	mS	**A**			X	BE	NC	....	....	....	....	....	50.0	M2	'97	108⅜	95⅜	95⅜	7.02	7.02
M-T Nts 'B' 7.20s 2027	mS	**A**			X	BE	NC	....	....	....	....	....	75.0	M2	'97	110½	90⅞	91	7.91	7.91
M-T Nts 'B' 7.11s 2037	[1]ms	**A**			X	BE	NC	....	....	....	....	....	100	M2	'97	114¼	97⅜	97⅜	7.30	7.30
LTV Corp	***66a***	***n/a***	***n/a***	***n/a***		***Dc***	***167.0***	***1521***	***871.0***	***9-30-99***	***402.0***		***2063***	***17.5***						
Sub Deb[2] 8.20s 2007	mS15	**BB–**	2/99	BB	Y	BE	104.10	(9-15-02)	....	....	[3]Z108.20	9-15-00	300	Exch.	'98	97½	85	90	9.11	9.11
Lubrizol Corp	***14***	***18.62***	***21.95***	***8.22***		***Dc***	***163.7***	***763.1***	***277.5***	***9-30-99***	***390.0***		***1206***	***33.7***						
Deb 7¼s 2025	Jd15	**A+**	10/98	AA–	X	BE	NC	....	....	....	....	....	100	M6	'95	109	94⅛	94⅝	7.66	7.66
Lucent Technologies	***67f***	***2.63***	***9.17***	***7.91***		***Sp***	***1495***	***20810***	***11956***	***6-30-99***	***3712***		***19195***	***35.4***						
• Deb 6½s 2028	Jj15	**A**			X	BE	NC	....	....	....	....	....	300	G1	'98	99	87⅛	87¼	7.45	7.45
• Deb 6.45s 2029	Ms15	**A**			X	BE	NC	....	....	....	....	....	1360	B7	'99	100¼	98½	87½	7.37	7.37
• Nts 6.90s 2001	jJ15	**A**			X	BE	NC	....	....	....	....	....	750	G1	'96	104¼	100⅜	100¼	6.88	6.88
• Nts 7¼s 2006	jJ15	**A**			X	BE	NC	....	....	....	....	....	750	G1	'96	110⅛	98¼	100⅜	7.22	7.22
• Nts 5½s 2008	mN15	**A**			X	BE	NC	....	....	....	....	....	500	G1	'98	93	89½	88	6.25	6.25
Lukens Inc	***66d***	***Merged into Bethlehem Steel,see***																		
Nts 7⅝s 2004	fA	**BB–**	6/98	BBB	Y	R	NC	....	....	....	....	....	150	F1	'92	103⅛	92⅝	92⅝	8.23	8.23
Lyondell Chemical	***49g***	***3.05***	***5.85***	***0.70***		***Dc***	***258.0***	***1375***	***748.0***	***9-30-99***	***6256***		***7638***	***82.2***						
Sr Sec Nts[2]'A' 9⅝s 2007	Mn	**BB**			Y	BE	[4]Z100	....	....	....	....	....	900	Exch.	'99	103½	98½	102¼	9.41	9.41
Sr Sec Nts[2]'B' 9⅞s 2007	Mn	**BB**			Y	BE	104.938	(5-1-04)	....	....	....	....	1000	Exch.	'99	103½	98½	102	9.68	9.68
Sr Sub Nts 10⅞s 2009	Mn	**B+**			Y	BE	105.438	(5-1-04)	....	....	[5]Z110.875	5-1-02	500	Exch.	'99	104¾	97⅞	103	10.56	10.56
Mack-Cali Realty	***57***	***1.55***	***0.64***	***2.72***		***Dc***				***9-30-99***	***[6]1579***		***3475***	***58.6***						
Nts 7s 2004	Ms15	**BBB**			X	BE	[4]Z100	....	....	....	....	....	300	M5	'99	100¾	96¼	96⅜	7.26	7.26
Nts 7¼s 2009	Ms15	**BBB**			X	BE	[4]Z100	....	....	....	....	....	300	M5	'99	100½	92	92¼	7.86	7.86
MacSaver Financial Svcs	***25***	***2.29***	***d0.17***	***0.97***		***Fb***	***4.91***	***976.2***	***425.8***	***8-31-99***	***536.0***		***1523***	***58.4***						
Nts[7] 7.40s 2002	Fa15	**BB–**	6/99	BB+	Y	BE	NC	....	....	....	....	....	100	G1	'97	88	63	63	11.75	11.74
Nts[7] 7⅞s 2003	fA	**BB–**	6/99	BB+	Y	BE	NC	....	....	....	....	....	200	G1	'96	86	61	61	12.91	12.90
Nts[7] 7.60s 2007	fA	**BB–**	6/99	BB+	Y	BE	NC	....	....	....	....	....	175	G1	'97	82	59	59	12.88	12.88
Madison Gas & Electric	***75***	***2.74***	***4.36***	***4.22***		***Dc***	***5.55***	***64.60***	***34.90***	***9-30-99***	***160.0***		***346.0***	***46.2***						
1st 8½s 2022	Ao15	**AA**			X	R	104.25	(4-1-02)	....	....	....	....	40.0	F1	'92	110¾	100¾	100⅞	8.43	8.43
1st 7.70s 2028	Fa15	**AA**			X	R	104.26	(2-15-03)	....	....	....	....	21.2	F1	'93	107¾	93⅜	93½	8.24	8.23
Nts 6.02s 2008	[8]ms	**AA–**			X	BE	[9]Z100	....	....	....	....	....	30.0		'98	100⅞	89⅛	89⅛	6.75	6.75
Magellan Health Svcs[10]	***30***	***2.10***	***2.55***	***1.75***		***Sp***	***40.31***	***333.1***	***486.1***	***6-30-99***	***1102***		***1425***	***86.1***						
Sr Suub Nts[2] 'A' 9s 2008	Fa15	**B–**			Y	BE	104.50	(2-15-03)	....	....	[11]Z109	2-15-01	625	Exch.	'98	91	80	81	11.11	11.11
Magma Copper[12]	***45b***	***2.76***	***3.47***	***0.42***		***My***	***1152***	***7218***	***6175***	***:5-31-98***	***6175***		***26748***	***53.6***						
Sr Sub Nts 8.70s 2005	Mn15	**A–**	1/99	NR	X	BE	NC	....	....	....	....	....	200	G1	'95	109⅜	100¼	100¼	8.68	8.68
Majestic Star Casino/Cap[13]	***40i***	***d2.06***	***d2.20***	***d1.43***		***Dc***	***18.40***	***27.70***	***18.70***	***9-30-99***	***129.0***		***121.0***	***114.0***						
Sr Sec[2]Nts[14]'B' 10⅞s 2006	jJ	**B**			Y	BE	105.438	(7-1-03)	....	....	[15]Z110.875	6-30-02	130	Exch.	'99	97¾	95	96½	11.27	11.27
Magnum Hunter Resources	***49a***	***1.34***	***0.75***	***0.02***		***Dc***	***3.32***	***16.62***	***15.20***	***9-30-99***	***230.0***		***286.0***	***80.4***						
◆Sr Nts[2] 10s 2007	Jd	**B**	5/99	B–	Y	BE	105	(6-1-02)	....	....	[16]Z110	6-1-00	140	Exch.	'97	99	80	85	11.76	11.76
[17]Mallinckrodt Group[18]	***43***	***△6.89***	***△1.57***	***△3.99***		***Je***	***26.00***	***1171***	***1140***	***9-30-99***	***742.0***		***2187***	***51.5***						
Nts 6¾s 2005	mS15	**BBB**	9/97	A–	X	BE	NC	....	....	....	....	....	100	G1	'95	101⅛	93½	94¼	7.16	7.16

Uniform Footnote Explanations-See Page 260. Other: [1] Due 5-15-37. [2] (HRO)On Chge of Ctrl at 101. [3] Max $105M red w/proceeds of Pub Eq Off'g. [4] Plus Make-Whole Amt. [5] Max $175M red w/proceeds of Pub Eq Off'g. [6] Incl current amts. [7] Gtd by Heilig-Meyers Co. [8] Due 9-15-08. [9] Red at greater of 100 or amt based on formula. [10] Was Charter Medical. [11] Max $219M red w/proceeds of Equity Off'g. [12] Subsid & data of Broken Hill Prop. [13] Data of Majectic Star Casino. [14] Co may redeem at 100 for Req Reg Redeem. [15] Max $45M red w/proceeds of Pub Eq Off'g. [16] Max $49M red w/proceeds of Pub Eq Off'g. [17] See IMCERA Grp,Int'l Minerals & Chem. [18] Now Mallinckrodt Inc.

Title-Industry Code & Co. Finances (In Italics) / Individual Issue Statistics (Exchange)	Ind / Interest Dates	Fixed Charge Coverage 1996 / S&P Rating	1997 / Date of Last Rating Change	1998 / Prior Rating	Eligible	Year End / Bond Form	Cash & Equiv. (Million $) / Regular Price	Curr. Assets (Million $) / Regular (Begins) Thru	Curr. Liab. (Million $) / Sinking Fund Price	Balance Sheet Date / Sinking Fund (Begins) Thru	L. Term Debt (Mil $) / Refund/Other Restriction Price	Refund/Other Restriction (Begins) Thru	Capital-ization (Mil $) / Outst'g (Mil $)	Total Debt % Capital / Underwriting Firm	Underwriting Year	Price Range 1999 High	Price Range 1999 Low	Mo. End Price Sale(s) or Bid	Curr. Yield	Yield to Mat.
***Mallinckrodt Group** (Cont.)*																				
Nts 6½s 2007	mN15	BBB	9/97	A–	X	BE	NC	....	....	....	....	....	100	M5	'95	98¾	90	90¼	7.20	7.20
Manor Care	*30*	*5.08*	*4.42*	*[1]5.66*		*Dc*	*91.80*	*519.0*	*460.0*	*9-30-99*	*696.0*		*2059*	*43.8*						
Sr Nts[2] 7½s 2006	Jd15	BBB			X	BE	[3]Z100	....	....	....	....	....	150	L3	'96	105½	96	96	7.81	7.81
[4]Manufacturers & Traders Trust	*10*	*4.40*	*3.82*	*3.00*		*Dc*				*9-30-99*	*1775*		*3384*	*50.7*						
Sub Nts[5] 8⅛s 2002	jD	BBB+			X	BE	NC	....	....	....	....	....	75.0	L3	'92	108¼	102	102	7.97	7.96
Sub Nts[5] 7s 2005	jJ	BBB+			X	BE	NC	....	....	....	....	....	100	M2	'95	105	96⅜	96⅜	7.26	7.26
MAPCO Inc.	*73d*	*Merged into Williams Cos,see*																		
Deb 7.70s 2027	Ms	BBB–	4/98	BBB	X	BE	NC	....	....	....	....	....	100	M5	'97	109⅜	93⅛	93⅛	8.27	8.27
Nts 7¼s 2009	Ms	BBB–	4/98	BBB	X	BE	NC	....	....	....	....	....	100	C1	'97	107¾	95¼	95¼	7.61	7.61
Marathon Oil Co.	*49b*	*Gtd by USX Corp, see*																		
•[6]Gtd[7]Nts[8] 7s 2002	[9]Jun	BBB–	11/96	BB+	X	R	NC	....	....	....	....	....	135	Exch.	'93	101¾	98	s98⅝	7.12	7.11
Margaretten Financial	*25h*	*Merged into Chem'l Bkg,see Chase Manhattan*																		
Nts 6¾s 2000	Jd15	AA–	5/98	A+	X	BE	NC	....	....	....	....	....	150	G1	'93	102⅛	100⅛	100⅛	6.74	6.74
Mark IV Industries	*8*	*3.78*	*3.87*	*2.46*		*Fb*	*2.20*	*1002*	*576.0*	*8-31-99*	*794.0*		*1613*	*62.1*						
Sr Sub Nts[10] 7¾s 2006	Ao	BB–	12/98	BB+	Y	R	NC	....	....	....	....	....	248	B7	'96	99¼	93¼	93½	8.29	8.29
Sub Nts 7½s 2007	mS	BB–	12/98	BB+	Y	BE	NC	....	....	....	....	....	250	Exch.	'97	96⅞	90⅜	90⅜	8.30	8.30
Markel Corp	*35b*	*6.91*	*4.30*	*4.69*		*Dc*	*1.53*			*9-30-99*	*389.0*		*762.0*	*45.7*						
Nts 7¼s 2003	mN	DDD	8/98	BBB	X	BE	NC	....	....	....	....	....	100	S7	'93	103¾	98¾	98⅞	7.33	7.33
Market Hub Ptnrs Storage/Fin	*49e*	*3.36*	*3.79*	*1.73*		*Dc*	*16.70*	*30.40*	*6.78*	*9-30-99*	*115.0*		*201.0*	*57.2*						
Sr Nts[10] 8¼s 2008	Ms	BB+			Y	BE	104.125	(3-1-03)	....	....	[11]Z108.25	3-1-01	115	Exch.	'98	102½	93⅜	95¼	8.66	8.66
[12]Marriott Corp	*32*	*0.98*	*1.34*	*1.76*		*Dc*				*9-10-99*	*5700*		*7175*	*74.2*						
Deb 9⅜s 2007	Jd15	B	5/93	BBB	Y	R	NC	....	....	....	....	....	9.00	M2	'87	108¾	94⅝	96⅝	9.70	9.70
Sr Nts K 10¼s 2001	jJ18	B	5/93	BBB	Y	R	NC	....	....	....	....	....	7.99	M2	'91	107¾	101⅛	101⅝	10.09	10.08
Sr Nts L 10s 2012	Mn	B	5/93	BBB	Y	R	NC	....	....	....	....	....	6.90	S1	'92	114	95½	99⅛	10.09	10.09
Sr Nts M 9½s 2002	Mn	B	5/93	BBB	Y	R	NC	....	....	....	....	....	14.0	S1	'92	107¼	99⅝	100⅜	9.46	9.46
Marriott Int'l	*32*	*6.91*	*6.24*	*7.07*		*Dc*	*240.0*	*1239*	*1421*	*6-18-99*	*1178*		*4051*	*29.1*						
Nts 'A' 6⅝s 2003	mN15	BBB+			X	BE	NC	....	....	....	....	....	200	Exch.	'99	100⅝	95⅝	96	6.90	6.90
Nts 'B' 6⅞s 2005	mN15	BBB+			X	BE	NC	....	....	....	....	....	200	Exch.	'99	100½	94⅛	94½	7.28	7.27
Nts 'C' 7⅞s 2009	mS15	BBB+			X	BE	NC	....	....	....	....	....	300	L3	'99	101¼	98¼	98¼	8.02	8.01
Marsh & McLennan	*35b*	*11.95*	*7.68*	*10.32*		*Dc*	*641.0*	*3403*	*3559*	*9-30-99*	*2591*		*7878*	*45.8*						
Sr Nts 6⅝s 2004	Jd15	AA–			X	BE	[13]Z100	....	....	....	....	....	600	C1	'99	100⅜	97⅝	97⅝	6.79	6.79
Sr Nts 7⅛s 2009	Jd15	AA–			X	BE	[13]Z100	....	....	....	....	....	400	C1	'99	101¾	96¾	96¾	7.36	7.36
Marsh Supermkts	*59c*	*0.94*	*1.70*	*1.72*		*Mr*	*24.30*	*178.0*	*123.0*	*6-19-99*	*232.0*		*362.0*	*65.0*						
Sr Sub Nts[10]'B' 8⅞s 2007	fA	B+			Y	BE	104.438	(8-1-02)	....	....	....	....	150	M2	'97	106½	88	92	9.65	9.64
Marshall & Ilsley	*10*	*3.99*	*3.47*	*3.53*		*Dc*				*9-30-99*	*569.0*		*3112*	*31.4*						
M-T[14]Nts 'D' 6.33s 2001	[15]mn	A+			X	BE	NC	....	....	....	....	....	25.0		'97	101⅞	99	99	6.39	6.39
Sub Nts 6⅝s 2003	jJ15	A			X	BE	NC	....	....	....	....	....	99.0	G1	'93	103¾	98	98	6.51	6.50
Martin Marietta Materials	*13a*	*12.75*	*9.95*	*8.32*		*Dc*	*0.60*	*429.7*	*219.3*	*9-30-99*	*603.0*		*1272*	*47.3*						
Deb 7s 2025	jD	A			X	BE	NC	....	....	....	....	....	125	G1	'95	104⅛	89⅞	90	7.78	7.78
Martin Marietta Technologies	*2a*	*Gtd by Lockheed Martin,see Lockheed Corp*																		
Nts 6.90s 2007	fA15	A			X	BE	NC	....	....	....	....	....	125	G1	'97	106⅜	96⅞	96⅞	7.12	7.12
Deb 7s 2011	Ms15	BBB–	11/99	BBB	X	R	100	....	....	....	....	....	[16]175	G1	'81	108¾	89	89	7.87	7.86
Deb[17] 7⅜s 2013	Ao15	BBB–	11/99	BBB	X	R	NC	....	....	....	....	....	150	G1	'93	110⅛	92¼	92¼	7.99	7.99
Deb[17] 7¾s 2023	Ao15	BBB–	11/99	BBB	X	R	103.735	(4-15-03)	....	....	....	....	150	G1	'93	107⅛	88¼	88¼	8.78	8.78

Uniform Footnote Explanations-See Page 260. Other: [1] Fiscal May'98 & prior. [2] Gtd by HCR Manor Care. [3] Greater of 100 or amt based on formula. [4] Subsid & data of M & T Bank. [5] Issued in min denom $250T. [6] Int at 9.75% to 3-1-94,7% aft. [7] Gtd by USX Corp. [8] (HRO)On Chge of Ctrl at 100. [9] Int pd monthly. [10] (HRO)On Chge of Ctrl at 101. [11] Max $40.3M red w/proceeds of Equity Off'g. [12] Now Host Marriott. [13] Red at greater of 100 or amt based on formula. [14] Issued in min denom $25T. [15] Due 6-1-01. [16] Incl disc. [17] Gtd by Martin Marietta Corp.

Title-Industry Code & Co. Finances (In Italics) / Individual Issue Statistics: Exchange, Interest Dates	Fixed Charge Coverage 1996 / S&P Rating	1997 / Date of Last Rating Change	1998 / Prior Rating	Eligible	Year End / Bond Form	Cash & Equiv. / Regular Price	Million $ Curr. Assets / Regular (Begins) Thru	Million $ Curr. Liab. / Sinking Fund Price	Balance Sheet Date / Sinking Fund (Begins) Thru	L. Term Debt (Mil $) / Refund/Other Restriction Price	Refund/Other Restriction (Begins) Thru	Capital-ization (Mil $) / Outst'g (Mil $)	Total Debt % Capital / Underwriting Firm	Underwriting Year	Price Range 1999 High	Price Range 1999 Low	Mo. End Price Sale(s) or Bid	Curr. Yield	Yield to Mat.
Martin Marietta Technologies (Cont.)																			
Nts 9s 2003 Ms	BBB–	11/99	BBB	X	R	NC	....	....	....	....	....	100	G1	'91	112¾	103⅜	103⅜	8.71	8.70
Nts[1] 6½s 2003 Ao15	BBB–	11/99	BBB	X	R	NC	....	....	....	....	....	400	G1	'93	103⅞	96⅝	96⅝	6.73	6.73
Masco Corp. ***13f***	*6.55*	*8.23*	*9.51*		*Dc*	*145.5*	*2160*	*970.3*	*9-30-99*	*2420*		*4353*	*36.9*						
Deb 7⅛s 2013 fA15	A–	3/98	BBB+	X	R	NC	....	....	....	....	....	200	S1	'93	106⅞	93	93	7.66	7.66
Deb 6⅝s 2018 Ao15	A–			X	BE	NC	....	....	....	....	....	250	S4	'98	101⅞	87⅝	88¼	7.51	7.51
Deb 7¾s 2029 fA	A–			X	BE	NC	....	....	....	....	....	300	M2	'99	102¾	97¼	98½	7.87	7.87
Nts 9s 2001 aO	A–	3/98	BBB+	X	R	NC	....	....	....	....	....	175	S1	'91	108⅞	96½	103⅜	8.69	8.68
Nts 6⅛s 2003 mS15	A–	3/98	BBB+	X	R	NC	....	....	....	....	....	200	S1	'93	102½	97½	97½	6.28	6.28
Nts 5¾s 2008 aO15	A–			X	BE	NC	....	....	....	....	....	100	M2	'98	99⅝	88⅞	89⅝	6.43	6.43
Massachusetts Electric[2] ***72a***	*2.80*	*4.07*	*3.50*		*Dc*	*7.49*	*225.0*	*310.0*	*9-30-99*	*332.0*		*910.0*	*44.8*						
1st T(93-2) 7.09s 2003 [3]jj	AA–	10/97	A+	X	BE	NC	....	....	....	....	....	20.0	K2	'93	105¼	99¼	99¼	7.14	7.14
1st T(93-4) 7.69s 2023 [4]jj	AA–	10/97	A+	X	BE	103.84	(2-1-03)	Z100	(2-1-03)	....	....	10.0	C5	'93	107½	94½	94⅝	8.13	8.13
1st T(93-5) 6.40s 2003 [5]jj	AA–	10/97	A+	X	BE	NC	....	....	....	....	....	10.0	K2	'93	103	97	97	6.60	6.60
1st T(93-7) 6.66s 2008 [6]jj	AA–	10/97	A+	X	BE	NC	....	....	....	....	....	5.00	K2	'93	106¼	93⅞	93⅞	7.09	7.09
1st T(93-8) 6.66s 2008 [7]jj	AA–	10/97	A+	X	BE	NC	....	....	....	....	....	5.00	C5	'93	106¼	93⅞	93⅞	7.09	7.09
1st T(93-9) 7½s 2023 [8]jj	AA–	10/97	A+	X	BE	103.75	(6-30-03)	Z100	(6-30-03)	....	....	7.00	K2	'93	106	92½	92⅝	8.10	8.10
1st T(93-10) 6.11s 2008 [9]jj	AA–	10/97	A+	X	BE	NC	....	....	....	....	....	10.0	K2	'93	102⅛	90¼	90¼	6.77	6.77
1st T(93-11) 6⅝s 2008 [10]jj	AA–	10/97	A+	X	BE	NC	....	....	....	....	....	10.0	K2	'93	104⅛	91¾	91¾	6.95	6.95
1st U(93-1) 6.24s 2003 [11]ms	AA–	10/97	A+	X	BE	NC	....	....	....	....	....	5.00	C5	'93	102½	96	96	6.50	6.50
1st U(93-2) 7.20s 2023 [12]ms	AA–	10/97	A+	X	BE	103.60	(11-1-03)	Z100	(11-1-03)	....	....	10.0	C5	'93	103¾	89⅝	89½	8.04	8.04
1st U(94-1) 7.05s 2024 [13]ms	AA–	10/97	A+	X	BE	103.53	(2-2-04)	Z100	(2-2-04)	....	....	10.0	C5	'94	105½	88⅛	88¼	7.99	7.99
1st U(94-2) 8.08s 2024 [14]ms	AA–	10/97	A+	X	BE	104.04	(5-2-04)	Z100	(5-2-04)	....	....	5.00	C5	'94	111⅜	97⅞	97⅞	8.26	8.25
1st U(94-3) 8.03s 2024 [15]ms	AA–	10/97	A+	X	BE	104.02	(6-14-04)	Z100	(6-14-04)	....	....	5.00	C5	'94	111	97½	97½	8.24	8.23
1st U(94-4) 8.16s 2024 [16]ms	AA–	10/97	A+	X	BE	104.08	(8-9-04)	Z100	(8-9-04)	....	....	5.00	C5	'94	119⅜	99⅞	99⅞	8.17	8.17
MasTec Inc. ***67***	*4.72*	*5.83*	*1.09*		*Dc*	*28.70*	*411.0*	*168.0*	*9-30-99*	*290.0*		*547.0*	*59.5*						
Sr Sub Nts[17]'B' 7¾s 2008 Fa	BB–			Y	BE	103.875	(2-1-03)	....	....	[18]Z107.75	2-1-01	200	Exch.	'98	98	91½	94	8.24	8.24
Mattel,Inc. ***40h***	*8.23*	*8.77*	*5.59*		*Dc*	*92.71*	*3307*	*2486*	*9-30-99*	*1084*		*4167*	*51.9*						
Nts 6¾s 2000 Mn15	A–	7/99	A	X	R	NC	....	....	....	....	....	100	M6	'93	101½	99⅞	99⅞	6.76	6.76
Nts 6s 2003 jJ15	A–	7/99	A	X	BE	[19]Z100	....	....	....	....	....	150	C6	'98	101⅜	94⅜	94⅜	6.36	6.36
Nts 6⅛s 2005 jJ15	A–	7/99	A	X	BE	[19]Z100	....	....	....	....	....	150	C6	'98	101⅞	91⅜	91⅜	6.70	6.70
M-T Nts 'A' 8½s 2001 [20]mn15	A–	7/99	A	X	BE	NC	....	....	....	....	....	20.5	M6	'94	108⅛	102⅛	102⅛	8.32	8.32
M-T Nts 'A' 8.48s 2001 [21]mn15	A–	7/99	A	X	BE	NC	....	....	....	....	....	10.0	M6	'94	108	102⅛	102⅛	8.30	8.30
M-T Nts 'A' 7.65s 2002 [22]mn15	A–	7/99	A	X	BE	NC	....	....	....	....	....	30.0	M6	'95	106¼	100⅝	100⅝	7.60	7.60
M-T Nts 'A' 7.44s 2003 [23]mn15	A–	7/99	A	X	BE	NC	....	....	....	....	....	15.0	M6	'95	107	100	100	7.44	7.44
M-T Nts 'A' 8.55s 2004 [24]mn15	A–	7/99	A	X	BE	NC	....	....	....	....	....	20.0	M6	'94	113⅞	103¾	103¾	8.24	8.24
M-T Nts 'A' 7.17s 2006 [25]mn15	A–	7/99	A	X	BE	NC	....	....	....	....	....	15.0	M6	'95	108⅛	96⅜	96⅜	7.44	7.44
M-T Nts 'A' 7.20s 2006 [25]mn15	A–	7/99	A	X	BE	NC	....	....	....	....	....	15.0	M6	'95	108⅜	96½	96½	7.46	7.46
M-T Nts 'A' 7.20s 2007 [26]mn15	A–	7/99	A	X	BE	NC	....	....	....	....	....	30.0	M6	'95	109⅛	96	96	7.50	7.50
M-T Nts 'B' 7¼s 2012 [27]mn15	A–	7/99	A	X	BE	NC	....	....	....	....	....	50.0	C5	'97	113⅜	94¾	94¾	7.65	7.65
M-T Nts 'C' 6½s 2013 [28]mn15	A–	7/99	A	X	BE	NC	....	....	....	....	....	35.0	C6	'98	106⅞	88⅛	88⅛	7.38	7.38
Maxus Energy ***49a***	***Acquired by YPF S.A.***																		
Nts 9⅞s 2002 aO15	BBB–	4/97	BB	X	BE	100	....	....	....	....	....	25.4	F1	'92	105	100¼	100½	9.83	9.83
Nts 9½s 2003 Fa15	BBB–	4/97	BB	X	BE	100	(2-15-00)	....	....	....	....	11.1	M2	'93	108⅜	100	100	9.50	9.50
Nts'B' 9⅜s 2003 mN	BBB–	4/97	BB	X	BE	NC	....	....	....	....	....	3.03	C5	'94	105	98	98	9.57	9.57

Uniform Footnote Explanations-See Page 260. Other: [1] Gtd by Martin Marietta Corp. [2] Contr by New Eng Elec Sys. [3] Due 1-27-03. [4] Due 2-24-23. [5] Due 6-24-03. [6] Due 6-23-08. [7] Due 6-30-08. [8] Due 6-29-23. [9] Due 9-8-08. [10] Due 11-17-08. [11] Due 11-17-03. [12] Due 11-15-23. [13] Due 2-2-24. [14] Due 5-2-24. [15] Due 6-14-24. [16] Due 8-9-24. [17] (HRO)On Chge of Ctrl at 101. [18] Max $67M red w/proceeds of Pub Eq Off'g. [19] Red at greater of 100 or amt based on formula. [20] Due 12-10-01. [21] Due 12-12-01. [22] Due 4-4-02. [23] Due 5-12-03. [24] Due 12-13-04. [25] Due 5-16-06. [26] Due 5-24-07. [27] Due 7-9-12. [28] Due 11-18-13.

Title-Industry Code & Co. Finances (In Italics) / Individual Issue Statistics (Exchange ↓)	Ind / Interest Dates	Fixed Charge Coverage 1996 / S&P Rating	1997 / Date of Last Rating Change	Prior Rating	1998 / Eligible ↓	Year End / Bond Form	Cash & Equiv. / Redemption Provisions: Regular Price	Million $ Curr. Assets / Regular (Begins) Thru	Curr. Liab. / Sinking Fund Price	Balance Sheet Date / Sinking Fund (Begins) Thru	Refund/Other Restriction Price	L. Term Debt (Mil $) / Refund/Other Restriction (Begins) Thru	Capital-ization (Mil $) / Outst'g (Mil $)	Underwriting Firm	Total Debt % Capital / Underwriting Year	Price Range 1999 High	Price Range 1999 Low	Mo. End Price Sale(s) or Bid	Curr. Yield	Yield to Mat.
Maxus Energy (Cont.)																				
M-T Nts 'C' 10.83s 2004	[1]fa15	BBB−	4/97	BB	X	BE	NC	....	....	....	....	....	40.0	L3	'94	120⅝	104	104	10.41	10.41
[2]MAXXAM Group Hldgs[3]	***5***	***0.91***	***1.42***		***0.97***	***Dc***	***209.1***	***1272***	***683.9***	***9-30-99***		***1978***	***2758***		***94.6***					
Sr Nts[4]'B' 12s 2003	fA	CCC+			Y	BE	106	(8-1-00)	....	....	[5]Z110	8-1-00	130	Exch.	'97	107	90	93	12.90	12.90
May Department Stores[6]	***59f***	***5.44***	***5.28***		***6.02***	***Ja***	***34.00***	***5303***	***2775***	***10-30-99***		***3567***	***7694***		***49.9***					
Deb 9⅞s 2000	Jd15	A+	7/99	A	X	R	NC	....	....	....	....	....	200	M6	'88	106⅛	101½	101½	9.73	9.73
Deb 9⅜s 2002	jD	A+	7/99	A	X	R	NC	....	....	....	....	....	175	M6	'90	115⅛	107½	107½	9.19	9.18
Deb 6⅞s 2005	mN	A+	7/99	A	X	BE	NC	....	....	....	....	....	125	M6	'96	107	97⅞	97⅞	7.02	7.02
Deb 10⅝s 2010	mN	A+	7/99	A	X	R	NC	....	....	....	....	....	150	M6	'90	139¾	120¾	121⅝	8.74	8.73
Deb 7.45s 2011	mS15	A+	7/99	A	X	BE	NC	....	....	....	....	....	150	M6	'96	115¾	99½	99⅝	7.48	7.48
Deb 7⅝s 2013	fA15	A+	7/99	A	X	R	NC	....	....	....	....	....	125	M6	'95	115⅛	100	100	7.63	7.62
Deb 7½s 2015	Jd	A+	7/99	A	X	R	NC	....	....	....	....	....	100	M6	'95	112½	100⅛	101	7.43	7.42
Deb 7.45s 2016	aO15	A+	7/99	A	X	BE	NC	....	....	....	....	....	125	M6	'96	112½	97½	98⅛	7.59	7.59
Deb 10¼s 2021	Jj	A+	7/99	A	X	R	NC	....	....	....	....	....	100	M6	'91	144⅜	122	122¾	8.35	8.35
Deb 9⅞s 2021	Jd15	A+	7/99	A	X	R	104.563	(6-15-01)	100	(6-15-02)	....	....	100	M6	'91	113⅝	107⅝	107¾	9.16	9.16
Deb 8⅜s 2022	aO	A+	7/99	A	X	R	104.044	(10-1-02)	100	(10-1-03)	....	....	200	M6	'92	113⅞	101½	101½	8.25	8.25
Deb 8⅜s 2024	fA	A+	7/99	A	X	R	104.188	(8-1-04)	[7]100	7-31-05	....	....	200	M6	'94	114	99	99	8.46	8.46
Deb 7.60s 2025	Jd	A+	7/99	A	X	R	NC	....	....	....	....	....	100	M6	'95	114⅞	96⅞	97⅝	7.78	7.78
Deb 8.30s 2026	jJ15	A+	7/99	A	X	BE	104.15	(7-15-06)	....	....	....	....	200	M6	'96	113	99¼	99⅞	8.31	8.31
Deb 6.70s 2028	mS15	A+	7/99	A	X	BE	[8]Z100	....	....	....	....	....	200	M7	'98	105⅞	87¼	87⅞	7.62	7.62
Deb 8⅛s 2035	fA15	A+	7/99	A	X	R	100	(8-15-15)	....	....	....	....	150	M6	'95	115⅞	98⅝	99⅜	8.18	8.17
Deb 7⅞s 2036	fA15	A+	7/99	A	X	BE	100	....	....	....	....	....	200	M6	'96	112⅝	96½	97¼	8.10	8.10
[9]Amortizing Deb 9¾s 2021	Fa15	A+	7/99	A	X	R	NC	....	....	....	....	....	125	M6	'91	127⅞	113⅛	113⅛	8.62	....
[10]Amortizing Deb 9½s 2021	Ao15	A+	7/99	A	X	R	NC	....	....	....	....	....	150	M6	'91	128½	110⅝	110⅝	8.59	....
Nts 7.15s 2004	fA15	A+	7/99	A	X	R	NC	....	....	....	....	....	125	M6	'95	107½	100⅛	100¼	7.13	7.13
Nts 5.95s 2008	mN	A+	7/99	A	X	BE	[8]Z100	....	....	....	....	....	150	M7	'98	102¾	90¼	90¾	6.56	6.56
Maytag Corp	***23d***	***7.24***	***6.09***		***8.50***	***Dc***	***27.40***	***1103***	***939.0***	***9-30-99***		***415.0***	***1560***		***53.1***					
Nts 9¾s 2002	Mn15	A−	5/98	BBB+	X	R	NC	....	....	....	....	....	177	G1	'90	112⅞	105⅝	105⅝	9.23	9.23
MBIA Inc.	***35c***	***13.20***	***13.81***		***13.66***	***Dc***				***9-30-99***		***689.0***	***4231***		***16.3***					
Deb 8.20s 2022	aO	AA	8/95	AA+	X	BE	103.988	(10-1-02)	....	....	....	....	100	D6	'92	109¼	99½	100	8.20	8.20
Deb 7s 2025	jD15	AA			X	BE	NC	....	....	....	....	....	75.0	L3	'95	105⅛	88¼	89⅜	7.83	7.83
Deb 7.15s 2027	jJ15	AA			X	BE	NC	....	....	....	....	....	100	D6	'97	107⅛	89¾	90¾	7.88	7.88
Deb 6⅝s 2028	aO	AA			X	BE	NC	....	....	....	....	....	150	G1	'98	100⅛	83¾	84⅞	7.81	7.81
Nts 9s 2001	Fa15	AA	8/95	AA+	X	R	NC	....	....	....	....	....	100	D6	'91	107	102¼	102¼	8.80	8.80
Nts 9⅜s 2011	Fa15	AA	8/95	AA+	X	BE	NC	....	....	....	....	....	100	D6	'91	129¾	112¾	112¾	8.31	8.31
MBNA America Bank,NA	***10***	***Subsid of MBNA Corp,see***																		
Sub Nts[11] 7¼s 2002	mS15	BBB	8/97	BBB+	Y	BE	NC	....	....	....	....	....	200	M2	'92	103⅝	98½	98½	7.36	7.36
MBNA Corp[12]	***10***	***4.66***	***4.15***		***4.08***	***Dc***				***9-30-99***		***6096***	***9899***		***61.9***					
Sr Nts 6⅞s 2005	Jd	BBB	8/97	BBB+	X	BE	NC	....	....	....	....	....	100	M2	'95	105⅝	95¼	95¼	7.22	7.22
F/R[13]Sr M-T Nts[11] 2000	QMar9	BBB	8/97	BBB+	X	BE	NC	....	....	....	....	....	75.0	B7	'95	100⅛	99⅞	100	....	....
M-T Sr Nts[11] 6.15s 2003	[14]fa15	BBB	8/97	BBB+	X	BE	NC	....	....	....	....	....	100	B7	'93	98¾	93⅝	94⅜	6.52	6.52
Sr[11]M-T Nts 6.963s 2002	mS12	BBB			X	BE	NC	....	....	....	....	....	30.0	C5	'97	101⅞	97¾	98	7.11	7.10
Sr M-T Nts[11] 6⅞s 2002	mN15	BBB			X	BE	NC	....	....	....	....	....	100	M5	'97	101⅝	97¼	97⅝	7.04	7.04
Sr M-T Nts 7⅛s 2004	mS15	BBB			X	BE	NC	....	....	....	....	....	35.0	M5	'97	102⅞	96	96⅝	7.37	7.37
McCaw International Ltd	***67g***	***Merged into NEXTEL Commun's,see***																		
Sr[15]Disc Nts[16] 13s 2007	Ao15	B−	4/99	B−	Y	BE	106.50	(4-15-02)	....	....	[17]Z113	4-15-00	[18]939	Exch.	'97	70	53	69	....	Flat

Uniform Footnote Explanations-See Page 260. Other: [1] Due 9-1-04. [2] Was McCulloch Oil,MCO Hldgs. [3] Now MAXXAM Inc. [4] (HRO)On Chge of Ctrl at 101. [5] Max $45.5M red w/proceeds of Pub Eq Off'g. [6] See Assoc Dry Goods,Strawbridge & Clothier. [7] Fr 8-1-05. [8] Red at greater of 100 or amt based on formula. [9] Deb prin will amortize ea F&A 15 fr 8-15-01. [10] Deb prin will amortize ea A&O 15 fr 10-15-01. [11] Issued in min denom $100T. [12] See MBNA America Bank,NA. [13] Int adj qtrly(3 Mo LIBOR & 0.30%). [14] Due 10-1-03. [15] Int accrues at 13% fr 4-15-02. [16] (HRO)On Chge of Ctrl at 101(Accreted Amt). [17] Fr 4-15-02. [18] Incl disc.

Title-Industry Code & Co. Finances (In Italics) / Individual Issue Statistics: Exchange	Ind / Interest Dates	Fixed Charge Coverage 1996 / S&P Rating	1997 / Date of Last Rating Change	1998 / Prior Rating	Eligible	Year End / Bond Form	Cash & Equiv. (Million $) / Regular Price	Curr. Assets (Million $) / Regular (Begins) Thru	Curr. Liab. (Million $) / Sinking Fund Price	Balance Sheet Date / Sinking Fund (Begins) Thru	L. Term Debt (Mil $) / Refund/Other Restriction Price	Refund/Other Restriction (Begins) Thru	Capital-ization (Mil $) / Outst'g (Mil $)	Total Debt % Capital / Underwriting Firm	Underwriting Year	Price Range 1999 High	Price Range 1999 Low	Mo. End Price Sale(s) or Bid	Curr. Yield	Yield to Mat.
McCormick & Co	***26***	***4.54***	***4.83***	***5.20***		***Nv***	***13.86***	***506.4***	***533.7***	***8-31-99***	***242.0***		***882.0***	***46.9***						
Nts 8.95s 2001	jJ	A			X	BE	NC	....	....	....	....	....	75.0	F1	'91	108⅜	102⅞	102⅞	8.70	8.70
[1] ***McDermott Inc***	***49e***	***d1.26***	***5.17***	***4.69***		***Mr***	***225.0***	***1406***	***1251***	***9-30-99***	***323.0***		***1278***	***35.8***						
Nts 9⅜s 2002	Ms15	BBB–	7/98	BB+	X	BE	NC	....	....	....	....	....	225	G1	'92	106¾	102¼	102¼	9.17	9.17
McDonald's Corp	***27b***	***6.98***	***6.89***	***6.86***		***Dc***	***425.0***	***1394***	***2355***	***9-30-99***	***6289***		***15971***	***43.3***						
• Deb 8⅞s 2011	Ao	AA			X	R	NC	....	....	....	....	....	100	M5	'91	119	108¼	107	8.29	8.29
• Deb 7.05s 2025	mN15	AA			X	BE	103.26	(11-15-05)	....	....	....	....	150	M5	'95	106⅛	93	93	7.58	7.58
• Deb 6⅜s 2028	Jj8	AA			X	BE	[2]Z100	....	....	....	....	....	150	M2	'98	96	96	85⅞	7.42	7.42
• Deb 7⅜s 2033	jJ15	AA			X	R	104.635	(7-15-03)	....	....	....	....	200	S1	'93	105⅞	92	95	7.76	7.76
• Nts 6¾s 2003	Fa15	AA			X	R	100	(2-15-00)	....	....	....	....	125	M5	'93	102½	98½	98½	6.85	6.85
• Nts 6⅝s 2005	mS	AA			X	BE	100	(9-1-02)	....	....	....	....	150	M6	'95	102⅝	98	97½	6.79	6.79
M-T Nts 'E' 5.95s 2008	Jj15	AA			X	BE	Z100	....	....	....	....	....	200	M5	'98	105¼	92⅛	92⅛	6.46	6.46
M-T Nts 'F' 5.35s 2008	mS15	AA			X	BE	[2]Z100	....	....	....	....	....	150	M5	'98	100⅝	87⅝	87⅝	6.11	6.11
• Sub[3]Deferrable Int Deb 7.31s 2027	mS15	A+	8/99	AA–	X	BE	100	(9-15-07)	....	....	....	....	150	M6	'97	106	106	92⅛	7.93	7.93
McDonnell Douglas	***2a***	***Acq by Boeing Co, see***																		
• Deb 9¾s 2012	Ao	AA–	12/98	AA	X	R	NC	....	....	....	....	....	350	M2	'92	133¼	126¼	114¼	8.53	8.53
• Nts 8¼s 2000	jJ	AA–	12/98	AA	X	BE	NC	....	....	....	....	....	200	M2	'93	103¾	102⅞	100⅞	8.18	8.18
• Nts 9¼s 2002	Ao	AA–	12/98	AA	X	R	NC	....	....	....	....	....	120	M2	'92	110½	108⅜	104⅜	8.86	8.86
Nts 6⅞s 2006	mN	AA–	12/98	AA	X	BE	NC	....	....	....	....	....	250	M2	'96	107¼	96⅝	96⅝	7.12	7.11
McDonnell Douglas Finance	***25***	***Subsid of Boeing Capital, see***																		
Sr M-T Nts 'IX'[4] 7.42s 2000	[5]ms15	A+	12/98	AA–	X	BE	NC	....	....	....	....	....	20.0	M2	'95	101⅞	100	100	7.42	Mat.
Sub M-T Nts 'IX'[4] 8.31s 2004	[6]jj15	A	12/98	A+	X	BE	NC	....	....	....	....	....	20.0	C1	'94	112⅞	103½	103½	8.03	8.03
McGraw-Hill Companies	***54***	***9.31***	***9.58***	***12.13***		***Dc***	***15.40***	***1774***	***1695***	***9-30-99***	***407.0***		***2431***	***32.3***						
Nts[7] 9.43s 2000	mS	[8]...				BE	NC	....	....	....	....	....	95.0	M6	'90	106¾	102	102	9.25	9.24
[9] ***MCI Communications***	***67b***	***7.46***	***2.27***	***4.38***		***Dc***	***307.0***	***9707***	***15553***	***9-30-99***	***14043***		***69405***	***25.5***						
Sr Deb 8¼s 2023	Jj20	A–	7/99	BBB+	X	BE	103.74	(1-20-03)	....	....	....	....	200	M2	'93	107	97¾	98	8.42	8.42
Sr Deb 7¾s 2024	Ms15	A–	7/99	BBB+	X	BE	103.665	(3-15-03)	....	....	....	....	240	M2	'93	104½	93¾	93¾	8.27	8.27
Sr Deb 7¾s 2025	Ms23	A–	7/99	BBB+	X	BE	103.469	(3-23-04)	....	....	....	....	450	M2	'94	108⅛	93⅝	93¾	8.27	8.27
Deb[10] 7⅛s 2027	Jd15	A–	7/99	BBB+	X	BE	NC	....	....	....	....	....	500	M5	'96	110½	99¾	99¾	7.14	7.14
Sr Nts 7⅛s 2000	Jj20	A–	7/99	BBB+	X	BE	NC	....	....	....	....	....	200	M2	'93	101½	100	100	7.13	7.12
Sr Nts 7½s 2004	fA20	A–	7/99	BBB+	X	BE	NC	....	....	....	....	....	400	M2	'92	109⅛	101⅛	101⅛	7.42	7.42
Sr Nts 6.95s 2006	fA15	A–	7/99	BBB+	X	BE	NC	....	....	....	....	....	300	M2	'96	108¼	97½	97½	7.13	7.13
Sr Nts 6½s 2010	Ao15	A–	7/99	BBB+	X	BE	[2]Z100	....	....	....	....	....	500	L3	'98	105	93⅛	93⅛	6.98	6.98
[11] ***McKesson Corp***	***19***	***1.66***	***3.52***	***2.68***		***Mr***	***361.0***	***6696***	***4981***	***6-30-99***	***1133***		***4880***	***39.4***						
Deb 7.65s 2027	Ms	BBB	12/99	BBB+	X	BE	[12]Z100	....	....	....	....	....	175	Exch.		113⅝	89¼	89⅝	8.54	8.53
Nts 6.60s 2000	Ms	BBB	12/99	BBB+	X	BE	NC	....	....	....	....	....	175	Exch.		101⅜	100	100⅛	6.59	6.59
Nts 6⅞s 2002	Ms	BBB	12/99	BBB+	X	BE	NC	....	....	....	....	....	175	Exch.	'97	103⅝	98⅝	98⅝	6.97	6.97
Nts 6.30s 2005	Ms	BBB	12/99	BBB+	X	BE	[2]Z100	....	....	....	....	....	150	Exch.	'98	101¾	93	93	6.77	6.77
Nts 6.40s 2008	Ms	BBB	12/99	BBB+	X	BE	[2]Z100	....	....	....	....	....	150	Exch.	'98	102⅞	89⅛	89⅛	7.18	7.18
McLeodUSA Inc	***67a***	***n/a***	***n/a***	***n/a***		***Dc***	***1463***	***1752***	***272.0***	***9-30-99***	***1801***		***1443***	***66.5***						
Sr[13]Disc[14]Nts 10½s 2007	Ms	B+	3/98	B	Y	BE	105.25	(3-1-02)	....	....	[15][16]110.50	3-1-00	[17]500	Exch.	'97	82	73½	82	....	Flat
Sr Nts[18] 9¼s 2007	jJ15	B+	3/98	B	Y	BE	104.625	(7-15-02)	....	....	[19]Z109.25	7-15-00	225	Exch.	'97	106½	96¼	99⅞	9.26	9.26
Sr Nts[18] 8⅜s 2008	Ms15	B+			Y	BE	104.188	(3-15-03)	....	....	[20]Z108.375	3-15-01	300	Exch.	'98	102½	91½	94½	8.86	8.86
Sr Nts[18] 9½s 2008	mN	B+			Y	BE	106.75	(11-1-03)	....	....	[21]Z111.50	11-1-01	300	Exch.	'98	110	97	101¼	9.38	9.38
Sr Nts[18] 8⅛s 2009	Fa15	B+			Y	BE	104.063	(2-15-04)	....	....	[15]Z108.125	2-14-02	500	Exch.	'99	94¼	89	93¼	8.71	8.71

Uniform Footnote Explanations-See Page 260. Other: [1] Subsid & data of McDermott Int'l. [2] Red at greater of 100 or amt based on formula. [3] Co may red in whole,at 100,for tax law chge. [4] Issued in min denom $100T. [5] Due 1-10-00. [6] Due 8-16-04. [7] Int subj to adj for Designated Event&Rat'g Chge. [8] S&P is a div of McGraw-Hill Cos, debt not rated. [9] Now MCI WorldCom. [10] (HRO)On 6-15-03 at 100. [11] Now Mckesson HBOC Inc. [12] Plus Make-Whole Amt. [13] Int accrues at 13% fr 3-1-02. [14] (HRO)On Chge of Ctrl at 101(Accreted Val). [15] Max $167M red w/proceeds of Pub Eq Off'g. [16] Accreted Val. [17] Incl disc. [18] (HRO)On Chge of Ctrl at 101. [19] Max $75M red w/proceeds of Pub Eq Off'g. [20] Max $105M red w/proceeds of Pub Eq Off'g. [21] Max $100M red w/proceeds of Equity Off'g.

Title-Industry Code & Co. Finances (In Italics) / Individual Issue Statistics (Exchange)	Ind / Interest Dates	1996 / S&P Rating	1997 / Date of Last Rating Change	1998 / Prior Rating	Eligible	Year End / Bond Form	Cash & Equiv. (Million $) / Regular Price	Curr. Assets (Million $) / Regular (Begins) Thru	Curr. Liab. (Million $) / Sinking Fund Price	Balance Sheet Date / Sinking Fund (Begins) Thru	L. Term Debt (Mil $) / Refund/Other Restriction Price	Refund/Other Restriction (Begins) Thru	Capital-ization (Mil $) / Outst'g (Mil $)	Total Debt % Capital / Underwriting Firm	Underwriting Year	Price Range 1999 High	Price Range 1999 Low	Mo. End Price Sale(s) or Bid	Curr. Yield	Yield to Mat.
[1]MCN Investment Corp	***73c***	***2.39***	***3.25***	***1.15***		***Dc***	***30.35***	***687.7***	***957.3***	***9-30-99***	***1864***		***3246***	***72.7***						
M-T Nts 6.03s 2001	Fa	BBB	9/98	BBB+	X	BE	NC	....	....	....	....	....	60.0	M2	'96	99⅞	98⅛	98⅛	6.15	6.14
M-T Nts 6.32s 2003	Fa	BBB	9/98	BBB+	X	BE	NC	....	....	....	....	....	60.0	M2	'96	100¼	94⅞	94⅞	6.66	6.66
M.D.C. Hldgs	***13h***	***0.82***	***1.03***	***3.18***		***Dc***				***9-30-99***	***207.0***		***547.0***	***37.8***						
• Sr Nts[2] 8⅜s 2008	Fa	BB	12/99	BB–	Y	BE	104.188	(2-1-03)	....	....	[3]Z108.375	2-1-01	175	S4	'98	103¼	88⅛	91½	9.15	9.15
Mead Corp	***50***	***6.09***	***3.39***	***2.82***		***Dc***	***139.0***	***1179***	***686.0***	***10-3-99***	***1333***		***3669***	***37.4***						
Deb 7.35s 2017	Ms	A–			X	BE	NC	....	....	....	....	....	150	G1	'97	107⅛	93¾	93⅞	7.83	7.83
Deb 8⅛s 2023	Fa	A–	11/94	BBB+	X	BE	103.68	(2-1-03)	....	....	....	....	150	G1	'93	107	97¾	97¾	8.31	8.31
Deb 7⅛s 2025	fA	A–	11/94	BBB+	X	BE	103	(8-1-03)	....	....	....	....	150	S7	'93	100¼	89⅜	89½	7.96	7.96
Deb 6.84s 2037	Ms	A–			X	BE	NC	....	....	....	....	....	150	G1	'97	102⅞	94½	94½	7.24	7.24
Deb[4] 7.55s 2047	Ms	A–			X	BE	NC	....	....	....	....	....	150	G1	'97	107⅛	90⅝	90¾	8.32	8.32
Nts 6.60s 2002	Ms	A–			X	BE	NC	....	....	....	....	....	100	G1	'97	102¾	99⅛	99⅛	6.66	6.66
[5]Medaphis Corp	***63***	***n/a***	***n/a***	***n/a***		***Dc***	***38.10***	***140.7***	***75.56***	***9-30-99***	***175.0***		***146.0***	***82.7***						
Sr Nts[2] 'B' 9½s 2005	Fa15	B	11/98	B+	Y	BE	104.75	(2-15-02)	....	....	[6]Z109.50	2-15-01	175	Exch.	'98	99¼	73	77½	12.26	12.25
[7]Mediacomn LLC/Capital	***12a***	***n/a***	***n/a***	***n/a***		***Dc***				***9-30-99***	***378.0***		***418.0***	***90.3***						
Sr Nts[2]'B' 8½s 2008	Ao15	B+			Y	BE	104.25	(4-15-03)	....	....	[8]Z108.50	4-15-01	200	Exch.	'98	103½	91½	93	9.14	9.14
Sr Nts[2] 7⅞s 2011	Fa15	B+			Y	BE	103.938	(2-15-06)	....	....	[9]Z108.875	2-15-02	125	Exch.	'99	100¼	85½	88	8.95	8.95
MediaOne Group[10]	***25***	***4.12***	***2.32***	***d0.31***		***Dc***	***1182***	***2373***	***2765***	***9-30-99***	***8501***		***22543***	***44.4***						
Deb[10] 7.90s 2027	Fa	BBB	5/98	BBB+	X	BE	NC	....	....	....	....	....	1100	M2	'97	112¼	96⅜	96½	8.19	8.18
Deb[10] 8.15s 2032	Fa	BBB	5/98	BBB+	X	BE	104.075	(2-1-07)	....	....	....	....	200	M2	'97	112	96⅜	96½	8.45	8.44
Deb[10] 6.95s 2037	Jj15	BBB	5/98	BBB+	X	BE	NC	....	....	....	....	....	600	M2	'97	107	92¾	99⅛	7.01	7.01
[10]Deb[11] 7.95s 2097	Fa	BBB	5/98	BBB+	X	BE	NC	....	....	....	....	....	0.10	M2	'97	114½	96⅛	96¼	8.26	8.26
Nts[10] 6.85s 2002	Jj15	BBB	5/98	BBB+	X	BE	NC	....	....	....	....	....	600	M2	'97	103¼	99⅜	99⅜	6.89	6.89
Gtd[10]Nts 6¾s 2005	aO	BBB	5/98	BBB+	X	BE	NC	....	....	....	....	....	300	G1	'95	104⅞	96⅜	96⅜	7.00	7.00
Nts[10] 6.31s 2005	mN	BBB	5/98	BBB+	X	BE	NC	....	....	....	....	....	250	M2	'95	103½	96	99⅜	6.35	6.35
Nts[10] 7.30s 2007	Jj15	BBB	5/98	BBB+	X	BE	NC	....	....	....	....	....	39.9	M2	'97	107¼	96⅞	96⅞	7.54	7.53
Meditrust Corp[12]	***57***	***3.46***	***2.86***	***1.63***		***Dc***				***9-30-99***	***2708***		***5490***	***49.5***						
• Nts 7⅜s 2000	jJ15	BB	11/98	BBB–	Y	BE	[13]Z100	....	....	....	....	....	125	G1	'95	99½	86	91⅛	8.09	8.09
• Nts 7.60s 2001	jJ15	BB	11/98	BBB–	Y	BE	[13]Z100	....	....	....	....	....	80.0	G1	'95	No Sale		75	10.13	10.13
Nts 7s 2007	fA15	BB	11/98	BBB–	Y	BE	NC	....	....	....	....	....	160	M2	'97	82½	54⅜	54⅜	12.87	12.87
Nts[14] 7.82s 2026	mS10	BB	11/98	BBB–	Y	BE	[13]Z100	(9-10-03)	....	....	....	....	175	M2	'96	95⅛	75⅜	75⅜	10.37	10.37
[15]MedPartners Inc	***30a***	***9.92***	***d1.24***	***1.63***		***Dc***	***20.20***	***574.0***	***1224***	***9-30-99***	***680.0***		***77.80***	***152.0***						
Sr Nts 7⅜s 2006	aO	B	6/98	BB+	Y	R	NC	....	....	....	....	....	450	S7	'96	88	79	83	8.89	8.89
Sr Sub Nts 6⅞s 2000	mS	B	6/98	BB–	Y	BE	NC	....	....	....	....	....	420	S7	'97	96	87	96	7.16	7.16
Mellon Fin'l	***25***	***4.22***	***4.15***	***3.97***		***Dc***				***6-30-99***	***4294***		***9081***	***50.2***						
Sr[16]Nts 6.30s 2000	Jd	A+	5/98	A	X	BE	NC	....	....	....	....	....	200	L3	'95	101⅜	99⅞	99⅞	6.31	6.31
Sr Nts 5¾s 2003	mN15	A+			X	BE	NC	....	....	....	....	....	300	C6	'98	101	94¾	95	6.05	6.05
Sr[16]Nts 6s 2004	Ms	A+	5/98	A	X	BE	NC	....	....	....	....	....	200	G1	'98	102	95⅛	95⅜	6.29	6.29
Sub[16]Deb 9¾s 2001	Jd15	A	5/98	A–	X	BE	NC	....	....	....	....	....	100	L3	'91	109⅞	103¾	103¾	9.40	9.40
Sub[16]Deb 9¼s 2001	fA15	A	5/98	A–	X	BE	NC	....	....	....	....	....	100	F1	'91	109⅜	103⅜	103⅜	8.95	8.95
Sub[16]Deb 6⅞s 2003	Ms	A	5/98	A–	X	BE	NC	....	....	....	....	....	150	G1	'93	105	98⅞	99	6.94	6.94
Sub[16]Deb 6.70s 2008	Ms	A			X	BE	NC	....	....	....	....	....	250	G1	'96	107¼	94¾	95	7.05	7.05
Sub[16]Deb 6⅜s 2010	Fa15	A	5/98	A–	X	BE	NC	....	....	....	....	....	350	M5	'98	105¼	91⅛	91⅛	7.00	7.00
Mercantile Bancorp	***10***	***Acqd by Firstar Corp,see***																		
Sr Nts 6.80s 2001	Jd15	A–	10/99	BBB+	X	BE	NC	....	....	....	....	....	150	S1	'97	102¾	99⅝	99⅝	6.83	6.82

Uniform Footnote Explanations-See Page 260. Other: [1] Subsid & data of MCN Energy Gr. [2] (HRO)On Chge of Ctrl at 101. [3] Max $58.3M red w/proceeds of Pub Eq Off'g. [4] Co may shorten mty for Tax Event. [5] Now Per-Se Technologies. [6] Max $61.3M red w/proceeds of Equity Off'g. [7] Data of Mediacom LLC. [8] Max $70M red w/proceeds of Pub Eq Off'g. [9] Max $43.8M red w/proceeds of Pub Eq Off'g. [10] Was US WEST Cap Fndg. [11] Co may red in whole,at 100(min),for tax law chge. [12] See La Quinta Inns. [13] Plus Make-Whole Amt. [14] (HRO)On 9-10-03 at 100. [15] Now Caremark Rx. [16] Gtd by Mellon Bank Corp.

Title-Industry Code & Co. Finances (In Italics) / Individual Issue Statistics — Exchange, Interest Dates	Fixed Charge Coverage 1996 / S&P Rating	1997 / Date of Last Rating Change	1998 / Prior Rating	Eligible	Year End / Bond Form	Cash & Equiv. (Million $) / Redemption Provisions: Regular Price	Curr. Assets (Million $) / Regular (Begins) Thru	Curr. Liab. (Million $) / Sinking Fund Price	Balance Sheet Date / Sinking Fund (Begins) Thru	L. Term Debt (Mil $) / Refund/Other Restriction Price	Capital-ization (Mil $) / Refund/Other Restriction (Begins) Thru	Outst'g (Mil $)	Total Debt % Capital / Underwriting Firm	Underwriting Year	Price Range 1999 High	Price Range 1999 Low	Mo. End Price Sale(s) or Bid	Curr. Yield	Yield to Mat.
***Mercantile Bancorp** (Cont.)*																			
Sr Nts 7.05s 2004 ....Jd15	A–	10/99	BBB+	X	BE	NC	....	....	....	....	....	150	S1	'97	106	98⅜	98⅜	7.17	7.17
Sub Nts 7⅝s 2002 ....aO15	BBB+	10/99	BBB	X	BE	NC	....	....	....	....	....	150	S1	'92	106¾	100⅞	100⅞	7.56	7.56
Sub Nts 7.30s 2007 ....Jd15	BBB+	10/99	BBB	X	BE	NC	....	....	....	....	....	200	S1	'97	109¼	96¾	96¾	7.55	7.54
***Mercantile Stores** 59f*	*Now Dillard's Inc,see*																		
Deb 8.20s 2022 ....mS15	BBB	8/98	A+	X	BE	100	(9-15-02)	100	(9-15-03)	....	....	100	G1	'92	107¾	101½	101½	8.08	8.08
***Merck & Co** 21a*	*37.58*	*58.17*	*33.24*		*Dc*	*3780*	*11015*	*7670*	*9-30-99*	*3214*	*20917*		*18.4*						
Deb 6.30s 2026 ....Jj	AAA			X	BE	NC	....	....	....	....	....	250	M6	'96	106⅛	86⅞	87⅛	7.23	7.23
M-T Nts 'B'[1] 5.76s 2037 ....[2]mn13	AAA			X	BE	[3]NC	....	....	....	....	....	500	M6	'97	104¼	95⅝	99⅞	5.77	5.77
***Meridian Bancorp**[4] 10*	*Merged into CoreStates Fin'l*																		
Nts 6⅝s 2000 ....Jd15	A	4/96	BBB+	X	BE	NC	....	....	....	....	....	150	C5	'95	101½	99⅞	100	6.63	6.62
Sub Deb 7⅞s 2002 ....jJ15	A–	4/96	BBB	X	BE	NC	....	....	....	....	....	100	F1	'92	107¼	101⅛	101⅛	7.79	7.79
***Merisel, Inc.** 20a*	*d0.69*	*0.57*	*2.29*		*Dc*	*9.26*	*797.2*	*656.3*	*9-30-99*	*133.0*	*270.0*		*50.0*						
Sr Nts[5] 12½s 2004 ....jD31	CCC+	1/98	CCC–	Y	R	106.25	12-30-00	....	....	....	....	125	C4	'94	109	65	65	19.23	19.21
***MeriStar Hospitality** 57*	*1.51*	*2.87*	*2.05*		*Dc*				*9-30-99*	*1662*	*2931*		*57.4*						
Sr Sub Nts[5] 8¾s 2007 ....fA15	B			Y	BE	104.375	(8-15-02)	....	....	[6]Z108.75	8-15-00	55.0	Exch.	'99	96½	89	92	9.51	9.51
***Meritor Automotive** 8*	*n/a*	*n/a*	*n/a*		*Sp*	*45.00*	*1389*	*1115*	*6-30-99*	*878.0*	*1263*		*75.3*						
Nts 6.80s 2009 ....Fa15	BBB			X	BE	[7]Z100	....	....	....	....	....	500	M7	'99	100½	91⅛	91⅛	7.46	7.46
***Merrill Lynch** 62*	*1.22*	*1.19*	*1.14*		*Dc*				*9-24-99*	*★55400*	*67500*		*82.1*						
Nts 8⅜s 2000 ....Fa9	AA–	12/96	A+	X	BE	NC	....	....	....	....	....	150	M2	'95	103⅛	100¼	100¼	8.35	8.35
Nts 6.70s 2000 ....fA	AA–	12/96	A+	X	BE	NC	....	....	....	....	....	150	M2	'95	101⅞	100	100⅛	6.69	6.69
Nts 6s 2001 ....Jj15	AA–	12/96	A+	X	BE	NC	....	....	....	....	....	500	M2	'96	101⅛	99⅛	99⅛	6.05	6.05
Nts 6s 2001 ....Ms	AA–	12/96	A+	X	BE	NC	....	....	....	....	....	250	M2	'96	101⅛	98⅞	98⅞	6.07	6.07
Nts 6½s 2001 ....Ao	AA–	12/96	A+	X	BE	NC	....	....	....	....	....	300	M2	'96	102¼	99⅜	99⅜	6.54	6.54
Nts 8s 2002 ....Fa	AA–	12/96	A+	X	R	NC	....	....	....	....	....	225	M2	'92	107⅛	101¾	101⅞	7.85	7.85
Nts 7⅜s 2002 ....fA17	AA–	12/96	A+	X	BE	NC	....	....	....	....	....	150	M2	'92	106⅛	100⅝	100⅝	7.33	7.33
Nts 6.64s 2002 ....mS19	AA–	12/96	A+	X	BE	NC	....	....	....	....	....	250	M2	'95	103⅞	98⅞	99	6.71	6.71
Nts 8.30s 2002 ....mN	AA–	12/96	A+	X	R	NC	....	....	....	....	....	150	M2	'92	109¼	102⅞	103	8.06	8.06
Nts 6⅞s 2003 ....Ms	AA–	12/96	A+	X	BE	NC	....	....	....	....	....	200	M2	'93	104⅞	99⅛	99⅛	6.94	6.94
F/R[9]Nts 5.825s 2003 ....QFeb4	AA–			X	BE	NC	....	....	....	....	....	300	M2	'98	100⅝	99⅜	99⅝	5.85	....
Nts 6.55s 2004 ....fA	AA–			X	BE	NC	....	....	....	....	....	500	M2	'97	104½	97⅛	97⅛	6.74	6.74
Nts[10] 6s 2004 ....mn15	AA–			X	BE	NC	....	....	....	....	....	500	M2	'98	102¼	94¾	94¾	6.33	6.33
Nts 6s 2005 ....jJ15	AA–			X	BE	NC	....	....	....	....	....	500	M2	'98	101⅞	93¾	93¾	6.40	6.40
Nts 6¼s 2006 ....Jj15	AA–	12/96	A+	X	BE	NC	....	....	....	....	....	200	M2	'94	103⅛	93½	93½	6.68	6.68
Nts 7s 2006 ....Ms15	AA–	12/96	A+	X	BE	NC	....	....	....	....	....	200	M2	'96	107⅜	97⅜	97⅜	7.19	7.19
Nts 7⅜s 2006 ....Mn15	AA–	12/96	A+	X	BE	NC	....	....	....	....	....	350	M2	'96	109⅝	99⅛	99⅛	7.44	7.44
Nts 6⅜s 2006 ....mS8	AA–	12/96	A+	X	BE	100	(9-8-03)	....	....	....	....	125	M2	'93	102¼	92¾	92¾	6.87	6.87
Nts 7s 2007 ....Jj15	AA–			X	BE	NC	....	....	....	....	....	500	M2	'97	106½	95⅞	96¾	7.24	7.23
Nts 8s 2007 ....Jd	AA–	12/96	A+	X	R	NC	....	....	....	....	....	150	M2	'92	114⅜	101⅛	101⅞	7.85	7.85
Nts 6.56s 2007 ....jD16	AA–			X	BE	NC	....	....	....	....	....	250	M2	'97	105¼	93⅞	93⅞	6.99	6.99
Nts 7s 2008 ....Ao27	AA–	12/96	A+	X	BE	NC	....	....	....	....	....	250	M2	'93	108¼	96¼	96¼	7.27	7.27
Nts 6¼s 2008 ....aO15	AA–	12/96	A+	X	BE	NC	....	....	....	....	....	150	M2	'93	103⅛	91¼	91¼	6.85	6.85
Nts 6⅜s 2008 ....aO15	AA–			X	BE	NC	....	....	....	....	....	500	M2	'98	104¼	92¼	92¼	6.91	6.91
Nts 6s 2009 ....Fa17	AA–			X	BE	NC	....	....	....	....	....	2000	M2	'99	99½	89⅝	89⅝	6.69	6.69
Nts[10] 6½s 2018 ....jJ15	AA–			X	BE	NC	....	....	....	....	....	700	M2	'98	100⅝	86⅞	87	7.47	7.47

Uniform Footnote Explanations-See Page 260. Other: [1] (HRO)Ea May 3 fr'99 to'36 at 100. [2] Due 5-3-37. [3] Callable at 100 if less than $25M outstanding. [4] See CoreStates Capital. [5] (HRO)On Chge of Ctrl at 101. [6] Max $19.3M red w/proceeds of equity off'g. [7] Red at greater of 100 or amt based on formula. [8] Total Issue Amt. [9] Int adj qtrly(3 Mo LIBOR & 0.20%). [10] Co may red in whole,at 100,for tax law chge.

Title-Industry Code & Co. Finances (In Italics) / Individual Issue Statistics (Exchange)	Ind / Interest Dates	1996 / S&P Rating	1997 / Date of Last Rating Change	1998 / Prior Rating	Eligible	Year End / Bond Form	Cash & Equiv. (Million $) / Regular Price	Curr. Assets / Regular (Begins) Thru	Curr. Liab. / Sinking Fund Price	Balance Sheet Date / Sinking Fund (Begins) Thru	L. Term Debt (Mil $) / Refund/Other Restriction Price	Refund/Other Restriction (Begins) Thru	Capital-ization (Mil $) / Outst'g (Mil $)	Total Debt % Capital / Underwriting Firm	Underwriting Year	Price Range 1999 High	Price Range 1999 Low	Mo. End Price Sale(s) or Bid	Curr. Yield	Yield to Mat.
***Merrill Lynch** (Cont.)*																				
Nts[1] 6⅞s 2018	mN15	AA–			X	BE	NC	....	....	....	....	....	1000	M2	'98	104½	90⅜	90⅝	7.59	7.59
Nts 8.40s 2019	mN	AA–	12/96	A+	X	R	NC	....	....	....	....	....	200	M2	'89	122⅞	102⅛	105	8.00	8.00
Nts 6¾s 2028	Jd	AA–			X	BE	NC	....	....	....	....	....	250	M2	'98	103⅞	85⅝	86¾	7.78	7.78
◆[2]SMART([3]Reset)Nts[4] 2000	[5]jd31	AA–	12/96	A+	X	BE	NC	....	....	....	....	....	25.0	M2	'94	112	99¾	100	....	....
M-T Nts 'B' 6.62s 2000	[6]mn15	AA–			X	BE	NC	....	....	....	....	....	100	M2	'97	101½	100⅛	100¼	6.60	6.60
M-T Nts 'B' 6.61s 2000	[7]mn15	AA–			X	BE	NC	....	....	....	....	....	25.0	M2	'97	101⅜	100⅛	100¼	6.59	6.59
F/R[8]M-T Nts 'B' 2000	QJun27	AA–			X	BE	NC	....	....	....	....	....	62.0	M2	'97	99¾	99⅛	99¾	....	....
M-T Nts 'B' 6.47s 2000	[9]mn15	AA–			X	BE	NC	....	....	....	....	....	75.0	M2	'97	101¼	100⅛	100⅛	6.46	6.46
M-T Nts 'B' 6.38s 2000	[10]mn15	AA–			X	BE	NC	....	....	....	....	....	100	M2	'97	101¼	100	100⅛	6.37	6.37
M-T Nts 'B' 6.35s 2000	[11]mn15	AA–			X	BE	NC	....	....	....	....	....	30.0	M2	'97	101⅛	100	100	6.35	6.35
F/R[12]M-T Nts 'B' 2000	QAug14	AA–			X	BE	NC	....	....	....	....	....	100	M2	'98	100⅛	99⅝	99⅞	....	....
M-T Nts 'B' 6.45s 2000	[13]mn15	AA–			X	BE	NC	....	....	....	....	....	50.0	M2	'97	101⅜	100	100	6.45	6.45
M-T Nts 'B' 6¼s 2000	[14]mn15	AA–			X	BE	NC	....	....	....	....	....	75.0	M2	'97	101	100	100	6.25	6.25
F/R[15]M-T Nts 'B' 2000	QSep5	AA–			X	BE	NC	....	....	....	....	....	25.0	M2	'97	100	99¾	99⅞	....	....
M-T Nts 'B' 6.46s 2001	[16]mn15	AA–			X	BE	NC	....	....	....	....	....	37.3	M2	'97	102⅛	99½	99½	6.49	6.49
M-T Nts 'B' 6⅝s 2001	aO	AA–			X	BE	NC	....	....	....	....	....	100	M2	'97	102	99¼	99¼	6.42	6.42
M-T Nts 'B' 6.06s 2001	ao15	AA–			X	BE	NC	....	....	....	....	....	100	M2	'98	101¼	98¾	98¾	6.14	6.14
F/R[17]M-T Nts 'D' 2002	QApr22	AA			X	BE	NC	....	....	....	....	....	200	M2	'98	100⅜	99¼	99½	....	....
M-T Nts 'B' 6.07s 2001	aO15	AA–			X	BE	NC	....	....	....	....	....	115	M2	'98	101¼	98¾	98¾	6.15	6.15
M-T Nts 'B' 6.81s 2002	[18]mn15	AA–			X	BE	NC	....	....	....	....	....	50.0	M2	'97	103⅝	99¾	99¾	6.83	6.83
F/R[19]M-T Nts 'B' 2003	[20]Aug13	AA–			X	BE	NC	....	....	....	....	....	30.0	M2	'98	100¼	99⅜	99½	....	....
M-T Nts 'B' 6.18s 2004	Ao20	AA–			X	BE	NC	....	....	....	....	....	100	M2	'98	102	96¼	96¼	6.42	6.42
M-T Nts 'B' 7.09s 2007	[21]mn15	AA–			X	BE	NC	....	....	....	....	....	50.0	M2	'97	107⅞	97⅜	97⅜	7.28	7.28
M-T Nts 'B' 7.15s 2012	jJ30	AA–			X	BE	[22]100	7-30-02	....	....	....	....	100	M2	'97	104	94⅝	94⅝	7.56	7.55
M-T Nts 'B' 7.20s 2012	aO15	AA–			X	BE	[23]100	10-15-01	....	....	....	....	50.0	M2	'97	102⅞	93¾	94	7.66	7.66
Merry Land & Invest	***57***	*Mgr w/Equity Resid Prop,see Evans Withcombe Residential*																		
Sr Nts 7¼s 2002	aO	BBB+			X	BE	NC	....	....	....	....	....	40.0	M5	'95	102¾	99	99	7.32	7.32
Nts 7¼s 2005	Jd15	BBB+			X	BE	Z100	(6-15-02)	....	....	....	....	120	M5	'95	102¾	97	97	7.47	7.47
Nts 6⅞s 2003	mN	BBB+			X	BE	NC	....	....	....	....	....	40.0	M5	'95	101¾	97	97	7.09	7.09
Nts 6⅞s 2004	mN	BBB+			X	BE	NC	....	....	....	....	....	40.0	M5	'95	101⅝	95⅞	95⅞	7.17	7.17
Nts 6.69s 2006	[24]mn	BBB+			X	BE	[25]Z100	....	....	....	....	....	50.0		'97	99½	93¼	93¼	7.17	7.17
Nts 6.90s 2007	fA	BBB+			X	BE	[25]Z100	....	....	....	....	....	50.0	M5	'97	100⅞	93⅛	93⅛	7.41	7.41
Metallurg Inc	***44d***	*n/a*	*n/a*	*n/a*		*Ja*	*48.40*	*229.0*	*84.20*	*10-31-99*	*108.0*		*143.0*	*76.2*						
Sr Nts[26] 'B' 11s 2007	jD	B–			Y	BE	105.50	(12-1-02)	....	....	[27]Z111	12-1-00	100	Exch.	'98	99	88½	90	12.22	12.22
Metals USA	***59***	*n/a*	*5.36*	*3.27*		*Dc*	*8.00*	*493.0*	*169.0*	*9-30-99*	*443.0*		*815.0*	*54.8*						
Sr Sub Nts[26] 8⅝s 2008	Fa15	B			Y	BE	104.313	(2-15-03)	....	....	[28]Z108.625	2-15-01	200	Exch.	'98	100	89⅛	95	9.08	9.08
Metris Cos.	***63***	*8.93*	*6.18*	*4.06*		*Dc*				*9-30-99*	*345.0*		*934.0*	*36.9*						
Sr Nts[26] 10s 2004	mN	B+			Y	BE	107.50	(11-1-01)	....	....	....	....	99.9	Exch.	'98	102¾	90	95½	10.47	10.47
Metrocall Inc[29]	***67g***	*d1.28*	*d0.58*	*d1.70*		*Dc*	*4.80*	*65.43*	*105.5*	*9-30-99*	*783.0*		*728.0*	*108.0*						
Sr Sub[26]Nts 10⅜s 2007	aO	CCC+	12/98	CCC	Y	R	105.188	(10-1-00)	....	....	....	....	150	L3	'95	99	57	62	16.73	16.73
Sr Sub Nts[26] 9¾s 2007	[30]jj15	CCC+	12/98	CCC	Y	BE	104.875	(10-31-02)	....	....	....	....	200	Exch.	'98	96¼	55½	59	16.53	16.52
Metromedia Fiber Network	***67f***	*d2.91*	*d34.44*	*1.66*		*Dc*	*383.0*	*559.0*	*166.0*	*9-30-99*	*689.0*		*2675*	*26.0*						
Sr Nts[26] 10s 2009	jD15	B+			Y	BE	105	(12-15-04)	....	....	[31]Z110	12-14-02	750	S4	'99	102½	99¼	102½	9.76	9.75
Metropolitan Edison[32]	***72a***	*3.50*	*4.30*	*2.63*		*Dc*	*44.90*	*240.0*	*364.0*	*9-30-99*	*497.0*		*1571*	*39.0*						
Sec M-T Nts 'A'[33] 9.48s 2000	[34]jj	A+	1/99	A–	X	BE	NC	....	....	....	....	....	20.0	G1	'90	105	101	101	9.39	9.38

Uniform Footnote Explanations-See Page 260. Other: [1] Co may red in whole,at 100,for tax law chge. [2] SMART-Stk Mkt Annual Reset Term. [3] Int(min 2%)adj annually. [4] Int pd:50% min amt in Jul,bal Dec. [5] Due 12-29-00. [6] Due 6-13-00. [7] Due 6-15-00. [8] Int adj qtrly(3 Yr CMT & 0.03%). [9] Due 6-27-00. [10] Due 7-18-00. [11] Due 7-24-00. [12] Int adj qtrly(3 Mo LIBOR). [13] Due 8-30-00. [14] Due 7-25-00. [15] Int reset dailty. [16] Due 8-8-01. [17] Int adj qtrly(3 Mo LIBOR & 0.12%). [18] Due 6-13-02. [19] Int adj monthly. [20] Int pd mthly ea 13th. [21] Due 6-13-07. [22] On 7-30-02. [23] On 10-15-01 only. [24] Due 10-30-06. [25] Plus Make-Whole Amt. [26] (HRO)On Chge of Ctrl at 101. [27] Max $34M red w/proceeds of Equity Off'g. [28] Max $70M red w/proceeds of Equity Off'g. [29] See ProNet Inc. [30] Due 11-1-07. [31] Max $262M red w/proceeds of Pub Eq Off'g. [32] Subsid of Gen'l Public Util. [33] Issued in min denom $100T. [34] Due 5-22-00.

Title-Industry Code & Co. Finances (In Italics) / Individual Issue Statistics / Exchange	Ind / Interest Dates	Fixed Charge Coverage 1996 / S&P Rating	1997 / Date of Last Rating Change	1998 / Prior Rating	Eligible	Year End / Bond Form	Million $ Cash & Equiv. / Redemption Provisions: Regular Price	Curr. Assets / Regular (Begins) Thru	Curr. Liab. / Sinking Fund Price	Balance Sheet Date / Sinking Fund (Begins) Thru	L. Term Debt (Mil $) / Refund/Other Restriction Price	Refund/Other Restriction (Begins) Thru	Capital-ization (Mil $) / Outst'g (Mil $)	Total Debt % Capital / Underwriting Firm	Underwriting Year	Price Range 1999 High	Price Range 1999 Low	Mo. End Price Sale(s) or Bid	Curr. Yield	Yield to Mat.
***Metropolitan Edison** (Cont.)*																				
Sec M-T Nts 'A'[1] 9.10s 2003	[2]jj	**A+**	1/99	A–	X	BE	100	(3-19-01)	....	....	....	....	30.0	G1	'91	107½	102⅜	102⅜	8.89	8.89
Sec M-T Nts 'A'[1] 8.60s 2022	[3]jj	**A+**	1/99	A–	X	BE	104.30	(1-24-02)	100	....	....	....	30.0	G1	'92	122⅛	102⅜	102½	8.39	8.39
Sec M-T Nts 'A'[1] 8.80s 2022	[4]jj	**A+**	1/99	A–	X	BE	104.40	(4-9-02)	....	....	....	....	30.0	G1	'92	124½	104⅜	104½	8.42	8.42
Sec M-T Nts 'B'[1] 6.20s 2000	[5]fa	**A+**	1/99	A–	X	BE	NC	....	....	....	....	....	30.0	M6	'93	100¾	99⅝	99¾	6.22	6.21
Sec M-T Nts 'B'[1] 7.22s 2003	[6]fa	**A+**	1/99	A–	X	BE	NC	....	....	....	....	....	40.0	M6	'93	100⅛	98⅝	98⅝	7.32	7.32
Sec M-T Nts 'B'[1] 6.60s 2003	[7]fa	**A+**	1/99	A–	X	BE	NC	....	....	....	....	....	20.0	M6	'93	103⅛	96⅞	96⅞	6.81	6.81
Sec M-T Nts 'B'[1] 6.34s 2004	[8]fa	**A+**	1/99	A–	X	BE	NC	....	....	....	....	....	40.0	M6	'93	102⅜	94⅞	94⅞	6.68	6.68
Sec M-T Nts 'B'[1] 7.35s 2005	Fa	**A+**	1/99	A–	X	BE	100	(1-29-03)	....	....	....	....	20.0	M6	'93	107½	98½	98½	7.46	7.46
Sec M-T Nts 'B'[1] 8.15s 2023	[9]fa	**A+**	1/99	A–	X	BE	104.08	(1-29-03)	....	....	....	....	60.0	M6	'93	109⅛	96⅜	96⅜	8.46	8.45
Sec M-T Nts 'B'[1] 7.65s 2023	[10]fa	**A+**	1/99	A–	X	BE	103.83	(6-18-03)	....	....	....	....	30.0	M6	'93	106⅛	92⅛	92⅛	8.30	8.30
Sec M-T Nts 'B'[1] 6.97s 2023	[11]fa	**A+**	1/99	A–	X	BE	103.49	(10-19-03)	....	....	....	....	30.0	M6	'93	100¾	85⅜	85½	8.15	8.15
Sec M-T Nts 'C'[1] 6.36s 2006	[12]mn	**A+**	1/99	A–	X	BE	100	(2-8-04)	....	....	....	....	17.0	M2	'94	101⅞	92¾	92¾	6.86	6.86
Sec M-T Nts 'C'[1] 6.40s 2006	[13]mn	**A+**	1/99	A–	X	BE	100	(2-8-04)	....	....	....	....	33.0	M2	'94	102⅛	92⅞	92⅞	6.89	6.89
Meyer (Fred) Inc	***59f***	***Acq by Kroger Co,see***																		
Nts 7.15s 2003	Ms	**BBB–**	6/99	BB+	X	BE	[14]Z100	....	....	....	....	....	250	S4	'98	104⅝	99	99	7.22	7.22
Nts 7⅜s 2005	Ms	**BBB–**	6/99	BB+	X	BE	[14]Z100	....	....	....	....	....	750	S4	'98	107⅛	98¾	98¾	7.47	7.47
Nts 7.45s 2008	Ms	**BBB–**	6/99	BB+	X	BE	[14]Z100	....	....	....	....	....	750	S4	'98	109¾	97⅛	97⅛	7.67	7.67
MGC Communications	***67***	***n/a***	***d0.94***	***d0.59***		***Dc***	***143.0***	***191.0***	***43.40***	***9-30-99***	***157.0***		***236.0***	***66.6***						
Sr Nts[15] 'B' 13s 2004	aO	**B–**			Y	BE	106.50	(10-1-01)	....	....	[16]Z113	10-1-00	160	Exch.	'98	101	66½	100⅜	12.95	12.95
MGM Grand	***40i***	***4.47***	***11.62***	***2.94***		***Dc***	***108.0***	***262.0***	***249.0***	***9-30-99***	***1349***		***2367***	***57.7***						
Sr Coll Nts 6.95s 2005	Fa	**BBB–**			X	BE	Z100	....	....	....	....	....	300	B2	'98	96⅝	92½	92⅞	7.48	7.48
Sr Coll Nts 6⅞s 2008	Fa6	**BBB–**			X	BE	[14]Z100	....	....	....	....	....	200	D5	'98	94½	88⅜	88⅝	7.76	7.76
Michaels Stores	***59l***	***d0.95***	***3.07***	***4.10***		***Ja***	***21.60***	***727.1***	***341.7***	***10-30-99***	***222.0***		***702.0***	***35.9***						
Sr Nts 10⅞s 2006	Jd15	**BB–**	10/96	BB	Y	BE	105.438	(6-15-01)	....	....	....	....	125	C5	'96	107¾	104	106	10.26	10.26
Michigan Bell Telephone[17]	***67a***	***11.79***	***12.66***	***12.19***		***Dc***	***13.10***	***689.0***	***1008***	***6-30-99***	***513.0***		***2439***	***34.0***						
Deb 7.85s 2022	Jj15	**AAA**			X	BE	NC	....	....	....	....	....	200	G1	'92	118⅝	100⅝	101⅛	7.76	7.76
Deb 7½s 2023	Fa15	**AAA**			X	BE	103.483	(2-15-03)	....	....	....	....	200	G1	'93	106⅞	94⅜	94½	7.94	7.94
Nts 6⅜s 2002	mS15	**AAA**			X	BE	NC	....	....	....	....	....	100	L3	'92	103⅝	98⅞	98⅞	6.45	6.45
Michigan Consol Gas[18]	***73b***	***3.49***	***3.31***	***2.84***		***Dc***	***11.90***	***317.0***	***405.0***	***9-30-99***	***683.0***		***1552***	***54.4***						
1st 5¾s 2001	Mn	**A–**	9/98	A	X	BE	NC	....	100	....	....	....	60.0	M2	'93	100⅝	98¾	98¾	5.82	5.82
1st 8s 2002	Mn	**A–**	9/98	A	X	R	NC	....	....	....	....	....	70.0	M2	'92	107½	101¾	101¾	7.86	7.86
1st 8¼s 2014	Mn	**A–**	9/98	A	X	BE	NC	....	....	....	....	....	80.0	M2	'94	117½	101½	101⅝	8.12	8.12
1st 6¾s 2023	mN	**A–**	9/98	A	X	BE	Z104	10-31-00	....	....	....	....	17.7	B3	'93	104⅛	97⅝	97⅝	6.91	6.91
1st 7s 2025	Mn	**A–**	9/98	A	X	BE	102.88	(5-1-03)	....	....	....	....	40.0	M2	'93	101⅞	85⅝	85⅝	8.18	8.17
Sec M-T Nts 'B' 7.06s 2012	[19]fa	**A–**	9/98	A	X	BE	NC	....	....	....	....	....	40.0	M2	'97	111½	98½	98½	7.17	7.17
Sec M-T Nts 'A'[20] 7½s 2020	Mn	**A–**	9/98	A	X	BE	105	(5-1-00)	....	....	....	....	10.0	J2	'95	107	91⅛	91¼	8.22	8.22
Sec M-T Nts 'B'[20] 7½s 2020	Mn	**A–**	9/98	A	X	BE	105	(5-1-00)	....	....	....	....	20.0	J2	'95	107⅛	91⅝	91¾	8.17	8.17
MidAmerican Energy	***75***	***3.19***	***3.14***	***3.04***		***Dc***	***1.22***	***265.0***	***554.0***	***9-30-99***	***760.0***		***2150***	***43.3***						
Nts 6½s 2001	jD15	**A–**	3/99	A	X	BE	NC	....	....	....	....	....	100	P1	'96	102⅛	98⅝	98⅝	6.59	6.59
Nts 6⅜s 2006	Jd15	**A–**	3/99	A	X	BE	[14]Z100	....	....	....	....	....	155	L3	'98	102⅝	93	93⅛	6.85	6.85
Midland Enterprises[21]	***64***	***4.27***	***2.85***	***2.68***		***Dc***	***0.06***	***100.0***	***48.50***	***9-30-99***	***144.0***		***316.0***	***47.2***						
1st Pfd Ship Mtg 6¼s 2008	aO	**A–**			X	BE	[14]Z100	....	....	....	....	....	75.0	D6	'98	100⅞	91¼	91⅜	6.84	6.84
Midlantic Corp	***10***	***Merged into PNC Bank,see PNC Funding***																		
Sub[22]Cap Nts 9.20s 2001	fA	**BBB+**	1/96	BBB–	X	R	NC	....	....	....	[23]Z100	....	100	F1	'89	108⅜	102⅞	102⅞	8.94	8.94

Uniform Footnote Explanations-See Page 260. Other: [1] Issued in min denom $100T. [2] Due 9-18-03. [3] Due 1-24-22. [4] Due 4-15-22. [5] Due 6-19-00. [6] Due 1-30-03. [7] Due 6-18-03. [8] Due 8-27-04. [9] Due 1-30-23. [10] Due 6-19-03. [11] Due 10-19-23. [12] Due 2-8-06. [13] Due 2-9-06. [14] Red at greater of 100 or amt based on formula. [15] (HRO)On Chge of Ctrl at 101. [16] Max $56M red w/proceeds of Pub Eq Off'g. [17] Subsid of Ameritech Corp. [18] Subsid of MCN Corp. [19] Due 5-1-12. [20] Death redemp benefit,ltd,as defined. [21] Subsid of East'n Enterprises. [22] Co may exch for Cap Sec when due. [23] For certain events relating to Fed Inc Tax.

Individual Issue Statistics / Exchange	Interest Dates	S&P Rating	Date of Last Rating Change	Prior Rating	Eligible	Bond Form	Regular Price	Regular (Begins) Thru	Sinking Fund Price	Sinking Fund (Begins) Thru	Refund/Other Restriction Price	Refund/Other Restriction (Begins) Thru	Outst'g (Mil $)	Underwriting Firm	Underwriting Year	Price Range 1999 High	Price Range 1999 Low	Mo. End Price Sale(s) or Bid	Curr. Yield	Yield to Mat.
Title-Industry Code & Co. Finances (In Italics)	*Ind*		*Fixed Charge Coverage 1996*	*1997*	*1998*	*Year End*	*Million $ Cash & Equiv.*	*Curr. Assets*	*Curr. Liab.*	*Balance Sheet Date*	*L. Term Debt (Mil $)*		*Capital-ization (Mil $)*	*Total Debt % Capital*						
Midwest Power Systems	***75***	***Merged with Iowa-Ill Gas & El,see***																		
Gen Mtg 6¾s 2000	Fa	**A+**	3/99	AA–	X	R	NC	....	....	....	....	....	75.0	P1	'93	101⅝	100	100	6.75	6.75
Gen Mtg 7⅛s 2003	Fa	**A+**	3/99	AA–	X	R	NC	....	....	....	....	....	100	P1	'93	106⅛	99⅝	99⅝	7.15	7.15
Gen Mtg 7s 2005	Fa15	**A+**	3/99	AA–	X	R	NC	....	....	....	....	....	90.5	P1	'93	107½	98⅛	98⅛	7.13	7.13
Gen Mtg 7⅜s 2008	Fa	**A+**	3/99	AA–	X	R	101.55	(2-1-03)	....	....	....	....	75.0	P1	'93	108⅜	97½	97½	7.56	7.56
Millenium America Inc	***14***		***n/a***	***n/a***	***3.63***	***Dc***	***78.00***	***781.0***	***380.0***	***9-30-99***	***993.0***		***2480***	***42.7***						
Sr[1]Deb[2] 7⅝s 2026	mN15	**BBB–**			X	BE	NC	....	....	....	....	....	250	G1	'96	90⅛	83⅛	83¼	9.16	9.16
Sr[1]Nts[2] 7s 2006	mN15	**BBB–**			X	BE	NC	....	....	....	....	....	500	G1	'96	95⅜	90⅛	90⅛	7.77	7.77
Millipore Corp	***23g***		***5.50***	***0.13***	***1.62***	***Dc***	***52.45***	***354.5***	***290.4***	***9-30-99***	***308.0***		***591.0***	***79.4***						
Nts 7.20s 2002	Ao	**BB+**	12/98	BBB–	Y	BE	NC	....	....	....	....	....	100	M5	'97	101⅜	97¾	97¾	7.37	7.37
Nts 7½s 2007	Ao	**BB+**	12/98	BBB–	Y	BE	NC	....	....	....	....	....	100	M5	'97	103⅜	93	93	8.06	8.06
Minnesota Min'g/Mfg	***17***		***32.38***	***37.60***	***18.58***	***Dc***	***490.0***	***6583***	***3865***	***9-30-99***	***1550***		***8479***	***27.2***						
Deb 6⅜s 2028	Fa15	**AA**			X	BE	[3]Z100	....	....	....	....	....	330	M2	'98	100⅝	87	87	7.33	7.33
F/R[4]M-T Nts[5]'B'[6] 2027	[7]mS30	**AA**	2/98	AAA	X	BE	NC	....	....	....	....	....	29.4	P1	'97	98⅝	98⅜	98⅝	....	....
[8]Minnesota Power & Light	***72a***		***2.15***	***2.56***	***2.72***	***Dc***	***312.0***	***698.0***	***551.0***	***9-30-99***	***790.0***		***1609***	***49.7***						
1st 6¼s 2003	jJ	**A**	10/97	BBB+	X	R	NC	....	....	....	....	....	25.0	P1	'93	103⅛	96¾	96¾	6.46	6.46
1st 7s 2007	Fa15	**A**	10/97	BBB+	X	BE	NC	....	....	....	....	....	60.0	P1	'97	108⅜	95¾	95¾	7.31	7.31
1st 7¾s 2007	Jd	**A**	10/97	BBB+	X	R	101.31	(6-1-02)	....	....	....	....	55.0	P1	'92	107⅝	98⅞	98⅞	7.84	7.84
1st 7½s 2007	fA	**A**	10/97	BBB+	X	R	100	(8-1-05)	....	....	....	....	35.0	P1	'92	109	97¼	97¼	7.71	7.71
1st 6.68s 2007	mN15	**A**			X	BE	NC	....	....	....	....	....	20.0	P1	'96	106¾	94⅞	94⅞	7.04	7.04
1st 7s 2008	Ms	**A**	10/97	BBB+	X	R	100	(3-1-06)	....	....	....	....	50.0	P1	'93	107⅝	95⅜	95⅜	7.34	7.34
Mirage Resorts	***40i***		***10.46***	***5.62***	***1.29***	***Dc***	***101.3***	***428.9***	***299.5***	***9-30-99***	***2117***		***4147***	***50.3***						
Deb[9] 7¼s 2017	fA	**BBB**	7/99	BBB+	X	BE	[3]Z100	....	....	....	....	....	100	C5	'97	97⅛	82⅛	82¼	8.81	8.81
Sr[10]Nts 7¼s 2006	aO15	**BBB**	7/99	BBB+	X	BE	[3]Z100	....	....	....	....	....	250	G1	'96	102⅛	91⅛	91⅛	7.96	7.96
Nts 6⅝s 2005	Fa	**BBB**	7/99	BBB+	X	BE	[3]Z100	....	....	....	....	....	200	C6	'98	98⅞	91	91	7.28	7.28
Nts[9] 6¾s 2007	fA	**BBB**	7/99	BBB+	X	BE	[3]Z100	....	....	....	....	....	200	C5	'97	98¾	87⅜	87⅜	7.73	7.72
Nts 6¾s 2008	Fa	**BBB**	7/99	BBB+	X	BE	[3]Z100	....	....	....	....	....	200	C6	'98	98⅛	86⅝	86⅝	7.79	7.79
Mississippi Chemical	***14a***		***n/a***	***10.61***	***2.41***	***Je***	***1.72***	***157.9***	***59.80***	***9-30-99***	***323.0***		***749.0***	***43.4***						
Sr Nts[11] 7¼s 2017	mN15	**BBB–**			X	BE	[12]Z100	....	....	....	....	....	200	D6	'97	98¼	87½	87½	8.29	8.28
Mississippi Power Co.[13]	***72a***		***4.82***	***5.15***	***4.98***	***Dc***	***0.16***	***137.0***	***214.0***	***9-30-99***	***328.0***		***809.0***	***46.7***						
1st 6.60s 2004	Ms	**AA–**	12/97	A+	X	R	101.40	2-29-00	Z100	....	....	....	35.0	C4	'94	101¾	97⅜	97⅜	6.78	6.78
1st 7.45s 2023	Jd	**AA–**	12/97	A+	X	R	104.49	5-31-00	Z100	....	....	....	35.0	G1	'93	104⅞	92¾	92¾	8.03	8.03
1st 6⅞s 2025	jD	**AA–**	12/97	A+	X	R	102.97	(12-1-05)	Z100	(12-1-05)	....	....	30.0	S1	'95	104⅜	86⅛	86¼	7.97	7.97
Sr Nts 'B' 6.05s 2003	Mn	**A**			X	BE	NC	....	....	....	....	....	35.0		'98	102⅝	96⅜	96⅜	6.28	6.28
Mississippi Power & Lt.	***72a***	***Now Entergy Mississippi,see***																		
Gen & Ref 8¼s 2004	jJ	**BBB+**	10/97	BBB	X	BE	102	6-30-00	Z100	....	....	....	25.0	B7	'94	103⅜	100¼	100¾	8.19	8.19
Gen & Ref 6⅝s 2003	mN	**BBB+**	10/97	BBB	X	BE	100.93	10-31-00	Z100	....	....	....	65.0	K2	'93	102	97⅝	97⅝	6.79	6.79
Missouri-Kan-Tex RR	***55***	***Subsid of Union Pacific Corp,see***																		
• Sub[14]Inc[15]Deb[16] 5½s 2033	Anapr	**CI**	5/89	C	Y	CR	100	....	100	....	....	....	27.1	Exch.	'58	89¼	69¼	80⅜	....	Flat
Missouri Pacific RR.	***55***	***Merged into Union Pacific RR,see***																		
• 1st C 4¼s 2005	Jj	**BBB+**	7/98	BBB–	X	CR	102	12-31-01	100	....	....	....	93.0	Reorg	'56	91¼	83⅛	83¼	5.11	5.11
• Gen[17]Inc[16]A 4¾s 2020	AnApr	**NR**	2/95	A		R	100	....	100	....	....	....	33.1	Reorg	'56	75	55	63¼	....	Flat
• Gen[17]Inc[16]B 4¾s 2030	AnApr	**NR**	2/95	A		R	100	....	100	....	....	....	34.7	Reorg	'56	74	58	s61⅛	....	Flat
• Inc [18]Deb[16] 5s 2045	Anapr	**NR**	2/95	A		R	100	....	....	....	....	....	100	Reorg	'56	68	50¾	51⅜	....	Flat
Mitchell Energy & Devel	***49***		***3.41***	***4.05***	***0.38***	***Ja***	***20.60***	***76.10***	***150.0***	***10-31-99***	***394.0***		***787.0***	***58.7***						
Sr Nts 9¼s 2002	Jj15	**BBB–**			X	R	NC	....	....	....	....	....	250	F1	'92	106	102⅛	102⅛	9.06	9.06

Uniform Footnote Explanations-See Page 260. Other: [1] Co may red in whole,at 100,for tax law chge. [2] Gtd by Millenium Chemicals Inc. [3] Red at greater of 100 or amt based on formula. [4] (HRO)On 9-30-07('10,'13)at 99.39(99.60,99.87). [5] Int adj qtrly(3 Mo LIBOR less 0.6%). [6] (HRO)On 9-30-16('19,'22,'25) at 100. [7] Issued in min denom $100T. [8] Now Minnesota Power. [9] Gaming laws may req sale/red by hldr. [10] (HRO)On Chge of Ctrl at 101. [11] (HRO)On 11-15-07 at 100. [12] Plus Make-Whole Amt. [13] Subsid of Southern Co. [14] Int non-cum contg. [15] If int not pd it is cum to max 16.5%. [16] Due Jan 1. [17] Int contingent cum to 13.50%. [18] Int non-cum contingent.

Title-Industry Code & Co. Finances (In Italics) / Individual Issue Statistics (Exchange)	Ind / Interest Dates	Fixed Charge Coverage 1996 / S&P Rating	1997 / Date of Last Rating Change	Prior Rating	1998 / Eligible	Year End / Bond Form	Cash & Equiv. (Million $) / Regular Price	Curr. Assets (Million $) / Regular (Begins) Thru	Curr. Liab. / Sinking Fund Price	Balance Sheet Date / Sinking Fund (Begins) Thru	L. Term Debt (Mil $) / Refund/Other Restriction Price	Refund/Other Restriction (Begins) Thru	Capitalization (Mil $) / Outst'g (Mil $)	Total Debt % Capital / Underwriting Firm	Underwriting Year	Price Range 1999 High	Price Range 1999 Low	Mo. End Price Sale(s) or Bid	Curr. Yield	Yield to Mat.
***Mitchell Energy & Devel** (Cont.)*																				
Sr[1]Nts 6¾s 2004	Fa15	BBB–			X	R	NC	....	....	....	....	....	250	C5	'94	98	94⅝	95⅛	7.10	7.10
MJD Communications	*67a*	*1.15*	*1.50*		*0.72*	*Dc*	*8.74*	*36.40*	*36.70*	*9-30-99*	*371.0*		*382.0*	*98.4*						
F/R[2]Sub Nts[3]'B' 2008	Mn	B–			Y	BE	104	4-30-00	....	....	....	....	75.0	Exch.	'98	101	93½	93⅝	....	....
Sr Sub Nts[2] 9½s 2008	Mn	B–			Y	BE	104.75	(5-1-03)	....	....	[4]Z109.50	5-1-01	125	Exch.	'98	102½	90	94½	10.05	10.05
MMI Products	*13*	*2.42*	*1.99*		*2.06*	*Dc*	*3.16*	*148.0*	*66.30*	*10-2-99*	*171.0*		*177.0*	*98.3*						
Sr Sub Nts[2] 11¼s 2007	Ao15	B–			Y	BE	105.625	(4-15-02)	....	....	[5]Z111.25	4-15-00	150	Exch.	'97	108	100½	103	10.92	10.92
Mobil Corp	*49c*	***Mgr w/Exxon Corp,see Exxon Cap***																		
Deb 8⅝s 2021	fA15	AAA	12/99	AA	X	R	NC	....	....	....	....	....	250	M2	'91	127⅜	110	109	7.91	7.91
Deb 8s 2032	fA12	AAA	12/99	AA	X	R	105.007	(8-12-02)	....	....	....	....	164	M2	'92	113	100	100⅝	7.97	7.97
Deb 7⅝s 2033	Fa23	AAA	12/99	AA	X	R	104.384	(2-23-03)	....	....	....	....	250	F1	'93	108	98½	98½	7.74	7.74
Nts 8⅜s 2001	Fa12	AAA	12/99	AA	X	R	NC	....	....	....	....	....	200	S1	'91	107⅛	101⅝	102	8.21	8.21
[6]***Mobile Telecommun Tech***	*67g*	*d2.70*	*d0.53*		*0.63*	*Dc*	*10.79*	*76.63*	*129.3*	*9-30-99*	*327.0*		*534.0*	*72.3*						
Sr Nts[2] 13½s 2002	jD15	B–	7/96	BB–	Y	R	103.375	12-14-00	....	....	....	....	265	B7	'95	115	111¼	113¼	11.92	11.92
MobileMedia Communications[7]	*67g*	....	....		....	*Dc*	***Bankruptcy Chapt 11***				*427.0*		*561.0*	*78.8*						
Sr Sub Defr[8]Cpn[9]Nts 10½s 2003	§jD	NR	6/99	D	Z	R			Default 6-1-99 int				[10]210	D6	'93	12	8	9	....	Flat
Sub Nts[2] 9⅝s 2007	§mN	NR	6/99	D	Z	R			Default 11-1-96 int				250	L3	'95	14	11	12	....	Flat
Mohegan Tribal Gaming	*40i*	*n/a*	*1.81*		*2.75*	*Sp*	*279.0*	*428.0*	*208.0*	*6-30-99*	*510.0*		*127.0*	*410.0*						
Sr Exch[2]Nts[11] 8⅛s 2006	Jj	BB			Y	BE	Z100	....	....	....	....	....	200	Exch.	'99	101½	95½	97	8.38	8.37
Sr Sub Exch[2]Nts[11] 8¾s 2009	Jj	BB–			Y	BE	104.375	(1-1-05)	....	....	....	....	300	Exch.	'99	105	96¼	98½	8.88	8.88
Money Store	*25h*	***Merged into First Union,see***																		
Sr Nts 8.05s 2002	Ao15	A+	6/98	BBB	X	BE	NC	....	....	....	....	....	175	B7	'97	106⅞	101¾	101¾	7.91	7.91
Sr Nts 8⅜s 2004	Ao15	A+	6/98	BBB	X	BE	NC	....	....	....	....	....	125	B7	'97	111⅝	103⅛	103⅛	8.12	8.12
Sub Nts 7.30s 2002	jD	A	6/98	BBB–	X	BE	NC	....	....	....	....	....	150	P4	'97	105½	99¾	99¾	7.32	7.32
Sub Nts 7.95s 2007	jD	A	6/98	BBB–	X	BE	NC	....	....	....	....	....	100	P4	'97	113	101¾	101¾	7.81	7.81
Monon R.R.	*55*	***See Seaboard Coast Line RR***																		
• Inc[12]SF[13]Deb[14] 6s 2007	Anapr	NR	7/94	BBB		CR	100	....	100	....	....	....	4.08	Exch.	'58	99	88½	85	....	Flat
Monongahela Power Co.[15]	*72a*	*3.48*	*4.27*		*4.62*	*Dc*	*2.90*	*204.0*	*225.0*	*9-30-99*	*397.0*		*1117*	*41.4*						
1st 5⅝s 2000	Ao	A+	4/94	AA–	X	R	NC	....	Z100	....	....	....	65.0	G1	'93	100	99⅝	99⅞	5.63	5.63
1st 7⅜s 2002	jJ	A+	4/94	AA–	X	R	NC	....	Z100	....	....	....	25.0	M6	'92	106⅛	100¼	100¼	7.36	7.36
1st 7¼s 2007	mS	A+	4/94	AA–	X	R	100	(9-1-02)	Z100	....	....	....	25.0	M6	'92	105	96	96	7.55	7.55
1st 8⅝s 2021	mN	A+	4/94	AA–	X	R	105.02	10-31-00	Z100	....	®104.19	10-31-01	50.0	S1	'91	106½	103⅜	103½	8.33	8.33
1st 8⅜s 2022	jJ	A+	4/94	AA–	X	R	104.12	(7-1-02)	Z100	....	....	....	40.0	M6	'92	109⅞	96½	97½	8.59	8.59
1st 7⅝s 2025	Mn	A+			X	R	102.953	(5-1-05)	Z100	....	....	....	70.0	G1	'95	104⅞	90⅞	91	8.38	8.38
M-T Nts 'A' 5.63s 2003	[16]ms	A			X	BE	NC	....	....	....	....	....	20.5	G1	'98	99⅛	94⅜	94½	5.96	5.96
M-T Nts 'A' 5.56s 2003	[17]ms	A			X	BE	NC	....	....	....	....	....	15.0	G1	'98	98⅞	94⅛	94¼	5.90	5.90
M-T Nts 'A' 7.36s 2010	[18]ms	A			X	BE	NC	....	....	....	....	....	110	G1	'99	100¼	97⅛	97⅛	7.58	7.58
Monsanto Co	*14*	*7.26*	*6.63*		*2.27*	*Dc*	*84.00*	*5635*	*3555*	*9-30-99*	*5961*		*13084*	*62.7*						
Deb[19] 8⅞s 2009	jD15	A			X	R	NC	....	....	....	....	....	100	M2	'89	124⅜	108¾	108¾	8.16	8.16
Deb 8.70s 2021	aO15	A			X	BE	NC	....	....	....	....	....	100	G1	'91	126¾	106¼	107½	8.09	8.09
Deb 8.20s 2025	Ao15	A			X	BE	104.064	(4-15-05)	....	....	....	....	150	S1	'95	109⅛	95¾	97⅛	8.44	8.44
Deb 6¾s 2027	jD15	A			X	BE	NC	....	....	....	....	....	200	G1	'97	103	86¼	87½	7.71	7.71
Nts 6s 2000	jJ	A			X	BE	NC	....	....	....	....	....	150	M2	'93	100⅞	99⅝	100	6.00	6.00
M-T Nts 'D' 6.11s 2005	[20]ao15	A			X	BE	NC	....	....	....	....	....	45.4	G1	'98	103⅞	94⅝	95⅛	6.42	6.42
M-T Nts 'D' 6.21s 2008	ao15	A			X	BE	NC	....	....	....	....	....	21.5	G1	'98	105⅞	92¼	92½	6.71	6.71

Uniform Footnote Explanations-See Page 260. Other: [1] (HRO)On Special Redemption Event at 100. [2] (HRO)On Chge of Ctrl at 101. [3] Int adj semi-anly(6 Mo LIBOR&4.1875%). [4] Max $44M red w/proceeds of Equity Off'g. [5] Max $52.5M red w/proceeds Pub Eq Off'g. [6] Now SkyTel Communications. [7] Subsid & data of MobileMedia Corp. [8] Int accrues at 10.5% fr 12-1-98. [9] Co must offer repurch at 101 on Chge of Ctrl(Accreted Val). [10] Incl disc. [11] State gaming laws may req hldr's sale/Co red. [12] Int pay extent earned, cum to 12%. [13] Due 1-1-07. [14] Arrears cleared 10-1-65. [15] Contr by Allegheny Pwr Sys. [16] Due 9-29-03. [17] Due 9-30-03. [18] Due 1-15-10. [19] (HRO)At 100 for DesignatedEvent&Rat'gDecline. [20] Due 2-3-05.

Title-Industry Code & Co. Finances (In Italics) / Individual Issue Statistics (Exchange)	Ind / Interest Dates	Fixed Charge Coverage 1996 / S&P Rating	1997 / Date of Last Rating Change	1998 / Prior Rating	Eligible	Year End / Bond Form	Million $ Cash & Equiv. / Redemption Provisions: Regular Price	Million $ Curr. Assets / Regular (Begins) Thru	Million $ Curr. Liab. / Sinking Fund Price	Balance Sheet Date / Sinking Fund (Begins) Thru	L. Term Debt (Mil $) / Refund/Other Restriction Price	Refund/Other Restriction (Begins) Thru	Capital-ization (Mil $) / Outst'g (Mil $)	Total Debt % Capital / Underwriting Firm	Underwriting Year	Price Range 1999 High	Price Range 1999 Low	Mo. End Price Sale(s) or Bid	Curr. Yield	Yield to Mat.
Montana Power Co.	***75***	***4.92***	***4.17***	***4.68***		***Dc***				***9-30-99***	***650.0***		***2786***	***29.9***						
1st 7½s 2001	Ao	A–	10/97	BBB+	X	R	100.26	3-31-00	100	....	....	....	25.0	K2	'71	100½	100⅛	100⅛	7.49	7.49
1st 7s 2005	Ms	A–	10/97	BBB+	X	R	NC	....	....	....	....	....	50.0	G1	'93	106¾	97½	97½	7.18	7.18
1st 8¼s 2007	Fa	A–	10/97	BBB+	X	R	NC	....	....	....	....	....	55.0	G1	'91	116⅛	102¼	102¼	8.07	8.07
1st 8.95s 2022	Fa	A–	10/97	BBB+	X	R	104.449	(2-1-02)	....	....	....	....	50.0	G1	'91	111¾	101½	101½	8.82	8.82
F/R[1]M-T Nts 'B' 2001	QApr6	BBB			X	BE	100	....	....	....	....	....	60.0	G1	'98	100¼	99⅝	99⅞	....	....
Moog, Inc	***41g***	***1.89***	***1.86***	***2.48***		***Sp***	***8.92***	***398.0***	***170.0***	***6-30-99***	***357.0***		***397.0***	***51.9***						
Sr Sub Nts 'B'[2] 10s 2006	Mn	B			Y	R	105	(5-1-01)	....	....	....	....	120		'96	104	101⅛	101⅞	9.82	9.81
Morgan (J.P.)& Co[3]	***10***	***1.36***	***1.28***	***1.17***		***Dc***				***9-30-99***	***25402***		***41083***	***71.3***						
Nts 5¾s 2004	Fa25	AA–	10/99	AA	X	BE	NC	....	....	....	....	....	1000	M5	'99	99⅝	94¾	94⅞	6.06	6.06
M-T Nts 'A'[4] 6⅛s 2000	aO2	AA–	10/99	AA	X	BE	NC	....	....	....	....	....	200	M5	'97	100⅞	99½	99½	6.16	6.16
Sub Nts 6.61s 2010	[5]Dec15	A+	10/99	AA–	X	BE	[6]■100	(12-15-00)	....	....	....	....	100	M5	'95	100⅝	90	90	7.34	7.34
Sub Nts 7¼s 2002	Jj15	A+	10/99	AA–	X	BE	NC	....	....	....	....	....	200	F1	'92	105¼	100⅛	100⅛	7.24	7.24
Sub Nts 8½s 2003	fA15	A+	10/99	AA–	X	BE	NC	....	....	....	....	....	150	F1	'91	112	104¼	104¼	8.15	8.15
Sub Nts 7⅝s 2004	mS15	A+	10/99	AA–	X	BE	NC	....	....	....	....	....	500	M5	'94	109⅜	101¾	101¾	7.49	7.49
Sub Nts 6¼s 2005	jD15	A+	10/99	AA–	X	BE	NC	....	....	....	....	....	300	M5	'95	103	94⅝	95⅛	6.57	6.57
Sub Nts 6⅞s 2007	Jj15	A+	10/99	AA–	X	BE	NC	....	....	....	....	....	300	M5	'97	106¾	96½	96½	7.12	7.12
Sub Nts 6.70s 2007	mN	A+	10/99	AA–	X	BE	NC	....	....	....	....	....	350	M5	'97	106	95¼	95¼	7.03	7.03
Sub Nts 5¾s 2008	aO15	A+	10/99	AA–	X	BE	NC	....	....	....	....	....	150	K2	'93	99⅞	88⅛	88⅛	6.52	6.53
Sub Nts 6¼s 2009	Jj15	A+	10/99	AA–	X	BE	NC	....	....	....	....	....	300	M5	'94	103¼	91⅛	91⅛	6.86	6.86
Sub Nts[4] 6¼s 2011	Fa15	A+	10/99	AA–	X	BE	NC	....	....	....	....	....	100	M5	'96	102⅜	89	89	7.02	7.02
Sub[4]F/R[7]Nts 2000	QMar13	A+	10/99	AA–	X	BE	NC	....	....	....	....	....	200	L3	'93	99¼	99	99¼	....	....
Sub M-T Nts 'A' 7.15s 2011	[5]Mar15	A+	10/99	AA–	X	BE	100	(3-15-01)	....	....	....	....	75.0	M5	'96	101⅜	93¼	96⅞	7.38	7.38
Sub M-T Nts 'A' 7s 2012	mN15	A+	10/99	AA–	X	BE	*100	(11-15-02)	....	....	....	....	100	M5	'97	100¾	92⅛	93⅝	7.48	7.48
Sub M-T Nts 'A' 6½s 2013	[5]Feb11	A+	10/99	AA–	X	BE	[8]Z100	(2-11-02)	....	....	....	....	40.0	M5	'98	98⅛	87¾	88⅝	7.33	7.33
Sub M-T Nts 'A' 7s 2017	[5]Dec15	A+	10/99	AA–	X	BE	[9]■100	(12-15-02)	....	....	....	....	85.0	M5	'97	101	89	89	7.87	7.86
Morgan Guaranty Trust N.Y.	***10***	***Subsid of Morgan (J.P.) & Co,see***																		
Sub Nts[4] 7⅜s 2002	Fa	AA–	10/99	AA–	X	R	NC	....	....	....	....	....	200	F1	'92	105⅜	100⅝	100⅝	7.33	7.33
Morgan Stan Dean Witter[10]	***25e***	***[11]1.99***	***1.40***	***1.35***		***Nv***				***8-31-99***	***29038***		***45466***	***63.9***						
Deb 8.33s 2007	Jj15	A+			X	BE	NC	....	....	....	....	....	100	M6	'92	115⅛	103⅜	103⅜	8.06	8.06
Deb[12] 10s 2008	Jd15	A+			X	R	NC	....	....	....	....	....	100	M6	'88	128⅜	114½	114½	8.73	8.73
Deb 7s 2013	aO	A+			X	BE	NC	....	....	....	....	....	175	M6	'93	106	91½	91½	7.65	7.65
Deb 7½s 2024	Fa	A+			X	BE	103.688	(2-1-04)	....	....	....	....	250	M6	'94	103	92¼	92⅜	8.12	8.12
Nts 9⅜s 2001	Jd15	A+			X	BE	NC	....	....	....	....	....	125	M6	'91	108⅜	103¼	103¼	9.08	9.08
Nts 8⅞s 2001	aO15	A+			X	BE	NC	....	....	....	....	....	200	M6	'91	108⅛	103⅛	103⅛	8.61	8.61
Nts 8.10s 2002	Jd24	A+			X	BE	NC	....	....	....	....	....	300	M6	'92	107½	102⅛	102⅛	7.93	7.93
Nts 6⅜s 2002	fA	A+			X	BE	NC	....	....	....	....	....	350	M6	'97	102¼	98¼	98¼	6.49	6.49
Nts 6¾s 2003	Ms4	A+			X	BE	NC	....	....	....	....	....	100	M6	'93	103¾	98⅞	98⅞	6.83	6.83
Nts 6⅛s 2003	aO	A+			X	BE	NC	....	....	....	....	....	150	M6	'93	101⅝	96½	96½	6.35	6.35
Nts 6⅜s 2003	jD15	A+			X	BE	NC	....	....	....	....	....	150	M6	'93	102¾	97⅛	97⅛	6.56	6.56
• Nts[13] 5⅝s 2004	Jj20	A+			X	BE	NC	....	....	....	....	....	2000	M5	'99	100	94	94	5.98	5.98
Nts 6⅞s 2007	Ms	A+			X	BE	NC	....	....	....	....	....	1000	M6	'97	107	96¼	96¼	7.14	7.14
M-T Nts 'C' 5⅞s 2000	Jd23	A+			X	BE	NC	....	....	....	....	....	200	M7	'98	100½	99¾	99⅞	5.88	5.88
M-T Nts 'C' 5¾s 2001	Fa15	A+			X	BE	NC	....	....	....	....	....	250	M6	'96	100½	99	99	5.81	5.81
M-T Nts 'C' 5⅞s 2001	Fa28	A+			X	BE	NC	....	....	....	....	....	150	M7	'98	100⅝	99⅛	99⅛	5.93	5.93

Uniform Footnote Explanations-See Page 260. Other: [1] Int adj qtrly(3 Mo LIBOR & 0.25%). [2] Co must offer repurch at 101 on Chge of Ctrl. [3] See Morgan Gty & Morgan(J.P.)Delaware. [4] Issued in min denom $250T. [5] Int pd monthly. [6] Red ea Jun & Dec 15th. [7] Int(min 5.30%)adj qtrly. [8] Red on any Feb or Aug 11. [9] On ea Jun & Dec 15. [10] Was Morgan Stanley Group,see Dean Witter. [11] Fiscal Dec'96 & prior. [12] Negative Pledge,as defined. [13] Co may red in whole,at 100,for tax law chge.

Individual Issue Statistics / Exchange ↓	Interest Dates	S&P Rating	Date of Last Rating Change	Prior Rating	Eligible ↓	Bond Form	Redemption Provisions: Regular Price	Regular (Begins) Thru	Sinking Fund Price	Sinking Fund (Begins) Thru	Refund/Other Restriction Price	Refund/Other Restriction (Begins) Thru	Outst'g (Mil $)	Underwriting Firm	Underwriting Year	Price Range 1999 High	Price Range 1999 Low	Mo. End Price Sale(s) or Bid	Curr. Yield	Yield to Mat.
Title-Industry Code & Co. Finances (In Italics)	*Ind*	*Fixed Charge Coverage 1996*	*1997*	*1998*		*Year End*	*Million $ Cash & Equiv.*	*Curr. Assets*	*Curr. Liab.*	*Balance Sheet Date*	*L. Term Debt (Mil $)*		*Capital-ization (Mil $)*	*Total Debt % Capital*						
***Morgan Stan Dean Witter** (Cont.)*																				
M-T Nts 'C' 7.115s 2012	fA6	A+			X	BE	[1]■100	8-6-02	....	....	....	....	40.0	M6	'97	102¾	94⅛	94⅛	7.56	7.56
M-T Nts 'C' 7s 2012	aO21	A+			X	BE	■100	....	....	....	....	....	30.0	M6	'97	100	92⅝	93⅛	7.52	7.52
Morton International	***14***	***Acqd by Rohm & Haas,see***																		
[2]Deb[3] 9¼s 2020	Jd	A–	3/99	AA–	X	R	NC	....	....	....	....	....	200	G1	'90	136⅜	110¾	110⅞	8.34	8.34
Mosler Inc	***63***	***△0.29***	***△1.20***	***△0.27***		***Je***	***0.73***	***145.0***	***80.70***	***9-24-99***	***202.0***		***105.0***	***192.0***						
Sr Nts[4] 11s 2003	[5]jj15	NR	8/96	CCC–		R	102.75	7-14-00	....	....	....	....	115	F1	'93	87½	77	79	13.92	13.92
Motorola, Inc.	***23a***	***8.13***	***9.40***	***3.01***		***Dc***	***3527***	***16015***	***11898***	***10-2-99***	***3598***		***19529***	***26.1***						
Deb 7½s 2025	Mn15	A+	6/99	AA–	X	R	NC	....	....	....	....	....	398	G1	'95	115⅛	96⅞	97⅜	7.70	7.70
Deb[6] 6½s 2025	mS	A+	6/99	AA–	X	BE	NC	....	....	....	....	....	397	G1	'95	105⅞	96⅛	96⅛	6.76	6.76
Deb 6½s 2028	mN15	A+	6/99	AA–	X	BE	[7]Z100	....	....	....	....	....	445	M2	'98	102⅝	85⅛	85⅞	7.57	7.57
Deb[8] 8.40s 2031	fA15	A+	6/99	AA–	X	R	NC	....	....	....	[9]Z100	....	200	G1	'91	126	107⅛	107⅛	7.84	7.84
Deb[10] 5.22s 2097	aO	A+	6/99	AA–	X	BE	[11]Z100	....	....	....	....	....	225	M2	'97	80⅜	63⅞	63⅞	8.17	8.17
Nts 7.60s 2007	Jj	A+	6/99	AA–	X	R	NC	....	....	....	....	....	300	G1	'92	112⅜	100¼	100¼	7.58	7.58
Nts 6½s 2008	Ms	A+	6/99	AA–	X	R	NC	....	....	....	....	....	199	M2	'93	106⅞	94⅜	94⅜	6.89	6.89
Nts 5.80s 2008	aO15	A+	6/99	AA–	X	BE	NC	....	....	....	....	....	325	G1	'98	102¼	89⅝	89⅝	6.47	6.47
Motors & Gears	***23c***	***2.11***	***1.26***	***1.30***		***Dc***	***7.49***	***111.0***	***47.00***	***9-30-99***	***310.0***		***336.0***	***92.6***						
Nts[12]'D' 10¾s 2006	mN15	B			Y	BE	105.35	11-14-01	....	....	....	....	270	Exch.	'98	103¾	93½	99¼	10.83	10.83
[13]Mountain Fuel Supply[14]	***73b***	***3.55***	***3.22***	***3.03***		***Dc***	***15.70***	***53.40***	***70.50***	***9-30-99***	***225.0***		***512.0***	***48.9***						
M-T Nts 'C' 6.89s 2011	[15]ao	A+			X	BE	NC	....	....	....	....	....	2.00	M2	'97	108	92½	92½	7.45	7.45
M-T Nts 'C' 6.89s 2012	aO	A+			X	BE	NC	....	....	....	....	....	3.00	M2	'97	109	92⅝	92⅝	7.44	7.44
M-T Nts 'C' 6.85s 2012	aO	A+			X	BE	NC	....	....	....	....	....	3.50	M2	'97	108⅞	92½	92½	7.41	7.41
M-T Nts 'C' 6.89s 2013	[16]ao	A+			X	BE	NC	....	....	....	....	....	2.00	M2	'97	109¼	91⅞	91⅞	7.50	7.50
Mountain States Tel&Tel	***67a***	***Now U S WEST Commun,see***																		
Deb 5s 2000	Ao	A+	5/98	A	X	CR	100	....	....	....	....	....	40.0	H1	'60	99¾	99¼	99¾	5.01	5.01
Deb 4½s 2002	Jd	A+	5/98	A	X	CR	100	....	....	....	....	....	50.0	F1	'62	97⅜	94¼	94¼	4.77	4.78
Deb 5½s 2005	Jd	A+	5/98	A	X	R	100.17	5-31-00	....	....	....	....	40.7	M2	'66	98¾	91⅛	91⅛	6.04	6.04
Deb 6s 2007	fA	A+	5/98	A	X	R	100.45	7-31-00	....	....	....	....	70.2	F1	'67	99⅞	91¾	91¾	6.54	6.54
Deb 7⅜s 2030	Mn	A+	5/98	A	X	BE	NC	....	....	....	....	....	55.1	M6	'90	114½	91⅛	91¼	8.08	8.08
Nts 9½s 2000	Mn	A+	5/98	A	X	BE	NC	....	....	....	....	....	100	M6	'90	105⅜	101	101	9.41	9.40
Movie Star Inc[17]	***68c***	***d0.10***	***1.21***	***1.40***		***Je***	***0.67***	***31.91***	***11.23***	***9-30-99***	***17.90***		***30.30***	***70.3***						
◆Sub Deb 12⅞s 2001	aO	CCC–	10/95	B–	Y	R	100.89	9-30-00	100	....	....	....	10.0	B7	'86	99¾	86⅛	96	13.41	13.41
MSX International	***63***	***n/a***	***n/a***	***n/a***		***Dc***	***9.13***	***265.0***	***179.0***	***10-3-99***	***227.0***		***248.0***	***93.1***						
Sr Sub Nts[12] 11⅜s 2008	Jj15	B–			Y	BE	105.6875	(1-15-03)	....	....	[18]Z111.375	1-15-01	100	Exch.	'98	98	93	93	12.23	12.23
Multicare Cos[19]	***30***	***Acq by Genesis Health Ventures,see***																		
Sr Sub Nts[12] 9s 2007	fA	CCC+	3/99	B–	Y	BE	104.50	(8-1-03)	....	....	....	....	250	Exch.	'98	92½	20	20	....	....
Murphy Oil	***49b***	***n/a***	***n/a***	***n/a***		***Dc***	***43.98***	***546.5***	***453.7***	***9-30-99***	***427.0***		***1435***	***29.8***						
Nts 7.05s 2029	Mn	A–			X	BE	[20]Z100	....	....	....	....	....	250	S4	'99	99⅝	89½	89⅝	7.87	7.87
[21]Musicland Group Inc	***59l***	***d0.29***	***1.45***	***2.78***		***Dc***	***65.96***	***515.0***	***383.7***	***9-30-99***	***259.0***		***328.0***	***79.0***						
Sr Sub[22]Nts[12] 9s 2003	Jd15	B–	11/98	CCC+	Y	R	102.25	6-14-00	....	....	....	....	110	D6	'93	101½	90	97	9.28	9.28
Sr Sub Nts[22]'B' 9⅞s 2008	Ms15	B–	11/98	CCC+	Y	BE	104.938	(3-15-03)	....	....	[23,24]Z109.875	3-15-01	150	Exch.	'98	103	83	92½	10.68	10.67
Muzak L.P./Capital[25]	***12***	***d0.03***	***d0.25***	***....***		***Dc***	***3.35***	***52.60***	***51.80***	***9-30-99***	***327.0***		***400.0***	***86.5***						
Sr Nts 10s 2003	aO	NR	3/99	B+	Y	R	105	(10-1-00)	....	....	....	....	100	D6	'96	109¼	103½	105¾	9.46	9.46
Nabisco, Inc[26]	***69a***	***2.64***	***3.22***	***0.90***		***Dc***	***76.00***	***1671***	***1581***	***9-30-99***	***3753***		***7824***	***50.7***						
Deb 7.55s 2015	Jd15	BBB			X	BE	NC	....	....	....	....	....	400	G1	'95	105	94⅜	94½	7.99	7.99

Uniform Footnote Explanations-See Page 260. Other: [1] On 8-6-02. [2] Credit Sensitive Deb. [3] Int subj to adj for rating chge. [4] (HRO)On Chge in Ctrl at 101. [5] Due 4-15-03. [6] (HRO)On 9-1-05 at 100. [7] Red at greater of 100 or amt based on formula. [8] (HRO)On 8-15-01 at 100. [9] On 8-15-01,if 95% or more put. [10] Co may red in whole,at 100,for Tax Event. [11] Greater of 100 or amt based on formula. [12] (HRO)On Chge of Ctrl at 101. [13] Subsid of Questar Corp. [14] Now Questar Gas. [15] Due 9-29-11. [16] Due 9-30-13. [17] Was Sanmark-Stardust. [18] Max $35M red w/proceeds of Pub Eq Off'g. [19] Acq by Genesis ElderCare. [20] Plus Make-Whole Amt. [21] Subsid & data of Musicland Stores. [22] Gtd by Musicland Stores. [23] Max $60M red w/proceeds of Pub Eq Off'g. [24] Max $60M red w/proceeds of Equity Off'g. [25] Data of Muzak Holdings LLC. [26] Subsid of Nabisco Hldgs.

Title-Industry Code & Co. Finances (In Italics) / Individual Issue Statistics (Exchange)	Ind / Interest Dates	S&P Rating	Fixed Charge Coverage 1996 / Date of Last Rating Change	1997 / Prior Rating	1998 / Eligible	Year End / Bond Form	Cash & Equiv. (Million $) / Regular Price	Curr. Assets (Million $) / Regular (Begins) Thru	Curr. Liab. (Million $) / Sinking Fund Price	Balance Sheet Date / Sinking Fund (Begins) Thru	L. Term Debt (Mil $) / Refund/Other Restriction Price	Refund/Other Restriction (Begins) Thru	Capital-ization (Mil $) / Outst'g (Mil $)	Total Debt % Capital / Underwriting Firm	Underwriting Year	Price Range 1999 High	Price Range 1999 Low	Mo. End Price Sale(s) or Bid	Curr. Yield	Yield to Mat.
***Nabisco, Inc** (Cont.)*																				
• Nts 8s 2000	Jj15	**BBB**			X	BE	NC	....	....	....	....	....	149	Exch.		102⅝	99⅞	99¾	8.02	8.02
Nts[1] 6.80s 2001	mS	**BBB**			X	BE	NC	....	....	....	....	....	93.9	Exch.	'95	101⅞	99⅛	99⅛	6.86	6.86
Nts 6.70s 2002	Jd15	**BBB**			X	BE	NC	....	....	....	....	....	400	G1	'95	101⅜	98	98	6.84	6.84
Nts 6.85s 2005	Jd15	**BBB**			X	BE	NC	....	....	....	....	....	400	G1	'95	102¼	95½	95½	7.17	7.17
Nts 7.05s 2007	jJ15	**BBB**			X	BE	NC	....	....	....	....	....	400	G1	'95	103½	94⅜	94⅞	7.43	7.43
Nts[2] 6s 2011	Fa15	**BBB**			X	BE	[3]■100	2-15-01	....	....	....	....	400	M7	'98	100¼	98½	98¾	6.08	6.08
Nts[4] 6⅛s 2033	Fa	**BBB**			X	BE	[5]■100	2-1-03	....	....	....	....	300	M7	'98	98¾	96	96	6.38	6.38
Nts[6] 6⅜s 2035	Fa	**BBB**			X	BE	[7]■100	2-1-05	....	....	....	....	300	M7	'98	98⅞	93¾	94	6.78	6.78
Nabors Industries[8]	***49e***		*n/a*	*n/a*	*n/a*	***Dc***	***175.0***	***354.0***	***151.0***	***9-30-99***	***325.0***		***1145***	***25.7***						
Nts 6.80s 2004	Ao15	**A−**	11/99	BBB+	X	BE	[9]Z100	....	....	....	....	....	325	L3	'99	101⅞	96⅜	96⅜	7.06	7.06
[10]***NAC Re Corp***	***35c***		***4.99***	***6.65***	***5.04***	***Dc***				***9-30-99***	***411.0***		***5775***	***0.1***						
Nts 7.15s 2005	mN15	**A−**			X	BE	NC	....	....	....	....	....	100	D4	'95	105⅜	96⅝	96⅝	7.40	7.40
Nalco Chemical[11]	***14***		***15.23***	***15.91***	***14.10***	***Dc***	***48.10***	***539.5***	***297.8***	***9-30-99***	***464.0***		***1215***	***40.3***						
Nts 6¼s 2008	Mn15	**NR**	12/99	A		BE	NC	....	....	....	....	....	27.9	C1	'98	102⅝	91⅝	91⅝	6.82	6.82
Narragansett Electric Co[12]	***72a***		***2.68***	***3.23***	***3.62***	***Dc***	***2.38***	***92.20***	***122.0***	***9-30-99***	***154.0***		***491.0***	***43.2***						
1st S 9⅛s 2021	Mn	**AA−**	10/97	A+	X	R	104.04	(5-1-01)	Z100	....	....	....	22.2	K2	'91	109⅞	102⅜	102½	8.90	8.90
1st T 8⅞s 2021	fA	**AA−**	10/97	A+	X	R	103.79	(8-1-01)	100	....	....	....	22.0	M2	'91	110⅞	102	102⅛	8.69	8.69
1st U(93-5) 7.05s 2023	[13]fa	**AA−**	10/97	A+	X	BE	103.52	(9-1-03)	Z100	(9-1-03)	....	....	5.00	C5	'93	101¼	86½	86⅝	8.14	8.14
1st U(94-1) 7.05s 2024	[14]fa	**AA−**	10/97	A+	X	BE	103.53	(2-2-04)	Z100	(2-2-04)	....	....	5.00	K2	'94	103¼	86½	86⅝	8.14	8.14
1st V(94-1) 8.08s 2024	[15]ms	**AA−**	10/97	A+	X	BE	104.04	(5-2-04)	Z100	(5-2-04)	....	....	5.00	C5	'94	110¼	96⅝	96¾	8.35	8.35
1st V(94-4) 7.42s 2004	[16]ms	**AA−**	10/97	A+	X	BE	NC	....	....	....	....	....	5.00	C5	'94	107¾	99½	99½	7.46	7.46
1st V(94-5) 8.16s 2024	[17]ms	**AA−**	10/97	A+	X	BE	104.08	(8-9-04)	Z100	(8-9-04)	....	....	5.00	C5	'94	116⅞	98	98⅛	8.32	8.31
Nash Finch Co	***26***		***3.26***	***1.94***	***d1.01***	***Dc***	***1.30***	***486.0***	***360.6***	***10-9-99***	***348.0***		***493.0***	***68.2***						
Sr Sub Nts[18] 8½s 2008	Mn	**B+**	9/99	BB+	Y	BE	104.25	(5-1-03)	....	....	[19]Z110	5-1-01	165	Exch.	'98	95	79	83	10.24	10.24
National City Corp[21]	***10***		***3.13***	***3.01***	***2.65***	***Dc***				***9-30-99***	***14805***		***21777***	***71.3***						
Sub Nts 6⅝s 2004	Ms	**A−**			X	BE	NC	....	....	....	....	....	250	S1	'94	104⅞	97	97	6.83	6.83
Sub Nts 7.20s 2005	Mn15	**A−**			X	BE	NC	....	....	....	....	....	250	M2	'95	108¾	98⅝	98⅝	7.30	7.30
Sub Nts 5¾s 2009	Fa	**A−**			X	BE	NC	....	....	....	....	....	300	M2	'99	99½	87⅝	87⅝	6.56	6.56
Sub Nts 6⅞s 2019	Mn15	**A−**			X	BE	NC	....	....	....	....	....	700	M2	'99	99¾	89⅜	89⅝	7.67	7.67
National Fuel Gas	***73b***		***4.02***	***4.22***	***3.11***	***Sp***	***35.80***	***258.0***	***703.0***	***6-30-99***	***726.0***		***2214***	***56.3***						
Deb 7¾s 2004	Fa	**A−**	10/92	BBB+	X	R	NC	....	....	....	....	....	125	K2	'92	109⅜	100⅞	100⅞	7.68	7.68
M-T Nts 'D' 6.82s 2004	fA	**A−**			X	BE	NC	....	....	....	....	....	100	P1	'99	101¼	96¾	96¾	7.05	7.05
M-T Nts 'D' 6.303s 2008	[22]mn	**A−**			X	BE	NC	....	....	....	....	....	200	P1	'98	103⅞	90⅝	90⅝	6.96	6.95
M-T Nts 'D' 6s 2009	Ms	**A−**			X	BE	NC	....	....	....	....	....	100	L3	'99	99⅜	87⅞	87⅞	6.83	6.83
M-T[23]Nts 'D' 6.214s 2027	[24]mn	**A−**			X	BE	NC	....	....	....	....	....	100	B7	'97	105	96½	96½	6.44	6.44
Nat'l Health Investors	***57***		***4.26***	***4.39***	***4.64***	***Dc***				***9-30-99***	***360.0***		***771.0***	***46.7***						
Nts 7.30s 2007	[25]jj15	**BBB−**			X	BE	[26]Z100		....	....	....	....	100	S7	'97	100¾	96⅝	96⅞	7.54	7.53
Natl-Oilwell Inc	***49e***		***3.72***	***16.03***	***11.04***	***Dc***	***15.60***	***437.0***	***140.0***	***9-30-99***	***195.0***		***587.0***	***33.2***						
Nts 6⅞s 2005	jJ	**BBB+**			X	BE	[9]Z100	....	....	....	....	....	150	Exch.	'99	102¾	94¾	94¾	7.26	7.26
Natl Re Corp	***35c***	***Acquired by General Re,see***																		
Sr Nts 8.85s 2005	Jj15	**AA**	10/96	A+	X	BE	NC	....	....	....	....	....	100	M2	'95	116⅜	105⅝	105⅝	8.38	8.38
Sr Nts 7½s 2005	jJ31	**AA**	10/96	A+	X	BE	NC	....	....	....	....	....	25.0	M2	'95	110¼	100	100	7.50	7.50
Nat'l Rural Util.Co-opFin	***25***		***△1.12***	***△1.11***	***△1.12***	***My***				***8-31-99***	***8140***		***14457***	***95.5***						
• CT Bonds V 9s 2021	mS	**AA**	5/94	AA−	X	R	104	(9-1-01)	....	....	....	....	150	L3	'91	106⅛	105⅛	103¼	8.72	8.72

Uniform Footnote Explanations-See Page 260. Other: [1] Issued in min denom $100T. [2] Put on 2-15-01, as defined. [3] On 2-15-01 only. [4] Put on 2-1-03, as defined. [5] On 2-1-03 only. [6] Put on 2-1-05, as defined. [7] On 2-1-05 only. [8] See Pool Energy Services. [9] Red at greater of 100 or amt based on formula. [10] Acq by & data of XL Capital. [11] Acq by Suez Lyonnaise des Eaux. [12] Contr by New England Elec System. [13] Due 9-1-23. [14] Due 2-2-24. [15] Due 5-2-24. [16] Due 6-15-04. [17] Due 8-9-24. [18] (HRO)On Chge of Ctrl at 101. [19] Max $58M red w/proceeds of Pub Eq Off'g. [21] See First of Am Bank,Integra Finl. [22] Due 5-27-08. [23] (HRO)On 8-12-02 at 100. [24] Due 8-12-28. [25] Due 7-16-07. [26] Plus Make-Whole Amt.

Title-Industry Code & Co. Finances (In Italics) / Individual Issue Statistics (Exchange)	Ind / Interest Dates	Fixed Charge Coverage 1996 / S&P Rating	1997 / Date of Last Rating Change	1998 / Prior Rating	Eligible	Year End / Bond Form	Million $ Cash & Equiv. / Redemption Provisions: Regular Price	Curr. Assets / Regular (Begins) Thru	Curr. Liab. / Sinking Fund Price	Balance Sheet Date / Sinking Fund (Begins) Thru	L. Term Debt (Mil $) / Refund/Other Restriction Price	Refund/Other Restriction (Begins) Thru	Capital-ization (Mil $) / Outst'g (Mil $)	Total Debt % Capital / Underwriting Firm	Underwriting Year	Price Range 1999 High	Price Range 1999 Low	Mo. End Price Sale(s) or Bid	Curr. Yield	Yield to Mat.
***Nat'l Rural Util.Co-opFin** (Cont.)*																				
• CT Bonds 6.45s 2001	Ao	**AA**			X	BE	NC	....	....	....	....	....	100	L3	'96	99	99	97	6.65	6.65
• CT Bonds 6¾s 2001	mS	**AA**			X	BE	NC	....	....	....	....	....	100	L3	'96	99	98	98	6.89	6.89
• CT Bonds 6.70s 2002	Jd15	**AA**			X	BE	NC	....	....	....	....	....	100	L3	'97	98	98	96¼	6.96	6.96
• CT Bonds 6½s 2002	mS15	**AA**			X	BE	NC	....	....	....	....	....	100	L3	'95	98	96¾	96¾	6.72	6.72
• CT Bonds 5½s 2005	Jj15	**AA**			X	BE	NC	....	....	....	....	....	200	L3	'99	100⅝	90⅛	90⅛	6.10	6.10
• CT Bonds 5s 2002	aO	**AA**			X	BE	NC	....	....	....	....	....	200	L3	'98	94½	94½	92½	5.41	5.41
• CT Bonds 5.95s 2003	Jj15	**AA**			X	BE	NC	....	....	....	....	....	100	L3	'96	98	94	94	6.33	6.33
• CT Bonds 5.30s 2003	mS25	**AA**			X	BE	NC	....	....	....	....	....	100	L3	'98	100½	100½	91⅝	5.78	5.79
• CT Bonds 6s 2004	Jj15	**AA**			X	BE	NC	....	....	....	....	....	200	L3	'98	103¼	103¼	92⅞	6.46	6.46
• CT Bonds 6⅜s 2004	aO15	**AA**			X	BE	NC	....	....	....	....	....	100	L3	'97	105⅛	96	93½	6.82	6.82
• CT Bonds 6⅛s 2005	Mn15	**AA**			X	BE	NC	....	....	....	....	....	200	L3	'98	104	96	91	6.73	6.73
• CT Bonds 6.65s 2005	aO	**AA**			X	BE	NC	....	....	....	....	....	50.0	L3	'95	107⅛	107⅛	97¼	6.84	6.84
• CT Bonds 7.30s 2006	mS15	**AA**			X	BE	NC	....	....	....	....	....	100	L3	'96	110⅞	96¼	94½	7.72	7.72
• CT Bonds 6.20s 2008	Fa	**AA**			X	BE	NC	....	....	....	....	....	300	L3	'98	105⅝	90	85	7.29	7.29
• CT Bonds 5¾s 2008	mN	**AA**			X	BE	[1]Z100	....	....	....	....	....	225	L3	'98	100	88	82	7.01	7.01
• CT Bonds 5.70s 2010	Jj15	**AA**			X	BE	NC	....	....	....	....	....	200	L3	'99	101	98⅞	80	7.13	7.12
• CT Bonds 7.20s 2015	aO	**AA**			X	BE	NC	....	....	....	....	....	50.0	L3	'95	99	96	88	8.18	8.18
• CT Bonds 6.55s 2018	mN	**AA**			X	BE	[1]Z100	....	....	....	....	....	175	L3	'98	103⅝	95	80	8.19	8.19
• CT Bonds 7.35s 2026	mN	**AA**			X	BE	NC	....	100	(11-1-07)	....	....	100	L3	'96	113	97	86	8.55	8.55
Nts 5¾s 2008	jD	**AA–**			X	BE	NC	....	....	....	....	....	230	L3	'98	101	88⅝	88⅝	6.49	6.49
Natl Service Indus	***17a***	*△n/a*	*△n/a*	*△15.76*		***Au***	***2.25***	***680.0***	***424.0***	***8-31-99***	***435.0***		***1063***	***42.1***						
Nts 6s 2009	Fa	**A**			X	BE	[1]Z100	....	....	....	....	....	160	S4	'99	99⅝	88⅜	88⅜	6.79	6.79
National Steel[2]Corp[3]	***66a***	***1.45***	***5.33***	***2.76***		***Dc***	***148.0***	***1040***	***542.0***	***9-30-99***	***561.0***		***1389***	***42.5***						
• 1st 8⅜s 2006	fA	**B+**	10/98	BB–	Y	R	100.67	7-31-00	100	....	....	....	75.0	M2	'76	101¾	86½	89⅝	9.37	9.37
1st[4] 'D' 9⅞s 2009	Ms	**B+**			Y	BE	104.938	(3-1-04)	....	....	[5]Z109.875	3-1-02	300	Exch.	'99	103½	97	103	9.59	9.59
Natl Wine & Spirits	***11c***	***1.18***	***1.31***	***1.12***		***Mr***	***2.56***	***131.0***	***55.40***	***9-30-99***	***128.0***		***148.0***	***87.0***						
Sr Nts[4] 10⅛s 2009	Jj15	**B**			Y	BE	105.0625	(1-15-04)	....	....	[6]Z110.125	1-19-02	110	Exch.	'99	102	97¼	99½	10.18	10.17
NationsBank[7]Corp[8]	***10***	***Merged w/BankAmerica Corp***																		
Sr Nts 5⅝s 2000	aO15	**A+**	12/96	A	X	R	NC	....	....	....	....	....	400		'93	100¼	99½	99¾	5.39	5.39
Sr Nts 5¾s 2001	Ms15	**A+**			X	BE	NC	....	....	....	....	....	600	N2	'98	100¾	98⅝	98⅝	5.83	5.83
Sr Nts 7s 2001	mS15	**A+**	12/96	A	X	BE	NC	....	....	....	....	....	500		'96	104⅛	99⅞	100	7.00	7.00
Sr Nts 7s 2003	Mn15	**A+**	12/96	A	X	BE	NC	....	....	....	....	....	500		'96	105¾	99⅛	99⅝	7.03	7.03
Sr Nts 6⅛s 2004	jJ15	**A+**			X	BE	NC	....	....	....	....	....	450	N2	'98	102⅞	95⅜	95⅞	6.39	6.39
Sr Nts 6⅜s 2005	Mn15	**A+**			X	BE	NC	....	....	....	....	....	500	N2	'98	104¼	94⅞	96⅛	6.63	6.63
M-T Nts 'E' 5.76s 2001	[9]jj15	**A+**	12/96	A	X	BE	NC	....	....	....	....	....	25.4	B7	'96	100⅝	99	99	5.82	5.82
M-T Nts 'E' 5.85s 2001	Jj17	**A+**	12/96	A	X	BE	NC	....	....	....	....	....	50.0	S1	'96	100¾	99	99	5.91	5.91
M-T Nts 'E' 5¾s 2001	Jj17	**A+**	12/96	A	X	BE	NC	....	....	....	....	....	35.0	M5	'96	100⅝	99	99	5.81	5.81
M-T Nts 'E' 5¾s 2001	Jj25	**A+**	12/96	A	X	BE	NC	....	....	....	....	....	42.0	M2	'96	100⅝	98⅞	98⅞	5.82	5.82
M-T Nts 'E' 5.60s 2001	Fa7	**A+**	12/96	A	X	BE	NC	....	....	....	....	....	40.0	B7	'96	100⅜	98¾	98¾	5.67	5.67
M-T Nts 'E' 5.85s 2002	Fa5	**A+**	12/96	A	X	BE	NC	....	....	....	....	....	50.0	D6	'96	101	97⅞	97⅞	5.98	5.98
M-T Nts 'F' 7.04s 2012	[10]Aug15	**A+**			X	BE	Z100	(8-15-01)	....	....	....	....	50.0	M2	'97	101¾	94¾	95½	7.37	7.37
M-T Nts 'F' 7s 2012	[10]Aug15	**A+**			X	BE	*100	(8-15-01)	....	....	....	....	25.0	S7	'97	101½	93⅜	94⅛	7.44	7.44
M-T Nts 'G' 7s 2023	[11]fa11	**A+**			X	BE	*100	(2-11-02)	....	....	....	....	25.0	S1	'98	99⅜	90¼	91⅝	7.64	7.64
Sub Nts 8⅛s 2002	Jd15	**A**	12/96	A–	X	R	NC	....	....	....	....	....	350	M2	'92	108	102⅜	102⅜	7.94	7.94

Uniform Footnote Explanations-See Page 260. Other: [1] Red at greater of 100 or amt based on formula. [2] Subsid of Nat'l Intergroup. [3] Was Granite City Steel. [4] (HRO)On Chge of Ctrl at 101. [5] Max $105M red w/proceeds of Pub Eq Off'g. [6] Max $36M red w/proceeds of Pub Eq Off'g. [7] See NCNB Corp,NCNB Tex Natl Bk. [8] See Bank South,Boatmen's Bancshares. [9] Due 1-16-01. [10] Int pd monthly. [11] Due 2-10-23.

Title-Industry Code & Co. Finances (In Italics) / Individual Issue Statistics, Exchange	Ind / Interest Dates	Fixed Charge Coverage 1996 / S&P Rating	1997 / Date of Last Rating Change	1998 / Prior Rating	Eligible	Year End / Bond Form	Cash & Equiv. (Million $) / Regular Price	Curr. Assets (Million $) / Regular (Begins) Thru	Curr. Liab. / Sinking Fund Price	Balance Sheet Date / Sinking Fund (Begins) Thru	L. Term Debt (Mil $) / Refund/Other Restriction Price	Capital-ization (Mil $) / Refund/Other Restriction (Begins) Thru	Total Debt % Capital / Outst'g (Mil $)	Underwriting Firm	Underwriting Year	Price Range 1999 High	Price Range 1999 Low	Mo. End Price Sale(s) or Bid	Curr. Yield	Yield to Mat.
***NationsBank Corp** (Cont.)*																				
Sub Nts 6½s 2003	fA15	A	12/96	A–	X	R	NC	....	....	....	....	....	600	M2	'93	103¾	98⅛	98⅛	6.62	6.62
Sub Nts 7¾s 2004	fA15	A	12/96	A–	X	R	NC	....	....	....	....	....	300		'94	110⅝	101⅞	101⅞	7.61	7.61
Sub Nts 6⅞s 2005	Fa15	A	12/96	A–	X	R	NC	....	....	....	....	....	400	M2	'93	106	97⅞	98½	6.98	6.98
Sub Nts 7⅝s 2005	Ao15	A	12/96	A–	X	BE	NC	....	....	....	....	....	300		'95	110½	101	101⅜	7.52	7.52
Sub Nts 6½s 2006	Ms15	A	12/96	A–	X	BE	NC	....	....	....	....	....	300		'96	105⅛	95	95⅞	6.78	6.78
Sub Nts 7½s 2006	mS15	A	12/96	A–	X	BE	NC	....	....	....	....	....	500		'96	111¾	100	100¾	7.44	7.44
Sub Nts 6⅜s 2008	Fa15	A			X	BE	NC	....	....	....	....	....	350	N2	'98	105	92⅛	93¼	6.84	6.84
Sub Nts 6.60s 2010	Mn15	A			X	BE	NC	....	....	....	....	....	300	N2	'98	106⅜	91⅜	93	7.10	7.10
Sub M-T Nts 'F' 7.19s 2012	jJ30	A			X	BE	*100	7-30-02	....	....	....	....	50.0		'97	102½	94¼	94⅝	7.60	7.60
Sub Nts 7¾s 2015	fA15	A	12/96	A–	X	BE	NC	....	....	....	....	....	350		'95	114¼	97⅜	99¼	7.81	7.81
Sub Nts 7.80s 2016	mS15	A	12/96	A–	X	BE	NC	....	....	....	....	....	450		'96	115⅝	99⅝	100	7.80	7.80
Sub Nts 7¼s 2025	aO15	A	12/96	A–	X	BE	NC	....	....	....	....	....	450		'95	110⅝	91⅞	92⅝	7.83	7.83
Sub Nts 6.80s 2028	Ms15	A			X	BE	NC	....	....	....	....	....	400	N2	'98	105½	87⅜	87½	7.77	7.77
Nationwide Credit	*63*	*n/a*	*n/a*	*d0.84*		*Dc*	*1.27*	*21.50*	*12.00*	*9-30-99*	*122.0*	*124.0*	*98.4*							
Sr Nts[1] 10¼s 2008	Jj15	B–			Y	BE	105.125	(1-15-03)	....	....	[2]Z110.25	1-15-01	100	Exch.	'98	83	53	60	17.08	17.07
Nationwide Finl Svcs	*35*	*n/a*	*n/a*	*n/a*		*Dc*				*9-30-99*	*598.0*	*3016*	*19.8*							
•Sr Nts 8s 2027	Ms	A+			X	BE	103.728	(3-1-07)	....	....	....	....	300	C5	'97	94	94	94	8.51	8.51
Nationwide Health Prop	*57*	*3.64*	*3.18*	*2.93*		*Dc*				*9-30-99*	*778.0*	*1336*	*55.1*							
M-T Nts 'B' 6.65s 2002	[3]ao	BBB			X	BE	NC	....	....	....	....	....	25.0	M2	'97	100½	92⅝	94½	7.04	7.04
M-T Nts 7.06s 2006	[4]ao	BBB			X	BE	NC	....	....	....	....	....	20.0	G1	'96	101⅞	82⅝	85¾	8.23	8.23
M-T Nts[5] 'C' 6.90s 2037	aO	BBB			X	BE	NC	....	....	....	....	....	55.0	G1	'97	99⅛	85¼	88½	7.80	7.80
M-T Nts 7.28s 2007	[6]ao	BBB			X	BE	NC	....	....	....	....	....	40.0	M2	'97	103½	83⅛	86¼	8.44	8.44
Navistar Fin'l Corp[7]	*25d*	*1.99*	*2.02*	*1.97*		*Oc*				*7-31-99*	*1505*	*1806*	*84.4*							
Sub Nts[1]'B' 9s 2002	Jd	BB–			Y	BE	NC	....	....	....	....	....	100	Exch.	'97	104½	100	100¼	8.98	8.98
Navistar Intl	*9a*	*2.27*	*4.27*	*4.90*		*Oc*				*7-31-99*	*2060*	*3090*	*66.7*							
Sr Nts[1]'B' 7s 2003	Fa	BB+			Y	BE	NC	....	....	....	....	....	100	Exch.	'98	102⅝	95¾	95¾	7.31	7.31
Sr Sub Nts[1]'B' 8s 2008	Fa	BB–			Y		104	(2-1-03)	....	....	[8]Z108	2-1-01	250	Exch.	'98	104¼	94	95	8.42	8.42
NBD Bancorp	*10*	*Now First Chicago NBD,see*																		
Sub Nts 7⅛s 2007	Mn15	A	12/95	A+	X	BE	NC	....	....	....	....	....	200	L3	'95	108¼	96½	96½	7.38	7.38
NBTY Inc	*21*	*13.91*	*8.58*	*4.72*		*Sp*	*23.60*	*201.0*	*102.0*	*6-30-99*	*199.0*	*408.0*	*48.8*							
Sr Sub Nts[1] 8⅝s 2007	mS15	B+			Y	BE	104.313	(9-15-02)	....	....	[9]Z108.625	9-15-00	150	Exch.	'98	98	80½	92½	9.32	9.32
NCI Building Systems	*13h*	*n/a*	*n/a*	*3.94*		*Oc*	*5.30*	*201.0*	*146.0*	*7-31-99*	*411.0*	*704.0*	*63.1*							
Sr Sub Nts[1]'B' 9¼s 2009	Mn	B			Y	BE	104.625	(5-1-04)	....	....	[10]Z109.25	5-1-02	125	Exch.	'99	96⅞	91¾	95	9.74	9.74
NCNB Corp	*10*	*Now NationsBank Corp,see*																		
◆Deb 7¾s 2002	fA	A+	12/96	A	X	R	100	....	....	....	....	....	[11]27.5	S1	'82	102	99	100⅛	7.74	7.74
Sub Nts 9⅛s 2001	aO15	A	12/96	A–	X	R	NC	....	....	....	....	....	300	M2	'91	109⅛	103⅜	103⅜	8.83	8.83
Sub Nts 9⅜s 2009	mS15	A	12/96	A–	X	R	NC	....	....	....	....	....	400	M2	'89	127	111⅜	111⅜	8.42	8.42
Sub Nts 10.20s 2015	jJ15	A	12/96	A–	X	R	NC	....	....	....	....	....	200	M2	'90	135½	119⅛	119⅛	8.56	8.56
[12]***NCNB Texas Nat'l Bank***	*10*	*Subsid of NationsBank Corp,see*																		
Cap Nts Oblig 9½s 2004	Jd	A+	12/96	A	X	R	NC	....	....	....	....	....	300	S10	'89	117⅝	108¼	108¼	8.78	8.77
NE Restaurant Co	*27c*	*3.52*	*2.60*	*0.64*		*Dc*	*1.58*	*16.00*	*33.80*	*9-29-99*	*134.0*	*144.0*	*93.2*							
Sr Nts[1] 10¾s 2008	jJ15	B			Y	BE	105.375	(7-15-03)	....	....	[2]Z110.75	7-15-01	100	Exch.	'98	100½	88½	88½	12.15	12.14
Nebraska Book Co	*67d*	*1.54*	*0.93*	*1.21*		*Mr*	*22.60*	*111.0*	*43.10*	*9-30-99*	*165.0*	*138.0*	*122.0*							
Sr Sub Nts[1] 8¾s 2008	Fa15	B–			Y	BE	104.375	(2-15-03)	....	....	[13]Z108.75	2-15-01	110	Exch.	'98	96	80	88	9.94	9.94

Uniform Footnote Explanations-See Page 260. Other: [1] (HRO)On Chge of Ctrl at 101. [2] Max $35M red w/proceeds of Equity Off'g. [3] Due 7-29-02. [4] Due 12-5-06. [5] (HRO)On 10-1-04('07,'09,'12,'17&,'27)at 100. [6] Due 6-18-07. [7] Subsid of Navistar Int'l. [8] Max $87.5M red w/proceeds Eq Off'g. [9] Max $50M red w/proceeds of Pub Eq off'g. [10] Max $43M red w/proceeds of Pub Eq Off'g. [11] Incl disc. [12] Now NationsBank of Texas N.A. [13] Max $38.5M red w/proceeds of Equity Off'g.

Title-Industry Code & Co. Finances (In Italics) / Individual Issue Statistics (Exchange)	Ind / Interest Dates	Fixed Charge Coverage 1996 / S&P Rating	1997 / Date of Last Rating Change	Prior Rating	1998 / Eligible	Year End / Bond Form	Cash & Equiv. (Million $) / Redemption Provisions: Regular Price	Curr. Assets (Million $) / Regular (Begins) Thru	Curr. Liab. (Million $) / Sinking Fund Price	Balance Sheet Date / Sinking Fund (Begins) Thru	L. Term Debt (Mil $) / Refund/Other Restriction Price	Capital-ization (Mil $) / Refund/Other Restriction (Begins) Thru	Outst'g (Mil $)	Total Debt % Capital / Underwriting Firm	Underwriting Year	Price Range 1999 High	Price Range 1999 Low	Mo. End Price Sale(s) or Bid	Curr. Yield	Yield to Mat.
Neenah Foundary Co	***42b***	*n/a*	*n/a*		*1.81*	*Sp*	*11.60*	*155.0*	*60.90*	*6-30-99*	*426.0*	*494.0*		*87.0*						
Sr Sub Nts[1]'B' 11⅛s 2007	Mn	B–			Y	BE	[2]Z100	....	....	....	[3]Z111.125	5-1-00	149	C1	'97	106¾	91½	92½	12.03	12.02
Neff Corp	***59l***	*0.85*	*0.43*		*1.06*	*Dc*				*9-30-99*	*226.0*	*330.0*		*68.3*						
Sr Sub Nts[1] 10¼s 2008	Jd	B			Y	BE	105.125	(6-1-03)	....	....	[4]Z110.25	6-1-01	100	Exch.	'98	104	96	96	10.68	10.67
Neiman-Marcus Group	***59f***	*5.65*	*6.87*		*9.11*	*Jl*	*214.7*	*1037*	*486.3*	*10-30-99*	*340.0*	*1124*		*30.3*						
Sr Deb 7⅛s 2028	Jd	BBB			X	BE	Z100	....	....	....	....	....	125	S4	'98	97⅞	84½	84½	8.43	8.43
Sr Nts 6.65s 2008	Jd	BBB			X	BE	[5]Z100	....	....	....	....	....	125	S4	'98	100⅞	90½	90½	7.35	7.35
[6]Nevada Power	***72a***	*3.28*	*3.34*		*2.51*	*Dc*	*19.80*	*166.0*	*198.0*	*9-30-99*	*777.0*	*1634*		*51.6*						
1st L 7⅝s 2002	mN	A	4/99	A–	X	R	100.55	10-31-00	100.07	10-31-00	....	....	15.0	B8	'72	101	99⅞	99⅞	7.63	7.63
1st Z 8½s 2023	Jj	A	4/99	A–	X	R	103.71	(1-1-03)	....	....	....	....	45.0	P1	'93	111⅞	99¼	99⅜	8.55	8.55
1st 7.06s 2000	Mn	A	4/99	A–	X	R	NC	....	....	....	....	....	85.0	P1	'95	102⅛	100⅛	100⅛	7.05	7.05
New England Power Co.[7]	***72a***	*5.33*	*5.63*		*5.85*	*Dc*	*242.0*	*399.0*	*153.0*	*9-30-99*	*372.0*	*967.0*		*42.4*						
Gen & Ref U 8s 2022	fA	A+	12/97	A	X	R	103.61	(8-1-02)	Z100	(8-1-02)	....	....	134	G1	'92	109¾	100⅝	100¾	7.94	7.94
Gen & Ref W(93-1) 7s 2003	[8]mn	A+	12/97	A	X	BE	NC	....	....	....	....	....	25.0	C5	'93	104¾	99	99	7.07	7.07
Gen & Ref W(93-6) 6.58s 2000	[9]mn	A+	12/97	A	X	BE	NC	....	....	....	....	....	5.00	C5	'93	101⅛	100	100	6.58	6.58
Gen & Ref Y(94-1) 8.53s 2024	[10]mn	A+	12/97	A	X	BE	104.27	(9-23-04)	Z100	(9-23-04)	....	....	5.00	C5	'94	114	100½	100½	8.49	8.49
New England Tel. & Tel.[11]	***67a***	*8.44*	*7.47*		*7.69*	*Dc*	*66.60*	*1487*	*2239*	*6-30-99*	*1806*	*4426*		*55.3*						
• Deb 4½s 2002	jJ	AA	4/97	AA–	X	CR	100	....	....	....	....	....	50.0	F1	'62	98¼	93½	93¾	4.80	4.80
• Deb 4⅝s 2005	jJ	AA	4/97	AA–	X	R	100.14	6-30-00	....	....	....	....	60.0	H1	'65	97½	88⅛	86⅝	5.34	5.34
• Deb 6⅛s 2006	aO	AA	4/97	AA–	X	R	100.38	9-30-00	....	....	....	....	100	L3	'67	101	92⅛	s92¾	6.60	6.60
• Deb 6⅜s 2008	mS	AA	4/97	AA–	X	R	100.65	8-31-00	....	....	....	....	125	F1	'68	101	91¾	92	6.93	6.93
• Deb 7⅞s 2022	mS	AA	4/97	AA–	X	BE	103.551	(9-1-02)	....	....	....	....	100	L3	'92	107⅞	99	98¼	8.02	8.01
• Deb 6⅞s 2023	aO	AA	4/97	AA–	X	BE	102.75	(10-1-03)	....	....	....	....	250	F1	'93	104½	88¼	88¼	7.79	7.79
• Deb 7⅞s 2029	mN15	AA	4/97	AA–	X	R	NC	....	....	....	....	....	350	S1	'89	118	101	101	7.80	7.80
• Deb 9s 2031	fA	AA	4/97	AA–	X	BE	106	(8-1-01)	....	....	....	....	100	G1	'91	108½	108⅛	106½	8.45	8.45
• Nts 5¾s 2000	Mn	AA	4/97	AA–	X	BE	NC	....	....	....	....	....	100	M5	'93	101¼	99¼	99½	5.78	5.78
• Nts 8⅝s 2001	fA	AA	4/97	AA–	X	BE	NC	....	....	....	....	....	100	G1	'91	108	101⅛	101⅛	8.53	8.53
• Nts 6¼s 2003	Ms15	AA	4/97	AA–	X	BE	NC	....	....	....	....	....	225	M6	'93	103⅞	96½	97⅜	6.42	6.42
Nts 5⅞s 2009	Ao15	AA			X	BE	[5]Z100	....	....	....	....	....	200	M2	'99	99⅛	89¼	89¼	6.58	6.58
New Jersey Bell Tel[12]	***67a***	***Now Bell Atlantic-N.J.,see***																		
Deb 4⅞s 2000	mN	AA	4/97	AA+	X	CR	100	....	....	....	....	....	20.0	M6	'60	99¼	98¼	98½	4.95	4.95
Deb 7¼s 2002	Jd	AA	4/97	AA+	X	BE	NC	....	....	....	....	....	100	S1	'92	106¼	100¾	100¾	7.20	7.20
Deb 4⅝s 2005	Jd	AA	4/97	AA+	X	R	100.16	5-31-00	....	....	....	....	40.0	W5	'65	97⅝	88⅜	88⅜	5.23	5.24
Deb 5⅞s 2006	jD	AA	4/97	AA+	X	R	100.32	11-30-00	....	....	....	....	55.0	S1	'66	99⅜	91¾	91¾	6.40	6.40
Deb 6⅝s 2008	Ao	AA	4/97	AA+	X	R	100.65	3-31-00	....	....	....	....	50.0	M2	'68	100⅞	97½	97½	6.79	6.79
• Deb 7¼s 2011	Ao	AA	4/97	AA+	X	R	101.58	3-31-00	....	....	....	....	125	M6	'71	102⅝	95	97¼	7.46	7.45
• Deb 7⅜s 2012	Jd	AA	4/97	AA+	X	R	101.47	5-31-00	....	....	....	....	75.0	H1	'72	102½	95	96⅝	7.63	7.63
Deb 8s 2022	Jd	AA	4/97	AA+	X	BE	NC	....	....	....	....	....	200	G1	'92	122⅝	101	101⅛	7.91	7.91
Deb 7¼s 2023	Ms	AA	4/97	AA+	X	BE	103.42	(3-1-03)	....	....	....	....	100	F1	'93	108⅜	90⅜	90⅜	8.02	8.02
Deb 6.80s 2024	jD15	AA	4/97	AA+	X	BE	101.536	(12-15-08)	....	....	....	....	100	M6	'93	103⅜	85⅝	85½	7.95	7.95
Deb 7.85s 2029	mN15	AA	4/97	AA+	X	R	NC	....	....	....	....	....	150	M2	'89	122⅞	100⅛	100⅛	7.84	7.84
New Orleans Public Serv[13]	***75***	*3.60*	*2.76*		*2.74*	*Dc*	*13.40*	*124.0*	*76.60*	*6-30-99*	*169.0*	*336.0*		*50.3*						
Gen & Ref[14] 7s 2003	Ms	BBB			X	BE	100.99	2-29-00	100	....	....	....	25.0	G1	'93	104⅝	98⅜	98⅜	7.12	7.11
Gen & Ref[14] 8s 2006	Ms	BBB			X	BE	100	(3-1-01)	Z100	(3-1-01)	....	....	40.0	S1	'96	105	99	99	8.08	8.08
Gen & Ref[14] 8s 2023	Ms	BBB			X	BE	104.03	2-29-00	100	....	....	....	45.0	G1	'93	104⅝	94⅜	94½	8.47	8.46

Uniform Footnote Explanations-See Page 260. Other: [1] (HRO)On Chge of Ctrl at 101. [2] On Chge of Ctrl,plus premium. [3] Max $60M red w/proceeds of Pub Eq Off'g. [4] Max $30M red w/proceeds of Equity Off'g. [5] Red at greater of 100 or amt based on formula. [6] Now Sierra Pacific Power. [7] Subsid of New England Elec System. [8] Due 2-3-03. [9] Due 2-10-00. [10] Due 9-23-24. [11] Subsid of NYNEX Corp. [12] Subsid of Bell Atlantic Corp. [13] Subsid of Entergy Corp,now Entergy New Orleans. [14] (HRO)On Chge of Ctrl at prices,as defined.

Title-Industry Code & Co. Finances (In Italics)	Ind	Fixed Charge Coverage 1996	1997	1998		Year End	Million $ Cash & Equiv.	Curr. Assets	Curr. Liab.	Balance Sheet Date	L. Term Debt (Mil $)		Capital-ization (Mil $)	Total Debt % Capital						
Individual Issue Statistics Exchange	**Interest Dates**	**S&P Rating**	**Date of Last Rating Change**	**Prior Rating**	**Eligible**	**Bond Form**	**Redemption Provisions: Regular Price**	**Regular (Begins) Thru**	**Sinking Fund Price**	**Sinking Fund (Begins) Thru**	**Refund/Other Restriction Price**	**Refund/Other Restriction (Begins) Thru**	**Outst'g (Mil $)**	**Underwriting Firm**	**Underwriting Year**	**Price Range 1999 High**	**Price Range 1999 Low**	**Mo. End Price Sale(s) or Bid**	**Curr. Yield**	**Yield to Mat.**
New Orleans Public Serv *(Cont.)*																				
Gen & Ref[1] 7.55s 2023	mS	**BBB**			X	BE	105.20	8-31-00	Z100	....	....	....	30.0	K2	'93	101¾	88⅞	89	8.48	8.48
New Plan Excel[2] Realty Tr	***57***	***4.99***	***3.73***	***[3]3.46***		***Dc***				***9-30-99***	***968.0***		***2626***	***36.9***						
M-T Nts 7.40s 2009	mS15	**A**			X	BE	NC	....	....	....	....	....	150	S4	'99	9975	94⅝	94⅝	7.82	7.82
M-T Nts 7½s 2029	jJ30	**A**			X	BE	NC	....	....	....	....	....	25.0	L3	'99	100	84¼	86⅛	8.71	8.71
New Plan Realty Tr	***57***	***Now New Plan Excel Realty Tr,see***																		
Sr Nts 6.80s 2002	Mn15	**A**	3/99	A+	X	BE	NC	....	....	....	....	....	81.0	L3	'95	101¼	97¾	97¾	6.96	6.96
Sr Nts 7¾s 2005	Ao6	**A**	3/99	A+	X	BE	NC	....	....	....	....	....	100	M2	'95	105¼	98⅞	98⅞	7.84	7.84
M-T Nts 6.90s 2028	Fa15	**A**	3/99	A+	X	BE	NC	....	....	....	....	....	25.0	B4	'98	90¼	78⅛	80⅛	8.61	8.61
M-T Nts 6.90s 2028	Fa15	**A**	3/99	A+	X	BE	NC	....	....	....	....	....	25.0	P4	'98	90¼	78⅛	80⅛	8.61	8.61
[4]New York St. Elec & Gas	***75***	***3.33***	***3.45***	***3.85***		***Dc***	***1167***	***1490***	***449.0***	***9-30-99***	***1387***		***3335***	***52.1***						
1st 6¾s 2002	aO15	**A**	5/99	BBB+	X	R	NC	....	....	....	Z100	....	150	M2	'92	104⅜	99	99	6.82	6.82
1st 9⅞s 2020	Mn	**A**	5/99	BBB+	X	R	104.18	(5-1-00)	Z100	....	....	....	100	S1	'90	108⅞	105⅛	105⅛	9.39	9.39
1st 9⅞s 2020	mN	**A**	5/99	BBB+	X	R	104.34	(11-1-00)	Z100	....	....	....	100	S1	'90	110¾	106⅛	106⅛	9.31	9.30
1st 8⅞s 2021	mN	**A**	5/99	BBB+	X	R	103.79	(11-1-01)	Z100	....	....	....	150	M2	'91	110⅛	98⅝	98¾	8.99	8.99
1st 8.30s 2022	jD15	**A**	5/99	BBB+	X	R	103.43	(12-15-02)	Z100	(12-15-02)	Z100	....	100	M2	'92	108⅞	96⅝	96⅝	8.59	8.59
1st 7.55s 2023	Ao	**A**	5/99	BBB+	X	R	102.78	(4-1-03)	Z100	....	....	....	50.0	M2	'93	105	90¾	90⅞	8.31	8.31
1st 7.45s 2023	jJ15	**A**	5/99	BBB+	X	R	103.50	(7-15-03)	Z100	(7-15-03)	Z100	....	100	M2	'93	104½	89⅝	89¾	8.30	8.30
New York Telephone Co[5]	***67a***	***5.00***	***2.92***	***2.33***		***Dc***	***135.0***	***2178***	***3951***	***6-30-99***	***3653***		***6641***	***73.4***						
• Ref M 4⅝s 2002	Jj	**A+**	4/97	A	X	CR	100	....	....	....	....	....	60.0	H1	'62	98¾	94⅜	94¾	4.88	4.88
• Ref N 4¼s 2000	Jj	**A+**	4/97	A	X	CR	100	....	....	....	....	....	70.0	H1	'63	99⅝	98¼	99⅝	4.27	Mat.
• Ref O 4⅝s 2004	Jj	**A+**	4/97	A	X	CR	100	....	....	....	....	....	130	M6	'64	97⅛	91	s91	5.08	5.08
• Ref P 4⅞s 2006	Jj	**A+**	4/97	A	X	R	100.15	12-31-00	....	....	....	....	100	M6	'66	96¼	86¼	86¼	5.65	5.65
• Ref Q 6s 2007	mS	**A+**	4/97	A	X	R	100.53	8-31-00	....	....	....	....	75.0	H1	'67	100¾	91¼	s91⅞	6.53	6.53
• Ref V 7⅜s 2011	jD15	**A+**	4/97	A	X	R	101.72	12-14-00	....	....	....	....	200	M6	'71	103	96	96	7.68	7.68
• Deb 6½s 2005	Ms	**A+**	4/97	A	X	BE	NC	....	....	....	....	....	200	S1	'93	104½	97⅛	96⅛	6.76	6.76
Deb 6s 2008	Ao15	**A+**			X	BE	NC	....	....	....	....	....	250	B7	'98	104⅝	90⅛	90⅛	6.66	6.66
• Deb 6⅛s 2010	Jj15	**A+**			X	BE	NC	....	....	....	....	....	250	B7	'98	105	91	90⅛	6.80	6.80
• Deb 8⅝s 2010	mN15	**A+**	4/97	A	X	R	NC	....	....	....	....	....	150	M6	'89	116⅛	104	104⅜	8.26	8.26
• Deb 7s 2013	Mn	**A+**	4/97	A	X	BE	NC	....	....	....	....	....	100	S1	'93	104	96	95½	7.33	7.33
• Deb 7s 2013	Jd15	**A+**	4/97	A	X	BE	NC	....	....	....	....	....	100	S1	'93	106½	96	94⅛	7.44	7.44
• Deb 7⅝s 2023	Fa	**A+**	4/97	A	X	BE	102.879	(2-1-03)	....	....	....	....	100	K2	'93	108⅜	94¾	s96¾	7.88	7.88
Deb 6.70s 2023	mN	**A+**	4/97	A	X	BE	100	(11-1-13)	....	....	....	....	250	S1	'93	102½	85¼	85¼	7.86	7.86
• Deb 7¼s 2024	Fa15	**A+**	4/97	A	X	BE	103.061	(2-15-04)	....	....	....	....	450	M6	'94	104⅛	96	96⅝	7.50	7.50
• Deb 7s 2025	fA15	**A+**	4/97	A	X	BE	102.34	(8-15-03)	....	....	....	....	250	G1	'93	104⅜	87⅜	87¾	7.98	7.98
Deb 6½s 2028	Ao15	**A+**			X	BE	NC	....	....	....	....	....	100	M7	'98	104⅛	82¾	82⅞	7.84	7.84
• Deb 9⅜s 2031	jJ15	**A+**	4/97	A	X	BE	106.08	(7-15-01)	....	....	....	....	200	S1	'91	111	107⅛	s108	8.68	8.68
• Deb 7s 2033	jD	**A+**	4/97	A	X	BE	100	(12-1-13)	....	....	....	....	200	K2	'93	106⅝	87	s89	7.87	7.86
• Nts 5⅞s 2003	mS	**A+**	4/97	A	X	BE	NC	....	....	....	....	....	200	C4	'93	102½	95½	95¾	6.14	6.14
Nts 5⅝s 2003	mN	**A+**	4/97	A	X	BE	NC	....	....	....	....	....	150	M6	'93	102⅜	94⅛	94½	5.95	5.95
• Nts 6¼s 2004	Fa15	**A+**	4/97	A	X	BE	NC	....	....	....	....	....	150	G1	'94	106⅞	91	91¼	6.85	6.85
New York Times	***54c***	***6.05***	***9.08***	***11.02***		***Dc***	***43.58***	***529.2***	***851.2***	***9-26-99***	***598.0***		***2298***	***40.0***						
Deb 8¼s 2025	Ms15	**A+**			X	R	103.76	(3-15-05)	....	....	....	....	150	C5	'95	113¼	101⅝	101⅝	8.12	8.12
Nts 7⅝s 2005	Ms15	**A+**			X	R	NC	....	....	....	....	....	250	C5	'95	111⅜	102⅛	102⅛	7.47	7.47
M-T Nts 2003	[6]fa15	**A+**			X	BE	[7]100	(9-8-01)	....	....	....	....	49.5	C1	'98	98⅜	93	93	....	....

Uniform Footnote Explanations-See Page 260. Other: [1] (HRO)On Chge of Ctrl at prices,as defined. [2] See Excel Realty Trust,New Plan Rlty Tr. [3] Fiscal Jul'98 & prior. [4] Now Energy East. [5] Subsid of NYNEX Corp. [6] Due 10-8-03. [7] On any Mar or Sep 8.

Title-Industry Code & Co. Finances (In Italics) / Individual Issue Statistics (Exchange)	Ind / Interest Dates	Fixed Charge Coverage 1996 / S&P Rating	1997 / Date of Last Rating Change	1998 / Prior Rating	Eligible	Year End / Bond Form	Cash & Equiv. (Million $) / Regular Price	Curr. Assets (Million $) / Regular (Begins) Thru	Curr. Liab. (Million $) / Sinking Fund Price	Balance Sheet Date / Sinking Fund (Begins) Thru	L. Term Debt (Mil $) / Refund/Other Restriction Price	Refund/Other Restriction (Begins) Thru	Capitalization (Mil $) / Outst'g (Mil $)	Total Debt % Capital / Underwriting Firm	Underwriting Year	Price Range 1999 High	Price Range 1999 Low	Mo. End Price Sale(s) or Bid	Curr. Yield	Yield to Mat.
[1]Newell Co[2]	*34*	*8.37*	*7.44*	*9.81*		*Dc*	*34.00*	*2539*	*1415*	*9-30-99*	*1362*		*4640*	*31.1*						
M-T Nts 'A' 5.70s 2003	[3]jj	A			X	BE	NC	....	....	....	....	....	100	M7	'98	100⅝	95⅜	95⅜	5.98	5.98
Newfield Exploration	*49a*	*n/a*	*21.40*	*2.74*		*Dc*	*30.40*	*85.50*	*55.70*	*9-30-99*	*125.0*		*624.0*	*20.0*						
Sr Nts 'B' 7.45s 2007	aO15	BB			Y	BE	[4]Z100	....	....	....	....	....	125	Exch.	'97	98⅜	91½	91½	8.14	8.14
Newmont Mining[5]	*45e*	*1.48*	*2.71*	*2.51*		*Dc*	*31.43*	*490.9*	*193.0*	*9-30-99*	*1073*		*2827*	*44.9*						
Nts 8⅝s 2002	Ao	BBB	2/98	BBB+	X	R	NC	....	....	....	....	....	150	L1	'92	107⅞	102½	102½	8.41	8.41
Newpark Resources	*49e*	*9.15*	*15.19*	*d0.11*		*Dc*	*2.95*	*110.6*	*41.22*	*9-30-99*	*207.0*		*477.0*	*39.0*						
• Sr Sub Nts[6] 8⅝s 2007	jD15	B+			Y	BE	104.313	(12-15-02)	....	....	[7]Z108.625	12-1-00	125	Exch.	'97	No Sale		85	10.15	10.14
NEXTEL Communic'ns[8]	*67*	*d2.79*	*d2.21*	*d1.61*		*Dc*	*1379*	*2069*	*1542*	*9-30-99*	*8991*		*10682*	*83.3*						
Sr[9]Red[6]Disc Nts 11½s 2003	mS	B	12/99	B–	Y	R	103.40	8-31-00	....	....	....	....	[10]526	M2	'93	104	100	103	11.17	11.16
Sr Red[11]Disc Nts[12] 9¾s 2004	fA15	B	12/99	B–	Y	R	104.875	2-14-00	....	....	....	....	[10]1126	M2	'94	104¼	97	103	9.47	9.46
Sr Disc[13]Nts[11] 10.65s 2007	mS15	B	12/99	B–	Y	BE	105.325	(9-15-02)	....	....	[14]Z110.65	9-15-00	[10]840	Exch.	'98	80½	63¾	74½	14.30	14.29
Sr Disc[11]Nts[15] 9¾s 2007	aO31	B	12/99	B–	Y	BE	104.875	(10-31-02)	....	....	[16]Z109.75	10-31-00	[10]1129	Exch.	'98	76¾	60½	71½	....	Flat
Sr Disc[17]Nts 9.95s 2008	Fa15	B	12/99	B–	Y	BE	104.975	(2-15-03)	....	....	[18]Z109.95	2-15-01	[10]1627	Exch.	'98	76	59¼	70	14.21	14.21
Nextel Partners	*67g*	*n/a*	*n/a*	*n/a*		*Dc*	*407.0*	*593.0*	*25.50*	*9-30-99*	*770.0*		*909.0*	*84.7*						
Sr[19]Disc Nts[6] 14s 2009	Fa	CCC+			Y	BE	107	(2-1-04)	....	....	[20]Z114	2-1-02	[10]800	Exch.	'99	67	50½	67	20.90	20.87
NEXTLINK Communications	*67f*	*n/a*	*n/a*	*d0.93*		*Dc*	*1644*	*1738*	*202.0*	*9-30-99*	*3057*		*3359*	*90.5*						
Sr Nts[6] 12½s 2006	Ao15	B			Y	BE	106.25	(4-15-01)	....	....	....	....	350	Exch.	'96	111⅞	103	107¾	11.60	11.60
Sr Nts[6] 9s 2008	Ms15	B			Y	BE	104.50	(3-15-03)	....	....	[21]Z109	3-15-01	335	Exch.	'98	101	90¾	94	9.57	9.57
Sr Nts[6] 9⅝s 2007	aO	B			Y	BE	104.813	(10-1-02)	....	....	[22]109.625	10-1-00	400	S1	'97	103	94	97½	9.87	9.87
Sr[6]Nts 10¾s 2009	Jd	B			Y	BE	105.375	(6-1-04)	....	....	[23]Z110.75	6-1-02	675	S4	'99	104½	98¾	102¾	10.46	10.46
Sr Disc[24]Nts[6] 12¼s 2009	Jd	B			Y	BE	106.125	(6-1-04)	....	....	[25]Z112.25	6-1-02	589	S4	'99	62¾	55⅛	61½	....	Flat
NGC Corp	*73e*	*Now Dynegy Inc,see*																		
Sr Deb 7⅛s 2018	Mn15	BBB+			X	BE	[26]Z100	....	....	....	....	....	175	S4	'98	98⅛	87⅝	87¾	8.12	8.12
Sr Deb 7⅝s 2026	aO15	BBB+			X	BE	[27]Z100	....	....	....	....	....	175	L3	'96	102¼	89¾	89⅞	8.48	8.48
Sr Nts 6¾s 2005	jD15	BBB+	9/96	BBB–	X	BE	NC	....	....	....	....	....	150	L3	'95	103¼	94⅝	94⅝	7.13	7.13
Niagara Mohawk Power[28]	*75*	*1.97*	*1.44*	*1.14*		*Dc*	*102.0*	*787.0*	*780.0*	*9-30-99*	*5383*		*9131*	*62.0*						
1st 9½s 2000	Jd	BBB+	6/99	BBB	X	R	NC	....	....	....	....	....	150	M2	'90	104⅞	101¼	101¼	9.38	9.38
1st 6⅞s 2001	Ms	BBB+	6/99	BBB	X	R	NC	....	....	....	....	....	210	M2	'94	102⅜	99⅝	99⅝	6.90	6.90
1st 9¼s 2001	aO	BBB+	6/99	BBB	X	R	NC	....	....	....	....	....	100	M2	'89	108½	102⅞	102⅞	8.99	8.99
1st 5⅞s 2002	mS	BBB+	6/99	BBB	X	R	NC	....	....	....	....	....	230	M2	'93	100⅜	96½	96½	6.09	6.09
1st 6⅞s 2003	Ao	BBB+	6/99	BBB	X	R	NC	....	....	....	....	....	85.0	G1	'93	104⅜	98⅜	98½	6.98	6.98
1st 7⅜s 2003	fA	BBB+	6/99	BBB	X	R	NC	....	....	....	....	....	220	M2	'92	105⅞	99⅝	99¾	7.39	7.39
1st 8s 2004	Jd	BBB+	6/99	BBB	X	R	NC	....	....	....	....	....	300	M2	'92	110¾	101¼	101¼	7.90	7.90
1st 6⅝s 2005	jJ	BBB+	6/99	BBB	X	R	NC	....	....	....	....	....	110	M2	'93	104⅜	95¼	95¼	6.96	6.95
1st 9¾s 2005	mN	BBB+	6/99	BBB	X	R	NC	....	....	....	....	....	150	M2	'90	120⅝	109	109	8.94	8.94
1st 7¾s 2006	Mn15	BBB+	6/99	BBB	X	R	NC	....	....	....	....	....	275	P1	'95	110⅝	99	99	7.83	7.83
1st 8¾s 2022	Ao	BBB+	6/99	BBB	X	R	104	(4-1-02)	□100	(4-1-02)	....	....	150	M2	'92	112½	99⅞	100	8.75	8.75
1st 8½s 2023	jJ	BBB+	6/99	BBB	X	R	103.894	(7-2-03)	□100	(7-2-02)	....	....	165	G1	'92	111⅛	96⅞	96⅞	8.77	8.77
1st 7⅞s 2024	Ao	BBB+	6/99	BBB	X	R	102.999	(4-1-03)	□100	....	....	....	210	G1	'93	105⅜	92⅛	92¼	8.54	8.54
Sr Nts[6] 'B' 7s 2000	aO	BBB–	6/99	BB+	X	BE	[29]Z100	....	....	....	Z100	12-31-00	450	D6	'98	101⅜	100	100⅛	6.99	6.99
Sr Nts[6] 'C' 7⅛s 2001	jJ	BBB–	6/99	BB+	X	BE	[29]Z100	....	....	....	Z100	12-31-00	400	D6	'98	102	99¾	99¾	7.14	7.14
Sr Nts 'D' 7¼s 2002	aO	BBB–	6/99	BB+	X	BE	[29]Z100	....	....	....	Z100	12-31-00	400	D6	'98	102⅞	99⅜	99⅝	7.28	7.28
Sr Nts[6] 'E' 7⅜s 2003	jJ	BBB–	6/99	BB+	X	BE	[29]Z100	....	....	....	Z100	12-31-00	400	D6	'98	103⅝	99⅛	99⅝	7.40	7.40
Sr Nts[6] 'F' 7⅝s 2005	aO	BBB–	6/99	BB+	X	BE	[29]Z100	....	....	....	Z100	12-31-00	400	D6	'98	105⅝	98⅞	100⅛	7.62	7.62

Uniform Footnote Explanations-See Page 260. Other: [1] See Rubbermaid, Inc. [2] Now Newell Rubbermaid. [3] Due 9-22-03. [4] Plus make-Whole Amt. [5] See Santa Fe Pacific Gold. [6] (HRO)On Chge of Ctrl at 101. [7] Max $44M red w/proceeds of Pub Eq Off'g. [8] See Cencall Communications,McCaw Int'l Ltd. [9] Int accr at 11.50% fr 9-1-98. [10] Incl disc. [11] (HRO)On Chge of Ctrl at 101(Accreted Val). [12] Int accr at 9.75% fr 2-15-99. [13] Int accrues at 10.65% fr 9-15-02. [14] Accreted Val:Max $280M red w/proceeds Pub Eq Off'g. [15] Int accrues at 9.75% fr 10-31-02. [16] Accreted Val:Max $376M red w/proceeds of Pub Eq Off'g. [17] (GRO)On Chge of Ctrl at 101(Accreted Val). [18] Accr Val: Max $569M red/wproceeds of Pub Eq Off'g. [19] Int accrues at 14% fr 2-1-04. [20] Accreted:Max $280M red w/proceeds Pub Eq Off'g. [21] Max $112M red w/proceeds of Pub Eq Off'g. [22] Max $133M red w/proceeds of Com Sales. [23] Max $225M red w/proceeds of Equity Off'g. [24] Int accrues at 12.25% fr 6-1-04. [25] Max $196M red w/proceeds of Equity Off'g. [26] Red at greater of 100 or amt based on formula. [27] Greater of 100 or amt based on formula. [28] Subsid of Niagara Mohawk Holdings. [29] Plus Make-Whole Premium.

Title-Industry Code & Co. Finances (In Italics) / Exchange ↓ Individual Issue Statistics	Ind / Interest Dates	Fixed Charge Coverage 1996 / S&P Rating	1997 / Date of Last Rating Change	1998 / Prior Rating	Eligible ↓	Year End / Bond Form	Million $ Cash & Equiv. / Redemption Provisions: Regular Price	Curr. Assets / Regular (Begins) Thru	Curr. Liab. / Sinking Fund Price	Balance Sheet Date / Sinking Fund (Begins) Thru	L. Term Debt (Mil $) / Refund/Other Restriction Price	Refund/Other Restriction (Begins) Thru	Capital-ization (Mil $) / Outst'g (Mil $)	Total Debt % Capital / Underwriting Firm	Underwriting Year	Price Range 1999 High	Price Range 1999 Low	Mo. End Price Sale(s) or Bid	Curr. Yield	Yield to Mat.
***Niagara Mohawk Power** (Cont.)*																				
Sr Nts[1] 'G' 7¾s 2008	aO	**BBB−**	6/99	BB+	X	BE	[2]Z100	....	....	....	Z100	12-31-00	600	D6	'98	110¼	99¾	99⅞	7.76	7.76
Sr[3]Disc Nts[4] 8½s 2010	jJ	**BBB−**	6/99	BB+	X	BE	[5]Z100	....	....	....	....	....	[6]500	D6	'98	78½	72½	75½	11.26	11.25
***Nielsen Media Research**[7]*	*63*	*n/a*	*n/a*	*12.55*		*Dc*	*18.00*	*77.30*	*62.90*	*9-30-99*	*200.0*		*115.0*	*174.0*						
Nts 7.60s 2009	Jd15	**NR**	11/99	BBB		BE	[8]Z100	....	....	....	....	....	150	M7	'99	103¾	97¼	97¼	7.81	7.81
Nike Inc	*39a*	*△26.92*	*△14.05*	*△17.93*		*My*	*226.0*	*3457*	*1808*	*8-31-99*	*462.0*		*4355*	*23.0*						
M-T Nts 6.51s 2000	[9]jd	**A**	4/99	A+	X	BE	NC	....	....	....	....	....	50.0	M2	'97	101⅛	99⅞	100	6.51	6.51
M-T Nts 6.69s 2002	[10]jd	**A**	4/99	A+	X	BE	NC	....	....	....	....	....	50.0	M2	'97	103	98⅝	98⅝	6.78	6.78
Nts 6⅜s 2003	jD	**A**	4/99	A+	X	BE	[11]Z100	....	....	....	....	....	200	G1	'96	102⅜	96⅜	96⅜	6.61	6.61
*[12]**Nine West Group***	*39a*	*n/a*	*n/a*	*n/a*		*Dc*	*36.50*	*1361*	*893.0*	*10-3-99*	*839.0*		*2483*	*51.2*						
Sr Nts[1]'B' 8⅜s 2005	fA15	**BBB−**	6/99	BB−	X	BE	NC	....	....	....	....	....	131	Exch.	'98	106	95	98⅞	8.47	8.47
NIPSCO Capital Markets	*25*	***Subsid of NiSource Inc***																		
Sr Nts[13] 6.78s 2027	jD	**A−**			X	BE	NC	....	....	....	....	....	75.0	G1	'97	110¾	91	93⅜	7.26	7.26
NL Industries	*14*	*1.22*	*0.54*	*2.85*		*Dc*	*181.0*	*542.8*	*312.9*	*9-30-99*	*244.0*		*615.0*	*55.4*						
Sr Sec Nts[1] 11¾s 2003	aO15	**B**			Y	R	101.50	(10-15-00)	....	....	....	....	250	S1	'93	107½	103	103½	11.35	11.35
Noble Affiliates	*49a*	*4.49*	*3.86*	*1.00*		*Dc*	*65.54*	*193.5*	*135.3*	*9-30-99*	*670.0*		*1358*	*53.0*						
Deb 7¼s 2097	fA	**BBB**			X	BE	[11]Z100	....	....	....	....	....	100	M6	'97	94⅝	84	84	8.63	8.63
Nts 7¼s 2023	aO15	**BBB**			X	R	NC	....	....	....	....	....	100	K2	'93	98⅛	89¼	90	8.06	8.06
Sr Nts 8s 2027	Ao	**BBB**			X	BE	NC	....	....	....	....	....	250	M6	'97	107⅛	96⅝	97⅜	8.22	8.22
Noble Drilling Corp	*49e*	*6.44*	*15.09*	*45.57*		*Dc*	*153.0*	*329.2*	*249.1*	*9-30-99*	*748.0*		*2169*	*37.3*						
Sr Nts 6.95s 2009	Ms15	**A−**			X	BE	[14]Z100	....	....	....	....	....	150	M2	'99	103½	94⅝	95¼	7.30	7.30
Sr Nts 7½s 2019	Ms15	**A−**			X	BE	[14]Z100	....	....	....	....	....	250	M2	'99	104	94¾	95½	7.85	7.85
***NorAm Energy Corp**[15]*	*73*	***Merged into Houston Indus,see***																		
Deb 6½s 2008	Fa	**BBB**			X	BE	NC	....	....	....	....	....	300	M2	'98	104¾	92	92	7.07	7.06
Nts 7½s 2000	fA	**BBB**	10/96	BBB−	X	BE	NC	....	....	....	....	....	200	M2	'95	103¼	100⅜	100⅜	7.47	7.47
Nordstrom Credit	*25d*	*2.21*	*2.18*	*2.51*		*Ja*				*7-31-99*	*430.0*		*571.0*	*75.3*						
Nts 6.70s 2005	jJ	**A**	5/98	A+	X	BE	NC	....	....	....	....	....	100	G1	'95	105⅝	97⅛	97⅛	6.90	6.90
Nordstrom, Inc.	*59f*	*6.20*	*7.82*	*7.12*		*Ja*	*40.00*	*1732*	*984.1*	*10-31-99*	*747.0*		*2154*	*40.1*						
Sr Deb 6.95s 2028	Ms15	**A**	5/98	A+	X	BE	NC	....	....	....	....	....	300	G1	'98	107⅛	87¾	87⅞	7.91	7.91
Sr Nts 5⅝s 2009	Jj15	**A**			X	BE	NC	....	....	....	....	....	250	G1	'99	99⅝	86¾	86¾	6.48	6.48
***Norfolk Southern**[16]*	*55*	*8.45*	*3.34*	*2.17*		*Dc*	*56.00*	*1316*	*2054*	*9-30-99*	*7329*		*13960*	*57.2*						
Nts 6.70s 2000	Mn	**BBB+**			X	BE	NC	....	....	....	....	....	400	M2	'97	101⅝	100	100⅛	6.69	6.69
Nts 6⅞s 2001	Mn	**BBB+**			X	BE	NC	....	....	....	....	....	200	M2	'97	103¼	99⅝	99⅝	6.90	6.90
Nts 6.95s 2002	Mn	**BBB+**			X	BE	NC	....	....	....	....	....	500	M2	'97	104⅜	99¼	99¼	7.00	7.00
Nts 7⅞s 2004	Fa15	**BBB+**	5/97	AA−	X	R	NC	....	....	....	....	....	250	M5	'92	110¼	101⅜	101⅜	7.77	7.77
Nts 7.35s 2007	Mn15	**BBB+**			X	BE	NC	....	....	....	....	....	750	M2	'97	110⅝	97¾	97¾	7.52	7.52
Sr Nts[17] 6.20s 2009	Ao15	**BBB+**			X	BE	[8]Z100	....	....	....	....	....	400	M5	'99	99⅝	90	90	6.89	6.89
Nts 7.70s 2017	Mn15	**BBB+**			X	BE	[11]Z100	....	....	....	....	....	550	M2	'97	114¾	97½	97⅝	7.89	7.89
Nts 9s 2021	Ms	**BBB+**	5/97	AA−	X	R	NC	....	....	....	....	....	250	G1	'91	130¾	106⅞	107⅛	8.40	8.40
Nts 7.80s 2027	Mn15	**BBB+**			X	BE	[18]Z100	....	....	....	....	....	800	M2	'97	118¼	97½	97⅝	7.99	7.99
Nts[19] 7.05s 2037	Mn	**BBB+**			X	BE	[11]Z100	(5-1-04)	....	....	....	....	750	M2	'97	106⅝	98⅜	98⅜	7.17	7.17
Nts[20] 7.90s 2097	Mn15	**BBB+**			X	BE	[11]Z100	....	....	....	....	....	350	M2	'97	118½	94½	95⅜	8.28	8.28
M-T Nts 'A' 7.40s 2006	mS15	**BBB+**	5/97	AA−	X	BE	NC	....	....	....	....	....	100	M2	'96	110¼	98	98	7.55	7.55
M-T Nts 'A' 7.22s 2006	mS15	**BBB+**	5/97	AA−	X	BE	NC	....	....	....	....	....	100	M5	'96	109⅛	97	97	7.44	7.44
Norfolk & Western Ry	*55*	***Subsid of Norfolk Southern, see***																		
• Sub Inc Deb 4.85s 2015	mN15	**NR**	2/96	AA−		CR	100.75	11-14-00	100.375	11-14-00	....	....	1.75	Exch.	'65	84	70¼	70½	6.88	6.88

Uniform Footnote Explanations-See Page 260. Other: [1] (HRO)On Chge of Ctrl at 101. [2] Plus Make-Whole Premium. [3] Int accrues at 8.5% fr 7-1-03. [4] (HRO)On Chge of Ctrl at 101(Accreted Amt). [5] Percent Accreted Amt:Plus Make-Whole Premium. [6] Incl disc. [7] Acq by VNU NV. [8] Red at greater of 100 or amt based on formula. [9] Due 6-16-00. [10] Due 6-17-02. [11] Greater of 100 or amt based on formula. [12] Acq by & data of Jones Apparel Group. [13] (HRO)On 12-1-07 at 100. [14] Plus Make-Whole Amt. [15] See Arkla Inc. [16] See Consol Rail, Norfolk&West'n Ry,So'n Ry. [17] Issued in min denom $100T. [18] Greater of 100 or amt based or formula. [19] (HRO)On 5-1-04 at 100. [20] Co may shorten mty for Tax Event.

Individual Issue Statistics / Exchange ↓	Interest Dates	S&P Rating	Date of Last Rating Change	Prior Rating	Eligible ↓	Bond Form	Redemption Provisions: Regular Price	Regular (Begins) Thru	Sinking Fund Price	Sinking Fund (Begins) Thru	Refund/Other Restriction Price	Refund/Other Restriction (Begins) Thru	Outst'g (Mil $)	Underwriting Firm	Underwriting Year	Price Range 1999 High	Price Range 1999 Low	Mo. End Price Sale(s) or Bid	Curr. Yield	Yield to Mat.
Title-Industry Code & Co. Finances (In Italics)	*Ind*	*Fixed Charge Coverage 1996*	*1997*	*1998*		*Year End*	*Million $ Cash & Equiv.*	*Curr. Assets*	*Curr. Liab.*	*Balance Sheet Date*	*L. Term Debt (Mil $)*		*Capital-ization (Mil $)*	*Total Debt % Capital*						
Nortek, Inc.	***42***	***2.17***	***1.85***	***1.66***		***Dc***	***97.00***	***713.0***	***381.0***	***10-2-99***	***1021***		***1264***	***80.9***						
Sr Nts 'B' 9¼s 2007	Ms15	B+			Y	BE	104.625	(3-15-02)	....	....	....	....	175	Exch.	'97	105⅛	96¾	97½	9.49	9.49
Sr Sub Nts[1] 9⅞s 2004	Ms	B–	10/96	CCC+	Y	R	104.214	2-29-00	....	....	....	....	190	B7	'94	104½	97½	98½	10.03	10.02
North Atlantic Energy[2]	***72a***	***n/a***	***n/a***	***n/a***		***Dc***		***72.00***	***93.20***	***9-30-99***	***335.0***		***578.0***	***70.6***						
1st 'A' 9.05s 2002	Jd	BB+	12/99	BB–	Y	R	[3]Z102.715	5-31-00	100	....	....	....	205	M6	'92	104⅞	99¾	99¾	9.07	9.07
North Shore Gas (Ill)[4]	***73b***	***5.64***	***5.74***	***3.53***		***Sp***	***15.40***	***33.90***	***33.40***	***6-30-99***	***69.70***		***170.0***	***41.0***						
1st[5]J 8s 2020	mN	AA–			X	R	104	10-31-00	▲100	....	....	....	24.9	J2	'90	104¼	101⅛	101¼	7.90	7.90
NorthEast Optic Network	***67b***	***n/a***	***n/a***	***d0.48***		***Dc***	***28.00***	***104.0***	***21.50***	***9-30-99***	***180.0***		***255.0***	***70.7***						
Sr Nts[1] 12.65s 2008	fA15	NR				BE	106.375	(8-15-03)	....	....	....	....	180	C6	'98	107	98	107	11.82	11.82
Northeast Utilities	***72b***	***1.30***	***0.49***	***0.93***		***Dc***	***402.0***	***1177***	***1444***	***9-30-99***	***2947***		***6163***	***61.9***						
[6]Amortizing[7]Nts'A'[8] 8.58s 2006	jD	BB+	12/99	BB–	Y	BE	NC	....	....	....	....	....	124	M6	'91	100¾	96⅞	96⅞	8.86	....
Northern Illinois[9]Gas[10]	***73b***	***4.74***	***4.58***	***4.81***		***Dc***	***73.50***	***273.0***	***389.0***	***6-30-99***	***471.0***		***1209***	***43.2***						
1st 6.45s 2001	fA	AA			X	R	100	(8-1-00)	....	....	....	....	75.0	P1	'96	101½	99	99	6.52	6.51
1st 5¾s 2003	Jd	AA			X	BE	NC	....	....	....	....	....	50.0	A3	'98	101⅞	96¼	96¼	5.97	5.97
1st 8⅞s 2021	fA15	AA			X	R	105.11	8-14-00	....	....	....	....	50.0	M6	'91	105¾	105¼	105¼	8.43	8.43
1st 7.26s 2025	aO15	AA			X	R	105.09	(10-15-00)	....	....	....	....	50.0	M6	'95	103½	90	90⅛	8.06	8.06
1st 7⅜s 2027	aO15	AA			X	R	105.16	(10-15-02)	....	....	....	....	50.0	M2	'97	104½	89⅝	89¾	8.22	8.22
1st 6.58s 2028	Fa15	AA			X	R	NC	....	....	....	....	....	50.0	S4	'98	104	85	85⅛	7.73	7.73
Northern Ind Pub Svc[11]	***75***	***4.63***	***4.70***	***3.81***		***Dc***	***7.81***	***309.0***	***649.0***	***9-30-99***	***923.0***		***2323***	***50.3***						
1st T 7½s 2002	Ao	A+	10/97	A	X	R	100.61	3-31-00	100.25	9-30-00	....	....	38.5	F1	'72	100⅞	99⅝	99⅝	7.53	7.53
M-T Nts 'E' 7.69s 2027	[12]ms15	A			X	BE	NC	....	....	....	....	....	53.0	M6	'97	111	92⅜	92½	8.31	8.31
Northern Pac.Ry	***55***	***Merged into Burlington No'n RR see***																		
• Gen[13]Ln Mtg[14] 3s 2047	[15]Qfeb	A	12/98	A–	X	CR	NC	....	....	....	....	....	[16]34.5		1896	79	77¼	70½	4.26	4.26
• Gen Ln[14]Mtg-Stpd 3s 2047	[15]Qfeb	A	12/98	A–	X	CR	NC	....	....	....	....	....	[17]35.0		1896	47	37	s37	8.11	8.11
Northern Sts Pwr (Minn)	***75***	***3.82***	***2.80***	***2.72***		***Dc***	***86.70***	***892.0***	***1919***	***9-30-99***	***2593***		***6652***	***57.1***						
1st 5¾s 2000	jD	AA	10/97	AA–	X	R	NC	....	....	....	....	....	100	K2	'93	101⅛	99⅛	99¼	5.79	5.79
1st 7⅞s 2001	aO	AA	10/97	AA–	X	BE	NC	....	....	....	....	....	150	K2	'94	106⅝	101⅝	101⅝	7.75	7.75
1st 5⅞s 2003	Ms	AA			X	BE	NC	....	....	....	....	....	100	S4	'98	102⅜	97⅛	97⅛	6.05	6.05
1st 6⅜s 2003	Ao	AA	10/97	AA–	X	R	NC	....	....	....	....	....	80.0	K2	'93	104⅛	98¼	98¼	6.49	6.49
1st 6⅛s 2005	jD	AA	10/97	AA–	X	R	NC	....	....	....	....	....	70.0	K2	'93	104⅜	94⅛	94⅛	6.51	6.51
1st 7⅛s 2025	jJ	AA	10/97	AA–	X	BE	NC	....	....	....	....	....	250	P1	'95	110⅝	92⅜	92½	7.70	7.70
1st 6½s 2028	Ms	AA			X	BE	NC	....	....	....	....	....	150	S4	'98	105⅝	85⅛	85¼	7.62	7.62
Sr Nts 6⅞s 2009	fA	A+			X	BE	[18]Z100	....	....	....	....	....	250	S4	'99	99⅛	96⅛	96⅛	7.15	7.15
North'n Sts Pwr (Wisc)[19]	***75***	***4.24***	***4.38***	***3.84***		***Dc***	***0.15***	***54.30***	***87.10***	***6-30-99***	***232.0***		***624.0***	***43.6***						
1st 5¾s 2003	a0	AA			X	BE	NC	....	....	....	....	....	40.0	K2	'93	102⅜	95¾	95¾	6.01	6.01
1st 7¼s 2023	Ms	AA			X	R	102.84	(3-1-03)	100	....	....	....	110	G1	'93	105⅜	90⅞	90⅞	7.98	7.98
1st 7⅜s 2026	jD	AA			X	BE	103.481	(12-1-06)	....	....	....	....	65.0	B7	'96	108¼	91	91⅛	8.09	8.09
Northern Trust	***10***	***2.23***	***2.27***	***2.22***		***Dc***				***9-30-99***	***1313***		***3436***	***38.2***						
Sub Nts 6½s 2003	Mn	A+			X	BE	NC	....	....	....	....	....	100	M2	'93	102⅞	97⅞	97⅞	6.64	6.64
Sub Nts[20] 6.70s 2005	mS15	A+			Y	BE	NC	....	....	....	....	....	100	G1	'95	104¾	96⅝	96⅝	6.93	6.93
Sub Nts[20] 7.30s 2006	mS15	A+			X	BE	NC	....	....	....	....	....	100	M5	'96	108⅞	98¾	98¾	7.39	7.39
Sub Nts[20] 6¼s 2008	Jd2	A+			X	BE	NC	....	....	....	....	....	100	M2	'98	102½	92⅜	92⅜	6.77	6.77
Northland Cable TV[21]	***12a***	***0.49***	***1.54***	***0.56***		***Dc***	***3.75***	***6.74***	***13.60***	***9-30-99***	***173.0***		***137.0***	***128.0***						
Sr Sub Nts[1] 10¼s 2007	mN15	B–			Y	BE	105.125	(11-15-02)	....	....	Z110.25	11-15-00	100	Exch.	'98	108	99	100¼	10.22	10.22
Northrop Grumman	***2a***	***2.42***	***3.53***	***2.34***		***Dc***	***37.00***	***2876***	***2443***	***9-30-99***	***2300***		***6171***	***50.9***						
Deb 7¾s 2016	Ms	BBB–	7/98	BBB+	X	BE	NC	....	....	....	....	....	300	Exch.	'96	109	93	94⅜	8.21	8.21

Uniform Footnote Explanations-See Page 260. Other: [1] (HRO)On Chge of Ctrl at 101. [2] Subsid of Northeast Utilities. [3] Red w/proceeds of property sales. [4] Subsid of Peoples Energy. [5] (HRO)At 100, ltd as defined. [6] Princ pyts due ea Dec 1. [7] Issued in min denom $100T. [8] Prin amt $708.57 at 12-1-99. [9] Subsid of Nicor, Inc. [10] D/B/A Nicor Gas. [11] Subsid of NIPSCO Industries. [12] Due 6-7-27. [13] Unstpd. [14] Red thru purch fund at 100. [15] Due 1-1-47. [16] Incl amt of stpd issue. [17] Incl amt of unstpd issue. [18] Red at greater of 100 or amt based on formula. [19] Contr by No'n Sts Pwr (Minn). [20] Issued in min denom $250T. [21] Subsid of Northland Telecommunications.

Title-Industry Code & Co. Finances (In Italics) / Individual Issue Statistics, Exchange	Ind / Interest Dates	Fixed Charge Coverage 1996 / S&P Rating	1997 / Date of Last Rating Change	1998 / Prior Rating	Eligible	Year End / Bond Form	Million $ Cash & Equiv. / Redemption Provisions Regular Price	Curr. Assets / Regular (Begins) Thru	Curr. Liab. / Sinking Fund Price	Balance Sheet Date / Sinking Fund (Begins) Thru	L. Term Debt (Mil $) / Refund/Other Restriction Price	Refund/Other Restriction (Begins) Thru	Capital-ization (Mil $) / Outst'g (Mil $)	Total Debt % Capital / Underwriting Firm	Underwriting Year	Price Range 1999 High	Price Range 1999 Low	Mo. End Price Sale(s) or Bid	Curr. Yield	Yield to Mat.
***Northrop Grumman** (Cont.)*																				
Deb 9⅜s 2024	aO15	**BBB−**	7/98	BBB+	X	BE	104.363	(10-15-04)	....	....	....	....	250	C5	'94	116½	104¼	105½	8.89	8.89
Deb 7⅞s 2026	Ms	**BBB−**	7/98	BBB+	X	BE	NC	....	....	....	....	....	300	Exch.	'96	112	92¾	93⅞	8.39	8.39
Nts 8⅝s 2004	aO15	**BBB−**	7/98	BBB+	X	BE	NC	....	....	....	....	....	350	C5	'94	112½	102⅞	103	8.37	8.37
Nts 7s 2006	Ms	**BBB−**	7/98	BBB+	X	BE	NC	....	....	....	....	....	400	Exch.	'96	105⅛	94½	94½	7.41	7.41
Northwest Airlines	***4***	***n/a***	***4.98***	***d0.31***		***Dc***	***757.0***	***2284***	***3822***	***9-30-99***	***4728***		***5506***	***104.0***						
Nts 8⅜s 2004	Ms15	**BB**	1/98	BB−	Y	BE	[1]Z100	....	....	....	....	....	150	G1	'97	101¾	93¾	93¾	8.93	8.93
Nts 8.52s 2004	Ao7	**BB**			Y	BE	[2]Z100	....	....	....	....	....	200	C6	'99	99⅜	93	93	9.16	9.16
Nts 8.70s 2007	Ms15	**BB**	1/98	BB−	Y	BE	[1]Z100	....	....	....	....	....	100	G1	'97	102⅞	91	91	9.56	9.56
Northwest Natural Gas	***73b***	***3.67***	***3.03***	***2.19***		***Dc***	***18.00***	***122.0***	***197.0***	***9-30-99***	***386.0***		***835.0***	***44.0***						
1st 9¾s 2015	jJ	**A**			X	BE	104.63	(7-1-00)	....	....	....	....	50.0	P3	'90	109⅛	106⅛	106⅛	9.19	9.18
Sec M-T Nts A 8.05s 2002	[3]jd	**A**			X	BE	NC	....	....	....	....	....	10.0	M2	'92	107⅜	101⅝	101⅝	7.92	7.92
Sec M-T Nts A 9.05s 2021	[4]jd	**A**			X	BE	NC	....	....	....	....	....	10.0	M2	'91	129⅞	109½	109⅝	8.26	8.25
Sec M-T Nts B 5.96s 2000	[5]jd	**A**			X	BE	NC	....	....	....	....	....	5.00	M2	'93	100⅞	99	99	6.02	6.02
Sec M-T Nts B 5.98s 2000	[5]jd	**A**			X	BE	NC	....	....	....	....	....	5.00	M2	'93	101	99	99	6.04	6.04
Sec M-T Nts B 6.40s 2003	[6]jd	**A**			X	BE	NC	....	....	....	....	....	20.0	M2	'93	103	96⅞	96⅞	6.61	6.61
Sec M-T Nts B 6.34s 2005	[7]jd	**A**			X	BE	NC	....	....	....	....	....	5.00	M2	'93	103⅜	94½	94½	6.71	6.71
Sec M-T Nts B 6.38s 2005	[8]jd	**A**			X	BE	NC	....	....	....	....	....	5.00	M2	'93	103½	94⅝	94⅝	6.74	6.74
Sec M-T Nts B 6.45s 2005	[9]jd	**A**			X	BE	NC	....	....	....	....	....	5.00	M2	'93	103⅞	94⅞	94⅛	6.80	6.80
Sec M-T Nts B 6½s 2008	[10]jd	**A**			X	BE	NC	....	....	....	....	....	5.00	M2	'93	105⅛	92¾	92¾	7.01	7.01
Sec M-T Nts B 8.26s 2014	[11]jd	**A**			X	BE	NC	....	....	....	....	....	10.0		'94	119⅞	103⅝	103⅝	7.97	7.97
Sec M-T Nts B 7s 2017	[12]jd	**A**			X	BE	NC	....	....	....	....	....	40.0	M2	'97	105⅜	89⅞	89⅞	7.79	7.79
Sec M-T Nts B 8.31s 2019	[13]jd	**A**			X	BE	[2]Z100	....	....	....	....	....	10.0		'94	120½	102	102⅛	8.14	8.14
Sec M-T Nts B 7.63s 2019	[14]jd	**A**			X	BE	NC	....	....	....	....	....	20.0	M2	'99	100	95¼	95⅜	8.00	8.00
Sec M-T Nts B 7½s 2023	[15]jd	**A**			X	BE	103.75	(7-1-03)	....	....	....	....	4.00	M2	'93	111¼	93¼	93¼	8.04	8.04
Sec M-T Nts B 7.52s 2023	[15]jd	**A**			X	BE	103.76	(7-1-03)	....	....	....	....	11.0	M2	'93	111½	93⅜	93½	8.04	8.04
Sec M-T Nts B 7¼s 2023	[16]jd	**A**			X	BE	103.65	(8-18-03)	....	....	....	....	20.0	M2	'93	104⅜	90¼	90⅜	8.02	8.02
Unsec M-T Nts A 8.47s 2001	[17]jd	**A−**			X	BE	NC	....	....	....	....	....	5.00	M2	'91	107¼	102	102	8.30	8.30
Northwest Pipeline[18]	***73a***	***3.30***	***3.16***	***3.84***		***Dc***	***0.37***	***79.10***	***88.40***	***6-30-99***	***371.0***		***827.0***	***45.0***						
Deb 9s 2022	fA	**BBB**	2/95	BBB+	X	R	104.24	(8-1-02)	100	(8-1-03)	....	....	33.0	F1	'92	111⅛	105⅛	105⅛	8.56	8.56
Deb 7⅛s 2025	jD	**BBB**			X	BE	NC	....	....	....	....	....	85.0	M2	'95	102⅜	86¼	86⅜	8.25	8.25
Northwestern Bell Tel	***67a***	***Merged into U S WEST Commun***																		
Deb 6s 2001	mS	**A+**	5/98	A	X	R	100	....	....	....	....	....	50.0	B8	'66	100⅝	98⅝	98⅝	6.08	6.08
Deb 4⅜s 2003	Ms	**A+**	5/98	A	X	CR	100	....	....	....	....	....	[19]40.0	F1	'63	95¼	90¾	92½	4.73	4.73
Deb 6¼s 2007	Jj	**A+**	5/98	A	X	R	100.31	12-31-00	....	....	....	....	89.7	H1	'68	100½	92¾	92¾	6.74	6.74
Deb 7¾s 2030	Mn	**A+**	5/98	A	X	BE	NC	....	....	....	....	....	42.9	M6	'99	120⅜	96½	96⅝	8.02	8.02
Nts 9½s 2000	Mn	**A+**	5/98	A	X	BE	NC	....	....	....	....	....	75.0	M6	'90	105⅜	101	101	9.41	9.40
NorthWestern Corp[20]	***75***	***3.19***	***2.27***	***2.24***		***Dc***	***38.54***	***355.7***	***270.2***	***9-30-99***	***286.0***		***1431***	***45.6***						
Sr Deb 6.95s 2028	mN15	**A**			X	BE	[21]Z100	....	....	....	....	....	105	M7	'98	101⅛	83¾	83⅞	8.29	8.29
Northwestern Pub. Serv.	***75***	***Now NorthWestern Corp,see***																		
Mtg Bonds 7.10s 2005	fA	**A+**	12/96	A	X	BE	NC	....	....	....	....	....	60.0	M6	'95	108⅞	98⅜	98⅜	7.22	7.22
New Mtg 7s 2023	fA15	**A+**	12/96	A	X	BE	103.163	(8-15-03)	....	....	....	....	55.0	M6	'93	103¾	86¼	86⅜	8.10	8.10
Northwestern Steel & Wire	***66h***	***1.92***	***d3.91***	***5.21***		***Jl***	***10.36***	***107.6***	***56.67***	***10-31-99***	***116.0***		***173.0***	***67.1***						
Sr Nts[22] 9½s 2001	Jd15	**CC**	9/99	CCC+	Y	R	100	....	....	....	....	....	115	L3	'93	68	44	45	21.11	21.09
Norwest Corp[23]	***10***	***Now Wells Fargo & Co,see***																		
Sr Nts 6s 2000	Ms15	**A+**	11/98	AA−	X	R	NC	....	....	....	....	....	200	M2	'93	100⅝	99⅞	99⅞	6.01	6.01

Uniform Footnote Explanations-See Page 260. Other: [1] Plus Make Whole Amt. [2] Plus Make-Whole Amt. [3] Due 4-15-02. [4] Due 8-13-21. [5] Due 12-15-00. [6] Due 6-30-03. [7] Due 7-25-05. [8] Due 7-27-05. [9] Due 7-29-05. [10] Due 7-30-08. [11] Due 9-21-14. [12] Due 8-1-17. [13] Due 9-21-19. [14] Due 12-9-19. [15] Due 6-30-23. [16] Due 8-18-23. [17] Due 9-17-01. [18] Subsid of Northwest Energy Co. [19] Defeased, fds deposited w/trustee. [20] Was Northwestern Public Serv,see. [21] Red at greater of 100 or amt based on formula. [22] (HRO)On Chge of Ctrl at 101. [23] Was Northwest Bancorp.

Title-Industry Code & Co. Finances (In Italics) / Ind	*Fixed Charge Coverage 1996*	*1997*	*1998*		*Year End*	*Cash & Equiv.*	*Million $ Curr. Assets*	*Curr. Liab.*	*Balance Sheet Date*	*L. Term Debt (Mil $)*		*Capital-ization (Mil $)*	*Total Debt % Capital*						
Individual Issue Statistics Exchange ↓ / Interest Dates	S&P Rating	Date of Last Rating Change	Prior Rating	Eligible ↓	Bond Form	Redemption Provisions: Regular Price	Regular (Begins) Thru	Sinking Fund Price	Sinking Fund (Begins) Thru	Refund/Other Restriction Price	Refund/Other Restriction (Begins) Thru	Outst'g (Mil $)	Underwriting Firm	Underwriting Year	Price Range 1999 High	Price Range 1999 Low	Mo. End Price Sale(s) or Bid	Curr. Yield	Yield to Mat.
***Norwest Corp** (Cont.)*																			
M-T Nts 'D' 8.15s 2001 .... mN	**A+**	11/98	AA–	X	BE	NC	....	....	....	....	....	100	M6	'94	106⅞	102⅛	102⅛	7.98	7.98
M-T Nts 'E' 7¾s 2002 .... Ms	**A+**	11/98	AA–	X	BE	NC	....	....	....	....	....	125	M5	'95	106⅜	101½	101½	7.64	7.63
M-T Nts 'F' 7⅛s 2000 .... Ao	**A+**	11/98	AA–	X	BE	NC	....	....	....	....	....	200	B7	'95	101⅞	100¼	100¼	7.11	7.11
M-T Nts 'F' 6¾s 2000 .... Mn12	**A+**	11/98	AA–	X	BE	NC	....	....	....	....	....	200	M2	'95	101⅝	100¼	100¼	6.73	6.73
M-T Nts 'F' 6.80s 2002 .... Mn15	**A+**	11/98	AA–	X	BE	NC	....	....	....	....	....	200	M6	'95	103¾	99⅝	99⅝	6.83	6.83
M-T Nts 'F' 7.65s 2005 .... Ms15	**A+**	11/98	AA–	X	BE	NC	....	....	....	....	....	100	M6	'95	110	101½	101½	7.54	7.54
M-T Nts 'F' 6½s 2005 .... Jd	**A+**	11/98	AA–	X	BE	NC	....	....	....	....	....	200	S7	'95	104⅛	96¼	96⅜	6.74	6.74
M-T Nts 'G' 6⅛s 2000 .... aO15	**A+**	11/98	AA–	X	BE	NC	....	....	....	....	....	200	S1	'95	101⅛	99⅝	99⅝	6.15	6.15
M-T Nts 'G' 6⅜s 2002 .... mS15	**A+**	11/98	AA–	X	BE	NC	....	....	....	....	....	200	M6	'95	102½	98⅜	98⅜	6.48	6.48
M-T Nts 'G' 5¾s 2003 .... Fa	**A+**	11/98	AA–	X	BE	NC	....	....	....	....	....	200	U1	'96	100⅜	96⅜	96⅜	5.97	5.97
M-T Nts 'G' 6.20s 2005 .... jD	**A+**	11/98	AA–	X	BE	NC	....	....	....	....	....	200	M6	'95	102⅝	94	94½	6.56	6.56
M-T Nts 'G' 6⅞s 2006 .... fA8	**A+**	11/98	AA–	X	BE	NC	....	....	....	....	....	200		'96	106¾	96½	97⅜	7.06	7.06
M-T Nts 'H' 5⅝s 2001 .... Fa5	**A+**	11/98	AA–	X	BE	NC	....	....	....	....	....	200	L3	'96	100⅜	98¾	98⅞	5.69	5.69
M-T Nts 'H' 6¾s 2007 .... Jd15	**A+**	11/98	AA–	X	BE	NC	....	....	....	....	....	200	U1	'97	106⅜	95⅞	96½	6.99	6.99
M-T Nts 'J' 6¾s 2027 .... jD15	**A+**	11/98	AA–	X	BE	NC	....	....	....	....	....	200	M5	'97	102⅞	86⅛	87⅝	7.70	7.70
M-T Nts 'J' 6.55s 2006 .... [1]jd2	**A+**	11/98	AA–	X	BE	NC	....	....	....	....	....	200	L3	'96	104⅞	94½	95⅝	6.85	6.85
Sub Deb 6.65s 2023 .... aO15	**A**	11/98	A+	X	BE	NC	....	....	....	....	....	200	M6	'93	99⅜	84⅝	87¼	7.62	7.62
Sub Nts 6⅝s 2003 .... Ms15	**A**	11/98	A+	X	R	NC	....	....	....	....	....	200	M2	'93	103½	98¼	98¼	6.74	6.74
***Norwest Fin'l** 25a*	*2.14*	*2.03*	*1.74*		*Dc*				*6-30-99*	*5645*		*10110*	*84.3*						
Sr Nts 7¼s 2000 .... Ms15	**A+**	11/98	AA–	X	R	NC	....	....	....	....	....	150	M2	'95	102	100⅛	100¼	7.23	7.23
Sr Nts 5⅛s 2000 .... Ao15	**A+**	11/98	AA–	X	R	NC	....	....	....	....	....	150	M2	'93	100	99½	99⅝	5.14	5.14
Sr Nts 6⅞s 2000 .... Jd15	**A+**	11/98	AA–	X	R	NC	....	....	....	....	....	150	M2	'94	102	100¼	100¼	6.86	6.86
Sr Nts 6.10s 2000 .... aO	**A+**	11/98	AA–	X	BE	NC	....	....	....	....	....	150		'97	101¼	99⅝	99⅝	6.12	6.12
Sr Nts 5½s 2001 .... Ms19	**A+**			X	R	NC	....	....	....	....	....	150	M2	'99	100⅜	98⅜	98⅜	5.59	5.59
Sr Nts 7¾s 2001 .... fA15	**A+**	11/98	AA–	X	R	NC	....	....	....	....	....	100	M2	'94	105½	101⅛	101⅛	7.66	7.66
Sr Nts 6⅜s 2001 .... mN15	**A+**	11/98	AA–	X	R	NC	....	....	....	....	....	150	M2	'96	102⅜	99	99	6.44	6.44
Sr Nts 7⅞s 2002 .... Fa15	**A+**	11/98	AA–	X	R	NC	....	....	....	....	....	150	M2	'95	106¾	101⅜	101⅜	7.77	7.77
Sr Nts 7.95s 2002 .... Mn15	**A+**	11/98	AA–	X	R	NC	....	....	....	....	....	100	M2	'92	107½	101⅝	101⅝	7.82	7.82
Sr Nts 6⅜s 2002 .... jJ16	**A+**			X	BE	NC	....	....	....	....	....	250	M2	'99	100⅛	98⅛	98⅛	6.50	6.50
Sr Nts 6⅜s 2002 .... mS15	**A+**	11/98	AA–	X	R	NC	....	....	....	....	....	200	M2	'97	102¾	98⅛	98⅛	6.50	6.50
Sr Nts 6¼s 2002 .... mN	**A+**	11/98	AA–	X	R	NC	....	....	....	....	....	200	M2	'95	102⅜	97⅝	97⅝	6.40	6.40
• Sr Nts 7s 2003 .... Jj15	**A+**	11/98	AA–	X	R	NC	....	....	....	....	....	150	M2	'93	102	98⅛	98⅜	7.12	7.11
Sr Nts 6⅛s 2003 .... fA	**A+**	11/98	AA–	X	R	NC	....	....	....	....	....	150	M2	'93	102¼	96⅜	96⅜	6.36	6.36
Sr Nts 5⅜s 2003 .... mS30	**A+**	11/98	AA–	X	R	NC	....	....	....	....	....	200	M2	'98	99⅜	94	94	5.72	5.72
Nts 6⅜s 2003 .... mN15	**A+**			X	R	NC	....	....	....	....	....	150	M2	'96	103⅜	97¼	97¼	6.56	6.55
Sr Nts 6s 2004 .... Fa	**A+**	11/98	AA–	X	R	NC	....	....	....	....	....	150	M2	'94	102⅛	95⅝	95⅝	6.27	6.27
Sr Nts 7.20s 2004 .... Ao	**A+**	11/98	AA–	X	R	NC	....	....	....	....	....	100	M2	'97	107⅛	99⅝	99⅝	7.23	7.23
Sr Nts 6⅝s 2004 .... jJ15	**A+**	11/98	AA–	X	R	NC	....	....	....	....	....	250	M2	'97	105	97⅝	97⅝	6.79	6.79
Sr Nts 6.70s 2004 .... mS22	**A+**			X	R	NC	....	....	....	....	....	300	M2	'99	100⅛	97⅞	97⅞	6.85	6.85
Sr Nts 7½s 2005 .... Ao15	**A+**	11/98	AA–	X	R	NC	....	....	....	....	....	150	M2	'95	109½	100½	100½	7.46	7.46
Sr Nts 6¾s 2005 .... Jd	**A+**	11/98	AA–	X	R	NC	....	....	....	....	....	150	M2	'95	106⅛	97¼	97¼	6.94	6.94
Sr Nts 7.20s 2007 .... Mn	**A+**	11/98	AA–	X		NC	....	....	....	....	....	150	M2	'97	109½	98	98	7.35	7.35
Sr Nts 6⅜s 2007 .... jD	**A+**	11/98	AA–	X	R	NC	....	....	....	....	....	100	M2	'97	104⅞	93⅜	93⅜	6.83	6.83
Sr Nts 6¼s 2007 .... jD15	**A+**	11/98	AA–	X	R	NC	....	....	....	....	....	100	M2	'95	104	92½	92½	6.76	6.76

Uniform Footnote Explanations-See Page 260. Other: [1] Due 12-1-06.

Title-Industry Code & Co. Finances (In Italics)	Ind	Fixed Charge Coverage 1996	1997	1998		Year End	Million $ Cash & Equiv.	Curr. Assets	Curr. Liab.	Balance Sheet Date	L. Term Debt (Mil $)	Capital-ization (Mil $)	Total Debt % Capital							
Exchange ↓ Individual Issue Statistics	Interest Dates	S&P Rating	Date of Last Rating Change	Prior Rating	Eligible ↓	Bond Form	Redemption Provisions: Regular Price	Regular (Begins) Thru	Sinking Fund Price	Sinking Fund (Begins) Thru	Refund/Other Restriction Price	Refund/Other Restriction (Begins) Thru	Outst'g (Mil $)	Underwriting Firm	Underwriting Year	Price Range 1999 High	Price Range 1999 Low	Mo. End Price Sale(s) or Bid	Curr. Yield	Yield to Mat.
***Norwest Fin'l** (Cont.)*																				
Sr Nts 5⅝s 2009	Fa3	A+			X	R	NC	....	....	....	....	....	200	M2	'99	99¾	87½	87½	6.43	6.43
Sr Nts 6.85s 2009	jJ15	A+	11/98	AA–	X	R	NC	....	....	....	....	....	250	M2	'97	107⅞	95⅛	95⅛	7.20	7.20
M-T Nts 'B' 6.20s 2001	[1]ao	A+	11/98	AA–	X	BE	NC	....	....	....	....	....	125		'97	101½	99½	99½	6.23	6.23
NRG Energy	***75***	*n/a*	*n/a*	*n/a*		*Dc*	*25.20*	*232.0*	*960.0*	*9-30-99*	*797.0*	*2368*	*69.5*							
Sr Nts[2] 7½s 2009	Jd	BBB–			X	BE	[3]Z100	....	....	....	....	....	300	S4	'99	100¾	92¾	92¾	8.09	8.09
***NTL Inc**[4]*	***67a***	*n/a*	*d0.60*	*d0.56*		*Dc*	*1568*	*1969*	*1030*	*9-30-99*	*7483*	*10023*	*75.8*							
Sr Nts[2] 10s 2007	Fa15	B–			Y	BE	105	2-14-02	....	....	....	....	400	Exch.	'97	108⅜	99	102¾	9.73	9.73
Sr Nts[2]'B' 11½s 2008	aO	B–			Y	BE	105.75	(10-1-03)	....	....	....	....	625	Exch.	'99	113¾	105	108½	10.60	10.60
Sr[5]Dfrd Cpn Nts[6]'B' 12⅜s 2008	aO	B–			Y	BE	106.188	(10-1-03)	....	....	....	....	450	Exch.	'99	73	66¼	70¾	....	Flat
Numatics Inc	***42b***	*1.23*	*1.13*	*1.32*		*Dc*	*1.21*	*64.00*	*26.30*	*9-30-99*	*156.0*	*863.0*	*185.0*							
Sr Sub Nts[7]'B' 9⅝s 2008	Ao	CCC+	6/99	B–	Y	BE	104.8125	(4-1-03)	....	....	[8]Z109.625	4-1-01	115	Exch.	'98	93¾	74½	75	12.83	12.83
NVR Inc	***13h***	*3.58*	*3.70*	*5.67*		*Dc*	*9.39*			*9-30-99*	*190.0*	*547.0*	*64.2*							
♦Sr Nts[2] 8s 2005	Jd	BB–			Y	BE	104	(6-1-03)	....	....	[9]Z108	6-1-01	145	S4	'98	100	95	94	8.51	8.51
NYNEX Capital Funding	***25***	***Subsid of & Gtd by NYNEX Corp,see***																		
(Gtd[10])M-T Nts 'B' 8.06s 2001	[11]ms15	A+	4/97	A–	X	BE	NC	....	....	....	....	....	10.0	S1	'94	106½	101¾	101¾	7.92	7.92
(Gtd[10])M-T Nts 'B' 8.22s 2001	[11]ms15	A+	4/97	A–	X	BE	NC	....	....	....	....	....	65.0	M6	'94	106⅞	102⅛	102⅛	8.05	8.05
(Gtd[10])M-T Nts 'B' 8.40s 2001	jD13	A+	4/97	A–	X	BE	NC	....	....	....	....	....	10.0	L3	'94	107¾	102½	102½	8.20	8.19
(Gtd[10])M-T Nts 'B' 8.32s 2004	[12]ms15	A+	4/97	A–	X	BE	NC	....	....	....	....	....	10.0	S1	'94	112¾	103⅞	103⅞	8.01	8.01
(Gtd[10])M-T Nts'B' 8¾s 2004	jD	A+	4/97	A–	X	BE	NC	....	....	....	....	....	150	S1	'94	115	105⅝	105¾	8.27	8.27
(Gtd[10])M-T Nts 'B' 8.61s 2006	Mn15	A+	4/97	A–	X	BE	NC	....	....	....	....	....	10.0	M6	'94	116⅞	105⅛	105⅛	8.19	8.19
*[13]**NYNEX Corp***	***67a***	*4.28*	*4.34*	*5.06*		*Dc*	*299.0*	*8897*	*11369*	*9-30-99*	*17463*	*36410*	*57.5*							
([14]Amort) Deb 9.55s 2010	Mn	A+	4/97	A–	X	BE	NC	....	....	....	....	....	369	F1	'90	116¼	108⅜	108⅜	8.81	....
Oakwood Homes	***46***	*5.95*	*7.72*	*4.67*		*Sp*				*6-30-99*	*356.0*	*935.0*	*38.8*							
Reset[15]Deb[16]'B' 8s 2007	QJun	BB–	11/99	BBB–	Y	R	[17]100	....	....	....	....	....	23.0	B9	'92	106¼	85	85⅝	9.34	....
Sr Nts[2] 7⅞s 2004	Ms	BB–	11/99	BBB–	Y	BE	[18]Z100	....	....	....	....	....	125	N2	'99	100¾	54½	56	14.06	14.06
Sr Nts 8⅛s 2009	Ms	BB–	11/99	BBB–	Y	BE	[18]Z100	....	....	....	....	....	175	N2	'99	100⅛	45½	51	15.93	15.92
Oasis Residential Inc	***57***	***Acq by Camden Prop Trust,see***																		
Nts[19] 6¾s 2001	mN15	BBB	11/98	BBB–	X	BE	[3]Z100	....	....	....	....	....	50.0	M5	'96	99⅛	97⅞	97⅞	6.90	6.90
Nts[19] 7s 2003	mN15	BBB	11/98	BBB–	X	BE	[3]Z100	....	....	....	....	....	50.0	M5	'96	101⅝	95⅞	95⅞	7.30	7.30
Nts[19] 7¼s 2006	mN15	BBB	11/98	BBB–	X	BE	[3]Z100	....	....	....	....	....	50.0	M5	'96	99⅛	91⅝	91⅝	7.91	7.91
***Occidental Petroleum**[20]*	***49b***	*3.39*	*2.22*	*1.29*		*Dc*	*151.0*	*1491*	*1577*	*9-30-99*	*5653*	*9146*	*62.2*							
• Sr Deb 10⅛s 2009	mS15	BBB	1/91	BBB–	X	R	NC	....	....	....	....	....	276	S5	'89	128	112	114¾	8.82	8.82
• Sr Deb 11⅛s 2019	Jd	BBB	1/91	BBB–	X	R	105.563	5-31-00	100	(6-1-00)	....	....	144	D7	'89	110⅜	105⅝	106½	10.45	10.44
• Sr Deb[21] 9¼s 2019	fA	BBB	1/91	BBB–	X	R	NC	....	....	....	....	....	300	M2	'89	125	103⅛	105	8.81	8.81
Sr Deb 7.20s 2022	Ao	BBB			X	BE	[18]Z100	....	....	....	....	....	200	M5	'98	94¾	87⅜	89⅝	8.03	8.03
Sr Nts 8½s 2001	mN9	BBB			X	BE	NC	....	....	....	....	....	150	M2	'94	105⅜	102⅛	102⅛	8.32	8.32
• Sr Nts 10⅛s 2001	mN15	BBB	1/91	BBB–	X	R	NC	....	....	....	....	....	89.7	D6	'89	110	104	s104½	9.69	9.69
Sr Nts 6¾s 2002	mN15	BBB			X	BE	[18]Z100	....	....	....	....	....	200	M2	'98	100½	98⅜	98⅜	6.86	6.86
Sr Nts 6½s 2005	Ao	BBB			X	BE	[18]Z100	....	....	....	....	....	250	M5	'98	99⅛	94¾	95¼	6.82	6.82
Sr Nts 7.65s 2006	Fa15	BBB			X	BE	[18]Z100	....	....	....	....	....	450	M5	'99	103⅝	99¼	99½	7.69	7.69
Sr Nts 7⅜s 2008	mN15	BBB			X	BE	Z100	....	....	....	Z100	....	400	M2	'98	102⅝	96⅞	97⅜	7.57	7.57
Sr Nts[22] 11⅛s 2010	fA	BBB	1/91	BBB–	X	BE	NC	....	....	....	....	....	150	D6	'90	131⅜	119⅞	119⅞	9.28	9.28
Sr[23]Nts 6.40s 2013	Ao	BBB			X	BE	NC	....	....	....	....	....	450	M2	'98	100	95¾	96¼	6.65	6.65
Sr Nts 8¾s 2023	Jj15	BBB			X	BE	NC	....	....	....	....	....	100	M5	'93	109⅜	98⅝	105¾	8.27	8.27

Uniform Footnote Explanations-See Page 260. Other: [1] Due 2-15-01. [2] (HRO)On Chge of Ctrl at 101. [3] Plus Make-Whole Amt. [4] See Int'l CableTel Inc. [5] Int accrues at 12.375% fr 10-1-03. [6] (HRO)On Chge of Ctrl at 101(Accreted Val). [7] (HRO)On Chge of Ctrl at 1010. [8] Max $40M red w/proceeds of Pub Eq Off'g. [9] Max $50.75M red w/proceeds of Pub Eq Off'g. [10] Gtd by NYNEX Corp. [11] Due 10-17-01. [12] Due 10-19-04. [13] Subsid & data of Bell Atlantic Corp. [14] Princ pyts due ea May 1 fr 1991. [15] Int to be reset 6-1-02. [16] Death red benefit,ltd,as defined. [17] Min $10M. [18] Red at greater of 100 or amt based on formula. [19] Asmd by Camden Property Trust. [20] See OXY O&G USA. [21] (HRO)On 8-1-04 at 100. [22] Issued in min denom $100T. [23] Mandatory put/call at 100 on 4-1-03.

Exchange / Individual Issue Statistics / Interest Dates	S&P Rating	Date of Last Rating Change	Prior Rating	Eligible	Bond Form	Redemption Provisions: Regular Price	Regular (Begins) Thru	Sinking Fund Price	Sinking Fund (Begins) Thru	Refund/Other Restriction Price	Refund/Other Restriction (Begins) Thru	Outst'g (Mil $)	Underwriting Firm	Underwriting Year	Price Range 1999 High	Price Range 1999 Low	Mo. End Price Sale(s) or Bid	Curr. Yield	Yield to Mat.
Title-Industry Code & Co. Finances (In Italics) / Ind	*Fixed Charge Coverage 1996*	*1997*		*1998*	*Year End*	*Million $ Cash & Equiv.*	*Curr. Assets*	*Curr. Liab.*	*Balance Sheet Date*	*L. Term Debt (Mil $)*	*Capital-ization (Mil $)*	*Total Debt % Capital*							
***Occidental Petroleum** (Cont.)*																			
Sr Nts 8.45s 2029 .... Fa15	**BBB**			X	BE	[1]Z100	....	....	....	....	....	350	M5	'99	108⅛	99¾	103¾	8.14	8.14
Ocean[2] Energy[3] 49a	***2.03***	***2.81***		***0.40***	***Dc***	***53.90***	***252.0***	***288.0***	***9-30-99***	***1539***	***2478***	***62.1***							
Sr Nts[4] 'B' 7⅝s 2005 .... jJ	**BB+**			Y	BE	[5]Z100	....	....	....	....	....	125	Exch.	'98	99	91	95	8.03	8.02
Sr Nts[4] 'B' 8¼s 2018 .... jJ	**BB+**			Y	BE	[5]Z100	....	....	....	....	....	125	Exch.	'98	97½	88	91	9.07	9.06
Sr Sub Nts[4]'B' 8⅞s 2007 .... jJ15	**BB–**	4/98	B–	Y	BE	104.438	(7-15-02)	....	....	Z108.875	7-15-00	200	Exch.	'97	103½	89	99	8.96	8.96
Sr Sub Nts[4] 'B' 8⅜s 2008 .... jJ	**BB–**	4/99	B–	Y	BE	[5]Z100	6-30-01	....	....	[6]Z108.375	7-1-01	250	Exch.	'98	100½	91	96	8.72	8.72
Ocwen Asset Investment 57	***Subsid of Ocwen Fin'l,see***																		
Sr[4]Nts 11½s 2005 .... jJ	**NR**				BE	105.75	(7-1-02)	....	....	[7]Z111.50	7-1-01	150	Exch.	'98	87	77	84	13.69	13.68
Ocwen Financial[8] 10	***3.74***	***4.00***		***0.70***	***Dc***				***9-30-99***	***222.0***	***659.0***	***33.7***							
Nts[4] 11⅞s 2003 .... aO	**B+**	7/99	BB–	Y	BE	105.938	(10-1-01)	....	....	....	....	125		'96	96	82	94	12.63	12.63
Ogden Corp 17a	***1.67***	***1.67***		***1.63***	***Dc***	***119.1***	***1178***	***466.1***	***9-30-99***	***1850***	***2749***	***78.6***							
Deb 9¼s 2022 .... Ms	**BBB+**			X	BE	NC	....	....	....	....	....	100	G1	'92	127⅝	109¾	109⅞	8.42	8.42
Ohio Bell Tel. Co.[9] 67a	***8.78***	***7.99***		***8.18***	***Dc***	***13.80***	***469.0***	***1061***	***6-30-99***	***397.0***	***2021***	***48.4***							
Deb 5s 2006 .... Fa	**AAA**	8/88	AA	X	R	100.30	1-31-00	....	....	....	....	60.0	S1	'66	96½	88⅛	88⅛	5.67	5.68
Deb 5⅜s 2007 .... Ms	**AAA**	8/88	AA	X	R	100.45	2-28-00	....	....	....	....	75.0	E1	'67	97⅞	88¼	88¼	6.09	6.09
Deb 7.85s 2022 .... jD15	**AAA**			X	BE	103.764	(12-15-02)	....	....	....	....	100	L3	'92	110¾	94⅝	94¾	8.28	8.28
Nts 5¾s 2000 .... Mn	**AAA**			X	BE	NC	....	....	....	....	....	100	M2	'93	100⅞	99¾	99⅞	5.76	5.76
Nts 6⅛s 2003 .... Mn15	**AAA**			X	BE	NC	....	....	....	....	....	150	K2	'93	103⅝	97	97	6.31	6.31
Ohio Edison Co.[10] 72a	***3.01***	***2.16***		***3.08***	***Dc***	***11.00***	***746.0***	***1448***	***9-30-99***	***2094***	***5817***	***52.0***							
1st('93) 6⅜s 2000 .... Ao	**BBB–**	10/97	BB+	X	BE	NC	....	....	....	....	....	80.0	M6	'93	101⅛	99⅞	100	6.38	6.37
1st 8¼s 2002 .... Ao	**BBB–**	10/97	BB+	X	BE	NC	....	....	....	....	....	125	M6	'92	107½	102	102	8.09	8.09
1st 7½s 2002 .... fA	**BBB–**	10/97	BB+	X	R	100	....	Z100	....	....	....	34.3	F1	'72	100⅜	98½	98½	7.61	7.61
1st ('92) 7⅜s 2002 .... mS15	**BBB–**	10/97	BB+	X	BE	NC	....	....	....	....	....	120	M6	'92	105⅞	100⅜	100⅜	7.35	7.35
1st ('91) 8⅝s 2003 .... mS15	**BBB–**	10/97	BB+	X	BE	NC	....	....	....	....	....	150	M6	'91	111⅝	103¾	103¾	8.31	8.31
1st('93) 6⅞s 2005 .... Ao	**BBB–**	10/97	BB+	X	BE	NC	....	....	....	....	....	80.0	M6	'93	105¾	97¼	97¼	7.07	7.07
1st ('92) 8¾s 2022 .... Jd15	**BBB–**	10/97	BB+	X	BE	105.42	6-14-00	Z100	....	....	....	100	M6	'92	106	101⅝	101¾	8.60	8.60
1st ('93) 7⅞s 2023 .... Ao	**BBB–**	10/97	BB+	X	BE	103.38	(4-1-03)	Z100	(4-1-03)	....	....	100	M6	'93	105¼	93	93⅛	8.46	8.46
1st ('93) 7⅝s 2023 .... Jd15	**BBB–**	10/97	BB+	X	BE	103.34	(6-15-03)	Z100	(6-15-03)	....	....	75.0	M6	'93	105⅝	89⅜	89½	8.52	8.52
Ohio Power Co.[11] 72a	***4.92***	***5.00***		***5.13***	***Dc***	***137.0***	***947.0***	***799.0***	***9-30-99***	***1143***	***2676***	***48.0***							
1st[12] 8.10s 2002 .... Fa15	**A–**			X	BE	100	....	□100	....	....	....	50.0	S1	'92	101⅛	99⅞	100	8.10	8.10
1st[12] 8¼s 2002 .... [13]jd	**A–**			X	BE	100	....	100	....	....	....	50.0	S1	'92	101¼	100⅛	100½	8.21	8.21
1st 6¾s 2003 .... Ao	**A–**			X	BE	NC	....	....	....	....	....	40.0	S1	'93	103⅝	97¾	97¾	6.91	6.91
1st 6s 2003 .... [14]ao	**A–**			X	BE	100.86	10-31-00	□100	....	....	....	25.0	S1	'93	99½	94¾	94¾	6.33	6.33
1st 6.15s 2003 .... [15]ao	**A–**			X	BE	100.88	11-30-00	□100	....	....	....	50.0	S1	'93	101½	95⅛	95⅛	6.47	6.46
1st[12] 8.80s 2022 .... [16]jd	**A–**			X	BE	104.40	(2-1-01)	100	(2-10-02)	....	....	50.0	S1	'92	108½	98⅝	98⅝	8.92	8.92
1st 7¾s 2023 .... Ao	**A–**			X	BE	103.88	(4-1-03)	100	....	....	....	40.0	S1	'93	106	92⅞	93	8.33	8.33
1st 7.10s 2023 .... [17]ao	**A–**			X	BE	103.55	(11-1-03)	□100	(11-1-03)	....	....	25.0	S1	'93	100¾	86¼	86⅜	8.22	8.22
Sr Nts 'B' 6¾s 2004 .... jJ	**BBB+**			X	BE	[1]Z100	....	....	....	....	....	100	S4	'99	100⅞	97½	97½	6.92	6.92
Sr Nts 'C' 7s 2004 .... jJ	**BBB+**			X	BE	[1]Z100	....	....	....	....	....	75.0	M2	'99	100¼	97¼	97¼	7.20	7.20
M-T Nts 'A' 6.73s 2004 .... mN	**BBB+**			X	BE	NC	....	....	....	....	....	48.0	M6	'97	104¼	96½	96½	6.97	6.97
M-T Nts 'A' 6.24s 2008 .... [18]mn	**BBB+**			X	BE	[1]Z100	....	....	....	....	....	50.0	M7	'98	101	89⅛	89⅛	7.00	7.00
[19]Oklahoma Gas & Electric 72a	***4.08***	***4.08***		***6.32***	***Dc***	***16.70***	***589.0***	***1256***	***9-30-99***	***1051***	***2100***	***50.3***							
Sr[20]Nts 6¼s 2000 .... aO15	**A+**	8/99	AA–	X	BE	NC	....	....	....	....	....	110	B7	'95	101⅜	99½	99½	6.28	6.28
Sr[20]Nts[21] 6½s 2017 .... jJ15	**A+**	8/99	AA–	X	BE	[1]Z100	(8-15-04)	....	....	....	....	125	L3	'97	104½	96¾	96¾	6.72	6.72

Uniform Footnote Explanations-See Page 260. Other: [1] Red at greater of 100 or amt based on formula. [2] Was Unite Meridian. [3] See Flores & Rucks. [4] (HRO)On Chge of Ctrl at 101. [5] Plus Make-Whole Amt. [6] Max $83.3M red w/proceeds of Equity Off'g. [7] Max $37M red w/proceeds of Equity Off'g. [8] See Ocwen Asset Inv. [9] Subsid of Ameritech Corp. [10] Merged w/Centerior to form First Energy. [11] Contr. by Amer Elec Pwr. [12] Issued in min denom $100T. [13] Due 3-15-02. [14] Due 11-1-03. [15] Due 12-1-03. [16] Due 2-10-22. [17] Due 11-1-23. [18] Due 12-4-08. [19] Now OGE Energy. [20] Secured until Release Date. [21] (HRO)On 7-15-04 at 100.

Title-Industry Code & Co. Finances (In Italics) / Individual Issue Statistics (Exchange)	Ind / Interest Dates	Fixed Charge Coverage 1996 / S&P Rating	1997 / Date of Last Rating Change	1998 / Prior Rating	Eligible	Year End / Bond Form	Million $ Cash & Equiv. / Redemption Provisions: Regular Price	Curr. Assets / Regular (Begins) Thru	Curr. Liab. / Sinking Fund Price	Balance Sheet Date / Sinking Fund (Begins) Thru	L. Term Debt (Mil $) / Refund/Other Restriction Price	Refund/Other Restriction (Begins) Thru	Capital-ization (Mil $) / Outst'g (Mil $)	Total Debt % Capital / Underwriting Firm	Underwriting Year	Price Range 1999 High	Price Range 1999 Low	Mo. End Price Sale(s) or Bid	Curr. Yield	Yield to Mat.
***Oklahoma Gas & Electric** (Cont.)*																				
Sr[1]Nts 7.30s 2025	aO15	**A+**	8/99	AA−	X	BE	103.261	(10-15-05)	....	....	....	....	110	M2	'95	107½	90⅛	90¼	8.09	8.09
Sr[1]Nts[2] 6.65s 2027	jJ15	**A+**	8/99	AA−	X	BE	[3]Z100	(8-15-07)	....	....	....	....	125	M2	'97	106⅝	94⅞	94⅞	7.01	7.01
Sr (Unsec) Nts 6½s 2028	Ao15	**A+**	8/99	AA−	X	BE	[3]Z100	....	....	....	....	....	100	M2	'98	102⅝	83¼	83⅜	7.80	7.80
Old Kent Fin'l	***10***	***4.38***	***3.75***	***3.68***		***Dc***				***9-30-99***	***200.0***		***1272***	***15.7***						
Sub Nts 6⅝s 2005	mN15	**A−**			X	BE	NC	....	....	....	....	....	100	C5	'95	104½	95⅞	95⅞	6.91	6.91
Old Republic Int'l	***35c***	***14.10***	***32.84***	***33.65***		***Dc***				***9-30-99***	***150.0***		***2394***	***6.3***						
• Deb 7s 2007	Jd15	**A+**	10/99	AA−	X	BE	NC	....	....	....	....	....	115	L3	'97	No Sale		95⅝	7.32	7.32
Olin Corp	***14***	***15.32***	***9.96***	***7.32***		***Dc***	***56.40***	***509.3***	***261.8***	***9-30-99***	***229.0***		***554.0***	***41.5***						
Nts 8s 2002	Jd15	**BBB**			X	R	NC	....	....	....	....	....	100	L3	'92	107⅛	101⅝	101⅝	7.87	7.87
Olsten Corp	***63***	***9.19***	***7.28***	***1.61***		***Dc***	***13.88***	***1337***	***530.0***	***10-3-99***	***774.0***		***1513***	***49.3***						
Sr Nts 7s 2006	Ms15	**BBB−**	9/98	BBB+	X	BE	NC	....	....	....	....	....	200	S7	'96	98½	90½	93⅞	7.46	7.46
Olympic Financial Ltd	***25a***	***Now Arcadia Fin'l Ltd,see***																		
xwSr Nts[4] 11½s 2007	Ms15	**B**	7/98	BB−	Y	R	105.75	(3-15-02)	....	....	....	....	300	D6	'97	104	61⅞	104	11.06	11.06
Sub Nts 10⅛s 2001	[5]Mar15	**NR**				BE	100	....	....	....	....	....	30.0		'96	94	72	94	10.77	10.77
[6]Olympus Communications/Cap	***12a***	***0.71***	***0.63***	***0.63***		***Dc***				***9-30-99***	***382.0***		***179.0***	***214.0***						
Sr Nts[4]'B' 10⅝s 2006	mN15	**B+**	3/99	B	Y	BE	105.3125	(11-15-01)	....	....	....	....	200	Exch.	'99	111¾	104½	105½	10.07	10.07
Omega Cabinets	***42a***	***2.14***	***1.21***	***1.72***		***Dc***	***1.88***	***50.40***	***38.90***	***10-2-99***	***164.0***		***167.0***	***105.0***						
Sr Sub Nts 10½s 2007	Jd15	**B**			Y	BE	105.25	(6-15-02)		....	[7]Z110	6-15-00	100	G1	'97	103	93	99	10.61	10.60
Omega Healthcare Investors	***57***	***2.66***	***2.83***	***2.57***		***Dc***				***9-30-99***	***587.0***		***1081***	***54.3***						
Nts 6.95s 2002	Jd15	**BB+**	12/99	BBB−	Y	BE	NC	....	....	....	....	....	125	M5	'98	99⅜	92	92	7.55	7.55
Nts 6.95s 2007	fA	**BB+**	12/99	BBB−	Y	BE	[8]Z100	....	....	....	....	....	100	M5	'97	94	78¼	78¼	8.88	8.88
Omnipoint Corp	***67f***	***d2.41***	***d2.53***	***d2.42***		***Dc***	***369.1***	***498.4***	***418.7***	***9-30-99***	***2710***		***1472***	***150.0***						
Sr Nts[4] 11⅝s 2006	fA15	**CCC+**			Y	BE	105.81	(8-15-01)	....	....	....	....	250	Exch.	'96	109½	69½	106	10.97	10.96
Sr Nts[4] 11½s 2009	mS15	**CCC+**			Y	BE	105.75	(9-15-04)	....	....	[9]Z111.50	9-15-02	205	Exch.	'99	109½	100	107¼	10.72	10.72
ONEOK Inc	***73b***	***△3.65***	***△5.89***	***△2.51***		***Au***	***4.40***	***439.0***	***544.0***	***8-31-99***	***810.0***		***2271***	***48.3***						
Deb 6s 2009	Fa	**A**			X	BE	[3]Z100	....	....	....	....	....	100	P1	'99	101⅝	87⅞	88⅜	6.79	6.79
Deb 9.70s 2019	jD	**A**	7/98	A−	X	R	104.75	11-30-00	100	(6-1-00)	....	....	125	P1	'89	107½	104⅜	104⅜	9.29	9.29
Deb 9¾s 2020	jD	**A**	7/98	A−	X	R	104.35	(12-1-00)	100	(6-1-01)	....	....	75.0	P1	'90	110⅛	105	105	9.29	9.28
Deb 6⅞s 2028	[10]ao	**A**			X	BE	[3]Z100	....	....	....	....	....	100		'98	98⅜	83¾	85	8.09	8.09
Nts 7¾s 2006	fA15	**A**			X	BE	[3]Z100	....	....	....	....	....	300	P1	'99	103⅝	98¾	99¾	7.77	7.77
OPI Int'l[11]	***49e***	***1.02***	***n/a***	***8.44***		***Mr***	***225.0***	***1406***	***1251***	***9-30-99***	***323.0***		***1278***	***35.8***						
Gtd[12]Sr Nts[13] 12⅞s 2002	jJ15	**NR**	10/97	BB+		R	101.60	7-14-00	100	(7-20-00)	....	....	70.0	B7	'92	104½	102⅛	102¼	12.59	12.59
Optel Inc	***67***	***d2.07***	***d0.55***	***d0.40***		***Au***				***5-31-99***	***429.0***		***520.0***	***82.5***						
Sr Nts[4] 'B' 11½s 2008	jJ	**D**	10/99	B−		BE	105.75	(7-1-03)	....	....	[14]Z111.50	7-1-01	200	Exch.	'98	105⅜	25	71	....	Flat
Oracle Corp	***20d***	***△n/a***	***△n/a***	***△93.52***		***My***	***2721***	***4788***	***2549***	***8-31-99***	***301.0***		***4003***	***7.7***						
Sr Nts 6.72s 2004	Fa15	**A−**	11/99	BBB+	X	BE	[15]Z100	....	....	....	....	....	150	M6	'97	103⅞	97⅜	97½	6.89	6.89
Sr Nts 6.91s 2007	Fa15	**A−**	11/99	BBB+	X	BE	[15]Z100	....	....	....	....	....	150	M6	'97	105¼	94⅞	94⅞	7.28	7.28
Orange & Rockland Utils[16]	***75***	***3.27***	***3.09***	***2.94***		***Dc***	***6.82***	***239.0***	***281.0***	***9-30-99***	***401.0***		***916.0***	***58.2***						
Deb 'A' 9⅜s 2000	Ms15	**A+**	4/99	A−	X	R	NC	....	....	....	....	....	80.0	G1	'90	104⅝	100½	100½	9.33	9.33
Deb 'C' 6.14s 2000	Ms	**A+**	4/99	A−	X	BE	NC	....	....	....	....	....	20.0	S7	'93	106⅝	99⅞	100	6.14	6.14
Deb 'D' 6.56s 2003	Ms	**A+**	4/99	A−	X	BE	NC	....	....	....	....	....	35.0	S7	'93	103¾	97⅝	97⅝	6.72	6.72
Deb 'G' 7s 2029	Ms	**A+**	4/99	A−	X	BE	104.586	(3-1-09)	....	....	....	....	45.0	B7	'99	99½	87⅜	87½	8.00	8.00
ORBCOMM Global L.P./Cap	***67f***	***47.46***	***d26.64***	***d22.06***		***Dc***	***6.15***	***26.70***	***103.0***	***9-30-99***	***170.0***		***270.0***	***63.0***						
Sr Nts[4]'B' 14s 2004	fA15	**CCC+**	11/99	B−	Y	BE	115	(8-15-01)	....	....	....	....	170	Exch.	'97	110	65	72	19.44	19.43

Uniform Footnote Explanations-See Page 260. Other: [1] Secured until Release Date. [2] (HRO)On 8-15-07 at 100. [3] Red at greater of 100 or amt based on formula. [4] (HRO)On Chge of Ctrl at 101. [5] Int pd monthly. [6] Data of Olympus LP. [7] Max $35M red w/proceeds of Pub Eq Off'g. [8] Plus Make-Whole Amt. [9] Max $71.8M red w/proceeds of Pub Eq Off'g. [10] Due 9-30-28. [11] Acqd by & data of McDermott Intl. [12] Gtd by Offshore Pipelines. [13] Co must offer repurch at 101 On Chge of Ctrl. [14] Max $70M red w/proceeds of Equity Off'g. [15] Plus make-whole amt. [16] See Rockland Electric.

Title-Industry Code & Co. Finances (In Italics) / Exchange ↓ Individual Issue Statistics	Ind / Interest Dates	Fixed Charge Coverage 1996 / S&P Rating	1997 / Date of Last Rating Change	1998 / Prior Rating	Eligible ↓	Year End / Bond Form	Million $ Cash & Equiv. / Redemption Provisions Regular Price	Curr. Assets / Regular (Begins) Thru	Curr. Liab. / Sinking Fund Price	Balance Sheet Date / Sinking Fund (Begins) Thru	L. Term Debt (Mil $) / Refund/Other Restriction Price	Refund/Other Restriction (Begins) Thru	Capital-ization (Mil $) / Outst'g (Mil $)	Total Debt % Capital / Underwriting Firm	Underwriting Year	Price Range 1999 High	Price Range 1999 Low	Mo. End Price Sale(s) or Bid	Curr. Yield	Yield to Mat.
Orbital Imaging	***67f***	*n/a*	*n/a*	*d0.76*		*Dc*	*57.50*	*75.50*	*15.40*	*9-30-99*	*213.0*		*251.0*	*85.0*						
Sr Nts[1]'B' 11⅝s 2005	Ms	**CCC+**			Y	BE	105.8125	2-28-02	....	....	[2]Z111.625	3-1-01	150	Exch.	'98	102	65	69	16.85	16.84
Sr Nts[1]'D' 11⅝s 2005	Ms	**CCC+**			Y	BE	105.8125	(3-1-02)	....	....	[3]Z111.625	3-1-01	75.0	Exch.	'99	78	65	66	17.61	17.60
Oregon Steel Mills	***66***	*4.01*	*3.40*	*1.33*		*Dc*	*0.68*	*240.2*	*130.5*	*9-30-99*	*303.0*		*668.0*	*46.5*						
1st[4] 11s 2003	Jd15	**BB**	12/96	BB+	Y	BE	105.50	(6-15-00)	....	....	....	....	235	S7	'96	107¼	102¼	103	10.68	10.68
Oriole Homes Corp	***13h***	*0.18*	*d2.24*	*Nil*		*Dc*	*20.70*			*6-30-99*	*[5]47.80*		*101.0*	*52.2*						
Sr Nts[6] 12½s 2003	Jj15	**CCC+**	8/97	B–	Y	R	101.625	1-14-01	100	(1-15-01)	....	....	70.0	B7	'93	96	87	93	13.44	13.43
Orion Capital[7]	***35c***	*6.14*	*7.78*	*8.33*		*Dc*				*9-30-99*	*459.0*		*1090*	*42.1*						
Sr Nts 9⅛s 2002	mS	**A–**	11/99	BBB	X	R	NC	....	....	....	....	....	110	M2	'92	110¼	103⅛	104	8.77	8.77
Sr Nts 7¼s 2005	jJ15	**A–**	11/99	BBB	X	BE	NC	....	....	....	....	....	100	L3	'95	105⅜	94½	98	7.40	7.40
[8]Orion Network Systems	***67e***	*n/a*	*n/a*	*n/a*		*Dc*	*16.52*	*239.6*	*263.7*	*9-30-99*	*947.0*		*1365*	*73.6*						
Sr Nts[1] 11¼s 2007	Jj15	**B+**	3/98	B	Y	BE	105.625	(1-15-02)	....	....	....	....	443	M6	'97	99	72	75	15.00	14.99
Sr[9]Disc Nts[10] 12½s 2007	Jj15	**B+**	3/98	B	Y	BE	106.25	(1-15-02)	....	....	....	....	[11]484	M6	'97	64½	42	46	....	Flat
Oryx Energy Co[12]	***49a***	***Merged into Kerr-McGee,see***																		
Nts 10s 2001	Ao	**BBB**	3/99	BB+	X	R	NC	....	....	....	....	....	150	M2	'91	107½	103⅛	103⅛	9.70	9.70
Nts 8s 2003	aO15	**BBB**	3/99	BB+	X	BE	NC	....	....	....	....	....	100	C5	'95	105⅞	101⅜	101⅜	7.89	7.89
Nts 8⅜s 2004	jJ15	**BBB**	3/99	BB+	X	BE	NC	....	....	....	....	....	150	C1	'96	108¼	102¾	102¾	8.15	8.15
Nts 8⅛s 2005	aO15	**BBB**	3/99	BB+	X	BE	NC	....	....	....	....	....	150	C5	'95	108⅛	101½	101½	8.00	8.00
Otter Tail Power	***72a***	*3.65*	*3.52*	*4.72*		*Dc*	*12.70*	*102.0*	*68.20*	*9-30-99*	*190.0*		*457.0*	*41.6*						
1st 7¼s 2002	fA	**AA–**			X	R	NC	....	100	....	....	....	19.4	S7	'92	105⅞	99⅞	99⅞	7.26	7.26
1st 7⅝s 2003	Fa	**AA–**	6/90	A+	X	R	100.82	1-31-00	100.09	1-31-00	....	....	9.24	W5	'73	101⅜	100¾	100¾	7.57	7.57
1st 8¾s 2021	mS15	**AA–**			X	R	103.54	(9-15-01)	Z100	....	....	....	19.0	P2	'91	110	100⅝	100¾	8.68	8.68
1st 8¼s 2022	fA	**AA–**			X	R	104.13	(8-1-02)	100	....	....	....	28.8	S7	'92	110¾	97⅞	97⅞	8.43	8.43
Sr Deb 6⅜s 2007	jD	**A+**			X	BE	NC	....	....	....	....	....	50.0	E2	'97	105⅜	93⅜	93⅜	6.83	6.83
Outboard Marine Corp	***40a***	*2.08*	*d3.48*	*d0.71*		*Sp*	*22.80*	*342.0*	*324.1*	*9-30-99*	*248.0*		*354.0*	*73.2*						
SF Deb 9⅛s 2017	Ao15	**B**	5/98	BB–	Y	R	103.55	4-14-00	100	....	....	....	62.8	S1	'87	80	50	50	18.25	18.25
Sr Nts[1] 'B' 10¾s 2008	Jd	**B**			Y	BE	105.375	(6-1-03)	....	....	[13]Z110.75	6-1-01	160	Exch.	'98	97½	67	76	14.14	14.14
[14]Outdoor Systems	***1***	*1.76*	*6.92*	*1.52*		*Dc*	*129.0*	*732.0*	*325.0*	*9-30-99*	*248.0*									
Sr Sub Nts[1] 9⅜s 2006	aO15	**BB+**	12/99	B	Y	R	104.688	(10-15-01)	....	....	....	....	250	W6	'96	107½	103	104	9.01	9.01
Sr Sub Nts[1] 8⅞s 2007	Jd15	**BB+**	12/99	B	Y	BE	104.438	(6-15-02)	....	....	[15]Z108.875	6-15-00	500	Exch.	'97	108⅜	101	103	8.62	8.61
Outsourcing Solutions	***25d***	*n/a*	*n/a*	*n/a*		*Dc*	*4.83*	*116.0*	*110.0*	*9-30-99*	*510.0*		*489.0*	*108.0*						
Sr Sub Nts[1]'B' 11s 2006	mN	**B–**			Y	BE	105.50	(11-1-01)	....	....	....	....	100	Exch.	'97	99	93½	94	11.70	11.70
Overseas Shipholding Gr	***64***	*1.05*	*1.37*	*1.72*		*Dc*	*48.26*	*97.81*	*52.55*	*9-30-99*	*795.0*		*923.0*	*90.4*						
Deb 8¾s 2013	jD	**BB+**	6/99	BBB–	Y	BE	[16]Z100	....	....	....	....	....	100	G1	'93	101⅛	89⅜	89⅜	9.79	9.79
Nts 8s 2003	jD	**BB+**	6/99	BBB–	Y	BE	[16]Z100	....	....	....	....	....	100	G1	'93	99⅛	94½	94½	8.47	8.46
Owens Corning[17]	***28***	*5.31*	*4.25*	*2.49*		*Dc*	*99.00*	*1532*	*2021*	*9-30-99*	*2189*		*1204*	*187.0*						
Deb 7½s 2018	fA	**BBB–**			X	BE	[18]Z100	....	....	....	....	....	400	C6	'98	101⅜	82⅞	85¼	8.80	8.80
Nts 7½s 2005	Mn	**BBB–**			X	BE	[18]Z100	....	....	....	....	....	300	G1	'98	104⅜	94	95	7.89	7.89
Nts 7.70s 2008	Mn	**BBB–**			X	BE	[18]Z100	....	....	....	....	....	250	G1	'98	106⅝	91⅝	93¼	8.26	8.26
Nts 7s 2009	Ms15	**BBB–**			X	BE	[18]Z100	....	....	....	....	....	250	C6	'99	99¾	87	88⅜	7.92	7.92
Owens-Corning Fiberglas	***28***	***Now Owens Corning,see***																		
Deb 8⅞s 2002	Jd	**BBB–**			X	BE	NC	....	....	....	....	....	150	G1	'92	106½	101	101	8.79	8.79
Deb 9⅜s 2012	Jd	**BBB–**			X	BE	NC	....	....	....	....	....	150	G1	'92	122¼	104	104	9.01	9.01
Owens-Illinois	***16***	*2.07*	*2.44*	*1.51*		*Dc*	*235.0*	*2168*	*1316*	*9-30-99*	*5505*		*8451*	*68.1*						
Sr Deb 7½s 2010	Mn15	**BB+**			Y	BE	NC	....	....	....	....	....	250	M7	'98	104⅛	88⅞	88⅞	8.44	8.44

Uniform Footnote Explanations-See Page 260. Other: [1] (HRO)On Chge of Ctrl at 101. [2] Max $52.5M red w/proceeds of Equity Off'g. [3] Max $26.3M red w/proceeds of Equity Off'g. [4] Co must offer repurch at 101 on Chge of Ctrl. [5] Incl current amts. [6] (HRO)On Chge in Ctrl at 101. [7] Acq by Royal & Sun Alliance Ins plc. [8] Now Loral Orion Inc(Subsid Loral Space & Commun). [9] Int accr at 12.5% fr 1-15-02. [10] (HRO)On Chge of Ctrl at 101(Accreted Val). [11] Incl disc. [12] Was Sun Explor'n & Prod'n. [13] Max $56M red w/proceeds of Equity Off'g. [14] Acq by & data of Infinity Broadcasting. [15] Max $175M red w/proceeds of Pub Eq Off'g. [16] Plus Make-Whole Premium. [17] Was Owens-Corning Fiberglas,see. [18] Red at greater of 100 or amt based on formula.

Title-Industry Code & Co. Finances (In Italics) / Exchange ↓ Individual Issue Statistics	Ind / Interest Dates	Fixed Charge Coverage 1996 / S&P Rating	1997 / Date of Last Rating Change	1998 / Prior Rating	Eligible ↓	Year End / Bond Form	Million $ Cash & Equiv. / Redemption Provisions Regular Price	Curr. Assets / Regular (Begins) Thru	Curr. Liab. / Sinking Fund Price	Balance Sheet Date / Sinking Fund (Begins) Thru	L. Term Debt (Mil $) / Refund/Other Restriction Price	Refund/Other Restriction (Begins) Thru	Capitalization (Mil $) / Outst'g (Mil $)	Total Debt % Capital / Underwriting Firm	Underwriting Year	Price Range 1999 High	Price Range 1999 Low	Mo. End Price Sale(s) or Bid	Curr. Yield	Yield to Mat.
Owens-Illinois (Cont.)																				
Sr Deb 7.80s 2018	Mn15	**BB+**			Y	BE	NC	....	....	....	....	....	250	M7	'98	102⅝	85¾	85⅞	9.08	9.08
Sr Nts 7.85s 2004	Mn15	**BB+**			Y	BE	NC	....	....	....	....	....	300	M6	'97	105⅛	96¾	96¾	8.11	8.11
Sr nts 7.15s 2004	Mn15	**BB+**			Y	BE	NC	....	....	....	....	....	350	M7	'98	102⅛	92⅞	92⅞	7.70	7.70
Sr Nts 8.10s 2007	Mn15	**BB+**			Y	BE	NC	....	....	....	....	....	300	M6	'97	107¾	95⅛	95⅛	8.52	8.51
Sr Nts 7.35s 2008	Mn15	**BB+**			Y	BE	NC	....	....	....	....	....	250	M7	'98	103¼	90¼	90¼	8.14	8.14
Owens & Minor	***43***	***1.98***	***1.81***	***3.69***		***Dc***	***0.58***	***518.4***	***327.1***	***9-30-99***	***150.0***		***320.0***	***46.9***						
• Sr Sub Nts[1] 10⅞s 2006	Jd	**B+**			Y	R	105.4375	(6-1-01)	....	....	....	....	150	M5	'96	109½	106	103	10.56	10.56
OXY USA Inc[2]	***49a***	***Gtd by Occidental Petroleum, see***																		
Deb[3] 7s 2011	Ao15	**BBB**	1/91	BBB–	X	R	100	....	....	....	....	....	[4]274	F1	'81	108⅛	90⅞	100	7.00	7.00
P&L Coal Holdings	***45a***	***n/a***	***n/a***	***1.12***		***Mr***	***126.0***	***1790***	***1346***	***9-30-99***	***2433***		***3032***	***83.3***						
Sr Nts[5]'B' 8⅞s 2008	Mn15	**B+**			Y	BE	[6]Z100	5-14-03	....	....	Z108.875	5-15-01	400	Exch.	'98	104⅝	96	97¾	9.08	9.08
Sr Sub Nts[5] 9⅝s 2008	Mn15	**B**			Y	BE	104.813	(5-15-03)	....	....	109.625	5-15-01	499	Exch.	'98	104⅝	95¾	98½	9.77	9.77
Pac-West Telecommun	***67***	***n/a***	***n/a***	***n/a***		***Dc***	***59.00***	***77.90***	***29.40***	***9-30-99***	***150.0***		***133.0***	***113.0***						
Sr Nts[5] 13½s 2009	Fa	**B**			Y	BE	106.75	(2-1-04)	....	....	[7]Z113.50	2-1-02	150	Exch.	'99	112⅝	101	103½	13.04	13.04
Paccar Financial	***25***	***1.52***	***1.50***	***1.36***		***Dc***				***9-30-99***	***1298***		***2994***	***86.1***						
• M-T Nts 'H' 6.30s 2000	[8]ms15	**AA–**			X	BE	NC	....	....	....	....	....	5.00	M2	'96	No Sale		99¾	6.32	6.32
M-T Nts 'H' 6.04s 2001	[9]ms15	**AA–**			X	BE	NC	....	....	....	....	....	20.0	M2	'98	101¼	99⅛	99⅛	6.09	6.09
M-T Nts 'H' 6.055s 2001	[10]ms15	**AA–**			X	BE	NC	....	....	....	....	....	20.0	M2	'98	101¼	99	99	6.12	6.12
F/R[11]Nts 'I' 2000	QDec4	**AA–**			X	BE	NC	....	....	....	....	....	20.0	M2	'99	100	99¾	100	....	....
F/R[12]M-T Nts 'I' 2001	[13]	**AA–**			X	BE	NC	....	....	....	....	....	30.0	L3	'99	100	99¾	100	....	....
M-T Nts 'I' 6.39s 2001	Ms15	**AA–**			X	BE	NC	....	....	....	....	....	30.0	M2	'99	100¼	99¼	99¼	6.44	6.44
PacifiCorp[14]	***72b***	***2.67***	***2.21***	***2.16***		***Dc***	***273.0***	***1125***	***1189***	***9-30-99***	***4410***		***9197***	***54.4***						
1st & CT 6¾s 2005	Ao	**A+**	4/98	A	X	R	NC	....	....	....	....	....	150	G1	'93	105⅞	97¼	97¼	6.94	6.94
1st 6¾s 2004	jJ15	**A+**	4/98	A	X	BE	[15]Z100	....	....	....	....	....	167	G1	'97	105¼	97½	97½	6.92	6.92
1st 5.65s 2006	mN	**A+**			X	BE	NC	....	....	....	....	....	200	G1	'98	100⅝	90	90	6.28	6.28
1st 7s 2009	jJ15	**A+**	4/98	A	X	BE	[15]Z100	....	....	....	....	....	115	G1	'97	106⅜	93⅞	93⅞	7.46	7.46
Sec M-T Nts 'G' 6.12s 2006	Jj15	**A+**	4/98	A	X	R	[16]Z100	....	....	....	....	....	100	M6	'96	102½	93⅛	93⅛	6.57	6.57
Sec M-T Nts 'H' 6⅜s 2008	Mn15	**A+**			X	BE	[17]NC	....	....	....	....	....	200	G1	'98	104⅛	92⅝	92⅝	6.88	6.88
Pacific[18]Bell[19]	***67a***	***5.62***	***1.12***	***5.39***		***Dc***	***12.00***	***2592***	***4371***	***6-30-99***	***4490***		***9656***	***61.5***						
Deb 5⅞s 2006	Fa15	**AA–**			X	BE	NC	....	....	....	....	....	250	S1	'96	102⅞	93⅝	93⅝	6.28	6.28
Deb 6⅞s 2006	fA15	**AA–**			X	BE	NC	....	....	....	....	....	250	S1	'96	109⅛	97⅝	97⅝	7.04	7.04
Deb 6⅞s 2023	fA15	**AA–**			X	R	101.57	(8-15-03)	....	....	....	....	100	L3	'93	103⅝	86⅛	86¼	7.97	7.97
Deb 7⅜s 2025	Jd15	**AA–**			X	R	103.367	(6-15-03)	....	....	....	....	350	G1	'93	106	90¾	90⅞	8.12	8.11
Deb 7⅛s 2026	Ms15	**AA–**			X	R	NC	....	....	....	....	....	625	L3	'93	112½	91⅞	92	7.74	7.74
Deb 7¼s 2027	mN	**AA–**			X	BE	103.2035	(11-1-07)	....	....	....	....	100	M2	'97	105⅞	88⅛	88¼	8.22	8.21
Deb 8½s 2031	fA15	**AA–**			X	R	102.76	(8-15-01)	....	....	....	....	225	M2	'91	107⅛	98¼	101⅜	8.38	8.38
Deb 7¾s 2032	mS15	**AA–**			X	R	103.92	(9-15-02)	....	....	....	....	300	M2	'92	110¼	94	94⅛	8.23	8.23
Deb 7½s 2033	Fa	**AA–**			X	R	102.94	(2-1-03)	....	....	....	....	149	L3	'93	106⅞	90⅝	90¾	8.26	8.26
Deb 6⅝s 2034	aO15	**AA–**			X	R	101.12	(10-15-13)	....	....	....	....	550	L3	'93	103¼	82⅞	83	7.98	7.98
Deb 7⅜s 2043	jJ15	**AA–**			X	R	102.89	(7-15-13)	....	....	....	....	300	S1	'93	109	90⅜	90½	8.15	8.15
Nts 8.70s 2001	Jd15	**AA–**			X	R	NC	....	....	....	....	....	200	L3	'91	107½	102⅜	102⅜	8.50	8.50
Nts 7¼s 2002	jJ	**AA–**			X	R	NC	....	....	....	....	....	300	L3	'92	105⅝	100¼	100¾	7.20	7.19
Nts 7s 2004	jJ15	**AA–**			X	R	NC	....	....	....	....	....	325	S1	'92	108	99⅛	99⅛	7.06	7.06
Nts 6¼s 2005	Ms	**AA–**			X	R	NC	....	....	....	....	....	325	L3	'93	104¾	95⅝	96⅛	6.50	6.50

Uniform Footnote Explanations-See Page 260. Other: [1] Co must offer repurch at 101 on Chge of Ctrl. [2] Was Cities Service Co,then OXY Oil&Gas USA. [3] Not gtd by Occidental Petroleum. [4] Incl disc. [5] (HRO)On Chge of Ctrl at 101. [6] Plus Make-Whole Amt. [7] Max $52.5M red w/proceeds Pub Eq Off'g. [8] Due 12-15-00. [9] Due 1-16-01. [10] Due 2-15-01. [11] Int adj qtrly(3 Mo LIBOR & 0.10%). [12] Int adj qtrly (3 Mo LIBOR & 0.22%). [13] Due 8-31-01:Int pd qtrly, Sep 1, etc. [14] Acq by Scottish Power. [15] Red at greater of 100 or amt based on formula. [16] Greater of 100 or amt based on formula. [17] Red at greater of 100 or based on formula. [18] Subsid of Pacific Telesis Gr. [19] See Pacific Tel & Tel.

Title-Industry Code & Co. Finances (In Italics) / Individual Issue Statistics (Exchange)	Ind / Interest Dates	Fixed Charge Coverage 1996 / S&P Rating	1997 / Date of Last Rating Change	Prior Rating	1998 / Eligible	Year End / Bond Form	Cash & Equiv. (Million $) / Redemption Provisions: Regular Price	Curr. Assets (Million $) / Regular (Begins) Thru	Curr. Liab. (Million $) / Sinking Fund Price	Balance Sheet Date / Sinking Fund (Begins) Thru	L. Term Debt (Mil $) / Refund/Other Restriction Price	Refund/Other Restriction (Begins) Thru	Capital-ization (Mil $) / Outst'g (Mil $)	Total Debt % Capital / Underwriting Firm	Underwriting Year	Price Range 1999 High	Price Range 1999 Low	Mo. End Price Sale(s) or Bid	Curr. Yield	Yield to Mat.
***Pacific Bell** (Cont.)*																				
Nts 6⅛s 2008	Fa15	**AA–**			X	BE	NC	....	....	....	....	....	200	B7	'98	105⅛	92¼	92¼	6.64	6.64
Nts 6⅝s 2009	mN	**AA–**			X	BE	NC	....	....	....	....	....	150	M2	'97	109⅜	94½	94½	7.01	7.01
[1]Pacific Gas & Electric	***75***	***3.05***	***2.90***		***2.65***	***Dc***	***321.0***	***3947***	***6505***	***6-30-99***	***9376***		***18402***	***55.5***						
1st & Ref QQ 6⅝s 2000	Jd	**AA–**	10/97	A+	X	CR	100	....	*100	....	....	....	49.9	F1	'68	100⅜	99⅞	100	6.63	6.62
1st & Ref RR 6¾s 2000	jD	**AA–**	10/97	A+	X	CR	100	....	*100	....	....	....	59.8	B8	'68	100½	99¾	99¾	6.77	6.77
1st & Ref 90B 8¾s 2001	[2]jd	**AA–**	10/97	A+	X	R	NC	....	....	....	....	....	100	F1	'90	106⅝	101¾	101¾	8.60	8.60
1st & Ref 91A 8.80s 2024	[3]jd	**AA–**	10/97	A+	X	R	NC	....	....	....	....	....	200	G1	'91	130¾	108½	108⅝	8.10	8.10
1st & Ref 92A 7⅞s 2002	[4]jd	**AA–**	10/97	A+	X	R	NC	....	....	....	....	....	400	G1	'92	107½	97¼	101⅝	7.75	7.75
1st & Ref 92B 8⅜s 2025	[3]jd	**AA–**	10/97	A+	X	R	102.51	(6-1-02)	‡102.51	(6-1-02)	....	....	200	M6	'92	111	99¼	99⅜	8.43	8.43
1st & Ref 92D 8¼s 2022	[5]jd	**AA–**	10/97	A+	X	R	103.14	(12-1-02)	‡103.14	(12-1-02)	....	....	400	F1	'92	110⅝	97⅞	97⅞	8.43	8.43
1st & Ref 93A 7¼s 2026	[4]jd	**AA–**	10/97	A+	X	R	102.02	(6-1-03)	‡102.02	(6-1-03)	....	....	300	F1	'93	104½	89⅜	89⅜	8.11	8.11
1st & Ref 93C 6¼s 2003	[6]jd	**AA–**	10/97	A+	X	R	NC	....	....	....	....	....	400	G1	'93	104⅛	97⅛	97⅛	6.44	6.43
1st & Ref 93D 7¼s 2026	[6]jd	**AA–**	10/97	A+	X	R	103.63	(6-1-03)	*103.63	(6-1-03)	....	....	402	G1	'93	106½	89¼	89⅜	8.11	8.11
1st & Ref 93E 5⅞s 2005	jd	**AA–**	10/97	A+	X	R	NC	....	....	....	....	....	300	F1	'93	103⅛	93⅛	93⅛	6.31	6.31
1st & Ref 93F 6¾s 2023	[7]jd	**AA–**	10/97	A+	X	R	102.74	(12-1-03)	‡102.74	(12-1-03)	....	....	400	F1	'93	105¼	86⅝	86¾	7.78	7.78
1st & Ref 93G 6¼s 2004	[4]jd	**AA–**	10/97	A+	X	R	NC	....	....	....	....	....	338	M6	'93	104¼	96⅝	96⅝	6.47	6.47
1st & Ref 93H 7.05s 2024	[4]jd	**AA–**	10/97	A+	X	R	NC	....	....	....	....	....	350	M6	'93	111⅜	91⅜	91½	7.70	7.70
[8]Pacific Gas Transmission[9]	***73a***	***3.05***	***2.44***		***3.26***	***Dc***	***0.05***	***33.50***	***31.90***	***6-30-99***	***580.0***		***922.0***	***62.9***						
• Sr Deb 7.80s 2025	Jd	**A–**			X	BE	103.036	(6-1-05)	....	....	....	....	150	M6	'95	No Sale		93⅜	8.35	8.35
• Sr Nts 7.10s 2005	Jd	**A–**			X	BE	NC	....	....	....	....	....	250	M6	'95	No Sale		98½	7.21	7.21
Pacific NorthwestBellTel	***67a***	***Merged into U S WEST Commun, see***																		
Deb 4½s 2000	jD	**A+**	5/98	A	X	CR	100	....	....	....	....	....	50.0	M6	'63	98¾	97⅝	98	4.59	4.59
Deb 4⅜s 2002	mS	**A+**	5/98	A	X	CR	100	....	....	....	....	....	50.0	M6	'62	96⅞	93½	93½	4.68	4.68
Deb 4½s 2003	Ao	**A+**	5/98	A	X	CR	100	....	....	....	....	....	50.0	M6	'63	96½	92⅜	92⅜	4.87	4.87
Pacific Telephone & Tel[10]	***67a***	***Now Pacific Bell, see***																		
Deb 4⅝s 2000	Mn	**AA–**	2/90	A+	X	CR	100	....	....	....	....	....	125	M2	'65	99½	98¾	99½	4.65	4.65
Deb 6s 2002	mN	**AA–**	2/90	A+	X	R	100	....	....	....	....	....	130	L3	'66	99⅞	97	97	6.19	6.19
Deb 6½s 2003	jJ	**AA–**	2/90	A+	X	R	100	....	....	....	....	....	165	H1	'68	100⅛	97⅝	97⅝	6.66	6.66
Packaged Ice	***26j***	***d6.62***	***d0.28***		***0.30***	***Dc***	***2.40***	***41.90***	***34.60***	***9-30-99***	***316.0***		***448.0***	***72.5***						
Sr Nts[11] 'B' 9¾s 2005	Fa	**B**			Y	BE	104.875	(2-1-02)	....	....	[12]Z109.75	2-1-01	270	Exch.	'98	104¼	80	91½	10.66	10.65
Packard BioScience	***43a***	***n/a***	***1.32***		***1.21***	***Dc***	***6.18***	***112.0***	***58.70***	***9-30-99***	***237.0***		***138.0***	***176.0***						
Sr Sub Nts[11] 'B' 9⅜s 2007	Ms	**B–**			Y	BE	104.688	(3-1-02)	....	....	[13]Z109.375	2-29-00	150	Exch.	'97	100½	83	85	11.03	11.03
Packaging Corp America	***17***	***n/a***	***n/a***		***n/a***		***64.30***	***431.0***	***218.0***	***p6-30-99***	***1678***		***2124***	***79.4***						
Sr Sub Nts 'B' 9⅝s 2009	Ao	**B**			Y	BE	[14]Z100	3-31-04	....	....	[15]Z109.625	3-31-02	550	Exch.	'99	104⅜	99	102⅛	9.42	9.42
Packaging Resources	***52***	***1.06***	***1.08***		***1.31***	***Fb***	***0.56***	***47.30***	***26.80***	***8-31-99***	***138.0***		***130.0***	***107.0***						
Sr Sec Nts[11] 11⅝s 2003	Mn	**B+**			Y	BE	105.813	(5-1-00)	....	....	....	....	110	Exch.	'96	105½	98	98	11.86	11.86
PageMart Nationwide	***63***	***See PageMart Wireless***																		
SrDisc Nts 15s 2005	Fa	**NR**				BE	105	(2-1-00)	....	....	....	....	[16]207	Exch.	'95	95½	84	89	....	Flat
[17]PageMart Wireless	***63***	***d0.39***	***d0.14***		***0.05***	***Dc***	***6.21***	***70.10***	***110.0***	***9-30-99***	***523.0***		***358.0***	***146.0***						
Sr Disc[18]Nts[19] 11¼s 2008	Fa	**NR**				BE	105.625	(2-1-03)	....	....	[20]Z111.25	2-1-01	[16]432	Exch.	'98	46½	27	34	....	Flat
Paging Network	***67g***	***0.34***	***0.16***		***0.40***	***Dc***	***102.9***	***203.4***	***233.2***	***9-30-99***	***1999***		***1189***	***157.0***						
Sr Sub Nts[21] 8⅞s 2006	Fa	**CC**	11/99	B–	Y	R	104.438	1-31-00	....	....	....	....	300	G1	'94	93	23	29	....	....
Sr Sub Nts[21] 10⅛s 2007	fA	**CC**	11/99	B–	Y	BE	105.0625	(8-1-07)	....	....	....	....	400	G1	'95	97⅛	23½	29	....	....
Sr Sub Nts[11] 10s 2008	aO15	**CC**	11/99	B–	Y	BE	105	(10-15-01)	....	....	....	....	482	Exch.	'97	97	24	29	....	....

Uniform Footnote Explanations-See Page 260. Other: [1] Now PG&E Corp. [2] Due Jan 1. [3] Due May 1. [4] Due Mar 1. [5] Due Nov 1. [6] Due Aug 1. [7] Due Oct 1. [8] Subsid of Pacific Gas & Elec. [9] Now PG&E Transmission Nthwst. [10] Subsid of Pacific Telesis Group. [11] (HRO)On Chge of Ctrl at 101. [12] Max $94.5M red w/proceeds of Equity Off'g. [13] Max $45M red w/proceeds of Pub Eq Off'g. [14] On Chge of Ctrl. [15] Max $192M red w/proceeds of Pub Eq Off'g. [16] Incl disc. [17] Now WebLink Wireless. [18] Int accrues at 11.25% fr 2-1-03. [19] On Chge of Ctrl at 101(Accreted Val). [20] Accr Val:Max $151m red w/proceeds of Eq Off'g. [21] Co must offer repurch at 101 on Chge of Ctrl.

Exchange ↓ Individual Issue Statistics	Interest Dates	S&P Rating	Date of Last Rating Change	Prior Rating	Eligible ↓	Bond Form	Redemption Provisions: Regular Price	Regular (Begins) Thru	Sinking Fund Price	Sinking Fund (Begins) Thru	Refund/Other Restriction Price	Refund/Other Restriction (Begins) Thru	Outst'g (Mil $)	Underwriting Firm	Underwriting Year	Price Range 1999 High	Price Range 1999 Low	Mo. End Price Sale(s) or Bid	Curr. Yield	Yield to Mat.
Title-Industry Code & Co. Finances (In Italics)	*Ind*	*Fixed Charge Coverage 1996*	*1997*	*1998*		*Year End*	*Million $ Cash & Equiv.*	*Curr. Assets*	*Curr. Liab.*	*Balance Sheet Date*	*L. Term Debt (Mil $)*		*Capital-ization (Mil $)*	*Total Debt % Capital*						
Paine Webber Group	***62***	***1.29***	***1.26***		***1.25***	***Dc***	***171.0***			***9-30-99***	***5362***		***6957***	***62.8***						
Nts 7s 2000	Ms	BBB+			X	R	NC	....	....	....	....	....	200	P1	'93	101¼	100	100⅛	6.99	6.99
Nts 9¼s 2001	jD15	BBB+			X	R	NC	....	....	....	....	....	150	P1	'91	108⅜	103½	103½	8.94	8.94
Nts 8¼s 2002	Mn	BBB+			X	R	NC	....	....	....	....	....	125	P1	'95	106½	101½	101½	8.13	8.13
Nts 7⅞s 2003	Fa15	BBB+			X	R	NC	....	....	....	....	....	100	P1	'93	106¼	100½	100½	7.84	7.83
Nts 6.45s 2003	jD	BBB+			X	BE	NC	....	....	....	....	....	340	P1	'98	101½	95⅞	95⅞	6.73	6.73
Nts 6⅜s 2004	Mn15	BBB+			X	BE	NC	....	....	....	....	....	525	P1	'99	99½	95⅛	95⅛	6.70	6.70
Nts 8⅞s 2005	Ms15	BBB+			X	R	NC	....	....	....	....	....	125	P1	'95	112½	104⅜	104⅜	8.50	8.50
Nts 6½s 2005	mN	BBB+			X	R	NC	....	....	....	....	....	200	P1	'93	100¾	94	94	6.91	6.91
Nts 6¾s 2006	Fa	BBB+			X	R	NC	....	....	....	....	....	100	P1	'96	101⅝	94⅞	94⅞	7.11	7.11
Nts 6.55s 2008	Ao15	BBB+			X	R	NC	....	....	....	....	....	250	P1	'98	100¼	91⅛	91⅛	7.19	7.19
Nts 7⅝s 2008	aO15	BBB+			X	R	NC	....	....	....	....	....	150	P1	'96	107⅞	97⅜	97⅜	7.83	7.83
Nts 7⅝s 2009	jD	BBB+			X	BE	NC	....	....	....	....	....	275	P1	'99	99¾	97⅜	97⅜	7.83	7.83
Nts 7⅝s 2014	Fa15	BBB+			X	R	NC	....	....	....	....	....	200	P1	'94	104⅝	94⅛	94⅛	8.10	8.10
F/R[1]M-T Sr Nts[2]'C' 2000	[3]	BBB+			X	BE	NC	....	....	....	....	....	25.0	P1	'97	99¾	98⅞	99¾	....	....
F/R[4]M-T Sr Nts 'C' 2002	[5]	BBB+			X	BE	NC	....	....	....	....	....	25.0	P1	'97	99¼	97⅝	99⅛	....	....
M-T Nts[2]'C' 6.65s 2002	[6]ms	BBB+			X	BE	NC	....	....	....	....	....	25.0	P1	'97	101¼	97¾	97¾	6.80	6.80
M-T Sr Nts[2]'C' 6¼s 2003	[7]ms	BBB+			X	BE	NC	....	....	....	....	....	25.0	P1	'98	100	96	96⅜	6.49	6.48
M-T Sr Nts[2]'C' 6.331s 2003	[8]ms	BBB+			X	BE	NC	....	....	....	....	....	25.0	P1	'98	100¼	96	96⅛	6.59	6.59
M-T Sr Nts 'C' 6.785s 2003	[9]ms	BBB+			X	BE	NC	....	....	....	....	....	30.0	P1	'97	101½	97⅜	97⅝	6.97	6.97
M-T Nts[2] 'C' 6.52s 2005	[10]ms	BBB+			X	BE	NC	....	....	....	....	....	30.0	P1	'98	100	93⅝	94⅜	6.91	6.91
F/R[11]M-T Nts 'C' 6.1375s 2007	[12]	BBB+			X	BE	NC	....	....	....	....	....	25.0	P1	'97	99¼	95⅛	95¼	6.44	....
M-T Sr Nts 'C' 6.72s 2008	[13]ms	BBB+			X	BE	NC	....	....	....	....	....	35.0	P1	'98	100⅝	92⅜	92⅜	7.27	7.27
M-T Sr Nts 'C' 6.73s 2008	[14]ms	BBB+			X	BE	NC	....	....	....	....	....	42.5	P1	'98	100⅝	92⅜	92⅜	7.29	7.29
M-T Nts[2] 'C' 6.64s 2009	[15]ms	BBB+			X	BE	NC	....	....	....	....	....	25.0	P1	'99	100	91	91	7.30	7.30
M-T Sr Nts 'C' 6.65s 2010	[16]ms	BBB+			X	BE	NC	....	....	....	....	....	25.0	P1	'98	99¼	88¼	89¾	7.41	7.41
M-T Sr Nts 'C' 6.64s 2010	[17]ms	BBB+			X	BE	NC	....	....	....	....	....	30.0	P1	'98	99⅛	88	89¾	7.40	7.40
M-T Sr Nts 'C' 7.39s 2017	[18]ms	BBB+			X	BE	NC	....	....	....	....	....	25.0	P1	'97	102⅛	89⅞	90	8.21	8.21
Sub Nts 7¾s 2002	mS	BBB			X	R	NC	....	....	....	....	....	175	P1	'92	105¼	100½	100½	7.71	7.71
PanEnergy Corp	***73a***	***Subsid of Duke Energy,see***																		
Nts 7⅜s 2003	mS15	A	4/98	A–	X	BE	NC	....	....	....	....	....	100	M5	'96	106¾	100¾	100¾	7.32	7.32
Nts 7s 2006	aO15	A	4/98	A–	X	BE	NC	....	....	....	....	....	150	C1	'96	107⅛	97⅜	97⅜	7.19	7.19
Panhandle East'n Corp	***73a***	***Subsid of Duke Energy,see***																		
Deb 8⅝s 2025	Ao15	A	4/98	A–	X	R	104.03	(4-15-05)	....	....	....	....	100	M6	'95	113¾	101⅜	101⅞	8.47	8.47
Nts 7¼s 2005	Mn15	A	4/98	A–	X	R	NC	....	....	....	....	....	100	M2	'95	108⅝	99½	99½	7.29	7.29
Panhandle East'n P.L.[19]	***73a***	***3.09***	***2.76***		***2.92***	***Dc***		***214.0***	***138.0***	***6-30-99***	***1094***		***2224***	***49.2***						
• Deb 7.95s 2023	Ms15	BBB–	3/99	A	X	R	103.975	(3-15-03)	....	....	....	....	100	K2	'93	No Sale		92⅛	8.63	8.63
Deb 7.20s 2024	fA15	BBB–	3/99	A	X	R	103.225	(8-15-03)	....	....	....	....	100	K2	'93	101⅞	88⅜	88½	8.14	8.13
Nts 7⅞s 2004	fA15	BBB–	3/99	A	X	R	NC	....	....	....	....	....	100	D4	'94	110⅜	101⅞	101⅞	7.73	7.73
Pantry Inc	***59b***	***1.20***	***0.93***		***0.54***	***Sp***	***61.20***	***155.0***	***153.0***	***6-24-99***	***425.0***		***533.0***	***81.9***						
Sr Sub Nts[20] 10¼s 2007	aO15	B	9/99	B–	Y		105.125	(10-15-02)	....	....	[21]Z110.25	10-15-00	200	Exch.	'98	105½	95	97	10.57	10.57
Paracelsus Healthcare	***30***	***d4.68***	***0.85***		***0.92***	***Dc***	***5.54***	***112.4***	***88.26***	***9-30-99***	***556.0***		***589.0***	***95.4***						
Sr Sub Nts 10s 2006	fA15	B–	4/97	B	Y	R	105	(8-15-01)	....	....	....	....	325	D6	'96	90	55	55	18.18	18.17
Paramount Communications[22]	***24***	***Merged with Viacom Inc, see Viacom Int'l***																		
Sr Deb 8¼s 2022	fA	BBB–	10/98	BB+	X	R	103.467	(8-1-02)	....	....	....	....	250	F1	'92	110⅜	98¾	98⅞	8.34	8.34

Uniform Footnote Explanations-See Page 260. Other: [1] Int adj qtrly(3 Mo LIBOR&0.26%). [2] Issued in min denom $100T. [3] Due 7-30-00:Int pd qtrly ea 3rd Wed Mar,etc. [4] Int adj qtrly(3 Mo LIBOR & 0.35%). [5] Due 9-19-02:Int pd ea 3rd Wed Mar, etc. [6] Due 10-15-02. [7] Due 2-4-03. [8] Due 5-20-03. [9] Due 7-1-03. [10] Due 4-6-05. [11] Int adj qtrly(3 Mo LIBOR&0.45%). [12] Due 10-22-07:Int pd qtrly ea 3rd Wed,Mar,etc. [13] Due 4-1-08. [14] Due 4-3-08. [15] Due 2-5-09. [16] Due 4-13-10. [17] Due 4-14-10. [18] Due 10-16-17. [19] Subsid of CMS Energy. [20] (HRO)On Chge of Ctrl at 101. [21] Max $70M red w/proceeds Pub Eq Off'g. [22] Was Gulf & Western.

Title-Industry Code & Co. Finances (In Italics) / Individual Issue Statistics, Exchange	Ind / Interest Dates	Fixed Charge Coverage 1996 / S&P Rating	1997 / Date of Last Rating Change	1998 / Prior Rating	Eligible	Year End / Bond Form	Cash & Equiv. (Million $) / Regular Price	Curr. Assets (Million $) / Regular (Begins) Thru	Curr. Liab. (Million $) / Sinking Fund Price	Balance Sheet Date / Sinking Fund (Begins) Thru	L. Term Debt (Mil $) / Refund/Other Restriction Price	Refund/Other Restriction (Begins) Thru	Capital-ization (Mil $) / Outst'g (Mil $)	Total Debt % Capital / Underwriting Firm	Underwriting Year	Price Range 1999 High	Price Range 1999 Low	Mo. End Price Sale(s) or Bid	Curr. Yield	Yield to Mat.
***Paramount Communications** (Cont.)*																				
Sr Deb 7½s 2023	jJ15	BBB–	10/98	BB+	X	R	103.564	(7-15-03)	....	....	....	....	150	S1	'93	102¾	89½	89½	8.38	8.38
Sr Nts 5⅞s 2000	jJ15	BBB–	10/98	BB+	X	R	NC	....	....	....	....	....	150	S1	'93	100½	99⅜	99⅝	5.90	5.90
Sr Nts 7½s 2002	Jj15	BBB–	10/98	BB+	X	R	NC	....	....	....	....	....	250	F1	'92	105¼	100⅝	100⅝	7.45	7.45
[1]Park'N View	*67*	*n/a*	*n/a*	*d2.78*		*Je*	*37.10*	*48.70*	*5.17*	*p6-30-99*	*71.10*									
Sr[2]Nts'B' 13s 2008	Mn15	CCC+	3/99	B–	Y	BE	106.50	(5-15-03)	....	....	[3]Z113	5-14-01	75.0	Exch.	'98	78	29¾	41	....	....
Park Place Entertainment	*40i*	*n/a*	*n/a*	*n/a*		*Dc*	*215.0*	*532.0*	*423.0*	*9-30-99*	*2521*		*6249*	*40.4*						
Sr[2]Nts[4] 7.95s 2003	fA	BBB–			X	BE	Z100	....	....	....	....	....	300	Exch.	'99	99⅜	98	99	8.03	8.03
Sr Nts[5] 8½s 2006	mN15	BBB–			X	BE	[6]Z100	....	....	....	....	....	400	M2	'99	99⅜	98¼	98⅝	8.62	8.62
Sr Sub Nts 'B' 7⅞s 2005	jD15	BB+			Y	BE	[6]Z100	....	....	....	....	....	400	Exch.	'99	99	93	95¾	8.22	8.22
Park-Ohio Industries[7]	*42b*	*3.51*	*3.11*	*2.30*		*Dc*	*1.90*	*311.0*	*123.0*	*9-30-99*	*328.0*		*481.0*	*481.0*						
Sr Sub Nts[2] 9¼s 2007	jD	B+			Y	BE	104.625	(12-1-02)	....	....	[8]Z109.25	12-1-00	150	Exch.	'98	104¼	91½	96¼	9.61	9.61
Parker Drilling	*49e*	*n/a*	*1.72*	*[9]1.90*		*Dc*	*20.80*	*135.0*	*78.00*	*9-30-99*	*629.0*		*971.0*	*64.9*						
Sr Nts[2]'D' 9¾s 2006	mN15	B+			Y	BE	104.875	(11-15-01)	....	....	....	....	450	Exch.	'98	99	73	97¾	9.97	9.97
Parker & Parsley Petrol	*49a*	*Now Pioneer Natural Res,see*																		
Sr Nts[10] 8⅞s 2005	Ao15	BB+	1/99	BBB–	Y	BE	NC	....	....	....	....	....	150	S1	'95	107¾	91¼	99⅞	8.89	8.89
Sr Nts[10] 8¼s 2007	fA15	BB+	1/99	BBB–	Y	BE	NC	....	....	....	....	....	150	S1	'95	105½	85⅝	95½	8.64	8.64
Parker-Hannifin	*41h*	*△10.04*	*△10.55*	*△8.54*		*Je*	*64.42*	*1811*	*741.0*	*9-30-99*	*718.0*		*2707*	*28.7*						
Deb 9¾s 2021	Fa15	A			X	R	104.585	(2-15-01)	100	(2-15-02)	....	....	100	K2	'91	110⅜	105⅞	105⅞	9.21	9.21
Nts 7.30s 2011	Mn15	A			X	BE	NC	....	....	....	....	....	100	M6	'96	112⅞	97⅛	97⅛	7.52	7.52
M-T Nts 6.35s 2003	jD16	A			X	BE	NC	....	....	....	....	....	50.0	M6	'97	103⅞	96¾	96¾	6.56	6.56
M-T Nts 6.55s 2018	jJ15	A			X	BE	[11]Z100	....	....	....	....	....	100	M7	'98	99⅛	86½	86⅝	7.56	7.56
Pathmark Stores, Inc	*59c*	*0.79*	*0.73*	*0.83*		*Ja*	*8.31*	*260.0*	*353.0*	*7-31-99*	*1409*		*358.0*	*420.0*						
Sr Sub Nts[2] 9⅝s 2003	Mn	CCC+	12/97	B–	Y	R	102.41	10-30-00	....	....	....	....	440	M2	'93	103	73	75	12.83	12.83
Sub Deb 12⅝s 2002	Jd15	CCC+	12/97	B–	Y	R	101.80	6-14-00	....	....	....	....	95.8	Exch.	'93	103	33	33	....	....
Sub Nts[2] 11⅝s 2002	Jd15	CCC+	12/97	B–	Y	R	101.9375	6-14-00	100	(6-15-00)	....	....	200	Exch.	'93	103½	30	33	....	....
• Jr Sub[12]Dfr Cpn Nts[13] 10⅜s 2003	mN	CCC+	12/97	B–	Y	R	[14]105	10-30-00	....	....	....	....	225	M2	'93	100	17	12¼	....	....
Pathnet, Inc	*67*	*n/a*	*n/a*	*d0.07*		*Dc*	*98.90*	*170.0*	*33.10*	*9-30-99*	*347.0*		*305.0*	*114.0*						
Sr Nts[2] 12¼s 2008	Ao15	NR				BE	106.125	(4-15-03)	....	....	[15]Z112.25	4-15-01	[16]350	Exch.	'98	70	50	63	19.44	19.44
Paxson Communications	*12*	*0.16*	*d0.22*	*d2.94*		*Dc*	*435.1*	*535.0*	*167.9*	*9-30-99*	*498.0*		*1577*	*31.6*						
◆Sr Sub Nts[17] 11⅝s 2002	aO	CCC+	7/98	B–	Y	R	104	9-30-01	....	....	[18]Z110	....	230	Exch.	'96	106	101½	103	11.29	11.29
Pegasus Communications	*12c*	*d0.79*	*d0.36*	*d1.35*		*Dc*	*22.80*	*69.80*	*86.50*	*9-30-99*	*611.0*		*753.0*	*83.0*						
Sr Nts[2]'B' 9⅝s 2006	jD	CCC+	9/99	B–	Y	BE	104.875	(12-1-02)	....	....	[19]Z109.75	12-1-01	100	Exch.	'98	104¾	96	101	9.65	9.65
Pen Holdings	*45a*	*1.61*	*2.23*	*1.31*		*Dc*	*2.30*	*32.00*	*19.00*	*9-30-99*	*105.0*		*170.0*	*62.4*						
Sr[2]Nts'B' 9⅞s 2008	Jd15	B+			Y	BE	104.938	(6-15-03)	....	....	[19]Z109.875	6-15-01	100	Exch.	'98	103½	93½	94½	10.45	10.45
Penda Corp		*2.26*	*0.32*	*1.59*		*Dc*	*11.40*	*31.50*	*8.23*	*9-30-99*	*79.10*		*126.0*	*63.4*						
Sr Nts 'B' 10¾s 2004	Ms	B	6/99	B–	Y	BE	105.375	2-29-00	....	....	....	....	80.0	Exch.	'94	102½	95½	95½	11.26	11.25
Pen-Tab Industries	*42a*	*n/a*	*0.89*	*0.91*		*Dc*		*109.0*	*29.70*	*7-3-99*	*185.0*		*206.0*	*93.2*						
Sr Sub Nts[2] 10⅞s 2007	Fa	B–			Y	BE	105.438	(2-1-02)	....	....	[20]Z110.875	2-1-00	75.0	Exch.	'97	88½	25	25	....	....
Penn Central	*35c*	*Now Amer Fin'l Group,see*																		
Sub Nts[21] 10⅝s 2000	Ao15	BBB	10/98	BBB–	X	R	NC	....	....	....	....	....	43.0	S5	'90	105⅛	100⅝	100⅝	10.56	10.56
Sub Nts[21] 10⅞s 2011	Mn	BBB	10/98	BBB–	X	R	NC	....	....	....	....	....	16.5	D6	'91	127⅝	109¾	109¾	9.91	9.91
PennCorp Financial Group	*35*	*7.52*	*3.02*	*d0.55*		*Dc*				*9-30-99*	*280.0*		*567.0*	*49.4*						
Sr[22]Sub Nts 9¼s 2003	jD15	CCC–	12/98	B–	Y	R	103.09	12-14-00	....	....	....	....	150	S7	'93	88	51¾	85	10.88	10.88
Penney (J.C.) Co.	*59f*	*4.15*	*3.12*	*2.56*		*Ja*	*853.0*	*12430*	*7787*	*10-30-99*	*6504*		*16915*	*55.4*						
SF Deb 9¾s 2021	Jd15	BBB+	6/99	A	X	R	104.57	(6-15-01)	100	(6-15-02)	....	....	154	F1	'91	111⅜	106¼	106⅜	9.17	9.16

Uniform Footnote Explanations-See Page 260. Other: [1] Now PNV Inc. [2] (HRO)On Chge of Ctrl at 101. [3] Max \$26.3M red w/proceeds of Equity Off'g. [4] State gaming laws may req hldr's sale/Co red. [5] State gaming laws may reg hldr's sale/Co red. [6] Plus Make-Whole Amt. [7] Subsid of Park-Ohio Hldgs. [8] Max \$52.5M red w/proceeds of Pub Eq Off'g. [9] Fiscal Aug'98 & prior. [10] Asmd by Parker Natural Res USA, Inc. [11] Red at greater of 100 or amt based on formula. [12] (HRO)On Chge of Ctrl at 101(Acrreted Val). [13] Int accr at 10.75% fr 11-1-99. [14] Percent of Accreted Val. [15] Max \$123M red w/proceeds of Pub Eq Off'g. [16] Incl disc. [17] Co must offer repurch at 101 on Chge of Ctrl. [18] Max \$57.5 red w/proceeds of Pub Equity Off'g. [19] Max \$35M red w/proceeds of Equity Off'g. [20] Max \$26M red w/proceeds of Pub Eq Off'g. [21] (HRO)For Designated Event&Rat'g Decline at 100. [22] Co must offer repurch,at 101,on Chge of Ctrl.

Exchange / Individual Issue Statistics	Interest Dates	S&P Rating	Date of Last Rating Change	Prior Rating	Eligible	Bond Form	Redemption Provisions: Regular Price	Regular (Begins) Thru	Sinking Fund Price	Sinking Fund (Begins) Thru	Refund/Other Restriction Price	Refund/Other Restriction (Begins) Thru	Outst'g (Mil $)	Underwriting Firm	Underwriting Year	Price Range 1999 High	Price Range 1999 Low	Mo. End Price Sale(s) or Bid	Curr. Yield	Yield to Mat.
Title-Industry Code & Co. Finances (In Italics)	*Ind*	*Fixed Charge Coverage 1996*		*1997*	*1998*	*Year End*	*Million $ Cash & Equiv.*	*Curr. Assets*	*Curr. Liab.*	*Balance Sheet Date*	*L. Term Debt (Mil $)*		*Capitalization (Mil $)*	*Total Debt % Capital*						
***Penney (J.C.) Co.** (Cont.)*																				
SF Deb 8¼s 2022	fA15	**BBB+**	6/99	A	X	R	103.87	(8-15-02)	100	(8-15-03)	....	....	250	F1	'92	108½	89	89	9.27	9.27
Deb 6s 2006	Mn	**BBB+**	6/99	A	X	R	100	....	....	....	....	....	[1]117	F1	'81	99⅞	86½	86½	6.94	6.94
Deb 7.65s 2016	fA15	**BBB+**	6/99	A	X	R	NC	....	....	....	....	....	200	C5	'96	107½	85⅜	85¾	8.92	8.92
Deb 7.95s 2017	Ao	**BBB+**	6/99	A	X	BE	NC	....	....	....	....	....	300	C5	'97	110⅞	88	89	8.93	8.93
Deb 7⅛s 2023	mN15	**BBB+**	6/99	A	X	R	NC	....	....	....	....	....	275	C5	'93	102⅞	79⅝	80⅛	8.89	8.89
Deb 6.90s 2026	fA15	**BBB+**	6/99	A	X	R	NC	....	....	....	....	....	200	C5	'96	104¼	95½	95½	7.23	7.22
Deb 8⅛s 2027	Ao	**BBB+**	6/99	A	X	BE	102.839	(4-1-07)	....	....	....	....	350	C5	'97	107⅝	86	86½	9.39	9.39
Deb 7.40s 2037	Ao	**BBB+**	6/99	A	X	BE	NC	....	....	....	....	....	400	C5	'97	107¾	94⅞	94⅞	7.80	7.80
Deb[2] 7⅝s 2097	Ms	**BBB+**	6/99	A	X	BE	[3]Z100	....	....	....	....	....	500	C5	'97	102⅛	77½	77⅞	9.79	9.79
Nts 6.95s 2000	Ao	**BBB+**	6/99	A	X	BE	NC	....	....	....	....	....	325	C5	'97	101½	99⅞	100	6.95	6.95
Nts 9.05s 2001	Ms	**BBB+**	6/99	A	X	R	NC	....	....	....	....	....	250	F1	'91	106⅝	101	101⅛	8.95	8.95
Nts 7¼s 2002	Ao	**BBB+**	6/99	A	X	BE	NC	....	....	....	....	....	700	C5	'97	104⅛	98	98	7.40	7.40
Nts 9.45s 2002	jJ15	**BBB+**	6/99	A	X	R	100	(7-15-00)	....	....	....	....	180	F1	'90	105	98¾	98¾	9.57	9.57
Nts 6⅛s 2003	mN15	**BBB+**	6/99	A	X	R	NC	....	....	....	....	....	325	C5	'93	101¼	92⅞	92⅞	6.59	6.59
Nts 7⅜s 2004	Jd15	**BBB+**	6/99	A	X	R	NC	....	....	....	....	....	275	F1	'94	106½	95⅞	95⅞	7.69	7.69
Nts 7.60s 2007	Ao	**BBB+**	6/99	A	X	BE	NC	....	....	....	....	....	425	C5	'97	109½	92⅛	92⅛	8.25	8.25
Nts 7⅜s 2008	fA15	**BBB+**	6/99	A	X	R	NC	....	....	....	....	....	200	C5	'96	109	90¾	90¾	8.13	8.13
M-T Nts 'A' 6⅜s 2000	mS15	**BBB+**	6/99	A	X	BE	NC	....	....	....	....	....	300	C5	'95	101⅜	99	99	6.44	6.44
M-T Nts 'A' 6½s 2007	jD15	**BBB+**	6/99	A	X	BE	NC	....	....	....	....	....	100	C5	'95	103⅞	86⅝	86⅝	7.50	7.50
M-T Nts 'A' 6⅞s 2015	aO15	**BBB+**	6/99	A	X	BE	NC	....	....	....	....	....	200	C5	'95	101⅝	80⅜	80½	8.54	8.54
***Pennsylvania Electric**[4]*	*72a*	*3.15*		*3.46*	*2.60*	*Dc*	*22.30*	*204.0*	*294.0*	*9-30-99*	*425.0*		*1039*	*42.6*						
Sr Nts 'A' 5¾s 2004	Ao	**A**			X	BE	[5]Z100	....	....	....	....	....	125	S4	'99	99⅞	94⅝	94⅝	6.08	6.08
Sr Nts 'B' 6⅛s 2009	Ao	**A**			X	BE	[5]Z100	....	....	....	....	....	100	S4	'99	100⅛	90⅝	90⅝	6.76	6.76
Sr Nts 'C' 6⅝s 2019	Ao	**A**			X	BE	[5]Z100	....	....	....	....	....	125	S4	'99	99⅞	86⅞	87	7.61	7.61
***Pennsylvania Power Co**[6]*	*72a*	*2.44*		*3.52*	*4.44*	*Dc*	*1.98*	*129.0*	*92.30*	*6-30-99*	*288.0*		*577.0*	*52.0*						
1st 7½s 2003	fA	**BB+**	7/97	BBB–	Y	BE	NC	....	....	....	....	....	40.0	M6	'92	107	99½	99½	7.54	7.54
1st 6⅝s 2004	jJ	**BB+**	7/97	BBB–	Y	BE	NC	....	....	....	....	....	14.0	M6	'93	104	96⅝	96⅝	6.86	6.86
1st 6⅜s 2004	mS	**BB+**	7/97	BBB–	Y	BE	NC	....	....	....	....	....	50.0	M6	'93	103¼	95⅛	95⅛	6.70	6.70
1st 8½s 2022	jJ15	**BB+**	7/97	BBB–	Y	BE	104.15	(7-15-02)	Z100	....	....	....	50.0	M6	'92	111¼	96⅛	96¼	8.83	8.83
1st 7⅝s 2023	jJ	**BB+**	7/97	BBB–	Y	BE	103.32	(7-1-03)	Z100	....	....	....	40.0	M6	'93	104¾	89	89	8.57	8.57
***Pennsylvania Pwr & Light**[7]*	*72b*	*3.85*		*2.92*	*4.47*	*Dc*	*340.0*	*1479*	*1900*	*9-30-99*	*3900*		*6259*	*68.3*						
1st 6s 2000	Jd	**A–**	7/94	A	X	R	NC	....	....	....	....	....	125	F1	'93	101	99⅞	99⅞	6.01	6.01
1st 7¾s 2002	Mn	**A–**	7/94	A	X	R	NC	....	....	....	....	....	150	F1	'92	106½	101¼	101¼	7.65	7.65
1st 6⅞s 2003	Fa	**A–**	7/94	A	X	R	NC	....	....	....	....	....	100	F1	'93	105⅛	98⅞	98⅞	6.95	6.95
1st 6⅞s 2004	Ms	**A–**	7/94	A	X	R	NC	....	....	....	....	....	150	C5	'94	106¼	98¼	98¼	7.00	7.00
1st 6½s 2005	Ao	**A–**	7/94	A	X	R	NC	....	....	....	....	....	125	F1	'93	105	96¼	96¼	6.75	6.75
1st 6.55s 2006	Ms	**A–**	7/94	A	X	R	NC	....	....	....	....	....	150	C5	'94	105⅝	95⅛	95⅛	6.89	6.89
1st 7⅜s 2014	Ms	**A–**	7/94	A	X	R	NC	....	....	....	....	....	100	C5	'94	111⅜	95⅝	95⅝	7.71	7.71
1st 9¼s 2019	aO	**A–**	7/94	A	X	R	104.53	9-30-00	Z100	....	....	....	250	F1	'89	107⅜	102⅛	104⅝	8.84	8.84
1st 9⅜s 2021	jJ	**A–**	7/94	A	X	R	104.46	(7-1-01)	Z100	(7-1-01)	....	....	150	F1	'91	112¾	104⅝	104⅝	8.96	8.96
1st 8½s 2022	Mn	**A–**	7/94	A	X	R	104.14	(5-1-02)	Z100	....	....	....	150	F1	'92	112	99¾	100	8.50	8.50
1st 7⅞s 2023	Fa	**A–**	7/94	A	X	R	103.57	(2-1-03)	Z100	(2-1-03)	....	....	200	F1	'93	108⅝	95⅛	95¼	8.27	8.27
1st 6¾s 2023	aO	**A–**	7/94	A	X	R	102.86	(10-1-03)	Z100	(10-1-03)	....	....	150	F1	'93	102¾	84	84	8.04	8.04
1st 7.30s 2024	Ms	**A–**	7/94	A	X	R	103.41	(3-1-04)	Z100	(3-1-04)	....	....	150	C5	'94	105¼	89	89⅛	8.19	8.19

Uniform Footnote Explanations-See Page 260. Other: [1] Incl disc. [2] Co may shorten mty for Tax Event. [3] Plus make-whole amt. [4] Subsid of Gen'l Public Util. [5] Red at greater of 100 or amt based on formula. [6] Subsid of Ohio Edison. [7] Subsid of PP&L Resources,now PP&L Inc.

Title-Industry Code & Co. Finances (In Italics) / Individual Issue Statistics / Exchange	Ind / Interest Dates	Fixed Charge Coverage 1996 / S&P Rating	1997 / Date of Last Rating Change	1998 / Prior Rating	Eligible	Year End / Bond Form	Million $ Cash & Equiv. / Regular Price	Curr. Assets / Regular (Begins) Thru	Curr. Liab. / Sinking Fund Price	Balance Sheet Date / Sinking Fund (Begins) Thru	L. Term Debt (Mil $) / Refund/Other Restriction Price	Refund/Other Restriction (Begins) Thru	Capital-ization (Mil $) / Outst'g (Mil $)	Total Debt % Capital / Underwriting Firm	Underwriting Year	Price Range 1999 High	Price Range 1999 Low	Mo. End Price Sale(s) or Bid	Curr. Yield	Yield to Mat.
[1]Pennzoil Co[2]	***49b***	***n/a***	***n/a***	***n/a***		***Dc***	***380.0***	***597.0***	***541.0***	***9-30-99***	***1933***		***3952***	***54.0***						
Deb 10¼s 2005	mN	**BBB+**	8/99	BB	X	R	NC	....	....	....	....	....	250	L3	'90	113	104⅝	110	9.32	9.32
Deb 10⅛s 2009	mN15	**BBB+**	8/99	BB	X	R	NC	....	....	....	....	....	200	S5	'89	116½	102⅜	113⅜	8.93	8.93
Pennzoil-Quaker State	***49d***	***n/a***	***n/a***	***d2.18***		***Dc***	***19.10***	***769.0***	***422.0***	***9-30-99***	***1060***		***2374***	***44.7***						
Deb 7⅜s 2029	Ao	**BBB–**			X	BE	[3]Z100	....	....	....	....	....	400	C1	'99	100¼	88⅜	88½	8.33	8.33
Nts 6¾s 2009	Ao	**BBB–**			X	BE	[3]Z100	....	....	....	....	....	200	C1	'99	100⅞	91¼	91¼	7.40	7.40
Pentair Inc	***17a***	***7.38***	***7.65***	***8.12***		***Dc***	***30.27***	***1096***	***778.9***	***9-25-99***	***1045***		***1143***	***36.6***						
Sr Nts 7.85s 2009	aO15	**BBB**			X	BE	[3]Z100	....	....	....	....	....	250	G1	'99	102⅝	96¾	96¾	8.11	8.11
People's Bank	***10a***	***2.22***	***2.56***	***2.79***		***Dc***				***12-31-98***	***1234***		***1379***	***48.5***						
Sub Nts[4] 7.20s 2006	jD	**BBB–**			X	BE	NC	....	....	....	....	....	150	L3	'96	105⅞	93¾	96⅛	7.49	7.49
Pep Boys-Manny,Mo,Ja	***59l***	***5.59***	***2.90***	***1.13***		***Ja***	***46.84***	***677.4***	***507.4***	***10-30-99***	***773.0***		***1441***	***53.6***						
Nts 6⅝s 2003	Mn15	**BBB–**	1/99	BBB+	X	R	NC	....	....	....	....	....	75.0	F1	'93	99¾	94⅛	94⅛	7.04	7.04
Nts 7s 2005	Jd	**BBB–**	1/99	BBB+	X	BE	NC	....	....	....	....	....	100	C5	'95	100¼	91¾	91¾	7.63	7.63
M-T Nts 'A' 6.71s 2004	mN3	**BBB–**	1/99	BBB+	X	BE	NC	....	....	....	....	....	35.0	C5	'97	99¾	91½	91½	7.33	7.33
M-T Nts[5] 'A' 6.40s 2007	mS19	**BBB–**	1/99	BBB+	X	BE	NC	....	....	....	....	....	49.0	C5	'97	100½	94½	94½	6.77	6.77
M-T Nts 'B' 6¾s 2004	Ms10	**BBB–**	1/99	BBB+	X	BE	NC	....	....	....	....	....	32.0	C6	'98	100¼	92⅝	92⅝	7.29	7.29
M-T Nts 'B' 6.88s 2006	Ms6	**BBB–**	1/99	BBB+	X	BE	NC	....	....	....	....	....	43.0	C6	'98	100¼	89¾	89¾	7.67	7.67
Pepsi Bottling Group	***11e***	***n/a***	***n/a***	***n/a***		***Dc***	***164.0***	***1717***	***1087***	***9-4-99***	***3272***		***4997***	***66.0***						
Sr Nts 7s 2029	Ms	**A–**			X	BE	Z100	....	....	....	....	....	1000	Exch.	'99	94⅝	90¼	90¼	7.76	7.76
PepsiCo Capital Resources	***25***	***Gtd by PepsiCo Inc,see***																		
Gtd[6]Deb[7]Zero Cpn 2000	[8]	**A**	7/89	A+	X	R	100	....	....	....	....	....	[9]25.0	F1	'82	98½	93⅜	98½	....	0.02
Gtd[6]Deb[7]Zero Cpn 2001	[8]	**A**	7/89	A+	X	R	100	....	....	....	....	....	[9]25.0	F1	'82	92	87¾	92	....	0.08
Gtd[6]Deb[7]Zero Cpn 2002	[8]	**A**	7/89	A+	X	R	100	....	....	....	....	....	[9]25.0	F1	'82	85¾	82¼	85⅜	....	0.16
Gtd[6]Deb[7]Zero Cpn 2003	[8]	**A**	7/89	A+	X	R	100	....	....	....	....	....	[9]25.0	F1	'82	79⅞	77	79¼	....	0.23
Gtd[6]Deb[7]Zero Cpnb 2004	[8]	**A**	7/89	A+	X	R	100	....	....	....	....	....	[9]25.0	F1	'82	74½	71⅞	73⅝	....	0.30
Gtd[6]Deb[7]Zero Cpn 2005	[8]	**A**	7/89	A+	X	R	100	....	....	....	....	....	[9]25.0	F1	'82	70½	66⅝	68⅛	....	0.37
Gtd[6]Deb[7]Zero Cpn 2006	[8]	**A**	7/89	A+	X	R	100	....	....	....	....	....	[9]25.0	F1	'82	66⅝	61¾	62⅞	....	0.44
Gtd[6]Deb[7]Zero Cpn 2007	[8]	**A**	7/89	A+	X	R	100	....	....	....	....	....	[9]25.0	F1	'82	62⅜	57⅜	58¼	....	0.51
Gtd[6]Deb[7]Zero Cpn 2008	[8]	**A**	7/89	A+	X	R	100	....	....	....	....	....	[9]75.0	F1	'82	58⅞	52⅞	54	....	0.58
Gtd[6]Deb[7]Zero Cpn 2009	[8]	**A**	7/89	A+	X	R	100	....	....	....	....	....	[9]75.0	F1	'82	55½	49¾	50	....	0.64
Gtd[6]Deb[7]Zero Cpn 2010	[8]	**A**	7/89	A+	X	R	100	....	....	....	....	....	[9]75.0	F1	'82	52¼	46¼	46¼	....	0.71
Gtd[6]Deb[7]Zero Cpn 2011	[8]	**A**	7/89	A+	X	R	100	....	....	....	....	....	[9]75.0	F1	'82	48⅞	42⅝	42⅝	....	0.78
Gtd[6]Deb[7]Zero Cpn 2012	[8]	**A**	7/89	A+	X	R	100	....	....	....	....	....	[9]75.0	F1	'82	45¾	39¼	39¼	....	0.84
PepsiCo Inc[10]	***11e***	***5.78***	***6.44***	***7.46***		***Dc***	***550.0***	***3597***	***3402***	***9-4-99***	***2641***		***9617***	***28.4***						
Debt Securities 6.80s 2000	Mn15	**A**			X	BE	NC	....	....	....	....	....	200	L3	'95	102	100¼	100¼	6.78	6.78
Debt Securities 5⅞s 2000	Jd	**A**			X	BE	NC	....	....	....	....	....	200	U1	'95	100⅞	99⅞	99⅞	5.88	5.88
Debt Securities 6.65s 2000	Jd6	**A**			X	BE	■100	....	....	....	....	....	25.0	B7	'95	100½	100⅛	100¼	6.63	6.63
Debt[7]Securities 5¾s 2003	Jj	**A**			X	BE	NC	....	....	....	....	....	250	C6	'98	101¼	96⅞	96⅞	5.94	5.94
Debt Securities 7.05s 2006	Mn15	**A**			X	BE	*100	(5-15-03)	....	....	....	....	100	U1	'96	106⅜	98	98	7.19	7.19
Debt Securities 7.13s 2007	[11]Aug17	**A**			X	BE	[12]100	....	....	....	....	....	25.0	M2	'95	101½	97	97	7.35	7.35
Debt Securities 7.425s 2007	fA17	**A**			X	BE	*100	....	....	....	....	....	25.0	M2	'95	101⅝	98⅛	98⅛	7.57	7.57
Deb Securities[7] 5¾s 2008	Jj15	**A**			X	BE	NC	....	....	....	....	....	250	B7	'98	102¼	90½	90½	6.35	6.35
Debt Securities 7½s 2011	[11]Sep19	**A**			X	BE	[13]100	(9-19-00)	....	....	....	....	25.0	M2	'96	104⅛	97¼	97¼	7.71	7.71
Debt Securities 6½s 2013	[11]Jan28	**A**			X	BE	*■100	....	....	....	....	....	25.0	B7	'98	99¾	91⅛	91⅛	7.13	7.13
Debt Securities 6½s 2013	[11]May22	**A**			X	BE	*100	(5-22-13)	....	....	....	....	25.0	S4	'98	100½	90⅞	90⅞	7.15	7.15

Uniform Footnote Explanations-See Page 260. Other: [1] Mgr into & data of Devon Energy. [2] See Quaker State Corp. [3] Red at greater of 100 or amt based on formula. [4] Issued in min denom $100T. [5] (HRO)On 9-19-02 at 100. [6] Gtd by PepsiCo Inc. [7] Issued in min denom $10T. [8] Due Apr 1. [9] Incl disc. [10] See PepsiCo Capital Resources. [11] Int pd monthly. [12] Ea Feb & Aug 17. [13] Red ea Mar & Sep 19.

Title-Industry Code & Co. Finances (In Italics) / Individual Issue Statistics (Exchange)	Ind / Interest Dates	S&P Rating / Fixed Charge Coverage 1996	Date of Last Rating Change / 1997	Prior Rating / 1998	Eligible	Bond Form / Year End	Redemption Provisions: Regular Price / Cash & Equiv. (Million $)	Regular (Begins) Thru / Curr. Assets (Million $)	Sinking Fund Price / Curr. Liab. (Million $)	Sinking Fund (Begins) Thru / Balance Sheet Date	Refund/Other Restriction Price / L. Term Debt (Mil $)	Refund/Other Restriction (Begins) Thru	Outst'g (Mil $) / Capital-ization (Mil $)	Underwriting Firm / Total Debt % Capital	Underwriting Year	Price Range 1999 High	Price Range 1999 Low	Mo. End Price Sale(s) or Bid	Curr. Yield	Yield to Mat.
Perkins Family Restautants	***27c***	***3.48***	***4.06***	***1.22***		***Dc***	***2.50***	***17.50***	***36.20***	***9-30-99***	***136.0***		***165.0***	***83.0***						
Sr Nts[1]'A' 10⅛s 2007	jD15	B+			Y	BE	105.063	(12-15-02)	....	....	[2]Z110.125	12-15-00	130	Exch.	'98	108⅜	99¼	101	10.02	10.02
[3]Perry-Judd's Inc	***54***	***n/a***	***n/a***	***n/a***		***Dc***	***3.81***	***83.20***	***46.20***	***9-30-99***	***130.0***		***163.0***	***83.4***						
Sr Sub Nts[1] 10⅝s 2007	jD15	B–			Y	BE	105.313	(12-15-02)	....	....	[4]Z110.625	12-15-00	115	Exch.	'98	105	89	90	11.81	11.80
Pet Inc[5]	***26***	***[6]2.31***	***n/a***	....		***Je***	***1097***	***6558***	***7437***	***:6-30-99***	***3395***		***12439***	***58.5***						
Nts 6½s 2003	jJ	A+	5/95	BBB+	X	R	NC	....	....	....	....	....	91.5	F1	'93	104½	98¼	98⅜	6.61	6.61
[7]Peters(J.M.)Co	***13h***	***1.23***	***0.76***	***1.14***		***Fb***				***8-31-99***	***206.0***		***304.0***	***67.8***						
Sr Nts[1] 12¾s 2002	Mn	B–			Y	BE	106.375	4-30-00	....	....	....	....	100	Exch.	'94	100	81	83	15.36	15.36
[8]Petro Shopping Ctrs/Fin	***57***	***n/a***	***n/a***	***n/a***		***Dc***	***14.50***	***54.90***	***54.20***	***9-30-99***	***181.0***		***214.0***	***92.5***						
Sr Nts[1] 10½s 2007	fA	B			Y	BE	105.25	(2-1-02)	....	....	[9]Z110.50	2-1-00	135	Exch.	'97	107¼	92½	92¾	11.32	11.32
PharMerica Inc.		***Mgr w/Bergen Brunswig,see***																		
Sr Sub Nts[1] 8⅜s 2008	Ao	BB+	12/99	BBB	Y	BE	104.19	(4-1-03)	....	....	[10]Z108.375	4-1-01	308	Exch.	'98	108½	62	74	11.32	11.32
Phelps Dodge Corp.	***45b***	***11.24***	***9.32***	***2.51***		***Dc***	***165.0***	***1013***	***754.7***	***9-30-99***	***807.0***		***3537***	***30.5***						
Deb 7⅛s 2027	mN	A–	2/99	A	X	BE	[11]Z100	....	....	....	....	....	150	M6	'97	103⅛	86⅜	87½	8.14	8.14
Nts 7¾s 2002	Jj	A–	2/99	A	X	BE	NC	....	....	....	....	....	100	M6	'92	105⅝	101⅛	101⅛	7.66	7.66
PG Energy[12]	***75***	***Mgr w/Southern Union,see***																		
1st 8⅜s 2002	jD	A	11/99	A–	X	R	NC	....	....	....	....	....	30.0	L2	'92	109	102⅛	102⅛	8.20	8.20
Nts 6⅜s 2004	mN	A–	2/99	A	X	BE	NC	....	....	....	....	....	100	M6	'97	101⅞	96½	96½	6.61	6.61
PHH Corp[13]	***63***	***n/a***	***n/a***	***2.34***		***Dc***	***130.0***	***1743***	***934.0***	***9-30-99***	***[14]294.0***		***3959***	***70.6***						
Nts 6½s 2000	Fa	A–	10/98	A+	X	BE	NC	....	....	....	....	....	100	F1	'93	100¾	99⅞	100	6.50	6.50
M-T Nts 5.92s 2000	mS18	A–			X	BE	NC	....	....	....	....	....	75.0	G1	'99	100¼	99¼	99⅝	5.94	5.94
F/R[15]M-T Nts 2000	[16]Sep18	A–			X	BE	NC	....	....	....	....	....	86.0	C1	'99	100	99¾	99⅞	....	....
M-T Nts 7.02s 2001	mN9	A–			X	BE	NC	....	....	....	....	....	56.6	M2	198	103⅞	100	100	7.02	7.02
[17]Philadelphia Electric	***75***	***3.05***	***2.52***	***3.66***		***Dc***	***642.0***	***1525***	***1178***	***9-30-99***	***6051***		***8513***	***74.2***						
• 1st & Ref 5⅝s 2001	mN	A	5/99	BBB+	X	R	NC	....	....	....	....	....	250	C4	'93	101	96½	96⅞	5.81	5.81
• 1st & Ref 7⅜s 2001	jD15	A	5/99	BBB+	X	R	100.30	12-14-00	....	....	....	....	80.0	M2	'71	103⅜	99¾	99¾	7.39	7.39
1st & Ref 8s 2002	Ao	A	5/99	BBB+	X	R	NC	....	....	....	....	....	200	L3	'92	107½	101¼	101¼	7.90	7.90
1st & Ref 7½s 2002	jJ15	A	5/99	BBB+	X	R	NC	....	....	....	....	....	100	F1	'92	106½	100½	100½	7.46	7.46
1st & Ref 7⅛s 2002	mS	A	5/99	BBB+	X	R	NC	....	....	....	....	....	200	F1	'92	105⅝	99½	99½	7.16	7.16
1st & Ref 6⅝s 2003	Ms	A	5/99	BBB+	X	R	NC	....	....	....	....	....	250	L3	'93	104⅜	97⅞	97⅞	6.77	6.77
• 1st & Ref 6½s 2003	Mn	A	5/99	BBB+	X	R	NC	....	....	....	....	....	200	G1	'93	104½	97	97	6.70	6.70
• 1st & Ref 6⅜s 2005	fA15	A	5/99	BBB+	X	R	102.44	8-14-00	....	....	....	....	75.0	M6	'93	104⅞	94⅞	94⅝	6.74	6.74
Philip Morris Cos[18]	***69a***	***10.03***	***11.18***	***11.90***		***Dc***	***5876***	***21893***	***18023***	***9-30-99***	***13123***		***30626***	***48.1***						
SF Deb 8⅜s 2017	Jj15	A			X	R	102.931	1-14-01	100	....	....	....	200	F1	'87	108⅜	99⅞	99⅞	8.39	8.38
Deb 7¾s 2027	Jj15	A			X	BE	NC	....	....	....	....	....	750	M2	'97	114	90¼	90¼	8.59	8.59
Nts 9¼s 2000	Fa15	A			X	R	NC	....	....	....	....	....	350	M2	'90	104⅛	100¼	100¼	9.23	9.22
Nts 9s 2001	Jj	A			X	R	NC	....	....	....	....	....	350	M2	'91	106½	101¼	101¼	8.89	8.89
Nts 8¾s 2001	Jd	A			X	BE	NC	....	....	....	....	....	300	S1	'91	107⅛	101⅜	101⅜	8.63	8.63
Nts 7¼s 2001	mS15	A			X	BE	NC	....	....	....	....	....	650	M6	'96	104¼	99¼	99¼	7.30	7.30
Nts 7½s 2002	Jj15	A			X	BE	NC	....	....	....	....	....	500	L3	'92	105¼	99¼	99½	7.54	7.54
Nts 7⅝s 2002	Mn15	A			X	BE	NC	....	....	....	....	....	300	L3	'92	106⅛	99⅜	99⅝	7.65	7.65
Nts 7⅛s 2002	fA15	A			X	BE	NC	....	....	....	....	....	350	S1	'92	105	98⅛	98⅜	7.24	7.24
Nts 7¼s 2003	Jj15	A			X	BE	NC	....	....	....	....	....	350	L3	'93	105½	98⅛	98⅜	7.37	7.37
Nts 8¼s 2003	aO15	A			X	BE	NC	....	....	....	....	....	350	M2	'91	110⅜	100⅝	100⅝	8.20	8.20
Nts 6.80s 2003	jD	A			X	BE	NC	....	....	....	....	....	500	G1	'96	104¾	95⅞	96¼	7.06	7.06

Uniform Footnote Explanations-See Page 260. Other: [1] (HRO)On Chge of Ctrl at 101. [2] Max $45M red w/proceeds of Pub Eq Off'g. [3] Subsid & data of Perry-Judd's Hldgs. [4] Max $40.3M red w/proceeds of Pub Eq Off'g. [5] Merged into & data of Diageo plc ADS. [6] Fiscal Sep,'96 & prior. [7] Now Capital Pacific Hldg. [8] Data of Petro Shopping Centers L.P. [9] Max $47.25M red w/proceeds of Pub Eq Off'g. [10] Max $108M red w/proceeds of Equity Off'g. [11] Red at greater of 100 or amt based on formula. [12] Was Pennsylvania Gas & Water. [13] Subsid of Cendant Corp. [14] Incl liabs under mgmt programs. [15] Int adj monthly(1 Mo LIBOR&0.50%). [16] Int pd monthly. [17] Now PECO Energy. [18] See Gen'l Foods,Philip Morris Inc.

Exchange / Individual Issue Statistics	Interest Dates	S&P Rating	Date of Last Rating Change	Prior Rating	Eligible	Bond Form	Regular Price	Regular (Begins) Thru	Sinking Fund Price	Sinking Fund (Begins) Thru	Refund/Other Restriction Price	Refund/Other Restriction (Begins) Thru	Outst'g (Mil $)	Underwriting Firm	Underwriting Year	Price Range 1999 High	Price Range 1999 Low	Mo. End Price Sale(s) or Bid	Curr. Yield	Yield to Mat.
Title-Industry Code & Co. Finances (In Italics)	Ind	*Fixed Charge Coverage 1996*		*1997*	*1998*	*Year End*	*Cash & Equiv. (Million $)*	*Curr. Assets*	*Curr. Liab.*	*Balance Sheet Date*	*L. Term Debt (Mil $)*		*Capital-ization (Mil $)*	*Total Debt % Capital*						
Philip Morris Cos *(Cont.)*																				
Nts 7½s 2004	Ao	A			X	BE	NC	....	....	....	....	....	500	G1	'97	107⅞	97⅞	97⅞	7.66	7.66
Nts 7⅛s 2004	aO	A			X	BE	NC	....	....	....	....	....	250	M6	'92	106⅝	96¼	96⅜	7.39	7.39
Nts[1] 7s 2005	jJ15	A			X	BE	NC	....	....	....	....	....	1000	M2	'97	106⅝	94¾	94¾	7.39	7.39
Nts 6⅜s 2006	Fa	A			X	BE	NC	....	....	....	....	....	400	M2	'96	103¼	90⅞	91	7.01	7.01
Nts[2] 6.95s 2006	Jd	A			X	BE	NC	....	....	....	....	....	500	L3	'96	104⅜	98⅛	98¾	7.04	7.04
Nts 7.20s 2007	Fa	A			X	BE	NC	....	....	....	....	....	500	L3	'97	108½	93⅝	94	7.66	7.66
Nts 7⅝s 2008	jJ	A			X	BE	NC	....	....	....	....	....	350	G1	'96	112½	95½	95½	7.98	7.98
Philip Morris Inc.	**69a**	***Subsid Philip Morris Cos, see***																		
Deb 6s 2001	jJ15	A	10/85	A+	X	R	100	....	....	....	....	....	[3]250	L3	'81	101⅛	98⅜	98⅜	6.10	6.10
Phillips Petroleum	**49b**	***6.27***		***6.05***	***1.84***	***Dc***	***180.0***	***2779***	***2590***	***9-30-99***	***5093***		***9577***	***49.1***						
• Deb 6.65s 2018	jJ15	A–			X	R	[4]Z100	....	....	....	....	....	300	M5	'98	No Sale		88⅛	7.55	7.54
• Deb 7⅛s 2028	Ms15	A–			X	R	102.70	(3-15-08)	....	....	....	....	300	G1	'98	103	87½	84	8.48	8.48
• Deb 7s 2029	Ms30	A–			X	BE	[4]Z100	....	....	....	....	....	200	M2	'99	101⅞	98⅝	86	8.14	8.14
• Nts 9s 2001	Jd	A–	7/96	BBB	X	R	NC	....	....	....	....	....	250	M6	'91	107	102	102½	8.78	8.78
• Nts 6.65s 2003	Ms	A–	7/96	BBB	X	R	NC	....	....	....	....	....	100	M2	'93	101⅝	97¾	96⅝	6.90	6.90
• Nts 6⅜s 2009	Ms30	A–			X	BE	Z100	....	....	....	....	....	300	M2	'99	101⅛	99⅛	84	7.59	7.59
• Nts 9⅜s 2011	Fa15	A–	7/96	BBB	X	R	NC	....	....	....	....	....	350	M6	'91	116	110¾	107	8.76	8.76
• Nts 9.18s 2021	mS15	A–	7/96	BBB	X	R	104.59	(9-15-01)	....	....	....	....	300	G1	'91	109⅝	103	103¼	8.89	8.89
• Nts 8.86s 2022	Mn15	A–	7/96	BBB	X	R	104.43	(5-15-02)	....	....	....	....	250	G1	'92	No Sale		100	8.86	8.86
• Nts 8.49s 2023	Jj	A–	7/96	BBB	X	R	104.245	(1-1-03)	....	....	....	....	250	M6	'93	109¼	102⅛	87	9.76	9.76
• Nts 7.92s 2023	Ao15	A–	7/96	BBB	X	R	103.96	(4-15-03)	....	....	....	....	250	M6	'93	106½	96	s97	8.16	8.16
• Nts 7.20s 2023	mN	A–	7/96	BBB	X	R	103.60	(11-1-03)	....	....	....	....	250	M2	'93	104	85⅝	s87½	8.23	8.23
Phillips-Van Heusen	**68c**	***2.06***		***d4.22***	***1.67***	***Ja***	***41.30***	***417.3***	***117.5***	***10-31-99***	***249.0***		***477.0***	***52.2***						
Deb[5] 7¾s 2023	mN15	BB	3/98	BB+	Y	BE	NC	....	....	....	....	....	100	G1	'93	89½	76	76	10.20	10.20
PhoneTel Technologies	**67**	***n/a***		***0.17***	***d1.22***	***Dc***	***6.33***	***19.97***	***14.68***	***9-30-99***	***138.0***		***141.0***	***117.0***						
Sr Nts 12s 2006	$§d	D	12/98	CCC	Z	BE			Default 12-15-98 int				125	M5	'96	51½	16	17	....	Flat
[6]Physician Sales & Service	**43**	***7.80***		***6.33***	***7.82***	***Mr***	***45.30***	***575.0***	***198.0***	***9-30-99***	***186.0***									
Sr Sub Nts 8½s 2007	aO	B+	4/98	B	Y	BE	104.25	(10-1-02)	....	....	[7]Z108.50	10-1-00	125	Exch.	'97	106	95	96	8.85	8.85
Piedmont Natural Gas	**73b**	***3.47***		***3.54***	***3.84***	***Oc***	***49.40***	***152.0***	***229.0***	***7-31-99***	***333.0***		***945.0***	***46.3***						
M-T Nts[8]'C' 7.35s 2009	[9]jj	A			X	BE	NC	....	....	....	....	....	30.0	G1	'99	102	97½	97½	7.54	7.54
M-T Nts[8]'C' 7.95s 2029	[10]jj	A			X	BE	NC	....	....	....	....	....	60.0	G1	'99	102⅝	96⅝	96¾	8.22	8.22
Pierce Leahy	**63**	***1.17***		***0.94***	***0.82***	***Dc***	***2.03***	***66.80***	***86.10***	***9-30-99***	***564.0***		***641.0***	***89.1***						
• Sr Sub Nts 11⅛s 2006	jJ15	B–			Y	BE	105.563	(7-15-01)	....	....	....	....	200	Exch.	'97	No Sale		106	10.50	10.49
• Sr Sub Nts[11] 9⅛s 2007	jJ15	B–			Y	BE	104.563	(7-15-02)	....	....	Z109.125	7-15-00	120	S7	'97	104¾	99	98	9.31	9.31
Pilgrim's Pride Corp	**26e**	***Δ2.92***		***Δ3.81***	***Δ5.15***	***Sp***	***15.70***	***278.0***	***124.0***	***9-30-99***	***184.0***		***482.0***	***39.0***						
Sr Sub Nts[12] 10⅞s 2003	fA	B+	5/99	B	Y	R	102.719	7-31-00	....	....	....	....	100	D6	'93	103	100½	101	10.77	10.76
Pillowtex Corp	**31**	***2.73***		***1.88***	***1.99***	***Dc***	***7.67***	***822.0***	***948.0***	***10-2-99***	***400.0***		***1356***	***80.0***						
Sr Sub Nts[11] 10s 2006	mN15	CC	11/99	CCC+	Y	BE	105	(11-15-01)	....	....	....	....	125	Exch.	'97	108	28	46	21.74	21.72
Sr Sub Nts 'B' 9s 2007	jD15	CC	11/99	CCC+	Y		104.50	(12-15-02)	....	....	....	....	185	Exch.	'98	104	28	43	20.93	20.91
[13]Pioneer Americas Acquis[14]	**14**	***n/a***		***n/a***	***n/a***	***Dc***	***4.94***	***80.00***	***71.60***	***9-30-99***	***566.0***		***580.0***	***98.0***						
Sr Sec Nts[11]'B' 9¼s 2007	Jd15	B+			Y	BE	104.625	(6-15-02)	....	....	Z109.25	6-15-00	200	Exch.	'97	88	68	79	11.71	11.70
Pioneer Hi-Bred Intl	**26**	***n/a***		***n/a***	***n/a***	***Au***	***88.00***	***1593***	***596.0***	***5-31-99***	***205.0***		***1392***	***20.5***						
Sr Nts 5¾s 2009	Jj15	AA–	10/99	A+	X	BE	[4]Z100	....	....	....	....	....	200	L1	'99	101½	89¼	89½	6.42	6.42
Pioneer Natural Res[15]	**49a**	***3.24***		***d16.76***	***d3.64***	***Dc***	***33.25***	***165.6***	***187.0***	***9-30-99***	***1714***		***2478***	***69.2***						
Sr Nts[16] 6½s 2008	Jd15	BB+	12/98	BBB–	Y	BE	[17]Z100	....	....	....	....	....	350	S4	'98	87¼	80½	84⅞	7.66	7.66

Uniform Footnote Explanations-See Page 260. Other: [1] Co may red in whole for tax law chge. [2] (HRO)On 6-1-01 at 100. [3] Incl disc. [4] Red at greater of 100 or amt based on formula. [5] (HRO)At 100 for a Designated Event. [6] Now PSS World Medical. [7] Max $50M red w/proceeds of Pub Eq Off'g. [8] Issued in min denom $100T. [9] Due 9-25-09. [10] Due 9-14-29. [11] (HRO)On Chge of Ctrl at 101. [12] Co must offer repurch at 101 on Chge in Ctrl. [13] Now Pioneer Americas Inc. [14] Subsid of Pioneer Cos Inc. [15] See Mesa Operating Co.,Parker & Parsley Petrol. [16] Gtd by Pioneer Resources USA,Inc. [17] Plus Make-Whole Premium.

Title-Industry Code & Co. Finances (In Italics) / Exchange, Individual Issue Statistics	Ind / Interest Dates	Fixed Charge Coverage 1996 / S&P Rating	1997 / Date of Last Rating Change	1998 / Prior Rating	Eligible	Year End / Bond Form	Cash & Equiv. (Million $) / Redemption Provisions: Regular Price	Curr. Assets / Regular (Begins) Thru	Curr. Liab. / Sinking Fund Price	Balance Sheet Date / Sinking Fund (Begins) Thru	L. Term Debt (Mil $) / Refund/Other Restriction Price	Refund/Other Restriction (Begins) Thru	Capital-ization (Mil $) / Outst'g (Mil $)	Total Debt % Capital / Underwriting Firm	Underwriting Year	Price Range 1999 High	Price Range 1999 Low	Mo. End Price Sale(s) or Bid	Curr. Yield	Yield to Mat.
Pioneer Natural Res (Cont.)																				
Sr Nts[1] 7.20s 2028	Jj15	BB+	12/98	BBB–	Y	BE	[2]Z100	....	....	....	....	....	250	S4	'98	80¼	70⅝	75¾	9.50	9.50
Pioneer Std Electr	*23b*	*3.36*	*3.52*	*3.03*		*Mr*	*39.11*	*767.6*	*267.5*	*9-30-99*	*333.0*		*746.0*	*42.8*						
Sr Nts[3] 8½s 2003	fA	BB	12/97	BB–	Y	BE	NC	....	....	....	....	....	150	L1	'96	98	90⅛	91⅞	9.25	9.25
Pitney Bowes	*48*	*4.36*	*4.84*	*6.13*		*Dc*	*152.9*	*2630*	*2745*	*9-30-99*	*1899*		*5041*	*62.7*						
Nts 5½s 2004	Ao15	AA			X	BE	[4]Z100	....	....	....	....	....	200	C6	'99	100	94⅜	94⅜	5.83	5.83
Nts 5.95s 2005	Fa	AA			X	BE	[4]Z100	....	....	....	....	....	300	C6	'98	103½	94⅞	94⅞	6.27	6.27
Pitney Bowes Credit	*25*	*2.32*	*2.41*	*3.41*		*Dc*	*32.50*			*6-30-99*	*2928*		*4200*	*70.6*						
Nts 6⅝s 2002	Jd	AA			X	BE	NC	....	....	....	....	....	100	C5	'95	103¾	99⅝	99⅝	6.67	6.67
Nts 5.65s 2003	Jj15	AA			X	BE	NC	....	....	....	....	....	250	G1	'98	100⅞	96⅜	96⅜	5.86	5.86
Nts 8.80s 2003	Fa15	AA			X	R	NC	....	....	....	....	....	150	G1	'91	112⅛	104⅞	104⅞	8.39	8.39
Nts 8⅜s 2008	Fa15	AA	8/88	AA–	X	R	NC	....	....	....	....	....	100	F1	'88	120½	107¼	107¼	8.04	8.04
Nts 9¼s 2008	Jd15	AA	8/88	AA–	X	R	NC	....	....	....	....	....	100	G1	'88	125¾	110½	110½	8.37	8.37
Nts 8.55s 2009	mS15	AA			X	R	NC	....	....	....	....	....	150	G1	'89	122⅛	106¾	106¾	8.01	8.01
Plains Resources	*49a*	*2.26*	*2.03*	*1.38*		*Dc*	*3.87*	*539.0*	*528.0*	*9-30-99*	*653.0*		*803.0*	*79.0*						
Sr Sub Nts[5]'B' 10¼s 2006	Ms15	B–	12/99	B	Y	BE	105.125	(3-15-01)	....	....	....	....	150	Exch.	'96	105	93	97	10.57	10.57
Players International	*40i*	*d3.09*	*1.55*	*1.62*		*Mr*	*35.33*	*46.01*	*69.15*	*9-30-99*	*150.0*		*313.0*	*47.9*						
Sr[6]Nts 10⅞s 2005	Ao15	BB–	4/97	BB	Y	R	104.078	(4-15-00)	....	....	....	....	150	S1	'95	108	104	105	10.36	10.36
[7]Playtex Products	*18*	*1.46*	*1.46*	*1.72*		*Dc*	*7.60*	*207.4*	*139.3*	*9-25-99*	*1030*		*665.0*	*122.0*						
Sr Nts[5]'B 8⅞s 2004	jJ15	B+			Y	BE	[8]Z100	7-14-01	....	....	[9]‡108.875	7-15-00	150	Exch.	'97	105¼	99	100¼	8.85	8.85
Sr[5]Sub Nts 9s 2003	jD15	B	1/96	B+	Y	R	103	12-14-00	....	....	....	....	360	M2	'94	104½	97¼	99	9.09	9.09
PMI Group	*35*	*n/a*	*36.90*	*40.16*		*Dc*				*9-30-99*	*244.0*		*1253*	*15.8*						
Nts 6¾s 2006	mN15	AA–	10/99	A+	X	BE	NC	....	....	....	....	....	100	G1	'96	106⅝	96⅜	96⅜	7.00	7.00
[10]PNC Funding[11]	*25*	*2.43*	*2.47*	*2.35*		*Dc*				*9-30-99*	*17569*		*24288*	*72.3*						
Nts[12] 6.95s 2002	mS	A–			X	BE	NC	....	....	....	....	....	300	S4	'99	100⅝	99¼	99¼	7.00	7.00
Nts[12] 7s 2004	mS	A–			X	BE	NC	....	....	....	....	....	300	S4	'99	100⅝	98⅜	98⅜	7.12	7.11
Sub Nts[12] 9⅞s 2001	Ms	BBB+	2/95	A–	X	BE	NC	....	....	....	....	....	100	S1	'91	109	102⅞	102⅞	9.60	9.60
Sub Nts[12] 6⅞s 2003	Ms	BBB+	2/95	A–	X	BE	NC	....	....	....	....	....	200	S1	'93	104⅝	98¾	98¾	6.96	6.96
Sub Nts[12] 6⅛s 2003	mS	BBB+	2/95	A–	X	BE	NC	....	....	....	....	....	250	S7	'93	102⅛	96	96	6.38	6.38
Sub Nts[12] 7¾s 2004	Jd	BBB+	2/95	A–	X	BE	NC	....	....	....	....	....	200	S7	'94	109⅝	101¼	101¼	7.65	7.65
Sub Nts[12] 6⅞s 2007	jJ15	BBB+			X	BE	NC	....	....	....	....	....	350	S7	'97	107¾	95⅝	95⅝	7.21	7.21
Sub Nts[12] 6⅛s 2009	Fa15	BBB+			X	BE	NC	....	....	....	....	....	250	S4	'99	100⅝	89¾	89¾	6.82	6.82
Sub Nts[12] 7½s 2009	mN	BBB+			X	BE	NC	....	....	....	....	....	400	S4	'99	101½	98½	98½	7.61	7.61
Sub M-T Nts[12] 6½s 2008	Mn	BBB+			X	BE	NC	....	....	....	....	....	140	S4	'98	104⅝	93¼	93¼	6.97	6.97
Pogo Producing	*49a*	*4.66*	*3.24*	*d2.25*		*Dc*	*28.40*	*104.0*	*62.90*	*9-30-99*	*365.0*		*771.0*	*47.4*						
Sub Sub Nts[5]'B' 8¾s 2007	Mn15	BB–	11/99	B+	Y	BE	104.375	(5-15-02)	....	....	....	....	100	Exch.	'97	97¾	88	95	9.21	9.21
Sr Sub Nts[5]'B' 10⅝s 2009	Fa15	BB–	11/99	B+	Y	BE	105.188	(2-15-04)	....	....	....	....	150	Exch.	'99	106	96½	103	10.07	10.07
Poindexter(J.B.) & Co, Inc.	*8*	*0.56*	*0.64*	*0.49*		*Dc*	*1.59*	*74.40*	*57.90*	*6-30-99*	*85.90*		*95.40*	*111.0*						
Sr Nts[5] 12½s 2004	Mn15	B	11/99	B–	Y	R	106.25	5-14-00	....	....	....	....	100	M6	'94	97	92	96	13.02	13.02
Polaroid Corp	*40d*	*4.22*	*3.56*	*1.15*		*Dc*	*88.00*	*1214*	*792.8*	*9-26-99*	*573.0*		*1212*	*71.9*						
• Nts[5] 11½s 2006	Fa15	BB–			Y	BE	[13]Z100	....	....	....	[14]111.50	2-14-02	275	L3	'99	108⅛	97½	s98¾	11.65	11.64
M-T Nts 6¾s 2002	Jj15	BB–	12/98	BBB–	Y	BE	NC	....	....	....	....	....	150	L3	'97	97½	91⅛	93½	7.22	7.22
M-T Nts 7¼s 2007	Jj15	BB–	12/98	BBB–	Y	BE	NC	....	....	....	....	....	150	L3	'97	95	81⅞	81⅞	8.85	8.85
Polymer Group	*42b*	*n/a*	*1.94*	*1.55*		*Dc*	*39.49*	*318.0*	*140.7*	*10-2-99*	*936.0*		*1129*	*80.2*						
Sr Sub Nts 'B'[5] 9s 2007	jJ	B			Y	BE	104.625	(7-1-02)	....	....	[15]Z109.25	7-1-00	400	Exch.	'97	102½	94½	97	9.28	9.28

Uniform Footnote Explanations-See Page 260. Other: [1] Gtd by Pioneer Resources USA,Inc. [2] Plus Make-Whole Premium. [3] (HRO)On Chge of Ctrl at 100. [4] Red at greater of 100 or amt based on formula. [5] (HRO)On Chge of Ctrl at 101. [6] State gaming laws may req hldr's sale/Co red. [7] Was Playtex Family Products. [8] On Chge of Ctrl. [9] Max $52.5M red w/proceeds of Pub Eq Off'g. [10] Gtd by & data of PNC Bank Corp. [11] See Midlantic Corp. [12] Gtd by PNC Bank Corp. [13] Plus Make-Whole Amt. [14] Max $96.25M red w/proceeds of Equity Off'g. [15] Max $140M red w/proceeds of Pub Eq Off'g.

Title-Industry Code & Co. Finances (In Italics) / Individual Issue Statistics (Exchange)	Ind / Interest Dates	Fixed Charge Coverage 1996 / S&P Rating	1997 / Date of Last Rating Change	1998 / Prior Rating	Eligible	Year End / Bond Form	Million $ Cash & Equiv. / Redemption Provisions: Regular Price	Million $ Curr. Assets / Regular (Begins) Thru	Million $ Curr. Liab. / Sinking Fund Price	Balance Sheet Date / Sinking Fund (Begins) Thru	L. Term Debt (Mil $) / Refund/Other Restriction Price	Capital-ization (Mil $) / Refund/Other Restriction (Begins) Thru	Outst'g (Mil $)	Total Debt % Capital / Underwriting Firm	Underwriting Year	Price Range 1999 High	Price Range 1999 Low	Mo. End Price Sale(s) or Bid	Curr. Yield	Yield to Mat.
***Polymer Group** (Cont.)*																				
Sr Sub Nts[1] 'B' 8¾s 2008	Ms	B			Y	BE	104.375	(3-1-03)	....	....	[2]Z108.75	3-1-01	200	Exch.	'98	102½	93	96	9.11	9.11
Pool Energy Services	*49e*	***Acq by Nabors Indus,see***																		
Sr Sub Nts'B' 8⅝s 2008	Ao	BBB	12/99	B+	X	BE	104.313	(4-1-03)	....	....	[3]Z108.625	4-1-01	150	Exch.	'98	104½	88⅞	101	8.54	8.54
Pope & Talbot	*50*	*1.08*	*2.11*	*d2.46*		*Dc*	*114.0*	*275.0*	*102.0*	*9-30-99*	*199.0*	*416.0*		*50.7*						
Deb 8⅜s 2013	Jd	BB	12/98	BB+	Y	R	NC	....	....	....	....	....	75.0	F1	'93	94⅞	84½	88	9.52	9.51
***Popular Inc**[4]*	*10*	*2.06*	*1.83*	*1.84*		*Dc*				*9-30-99*	*1784*	*5305*		*67.9*						
M-T Nts '3' 6.40s 2000	[5]jd15	BBB+			X	BE	NC	....	....	....	....	....	100	C5	'97	101	99⅝	99¾	6.42	6.42
M-T Nts '3' 6.20s 2001	Ao30	BBB+			X	BE	NC	....	....	....	....	....	200	M2	'99	100	98⅝	98⅝	6.29	6.29
M-T Nts '3' 6⅜s 2003	mS15	BBB+			X	BE	NC	....	....	....	....	....	115	M2	'98	99⅜	94¼	95⅞	6.65	6.65
Popular N.A.	*10*	***Gtd by Popular Inc,see***																		
M-T Nts 'D' 6⅞s 2001	Jd15	BBB+			X	BE	NC	....	....	....	....	....	200	C1	'99	100¼	99⅜	99⅜	6.92	6.92
M-T Nts 'D' 6⅝s 2002	[6]jd15	BBB+			X	BE	NC	....	....	....	....	....	100	C5	'97	102⅝	97⅝	97⅝	6.79	6.79
M-T Nts 'D' 6⅝s 2004	Jj15	BBB+			X	BE	NC	....	....	....	....	....	255	C1	'99	100¾	96¼	96¼	6.88	6.88
M-T Nts 'E' 7⅜s 2001	mS15	BBB+			X	BE	NC	....	....	....	....	....	250	C6	'99	101⅛	99⅞	100	7.38	7.37
***Portland General Elec**[7]*	*72a*	*4.44*	*3.82*	*3.92*		*Dc*	*13.00*	*291.0*	*499.0*	*9-30-99*	*709.0*	*2006*		*47.2*						
1st 7¾s 2023	Ao15	A	3/96	A–	X	R	103.751	(4-15-03)	Z100	....	....	....	125	G1	'93	109⅛	94⅝	94¾	8.18	8.18
M-T Nts[8] 9.07s 2005	[9]ao15	A	3/96	A–	X	BE	NC	....	....	....	....	....	18.0	M2	'91	118⅜	106⅞	106⅞	8.49	8.48
M-T Nts[8] 9.31s 2021	[10]ao15	A	3/96	A–	X	BE	NC	....	....	....	....	....	20.0	M2	'91	132½	111⅝	111¾	8.33	8.33
M-T Nts[8] 9.46s 2021	[11]ao15	A	3/96	A–	X	BE	104.73	(8-12-01)	....	....	....	....	25.0	M2	'91	134¼	113¼	113¼	8.35	8.35
M-T Nts 'I'[8] 7.66s 2002	[12]jj15	A	3/96	A–	X	BE	NC	....	....	....	....	....	15.0	S1	'92	106	100⅞	100⅞	7.59	7.59
M-T Nts 'I'[8] 7.61s 2004	[13]jj15	A	3/96	A–	X	BE	NC	....	....	....	....	....	11.0	S1	'92	109¼	100¾	100¾	7.55	7.55
M-T Nts 'I'[8] 7.61s 2004	[14]jj15	A	3/96	A–	X	BE	NC	....	....	....	....	....	26.0	S1	'92	109¼	100¾	100¾	7.55	7.55
M-T Nts 'I'[8] 7.60s 2004	[15]jj15	A	3/96	A–	X	BE	NC	....	....	....	....	....	8.00	S1	'92	109¼	100¾	100¾	7.54	7.54
M-T Nts 'II'[8] 6.47s 2003	fA15	A	3/96	A–	X	BE	NC	....	....	....	....	....	40.0	S1	'93	103½	97¼	97¼	6.65	6.65
M-T Nts 'III'[8] 7.40s 2001	mS15	A	3/96	A–	X	BE	NC	....	....	....	....	....	45.0	U1	'94	104⅞	100⅜	100⅜	7.37	7.37
Portola Packaging, Inc	*16d*	*△0.58*	*△0.87*	*△0.93*		*Au*	*2.37*	*44.60*	*27.60*	*8-31-99*	*136.0*	*124.0*		*110.0*						
Sr[1]Nts 10⅜s 2005	aO	B			Y	R	105.375	(10-1-00)	....	....	....	....	110	C1	'95	103½	100	100	10.75	10.75
Post Apartment Homes, L.P.	*57*	*3.24*	*3.51*	*4.27*		*Dc*				*9-30-99*	*893.0*	*2141*		*41.7*						
Nts 7¼s 2003	aO	BBB+			X	BE	[16]Z100	....	....	....	....	....	100	M2	'96	102½	97⅝	97⅝	7.43	7.43
Nts 7½s 2006	aO	BBB+			X	BE	[16]Z100	....	....	....	....	....	25.0	M2	'96	106⅜	96	96⅛	7.80	7.80
M-T Nts 6.78s 2005	[17]mn	BBB+			X	BE	NC	....	....	....	....	....	25.0	L3	'97	102½	95¼	95¼	7.12	7.12
Potlatch Corp.	*50*	*2.40*	*1.93*	*1.97*		*Dc*	*11.34*	*392.4*	*337.6*	*9-30-99*	*702.0*	*1715*		*46.4*						
[18]Deb[19] 9⅛s 2009	jD	BBB+	3/99	A–	X	R	NC	....	....	....	....	....	100	G1	'89	121⅛	108	108	8.45	8.45
Deb[8] 6.95s 2015	jD15	BBB+	3/99	A–	X	R	NC	....	....	....	....	....	100	G1	'95	99¼	88¾	89	7.81	7.81
***Potomac Edison Co.**[20]*	*72a*	*3.71*	*3.56*	*4.18*		*Dc*	*8.47*	*277.0*	*104.0*	*6-30-99*	*588.0*	*1389*		*42.3*						
1st 5⅞s 2000	Ms	A+	4/94	AA–	X	R	NC	....	Z100	....	....	....	75.0	G1	'93	100½	99⅞	100	5.88	5.87
1st 8s 2006	Jd	A+	4/94	AA–	X	R	101.59	11-30-00	Z100	....	®100	11-30-01	50.0	G1	'91	102½	99⅝	100¼	7.98	7.98
1st 8s 2022	jD	A+	4/94	AA–	X	R	103.398	(12-1-02)	Z100	....	....	....	50.0		'92	107⅛	96⅛	96⅞	8.26	8.26
1st 7¾s 2023	Fa	A+	4/94	AA–	X	R	103.475	(2-1-03)	Z100	....	....	....	45.0	G1	'93	107⅝	94	94⅛	8.23	8.23
1st 8s 2024	Jd	A+			X	R	103.597	(6-1-04)	Z100	....	....	....	75.0	G1	'94	109½	97	97⅝	8.19	8.19
1st 7¾s 2025	Mn	A+			X	R	103.084	(5-1-05)	Z100	....	....	....	65.0	G1	'95	109⅛	95⅛	95¼	8.14	8.14
1st 7⅝s 2025	Mn	A+			X	R	103.263	(5-1-05)	Z100	....	....	....	80.0	P4	'95	107⅝	93⅜	93¾	8.13	8.13
Potomac Electric Power	*72a*	*3.47*	*3.30*	*3.44*		*Dc*	*31.20*	*551.0*	*444.0*	*9-30-99*	*2763*	*5340*		*57.9*						
1st 5⅛s 2001	Ao	A	1/95	A+	X	R	100.19	3-31-00	....	....	....	....	15.0	K2	'66	99⅛	97⅝	97¾	5.24	5.24

Uniform Footnote Explanations-See Page 260. Other: [1] (HRO)On Chge of Ctrl at 101. [2] Max $70M red w/proceeds of Equity Off'g. [3] Max $52M red w/proceeds of Pub Eq Off'g. [4] See BanPonce Corp,Popular N.A. [5] Due 8-25-00. [6] Due 10-27-02. [7] Subsid of Portland Gen'l Corp. [8] Issued in min denom $100T. [9] Due 8-15-05. [10] Due 8-11-21. [11] Due 8-12-21. [12] Due 1-14-02. [13] Due 7-14-04. [14] Due 7-20-04. [15] Due 7-21-04. [16] Plus Make Whole Amt. [17] Due 9-22-05. [18] Credit Sensitive Deb. [19] Int(min8.825%,max14%)subj to adj for Rat'g chge. [20] Subsid of Allegheny Power Systems.

Title-Industry Code & Co. Finances (In Italics) / Exchange, Individual Issue Statistics	Ind / Interest Dates	S&P Rating	Fixed Charge Coverage 1996 / Date of Last Rating Change	1997 / Prior Rating	1998 / Eligible	Year End / Bond Form	Cash & Equiv. (Million $) / Redemption Provisions: Regular Price	Curr. Assets (Million $) / Regular (Begins) Thru	Curr. Liab. / Sinking Fund Price	Balance Sheet Date / Sinking Fund (Begins) Thru	L. Term Debt (Mil $) / Refund/Other Restriction Price	Refund/Other Restriction (Begins) Thru	Capital-ization (Mil $) / Outst'g (Mil $)	Total Debt % Capital / Underwriting Firm	Underwriting Year	Price Range 1999 High	Price Range 1999 Low	Mo. End Price Sale(s) or Bid	Curr. Yield	Yield to Mat.
***Potomac Electric Power** (Cont.)*																				
1st 5⅞s 2002	Mn	A	1/95	A+	X	R	100.46	4-30-00	....	....	....	....	35.0	K2	'67	100⅛	97¼	97¼	6.04	6.04
1st 6⅝s 2003	Fa15	A	1/95	A+	X	R	100.74	2-14-00	....	....	....	....	40.0	K2	'68	101⅛	98⅞	98⅞	6.70	6.70
1st 5⅝s 2003	aO15	A	1/95	A+	X	R	NC	....	....	....	....	....	50.0	G1	'93	101⅛	95	95	5.92	5.92
1st 6s 2004	[1]Apr	A			X	BE	100	(7-1-00)	....	....	....	....	270	L2	'99	100	95⅛	95⅛	6.31	6.31
1st 6½s 2005	mS15	A			X	R	NC	....	....	....	....	....	100	S1	'95	105¾	95¾	95¾	6.79	6.79
1st 6½s 2008	Ms15	A	1/95	A+	X	R	NC	....	....	....	....	....	78.0	B7	'93	105⅞	93⅞	93⅞	6.92	6.92
1st 5⅞s 2008	aO15	A	1/95	A+	X	R	NC	....	....	....	....	....	50.0	M6	'93	102⅜	90⅛	90⅛	6.52	6.52
1st 9s 2021	Jd	A	1/95	A+	X	R	103.61	(6-1-01)	....	....	....	....	100	M2	'91	109⅞	101⅝	101⅝	8.86	8.85
1st 7¼s 2023	jJ	A	1/95	A+	X	R	102.99	(6-30-03)	....	....	....	....	100	M2	'93	104	88¾	88⅞	8.16	8.16
1st 6⅞s 2023	mS	A	1/95	A+	X	R	102.66	(9-1-03)	....	....	....	....	100	F1	'93	102⅝	86	86⅛	7.98	7.98
1st 6⅞s 2024	aO15	A	1/95	A+	X	R	103.10	(10-15-03)	....	....	....	....	75.0	L3	'93	101¾	85⅛	85¼	8.06	8.06
1st 7⅜s 2025	mS15	A			X	R	103.38	(9-15-05)	....	....	....	....	75.0	C5	'95	106¾	89¾	89¾	8.22	8.22
1st 8½s 2027	Mn15	A	1/95	A+	X	R	103.21	(5-15-02)	....	....	....	....	75.0	S1	'92	111	100	100⅛	8.49	8.49
1st 7½s 2028	Ms15	A	1/95	A+	X	R	103.45	(3-15-03)	....	....	....	....	40.0	S1	'93	106⅛	90⅛	90¼	8.31	8.31
[4]PP&L Capital Funding	***25***		***3.77***	***3.24***	***3.45***	***Dc***	***340.0***	***1479***	***1900***	***9-30-99***	***3983***		***6651***	***74.6***						
M-T Nts[5]'A' 5.86s 2000	[6]ms15	BBB	10/99	BBB+	X	BE	NC	....	....	....	....	....	50.0	M2	'98	99¾	98⅝	99⅛	5.91	5.91
M-T Nts[5]'A' 5.81s 2001	[7]ms15	BBB	10/99	BBB+	X	BE	NC	....	....	....	....	....	25.0	M2	'98	99¼	97	97⅝	5.95	5.95
M-T Nts[5]'A' 6⅜s 2003	[8]fa15	BBB	10/99	BBB+	X	BE	NC	....	....	....	....	....	60.0	M2	'98	102	98¼	99⅛	6.43	6.43
M-T Nts[5]'A' 6.79s 2004	[9]fa15	BBB	10/99	BBB+	X	BE	NC	....	....	....	....	....	100	M2	'97	101½	94⅝	96¼	7.05	7.05
PPG Indus	***15***		***12.94***	***13.16***	***11.09***	***Dc***	***164.0***	***3141***	***2291***	***9-30-99***	***1849***		***4788***	***36.8***						
Deb 7.40s 2019	fA15	A			X	BE	[10]Z100	....	....	....	....	....	200	G1	'99	100¾	96¾	97	7.63	7.63
Deb 9s 2021	Mn	A			X	BE	NC	....	....	....	....	....	148	F1	'91	128¼	111⅝	111¾	8.05	8.05
Nts 6¼s 2002	Fa15	A			X	BE	[11]Z100	....	....	....	....	....	100	C5	'97	101⅞	98⅝	98⅝	6.34	6.34
Nts 6¾s 2004	fA15	A			X	BE	NC	....	....	....	....	....	300	G1	'99	100½	98⅝	98⅝	6.84	6.84
Nts 6⅞s 2005	fA	A			X	BE	NC	....	....	....	....	....	100	C5	'95	106⅛	98	98	7.02	7.01
Nts 6½s 2007	mN	A			X	BE	[12]Z100	....	....	....	....	....	150	C5	'97	103⅞	94⅝	94⅝	6.87	6.87
Nts 7.05s 2009	fA15	A			X	BE	[10]Z100	....	....	....	....	....	300	G1	'99	100⅝	97¼	97¼	7.25	7.25
Nts 6⅞s 2012	Fa15	A			X	BE	NC	....	....	....	....	....	100	C5	'97	108⅝	95½	95½	7.20	7.20
Nts 7⅜s 2016	Jd	A			X	BE	[12]Z100	....	....	....	....	....	150	C5	'96	109½	97⅝	97¾	7.54	7.54
Nts 6⅞s 2017	mn	A			X	BE	[12]Z100	....	....	....	....	....	100	C5	'97	104⅛	91⅞	92	7.47	7.47
Praxair, Inc[13]	***14b***		***3.33***	***3.42***	***2.98***	***Dc***	***35.00***	***1283***	***1001***	***9-30-99***	***2745***		***6168***	***53.1***						
Deb 8.70s 2022	jJ15	BBB+	6/95	BBB	X	BE	104.35	(7-15-02)	....	....	....	....	300	G1	'92	115½	103⅝	106⅞	8.14	8.14
Nts 6.70s 2001	Ao15	BBB+			X	BE	NC	....	....	....	....	....	250	M5	'96	101¼	99⅜	99⅜	6.74	6.74
Nts 6¾s 2003	Ms	BBB+	6/95	BBB	X	BE	NC	....	....	....	....	....	300	M6	'93	102	98⅛	98⅛	6.88	6.88
Nts 6.15s 2003	Ao15	BBB+			X	BE	NC	....	....	....	....	....	250	M5	'98	100⅛	96⅜	96⅜	6.38	6.38
Nts 6.85s 2005	Jd15	BBB+			X	BE	NC	....	....	....	....	....	150	M6	'95	103⅛	96½	96½	7.10	7.10
Nts 6.90s 2006	mN	BBB+			X	BE	NC	....	....	....	....	....	250	M6	'96	103⅝	94¾	94¾	7.28	7.28
Nts 6⅝s 2007	aO15	BBB+			X	BE	NC	....	....	....	....	....	250	M5	'97	102	93	93	7.12	7.12
Precise Technologies[14]	***52***		***1.28***	***0.78***	***0.84***	***Dc***	***0.31***	***33.50***	***27.70***	***9-30-99***	***84.10***		***78.30***	***116.0***						
Sub Nts[2]'B' 11⅛s 2007	Jd15	B−			Y	BE	[15]Z100	6-14-02	....	....	111.125	....	75.0	Exch.	'97	96½	90	90	12.36	12.36
Precision Castparts	***3***		***6.93***	***7.95***	***6.94***	***Mr***	***31.60***	***567.0***	***288.0***	***9-26-99***	***342.0***		***1143***	***35.2***						
Nts 6¾s 2007	jD15	BBB−	6/99	BBB	X	BE	[10]100	....	....	....	....	....	150	G1	'97	104¼	90⅝	90⅝	7.45	7.45
Premark Int'l	***34***		***10.51***	***15.44***	***15.64***	***Dc***	***175.9***	***1204***	***659.4***	***9-25-99***	***157.0***		***1285***	***21.9***						
Nts 10½s 2000	mS15	AA−	12/99	BBB+	X	R	NC	....	....	....	....	....	100	G1	'90	107⅞	102½	102½	10.24	10.24

Uniform Footnote Explanations-See Page 260. Other: [1] Int pd monthly. [2] (HRO)On Chge of Ctrl at 101. [3] Max $105M red w/proceeds of Pub Eq Off'g. [4] Gtd by & data of PP&L Resources. [5] Gtd by PP&L Resources. [6] Due 10-17-00. [7] Due 9-17-01. [8] Due 3-24-03. [9] Due 11-24-04. [10] Red at greater of 100 or amt based on formula. [11] Plus make-whole amt. [12] Greater of 100 or amt based on formula. [13] See CBI Indus. [14] Subsid of Precise Hldg. [15] Plus Make-Whole Premium.

Title-Industry Code & Co. Finances (In Italics) / Individual Issue Statistics (Exchange)	Ind / Interest Dates	Fixed Charge Coverage 1996 / S&P Rating	1997 / Date of Last Rating Change	Prior Rating	1998 / Eligible	Year End / Bond Form	Cash & Equiv. (Million $) / Regular Price	Curr. Assets (Million $) / Regular (Begins) Thru	Curr. Liab. (Million $) / Sinking Fund Price	Balance Sheet Date / Sinking Fund (Begins) Thru	L. Term Debt (Mil $) / Refund/Other Restriction Price	Refund/Other Restriction (Begins) Thru	Capital-ization (Mil $) / Outst'g (Mil $)	Total Debt % Capital / Underwriting Firm	Underwriting Year	Price Range 1999 High	Price Range 1999 Low	Mo. End Price Sale(s) or Bid	Curr. Yield	Yield to Mat.
***Premark Int'l** (Cont.)*																				
Nts 6⅞s 2008	mN15	**AA–**	12/99	BBB+	X	BE	NC	....	....	....	....	....	150	G1	'98	101¾	91⅜	92½	7.43	7.43
Premier Parks	***40***	***1.29***	***2.33***		***1.52***	***Dc***	***171.0***	***513.0***	***374.0***	***9-30-99***	***1888***		***3487***	***54.2***						
(Oper)Sr Nts 9¾s 2007	Jj15	**B**	3/98	B+	Y	BE	104.875	(1-15-02)	....	....	....	....	125	L3	'97	109	99¾	102¼	9.54	9.53
Sr Nts 9¼s 2006	Ao	**B–**			Y	BE	104.625	(4-1-02)	....	....	....	....	280	L3	'98	107¾	94½	98¼	9.41	9.41
Sr Nts[1] 9¾s 2007	Jd15	**B–**			Y	BE	104.875	(6-15-03)	....	....	[2]Z109.75	6-15-02	430	L3	'99	103¾	96½	99½	9.80	9.80
Sr Disc[3]Nts 10s 2008	Ao	**B–**			Y		105	(4-1-03)	....	....	[4]Z110	4-1-01	410	L3	'98	71	63½	69	14.49	14.49
[5]President Riverboat Casinos	***40i***	***0.41***	***0.21***		***0.33***	***Fb***	***21.20***	***27.70***	***65.70***	***12-15-99***	***105.0***		***146.0***	***97.0***						
Sr Nts 13s 2001	mS15	**CCC+**	11/99	B	Y	BE	102	9-14-00	....	....	....	....	75.0	Exch.	'95	94	85	85	15.29	15.29
Presidential Life	***35a***	***11.31***	***15.20***		***15.39***	***Dc***				***9-30-99***	***100.0***		***317.0***	***21.1***						
Sr Nts[6] 7⅞s 2009	Fa15	**BBB**			X	BE	[7]Z100	....	....	....	....	....	100	B4	'99	99⅛	91⅛	91⅛	8.64	8.64
Presley Cos	***13h***	***0.08***	***d0.25***		***6.13***	***Dc***				***p6-30-99***	***292.0***		***204.0***	***88.7***						
Sr Nts[1] 12½s 2001	jJ	**CCC**	3/96	B–	Y	R	104	6-30-00	....	....	....	....	180	D6	'94	89	82	85	14.71	14.70
Prestolite Electric	***23b***	***n/a***	***1.95***		***1.30***	***Dc***	***0.83***	***113.0***	***53.10***	***10-2-99***	***147.0***		***145.0***	***93.2***						
Sr[1]Nts[8] 9⅝s 2008	Fa	**B+**			Y	BE	104.8125	(2-1-03)	....	....	[9]Z110	2-1-01	125	Exch.	'98	101	78	78	12.34	12.33
[10]Price Commun'ns Wireless	***12***	***n/a***	***0.43***		***1.25***	***Dc***	***206.1***	***237.3***	***57.95***	***9-30-99***	***700.0***		***834.0***	***79.0***						
Sr Sec Nts[1]'B' 9⅛s 2006	jD15	**B+**	10/99	B	Y	BE	[11]Z100	6-14-02	....	....	[12]Z109.125	6-15-01	525	Exch.	'99	105½	100	101¼	9.01	9.01
Sr Sub Nts[1] 11¾s 2007	jJ15	**B–**	10/99	CCC+	Y	BE	105.875	(7-15-02)	....	....	[13]Z111.75	7-10-02	175	Exch.	'97	112	105½	109	10.78	10.78
Price/Costco Inc[14]	***59m***	***6.56***	***8.80***		***17.12***	***Au***	***661.1***	***3081***	***2662***	***5-9-99***	***912.0***		***4394***	***20.8***						
Sr Nts 7⅛s 2005	Jd15	**A–**	8/97	BBB+	X	R	NC	....	....	....	....	....	300	D6	'95	107⅝	99	99	7.20	7.20
Price Development Co L.P.	***57***	***5.64***	***p4.10***		***5.09***	***Dc***				***9-30-99***	***393.0***		***730.0***	***53.9***						
Sr([15]Amort)Nts 7.29s 2008	Ms11	**BBB–**			X	BE	[7]Z100	....	....	....	....	....	100	M2	'98	102¾	90¼	90¼	8.08	....
Price REIT	***57***	***Acq by Kimco Realty, see***																		
Sr Nts 7¼s 2000	mN	**A–**	6/98	BBB–	X	BE	NC	....	....	....	....	....	100	M2	'95	102⅜	100⅛	100⅛	7.24	7.24
Sr Nts 7⅛s 2004	Jd15	**A–**	6/98	BBB–	X	BE	[7]Z100	....	....	....	....	....	50.0	M2	'97	101⅝	97	97	7.35	7.34
Sr Nts 7½s 2006	mN5	**A–**	6/98	BBB–	X	BE	Z100	(11-5-01)	....	....	....	....	55.0	M2	'96	103¼	96⅛	96⅛	7.80	7.80
Pride International[16]	***49e***	***n/a***	***5.53***		***6.11***	***Dc***	***195.4***	***428.9***	***263.3***	***9-30-99***	***1189***		***2029***	***60.8***						
Sr Nts[1] 10s 2009	Jd	**BB**			Y	BE	105	(6-1-04)	....	....	[17]Z110	6-1-04	200	S4	'99	103	100	102	9.80	9.80
Pride Petroleum Services	***49e***	***Now Pride Int'l,see***																		
Sr Nts[1] 9⅜s 2007	Mn	**BB**	4/98	BB–	Y	BE	104.688	(5-1-02)	....	....	[18]Z109.375	4-30-00	325	D6	'97	102	91¾	99½	9.42	9.42
Prime Hospitality	***32***	***3.54***	***3.57***		***5.40***	***Dc***	***32.80***	***78.20***	***70.30***	***9-30-99***	***566.0***		***1210***	***47.4***						
• 1st[1] 9¼s 2006	Jj15	**BB**	12/96	BB–	Y	R	104.625	(1-15-01)	....	....	....	....	120	S7	'96	105	95	96	9.64	9.63
Sr Sub Nts[1] 9¾s 2007	Ao	**B+**			Y	BE	104.875	(4-1-02)	....	....	[19]Z109.75	4-1-00	200	Exch.	'97	105	91	99	9.85	9.85
Prime Medical Services	***30a***	***6.10***	***7.11***		***6.26***	***Dc***	***21.00***	***54.90***	***16.70***	***9-30-99***	***103.0***		***224.0***	***46.8***						
Sr Sub Nts[20] 8¾s 2008	Ao	**B**			Y	BE	104.375	(4-1-03)	....	....	[21]Z108.75	4-1-01	100	Exch.	'98	99	91½	92	9.51	9.51
Prime Succession[22]	***63***	***n/a***	***1.01***		***0.73***	***Dc***	***4.83***	***12.70***	***16.40***	***9-30-99***	***220.0***		***339.0***	***66.9***						
Sr Sub Nts[1] 10¾s 2004	fA15	**CC**	11/99	CCC	Y	BE	105.375	(8-15-00)	....	....	....	....	100	S7	'96	99	30	30	....	....
PRIMEDIA Inc[23]	***54***	***0.72***	***0.85***		***0.71***	***Dc***	***30.00***	***499.0***	***558.0***	***9-30-99***	***2099***		***2489***	***85.3***						
Sr Nts[1] 7⅝s 2008	Ao	**BB–**			Y	BE	103.813	(4-1-03)	....	....	[24]Z100	....	250	Exch.	'98	100¼	92½	93½	8.16	8.15
Primus Telecomm Grp	***67b***	***d9.00***	***d1.80***		***d0.59***	***Dc***	***84.50***	***307.0***	***271.0***	***9-30-99***	***648.0***		***706.0***	***92.6***						
Sr Nts[1] 11¾s 2004	fA	**B–**			Y	BE	105.875	(8-1-01)	....	....	[25]Z111.75	8-1-00	225	L3	'97	106½	96	100	11.75	11.75
Printpack Inc.	***20b***	***△0.64***	***△0.81***		***△0.92***	***Je***	***1.03***	***177.0***	***88.60***	***9-25-99***	***479.0***		***479.0***	***102.0***						
Sr Nts[1]'B' 9⅞s 2004	fA15	**B+**	12/98	BB–	Y	BE	104.938	8-14-00	....	....	....	....	100	Exch.	'97	101	95½	100	9.88	9.87
Sr Sub Nts[1]'B' 10⅝s 2006	fA15	**B**	12/98	B+	Y	BE	105.313	(8-15-01)	....	....	....	....	200	Exch.	'97	98	91	96	11.07	11.06
Prison Realty Trust	***57***	***n/a***	***n/a***		***n/a***	***Dc***				***9-30-99***	***1016***		***2012***	***34.3***						
Sr[1]Nts 12s 2006	Jd	**B+**			Y	BE	NC	....	....	....	[26]Z112	5-31-02	100	L3	'99	101	95	96	12.50	12.50

Uniform Footnote Explanations-See Page 260. Other: [1] (HRO)On Chge of Ctrl at 101. [2] Max $150.5M red w/proceeds of Pub Eq Off'g. [3] (HRO)On Chge of Ctrl at 101(Accreted Val). [4] Accreted Val:Max $143M red w/proceeds of Pub Eq Off'g. [5] Now President Casinos. [6] (HRO)On Sale of certain subsid at 100. [7] Plus Make-Whole Amt. [8] Gtd by Prestolite Electric Hldg. [9] Max $43.8M red w/proceeds of Equity Off'g. [10] Now Price Communications. [11] On Chge of Ctrl,plus premium. [12] Max $184M red w/proceeds of Equity Off'g. [13] Max $61M red/w proceeds of Pub Eq Off'g. [14] Now Costco Cos. [15] Prin pyts:$250/note ea 3-11 fr 2005. [16] Was Pride Petroleum,see. [17] Max $66.6M red w/proceeds of Pub Eq Off'g. [18] Max $108.3M red w/proceeds of Pub Eq Off'g. [19] Max $70M red w/proceeds of Pub Eq Off'g. [20] (HRO)On Chge of Ctrl at 100. [21] Max $35M red w/proceeds Pub Eq Off'g. [22] Was Prime Succession Acq. [23] Was K-III Communications. [24] On Chge of Ctrl,plus Applicable Premium. [25] Max $78.75M red w/proceeds of Pub Eq Off'g. [26] Max $35M red w/proceeds of Pub Eq Off'g.

Title-Industry Code & Co. Finances (In Italics)	Ind	Fixed Charge Coverage 1996	1997	1998	Year End		Million $ Cash & Equiv.	Curr. Assets	Curr. Liab.	Balance Sheet Date	L. Term Debt (Mil $)		Capital-ization (Mil $)	Total Debt % Capital						
Individual Issue Statistics Exchange ↓	Interest Dates	S&P Rating	Date of Last Rating Change	Prior Rating	Eligible ↓	Bond Form	Redemption Provisions: Regular Price	Regular (Begins) Thru	Sinking Fund Price	Sinking Fund (Begins) Thru	Refund/Other Restriction Price	Refund/Other Restriction (Begins) Thru	Outst'g (Mil $)	Underwriting Firm	Underwriting Year	Price Range 1999 High	Price Range 1999 Low	Mo. End Price Sale(s) or Bid	Curr. Yield	Yield to Mat.
Private Export Funding	***25***	***Gtd by Export-Import Bank of U.S.***																		
Sec[1]Nts'B' 6.49s 2007	jJ15	**AAA**			X	BE	NC	....	....	....	....	....	100	C4	'96	108⅝	96⅝	96⅝	6.71	6.71
Sec[1]Nts 'D' 5.87s 2008	jJ31	**AAA**			X	BE	NC	....	....	....	....	....	200	C1	'98	104	92⅛	92¼	6.36	6.36
Sec[1]Nts E 5.73s 2004	Jj15	**AAA**			X	BE	NC	....	....	....	....	....	200	C1	'98	103	96¼	96¼	5.95	5.95
Sec[1]Nts 'F' 5¼s 2005	Mn15	**AAA**			X	BE	NC	....	....	....	....	....	150	C1	'98	100⅛	92⅝	92⅝	5.67	5.67
Sec[1]Nts HH 8.35s 2001	Jj31	**AAA**			X	R	NC	....	....	....	....	....	100		'91	106½	101⅞	101⅞	8.19	8.19
Sec[1]Nts II 8.40s 2001	jJ31	**AAA**			X	R	NC	....	....	....	....	....	200	B11	'91	108	102¾	102¾	8.18	8.17
Sec[1]Nts KK 8¾s 2003	Jd30	**AAA**			X	R	NC	....	....	....	....	....	100	M5	'91	114	105⅞	105⅞	8.26	8.26
Sec[1]Nts LL 7.90s 2000	Ms31	**AAA**			X	R	NC	....	....	....	....	....	150		'91	103⅜	100⅜	100⅜	7.87	7.87
Sec[1]Nts NN 7.30s 2002	Jj31	**AAA**			X	R	NC	....	....	....	....	....	99.0	B11	'92	106⅛	101¼	101¼	7.21	7.20
Sec[1]Nts PP 6.90s 2003	Jj31	**AAA**			X	BE	NC	....	....	....	....	....	93.0	B5	'93	106½	100½	100½	6.86	6.86
Sec([2]Amort)[1]Nts QQ 5.65s 2003	Ms15	**AAA**			X	BE	NC	....	....	....	....	....	63.0	M5	'93	100¾	97¾	97¾	5.78	....
Sec([2]Amort)[1]Nts RR 5.48s 2003	mS15	**AAA**			X	BE	NC	....	....	....	....	....	87.0	B11	'93	100¼	97⅜	97⅜	5.63	....
Sec([3]Amort)[1]Nts SS 5.80s 2004	Fa	**AAA**			X	BE	NC	....	....	....	....	....	85.0	B11	'94	102¼	97⅛	98⅛	5.91	....
Sec([4]Amort)[1]Nts TT 6.86s 2004	Ao31	**AAA**			X	BE	NC	....	....	....	....	....	183	B11	'94	107⅝	99⅞	99⅞	6.86	....
Sec[1]Nts UU 7.95s 2006	mN	**AAA**			X	BE	100	(11-1-04)	....	....	....	....	94.0	B11	'94	113¼	103	103	7.71	7.71
Sec[1]Nts VV 6.24s 2002	Mn15	**AAA**			X	BE	NC	....	....	....	....	....	125	C2	'95	103½	99⅛	99⅛	6.29	6.29
◆Sec[1]Nts WW 6.62s 2005	aO	**AAA**			X	BE	NC	....	....	....	....	....	125	C2	'95	No Sale		98⅜	6.72	6.72
Sec Nts XX 5⅛s 2001	Ms15	**AAA**			X	BE	NC	....	....	....	....	....	116	D4	'96	101	98⅞	98⅞	5.56	5.56
Sec Nts YY 7.03s 2003	aO31	**AAA**			X	BE	NC	....	....	....	....	....	125	C1	'96	107¾	100⅝	100⅝	6.99	6.99
Sec Nts ZZ[1] 7.11s 2007	Ao15	**AAA**			X	BE	NC	....	....	....	....	....	100		'97	112¼	100¼	100¼	7.09	7.09
Sec Nts AAA[1] 7.01s 2004	Ao30	**AAA**			X	BE	NC	....	....	....	....	....	125	C1	'97	108⅛	100½	100½	6.98	6.97
Procter & Gamble Co.	***33***	***△12.49***	***△11.42***	***△9.98***	***Je***		***2471***	***11826***	***12675***	***9-30-99***	***7212***		***24480***	***49.5***						
Deb 7⅝s 2023	Ms	**AA**			X	BE	103.608	(3-1-03)	....	....	....	....	175	G1	'93	106⅝	94¾	95	7.76	7.76
Deb 6.45s 2026	Jj15	**AA**			X	BE	[5]Z100	....	....	....	....	....	300	G1	'96	105⅝	88⅛	88¼	7.31	7.31
Deb 8¾s 2022	Jd	**AA**			X	BE	NC	....	....	....	....	....	100		'97	133	114⅛	114⅜	7.65	7.65
Deb 8s 2029	aO26	**AA**	4/91	AA+	X	R	NC	....	....	....	....	....	100	M6	'89	127⅛	105½	105¾	7.57	7.56
Nts 8.70s 2001	fA	**AA**			X	BE	NC	....	....	....	....	....	175	M5	'91	108⅞	103⅛	103⅛	8.44	8.43
Nts 5¼s 2003	mS15	**AA**			X	BE	NC	....	....	....	....	....	750	G1	'98	100¾	94⅞	94⅞	5.53	5.53
Nts 8s 2003	mN15	**AA**			X	BE	NC	....	....	....	....	....	200	G1	'91	111⅞	103⅝	103⅝	7.72	7.72
Nts[6] 8½s 2009	fA10	**AA**	4/91	AA+	X	R	NC	....	....	....	....	....	150	M2	'89	124⅞	108⅝	108⅝	7.83	7.82
Nts 6⅞s 2009	mS15	**AA**			X	BE	NC	....	....	....	....	....	1000	G1	'99	101½	97¾	97¾	7.03	7.03
[7]***Production Resources/PRG Fin***	***63***	***n/a***	***1.17***	***0.88***	***Dc***		***5.23***	***91.20***	***51.70***	***9-30-99***	***179.0***		***187.0***	***96.4***						
Sr Sub Nts[8] 11½s 2008	Jj15	**B–**			Y	BE	105.75	(1-15-03)	....	....	[9]Z110	1-15-01	100	Exch.	'98	102	88	89	12.92	12.91
Progressive Corp	***35c***	***8.18***	***9.96***	***11.80***	***Dc***					***9-30-99***	***1041***		***3757***	***28.5***						
Nts 10s 2000	jD15	**A+**	2/95	A–	X	R	NC	....	....	....	....	....	150	B7	'88	107¾	102⅞	102⅞	9.72	9.72
Nts 6.60s 2004	Jj15	**A+**	2/95	A–	X	BE	NC	....	....	....	....	....	200	M5	'94	102⅝	96⅞	96⅞	6.81	6.81
Nts 7.30s 2006	Jd	**A+**			X	BE	NC	....	....	....	....	....	100	M5	'96	108	98	98	7.45	7.45
Nts 7s 2013	aO	**A+**	2/95	A–	X	BE	NC	....	....	....	....	....	150	F1	'93	105¼	92½	92½	7.57	7.57
Sr Nts 6⅝s 2029	Ms	**A+**			X	BE	[10]Z100	....	....	....	....	....	300	D6	'99	98¾	83¼	84¾	7.82	7.82
Sub Nts 10⅛s 2000	jD15	**A**	2/95	BBB+	X	R	NC	....	....	....	....	....	150	B7	'88	108	103	103	9.83	9.83
ProLogis Trust[11]	***57***	***2.21***	***2.31***	***1.74***	***Dc***					***9-30-99***	***2484***		***5761***	***46.7***						
Nts 7s 2003	aO	**BBB+**			X	BE	[12]Z100	....	....	....	....	....	125	G1	'98	99⅜	94⅞	96⅞	7.23	7.23
Nts 6.70s 2004	Ao15	**BBB+**			X	BE	[12]Z100	....	....	....	....	....	250	G1	'99	99¾	95¼	95⅜	7.02	7.03
Nts 7.05s 2006	jJ15	**BBB+**			X	BE	[10]Z100	....	....	....	....	....	250	G1	'98	99¾	92	94½	7.46	7.46

Uniform Footnote Explanations-See Page 260. Other: [1] Gtd by Export-Import Bank of U.S. [2] Prin due in 20 equal pyts ea Mar & Sep 15. [3] Prin due in 10 equals pyts ea Feb & Aug 1. [4] Prin due in 20 equal pyts ea Apr 30 & Oct 31. [5] Greater of 100 or amt based on forumla. [6] Min denom $10T. [7] Data of Production Resource Group. [8] (HRO)On Chge of Ctrl at 101. [9] Max $35M red w/proceeds of Pub Eq Off'g. [10] Red at greater of 100 or amt based on formula. [11] See Security Capital Ind Tr. [12] Plus Make-Whole Amt.

Title-Industry Code & Co. Finances (In Italics) / Exchange ↓ Individual Issue Statistics	Ind / Interest Dates	Fixed Charge Coverage 1996 / S&P Rating	1997 / Date of Last Rating Change	1998 / Prior Rating	Eligible ↓	Year End / Bond Form	Million $ Cash & Equiv. / Redemption Provisions Regular Price	Curr. Assets / Regular (Begins) Thru	Curr. Liab. / Sinking Fund Price	Balance Sheet Date / Sinking Fund (Begins) Thru	L. Term Debt (Mil $) / Refund/Other Restriction Price	Refund/Other Restriction (Begins) Thru	Capital-ization (Mil $) / Outst'g (Mil $)	Total Debt % Capital / Underwriting Firm	Underwriting Year	Price Range 1999 High	Price Range 1999 Low	Mo. End Price Sale(s) or Bid	Curr. Yield	Yield to Mat.
ProLogis Trust (Cont.)																				
Nts 7.10s 2008	Ao15	**BBB+**			X	BE	[1]Z100	....	....	....	....	....	250	G1	'99	99⅞	92½	92½	7.68	7.68
ProNet Inc	***67f***	***Mgr w/Metrocall Inc,see***																		
Sr[2]Sub Nts[3] 11⅞s 2005	Jd15	**CCC+**	12/98	CCC	Y	BE	105.938	(6-15-00)	....	....	....	....	100	Exch.	'95	106	68	68	17.46	17.45
Protection One[4] Alarm Monitoring	***63***	***n/a***	***n/a***	***n/a***		***Dc***	***28.70***	***219.0***	***239.0***	***9-30-99***	***1075***		***2400***	***46.3***						
Sr[2]Nts 7⅜s 2005	fA15	**BB–**	12/99	BB	Y	BE	[5]100	....	....	....	....	....	250	Exch.	'98	101	55	79½	9.28	9.27
Sr Sub[2]Disc Nts[6] 13⅝s 2005	Jd31	**B**	12/99	B+	Y	R	106.813	(6-30-00)	....	....	....	....	[7]108	Exch.	'95	114	23	63	21.63	21.60
Protective Life Corp	***35a***	***1.41***	***1.56***	***1.98***		***Dc***				***9-30-99***	***426.0***		***1321***	***35.1***						
Sr Nts 7.95s 2004	jJ	**A**			X	BE	NC	....	....	....	....	....	75.0	G1	'94	108⅞	102	102	7.79	7.79
Provident Companies	***35a***	***Mgr with UNUM Corp,see***																		
Sr Nts 6⅜s 2005	jJ15	**A**	7/99	BBB+	X	BE	NC	....	....	....	....	....	200	M2	'98	103½	93¼	93¼	6.84	6.84
Sr Nts 7s 2018	jJ15	**A**	7/99	BBB+	X	BE	NC	....	....	....	....	....	200	M2	'98	103⅜	86⅜	87⅛	8.03	8.03
Sr Nts 7¼s 2028	Ms15	**A**	7/99	BBB+	X	BE	[5]Z100	....	....	....	....	....	200	M7	'98	105⅞	86¼	87¼	8.31	8.31
PSI Energy	***72a***	***Subsid of CINergy,see Cin Gas & El***																		
Deb[8] 6.35s 2006	mN15	**BBB+**			X	BE	NC	....	....	....	....	....	100	S1	'96	104⅝	95	95	6.68	6.68
Deb 7.85s 2007	aO15	**BBB+**			X	BE	[1]Z100	....	....	....	....	....	265	M7	'99	102	98½	98½	7.97	7.97
PSINet Inc	***20c***	***d10.00***	***d7.59***	***d1.24***		***Dc***	***1543***	***1830***	***341.0***	***9-30-99***	***2403***		***2980***	***83.6***						
Sr Nts[2]'B' 10s 2005	Fa15	**B–**			Y	BE	105	(2-15-02)	....	....	[9]Z110	2-15-01	600	Exch.	'98	107	94¼	98⅞	10.11	10.11
Public Serv, Colorado[10]	***75***	***2.84***	***2.91***	***3.12***		***Dc***	***38.60***	***424.0***	***1077***	***6-30-99***	***1647***		***3962***	***58.7***						
1st 8⅛s 2004	Ms	**A**	10/97	A–	X	BE	NC	....	....	....	....	....	100	K2	'92	110⅝	102½	102½	7.93	7.93
1st 9⅞s 2020	jJ	**A**	10/97	A–	X	R	104.61	(7-1-00)	....	....	....	....	75.0	M2	'90	109¼	105⅝	105⅝	9.35	9.35
1st 8¾s 2022	Ms	**A**	10/97	A–	X	BE	104.18	(3-1-02)	100	(3-1-02)	....	....	150	K2	'92	110⅜	101	101⅛	8.65	8.65
1st Coll Tr Ser 1 6⅜s 2005	mN	**A**	10/97	A–	X	BE	NC	....	....	....	....	....	134	M2	'93	104⅝	95¼	95¼	6.69	6.69
1st Coll Tr Ser 2 6s 2001	Jj	**A**	10/97	A–	X	BE	NC	....	....	....	....	....	103	M2	'94	101⅜	99¼	99¼	6.05	6.04
1st Coll Tr Ser 2 7¼s 2024	Jj	**A**	10/97	A–	X	BE	102.87	(1-1-04)	....	....	....	....	110	M2	'94	103¾	87⅝	87¾	8.26	8.26
1st Coll Tr Ser 3 7⅛s 2006	Jd	**A**	10/97	A–	X	BE	NC	....	....	....	....	....	125	M2	'96	108¾	98	98	7.27	7.27
1st Coll Tr Ser 6 6s 2003	Ao15	**A**			X	BE	NC	....	....	....	....	....	250	S4	'98	102⅜	96⅝	96⅝	6.21	6.21
Sr Nts 'A' 6⅞s 2009	jJ15	**BBB+**			X	BE	[5]Z100	....	....	....	....	....	200	M2	'99	99⅞	95¼	95⅜	7.21	7.21
Public Serv, New Mexico	***72a***	***3.07***	***3.27***	***3.40***		***Dc***	***88.60***	***354.0***	***199.0***	***9-30-99***	***977.0***		***1878***	***52.0***						
Sr Unsec Nts 'A' 7.10s 2005	fA	**BBB–**	8/99	BB+	X	BE	[5]Z100	....	....	....	....	....	300	S4	'98	102¼	96¼	96¼	7.38	7.38
Sr Unsec Nts 'B' 7½s 2018	fA	**BBB–**	8/99	BB+	X	BE	[5]Z100	....	....	....	....	....	135	S4	'98	102½	92⅛	92⅝	8.10	8.10
1st 8⅛s 2001	mS15	**NR**	3/98	BB+		R	100.28	9-14-00	100	....	....	....	15.7	B8	'71	101	100½	100½	8.08	8.08
1st 9⅛s 2005	Ms15	**NR**	3/98	BB+		R	101.58	3-14-00	100	....	....	....	21.8	K2	'75	102¼	101¾	101¾	8.97	8.97
1st 8⅛s 2007	Jd15	**NR**	3/98	BB+		R	101.90	6-14-00	100	....	....	....	26.7	F1	'77	102⅛	99⅝	99⅝	8.16	8.15
1st 9s 2008	Mn	**NR**	3/98	BB+		R	102.21	4-30-00	100	....	....	....	54.4	M5	'78	103	102⅛	102⅛	8.81	8.81
Public Svc No Car	***73b***	***4.13***	***3.88***	***3.15***		***Sp***	***23.10***	***86.60***	***150.0***	***6-30-99***	***157.0***		***493.0***	***54.6***						
Sr Deb 6.99s 2026	Jj15	**A–**			X	BE	NC	....	....	....	....	....	50.0	M6	'96	104¾	86¼	86⅜	8.09	8.09
Sr Deb 7.45s 2026	jD15	**A–**			X	BE	NC	....	....	....	....	....	50.0	M6	'96	112⅛	92½	94½	7.88	7.88
Public Serv, Oklahoma[11]	***72a***	***3.85***	***2.97***	***4.93***		***Dc***	***3.23***	***99.10***	***205.0***	***6-30-99***	***449.0***		***977.0***	***49.2***						
1st S 7¼s 2003	jJ	**AA–**	10/97	A+	X	R	NC	....	....	....	....	....	65.0	M2	'92	107¼	100½	100½	7.21	7.21
1st T 7⅜s 2004	jD	**AA–**	10/97	A+	X	R	NC	....	□100	....	....	....	50.0	M6	'92	109½	100¾	100¾	7.32	7.32
1st U 6¼s 2003	Ao	**AA–**	10/97	A+	X	R	NC	....	□100	....	....	....	35.0	M2	'93	103½	97¾	97¾	6.39	6.39
1st V 7⅜s 2023	Ao	**AA–**	10/97	A+	X	R	102.97	(4-1-03)	□100	....	....	....	100	M2	'93	107	90½	90⅝	8.14	8.14
1st W 6½s 2005	Jd	**AA–**	10/97	A+	X	R	NC	....	Z100	....	....	....	50.0	M6	'93	105½	96⅝	96⅝	6.73	6.73
Public Serv Elec & Gas[12]	***75***	***3.03***	***3.31***	***3.28***		***Dc***	***24.00***	***1682***	***2750***	***9-30-99***	***3261***		***9416***	***52.9***						
• 1st & Ref BB 9⅛s 2005	jJ	**A–**	1/94	A	X	R	NC	....	Z100	....	....	....	125	P1	'90	114⅝	100⅝	101⅛	9.02	9.02

Uniform Footnote Explanations-See Page 260. Other: [1] Plus Make-Whole Amt. [2] (HRO)On Chge of Ctrl at 101. [3] Asmd by Metrocall Inc. [4] Subsid of Western Resources. [5] Red at greater of 100 or amt based on formula. [6] Int accrues at 13.625% fr 6-30-98. [7] Incl disc. [8] (HRO)On 11-15-00 at 100. [9] Max $210M red w/proceeds of Pub Eq Off'g. [10] Subsid of New Century Energies. [11] Contr by Central & South West Corp. [12] Subsid of Public Serv Enterprise Gr.

Title-Industry Code & Co. Finances (In Italics)	Ind	Fixed Charge Coverage 1996	1997	1998	Year End		Million $ Cash & Equiv.	Curr. Assets	Curr. Liab.	Balance Sheet Date	L. Term Debt (Mil $)		Capital-ization (Mil $)	Total Debt % Capital						
Exchange ↓ Individual Issue Statistics	Interest Dates	S&P Rating	Date of Last Rating Change	Prior Rating	Eligible ↓	Bond Form	Redemption Provisions: Regular Price	Regular (Begins) Thru	Sinking Fund Price	Sinking Fund (Begins) Thru	Refund/Other Restriction Price	Refund/Other Restriction (Begins) Thru	Outst'g (Mil $)	Underwriting Firm	Underwriting Year	Price Range 1999 High	Price Range 1999 Low	Mo. End Price Sale(s) or Bid	Curr. Yield	Yield to Mat.
***Public Serv Elec & Gas** (Cont.)*																				
• 1st & Ref CC 9¼s 2021	Jd	A–	1/94	A	X	R	NC	....	Z100	....	....	....	150	F1	'91	110	109	108	8.56	8.56
• 1st & Ref DD 8⅞s 2003	Jd	A–	1/94	A	X	R	NC	....	Z100	....	....	....	150	M2	'91	109⅛	103⅞	102⅛	8.69	8.69
• 1st & Ref FF 7⅞s 2001	mN	A–	1/94	A	X	R	NC	....	Z100	....	....	....	100	K2	'91	105¼	100¼	102	7.72	7.72
• 1st & Ref II 7⅝s 2000	Fa	A–	1/94	A	X	R	NC	....	Z100	....	....	....	100	S1	'92	102½	99¾	99¾	7.64	7.64
• 1st & Ref MM 6⅞s 2003	Jj	A–	1/94	A	X	R	NC	....	Z100	....	....	....	150	G1	'93	104⅞	99⅝	98⅜	6.99	6.99
• 1st & Ref PP 6½s 2004	Mn	A–	1/94	A	X	R	NC	....	Z100	....	....	....	300	F1	'93	104⅝	96¼	97⅛	6.69	6.69
• 1st & Ref QQ 6s 2000	Mn	A–	1/94	A	X	R	NC	....	Z100	....	....	....	300	M5	'93	100⅞	99	99½	6.03	6.03
• 1st & Ref RR 6⅛s 2002	fA	A–	1/94	A	X	R	NC	....	Z100	....	....	....	300	M5	'93	102⅜	97½	97⅜	6.29	6.29
• 1st & Ref SS 7s 2024	mS	A–	1/94	A	X	R	102.74	(9-1-03)	Z100	....	....	....	300	G1	'93	104	90	89¾	7.80	7.80
• 1st & Ref TT 7⅜s 2014	Ms	A–			X	R	102.13	(3-1-04)	Z100	....	....	....	175	K2	'94	105	95½	95⅛	7.75	7.75
• 1st & Ref UU 6¾s 2006	Ms	A–			X	R	NC	....	Z100	....	....	....	175	C5	'94	106¾	97¼	96⅝	6.99	6.99
• 1st & Ref VV 6¾s 2016	Jj	A–			X	R	[1]Z100	....	Z100	....	....	....	200	M2	'96	100	93	91⅛	7.41	7.41
• 1st & Ref WW 6¼s 2007	Jj	A–			X	R	[1]Z100	....	....	....	....	....	150	S1	'96	101¾	93⅝	93⅞	6.66	6.66
• 1st & Ref XX 6½s 2000	Jd	A–			X	R	[2]Z100	....	....	....	....	....	235	M6	'97	100⅛	99½	99½	6.53	6.53
• 1st & Ref YY[3] 6⅝s 2023	Mn	A–			X	BE	NC	....	....	....	....	....	250	C4	'98	99⅞	88	88	7.24	7.24
• 1st & Ref 5s 2037	jJ	A–	1/94	A	X	CR	NC	....	....	....	....	....	7.54	Exch.	'38	83	73¾	74½	6.71	6.71
• 1st & Ref 8s 2037	Jd	A–	1/94	A	X	CR	NC	....	....	....	....	....	7.46	Exch.	'38	110¼	100	104	7.69	7.69
Sec M-T Nts 'A' 8.16s 2009	[4]jj	A–			X	BE	NC	....	....	....	....	....	16.5	M2	'94	117¾	102	102	8.00	8.00
Sec M-T Nts 'A' 8.10s 2009	[4]jj	A–			X	BE	NC	....	....	....	....	....	43.5	M2	'94	117¼	101⅝	101⅝	7.97	7.97
Pueblo Xtra Int'l	***59c***	***0.04***	***0.92***	***1.63***	***Ja***		***50.30***	***137.0***	***96.50***	***8-14-99***	***283.0***	***327.0***		***86.8***						
Sr Nts[5] 9½s 2003	fA	CCC+	12/99	B–	Y	R	102.375	7-31-00	....	....	....	....	180	M6	'93	99¼	60	60	15.83	15.82
Sr[5]Nts'C' 9½s 2003	fA	CCC+	12/99	B–	Y	BE	102.375	7-31-00	....	....	....	....	85.0	Exch.	'97	99¼	60	60	15.83	15.82
Puget Sound Energy[6]	***72a***	***3.69***	***2.02***	***3.28***	***Dc***		***72.20***	***410.0***	***79.00***	***9-30-99***	***1790***	***3759***		***60.9***						
Sr M-T Nts 'A' 6.74s 2018	ms15	A–			X	BE	[2]Z100	....	....	....	....	....	200	M2	'98	101	87⅜	87½	7.70	7.70
Sr M-T Nts 'B' 6.46s 2009	[7]ao15	A–			X	BE	[2]Z100	....	....	....	....	....	150	M2	'99	102⅞	91⅝	91⅝	7.05	7.05
Puget Sound Pwr & Lt	***72a***	**Now Puget Sound Energy,see**																		
Sec M-T Nts 'A'[8] 7.15s 2002	[9]ao15	A–	12/97	BBB+	X	BE	NC	....	....	....	....	....	5.00	S1	'92	104¾	99⅝	99⅝	7.18	7.18
Sec M-T Nts 'A'[8] 7.85s 2002	[10]ao15	A–	12/97	BBB+	X	BE	NC	....	....	....	....	....	30.0	S1	'92	106⅝	101¼	101¼	7.75	7.75
Sec M-T Nts 'A'[8] 7.07s 2002	[11]ao15	A–	12/97	BBB+	X	BE	NC	....	....	....	....	....	27.0	S1	'92	104⅜	99⅜	99⅜	7.11	7.11
Sec M-T Nts 'A'[8] 8.06s 2006	[12]ao15	A–	12/97	BBB+	X	BE	NC	....	....	....	....	....	46.0	S1	'92	113¼	101¾	101¾	7.92	7.92
Sec M-T Nts 'A'[8] 8.14s 2006	[13]ao15	A–	12/97	BBB+	X	BE	NC	....	....	....	....	....	25.0	S1	'91	114⅜	102⅛	102⅛	7.97	7.97
Sec M-T Nts 'A'[8] 7¾s 2007	[14]ao15	A–	12/97	BBB+	X	BE	NC	....	....	....	....	....	100	S1	'92	112	99⅞	99⅞	7.76	7.76
Sec M-T Nts 'A'[8] 8.40s 2007	[15]ao15	A–	12/97	BBB+	X	BE	100	(5-1-02)	....	....	....	....	10.0	S1	'92	116⅝	103¾	103¾	8.10	8.10
Sec M-T Nts 'A'[8] 8.59s 2012	[16]ao15	A–	12/97	BBB+	X	BE	102.89	(4-9-02)	....	....	....	....	5.00	S1	'92	124⅛	106⅝	106⅝	8.06	8.06
Sec M-T Nts 'B'[8] 6.61s 2000	[17]jj15	A–	12/97	BBB+	X	BE	NC	....	....	....	....	....	10.0	K2	'93	101⅛	100	100	6.61	6.61
Sec M-T Nts 'B'[8] 7⅝s 2002	[18]jj15	A–	12/97	BBB+	X	BE	NC	....	....	....	....	....	25.0	K2	'92	106⅝	100¾	100¾	7.57	7.57
Sec M-T Nts 'B'[8] 7.02s 2003	[19]jj15	A–	12/97	BBB+	X	BE	NC	....	....	....	....	....	30.0	K2	'93	104⅝	99	99	7.09	7.09
Sec M-T Nts 'B'[8] 6.20s 2003	[20]jj15	A–	12/97	BBB+	X	BE	NC	....	....	....	....	....	3.00	K2	'93	101⅞	95¾	95¾	6.48	6.47
Sec M-T Nts 'B'[8] 6.40s 2003	[21]jj15	A–	12/97	BBB+	X	BE	NC	....	....	....	....	....	11.0	K2	'93	102¾	96⅜	96⅜	6.64	6.64
Sec M-T Nts 'B'[8] 7.80s 2004	[22]jj15	A–	12/97	BBB+	X	BE	NC	....	....	....	....	....	30.0		'94	109¼	101⅛	101⅛	7.71	7.71
Sec M-T Nts 'B'[8] 7.70s 2004	[23]jj15	A–	12/97	BBB+	X	BE	NC	....	....	....	....	....	50.0	K2	'92	109⅜	100⅞	100⅞	7.63	7.63
Sec M-T Nts 'B'[8] 8.20s 2012	[24]ao15	A–	12/97	BBB+	X	BE	102.70	(12-21-02)	....	....	....	....	30.0	K2	'92	121⅛	103⅝	103⅝	7.91	7.91
Sec M-T Nts 'B'[8] 7.35s 2024	[25]ao15	A–	12/97	BBB+	X	BE	103.68	(2-1-04)	....	....	....	....	55.0	S1	'94	104⅝	91⅜	91½	8.03	8.03
Pulte Corp	***13h***	***3.89***	***4.80***	***2.98***	***Dc***					***9-30-99***	***518.0***	***1709***		***46.1***						
Sr Nts[26] 7s 2003	jD15	BBB			X	BE	NC	....	....	....	....	....	100	M2	'93	100⅛	95	95	7.37	7.37

Uniform Footnote Explanations-See Page 260. Other: [1] Greater of 100 or amt based on formula. [2] Red at greater of 100 or amt based on formula. [3] Mandatory Put/Call on 5-1-08 at 100. [4] Due 5-26-09. [5] (HRO)On Chge of Ctrl at 101. [6] Was Puget Sound Power & Lt,see. [7] Due 3-9-09. [8] Issued in min denom $100T. [9] Due 9-11-02. [10] Due 5-29-02. [11] Due 8-28-02. [12] Due 6-19-06. [13] Due 11-30-06. [14] Due 2-1-07. [15] Due 5-7-07. [16] Due 4-9-12. [17] Due 2-9-00. [18] Due 12-10-02. [19] Due 2-10-03. [20] Due 12-1-03. [21] Due 12-2-03. [22] Due 5-27-04. [23] Due 12-10-04. [24] Due 12-21-12. [25] Due 2-1-24. [26] (HRO)On Chge of Ctrl at 100.

Title-Industry Code & Co. Finances (In Italics) / Individual Issue Statistics (Exchange)	Ind / Interest Dates	Fixed Charge Coverage 1996 / S&P Rating	1997 / Date of Last Rating Change	1998 / Prior Rating	Eligible	Year End / Bond Form	Million $ Cash & Equiv. / Redemption Provisions: Regular Price	Curr. Assets / Regular (Begins) Thru	Curr. Liab. / Sinking Fund Price	Balance Sheet Date / Sinking Fund (Begins) Thru	L. Term Debt (Mil $) / Refund/Other Restriction Price	Capital-ization (Mil $) / Refund/Other Restriction (Begins) Thru	Outst'g (Mil $)	Total Debt % Capital / Underwriting Firm	Underwriting Year	Price Range 1999 High	Price Range 1999 Low	Mo. End Price Sale(s) or Bid	Curr. Yield	Yield to Mat.
Pulte Corp (Cont.)																				
Sr Nts[1] 8⅜s 2004	fA15	**BBB**			X	BE	NC	....	....	....	....	....	115	M2	'94	106¼	99⅜	99⅜	8.43	8.43
Sr Nts 7.30s 2005	aO24	**BBB**			X	BE	NC	....	....	....	....	....	125	M2	'95	101¼	93⅜	93⅜	7.82	7.82
Sr Nts 7⅝s 2017	aO15	**BBB**			X	BE	NC	....	....	....	....	....	150	M2	'97	98	85⅜	85½	8.92	8.92
Quaker Oats	***26***	***3.83***	***5.91***	***8.50***		***Dc***	***431.0***	***1222***	***1071***	***9-30-99***	***715.0***	***1113***		***75.7***						
M-T Nts 'D' 6.47s 2000	ms15	**BBB+**	11/96	A–	X	BE	NC	....	....	....	....	....	20.0	L3	'95	101⅛	100	100⅛	6.46	6.46
M-T Nts 'D' 7½s 2005	[2]ms15	**BBB+**	11/96	A–	X	BE	NC	....	....	....	....	....	25.0	L3	'95	108⅛	100¼	100¼	7.48	7.48
M-T Nts 'D' 7.78s 2011	ms15	**BBB+**	11/96	A–	X	BE	NC	....	....	....	....	....	15.0	M6	'95	114⅜	100¼	100¼	7.76	7.76
M-T Nts 'D' 7.77s 2025	ms15	**BBB+**	11/96	A–	X	BE	NC	....	....	....	....	....	30.0	L1	'95	111½	97⅛	97⅛	8.00	8.00
M-T Nts 'D' 7.28s 2015	ms15	**BBB+**	11/96	A–	X	BE	NC	....	....	....	....	....	27.0	M6	'95	104⅞	93⅞	94	7.74	7.74
Quaker State Corp[3]	***49d***	***Gtd by Pennzoil-Quaker State,see***																		
• Nts[4] 6⅝s 2005	aO15	**BBB–**	9/98	BBB	X	BE	[5]Z100	....	....	....	....	....	100	C5	'95	No Sale		85	7.79	7.79
Quality Food Centers	***59c***	***Merged into Meyer (Fred) Inc,see***																		
Sr Sub Nts 'B' 8.70s 2007	Ms15	**BB+**	6/99	BB	Y	BE	104.35	(3-15-02)	....	....	[6]Z108	3-15-00	135	Exch.	'97	108	105	106	8.21	8.21
Quest Diagnostics Inc	***43a***	***n/a***	***n/a***	***2.22***		***Dc***	***36.80***	***875.0***	***638.8***	***9-30-99***	***1230***	***2123***		***59.7***						
• Sr Sub Nts[7] 10¾s 2006	jD15	**B+**	11/99	NR	Y	R	105.375	(12-15-01)	....	....	....	....	150	M5	'96	114½	105	105	10.24	10.24
Questar Pipeline Co	***73b***	***4.37***	***4.17***	***3.96***		***Dc***		***15.40***	***72.60***	***6-30-99***	***203.0***	***457.0***		***56.0***						
Deb[8] 9⅞s 2020	Jd	**A+**	9/93	A	X	R	104.67	(6-1-00)	100	(6-1-01)	[9]Z100	....	50.0	F1	'90	109⅝	105⅝	105⅝	9.35	9.35
Deb 9⅜s 2021	Jd	**A+**	9/93	A	X	R	104.51	(6-1-01)	100	(6-1-02)	....	....	85.0	M2	'91	111½	106¼	106⅜	8.81	8.81
Quorum Health Group	***30a***	***△4.06***	***△5.05***	***△2.50***		***Je***	***16.56***	***442.0***	***211.7***	***9-30-99***	***844.0***	***1558***		***56.0***						
Sr Sub Nts[10] 8¾s 2005	mN	**B+**	1/99	BB–	Y	R	104.375	(11-1-00)	....	....	....	....	150	G1	'95	100¼	89½	95¾	9.14	9.14
Qwest Communications[11]	***67a***	***n/a***	***n/a***	***d7.61***		***Dc***	***860.0***	***1909***	***955.0***	***9-30-99***	***2352***	***8865***		***26.5***						
Sr Nts[7]'B' 10⅞s 2007	Ao	**BB+**	6/98	B+	Y	BE	105.438	(4-1-02)	....	....	[12]Z110.875	4-1-00	163	Exch.	'97	117½	111	112	9.71	9.71
Sr Nts[7]'B' 7½s 2008	mN	**BB+**			Y	BE	[13]Z100	....	....	....	....	....	750	Exch.	'98	106½	95¾	98	7.65	7.65
Sr Nts[7]'B' 7¼s 2008	mN	**BB+**			Y	BE	[13]Z100	....	....	....	....	....	300	Exch.	'98	103¾	94	96⅜	7.52	7.52
Sr Disc[14]Nts[15]'B' 9.47s 2007	aO15	**BB+**			Y	BE	104.735	(10-15-02)	....	....	[16]Z109.47	10-15-02	[17]556	Exch.	'98	82½	75⅞	81	....	Flat
Sr Disc[18]Nts[19]'B' 8.29s 2008	Fa	**BB+**			Y	BE	[20]104.145	(2-1-03)	....	....	[21]Z108.29	2-1-01	[17]451	Exch.	'98	80⅜	72	77¼	....	Flat
R&B Falcon	***49e***	***3.74***	***4.19***	***2.11***		***Dc***	***678.0***	***1000***	***276.0***	***9-30-99***	***2943***	***6739***		***40.4***						
Sr Nts 'B' 6½s 2003	Ao15	**B+**	3/99	BB+	Y	BE	NC	....	....	....	....	....	250	Exch.	'98	92⅞	80⅛	91½	7.10	7.10
Sr Nts 9⅛s 2003	jD15	**B+**			Y	BE	[13]Z100	....	....	....	....	....	98.0	Exch.	'99	102⅜	92½	98¾	9.24	9.24
Sr Nts 'B' 6¾s 2005	Ao15	**B+**	3/99	BB+	Y	BE	[13]Z100	....	....	....	....	....	350	Exch.	'98	91⅜	73⅞	89¾	7.52	7.52
Sr Nts[7] 12¼s 2006	Ms15	**B+**			Y	BE	[13]Z100	....	....	....	....	....	200	Exch.	'99	109⅞	103½	109	11.24	11.24
Sr Nts 'B' 6.95s 2008	Ao15	**B+**	3/99	BB+	Y	BE	[13]Z100	....	....	....	....	....	250	Exch.	'98	89⅛	67	86⅝	8.02	8.02
Sr Nts'B' 9½s 2008	jD15	**B+**			Y	BE	[13]Z100	....	....	....	....	....	300	Exch.	'99	101⅛	88½	100¼	9.48	9.47
Sr Nts'B' 7⅜s 2018	Ao15	**B+**	3/99	BB+	Y	BE	[13]Z100	....	....	....	....	....	250	Exch.	'98	81½	61⅜	77½	9.52	9.52
Radnor Holdings	***14***	***1.84***	***1.08***	***1.46***		***Dc***	***3.82***	***79.90***	***66.90***	***9-24-99***	***208.0***	***220.0***		***95.9***						
Sr Nts[7]'A' 10s 2003	jD	**BB–**			Y	BE	105	(12-1-00)	....	....	....	....	100	Exch.	'97	104½	99½	100	10.00	10.00
Raintree Resorts Intl	***40g***	***n/a***	***n/a***	***n/a***		***Dc***				***9-30-99***	***119.0***	***114.0***		***104.0***						
Sr[7]Nts 'B' 13s 2004	jD	**B–**			Y	BE	107.429	(12-1-00)	....	....	[22]Z113	12-1-00	99.8	Exch.	'98	65½	49	60	21.67	21.64
Rally's Hamburgers[23]	***27b***	***0.54***	***0.45***	***0.73***		***Dc***	***11.60***	***17.05***	***21.68***	***6-14-99***	***65.40***	***100.0***		***67.1***						
• Sr Nts[24] 9⅞s 2000	Jd15	**NR**	11/98	B–		R	100	....	100	....	....	....	56.7	P1	'93	97½	75¼	s94½	10.45	10.45
Ralphs Grocery Co	***59c***	***Acq by Meyer(Fred),see***																		
Sr Nts[7] 10.45s 2004	Jd15	**BBB–**	6/99	BB+	Y	R	105.225	(6-15-00)	....	....	....	....	350	B11	'95	110½	106⅝	106⅝	9.80	9.80
Sr Sub Nts[7] 11s 2005	Jd15	**BB+**	6/99	BB–	Y	R	105.50	(6-15-00)	....	....	....	....	524	Exch.	'95	114	107⅛	107⅛	10.27	10.27
Ralston Purina Co	***26***	***4.05***	***3.72***	***4.26***		***Sp***	***85.00***	***1473***	***1913***	***9-30-99***	***1252***	***3950***		***65.9***						
• Deb[25] 9¼s 2009	aO15	**A–**			X	R	NC	....	....	....	....	....	181	S1	'89	123⅜	109½	110⅝	8.36	8.36

Uniform Footnote Explanations-See Page 260. Other: [1] (HRO)On Chge of Ctrl at 100. [2] Due 5-2-05. [3] Was Quaker St Oil Ref. [4] Gtd by Pennzoil-Quaker State. [5] Co may red at greater of 100 or amt based on formula. [6] Max $30M red w/proceeds of Pub Eq Off'g. [7] (HRO)On Chge of Ctrl at 101. [8] (HRO)To 6-1-00 at 100 for Rat'g Decline. [9] Co may redeem upon repurch of 80% deb. [10] Co must offer repurch at 101 on Chge in Ctrl. [11] See LCI Int'l. [12] Max $87.5M red w/proceeds of Pub Equity Off'g. [13] Plus Make-Whole Amt. [14] (HRO)On Chge of Ctrl agt 101(Accreted Amt). [15] Int accrues at 9.47% fr 10-15-02. [16] Accreted:Max $195M red w/proceeds Equity Off'g. [17] Incl disc. [18] Int accrues at 8.29% fr 2-1-03. [19] (HRO)On Chge of Ctrl at 101(Accreted Amt). [20] Percent Accreted Val. [21] Accreted:Max $158M red w/proceeds Eq Off'g. [22] Max $35M red w/proceeds of Equity Off'g. [23] Was Rally's Inc. [24] Co must offer repurch at 101 on Chge of Ctrl. [25] (HRO)At 100 for Designated Event&Rat'g Decline.

Title-Industry Code & Co. Finances (In Italics) / Exchange ↓ Individual Issue Statistics	Ind / Interest Dates	Fixed Charge Coverage 1996 / S&P Rating	1997 / Date of Last Rating Change	1998 / Prior Rating	Eligible ↓	Year End / Bond Form	Million $ Cash & Equiv. / Redemption Provisions: Regular Price	Curr. Assets / Regular (Begins) Thru	Curr. Liab. / Sinking Fund Price	Balance Sheet Date / Sinking Fund (Begins) Thru	L. Term Debt (Mil $) / Refund/Other Restriction Price	Refund/Other Restriction (Begins) Thru	Capital-ization (Mil $) / Outst'g (Mil $)	Total Debt % Capital / Underwriting Firm	Underwriting Year	Price Range 1999 High	Low	Mo. End Price Sale(s) or Bid	Curr. Yield	Yield to Mat.
***Ralston Purina Co** (Cont.)*																				
• Deb 7¾s 2015	aO	**A–**			X	BE	NC	....	....	....	....	....	175	M6	'95	103	102¾	98	7.91	7.91
• Deb[1] 9.30s 2021	Mn	**A–**			X	R	NC	....	....	....	....	....	200	G1	'91	No Sale		100	9.30	9.30
• Deb[1] 8⅝s 2022	Fa15	**A–**			X	BE	NC	....	....	....	....	....	250	G1	'92	119¾	103⅛	s106	8.14	8.14
• Deb[1] 8⅛s 2023	Fa	**A–**			X	BE	NC	....	....	....	....	....	175	M5	'93	109	99¼	94	8.64	8.64
• Deb 7⅞s 2025	Jd15	**A–**			X	BE	NC	....	....	....	....	....	225	L3	'95	111	98	90	8.75	8.75
Rayovac Corp	***42***	***Δ1.39***	***Δ1.97***	***Δ3.30***		***Sp***	***11.10***	***257.0***	***152.0***	***9-30-99***	***307.0***		***377.0***	***87.5***						
Sub Nts[2]'B' 10¼s 2006	mN	**B**			Y	BE	105.125	(11-1-01)	....	....	....	....	65.0	Exch.	'97	110	102	102	10.05	10.05
Raytheon Co	***23i***	***5.36***	***4.24***	***2.99***		***Dc***	***113.0***	***9220***	***7890***	***10-3-99***	***7296***		***21079***	***46.9***						
Deb 7⅜s 2025	jJ15	**BBB–**	10/99	BBB	X	BE	102.881	(7-15-05)	....	....	....	....	375	C5	'95	104⅝	86	86⅜	8.54	8.54
Deb 7.20s 2027	fA15	**BBB–**	10/99	BBB	X	BE	[3]Z100	....	....	....	....	....	500	M6	'97	109⅞	88½	89¼	8.07	8.07
Deb 7s 2028	mN	**BBB–**	10/99	BBB	X	BE	[4]Z100	....	....	....	....	....	250	C6	'98	108⅛	86¼	86⅞	8.06	8.06
Deb 6s 2010	jD15	**BBB–**	10/99	BBB	X	BE	[4]Z100	....	....	....	....	....	250	Exch.	'98	101½	85⅛	85⅜	7.03	7.03
Deb 6.40s 2018	jD15	**BBB–**	10/99	BBB	X	BE	[4]Z100	....	....	....	....	....	550	Exch.	'98	100⅞	82¾	83⅜	7.68	7.68
Nts 6.30s 2000	fA15	**BBB**			X	BE	NC	....	....	....	....	....	500	M6	'97	101⅝	99½	99⅝	6.32	6.32
Nts 6.45s 2002	fA15	**BBB–**	10/99	BBB	X	BE	NC	....	....	....	....	....	1000	M6	'97	103⅛	97¾	97¾	6.60	6.60
Nts 5.70s 2003	mN	**BBB–**	10/99	BBB	X	BE	NC	....	....	....	....	....	400	C6	'98	100½	93⅞	93⅞	6.07	6.07
Nts 6½s 2005	jJ15	**BBB–**	10/99	BBB	X	BE	NC	....	....	....	....	....	750	C5	'95	105⅝	94	94	6.91	6.91
Nts 6¾s 2007	fA15	**BBB–**	10/99	BBB	X	BE	[3]Z100	....	....	....	....	....	1000	M6	'97	106⅞	93⅛	93⅛	7.25	7.25
Nts 6.15s 2008	mN	**BBB–**	10/99	BBB	X	BE	[4]Z100	....	....	....	....	....	750	C6	'98	102⅞	88¾	88⅞	6.92	6.92
RBF Finance	***25b***	***Gtd by R&B Falcon***																		
Sr Sec[2]Nts[5] 11s 2006	Ms15	**BB–**			Y	BE	[3]100	....	....	....	....	....	400	Exch.	'99	108	101	106½	10.33	10.33
Sr Sec[5]Nts[2] 11⅜s 2009	Ms15	**BB–**			Y	BE	105.6875	(3-15-04)	....	....	....	....	400	Exch.	'99	108½	101½	107	10.63	10.63
RBX Corp[6]	***41c***	***1.32***	***0.27***	***d4.39***		***Dc***	***0.13***	***61.50***	***46.00***	***9-30-99***	***209.0***		***51.90***	***404.0***						
Sr Sub Nts[2]'B' 11¼s 2005	aO15	**B–**			Y	BE	105.625	(10-15-00)	....	....	....	....	100	Exch.	'96	43½	16	20	....	....
RCN Corp	***67***	***0.85***	***d0.49***	***d0.86***		***Dc***	***1592***	***1704***	***193.0***	***9-30-99***	***1743***		***2639***	***66.1***						
Sr Nts[2] 'B' 10s 2007	aO15	**B–**			Y	BE	105	(10-15-02)	....	....	[7]Z110	10-15-00	225	Exch.	'98	105¾	93	99⅜	10.06	10.06
Sr Disc[8]Nts[9] 9.80s 2008	Fa15	**B–**			Y	BE	104.90	(2-15-03)	....	....	[10]Z109.80	2-15-01	[11]567	Exch.	'98	67	52	65½	....	Flat
Sr[12]Disc Nts[2] 11s 2008	jJ	**B–**			Y	BE	105.50	(7-1-03)	....	....	[13]Z111	7-1-03	[11]257	M2	'98	67	51½	65½	....	Flat
Realty Income	***57***	***n/a***	***5.09***	***3.84***		***Dc***				***9-30-99***	***230.0***		***746.0***	***39.5***						
Nts 7¾s 2007	Mn6	**BBB–**			X		[3]Z100	....	....	....	....	....	110	M2	'97	111¼	91⅞	91⅞	8.44	8.43
Reckson Operating Ptnrshp	***57***	***2.88***	***3.12***	***2.37***		***Dc***				***9-30-99***	***1239***		***2600***	***47.7***						
Nts 7.40s 2000		**BBB–**			X	BE	[3]Z100	....	....	....	....	....	100	G1	'99	99¾	96⅝	96⅝	7.68	7.68
Nts 7¾s 2009	Ms15	**BBB–**			X	BE	[3]Z100	....	....	....	....	....	200	G1	'99	100¼	92⅜	92⅜	8.39	8.39
Reebok Int'l	***39a***	***6.63***	***4.36***	***2.19***		***Dc***	***143.0***	***1304***	***665.7***	***9-30-99***	***400.0***		***1262***	***54.6***						
Deb 6¾s 2005	mS15	**BBB–**	1/99	BBB	X	BE	NC	....	....	....	....	....	100	C5	'95	102½	94	94	7.18	7.18
Regency Centers L.P.	***57***	....	***2.64***	***2.62***		***Dc***				***9-30-99***	***724.0***		***2294***	***31.5***						
Nts[14] 7.40s 2004	Ao	**BBB–**			X	BE	[3]Z100	....	....	....	....	....	200	G1	'99	99⅞	95¾	95¾	7.73	7.73
Nts[14] 7¾s 2009	Ao	**BBB–**			X	BE	[3]Z100	....	....	....	....	....	50.0	G1	'99	100	92	92	8.42	8.42
Regions Financial[15]	***10***	***4.77***	***4.51***	***4.06***		***Dc***				***9-30-99***	***388.0***		***3623***	***13.7***						
Sub Nts 7.65s 2001	fA15	**A–**	7/98	A	X	BE	NC	....	....	....	....	....	25.0	B7	'94	104⅞	100¾	100¾	7.59	7.59
Sub Nts[15] 7.80s 2002	jD	**A–**	7/98	A	X	BE	NC	....	....	....	....	....	75.0	B7	'92	107⅜	101½	101½	7.68	7.68
Sub Nts[16] 7¾s 2024	mS15	**A–**	7/98	A	X	BE	NC	....	....	....	....	....	100	C5	'94	113¼	100	100¼	7.73	7.73
Reliance Electric	***23c***	***Mgr into Rockwell Int'l, see***																		
Nts[17] 6.80s 2003	Ao15	**A+**	10/98	AA–	X	R	NC	....	....	....	....	....	150	G1	'93	105⅝	99⅜	99⅜	6.84	6.84

Uniform Footnote Explanations-See Page 260. Other: [1] Issued in min denom $100T. [2] (HRO)On Chge of Ctrl at 101. [3] Plus Make-Whole Amt. [4] Red at greater of 100 or amt based on formula. [5] Gtd by R&B Falcon. [6] Subsid of RBX Group. [7] Max $78.M red w/proceeds of Pub Equity Off'g. [8] (HRO)On Chge of Ctrl at 101(accreted val). [9] Int accrues at 9.8% fr 2-15-03. [10] Max 35% red w/proceeds of Pub Eq Off'g(accreted val). [11] Incl disc. [12] Int accrues at 11% fr 1-1-03. [13] Max $89.9M red w/proceeds of Pub Eq Off'g. [14] Gtd by Regency Realty & subsid. [15] Was First Alabama Bancshrs. [16] (HRO)On 9-15-04 at 100. [17] (HRO)For a Designated Event at 100.

Title-Industry Code & Co. Finances (In Italics) / Individual Issue Statistics, Exchange	Ind / Interest Dates	Fixed Charge Coverage 1996 / S&P Rating	Date of Last Rating Change	1997 / Prior Rating	1998 / Eligible	Year End / Bond Form	Cash & Equiv. / Regular Price	Curr. Assets / Regular (Begins) Thru	Curr. Liab. / Sinking Fund Price	Balance Sheet Date / Sinking Fund (Begins) Thru	L. Term Debt (Mil $) / Refund/Other Restriction Price	Refund/Other Restriction (Begins) Thru	Capitalization (Mil $) / Outst'g (Mil $)	Total Debt % Capital / Underwriting Firm	Underwriting Year	Price Range 1999 High	Price Range 1999 Low	Mo. End Price Sale(s) or Bid	Curr. Yield	Yield to Mat.
Reliance Group Hldgs	***35d***	***1.53***		***3.71***	***6.58***	***Dc***				***9-30-99***	***456.0***		***1953***	***37.2***						
• Sr Nts 9s 2000	mN15	BBB–	8/98	BB+	Y	BE	NC	....	....	....	....	....	400	D6	'93	104⅞	71¾	s90	10.00	10.00
• Sr Sub Deb[1] 9¾s 2003	mN15	BB+	8/98	BB–	Y	BE	102.438	11-14-00	....	....	....	....	250	D6	'93	104½	45	s74	13.18	13.17
ReliaStar Financial[2]	***35d***	***11.60***		***11.31***	***10.39***	***Dc***				***9-30-99***	***909.0***		***2754***	***22.4***						
• Nts 7⅛s 2003	Ms	A	10/98	A–	X	BE	NC	....	....	....	....	....	75.0	M2	'96	No Sale		98	7.27	7.27
• Nts 6⅝s 2003	mS15	A	10/98	A–	X	BE	NC	....	....	....	....	....	120	M2	'93	99¾	96½	95	6.97	6.97
• Nts 8⅝s 2005	Fa15	A	10/98	A–	X	BE	NC	....	....	....	....	....	110	S1	'95	100	100	100	8.63	8.62
Nts 8s 2006	aO30	A			X	BE	NC	....	....	....	....	....	200	M2	'99	102⅝	99⅝	100⅜	7.97	7.97
Nts 6½s 2008	mN15	A			X	BE	NC	....	....	....	....	....	200	M2	'98	102⅞	90⅜	90½	7.18	7.18
[3]Remington Arms	***40f***	***0.55***		***1.38***	***2.46***	***Dc***	***2.20***	***200.0***	***100.0***	***p9-30-99***	***★97.90***		***254.0***	***49.8***						
Sr[4]Nts[5]'B' 9½s 2003	jD	B	2/99	NR	Y	BE	103	11-30-00	....	....	....	....	87.4	M2	'93	102½	96	100	9.50	9.50
Sr Sub Nts[4] 11s 2006	Mn15	CCC+			Y	BE	105.50	(5-15-01)	....	....	....	....	130	Exch.	'96	84	68	77	14.29	14.28
Renaissance Media Group	***12a***	***n/a***		***n/a***	***1.89***	***Dc***				***9-30-99***	***83.80***		***464.0***	***18.1***						
Sr[4]Disc[6]Nts 10s 2008	Ao15	B–			Y	BE	105	(4-15-03)	....	....	[7]Z110	4-15-01	114	Exch.	'98	73	68¼	70	....	Flat
Remington Products LLC	***42a***	***n/a***		***0.71***	***0.60***	***Dc***	***4.27***	***149.0***	***51.60***	***9-30-99***	***213.0***		***174.0***	***123.0***						
Renco Metals, Inc.	***44***	***4.01***		***1.89***	***1.78***	***Oc***	***7.38***	***78.80***	***16.40***	***7-31-99***	***154.0***		***94.90***	***162.0***						
Sr Nts[4] 11½s 2003	jJ	B			Y	R	105.75	(7-1-00)	....	....	....	....	150	D6	'96	106	84	84	13.69	13.68
Renco Steel Holdings	***66d***	***2.89***		***2.08***	***1.46***	***Oc***	***7.20***	***228.0***	***109.0***	***7-31-99***	***421.0***		***289.0***	***146.0***						
Sr Nts[4] 10⅞s 2005	Fa	B–			Y	BE	105.438	(2-1-02)	....	....	[8]Z111	2-1-01	120	Exch.	'98	90	80	81	13.43	13.42
Republic N.Y. Corp	***10***	***2.00***		***1.87***	***1.46***	***Dc***				***9-30-99***	***4140***		***7692***	***57.5***						
• Deb 8⅜s 2007	Fa15	A+	11/98	AA	X	R	NC	....	....	....	....	....	100	S1	'87	110⅜	101¼	100⅛	8.36	8.36
Sub Deb 9½s 2014	Ao15	A	11/98	AA–	X	R	NC	....	....	....	....	....	150	S1	'89	129½	110½	110½	8.60	8.60
Sub Deb[9] 7.20s 2097	jJ15	A	11/98	AA–	X	BE	NC	....	....	....	....	....	250	B7	'97	103⅞	83	84⅞	8.48	8.48
Sub Nts 9½s 2000	jJ	A	11/98	AA–	X	R	NC	....	....	....	....	....	100	G1	'90	105¼	101⅜	101⅜	9.37	9.37
Sub Nts 9¾s 2000	jD	A	11/98	AA–	X	R	NC	....	....	....	....	....	100	G1	'90	107¼	102½	102½	9.51	9.51
Sub Nts 8⅞s 2001	Fa15	A	11/98	AA–	X	R	NC	....	....	....	....	....	100	L3	'91	106⅛	101¾	101¾	8.72	8.72
Sub Nts 8¼s 2001	mN	A	11/98	AA–	X	R	NC	....	....	....	....	....	150	L3	'91	106½	101½	101½	8.13	8.13
Sub Nts 7⅞s 2001	jD12	A	11/98	AA–	X	R	NC	....	....	....	....	....	100	M2	'91	105¾	100⅞	100⅞	7.81	7.81
Sub Nts 7¾s 2002	Mn15	A	11/98	AA–	X	R	NC	....	....	....	....	....	150	S1	'92	106¼	100½	100½	7.71	7.71
Sub Nts 7¼s 2002	jJ15	A	11/98	AA–	X	BE	NC	....	....	....	....	....	250	L3	'92	105	99⅜	99⅜	7.30	7.29
Sub Nts 5⅞s 2008	aO15	A	11/98	AA–	X	BE	NC	....	....	....	....	....	250	S1	'93	100⅜	87½	87⅝	6.70	6.71
Sub Nts 9.70s 2009	Fa	A	11/98	AA–	X	R	NC	....	....	....	....	....	150	G1	'89	127⅞	110⅞	111⅜	8.71	8.71
Sub Nts 7¾s 2009	Mn15	A	11/98	AA–	X	BE	NC	....	....	....	....	....	200	L3	'94	114⅜	98⅞	99¼	7.81	7.81
Sub Nts 7s 2011	Ms22	A	11/98	AA–	X	BE	NC	....	....	....	....	....	100	B7	'96	108½	92¼	92¼	7.59	7.59
Sub Nts 9⅛s 2021	Mn15	A	11/98	AA–	X	R	NC	....	....	....	....	....	100	L3	'91	127¾	106⅝	106⅝	8.56	8.56
Sub Nts 9.30s 2021	Jd	A	11/98	AA–	X	R	NC	....	....	....	....	....	100	M2	'91	129¾	108¼	108⅜	8.58	8.58
F/R[10]Sub Nts 2002	QAug7	A	11/98	AA–	X	BE	NC	....	....	....	....	....	100	L3	'92	99⅛	98	98¾	....	....
F/R[11]Sub Nts 2002	QOct28	A	11/98	AA–	X	BE	NC	....	....	....	....	....	150	L3	'92	99	97⅞	98¾	....	....
Republic Services	***53***	***4.32***		***8.03***	***6.37***	***Dc***	***9.80***	***322.1***	***421.7***	***9-30-99***	***1154***		***2287***	***41.2***						
Nts 6⅝s 2004	Mn15	BBB			X	BE	[12]Z100	....	....	....	....	....	225	M2	'99	99⅝	92¾	93¼	7.10	7.10
Nts 7⅛s 2009	Mn15	BBB			X	BE	[12]Z100	....	....	....	....	....	375	M2	'99	100⅛	89	89¾	7.94	7.94
Resource America	***49a***	***9.43***		***3.83***	***3.33***	***Sp***				***6-30-99***	***524.0***		***779.0***	***67.3***						
Sr Nts[4] 12s 2004	fA	B–			Y	BE	106	(1-1-02)	....	....	....	....	113	Exch.	'98	92½	82	82½	14.55	14.54
Revlon Consumer Pr[13]	***18***	***1.38***		***1.52***	***0.85***	***Dc***	***26.80***	***836.0***	***489.0***	***6-30-99***	***1712***		***1037***	***169.0***						
Sr Exch[4]Nts[14] 8⅛s 2006	Fa	B–	11/99	B	Y	BE	104.063	(2-1-02)	....	....	[15]Z108.125	2-1-01	250	Exch.	'98	99	73½	73½	11.05	11.05

Uniform Footnote Explanations-See Page 260. Other: [1] (HRO)On Chge of Ctrl at 100. [2] Was NWNL Cos. [3] Gtd by & data of RACI Hldg. [4] (HRO)On Chge of Ctrl at 101. [5] Gtd by RACI Hldg. [6] Int accrues at 10% fr 4-15-03. [7] Accreted:Max $57.1M red w/proceeds Equity Off'g. [8] Max $40M red w/proceeds of Pub Eq Off'g. [9] Co may shorten mty for Tax Event. [10] Int(min 5%,max 10%)adj qtrly. [11] Int(min 5%,max 9.50%)adj qtrly. [12] Red at greater of 100 or amt based on formula. [13] Was Revlon, Inc. [14] Co may red in whole,at 100 & prem,on Ctrl Chge. [15] Max $87.5 red w/proceeds Pub Eq Off'g.

Title-Industry Code & Co. Finances (In Italics)	Ind	Fixed Charge Coverage 1996	1997	1998		Year End	Million $ Cash & Equiv.	Curr. Assets	Curr. Liab.	Balance Sheet Date	L. Term Debt (Mil $)		Capital-ization (Mil $)	Total Debt % Capital						
Individual Issue Statistics Exchange ↓	Interest Dates	S&P Rating	Date of Last Rating Change	Prior Rating	Eligible ↓	Bond Form	Redemption Provisions: Regular Price	Regular (Begins) Thru	Sinking Fund Price	Sinking Fund (Begins) Thru	Refund/Other Restriction Price	Refund/Other Restriction (Begins) Thru	Outst'g (Mil $)	Underwriting Firm	Underwriting Year	Price Range 1999 High	Price Range 1999 Low	Mo. End Price Sale(s) or Bid	Curr. Yield	Yield to Mat.
***Revlon Consumer Pr** (Cont.)*																				
Sr Sub Exch[1]Nts[2] 8⅝s 2008	Fa	**CCC+**	11/99	B–	Y	BE	104.313	(2-1-03)	....	....	[3]Z108.625	2-1-01	650	Exch.	'98	96½	42½	50	17.25	17.24
[4]Revlon Worldwide	***18***	***1.53***	***0.92***	***0.57***		***Dc***	***97.70***	***908.0***	***602.0***	***9-30-99***	***2496***		***961.0***	***260.0***						
Sr[5]Sec Disc (Zero Cpn) Nts 2001	[6]	**B–**			Y	BE	[7]Z102.6875	(3-15-00)	....	....	....	....	[8]770	Exch.	'97	69¾	16	20	....	1.62
Reynolds Metals Co	***5***	***2.02***	***2.91***	***3.61***		***Dc***	***62.00***	***1368***	***1258***	***9-30-99***	***1009***		***3552***	***41.0***						
Deb[9] 9s 2003	fA15	**BBB**	5/98	BBB+	X	BE	NC	....	....	....	....	....	100	G1	'91	112⅜	104½	104½	8.61	8.61
Reynolds & Reynolds	***48b***	***n/a***	***14.50***	***13.37***		***Sp***	***123.0***	***459.0***	***227.0***	***6-30-99***	***382.0***		***833.0***	***45.9***						
M-T Nts 6.12s 2001	[10]fa15	**BBB+**			X	BE	NC	....	....	....	....	....	40.0	G1	'98	101	98⅝	98⅝	6.21	6.21
Sr Nts 7s 2006	jD15	**BBB+**			X	BE	NC	....	....	....	....	....	100	G1	'96	107⅞	95⅞	95⅞	7.30	7.30
Reynolds(RJ)Tobacco Hldgs	***69a***	***n/a***	***n/a***	***n/a***		***Dc***	***2503***	***3477***	***3771***	***9-30-99***	***1983***		***9235***	***21.9***						
• Deb[11] 9¼s 2013	fA15	**BB+**	4/99	BBB–	X	BE	NC	....	....	....	....	....	60.1	L3	'93	118⅛	90	s90	10.28	10.27
• Nts[11] 8s 2000	Jj15	**BB+**	4/99	BBB–	X	BE	NC	....	....	....	....	....	23.1	M2	'93	102¼	98⅜	98¾	8.10	8.10
• Sr Nts[12] 8¾s 2004	Ao15	**BB+**	4/99	BBB–	X	R	NC	....	....	....	....	....	53.1	G1	'92	111	91⅜	91½	9.56	9.56
• Nts[11] 8s 2001	jJ15	**BB+**	4/99	BBB–	X	BE	NC	....	....	....	....	....	23.9	M2	'95	105	95¾	94⅛	8.50	8.50
• Nts[11] 7⅝s 2003	mS15	**BB+**	4/99	BBB–	X	BE	NC	....	....	....	....	....	93.2	S1	'92	106	89	s90	8.47	8.47
• Nts[11] 8¾s 2007	jJ15	**BB+**	4/99	BBB–	X	BE	NC	....	....	....	....	....	22.0	M2	'95	114½	88¾	s89¼	9.80	9.80
• Nts[11] 8¾s 2005	fA15	**BB+**	4/99	BBB–	X	BE	NC	....	....	....	....	....	78.2	L3	'93	112¼	90⅜	s92⅛	9.50	9.50
• Nts[11] 8⅝s 2002	jD	**BB+**	4/99	BBB–	X	BE	NC	....	....	....	....	....	42.8	M6	'92	108½	94⅛	s94⅛	9.16	9.16
[13]Richmont Mktg Specialists	***63***	***n/a***	***n/a***	***n/a***		***Dc***	***4.44***	***76.20***	***75.90***	***9-30-99***	***246.0***		***392.0***	***69.0***						
Sr Sub[1]Nts 10⅛s 2007	jD15	**CCC**			Y	BE	Z105.063	(12-15-02)	....	....	[14]Z110.125	12-14-00	100	Exch.	'99	83⅜	60	60	16.88	16.86
Riddell Sports	***40f***	***2.07***	***0.95***	***0.51***		***Dc***	***0.37***	***93.10***	***28.00***	***9-30-99***	***145.0***		***179.0***	***81.0***						
Sr Nts[1] 10½s 2007	jJ15	**B**			Y	BE	105.25	(7-2-02)	....	....	[15]Z110.50	7-15-00	115	Exch.	'97	95	83	86½	12.14	12.13
Riggs National Corp	***10***	***3.42***	***3.92***	***3.97***		***Dc***				***9-30-99***	***416.0***		***1028***	***52.7***						
Sub Deb 9.65s 2009	Jd15	**BB+**	8/98	BB–	Y	R	NC	....	....	....	....	....	66.5	P4	'89	111	96½	100⅛	9.64	9.64
Rio Hotel & Casino	***40i***	***Acqd by Harrah's Ent,see Harrah's Op***																		
Sr[1]Sub[16]Nts[17] 10⅝s 2005	jJ15	**BB+**	1/99	B+	Y	R	103.98	(7-15-00)	....	....	....	....	100	S1	'95	110	107	109⅝	9.69	9.69
Rite Aid	***59e***	***4.36***	***4.21***	***3.35***		***Fb***	***98.57***	***4002***	***2297***	***8-28-99***	***5413***		***7873***	***69.0***						
Sr Deb 6⅞s 2013	fA15	**BB**	10/99	BBB–	Y	BE	NC	....	....	....	....	....	200	B7	'93	103⅞	55	68	10.11	10.11
Deb 7.70s 2027	Fa15	**BB**	10/99	BBB–	Y	BE	NC	....	....	....	....	....	300	G1	'96	113⅛	54	68	11.32	11.32
Nts 6.70s 2001	jD15	**BB**	10/99	BBB	Y	BE	NC	....	....	....	....	....	350	G1	'96	102¾	70	84	7.98	7.98
Sr Nts 7⅝s 2005	Ao15	**BB**	10/99	BBB–	Y	BE	NC	....	....	....	....	....	200	D6	'95	108⅝	62	77½	9.84	9.84
Nts 7⅛s 2007	Jj15	**BB**	10/99	BBB	Y	BE	NC	....	....	....	....	....	350	G1	'96	107⅛	61½	75½	9.44	9.43
Riverwood Int'l[18]	***16c***	***0.01***	***0.05***	***0.16***		***Dc***	***9.50***	***364.0***	***261.0***	***9-30-99***	***1727***		***2026***	***85.7***						
Sr Nts 10¼s 2006	Ao	**B–**	11/96	B	Y	R	105.125	(4-1-01)	....	....	....	....	250	C2	'96	104½	97¼	101¼	10.12	10.12
Sr[19]Nts[20] 10⅝s 2007	fA	**B–**			Y	BE	105.313	(8-1-02)	....	....	[21]Z110.625	8-1-00	250	Exch.	'97	106¾	99	103	10.32	10.31
Sr Sub Nts 10⅞s 2008	Ao	**CCC+**	7/97	B–	Y	R	105.4375	(4-1-01)	....	....	....	....	400	C2	'96	100½	90	98½	11.04	11.04
Riviera Holdings	***40i***	***2.06***	***1.14***	***0.82***		***Dc***	***44.40***	***85.10***	***31.40***	***9-30-99***	***223.0***		***254.0***	***88.0***						
1st[1] 10s 2004	fA15	**B+**			Y		105	(8-15-01)	....	....	[22]Z110	8-15-00	175	Exch.	'98	95	85	92¼	10.84	10.84
RJR[23]Nabisco[24]Inc[25]	***69a***	***3.06***	***2.72***	***2.96***		***Dc***	***246.0***	***4487***	***4534***	***3-31-99***	***8630***		***18911***	***47.8***						
Nts[26] 7⅝s 2000	mS	**BB+**	4/99	BBB–	X	BE	NC	....	....	....	....	....	19.1	D6	'92	102¾	99⅜	100	7.63	7.62
Sr Nts 8¼s 2004	jJ	**BB+**	4/99	BBB–	X	BE	[27]Z100	....	....	....	....	....	2.83	M2	'97	109¼	95⅞	96¾	8.53	8.53
Sr Nts 8½s 2007	jJ	**BB+**	4/99	BBB–	X	BE	[27]Z100	....	....	....	....	....	8.67	M6	'97	112⅛	93⅞	95	8.95	8.95
[28]Rochester Gas & Electric	***75***	***3.79***	***4.50***	***3.91***		***Dc***	***4.55***	***199.0***	***223.0***	***9-30-99***	***720.0***		***1658***	***49.1***						
1st PP 9⅜s 2021	Ao	**A–**	4/98	BBB+	X	R	104.47	(4-1-01)	Z100	(4-1-01)	....	....	100	F1	'91	110⅞	104⅛	104⅛	9.00	9.00
1st QQ 8¼s 2002	Ms15	**A–**	4/98	BBB+	X	R	NC	....	Z100	....	....	....	100	F1	'92	108⅜	101⅝	101⅝	8.12	8.12

Uniform Footnote Explanations-See Page 260. Other: [1] (HRO)On Chge of Ctrl at 101. [2] Co may red in whole,at 100 & prem,on Ctrl Chge. [3] Max $227M red w/proceeds of Pub Eq Off'g. [4] Now REV Holdings. [5] Red in whole,at 100(Accreted)&prem on Ctrl Chge. [6] Due 3-15-01. [7] Accreted Val. [8] Incl disc. [9] (HRO)For Designated Event&Rat'g Decline at 100. [10] Due 3-2-01. [11] Was RJR Nabisco. [12] Was RJR Nabisco Capital,then RJR Nabisco. [13] No Marketing Specialists. [14] Max $35M red w/proceeds of Pub Eq Off'g. [15] Max $40.25M red w/proceeds Pub Eq Off'g. [16] State gaming laws may req hldr's sale/Co red. [17] Gtd by Rio Properties, Inc. [18] Now Riverwood Holding. [19] (HRO)On Chge of Ctrl at 100. [20] Gtd by RTC Holdings. [21] Max $87M red w/proceeds of Pub Eq Off'g. [22] Max $58.3M red w/proceeds Pub Eq Off'g. [23] See Nabisco. [24] Was Reynold(RJ)Indus. [25] Subsid of RJR Nabisco Hldgs Corp. [26] Issued in min denom $100T. [27] Plus Make-Whole Amt. [28] Now RGS Energy Group.

Title-Industry Code & Co. Finances (In Italics) / Exchange, Individual Issue Statistics	Ind / Interest Dates	Fixed Charge Coverage 1996 / S&P Rating	1997 / Date of Last Rating Change	1998 / Prior Rating	Eligible	Year End / Bond Form	Million $ Cash & Equiv. / Redemption Provisions: Regular Price	Million $ Curr. Assets / Regular (Begins) Thru	Million $ Curr. Liab. / Sinking Fund Price	Balance Sheet Date / Sinking Fund (Begins) Thru	L. Term Debt (Mil $) / Refund/Other Restriction Price	Refund/Other Restriction (Begins) Thru	Capital-ization (Mil $) / Outst'g (Mil $)	Total Debt % Capital / Underwriting Firm	Underwriting Year	Price Range 1999 High	Price Range 1999 Low	Mo. End Price Sale(s) or Bid	Curr. Yield	Yield to Mat.
***Rochester Gas & Electric** (Cont.)*																				
Sec[1]M-T Nts 'B' 5.84s 2008	[2]fa15	**A–**			X	BE	NC	....	....	....	....	....	50.0	M5	'98	99¼	86⅝	86⅝	6.74	6.74
Sec[1]M-T Nts 'B' 7.60s 2009	[3]fa15	**A–**			X	BE	NC	....	....	....	....	....	100	M7	'99	102⅛	97½	97½	7.79	7.79
[4]Rochester Telephone Corp[5]	***67a***	***10.16***	***39.80***	***55.50***		***Dc***	***53.60***	***120.0***	***58.10***	***6-30-99***	***40.00***		***421.0***	***9.5***						
Deb 9s 2021	fA15	**A**			X	R	104.50	(8-15-01)	....	....	....	....	100	S1	'91	111½	94½	94⅝	9.51	9.51
Rock-Tenn Co	***16c***	***8.51***	***3.00***	***3.28***		***Sp***	***3.12***	***236.7***	***146.4***	***6-30-99***	***476.0***		***923.0***	***54.3***						
Nts 7¼s 2005	fA	**BBB**			X	BE	NC	....	....	....	....	....	100	M5	'95	107⅝	98⅜	98⅜	7.37	7.37
Rockland Electric Co.	***72a***	***Subsid of Orange & Rockland Util,see***																		
1st I 6s 2000	jJ	**A+**	4/99	A–	X	R	NC	....	▲100	....	....	....	20.0	D6	'93	101	99⅝	99¾	6.02	6.01
Rockwell Intl(New)[6]	***23***	***△35.19***	***△13.50***	***△11.60***		***Sp***	***356.0***	***3582***	***2108***	***9-30-99***	***911.0***		***3737***	***29.4***						
Nts 6.15s 2008	Jj15	**A+**	10/98	AA–	X	BE	[7]Z100	....	....	....	....	....	350	M7	'98	104⅛	91⅞	91⅞	6.69	6.69
Deb 6.70s 2028	Jj15	**A+**	10/98	AA–	X	BE	[7]Z100	....	....	....	....	....	250	M7	'98	104¾	87¾	87¾	7.64	7.63
[8]Rockwell Intl(Old)	***23***	***Gtd by Boeing Co,see***																		
Nts[9] 8⅜s 2001	Fa15	**AA–**	12/98	AA	X	R	NC	....	....	....	....	....	180	G1	'91	106⅛	101⅝	101⅝	8.24	8.24
Nts[9] 6¾s 2002	mS15	**AA–**	12/98	AA	X	R	NC	....	....	....	....	....	300	U1	'92	104⅞	99⅛	99¼	6.80	6.80
Nts[9] 7⅞s 2005	Fa15	**AA–**	12/98	AA	X	R	NC	....	....	....	....	....	200	M6	'95	112½	102⅜	102⅜	7.69	7.69
Nts[9] 6⅝s 2005	Jd	**AA–**	12/98	AA	X	R	NC	....	....	....	....	....	300	M6	'95	106½	96¾	96⅞	6.84	6.84
Rogers Cablesystems Ltd	***12a***	***Subsid of Rogers Communications,see***																		
Sr[10]Sec[11]2nd Pr'ty Deb[12] 10⅛s 2012	$mS	**BB+**			Q	R	104	(9-1-02)	....	....	....	....	200	M2	'92	112¼	105	105½	9.60	9.60
Sr[10]Sec[11]2nd Pr'ty Deb[12] 10s 2007	jD	**BB+**			Q	R	105	(12-1-02)	....	....	....	....	150	M2	'95	115	105	106⅝	9.38	9.38
Sr[12]Sec[10]2nd Pr'ty Nts[11] 9⅝s 2002	$fA	**BB+**			Q	R	NC	....	....	....	....	....	250	M2	'92	108½	102	102	9.44	9.43
Sr Sec 2nd[10]Pr'ty Nts[11] 10s 2005	$Ms15	**BB+**			Q	R	NC	....	....	....	....	....	450	M2	'95	115⅛	105¼	107¾	9.28	9.28
Sr[10]Sub[11]Gtd Deb[12] 11s 2015	jD	**BB–**			Q	R	105.50	(12-1-05)	....	....	....	....	125	M2	'95	118	110	110	10.00	10.00
Rogers Communications[13]	***12a***	***0.55***	***0.66***	***0.58***		***Dc***				***:12-31-98***	***5254***		***5212***	***101.0***						
Sr[14]Nts[11] 9⅛s 2006	$Jj15	**BB–**			Q	R	104.563	(1-15-01)	....	....	....	....	100	M2	'96	105¼	100¾	100¾	9.06	9.05
SrNts 8¾s 2007	©jJ15	**BB–**			Q	R	104.375	(7-15-02)	....	....	....	....	165	S3	'97	71¼	62¾	69⅜	12.60	12.59
Sr[10]Nts[11] 8⅞s 2007	$jJ15	**BB–**			Q	R	104.438	(7-15-02)	....	....	....	....	330	M2	'97	105¼	100	100	8.88	8.87
Rohm & Haas	***14***	***10.59***	***12.98***	***18.29***		***Dc***	***83.00***	***2427***	***2189***	***9-30-99***	***3242***		***7654***	***54.8***						
[15]**(Hldgs)**[16]Deb[17] 9.80s 2020	Ao15	**A–**	3/99	A	X	R	NC	....	....	....	....	....	150	G1	'90	120⅛	106⅛	107¾	9.10	9.09
Deb[1] 7.85s 2029	jJ15	**A–**			X	BE	[7]Z100	....	....	....	....	....	1000	Exch.	'99	105¼	98½	100½	7.81	7.81
Nts[18] 9⅞s 2000	mS	**A–**	3/99	A–	X	R	[19]Z100	....	....	....	....	....	100	G1	'90	107⅛	102¼	102¼	9.66	9.66
Nts[1] 6.95s 2004	jJ15	**A–**			X	BE	[7]Z100	....	....	....	....	....	500	Exch.	'99	100⅞	98⅞	98⅞	7.03	7.03
Nts[1] 7.40s 2009	jJ15	**A–**			X	BE	[7]Z100	....	....	....	....	....	500	Exch.	'99	101⅝	99¼	99¼	7.46	7.45
Rollins Truck Leasing	***25c***	***△2.43***	***△2.65***	***△2.37***		***Sp***	***34.30***	***150.0***	***80.00***	***9-30-99***	***802.0***		***1122***	***71.5***						
CT Deb I 10.35s 2000	Mn15	**BBB+**			X	R	NC	....	....	....	....	....	50.0	G1	'90	106	101¼	101¼	10.22	10.22
CT Deb L 7s 2003	Ms15	**BBB+**			X	R	NC	....	....	....	....	....	70.0	G1	'93	104¼	98⅝	98⅝	7.10	7.10
CT Deb M 7s 2001	Ms15	**BBB+**			X	R	NC	....	....	....	....	....	60.0	M2	'94	102¾	99¾	99¾	7.02	7.02
CT Deb O 7¼s 2005	Ms15	**BBB+**			X	R	NC	....	....	....	....	....	50.0	M2	'95	107¼	98¼	98¼	7.38	7.38
CT Deb Q 6⅞s 2001	fA	**BBB+**			X	R	NC	....	....	....	....	....	60.0	M2	'96	102¾	99⅜	99⅜	6.92	6.92
CT Deb R 7.30s 2007	Ms	**BBB+**			X	BE	NC	....	....	....	....	....	75.0	G1	'97	108½	97	97	7.53	7.52
CT Deb T 6¾s 2006	Ao5	**BBB+**			X	BE	NC	....	....	....	....	....	100	M2	'99	102⅜	95⅛	95⅛	7.10	7.10
Rouse Co	***38***	***1.21***	***1.24***	***1.09***		***Dc***				***9-30-99***	***3505***		***4149***	***84.5***						
Nts 8½s 2003	Jj15	**BBB–**	2/95	BBB	X	R	[20]100	....	....	....	....	....	120	G1	'93	108⅛	101⅛	101⅛	8.41	8.40
Nts 8s 2009	Ao30	**BBB–**			X	BE	[20]Z100	....	....	....	....	....	200	B4	'99	100½	94⅝	94⅞	8.43	8.43
Royal Caribbean Cruises	***40g***	***2.97***	***2.42***	***2.97***		***Dc***	***172.0***	***286.0***	***890.0***	***12-31-98***	***2341***		***4924***	***50.1***						
Sr Deb 7¼s 2018	Ms15	**BBB**	10/99	BBB–	X	BE	NC	....	....	....	....	....	150	G1	'98	103	89¾	90¼	8.03	8.03

Uniform Footnote Explanations-See Page 260. Other: [1] Issued in min denom $100T. [2] Due 12-22-08. [3] Due 10-27-09. [4] Subsid of Frontier Corp. [5] Now Frontier Telephone Rochester. [6] See Reliance Electric. [7] Red at greater of 100 or amt based on formula. [8] Now Boeing North American Inc. [9] Now Boeing North America Inc. [10] Co may offer repurch at 101 on Chge of Ctrl. [11] Co may red in whole,at 100,for tax law chge. [12] Gtd by Rogers Cable TV Ltd. [13] See Roger Cablesystems Ltd. [14] Co must offer repurch at 101 on Chge of Ctrl. [15] Mand pyt 2.5% of issued on int dates fr10-15-00. [16] (HRO)For Trigger Event at 100. [17] Gtd by Rohm&Haas Co. [18] (HRO)At 100 for a Trigger Event. [19] Red in whole if 80% Nts put. [20] Plus Make-Whole Premium.

Title-Industry Code & Co. Finances (In Italics) / Individual Issue Statistics (Exchange)	Ind / Interest Dates	Fixed Charge Coverage 1996 / S&P Rating	1997 / Date of Last Rating Change	1998 / Prior Rating	Eligible	Year End / Bond Form	Cash & Equiv. (Million $) / Redemption Provisions: Regular Price	Curr. Assets (Million $) / Regular (Begins) Thru	Curr. Liab. (Million $) / Sinking Fund Price	Balance Sheet Date / Sinking Fund (Begins) Thru	L. Term Debt (Mil $) / Refund/Other Restriction Price	Refund/Other Restriction (Begins) Thru	Capital-ization (Mil $) / Outst'g (Mil $)	Total Debt % Capital / Underwriting Firm	Underwriting Year	Price Range 1999 High	Price Range 1999 Low	Mo. End Price Sale(s) or Bid	Curr. Yield	Yield to Mat.
***Royal Caribbean Cruises** (Cont.)*																				
Sr Nts 7⅛s 2002	mS18	**BBB**	10/99	BBB–	X	BE	NC	....	....	....	....	....	150	M2	'95	102¾	99	99	7.20	7.20
Sr Nts 8⅛s 2004	jJ28	**BBB**	10/99	BBB–	X	BE	NC	....	....	....	....	....	125	M2	'94	107⅜	101⅛	101⅛	8.03	8.03
Sr Nts 8¼s 2005	Ao	**BBB**	10/99	BBB–	X	BE	NC	....	....	....	....	....	150	G1	'95	108⅛	101½	101½	8.13	8.13
Sr Nts 7¼s 2006	fA15	**BBB**	10/99	BBB–	X	BE	NC	....	....	....	....	....	175	M2	'96	103⅞	96	96	7.55	7.55
Sr Nts 7s 2007	aO15	**BBB**	10/99	BBB–	X	BE	NC	....	....	....	....	....	200	M2	'97	102¼	93⅜	93¾	7.47	7.47
Sr Nts 6¾s 2008	Ms15	**BBB**	10/99	BBB–	X	BE	NC	....	....	....	....	....	150	G1	'98	101⅜	91⅝	92	7.34	7.34
Sr Nts 7½s 2027	aO15	**BBB**	10/99	BBB–	X	BE	NC	....	....	....	....	....	300	M2	'97	102⅞	88⅞	89⅞	8.34	8.34
RPM, Inc	***15***	*△4.92*	*△4.66*	*△5.87*		***My***	*34.49*	*772.3*	*350.3*	*8-31-99*	*866.0*		*1433*	*48.3*						
Sr Nts 7s 2005	Jd15	**BBB**			X	R	NC	....	....	....	....	....	150	Exch.	'95	106⅝	94¾	94¾	7.39	7.39
Rubbermaid, Inc	***34***	***Now Newell Rubbermaid, see Newell Co***																		
Sr Nts 6.60s 2006	mN15	**A**	9/97	A+	X	BE	NC	....	....	....	....	....	150	M5	'96	107⅝	96⅛	96⅛	6.87	6.87
Ryder System	***7***	*0.92*	*2.40*	*2.30*		***Dc***	*315.0*	*1353*	*1806*	*9-30-99*	*1875*		*4049*	*73.3*						
Deb 6.95s 2025	jD	**BBB+**	6/97	A–	X	BE	[1]Z100	....	....	....	....	....	150	M6	'95	102⅝	85¾	85⅞	8.09	8.09
• Bonds G 9s 2016	Mn15	**BBB+**	6/97	A–	X	R	103	(5-15-06)	100	(5-15-07)	....	....	100	S1	'86	115	99	103	8.74	8.74
• Bonds H 8⅜s 2017	Fa15	**BBB+**	6/97	A–	X	R	103.35	2-14-00	100	....	....	....	123	S1	'87	104	98¼	100¾	8.31	8.31
• Bonds J 8¾s 2017	Ms15	**BBB+**	6/97	A–	X	R	103.34	3-14-00	100	....	....	....	95.0	S1	'87	108	99	100	8.75	8.75
• Bonds K 9⅞s 2017	Mn15	**BBB+**	6/97	A–	X	R	101.925	(5-15-07)	100	(5 15 08)	....	....	100	S1	'87	120	119	100	9.88	9.87
Nts N 9¼s 2001	Mn15	**BBB+**	6/97	A–	X	BE	NC	....	....	....	....	....	100	S1	'91	108¼	102¼	102¼	9.05	9.05
Nts O 6½s 2005	ms15	**BBB+**			X	BE	NC	....	....	....	....	....	100	M7	'98	103¼	94⅜	94⅜	6.89	6.89
M-T Nts '11' 7.52s 2000	[2]mn	**BBB+**	6/97	A–	X	BE	NC	....	....	....	....	....	20.0	S1	'95	102¼	100¼	100¼	7.50	7.50
M-T Nts '12' 7.30s 2000	Mn	**BBB+**	6/97	A–	X	BE	NC	....	....	....	....	....	35.0	S1	'95	101⅝	100⅛	100⅛	7.29	7.29
M-T Nts '12' 7.30s 2000	[3]mn	**BBB+**	6/97	A–	X	BE	NC	....	....	....	....	....	15.0	M6	'95	102¼	99⅞	99⅞	7.31	7.31
M-T Nts '12' 7.34s 2000	mN	**BBB+**	6/97	A–	X	BE	NC	....	....	....	....	....	26.0	S1	'95	102⅜	100	100	7.34	7.34
M-T Nts '12' 7.33s 2000	mN	**BBB+**	6/97	A–	X	BE	NC	....	....	....	....	....	22.0	M2	'95	102⅜	99⅞	99⅞	7.34	7.34
M-T Nts '12' 7.08s 2001	[4]mn	**BBB+**	6/97	A–	X	BE	NC	....	....	....	....	....	20.0	M6	'95	102¼	99½	99½	7.12	7.11
M-T Nts '12' 6.80s 2001	mn	**BBB+**	6/97	A–	X	BE	NC	....	....	....	....	....	15.0	S1	'95	101¾	99⅛	99⅛	6.86	6.86
M-T Nts '12' 6.77s 2001	[5]mn	**BBB+**	6/97	A–	X	BE	NC	....	....	....	....	....	25.0	M2	'95	101¾	99	99	6.84	6.84
M-T Nts '12' 6.38s 2002	[6]mn	**BBB+**	6/97	A–	X	BE	NC	....	....	....	....	....	40.0	M5	'95	101	96⅜	96⅜	6.62	6.62
M-T Nts '13' 6.30s 2003	[7]mn	**BBB+**			X	BE	NC	....	....	....	....	....	50.0	M5	'98	100	94½	94½	6.67	6.67
Ryerson Intl	***66a***	*0.32*	*3.52*	*3.29*		***Dc***		*846.0*	*252.0*	*9-30-99*	*259.0*		*940.0*	*27.6*						
Nts 8½s 2001	jJ15	**BBB**			X	BE	[1]Z100	....	....	....	....	....	150	G1	'96	105¼	101½	101½	8.37	8.37
Nts 9⅛s 2006	jJ15	**BBB**			X	BE	[1]Z100	....	....	....	....	....	100	G1	'96	113¾	105	105	8.69	8.69
Ryland Group	***13h***	*1.57*	*1.87*	*3.19*		***Dc***				*9-30-99*	*368.0*		*908.0*	*58.7*						
Sr Nts[8] 10½s 2006	jJ	**BB**			Y	BE	105.25	(7-1-01)	....	....	....	....	100	D4	'96	109¾	102¼	103	10.19	10.19
Sr Sub Nts[8] 9⅝s 2004	jD	**B+**	6/96	BB–	Y	R	100	(12-1-00)	....	....	....	....	100	D4	'93	103	95¾	98½	9.77	9.77
Sr Sub Nts[8] 8¼s 2008	Ao	**B+**			Y	BE	104.125	(4-1-03)	....	....	....	....	100	N2	'98	97	88	91	9.07	9.07
Rythems NetConncetions	***20c***	*n/a*	*n/a*	*d2.64*		***Dc***	*445.0*	*493.0*	*56.70*	*9-30-99*	*500.0*		*702.0*	*71.3*						
Sr Nts[8] 12¾s 2009	Ao15	**CCC+**			Y	BE	106.375	(4-15-04)	....	....	[9]Z112.75	4-15-02	325	Exch.	'99	100½	88¾	96¾	13.18	13.18
SAFECO Corp.	***35c***	*8.26*	*6.63*	*2.94*		***Dc***				*9-30-99*	*1313*		*8197*	*39.4*						
Nts 7⅞s 2005	Ao	**A–**	11/99	A+	X	BE	100	(4-1-03)	....	....	....	....	200	G1	'95	107¾	98½	98½	7.99	7.99
Nts 6⅞s 2007	jJ15	**A–**	11/99	A+	X	BE	NC	....	....	....	....	....	200	Exch.	'97	106½	92¼	92¼	7.45	7.45
Safety Components Intl	***8***	*n/a*	*1.53*	*0.02*		***Mr***	*9.48*	*75.70*	*41.60*	*9-25-99*	*146.0*		*171.0*	*87.5*						
Sr Sub Nts[8]'B' 10⅛s 2007	jJ15	**CCC–**	12/99	B–	Y	BE	105.063	(7-15-02)	....	....	[10]Z110.125	7-15-00	90.0	Exch.	'97	101	40	40	....	....
Safeway Inc[11]	***59c***	*4.90*	*5.19*	*6.57*		***Dc***	*83.30*	*2754*	*3209*	*9-11-99*	*5950*		*8054*	*61.7*						
• Sr Sec Deb[12] 9.30s 2007	Fa	**BBB**	10/96	BBB–	X	R	NC	....	....	....	[13]Z100	....	24.3	S1	'92	118	108⅝	109	8.53	8.53

Uniform Footnote Explanations-See Page 260. Other: [1] Red at greater of 100 or amt based on formula. [2] Due 8-1-00. [3] Due 10-30-00. [4] Due 3-1-01. [5] Due 4-20-01. [6] Due 12-2-02. [7] Due 7-21-03. [8] (HRO)On Chge of Ctrl at 101. [9] Max $114M red w/proceeds of Pub Eq Off'g. [10] Max $22.5M red w/proceeds Pub Eq Off'g. [11] See Allied Supermarkets. [12] (HRO)At 100 for certain chge in collateral. [13] In whole,for certain chge in collateral.

Title-Industry Code & Co. Finances (In Italics)	Ind	Fixed Charge Coverage 1996	1997	1998		Year End	Million $ Cash & Equiv.	Curr. Assets	Curr. Liab.	Balance Sheet Date	L. Term Debt (Mil $)		Capital-ization (Mil $)	Total Debt % Capital						
Individual Issue Statistics — Exchange	*Interest Dates*	*S&P Rating*	*Date of Last Rating Change*	*Prior Rating*	*Eligible*	*Bond Form*	*Redemption Provisions — Regular Price*	*Regular (Begins) Thru*	*Sinking Fund Price*	*Sinking Fund (Begins) Thru*	*Refund/Other Restriction Price*	*Refund/Other Restriction (Begins) Thru*	*Outst'g (Mil $)*	*Underwriting Firm*	*Underwriting Year*	*Price Range 1999 High*	*Price Range 1999 Low*	*Mo. End Price Sale(s) or Bid*	*Curr. Yield*	*Yield to Mat.*
Safeway Inc (Cont.)																				
• Sr Deb 7.45s 2027	mS15	**BBB**			X	BE	[1]Z100	....	....	....	....	....	150	G1	'97	No Sale		93¼	7.99	7.99
Nts 5¾s 2000	mN15	**BBB**			X	BE	NC	....	....	....	....	....	400	M7	'98	100½	98⅞	99⅛	5.80	5.80
Nts 5⅞s 2001	mN15	**BBB**			X	BE	NC	....	....	....	....	....	400	M7	'98	100¾	97¾	97⅞	6.00	6.00
Nts 7s 2002	mS15	**BBB**			X	BE	NC	....	....	....	....	....	600	M7	'99	100⅜	99⅜	99⅜	7.04	7.04
• Sr Nts 10s 2002	mN	**BBB**	10/96	BBB–	X	BE	NC	....	....	....	....	....	6.12	S1	'92	121⅞	107	106¾	9.37	9.37
Nts 6.05s 2003	mN15	**BBB**			X	BE	[2]Z100	....	....	....	....	....	350	M7	'98	101¾	95½	95½	6.34	6.34
Nts 7¼s 2004	mS15	**BBB**			X	BE	[2]Z100	....	....	....	....	....	400	M7	'99	100¾	99⅜	99⅜	7.30	7.30
• Sr Nts 6.85s 2004	mS15	**BBB**			X	BE	[1]Z100	....	....	....	....	....	200	G1	'97	101½	99½	94½	7.25	7.25
• Sr Nts 7s 2007	mS15	**BBB**			X	BE	[1]Z100	....	....	....	....	....	250	G1	'97	102	96½	93	7.53	7.53
Nts 6½s 2008	mN15	**BBB**			X	BE	[2]Z100	....	....	....	....	....	250	M7	'98	105⅜	92¼	92¼	7.05	7.05
Nts 7½s 2009	mS15	**BBB**			X	BE	[2]Z100	....	....	....	....	....	500	M7	'99	101⅝	98¾	98¾	7.59	7.59
• Sr Sub Deb 9.65s 2004	Jj15	**BBB–**	10/96	BB+	X	R	NC	....	....	....	....	....	80.6	G1	'92	115¾	104⅝	104⅝	9.22	9.22
• Sr Sub Deb 9⅞s 2007	Ms15	**BBB–**	10/96	BB+	X	R	NC	....	....	....	....	....	23.8	G1	'92	122	110	111⅜	8.87	8.87
• Sr Sub Nts 10s 2001	jD	**BBB–**	10/96	BB+	X	R	NC	....	....	....	....	....	79.5	G1	'91	110½	103⅝	103¾	9.64	9.64
St Louis-San Fran Ry	***55***	***Merged into Burlington No'n RR, see***																		
• Inc Deb A 5s 2006	[3]mn	**NR**	7/95	BBB		CR	100	....	100	....	....	....	8.00	E1	'56	92	81¾	78⅜	....	Flat
[4]St. Paul Bancorp	***10a***	***n/a***	***n/a***	***n/a***		***Dc***				***9-30-99***	***7930***		***9893***	***80.2***						
Sr Nts 7⅛s 2004	Fa15	**NR**	10/99	BBB–		BE	NC	....	....	....	....	....	100		'97	104½	97⅜	97⅜	7.32	7.32
St Paul Cos	***35c***	***15.56***	***20.60***	***0.37***		***Dc***				***9-30-99***	***1793***		***8294***	***24.2***						
M-T Nts 'B' 6.60s 2005	[5]mn15	**A+**	6/98	AA	X	BE	NC	....	....	....	....	....	10.0	G1	'95	103⅞	96¼	96¼	6.86	6.86
M-T Nts 'B' 6.71s 2005	[5]mn15	**A+**	6/98	AA	X	BE	NC	....	....	....	....	....	10.0	M5	'95	104⅜	96¾	96¾	6.94	6.93
M-T Nts 'B' 6.72s 2005	[5]mn15	**A+**	6/98	AA	X	BE	NC	....	....	....	....	....	10.0	G1	'95	104½	96⅞	96⅞	6.94	6.94
M-T Nts 'B' 6.82s 2005	[6]mn15	**A+**	6/98	AA	X	BE	NC	....	....	....	....	....	10.0	M5	'95	105	97¼	97¼	7.01	7.01
M-T Nts 'B' 7.09s 2005	[7]mn15	**A+**	6/98	AA	X	BE	NC	....	....	....	....	....	10.0	G1	'95	106½	98⅜	98⅜	7.21	7.21
M-T Nts 'B' 7.33s 2006	[8]mn15	**A+**	6/98	AA	X	BE	NC	....	....	....	....	....	10.0	G1	'95	108⅝	98⅞	98⅞	7.41	7.41
M-T Nts 'B' 7.20s 2007	[9]mn15	**A+**	6/98	AA	X	BE	NC	....	....	....	....	....	10.0	G1	'95	108⅜	98⅛	98⅛	7.34	7.34
M-T Nts 'C' 6.38s 2008	jD15	**A+**			X	BE	NC	....	....	....	....	....	150	G1	'98	102⅞	92¾	92¾	6.88	6.88
Saks Inc.	***59f***	***n/a***	***n/a***	***3.22***		***Ja***	***20.90***	***2219***	***1101***	***10-30-99***	***2090***		***4162***	***50.4***						
Nts 7s 2004	jJ15	**BB+**			Y	BE	[2]Z100	....	....	....	....	....	350	B5	'99	98½	93¼	94⅝	7.40	7.40
Nts 7¼s 2004	jD	**BB+**			X	BE	[2]Z100	....	....	....	....	....	350	L3	'98	103	93⅝	95¼	7.61	7.61
Nts 8¼s 2008	mN15	**BB+**			Y	BE	[2]Z100	....	....	....	....	....	500	S4	'98	111	95¼	97¼	8.48	8.48
Nts 7½s 2010	jD	**BB+**			Y	BE	[2]Z100	....	....	....	....	....	250	S4	'98	104⅞	89⅛	91¼	8.22	8.22
Nts 7⅜s 2019	Fa15	**BB+**			X	BE	[2]Z100	....	....	....	....	....	200	S4	'99	101	81⅞	84½	8.73	8.73
Salem Communications	***12b***	***3.64***	***0.91***	***0.88***		***Dc***	***37.30***	***60.80***	***8.84***	***9-30-99***	***100.0***		***246.0***	***42.0***						
Sr Sub Nts[10]'B' 9½s 2007	aO	**B–**			Y	BE	104.75	(10-1-07)	....	....	[11]Z109.50	10-1-00	150	Exch.	'98	108¼	98¾	100⅛	9.49	9.49
Salomon Smith Barney Hldgs[12]	***62***	***1.34***	***1.25***	***1.11***		***Dc***				***9-30-99***	***19864***		***29743***	***66.8***						
• Nts[13] 6⅝s 2000	Jd	**A**	4/97	A–	X	BE	NC	....	....	....	....	....	150	Exch.	'93	No Sale		100⅛	6.62	6.62
• Sr[14]F/R Nts 2003	[15]Sep30	**A**	12/97	BBB	X	BE	NC	....	....	....	....	....	50.0	P1	'93	92	88	86½	....	....
Nts 6¼s 2005	Jj15	**A**			X	BE	NC	....	....	....	....	....	300	S4	'98	101⅝	94¾	94¾	6.60	6.60
Sr Nts 7¼s 2000	Jj15	**A**	12/97	BBB	X	BE	NC	....	....	....	....	....	150	S1	'93	101⅝	100	100	7.25	7.25
Nts[13] 7.98s 2000	Ms	**A**	4/97	A–	X	BE	NC	....	....	....	....	....	200	S7	'95	102⅝	100¼	100¼	7.96	7.96
Nts 6½s 2000	Ms	**A**	12/97	BBB	X	BE	NC	....	....	....	....	....	750	S1	'97	101	100	100	6.50	6.50
Sr Nts 7¾s 2000	Mn15	**A**	12/97	BBB	X	BE	NC	....	....	....	....	....	150	S1	'95	102¾	100½	100½	7.71	7.71
Nts[13] 7s 2000	Mn15	**A**	4/97	A–	X	BE	NC	....	....	....	....	....	150	S7	'95	101⅞	100⅛	100¼	6.98	6.98

Uniform Footnote Explanations-See Page 260. Other: [1] Greater of 100 or amt based on formula. [2] Red at greater of 100 or amt based on formula. [3] Due 1-1-06. [4] Acq by & data of Charter One Fin'l. [5] Due 6-9-05. [6] Due 6-30-05. [7] Due 8-1-05. [8] Due 8-18-06. [9] Due 8-1-07. [10] (HRO)On Chge of Ctrl at 101. [11] Max $50M red w/proceeds Pub Eq Off'g. [12] Subsid of Travelers Group Inc. [13] Was Smith Barney Hldgs. [14] Int(min 4%)adj mthly. [15] Int pd monthly.

Title-Industry Code & Co. Finances (In Italics) / Individual Issue Statistics (Exchange)	Ind / Interest Dates	Fixed Charge Coverage 1996 / S&P Rating	1997 / Date of Last Rating Change	1998 / Prior Rating	Eligible	Year End / Bond Form	Million $ Cash & Equiv. / Redemption Provisions: Regular Price	Curr. Assets / Regular (Begins) Thru	Curr. Liab. / Sinking Fund Price	Balance Sheet Date / Sinking Fund (Begins) Thru	L. Term Debt (Mil $) / Refund/Other Restriction Price	Refund/Other Restriction (Begins) Thru	Capital-ization (Mil $) / Outst'g (Mil $)	Total Debt % Capital / Underwriting Firm	Underwriting Year	Price Range 1999 High	Price Range 1999 Low	Mo. End Price Sale(s) or Bid	Curr. Yield	Yield to Mat.
***Salomon Smith Barney Hldgs** (Cont.)*																				
Sr Nts 6.70s 2000	jJ15	**A**	12/97	BBB	X		NC	....	....	....	....	....	400	S1	'97	101⅝	100⅛	100⅛	6.69	6.69
Nts[1] 5⅞s 2001	Fa	**A**	4/97	A–	X	BE	NC	....	....	....	....	....	250	S7	'96	100⅝	99	99	5.93	5.93
Sr Nts 9¼s 2001	Mn	**A**	12/97	BBB	X	BE	NC	....	....	....	....	....	61.6	S1	'91	107⅞	102⅞	102⅞	8.99	8.99
Sr Nts 7¼s 2001	Mn	**A**	12/97	BBB	X	BE	NC	....	....	....	....	....	250	S1	'96	103⅝	100⅜	100⅜	7.22	7.22
Sr Nts 6.65s 2001	jJ15	**A**	12/97	BBB	X	BE	NC	....	....	....	....	....	350	S1	'97	102⅜	99½	99½	6.68	6.68
Nts[1] 7½s 2002	Mn	**A**	4/97	A–	X	BE	NC	....	....	....	....	....	150	S7	'95	105¼	101	101	7.43	7.43
Sr Nts 7.30s 2002	Mn15	**A**	12/97	BBB	X	BE	NC	....	....	....	....	....	500	S1	'97	104⅝	100⅝	100⅝	7.25	7.25
Nts[1] 6⅝s 2002	jJ	**A**			X	BE	NC	....	....	....	....	....	250	S7	'97	102¾	99	99	6.69	6.69
Nts[1] 6½s 2002	aO15	**A**	4/97	A–	X	BE	NC	....	....	....	....	....	150	S7	'95	102½	98½	98½	6.60	6.60
Nts 6⅛s 2003	Jj15	**A**			X	BE	NC	....	....	....	....	....	300	S4	'98	101	97	97	6.31	6.31
Sr Nts 7½s 2003	Fa	**A**	12/97	BBB	X	BE	NC	....	....	....	....	....	200	S1	'93	105⅞	100⅜	100⅜	7.47	7.47
Sr Nts 6¾s 2003	Fa15	**A**	12/97	BBB	X	BE	NC	....	....	....	....	....	500	S1	'96	103¼	98⅜	98⅜	6.86	6.86
Nts 6¼s 2003	Mn15	**A**			X	BE	NC	....	....	....	....	....	500	S4	'98	101½	97	97	6.44	6.44
Sr Nts 7s 2003	Jd15	**A**	12/97	BBB	X	BE	NC	....	....	....	....	....	150	S1	'93	104½	98⅞	98⅞	7.08	7.08
Sr Nts 6¾s 2003	fA15	**A**	12/97	BBB	X	BE	NC	....	....	....	....	....	200	S1	'93	103⅝	98⅛	98⅛	6.88	6.88
Nts[1] 6⅝s 2003	mN15	**A**	4/97	A–	X	BE	NC	....	....	....	....	....	200	S7	'96	103⅛	97⅞	97⅞	6.77	6.77
Sr Nts 6⅞s 2003	jD15	**A**	12/97	BBB	X	BE	NC	....	....	....	....	....	150	S1	'93	104⅜	98⅜	98⅜	6.99	6.99
Sr Nts 7.20s 2004	Fa	**A**	12/97	BBB	X	BE	NC	....	....	....	....	....	500	S1	'97	105¾	99⅛	99⅛	7.26	7.26
Nts[1] 7s 2004	Ms15	**A**	4/97	A–	X	BE	NC	....	....	....	....	....	250	S7	'97	104⅞	98⅜	98⅜	7.12	7.12
Nts[1] 6⅜s 2004	aO	**A**			X	BE	NC	....	....	....	....	....	200	S7	'97	102⅜	95¾	95¾	6.66	6.66
Nts[1] 6⅞s 2005	Jd15	**A**	4/97	A–	X	BE	NC	....	....	....	....	....	175	S7	'95	105	97⅛	97⅛	7.08	7.08
Nts 6¼s 2005	Jd15	**A**			X	BE	NC	....	....	....	....	....	300	S4	'98	101⅝	94⅛	94⅛	6.64	6.64
Sr Nts 6¾s 2006	Jj15	**A**	12/97	BBB	X	BE	NC	....	....	....	....	....	150	S1	'94	104½	95⅞	95⅞	7.04	7.04
Nts[1] 7⅛s 2006	aO	**A**	4/97	A–	X	BE	NC	....	....	....	....	....	200	S7	'96	106¾	97⅜	97½	7.31	7.31
Nts[1] 7⅜s 2007	Mn15	**A**			X	BE	NC	....	....	....	....	....	200	S7	'97	109	98⅝	98⅝	7.48	7.48
M-T Nts 'D' 9.15s 2001	[2]ms15	**A**	12/97	BBB	X	BE	NC	....	....	....	....	....	35.0	S1	'95	106¾	102½	102½	8.93	8.92
M-T Nts 'D' 7.66s 2001	[3]ms15	**A**	12/97	BBB	X	BE	NC	....	....	....	....	....	18.0	S1	'95	104½	101¼	101¼	7.57	7.56
***Salton Inc**[4]*	***23d***	*n/a*	*n/a*	*n/a*		*Je*	*8.34*	*335.0*	*155.0*	*9-25-99*	*182.0*		*315.0*	*79.2*						
[5]Sr Sub Nts[4] 10¾s 2005	jD15	**B–**			Y	BE	105.375	(12-17-02)	....	....	[6]Z110.75	12-16-01	125	Exch.	'98	106	100	102¼	10.51	10.51
***San Diego Gas & Electric**[7]*	***75***	*5.38*	*n/a*	*3.76*		*Dc*	*355.0*	*1097*	*533.0*	*6-30-99*	*1486*		*2879*	*53.9*						
1st JJ 9⅝s 2020	Ao15	**AA–**	1/99	A+	X	R	104.04	(4-15-00)	....	....	....	....	100	M2	'90	107¾	103¾	104⅝	9.20	9.20
1st LL 8½s 2022	Ao	**AA–**	1/99	A+	X	BE	103.66	(4-1-02)	....	....	Z100	....	60.0	D6	'92	110⅞	101¼	101¼	8.40	8.39
1st MM 7⅝s 2002	Jd15	**AA–**	1/99	A+	X	BE	NC	....	....	....	....	....	80.0	S1	'92	106⅜	101	101	7.55	7.55
Santa Fe Hotel	***40j***	***Mgr into Sahara Gaming,see Hacienda Res***																		
xw 1st[8] 11s 2000	jD15	**NR**	3/97	B–		R	100	....	....	....	....	....	99.4	D6	'93	99	91½	97	11.34	11.34
Santa Fe Pacific Corp	***55***	***Subsid of Burlington No'n Santa Fe,see***																		
Nts 8⅜s 2001	mN	**BBB+**	12/98	BBB	X	BE	NC	....	....	....	....	....	100	M5	'94	107	101⅞	101⅞	8.22	8.22
Nts 8⅝s 2004	mN	**BBB+**	12/98	BBB	X	BE	NC	....	....	....	....	....	100	M5	'94	113⅞	104½	104½	8.25	8.25
Santa Fe Pacific Gold	***45e***	***Acquired by Newmont Mining,see***																		
Sr Deb 8⅜s 2005	jJ	**BBB**	2/98	BBB+	X	BE	NC	....	....	....	....	....	200	M5	'95	112	102⅝	102⅝	8.16	8.16
***Sara Lee**[9]*	***26***	*△8.35*	*△8.13*	*△7.79*		*Je*	*169.0*	*5250*	*5904*	*10-2-99*	*2140*		*5958*	*65.0*						
M-T Nts 'C' 5.95s 2005	[10]ms15	**AA–**			X	BE	NC	....	....	....	....	....	34.0	L3	'98	102¼	94⅞	94⅞	6.27	6.27
M-T Nts 'C' 6s 2008	[11]ms15	**AA–**			X	BE	NC	....	....	....	....	....	49.0		'98	102¾	91⅝	91⅝	6.55	6.55
M-T Nts 'C' 6s 2008	ms15	**AA–**			X	BE	NC	....	....	....	....	....	35.0	L3	'98	102¾	91⅝	91⅝	6.55	6.55

Uniform Footnote Explanations-See Page 260. Other: [1] Was Smith Barney Hldgs. [2] Due 2-13-01. [3] Due 6-14-01. [4] Was Salton/Maxim Housewares. [5] (HR)On Chge of Ctrl at 101. [6] Max 35% red w/proceeds of Equity Off'g. [7] Subsid of Enova Corp. [8] Co must offer repurch,at 101,on Chge of Ctrl. [9] Was Consolidated Foods. [10] Due 1-20-05. [11] Due 1-15-08.

Title-Industry Code & Co. Finances (In Italics)	Ind		Fixed Charge Coverage 1996	1997	1998	Year End	Million $ Cash & Equiv.	Curr. Assets	Curr. Liab.	Balance Sheet Date		L. Term Debt (Mil $)		Capital-ization (Mil $)	Total Debt % Capital					
Individual Issue Statistics Exchange	Interest Dates	S&P Rating	Date of Last Rating Change	Prior Rating	Eligible	Bond Form	Redemption Provisions: Regular Price	Regular (Begins) Thru	Sinking Fund Price	Sinking Fund (Begins) Thru	Refund/Other Restriction Price	Refund/Other Restriction (Begins) Thru	Outst'g (Mil $)	Underwriting Firm	Underwriting Year	Price Range 1999 High	Price Range 1999 Low	Mo. End Price Sale(s) or Bid	Curr. Yield	Yield to Mat.
Sara Lee (Cont.)																				
M-T Nts 'D' 6.05s 2008	[1]ms15	AA–			X	BE	NC	....	....	....	....	....	49.0	G1	'98	103⅛	91¾	91¾	6.59	6.59
M-T Nts 'D' 6.15s 2008	[2]ms15	AA–			X	BE	NC	....	....	....	....	....	100	G1	'98	103¾	92⅛	92⅛	6.68	6.68
Savannah Electric&Power[3]	72a		4.20	4.36	4.45	Dc	3.43	71.10	3.30	6-30-99		187.0	393.0	56.7						
1st 6⅝s 2003	jJ	AA–	10/97	A+	X	R	100.87	6-30-00	Z100	....	....	....	20.0	S1	'93	100¾	97	97	6.57	6.57
1st 6.90s 2006	Mn	AA–	10/97	A+	X	R	NC	....	....	....	....	....	20.0	F4	'96	108⅜	96⅝	96⅝	7.14	7.14
1st 7.40s 2023	jJ	AA–	10/97	A+	X	R	104.15	6-30-00	Z100	....	....	....	25.0	L3	'93	104	90⅞	91	8.13	8.13
1st 7⅞s 2025	Mn	AA–	10/97	A+	X	R	105.43	(5-1-00)	Z100	(5-1-00)	....	....	15.0	D6	'95	107⅞	95¼	95⅜	8.26	8.26
[4]SBC Communications Capital[5]	25		7.09	3.26	7.42	Dc	267.0	7533	11243	9-30-99		11266	27765	44.5						
M-T Nts 'E' 7s 2012	[6]fa	AA–			X	BE	101.50	(10-1-07)	....	....	....	....	60.0	B7	'97	108¾	94	94	7.45	7.45
SCANA Corp	75		3.40	3.15	3.40	Dc	57.00	516.0	824.0	9-30-99		1610	3827	51.6						
M-T Nts 'B' 6.05s 2003	[7]ao	A	7/98	A–	X	BE	NC	....	....	....	....	....	60.0	P1	'98	101¼	96⅜	96⅜	6.28	6.28
Scherer (R.P.) Corp	21	Acq by Cardinal Health,see																		
Sr Nts 6¾s 2004	Fa	NR	11/99	A	X	BE	NC	....	....	....	....	....	100	L3	'94	104⅛	97½	97½	6.92	6.92
Scholastic Corp	54		△1.06	△2.86	△4.10	My	2.87	551.2	274.1	8-31-99		329.0	689.0	50.9						
Nts 7s 2003	jD15	BBB			X	BE	NC	....	....	....	....	....	125	G1	'96	104½	97⅞	97⅞	7.15	7.15
[8]Scotsman Group	25c		1.59	1.17	1.19	Dc	0.69			9-30-99		915.0	866.0	106.0						
Sr Sub[9]Nts[10] 8⅝s 2007	jD15	B+			Y	BE	104.3125	(12-15-02)	....	....	[11]Z108.625	12-15-00	100	M7	'97	108½	99	108	7.99	7.98
Scott Paper	33	Merged into Kimberly-Clark,see																		
Deb 10s 2002	Ms	AA	1/96	A–	X	R	NC	....	....	....	....	....	[12]52.8	G1	'90	113¾	106½	106½	9.39	9.39
Deb 8.30s 2004	Ms15	AA	1/96	A–	X	R	NC	....	....	....	....	....	63.2	G1	'92	112¾	104½	104½	7.94	7.94
Deb 10s 2005	Ms15	AA	1/96	A–	X	R	NC	....	....	....	....	....	51.1	G1	'90	123⅜	112¼	112¼	8.91	8.91
Deb 8.80s 2022	Mn15	AA	1/96	A–	X	R	104.106	(5-15-02)	....	....	....	....	11.4	G1	'92	115½	107⅜	108¾	8.09	8.09
Deb 7s 2023	fA15	AA	1/96	A–	X	BE	102.116	(8-15-03)	....	....	....	....	200	S1	'93	101½	90⅝	90¾	7.71	7.71
Scripps(E.W.)Co	54c		22.19	15.19	5.86	Dc	12.80	423.0	524.0	6-30-99		631.0	2011	44.9						
Nts 6⅜s 2002	aO15	A			X	BE	NC	....	....	....	....	....	100	C5	'97	103	98⅜	98⅜	6.48	6.48
Sea Containers Ltd[13]	70		1.32	1.40	1.53	Dc	134.0			12-31-98		1056	1531	69.0						
• Sr[9]Nts[14] 9½s 2003	jJ	BB–			Y	R	102.375	6-30-00	....	....	....	....	100	Exch.	'93	104	95	s95	10.00	10.00
• Sr Nts 10½s 2003	jJ	BB–			Y	BE	105.25	(7-1-00)	....	....	....	....	65.0	L1	'96	108	100	96⅛	10.92	10.92
• Sr Sub[15]Deb[14] 12½s 2004	jD	BB–			Y	R	106.25	11-30-00	....	....	....	....	100	L1	'92	111	100⅛	102	12.25	12.25
• Sr Sub[14]Deb[16]'B' 12½s 2004	jD	BB–			Y	R	106.25	11-30-00	....	....	....	....	25.0	Exch.	'93	110	102¼	102	12.25	12.25
Seagate Technology	20e		△31.24	△d1.63	△10.58	Je	1415	3031	1565	10-1-99		703.0	4267	16.5						
Sr Deb 7⅞s 2017	Ms	BBB			X	BE	[17]Z100	....	....	....	....	....	100	M6	'97	95⅜	83⅜	83½	9.43	9.43
Sr Deb 7.45s 2037	Ms	BBB			X	BE	[17]Z100	....	....	....	....	....	200	M6	'97	99⅜	86⅞	86⅞	8.58	8.57
Sr Nts 7⅛s 2004	Ms	BBB			X	BE	[17]Z100	....	....	....	....	....	200	M6	'97	99¼	92⅜	92⅜	7.71	7.71
Sr Nts 7.37s 2007	Ms	BBB			X	BE	[17]Z100	....	....	....	....	....	200	M6	'97	98⅝	88⅛	88⅛	8.36	8.36
Seagram(Jos.E.)& Sons	11b	Gtd by Seagram Co. Ltd,see																		
Gtd[18]Deb 7s 2008	Ao15	BBB–	10/98	A	X	BE	NC	....	....	....	....	....	200	G1	'93	103¾	95⅛	95⅛	7.36	7.36
Gtd[18]Deb 8⅜s 2007	Fa15	BBB–	10/98	A	X	R	NC	....	....	....	....	....	200	G1	'87	111⅞	101⅞	101⅞	8.22	8.22
Gtd[18]Deb 8⅞s 2011	mS15	BBB–	10/98	A	X	R	NC	....	....	....	....	....	225	G1	'91	117⅜	105⅝	106	8.37	8.37
Gtd[18]Deb[19] 9.65s 2018	fA15	BBB–	10/98	A	X	R	NC	....	....	....	....	....	250	G1	'88	134⅛	113¾	113¾	8.48	8.48
Gtd[18]Sr Deb 7½s 2018	jD15	BBB–			X	BE	NC	....	....	....	....	....	875	B7	'98	9975	93¾	94½	7.94	7.94
Gtd[18]Deb 9s 2021	fA15	BBB–	10/98	A	X	R	NC	....	....	....	....	....	200	G1	'91	119⅛	106½	106⅞	8.42	8.42
Gtd[18]Sr Deb 7.60s 2028	jD15	BBB–			X	BE	NC	....	....	....	....	....	700	B7	'98	105⅞	93⅛	94¼	8.06	8.06
Gtd[18]Sr Nts 5.79s 2000	Ao15	BBB–			X	BE	NC	....	....	....	....	....	250	M7	'99	100⅛	98	98⅛	5.90	5.90

Uniform Footnote Explanations-See Page 260. Other: [1] Due 4-14-08. [2] Due 6-19-08. [3] Subsid of Southern Co. [4] Subsid & data of SBC Communications. [5] See Southwestern Bell Cap. [6] Due 10-1-12. [7] Due 1-13-03. [8] Now Williams Scotsman. [9] (HRO)On Chge of Ctrl at 101. [10] Gtd by Scotsman Indus. [11] Max $35M red w/proceeds of Pub Eq Off'g. [12] Defeased,fds deposited w/trustee. [13] See Orient Express Hotels. [14] Co may red in whole at 100 for certain tax chge. [15] Co must offer repurch at 101 on Chge in Ctrl. [16] Co must offer repurch at 101 on Chge of Ctrl. [17] Greater of 100 or amt based on formula. [18] Gtd by Seagram Co Ltd. [19] (HRO)On 8-15-03 at 100.

Title-Industry Code & Co. Finances (In Italics)	Ind	Fixed Charge Coverage 1996	1997	1998		Year End	Million $ Cash & Equiv.	Curr. Assets	Curr. Liab.	Balance Sheet Date	L. Term Debt (Mil $)		Capital-ization (Mil $)	Total Debt % Capital						
Exchange ↓ Individual Issue Statistics	**Interest Dates**	**S&P Rating**	**Date of Last Rating Change**	**Prior Rating**	**Eligible ↓**	**Bond Form**	**Redemption Provisions: Regular Price**	**Regular (Begins) Thru**	**Sinking Fund Price**	**Sinking Fund (Begins) Thru**	**Refund/Other Restriction Price**	**Refund/Other Restriction (Begins) Thru**	**Outst'g (Mil $)**	**Underwriting Firm**	**Year**	**Price Range 1999 High**	**Low**	**Mo. End Price Sale(s) or Bid**	**Curr. Yield**	**Yield to Mat.**
***Seagram(Jos.E.)& Sons** (Cont.)*																				
Gtd[1]Sr Nts 6¼s 2001	jD15	BBB–			X	BE	NC	....	....	....	....	....	600	B7	'98	100¾	97⅞	97⅞	6.39	6.39
Gtd[1]Sr Nts 6.40s 2003	jD15	BBB–			X	BE	NC	....	....	....	....	....	400	B7	'98	101⅛	95⅞	96⅜	6.64	6.64
Gtd[1]Sr Nts 6⅝s 2005	jD15	BBB–			X	BE	NC	....	....	....	....	....	475	B7	'98	101⅝	94⅝	95¼	6.96	6.95
Gtd[1]Sr Nts 6.80s 2008	jD15	BBB–			X	BE	NC	....	....	....	....	....	450	B7	'98	102⅜	93½	93¾	7.25	7.25
***Seagram Co. Ltd**[2]*	***11b***	*△3.09*	*△1.87*	*△0.51*		*Je*	*1420*	*8965*	*7877*	*9-30-99*	*7561*		*23079*	*36.2*						
Deb 6½s 2003	aO	BBB–	10/98	A	X	BE	NC	....	....	....	....	....	200	G1	'93	101⅛	97¼	97¼	6.68	6.68
Deb 8.35s 2006	mN15	BBB–	10/98	A	X	BE	NC	....	....	....	....	....	200	G1	'91	111	102½	102½	8.15	8.15
Deb 8.35s 2022	Jj15	BBB–	10/98	A	X	BE	NC	....	....	....	....	....	200	G1	'92	111½	101¼	101⅜	8.24	8.24
Deb 6⅞s 2023	mS	BBB–	10/98	A	X	BE	NC	....	....	....	....	....	200	G1	'93	94⅞	85¾	85⅞	8.01	8.00
Seagull Energy	***73a***	*2.29*	*2.74*	*d0.37*		*Dc*	*53.88*	*251.8*	*288.2*	*9-30-99*	*582.0*		*1160*	*50.8*						
Sr Nts[3] 7⅞s 2003	fA	BB+	4/99	BBB–	Y	R	NC	....	....	....	....	....	100	D4	'93	103¼	92½	100	7.88	7.87
Sr Nts 7½s 2027	mS15	BB+	4/99	BBB–	Y	BE	NC	....	....	....	....	....	150	M2	'97	88½	77⅝	82⅛	9.13	9.13
Sr Sub Nts[3] 8⅝s 2005	fA	BB–	4/99	BB+	Y	R	102.59	(8-1-00)	....	....	....	....	150	D4	'93	102	95	99¾	8.65	8.64
***Seariver Maritime Fin'l Hldgs**[4]*	***64***	*Subsid of Exxon Corp,see Exxon Capital*																		
Gtd[5]Defrd Int Deb 2012	[6]	AAA			X	R	[7]100	....	....	....	....	....	[8]771	Co.	'82	46	38¾	38¾	....	Flat
Sears Roebuck Acceptance	***25***	*2.54*	*1.25*	*1.26*		*Dc*	*60.00*			*10-2-99*	*11271*		*14164*	*79.6*						
Nts 6½s 2000	Jd15	A–	5/96	BBB	X	R	NC	....	....	....	....	....	250	M6	'95	101⅜	100	100	6.50	6.50
Nts 6.95s 2002	Mn15	A–			X	R	NC	....	....	....	....	....	300	M6	'97	104	98⅞	98⅞	7.03	7.03
Nts 6.90s 2003	fA	A–			X	R	NC	....	....	....	....	....	250	M6	'96	104½	97⅞	97⅞	7.05	7.05
• Nts 6¾s 2005	mS15	A–	5/96	BBB	X	R	NC	....	....	....	....	....	250	G1	'95	101¼	96	94⅛	7.17	7.17
Nts 6⅛s 2006	Jj15	A–	5/96	BBB	X	R	NC	....	....	....	....	....	250	G1	'96	102	91½	91½	6.69	6.69
Nts 6.70s 2006	mN15	A–			X	R	NC	....	....	....	....	....	300	G1	'96	105⅝	93⅜	93⅜	7.18	7.17
Nts[9] 7s 2007	Jd15	A–			X	BE	NC	....	....	....	....	....	500	G1	'97	107¾	94½	94½	7.41	7.41
Nts 6.70s 2007	mS18	A–			X	BE	NC	....	....	....	....	....	150	M2	'97	106	92¾	92¾	7.22	7.22
Nts[10] 6¼s 2009	Mn	A–			X	BE	NC	....	....	....	....	....	750	G1	'99	99	88	88	7.10	7.10
Nts 6⅞s 2017	aO15	A–			X	BE	[11]Z100	....	....	....	....	....	300	G1	'97	102½	85⅞	85⅞	8.01	8.01
Nts 7½s 2027	aO15	A–			X	BE	103.676	(10-15-07)	....	....	....	....	250	M6	'97	108¼	90¼	90⅜	8.30	8.30
Nts 6¾s 2028	Jj15	A–			X	BE	[12]Z100	....	....	....	....	....	200	G1	'98	101½	81½	81½	8.28	8.28
Deb 6½s 2028	jD	A–			X	BE	[12]Z100	....	....	....	....	....	300	M2	'98	98⅞	78¾	78¾	8.25	8.25
M-T Nts 'I' 6.65s 2000	[13]mn15	A–	5/96	BBB	X	BE	NC	....	....	....	....	....	24.0	G1	'95	101¼	100	100	6.65	6.65
M-T Nts 'I' 6.34s 2000	[14]mn15	A–	5/96	BBB	X	BE	NC	....	....	....	....	....	20.0	G1	'95	101⅜	99⅝	99⅝	6.36	6.36
M-T Nts 'I' 6½s 2000	[15]mn15	A–	5/96	BBB	X	BE	NC	....	....	....	....	....	40.0	G1	'95	101⅝	99⅝	99⅝	6.52	6.52
M-T Nts 'I' 6.40s 2000	[16]mn15	A–	5/96	BBB	X	BE	NC	....	....	....	....	....	20.0	G1	'95	101½	99½	99½	6.43	6.43
M-T Nts 'I' 6.34s 2000	[17]mn15	A–	5/96	BBB	X	BE	NC	....	....	....	....	....	25.0	G1	'95	101⅜	99½	99½	6.37	6.37
M-T Nts 'I' 6.29s 2000	[18]mn15	A–	5/96	BBB	X	BE	NC	....	....	....	....	....	25.0	G1	'95	101¼	99⅜	99⅜	6.33	6.33
M-T Nts 'I' 6.19s 2000	[19]mn15	A–	5/96	BBB	X	BE	NC	....	....	....	....	....	20.0	G1	'95	101¼	99⅛	99⅛	6.24	6.24
M-T Nts 'I' 6.18s 2000	[20]mn15	A–	5/96	BBB	X	BE	NC	....	....	....	....	....	45.0	G1	'95	101¼	99⅛	99⅛	6.23	6.23
M-T Nts 'I' 5.96s 2000	[21]mn15	A–	5/96	BBB	X	BE	NC	....	....	....	....	....	25.0	G1	'95	100⅞	98⅞	98⅞	6.03	6.03
M-T Nts 'I 5.99s 2000	[22]mn15	A–	5/96	BBB	X	BE	NC	....	....	....	....	....	20.0	G1	'95	100⅞	98⅞	98⅞	6.06	6.06
M-T Nts 'I' 5.99s 2000	[23]mn15	A–	5/96	BBB	X	BE	NC	....	....	....	....	....	25.0	G1	'95	100⅞	98⅞	98⅞	6.06	6.06
M-T Nts 'I' 5.71s 2001	[24]mn15	A–	5/96	BBB	X	BE	NC	....	....	....	....	....	53.3	G1	'96	100½	98⅜	98⅜	5.80	5.80
M-T Nts 'I' 5.63s 2001	[25]mn15	A–	5/96	BBB	X	BE	NC	....	....	....	....	....	50.0	G1	'96	100¼	98⅜	98⅜	5.72	5.72
M-T Nts 'I' 5.65s 2001	[25]mn15	A–	5/96	BBB	X	BE	NC	....	....	....	....	....	68.8	G1	'96	100⅜	98⅜	98⅜	5.74	5.74
M-T Nts 'I' 5.67s 2001	[25]mn15	A–	5/96	BBB	X	BE	NC	....	....	....	....	....	30.0	G1	'96	100⅜	98⅜	98⅜	5.76	5.76

Uniform Footnote Explanations-See Page 260. Other: [1] Gtd by Seagram Co Ltd. [2] See Seagram (Jos.E.)& Sons. [3] (HRO)On Chge of Ctrl at 101. [4] Was Seariver Maritime Inc. [5] At mat:$270 prin&$730 defrd int to be pd. [6] Due 9-1-12. [7] Percent of Accreted Value. [8] Incl disc. [9] Co may red in whole,at 100,for tax law chge. [10] Co may red in whole, at 100, for tax law chge. [11] Plus Make-Whole Amt. [12] Red at greater of 100 or amt based on formula. [13] Due 1-20-00. [14] Due 9-19-00. [15] Due 10-4-00. [16] Due 10-11-00. [17] Due 10-12-00. [18] Due 10-18-00. [19] Due 11-30-00. [20] Due 12-1-00. [21] Due 12-7-00. [22] Due 12-13-00. [23] Due 12-26-00. [24] Due 2-6-01. [25] Due 2-7-01.

Title-Industry Code & Co. Finances (In Italics)	Ind	Fixed Charge Coverage 1996	1997	1998		Year End	Million $ Cash & Equiv.	Curr. Assets	Curr. Liab.	Balance Sheet Date	L. Term Debt (Mil $)		Capital-ization (Mil $)	Total Debt % Capital						
Individual Issue Statistics Exchange	Interest Dates	S&P Rating	Date of Last Rating Change	Prior Rating	Eligible	Bond Form	Redemption Provisions: Regular Price	Regular (Begins) Thru	Sinking Fund Price	Sinking Fund (Begins) Thru	Refund/Other Restriction Price	Refund/Other Restriction (Begins) Thru	Outst'g (Mil $)	Underwriting Firm	Underwriting Year	Price Range 1999 High	Price Range 1999 Low	Mo. End Price Sale(s) or Bid	Curr. Yield	Yield to Mat.
Sears Roebuck Acceptance (Cont.)																				
M-T Nts 'I' 6.12s 2001	[1]mn15	A–	5/96	BBB	X	BE	NC	....	....	....	....	....	20.0	G1	'95	101½	97⅝	97⅝	6.27	6.27
M-T Nts 'I'[2] 6.11s 2005	mN15	A–	5/96	BBB	X	BE	NC	....	....	....	....	....	25.8	G1	'95	103¼	98⅞	98⅞	6.18	6.18
M-T Nts 'I'[2] 6.13s 2005	mN15	A–	5/96	BBB	X	BE	NC	....	....	....	....	....	50.0	G1	'95	103¼	99⅛	99⅛	6.18	6.18
M-T Nts 'I'[2] 6.15s 2005	mN15	A–	5/96	BBB	X	BE	NC	....	....	....	....	....	55.0	G1	'95	102⅞	98¾	99¼	6.20	6.20
M-T Nts 'III' 6.76s 2003	[3]mn15	A–			X	BE	NC	....	....	....	....	....	38.0	M2	'97	104⅛	97⅜	97⅜	6.94	6.94
M-T Nts 'III' 6.95s 2004	[4]mn15	A–			X	BE	NC	....	....	....	....	....	26.0	G1	'97	105⅝	97⅛	97⅛	7.16	7.15
M-T Nts 'III' 6.92s 2004	[4]mn15	A–			X	BE	NC	....	....	....	....	....	50.0	G1	'97	105½	97	97	7.13	7.13
M-T Nts 'IV' 6.23s 2000	[5]fa15	A–			X	BE	NC	....	....	....	....	....	40.0	M6	'97	101	99¾	99⅞	6.24	6.24
M-T Nts 'IV' 6.22s 2000	[6]fa15	A–			X	BE	NC	....	....	....	....	....	25.0	M6	'97	101	99⅝	99¾	6.24	6.23
M-T Nts 'IV' 6.16s 2000	[7]fa15	A–			X	BE	NC	....	....	....	....	....	200	G1	'97	101	99⅜	99½	6.19	6.19
M-T Nts 'IV' 6.22s 2000	[8]fa15	A–			X	BE	NC	....	....	....	....	....	48.0	M2	'97	101¼	99¼	99¼	6.27	6.27
M-T Nts 'IV' 6.37s 2001	[9]fa15	A–			X	BE	NC	....	....	....	....	....	52.0	M6	'97	102⅛	98⅛	98⅛	6.49	6.49
M-T Nts 'IV' 6.36s 2001	[10]fa15	A–			X	BE	NC	....	....	....	....	....	100	M6	'97	102⅛	98⅛	98⅛	6.48	6.48
M-T Nts 'IV' 6.63s 2002	[11]fa15	A–			X	BE	NC	....	....	....	....	....	90.7	M2	'97	103⅛	98	98	6.77	6.76
M-T Nts 'IV' 6.38s 2002	[12]fa15	A–			X	BE	NC	....	....	....	....	....	45.0	S1	'97	102⅜	97⅛	97⅛	6.57	6.57
M-T Nts 'IV' 6.72s 2003	[13]fa15	A–			X	BE	NC	....	....	....	....	....	27.5	G1	'97	104⅛	97	97	6.93	6.93
M-T Nts 'V 5.88s 2000	[14]fa15	A–			X	BE	NC	....	....	....	....	....	150	C1	'98	100½	99¾	99⅞	5.89	5.89
Sears, Roebuck & Co.[15]	***59f***	***2.51***	***2.75***	***2.56***		***Dc***	***281.0***	***27434***	***12492***	***10-2-99***	***13245***		***23360***	***77.2***						
Deb 9⅜s 2011	mN	A–	5/96	BBB	X	R	NC	....	....	....	Z100	....	300	D3	'91	129¼	106⅞	106⅞	8.77	8.77
Nts 6¼s 2004	Jj15	A–	5/96	BBB	X	R	NC	....	....	....	Z100	....	300	M6	'94	103	94¾	94¾	6.60	6.60
M-T Nts 'VII'[16] 7.35s 2000	[17]ao	A–	5/96	BBB	X	BE	NC	....	....	....	....	....	20.0	D3	'95	101¾	100⅛	100⅛	7.34	7.34
M-T Nts 'VII'[16] 7.41s 2000	[18]ao	A–	5/96	BBB	X	BE	NC	....	....	....	....	....	15.0	D3	'95	101⅞	100⅛	100⅛	7.40	7.40
M-T Nts 'VII'[16] 7.38s 2000	[19]ao	A–	5/96	BBB	X	BE	NC	....	....	....	....	....	20.0	D3	'95	102	100⅛	100¼	7.36	7.36
M-T Nts 'VII'[16] 6.58s 2000	[20]ao	A–	5/96	BBB	X	BE	NC	....	....	....	....	....	5.00	D3	'93	101⅛	99¾	99⅞	6.59	6.59
M-T Nts 'VII'[16] 6.70s 2000	[20]ao	A–	5/96	BBB	X	BE	NC	....	....	....	....	....	5.00	D3	'93	101¼	99⅞	100	6.70	6.70
M-T Nts 'VII'[16] 6¼s 2000	[21]ao	A–	5/96	BBB	X	BE	NC	....	....	....	....	....	20.0	D3	'93	100¾	99½	99⅝	6.27	6.27
M-T Nts 'VII'[16] 6.27s 2000	[22]ao	A–	5/96	BBB	X	BE	NC	....	....	....	....	....	36.0	D3	'93	100¾	99½	99⅝	6.29	6.29
M-T Nts 'VII'[16] 6.28s 2000	[23]ao	A–	5/96	BBB	X	BE	NC	....	....	....	....	....	7.50	D3	'93	100⅞	99½	99⅝	6.30	6.30
M-T Nts 'VII'[16] 5.81s 2000	[24]ao	A–	5/96	BBB	X	BE	NC	....	....	....	....	....	10.0	D3	'93	100⅛	98⅞	98⅞	5.88	5.88
M-T Nts 'VII'[16] 6.56s 2003	[25]ao	A–	5/96	BBB	X	BE	NC	....	....	....	....	....	25.0	D3	'93	102½	97	97	6.76	6.76
M-T Nts 'VII'[16] 6.57s 2003	[26]ao	A–	5/96	BBB	X	BE	NC	....	....	....	....	....	5.00	D3	'93	102¾	96¼	96¼	6.83	6.83
M-T Nts 'VII'[16] 6.67s 2003	[27]ao	A–	5/96	BBB	X	BE	NC	....	....	....	....	....	40.0	D3	'93	103⅛	96¾	96¾	6.89	6.89
M-T Nts 'VII'[16] 6.65s 2003	[25]ao	A–	5/96	BBB	X	BE	NC	....	....	....	....	....	10.0	D3	'93	102⅞	97⅛	97⅛	6.85	6.85
M-T Nts 'VII'[16] 6.76s 2003	[25]ao	A–	5/96	BBB	X	BE	NC	....	....	....	....	....	10.0	D3	'93	103¼	97½	97½	6.93	6.93
M-T Nts 'VII'[16] 6.66s 2003	[28]ao	A–	5/96	BBB	X	BE	NC	....	....	....	....	....	25.0	D3	'93	103⅛	96⅝	96⅝	6.89	6.89
M-T Nts 'VII'[16] 6.65s 2003	[29]ao	A–	5/96	BBB	X	BE	NC	....	....	....	....	....	5.00	D3	'93	102⅝	96¼	96¼	6.91	6.91
M-T Nts 'VII'[16] 6.34s 2004	[30]ao	A–	5/96	BBB	X	BE	NC	....	....	....	....	....	5.00	D3	'93	102	94⅜	94⅜	6.72	6.72
Security Capital Grp	***36***	***n/a***	***n/a***	***n/a***		***Dc***				***9-30-99***	***1585***		***4248***	***43.8***						
M-T Nts 'A' 7¾s 2003	mN15	BBB			X	BE	NC	....	....	....	....	....	100	M5	'98	100¾	97	97	7.99	7.99
Security Capital Ind Tr	***57***	***Now ProLogis Trust, see***																		
Nts 7¼s 2000	Mn15	BBB+			X	BE	[31]Z100	....	....	....	....	....	17.5	M5	'95	107⅛	100¼	100¼	7.23	7.23
Nts 7.30s 2001	Mn15	BBB+			X	BE	[31]Z100	....	....	....	....	....	17.5	M5	'95	103¼	100⅛	100⅛	7.29	7.29
([32]Amort)Nts 7⅞s 2009	Mn15	BBB+			X	BE	[31]Z100	....	....	....	....	....	75.0	M5	'95	108⅛	96⅜	96⅜	8.17	....
([33]Amort)Nts 8.65s 2016	Mn15	BBB+			X	BE	[31]Z100	....	....	....	....	....	50.0	M5	'96	107⅜	97⅛	97⅛	8.91	....

Uniform Footnote Explanations-See Page 260. Other: [1] Due 12-13-01. [2] (HRO)On 11-15-00 at 100. [3] Due 6-25-03. [4] Due 6-17-04. [5] Due 7-12-00. [6] Due 8-10-00. [7] Due 9-20-00. [8] Due 11-8-00. [9] Due 11-21-01. [10] Due 12-4-01. [11] Due 7-9-02. [12] Due 10-7-02. [13] Due 9-17-03. [14] Due 5-8-00. [15] See Orchard Supply Hardware Corp. [16] Issued in min denom $100T. [17] Due 3-23-00. [18] Due 3-30-00. [19] Due 4-19-00. [20] Due 6-15-00. [21] Due 7-17-00. [22] Due 7-20-00. [23] Due 8-09-00. [24] Due 10-25-00. [25] Due 2-20-03. [26] Due 8-19-03. [27] Due 7-07-03. [28] Due 7-29-03. [29] Due 8-06-03. [30] Due 6-15-04. [31] Plus Make-Whole Amt. [32] Princ pyts of $125/bond due ea 5-15(fr 5-15-02). [33] Prin pyts due ea 5-15:'13,$100,incr$50 anly aft.

Title-Industry Code & Co. Finances (In Italics)	Ind	Fixed Charge Coverage 1996	1997	1998		Year End	Million $ Cash & Equiv.	Curr. Assets	Curr. Liab.	Balance Sheet Date	L. Term Debt (Mil $)		Capital-ization (Mil $)	Total Debt % Capital						
Exchange ↓ Individual Issue Statistics	**Interest Dates**	**S&P Rating**	**Date of Last Rating Change**	**Prior Rating**	**Eligible ↓**	**Bond Form**	**Redemption Provisions — Regular Price**	**Regular (Begins) Thru**	**Sinking Fund Price**	**Sinking Fund (Begins) Thru**	**Refund/Other Restriction Price**	**Refund/Other Restriction (Begins) Thru**	**Outst'g (Mil $)**	**Underwriting Firm**	**Underwriting Year**	**Price Range 1999 High**	**Price Range 1999 Low**	**Mo. End Price Sale(s) or Bid**	**Curr. Yield**	**Yield to Mat.**
***Security Capital Ind Tr** (Cont.)*																				
Nts 7⅝s 2017	jJ	**BBB+**			X	BE	[1]Z100	....	....	....	....	....	100	G1	'97	97⅜	88½	88½	8.62	8.61
Security Pacific Corp	***10***	***Merged into BankAmer Corp,see***																		
Sub Nts 11½s 2000	mN15	**A**	10/95	A–	X	R	NC	....	....	....	....	....	150	M2	'90	110	103¾	103¾	11.08	11.08
Sub Nts 11s 2001	Ms	**A**	10/95	A–	X	R	NC	....	....	....	....	....	250	M2	'91	110⅜	104½	104½	10.53	10.52
Sequa Corp[2]	***2***	***1.25***	***1.78***	***2.11***		***Dc***	***400.3***	***1080***	***666.1***	***9-30-99***	***500.0***		***1160***	***43.4***						
• Sr[3]Nts 9s 2009	fA	**BB**			Y	BE	[4]Z100	....	....	....	....	....	500	B7	'99	99⅝	97¼	92	9.78	9.78
Service Corp Int'l[5]	***63***	***4.06***	***5.31***	***3.93***		***Dc***	***206.0***	***1092***	***788.3***	***9-30-99***	***4111***		***7908***	***53.1***						
Deb 7⅞s 2013	Fa	**BBB–**	11/99	BBB	X	R	NC	....	....	....	....	....	150	M2	'93	117⅞	72⅞	73¼	10.75	10.75
Nts 6⅜s 2000	aO	**BBB–**	11/99	BBB	X	BE	NC	....	....	....	....	....	150	M5	'95	101⅜	94¼	94⅝	6.74	6.74
Nts 6¾s 2001	Jd	**BBB–**	11/99	BBB	X	BE	NC	....	....	....	....	....	150	M5	'96	102⅝	91⅜	91½	7.38	7.38
Nts 7⅜s 2004	Ao15	**BBB–**	11/99	BBB	X	BE	NC	....	....	....	....	....	250	M5	'97	107⅛	82¾	84¼	8.75	8.75
Nts 8⅜s 2004	jD15	**BBB–**	11/99	BBB	X	BE	NC	....	....	....	....	....	51.8	M5	'94	112⅜	84¼	84¼	9.94	9.94
Nts 6s 2005	jD15	**BBB–**	11/99	BBB	X	BE	[4]Z100	....	....	....	....	....	600	C1	'98	100⅛	74⅜	74⅜	8.07	8.07
Nts 7.20s 2006	Jd	**BBB–**	11/99	BBB	X	BE	NC	....	....	....	....	....	150	M5	'96	106⅞	77⅝	77⅝	9.28	9.27
Nts 6⅞s 2007	aO	**BBB–**	11/99	BBB	X	BE	NC	....	....	....	....	....	150	M5	'95	106⅛	73⅞	73⅞	9.31	9.31
Nts 7.70s 2009	Ao15	**BBB–**	11/99	BBB	X	BE	NC	....	....	....	....	....	200	M5	'97	112⅝	76	76	10.13	10.13
Nts[6] 7s 2015	Jd	**BBB–**	11/99	BBB	X	BE	NC	....	....	....	....	....	300	M5	'95	103¼	88⅝	88⅝	7.90	7.90
Service Merchandise	***59i***	***1.86***	***0.84***	***0.01***		***Dc***	***Bankruptcy Chapt 11***				***[7]960.0***		***1119***	***79.8***						
Sr Nts[3] 8⅜s 2001	§Jj15	**D**	3/99	C	Z	R			Default 7-15-99 int				21.6	M2	'93	73	43	60¼	....	Flat
Sr Sub Deb[3] 9s 2004	§jD15	**D**	3/99	C	Z	R			Default 6-15-99 int				300	M2	'93	41	8⅜	8¾	....	Flat
ServiceMaster Co[8]	***63***	***7.21***	***4.69***	***4.43***		***Dc***	***76.91***	***927.6***	***766.5***	***9-30-99***	***1688***		***2884***	***58.6***						
(L.P.) Nts 6.95s 2007	fA15	**BBB**			X	BE	[4]Z100	....	....	....	....	....	100	M5	'97	104⅞	93	93	7.47	7.47
Nts 7.10s 2018	Ms	**BBB**			X	BE	[4]Z100	....	....	....	....	....	150	M5	'98	98¾	85½	85⅝	8.29	8.29
(L.P.)Nts 7.45s 2027	fA15	**BBB**			X	BE	[4]Z100	....	....	....	....	....	200	M5	'97	107⅛	86¾	86¾	8.59	8.59
Nts 7¼s 2038	Ms	**BBB**			X	BE	[4]Z100	....	....	....	....	....	150	M5	'98	98⅛	82¾	82⅞	8.75	8.75
SFX Entertainment	***12e***	***n/a***	***n/a***	***d0.18***		***Dc***	***550.0***	***772.0***	***358.0***	***9-30-99***	***1391***		***2558***	***54.4***						
Sr Sub Nts[3] 9⅛s 2008	Fa	**B**	8/99	B–	Y	BE	104.563	(2-2-03)	....	....	[9]Z109.125	2-1-01	350	Exch.	'98	104	91½	94¼	9.68	9.68
Shared Tech Fairchild Commun	***67***	***Acquired by Intermedia Commun's,see***																		
Sr[10]Sub[11]Disc[12]Nts 12¼s 2006	Ms	**B–**			Y	BE	106.125	(3-1-01)	....	....	....	....	[13]164		'96	100½	94	97½	12.56	12.56
Shawmut Nat'l	***10***	***Merged into Fleet Fin'l Group,see***																		
Sub Nts 7.20s 2003	Ao15	**A–**	5/98	BBB+	X	BE	NC	....	....	....	....	....	150	M6	'93	105⅞	99⅝	99⅝	7.23	7.23
Shell Oil Co[14]	***49a***	***12.83***	***15.77***	***d5.41***		***Dc***	***284.0***	***4932***	***9709***	***6-30-99***	***476.0***		***19013***	***32.5***						
Nts 6.70s 2002	fA15	**AAA**			X	BE	NC	....	....	....	....	....	250	M5	'92	105⅛	99⅞	99⅞	6.71	6.71
Sherwin-Williams[15]	***15***	***17.15***	***6.34***	***7.46***		***Dc***	***5.01***	***1665***	***1309***	***9-30-99***	***624.0***		***2564***	***33.1***						
Deb 7⅜s 2027	Fa	**A**			X	BE	[1]Z100	....	....	....	....	....	150	Exch.	'97	112⅞	94½	94½	7.80	7.80
Nts 6¼s 2000	Fa	**A**			X	BE	NC	....	....	....	....	....	100	S1	'97	101	100	100	6.25	6.25
Nts 6½s 2002	Fa	**A**			X	BE	NC	....	....	....	....	....	100	S1	'97	103	98⅞	98⅞	6.57	6.57
Nts 6.85s 2007	Fa	**A**			X	BE	[16]Z100	....	....	....	....	....	200	S1	'97	107⅝	96⅝	96⅝	7.09	7.09
M-T Nts[17] 5½s 2027	aO15	**A**			X	BE	NC	....	....	....	....	....	50.0	S4	'97	101¼	99⅜	99⅜	5.53	5.53
Sherwin-Willians Devel	***15***	***Controlled by Sherwin Williams Co,see***																		
Gtd[18]Deb 9⅞s 2016	Jd15	**A**	2/97	A+	X	R	100	(6-15-06)	100	(6-15-07)	....	....	15.9	S1	'86	122¾	111	111	8.90	8.89
Shop At Home	***59h***	***Δn/a***	***Δn/a***	***Δ0.89***		***Je***	***22.50***	***49.02***	***29.05***	***9-30-99***	***75.80***		***164.0***	***46.2***						
Sr Sec Nts[3] 11s 2005	Ao	**B**			Y	BE	105.50	(4-1-02)	....	....	....	....	75.0	N2	'98	105	97	100	11.00	11.00
ShopKo Stores	***59g***	***[19]3.33***	***3.72***	***3.54***		***Ja***	***34.06***	***1006***	***942.2***	***10-30-99***	***444.0***		***1331***	***50.8***						
Sr Nts 8½s 2002	[20]jd15	**BBB–**	6/97	BBB	X	R	NC	....	....	....	....	....	100	G1	'92	107½	101	101	8.42	8.41

Uniform Footnote Explanations-See Page 260. Other: [1] Plus Make-Whole Amt. [2] Was Sun Chemical. [3] (HRO)On Chge of Ctrl at 101. [4] Red at greater of 100 or amt based on formula. [5] Was IFS Indus. [6] (HRO)On 6-1-02 at 100. [7] Incl liabs subj to compromise. [8] Was ServiceMaster Co L.P. [9] Max $122.5M red w/proceeds Pub Eq Off'g. [10] Int accrues at 12.25% fr 3-1-99. [11] Gtd by Shared Tech Fairchild Inc. [12] (HRO)On Chge of Ctrl at 101(Accreted Val). [13] Incl disc. [14] Subsid of SPNV Hldg. [15] See Sherwin-Williams Devel. [16] Greater of 100 or amt based on formula. [17] (HRO)On ea 10-15 at 100 fr 1999. [18] Gtd by Sherwin-Williams Co. [19] Fiscal Feb'97 & prior. [20] Due 3-15.

Title-Industry Code & Co. Finances (In Italics) / Individual Issue Statistics (Exchange)	Ind / Interest Dates	Fixed Charge Coverage 1996 / S&P Rating	1997 / Date of Last Rating Change	1998 / Prior Rating	Eligible	Year End / Bond Form	Cash & Equiv. (Million $) / Redemption Provisions: Regular Price	Curr. Assets (Million $) / Regular (Begins) Thru	Curr. Liab. (Million $) / Sinking Fund Price	Balance Sheet Date / Sinking Fund (Begins) Thru	L. Term Debt (Mil $) / Refund/Other Restriction Price	Capitalization (Mil $) / Refund/Other Restriction (Begins) Thru	Total Debt % Capital / Outst'g (Mil $)	Underwriting Firm	Underwriting Year	Price Range 1999 High	Price Range 1999 Low	Mo. End Price Sale(s) or Bid	Curr. Yield	Yield to Mat.
***ShopKo Stores** (Cont.)*																				
Sr Nts 6½s 2003	fA15	BBB–	6/97	BBB	X	BE	NC	....	....	....	....	....	100	G1	'93	102¼	94⅞	94⅞	6.85	6.85
Sr Nts 9s 2004	mN15	BBB–	6/97	BBB	X	BE	NC	....	....	....	....	....	100	G1	'94	112¼	101¾	101¾	8.85	8.84
Sr Nts 9¼s 2022	[1]jd15	BBB–	6/97	BBB	X	R	NC	....	....	....	....	....	100	G1	'92	127⅛	100⅞	101	9.16	9.16
Shurgard Storage Centers	***57***	*n/a*	*n/a*	*3.12*		*Dc*				*9-30-99*	*547.0*	*1222*	*44.8*							
Nts 7⅝s 2007	Ao25	BBB			X	BE	[2]Z100	....	....	....	....	....	50.0	M2	'97	109⅞	94¼	94¼	8.09	8.09
Silverleaf Resorts	***38***	*2.77*	*5.07*	*3.75*		*Dc*				*9-30-99*	*229.0*	*387.0*	*59.2*							
Sr Sub Nts[3] 10½s 2008	Ao	B–			Y	BE	105.25	(4-1-03)	....	....	[4]Z110.50	4-1-01	75.0	C6	'98	85¾	64	67½	15.56	15.55
Simon DeBartolo Group	***57***	***Now Simon Property Group,see***																		
Nts 6¾s 2004	jJ15	BBB+	6/98	BBB	X	BE	[2]Z100	....	....	....	....	....	100	M2	'97	100⅛	94½	94½	7.14	7.14
Nts 6⅞s 2005	[5]ao15	BBB+	6/98	BBB	X	BE	[2]Z100	....	....	....	....	....	150	M2	'97	100	93⅛	93⅜	7.36	7.36
Nts 6⅞s 2006	mN15	BBB+	6/98	BBB	X	BE	[6]Z100	....	....	....	....	....	250	M2	'96	99¾	91⅞	91⅞	7.48	7.48
M-T Nts 7⅛s 2007	mn15	BBB+	6/98	BBB	X	BE	[2]Z100	....	....	....	....	....	180	C1	'97	105⅛	92	92	7.74	7.74
Nts 7s 2009	jJ15	BBB+	6/98	BBB	X	BE	[2]Z100	....	....	....	....	....	150	M2	'97	99⅝	90	90⅛	7.77	7.77
Simon Property Group[7]	***57***	*1.64*	*1.04*	*1.37*		*Dc*				*9-30-99*	*8542*	*13223*	*64.6*							
Nts 6¾s 2004	Fa9	BBB+			X	BE	[2]Z100	....	....	....	....	....	300	M2	'99	100⅜	94¾	94¾	7.12	7.12
Nts 7⅛s 2009	Fa9	BBB+			X	BE	[2]Z100	....	....	....	....	....	300	M2	'99	101	91⅛	91⅛	7.82	7.82
Sinclair Broadcast Group	***12c***	*1.10*	*1.31*	*1.30*		*Dc*	*8.36*	*1043*	*295.0*	*9-30-99*	*2339*	*1828*	*70.1*							
Sr Sub Nts[3] 10s 2005	mS30	B	5/96	B+	Y	R	105	(9-30-00)	....	....	....	....	300	C1	'95	107	98½	99	10.10	10.10
Sr Sub Nts 8¾s 2007	jD15	B			Y	BE	104.375	(12-15-02)	....	....	[8]Z108.75	12-15-00	250	S1	'97	103	91½	92¼	9.49	9.48
Smith Intl	***49e***	*7.22*	*8.17*	*4.58*		*Dc*	*28.29*	*1009*	*426.5*	*9-30-99*	*331.0*	*1370*	*49.9*							
Sr Nts 7s 2007	mS15	BBB+			X	BE	[9]Z100	....	....	....	....	....	150	M6	'97	102½	94¼	94¾	7.39	7.39
Snap-On Inc	***8***	*17.50*	*14.52*	*5.71*		*Dc*	*42.69*	*1265*	*504.2*	*10-2-99*	*670.0*	*1102*	*30.9*							
Nts 6⅝s 2005	aO	A+	6/99	AA–	X	BE	NC	....	....	....	....	....	100	M2	'95	106⅞	97¼	97¼	6.81	6.81
Snyder Oil	***49a***	***Mrg w/Santa Fe Snyder***																		
Sr Sub Nts 8¾s 2007	Jd15	BB–	5/99	B+	Y	BE	104.375	(6-15-02)	....	....	[10]Z108.75	6-15-00	175		'97	102¼	96½	100¼	8.73	8.73
Society Corp	***10***	***Merged with KeyCorp, see***																		
Sub Nts 8⅛s 2002	Jd15	BBB+			X	BE	NC	....	....	....	....	....	200	G1	'92	107⅞	102⅜	102⅜	7.94	7.94
Sola Group Ltd	***43***	***Now Sola International,see***																		
Sr[11]Sub[12]Nts 9⅝s 2003	jD15	NR	11/97	BB+		R	102.406	12-14-00	....	....	....	....	[13]117	M6	'93	102	100	102	9.44	9.43
Sola International	***43***	*4.07*	*4.00*	*3.65*		*Mr*	*22.80*	*354.0*	*143.0*	*9-30-99*	*206.0*	*563.0*	*40.9*							
Nts 6⅞s 2008	Ms15	BBB–			X	BE	[9]Z100	....	....	....	....	....	100	M2	'98	95⅛	86⅛	86⅛	7.98	7.98
Solectron Corp	***23b***	*△10.13*	*△13.08*	*△12.84*		*Au*	*1688*	*3994*	*1113*	*8-31-99*	*923.0*	*3737*	*25.3*							
Sr Nts'B' 7⅜s 2006	Ms	BBB	10/97	BBB–	X	R	NC	....	....	....	....	....	150		'96	105½	95⅜	95⅜	7.73	7.73
Solutia Inc	***14***	*1.33*	*7.32*	*9.14*		*Dc*	*7.00*	*1020*	*899.0*	*9-30-99*	*597.0*	*573.0*	*104.0*							
Deb 7⅜s 2027	aO15	BBB			X	BE	[9]Z100	....	....	....	....	....	300	G1	'97	100⅜	87⅝	87¾	8.40	8.40
Deb 6.72s 2037	aO15	BBB			X	BE	[9]Z100	(10-15-04)	....	....	....	....	150	G1	'97	101⅝	94½	94½	7.11	7.11
Nts 6½s 2002	aO15	BBB			X	BE	NC	....	....	....	....	....	150	G1	'97	101⅛	96¾	96¾	6.72	6.72
Sonat Inc	***73a***	***Acq by El Paso Energy,see***																		
Nts 9s 2001	Mn	BBB	9/99	BBB+	X	R	NC	....	....	....	....	....	100	G1	'91	106¾	102⅛	102⅛	8.81	8.81
Nts 6⅞s 2005	Jd	BBB	9/99	BBB+	X	BE	NC	....	....	....	....	....	200	G1	'95	105¼	95¾	96½	7.12	7.12
Nts 6¾s 2007	aO	BBB	9/99	BBB+	X	BE	NC	....	....	....	....	....	100	G1	'97	105⅛	93⅝	94⅛	7.17	7.17
Nts 6⅝s 2008	Fa	BBB	9/99	BBB+	X	BE	[9]Z100	....	....	....	....	....	100	S4	'98	104⅛	93	93	7.12	7.12
Nts 7⅝s 2011	jJ15	BBB	9/99	BBB+	X	BE	[9]Z100	....	....	....	....	....	600	D6	'99	102¼	96⅞	98¼	7.76	7.76
Nts 7s 2018	Fa	BBB	9/99	BBB+	X	BE	[9]Z100	....	....	....	....	....	100	S4	'98	103⅝	88⅞	90¼	7.76	7.76

Uniform Footnote Explanations-See Page 260. Other: [1] Due 3-15-22. [2] Plus Make-Whole Amt. [3] (HRO)On Chge of Ctrl at 101. [4] Max $25 red w/proceeds of Pub Eq Off'g. [5] Due 10-27-05. [6] Plus Make Whole Amt. [7] See Simon DeBartolo Group. [8] Max $62M red w/procees of Pub Eq Off'g. [9] Red at greater of 100 or amt based on formula. [10] Max $52.5M red w/proceeds of Pub Eq Off'g. [11] (HRO)On Chge of Ctrl at 101(Accreted Val). [12] Int 9.625 aft. [13] Incl disc.

Title-Industry Code & Co. Finances (In Italics) / Individual Issue Statistics	Ind / Exchange Interest Dates	Fixed Charge Coverage 1996 / S&P Rating	1997 / Date of Last Rating Change	1998 / Prior Rating	Year End / Eligible	Bond Form	Million $ Cash & Equiv. / Regular Price	Curr. Assets / Regular (Begins) Thru	Curr. Liab. / Sinking Fund Price	Balance Sheet Date / Sinking Fund (Begins) Thru	L. Term Debt (Mil $) / Refund/Other Restriction Price	Refund/Other (Begins) Thru	Capital-ization (Mil $) / Outst'g (Mil $)	Total Debt % Capital / Underwriting Firm	Year	Price Range 1999 High	Low	Mo. End Price Sale(s) or Bid	Curr. Yield	Yield to Mat.
Sonoco Products	***16c***	***6.05***	***6.07***	***5.37***	***Dc***		***52.12***	***721.0***	***454.0***	***9-26-99***	***791.0***		***1778***	***50.4***						
Deb 6¾s 2010	mN	A	7/96	A+	X	BE	NC	....	....	....	....	....	100	M5	'95	110	93¼	93¼	7.24	7.24
Deb 9.20s 2021	fA	A	7/96	A+	X	R	NC	....	....	....	....	....	100	M5	'91	134¼	111⅝	111⅝	8.24	8.24
Nts 5⅞s 2003	mN	A	7/96	A+	X	BE	NC	....	....	....	....	....	100	M5	'93	102⅛	95⅝	95⅝	6.16	6.16
Nts 7s 2004	mN15	A			X	BE	NC	....	....	....	....	....	150	C6	'99	100⅛	98⅛	98⅛	7.13	7.13
Sotheby's Hldgs	***63***	***n/a***	***n/a***	***9.44***	***Dc***		***3.82***	***441.5***	***297.3***	***9-30-99***	***100.0***		***429.0***	***23.3***						
Nts 6⅞s 2009	Fa	A			X	BE	[1]Z100	....	....	....	....	....	100	M7	'99	106	93⅞	94¼	7.29	7.29
Source One Mortgage Svcs	***25h***	***Acq by Citicorp Mortgage Inc***																		
Deb[2] 9s 2012	Jd	AA–	5/99	BBB–	X	BE	NC	....	....	....	....	....	100	S1	'92	118½	95⅞	111¼	8.09	8.09
South Carolina El. & Gas[3]	***75***	***3.76***	***3.76***	***4.25***	***Dc***		***57.00***	***516.0***	***824.0***	***9-30-99***	***1660***		***4026***	***49.4***						
1st & Ref 9s 2006	jJ15	A+	7/98	A	X	R	NC	....	....	....	[4]Z100	....	130	S1	'91	120⅛	106⅛	106⅛	8.48	8.48
1st & Ref 8⅞s 2021	fA15	A+	7/98	A	X	R	103.79	(8-15-01)	Z100	....	....	....	114	P1	'91	111⅛	102	102⅛	8.69	8.69
1st 6s 2000	Jd15	A+	7/98	A	X	R	NC	....	....	....	....	....	100	P1	'93	101⅛	99¾	99¾	6.02	6.01
1st 6¼s 2003	jD15	A+	7/98	A	X	R	NC	....	....	....	....	....	100	P1	'93	103⅝	96⅛	96⅛	6.50	6.50
1st 7.70s 2004	jJ15	A+	7/98	A	X	R	NC	....	....	....	....	....	100	P1	'94	110½	101⅛	101⅛	7.61	7.61
1st 6⅛s 2009	Ms	A+			X	BE	[5]Z100	....	....	....	....	....	100	C6	'99	101¾	90⅞	90⅞	6.74	6.74
1st 7⅛s 2013	Jd15	A+	7/98	A	X	R	NC	....	....	....	....	....	150	P1	'93	112¼	95⅛	95⅛	7.49	7.49
1st 7⅝s 2023	Jd	A+	7/98	A	X	R	103.66	(6-1-03)	....	....	....	....	100	P1	'93	106⅝	92⅜	92½	8.24	8.24
1st 7½s 2023	Jd15	A+	7/98	A	X	R	103.44	(6-15-03)	....	....	....	....	150	P1	'93	105¾	91⅛	91¼	8.22	8.22
1st[6] 7⅝s 2025	Ao	A+	7/98	A	X	R	102	(4-1-05)	....	....	....	....	100	P1	'95	111⅝	101¾	101¾	7.49	7.49
Southern Bell Tel. & Tel	***67a***	***Now BellSouth Telecommunications, see***																		
• Deb[7] 4¾s 2000	mS	AAA	6/88	AA+	X	R	100	....	....	....	....	....	100	M6	'65	99¾	98	98⅝	4.82	4.82
• Deb 4⅜s 2001	Ao	AAA	6/88	AA+	X	CR	100	....	....	....	....	....	75.0	M6	'62	98⅝	96¼	96⅝	4.53	4.53
• Deb[7] 4⅜s 2003	fA	AAA	6/88	AA+	X	CR	100	....	....	....	....	....	70.0	L3	'63	97¼	91⅛	91⅛	4.80	4.80
• Deb 6s 2004	aO	AAA	6/88	AA+	X	R	100	....	....	....	....	....	100	H1	'66	101⅜	95⅝	95	6.32	6.32
Southern Calif Edison[8]	***72a***	***3.50***	***3.47***	***2.96***	***Dc***		***72.40***	***2518***	***3430***	***6-30-99***	***5297***		***9469***	***66.2***						
1st & Ref '93A 6¾s 2000	Jj15	A+			X	R	NC	....	....	....	....	....	225	S1	'93	101⅝	100	100	6.75	6.75
1st & Ref '93C 7¼s 2026	Ms	A+			X	R	102.43	(3-1-03)	....	....	....	....	300	G1	'93	103⅛	89⅜	89½	8.10	8.10
1st & Ref '93F 6¼s 2003	Jd15	A+			X	R	NC	....	....	....	....	....	125	S1	'93	103¼	97½	97½	6.41	6.41
1st & Ref '93G 7⅛s 2025	jJ15	A+			X	R	102.09	(7-15-03)	....	....	....	....	225	L3	'93	101¾	88¾	88⅞	8.02	8.02
1st & Ref '93H 5⅞s 2004	mS	A+			X	R	NC	....	....	....	....	....	125	F1	'93	102⅛	94⅞	94⅞	6.19	6.19
1st & Ref '93I 6.90s 2018	aO	A+			X	R	103.16	9-30-00	....	....	....	....	200	L3	'93	100⅝	90⅝	90¾	7.60	7.60
1st & Ref '93J 5⅝s 2002	aO	A+			X	R	NC	....	....	....	....	....	200	S1	'93	100⅞	96⅜	96⅜	5.84	5.84
Deb 5⅞s 2001	Jj15	A			X	R	NC	....	....	....	....	....	200	G1	'96	101	99⅛	99⅛	5.93	5.93
Nts 8¼s 2000	Fa	A			X	R	NC	....	....	....	....	....	100	M2	'95	102¾	100⅛	100⅛	8.24	8.24
Nts 6½s 2001	Jd	A			X	R	NC	....	....	....	....	....	200	S1	'95	102½	99½	99½	6.53	6.53
Nts 6⅜s 2006	Jj15	A			X	R	NC	....	....	....	....	....	200	S1	'96	104¾	95	95	6.71	6.71
Nts 6.65s 2029	Ao	A			X	BE	[1]Z100	....	....	....	....	....	300	S4	'99	99¾	84½	84⅝	7.86	7.86
Southern California Gas[9]	***73b***	***4.90***	***5.69***	***4.56***	***Dc***		***110.0***	***865.0***	***1074***	***9-30-99***	***939.0***		***2289***	***45.6***						
• 1st Y 8¾s 2021	aO	AA–	4/95	A+	X	R	103.59	(10-1-01)	Z103.59	(10-1-01)	....	....	150	L3	'91	106⅜	106⅜	101⅛	8.65	8.65
• 1st Z 6⅞s 2002	fA15	AA–	4/95	A+	X	R	NC	....	....	....	....	....	100	M5	'92	101⅝	101	97	7.09	7.09
• 1st BB 7⅜s 2023	Ms	AA–	4/95	A+	X	R	103.53	(3-1-03)	Z103.53	(3-1-03)	....	....	100	F1	'93	102½	94	91	8.10	8.10
• 1st DD 7½s 2023	Jd15	AA–	4/95	A+	X	R	103.15	(6-15-03)	Z103.15	(6-15-03)	....	....	125	M6	'93	102	92	94½	7.94	7.94
• 1st EE 6⅞s 2025	mN	AA–	4/95	A+	X	R	101.96	(11-1-03)	Z101.96	(11-1-03)	....	....	175	C5	'93	103	81	83½	8.23	8.23
• 1st FF 5¾s 2003	mN15	AA–	4/95	A+	X	R	NC	....	....	....	....	....	100	M2	'93	102⅜	94⅜	94½	6.08	6.08

Uniform Footnote Explanations-See Page 260. Other: [1] Red at greater of 100 or amt based on formula. [2] Issued in min denom $100T. [3] Subsid of SCANA Corp. [4] Co may red for mgrs/consol. [5] Plus Make-Whole Amt. [6] (HRO)On 4-1-05 at 100. [7] Oblig of So Cent Bell Tel,contingently liable. [8] Subsid of Edison Intl. [9] Subsid of Pacific Enterprises.

Title-Industry Code & Co. Finances (In Italics) / Exchange ↓ Individual Issue Statistics	Ind / Interest Dates	Fixed Charge Coverage 1996 / S&P Rating	1997 / Date of Last Rating Change	Prior Rating	1998 / Eligible ↓	Year End / Bond Form	Million $ Cash & Equiv. / Redemption Provisions Regular Price	Million $ Curr. Assets / Regular (Begins) Thru	Curr. Liab. / Sinking Fund Price	Balance Sheet Date / Sinking Fund (Begins) Thru	L. Term Debt (Mil $) / Refund/Other Restriction Price	Refund/Other Restriction (Begins) Thru	Capital-ization (Mil $) / Outst'g (Mil $)	Total Debt % Capital / Underwriting Firm	Underwriting Year	Price Range 1999 High	Price Range 1999 Low	Mo. End Price Sale(s) or Bid	Curr. Yield	Yield to Mat.
***Southern California Gas** (Cont.)*																				
M-T Nts[1] 6.38s 2001	[2]ms	**A+**			X	BE	NC	....	....	....	....	....	120		'97	102⅜	98¾	98¾	6.46	6.46
M-T Nts[3] 5.67s 2028	[4]ms	**A+**			X	BE	NC	....	....	....	....	....	75.0		'98	100½	95⅜	95⅜	5.94	5.94
Southern Calif Water[5]	***74***	***n/a***	***n/a***		***3.14***	***Dc***	***2.99***	***51.40***	***51.60***	***9-30-99***	***160.0***		***322.0***	***50.0***						
M-T Nts 'C' 6.59s 2029	[6]jd	**A+**			X	BE	NC	....	....	....	....	....	40.0	E2	'99	100½	82⅝	82⅝	7.98	7.97
Southern Indiana Gas & El[7]	***75***	***4.12***	***4.67***		***4.25***	***Dc***	***0.34***	***90.90***	***209.0***	***6-30-99***	***170.0***		***673.0***	***48.9***						
1st 8⅞s 2016	Jd	**AA**			X	R	NC	....	....	....	....	....	25.0	G1	'86	127¼	108⅝	108¾	8.16	8.16
1st 7.60s 2023	Ao	**AA**			X	R	103.745	(4-1-03)	Z100	(4-1-03)	....	....	45.0	G1	'93	107¼	93⅛	93¼	8.15	8.15
Sr Nts[8] 6.72s 2029	fA	**AA**			X	BE	[9]Z100	....	....	....	....	....	80.0	G1	'99	102⅝	93⅝	93⅝	7.18	7.18
Southern National	***10***	***Now BB & T Corp,see***																		
Sub Nts 7.05s 2003	Mn23	**BBB+**			X	BE	NC	....	....	....	....	....	250	M2	'96	105¼	99⅜	99⅜	7.09	7.09
Southern Natural Gas[10]	***73a***	***5.69***	***6.20***		***5.12***	***Dc***	***0.04***	***165.0***	***84.70***	***6-30-99***	***500.0***		***1296***	***38.6***						
Nts 8⅞s 2001	Fa15	**BBB+**	9/99	A–	X	R	NC	....	....	....	....	....	100	G1	'91	106⅛	101¾	101¾	8.72	8.72
• Nts 7.85s 2002	Jj15	**BBB+**	9/99	A–	X	R	NC	....	....	....	....	....	100	G1	'92	104¼	100	100½	7.81	7.81
Nts 8⅝s 2002	Mn	**BBB+**	9/99	A–	X	R	NC	....	....	....	....	....	100	G1	'92	108⅜	102⅝	102⅝	8.40	8.40
Nts 6.70s 2007	aO	**BBB+**	9/99	A–	X	BE	NC	....	....	....	....	....	100	G1	'97	104⅞	93¾	93¾	7.15	7.15
Nts 6⅛s 2008	mS15	**BBB+**	9/99	A–	X	BE	NC	....	....	....	....	....	100	G1	'98	100⅝	89⅞	89⅞	6.82	6.82
Southern New Eng Telecom	***67a***	***Mgr w/SBC Communications,see***																		
M-T[1]Nts '2' 6½s 2000	fA15	**AA–**	1/99	A+	X	BE	NC	....	....	....	....	....	100	L3	'95	101¾	100	100	6.50	6.50
M-T Nts '2' 6½s 2002	Fa15	**AA–**	1/99	A+	X	BE	NC	....	....	....	....	....	100	L3	'97	103¼	99	99	6.57	6.57
M-T[1]Nts '2' 7s 2005	fA15	**AA–**	1/99	A+	X	BE	NC	....	....	....	....	....	200	L3	'95	108⅛	98⅝	98⅝	7.10	7.10
Southern New Eng Telephone	***67a***	***Subsid of SBC Communications,see***																		
Deb 4⅜s 2001	jD	**AA**	5/91	AA+	X	CR	100	....	....	....	....	....	45.0	F1	'66	97⅞	95⅝	95⅝	4.58	4.58
M-T Nts[1]'B' 7s 2004	fA	**AA**			X	BE	NC	....	....	....	....	....	70.0	G1	'92	107	99¼	99¼	7.05	7.05
M-T Nts[1]'B' 7⅛s 2007	fA	**AA**			X	BE	NC	....	....	....	....	....	110	G1	'92	110⅜	98¼	98¼	7.25	7.25
M-T Nts[1]'C' 6⅛s 2003	jD15	**AA**			X	BE	NC	....	....	....	....	....	200	L3	'93	102¾	96½	96½	6.35	6.35
M-T Nts[1]'C' 7¼s 2033	jD15	**AA**			X	BE	NC	....	....	....	....	....	245	L3	'93	105¾	91	91⅛	7.96	7.95
Southern Pacific Funding	***25a***	***n/a***	***4.33***		....	***Dc***	***Bankruptcy Chapt 11***				***[11]472.0***		***638.0***	***74.0***						
Sr Nts[12] 11½s 2004	§mN	**D**	10/98	CCC–	Z	BE			Default 11-1-98 int				100	D6	'97	56	26½	47	....	Flat
Southern Railway[13]	***55***	***Now Norfolk So'n Ry,see***																		
Southern Union	***73b***	***△1.73***	***△1.64***		***△1.39***	***Je***	***0.60***	***84.70***	***165.0***	***6-30-99***	***490.0***		***809.0***	***63.5***						
Sr Nts 7.60s 2024	Fa	**BBB+**	4/98	BBB	X	R	NC	....	....	....	....	....	475	M2	'94	108⅞	92¾	93⅝	8.12	8.12
Sr Nts 8¼s 2029	mN15	**BBB+**			X	BE	NC	....	....	....	....	....	300	D6	'99	103⅝	99⅜	100	8.25	8.25
[14]Southland Corp	***59b***	***2.45***	***2.28***		***1.62***	***Dc***	***4.09***	***411.0***	***730.0***	***9-30-99***	***2205***		***1822***	***131.0***						
1st Pr'ty Sr Sub Deb[15] 5s 2003	jD15	**BB+**	6/93	B	Y	R	100	....	100	....	....	....	364	Reorg	'91	89	83½	84½	5.92	5.92
2nd Pr'ty Sr Sub Deb'B'[15] 4s 2004	Jd15	**BB+**	6/93	B	Y	R	100	....	....	....	....	....	24.4	Reorg	'91	78	74¾	77⅞	5.14	5.14
2nd Pr'ty Sr Sub[16]Deb'A' 4½s 2004	Jd15	**BB+**	6/93	B	Y	R	100	....	....	....	....	....	165	Reorg	'91	85	79½	81	5.56	5.56
SouthTrust Corp	***10***	***2.32***	***2.08***		***2.12***	***Dc***				***9-30-99***	***4606***		***8769***	***67.1***						
Sub Nts 7s 2003	Mn15	**BBB+**			X	BE	NC	....	....	....	....	....	100	F1	'93	105	98	98	7.14	7.14
Sub Nts 7⅝s 2004	Mn	**BBB+**			X	BE	NC	....	....	....	....	....	100	M2	'94	108½	99¼	99¼	7.68	7.68
Sub Nts 8⅝s 2004	Mn15	**BBB+**			X	BE	NC	....	....	....	....	....	100	F1	'92	113	102⅞	102⅞	8.38	8.38
Southwest Airlines	***4***	***6.38***	***8.84***		***13.07***	***Dc***	***266.6***	***488.4***	***1001***	***9-30-99***	***617.0***		***3425***	***18.2***						
Deb 7⅞s 2007	mS	**A–**			X	R	NC	....	....	....	....	....	100	L3	'92	114⅝	101	101	7.80	7.80
Deb 7⅜s 2027	Ms	**A–**			X	BE	[17]Z100	....	....	....	....	....	100	L3	'97	111⅝	92⅝	92¾	7.95	7.95
Nts 9.40s 2001	jJ	**A–**			X	R	NC	....	....	....	....	....	100	M2	'91	109⅜	103¼	103¼	9.10	9.10

Uniform Footnote Explanations-See Page 260. Other: [1] Issued in min denom $100T. [2] Due 10-22-01. [3] (HRO)On 1-15-03 at 100. [4] Due 1-28-28. [5] Subsid of Amer States Water. [6] Due 1-25-09. [7] Subsid of SIGCORP Inc. [8] (HRO)On 8-3-05 at 95.5. [9] Red at greater of 100 or amt based on formula. [10] Subsid of Sonat Inc. [11] Incl currents amts. [12] (HRO)On Chge of Ctrl at 101. [13] See Va & So'w'n Ry. [14] Now 7-Eleven Inc. [15] (HRO)On Chge of Ctrl at the Put Price. [16] On Chge of Ctrl at the Put Price. [17] Plus make-whole amt.

Title-Industry Code & Co. Finances (In Italics)	Ind	Fixed Charge Coverage 1996	1997	1998		Year End	Million $ Cash & Equiv.	Curr. Assets	Curr. Liab.	Balance Sheet Date	L. Term Debt (Mil $)		Capital-ization (Mil $)	Total Debt % Capital						
Individual Issue Statistics Exchange ↓	Interest Dates	S&P Rating	Date of Last Rating Change	Prior Rating	Eligible ↓	Bond Form	Redemption Provisions: Regular Price	Regular (Begins) Thru	Sinking Fund Price	Sinking Fund (Begins) Thru	Refund/Other Restriction Price	Refund/Other Restriction (Begins) Thru	Outst'g (Mil $)	Underwriting Firm	Underwriting Year	Price Range 1999 High	Price Range 1999 Low	Mo. End Price Sale(s) or Bid	Curr. Yield	Yield to Mat.
***Southwest Airlines** (Cont.)*																				
Nts 8¾s 2003	aO15	**A–**			X	R	NC	....	....	....	....	....	100	F1	'91	113⅝	104⅝	104⅝	8.36	8.36
Nts 8s 2005	Ms	**A–**			X	BE	NC	....	....	....	....	....	100	S1	'95	113	102⅝	102⅝	7.80	7.79
Southwest Gas	***73b***	*1.17*	*1.39*	*2.22*		*Dc*	*5.83*	*124.0*	*214.0*	*9-30-99*	*820.0*		*1402*	*61.6*						
Deb 7½s 2006	fA	**BBB–**			X	BE	NC	....	....	....	....	....	75.0	M2	'96	108⅜	97⅝	97⅝	7.68	7.68
Deb F 9¾s 2002	Jd15	**BBB–**			X	BE	NC	....	....	....	....	....	100	S1	'92	111½	104¾	104¾	9.31	9.31
Deb 8s 2026	fA	**BBB–**			X	BE	NC	....	....	....	....	....	75.0	M2	'96	113	95¼	95⅜	8.39	8.39
Southwestern Bell Cap	***25***	***See SBC Communications Capital***																		
M-T Nts 'D' 6¾s 2000	[1]ms	**AA–**	3/97	A+	X	BE	NC	....	....	....	....	....	20.0	S1	'93	101⅜	100	100	6.75	6.75
M-T Nts 'D' 6¾s 2000	[2]ms	**AA–**	3/97	A+	X	BE	NC	....	....	....	....	....	15.0	M2	'93	101⅜	100	100	6.75	6.75
M-T Nts 'D' 7.83s 2000	[3]ms	**AA–**	3/97	A+	X	BE	NC	....	....	....	....	....	19.0	M2	'95	102⅝	100¼	100¼	7.81	7.81
M-T Nts 'D' 7.84s 2000	[3]ms	**AA–**	3/97	A+	X	BE	NC	....	....	....	....	....	18.0	C5	'95	102⅝	100¼	100¼	7.82	7.82
M-T Nts 'D' 7.57s 2000	[4]ms	**AA–**	3/97	A+	X	BE	NC	....	....	....	....	....	15.0	S1	'95	102⅜	100¼	100¼	7.55	7.55
M-T Nts 'D' 7.37s 2002	[5]ms	**AA–**	3/97	A+	X	BE	NC	....	....	....	....	....	15.0	M2	'95	105½	100¼	100¼	7.35	7.35
M-T Nts 'D' 7¼s 2003	[6]ms	**AA–**	3/97	A+	X	BE	NC	....	....	....	....	....	11.0	S1	'93	105⅞	99⅞	99⅞	7.26	7.26
M-T Nts 'D' 7.30s 2003	[6]ms	**AA–**	3/97	A+	X	BE	NC	....	....	....	....	....	10.0	S1	'93	106⅛	100	100	7.30	7.30
M-T Nts 'D' 7.10s 2003	[7]ms	**AA–**	3/97	A+	X	BE	NC	....	....	....	....	....	5.00	C5	'93	105⅜	99⅜	99⅜	7.14	7.14
M-T Nts 'D' 7.30s 2003	[8]ms	**AA–**	3/97	A+	X	BE	NC	....	....	....	....	....	6.00	C5	'93	106¼	99⅞	99⅞	7.31	7.31
M-T Nts 'D' 7.05s 2004	[9]ms	**AA–**	3/97	A+	X	BE	NC	....	....	....	....	....	10.0	S1	'93	106¾	98½	98½	7.16	7.16
M-T Nts 'D' 8.15s 2005	[10]ms	**AA–**	3/97	A+	X	BE	102	(3-2-00)	....	....	....	....	16.0	C5	'95	104⅞	101	101	8.07	8.07
M-T Nts 'D' 7.35s 2010	[11]ms	**AA–**	3/97	A+	X	BE	NC	....	....	....	....	....	20.0	M2	'95	112¾	97⅝	97⅝	7.53	7.53
Southwest'n Bell Tel[12]	***67a***	*7.63*	*6.50*	*7.44*		*Dc*	*67.00*	*2491*	*5176*	*6-30-99*	*4210*		*9739*	*66.4*						
Deb 5⅞s 2003	Jd	**AA**	6/95	A+	X	R	100	....	....	....	....	....	150	S1	'67	99¾	96⅛	96½	6.09	6.09
Deb 5⅜s 2006	Jd	**AA**	6/95	A+	X	R	100.27	5-31-00	....	....	....	....	150	M6	'66	99½	90⅜	90⅜	5.95	5.95
Deb 6¾s 2008	Jd	**AA**	6/95	A+	X	R	100.60	5-31-00	....	....	....	....	150	H1	'68	102⅜	95⅝	96	7.03	7.03
◆Deb 6⅞s 2011	Fa	**AA**	6/95	A+	X	R	101.58	1-31-00	....	....	....	....	200	H1	'71	101⅞	93¾	94¼	7.29	7.29
Deb 7s 2015	jJ	**AA**	6/95	A+	X	BE	NC	....	....	....	....	....	250	G1	'93	109¼	92½	93⅜	7.50	7.50
Deb 7⅝s 2023	Ms	**AA**	6/95	A+	X	BE	103.735	(3-1-03)	....	....	....	....	200	S1	'93	108⅜	94⅝	95¼	8.01	8.00
Deb 6⅝s 2024	mS	**AA**	6/95	A+	X	BE	102.188	(9-1-03)	....	....	....	....	200	S1	'93	100⅞	82¼	82⅞	7.99	7.99
Deb 7¼s 2025	jJ15	**AA**	6/95	A+	X	BE	102.8605	(7-15-03)	....	....	....	....	150	G1	'93	105⅝	89½	90	8.06	8.05
Deb 7.20s 2026	aO15	**AA**			X	BE	103.5375	(10-15-05)	....	....	....	....	300	M2	'95	107¼	88⅝	89¼	8.07	8.07
Deb 7⅜s 2027	jJ15	**AA**			X	BE	103.465	(7-15-07)	....	....	....	....	150	G1	'97	111⅜	89⅝	90¼	8.17	8.17
Deb 7s 2027	mN15	**AA**			X	BE	102.58	(11-15-07)	....	....	....	....	100	M6	'97	105⅞	85⅝	86¼	8.12	8.11
Nts 6⅛s 2000	Ms	**AA**	6/95	A+	X	BE	NC	....	....	....	....	....	150	S1	'93	101⅛	99⅝	100	6.13	6.12
Nts 6⅜s 2001	Ao	**AA**	6/95	A+	X	BE	NC	....	....	....	....	....	200	M2	'93	103⅜	99	99¼	6.42	6.42
Nts 6¼s 2002	aO15	**AA**			X	BE	NC	....	....	....	....	....	150	M2	'95	103⅜	97¾	97⅞	6.39	6.39
Nts 5¾s 2004	mS	**AA**	6/95	A+	X	BE	100.674	(9-1-00)	....	....	....	....	200	S1	'93	100½	93¾	93⅞	6.13	6.13
Nts 6⅝s 2005	Ao	**AA**	6/95	A+	X	BE	NC	....	....	....	....	....	150	M2	'93	107½	96¾	97⅛	6.82	6.82
Nts 6⅝s 2007	jJ15	**AA**			X	BE	NC	....	....	....	....	....	250	G1	'97	108⅜	95⅜	95½	6.94	6.94
Nts 6⅜s 2007	mN15	**AA**			X	BE	NC	....	....	....	....	....	100	M6	'97	106⅞	93⅞	94⅛	6.77	6.77
M-T Nts 'C' 7¼s 2010	[13]mn15	**AA**	6/95	A+	X	BE	NC	....	....	....	....	....	15.0	M6	'95	112½	97⅞	97⅞	7.41	7.41
M-T Nts 'C' 7.55s 2005	[14]mn15	**AA**	6/95	A+	X	BE	NC	....	....	....	....	....	15.0	M6	'95	110¼	100⅞	100⅞	7.48	7.48
M-T Nts 'C' 7½s 2005	[15]mn15	**AA**	6/95	A+	X	BE	NC	....	....	....	....	....	15.0	G1	'95	110	100⅝	100⅝	7.45	7.45
M-T Nts 'C' 7.67s 2007	[16]mn15	**AA**	6/95	A+	X	BE	NC	....	....	....	....	....	15.0	M2	'95	113¼	100¾	100¾	7.61	7.61
M-T Nts 'C' 6.55s 2008	[17]mn15	**AA**			X	BE	NC	....	....	....	....	....	30.0	M2	'97	106⅜	94	94	6.97	6.97

Uniform Footnote Explanations-See Page 260. Other: [1] Due 2-1-00. [2] Due 2-2-00. [3] Due 2-28-00. [4] Due 3-2-00. [5] Due 5-1-02. [6] Due 1-13-03. [7] Due 2-3-03. [8] Due 3-1-03. [9] Due 9-22-04. [10] Due 3-2-05. [11] Due 5-24-10. [12] Subsid of SBC Communications. [13] Due 5-17-10. [14] Due 4-12-05. [15] Due 4-26-05. [16] Due 4-12-07. [17] Due 10-7-08.

Title-Industry Code & Co. Finances (In Italics)	Ind	Fixed Charge Coverage 1996	1997	1998		Year End	Million $ Cash & Equiv.	Curr. Assets	Curr. Liab.	Balance Sheet Date	L. Term Debt (Mil $)		Capital-ization (Mil $)	Total Debt % Capital						
Individual Issue Statistics Exchange	Interest Dates	S&P Rating	Date of Last Rating Change	Prior Rating	Eligible	Bond Form	Redemption Provisions: Regular Price	Regular (Begins) Thru	Sinking Fund Price	Sinking Fund (Begins) Thru	Refund/Other Restriction Price	Refund/Other Restriction (Begins) Thru	Outst'g (Mil $)	Underwriting Firm	Underwriting Year	Price Range 1999 High	Price Range 1999 Low	Mo. End Price Sale(s) or Bid	Curr. Yield	Yield to Mat.
***Southwest'n Bell Tel** (Cont.)*																				
M-T Nts 'C' 7.60s 2007	[1]mn15	**AA**	6/95	A+	X	BE	NC	....	....	....	....	....	18.0	G1	'95	112⅞	100⅜	100⅜	7.57	7.57
M-T Nts 'C' 7.21s 2010	[2]mn15	**AA**	6/95	A+	X	BE	NC	....	....	....	....	....	50.0	G1	'95	112⅛	97⅝	97⅝	7.39	7.38
M-T Nts 'C' 7.18s 2010	[2]mn15	**AA**	6/95	A+	X	BE	NC	....	....	....	....	....	20.0	G1	'95	111⅞	97⅜	97⅜	7.37	7.37
M-T Nts 'C' 7.22s 2010	[2]mn15	**AA**	6/95	A+	X	BE	NC	....	....	....	....	....	23.0	M2	'95	112¼	97¾	97¾	7.39	7.39
Southwest'n Elec Power[3]	***72a***	***3.23***	***3.48***	***3.53***		***Dc***	***3.78***	***168.0***	***262.0***	***6-30-99***	***606.0***		***1362***	***51.1***						
1st V 7¾s 2004	Jd	**AA–**	10/97	A+	X	R	NC	....	□100	....	....	....	40.0	M6	'92	110¾	101⅜	101⅜	7.64	7.64
1st X 7s 2007	mS	**AA–**	10/97	A+	X	R	NC	....	□100	....	....	....	90.0	F1	'92	110⅝	96⅝	96⅝	7.24	7.24
1st Y 6⅝s 2003	Fa	**AA–**	10/97	A+	X	R	NC	....	□100	....	....	....	55.0	M2	'93	105⅛	98⅝	98⅝	6.72	6.72
1st Z 7⅛s 2023	jJ	**AA–**	10/97	A+	X	R	103.06	(7-1-03)	□100	....	....	....	45.0	G1	'93	104¼	89⅞	90	8.06	8.05
1st AA 5¼s 2000	Ao	**AA–**	10/97	A+	X	R	NC	....	....	....	....	....	45.0	M6	'93	100⅛	99⅜	99¾	5.26	5.26
1st BB 6⅞s 2025	aO	**AA–**	10/97	A+	X	R	103.08	(10-1-03)	....	....	....	....	80.0	M6	'93	102¼	85½	85½	8.04	8.04
Southwestern Energy	***73b***	***2.56***	***2.25***	***1.59***		***Dc***	***1.56***	***69.84***	***56.48***	***9-30-99***	***283.0***		***471.0***	***60.3***						
Sr Nts 6.70s 2005	jD	**BBB+**			X	BE	NC	....	....	....	....	....	125	M6	'95	100⅞	92⅜	92⅜	7.25	7.25
Southwestern Public Serv[4]	***72a***	***4.23***	***3.45***	***4.40***		***Dc***	***6.90***	***141.0***	***316.0***	***6-30-99***	***731.0***		***1622***	***54.3***						
1st 7¼s 2004	jJ15	**A**	4/97	AA	X	R	NC	....	....	....	....	....	135	D4	'92	108⅞	99⅞	99⅞	7.26	7.26
1st 6½s 2006	Ms	**A**	4/97	AA	X	BE	NC	....	....	....	....	....	60.0	D4	'96	105⅞	94¾	94¾	6.86	6.86
1st 8¼s 2022	jJ15	**A**	4/97	AA	X	R	103.575	(7-15-02)	▲100	....	....	....	40.0	D4	'92	111¾	99½	99⅝	8.28	8.28
1st 8.20s 2022	jD	**A**	4/97	AA	X	BE	104.038	(12-1-02)	Z100	....	....	....	100	D4	'92	111½	98¾	98⅞	8.29	8.29
1st 8½s 2025	Fa15	**A**	4/97	AA	X	BE	104.225	(2-15-05)	▲100	....	....	....	70.0	D4	'95	115½	100¼	100¼	8.48	8.48
Sr Nts 'A' 6.20s 2009	Ms	**A–**			X	BE	[5]Z100	....	....	....	....	....	100	S4	'99	101⅝	91¼	91¼	6.79	6.79
Sovereign Bancorp	***10a***	***1.44***	***1.56***	***1.62***		***Dc***				***9-30-99***	***4382***		***12247***	***88.2***						
Sr Nts 6¾s 2000	jJ	**BB+**	11/99	BBB–	Y	BE	NC	....	....	....	....	....	50.0	M2	'95	101½	99¼	99⅜	6.79	6.79
Sr Nts[6] 6⅝s 2001	Ms15	**BB+**	11/99	BBB–	Y	BE	[7]Z100	....	....	....	....	....	240	L3	'99	100½	97½	97½	6.79	6.79
Sr Nts 10¼s 2004	Mn15	**BB+**			Y	BE	[7]Z100						200	S4	'99	102⅛	100	101	10.15	10.15
Sr Nts 10½s 2006	mN15	**BB+**			Y	BE	[7]Z100	....	....	....	....	....	500	S4	'99	102⅞	100	102	10.29	10.29
Sub Deb 6¾s 2000	mS	**BB–**	11/99	BB+	Y	BE	NC	....	....	....	....	....	99.0	B7	'93	101¼	98⅞	99⅛	6.81	6.81
Sub Deb 8½s 2002	mS15	**NR**				R	101.70	9-14-00	....				20.0	W4	'92	104¾	98¼	98¼	8.65	8.65
Sovran Financial[8]	***10***	***Now NationsBank Corp,see NCNB Corp***																		
Nts 9¼s 2006	Jd15	**A+**	12/96	A	X	R	NC	....	....	....	....	....	125	F1	'86	118⅝	107½	107½	8.60	8.60
Spieker Properties L.P.	***57***	***2.76***	***3.56***	***2.60***		***Dc***				***9-30-99***	***1966***		***3986***	***49.3***						
Deb 7.35s 2017	jD	**BBB**			X	BE	[7]Z100	....	....	....	....	....	200	G1	'97	98¾	87½	87⅝	8.39	8.39
Deb 7½s 2027	aO	**BBB**			X	BE	[7]Z100	....	....	....	....	....	150	G1	'97	96¼	84⅝	86⅝	8.66	8.66
Nts 6.65s 2000	jD15	**BBB**			X	BE	[7]Z100	....	....	....	....	....	100	G1	'95	100⅝	99¼	99¼	6.70	6.70
Nts 6.80s 2001	jD15	**BBB**			X	BE	[7]Z100	....	....	....	....	....	50.0	G1	'95	101	98½	98½	6.90	6.90
Nts 6.95s 2002	jD15	**BBB**			X	BE	[7]Z100	....	....	....	....	....	110	G1	'95	101⅝	97¾	97¾	7.11	7.11
Nts 6.80s 2004	Mn	**BBB**			X	BE	[7]Z100	....	....	....	....	....	200	G1	'99	100⅜	96	96	7.08	7.08
Nts 6⅞s 2005	Fa	**BBB**			X	BE	[7]Z100	....	....	....	....	....	125	M7	'98	101⅜	95¼	95¼	7.22	7.22
Nts 7⅛s 2006	jD	**BBB**			X	BE	[7]Z100	....	....	....	....	....	100	G1	'96	102½	93⅞	94⅝	7.53	7.53
Nts 6¾s 2008	Jj15	**BBB**			X	BE	[7]Z100	....	....	....	....	....	150	G1	'98	99⅞	91½	91½	7.38	7.38
Nts 7¼s 2009	Mn	**BBB**			X		[7]Z100	....	....	....	....	....	200	G1	'99	100⅝	93⅝	93⅝	7.74	7.74
Nts 7⅛s 2009	jJ	**BBB**			X	BE	[7]Z100	....	....	....	....	....	150	G1	'97	100½	92	92¾	7.68	7.68
Nts 7⅞s 2016	jD	**BBB**			X	BE	[7]Z100	....	....	....	....	....	25.0	G1	'96	104	92¼	92⅜	8.53	8.52
Sprint Capital	***25***	***Subsid of & gtd by Sprint Corp,see***																		
Nts[9] 5.70s 2003	mN15	**BBB+**	4/99	A–	X	BE	[5]Z100	....	....	....	....	....	1000	S4	'98	100¾	94⅞	95	6.00	6.00

Uniform Footnote Explanations-See Page 260. Other: [1] Due 4-26-07. [2] Due 5-17-10. [3] Contr by Central & South West Corp. [4] Subsid of New Century Energies. [5] Red at greater of 100 or amt based on formula. [6] Issued in min denom $100T. [7] Plus Make-Whole Amt. [8] Was Virginia Nat'l Bankshrs. [9] Gtd by Sprint Corp.

Title-Industry Code & Co. Finances (In Italics) / Exchange Individual Issue Statistics	Ind / Interest Dates	Fixed Charge Coverage 1996 / S&P Rating	1997 / Date of Last Rating Change	1998 / Prior Rating	Eligible	Year End / Bond Form	Cash & Equiv. / Regular Price	Curr. Assets / Regular (Begins) Thru	Curr. Liab. / Sinking Fund Price	Balance Sheet Date / Sinking Fund (Begins) Thru	L. Term Debt (Mil $) / Refund/Other Restriction Price	Refund/Other Restriction (Begins) Thru	Capital-ization (Mil $) / Outst'g (Mil $)	Total Debt % Capital / Underwriting Firm	Underwriting Year	Price Range 1999 High	Price Range 1999 Low	Mo. End Price Sale(s) or Bid	Curr. Yield	Yield to Mat.
***Sprint Capital** (Cont.)*																				
Nts 5⅞s 2004	Mn	**BBB+**			X	BE	[1]Z100	....	....	....	....	....	1000	S4	'99	99½	94⅞	94⅞	6.19	6.19
Nts[2] 6⅛s 2008	mN15	**BBB+**	4/99	A–	X	BE	[1]Z100	....	....	....	....	....	1500	S4	'98	102½	90⅝	90⅝	6.76	6.76
Nts 6⅜s 2009	Mn	**BBB+**			X	BE	[1]Z100	....	....	....	....	....	750	S4	'99	99⅜	92	92	6.93	6.93
Nts 6.90s 2019	Mn	**BBB+**			X	BE	Z100	....	....	....	....	....	1750	S4	'99	99⅝	90⅝	91¼	7.56	7.56
• Nts[2] 6⅞s 2028	mN15	**BBB+**	4/99	A–	X	BE	[3]Z100	....	....	....	....	....	2500	S4	'98	96⅝	90	89½	7.68	7.68
M-T[2]Nts 6½s 2001	mN15	**BBB+**			X	BE	NC	....	....	....	....	....	500	L3	'99	99⅞	98⅞	99⅛	6.56	6.56
[4]Sprint[5]Corp[6]	***67b***	*7.01*	*6.33*	*7.87*		*Dc*	*16.00*	*1333*	*2802*	*9-30-99*	*9630*		*27473*	*49.1*						
Deb 9¼s 2022	Ao15	**BBB+**	4/99	A–	X	R	NC	....	....	....	....	....	200	D6	'92	135⅝	114	114⅛	8.11	8.10
Nts 8⅛s 2002	jJ15	**BBB+**	4/99	A–	X	R	NC	....	....	....	....	....	150	L3	'92	109	102⅛	102⅛	7.96	7.95
Standard Fedl Bancorp'n	***10a***	*Acquired by ABN AMRO Holding*																		
Sub Nts 7¾s 2006	jJ17	**A+**	5/97	BBB–	X	BE	NC	....	....	....	....	....	100	M2	'96	110⅜	99½	99½	7.79	7.79
Standard Pacific	***13h***	*1.06*	*9.19*	*2.69*		*Dc*				*9-30-99*	*418.0*		*765.0*	*54.0*						
• Sr Nts[7] 8½s 2007	Jd15	**BB**			Y	BE	104.25	(6-15-02)	....	....	....	....	100	S1	'97	103⅞	90	92½	9.19	9.19
Sr Nts[7] 8½s 2009	Ao	**BB**			Y	BE	104.24	3-31-03	....	....	....	....	100	D6	'99	100½	88	94½	8.99	8.99
Stanley Works	***13e***	*8.93*	*9.90*	*7.95*		*Dc*	*131.5*	*1149*	*735.6*	*10-2-99*	*299.0*		*991.0*	*31.3*						
Nts 7⅜s 2002	jD15	**A**			X	BE	NC	....	....	....	....	....	100	F1	'92	107⅛	100⅛	100⅛	7.37	7.36
Nts 5¾s 2004	Ms	**A**			X	BE	NC	....	....	....	....	....	120	G1	'99	100	94	94	6.12	6.12
Staples Inc	***59l***	*n/a*	*11.78*	*24.40*		*Ja*	*91.38*	*2173*	*1496*	*10-30-99*	*493.0*		*2203*	*23.4*						
Sr Nts 7⅛s 2007	fA15	**BBB–**	6/98	BB+	X	BE	NC	....	....	....	....	....	200	G1	'97	106	95¼	95¼	7.48	7.48
Star Banc Corp	***10***	*Now Firststar Corp,see*																		
Nts 5⅞s 2003	mN	**A–**			X	BE	NC	....	....	....	....	....	100	M7	'98	100⅝	95⅜	95⅜	6.16	6.16
[8]State St Boston	***10***	*1.96*	*1.51*	*1.44*		*Dc*				*9-30-99*	*922.0*		*3233*	*28.5*						
Nts 5.95s 2003	mS15	**AA–**			X	BE	NC	....	....	....	....	....	100	G1	'93	100⅞	96⅝	96⅝	6.16	6.16
Nts 7.35s 2026	Jd15	**AA–**			X	BE	NC	....	....	....	....	....	150	G1	'96	112½	101½	101½	7.24	7.24
Station Casinos	***40i***	*1.58*	*[9]0.92*	*[10]0.90*		*Dc*	*53.74*	*100.5*	*125.5*	*9-30-99*	*887.0*		*1185*	*75.7*						
Sr Sub[11]Nts[7] 10⅛s 2006	Ms15	**B+**			Y	R	103.79	(3-15-01)	....	....	....	....	198	S1	'96	107½	101¾	102	9.93	9.93
STC Broadcasting	***12c***	*n/a*	*n/a*	*0.11*		*Dc*	*2.84*	*27.70*	*23.10*	*9-30-99*	*223.0*		*304.0*	*75.6*						
Sr Sub Nts[7] 11s 2007	Ms15	**B–**			Y	BE	105.50	(3-15-02)	....	....	[12]Z111	3-15-00	100	Exch.	'97	107	99¼	99¾	11.03	11.03
Stewart Enterprises	***63***	*4.15*	*3.80*	*2.48*		*Oc*	*69.90*	*334.5*	*117.9*	*7-31-99*	*921.0*		*2075*	*45.0*						
Nts 6.70s 2003	jD	**BBB**			X	BE	NC	....	....	....	....	....	100		'96	102½	84¼	84¼	7.95	7.95
[13]Stone Container	***16c***	*0.54*	*d0.32*	*0.80*		*Dc*	*86.00*	*1910*	*1613*	*9-30-99*	*5631*		*7605*	*78.4*						
• 1st Mtg Nts[7] 10¾s 2002	aO	**B+**	4/97	BB–	Y	R	103.07	9-30-00	....	....	....	....	500	S1	'94	105⅞	102⅛	102	10.54	10.54
• Sr Nts[7] 9⅞s 2001	Fa	**B**	4/97	B+	Y	R	101.646	1-31-00	....	....	....	....	571	S1	'94	102⅝	99¾	s99⅞	9.89	9.88
• Sr Nts[7] 11½s 2004	aO	**B**	4/97	B+	Y	R	104.31	9-30-00	....	....	....	....	200	S1	'94	107⅜	100⅜	s103⅜	11.12	11.12
• [14]Sr[15]Nts[7] 11⅞s 2016	[16]fA	**B**	4/97	B+	Y	R	105.938	(8-1-01)	....	....	....	....	125	Exch.	'96	No Sale		102½	11.59	11.58
• Sr Sub[17]Deb[7] 10⅜s 2002	Ao	**B–**	4/97	B	Y	R	100	....	....	....	....	....	200	B7	'92	101⅞	99	s100⅜	10.71	10.71
• Sr Sub Deb(Unit)[7] 10¾s 2002	Ao	**B–**			Y	BE	100	....	....	....	....	....	275	D6	'97	103¾	99½	99⅞	10.76	10.76
Stop & Shop Cos[18]	***59c***	*n/a*	*n/a*	*n/a*		*Dc*	*1145*	*8869*	*10153*	*1-3-99*	*8646*		*4678*	*66.4*						
Sr Sub Nts 9¾s 2002	Fa	**NR**	9/96	BB+	Y	R	NC	....	....	....	....	....	195	B11	'92	111	104⅝	104⅝	9.32	9.32
Strawbridge & Clothier	***59f***	*Assumed by May Department Stores,see*																		
Nts[19] 6⅝s 2003	aO15	**A**	7/96	BBB–	X	R	NC	....	....	....	....	....	50.0	K2	'93	104⅞	98¼	98¼	6.74	6.74
[20]Student Loan Mktg Assn	***25b***	*1.22*	*1.30*	*1.39*		*Dc*				*9-30-99*	*5675*		*42769*	*98.0*						
Nts 7.30s 2012	fA	**NR**				BE	NC	....	....	....	....	....	131	L3	'92	117½	100⅝	100⅝	7.25	7.25
F/R[21]Nts 'CQ' 2001	QMar7	**NR**				BE	■100	....	....	....	....	....	500	M2	'94	99½	99	99½	....	....

Uniform Footnote Explanations-See Page 260. Other: [1] Red at greater of 100 or amt based on formula. [2] Gtd by Sprint Corp. [3] Red at greater or 100 or amt based on formula.
[4] See United Tel(Ohio),United Tel(Penna). [5] Now Sprint Corp(FON Group). [6] See Centel Cap,United Telecommun,Carolina Tel&Tel. [7] (HRO)On Chge of Ctrl at 101. [8] Now State Street Corp.
[9] Fiscal Mar'98 & prior. [10] 9 Mo Dec'98. [11] State gaming laws may req hldrs sale/Co red. [12] Man $25M red w/proceeds of Pub Eq Off'g. [13] Now Smurfit-Stone Container. [14] Int 11.875% to 8-1-97.
[15] To 8-1-06,repurch at 100 for certain events. [16] Int(7.76%-13.08%)subj to rtg chge. [17] Int may be reset if below min Net Worth levels. [18] Subsid & data of Ahold nv. [19] Assumed by May Dept Stores.
[20] Now SLM Holding. [21] Int adj weekly, as defined.

Title-Industry Code & Co. Finances (In Italics)	Ind	Fixed Charge Coverage 1996	1997	1998		Year End	Million $ Cash & Equiv.	Curr. Assets	Curr. Liab.	Balance Sheet Date	L. Term Debt (Mil $)		Capital-ization (Mil $)	Total Debt % Capital						
Individual Issue Statistics Exchange ↓	Interest Dates	S&P Rating	Date of Last Rating Change	Prior Rating	Eligible ↓	Bond Form	Redemption Provisions Regular Price	Regular (Begins) Thru	Sinking Fund Price	Sinking Fund (Begins) Thru	Refund/Other Restriction Price	Refund/Other Restriction (Begins) Thru	Outst'g (Mil $)	Underwriting Firm	Underwriting Year	Price Range 1999 High	Price Range 1999 Low	Mo. End Price Sale(s) or Bid	Curr. Yield	Yield to Mat.
Summit Bancorp[1]	***10***	***4.12***	***3.75***	***3.06***		***Dc***				***9-30-99***	***3971***		***6603***	***60.6***						
• Sub Nts 8⅝s 2002	jD10	**BBB+**	3/98	BBB	X	BE	NC	....	....	....	....	....	175	M2	'92	106	102	103	8.37	8.37
Summit Properties Ptnrshp[2]	***57***	***2.25***	***2.26***	***1.59***		***Dc***	***4.82***			***9-30-99***	***620.0***		***956.0***	***64.8***						
Nts 6⅝s 2003	jD15	**BBB–**			X	BE	[3]Z100	....	....	....	....	....	30.0	M5	'97	98	92⅞	92⅞	7.13	7.13
Nts 7.20s 2007	fA15	**BBB–**			X	BE	[4]Z100	....	....	....	....	....	50.0	M5	'97	97¼	89⅜	89⅜	8.06	8.05
M-T Nts 6.71s 2000	[5]ao15	**BBB–**			X	BE	NC	....	....	....	....	....	25.0	M5	'98	99⅜	97¾	99¼	6.76	6.76
M-T Nts 6¾s 2001	jJ30	**BBB–**			X	BE	NC	....	....	....	....	....	30.0	M7	'98	99⅛	97⅛	98	6.89	6.89
Sun Communities Oper LP	***57***	***2.95***	***2.92***	***2.30***		***Dc***				***9-30-99***	***388.0***		***866.0***	***44.8***						
Sr Nts 7⅜s 2001	Mn	**BBB**	7/97	BBB–	X	BE	[4]Z100	....	....	....	....	....	65.0	L3	'96	101⅞	99¼	99½	7.41	7.41
Sr Nts 7⅝s 2003	Mn	**BBB**	7/97	BBB–	X	BE	[4]Z100	....	....	....	....	....	85.0	L3	'96	102¼	98½	98½	7.74	7.74
Sun Co	***49d***	***Now Sunoco Inc,see***																		
• SF Deb 9⅜s 2016	Jd	**BBB**	12/96	BBB+	X	R	100	(6-1-06)	100	(6-1-07)	....	....	200	F1	'86	109	106	102	9.19	9.19
Deb 9s 2024	mN	**BBB**	12/96	BBB+	X	R	NC	....	....	....	....	....	100	C5	'94	123⅞	105	105⅛	8.56	8.56
• Nts 7.95s 2001	jD15	**BBB**	12/96	BBB+	X	R	NC	....	....	....	....	....	150	L3	'91	105	100¼	100⅜	7.92	7.92
Nts 7⅛s 2004	Ms15	**BBB**	12/96	BBB+	X	R	NC	....	....	....	....	....	100	L3	'94	105	98	98	7.27	7.27
Sun Microsystems	***2b***	***n/a***	***n/a***	***n/a***		***Je***	***4113***	***7662***	***3128***	***9-26-99***	***★1500***		***4429***	***4.0***						
Sr Nts 7s 2002	fA15	**BBB+**			X	BE	[6]Z100	....	....	....	....	....	200	G1	'99	100⅞	99⅜	99½	7.04	7.03
Sr Nts 7.35s 2004	fA15	**BBB+**			X	BE	[6]Z100	....	....	....	....	....	250	G1	'99	101⅞	99¼	99⅝	7.38	7.38
Sr Nts 7½s 2006	fA15	**BBB+**			X	BE	Z100	....	....	....	....	....	500	G1	'99	102½	98⅝	100⅜	7.47	7.47
Sr Nts 7.65s 2009	fA15	**BBB+**			X	BE	[6]Z100	....	....	....	....	....	550	G1	'99	103	98¼	100⅛	7.64	7.64
SunAmerica[7]Inc[8]	***35a***	***n/a***	***n/a***	***n/a***		***Sp***				***6-30-99***	***19149***		***51021***	***37.5***						
Deb 9.95s 2012	Fa	**AAA**	1/99	A	X	R	NC	....	....	....	....	....	100	M2	'92	140⅜	119⅛	119⅛	8.35	8.35
Deb 8⅛s 2023	Ao28	**AAA**	1/99	A	X	R	NC	....	....	....	....	....	100	M2	'93	125¼	102⅞	103	7.89	7.89
Nts 6¾s 2007	aO	**AAA**	1/99	A	X	BE	NC	....	....	....	....	....	100	S7	'97	109	96¼	96¼	7.01	7.01
Sunoco Inc	***49b***	***d0.17***	***5.78***	***5.46***		***Dc***	***84.00***	***1424***	***1642***	***9-30-99***	***872.0***		***2498***	***39.2***						
Nts 7¾s 2009	mS	**BBB**			X	BE	[6]Z100	....	....	....	....	....	200	C6	'99	101⅛	97⅞	97⅞	7.92	7.92
SunTrust Banks Inc	***10***	***3.38***	***2.70***	***2.47***		***Dc***		***6325***		***9-30-99***	***6325***		***14163***	***44.7***						
Sr Deb[9] 6s 2028	Jj15	**A+**			X	BE	NC	....	....	....	....	....	250	L3	'98	100⅜	90½	90½	6.63	6.63
Nts 7⅜s 2002	jJ	**A+**			X	BE	NC	....	....	....	....	....	200	L3	'92	106¼	100½	100½	7.34	7.34
Sr Nts 6¼s 2008	Jd	**A+**			X	BE	NC	....	....	....	....	....	300	S4	'98	104⅜	92¼	92¼	6.78	6.77
F/R[10]Nts 2002	QApr22	**A+**			X	BE	NC	....	....	....	....	....	250	S1	'97	100⅜	99¼	99⅝	....	....
Sub Nts[11] 6s 2026	Fa15	**A**			X	BE	NC	....	....	....	....	....	200	M6	'96	100⅝	92⅛	92⅛	6.51	6.51
Sub Nts 6⅛s 2004	Fa15	**A**			X	BE	NC	....	....	....	....	....	200	L3	'94	102⅝	95⅞	95⅞	6.39	6.39
Sub Nts 7⅜s 2006	jJ	**A**			X	BE	NC	....	....	....	....	....	200	L3	'96	110⅞	99¼	99¾	7.39	7.39
Super Value Stores	***26g***	***Now Supervalu Inc,see***																		
SF Deb[12] 8⅞s 2016	Ao	**BBB+**	6/95	A	X	R	103.014	3-31-00	100	....	....	....	7.11	G1	'86	104⅛	101	101¼	8.77	8.77
Supervalu Inc[13]	***26g***	***2.90***	***3.17***	***3.55***		***Fb***	***11.30***	***1975***	***2203***	***9-11-99***	***1851***		***4172***	***56.5***						
Nts 7.80s 2002	mN15	**BBB+**	6/95	A	X	BE	NC	....	....	....	....	....	300	G1	'92	107¼	101⅛	101⅛	7.71	7.71
Nts 8⅞s 2022	mN15	**BBB+**	6/95	A	X	BE	104.396	(11-15-02)	....	....	....	....	100	G1	'92	113½	102¼	102¾	8.64	8.64
SUSA Partnership, L.P.	***57***	***6.59***	***4.33***	***2.89***		***Dc***				***6-30-99***	***738.0***		***1713***	***43.1***						
Deb 7½s 2027	jD	**BBB**			X	BE	[4]Z100	....	....	....	....	....	100	G1	'97	93	81¾	81⅞	9.16	9.16
Nts 7s 2007	jD	**BBB**			X	BE	[4]Z100	....	....	....	....	....	100	G1	'97	99⅛	90	90	7.78	7.78
Nts 8.20s 2017	Jd	**BBB**	12/97	BBB–	X	BE	[4]Z100	....	....	....	....	....	100	G1	'97	102⅛	90⅝	91⅛	9.00	9.00
Susquehanna Bancshares	***10***	***4.72***	***3.65***	***3.43***		***Dc***				***9-30-99***	***404.0***		***813.0***	***49.7***						
Sr Nts 6.30s 2003	Fa	**BBB**			X	BE	NC	....	....	....	....	....	35.0	O3	'96	102¼	97½	97½	6.46	6.46

Uniform Footnote Explanations-See Page 260. Other: [1] Was UJB Fin'l. [2] Data of Summit Properties Inc. [3] Make Make-Whole Amt. [4] Plus Make-Whole Amt. [5] Due 10-5-00. [6] Red at greater of 100 or amt based on formula. [7] Was Broad Inc, see. [8] Subsid & data of Amer Intl Grp. [9] (HRO)On 1-15-08 at 100. [10] Int adj qtrly(3 Mo LIBOR&0.08%). [11] (HRO)On 2-15-06 at 100. [12] Issued in min denom $5T. [13] Was Super Valu Stores,see.

Company rows (Title-Industry Code & Co. Finances, in italics): Ind; Fixed Charge Coverage 1996, 1997, 1998; Year End; Million $ Cash & Equiv., Curr. Assets, Curr. Liab.; Balance Sheet Date; L. Term Debt (Mil $); Capital-ization (Mil $); Total Debt % Capital.

Exchange / Individual Issue Statistics	Interest Dates	S&P Rating	Date of Last Rating Change	Prior Rating	Eligible	Bond Form	Regular Price	Regular (Begins) Thru	Sinking Fund Price	Sinking Fund (Begins) Thru	Refund/Other Restriction Price	Refund/Other Restriction (Begins) Thru	Outst'g (Mil $)	Underwriting Firm	Underwriting Year	Price Range 1999 High	Price Range 1999 Low	Mo. End Price Sale(s) or Bid	Curr. Yield	Yield to Mat.
Susquehanna Bancshares (Cont.)																				
Sub Nts 9s 2005	Fa	BBB–			X	BE	NC	....	....	....	....	....	50.0		'95	113⅝	104¼	104¼	8.63	8.63
[1]Sweetheart Cup Co.	***50***	***1.25***	***d0.82***	***d0.56***		***Sp***	***4.06***	***265.0***	***163.0***	***6-27-99***	***408.0***		***422.0***	***96.9***						
Sr Sec[2]Nts[3] 9⅝s 2000	mS	B+			Y	R	100	....	....	....	....	....	190	D6	'93	100	90	99	9.72	9.72
Sr Sub[2]Nts[3] 10½s 2003	mS	B–			Y	R	102.625	8-31-00	....	....	....	....	110	D6	'93	97½	47	97	10.82	10.82
Swift Energy Co	***49a***	***13.14***	***5.19***	***2.07***		***Dc***	***42.14***	***69.10***	***32.48***	***9-30-99***	***239.0***		***402.0***	***59.5***						
Sr Sub[2]Nts 10¼s 2009	fA	B–			Y	BE	Z105.125	(8-1-04)	....	....	[4]Z110.25	7-31-02	125	S4	'99	102½	98	100¾	10.17	10.17
Synovus Financial	***10***	***11.98***	***11.30***	***14.46***		***Dc***				***9-30-99***	***229.0***		***1358***	***14.1***						
Sr Nts 6⅛s 2003	aO15	A			X	BE	NC	....	....	....	....	....	75.0	S1	'93	102	96⅝	96⅝	6.36	6.36
Sysco Corp	***26g***	***△11.55***	***△10.19***	***△9.14***		***Je***	***143.8***	***2575***	***1673***	***10-2-99***	***1055***		***2509***	***42.0***						
Deb[5] 7¼s 2007	Ao15	AA–			X	BE	NC	....	....	....	....	....	100	C1	'97	111½	99⅝	99⅝	7.28	7.28
Deb[5] 7.16s 2027	Ao15	AA–			X	BE	NC	....	....	....	....	....	50.0	M2	'97	117¾	101	101⅜	7.06	7.06
Deb 6½s 2028	fA	AA–			X	BE	[6]Z100	....	....	....	....	....	225	M2	'98	103½	85¾	85⅝	7.57	7.57
Sr Nts 6½s 2005	Jd15	AA–			X	BE	NC	....	....	....	....	....	150	M2	'95	106⅛	96½	96½	6.74	6.74
Sr Nts 7s 2006	Mn	AA–			X	BE	NC	....	....	....	....	....	200	G1	'96	109⅝	98	98	7.14	7.14
System Energy Resources[7]	***72***	***2.24***	***2.36***	***2.59***		***Dc***	***360.0***	***541.0***	***376.0***	***6-30-99***	***1227***		***2254***	***60.9***						
1st 7.71s 2001	fA	BBB–			X	BE	NC	....	....	....	....	....	135	M6	'96	101¾	100⅜	100⅜	7.68	7.68
1st 8¼s 2002	aO	BBB–			X	R	102.05	9-30-00	Z100	....	....	....	70.0	M6	'92	102¼	100½	100½	8.21	8.21
Deb 7.80s 2000	fA	BBB–			X	BE	NC	....	....	....	....	....	45.0	B7	'96	102⅜	100⅛	100⅛	7.79	7.79
Tampa Electric Co.[8]	***72a***	***4.54***	***4.55***	***4.67***		***Dc***	***1.60***	***303.0***	***421.0***	***6-30-99***	***774.0***		***2232***	***40.1***						
1st 5¾s 2000	Mn	AA			X	BE	NC	....	....	....	....	....	80.0	C1	'93	100¾	99¾	99⅞	5.76	5.76
1st 6⅛s 2003	Mn	AA			X	BE	NC	....	....	....	....	....	75.0	C1	'93	103⅛	97⅛	97⅛	6.31	6.31
1st 7¾s 2022	mN	AA			X	R	101.46	(11-1-02)	100	....	....	....	75.0	C1	'92	108	93⅞	94	8.24	8.24
Tandy Corp	***59l***	***4.55***	***7.59***	***7.40***		***Dc***	***54.30***	***1379***	***880.2***	***9-30-99***	***325.0***		***1456***	***39.8***						
M-T Nts 'B' 6⅛s 2003	[9]ao	A–			X	BE	NC	....	....	....	....	....	20.0	B7	'98	101⅛	95⅞	96¼	6.36	6.36
Nts 6.95s 2007	mS	A–			X	BE	NC	....	....	....	....	....	150	B7	'97	105¾	94⅝	94⅝	7.34	7.34
[10]Tanger Properties LP	***57***	***2.01***	***2.04***	***2.37***		***Dc***				***9-30-99***	***307.0***		***447.0***	***68.7***						
Gtd[11]Nts 8¾s 2001	Ms11	BB+			Y	BE	NC	....	....	....	....	....	75.0	M2	'96	101⅞	98	98¼	8.91	8.90
[11]Nts 7⅞s 2004	aO24	BB+			Y	BE	NC	....	....	....	....	....	75.0	M2	'97	95¼	92	92¼	8.54	8.54
TCA Cable TV[12]	***12a***	***Acq by Cox Commun,see***																		
[13]Deb[14] 6.53s 2028	Fa	BBB+			X	BE	[6]Z100	....	....	....	....	....	200	C1	'98	101¾	91¼	91¼	7.16	7.16
TCI Communications	***12a***	***Merged into AT&T Corp***																		
Sr Deb[15] 8¾s 2015	fA	AA–	2/99	BBB–	X	R	NC	....	....	....	....	....	750	M2	'95	127¾	109	109⅛	8.02	8.02
Sr Deb[15] 7⅞s 2026	Fa15	AA–	2/99	BBB–	X	R	NC	....	....	....	....	....	600	S1	'96	121	100¼	100¼	7.86	7.85
Sr Nts[16] 6⅜s 2003	Mn	AA–	2/99	BBB–	X	BE	NC	....	....	....	....	....	750	C6	'98	104	97⅞	97⅞	6.51	6.51
Sr Nts[15] 8.65s 2004	mS15	AA–	2/99	BBB–	X	R	NC	....	....	....	....	....	300	M6	'94	115½	105½	105½	8.20	8.20
Sr Nts[15] 8s 2005	fA	AA–	2/99	BBB–	X	R	NC	....	....	....	....	....	350	M2	'95	113¾	103⅛	103⅛	7.76	7.76
Sr Nts[15] 6⅞s 2006	Fa15	AA–	2/99	BBB–	X	R	NC	....	....	....	....	....	400	S1	'96	108	97⅜	97⅜	7.06	7.06
F/R[17]Sr M-T Nts 'C' 2000	QFeb2	AA–	2/99	BBB–	X	BE	NC	....	....	....	....	....	95.0	L3	'98	100	99½	100	....	....
Sr Nts 7⅛s 2028	Fa15	AA–	2/99	BBB–	X	R	NC	....	....	....	....	....	300	M2	'98	111¾	91⅝	91¾	7.77	7.76
TE Products Pipeline Co	***49***	***Subsid of Duke Energy, see***																		
• Sr Nts 6.45s 2008	Jj15	BBB+			X	BE	NC	....	....	....	....	....	180	M2	'98	No Sale		92⅛	7.00	7.00
• Sr Nts 7.51s 2028	Jj15	BBB+			X	BE	103.755	(1-15-08)	....	....	....	....	210	M2	'98	No Sale		90⅝	8.29	8.29
Tektronix Inc.	***65***	***△13.62***	***△2.19***	***△1.61***		***My***	***43.06***	***732.5***	***517.1***	***8-28-99***	***151.0***		***888.0***	***30.0***						
Nts 7½s 2003	fA	BBB–			X	BE	NC	....	....	....	....	....	100	M5	'93	107	100⅜	100⅜	7.47	7.47

Uniform Footnote Explanations-See Page 260. Other: [1] Subsid & data of Sweetheart Holdings. [2] (HRO)On Chge of Ctrl at 101. [3] Gtd by Sweetheart Holdings. [4] Max $41M red w/proceeds of Pub Eq Off'g. [5] (HRO)On 4-15-07 at 100. [6] Red at greater of 100 or amt based on formula. [7] Subsid of Entergy Corp. [8] Subsid of TECO Energy, Inc. [9] Due 1-15-03. [10] Subsid & data of Tanger Factory Outlet Ctrs. [11] Gtd by Tanger Factory Outlet Ctrs, Inc. [12] Acq by Cox Commun. [13] (HRO)On 2-1-08 at 100. [14] Asmd by Cox Communic sub. [15] (HRO)On Chge of Ctrl at 100. [16] Co may red in whole,at 100,for tax law chge. [17] Int adj qtrly(2 Yr CMT & 0.50%).

Title-Industry Code & Co. Finances (In Italics)	Ind	Fixed Charge Coverage 1996	1997	1998		Year End	Million $ Cash & Equiv.	Curr. Assets	Curr. Liab.	Balance Sheet Date	L. Term Debt (Mil $)		Capital-ization (Mil $)	Total Debt % Capital						
Individual Issue Statistics / Exchange	Interest Dates	S&P Rating	Date of Last Rating Change	Prior Rating	Eligible	Bond Form	Redemption Provisions: Regular Price	Regular (Begins) Thru	Sinking Fund Price	Sinking Fund (Begins) Thru	Refund/Other Restriction Price	Refund/Other Restriction (Begins) Thru	Outst'g (Mil $)	Underwriting Firm	Underwriting Year	Price Range 1999 High	Price Range 1999 Low	Mo. End Price Sale(s) or Bid	Curr. Yield	Yield to Mat.
***Tektronix Inc** (Cont.)*																				
Nts 7⅝s 2002	fA15	**BBB–**			X	BE	NC	....	....	....	....	....	50.0	M5	'95	106¼	100⅞	100⅞	7.56	7.56
Tele-Communications(Old)	***12a***	***Now TCI Commmunications,see***																		
Sr Deb[1] 9.80s 2012	Fa	**AA–**	2/99	BBB–	X	R	NC	....	....	....	....	....	600	M2	'92	135⅞	116¾	116¾	8.39	8.39
Sr Deb 7⅞s 2013	fA	**AA–**	2/99	BBB–	X	R	NC	....	....	....	....	....	550	M2	'93	118½	101¼	101¼	7.78	7.78
Sr Deb 10⅛s 2022	Ao15	**AA–**	2/99	BBB–	X	R	NC	....	....	....	....	....	65.0	F1	'92	145	122¼	122⅜	8.27	8.27
Sr Deb[1] 9⅞s 2022	Jd15	**AA–**		BBB–	X	R	NC	....	....	....	....	....	100	F1	'92	142¾	120	120⅛	8.22	8.22
Sr Deb[1] 9¼s 2023	Jj15	**AA–**	2/99	BBB–	X	R	104.42	(1-15-03)	....	....	....	....	500	F1	'93	116⅛	107¼	107⅝	8.59	8.59
Sr Deb[1] 8¾s 2023	Fa15	**AA–**	2/99	BBB–	X	R	103.65	(2-15-03)	....	....	....	....	250	F1	'93	111⅛	93	102⅜	8.55	8.55
Sr Nts[1] 7⅜s 2000	Fa15	**AA–**	2/99	BBB–	X	R	NC	....	....	....	....	....	300	F1	'93	102¼	100⅛	100⅛	7.37	7.36
Sr Nts[1] 10⅛s 2001	fA	**AA–**	2/99	BBB–	X	R	NC	....	....	....	....	....	100	F1	'91	111¼	104¾	104¾	9.67	9.66
Sr Nts 9¼s 2002	Ao15	**AA–**	2/99	BBB–	X	R	NC	....	....	....	....	....	200	F1	'92	111⅜	104¾	104¾	8.83	8.83
Sr Nts[1] 8¼s 2003	Jj15	**AA–**	2/99	BBB–	X	R	NC	....	....	....	....	....	550	F1	'93	110	103⅛	103⅛	8.00	8.00
Sr Nts 9.65s 2003	aO	**AA–**	2/99	BBB–	X	R	NC	....	100	....	....	....	150	M2	'91	109⅞	104⅛	104⅛	9.27	9.27
Sr Nts 7¼s 2005	fA	**AA–**	2/99	BBB–	X	R	NC	....	....	....	....	....	300	M2	'93	109½	99⅝	99⅝	7.28	7.28
Telephone & Data Sys	***67a***	***6.88***	***1.21***	***2.02***		***Dc***	***86.50***	***447.0***	***484.0***	***9-30-99***	***1581***		***4672***	***36.9***						
Nts 7s 2006	fA	**BBB**			X	BE	[2]Z100	....	....	....	....	....	200	M2	'98	100	92⅜	93¼	7.51	7.51
Teligent Inc	***67***	***n/a***	***n/a***	***1.51***		***Dc***	***227.4***	***291.0***	***198.8***	***9-30-99***	***800.0***		***500.0***	***160.0***						
Sr Nts[3] 11½s 2007	jD	**CCC**			Y	BE	105.75	(12-1-02)	....	....	....	....	300	M2	'97	101	91	96½	11.92	11.91
Sr[4]Disc Nts[5] 'B' 11½s 2008	Ms	**CCC**			Y	BE	105.75	(3-1-03)	....	....	....	....	[6]440	Exch.	'98	61	48	59	....	Flat
Temple-Inland	***16c***	***2.35***	***1.59***	***2.61***		***Dc***				***9-30-99***	***4564***		***6774***	***67.4***						
Deb[7] 8¼s 2022	mS15	**BBB+**	12/98	A–	X	BE	104.125	(9-15-02)	....	....	....	....	150	S1	'92	109⅛	98	98¼	8.40	8.40
Nts[7] 9s 2001	Mn	**BBB+**	12/98	A–	X	BE	NC	....	....	....	....	....	200	S1	'91	107¼	102	102	8.82	8.82
Nts[7] 7¼s 2004	mS15	**BBB+**	12/98	A–	X	BE	NC	....	....	....	....	....	100	S1	'92	107⅛	98¼	98¼	7.38	7.38
Tenet Healthcare	***30***	***△2.77***	***△2.95***	***△2.74***		***My***	***143.0***	***3951***	***1767***	***8-31-99***	***6525***		***10504***	***62.2***						
• Sr Nts[3] 8⅝s 2003	jD	**BB+**	2/98	BB	Y	R	NC	....	....	....	....	....	500	D6	'95	105¾	97⅝	s98¼	8.78	8.78
• Sr Nts[3] 7⅞s 2003	Jj15	**BB+**	2/98	BB	Y	BE	NC	....	....	....	....	....	400	D6	'97	102	95	95⅜	8.26	8.26
• Sr Nts[3] 8s 2005	Jj15	**BB+**	2/98	BB	Y	BE	NC	....	....	....	....	....	900	D6	'97	105¼	93⅝	95¼	8.40	8.40
• Sr Nts[3]'B' 7⅝s 2008	Jd	**BB+**			Y	BE	[8]Z100	....	....	....	....	....	350	Exch.	'98	103½	96	92	8.29	8.29
• Sr Sub Nts[3] 8⅝s 2007	Jj15	**BB–**	2/98	B+	Y	BE	104.313	(1-15-02)	....	....	....	....	700	D6	'97	106⅞	93¼	s95⅛	9.07	9.06
• Sr Sub Nts[3]'B' 8⅛s 2008	jD	**BB–**			Y	BE	104.063	(6-1-03)	....	....	....	....	1000	Exch.	'98	103¼	95½	80	10.16	10.15
Tennessee Gas[9]Pipeline[10]	***49***	***2.94***	***3.79***	***1.87***		***Dc***	***3.00***	***224.0***	***556.0***	***6-30-99***	***1353***		***2958***	***49.5***						
Deb 7½s 2017	Ao	**BBB+**	9/99	BBB	X	BE	NC	....	....	....	....	....	300	D6	'97	107¾	94¼	94¼	7.96	7.96
Deb 7s 2027	Ms15	**BBB+**	9/99	BBB	X	BE	[8]Z100	(3-15-07)	....	....	....	....	300	D6	'97	107⅛	95⅜	95⅜	7.34	7.34
Deb 7s 2028	aO15	**BBB+**	9/99	BBB	X	BE	[2]Z100	....	....	....	....	....	400	D6	'98	102⅛	86½	86½	8.09	8.09
Deb 7⅝s 2037	Ao	**BBB+**	9/99	BBB	X	BE	NC	....	....	....	....	....	300	D6	'97	107½	91⅛	91¼	8.36	8.36
Tennessee Valley[11]Auth[12]	***72***	***1.10***	***1.10***	***1.12***		***Sp***	***32.00***	***1146***	***3430***	***6-30-99***	***23349***		***29869***	***86.5***						
• Pwr Bonds '96B 6½s 2001	fA20	**AAA**			X	BE	NC	....	....	....	....	....	300		'96	100⅞	100½	96	6.77	6.77
• Pwr Bonds '92D 8¼s 2042	Ao15	**NR**			X	BE	■106	(4-15-12)	....	....	....	....	1000	G1	'92	123	107⅜	107⅝	7.67	7.67
• Pwr Bonds '93C 6⅛s 2003	jJ15	**NR**			X	BE	■101.614	7-14-00	....	....	....	....	1250	L3	'93	101¾	96⅝	97⅜	6.29	6.29
• Pwr Bonds '93D 7¼s 2043	jJ15	**NR**			X	BE	■105.438	(7-15-03)	....	....	....	....	750	F1	'93	107½	95½	s95½	7.59	7.59
• Pwr Bonds '93F 6⅞s 2043	jD15	**NR**			X	BE	■104.50	(12-15-03)	....	....	....	....	500	S1	'93	104½	89⅝	s89⅝	7.67	7.67
• Pwr Bonds '94A 7.85s 2044	Jd15	**NR**			X	BE	■106.729	6-14-00	....	....	....	....	850	M6	'94	107⅛	98⅝	100⅛	7.84	7.84
• Pwr Bonds '94C 8¼s 2034	mS15	**NR**			X	BE	■100	....	....	....	....	....	500	C5	'94	102	99	s99¾	8.27	8.27
• Global Pwr Bonds '95A 6⅜s 2005	Jd15	**AAA**			X	BE	NC	....	....	....	....	....	2000	L3	'95	105½	97	97⅜	6.55	6.55

Uniform Footnote Explanations-See Page 260. Other: [1] (HRO)On Chge of Ctrl at 100. [2] Red at greater of 100 or amt based on formula. [3] (HRO)On Chge of Ctrl at 101. [4] Int accrues at 11.5% fr 3-1-03. [5] (HRO)On Chge of Ctrl at 101(Accreted Amt). [6] Incl disc. [7] Issued in min denom $100T. [8] Plus Make-Whole Amt. [9] Was Tenneco Inc. [10] Subsid of Tenneco Inc. [11] Gvt agency:Int exempt state,local tax. [12] Balance sheet data of Pwr program.

Title-Industry Code & Co. Finances (In Italics) / Individual Issue Statistics — Exchange, Interest Dates	Fixed Charge Coverage 1996 / S&P Rating	1997 / Date of Last Rating Change	1998 / Prior Rating	Eligible	Year End / Bond Form	Million $ Cash & Equiv. / Redemption Provisions: Regular Price	Million $ Curr. Assets / Regular (Begins) Thru	Million $ Curr. Liab. / Sinking Fund Price	Balance Sheet Date / Sinking Fund (Begins) Thru	L. Term Debt (Mil $) / Refund/Other Restriction Price	Refund/Other Restriction (Begins) Thru	Capital-ization (Mil $) / Outst'g (Mil $)	Total Debt % Capital / Underwriting Firm	Underwriting Year	Price Range 1999 High	Price Range 1999 Low	Mo. End Price Sale(s) or Bid	Curr. Yield	Yield to Mat.
***Tennessee Valley Auth** (Cont.)*																			
• Global Pwr Bonds'95D 6s 2000.....mN	**AAA**			X	BE	NC	....	....	....	....	....	1000	L3	'95	101¾	98½	99⅝	6.02	6.02
• Global Pwr Bonds'95E 6¾s 2025..........mN	**AAA**			X	BE	NC	....	....	....	....	....	1350	L3	'95	100	92	92½	7.30	7.30
• Pwr Bonds '96A[1] 5.98s 2036...........Ao	**NR**			X	BE	NC	....	....	....	....	....	121	M6	'96	No Sale		98¾	6.06	6.06
• Pwr Bonds '97E 6¼s 2017 ....jD15	**AAA**			X	BE	NC	....	....	....	....	....	750	S4	'97	95½	95½	89⅛	7.01	7.01
• Pwr Bonds[2]'98A 6.35s 2018....QJan15	**AAA**			X	BE	100	(1-15-01)	....	....	....	....	250	J2	'98	100	89	89	7.13	7.13
• Global Pwr Bonds '98C 6s 2013........Ms15	**AAA**			X	BE	NC	....	....	....	....	....	1000	C6	'98	95½	90⅝	88¾	6.76	6.76
• Global Pwr Bonds'98G 5⅝s 2008.....mN10	**NR**			X	BE	NC	....	....	....	....	....	2000	L3	'98	92⅝	90⅛	89	6.04	6.04
Terex Cor*...................................... *41b	***0.11***	***1.74***	***2.51***		***Dc***	***154.1***	***1338***	***611.1***	***9-30-99***	***1066***		***1474***	***76.1***						
Sr Sub Nts[3] 8⅞s 2008 ....Ao	**B**	9/99	B–	Y	R	104.43	3-31-03	....	....	Z108.875	4-1-01	150	Exch.	'98	101¼	92	94½	9.39	9.39
Terminal RR Assn. St. L*.................. *55	***No Recent Fin'ls***																		
• Imp C 4s 2019 ....jJ	**NR**	6/87	AA		CR	[4]....	....	....	....	....	....	7.79	Exch.	'45	85¼	72½	67½	5.93	5.93
Texaco Capital*[5]................................ *25	***7.82***	***8.81***	***2.47***		***Dc***	***219.0***	***5973***	***5194***	***9-30-99***	***6626***		***19962***	***36.5***						
Gtd[6]Deb 8¼s 2006..........................aO	**A+**			X	R	NC	....	....	....	....	....	150	F1	'91	117⅛	105	105	7.86	7.86
• Gtd[6]Deb 8⅝s 2010.......................Jd30	**A+**			X	R	NC	....	....	....	....	....	150	M6	'90	115⅛	107	105⅝	8.17	8.16
• Gtd[6]Deb 9¾s 2020......................Ms15	**A+**			X	R	NC	....	....	....	....	....	250	S1	'90	120	120	118⅛	8.25	8.25
Gtd[6]Deb 8⅞s 2021........................mS	**A+**			X	R	NC	....	....	....	....	....	150	S1	'91	129¼	110⅞	111	8.00	7.99
Gtd[6]Deb 8⅜s 2022.........................jJ15	**A+**			X	R	103.672	(7-15-02)	....	....	....	....	200	F1	'92	110	101¾	102⅝	8.16	8.16
Gtd[6]Deb 6⅞s 2023......................fA15	**A+**			X	R	102.109	(8-15-03)	....	....	....	....	200	F1	'93	100½	86¾	86⅞	7.91	7.91
Gtd[6]Deb 8⅝s 2031.....................mN15	**A+**			X	R	NC	....	....	....	....	....	200	M6	'91	129⅛	107⅝	107¾	8.00	8.00
Gtd[6]Deb 8⅝s 2032..........................Ao	**A+**			X	R	NC	....	....	....	....	....	200	S1	'92	129⅛	107⅝	107¾	8.00	8.00
Gtd[6]Deb 8s 2032...............................fA	**A+**			X	R	NC	....	....	....	....	....	150	M6	'92	120⅝	100¾	100⅞	7.93	7.93
Gtd[6]Deb 7¾s 2033...................... Fa15	**A+**			X	R	104.635	(2-15-03)	....	....	....	....	200	F1	'93	106¼	96⅛	96¼	8.05	8.05
Gtd[6]Deb 7½s 2043...........................Ms	**A+**			X	R	102.717	(3-1-13)	....	....	....	....	200	S1	'93	111⅛	93⅛	93¼	8.04	8.04
• Gtd[7]Ext'd[6]Nts 9.45s 2000 ....Ms	**A+**	3/90	A	X	R	NC	....	....	....	....	....	50.8	S1	'85	106⅛	100½	100½	9.40	9.40
• Gtd[6]Nts 8½s 2003...................... Fa15	**A+**			X	R	NC	....	....	....	....	....	200	M6	'91	112	102¼	104⅛	8.16	8.16
Gtd[6]Nts 6s 2005 ....Jd15	**A+**			X	BE	[8]Z100	....	....	....	....	....	300	S4	'98	103¼	94¾	94¾	6.33	6.33
Gtd Nts[6] 7.09s 2007 .... Fa	**A+**			X	BE	NC	....	....	....	....	....	150		'97	110½	98½	98½	7.20	7.20
Gtd[6]M-T Nts 6¼s 2008 ....Jd28	**A+**			X	BE	*100	....	....	....	....	....	25.0	G1	'98	98⅞	93	93	6.72	6.72
Gtd[6]Nts 5.70s 2008...........................jD	**A+**			X	BE	100	(12-1-05)	....	....	....	....	200	G1	'98	101⅛	89¼	89¼	6.39	6.39
Gtd[6]Nts 5½s 2009.........................Jj15	**A+**			X	BE	[9]Z100	....	....	....	....	....	400	S4	'99	100	87¾	87¾	6.27	6.27
Texas Eastern Transm.*[10]................ *73a	***2.75***	***3.01***	***3.62***		***Dc***		***231.0***	***304.0***	***6-30-99***	***1156***		***3320***	***36.3***						
Nts 10⅜s 2000 ....mN15	**A**	6/97	BBB+	X	R	NC	....	....	....	....	....	200	F1	'90	108⅝	103	103	10.07	10.07
Nts 10s 2001..................................fA15	**A**	6/97	BBB+	X	R	NC	....	....	....	....	....	100	D4	'91	110⅞	104½	104½	9.57	9.57
Nts 8s 2002.....................................jJ15	**A**	6/97	BBB+	X	R	NC	....	....	....	....	....	100	K2	'92	107¾	102	102	7.84	7.84
• Nts 8¼s 2004.................................aO15	**A**	6/97	BBB+	X	R	NC	....	....	....	....	....	100	M2	'94	No Sale		101⅝	8.12	8.12
Texas Gas Transmission*[11]............. *73a	***4.44***	***4.57***	***4.50***		***Dc***	***0.11***	***123.0***	***109.0***	***6-30-99***	***251.0***		***890.0***	***28.2***						
Deb 7¼s 2027..................................jJ15	**BBB**			X	BE	[8,12]Z100	....	....	....	....	....	100	C1	'97	107⅜	90¾	90⅞	7.98	7.98
Nts 8⅝s 2004....................................Ao	**BBB**	2/95	BB	X	R	NC	....	....	....	....	....	150	M2	'93	113	104⅜	104⅜	8.26	8.26
Texas Instruments*........................ *23h	***0.46***	***7.08***	***8.14***		***Dc***	***2015***	***5488***	***2438***	***9-30-99***	***1159***		***7944***	***15.4***						
Nts 6⅞s 2000...................................jJ15	**A**			X	BE	NC	....	....	....	....	....	200	M6	'96	102½	100⅛	100⅛	6.87	6.87
Nts 9¼s 2003..................................Jd15	**A**			X	R	NC	....	....	....	....	....	104	M6	'91	115⅜	106⅛	106⅛	8.72	8.71
Nts 6⅛s 2006...................................... Fa	**A**			X	BE	NC	....	....	....	....	....	300	M6	'96	104⅛	92½	93¼	6.57	6.57
Nts 8¾s 2007.......................................Ao	**A**			X	R	NC	....	....	....	....	....	43.0	M6	'92	120⅞	105¾	105¾	8.27	8.27
Texas-New Mexico Pwr*[13] *72a	***1.53***	***2.16***	***1.95***		***Dc***	***10.00***	***31.70***	***69.30***	***6-30-99***	***460.0***		***782.0***	***58.8***						
1st U[3] 9¼s 2000 ....mS15	**BBB**	10/97	BB+	X	R	NC	....	....	....	....	....	100	D4	'93	105⅝	101¼	101¼	9.14	9.13

Uniform Footnote Explanations-See Page 260. Other: [1] (HRO)On 4-3-06 at 100. [2] Death red benefit,ltd,as defined. [3] (HRO)On Chge of Ctrl at 101. [4] At price to yield 3% at maturity. [5] Gtd by & data of Texaco Inc. [6] Gtd by Texaco Inc. [7] Int arrears pd 4-8-88. [8] Red at greater of 100 or amt based on formula. [9] Plus Make-Whole Amt. [10] Subsid of Texas Eastern Corp. [11] Subsid of Texas Gas Co(Transco Energy). [12] Plus Make-Whole Premium. [13] Subsid of TNP Enterprises.

Title-Industry Code & Co. Finances (In Italics) / Individual Issue Statistics (Exchange)	Ind / Interest Dates	Fixed Charge Coverage 1996 / S&P Rating	1997 / Date of Last Rating Change	1998 / Prior Rating	Eligible	Year End / Bond Form	Cash & Equiv. (Million $) / Redemption Provisions: Regular Price	Curr. Assets (Million $) / Regular (Begins) Thru	Curr. Liab. (Million $) / Sinking Fund Price	Balance Sheet Date / Sinking Fund (Begins) Thru	L. Term Debt (Mil $) / Refund/Other Restriction Price	Refund/Other Restriction (Begins) Thru	Capital-ization (Mil $) / Outst'g (Mil $)	Total Debt % Capital / Underwriting Firm	Underwriting Year	Price Range 1999 High	Price Range 1999 Low	Mo. End Price Sale(s) or Bid	Curr. Yield	Yield to Mat.
***Texas-New Mexico Pwr** (Cont.)*																				
Sr Nts 6¼s 2009	Jj15	**BBB**			X	BE	[1]Z100	....	....	....	....	....	175	D6	'99	100⅞	85⅛	85⅛	7.34	7.34
Sec Deb[2] 10¾s 2003	mS15	**BB+**	8/98	BB−	Y	R	100	(9-15-00)	....	....	....	....	140	D4	'93	107½	102⅛	102⅛	10.53	10.52
Texas & Pacific Ry	***55***	***Merged into Missouri Pacific RR, see***																		
• 1st 5s 2000	Jd	**BBB+**	7/98	BBB−	X	CR	NC	....	....	....	....	....	19.0	L3	1883	98¾	98	98⅞	5.06	5.06
Texas Utilities Electric[3]	***72a***	***3.17***	***3.35***	***3.34***		***Dc***	***47.00***	***667.0***	***1652***	***9-30-99***	***5604***		***13161***	***47.7***						
1st & CT 7⅜s 2001	fA	**BBB+**	7/95	BBB	X	R	NC	....	....	....	....	....	150	G1	'92	104¾	100½	100½	7.34	7.34
1st & CT 8⅛s 2002	Fa	**BBB+**	7/95	BBB	X	R	NC	....	....	....	....	....	150	M2	'92	107½	101⅞	102⅛	7.96	7.95
1st & CT 8s 2002	Jd	**BBB+**	7/95	BBB	X	R	NC	....	....	....	....	....	147	S1	'92	107¾	101¾	101¾	7.86	7.86
1st & CT 6¾s 2003	Ms	**BBB+**	7/95	BBB	X	R	NC	....	....	....	....	....	200	G1	'93	105⅛	98⅝	98⅝	6.84	6.84
1st & CT 6¾s 2003	Ao	**BBB+**	7/95	BBB	X	R	NC	....	....	....	....	....	100	M6	'93	105¼	98¾	98¾	6.84	6.84
1st & CT 8¼s 2004	Ao	**BBB+**	7/95	BBB	X	R	NC	....	....	....	....	....	100	G1	'92	112¼	102⅝	102⅝	8.04	8.04
1st & CT 6¼s 2004	aO	**BBB+**	7/95	BBB	X	R	NC	....	....	....	....	....	125	M2	'93	104½	95¾	95¾	6.53	6.53
1st & CT 6¾s 2005	jJ	**BBB+**	7/95	BBB	X	R	NC	....	....	....	....	....	100	S1	'93	107¼	96¾	96¾	6.98	6.98
1st & CT 9¾s 2021	Mn	**BBB+**	7/95	BBB	X	R	104.87	(5-1-01)	....	....	....	....	300	S1	'91	112	107⅛	107⅛	9.10	9.10
1st & CT 8⅞s 2022	Fa	**BBB+**	7/95	BBB	X	R	104.26	(2-1-02)	....	....	....	....	175	M2	'92	112¾	101½	101⅞	8.71	8.71
1st & CT 7⅞s 2023	Ms	**BBB+**	7/95	BBB	X	R	103.84	(3-1-03)	....	....	....	....	300	G1	'93	108	94⅛	94¼	8.36	8.35
1st & CT 8¾s 2023	mN	**BBB+**	7/95	BBB	X	R	104.01	(11-1-02)	....	....	....	....	200	M6	'92	112	100¾	100⅞	8.67	8.67
1st & CT 8½s 2024	fA	**BBB+**	7/95	BBB	X	R	104.05	(8-1-02)	....	....	....	....	175	G1	'92	109⅞	98½	98⅝	8.62	8.62
1st & CT 7⅞s 2024	Ao	**BBB+**	7/95	BBB	X	R	103.85	(4-1-03)	....	....	....	....	225	M6	'93	107⅛	93⅛	93¼	8.45	8.44
1st & CT 7⅝s 2025	jJ	**BBB+**	7/95	BBB	X	R	102.69	(7-1-03)	....	....	....	....	250	S1	'93	107⅝	91¼	91⅜	8.34	8.34
1st & CT 7⅜s 2025	aO	**BBB+**	7/95	BBB	X	R	103.35	(10-1-03)	....	....	....	....	300	G1	'93	105¾	89⅛	89¼	8.26	8.26
Sec M-T Nts 'D' 6¼s 2000	[4]ms	**BBB+**			X	BE	NC	....	....	....	....	....	16.0	M6	'95	100¾	100	100	6.25	6.25
Sec M-T Nts 'D' 6.27s 2000	[5]ms	**BBB+**			X	BE	NC	....	....	....	....	....	25.0	B7	'95	100¾	100	100	6.27	6.27
Sec M-T Nts 'D' 6.27s 2000	[6]ms	**BBB+**			X	BE	NC	....	....	....	....	....	40.0	B7	'95	101⅜	99⅜	99⅜	6.31	6.31
Deb 7.17s 2007	fA	**BBB**			X	BE	[7]Z100	....	....	....	....	....	300	M6	'97	109⅝	97⅝	97⅝	7.34	7.34
Textran Financial	***25c***	***n/a***	***n/a***	***n/a***		***Dc***				***9-30-99***	***2426***		***4131***	***87.2***						
• F/R[8]Nts[9] 2002	QDec9	**A−**			X	BE	NC	....	....	....	....	....	400	M2	'99	100	100	99¼	....	....
• Nts[8] 7⅛s 2004	jD9	**A−**			X	BE	NC	....	....	....	....	....	600	M2	'99	100¼	99¼	98¾	7.22	7.21
Textron, Inc.	***17***	***2.13***	***2.31***	***3.42***		***Dc***				***10-2-99***	***5181***		***8521***	***48.6***						
Deb 8¾s 2022	jJ	**A**	7/99	A−	X	BE	104.07	(7-1-02)	....	....	....	....	200	M6	'92	110½	101⅛	101¾	8.60	8.60
Nts 6¾s 2002	mS15	**A**			X	BE	NC	....	....	....	....	....	500	G1	'99	100⅜	98⅞	98⅞	6.83	6.83
Nts 6⅜s 2004	jJ15	**A**			X	BE	[10]Z100	....	....	....	....	....	300	M5	'99	99¾	96½	96½	6.61	6.61
Nts 6⅝s 2007	mN15	**A**	7/99	A−	X	BE	NC	....	....	....	....	....	200	S1	'97	106⅞	94¾	94¾	6.99	6.99
[11]Thiokol Corp	***2b***	***27.40***	***46.57***	***4.44***		***Dc***	***20.30***	***606.0***	***766.0***	***9-30-99***	***357.0***		***15376***	***47.7***						
Sr Nts 6⅝s 2008	Ms	**BBB**			X	BE	[10]Z100	....	....	....	....	....	150	M7	'98	102⅝	89⅞	89⅞	7.37	7.37
Thomas & Betts	***23b***	***3.49***	***5.35***	***4.83***		***Dc***	***85.70***	***1142***	***595.0***	***10-3-99***	***837.0***		***1058***	***46.4***						
Nts 8¼s 2004	Jj15	**BBB**	12/95	BBB+	X	R	NC	....	....	....	....	....	125	M2	'92	109⅜	102¾	102¾	8.03	8.03
Nts 6½s 2006	Jj15	**BBB**			X	BE	NC	....	....	....	....	....	150	Exch.	'96	102⅛	94½	94½	6.88	6.88
360(Degrees)Commun	***67g***	***Acq by ALLTEL Corp,see***																		
Sr[12]Nts[13] 7⅛s 2003	Ms	**A**	5/98	BBB−	X	BE	NC	....	....	....	....	....	450	S1	'96	105½	99⅞	99⅞	7.13	7.13
Sr[12]Nts[13] 7½s 2006	Ms	**A**	5/98	BBB−	X	BE	[7]Z100	....	....	....	....	....	450	S1	'96	110⅛	100⅝	100⅝	7.45	7.45
Sr[2]Nts[13] 6.65s 2008	Jj15	**A**	5/98	BBB−	X	BE	[10]Z100	....	....	....	....	....	100	S4	'98	106⅛	94⅞	94⅞	7.01	7.01
Sr[12]Nts[13] 7.60s 2009	Ao	**A**	5/98	BBB−	X	BE	[1]Z100	....	....	....	....	....	200	S1	'97	113¼	100⅛	100⅛	7.59	7.59
TIG Holdings	***35c***	***Acq by Fairfax Fin'l Hldgs Ltd***																		
Nts 8⅛s 2005	Ao15	**BBB−**	4/99	BBB	X	BE	NC	....	....	....	....	....	100	S1	'95	109⅜	93½	93½	8.69	8.69

Uniform Footnote Explanations-See Page 260. Other: [1] Plus Make-Whole Amt. [2] (HRO)On Chge of Ctrl at 101. [3] Subsid of Texas Utilities. [4] Due 1-31-00. [5] Due 2-1-00. [6] Due 11-13-00. [7] Greater of 100 or amt based on formula. [8] Co may red in whole, at 100, for tax law chge. [9] Int adj qtrly(3 Mo LIBOR & 0.35%). [10] Red at greater of 100 or amt based on formula. [11] Now Cordant Technologies. [12] (HRO)On Chge of Ctrl Trigger'g Event at 101. [13] Gtd by ALLTEL Corp.

Title-Industry Code & Co. Finances (In Italics) / Individual Issue Statistics, Exchange	Ind / Interest Dates	Fixed Charge Coverage 1996 / S&P Rating	1997 / Date of Last Rating Change	1998 / Prior Rating	Eligible	Year End / Bond Form	Million $ Cash & Equiv. / Redemption Provisions: Regular Price	Curr. Assets / Regular (Begins) Thru	Curr. Liab. / Sinking Fund Price	Balance Sheet Date / Sinking Fund (Begins) Thru	L. Term Debt (Mil $) / Refund/Other Restriction Price	Refund/Other Restriction (Begins) Thru	Capital-ization (Mil $) / Outst'g (Mil $)	Total Debt % Capital / Underwriting Firm	Underwriting Year	Price Range 1999 High	Price Range 1999 Low	Mo. End Price Sale(s) or Bid	Curr. Yield	Yield to Mat.
Time Warner Entertainment	***54***	***Subsid of Time Warner,see***																		
• Sr Deb 7¼s 2008	Ms	**BBB**	11/98	BBB–	X	R	NC	....	....	....	....	....	600	Exch.	'94	109	96¾	95⅞	7.56	7.56
Sr Deb 8⅜s 2023	Ms15	**BBB**	11/98	BBB–	X	R	NC	....	....	....	Z100	....	990	Exch.	'93	123⅝	104⅛	104¼	8.03	8.03
Time Warner Inc[1]	***54***	***0.75***	***1.15***	***1.03***		***Dc***	***645.0***	***8600***	***8576***	***9-30-99***	***18387***		***30374***	***60.6***						
• Deb 8.11s 2006	fA15	**BBB**	11/98	BBB–	X	R	NC	....	....	....	....	....	548	Exch.	'95	114	101⅛	101⅜	8.00	8.00
• Deb 8.18s 2007	fA15	**BBB**	11/98	BBB–	X	R	NC	....	....	....	....	....	548	Exch.	'95	114	101⅞	100⅞	8.11	8.11
• Deb 7.48s 2008	Jj15	**BBB**	11/98	BBB–	X	BE	NC	....	....	....	....	....	166	M6	'96	112	98½	99	7.56	7.55
• Deb 9⅛s 2013	Jj15	**BBB**	11/98	BBB–	X	BE	NC	....	....	....	....	....	1000	M2	'93	126⅛	107⅜	s108	8.45	8.45
• Deb 8.05s 2016	Jj15	**BBB**	11/98	BBB–	X	BE	NC	....	....	....	....	....	150	M6	'96	107⅜	104	101⅜	7.94	7.94
Deb 7¼s 2017	aO15	**BBB**	11/98	BBB–	X	BE	NC	....	....	....	....	....	500	M2	'97	110¼	93⅜	93½	7.75	7.75
Deb[2] 6⅞s 2018	Jd15	**BBB**	11/98	BBB–	X	BE	NC	....	....	....	....	....	600	M2	'98	105⅞	89⅞	90	7.64	7.64
• Deb 9.15s 2023	Fa	**BBB**	11/98	BBB–	X	BE	NC	....	....	....	....	....	1000	M2	'93	130	109⅛	s110⅞	8.25	8.25
Deb 7.57s 2024	Fa	**BBB**	11/98	BBB–	X	BE	NC	....	....	....	....	....	450	M6	'97	114⅛	96⅛	96¼	7.86	7.86
• Deb[3] 6.85s 2026	Jj15	**BBB**	11/98	BBB–	X	BE	NC	....	....	....	....	....	400	M6	'96	95	95	96	7.14	7.13
Deb[2] 6⅝s 2029	Mn15	**BBB**			X	BE	[4]Z100	....	....	....	....	....	1000	M7	'98	103⅜	85	85⅛	7.78	7.78
• Disc[5]Deb 8.30s 2036	Jj15	**BBB**	11/98	BBB–	X	BE	NC	....	....	....	....	....	200	M6	'96	29	25	18⅛	....	Flat
• Nts 7.95s 2000	Fa	**BBB**	11/98	BBB–	X	BE	NC	....	....	....	....	....	500	S1	'93	102⅜	99⅞	99⅞	7.96	7.96
• Nts 7.975s 2004	fA15	**BBB**	11/98	BBB–	X	R	NC	....	....	....	....	....	274	Exch.	'95	110½	100⅜	101	7.90	7.89
• Nts 7¾s 2005	Jd15	**BBB**	11/98	BBB–	X	BE	NC	....	....	....	....	....	500	M6	'95	111	101	101	7.67	7.67
Time Warner Telecom LLC/Inc	***67***	***n/a***	***n/a***	***n/a***		***Dc***	***324.0***	***362.0***	***128.0***	***6-30-99***	***438.0***		***866.0***	***50.6***						
Sr Nts[6] 9¾s 2008	jJ15	**B**	10/99	B–	Y	BE	104.875	(7-15-03)	....	....	[7]Z109.75	7-15-01	400	M7	'98	109	100½	103	9.47	9.46
Times Mirror	***54c***	***13.78***	***8.74***	***6.38***		***Dc***	***180.1***	***817.7***	***938.9***	***9-30-99***	***1493***		***2233***	***84.1***						
Nts 6.65s 2001	aO15	**A**			X	BE	NC	....	....	....	....	....	200	G1	'99	100⅜	99½	99½	6.68	6.68
Nts 7.45s 2009	aO15	**A**			X	BE	[4]Z100	....	....	....	....	....	400	G1	'99	101⅞	98⅜	98⅜	7.57	7.57
Deb 7¼s 2013	Ms	**A**	10/99	A+	X	R	NC	....	....	....	....	....	141	Exch.	'95	114¼	96	96	7.55	7.55
Deb 7½s 2023	jJ	**A**	10/99	A+	X	R	NC	....	....	....	....	....	98.7	Exch.	'95	113¾	94⅝	94¾	7.92	7.91
Deb 7¼s 2096	mN15	**A**	10/99	A+	X	BE	NC	....	....	....	....	....	148	M2	'96	111⅞	91	91⅛	7.96	7.96
Nts 6.61s 2027	mS15	**A**	10/99	A+	X	BE	[8]Z100	(9-15-04)	....	....	....	....	250	G1	'97	104½	96¾	96¾	6.83	6.83
Timken Co	***41i***	***13.59***	***13.44***	***7.99***		***Dc***	***18.38***	***839.4***	***507.0***	***9-30-99***	***328.0***		***1563***	***32.4***						
M-T Nts 'A' 6.40s 2004	[9]fa15	**A**			X	BE	NC	....	....	....	....	....	5.00	M5	'97	103⅞	96¼	96¼	6.65	6.65
M-T Nts[10] 'A' 7.08s 2006	[11]Fa15	**A**			X	BE	NC	....	....	....	....	....	5.00	M5	'96	108⅞	97⅜	97⅜	7.27	7.27
M-T Nts 'A' 6.99s 2006	[12]fa15	**A**	9/97	A–	X	BE	NC	....	....	....	....	....	10.0	M5	'96	108⅜	96⅞	96⅞	7.22	7.22
M-T Nts 'A' 6.78s 2006	[13]fa15	**A**	9/97	A–	X	BE	NC	....	....	....	....	....	5.00	M5	'96	107⅛	95⅝	95⅝	7.09	7.09
M-T Nts 'A' 7.68s 2016	[14]fa15	**A**	9/97	A–	X	BE	NC	....	....	....	....	....	5.00	M5	'96	113	97¾	97⅞	7.85	7.85
M-T Nts 'A' 7.49s 2016	[15]fa15	**A**	9/97	A–	X	BE	NC	....	....	....	....	....	10.0	M5	'96	111	96	96⅛	7.79	7.79
M-T Nts[10]'A' 7.01s 2017	[16]fa15	**A**	9/97	A–	X	BE	NC	....	....	....	....	....	5.00	M5	'97	105⅞	91⅛	91¼	7.68	7.68
M-T Nts 'A' 7.76s 2026	[17]fa15	**A**	9/97	A–	X	BE	NC	....	....	....	....	....	5.00	M5	'96	114½	96½	96⅝	8.03	8.03
M-T Nts 'A' 7.61s 2026	[18]fa15	**A**	9/97	A–	X	BE	NC	....	....	....	....	....	5.00	M5	'96	112⅝	94⅞	95	8.01	8.01
M-T Nts 'A' 7.16s 2027	[19]fa15	**A**			X	BE	NC	....	....	....	....	....	10.0	M6	'97	106¾	89⅝	89¾	7.98	7.98
M-T Nts 'A' 6⅞s 2028	fa15	**A**			X	BE	NC	....	....	....	....	....	100	M7	'98	103	86⅜	86½	7.95	7.95
[20]Titan Wheel Intl	***66d***	***6.51***	***3.68***	***1.72***		***Dc***	***12.83***	***289.6***	***142.4***	***9-30-99***	***250.0***		***520.0***	***54.0***						
Sr Sub Nts[6] 8¾s 2007	Ao	**B+**	12/99	BB–	Y	BE	104.375	(4-1-02)	....	....	....	....	150	M2	'97	100⅜	81	82⅛	10.65	10.65
TJX Cos[21]	***59g***	***10.89***	***117.01***	***418.56***		***Ja***	***24.56***	***1852***	***1628***	***10-30-99***	***120.0***		***1507***	***18.6***						
Nts 6⅝s 2000	Jd15	**A–**	1/99	BBB+	X	BE	NC	....	....	....	....	....	100	S1	'95	101⅜	100	100⅛	6.62	6.62
Nts 7s 2005	Jd15	**A–**	1/99	BBB+	X	BE	NC	....	....	....	....	....	100	S1	'95	105⅞	97⅞	97⅞	7.15	7.15

Uniform Footnote Explanations-See Page 260. Other: [1] See Time Warner Entmt,Turner Broadcast'g Sys. [2] Gtd by Time Warner Cos & Turner Broadcast'g Sys. [3] (HRO)On 1-15-03 at 100. [4] Red at greater of 100 or amt based on formula. [5] Int accrues at 8.30% fr 1-15-16. [6] (HRO)On Chge of Ctrl at 101. [7] Max $140M red w/proceeds of Pub Eq Off'g. [8] Plus Make-Whole Amt. [9] Due 11-12-04. [10] Issued in min denom $100T. [11] Due 10-10-06. [12] Due 11-1-06. [13] Due 12-13-06. [14] Due 7-5-16. [15] Due 8-8-16. [16] Due 11-6-17. [17] Due 7-6-26. [18] Due 10-13-26. [19] Due 11-3-27. [20] Now Titan Intl. [21] Was Zayre Corp.

Title-Industry Code & Co. Finances (In Italics) / Individual Issue Statistics Exchange	Ind / Interest Dates	Fixed Charge Coverage 1996 / S&P Rating	1997 / Date of Last Rating Change	1998 / Prior Rating	Eligible	Year End / Bond Form	Million $ Cash & Equiv. / Redemption Provisions Regular Price	Curr. Assets / Regular (Begins) Thru	Curr. Liab. / Sinking Fund Price	Balance Sheet Date / Sinking Fund (Begins) Thru	L. Term Debt (Mil $) / Refund/Other Restriction Price	Refund/Other Restriction (Begins) Thru	Capital-ization (Mil $) / Outst'g (Mil $)	Total Debt % Capital / Underwriting Firm	Underwriting Year	Price Range 1999 High	Price Range 1999 Low	Mo. End Price Sale(s) or Bid	Curr. Yield	Yield to Mat.
TJX Cos (Cont.)																				
Nts 7.45s 2009	jD15	A–			X	BE	[1]Z100	....	....	....	....	....	200	G1	'99	99¾	97	97⅝	7.63	7.63
TNT Freightways	***71***	***Now USFreigtways,see***																		
Nts 6⅝s 2000	Mn	A–	7/97	BBB+	X	BE	NC	....	....	....	....	....	100	M2	'93	101¼	100	100	6.63	6.62
Toledo Edison Co.[2]	***72a***	***2.07***	***1.87***	***2.98***		***Dc***	***4.72***	***206.0***	***310.0***	***6-30-99***	***1040***		***1967***	***60.8***						
• 1st 8s 2003	mN	BB+	7/97	BB	Y	R	100.83	10-31-00	100	....	....	....	35.7	B8	'73	103½	99⅛	98⅝	8.11	8.11
1st 7⅞s 2004	fA	BB+	7/97	BB	Y	R	NC	....	....	....	....	....	145	M6	'92	107⅝	100⅛	100⅛	7.87	7.86
Deb 8.70s 2002	mS	BB–	7/97	B+	Y	R	NC	....	....	....	....	....	135	M6	'92	106⅝	101⅜	101⅜	8.58	8.58
[3]Toll Corp	***13h***	***4.55***	***4.66***	***4.74***		***Oc***	***63.90***			***7-31-99***	***707.0***		***1294***	***54.6***						
• Sr Sub Nts[4] 8¾s 2006	mN15	BB+	4/97	BB–	Y	R	104.375	(11-15-01)	....	....	....	....	100	S1	'96	106⅜	96⅝	s98⅛	8.92	8.92
Sr Sub Nts[4] 7¾s 2007	mS15	BB+			Y	BE	103.875	(9-15-02)	....	....	....	....	100	S7	'97	100	90⅜	91⅝	8.46	8.46
Sr Sub Nts[4] 8⅛s 2009	Fa	BB+			Y	BE	104.063	(2-1-04)	....	....	....	....	170	S4	'99	101¾	90	93	8.74	8.73
Sr Sub Nts[4] 8s 2009	Mn	BB+			Y	BE	104	(5-1-04)	....	....	....	....	100	G1	'99	100¾	89½	92¾	8.63	8.62
[5]Tommy Hilfiger U.S.A.	***60***	***n/a***	***n/a***	***n/a***		***Mr***	***242.0***	***700.0***	***257.0***	***3-31-99***	***609.0***		***1631***	***40.2***						
• [6]Nts[7] 6½s 2003	Jd	BBB–			X	BE	[1]Z100	....	....	....	....	....	250	M7	'98	98	98	95⅝	6.80	6.80
• [6]Nts[7] 6.85s 2008	Jd	BBB–			X	BE	[8]Z100	....	....	....	....	....	200	M7	'98	95¾	95¾	91	7.53	7.53
Torchmark Corp	***35a***	***7.73***	***8.27***	***8.57***		***Dc***				***9-30-99***	***372.0***		***2978***	***26.0***						
Deb 8¼s 2009	fA15	A	6/95	A+	X	R	NC	....	....	....	....	....	100	S1	'89	115½	99⅞	99⅞	8.26	8.26
Nts 7⅜s 2013	fA	A	6/95	A+	X	R	NC	....	....	....	....	....	100	M6	'93	101¾	90⅜	90⅜	8.16	8.16
Nts 7⅞s 2023	Mn15	A	6/95	A+	X	R	NC	....	....	....	....	....	200	M6	'93	102⅜	91¾	91⅞	8.57	8.57
Toro Co	***42a***	***5.43***	***4.03***	***1.27***		***Oc***	***1.92***	***583.3***	***351.2***	***7-30-99***	***196.0***		***597.0***	***52.3***						
Nts 7⅛s 2007	Jd15	BBB–			X	BE	[9]Z100	....	....	....	....	....	75.0	G1	'97	100¾	89¾	89¾	7.94	7.94
Deb 7.80s 2027	Jd15	BBB–			X	BE	[9]Z100	....	....	....	....	....	100	G1	'97	95¾	87½	90½	8.62	8.62
Tosco Corp	***49d***	***3.87***	***3.99***	***4.42***		***Dc***	***83.20***	***1625***	***1583***	***9-30-99***	***1560***		***3881***	***46.7***						
• 1st 'B' 9⅝s 2002	Ms15	BBB	2/99	BBB–	X	R	NC	....	....	....	....	....	200	L3	'92	104⅝	103	104½	9.21	9.21
1st 'B' 8¼s 2003	Mn15	BBB	2/99	BBB–	X	BE	NC	....	....	....	....	....	150	Exch.	'93	106¾	101¾	101¾	8.11	8.11
Nts 7s 2000	jJ15	BBB	2/99	BBB–	X	BE	NC	....	....	....	....	....	125	M6	'95	101	100	100	7.00	7.00
Nts 7⅝s 2006	Mn15	BBB	2/99	BBB–	X	BE	[9]Z100	....	....	....	....	....	240	M6	'96	106⅛	97⅝	97⅝	7.81	7.81
Town Sports Intl	***59l***	***n/a***	***n/a***	***n/a***		***Dc***	***33.60***	***37.10***	***29.20***	***9-30-99***	***129.0***		***166.0***	***78.9***						
Sr Nts[10]'B' 9¾s 2004	aO15	B			Y	BE	104.875	(10-15-00)	....	....	[11]Z109.75	10-15-00	85.0	Exch.	'98	101	92	97½	10.00	10.00
Toyota Motor Credit	***25d***	***1.31***	***1.30***	***1.25***		***Sp***				***6-30-99***	***17565***		***19907***	***88.2***						
Nts 5½s 2001	mS17	AAA			X	BE	NC	....	....	....	....	....	400	M2	'98	100¼	97⅞	97⅞	5.62	5.62
Nts 5⅝s 2003	mN13	AAA			X	BE	NC	....	....	....	....	....	1000	M7	'98	101¼	95¼	95¼	5.91	5.91
Nts 5½s 2008	jD15	AAA			X	BE	NC	....	....	....	....	....	300	B7	'98	99⅜	87⅜	87⅜	6.29	6.30
• M-T Nts 5¼s 2001	Jj19	AAA			X	BE	NC	....	....	....	....	....	5.00	M2	'99	100	99¾	98⅜	5.34	5.34
Toys R Us	***59g***	***8.16***	***10.08***	***2.84***		***Ja***	***297.0***	***3700***	***3969***	***10-30-99***	***1240***		***4781***	***25.5***						
Deb 8¼s 2017	Fa	A–	5/99	A+	X	R	103.30	1-31-00	100	....	....	....	87.9	S1	'87	109⅜	100⅛	100⅛	8.24	8.24
Deb 8¾s 2021	mS	A–	5/99	A+	X	BE	NC	....	....	....	....	....	200	G1	'91	129⅜	98⅜	98½	8.88	8.88
Trans Fin'l Bancorp	***10***	***Mgr w/Firstar Corp,see***																		
Sub[12]Nts 7¼s 2003	[13]Qoct	NR				BE	NC	....	....	....	....	....	32.7	M4	'93	100¾	95⅝	99½	7.29	7.29
Trans Ocean Container	***16b***	***Acquired by Transamerica Corp,see***																		
Sr Sub Nts[10] 12¼s 2004	jJ	A	2/99	A+	X	R	106.15	6-30-00	....	....	....	....	74.6	M2	'94	109¼	106⅛	106⅝	11.49	11.48
Trans World Airlines Inc	***4***	***0.68***	***0.22***	***0.08***		***Dc***	***239.9***	***675.1***	***1125***	***9-30-99***	***674.0***		***997.0***	***83.8***						
◆Sr Nts 11½s 2004	jD15	CCC			Y	BE	105.75	(12-15-01)	....	....	Z111.50	12-15-00	140	Exch.	'97	90⅞	61	s65	17.69	17.68
Transamerica Corp[14]	***25g***	***n/a***	***n/a***	***n/a***		***Dc***				***12-31-98***	***2210***									
Deb 9⅜s 2008	Ms	AA	8/99	A	X	R	NC	....	....	....	....	....	100	G1	'88	122¾	109⅜	109⅜	8.57	8.57

Uniform Footnote Explanations-See Page 260. Other: [1] Red at greater of 100 or amt based on formula. [2] Subsid of Centerior Energy. [3] Gtd by & data of Toll Bros. [4] Gtd by Toll Bros. [5] Subsid&data of Tommy Hilfiger Corp. [6] Red in whole,at 100,for tax law chge. [7] Gtd by Tommy Hilfiger Corp. [8] Red at greter of 100 or amt based on formula. [9] Greater of 100 or amt based on formula. [10] (HRO)On Chge of Ctrl at 101. [11] Max $29.8M red w/proceeds Pub Eq Off'g. [12] Death red benefit,ltd,as defined. [13] Due 9-15-03. [14] Acq by & data of AEGON NV.

Title-Industry Code & Co. Finances (In Italics) / Individual Issue Statistics (Exchange)	Ind / Interest Dates	Fixed Charge Coverage 1996 / S&P Rating	1997 / Date of Last Rating Change	Prior Rating	1998 / Eligible	Year End / Bond Form	Cash & Equiv. / Regular Price	Million $ Curr. Assets / Regular (Begins) Thru	Curr. Liab. / Sinking Fund Price	Balance Sheet Date / Sinking Fund (Begins) Thru	L. Term Debt (Mil $) / Refund/Other Restriction Price	Refund/Other Restriction (Begins) Thru	Capital-ization (Mil $) / Outst'g (Mil $)	Total Debt % Capital / Underwriting Firm	Underwriting Year	Price Range 1999 High	Price Range 1999 Low	Mo. End Price Sale(s) or Bid	Curr. Yield	Yield to Mat.
***Transamerica Corp** (Cont.)*																				
Nts 6¾s 2006	mN15	**AA**	8/99	A	X	BE	NC	....	....	....	....	....	200	M6	'96	104⅞	94⅝	94⅝	7.13	7.13
Transamerica Finance[1] Corp[2]	***25a***	***1.24***	***1.54***		***1.56***	***Dc***	***119.0***			***9-30-99***	***8563***		***10234***	***83.7***						
Deb[3] 6½s 2011	Ms15	**A**	6/98	A+	X	R	100	....	....	....	....	....	[4]102	G1	'81	98⅛	90⅜	90⅜	7.19	7.19
Sr Nts 6⅜s 2001	mN15	**A**	6/98	A+	X	BE	NC	....	....	....	....	....	200	G1	'96	101⅜	98⅜	98⅜	6.48	6.48
Sr Nts 7¼s 2002	fA15	**A**			X	BE	NC	....	....	....	....	....	1000	S4	'99	101⅛	99½	99¾	7.27	7.27
Sr Nts 7½s 2004	Ms15	**A**	6/98	A+	X	BE	NC	....	....	....	....	....	56.2	G1	'94	107⅛	99⅜	99⅜	7.55	7.55
• Nts[5] 8½s 2001	jJ	**A**	6/98	A+	X	R	NC	....	....	....	....	....	0.75	M2	'76	No Sale		101	8.42	8.41
M-T Nts 'D'[6] 7.60s 2001	[7]ms	**A**	6/98	A+	X	BE	NC	....	....	....	....	....	25.0	S1	'94	104⅜	100½	100½	7.56	7.56
M-T Nts 'E' 6⅛s 2001	mN	**A**			X	BE	NC	....	....	....	....	....	625	G1	'98	101	97⅞	98⅛	6.24	6.24
M-T Nts 'F' 5.89s 2001	[8]ms	**A**			X	BE	NC	....	....	....	....	....	100	C1	'99	100½	98½	98⅝	5.97	5.97
M-T Nts 'F' 5.93s 2002	[9]ms	**A**			X	BE	NC	....	....	....	....	....	100	S1	'99	100½	96⅞	97⅛	6.11	6.11
M-T Nts 'F' 5.92s 2002	ms	**A**			X	BE	NC	....	....	....	....	....	212	S4	'99	100⅛	96⅞	97⅛	6.10	6.10
Sub Nts 6¾s 2000	Jd	**A–**	6/98	A	X	BE	NC	....	....	....	....	....	100	S1	'95	101⅛	100	100⅛	6.74	6.74
Sub M-T Nts 'D'[6] 6.05s 2000	[10]ms	**A–**	6/98	A	X	BE	NC	....	....	....	....	....	6.00	M5	'93	100¾	99	99¼	6.10	6.10
Sub M-T Nts 'D'[6] 6.51s 2003	[11]ms	**A–**	6/98	A	X	BE	NC	....	....	....	....	....	10.0	G1	'93	102½	96½	96⅝	6.74	6.74
Sub M-T Nts 'D'[6] 6.49s 2003	[11]ms	**A–**	6/98	A	X	BE	NC	....	....	....	....	....	5.00	M6	'93	102⅜	96½	96⅝	6.72	6.72
Transco Energy Co	***73a***	***Merged into Williams Cos, see***																		
Deb 9⅞s 2020	Jd15	**BBB–**	2/95	B+	X	R	NC	....	....	....	....	....	26.8	M2	'90	130⅝	114⅞	116½	8.48	8.47
Nts 9⅝s 2000	Jd15	**BBB–**	2/95	B+	X	R	NC	....	....	....	....	....	23.2	M2	'90	105	101⅜	101⅜	9.49	9.49
Nts 9⅜s 2001	fA15	**BBB–**	2/95	B+	X	BE	NC	....	....	....	....	....	47.9	M2	'91	107⅞	103½	103½	9.06	9.06
Transcont'l Gas PipeLine[12]	***73a***	***3.29***	***3.44***		***3.35***	***Dc***	***1.35***	***709.0***	***442.0***	***6-30-99***	***976.0***		***3123***	***31.3***						
Deb 7.08s 2026	jJ15	**BBB**			X	R	[13]100	(7-15-01)	....	....	....	....	200	M2	'96	103⅜	99⅜	99⅜	7.12	7.12
Deb 7¼s 2026	jD	**BBB**			X	R	[13]Z100	....	....	....	....	....	200	S7	'96	105⅜	88⅜	88½	8.19	8.19
Nts 8⅞s 2002	mS15	**BBB**	2/95	BB	X	R	NC	....	....	....	....	....	125	F1	'92	109⅞	103¼	103¼	8.60	8.59
Nts 6⅛s 2005	Jj15	**BBB**			X	BE	NC	....	....	....	....	....	200	S4	'98	101	93⅝	93⅝	6.54	6.54
Nts 6¼s 2008	Jj15	**BBB**			X	BE	NC	....	....	....	....	....	100	S4	'98	101½	90¼	90¼	6.93	6.92
Transocean Offshore	***49e***	***n/a***	***n/a***		***n/a***	***Dc***	***26.40***	***243.0***	***237.0***	***9-30-99***	***711.0***		***2900***	***25.6***						
Deb 8s 2027	Ao15	**A–**			X	BE	[14]Z100	....	....	....	....	....	200	G1	'97	116⅝	99⅛	99¼	8.06	8.06
Nts[15] 7.45s 2027	Ao15	**A–**			X	BE	[16]Z100	(4-15-07)	....	....	....	....	100	G1	'97	109¾	98¼	98¼	7.58	7.58
Travelers Property Casualty[17]	***35c***	***n/a***	***11.75***		***12.41***	***Dc***				***9-30-99***	***2326***		***11197***	***19.2***						
• Nts 6¾s 2001	Ao15	**A+**	4/97	A	X	BE	NC	....	....	....	....	....	500	S7	'96	102½	97	99	6.82	6.82
Nts 7¾s 2026	Ao15	**A+**	4/97	A	X	BE	NC	....	....	....	....	....	200	S7	'96	112¼	95⅜	97½	7.95	7.95
Tribune Co	***54c***	***10.93***	***7.73***		***8.01***	***Dc***	***1173***	***2186***	***850.7***	***9-26-99***	***2275***		***5475***	***42.1***						
Nts 7⅞s 2006	mN	**A**			X	BE	NC	....	....	....	....	....	250	M2	'96	106⅞	96	96	8.20	8.20
M-T Nts 'E' 5¼s 2005	[18]mn15	**A**			X	BE	NC	....	....	....	....	....	67.2	S4	'98	97⅞	89¾	89¾	5.85	5.85
Tricon Global Restaurants	***27b***	***n/a***	***n/a***		***3.77***	***Dc***	***316.0***	***752.0***	***1473***	***9-4-99***	***2605***		***1989***	***131.0***						
Sr Nts 7.45s 2005	Mn15	**BB**			Y	BE	[19]Z100	....	....	....	....	....	350	G1	'98	104⅜	95	96⅛	7.75	7.75
Sr Nts 7.65s 2008	Mn15	**BB**			Y	BE	[19]Z100	....	....	....	....	....	250	G1	'98	105	94¼	94⅝	8.08	8.08
TriNet Corporate Rlty Tr[20]	***57***	***2.20***	***3.06***		***2.83***	***Dc***				***9-30-99***	***622.0***		***1433***	***43.4***						
Nts 7.30s 2001	Mn15	**BB**	11/99	BBB–	Y	BE	[21]Z100	....	....	....	....	....	100	M5	'96	100⅞	95½	95⅝	7.63	7.63
Nts 7.95s 2001	Mn15	**BB**	11/99	BBB–	Y	BE	[21]Z100	....	....	....	....	....	50.0	M5	'96	103⅛	83¾	84	9.46	9.46
Nts 7.70s 2017	jJ15	**BB**	11/99	BBB–	Y	BE	[22]Z100	....	....	....	....	....	100	M5	'97	97	68⅝	69¼	11.12	11.11
TRINOVA Corp	***41h***	***Now Aeroquip-Vickers Inc,see***																		
Deb 7⅞s 2026	Jd	**A**	3/99	BBB+	X	BE	NC	....	....	....	....	....	100	M6	'96	109½	92½	92½	8.51	8.51

Uniform Footnote Explanations-See Page 260. Other: [1] Was Transmer Fin'l,then Transamer Finance Group. [2] Subsid of Transamerica Corp. [3] Trades as Transamer Fin'l. [4] Incl disc. [5] (HRO)Ea Jul 1 to 2000 at 100. [6] Issued in min denom $100T. [7] Due 8-23-01. [8] Due 3-5-01. [9] Due 3-25-02. [10] Due 11-22-00. [11] Due 12-9-03. [12] Subsid of Transco Energy. [13] Greater of 100 or amt based on formula. [14] Plus Make-Whole Premium. [15] (HRO)On 4-15-07 at 100. [16] Plus Make-Whole premium. [17] Was Travelers/Aetna Prop Casualty. [18] Due 10-11-05. [19] Red at greater of 100 or amt based on formula. [20] Acq by Starwood Fin'l. [21] Plus make-whole amt. [22] Plus Make-Whole Amt.

Exchange ↓ Individual Issue Statistics	Interest Dates	S&P Rating	Date of Last Rating Change	Prior Rating	Eligible ↓	Bond Form	Redemption Provisions: Regular Price	Regular (Begins) Thru	Sinking Fund Price	Sinking Fund (Begins) Thru	Refund/Other Restriction Price	Refund/Other Restriction (Begins) Thru	Outst'g (Mil $)	Underwriting Firm	Underwriting Year	Price Range 1999 High	Price Range 1999 Low	Mo. End Price Sale(s) or Bid	Curr. Yield	Yield to Mat.
Title-Industry Code & Co. Finances (In Italics)	*Ind*	*Fixed Charge Coverage 1996*	*1997*	*1998*		*Year End*	*Million $ Cash & Equiv.*	*Curr. Assets*	*Curr. Liab.*	*Balance Sheet Date*	*L. Term Debt (Mil $)*		*Capital-ization (Mil $)*	*Total Debt % Capital*						
Triton Energy	***49a***	***1.25***	***1.02***	***3.50***		***Dc***	***203.0***	***261.0***	***81.10***	***9-30-99***	***404.0***		***868.0***	***47.6***						
Sr Nts 8¾s 2002	Ao15	**BB–**	11/99	B+	Y	BE	[1]Z100	....	....	....	....	....	200	S7	'97	101⅛	87	100¼	8.73	8.73
Sr Nts 9¼s 2005	Ao15	**BB–**	11/99	B+	Y	BE	[1]Z100	....	....	....	....	....	200	S7	'97	101¾	91	101¼	9.14	9.14
Trump Atlantic City Assoc/Funding[2]	***32***	***n/a***	***n/a***	***1.93***		***Dc***	***79.40***	***199.0***	***113.0***	***6-30-99***	***1300***		***1559***	***83.6***						
1st[3]Mtg Nts[4] 11¼s 2006	Mn	**B**	12/97	BB–	Y	R	105.625	(5-1-01)	....	....	....	....	1200	D6	'96	92½	80	81	13.89	13.89
[5]Trump's Castle Funding	***25***	***[6]d0.18***	***0.44***	***0.55***		***Dc***	***17.70***	***36.00***	***56.80***	***6-30-99***	***377.0***		***475.0***	***79.4***						
◆Mtg[7]Nts[8] 11¾s 2003	mN15	**NR**				R	103.917	12-30-00	....	....	....	....	242	Exch.	'94	92	78½	s82½	....	Flat
◆Sub[7]PIK[9]Nts[8] 13⅞s 2005	mN15	**NR**				R	100	....	....	....	....	....	92.5	Exch.	'94	93	80	s83	....	Flat
Trump Hotels & Casino Res	***40i***	***0.80***	***0.70***	***0.73***		***Dc***	***179.6***	***289.7***	***239.1***	***9-30-99***	***1847***		***2217***	***83.6***						
Sr Sec Nts[7] 15½s 2005	Jd15	**B–**			Y	R	107.75	(6-15-00)	....	....	....	....	145	D6	'95	107	81⅝	82¼	18.84	18.83
TRW, Inc	***17***	***5.08***	***5.54***	***7.60***		***Dc***	***294.0***	***5199***	***7452***	***9-30-99***	***5530***		***11184***	***81.3***						
Deb 6.65s 2028	Jj15	**BBB**	3/99	A	X	BE	[10]Z100	....	....	....	....	....	150	M7	'98	100⅝	82½	83⅜	7.98	7.97
Nts 6.05s 2005	Jj15	**BBB**	3/99	A	X	BE	[10]Z100	....	....	....	....	....	200	M7	'98	101⅝	93¾	94⅛	6.43	6.43
Nts 6¼s 2010	Jj15	**BBB**	3/99	A	X	BE	[10]Z100	....	....	....	....	....	150	M7	'98	102¾	88¼	88¼	7.08	7.08
M-T[11]Nts'A'[12] 9.35s 2020	[13]fa15	**BBB**	3/99	A	X	R	NC	....	....	....	....	....	100	M2	'90	133¾	112⅝	114	8.20	8.20
Nts[11] 9⅜s 2021	Ao15	**BBB**	3/99	A	X	BE	NC	....	....	....	....	....	100	S1	'91	133⅝	110¾	112½	8.33	8.33
M-T Nts 'D' 6.30s 2008	Mn15	**BBB**	3/99	A	X	BE	NC	....	....	....	....	....	100	B7	'98	104	90⅝	91¼	6.90	6.90
[14]Tucson Elec Pwr[15]	***72a***	***1.38***	***1.31***	***1.50***		***Dc***	***132.0***	***347.0***	***229.0***	***9-30-99***	***1989***		***2372***	***87.5***						
1st 8½s 2009	aO	**BB+**	10/97	BB–	Y	R	102.47	9-30-00	100	....	....	....	60.0	M2	'77	103	102	102	8.33	8.33
Tultex Corp	***68c***	***2.24***	***1.20***	***d0.41***		***Dc***	***Bankruptcy Chapt 11***				***129.0***		***393.0***	***64.4***						
Sr Nts[16] 10⅝s 2005	[17]§jd15	**D**	12/99	C	Z	R			Default 12-15-99 int				70.0	M5	'95	43	17½	17½	....	Flat
Turner Broadcast'g Sys	***12e***	***Merged into Time Warner Inc,see***																		
Sr Deb[18] 8.40s 2024	Fa	**BBB**	11/98	BBB–	X	R	104.161	(2-1-04)	....	....	....	....	200	G1	'94	111¼	98½	98⅝	8.52	8.52
Sr Nts[18] 7.40s 2004	Fa	**BBB**	11/98	BBB–	X	R	NC	....	....	....	....	....	250	G1	'94	107⅛	99⅞	99⅞	7.41	7.41
Sr Nts[19] 8⅜s 2013	jJ	**BBB**	11/98	BBB–	X	R	NC	....	....	....	....	....	300	F1	'93	121½	103¼	103¼	8.11	8.11
TV Guide Inc	***54b***	***29.11***	***43.15***	***68.89***		***Dc***	***102.8***	***443.1***	***494.7***	***9-30-99***	***625.0***		***2093***	***28.8***						
Sr Sub Nts[7]'B' 8⅛s 2009	Ms	**B+**			Y	BE	104.063	(3-1-04)	....	....	[20]Z108.125	3-1-02	400		'99	100	93½	99¾	8.15	8.14
Tyco International[21] (New)[22]	***13***	***[23]9.40***	***[24]7.09***	***8.28***		***Sp***	***1625***	***10522***	***8421***	***6-30-99***	***8293***		***19005***	***47.1***						
Deb 9½s 2022	Mn	**A–**	7/97	BBB+	X	BE	NC	....	....	....	....	....	49.0	M5	'92	131⅝	113	113⅛	8.40	8.40
Deb 8s 2023	Ms	**A–**	7/97	BBB+	X	BE	NC	....	....	....	....	....	50.0	M5	'93	113⅝	97¾	97⅞	8.17	8.17
Nts 6½s 2001	mN	**A–**	7/97	BBB+	X	BE	NC	....	....	....	....	....	300	M5	'96	102¼	99⅛	99⅛	6.56	6.56
Nts 6⅜s 2004	Jj15	**A–**	7/97	BBB+	X	BE	NC	....	....	....	....	....	105	M5	'94	102½	97	97	6.57	6.57
Tyson Foods	***26e***	***△3.99***	***△2.50***	***△4.61***		***Sp***	***30.00***	***1727***	***987.0***	***9-30-99***	***1515***		***4057***	***48.0***						
Nts 6s 2003	Jj15	**A–**			X	BE	NC	....	....	....	....	....	150	M5	'98	101½	96⅝	96⅝	6.21	6.21
Nts 6¾s 2005	Jd	**A–**			X	BE	NC	....	....	....	....	....	150	M5	'95	105⅞	96⅜	96⅜	7.00	7.00
Nts 7s 2018	Mn	**A–**			X	BE	NC	....	....	....	....	....	240	M5	'98	102⅝	91⅜	91⅜	7.66	7.66
Nts 7s 2028	Jj15	**A–**			X	BE	NC	....	....	....	....	....	150	M5	'98	102¾	88⅜	88½	7.91	7.91
M-T Nts 6⅝s 2005	[25]jd	**A–**			X	BE	NC	....	....	....	....	....	150	M2	'95	105½	96¼	96¼	6.88	6.88
UCC Investors Holdings	***14***	***Now Uniroyal Chemical,see***																		
Sr Nts[7] 10½s 2002	Mn	**B–**			Y	R	NC	....	....	....	....	....	283	M6	'93	110	100	109¼	9.61	9.61
UGI Utilities[26]	***73b***	***4.84***	***4.75***	***4.24***		***Sp***	***1.43***	***75.60***	***145.0***	***6-30-99***	***180.0***		***489.0***	***50.5***						
M-T Nts[11] 'B' 7¼s 2017	mn15	**A–**			X	BE	NC	....	....	....	....	....	20.0	D6	'97	107¾	90¼	90⅜	8.02	8.02
Ultramar Credit	***25***	***Gtd by Ultramar Diamond Shamrock,see***																		
Gtd[27]Nts[28] 8⅝s 2002	jJ	**BBB**			X	BE	NC	....	....	....	....	....	275	G1	'92	107¼	102¼	102¼	8.44	8.43
Ultramar Diamond Shamrock[29]	***49g***	***1.21***	***2.83***	***1.45***		***Dc***	***136.7***	***1304***	***1217***	***9-30-99***	***1492***		***2981***	***50.3***						
Sr Nts 7.20s 2017	aO15	**BBB**			X	BE	[10]Z100	....	....	....	....	....	200	M5	'97	100¾	89⅜	89½	8.04	8.04

Uniform Footnote Explanations-See Page 260. Other: [1] Plus Make-Whole Premium. [2] Data of Trump Atlantic City Assoc. [3] (HRO)On Cjge of Ctrl at 101. [4] State gaming laws may req hldr's sale/Co red. [5] Subsid & data of Trump's Castle Assoc. [6] 7 Mo Dec'96. [7] (HRO)On Chge of Ctrl at 101. [8] Gtd by Trumps Castle Assoc. [9] Int 7% to 9-30-94,13.875% aft. [10] Red at greater of 100 or amt based on formula. [11] Issued in min denom $100T. [12] (HRO)On 8-15-00 at 100. [13] Due 6-4-20. [14] Was Tucson Gas & Elec. [15] Now Unisource Energy. [16] Co must offer repurch at 101 on Chge of Ctrl. [17] Due 3-15-05. [18] (HRO)For Triggering Event at 101. [19] (HRO)For a Triggering Event at 101. [20] Max $140M red w/proceeds of Pub Eq Off'g. [21] Was Tyco Labs. [22] See ADT Operations,U.S. Surgical. [23] Fiscal Jun'96 & prior. [24] 9 Mo Sep'97. [25] Due 10-17-05. [26] Subsid of UGI Corp. [27] Co must offer repurch at 100 for certain asset sales. [28] Co may offer 101 on Chge of Ctrl Trigger'g Event. [29] See Diamond Shamrock & Ultramar Credit.

Title-Industry Code & Co. Finances (In Italics) / Individual Issue Statistics (Exchange)	Ind / Interest Dates	Fixed Charge Coverage 1996 / S&P Rating	1997 / Date of Last Rating Change	1998 / Prior Rating	Eligible	Year End / Bond Form	Million $ Cash & Equiv. / Redemption Provisions Regular Price	Curr. Assets / Regular (Begins) Thru	Curr. Liab. / Sinking Fund Price	Balance Sheet Date / Sinking Fund (Begins) Thru	L. Term Debt (Mil $) / Refund/Other Restriction Price	Refund/Other Restriction (Begins) Thru	Capital-ization (Mil $) / Outst'g (Mil $)	Total Debt % Capital / Underwriting Firm	Underwriting Year	Price Range 1999 High	Price Range 1999 Low	Mo. End Price Sale(s) or Bid	Curr. Yield	Yield to Mat.
***Ultramar Diamond Shamrock** (Cont.)*																				
Sr Nts[1] 6¾s 2037	aO15	**BBB**			X	BE	[2]Z100	(10-15-09)	....	....	....	....	100	M5	'97	103¼	91⅜	91⅜	7.39	7.39
Sr Nts 7.45s 2097	aO15	**BBB**			X	BE	[2]Z100	....	....	....	....	....	100	M5	'97	102½	87⅝	87¾	8.49	8.49
Unilab Corp[3]	***43a***	***d0.60***	***1.03***	***1.79***		***Dc***	***31.25***	***93.40***	***35.34***	***9-30-99***	***161.0***		***157.0***	***104.0***						
Sr Nts[4] 11s 2006	Ao	**NR**	9/99	B+		R	105.50	(4-1-01)	....	....	....	....	120	D4	'96	112½	103½	112¼	9.80	9.80
Union Camp Corp	***50***	***Acq by Int'l Paper,see***																		
• SF Deb 8⅝s 2016	Ao15	**BBB+**	5/99	A–	X	R	103.019	4-14-00	100	....	....	....	100	G1	'86	102½	100⅜	100⅛	8.61	8.61
SF Deb 10s 2019	Mn	**BBB+**	5/99	A–	X	R	105	4-30-00	100	(5-1-00)	....	....	100	M6	'89	105⅜	105	105	9.52	9.52
SF Deb 9¼s 2021	fA15	**BBB+**	5/99	A–	X	R	104.283	(8-16-01)	100	(8-15-02)	....	....	125	G1	'91	106⅞	103¼	103¼	8.96	8.96
Deb 9½s 2002	Ms15	**BBB+**	5/99	A–	X	R	NC	....	....	....	....	....	100	S1	'90	110⅞	104¾	104¾	9.07	9.07
Deb 9¼s 2011	Fa	**BBB+**	5/99	A–	X	R	NC	....	....	....	....	....	125	F1	'91	126⅜	109½	109½	8.45	8.45
Deb 8½s 2022	Mn15	**BBB+**	5/99	A–	X	R	104.25	(5-15-02)	....	....	....	....	100	S1	'92	108⅜	101½	102	8.33	8.33
Nts 7s 2006	fA15	**BBB+**	5/99	A–	X	BE	NC	....	....	....	....	....	150	G1	'96	106¼	97	97	7.22	7.22
Nts 6½s 2007	mN15	**BBB+**	5/99	A–	X	BE	NC	....	....	....	....	....	150	G1	'97	103⅜	93⅞	93⅞	6.92	6.92
Union Carbide[5]	***14***	***7.61***	***8.04***	***3.91***		***Dc***	***36.00***	***2013***	***1624***	***9-30-99***	***1868***		***5066***	***49.4***						
Deb 7½s 2025	Jd	**BBB**			X	BE	NC	....	....	....	....	....	150	M6	'95	102⅛	94¼	96⅛	7.80	7.80
Deb[6] 6.79s 2025	Jd	**BBB**			X	BE	NC	....	....	....	....	....	250	M6	'95	101⅞	95½	96½	7.04	7.04
Deb[7] 7¾s 2096	aO	**BBB**			X	BE	NC	....	....	....	....	....	200	M6	'96	103½	92¾	93¾	8.27	8.27
Nts 6¼s 2003	Jd15	**BBB**			X	BE	NC	....	....	....	....	....	250	G1	'98	100⅜	96⅞	97⅛	6.44	6.43
Union Carbide Chem & Plastics	***14***	***Gtd by Union Carbide,see***																		
Deb[8] 8¾s 2022	fA	**BBB**			X	BE	104.337	(8-1-02)	....	....	....	....	125	M6	'92	108¾	101⅛	102⅜	8.55	8.55
Deb 7⅞s 2023	Ao	**BBB**			X	BE	NC	....	....	....	....	....	175	M6	'93	106¼	97½	100¼	7.86	7.86
Nts 6¾s 2003	Ao	**BBB**			X	BE	NC	....	....	....	....	....	125	M6	'93	102	97⅝	98⅝	6.84	6.84
[9]Union Electric Co[10]	***72a***	***3.20***	***n/a***	***4.63***		***Dc***	***331.0***	***1150***	***1198***	***9-30-99***	***2302***		***6893***	***40.4***						
1st 7.65s 2003	Jj15	**AA–**	4/92	A+	X	BE	NC	....	....	....	....	....	100	S1	'92	109¾	102	102	7.50	7.50
1st 7⅜s 2004	jD15	**AA–**			X	BE	NC	....	....	....	....	....	85.0	S1	'92	110¼	100⅞	100⅞	7.31	7.31
1st 6⅞s 2004	fA	**AA–**			X	BE	NC	....	....	....	....	....	188	S1	'93	107⅜	98⅞	98⅞	6.95	6.95
1st 6¾s 2008	mN	**AA–**			X	BE	NC	....	....	....	....	....	148	S1	'93	108¾	96½	96½	6.99	6.99
1st 8¾s 2021	jD	**AA–**	4/92	A+	X	BE	104.38	(12-1-01)	....	....	....	....	125	S1	'91	111	100¾	100⅞	8.67	8.67
1st 8¼s 2022	aO15	**AA–**			X	BE	103.61	(10-15-02)	....	....	....	....	104	S1	'92	110⅜	99⅛	99¼	8.31	8.31
1st 8s 2022	jD15y	**AA–**			X	BE	103.38	(12-15-02)	....	....	....	....	85.0	S1	'92	108⅜	96⅞	96⅞	8.26	8.26
1st 7.15s 2023	fA	**AA–**			X	BE	103.01	(8-1-03)	....	....	....	....	75.0	S1	'93	104⅛	88¾	88⅞	8.05	8.04
1st 7s 2024	Jj15	**AA–**			X	BE	103.41	(1-15-04)	....	....	....	....	100	S1	'94	104	87½	87⅝	7.99	7.99
Union Light Heat & Pwr[11]	***72a***	***6.24***	***5.30***	***5.63***		***Dc***	***5.73***	***21.50***	***61.10***	***9-30-99***	***74.50***		***238.0***	***44.1***						
1st 9½s 2008	jD	**A–**	7/95	BBB+	X	R	102.90	11-30-00	100.66	11-30-00	....	....	10.0	H4	'78	103⅞	103⅛	103⅜	9.19	9.19
Deb 6.11s 2003	jD8	**BBB+**			X	BE	[2]Z100	....	....	....	....	....	20.0	F2	'98	102½	95⅝	95⅝	6.39	6.39
[12]Union Oil of California	***49a***	***2.92***	***3.67***	***0.86***		***Dc***	***209.0***	***1360***	***1346***	***9-30-99***	***3356***		***5909***	***56.8***						
Deb[13] 9¼s 2003	Fa	**BBB+**	4/97	BBB	X	R	NC	....	....	....	....	....	89.0	M2	'91	111⅛	104⅞	104⅞	8.82	8.82
Deb[13] 9⅛s 2006	Fa15	**BBB+**	4/97	BBB	X	R	NC	....	....	....	....	....	200	M2	'91	116⅛	105⅞	105⅞	8.62	8.62
Deb[13] 7s 2028	Mn	**BBB+**			X	BE	[2]Z100	....	....	....	....	....	200	M7	'98	98½	87⅞	88⅛	7.94	7.94
Deb 7½s 2029	Fa15	**BBB+**			X	BE	[2]Z100	....	....	....	....	....	350	M7	'99	104½	93¼	93¼	8.04	8.04
Nts[13] 9¾s 2000	jD	**BBB+**	4/97	BBB	X	R	NC	....	....	....	....	....	65.1	M2	'90	106¾	102¼	102¼	9.54	9.53
Nts[13] 8¾s 2001	fA15	**BBB+**	4/97	BBB	X	R	NC	....	....	....	....	....	38.5	F1	'91	106⅜	102¼	102¼	8.56	8.56
Nts[13] 6⅜s 2004	Fa	**BBB+**	4/97	BBB	X	R	NC	....	....	....	....	....	200	G1	'94	101⅛	95⅞	95⅞	6.65	6.65
Nts[13] 7.20s 2005	Mn15	**BBB+**	4/97	BBB	X	BE	NC	....	....	....	....	....	200	G1	'95	104¾	98⅝	98⅝	7.30	7.30

Uniform Footnote Explanations-See Page 260. Other: [1] (HRO)On 10-15-09 at 100. [2] Red at greater of 100 or amt based on formula. [3] Acq by Kelso & Co. [4] (HRO)On Chge of Ctrl at 101. [5] See Union Carbide Chem & Plastics. [6] (HRO)On 6-1-05 at 100. [7] Co may shorten mty for tax law chge. [8] Gtd by Union Carbide. [9] See Missouri Pwr & Lt. [10] Now Ameren Corp. [11] Subsid of Cinn Gas & Elec. [12] Subsid & data of Unocal Corp. [13] Gtd by Unocal Corp.

Exchange / Individual Issue Statistics	Interest Dates	S&P Rating	Date of Last Rating Change	Prior Rating	Eligible	Bond Form	Regular Price	Regular (Begins) Thru	Sinking Fund Price	Sinking Fund (Begins) Thru	Refund/Other Restriction Price	Refund/Other Restriction (Begins) Thru	Outst'g (Mil $)	Underwriting Firm	Underwriting Year	Price Range 1999 High	Price Range 1999 Low	Mo. End Price Sale(s) or Bid	Curr. Yield	Yield to Mat.
Title-Industry Code & Co. Finances (In Italics)	*Ind*	*Fixed Charge Coverage 1996*	*1997*	*1998*		*Year End*	*Million $ Cash & Equiv.*	*Curr. Assets*	*Curr. Liab.*	*Balance Sheet Date*	*L. Term Debt (Mil $)*		*Capital-ization (Mil $)*	*Total Debt % Capital*						
***Union Oil of California** (Cont.)*																				
Nts[1] 6½s 2008	Mn	**BBB+**			X	BE	[2]Z100	....	....	....	....	....	100	M7	'98	100¼	92⅛	92⅛	7.06	7.06
Nts[1] 7.35s 2009	Jd15	**BBB+**			X	BE	[2]Z100	....	....	....	....	....	350	G1	'99	102¼	96⅞	96⅞	7.59	7.59
M-T Nts 'C' 7.64s 2002	[3]jj31	**BBB+**	4/97	BBB	X	BE	NC	....	....	....	....	....	30.0	S1	'95	104½	101	101	7.56	7.56
M-T Nts 'C' 7.68s 2005	[4]jj31	**BBB+**	4/97	BBB	X	BE	NC	....	....	....	....	....	26.0	C5	'95	107	100⅝	100⅝	7.63	7.63
M-T Nts 'C' 6.70s 2007	[5]jj31	**BBB+**	4/97	BBB	X	BE	NC	....	....	....	....	....	100	U1	'95	101⅞	94	94	7.13	7.13
Union Pacific Corp[6]	***55***	***3.04***	***1.95***	***0.64***		***Dc***	***198.0***	***1380***	***2889***	***9-30-99***	***8502***		***18028***	***48.3***						
SF Deb 8½s 2017	Jj15	**BBB–**	5/98	BBB	X	R	102.975	1-14-01	100	....	....	....	200	F1	'87	103⅝	101⅞	101⅞	8.34	8.34
SF Deb 8⅝s 2022	Mn15	**BBB–**	5/98	BBB	X	BE	103.93	(5-15-02)	100	(5-15-03)	....	....	150	F1	'92	108	103	103	8.37	8.37
SF Deb 8.35s 2025	Mn	**BBB–**	5/98	BBB	X	BE	104.12	(5-1-05)	100	(5-1-06)	....	....	275	C5	'95	110⅞	96⅛	96⅛	8.69	8.69
Deb 7s 2016	Fa	**BBB–**	5/98	BBB	X	BE	NC	....	....	....	....	....	250	C5	'96	103⅝	91	91¼	7.67	7.67
Deb 7⅞s 2023	Fa	**BBB–**	5/98	BBB	X	BE	103.37	(2-1-03)	....	....	....	....	150	F1	'93	106⅜	94⅞	96⅛	8.19	8.19
Deb 7⅛s 2028	Fa	**BBB–**	5/98	BBB	X	BE	NC	....	....	....	....	....	250	C6	'98	106¾	89½	89⅞	7.93	7.93
Deb 6⅝s 2029	Fa	**BBB–**			X	BE	[2]Z100	....	....	....	....	....	600	C6	'99	98⅞	83⅞	84½	7.84	7.84
Nts 7s 2000	Jd15	**BBB–**	5/98	BBB	X	BE	NC	....	....	....	....	....	150	F1	'94	102	100¼	100¼	6.98	6.98
Nts 7⅜s 2001	Mn15	**BBB–**	5/98	BBB	X	BE	NC	....	....	....	....	....	150	G1	'95	103⅞	100⅜	100⅜	7.35	7.35
Nts 5.78s 2001	aO15	**BBB–**			X	BE	NC	....	....	....	....	....	225	M7	'98	100⅝	97¾	97¾	5.91	5.91
Nts 7⅞s 2002	Fa15	**BBB–**	5/98	BBB	X	BE	NC	....	....	....	....	....	200	F1	'92	106½	101½	101½	7.76	7.76
Nts 9⅝s 2002	jD15	**BBB–**	5/98	BBB	X	BE	NC	....	....	....	....	....	100	F1	'90	114	106½	106½	9.04	9.04
Nts 6s 2003	mS	**BBB–**	5/98	BBB	X	BE	100	(9-1-00)	....	....	....	....	150	F1	'93	100	95¾	96⅛	6.24	6.24
Nts 6⅛s 2004	Jj15	**BBB–**	5/98	BBB	X	BE	100	(1-15-01)	....	....	....	....	150	C5	'94	100½	96	96¼	6.36	6.36
Nts 7.60s 2005	Mn	**BBB–**	5/98	BBB	X	BE	NC	....	....	....	....	....	425	C5	'95	108¾	100	100	7.60	7.60
Nts 6.40s 2006	Fa	**BBB–**	5/98	BBB	X	BE	NC	....	....	....	....	....	250	C5	'96	102½	94	94¼	6.79	6.79
Nts 6.70s 2006	jD	**BBB–**	5/98	BBB	X	BE	NC	....	....	....	....	....	250	M6	'96	104⅜	94⅜	94½	7.09	7.09
Nts 6⅝s 2008	Fa	**BBB–**	5/98	BBB	X	BE	NC	....	....	....	....	....	300	C6	'98	104¼	93⅜	93⅜	7.10	7.09
Nts 7¼s 2008	mN	**BBB–**	5/98	BBB	X	BE	NC	....	....	....	....	....	250	C5	'96	109	96¾	96¾	7.49	7.49
Nts 7⅜s 2009	mS15	**BBB–**			X	BE	[2]Z100	....	....	....	....	....	150	C6	'99	100¼	97½	97½	7.56	7.56
M-T Nts 'E' 6.34s 2003	[7]mn	**BBB–**			X	BE	NC	....	....	....	....	....	180	C6	'98	101⅜	96⅛	96¼	6.59	6.59
M-T Nts 'E' 6.79s 2007	[8]mn	**BBB–**			X	BE	NC	....	....	....	....	....	300	C6	'98	104¼	94⅜	94⅜	7.19	7.19
Union Pacific Resources Group	***49b***	***10.34***	***9.78***	***d4.89***		***Dc***	***137.0***	***565.0***	***733.0***	***9-30-99***	***2966***		***3906***	***77.6***						
Deb 7.05s 2018	Mn15	**BBB–**	4/99	BBB	X	BE	[2]Z100	....	....	....	....	....	200	S4	'98	93⅜	88⅛	89⅞	7.84	7.84
Deb 7½s 2026	aO15	**BBB–**	4/99	BBB	X	BE	NC	....	....	....	....	....	200	S7	'96	96½	89⅛	92⅞	8.08	8.08
Deb 7.15s 2028	Mn15	**BBB–**	4/99	BBB	X	BE	[2]Z100	....	....	....	....	....	425	S4	'98	92½	86	88⅜	8.09	8.09
Deb 7.95s 2009	Ao15	**BBB–**			X	BE	[2]Z100	....	....	....	....	....	300	C6	'99	101¼	95¼	96⅞	8.21	8.21
Deb[9] 7½s 2096	mN	**BBB–**	4/99	BBB	X	BE	NC	....	....	....	....	....	150	S7	'96	92¼	83⅞	86⅜	8.68	8.68
Nts 6½s 2005	Mn15	**BBB–**	4/99	BBB	X	BE	[2]Z100	....	....	....	....	....	200	S4	'98	97½	93⅞	94¾	6.86	6.86
Nts 7s 2006	aO15	**BBB–**	4/99	BBB	X	BE	NC	....	....	....	....	....	200	S7	'96	99¾	94½	95⅜	7.34	7.34
Nts 6¾s 2008	Mn15	**BBB–**	4/99	BBB	X	BE	[2]Z100	....	....	....	....	....	200	S4	'98	97¼	91¾	92¾	7.28	7.28
Nts 7.30s 2009	Ao15	**BBB–**			X	BE	[2]Z100	....	....	....	....	....	200	C6	'99	99¾	95⅜	95⅝	7.63	7.63
Union Planters	***10***	***2.79***	***3.11***	***2.76***		***Dc***				***9-30-99***	***1133***		***8131***	***63.7***						
Sub Nts 6¼s 2003	mN	**BBB–**			X	R	NC	....	....	....	....	....	75.0	M2	'93	101	94⅜	94⅜	6.62	6.62
Sub Nts 6¾s 2005	mN	**BBB–**			X	BE	NC	....	....	....	....	....	100	S1	'95	103⅜	93⅛	93⅛	7.25	7.25
Union Tank Car[10]	***56a***	***3.25***	***3.10***	***3.82***		***Dc***	***70.70***			***9-30-99***	***1002***		***1661***	***60.3***						
Eq Tr '24' 6.60s 2009	Fa15	**AA–**	7/98	A+	X	BE	NC	....	....	....	....	....	94.3	S1	'94	103⅜	92⅛	92⅛	7.16	7.16
Sr Sec Nts 6.79s 2010	Mn	**AA–**			X	BE	[11]Z100	....	....	....	....	....	100	S4	'99	101	94⅜	94⅜	7.19	7.19

Uniform Footnote Explanations-See Page 260. Other: [1] Gtd by Unocal Corp. [2] Red at greater of 100 or amt based on formula. [3] Due 4-22-02. [4] Due 4-25-05. [5] Due 10-15-07. [6] See Southern Pac Rail. [7] Due 11-25-03. [8] Due 11-09-07. [9] Co may shorten maturity for Tax Event. [10] Subsid of Marmon Indus. [11] Plus Make-Whole Amt.

Individual Issue Statistics / Exchange	Interest Dates	S&P Rating	Date of Last Rating Change	Prior Rating	Eligible	Bond Form	Regular Price	Regular (Begins) Thru	Sinking Fund Price	Sinking Fund (Begins) Thru	Refund/Other Restriction Price	Refund/Other Restriction (Begins) Thru	Outst'g (Mil $)	Underwriting Firm	Underwriting Year	Price Range 1999 High	Price Range 1999 Low	Mo. End Price Sale(s) or Bid	Curr. Yield	Yield to Mat.
Title-Industry Code & Co. Finances (In Italics)	*Ind*	*Fixed Charge Coverage 1996*	*1997*	*1998*		*Year End*	*Million $ Cash & Equiv.*	*Curr. Assets*	*Curr. Liab.*	*Balance Sheet Date*	*L. Term Debt (Mil $)*		*Capital-ization (Mil $)*	*Total Debt % Capital*						
Union Tank Car (Cont.)																				
Nts 7⅛s 2007	Fa	**A**			X	BE	NC	....	....	....	....	....	150	S1	'97	107¼	94¾	94¾	7.52	7.52
Nts 7.45s 2009	Jd	**A**			X	BE	NC	....	....	....	....	....	150	S1	'97	111	96⅞	96⅞	7.69	7.69
M-T Nts 'A' 6.63s 2004	[1]ms	**A**			X	BE	NC	....	....	....	....	....	30.0		'97	103¾	96¾	96¾	6.85	6.85
M-T Nts 'A' 6¾s 2007	[2]ms	**A**			X	BE	NC	....	....	....	....	....	20.0		'97	105⅝	94½	94½	7.14	7.14
M-T Nts 'A' 6.68s 2008	[3]ms	**A**			X	BE	NC	....	....	....	....	....	50.0	M6	'97	105⅛	94⅛	94⅛	7.10	7.10
Union Texas Petroleum	***49a***	***Acq by Atlantic Richfield,see***																		
Sr Nts[4] 8⅜s 2005	Ms15	**A**	7/98	BBB–	X	BE	[5]Z100	....	....	....	....	....	125	G1	'95	113⅜	104¼	104¼	8.03	8.03
Sr Nts[4] 8½s 2007	Ao15	**A**	7/98	BBB–	X	BE	[5]Z100	....	....	....	....	....	75.0	G1	'95	118⅛	105⅝	105⅝	8.05	8.05
M-T Nts 6.70s 2002	[6]jd15	**A**	7/98	BBB–	X	BE	NC	....	....	....	....	....	20.0	S1	'95	103½	99⅛	99⅛	6.76	6.76
M-T Nts 6.81s 2007	[7]jd15	**A**	7/98	BBB–	X	BE	NC	....	....	....	....	....	20.0	S1	'95	105⅞	95¾	95¾	7.11	7.11
Uniroyal Chemical Co, Inc	***14***	***Subsid of CK Witco Corp***																		
Sr[8]Nts 9s 2000	mS	**BBB–**	9/99	B+	X	R	NC	....	....	....	....	....	270	M6	'93	106½	100	102	8.82	8.82
Unisys Corp[9]	***20b***	***1.38***	***1.54***	***4.51***		***Dc***	***374.0***	***2631***	***2507***	***9-30-99***	***951.0***		***2676***	***43.3***						
Sr Nts[8]'B' 12s 2003	Ao15	**BB+**	8/99	BB–	Y	BE	106	(4-15-00)	....	....	....	....	425	Exch.	'96	112½	106½	106¾	11.24	11.24
Sr Nts 11¾s 2004	aO15	**BB+**	8/99	BB–	Y	BE	103.917	(10-15-01)	....	....	....	....	450	B7	'96	116	109¼	109¼	10.76	10.75
Sr Nts[8] 7⅞s 2008	Ao	**BB+**	8/99	BB–	Y	R	103.938	(4-1-03)	....	....	....	....	200	B7	'98	108½	94½	96½	8.16	8.16
United Air Lines[10]	***4***	***4.08***	***4.39***	***3.97***		***Dc***	***1309***	***3734***	***6136***	***6-30-99***	***5066***		***11618***	***47.2***						
Eq Tr '91A 10.11s 2006	Jj5	**BBB**	4/97	BBB–	X	R	[11]Z100	....	100	....	....	....	36.2	M2	'91	115¾	106	106	9.54	9.54
Eq Tr '91A 10.85s 2014	jJ5	**BBB**	4/97	BBB–	X	R	[12]Z100	....	100	(1-5-08)	....	....	62.1	M2	'91	134⅝	113⅞	113⅞	9.53	9.53
Eq Tr '91B 10.11s 2006	Fa19	**BBB**	4/97	BBB–	X	R	[11]Z100	....	100	....	....	....	35.3	M2	'91	116	106¼	106¼	9.52	9.51
Eq Tr '91B 10.85s 2015	Fa19	**BBB**	4/97	BBB–	X	R	[12]Z100	....	100	(2-19-07)	....	....	65.6	M2	'91	134⅝	113⅞	113⅞	9.53	9.53
Eq Tr '91C 9.76s 2006	Mn13	**BBB**	4/97	BBB–	X	R	[12]Z100	....	[13]100	....	....	....	25.4	M2	'91	114⅜	104¾	104¾	9.32	9.32
Eq Tr '91E 9.76s 2006	Mn27	**BBB**	4/97	BBB–	X	R	[12]Z100	....	[13]100	....	....	....	24.9	M2	'91	114⅜	104¾	104¾	9.32	9.32
Eq Tr '91E 10.36s 2012	mN27	**BBB**	4/97	BBB–	X	R	[12]Z100	....	[13]100	(5-27-07)	....	....	35.1	M2	'91	128¾	110⅞	110⅞	9.34	9.34
• Deb 'A' 10.67s 2004	Mn	**BB+**	4/97	BB	Y	R	NC	....	....	....	....	....	370	M2	'94	118	110	110	9.70	9.70
Deb 9⅛s 2012	Jj15	**BB+**	4/97	BB	Y	R	NC	....	....	....	....	....	200	M2	'92	115⅞	103⅛	103⅛	8.85	8.85
• Deb 'B' 11.21s 2014	Mn	**BB+**	4/97	BB	Y	R	NC	....	....	....	....	....	371	M2	'94	120	118⅛	117½	9.54	9.54
Deb 10¼s 2021	jJ15	**BB+**	4/97	BB	Y	R	NC	....	....	....	....	....	300	F1	'91	127⅛	113⅛	113¼	9.05	9.05
Deb 9¾s 2021	fA15	**BB+**	4/97	BB	Y	R	NC	....	....	....	....	....	250	S1	'91	122⅝	108⅛	108⅛	9.02	9.02
Nts 9s 2003	jD15	**BB+**	4/97	BB	Y	R	NC	....	....	....	....	....	150	S1	'91	110⅜	102⅜	102⅜	8.79	8.79
United Cos Financial	***35a***	***4.47***	***3.07***	**....**		***Dc***	***Bankruptcy Chapt 11***				***1026***		***1531***	***67.0***						
Sr Nts 9.35s '99	§mN	**D**	3/99	CCC	Z	BE			Default 5-1-99 int				125	M2	'94	89⅛	15	34½	....	Flat
Sub Nts 8⅜s 2005	§jJ	**D**	3/99	CC	Z	BE			Default 7-1-99 int				150	M2	'97	55¼	2	2½	....	Flat
United Dominion Rlty Tr.	***57***	***1.67***	***1.73***	***1.59***		***Dc***				***9-30-99***	***2177***		***3618***	***60.2***						
Deb 7¼s 2007	Jj15	**BBB**	9/98	BBB+	X	BE	[14]Z100	....	....	....	....	....	125	G1	'97	95¾	90	90⅞	7.98	7.98
Deb[15] 8½s 2024	mS15	**BBB**	9/98	BBB+	X	BE	NC	....	....	....	....	....	150	G1	'94	103¼	90¼	99¼	8.56	8.56
United Healthcare	***30a***	***n/a***	***n/a***	***d10.50***		***Dc***	***1174***	***3623***	***5469***	***9-30-99***	***250.0***		***4807***	***13.5***						
Nts 6.60s 2003	jD	**A**			X		NC	....	....	....	....	....	244	Exch.	'99	100⅜	96½	96½	6.84	6.84
United Illuminating	***72a***	***2.20***	***2.50***	***2.80***		***Dc***	***18.00***	***227.0***	***249.0***	***9-30-99***	***622.0***		***1334***	***62.5***						
Nts 6¼s 2002	[16]jj	**BBB+**	5/99	BBB–	X	BE	[17]Z100	....	....	....	....	....	100	M7	'98	101	96⅛	96⅛	6.50	6.50
Nts 6s 2003	jD15	**BBB+**	5/99	BBB–	X	BE	NC	....	....	....	....	....	100	M7	'98	101⅝	93⅝	93⅝	6.41	6.41
United Parcel Service of Amer	***70b***	***n/a***	***n/a***	***13.78***		***Dc***	***3243***	***6604***	***6170***	***6-30-99***	***2138***		***9355***	***34.6***						
Deb 8⅜s 2020	Ao	**AAA**			X	R	NC	....	....	....	....	....	700	M2	'89	127⅞	108¼	108⅜	7.73	7.73
U.S. Bancorp[18]	***10***	***3.94***	***3.41***	***3.42***		***Dc***				***9-30-99***	***16155***		***23824***	***67.8***						
Sr M-T Nts'J' 6s 2004	Mn15	**A**			X	BE	NC	....	....	....	....	....	200	L3	'99	99¾	95⅝	95⅝	6.27	6.27

Uniform Footnote Explanations-See Page 260. Other: [1] Due 10-3-04. [2] Due 10-3-07. [3] Due 1-15-08. [4] Gtd by Atlantic Richfield. [5] Plus Make-Whole Premium. [6] Due 11-18-02. [7] Due 12-5-07. [8] (HRO)On Chge of Ctrl at 101. [9] Was Sperry Rand Corp. [10] Subsid of UAL Corp. [11] In whole, plus red premium:dates&circum.,as def. [12] In whole,plus red premium:dates&circum.,as def. [13] Prin pyts due,made pro rata among all hldrs. [14] Greater of 100 or amt based on formula. [15] (HRO)On 9-15-04 at 100. [16] Due 12-15-02. [17] Red at greater of 100 or amt based on formula. [18] See First Bank Sys & First Bank N.A.

Title-Industry Code & Co. Finances (In Italics) / Exchange ↓ Individual Issue Statistics	Ind / Interest Dates	Fixed Charge Coverage 1996 / S&P Rating	1997 / Date of Last Rating Change	1998 / Prior Rating	Eligible ↓	Year End / Bond Form	Million $ Cash & Equiv. / Redemption Provisions Regular Price	Curr. Assets / Regular (Begins) Thru	Curr. Liab. / Sinking Fund Price	Balance Sheet Date / Sinking Fund (Begins) Thru	L. Term Debt (Mil $) / Refund/Other Restriction Price	Refund/Other Restriction (Begins) Thru	Capital-ization (Mil $) / Outst'g (Mil $)	Total Debt % Capital / Underwriting Firm	Underwriting Year	Price Range 1999 High	Price Range 1999 Low	Mo. End Price Sale(s) or Bid	Curr. Yield	Yield to Mat.
U.S. Bancorp *(Cont.)*																				
Sr M-T Nts 'J' 6⅞s 2004	jD	**A**			X	BE	NC	....	....	....	....	....	200	L3	'99	100⅛	98⅝	98⅝	6.97	6.97
Sub Deb[1] 7½s 2026	Jd	**A–**			X	BE	NC	....	....	....	....	....	200	G1	'96	114¾	97⅛	99⅞	7.51	7.51
Sub Nts 8⅛s 2002	Mn15	**A–**			X	BE	NC	....	....	....	....	....	150	G1	'92	107⅞	102⅛	102⅛	7.96	7.95
Sub Nts 7s 2003	Ms15	**A–**			X	R	NC	....	....	....	....	....	150	G1	'93	104⅞	99⅛	99⅛	7.06	7.06
Sub Nts 6¾s 2005	aO15	**A–**			X	BE	NC	....	....	....	....	....	300	C5	'95	105⅝	96⅞	96⅞	6.97	6.97
U.S. Banknote[2]	***29a***	***Now Amer Banknote,see***																		
Sr(Sec)Nts[3] 10⅜s 2002	Jd	**CC**	6/99	CCC–	Y	R	101.7292	5-31-00	100	(6-1-00)	....	....	56.5	B7	'92	78	55	63½	16.34	16.33
U.S. Can Corp	***16b***	***2.05***	***0.15***	***0.60***		***Dc***	***32.15***	***230.9***	***161.1***	***10-4-99***	***280.0***		***360.0***	***85.6***						
Sr Sub Nts[3]'B' 10⅛s 2006	aO15	**B**			Y	BE	105.063	(10-15-01)	....	....	....	....	275	Exch.	'96	106½	101	102	9.93	9.93
U.S. Home Corp(New)	***13h***	***1.55***	***2.01***	***1.49***		***Dc***				***9-30-99***	***801.0***		***1361***	***58.9***						
Sr Nts[3] 7.95s 2001	Ms	**BB+**	8/97	BB	Y	BE	NC	....	....	....	....	....	75.0	D4	'96	103	99⅞	100¼	7.93	7.93
Sr Nts[3] 8¼s 2004	fA15	**BB+**			Y	BE	NC	....	....	....	....	....	100	D4	'97	101⅝	92	95⅜	8.65	8.65
Sr Nts[3] 7¾s 2005	Jj15	**BB+**			Y	BE	101.29	(1-15-03)	....	....	....	....	100	S6	'98	99¾	91	93¾	8.27	8.27
Sr Sub Nts 8.88s 2007	fA15	**BB–**			Y	BE	104.44	(8-15-02)	....	....	....	....	125	D4	'97	102½	89½	92¼	9.63	9.62
Sr Sub Nts[3] 8⅞s 2009	Fa15	**BB–**			Y	BE	104.438	(2-15-04)	....	....	....	....	125		'99	101	87¼	91½	9.70	9.70
U.S. Leasing Int'l	***25***	***Now USL Capital,see***																		
Sr Nts[4] 8¾s 2001	jD	**A**	10/97	A+	X	BE	NC	....	....	....	....	....	200	L3	'91	108⅛	102⅝	102⅝	8.53	8.52
Sr Nts 6⅝s 2003	Mn15	**A**	10/97	A+	X	BE	NC	....	....	....	....	....	150	L3	'93	103¼	97⅝	97⅝	6.79	6.79
Sr Nts 5.95s 2003	aO15	**A**	10/97	A+	X	BE	NC	....	....	....	....	....	150	G1	'93	100¾	95⅛	95⅛	6.25	6.26
U.S. Surgical	***43***	***Acq by Tyco Int'l,see***																		
Sr Nts 7¼s 2008	Ms15	**A–**	10/98	BBB–	X	BE	NC	....	....	....	....	....	300	S4	'98	108½	97⅛	97⅛	7.46	7.46
U.S. Timberlands	***50***	***n/a***	***0.95***	***0.72***		***Dc***	***5.74***	***14.00***	***11.40***	***9-30-99***	***225.0***		***329.0***	***68.4***						
• Sr Nts[3] 9⅝s 2007	mN15	**B+**			Y	BE	104.8125	(11-15-02)	....	....	[5]Z109.625	11-15-00	225	S1	'97	103	90	s91½	10.52	10.52
United Technologies	***17***	***7.52***	***9.51***	***10.62***		***Dc***	***1115***	***10316***	***8141***	***9-30-99***	***2110***		***7312***	***22.9***						
Deb[6] 8⅞s 2019	mN15	**A+**	1/92	AA–	X	R	NC	....	....	....	....	....	265	B7	'89	133⅛	112¼	112⅜	7.90	7.90
Deb 8¾s 2021	Ms	**A+**	1/92	AA–	X	BE	NC	....	....	....	....	....	250	S1	'91	132⅜	111⅛	111¼	7.87	7.86
Nts 6.40s 2001	mS15	**A+**			X	BE	NC	....	....	....	....	....	200	S4	'99	100⅜	99½	99½	6.43	6.43
Nts 6⅝s 2004	mN15	**A+**			X	BE	NC	....	....	....	....	....	325	S4	'99	99⅞	97⅞	97⅞	6.77	6.77
Nts 7s 2006	mS15	**A+**			X	BE	[7]Z100	....	....	....	....	....	250	G1	'99	101½	98½	98½	7.11	7.11
Nts 6½s 2009	Jd	**A+**			X	BE	[7]Z100	....	....	....	....	....	400	S4	'99	99¾	94⅛	94⅛	6.91	6.91
Nts 6.70s 2028	fA	**A+**			X	BE	NC	....	....	....	....	....	400	G1	'98	107⅞	88⅝	88¾	7.55	7.55
Nts 7½s 2029	mS15	**A+**			X	BE	[7]Z100	....	....	....	....	....	550	G1	'99	103	97¾	97⅞	7.66	7.66
United Telecommunications	***67b***	***Now Sprint Corp,see***																		
Nts 9¾s 2000	Ao	**BBB+**	4/99	A–	X	R	NC	....	....	....	....	....	250	D4	'90	105	100¾	100¾	9.68	9.68
Nts 9½s 2003	Ao	**BBB+**	4/99	A–	X	R	NC	....	....	....	....	....	200	D4	'91	114¾	106⅝	106⅝	8.91	8.91
United Tel Co(Florida)	***67a***	***Now Sprint-florida,see Sprint Corp***																		
1st DD 7¼s 2004	jD15	**A–**	4/99	A	X	R	NC	....	Z100	....	....	....	50.0	C4	'92	107⅞	99½	99½	7.29	7.29
1st EE 6¼s 2003	Mn15	**A–**	4/99	A	X	R	NC	....	Z100	....	....	....	70.0	D6	'93	103	97¼	97¼	6.43	6.43
1st FF 6⅞s 2013	jJ15	**A–**	4/99	A	X	BE	NC	....	Z100	....	....	....	60.0	L3	'93	108⅜	93	93⅛	7.38	7.38
1st GG 7⅛s 2023	jJ15	**A–**	4/99	A	X	BE	NC	....	Z100	....	....	....	75.0	M2	'93	109	90⅝	90¾	7.85	7.85
1st HH 8⅜s 2025	Jj15	**A–**	4/99	A	X	BE	NC	....	▲100	....	....	....	70.0	D4	'95	122⅞	102⅜	102½	8.17	8.17
United Tel Co (Ohio)	***67a***	***Subsid of Sprint Corp,see***																		
1st BB 6⅝s 2002	aO	**A**	4/99	A+	X	R	NC	....	Z100	....	....	....	60.0	K2	'92	102⅝	98⅜	98⅜	6.73	6.73
1st DD 5⅞s 2000	Jd	**A**	4/99	A+	X	BE	NC	....	Z100	....	....	....	30.0	L3	'93	100¾	99¾	99⅞	5.88	5.88

Uniform Footnote Explanations-See Page 260. Other: [1] (HRO)On 6-1-06 at 100. [2] Was Intl Banknote. [3] (HRO)On Chge of Ctrl at 101. [4] Issued in min denom $100T. [5] Max $78.8M red w/proceeds Pub Eq Off'g. [6] Int(min 8.875%)may be adj for certain events. [7] Red at greater of 100 or amt based on formula.

Title-Industry Code & Co. Finances (In Italics) / Individual Issue Statistics (Exchange)	Ind / Interest Dates	S&P Rating / Fixed Charge Coverage 1996	Date of Last Rating Change / 1997	Prior Rating / 1998	Eligible	Bond Form / Year End	Regular Price / Cash & Equiv. (Million $)	Regular (Begins) Thru / Curr. Assets	Sinking Fund Price / Curr. Liab.	Sinking Fund (Begins) Thru / Balance Sheet Date	Refund/Other Restriction Price / L. Term Debt (Mil $)	Refund/Other Restriction (Begins) Thru	Outst'g (Mil $) / Capital-ization (Mil $)	Underwriting Firm / Total Debt % Capital	Underwriting Year	Price Range 1999 High	Low	Mo. End Price Sale(s) or Bid	Curr. Yield	Yield to Mat.
United Tel Co (Ohio) *(Cont.)*																				
1st EE 6½s 2005	Jd	**A**	4/99	A+	X	BE	NC	....	Z100	....	....	....	35.0	L3	'93	105½	96¼	96¼	6.75	6.75
United Tel Co (Penna)	***67a***	***Subsid of Sprint Corp,see***																		
1st Y 7⅜s 2002	jD	**NR**	8/96	A	X	R	NC	....	Z100	....	....	....	55.0	K2	'92	106¾	100⅝	100⅝	7.33	7.33
UNOVA Inc	***42b***	***n/a***	***n/a***	***5.15***		***Dc***	***3.24***	***1124***	***717.0***	***9-30-99***	***366.0***		***1109***	***41.4***						
Nts 6⅞s 2005	Ms15	**BBB–**			X	BE	[1]Z100	....	....	....	....	....	100	G1	'98	102½	94½	94½	7.28	7.27
Nts 7s 2008	Ms15	**BBB–**			X	BE	[1]Z100	....	....	....	....	....	100	G1	'98	103	91⅝	91⅝	7.64	7.64
Universal Corp	***69c***	***Δ3.65***	***Δ4.61***	***Δ4.41***		***Je***	***82.81***	***1276***	***1029***	***9-30-99***	***202.0***		***1323***	***56.5***						
Nts 9¼s 2001	Fa15	**A–**			X	BE	NC	....	....	....	....	....	100	G1	'91	106¾	102	102	9.07	9.07
Nts 6½s 2006	Fa15	**A–**			X	BE	NC	....	....	....	....	....	100	D4	'96	102⅝	93¼	93¼	6.97	6.97
Univl Foods	***26***	***n/a***	***n/a***	***n/a***		***Sp***	***7.53***	***396.8***	***202.3***	***6-30-99***	***392.0***		***818.0***	***48.8***						
Nts 6½s 2009	Ao	**BBB**			X	BE	NC	....	....	....	....	....	150	G1	'99	99¼	90⅝	90⅝	7.17	7.17
Univl Health Svcs	***30***	***4.76***	***6.47***	***5.45***		***Dc***	***7.09***	***371.0***	***205.5***	***9-30-99***	***400.0***		***1043***	***38.7***						
Sr Nts[2] 8¾s 2005	fA15	**BBB–**	5/98	BB+	X	BE	102.265	(8-15-00)	....	....	....	....	135	D4	'95	105	98⅜	98⅜	8.89	8.89
[3]UNUM Corp	***35a***	***9.39***	***13.65***	***11.37***		***Dc***				***9-30-99***	***1516***		***6986***	***29.3***						
Nts 6¾s 2028	jD15	**A**	7/99	A+	X	BE	[1]Z100	....	....	....	....	....	250	G1	'98	99¼	81⅛	81¼	8.31	8.31
M-T Nts 'B'[4] 7.08s 2024	[5]mn15	**A**	7/99	A+	X	BE	NC	....	....	....	....	....	10.0	M6	'94	104	91⅛	91¼	7.76	7.76
M-T Nts 'C' 7.19s 2028	[6]mn15	**A**	7/99	A+	X	BE	NC	....	....	....	....	....	50.0	G1	'98	104⅞	91	91	7.90	7.90
[7]Upjohn Co	***21a***	***25.43***	***13.91***	***18.60***		***Dc***	***1382***	***4696***	***3246***	***9-30-99***	***339.0***		***6582***	***18.4***						
Nts 5⅞s 2000	Ao15	**AA–**	4/95	AA	X	BE	NC	....	....	....	....	....	200	M6	'93	100⅞	99⅞	100	5.88	5.87
URS Corp[8]	***63***	***4.09***	***5.00***	***5.73***		***Oc***	***19.70***	***680.0***	***293.0***	***7-31-99***	***667.0***		***987.0***	***70.4***						
• Sr Sub Deb[9] 8⅝s 2004	Jj15	**NR**				R	100	....	....	....	....	....	6.46	Exch.	'89	101½	90	92½	9.32	9.32
USA Mobile Communications II	***67g***	***Merged into Arch Commun,see***																		
Sr Nts[10] 9½s 2004	Fa	**B–**	2/99	CCC+	Y	R	104.75	1-31-00	....	....	....	....	125	N3	'94	90	74	81⅝	11.64	11.63
Sr Nts[11] 14s 2004	mN	**B–**	2/99	CCC+	Y	R	107	10-31-00	....	....	....	....	100	M6	'94	104	86	91½	15.30	15.30
USA Waste Services	***52***	***Now Waste Management,see***																		
Sr Nts 6½s 2002	jD15	**BBB**	8/99	BBB+	X	BE	NC	....	....	....	....	....	350	D6	'97	102½	88⅛	92⅜	7.04	7.04
Sr Nts 7s 2004	aO	**BBB**	8/99	BBB+	X	BE	[12]Z100	....	....	....	....	....	300	D6	'97	105⅛	85⅛	90⅛	7.77	7.77
Sr Nts 7⅛s 2007	aO	**BBB**	8/99	BBB+	X	BE	[12]Z100	....	....	....	....	....	300	D6	'97	107⅝	82½	87⅜	8.15	8.15
Sr Nts 7⅛s 2017	jD15	**BBB**	8/99	BBB+	X	BE	[12]Z100	....	....	....	....	....	150	D6	'97	106	73¼	78⅜	9.09	9.09
Sr Nts 7s 2028	jJ15	**BBB**	8/99	BBB+	X	BE	[12]Z100	....	....	....	....	....	600	D6	'98	104⅜	68½	74½	9.40	9.39
USAir,[13]Inc[14]	***4***	***1.86***	***2.90***	***5.18***		***Dc***	***1151***	***2297***	***2457***	***6-30-99***	***1878***		***2048***	***94.9***						
Sr[15]Nts 9⅝s 2001	Fa	**B**	4/98	CCC+	Y	BE	NC	....	....	....	....	....	175	L3	'94	103¾	99⅝	99⅝	9.66	9.66
USEC Inc	***42b***	***n/a***	***n/a***	***n/a***		***Je***	***37.70***	***1192***	***373.7***	***9-30-99***	***500.0***		***1747***	***34.3***						
Sr Nts 6⅝s 2006	Jj20	**BBB**	8/99	BBB+	X	BE	[12]Z100	....	....	....	....	....	350	M2	'99	100	90	90	7.36	7.36
Sr Nts 6¾s 2009	Jj20	**BBB**	8/99	BBB+	X	BE	[12]Z100	....	....	....	....	....	150	M2	'99	99½	86⅞	86⅞	7.77	7.77
USF&G Corp	***35c***	***Acquired by St. Paul Cos, see***																		
Sr Nts 8⅜s 2001	Jd15	**A+**	8/98	BBB	X	BE	NC	....	....	....	....	....	149	M2	'94	106¼	101⅞	101⅞	8.22	8.22
Sr Nts 7⅛s 2005	Jd	**A+**	8/98	BBB	X	BE	NC	....	....	....	....	....	80.0	M2	'95	105⅝	97⅜	97⅜	7.32	7.32
USFreightways[16]	***71***	***3.93***	***12.52***	***14.83***		***Dc***	***6.28***	***352.5***	***387.6***	***10-2-99***	***103.0***		***749.0***	***29.2***						
Gtd Nts 6½s 2009	Mn	**A–**			X	BE	[1]Z100	....	....	....	....	....	100	M2	'99	101¼	92	92	7.07	7.07
USG Corp	***13g***	***2.76***	***6.32***	***11.08***		***Dc***	***273.0***	***972.0***	***476.0***	***9-30-99***	***577.0***		***1114***	***53.5***						
Sr Nts 9¼s 2001	mS15	**BBB+**	6/99	BBB	X	R	NC	....	....	....	....	....	150	Exch.	'94	107⅛	103	103	8.98	8.98
• Sr Nts[17] 8½s 2005	fA	**BBB+**	6/99	BBB	X	R	NC	....	....	....	....	....	150	S1	'95	No Sale		101	8.42	8.41
USL Capital[18]Corp	***25***	***Subsid of Ford Holdings Inc***																		
Sr Nts 6½s 2003	jD	**A**	10/97	A+	X	BE	NC	....	....	....	....	....	250	M2	'93	103½	96¾	96¾	6.72	6.72

Uniform Footnote Explanations-See Page 260. Other: [1] Red at greater of 100 or amt based on formula. [2] (HRO)On Chge of Ctrl at 100. [3] UNUMProvident Corp. [4] Issued in min denom $100T. [5] Due 2-1-24. [6] Due 2-1-28. [7] Merged into & data of Pharmacia & Upjohn. [8] Was Thortec Int'l. [9] Mand offer:red(10%)at 100 when Net Worth low. [10] (HRO)On Chge of Ctrl at 101. [11] (HRO)On Chge of Ctrl at 102. [12] Plus Make-Whole Amt. [13] Was Allegheny Airlines,now US Airways,Inc. [14] Subsid of US Airways Group. [15] Gtd by USAir Group. [16] Was TNT Freightways. [17] Co must offer repurch at 100 on Chge of Ctrl. [18] Formerly U.S. Leasing Int'l,see.

Title-Industry Code & Co. Finances (In Italics)	Ind		1996	1997	1998	Year End	Cash & Equiv. (Million $)	Curr. Assets (Million $)	Curr. Liab. (Million $)	Balance Sheet Date	L. Term Debt (Mil $)		Capital-ization (Mil $)	Total Debt % Capital						
Exchange ↓ Individual Issue Statistics	Interest Dates	S&P Rating	Date of Last Rating Change	Prior Rating	Eligible ↓	Bond Form	Redemption Provisions: Regular Price	Regular (Begins) Thru	Sinking Fund Price	Sinking Fund (Begins) Thru	Refund/Other Restriction Price	Refund/Other Restriction (Begins) Thru	Outst'g (Mil $)	Underwriting Firm	Underwriting Year	Price Range 1999 High	Price Range 1999 Low	Mo. End Price Sale(s) or Bid	Curr. Yield	Yield to Mat.
USLIFE Corp	***35a***	***Acquired by Amer Gen'l Corp, See***																		
Nts 6⅜s 2000	Jd15	AA–	6/97	A+	X	R	NC	....	....	....	....	....	150	B7	'93	101⅜	100	100⅛	6.37	6.37
U S WEST Cap Fndg	***25***	***Now MediaOne Group,see***																		
Deb 6½s 2018	mN15	A–			X	BE	[1]Z100	....	....	....	....	....	400	M5	'98	104¼	85½	85⅞	7.57	7.57
Deb[2] 6⅞s 2028	jJ15	A–			X	BE	[1]Z100	....	....	....	....	....	1500	M2	'98	108⅞	86¾	87⅝	7.85	7.84
• Nts[2] 6⅛s 2002	jJ15	A–			X	BE	[1]Z100	....	....	....	....	....	500	M2	'98	No Sale		94	6.52	6.52
Nts[2] 6¼s 2005	jJ15	A–			X	BE	[1]Z100	....	....	....	....	....	500	M2	'98	104⅝	93⅞	94½	6.61	6.61
Nts[2] 6⅜s 2008	jJ15	A–			X	BE	[1]Z100	....	....	....	....	....	600	M2	'98	106¼	91⅝	91¾	6.95	6.95
U S WEST[3]Communications[4]	***67a***		***5.29***	***5.74***	***5.59***	***Dc***	***66.00***	***2124***	***4729***	***6-30-99***	***4970***		***10774***	***58.6***						
Deb 7½s 2023	Jd15	A+	5/98	A	X	BE	103.3605	(6-15-03)	....	....	....	....	484	S1	'93	107	90⅝	90¾	8.26	8.26
Deb 7¼s 2025	mS15	A+	5/98	A	X	BE	NC	....	....	....	....	....	250	S1	'95	110⅞	90⅞	91	7.97	7.97
Deb 7.20s 2026	mN10	A+	5/98	A	X	BE	103.038	(11-10-05)	....	....	....	....	250	M2	'95	105⅛	86⅝	86¾	8.30	8.30
Deb 8⅞s 2031	Jd	A+	5/98	A	X	BE	105.917	(6-1-01)	....	....	....	....	250	G1	'91	112⅝	101½	102	8.70	8.70
Deb 6⅞s 2033	mS15	A+	5/98	A	X	BE	101.951	(9-15-03)	....	....	....	....	1000	L3	'93	101	82⅞	83⅛	8.27	8.27
Deb 7¼s 2035	aO15	A+	5/98	A	X	BE	101.94	(10-15-15)	....	....	....	....	250	L3	'95	108⅜	87	87⅛	8.32	8.32
Deb 7⅛s 2043	mN15	A+	5/98	A	X	BE	102.74	(11-15-13)	....	....	....	....	250	M2	'93	107⅜	86½	86⅝	8.23	8.22
Nts 6⅜s 2002	aO15	A+	5/98	A	X	BE	NC	....	....	....	....	....	250	L3	'95	104	98¼	98¼	6.49	6.49
Nts 5.65s 2004	mN	A+	5/98	A	X	BE	100.66	(11-1-00)	....	....	....	....	100	S1	'93	100⅞	93⅝	93⅝	6.03	6.04
Nts 6⅝s 2005	mS15	A+	5/98	A	X	BE	NC	....	....	....	....	....	250	S1	'95	107⅝	96½	96½	6.87	6.87
Nts 6⅛s 2005	mN15	A+	5/98	A	X	BE	NC	....	....	....	....	....	150	M2	'93	104⅝	94¼	94¼	6.50	6.50
• Nts 5⅝s 2008	mN15	A+			X	BE	[1]Z100	....	....	....	....	....	320	M5	'98	No Sale		86⅞	6.47	6.48
USX Corp[5]	***49b***		***3.60***	***4.22***	***3.38***	***Dc***	***87.00***	***4002***	***2803***	***9-30-99***	***3497***		***12189***	***35.5***						
Deb 9⅜s 2012	Fa15	BBB–	11/96	BB+	X	R	NC	....	....	....	....	....	200	F1	'92	122¼	109	110	8.52	8.52
Deb 9⅛s 2013	Jj15	BBB–	11/96	BB+	X	BE	NC	....	....	....	....	....	300	M5	'92	120	107⅝	108⅜	8.42	8.42
Deb 9⅜s 2022	Mn15	BBB–	11/96	BB+	X	R	NC	....	....	....	....	....	150	S1	'92	121⅜	108¼	111¾	8.39	8.39
Deb 8½s 2023	Ms	BBB–	11/96	BB+	X	BE	NC	....	....	....	....	....	150	M6	'93	111⅛	102	103⅝	8.20	8.20
Deb 8⅛s 2023	jJ15	BBB–	11/96	BB+	X	BE	NC	....	....	....	....	....	250	F1	'93	107¼	98¼	99⅞	8.14	8.13
Nts 9.80s 2001	jJ	BBB–	11/96	BB+	X	R	NC	....	....	....	....	....	250	G1	'91	108⅞	103¾	103¾	9.45	9.44
Nts 9⅝s 2003	fA15	BBB–	11/96	BB+	X	R	NC	....	....	....	....	....	150	F1	'91	113½	106⅜	106⅜	9.05	9.05
Nts 7.20s 2004	Fa15	BBB–	11/96	BB+	X	BE	NC	....	....	....	....	....	300	S1	'94	103¾	98⅝	98⅝	7.30	7.30
Nts 6.65s 2006	Fa	BBB–			X	BE	NC	....	....	....	....	....	300	M5	'99	99¾	94⅝	94⅝	7.03	7.03
Nts 6.85s 2008	Ms	BBB–			X	BE	NC	....	....	....	....	....	400	G1	'98	101⅛	94⅛	94⅛	7.28	7.28
UtiliCorp United	***75***		***1.70***	***2.84***	***1.96***	***Dc***	***181.0***	***3302***	***3510***	***9-30-99***	***2234***		***4335***	***60.4***						
Sr Nts 7s 2004	jJ15	BBB			X	BE	NC	....	....	....	....	....	250	G1	'99	100⅞	96⅝	96⅝	7.24	7.24
Sr Nts 6⅞s 2004	aO	BBB			X	BE	NC	....	....	....	....	....	150	G1	'97	105	96	96	7.16	7.16
Sr Nts[6] 6⅜s 2005	Jd	BBB			X	R	NC	....	....	....	....	....	100	D6	'95	103	99⅞	99⅞	6.38	6.38
Sr Nts[7] 6.70s 2006	aO15	BBB			X	BE	NC	....	....	....	....	....	100	D6	'96	104½	98⅞	98⅞	6.78	6.78
Sr Nts 8.20s 2007	Jj15	BBB			X	R	NC	....	....	....	....	....	130	S7	'92	113¾	99⅞	99⅞	8.21	8.21
Sr Nts 10½s 2020	jD	BBB	10/91	BBB–	X	R	104.80	(12-1-00)	....	....	....	....	55.9	D6	'90	111½	107⅛	107⅛	9.80	9.80
Sr Nts 9s 2021	mN15	BBB			X	R	104.027	(11-15-01)	....	....	....	....	150	G1	'91	110½	101¾	101⅞	8.83	8.83
Sr Nts 8s 2023	Ms	BBB			X	R	103.752	(3-1-03)	....	....	....	....	125	G1	'93	105⅞	91	91⅛	8.78	8.78
Valassis Communications[8]	***54***		***2.79***	***4.00***	***4.96***	***Dc***	***7.70***	***147.0***	***160.0***	***9-30-99***	***304.0***		***76.60***	***397.0***						
Sr Nts 9.55s 2003	jD	BBB–	12/98	BB+	X	R	NC	....	....	....	....	....	255	S1	'94	114⅜	105¾	105¾	9.03	9.03
Valero Energy	***49g***		***n/a***	***n/a***	***n/a***	***Dc***	***7.82***	***862.0***	***702.0***	***9-30-99***	***846.0***		***1934***	***44.4***						
Nts 7⅜s 2006	Ms15	BBB–			X	BE	[1]Z100	....	....	....	....	....	300	M5	'99	101½	94⅞	94⅞	7.77	7.77

Uniform Footnote Explanations-See Page 260. Other: [1] Red at greater of 100 or amt based on formula. [2] Gtd by US WEST, Inc. [3] Subsid of US WEST Commun Gr. [4] See Mountain St T&T,No'w'n Bell & Pac NW Bell. [5] Was U.S. Steel,See Marathon Oil. [6] (HRO)On 6-1-00 at 100. [7] (HRO)On 10-15-01 at 100. [8] Was Valassis Inserts.

Title-Industry Code & Co. Finances (In Italics) / Individual Issue Statistics (Exchange)	Ind / Interest Dates	Fixed Charge Coverage 1996 / S&P Rating	1997 / Date of Last Rating Change	1998 / Prior Rating	Eligible	Year End / Bond Form	Million $ Cash & Equiv. / Redemption Provisions: Regular Price	Million $ Curr. Assets / Regular (Begins) Thru	Million $ Curr. Liab. / Sinking Fund Price	Balance Sheet Date / Sinking Fund (Begins) Thru	L. Term Debt (Mil $) / Refund/Other Restriction Price	Refund/Other Restriction (Begins) Thru	Capital-ization (Mil $) / Outst'g (Mil $)	Total Debt % Capital / Underwriting Firm	Underwriting Year	Price Range 1999 High	Price Range 1999 Low	Mo. End Price Sale(s) or Bid	Curr. Yield	Yield to Mat.
Vanguard Cellular Sys	***67g***	***Acq by AT&T Corp,see***																		
Sr[1]Deb 9⅜s 2006	Ao15	B+			Y	BE	104.69	(4-15-01)	....	....	....	....	200	S1	'96	112	109	112	8.37	8.37
Vastar Resources	***49b***	***5.07***	***5.91***	***1.85***		***Dc***	***10.50***	***323.4***	***268.6***	***9-30-99***	***1068***		***1904***	***67.7***						
Nts 8¾s 2005	Fa	BBB+	8/97	BBB	X	BE	NC	....	....	....	....	....	150	G1	'95	113⅜	105½	105½	8.29	8.29
Nts 6½s 2009	Ao	BBB+			X	BE	NC	....	....	....	....	....	300	C6	'99	103½	92⅞	92⅞	7.00	7.00
M-T Nts 'A' 6.95s 2006	[2]jd15	BBB+	8/97	BBB	X	BE	NC	....	....	....	....	....	75.0	L3	'96	105⅛	96¼	96¼	7.22	7.22
M-T Nts 'A' 6.96s 2007	[3]jd15	BBB+	8/97	BBB	X	BE	NC	....	....	....	....	....	75.0	M2	'97	105¼	96⅛	96⅛	7.24	7.24
M-T Nts 'A' 6.39s 2008	[4]jd15	BBB+			X	BE	NC	....	....	....	....	....	50.0	M2	'98	101½	92⅝	92⅝	6.90	6.90
Veritas DGC Inc	***49e***	***△5.17***	***△14.69***	***△3.39***		***Jl***	***35.30***	***174.9***	***78.03***	***10-31-99***	***130.0***		***451.0***	***29.9***						
Sr Nts[1] 9¾s 2003	aO15	BB+	2/98	BB	Y	BE	104.875	(10-15-00)	....	....	....	....	75.0	D4	'96	104¼	98½	101½	9.61	9.61
Vesta Insurance Group	***35c***	***8.48***	***10.31***	***d7.43***		***Dc***				***9-30-99***	***98.30***		***315.0***	***48.9***						
Sr Deb 8¾s 2025	jJ15	BBB−	6/98	BBB+	X	BE	NC	....	....	....	....	....	100	M6	'95	93	58⅜	58⅞	14.86	14.85
V.F. Corp	***68c***	***9.06***	***12.70***	***11.20***		***Dc***	***81.78***	***2071***	***1283***	***10-2-99***	***523.0***		***2713***	***19.3***						
Nts 9½s 2001	Mn	A−	10/92	BBB+	X	R	NC	....	....	....	....	....	100	G1	'91	108½	103¼	103¼	9.20	9.20
Nts 6⅝s 2003	Ms15	A−			X	R	100	(3-15-00)	....	....	....	....	100	G1	'93	101½	98¼	98⅜	6.73	6.73
Nts 6¾s 2005	Jd	A−			X	BE	NC	....	....	....	....	....	100	G1	'95	106	97⅛	97⅛	6.95	6.95
Deb 9¼s 2022	Mn	A−	10/92	BBB+	X	R	104.52	(5-1-02)	....	....	....	....	100	G1	'92	115⅝	107	107⅜	8.61	8.61
Viacom Inc[5]	***12***	***1.68***	***2.56***	***1.22***		***Dc***	***674.0***	***4982***	***4185***	***9-30-99***	***6142***		***17191***	***36.5***						
◆Sr Deb 7⅝s 2016	Jj15	BBB−	10/98	BB+	X	BE	NC	....	....	....	....	....	200	G1	'95	101	98¼	100	7.63	7.62
◆Sr Nts 6¾s 2003	Jj15	BBB−	10/98	BB+	X	BE	NC	....	....	....	....	....	350	G1	'95	100¾	98⅝	96	7.03	7.03
◆Sr Nts[6] 7¾s 2005	Jd	BBB−	10/98	BB+	X	BE	NC	....	....	....	....	....	1000	B7	'95	109½	98	100	7.75	7.75
Viacom Int'l Inc	***12***	***Subsid of Viacom Inc,see***																		
◆Sr Sub Nts[7] 10¼s 2001	mS15	BB+	10/98	BB−	Y	R	NC	....	....	....	....	....	200	G1	'91	110¼	103¾	104½	9.81	9.81
Vintage Petroleum	***49a***	***2.88***	***3.44***	***d0.38***		***Dc***	***5.94***	***110.3***	***100.6***	***9-30-99***	***652.0***		***946.0***	***71.1***						
Sr Sub Nts[1] 9s 2005	jD15	B+			Y	BE	104.50	(12-15-00)	....	....	....	....	125	S1	'95	101¾	92	99¾	9.02	9.02
Sr Sub Nts[1] 8⅝s 2009	Fa	B+			Y	BE	104.313	(2-1-02)	....	....	....	....	100	S1	'97	99½	90	96¼	8.96	8.96
Sr Sub Nts[1] 9¾s 2009	Jd30	B+			Y	BE	104.875	(2-1-04)	....	....	[8]Z109.75	1-31-02	150	Exch.	'99	105	96	102¼	9.54	9.53
Virginia Electric & Pwr[9]	***72a***	***3.57***	***3.36***	***2.22***		***Dc***	***115.0***	***1731***	***2108***	***9-30-99***	***3487***		***8579***	***48.0***						
1st & Ref '91A 8¾s 2021	Ao	A	11/91	A+	X	R	102.20	(4-1-01)	Z100	....	....	....	100	M2	'91	108⅝	100½	102	8.58	8.58
1st & Ref '92C 8s 2004	Ms	A			X	R	NC	....	....	....	....	....	250	M2	'92	111¾	101⅝	101⅝	7.87	7.87
1st & Ref '92D 7⅝s 2007	jJ	A			X	R	NC	....	....	....	....	....	215	L3	'92	113⅝	100	100	7.63	7.62
1st & Ref '92E 7⅜s 2002	jJ	A			X	R	NC	....	....	....	....	....	155	L3	'92	106⅜	100¼	100¼	7.36	7.36
1st & Ref '93A 7¼s 2023	Fa	A			X	R	100.44	(2-1-03)	Z100	....	....	....	100	L3	'93	104⅝	88⅝	88⅝	8.18	8.18
1st & Ref '93B 6⅝s 2003	Ao	A			X	R	NC	....	....	....	....	....	200	M6	'93	104⅞	98¼	98¼	6.74	6.74
1st & Ref '93C 5⅞s 2000	Ao	A			X	R	NC	....	....	....	....	....	135	F1	'93	100⅞	99¾	99⅞	5.88	5.88
1st & Ref '93D 7½s 2023	Jd	A			X	R	103.16	(6-1-03)	Z100	5-31-03	....	....	200	G1	'93	106⅜	90⅞	91	8.24	8.24
1st & Ref '93E 6s 2001	fA	A			X	R	NC	....	....	....	....	....	100	M2	'93	101⅝	98⅜	98⅜	6.10	6.10
1st & Ref '93F 6s 2002	fA	A			X	R	NC	....	....	....	....	....	100	M6	'93	102½	97½	97½	6.15	6.15
1st & Ref '93G 6¾s 2023	aO	A			X	R	102.77	(10-1-03)	Z100	(10-1-03)	....	....	200	F1	'93	101⅝	83⅝	83¾	8.06	8.06
1st & Ref '94A 7s 2024	Jj	A			X	R	102.82	(1-1-04)	Z100	(1-1-04)	....	....	125	S1	'94	102½	86	86⅛	8.13	8.13
1st & Ref '94B 8⅝s 2024	aO	A			X	R	103.86	(10-1-04)	Z100	(10-1-04)	....	....	200	L3	'94	113⅝	99⅝	99¾	8.65	8.65
1st & Ref '95A 8¼s 2025	Ms	A			X	R	103.48	(3-1-05)	Z100	(3-1-05)	....	....	200	S1	'95	112½	96½	96⅝	8.54	8.54
1st & Ref '97A 6¾s 2007	Fa	A			X	R	102.74	(2-1-02)	Z100	(2-1-02)	....	....	200	M5	'97	105⅜	94⅝	94⅝	7.13	7.13
M-T Nts 'F' 5.73s 2008	[10]jj	A−			X	BE	NC	....	....	....	....	....	120	G1	'98	100	87⅞	87⅞	6.52	6.52
M-T Nts'G' 6.30s 2001	[11]mn	A−			X	BE	NC	....	....	....	....	....	80.0	G1	'99	100⅛	99	99	6.36	6.36

Uniform Footnote Explanations-See Page 260. Other: [1] (HRO)On Chge of Ctrl at 101. [2] Due 11-8-06. [3] Due 2-26-07. [4] Due 1-15-08. [5] See Viacom Int'l Inc. [6] Gtd by Viacom Int'l. [7] Gtd by Viacom Inc. [8] Max $50M red w/proceeds of Pub Eq Off'g. [9] Subsid of Dominion Resources. [10] Due 11-25-08. [11] Due 6-21-01.

Title-Industry Code & Co. Finances (In Italics) / Individual Issue Statistics / Exchange	Ind / Interest Dates	Fixed Charge Coverage 1996 / S&P Rating	1997 / Date of Last Rating Change	1998 / Prior Rating	Eligible	Year End / Bond Form	Million $ Cash & Equiv. / Redemption Provisions: Regular Price	Curr. Assets / Regular (Begins) Thru	Curr. Liab. / Sinking Fund Price	Balance Sheet Date / Sinking Fund (Begins) Thru	L. Term Debt (Mil $) / Refund/Other Restriction Price	Refund/Other Restriction (Begins) Thru	Capital-ization (Mil $) / Outst'g (Mil $)	Total Debt % Capital / Underwriting Firm	Underwriting Year	Price Range 1999 High	Price Range 1999 Low	Mo. End Price Sale(s) or Bid	Curr. Yield	Yield to Mat.
Virginia & Southwestn Ry	***55***	***Sub of Norfolk So'n Ry, see So'n Ry***																		
• 1st 5s 2003	Jj	**NR**			X	C	NC	....	....	....	....	....	1.48		'02	96½	93	92	5.43	5.44
Virginian Ry	***55***	***Asmd by Norfolk & Western Ry,see***																		
• Sub Inc Deb 6s 2008	fA	**AA–**	12/80	BBB+	X	CR	102	7-31-00	101.50	7-31-00	....	....	4.79	Exch.	'58	98	89⅜	89	6.74	6.74
Vulcan Materials	***13a***	***n/a***	***n/a***	***n/a***		***Dc***	***84.62***	***703.5***	***494.7***	***9-30-99***	***688.0***		***1873***	***37.4***						
Nts 2004	Ao	**A+**			X	BE	NC	....	....	....	....	....	250	G1	'99	99⅞	95¼	95¼	....	....
Nts 6s 2009	Ao	**A+**			X	BE	NC	....	....	....	....	....	250	G1	'99	99⅜	90⅜	90⅜	6.64	6.64
Wachovia Corp[1]	***10***	***2.18***	***2.34***	***2.46***		***Dc***				***9-30-99***	***8576***		***14204***	***60.4***						
Sr Nts 6⅝s 2006	mN15	**AA–**	10/98	AA	X	BE	NC	....	....	....	....	....	200	S7	'96	106¾	95⅞	96¼	6.88	6.88
Sub Nts 6⅜s 2003	Ao15	**A+**	10/98	AA–	X	BE	NC	....	....	....	....	....	250	M2	'93	103⅜	97⅞	98⅛	6.50	6.50
Sub Nts 6.80s 2005	Jd	**A+**	10/98	AA–	X	BE	NC	....	....	....	....	....	250	M2	'95	106⅝	97⅞	97⅞	6.95	6.95
Sub Nts 6¼s 2008	fA4	**A+**	10/98	AA–	X	BE	NC	....	....	....	....	....	350	M2	'98	104⅝	92¼	92¼	6.78	6.77
Sub Nts 5⅝s 2008	jD15	**A+**			X	BE	NC	....	....	....	....	....	400	M2	'98	100½	88	88	6.39	6.39
Sub Nts 6.735s 2009	Fa	**A+**	10/98	AA–	X	BE	NC	....	....	....	....	....	250	M2	'94	105¼	92⅝	92⅝	7.27	7.27
Sub Nts 6.15s 2009	Ms15	**A+**			X	BE	NC	....	....	....	....	....	400	S4	'99	100½	91⅛	91⅛	6.75	6.75
Sub Nts[2] 6.605s 2025	Ao	**A+**	10/98	AA–	X	BE	NC	....	....	....	....	....	250	C5	'95	105⅝	95⅞	95⅞	6.89	6.89
Wal-Mart Stores	***59g***	***6.41***	***7.96***	***9.69***		***Ja***	***1435***	***26955***	***28992***	***10-31-99***	***16559***		***40838***	***40.5***						
Deb 7¼s 2013	Jd	**AA**			X	R	NC	....	....	....	....	....	500	G1	'93	116½	98⅜	98⅜	7.37	7.37
Deb 6¾s 2023	aO15	**AA**			X	R	NC	....	....	....	....	....	250	G1	'93	109½	90⅛	90⅜	7.47	7.47
Deb 8½s 2024	mS15	**AA**			X	R	103.7655	(9-15-04)	....	....	....	....	250	G1	'94	118	104¾	106	8.02	8.02
Nts 6½s 2003	Jd	**AA**			X	R	NC	....	....	....	....	....	500	G1	'93	105½	99	99	6.57	6.57
Nts 9.10s 2000	jJ15	**AA**			X	R	NC	....	....	....	....	....	500	G1	'90	106	101½	101½	8.97	8.96
Nts 8⅝s 2001	Ao	**AA**			X	R	NC	....	....	....	....	....	750	G1	'91	107⅝	102¼	102¼	8.44	8.43
Nts 6.15s 2001	fA10	**AA**			X	BE	[3]NC	....	....	....	....	....	1250	L3	'99	100¼	99¼	99¼	6.20	6.20
Nts 6¾s 2002	Mn15	**AA**			X	R	NC	....	....	....	....	....	300	G1	'95	104¾	99⅞	99⅞	6.76	6.76
Nts 6⅜s 2003	Ms	**AA**			X	R	NC	....	....	....	....	....	250	G1	'93	104¾	98¾	98¾	6.46	6.46
Nts 7½s 2004	Mn15	**AA**			X	R	NC	....	....	....	....	....	500	G1	'94	111	102⅛	102⅛	7.34	7.34
Nts[4] 6.55s 2004	fA10	**AA**			X	BE	NC	....	....	....	....	....	1250	L3	'99	101	98⅜	98⅜	6.66	6.66
Nts 5⅞s 2005	aO15	**AA**			X	R	NC	....	....	....	....	....	750	G1	'93	103¾	94⅜	94⅜	6.23	6.23
Nts 8s 2006	mS15	**AA**			X	R	NC	....	....	....	....	....	250	G1	'94	117¼	103¾	104	7.69	7.69
Nts[4] 6⅞s 2009	fA10	**AA**			X	BE	NC	....	....	....	....	....	3500	L3	'99	101⅜	97⅜	97⅜	7.06	7.06
Warner-Lambert	***21a***	***5.73***	***8.01***	***14.23***		***Dc***	***1600***	***5049***	***3378***	***9-30-99***	***1281***		***6097***	***24.8***						
Nts 6⅝s 2002	mS15	**AA**	7/98	AA–	X	BE	NC	....	....	....	....	....	200	G1	'92	105⅜	99⅝	99⅝	6.65	6.65
Nts 5¾s 2003	Jj15	**AA**	7/98	AA–	X	BE	NC	....	....	....	....	....	250	B7	'98	102⅜	97⅛	97⅛	5.92	5.92
Nts 6s 2008	Jj15	**AA**	7/98	AA–	X	BE	NC	....	....	....	....	....	250	B7	'98	105½	93⅜	93⅜	6.43	6.43
Washington Gas Light	***73b***	***△4.80***	***△3.74***	***△3.98***		***Sp***	***26.90***	***250.0***	***285.0***	***9-30-99***	***506.0***		***1332***	***46.5***						
M-T Nts 'C'[5] 6.82s 2026	[6]ms15	**AA–**			X	BE	NC	....	....	....	....	....	25.0	S1	'96	111½	96⅝	96⅝	7.06	7.06
M-T Nts[7] 'D' 6.49s 2027	[8]ms15	**AA–**			X	BE	NC	....	....	....	....	....	30.0	M2	'97	107⅞	94⅝	94⅝	6.86	6.86
M-T Nts 'E' 6.92s 2009	[9]ms15	**AA–**			X	BE	[10]Z100	....	....	....	....	....	50.0	G1	'99	102	95½	95½	7.25	7.25
Washington Mutual[11]	***10a***	***1.39***	***1.45***	***1.61***		***Dc***				***9-30-99***	***52532***		***67288***	***86.8***						
Sr Nts 7¼s 2005	fA15	**BBB+**	7/97	BBB	X	BE	NC	....	....	....	....	....	150	L3	'95	106½	98⅛	98⅛	7.39	7.39
Sr Nts 7½s 2006	fA15	**BBB+**			X	BE	NC	....	....	....	....	....	1000	L3	'99	99¾	98⅞	98⅞	7.59	7.58
Washington Post	***54c***	***n/a***	***n/a***	***56.56***		***Dc***	***47.40***	***379.0***	***416.0***	***10-3-99***	***398.0***		***2051***	***19.4***						
Nts 5½s 2009	Fa15	**AA**			X	BE	Z100	....	....	....	....	....	400	G1	'99	99¼	87⅞	87⅞	6.26	6.26
Washington REIT	***57***	***6.11***	***4.11***	***3.01***		***Dc***				***9-30-99***	***326.0***		***564.0***	***54.1***						
Sr Nts 7⅛s 2003	fA13	**A–**	12/97	BBB+	X	BE	[12]Z100	....	....	....	....	....	50.0	M2	'96	102	97⅞	97⅞	7.28	7.28

Uniform Footnote Explanations-See Page 260. Other: [1] See Central Fidelity Banks. [2] (HRO)On 10-1-05 at 100. [3] Co may red in whole,at 100,for tax law chge. [4] Co may red in whole, at 100, for tax law chge. [5] (HRO)On 10-9-06 at 100. [6] Due 10-9-26. [7] (HRO)On 9-27-07 at 100. [8] Due 9-27-27. [9] Due 7-9-09. [10] Red at greater of 100 or amt based on formula. [11] See Ahmanson(H.F.) & Co,Great West'n Finl. [12] Greater of 100 or amt based on formula.

Title-Industry Code & Co. Finances (In Italics) / Individual Issue Statistics (Exchange)	Ind / Interest Dates	Fixed Charge Coverage 1996 / S&P Rating	1997 / Date of Last Rating Change	1998 / Prior Rating	Eligible	Year End / Bond Form	Million $ Cash & Equiv. / Redemption Provisions: Regular Price	Million $ Curr. Assets / Regular (Begins) Thru	Curr. Liab. / Sinking Fund Price	Balance Sheet Date / Sinking Fund (Begins) Thru	L. Term Debt (Mil $) / Refund/Other Restriction Price	Refund/Other Restriction (Begins) Thru	Capital-ization (Mil $) / Outst'g (Mil $)	Total Debt % Capital / Underwriting Firm	Underwriting Year	Price Range 1999 High	Price Range 1999 Low	Mo. End Price Sale(s) or Bid	Curr. Yield	Yield to Mat.
Washington REIT (Cont.)																				
Sr Nts 7¼s 2006	fA13	A–	12/97	BBB+	X	BE	[1]Z100	....	....	....	....	....	50.0	M2	'96	103	95½	95½	7.59	7.59
[2]Washinton Water Power	***75***	***2.96***	***3.47***	***2.34***		***Dc***	***180.0***	***1350***	***1218***	***9-30-99***	***788.0***		***1535***	***49.0***						
Sec M-T Nts'A'[3] 6.13s 2000	[4]mn	A	7/96	A–	X	BE	NC	....	....	....	....	....	5.00	G1	'93	100¾	99⅞	99⅞	6.14	6.14
Sec M-T Nts'A'[3] 6.15s 2000	[4]mn	A	7/96	A–	X	BE	NC	....	....	....	....	....	15.0	G1	'93	100¾	99⅞	99⅞	6.16	6.16
Sec M-T Nts'A'[3] 6.28s 2002	[5]mn	A	7/96	A–	X	BE	NC	....	....	....	....	....	5.00	G1	'93	102⅛	97¾	97¾	6.42	6.42
Sec M-T Nts'A'[3] 6.32s 2002	[6]mn	A	7/96	A–	X	BE	NC	....	....	....	....	....	15.0	G1	'93	102¼	97¾	97¾	6.47	6.46
Sec M-T Nts'A'[3] 6.28s 2002	[7]mn	A	7/96	A–	X	BE	NC	....	....	....	....	....	5.00	G1	'93	102⅛	97¾	97¾	6.42	6.42
Sec M-T Nts'A'[3] 6¼s 2003	[8]mn	A	7/96	A–	X	BE	NC	....	....	....	....	....	5.00	G1	'93	102⅜	96⅛	96⅛	6.50	6.50
Sec M-T Nts'A'[3] 6¼s 2003	[9]mn	A	7/96	A–	X	BE	NC	....	....	....	....	....	10.0	G1	'93	102⅜	96⅛	96⅛	6.50	6.50
Sec M-T Nts'A'[3] 6.95s 2008	[10]mn	A	7/96	A–	X	BE	NC	....	....	....	....	....	10.0	G1	'93	107¾	95⅜	95⅜	7.29	7.29
Sec M-T Nts'A'[3] 6.89s 2008	[11]mn	A	7/96	A–	X	BE	NC	....	....	....	....	....	10.0	G1	'93	107⅜	95	95	7.25	7.25
Sec M-T Nts'A'[3] 6.67s 2010	[12]mn	A	7/96	A–	X	BE	NC	....	....	....	....	....	5.00	G1	'93	106⅜	92¼	92¼	7.23	7.23
Sec M-T Nts'A'[3] 7.37s 2012	[13]mn	A	7/96	A–	X	BE	NC	....	....	....	....	....	7.00	G1	'93	113⅛	96¾	96¾	7.62	7.62
Sec M-T Nts'A'[3] 7.39s 2018	[14]mn	A	7/96	A–	X	BE	NC	....	....	....	....	....	7.00	G1	'93	108⅝	92⅝	92¾	7.97	7.97
Sec M-T Nts'A'[3] 7.45s 2018	[15]mn	A	7/96	A–	X	BE	NC	....	....	....	....	....	15.5	G1	'93	109¼	93¼	93¼	7.99	7.99
Sec M-T Nts'A'[3] 7.26s 2018	[16]mn	A	7/96	A–	X	BE	103.23	(7-22-03)	....	....	....	....	5.00	G1	'93	104¼	91⅛	91¼	7.96	7.95
Sec M-T Nts'A'[3] 7s 2019	[17]mn	A	7/96	A–	X	BE	103.11	(10-13-03)	....	....	....	....	10.0	G1	'93	104⅛	88⅜	88½	7.91	7.91
Sec M-T Nts'A'[3] 7.53s 2023	[18]mn	A	7/96	A–	X	BE	NC	....	....	....	....	....	6.00	G1	'93	110¾	93⅛	93¼	8.08	8.07
Sec M-T Nts'A'[3] 7.40s 2023	[19]mn	A	7/96	A–	X	BE	103.70	(8-2-03)	....	....	....	....	10.0	G1	'93	105	91¼	91⅜	8.10	8.10
Sec M-T Nts'A'[3] 7.18s 2023	[20]mn	A	7/96	A–	X	BE	NC	....	....	....	....	....	10.0	G1	'93	106½	89⅜	89½	8.02	8.02
Sec M-T Nts'A'[3] 7.30s 2023	[20]mn	A	7/96	A–	X	BE	103.65	(8-12-03)	....	....	....	....	20.0	G1	'93	104¼	90¼	90⅜	8.08	8.08
Sec M-T Nts'A'[3] 7.06s 2023	[21]mn	A	7/96	A–	X	BE	103.53	(10-13-03)	....	....	....	....	5.00	G1	'93	105	88⅛	88¼	8.00	8.00
Sec M-T Nts 'B' 6.61s 2002	jj	A	7/96	A–	X	BE	NC	....	....	....	....	....	15.0	G1	'95	103⅛	98½	98½	6.71	6.71
Sec M-T Nts'B'[3] 7.89s 2006	[22]fa	A	7/96	A–	X	BE	NC	....	....	....	....	....	26.0	G1	'94	112¾	100⅞	100⅞	7.82	7.82
M-T Nts 'C' 6.88s 2028	[23]ao	A–			X	BE	NC	....	....	....	....	....	20.0	M2	'98	102⅝	85¼	85⅜	8.06	8.06
M-T Nts 'C' 6.06s 2008	[24]ao	A–			X	BE	NC	....	....	....	....	....	25.0	M7	'98	100⅜	88⅝	88⅝	6.84	6.84
Waste[25]Management[26]	***53***	***4.34***	***d1.19***	***3.93***		***Dc***	***222.0***	***4797***	***5883***	***9-30-99***	***8713***		***15161***	***68.8***						
Deb 8¾s 2018	Mn	BBB	8/99	BBB+	X	R	100	(5-1-08)	....	....	....	....	250	M2	'88	114⅛	81⅞	84⅛	10.40	10.40
Deb 7.65s 2011	Ms15	BBB	8/99	BBB+	X	BE	NC	....	....	....	....	....	150	M2	'91	112⅜	81	86¼	8.87	8.87
Nts 6⅝s 2002	jJ15	BBB	8/99	BBB+	X	BE	NC	....	....	....	....	....	300	M2	'97	103	91	93¾	7.07	7.07
Step-Up[27]Nts 7.70s 2002	aO	BBB	8/99	BBB+	X	BE	NC	....	....	....	....	....	300	M2	'92	106	92¾	95¾	8.04	8.04
Watson Pharmaceuticals	***21***	***n/a***	***n/a***	***n/a***		***Dc***	***113.6***	***373.7***	***91.99***	***9-30-99***	***150.0***		***1053***	***14.8***						
Sr Nts 7⅛s 2008	Mn15	BBB–			X	BE	[28]Z100	....	....	....	....	....	150	D6	'98	103¾	93	93	7.66	7.66
Watts Industries	***41h***	***△8.20***	***△8.79***	***△8.30***		***Je***	***5.04***	***379.5***	***106.4***	***9-30-99***	***117.0***		***523.0***	***22.8***						
Nts 8⅜s 2003	jD	BBB	9/99	BBB+	X	R	NC	....	....	....	....	....	75.0	D6	'91	111⅛	103⅛	103⅛	8.12	8.12
[29]Weatherford Enterra	***49e***	***4.32***	***7.91***	***5.42***		***Dc***	***21.20***	***852.0***	***608.0***	***9-30-99***	***628.0***		***2584***	***34.3***						
Nts 7¼s 2006	Mn15	BBB+			X	BE	NC	....	....	....	....	....	200	M2	'96	109	95⅜	95⅜	7.60	7.60
Webb (Del) Corp	***38***	***1.02***	***1.19***	***1.08***		***Je***				***9-30-99***	***1108***		***1528***	***72.5***						
• Sr Sub Deb[30] 9¾s 2003	Ms	B–	2/94	B	Y	R	102.4375	2-29-00	....	....	....	....	100	G1	'93	103⅜	96	s99⅛	9.84	9.83
• Sr Sub Deb[31] 9s 2006	Fa15	B–			Y	R	104.50	2-14-00	....	....	....	....	100	G1	'94	103½	87⅛	s89⅞	10.01	10.01
• Sr Sub Deb[30] 9⅜s 2009	Mn	B–			Y	BE	104.688	(5-1-03)	....	....	....	....	200	S6	'98	100	84	91⅛	10.29	10.29
• Sr Sub Deb[30] 10¼s 2010	Fa15	B–			Y	BE	105.125	(2-15-04)	....	....	....	....	150		'99	105⅝	89⅛	s97⅞	10.47	10.47
• Sr Sub Nts[31] 9¾s 2008	Jj15	B–			Y	R	104.875	(1-15-02)	....	....	....	....	150	D4	'97	103	89½	s93½	10.43	10.42
Webster Fin'l Corp	***10a***	***2.28***	***1.63***	***1.72***		***Dc***				***9-30-99***	***1754***		***2377***	***73.8***						
Sr Nts 8¾s 2000	Jd30	BBB–	2/99	BB+	X	R	NC	....	....	....	....	....	40.0	M2	'93	103	98⅛	100⅞	8.67	8.67

Uniform Footnote Explanations-See Page 260. Other: [1] Greater of 100 or amt based on formula. [2] Now Avista Corp. [3] Issued in min denom $100T. [4] Due 5-8-00. [5] Due 6-28-02. [6] Due 7-8-02. [7] Due 7-9-02. [8] Due 11-19-03. [9] Due 11-24-03. [10] Due 6-3-08. [11] Due 6-4-08. [12] Due 7-12-10. [13] Due 5-10-12. [14] Due 5-11-18. [15] Due 6-11-18. [16] Due 7-23-18. [17] Due 10-14-19. [18] Due 5-5-23. [19] Due 8-2-23. [20] Due 8-11-23. [21] Due 10-13-23. [22] Due 8-25-06. [23] Due 6-5-28. [24] Due 12-10-08. [25] Was WMX Technologies. [26] See USA Waste Services,WMX Technologies. [27] Int incr fr 4.10% on 10-1-94. [28] Red at greater of 100 or amt based on formula. [29] Now Weatherford Intl. [30] (HRO)On Chge of Ctrl at 101. [31] Co must offer repurch at 101 on Chge of Ctrl.

Title-Industry Code & Co. Finances (In Italics)	I n d	Fixed Charge Coverage 1996	1997		1998	Year End	Million $ Cash & Equiv.	Curr. Assets	Curr. Liab.	Balance Sheet Date	L. Term Debt (Mil $)		Capital-ization (Mil $)	Total Debt % Capital						
Exchange ↓ Individual Issue Statistics	Interest Dates	S&P Rating	Date of Last Rating Change	Prior Rating	Eligible ↓	Bond Form	Redemption Provisions: Regular Price	Regular (Begins) Thru	Sinking Fund Price	Sinking Fund (Begins) Thru	Refund/Other Restriction Price	Refund/Other Restriction (Begins) Thru	Outst'g (Mil $)	Underwriting Firm	Year	Price Range 1999 High	Low	Mo. End Price Sale(s) or Bid	Curr. Yield	Yield to Mat.
Weingarten Rlty Inv	***57***	***2.97***	***2.62***		***2.69***	***Dc***				***9-30-99***	***564.0***		***979.0***	***54.1***						
M-T Nts'A' 6.82s 2000	[1]ms15	**A**			X	BE	NC	....	....	....	....	....	25.0	G1	'95	100⅞	99⅞	100	6.82	6.82
M-T Nts[2] 'A' 6.46s 2028	[3]ms15	**A**			X	BE	NC	....	....	....	....	....	25.0	G1	'98	100	91⅛	91⅛	7.09	7.09
Weirton Steel Corp	***66a***	***d0.44***	***0.90***		***0.95***	***Dc***	***75.30***	***425.0***	***256.0***	***9-30-99***	***305.0***		***545.0***	***71.4***						
• Sr[4]Nts 11⅜s 2004	jJ	**B**			Y	BE	105.6875	(7-1-00)	....	....	....	....	[5]125	L3	'96	102⅛	88⅛	98¼	11.58	11.57
• Sr Nts[6] 10¾s 2005	Jd	**B**			Y	BE	105.375	(6-1-01)	....	....	....	....	125		'95	101	82	98	10.97	10.97
Wells Fargo & Co.[7]	***10***	***5.76***	***4.67***		***2.69***	***Dc***				***9-30-99***	***25696***		***43428***	***50.8***						
Nts 6⅝s 2004	jJ15	**A+**			X	BE	NC	....	....	....	....	....	1500	C6	'99	99⅞	97¾	97¾	6.78	6.78
Sub Nts 8¾s 2002	Mn	**A**	11/98	A–	X	BE	NC	....	....	....	....	....	200	G1	'92	109¾	103¼	103¼	8.47	8.47
Sub Nts 8⅜s 2002	Mn15	**A**	11/98	A–	X	BE	NC	....	....	....	....	....	150	S1	'92	108¾	102½	102½	8.17	8.17
Sub Nts 6⅞s 2003	Ao15	**A**	11/98	A–	X	BE	NC	....	....	....	....	....	150	M6	'93	105⅛	99¼	99¼	6.93	6.93
Sub Nts 6⅛s 2003	mN	**A**	11/98	A–	X	BE	NC	....	....	....	....	....	250	S1	'93	102⅝	96½	96½	6.35	6.35
Sub Nts 6⅞s 2006	Ao	**A**	11/98	A–	X	BE	NC	....	....	....	....	....	500	C5	'96	107¾	96¾	96¾	7.11	7.11
Sub Nts 7⅛s 2006	fA15	**A**	11/98	A–	X	BE	NC	....	....	....	....	....	300	S1	'96	109⅜	98	98	7.27	7.27
Sub Nts 6¼s 2008	Ao15	**A**	11/98	A–	X	BE	NC	....	....	....	....	....	200	G1	'98	104⅜	92	92	6.79	6.79
[8]***Wellsford Residential Prop Tr***	***57***	***n/a***	***n/a***		***2.05***	***Dc***				***9-30-99***	***4846***		***10640***	***45.5***						
Nts 9⅜s 2002	Fa	**BBB+**	8/97	BBB	X	BE	Z100	(2-1-00)	....	....	....	....	100	M5	'95	107⅜	102	103⅜	9.07	9.07
Sr Nts 7¼s 2000	fA15	**BBB+**	8/97	BBB	X	BE	NC	....	....	....	....	....	55.0	M2	'95	104¼	98¾	99⅜	7.30	7.29
Sr Nts 7¾s 2005	fA15	**BBB+**	8/97	BBB	X	BE	Z100	(8-24-02)	....	....	....	....	70.0	M2	'95	101¼	100	100⅛	7.74	7.74
Wendy's Int'l	***27b***	***13.72***	***12.12***		***9.05***	***Dc***	***238.6***	***358.5***	***217.7***	***10-3-99***	***447.0***		***1549***	***29.2***						
Deb 7s 2025	jD15	**BBB+**			X	BE	NC	....	....	....	....	....	100	G1	'95	101½	86⅛	88⅝	7.90	7.90
Nts 6.35s 2005	jD15	**BBB+**			X	BE	NC	....	....	....	....	....	100	G1	'95	102⅞	94	94⅛	6.75	6.75
West Penn Power Co.[9]	***72a***	***3.62***	***3.93***		***3.59***	***Dc***	***9.14***	***344.0***	***410.0***	***6-30-99***	***859.0***		***1747***	***56.9***						
1st MM 7¾s 2025	Mn	**A+**			X	R	103.073	(5-1-05)	Z100	....	....	....	30.0	P4	'95	109⅞	95⅜	95½	8.12	8.11
M-T Nts 6⅜s 2004	Jd	**A**			X	BE	NC	....	....	....	....	....	84.0	M2	'99	100	95⅞	95⅞	6.65	6.65
West Texas Utilities[10]	***72a***	***2.49***	***3.18***		***3.49***	***Dc***	***8.40***	***71.40***	***122.0***	***6-30-99***	***264.0***		***560.0***	***54.3***						
1st P 7¾s 2007	Jd	**A**	4/97	A+	X	R	NC	....	....	....	....	....	25.0	M6	'92	112⅞	99½	99½	7.79	7.79
1st Q 6⅞s 2002	aO	**A**	4/97	A+	X	R	NC	....	....	....	....	....	35.0	F1	'92	105⅛	99½	99½	6.91	6.91
1st R 7s 2004	aO	**A**	4/97	A+	X	R	NC	....	....	....	....	....	40.0	F1	'92	107	98¼	98¼	7.12	7.12
1st S 6⅛s 2004	Fa	**A**	4/97	A+	X	R	NC	....	....	....	....	....	40.0	S7	'94	103⅛	95¾	95¾	6.40	6.40
1st U 6⅜s 2005	aO	**A**	4/97	A+	X	R	NC	....	....	....	....	....	80.0	M5	'95	104⅝	94⅝	94⅝	6.74	6.74
1st T 7½s 2000	Ao	**A**	4/97	A+	X	R	NC	....	....	....	....	....	40.0	M6	'95	102½	100¼	100¼	7.48	7.48
Western Atlas Inc	***49e***	***Merged into Baker Hughes,see***																		
Deb 8.55s 2024	Jd15	**A**	8/98	A–	X	BE	NC	....	....	....	....	....	150	M2	'94	119	104⅝	105¼	8.12	8.12
Nts 7⅞s 2004	Jd15	**A**	8/98	A–	X	BE	NC	....	....	....	....	....	250	M2	'94	108	101⅞	101⅞	7.73	7.73
[11]***Western Fin'l Savings Bk***	***10a***	***2.68***	***2.36***		***0.80***	***Dc***				***9-30-99***	***207.0***		***576.0***	***35.9***						
Sub Cap Deb 8½s 2003	jJ	**BB–**	4/98	BB+	Y	BE	100	(7-1-00)	....	....	....	....	104	D6	'93	91½	81⅜	90⅛	9.43	9.43
[12]***Western Inv RE Tr***	***57***	***1.98***	***1.99***		***1.83***	***Dc***				***9-30-99***	***212.0***		***388.0***	***54.1***						
Sr Nts[4] 7⅞s 2004	Fa15	**BBB–**	7/97	BBB	X	BE	NC	....	....	....	....	....	50.0	D6	'94	101½	97	97	8.12	8.12
Sr Nts 7.10s 2006	mS15	**BBB–**			X	BE	[13]Z100	....	....	....	....	....	25.0	P1	'97	96⅝	90¾	90¾	7.82	7.82
Sr Nts 7.20s 2008	mS15	**BBB–**			X	BE	[13]Z100	....	....	....	....	....	25.0	P1	'97	102½	89½	89½	8.04	8.04
Sr Nts 7.30s 2010	mS15	**BBB–**			X	BE	[13]Z100	....	....	....	....	....	25.0	P1	'97	95½	86⅛	86⅛	8.48	8.48
Western Mass. Electric[14]	***72a***	***1.35***	***d0.62***		***0.50***	***Dc***	***0.50***	***100.0***	***214.0***	***9-30-99***	***300.0***		***755.0***	***61.3***						
1st V 7¾s 2002	jD	**BBB–**	5/99	BB+	X	R	100.96	11-30-00	100	....	....	....	85.0	M6	'92	100⅞	98⅝	99⅜	7.80	7.80
1st W 6⅞s 2000	Jj	**BBB–**	5/99	BB+	X	R	NC	....	Z100	....	....	....	60.0	S1	'93	100¾	100	100	6.88	Mat.

Uniform Footnote Explanations-See Page 260. Other: [1] Due 6-1-00. [2] (HRO)On 2-10-06,8-11-08,'10,&'18 at 100. [3] Due 8-11-28. [4] (HRO)On Chge of Ctrl at 101. [5] Incl disc. [6] (HRO)On Chge of Ctrl at 100. [7] See First Interstate Bancorp. [8] Subsid & data of Equity Residential Prop Tr. [9] Subsid of Allegheny Pwr System. [10] Contr by Central & South West Corp. [11] Subsid & data of Westcorp, Inc. [12] Now Western Properties Trust. [13] Plus Make-Whole Amt. [14] Subsid of Northeast Util.

Title-Industry Code & Co. Finances (In Italics) / Individual Issue Statistics (Exchange)	Ind / Interest Dates	Fixed Charge Coverage 1996 / S&P Rating	1997 / Date of Last Rating Change	1998 / Prior Rating	Year End / Eligible	Bond Form	Million $ Cash & Equiv. / Redemption Provisions Regular Price	Curr. Assets / Regular (Begins) Thru	Curr. Liab. / Sinking Fund Price	Balance Sheet Date / Sinking Fund (Begins) Thru	L. Term Debt (Mil $) / Refund/Other Restriction Price	Capital-ization (Mil $) / Refund/Other Restriction (Begins) Thru	Total Debt % Capital / Outst'g (Mil $)	Underwriting Firm	Underwriting Year	Price Range 1999 High	Price Range 1999 Low	Mo. End Price Sale(s) or Bid	Curr. Yield	Yield to Mat.
***Western Mass. Electric** (Cont.)*																				
1st Y 7¾s 2024	Ms	**BBB–**	5/99	BB+	X	BE	104.65	2-29-00	Z100	....	....	....	50.0	M6	'94	105⅛	91¼	91¼	8.49	8.49
1st '97B 7⅜s 2001	jJ	**BBB–**	5/99	BB+	X	BE	[1]Z100	....	....	....	....	....	60.0	M6	'97	102⅝	99⅜	99⅜	7.42	7.42
Western Natl Corp	***35a***	***Merged into Amer Genl,see***																		
Sr Nts 7⅛s 2004	Fa15	**AA–**	10/98	A–	X	BE	NC	....	....	....	....	....	150	M2	'94	106	99¼	99⅝	7.15	7.15
Western Resources, Inc[2]	***75***	***2.94***	***1.34***	***1.70***	***Dc***		***208.9***	***635.9***	***1173***	***9-30-99***	***3366***	***5898***	***67.1***							
1st 7¼s 2002	fA15	**A–**	10/97	BBB+	X	R	NC	....	....	....	....	....	100	D4	'92	105⅛	97¾	98	7.40	7.40
1st 8½s 2022	jJ	**A–**	10/97	BBB+	X	R	103.73	(7-1-02)	....	....	....	....	125	D4	'92	110¾	92½	93⅝	9.08	9.08
1st 7.65s 2023	Ao15	**A–**	10/97	BBB+	X	R	103.72	(4-15-03)	....	....	....	....	100	D4	'93	107¼	85¼	86⅛	8.88	8.88
Sr Nts[3] 6⅞s 2004	fA	**BBB**	11/97	A–	X	R	NC	....	....	....	....	....	370	D4	'97	105	94¾	95¼	7.22	7.22
Sr Nts[3] 7⅛s 2009	fA	**BBB**	11/97	A–	X	R	NC	....	....	....	....	....	150	D4	'97	108¾	90¾	91¾	7.77	7.76
Western Wireless	***67f***	***d1.91***	***d1.57***	***d0.88***	***Dc***		***8.86***	***107.5***	***83.35***	***9-30-99***	***1195***	***1008***	***119.0***							
Sr Sub Nts[4] 10½s 2006	Jd	**B–**			Y	BE	[5]Z100	5-31-01	....	....	....	....	200	G1	'96	112	103¼	105	10.00	10.00
Sr Sub Nts 10½s 2007	Fa	**B–**			Y	BE	[5]100	1-31-02	....	....	....	....	199	Exch.	'97	112	103¼	105	10.00	10.00
Westinghouse Air Brake	***56b***	***3.19***	***3.04***	***3.32***	***Dc***		***7.49***	***267.0***	***150.1***	***9-30-99***	***414.0***	***299.0***	***122.0***							
Sr Nts[4] 9⅜s 2005	Jd15	**B+**			Y	R	104.688	(6-15-00)	....	....	....	....	100	M6	'95	104¼	98½	100	9.38	9.37
Westinghouse Credit	***25***	***Assmd by Westinghouse Elec,see***																		
[6]Nts[7] 8⅞s 2014	Jd14	**BBB–**	12/98	BB+	X	R	[8]NC	....	....	....	....	....	150	M2	'90	121⅛	104¾	104¾	8.47	8.47
Westinghouse Electric	***23a***	***Merged w/CBS Inc,see CBS Corp***																		
Deb 8⅝s 2012	fA	**BBB–**	12/98	BB+	X	BE	NC	....	....	....	....	....	275	G1	'92	117½	103⅜	105⅝	8.19	8.18
Deb 7⅞s 2023	mS	**BBB–**	12/98	BB+	X	BE	NC	....	....	....	....	....	325	L3	'93	111⅜	96⅜	98¼	8.02	8.01
Nts 8⅞s 2001	Jd	**BBB–**	12/98	BB+	X	BE	NC	....	....	....	....	....	250	L3	'91	106¾	102¼	102¼	8.68	8.68
Nts 8⅜s 2002	Jd15	**BBB–**	12/98	BB+	X	BE	NC	....	....	....	....	....	350	M6	'92	108	102⅛	102⅛	8.20	8.20
Nts 6⅞s 2003	mS	**BBB–**	12/98	BB+	X	BE	NC	....	....	....	....	....	275	L3	'93	105⅛	98⅛	98⅛	7.01	7.01
Westvaco Corp	***50***	***△2.76***	***△2.41***	***△2.51***	***Oc***		***109.0***	***738.0***	***425.0***	***10-31-99***	***1502***	***3815***	***42.8***							
• SF Deb 8⅛s 2007	fA15	**A–**	10/99	A	X	R	100.89	8-14-00	100	....	....	....	24.1	M2	'77	101	100⅜	99½	8.17	8.16
• SF Deb 10¼s 2018	jJ	**A–**	10/99	A	X	R	104.6125	6-30-00	100	....	....	....	100	G1	'88	109	103⅝	104⅜	9.82	9.82
SF Deb 10.30s 2019	Jj15	**A–**	10/99	A	X	R	104.635	1-14-01	100	....	....	....	100	M2	'89	106	105⅜	105⅜	9.77	9.77
SF Deb 10⅛s 2019	Jd	**A–**	10/99	A	X	R	105.0625	5-31-00	100	(6-1-00)	....	....	100	M2	'89	106¾	104¾	104¾	9.67	9.66
SF Deb 8.30s 2022	fA	**A–**	10/99	A	X	R	104.15	(8-1-02)	100	(8-1-03)	....	....	125	M2	'92	112¼	100⅜	100⅜	8.27	8.27
SF Deb 7¾s 2023	Fa15	**A–**	10/99	A	X	R	103.619	(2-15-03)	100	(2-15-04)	....	....	150	G1	'93	110⅛	96⅛	96⅛	8.06	8.06
SF Deb 7s 2023	fA15	**A–**	10/99	A	X	R	103.025	(8-15-03)	100	(8-15-04)	....	....	150	M2	'93	103⅛	89¾	89⅞	7.79	7.79
SF Deb 7.65s 2027	Ms15	**A–**	10/99	A	X	BE	NC	....	100	(3-15-08)	....	....	150	G1	'97	111½	95⅛	95¼	8.03	8.03
SF Deb 7½s 2027	Jd15	**A–**	10/99	A	X	BE	NC	....	100	(6-15-08)	....	....	150	M2	'97	111⅛	94⅞	95	7.89	7.89
Deb 9.65s 2002	Ms	**A–**	10/99	A	X	R	NC	....	....	....	....	....	100	G1	'90	112⅛	105⅛	105⅛	9.18	9.18
Deb 9¾s 2020	Jd15	**A–**	10/99	A	X	R	NC	....	....	....	....	....	100	G1	'90	135½	115⅜	115½	8.44	8.44
Nts 6.85s 2004	mN15	**A–**			X	BE	NC	....	....	....	....	....	200	G1	'99	99¾	97¾	97¾	7.01	7.01
Nts 7.10s 2009	mN15	**A–**			X	BE	NC	....	....	....	....	....	200	G1	'99	99½	95⅞	95⅞	7.41	7.40
Weyerhaeuser Co	***50***	***2.57***	***2.43***	***2.37***	***Dc***					***9-26-99***	***4243***	***9125***	***47.6***							
Deb 8⅜s 2007	Fa15	**A**	8/92	A+	X	R	NC	....	....	....	....	....	150	M6	'87	115	104¼	104¼	8.03	8.03
Deb 7½s 2013	Ms	**A**			X	R	NC	....	....	....	....	....	250	M6	'93	113¼	98⅛	99	7.58	7.57
Deb 7¼s 2013	jJ	**A**			X	R	NC	....	....	....	....	....	250	M6	'93	111⅜	95⅜	96¼	7.53	7.53
Deb 6.95s 2017	fA	**A**			X		NC	....	....	....	....	....	300	M6	'97	104⅛	92⅛	92⅛	7.54	7.54
Deb 7⅛s 2023	jJ15	**A**			X	R	NC	....	....	....	....	....	250	M6	'93	105⅞	91⅞	92⅛	7.73	7.73
Deb 8½s 2025	Jj15	**A**			X	R	NC	....	....	....	....	....	300	M6	'95	122⅝	106¼	106¼	8.00	8.00

Uniform Footnote Explanations-See Page 260. Other: [1] Red at greater of 100 or amt based on formula. [2] Was Kansas P&L,see. [3] Was 1st Mtg. [4] (HRO)On Chge of Ctrl at 101. [5] Plus Make-Whole Amt. [6] (HRO)On 6-14-04 at 100. [7] Assmd by Westinghouse Elec. [8] Red at 100 if less than $10M outstg.

Title-Industry Code & Co. Finances (In Italics) / Individual Issue Statistics (Exchange ↓)	Ind / Interest Dates	Fixed Charge Coverage 1996 / S&P Rating	1997 / Date of Last Rating Change	1998 / Prior Rating	Eligible ↓	Year End / Bond Form	Million $ Cash & Equiv. / Regular Price	Million $ Curr. Assets / Regular (Begins) Thru	Million $ Curr. Liab. / Sinking Fund Price	Balance Sheet Date / Sinking Fund (Begins) Thru	L. Term Debt (Mil $) / Refund/Other Restriction Price	Refund/Other Restriction (Begins) Thru	Capital-ization (Mil $) / Outst'g (Mil $)	Total Debt % Capital / Underwriting Firm	Underwriting Year	Price Range 1999 High	Price Range 1999 Low	Mo. End Price Sale(s) or Bid	Curr. Yield	Yield to Mat.
Weyerhaeuser Co *(Cont.)*																				
Deb 7.95s 2025	Ms15	**A**			X	R	NC	....	....	....	....	....	250	M6	'95	115¾	100⅜	100⅜	7.92	7.92
Deb 6.95s 2027	aO	**A**			X	BE	NC	....	....	....	....	....	300	M6	'97	103¾	89¾	89⅞	7.73	7.73
Nts 9.05s 2003	Fa	**A**	8/92	A+	X	R	NC	....	....	....	....	....	200	M6	'91	111⅞	104¾	104¾	8.64	8.64
[1]***Wheeling Pittsburgh***	***66b***	***0.46***	***d4.60***	***1.69***		***Dc***	***196.5***	***855.9***	***528.1***	***9-30-99***	***864.0***		***1904***	***76.3***						
• Sr[2]Nts[3] 9⅜s 2003	mN15	**AAA**	3/98	BB–	X	R	102.50	(11-15-00)	....	....	....	....	266	M2	'93	109½	104⅛	s104⅛	9.00	9.00
Whirlpool Corp.	***23d***	***1.68***	***2.02***	***3.17***		***Dc***	***230.0***	***3389***	***3130***	***9-30-99***	***772.0***		***3464***	***49.0***						
Deb 7¾s 2016	jJ15	**BBB+**	4/99	A–	X	BE	NC	....	....	....	....	....	244	G1	'96	114⅜	95⅞	96½	8.03	8.03
Nts 9½s 2000	Jd15	**BBB+**	4/99	A–	X	R	NC	....	....	....	....	....	200	G1	'90	105⅝	101¼	101¼	9.38	9.38
Nts 9s 2003	Ms	**BBB+**	4/99	A–	X	R	NC	....	....	....	....	....	200	G1	'91	112½	104⅜	104⅜	8.62	8.62
Nts 9.10s 2008	Fa	**BBB+**	4/99	A–	X	R	NC	....	....	....	....	....	125	G1	'88	123	107½	107¾	8.45	8.44
Whitman Corp.	***11f***	***4.82***	***2.73***	***4.28***		***Dc***	***117.0***	***516.0***	***707.0***	***10-2-99***	***803.0***		***2325***	***48.8***						
Nts 7½s 2001	fA15	**A–**	2/99	BBB+	X	BE	NC	....	....	....	....	....	75.0	M2	'94	104⅝	100⅝	100⅝	7.45	7.45
Nts 7½s 2003	Fa	**A–**	2/99	BBB+	X	BE	NC	....	....	....	....	....	125	C6	'93	106½	100¾	100¾	7.44	7.44
Nts 6s 2004	Mn	**A–**			X	BE	[4]Z100	....	....	....	....	....	150	C6	'99	100	95	95	6.32	6.32
Nts 6½s 2006	Fa	**A–**	2/99	BBB+	X	BE	NC	....	....	....	....	....	100	M2	'94	104⅛	95⅛	95⅛	6.83	6.83
Nts 8¼s 2007	Fa15	**A–**	2/99	BBB+	X	BE	NC	....	....	....	....	....	9.00	M2	'95	115¼	103¼	103¼	7.99	7.99
Nts 6⅜s 2009	Mn	**A–**			X	BE	[4]Z100	....	....	....	....	....	150	C6	'99	99⅝	91¾	91¾	6.95	6.95
Nts 7⅝s 2015	Fa	**A–**	2/99	BBB+	X	BE	NC	....	....	....	....	....	9.00	F1	'95	109⅛	99½	99⅝	7.65	7.65
Nts 7.29s 2026	mS15	**A–**	2/99	BBB+	X	BE	NC	....	....	....	....	....	100	M2	'96	106⅞	100⅛	100⅛	7.28	7.28
Nts[5] 7.44s 2026	mS15	**A–**	2/99	BBB+	X	BE	NC	....	....	....	....	....	25.0	M2		112⅛	105	100	7.44	7.44
Wickes(Lumber)Inc	***59l***	***1.08***	***1.04***	***1.03***		***Dc***	***0.07***	***278.3***	***92.24***	***9-25-99***	***245.0***		***268.0***	***91.0***						
Sr Sub Nts[2] 11⅝s 2003	jD15	**CCC+**	3/96	B–	Y	R	105.8125	(12-15-00)	....	....	....	....	100	B11	'93	92½	83	85¼	13.64	13.63
Willamette Indus.	***50***	***3.86***	***1.68***	***1.82***		***Dc***	***20.15***	***881.6***	***447.8***	***9-30-99***	***1681***		***3865***	***44.7***						
Deb 6.45s 2005	Fa	**A–**			X	BE	NC	....	....	....	....	....	100	S4	'98	102	96⅛	96⅛	6.71	6.71
Deb 7s 2018	Fa	**A–**			X	BE	NC	....	....	....	....	....	100	S4	'98	102⅛	91⅛	91⅛	7.68	7.68
Deb 9s 2021	aO	**A–**	3/96	A	X	R	NC	....	....	....	....	....	150	G1	'91	125⅜	109⅛	109¼	8.24	8.24
Deb[6] 7.35s 2026	jJ	**A–**			X	BE	NC	....	....	....	....	....	200	G1	'96	108¾	98⅝	98⅝	7.45	7.45
Deb 7.85s 2026	jJ	**A–**			X	BE	NC	....	....	....	....	....	200	G1	'96	116¼	98⅛	98⅛	8.00	8.00
Nts 9⅝s 2000	fA15	**A–**	3/96	A	X	R	NC	....	....	....	....	....	150	S1	'90	106⅛	101¾	101¾	9.46	9.46
Nts 7¾s 2002	jJ15	**A–**	3/96	A	X	R	NC	....	....	....	....	....	100	S1	'92	106¾	101⅝	101⅝	7.63	7.62
Williams Communic	***67f***	***d0.01***	***d6.39***	***d10.25***		***Dc***	***119.0***	***1178***	***622.0***	***9-30-99***	***1915***		***2871***	***67.0***						
Sr Nts[2] 10.70s 2007	aO	**BB–**			Y	BE	[7]Z100	....	....	....	[8]Z110.70	10-1-02	500	M2	'99	106⅛	100	104⅞	10.20	10.20
Sr Nts[2] 10⅞s 2009	aO	**BB–**			Y	BE	[7]Z100	9-30-04	....	....	[9]Z110.875	10-1-02	1500	M2	'99	105¾	99⅛	104½	10.41	10.41
Williams Cos[10]	***73a***	***2.44***	***2.31***	***1.42***		***Dc***	***287.9***	***4256***	***5301***	***9-30-99***	***7773***		***13831***	***69.4***						
Deb 8⅞s 2012	mS15	**BBB–**	2/95	BBB	X	R	NC	....	....	....	....	....	37.0	F1	'92	125⅝	107½	107½	8.26	8.25
Deb 10¼s 2020	jJ15	**BBB–**	2/95	BBB	X	R	NC	....	....	....	....	....	24.9	F1	'90	140¼	119½	119⅝	8.57	8.57
Deb 9⅜s 2021	mN15	**BBB–**	2/95	BBB	X	R	NC	....	....	....	....	....	46.1	L3	'91	129¼	109⅝	109⅞	8.53	8.53
Nts 6⅛s 2001	Fa	**BBB–**			X	BE	NC	....	....	....	....	....	300	S4	'98	100¾	98⅞	99	6.19	6.19
Nts 6.20s 2002	fA	**BBB–**			X	BE	NC	....	....	....	....	....	350	L3	'98	101	97⅜	97½	6.36	6.36
Nts 6½s 2002	mN15	**BBB–**			X	BE	NC	....	....	....	....	....	150	S7	'97	102¼	97⅞	98	6.63	6.63
Nts 6⅝s 2004	mN15	**BBB–**			X	BE	NC	....	....	....	....	....	150	S7	'97	103⅛	96⅜	96⅜	6.87	6.87
Nts 6½s 2006	fA	**BBB–**			X	BE	[4]Z100	....	....	....	....	....	275	L3	'98	102	93⅛	93½	6.95	6.95
Nts 7⅝s 2019	jJ15	**BBB–**			X	BE	[4]Z100	....	....	....	....	....	700	L3	'99	99⅛	95⅛	96	7.94	7.94
Williams Holdings[11] ***of DE***	***73a***	***9.42***	***4.81***	***1.03***		***Dc***	***157.0***	***2619***	***3593***	***3-31-99***	***2839***		***8945***	***50.1***						
Sr Deb 6¼s 2006	Fa	**BBB–**			X	BE	[12]Z100	....	....	....	....	....	250	S1	'96	103⅞	92½	92⅞	6.73	6.73

Uniform Footnote Explanations-See Page 260. Other: [1] Now WHX Corp. [2] (HRO)On Chge of Ctrl at 101. [3] Co may offer repurch on Chge of Ctrl. [4] Red at greater of 100 or amt based on formula. [5] (HRO)On 9-15-08 at 100. [6] (HRO)On 7-1-06 at 100. [7] Plus Make-Whole Amt. [8] Max $175M red w/proceeds of Pub Eq Off'g. [9] Max $525M red w/proceeds of Pub Eq Off'g. [10] See Transco Energy,MAPCO Inc. [11] Subsid of Williams Cos. [12] Greater of 100 or amt based on formula.

Individual Issue Statistics / Exchange	Interest Dates	S&P Rating	Date of Last Rating Change	Prior Rating	Eligible	Bond Form	Redemption Provisions: Regular Price	Regular (Begins) Thru	Sinking Fund Price	Sinking Fund (Begins) Thru	Refund/Other Restriction Price	Refund/Other Restriction (Begins) Thru	Outst'g (Mil $)	Underwriting Firm	Underwriting Year	Price Range 1999 High	Price Range 1999 Low	Mo. End Price Sale(s) or Bid	Curr. Yield	Yield to Mat.
Title-Industry Code & Co. Finances (In Italics)	*Ind*	*Fixed Charge Coverage 1996*	*1997*	*1998*		*Year End*	*Million $ Cash & Equiv.*	*Curr. Assets*	*Curr. Liab.*	*Balance Sheet Date*	*L. Term Debt (Mil $)*		*Capital-ization (Mil $)*	*Total Debt % Capital*						
Williams Holdings of DE *(Cont.)*																				
Nts 6⅛s 2003	jD	**BBB–**			X	BE	NC	....	....	....	....	....	175	C1	'98	99⅞	95¼	95½	6.41	6.41
Nts 6½s 2008	jD	**BBB–**			X	BE	[1]Z100	....	....	....	....	....	250	C1	'98	100⅞	91¾	91¾	7.08	7.08
M-T Nts 'A' 6.91s 2002	[2]ms	**BBB–**			X	BE	NC	....	....	....	....	....	80.0	S1	'97	103¾	99⅛	99⅛	6.97	6.97
M-T Nts 'A' 6.68s 2000	[3]ms	**BBB–**			X	BE	NC	....	....	....	....	....	80.0	S1	'97	101⅜	100	100	6.68	6.68
Wilmington Trust Corp	***10***	***n/a***	***n/a***	***n/a***		***Dc***				***9-30-99***	***168.0***		***704.0***	***23.9***						
Sub Nts 6⅝s 2008	Mn	**A–**			X	BE	NC	....	....	....	....	....	125	S4	'97	103⅝	93¾	93¾	7.07	7.07
Wisconsin Bell [4]Inc[5]	***67a***	***11.98***	***7.53***	***10.54***		***Dc***	***1.90***	***241.0***	***339.0***	***6-30-99***	***291.0***		***926.0***	***33.1***						
Deb 6¾s 2024	fA15	**AAA**			X	BE	102.274	(8-15-03)	....	....	....	....	150	F1	'93	100¾	84¾	84⅞	7.95	7.95
Deb 6.35s 2026	jD	**AAA**			X	BE	NC	....	....	....	....	....	125	L3	'96	106⅝	95½	95½	6.65	6.65
Wisconsin Central Trans.	***55***	***n/a***	***5.38***	***7.32***		***Dc***	***3.62***	***118.5***	***142.2***	***9-30-99***	***331.0***		***805.0***	***41.5***						
Nts 6⅝s 2008	Ao15	**BBB–**			X	BE	[1]Z100	....	....	....	....	....	150	G1	'98	103¾	92⅞	92⅞	7.13	7.13
Wisconsin Electric Power[6]	***75***	***4.10***	***2.51***	***3.46***		***Dc***	***11.50***	***512.0***	***645.0***	***6-30-99***	***1525***		***3627***	***51.9***						
1st 7¼s 2004	fA	**AA+**			X	R	NC	....	....	....	....	....	140	S1	'92	108⅞	100⅝	100⅝	7.22	7.22
1st 7⅛s 2016	Ms15	**AA+**			X	BE	102.76	(3-15-03)	....	....	....	....	100	K2	'93	106¼	93⅜	93⅜	7.63	7.63
1st 7¾s 2023	Jj15	**AA+**			X	BE	102.72	(1-15-03)	....	....	....	....	100	G1	'93	108	94¼	94¼	8.22	8.22
1st 7.05s 2024	fA	**AA+**			X	BE	102.08	(8-1-03)	....	....	....	....	60.0	S1	'93	103¼	86⅝	86⅝	8.14	8.14
1st 9⅛s 2024	mS	**AA+**			X	R	105.25	8-31-00	....	....	....	....	3.44	S1	'89	105⅞	105⅜	105⅜	8.66	8.66
1st 8⅜s 2026	jD	**AA+**			X	R	102.92	(12-1-01)	....	....	....	....	100	G1	'91	109½	99¼	99¼	8.44	8.44
1st 7.70s 2027	jD15	**AA+**			X	BE	102.10	(12-15-02)	....	....	....	....	200	M6	'92	108	93⅜	93⅜	8.25	8.24
Deb 6⅝s 2002	jD	**AA**			X	BE	NC	....	....	....	....	....	150	B7	'99	99¾	98⅞	99	6.69	6.69
Deb 6½s 2028	Jd	**AA**			X	BE	NC	....	....	....	....	....	150	C1	'98	104	83⅞	83⅞	7.75	7.75
Deb 6⅞s 2095	jD	**AA**			X	BE	NC	....	....	....	....	....	100	M6	'95	108½	86	86	7.99	7.99
Wisconsin Gas Co.[7]	***73b***	***5.08***	***4.71***	***3.88***		***Dc***	***5.26***	***106.0***	***90.00***	***6-30-99***	***158.0***		***260.0***	***60.8***						
Deb 6.60s 2013	mS15	**AA–**			X	BE	NC	....	....	....	....	....	45.0	D3	'93	107⅛	90⅝	90⅝	7.28	7.28
Nts 6⅜s 2005	mN	**AA–**			X	BE	NC	....	....	....	....	....	65.0	D3	'95	105⅞	95	95	6.71	6.71
Nts 5½s 2009	Jj15	**AA–**			X	BE	[1]Z100	....	....	....	....	....	50.0	M7	'99	100	87½	87½	6.29	6.29
Wisconsin Natural Gas[6]	***73b***	***Merged into Wisc Elec Pwr,see***																		
Deb 8¼s 2022	jD15	**AA**			X	BE	103.80	(12-15-02)	....	....	....	....	25.0	K2	'92	111⅛	99½	99⅝	8.28	8.28
Wisconson Power & Light	***75***	***Merged to form Interstate Energy***																		
1st V 9.30s 2025	jD	**AA**			X	R	104.66	11-30-00	....	....	®104.36	11-30-00	50.0	G1	'90	105¼	104¾	104⅞	8.87	8.87
1st W 8.60s 2027	Ms15	**AA**			X	R	105.06	(3-15-02)	....	....	....	....	90.0	G1	'92	113	101⅞	102	8.43	8.43
1st X 7¾s 2004	Jd	**AA**			X	R	NC	....	....	....	....	....	62.0	G1	'92	110⅜	101¾	101¾	7.62	7.62
1st Y 7.60s 2005	jJ	**AA**			X	R	NC	....	....	....	....	....	72.0	G1	'92	111⅜	101⅜	101⅜	7.50	7.50
Deb 7s 2007	Jd15	**A+**	2/98	AA–	X	BE	NC	....	....	....	....	....	105	M2	'97	109¾	97⅛	97⅛	7.21	7.21
Deb 5.70s 2008	aO15	**A+**			X	BE	NC	....	....	....	....	....	60.0	M2	'98	101½	89⅜	89⅜	6.38	6.38
[8]Wisconsin Public Service	***75***	***4.64***	***4.72***	***3.48***		***Dc***	***5.62***	***155.0***	***117.0***	***6-30-99***	***376.0***		***946.0***	***43.0***						
1st 7.30s 2002	aO	**AA+**			X	R	NC	....	....	....	....	....	50.0	K2	'92	107⅛	101	101	7.23	7.23
1st 8.80s 2021	mS	**AA+**			X	R	104.40	(9-1-01)	100	(9-1-01)	....	....	60.0	G1	'91	113⅛	103¾	103⅞	8.47	8.47
1st 7⅛s 2023	jJ	**AA+**			X	R	102.705	(7-1-03)	....	....	....	....	50.0	K2	'93	104⅝	89⅛	89¼	7.98	7.98
Wisconsin Telephone Co	***67a***	***Now Wisconsin Bell,see***																		
Deb 4⅜s 2002	Mn	**AAA**			X	CR	100	....	....	....	....	....	20.0	H1	'62	97⅝	94⅝	94⅝	4.62	4.63
[9]Witco Corp[10]	***14***	***1.92***	***2.71***	***4.80***		***Dc***	***14.24***	***615.1***	***349.5***	***6-26-99***	***669.0***		***731.0***	***90.8***						
Deb 7¾s 2023	Ao	**BBB**	9/99	BBB+	X	R	103.776	(4-1-03)	....	....	....	....	110	G1	'93	94¾	81⅝	81¾	9.48	9.48
Deb 6⅞s 2026	Fa	**BBB**	9/99	BBB+	X	BE	NC	....	....	....	....	....	150	M5	'96	91⅝	74	74⅛	9.27	9.27

Uniform Footnote Explanations-See Page 260. Other: [1] Red at greater of 100 or amt based on formula. [2] Due 6-13-02. [3] Due 6-13-00. [4] Was Wisc Tel,see. [5] Subsid of Ameritech Corp. [6] Subsid of Wisc Energy. [7] Subsid of Wicor, Inc. [8] Subsid of WPS Resources. [9] Now CK Witco. [10] See Uniroyal Chemicals Co.

Title-Industry Code & Co. Finances (In Italics) / Exchange, Individual Issue Statistics	Ind / Interest Dates	S&P Rating / Fixed Charge Coverage 1996	Date of Last Rating Change / 1997	Prior Rating / 1998	Eligible	Bond Form / Year End	Redemption Provisions: Regular Price / Million $ Cash & Equiv.	Regular (Begins) Thru / Curr. Assets	Sinking Fund Price / Curr. Liab.	Sinking Fund (Begins) Thru / Balance Sheet Date	Refund/Other Restriction Price / L. Term Debt (Mil $)	Refund/Other Restriction (Begins) Thru	Outst'g (Mil $) / Capital-ization (Mil $)	Underwriting Firm / Total Debt % Capital	Underwriting Year	Price Range 1999 High	Price Range 1999 Low	Mo. End Price Sale(s) or Bid	Curr. Yield	Yield to Mat.
***Witco Corp** (Cont.)*																				
Nts 6.60s 2003	Ao	**BBB**	9/99	BBB+	X	R	NC	....	....	....	....	....	165	G1	'93	101¼	94⅝	94⅝	6.97	6.98
Nts 6⅛s 2006	Fa	**BBB**	9/99	BBB+	X	BE	NC	....	....	....	....	....	150	M5	'96	97½	87¼	87¼	7.02	7.02
***WMX Technologies**[1]*	*53*	*Now Waste Management,see*																		
Nts 6¼s 2000	aO15	**BBB−**	8/99	BBB+	X	BE	NC	....	....	....	....	....	250	D6	'95	100⅝	95¾	97¾	6.39	6.39
Nts 6.70s 2001	Mn	**BBB−**	8/99	BBB+	X	BE	NC	....	....	....	....	....	200	D6	'96	101⅞	94⅛	96⅝	6.93	6.93
Nts 7⅛s 2001	Jd15	**BBB−**	8/99	BBB+	X	BE	NC	....	....	....	....	....	200	M2	'96	102¾	94¼	96⅞	7.35	7.35
Nts 6⅜s 2003	jD	**BBB−**	8/99	BBB+	X	BE	NC	....	....	....	....	....	500	M2	'93	101¾	86⅛	89½	7.12	7.12
Nts[2] 6.65s 2005	Mn15	**BBB−**	8/99	BBB+	X	BE	NC	....	....	....	....	....	200	D6	'95	101⅛	98½	99⅛	6.71	6.71
Nts 7s 2005	Mn15	**BBB−**	8/99	BBB+	X	BE	NC	....	....	....	....	....	100	D6	'95	104⅞	85½	89¼	7.84	7.84
Nts 7s 2006	aO15	**BBB−**	8/99	BBB+	X	BE	NC	....	....	....	....	....	300	M2	'96	105¾	82⅛	87½	8.00	8.00
Nts[3] 7.10s 2026	fA	**BBB−**	8/99	BBB+	X	BE	NC	....	....	....	....	....	450	D6	'96	104⅜	90⅝	92⅛	7.71	7.71
Step-Up[4]Nts 8s 2004	Ao30	**BBB−**	8/99	BBB+	X	BE	NC	....	....	....	....	....	150	M2	'94	108	92½	94¼	8.49	8.49
*[5]**Woolworth Corp**[6]*	*59l*	*4.84*	*8.68*	*0.11*		*Ja*	*63.00*	*1364*	*1186*	*10-30-99*	*313.0*		*1851*	*46.0*						
Deb 8½s 2022	Jj15	**BB**	2/99	BBB−	Y	R	NC	....	....	....	....	....	200	M2	'92	101	65	65	13.08	13.07
Nts 7s 2000	Jd	**BB**	2/99	BBB−	Y	BE	NC	....	....	....	....	....	200	M5	'95	100	94	99⅛	7.06	7.06
WorldCom Inc	*67b*	*Mgr w/MCI Communications,see*																		
Sr Nts 6⅛s 2001	fA15	**A−**	7/99	BBB+	X	BE	[7]Z100	....	....	....	....	....	1500	S1	'98	101¾	98⅞	98⅞	6.19	6.19
Sr Nts 6¼s 2003	fA15	**A−**	7/99	BBB+	X	BE	[7]Z100	....	....	....	....	....	600	S1	'98	103	97¼	97¼	6.43	6.43
Sr Nts 7.55s 2004	Ao	**A−**	7/99	BBB+	X	BE	[8]Z100	....	....	....	....	....	600	S1	'97	108⅝	101¼	101¼	7.46	7.46
Sr Nts 6.40s 2005	fA15	**A−**	7/99	BBB+	X	BE	[7]Z100	....	....	....	....	....	2250	S1	'98	104⅝	96	96⅛	6.66	6.66
Sr Nts 8⅞s 2006	Jj15	**A−**	7/99	BBB+	X	BE	103.32	(1-15-02)	....	....	....	....	667	Exch.	'97	109⅛	104½	104½	8.49	8.49
Sr Nts 7¾s 2007	Ao	**A−**	7/99	BBB+	X	BE	[8]Z100	....	....	....	....	....	1100	S1	'97	113⅜	101⅞	102	7.60	7.60
Sr Nts[9] 7¾s 2027	Ao	**A−**	7/99	BBB+	X	BE	[8]Z100	(4-2-09)	....	....	....	....	300	S1	'97	116⅛	102	102	7.60	7.60
Sr Nts 6.95s 2028	fA15	**A−**	7/99	BBB+	X	BE	[7]Z100	....	....	....	....	....	1750	S1	'98	108¼	90⅝	91¼	7.62	7.62
Worthington Indus	*66g*	*Δ9.17*	*Δ5.35*	*Δ3.51*		*My*	*7.05*	*605.6*	*441.3*	*8-31-99*	*364.0*		*1283*	*42.6*						
Nts 7⅛s 2006	Mn15	**BBB**	5/99	A−	X	BE	NC	....	....	....	....	....	200	S1	'96	105⅞	95⅝	95⅝	7.45	7.45
WPS Resources	*75*	*3.53*	*3.77*	*3.56*		*Dc*	*6.62*	*214.0*	*220.0*	*9-30-99*	*415.0*		*1061*	*40.1*						
Sr Nts 7s 2009	mN	**AA**			X	BE	[10]Z100	....	....	....	....	....	150	E2	'99	99⅝	96⅝	96⅝	7.24	7.24
Xerox Corp	*48*	*4.65*	*5.12*	*5.02*		*Dc*	*106.0*	*12576*	*7690*	*9-30-99*	*12254*		*21661*	*75.1*						
Deb 7.20s 2016	Ao	**A**			X	BE	NC	....	....	....	....	....	250	S1	'96	109⅛	92⅛	92¼	7.80	7.80
Deb 6¼s 2026	mN15	**A**			X	BE	NC	....	....	....	....	....	350	M6	'96	105	94½	95⅝	6.55	6.55
Nts 9¾s 2000	Ms15	**A**	7/90	A+	X	R	NC	....	....	....	....	....	200	S1	'90	105⅛	100⅝	100⅝	9.69	9.69
Nts 8⅛s 2002	Ao15	**A**			X	R	NC	....	....	....	....	....	200	M5	'92	108¼	101⅝	101⅝	8.00	7.99
Nts 5½s 2003	mN15	**A**			X	BE	NC	....	....	....	....	....	600	M7	'98	100⅝	93¼	93¼	5.90	5.90
Nts 7.15s 2004	fA	**A**			X	R	NC	....	....	....	....	....	200	F1	'92	108¼	98¼	98¼	7.28	7.28
M-T Nts 'C'[11] 5⅞s 2037	Jd15	**A**			X	BE	[12]NC	....	....	....	....	....	150	M5	'97	103⅞	99⅜	100½	5.85	5.85
Xerox Credit	*25d*	*1.60*	*1.57*	*1.57*		*Dc*				*6-30-99*	*388.0*		*4578*	*87.9*						
F/R[13]Nts[14] 2048	fA15	**A**	7/90	A+	X	R	[15]Z100	....	....	....	....	....	60.0	G1	'88	99⅝	99½	99⅝	....	....
M-T Nts 'E' 7s 2012	Oct5	**A**			X	BE	*100	....	....	....	....	....	25.0	S7	'97	108	92⅝	92⅝	7.56	7.56
M-T Nts 'F' 5.83s 2000	[16]mn6	**A**			X	BE	NC	....	....	....	....	....	225	C1	'98	100⅜	99⅝	99⅞	5.84	5.84
M-T Nts 'F' 7s 2012	[17]Oct29	**A**			X	BE	*■100	....	....	....	....	....	25.0	S7	'97	101	92⅞	93⅛	7.52	7.52
M-T Nts 'F' 6½s 2013	Jj28	**A**			X	BE	*■100	....	....	....	....	....	25.0	S7	'98	99⅛	89¾	89¾	7.24	7.24
M-T Nts 'F' 7s 2018	Jj8	**A**			X	BE	*■100	....	....	....	....	....	25.0	S4	'97	98⅜	89⅜	89¾	7.80	7.80
*[18]**XTRA, Inc***	*25c*	*2.05*	*2.13*	*2.71*		*Sp*				*6-30-99*	*866.0*		*1231*	*65.1*						
M-T Nts[19]'C'[20] 6.925s 2000	[21]ao	**BBB+**			X	BE	NC	....	....	....	....	....	12.0	G1	'95	102⅛	99⅞	100	6.93	6.92

Uniform Footnote Explanations-See Page 260. Other: [1] Was Waste Management,see. [2] (HRO)On 5-15-00 at 100. [3] (HRO)On 8-1-03 at 100. [4] Int incr fr 6.22% on 4-30-97. [5] Was Woolworth (F.W.) Co. [6] Now Venator Group. [7] Plus Make-Whole Amt. [8] Plus Make-Whole Premium. [9] (HRO)On 4-1-09 at 100. [10] Red at greater of 100 or amt based on formula. [11] (HRO)Ea 6-15 at 100. [12] Co may red at 100 if amt outstanding is $15M or less. [13] (HRO)Min $0.1M ea Aug 15 to 2012. [14] Co may pay int mthly(15th day)/semi-anly fA15. [15] Red only if $5M or less outstdg. [16] Due 5-8-00. [17] Int pd monthly. [18] Gtd by & data of XTRA Corp. [19] Issued in min denom $100T. [20] Gtd by XTRA Corp. [21] Due 8-23-00.

Exchange / Individual Issue Statistics	Interest Dates	S&P Rating	Date of Last Rating Change	Prior Rating	Eligible	Bond Form	Redemption Provisions: Regular Price	Regular (Begins) Thru	Sinking Fund Price	Sinking Fund (Begins) Thru	Refund/Other Restriction Price	Refund/Other Restriction (Begins) Thru	Outst'g (Mil $)	Underwriting Firm	Underwriting Year	Price Range 1999 High	Price Range 1999 Low	Mo. End Price Sale(s) or Bid	Curr. Yield	Yield to Mat.
Title-Industry Code & Co. Finances (In Italics)	*Ind*	*Fixed Charge Coverage 1996*		*1997*	*1998*	*Year End*	*Million $ Cash & Equiv.*	*Curr. Assets*	*Curr. Liab.*	*Balance Sheet Date*	*L. Term Debt (Mil $)*		*Capital-ization (Mil $)*	*Total Debt % Capital*						
***XTRA, Inc** (Cont.)*																				
M-T[1]Nts 'C'[2] 6.68s 2001	[3]ao	**BBB+**			X	BE	NC	....	....	....	....	....	20.0	G1	'95	102⅞	98⅝	98⅝	6.77	6.77
M-T[1]Nts 'C'[2] 8.02s 2002	[4]ao	**BBB+**			X	BE	NC	....	....	....	....	....	12.0	G1	'95	106⅞	101	101	7.94	7.94
M-T Nts[2]'C'[5] 7.28s 2003	[6]ao	**BBB+**			X	BE	NC	....	....	....	....	....	10.0	G1	'95	106¼	98⅞	98⅞	7.36	7.36
M-T[1]Nts 'C'[2] 6¾s 2005	[7]ao	**BBB+**			X	BE	NC	....	....	....	....	....	10.0	G1	'95	103⅜	98¼	98¼	6.87	6.87
M-T Nts[2]'C'[1] 7.22s 2005	[8]ao	**BBB+**			X	BE	NC	....	....	....	....	....	25.0	G1	'95	107⅜	96¾	96¾	7.46	7.46
M-T[1]Nts 'C' 7.52s 2007	[9]jj15	**BBB+**			X	BE	NC	....	....	....	....	....	10.0	G1	'97	110¼	96⅞	96⅞	7.76	7.76
M-T[1]Nts 'C'[2] 7.53s 2007	[10]jj15	**BBB+**			X	BE	NC	....	....	....	....	....	35.0	G1	'97	110⅜	97	97	7.76	7.76
M-T Nts[2]'C'[1] 7.42s 2007	[11]ao	**BBB+**			X	BE	NC	....	....	....	....	....	25.0	G1	'95	109¾	96⅜	96⅜	7.70	7.70
M-T[1]Nts 'C'[2] 7.64s 2009	[12]jj15	**BBB+**			X	BE	NC	....	....	....	....	....	15.0	S7	'97	112⅛	97	97	7.88	7.88
York International	***13b***	***6.14***		***1.71***	***5.17***	***Dc***	***34.34***	***1473***	***968.6***	***9-30-99***	***921.0***		***1146***	***36.3***						
Sr Nts 6¾s 2003	Ms	**BBB+**	6/95	BBB	X	BE	NC	....	....	....	....	....	100	M6	'93	104¾	99	99	6.82	6.82
Sr Nts 6.70s 2008	Jd	**BBB+**			X	BE	[13]Z100	....	....	....	....	....	200	G1	'98	101½	92⅝	92⅝	7.23	7.23
Young Broadcasting Inc.	***12c***	***1.02***		***0.98***	***1.63***	***Dc***	***2.40***	***84.38***	***56.95***	***9-30-99***	***644.0***		***689.0***	***95.5***						
Sr Sub Nts[14] 11¾s 2004	mN15	**B**			Y	R	104.406	11-14-00	....	....	....	....	120	B11	'94	107¾	103¼	104⅜	11.26	11.25
Sr Sub Nts[14] 10⅛s 2005	Fa15	**B**			Y	R	105.063	(2-15-00)	....	....	....	....	125	B11	'95	106⅞	100½	102⅜	9.89	9.89
Sr Sub Nts[14] 'B' 9s 2006	Jj15	**B**			Y	BE	104.50	(1-15-01)	....	....	....	....	125	Exch.	'96	105	96	96¼	9.35	9.35
Sr Sub Nts[14] 'B' 8¾s 2007	Jd15	**B**			Y	BE	104.375	(6-15-02)	....	....	[15]Z108.75	6-15-00	200	Exch.	'97	104½	94¼	94¾	9.23	9.23
Zenith Nat'l Insurance	***35c***	***12.71***		***6.14***	***3.51***	***Dc***				***9-30-99***	***148.0***		***497.0***	***29.8***						
Sr Nts[16] 9s 2002	Mn	**A–**			X	R	NC	....	....	....	....	....	75.0	S1	'92	106⅞	101⅞	101⅞	8.83	8.83
Ziff-Davis ZD	***54e***	***n/a***		***n/a***	***0.64***	***Dc***	***0.49***	***38.60***	***18.10***	***9-30-99***	***1265***		***2900***	***53.3***						
Sr Sub Nts[14] 8½s 2008	Mn	**B**	12/98	B+	Y	BE	104.25	(5-1-03)	....	....	[17]Z108.50	5-1-01	250	M7	'98	102¾	92	102¾	8.27	8.27
ZiLOG, Inc	***23h***	***n/a***		***n/a***	***d1.59***	***Dc***	***47.60***	***118.8***	***66.62***	***10-3-99***	***280.0***		***232.0***	***121.0***						
Sr Sec Nts[14] 'B' 9½s 2005	Ms	**B–**			Y	BE	104.75	(3-1-02)	....	....	[18]Z109.50	3-1-01	277	Exch.	'98	92½	80	91	10.44	10.44
Zions Bancorp	***10***	***2.17***		***2.27***	***2.37***	***Dc***				***9-30-99***	***570.0***		***2540***	***56.2***						
Sub Nts 8⅝s 2002	aO15	**BBB–**	11/93	BB+	X	BE	NC	....	....	....	....	....	50.0	G1	'92	108¾	102⅝	102⅝	8.40	8.40

Uniform Footnote Explanations-See Page 260. Other: [1] Gtd by XTRA Corp. [2] Issued in min denom $100T. [3] Due 11-30-01. [4] Due 3-13-02. [5] Gtd XTRA Corp. [6] Due 8-8-03. [7] Due 7-5-05. [8] Due 8-11-05. [9] Due 5-30-07. [10] Due 6-1-07. [11] Due 8-15-07. [12] Due 6-2-09. [13] Red at greater of 100 or amt based on formula. [14] (HRO)On Chge of Ctrl at 101. [15] Max $66.6M red w/proceeds,Pub Eq Off'g. [16] (HRO)At 100 for Designated Event&Rat'g Decline. [17] Max $87.5M red w/proceeds of Pub Eq Off'g. [18] Max $90M red w/proceeds of Equity Off'g.

Exchange ↓ BONDS Description	Interest Rate	Due	Interest Dates	S&P Rating	Redemption Provisions: Regular	For Sinking Fund	Refund Earliest/ Other	Underwriting: Firm	Price	Year	Outstanding Mil-$ This Issue	Price Range 1988-1998 High	Low	1999 High	Low	Month End Price Sale(s) or Bid	Yield to Maturity
Abitibi-Consolidated Inc Deb	8½s	2029	$fA	BBB−	[1]Z100	....	....	G1	99.45	'99	250	....	....	99⅞	96	96	8.85
Abbey Nat'l 1st Capital B.V. [2]Sub[3]Notes[4]	8.20s	2004	$aO15	AA−	NC	....	....	M2	99.77	'94	500	113⅞	96¾	111⅞	102½	102½	8.00
Abbey Nat'l plc Perp Sub Reset[56]CapSecs	7.35s		$ao15	A+	NC	....	....	S1	99.95	'96	500	110⅞	97½	103¼	93⅞	95½	....
Abitibi-Consolidated Deb	7.40s	2018	$Ao	BBB−	NC	....	....	G1	99.29	'98	100	103¼	91	95⅞	87½	87½	8.46
Abitibi-Consolidated Deb	7½s	2028	$Ao	BBB−	NC	....	....	G1	99.18	'98	250	103⅞	90⅛	95¼	85½	85½	8.77
Abitibi-Consolidated Notes	6.95s	2008	$Ao	BBB−	NC	....	....	G1	99.81	'98	250	101½	97	99¼	91⅜	91⅜	7.61
ABN AMRO Bank N.V.[7] Sub[3]Notes[8]	7.55s	2006	$Jd28	AA−	NC	....	....		99.99	'96	750	109¾	99¾	109⅞	99¾	99⅞	7.56
ABN AMRO Bank N.V.[7] Global Sub[8]Notes[3]	7⅛s	2007	$Jd18	AA−	NC	....	....		99.95	'97	750	107¾	99⅞	108⅛	97¼	97¼	7.33
ABN AMRO Bank N.V.[7] Sub[8]Notes[3]	7s	2008	$Ao	AA−	NC	....	....		99.20	'96	250	107⅛	94½	107⅜	96	96¼	7.27
ABN AMRO Bank N.V.[7] Sub[8]Notes[9]	7.30s	2026	$jD	AA−	[10]100	....	....		97.79	'96	400	104	90	102	90¾	90⅞	8.03
ACE INA Holdings Inc Deb[11]	8⅞s	2029	$fA15	A−	....	....	....	M2	100	'99	100	....	....	114¼	100	100⅞	8.80
ACE INA Holdings Inc Notes[11]	8.20s	2004	$fA15	A−	NC	....	....	M2	100	'99	400	....	....	102⅝	99⅜	100½	8.16
ACE INA Holdings Inc Notes[11]	8.30s	2006	$fA15	A−	NC	....	....	M2	99.78	'99	300	....	....	102½	98¾	99⅞	8.31
Acetex Corp Sr Sec[12]Notes[3]	9¾s	2003	$aO	BB−	±104.875	....	....	Exch.	Exch.	'96	180	104½	91	100½	84	91	10.71
Acindar Industria Argentina [3]Notes[12]	11¼s	2004	$Fa15	B+	[13]105.625	....	....	C5	100	'97	100	110⅜	66¼	82½	66½	79	14.23
AEGON N.V. Sub Notes[3]	8s	2006	$fA15	AA−	NC	....	....	M5	99.09	'94	400	114⅞	94	113⅜	100⅞	100⅞	7.93
AES China Generating Co Ltd [12]Nts[3]	10⅛s	2006	$jD15	BB−	105.063	....	....	M6	99.90	'96	180	109	57¼	69¼	56	67½	14.99
African Development Bank Notes	6¾s	2004	$aO	AA+	NC	....	....	G1	98.28	'92	300	108⅜	88⅞	106	98½	98½	6.85
• African Development Bank Sub Notes ('88)	9¾s	2003	$jD15	AA−	NC	....	....	K2	100	'88	100	100	99¼	No Sale		100	9.75
African Development Bank Sub Notes ('90)	9.30s	2000	$jJ	AA−	NC	....	....	K2	99.55	'90	300	123½	95¼	105¾	101½	101½	9.16
African Development Bank Sub Notes ('91)	7¾s	2001	$jD15	AA−	NC	....	....	G1	99.31	'91	200	115⅜	97	106⅜	101⅞	101⅞	7.61
African Development Bank Sub Notes ('95)	6⅞s	2015	$aO15	AA−	NC	....	....	M2	99.29	'95	400	110⅝	90¾	111⅞	94⅜	94⅜	7.28
Agrium Inc Deb	7.70s	2017	$Fa	BBB	[14]Z100	....	....	M2	99.70	'97	100	112¾	96¼	103⅞	88¾	88⅞	8.66
Agrium Inc Deb[3]	7.80s	2027	$Fa	BBB	[14]Z100	....	....	M2	99.66	'97	125	116⅛	95½	100½	84⅞	85¼	9.15
Agrium Inc Notes[3]	7s	2004	$Fa	BBB	[14]Z100	....	....	M2	99.68	'97	75.0	107	97¼	100⅞	95⅜	95⅜	7.34
Ahold Finance U.S.A., Inc [3]Notes[15]	6¼s	2009	$Mn	A	[16]Z■100	....	....	C1	99.18	'99	500	....	....	99⅛	90¾	90¾	6.89
Ahold Finance U.S.A., Inc [3]Notes[17]	6⅞s	2029	$Mn	A	[16]Z■100	....	....	C1	99.20	'99	500	....	....	99⅛	87⅝	87¾	7.83
[18]Aktiebolaget SKF Sr[3]Notes	7⅝s	2003	$jJ15	BBB+	NC	....	....	M2	99.60	'93	100	108⅛	86½	105	98¾	98¾	7.72
Aktiebolaget SKF Sr Notes[3]	7⅛s	2007	$jJ	BBB+	NC	....	....	M2	99.35	'97	200	108⅞	99¼	104⅛	93⅝	93⅞	7.59
Alberta(Province of) Bonds[19]	4⅞s	2003	$aO29	AA+	NC	....	....		99.65	'98	500	100⅛	98⅛	99⅛	93⅜	93⅜	5.22
Alberta(Province of) Notes	9¼s	2000	$Ao	AA+	NC	....	....	M6	99⅞	'90	500	121¾	95⅞	104¾	100⅝	100⅝	9.19
Alcan Aluminium Ltd Deb	5⅞s	2000	$Ao	A−	NC	....	....	M6	99.39	'93	150	101⅝	89	100⅞	99⅞	99⅞	5.88
Alcan Aluminium Ltd Deb	6¼s	2008	$mN	A−	[1]Z100	....	....	M7	99.47	'98	200	100⅞	98	100⅝	91¼	91¼	6.85
Alcan Aluminium[20]Ltd[21] [22]Deb	9½s	2010	$Jj15	A−	103.494	....	....	M6	98.99	'89	100	121	92⅝	106¾	103½	103½	9.18
Alcan Aluminium Ltd Deb	8⅞s	2022	$Jj15	A−	[23]104.15	....	....	F1	99.42	'92	150	120¾	93⅝	111¼	107¼	107⅜	8.26
Alcan Aluminium Ltd[21] [24]SF[20]Deb[25]	9⅝s	2019	$jJ15	A−	±104.64	[26]100	....	F1	99.65	'89	18.0	121⅜	92	106⅝	104⅝	104⅝	9.20
Alcan Aluminium Ltd Deb	7¼s	2028	$mN	A−	[1]Z100	....	....	M7	99.11	'98	100	101¾	99	101¾	90¾	90⅞	7.98
Algoma Steel Inc 1st Mtg[3]Notes[12]	12⅜s	2005	$jJ15	B	NC	....	....	B11	90.15	'95	[27]306	119⅛	57	102	76	94	13.16
Altos Hornos De Mexico Sr Notes[3]'A'[28]	11⅜s	2002	$§Ao30	D	Default 4-30-99 int			Exch.	Exch.	'97	189	104¼	41	68	33	40	Flat
Altos Hornos De Mexico Sr Notes[3]'B'[28]	11⅞s	2004	$§Ao30	D	Default 4-30-99 int			Exch.	Exch.	'97	11.6	108¾	40	61	31½	41	Flat
Amoco Argentina Oil[29] Gtd[30]Negotiable[3]Oblig[8]	6⅝s	2005	$mS15	AA+	NC	....	....	C2	99.98	'95	100	108¾	94⅞	107½	97⅞	97⅞	6.77
Amoco Argentina Oil Gtd[30]Negotiable[31]Oblig[8]	6¾s	2007	$Fa	AA+	NC	....	....	C1	99.57	'97	100	110⅜	96¼	109⅜	97½	97½	6.92
Amoco Canada Petroleum Co Ltd Gtd[30]Deb	6¾s	2005	$Fa15	AA+	NC	....	....	G1	99.64	'93	300	108⅝	88⅜	107⅛	97¾	97¾	6.90
Amoco Canada Petroleum Co Ltd Gtd[30]Deb	7.95s	2022	$aO	AA+	[32]103.294	....	....	G1	98.64	'92	300	118⅞	92¾	109¾	99⅜	101⅜	7.84
Amoco Canada Petroleum Co Ltd Gtd[30]Deb	6¾s	2023	$mS	AA+	[33]102.742	....	....	G1	98.73	'93	300	108⅞	78	106⅞	95⅜	97	6.96
Amoco Canada Petroleum Co Ltd Gtd[30]Notes	7¼s	2002	$jD	AA+	NC	....	....	G1	99.65	'92	300	111¾	94⅛	106¼	100⅝	100⅝	7.20
Apache Finance Pty Ltd ([34]Gtd)Notes[3]	6½s	2007	$jD15	BBB+	[1]Z100	....	....	S4	99.25	'97	170	102¾	97¾	100¼	92⅛	92⅛	7.06
Apache Finance Pty Ltd ([3]Gtd)[12]Notes[34]	7s	2009	$Ms15	BBB+	NC	....	....	S4	99.34	'99	100	....	....	103⅜	94⅜	94⅜	7.42
APP Int'l Finance Gtd[35]Sec[28]Notes[3]	10¼s	2000	$aO	CCC+	NC	....	....	M6	100	'95	100	104½	53	95	83	94½	10.85
APP Int'l Finance Gtd[35]Sec[28]Notes[3]	11¾s	2005	$aO	CCC+	NC	....	....	M6	100	'95	450	110¼	52	84	60½	84	13.99
Argentina (Republic of) Bonds	9¼s	2001	$Fa23	BB	NC	....	....	M2	99.87	'96	1000	124⅞	74½	102¼	93½	98¾	9.37

Uniform Footnote Explanations-See Page 260. Other: [1] Red at greater of 100 or amt based on formula. [2] Gtd by Abbey Nat'l plc. [3] Co may red in whole,at 100,for tax law chge. [4] Issued in min denom U.S.$100T. [5] Int thru 10-15-06,adj every 5 yrs aft. [6] Red in whole,at 100,on reset dates fr 10-15-06 for tax chge. [7] Chicago Branch. [8] Issued in min denom $100T. [9] Company red in whole,at 100,for tax law chge. [10] Fr On 12-1-06. [11] Gtd by ACE Ltd. [12] (HRO)On Chge of Ctrl at 101. [13] Fr 2-15-02. [14] Greater of 100 or amt based on formula. [15] Gtd by Koninklijke Ahold(Royal Ahold). [16] Plus Make-Whole Amt. [17] Gtd by Koninklijke Ahold N.V.(Royal Ahold). [18] A/K/A SKF AB. [19] Red in whole,at 100,for tax law chge. [20] Co may reset int for certain events. [21] Co may red in whole at 100 if 90% outstg put. [22] (HRO)To 1-15-00 at 100 for certain events. [23] Fr 1-15-02. [24] Terms chge for Designated Event&Rat'g Decline. [25] (HRO)For certain events at 100. [26] Fr 7-15-00. [27] Incl disc. [28] (HRO)On Chge of Ctrl at 100. [29] Argentina Branch. [30] Gtd by Amoco Corp & Amoco Co. [31] Co may red in whole, at 100, for tax law chge. [32] Fr 10-1-02. [33] Fr 9-1-03. [34] Gtd by Apache Corp. [35] Gtd by Asia Pulp & Paper Co Ltd,et al.

Exchange ↓ BONDS Description	Interest Rate	Due	Interest Dates	S&P Rating	Redemption Provisions: Regular	Redemption Provisions: For Sinking Fund	Redemption Provisions: Refund Earliest/ Other	Underwriting: Firm	Underwriting: Price	Underwriting: Year	Out-standing Mil-$ This Issue	Price Range 1988-1998: High	Price Range 1988-1998: Low	1999: High	1999: Low	Month End Price Sale(s) or Bid	Yield to Maturity
Argentina (Republic of) .... Bonds	11¾s	2009	$Ao7	BB	NC	....	....	C1	97.64	'99	1500	....	....	103½	83⅝	100½	11.69
Argentina (Republic of) .... Bonds	11⅜s	2017	$Jj30	BB	NC	....	....	M2	99.42	'97	2000	118⅝	69¾	100¼	82	99½	11.43
Argentina(Republic of) .... Global Bonds	12⅛s	2019	$Fa25	BB	NC	....	....	M5	Unit	'99	1000	....	....	105½	85½	105½	11.49
Argentina (Republic of) .... Spread-Adj[1]Notes	9½s	2002	$mN30	BB	NC	....	....	M2	99.30	'97	500	100⅝	84	100	90¼	98¾	9.62
• Asian Development Bank .... Bonds	8s	2001	$Ao31	AAA	NC	....	....	M2	99.55	'86	56.2	....	....	No Sale		102	7.84
Asian Development Bank .... Global Bonds	5¾s	2003	$Mn19	AAA	NC	....	....	M7	99.34	'98	2000	105⅝	99¼	101½	96⅝	96⅝	5.95
Asian Development Bank .... Bonds[2]	6.22s	2027	fA15	AAA	[3]NC	....	....	M6	100	'97	300	110¾	98⅛	107	89½	96¼	6.46
Asian Development Bank .... Bonds[4]	5.593s	2018	$jJ16	AAA	[5]NC	....	....	M7	99.66	'98	700	105½	99⅝	102⅜	88	96¼	5.81
Asian Development Bank .... Bonds[6]	5.82s	2028	$Jd16	AAA	[7]NC	....	....	M7	99.48	'98	750	105½	91¼	103	90⅝	90⅝	6.42
Asian Development Bank .... Bonds[8]	6⅜s	2028	$aO	AAA	[9]NC	....	....	M7	106.10	'98	410	109⅜	106	109⅜	97¼	98⅛	6.50
Asian Development Bank .... Global Bonds	6¾s	2007	$Jd11	AAA	NC	....	....	G1	99.43	'97	1000	109½	99⅜	109½	97	97	6.96
Asian Development Bank .... Notes	9⅛s	2000	$Jd	AAA	NC	....	....	S5	99.19	'90	300	123	96¾	105⅜	101¼	101¼	9.01
Asian Development Bank .... Notes	8½s	2001	$Mn2	AAA	NC	....	....	S1	99.65	'91	300	119⅞	99	107⅛	102⅜	102⅜	8.30
Asian Development Bank .... Notes[10]	6½s	2002	$mS21	AAA	NC	....	....	L3	98.99	'92	300	107⅛	89⅞	104⅛	99½	99½	6.53
• Australia(Commonwealth) .... Bonds	9⅝s	2006	$Fa	AA+	NC	....	....	M6	99.20	'86	114	114½	100	No Sale		98	9.82
Australia(Commonwealth) .... Bonds	8⅜s	2017	$Ms15	AA+	NC	....	....	M6	99.87	'87	68.0	125	82⅝	122⅞	105¼	105¼	7.96
Australia & New Zealand Bkg .... Sub Notes[11]	6¼s	2004	$Fa	A+	NC	....	....	G1	99.70	'94	250	102⅝	84⅝	101⅛	95½	95⅞	6.52
Australia & New Zealand Bkg .... Sub Notes[11]	7.55s	2006	$mS15	A+	NC	....	....	M2	99.85	'96	500	111¼	99⅝	109⅛	99⅜	99⅜	7.60
• Aventis[12] .... Notes[11]	7¾s	2002	$Jj15	A–	NC	....	[13]Z100	B7	99.31	'92	500	109⅜	93	103⅞	98⅝	100	7.75
Baden-Wurttemberg L-Fin .... Global[14]Notes[15]	5¾s	2008	$Fa25	AAA	NC	....	....	L3	99.41	'98	100	102⅞	97¼	102⅞	90⅜	90⅜	6.36
Banco de Galicia .... Negotiable[11]Oblig[16]	9s	2003	$mN	BB	±102.25	....	....	G1	99.54	'93	200	105	73¾	98¾	86	93½	9.62
Banco Nacional de Obras .... Notes	9⅝s	2003	$mN15	BB	NC	....	....	M6	99.72	'96	200	106¼	76½	102	91	102	9.43
Banco Rio de la Plata .... Neg[11]Obligs	8¾s	2003	$jD15	BB+	NC	....	....	G1	99.84	'93	250	104¾	58	99	87½	93½	9.36
Banco Santiago .... Sub Notes	7s	2007	$jJ18	BBB	NC	....	....	U1	99.18	'97	300	102¾	77	92⅜	81⅞	89¾	7.80
Banesto Finance .... Gtd[17]Sub[18]Notes[19]	7½s	2007	Ms25	A	NC	....	....	L3	99.99	'97	150	108½	99⅞	107⅜	97¾	97¾	7.67
Bank of China .... [20]Bonds[21]	8¼s	2014	$Ms15	BB+	NC	....	....	M6	99.70	'94	100	106⅞	84⅞	94⅝	81¼	81¼	10.15
Bank of Montreal[22] .... Sub[23]Notes[24]	6.10s	2005	$mS15	A+	NC	....	....	M2	99¾	'93	300	102¼	82¼	102⅛	94⅜	94⅜	6.46
Bank of Montreal[22] .... Sub[23]Notes	7.80s	2007	$Ao	A+	[25]*Z100	....	....	G1	99.33	'95	300	113	99⅛	112⅞	100¾	100¾	7.74
Bank of Nova Scotia .... Sub[18]Deb[11]	6⅞s	2003	$Mn	A	NC	....	Z100	G1	....	'93	250	105¼	89⅝	104⅝	98¾	98¾	6.96
Bank of Nova Scotia .... F/R[11]Sub[26]Deb[18]	6½s	2007	$jJ15	A	[27]*100	....	....	G1	99⅞	'97	500	105¼	98¾	104⅜	94	94	....
Bank of Nova Scotia .... Sub[11]Deb[18]	6¼s	2008	$mS15	A	NC	....	....	S1	99.45	'93	250	102⅝	78¾	102⅝	90¾	90¾	6.89
Banque Centrale de Tunisie .... Bonds	8⅛s	2027	$mS19	BBB–	NC	....	....	M2	99.50	'97	150	101	75	88	80	81⅜	10.14
Banque Centrale de Tunisie .... Notes	7½s	2007	$mS19	BBB–	NC	....	....	M2	99.58	'97	250	100½	82¾	99⅛	90¼	91¼	8.22
Banque Paribas .... Sub[11]Notes	8.35s	2007	$Jd15	A–	NC	....	....	M2	100	'92	250	117¾	93¾	112⅝	102⅝	102⅞	8.12
Banque Paribas .... Sub[11]Notes[18]	6⅞s	2009	$Ms	A–	NC	....	....	M2	99.22	'94	300	106½	81⅜	103⅜	93⅝	93⅞	7.32
• Barclays Bank PLC .... Sub Notes	5⅞s	2000	$jJ15	A	NC	....	....		99.75	'98	225	99⅞	99⅝	No Sale		98	5.99
Barclays N. Amer Capital .... [28]Gtd Cap Notes[11]	9¾s	2021	$Ms15	AA–	[29]104.725	....	....	G1	99.70	'91	500	126⅝	96⅜	112⅜	106⅛	107⅜	9.08
Barrick Gold Finance Inc .... Gtd Deb[30]	7½s	2007	$Mn	A	[31]Z100	....	....	G1	99.90	'97	500	111¼	99⅞	107½	97⅛	97⅛	7.72
Basque Country[32] .... Notes[33]	8s	2004	$mS21	AA	NC	....	....	M2	99.86	'94	150	113⅞	99¾	112⅜	103	103	7.77
Bass America, Inc .... Gtd[34]Notes[11]	8⅛s	2002	$Ms31	A	NC	....	....	M6	99⅞	'92	350	115⅝	98⅛	107	101⅞	101⅞	7.98
Bass America, Inc .... Gtd[34]Notes[11]	6⅝s	2003	$Ms31	A	NC	....	....	M5	99.97	'93	300	106⅜	88¾	103⅞	98	98	6.76
Bayerische Landesbank(N.Y. Branch) .... Sub[11]Notes[18]	7⅜s	2002	$jD14	AAA	NC	....	....	M2	99.73	'92	250	111¾	94⅝	107⅜	100⅞	100⅞	7.31
BBV Int'l Finance Ltd .... Sub[35]Gtd[18]Notes[36]	6⅞s	2005	$jJ	A+	NC	....	....	L3	99.32	'95	150	106½	94½	104⅝	96¼	96½	7.12
BBV Int'l Finance Ltd .... Sub[35]Gtd[37]Notes[18]	7s	2025	$jD	A+	NC	....	....	U1	98.21	'95	200	104⅝	85¼	99⅝	86½	86½	8.09
BCH Cayman Islands Ltd .... Sub[38]Gtd[11]Deb	7½s	2005	$Jd15	A	NC	....	....	M6	99.11	'95	100	107⅛	97⅜	106⅞	98⅝	98⅝	7.60
BCH Cayman Islands Ltd .... Sub[11]Gtd[38]Notes	7.70s	2006	$jJ15	A	NC	....	....	M6	99.18	'96	225	108⅞	99⅛	108⅜	99	99	7.78
BCH Cayman Islands Ltd .... Sub[38]Gtd[11]Notes	8¼s	2004	$Jd15	A	NC	....	....	M6	99.26	'94	225	110⅜	93½	109⅜	102	102	8.09
Bell Cablemedia plc .... Sr[39]Disc[11]Notes[40]	11.95s	2004	$jJ15	BBB+	±104.48	....	....	S1	56.10	'94	[41]490	96¼	50½	89⅝	89½	89⅝	Flat
Bell Tel Canada[42] .... Deb EL	7¾s	2006	$Ao	A+	NC	....	....	G1	99.66	'92	200	115⅜	94⅛	112½	101⅜	101⅞	7.61
BET Icecalm B.V. .... Gtd[43]Notes[11]	8⅝s	2001	$aO15	NR	NC	....	....	M2	99.60	'91	200	115⅞	99	106⅜	101⅝	101⅝	8.49
BHP Finance(USA)Ltd .... Gtd[11]Deb[44]	7¼s	2016	$Ms	A–	NC	....	....	M6	100	'96	300	104½	93⅛	101⅛	89⅝	89¾	8.08

Uniform Footnote Explanations-See Page 260. Other: [1] Int adj semi-anly. [2] (HR)On 8-15-07('12,'17&'22)at 100. [3] Red in whole,at 100,if less than $15M outstg. [4] (HRO)On 7-16-03 at 100. [5] Red in whole,at 100,if less than $25M outstg. [6] (HRO)On 6-16-08 at 100. [7] Red in whole,at 100,if less than $37.5M outstg. [8] (HRO)On 10-4-04 at 100. [9] Red in whole,at 100,if less than $20.5M outstg. [10] Also issued as registered ctfs. [11] Co may red in whole,at 100,for tax law chge. [12] Was Rhone-Poulenc. [13] Mandatory,in whole,as defined. [14] May red in whole,at 100,for tax law chge. [15] Gtd by Landeskreditbanken Baden-Wurttemberg. [16] Issued in min denom $10T. [17] Gtd by Banesto(NY). [18] Issued in min denom $100T. [19] Fr 3-25-02,red in whole,at 100,for tax law chge. [20] (HRO)For a Redemp Event at 100. [21] Issued in min denom $5T. [22] Chicago Branch. [23] Issued in min denom $125T. [24] Co may red at 100 on,int dates for tax chge. [25] Fr 4-7-00. [26] Int to 7-15-02,adj qtrly(3 Mo LIBOR&1.00%). [27] Fr 7-15-02. [28] Gtd by Barclays Bank PLC. [29] Fr 5-15-01. [30] Gtd by Barrick Gold Corp. [31] Greater of 100 or amt based on formula. [32] An Autonomous Community in Spain. [33] Red in whole,at 100,for tax law chge. [34] Gtd by Bass PLC. [35] Gtd by Banco Bilbao Vizcaya,S.A.,N.Y. Branch. [36] Fr 7-1-00 Co may red in whole,at 100,for tax chge. [37] Fr 12-11-00 Co may red in whole,at 100,for tax law chge. [38] Gtd by Banco Central Hispanoamericano,S.A.(N.Y.). [39] Int accrues at 11.95% fr 1-15-00. [40] (HRO)On Chge of Ctrl at 101. [41] Incl disc. [42] Subsid of Bell Canada Enterprises. [43] Gtd by BET PLC. [44] Gtd by Broken Hill Proprietary Co Ltd.

Exchange ↓	BONDS Description	Interest Rate	Due	Interest Dates	S&P Rating	Redemption Provisions Regular	For Sinking Fund	Refund Earliest/ Other	Underwriting Firm	Price	Year	Outstanding Mil-$ This Issue	Price Range 1988-1998 High	Low	1999 High	Low	Month End Price Sale(s) or Bid	Yield to Maturity
	BHP Finance(USA)Ltd .... [1]Gtd[2]Deb[3]	6.42s	2026	$Ms	A–	NC	....	....	M6	100	'96	400	102⅛	94⅝	100⅞	96¼	96¼	6.67
	BHP Finance(USA)Ltd .... Gtd[1]Notes[2]	5⅝s	2000	$mN	A–	NC	....	....	M6	99¾	'93	300	100⅝	87	100⅛	98⅝	98¾	5.70
	BHP Finance(USA)Ltd .... Gtd[1]Notes[2]	7⅞s	2002	$jD	A–	NC	....	....	M6	99.22	'92	250	112¾	95⅝	107⅛	100⅝	100⅝	7.84
	BHP Finance(USA)Ltd .... [1]Gtd Notes[2]	6.69s	2006	$Ms	A–	NC	....	....	M6	100	'96	300	103	93¼	102⅛	94⅛	94⅛	7.11
	BHP Finance(USA)Ltd .... Gtd[1]Notes[2]	8½s	2012	$jD	A–	NC	....	....	M6	99.67	'92	250	123½	95	121⅝	102¾	102¾	8.27
	BHP Finance(USA)Ltd .... Gtd[1]Deb[2]	6¾s	2013	$mN	A–	NC	....	....	M6	99.55	'93	200	102¾	79⅛	99¾	89⅛	89⅛	7.57
	BP America .... [4]Gtd Deb[2]	8¾s	2003	$Fa	AA+	NC	....	Z100	M2	99¾	'91	350	121⅛	98	112½	105	105	8.33
	BP America .... [4]Gtd Deb[2]	9⅞s	2004	$Ms15	AA+	NC	....	Z100	G1	100	'89	250	130	98⅛	120⅜	110¼	110¼	8.96
	BP America .... [4]Gtd Notes[2]	9⅜s	2000	$mN	AA+	NC	....	....	G1	99.30	'90	350	122⅝	99¼	107⅜	102¼	102¼	9.17
	BP America .... [4]Gtd Notes[2]	8½s	2001	$Ao15	AA+	NC	....	....	S5	99.14	'91	200	118	96⅝	107⅛	102¼	102¼	8.31
•	BP America .... [4]Gtd[2]Notes	7⅞s	2002	$Mn15	AA+	NC	....	....	M2	99.44	'92	450	114	97⅛	107⅜	100⅝	101¼	7.78
	Brascan ltd .... Notes[2]	7⅜s	2002	$aO	BBB	NC	....	....	C5	99.60	'95	200	107	96⅜	104½	99¼	99¼	7.43
	Brazil(Fed Republic) .... Global Bonds	9⅜s	2008	$Ao7	B+	NC	....	....	M2	99.74	'98	1250	99¾	53	89½	57¼	88	10.65
	British Columbia (Prov of) ..... Bonds Ser BCUSD-1	7s	2003	$Jj15	AA–	NC	....	....	L3	99.26	'93	500	109⅞	92⅛	106⅛	100	100	7.00
	British Columbia (Prov of) ..... Bonds Ser BCUSD-2	6½s	2026	$Jj15	AA–	NC	....	....	L3	99.28	'96	500	105⅞	86⅞	106½	88⅝	88⅝	7.33
	British Columbia (Prov of) ..... Bonds Ser BCUSD-3	7¼s	2036	$mS	AA–	NC	....	....	L3	99.22	'96	300	115⅝	94⅞	116½	95½	95⅝	7.58
	British Columbia Prov of) .... Bonds[5]Ser BCUSG-1	5⅜s	2008	$aO29	AA–	NC	....	....	L3	99.48	'98	500	99⅞	98¼	99¾	88	88	6.11
	British Sky Broadcstg Gp .... Gtd[2]Notes[6]	7.30s	2006	$aO15	BBB–	NC	....	....	G1	99.83	'96	300	109¾	96⅞	103¼	92	92⅝	7.88
	Cable & Wireless Commun .... [2]Notes[7]	6⅜s	2003	$Ms6	A–	Z100	....	....	M2	99.54	'98	750	102⅝	99½	101½	97¾	99	6.44
	Cable & Wireless Commun .... [2]Notes[7]	6⅝s	2005	$Ms6	A–	Z100	....	....	M2	99.68	'98	650	104	99⅝	102⅞	96⅝	99	6.69
	Cable & Wireless Comm .... [2]Notes[7]	6¾s	2008	$Ms6	A–	Z100	....	....	M2	99.39	'98	400	104⅝	98¾	104⅝	95⅝	99⅛	6.81
	Canadian Airlines .... Sr Sec[8]Notes[2]	10s	2005	$Mn	CCC	[9]105	....	[10]Z110	L1	100	'98	175	101	85	88	70	76	13.16
	Canadian Airlines .... Sr[2]Notes[8]	12¼s	2006	$fA	CC	[11]106.25	....	[12]Z112.50	L1	98.76	'98	100	98¾	68	68	33	54	22.65
	Canadian Imperial Bank .... Notes	6.20s	2000	$fA	AA–	NC	....	....	C5	100	'97	750	101¾	99⅝	101¼	99¾	99¾	6.21
	Canada .... Bonds	5⅝s	2003	$Fa19	AA+	NC	....	....		99.72	'98	2000	103¼	69.72	102	96¾	96¾	5.81
	Canada .... Bonds	5¼s	2008	$mN5	AA+	NC	....	....		99.98	'98	2500	100⅞	97⅝	100⅝	88⅜	88⅜	5.94
	Canadian National Ry .... Deb	7⅝s	2023	$Mn15	BBB	NC	....	....	S1	98¾	'93	150	111¼	84¾	108⅛	98½	100⅛	7.61
	Canadian National Ry .... Notes	6⅝s	2003	$Mn15	BBB	NC	....	....	S1	100	'93	150	105¼	87½	103⅝	97⅝	97⅝	6.79
	Canadian National Ry .... Notes	6.80s	2018	$jJ15	BBB	NC	....	....	S1	99.24	'94	300	107¼	89¼	103	98¾	99⅝	6.82
	Canadian Occ Petrol .... Notes	7.40s	2028	$Mn	BBB	[13]Z100	....	....	M2	99.77	'98	200	102¾	90	93½	85⅞	88	8.41
	Canadian Pacific Ltd .... Deb	9.45s	2021	$fA	BBB+	NC	....	....	G1	99⅞	'91	250	133⅝	99⅞	128¼	111¾	112	8.44
	Canadian Pacific Ltd .... Deb	8.85s	2022	$Jd	BBB+	[14]104.335	....	....	G1	99.82	'92	250	124⅛	94⅛	119¼	106	107⅝	8.22
•	Canadian Pacific Ry .... Per Con Deb Stk	4s		$jj	AA–	NC	....	....		....	'21	178	80	39⅜	77	53	55	....
	Canadian Pacific Forest Prod .... Deb	10¼s	2003	$Jj15	BBB	NC	....	....	G1	100	'93	75.0	113¾	95½	109½	103¼	103¼	9.92
	Canadian Reynolds Metals Co,Ltd[15] ..... Gtd[16]Amort[17]Notes	6⅝s	2002	$jJ15	BBB	NC	....	....	M2	99.48	'93	285	103⅝	87½	98¾	95⅜	95⅜	....
	Carter Holt Harvey Ltd .... Sr Deb[2]	8⅜s	2015	$Ao15	BBB–	NC	....	....	C5	99.85	'95	125	118½	99	108½	98⅞	99⅞	8.39
	Carter Holt Harvey Ltd .... Sr Deb[2]	9½s	2024	$jD	BBB–	NC	....	....	C5	99.70	'94	150	134⅜	99⅝	116¾	107⅛	108¾	8.73
	Carter Holt Harvey Ltd .... Sr Notes[2]	7⅝s	2002	$Ao15	BBB–	NC	....	....	C5	99.55	'95	150	108⅛	99⅜	102⅝	100	100	7.62
	Carter Holt Harvey Ltd .... Sr Notes[2]	8⅞s	2004	$jD	BBB–	NC	....	....	C5	99⅝	'94	350	117½	99⅜	109	103⅞	103⅞	8.54
	Celulosa Araucoy Constitucion S.A. .... Notes[2]	6¾s	2003	$jD15	BBB+	NC	....	....	M5	99.81	'95	200	100¾	85	96⅛	87⅞	95	7.10
	Celulosa Araucoy Constiucion S.A. .... Notes[2]	7s	2007	$jD15	BBB+	NC	....	....	M5	99.75	'95	100	101⅝	75¼	92⅞	81¼	90⅝	7.72
	CF CABLE TV Inc .... Sr[2]Sec[8]1st Priority Notes	9⅛s	2007	$jJ15	BBB	[18]100	....	....	M2	100	'95	100	111½	97½	110	105½	106⅜	8.58
	CF CABLE TV INC .... Sr[2]Sec[8]2nd Priority Notes	11⅝s	2005	$Fa15	BBB–	[19]±105.8125	....	....	M2	100	'95	110	116	97	111	106⅜	106⅜	10.92
	Chile (Republic of) .... Bonds	6⅞s	2009	$Ao28	A–	NC	....	....	C1	99.86	'99	500	....	....	100⅛	91⅜	92¾	7.41
	Chilgener S.A. .... Notes[2]	6½s	2006	$Jj15	BBB+	NC	....	....	S7	99.13	'96	200	100½	80¾	94¾	86⅝	89¾	7.24
	China (People's Republic) .... Bonds	6½s	2004	$Fa17	BBB+	NC	....	....	M2	99.41	'94	1000	100⅛	83⅝	98⅞	95¼	96¼	6.75
	China (People's Republic) .... Bonds	7¾s	2006	$jJ5	BBB+	NC	....	....	C5	99.42	'96	300	107¾	90¾	103⅞	98½	99⅞	7.76
	China (People's Republic) .... Notes	7⅜s	2001	$jJ3	BBB+	NC	....	....	C5	99.56	'96	700	103⅜	97	101⅞	99⅞	100	7.37
	China (People's Republic) .... Notes	6⅝s	2003	Jj15	BBB+	NC	....	....	M5	99.68	'96	300	101¾	92¾	99½	96⅞	97⅞	6.77
	China (People's Republic) .... Bonds	9s	2096	Jj15	BBB+	NC	....	....	M5	98.62	'96	100	123⅝	93⅞	124¼	84½	91⅛	9.87
	China Int'l Trust & Investment .... [20]Bonds	6⅞s	2003	$fA	BB	NC	....	....	G1	99.71	'93	250	104¾	72¼	96¼	89¼	93⅜	7.36

Uniform Footnote Explanations-See Page 260. Other: [1] Gtd by Broken Hill Proprietary Co Ltd. [2] Co may red in whole,at 100,for tax law chge. [3] (HRO)On 3-1-03 at 100. [4] Subsid of & gtd by British Petroleum Co plc. [5] Red in whole,at 100,for tax law chge. [6] Gtd by British Sky Broadcstg Ltd & Sky Subscrib. [7] (HRO)On Chge of Ctrl at 100. [8] (HRO)On Chge of Ctrl at 101. [9] Fr 5-1-02. [10] Max $61.25M red w/proceeds of Eq Off'gs. [11] Fr 8-1-02. [12] Max $35M red w/proceeds of Pub Equity Off'gs. [13] Red at greater of 100 or amt based on formula. [14] Fr 6-1-02. [15] A/K/A Societe Canadienne de Metaux Reynolds,Lte. [16] Subsid of & gtd by Reynolds Metals Co. [17] Princ pyts:$200 prin amt due ea 7-15 '98-'02. [18] Fr 7-15-05. [19] Fr 2-15-00. [20] Issued in min denom U.S. $5T.

Exchange	BONDS Description	Interest Rate	Due	Interest Dates	S&P Rating	Redemption Provisions: Regular	For Sinking Fund	Refund Earliest/ Other	Underwriting: Firm	Price	Year	Outstanding Mil-$ This Issue	Price Range 1988-1998: High	Low	1999: High	Low	Month End Price Sale(s) or Bid	Yield to Maturity
	China Int'l Trust&Investment ... Bonds[1]	9s	2006	$aO15	BB	NC	....	....	M5	99.50	'94	200	112⅜	75½	100¾	84⅛	84⅛	10.70
	China Light & Pwr ... Notes[2]	7½s	2006	Ao15	A	NC	....	....	M5	99.36	'96	300	106⅝	93⅜	104⅝	97⅛	99⅝	7.55
	Clearnet Communications Inc ... Sr[3]Disc Notes[4]	14¾s	2005	$jD15	NR	[5]±107.375	....	....	M6	Unit	'95	[6]367	87	57⅛	98½	85¼	98⅛	Flat
•	Coca-Cola FEMSA,S.A. de C.V. ... [7]Notes[2]	8.95s	2006	$mN	A	NC	....	....	M5	99.96	'96	200	106½	84	102	96¼	99⅝	9.01
	Colombia (Republic of) ... Bonds	8.70s	2016	$Fa15	BB+	NC	....	....	G1	99.87	'96	200	106¾	54¾	86½	66	78	11.15
	Colombia(Republic of) ... Bonds	7⅝s	2007	$Fa15	BB+	NC	....	....	M2	99.71	'97	750	100¾	62¾	89	73	84	9.08
	Colombia(Republic of) ... Bonds	8⅜s	2027	$Fa15	BB+	NC	....	....	M2	99.88	'97	250	103	56¼	81⅜	64¼	76½	10.94
	Colombia (Republic of) ... Notes	7¼s	2003	$Fa15	BB+	NC	....	....	G1	99.76	'96	200	100⅛	75⅝	92⅜	82⅞	92¼	7.86
	COLT Telecom Group plc ... Sr[8]Disc[2]Notes[9]	12s	2006	$jD15	B	[10]106	....	....	M6	55⅞	'96	[6]314	84½	72	87⅜	80	86	Flat
	Comcast UK Cable Ptnrs Ltd ... Sr[2]Disc[8]Deb[11]	11.20s	2007	$mN15	B−	±104.20	....	....	D6	57.99	'95	[6]517	86	57¼	95⅝	83¼	95¼	Flat
	Cominco Ltd ... Deb	6⅞s	2006	$Fa15	BB+	NC	....	....	G1	99.76	'96	150	101⅞	87	91¼	86⅛	87	7.90
	Commun Urb de Montreal ... Deb[12]	9⅛s	2001	$Ms15	A+	NC	....	....	M2	99.38	'91	135	120¼	98⅞	107½	101¼	101¼	9.01
	Compania de Telecom de Chile ... Notes[2]	7⅝s	2006	$jJ15	A−	NC	....	....	M5	99.76	'96	200	108¼	87	100⅝	92¼	94⅝	8.06
	Corporacion Andina de Fomento ... Notes[2]	7⅜s	2000	$jJ21	A	NC	....	....	M2	99.89	'95	250	103⅜	98⅝	101	99⅝	100⅜	7.35
	Corporacion Andina de Fomento ... Bonds	7.10s	2003	$Fa	A	NC	....	....	G1	99.93	'96	200	102⅜	94⅝	100⅛	96⅞	98⅝	7.20
	Corporacion Andina de Fomento ... Bonds	7¼s	2007	$Ms	A	NC	....	....	M2	99.37	'97	150	104⅝	89⅛	99¼	93⅜	94⅞	7.64
	Cott Corp ... Sr[2]Notes[13]	9⅜s	2005	$jJ	B+	[14]±104.688	....	....	M6	100	'95	160	105½	95	100	91½	98½	9.52
	Cott Corp ... Sr[8]Notes[2]	8½s	2007	Mn	B+	[14]±107	....	....	M6	100	'97	125	102¼	89	95	84	93¼	9.11
	CRA Finance(USA)Ltd ... [15]Gtd[2]Nts	6½s	2003	$jD	AA−	NC	....	....	M6	99.85	'93	200	106⅜	85⅝	104⅜	96¾	96¾	6.72
	CRA Finance(USA)Ltd ... [15]Gtd[2]Nts	7⅛s	2013	$jD	AA−	NC	....	....	M6	99.42	'93	100	109	82½	108⅝	91⅝	91⅝	7.78
	CSR America, Inc ... [2]Notes	6⅞s	2005	$jJ21	A−	NC	....	....	M2	99.42	'95	250	109¼	94⅞	105½	95	95	7.24
	CSR Finance Ltd ... [2]Notes[16]	7.70s	2025	$jJ21	A−	NC	....	....	M2	99.61	'95	150	114⅝	95⅛	112⅞	93⅛	93¼	8.26
•	Daimler-Benz N.A. ... M-T Notes'A'[17]	7⅜s	2006	$mS15	A+	NC	....	....	M5	99.96	'96	500	103¾	97¾	No Sale		96	7.68
	Deutsche Bank Fin'l ... Sub[2]Notes[18]	6.70s	2006	jD13	AA−	NC	....	....		99.69	'96	1100	106¼	94¼	105¾	94¾	94¾	7.07
	Deutsche Bank Fin'l ... Sub[19]Notes[2]	7½s	2009	$Ao25	AA−	NC	....	....		99.59	'97	550	113¾	99½	111⅝	98⅜	98⅜	7.62
	Diamond Cable Commun PLC ... Sr[20]Disc[21]Notes[22]	13¼s	2004	$mS30	B−	±107.125	....	....	G1	52.61	'94	[6]285	98½	52½	107⅞	98½	107⅛	12.37
	Diamond Cable Commun ... [13]Sr Disc[23]Notes[2]	11¾s	2005	jD15	B−	[5]±104.406	....	....	G1	56.50	'95	530	86	56½	94¾	82½	94½	Flat
	Diamond Holdings Plc ... Sr Notes	9⅛s	2008	$Fa	B−	[24]104.562	....	....	Exch.	Exch.	'98	110	104	92¾	105¾	95½	99	9.21
	Doman Industries Ltd ... Sr Notes[8]	8¾s	2004	$Ms15	B	±104.375	....	....	B7	100	'94	425	100¼	64	86¼	58	85¼	10.26
	Dominion Textile(USA) ... Gtd[25]Sr Nts[8]	8⅞s	2003	$mN	NR	±102.1875	....	....	G1	99.51	'93	150	106¼	89¼	99½	99⅜	99⅜	8.93
	Dominion Textile(USA) ... Sr[26]Gtd[27]Notes[2]	9¼s	2006	$Ao	NR	[28]104.625	....	....	G1	100	'96	125	111¾	96	105	104⅞	104⅞	8.82
	Domtar Inc ... [2]Deb[29]	9½s	2016	fA	BBB−	[30]Z100	....	....	S1	99.64	'96	125	113¼	94	109½	103	107	8.88
	Domtar Inc ... [2]Notes[29]	8¾s	2006	fA	BBB−	[30]Z100	....	....	S1	99.74	'96	150	107¼	95¼	105½	101	102	8.58
	Donohue Forest Products ... Gtd[31]Notes[2]	7⅝s	2007	$Mn15	BBB	[32]Z100	....	....	D6	99.73	'97	200	111⅛	99½	109¾	96⅞	96⅞	7.87
	Dresdner Bank AG[33] ... Sub Notes[2]	6⅝s	2005	$mS	AA−	NC	....	....	M5	99.59	'95	500	104⅛	93⅝	104⅝	95½	95½	6.94
	Dresdner Bank AG[33] ... Sub Deb[2]	7¼s	2015	$mS15	AA−	NC	....	....	M5	99.80	'95	500	106⅞	93⅞	105⅝	93⅝	94	7.71
	Dynacare Inc ... Sr Notes[13]	10¾s	2006	$Jj15	B+	[34]105.375	....	....	C4	100	'96	125	107	96½	103	96¼	97	11.08
	Embotelladora Andina S.A. ... Notes[2]'A'	7s	2007	$aO	BBB+	NC	....	....	C5	99.86	'97	150	101⅜	80⅜	96⅝	83⅜	92⅝	7.58
	Embotelladora Andina S.A. ... Notes[2]'B'	7⅞s	2027	$aO	BBB+	NC	....	....	C5	99.77	'97	100	101⅞	69⅛	90¾	75	84½	9.02
	Empresa Electrica Pehuenche S.A. ... [2]Notes	7.30s	2003	$Mn	BBB+	[35]■100	....	....	M5	99.72	'96	170	104⅜	90¼	98⅛	91⅞	97¼	7.51
	Endesa-Chile ... Notes[2]	7⅞s	2027	$Fa	A−	NC	....	....	C1	99.60	'97	230	108⅝	69⅜	94⅜	79⅜	86⅞	9.06
	Endesa-Chile ... [2]Notes[36]	7.325s	2037	$Fa	A−	NC	....	....	C1	100	'97	220	105	81¾	98¾	88½	91¼	8.03
	Endesa-Chile Overseas ... Gtd[37]Notes[2]	7.20s	2006	$Ao	A−	NC	....	....	M5	99.95	'96	150	105¼	84⅝	98⅞	90⅝	93⅝	7.69
	English China Clays Del Inc ... Gtd[38]Notes[2]	7⅜s	2002	$aO	NR	NC	....	....	M2	100	'92	250	109	93	106½	100⅜	100¾	7.32
	Enterprise Oil plc ... Notes[2]	6½s	2005	$Mn	BBB+	NC	....	....	L3	99.52	'98	100	106	99½	100½	93⅜	93⅜	6.96
	Enterprise Oil plc ... Notes[2]	6.70s	2007	$mS15	BBB+	NC	....	....	L3	99.71	'97	350	107⅜	99⅝	99⅝	92⅛	92¾	7.22
	Esprit Telecom Group plc ... Sr[8]Notes[2]	11½s	2007	$jD15	B−	[39]105.75	....	[40]Z111.50	L3	100	'97	230	110	89½	110	99½	100¼	11.47
•	European Invest Bank ... Notes	10⅛s	2000	$aO	AAA	NC	....	....	S5	99¼	'87	200	124	100¼	106	100	100⅛	10.11
•	European Invest Bank ... Notes	8⅞s	2001	$Ms	AAA	NC	....	....	S1	99.92	'90	300	116⅝	97⅝	101	100	100	8.87
•	European Invest Bank ... Notes	9⅛s	2002	$Jd	AAA	NC	....	....	F1	99.32	'90	300	102½	99¼	No Sale		100	9.12
	European Invest Bank ... Notes	7⅛s	2006	$mS18	AAA	NC	....	....	L3	99.98	'96	1000	112⅞	99½	111½	101	101	7.05

Uniform Footnote Explanations-See Page 260. Other: [1] Issued in min denom U.S.$5T. [2] Co may red in whole,at 100,for tax law chge. [3] Co may red in whole,at 100(Accreted Val),for tax law chge. [4] Int accrues at 14.75% fr 12-16-00. [5] Fr 12-15-00. [6] Incl disc. [7] (HRO)On Chge of Ctrl at 100. [8] (HRO)On Chge of Ctrl at 101. [9] Int accrues at 12% fr 12-15-01. [10] Fr 12-15-01. [11] Int accrues at 11.20% fr 11-15-00. [12] A/K/A Montreal Urban Community. [13] Co must offer repurch at 101 on Chge of Ctrl. [14] Fr 7-1-00. [15] Gtd by CRA Ltd. [16] Gtd by CSR Ltd. [17] Gtd by Daimler-Benz AG. [18] Gtd by Deutche Bank AG-NY Branch. [19] Gtd by Deutsche Bank AG-NY Branch. [20] Int accrues at 13.25% fr 9-30-98. [21] (HRO)On Chge of Ctrl at 101(Accreted Val). [22] Co may red in whole at 100(Accreted Val)for tax chge. [23] Int accrues at 11.75% fr 12-15-00. [24] Fr 2-1-03. [25] Subsid of & gtd by Dominion Textile Inc. [26] Gtd by Dominion Textile Inc. [27] Co must offer repurch at 101 for Chge of Ctrl. [28] Fr 4-1-01. [29] (HRO)On Chge of Ctrl Triggering Event at 101. [30] Greater of 100 or amt based on formula. [31] Gtd by Donohue Inc. [32] Plus Make-Whole Amt. [33] N.Y. Branch. [34] Fr 1-15-01. [35] On 11-1-02,plus Make Whole Amt. [36] (HRO)On 2-1-09 at 100. [37] Gtd by Empresa Nacional de Electricidad S.A. [38] Gtd by English China Clays plc. [39] Fr 12-15-02. [40] Max $80.5M red w/proceeds Pub Eq Off'g.

Exchange ↓ BONDS Description, Interest Rate, Due and Interest Dates				S&P Rating	Redemption Provisions Regular	For Sinking Fund	Refund Earliest/ Other	Underwriting Firm	Price	Year	Out-standing Mil-$ This Issue	Price Range 1988-1998 High	Low	1999 High	Low	Month End Price Sale(s) or Bid	Yield to Matur-ity
Export-Import Bank,Korea .... Bonds	6¼s	2000	$Mn15	BBB	NC	....	....	F1	99.56	'93	200	105¼	80⅝	99¾	96	99½	6.53
Export-Import Bank,Korea .... Bonds	6⅜s	2006	$Fa15	BBB	NC	....	....	L3	99.45	'96	500	99⅜	55⅞	93⅝	85	91¼	6.99
Export-Import Bank, Korea .... Notes	6½s	2006	$mN15	BBB	NC	....	....	L3	99.84	'96	350	100½	68⅝	96⅜	87⅛	94¾	6.86
Export-Import Bank,Korea .... Notes[1]	7.10s	2007	$Ms15	BBB	NC	....	....	L3	99.85	'97	650	103½	74⅛	99¼	92	98¼	7.23
Fairfax Financial Hldgs .... Notes	7¾s	2003	$jD15	BBB+	NC	....	....	M5	99.81	'93	100	107½	92¾	105½	95¾	95¾	8.09
Fairfax Financial Hldgs .... Notes	8¼s	2015	$aO	BBB+	NC	....	....	M5	99.85	'95	100	112	97½	103⅝	87⅛	87¼	9.46
Fairfax Financial Hldgs .... Notes	8.30s	2026	$Ao15	BBB+	NC	....	....	M5	99.30	'96	125	115	95	107⅝	84⅛	84¼	9.85
Falconbridge Ltd .... Deb	7⅜s	2005	$mS	BBB	NC	....	....	G1	100	'95	200	107½	96¾	100⅛	94½	95¾	7.70
Falconbridge Ltd .... Deb	7.35s	2006	$mN	BBB	NC	....	....	G1	99.86	'96	250	107⅞	97¼	100	93¼	94⅝	7.79
Finland (Republic of) .... Bonds	6.95s	2026	$Fa15	AA+	[2]Z100	....	....	G1	99.56	'96	300	113⅞	90½	111⅝	95	95	7.31
Finland (Republic of) .... Notes	7⅞s	2004	$jJ28	AA+	NC	....	....	M2	99.27	'94	1500	114¼	95⅞	112¾	104⅜	104⅜	7.54
Fletcher Challenge Cap Cda .... [3]Notes[4]	7¾s	2006	$Jd20	BBB	NC	....	....	M2	99.86	'96	300	110¼	98⅞	103⅝	96⅛	96⅛	8.06
Fletcher Challenge Cap Cda .... [3]Notes[4]	8¼s	2016	$Jd20	BBB	NC	....	....	M2	....	'96	150	115½	96⅛	110⅝	96⅛	96⅛	8.58
fONOROLA .... Sr Sec[5]Notes[3]	12½s	2002	$fA15	NR	±106.25	....	....	D6	100	'95	120	113¼	100	108¾	105¾	106	11.79
Fundy Cable Ltd/Ltee ..... Sr Sec 2nd Priority[3]Notes[6]	11s	2005	$mN15	BBB	[7]±105.50	....	....	B7	100	'95	100	112	100	109¾	105	107¾	10.21
Gearbulk Holding Ltd .... Sr[8]Notes[3]	11¼s	2004	$jD	B+	±105.625	....	....		100	'94	175	112	100	106	100½	102¾	10.95
Generalitat de Catalunya .... Notes[3]	6⅜s	2007	$jD15	AA−	NC	....	....	M2	99.36	'95	165	107¼	89½	107¼	94¾	94¾	6.73
Grand Metropolitan Investment .... Zero Cpn[10]Bonds[11]		2004	[9]	A+	NC	....	....	G1	46.55	'94	[12]1224	74⅝	45⅛	75¾	72⅞	74⅞	0.28
Grand Metropolitan Investment .... Gtd[10]Deb[3]	9s	2011	$fA15	A+	NC	....	....	M6	99.17	'91	300	129	99⅛	127⅞	108⅝	109¾	8.20
Grand Metropolitan Investment .... Gtd[10]Deb[3]	8s	2022	$mS15	A+	NC	....	....	G1	99½	'92	300	117¼	90⅝	117⅛	100⅛	100¼	7.98
Grand Metropolitan Investment .... Gtd[10]Notes[3]	8⅝s	2001	$fA15	A+	NC	....	....	M6	99.70	'91	300	117⅛	99⅝	107½	102⅜	102⅜	8.42
Grand Metropolitan Investment .... Gtd[10]Notes[3]	7⅛s	2004	$mS15	A+	NC	....	....	G1	100	'92	200	109	90¼	107⅜	99½	99½	7.16
Grand Metropolitan Investment .... Gtd[10]Sr[3]Notes[13]	7.45s	2035	$Ao15	A+	NC	....	....	L3	100	'95	400	117⅝	92	114⅞	99⅝	99⅝	7.48
Great Lakes Power Inc .... Notes[3]	9s	2004	$fA	BBB−	NC	....	....	G1	99.53	'94	175	115¾	95¼	113¾	102⅛	102⅛	8.81
Grupo Industrial Durango .... [3]Notes[6]	12s	2001	$jJ15	BB−	NC	....	....	M6	100	'94	150	110⅞	66¾	100½	85	100	11.99
Gulf Canada Resources Ltd .... Sr[3]Sub Deb	9¼s	2004	$Jj	BB−	102.31	....	....	S1	99.37	'94	300	106½	88¼	102¾	99	101	9.16
Hanson Overseas B.V. .... Gtd[14]Sr[3]Notes[15]	7⅜s	2003	$Jj15	A	NC	....	....	F1	99.47	'93	750	110⅛	93⅛	105⅝	100	100	7.37
Hanson Overseas B.V. .... Gtd[14]Sr[3]Notes[15]	6¾s	2005	$mS15	A	NC	....	....	C5	99.96	'95	750	106⅞	93⅞	104½	95¾	95¾	7.05
Household Fin'l Corp Ltd .... Sr Notes[16]	7.45s	2000	$Ao	A	NC	....	....	M6	99.82	'95	100	105⅞	99¾	102½	100¼	100¼	7.43
Hydro-Quebec .... Deb[17]'FG'	13⅜s	2013	$Fa15	A+	104.75	[18]Z100	....	F1	100	'83	17.6	135¾	104¾	106	105½	105½	12.67
Hydro-Quebec .... Deb[19]'FU'[17]	11¾s	2012	$Fa	A+	NC	....	....	F1	99.60	'85	200	152¾	110¾	152	131⅛	131⅛	8.96
Hydro-Quebec .... [20]Deb[21]'GF'[17]	8⅞s	2026	$Ms	A+	NC	....	....	F1	99.73	'86	250	132⅞	87¾	132½	110¾	111	7.99
Hydro-Quebec .... [20]Deb[22]'GH'[17]	8¼s	2026	$Ao15	A+	NC	....	....	M2	99⅜	'86	250	124⅞	82⅛	124½	103⅞	104⅛	7.92
Hydro-Quebec .... Deb[23]'GQ'[17]	8¼s	2027	$Jj15	A+	NC	....	....	M2	99.55	'87	250	124¾	82	124⅝	103⅞	104	7.93
Hydro-Quebec .... Deb[23]'GW'[17]	9¾s	2018	$Jj15	A+	[24]100	....	....	M2	100	'88	250	130⅞	94⅞	114	106⅛	106⅛	9.18
Hydro-Quebec .... Deb[23]'HH'[17]	8½s	2029	$jD	A+	NC	....	....	F1	99.70	'89	500	128⅜	86¼	128½	106⅝	107	7.94
Hydro-Quebec .... Deb[23]'HK'[17]	9⅜s	2030	$Ao15	A+	NC	....	....	M2	99.87	'90	500	140	94	140¼	116¼	116⅝	8.04
Hydro-Quebec .... Deb[17]'HQ'	9½s	2030	$mN15	A+	NC	....	....	F1	99.42	'90	500	142	99⅜	142⅛	117⅞	118⅛	8.04
Hydro-Quebec .... Deb[17]'HS'	9.40s	2021	$Fa	A+	NC	....	....	M2	99.17	'91	900	136	99	136⅛	115½	115⅝	8.13
Hydro-Quebec .... Deb[17]'HY'	8.40s	2022	$Jj15	A+	NC	....	....	F1	99.27	'92	1000	124⅝	91⅞	124⅞	105⅜	105¾	7.94
Hydro-Quebec .... Deb[17]'IF'	7⅜s	2003	$Fa	A+	NC	....	....	M2	100	'93	500	110¼	92½	106¾	100⅝	100⅝	7.33
Hydro-Quebec .... Deb[17]'IF'	8s	2013	$Fa	A+	NC	....	....	M2	99.49	'93	1000	118¾	90¼	119⅝	102⅝	102⅝	7.79
Hydro-Quebec .... Deb[17]	7½s	2016	$Ao	A+	NC	....	....	C5	99.33	'96	400	113⅞	94¾	113½	97⅝	97⅝	7.68
Hydro-Quebec .... Deb[17]'IO'[25]	8.05s	2024	$jJ7	A+	NC	....	....	F1	100	'94	1000	121⅝	94¾	122	104⅜	104½	7.70
ICI Wilmington Inc[26] .... Gtd[27]Notes[3]	9½s	2000	$mN15	A−	NC	....	....	G1	99.82	'90	300	117½	99	105⅝	102	102	9.31
ICI Wilmington Inc .... Gtd[27]Notes[3]	8¾s	2001	$Mn	A−	NC	....	....	M2	99.91	'91	250	117	95⅛	105¼	101⅞	101⅞	8.59
ICI Wilmington Inc .... Gtd[27]Notes[3]	7½s	2002	$J15	A−	NC	....	....	G1	99¾	'92	200	112⅜	95⅜	103½	100⅜	100⅜	7.47
ICI North Amer .... [28]Gtd Deb	8⅞s	2006	$mN15	A−	NC	....	....	G1	100	'86	250	124¼	88⅝	114⅝	104⅝	104¾	8.47
Imperial Oil Ltd .... SF Deb	8¾s	2019	$aO15	AA+	±103.7755	[29]100	....	F1	98.80	'89	135	124	87¾	106⅛	103¾	103¾	8.43
Imperial Oil Ltd .... Notes	8.30s	2001	$fA20	AA+	NC	....	....	M5	99.80	'91	200	117⅞	98¾	106⅜	101⅞	101⅞	8.15
Inco Ltd .... SF Deb[30]	9⅞s	2019	$Jd15	BB+	±103.638	[31]100	[32]Z100	M6	97.40	'89	150	119⅛	89⅝	105⅛	103⅝	103⅝	9.53

Uniform Footnote Explanations-See Page 260. Other: [1] (HRO)On 3-15-02 at 100. [2] Greater of 100 or amt based on formula. [3] Co may red in whole,at 100,for tax law chge.
[4] Gtd by Fletcher Challenge Ltd/Indus Ltd. [5] Co must offer repurch at 101 on Chge of Ctrl. [6] (HRO)On Chge of Ctrl at 101. [7] Fr 11-15-00. [8] Co may offer repurch at 101 on Chge of Ctrl.
[9] Due 1-6-04:payable in U.S.$. [10] Gtd by Grand Metropolitan PLC. [11] Red in whole for certain tax chge. [12] Incl disc. [13] (HRO)On Chge of Ctrl at 100. [14] Gtd by Hanson PLC. [15] Issued in min denom $100T.
[16] Gtd by Household Int'l. [17] Gtd by Quebec(Prov). [18] Fr gen'l fds. [19] Invested SF fr gen'l fds. [20] Issued in min denom U.S. $5T. [21] Invested SF,fr gen'l fds ea Mar 1 to 2006.
[22] Invested SF,fr gen'l fds ea Apr 15 to 2006. [23] Issued in min denom U.S.$5T. [24] Fr 1-15-03. [25] (HRO)On 7-7-06 at 100. [26] Was ICI Financial. [27] Gtd by Imperial Chemical Indus PLC.
[28] Subsid of & gtd by Imperial Chemical Indus. [29] Fr 10-15-00. [30] Terms chge for Designated Event&Rat'g Decline. [31] Fr 6-15-00. [32] Co may red in whole if 90% of outstg are put.

Exchange ↓ BONDS Description	Interest Rate	Due	Interest Dates	S&P Rating	Redemption Provisions Regular	Redemption Provisions For Sinking Fund	Redemption Provisions Refund Earliest/ Other	Underwriting Firm	Underwriting Price	Underwriting Year	Out-standing Mil-$ This Issue	Price Range 1988-1998 High	Price Range 1988-1998 Low	1999 High	1999 Low	Month End Price Sale(s) or Bid	Yield to Matur-ity
Inco Ltd ... Deb	9.60s	2022	$Jd15	BB+	[1]104.80	....	....	M6	100	'92	187	117¼	96⅜	112⅝	87⅞	97	9.89
Indah Kiat Int'l Fin Co B.V. ... Gtd[2]Sec[3]Notes[4]	11⅞s	2002	$Jd15	CCC+	NC	....	....	M6	100	'94	200	112½	49	88½	63½	88½	13.41
Indah Kiat Int'l Fin Co B.V. ... Gtd[2]Sec[3]Notes[4]	12½s	2006	$Jd15	CCC+	[5]106.25	....	....	M6	100	'94	150	114	48½	82	62	82	15.23
• Inter-Amer Devel Bank ... Bonds	6⅛s	2006	$Ms8	AAA	NC	....	....	M2	99.12	'96	1000	99	99	No Sale		95.72	6.40
• Inter-Amer Devel Bank ... Bonds	12¼s	2008	$jD15	AAA	NC	....	....	S1	99.30	'83	200	162¼	106½	No Sale		133.94	9.14
Inter-Amer Devel Bank ... bonds	8⅞s	2009	$Jd	AAA	NC	....	....	S1	99.45	'89	300	131.53	96⅝	127.72	111½	111½	7.96
Inter-Amer Devel Bank ... Bonds[6]	8.40s	2009	$mS	AAA	NC	....	....	M2	99.57	'89	300	128.84	93⅜	124.34	108¾	108¾	7.72
• Inter-Amer Devel Bank ... Bonds	8½s	2011	$Ms15	AAA	NC	....	....	S1	99	'86	300	124⅞	85½	No Sale		110.16	7.72
Inter-Amer Devel Bank ... Bonds[7]	7s	2025	$Jd15	AAA	NC	....	....	L3	99.87	'95	300	119⅛	91.66	117.47	95.28	95.28	7.35
Inter-Amer Devel Bank ... Notes	8½s	2001	$Mn	AAA	NC	....	....	G1	99.93	'91	300	119.94	97⅞	107.53	102.47	102.47	8.29
• Int'l Bank for Reconstr[8] ... Bonds	8⅛s	2001	$Ms	AAA	NC	....	....	M2	98.83	'91	1500	107⅝	96⅜	No Sale		101.81	7.98
• Int'l Bank for Reconstr[8] ... Bonds	6¾s	2002	$Jj16	AAA	NC	....	....	M2	99.07	'92	1500	111⅛	93¼	No Sale		100.28	6.73
• Int'l Bank for Reconstr[8] ... Bonds	7⅝s	2023	$Jj19	AAA	NC	....	....	G1	99.49	'93	1250	99⅜	99⅜	No Sale		102¼	7.46
• Int'l Bank for Reconstr ... Global Bonds[8]	6⅜s	2005	$jJ21	AAA	NC	....	....	L3	99.65	'95	1500	99⅝	99⅝	No Sale		97.47	6.54
• Int'l Bank for Reconstr ... Global Bonds	6⅝s	2006	$fA21	AAA	NC	....	....	M2	99.19	'96	1000	99⅛	99⅛	No Sale		98½	6.73
Ireland ... Bonds	8⅝s	2001	$Ao15	AA+	NC	....	....	G1	99⅜	'91	200	119⅛	97⅛	107¼	102¾	102¾	8.39
Ireland ... Bonds	7⅞s	2001	$jD	AA+	NC	....	....	M2	99.15	'91	200	115⅜	97⅜	107⅛	102⅜	102⅜	7.69
Ireland ... Bonds	7⅛s	2002	$jJ15	AA+	NC	....	....	L3	99	'92	300	109½	93⅛	106¼	101	101	7.05
Israel (State of) ... Bonds	6⅜s	2005	$jD15	A−	NC	....	....	S1	99.16	'95	250	104⅜	91⅛	101⅜	91⅝	91⅝	6.96
• Ivaco Inc ... Sr[3]Notes[9]	11½s	2005	$mS15	NR	±105.75	....	....	P1	100	'95	[10]150	113	95⅛	108⅞	96⅛	104⅛	11.04
Japan Fin for Muni Ent ... Gtd Bonds[11]	9⅛s	2000	$Ms13	AAA	NC	....	....	F1	99.71	'90	150	118¾	97	104¼	100½	100½	9.08
Japan Fin for Muni Ent ... Gtd Bonds[11]	9⅛s	2000	$aO11	AAA	NC	....	....	M6	99.52	'90	150	121⅜	97⅞	106¼	102	102	8.95
Japan Fin for Muni Ent ... Gtd Bonds[11]	8.70s	2001	$jJ30	AAA	NC	....	....	G1	99⅞	'91	150	121⅛	99⅞	107⅞	102⅞	102⅞	8.46
Japan Fin for Muni Ent ... Gtd[11]Bonds	7⅜s	2005	$Ao27	AAA	NC	....	....	M2	99.95	'95	300	112	99⅝	109½	100⅛	100⅛	7.37
Kansallis-Osake-Parkki ... Sub Notes[3]	10s	2002	$Mn	A−	NC	....	....	M5	99⅜	'92	200	124¼	99⅜	113¼	106	106	9.43
KfW Int'l Finance ... [12]Gtd[13]Deb[3]	8s	2010	$Fa15	AAA	NC	....	....	M2	99.87	'95	250	123⅞	99¾	122⅛	105⅝	105⅝	7.57
KfW Int'l Finance ... [12]Gtd[13]Deb[3]	7.20s	2014	$Ms15	AAA	NC	....	....	M2	99.53	'94	250	115¼	85⅞	112⅜	98¾	98¾	7.29
KfW Int'l Finance ... [12]Gtd[13]Notes[3]	9½s	2000	$jD15	AAA	NC	....	....	F1	99¾	'88	200	124⅝	95¾	108¼	102⅞	102⅞	9.23
KfW Int'l Finance ... [12]Gtd[13]Notes[3]	9⅛s	2001	$Mn15	AAA	NC	....	....	M6	100	'90	200	123⅛	99⅞	108½	103⅛	103⅛	8.85
KfW Int'l Finance ... [12]Gtd[13]Notes[3]	7⅝s	2004	$Fa15	AAA	NC	....	....	M6	99.34	'92	200	114¾	94⅞	110½	102¼	102¼	7.46
KfW Int'l Finance ... [12]Gtd[3]Notes[13]	7s	2013	$Ms	AAA	NC	....	....	M2	98.89	'93	250	113⅞	84⅜	110½	96⅞	96⅞	7.23
Korea Development Bank ... Bonds	8.65s	2000	$Jj26	BBB	NC	....	....	C5	99.94	'95	500	110	93	101¼	99	100	8.65
Korea Development Bank ... Bonds	6¼s	2000	$Mn	BBB	NC	....	....	S1	99.33	'93	300	103¾	85½	99¾	95⅞	99⅝	6.27
Korea Development Bank ... Bonds[14]	9.60s	2000	$jD	BBB	NC	....	....	G1	99.90	'90	300	122⅜	93¼	103⅝	99⅞	102	9.41
Korea Development Bank ... Bonds[14]	7.90s	2002	$Fa	BBB	NC	....	....	M2	98.61	'92	500	112⅜	85¼	101⅝	95¼	100⅜	7.87
Korea Development Bank ... Bonds	6¾s	2005	$jD	BBB	NC	....	....	M2	99.62	'93	200	104⅜	60⅛	96¼	82⅜	94¼	7.16
Korea Development Bank ... Bonds	6½s	2002	$mN15	BBB	NC	....	....	L3	99.65	'95	500	101⅛	74¾	97⅝	89⅜	96⅞	6.71
Korea Development Bank ... Bonds	7¼s	2006	$Mn15	BBB	NC	....	....	C5	99.24	'96	750	103½	64⅝	98½	89⅜	96⅛	7.54
Korea Development Bank ... Notes	8.09s	2004	$aO6	BBB	NC	....	....	C5	100	'94	500	112⅜	82¼	102¾	97⅝	100⅜	8.06
Korea Electric Power ... Deb[15]	7¾s	2013	$Ao	BBB	NC	....	....	L3	99.35	'93	350	111¼	56¾	97⅜	81⅞	93⅜	8.30
Korea Electric Power ... [16]Deb[17]	6s	2026	$jD	BBB	NC	....	....	G1	100	'96	100	100	74⅞	97¼	86¾	96¾	6.20
Korea Electric Power ... [4]Deb[3]	7s	2027	$Fa	BBB	NC	....	....	G1	100	'97	300	106⅛	62½	94⅞	81⅞	92	7.61
Korea Electric Power ... Deb[3]	6¾s	2027	$fA	BBB	NC	....	....	L3	99.67	'97	200	99⅝	65⅛	95½	85⅛	94⅞	7.11
Korea Electric Power ... [3]Notes[4]	7s	2002	$aO	BBB	NC	....	....	U1	99.32	'97	150	100½	72¾	98⅝	89¾	97⅞	7.15
Korea Electric Power ... Notes[15]	8s	2002	$jJ	BBB	NC	....	....	L3	99.26	'92	300	113⅝	84¼	101⅜	92¼	100⅜	7.97
Korea Electric Power ... Notes[15]	6⅜s	2003	$jD	BBB	NC	....	....	L3	98.55	'93	1350	100⅝	64⅛	95⅞	85⅛	94⅝	6.74
Korea Electric Power ... [18]Amortizing[3]Deb[19]	7.40s	2016	$Ao	BBB	NC	....	....	S1	99.66	'96	171	104⅛	71¾	96	83⅜	92⅛	....
Korea Electric Power ... Dfrd[3]Int[20]Deb[21]	7.95s	2096	$Ao	BBB	NC	....	....	S1	14.00	'96	208	102⅝	4⅝	20¼	9⅝	17¼	Flat
Korea Telecom ... Notes[3]	7½s	2006	$Jd	BBB	NC	....	....	M6	99.53	'96	150	105	68⅞	97½	86¾	96¾	7.75
Landeskreditbank Baden-Wurt ... Sub Notes[3]	7⅝s	2023	$Fa	AAA	NC	....	....	S1	99.05	'93	300	117⅞	87¾	117¾	97⅞	97⅞	7.79
• Landesbank Baden-Wurttemberg[22] ... Sub Notes[3]	7⅞s	2004	$Ao15	AAA	NC	....	....	M5	99.27	'92	250	99¼	99¼	No Sale		100	7.87

Uniform Footnote Explanations-See Page 260. Other: [1] Fr 6-15-02. [2] Gtd by P.T. Indah Kiat Pulp & Paper Corp. [3] Co may red in whole,at 100,for tax law chge. [4] (HRO)On Chge of Ctrl at 100. [5] Fr 6-15-01. [6] (HRO)On 9-1-04 at 100. [7] Also issuable in regis form. [8] A/K/A World Bank. [9] (HRO)On Chge of Ctrl at 101. [10] Defeased,fds deposited w/trustee. [11] Gtd by Japan. [12] Gtd by Kreditanstalt fur Wiederaufbau. [13] (HRO)On or aft a Redemption Event at 100. [14] Issued in min denom U.S. $5T. [15] Co may red,in whole,at 100 for tax law chge. [16] (HRO)On 12-1-01(06) at 100. [17] Co may red in whole, at 100,for tax law chge. [18] Amortizing pyts due on int dates. [19] (HRO)On Chge of Ctrl at Amortized Val. [20] (HRO)On Chge of Ctrl at Accreted Val. [21] Int accrues at 7.95% fr 4-1-16. [22] Was Landeskeditbank Baden-Wurt.

Exchange ↓ BONDS Description	Issue	Interest Rate	Due	Interest Dates	S&P Rating	Redemption Provisions Regular	For Sinking Fund	Refund Earliest/ Other	Underwriting Firm	Price	Year	Out-standing Mil-$ This Issue	Price Range 1988-1998 High	Low	1999 High	Low	Month End Price Sale(s) or Bid	Yield to Matur-ity
LASMO(USA) Inc	Gtd[1]Deb[2]	7.30s	2027	$mN15	BBB	[3]Z100	....	....	C1	99⅜	'97	400	105⅛	85⅞	96⅜	88¼	91⅛	8.01
LASMO(USA) Inc	Gtd[2]Notes[1]	7⅛s	2003	$Jd	BBB	NC	....	....	M2	99.14	'93	200	105⅞	88½	101½	98⅛	98⅜	7.24
LASMO(USA) Inc	Gtd[1]Notes[2]	7½s	2006	$Jd30	BBB	NC	....	....		99.37	'96	300	109⅜	98⅜	102⅞	97¼	98⅜	7.62
LASMO(USA) Inc	Gtd[2]Notes[1]	6¾s	2007	$jD15	BBB	NC	....	....	C1	99.75	'97	200	103⅞	95¼	98⅜	90⅛	94¼	7.16
LASMO(USA) Inc	Gtd[2]Notes[1]	8⅜s	2023	$Jd	BBB	[4]*103.9375	....	....	M2	99½	'93	150	117⅛	87	109	100⅜	101	8.29
Le Groupe Videotron Ltee	Sr Notes[5]	10⅝s	2005	$Fa15	BBB–	[6]±104.80	....	....	M2	99⅜	'95	200	112¾	99⅜	109	104	105¼	10.09
Legrand S.A.	[7]Deb[1]	8½s	2025	$Fa15	A	NC	....	Z100	M5	99.15	'95	400	127⅝	99	119¼	102¼	104	8.17
• London Insurance Group	Notes[1]	6⅞s	2005	$mS15	AA	NC	....	....	L3	99.58	'95	150	99½	99½	No Sale		95	7.24
MacMillan Bloedel(Del)	Gtd[8]Deb	8½s	2004	$Jj15	A	NC	....	....	G1	99.85	'92	150	112¾	90¾	107¼	101⅝	101⅝	8.36
MacMillan Bloedel Ltd	Deb[1]	7.70s	2026	$Fa15	A	NC	....	....	S1	99.68	'96	150	112¾	87⅝	98⅞	88⅝	88¾	8.67
MacMillan Bloedel Ltd	Notes[1]	6¾s	2006	$Fa15	A	NC	....	....	S1	99.97	'96	150	101¾	91	99½	92¼	92⅜	7.31
Malayan Banking Berhad[9]	Sub[1]Notes[10]	7⅛s	2005	$mS15	BB+	NC	....	....	M6	99.36	'95	250	104⅜	65⅜	93¾	65⅛	93⅝	7.61
Malaysia	Bonds[11]	9⅞s	2000	$mS27	BBB	NC	....	....	S1	99	'90	200	123⅛	99	104⅝	101	101	9.78
Manitoba (Prov of)	Ser AZ Deb[11]	7¾s	2016	$jJ17	AA–	NC	....	....	S1	99.65	'86	150	119⅛	86⅞	119½	101⅝	101⅝	7.62
Manitoba (Prov of)	Ser BM Deb[11]	9⅛s	2018	$Jj15	AA–	NC	....	....	M2	99.32	'88	200	134¾	93⅛	135	116	116	7.86
Manitoba (Prov of)	Ser BU[11]Deb	9⅝s	2018	$jD	AA–	NC	....	....	S1	99.08	'88	300	141¼	96	141½	121¼	121¼	7.94
Manitoba (Prov of)	Ser CB[11]Deb	8.80s	2020	$Jj15	AA–	NC	....	....	F1	99.68	'90	250	132⅜	87¾	132⅝	113⅛	113⅛	7.78
Manitoba (Prov of)	Ser CD Deb	9¼s	2020	$Ao	AA–	NC	....	....	S1	99.40	'90	300	137¾	93⅜	138⅛	117¾	117¾	7.86
Manitoba (Prov of)	Ser CJ Deb	9½s	2000	$aO	AA–	NC	....	....	M2	99.73	'90	350	122⅞	99⅝	107	102⅛	102⅛	9.30
Manitoba (Prov of)	Ser CK Deb	9s	2000	$jD15	AA–	NC	....	....	F1	99.42	'90	250	120¾	99⅜	106⅞	102⅛	102⅛	8.81
Manitoba (Prov of)	Ser CN Deb	8¾s	2001	$Mn15	AA–	NC	....	....	S1	99.55	'91	300	119⅜	98	107⅝	102⅜	102⅜	8.55
Manitoba (Prov of)	Ser CO Deb	8⅞s	2021	$mS15	AA–	NC	....	....	M2	99.62	'91	300	134½	98¾	134¾	114¼	114¼	7.77
Manitoba (Prov of)	Ser CQ Deb	8s	2002	$Ao15	AA–	NC	....	....	S1	99.53	'92	300	115	97¾	108¼	100¼	100¼	7.98
Manitoba (Prov of)	Ser CP Deb	7¾s	2002	$Fa	AA–	NC	....	....	F1	99.93	'92	500	113⅛	96½	107	99¾	99¾	7.77
Manitoba (Prov of)	Ser CT Deb	6⅞s	2002	$mS15	AA–	NC	....	....	M2	99.29	'92	300	107¼	90⅞	105½	99⅝	99⅝	6.90
Manitoba (Prov of)	Ser CZ Deb	6¾s	2003	$Ms	AA–	NC	....	....	S1	100	'93	300	106¾	89⅝	105⅝	99¼	99¼	6.80
Manitoba (Prov of)	Ser DH Deb	6⅛s	2004	$Jj19	AA–	NC	....	....	C5	99.90	'94	350	104⅝	84¾	103⅝	96½	96½	6.35
Mass Transit Railway Corp	Notes[1]	7¼s	2005	$aO	A	NC	....	....	G1	99.90	'95	300	105⅝	93½	105⅝	98	98½	7.36
Matsushita Elec Industrial	Bonds[1]	7¼s	2002	$fA	AA–	NC	....	....	L3	99.32	'92	1000	110⅜	93½	105⅝	100⅜	100⅜	7.22
Mayne Nickless Ltd	Notes[1]	6¼s	2006	$Fa	BBB+	NC	....	....	M2	99.58	'96	350	103⅝	90¼	102⅞	89⅛	89⅛	7.01
MDC Communications	Sr Sub Notes[1]	10½s	2006	$jD	B	[12]105.25	....	....	G1	100	'96	125	108⅜	94½	104	97	98¾	10.63
Merita Bank Ltd[9]	Sub Notes[1]	6½s	2006	$Jj15	A–	NC	....	....	M5	99.37	'96	250	102⅝	91¼	102½	93¾	93⅞	6.92
Methanex Corp	Notes[1]	7.40s	2002	$fA15	BBB	NC	....	....	G1	99.52	'95	150	105¼	97¼	104⅛	90¾	90¾	8.15
Methanex Corp	Notes[1]	7¾s	2005	$fA15	BBB	NC	....	....	G1	99.45	'95	250	109⅜	96⅞	107⅞	82⅝	82⅝	9.38
Midland Bank plc	Sub[13]Notes[1]	8⅝s	2004	$jD15	A+	NC	....	....	M5	99⅝	'94	400	115¾	98⅞	114⅛	103¾	103¾	8.31
• Midland Bank plc	Sub Notes[1]	7⅝s	2006	$Jd15	A+	NC	....	....		99.76	'96	500	102⅞	98⅞	No Sale		99⅝	7.65
• Midland Bank plc	Sub Notes	6.95s	2011	$Ms15	A+	NC	....	....		99.72	'96	300	99⅝	90⅞	No Sale		92½	7.51
Midland Bank plc	[13]Sub[1]Notes[14]	7.65s	2025	$Mn	A+	NC	....	....	L3	99.83	'95	300	118⅝	99	110¾	97⅜	100	7.65
Multicanal S.A.	[1]Notes[5]	9¼s	2002	$Fa	BB+	NC	....	[15]Z109.25	Exch.	Exch.	'97	103	104	75½	93½	82½	93	9.94
Multicanal S.A.	[1]Notes[5]	10½s	2007	$Fa	BB+	NC	....	[15]Z110.50	Exch.	Exch.	'97	86.3	109½	64¼	91½	74½	86	12.20
Murrin Murrin Hldgs Pty	Sr Notes[5]	9⅜s	2007	[16]$ms	BB–	[17]104.34375	....	[18]Z109.375	Exch.	Exch.	'98	340	100⅛	74	92⅛	85	88	10.65
• Naples (City of)	(Amort[19])Notes[1]	7.52s	2006	$jJ15	A–	NC	....	....	M2	100	'96	195	100	100	No Sale		80	....
Nat'l Bank of Canada[20]	Sub[1]Notes 'B'[10]	8⅛s	2004	$fA15	A–	NC	....	....	G1	99.98	'94	250	114⅝	95¼	111¼	102⅝	102⅝	7.92
National Bank of Hungary	Bonds	8⅞s	2013	$mN	BBB	NC	....	....	M6	100	'93	200	121⅛	89	119¾	104⅝	104⅝	8.48
Nat'l Westminster Bancorp[21]	[22]Gtd Cap Notes[1]	9⅜s	2003	$mN15	AA–	NC	....	....	M2	99.48	'88	500	124½	94	114⅝	106¼	106¼	8.82
Nat'l Westminster Bank[9]PLC	Sub[1]Notes	9.45s	2001	$Mn	AA–	NC	....	....	G1	100	'91	750	122¾	98¼	108⅛	103⅜	103⅜	9.14
New Brunswick (Prov of)	Ser DM Deb	9½s	2018	$Ms3	AA–	[23]100	....	....	F1	99.80	'88	139	129	92⅛	115¼	106⅞	106⅞	8.89
New Brunswick (Prov of)	Ser DU Deb	9¾s	2020	$Mn15	AA–	NC	....	....	S1	98.85	'90	200	142⅜	96¼	144	122¾	122¾	7.94
New Brunswick (Prov of)	Deb	7⅛s	2002	$aO	AA–	NC	....	....	S1	99.68	'92	225	109⅝	92½	106¼	100⅛	100⅛	7.12
New Brunswick (Prov of)	Deb[24]	7⅝s	2004	$Jd29	AA–	NC	....	....	F1	99.35	'94	200	112¼	94	110⅜	101⅝	101⅝	7.50
New Brunswick (Prov of)	Deb	7⅝s	2013	$Fa15	AA–	NC	....	....	F1	99.85	'93	200	119¼	89	117⅛	100⅜	100⅜	7.60

Uniform Footnote Explanations-See Page 260. **Other:** [1] Co may red in whole,at 100,for tax law chge. [2] Gtd by LASMO plc. [3] Red at greater of 100 or amt based on formula. [4] Fr 6-1-03. [5] (HRO)On Chge of Ctrl at 101. [6] Fr 2-15-00. [7] (HRO)On Chge of Ctrl at 100. [8] Gtd by MacMillan Bloedel Ltd. [9] N.Y. Branch. [10] Issued in min denom $100T. [11] Issued in min denom U.S. $5T. [12] Fr 12-1-01. [13] Issued in min denom $150T. [14] (HRO)On 5-1-07 at 100. [15] Max $25M red w/proceeds of Pub Eq Off'g. [16] Due 8-31-07. [17] Fr 9-1-02. [18] Max $119M red w/procceds of Pub Eq Off'g. [19] Princ pyts of $50 due ea Jan&Jul 15. [20] NY Branch. [21] Was NatWest Capital. [22] Gtd by Nat'l Westminster Bank PLC. [23] Fr 3-3-03. [24] Invested SF,fds set aside.

Exchange ↓ BONDS Description	Interest Rate	Due	Interest Dates	S&P Rating	Redemption Provisions Regular	For Sinking Fund	Refund Earliest/ Other	Underwriting Firm	Price	Year	Out-standing Mil-$ This Issue	Price Range 1988-1998 High	Low	1999 High	Low	Month End Price Sale(s) or Bid	Yield to Maturity
New Brunswick (Prov of) Deb[1]	8¾s	2022	$Mn	AA−	NC	....	....	F1	99.70	'92	200	132⅛	97¾	133½	112⅞	112⅞	7.75
New Zealand (Govt) Notes[2]	8¾s	2006	$jD15	AA+	NC	....	....	F1	100	'86	300	125¾	87¾	121⅞	109⅝	109⅝	7.98
• New Zealand (Govt) Notes	9⅞s	2011	$Jj15	AA+	NC	....	....	K2	99¼	'86	150	107	98	No Sale		100	9.87
New Zealand (Govt) Notes	8¾s	2016	$Ao	AA+	NC	....	....	M2	99.57	'86	200	130½	86⅛	128⅛	110½	110½	7.92
New Zealand (Govt) Notes[2]	9⅛s	2016	$mS25	AA+	NC	....	....	G1	99	'86	150	135	89⅛	132⅝	114⅛	114⅛	8.00
Newfoundland (Prov) SF[1]Deb	11⅝s	2007	$aO15	A−	NC	....	....	M2	100	'87	100	147¾	107¼	140½	123⅛	123⅛	9.44
Newfoundland (Prov) SF[1]Deb	9⅞s	2020	$Jd	A−	NC	....	....	M2	99.76	'90	150	140¾	95¼	141	119⅝	119⅝	8.25
Newfoundland (Prov) SF[1]Deb	10s	2020	$jD	A−	NC	....	....	M2	99.74	'90	150	142¾	99¾	143	120¾	121⅛	8.25
Newfoundland (Prov) SF Deb[1]	9s	2021	$aO15	A−	NC	....	....	G1	100	'91	200	131½	96¼	131¾	110⅞	111⅛	8.10
Newfoundland (Prov) SF[1]Deb	8.65s	2022	$aO22	A−	NC	....	....	M2	100	'92	200	127¾	91⅞	128⅛	107⅜	107⅝	8.04
Newfoundland(Prov) SF[1]Deb	7.32s	2023	$aO	A−	NC	....	....	M2	100	'93	200	111⅞	79⅝	112¼	93⅜	93⅝	7.82
News Amer Holdings Inc [3]Sr[4]Deb[5]	10⅛s	2012	$aO5	BBB−	[6]104.50	....	....	M2	100	'92	300	123½	98¾	119⅛	108⅜	110	9.20
News Amer Holdings Inc [5]Sr[3]Deb[4]	9¼s	2013	$Fa	BBB−	NC	....	....	M2	99.24	'93	500	126⅛	95	127¼	108	108¼	8.54
News Amer Holdings Inc [3]Sr[4]Deb[5]	7.60s	2015	$aO11	BBB−	NC	....	....		99.69	'95	200	106⅞	91	110	93⅞	95⅞	7.93
News Amer Holdings Inc [5]Sr[4]Deb[3]	8¼s	2018	$FA10	BBB−	NC	....	....	M2	100	'93	250	114¼	85¾	117½	98⅜	100¼	8.23
News Amer Holdings Inc [5]Sr[3]Deb[4]	8⅞s	2023	$Ao26	BBB−	NC	....	....	M2	98.09	'93	250	121¼	90⅛	125⅝	103⅞	105¾	8.39
News Amer Holdings Inc [3]Sr[3]Deb[5]	7¾s	2024	$Jj20	BBB−	NC	....	....	M2	100	'94	200	108¼	79⅞	111½	92½	94⅝	8.21
News Amer Holdings Inc [4]Sr[3]Deb[5]	9½s	2024	$jJ15	BBB−	NC	....	....	M2	99.90	'94	200	128⅛	98	132	109¼	112	8.48
News Amer Holdings[5]Inc [3]Sr[7]Deb[4]	8½s	2025	$Fa23	BBB−	NC	....	....	M2	100	'95	200	123¼	99⅞	116⅞	102¾	102¾	8.27
News Amer Holdings Inc [3]Sr[4]Deb[5]	7.70s	2025	$aO30	BBB−	NC	....	....		99.54	'95	250	108	89⅛	111⅞	91¾	93¼	8.26
News Amer Holdings Inc [3]Sr[4]Deb[5]	8.45s	2034	$fA	BBB−	NC	....	....	G1	100	'94	200	126½	91¼	116¼	101⅞	101⅞	8.29
News Amer Holdings Inc [3]Sr[4]Deb[8]	7¾s	2045	$jD	BBB−	NC	....	....	G1	98⅞	'95	600	107⅜	86¾	111⅞	88⅛	91⅛	8.50
News Amer Holdings Inc [9]Sr[4]Deb[5]	7.90s	2095	$jD	BBB−	NC	....	....	G1	99.50	'95	150	109	86½	112¼	88¾	91¼	8.66
News Amer Holdings Inc [5]Sr[3]Notes[4]	7½s	2000	$Ms	BBB−	NC	....	....	M2	100	'93	500	106¼	94	102⅛	100⅛	100⅛	7.49
News Amer Holdings Inc [5]Sr[3]Notes[4]	7.45s	2000[10]	$ms15	BBB−	NC	....	....	C4	100	'93	100	105⅝	93½	102½	100⅜	100⅜	7.42
News Amer Holdings Inc [5]Sr[3]Notes[4]	8⅝s	2003	$Fa	BBB−	NC	....	....	M2	99.85	'93	500	113	96½	111	103⅜	103⅜	8.34
News Amer Holdings Inc [5]Sr[3]Notes[4]	8½s	2005	$Fa15	BBB−	NC	....	....	M5	100	'93	500	113¾	94⅝	114	103½	103¾	8.19
Noranda Inc F/R[11]Deb		2000	$QAug18	BBB	NC	....	....	U1	100	'93	100	101⅞	99	101	100¼	100⅜	....
Noranda Inc Deb	8s	2003	$Jd	BBB	NC	....	....	G1	100	'93	200	110⅛	94⅞	103½	100	100	8.00
Noranda Inc Deb	8⅛s	2004	$Jd15	BBB	NC	....	....	F1	99.90	'94	300	111⅜	92¾	104⅝	92½	100¼	8.10
Noranda Inc Deb	7s	2005	$jJ15	BBB	NC	....	....	G1	99.89	'95	200	105	94⅝	98⅛	94⅝	94⅝	7.40
Noranda Forest Inc Deb	7½s	2003	$jJ15	BBB	NC	....	....	F1	99.24	'93	150	107⅝	90¾	102½	98⅜	99⅛	7.56
Noranda Forest Deb	6⅞s	2005	$mN15	BBB	[12]Z100	....	....	C5	99.91	'95	200	105	92⅞	168⅛	93½	94½	7.27
• Norcen Energy Resources Ltd Deb	7⅜s	2006	$Mn15	BBB−	NC	....	....	G1	99.38	'96	250	99⅜	99⅜	No Sale		95¼	7.74
• Norcen Energy Resources Ltd Deb	7.80s	2008	$jJ2	BBB−	NC	....	....	G1	100	'96	150	101	100	No Sale		97	8.04
Norsk Hydro a.s Deb[3]	9s	2012	$Ao15	A	NC	....	....	G1	100	'92	350	130¾	99½	124¾	108⅞	108⅞	8.27
Norsk Hydro a.s Deb[3]	7¾s	2023	$Jd15	A	NC	....	....	M6	99.53	'93	300	116⅛	85½	111⅜	95⅞	97½	7.95
Norsk Hydro a.s. Deb[3]	7.15s	2025	$mN15	A	[12]*100	....	....	G1	99.58	'95	250	107⅞	90⅞	103⅜	89⅝	90⅜	7.91
Northern Telecom Capital Gtd[13]Notes	7.40s	2006	$Jd15	A	NC	....	....	G1	99.33	'96	150	113¾	99¼	109¼	100¼	100¼	7.38
Northern Telecom Capital GtdNotes	7⅞s	2026	$Jd15	A	NC	....	....	G1	99.53	'96	150	121½	98¾	116⅝	99¼	99¼	7.93
Northern Telecom Ltd. Notes	8¾s	2001	$Jd12	A	NC	....	....	S1	99.56	'91	231	118½	98⅝	107⅝	102½	102½	8.53
Northern Telecom Ltd. Notes	6⅞s	2002	$aO	A	NC	....	....	G1	100	'92	300	109⅛	90⅞	105¼	99⅝	99⅝	6.92
Northern Telecom Ltd. Notes	6s	2003	$mS	A	NC	....	....	G1	99.51	'93	200	103½	84¼	102⅞	96⅝	96⅜	6.23
Northern Telecom Ltd. Notes	6⅞s	2023	$mS	A	NC	....	....	G1	98.71	'93	200	105⅝	78⅜	100⅞	89⅞	90⅞	7.56
NOVA Chemicals corp Notes	7.40s	2009	$Ao	BBB+	[14]Z100	....	....	M7	99.87	'99	250	....	....	103¾	93¾	93¾	7.89
NOVA Chemicals Ltd[15] Deb	7⅞s	2025	$mS15	BBB	[16]103.174	....	....	C5	98.47	'95	100	99¼	93½	102⅝	96	97¼	8.10
NOVA Chemicals Ltd Deb[17]	7s	2026	$fA15	BBB	NC	....	....	C5	100	'96	150	100	100	105⅝	96⅝	96⅝	7.24
NOVA Chemicals Ltd Deb[18]	7¼s	2028	$fA15	BBB	NC	....	....	C5	99.05	'96	125	102¾	96⅞	99¼	89⅞	89⅞	8.07
NOVA Chemicals Ltd[15] Notes	6½s	2000	$mS22	BBB	NC	....	....	C5	99.62	'95	150	100¾	96¾	100⅝	99¼	99¼	6.55
NOVA Chemicals Ltd[15] Notes	7s	2005	$mS22	BBB	NC	....	....	C5	100	'95	100	102⅞	93¾	102⅞	94¼	94¼	7.43
NOVA Gas Transmission[19] Deb	8½s	2012	$jD15	A−	NC	....	....	G1	99.22	'92	175	127⅛	94	122¼	110½	112¼	7.57

Uniform Footnote Explanations-See Page 260. Other: [1] Invested SF,fds set aside. [2] Issued in min denom U.S. $5T. [3] Co may red in whole,at 100,for tax law chge. [4] (HRO)On Chge of Ctrl Triggering Event at 101. [5] Gtd by News Corp Ltd. [6] Fr 10-15-02. [7] (HRO)On 2-23-07 at 100. [8] Gtd by NewsCorp Ltd. [9] Co may red in whole,at 100, for tax law chge. [10] Due 6-1-00. [11] Int(min 5%)adj qtrly(3 Mo LIBOR&0.75%). [12] Greater of 100 or amt based on formula. [13] Gtd by Northern Telecom Ltd. [14] Red at greater of 100 or amt based on formula. [15] Was Novacor Chemicals Ltd. [16] Fr 9-15-05. [17] (HRO)On 8-15-03 at 100. [18] (HRO)On 8-15-08 at 100. [19] Was NOVA Corp of Alberta.

Exchange	BONDS Description	Interest Rate	Due	Interest Dates	S&P Rating	Redemption Provisions: Regular	For Sinking Fund	Refund Earliest/ Other	Underwriting: Firm	Price	Year	Out-standing Mil-$ This Issue	Price Range 1988-1998: High	Low	1999: High	Low	Month End Price Sale(s) or Bid	Yield to Matur-ity
•	NOVA Gas Transmission[1] Deb	7⅞s	2023	$Ao	A−	NC	....	....	G1	99.36	'93	200	109½	97⅛	No Sale		121⅛	6.50
	NOVA Gas Transmission[1] Notes	7⅞s	2002	$jD15	A−	NC	....	....	G1	99.85	'92	125	112½	94⅛	107¾	102⅜	103	7.64
	NOVA Gas Transmission Notes	8½s	2004	$jD8	A−	NC	....	....	M6	99.74	'94	125	115⅞	97½	112½	106⅜	107¼	7.92
	Nova Scotia Pwr SF Deb	9.40s	2021	$Ao	A−	NC	....	....	M2	99.90	'91	300	135¼	97⅞	133⅛	133⅛	133⅛	7.06
	Nova Scotia (Prov) SF[2] Deb '8V'	8⅞s	2016	$Ms15	A−	NC	....	....	M2	99¼	'86	150	129¼	87⅛	129⅞	110⅝	110⅝	8.02
	Nova Scotia (Prov) SF[2]Deb '9B'	9½s	2019	$Fa	A−	NC	....	....	M2	99.90	'89	200	138	94⅜	138¾	117⅜	117⅜	8.09
	Nova Scotia (Prov) SF[3]Deb[2] '9D'	8¼s	2019	$mN15	A−	NC	....	....	M2	99.78	'89	250	124¼	83⅝	125	105⅛	105⅛	7.85
	Nova Scotia (Prov) SF Deb[4] '9E'	9¼s	2020	$Ms	A−	NC	....	....	M2	99.07	'90	300	136	92½	136¾	115⅜	115⅜	8.02
	Nova Scotia (Prov) Deb '9F'	9⅜s	2002	$jJ15	A−	NC	....	....	M2	99.36	'90	300	123⅛	95⅜	112⅝	105⅛	105⅛	8.92
	Nova Scotia (Prov) Deb[4] '9J'	9⅛s	2021	$Mn	A−	NC	....	....	M2	98.82	'91	300	135⅜	95¼	136⅛	114⅜	114⅜	7.98
	Nova Scotia (Prov) Deb[4]	7¼s	2013	$jJ27	A−	NC	....	....	M2	98.96	'93	300	114¼	82¾	111¾	95⅞	95⅞	7.56
	Nova Scotia (Prov) Deb[4]	8¾s	2022	$Ao	A−	NC	....	....	M2	98.30	'92	300	131½	95¼	132¼	110⅝	110⅝	7.91
	Nova Scotia (Prov) Deb[4]	8¼s	2022	$jJ30	A−	NC	....	....	M2	98.20	'92	300	125½	90⅜	126¼	105⅜	105⅜	7.83
	Ontario (Prov) Bonds[5]	7¾s	2002	$Jd4	AA−	NC	....	....	M5	99.49	'92	2000	113⅛	96	107⅝	101¾	101¾	7.62
	Ontario (Prov) Bonds[5]	7⅝s	2004	$Jd22	AA−	NC	....	....	G1	99.86	'94	1000	112¼	94	110¾	102	102	7.47
	Ontario (Prov) Bonds[5]	7s	2005	$fA4	AA−	NC	....	....	L3	99.61	'95	1000	110	96¾	109⅛	99⅝	99⅝	7.03
	Ontario (Prov) Notes	8s	2001	$aO17	AA−	NC	....	....	M6	99.92	'91	750	115⅜	97¾	107	101¾	101¾	7.86
	Pacific Dunlop USA Inc (⁶Gtd) Notes[7]	9¾s	2000	$jD15	A−	NC	....	....	M2	99.80	'90	100	125⅛	99¼	108	102⅝	102⅝	9.50
•	Panamerican Beverages Sr Notes[7]	8⅛s	2003	$Ao	BBB−	NC	....	....	L1	99.45	'96	150	99⅜	98½	98	91	92¼	8.81
•	PDV America, Inc Sr[8]Notes[9]	7¾s	2000	$fA	B+	NC	....	....	S1	100	'93	250	100	100	No Sale		99	7.83
	Petro-Canada Deb	9¼s	2021	$aO15	BBB+	NC	....	....	M6	100	'91	300	131	100	125¼	106⅜	106⅜	8.70
	Petro-Canada Deb	7⅞s	2026	$Jd15	BBB+	[10]Z100	....	....	M2	99.55	'96	275	115¾	98¼	108	94	96	8.20
	Petro-Canada Notes	8.60s	2001	$aO15	BBB+	NC	....	....	M6	100	'91	300	117⅛	97⅝	106¼	102¼	102¼	8.41
	Petro-Canada(Ltd) ([11]Gtd) Deb	9½s	2003	$Jd30	AA+	NC	....	....	M6	100	'88	[12]96.4	130	95⅝	117⅛	109⅞	110½	8.60
	Petro-Canada(Ltd) ([11]Gtd) Deb	8.60s	2010	$Jj15	AA+	NC	....	....	M6	100	'90	[12]158	129¼	90¾	127⅜	110	110	7.82
	Petro-Canada(Ltd) ([11]Gtd) Deb	8¼s	2016	$jD15	AA+	NC	....	....	M6	98⅛	'86	[12]38.2	128⅜	83⅛	128⅝	107¼	107⅜	7.68
	Petro-Canada(Ltd) ([11]Gtd) Deb	9.70s	2018	$Jd30	AA+	NC	....	....	M6	100	'88	[12]16.1	142	96⅛	139¼	125	126⅝	7.66
	Petro-Canada(Ltd) ([11]Gtd)[13]Deb	8.80s	2019	$Jd	AA+	NC	....	....	M2	100	'89	[12]3.50	129⅜	95¾	119⅝	102¼	102¼	8.60
	Philippine Long Distance Tel Notes	10⅝s	2004	$Jd2	BB+	NC	....	....	B11	99.48	'94	250	116¼	83⅛	103⅝	99⅛	102⅝	10.35
	Philips Electronics NV Deb[7]	7¼s	2013	$fA15	BBB+	NC	....	....	G1	99.15	'93	250	109½	82¾	107⅞	96⅜	96⅜	7.52
	Philips Electronics N.V. Deb[7]'A'	7⅛s	2025	$Mn15	BBB+	NC	....	....	C5	99.39	'95	175	112⅜	95	110⅜	95	95½	7.46
	Philips Electronics N.V. Deb[7]'B'	7¾s	2025	$Mn15	BBB+	NC	....	....	C5	99.66	'95	175	118¾	94½	112⅜	96½	96½	8.03
	Philips Electronics NV Notes[7]	6¾s	2003	$fA15	BBB+	NC	....	....	G1	99.72	'93	250	105⅝	87⅞	104⅞	97½	97¾	6.90
	Philips Electronics NV Notes[7]	7¾s	2004	$Ao15	BBB+	NC	....	....	M5	100	'94	250	111	93⅞	110	100⅞	100⅞	7.68
	Philips Electronics N.V. Notes[7]	8⅜s	2006	$mS15	BBB+	NC	....	....	M6	99.58	'94	400	116⅜	96⅜	116⅜	103¾	103¾	8.07
	Philips Electronics NV [7]Notes[14]	7.20s	2026	$Jd	BBB+	NC	....	....	M5	99.77	'96	300	111½	97⅜	110¼	96¼	96¼	7.48
	Placer Dome Inc Notes	7⅛s	2003	$Mn15	BBB	NC	....	....	M5	99.81	'93	200	106½	89⅞	99⅜	96	97	7.34
	Placer Dome Inc Notes	7⅛s	2007	$Jd15	BBB	NC	....	....	M5	99.54	'95	100	106⅜	94⅜	97¾	91¼	91¾	7.76
	Placer Dome Inc Notes	7¾s	2015	$Jd15	BBB	NC	....	....	M5	99.03	'95	100	110½	93½	99½	90⅛	90⅛	8.60
	Pohang Iron & Steel Co. Ltd Notes[7]	7½s	2002	$fA	BBB−	NC	....	....	G1	99.37	'92	250	109⅛	66½	99⅝	92¼	98¾	7.59
	Pohang Iron & Steel Co. Ltd Notes[7]	6⅝s	2003	$jJ	BBB−	NC	....	....	S1	99.20	'93	200	103½	65¼	96¼	85⅝	95¼	6.95
	Pohang Iron & Steel Co. Ltd Notes[7]	7⅜s	2005	$Mn15	BBB−	NC	....	....	M6	99.60	'95	250	106¾	65¼	98⅛	86¾	95½	7.72
	Portugal (Republic of) Bonds	5¾s	2003	$aO8	AA	NC	....	....	M2	99.35	'93	1000	103½	82⅞	102½	96⅜	96⅜	5.97
•	P.T. ALatieF Freeport Fin B.V. Sr[7]Notes[15]	9¾s	2001	$Ao15	CCC	NC	....	....	C5	99.90	'94	120	100	100	100	97	87	11.21
	Quebec (Prov) Deb[16]	9⅛s	2000	$Ms	A+	NC	....	....	M2	99.85	'90	500	119⅞	96⅜	104⅛	100⅜	100⅜	9.09
	Quebec (Prov) Deb	7½s	2002	$jJ15	A+	NC	....	....	M2	99.77	'92	750	111½	93¼	106⅜	101	101	7.42
	Quebec (Prov) Deb	8.80s	2003	$Ao15	A+	NC	....	....	F1	99.69	'91	500	121	96⅞	112⅜	104¾	104¾	8.40
	Quebec (Prov) [16]Deb[4]	11s	2015	$Jd15	A+	[17]±103.75	....	....	M2	99¾	'85	200	132¼	105½	110⅞	105⅜	105⅜	10.44
	Quebec (Prov) Deb[4]NJ	7½s	2023	$jJ15	A+	NC	....	....	F1	99.69	'93	1000	114¾	82½	115⅛	96⅞	96⅞	7.74
	Quebec (Prov) Deb[18]NN	7⅛s	2024	$Fa	A+	NC	....	....	M2	99.48	'94	1000	110⅛	78⅝	110½	92¾	92⅞	7.67
	Quebec (Prov) Deb NS	8⅝s	2005	$Jj19	A+	NC	....	....	C5	99.30	'95	500	116	97½	115	105¾	105¾	8.15

Uniform Footnote Explanations-See Page 260. Other: [1] Was NOVA Corp of Alberta. [2] Invested SF. [3] (HRO)On 11-15-01 at 100. [4] Invested SF,fds set aside. [5] Red in whole,at 100,for tax law chge. [6] Gtd by Pacific Dunlop Ltd. [7] Co may red in whole,at 100,for tax law chge. [8] Gtd by Properyn B.V. & Petroleos de Venezuela, S.A. [9] (HRO)On Chge of Ctrl at 101. [10] Greater of 100 or amt based on formula. [11] Gtd by Canada. [12] Defeased,fds deposited w/trustee. [13] (HRO)On 6-1-04 at 100. [14] (HRO)On 6-1-06 at 100. [15] Gtd by Freeport-McMoRan Copper & Gold Inc. [16] Issued in min denom U.S. $5T. [17] Fr 6-15-00. [18] Invested SF, fds set aside.

Exchange ↓ BONDS Description, Interest Rate, Due and Interest Dates				S&P Rating	Redemption Provisions Regular	For Sinking Fund	Refund Earliest/ Other	Underwriting Firm	Price	Year	Out-standing Mil-$ This Issue	Price Range 1988-1998 High	Low	1999 High	Low	Month End Price Sale(s) or Bid	Yield to Matur-ity
Quebec (Prov)....Deb NY	6½s	2006	$Jj17	A+	NC	....	....	M2	99.54	'96	500	105¼	92	104¾	95⅞	95⅞	6.78
Quebec (Prov)....Deb[1]	8⅝s	2026	$jD	A+	NC	....	....	F1	99.60	'86	300	130⅛	84⅜	129¾	108	108¼	7.97
QUNO Corp....Sr[2]Notes[3]	9⅛s	2005	$Mn15	BBB	[4]±104.50	....	....	M2	99⅞	'95	150	110¼	96½	108	105¼	105¼	8.67
RBSG Capital Corp....[5]Gtd Cap[2]Notes	10⅛s	2004	$Ms	A	NC	....	....	M2	99¼	'89	250	129	96¼	118⅝	109⅛	109⅛	9.28
Reed Elsevier Capital Inc....Deb[2]	7½s	2025	$Mn15	AA−	NC	....	....	L3	98.88	'95	150	113¾	95¾	110	94⅛	96⅝	7.76
Reed Elsevier Capital Inc....Notes[2]	6⅝s	2000	$Mn15	AA−	NC	....	....	L3	99.92	'95	150	104¼	98⅝	101⅝	100⅛	100¼	6.61
Reed Elsevier Capital Inc....Notes[2]	7s	2005	$Mn15	AA−	NC	....	....	L3	100	'95	150	109¼	96⅞	107	98⅜	98⅞	7.08
Repsol Int'l Finance B.V....[6]Gtd[7]Notes[8]	7s	2005	$fA	A−	NC	....	....	M5	99.95	'95	300	109½	96¾	108¼	97⅜	97⅜	7.19
Rio Algom Ltd....Deb	7.05s	2005	$mN	BBB−	NC	....	....	G1	99.69	'95	150	105⅛	93⅜	101	94	94⅛	7.49
Rodamco N.V....Notes[2]	7.30s	2005	$Mn15	NR	NC	....	....	L1	100	'95	350	109¾	97¼	108⅛	99¼	99¼	7.35
Saga Petroleum a.s....Deb[2]	9⅛s	2014	$jJ15	A	NC	....	....	G1	99.93	'94	100	121⅜	95¾	117¾	108¾	110½	8.26
Saga Petroleum a.s....Notes[2]	8.40s	2004	$jJ15	A	NC	....	....	G1	99.74	'94	100	111¾	95¾	107⅝	103⅛	103½	8.11
Santander Fin'l Issuances Ltd....Sub[9]Gtd[2]Notes[10]	7⅞s	2005	$Ao15	A	NC	....	....	M2	99.59	'95	300	110¾	99½	108⅜	100⅝	100¾	7.82
Santander Fin'l Issuances Ltd....Sub[11]Gtd[12]Notes[13]	7¼s	2006	$Mn30	A	NC	....	....	M2	99.59	'96	200	105¾	96⅛	105¾	97	97⅜	7.44
Santander Fin'l Issuances Ltd....Sub[14]Gtd[15]Notes[10]	7¾s	2005	$Mn15	A	NC	....	....	P1	99.76	'95	150	109¾	99¾	107¾	100	100⅛	7.74
Santander Fin'l Issuances Ltd....Sub[16]Gtd[17]Notes[7]	6.80s	2005	$jJ15	A	NC	....	....	S1	99.14	'95	200	103¼	93⅝	103	95½	95⅞	7.09
Santander Fin'l Issuances Ltd....Sub[18]Gtd[12]Notes[19]	6⅜s	2011	$Fa15	A	NC	....	....	L3	99.14	'96	300	99⅝	85⅝	97¾	87⅝	88¾	7.18
Santander Fin'l Issuances Ltd....Sub[7]Gtd[20]Notes[21]	7¼s	2015	$mN	A	NC	....	....	S1	99.90	'95	200	106⅜	85½	101⅜	91	93¼	7.77
Saskatchewan (Prov)....Deb	9⅜s	2020	$jD15	A	NC	....	....	S1	99.33	'90	300	139¼	96⅛	139⅜	117¼	117¼	7.99
Saskatchewan (Prov)....Deb	9⅛s	2021	$Fa15	A	NC	....	....	S1	99.14	'91	200	136⅜	96⅜	136½	114⅝	114⅝	7.96
Saskatchewan (Prov)....Deb	8s	2013	$Fa	A	NC	....	....	S1	98.33	'93	400	122⅝	91¼	120¾	102⅞	102⅞	7.78
Saskatchewan (Prov)....Deb	7⅜s	2013	$jJ15	A	NC	....	....	S1	99.10	'93	300	116⅞	84¾	115⅛	97¾	97¾	7.54
Saskatchewan (Prov)....Deb	8½s	2022	$jJ15	A	NC	....	....	S1	99.84	'92	300	129⅝	93¾	129⅞	108⅜	108⅜	7.84
Saskatchewan (Prov)....Notes	6⅝s	2003	$jJ15	A	NC	....	....	S1	99.83	'93	200	106⅝	88	105⅜	98¾	98¾	6.71
Shell Canada Ltd....Notes	8⅞s	2001	$Jj14	AA	NC	....	....	G1	99.92	'91	300	119⅛	99¼	107½	102⅛	102⅛	8.69
Singer Co N.V.[22]....Notes[2]	7s	2003	$§Ao	D	Default 10-1-99 int			M2	99.55	'93	150	102⅝	51	54	6	6	Flat
SK Telecom Co Ltd....Notes[23]	7¾s	2004	$Ao29	BBB	NC	....	....	M2	99.56	'97	230	99½	78⅛	99½	89¾	98⅝	7.86
Skandinaviska Enskilda Banken....Sub[12]Notes[2]	8.45s	2002	$Mn15	BBB+	NC	....	....	G1	99.84	'92	400	115⅝	98¾	108⅛	102½	102½	8.24
SmithKline Beecham plc....M-T Notes 'A'	7⅛s	2002	$Mn	AA−	NC	....	....	M5	99.59	'95	110	107¼	99⅜	105⅞	100¾	100¾	7.07
SmithKline Beecham plc....M-T Notes 'A'	7⅜s	2005	$Ao15	AA−	NC	....	....	C5	100	'95	100	112⅝	99⅜	110⅝	101¼	101¼	7.28
Smurfit Capital Funding plc....Gtd[2]Deb[24]	7½s	2025	$mN20	BBB+	NC	....	....	M2	99.54	'95	350	109⅝	90¼	100⅛	89⅝	89⅝	8.37
Smurfit Capital Funding plc....Gtd[2]Notes[24]	6¾s	2005	$mN20	BBB+	NC	....	....	M2	99.57	'95	250	104	93	103¼	94½	94½	7.14
Societe Generale....Sub[7]Notes[2]	7.40s	2006	$Jd	A+	NC	....	....	S1	99.78	'96	800	108⅜	97¾	108¼	98	98⅜	7.52
Societe Nat'l Elf Aquitaine....Notes[2]	8s	2001	$aO15	AA−	NC	....	....	G1	99.66	'91	300	114	97⅜	107⅛	102¼	102¼	7.82
Sony Corp....Notes	6⅛s	2004	$Mn4	A+	NC	....	....	G1	99.79	'98	1500	103½	99⅜	102⅝	97⅝	97¾	6.27
South Africa (Republic of)....Notes	8⅜s	2006	$aO17	BB+	NC	....	....	M2	99.16	'96	300	105¾	81	102⅝	90	99½	8.42
Spain (Kingdom of)....Notes	9⅛s	2000	$fA	AA+	NC	....	....	M6	100	'90	300	120⅝	99⅞	105¾	101⅜	101⅜	9.00
Stena AB....Sr[2]Notes[25]	10½s	2005	$jD15	BB	[26]±105.25	....	....	C2	100	'95	175	110¾	97¾	104	91	91	11.53
Sunclipse, Inc....Gtd[27]Notes[2]	6¾s	2003	$Jd15	BBB+	NC	....	....	M6	99.45	'93	125	107	89¼	105¼	99	99	6.82
Svenska Handelsbanken[28]....Sub[2]Notes[12]	8.35s	2004	$jJ15	A	NC	....	....	M2	100	'92	400	117⅝	96⅞	111¼	103⅛	103¾	8.05
Svenska Handelsbanken[28]....Sub[2]Notes[12]	8⅛s	2007	$fA15	A	NC	....	....	M2	98.90	'92	100	117⅝	93½	114	101¼	101⅝	7.99
• Sweden (Kingdom of)....Bonds	12s	2010	$Fa	AA+	NC	....	....	S1	99.60	'85	55.2	136	126½	144½	143	134	8.95
Sweden (Kingdom of)....Bonds	11⅛s	2015	$Jd	AA+	NC	....	....	M2	Unit	'85	331	157	109	154⅛	131⅞	131⅞	8.43
Sweden (Kingdom of)....Bonds	10¼s	2015	$mN	AA+	[29]100	....	....	M6	99⅜	'85	135	142¾	101⅜	138⅞	121¼	121¼	8.45
Swedish Export Cr....Deb	8¼s	2003	$Jj15	AA+	[30]103.665	....	....	L3	99.08	'93	150	119⅛	91½	117	101¼	101¼	8.15
Swiss Bank Corp(N.Y. Branch)....Sub[7]Deb	7⅜s	2015	$jJ15	AA	NC	....	....	M2	99.38	'95	150	108¾	95⅜	106⅞	95¾	96	7.68
Swiss Bank Corp(N.Y. Branch)....Sub[7]Deb[31]	7s	2015	$aO15	AA	NC	....	....	M2	99.35	'95	300	105	91¾	103⅛	92½	92⅝	7.56
Swiss Bank Corp(N.Y. Branch)....Sub[7]Deb	7½s	2025	$jJ15	AA	NC	....	....	M2	99.52	'95	350	111⅜	94⅝	109¼	95⅜	95⅞	7.82
Swiss Bank Corp(N.Y. Branch)....Sub Deb[2]	7¾s	2026	$mS	AA	NC	....	....	M2	99.61	'96	300	114¼	97⅜	112¼	97¾	98½	7.87
Swiss Bank Corp(N.Y. Branch)....Sub[7]Notes	6¾s	2005	$jJ15	AA	NC	....	....	M2	99.35	'95	200	106⅞	94¾	106⅜	96⅜	96⅜	7.00
Swiss Bank Corp(N.Y. Branch)....Sub Notes[2]	7¼s	2006	$mS	AA	NC	....	....	M2	99.65	'96	150	110⅛	97⅞	109⅛	97¾	98⅜	7.37

Uniform Footnote Explanations-See Page 260. Other: [1] Invested SF,fds set aside. [2] Co may red in whole,at 100,for tax law chge. [3] (HRO)On Chge of Ctrl at 101. [4] Fr 5-15-00. [5] Gtd by Royal Bank of Scotland Group plc. [6] Co may redeem in whole,at 100,for tax law chge. [7] Issued in min denom $100T. [8] Gtd by Repsol S.A. [9] Gtd by Banco Santander, S.A., N.Y. Branch. [10] Issued in min denom U.S.$100T. [11] Co may red in whole,at 100,for tax law chge,fr 6-1-01. [12] Issued in min denom U.S. $100T. [13] Gtd by BancoSantander, S.A. [14] Gtd by Banco Santander, S.A.,N.Y. Branch. [15] Co may red in whole,at 100,for tax law chge fr 5-15-00. [16] Gtd by Banco Santander,S.A., N.Y. Branch. [17] Fr 7-15-00,Co may red in whole,at 100,for tax chge. [18] Gtd by Banco Santander S.A. N.Y. Branch. [19] Fr 2-17-01,red in whole,at 100 for tax law chge. [20] Gtd by Banco Santander,S.A. NY Br. [21] Co my red in whole,at 100,for tax law chge fr 11-10-00. [22] Filed bankruptcy Chapt 11. [23] Co may red in whole at 100. [24] Gtd by Jefferson Smurfit Group plc. [25] Co must offer repurch at 101 on Chge of Ctrl. [26] Fr 12-15-00. [27] Gtd by Amcor Ltd. [28] N.Y. Branch. [29] Fr 11-1-10. [30] Fr 1-15-03. [31] Co may red,at 100,for tax law chge.

Exchange ↓	BONDS Description	Interest Rate	Due	Interest Dates	S&P Rating	Redemption Provisions Regular	For Sinking Fund	Refund Earliest/ Other	Underwriting Firm	Price	Year	Outstanding Mil-$ This Issue	Price Range 1988-1998 High	Low	1999 High	Low	Month End Price Sale(s) or Bid	Yield to Maturity
	Talisman Energy Inc .... Deb	7⅛s	2007	$Jd	BBB+	NC	....	....	M2	99.76	'95	175	105⅝	94⅝	106	95¾	96	7.42
	Teck Corp .... Deb	8.70s	2002	$Mn	BBB	NC	....	....	G1	99.87	'92	125	114⅜	98	109⅛	103⅛	103⅛	8.44
	Telecom Argentina STET-France .... Notes[1]	12s	2002	$mN15	NR	NC	....	....	M5	99.97	'95	128	118⅞	91	108½	98	102½	11.70
•	Telefonica de Argentina S.A. .... Notes[1]	11⅞s	2004	$mN	BBB–	NC	....	....	S1	98.01	'94	300	123⅞	73¼	112	100	s101⅝	11.68
	Tembec Finance Corp .... [2]Sr[1]Notes[3]	9⅞s	2005	$mS30	BB+	[4]±104.938	....	....	G1	100	'95	250	107	88	106½	103	103¾	9.52
	TeleWest plc .... Sr[1]Deb	9⅝s	2006	$aO	B+	[5]±104.813	....	....	M6	100	'95	300	107⅝	96	107½	99¾	101	9.53
	TeleWest plc .... Sr[1]Disc[6]Deb[7]	11s	2007	$aO	B+	[5]100	....	....	M6	58.58	'95	[8]1536	84½	57¾	93½	83½	93¼	Flat
	Thailand (Kingdom of) .... Bonds	8¼s	2002	$Ms15	BBB–	NC	....	....	S1	99.67	'92	300	113⅜	77⅛	104¼	100½	101¼	8.15
	Tjiwi Kimia Int'l Fin.B.V. .... [9]Gtd[1]Sr Notes[2]	13¼s	2001	$fA	BB	NC	....	....	C5	100	'94	200	114½	43½	89	58½	89	14.88
	Tokyo (Metropolis) .... Gtd[10]Bonds	9¼s	2000	$mN8	AAA	NC	....	....	F1	99.78	'90	200	122⅞	99¾	106⅞	102⅛	102⅛	9.06
	Tokyo (Metropolis) .... Gtd[10]Bonds	8.65s	2001	$jJ18	AAA	NC	....	....	G1	99.70	'91	200	120⅛	99¼	107½	102½	102½	8.44
	TOLMEX S.A. de C.V. .... [11]Gtd[1]Notes[2]	8⅜s	2003	$mN	BB+	NC	....	....	G1	99.77	'93	250	105¾	35	99¼	89½	97	8.63
	Toronto-Dominion Bank .... F/R[1]Sub[12]Notes		2003	QAug4	A+	NC	....	....	M6	100	'93	150	100½	98	99⅞	98⅜	99¼	....
	Toronto-Dominion Bank .... Sub[13]Notes[1]	6.45s	2009	$Jj15	A+	NC	....	....	U1	99.85	'94	150	104½	80⅝	104⅜	92½	92½	6.97
	Toronto-Dominion Bank .... [13]Sub[1]Notes	6½s	2008	$fA15	A+	NC	....	....	K2	99.72	'93	150	104¾	81	104¾	93	93	6.99
	Toronto-Dominion Bank .... [1]Sub[13]Notes	6.15s	2008	$aO15	A+	NC	....	....	M6	99.64	'93	150	102¼	78⅜	102⅛	90¾	90¾	6.78
	TransCanada P.L. .... Deb	8⅝s	2012	$Mn15	A–	NC	....	....	M6	99.44	'92	200	127⅛	96¼	122¼	106½	106½	8.10
	TransCanada P.L. .... Deb	9⅞s	2021	$Jj	A–	NC	....	....	M6	99⅞	'91	400	137⅞	99⅞	137	117⅛	117½	8.40
	TransCanada P.L. .... Deb	8½s	2023	$Ms20	A–	[14]104.138	....	....	M6	99.78	'92	200	118⅞	93⅛	113½	99⅞	101⅜	8.38
	TransCanada P.L. .... Sub Deb	9⅛s	2006	$Ao20	BBB	NC	....	....	M6	99.08	'91	200	124	95⅝	116	106¼	107¼	8.51
•	Transportacion Maritima Mex .... [2]Notes[1]	8½s	2000	$aO15	BB–	NC	....	....	B7	99.35	'93	150	101	62½	96½	84¾	89	9.55
•	Transportacion Maritima Mex .... [2]Notes[1]	9¼s	2003	$Mn15	BB–	±103.083	....	....	B7	99.77	'93	200	103⅛	60	86½	63	77¼	11.97
•	Transportacion Martima Mex .... Sr Notes[15]	10s	2006	$mN15	BB–	NC	....	....	M6	99⅝	'96	200	105	73	86⅞	62	78⅞	12.67
	Transportadora de Gas del Sur S.A. .... Notes[1]	10¼s	2001	$Ao25	BBB–	NC	....	....	M2	99.94	'96	150	109	91	102½	95	100	10.25
	Tri Polyta Finance BV .... Gtd[16]Sec Notes	11⅜s	2003	$§jD	D	Default 6-1-99 int			M2	99.40	'96	185	104¼	15	34	19	31	Flat
•	Trizec Finance Ltd .... Sr[17]Notes[1]	10⅞s	2005	$aO15	BB+	[18]±105.438	....	[19]Z109	G1	99.25	'95	250	112½	99¼	106	100⅛	106	10.26
	Union Bank of Switzerland[20] .... Sub[1]Notes[13]	7¼s	2006	$jJ15	AA	NC	....	....	U1	99.71	'96	500	111	98	109¾	98¾	98¾	7.34
	United Mexican States .... Global Bonds	8⅝s	2008	$Ms12	BB	NC	....	....	M7	100	'98	1000	100⅝	74	98¼	88	98	8.80
	United Mexican States .... Notes	8½s	2002	$mS15	BB	NC	....	....	G1	99¾	'92	250	107¼	46	103¼	97¼	101¾	8.35
	United News & Media plc .... Notes[1]	7¼s	2004	$jJ	BBB	[21]Z100	....	....	M7	99.13	'99	25.0	....	....	101⅝	97⅜	97⅝	7.44
	United News & Media plc .... Notes[1]	7¾s	2009	$jJ	BBB	[21]Z100	....	....	M7	98.80	'99	250	....	....	102⅜	96	96	8.07
	United Utilities PLC .... Notes[1]	6¼s	2005	$fA15	A	[21]Z100	....	....	M5	99.52	'98	350	102¼	99⅝	102¼	93	93¾	6.67
	United Utilities PLC .... Notes[1]	6⅞s	2028	$fA15	A	[21]Z100	....	....	M5	99.44	'98	400	102¾	94⅛	101⅞	83⅛	85	8.09
	Usinor Salicor .... Bonds[1]	7¼s	2006	$fA	BBB	NC	....	[22]Z■100	C5	99.19	'96	300	110⅜	96⅝	101⅛	94¼	94¼	7.69
	Victorian Pub Auth Fin Agy .... [23]Gtd[24]Bonds[25]	8.45s	2001	$aO	AA+	NC	....	....	S1	99.93	'91	350	117¾	99⅞	108	102¾	102¾	8.22
	Westdeutsche Landesbank Giro ...... Sub[13]Notes[1]	6.05s	2009	$Jj15	AA+	NC	....	....	G1	99.75	'99	750	....	....	101	89⅜	89½	6.76
	Westpac Banking Corp .... Sub[26]Deb[1]	9⅛s	2001	$fA15	A+	NC	....	....	F1	99.60	'89	400	119¼	86⅞	108	102⅞	102⅞	8.87
	Westpac Banking Corp .... Sub[26]Deb[1]	7⅞s	2002	$aO15	A+	NC	....	....	F1	99.26	'92	350	111¾	95	106⅞	101⅜	101⅜	7.77
	WPP Finance(USA) Corp .... Gtd[1]Notes[27]	6⅞s	2008	$jJ15	BBB+	NC	....	....	M5	99.73	'98	100	102½	99⅝	101⅛	90⅛	90¾	7.57
	WMC Finance(USA)Ltd .... Gtd[28]Notes[1]	6½s	2003	$mN15	A	NC	....	....	G1	99.78	'93	250	105⅛	87⅜	103⅞	96⅜	96⅝	6.74
	WMC Finance(USA)Ltd .... Gtd[28]Notes[1]	6¾s	2006	$jD	A	NC	....	....	M2	99.38	'96	200	99⅜	99⅛	101⅜	94	94	7.18
	WMC Finance(USA)Ltd .... Gtd[28]Notes[1]	7.35s	2026	$jD	A	NC	....	....	M2	99.74	'96	200	114⅛	93	111⅜	89⅜	89⅜	8.22
	WMC Finance(USA)Ltd .... Gtd[28]Deb[1]	7¼s	2013	$mN15	A	NC	....	....	G1	99.68	'93	150	111½	82⅝	108¼	95	95	7.63
	Xerox Capital(Europe)plc .... Notes[1]	5¾s	2002	$Mn15	A	NC	....	....	C1	99.81	'99	500	....	....	99¾	96½	96½	5.96
	WPP Finance (USA) Corp .... Gtd[1]Notes[27]	6⅝s	2005	$jJ15	BBB+	NC	....	....	M5	99.31	'98	200	102½	99¼	101½	92¾	92¾	7.14
	Xerox Capital(Europe)plc .... Notes[1]	5⅞s	2004	$Mn15	A	NC	....	....	C1	99.50	'99	500	....	....	99½	93½	93½	6.28
	YPF Sociedad Anonima .... [29]Negotiable[1]Oblig[30]	8s	2004	$Fa15	BBB–	NC	....	....	C5	99.77	'94	350	103¾	80	103¼	93	98¾	8.10
	YPF Sociedad Anonima .... [1]Notes[30]	7¼s	2003	$Ms15	BBB–	NC	....	....	C6	99.84	'98	350	100⅜	75⅝	100⅞	90½	97⅛	7.46
•	YPF Sociedad Anonima .... Notes[1]	7¾s	2007	$fA27	BBB–	NC	....	....	M2	99.19	'97	300	99⅛	99⅛	99½	94½	93	8.33
	YPF Sociedad Anonima .... Notes[1]	9⅛s	2009	$Fa24	BBB–	NC	....	....	M2	99.68	'99	225	....	....	110⅞	98¼	103⅛	8.85
	Zeneca Wilmington Inc .... Gtd[1]Deb[31]	7s	2023	$mN15	AA+	NC	....	....	G1	99.09	'93	300	109¾	80⅜	108¾	91¼	91⅜	7.66

Uniform Footnote Explanations-See Page 260. Other: [1] Co may red in whole,at 100,for tax law chge. [2] (HRO)On Chge of Ctrl at 101. [3] Gtd by Tembec, Inc. [4] Fr 9-30-00. [5] Fr 10-1-00. [6] Int accrues at 11% fr 10-1-00. [7] (HRO)On Chge of Ctrl at 101(of Accreted Val). [8] Incl disc. [9] Gtd by P.T. Pabrik Kertas Tjiwi Kimia. [10] Gtd by Japan. [11] Gtd by Empresas Tolteca & Cegusa SA. [12] Int(min 4.10%)adj qtrly(3 Mo LIBOR). [13] Issued in min denom $100T. [14] Fr 9-20-02. [15] Co may red in whole,at,100 for tax law chge. [16] Gtd by Pt. Tri Polyta Indonesia Tbk. [17] Gtd by Trizec Corp Ltd. [18] Fr 10-15-00. [19] Max $82.5M red w/proceeds of Pub Equity Off'g. [20] N.Y. Branch. [21] Red at greater of 100 or amt based on formula. [22] Mandatory if add'l amts due. [23] Issued in min denom U.S. $5T. [24] Gtd by gov't of Victoria,Australia. [25] Red in whole,at 100,for tax law chge. [26] Issued in min denom U.S. $100T. [27] Gtd by WPP Group plc. [28] Gtd by Western Mining Corp Hldg Ltd. [29] Issued in min denom $10T. [30] (HRO)On Chge of Ctrl at 100. [31] Gtd by Zeneca Group.

Convertible Bonds

EXPLANATION OF COLUMN HEADINGS AND FOOTNOTES

EXCHANGE: Unlisted except where symbols are used:
● —New York Stock Exchange ◆—American Stock Exchange.

ISSUE TITLE: Name of Bond at time of offering; otherwise issue footnoted with name change of obligor. Minor changes with old title indicated in brackets, i.e. Midlantic (Banks) Corp.
§ Int. and/or prin. in default.

S&P RATING: See pages xxi & xxiii for definitions.

BOND FORM: Letters are used to indicate form of bond: BE – Book-Entry; C – Coupon only; CR – Coupon or Registered, interchangeable; R – Registered only.

CONVERSION EXPIRES: Denotes the year in which the conversion privilege expires. When privilege will expire within the next 12 months, the month, day and year are given.

DIVIDEND INCOME PER BOND: If $1,000 Bond were converted, the annual amount of dividends expected to be paid by the company on the stock based on most recent indication of annual rate of payment.

STOCK VALUE OF BOND: Price at which the bond must sell to equal the price of the stock, i.e., number of shares received on conversion times price of the stock.

CONVERSION PARITY: Price at which stock must sell to equal bond price, i.e., price of bond divided by number of shares received on conversion.

P/E RATIO: (Price-Earnings Ratio) Ratio is derived by dividing current stock price by estimated new year earnings or last 12 months if no estimate is available.

EARNINGS, in general, are per share as reported by company. **FOR YEARS INDICATED:** Fiscal years ending prior to March 31 are shown under preceding year. Foreign issues traded ADR are dollars per share, converted at prevailing exchange rate. Specific footnotes used:

△ – Excl extra-ord income
▲ – Incl extra-ord income
□ – Excl extra-ord charges
■ – Incl extra-ord charges
✳ – Excl tax credits
± – Combined various classes

⁑ – Partial Year
ǂ – New Year Earns
d – Deficit
E – S&P Estimate
j – Currency of origin
n/a – Not available

P – Preliminary
p – Pro forma
R – Fully diluted
n/r – Not reported
v – Diluted

LAST 12 Mos. indicates earnings through period indicated by superior number preceding figure: [1] for Jan., [2] for Feb., etc. Figure without superior number indicates fiscal year end.

Exchange ↓ Issue, Rate, Interest Dates and Maturity	S&P Rating	Bond Form	Outstdg. Mil-$	Conv. Ex-pires	Shares per $1,000 Bond	Price per Share	Div. Income per Bond	1999 Price Range High	1999 Price Range Low	Curr Bid Sale(s) Ask(A)	Curr. Yield	Yield to Mat	Stock Value of Bond	Conv Parity	Stock Data Month End	Stock Data P/E Ratio	Earnings Per Share Yr. End	1998	1999	Last 12 Mos
Aames Financial........ 5½s Ms15 2006	NR	R	114	2006	53.56	18.67	....	43⅜	33⅛	42⅜	12.98	12.98	4⅛	8	•¾	d	Je	v1.23	vd8.00	[9]d7.95
Acclaim Entertainment........ 10s Ms 2002	NR	R	50.0	2002	193.05	5.18	....	251	100	A100	10.00	10.00	99	5¼	5⅛	9	Au	v0.37	v0.57	0.57
Action Performance Cos[1]........ 4¾s Ao 2005	NR	R	100	2005	20.75	48.20	....	106⅛	52	53¼	8.92	8.92	23⅞	25¾	11½	7	Sp	v1.48	Pv1.65	1.65
Activision Inc........ 6¾s Jj 2005	NR	R	60.0	2004	52.98	18.875	....	111⅛	85⅛	99¾	6.77	6.77	81⅛	18⅞	15⁵⁄₁₆	19	Mr	v0.66	....	[9]0.77
Adaptec Inc[2]........ 4¾s Fa 2004	BB−	BE	230	2004	19.36	51.66	....	143¾	77⅜	108⅛	4.39	4.39	96⅝	55⅞	49⅞	27	Mr	vd0.12	E1.80	[9]1.51
Adaptive[3]Broadband[4]........ 5¼s jD15 2003	B	R	57.5	2003	35.16	28.4375	....	269½	60	259⅝	2.02	1.82	259⅝	73⅞	73¹³⁄₁₆	63	Je	vd0.47	v0.78	[9]1.17
• [5]ADT[6]Operations[7](Zero)........ [8] 2010	BBB+	R	[9]238	2010	[10]54.352	....	2.72	250	190	212	....	Flat	212	39⅛	•39	25	Sp	v□1.01	vP1.53	1.53
Advanced Energy Indus[11]........ 5¼s mN15 2006	NR	BE	135	2006	20.19	49.53	....	119	93⅝	119	4.41	4.40	99½	59	49¼	..	Dc	vd0.36	....	[9]0.17
♦Advanced Medical[3]Inc........ 7¼s Jj15 2002	B−	R	16.2	2002	55.13	18.14	....	87	27	45	16.11	16.10	10⅜	8¼	♦1⅞	d	Dc	vd0.42	....	[9]d0.18
Advanced Micro Dev........ 6s Mn15 2005	CCC+	BE	45.0	2005	27.03	37.00	....	103¼	71	95⅜	6.29	6.29	78¼	35⅜	•28¹⁵⁄₁₆	d	Dc	vd0.72	Ed3.11	[9]d0.89
• AES Corp[3]........ 4½s fA15 2005	B+	R	150	2005	18.52	54.00	....	137	90	138½	3.25	3.22	138½	74⅞	•74¾	55	Dc	v△1.67	E1.34	[9]1.10
Agnico-Eagle Mines[12](Sr)[13]........ 5¾s $Jj27 2004	B	R	[9]127	2004	55.762	....	1.12	72	58½	66¼	8.68	8.68	41½	12	•7⁷⁄₁₆	..	Dc	vd0.23	....	[9]....
• Alpharma Inc[3]........ 5¾s Ao 2005	B	R	125	2005	34.97	28.59	6.29	No Sale		114⅝	5.02	5.01	107⅝	32⅞	•30¾	24	Dc	v±0.92	....	[9]1.26
Alpharma Inc[14]........ 3s Jd 2006	B	BE	[15]170	2006	[16]31.14	32.11	5.61	135⅛	100⅞	107¼	2.80	2.79	95⅞	34½	•30¾	24	Dc	v±0.92	....	[9]1.26
♦Alternative Living Services........ 5¼s jD15 2002	NR	R	125	2002	34.78	28.75	....	122½	55	s64½	8.14	8.14	29	18⅝	♦8⁵⁄₁₆	8	Dc	v0.92	....	[9]0.96
• ALZA Corp[3]........ 5s Mn 2006	BBB−	R	435	2006	26.18	38.19	....	150	100⅛	s105¾	4.73	4.73	90¾	40½	•34⅝	22	Dc	v1.26	E1.55	[9]1.21
• ALZA Corp[17](Zero)........ 2014	BBB−	R	[9]825	2014	12.987	....	....	70	45½	48¼	....	Flat	45	37¼	•34⅝	22	Dc	v1.26	E1.55	[9]1.21
Amazon.com........ 6.408s Fa 2009	CCC+	BE	1250	2009	12.82	78.03	....	151¼	76	113⅛	5.66	5.66	97⅝	88¼	76⅛	d	Dc	vd0.42	Ed1.05	[9]d1.38
America Online........ 4s mN15 2002	BB−	BE	350	2002	153.28	6.524	....	1468⅝	498¼	1163⅛	0.34	....	1163⅛	76	•75⅞	..	Je	v0.04	v0.30	[9]0.34
America Online[18](Zero)[19]........ [20] 2019	BB−	BE	[9]2268	2019	5.833	....	....	63	55⅛	56½	....	Flat	44⅜	96⅞	•75⅞	..	Je	v0.04	v0.30	[9]0.34
[21]Amer Residential Services.... 7¼s Ao15 2004	NR	BE	1.17	2004	Conv into $225.49			99¼	29½	98½	7.36	7.36	....	....	....	..		....	....	....
• Amer Retirement[2]........ 5¾s aO 2002	NR	R	138	2002	41.67	24.00	....	90½	57	s72	7.99	7.99	33⅛	17⅜	•7¹⁵⁄₁₆	12	Dc	v□0.51	....	[9]0.62
AmeriTrade Holding[3]........ 5¾s fA 2004	CCC+	BE	200	2004	[22]30.71	32.56	....	192⅞	69½	87⅜	6.58	6.58	66⅝	28½	21¹¹⁄₁₆	..	Sp	vNil	Pv0.07	0.07
AMF[23]Bowling(Zero)[24]........ [25] 2018	C	BE	[9]1125	2018	8.67	115.34	....	14¼	4⅝	4¾	....	Flat	2¾	5½	•3⅛	d	Dc	vd2.11	....	[9]d3.69
Amkor Technology[2]........ 5¾s Mn 2003	B	BE	180	2003	74.07	13.50	....	219	82¼	209¼	2.75	2.65	209¼	28⅜	28¼	44	Dc	vp0.66	....	[9]0.64
ANTEC Corp[3]........ 4½s Mn15 2003	B−	BE	115	2003	41.67	24.00	....	251⅛	93	152⅛	2.96	2.90	152⅛	36⅝	36½	25	Dc	v0.15	....	[9]1.43
• APP[26]Fin(VI)[27]Mauritius(Zero)[28]..... [29] 2012	CCC+	R	[9]1250	2012	[30]16.146	....	....	22	12	s17⅝	....	Flat	12¾	11	•7⅞	13	Dc	v0.60	....	0.60
Arbor Software[31]........ 4½s Ms15 2005	NR	BE	100	2005	17.74	56.357	....	96½	64	96½	4.66	4.66	77¼	54½	43½	55	Je	v0.67	v0.26	[9]0.78
ARV Assisted Living[32]........ 6¾s Ao 2006	NR	BE	57.5	2006	53.85	18.57	....	53⅞	21⅞	21⅞	....	....	8⅛	4⅛	♦1½	d	Dc	vd2.90	....	[9]d3.39
• Ashanti[33]Capital[34]Ltd[35]........ 5½s Ms15 2003	NR	BE	250	2003	[36]37.04	27.00	3.33	86¼	65	A67	8.21	8.21	9¾	18⅛	•2⅝	4	Dc	v0.37	....	[9]0.58
[37]Aspect[38]Telecommun[39](Zero)..... [40] 2018	B−	BE	[9]490	2018	8.713	....	....	43⅛	18½	39½	....	Flat	34⅛	45⅜	39⅛	d	Dc	v0.61	Ed0.68	[9]d0.50
Aspen Technology[3]........ 5¼s Jd15 2005	B−	BE	86.3	2005	18.88	52.97	....	82⅜	55½	78¼	6.71	6.71	50	41½	26⁷⁄₁₆	d	Je	v0.59	vd1.04	[9]d0.89
Assisted Living Concepts[2]........ 6s mN 2002	NR	BE	86.2	2002	44.31	22.57	....	84	51	59	10.17	10.17	9½	13⅜	♦2⅛	d	Dc	v□d1.18	....	[9]d1.78
At Home [41]Corp[42]........ .5246s jD28 2018	NR	BE	[9]437	2018	[43]13.10	....	....	129¾	56⅝	64¾	....	Flat	56¼	49½	42⅞	d	Dc	pvd0.63	Ed0.04	[9]d2.75
Atmel Corp[44](Zero)[45]........ [46] 2018	NR	BE	[9]340	2018	27.966	....	....	88⅛	52¾	84⅝	....	Flat	82¾	30⅜	29⁹⁄₁₆	79	Dc	vd0.25	E0.37	[9]0.29
Atrix Laboratories[1]........ 7s jD 2004	NR	R	50.0	2004	52.63	19.00	....	97½	56⅜	57⅝	12.15	12.14	27⅜	11	5³⁄₁₆	d	Dc	△v0.13	....	[9]d1.16
♦Audiovox Corp[47]........ 6¼s Ms15 2001	CCC+	BE	23.8	2001	[48]56.50	17.70	....	140	92¾	11	....	....	171	2	♦30¼	30	Nv	v±0.16	....	[8]1.00
• Automatic Data Proc (Zero)[49]........ [50] 2012	AAA	R	[9]291	2012	25.844	....	9.05	135	96	139¼	....	Flat	139¼	54	•53⅞	47	Je	v0.99	v1.10	[9]1.13

Uniform Footnote Explanations—See Page 260. Other: [1] (HRO)For Repurch Event at 100. [2] (HRO)On Chge of Ctrl at 101. [3] (HRO)On Chge of Ctrl at 100. [4] Was California Microwave. [5] Gtd by & data of Tyco Int'l. [6] (HRO)To 7-6-02,Chge of Ctr at $383.09&accr OID. [7] (HRO)On 7-2-02 at $599.46. [8] Due 7-6-10. [9] Incl disc. [10] Conv into Tyco Int'l. [11] (HRO)On Chge of Crtl at 100. [12] Co must offer repurch on Chge of Ctrl. [13] Int of 3.5% pd Jan & Jul 27,bal pd at maturity. [14] (HRO)On Chge of Ctrl at curr red price. [15] At maturity co to pay 134.104% times princ amt. [16] Into Cl A. [17] (HRO)On 7-14-04(09) $595.58($771.74). [18] (HRO)On 12-6-04 at $551.26 & accr OID. [19] (HRO)For Fundamental Chge at $551.26 & accr OID. [20] Due 12-6-19. [21] Mgr into ServiceMaster Co. [22] Into Cl'A' com. [23] (HRO)On chge of Ctrl at 25.257 & accr OID. [24] (HRO)On 5-12-03('08&'12)at 25.257 & accr OID. [25] Due 5-12-18. [26] Subsid & data of Asia Pulp & Paper(guarantor). [27] May red in whole for tax event,$204.24&accr OID. [28] (HRO)11-18-02(07)&Ctrl Chge at $204.24&accr OID. [29] Due 11-18-12. [30] Conv into Asia Pulp & Paper ADS. [31] (HRO)For Fundamental Chge at 103.857 - 100,as defined. [32] (HRO)For Designated Event at 101. [33] Gtd by & data of Ashanti Goldfields Ltd GDS. [34] (HRO)For a Fundamental Chge at 100. [35] Co may red in whole,at 100,for tax law chge. [36] Exch for Ashanti Goldfields Ltd GDS shrs. [37] (HRO)On 8-10-03('08&'13)at $306.56 & accr OID. [38] (HRO)For Fundamental Chge at $306.56 & accr OID. [39] Now Aspect Communications. [40] Due 8-10-18. [41] (HRO)On 12-28-03(08&13)at $610.81($715.86&$843.91). [42] (HRO)On Chge of Ctrl at $524.64 & accr OID. [43] Into Ser'A' com. [44] (HRO)On 4-21-03(08&13)at $337.85 & accr OID. [45] (HRO)For Fundamental Chge at $337.85 & accr OID. [46] Due 4-21-18. [47] Co must offer repurch at 101 on Chge of Ctrl. [48] Conv into Cl'A' com. [49] (HRO)2-20-02(07)at$595.58($771.74). [50] Due 2-20-12.

Exchange ↓ Issue, Rate, Interest Dates and Maturity	S&P Rating	Bond Form	Outstdg. Mil-$	Conv. Ex-pires	Shares per $1,000 Bond	Price per Share	Div. Income per Bond	1999 Price Range High	1999 Price Range Low	Curr Bid Sale(s) Ask(A)	Curr. Yield	Yield to Mat	Stock Value of Bond	Conv Parity	Stock Data Month End	Stock Data P/E Ratio	EPS Yr. End	EPS 1998	EPS 1999	EPS Last 12 Mos
◆Avatar Hldgs[1] .... 7s Ao 2005	NR	BE	86.2	2005	31.45	31.80	....	90¾	82¼	86	8.14	8.14	57⅛	27⅜	18⅛	2	Dc	v□d2.23	....	[9]9.16
Aviron[1] .... 5¾s Ao 2005	NR	BE	100	2005	32.358	30.904	....	110¼	68⅜	68¾	8.36	8.36	51¼	21¼	15 13/16	d	Dc	vd3.49	....	[9]d3.52
• Baker Hughes (Sr)[2] (Zero) .... [3] 2008	A	R	385	2008	18.599	....	8.56	76½	63	70⅛	....	Flat	39¼	37¾	•21 1/16	..	Dc	vd0.92	E0.21	[9]0.40
Baker (J.) Inc[4] .... 7s Jd 2002	B–	R	70.0	2002	62.02	16.125	3.72	86	65	74½	9.40	9.39	37¼	12⅛	6	22	Ja	v0.14	....	[10]0.27
BankAtlantic Bancorp .... 6¾s jJ 2006	NR	R	50.0	2006	[5]175.438	5.70	17.54	137⅜	86	86¼	7.83	7.83	72⅜	5	•4⅛	14	Dc	vd0.19	....	[9]0.29
BankAtlantic Bancorp .... 5⅝s jD 2007	NR	BE	100	2007	88.888	11.25	8.00	75½	75½	60	9.38	9.37	45⅝	6¾	5⅛	17	Dc	vd0.19	....	[9]0.29
[6]BBN Corp[7] .... 6s Ao 2012	NR	R	73.2	2012	Conv into $966.67			96⅝	96¼	96⅝	6.21	6.21	....	....	....	..		....	....	....
BEA Systems[1] 4s Jd15 2005	NR	BE	250	2005	75.73	13.21	....	565¼	64½	529¾	0.76	....	529¾	70	69 15/16	d	Ja	v±d0.37	....	[10]d0.06
Bell Sports Corp[8] 4¼s mN15 2000	B–	R	23.7	11-15-00	Conv into $189.63			90	76	90	4.72	4.73	....	....	....	..	Je	....	....	....
◆Bentley Pharmaceuticals ..... 12s [9]Qjan 2006	NR		6.90	2006	400.00	2.50	....	250	101	247½	4.85	4.83	247½	6¼	◆6 3/16	d	Dc	vd0.35	....	[9]d0.20
• Bergen Brunswig 6⅞s jJ15 2011	BB+	R	10.6	2011	Conv into apx $520.83			100¼	84	s84	8.18	8.18	....	....	....	..		....	....	....
• Berkshire Hathaway 1s jD2 2001	NR	R	[10]500	2001	[11]17.65	56.66	11.30	No Sale		232	0.43	....	....	131½	•....	12	Dc	E5.60	....	[9]4.36
Beyond.com Corp[1] .... 7¼s jD 2003	NR	BE	63.3	2003	54.53	18.34	....	225⅜	57⅞	57⅞	12.53	12.52	42⅝	10⅝	7 13/16	..	Dc	vpd1.28	....	[9]....
• Bluegreen Corp[12] 8¼s Mn15 2012	CCC+	R	34.7	2012	121.36	8.24	....	103	80	80½	10.25	10.25	60¾	6¾	•5	7	Mr	□v0.72	....	[9]0.67
Brightpoint[13]Inc[14](Zero) .... [15] 2018	B	BE	[10]380	2018	19.109	....	....	43⅜	23⅞	32⅛	....	Flat	25⅛	16⅞	13⅛	d	Dc	v0.38	....	[9]d1.80
BroadBand Technologies 5s Mn15 2001	NR	R	115	2001	24.108	41.48	....	62½	35¾	52½	9.52	9.52	21⅝	21⅞	8 15/16	d	Dc	vd0.21	....	[9]d0.67
C-Cube Microsystems[16] .... 5⅞s mN 2005	NR	R	65.7	2005	32.57	30.70	....	213	88⅜	202¾	2.90	2.82	202¾	62⅜	62¼	50	Dc	v∆1.11	....	[9]1.23
• Camden Property Trust .... 7.33s Ao 2001	NR	R	47.8	2001	41.67	24.00	86.67	115	102⅛	115¾	6.33	6.33	115¾	27⅞	•27¾	21	Dc	v1.12	....	[9]1.27
• [1]CapStar Hotels[17] 4¾s aO15 2004	B	BE	172	2004	29.41	34.00	59.41	80	67	67	7.09	7.09	47⅛	22⅞	•16	10	Dc	□v1.40	....	[9]1.49
CareMatrix Corp 6¼s fA15 2004	B–	R	115	2004	34.63	28.875	....	117¼	20½	34⅛	18.32	18.30	8¾	9⅞	2½	2	Dc	v0.99	....	[9]0.91
[1]CD Radio Inc[18] 8¾s mS29 2009	NR	BE	125	2009	35.134	28.4625	....	170½	99⅝	156⅜	5.60	5.59	156⅜	44⅝	44½	d	Dc	vd4.79	....	[9]d4.07
CellStar Corp[19] 5s aO15 2002	B	BE	150	2002	36.14	27.67	....	78⅞	64	76¾	6.51	6.52	35¾	21¼	9⅞	23	Nv	v0.24	....	[8]0.42
Central Garden & Pet .... 6s [20]ms15 2003	B	BE	115	2003	35.71	28.00	....	89⅞	71½	75⅝	7.96	7.96	37⅛	21⅛	10⅜	11	Sp	±v1.15	±vP0.89	0.89
• Center Trust Retail Prop[21] ... 7½s jJ15 2001	NR	R	75.0	1-15-01	55.56	18.00	80.01	98⅜	91	s94	7.98	7.98	53⅞	17	•9 11/16	25	Dc	vd0.38	....	[9]0.38
[22]Centocor Inc[23] 4¾s Fa15 2005	AAA	BE	460	2005	[24]12.97	77.09	14.53	146⅛	99⅞	121	3.93	3.91	121	93⅜	•93¼	30	Dc	v2.23	E3.05	[9]2.52
Charming Shoppes 7½s jJ15 2006	B	BE	138	2006	134.05	7.46	....	105⅝	85⅜	101⅞	7.36	7.36	88⅞	7⅝	6⅝	26	Ja	vd0.20	....	[10]0.25
Chesapeake Utilities[25] .... 8¼s Ms 2014	NR	R	3.93	2014	58.77	17.01	61.12	116½	101	111⅛	7.42	7.42	108	19	•18⅜	13	Dc	v1.04	....	[9]1.39
[26]CII Financial[1] 7½s mS15 2001	NR	R	54.5	2001	[27]25.38	39.40	....	95⅛	63⅛	70½	10.64	10.64	17	27⅞	•6 11/16	3	Dc	v1.43	E2.17	[9]0.71
Cincinnati Fin'l(Sr)[28] .... 5½s Mn 2002	AA–	R	58.4	2002	67.23	14.88	45.72	285¾	206¾	209¾	2.62	2.51	209¾	31¼	31 3/16	20	Dc	v1.41	E1.50	[9]1.50
Cirrus Logic 6s jD15 2003	CCC+	R	300	2003	41.29	24.22	....	83½	62¼	83½	7.19	7.19	55	20¼	13 5/16	..	Mr	vd6.77	E0.03	[9]d7.18
Citrix System[29](Zero)[30] .... [31] 2019	NR	BE	[10]850	2019	7.03	....	....	91½	35⅜	88¼	....	Flat	86½	125⅝	123	93	Dc	v0.67	E1.32	[9]1.11
CKE Restaurants[1] 4¼s Ms15 2004	B	BE	159	2004	22.82	43.82	1.83	88⅛	51	53	8.02	8.02	13½	23¼	•5⅞	6	Ja	v∆1.39	....	[10]0.86
Clear Channel Commun[1] .... 1½s jD 2002	BBB–	BE	900	2002	9.45	105.78	....	102¼	98	102¼	1.47	1.46	84⅜	108¼	•89¼	..	Dc	v0.22	E0.68	[9]0.34
Clear Channel Commun[1] .... 2⅝s Ao 2003	BBB–	BE	575	2003	16.14	61.95	....	150	110⅞	144⅛	1.82	1.71	144⅛	89⅜	•89¼	..	Dc	v0.22	E0.68	[9]0.34
CNET Inc[1] .... 5s Ms 2006	NR	BE	173	2006	26.73	37.4062	....	216⅞	103⅛	151¾	3.29	3.26	151¾	56⅞	56¾	70	Dc	v0.03	....	[9]0.81
• Coeur d'Alene Mines[32] 6⅜s Jj31 2004	CCC+	BE	95.0	2004	38.80	25.77	....	65¼	51¼	s53¼	11.97	11.97	13⅜	13¾	•3 7/16	d	Dc	vd11.73	Ed1.05	[9]d8.87
• Coeur d'Alene Mines[33] 7¼s aO31 2005	CCC+	BE	144	2005	57.31	17.45	....	65¾	54	s55¾	13.00	13.00	19¾	9¾	•3 7/16	d	Dc	vd11.73	Ed1.05	[9]d8.87
Colonial BancGroup[34] 7½s Ms31 2011	NR	R	3.88	2011	142.86	7.00	54.29	214⅜	147⅜	148¼	5.06	5.05	148¼	10½	•10⅜	13	Dc	v0.49	....	[9]0.75

Uniform Footnote Explanations—See Page 260. Other: [1](HRO)On Chge of Ctrl at 100. [2] (HRO)On 5-5-03 at $840.73. [3] Due 5-5-08. [4] (HRO)For a Redemp at 100. [5] Into non-vtg Cl A com. [6] Was Bolt Beranek/Newman. [7] Acq by GTE Corp. [8] (HRO)For a Risk Event at 100. [9] Due 2-13-06. [10] Incl disc. [11] Into Salomon Inc com on last trade day qtrly,Jan,etc. [12] Was Patten Corp. [13] (HRO)On3-11-03(08&13)at$552.07($672.97&$820.35). [14] (HRO)To 3-11-03,Ctr Chge at $452.89 & accr OID. [15] Due 3-11-18. [16] (HRO)For a Fundamental Chge at declining prices. [17] Now MeriStar Hospitality. [18] Now Sirius Satellite Radio. [19] (HRO)On Chge of Ctrl at 101. [20] Due 11-15-03. [21] Was CenterTrust Retail Prop,then Alexander Haagen Prop. [22] (HRO)for Fundamental Chge at 100. [23] Acq by & data of Johnson & Johnson. [24] Into Johnson & Johnson com. [25] (HRO)For a Designated Event,as defined. [26] Merged into&data of Sierra Health Services. [27] Into Sierra Health Services Com. [28] Co must offer to redeem on sale of certain ops. [29] (HRO)On 3-22-04(09&14)at $459.63($595.58&$771.74). [30] (HRO)On Chge of Ctrl at $354.71 & accr OID. [31] Due 3-22-19. [32] (HRO)For a Designated Event at 100. [33] (HRO)For Designated Event at 100. [34] Into Cl'A'.

Exchange ↓ Issue, Rate, Interest Dates and Maturity	S&P Rating	Bond Form	Outstdg. Mil-$	Conv. Ex-pires	Shares per $1,000 Bond	Price per Share	Div. Income per Bond	1999 Price Range High	1999 Price Range Low	Curr Bid Sale(s) Ask(A)	Curr. Yield	Yield to Mat	Stock Value of Bond	Conv Parity	Stock Data Month End	Stock Data P/E Ratio	Earnings Per Share Yr. End	1998	1999	Last 12 Mos
• Compania de Telecom Chile[1] 4½s $Jj15 2003	NR	BE	35.9	2003	[2]12.28	81.43	1.72	No Sale		109¾	4.10	....	22½	89⅜	•18¼	8	Dc	v1.03	E2.25	1.03
Comverse Technology 4½s jJ 2005	B	BE	300	2005	23.26	43.00	....	340⅝	120¼	336¾	1.34	0.94	336¾	144⅞	144¾	68	Ja	v1.55	E2.13	[10]1.96
Conexant Systems[3] 4¼s Mn 2006	B	BE	350	2006	43.29	23.10	....	329⅞	100⅛	287⅜	1.48	1.16	287⅜	66½	66⅜	..	Sp	vpd1.33	Pv0.07	0.07
• Consorcio G Grupo[4]Dina[5] 8s §jj15 2004	NR	R	164	2004	[6]56.88	17.58	....	57¼	38	s51¾	....	Flat	3⅝	9⅛	•⅝	..	Dc	....	....	....
• Converse Inc[7] 7s Jd 2004	NR	BE	80.0	2004	45.81	21.83	....	52	6	s25	....	....	6⅜	5½	•1⅜	d	Dc	vΔd1.36	....	[9]d1.92
Cooker[7]Restaurant[8] 6¾s QOct 2002	NR	R	13.7	2002	46.38	21.5625	4.64	92	80	A80	8.44	8.44	13⅜	17¼	•2⅞	d	Dc	v0.65	....	[9]d0.38
CoreComm[9]Ltd[4] 6s aO 2006	NR	BE	....	2006	24.336	41.09	....	156	121⅜	144½	4.15	4.13	144½	59½	59⅜	d	Dc	‡d0.82	....	[9]d3.16
Cray Research[10] 6⅛s Fa 2011	B–	R	105	2011	[11]12.82	78.00	....	73	60⅜	60½	10.12	10.12	12½	47¼	•9¹¹⁄₁₆	d	Je	vd2.47	v0.28	[9]d0.65
Credence Systems[12] 5¼s mS15 2002	NR	BE	115	2002	14.46	69.15	....	140⅝	67⅜	125⅛	4.20	4.18	125⅛	86⅝	86½	d	Oc	vd1.22	□Pd0.12	d0.12
Cymer[13]Inc([14]Step-Up) 3½s fA6 2004	BBB–	BE	173	2004	21.28	47.00	....	112⅝	73⅝	110¾	3.16	....	....	52⅛	46	..	Dc	....	....	....
Cypress[15]Semiconductor[16] 6s aO 2002	B	BE	160	2002	42.33	23.625	....	143⅞	86¼	137⅛	4.38	4.36	137⅛	32½	•32⅜	46	Dc	vd1.24	E0.69	[9]0.17
Datapoint Corp 8⅞s Jd 2006	NR	R	64.4	2006	55.231	18.11	....	40½	37	37	....	Flat	2	6¾	⅜	..	Jl	vΔd0.11	vn/a	[10]....
• Deere & Co. 5½s Jj15 2001	A	R	2.00	1-15-01	91.58	10.92	80.59	No Sale		397¼	1.38	0.93	397¼	43½	•43⅜	42	Oc	v4.16	vP1.02	1.02
• [17]Devon Energy[18] 4.90s fA15 2008	BBB+	BE	444	2008	[19]9.328	....	24.25	106	94⅛	95	5.16	5.16	80⅞	101⅞	•86⅝	25	Dc	v2.04	E3.35	[9]1.60
• [17]Devon Energy[18] 4.95s fA15 2008	BBB+	BE	317	2008	[19]9.328	....	24.25	106⅛	94⅛	96¼	5.14	5.14	80⅞	103¼	•86⅝	25	Dc	v2.04	E3.35	[9]1.60
Diamond Offshore Drilling[7] 3¾s Fa15 2007	A–	R	350	2007	12.35	81.00	6.18	116⅛	89⅛	101	3.71	3.71	37¾	81⅞	•30⁹⁄₁₆	25	Dc	v2.66	E1.20	[9]1.60
Dixie Group[20] 7s Mn15 2012	B+	R	44.8	2012	31.06	32.20	....	78	69	69	10.14	10.14	23	22¼	7⅜	36	Dc	vd1.78	....	[9]0.20
DoubleClick Inc[7] 4¾s Ms15 2006	NR	BE	200	2006	12.12	82.50	....	310¼	99½	306¾	1.55	1.23	306¾	253⅛	253¹⁄₁₆	d	Dc	vd0.56	....	[9]d0.57
◆DRS[7]Technologies[21] 9s aO 2003	NR	R	25.0	2003	113.00	8.85	....	120½	101	108⅞	8.27	8.27	108⅞	9¾	◆9⅝	16	Mr	v□0.44	....	[9]0.60
Drug Emporium 7¾s aO 2014	NR	R	50.8	2014	65.146	15.35	....	89	55	55	14.09	14.09	29	8½	4⁷⁄₁₆	d	Fb	v0.29	....	[11]d0.58
Dura Pharmaceutials[7] 3½s jJ15 2002	B	R	250	2002	19.75	50.635	....	80¾	73	80¾	4.33	4.35	27⅝	41	13¹⁵⁄₁₆	19	Dc	v0.06	E0.71	[9]0.10
EDO Corp[22] 7s jD15 2011	NR	R	29.3	2011	45.45	22.00	5.45	85	68⅜	77	9.09	9.09	26¾	17	•5⅞	22	Dc	v0.94	....	[9]0.26
• EMC Corp[9] 3¼s Ms15 2002	BBB–	BE	517	2002	88.28	11.3275	....	404	400	964½	0.34	....	964½	109⅜	•109¼	..	Dc	v0.74	E1.05	[9]0.99
• EMC Corp[23] 6s Mn15 2004	B	R	213	2004	11.93	83.82	....	135	79½	s131	4.58	4.57	130⅜	109⅞	•109¼	..	Dc	v0.74	E1.05	[9]0.99
EMCOR Group 5¾s Ao 2005	BB–	R	100	2005	37.58	27.34	....	103	84	87	6.61	6.61	68⅝	23¼	18¼	9	Dc	v□1.46	....	[9]1.89
• Empresas ICA Sociedad 5s $Ms15 2004	B	BE	375	2004	[24]30.17	33.15	6.94	74	50	58⅜	8.57	8.57	9⅞	19⅜	•3¼	d	Dc	v0.18	....	[6]d1.00
[25]Environmental Systems 6¾s Mn 2011	NR	R	21.4	2011	Conv into $693.07			82	69⅜	69⅜	9.73	9.73	....	....	....	..		....	....	....
E'town Corp 6¾s Fa 2012	BBB+	R	12.2	2012	25.00	40.00	51.00	158½	101⅜	155⅝	4.34	4.32	155⅝	62¼	•62¼	22	Dc	v2.66	....	[9]2.82
Evans&Southerl'd Comp 6s Ms 2012	NR	R	37.1	2012	23.752	42.10	....	89½	69	69	8.70	8.69	27¼	29⅛	11⁷⁄₁₆	d	Dc	vd1.70	....	[9]d2.06
ESC Medical Systems[26] 6s mS 2002	CCC+	R	115	2002	21.48	46.55	....	73⅝	56⅞	72⅝	8.26	8.26	20⅝	33⅞	9⁹⁄₁₆	d	Dc	Pv0.15	....	[9]d4.72
Executone Info Systems[27] 7½s Ms15 2011	NR	R	11.9	2011	94.12	10.625	....	113	56	82	9.15	9.15	51¼	8¾	5⁷⁄₁₆	d	Dc	vd0.74	....	[9]d0.79
Exodus Communications[7] 5s Ms15 2006	NR	BE	250	2006	87.57	11.42	....	818¼	190¾	777¾	0.64	....	777¾	88⅞	88¹³⁄₁₆	d	Dc	vd0.55	....	[9]d0.57
Family Golf Ceters[9] 5¾s aO15 2004	C	BE	115	2004	40.27	24.83	....	90¼	22⅝	25½	22.55	22.55	5¾	6⅝	1⅜	d	Dc	v□0.08	....	[9]d2.44
Farm Fresh[28]Inc[29] 7½s §Ms 2010	NR	R	15.0	2010	Conv into cash & deb[30]			3	3	3	....	Flat	....	....	....	..		....	....	....
[31]Fieldcrest Cannon 6s Ms15 2012	B+	R	104	2012	Conv into cash & com[32]			85¼	37¼	38	15.79	15.78	....	....	•6³⁄₁₆	29	Dc	v2.52	....	[9]0.21
• Financial Federal[12] 4½s Mn 2005	NR	BE	95.5	2005	33.16	30.1562	....	96	80	84	5.36	5.36	75¾	25⅝	•22¹³⁄₁₆	16	Jl	v1.03	v1.30	[10]1.36
Fischbach[33] 8½s aO 2005	NR	R	5.30	2005	Conv into $305.56			107⅝	99⅛	100	8.50	8.50	....	....	....	..		....	....	....
• Fremont Gen'l[34](Zero) [35] 2013	NR	BE	[36]21.6	2013	38.573	....	12.34	89½	33	33	....	Flat	28½	8⅝	•7⅜	30	Dc	v1.90	....	[9]0.24

Uniform Footnote Explanations—See Page 260. Other: [1]At maturity Deb red at 112.660% of par. [2] Into ADSs (rep 208.77 Cl A com). [3] (HRO)For Fundamental Chge at 100. [4] Co may red in whole,at 100,for tax law chge. [5] Default 7-15-99 int. [6] Into Grupo Dina Ser L ADSs. [7] (HRO)On Chge of Ctrl at 100. [8] (HRO)On ea 11-1 at 100,ltd,as defined. [9] (HRO)On Chge of Ctrl at 101. [10] Subsid & data of Silicon Graphics. [11] Cv into Silicon Graphics com. [12] (HRO)For Repurch Event at 100. [13] (HRO)On 8-6-00 at 101. [14] Int at 3.5% to 8-5-00,7.25% aft. [15] (HRO)For Fundamental Chge at various prices. [16] Co may repurch in whole,at 100,for tax law chge. [17] Cv into & data of Chevron Corp. [18] Was Pennzoil Co,then PennzEnergy Co. [19] Into Chevron Com. [20] Was Dixie Yarns. [21] Was Diagnostic/Retrieval Sys. [22] (HRO)On Chge of Ctrl at curr red prices. [23] Was Data General. [24] Into ADSs. [25] Acq by Brambles USA. [26] (HRO)for Repurch Event at 100. [27] Was Vodavi Technology. [28] Filed bankruptcy Chapt 11. [29] Default 3-1-98 int. [30] Cv into $416 & $119 16.5% Sub Deb'04. [31] Acq by & data of Pillowtex Corp. [32] Conv into $610.20 cash & 6.079 com of Pillowtex Corp. [33] Merged into American Int'l Group. [34] (HRO)On 10-12-03(08)at $610.26(781.19). [35] Due 10-12-13. [36] Incl disc.

Exchange ↓ Issue, Rate, Interest Dates and Maturity	S&P Rating	Bond Form	Outstdg. Mil-$	Conv. Ex-pires	Shares per $1,000 Bond	Price per Share	Div. Income per Bond	1999 Price Range High	Low	Curr Bid Sale(s) Ask(A)	Curr. Yield	Yield to Mat	Stock Value of Bond	Conv Parity	Stock Data Month End	P/E Ratio	Earnings Per Share Yr. End	1998	1999	Last 12 Mos
◆Friede Goldman[1]Halter[2]...... 4½s mS15 2004	B	BE	185	2004	18.10	55.26	....	68	50	61	7.38	7.38	12⅝	33¾	•6[15]⁄16	7	Dc	v1.43	....	[9]0.88
Genesco Inc[1] 5½s Ao15 2005	B	BE	104	2005	47.517	21.045	....	91⅜	68⅜	84½	6.51	6.51	61⅞	17⅞	•13	6	Ja	v□1.90	....	[10]1.89
Genzyme Corp[3] .... 5¼s Jd 2005	NR	BE	250	2005	[4]25.25	39.60	....	167½	109½	127⅜	4.12	4.11	113⅝	50½	45	24	Dc	v1.48	E1.85	[9]1.29
Getty Images[1] .... 4¾s Jd 2003	B–	BE	75.0	2003	35.08	28.5075	....	197	78⅜	171½	2.77	2.69	171½	49	48⅞	d	Dc	v□d1.22	....	[9]d1.62
[5]Glycomed Inc[6] .... 7½s Jj 2003	NR	BE	50.0	2003	[7]37.71	26.52	....	83	73½	80¼	9.35	9.34	48⅝	21⅜	12⅞	d	Dc	vd2.92	....	[9]d2.06
[8]Greenery Rehab Group...... 6½s Jd15 2011	NR	R	5.68	2011	[9]12.166	82.19	....	96⅞	55	A55	11.82	11.81	6⅝	45¼	•5⅜	6	Dc	v0.11	E0.86	[9]0.08
[8]Greenery Rehab Group.......... 8¾s Ao 2015	NR	R	5.70	2015	[9]15.618	64.03	....	94½	75	A75	11.67	11.67	8½	48⅛	•5⅜	6	Dc	v0.11	E0.86	[9]0.08
◆[1]Greyhound Lines[10] 8½s Ms31 2007	NR	R	9.80	2007	Conv into $525.25			103	97	95	8.95	8.95	....	....	◆....	13	Dc	Pv0.47	....	0.47
• Healthcare Realty[11]Tr 6.55s Ms14 2002	NR	BE	[12]74.8	2002	33.63	29.74	73.31	104	82	85	7.71	7.71	52⅝	25⅜	•15⅝	7	Dc	v1.65	....	[9]2.04
• Healthcare Realty[1]Tr[11] ....10½s Ao 2002	NR	R	4.97	2002	52.82	18.93	115.15	106	89	82⅝	12.71	12.71	82⅝	15¾	•15⅝	7	Dc	v1.65	....	[9]2.04
HEALTHSOUTH Corp[13]........... 3¼s Ao 2003	BBB–	BE	458	2003	27.30	36.625	....	86⅛	75⅛	77⅛	4.21	4.23	14¾	28⅜	•5⅜	6	Dc	v0.11	E0.86	[9]0.08
Heartport Inc[14]......................... 7¼s Mn 2004	CCC	BE	86.2	2004	34.53	28.96	....	67⅛	46½	46⅞	15.47	15.46	16½	13⅝	4¾	d	Dc	vΔd2.39	....	[9]d0.95
• Hercules Inc........................... 8s fA15 2010	NR	R	5.97	2010	67.11	14.90	72.48	No Sale		187⅛	4.28	4.25	187⅛	28	•27⅞	13	Dc	v0.10	E2.07	[9]d0.23
• Hewlett-Packard(Zero)[15] .... [16] 2017	A+	R	[12]2000	2017	5.43	....	3.48	68	51⅜	66½	....	Flat	61⅞	122½	•113¾	34	Oc	v2.77	vP3.34	3.34
• Hexcel Corp[1]................................ 7s fA 2003	B+	R	114	2003	63.25	15.81	....	97	65	s70	10.00	10.00	35¼	11⅛	•5⁹⁄16	d	Dc	v1.24	....	[9]d0.47
Hexcel Corp .... 7s fA 2011	NR	R	25.6	2011	32.55	30.72	....	82½	63	76	9.21	9.21	18⅛	23⅜	•5⁹⁄16	d	Dc	v1.24	....	[9]d0.47
• Hilton[17]Hotels[18] 5s Mn15 2006	BB+	BE	500	2006	45.12	22.1654	3.61	99¾	72	s75¾	6.60	6.60	43¼	16⅞	•9⁹⁄16	12	Dc	v1.12	E0.79	[9]0.71
HMT Technology[19] 5¾s Jj15 2004	B–	R	230	2004	42.11	23.75	....	84½	30	39	14.74	14.73	16⅞	9⅜	4	d	Mr	vd0.48	....	[9]d1.24
HNC Software[20] .... 5¾s Ms 2003	NR	R	100	2003	22.30	44.85	....	290	76	235⅞	2.44	2.29	235⅞	105⅞	105¾	..	Dc	v0.39	....	[9]0.43
[6]HomeTown[21]Buffets .... 7s jD 2002	NR	R	41.5	2002	[22]85.71	11.67	....	107	95	99	7.07	7.07	85¾	11⅝	10	11	Dc	v0.83	....	[9]0.91
[23]Hospital Corp Amer .... 8½s Ms 2008	NR	R	7.59	2008	Conv into $983			257¾	99⅝	100¼	8.48	8.48	....	....	....	..		....	....	....
• HRPT Properties Trust[24]('A')........ 7½s aO 2003	BBB–	BE	171	2003	55.56	18.00	71.12	100½	86	s88	8.52	8.52	50⅛	15⅞	•9	8	Dc	v□1.22	....	[9]1.08
• Huaneng Power Int'l[25](Sr).. 1¾s Mn21 2004	BBB	BE	230	2004	[26]34.25	29.20	....	No Sale		102⅛	1.71	1.71	36¼	29⅞	•10⁹⁄16	6	Dc	Pv1.59	....	[6]1.66
Hutchinson Technology[13] 6s Ms15 2005	NR	BE	150	2005	35.27	28.35	....	180⅞	86⅞	94¾	6.33	6.33	75	26⅞	21¼	28	Sp	vd2.46	Pv0.75	0.75
IDEC Pharmaceuticals[27](Zero)[28] .... [29] 2019	NR	BE	345	2019	13.468	....	....	141½	33¾	132⅛	....	Flat	132⅜	98⅛	98¼	..	Dc	v0.46	E0.97	[9]0.84
• Inco Ltd (Sr)....................... 7¾s $Ms15 2016	BB+	R	173	2016	26.14	38.25	....	99	83½	s86	9.01	9.01	61½	33	•23½	d	Dc	vd0.63	Ed0.15	[9]d0.30
• Inco Ltd (Sr)............................ 5¾s $jJ 2004	BB+	R	172	2004	33.33	30.00	....	97¼	86½	s95⅜	6.03	6.03	78⅜	28⅝	•23½	d	Dc	vd0.63	Ed0.15	[9]d0.30
Ingram[30]Micro(Sr-Zero)[31] .... [32] 2018	BBB	R	[12]1330	2018	5.495	....	....	34¾	29½	32⅜	....	Flat	7¼	59	•13⅛	11	Dc	±v1.64	....	[9]1.19
Integrated Device Tech[33]......... 5½s Jd 2002	B–	R	175	2002	34.93	28.625	....	109¾	68½	109¾	5.01	5.01	101⅜	31½	29	27	Mr	vd3.45	E1.06	[9]0.39
Integrated Health[34]Svcs[35]......... 5¾s Jj 2001	NR	R	125	1-1-01	30.675	32.60	....	87	¼	⅝	....	Flat	½	¼	⅛	d	Dc	vd1.08	....	[9]d36.08
[18]Integrated Process Equip[36] 6¼s mS15 2004	B–	BE	115	2004	18.20	54.93	....	78⅛	69⅞	71⅝	8.73	8.73	23⅝	39⅜	12[15]⁄16	d	My	v0.83	vd4.84	[11]d4.54
Interim Services .... 4½s Jd 2005	BB+	BE	207	2005	26.81	37.31	....	91¼	76¼	88	5.11	5.12	66⅜	32⅞	•24¾	19	Dc	□v1.29	....	[9]1.27
Interpublic Grp Cos[37].........1.80s mS16 2004	NR	BE	[12]250	2004	26.772	....	9.10	157	105⅜	154½	1.17	0.97	154½	57¾	•57[11]⁄16	44	Dc	v1.10	E1.30	[9]1.24
Interpublic Grp Cos[38]..............1.87s Jd 2006	NR	BE	[12]361	2006	17.62	....	5.99	113¼	88⅜	113⅛	1.65	1.61	101¾	64¼	•57[11]⁄16	44	Dc	v1.10	E1.30	[9]1.24
Intevac Inc[19]............................ 6½s Ms 2004	NR	R	57.5	2004	48.48	20.63	....	72⅝	50⅜	54½	11.93	11.92	17	11¼	3½	d	Dc	v0.03	....	[9]d1.14
• Iomega Corp[34] 6¾s Ms15 2001	NR	R	40.0	2001	202.54	4.94	....	145	87	95⅛	7.10	7.10	68⅜	4¾	•3⅜	d	Dc	vd0.20	Ed0.41	[9]d0.38
• IRT Property........................ 7.30s fA15 2003	BB+	R	84.9	2003	88.89	11.25	83.56	99¾	90	s93¾	7.79	7.79	69½	10⅝	•7[13]⁄16	9	Dc	v□0.78	....	[9]0.82
Itron Inc[1]............................. 6¾s Ms31 2004	NR	R	63.4	2004	42.19	23.70	....	71⅜	54⅞	56⅝	11.92	11.92	25⅞	13½	6⅛	d	Dc	vd0.42	....	[9]d0.47

Uniform Footnote Explanations—See Page 260. Other: [1](HRO)On Chge of Ctrl at 100. [2] Was Halter Marine Group. [3] (HRO)For Fundamental Chge at 100. [4] Into Genzyme Corp-Genl Division com. [5] Subsid&data of Ligand Pharmaceuticals. [6] (HRO)For a Risk Event at 100. [7] Into Ligand Pharm com. [8] Now HEALTHSOUTH Corp. [9] Into HEALTHSOUTH Corp. [10] Acquired by Laidlaw. [11] Was Capstone Capital. [12] Incl disc. [13] (HRO)For Repurch Event at 100. [14] (HRO)For Fundamental Chge,see prosp. [15] (HRO)On 10-14-00 at $590.29. [16] Due 10-14-17. [17] State gaming laws may req hldr's sale/co red. [18] (HRO)On Chge of Ctrl at 101. [19] (HRO)For Designated Event at 101. [20] (HRO)For Fundamental Chge. [21] Gtd by & data of Buffets Inc. [22] Into Buffets Inc com. [23] Merged into Columbia Hlthcare. [24] Was Health & Retirement Prop. [25] (HRO)On 5-21-02 at 128.575. [26] Cv into ADS. [27] (HRO)On 2-16-04(09&14)at $337.85 & arrc OID. [28] (HRO)Chge of Ctrl,$337.85&accr OID to 2-16-04. [29] Due 2-16-19. [30] (HRO)On 6-9-01(03,08,13)at $451.32&accr OID. [31] (HRO)On Chge of Ctrl at $451.32 & accr OID. [32] Due 6-9-18. [33] (HRO)For Designated Event at declining prices. [34] (HRO)For a Repurch Event at 100. [35] May default 1-1-00 int. [36] Acq by & data of SpeedFam-IPEC Inc. [37] (HRO)For Fundamental Chge at $800.07 accr OID. [38] (HRO)For Fundamental Chge at $830.18 & accr OID.

Exchange ↓ Issue, Rate, Interest Dates and Maturity	S&P Rating	Bond Form	Outstdg. Mil-$	Conv. Ex-pires	Shares per $1,000 Bond	Price per Share	Div. Income per Bond	1999 Price Range High	Low	Curr Bid Sale(s) Ask(A)	Curr. Yield	Yield to Mat	Stock Value of Bond	Conv Parity	Stock Data Month End	P/E Ratio	Earnings Per Share Yr. End	1998	1999	Last 12 Mos
J. Alexander's Corp[1] .... 8¼s Jd 2003	NR	R	15.6	2003	56.34	17.75	....	92⅜	83⅜	92	8.97	8.97	17⅝	16⅝	•3⅛	d	Dc	vd0.27	....	[9]d0.04
Jacobson Stores 6¾s jD15 2011	NR	R	32.8	2011	30.61	32.67	....	82½	63⅛	67¾	9.96	9.96	18	22¼	5⅞	9	Ja	v0.28	....	[10]0.62
[2]Jacor[3]Communiations[4](Zero) .... [5] 2011	BB+	BE	[6]250	2011	[7]15.521	....	....	142⅛	86⅝	138⅝	....	Flat	138⅝	89⅝	•89¼	..	Dc	v0.22	E0.68	[9]0.34
[8]Jacor[9]Communiations(Zero)[4] .... [10] 2018	BB+	BE	[6]427	2018	[11]7.227	....	....	67⅞	45½	66¾	....	Flat	64⅝	92⅜	•89¼	..	Dc	v0.22	E0.68	[9]0.34
Kaman Corp 6s Ms15 2012	BBB–	R	33.2	2012	[12]42.81	23.36	18.84	98	90	90	6.67	6.67	55⅛	21⅛	12⅞	10	Dc	v1.23	....	[9]1.29
[13]Kelley Oil & Gas Ptnrs[14] .... 8½s Ao 2000	CC	R	9.69	4-1-00	Conv into com/com & pfd[15]			88½	24	85⅝	9.93	9.93	....	....	½	d	Dc	vd4.90	....	[9]d4.09
Kellstrom Industries[17] 5¾s aO15 2002	B–	BE	54.0	2002	36.36	27.50	....	111¾	65⅛	66⅞	8.60	8.60	33¼	18½	9⅛	5	Dc	v1.53	....	[9]1.64
Kellstrom Industries[18] 5½s Jd15 2003	B–	BE	86.2	2003	30.77	32.50	....	103¾	63⅝	64¾	8.49	8.49	28⅛	21⅛	9⅛	5	Dc	v1.53	....	[9]1.64
• Kent Electronics[19] .... 4½s mS 2004	B	BE	207	2004	20.19	49.53	....	82⅛	72	s79½	5.66	5.66	46	39½	•22¾	..	Mr	v0.01	....	[9]0.19
• [20]Kerr-McGee[21] 7½s Mn15 2014	BBB–	R	190	2014	9.43	106.03	16.97	100⅝	90⅝	s93¼	8.04	8.04	58½	99	•62	20	Dc	v1.06	E3.01	[9]d1.47
• Kollmorgen Corp .... 8¾s Mn 2009	NR	R	32.8	2009	29.11	34.35	2.33	105	96½	97	9.02	9.02	35⅞	33⅜	•12⁹⁄₁₆	34	Dc	v□1.40	....	[9]0.36
• Korea Electric Power[22](Sr) .... 5s [23]dec31 2001	BBB	BE	200	2001	[24]40.816	24.50	8.98	99	91	97¼	5.14	5.14	68⅝	23⅞	•16¾	20	Dc	v0.82	....	0.82
Key Energy Group 5s mS15 2004	NR	R	216	2004	25.97	38.50	....	69⅝	44	68⅜	7.31	7.31	13½	26⅜	•5⁵⁄₁₆	d	Je	v1.23	vd1.94	[9]d1.93
Lam Research .... 5s mS 2002	B	BE	310	2002	11.39	87.77	....	136⅞	78⅝	127⅛	3.93	3.92	127⅛	111⅝	111⁹⁄₁₆	d	Je	vd3.80	vd2.93	[9]d1.65
Lamar Advertising[18](Sr) 5¼s mS15 2006	B	BE	250	2006	21.62	46.25	....	151¾	100	131	4.01	3.99	131	60⅝	60⁹⁄₁₆	d	Dc	vd0.24	....	[9]d0.45
Leasing[18]Solutions[25]Inc[26] .... 6⅞s §aO 2003	NR	R	71.9	2003	28.65	34.90	....	31	1⅛	3	....	Flat	....	1⅛	....	d	Dc	vd6.84	....	d6.84
[27]Level One[28]Communications .... 4s mS 2004	A	R	115	2004	[29]32.25	31.01	3.87	288¾	161¾	265½	1.51	1.20	265½	82⅜	82⁵⁄₁₆	35	Dc	v1.72	E2.30	[9]2.09
Level 3[30]Communications[18] 6s mS15 2009	CCC+	BE	750	2009	15.34	65.19	....	153⅝	99	125⅝	4.78	4.77	125⅝	82	81⅞	d	Dc	v2.66	Ed1.65	[9]d1.04
• [31]Liberty Property L.P. .... 8s jJ 2001	BB+	BE	200	2001	[32]50.00	20.00	104.00	126½	103¼	123¾	6.46	6.46	123¾	24¾	•24¾	13	Dc	v1.59	....	[9]1.89
[33]Liebert Corp 8s mN15 2010	AA	R	9.50	2010	[34]74.16	13.48	106.05	529⅞	392⅛	425½	1.88	1.63	425½	57½	•57⅜	19	Sp	v2.77	v3.00	3.00
• [35]Loews Corp 3⅛s mS15 2007	A+	BE	1150	2007	[36]15.38	65.04	7.69	90⅞	78⅛	s80½	3.88	3.90	47⅛	52⅜	•30⁹⁄₁₆	25	Dc	v2.66	E1.20	[9]1.60
LSI Logic[37] 4¼s Ms15 2004	B	BE	345	2004	31.875	31.353	....	227⅝	152⅞	215¼	1.97	1.79	215¼	67⅝	•67½	79	Dc	vd0.93	E0.85	[9]0.54
• LTC Properties .... 8¼s jJ 2001	NR	R	19.5	2001	57.97	17.25	90.43	109⅝	85	87⅝	9.42	9.41	49	15⅛	•8⁷⁄₁₆	6	Dc	v1.39	....	[9]1.26
LTC Properties .... 7¾s Jj 2002	NR	R	7.52	2001	60.606	16.50	94.55	103⅞	71	75⅝	10.25	10.24	51¼	12½	•8⁷⁄₁₆	6	Dc	v1.39	....	[9]1.26
LTX Corp 7¼s Ao15 2011	NR	R	7.31	2011	55.56	18.00	....	127⅛	60	124⅝	5.83	5.83	124⅝	22½	22⅜	60	Jl	vd2.15	v0.01	[10]0.37
• Magna[22]Intl[18] 5s $aO15 2002	A–	BE	344	2002	[38]13.382	54.40	13.38	119½	93½	93¾	5.33	5.33	56¾	70⅛	•42⅜	8	Dc	v‡1.55	E4.77	[6]....
• Mail-Well Inc .... 5s mN 2002	B+	BE	152	2002	52.63	19.00	....	107	90	88⅝	5.64	5.64	71⅛	16⅞	•13½	18	Dc	v□0.53	....	[9]0.74
• Malan Realty Investors 9½s jJ15 2004	NR	R	64.0	2004	58.82	17.00	99.99	100	85⅛	88⅝	10.72	10.72	78¾	15⅛	•13⅜	11	Dc	v□0.45	....	[9]1.12
Marsh Supermarkets[18] 7s Fa15 2003	NR	R	19.9	2003	[39]64.52	15.50	28.39	104½	90	90	7.78	7.78	65⅝	14	10⅛	7	Mr	±v1.28	....	[9]1.32
• MascoTech, Inc 4½s jD15 2003	B+	R	345	2003	32.26	31.00	10.32	83⅜	70	s73⅝	6.13	6.14	41	22¾	•12¹¹⁄₁₆	7	Dc	v1.83	....	[9]1.75
Maxtor Corp[40] .... 5¾s Ms 2012	NR	R	100	2012	Conv into $167.50			111⅝	65	70	8.21	8.21	....	....	....	..	....	....	....	....
• [41]MBL[37]Int'l[22]Finance(Bermuda) 3s mN31 2002	A–	BE	1999	2002	45.45	20.95	2.73	125	93	109	2.75	2.74	63⅝	24	•13¹⁵⁄₁₆	d	Mr	vd0.62	....	d0.62
[42]McKesson Corp .... 4½s Ms 2004	BBB–	R	67.7	2004	Conv into $610.25			95¾	85	85	5.29	5.30	....	....	....	..	Mr	....	....	....
[43]Medco Containment Svc[44] .... 6s mS 2001	AAA	R	28.7	2001	Cv into Cash & Com[45]			408⅝	301	386½	1.55	1.16	....	....	•67⁹⁄₁₆	27	Dc	v2.15	E2.45	[9]2.37
• Meditrust Corp .... 7½s Ms 2001	BB	R	88.4	2001	33.21	30.11	....	100	63	s83	9.04	9.03	18⅝	25	•5½	2	Dc	vd1.29	E2.00	[9]0.40
Meridian Diagnostics .... 7s mS 2006	NR	R	20.0	2006	62.14	16.09	12.43	85	42	A75	9.33	9.33	45⅛	12⅛	7¼	45	Sp	v0.34	Pv0.16	0.16
♦[46]Merrill Lynch[47] 0¼s Mn10 2006	AA–	BE	200	2006	[48]12.151	....	2.19	100⅛	100	94⅝	0.26	0.31	87⅞	77¾	•72⁵⁄₁₆	93	Dc	vd0.31	E0.77	[9]0.64
Metamor Worldwide[49] 2.94s fA15 2004	NR	R	[6]230	2004	23.74	35.38	....	98⅞	62	83½	3.52	3.54	69¼	35¼	29⅛	18	Dc	v±1.88	....	[9]1.61

Uniform Footnote Explanations—See Page 260. Other: [1]Was Winners Corp. [2] (HRO)6-12-01 at $581.25 & 6-12-06 at $762.39. [3] (HRO)To 6-12-01 on Chge of Ctrl. [4] Acq by & data of Clear Channel Commun. [5] Due 6-12-11. [6] Incl disc. [7] Cv into Clear Channel Commun com. [8] (HRO)To 2-9-03 on Chge of Ctrl. [9] (HRO)2-9-03('08&'13)at $494.52($625.35&$790.79). [10] Due 2-9-18. [11] Cv into Clear Channel Commun. [12] Into Cl A com. [13] (HRO)For a Redemp Event at 100. [14] Now Contour Energy. [15] Into 5.1864 com or 2.5932 com & 5.411 $2.625 Pfd. [16] Into 5.1864 com or 2.5932 com & 5.411 $2.625 Pfd. [17] (HRO)On Chge of Ctrl at 101. [18] (HRO)On Chge of Ctrl at 100. [19] (HRO)At 100 for a Repurch Event. [20] (HRO)For a Risk Event at 100. [21] Was Oryx Energy Co. [22] Co may red in whole,at 100,for tax law chge. [23] Due 8-1-01:Int pd annually. [24] Cv into ADS. [25] Default 10-1-99. [26] Filed bankruptcy Chapt 11. [27] (HRO)For Repurchase Event at 105. [28] Mgr into & data of Intel Corp. [29] Cv into Intel Corp com. [30] Co may terminate conv rts aft 9-15-02. [31] Exch for & data of Liberty Prop Trust. [32] Into Liberty Property Trust com. [33] Subsid & data of Emerson Electric. [34] Into Emerson Electric com. [35] Exch for & data of Diamond Offshore Drilling. [36] Into com of Diamond Offshore. [37] (HRO)For Fundamental Chge at 100. [38] Into Cl A Vtg Shrs. [39] Conv into Cl B com. [40] Merged into Hyundai Electr Indus Co Ltd. [41] Conv into & data of Bank of Tokyo-Mitsubishi. [42] Exch for & data of Armor All Products. [43] (HRO)For a Designated Event at 100. [44] Cv into & data of Merck & Co. [45] Into $532.79 & 49.754 com of Merck & Co. [46] On 5-10-06 hldr's rec greater of 100 or formulated amt. [47] Exch for & data of Time Warner. [48] Exch for Time Warner com. [49] Was COREStaff Inc.

Exchange ↓ Issue, Rate, Interest Dates and Maturity	S&P Rating	Bond Form	Outstdg. Mil-$	Conv. Ex-pires	Shares per $1,000 Bond	Price per Share	Div. Income per Bond	1999 Price Range High	1999 Price Range Low	Curr Bid Sale(s) Ask(A)	Curr. Yield	Yield to Mat	Stock Value of Bond	Conv Parity	Stock Data Month End	Stock Data P/E Ratio	Earnings Per Share Yr. End	1998	1999	Last 12 Mos
Michaels[1]Stores[2] 4¾s Jj15 2003	B	BE	96.9	2003	26.32	38.00	....	103⅝	86	94½	5.03	5.03	75⅛	36	28½	16	Ja	v1.43	E1.75	[10]1.52
Micron Technology[2] 7s jJ 2004	B	BE	500	2004	14.83	67.44	....	130¾	98⅝	128⅝	5.44	5.44	115⅜	86¾	•77¾	69	Au	vd1.10	vd0.26	[11]1.12
• Mid-Atlantic Realty Trust 7⅝s mS15 2003	NR	R	60.0	2003	95.24	10.50	102.86	100	100	103⅝	7.36	7.36	95⅞	11	•10 1/16	11	Dc	□v0.84	....	[9]0.87
MindSpring Enterprises[2] 5s Ao15 2006	B–	BE	180	2006	16.00	62.50	....	121¼	71⅛	95¾	5.22	5.22	42¼	59⅞	26⅜	d	Dc	v0.20	Ed0.60	[9]d0.28
• [3]Moran Energy 8¾s Jj15 2008	NR	R	23.7	2008	[4]57.01	17.54	....	99½	84	85	....	Flat	25	15	•4⅜	5	Dc	v0.40	....	[9]0.78
• Motorola, Inc[5](Zero) [6] 2009	A	R	[7]62.0	2009	18.268	....	8.77	264¼	115	269	....	Flat	269	147⅜	•147¼	71	Dc	vd1.61	E2.05	[9]1.01
• Motorola,Inc[8](Zero) [9] 2013	A	R	[7]480	2013	11.178	....	5.37	160	75	164⅝	....	Flat	164⅝	147⅜	•147¼	71	Dc	vd1.61	E2.05	[9]1.01
• MSC.Software Corp[10] 7⅞s [11]ms15 2004	NR	R	56.6	2004	[12]66.006	15.15	....	95	82	s87½	9.00	9.00	66⅞	13⅜	•10⅛	d	Dc	vd0.95	....	[9]d1.43
NABI Inc[2] 6½s Fa 2003	CCC–	R	80.5	2003	71.43	14.00	....	82½	60⅞	74⅜	8.74	8.74	33⅛	10½	4⅝	d	Dc	vd0.62	....	[9]d0.38
• Natl Data 5s mN 2003	BB–	BE	144	2003	19.15	52.23	5.75	115	81	91	5.49	5.50	65	47⅝	•33 15/16	28	My	vd1.90	v2.02	[11]1.19
• National Education[13] 6½s Mn15 2011	BBB	R	48.6	2011	Conv into $840			95	83⅞	83¾	7.76	7.76	....	....	....	..		....	....	....
• Nat'l Health Investors 7¾s Jj 2001	NR	R	74.9	1-1-01	31.62	31.625	93.60	98	85	88	8.81	8.80	47⅛	27⅞	•14⅞	5	Dc	v2.69	....	[9]2.55
◆Nat'l Healthcare[14]L.P.[15] 6s [16]Qmar31 2000	NR	BE	0.01	7-1-00	Conv int com of 2 Cos.[17]			No Sale		61	9.84	9.83	34⅝	9⅜	◆5¼	d	Dc	vd0.58	....	[9]d0.77
Net.Bank Inc[2] 4¾s Jd 2004	B–	BE	115	2004	28.03	35.67	....	232¾	77⅝	78⅝	6.04	6.04	51⅞	28⅛	18½	..	Dc	v0.23	....	[9]0.13
Network Equip Tech 7¼s Mn15 2014	NR	R	33.5	2014	31.75	31.50	....	82	61½	72	10.07	10.07	37⅝	22¾	•11 13/16	d	Mr	vΔd0.33	....	[9]d0.59
• [19]News America Hldgs(Zero) [20] 2002	BB+	R	[7]60.0	2002	[21]30.084	....	2.11	No Sale		165½	....	Flat	115⅛	55⅛	•38¼	43	Je	v1.04	vΔP0.92	[9]0.88
[2]NeXstar[22]Pharmaceuticals 6¼s fA 2004	NR	BE	80.0	2004	[23]22.44	44.56	....	191⅞	77¼	151½	4.13	4.10	151½	67⅝	•67½	79	Dc	vd0.93	E0.85	[9]0.54
• [24]NorAm Energy 6s QMar15 2012	BBB–	R	116	2012	Conv into cash & common[25]			98½	84½	s86	6.98	6.98	....	....	•22⅞	4	Dc	vd0.50	E5.70	[9]4.01
Northwest Natural Gas (Sr) 7¼s Ms 2012	A–	R	10.3	2012	50.25	19.90	61.31	140⅛	108½	131⅜	5.52	5.52	110¼	26¼	21 15/16	15	Dc	v1.02	....	[9]1.39
NovaCare, Inc[2] 5½s Jj15 2000	CC	R	175	1-15-00	37.52	26.65	....	99⅛	63⅞	98½	5.58	5.58	¾	26⅜	3/16	d	Je	v0.91	vd3.02	[9]d8.17
NTL Inc[27] 7s jD15 2008	CCC+	BE	600	2008	16.33	61.25	....	208⅞	123⅛	203¾	3.44	3.39	203¾	124⅞	124¾	d	Dc	v□d10.15	....	[9]d12.64
Oak Indus[2] 4⅞s Ms 2008	B	BE	100	2008	25.87	38.66	....	276¼	95	274⅝	1.78	1.54	274⅝	106¼	•106⅛	61	Dc	v1.46	E1.73	[9]1.57
• Office Depot[28](Zero) [29] 2007	BBB–	BE	[7]314	2007	43.895	....	....	110½	62¼	s62⅜	....	Flat	48⅜	14¼	•11	16	Dc	v0.61	E0.66	[9]0.63
• Office[30]Depot[31](Zero) [32] 2008	BBB–	BE	[7]345	2008	31.851	....	....	90	63	66	....	Flat	35⅛	20¾	•11	16	Dc	v0.61	E0.66	[9]0.63
Offshore Logistics 6s jD15 2003	B+	R	80.0	2003	43.74	22.86	....	90⅛	80⅜	81⅞	7.33	7.33	41⅛	18¾	9⅜	26	Mr	v0.97	....	[9]0.36
[33]OHM Corp[34] 8s aO 2006	B+	R	44.5	2006	Conv into cash & common[35]			94½	86	87½	9.14	9.14	41⅛	19½	•9⅛	4	Dc	v‡d0.63	....	[9]2.18
Old Nat'l Bancorp(Ind) 8s mS15 2012	BBB	R	22.0	2012	77.52	12.90	52.71	285⅝	217¼	251½	3.18	3.12	251½	32½	32 7/16	21	Dc	v1.39	....	[9]1.54
• Omega Healthcare Investors 8½s Fa 2001	NR	R	95.0	2001	34.93	28.625	....	No Sale		85⅝	9.93	9.92	44⅜	24⅝	•12 11/16	7	Dc	v3.39	....	[9]1.82
Omnicare, Inc[37] 5s jD 2007	BBB–	BE	345	2007	25.25	39.60	2.27	110⅞	61⅛	67	7.46	7.46	30⅜	26⅝	•12	10	Dc	v0.90	E1.10	[9]0.80
Omnicom[38]Group[39] 4¼s Jj3 2007	A	BE	218	2007	31.75	31.50	22.23	341⅜	177⅝	317½	1.34	0.96	317½	100	•100	49	Dc	v1.68	E2.02	[9]1.94
Omnicom[40]Group[41] 2¼s Jj6 2013	A	BE	230	2013	20.07	49.83	14.05	215⅞	122⅞	200¾	1.12	0.85	200¾	100⅛	•100	49	Dc	v1.68	E2.02	[9]1.94
[42]On-Line Software Intl 6¼s Ms15 2002	NR	R	11.3	2002	Conv into $855.67			90	85½	85½	7.31	7.31	....	....	....	..		....	....	....
Orbital Sciences[43]Corp 5s aO 2002	B–	BE	100	2002	35.71	28.00	....	172¼	66⅞	85⅛	5.87	5.88	66⅜	23⅞	•18 9/16	d	Dc	vd0.18	Ed1.00	[9]....
• [2]Outboard Marine[44] 7s jJ 2002	B–	R	7.10	2002	Conv in $808.99			85½	76	84	8.33	8.33	....	....	....	..		....	....	....
P-Com Inc[2] 4¼s mN 2002	NR	BE	60.1	2002	36.42	27.46	....	74⅛	39¾	65	6.54	6.54	32¼	17⅞	8⅞	13	Dc	vΔd1.44	E0.66	[9]d2.34
Paco Pharm'l Svs 6½s Ms 2007	NR	R	4.30	2007	Conv into $505.69			88	83	83	7.83	7.83	....	....	....	..		....	....	....
• Park Electrochemical[45] 5½s Ms 2006	B–	R	100	2007	23.703	42.188	7.58	103½	83¼	s89½	6.15	6.15	63	37⅞	•26 9/16	13	Fb	v1.38	....	[11]2.04
• Parker Drilling 5½s fA 2004	B–	BE	175	2004	64.97	15.39	....	79	53⅝	s68	8.09	8.09	20¾	10½	•3 3/16	..	Dc	v0.36	....	[9]....

Uniform Footnote Explanations—See Page 260. Other: [1] Int at 4.75% to 1-15-96,6.75% aft. [2] (HRO)On Chge of Ctrl at 100. [3] Now Kaneb Services. [4] Into Kaneb Services com. [5] (HRO)On 9-7-04 at $744.10. [6] Due 9-7-09. [7] Incl disc. [8] (HRO)On 9-27-03(08)at $799.52($894.16). [9] Due 9-27-13. [10] Now MSC.Software Corp. [11] Due 8-18-04. [12] Into MSC.Software Corp com. [13] Subsid of & assumed by Harcourt Gen'l. [14] (HRO)On Chge of Ctrl at 125. [15] Asmd by Nat'l Healthcare Corp. [16] Due 7-1-00. [17] Into 65.76 com of Natl Healthcare & Natl Hlth Rlty. [18] Into 65.76 com of Natl Healthcare & Natl Hlth Rlty. [19] Gtd by & conv into News Corp Ltd. [20] Due 3-31-02. [21] Into News Corp Ltd ADSs. [22] Cv into & data of Gilead Sciences. [23] Into Gilead Sciences com. [24] Merged into & data of Houston Indus. [25] Cv into $284.80 cash&13 Houston Ind com. [26] Cv into $284.80 cash&13 Houston Ind com. [27] (HRO)On Chge of Ctrl at 101. [28] (HRO)On 12-11-02 at $781.19. [29] Due 12-11-07. [30] (HRO)To 11-1-00 on Chge of Ctrl at $552.07 & accr OID. [31] (HRO)On 11-1-00 at $728.41. [32] Due 11-1-08. [33] Was Environmental Treat/Tech. [34] Gtd by & data of Int'l Technology. [35] Into $107.50 cash & 45.04 Int'l Technol com. [36] Into $107.50 cash & 45.04 Int'l Technol com. [37] (HRO)For Fundamental Chge as defined. [38] (HRO)On 1-3-03 at 112.418. [39] (HRO)For Fundamental chge at incr prices. [40] (HRO)For Fundamental Chge at various incr prices. [41] (HRO)On 1-6-04 at 118.968. [42] Acq by Computer Assoc Int'l. [43] (HRO)Fundament'l Chge at 102(101,100)to 9-30-00(01,02). [44] Acquired by Geenmarine Hldgs LLC. [45] (HRO)On Fundamental Chge at 102.75 to 3-1-98,declining aft.

Exchange ↓ Issue, Rate, Interest Dates and Maturity	S&P Rating	Bond Form	Outstdg. Mil-$	Conv. Ex-pires	Shares per $1,000 Bond	Price per Share	Div. Income per Bond	1999 Price Range High	1999 Price Range Low	Curr Bid Sale(s) Ask(A)	Curr. Yield	Yield to Mat	Stock Value of Bond	Conv Parity	Stock Data Month End	Stock Data P/E Ratio	Earnings Per Share Yr. End	1998	1999	Last 12 Mos
Penn Treaty American[1] .... 6¼s jD 2003	BB+	BE	74.8	2003	35.16	28.44	....	110⅞	72⅞	76	8.22	8.22	55½	21⅝	•15¾	6	Dc	v2.64	....	[9]2.39
• Pep Boys-Man,Mo,Jack(Zero) .... [2] 2011	BB+	R	[3]237	2011	12.929	....	3.49	56	51	50	....	Flat	11⅝	38¾	•8 15/16	9	Ja	v0.08	E0.94	[10]0.48
Personal Group of America[4].... 5¾s jJ 2004	B+	R	115	2004	28.07	35.62	....	117⅜	69⅛	81⅛	7.09	7.09	28⅞	29	•10¼	10	Dc	v0.96	....	[9]1.03
PETsMART Inc[5] .... 6¾s mN 2004	B–	BE	200	2004	114.29	8.75	....	131¼	64⅛	79¾	8.46	8.46	65¾	7	5¾	23	Ja	v0.20	E0.25	[10]d0.06
• Phoenix Investment Ptnrs[6] 6s Qmar10 2015	NR	R	76.4	2015	124.38	8.04	29.85	130¾	95	101⅛	5.93	5.93	101⅛	8¼	•8⅛	11	Dc	v0.68	....	[9]0.71
Photronics Inc .... 6s Jd 2004	B	BE	103	2004	17.88	55.94	....	119½	93½	116¼	5.16	5.16	51¼	65⅛	28⅝	63	Oc	v0.84	vP0.45	0.45
[5]PHP[7]Healthcare[8] .... 6½s §jD15 2002	NR	R	69.0	2002	36.70	27.25	....	3	1½	3	....	Flat	⅛	⅞	1/32	d	Ap	vd3.30	....	[7]d4.95
PhyCor Inc[5] 4½s Fa15 2003	B+	R	175	2003	25.86	38.67	....	75½	38¼	52	8.65	8.65	4⅞	20⅛	1⅞	4	Dc	vd1.55	E0.43	[9]d6.64
[9]PhyMatrix Corp 6¾s Jd15 2003	B–	R	100	2003	35.46	28.20	....	50½	26½	26½	....	....	1	7½	¼	d	Ja	v□d1.02	....	[10]d2.35
• Pier 1 Imports[10] .... 5¾s aO 2003	BB+	R	86.3	2003	121.65	8.22	14.60	117¾	92	93⅜	6.16	6.16	77⅝	7¾	•6⅜	9	Fb	v0.77	E0.66	[11]0.68
[11]PLATINUM technology..... 6¾s mN15 2001	NR	BE	25.8	2001	Conv into apx $2096.77			209¾	80	209	3.23	3.16	....	....	....	..	Dc	....	....	....
Pogo Producing 5½s Jd15 2006	BB–	R	115	2006	23.71	42.18	2.85	83¼	69⅞	79½	6.92	6.92	48⅜	33⅝	•20⅜	46	Dc	vd1.14	E0.44	[9]d0.50
• Potomac Elec Pwr (Sr) .... 5s mS 2002	A–	R	[3]115	2002	29.50	....	48.97	99¼	91¾	93¼	5.36	5.36	67¾	31⅝	•22 15/16	11	Dc	v1.73	E2.00	[9]2.05
Premiere Technologies............ 5¾s jJ 2004	NR	R	172	2004	30.303	33.00	....	82½	51½	57⅛	10.07	10.06	21¼	18⅞	7	d	Dc	vd1.67	....	[9]d2.65
[12]Preston Corp.......................... 7s Mn 2011	NR	R	27.8	2011	Conv into apx $158.65			85½	62¼	76	9.21	9.21	....	....	....	..		....	....	....
Pride International[13](Zero)[14].......... [15] 2018	B+	R	[3]511	2018	13.794	....	....	35⅜	22	33⅛	....	Flat	20¼	24⅛	•14⅝	d	Dc	v1.39	Ed1.03	[9]d0.80
◆Professional Bancorp........... 7.21s Ms 2004	NR	R	1.15	2004	78.75	12.70	....	165	100	100	7.21	7.21	57⅛	12¾	◆7¼	d	Dc	v0.74	....	[9]d0.92
• [16]Protection One Alarm 6¾s mS15 2003	B	R	90.0	2003	[17]55.71	17.95	....	No Sale		48¾	13.85	13.84	10⅞	8⅞	•1 15/16	d	Dc	vΔd0.04	....	[9]d0.47
• Quanex Corp[18]..................... 6.88s Jd31 2007	BB–	R	83.4	2007	31.75	31.50	20.32	105¾	85⅜	s97¾	7.04	7.04	81	30⅞	•25½	10	Oc	v0.65	vP2.56	2.56
Quantum Corp[19] .... 7s fA 2004	B+	BE	287	2004	Cv into Quantum Corp DSSG & HDDG[20]			101½	75½	75½	9.27	9.27	46¾	24½	•15⅛	11	Mr	pv0.73	E1.30	[9]0.56
[22]Quantum Hlth Resources[23]........ 4¾s aO 2000	BB+	R	86.3	10-1-00	[24]19.14	52.26	....	91⅞	84½	91⅞	5.17	5.17	21¾	48⅛	•11 5/16	53	Dc	v±0.05	....	[9]0.21
Quintiles[5]Transnational[25] ... 4¼s Mn31 2000	BB+	R	144	5-31-00	24.17	41.375	....	136	95⅝	96⅝	4.40	4.40	45¼	40	18 11/16	13	Dc	v1.06	E1.40	[9]1.14
Remington[5]Oil & Gas[26] .... 8¼s jD 2002	NR	R	6.00	2002	[27]90.909	11.00	....	98½	83	83	9.94	9.94	35¼	9¼	3⅞	2	Dc	v0.66	....	[9]1.33
[5]Renal Treatment Centers[28] 5⅝s jJ15 2006	B	R	125	2006	[29]39.03	25.62	....	120½	62	62¼	9.04	9.03	26⅛	16	•6 11/16	31	Dc	v□0.19	....	[9]0.21
Rent-Way Inc .... 7s Fa 2007	NR	R	23.0	2007	74.80	13.37	....	224½	119⅛	139⅞	5.00	5.00	139⅞	18¾	•18 11/16	27	Sp	v1.08	P□v0.68	0.68
Reptron Electronics[5]................ 6¾s fA 2004	CCC+	R	115	2004	35.09	28.50	....	52½	38⅝	52½	12.86	12.85	30¾	15	8¾	d	Dc	vd2.15	....	[9]d2.72
Res-Care Inc[30] .... 6s jD 2004	B–	BE	109	2004	53.168	18.81	....	143¾	72⅝	81½	7.36	7.36	67⅞	15⅜	12¾	19	Dc	v0.94	....	[9]0.65
Richardson Elecr................. 8¼s Jd15 2006	NR	R	40.0	2006	55.56	18.00	8.89	88⅜	78⅝	81¼	10.15	10.15	41¾	14⅝	7½	11	My	v0.77	v0.60	[8]0.64
Richardson Electr 7¼s jD15 2006	NR	R	30.8	2006	47.30	21.14	7.57	78¼	71⅝	72⅜	10.02	10.01	35½	15⅜	7½	11	My	v0.77	v0.60	[8]0.64
Rite Aid[5] 5¼s mS15 2002	B+	R	650	2002	27.67	36.14	12.73	149½	45⅛	67¾	7.75	7.75	30⅞	24½	•11⅛	53	Fb	v0.54	E0.21	[8]0.73
• Robbins & Meyers[5] .... 6½s mS 2003	NR	R	65.0	2003	36.70	27.25	8.07	104	81⅞	97	6.70	6.70	83⅛	26½	•22⅝	22	Au	v2.43	v1.06	[11]0.99
◆Rogers Commun'n([31]Drfd)(Sr).... 5¾s $mN26 2005	BB–	R	225	2005	[32]34.368	....	....	76	56½	85⅛	6.75	6.76	85⅛	24⅞	•24¾	4	Dc	v±2.92	....	[9]j3.96
[5]RoTech Medical[33]................... 5¼s Jd 2003	NR	BE	2.03	2003	[34]22.12	45.21	....	86¾	64⅛	64½	8.14	8.14	⅜	29¼	⅛	d	Dc	vd1.08	....	[9]d36.08
S3 Inc...................................... 5¾s aO 2003	NR	R	104	2003	52.03	19.22	....	92⅞	70⅜	92⅞	6.19	6.19	60¼	17⅞	11 9/16	d	Dc	vd2.22	....	[9]d1.83
Savoy Pictures Entertainment.... 7s jJ 2003	B	R	26.0	2003	[35]15.06	66.40	....	98	94	97	7.22	7.22	83¼	64½	55¼	..	Dc	v0.43	....	[9]0.23
[36]Scan-Tron Corp .... 6¾s Jd 2011	NR	R	10.2	2011	[37]39.73	25.17	11.92	90¼	75½	78¾	8.57	8.57	72⅞	19⅞	•18 5/16	15	Dc	vd0.66	E1.20	[9]d0.08
Schuler Homes[22] 6½s Jj15 2003	B–	R	50.0	2003	45.81	21.83	....	81	76½	78	8.33	8.33	29⅞	17⅛	6½	5	Dc	v0.63	....	[9]1.12
[30]Seacor Holdings Inc[38]...... 5⅜s mN15 2006	BBB–	BE	172	2006	15.15	66.00	....	101⅝	89⅞	95¾	5.61	5.61	78½	63¼	•51¾	13	Dc	vΔ8.17	....	[9]3.82

Uniform Footnote Explanations—See Page 260. Other: [1](HRO)On Chge of Ctrl at 101. [2] Due 9-20-11. [3] Incl disc. [4] (HRO)For Repurchase Event at 100. [5] (HRO)On Chge of Ctrl at 100. [6] Was Phoenix Duff & Phelps. [7] Filed bankruptcy Chapt 11. [8] Default 12-15-98 int. [9] Now Innovative Clinical Solutions. [10] Co must offer repurch at 100 on Chge of Ctrl. [11] Acq by Computer Assoc. [12] Merged into Yellow Corp. [13] (HRO)On 4-24-03('08&'13)at$494.52($625.35&$790). [14] (HRO)On Chge of Ctrl at $391.06 & accr OID. [15] Due 4-24-19. [16] Gtd by & data of Protection One. [17] Into Protection One, Inc com. [18] (HRO)On Chge of Ctrl at curr redemp price. [19] (HRO)For a Fundamental Chge. [20] Into 30.88 DSSG & 10.793 HDDG com. [21] Into 30.88 DSSG & 10.793 HDDG com. [22] (HRO)For a Risk Event at 100. [23] Cv into & data of Olsten Corp. [24] Conv into Olsten Corp com. [25] Co may red in whole,at 100,for tax law chge. [26] Was Box Energy. [27] Into Cl'B' com. [28] Acq by&data of Total Renal Care Hldgs. [29] Conv into Total Renal Care Hldgs com. [30] (HRO)For Repurch Event at 100. [31] Int of 2% pd in cash, bal deferred. [32] Conv into Cl'B' com. [33] Merged into&data if Integrated Health Svcs. [34] Conv into Integrated Health Com. [35] Into USA Networks com. [36] Now Scantron Corp sub&data of Harland(John H.). [37] Into Harland (John H.)com. [38] Now Seacor SMIT Inc.

Exchange ↓ Issue, Rate, Interest Dates and Maturity			S&P Rating	Bond Form	Outstdg. Mil-$	Conv. Ex-pires	Shares per $1,000 Bond	Price per Share	Div. Income per Bond	1999 Price Range High	Low	Curr Bid Sale(s) Ask(A)	Curr. Yield	Yield to Mat	Stock Value of Bond	Conv Parity	Stock Data Month End	P/E Ratio	Earnings Per Share Yr. End	1998	1999	Last 12 Mos
• [1]Seagram & Sons[2](Zero)	[3]	2006	BB+	R	[4]70.7	2006	[5]18.44	....	12.17	110	71⅝	82⅝	....	Flat	82⅝	44⅞	•44¾	d	Je	v2.68	v1.81	[9]d1.61
[6]Security First[7]	6¼s QMay	2008	NR	R	1.35	2008	[8]113.67	8.80	90.94	374	260¾	261½	2.39	2.25	261½	23⅛	23	18	Dc	v1.34	....	[9]1.27
Sepracor Inc[9]	7s jD15	2005	CCC+	BE	300	2005	8.01	124.875	....	133¼	84⅝	105¼	6.65	6.65	79½	131½	99 9/16	d	Dc	vd3.23	Ed4.90	[9]d4.86
Sholodge, Inc[6]	7½s Mn	2004	CCC	R	54.0	2004	42.90	23.31	....	64⅝	54⅝	62⅝	12.02	12.02	19⅜	14⅝	4½	14	Dc	v□1.07	....	[9]0.32
• Shoney's, Inc(Zero)	[10]	2004	NR	R	[4]201	2004	29.349	....	....	32	15	15⅝	....	Flat	4⅛	5⅜	•1⅜	d	Oc	v□d2.18	....	[7]d0.83
Signature Resorts[6]	5¾s Jj15	2007	B	BE	138	2007	32.88	30.417	....	74¼	59¼	61⅛	9.41	9.40	37⅞	18⅝	•11½	8	Dc	□v1.20	....	[9]1.44
• SiliconGraphics(Sr)	5¼s mS	2004	B+	BE	231	2004	27.59	36.25	....	94½	70⅛	72	7.29	7.29	26¾	26⅛	•9 11/16	d	Je	vd2.47	v0.28	[9]d0.65
• Simula Inc[6]	8s Mn	2004	NR	R	34.5	2004	56.98	17.55	....	89	63	63⅛	12.67	12.67	31	11⅛	•5 7/16	d	Dc	vd2.80	....	[9]d1.95
• Sizeler Property Inv	8s jJ15	2003	NR	R	65.0	2003	76.92	13.00	67.69	96	90½	92	8.70	8.69	62½	12	•8⅛	25	Dc	v0.33	....	[9]0.32
SmarTalk[11]TeleServices[12]	5¾s $mS15	2004	NR	R	150	2004	38.10	26.25	....	50½	10⅝	32½	....	Flat	....	8⅝	....	..	Dc	....	....	[9]d6.63
Solectron[13]Corp[14](Sr-Zero)	[15]	2019	BBB	BE	[4]1656	2019	7.472	....	....	75⅛	50¼	75⅛	....	Flat	71⅛	100⅝	•95⅛	77	Au	v0.82	v1.13	[11]1.23
Southern Mineral[6]	6⅞s aO	2007	NR	BE	41.4	2007	121.07	8.26	....	38	18	33½	20.52	20.52	2¼	2⅞	3/16	d	Dc	vd1.32	....	[9]d0.62
Southern[6]Pacific[16]Funding[17]	6¾s §aO15	2006	NR	R	75.0	2006	28.01	35.70	....	48	2	8½	....	Flat	⅛	3⅛	1/32	..	Dc	....	....	[6]2.29
• Speedway Motorsports[6]	5¾s mS31	2003	B+	BE	74.0	2003	32.14	31.11	....	No Sale		102¼	5.62	5.62	89½	31⅞	•27 13/16	27	Dc	v1.00	....	[9]1.02
Sports Authority[6]	5¼s mS15	2001	CCC+	R	149	2001	30.641	32.635	....	77⅝	43½	59½	8.82	8.82	6¼	19½	•2	d	Ja	vd2.01	Ed0.05	[10]d0.28
SportsLine.com Inc[6]	5s Ao	2006	NR	R	20.0	2006	15.355	65.125	....	127⅞	59¾	99⅛	5.04	5.04	77	64⅝	50⅛	d	Dc	vd1.94	....	[9]d2.26
[18]SRI Corp	8¾s Jj	2008	BBB	R	7.83	2008	[19]141.14	7.08	84.68	317⅝	236¾	242⅝	3.61	3.56	242⅝	17¼	17 3/16	9	Dc	v1.74	....	[9]1.88
• Standard Commercial[20]	7¼s Ms31	2007	B	R	69.0	2007	34.04	29.38	6.81	73	46⅞	s48¼	15.03	15.02	12¼	14¼	•3 9/16	7	Mr	v0.66	....	[9]0.46
[21]State St Boston	7¾s Mn	2008	A+	R	2.38	2008	347.83	2.875	222.61	3313⅛	2065¼	2541⅜	0.30	....	2541⅜	73⅛	•73 1/16	24	Dc	v2.66	E3.00	[9]2.94
Standard Motor Prod[22]	6¾s jJ15	2009	B+	BE	90.0	2009	31.068	32.1875	11.18	101	79½	79½	8.49	8.49	50⅛	25⅝	•16⅛	8	Dc	v1.69	....	[9]1.97
Statesman Group[6]	6¼s Mn	2003	NR	R	12.9	2003	Conv into $1000.78[23]			104⅞	100	100	6.25	6.25	....	....	....	..	Dc	....	....	....
• STMicroelectronics[24]NV[25](Zero)	[26]	2008	BBB	BE	[4]447	2008	17.904	....	....	173⅜	84	271¼	....	Flat	271¼	151⅝	•151 7/16	85	Dc	v1.45	E1.77	[9]1.66
• [6]Stone Container[27]	6¾s Fa15	2007	B–	R	45.0	2007	29.17	34.28	....	93¾	82	85½	7.89	7.89	71½	29⅜	24½	d	Dc	v□d1.48	Ed0.40	[9]d2.34
• Sun Co.	6¾s Jd15	2012	BBB–	R	10.0	2012	24.50	40.81	24.50	107	85	91½	7.38	7.38	57⅝	37⅜	•23½	33	Dc	v2.95	E0.70	[9]1.21
Sunrise Assisted Living[6]	5½s Jd15	2002	B–	BE	150	2002	26.89	37.19	....	141¼	73½	76¾	7.17	7.17	37	28⅝	13¾	12	Dc	v1.11	....	[9]1.14
• Swift Energy Co[28]	6¼s mN15	2006	B–	BE	115	2006	31.71	31.54	....	85	69	s77¼	....	Flat	36½	24⅜	•11½	13	Dc	vd2.93	....	[9]0.85
Synetic Inc[6]	5s Fa15	2007	NR	BE	165	2007	16.67	60.00	....	188	86¼	140½	3.56	3.53	140½	84⅜	84¼	..	Je	v0.46	vp0.48	[9]Nil
System Software[6]	7s mS15	2002	NR	BE	120	2002	13.84	72.24	....	72	29⅞	29⅞	23.43	23.41	2⅞	21⅝	2	d	Oc	vd11.20	vPd7.46	d7.46
Systems & Computer Tech[6]	5s aO15	2004	NR	R	74.8	2004	37.91	26.375	....	82⅛	68½	84	5.95	5.95	61⅝	22¼	16¼	28	Sp	v0.59	vP0.58	0.58
Telxon Corp[6]	5¾s Jj	2003	CCC+	BE	82.5	2003	36.36	27.50	0.36	90¼	57	83¼	6.91	6.91	58¼	23	16	d	Mr	vd8.50	....	[9]d8.21
[22]Tel-Save Holdings[29]	4½s mS15	2002	B+	R	300	2002	40.62	24.62	....	94¾	59⅝	86¼	5.22	5.22	72⅛	21¼	17¾	d	Dc	vΔd5.20	....	[9]d0.86
Telxon Corp	7½s Jd	2012	NR	R	24.7	2012	37.38	26.75	0.37	88¾	55	85	8.82	8.82	59⅞	22¾	16	d	Mr	vd8.50	....	[9]d8.21
• [30]Tenet Healthcare	6s jD	2005	BB–	R	320	2005	[31]25.94	38.55	....	86	75	s80¾	7.43	7.43	¼	31¼	1/16	..	Dc	v□d8.39	E0.50	[9]d10.27
◆Thermo Instrument Sys[32]	4s Jj15	2005	BBB	R	250	2005	28.05	35.65	....	85	73	73	5.48	5.49	31¼	26⅛	◆11⅛	18	Dc	Δv0.78	....	[9]0.61
◆ThermoTrex Corp[6]	3¼s mN	2007	BBB	BE	88.9	2007	37.04	27.00	....	75	65⅛	65	5.00	5.01	29¼	17⅝	◆7⅞	d	Sp	vΔd0.30	....	[6]d7.17
Times Mirror[33](Zero)[34]	[35]	2017	A–	BE	[4]500	2017	[36]5.828	....	4.66	50¼	45	48⅜	....	Flat	39⅛	83⅛	•67	19	Dc	v±16.06	E3.37	[9]5.47
Tops Appliance City[37]	6½s [38]	2003	NR	R	20.3	2003	44.94	22.25	....	60½	29½	35	18.57	18.56	2¼	7⅞	½	d	Dc	vΔd0.26	....	[9]d0.36
[6]TPI[39]Enterprises[40]	8¼s jJ15	2002	NR	R	51.6	2002	[41]50.51	19.80	....	62½	48⅛	48⅛	17.14	17.13	7	9⅝	•1⅜	d	Oc	v□d2.18	....	[7]d0.83

Uniform Footnote Explanations—See Page 260. Other: [1]Sub & data of Seagram Co Ltd(guarantor). [2] (HRO)On ea Sep 15. [3] Due 3-5-06. [4] Incl disc. [5] Into Seagram Co Ltd. [6] (HRO)On Chge of Ctrl at 100. [7] Acq by FirstMerit Corp. [8] Into FirstMerit Corp com. [9] (HRO)For Fundamental Chge at 100. [10] Due 4-11-04. [11] Filed bankruptcy Chapt 11. [12] Default 3-15-99 int. [13] (HRO)On 1-27-02(09)at $510.03($672.97). [14] (HRO)On Chge of Ctrl to 1-27-02. [15] Due 1-27-19. [16] Filed bankruptcy Chapt XI. [17] Default 10-15-98 int. [18] Now Selective Insurance Group. [19] Into Selective Insurance Group com. [20] (HRO)For a Special Redemp Event at 100. [21] Now State Street Corp. [22] (HRO)On Chge of Ctrl at 101. [23] Excl $131.25 for pending litigation settlement. [24] (HRO)On 6-10-03 at $916.57. [25] (HRO)On Chge of Ctrl at $840.10 & accr OID. [26] Due 6-10-08. [27] Now Smurfitt-Stone Container. [28] (HRO)For Designated Event at 101. [29] Now Talk.com Inc. [30] Exch for & data of Vencor Inc. [31] Into 25.9403 com of Vencor Inc. [32] Co may red in whole,at 100,for tax law chge. [33] (HRO)On 4-15-02(07&12)at $494.52($625.35 & $790.79). [34] (HRO)On Chge of Ctrl to 4-15-02 at $391.06 plus accr OID. [35] Due 4-15-07. [36] Into Cl. A com. [37] (HRO)For Red Event at 101. [38] Due 11-30-03:Int pd Feb 28 & Aug 31. [39] Gtd by TPI Restaurants. [40] Merged into & data of Shoney's Inc. [41] Into Shoney's Inc com.

Exchange ↓ Issue, Rate, Interest Dates and Maturity	S&P Rating	Bond Form	Outstdg. Mil-$	Conv. Ex-pires	Shares per $1,000 Bond	Price per Share	Div. Income per Bond	1999 Price Range High	1999 Price Range Low	Curr Bid Sale(s) Ask(A)	Curr. Yield	Yield to Mat	Stock Value of Bond	Conv Parity	Stock Data Month End	Stock Data P/E Ratio	Earnings Per Share Yr. End	1998	1999	Last 12 Mos
◆Trans-Lux[1] .... 7½s jD 2006	NR	R	27.5	2006	71.36	14.013	9.99	100	84¾	s86	8.72	8.72	50½	12⅛	◆7 1/16	9	Dc	v±0.85	....	[9]0.73
[2]TransAmerican Waste Indus...... 10s jJ29 2003	NR	R	[3]4.01	2003	[4]8.18	123.24	0.16	107	90	A90	11.11	11.11	14⅛	110⅛	•17 3/16	9	Dc	v□d1.31	E1.90	[9]d0.33
Triarc Cos[5](Zero)[6] .... [7] 2018	NR	BE	[3]360	2018	9.465	....	....	27⅜	21¼	22½	....	Flat	17½	23⅞	•18⅜	29	Dc	v0.46	....	[9]0.63
◆U.S. Cellular[8](Zero)[9] .... [10] 2015	BBB−	R	[3]745	2015	9.475	....	....	109¼	40½	95¾	....	Flat	95¾	101⅛	◆100 15/16	30	Dc	v2.48	....	[9]3.34
U.S. Office Products[11] .... 5½s Fa 2001	NR	R	12.8	2001	13.16	76.00	....	71¾	69¼	69¼	7.94	7.94	4⅛	52⅝	3⅛	d	Ap	v2.20	vd5.48	[10]d4.49
UroMed Corp 6s aO15 2003	NR	R	69.0	2003	15.06	66.41	....	57	37	57	10.53	10.53	1¾	37⅞	1⅛	d	Dc	vΔd3.59	....	[9]d1.60
•URS Corp[12] 6½s Fa15 2012	NR	R	2.15	2012	4.85	206.30	....	85	71	71	9.15	9.15	10⅝	146½	•21 11/16	11	Oc	v1.43	Pv1.98	1.98
[13]USF&G Corp(Zero)[14] .... [15] 2009	A	R	[3]175	2009	16.64	....	17.31	67⅝	60½	64⅛	....	Flat	56⅛	38⅝	•33 11/16	13	Dc	v0.32	E2.60	[9]3.37
•UtiliCorp United[16] .... 6⅝s [17]mn 2011	BBB−	R	5.80	2011	63.33	15.79	76.00	150	135	123⅛	5.38	5.38	123⅛	19½	•19 7/16	10	Dc	v1.63	E1.78	[9]1.75
[18]UTL Corp .... 6½s jJ 2011	NR	R	28.0	2011	Conv into $158.33			85	85	85	7.65	7.65	....	....	....	..		....	....	....
•[19]Valhi[20]Inc(Zero)[21](Sr Sec) .... [22] 2007	B	R	[3]186	2007	[23]14.43	....	7.22	66⅝	50	58⅛	....	Flat	58⅛	40⅜	•40¼	66	Dc	vd0.03	E0.61	[9]0.65
[24]Ventritex Inc[25] 5¾s fA15 2001	NR	BE	30.0	2001	[26]29.09	34.375	....	118⅝	98⅞	102¼	5.62	5.62	89⅜	35¼	•30 11/16	26	Dc	v1.50	E1.16	[9]0.22
VERITAS Software[27] .... 5¼s mN 2004	NR	BE	100	2004	69.77	14.33	....	1031¾	164¼	998⅝	0.53	....	998⅝	143¼	143⅛	d	Dc	v0.33	Evd0.01	[9]d1.58
•Waste[24]Management[28] .... 4s Fa 2002	BBB−	R	535	2002	22.96	43.56	0.46	142	81¼	s87	4.60	4.60	39½	38	•17 3/16	9	Dc	v□d1.31	E1.90	[9]d0.33
Western[29]Digital[30](Zero) .... [31] 2018	B−	R	[3]1297	2018	14.935	....	....	37⅝	10½	13⅞	....	Flat	6⅜	9⅜	•4 3/16	d	Je	vd3.32	vd5.51	[9]d5.36
Weston(Roy F.),Inc 7s Ao15 2002	NR	R	18.1	2002	[32]47.33	21.13	....	96½	86¾	87	8.05	8.05	9⅞	18½	2 1/16	20	Dc	v0.09	....	[9]0.10
Wind River[33]Systems[34] .... 5s fA 2002	B−	BE	140	2002	30.93	32.333	....	139¼	82⅛	126¼	3.96	3.94	113⅜	40⅞	36⅝	67	Ja	v0.61	....	[10]0.54
[35]WMX Technologies[36] 2s Jj24 2005	BBB−	R	[3]550	2005	18.906	....	0.38	113½	81¼	82	2.44	2.48	32½	43⅜	•17 3/16	9	Dc	v□d1.31	E1.90	[9]d0.33
[37]World Color Press[38] .... 6s aO 2007	BB−	R	132	2007	Cv into cash & common[39]			105½	88	97⅞	6.13	6.13	....	....	•22¼	15	Dc	v±1.29	....	[9]1.44
[41]WorldWay Corp[42] 6¼s Ao15 2011	B+	R	50.0	2011	Cv into $231.55			82	75	81	7.72	7.72	....	....	....	..		....	....	....
Xerox[43]Corp[44] .... .57s Ao21 2018	A−	BE	[3]1012	2018	7.808	....	6.25	63⅞	52	53¼	....	Flat	17¾	68¼	•22 11/16	10	Dc	v0.52	E2.22	[9]2.46

Uniform Footnote Explanations-See Page 260. Other: [1] (HRO)For a Repurch Event at 100. [2] Conv into&data of Waste Management. [3] Incl disc. [4] Into Waste Management com. [5] (HRO)On 2-9-03(08&13)at $278.23&accr OID. [6] (HRO)For Fundamental Chge at $278.23&accr OID. [7] Due 2-9-18. [8] (HRO)To 6-15-00 on Ctrl Chge at $306.46 & accr OID. [9] (HRO)On 6-15-00 at $411.99. [10] Due 6-15-15. [11] (HRO)At 100 for Designated Event. [12] Was Thortec Int'l. [13] (HRO)On 3-3-04 at $800.51. [14] Now St Paul Cos. [15] Due 3-3-09. [16] (HRO)Ea May 1, limited,as defined. [17] Due 7-1-11. [18] Acquired by Boeing Co. [19] Exch for & data of Halliburton Co com. [20] (HRO)On 10-20-02 at $636.27. [21] (HRO)On Chge in Ctrl at $257.59 & accr OID. [22] Due 10-20-07. [23] Into Halliburton Co com. [24] (HRO)On Chge of Ctrl at 100. [25] Now St Jude Medical. [26] Into St Jude Medical com. [27] (HRO)For a Fundamental Chge at 101. [28] Was USA Waste Services. [29] (HRO)For Fundamental Chge at $354.71&accr OID. [30] (HRO)On 2-18-03(08&13)at $354.71&accr OID. [31] Due 2-18-18. [32] Into Cl A com. [33] (HRO)On Chge of Ctrl at various prices. [34] Co may red in whole,at 100,for tax law chge. [35] (HRO)On 3-15-00 at $843.03. [36] Now Waste Management. [37] (HRO) Chge of Ctrl at 100. [38] Merged into & data of Quebecor Printing. [39] Into $197.25 cash & 30.588 Quebecor Printing. [40] Into $197.25 cash & 30.588 Quebecor Printing. [41] Was Carolina Freight. [42] Mgr into & data of Arkansas Best. [43] (HRO)On 4-21-03 at $648.91. [44] (HRO)On Chge of Ctrl to 4-21-03.